SPANISH DICTIONARY Plus GRAMMAR

Collins
An Imprint of HarperCollins*Publishers*

second edition 2000

latest reprint 2000

HarperCollins Publishers
Westerhill Road, Bishopbriggs, Glasgow G64 2QT, Great Britain

The HarperCollins website address is
www.**fire**and**water**.com

ISBN 0-00-470787-7

HarperCollins Publishers, Inc.
10 East 53rd Street, New York, NY 10022

ISBN 0-06-095692-5

Library of Congress Catalog Card Number: 99-76599*
*Published in the U.S. as *HarperCollins Spanish Concise Dictionary*

The HarperCollins USA website address is
www.harpercollins.com

First HarperCollins edition published 1998

00 01 02 03 04 CIBM 10 9 8 7 6 5 4 3 2

Dictionary text typeset by Morton Word Processing Ltd, Scarborough
Grammar text typeset by Wordcraft, Glasgow

A catalogue record for this book is available from the British Library

Printed and bound in Great Britain by
Omnia Books Ltd, Glasgow, G64

ÍNDICE DE MATERIAS

CONTENTS

Jeremy Butterfield, Mike Gonzalez, Gerry Breslin
Teresa Alvarez García, Brian Steel
Ana Cristina Llompart, José Miguel Galván Déniz

editorial staff
Megan Thomson, Val McNulty, Irene Lakhani, Sharon Hunter
Tracy Lomas, Claire Evans, Jane Horwood, Linda Chestnutt
Enrique González Sandinero, Caitlin McMahon

series editor
Lorna Sinclair

editorial management
Vivian Marr

INTRODUCTION

You may be starting Spanish for the first time, or you may wish to extend your knowledge of the language. Perhaps you want to read and study Spanish books, newspapers and magazines, or perhaps simply have a conversation with Spanish speakers. Whatever the reason, whether you're a student, a tourist or want to use Spanish for business, this is the ideal book to help you understand and communicate. This modern, user-friendly dictionary gives priority to everyday vocabulary and the language of current affairs, business, computing and tourism, and, as in all Collins dictionaries, the emphasis is firmly placed on contemporary language and expressions.

HOW TO USE THE DICTIONARY

Below you will find an outline of how information is presented in your dictionary. Our aim is to give you the maximum amount of detail in the clearest and most helpful way.

Entries

A typical entry in your dictionary will be made up of the following elements:

Phonetic transcription

Phonetics appear in square brackets immediately after the headword. They are shown using the International Phonetic Alphabet (IPA), and a complete list of the symbols used in this system can be found on page xiv. The pronunciation given is for Castilian Spanish except where a word is solely used in Latin America, when we give the Latin American pronunciation. A further guide to the differences in types of Spanish pronunciation is given on page xiv.

Grammatical information

All words belong to one of the following parts of speech: noun, verb, adjective, adverb, pronoun, article, conjunction, preposition, abbreviation. Nouns can be singular or plural and, in Spanish, masculine or feminine. Verbs can be transitive, intransitive, reflexive or impersonal. Parts of speech appear in *italics* immediately after the phonetic spelling of the headword. The gender of the translation also appears in *italics* immediately following the key element of the translation, except where this is a regular masculine singular noun ending in "o", or a regular feminine singular noun ending in "a".

Often a word can have more than one part of speech. Just as the English word **chemical** can be an adjective or a noun, the Spanish word **conocido** can be an adjective ("(well-)known") or a noun ("acquaintance"). In the same way the verb **to walk** is sometimes transitive, ie it takes an object ("to walk the dog") and sometimes intransitive, ie it doesn't take an object ("to walk to school"). To help you find the meaning you are looking for quickly and for clarity of presentation, the different part of speech categories are separated by a black lozenge ♦.

Meaning divisions

Most words have more than one meaning. Take, for example, **punch** which can be, amongst other things, a blow with the fist or an object used for making holes. Other words are translated differently depending on the context in which they are used. The transitive verb **to put on**, for example, can be translated by "ponerse", "encender" etc depending on *what* it is you are putting on. To help you select the most appropriate translation in every context, entries are divided according to meaning. Each different meaning is introduced by an "indicator" in *italics* and in brackets. Thus, the examples given above will be shown as follows:

punch *n* (*blow*) golpe *m*, puñetazo; (*tool*) punzón *m*

put on *vt* (*clothes, lipstick etc*) ponerse; (*light etc*) encender

Likewise, some words can have a different meaning when used to talk about a specific subject area or field. For example **bishop**, which in a religious context means a high-ranking clergyman, is also the name of a chess piece. To show English speakers which translation to use, we have added "subject field labels" in capitals and in brackets, in this case (*CHESS*):

bishop *n* obispo; (*CHESS*) alfil *m*

Field labels are often shortened to save space. You will find a complete list of abbreviations used in the dictionary on page xii.

Translations

Most English words have a direct translation in Spanish and vice versa, as shown in the examples given above. Sometimes, however, no exact equivalent exists in the target language. In such cases we have given an approximate equivalent, indicated by the sign ≈. An example is **British Rail**, the Spanish equivalent of which is "RENFE". There is no exact equivalent since the bodies in the two countries are quite different:

British Rail (BR) *n* ≈ RENFE *f* (*SP*)

On occasion it is impossible to find even an approximate equivalent. This may be the case, for example, with the names of types of food:

fabada *nf bean and sausage stew*

Here the translation (which doesn't exist) is replaced by an explanation. For increased clarity the explanation, or "gloss", is shown in *italics*.

It is often the case that a word, or a particular meaning of a word, cannot be translated in isolation. The translation of **Dutch**, for example, is "holandés/esa". However, the phrase **to go Dutch** is rendered by "pagar cada uno lo suyo". Even an expression as simple as **washing powder** needs a separate translation since it translates as "detergente (en polvo)", not "polvo para lavar". This is where your dictionary will prove to be particularly informative and useful since it contains an abundance of compounds, phrases and idiomatic expressions.

Levels of formality and familiarity

In English you instinctively know when to say **I'm broke** or **I'm a bit short of cash** and when to say **I don't have any money**. When you are trying to understand someone who is speaking Spanish, however, or when you yourself try to speak Spanish, it is important to know what is polite and what is less so, and what you can say in a relaxed situation but not in a formal context. To help you with this, on the Spanish-English side we have added the label (*fam*) to show that a Spanish meaning or expression is colloquial, while those meanings or expressions which are vulgar are given an exclamation mark (*fam!*), warning you they can cause serious offence. Note also that on the English-Spanish side, translations which are vulgar are followed by an exclamation mark in brackets.

Keywords

Words labelled in the text as *KEYWORD*s, such as **have** and **do** or their Spanish equivalents **tener** and **hacer**, have been given special treatment because they form the basic elements of the language. This extra help will ensure that you know how to use these complex words with confidence.

Cultural information

Entries which appear separated from the main text by a line above and below them explain aspects of culture in Spanish and English-speaking countries. Subject areas covered include politics, education, media and national festivals.

Spanish alphabetical order

In 1994 the **Real Academia Española** and the Spanish American language academies jointly decided to stop treating CH and LL as separate letters in Spanish, thereby bringing it into line with European spelling norms. This means that **chapa** and **lluvia** will be filed in letters C and L respectively. Of course, it should also be remembered that words like **cancha** and **callar**, with **ch** and **ll** in the middle of the words, will also have changed places alphabetically, now being found after **cáncer** and **cáliz** respectively. Spanish however still has one more letter than English with Ñ treated separately, between N and O.

ABREVIATURAS		ABBREVIATIONS
abreviatura	***ab(b)r***	abbreviation
adjetivo, locución adjetiva	***adj***	adjective, adjectival phrase
administración, lengua administrativa	***ADMIN***	administration
adverbio, locución adverbial	***adv***	adverb, adverbial phrase
agricultura	***AGR***	agriculture
alguien	***algn***	
América Latina	***AM***	Latin America
anatomía	***ANAT***	anatomy
arquitectura	***ARQ, ARCH***	architecture
astrología, astronomía	***ASTRO***	astrology, astronomy
el automóvil	***AUT(O)***	the motor car and motoring
aviación, viajes aéreos	***AVIAT***	flying, air travel
biología	***BIO(L)***	biology
botánica, flores	***BOT***	botany
inglés británico	***BRIT***	British English
química	***CHEM***	chemistry
	CINE	cinema
lengua familiar (! vulgar)	***col (!)***	colloquial usage (! particularly offensive)
comercio, finanzas, banca	***COM(M)***	commerce, finance, banking
informática	***COMPUT***	computing
conjunción	***conj***	conjunction
construcción	***CONSTR***	building
compuesto	***cpd***	compound element
cocina	***CULIN***	cookery
economía	***ECON***	economics
electricidad, electrónica	***ELEC***	electricity, electronics
enseñanza, sistema escolar	***ESCOL***	schooling, schools
España	***ESP***	Spain
especialmente	***esp***	especially
exclamación, interjección	***excl***	exclamation, interjection
femenino	***f***	feminine
lengua familiar (! vulgar)	***fam (!)***	colloquial usage (! particularly offensive)
ferrocarril	***FERRO***	railways
uso figurado	***fig***	figurative use
fotografía	***FOTO***	photography
(verbo inglés) del cual la partícula es inseparable	***fus***	(phrasal verb) where the particle is inseparable
generalmente	***gen***	generally
geografía, geología	***GEO***	geography, geology
geometría	***GEOM***	geometry
informática	***INFORM***	computing
invariable	***inv***	invariable
irregular	***irreg***	irregular
lo jurídico	***JUR***	law
América Latina	***LAM***	Latin America
gramática, lingüística	***LING***	grammar, linguistics
literatura	***LIT***	literature
masculino	***m***	masculine
matemáticas	***MAT(H)***	mathematics
medicina	***MED***	medical term, medicine
masculino/femenino	***m/f***	masculine/feminine

ABREVIATURAS — *ABBREVIATIONS*

lo militar, ejército	***MIL***	military matters
música	***MUS***	music
sustantivo, nombre	***n***	noun
navegación, náutica	***NAUT***	sailing, navigation
sustantivo no empleado en el plural	***no pl***	collective (uncountable) noun, not used in plural
sustantivo numérico	***num***	numeral noun
complemento	***obj***	(grammatical) object
	o.s.	oneself
peyorativo	***pey, pej***	derogatory, pejorative
fotografía	***PHOT***	photography
fisiología	***PHYSIOL***	physiology
plural	***pl***	plural
política	***POL***	politics
participio de pasado	***pp***	past participle
prefijo	***pref***	prefix
preposición	***prep***	preposition
pronombre	***pron***	pronoun
psicología, psiquiatría	***PSICO, PSYCH***	psychology, psychiatry
tiempo pasado	***pt***	past tense
ferrocarril	***RAIL***	railways
religión, lo eclesiástico	***REL***	religion, church service
	sb	somebody
enseñanza, sistema escolar	***SCOL***	schooling, schools
singular	***sg***	singular
España	***SP***	Spain
	sth	something
subjuntivo	***subjun***	subjunctive
sujeto	***su(b)j***	(grammatical) subject
sufijo	***suff***	suffix
tauromaquia	***TAUR***	bullfighting
también	***tb***	also
teatro	***TEAT***	
técnica, tecnología	***TEC(H)***	technical term, technology
telecomunicaciones	***TELEC, TEL***	telecommunications
	THEAT	theatre
imprenta, tipografía	***TIP, TYP***	typography, printing
televisión	***TV***	television
sistema universitario	***UNIV***	universities
inglés norteamericano	***US***	American English
verbo	***vb***	verb
verbo intransitivo	***vi***	intransitive verb
verbo pronominal	***vr***	reflexive verb
verbo transitivo	***vt***	transitive verb
zoología, animales	***ZOOL***	zoology
marca registrada	®	registered trademark
indica un equivalente cultural	≈	introduces a cultural equivalent

SPANISH PRONUNCIATION

Consonants

b	[b] [ß]	bomba labor	see notes on *v* below
c	[k]	caja	*c* before *a*, *o* or *u* is pronounced as in *c*at
ce, ci	[θe, θi] [se, si][1]	cero cielo vocero noticiero	*c* before *e* or *i* is pronounced as in *th*in and as *s* in *s*in in Latin America and parts of Spain
ch	[tʃ]	chiste	*ch* is pronounced as *ch* in *ch*air
d	[d] [ð]	danés ciudad	at the beginning of a word or after *l* or *n*, *d* is pronounced as in English. In any other position it is like *th* in *th*e
g	[g] [ɣ]	gafas guerra paga	*g* before *a*, *o* or *u* is pronounced as in *g*ap, if at the beginning of a word or after *n*. In other positions the sound is softened
ge, gi	[xe, xi]	gente girar	*g* before *e* or *i* is pronounced similar to *ch* in Scottish lo*ch*
h		haber	*h* is always silent in Spanish
j	[x]	jugar	*j* is pronounced like *ch* in Scottish lo*ch*
ll	[ʎ]	talle	*ll* is pronounced like the *lli* in mi*lli*on
ñ	[ɲ]	niño	*ñ* is pronounced like the *ni* in o*ni*on
q	[k]	que	*q* is pronounced as *k* in *k*ing
r, rr	[r] [rr]	quitar garra	*r* is always pronounced in Spanish, unlike the silent *r* in dance*r*. *rr* and *r* at the beginning of a word are trilled, like a Scottish *r*
s	[s]	quizás isla	*s* is usually pronounced as in pa*ss*, but before *b*, *d*, *g*, *l*, *m* or *n* it is pronounced as in ro*s*e
v	[b] [ß]	vía dividir	*v* is pronounced something like *b*. At the beginning of a word or after *m* or *n* it is pronounced as *b* in *b*oy. In any other position it is pronounce with the lips in position to pronounce *b* of *b*oy, but not meeting
w	[b] [w]	wáter whiskey	pronounced either like Spanish *b*, or like English *w*
z	[θ] [s][1]	tenaz izada	*z* is pronounced as *th*in *th*in and as *s* in *s*in in Latin America and parts of Spain
	[ks] [s]	tóxico xenofobia	*x* is pronounced as in to*x*in except in informal Spanish or at the beginning of a word

f, k, l, m, n, p and t are pronounced as in English.

[1]Only shown in Latin American entries.

Vowels

a	[a]	pata	not as long as *a* in f*a*r. When followed by a consonant in the same syllable (i.e. in a closed syllable), as in am*a*nte, the *a* is short, as in b*a*t
e	[e]	me	like *e* in th*e*y. In a closed syllable, as in *gente*, the *e* is short as in p*e*t
i	[i]	pino	as in m*ea*n or mach*i*ne
o	[o]	lo	as in l*o*cal. In a closed syllable, as in *control*, the *o* is short as in c*o*t
u	[u]	lunes	as in r*u*le. It is silent after *q*, and in *gue*, *gui*, unless marked *güe*, *güi* e.g. antig*üe*dad, when it is pronounced like *w* in *w*olf

Semivowels

i, y	[j]	bien hielo yunta	pronounced like *y* in *y*es
u	[w]	huevo fuente antigüedad	unstressed *u* between consonant and vowel is pronounced like *w* in *w*ell. See also notes on *u* above

Dipthongs

ai, ay	[ai]	baile	as *i* in r*i*de
au	[au]	auto	as *ou* in sh*ou*t
ei, ey	[ei]	buey	as *ey* in gr*ey*
eu	[eu]	deuda	both elements pronounced independently [e] + [u]
oi, oy	[oi]	hoy	as *oy* in t*oy*

Stress

The rules of stress in Spanish are as follows:

(a) when a word ends in a vowel or in *n* or *s*, the second last syllable is stressed: pat*a*ta, pat*a*tas, c*o*me, c*o*men

(b) when a word ends in a consonant other than *n* or *s*, the stress falls on the last syllable: par*e*d, habl*a*r

(c) when the rules set out in a and b are not applied, an acute accent appears over the stressed vowel: com*ú*n, geograf*í*a, ingl*é*s

In the phonetic transcription, the symbol ['] precedes the syllable on which the stress falls.

In general, we give the pronunciation of each entry in square brackets after the word in question.

SPANISH VERB FORMS

1 Gerund *2* Imperative *3* Present *4* Preterite *5* Future *6* Present subjunctive *7* Imperfect subjunctive *8* Past participle *9* Imperfect

acertar *2* acierta *3* acierto, aciertas, acierta, aciertan *6* acierte, aciertes, acierte, acierten
acordar *2* acuerda *3* acuerdo, acuerdas, acuerda, acuerdan *6* acuerde, acuerdes, acuerde, acuerden
advertir *1* advirtiendo *2* advierte *3* advierto, adviertes, advierte, advierten *4* advirtió, advirtieron *6* advierta, adviertas, advierta, advirtamos, advirtáis, adviertan *7* advirtiera *etc*
agradecer *3* agradezco *6* agradezca *etc*
aparecer *3* aparezco *6* aparezca *etc*
aprobar *2* aprueba *3* apruebo, apruebas, aprueba, aprueban *6* apruebe, apruebes, apruebe, aprueben
atravesar *2* atraviesa *3* atravieso, atraviesas, atraviesa, atraviesan *6* atraviese, atravieses, atraviese, atraviesen
caber *3* quepo *4* cupe, cupiste, cupo, cupimos, cupisteis, cupieron *5* cabré *etc* *6* quepa *etc* *7* cupiera *etc*
caer *1* cayendo *3* caigo *4* cayó, cayeron *6* caiga *etc* *7* cayera *etc*
calentar *2* calienta *3* caliento, calientas, calienta, calientan *6* caliente, calientes, caliente, calienten
cerrar *2* cierra *3* cierro, cierras, cierra, cierran *6* cierre, cierres, cierre, cierren
COMER *1* comiendo *2* come, comed *3* como, comes, come, comemos, coméis, comen *4* comí, comiste, comió, comimos, comisteis, comieron *5* comeré, comerás, comerá, comeremos, comeréis, comerán *6* coma, comas, coma, comamos, comáis, coman *7* comiera, comieras, comiera, comiéramos, comierais, comieran *8* comido *9* comía, comías, comía, comíamos comíais, comían
conocer *3* conozco *6* conozca *etc*
contar *2* cuenta *3* cuento, cuentas, cuenta, cuentan *6* cuente, cuentes, cuente, cuenten
costar *2* cuesta *3* cuesto, cuestas, cuesta, cuestan *6* cueste, cuestes, cueste, cuesten
dar *3* doy *4* di, diste, dio, dimos, disteis, dieron *7* diera *etc*
decir *2* di *3* digo *4* dije, dijiste, dijo, dijimos, dijisteis, dijeron *5* diré *etc* *6* diga *etc* *7* dijera *etc* *8* dicho
despertar *2* despierta *3* despierto, despiertas, despierta, despiertan *6* despierte, despiertes, despierte, despierten
divertir *1* divirtiendo *2* divierte *3* divierto, diviertes, divierte, divierten *4* divirtió, divirtieron *6* divierta, diviertas, divierta, divirtamos, divirtáis, diviertan *7* divirtiera *etc*
dormir *1* durmiendo *2* duerme *3* duermo, duermes, duerme, duermen *4* durmió, durmieron *6* duerma, duermas, duerma, durmamos, durmáis, duerman *7* durmiera *etc*
empezar *2* empieza *3* empiezo, empiezas, empieza, empiezan *4* empecé *6* empiece, empieces, empiece, empecemos, empecéis, empiecen
entender *2* entiende *3* entiendo, entiendes, entiende, entienden *6* entienda, entiendas, entienda, entiendan
ESTAR *2* está *3* estoy, estás, está, están *4* estuve, estuviste, estuvo, estuvimos, estuvisteis, estuvieron *6* esté, estés, esté, estén *7* estuviera *etc*
HABER *3* he, has, ha, hemos, han *4* hube, hubiste, hubo, hubimos, hubisteis, hubieron *5* habré *etc* *6* haya *etc* *7* hubiera *etc*
HABLAR *1* hablando *2* habla, hablad *3* hablo, hablas, habla, hablamos, habláis, hablan *4* hablé, hablaste, habló, hablamos, hablasteis, hablaron *5* hablaré, hablarás, hablará, hablaremos, hablaréis, hablarán *6* hable, hables, hable, hablemos, habléis, hablen *7* hablara, hablaras, hablara, habláramos, hablarais, hablaran *8* hablado *9* hablaba, hablabas, hablaba, hablábamos, hablabais, hablaban
hacer *2* haz *3* hago *4* hice, hiciste, hizo, hicimos, hicisteis, hicieron *5* haré *etc* *6* haga *etc* *7* hiciera *etc* *8* hecho
instruir *1* instruyendo *2* instruye *3* instruyo, instruyes, instruye, instruyen *4* instruyó, instruyeron *6* instruya *etc* *7* instruyera *etc*
ir *1* yendo *2* ve *3* voy, vas, va, vamos, vais, van *4* fui, fuiste, fue, fuimos, fuisteis, fueron *6* vaya, vayas, vaya, vayamos,

vayáis, vayan *7* fuera *etc* *8* iba, ibas, iba, íbamos, ibais, iban
jugar *2* juega *3* juego, juegas, juega, juegan *4* jugué *6* juegue *etc*
leer *1* leyendo *4* leyó, leyeron *7* leyera *etc*
morir *1* muriendo *2* muere *3* muero, mueres, muere, mueren *4* murió, murieron *6* muera, mueras, muera, muramos, muráis, mueran *7* muriera *etc* *8* muerto
mostrar *2* muestra *3* muestro, muestras, muestra, muestran *6* muestre, muestres, muestre, muestren
mover *2* mueve *3* muevo, mueves, mueve, mueven *6* mueva, muevas, mueva, muevan
negar *2* niega *3* niego, niegas, niega, niegan *4* negué *6* niegue, niegues, niegue, neguemos, neguéis, nieguen
ofrecer *3* ofrezco *6* ofrezca *etc*
oír *1* oyendo *2* oye *3* oigo, oyes, oye, oyen *4* oyó, oyeron *6* oiga *etc* *7* oyera *etc*
oler *2* huele *3* huelo, hueles, huele, huelen *6* huela, huelas, huela, huelan
parecer *3* parezco *6* parezca *etc*
pedir *1* pidiendo *2* pide *3* pido, pides, pide, piden *4* pidió, pidieron *6* pida *etc* *7* pidiera *etc*
pensar *2* piensa *3* pienso, piensas, piensa, piensan *6* piense, pienses, piense, piensen
perder *2* pierde *3* pierdo, pierdes, pierde, pierden *6* pierda, pierdas, pierda, pierdan
poder *1* pudiendo *2* puede *3* puedo, puedes, puede, pueden *4* pude, pudiste, pudo, pudimos, pudisteis, pudieron *5* podré *etc* *6* pueda, puedas, pueda, puedan *7* pudiera *etc*
poner *2* pon *3* pongo *4* puse, pusiste, puso, pusimos, pusisteis, pusieron *5* pondré *etc* *6* ponga *etc* *7* pusiera *etc* *8* puesto
preferir *1* prefiriendo *2* prefiere *3* prefiero, prefieres, prefiere, prefieren *4* prefirió, prefirieron *6* prefiera, prefieras, prefiera, prefiramos, prefiráis, prefieran *7* prefiriera *etc*
querer *2* quiere *3* quiero, quieres, quiere, quieren *4* quise, quisiste, quiso, quisimos, quisisteis, quisieron *5* querré *etc* *6* quiera, quieras, quiera, quieran *7* quisiera *etc*
reír *2* ríe *3* río, ríes, ríe, ríen *4* rio, rieron *6* ría, rías, ría, riamos, riáis, rían *7* riera *etc*
repetir *1* repitiendo *2* repite *3* repito, repites, repite, repiten *4* repitió, repitieron *6* repita *etc* *7* repitiera *etc*
rogar *2* ruega *3* ruego, ruegas, ruega, ruegan *4* rogué *6* ruegue, ruegues, ruegue, roguemos, roguéis, rueguen
saber *3* sé *4* supe, supiste, supo, supimos, supisteis, supieron *5* sabré *etc* *6* sepa *etc* *7* supiera *etc*
salir *2* sal *3* salgo *5* saldré *etc* *6* salga *etc*
seguir *1* siguiendo *2* sigue *3* sigo, sigues, sigue, siguen *4* siguió, siguieron *6* siga *etc* *7* siguiera *etc*
sentar *2* sienta *3* siento, sientas, sienta, sientan *6* siente, sientes, siente, sienten
sentir *1* sintiendo *2* siente *3* siento, sientes, siente, sienten *4* sintió, sintieron *6* sienta, sientas, sienta, sintamos, sintáis, sientan *7* sintiera *etc*
SER *2* sé *3* soy, eres, es, somos, sois, son *4* fui, fuiste, fue, fuimos, fuisteis, fueron *6* sea *etc* *7* fuera *etc* *9* era, eras, era, éramos, erais, eran
servir *1* sirviendo *2* sirve *3* sirvo, sirves, sirve, sirven *4* sirvió, sirvieron *6* sirva *etc* *7* sirviera *etc*
soñar *2* sueña *3* sueño, sueñas, sueña, sueñan *6* sueñe, sueñes, sueñe, sueñen
tener *2* ten *3* tengo, tienes, tiene, tienen *4* tuve, tuviste, tuvo, tuvimos, tuvisteis, tuvieron *5* tendré *etc* *6* tenga *etc* *7* tuviera *etc*
traer *1* trayendo *3* traigo *4* traje, trajiste, trajo, trajimos, trajisteis, trajeron *6* traiga *etc* *7* trajera *etc*
valer *2* val *3* valgo *5* valdré *etc* *6* valga *etc*
venir *2* ven *3* vengo, vienes, viene, vienen *4* vine, viniste, vino, vinimos, vinisteis, vinieron *5* vendré *etc* *6* venga *etc* *7* viniera *etc*
ver *3* veo *6* vea *etc* *8* visto *9* veía *etc*
vestir *1* vistiendo *2* viste *3* visto, vistes, viste, visten *4* vistió, vistieron *6* vista *etc* *7* vistiera *etc*
VIVIR *1* viviendo *2* vive, vivid *3* vivo, vives, vive, vivimos, vivís, viven *4* viví, viviste, vivió, vivimos, vivisteis, vivieron *5* viviré, vivirás, vivirá, viviremos, viviréis, vivirán *6* viva, vivas, viva, vivamos, viváis, vivan *7* viviera, vivieras, viviera, viviéramos, vivierais, vivieran *8* vivido *9* vivía, vivías, vivía, vivíamos, vivías, vivían
volver *2* vuelve *3* vuelvo, vuelves, vuelve, vuelven *6* vuelva, vuelvas, vuelva, vuelvan *8* vuelto

For additional information on Spanish verb formation, see pp 6-162 of Grammar section

NÚMEROS		*NUMBERS*
uno (un, una)*	**1**	one
dos	**2**	two
tres	**3**	three
cuatro	**4**	four
cinco	**5**	five
seis	**6**	six
siete	**7**	seven
ocho	**8**	eight
nueve	**9**	nine
diez	**10**	ten
once	**11**	eleven
doce	**12**	twelve
trece	**13**	thirteen
catorce	**14**	fourteen
quince	**15**	fifteen
dieciséis	**16**	sixteen
diecisiete	**17**	seventeen
dieciocho	**18**	eighteen
diecinueve	**19**	nineteen
veinte	**20**	twenty
veintiuno(-un, -una)*	**21**	twenty-one
veintidós	**22**	twenty-two
treinta	**30**	thirty
treinta y uno(un, una)*	**31**	thirty-one
treinta y dos	**32**	thirty-two
cuarenta	**40**	forty
cincuenta	**50**	fifty
sesenta	**60**	sixty
setenta	**70**	seventy
ochenta	**80**	eighty
noventa	**90**	ninety
cien(ciento)**	**100**	a hundred, one hundred
ciento uno(un, una)*	**101**	a hundred and one
ciento dos	**102**	a hundred and two
ciento cincuenta y seis	**156**	a hundred and fifty-six
doscientos(as)	**200**	two hundred
trescientos(as)	**300**	three hundred
quinientos(as)	**500**	five hundred
mil	**1,000**	a thousand
mil tres	**1,003**	a thousand and three
dos mil	**2,000**	two thousand
un millón	**1,000,000**	a million

* 'uno' (+ 'veintiuno' etc) agrees in gender (but not number) with its noun: treinta y un**a** person**as**; the masculine form is shortened to 'un' unless it stands alone: veinti**ún** caballos, veinti**uno**.

** 'ciento' is used in compound numbers, except when it multiplies: ciento diez, but cien mil. 'Cien' is used before nouns: cien hombres, cien casas.

NÚMEROS	*NUMBERS*
primero(primer, primera), 1°, $1^{er}/1^{a}$, 1^{era}	first, 1st
segundo(a), $2^{o}/2^{a}$	second, 2nd
tercero(tercer, tercera), 3°, $3^{er}/3^{a}$, 3^{era}	third, 3rd
cuarto(a), $4^{o}/4^{a}$	fourth, 4th
quinto(a)	fifth, 5th
sexto(a)	sixth, 6th
séptimo(a)	seventh
octavo(a)	eighth
noveno(a); nono(a)	ninth
décimo(a)	tenth
undécimo(a)	eleventh
duodécimo(a)	twelfth
decimotercio(a)	thirteenth
decimocuarto(a)	fourteenth
decimoquinto(a)	fifteenth
decimosexto(a)	sixteenth
decimoséptimo(a)	seventeenth
decimoctavo(a)	eighteenth
decimonono(a)	nineteenth
vigésimo(a)	twentieth
vigésimo primero(a)	twenty-first
vigésimo segundo(a)	twenty-second
trigésimo(a)	thirtieth
trigésimo primero(a)	thirty-first
trigésimo segundo(a)	thirty-second
cuadragésimo(a)	fortieth
quincuagésimo(a)	fiftieth
sexagésimo(a)	sixtieth
septuagésimo(a)	seventieth
octogésimo(a)	eightieth
nonagésimo(a)	ninetieth
centésimo(a)	hundredth
centésimo primero(a)	hundred-and-first
milésimo(a)	thousandth

LA HORA / *THE TIME*

¿qué hora es?	*what time is it?*
es la una	it's one o'clock
son las cuatro	it's four o'clock
medianoche, las doce de la noche	midnight
la una (de la madrugada)	one o'clock (in the morning), one (a.m.)
la una y cinco	five past one
la una y diez	ten past one
la una y cuarto *or* quince	a quarter past one, one fifteen
la una y veinticinco	twenty-five past one, one twenty-five
la una y media *or* treinta	half-past one, one thirty
las dos menos veinticinco, la una treinta y cinco	twenty-five to two, one thirty-five
las dos menos veinte, la una cuarenta	twenty to two, one forty
las dos menos cuarto, la una cuarenta y cinco	a quarter to two, one forty-five
las dos menos diez, la una cincuenta	ten to two, one fifty
mediodía, las doce (de la mañana)	twelve o'clock, midday, noon
las dos (de la tarde)	two o'clock (in the afternoon), two (p.m.)
las siete (de la tarde)	seven o'clock (in the evening), seven (p.m.)
¿a qué hora?	*at what time?*
a medianoche	at midnight
a las siete	at seven o'clock
a las una	at one o'clock
en veinte minutos	in twenty minutes
hace diez minutos	ten minutes ago

LA FECHA / *THE DATE*

hoy	today
mañana	tomorrow
pasado mañana	the day after tomorrow
ayer	yesterday
antes de ayer, anteayer	the day before yesterday
la víspera	the day before, the previous day
el día siguiente	the next *or* following day

la mañana	morning
la tarde	evening
esta mañana	this morning
esta tarde	this evening
esta tarde	this afternoon
ayer por la mañana	yesterday morning
ayer por la tarde	yesterday evening
mañana por la mañana	tomorrow morning
mañana por la tarde	tomorrow evening
en la noche del sábado al domingo	during Saturday night, during the night of Saturday to Sunday
vendrá el sábado	he's coming on Saturday
los sábados	on Saturdays
todos los sábados	every Saturday
el sábado pasado	last Saturday
el sábado que viene, el próximo sábado	next Saturday
del sábado en ocho días	a week on Saturday
del sábado en quince días	a fortnight *or* two weeks on Saturday
de lunes a sábado	from Monday to Saturday
todos los días	every day
una vez a la semana	once a week
una vez ala mes	once a month
dos veces a la semana	twice a week
hace una semana *o* ocho días	a week ago
hace quince días	a fortnight *or* two weeks ago
el año pasado	last year
dentro de dos días	in two days
dentro de ocho días *o* una semana	in a week
dentro de quince días	in a fortnight *or* two weeks
el mes que viene, el próximo mes	next month
el año que viene, el próximo año	next year

¿a qué o a cuántos estamos?	*what day is it?*
el 1/24 octubre de 1996	the 1st/24th of October 1996, October 1st/24th 1996
en 1996	in 1996
mil novecientos noventa y cinco	nineteen ninety-five
44 a. de J.C.	44 BC
14 d. de J.C.	14 AD
en el (siglo) XIX	in the nineteenth century
en los años treinta	in the thirties
érase una vez ...	once upon a time ...

Español-Inglés
Spanish-English

A a

A, a [a] *nf* (*letra*) A, a; **A de Antonio** A for Andrew (*BRIT*) *o* Able (*US*).

PALABRA CLAVE

a [a] (*a+él = al*) *prep* **1** (*dirección*) to; **fueron ~ Madrid/Grecia** they went to Madrid/ Greece; **me voy ~ casa** I'm going home
2 (*distancia*): **está ~ 15 km de aquí** it's 15 kms from here
3 (*posición*): **estar ~ la mesa** to be at table; **al lado de** next to, beside; **~ la derecha/izquierda** on the right/left; *V tb* **puerta**
4 (*tiempo*): **~ las 10/~ medianoche** at 10/midnight; **¿~ qué hora?** (at) what time?; **~ la mañana siguiente** the following morning; **~ los pocos días** after a few days; **estamos ~ 9 de julio** it's the 9th of July; **~ los 24 años** at the age of 24; **ocho horas al día** eight hours a day; **al año/~ la semana** (*AM*) a year/ week later
5 (*manera*): **~ la francesa** the French way; **~ caballo** on horseback; **~ oscuras** in the dark; **~ rayas** striped; **le echaron ~ patadas** they kicked him out
6 (*medio, instrumento*): **~ lápiz** in pencil; **~ mano** by hand; **cocina ~ gas** gas stove
7 (*razón*): **~ 30 ptas el kilo** at 30 pesetas a kilo; **~ más de 50 kms por hora** at more than 50 kms per hour; **poco ~ poco** little by little
8 (*dativo*): **se lo di ~ él** I gave it to him; **se lo compré ~ él** I bought it from him
9 (*complemento directo*): **vi al policía** I saw the policeman
10 (*tras ciertos verbos*): **voy ~ verle** I'm going to see him; **empezó ~ trabajar** he started working *o* to work; **sabe ~ queso** it tastes of cheese
11 (*+infin*): **al verle, le reconocí inmediatamente** when I saw him I recognized him at once; **el camino ~ recorrer** the distance we (*etc*) have to travel; **¡~ callar!** keep quiet!; **¡~ comer!** let's eat!
12 (*a+que*): **¡~ que llueve!** I bet it's going to rain!; **¿~ qué viene eso?** what's the meaning of this?; **¿~ que sí va a venir?** he IS coming, isn't he?; **¿~ que no lo haces? – ¡~ que sí!** bet you don't do it! – yes, I WILL!

A. *abr* (*ESCOL: = aprobado*) pass.
AA *nfpl abr = Aerolíneas Argentinas.*
AA EE *abr* (*= Asuntos Exteriores*): **Min. de AA EE** ≈ FO (*BRIT*).
ab. *abr* (*= abril*) Apr.
abad, esa [a'ßað, 'ðesa] *nm/f* abbot/abbess.
abadía [aßa'ðia] *nf* abbey.
abajo [a'ßaxo] *adv* (*situación*) (down) below, underneath; (*en edificio*) downstairs; (*dirección*) down, downwards; **~ de** *prep* below, under; **el piso de ~** the downstairs flat; **la parte de ~** the lower part; **¡~ el gobierno!** down with the government!; **cuesta/río ~** downhill/downstream; **de arriba ~** from top to bottom; **el ~ firmante** the undersigned; **más ~** lower *o* further down.
abalance [aßa'lanθe] *etc vb V* **abalanzarse.**
abalanzarse [aßalan'θarse] *vr*: **~ sobre** *o* **contra** to throw o.s. at.
abalear [aßale'ar] *vt* (*AM fam*) to shoot.
abalorios [aßa'lorjos] *nmpl* (*chucherías*)

trinkets.
abanderado [aβande'raðo] *nm* standard bearer.
abandonado, a [aβando'naðo, a] *adj* derelict; (*desatendido*) abandoned; (*desierto*) deserted; (*descuidado*) neglected.
abandonar [aβando'nar] *vt* to leave; (*persona*) to abandon, desert; (*cosa*) to abandon, leave behind; (*descuidar*) to neglect; (*renunciar a*) to give up; (*INFORM*) to quit; **~se** *vr*: **~se a** to abandon o.s. to; **~se al alcohol** to take to drink.
abandono [aβan'dono] *nm* (*acto*) desertion, abandonment; (*estado*) abandon, neglect; (*renuncia*) withdrawal, retirement; **ganar por ~** to win by default.
abanicar [aβani'kar] *vt* to fan.
abanico [aβa'niko] *nm* fan; (*NAUT*) derrick; **en ~** fan-shaped.
abanique [aβa'nike] *etc vb V* **abanicar**.
abaratar [aβara'tar] *vt* to lower the price of ♦ *vi*, **~se** *vr* to go *o* come down in price.
abarcar [aβar'kar] *vt* to include, embrace; (*contener*) to comprise; (*AM*) to monopolize; **quien mucho abarca poco aprieta** don't bite off more than you can chew.
abarque [a'βarke] *etc vb V* **abarcar**.
abarrotado, a [aβarro'taðo, a] *adj* packed; **~ de** packed *o* bursting with.
abarrote [aβa'rrote] *nm* packing; **~s** *nmpl* (*AM*) groceries, provisions.
abarrotería [aβarrote'ria] *nf* (*AM*) grocery store.
abarrotero, a [aβarro'tero, a] *nm/f* (*AM*) grocer.
abastecedor, a [aβasteθe'ðor, a] *adj* supplying ♦ *nm/f* supplier.
abastecer [aβaste'θer] *vt*: **~ (de)** to supply (with).
abastecimiento [aβasteθi'mjento] *nm* supply.
abastezca [aβas'teθka] *etc vb V* **abastecer**.
abasto [a'βasto] *nm* supply; (*abundancia*) abundance; **no dar ~ a algo** not to be able to cope with sth.
abatible [aβa'tiβle] *adj*: **asiento ~** tip-up seat.
abatido, a [aβa'tiðo, a] *adj* dejected, downcast; **estar muy ~** to be very depressed.
abatimiento [aβati'mjento] *nm* (*depresión*) dejection, depression.
abatir [aβa'tir] *vt* (*muro*) to demolish; (*pájaro*) to shoot *o* bring down; (*fig*) to depress; **~se** *vr* to get depressed; **~se sobre** to swoop *o* pounce on.
abdicación [aβðika'θjon] *nf* abdication.
abdicar [aβði'kar] *vi* to abdicate; **~ en algn** to abdicate in favour of sb.
abdique [aβ'ðike] *etc vb V* **abdicar**.
abdomen [aβ'ðomen] *nm* abdomen.
abdominal [aβðomi'nal] *adj* abdominal ♦ *nm*: **~es** (*DEPORTE*) abdominals; (*ANAT*) abdominals, stomach muscles.
abecedario [aβeθe'ðarjo] *nm* alphabet.
abedul [aβe'ðul] *nm* birch.
abeja [a'βexa] *nf* bee; (*fig*: *hormiguita*) hard worker.
abejorro [aβe'xorro] *nm* bumblebee.
aberración [aβerra'θjon] *nf* aberration.
aberrante [aβe'rrante] *adj* (*disparatado*) ridiculous.
abertura [aβer'tura] *nf* = **apertura**.
abertzale [aβer'tʃale] *adj, nm/f* Basque nationalist.
abeto [a'βeto] *nm* fir.
abierto, a [a'βjerto, a] *pp de* **abrir** ♦ *adj* open; (*fig*: *carácter*) frank.
abigarrado, a [aβiɣa'rraðo, a] *adj* multicoloured; (*fig*) motley.
abismal [aβis'mal] *adj* (*fig*) vast, enormous.
abismar [aβis'mar] *vt* to humble, cast down; **~se** *vr* to sink; (*AM*) to be amazed; **~se en** (*fig*) to be plunged into.
abismo [a'βismo] *nm* abyss; **de sus ideas a las mías hay un ~** our views are worlds apart.
abjurar [aβxu'rar] *vt* to abjure, forswear ♦ *vi*: **~ de** to abjure, forswear.
ablandar [aβlan'dar] *vt* to soften up; (*conmover*) to touch; (*CULIN*) to tenderize ♦ *vi*, **~se** *vr* to get softer.
abnegación [aβneɣa'θjon] *nf* self-denial.
abnegado, a [aβne'ɣaðo, a] *adj* self-sacrificing.
abobado, a [aβo'βaðo, a] *adj* silly.
abobamiento [aβoβa'mjento] *nm* (*asombro*) bewilderment.
abocado, a [aβo'kaðo, a] *adj*: **verse ~ al desastre** to be heading for disaster.
abochornar [aβotʃor'nar] *vt* to embarrass; **~se** *vr* to get flustered; (*BOT*) to wilt; **~se de** to get embarrassed about.
abofetear [aβofete'ar] *vt* to slap (in the face).
abogacía [aβoɣa'θia] *nf* legal profession; (*ejercicio*) practice of the law.
abogado, a [aβo'ɣaðo, a] *nm/f* lawyer; (*notario*) solicitor; (*asesor*) counsel; (*en tribunal*) barrister, advocate, attorney (*US*); **~ defensor** defence lawyer *o* attorney (*US*); **~ del diablo** devil's

advocate.
abogar [aβo'ɣar] *vi*: ~ **por** to plead for; (*fig*) to advocate.
abogue [a'βoɣe] *etc vb V* **abogar**.
abolengo [aβo'lengo] *nm* ancestry, lineage.
abolición [aβoli'θjon] *nf* abolition.
abolir [aβo'lir] *vt* to abolish; (*cancelar*) to cancel.
abolladura [aβoʎa'ðura] *nf* dent.
abollar [aβo'ʎar] *vt* to dent.
abominable [aβomi'naβle] *adj* abominable.
abominación [aβomina'θjon] *nf* abomination.
abonado, a [aβo'naðo, a] *adj* (*deuda*) paid(-up) ♦ *nm/f* subscriber.
abonar [aβo'nar] *vt* to pay;(*deuda*) to settle; (*terreno*) to fertilize; (*idea*) to endorse; ~**se** *vr* to subscribe; ~ **dinero en una cuenta** to pay money into an account, credit money to an account.
abono [a'βono] *nm* payment; fertilizer; subscription.
abordable [aβor'ðaβle] *adj* (*persona*) approachable.
abordar [aβor'ðar] *vt* (*barco*) to board; (*asunto*) to broach; (*individuo*) to approach.
aborigen [aβo'rixen] *nm/f* aborigine.
aborrecer [aβorre'θer] *vt* to hate, loathe.
aborrezca [aβo'rreθka] *etc vb V* **aborrecer**.
abortar [aβor'tar] *vi* (*malparir*) to have a miscarriage; (*deliberadamente*) to have an abortion.
aborto [a'βorto] *nm* miscarriage; abortion.
abotagado, a [aβota'ɣaðo, a] *adj* swollen.
abotonar [aβoto'nar] *vt* to button (up), do up.
abovedado, a [aβoβe'ðaðo, a] *adj* vaulted, domed.
abr. *abr* (= *abril*) Apr.
abrace [a'βraθe] *etc vb V* **abrazar**.
abrasar [aβra'sar] *vt* to burn (up); (*AGR*) to dry up, parch.
abrazadera [aβraθa'ðera] *nf* bracket.
abrazar [aβra'θar] *vt* to embrace, hug; ~**se** *vr* to embrace, hug each other.
abrazo [a'βraθo] *nm* embrace, hug; **un** ~ (*en carta*) with best wishes.
abrebotellas [aβreβo'teʎas] *nm inv* bottle opener.
abrecartas [aβre'kartas] *nm inv* letter opener.
abrelatas [aβre'latas] *nm inv* tin (*BRIT*) *o* can (*US*) opener.
abrevadero [aβreβa'ðero] *nm* watering place.
abreviar [aβre'βjar] *vt* to abbreviate; (*texto*) to abridge; (*plazo*) to reduce ♦ *vi*: **bueno, para** ~ well, to cut a long story short.
abreviatura [aβreβja'tura] *nf* abbreviation.
abridor [aβri'ðor] *nm* (*de botellas*) bottle opener; (*de latas*) tin (*BRIT*) *o* can (*US*) opener.
abrigar [aβri'ɣar] *vt* (*proteger*) to shelter; (*suj*: *ropa*) to keep warm; (*fig*) to cherish; ~**se** *vr* to take shelter, protect o.s (*de* from); (*con ropa*) to cover (o.s.) up; **¡abrígate bien!** wrap up well!
abrigo [a'βriɣo] *nm* (*prenda*) coat, overcoat; (*lugar protegido*) shelter; **al** ~ **de** in the shelter of.
abrigue [a'βriɣe] *etc vb V* **abrigar**.
abril [a'βril] *nm* April.
abrillantar [aβriʎan'tar] *vt* (*pulir*) to polish; (*fig*) to enhance.
abrir [a'βrir] *vt* to open (up); (*camino etc*) to open up; (*apetito*) to whet; (*lista*) to head ♦ *vi* to open; ~**se** *vr* to open (up); (*extenderse*) to open out; (*cielo*) to clear; ~ **un negocio** to start up a business; **en un** ~ **y cerrar de ojos** in the twinkling of an eye; ~**se paso** to find *o* force a way through.
abrochar [aβro'tʃar] *vt* (*con botones*) to button (up); (*zapato, con broche*) to do up; ~**se** *vr*: ~**se los zapatos** to tie one's shoelaces.
abrogación [aβroɣa'θjon] *nf* repeal.
abrogar [aβro'ɣar] *vt* to repeal.
abrumador, a [aβruma'ðor, a] *adj* (*mayoría*) overwhelming.
abrumar [aβru'mar] *vt* to overwhelm; (*sobrecargar*) to weigh down.
abrupto, a [a'βrupto, a] *adj* abrupt; (*empinado*) steep.
absceso [aβs'θeso] *nm* abscess.
absentismo [aβsen'tismo] *nm* (*de obreros*) absenteeism.
absolución [aβsolu'θjon] *nf* (*REL*) absolution; (*JUR*) acquittal.
absoluto, a [aβso'luto, a] *adj* absolute; (*total*) utter, complete; **en** ~ *adv* not at all.
absolver [aβsol'βer] *vt* to absolve; (*JUR*) to pardon; (: *acusado*) to acquit.
absorbente [aβsor'βente] *adj* absorbent; (*interesante*) absorbing, interesting; (*exigente*) demanding.
absorber [aβsor'βer] *vt* to absorb; (*embeber*) to soak up; ~**se** *vr* to become absorbed.
absorción [aβsor'θjon] *nf* absorption; (*COM*) takeover.
absorto, a [aβ'sorto, a] *pp de* **absorber** ♦ *adj*

absorbed, engrossed.
abstemio, a [aβs'temjo, a] *adj* teetotal.
abstención [aβsten'θjon] *nf* abstention.
abstendré [aβsten'dre] *etc vb V* **abstenerse**.
abstenerse [aβste'nerse] *vr*: ~ **(de)** to abstain *o* refrain (from).
abstenga [aβs'tenga] *etc vb V* **abstenerse**.
abstinencia [aβsti'nenθja] *nf* abstinence; (*ayuno*) fasting.
abstracción [aβstrak'θjon] *nf* abstraction.
abstracto, a [aβ'strakto, a] *adj* abstract; **en** ~ in the abstract.
abstraer [aβstra'er] *vt* to abstract; ~**se** *vr* to be *o* become absorbed.
abstraído, a [aβstra'iðo, a] *adj* absent-minded.
abstraiga [aβs'traiɣa] *etc*, **abstraje** [aβs'traxe] *etc*, **abstrayendo** [aβstra'jendo] *etc vb V* **abstraer**.
abstuve [aβs'tuβe] *etc vb V* **abstenerse**.
absuelto [aβ'swelto] *pp de* **absolver**.
absurdo, a [aβ'surðo, a] *adj* absurd; **lo ~ es que** ... the ridiculous thing is that ... ♦ *nm* absurdity.
abuchear [aβutʃe'ar] *vt* to boo.
abucheo [aβu'tʃeo] *nm* booing; **ganarse un** ~ (*TEAT*) to be booed.
abuela [a'βwela] *nf* grandmother; **¡cuéntaselo a tu ~!** (*fam!*) do you think I was born yesterday? (*fam*); **no tener/necesitar** ~ (*fam*) to be full of o.s./blow one's own trumpet.
abuelita [aβwe'lita] *nf* granny.
abuelo [a'βwelo] *nm* grandfather; (*antepasado*) ancestor; ~**s** *nmpl* grandparents.
abulense [aβu'lense] *adj* of Ávila ♦ *nm/f* native *o* inhabitant of Ávila.
abulia [a'βulja] *nf* lethargy.
abúlico, a [a'βuliko, a] *adj* lethargic.
abultado, a [aβul'taðo, a] *adj* bulky.
abultar [aβul'tar] *vt* to enlarge; (*aumentar*) to increase; (*fig*) to exaggerate ♦ *vi* to be bulky.
abundancia [aβun'danθja] *nf*: **una ~ de** plenty of; **en** ~ in abundance.
abundante [aβun'dante] *adj* abundant, plentiful.
abundar [aβun'dar] *vi* to abound, be plentiful; ~ **en una opinión** to share an opinion.
aburguesarse [aβurɣe'sarse] *vr* to become middle-class.
aburrido, a [aβu'rriðo, a] *adj* (*hastiado*) bored; (*que aburre*) boring.
aburrimiento [aβurri'mjento] *nm* boredom, tedium.
aburrir [aβu'rrir] *vt* to bore; ~**se** *vr* to be bored, get bored; ~**se como una almeja** *u* **ostra** to be bored stiff.
abusar [aβu'sar] *vi* to go too far; ~ **de** to abuse.
abusivo, a [aβu'siβo, a] *adj* (*precio*) exorbitant.
abuso [a'βuso] *nm* abuse; ~ **de confianza** betrayal of trust.
abyecto, a [aβ'jekto, a] *adj* wretched, abject.
A.C. *abr* (= *Año de Cristo*) A.D.
a/c *abr* (= *al cuidado de*) c/o; (= *a cuenta*) on account.
acá [a'ka] *adv* (*lugar*) here; **pasearse de ~ para allá** to walk up and down; **¡vente para ~!** come over here!; **¿de cuándo ~?** since when?
acabado, a [aka'βaðo, a] *adj* finished, complete; (*perfecto*) perfect; (*agotado*) worn out; (*fig*) masterly ♦ *nm* finish.
acabar [aka'βar] *vt* (*llevar a su fin*) to finish, complete; (*consumir*) to use up; (*rematar*) to finish off ♦ *vi* to finish, end; (*morir*) to die; ~**se** *vr* to finish, stop; (*terminarse*) to be over; (*agotarse*) to run out; ~ **con** to put an end to; ~ **mal** to come to a sticky end; **esto acabará conmigo** this will be the end of me; ~ **de llegar** to have just arrived; **acababa de hacerlo** I had just done it; ~ **haciendo** *o* **por hacer algo** to end up (by) doing sth; **¡se acabó!** (*¡basta!*) that's enough!; (*se terminó*) it's all over!; **se me acabó el tabaco** I ran out of cigarettes.
acabóse [aka'βose] *nm*: **esto es el ~** this is the limit.
acacia [a'kaθja] *nf* acacia.
academia [aka'ðemja] *nf* academy; (*ESCOL*) private school; *V tb* **colegio**.
académico, a [aka'ðemiko, a] *adj* academic.
acaecer [akae'θer] *vi* to happen, occur.
acaezca [aka'eθka] *etc vb V* **acaecer**.
acallar [aka'ʎar] *vt* (*silenciar*) to silence; (*calmar*) to pacify.
acalorado, a [akalo'raðo, a] *adj* (*discusión*) heated.
acalorarse [akalo'rarse] *vr* (*fig*) to get heated.
acampada [akam'paða] *nf*: **ir de** ~ to go camping.
acampanado, a [akampa'naðo, a] *adj* flared.
acampar [akam'par] *vi* to camp.
acanalado, a [akana'laðo, a] *adj* (*hierro*) corrugated.
acanalar [akana'lar] *vt* to groove; (*ondular*) to corrugate.

acantilado [akanti'laðo] *nm* cliff.
acaparador, a [akapara'ðor, a] *nm/f* monopolizer.
acaparar [akapa'rar] *vt* to monopolize; (*acumular*) to hoard.
acápite [a'kapite] *nm* (*AM*) paragraph; **punto ~** full stop, new paragraph.
acaramelado, a [akarame'laðo, a] *adj* (*CULIN*) toffee-coated; (*fig*) sugary.
acariciar [akari'θjar] *vt* to caress; (*esperanza*) to cherish.
acarrear [akarre'ar] *vt* to transport; (*fig*) to cause, result in; **le acarreó muchos disgustos** it brought him lots of problems.
acaso [a'kaso] *adv* perhaps, maybe ♦ *nm* chance; **¿~ es mi culpa?** (*AM fam*) what makes you think it's my fault?; **(por) si ~** (just) in case.
acatamiento [akata'mjento] *nm* respect; (*de la ley*) observance.
acatar [aka'tar] *vt* to respect; (*ley*) to obey, observe.
acatarrarse [akata'rrarse] *vr* to catch a cold.
acaudalado, a [akauða'laðo, a] *adj* well-off.
acaudillar [akauði'ʎar] *vt* to lead, command.
acceder [akθe'ðer] *vi* to accede, agree; **~ a** (*INFORM*) to access.
accesible [akθe'siβle] *adj* accessible; **~ a** open to.
accésit, *pl* **accésits** [ak'θesit, ak'θesits] *nm* consolation prize.
acceso [ak'θeso] *nm* access, entry; (*camino*) access road; (*MED*) attack, fit; (*de cólera*) fit; (*POL*) accession; (*INFORM*) access; **~ aleatorio/directo/secuencial** *o* **en serie** (*INFORM*) random/direct/sequential *o* serial access; **de ~ múltiple** multi-access.
accesorio, a [akθe'sorjo, a] *adj* accessory ♦ *nm* accessory; **~s** *nmpl* (*AUTO*) accessories, extras; (*TEAT*) props.
accidentado, a [akθiðen'taðo, a] *adj* uneven; (*montañoso*) hilly; (*azaroso*) eventful ♦ *nm/f* accident victim.
accidental [akθiðen'tal] *adj* accidental; (*empleo*) temporary.
accidentarse [akθiðen'tarse] *vr* to have an accident.
accidente [akθi'ðente] *nm* accident; **por ~** by chance; **~s** *nmpl* unevenness *sg*, roughness *sg*.
acción [ak'θjon] *nf* action; (*acto*) action, act; (*TEAT*) plot; (*COM*) share; (*JUR*) action, lawsuit; **capital en acciones** share capital; **~ liberada/ordinaria/preferente** fully-paid/ordinary/preference share.
accionamiento [akθjona'mjento] *nm* (*de máquina*) operation.
accionar [akθjo'nar] *vt* to work, operate; (*INFORM*) to drive.
accionista [akθjo'nista] *nm/f* shareholder.
acebo [a'θeβo] *nm* holly; (*árbol*) holly tree.
acechanza [aθe'tʃanθa] *nf* = **acecho.**
acechar [aθe'tʃar] *vt* to spy on; (*aguardar*) to lie in wait for.
acecho [a'θetʃo] *nm*: **estar al ~ (de)** to lie in wait (for).
acedera [aθe'ðera] *nf* sorrel.
aceitar [aθei'tar] *vt* to oil, lubricate.
aceite [a'θeite] *nm* oil; (*de oliva*) olive oil; **~ de hígado de bacalao** cod-liver oil.
aceitera [aθei'tera] *nf* oilcan.
aceitoso, a [aθei'toso, a] *adj* oily.
aceituna [aθei'tuna] *nf* olive.
aceitunado, a [aθeitu'naðo, a] *adj* olive *cpd*; **de tez aceitunada** olive-skinned.
acelerador [aθelera'ðor] *nm* accelerator.
acelerar [aθele'rar] *vt* to accelerate; **~se** *vr* to hurry.
acelga [a'θelɣa] *nf* chard, beet.
acendrado, a [aθen'draðo, a] *adj*: **de ~ carácter español** typically Spanish.
acendrar [aθen'drar] *vt* to purify.
acento [a'θento] *nm* accent; (*acentuación*) stress; **~ cerrado** strong *o* thick accent.
acentuar [aθen'twar] *vt* to accent; to stress; (*fig*) to accentuate; (*INFORM*) to highlight.
acepción [aθep'θjon] *nf* meaning.
aceptación [aθepta'θjon] *nf* acceptance; (*aprobación*) approval.
aceptar [aθep'tar] *vt* to accept; to approve.
acequia [a'θekja] *nf* irrigation ditch.
acera [a'θera] *nf* pavement (*BRIT*), sidewalk (*US*).
acerado, a [aθe'raðo, a] *adj* steel; (*afilado*) sharp; (*fig*: *duro*) steely; (: *mordaz*) biting.
acerbo, a [a'θerβo, a] *adj* bitter; (*fig*) harsh.
acerca [a'θerka]: **~ de** *prep* about, concerning.
acercar [aθer'kar] *vt* to bring *o* move nearer; **~se** *vr* to approach, come near.
acerico [aθe'riko] *nm* pincushion.
acero [a'θero] *nm* steel; **~ inoxidable** stainless steel.
acerque [a'θerke] *etc vb V* **acercar.**
acérrimo, a [a'θerrimo, a] *adj* (*partidario*) staunch; (*enemigo*) bitter.
acertado, a [aθer'taðo, a] *adj* correct; (*apropiado*) apt; (*sensato*) sensible.
acertar [aθer'tar] *vt* (*blanco*) to hit; (*solución*) to get right; (*adivinar*) to guess

♦ *vi* to get it right, be right; ~ **a** to manage to; ~ **con** to happen *o* hit on.
acertijo [aθer'tixo] *nm* riddle, puzzle.
acervo [a'θerβo] *nm* heap; ~ **común** undivided estate.
achacar [atʃa'kar] *vt* to attribute.
achacoso, a [atʃa'koso, a] *adj* sickly.
achantar [atʃan'tar] *vt* (*fam*) to scare, frighten; ~**se** *vr* to back down.
achaque [a'tʃake] *etc vb V* **achacar** ♦ *nm* ailment.
achatar [atʃa'tar] *vt* to flatten.
achicar [atʃi'kar] *vt* to reduce; (*humillar*) to humiliate; (*NAUT*) to bale out; ~**se** (*ropa*) to shrink; (*fig*) to humble o.s.
achicharrar [atʃitʃa'rrar] *vt* to scorch, burn.
achicoria [atʃi'korja] *nf* chicory.
achinado, a [atʃi'naðo, a] *adj* (*ojos*) slanting; (*AM*) half-caste.
achique [a'tʃike] *etc vb V* **achicar**.
acholado, a [atʃo'laðo, a] *adj* (*AM*) half-caste.
achuchar [atʃu'tʃar] *vt* to crush.
achuchón [atʃu'tʃon] *nm* shove; **tener un** ~ (*MED*) to be poorly.
achuras [a'tʃuras] *nf* (*AM CULIN*) offal.
aciago, a [a'θjaɣo, a] *adj* ill-fated, fateful.
acicalar [aθika'lar] *vt* to polish; (*adornar*) to bedeck; ~**se** *vr* to get dressed up.
acicate [aθi'kate] *nm* spur; (*fig*) incentive.
acidez [aθi'ðeθ] *nf* acidity.
ácido, a ['aθiðo, a] *adj* sour, acid ♦ *nm* acid; (*fam*: *droga*) LSD.
acierto [a'θjerto] *etc vb V* **acertar** ♦ *nm* success; (*buen paso*) wise move; (*solución*) solution; (*habilidad*) skill, ability; (*al adivinar*) good guess; **fue un** ~ **suyo** it was a sensible choice on his part.
aclamación [aklama'θjon] *nf* acclamation; (*aplausos*) applause.
aclamar [akla'mar] *vt* to acclaim; to applaud.
aclaración [aklara'θjon] *nf* clarification, explanation.
aclarar [akla'rar] *vt* to clarify, explain; (*ropa*) to rinse ♦ *vi* to clear up; ~**se** *vr* (*suj*: *persona*: *explicarse*) to understand; (*fig*: *asunto*) to become clear; ~**se la garganta** to clear one's throat.
aclaratorio, a [aklara'torjo, a] *adj* explanatory.
aclimatación [aklimata'θjon] *nf* acclimatization.
aclimatar [aklima'tar] *vt* to acclimatize; ~**se** *vr* to become *o* get acclimatized; ~**se a algo** to get used to sth.
acné [ak'ne] *nm* acne.
acobardar [akoβar'ðar] *vt* to daunt, intimidate; ~**se** *vr* (*atemorizarse*) to be intimidated; (*echarse atrás*): ~**se (ante)** to shrink back (from).
acodarse [ako'ðarse] *vr*: ~ **en** to lean on.
acogedor, a [akoxe'ðor, a] *adj* welcoming; (*hospitalario*) hospitable.
acoger [ako'xer] *vt* to welcome; (*abrigar*) to shelter; ~**se** *vr* to take refuge; ~**se a** (*pretexto*) to take refuge in; (*ley*) to resort to.
acogida [ako'xiða] *nf* reception; refuge.
acoja [a'koxa] *etc vb V* **acoger**.
acojonante [akoxo'nante] *adj* (*ESP fam*) tremendous.
acolchar [akol'tʃar] *vt* to pad; (*fig*) to cushion.
acólito [a'kolito] *nm* (*REL*) acolyte; (*fig*) minion.
acometer [akome'ter] *vt* to attack; (*emprender*) to undertake.
acometida [akome'tiða] *nf* attack, assault.
acomodado, a [akomo'ðaðo, a] *adj* (*persona*) well-to-do.
acomodador, a [akomoða'ðor, a] *nm/f* usher(ette).
acomodar [akomo'ðar] *vt* to adjust; (*alojar*) to accommodate; ~**se** *vr* to conform; (*instalarse*) to install o.s.; (*adaptarse*) to adapt o.s.; **¡acomódese a su gusto!** make yourself comfortable!
acomodaticio, a [akomoða'tiθjo, a] *adj* (*pey*) accommodating, obliging; (*manejable*) pliable.
acompañamiento [akompaɲa'mjento] *nm* (*MUS*) accompaniment.
acompañante, a [akompa'ɲante, a] *nm/f* companion.
acompañar [akompa'ɲar] *vt* to accompany, go with; (*documentos*) to enclose; **¿quieres que te acompañe?** do you want me to come with you?; ~ **a algn a la puerta** to see sb to the door *o* out; **le acompaño en el sentimiento** please accept my condolences.
acompasar [akompa'sar] *vt* (*MUS*) to mark the rhythm of.
acomplejado, a [akomple'xaðo, a] *adj* neurotic.
acomplejar [akomple'xar] *vt* to give a complex to; ~**se** *vr*: ~**se (con)** to get a complex (about).
acondicionado, a [akondiθjo'naðo, a] *adj* (*TEC*) in good condition.
acondicionador [akondiθjona'ðor] *nm* conditioner.
acondicionar [akondiθjo'nar] *vt* to get

ready, prepare; (*pelo*) to condition.
acongojar [akongo'xar] *vt* to distress, grieve.
aconsejable [akonse'xaßle] *adj* advisable.
aconsejar [akonse'xar] *vt* to advise, counsel; **~se** *vr*: **~se con** *o* **de** to consult.
acontecer [akonte'θer] *vi* to happen, occur.
acontecimiento [akonteθi'mjento] *nm* event.
acontezca [akon'teθka] *etc vb V* **acontecer**.
acopiar [ako'pjar] *vt* (*recoger*) to gather; (*COM*) to buy up.
acopio [a'kopjo] *nm* store, stock.
acoplador [akopla'ðor] *nm*: **~ acústico** (*INFORM*) acoustic coupler.
acoplamiento [akopla'mjento] *nm* coupling, joint.
acoplar [ako'plar] *vt* to fit; (*ELEC*) to connect; (*vagones*) to couple.
acoquinar [akoki'nar] *vt* to scare; **~se** *vr* to get scared.
acorazado, a [akora'θaðo, a] *adj* armour-plated, armoured ♦ *nm* battleship.
acordar [akor'ðar] *vt* (*resolver*) to agree, resolve; (*recordar*) to remind; **~se** *vr* to agree; **~se (de algo)** to remember (sth).
acorde [a'korðe] *adj* (*MUS*) harmonious; **~ con** (*medidas etc*) in keeping with ♦ *nm* chord.
acordeón [akorðe'on] *nm* accordion.
acordonado, a [akorðo'naðo, a] *adj* (*calle*) cordoned-off.
acorralar [akorra'lar] *vt* to round up, corral; (*fig*) to intimidate.
acortar [akor'tar] *vt* to shorten; (*duración*) to cut short; (*cantidad*) to reduce; **~se** *vr* to become shorter.
acosar [ako'sar] *vt* to pursue relentlessly; (*fig*) to hound, pester; **~ a algn a preguntas** to pester sb with questions.
acoso [a'koso] *nm* relentless pursuit; (*fig*) hounding; **~ sexual** sexual harassment.
acostar [akos'tar] *vt* (*en cama*) to put to bed; (*en suelo*) to lay down; (*barco*) to bring alongside; **~se** *vr* to go to bed; to lie down.
acostumbrado, a [akostum'braðo, a] *adj* (*habitual*) usual; **estar ~ a (hacer) algo** to be used to (doing) sth.
acostumbrar [akostum'brar] *vt*: **~ a algn a algo** to get sb used to sth ♦ *vi*: **~ (a hacer algo)** to be in the habit (of doing sth); **~se** *vr*: **~se a** to get used to.
acotación [akota'θjon] *nf* (*apunte*) marginal note; (*GEO*) elevation mark; (*de límite*) boundary mark; (*TEAT*) stage direction.
acotar [ako'tar] *vt* (*terreno*) to mark out; (*fig*) to limit; (*caza*) to protect.
acotejar [akote'xar] *vt* (*AM*) to put in order, arrange.
ácrata ['akrata] *adj*, *nm/f* anarchist.
acre ['akre] *adj* (*sabor*) sharp, bitter; (*olor*) acrid; (*fig*) biting ♦ *nm* acre.
acrecentar [akreθen'tar] *vt* to increase, augment.
acreciente [akre'θjente] *etc vb V* **acrecentar**.
acreditado, a [akreði'taðo, a] *adj* (*POL*) accredited; (*COM*): **una casa acreditada** a reputable firm.
acreditar [akreði'tar] *vt* (*garantizar*) to vouch for, guarantee; (*autorizar*) to authorize; (*dar prueba de*) to prove; (*COM*: *abonar*) to credit; (*embajador*) to accredit; **~se** *vr* to become famous; (*demostrar valía*) to prove one's worth; **~se de** to get a reputation for.
acreedor, a [akree'ðor, a] *adj*: **~ a** worthy of ♦ *nm/f* creditor; **~ común/diferido/con garantía** (*COM*) unsecured/deferred/secured creditor.
acribillar [akrißi'ʎar] *vt*: **~ a balazos** to riddle with bullets.
acrimonia [akri'monja], **acritud** [akri'tuð] *nf* acrimony.
acrobacia [akro'ßaθja] *nf* acrobatics; **~ aérea** aerobatics.
acróbata [a'kroßata] *nm/f* acrobat.
acta ['akta] *nf* certificate; (*de comisión*) minutes *pl*, record; **~ de nacimiento/de matrimonio** birth/marriage certificate; **~ notarial** affidavit; **levantar ~** (*JUR*) to make a formal statement *o* deposition.
actitud [akti'tuð] *nf* attitude; (*postura*) posture; **adoptar una ~ firme** to take a firm stand.
activar [akti'ßar] *vt* to activate; (*acelerar*) to speed up.
actividad [aktißi'ðað] *nf* activity; **estar en plena ~** to be in full swing.
activo, a [ak'tißo, a] *adj* active; (*vivo*) lively ♦ *nm* (*COM*) assets *pl*; **~ y pasivo** assets and liabilities; **~ circulante/fijo/inmaterial/invisible** (*COM*) current/fixed/intangible/invisible assets; **~ realizable** liquid assets; **~s congelados** *o* **bloqueados** frozen assets; **estar en ~** (*MIL*) to be on active service.
acto ['akto] *nm* act, action; (*ceremonia*) ceremony; (*TEAT*) act; **en el ~** immediately; **hacer ~ de presencia** (*asistir*) to attend (formally).
actor [ak'tor] *nm* actor; (*JUR*) plaintiff.
actora [ak'tora] *adj*: **parte ~** prosecution;

(*demandante*) plaintiff.
actriz [ak'triθ] *nf* actress.
actuación [aktwa'θjon] *nf* action; (*comportamiento*) conduct, behaviour; (*JUR*) proceedings *pl*; (*desempeño*) performance.
actual [ak'twal] *adj* present(-day), current; **el 6 del ~** the 6th of this month.
actualice [aktwa'liθe] *etc vb V* **actualizar**.
actualidad [aktwali'ðað] *nf* present; **~es** *nfpl* news *sg*; **en la ~** nowadays, at present; **ser de gran ~** to be current.
actualización [aktwaliθa'θjon] *nf* updating, modernization.
actualizar [aktwali'θar] *vt* to update, modernize.
actualmente [aktwal'mente] *adv* at present; (*hoy día*) nowadays.
actuar [ak'twar] *vi* (*obrar*) to work, operate; (*actor*) to act, perform ♦ *vt* to work, operate; **~ de** to act as.
actuario, a [ak'twarjo] *nm/f* clerk; (*COM*) actuary.
acuarela [akwa'rela] *nf* watercolour.
acuario [a'kwarjo] *nm* aquarium; **A~** (*ASTRO*) Aquarius.
acuartelar [akwarte'lar] *vt* (*MIL*: *alojar*) to quarter.
acuático, a [a'kwatiko, a] *adj* aquatic.
acuchillar [akutʃi'ʎar] *vt* (*TEC*) to plane (down), smooth.
acuciar [aku'θjar] *vt* to urge on.
acuclillarse [akukli'ʎarse] *vr* to crouch down.
ACUDE [a'kuðe] *nf abr* = *Asociación de Consumidores y Usuarios de España*.
acudir [aku'ðir] *vi* to attend, turn up; **~ a** to turn to; **~ en ayuda de** to go to the aid of; **~ a una cita** to keep an appointment; **~ a una llamada** to answer a call; **no tener a quién ~** to have nobody to turn to.
acuerdo [a'kwerðo] *etc vb V* **acordar** ♦ *nm* agreement; (*POL*) resolution; **~ de pago respectivo** (*COM*) knock-for-knock agreement; **A~ general sobre aranceles aduaneros y comercio** (*COM*) General Agreement on Tariffs and Trade; **tomar un ~** to pass a resolution; **¡de ~!** agreed!; **de ~ con** (*persona*) in agreement with; (*acción, documento*) in accordance with; **de común ~** by common consent; **estar de ~** (*persona*) to agree; **llegar a un ~** to come to an understanding.
acueste [a'kweste] *etc vb V* **acostar**.
acullá [aku'ʎa] *adv* over there.
acumular [akumu'lar] *vt* to accumulate, collect.
acunar [aku'nar] *vt* to rock (to sleep).
acuñar [aku'ɲar] *vt* (*moneda*) to mint; (*frase*) to coin.
acuoso, a [a'kwoso, a] *adj* watery.
acupuntura [akupun'tura] *nf* acupuncture.
acurrucarse [akurru'karse] *vr* to crouch; (*ovillarse*) to curl up.
acurruque [aku'rruke] *etc vb V* **acurrucarse**.
acusación [akusa'θjon] *nf* accusation.
acusado, a [aku'saðo, a] *adj* (*JUR*) accused; (*marcado*) marked; (*acento*) strong.
acusar [aku'sar] *vt* to accuse; (*revelar*) to reveal; (*denunciar*) to denounce; (*emoción*) to show; **~ recibo** to acknowledge receipt; **su rostro acusó extrañeza** his face registered surprise; **~se** *vr*: **~se (de)** to confess (to).
acuse [a'kuse] *nm*: **~ de recibo** acknowledgement of receipt.
acústico, a [a'kustiko, a] *adj* acoustic ♦ *nf* (*de una sala etc*) acoustics *pl*; (*ciencia*) acoustics *sg*.
ADA ['aða] *nf abr* (*ESP*: = *Ayuda del Automovilista*) ≈ AA, RAC (*BRIT*), AAA (*US*).
adagio [a'ðaxjo] *nm* adage; (*MUS*) adagio.
adalid [aða'lið] *nm* leader, champion.
adaptación [aðapta'θjon] *nf* adaptation.
adaptador [aðapta'ðor] *nm* (*ELEC*) adapter.
adaptar [aðap'tar] *vt* to adapt; (*acomodar*) to fit; (*convertir*): **~ (para)** to convert (to).
adecentar [aðeθen'tar] *vt* to tidy up.
adecuado, a [aðe'kwaðo, a] *adj* (*apto*) suitable; (*oportuno*) appropriate; **el hombre ~ para el puesto** the right man for the job.
adecuar [aðe'kwar] *vt* (*adaptar*) to adapt; (*hacer apto*) to make suitable.
adefesio [aðe'fesjo] *nm* (*fam*): **estaba hecha un ~** she looked a sight.
a. de J.C. *abr* (= *antes de Jesucristo*) B.C.
adelantado, a [aðelan'taðo, a] *adj* advanced; (*reloj*) fast; **pagar por ~** to pay in advance.
adelantamiento [aðelanta'mjento] *nm* advance, advancement; (*AUTO*) overtaking.
adelantar [aðelan'tar] *vt* to move forward; (*avanzar*) to advance; (*acelerar*) to speed up; (*AUTO*) to overtake ♦ *vi* (*ir delante*) to go ahead; (*progresar*) to improve; (*tb*: **~se** *vr*: *tomar la delantera*) to go forward, advance; **~se a algn** to get ahead of sb; **~se a los deseos de algn** to anticipate sb's wishes.
adelante [aðe'lante] *adv* forward(s),

onward(s), ahead ♦ *excl* come in!; **de hoy en** ~ from now on; **más** ~ later on; (*más allá*) further on.
adelanto [aðe'lanto] *nm* advance; (*mejora*) improvement; (*progreso*) progress; (*dinero*) advance; **los ~s de la ciencia** the advances of science.
adelgace [aðel'ɣaθe] *etc vb V* **adelgazar**.
adelgazar [aðelɣa'θar] *vt* to thin (down); (*afilar*) to taper ♦ *vi* to get thin; (*con régimen*) to slim down, lose weight.
ademán [aðe'man] *nm* gesture; **ademanes** *nmpl* manners; **en** ~ **de** as if to.
además [aðe'mas] *adv* besides; (*por otra parte*) moreover; (*también*) also; ~ **de** besides, in addition to.
ADENA [a'ðena] *nf abr* (*ESP:* = *Asociación para la Defensa de la Naturaleza*) *organization for nature conservation.*
adentrarse [aðen'trarse] *vr*: ~ **en** to go into, get inside; (*penetrar*) to penetrate (into).
adentro [a'ðentro] *adv* inside, in; **mar** ~ out at sea; **tierra** ~ inland ♦ *nm*: **dijo para sus ~s** he said to himself.
adepto, a [a'ðepto, a] *nm/f* supporter.
aderece [aðe'reθe] *etc vb V* **aderezar**.
aderezar [aðere'θar] *vt* (*ensalada*) to dress; (*comida*) to season.
aderezo [aðe'reθo] *nm* dressing; seasoning.
adeudar [aðeu'ðar] *vt* to owe; **~se** *vr* to run into debt; ~ **una suma en una cuenta** to debit an account with a sum.
a.D.g. *abr* (= *a Dios gracias*) D.G. (= *Deo gratias: thanks be to God*).
adherirse [aðe'rirse] *vr*: ~ **a** to adhere to; (*fig*) to follow.
adhesión [aðe'sjon] *nf* adhesion; (*fig*) adherence.
adhesivo, a [aðe'siβo, a] *adj* adhesive ♦ *nm* sticker.
adhiera [a'ðjera] *etc*, **adhiriendo** [aði'rjendo] *etc vb V* **adherirse**.
adicción [aðik'θion] *nf* addiction.
adición [aði'θjon] *nf* addition.
adicional [aðiθjo'nal] *adj* additional; (*INFORM*) add-on.
adicionar [aðiθjo'nar] *vt* to add.
adicto, a [a'ðikto, a] *adj*: ~ **a** (*droga etc*) addicted to; (*dedicado*) devoted to ♦ *nm/f* supporter, follower; (*toxicómano etc*) addict.
adiestrar [aðjes'trar] *vt* to train, teach; (*conducir*) to guide, lead; **~se** *vr* to practise; (*enseñarse*) to train o.s.
adinerado, a [aðine'raðo, a] *adj* wealthy.
adiós [a'ðjos] *excl* (*para despedirse*) goodbye!, cheerio!; (*al pasar*) hello!
aditivo [aði'tiβo] *nm* additive.
adivinanza [aðiβi'nanθa] *nf* riddle.
adivinar [aðiβi'nar] *vt* (*profetizar*) to prophesy; (*conjeturar*) to guess.
adivino, a [aði'βino, a] *nm/f* fortune-teller.
adj *abr* (= *adjunto*) encl.
adjetivo [aðxe'tiβo] *nm* adjective.
adjudicación [aðxuðika'θjon] *nf* award; (*COM*) adjudication.
adjudicar [aðxuði'kar] *vt* to award; **~se** *vr*: **~se algo** to appropriate sth.
adjudique [aðxu'ðike] *etc vb V* **adjudicar**.
adjuntar [aðxun'tar] *vt* to attach, enclose.
adjunto, a [að'xunto, a] *adj* attached, enclosed ♦ *nm/f* assistant.
adminículo [aðmi'nikulo] *nm* gadget.
administración [aðministra'θjon] *nf* administration; (*dirección*) management; ~ **pública** civil service; **A~ de Correos** General Post Office.
administrador, a [aðministra'ðor, a] *nm/f* administrator; manager(ess).
administrar [aðminis'trar] *vt* to administer.
administrativo, a [aðministra'tiβo, a] *adj* administrative.
admirable [aðmi'raβle] *adj* admirable.
admiración [aðmira'θjon] *nf* admiration; (*asombro*) wonder; (*LING*) exclamation mark.
admirar [aðmi'rar] *vt* to admire; (*extrañar*) to surprise; **~se** *vr* to be surprised; **se admiró de saberlo** he was amazed to hear it; **no es de** ~ **que** ... it's not surprising that ...
admisible [aðmi'siβle] *adj* admissible.
admisión [aðmi'sjon] *nf* admission; (*reconocimiento*) acceptance.
admitir [aðmi'tir] *vt* to admit; (*aceptar*) to accept; (*dudas*) to leave room for; **esto no admite demora** this must be dealt with immediately.
admón. *abr* (= *administración*) admin.
admonición [aðmoni'θjon] *nf* warning.
ADN *nm abr* (= *acido desoxirribonucleico*) DNA.
adobar [aðo'βar] *vt* (*preparar*) to prepare; (*cocinar*) to season.
adobe [a'ðoβe] *nm* adobe, sun-dried brick.
adocenado, a [aðoθe'naðo, a] *adj* (*fam*) mediocre.
adoctrinar [aðoktri'nar] *vt* to indoctrinate.
adolecer [aðole'θer] *vi*: ~ **de** to suffer from.
adolescente [aðoles'θente] *nm/f* adolescent, teenager ♦ *adj* adolescent, teenage.

adolezca [aðo'leθka] *etc vb V* **adolecer**.
adonde [a'ðonde] *adv* (to) where.
adónde [a'ðonde] *adv* = **dónde**.
adondequiera [aðonde'kjera] *adv* wherever.
adopción [aðop'θjon] *nf* adoption.
adoptar [aðop'tar] *vt* to adopt.
adoptivo, a [aðop'tiβo, a] *adj* (*padres*) adoptive; (*hijo*) adopted.
adoquín [aðo'kin] *nm* paving stone.
adorar [aðo'rar] *vt* to adore.
adormecer [aðorme'θer] *vt* to put to sleep; ~**se** *vr* to become sleepy; (*dormirse*) to fall asleep.
adormezca [aðor'meθka] *etc vb V* **adormecer**.
adormilarse [aðormi'larse] *vr* to doze.
adornar [aðor'nar] *vt* to adorn.
adorno [a'ðorno] *nm* adornment; (*decoración*) decoration.
adosado, a [aðo'saðo, a] *adj* (*casa*) semidetached.
adquiera [að'kjera] *etc vb V* **adquirir**.
adquirir [aðki'rir] *vt* to acquire, obtain.
adquisición [aðkisi'θjon] *nf* acquisition; (*compra*) purchase.
adrede [a'ðreðe] *adv* on purpose.
Adriático [að'rjatiko] *nm*: **el (Mar)** ~ the Adriatic (Sea).
adscribir [aðskri'βir] *vt* to appoint; **estuvo adscrito al servicio de ...** he was attached to ...
adscrito [að'skrito] *pp de* **adscribir**.
aduana [a'ðwana] *nf* customs *pl*; (*impuesto*) (customs) duty.
aduanero, a [aðwa'nero, a] *adj* customs *cpd* ♦ *nm/f* customs officer.
aducir [aðu'θir] *vt* to adduce; (*dar como prueba*) to offer as proof.
adueñarse [aðwe'ɲarse] *vr*: ~ **de** to take possession of.
adulación [aðula'θjon] *nf* flattery.
adular [aðu'lar] *vt* to flatter.
adulterar [aðulte'rar] *vt* to adulterate ♦ *vi* to commit adultery.
adulterio [aðul'terjo] *nm* adultery.
adúltero, a [a'ðultero, a] *adj* adulterous ♦ *nm/f* adulterer/adulteress.
adulto, a [a'ðulto, a] *adj, nm/f* adult.
adusto, a [a'ðusto, a] *adj* stern; (*austero*) austere.
aduzca [a'ðuθka] *etc vb V* **aducir**.
advenedizo, a [aðβene'ðiθo, a] *nm/f* upstart.
advenimiento [aðβeni'mjento] *nm* arrival; (*al trono*) accession.
adverbio [að'βerβjo] *nm* adverb.
adversario, a [aðβer'sarjo, a] *nm/f* adversary.
adversidad [aðβersi'ðað] *nf* adversity; (*contratiempo*) setback.
adverso, a [að'βerso, a] *adj* adverse; (*suerte*) bad.
advertencia [aðβer'tenθja] *nf* warning; (*prefacio*) preface, foreword.
advertir [aðβer'tir] *vt* (*observar*) to notice; (*avisar*): ~ **a algn de** to warn sb about *o* of.
Adviento [að'βjento] *nm* Advent.
advierta [að'βjerta] *etc*, **advirtiendo** [aðβir'tjendo] *etc vb V* **advertir**.
adyacente [aðja'θente] *adj* adjacent.
aéreo, a [a'ereo, a] *adj* aerial; (*tráfico*) air *cpd*.
aerobic [ae'roβik] *nm* aerobics *sg*.
aerodeslizador [aeroðesliθa'ðor] *nm* hovercraft.
aerodinámico, a [aeroði'namiko, a] *adj* aerodynamic.
aeródromo [ae'roðromo] *nm* aerodrome.
aerograma [aero'ɣrama] *nm* airmail letter.
aeromodelismo [aeromoðe'lismo] *nm* model aircraft making, aeromodelling.
aeromozo, a [aero'moso, a] *nm/f* (*AM*) flight attendant, air steward(ess).
aeronáutico, a [aero'nautiko, a] *adj* aeronautical.
aeronave [aero'naβe] *nm* spaceship.
aeroplano [aero'plano] *nm* aeroplane.
aeropuerto [aero'pwerto] *nm* airport.
aerosol [aero'sol] *nm* aerosol, spray.
a/f *abr* (= *a favor*) in favour.
afabilidad [afaβili'ðað] *nf* affability, pleasantness.
afable [a'faβle] *adj* affable, pleasant.
afamado, a [afa'maðo, a] *adj* famous.
afán [a'fan] *nm* hard work; (*deseo*) desire; **con** ~ keenly.
afanar [afa'nar] *vt* to harass; (*fam*) to pinch; ~**se** *vr*: ~**se por** to strive to.
afanoso, a [afa'noso, a] *adj* (*trabajo*) hard; (*trabajador*) industrious.
AFE ['afe] *nf abr* (= *Asociación de Futbolistas Españoles*) ≈ F.A.
afear [afe'ar] *vt* to disfigure.
afección [afek'θjon] *nf* affection; (*MED*) disease.
afectación [afekta'θjon] *nf* affectation.
afectado, a [afek'taðo, a] *adj* affected.
afectar [afek'tar] *vt* to affect, have an effect on; (*AM*: *dañar*) to hurt; **por lo que afecta a esto** as far as this is concerned.
afectísimo , **a** [afek'tisimo, a] *adj* affectionate; **suyo** ~ yours truly.
afectivo, a [afek'tiβo, a] *adj* affective.
afecto, a [a'fekto, a] *adj*: ~ **a** fond of; (*JUR*)

subject to ♦ *nm* affection; **tenerle ~ a algn** to be fond of sb.
afectuoso, a [afek'twoso, a] *adj* affectionate.
afeitar [afei'tar] *vt* to shave; **~se** *vr* to shave.
afeminado, a [afemi'naðo, a] *adj* effeminate.
aferrar [afe'rrar] *vt* to moor; (*fig*) to grasp ♦ *vi* to moor; **~se** *vr* (*agarrarse*) to cling on; **~se a un principio** to stick to a principle; **~se a una esperanza** to cling to a hope.
affmo., a. *abr* (= *afectísimo, a*) Yours.
Afganistán [afɣanis'tan] *nm* Afghanistan.
afgano, a [af'ɣano, a] *adj, nm/f* Afghan.
afiance [a'fjanθe] *etc vb V* **afianzar**.
afianzamiento [afjanθa'mjento] *nm* strengthening; security.
afianzar [afjan'θar] *vt* to strengthen, secure; **~se** *vr* to steady o.s.; (*establecerse*) to become established.
afiche [a'fitʃe] *nm* (*AM*) poster.
afición [afi'θjon] *nf*: **~ a** fondness *o* liking for; **la ~** the fans *pl*; **pinto por ~** I paint as a hobby.
aficionado, a [afiθjo'naðo, a] *adj* keen, enthusiastic; (*no profesional*) amateur ♦ *nm/f* enthusiast, fan; amateur.
aficionar [afiθjo'nar] *vt*: **~ a algn a algo** to make sb like sth; **~se** *vr*: **~se a algo** to grow fond of sth.
afilado, a [afi'laðo, a] *adj* sharp.
afilador [afila'ðor] *nm* (*persona*) knife grinder.
afilalápices [afila'lapiθes] *nm inv* pencil sharpener.
afilar [afi'lar] *vt* to sharpen; **~se** *vr* (*cara*) to grow thin.
afiliación [afilja'θjon] *nf* (*de sindicatos*) membership.
afiliado, a [afi'ljaðo, a] *adj* subsidiary ♦ *nm/f* affiliate.
afiliarse [afi'ljarse] *vr* to affiliate.
afín [a'fin] *adj* (*parecido*) similar; (*conexo*) related.
afinar [afi'nar] *vt* (*TEC*) to refine; (*MUS*) to tune ♦ *vi* to play/sing in tune.
afincarse [afin'karse] *vr* to settle.
afinidad [afini'ðað] *nf* affinity; (*parentesco*) relationship; **por ~** by marriage.
afirmación [afirma'θjon] *nf* affirmation.
afirmar [afir'mar] *vt* to affirm, state; (*sostener*) to strengthen; **~se** *vr* (*recuperar el equilibrio*) to steady o.s.; **~se en lo dicho** to stand by what one has said.
afirmativo, a [afirma'tiβo, a] *adj* affirmative.
aflicción [aflik'θjon] *nf* affliction; (*dolor*) grief.
afligir [afli'xir] *vt* to afflict; (*apenar*) to distress; **~se** *vr*: **~se (por *o* con *o* de)** to grieve (about *o* at); **no te aflijas tanto** you must not let it affect you like this.
aflija [a'flixa] *etc vb V* **afligir**.
aflojar [aflo'xar] *vt* to slacken; (*desatar*) to loosen, undo; (*relajar*) to relax ♦ *vi* (*amainar*) to drop; (*bajar*) to go down; **~se** *vr* to relax.
aflorar [aflo'rar] *vi* (*GEO, fig*) to come to the surface, emerge.
afluencia [aflu'enθja] *nf* flow.
afluente [aflu'ente] *adj* flowing ♦ *nm* (*GEO*) tributary.
afluir [aflu'ir] *vi* to flow.
afluya [a'fluja] *etc*, **afluyendo** [aflu'jendo] *etc vb V* **afluir**.
afmo., a. *abr* (= *afectísimo, a suyo, a*) Yours.
afónico, a [a'foniko, a] *adj*: **estar ~** to have a sore throat; to have lost one's voice.
aforar [afo'rar] *vt* (*TEC*) to gauge; (*fig*) to value.
aforo [a'foro] *nm* (*TEC*) gauging; (*de teatro etc*) capacity; **el teatro tiene un ~ de 2,000** the theatre can seat 2,000.
afortunado, a [afortu'naðo, a] *adj* fortunate, lucky.
afrancesado, a [afranθe'saðo, a] *adj* francophile; (*pey*) Frenchified.
afrenta [a'frenta] *nf* affront, insult; (*deshonra*) dishonour (*BRIT*), dishonor (*US*), shame.
afrentoso, a [afren'toso, a] *adj* insulting; shameful.
África ['afrika] *nf* Africa; **~ del Sur** South Africa.
africano, a [afri'kano, a] *adj, nm/f* African.
afrontar [afron'tar] *vt* to confront; (*poner cara a cara*) to bring face to face.
afuera [a'fwera] *adv* out, outside; **por ~** on the outside; **~s** *nfpl* outskirts.
ag. *abr* (= *agosto*) Aug.
agachar [aɣa'tʃar] *vt* to bend, bow; **~se** *vr* to stoop, bend.
agalla [a'ɣaʎa] *nf* (*ZOOL*) gill; **~s** *nfpl* (*MED*) tonsillitis *sg*; (*ANAT*) tonsils; **tener ~s** (*fam*) to have guts.
agarradera [aɣarra'ðera] *nf* (*AM*), **agarradero** [aɣarra'ðero] *nm* handle; **~s** *nfpl* pull *sg*, influence *sg*.
agarrado, a [aɣa'rraðo, a] *adj* mean, stingy.
agarrar [aɣa'rrar] *vt* to grasp, grab; (*AM*) to take, catch ♦ *vi* (*planta*) to take root; **~se** *vr* to hold on (tightly); (*meterse uno con otro*) to grapple (with each other);

agarrársela con algn (*AM*) to pick on sb; **agarró y se fue** (*esp AM fam*) he upped and went.

agarrotar [aɣarro'tar] *vt* (*lío*) to tie tightly; (*persona*) to squeeze tightly; (*reo*) to garrotte; ~**se** *vr* (*motor*) to seize up; (*MED*) to stiffen.

agasajar [aɣasa'xar] *vt* to treat well, fête.

agave [a'ɣaβe] *nf* agave.

agazapar [aɣaθa'par] *vt* (*coger*) to grab hold of; ~**se** *vr* (*agacharse*) to crouch down.

agencia [a'xenθja] *nf* agency; ~ **de créditos/publicidad/viajes** credit/advertising/travel agency; ~ **inmobiliaria** estate agent's (office) (*BRIT*), real estate office (*US*); ~ **matrimonial** marriage bureau.

agenciar [axen'θjar] *vt* to bring about; ~**se** *vr* to look after o.s.; ~**se algo** to get hold of sth.

agenda [a'xenda] *nf* diary; ~ **telefónica** telephone directory.

agente [a'xente] *nm* agent; (*de policía*) policeman; ~ **femenino** policewoman; ~ **acreditado** (*COM*) accredited agent; ~ **de bolsa** stockbroker; ~ **inmobiliario** estate agent (*BRIT*), realtor (*US*); ~ **de negocios** (*COM*) business agent; ~ **de seguros** insurance broker; ~ **de viajes** travel agent; ~**s sociales** social partners.

ágil ['axil] *adj* agile, nimble.

agilidad [axili'ðað] *nf* agility, nimbleness.

agilizar [axili'θar] *vt* to speed up.

agitación [axita'θjon] *nf* (*de mano etc*) shaking, waving; (*de líquido etc*) stirring; agitation.

agitar [axi'tar] *vt* to wave, shake; (*líquido*) to stir; (*fig*) to stir up, excite; ~**se** *vr* to get excited; (*inquietarse*) to get worried *o* upset.

aglomeración [aɣlomera'θjon] *nf*: ~ **de tráfico/gente** traffic jam/mass of people.

aglomerar [aɣlome'rar] *vt*, ~**se** *vr* to crowd together.

agnóstico, a [aɣ'nostiko, a] *adj, nm/f* agnostic.

ag.º *abr* = **ag.**

agobiante [aɣo'βjante] *adj* (*calor*) oppressive.

agobiar [aɣo'βjar] *vt* to weigh down; (*oprimir*) to oppress; (*cargar*) to burden; **sentirse agobiado por** to be overwhelmed by.

agobio [a'ɣoβjo] *nm* (*peso*) burden; (*fig*) oppressiveness.

agolpamiento [aɣolpa'mjento] *nm* crush.

agolparse [aɣol'parse] *vr* to crowd together.

agonía [aɣo'nia] *nf* death throes *pl*; (*fig*) agony, anguish.

agonice [aɣo'niθe] *etc vb V* **agonizar**.

agonizante [aɣoni'θante] *adj* dying.

agonizar [aɣoni'θar] *vi* (*tb:* **estar agonizando**) to be dying.

agorero, a [aɣo'rero, a] *adj* ominous ♦ *nm/f* soothsayer; **ave agorera** bird of ill omen.

agostar [aɣo'star] *vt* (*quemar*) to parch; (*fig*) to wither.

agosto [a'ɣosto] *nm* August; (*fig*) harvest; **hacer su** ~ to make one's pile.

agotado, a [aɣo'taðo, a] *adj* (*persona*) exhausted; (*acabado*) finished; (*COM*) sold out; (*: libros*) out of print; (*pila*) flat.

agotador, a [aɣota'ðor, a] *adj* exhausting.

agotamiento [aɣota'mjento] *nm* exhaustion.

agotar [aɣo'tar] *vt* to exhaust; (*consumir*) to drain; (*recursos*) to use up, deplete; ~**se** *vr* to be exhausted; (*acabarse*) to run out; (*libro*) to go out of print.

agraciado, a [aɣra'θjaðo, a] *adj* (*atractivo*) attractive; (*en sorteo etc*) lucky.

agraciar [aɣra'θjar] *vt* (*JUR*) to pardon; (*con premio*) to reward; (*hacer más atractivo*) to make more attractive.

agradable [aɣra'ðaβle] *adj* pleasant, nice.

agradar [aɣra'ðar] *vt, vi* to please; ~**se** *vr* to like each other.

agradecer [aɣraðe'θer] *vt* to thank; (*favor etc*) to be grateful for; **le agradecería me enviara** ... I would be grateful if you would send me ...; ~**se** *vr*: **¡se agradece!** much obliged!

agradecido, a [aɣraðe'θiðo, a] *adj* grateful; **¡muy** ~! thanks a lot!

agradecimiento [aɣraðeθi'mjento] *nm* thanks *pl*; gratitude.

agradezca [aɣra'ðeθka] *etc vb V* **agradecer**.

agrado [a'ɣraðo] *nm*: **ser de tu** *etc* ~ to be to your *etc* liking.

agrandar [aɣran'dar] *vt* to enlarge; (*fig*) to exaggerate; ~**se** *vr* to get bigger.

agrario, a [a'ɣrarjo, a] *adj* agrarian, land *cpd*; (*política*) agricultural, farming *cpd*.

agravante [aɣra'βante] *adj* aggravating ♦ *nf* complication; **con la** ~ **de que** ... with the further difficulty that ...

agravar [aɣra'βar] *vt* (*pesar sobre*) to make heavier; (*irritar*) to aggravate; ~**se** *vr* to worsen, get worse.

agraviar [aɣra'βjar] *vt* to offend; (*ser injusto con*) to wrong; ~**se** *vr* to take offence.

agravio [a'ɣraβjo] *nm* offence; wrong;

(*JUR*) grievance.
agraz [a'ɣraθ] *nm* (*uva*) sour grape; **en ~** (*fig*) immature.
agredir [aɣre'ðir] *vt* to attack.
agregado [aɣre'ɣaðo] *nm* aggregate; (*persona*) attaché; (*profesor*) assistant professor.
agregar [aɣre'ɣar] *vt* to gather; (*añadir*) to add; (*persona*) to appoint.
agregue [a'ɣreɣe] *etc vb V* **agregar**.
agresión [aɣre'sjon] *nf* aggression; (*ataque*) attack.
agresivo, a [aɣre'siβo, a] *adj* aggressive.
agreste [a'ɣreste] *adj* (*rural*) rural; (*fig*) rough.
agriar [a'ɣrjar] *vt* (*fig*) to (turn) sour; **~se** *vr* to turn sour.
agrícola [a'ɣrikola] *adj* farming *cpd*, agricultural.
agricultor, a [aɣrikul'tor, a] *nm/f* farmer.
agricultura [aɣrikul'tura] *nf* agriculture, farming.
agridulce [aɣri'ðulθe] *adj* bittersweet; (*CULIN*) sweet and sour.
agrietarse [aɣrje'tarse] *vr* to crack; (*la piel*) to chap.
agrimensor, a [aɣrimen'sor, a] *nm/f* surveyor.
agringado, a [aɣrin'gaðo, a] *adj* gringolike.
agrio, a ['aɣrjo, a] *adj* bitter.
agronomía [aɣrono'mia] *nf* agronomy, agriculture.
agrónomo, a [a'ɣronomo, a] *nm/f* agronomist, agricultural expert.
agropecuario, a [aɣrope'kwarjo, a] *adj* farming *cpd*, agricultural.
agrupación [aɣrupa'θjon] *nf* group; (*acto*) grouping.
agrupar [aɣru'par] *vt* to group; (*INFORM*) to block; **~se** *vr* (*POL*) to form a group; (*juntarse*) to gather.
agua ['aɣwa] *nf* water; (*NAUT*) wake; (*ARQ*) slope of a roof; **~s** *nfpl* (*de joya*) water *sg*, sparkle *sg*; (*MED*) water *sg*, urine *sg*; (*NAUT*) waters; **~s abajo/arriba** downstream/upstream; **~ bendita/ destilada/potable** holy/distilled/drinking water; **~ caliente** hot water; **~ corriente** running water; **~ de colonia** eau de cologne; **~ mineral (con/sin gas)** (fizzy/ non-fizzy) mineral water; **~s jurisdiccionales** territorial waters; **~s mayores** excrement *sg*; **~ pasada no mueve molino** it's no use crying over spilt milk; **estar con el ~ al cuello** to be up to one's neck; **venir como ~ de mayo** to be a godsend.
aguacate [aɣwa'kate] *nm* avocado (pear).
aguacero [aɣwa'θero] *nm* (heavy) shower, downpour.
aguachirle [aɣwa'tʃirle] *nm* (*bebida*) slops *pl*.
aguado, a [a'ɣwaðo, a] *adj* watery, watered down ♦ *nf* (*AGR*) watering place; (*NAUT*) water supply; (*ARTE*) watercolour.
aguafiestas [aɣwa'fjestas] *nm/f inv* spoilsport.
aguafuerte [aɣwa'fwerte] *nf* etching.
aguaitar [aɣwai'tar] *vt* (*AM*) to watch.
aguanieve [aɣwa'njeβe] *nf* sleet.
aguantable [aɣwan'taβle] *adj* bearable, tolerable.
aguantar [aɣwan'tar] *vt* to bear, put up with; (*sostener*) to hold up ♦ *vi* to last; **~se** *vr* to restrain o.s.; **no sé cómo aguanta** I don't know how he can take it.
aguante [a'ɣwante] *nm* (*paciencia*) patience; (*resistencia*) endurance; (*DEPORTE*) stamina.
aguar [a'ɣwar] *vt* to water down; (*fig*): **~ la fiesta a algn** to spoil sb's fun.
aguardar [aɣwar'ðar] *vt* to wait for.
aguardentoso, a [aɣwarðen'toso, a] *adj* (*pey: voz*) husky, gruff.
aguardiente [aɣwar'ðjente] *nm* brandy, liquor.
aguarrás [aɣwa'rras] *nm* turpentine.
aguce [a'ɣuθe] *etc vb V* **aguzar**.
agudeza [aɣu'ðeθa] *nf* sharpness; (*ingenio*) wit.
agudice [aɣu'ðiθe] *etc vb V* **agudizar**.
agudizar [aɣuði'θar] *vt* to sharpen; (*crisis*) to make worse; **~se** *vr* to worsen, deteriorate.
agudo, a [a'ɣuðo, a] *adj* sharp; (*voz*) high-pitched, piercing; (*dolor, enfermedad*) acute.
agüe ['aɣwe] *etc vb V* **aguar**.
agüero [a'ɣwero] *nm*: **buen/mal ~** good/ bad omen; **ser de buen ~** to augur well; **pájaro de mal ~** bird of ill omen.
aguerrido, a [aɣe'rriðo, a] *adj* hardened; (*fig*) experienced.
aguijar [aɣi'xar] *vt* to goad; (*incitar*) to urge on ♦ *vi* to hurry along.
aguijón [aɣi'xon] *nm* sting; (*fig*) spur.
aguijonear [aɣixone'ar] *vt* = **aguijar**.
águila ['aɣila] *nf* eagle; (*fig*) genius.
aguileño, a [aɣi'leɲo, a] *adj* (*nariz*) aquiline; (*rostro*) sharp-featured.
aguinaldo [aɣi'naldo] *nm* Christmas box.
aguja [a'ɣuxa] *nf* needle; (*de reloj*) hand; (*ARQ*) spire; (*TEC*) firing-pin; **~s** *nfpl* (*ZOOL*) ribs; (*FERRO*) points.

agujerear [aɣuxere'ar] *vt* to make holes in; (*penetrar*) to pierce.
agujero [aɣu'xero] *nm* hole; (*COM*) deficit.
agujetas [aɣu'xetas] *nfpl* stitch *sg*; (*rigidez*) stiffness *sg*.
aguzar [aɣu'θar] *vt* to sharpen; (*fig*) to incite; ~ **el oído** to prick up one's ears.
aherrumbrarse [aerrum'brarse] *vr* to get rusty.
ahí [a'i] *adv* there; (*allá*) over there; **de ~ que** so that, with the result that; ~ **llega** here he comes; **por ~** (*dirección*) that way; **¡hasta ~ hemos llegado!** so it has come to this!; **¡~ va!** (*objeto*) here it comes!; (*individuo*) there he goes!; ~ **donde le ve** as sure as he's standing there.
ahijado, a [ai'xaðo, a] *nm/f* godson/daughter.
ahijar [ai'xar] *vt*: ~ **algo a algn** (*fig*) to attribute sth to sb.
ahínco [a'inko] *nm* earnestness; **con ~** eagerly.
ahíto, a [a'ito, a] *adj*: **estoy ~** I'm full up.
ahogado, a [ao'ɣaðo, a] *adj* (*en agua*) drowned; (*emoción*) pent-up; (*grito*) muffled.
ahogar [ao'ɣar] *vt* (*en agua*) to drown; (*asfixiar*) to suffocate, smother; (*fuego*) to put out; **~se** *vr* (*en agua*) to drown; (*por asfixia*) to suffocate.
ahogo [a'oɣo] *nm* (*MED*) breathlessness; (*fig*) distress; (*problema económico*) financial difficulty.
ahogue [a'oɣe] *etc vb V* **ahogar**.
ahondar [aon'dar] *vt* to deepen, make deeper; (*fig*) to go deeply into ♦ *vi*: ~ **en** to go deeply into.
ahora [a'ora] *adv* now; (*hace poco*) a moment ago, just now; (*dentro de poco*) in a moment; ~ **voy** I'm coming; ~ **mismo** right now; ~ **bien** now then; **por ~** for the present.
ahorcado, a [aor'kaðo, a] *nm/f* hanged person.
ahorcar [aor'kar] *vt* to hang; **~se** *vr* to hang o.s.
ahorita [ao'rita], **ahoritita** [aori'tita] *adv* (*esp AM*: *fam*) right now.
ahorque [a'orke] *etc vb V* **ahorcar**.
ahorrar [ao'rrar] *vt* (*dinero*) to save; (*esfuerzos*) to save, avoid; **~se** *vr*: **~se molestias** to save o.s. trouble.
ahorrativo, a [aorra'tiβo, a] *adj* thrifty.
ahorro [a'orro] *nm* (*acto*) saving; (*frugalidad*) thrift; **~s** *nmpl* savings.
ahuecar [awe'kar] *vt* to hollow (out); (*voz*) to deepen ♦ *vi*: **¡ahueca!** (*fam*) beat it! (*fam*); **~se** *vr* to give o.s. airs.
ahueque [a'weke] *etc vb V* **ahuecar**.
ahumar [au'mar] *vt* to smoke, cure; (*llenar de humo*) to fill with smoke ♦ *vi* to smoke; **~se** *vr* to fill with smoke.
ahuyentar [aujen'tar] *vt* to drive off, frighten off; (*fig*) to dispel.
AI *nf abr* (= *Amnistía Internacional*) AI.
aimara [ai'mara], **aimará** [aima'ra] *adj, nm/f* Aymara.
aindiado, a [aindi'aðo, a] *adj* (*AM*) Indian-like.
airado, a [ai'raðo, a] *adj* angry.
airar [ai'rar] *vt* to anger; **~se** *vr* to get angry.
aire ['aire] *nm* air; (*viento*) wind; (*corriente*) draught; (*MUS*) tune; **~s** *nmpl*: **darse ~s** to give o.s. airs; **al ~ libre** in the open air; ~ **acondicionado** air conditioning; **tener ~ de** to look like; **estar de buen/mal ~** to be in a good/bad mood; **estar en el ~** (*RADIO*) to be on the air; (*fig*) to be up in the air.
airear [aire'ar] *vt* to ventilate; (*fig*: *asunto*) to air; **~se** *vr* to take the air.
airoso, a [ai'roso, a] *adj* windy; draughty; (*fig*) graceful.
aislado, a [ais'laðo, a] *adj* (*remoto*) isolated; (*incomunicado*) cut off; (*ELEC*) insulated.
aislante [ais'lante] *nm* (*ELEC*) insulator.
aislar [ais'lar] *vt* to isolate; (*ELEC*) to insulate; **~se** *vr* to cut o.s. off.
ajar [a'xar] *vt* to spoil; (*fig*) to abuse; **~se** *vr* to get crumpled; (*fig*: *piel*) to get wrinkled.
ajardinado, a [axarði'naðo, a] *adj* landscaped.
ajedrez [axe'ðreθ] *nm* chess.
ajenjo [a'xenxo] *nm* (*bebida*) absinth(e).
ajeno, a [a'xeno, a] *adj* (*que pertenece a otro*) somebody else's; ~ **a** foreign to; ~ **de** free from, devoid of; **por razones ajenas a nuestra voluntad** for reasons beyond our control.
ajetreado, a [axetre'aðo, a] *adj* busy.
ajetrearse [axetre'arse] *vr* (*atarearse*) to bustle about; (*fatigarse*) to tire o.s. out.
ajetreo [axe'treo] *nm* bustle.
ají [a'xi] *nm* chil(l)i, red pepper; (*salsa*) chil(l)i sauce.
ajiaco [axi'ako] *nm* (*AM*) potato and chil(l)i stew.
ajilimoje [axili'moxe] *nm* sauce of garlic and pepper; **~s** *nmpl* (*fam*) odds and ends.
ajo ['axo] *nm* garlic; ~ **porro** *o* **puerro** leek; **(tieso) como un ~** (*fam*) snobbish; **estar**

en el ~ to be mixed up in it.
ajorca [a'xorka] *nf* bracelet.
ajuar [a'xwar] *nm* household furnishings *pl*; (*de novia*) trousseau; (*de niño*) layette.
ajustado, a [axus'taðo, a] *adj* (*tornillo*) tight; (*cálculo*) right; (*ropa*) tight(-fitting); (*DEPORTE*: *resultado*) close.
ajustar [axus'tar] *vt* (*adaptar*) to adjust; (*encajar*) to fit; (*TEC*) to engage; (*TIP*) to make up; (*apretar*) to tighten; (*concertar*) to agree (on); (*reconciliar*) to reconcile; (*cuenta*) to settle ♦ *vi* to fit.
ajuste [a'xuste] *nm* adjustment; (*COSTURA*) fitting; (*acuerdo*) compromise; (*de cuenta*) settlement; (*INFORM*) patch.
al [al] = **a + el**; *V* **a**.
ala ['ala] *nf* wing; (*de sombrero*) brim; (*futbolista*) winger; ~ **delta** hang-glider; **andar con el** ~ **caída** to be downcast; **cortar las** ~**s a algn** to clip sb's wings; **dar** ~**s a algn** to encourage sb.
alabanza [ala'βanθa] *nf* praise.
alabar [ala'βar] *vt* to praise.
alacena [ala'θena] *nf* cupboard (*BRIT*), closet (*US*).
alacrán [ala'kran] *nm* scorpion.
ALADI [a'laði] *nf abr* = *Asociación Latinoamericana de Integración*.
alado, a [a'laðo, a] *adj* winged.
ALALC [a'lalk] *nf abr* (= *Asociación Latinoamericana de Libre Comercio*) LAFTA.
alambicado, a [alambi'kaðo, a] *adj* distilled; (*fig*) affected.
alambicar [alambi'kar] *vt* to distil.
alambique [alam'bike] *etc vb V* **alambicar** ♦ *nm* still.
alambrada [alam'braða] *nf*, **alambrado** [alam'braðo] *nm* wire fence; (*red*) wire netting.
alambre [a'lambre] *nm* wire; ~ **de púas** barbed wire.
alambrista [alam'brista] *nm/f* tightrope walker.
alameda [ala'meða] *nf* (*plantío*) poplar grove; (*lugar de paseo*) avenue, boulevard.
álamo ['alamo] *nm* poplar; ~ **temblón** aspen.
alano [a'lano] *nm* mastiff.
alarde [a'larðe] *nm* show, display; **hacer** ~ **de** to boast of.
alardear [alarðe'ar] *vi* to boast.
alargador [alarɣa'ðor] *nm* extension cable *o* lead.
alargar [alar'ɣar] *vt* to lengthen, extend; (*paso*) to hasten; (*brazo*) to stretch out; (*cuerda*) to pay out; (*conversación*) to spin out; ~**se** *vr* to get longer.
alargue [a'larɣe] *etc vb V* **alargar**.
alarido [ala'riðo] *nm* shriek.
alarma [a'larma] *nf* alarm; **voz de** ~ warning note; **dar la** ~ to raise the alarm.
alarmante [alar'mante] *adj* alarming.
alarmar [alar'mar] *vt* to alarm; ~**se** *vr* to get alarmed.
alavés, esa [ala'βes, esa] *adj* of Álava ♦ *nm/f* native *o* inhabitant of Álava.
alazán [ala'θan] *nm* sorrel.
alba ['alβa] *nf* dawn.
albacea [alβa'θea] *nm/f* executor/executrix.
albaceteño, a [alβaθe'teɲo, a] *adj* of Albacete ♦ *nm/f* native *o* inhabitant of Albacete.
albahaca [al'βaka] *nf* (*BOT*) basil.
Albania [al'βanja] *nf* Albania.
albañal [alβa'ɲal] *nm* drain, sewer.
albañil [alβa'ɲil] *nm* bricklayer; (*cantero*) mason.
albarán [alβa'ran] *nm* (*COM*) invoice.
albarda [al'βarða] *nf* packsaddle.
albaricoque [alβari'koke] *nm* apricot.
albedrío [alβe'ðrio] *nm*: **libre** ~ free will.
alberca [al'βerka] *nf* reservoir; (*AM*) swimming pool.
albergar [alβer'ɣar] *vt* to shelter; (*esperanza*) to cherish; ~**se** *vr* (*refugiarse*) to shelter; (*alojarse*) to lodge.
albergue [al'βerɣe] *etc vb V* **albergar** ♦ *nm* shelter, refuge; ~ **de juventud** youth hostel.
albis ['alβis] *adv*: **quedarse en** ~ not to have a clue.
albóndiga [al'βondiɣa] *nf* meatball.
albor [al'βor] *nm* whiteness; (*amanecer*) dawn.
alborada [alβo'raða] *nf* dawn; (*diana*) reveille.
alborear [alβore'ar] *vi* to dawn.
albornoz [alβor'noθ] *nm* (*de los árabes*) burnous; (*para el baño*) bathrobe.
alboroce [alβo'roθe] *etc vb V* **alborozar**.
alborotar [alβoro'tar] *vi* to make a row ♦ *vt* to agitate, stir up; ~**se** *vr* to get excited; (*mar*) to get rough.
alboroto [alβo'roto] *nm* row, uproar.
alborozar [alβoro'θar] *vt* to gladden; ~**se** *vr* to rejoice, be overjoyed.
alborozo [alβo'roθo] *nm* joy.
albricias [al'βriθjas] *nfpl*: ¡~! good news!
álbum, *pl* **álbums** *o* **álbumes** ['alβum] *nm* album.
albumen [al'βumen] *nm* egg white, albumen.
alcabala [alka'βala] *nf* (*AM*) roadblock.

alcachofa [alka'tʃofa] *nf* (globe) artichoke; (*TIP*) golf ball; (*de ducha*) shower head.
alcahueta [alka'weta] *nf* procuress.
alcahuete [alka'wete] *nm* pimp.
alcalde, esa [al'kalde, alkal'desa] *nm/f* mayor(ess).
alcaldía [alkal'dia] *nf* mayoralty; (*lugar*) mayor's office.
álcali ['alkali] *nm* (*QUÍMICA*) alkali.
alcance [al'kanθe] *etc vb V* **alcanzar** ♦ *nm* (*MIL, RADIO*) range; (*fig*) scope; (*COM*) adverse balance, deficit; **estar al/fuera del ~ de algn** to be within/beyond one's reach; (*fig*) to be within one's powers/ over one's head; **de gran ~** (*MIL*) long-range; (*fig*) far-reaching.
alcancía [alkan'θia] *nf* money box.
alcanfor [alkan'for] *nm* camphor.
alcantarilla [alkanta'riʎa] *nf* (*de aguas cloacales*) sewer; (*en la calle*) gutter.
alcanzar [alkan'θar] *vt* (*algo: con la mano, el pie*) to reach; (*alguien: en el camino etc*) to catch up (with); (*autobús*) to catch; (*suj: bala*) to hit, strike ♦ *vi* (*ser suficiente*) to be enough; **~ algo a algn** to hand sth to sb; **alcánzame la sal, por favor** pass the salt please; **~ a hacer** to manage to do.
alcaparra [alka'parra] *nf* (*BOT*) caper.
alcatraz [alka'traθ] *nm* gannet.
alcayata [alka'jata] *nf* hook.
alcázar [al'kaθar] *nm* fortress; (*NAUT*) quarter-deck.
alce ['alθe] *etc vb V* **alzar**.
alcista [al'θista] *adj* (*COM, ECON*): **mercado ~** bull market; **la tendencia ~** the upward trend ♦ *nm* speculator.
alcoba [al'koβa] *nf* bedroom.
alcohol [al'kol] *nm* alcohol; **no bebe ~** he doesn't drink (alcohol).
alcoholemia [alkoo'lemia] *nf* blood alcohol level; **prueba de la ~** breath test.
alcoholice [alko'liθe] *etc vb V* **alcoholizarse**.
alcohólico, a [al'koliko, a] *adj, nm/f* alcoholic.
alcoholímetro [alko'limetro] *nm* Breathalyser ®, drunkometer (*US*).
alcoholismo [alko'lismo] *nm* alcoholism.
alcoholizarse [alkoli'θarse] *vr* to become an alcoholic.
alcornoque [alkor'noke] *nm* cork tree; (*fam*) idiot.
alcotana [alko'tana] *nf* pickaxe; (*DEPORTE*) ice-axe.
alcurnia [al'kurnja] *nf* lineage.
alcuza [al'kusa] *nf* (*AM*) cruet.
aldaba [al'daβa] *nf* (door) knocker.
aldea [al'dea] *nf* village.
aldeano, a [alde'ano, a] *adj* village *cpd* ♦ *nm/f* villager.
ale ['ale] *excl* come on!, let's go!
aleación [alea'θjon] *nf* alloy.
aleatorio, a [alea'torjo, a] *adj* random, contingent; **acceso ~** (*INFORM*) random access.
aleccionador, a [alekθjona'ðor, a] *adj* instructive.
aleccionar [alekθjo'nar] *vt* to instruct; (*adiestrar*) to train.
aledaño, a [ale'ðaɲo, a] *adj*: **~ a** bordering on ♦ *nmpl*: **~s** outskirts.
alegación [aleɣa'θjon] *nf* allegation.
alegar [ale'ɣar] *vt* (*dificultad etc*) to plead; (*JUR*) to allege ♦ *vi* (*AM*) to argue; **~ que ...** to give as an excuse that ...
alegato [ale'ɣato] *nm* (*JUR*) allegation; (*escrito*) indictment; (*declaración*) statement; (*AM*) argument.
alegoría [aleɣo'ria] *nf* allegory.
alegrar [ale'ɣrar] *vt* (*causar alegría*) to cheer (up); (*fuego*) to poke; (*fiesta*) to liven up; **~se** *vr* (*fam*) to get merry *o* tight; **~se de** to be glad about.
alegre [a'leɣre] *adj* happy, cheerful; (*fam*) merry, tight; (*licencioso*) risqué, blue.
alegría [ale'ɣria] *nf* happiness; merriment; **~ vital** joie de vivre.
alegrón [ale'ɣron] *nm* (*fig*) sudden joy.
alegue [a'leɣe] *etc vb V* **alegar**.
alejamiento [alexa'mjento] *nm* removal; (*distancia*) remoteness.
alejar [ale'xar] *vt* to move away, remove; (*fig*) to estrange; **~se** *vr* to move away.
alelado, a [ale'laðo, a] *adj* (*bobo*) foolish.
alelar [ale'lar] *vt* to bewilder.
aleluya [ale'luja] *nm* (*canto*) hallelujah.
alemán, ana [ale'man, ana] *adj, nm/f* German ♦ *nm* (*lengua*) German.
Alemania [ale'manja] *nf* Germany; **~ Occidental/Oriental** West/East Germany.
alentador, a [alenta'ðor, a] *adj* encouraging.
alentar [alen'tar] *vt* to encourage.
alergia [a'lerxja] *nf* allergy.
alero [a'lero] *nm* (*de tejado*) eaves *pl*; (*de foca, DEPORTE*) flipper; (*AUTO*) mudguard.
alerta [a'lerta] *adj inv, nm* alert.
aleta [a'leta] *nf* (*de pez*) fin; (*de ave*) wing; (*de coche*) mudguard.
aletargar [aletar'ɣar] *vt* to make drowsy; (*entumecer*) to make numb; **~se** *vr* to grow drowsy; to become numb.
aletargue [ale'tarɣe] *etc vb V* **aletargar**.
aletear [alete'ar] *vi* to flutter; (*ave*) to flap its wings; (*individuo*) to wave one's arms.

alevín [ale'βin] *nm* fry, young fish.
alevosía [aleβo'sia] *nf* treachery.
alfabetización [alfaβetiθa'θjon] *nf*: **campaña de ~** literacy campaign.
alfabeto [alfa'βeto] *nm* alphabet.
alfajor [alfa'xor] *nm* (*ESP*: *polvorón*) *cake eaten at Christmas time*.
alfalfa [al'falfa] *nf* alfalfa, lucerne.
alfaque [al'fake] *nm* (*NAUT*) bar, sandbank.
alfar [al'far] *nm* (*taller*) potter's workshop; (*arcilla*) clay.
alfarería [alfare'ria] *nf* pottery; (*tienda*) pottery shop.
alfarero [alfa'rero] *nm* potter.
alféizar [al'feiθar] *nm* window-sill.
alférez [al'fereθ] *nm* (*MIL*) second lieutenant; (*NAUT*) ensign.
alfil [al'fil] *nm* (*AJEDREZ*) bishop.
alfiler [alfi'ler] *nm* pin; (*broche*) clip; (*pinza*) clothes peg (*BRIT*) *o* pin (*US*); **~ de gancho** (*AM*) safety pin; **prendido con ~es** shaky.
alfiletero [alfile'tero] *nm* needle case.
alfombra [al'fombra] *nf* carpet; (*más pequeña*) rug.
alfombrar [alfom'brar] *vt* to carpet.
alfombrilla [alfom'briʎa] *nf* rug, mat; (*INFORM*) mouse mat *o* pad.
alforja [al'forxa] *nf* saddlebag.
alforza [al'forθa] *nf* pleat.
algarabía [alɣara'βia] *nf* (*fam*) gibberish; (*griterío*) hullabaloo.
algarada [alɣa'raða] *nf* outcry; **hacer** *o* **levantar una ~** to kick up a tremendous fuss.
Algarbe [al'ɣarβe] *nm*: **el ~** the Algarve.
algarroba [alɣa'rroβa] *nf* carob.
algarrobo [alɣa'rroβo] *nm* carob tree.
algas ['alɣas] *nfpl* seaweed *sg*.
algazara [alɣa'θara] *nf* din, uproar.
álgebra ['alxeβra] *nf* algebra.
álgido, a ['alxiðo, a] *adj* icy; (*momento etc*) crucial, decisive.
algo ['alɣo] *pron* something; (*en frases interrogativas*) anything ♦ *adv* somewhat, rather; **por ~ será** there must be some reason for it; **es ~ difícil** it's a bit awkward.
algodón [alɣo'ðon] *nm* cotton; (*planta*) cotton plant; **~ de azúcar** candy floss (*BRIT*), cotton candy (*US*); **~ hidrófilo** cotton wool (*BRIT*), absorbent cotton (*US*).
algodonero, a [alɣoðo'nero, a] *adj* cotton *cpd* ♦ *nm/f* cotton grower ♦ *nm* cotton plant.
algoritmo [alɣo'ritmo] *nm* algorithm.
alguacil [alɣwa'θil] *nm* bailiff; (*TAUR*) mounted official.
alguien ['alɣjen] *pron* someone, somebody; (*en frases interrogativas*) anybody.
alguno, a [al'ɣuno, a] *adj* (*delante de nm*: **algún**) some; (*después de n*): **no tiene talento alguno** he has no talent, he hasn't any talent ♦ *pron* (*alguien*) someone, somebody; **algún que otro libro** some book or other; **algún día iré** I'll go one *o* some day; **sin interés alguno** without the slightest interest; **alguno que otro** an occasional one; **algunos piensan** some (people) think; **alguno de ellos** one of them.
alhaja [a'laxa] *nf* jewel; (*tesoro*) precious object, treasure.
alhelí [ale'li] *nm* wallflower, stock.
aliado, a [a'ljaðo, a] *adj* allied.
alianza [a'ljanθa] *nf* (*POL etc*) alliance; (*anillo*) wedding ring.
aliar [a'ljar] *vt* to ally; **~se** *vr* to form an alliance.
alias ['aljas] *adv* alias.
alicaído, a [alika'iðo, a] *adj* (*MED*) weak; (*fig*) depressed.
alicantino, a [alikan'tino, a] *adj* of Alicante ♦ *nm/f* native *o* inhabitant of Alicante.
alicatar [alika'tar] *vt* to tile.
alicate(s) [ali'kate(s)] *nm(pl)* pliers *pl*; **~ de uñas** nail clippers.
aliciente [ali'θjente] *nm* incentive; (*atracción*) attraction.
alienación [aljena'θjon] *nf* alienation.
aliento [a'ljento] *etc vb V* **alentar** ♦ *nm* breath; (*respiración*) breathing; **sin ~** breathless; **de un ~** in one breath; (*fig*) in one go.
aligerar [alixe'rar] *vt* to lighten; (*reducir*) to shorten; (*aliviar*) to alleviate; (*mitigar*) to ease.
alijo [a'lixo] *nm* (*NAUT*) unloading; (*contrabando*) smuggled goods.
alimaña [ali'maɲa] *nf* pest.
alimentación [alimenta'θjon] *nf* (*comida*) food; (*acción*) feeding; (*tienda*) grocer's (shop); **~ continua** (*en fotocopiadora etc*) stream feed.
alimentador [alimenta'ðor] *nm*: **~ de papel** sheet-feeder.
alimentar [alimen'tar] *vt* to feed; (*nutrir*) to nourish; **~se** *vr*: **~se (de)** to feed (on).
alimenticio, a [alimen'tiθjo, a] *adj* food *cpd*; (*nutritivo*) nourishing, nutritious.
alimento [ali'mento] *nm* food; (*nutrición*) nourishment; **~s** *nmpl* (*JUR*) alimony *sg*.
alimón [ali'mon]: **al ~** *adv* jointly, together.
alineación [alinea'θjon] *nf* alignment; (*DEPORTE*) line-up.

alineado, a [aline'aðo, a] *adj* (*TIP*): **(no) ~** (un)justified; **~ a la izquierda/derecha** ranged left/right.
alinear [aline'ar] *vt* to align; (*TIP*) to justify; **~se** *vr* to line up; **~se en** to fall in with.
aliñar [ali'ɲar] *vt* (*CULIN*) to dress.
aliño [a'liɲo] *nm* (*CULIN*) dressing.
alisar [ali'sar] *vt* to smooth.
aliso [a'liso] *nm* alder.
alistamiento [alista'mjento] *nm* recruitment.
alistar [ali'star] *vt* to recruit; **~se** *vr* to enlist; (*inscribirse*) to enrol; (*AM*: *prepararse*) to get ready.
aliviar [ali'ßjar] *vt* (*carga*) to lighten; (*persona*) to relieve; (*dolor*) to relieve, alleviate.
alivio [a'lißjo] *nm* alleviation, relief; **~ de luto** half-mourning.
aljibe [al'xiße] *nm* cistern.
allá [a'ʎa] *adv* (*lugar*) there; (*por ahí*) over there; (*tiempo*) then; **~ abajo** down there; **más ~** further on; **más ~ de** beyond; **¡~ tú!** that's your problem!
allanamiento [aʎana'mjento] *nm* (*AM POLICÍA*) raid, search; **~ de morada** housebreaking.
allanar [aʎa'nar] *vt* to flatten, level (out); (*igualar*) to smooth (out); (*fig*) to subdue; (*JUR*) to burgle, break into; (*AM POLICÍA*) to raid, search; **~se** *vr* to fall down; **~se a** to submit to, accept.
allegado, a [aʎe'ɣaðo, a] *adj* near, close ♦ *nm/f* relation.
allende [a'ʎenðe] *adv* on the other side ♦ *prep*: **~ los mares** beyond the seas.
allí [a'ʎi] *adv* there; **~ mismo** right there; **por ~** over there; (*por ese camino*) that way.
alma ['alma] *nf* soul; (*persona*) person; (*TEC*) core; **se le cayó el ~ a los pies** he became very disheartened; **entregar el ~** to pass away; **estar con el ~ en la boca** to be scared to death; **lo siento en el ~** I am truly sorry; **tener el ~ en un hilo** to have one's heart in one's mouth; **estar como ~ en pena** to suffer; **ir como ~ que lleva el diablo** to go at breakneck speed.
almacén [alma'θen] *nm* (*depósito*) warehouse, store; (*MIL*) magazine; (*AM*) grocer's shop, foodstore, grocery store (*US*); **(grandes) almacenes** *nmpl* department store *sg*; **~ depositario** (*COM*) depository.
almacenaje [almaθe'naxe] *nm* storage; **~ secundario** (*INFORM*) backing storage.
almacenamiento [almaθena'mjento] *nm* (*INFORM*) storage; **~ temporal en disco** disk spooling.
almacenar [almaθe'nar] *vt* to store, put in storage; (*INFORM*) to store; (*proveerse*) to stock up with.
almacenero [almaθe'nero] *nm* warehouseman; (*AM*) grocer, shopkeeper.
almanaque [alma'nake] *nm* almanac.
almeja [al'mexa] *nf* clam.
almenas [al'menas] *nfpl* battlements.
almendra [al'mendra] *nf* almond.
almendro [al'mendro] *nm* almond tree.
almeriense [alme'rjense] *adj* of Almería ♦ *nm/f* native *o* inhabitant of Almería.
almiar [al'mjar] *nm* haystack.
almíbar [al'mißar] *nm* syrup.
almidón [almi'ðon] *nm* starch.
almidonado, a [almiðo'naðo, a] *adj* starched.
almidonar [almiðo'nar] *vt* to starch.
almirantazgo [almiran'taθɣo] *nm* admiralty.
almirante [almi'rante] *nm* admiral.
almirez [almi'reθ] *nm* mortar.
almizcle [al'miθkle] *nm* musk.
almizclero [almiθ'klero] *nm* musk deer.
almohada [almo'aða] *nf* pillow; (*funda*) pillowcase.
almohadilla [almoa'ðiʎa] *nf* cushion; (*TEC*) pad; (*AM*) pincushion.
almohadillado, a [almoaði'ʎaðo, a] *adj* (*acolchado*) padded.
almohadón [almoa'ðon] *nm* large pillow.
almorcé [almor'θe], **almorcemos** [almor'θemos] *etc vb V* **almorzar**.
almorranas [almo'rranas] *nfpl* piles, haemorrhoids (*BRIT*), hemorrhoids (*US*).
almorzar [almor'θar] *vt*: **~ una tortilla** to have an omelette for lunch ♦ *vi* to (have) lunch.
almuerce [al'mwerθe] *etc vb V* **almorzar**.
almuerzo [al'mwerθo] *etc vb V* **almorzar** ♦ *nm* lunch.
aló [a'lo] *excl* (*esp AM TELEC*) hello!
alocado, a [alo'kaðo, a] *adj* crazy.
alojamiento [aloxa'mjento] *nf* lodging(s) (*pl*); (*viviendas*) housing.
alojar [alo'xar] *vt* to lodge; **~se** *vr*: **~se en** to stay at; (*bala*) to lodge in.
alondra [a'londra] *nf* lark, skylark.
alpaca [al'paka] *nf* alpaca.
alpargata [alpar'ɣata] *nf* espadrille.
Alpes ['alpes] *nmpl*: **los ~** the Alps.
alpinismo [alpi'nismo] *nm* mountaineering, climbing.
alpinista [alpi'nista] *nm/f* mountaineer, climber.

alpino, a [al'pino, a] *adj* alpine.
alpiste [al'piste] *nm* (*semillas*) birdseed; (*AM fam: dinero*) dough; (*fam: alcohol*) booze.
alquería [alke'ria] *nf* farmhouse.
alquilar [alki'lar] *vt* (*suj: propietario: inmuebles*) to let, rent (out); (*: coche*) to hire out; (*: TV*) to rent (out); (*suj: alquilador: inmuebles, TV*) to rent; (*: coche*) to hire; **"se alquila casa"** "house to let (*BRIT*) *o* to rent (*US*)".
alquiler [alki'ler] *nm* renting, letting; hiring; (*arriendo*) rent; hire charge; **de ~** for hire; **~ de automóviles** car hire.
alquimia [al'kimja] *nf* alchemy.
alquitrán [alki'tran] *nm* tar.
alrededor [alreðe'ðor] *adv* around, about; **~es** *nmpl* surroundings; **~ de** *prep* around, about; **mirar a su ~** to look (round) about one.
Alsacia [al'saθja] *nf* Alsace.
alta ['alta] *nf* (certificate of) discharge; **dar a algn de ~** to discharge sb; **darse de ~** (*MIL*) to join, enrol; (*DEPORTE*) to declare o.s. fit.
altanería [altane'ria] *nf* haughtiness, arrogance.
altanero, a [alta'nero, a] *adj* haughty, arrogant.
altar [al'tar] *nm* altar.
altavoz [alta'ßoθ] *nm* loudspeaker; (*amplificador*) amplifier.
alteración [altera'θjon] *nf* alteration; (*alboroto*) disturbance; **~ del orden público** breach of the peace.
alterar [alte'rar] *vt* to alter; to disturb; **~se** *vr* (*persona*) to get upset.
altercado [alter'kaðo] *nm* argument.
alternar [alter'nar] *vt* to alternate ♦ *vi*, **~se** *vr* to alternate; (*turnar*) to take turns; **~ con** to mix with.
alternativo, a [alterna'tißo, a] *adj* alternative; (*alterno*) alternating ♦ *nf* alternative; (*elección*) choice; **alternativas** *nfpl* ups and downs; **tomar la alternativa** (*TAUR*) to become a fully-qualified bullfighter.
alterno, a [al'terno, a] *adj* (*BOT, MAT*) alternate; (*ELEC*) alternating.
alteza [al'teθa] *nf* (*tratamiento*) highness.
altibajos [alti'ßaxos] *nmpl* ups and downs.
altillo [al'tiʎo] *nm* (*GEO*) small hill; (*AM*) attic.
altiplanicie [altipla'niθje] *nf*, **altiplano** [alti'plano] *nm* high plateau.
altisonante [altiso'nante] *adj* high-flown, high-sounding.
altitud [alti'tuð] *nf* altitude, height; **a una ~ de** at a height of.
altivez [alti'ßeθ] *nf* haughtiness, arrogance.
altivo, a [al'tißo, a] *adj* haughty, arrogant.
alto, a ['alto, a] *adj* high; (*persona*) tall; (*sonido*) high, sharp; (*noble*) high, lofty; (*GEO, clase*) upper ♦ *nm* halt; (*MUS*) alto; (*GEO*) hill; (*AM*) pile ♦ *adv* (*estar*) high; (*hablar*) loud, loudly ♦ *excl* halt!; **la pared tiene 2 metros de ~** the wall is 2 metres high; **en alta mar** on the high seas; **en voz alta** in a loud voice; **las altas horas de la noche** the small (*BRIT*) *o* wee (*US*) hours; **en lo ~ de** at the top of; **pasar por ~** to overlook; **~s y bajos** ups and downs; **poner la radio más ~** to turn the radio up; **¡más ~, por favor!** louder, please!
altoparlante [altopar'lante] *nm* (*AM*) loudspeaker.
altramuz [altra'muθ] *nm* lupin.
altruismo [al'truismo] *nm* altruism.
altura [al'tura] *nf* height; (*NAUT*) depth; (*GEO*) latitude; **la pared tiene 1.80 de ~** the wall is 1 metre 80 (cm) high; **a esta ~ del año** at this time of the year; **estar a la ~ de las circunstancias** to rise to the occasion; **ha sido un partido de gran ~** it has been a terrific match.
alubia [a'lußja] *nf* French bean, kidney bean.
alucinación [aluθina'θjon] *nf* hallucination.
alucinante [aluθi'nante] *adj* (*fam: estupendo*) great, super.
alucinar [aluθi'nar] *vi* to hallucinate ♦ *vt* to deceive; (*fascinar*) to fascinate.
alud [a'luð] *nm* avalanche; (*fig*) flood.
aludir [alu'ðir] *vi*: **~ a** to allude to; **darse por aludido** to take the hint; **no te des por aludido** don't take it personally.
alumbrado [alum'braðo] *nm* lighting.
alumbramiento [alumbra'mjento] *nm* lighting; (*MED*) childbirth, delivery.
alumbrar [alum'brar] *vt* to light (up) ♦ *vi* (*iluminar*) to give light; (*MED*) to give birth.
aluminio [alu'minjo] *nm* aluminium (*BRIT*), aluminum (*US*).
alumnado [alum'naðo] *nm* (*UNIV*) student body; (*ESCOL*) pupils *pl*.
alumno, a [a'lumno, a] *nm/f* pupil, student.
alunice [alu'niθe] *etc vb V* **alunizar**.
alunizar [aluni'θar] *vi* to land on the moon.
alusión [alu'sjon] *nf* allusion.
alusivo, a [alu'sißo, a] *adj* allusive.
aluvión [alu'ßjon] *nm* (*GEO*) alluvium; (*fig*) flood; **~ de improperios** torrent of abuse.
alvéolo [al'ßeolo] *nm* (*ANAT*) alveolus; (*fig*)

network.

alza ['alθa] *nf* rise; (*MIL*) sight; **~s fijas/graduables** fixed/adjustable sights; **al** *o* **en** ~ (*precio*) rising; **jugar al** ~ to speculate on a rising *o* bull market; **cotizarse** *o* **estar en** ~ to be rising.

alzado, a [al'θaðo, a] *adj* (*gen*) raised; (*COM*: *precio*) fixed; (: *quiebra*) fradulent; **por un tanto** ~ for a lump sum ♦ *nf* (*de caballos*) height; (*JUR*) appeal.

alzamiento [alθa'mjento] *nm* (*aumento*) rise, increase; (*acción*) lifting, raising; (*mejor postura*) higher bid; (*rebelión*) rising; (*COM*) fraudulent bankruptcy.

alzar [al'θar] *vt* to lift (up); (*precio, muro*) to raise; (*cuello de abrigo*) to turn up; (*AGR*) to gather in; (*TIP*) to gather; **~se** *vr* to get up, rise; (*rebelarse*) to revolt; (*COM*) to go fraudulently bankrupt; (*JUR*) to appeal; **~se con el premio** to carry off the prize.

a.m. *abr* (*AM*: = *ante meridiem*) a.m.

ama ['ama] *nf* lady of the house; (*dueña*) owner; (*institutriz*) governess; (*madre adoptiva*) foster mother; ~ **de casa** housewife; ~ **de cría** *o* **de leche** wet-nurse; ~ **de llaves** housekeeper.

amabilidad [amaβili'ðað] *nf* kindness; (*simpatía*) niceness.

amabilísimo, a [amaβi'lisimo, a] *adj superlativo de* **amable**.

amable [a'maβle] *adj* kind; nice.

amaestrado, a [amaes'traðo, a] *adj* (*animal*) trained; (: *en circo etc*) performing.

amaestrar [amaes'trar] *vt* to train.

amagar [ama'ɣar] *vt, vi* to threaten.

amago [a'maɣo] *nm* threat; (*gesto*) threatening gesture; (*MED*) symptom.

amague [a'maɣe] *etc vb V* **amagar**.

amainar [amai'nar] *vt* (*NAUT*) to lower, take in; (*fig*) to calm ♦ *vi*, **~se** *vr* to drop, die down; **el viento amaina** the wind is dropping.

amalgama [amal'ɣama] *nf* amalgam.

amalgamar [amalɣa'mar] *vt* to amalgamate; (*combinar*) to combine, mix.

amamantar [amaman'tar] *vt* to suckle, nurse.

amancebarse [amanθe'βarse] *vr* (*pareja*) to live together.

amanecer [amane'θer] *vi* to dawn; (*fig*) to appear, begin to show ♦ *nm* dawn; **el niño amaneció afiebrado** the child woke up with a fever.

amanerado, a [amane'raðo, a] *adj* affected.

amanezca [ama'neθka] *etc vb V* **amanecer**.

amansar [aman'sar] *vt* to tame; (*persona*) to subdue; **~se** *vr* (*persona*) to calm down.

amante [a'mante] *adj*: ~ **de** fond of ♦ *nm/f* lover.

amanuense [ama'nwense] *nm* (*escribiente*) scribe; (*copista*) copyist; (*POL*) secretary.

amañar [ama'ɲar] *vt* (*gen*) to do skilfully; (*pey: resultado*) to alter.

amaño [a'maɲo] *nm* (*habilidad*) skill; **~s** *nmpl* (*TEC*) tools; (*fig*) tricks.

amapola [ama'pola] *nf* poppy.

amar [a'mar] *vt* to love.

amargado, a [amar'ɣaðo, a] *adj* bitter; embittered.

amargar [amar'ɣar] *vt* to make bitter; (*fig*) to embitter; **~se** *vr* to become embittered.

amargo, a [a'marɣo, a] *adj* bitter.

amargor [amar'ɣor] *nm* (*sabor*) bitterness; (*fig*) grief.

amargue [a'marɣe] *etc vb V* **amargar**.

amargura [amar'ɣura] *nf* = **amargor**.

amarillento, a [amari'ʎento, a] *adj* yellowish; (*tez*) sallow.

amarillismo [amari'ʎismo] *nm* (*de prensa*) sensationalist journalism.

amarillo, a [ama'riʎo, a] *adj, nm* yellow.

amarra [a'marra] *nf* (*NAUT*) mooring line; **~s** *nfpl* (*fig*) protection *sg*; **tener buenas ~s** to have good connections; **soltar ~s** to set off.

amarrar [ama'rrar] *vt* to moor; (*sujetar*) to tie up.

amartillar [amarti'ʎar] *vt* (*fusil*) to cock.

amasar [ama'sar] *vt* to knead; (*mezclar*) to mix, prepare; (*confeccionar*) to concoct.

amasijo [ama'sixo] *nm* kneading; mixing; (*fig*) hotchpotch.

amateur ['amatur] *nm/f* amateur.

amatista [ama'tista] *nf* amethyst.

amazacotado, a [amaθako'taðo, a] *adj* (*terreno, arroz etc*) lumpy.

amazona [ama'θona] *nf* horsewoman.

Amazonas [ama'θonas] *nm*: **el (Río)** ~ the Amazon.

ambages [am'baxes] *nmpl*: **sin** ~ in plain language.

ámbar ['ambar] *nm* amber.

Amberes [am'beres] *nm* Antwerp.

ambición [ambi'θjon] *nf* ambition.

ambicionar [ambiθjo'nar] *vt* to aspire to.

ambicioso, a [ambi'θjoso, a] *adj* ambitious.

ambidextro, a [ambi'ðekstro, a] *adj* ambidextrous.

ambientación [ambjenta'θjon] *nf* (*CINE, LIT etc*) setting; (*RADIO etc*) sound effects *pl*.

ambientador [ambjenta'ðor] *nm* air freshener.
ambientar [ambjen'tar] *vt* (*gen*) to give an atmosphere to; (*LIT etc*) to set.
ambiente [am'bjente] *nm* (*tb fig*) atmosphere; (*medio*) environment; (*AM*) room.
ambigüedad [ambiɣwe'ðað] *nf* ambiguity.
ambiguo, a [am'biɣwo, a] *adj* ambiguous.
ámbito ['ambito] *nm* (*campo*) field; (*fig*) scope.
ambos, as ['ambos, as] *adj pl, pron pl* both.
ambulancia [ambu'lanθja] *nf* ambulance.
ambulante [ambu'lante] *adj* travelling, itinerant; (*biblioteca*) mobile.
ambulatorio [ambula'torio] *nm* state health-service clinic.
ameba [a'meβa] *nf* amoeba.
amedrentar [ameðren'tar] *vt* to scare.
amén [a'men] *excl* amen; ~ **de** *prep* besides, in addition to; **en un decir** ~ in the twinkling of an eye; **decir** ~ **a todo** to have no mind of one's own.
amenace [ame'naθe] *etc vb V* **amenazar**.
amenaza [ame'naθa] *nf* threat.
amenazar [amena'θar] *vt* to threaten ♦ *vi*: ~ **con hacer** to threaten to do.
amenidad [ameni'ðað] *nf* pleasantness.
ameno, a [a'meno, a] *adj* pleasant.
América [a'merika] *nf* (*continente*) America, the Americas; (*EEUU*) America; (*Hispanoa~*) Latin *o* South America; ~ **del Norte/del Sur** North/South America; ~ **Central/Latina** Central/Latin America.
americanismo [amerika'nismo] *nm* Americanism.
americano, a [ameri'kano, a] *adj, nm/f* (*V* **América**) American; Latin *o* South American ♦ *nf* coat, jacket.
americe [ame'riθe] *etc vb V* **amerizar**.
amerindio, a [ame'rindjo, a] *adj, nm/f* Amerindian, American Indian
amerizaje [ameri'θaxe] *nm* (*AVIAT*) landing (on the sea).
amerizar [ameri'θar] *vi* (*AVIAT*) to land (on the sea).
ametralladora [ametraʎa'ðora] *nf* machine gun.
amianto [a'mjanto] *nm* asbestos.
amigable [ami'ɣaβle] *adj* friendly.
amígdala [a'miɣðala] *nf* tonsil.
amigdalitis [amiɣða'litis] *nf* tonsillitis.
amigo, a [a'miɣo, a] *adj* friendly ♦ *nm/f* friend; (*amante*) lover; ~ **de lo ajeno** thief; ~ **corresponsal** penfriend; **hacerse** ~**s** to become friends; **ser** ~ **de** to like, be fond of; **ser muy** ~**s** to be close friends.
amigote [ami'ɣote] *nm* mate (*BRIT*), buddy.
amilanar [amila'nar] *vt* to scare; ~**se** *vr* to get scared.
aminorar [amino'rar] *vt* to diminish; (*reducir*) to reduce; ~ **la marcha** to slow down.
amistad [amis'tað] *nf* friendship; ~**es** *nfpl* friends.
amistoso, a [ami'stoso, a] *adj* friendly.
amnesia [am'nesja] *nf* amnesia.
amnistía [amnis'tia] *nf* amnesty.
amnistiar [amni'stjar] *vt* to amnesty, grant an amnesty to.
amo ['amo] *nm* owner; (*jefe*) boss.
amodorrarse [amoðo'rrarse] *vr* to get sleepy.
amolar [amo'lar] *vt* to annoy.
amoldar [amol'dar] *vt* to mould; (*adaptar*) to adapt.
amonestación [amonesta'θjon] *nf* warning; **amonestaciones** *nfpl* marriage banns.
amonestar [amone'star] *vt* to warn; to publish the banns of.
amoniaco [amo'njako] *nm* ammonia.
amontonar [amonto'nar] *vt* to collect, pile up; ~**se** *vr* (*gente*) to crowd together; (*acumularse*) to pile up; (*datos*) to accumulate; (*desastres*) to come one on top of another.
amor [a'mor] *nm* love; (*amante*) lover; **hacer el** ~ to make love; ~ **interesado** cupboard love; ~ **propio** self-respect; **por (el)** ~ **de Dios** for God's sake; **estar al** ~ **de la lumbre** to be close to the fire.
amoratado, a [amora'taðo, a] *adj* purple, blue with cold; (*con cardenales*) bruised.
amordace [amor'ðaθe] *etc vb V* **amordazar**.
amordazar [amorða'θar] *vt* to muzzle; (*fig*) to gag.
amorfo, a [a'morfo, a] *adj* amorphous, shapeless.
amorío [amo'rio] *nm* (*fam*) love affair.
amoroso, a [amo'roso, a] *adj* affectionate, loving.
amortajar [amorta'xar] *vt* (*fig*) to shroud.
amortice [amor'tiθe] *etc vb V* **amortizar**.
amortiguador [amortiɣwa'ðor] *nm* shock absorber; (*parachoques*) bumper; (*silenciador*) silencer; ~**es** *nmpl* (*AUTO*) suspension *sg*.
amortiguar [amorti'ɣwar] *vt* to deaden; (*ruido*) to muffle; (*color*) to soften.
amortigüe [amor'tiɣwe] *etc vb V* **amortiguar**.
amortización [amortiθa'θjon] *nf* redemption; repayment; (*COM*) capital allowance.

amortizar [amorti'θar] *vt* (*ECON*: *bono*) to redeem; (: *capital*) to write off; (: *préstamo*) to pay off.
amoscarse [amos'karse] *vr* to get cross.
amosque [a'moske] *etc vb V* **amoscarse.**
amotinar [amoti'nar] *vt* to stir up, incite (to riot); **~se** *vr* to mutiny.
amparar [ampa'rar] *vt* to protect; **~se** *vr* to seek protection; (*de la lluvia etc*) to shelter.
amparo [am'paro] *nm* help, protection; **al ~ de** under the protection of.
amperímetro [ampe'rimetro] *nm* ammeter.
amperio [am'perjo] *nm* ampère, amp.
ampliable [am'pljaßle] *adj* (*INFORM*) expandable.
ampliación [amplja'θjon] *nf* enlargement; (*extensión*) extension.
ampliar [am'pljar] *vt* to enlarge; to extend.
amplificación [amplifika'θjon] *nf* enlargement.
amplificador [amplifika'ðor] *nm* amplifier.
amplificar [amplifi'kar] *vt* to amplify.
amplifique [ampli'fike] *etc vb V* **amplificar.**
amplio, a ['ampljo, a] *adj* spacious; (*falda etc*) full; (*extenso*) extensive; (*ancho*) wide.
amplitud [ampli'tuð] *nf* spaciousness; extent; (*fig*) amplitude; **~ de miras** broadmindedness; **de gran ~** far-reaching.
ampolla [am'poʎa] *nf* blister; (*MED*) ampoule.
ampolleta [ampo'ʎeta] *nf* (*AM*) (light) bulb.
ampuloso, a [ampu'loso, a] *adj* bombastic, pompous.
amputar [ampu'tar] *vt* to cut off, amputate.
amueblar [amwe'ßlar] *vt* to furnish.
amuleto [amu'leto] *nm* (lucky) charm.
amurallar [amura'ʎar] *vt* to wall up *o* in.
anacarado, a [anaka'raðo, a] *adj* mother-of-pearl *cpd.*
anacardo [ana'karðo] *nm* cashew (nut).
anaconda [ana'konda] *nf* anaconda.
anacronismo [anakro'nismo] *nm* anachronism.
ánade ['anaðe] *nm* duck.
anagrama [ana'ɣrama] *nm* anagram.
anales [a'nales] *nmpl* annals.
analfabetismo [analfaße'tismo] *nm* illiteracy.
analfabeto, a [analfa'ßeto, a] *adj, nm/f* illiterate.
analgésico [anal'xesiko] *nm* painkiller, analgesic.
analice [ana'liθe] *etc vb V* **analizar.**
análisis [a'nalisis] *nm inv* analysis; **~ de costos-beneficios** cost-benefit analysis; **~ de mercados** market research; **~ de sangre** blood test.
analista [ana'lista] *nm/f* (*gen*) analyst; (*POL, HISTORIA*) chronicler; **~ de sistemas** (*INFORM*) systems analyst.
analizar [anali'θar] *vt* to analyse.
analogía [analo'xia] *nf* analogy; **por ~ con** on the analogy of.
analógico, a [ana'loxico, a] *adj* analogue.
análogo, a [a'naloɣo, a] *adj* analogous, similar.
ananá(s) [ana'na(s)] *nm* pineapple.
anaquel [ana'kel] *nm* shelf.
anaranjado, a [anaran'xaðo, a] *adj* orange (-coloured).
anarquía [anar'kia] *nf* anarchy.
anarquismo [anar'kismo] *nm* anarchism.
anarquista [anar'kista] *nm/f* anarchist.
anatematizar [anatemati'θar] *vt* (*REL*) to anathematize; (*fig*) to curse.
anatemice [anate'miθe] *etc vb V* **anatemizar.**
anatomía [anato'mia] *nf* anatomy.
anca ['anka] *nf* rump, haunch; **~s** *nfpl* (*fam*) behind *sg*; **llevar a algn en ~s** to carry sb behind one.
ancestral [anθes'tral] *adj* (*costumbre*) age-old.
ancho, a ['antʃo, a] *adj* wide; (*falda*) full; (*fig*) liberal ♦ *nm* width; (*FERRO*) gauge; **le viene muy ~ el cargo** (*fig*) the job is too much for him; **ponerse ~** to get conceited; **quedarse tan ~** to go on as if nothing had happened; **estar a sus anchas** to be at one's ease.
anchoa [an'tʃoa] *nf* anchovy.
anchura [an'tʃura] *nf* width; (*extensión*) wideness.
anchuroso, a [antʃu'roso, a] *adj* wide.
anciano, a [an'θjano, a] *adj* old, aged ♦ *nm/f* old man/woman ♦ *nm* elder.
ancla ['ankla] *nf* anchor; **levar ~s** to weigh anchor.
ancladero [ankla'ðero] *nm* anchorage.
anclar [an'klar] *vi* to (drop) anchor.
andadas [an'daðas] *nfpl* (*aventuras*) adventures; **volver a las ~** to backslide.
andaderas [anda'ðeras] *nfpl* baby-walker *sg.*
andadura [anda'ðura] *nf* gait; (*de caballo*) pace.
Andalucía [andalu'θia] *nf* Andalusia.
andaluz, a [anda'luθ, a] *adj, nm/f* Andalusian.
andamio [an'damjo] *nm*, **andamiaje** [anda'mjaxe] *nm* scaffold(ing).

andanada [anda'naða] *nf* (*fig*) reprimand; **soltarle a algn una** ~ to give sb a rocket.
andante [an'dante] *adj*: **caballero** ~ knight errant.
andar [an'dar] *vt* to go, cover, travel ♦ *vi* to go, walk, travel; (*funcionar*) to go, work; (*estar*) to be ♦ *nm* walk, gait, pace; ~**se** *vr* (*irse*) to go away *o* off; ~ **a pie/a caballo/en bicicleta** to go on foot/on horseback/by bicycle; **¡anda!** (*sorpresa*) go on!; **anda en** *o* **por los 40** he's about 40; **¿en qué andas?** what are you up to?; **andamos mal de dinero/tiempo** we're badly off for money/we're short of time; ~**se por las ramas** to beat about the bush; **no** ~**se con rodeos** to call a spade a spade (*fam*); **todo se andará** all in good time; **anda por aquí** it's round here somewhere; ~ **haciendo algo** to be doing sth.
andariego, a [anda'rjeɣo, a] *adj* fond of travelling.
andas ['andas] *nfpl* stretcher *sg*.
andén [an'den] *nm* (*FERRO*) platform; (*NAUT*) quayside; (*AM*: *acera*) pavement (*BRIT*), sidewalk (*US*).
Andes ['andes] *nmpl*: **los** ~ the Andes.
andinismo [andin'ismo] *nm* (*AM*) mountaineering, climbing.
andino, a [an'dino, a] *adj* Andean, of the Andes.
Andorra [an'dorra] *nf* Andorra.
andrajo [an'draxo] *nm* rag.
andrajoso, a [andra'xoso, a] *adj* ragged.
andurriales [andu'rrjales] *nmpl* out-of-the-way place *sg*, the sticks; **en esos** ~ in that godforsaken spot.
anduve [an'duβe], **anduviera** [andu'βjera] *etc vb V* **andar**.
anécdota [a'nekðota] *nf* anecdote, story.
anegar [ane'ɣar] *vt* to flood; (*ahogar*) to drown; ~**se** *vr* to drown; (*hundirse*) to sink.
anegue [a'neɣe] *etc vb V* **anegar**.
anejo, a [a'nexo, a] *adj* attached ♦ *nm* (*ARQ*) annexe.
anemia [a'nemja] *nf* anaemia.
anestesia [anes'tesja] *nf* anaesthetic; ~ **general/local** general/local anaesthetic.
anestesiar [aneste'sjar] *vt* to anaesthetize (*BRIT*) anesthetize (*US*).
anestésico [anes'tesiko] *nm* anaesthetic.
anexar [anek'sar] *vt* to annex; (*documento*) to attach; (*INFORM*) to append.
anexión [anek'sjon] *nf*, **anexionamiento** [aneksjona'mjento] *nm* annexation.
anexionar [aneksjo'nar] *vt* to annex; ~**se** *vr*: ~ **un país** to annex a country.
anexo, a [a'nekso, a] *adj* attached ♦ *nm* annexe.
anfetamina [anfeta'mina] *nf* amphetamine.
anfibio, a [an'fiβjo, a] *adj* amphibious ♦ *nm* amphibian.
anfiteatro [anfite'atro] *nm* amphitheatre; (*TEAT*) dress circle.
anfitrión, ona [anfi'trjon, ona] *nm/f* host(ess).
ángel ['anxel] *nm* angel; ~ **de la guarda** guardian angel; **tener** ~ to have charm.
Ángeles ['anxeles] *nmpl*: **los** ~ Los Angeles.
angélico, a [an'xeliko, a], **angelical** [anxeli'kal] *adj* angelic(al).
angina [an'xina] *nf* (*MED*): ~ **de pecho** angina; **tener** ~**s** to have a sore throat *o* throat infection.
anglicano, a [angli'kano, a] *adj, nm/f* Anglican.
anglicismo [angli'θismo] *nm* anglicism.
anglosajón, ona [anglosa'xon, 'xona] *adj, nm/f* Anglo-Saxon.
Angola [an'gola] *nf* Angola.
angoleño, a [ango'leɲo, a] *adj, nm/f* Angolan.
angosto, a [an'gosto, a] *adj* narrow.
anguila [an'gila] *nf* eel; ~**s** *nfpl* slipway *sg*.
angula [an'gula] *nf* elver, baby eel.
ángulo ['angulo] *nm* angle; (*esquina*) corner; (*curva*) bend.
angustia [an'gustja] *nf* anguish.
angustiar [angus'tjar] *vt* to distress, grieve; ~**se** *vr* to be distressed (*por* at, on account of).
anhelante [ane'lante] *adj* eager; (*deseoso*) longing.
anhelar [ane'lar] *vt* to be eager for; to long for, desire ♦ *vi* to pant, gasp.
anhelo [a'nelo] *nm* eagerness; desire.
anhídrido [a'niðriðo] *nm*: ~ **carbónico** carbon dioxide.
anidar [ani'ðar] *vt* (*acoger*) to take in, shelter ♦ *vi* to nest; (*fig*) to make one's home.
anilina [ani'lina] *nf* aniline.
anilla [a'niʎa] *nf* ring; **(las)** ~**s** (*DEPORTE*) the rings.
anillo [a'niʎo] *nm* ring; ~ **de boda** wedding ring; ~ **de compromiso** engagement ring; **venir como** ~ **al dedo** to suit to a tee.
ánima ['anima] *nf* soul; **las** ~**s** the Angelus (bell) *sg*.
animación [anima'θjon] *nf* liveliness; (*vitalidad*) life; (*actividad*) bustle.
animado, a [ani'maðo, a] *adj* (*vivo*) lively;

(*vivaz*) animated; (*concurrido*) bustling; (*alegre*) in high spirits; **dibujos ~s** cartoon *sg*.
animador, a [anima'ðor, a] *nm/f* (*TV*) host(ess) ♦ *nf* (*DEPORTE*) cheerleader.
animadversión [animaðßer'sjon] *nf* ill-will, antagonism.
animal [ani'mal] *adj* animal; (*fig*) stupid ♦ *nm* animal; (*fig*) fool; (*bestia*) brute.
animalada [anima'laða] *nf* (*gen*) silly thing (to do *o* say); (*ultraje*) disgrace.
animar [ani'mar] *vt* (*BIO*) to animate, give life to; (*fig*) to liven up, brighten up, cheer up; (*estimular*) to stimulate; **~se** *vr* to cheer up, feel encouraged; (*decidirse*) to make up one's mind.
ánimo ['animo] *nm* soul, mind; (*valentía*) courage ♦ *excl* cheer up!; **cobrar ~** to take heart; **dar ~(s) a** to encourage.
animoso, a [ani'moso, a] *adj* brave; (*vivo*) lively.
aniñado, a [ani'ɲaðo, a] *adj* (*facción*) childlike; (*carácter*) childish.
aniquilar [aniki'lar] *vt* to annihilate, destroy.
anís [a'nis] *nm* (*grano*) aniseed; (*licor*) anisette.
aniversario [anißer'sarjo] *nm* anniversary.
Ankara [an'kara] *nf* Ankara.
ano ['ano] *nm* anus.
anoche [a'notʃe] *adv* last night; **antes de ~** the night before last.
anochecer [anotʃe'θer] *vi* to get dark ♦ *nm* nightfall, dark; **al ~** at nightfall.
anochezca [ano'tʃeθka] *etc vb V* **anochecer**.
anodino, a [ano'ðino, a] *adj* dull, anodyne.
anomalía [anoma'lia] *nf* anomaly.
anonadado, a [anona'ðaðo, a] *adj* stunned.
anonimato [anoni'mato] *nm* anonymity.
anónimo, a [a'nonimo, a] *adj* anonymous; (*COM*) limited ♦ *nm* (*carta*) anonymous letter; (*: maliciosa*) poison-pen letter.
anorak [ano'rak], *pl* **anoraks** *nm* anorak.
anorexia [ano'reksja] *nf* anorexia.
anormal [anor'mal] *adj* abnormal.
anotación [anota'θjon] *nf* note; annotation.
anotar [ano'tar] *vt* to note down; (*comentar*) to annotate.
anquilosado, a [ankilo'saðo, a] *adj* (*fig*) stale, out of date.
anquilosamiento [ankilosa'mjento] *nm* (*fig*) paralysis, stagnation.
ansia ['ansja] *nf* anxiety; (*añoranza*) yearning.
ansiar [an'sjar] *vt* to long for.
ansiedad [ansje'ðað] *nf* anxiety.
ansioso, a [an'sjoso, a] *adj* anxious; (*anhelante*) eager; **~ de** *o* **por algo** greedy for sth.
antagónico, a [anta'ɣoniko, a] *adj* antagonistic; (*opuesto*) contrasting.
antagonista [antaɣo'nista] *nm/f* antagonist.
antaño [an'taɲo] *adv* long ago.
Antártico [an'tartiko] *nm*: **el (océano) ~** the Antarctic (Ocean).
Antártida [an'tartiða] *nf* Antarctica.
ante ['ante] *prep* before, in the presence of; (*encarado con*) faced with ♦ *nm* suede; **~ todo** above all.
anteanoche [antea'notʃe] *adv* the night before last.
anteayer [antea'jer] *adv* the day before yesterday.
antebrazo [ante'ßraθo] *nm* forearm.
antecámara [ante'kamara] *nf* (*ARQ*) anteroom; (*antesala*) waiting room; (*POL*) lobby.
antecedente [anteθe'ðente] *adj* previous ♦ *nm*: **~s** *nmpl* (*profesionales*) background *sg*; **~s penales** criminal record; **no tener ~s** to have a clean record; **estar en ~s** to be well-informed; **poner a algn en ~s** to put sb in the picture.
anteceder [anteθe'ðer] *vt* to precede, go before.
antecesor, a [anteθe'sor, a] *nm/f* predecessor.
antedicho, a [ante'ðitʃo, a] *adj* aforementioned.
antelación [antela'θjon] *nf*: **con ~** in advance.
antemano [ante'mano]: **de ~** *adv* beforehand, in advance.
antena [an'tena] *nf* antenna; (*de televisión etc*) aerial.
anteojeras [anteo'xeras] *nfpl* blinkers (*BRIT*), blinders (*US*).
anteojo [ante'oxo] *nm* eyeglass; **~s** *nmpl* (*esp AM*) glasses, spectacles.
antepasados [antepa'saðos] *nmpl* ancestors.
antepecho [ante'petʃo] *nm* guardrail, parapet; (*repisa*) ledge, sill.
antepondré [antepon'dre] *etc vb V* **anteponer**.
anteponer [antepo'ner] *vt* to place in front; (*fig*) to prefer.
anteponga [ante'ponɣa] *etc vb V* **anteponer**.
anteproyecto [antepro'jekto] *nm* preliminary sketch; (*fig*) blueprint; (*POL*): **~ de ley** draft bill.
antepuesto, a [ante'pwesto, a] *pp de* **anteponer**.
antepuse [ante'puse] *etc vb V* **anteponer**.

anterior [ante'rjor] *adj* preceding, previous.
anterioridad [anterjori'ðað] *nf*: **con ~ a** prior to, before.
anteriormente [anterjor'mente] *adv* previously, before.
antes ['antes] *adv* sooner; (*primero*) first; (*con prioridad*) before; (*hace tiempo*) previously, once; (*más bien*) rather ♦ *prep*: **~ de** before ♦ *conj*: **~ (de) que** before; **~ bien** (but) rather; **dos días ~** two days before *o* previously; **mucho/poco ~** long/shortly before; **~ muerto que esclavo** better dead than enslaved; **tomo el avión ~ que el barco** I take the plane rather than the boat; **cuanto ~, lo ~ posible** as soon as possible; **cuanto ~ mejor** the sooner the better.
antesala [ante'sala] *nf* anteroom.
antiadherente [antiaðe'rente] *adj* non-stick.
antiaéreo, a [antia'ereo, a] *adj* anti-aircraft.
antialcohólico, a [antial'koliko, a] *adj*: **centro ~** (*MED*) detoxification unit.
antibalas [anti'βalas] *adj inv*: **chaleco ~** bulletproof jacket.
antibiótico [anti'βjotiko] *nm* antibiotic.
anticiclón [antiθi'klon] *nm* (*METEOROLOGÍA*) anti-cyclone.
anticipación [antiθipa'θjon] *nf* anticipation; **con 10 minutos de ~** 10 minutes early.
anticipado, a [antiθi'paðo, a] *adj* (in) advance; **por ~** in advance.
anticipar [antiθi'par] *vt* to anticipate; (*adelantar*) to bring forward; (*COM*) to advance; **~se** *vr*: **~se a su época** to be ahead of one's time.
anticipo [anti'θipo] *nm* (*COM*) advance; *V tb* **anticipación**.
anticonceptivo, a [antikonθep'tiβo, a] *adj, nm* contraceptive; **métodos ~s** contraceptive devices.
anticongelante [antikonxe'lante] *nm* antifreeze.
anticonstitucional [antikonstituθjo'nal] *adj* unconstitutional.
anticuado, a [anti'kwaðo, a] *adj* out-of-date, old-fashioned; (*desusado*) obsolete.
anticuario [anti'kwarjo] *nm* antique dealer.
anticuerpo [anti'kwerpo] *nm* (*MED*) antibody.
antidemocrático, a [antiðemo'kratiko, a] *adj* undemocratic.
antideportivo, a [antiðepor'tiβo, a] *adj* unsporting.
antidepresivo [antiðepre'siβo] *nm* antidepressant.
antideslumbrante [antiðeslum'brante] *adj* (*INFORM*) anti-dazzle.
antidoping [anti'ðopin] *adj inv* anti-drug.
antídoto [an'tiðoto] *nm* antidote.
antidroga [anti'ðroɣa] *adj inv* anti-drug; **brigada ~** drug squad.
antiestético, a [anties'tetiko, a] *adj* unsightly.
antifaz [anti'faθ] *nm* mask; (*velo*) veil.
antigás [anti'gas] *adj inv*: **careta ~** gasmask.
antigualla [anti'ɣwaʎa] *nf* antique; (*reliquia*) relic; **~s** *nfpl* old things.
antiguamente [antiɣwa'mente] *adv* formerly; (*hace mucho tiempo*) long ago.
antigüedad [antiɣwe'ðað] *nf* antiquity; (*artículo*) antique; (*rango*) seniority.
antiguo, a [an'tiɣwo, a] *adj* old, ancient; (*que fue*) former; **a la antigua** in the old-fashioned way.
antihigiénico, a [anti'xjeniko, a] *adj* unhygienic.
antihistamínico, a [antista'miniko, a] *adj, nm* antihistamine.
antiinflacionista [antinflaθjo'nista] *adj* anti-inflationary, counter-inflationary.
antillano, a [anti'ʎano, a] *adj, nm/f* West Indian.
Antillas [an'tiʎas] *nfpl*: **las ~** the West Indies, the Antilles; **el mar de las ~** the Caribbean Sea.
antílope [an'tilope] *nm* antelope.
antimonopolios [antimono'poljos] *adj inv*: **ley ~** anti-trust law.
antinatural [antinatu'ral] *adj* unnatural.
antiparras [anti'parras] *nfpl* (*fam*) specs.
antipatía [antipa'tia] *nf* antipathy, dislike.
antipático, a [anti'patiko, a] *adj* disagreeable, unpleasant.
Antípodas [an'tipoðas] *nfpl*: **las ~** the Antipodes.
antiquísimo, a [anti'kisimo, a] *adj* ancient.
antirreglamentario, a [antirreɣlamen'tarjo, a] *adj* (*gen*) unlawful; (*POL etc*) unconstitutional.
antirrobo [anti'rroβo] *adj inv*: **(dispositivo) ~** (*para casas etc*) burglar alarm; (*para coches*) car alarm.
antisemita [antise'mita] *adj* anti-Semitic ♦ *nm/f* anti-Semite.
antiséptico, a [anti'septiko, a] *adj, nm* antiseptic.
antiterrorista [antiterro'rista] *adj* antiterrorist; **la lucha ~** the fight against terrorism.
antítesis [an'titesis] *nf inv* antithesis.
antojadizo, a [antoxa'ðiθo, a] *adj*

capricious.
antojarse [anto'xarse] *vr* (*desear*): **se me antoja comprarlo** I have a mind to buy it; (*pensar*): **se me antoja que** I have a feeling that.
antojo [an'toxo] *nm* caprice, whim; (*rosa*) birthmark; (*lunar*) mole; **hacer a su ~** to do as one pleases.
antología [antolo'xia] *nf* anthology.
antonomasia [antono'masja] *nf*: **por ~** par excellence.
antorcha [an'tortʃa] *nf* torch.
antro ['antro] *nm* cavern; **~ de corrupción** (*fig*) den of iniquity.
antropófago, a [antro'pofaɣo, a] *adj, nm/f* cannibal.
antropología [antropolo'xia] *nf* anthropology.
antropólogo, a [antro'poloɣo, a] *nm/f* anthropologist.
anual [a'nwal] *adj* annual.
anualidad [anwali'ðað] *nf* annuity, annual payment; **~ vitalicia** life annuity.
anuario [a'nwarjo] *nm* yearbook.
anudar [anu'ðar] *vt* to knot, tie; (*unir*) to join; **~se** *vr* to get tied up; **se me anudó la voz** I got a lump in my throat.
anulación [anula'θjon] *nf* annulment; cancellation; repeal.
anular [anu'lar] *vt* to annul, cancel; (*suscripción*) to cancel; (*ley*) to repeal ♦ *nm* ring finger.
anunciación [anunθja'θjon] *nf* announcement; **A~** (*REL*) Annunciation.
anunciante [anun'θjante] *nm/f* (*COM*) advertiser.
anunciar [anun'θjar] *vt* to announce; (*proclamar*) to proclaim; (*COM*) to advertise.
anuncio [a'nunθjo] *nm* announcement; (*señal*) sign; (*COM*) advertisement; (*cartel*) poster; (*TEAT*) bill; **~s por palabras** classified ads.
anverso [am'berso] *nm* obverse.
anzuelo [an'θwelo] *nm* hook; (*para pescar*) fish hook; **tragar el ~** to swallow the bait.
añadido [aɲa'ðiðo] *nm* addition.
añadidura [aɲaði'ðura] *nf* addition, extra; **por ~** besides, in addition.
añadir [aɲa'ðir] *vt* to add.
añejo, a [a'ɲexo, a] *adj* old; (*vino*) vintage; (*jamón*) well-cured.
añicos [a'ɲikos] *nmpl*: **hacer ~** to smash, shatter; **hacerse ~** to smash, shatter.
añil [a'ɲil] *nm* (*BOT, color*) indigo.
año ['aɲo] *nm* year; **¡Feliz A~ Nuevo!** Happy New Year!; **tener 15 ~s** to be 15 (years old); **los ~s 80** the eighties; **~ bisiesto/escolar** leap/school year; **~ fiscal** fiscal *o* tax year; **estar de buen ~** to be in good shape; **en el ~ de la nana** in the year dot; **el ~ que viene** next year.
añoranza [aɲo'ranθa] *nf* nostalgia; (*anhelo*) longing.
añorar [aɲo'rar] *vt* to long for.
añoso, a [a'ɲoso, a] *adj* ancient, old.
aovado, a [ao'ßaðo, a] *adj* oval.
aovar [ao'ßar] *vi* to lay eggs.
apabullar [apaßu'ʎar] *vt* (*lit, fig*) to crush.
apacentar [apaθen'tar] *vt* to pasture, graze.
apacible [apa'θißle] *adj* gentle, mild.
apaciente [apa'θjente] *etc vb V* **apacentar**.
apaciguar [apaθi'ɣwar] *vt* to pacify, calm (down).
apacigüe [apa'θiɣwe] *etc vb V* **apaciguar**.
apadrinar [apaðri'nar] *vt* to sponsor, support; (*REL*) to act as godfather to.
apagado, a [apa'ɣaðo, a] *adj* (*volcán*) extinct; (*color*) dull; (*voz*) quiet; (*sonido*) muted, muffled; (*persona: apático*) listless; **estar ~** (*fuego, luz*) to be out; (*radio, TV etc*) to be off.
apagar [apa'ɣar] *vt* to put out; (*color*) to tone down; (*sonido*) to silence, muffle; (*sed*) to quench; (*INFORM*) to toggle off; **~se** *vr* (*luz, fuego*) to go out; (*sonido*) to die away; (*pasión*) to wither; **~ el sistema** (*INFORM*) to close *o* shut down.
apagón [apa'ɣon] *nm* blackout, power cut.
apague [a'paɣe] *etc vb V* **apagar**.
apaisado, a [apai'saðo, a] *adj* (*papel*) landscape *cpd*.
apalabrar [apala'ßrar] *vt* to agree to; (*obrero*) to engage.
Apalaches [apa'latʃes] *nmpl*: **(Montes) ~** Appalachians.
apalear [apale'ar] *vt* to beat, thrash; (*AGR*) to winnow.
apañado, a [apa'ɲaðo, a] *adj* (*mañoso*) resourceful; (*arreglado*) tidy; (*útil*) handy.
apañar [apa'ɲar] *vt* to pick up; (*asir*) to take hold of, grasp; (*reparar*) to mend, patch up; **~se** *vr* to manage, get along; **apañárselas por su cuenta** to look after number one (*fam*).
apaño [a'paɲo] *nm* (*COSTURA*) patch; (*maña*) skill; **esto no tiene ~** there's no answer to this one.
aparador [apara'ðor] *nm* sideboard; (*escaparate*) shop window.
aparato [apa'rato] *nm* apparatus; (*máquina*) machine; (*doméstico*) appliance; (*boato*) ostentation; (*INFORM*)

device; ~ **de facsímil** facsimile (machine), fax; ~ **respiratorio** respiratory system; ~**s de mando** (*AVIAT etc*) controls.

aparatoso, a [apara'toso, a] *adj* showy, ostentatious.

aparcamiento [aparka'mjento] *nm* car park (*BRIT*), parking lot (*US*).

aparcar [apar'kar] *vt, vi* to park.

aparear [apare'ar] *vt* (*objetos*) to pair, match; (*animales*) to mate; ~**se** *vr* to form a pair; to mate.

aparecer [apare'θer] *vi*, ~**se** *vr* to appear; **apareció borracho** he turned up drunk.

aparejado, a [apare'xaðo, a] *adj* fit, suitable; **ir** ~ **con** to go hand in hand with; **llevar** *o* **traer** ~ to involve.

aparejador, a [aparexa'ðor, a] *nm/f* (*ARQ*) quantity surveyor.

aparejar [apare'xar] *vt* to prepare; (*caballo*) to saddle, harness; (*NAUT*) to fit out, rig out.

aparejo [apa'rexo] *nm* preparation; (*de caballo*) harness; (*NAUT*) rigging; (*de poleas*) block and tackle.

aparentar [aparen'tar] *vt* (*edad*) to look; (*fingir*): ~ **tristeza** to pretend to be sad.

aparente [apa'rente] *adj* apparent; (*adecuado*) suitable.

aparezca [apa'reθka] *etc vb V* **aparecer**.

aparición [apari'θjon] *nf* appearance; (*de libro*) publication; (*fantasma*) spectre.

apariencia [apa'rjenθja] *nf* (outward) appearance; **en** ~ outwardly, seemingly.

aparque [a'parke] *etc vb V* **aparcar**.

apartado, a [apar'taðo, a] *adj* separate; (*lejano*) remote ♦ *nm* (*tipográfico*) paragraph; ~ **(de correos)** post office box.

apartamento [aparta'mento] *nm* apartment, flat (*BRIT*).

apartamiento [aparta'mjento] *nm* separation; (*aislamiento*) remoteness; (*AM*) apartment, flat (*BRIT*).

apartar [apar'tar] *vt* to separate; (*quitar*) to remove; (*MINERALOGÍA*) to extract; ~**se** *vr* (*separarse*) to separate, part; (*irse*) to move away; (*mantenerse aparte*) to keep away.

aparte [a'parte] *adv* (*separadamente*) separately; (*además*) besides ♦ *prep*: ~ **de** apart from ♦ *nm* (*TEAT*) aside; (*tipográfico*) new paragraph; **"punto y ~"** "new paragraph".

apasionado, a [apasjo'naðo, a] *adj* passionate; (*pey*) biassed, prejudiced ♦ *nm/f* admirer.

apasionante [apasjo'nante] *adj* exciting.

apasionar [apasjo'nar] *vt* to arouse passion in; ~**se** *vr* to get excited; **le apasiona el fútbol** she's crazy about football.

apatía [apa'tia] *nf* apathy.

apático, a [a'patiko, a] *adj* apathetic.

apátrida [a'patriða] *adj* stateless.

Apdo. *nm abr* (= *Apartado (de Correos)*) P.O. Box.

apeadero [apea'ðero] *nm* halt, stopping place.

apearse [ape'arse] *vr* (*jinete*) to dismount; (*bajarse*) to get down *o* out; (*de coche*) to get out, alight; **no** ~ **del burro** to refuse to climb down.

apechugar [apetʃu'ɣar] *vi*: ~ **con algo** to face up to sth.

apechugue [ape'tʃuɣe] *etc vb V* **apechugar**.

apedrear [apeðre'ar] *vt* to stone.

apegarse [ape'ɣarse] *vr*: ~ **a** to become attached to.

apego [a'peɣo] *nm* attachment, devotion.

apegue [a'peɣe] *etc vb V* **apegarse**.

apelación [apela'θjon] *nf* appeal.

apelar [ape'lar] *vi* to appeal; ~ **a** (*fig*) to resort to.

apelativo [apela'tiβo] *nm* (*LING*) appellative; (*AM*) surname.

apellidar [apeʎi'ðar] *vt* to call, name; ~**se** *vr*: **se apellida Pérez** her (sur)name's Pérez.

apellido [ape'ʎiðo] *nm* surname; *see boxed note.*

APELLIDO

In the Spanish-speaking world most people use two surnames, or ***apellidos;*** *the first is their father's first family name, and the second their mother's first family name. For example, if Juan García López married Carmen Pérez Rodríguez, their children's surname would be García Pérez. Married women retain their own surname(s) and sometimes add their husband's first surname to theirs: Carmen Pérez de García. This woman could also be referred to as (la) Señora de García. In Latin America the second surname is usually shortened to an initial in correspondence: Juan García L.*

apelmazado, a [apelma'θaðo, a] *adj* compact, solid.

apelotonar [apeloto'nar] *vt* to roll into a ball; ~**se** *vr* (*gente*) to crowd together.

apenar [ape'nar] *vt* to grieve, trouble; (*AM: avergonzar*) to embarrass; ~**se** *vr* to grieve; (*AM*) to be embarrassed.

apenas [a'penas] *adv* scarcely, hardly ♦ *conj* as soon as, no sooner.

apéndice [a'pendiθe] *nm* appendix.
apendicitis [apendi'θitis] *nf* appendicitis.
Apeninos [ape'ninos] *nmpl* Apennines.
apercibimiento [aperθiβi'mjento] *nm* (*aviso*) warning.
apercibir [aperθi'βir] *vt* to prepare; (*avisar*) to warn; (*JUR*) to summon; (*AM*) to notice, see; **~se** *vr* to get ready; **~se de** to notice.
aperitivo [aperi'tiβo] *nm* (*bebida*) aperitif; (*comida*) appetizer.
apero [a'pero] *nm* (*AGR*) implement; **~s** *nmpl* farm equipment *sg*.
apertura [aper'tura] *nf* (*gen*) opening; (*POL*) openness, liberalization; (*TEAT etc*) beginning; **~ de un juicio hipotecario** (*COM*) foreclosure.
aperturismo [apertu'rismo] *nm* (*POL*) (policy of) liberalization.
apesadumbrar [apesaðum'brar] *vt* to grieve, sadden; **~se** *vr* to distress o.s.
apestar [apes'tar] *vt* to infect ♦ *vi*: **~ (a)** to stink (of).
apestoso, a [apes'toso, a] *adj* (*hediondo*) stinking; (*asqueroso*) sickening.
apetecer [apete'θer] *vt*: **¿te apetece una tortilla?** do you fancy an omelette?
apetecible [apete'θiβle] *adj* desirable; (*comida*) tempting.
apetezca [ape'teθka] *etc vb V* **apetecer**.
apetito [ape'tito] *nm* appetite.
apetitoso, a [apeti'toso, a] *adj* (*gustoso*) appetizing; (*fig*) tempting.
apiadarse [apja'ðarse] *vr*: **~ de** to take pity on.
ápice ['apiθe] *nm* apex; (*fig*) whit, iota; **ni un ~** not a whit; **no ceder un ~** not to budge an inch.
apicultor, a [apikul'tor, a] *nm/f* beekeeper, apiarist.
apicultura [apikul'tura] *nf* beekeeping.
apiladora [apila'ðora] *nf* (*para máquina impresora*) stacker.
apilar [api'lar] *vt* to pile *o* heap up; **~se** *vr* to pile up.
apiñado, a [api'ɲaðo, a] *adj* (*apretado*) packed.
apiñar [api'ɲar] *vt* to crowd; **~se** *vr* to crowd *o* press together.
apio ['apjo] *nm* celery.
apisonadora [apisona'ðora] *nf* (*máquina*) steamroller.
aplacar [apla'kar] *vt* to placate; **~se** *vr* to calm down.
aplace [a'plaθe] *etc vb V* **aplazar**.
aplanamiento [aplana'mjento] *nm* smoothing, levelling.
aplanar [apla'nar] *vt* to smooth, level; (*allanar*) to roll flat, flatten; **~se** *vr* (*edificio*) to collapse; (*persona*) to get discouraged.
aplaque [a'plake] *etc vb V* **aplacar**.
aplastar [aplas'tar] *vt* to squash (flat); (*fig*) to crush.
aplatanarse [aplata'narse] *vr* to get lethargic.
aplaudir [aplau'ðir] *vt* to applaud.
aplauso [a'plauso] *nm* applause; (*fig*) approval, acclaim.
aplazamiento [aplaθa'mjento] *nm* postponement.
aplazar [apla'θar] *vt* to postpone, defer.
aplicación [aplika'θjon] *nf* application; (*esfuerzo*) effort; **aplicaciones de gestión** business applications.
aplicado, a [apli'kaðo, a] *adj* diligent, hard-working.
aplicar [apli'kar] *vt* (*gen*) to apply; (*poner en vigor*) to put into effect; (*esfuerzos*) to devote; **~se** *vr* to apply o.s.
aplique [a'plike] *etc vb V* **aplicar** ♦ *nm* wall light *o* lamp.
aplomo [a'plomo] *nm* aplomb, self-assurance.
apocado, a [apo'kaðo, a] *adj* timid.
apocamiento [apoka'mjento] *nm* timidity; (*depresión*) depression.
apocarse [apo'karse] *vr* to feel small *o* humiliated.
apocopar [apoko'par] *vt* (*LING*) to shorten.
apócope [a'pokope] *nf* apocopation; **gran es ~ de grande** "gran" is the shortened form of "grande".
apócrifo, a [a'pokrifo, a] *adj* apocryphal.
apodar [apo'ðar] *vt* to nickname.
apoderado [apoðe'raðo] *nm* agent, representative.
apoderar [apoðe'rar] *vt* to authorize, empower; (*JUR*) to grant (a) power of attorney to; **~se** *vr*: **~se de** to take possession of.
apodo [a'poðo] *nm* nickname.
apogeo [apo'xeo] *nm* peak, summit.
apolillado, a [apoli'ʎaðo, a] *adj* moth-eaten.
apolillarse [apoli'ʎarse] *vr* to get moth-eaten.
apología [apolo'xia] *nf* eulogy; (*defensa*) defence.
apoltronarse [apoltro'narse] *vr* to get lazy.
apoplejía [apople'xia] *nf* apoplexy, stroke.
apoque [a'poke] *etc vb V* **apocar**.
apoquinar [apoki'nar] *vt* (*fam*) to cough up, fork out.
aporrear [aporre'ar] *vt* to beat (up).
aportación [aporta'θjon] *nf* contribution.

aportar [apor'tar] *vt* to contribute ♦ *vi* to reach port.
aposentar [aposen'tar] *vt* to lodge, put up.
aposento [apo'sento] *nm* lodging; (*habitación*) room.
apósito [a'posito] *nm* (*MED*) dressing.
apostar [apos'tar] *vt* to bet, stake; (*tropas etc*) to station, post ♦ *vi* to bet.
aposta(s) [a'posta(s)] *adv* on purpose.
apostatar [aposta'tar] *vi* (*REL*) to apostatize; (*fig*) to change sides.
a posteriori [aposte'rjori] *adv* at a later date *o* stage; (*LÓGICA*) a posteriori.
apostilla [apos'tiʎa] *nf* note, comment.
apóstol [a'postol] *nm* apostle.
apóstrofo [a'postrofo] *nm* apostrophe.
apostura [apos'tura] *nf* neatness, elegance.
apoteósico, a [apote'osiko, a] *adj* tremendous.
apoyar [apo'jar] *vt* to lean, rest; (*fig*) to support, back; **~se** *vr*: **~se en** to lean on.
apoyo [a'pojo] *nm* support, backing.
apreciable [apre'θjaβle] *adj* considerable; (*fig*) esteemed.
apreciación [apreθja'θjon] *nf* appreciation; (*COM*) valuation.
apreciar [apre'θjar] *vt* to evaluate, assess; (*COM*) to appreciate, value ♦ *vi* (*ECON*) to appreciate.
aprecio [a'preθjo] *nm* valuation, estimate; (*fig*) appreciation.
aprehender [apreen'der] *vt* to apprehend, detain; (*ver*) to see, observe.
aprehensión [apreen'sjon] *nf* detention, capture.
apremiante [apre'mjante] *adj* urgent, pressing.
apremiar [apre'mjar] *vt* to compel, force ♦ *vi* to be urgent, press.
apremio [a'premjo] *nm* urgency; **~ de pago** demand note.
aprender [apren'der] *vt, vi* to learn; **~ a conducir** to learn to drive; **~se** *vr*: **~se algo** to learn sth (off) by heart.
aprendiz, a [apren'diθ, a] *nm/f* apprentice; (*principiante*) learner, trainee; **~ de comercio** business trainee.
aprendizaje [aprendi'θaxe] *nm* apprenticeship.
aprensión [apren'sjon] *nm* apprehension, fear.
aprensivo, a [apren'siβo, a] *adj* apprehensive.
apresar [apre'sar] *vt* to seize; (*capturar*) to capture.
aprestar [apres'tar] *vt* to prepare, get ready; (*TEC*) to prime, size; **~se** *vr* to get ready.
apresto [a'presto] *nm* (*gen*) preparation; (*sustancia*) size.
apresurado, a [apresu'raðo, a] *adj* hurried, hasty.
apresuramiento [apresura'mjento] *nm* hurry, haste.
apresurar [apresu'rar] *vt* to hurry, accelerate; **~se** *vr* to hurry, make haste; **me apresuré a sugerir que ...** I hastily suggested that ...
apretado, a [apre'taðo, a] *adj* tight; (*escritura*) cramped.
apretar [apre'tar] *vt* to squeeze, press; (*mano*) to clasp; (*dientes*) to grit; (*TEC*) to tighten; (*presionar*) to press together, pack ♦ *vi* to be too tight; **~se** *vr* to crowd together; **~ la mano a algn** to shake sb's hand; **~ el paso** to quicken one's step.
apretón [apre'ton] *nm* squeeze; **~ de manos** handshake.
aprieto [a'prjeto] *etc vb V* **apretar** ♦ *nm* squeeze; (*dificultad*) difficulty, jam; **estar en un ~** to be in a jam; **ayudar a algn a salir de un ~** to help sb out of trouble.
a priori [apri'ori] *adv* beforehand; (*LÓGICA*) a priori.
aprisa [a'prisa] *adv* quickly, hurriedly.
aprisionar [aprisjo'nar] *vt* to imprison.
aprobación [aproβa'θjon] *nf* approval.
aprobado [apro'βaðo] *nm* (*nota*) pass mark.
aprobar [apro'βar] *vt* to approve (of); (*examen, materia*) to pass ♦ *vi* to pass.
apropiación [apropja'θjon] *nf* appropriation.
apropiado, a [apro'pjaðo, a] *adj* appropriate.
apropiarse [apro'pjarse] *vr*: **~ de** to appropriate.
aprovechado, a [aproβe'tʃaðo, a] *adj* industrious, hardworking; (*económico*) thrifty; (*pey*) unscrupulous.
aprovechamiento [aproβetʃa'mjento] *nm* use, exploitation.
aprovechar [aproβe'tʃar] *vt* to use; (*explotar*) to exploit; (*experiencia*) to profit from; (*oferta, oportunidad*) to take advantage of ♦ *vi* to progress, improve; **~se** *vr*: **~se de** to make use of; (*pey*) to take advantage of; **¡que aproveche!** enjoy your meal!
aprovisionar [aproβisjo'nar] *vt* to supply.
aproximación [aproksima'θjon] *nf* approximation; (*de lotería*) consolation prize.
aproximadamente [aproksimaða'mente] *adv* approximately.

aproximado, a [aproksi'maðo, a] *adj* approximate.
aproximar [aproksi'mar] *vt* to bring nearer; **~se** *vr* to come near, approach.
apruebe [a'prweβe] *etc vb V* **aprobar**.
aptitud [apti'tuð] *nf* aptitude; (*capacidad*) ability; ~ **para los negocios** business sense.
apto, a ['apto, a] *adj* (*apropiado*) fit, suitable (*para* for, to); (*hábil*) capable; **~/no ~ para menores** (*CINE*) suitable/unsuitable for children.
apuesto, a [a'pwesto, a] *etc vb V* **apostar** ♦ *adj* neat, elegant ♦ *nf* bet, wager.
apuntador [apunta'ðor] *nm* prompter.
apuntalar [apunta'lar] *vt* to prop up.
apuntar [apun'tar] *vt* (*con arma*) to aim at; (*con dedo*) to point at *o* to; (*anotar*) to note (down); (*datos*) to record; (*TEAT*) to prompt; **~se** *vr* (*DEPORTE*: *tanto, victoria*) to score; (*ESCOL*) to enrol; ~ **una cantidad en la cuenta de algn** to charge a sum to sb's account; **~se en un curso** to enrol on a course; **¡yo me apunto!** count me in!
apunte [a'punte] *nm* note; (*TEAT*: *voz*) prompt; (: *texto*) prompt book.
apuñalar [apuɲa'lar] *vt* to stab.
apurado, a [apu'raðo, a] *adj* needy; (*difícil*) difficult; (*peligroso*) dangerous; (*AM*) hurried, rushed; **estar en una situación apurada** to be in a tight spot; **estar ~** to be in a hurry.
apurar [apu'rar] *vt* (*agotar*) to drain; (*recursos*) to use up; (*molestar*) to annoy; **~se** *vr* (*preocuparse*) to worry; (*esp AM*: *darse prisa*) to hurry.
apuro [a'puro] *nm* (*aprieto*) fix, jam; (*escasez*) want, hardship; (*vergüenza*) embarrassment; (*AM*) haste, urgency.
aquejado, a [ake'xaðo, a] *adj*: ~ **de** (*MED*) afflicted by.
aquejar [ake'xar] *vt* (*afligir*) to distress; **le aqueja una grave enfermedad** he suffers from a serious disease.
aquel, aquella, aquellos, as [a'kel, a'keʎa, a'keʎos, as] *adj* that; (*pl*) those.
aquél, aquélla, aquéllos, as [a'kel, a'keʎa, a'keʎos, as] *pron* that (one); (*pl*) those (ones).
aquello [a'keʎo] *pron* that, that business.
aquí [a'ki] *adv* (*lugar*) here; (*tiempo*) now; ~ **arriba** up here; ~ **mismo** right here; ~ **yace** here lies; **de ~ a siete días** a week from now.
aquietar [akje'tar] *vt* to quieten (down), calm (down).
Aquisgrán [akis'ɣran] *nm* Aachen, Aix-la-Chapelle.
A.R. *abr* (= *Alteza Real*) R.H.
ara ['ara] *nf* (*altar*) altar; **en ~s de** for the sake of.
árabe ['araβe] *adj* Arab, Arabian, Arabic ♦ *nm/f* Arab ♦ *nm* (*LING*) Arabic.
Arabia [a'raβja] *nf* Arabia; ~ **Saudí** *o* **Saudita** Saudi Arabia.
arábigo, a [a'raβiɣo, a] *adj* Arab, Arabian, Arabic.
arácnido [a'rakniðo] *nm* arachnid.
arado [a'raðo] *nm* plough.
aragonés, esa [araɣo'nes, esa] *adj, nm/f* Aragonese ♦ *nm* (*LING*) Aragonese
arancel [aran'θel] *nm* tariff, duty; ~ **de aduanas** (customs) duty.
arandela [aran'dela] *nf* (*TEC*) washer; (*chorrera*) frill.
araña [a'raɲa] *nf* (*ZOOL*) spider; (*lámpara*) chandelier.
arañar [ara'ɲar] *vt* to scratch.
arañazo [ara'ɲaθo] *nm* scratch.
arar [a'rar] *vt* to plough, till.
araucano, a [arau'kano, a] *adj, nm/f* Araucanian.
arbitraje [arβi'traxe] *nm* arbitration.
arbitrar [arβi'trar] *vt* to arbitrate in; (*recursos*) to bring together; (*DEPORTE*) to referee ♦ *vi* to arbitrate.
arbitrariedad [arβitrarje'ðað] *nf* arbitrariness; (*acto*) arbitrary act.
arbitrario, a [arβi'trarjo] *adj* arbitrary.
arbitrio [ar'βitrjo] *nm* free will; (*JUR*) adjudication, decision; **dejar al ~ de algn** to leave to sb's discretion.
árbitro ['arβitro] *nm* arbitrator; (*DEPORTE*) referee; (*TENIS*) umpire.
árbol ['arβol] *nm* (*BOT*) tree; (*NAUT*) mast; (*TEC*) axle, shaft.
arbolado, a [arβo'laðo, a] *adj* wooded; (*camino*) tree-lined ♦ *nm* woodland.
arboladura [arβola'ðura] *nf* rigging.
arbolar [arβo'lar] *vt* to hoist, raise.
arboleda [arβo'leða] *nf* grove, plantation.
arbusto [ar'βusto] *nm* bush, shrub.
arca ['arka] *nf* chest, box; **A~ de la Alianza** Ark of the Covenant; **A~ de Noé** Noah's Ark.
arcada [ar'kaða] *nf* arcade; (*de puente*) arch, span; **~s** *nfpl* retching *sg*.
arcaico, a [ar'kaiko, a] *adj* archaic.
arce ['arθe] *nm* maple tree.
arcén [ar'θen] *nm* (*de autopista*) hard shoulder; (*de carretera*) verge.
archiconocido, a [artʃikono'θiðo, a] *adj* extremely well-known.
archipiélago [artʃi'pjelaɣo] *nm*

archipelago.
archisabido, a [artʃisa'ßiðo, a] *adj* extremely well-known.
archivador [artʃißa'ðor] *nm* filing cabinet; ~ **colgante** suspension file.
archivar [artʃi'ßar] *vt* to file (away); (*INFORM*) to archive.
archivo [ar'tʃißo] *nm* archive(s) (*pl*); (*INFORM*) file, archive; **A~ Nacional** Public Record Office; **~s policíacos** police files; **nombre de ~** (*INFORM*) filename; ~ **maestro** (*INFORM*) master file; ~ **de transacciones** (*INFORM*) transactions file.
arcilla [ar'θiʎa] *nf* clay.
arco ['arko] *nm* arch; (*MAT*) arc; (*MIL, MUS*) bow; (*AM DEPORTE*) goal; ~ **iris** rainbow.
arcón [ar'kon] *nm* large chest.
arder [ar'ðer] *vt* to burn; ~ **sin llama** to smoulder; **estar que arde** (*persona*) to fume.
ardid [ar'ðið] *nm* ruse.
ardiente [ar'ðjente] *adj* ardent.
ardilla [ar'ðiʎa] *nf* squirrel.
ardor [ar'ðor] *nm* (*calor*) heat, warmth; (*fig*) ardour; ~ **de estómago** heartburn.
ardoroso, a [arðo'roso, a] *adj* passionate.
arduo, a ['arðwo, a] *adj* arduous.
área ['area] *nf* area; (*DEPORTE*) penalty area; ~ **de excedentes** (*INFORM*) overflow area.
ARENA [a'rena] *nf abr* (*El Salvador: POL*) = *Alianza Republicana Nacionalista*.
arena [a'rena] *nf* sand; (*de una lucha*) arena.
arenal [are'nal] *nm* (*arena movediza*) quicksand.
arenga [a'renga] *nf* (*fam*) sermon.
arengar [aren'gar] *vt* to harangue.
arengue [a'renge] *etc vb V* **arengar**.
arenillas [are'niʎas] *nfpl* (*MED*) stones.
arenisca [are'niska] *nf* sandstone; (*cascajo*) grit.
arenoso, a [are'noso, a] *adj* sandy.
arenque [a'renke] *nm* herring.
arepa [a'repa] *nf* (*AM*) corn pancake.
arete [a'rete] *nm* earring.
argamasa [arɤa'masa] *nf* mortar, plaster.
Argel [ar'xel] *n* Algiers.
Argelia [ar'xelja] *nf* Algeria.
argelino, a [arxe'lino, a] *adj, nm/f* Algerian.
Argentina [arxen'tina] *nf*: **(la)** ~ the Argentine, Argentina.
argentino, a [arxen'tino, a] *adj* Argentinian; (*de plata*) silvery ♦ *nm/f* Argentinian.
argolla [ar'ɤoʎa] *nf* (large) ring; (*AM: de matrimonio*) wedding ring.
argot [ar'ɤo] *nm, pl* **argots** [ar'ɤo, ar'ɤos] slang.
argucia [ar'ɤuθja] *nf* subtlety, sophistry.
argüir [ar'ɤwir] *vt* to deduce; (*discutir*) to argue; (*indicar*) to indicate, imply; (*censurar*) to reproach ♦ *vi* to argue.
argumentación [arɤumenta'θjon] *nf* (line of) argument.
argumentar [arɤumen'tar] *vt, vi* to argue.
argumento [arɤu'mento] *nm* argument; (*razonamiento*) reasoning; (*de novela etc*) plot; (*CINE, TV*) storyline.
arguyendo [arɤu'jendo] *etc vb V* **argüir**.
aria ['arja] *nf* aria.
aridez [ari'ðeθ] *nf* aridity, dryness.
árido, a ['ariðo, a] *adj* arid, dry; **~s** *nmpl* dry goods.
Aries ['arjes] *nm* Aries.
ariete [a'rjete] *nm* battering ram.
ario, a ['arjo, a] *adj* Aryan.
arisco, a [a'risko, a] *adj* surly; (*insociable*) unsociable.
aristocracia [aristo'kraθja] *nf* aristocracy.
aristócrata [aris'tokrata] *nm/f* aristocrat.
aristocrático, a [aristo'kratiko, a] *adj* aristocratic.
aritmética [arit'metika] *nf* arithmetic.
aritmético, a [arit'metiko, a] *adj* arithmetic(al) ♦ *nm/f* arithmetician.
arma ['arma] *nf* arm; **~s** *nfpl* arms; ~ **blanca** blade, knife; (*espada*) sword; ~ **de fuego** firearm; **~s cortas** small arms; **rendir las ~s** to lay down one's arms; **ser de ~s tomar** to be somebody to be reckoned with.
armada [ar'maða] *nf* armada; (*flota*) fleet; *V tb* **armado**.
armadillo [arma'ðiʎo] *nm* armadillo.
armado, a [ar'maðo, a] *adj* armed; (*TEC*) reinforced.
armador [arma'ðor] *nm* (*NAUT*) shipowner.
armadura [arma'ðura] *nf* (*MIL*) armour; (*TEC*) framework; (*ZOOL*) skeleton; (*FÍSICA*) armature.
armamentista [armamen'tista], **armamentístico, a** [armamen'tistiko, a] *adj* arms *cpd*.
armamento [arma'mento] *nm* armament; (*NAUT*) fitting-out.
armar [ar'mar] *vt* (*soldado*) to arm; (*máquina*) to assemble; (*navío*) to fit out; **~la, ~ un lío** to start a row; **~se** *vr*: **~se de valor** to summon up one's courage.
armario [ar'marjo] *nm* wardrobe.
armatoste [arma'toste] *nm* (*mueble*) monstrosity; (*máquina*) contraption.
armazón [arma'θon] *nf o m* body, chassis; (*de mueble etc*) frame; (*ARQ*) skeleton.
Armenia [ar'menja] *nf* Armenia.

armería [arme'ria] *nf* (*museo*) military museum; (*tienda*) gunsmith's.
armiño [ar'miɲo] *nm* stoat; (*piel*) ermine.
armisticio [armis'tiθjo] *nm* armistice.
armonía [armo'nia] *nf* harmony.
armónica [ar'monika] *nf* harmonica; *V tb* **armónico.**
armonice [armo'niθe] *etc vb V* **armonizar.**
armónico, a [ar'moniko, a] *adj* harmonic.
armonioso, a [armo'njoso, a] *adj* harmonious.
armonizar [armoni'θar] *vt* to harmonize; (*diferencias*) to reconcile ♦ *vi* to harmonize; ~ **con** (*fig*) to be in keeping with; (*colores*) to tone in with.
arnés [ar'nes] *nm* armour; **arneses** *nmpl* harness *sg.*
aro ['aro] *nm* ring; (*tejo*) quoit; (*AM: pendiente*) earring; **entrar por el** ~ to give in.
aroma [a'roma] *nm* aroma.
aromático, a [aro'matiko, a] *adj* aromatic.
arpa ['arpa] *nf* harp.
arpegio [ar'pexjo] *nm* (*MUS*) arpeggio.
arpía [ar'pia] *nf* (*fig*) shrew.
arpillera [arpi'ʎera] *nf* sacking, sackcloth.
arpón [ar'pon] *nm* harpoon.
arquear [arke'ar] *vt* to arch, bend; **~se** *vr* to arch, bend.
arqueo [ar'keo] *nm* (*gen*) arching; (*NAUT*) tonnage.
arqueología [arkeolo'xia] *nf* archaeology.
arqueológico, a [arkeo'loxiko, a] *adj* archaeological.
arqueólogo, a [arke'oloɣo, a] *nm/f* archaeologist.
arquero [ar'kero] *nm* archer, bowman; (*AM DEPORTE*) goalkeeper.
arquetipo [arke'tipo] *nm* archetype.
arquitecto, a [arki'tekto, a] *nm/f* architect; ~ **paisajista** *o* **de jardines** landscape gardener.
arquitectónico, a [arkitek'toniko, a] *adj* architectural.
arquitectura [arkitek'tura] *nf* architecture.
arrabal [arra'ßal] *nm* suburb; **~es** *nmpl* outskirts.
arrabalero, a [arraßa'lero, a] *adj* (*fig*) common, coarse.
arracimarse [arraθi'marse] *vr* to cluster together.
arraigado, a [arrai'ɣaðo, a] *adj* deep-rooted; (*fig*) established.
arraigar [arrai'ɣar] *vt* to establish ♦ *vi*, **~se** *vr* to take root; (*persona*) to settle.
arraigo [a'rraiɣo] *nm* (*raíces*) roots *pl*; (*bienes*) property; (*influencia*) hold; **hombre de** ~ man of property.
arraigue [a'rraiɣe] *etc vb V* **arraigar.**
arrancada [arran'kaða] *nf* (*arranque*) sudden start.
arrancar [arran'kar] *vt* (*sacar*) to extract, pull out; (*arrebatar*) to snatch (away); (*pedazo*) to tear off; (*página*) to rip out; (*suspiro*) to heave; (*AUTO*) to start; (*INFORM*) to boot; (*fig*) to extract ♦ *vi* (*AUTO, máquina*) to start; (*ponerse en marcha*) to get going; ~ **información a algn** to extract information from sb; ~ **de** to stem from.
arranque [a'rranke] *etc vb V* **arrancar** ♦ *nm* sudden start; (*AUTO*) start; (*fig*) fit, outburst.
arras ['arras] *nfpl* pledge *sg*, security *sg.*
arrasar [arra'sar] *vt* (*aplanar*) to level, flatten; (*destruir*) to demolish.
arrastrado, a [arras'traðo, a] *adj* poor, wretched.
arrastrador [arrastra'ðor] *nm* (*en máquina impresora*) tractor.
arrastrar [arras'trar] *vt* to drag (along); (*fig*) to drag down, degrade; (*suj: agua, viento*) to carry away ♦ *vi* to drag, trail on the ground; **~se** *vr* to crawl; (*fig*) to grovel; **llevar algo arrastrado** to drag sth along.
arrastre [a'rrastre] *nm* drag, dragging; (*DEPORTE*) crawl; **estar para el** ~ (*fig*) to have had it; ~ **de papel por fricción/por tracción** (*en máquina impresora*) friction/tractor feed.
array [a'rrai] *nm* (*INFORM*) array; ~ **empaquetado** (*INFORM*) packed array.
arrayán [arra'jan] *nm* myrtle.
arre ['arre] *excl* gee up!
arrear [arre'ar] *vt* to drive on, urge on ♦ *vi* to hurry along.
arrebañar [arreßa'ɲar] *vt* (*juntar*) to scrape together.
arrebatado, a [arreßa'taðo, a] *adj* rash, impetuous; (*repentino*) sudden, hasty.
arrebatar [arreßa'tar] *vt* to snatch (away), seize; (*fig*) to captivate; **~se** *vr* to get carried away, get excited.
arrebato [arre'ßato] *nm* fit of rage, fury; (*éxtasis*) rapture; **en un** ~ **de cólera** in an outburst of anger.
arrebolar [arreßo'lar] *vt* to redden; **~se** *vr* (*enrojecer*) to blush.
arrebujar [arreßu'xar] *vt* (*objetos*) to jumble together; **~se** *vr* to wrap o.s. up.
arrechar [arre'tʃar] (*AM*) *vt* to arouse, excite; **~se** *vr* to become aroused.
arrechucho [arre'tʃutʃo] *nm* (*MED*) turn.
arreciar [arre'θjar] *vi* to get worse; (*viento*) to get stronger.

arrecife [arre'θife] *nm* reef.
arredrar [arre'ðrar] *vt* (*hacer retirarse*) to drive back; **~se** *vr* (*apartarse*) to draw back; **~se ante algo** to shrink away from sth.
arreglado, a [arre'ɣlaðo, a] *adj* (*ordenado*) neat, orderly; (*moderado*) moderate, reasonable.
arreglar [arre'ɣlar] *vt* (*poner orden*) to tidy up; (*algo roto*) to fix, repair; (*problema*) to solve; **~se** *vr* to reach an understanding; **arreglárselas** (*fam*) to get by, manage.
arreglo [a'rreɣlo] *nm* settlement; (*orden*) order; (*acuerdo*) agreement; (*MUS*) arrangement, setting; (*INFORM*) array; **con ~ a** in accordance with; **llegar a un ~** to reach a compromise.
arrellanarse [arreʎa'narse] *vr* to sprawl; **~ en el asiento** to lie back in one's chair.
arremangar [arreman'gar] *vt* to roll up, turn up; **~se** *vr* to roll up one's sleeves.
arremangue [arre'mange] *etc vb V* **arremangar.**
arremeter [arreme'ter] *vt* to attack, assault; **~ contra algn** to attack sb.
arremetida [arreme'tiða] *nf* assault.
arremolinarse [arremoli'narse] *vr* to crowd around, mill around; (*corriente*) to swirl, eddy.
arrendador, a [arrenda'ðor, a] *nm/f* landlord/lady.
arrendamiento [arrenda'mjento] *nm* letting; (*el alquilar*) hiring; (*contrato*) lease; (*alquiler*) rent.
arrendar [arren'dar] *vt* to let; to hire; to lease; to rent.
arrendatario, a [arrenda'tarjo, a] *nm/f* tenant.
arreos [a'rreos] *nmpl* harness *sg*, trappings.
arrepentido, a [arrepen'tiðo, a] *nm/f* (*POL*) reformed terrorist.
arrepentimiento [arrepenti'mjento] *nm* regret, repentance.
arrepentirse [arrepen'tirse] *vr* to repent; **~ de (haber hecho) algo** to regret (doing) sth.
arrepienta [arre'pjenta] *etc*, **arrepintiendo** [arrepin'tjendo] *etc vb V* **arrepentirse.**
arrestar [arres'tar] *vt* to arrest; (*encarcelar*) to imprison.
arresto [a'rresto] *nm* arrest; (*MIL*) detention; (*audacia*) boldness, daring; **~ domiciliario** house arrest.
arriar [a'rrjar] *vt* (*velas*) to haul down; (*bandera*) to lower, strike; (*un cable*) to pay out.
arriate [a'rrjate] *nm* (*BOT*) bed; (*camino*) road.

PALABRA CLAVE

arriba [a'rriβa] *adv* **1** (*posición*) above; **desde ~** from above; **~ del todo** at the very top, right on top; **Juan está ~** Juan is upstairs; **lo ~ mencionado** the aforementioned; **aquí/allí ~** up here/there; **está hasta ~ de trabajo** (*fam*) he's up to his eyes in work (*fam*)
2 (*dirección*) up, upwards; **más ~** higher *o* further up; **calle ~** up the street
3: **de ~ abajo** from top to bottom; **mirar a algn de ~ abajo** to look sb up and down
4: **para ~**: **de 5000 pesetas para ~** from 5,000 pesetas up(wards); **de la cintura (para) ~** from the waist up
♦ *adj*: **de ~**: **el piso de ~** the upstairs flat (*BRIT*) *o* apartment; **la parte de ~** the top *o* upper part
♦ *prep*: **~ de** (*AM*) above; **~ de 200 dólares** more than 200 dollars
♦ *excl*: **¡~!** up!; **¡manos ~!** hands up!; **¡~ España!** long live Spain!

arribar [arri'βar] *vi* to put into port; (*esp AM*: *llegar*) to arrive.
arribista [arri'βista] *nm/f* parvenu(e), upstart.
arribo [a'rriβo] *nm* (*esp AM*) arrival.
arriendo [a'rrjendo] *etc vb V* **arrendar** ♦ *nm* = **arrendamiento.**
arriero [a'rrjero] *nm* muleteer.
arriesgado, a [arrjes'ɣaðo, a] *adj* (*peligroso*) risky; (*audaz*) bold, daring.
arriesgar [arrjes'ɣar] *vt* to risk; (*poner en peligro*) to endanger; **~se** *vr* to take a risk.
arriesgue [a'rrjesɣe] *etc vb V* **arriesgar.**
arrimar [arri'mar] *vt* (*acercar*) to bring close; (*poner de lado*) to set aside; **~se** *vr* to come close *o* closer; **~se a** to lean on; (*fig*) to keep company with; (*buscar ayuda*) to seek the protection of; **arrímate a mí** cuddle up to me.
arrinconado, a [arrinko'naðo, a] *adj* forgotten, neglected.
arrinconar [arrinko'nar] *vt* to put in a corner; (*fig*) to put on one side; (*abandonar*) to push aside.
arriscado, a [arris'kaðo, a] *adj* (*GEO*) craggy; (*fig*) bold, resolute.
arroba [a'rroβa] *nf* (*peso*) 25 pounds; (*INFORM*: *en dirección electrónica*) at; **tiene talento por ~s** he has loads *o* bags of talent.
arrobado, a [arro'βaðo, a] *adj* entranced, enchanted.

arrobamiento [arroβa'mjento] *nm* ecstasy.
arrobar [arro'βar] *vt* to enchant; ~**se** *vr* to be enraptured; (*místico*) to go into a trance.
arrodillarse [arroði'ʎarse] *vr* to kneel (down).
arrogancia [arro'ɣanθja] *nf* arrogance.
arrogante [arro'ɣante] *adj* arrogant.
arrojar [arro'xar] *vt* to throw, hurl; (*humo*) to emit, give out; (*COM*) to yield, produce; ~**se** *vr* to throw *o* hurl o.s.
arrojo [a'rroxo] *nm* daring.
arrollador, a [arroʎa'ðor, a] *adj* crushing, overwhelming.
arrollar [arro'ʎar] *vt* (*enrollar*) to roll up; (*suj*: *inundación*) to wash away; (*AUTO*) to run over; (*DEPORTE*) to crush.
arropar [arro'par] *vt* to cover (up), wrap up; ~**se** *vr* to wrap o.s. up.
arrostrar [arros'trar] *vt* to face (up to); ~**se** *vr*: ~**se con algn** to face up to sb.
arroyo [a'rrojo] *nm* stream; (*de la calle*) gutter; **poner a algn en el** ~ to turn sb onto the streets.
arroz [a'rroθ] *nm* rice; ~ **con leche** rice pudding.
arrozal [arro'θal] *nm* paddy field.
arruga [a'rruɣa] *nf* fold; (*de cara*) wrinkle; (*de vestido*) crease.
arrugar [arru'ɣar] *vt* to fold; to wrinkle; to crease; ~**se** *vr* to get wrinkled; to get creased.
arrugue [a'rruɣe] *etc vb V* **arrugar**.
arruinar [arrwi'nar] *vt* to ruin, wreck; ~**se** *vr* to be ruined.
arrullar [arru'ʎar] *vi* to coo ♦ *vt* to lull to sleep.
arrumaco [arru'mako] *nm* (*caricia*) caress; (*halago*) piece of flattery.
arrumbar [arrum'bar] *vt* (*objeto*) to discard; (*individuo*) to silence.
arrurruz [arru'rruθ] nm arrowroot.
arsenal [arse'nal] *nm* naval dockyard; (*MIL*) arsenal.
arsénico [ar'seniko] *nm* arsenic.
arte ['arte] *nm* (*gen m en sg y siempre f en pl*) art; (*maña*) skill, guile; **por** ~ **de magia** (as if) by magic; **no tener** ~ **ni parte en algo** to have nothing whatsoever to do with sth; ~**s** *nfpl* arts; **Bellas A**~**s** Fine Art *sg*; ~**s y oficios** arts and crafts.
artefacto [arte'fakto] *nm* appliance; (*ARQUEOLOGÍA*) artefact.
arteria [ar'terja] *nf* artery.
arterial [arte'rjal] *adj* arterial; (*presión*) blood *cpd*.
arterio(e)sclerosis [arterjo(e)skle'rosis] *nf inv* hardening of the arteries, arteriosclerosis.
artesa [ar'tesa] *nf* trough.
artesanía [artesa'nia] *nf* craftsmanship; (*artículos*) handicrafts *pl*.
artesano, a [arte'sano, a] *nm/f* artisan, craftsman/woman.
ártico, a ['artiko, a] *adj* Arctic ♦ *nm*: **el (océano) Á**~ the Arctic (Ocean).
articulación [artikula'θjon] *nf* articulation; (*MED, TEC*) joint.
articulado, a [artiku'laðo, a] *adj* articulated; jointed.
articular [artiku'lar] *vt* to articulate; to join together.
articulista [artiku'lista] *nm/f* columnist, contributor (to a newspaper).
artículo [ar'tikulo] *nm* article; (*cosa*) thing, article; (*TV*) feature, report; ~ **de fondo** leader, editorial; ~**s** *nmpl* goods; ~**s de marca** (*COM*) proprietary goods.
artífice [ar'tifiθe] *nm* artist, craftsman; (*fig*) architect.
artificial [artifi'θjal] *adj* artificial.
artificio [arti'fiθjo] *nm* art, skill; (*artesanía*) craftsmanship; (*astucia*) cunning.
artillería [artiʎe'ria] *nf* artillery.
artillero [arti'ʎero] *nm* artilleryman, gunner.
artilugio [arti'luxjo] *nm* gadget.
artimaña [arti'maɲa] *nf* trap, snare; (*astucia*) cunning.
artista [ar'tista] *nm/f* (*pintor*) artist, painter; (*TEAT*) artist, artiste.
artístico, a [ar'tistiko, a] *adj* artistic.
artritis [ar'tritis] *nf* arthritis.
arveja [ar'βexa] *nf* (*AM*) pea.
Arz. *abr* (= *Arzobispo*) Abp.
arzobispo [arθo'βispo] *nm* archbishop.
as [as] *nm* ace; ~ **del fútbol** star player.
asa ['asa] *nf* handle; (*fig*) lever.
asado [a'saðo] *nm* roast (meat); (*AM*: *barbacoa*) barbecue.
asador [asa'ðor] *nm* (*varilla*) spit; (*aparato*) spit roaster.
asadura(s) [asa'ðura(s)] *nf(pl)* entrails *pl*, offal *sg*; (*CULIN*) chitterlings *pl*.
asaetear [asaete'ar] *vt* (*fig*) to bother.
asalariado, a [asala'rjaðo, a] *adj* paid, wage-earning, salaried ♦ *nm/f* wage earner.
asaltador, a [asalta'ðor, a], **asaltante** [asal'tante] *nm/f* assailant.
asaltar [asal'tar] *vt* to attack, assault; (*fig*) to assail.
asalto [a'salto] *nm* attack, assault; (*DEPORTE*) round.
asamblea [asam'blea] *nf* assembly; (*reunión*) meeting.

asar [a'sar] *vt* to roast; ~ **al horno/a la parrilla** to bake/grill; ~**se** *vr* (*fig*): **me aso de calor** I'm roasting; **aquí se asa uno vivo** it's boiling hot here.
asbesto [as'ßesto] *nm* asbestos.
ascendencia [asθen'denθja] *nf* ancestry; **de ~ francesa** of French origin.
ascender [asθen'der] *vi* (*subir*) to ascend, rise; (*ser promovido*) to gain promotion ♦ *vt* to promote; ~ **a** to amount to.
ascendiente [asθen'djente] *nm* influence ♦ *nm/f* ancestor.
ascensión [asθen'sjon] *nf* ascent; **la A~** the Ascension.
ascenso [as'θenso] *nm* ascent; (*promoción*) promotion.
ascensor [asθen'sor] *nm* lift (*BRIT*), elevator (*US*).
ascético, a [as'θetiko, a] *adj* ascetic.
ascienda [as'θjenda] *etc vb V* **ascender**.
asco ['asko] *nm*: **el ajo me da ~** I hate *o* loathe garlic; **hacer ~s de algo** to turn up one's nose at sth; **estar hecho un ~** to be filthy; **poner a algn de ~** to call sb all sorts of names *o* every name under the sun; **¡qué ~!** how revolting *o* disgusting!
ascua ['askwa] *nf* ember; **arrimar el ~ a su sardina** to look after number one; **estar en ~s** to be on tenterhooks.
aseado, a [ase'aðo, a] *adj* clean; (*arreglado*) tidy; (*pulcro*) smart.
asear [ase'ar] *vt* (*lavar*) to wash; (*ordenar*) to tidy (up).
asechanza [ase'tʃanθa] *nf* trap, snare.
asediar [ase'ðjar] *vt* (*MIL*) to besiege, lay siege to; (*fig*) to chase, pester.
asedio [a'seðjo] *nm* siege; (*COM*) run.
asegurado, a [aseɣu'raðo, a] *adj* insured.
asegurador, a [aseɣura'ðor, a] *nm/f* insurer.
asegurar [aseɣu'rar] *vt* (*consolidar*) to secure, fasten; (*dar garantía de*) to guarantee; (*preservar*) to safeguard; (*afirmar, dar por cierto*) to assure, affirm; (*tranquilizar*) to reassure; (*tomar un seguro*) to insure; ~**se** *vr* to assure o.s., make sure.
asemejarse [aseme'xarse] *vr* to be alike; ~ **a** to be like, resemble.
asentado, a [asen'taðo, a] *adj* established, settled.
asentar [asen'tar] *vt* (*sentar*) to seat, sit down; (*poner*) to place, establish; (*alisar*) to level, smooth down *o* out; (*anotar*) to note down ♦ *vi* to be suitable, suit.
asentimiento [asenti'mjento] *nm* assent, agreement.
asentir [asen'tir] *vi* to assent, agree.
aseo [a'seo] *nm* cleanliness; ~**s** *nmpl* toilet *sg* (*BRIT*), restroom *sg* (*US*), cloakroom *sg*.
aséptico, a [a'septiko, a] *adj* germ-free, free from infection.
asequible [ase'kißle] *adj* (*precio*) reasonable; (*meta*) attainable; (*persona*) approachable.
aserradero [aserra'ðero] *nm* sawmill.
aserrar [ase'rrar] *vt* to saw.
asesinar [asesi'nar] *vt* to murder; (*POL*) to assassinate.
asesinato [asesi'nato] *nm* murder; assassination.
asesino, a [ase'sino, a] *nm/f* murderer, killer; (*POL*) assassin.
asesor, a [ase'sor, a] *nm/f* adviser, consultant; (*COM*) assessor, consultant; ~ **administrativo** management consultant.
asesorar [aseso'rar] *vt* (*JUR*) to advise, give legal advice to; (*COM*) to act as consultant to; ~**se** *vr*: ~**se con** *o* **de** to take advice from, consult.
asesoría [aseso'ria] *nf* (*cargo*) consultancy; (*oficina*) consultant's office.
asestar [ases'tar] *vt* (*golpe*) to deal; (*arma*) to aim; (*tiro*) to fire.
aseverar [aseße'rar] *vt* to assert.
asfaltado, a [asfal'taðo, a] *adj* asphalted ♦ *nm* (*pavimiento*) asphalt.
asfalto [as'falto] *nm* asphalt.
asfixia [as'fiksja] *nf* asphyxia, suffocation.
asfixiar [asfik'sjar] *vt* to asphyxiate, suffocate.
asga ['asɣa] *etc vb V* **asir**.
así [a'si] *adv* (*de esta manera*) in this way, like this, thus; (*aunque*) although; (*tan pronto como*) as soon as; ~ **que** so; ~ **como** as well as; ~ **y todo** even so; **¿no es ~?** isn't it?, didn't you? *etc*; ~ **de grande** this big; **¡~ sea!** so be it!; ~ **es la vida** such is life, that's life.
Asia ['asja] *nf* Asia.
asiático, a [a'sjatiko, a] *adj, nm/f* Asian, Asiatic.
asidero [asi'ðero] *nm* handle.
asiduidad [asiðwi'ðað] *nf* assiduousness.
asiduo, a [a'siðwo, a] *adj* assiduous; (*frecuente*) frequent ♦ *nm/f* regular (customer).
asiento [a'sjento] *etc vb V* **asentar, asentir** ♦ *nm* (*mueble*) seat, chair; (*de coche, en tribunal etc*) seat; (*localidad*) seat, place; (*fundamento*) site; ~ **delantero/trasero** front/back seat.
asierre [a'sjerre] *etc vb V* **aserrar**.
asignación [asiɣna'θjon] *nf* (*atribución*)

assignment; (*reparto*) allocation; (*COM*) allowance; ~ **(semanal)** pocket money; ~ **de presupuesto** budget appropriation.
asignar [asiɣ'nar] *vt* to assign, allocate.
asignatura [asiɣna'tura] *nf* subject; (*curso*) course; ~ **pendiente** (*fig*) matter pending.
asilado, a [asi'laðo, a] *nm/f* refugee.
asilo [a'silo] *nm* (*refugio*) asylum, refuge; (*establecimiento*) home, institution; ~ **político** political asylum.
asimilación [asimila'θjon] *nf* assimilation.
asimilar [asimi'lar] *vt* to assimilate.
asimismo [asi'mismo] *adv* in the same way, likewise.
asintiendo [asin'tjendo] *etc vb V* **asentir**.
asir [a'sir] *vt* to seize, grasp; ~**se** *vr* to take hold; ~**se a** *o* **de** to seize.
asistencia [asis'tenθja] *nf* presence; (*TEAT*) audience; (*MED*) attendance; (*ayuda*) assistance; ~ **social** social *o* welfare work.
asistente, a [asis'tente, a] *nm/f* assistant ♦ *nm* (*MIL*) orderly ♦ *nf* daily help; **los** ~**s** those present; ~ **social** social worker.
asistido, a [asis'tiðo, a] *adj* (*AUTO*: *dirección*) power-assisted; ~ **por ordenador** computer-assisted.
asistir [asis'tir] *vt* to assist, help ♦ *vi*: ~ **a** to attend, be present at.
asma ['asma] *nf* asthma.
asno ['asno] *nm* donkey; (*fig*) ass.
asociación [asoθja'θjon] *nf* association; (*COM*) partnership.
asociado, a [aso'θjaðo, a] *adj* associate ♦ *nm/f* associate; (*COM*) partner.
asociar [aso'θjar] *vt* to associate; ~**se** *vr* to become partners.
asolar [aso'lar] *vt* to destroy.
asolear [asole'ar] *vt* to put in the sun; ~**se** *vr* to sunbathe.
asomar [aso'mar] *vt* to show, stick out ♦ *vi* to appear; ~**se** *vr* to appear, show up; ~ **la cabeza por la ventana** to put one's head out of the window.
asombrar [asom'brar] *vt* to amaze, astonish; ~**se** *vr*: ~**se (de)** (*sorprenderse*) to be amazed (at); (*asustarse*) to be frightened (at).
asombro [a'sombro] *nm* amazement, astonishment.
asombroso, a [asom'broso, a] *adj* amazing, astonishing.
asomo [a'somo] *nm* hint, sign; **ni por** ~ by no means.
asonancia [aso'nanθja] *nf* (*LIT*) assonance; (*fig*) connection; **no tener** ~ **con** to bear no relation to.
asorocharse [asoro'tʃarse] *vr* (*AM*) to get mountain sickness.
aspa ['aspa] *nf* (*cruz*) cross; (*de molino*) sail; **en** ~ X-shaped.
aspaviento [aspa'ßjento] *nm* exaggerated display of feeling; (*fam*) fuss.
aspecto [as'pekto] *nm* (*apariencia*) look, appearance; (*fig*) aspect; **bajo ese** ~ from that point of view.
aspereza [aspe'reθa] *nf* roughness; (*de fruta*) sharpness; (*de carácter*) surliness.
áspero, a ['aspero, a] *adj* rough; sharp; harsh.
aspersión [asper'sjon] *nf* sprinkling; (*AGR*) spraying.
aspersor [asper'sor] *nm* sprinkler.
aspiración [aspira'θjon] *nf* breath, inhalation; (*MUS*) short pause; **aspiraciones** *nfpl* aspirations.
aspiradora [aspira'ðora] *nf* vacuum cleaner, Hoover ®.
aspirante [aspi'rante] *nm/f* (*candidato*) candidate; (*DEPORTE*) contender.
aspirar [aspi'rar] *vt* to breathe in ♦ *vi*: ~ **a** to aspire to.
aspirina [aspi'rina] *nf* aspirin.
asquear [aske'ar] *vt* to sicken ♦ *vi* to be sickening; ~**se** *vr* to feel disgusted.
asquerosidad [askerosi'ðað] *nf* (*suciedad*) filth; (*dicho*) obscenity; (*truco*) dirty trick.
asqueroso, a [aske'roso, a] *adj* disgusting, sickening.
asta ['asta] *nf* lance; (*arpón*) spear; (*mango*) shaft, handle; (*ZOOL*) horn; **a media** ~ at half mast.
astado, a [as'taðo, a] *adj* horned ♦ *nm* bull.
asterisco [aste'risko] *nm* asterisk.
asteroide [aste'roiðe] *nm* asteroid.
astigmatismo [astiɣma'tismo] *nm* astigmatism.
astilla [as'tiʎa] *nf* splinter; (*pedacito*) chip; ~**s** *nfpl* firewood *sg*.
astillarse [asti'ʎarse] *vr* to splinter; (*fig*) to shatter.
astillero [asti'ʎero] *nm* shipyard.
astringente [astrin'xente] *adj, nm* astringent.
astro ['astro] *nm* star.
astrología [astrolo'xia] *nf* astrology.
astrólogo, a [as'troloɣo, a] *nm/f* astrologer.
astronauta [astro'nauta] *nm/f* astronaut.
astronave [astro'naße] *nm* spaceship.
astronomía [astrono'mia] *nf* astronomy.
astronómico, a [astro'nomiko, a] *adj* (*tb fig*) astronomical.
astrónomo, a [as'tronomo, a] *nm/f*

astronomer.
astroso, a [as'troso, a] *adj* (*desaliñado*) untidy; (*vil*) contemptible.
astucia [as'tuθja] *nf* astuteness; (*destreza*) clever trick.
asturiano, a [astu'rjano, a] *adj, nm/f* Asturian.
Asturias [as'turjas] *nfpl* Asturias; **Príncipe de ~** crown prince.
astuto, a [as'tuto, a] *adj* astute; (*taimado*) cunning.
asueto [a'sweto] *nm* holiday; (*tiempo libre*) time off; **día de ~** day off; **tarde de ~** (*trabajo*) afternoon off; (*ESCOL*) half-holiday.
asumir [asu'mir] *vt* to assume.
asunción [asun'θjon] *nf* assumption.
asunto [a'sunto] *nm* (*tema*) matter, subject; (*negocio*) business; **¡eso es ~ mio!** that's my business!; **~s exteriores** foreign affairs; **~s a tratar** agenda *sg.*
asustadizo, a [asusta'ðiθo, a] *adj* easily frightened.
asustar [asus'tar] *vt* to frighten; **~se** *vr* to be/become frightened.
atacante [ata'kante] *nm/f* attacker.
atacar [ata'kar] *vt* to attack.
atadura [ata'ðura] *nf* bond, tie.
atajar [ata'xar] *vt* (*gen*) to stop; (*ruta de fuga*) to cut off; (*discurso*) to interrupt ♦ *vi* to take a short cut.
atajo [a'taxo] *nm* short cut; (*DEPORTE*) tackle.
atalaya [ata'laja] *nf* watchtower.
atañer [ata'ɲer] *vi*: **~ a** to concern; **en lo que atañe a eso** with regard to that.
ataque [a'take] *etc vb V* **atacar** ♦ *nm* attack; **~ cardíaco** heart attack.
atar [a'tar] *vt* to tie, tie up; **~ la lengua a algn** (*fig*) to silence sb.
atardecer [atarðe'θer] *vi* to get dark ♦ *nm* evening; (*crepúsculo*) dusk.
atardezca [atar'ðeθka] *etc vb V* **atardecer**.
atareado, a [atare'aðo, a] *adj* busy.
atascar [atas'kar] *vt* to clog up; (*obstruir*) to jam; (*fig*) to hinder; **~se** *vr* to stall; (*cañería*) to get blocked up; (*fig*) to get bogged down; (*en discurso*) to dry up.
atasco [a'tasko] *nm* obstruction; (*AUTO*) traffic jam.
atasque [a'taske] *etc vb V* **atascar**.
ataúd [ata'uð] *nm* coffin.
ataviar [ata'ßjar] *vt* to deck, array; **~se** *vr* to dress up.
atavío [ata'ßio] *nm* attire, dress; **~s** *nmpl* finery *sg.*
ateísmo [ate'ismo] *nm* atheism.
atemorice [atemo'riθe] *etc vb V* **atemorizar**.
atemorizar [atemori'θar] *vt* to frighten, scare; **~se** *vr* to get frightened *o* scared.
Atenas [a'tenas] *nf* Athens.
atención [aten'θjon] *nf* attention; (*bondad*) kindness ♦ *excl* (be) careful!, look out!; **en ~ a esto** in view of this.
atender [aten'der] *vt* to attend to, look after; (*TEC*) to service; (*enfermo*) to care for; (*ruego*) to comply with ♦ *vi* to pay attention; **~ a** to attend to; (*detalles*) to take care of.
atendré [aten'dre] *etc vb V* **atenerse**.
atenerse [ate'nerse] *vr*: **~ a** to abide by, adhere to.
atenga [a'tenga] *etc vb V* **atenerse**.
ateniense [ate'njense] *adj, nm/f* Athenian.
atentado [aten'taðo] *nm* crime, illegal act; (*asalto*) assault; (*terrorista*) attack; **~ contra la vida de algn** attempt on sb's life; **~ golpista** (*POL*) attempted coup.
atentamente [atenta'mente] *adv*: **le saluda ~** Yours faithfully.
atentar [aten'tar] *vi*: **~ a** *o* **contra** to commit an outrage against.
atento, a [a'tento, a] *adj* attentive, observant; (*cortés*) polite, thoughtful; **su atenta (carta)** (*COM*) your letter.
atenuante [ate'nwante] *adj*: **circunstancias ~s** extenuating *o* mitigating circumstances ♦ *nfpl*: **~s** extenuating *o* mitigating circumstances.
atenuar [ate'nwar] *vt* to attenuate; (*disminuir*) to lessen, minimize.
ateo, a [a'teo, a] *adj* atheistic ♦ *nm/f* atheist.
aterciopelado, a [aterθjope'laðo, a] *adj* velvety.
aterido, a [ate'riðo, a] *adj*: **~ de frío** frozen stiff.
aterrador, a [aterra'ðor, a] *adj* frightening.
aterrar [ate'rrar] *vt* to frighten; (*aterrorizar*) to terrify; **~se** *vr* to be frightened; to be terrified.
aterrice [ate'rriθe] *etc vb V* **aterrizar**.
aterrizaje [aterri'θaxe] *nm* landing; **~ forzoso** forced landing.
aterrizar [aterri'θar] *vi* to land.
aterrorice [aterro'riθe] *etc vb V* **aterrorizar**.
aterrorizar [aterrori'θar] *vt* to terrify.
atesorar [ateso'rar] *vt* to hoard, store up.
atestado, a [ates'taðo, a] *adj* packed ♦ *nm* (*JUR*) affidavit.
atestar [ates'tar] *vt* to pack, stuff; (*JUR*) to attest, testify to.
atestiguar [atesti'ɣwar] *vt* to testify to, bear witness to.
atestigüe [ates'tiɣwe] *etc vb V* **atestiguar**.

atiborrar [atiβo'rrar] *vt* to fill, stuff; **~se** *vr* to stuff o.s.
atice [a'tiθe] *etc vb V* **atizar**.
ático ['atiko] *nm* attic; **~ de lujo** penthouse flat.
atienda [a'tjenda] *etc vb V* **atender**.
atildar [atil'dar] *vt* to criticize; (*TIP*) to put a tilde over; **~se** *vr* to spruce o.s. up.
atinado, a [ati'naðo, a] *adj* correct; (*sensato*) sensible.
atinar [ati'nar] *vi* (*acertar*) to be right; **~ con** *o* **en** (*solución*) to hit upon; **~ a hacer** to manage to do.
atípico, a [a'tipiko, a] *adj* atypical.
atiplado, a [ati'plaðo, a] *adj* (*voz*) high-pitched.
atisbar [atis'βar] *vt* to spy on; (*echar ojeada*) to peep at.
atizar [ati'θar] *vt* to poke; (*horno etc*) to stoke; (*fig*) to stir up, rouse.
atlántico, a [at'lantiko, a] *adj* Atlantic ♦ *nm*: **el (océano) A~** the Atlantic (Ocean).
atlas ['atlas] *nm* atlas.
atleta [at'leta] *nm/f* athlete.
atlético, a [at'letiko, a] *adj* athletic.
atletismo [atle'tismo] *nm* athletics *sg*.
atmósfera [at'mosfera] *nf* atmosphere.
atmosférico, a [atmos'feriko, a] *adj* atmospheric.
atol(e) [a'tol(e)] *nm* (*AM*) cornflour drink.
atolladero [atoʎa'ðero] *nm*: **estar en un ~** to be in a jam.
atollarse [ato'ʎarse] *vr* to get stuck; (*fig*) to get into a jam.
atolondrado, a [atolon'draðo, a] *adj* scatterbrained.
atolondramiento [atolondra'mjento] *nm* bewilderment; (*insensatez*) silliness.
atómico, a [a'tomiko, a] *adj* atomic.
atomizador [atomiθa'ðor] *nm* atomizer.
átomo ['atomo] *nm* atom.
atónito, a [a'tonito, a] *adj* astonished, amazed.
atontado, a [aton'taðo, a] *adj* stunned; (*bobo*) silly, daft.
atontar [aton'tar] *vt* to stun; **~se** *vr* to become confused.
atorar [ato'rar] *vt* to obstruct; **~se** *vr* (*atragantarse*) to choke.
atormentar [atormen'tar] *vt* to torture; (*molestar*) to torment; (*acosar*) to plague, harass.
atornillar [atorni'ʎar] *vt* to screw on *o* down.
atorón [ato'ron] *nm* (*AM*) traffic jam.
atosigar [atosi'ɣar] *vt* to harass.
atosigue [ato'siɣe] *etc vb V* **atosigar**.
atrabiliario, a [atraβi'ljarjo, a] *adj* bad-tempered.
atracadero [atraka'ðero] *nm* pier.
atracador, a [atraka'ðor, a] *nm/f* robber.
atracar [atra'kar] *vt* (*NAUT*) to moor; (*robar*) to hold up, rob ♦ *vi* to moor; **~se** *vr* (*hartarse*) to stuff o.s.
atracción [atrak'θjon] *nf* attraction.
atraco [a'trako] *nm* holdup, robbery.
atracón [atra'kon] *nm*: **darse** *o* **pegarse un ~ (de)** (*fam*) to pig out (on).
atractivo, a [atrak'tiβo, a] *adj* attractive ♦ *nm* attraction; (*belleza*) attractiveness.
atraer [atra'er] *vt* to attract; **dejarse ~ por** to be tempted by.
atragantarse [atraɣan'tarse] *vr*: **~ (con algo)** to choke (on sth); **se me ha atragantado el chico ese/el inglés** I don't take to that boy/English.
atraiga [a'traiɣa] *etc*, **atraje** [a'traxe] *etc vb V* **atraer**.
atrancar [atran'kar] *vt* (*con tranca, barra*) to bar, bolt.
atranque [a'tranke] *etc vb V* **atrancar**.
atrapar [atra'par] *vt* to trap; (*resfriado etc*) to catch.
atraque [a'trake] *etc vb V* **atracar**.
atrás [a'tras] *adv* (*movimiento*) back(wards); (*lugar*) behind; (*tiempo*) previously; **ir hacia ~** to go back(wards); to go to the rear; **estar ~** to be behind *o* at the back.
atrasado, a [atra'saðo, a] *adj* slow; (*pago*) overdue, late; (*país*) backward.
atrasar [atra'sar] *vi* to be slow; **~se** *vr* to remain behind; (*llegar tarde*) to arrive late.
atraso [a'traso] *nm* slowness; lateness, delay; (*de país*) backwardness; **~s** *nmpl* arrears.
atravesado, a [atraβe'saðo, a] *adj*: **un tronco ~ en la carretera** a tree trunk lying across the road.
atravesar [atraβe'sar] *vt* (*cruzar*) to cross (over); (*traspasar*) to pierce; (*período*) to go through; (*poner al través*) to lay *o* put across; **~se** *vr* to come in between; (*intervenir*) to interfere.
atraviese [atra'βjese] *etc vb V* **atravesar**.
atrayendo [atra'jendo] *vb V* **atraer**.
atrayente [atra'jente] *adj* attractive.
atreverse [atre'βerse] *vr* to dare; (*insolentarse*) to be insolent.
atrevido, a [atre'βiðo, a] *adj* daring; insolent.
atrevimiento [atreβi'mjento] *nm* daring; insolence.
atribución [atriβu'θjon] *nf* (*LIT*) attribution; **atribuciones** *nfpl* (*POL*) functions; (*ADMIN*)

responsibilities.
atribuir [atriβu'ir] *vt* to attribute; (*funciones*) to confer.
atribular [atriβu'lar] *vt* to afflict, distress.
atributo [atri'βuto] *nm* attribute.
atribuya [atri'βuja] *etc*, **atribuyendo** [atriβu'jendo] *etc vb V* **atribuir**.
atril [a'tril] *nm* lectern; (*MUS*) music stand.
atrincherarse [atrintʃe'rarse] *vr* (*MIL*) to dig (o.s.) in; ~ **en** (*fig*) to hide behind.
atrio ['atrjo] *nm* (*REL*) porch.
atrocidad [atroθi'ðað] *nf* atrocity, outrage.
atrofiado, a [atro'fjaðo, a] *adj* (*extremidad*) withered.
atrofiarse [atro'fjarse] *vr* (*tb fig*) to atrophy.
atronador, a [atrona'ðor, a] *adj* deafening.
atropellar [atrope'ʎar] *vt* (*derribar*) to knock over *o* down; (*empujar*) to push (aside); (*AUTO*) to run over *o* down; (*agraviar*) to insult; ~**se** *vr* to act hastily.
atropello [atro'peʎo] *nm* (*AUTO*) accident; (*empujón*) push; (*agravio*) wrong; (*atrocidad*) outrage.
atroz [a'troθ] *adj* atrocious, awful.
A.T.S. *nm/f abr* (= *Ayudante Técnico Sanitario*) nurse.
atto., a. *abr* (= *atento, a*) Yours faithfully.
attrezzo [a'treθo] *nm* props *pl*.
atuendo [a'twendo] *nm* attire.
atufar [atu'far] *vt* (*suj*: *olor*) to overcome; (*molestar*) to irritate; ~**se** *vr* (*fig*) to get cross.
atún [a'tun] *nm* tuna, tunny.
aturdir [atur'ðir] *vt* to stun; (*suj*: *ruido*) to deafen; (*fig*) to dumbfound, bewilder.
atur(r)ullar [atur(r)u'ʎar] *vt* to bewilder.
atusar [atu'sar] *vt* (*cortar*) to trim; (*alisar*) to smooth (down).
atuve [a'tuβe] *etc vb V* **atenerse**.
audacia [au'ðaθja] *nf* boldness, audacity.
audaz [au'ðaθ] *adj* bold, audacious.
audible [au'ðiβle] *adj* audible.
audición [auði'θjon] *nf* hearing; (*TEAT*) audition; ~ **radiofónica** radio concert.
audiencia [au'ðjenθja] *nf* audience; (*JUR*) high court; (*POL*): ~ **pública** public inquiry.
audífono [au'ðifono] *nm* hearing aid.
audiovisual [auðjoβi'swal] *adj* audio-visual.
auditivo, a [auði'tiβo, a] *adj* hearing *cpd*; (*conducto, nervio*) auditory.
auditor [auði'tor] *nm* (*JUR*) judge-advocate; (*COM*) auditor.
auditoría [auðito'ria] *nf* audit; (*profesión*) auditing.
auditorio [auði'torjo] *nm* audience; (*sala*) auditorium.
auge ['auxe] *nm* boom; (*clímax*) climax; (*ECON*) expansion; **estar en** ~ to thrive.
augurar [auɣu'rar] *vt* to predict; (*presagiar*) to portend.
augurio [au'ɣurjo] *nm* omen.
aula ['aula] *nf* classroom.
aullar [au'ʎar] *vi* to howl, yell.
aullido [au'ʎiðo] *nm* howl, yell.
aumentar [aumen'tar] *vt* to increase; (*precios*) to put up; (*producción*) to step up; (*con microscopio, anteojos*) to magnify ♦ *vi*, ~**se** *vr* to increase, be on the increase.
aumento [au'mento] *nm* increase; rise.
aún [a'un] *adv* still, yet.
aun [a'un] *adv* even.
aunque [a'unke] *conj* though, although, even though.
aúpa [a'upa] *excl* up!, come on!; (*fam*): **una función de** ~ a slap-up do; **una paliza de** ~ a good hiding.
aupar [au'par] *vt* (*levantar*) to help up; (*fig*) to praise.
aura ['aura] *nf* (*atmósfera*) aura.
aureola [aure'ola] *nf* halo.
auricular [auriku'lar] *nm* earpiece, receiver; ~**es** *nmpl* headphones.
aurora [au'rora] *nf* dawn; ~ **boreal(is)** northern lights *pl*.
auscultar [auskul'tar] *vt* (*MED*: *pecho*) to listen to, sound.
ausencia [au'senθja] *nf* absence.
ausentarse [ausen'tarse] *vr* to go away; (*por poco tiempo*) to go out.
ausente [au'sente] *adj* absent ♦ *nm/f* (*ESCOL*) absentee; (*JUR*) missing person.
auspiciar [auspi'sjar] *vt* (*AM*) to back, sponsor.
auspicios [aus'piθjos] *nmpl* auspices; (*protección*) protection *sg*.
austeridad [austeri'ðað] *nf* austerity.
austero, a [aus'tero, a] *adj* austere.
austral [aus'tral] *adj* southern ♦ *nm* *monetary unit of Argentina* (*1985-1991*).
Australia [aus'tralja] *nf* Australia.
australiano, a [austra'ljano, a] *adj, nm/f* Australian.
Austria ['austrja] *nf* Austria.
austriaco, a [aus'trjako, a], **austríaco, a** [aus'triako, a] *adj, nm/f* Austrian.
autenticar [autenti'kar] *vt* to authenticate.
auténtico, a [au'tentiko, a] *adj* authentic.
autentificar [autentifi'kar] *vt* to authenticate.
autentique [auten'tike] *etc vb V* **autenticar**.
auto ['auto] *nm* (*coche*) car; (*JUR*) edict, decree; (: *orden*) writ; ~**s** *nmpl* (*JUR*)

proceedings; (: *acta*) court record *sg*; ~ **de comparecencia** summons, subpoena; ~ **de ejecución** writ of execution.
autoadhesivo, a [autoaðe'siβo, a] *adj* self-adhesive; (*sobre*) self-sealing.
autoalimentación [autoalimenta'θjon] *nf* (*INFORM*): ~ **de hojas** automatic paper feed.
autobiografía [autoβjoɣra'fia] *nf* autobiography.
autobronceador [autoβronθea'ðor] *adj* self-tanning.
autobús [auto'βus] *nm* bus (*BRIT*), (passenger) bus (*US*).
autocar [auto'kar] *nm* coach; ~ **de línea** intercity coach.
autocomprobación [autokomproβa'θjon] *nf* (*INFORM*) self-test.
autóctono, a [au'toktono, a] *adj* native, indigenous.
autodefensa [autoðe'fensa] *nf* self-defence.
autodeterminación [autoðetermina'θjon] *nf* self-determination.
autodidacta [autoði'ðakta] *adj* self-taught ♦ *nm/f*: **ser un(a)** ~ to be self-taught.
autoescuela [autoes'kwela] *nf* driving school.
autofinanciado, a [autofinan'θjaðo, a] *adj* self-financing.
autogestión [autoxes'tjon] *nf* self-management.
autógrafo [au'toɣrafo] *nm* autograph.
automación [automa'θjon] *nf* = **automatización**.
autómata [au'tomata] *nm* automaton.
automáticamente [auto'matikamente] *adv* automatically.
automatice [automa'tiθe] *etc vb V* **automatizar**.
automático, a [auto'matiko, a] *adj* automatic ♦ *nm* press stud.
automatización [automatiθa'θjon] *nf*: ~ **de fábricas** factory automation; ~ **de oficinas** office automation.
automatizar [automati'θar] *vt* to automate.
automotor, triz [automo'tor, 'triz] *adj* self-propelled ♦ *nm* diesel train.
automóvil [auto'moβil] *nm* (motor) car (*BRIT*), automobile (*US*).
automovilismo [automoβi'lismo] *nm* (*DEPORTE*) (sports) car racing.
automovilista [automoβi'lista] *nm/f* motorist, driver.
automovilístico, a [automoβi'listiko, a] *adj* (*industria*) car *cpd*.
autonomía [autono'mia] *nf* autonomy; (*ESP POL*) autonomy, self-government; (: *comunidad*) autonomous region.
autonómico, a [auto'nomiko, a] *adj* (*ESP POL*) relating to autonomy, autonomous; **gobierno** ~ autonomous government.
autónomo, a [au'tonomo, a] *adj* autonomous; (*INFORM*) stand-alone, offline.
autopista [auto'pista] *nf* motorway (*BRIT*), freeway (*US*).
autopsia [au'topsja] *nf* autopsy.
autor, a [au'tor, a] *nm/f* author; **los ~es del atentado** those responsible for the attack.
autorice [auto'riθe] *etc vb V* **autorizar**.
autoridad [autori'ðað] *nf* authority; ~ **local** local authority.
autoritario, a [autori'tarjo, a] *adj* authoritarian.
autorización [autoriθa'θjon] *nf* authorization.
autorizado, a [autori'θaðo, a] *adj* authorized; (*aprobado*) approved.
autorizar [autori'θar] *vt* to authorize; to approve.
autorretrato [autorre'trato] *nm* self-portrait.
autoservicio [autoser'βiθjo] *nm* self-service shop *o* store; (*restaurante*) self-service restaurant.
autostop [auto'stop] *nm* hitch-hiking; **hacer** ~ to hitch-hike.
autostopista [autosto'pista] *nm/f* hitch-hiker.
autosuficiencia [autosufi'θjenθja] *nf* self-sufficiency.
autosuficiente [autosufi'θjente] *adj* self-sufficient; (*pey*) smug.
autosugestión [autosuxes'tjon] *nf* autosuggestion.
autovía [auto'βia] *nf* ≈ dual carriageway (*BRIT*), separated highway (*US*).
auxiliar [auksi'ljar] *vt* to help ♦ *nm/f* assistant.
auxilio [auk'siljo] *nm* assistance, help; **primeros ~s** first aid *sg*.
Av *abr* (= *Avenida*) Av(e).
a/v *abr* (*COM*: = *a vista*) at sight.
aval [a'βal] *nm* guarantee; (*persona*) guarantor.
avalancha [aβa'lantʃa] *nf* avalanche.
avalar [aβa'lar] *vt* (*COM etc*) to underwrite; (*fig*) to endorse.
avalista [aβa'lista] *nm* (*COM*) endorser.
avance [a'βanθe] *etc vb V* **avanzar** ♦ *nm* advance; (*pago*) advance payment; (*CINE*) trailer.
avanzado, a [aβan'θaðo, a] *adj* advanced; **de edad avanzada, ~ de edad** elderly.
avanzar [aβan'θar] *vt, vi* to advance.
avaricia [aβa'riθja] *nf* avarice, greed.

avaricioso, a [aβari'θjoso, a] *adj* avaricious, greedy.
avaro, a [a'βaro, a] *adj* miserly, mean ♦ *nm/f* miser.
avasallar [aβasa'ʎar] *vt* to subdue, subjugate.
avatar [aβa'tar] *nm* change; ~**es** ups and downs.
Avda *abr* (= *Avenida*) Av(e).
AVE ['aβe] *nm abr* (= *Alta Velocidad Española*) ≈ Bullet train.
ave ['aβe] *nf* bird; ~ **de rapiña** bird of prey.
avecinarse [aβeθi'narse] *vr* (*tormenta, fig*) to approach, be on the way.
avejentar [aβexen'tar] *vt, vi,* ~**se** *vr* to age.
avellana [aβe'ʎana] *nf* hazelnut.
avellano [aβe'ʎano] *nm* hazel tree.
avemaría [aβema'ria] *nm* Hail Mary, Ave Maria.
avena [a'βena] *nf* oats *pl*.
avendré [aβen'dre] *etc*, **avenga** [a'βenga] *etc vb V* **avenir.**
avenida [aβe'niða] *nf* (*calle*) avenue.
avenir [aβe'nir] *vt* to reconcile; ~**se** *vr* to come to an agreement, reach a compromise.
aventado, a [aβen'taðo, a] *adj* (*AM*) daring.
aventajado, a [aβenta'xaðo, a] *adj* outstanding.
aventajar [aβenta'xar] *vt* (*sobrepasar*) to surpass, outstrip.
aventar [aβen'tar] *vt* to fan, blow; (*grano*) to winnow; (*AM fam*: *echar*) to chuck out.
aventón [aβen'ton] *nm* (*AM*) push; **pedir** ~ to hitch a lift.
aventura [aβen'tura] *nf* adventure; ~ **sentimental** love affair.
aventurado, a [aβentu'raðo, a] *adj* risky.
aventurar [aβentu'rar] *vt* to risk; ~**se** *vr* to dare; ~**se a hacer algo** to venture to do sth.
aventurero, a [aβentu'rero, a] *adj* adventurous.
avergoncé [aβerɣon'θe], **avergoncemos** [aβerɣon'θemos] *etc vb V* **avergonzar.**
avergonzar [aβerɣon'θar] *vt* to shame; (*desconcertar*) to embarrass; ~**se** *vr* to be ashamed; to be embarrassed.
avergüence [aβer'ɣwenθe] *etc vb V* **avergonzar.**
avería [aβe'ria] *nf* (*TEC*) breakdown, fault.
averiado, a [aβe'rjaðo, a] *adj* broken-down.
averiar [aβe'rjar] *vt* to break; ~**se** *vr* to break down.
averiguación [aβeriɣwa'θjon] *nf* investigation; (*determinación*) ascertainment.
averiguar [aβeri'ɣwar] *vt* to investigate; (*descubrir*) to find out, ascertain.
averigüe [aβe'riɣwe] *etc vb V* **averiguar.**
aversión [aβer'sjon] *nf* aversion, dislike; **cobrar** ~ **a** to take a strong dislike to.
avestruz [aβes'truθ] *nm* ostrich.
aviación [aβja'θjon] *nf* aviation; (*fuerzas aéreas*) air force.
aviado, a [a'βjaðo, a] *adj*: **estar** ~ to be in a mess.
aviador, a [aβja'ðor, a] *nm/f* aviator, airman/woman.
aviar [a'βjar] *vt* to prepare, get ready.
avícola [a'βikola] *adj* poultry *cpd*.
avicultura [aβikul'tura] *nf* poultry farming.
avidez [aβi'ðeθ] *nf* avidity, eagerness.
ávido, a ['aβiðo, a] *adj* avid, eager.
aviente [a'βjente] *etc vb V* **aventar.**
avieso, a [a'βjeso, a] *adj* (*torcido*) distorted; (*perverso*) wicked.
avinagrado, a [aβina'ɣraðo, a] *adj* sour, acid.
avinagrarse [aβina'ɣrarse] *vr* to go *o* turn sour.
avine [a'βine] *etc vb V* **avenir.**
Aviñón [aβi'ɲon] *nm* Avignon.
avío [a'βio] *nm* preparation; ~**s** *nmpl* gear *sg*, kit *sg*.
avión [a'βjon] *nm* aeroplane; (*ave*) martin; ~ **de reacción** jet (plane); **por** ~ (*CORREOS*) by air mail.
avioneta [aβjo'neta] *nf* light aircraft.
avisar [aβi'sar] *vt* (*advertir*) to warn, notify; (*informar*) to tell; (*aconsejar*) to advise, counsel.
aviso [a'βiso] *nm* warning; (*noticia*) notice; (*COM*) demand note; (*INFORM*) prompt; ~ **escrito** notice in writing; **sin previo** ~ without warning; **estar sobre** ~ to be on the look-out.
avispa [a'βispa] *nf* wasp.
avispado, a [aβis'paðo, a] *adj* sharp, clever.
avispero [aβis'pero] *nm* wasp's nest.
avispón [aβis'pon] *nm* hornet.
avistar [aβis'tar] *vt* to sight, spot.
avitaminosis [aβitami'nosis] *nf inv* vitamin deficiency.
avituallar [aβitwa'ʎar] *vt* to supply with food.
avivar [aβi'βar] *vt* to strengthen, intensify; ~**se** *vr* to revive, acquire new life.
avizor [aβi'θor] *adj*: **estar ojo** ~ to be on the alert.
avizorar [aβiθo'rar] *vt* to spy on.
axila [ak'sila] *nf* armpit.
axioma [ak'sjoma] *nm* axiom.
ay [ai] *excl* (*dolor*) ow!, ouch!; (*aflicción*)

oh!, oh dear!; **¡~ de mí!** poor me!
aya ['aja] *nf* governess; (*niñera*) nanny.
ayer [a'jer] *adv, nm* yesterday; **antes de ~** the day before yesterday; **~ por la tarde** yesterday afternoon/evening.
aymara, aymará [ai'mara, aima'ra] *adj, nm/f* Aymara.
ayo ['ajo] *nm* tutor.
ayote [a'jote] *nm* (*AM*) pumpkin.
Ayto. *abr* = **Ayuntamiento.**
ayuda [a'juða] *nf* help, assistance; (*MED*) enema ♦ *nm* page; **~ humanitaria** humanitarian aid.
ayudante, a [aju'ðante, a] *nm/f* assistant, helper; (*ESCOL*) assistant; (*MIL*) adjutant.
ayudar [aju'ðar] *vt* to help, assist.
ayunar [aju'nar] *vi* to fast.
ayunas [a'junas] *nfpl*: **estar en ~** (*no haber comido*) to be fasting; (*ignorar*) to be in the dark.
ayuno [a'juno] *nm* fasting.
ayuntamiento [ajunta'mjento] *nm* (*consejo*) town/city council; (*edificio*) town/city hall; (*cópula*) sexual intercourse.
azabache [aθa'ßatʃe] *nm* jet.
azada [a'θaða] *nf* hoe.
azafata [aθa'fata] *nf* air hostess (*BRIT*) *o* stewardess.
azafate [asa'fate] *nm* (*AM*) tray.
azafrán [aθa'fran] *nm* saffron.
azahar [aθa'ar] *nm* orange/lemon blossom.
azalea [aθa'lea] *nf* azalea.
azar [a'θar] *nm* (*casualidad*) chance, fate; (*desgracia*) misfortune, accident; **por ~** by chance; **al ~** at random.
azaroso, a [aθa'roso, a] *adj* (*arriesgado*) risky; (*vida*) eventful.
Azerbaiyán [aθerba'jan] *nm* Azerbaijan.
azerbaiyano, a [aθerba'jano, a], **azerí** [aθe'ri] *adj, nm/f* Azerbaijani, Azeri.
azogue [a'θoɣe] *nm* mercury.
azor [a'θor] *nm* goshawk.
azoramiento [aθora'mjento] *nm* alarm; (*confusión*) confusion.
azorar [aθo'rar] *vt* to alarm; **~se** *vr* to get alarmed.
Azores [a'θores] *nfpl*: **las (Islas) ~** the Azores.
azotaina [aθo'taina] *nf* beating.
azotar [aθo'tar] *vt* to whip, beat; (*pegar*) to spank.
azote [a'θote] *nm* (*látigo*) whip; (*latigazo*) lash, stroke; (*en las nalgas*) spank; (*calamidad*) calamity.
azotea [aθo'tea] *nf* (flat) roof.
azteca [aθ'teka] *adj, nm/f* Aztec.
azúcar [a'θukar] *nm* sugar.
azucarado, a [aθuka'raðo, a] *adj* sugary, sweet.
azucarero, a [aθuka'rero, a] *adj* sugar *cpd* ♦ *nm* sugar bowl.
azuce [a'θuθe] *etc vb V* **azuzar.**
azucena [aθu'θena] *nf* white lily.
azufre [a'θufre] *nm* sulphur.
azul [a'θul] *adj, nm* blue; **~ celeste/marino** sky/navy blue.
azulejo [aθu'lexo] *nm* tile.
azulgrana [aθul'ɣrana] *adj inv* of Barcelona Football Club ♦ *nm*: **los A~** the Barcelona F.C. players *o* team.
azuzar [aθu'θar] *vt* to incite, egg on.

B b

B, b [(*ESP*) be, (*AM*) be'larɣa] *nf* (*letra*) B, b; **B de Barcelona** B for Benjamin (*BRIT*) *o* Baker (*US*).
baba ['baßa] *nf* spittle, saliva; **se le caía la ~** (*fig*) he was thrilled to bits.
babear [baße'ar] *vi* (*echar saliva*) to slobber; (*niño*) to dribble; (*fig*) to drool, slaver.
babel [ba'ßel] *nm o f* bedlam.
babero [ba'ßero] *nm* bib.
Babia ['baßja] *nf*: **estar en ~** to be daydreaming.
bable ['baßle] *nm* Asturian (dialect).
babor [ba'ßor] *nm* port (side); **a ~** to port.
babosada [baßo'saða] *nf*: **decir ~s** (*AM fam*) to talk rubbish.
baboso, a [ba'ßoso, a] *adj* slobbering; (*ZOOL*) slimy; (*AM*) silly ♦ *nm/f* (*AM*) fool.
babucha [ba'ßutʃa] *nf* slipper.
baca ['baka] *nf* (*AUTO*) luggage *o* roof rack.
bacalao [baka'lao] *nm* cod(fish).
bacanal [baka'nal] *nf* orgy.
bache ['batʃe] *nm* pothole, rut; (*fig*) bad patch.
bachillerato [batʃiʎe'rato] *nm* *2 year secondary school course*; *V tb* **sistema educativo.**
bacilo [ba'θilo] *nm* bacillus, germ.
bacinica [baθi'nika] *nf*, **bacinilla** [baθi'niʎa] *nf* chamber pot.
bacteria [bak'terja] *nf* bacterium, germ.
bacteriológico, a [bakterjo'loxico, a] *adj* bacteriological; **guerra ~a** germ warfare.

báculo ['bakulo] *nm* stick, staff; (*fig*) support.
badajo [ba'ðaxo] *nm* clapper (*of a bell*).
bádminton ['baðminton] *nm* badminton.
baf(f)le ['baf(f)le] *nm* (*ELEC*) speaker.
bagaje [ba'ɣaxe] *nm* baggage; (*fig*) background.
bagatela [baɣa'tela] *nf* trinket, trifle.
Bahama [ba'ama]: **las (Islas) ~, las ~s** *nfpl* the Bahamas.
bahía [ba'ia] *nf* bay.
bailar [bai'lar] *vt, vi* to dance.
bailarín, ina [baila'rin, ina] *nm/f* dancer; (*de ballet*) ballet dancer.
baile ['baile] *nm* dance; (*formal*) ball.
baja ['baxa] *nf* drop, fall; (*ECON*) slump; (*MIL*) casualty; (*paro*) redundancy; **dar de ~** (*soldado*) to discharge; (*empleado*) to dismiss, sack; **darse de ~** (*retirarse*) to drop out; (*MED*) to go sick; (*dimitir*) to resign; **estar de ~** (*enfermo*) to be off sick; (*BOLSA*) to be dropping *o* falling; **jugar a la ~** (*ECON*) to speculate on a fall in prices; *V tb* **bajo**.
bajada [ba'xaða] *nf* descent; (*camino*) slope; (*de aguas*) ebb.
bajamar [baxa'mar] *nf* low tide.
bajar [ba'xar] *vi* to go *o* come down; (*temperatura, precios*) to drop, fall ♦ *vt* (*cabeza*) to bow; (*escalera*) to go *o* come down; (*radio etc*) to turn down; (*precio, voz*) to lower; (*llevar abajo*) to take down; **~se** *vr* (*de vehículo*) to get out; (*de autobús*) to get off; **~ de** (*coche*) to get out of; (*autobús*) to get off; **~le los humos a algn** (*fig*) to cut sb down to size.
bajeza [ba'xeθa] *nf* baseness; (*una ~*) vile deed.
bajío [ba'xio] *nm* shoal, sandbank; (*AM*) lowlands *pl*.
bajista [ba'xista] *nm/f* (*MUS*) bassist ♦ *adj* (*BOLSA*) bear *cpd*.
bajo, a ['baxo, a] *adj* (*terreno*) low(-lying); (*mueble, número, precio*) low; (*piso*) ground *cpd*; (*de estatura*) small, short; (*color*) pale; (*sonido*) faint, soft, low; (*voz, tono*) deep; (*metal*) base ♦ *adv* (*hablar*) softly, quietly; (*volar*) low ♦ *prep* under, below, underneath ♦ *nm* (*MUS*) bass; **hablar en voz baja** to whisper; **~ la lluvia** in the rain.
bajón [ba'xon] *nm* fall, drop.
bajura [ba'xura] *nf*: **pesca de ~** coastal fishing.
bakalao [baka'lao] *nm* (*MUS*) rave music.
bala ['bala] *nf* bullet; **~ de goma** plastic bullet.
balacera [bala'sera] *nf* (*AM*) shoot-out.
balada [ba'laða] *nf* ballad.
baladí [bala'ði] *adj* trivial.
baladronada [balaðro'naða] *nf* (*dicho*) boast, brag; (*hecho*) piece of bravado.
balance [ba'lanθe] *nm* (*COM*) balance; (*: libro*) balance sheet; (*: cuenta general*) stocktaking; **~ de comprobación** trial balance; **~ consolidado** consolidated balance sheet; **hacer ~** to take stock.
balancear [balanθe'ar] *vt* to balance ♦ *vi*, **~se** *vr* to swing (to and fro); (*vacilar*) to hesitate.
balanceo [balan'θeo] *nm* swinging.
balandro [ba'landro] *nm* yacht.
balanza [ba'lanθa] *nf* scales *pl*, balance; **~ comercial** balance of trade; **~ de pagos/de poder(es)** balance of payments/of power; (*ASTRO*): **B~** Libra.
balar [ba'lar] *vi* to bleat.
balaustrada [balaus'traða] *nf* balustrade; (*pasamanos*) banister.
balazo [ba'laθo] *nm* (*tiro*) shot; (*herida*) bullet wound.
balboa [bal'ßoa] *nf* *Panamanian currency unit*.
balbucear [balßuθe'ar] *vi, vt* to stammer, stutter.
balbuceo [balßu'θeo] *nm* stammering, stuttering.
balbucir [balßu'θir] *vi, vt* to stammer, stutter.
balbuzca [bal'ßuθka] *etc vb V* **balbucir**.
Balcanes [bal'kanes] *nmpl*: **los (Montes) ~** the Balkans, the Balkan Mountains; **la Península de los ~** the Balkan Peninsula.
balcánico, a [bal'kaniko, a] *adj* Balkan.
balcón [bal'kon] *nm* balcony.
balda ['balda] *nf* (*estante*) shelf.
baldar [bal'dar] *vt* to cripple; (*agotar*) to exhaust.
balde ['balde] *nm* (*esp AM*) bucket, pail; **de ~** *adv* (for) free, for nothing; **en ~** *adv* in vain.
baldío, a [bal'dio, a] *adj* uncultivated; (*terreno*) waste; (*inútil*) vain ♦ *nm* wasteland.
baldosa [bal'dosa] *nf* (*azulejo*) floor tile; (*grande*) flagstone.
baldosín [baldo'sin] *nm* wall tile.
balear [bale'ar] *adj* Balearic, of the Balearic Islands ♦ *nm/f* native *o* inhabitant of the Balearic Islands ♦ *vt* (*AM*) to shoot (at).
Baleares [bale'ares] *nfpl*: **las (Islas) ~** the Balearics, the Balearic Islands.
balido [ba'liðo] *nm* bleat, bleating.
balín [ba'lin] *nm* pellet; **balines** *nmpl*

buckshot *sg.*
balística [ba'listika] *nf* ballistics *pl.*
baliza [ba'liθa] *nf* (*AVIAT*) beacon; (*NAUT*) buoy.
ballena [ba'ʎena] *nf* whale.
ballenero, a [baʎe'nero, a] *adj*: **industria ballenera** whaling industry ♦ *nm* (*pescador*) whaler; (*barco*) whaling ship.
ballesta [ba'ʎesta] *nf* crossbow; (*AUTO*) spring.
ballet, *pl* **ballets** [ba'le, ba'les] *nm* ballet.
balneario, a [balne'arjo, a] *adj*: **estación balnearia** (bathing) resort ♦ *nm* spa, health resort.
balompié [balom'pje] *nm* football.
balón [ba'lon] *nm* ball.
baloncesto [balon'θesto] *nm* basketball.
balonmano [balon'mano] *nm* handball.
balonvolea [balombo'lea] *nm* volleyball.
balsa ['balsa] *nf* raft; (*BOT*) balsa wood.
bálsamo ['balsamo] *nm* balsam, balm.
balsón [bal'son] *nm* (*AM*) swamp, bog.
báltico, a ['baltiko, a] *adj* Baltic; **el (Mar) B~** the Baltic (Sea).
baluarte [ba'lwarte] *nm* bastion, bulwark.
bambolearse [bambole'arse] *vr* to swing, sway; (*silla*) to wobble.
bamboleo [bambo'leo] *nm* swinging, swaying; wobbling.
bambú [bam'bu] *nm* bamboo.
banal [ba'nal] *adj* banal, trivial.
banana [ba'nana] *nf* (*AM*) banana.
bananal [bana'nal] *nm* (*AM*) banana plantation.
banano [ba'nano] *nm* (*AM*) banana tree.
banasta [ba'nasta] *nf* large basket, hamper.
banca ['banka] *nf* (*asiento*) bench; (*COM*) banking.
bancario, a [ban'karjo, a] *adj* banking *cpd*, bank *cpd*; **giro ~** bank draft.
bancarrota [banka'rrota] *nf* bankruptcy; **declararse en** *o* **hacer ~** to go bankrupt.
banco ['banko] *nm* bench; (*ESCOL*) desk; (*COM*) bank; (*GEO*) stratum; **~ comercial** *o* **mercantil** commercial bank; **~ por acciones** joint-stock bank; **~ de crédito/de ahorros** credit/savings bank; **~ de arena** sandbank; **~ de datos** (*INFORM*) data bank; **~ de hielo** iceberg.
banda ['banda] *nf* band; (*cinta*) ribbon; (*pandilla*) gang; (*MUS*) brass band; (*NAUT*) side, edge; **la B~ Oriental** Uruguay; **~ sonora** soundtrack; **~ transportadora** conveyor belt.
bandada [ban'daða] *nf* (*de pájaros*) flock; (*de peces*) shoal.
bandazo [ban'daθo] *nm*: **dar ~s** (*coche*) to veer from side to side.
bandeja [ban'dexa] *nf* tray; **~ de entrada/salida** in-tray/out-tray.
bandera [ban'dera] *nf* (*de tela*) flag; (*estandarte*) banner; (*INFORM*) marker, flag; **izar la ~** to hoist the flag.
banderilla [bande'riʎa] *nf* banderilla; (*tapa*) *savoury appetizer (served on a cocktail stick)*.
banderín [bande'rin] *nm* pennant, small flag.
banderola [bande'rola] *nf* (*MIL*) pennant.
bandido [ban'diðo] *nm* bandit.
bando ['bando] *nm* (*edicto*) edict, proclamation; (*facción*) faction; **pasar al otro ~** to change sides; **los ~s** (*REL*) the banns.
bandolera [bando'lera] *nf*: **bolsa de ~** shoulder bag.
bandolero [bando'lero] *nm* bandit, brigand.
bandoneón [bandone'on] *nm* (*AM*) large accordion.
BANESTO [ba'nesto] *nm abr* = *Banco Español de Crédito*.
banquero [ban'kero] *nm* banker.
banqueta [ban'keta] *nf* stool; (*AM*: *acera*) pavement (*BRIT*), sidewalk (*US*).
banquete [ban'kete] *nm* banquet; (*para convidados*) formal dinner; **~ de boda** wedding breakfast.
banquillo [ban'kiʎo] *nm* (*JUR*) dock, prisoner's bench; (*banco*) bench; (*para los pies*) footstool.
bañadera [baɲa'ðera] *nf* (*AM*) bath(tub).
bañado [baɲ'aðo] *nm* (*AM*) swamp.
bañador [baɲa'ðor] *nm* swimming costume (*BRIT*), bathing suit (*US*).
bañar [ba'ɲar] *vt* (*niño*) to bath, bathe; (*objeto*) to dip; (*de barniz*) to coat; **~se** *vr* (*en el mar*) to bathe, swim; (*en la bañera*) to have a bath.
bañero, a [ba'ɲero, a] *nmf* lifeguard ♦ *nf* bath(tub).
bañista [ba'ɲista] *nm/f* bather.
baño ['baɲo] *nm* (*en bañera*) bath; (*en río, mar*) dip, swim; (*cuarto*) bathroom; (*bañera*) bath(tub); (*capa*) coating; **ir a tomar los ~s** to take the waters.
baptista [bap'tista] *nm/f* Baptist.
baqueano, a, baquiano, a [bake'ano, a, baki'ano, a] *nm/f* (*AM*) guide.
baqueta [ba'keta] *nf* (*MUS*) drumstick.
bar [bar] *nm* bar.
barahúnda [bara'unda] *nf* uproar, hubbub.
baraja [ba'raxa] *nf* pack (of cards); *see boxed note.*

> **BARAJA ESPAÑOLA**
>
> *The* **baraja española** *is the traditional Spanish deck of cards, which differs from a standard poker deck. The four "palos" (suits) are "oros" (golden coins), "copas" (goblets), "espadas" (swords) and "bastos" ("clubs", but not the same as the ones in a poker pack). Every suit has nine numbered cards (although for certain games only seven are used), and three face cards: "sota" (jack), "caballo" (≈ queen) and "rey" (king).*

barajar [bara'xar] *vt* (*naipes*) to shuffle; (*fig*) to jumble up.
baranda [ba'randa], **barandilla** [baran'diʎa] *nf* rail, railing.
baratija [bara'tixa] *nf* trinket; (*fig*) trifle; **~s** *nfpl* (*COM*) cheap goods.
baratillo [bara'tiʎo] *nm* (*tienda*) junkshop; (*subasta*) bargain sale; (*conjunto de cosas*) second-hand goods *pl*.
barato, a [ba'rato, a] *adj* cheap ♦ *adv* cheap, cheaply.
baratura [bara'tura] *nf* cheapness.
baraúnda [bara'unda] *nf* = **barahúnda**.
barba ['barβa] *nf* (*mentón*) chin; (*pelo*) beard; **tener ~** to be unshaven; **hacer algo en las ~s de algn** to do sth under sb's very nose; **reírse en las ~s de algn** to laugh in sb's face.
barbacoa [barβa'koa] *nf* (*parrilla*) barbecue; (*carne*) barbecued meat.
barbaridad [barβari'ðað] *nf* barbarity; (*acto*) barbarism; (*atrocidad*) outrage; **una ~ de** (*fam*) loads of; **¡qué ~!** (*fam*) how awful!; **cuesta una ~** (*fam*) it costs a fortune.
barbarie [bar'βarje] *nf*, **barbarismo** [barβa'rismo] *nm* barbarism; (*crueldad*) barbarity.
bárbaro, a ['barβaro, a] *adj* barbarous, cruel; (*grosero*) rough, uncouth ♦ *nm/f* barbarian ♦ *adv*: **lo pasamos ~** (*fam*) we had a great time; **¡qué ~!** (*fam*) how marvellous!; **un éxito ~** (*fam*) a terrific success; **es un tipo ~** (*fam*) he's a great bloke.
barbecho [bar'βetʃo] *nm* fallow land.
barbero [bar'βero] *nm* barber, hairdresser.
barbilampiño [barβilam'piɲo] *adj* smooth-faced; (*fig*) inexperienced.
barbilla [bar'βiʎa] *nf* chin, tip of the chin.
barbitúrico [barβi'turiko] *nm* barbiturate.
barbo ['barβo] *nm*: **~ de mar** red mullet.
barbotar [barβo'tar], **barbotear** [barβote'ar] *vt, vi* to mutter, mumble.
barbudo, a [bar'βuðo, a] *adj* bearded.
barbullar [barβu'ʎar] *vi* to jabber away.
barca ['barka] *nf* (small) boat; **~ pesquera** fishing boat; **~ de pasaje** ferry.
barcaza [bar'kaθa] *nf* barge; **~ de desembarco** landing craft.
Barcelona [barθe'lona] *nf* Barcelona.
barcelonés, esa [barθelo'nes, esa] *adj* of *o* from Barcelona ♦ *nm/f* native *o* inhabitant of Barcelona.
barco ['barko] *nm* boat; (*buque*) ship; (*COM etc*) vessel; **~ de carga** cargo boat; **~ de guerra** warship; **~ de vela** sailing ship; **ir en ~** to go by boat.
baremo [ba'remo] *nm* scale; (*tabla de cuentas*) ready reckoner.
barítono [ba'ritono] *nm* baritone.
barman ['barman] *nm* barman.
Barna. *abr* = **Barcelona.**
barnice [bar'niθe] *etc vb V* **barnizar.**
barniz [bar'niθ] *nm* varnish; (*en la loza*) glaze; (*fig*) veneer.
barnizar [barni'θar] *vt* to varnish; (*loza*) to glaze.
barómetro [ba'rometro] *nm* barometer.
barón [ba'ron] *nm* baron.
baronesa [baro'nesa] *nf* baroness.
barquero [bar'kero] *nm* boatman.
barquilla [bar'kiʎa] *nf* (*NAUT*) log.
barquillo [bar'kiʎo] *nm* cone, cornet.
barra ['barra] *nf* bar, rod; (*JUR*) rail; (: *banquillo*) dock; (*de un bar, café*) bar; (*de pan*) French loaf; (*palanca*) lever; **~ de carmín** *o* **de labios** lipstick; **~ espaciadora** (*INFORM*) space bar; **~ inversa** backslash; **~ libre** free bar; **no pararse en ~s** to stick *o* stop at nothing.
barrabasada [barraβa'saða] *nf* (piece of) mischief.
barraca [ba'rraka] *nf* hut, cabin; (*en Valencia*) thatched farmhouse; (*en feria*) booth.
barracón [barra'kon] *nm* (*caseta*) big hut.
barragana [barra'ɣana] *nf* concubine.
barranca [ba'rranka] *nf* ravine, gully.
barranco [ba'rranko] *nm* ravine; (*fig*) difficulty.
barrena [ba'rrena] *nf* drill.
barrenar [barre'nar] *vt* to drill (through).
barrendero, a [barren'dero, a] *nm/f* street-sweeper.
barreno [ba'rreno] *nm* large drill.
barreño [ba'rreɲo] *nm* washing-up bowl.
barrer [ba'rrer] *vt* to sweep; (*quitar*) to sweep away; (*MIL, NAUT*) to sweep, rake (with gunfire) ♦ *vi* to sweep up.
barrera [ba'rrera] *nf* barrier; (*MIL*) barricade; (*FERRO*) crossing gate; **poner ~s a** to hinder; **~ arancelaria** (*COM*)

tariff barrier; ~ **comercial** (*COM*) trade barrier.

barriada [ba'rrjaða] *nf* quarter, district.

barricada [barri'kaða] *nf* barricade.

barrida [ba'rriða] *nf*, **barrido** [ba'rriðo] *nm* sweep, sweeping.

barriga [ba'rriɣa] *nf* belly; (*panza*) paunch; (*vientre*) guts *pl*; **echar** ~ to get middle-age spread.

barrigón, ona [barri'ɣon, ona], **barrigudo, a** [barri'ɣuðo, a] *adj* potbellied.

barril [ba'rril] *nm* barrel, cask; **cerveza de** ~ draught beer.

barrio ['barrjo] *nm* (*vecindad*) area, neighborhood (*US*); (*en las afueras*) suburb; ~**s bajos** poor quarter *sg*; ~ **chino** red-light district.

barriobajero, a [barrjobβa'xero, a] *adj* (*vulgar*) common.

barro ['barro] *nm* (*lodo*) mud; (*objetos*) earthenware; (*MED*) pimple.

barroco, a [ba'rroko, a] *adj* Baroque; (*fig*) elaborate ♦ *nm* Baroque.

barrote [ba'rrote] *nm* (*de ventana etc*) bar.

barruntar [barrun'tar] *vt* (*conjeturar*) to guess; (*presentir*) to suspect.

barrunto [ba'rrunto] *nm* guess; suspicion.

bartola [bar'tola]: **a la** ~ *adv*: **tirarse a la** ~ to take it easy, be lazy.

bártulos ['bartulos] *nmpl* things, belongings.

barullo [ba'ruʎo] *nm* row, uproar.

basa ['basa] *nf* (*ARQ*) base.

basamento [basa'mento] *nm* base, plinth.

basar [ba'sar] *vt* to base; ~**se** *vr*: ~**se en** to be based on.

basca ['baska] *nf* nausea.

báscula ['baskula] *nf* (platform) scales *pl*; ~ **biestable** (*INFORM*) flip-flop, toggle.

bascular [basku'lar] *vt* (*INFORM*) to toggle.

base ['base] *nf* base; **a** ~ **de** on the basis of, based on; (*mediante*) by means of; **a** ~ **de bien** in abundance; ~ **de conocimiento** knowledge base; ~ **de datos** database.

básico, a ['basiko, a] *adj* basic.

Basilea [basi'lea] *nf* Basle.

basílica [ba'silika] *nf* basilica.

basilisco [basi'lisco] *nm* (*AM*) iguana; **estar hecho un** ~ to be hopping mad.

basket, básquet ['basket] *nm* basketball.

PALABRA CLAVE

bastante [bas'tante] *adj* **1** (*suficiente*) enough; ~ **dinero** enough *o* sufficient money; ~**s libros** enough books

2 (*valor intensivo*): ~ **gente** quite a lot of people; **tener** ~ **calor** to be rather hot; **hace** ~ **tiempo que ocurrió** it happened quite *o* rather a long time ago

♦ *adv*: ~ **bueno/malo** quite good/rather bad; ~ **rico** pretty rich; **(lo)** ~ **inteligente (como) para hacer algo** clever enough *o* sufficiently clever to do sth; **voy a tardar** ~ I'm going to be a while *o* quite some time.

bastar [bas'tar] *vi* to be enough *o* sufficient; ~**se** *vr* to be self-sufficient; ~ **para** to be enough to; **¡basta!** (that's) enough!

bastardilla [bastar'ðiʎa] *nf* italics *pl*.

bastardo, a [bas'tarðo, a] *adj*, *nm/f* bastard.

bastidor [basti'ðor] *nm* frame; (*de coche*) chassis; (*ARTE*) stretcher; (*TEAT*) wing; **entre** ~**es** behind the scenes.

basto, a ['basto, a] *adj* coarse, rough ♦ *nmpl*: ~**s** (*NAIPES*) *one of the suits in the Spanish card deck*; *V tb* **Baraja Española**.

bastón [bas'ton] *nm* stick, staff; (*para pasear*) walking stick; ~ **de mando** baton.

bastonazo [basto'naθo] *nm* blow with a stick.

bastoncillo [baston'θiʎo] *nm* (*tb*: ~ **de algodón**) cotton bud.

basura [ba'sura] *nf* rubbish, refuse (*BRIT*), garbage (*US*).

basurero [basu'rero] *nm* (*hombre*) dustman (*BRIT*), garbage collector *o* man (*US*); (*lugar*) rubbish dump; (*cubo*) (rubbish) bin (*BRIT*), trash can (*US*).

bata ['bata] *nf* (*gen*) dressing gown; (*cubretodo*) smock, overall; (*MED, TEC etc*) lab(oratory) coat.

batacazo [bata'kaθo] *nm* bump.

batalla [ba'taʎa] *nf* battle; **de** ~ for everyday use.

batallar [bata'ʎar] *vi* to fight.

batallón [bata'ʎon] *nm* battalion.

batata [ba'tata] *nf* (*AM*: *CULIN*) sweet potato.

bate ['bate] *nm* (*DEPORTE*) bat.

batea [ba'tea] *nf* (*AM*) washing trough.

bateador [batea'ðor] *nm* (*DEPORTE*) batter, batsman.

batería [bate'ria] *nf* battery; (*MUS*) drums *pl*; (*TEAT*) footlights *pl*; ~ **de cocina** kitchen utensils *pl*.

batiburrillo [batiβu'rriʎo] *nm* hotchpotch.

batido, a [ba'tiðo, a] *adj* (*camino*) beaten, well-trodden ♦ *nm* (*CULIN*) batter; ~ **(de leche)** milk shake ♦ *nf* (*AM*) (police) raid.

batidora [bati'ðora] *nf* beater, mixer; ~ **eléctrica** food mixer, blender.

batir [ba'tir] *vt* to beat, strike; (*vencer*) to beat, defeat; (*revolver*) to beat, mix; (*pelo*) to back-comb; **~se** *vr* to fight; **~ palmas** to clap, applaud.
baturro, a [ba'turro, a] *nm/f* Aragonese peasant.
batuta [ba'tuta] *nf* baton; **llevar la ~** (*fig*) to be the boss.
baudio ['bauðjo] *nm* (*INFORM*) baud.
baúl [ba'ul] *nm* trunk; (*AM AUTO*) boot (*BRIT*), trunk (*US*).
bautice [bau'tiθe] *etc vb V* **bautizar**.
bautismo [bau'tismo] *nm* baptism, christening.
bautista [bau'tista] *adj, nm/f* Baptist.
bautizar [bauti'θar] *vt* to baptize, christen; (*fam: diluir*) to water down; (*dar apodo*) to dub.
bautizo [bau'tiθo] *nm* baptism, christening.
bávaro, a ['baβaro, a] *adj, nm/f* Bavarian.
Baviera [ba'βjera] *nf* Bavaria.
baya ['baja] *nf* berry; *V tb* **bayo**.
bayeta [ba'jeta] *nf* (*trapo*) floorcloth; (*AM: pañal*) nappy (*BRIT*), diaper (*US*).
bayo, a ['bajo, a] *adj* bay.
bayoneta [bajo'neta] *nf* bayonet.
baza ['baθa] *nf* trick; **meter ~** to butt in.
bazar [ba'θar] *nm* bazaar.
bazo ['baθo] *nm* spleen.
bazofia [ba'θofja] *nf* pigswill (*BRIT*), hogwash (*US*); (*libro etc*) trash.
BCE *nm abr* (= *Banco Central Europeo*) ECB.
beatificar [beatifi'kar] *vt* to beatify.
beato, a [be'ato, a] *adj* blessed; (*piadoso*) pious.
bebe (*AM*), *pl* **bebes**, **bebé**, *pl* **bebés** ['beβe, 'beβes, be'βe, be'βes] *nm* baby.
bebedero, a [beβe'ðero, a] *nm* (*para animales*) drinking trough.
bebedizo, a [beβe'ðiθo, a] *adj* drinkable ♦ *nm* potion.
bebedor, a [beβe'ðor, a] *adj* hard-drinking.
bebé-probeta [be'βe-pro'βeta], *pl* **bebés-probeta** *nm/f* test-tube baby.
beber [be'βer] *vt, vi* to drink; **~ a sorbos/tragos** to sip/gulp; **se lo bebió todo** he drank it all up.
bebido, a [be'βiðo, a] *adj* drunk ♦ *nf* drink.
beca ['beka] *nf* grant, scholarship.
becado, a [be'kaðo, a] *nm/f*, **becario, a** [be'karjo, a] *nm/f* scholarship holder.
becerro [be'θerro] *nm* yearling calf.
bechamel [betʃa'mel] *nf* = **besamel**.
becuadro [be'kwaðro] *nm* (*MUS*) natural sign.
bedel [be'ðel] *nm* porter, janitor.
beduino, a [be'ðwino, a] *adj, nm/f* Bedouin.
befarse [be'farse] *vr*: **~ de algo** to scoff at sth.
beige ['beix], **beis** ['beis] *adj, nm* beige.
béisbol ['beisβol] *nm* baseball.
bejuco [be'juko] *nm* (*AM*) reed, liana.
beldad [bel'dað] *nf* beauty.
Belén [be'len] *nm* Bethlehem; **b~** (*de Navidad*) nativity scene, crib.
belga ['belɣa] *adj, nm/f* Belgian.
Bélgica ['belxika] *nf* Belgium.
Belgrado [bel'ɣraðo] *nm* Belgrade.
Belice [be'liθe] *nm* Belize.
bélico, a ['beliko, a] *adj* (*actitud*) warlike.
belicoso, a [beli'koso, a] *adj* (*guerrero*) warlike; (*agresivo*) aggressive, bellicose.
beligerante [belixe'rante] *adj* belligerent.
bellaco, a [be'ʎako, a] *adj* sly, cunning ♦ *nm* villain, rogue.
belladona [beʎa'ðona] *nf* deadly nightshade.
bellaquería [beʎake'ria] *nf* (*acción*) dirty trick; (*calidad*) wickedness.
belleza [be'ʎeθa] *nf* beauty.
bello, a ['beʎo, a] *adj* beautiful, lovely; **Bellas Artes** Fine Art *sg*.
bellota [be'ʎota] *nf* acorn.
bemol [be'mol] *nm* (*MUS*) flat; **esto tiene ~es** (*fam*) this is a tough one.
bencina [ben'sina] *nf* (*AM*) petrol (*BRIT*), gas (*US*).
bendecir [bende'θir] *vt* to bless; **~ la mesa** to say grace.
bendición [bendi'θjon] *nf* blessing.
bendiga [ben'diɣa] *etc*, **bendije** [ben'dixe] *etc vb V* **bendecir**.
bendito, a [ben'dito, a] *pp de* **bendecir** ♦ *adj* (*santo*) blessed; (*agua*) holy; (*afortunado*) lucky; (*feliz*) happy; (*sencillo*) simple ♦ *nm/f* simple soul; **¡~ sea Dios!** thank goodness!; **es un ~** he's sweet; **dormir como un ~** to sleep like a log.
benedictino, a [beneðik'tino, a] *adj, nm* Benedictine.
benefactor, a [benefak'tor, a] *nm/f* benefactor/benefactress.
beneficencia [benefi'θenθja] *nf* charity.
beneficiar [benefi'θjar] *vt* to benefit, be of benefit to; **~se** *vr* to benefit, profit.
beneficiario, a [benefi'θjarjo, a] *nm/f* beneficiary; (*de cheque*) payee.
beneficio [bene'fiθjo] *nm* (*bien*) benefit, advantage; (*COM*) profit, gain; **a ~ de** for the benefit of; **en ~ propio** to one's own advantage; **~ bruto/neto** gross/net profit; **~ por acción** earnings *pl* per share.
beneficioso, a [benefi'θjoso, a] *adj* beneficial.
benéfico, a [be'nefiko, a] *adj* charitable;

sociedad ~a charity (organization).
benemérito, a [bene'merito, a] *adj* meritorious ♦ *nf*: **la Benemérita** (*ESP*) the Civil Guard; *V tb* **Guardia Civil**.
beneplácito [bene'plaθito] *nm* approval, consent.
benevolencia [beneβo'lenθja] *nf* benevolence, kindness.
benévolo, a [be'neβolo, a] *adj* benevolent, kind.
Bengala [ben'gala] *nf* Bengal; **el Golfo de ~** the Bay of Bengal.
bengala [ben'gala] *nf* (*MIL*) flare; (*fuego*) Bengal light; (*materia*) rattan.
bengalí [benga'li] *adj, nm/f* Bengali.
benignidad [beniɣni'ðað] *nf* (*afabilidad*) kindness; (*suavidad*) mildness.
benigno, a [be'niɣno, a] *adj* kind; (*suave*) mild; (*MED: tumor*) benign, non-malignant.
benjamín [benxa'min] *nm* youngest child.
beodo, a [be'oðo, a] *adj* drunk ♦ *nm/f* drunkard.
berberecho [berβe'retʃo] *nm* cockle.
berenjena [beren'xena] *nf* aubergine (*BRIT*), eggplant (*US*).
berenjenal [berenxe'nal] *nm* (*AGR*) aubergine bed; (*fig*) mess; **en buen ~ nos hemos metido** we've got ourselves into a fine mess.
bergantín [berɣan'tin] *nm* brig(antine).
Berlín [ber'lin] *nm* Berlin.
berlinés, esa [berli'nes, esa] *adj* of *o* from Berlin ♦ *nm/f* Berliner.
bermejo, a [ber'mexo, a] *adj* red.
bermellón [berme'ʎon] *nm* vermilion.
bermudas [ber'muðas] *nfpl* Bermuda shorts.
berrear [berre'ar] *vi* to bellow, low.
berrido [be'rriðo] *nm* bellow(ing).
berrinche [be'rrintʃe] *nm* (*fam*) temper, tantrum.
berro ['berro] *nm* watercress.
berza ['berθa] *nf* cabbage; **~ lombarda** red cabbage.
besamel [besa'mel], **besamela** [besa'mela] *nf* (*CULIN*) white sauce, bechamel sauce.
besar [be'sar] *vt* to kiss; (*fig: tocar*) to graze; **~se** *vr* to kiss (one another).
beso ['beso] *nm* kiss.
bestia ['bestja] *nf* beast, animal; (*fig*) idiot; **~ de carga** beast of burden; **¡~!** you idiot!; **¡no seas ~!** (*bruto*) don't be such a brute!; (*idiota*) don't be such an idiot!
bestial [bes'tjal] *adj* bestial; (*fam*) terrific.
bestialidad [bestjali'ðað] *nf* bestiality; (*fam*) stupidity.
besugo [be'suɣo] *nm* sea bream; (*fam*) idiot.
besuguera [besu'ɣera] *nf* (*CULIN*) fish pan.
besuquear [besuke'ar] *vt* to cover with kisses; **~se** *vr* to kiss and cuddle.
bético, a ['betiko, a] *adj* Andalusian.
betún [be'tun] *nm* shoe polish; (*QUÍMICA*) bitumen, asphalt.
Bib. *abr* = **Biblioteca**.
biberón [biβe'ron] *nm* feeding bottle.
Biblia ['biβlja] *nf* Bible.
bíblico, a ['biβliko, a] *adj* biblical.
bibliografía [biβljoɣra'fia] *nf* bibliography.
biblioteca [biβljo'teka] *nf* library; (*estantes*) bookcase, bookshelves *pl*; **~ de consulta** reference library.
bibliotecario, a [biβljote'karjo, a] *nm/f* librarian.
B.I.C. [bik] *nf abr* (= *Brigada de Investigación Criminal*) ≈ CID (*BRIT*), FBI (*US*).
bicarbonato [bikarβo'nato] *nm* bicarbonate.
bíceps ['biθeps] *nm inv* biceps.
bicho ['bitʃo] *nm* (*animal*) small animal; (*sabandija*) bug, insect; (*TAUR*) bull; **~ raro** (*fam*) queer fish.
bici ['biθi] *nf* (*fam*) bike.
bicicleta [biθi'kleta] *nf* bicycle, cycle; **~ estática/de montaña** exercise/mountain bike.
bicoca [bi'koka] *nf* (*ESP fam*) cushy job.
BID *n abbr* (= *Banco Interamericano de Desarrollo*) IDB.
bidé [bi'ðe] *nm* bidet.
bidireccional [biðirekθjo'nal] *adj* bidirectional.
bidón [bi'ðon] *nm* (*grande*) drum; (*pequeño*) can.
Bielorrusia [bjelo'rrusja] *nf* Belarus, Byelorussia.
bielorruso, a [bjelo'rruso, a] *adj, nm/f* Belarussian, Belorussian ♦ *nm* (*LING*) Belarussian, Belorussian.

PALABRA CLAVE

bien [bjen] *nm* **1** (*bienestar*) good; **te lo digo por tu ~** I'm telling you for your own good; **el ~ y el mal** good and evil
2 (*posesión*): **~es** goods; **~es de consumo/equipo** consumer/capital goods; **~es inmuebles** *o* **raíces/~es muebles** real estate *sg*/personal property *sg*
♦ *adv* **1** (*de manera satisfactoria, correcta etc*) well; **trabaja/come ~** she works/eats well; **contestó ~** he answered correctly; **oler ~** to smell nice *o* good; **me siento ~** I feel fine; **no me siento ~** I don't feel

very well; **se está ~ aquí** it's nice here
2 (*frases*): **hiciste ~ en llamarme** you were right to call me
3 (*valor intensivo*) very; **un cuarto ~ caliente** a nice warm room; **~ de veces** lots of times; **~ se ve que ...** it's quite clear that ...
4: **estar ~**: **estoy muy ~ aquí** I feel very happy here; **¿te encuentras ~?** are you all right?; **te está ~ la falda** (*ser la talla*) the skirt fits you; (*sentar*) the skirt suits you; **el libro está muy ~** the book is really good; **está ~ que vengan** it's all right for them to come; **¡está ~! lo haré** oh all right, I'll do it; **ya está ~ de quejas** that's quite enough complaining
5 (*de buena gana*): **yo ~ que iría pero ...** I'd gladly go but ...
♦ *excl*: **¡~!** (*aprobación*) O.K!; **¡muy ~!** well done!; **¡qué ~!** great!; **~, gracias, ¿y usted?** fine thanks, and you?
♦ *adj inv*: **niño ~** rich kid; **gente ~** posh people
♦ *conj* **1**: **~ ... ~**: **~ en coche ~ en tren** either by car or by train
2: **no ~** (*esp AM*): **no ~ llegue te llamaré** as soon as I arrive I'll call you
3: **si ~** even though; *V tb* **más.**

bienal [bje'nal] *adj* biennial.
bienaventurado, a [bjenaßentu'raðo, a] *adj* (*feliz*) happy; (*afortunado*) fortunate; (*REL*) blessed.
bienestar [bjenes'tar] *nm* well-being; **estado de ~** welfare state.
bienhechor, a [bjene'tʃor, a] *adj* beneficent ♦ *nm/f* benefactor/benefactress.
bienio ['bjenjo] *nm* two-year period.
bienvenido, a [bjembe'niðo, a] *adj* welcome ♦ *excl* welcome! ♦ *nf* welcome; **dar la bienvenida a algn** to welcome sb.
bies ['bjes] *nm*: **falda al ~** bias-cut skirt; **cortar al ~** to cut on the bias.
bifásico, a [bi'fasiko, a] *adj* (*ELEC*) two-phase.
bife ['bife] *nm* (*AM*) steak.
bifocal [bifo'kal] *adj* bifocal.
bifurcación [bifurka'θjon] *nf* fork; (*FERRO, INFORM*) branch.
bifurcarse [bifur'karse] *vr* to fork.
bigamia [bi'ɣamja] *nf* bigamy.
bígamo, a ['biɣamo, a] *adj* bigamous ♦ *nm/f* bigamist.
bígaro ['biɣaro] *nm* winkle.
bigote [bi'ɣote] *nm* (*tb*: **~s**) moustache.
bigotudo, a [biɣo'tuðo, a] *adj* with a big moustache.
bigudí [biɣu'ði] *nm* (hair-)curler.
bikini [bi'kini] *nm* bikini; (*CULIN*) toasted cheese and ham sandwich.
bilateral [bilate'ral] *adj* bilateral.
bilbaíno, a [bilßa'ino, a] *adj* of *o* from Bilbao ♦ *nm/f* native *o* inhabitant of Bilbao.
bilingüe [bi'lingwe] *adj* bilingual.
bilis ['bilis] *nf inv* bile.
billar [bi'ʎar] *nm* billiards *sg*; (*lugar*) billiard hall; (*galería de atracciones*) amusement arcade; **~ americano** pool.
billete [bi'ʎete] *nm* ticket; (*de banco*) banknote (*BRIT*), bill (*US*); (*carta*) note; **~ sencillo, ~ de ida solamente/~ de ida y vuelta** single (*BRIT*) *o* one-way (*US*) ticket/return (*BRIT*) *o* round-trip (*US*) ticket; **sacar (un) ~** to get a ticket; **un ~ de 5 libras** a five-pound note.
billetera [biʎe'tera] *nf*, **billetero** [biʎe'tero] *nm* wallet.
billón [bi'ʎon] *nm* billion.
bimensual [bimen'swal] *adj* twice monthly.
bimestral [bimes'tral] *adj* bimonthly.
bimestre [bi'mestre] *nm* two-month period.
bimotor [bimo'tor] *adj* twin-engined ♦ *nm* twin-engined plane.
binario, a [bi'narjo, a] *adj* (*INFORM*) binary.
bingo ['bingo] *nm* (*juego*) bingo; (*sala*) bingo hall.
binóculo [bi'nokulo] *nm* pince-nez.
binomio [bi'nomjo] *nm* (*MAT*) binomial.
biodegradable [bioðeɣra'ðaßle] *adj* biodegradable.
biodiversidad [bioðißersi'ðað] *nf* biodiversity.
biografía [bjoɣra'fia] *nf* biography.
biográfico, a [bio'ɣrafiko, a] *adj* biographical.
biógrafo, a [bi'oɣrafo, a] *nm/f* biographer.
biología [biolo'xia] *nf* biology.
biológico, a [bio'loxiko, a] *adj* biological; (*cultivo, producto*) organic; **guerra biológica** biological warfare.
biólogo, a [bi'oloɣo, a] *nm/f* biologist.
biombo ['bjombo] *nm* (folding) screen.
biopsia [bi'opsja] *nf* biopsy.
bioquímico, a [bio'kimiko, a] *adj* biochemical ♦ *nm/f* biochemist ♦ *nf* biochemistry.
biosfera [bios'fera] *nf* biosphere.
bióxido [bi'oksiðo] *nm* dioxide.
bipartidismo [biparti'ðismo] *nm* (*POL*) two-party system.
biquini [bi'kini] *nm* = **bikini.**
birlar [bir'lar] *vt* (*fam*) to pinch.
birlibirloque [birlißir'loke] *nm*: **por arte de**

~ (as if) by magic.
Birmania [bir'manja] *nf* Burma.
birmano, a [bir'mano, a] *adj nm/f* Burmese.
birrete [bi'rrete] *nm* (*JUR*) judge's cap.
birria ['birrja] *nf* (*fam*): **ser una** ~ to be rubbish; **ir hecho una** ~ to be *o* look a sight.
bis [bis] *excl* encore! ♦ *nm* encore ♦ *adv* (*dos veces*) twice; **viven en el 27** ~ they live at 27a.
bisabuelo, a [bisa'ßwelo, a] *nm/f* great-grandfather/mother; **~s** *nmpl* great-grandparents.
bisagra [bi'saɤra] *nf* hinge.
bisbisar [bisßi'sar], **bisbisear** [bisßise'ar] *vt* to mutter, mumble.
bisbiseo [bisßi'seo] *nm* muttering.
biselar [bise'lar] *vt* to bevel.
bisexual [bisek'swal] *adj, nm/f* bisexual.
bisiesto [bi'sjesto] *adj*: **año** ~ leap year.
bisnieto, a [bis'njeto, a] *nm/f* great-grandson/daughter; **~s** *nmpl* great-grandchildren.
bisonte [bi'sonte] *nm* bison.
bisoñé [biso'ɲe] *nm* toupée.
bisoño, a [bi'soɲo, a] *adj* green, inexperienced.
bistec [bis'tek], **bisté** [bis'te] *nm* steak.
bisturí [bistu'ri] *nm* scalpel.
bisutería [bisute'ria] *nf* imitation *o* costume jewellery.
bit [bit] *nm* (*INFORM*) bit; ~ **de parada** stop bit; ~ **de paridad** parity bit.
bitácora [bi'takora] *nf*: **cuaderno de** ~ logbook, ship's log.
bitio ['bitjo] *nm* (*INFORM*) bit.
bizantino, a [biθan'tino, a] *adj* Byzantine; (*fig*) pointless.
bizarría [biθa'rria] *nf* (*valor*) bravery; (*generosidad*) generosity.
bizarro, a [bi'θarro, a] *adj* brave; generous.
bizco, a ['biθko, a] *adj* cross-eyed.
bizcocho [biθ'kotʃo] *nm* (*CULIN*) sponge cake.
biznieto, a [biθ'nieto, a] *nm/f* = **bisnieto**.
bizquear [biθke'ar] *vi* to squint.
blanco, a ['blanko, a] *adj* white ♦ *nm/f* white man/woman, white ♦ *nm* (*color*) white; (*en texto*) blank; (*MIL, fig*) target ♦ *nf* (*MUS*) minim; **en** ~ blank; **cheque en** ~ blank cheque; **votar en** ~ to spoil one's vote; **quedarse en** ~ to be disappointed; **noche en** ~ sleepless night; **ser el** ~ **de las burlas** to be the butt of jokes; **estar sin blanca** to be broke.
blancura [blan'kura] *nf* whiteness.
blandengue [blan'denge] *adj* (*fam*) soft, weak.
blandir [blan'dir] *vt* to brandish.
blando, a ['blando, a] *adj* soft; (*tierno*) tender, gentle; (*carácter*) mild; (*fam*) cowardly ♦ *nm/f* (*POL etc*) soft-liner.
blandura [blan'dura] *nf* softness; tenderness; mildness.
blanquear [blanke'ar] *vt* to whiten; (*fachada*) to whitewash; (*paño*) to bleach; (*dinero*) to launder ♦ *vi* to turn white.
blanquecino, a [blanke'θino, a] *adj* whitish.
blanqueo [blan'keo] *nm* (*de pared*) whitewashing; (*de dinero*) laundering.
blasfemar [blasfe'mar] *vi* to blaspheme; (*fig*) to curse.
blasfemia [blas'femja] *nf* blasphemy.
blasfemo, a [blas'femo, a] *adj* blasphemous ♦ *nm/f* blasphemer.
blasón [bla'son] *nm* coat of arms; (*fig*) honour.
blasonar [blaso'nar] *vt* to emblazon ♦ *vi* to boast, brag.
bledo ['bleðo] *nm*: **(no) me importa un** ~ I couldn't care less.
blindado, a [blin'daðo, a] *adj* (*MIL*) armour-plated; (*antibalas*) bulletproof; **coche** *o* (*AM*) **carro** ~ armoured car; **puertas blindadas** security doors.
blindaje [blin'daxe] *nm* armour, armour-plating.
bloc, *pl* **blocs** [blok, blos] *nm* writing pad; (*ESCOL*) jotter; ~ **de dibujos** sketch pad.
bloque ['bloke] *nm* (*tb INFORM*) block; (*POL*) bloc; ~ **de cilindros** cylinder block.
bloquear [bloke'ar] *vt* (*NAUT etc*) to blockade; (*aislar*) to cut off; (*COM, ECON*) to freeze; **fondos bloqueados** frozen assets.
bloqueo [blo'keo] *nm* blockade; (*COM*) freezing, blocking.
bluejean [blu'jin] *nm* (*AM*) jeans *pl*, denims *pl*.
blusa ['blusa] *nf* blouse.
B.º *abr* (*FINANZAS*: = *banco*) bank; (*COM*: = *beneficiario*) beneficiary.
boa ['boa] *nf* boa.
boato [bo'ato] *nm* show, ostentation.
bobada [bo'ßaða] *nf* foolish action (*o* statement); **decir ~s** to talk nonsense.
bobalicón, ona [boßali'kon, ona] *adj* utterly stupid.
bobería [boße'ria] *nf* =**bobada**.
bobina [bo'ßina] *nf* (*TEC*) bobbin; (*FOTO*) spool; (*ELEC*) coil, winding.
bobo, a ['boßo, a] *adj* (*tonto*) daft, silly; (*cándido*) naïve ♦ *nm/f* fool, idiot ♦ *nm* (*TEAT*) clown, funny man.
boca ['boka] *nf* mouth; (*de crustáceo*)

pincer; (*de cañón*) muzzle; (*entrada*) mouth, entrance; (*INFORM*) slot; **~s** *nfpl* (*de río*) mouth *sg*; ~ **abajo/arriba** face down/up; **a ~ jarro** point-blank; **se me hace la ~ agua** my mouth is watering; **todo salió a pedir de ~** it all turned out perfectly; **en ~ de** (*esp AM*) according to; **la cosa anda de ~ en ~** the story is going the rounds; **¡cállate la ~!** (*fam*) shut up!; **quedarse con la ~ abierta** to be dumbfounded; **no abrir la ~** to keep quiet; ~ **del estómago** pit of the stomach; ~ **de metro** tube (*BRIT*) *o* subway (*US*) entrance.
bocacalle [boka'kaʎe] *nf* side street; **la primera ~** the first turning *o* street.
bocadillo [boka'ðiʎo] *nm* sandwich.
bocado [bo'kaðo] *nm* mouthful, bite; (*de caballo*) bridle; ~ **de Adán** Adam's apple.
bocajarro [boka'xarro]: **a ~** *adv* (*MIL*) at point-blank range; **decir algo a ~** to say sth bluntly.
bocanada [boka'naða] *nf* (*de vino*) mouthful, swallow; (*de aire*) gust, puff.
bocata [bo'kata] *nm* (*fam*) sandwich.
bocazas [bo'kaθas] *nm/f inv* (*fam*) bigmouth.
boceto [bo'θeto] *nm* sketch, outline.
bocha ['botʃa] *nf* bowl; **~s** *nfpl* bowls *sg*.
bochinche [bo'tʃintʃe] *nm* (*fam*) uproar.
bochorno [bo'tʃorno] *nm* (*vergüenza*) embarrassment; (*calor*): **hace ~** it's very muggy.
bochornoso, a [botʃor'noso, a] *adj* muggy; embarrassing.
bocina [bo'θina] *nf* (*MUS*) trumpet; (*AUTO*) horn; (*para hablar*) megaphone; **tocar la ~** (*AUTO*) to sound *o* blow one's horn.
bocinazo [boθi'naθo] *nm* (*AUTO*) toot.
bocio ['boθjo] *nm* (*MED*) goitre.
boda ['boða] *nf* (*tb:* **~s**) wedding, marriage; (*fiesta*) wedding reception; **~s de plata/de oro** silver/golden wedding *sg*.
bodega [bo'ðeɣa] *nf* (*de vino*) (wine) cellar; (*bar*) bar; (*restaurante*) restaurant; (*depósito*) storeroom; (*de barco*) hold.
bodegón [boðe'ɣon] *nm* (*ARTE*) still life.
bodrio [bo'ðrio] *nm*: **el libro es un ~** the book is awful *o* rubbish.
B.O.E. ['boe] *nm abr* = **Boletín Oficial del Estado**.
bofe ['bofe] *nm* (*tb:* **~s**: *de res*) lights *pl*; **echar los ~s** to slave (away).
bofetada [bofe'taða] *nf* slap (in the face); **dar de ~s a algn** to punch sb.
bofetón [bofe'ton] *nm* = **bofetada**.
boga ['boɣa] *nf*: **en ~** in vogue.
bogar [bo'ɣar] *vi* (*remar*) to row; (*navegar*) to sail.
bogavante [boɣa'βante] *nm* (*NAUT*) stroke, first rower; (*ZOOL*) lobster.
Bogotá [boɣo'ta] *n* Bogota.
bogotano, a [boɣo'tano, a] *adj* of *o* from Bogota ♦ *nm/f* native *o* inhabitant of Bogota.
bogue ['boɣe] *etc vb V* **bogar**.
bohemio, a [bo'emjo, a] *adj, nm/f* Bohemian.
boicot, *pl* **boicots** [boi'ko(t)] *nm* boycott.
boicotear [boikote'ar] *vt* to boycott.
boicoteo [boiko'teo] *nm* boycott.
boina ['boina] *nf* beret.
bola ['bola] *nf* ball; (*canica*) marble; (*NAIPES*) (grand) slam; (*betún*) shoe polish; (*mentira*) tale, story; **~s** *nfpl* (*AM*) bolas; ~ **de billar** billiard ball; ~ **de nieve** snowball.
bolchevique [boltʃe'βike] *adj, nm/f* Bolshevik.
boleadoras [bolea'ðoras] *nfpl* (*AM*) bolas *sg*.
bolera [bo'lera] *nf* skittle *o* bowling alley.
bolero [bo'lero] *nm* bolero.
boleta [bo'leta] *nf* (*AM: permiso*) pass, permit; (*: para votar*) ballot.
boletería [bolete'ria] *nf* (*AM*) ticket office.
boletero, a [bole'tero, a] *nm/f* (*AM*) ticket seller.
boletín [bole'tin] *nm* bulletin; (*periódico*) journal, review; ~ **escolar** (*ESP*) school report; ~ **de noticias** news bulletin; **B~ Oficial del Estado** (*ESP*) ≈ Hansard (*BRIT*), ≈ The Congressional Record (*US*); ~ **de pedido** application form; ~ **de precios** price list; ~ **de prensa** press release; *see boxed note*.

BOLETÍN OFICIAL DEL ESTADO

The **Boletín Oficial del Estado**, *or "BOE", is the official government record of all laws and resolutions passed by "las Cortes" (the Spanish Parliament). It is widely consulted, mainly because it also publishes details of the "oposiciones" (competitive public service examinations).*

boleto [bo'leto] *nm* (*esp AM*) ticket; ~ **de apuestas** betting slip.
boli ['boli] *nm* Biro ®.
boliche [bo'litʃe] *nm* (*bola*) jack; (*juego*) bowls *sg*; (*lugar*) bowling alley; (*AM: tienda*) small grocery store.
bólido ['boliðo] *nm* meteorite; (*AUTO*) racing car.
bolígrafo [bo'liɣrafo] *nm* ball-point pen, biro ®.
bolillo [bo'liʎo] *nm* (*COSTURA*) bobbin (for lacemaking).

bolívar [bo'lißar] *nm monetary unit of Venezuela.*
Bolivia [bo'lißja] *nf* Bolivia.
boliviano, a [boli'ßjano, a] *adj, nm/f* Bolivian.
bollo ['boʎo] *nm* (*pan*) roll; (*dulce*) scone; (*bulto*) bump, lump; (*abolladura*) dent; **~s** *nmpl* (*AM*) troubles.
bolo ['bolo] *nm* skittle; (*píldora*) (large) pill; **(juego de) ~s** skittles *sg.*
Bolonia [bo'lonja] *nf* Bologna.
bolsa ['bolsa] *nf* (*cartera*) purse; (*saco*) bag; (*AM*) pocket; (*ANAT*) cavity, sac; (*COM*) stock exchange; (*MINERÍA*) pocket; **~ de agua caliente** hot water bottle; **~ de aire** air pocket; **~ de (la) basura** bin-liner; **~ de dormir** (*AM*) sleeping bag; **~ de papel** paper bag; **~ de plástico** plastic (*o* carrier) bag; **"B~ de la propiedad"** "Property Mart"; **~ de trabajo** employment bureau; **jugar a la ~** to play the market.
bolsillo [bol'siʎo] *nm* pocket; (*cartera*) purse; **de ~** pocket *cpd*; **meterse a algn en el ~** to get sb eating out of one's hand.
bolsista [bol'sista] *nm/f* stockbroker.
bolso ['bolso] *nm* (*bolsa*) bag; (*de mujer*) handbag.
boludo, a [bo'luðo, a] (*AM fam!*) *adj* stupid ♦ *nm/f* prat (!)
bomba ['bomba] *nf* (*MIL*) bomb; (*TEC*) pump; (*AM: borrachera*) drunkenness ♦ *adj* (*fam*): **noticia ~** bombshell ♦ *adv* (*fam*): **pasarlo ~** to have a great time; **~ atómica/de humo/de retardo** atomic/ smoke/time bomb; **~ de gasolina** petrol pump; **~ de incendios** fire engine.
bombacho, a [bom'batʃo, a] *adj* baggy.
bombardear [bombarðe'ar] *vt* to bombard; (*MIL*) to bomb.
bombardeo [bombar'ðeo] *nm* bombardment; bombing.
bombardero [bombar'ðero] *nm* bomber.
bombear [bombe'ar] *vt* (*agua*) to pump (out *o* up); (*MIL*) to bomb; (*FÚTBOL*) to lob; **~se** *vr* to warp.
bombero [bom'bero] *nm* fireman; **(cuerpo de) ~s** fire brigade.
bombilla [bom'biʎa] *nf* (*ESP*), **bombillo** [bom'biʎo] *nm* (*AM*) (light) bulb.
bombín [bom'bin] *nm* bowler hat.
bombo ['bombo] *nm* (*MUS*) bass drum; (*TEC*) drum; (*fam*) exaggerated praise; **hacer algo a ~ y platillo** to make a great song and dance about sth; **tengo la cabeza hecha un ~** I've got a splitting headache.
bombón [bom'bon] *nm* chocolate; (*belleza*) gem.
bombona [bom'bona] *nf*: **~ de butano** gas cylinder.
bombonería [bombone'ria] *nf* sweetshop.
bonachón, ona [bona'tʃon, ona] *adj* good-natured.
bonaerense [bonae'rense] *adj* of *o* from Buenos Aires ♦ *nm/f* native *o* inhabitant of Buenos Aires.
bonancible [bonan'θißle] *adj* (*tiempo*) fair, calm.
bonanza [bo'nanθa] *nf* (*NAUT*) fair weather; (*fig*) bonanza; (*MINERÍA*) rich pocket *o* vein.
bondad [bon'dað] *nf* goodness, kindness; **tenga la ~ de** (please) be good enough to.
bondadoso, a [bonda'ðoso, a] *adj* good, kind.
bongo ['bonɣo] *nm* large canoe.
boniato [bo'njato] *nm* sweet potato, yam.
bonificación [bonifika'θjon] *nf* (*COM*) allowance, discount; (*pago*) bonus; (*DEPORTE*) extra points *pl.*
bonito, a [bo'nito, a] *adj* (*lindo*) pretty; (*agradable*) nice ♦ *adv* (*AM fam*) well ♦ *nm* (*atún*) tuna (fish).
bono ['bono] *nm* voucher; (*FIN*) bond; **~ de billetes de metro** booklet of metro tickets; **~ del Tesoro** treasury bill.
bonobús [bono'ßus] *nm* (*ESP*) bus pass.
Bono Loto, bonoloto [bono'loto] *nm o f* (*ESP*) *state-run weekly lottery; V tb* **lotería**.
boom, *pl* **booms** ['bum, 'bums] *nm* boom.
boquear [boke'ar] *vi* to gasp.
boquerón [boke'ron] *nm* (*pez*) (kind of) anchovy; (*agujero*) large hole.
boquete [bo'kete] *nm* gap, hole.
boquiabierto, a [bokia'ßjerto, a] *adj* open-mouthed (in astonishment); **quedar ~** to be left aghast.
boquilla [bo'kiʎa] *nf* (*para riego*) nozzle; (*para cigarro*) cigarette holder; (*MUS*) mouthpiece.
borbollar [borßo'ʎar], **borbollear** [borßoʎe'ar] *vi* to bubble.
borbollón [borßo'ʎon] *nm* bubbling; **hablar a borbollones** to gabble; **salir a borbollones** (*agua*) to gush out.
borbotar [borßo'tar] *vi* = **borbollar**.
borbotón [borßo'ton] *nm*: **salir a borbotones** to gush out.
borda ['borða] *nf* (*NAUT*) gunwale; **echar *o* tirar algo por la ~** to throw sth overboard.
bordado [bor'ðaðo] *nm* embroidery.

bordar [bor'ðar] *vt* to embroider.
borde ['borðe] *nm* edge, border; (*de camino etc*) side; (*en la costura*) hem; **al ~ de** (*fig*) on the verge *o* brink of; **ser ~** (*ESP fam*) to be a pain in the neck.
bordear [borðe'ar] *vt* to border.
bordillo [bor'ðiʎo] *nm* kerb (*BRIT*), curb (*US*).
bordo ['borðo] *nm* (*NAUT*) side; **a ~** on board.
Borgoña [bor'ɣoɲa] *nf* Burgundy.
borgoña [bor'ɣoɲa] *nm* burgundy.
boricua [bo'rikwa], **borinqueño, a** [borin'keɲo, a] *adj, nm/f* Puerto Rican.
borla ['borla] *nf* (*gen*) tassel; (*de gorro*) pompon.
borra ['borra] *nf* (*pelusa*) fluff; (*sedimento*) sediment.
borrachera [borra'tʃera] *nf* (*ebriedad*) drunkenness; (*orgía*) spree, binge.
borracho, a [bo'rratʃo, a] *adj* drunk ♦ *nm/f* (*que bebe mucho*) drunkard, drunk; (*temporalmente*) drunk, drunk man/woman ♦ *nm* (*CULIN*) *cake soaked in liqueur or spirit.*
borrador [borra'ðor] *nm* (*escritura*) first draft, rough sketch; (*cuaderno*) scribbling pad; (*goma*) rubber (*BRIT*), eraser; (*COM*) daybook; (*para pizarra*) duster; **hacer un nuevo ~ de** (*COM*) to redraft.
borrar [bo'rrar] *vt* to erase, rub out; (*tachar*) to delete; (*cinta*) to wipe out; (*INFORM: archivo*) to delete, erase; (*POL etc: eliminar*) to deal with.
borrasca [bo'rraska] *nf* (*METEOROLOGÍA*) storm.
borrascoso, a [borras'koso, a] *adj* stormy.
borrego, a [bo'rreɣo, a] *nm/f* lamb; (*oveja*) sheep; (*fig*) simpleton.
borricada [borri'kaða] *nf* foolish action/statement.
borrico, a [bo'rriko, a] *nm* donkey; (*fig*) stupid man ♦ *nf* she-donkey; (*fig*) stupid woman.
borrón [bo'rron] *nm* (*mancha*) stain; **~ y cuenta nueva** let bygones be bygones.
borroso, a [bo'rroso, a] *adj* vague, unclear; (*escritura*) illegible; (*escrito*) smudgy; (*FOTO*) blurred.
Bósforo ['bosforo] *nm*: **el (Estrecho del) ~** the Bosp(h)orus.
Bosnia ['bosnja] *nf* Bosnia.
bosnio, a ['bosnjo, a] *adj, nm/f* Bosnian.
bosque ['boske] *nm* wood; (*grande*) forest.
bosquejar [boske'xar] *vt* to sketch.
bosquejo [bos'kexo] *nm* sketch.
bosta ['bosta] *nf* dung, manure.
bostece [bos'teθe] *etc vb V* **bostezar**.
bostezar [boste'θar] *vi* to yawn.
bostezo [bos'teθo] *nm* yawn.
bota ['bota] *nf* (*calzado*) boot; (*saco*) leather wine bottle; **ponerse las ~s** (*fam*) to strike it rich.
botadura [bota'ðura] *nf* launching.
botanas [bo'tanas] *nfpl* (*AM*) hors d'œuvres.
botánico, a [bo'taniko, a] *adj* botanical ♦ *nm/f* botanist ♦ *nf* botany.
botar [bo'tar] *vt* to throw, hurl; (*NAUT*) to launch; (*esp AM fam*) to throw out ♦ *vi* to bounce.
botarate [bota'rate] *nm* (*imbécil*) idiot.
bote ['bote] *nm* (*salto*) bounce; (*golpe*) thrust; (*vasija*) tin, can; (*embarcación*) boat; **de ~ en ~** packed, jammed full; **~ salvavidas** lifeboat; **dar un ~** to jump; **dar ~s** (*AUTO etc*) to bump; **~ de la basura** (*AM*) dustbin (*BRIT*), trashcan (*US*).
botella [bo'teʎa] *nf* bottle; **~ de vino** (*contenido*) bottle of wine; (*recipiente*) wine bottle.
botellero [bote'ʎero] *nm* wine rack.
botellín [bote'ʎin] *nm* small bottle.
botica [bo'tika] *nf* chemist's (shop) (*BRIT*), pharmacy.
boticario, a [boti'karjo, a] *nm/f* chemist (*BRIT*), pharmacist.
botijo [bo'tixo] *nm* (earthenware) jug; (*tren*) excursion train.
botín [bo'tin] *nm* (*calzado*) half boot; (*polaina*) spat; (*MIL*) booty; (*de ladrón*) loot.
botiquín [boti'kin] *nm* (*armario*) medicine chest; (*portátil*) first-aid kit.
botón [bo'ton] *nm* button; (*BOT*) bud; (*de florete*) tip; **~ de arranque** (*AUTO etc*) starter; **~ de oro** buttercup; **pulsar el ~** to press the button.
botones [bo'tones] *nm inv* bellboy, bellhop (*US*).
botulismo [botu'lismo] *nm* botulism, food poisoning.
bóveda ['boβeða] *nf* (*ARQ*) vault.
bovino, a [bo'βino, a] *adj* bovine; (*AGR*): **ganado ~** cattle.
box ['boks] *nm* (*AM*) boxing.
boxeador [boksea'ðor] *nm* boxer.
boxear [bokse'ar] *vi* to box.
boxeo [bok'seo] *nm* boxing.
boya ['boja] *nf* (*NAUT*) buoy; (*flotador*) float.
boyante [bo'jante] *adj* (*NAUT*) buoyant; (*feliz*) buoyant; (*próspero*) prosperous.
bozal [bo'θal] *nm* (*de caballo*) halter; (*de perro*) muzzle.

bozo ['boθo] *nm* (*pelusa*) fuzz; (*boca*) mouth.
bracear [braθe'ar] *vi* (*agitar los brazos*) to wave one's arms.
bracero [bra'θero] *nm* labourer; (*en el campo*) farmhand.
braga ['braɣa] *nf* (*cuerda*) sling, rope; (*de bebé*) nappy, diaper (*US*); **~s** *nfpl* (*de mujer*) panties.
braguero [bra'ɣero] *nm* (*MED*) truss.
bragueta [bra'ɣeta] *nf* fly (*BRIT*), flies *pl* (*BRIT*), zipper (*US*).
braguetazo [braɣe'taθo] *nm* marriage of convenience.
braille [breil] *nm* braille.
bramante [bra'mante] *nm* twine, string.
bramar [bra'mar] *vi* to bellow, roar.
bramido [bra'miðo] *nm* bellow, roar.
branquias ['brankjas] *nfpl* gills.
brasa ['brasa] *nf* live *o* hot coal; **carne a la ~** grilled meat.
brasero [bra'sero] *nm* brazier; (*AM: chimenea*) fireplace.
Brasil [bra'sil] *nm*: (**el**) ~ Brazil.
brasileño, a [brasi'leɲo, a] *adj, nm/f* Brazilian.
bravata [bra'ßata] *nf* boast.
braveza [bra'ßeθa] *nf* (*valor*) bravery; (*ferocidad*) ferocity.
bravío, a [bra'ßio, a] *adj* wild; (*feroz*) fierce.
bravo, a ['braßo, a] *adj* (*valiente*) brave; (*bueno*) fine, splendid; (*feroz*) ferocious; (*salvaje*) wild; (*mar etc*) rough, stormy; (*CULIN*) hot, spicy ♦ *excl* bravo!
bravucón, ona [braßu'kon, ona] *adj* swaggering ♦ *nm/f* braggart.
bravura [bra'ßura] *nf* bravery; ferocity; (*pey*) boast.
braza ['braθa] *nf* fathom; **nadar a la ~** to swim (the) breast-stroke.
brazada [bra'θaða] *nf* stroke.
brazalete [braθa'lete] *nm* (*pulsera*) bracelet; (*banda*) armband.
brazo ['braθo] *nm* arm; (*ZOOL*) foreleg; (*BOT*) limb, branch; **~s** *nmpl* (*braceros*) hands, workers; **~ derecho** (*fig*) right-hand man; **a ~ partido** hand-to-hand; **cogidos** *etc* **del ~** arm in arm; **no dar su ~ a torcer** not to give way easily; **huelga de ~s caídos** sit-down strike.
brea ['brea] *nf* pitch, tar.
brebaje [bre'ßaxe] *nm* potion.
brecha ['bretʃa] *nf* breach; (*hoyo vacío*) gap, opening.
brécol ['brekol] *nm* broccoli.
brega ['breɣa] *nf* (*lucha*) struggle; (*trabajo*) hard work.
bregar [bre'ɣar] *vi* (*luchar*) to struggle; (*trabajar mucho*) to slog away.
bregue ['breɣe] *etc vb V* **bregar**.
breña ['breɲa] *nf* rough ground.
Bretaña [bre'taɲa] *nf* Brittany.
brete ['brete] *nm* (*cepo*) shackles *pl*; (*fig*) predicament; **estar en un ~** to be in a jam.
breteles [bre'teles] *nmpl* (*AM*) straps.
bretón, ona [bre'ton, ona] *adj, nm/f* Breton.
breva ['breßa] *nf* (*BOT*) early fig; (*puro*) flat cigar; **¡no caerá esa ~!** no such luck!
breve ['breße] *adj* short, brief; **en ~** (*pronto*) shortly; (*en pocas palabras*) in short ♦ *nf* (*MUS*) breve.
brevedad [breße'ðað] *nf* brevity, shortness; **con** *o* **a la mayor ~** as soon as possible.
breviario [bre'ßjarjo] *nm* (*REL*) breviary.
brezal [bre'θal] *nm* moor(land), heath.
brezo ['breθo] *nm* heather.
bribón, ona [bri'ßon, ona] *adj* idle, lazy ♦ *nm/f* (*vagabundo*) vagabond; (*pícaro*) rascal, rogue.
bricolaje [briko'laxe] *nm* do-it-yourself, DIY.
brida ['briða] *nf* bridle, rein; (*TEC*) clamp; **a toda ~** at top speed.
bridge [britʃ] *nm* (*NAIPES*) bridge.
brigada [bri'ɣaða] *nf* (*unidad*) brigade; (*trabajadores*) squad, gang ♦ *nm* warrant officer.
brigadier [briɣa'ðjer] *nm* brigadier (-general).
brillante [bri'ʎante] *adj* brilliant; (*color*) bright; (*joya*) sparkling ♦ *nm* diamond.
brillantez [briʎan'teθ] *nf* (*color etc*) brightness; (*fig*) brilliance.
brillar [bri'ʎar] *vi* (*tb fig*) to shine; (*joyas*) to sparkle; **~ por su ausencia** to be conspicuous by one's absence.
brillo ['briʎo] *nm* shine; (*brillantez*) brilliance; (*fig*) splendour; **sacar ~ a** to polish.
brilloso, a [bri'ʎoso, a] *adj* (*AM*) = **brillante**.
brincar [brin'kar] *vi* to skip about, hop about, jump about; **está que brinca** he's hopping mad.
brinco ['brinko] *nm* jump, leap; **a ~s** by fits and starts; **de un ~** at one bound.
brindar [brin'dar] *vi*: **~ a** *o* **por** to drink (a toast) to ♦ *vt* to offer, present; **le brinda la ocasión de** it offers *o* affords him the opportunity to; **~se** *vr*: **~se a hacer algo** to offer to do sth.
brindis ['brindis] *nm inv* toast; (*TAUR*) (ceremony of) dedication.
brinque ['brinke] *etc vb V* **brincar**.
brío ['brio] *nm* spirit, dash.

brioso, a [bri'oso, a] *adj* spirited, dashing.
brisa ['brisa] *nf* breeze.
británico, a [bri'taniko, a] *adj* British ♦ *nm/f* Briton, British person; **los ~s** the British.
brizna ['briθna] *nf* (*hebra*) strand, thread; (*de hierba*) blade; (*trozo*) piece.
broca ['broka] *nf* (*COSTURA*) bobbin; (*TEC*) drill bit; (*clavo*) tack.
brocado [bro'kaðo] *nm* brocade.
brocal [bro'kal] *nm* rim.
brocha ['brotʃa] *nf* (large) paintbrush; **~ de afeitar** shaving brush; **pintor de ~ gorda** painter and decorator; (*fig*) poor painter.
brochazo [bro'tʃaθo] *nm* brush-stroke; **a grandes ~s** (*fig*) in general terms.
broche ['brotʃe] *nm* brooch.
broma ['broma] *nf* joke; (*inocentada*) practical joke; **en ~** in fun, as a joke; **gastar una ~ a algn** to play a joke on sb; **tomar algo a ~** to take sth as a joke.
bromear [brome'ar] *vi* to joke.
bromista [bro'mista] *adj* fond of joking ♦ *nm/f* joker, wag.
bromuro [bro'muro] *nm* bromide.
bronca ['bronka] *nf* row; (*regañada*) ticking-off; **armar una ~** to kick up a fuss; **echar una ~ a algn** to tell sb off.
bronce ['bronθe] *nm* bronze; (*latón*) brass.
bronceado, a [bronθe'aðo, a] *adj* bronze *cpd*; (*por el sol*) tanned ♦ *nm* (sun)tan; (*TEC*) bronzing.
bronceador [bronθea'ðor] *nm* suntan lotion.
broncearse [bronθe'arse] *vr* to get a suntan.
bronco, a ['bronko, a] *adj* (*manera*) rude, surly; (*voz*) harsh.
bronquios ['bronkjos] *nmpl* bronchial tubes.
bronquitis [bron'kitis] *nf inv* bronchitis.
brotar [bro'tar] *vt* (*tierra*) to produce ♦ *vi* (*BOT*) to sprout; (*aguas*) to gush (forth); (*lágrimas*) to well up; (*MED*) to break out.
brote ['brote] *nm* (*BOT*) shoot; (*MED, fig*) outbreak.
broza ['broθa] *nf* (*BOT*) dead leaves *pl*; (*fig*) rubbish.
bruces ['bruθes]: **de ~** *adv*: **caer** *o* **dar de ~** to fall headlong, fall flat.
bruja ['bruxa] *nf* witch.
Brujas ['bruxas] *nf* Bruges.
brujería [bruxe'ria] *nf* witchcraft.
brujo ['bruxo] *nm* wizard, magician.
brújula ['bruxula] *nf* compass.
bruma ['bruma] *nf* mist.
brumoso, a [bru'moso, a] *adj* misty.
bruñendo [bru'ɲenðo] *etc vb V* **bruñir**.
bruñido [bru'ɲiðo] *nm* polish.
bruñir [bru'ɲir] *vt* to polish.
brusco, a ['brusko, a] *adj* (*súbito*) sudden; (*áspero*) brusque.
Bruselas [bru'selas] *nf* Brussels.
brusquedad [bruske'ðað] *nf* suddenness; brusqueness.
brutal [bru'tal] *adj* brutal.
brutalidad [brutali'ðað] *nf* brutality.
bruto, a ['bruto, a] *adj* (*idiota*) stupid; (*bestial*) brutish; (*peso*) gross ♦ *nm* brute; **a la bruta, a lo ~** roughly; **en ~** raw, unworked.
Bs. *abr* = **bolívares**.
Bs.As. *abr* = **Buenos Aires**.
bucal [bu'kal] *adj* oral; **por vía ~** orally.
bucanero [buka'nero] *nm* buccaneer.
bucear [buθe'ar] *vi* to dive ♦ *vt* to explore.
buceo [bu'θeo] *nm* diving; (*fig*) investigation.
buche ['butʃe] *nm* (*de ave*) crop; (*ZOOL*) maw; (*fam*) belly.
bucle ['bukle] *nm* curl; (*INFORM*) loop.
budín [bu'ðin] *nm* pudding.
budismo [bu'ðismo] *nm* Buddhism.
budista [bu'ðista] *adj, nm/f* Buddhist.
buen [bwen] *adj V* **bueno**.
buenamente [bwena'mente] *adv* (*fácilmente*) easily; (*voluntariamente*) willingly.
buenaventura [bwenaβen'tura] *nf* (*suerte*) good luck; (*adivinación*) fortune; **decir** *o* **echar la ~ a algn** to tell sb's fortune.

PALABRA CLAVE

bueno, a ['bweno, a] (*antes de nmsg*: **buen**) *adj* **1** (*excelente etc*) good; (*MED*) well; **es un libro ~, es un buen libro** it's a good book; **hace ~, hace buen tiempo** the weather is fine, it is fine; **es ~a persona** he's a good sort; **el ~ de Paco** good old Paco; **fue muy ~ conmigo** he was very nice *o* kind to me; **ya está ~** he's fine now
2 (*apropiado*): **ser ~ para** to be good for; **creo que vamos por buen camino** I think we're on the right track
3 (*irónico*): **le di un buen rapapolvo** I gave him a good *o* real ticking off; **¡buen conductor estás hecho!** some driver *o* a fine driver you are!; **¡estaría ~ que ...!** a fine thing it would be if ...!
4 (*atractivo, sabroso*): **está ~ este bizcocho** this sponge is delicious; **Julio está muy ~** (*fam*) Julio is a bit of alright
5 (*grande*) good, big; **un buen número de ...** a good number of ...; **un buen trozo**

de ... a nice big piece of ...
6 (*saludos*): **¡buen día!** (*AM*), **¡~s días!** (good) morning!; **¡buenas (tardes)!** good afternoon!; (*más tarde*) good evening!; **¡buenas noches!** good night!
7 (*otras locuciones*): **estar de buenas** to be in a good mood; **por las buenas o por las malas** by hook or by crook; **de buenas a primeras** all of a sudden
♦ *excl*: **¡~!** all right!; **~, ¿y qué?** well, so what?; **~, lo que pasa es que ...** well, the thing is ...; **pero ¡~!** well, I like that!; **~, pues ...** right, (then) ...

Buenos Aires [bweno'saires] *nm* Buenos Aires.
buey [bwei] *nm* ox.
búfalo ['bufalo] *nm* buffalo.
bufanda [bu'fanda] *nf* scarf.
bufar [bu'far] *vi* to snort.
bufete [bu'fete] *nm* (*despacho de abogado*) lawyer's office; **establecer su ~** to set up in legal practice.
buffer ['bufer] *nm* (*INFORM*) buffer.
bufón [bu'fon] *nm* clown.
bufonada [bufo'naða] *nf* (*dicho*) jest; (*hecho*) piece of buffoonery; (*TEAT*) farce.
buhardilla [buar'ðiʎa] *nf* attic.
búho ['buo] *nm* owl; (*fig*) hermit, recluse.
buhonero [buo'nero] *nm* pedlar.
buitre ['bwitre] *nm* vulture.
bujía [bu'xia] *nf* (*vela*) candle; (*ELEC*) candle (power); (*AUTO*) spark plug.
bula ['bula] *nf* (papal) bull.
bulbo ['bulβo] *nm* (*BOT*) bulb.
bulevar [bule'βar] *nm* boulevard.
Bulgaria [bul'ɣarja] *nf* Bulgaria.
búlgaro, a ['bulɣaro, a] *adj, nm/f* Bulgarian.
bulimia [bu'limja] *nf* bulimia.
bulla ['buʎa] *nf* (*ruido*) uproar; (*de gente*) crowd; **armar** *o* **meter ~** to kick up a row.
bullendo [bu'ʎendo] *etc vb V* **bullir**.
bullicio [bu'ʎiθjo] *nm* (*ruido*) uproar; (*movimiento*) bustle.
bullicioso, a [buʎi'θjoso, a] *adj* (*ruidoso*) noisy, (*calle etc*) busy; (*situación*) turbulent.
bullir [bu'ʎir] *vi* (*hervir*) to boil; (*burbujear*) to bubble; (*mover*) to move, stir; (*insectos*) to swarm; **~ de** (*fig*) to teem *o* seethe with.
bulo ['bulo] *nm* false rumour.
bulto ['bulto] *nm* (*paquete*) package; (*fardo*) bundle; (*tamaño*) size, bulkiness; (*MED*) swelling, lump; (*silueta*) vague shape; (*estatua*) bust, statue; **hacer ~** to take up space; **escurrir el ~** to make o.s. scarce; (*fig*) to dodge the issue.
buñuelo [bu'ɲwelo] *nm* ≈ doughnut, donut (*US*).
BUP [bup] *nm abr* (*ESP ESCOL*:= *Bachillerato Unificado y Polivalente*) *secondary education for 14-17 age group; V tb* **sistema educativo**.
buque ['buke] *nm* ship, vessel; **~ de guerra** warship; **~ mercante** merchant ship; **~ de vela** sailing ship.
burbuja [bur'βuxa] *nf* bubble; **hacer ~s** to bubble; (*gaseosa*) to fizz.
burbujear [burβuxe'ar] *vi* to bubble.
burdel [bur'ðel] *nm* brothel.
Burdeos [bur'ðeos] *nm* Bordeaux.
burdo, a ['burðo, a] *adj* coarse, rough.
burgalés, esa [burɣa'les, esa] *adj* of *o* from Burgos ♦ *nm/f* native *o* inhabitant of Burgos.
burgués, esa [bur'ɣes, esa] *adj* middle-class, bourgeois; **pequeño ~** lower middle-class; (*POL, pey*) petty bourgeois.
burguesía [burɣe'sia] *nf* middle class, bourgeoisie.
burla ['burla] *nf* (*mofa*) gibe; (*broma*) joke; (*engaño*) trick; **hacer ~ de** to make fun of.
burladero [burla'ðero] *nm* (bullfighter's) refuge.
burlador, a [burla'ðor, a] *adj* mocking ♦ *nm/f* mocker; (*bromista*) joker ♦ *nm* (*libertino*) seducer.
burlar [bur'lar] *vt* (*engañar*) to deceive; (*seducir*) to seduce ♦ *vi*, **~se** *vr* to joke; **~se de** to make fun of.
burlesco, a [bur'lesko, a] *adj* burlesque.
burlón, ona [bur'lon, ona] *adj* mocking.
buró [bu'ro] *nm* bureau.
burocracia [buro'kraθja] *nf* bureaucracy.
burócrata [bu'rokrata] *nm/f* bureaucrat.
buromática [buro'matika] *nf* office automation.
burrada [bu'rraða] *nf* stupid act; **decir ~s** to talk nonsense.
burro, a ['burro, a] *nm/f* (*ZOOL*) donkey; (*fig*) ass, idiot ♦ *adj* stupid; **caerse del ~** to realise one's mistake; **no ver tres en un ~** to be as blind as a bat.
bursátil [bur'satil] *adj* stock-exchange *cpd*.
bus [bus] *nm* bus.
busca ['buska] *nf* search, hunt ♦ *nm* bleeper, pager; **en ~ de** in search of.
buscador, a [buska'ðor, a] *nm/f* searcher.
buscapiés [buska'pjes] *nm inv* jumping jack (*BRIT*), firecracker (*US*).
buscapleitos [buska'pleitos] *nm/f inv* troublemaker.

buscar [bus'kar] *vt* to look for; (*objeto perdido*) to have a look for; (*beneficio*) to seek; (*enemigo*) to seek out; (*traer*) to bring, fetch; (*provocar*) to provoke; (*INFORM*) to search ♦ *vi* to look, search, seek; **ven a ~me a la oficina** come and pick me up at the office; **~le 3 *o* 4 pies al gato** to split hairs; **"~ y reemplazar"** (*INFORM*) "search and replace"; **se busca secretaria** secretary wanted; **se la buscó** he asked for it.
buscavidas [buska'βiðas] *nm/f inv* snooper; (*persona ambiciosa*) go-getter.
buscona [bus'kona] *nf* whore.
busilis [bu'silis] *nm inv* (*fam*) snag.
busque ['buske] *etc vb V* **buscar.**
búsqueda ['buskeða] *nf* = **busca.**
busto ['busto] *nm* (*ANAT, ARTE*) bust.
butaca [bu'taka] *nf* armchair; (*de cine, teatro*) stall, seat.
butano [bu'tano] *nm* butane (gas); **bombona de ~** gas cylinder.
butifarra [buti'farra] *nf* Catalan sausage.
buzo ['buθo] *nm* diver; (*AM: chandal*) tracksuit.
buzón [bu'θon] *nm* (*gen*) letter box; (*en la calle*) pillar box (*BRIT*); (*TELEC*) mailbox; **echar al ~** to post.
buzonear [buθone'ar] *vt* to leaflet.
byte [bait] *nm* (*INFORM*) byte.

C c

C, c [θe, se (*esp AM*)] *nf* (*letra*) C, c; **C de Carmen** C for Charlie.
C. *abr* (= *centígrado*) C.; (= *compañía*) Co.
c. *abr* (= *capítulo*) ch.
C/ *abr* (= *calle*) St, Rd.
c/ *abr* (*COM: = cuenta*) a/c.
ca [ka] *excl* not a bit of it!
c.a. *abr* (= *corriente alterna*) A.C.
cabal [ka'βal] *adj* (*exacto*) exact; (*correcto*) right, proper; (*acabado*) finished, complete; **~es** *nmpl*: **estar en sus ~es** to be in one's right mind.
cábala ['kaβala] *nf* (*REL*) cab(b)ala; (*fig*) cabal, intrigue; **~s** *nfpl* guess *sg*, supposition *sg*.
cabalgadura [kaβalɣa'ðura] *nf* mount, horse.
cabalgar [kaβal'ɣar] *vt, vi* to ride.
cabalgata [kaβal'ɣata] *nf* procession; *V tb* **Reyes Magos.**
cabalgue [ka'βalɣe] *etc vb V* **cabalgar.**
cabalístico, a [kaβa'listiko, a] *adj* (*fig*) mysterious.
caballa [ka'βaʎa] *nf* mackerel.
caballeresco, a [kaβaʎe'resko, a] *adj* noble, chivalrous.
caballería [kaβaʎe'ria] *nf* mount; (*MIL*) cavalry.
caballeriza [kaβaʎe'riθa] *nf* stable.
caballerizo [kaβaʎe'riθo] *nm* groom, stableman.
caballero [kaβa'ʎero] *nm* gentleman; (*de la orden de caballería*) knight; (*trato directo*) sir; **"C~s"** "Gents".
caballerosidad [kaβaʎerosi'ðað] *nf* chivalry.
caballete [kaβa'ʎete] *nm* (*AGR*) ridge; (*ARTE*) easel.
caballito [kaβa'ʎito] *nm* (*caballo pequeño*) small horse, pony; (*juguete*) rocking horse; **~s** *nmpl* merry-go-round *sg*; **~ de mar** seahorse; **~ del diablo** dragonfly.
caballo [ka'βaʎo] *nm* horse; (*AJEDREZ*) knight; (*NAIPES*) ≈ queen; **~ de vapor *o* de fuerza** horsepower; **es su ~ de batalla** it's his hobby-horse; **~ blanco** (*COM*) backer; *V tb* **Baraja Española.**
cabaña [ka'βaɲa] *nf* (*casita*) hut, cabin.
cabaré, cabaret, *pl* **cabarets** [kaβa're, kaβa'res] *nm* cabaret.
cabecear [kaβeθe'ar] *vi* to nod.
cabecera [kaβe'θera] *nf* (*gen*) head; (*de distrito*) chief town; (*de cama*) headboard; (*IMPRENTA*) headline.
cabecilla [kaβe'θiʎa] *nm* ringleader.
cabellera [kaβe'ʎera] *nf* (head of) hair; (*de cometa*) tail.
cabello [ka'βeʎo] *nm* (*tb*: **~s**) hair *sg*.
cabelludo [kaβe'ʎuðo] *adj V* **cuero.**
caber [ka'βer] *vi* (*entrar*) to fit, go; **caben 3 más** there's room for 3 more; **cabe preguntar si...** one might ask whether...; **cabe que venga más tarde** he may come later.
cabestrillo [kaβes'triʎo] *nm* sling.
cabestro [ka'βestro] *nm* halter.
cabeza [ka'βeθa] *nf* head; (*POL*) chief, leader ♦ *nm/f*: **~ rapada** skinhead; **caer de ~** to fall head first; **sentar la ~** to settle down; **~ de lectura/escritura** read/write head; **~ impresora *o* de impresión** printhead.
cabezada [kaβe'θaða] *nf* (*golpe*) butt; **dar una ~** to nod off.
cabezal [kaβe'θal] *nm*: **~ impresor** print head.

cabezazo [kaße'θaθo] *nm* (*golpe*) headbutt; (*FÚTBOL*) header.
cabezón, ona [kaße'θon, ona] *adj* with a big head; (*vino*) heady; (*obstinado*) obstinate, stubborn.
cabezota [kaße'θota] *adj inv* obstinate, stubborn.
cabezudo, a [kaße'θuðo, a] *adj* with a big head; (*obstinado*) obstinate, stubborn.
cabida [ka'ßiða] *nf* space; **dar ~ a** to make room for; **tener ~ para** to have room for.
cabildo [ka'ßildo] *nm* (*de iglesia*) chapter; (*POL*) town council.
cabina [ka'ßina] *nf* (*de camión*) cabin; **~ telefónica** (tele)phone box (*BRIT*) *o* booth.
cabizbajo, a [kaßiθ'ßaxo, a] *adj* crestfallen, dejected.
cable ['kaßle] *nm* cable; (*de aparato*) lead; **~ aéreo** (*ELEC*) overhead cable; **conectar con ~** (*INFORM*) to hardwire.
cabo ['kaßo] *nm* (*de objeto*) end, extremity; (*MIL*) corporal; (*NAUT*) rope, cable; (*GEO*) cape; (*TEC*) thread; **al ~ de 3 días** after 3 days; **de ~ a rabo** *o* **~** from beginning to end; (*libro*: *leer*) from cover to cover; **llevar a ~** to carry out; **atar ~s** to tie up the loose ends; **C~ de Buena Esperanza** Cape of Good Hope; **C~ de Hornos** Cape Horn; **las Islas de C~ Verde** the Cape Verde Islands.
cabra ['kaßra] *nf* goat; **estar como una ~** (*fam*) to be nuts.
cabré [ka'ßre] *etc vb V* **caber.**
cabrear [kaßre'ar] *vt* to annoy; **~se** *vr* to fly off the handle.
cabrío, a [ka'ßrio, a] *adj* goatish; **macho ~** (he-)goat, billy goat.
cabriola [ka'ßrjola] *nf* caper.
cabritilla [kaßri'tiʎa] *nf* kid, kidskin.
cabrito [ka'ßrito] *nm* kid.
cabrón [ka'ßron] *nm* (*fig*: *fam!*) bastard (*!*).
cabronada [kaßro'naða] *nf* (*fam!*): **hacer una ~ a algn** to be a bastard to sb.
caca ['kaka] *nf* (*palabra de niños*) pooh ♦ *excl*: **no toques,** ¡~! don't touch, it's dirty!
cacahuete [kaka'wete] *nm* (*ESP*) peanut.
cacao [ka'kao] *nm* cocoa; (*BOT*) cacao.
cacarear [kakare'ar] *vi* (*persona*) to boast; (*gallina*) to cackle.
cacatúa [kaka'tua] *nf* cockatoo.
cacereño, a [kaθe'reɲo, a] *adj* of *o* from Cáceres ♦ *nm/f* native *o* inhabitant of Cáceres.
cacería [kaθe'ria] *nf* hunt.
cacerola [kaθe'rola] *nf* pan, saucepan.
cacha ['katʃa] *nf* (*mango*) handle; (*nalga*) buttock.
cachalote [katʃa'lote] *nm* sperm whale.
cacharro [ka'tʃarro] *nm* (*vasija*) (earthenware) pot; (*cerámica*) piece of pottery; (*fam*) useless object; **~s** *nmpl* pots and pans.
cachear [katʃe'ar] *vt* to search, frisk.
cachemir [katʃe'mir] *nm* cashmere.
cacheo [ka'tʃeo] *nm* searching, frisking.
cachete [ka'tʃete] *nm* (*ANAT*) cheek; (*bofetada*) slap (in the face).
cachimba [ka'tʃimba] *nf*, **cachimbo** [ka'tʃimbo] *nm* (*AM*) pipe.
cachiporra [katʃi'porra] *nf* truncheon.
cachivache [katʃi'ßatʃe] *nm* piece of junk; **~s** *nmpl* trash *sg*, junk *sg*.
cacho, a ['katʃo, a] *nm* (small) bit; (*AM*: *cuerno*) horn.
cachondearse [katʃonde'arse] *vr*: **~ de algn** to tease sb.
cachondeo [katʃon'deo] *nm* (*fam*) farce, joke; (*guasa*) laugh.
cachondo, a [ka'tʃondo, a] *adj* (*ZOOL*) on heat; (*persona*) randy, sexy; (*gracioso*) funny.
cachorro, a [ka'tʃorro, a] *nm/f* (*perro*) pup, puppy; (*león*) cub.
cacique [ka'θike] *nm* chief, local ruler; (*POL*) local party boss; (*fig*) despot.
caco ['kako] *nm* pickpocket.
cacofonía [kakofo'nia] *nf* cacophony.
cacto ['kakto] *nm*, **cactus** ['kaktus] *nm inv* cactus.
cada ['kaða] *adj inv* each; (*antes de número*) every; **~ día** each day, every day; **~ dos días** every other day; **~ uno/a** each one, every one; **~ vez más/menos** more and more/less and less; **uno de ~ diez** one out of every ten; ¿**~ cuánto**? how often?
cadalso [ka'ðalso] *nm* scaffold.
cadáver [ka'ðaßer] *nm* (dead) body, corpse.
cadavérico, a [kaða'ßeriko, a] *adj* cadaverous; (*pálido*) deathly pale.
cadena [ka'ðena] *nf* chain; (*TV*) channel; **reacción en ~** chain reaction; **trabajo en ~** assembly line work; **~ midi/mini** (*MUS*) midi/mini system; **~ perpetua** (*JUR*) life imprisonment; **~ de caracteres** (*INFORM*) character string.
cadencia [ka'ðenθja] *nf* cadence, rhythm.
cadera [ka'ðera] *nf* hip.
cadete [ka'ðete] *nm* cadet.
Cádiz ['kaðiθ] *nm* Cadiz.
caducar [kaðu'kar] *vi* to expire.
caducidad [kaðuθi'ðað] *nf*: **fecha de ~** expiry date; (*de comida*) sell-by date.
caduco, a [ka'ðuko, a] *adj* (*idea etc*) outdated, outmoded; **de hoja caduca**

deciduous.
caduque [ka'ðuke] *etc vb V* **caducar.**
C.A.E. *abr* (= *cóbrese al entregar*) COD.
caer [ka'er] *vi* to fall; (*premio*) to go; (*sitio*) to be, lie; (*pago*) to fall due; **~se** *vr* to fall (down); **dejar ~** to drop; **estar al ~** to be due to happen; (*persona*) to be about to arrive; **me cae bien/mal** I like/don't like him; **~ en la cuenta** to catch on; **su cumpleaños cae en viernes** her birthday falls on a Friday; **se me ha caído el guante** I've dropped my glove.
café, *pl* **cafés** [ka'fe, ka'fes] *nm* (*bebida, planta*) coffee; (*lugar*) café ♦ *adj* (*color*) brown; **~ con leche** white coffee; **~ solo, ~ negro** (*AM*) (small) black coffee.
cafeína [kafe'ina] *nf* caffein(e).
cafetal [kafe'tal] *nm* coffee plantation.
cafetera [kafe'tera] *nf V* **cafetero.**
cafetería [kafete'ria] *nf* cafe.
cafetero, a [kafe'tero, a] *adj* coffee *cpd* ♦ *nf* coffee pot; **ser muy ~** to be a coffee addict.
cafre ['kafre] *nm/f*: **como ~s** (*fig*) like savages.
cagalera [kaɤa'lera] *nf* (*fam!*): **tener ~** to have the runs.
cagar [ka'ɤar] (*fam!*) *vt* to shit (*!*); (*fig*) to bungle, mess up ♦ *vi* to have a shit (*!*); **~se** *vr*: **¡me cago en diez** (*etc*)! Christ! (*!*).
cague ['kaɤe] *etc vb V* **cagar.**
caído, a [ka'iðo, a] *adj* fallen; (*INFORM*) down ♦ *nf* fall; (*declive*) slope; (*disminución*) fall, drop; **~ del cielo** out of the blue; **a la caída del sol** at sunset; **sufrir una caída** to have a fall.
caiga ['kaiɤa] *etc vb V* **caer.**
caimán [kai'man] *nm* alligator.
Cairo ['kairo] *nm*: **el ~** Cairo.
caja ['kaxa] *nf* box; (*ataúd*) coffin, casket (*US*); (*para reloj*) case; (*de ascensor*) shaft; (*COM*) cashbox; (*ECON*) fund; (*donde se hacen los pagos*) cashdesk; (*en supermercado*) checkout, till; (*TIP*) case; **~ de ahorros** savings bank; **~ de cambios** gearbox; **~ fuerte, ~ de caudales** safe, strongbox; **ingresar en ~** to be paid in.
cajero, a [ka'xero, a] *nm/f* cashier; (*en banco*) (bank) teller ♦ *nm*: **~ automático** cash dispenser, automatic telling machine, A.T.M.
cajetilla [kaxe'tiʎa] *nf* (*de cigarrillos*) packet.
cajista [ka'xista] *nm/f* typesetter.
cajón [ka'xon] *nm* big box; (*de mueble*) drawer.
cal [kal] *nf* lime; **cerrar algo a ~ y canto** to shut sth firmly.
cala ['kala] *nf* (*GEO*) cove, inlet; (*de barco*) hold.
calabacín [kalaβa'θin] *nm* (*BOT*) baby marrow, courgette, zucchini (*US*).
calabaza [kala'βaθa] *nf* (*BOT*) pumpkin; **dar ~s a** (*candidato*) to fail.
calabozo [kala'βoθo] *nm* (*cárcel*) prison; (*celda*) cell.
calado, a [ka'laðo, a] *adj* (*prenda*) lace *cpd* ♦ *nm* (*TEC*) fretwork; (*NAUT*) draught ♦ *nf* (*de cigarrillo*) puff; **estar ~ (hasta los huesos)** to be soaked (to the skin).
calamar [kala'mar] *nm* squid.
calambre [ka'lambre] *nm* (*tb*: **~s**) cramp.
calamidad [kalami'ðað] *nf* calamity, disaster; (*persona*): **es una ~** he's a dead loss.
calamina [kala'mina] *nf* calamine.
cálamo ['kalamo] *nm* (*BOT*) stem; (*MUS*) reed.
calaña [ka'laɲa] *nf* model, pattern; (*fig*) nature, stamp.
calar [ka'lar] *vt* to soak, drench; (*penetrar*) to pierce, penetrate; (*comprender*) to see through; (*vela, red*) to lower; **~se** *vr* (*AUTO*) to stall; **~se las gafas** to stick one's glasses on.
calavera [kala'βera] *nf* skull.
calcañal [kalka'ɲal], **calcañar** [kalka'ɲar] *nm* heel.
calcar [kal'kar] *vt* (*reproducir*) to trace; (*imitar*) to copy.
calce ['kalθe] *etc vb V* **calzar.**
calceta [kal'θeta] *nf* (knee-length) stocking; **hacer ~** to knit.
calcetín [kalθe'tin] *nm* sock.
calcinar [kalθi'nar] *vt* to burn, blacken.
calcio ['kalθjo] *nm* calcium.
calco ['kalko] *nm* tracing.
calcomanía [kalkoma'nia] *nf* transfer.
calculador, a [kalkula'ðor, a] *adj* calculating ♦ *nf* calculator.
calcular [kalku'lar] *vt* (*MAT*) to calculate, compute; **~ que ...** to reckon that ....
cálculo ['kalkulo] *nm* calculation; (*MED*) (gall)stone; (*MAT*) calculus; **~ de costo** costing; **~ diferencial** differential calculus; **obrar con mucho ~** to act cautiously.
caldear [kalde'ar] *vt* to warm (up), heat (up); (*metales*) to weld.
caldera [kal'dera] *nf* boiler.
calderero [kalde'rero] *nm* boilermaker.
calderilla [kalde'riʎa] *nf* (*moneda*) small change.
caldero [kal'dero] *nm* small boiler.
caldo ['kaldo] *nm* stock; (*consomé*)

consommé; ~ **de cultivo** (*BIO*) culture medium; **poner a ~ a algn** to tear sb off a strip; **los ~s jerezanos** sherries.
caldoso, a [kal'doso, a] *adj* (*guisado*) juicy; (*sopa*) thin.
calé [ka'le] *adj* gipsy *cpd.*
calefacción [kalefak'θjon] *nf* heating; ~ **central** central heating.
caleidoscopio [kaleiðos'kopjo] *nm* kaleidoscope.
calendario [kalen'darjo] *nm* calendar.
calentador [kalenta'ðor] *nm* heater.
calentamiento [kalenta'mjento] *nm* (*DEPORTE*) warm-up.
calentar [kalen'tar] *vt* to heat (up); (*fam: excitar*) to turn on; (*AM: enfurecer*) to anger; **~se** *vr* to heat up, warm up; (*fig: discusión etc*) to get heated.
calentura [kalen'tura] *nf* (*MED*) fever, (high) temperature; (*de boca*) mouth sore.
calenturiento, a [kalentu'rjento, a] *adj* (*mente*) overactive.
calibrar [kali'ßrar] *vt* to gauge, measure.
calibre [ka'lißre] *nm* (*de cañón*) calibre, bore; (*diámetro*) diameter; (*fig*) calibre.
calidad [kali'ðað] *nf* quality; **de** ~ quality *cpd*; ~ **de borrador** (*INFORM*) draft quality; ~ **de carta** *o* **de correspondencia** (*INFORM*) letter quality; ~ **texto** (*INFORM*) text quality; ~ **de vida** quality of life; **en ~ de** in the capacity of.
cálido, a ['kaliðo, a] *adj* hot; (*fig*) warm.
caliente [ka'ljente] *etc vb V* **calentar** ♦ *adj* hot; (*fig*) fiery; (*disputa*) heated; (*fam: cachondo*) randy.
califa [ka'lifa] *nm* caliph.
calificación [kalifika'θjon] *nf* qualification; (*de alumno*) grade, mark; ~ **de sobresaliente** first-class mark.
calificar [kalifi'kar] *vt* to qualify; (*alumno*) to grade, mark; ~ **de** to describe as.
calificativo, a [kalifika'tißo, a] *adj* qualifying ♦ *nm* qualifier, epithet.
califique [kali'fike] *etc vb V* **calificar**.
californiano, a [kalifor'njano, a] *adj, nm/f* Californian.
caligrafía [kaliɣra'fia] *nf* calligraphy.
calima [ka'lima] *nf* mist.
calina [ka'lina] *nf* haze.
cáliz ['kaliθ] *nm* (*BOT*) calyx; (*REL*) chalice.
caliza [ka'liθa] *nf* limestone.
callado, a [ka'ʎaðo, a] *adj* quiet, silent.
callar [ka'ʎar] *vt* (*asunto delicado*) to keep quiet about, say nothing about; (*omitir*) to pass over in silence; (*persona, oposición*) to silence ♦ *vi*, **~se** *vr* to keep quiet, be silent; (*dejar de hablar*) to stop talking; **¡calla!**, be quiet!; **¡cállate!**, **¡cállese!** shut up!; **¡cállate la boca!** shut your mouth!
calle ['kaʎe] *nf* street; (*DEPORTE*) lane; ~ **arriba/abajo** up/down the street; ~ **de sentido único** one-way street; **poner a algn (de patitas) en la ~** to kick sb out.
calleja [ka'ʎexa] *nf* alley, narrow street.
callejear [kaʎexe'ar] *vi* to wander (about) the streets.
callejero, a [kaʎe'xero, a] *adj* street *cpd* ♦ *nm* street map.
callejón [kaʎe'xon] *nm* alley, passage; (*GEO*) narrow pass; ~ **sin salida** cul-de-sac; (*fig*) blind alley.
callejuela [kaʎe'xwela] *nf* side-street, alley.
callista [ka'ʎista] *nm/f* chiropodist.
callo ['kaʎo] *nm* callus; (*en el pie*) corn; **~s** *nmpl* (*CULIN*) tripe *sg.*
callosidad [kaʎosi'ðað] *nf* (*de pie*) corn; (*de mano*) callus.
calloso, a [ka'ʎoso, a] *adj* horny, rough.
calma ['kalma] *nf* calm; (*pachorra*) slowness; (*COM, ECON*) calm, lull; ~ **chicha** dead calm; **¡~!**, **¡con ~!** take it easy!
calmante [kal'mante] *adj* soothing ♦ *nm* sedative, tranquillizer.
calmar [kal'mar] *vt* to calm, calm down; (*dolor*) to relieve ♦ *vi*, **~se** *vr* (*tempestad*) to abate; (*mente etc*) to become calm.
calmoso, a [kal'moso, a] *adj* calm, quiet.
caló [ka'lo] *nm* (*de gitanos*) gipsy language, Romany; (*argot*) slang.
calor [ka'lor] *nm* heat; (~ *agradable*) warmth; **entrar en ~** to get warm; **tener ~** to be *o* feel hot.
caloría [kalo'ria] *nf* calorie.
calorífero, a [kalo'rifero, a] *adj* heat-producing, heat-giving ♦ *nm* heating system.
calque ['kalke] *etc vb V* **calcar**.
calumnia [ka'lumnja] *nf* slander; (*por escrito*) libel.
calumniar [kalum'njar] *vt* to slander; to libel.
calumnioso, a [kalum'njoso, a] *a* slanderous; libellous.
caluroso, a [kalu'roso, a] *adj* hot; (*sin exceso*) warm; (*fig*) enthusiastic.
calva ['kalßa] *nf* bald patch; (*en bosque*) clearing.
calvario [kal'ßarjo] *nm* stations *pl* of the cross; (*fig*) cross, heavy burden.
calvicie [kal'ßiθje] *nf* baldness.
calvo, a ['kalßo, a] *adj* bald; (*terreno*) bare, barren; (*tejido*) threadbare ♦ *nm* bald

man.
calza ['kalθa] *nf* wedge, chock.
calzado, a [kal'θaðo, a] *adj* shod ♦ *nm* footwear ♦ *nf* roadway, highway.
calzador [kalθa'ðor] *nm* shoehorn.
calzar [kal'θar] *vt* (*zapatos etc*) to wear; (*un mueble*) to put a wedge under; (*TEC*: *rueda etc*) to scotch; **~se** *vr*: **~se los zapatos** to put on one's shoes; **¿qué (número) calza?** what size do you take?
calzón [kal'θon] *nm* (*tb*: **calzones**) shorts *pl*; (*AM*: *de hombre*) pants *pl*; (: *de mujer*) panties *pl*.
calzoncillos [kalθon'θiʎos] *nmpl* underpants.
cama ['kama] *nf* bed; (*GEO*) stratum; **~ individual/de matrimonio** single/double bed; **guardar ~** to be ill in bed.
camada [ka'maða] *nf* litter; (*de personas*) gang, band.
camafeo [kama'feo] *nm* cameo.
camaleón [kamale'on] *nm* chameleon.
cámara ['kamara] *nf* (*POL, TEC*) chamber; (*habitación*) room; (*sala*) hall; (*CINE*) cine camera; (*fotográfica*) camera; **~ de aire** inner tube; **~ alta/baja** upper/lower house; **~ de comercio** chamber of commerce; **~ digital** digital camera; **~ de gas** gas chamber; **~ de vídeo** video camera; **a ~ lenta** in slow motion.
camarada [kama'raða] *nm* comrade, companion.
camaradería [kamaraðe'ria] *nf* comradeship.
camarero, a [kama'rero, a] *nm* waiter ♦ *nf* (*en restaurante*) waitress; (*en casa, hotel*) maid.
camarilla [kama'riʎa] *nf* (*clan*) clique; (*POL*) lobby.
camarín [kama'rin] *nm* (*TEAT*) dressing room.
camarón [kama'ron] *nm* shrimp.
camarote [kama'rote] *nm* (*NAUT*) cabin.
cambiable [kam'bjaβle] *adj* (*variable*) changeable, variable; (*intercambiable*) interchangeable.
cambiante [kam'bjante] *adj* variable.
cambiar [kam'bjar] *vt* to change; (*trocar*) to exchange ♦ *vi* to change; **~se** *vr* (*mudarse*) to move; (*de ropa*) to change; **~(se) de** ... to change one's ...; **~ de idea/de ropa** to change one's mind/clothes.
cambiazo [kam'bjaθo] *nm*: **dar el ~ a algn** to swindle sb.
cambio ['kambjo] *nm* change; (*trueque*) exchange; (*COM*) rate of exchange; (*oficina*) bureau de change; (*dinero menudo*) small change; **en ~** on the other hand; (*en lugar de eso*) instead; **~ de divisas** (*COM*) foreign exchange; **~ de línea** (*INFORM*) line feed; **~ de página** (*INFORM*) form feed; **~ a término** (*COM*) forward exchange; **~ de velocidades** gear lever; **~ de vía** points *pl*.
cambista [kam'bista] *nm* (*COM*) exchange broker.
Camboya [kam'boja] *nf* Cambodia, Kampuchea.
camboyano, a [kambo'jano, a] *a, nm/f* Cambodian, Kampuchean.
camelar [kame'lar] *vt* (*con mujer*) to flirt with; (*persuadir*) to cajole.
camelia [ka'melia] *nf* camellia.
camello [ka'meʎo] *nm* camel; (*fam*: *traficante*) pusher.
camelo [ka'melo] *nm*: **me huele a ~** it smells fishy.
camerino [kame'rino] *nm* (*TEAT*) dressing room.
camilla [ka'miʎa] *nf* (*MED*) stretcher.
caminante [kami'nante] *nm/f* traveller.
caminar [kami'nar] *vi* (*marchar*) to walk, go; (*viajar*) to travel, journey ♦ *vt* (*recorrer*) to cover, travel.
caminata [kami'nata] *nf* long walk.
camino [ka'mino] *nm* way, road; (*sendero*) track; **a medio ~** halfway (there); **en el ~** on the way, en route; **~ de** on the way to; **~ particular** private road; **~ vecinal** country road; **C~s, Canales y Puertos** (*UNIV*) Civil Engineering; **C~ de Santiago** *see boxed note*; **ir por buen ~** (*fig*) to be on the right track.

CAMINO DE SANTIAGO

The **Camino de Santiago** *is a medieval pilgrim route stretching from the Pyrenees to Santiago de Compostela in north-west Spain, where tradition has it that the body of the Apostle James is buried. Nowadays it is a popular tourist route too. The "concha" (cockleshell) symbolizes the* **Camino de Santiago**, *because it is said that when St James's body was found it was covered in shells.*

camión [ka'mjon] *nm* lorry, truck (*US*); (*AM*: *autobús*) bus; **~ de bomberos** fire engine.
camionero [kamjo'nero] *nm* lorry *o* truck (*US*) driver, trucker (*esp US*).
camioneta [kamjo'neta] *nf* van, transit ®.
camisa [ka'misa] *nf* shirt; (*BOT*) skin; **~ de dormir** nightdress; **~ de fuerza**

straitjacket.
camisería [kamise'ria] *nf* outfitter's (shop).
camiseta [kami'seta] *nf* tee-shirt; (*ropa interior*) vest; (*de deportista*) top.
camisón [kami'son] *nm* nightdress, nightgown.
camomila [kamo'mila] *nf* camomile.
camorra [ka'morra] *nf*: **armar ~** to kick up a row; **buscar ~** to look for trouble.
camorrista [kamo'rrista] *nm/f* thug.
camote [ka'mote] *nm* (*AM*) sweet potato.
campal [kam'pal] *adj*: **batalla ~** pitched battle.
campamento [kampa'mento] *nm* camp.
campana [kam'pana] *nf* bell.
campanada [kampa'naða] *nf* peal.
campanario [kampa'narjo] *nm* belfry.
campanilla [kampa'niʎa] *nf* (*campana*) small bell.
campante [kam'pante] *adj*: **siguió tan ~** he went on as if nothing had happened.
campaña [kam'paɲa] *nf* (*MIL, POL*) campaign; **hacer ~ (en pro de/contra)** to campaign (for/against); **~ de venta** sales campaign.
campechano, a [kampe'tʃano, a] *adj* open.
campeón, ona [kampe'on, ona] *nm/f* champion.
campeonato [kampeo'nato] *nm* championship.
campesino, a [kampe'sino, a] *adj* country *cpd*, rural; (*gente*) peasant *cpd* ♦ *nm/f* countryman/woman; (*agricultor*) farmer.
campestre [kam'pestre] *adj* country *cpd*, rural.
camping ['kampin] *nm* camping; (*lugar*) campsite; **ir de** *o* **hacer ~** to go camping.
campiña [kam'piɲa] *nf* countryside.
campista [kam'pista] *nm/f* camper.
campo ['kampo] *nm* (*fuera de la ciudad*) country, countryside; (*AGR, ELEC, INFORM*) field; (*de fútbol*) pitch; (*de golf*) course; (*MIL*) camp; **~ de batalla** battlefield; **~ de minas** minefield; **~ petrolífero** oilfield; **~ visual** field of vision; **~ de concentración/de internación/de trabajo** concentration/ internment/labour camp.
camposanto [kampo'santo] *nm* cemetery.
CAMPSA ['kampsa] *nf abr* (*ESP COM*) = *Compañía Arrendataria del Monopolio de Petróleos, S.A.*
campus ['kampus] *nm inv* (*UNIV*) campus.
camuflaje [kamu'flaxe] *nm* camouflage.
camuflar [kamu'flar] *vt* to camouflage.
can [kan] *nm* dog, mutt (*fam*).
cana ['kana] *nf V* **cano.**
Canadá [kana'ða] *nm* Canada.
canadiense [kana'ðjense] *adj, nm/f* Canadian ♦ *nf* fur-lined jacket.
canal [ka'nal] *nm* canal; (*GEO*) channel, strait; (*de televisión*) channel; (*de tejado*) gutter; **C~ de la Mancha** English Channel; **C~ de Panamá** Panama Canal.
canalice [kana'liθe] *etc vb V* **canalizar.**
canalizar [kanali'θar] *vt* to channel.
canalla [ka'naʎa] *nf* rabble, mob ♦ *nm* swine.
canallada [kana'ʎaða] *nf* (*hecho*) dirty trick.
canalón [kana'lon] *nm* (*conducto vertical*) drainpipe; (*del tejado*) gutter; **canalones** *nmpl* (*CULIN*) cannelloni.
canapé, *pl* **canapés** [kana'pe, kana'pes] *nm* sofa, settee; (*CULIN*) canapé.
Canarias [ka'narjas] *nfpl*: **las (Islas) ~** the Canaries, the Canary Isles.
canario, a [ka'narjo, a] *adj* of *o* from the Canary Isles ♦ *nm/f* native *o* inhabitant of the Canary Isles ♦ *nm* (*ZOOL*) canary.
canasta [ka'nasta] *nf* (round) basket.
canastilla [kanas'tiʎa] *nf* small basket; (*de niño*) layette.
canasto [ka'nasto] *nm* large basket.
cancela [kan'θela] *nf* (wrought-iron) gate.
cancelación [kanθela'θjon] *nf* cancellation.
cancelar [kanθe'lar] *vt* to cancel; (*una deuda*) to write off.
cáncer ['kanθer] *nm* (*MED*) cancer; **C~** (*ASTRO*) Cancer.
cancerígeno, a [kanθe'rixeno, a] *adj* carcinogenic.
cancha ['kantʃa] *nf* (*de baloncesto, tenis etc*) court; (*AM: de fútbol etc*) pitch.
canciller [kanθi'ʎer] *nm* chancellor; **C~** (*AM*) Foreign Minister, ≈ Foreign Secretary (*BRIT*).
Cancillería [kansiʎe'ria] *nf* (*AM*) Foreign Ministry, ≈ Foreign Office (*BRIT*).
canción [kan'θjon] *nf* song; **~ de cuna** lullaby.
cancionero [kanθjo'nero] *nm* song book.
candado [kan'daðo] *nm* padlock.
candela [kan'dela] *nf* candle.
candelabro [kande'laβro] *nm* candelabra.
candelero [kande'lero] *nm* (*para vela*) candlestick; (*de aceite*) oil lamp.
candente [kan'dente] *adj* red-hot; (*tema*) burning.
candidato, a [kandi'ðato, a] *nm/f* candidate; (*para puesto*) applicant.
candidatura [kandiða'tura] *nf* candidature.
candidez [kandi'ðeθ] *nf* (*sencillez*) simplicity; (*simpleza*) naiveté.
cándido, a ['kandiðo, a] *adj* simple; naive.
candil [kan'dil] *nm* oil lamp.

candilejas [kandi'lexas] *nfpl* (*TEAT*) footlights.
candor [kan'dor] *nm* (*sinceridad*) frankness; (*inocencia*) innocence.
canela [ka'nela] *nf* cinnamon.
canelo [ka'nelo] *nm*: **hacer el** ~ to act the fool.
canelones [kane'lones] *nmpl* cannelloni.
cangrejo [kan'grexo] *nm* crab.
canguro [kan'guro] *nm* (*ZOOL*) kangaroo; (*de niños*) baby-sitter; **hacer de** ~ to baby-sit.
caníbal [ka'nißal] *adj, nm/f* cannibal.
canica [ka'nika] *nf* marble.
caniche [ka'nitʃe] *nm* poodle.
canícula [ka'nikula] *nf* midsummer heat.
canijo, a [ka'nixo, a] *adj* frail, sickly.
canilla [ka'niʎa] *nf* (*TEC*) bobbin.
canino, a [ka'nino, a] *adj* canine ♦ *nm* canine (tooth).
canje [kan'xe] *nm* exchange; (*trueque*) swap.
canjear [kanxe'ar] *vt* to exchange; (*trocar*) to swap.
cano, a ['kano, a] *adj* grey-haired, white-haired ♦ *nf* (*tb*: **canas**) white *o* grey hair; **tener canas** to be going grey.
canoa [ka'noa] *nf* canoe.
canon ['kanon] *nm* canon; (*pensión*) rent; (*COM*) tax.
canonice [kano'niθe] *etc vb V* **canonizar**.
canónico, a [ka'noniko, a] *adj*: **derecho** ~ canon law.
canónigo [ka'noniɣo] *nm* canon.
canonizar [kanoni'θar] *vt* to canonize.
canoro, a [ka'noro, a] *adj* melodious.
canoso, a [ka'noso, a] *adj* (*pelo*) grey (*BRIT*), gray (*US*); (*persona*) grey-haired.
cansado, a [kan'saðo, a] *adj* tired, weary; (*tedioso*) tedious, boring; **estoy** ~ **de hacerlo** I'm sick of doing it.
cansancio [kan'sanθjo] *nm* tiredness, fatigue.
cansar [kan'sar] *vt* (*fatigar*) to tire, tire out; (*aburrir*) to bore; (*fastidiar*) to bother; **~se** *vr* to tire, get tired; (*aburrirse*) to get bored.
cantábrico, a [kan'taßriko, a] *adj* Cantabrian; **Mar C~** Bay of Biscay; **(Montes) C~s, Cordillera Cantábrica** Cantabrian Mountains.
cántabro, a ['kantaßro, a] *adj, nm/f* Cantabrian.
cantante [kan'tante] *adj* singing ♦ *nm/f* singer.
cantaor, a [kanta'or, a] *nm/f* Flamenco singer.
cantar [kan'tar] *vt* to sing ♦ *vi* to sing; (*insecto*) to chirp; (*rechinar*) to squeak; (*fam*: *criminal*) to squeal ♦ *nm* (*acción*) singing; (*canción*) song; (*poema*) poem; ~ **a algn las cuarenta** to tell sb a few home truths; ~ **a dos voces** to sing a duet.
cántara ['kantara] *nf* large pitcher.
cántaro ['kantaro] *nm* pitcher, jug.
cantautor, a [kantau'tor, a] *nm/f* singer-songwriter.
cante ['kante] *nm*: ~ **jondo** flamenco singing.
cantera [kan'tera] *nf* quarry.
cántico ['kantiko] *nm* (*REL*) canticle; (*fig*) song.
cantidad [kanti'ðað] *nf* quantity, amount; (*ECON*) sum ♦ *adv* (*fam*) a lot; ~ **alzada** lump sum; ~ **de** lots of.
cantilena [kanti'lena] *nf* = **cantinela.**
cantimplora [kantim'plora] *nf* (*frasco*) water bottle, canteen.
cantina [kan'tina] *nf* canteen; (*de estación*) buffet; (*esp AM*) bar.
cantinela [kanti'nela] *nf* ballad, song.
canto ['kanto] *nm* singing; (*canción*) song; (*borde*) edge, rim; (*de un cuchillo*) back; ~ **rodado** boulder.
cantón [kan'ton] *nm* canton.
cantor, a [kan'tor, a] *nm/f* singer.
canturrear [kanturre'ar] *vi* to sing softly.
canutas [ka'nutas] *nfpl*: **pasarlas** ~ (*fam*) to have a rough time (of it).
canuto [ka'nuto] *nm* (*tubo*) small tube; (*fam*: *droga*) joint.
caña ['kaɲa] *nf* (*BOT*: *tallo*) stem, stalk; (*carrizo*) reed; (*vaso*) tumbler; (*de cerveza*) glass of beer; (*ANAT*) shinbone; (*AM*: *aguardiente*) cane liquor; ~ **de azúcar** sugar cane; ~ **de pescar** fishing rod.
cañada [ka'ɲaða] *nf* (*entre dos montañas*) gully, ravine; (*camino*) cattle track.
cáñamo ['kaɲamo] *nm* (*BOT*) hemp.
cañaveral [kaɲaße'ral] *nm* (*BOT*) reedbed; (*AGR*) sugar-cane field.
cañería [kaɲe'ria] *nf* piping; (*tubo*) pipe.
caño ['kaɲo] *nm* (*tubo*) tube, pipe; (*de aguas servidas*) sewer; (*MUS*) pipe; (*NAUT*) navigation channel; (*de fuente*) jet.
cañón [ka'ɲon] *nm* (*MIL*) cannon; (*de fusil*) barrel; (*GEO*) canyon, gorge.
cañonazo [kaɲo'naθo] *nm* (*MIL*) gunshot.
cañonera [kaɲo'nera] *nf* (*tb*: **lancha** ~) gunboat.
caoba [ka'oßa] *nf* mahogany.
caos ['kaos] *nm* chaos.
caótico, a [ka'otiko, a] *adj* chaotic.
C.A.P. *nm abr* (= *Certificado de Aptitud*

Pedagógica) teaching certificate.
cap. *abr* (= *capítulo*) ch.
capa ['kapa] *nf* cloak, cape; (*CULIN*) coating; (*GEO*) layer, stratum; (*de pintura*) coat; **de ~ y espada** cloak-and-dagger; **so ~ de** under the pretext of; **~ de ozono** ozone layer; **~s sociales** social groups.
capacho [ka'patʃo] *nm* wicker basket.
capacidad [kapaθi'ðað] *nf* (*medida*) capacity; (*aptitud*) capacity, ability; **una sala con ~ para 900** a hall seating 900; **~ adquisitiva** purchasing power.
capacitación [kapaθita'θjon] *nf* training.
capacitar [kapaθi'tar] *vt*: **~ a algn para algo** to qualify sb for sth; (*TEC*) to train sb for sth.
capar [ka'par] *vt* to castrate, geld.
caparazón [kapara'θon] *nm* (*ZOOL*) shell.
capataz [kapa'taθ] *nm* foreman, chargehand.
capaz [ka'paθ] *adj* able, capable; (*amplio*) capacious, roomy; **es ~ que venga mañana** (*AM*) he'll probably come tomorrow.
capcioso, a [kap'θjoso, a] *adj* wily, deceitful; **pregunta capciosa** trick question.
capea [ka'pea] *nf* (*TAUR*) bullfight with young bulls.
capear [kape'ar] *vt* (*dificultades*) to dodge; **~ el temporal** to weather the storm.
capellán [kape'ʎan] *nm* chaplain; (*sacerdote*) priest.
caperuza [kape'ruθa] *nf* hood; (*de bolígrafo*) cap.
capi ['kapi] *nf* (*esp AM fam*) capital (city).
capicúa [kapi'kua] *nm* *reversible number, e.g. 1441.*
capilar [kapi'lar] *adj* hair *cpd.*
capilla [ka'piʎa] *nf* chapel.
capital [kapi'tal] *adj* capital ♦ *nm* (*COM*) capital ♦ *nf* (*de nación*) capital (city); (*tb*: **~ de provincia**) provincial capital, ≈ county town; **~ activo/en acciones** working/share *o* equity capital; **~ arriesgado** venture capital; **~ autorizado** authorised capital; **~ emitido** issued capital; **~ improductivo** idle money; **~ invertido** *o* **utilizado** capital employed; **~ pagado** paid-up capital; **~ de riesgo** risk capital; **~ social** authorized *o* share capital; **inversión de ~es** capital investment; *V tb* **provincia**.
capitalice [kapita'liθe] *etc vb V* **capitalizar**.
capitalino, a [kapita'lino, a] *adj* (*AM*) of *o* from the capital ♦ *nm/f* native *o* inhabitant of the capital.
capitalismo [kapita'lismo] *nm* capitalism.
capitalista [kapita'lista] *adj, nm/f* capitalist.
capitalizar [kapitali'θar] *vt* to capitalize.
capitán [kapi'tan] *nm* captain; (*fig*) leader.
capitana [kapi'tana] *nf* flagship.
capitanear [kapitane'ar] *vt* to captain.
capitanía [kapita'nia] *nf* captaincy.
capitel [kapi'tel] *nm* (*ARQ*) capital.
capitolio [kapi'toljo] *nm* capitol.
capitulación [kapitula'θjon] *nf* (*rendición*) capitulation, surrender; (*acuerdo*) agreement, pact; **capitulaciones matrimoniales** marriage contract *sg.*
capitular [kapitu'lar] *vi* to come to terms, make an agreement; (*MIL*) to surrender.
capítulo [ka'pitulo] *nm* chapter.
capo [ka'po] *nm* drugs baron.
capó [ka'po] *nm* (*AUTO*) bonnet (*BRIT*), hood (*US*).
capón [ka'pon] *nm* capon.
caporal [kapo'ral] *nm* chief, leader.
capota [ka'pota] *nf* (*de mujer*) bonnet; (*AUTO*) hood (*BRIT*), top (*US*).
capote [ka'pote] *nm* (*abrigo: de militar*) greatcoat; (*de torero*) cloak.
capricho [ka'pritʃo] *nm* whim, caprice.
caprichoso, a [kapri'tʃoso, a] *adj* capricious.
Capricornio [kapri'kornjo] *nm* Capricorn.
cápsula ['kapsula] *nf* capsule; **~ espacial** space capsule.
captar [kap'tar] *vt* (*comprender*) to understand; (*RADIO*) to pick up; (*atención, apoyo*) to attract.
captura [kap'tura] *nf* capture; (*JUR*) arrest.
capturar [kaptu'rar] *vt* to capture; (*JUR*) to arrest; (*datos*) to input.
capucha [ka'putʃa] *nf* hood, cowl.
capullo [ka'puʎo] *nm* (*ZOOL*) cocoon; (*BOT*) bud; (*fam!*) berk (*BRIT*), jerk (*US*).
caqui ['kaki] *nm* khaki.
cara ['kara] *nf* (*ANAT, de moneda*) face; (*aspecto*) appearance; (*de disco*) side; (*fig*) boldness; (*descara*) cheek, nerve ♦ *prep*: **~ a** facing; **de ~ a** opposite, facing; **dar la ~** to face the consequences; **echar algo en ~ a algn** to reproach sb for sth; **¿~ o cruz?** heads or tails?; **¡qué ~ más dura!** what a nerve!; **de una ~** (*disquete*) single-sided.
carabina [kara'ßina] *nf* carbine, rifle; (*persona*) chaperone.
carabinero [karaßi'nero] *nm* (*de aduana*) customs officer; (*AM*) gendarme.
Caracas [ka'rakas] *nm* Caracas.
caracol [kara'kol] *nm* (*ZOOL*) snail; (*concha*) (sea)shell; **escalera de ~** spiral staircase.

caracolear [karakole'ar] *vi* (*caballo*) to prance about.
carácter, *pl* **caracteres** [ka'rakter, karak'teres] *nm* character; ~ **de cambio de página** (*INFORM*) form feed character; **caracteres de imprenta** (*TIP*) type(face) *sg*; ~ **libre** (*INFORM*) wildcard character; **tener buen/mal** ~ to be good-natured/bad tempered.
caracterice [karakte'riθe] *etc vb V* **caracterizar**.
característico, a [karakte'ristiko, a] *adj* characteristic ♦ *nf* characteristic.
caracterizar [karakteri'θar] *vt* (*distinguir*) to characterize, typify; (*honrar*) to confer (a) distinction on.
caradura [kara'ðura] *nm/f* cheeky person; **es un** ~ he's got a nerve.
carajillo [kara'xiʎo] *nm black coffee with brandy*.
carajo [ka'raxo] *nm* (*esp AM fam!*): ¡~! shit!(*!*); ¡**qué** ~! what the hell!; **me importa un** ~ I don't give a damn.
caramba [ka'ramba] *excl* well!, good gracious!
carámbano [ka'rambano] *nm* icicle.
carambola [karam'bola] *nf*: **por** ~ by a fluke.
caramelo [kara'melo] *nm* (*dulce*) sweet; (*azúcar fundido*) caramel.
carantoñas [karan'toɲas] *nfpl*: **hacer** ~ **a algn** to (try to) butter sb up.
caraqueño, a [kara'keɲo, a] *adj* of *o* from Caracas ♦ *nm/f* native *o* inhabitant of Caracas.
carátula [ka'ratula] *nf* (*máscara*) mask; (*TEAT*): **la** ~ the stage.
caravana [kara'ßana] *nf* caravan; (*fig*) group; (*de autos*) tailback.
carbón [kar'ßon] *nm* coal; ~ **de leña** charcoal; **papel** ~ carbon paper.
carbonatado, a [karßono'taðo, a] *adj* carbonated.
carbonato [karßo'nato] *nm* carbonate; ~ **sódico** sodium carbonate.
carboncillo [karßon'θiʎo] *nm* (*ARTE*) charcoal.
carbonice [karßo'niθe] *etc vb V* **carbonizar**.
carbonilla [karßo'niʎa] *nf* coal dust.
carbonizar [karßoni'θar] *vt* to carbonize; (*quemar*) to char; **quedar carbonizado** (*ELEC*) to be electrocuted.
carbono [kar'ßono] *nm* carbon.
carburador [karßura'ðor] *nm* carburettor.
carburante [karßu'rante] *nm* fuel.
carca ['karka] *adj, nm/f inv* reactionary.
carcajada [karka'xaða] *nf* (loud) laugh, guffaw.
carcajearse [karkaxe'arse] *vr* to roar with laughter.
cárcel ['karθel] *nf* prison, jail; (*TEC*) clamp.
carcelero, a [karθe'lero, a] *adj* prison *cpd* ♦ *nm/f* warder.
carcoma [kar'koma] *nf* woodworm.
carcomer [karko'mer] *vt* to bore into, eat into; (*fig*) to undermine; ~**se** *vr* to become worm-eaten; (*fig*) to decay.
carcomido, a [karko'miðo, a] *adj* worm-eaten; (*fig*) rotten.
cardar [kar'ðar] *vt* (*TEC*) to card, comb.
cardenal [karðe'nal] *nm* (*REL*) cardinal; (*MED*) bruise.
cárdeno, a ['karðeno, a] *adj* purple; (*lívido*) livid.
cardiaco, a [kar'ðjako, a], **cardíaco, a** [kar'ðiako, a] *adj* cardiac; (*ataque*) heart *cpd*.
cardinal [karði'nal] *adj* cardinal.
cardiólogo, a [karðj'oloɣo, a] *nm/f* cardiologist.
cardo ['karðo] *nm* thistle.
carear [kare'ar] *vt* to bring face to face; (*comparar*) to compare; ~**se** *vr* to come face to face, meet.
carecer [kare'θer] *vi*: ~ **de** to lack, be in need of.
carencia [ka'renθja] *nf* lack; (*escasez*) shortage; (*MED*) deficiency.
carente [ka'rente] *adj*: ~ **de** lacking in, devoid of.
carestía [kares'tia] *nf* (*escasez*) scarcity, shortage; (*COM*) high cost; **época de** ~ period of shortage.
careta [ka'reta] *nf* mask.
carey [ka'rei] *nm* (*tortuga*) turtle; (*concha*) tortoiseshell.
carezca [ka'reθka] *etc vb V* **carecer**.
carga ['karɣa] *nf* (*peso, ELEC*) load; (*de barco*) cargo, freight; (*FINANZAS*) tax, duty; (*MIL*) charge; (*INFORM*) loading; (*obligación, responsabilidad*) duty, obligation; ~ **aérea** (*COM*) air cargo; ~ **útil** (*COM*) payload; **la** ~ **fiscal** the tax burden.
cargadero [karɣa'ðero] *nm* goods platform, loading bay.
cargado, a [kar'ɣaðo, a] *adj* loaded; (*ELEC*) live; (*café, té*) strong; (*cielo*) overcast.
cargador, a [karɣa'ðor, a] *nm/f* loader; (*NAUT*) docker ♦ *nm* (*INFORM*): ~ **de discos** disk pack.
cargamento [karɣa'mento] *nm* (*acción*) loading; (*mercancías*) load, cargo.
cargante [kar'ɣante] *adj* (*persona*) trying.
cargar [kar'ɣar] *vt* (*barco, arma*) to load; (*ELEC*) to charge; (*impuesto*) to impose;

(*COM: algo en cuenta*) to charge, debit; (*MIL: enemigo*) to charge ♦ *vi* (*AUTO*) to load (up); (*inclinarse*) to lean; (*INFORM*) to load; ~ **con** to pick up, carry away; ~**se** *vr* (*fam: estropear*) to break; (*: matar*) to bump off; (*ELEC*) to become charged.
cargo ['karɣo] *nm* (*COM etc*) charge, debit; (*puesto*) post, office; (*responsabilidad*) duty, obligation; (*fig*) weight, burden; (*JUR*) charge; **altos ~s** high-ranking officials; **una cantidad en ~ a algn** a sum chargeable to sb; **hacerse ~ de** to take charge of *o* responsibility for.
cargue ['karɣe] *etc vb V* **cargar**.
Caribe [ka'riβe] *nm*: **el** ~ the Caribbean.
caribeño, a [kari'βeɲo, a] *adj* Caribbean.
caricatura [karika'tura] *nf* caricature.
caricia [ka'riθja] *nf* caress; (*a animal*) pat, stroke.
caridad [kari'ðað] *nf* charity.
caries ['karjes] *nf inv* (*MED*) tooth decay.
cariño [ka'riɲo] *nm* affection, love; (*caricia*) caress; (*en carta*) love ....
cariñoso, a [kari'ɲoso, a] *adj* affectionate.
carioca [ka'rjoka] *adj* (*AM*) of *o* from Rio de Janeiro ♦ *nm/f* native *o* inhabitant of Rio de Janeiro.
carisma [ka'risma] *nm* charisma.
carismático, a [karis'matiko, a] *adj* charismatic.
caritativo, a [karita'tiβo, a] *adj* charitable.
cariz [ka'riθ] *nm*: **tener** *o* **tomar buen/mal** ~ to look good/bad.
carmesí [karme'si] *adj, nm* crimson.
carmín [kar'min] *nm* (*color*) carmine; ~ **(de labios)** lipstick.
carnal [kar'nal] *adj* carnal; **primo** ~ first cousin.
carnaval [karna'βal] *nm* carnival; *see boxed note.*

CARNAVAL

The three days before "miércoles de ceniza" (Ash Wednesday), when fasting for Lent traditionally starts, are the signal for **carnaval**, *an exuberant celebration which dates back to pre-Christian times. Although in decline during the Franco years in Spain,* **carnaval** *has recently grown in popularity, Cádiz and Tenerife being particularly well known for their celebrations. "Martes de carnaval" (Shrove Tuesday) is the most important day, with colourful street parades, fancy dress, fireworks and a general party atmosphere.*

carne ['karne] *nf* flesh; (*CULIN*) meat; ~ **de cerdo/de cordero/de ternera/de vaca** pork/lamb/veal/beef; ~ **picada** mince; ~ **de gallina** (*fig*) gooseflesh.
carné [kar'ne] *nm* = **carnet**.
carnero [kar'nero] *nm* sheep, ram; (*carne*) mutton.
carnet, *pl* **carnets** [kar'ne, kar'nes] *nm*: ~ **de conducir** driving licence; ~ **de identidad** identity card; *V tb* **Documento Nacional de Identidad**.
carnicería [karniθe'ria] *nf* butcher's (shop); (*fig: matanza*) carnage, slaughter.
carnicero, a [karni'θero, a] *adj* carnivorous ♦ *nm/f* (*tb fig*) butcher ♦ *nm* carnivore.
carnívoro, a [kar'niβoro, a] *adj* carnivorous ♦ *nm* carnivore.
carnoso, a [kar'noso, a] *adj* beefy, fat.
caro, a ['karo, a] *adj* dear; (*COM*) dear, expensive ♦ *adv* dear, dearly; **vender** ~ to sell at a high price.
carpa ['karpa] *nf* (*pez*) carp; (*de circo*) big top; (*AM: de camping*) tent.
carpeta [kar'peta] *nf* folder, file.
carpintería [karpinte'ria] *nf* carpentry.
carpintero [karpin'tero] *nm* carpenter; **pájaro** ~ woodpecker.
carraca [ka'rraka] *nf* (*DEPORTE*) rattle.
carraspear [karraspe'ar] *vi* (*aclararse*) to clear one's throat.
carraspera [karras'pera] *nf* hoarseness.
carrera [ka'rrera] *nf* (*acción*) run(ning); (*espacio recorrido*) run; (*certamen*) race; (*trayecto*) course; (*profesión*) career; (*ESCOL, UNIV*) course; (*de taxi*) ride; (*en medias*) ladder; **a la** ~ at (full) speed; **caballo de ~(s)** racehorse; ~ **de armamentos** arms race.
carrerilla [karre'riʎa] *nf*: **decir algo de** ~ to reel sth off; **tomar** ~ to get up speed.
carreta [ka'rreta] *nf* wagon, cart.
carrete [ka'rrete] *nm* reel, spool; (*TEC*) coil.
carretera [karre'tera] *nf* (main) road, highway; ~ **nacional** ≈ A road (*BRIT*), state highway (*US*); ~ **de circunvalación** ring road.
carretilla [karre'tiʎa] *nf* trolley; (*AGR*) (wheel)barrow.
carril [ka'rril] *nm* furrow; (*de autopista*) lane; (*FERRO*) rail.
carril-bici, *pl* **carriles-bici** [karil'βiθi, kariles'βiθi] *nm* cycle lane, bikeway (*US*).
carrillo [ka'rriʎo] *nm* (*ANAT*) cheek; (*TEC*) pulley.
carro ['karro] *nm* cart, wagon; (*MIL*) tank; (*AM: coche*) car; (*TIP*) carriage; ~ **blindado** armoured car.

carrocería [karroθe'ria] *nf* body, bodywork *no pl* (*BRIT*).
carroña [ka'rroɲa] *nf* carrion *no pl.*
carroza [ka'rroθa] *nf* (*vehículo*) coach ♦ *nm/f* (*fam*) old fogey.
carruaje [ka'rrwaxe] *nm* carriage.
carrusel [karru'sel] *nm* merry-go-round, roundabout (*BRIT*).
carta ['karta] *nf* letter; (*CULIN*) menu; (*naipe*) card; (*mapa*) map; (*JUR*) document; ~ **de crédito** credit card; ~ **de crédito documentaria** (*COM*) documentary letter of credit; ~ **de crédito irrevocable** (*COM*) irrevocable letter of credit; ~ **certificada/urgente** registered/special delivery letter; ~ **marítima** chart; ~ **de pedido** (*COM*) order; ~ **verde** (*AUTO*) green card; ~ **de vinos** wine list; **echar una ~ al correo** to post a letter; **echar las ~s a algn** to tell sb's fortune.
cartabón [karta'ßon] *nm* set square.
cartearse [karte'arse] *vr* to correspond.
cartel [kar'tel] *nm* (*anuncio*) poster, placard; (*ESCOL*) wall chart; (*COM*) cartel.
cartelera [karte'lera] *nf* hoarding, billboard; (*en periódico etc*) listings *pl*, entertainments guide; **"en ~"** "showing".
cartera [kar'tera] *nf* (*de bolsillo*) wallet; (*de colegial, cobrador*) satchel; (*AM*: *de señora*) handbag (*BRIT*), purse (*US*); (*para documentos*) briefcase; **ministro sin ~** (*POL*) minister without portfolio; **ocupa la ~ de Agricultura** he is Minister of Agriculture; ~ **de pedidos** (*COM*) order book; **efectos en ~** (*ECON*) holdings.
carterista [karte'rista] *nm/f* pickpocket.
cartero [kar'tero] *nm* postman.
cartílago [kar'tilaɣo] *nm* cartilage.
cartilla [kar'tiʎa] *nf* (*ESCOL*) primer, first reading book; ~ **de ahorros** bank book.
cartografía [kartoɣgra'fia] *nf* cartography.
cartón [kar'ton] *nm* cardboard.
cartucho [kar'tutʃo] *nm* (*MIL*) cartridge; (*bolsita*) paper cone; ~ **de datos** (*INFORM*) data cartridge.
cartulina [kartu'lina] *nf* fine cardboard, card.
CASA ['kasa] *nf abr* (*ESP AVIAT*) = *Construcciones Aeronáuticas S.A.*
casa ['kasa] *nf* house; (*hogar*) home; (*edificio*) building; (*COM*) firm, company; ~ **consistorial** town hall; ~ **de huéspedes** ≈ guest house; ~ **de socorro** first aid post; ~ **de citas** (*fam*) brothel; **ir a ~** to go home; **salir de ~** to go out; (*para siempre*) to leave home; **echar la ~ por la ventana** (*gastar*) to spare no expense; *V tb* **hotel**.
casadero, a [kasa'ðero, a] *adj* marriageable.
casado, a [ka'saðo, a] *a* married ♦ *nm/f* married man/woman.
casamiento [kasa'mjento] *nm* marriage, wedding.
casar [ka'sar] *vt* to marry; (*JUR*) to quash, annul; **~se** *vr* to marry, get married; **~se por lo civil** to have a civil wedding, get married in a registry office (*BRIT*) .
cascabel [kaska'ßel] *nm* (small) bell; (*ZOOL*) rattlesnake.
cascada [kas'kaða] *nf* waterfall.
cascajo [kas'kaxo] *nm* gravel, stone chippings *pl.*
cascanueces [kaska'nweθes] *nm inv*: **un ~** a pair of nutcrackers.
cascar [kas'kar] *vt* to split; (*nuez*) to crack ♦ *vi* to chatter; **~se** *vr* to crack, split, break (open).
cáscara ['kaskara] *nf* (*de huevo, fruta seca*) shell; (*de fruta*) skin; (*de limón*) peel.
cascarón [kaska'ron] *nm* (broken) eggshell.
cascarrabias [kaska'rraßjas] *nm/f inv* (*fam*) hothead.
casco ['kasko] *nm* (*de bombero, soldado*) helmet; (*cráneo*) skull; (*NAUT*: *de barco*) hull; (*ZOOL*: *de caballo*) hoof; (*botella*) empty bottle; (*de ciudad*): **el ~ antiguo** the old part; **el ~ urbano** the town centre; **los ~s azules** the UN peace-keeping force, the blue berets.
cascote [kas'kote] *nm* piece of rubble; **~s** *nmpl* rubble *sg.*
caserío [kase'rio] *nm* hamlet, group of houses; (*casa*) country house.
casero, a [ka'sero, a] *adj*: **ser muy ~** (*persona*) to be homeloving; **"comida casera"** "home cooking" ♦ *nm/f* (*propietario*) landlord/lady; (*COM*) house agent.
caserón [kase'ron] *nm* large (ramshackle) house.
caseta [ka'seta] *nf* hut; (*para bañista*) cubicle; (*de feria*) stall.
casete [ka'sete] *nm o f* cassette: ~ **digital** digital audio tape, DAT.
casi ['kasi] *adv* almost; ~ **nunca** hardly ever, almost never; ~ **nada** next to nothing; ~ **te caes** you almost *o* nearly fell.
casilla [ka'siʎa] *nf* (*casita*) hut, cabin; (*TEAT*) box office; (*para cartas*) pigeonhole; (*AJEDREZ*) square; **C~ postal**

o **de Correo(s)** (*AM*) P.O. Box; **sacar a algn de sus ~ s** to drive sb round the bend (*fam*), make sb lose his temper.
casillero [kasi'ʎero] *nm* pigeonholes.
casino [ka'sino] *nm* club; (*de juego*) casino.
caso ['kaso] *nm* case; (*suceso*) event; **en ~ de ...** in case of ...; **el ~ es que** the fact is that; **en el mejor de los ~s** at best; **en ese ~** in that case; **en todo ~** in any case; **en último ~** as a last resort; **hacer ~ a** to pay attention to; **hacer ~ omiso de** to fail to mention, pass over; **hacer** *o* **venir al ~** to be relevant.
caspa ['kaspa] *nf* dandruff.
Caspio ['kaspjo] *adj*: **Mar ~** Caspian Sea.
casque ['kaske] *etc vb V* **cascar.**
casquillo [kas'kiʎo] *nm* (*de bombilla*) fitting; (*de bala*) cartridge case.
cassette [ka'set] *nf o m* = **casete.**
casta ['kasta] *nf* caste; (*raza*) breed.
castaña [kas'taɲa] *nf V* **castaño.**
castañetear [kastaɲete'ar] *vi* (*dientes*) to chatter.
castaño, a [kas'taɲo, a] *adj* chestnut (-coloured), brown ♦ *nm* chestnut tree ♦ *nf* chestnut; (*fam*: *golpe*) punch; **~ de Indias** horse chestnut tree.
castañuelas [kasta'ɲwelas] *nfpl* castanets.
castellano, a [kaste'ʎano, a] *adj* Castilian; (*fam*) Spanish ♦ *nm/f* Castilian; (*fam*) Spaniard ♦ *nm* (*LING*) Castilian, Spanish; *see boxed note.*

CASTELLANO

Castellano *is now the term most widely used in Spain and Spanish America to refer to the Spanish language, since "español" is too closely associated with the concept of Spain as a nation. Some purists maintain that* **castellano** *should only refer to the variety of Spanish spoken in Castille.*

castellonense [kasteʎo'nense] *adj* of *o* from Castellón de la Plana ♦ *nm/f* native *o* inhabitant of Castellón de la Plana.
castidad [kasti'ðað] *nf* chastity, purity.
castigar [kasti'ɣar] *vt* to punish; (*DEPORTE*) to penalize; (*afligir*) to afflict.
castigo [kas'tiɣo] *nm* punishment; (*DEPORTE*) penalty.
castigue [kas'tiɣe] *etc vb V* **castigar.**
Castilla [kas'tiʎa] *nf* Castile.
castillo [kas'tiʎo] *nm* castle.
castizo, a [kas'tiθo, a] *adj* (*LING*) pure; (*de buena casta*) purebred, pedigree; (*auténtico*) genuine.
casto, a ['kasto, a] *adj* chaste, pure.
castor [kas'tor] *nm* beaver.
castrar [kas'trar] *vt* to castrate; (*gato*) to doctor; (*BOT*) to prune.
castrense [kas'trense] *adj* army *cpd*, military.
casual [ka'swal] *adj* chance, accidental.
casualidad [kaswali'ðað] *nf* chance, accident; (*combinación de circunstancias*) coincidence; **¡qué ~!** what a coincidence!
casualmente [kaswal'mente] *adv* by chance.
cataclismo [kata'klismo] *nm* cataclysm.
catador [kata'ðor] *nm* taster.
catadura [kata'ðura] *nf* (*aspecto*) looks *pl.*
catalán, ana [kata'lan, ana] *adj, nm/f* Catalan ♦ *nm* (*LING*) Catalan; *V tb* **lenguas cooficiales.**
catalejo [kata'lexo] *nm* telescope.
catalizador [kataliθa'ðor] *nm* catalyst; (*AUTO*) catalytic converter.
catalogar [katalo'ɣar] *vt* to catalogue; **~ (de)** (*fig*) to classify (as).
catálogo [ka'taloɣo] *nm* catalogue.
catalogue [kata'loɣe] *etc vb V* **catalogar.**
Cataluña [kata'luɲa] *nf* Catalonia.
cataplasma [kata'plasma] *nf* (*MED*) poultice.
catapulta [kata'pulta] *nf* catapult.
catar [ka'tar] *vt* to taste, sample.
catarata [kata'rata] *nf* (*GEO*) (water)fall; (*MED*) cataract.
catarro [ka'tarro] *nm* catarrh; (*constipado*) cold.
catarsis [ka'tarsis] *nf* catharsis.
catastro [ka'tastro] *nm* property register.
catástrofe [ka'tastrofe] *nf* catastrophe.
catear [kate'ar] *vt* (*fam*) to flunk.
catecismo [kate'θismo] *nm* catechism.
cátedra ['kateðra] *nf* (*UNIV*) chair, professorship; (*ESCOL*) principal teacher's post; **sentar ~ sobre un argumento** to take one's stand on an argument.
catedral [kate'ðral] *nf* cathedral.
catedrático, a [kate'ðratiko, a] *nm/f* professor; (*ESCOL*) principal teacher.
categoría [kateɣo'ria] *nf* category; (*rango*) rank, standing; (*calidad*) quality; **de ~** (*hotel*) top-class; **de baja ~** (*oficial*) low-ranking; **de segunda ~** second-rate; **no tiene ~** he has no standing.
categórico, a [kate'ɣoriko, a] *adj* categorical.
catequesis [kate'kesis] *nf* catechism lessons.
caterva [ka'terβa] *nf* throng, crowd.
cateto, a [ka'teto, a] *nm/f* yokel.
cátodo ['katoðo] *nm* cathode.

catolicismo [katoli'θismo] *nm* Catholicism.
católico, a [ka'toliko, a] *adj, nm/f* Catholic.
catorce [ka'torθe] *num* fourteen.
catre ['katre] *nm* camp bed (*BRIT*), cot (*US*); (*fam*) pit.
Cáucaso ['kaukaso] *nm* Caucasus.
cauce ['kauθe] *nm* (*de río*) riverbed; (*fig*) channel.
caucho ['kautʃo] *nm* rubber; (*AM*: *llanta*) tyre.
caución [kau'θjon] *nf* bail.
caucionar [kauθjo'nar] *vt* (*JUR*) to bail (out), go bail for.
caudal [kau'ðal] *nm* (*de río*) volume, flow; (*fortuna*) wealth; (*abundancia*) abundance.
caudaloso, a [kauða'loso, a] *adj* (*río*) large; (*persona*) wealthy, rich.
caudillaje [kauði'ʎaxe] *nm* leadership.
caudillo [kau'ðiʎo] *nm* leader, chief.
causa ['kausa] *nf* cause; (*razón*) reason; (*JUR*) lawsuit, case; **a** *o* **por ~ de** because of, on account of.
causar [kau'sar] *vt* to cause.
cáustico, a ['kaustiko, a] *adj* caustic.
cautela [kau'tela] *nf* caution, cautiousness.
cauteloso, a [kaute'loso, a] *adj* cautious, wary.
cautivar [kauti'ßar] *vt* to capture; (*fig*) to captivate.
cautiverio [kauti'ßerjo] *nm*, **cautividad** [kautißi'ðað] *nf* captivity.
cautivo, a [kau'tißo, a] *adj, nm/f* captive.
cauto, a ['kauto, a] *adj* cautious, careful.
cava ['kaßa] *nf* (*bodega*) (wine) cellar ♦ *nm* (*vino*) *champagne-type wine.*
cavar [ka'ßar] *vt* to dig; (*AGR*) to dig over.
caverna [ka'ßerna] *nf* cave, cavern.
cavernoso, a [kaßer'noso, a] *adj* cavernous; (*voz*) resounding.
caviar [ka'ßjar] *nm* caviar(e).
cavidad [kaßi'ðað] *nf* cavity.
cavilación [kaßila'θjon] *nf* deep thought.
cavilar [kaßi'lar] *vt* to ponder.
cayado [ka'jaðo] *nm* (*de pastor*) crook; (*de obispo*) crozier.
cayendo [ka'jendo] *etc vb V* **caer.**
caza ['kaθa] *nf* (*acción*: *gen*) hunting; (: *con fusil*) shooting; (*una ~*) hunt, chase; (*animales*) game; **coto de ~** hunting estate ♦ *nm* (*AVIAT*) fighter.
cazabe [ka'saße] *nm* (*AM*) cassava bread *o* flour.
cazador, a [kaθa'ðor, a] *nm/f* hunter/ huntress ♦ *nf* jacket.
cazaejecutivos [kaθaexeku'tißos] *nm inv* (*COM*) headhunter.
cazar [ka'θar] *vt* to hunt; (*perseguir*) to chase; (*prender*) to catch; **~las al vuelo** to be pretty sharp.
cazasubmarinos [kaθasußma'rinos] *nm inv* (*NAUT*) destroyer; (*AVIAT*) anti-submarine craft.
cazo ['kaθo] *nm* saucepan.
cazuela [ka'θwela] *nf* (*vasija*) pan; (*guisado*) casserole.
cazurro, a [ka'θurro, a] *adj* surly.
CC *nm abr* (*POL*: = *Comité Central*) Central Committee.
c/c. *abr* (*COM*: = *cuenta corriente*) current account.
CC.AA. *abr* (*ESP*) = **Comunidades Autónomas.**
CCI *nf abr* (*COM*: = *Cámara de Comercio Internacional*) ICC.
CC.OO. *nfpl abr* = **Comisiones Obreras.**
CD *nm abr* (= *compact disc*) CD ♦ *abr* (*POL*: = *Cuerpo Diplomático*) CD.
c/d *abr* (= *en casa de*) c/o; (= *con descuento*) with discount.
CDN *nm abr* (= *Centro Dramático Nacional*) ≈ RADA (*BRIT*).
CDS *nm abr* (= *Centro Democrático y Social*) *political party.*
CE *nm abr* (= *Consejo de Europa*) Council of Europe ♦ *nf abr* (= *Comunidad Europea*) EC.
cebada [θe'ßaða] *nf* barley.
cebar [θe'ßar] *vt* (*animal*) to fatten (up); (*anzuelo*) to bait; (*MIL, TEC*) to prime; **~se** *vr*: **~se en** to vent one's fury on, take it out on.
cebo ['θeßo] *nm* (*para animales*) feed, food; (*para peces, fig*) bait; (*de arma*) charge.
cebolla [θe'ßoʎa] *nf* onion.
cebolleta [θebo'ʎeta] *nf* spring onion.
cebollino [θeßo'ʎino] *nm* spring onion.
cebón, ona [θe'ßon, ona] *adj* fat, fattened.
cebra ['θeßra] *nf* zebra; **paso de ~** zebra crossing.
CECA ['θeka] *nf abr* (= *Comunidad Europea del Carbón y del Acero*) ECSC.
ceca ['θeka] *nf*: **andar** *o* **ir de la ~ a la Meca** to chase about all over the place.
cecear [θeθe'ar] *vi* to lisp.
ceceo [θe'θeo] *nm* lisp.
cecina [θe'θina] *nf* cured *o* smoked meat.
cedazo [θe'ðaθo] *nm* sieve.
ceder [θe'ðer] *vt* (*entregar*) to hand over; (*renunciar a*) to give up, part with ♦ *vi* (*renunciar*) to give in, yield; (*disminuir*) to diminish, decline; (*romperse*) to give way; (*viento*) to drop; (*fiebre etc*) to abate; **"ceda el paso"** (*AUTO*) "give way".
cedro ['θeðro] *nm* cedar.
cédula ['θeðula] *nf* certificate, document;

~ **de identidad** (*AM*) identity card; ~ **en blanco** blank cheque; *V tb* **Documento Nacional de Identidad**.
CEE *nf abr* (= *Comunidad Económica Europea*) EEC.
cegar [θe'ɣar] *vt* to blind; (*tubería etc*) to block up, stop up ♦ *vi* to go blind; ~**se** *vr* to be blinded (*de* by).
cegué [θe'ɣe] *etc vb V* **cegar**.
ceguemos [θe'ɣemos] *etc vb V* **cegar**.
ceguera [θe'ɣera] *nf* blindness.
CEI *nf abr* (= *Comunidad de Estados Independientes*) CIS.
Ceilán [θei'lan] *nm* Ceylon, Sri Lanka.
ceja ['θexa] *nf* eyebrow; ~**s pobladas** bushy eyebrows; **arquear las** ~**s** to raise one's eyebrows; **fruncir las** ~**s** to frown.
cejar [θe'xar] *vi* (*fig*) to back down; **no** ~ to keep it up, stick at it.
cejijunto, a [θexi'xunto, a] *adj* with bushy eyebrows; (*fig*) scowling.
celada [θe'laða] *nf* ambush, trap.
celador, a [θela'ðor, a] *nm/f* (*de edificio*) watchman; (*de museo etc*) attendant; (*de cárcel*) warder.
celda ['θelda] *nf* cell.
celebérrimo, a [θele'ßerrimo, a] *adj superlativo de* **célebre**.
celebración [θeleßra'θjon] *nf* celebration.
celebrar [θele'ßrar] *vt* to celebrate; (*alabar*) to praise ♦ *vi* to be glad; ~**se** *vr* to occur, take place.
célebre ['θeleßre] *adj* celebrated, renowned.
celebridad [θeleßri'ðað] *nf* fame; (*persona*) celebrity.
celeridad [θeleri'ðað] *nf*: **con** ~ promptly.
celeste [θe'leste] *adj* sky-blue; (*cuerpo etc*) heavenly ♦ *nm* sky blue.
celestial [θeles'tjal] *adj* celestial, heavenly.
celibato [θeli'ßato] *nm* celibacy.
célibe ['θeliße] *adj, nm/f* celibate.
celo ['θelo] *nm* zeal; (*REL*) fervour; (*pey*) envy; ~**s** *nmpl* jealousy *sg*; **dar** ~**s a algn** to make sb jealous; **tener** ~**s de algn** to be jealous of sb; **en** ~ (*animales*) on heat.
celofán [θelo'fan] *nm* Cellophane ®.
celosía [θelo'sia] *nf* lattice (window).
celoso, a [θe'loso, a] *adj* (*envidioso*) jealous; (*trabajador*) zealous; (*desconfiado*) suspicious.
celta ['θelta] *adj* Celtic ♦ *nm/f* Celt.
célula ['θelula] *nf* cell.
celular [θelu'lar] *adj*: **tejido** ~ cell tissue.
celulitis [θelu'litis] *nf* (*enfermedad*) cellulitis; (*grasa*) cellulite.
celuloide [θelu'loiðe] *nm* celluloid.
celulosa [θelu'losa] *nf* cellulose.
cementerio [θemen'terjo] *nm* cemetery, graveyard; ~ **de coches** scrapyard.
cemento [θe'mento] *nm* cement; (*hormigón*) concrete; (*AM*: *cola*) glue.
CEN *nm abr* (*ESP*) = *Consejo de Economía Nacional*.
cena ['θena] *nf* evening meal, dinner.
cenagal [θena'ɣal] *nm* bog, quagmire.
cenar [θe'nar] *vt* to have for dinner, dine on ♦ *vi* to have dinner, dine.
cencerro [θen'θerro] *nm* cowbell; **estar como un** ~ (*fam*) to be round the bend.
cenicero [θeni'θero] *nm* ashtray.
ceniciento, a [θeni'θjento, a] *adj* ash-coloured, ashen.
cenit [θe'nit] *nm* zenith.
ceniza [θe'niθa] *nf* ash, ashes *pl*.
censar [θen'sar] *vt* to take a census of.
censo ['θenso] *nm* census; ~ **electoral** electoral roll.
censor [θen'sor] *nm* censor; ~ **de cuentas** (*COM*) auditor; ~ **jurado de cuentas** chartered (*BRIT*) *ou* certified public (*US*) accountant.
censura [θen'sura] *nf* (*POL*) censorship; (*moral*) censure, criticism.
censurable [θensu'raßle] *adj* reprehensible.
censurar [θensu'rar] *vt* (*idea*) to censure; (*cortar: película*) to censor.
centavo [θen'taßo] *nm* hundredth (part); (*AM*) cent.
centella [θen'teʎa] *nf* spark.
centellear [θenteʎe'ar] *vi* (*metal*) to gleam; (*estrella*) to twinkle; (*fig*) to sparkle.
centelleo [θente'ʎeo] *nm* gleam(ing); twinkling; sparkling.
centena [θen'tena] *nf* hundred.
centenar [θente'nar] *nm* hundred.
centenario, a [θente'narjo, a] *adj* one hundred years old ♦ *nm* centenary.
centeno [θen'teno] *nm* rye.
centésimo, a [θen'tesimo, a] *adj, nm* hundredth.
centígrado [θen'tiɣraðo] *adj* centigrade.
centigramo [θenti'ɣramo] *nm* centigramme.
centilitro [θenti'litro] *nm* centilitre (*BRIT*), centiliter (*US*).
centímetro [θen'timetro] *nm* centimetre (*BRIT*), centimeter (*US*).
céntimo, a ['θentimo, a] *adj* hundredth ♦ *nm* cent.
centinela [θenti'nela] *nm* sentry, guard.
centollo, a [θen'toʎo, a] *nm/f* large (*o* spider) crab.
central [θen'tral] *adj* central ♦ *nf* head

office; (*TEC*) plant; (*TELEC*) exchange; ~ **nuclear** nuclear power station.
centralice [θentra'liθe] *etc vb V* **centralizar.**
centralita [θentra'lita] *nf* (*TELEC*) switchboard.
centralización [θentraliθa'θjon] *nf* centralization.
centralizar [θentrali'θar] *vt* to centralize.
centrar [θen'trar] *vt* to centre.
céntrico, a ['θentriko, a] *adj* central.
centrifugar [θentrifu'ɣar] *vt* (*ropa*) to spin-dry.
centrífugo, a [θent'rifuɣo, a] *adj* centrifugal.
centrifugue [θentri'fuɣe] *etc vb V* **centrifugar.**
centrista [θen'trista] *adj* centre *cpd.*
centro ['θentro] *nm* centre; **ser de** ~ (*POL*) to be a moderate; ~ **de acogida (para niños)** children's home; ~ **de beneficios** (*COM*) profit centre; ~ **cívico** community centre; ~ **comercial** shopping centre; ~ **de computatión** computer centre; ~ **(de determinación) de costos** (*COM*) cost centre; ~ **delantero** (*DEPORTE*) centre forward; ~ **docente** teaching institution; ~ **juvenil** youth club; ~ **de llamadas** call centre; ~ **social** community centre.
centroafricano, a [θentroafri'kano, a] *adj*: **la República Centroafricana** the Central African Republic.
centroamericano, a [θentroameri'kano, a] *adj, nm/f* Central American.
centrocampista [θentrokam'pista] *nm/f* (*DEPORTE*) midfielder.
ceñido, a [θe'ɲiðo, a] *adj* tight.
ceñir [θe'ɲir] *vt* (*rodear*) to encircle, surround; (*ajustar*) to fit (tightly); (*apretar*) to tighten; ~**se** *vr*: ~**se algo** to put sth on; ~**se al asunto** to stick to the matter in hand.
ceño ['θeɲo] *nm* frown, scowl; **fruncir el** ~ to frown, knit one's brow.
CEOE *nf abr* (= *Confederación Española de Organizaciones Empresariales*) ≈ CBI (*BRIT*).
cepa ['θepa] *nf* (*de vid, fig*) stock; (*BIO*) strain.
CEPAL [θe'pal] *nf abr* (= *Comisión Económica de las Naciones Unidas para la América Latina*) ECLA.
cepillar [θepi'ʎar] *vt* to brush; (*madera*) to plane (down).
cepillo [θe'piʎo] *nm* brush; (*para madera*) plane; (*REL*) poorbox, alms box.
cepo ['θepo] *nm* (*caza*) trap.
CEPSA ['θepsa] *nf abr* (*COM*) = *Compañía Española de Petróleos, S.A.*
CEPYME *nf abr* = *Confederación Española de la Pequeña y Mediana Empresa.*
cera ['θera] *nf* wax; ~ **de abejas** beeswax.
cerámica [θe'ramika] *nf* pottery; (*arte*) ceramics *sg.*
ceramista [θera'mista] *nm/f* potter.
cerbatana [θerβa'tana] *nf* blowpipe.
cerca ['θerka] *nf* fence ♦ *adv* near, nearby, close; **por aquí** ~ nearby ♦ *prep*: ~ **de** (*cantidad*) nearly, about; (*distancia*) near, close to ♦ *nmpl*: ~**s** foreground *sg.*
cercado [θer'kaðo] *nm* enclosure.
cercanía [θerka'nia] *nf* nearness, closeness; ~**s** *nfpl* outskirts, suburbs; **tren de** ~**s** commuter *o* local train.
cercano, a [θer'kano, a] *adj* close, near; (*pueblo etc*) nearby; **C~ Oriente** Near East.
cercar [θer'kar] *vt* to fence in; (*rodear*) to surround.
cerciorar [θerθjo'rar] *vt* (*asegurar*) to assure; ~**se** *vr* (*descubrir*) to find out (*de* about); (*asegurarse*) to make sure (*de* of).
cerco ['θerko] *nm* (*AGR*) enclosure; (*AM*) fence; (*MIL*) siege.
cerda ['θerða] *nf* (*de cepillo*) bristle; (*ZOOL*) sow.
cerdada [θer'ðaða] *nf* (*fam*): **hacer una** ~ **a algn** to play a dirty trick on sb.
Cerdeña [θer'ðeɲa] *nf* Sardinia.
cerdo ['θerðo] *nm* pig; **carne de** ~ pork.
cereal [θere'al] *nm* cereal; ~**es** *nmpl* cereals, grain *sg.*
cerebral [θere'βral] *adj* (*tb fig*) cerebral; (*tumor*) brain *cpd.*
cerebro [θe'reβro] *nm* brain; (*fig*) brains *pl*; **ser un** ~ (*fig*) to be brilliant.
ceremonia [θere'monja] *nf* ceremony; **reunión de** ~ formal meeting; **hablar sin** ~ to speak plainly.
ceremonial [θeremo'njal] *adj, nm* ceremonial.
ceremonioso, a [θeremo'njoso, a] *adj* ceremonious; (*cumplido*) formal.
cereza [θe'reθa] *nf* cherry.
cerezo [θe'reθo] *nm* cherry tree.
cerilla [θe'riʎa] *nf*, **cerillo** [se'riʎo] *nm* (*AM*) match.
cerner [θer'ner] *vt* to sift, sieve; ~**se** *vr* to hover.
cero ['θero] *nm* nothing, zero; (*DEPORTE*) nil; **8 grados bajo** ~ 8 degrees below zero; **a partir de** ~ from scratch.
cerque ['θerke] *etc vb V* **cercar.**
cerrado, a [θe'rraðo, a] *adj* closed, shut; (*con llave*) locked; (*tiempo*) cloudy, overcast; (*curva*) sharp; (*acento*) thick, broad; **a puerta cerrada** (*JUR*) in camera.

cerradura [θerra'ðura] *nf* (*acción*) closing; (*mecanismo*) lock.
cerrajería [θerraxe'ria] *nf* locksmith's craft; (*tienda*) locksmith's (shop).
cerrajero, a [θerra'xero, a] *nm/f* locksmith.
cerrar [θe'rrar] *vt* to close, shut; (*paso, carretera*) to close; (*grifo*) to turn off; (*trato, cuenta, negocio*) to close ♦ *vi* to close, shut; (*la noche*) to come down; ~ **con llave** to lock; ~ **el sistema** (*INFORM*) to close *o* shut down the system; ~ **un trato** to strike a bargain; ~**se** *vr* to close, shut; (*herida*) to heal.
cerro ['θerro] *nm* hill; **andar por las ~s de Úbeda** to wander from the point, digress.
cerrojo [θe'rroxo] *nm* (*herramienta*) bolt; (*de puerta*) latch.
certamen [θer'tamen] *nm* competition, contest.
certero, a [θer'tero, a] *adj* (*gen*) accurate.
certeza [θer'teθa], **certidumbre** [θerti'ðumbre] *nf* certainty.
certificación [θertifika'θjon] *nf* certification; (*JUR*) affidavit.
certificado, a [θertifi'kaðo, a] *adj* certified; (*CORREOS*) registered ♦ *nm* certificate.
certificar [θertifi'kar] *vt* (*asegurar, atestar*) to certify.
certifique [θerti'fike] *etc vb V* **certificar**.
cervatillo [θerβa'tiʎo] *nm* fawn.
cervecería [θerβeθe'ria] *nf* (*fábrica*) brewery; (*taberna*) public house.
cerveza [θer'βeθa] *nf* beer; ~ **de barril** draught beer.
cervical [θerβi'kal] *adj* cervical.
cerviz [θer'βiθ] *nf* nape of the neck.
cesación [θesa'θjon] *nf* cessation, suspension.
cesante [θe'sante] *adj* redundant; (*AM*) unemployed; (*ministro*) outgoing; (*diplomático*) recalled ♦ *nm/f* redundant worker.
cesar [θe'sar] *vi* to cease, stop; (*de un trabajo*) to leave ♦ *vt* (*en el trabajo*) to dismiss; (*alto cargo*) to remove from office.
cesárea [θe'sarea] *nf* Caesarean (section).
cese ['θese] *nm* (*de trabajo*) dismissal; (*de pago*) suspension.
Cesid [θe'sið] *nm abr* (*ESP*: = *Centro Superior de Investigación de la Defensa Nacional*) *military intelligence service*.
cesión [θe'sjon] *nf*: ~ **de bienes** surrender of property.
césped ['θespeð] *nm* grass, lawn.
cesta ['θesta] *nf* basket.
cesto ['θesto] *nm* (large) basket, hamper.
cetrería [θetre'ria] *nf* falconry.
cetrino, a [θe'trino, a] *adj* (*tez*) sallow.
cetro ['θetro] *nm* sceptre.
Ceuta [θe'uta] *nf* Ceuta.
ceutí [θeu'ti] *adj* of *o* from Ceuta ♦ *nm/f* native *o* inhabitant of Ceuta.
C.F. *nm abr* (= *Club de Fútbol*) F.C.
CFC *nm abr* (= *clorofluorocarbono*) CFC.
cfr. *abr* (= *confróntese, compárese*) cf.
cg. *abr* (= *centígramo*) cg.
CGPJ *nm abr* (= *Consejo General del Poder Judicial*) *governing body of Spanish legal system*.
CGS *nf abr* (*Guatemala, El Salvador*) = *Confederación General de Sindicatos*.
CGT *nf abr* (*Colombia, México, Nicaragua, ESP*) = *Confederación General de Trabajadores*; (*Argentina*) = *Confederación General del Trabajo*.
Ch, ch [tʃe] *nf former letter in the Spanish alphabet*.
chabacano, a [tʃaβa'kano, a] *adj* vulgar, coarse.
chabola [tʃa'βola] *nf* shack; ~**s** *nfpl* shanty town *sg*.
chabolismo [tʃaβo'lismo] *nm*: **el problema del ~** the problem of substandard housing, the shanty town problem.
chacal [tʃa'kal] *nm* jackal.
chacarero [tʃaka'rero] *nm* (*AM*) small farmer.
chacha ['tʃatʃa] *nf* (*fam*) maid.
cháchara ['tʃatʃara] *nf* chatter; **estar de ~** to chatter away.
chacra ['tʃakra] *nf* (*AM*) smallholding.
chafar [tʃa'far] *vt* (*aplastar*) to crush, flatten; (*arruinar*) to ruin.
chaflán [tʃa'flan] *nm* (*TEC*) bevel.
chal [tʃal] *nm* shawl.
chalado, a [tʃa'laðo, a] *adj* (*fam*) crazy.
chalé, *pl* **chalés** [tʃa'le, tʃa'les] *nm* = **chalet**.
chaleco [tʃa'leko] *nm* waistcoat, vest (*US*); ~ **antibala** bulletproof vest; ~ **salvavidas** life jacket.
chalet, *pl* **chalets** [tʃa'le, tʃa'les] *nm* villa, ≈ detached house; ~ **adosado** semi-detached house.
chalupa [tʃa'lupa] *nf* launch, boat.
chamaco, a [tʃa'mako, a] *nm/f* (*AM*) boy/girl.
chamarra [tʃa'marra] *nf* sheepskin jacket; (*AM*: *poncho*) blanket.
champán [tʃam'pan] *nm*, **champaña** [tʃam'paɲa] *nm* champagne.
champiñón [tʃampi'ɲon] *nm* mushroom.
champú [tʃam'pu] (*pl* **champúes**,

champús) *nm* shampoo.
chamuscar [tʃamus'kar] *vt* to scorch, sear, singe.
chamusque [tʃa'muske] *etc vb V* **chamuscar**.
chamusquina [tʃamus'kina] *nf* singeing.
chance ['tʃanθe] *nm (a veces nf)* (*AM*) chance, opportunity.
chanchada [tʃan'tʃaðа] *nf* (*AM fam*) dirty trick.
chancho, a ['tʃantʃo, a] *nm/f* (*AM*) pig.
chanchullo [tʃan'tʃuʎo] *nm* (*fam*) fiddle, wangle.
chancla ['tʃankla] *nf*, **chancleta** [tʃan'kleta] *nf* flip-flop; (*zapato viejo*) old shoe.
chandal [tʃan'dal] *nm* tracksuit; ~ **(de tactel)** shellsuit.
chantaje [tʃan'taxe] *nm* blackmail; **hacer ~ a uno** to blackmail sb.
chanza ['tʃanθa] *nf* joke.
chao [tʃao] *excl* (*fam*) cheerio.
chapa ['tʃapa] *nf* (*de metal*) plate, sheet; (*de madera*) board, panel; (*de botella*) bottle top; (*insignia*) (lapel) badge; (*AM*: *AUTO*: ~ **de matrícula**) number (*BRIT*) *o* license (*US*) plate; (*AM cerradura*) lock; **de 3 ~s** (*madera*) 3-ply.
chapado, a [tʃa'paðo, a] *adj* (*metal*) plated; (*muebles etc*) finished.
chaparro, a [tʃa'parro, a] *adj* squat; (*AM*: *bajito*) short.
chaparrón [tʃapa'rron] *nm* downpour, cloudburst.
chapotear [tʃapote'ar] *vt* to sponge down ♦ *vi* (*fam*) to splash about.
chapucero, a [tʃapu'θero, a] *adj* rough, crude ♦ *nm/f* bungler.
chapurr(e)ar [tʃapurr(e)'ar] *vt* (*idioma*) to speak badly.
chapuza [tʃa'puθa] *nf* botched job.
chapuzón [tʃapu'θon] *nm*: **darse un ~** to go for a dip.
chaqué [tʃa'ke] *nm* morning coat.
chaqueta [tʃa'keta] *nf* jacket; **cambiar la ~** (*fig*) to change sides.
chaquetón [tʃake'ton] *nm* three-quarter-length coat.
charca ['tʃarka] *nf* pond, pool.
charco ['tʃarko] *nm* pool, puddle.
charcutería [tʃarkute'ria] *nf* (*tienda*) *shop selling chiefly pork meat products*; (*productos*) cooked pork meats *pl*.
charla ['tʃarla] *nf* talk, chat; (*conferencia*) lecture.
charlar [tʃar'lar] *vi* to talk, chat.
charlatán, ana [tʃarla'tan, ana] *nm/f* chatterbox; (*estafador*) trickster.
charol[1] [tʃa'rol] *nm* varnish; (*cuero*) patent leather.
charol[2] [tʃa'rol] *nm* (*AM*), **charola** [tʃa'rola] *nf* (*AM*) tray.
charqui ['tʃarki] *nm* (*AM*) dried beef, jerky (*US*).
charro, a ['tʃarro, a] *adj* Salamancan; (*AM*) Mexican; (*ropa*) loud, gaudy; (*AM*: *costumbres*) traditional ♦ *nm/f* Salamancan; Mexican.
chárter ['tʃarter] *adj inv*: **vuelo ~** charter flight.
chascarrillo [tʃaska'rriʎo] *nm* (*fam*) funny story.
chasco ['tʃasko] *nm* (*broma*) trick, joke; (*desengaño*) disappointment.
chasis ['tʃasis] *nm inv* (*AUTO*) chassis; (*FOTO*) plateholder.
chasquear [tʃaske'ar] *vt* (*látigo*) to crack; (*lengua*) to click.
chasquido [tʃas'kiðo] *nm* (*de lengua*) click; (*de látigo*) crack.
chatarra [tʃa'tarra] *nf* scrap (metal).
chato, a ['tʃato, a] *adj* flat; (*nariz*) snub ♦ *nm* wine tumbler; **beber unos ~s** to have a few drinks.
chau [tʃau], **chaucito** [tʃau'sito] *excl* (*fam*) cheerio.
chauvinismo [tʃoßi'nismo] *nm* chauvinism.
chauvinista [tʃoßi'nista] *adj, nm/f* chauvinist.
chaval, a [tʃa'ßal, a] *nm/f* kid (*fam*), lad/lass.
chavo ['tʃaßo] *nm* (*AM*: *fam*) bloke (*BRIT*), guy.
checo, a ['tʃeko, a] *adj, nm/f* Czech ♦ *nm* (*LING*) Czech.
checo(e)slovaco, a [tʃeko(e)slo'ßako, a] *adj, nm/f* Czech, Czechoslovak.
Checo(e)slovaquia [tʃeko(e)slo'ßakja] *nf* Czechoslovakia.
chepa ['tʃepa] *nf* hump.
cheque ['tʃeke] *nm* cheque (*BRIT*), check (*US*); ~ **abierto/en blanco/cruzado** open/blank/crossed cheque; ~ **al portador** cheque payable to bearer; ~ **caducado** stale cheque; ~ **de viajero** traveller's cheque.
chequeo [tʃe'keo] *nm* (*MED*) check-up; (*AUTO*) service.
chequera [tʃe'kera] *nf* (*AM*) chequebook (*BRIT*), checkbook (*US*).
chévere ['tʃeßere] *adj* (*AM*) great, fabulous (*fam*).
chicano, a [tʃi'kano, a] *adj, nm/f* chicano, Mexican-American.
chicha ['tʃitʃa] *nf* (*AM*) maize liquor.

chícharo ['tʃitʃaro] *nm* (*AM*) pea.
chicharra [tʃi'tʃarra] *nf* harvest bug, cicada.
chicharrón [tʃitʃa'rron] *nm* (pork) crackling.
chichón [tʃi'tʃon] *nm* bump, lump.
chicle ['tʃikle] *nm* chewing gum.
chico, a ['tʃiko, a] *adj* small, little ♦ *nm/f* child; (*muchacho*) boy; (*muchacha*) girl.
chicote [tʃi'kote] *nm* (*AM*) whip.
chiflado, a [tʃi'flaðo, a] *adj* (*fam*) crazy, round the bend ♦ *nm/f* nutcase.
chiflar [tʃi'flar] *vt* to hiss, boo ♦ *vi* (*esp AM*) to whistle.
Chile ['tʃile] *nm* Chile.
chile ['tʃile] *nm* chilli, pepper.
chileno, a [tʃi'leno, a] *adj, nm/f* Chilean.
chillar [tʃi'ʎar] *vi* (*persona*) to yell, scream; (*animal salvaje*) to howl; (*cerdo*) to squeal; (*puerta*) to creak.
chillido [tʃi'ʎiðo] *nm* (*de persona*) yell, scream; (*de animal*) howl; (*de frenos*) screech(ing).
chillón, ona [tʃi'ʎon, ona] *adj* (*niño*) noisy; (*color*) loud, gaudy.
chimenea [tʃime'nea] *nf* chimney; (*hogar*) fireplace.
chimpancé, *pl* **chimpancés** [tʃimpan'θe, tʃimpan'θes] *nm* chimpanzee.
China ['tʃina] *nf*: **(la)** ~ China.
china ['tʃina] *nf* pebble.
chinchar [tʃin'tʃar] (*fam*) *vt* to pester, annoy; ~**se** *vr* to get cross; **¡chínchate!** tough!
chinche ['tʃintʃe] *nf* bug; (*TEC*) drawing pin (*BRIT*), thumbtack (*US*) ♦ *nm/f* nuisance, pest.
chincheta [tʃin'tʃeta] *nf* drawing pin (*BRIT*), thumbtack (*US*).
chinchorro [tʃin'tʃorro] *nm* (*AM*) hammock.
chingado, a [tʃin'gaðo, a] *adj* (*esp AM fam!*) lousy, bloody (!); **hijo de la ~a** bastard (!), son of a bitch (*US!*).
chingar [tʃin'gar] *vt* (*AM: fam!*) to fuck (up) (*!*), screw (up) (*!*); ~**se** *vr* (*AM: emborracharse*) to get pissed (*BRIT*), get plastered; (*: fracasar*) to fail.
chingue ['tʃinge] *etc vb V* **chingar**.
chino, a ['tʃino, a] *adj, nm/f* Chinese ♦ *nm* (*LING*) Chinese; (*CULIN*) chinois, conical strainer.
chip [tʃip] *nm* (*INFORM*) chip.
chipirón [tʃipi'ron] *nm* squid.
Chipre ['tʃipre] *nf* Cyprus.
chipriota [tʃi'prjota], **chipriote** [tʃi'prjote] *adj* Cypriot, Cyprian ♦ *nm/f* Cypriot.
chiquillada [tʃiki'ʎada] *nf* childish prank; (*AM: chiquillos*) kids *pl*.
chiquillo, a [tʃi'kiʎo, a] *nm/f* kid (*fam*), youngster, child.
chiquito, a [tʃi'kito, a] *adj* very small, tiny ♦ *nm/f* kid (*fam*).
chirigota [tʃiri'ɣota] *nf* joke.
chirimbolo [tʃirim'bolo] *nm* thingummyjig (*fam*).
chirimoya [tʃiri'moja] *nf* custard apple.
chiringuito [tʃirin'gito] *nm* refreshment stall *o* stand.
chiripa [tʃi'ripa] *nf* fluke; **por** ~ by chance.
chirona [tʃi'rona], (*AM*) **chirola** [tʃi'rola] *nf* (*fam*) clink, jail.
chirriar [tʃi'rrjar] *vi* (*goznes*) to creak, squeak; (*pájaros*) to chirp, sing.
chirrido [tʃi'rriðo] *nm* creak(ing), squeak(ing); (*de pájaro*) chirp(ing).
chis [tʃis] *excl* sh!
chisme ['tʃisme] *nm* (*habladurías*) piece of gossip; (*fam: objeto*) thingummyjig.
chismoso, a [tʃis'moso, a] *adj* gossiping ♦ *nm/f* gossip.
chispa ['tʃispa] *nf* spark; (*fig*) sparkle; (*ingenio*) wit; (*fam*) drunkenness.
chispeante [tʃispe'ante] *adj* (*tb fig*) sparkling.
chispear [tʃispe'ar] *vi* to spark; (*lloviznar*) to drizzle.
chisporrotear [tʃisporrote'ar] *vi* (*fuego*) to throw out sparks; (*leña*) to crackle; (*aceite*) to hiss, splutter.
chistar [tʃistar] *vi*: **no** ~ not to say a word.
chiste ['tʃiste] *nm* joke, funny story; ~ **verde** blue joke.
chistera [tʃis'tera] *nf* top hat.
chistoso, a [tʃis'toso, a] *adj* (*gracioso*) funny, amusing; (*bromista*) witty.
chistu ['tʃistu] *nm* = **txistu**.
chivarse [tʃi'ßarse] *vr* (*fam*) to grass.
chivatazo [tʃißa'taθo] *nm* (*fam*) tip-off; **dar** ~ to inform.
chivo, a ['tʃißo, a] *nm/f* (billy/nanny-)goat; ~ **expiatorio** scapegoat.
chocante [tʃo'kante] *adj* startling; (*extraño*) odd; (*ofensivo*) shocking.
chocar [tʃo'kar] *vi* (*coches etc*) to collide, crash; (*MIL, fig*) to clash ♦ *vt* to shock; (*sorprender*) to startle; ~ **con** to collide with; (*fig*) to run into, run up against; **¡chócala!** (*fam*) put it there!
chochear [tʃotʃe'ar] *vi* to dodder, be senile.
chocho, a ['tʃotʃo, a] *adj* doddering, senile; (*fig*) soft, doting.
chocolate [tʃoko'late] *adj* chocolate ♦ *nm* chocolate; (*fam*) dope, marijuana.
chocolatería [tʃokolate'ria] *nf* chocolate

factory (*o* shop).
chófer ['tʃofer], **chofer** [tʃo'fer] (*esp AM*) *nm* driver.
chollo ['tʃoʎo] *nm* (*fam*) bargain, snip.
chomba ['tʃomba], **chompa** ['tʃompa] *nf* (*AM*) jumper, sweater.
chopo ['tʃopo] *nm* black poplar.
choque ['tʃoke] *etc vb V* **chocar** ♦ *nm* (*impacto*) impact; (*golpe*) jolt; (*AUTO*) crash; (*fig*) conflict.
chorizo [tʃo'riθo] *nm hard pork sausage,* (*type of*) salami; (*ladrón*) crook.
chorra ['tʃorra] *nf* luck.
chorrada [tʃo'rraða] *nf* (*fam*): **¡es una ~!** that's crap! (*!*); **decir ~s** to talk crap (*!*).
chorrear [tʃorre'ar] *vt* to pour ♦ *vi* to gush (out), spout (out); (*gotear*) to drip, trickle.
chorreras [tʃo'rreras] *nfpl* (*adorno*) frill *sg*.
chorro ['tʃorro] *nm* jet; (*caudalito*) dribble, trickle; (*fig*) stream; **salir a ~s** to gush forth; **con propulsión a ~** jet-propelled.
chotearse [tʃote'arse] *vr* to joke.
choto ['tʃoto] *nm* (*cabrito*) kid.
chovinismo [tʃoßi'nismo] *nm* = **chauvinismo**.
chovinista [tʃoßi'nista] *adj, nm/f* = **chauvinista**.
choza ['tʃoθa] *nf* hut, shack.
chubasco [tʃu'ßasko] *nm* squall.
chubasquero [tʃußas'kero] *nm* oilskins *pl*.
chuchería [tʃutʃe'ria] *nf* trinket.
chucho ['tʃutʃo] *nm* (*ZOOL*) mongrel.
chufa ['tʃufa] *nf* chufa, earth almond, tiger nut; **horchata de ~s** *drink made from chufas*.
chuleta [tʃu'leta] *nf* chop, cutlet; (*ESCOL etc*: *fam*) crib.
chulo, a ['tʃulo, a] *adj* (*encantador*) charming; (*aire*) proud; (*pey*) fresh; (*fam*: *estupendo*) great, fantastic ♦ *nm* (*pícaro*) rascal; (*madrileño*) working-class Madrilenian; (*rufián*: *tb*: **~ de putas**) pimp.
chumbera [tʃum'bera] *nf* prickly pear.
chungo, a ['tʃungo, a] (*fam*) *adj* lousy ♦ *nf*: **estar de chunga** to be in a merry mood.
chupa ['tʃupa] *nf* (*fam*) jacket.
chupado, a [tʃu'paðo, a] *adj* (*delgado*) skinny, gaunt; **está ~** (*fam*) it's simple, it's dead easy.
chupar [tʃu'par] *vt* to suck; (*absorber*) to absorb; **~se** *vr* to grow thin; **para ~se los dedos** mouthwatering.
chupatintas [tʃupa'tintas] *nm inv* penpusher.
chupe ['tʃupe] *nm* (*AM*) stew.
chupete [tʃu'pete] *nm* dummy (*BRIT*), pacifier (*US*).
chupetón [tʃupe'ton] *nm* suck.
churrasco [tʃu'rrasko] *nm* (*AM*) barbecue, barbecued meat.
churrería [tʃurre'ria] *nf stall or shop which sells "churros"*.
churrete [tʃu'rrete] *nm* grease spot.
churretón [tʃurre'ton] *nm* stain.
churrigueresco, a [tʃurrige'resko, a] *adj* (*ARQ*) baroque; (*fig*) excessively ornate.
churro, a ['tʃurro, a] *adj* coarse ♦ *nm* (*CULIN*) (type of) fritter; (*chapuza*) botch, mess; *see boxed note*.

CHURRO

Churros, *long golden fritters made from a flour and water batter, are very popular in much of Spain and are often eaten with very thick hot chocolate, either for breakfast or as a snack. The citizens of Madrid, eat a thicker variety of* **churro** *called "porra".*

churruscar [tʃurrus'kar] *vt* to fry crisp.
churrusque [tʃu'rruske] *etc vb V* **churruscar**.
churumbel [tʃurum'bel] *nm* (*fam*) kid.
chus [tʃus] *excl*: **no decir ni ~ ni mus** not to say a word.
chusco, a ['tʃusko, a] *adj* funny.
chusma ['tʃusma] *nf* rabble, mob.
chutar [tʃu'tar] *vi* (*DEPORTE*) to shoot (at goal); **esto va que chuta** it's going fine.
chuzo ['tʃuθo] *nm*: **llueve a ~s, llueven ~s de punta** it's raining cats and dogs.
C.I. *nm abr* = **coeficiente intelectual** *o* **de inteligencia**.
Cía *abr* (= *compañía*) Co.
cianuro [θja'nuro] *nm* cyanide.
ciática ['θjatika] *nf* sciatica.
cibercafé [θißerka'fe] *nm* cybercafe.
ciberespacio [θißereθ'paθjo] *nm* cyberspace.
cibernauta [θißer'nauta] *nmf* cybernaut.
cibernética [θißer'netika] *nf* cybernetics *sg*.
cicatrice [θika'triθe] *etc vb V* **cicatrizar**.
cicatriz [θika'triθ] *nf* scar.
cicatrizar [θikatri'θar] *vt* to heal; **~se** *vr* to heal (up), form a scar.
cíclico, a ['θikliko, a] *adj* cyclical.
ciclismo [θi'klismo] *nm* cycling.
ciclista [θi'klista] *nm/f* cyclist.
ciclo ['θiklo] *nm* cycle.
ciclomotor [θiklomo'tor] *nm* moped.
ciclón [θi'klon] *nm* cyclone.
cicloturismo [θiklotu'rismo] *nm* touring by bicycle.
cicuta [θi'kuta] *nf* hemlock.
ciego, a ['θjeɣo, a] *etc vb V* **cegar** ♦ *adj* blind ♦ *nm/f* blind man/woman; **a ciegas** blindly; **me puse ~ a mariscos** (*fam*) I stuffed myself with seafood.

ciegue ['θjeɣe] *etc vb V* **cegar**.
cielo ['θjelo] *nm* sky; (*REL*) heaven; (*ARQ*: *tb*: ~ **raso**) ceiling; ¡~**s**! good heavens!; **ver el ~ abierto** to see one's chance.
ciempiés [θjem'pjes] *nm inv* centipede.
cien [θjen] *num V* **ciento**.
ciénaga ['θjenaɣa] *nf* marsh, swamp.
ciencia ['θjenθja] *nf* science; ~**s** *nfpl* science *sg*; **saber algo a ~ cierta** to know sth for certain.
ciencia-ficción ['θjenθjafik'θjon] *nf* science fiction.
cieno ['θjeno] *nm* mud, mire.
científico, a [θjen'tifiko, a] *adj* scientific ♦ *nm/f* scientist.
ciento ['θjento], **cien** *num* hundred; **pagar al 10 por ciento** to pay at 10 per cent.
cierne ['θjerne] *etc vb V* **cerner** ♦ *nm*: **en ~** in blossom; **en ~(s)** (*fig*) in its infancy.
cierre ['θjerre] *etc vb V* **cerrar** ♦ *nm* closing, shutting; (*con llave*) locking; (*RADIO, TV*) close-down; ~ **de cremallera** zip (fastener); **precios de ~** (*BOLSA*) closing prices; ~ **del sistema** (*INFORM*) system shutdown.
cierto, a ['θjerto, a] *adj* sure, certain; (*un tal*) a certain; (*correcto*) right, correct; ~ **hombre** a certain man; **ciertas personas** certain *o* some people; **sí, es ~** yes, that's correct; **por ~** by the way; **lo ~ es que** ... the fact is that ...; **estar en lo ~** to be right.
ciervo ['θjerβo] *nm* (*ZOOL*) deer; (: *macho*) stag.
cierzo ['θjerθo] *nm* north wind.
CIES *nm abr* = *Consejo Interamericano Económico y Social*.
cifra ['θifra] *nf* number, figure; (*cantidad*) number, quantity; (*secreta*) code; ~ **global** lump sum; ~ **de negocios** (*COM*) turnover; **en ~s redondas** in round figures; ~ **de referencia** (*COM*) bench mark; ~ **de ventas** (*COM*) sales figures.
cifrado, a [θi'fraðo, a] *adj* in code.
cifrar [θi'frar] *vt* to code, write in code; (*resumir*) to abridge; (*calcular*) to reckon.
cigala [θi'ɣala] *nf* Norway lobster.
cigarra [θi'ɣarra] *nf* cicada.
cigarrera [θiɣa'rrera] *nf* cigar case.
cigarrillo [θiɣa'rriʎo] *nm* cigarette.
cigarro [θi'ɣarro] *nm* cigarette; (*puro*) cigar.
cigüeña [θi'ɣweɲa] *nf* stork.
cilíndrico, a [θi'lindriko, a] *adj* cylindrical.
cilindro [θi'lindro] *nm* cylinder.
cima ['θima] *nf* (*de montaña*) top, peak; (*de árbol*) top; (*fig*) height.
címbalo ['θimbalo] *nm* cymbal.
cimbrear [θimbre'ar] *vt* to brandish; ~**se** *vr* to sway.
cimentar [θimen'tar] *vt* to lay the foundations of; (*fig*: *reforzar*) to strengthen; (: *fundar*) to found.
cimiento [θi'mjento] *etc vb V* cimentar ♦ *nm* foundation.
cinc [θink] *nm* zinc.
cincel [θin'θel] *nm* chisel.
cincelar [θinθe'lar] *vt* to chisel.
cincha ['θintʃa] *nf* girth, saddle strap.
cincho ['θintʃo] *nm* sash, belt.
cinco ['θinko] *num* five; (*fecha*) fifth; **las ~** five o'clock; **no estar en sus ~** (*fam*) to be off one's rocker.
cincuenta [θin'kwenta] *num* fifty.
cincuentón, ona [θinkwen'ton, ona] *adj, nm/f* fifty-year-old.
cine ['θine] *nm* cinema; **el ~ mudo** silent films *pl*; **hacer ~** to make films.
cineasta [θine'asta] *nm/f* (*director de cine*) film-maker *o* director.
cine-club ['θine'klub] *nm* film club.
cinéfilo, a [θi'nefilo, a] *nm/f* film buff.
cinematográfico, a [θinemato'ɣrafiko, a] *adj* cine-, film *cpd*.
cínico, a ['θiniko, a] *adj* cynical; (*descarado*) shameless ♦ *nm/f* cynic.
cinismo [θi'nismo] *nm* cynicism.
cinta ['θinta] *nf* band, strip; (*de tela*) ribbon; (*película*) reel; (*de máquina de escribir*) ribbon; (*métrica*) tape measure; (*magnetofónica*) tape; ~ **adhesiva** sticky tape; ~ **aislante** insulating tape; ~ **de carbón** carbon ribbon; ~ **magnética** (*INFORM*) magnetic tape; ~ **métrica** tape measure; ~ **de múltiples impactos** (*en impresora*) multistrike ribbon; ~ **de tela** (*para máquina de escribir*) fabric ribbon; ~ **transportadora** conveyor belt.
cinto ['θinto] *nm* belt, girdle.
cintura [θin'tura] *nf* waist; (*medida*) waistline.
cinturón [θintu'ron] *nm* belt; (*fig*) belt, zone; ~ **salvavidas** lifebelt; ~ **de seguridad** safety belt.
ciña ['θiɲa] *etc*, **ciñendo** [θi'ɲendo] *etc vb V* **ceñir**.
CIP [θip] *nm abr* = *Club Internacional de Prensa* (*Madrid*).
ciprés [θi'pres] *nm* cypress (tree).
circo ['θirko] *nm* circus.
circuito [θir'kwito] *nm* circuit; (*DEPORTE*) lap; **TV por ~ cerrado** closed-circuit TV; ~ **experimental** (*INFORM*) breadboard; ~ **impreso** printed circuit; ~ **lógico** (*INFORM*) logical circuit.
circulación [θirkula'θjon] *nf* circulation;

(*AUTO*) traffic; **"cerrado a la ~ rodada"** "closed to vehicles".
circular [θirku'lar] *adj, nf* circular ♦ *vt* to circulate ♦ *vi* to circulate; (*dinero*) to be in circulation; (*AUTO*) to drive; (*autobús*) to run.
círculo ['θirkulo] *nm* circle; (*centro*) clubhouse; (*POL*) political group.
circuncidar [θirkunθi'dar] *vt* to circumcise.
circunciso, a [θrikun'θiso, a] *pp de* **circuncidar**.
circundante [θirkun'dante] *adj* surrounding.
circundar [θirkun'dar] *vt* to surround.
circunferencia [θirkunfe'renθja] *nf* circumference.
circunloquio [θirkun'lokjo] *nm* circumlocution.
circunscribir [θirkunskri'ßir] *vt* to circumscribe; **~se** *vr* to be limited.
circunscripción [θirkunskrip'θjon] *nf* division; (*POL*) constituency.
circunscrito [θirkuns'krito] *pp de* **circunscribir**.
circunspección [θirkunspek'θjon] *nf* circumspection, caution.
circunspecto, a [θirkuns'pekto, a] *adj* circumspect, cautious.
circunstancia [θirkuns'tanθja] *nf* circumstance; **~s agravantes/extenuantes** aggravating/extenuating circumstances; **estar a la altura de las ~s** to rise to the occasion.
circunvalación [θirkumbala'θjon] *nf*: **carretera de ~** ring road.
cirio ['θirjo] *nm* (wax) candle.
cirrosis [θi'rrosis] *nf* cirrhosis (of the liver).
ciruela [θi'rwela] *nf* plum; **~ pasa** prune.
ciruelo [θi'rwelo] *nm* plum tree.
cirugía [θiru'xia] *nf* surgery; **~ estética** *o* **plástica** plastic surgery.
cirujano [θiru'xano] *nm* surgeon.
cisco ['θisko] *nm*: **armar un ~** to kick up a row; **estar hecho ~** to be a wreck.
cisma ['θisma] *nm* schism; (*POL etc*) split.
cisne ['θisne] *nm* swan; **canto de ~** swan song.
cisterna [θis'terna] *nf* cistern, tank.
cistitis [θis'titis] *nf* cystitis.
cita ['θita] *nf* appointment, meeting; (*de novios*) date; (*referencia*) quotation; **acudir/faltar a una ~** to turn up for/miss an appointment.
citación [θita'θjon] *nf* (*JUR*) summons *sg*.
citadino, a [sita'ðino, a] (*AM*) *adj* urban ♦ *nm/f* urban *o* city dweller.
citar [θi'tar] *vt* to make an appointment with, arrange to meet; (*JUR*) to summons; (*un autor, texto*) to quote; **~se** *vr*: **~se con algn** to arrange to meet sb; **se citaron en el cine** they arranged to meet at the cinema.
cítara ['θitara] *nf* zither.
citología [θitolo'xia] *nf* smear test.
cítrico, a ['θitriko, a] *adj* citric ♦ *nm*: **~s** citrus fruits.
CiU *nm abr* (*POL*) = *Convergència i Unió*.
ciudad [θju'ðað] *nf* town; (*capital de país etc*) city; **~ universitaria** university campus; **C~ del Cabo** Cape Town; **la C~ Condal** Barcelona.
ciudadanía [θjuðaða'nia] *nf* citizenship.
ciudadano, a [θjuða'ðano, a] *adj* civic ♦ *nm/f* citizen.
ciudadrealeño, a [θjuðaðrea'leɲo, a] *adj* of *o* from Ciudad Real ♦ *nm/f* native *o* inhabitant of Ciudad Real.
cívico, a ['θißiko, a] *adj* civic; (*fig*) public-spirited.
civil [θi'ßil] *adj* civil ♦ *nm* (*guardia*) policeman.
civilice [θißi'liθe] *etc vb V* **civilizar**.
civilización [θißiliθa'θjon] *nf* civilization.
civilizar [θißili'θar] *vt* to civilize.
civismo [θi'ßismo] *nm* public spirit.
cizaña [θi'θaɲa] *nf* (*fig*) discord; **sembrar ~** to sow discord.
cl. *abr* (= *centilitro*) cl.
clamar [kla'mar] *vt* to clamour for, cry out for ♦ *vi* to cry out, clamour.
clamor [kla'mor] *nm* (*grito*) cry, shout; (*fig*) clamour, protest.
clamoroso, a [klamo'roso, a] *adj* (*éxito etc*) resounding.
clan ['klan] *nm* clan; (*de gángsters*) gang.
clandestinidad [klandestini'ðað] *nf* secrecy.
clandestino, a [klandes'tino, a] *adj* clandestine; (*POL*) underground.
clara ['klara] *nf* (*de huevo*) eggwhite.
claraboya [klara'ßoja] *nf* skylight.
clarear [klare'ar] *vi* (*el día*) to dawn; (*el cielo*) to clear up, brighten up; **~se** *vr* to be transparent.
clarete [kla'rete] *nm* rosé (wine).
claridad [klari'ðað] *nf* (*del día*) brightness; (*de estilo*) clarity.
clarificar [klarifi'kar] *vt* to clarify.
clarifique [klari'fike] *etc vb V* **clarificar**.
clarín [kla'rin] *nm* bugle.
clarinete [klari'nete] *nm* clarinet.
clarividencia [klarißi'ðenθja] *nf* clairvoyance; (*fig*) far-sightedness.
claro, a ['klaro, a] *adj* clear; (*luminoso*) bright; (*color*) light; (*evidente*) clear,

evident; (*poco espeso*) thin ♦ *nm* (*en bosque*) clearing ♦ *adv* clearly ♦ *excl* of course!; **hablar** ~ (*fig*) to speak plainly; **a las claras** openly; **no sacamos nada en** ~ we couldn't get anything definite.

clase ['klase] *nf* class; (*tipo*) kind, sort; (*ESCOL etc*) class; (: *aula*) classroom; ~ **alta/media/obrera** upper/middle/ working class; **dar ~s** to teach.

clásico, a ['klasiko, a] *adj* classical; (*fig*) classic.

clasificable [klasifi'kaβle] *adj* classifiable.

clasificación [klasifika'θjon] *nf* classification; (*DEPORTE*) league (table); (*COM*) ratings *pl*.

clasificador [klasifika'ðor] *nm* filing cabinet.

clasificar [klasifi'kar] *vt* to classify; (*INFORM*) to sort; **~se** *vr* (*DEPORTE*: *torneo*) to qualify.

clasifique [klasi'fike] *etc vb V* **clasificar**.

clasista [kla'sista] *adj* (*fam*: *actitud*) snobbish.

claudia ['klauðja] *nf* greengage.

claudicar [klauði'kar] *vi* (*fig*) to back down.

claudique [klau'ðike] *etc vb V* **claudicar**.

claustro ['klaustro] *nm* cloister; (*UNIV*) staff; (*junta*) senate.

claustrofobia [klaustro'foβja] *nf* claustrophobia.

cláusula ['klausula] *nf* clause; ~ **de exclusión** (*COM*) exclusion clause.

clausura [klau'sura] *nf* closing, closure.

clausurar [klausu'rar] *vt* (*congreso etc*) to close, bring to a close; (*POL etc*) to adjourn; (*cerrar*) to close (down).

clavado, a [kla'βaðo, a] *adj* nailed ♦ *excl* exactly!, precisely!

clavar [kla'βar] *vt* (*tablas etc*) to nail (together); (*con alfiler*) to pin; (*clavo*) to hammer in; (*cuchillo*) to stick, thrust; (*mirada*) to fix; (*fam*: *estafar*) to cheat.

clave ['klaβe] *nf* key; (*MUS*) clef ♦ *adj inv* key *cpd*; ~ **de búsqueda** (*INFORM*) search key; ~ **de clasificación** (*INFORM*) sort key.

clavel [kla'βel] *nm* carnation.

clavicémbalo [klaβi'θembalo] *nm* harpsichord.

clavicordio [klaβikor'ðjo] *nm* clavicord.

clavícula [kla'βikula] *nf* collar bone.

clavija [kla'βixa] *nf* peg, pin; (*MUS*) peg; (*ELEC*) plug.

clavo ['klaβo] *nm* (*de metal*) nail; (*BOT*) clove; **dar en el** ~ (*fig*) to hit the nail on the head.

claxon ['klakson], *pl* **claxons** *nm* horn; **tocar el** ~ to sound one's horn.

clemencia [kle'menθja] *nf* mercy, clemency.

clemente [kle'mente] *adj* merciful, clement.

cleptómano, a [klep'tomano, a] *nm/f* kleptomaniac.

clerical [kleri'kal] *adj* clerical.

clérigo ['kleriɣo] *nm* priest, clergyman.

clero ['klero] *nm* clergy.

clic [klik] *nm* click; **hacer ~/doble ~ en algo** to click/double-click on sth.

cliché [kli'tʃe] *nm* cliché; (*TIP*) stencil; (*FOTO*) negative.

cliente, a ['kljente, a] *nm/f* client, customer.

clientela [kljen'tela] *nf* clientele, customers *pl*; (*COM*) goodwill; (*MED*) patients *pl*.

clima ['klima] *nm* climate.

climatizado, a [klimati'θaðo, a] *adj* air-conditioned.

clímax ['klimaks] *nm inv* climax.

clínico, a ['kliniko, a] *adj* clinical ♦ *nf* clinic; (*particular*) private hospital.

clip, *pl* **clips** [klip, klis] *nm* paper clip.

clítoris ['klitoris] *nm inv* clitoris.

cloaca [klo'aka] *nf* sewer, drain.

clonación [klona'θjon] *nf* cloning.

clorhídrico, a [klo'ridriko, a] *adj* hydrochloric.

cloro ['kloro] *nm* chlorine.

clorofila [kloro'fila] *nf* chlorophyl(l).

cloroformo [kloro'formo] *nm* chloroform.

cloruro [klo'ruro] *nm* chloride; ~ **sódico** sodium chloride.

club, *pl* **clubs** *o* **clubes** [klub, klus, 'kluβes] *nm* club; ~ **de jóvenes** youth club.

cm *abr* (= *centímetro*) cm.

C.N.T. *nf abr* (*ESP*: *Confederación Nacional de Trabajo*) *Anarchist Union Confederation*; (*AM*) = *Confederación Nacional de Trabajadores*.

coacción [koak'θjon] *nf* coercion, compulsion.

coaccionar [koakθjo'nar] *vt* to coerce, compel.

coagular [koaɣu'lar] *vt*, **~se** *vr* (*sangre*) to clot; (*leche*) to curdle.

coágulo [ko'aɣulo] *nm* clot.

coalición [koali'θjon] *nf* coalition.

coartada [koar'taða] *nf* alibi.

coartar [koar'tar] *vt* to limit, restrict.

coba ['koβa] *nf*: **dar ~ a algn** to soft-soap sb.

cobarde [ko'βarðe] *adj* cowardly ♦ *nm/f* coward.

cobardía [koβar'ðia] *nf* cowardice.

cobaya [ko'βaja] *nf* guinea pig.

cobertizo [koβer'tiθo] *nm* shelter.

cobertor [koβer'tor] *nm* bedspread.

cobertura [koβer'tura] *nf* cover; (*COM*)

coverage; ~ **de dividendo** (*COM*) dividend cover.
cobija [ko'ßixa] *nf* (*AM*) blanket.
cobijar [koßi'xar] *vt* (*cubrir*) to cover; (*abrigar*) to shelter; ~**se** *vr* to take shelter.
cobijo [ko'ßixo] *nm* shelter.
cobra ['koßra] *nf* cobra.
cobrador, a [koßra'ðor, a] *nm/f* (*de autobús*) conductor/conductress; (*de impuestos, gas*) collector.
cobrar [ko'ßrar] *vt* (*cheque*) to cash; (*sueldo*) to collect, draw; (*objeto*) to recover; (*precio*) to charge; (*deuda*) to collect ♦ *vi* to draw one's pay; ~**se** *vr* to recover, get on well; **cóbrese al entregar** cash on delivery (COD) (*BRIT*), collect on delivery (COD) (*US*); **a** ~ (*COM*) receivable; **cantidades por** ~ sums due.
cobre ['koßre] *nm* copper; (*AM fam*) cent; ~**s** *nmpl* brass instruments.
cobrizo, a [ko'ßriθo, a] *adj* coppery.
cobro ['koßro] *nm* (*de cheque*) cashing; (*pago*) payment; **presentar al** ~ to cash; *V tb* **llamada**.
coca ['koka] *nf* coca; (*droga*) coke.
Coca-Cola ® ['koka'kola] *nf* Coca-Cola ®.
cocaína [koka'ina] *nf* cocaine.
cocainómano, a [kokai'nomano, a] *nm/f* cocaine addict.
cocción [kok'θjon] *nf* (*CULIN*) cooking; (*el hervir*) boiling.
cocear [koθe'ar] *vi* to kick.
cocer [ko'θer] *vt, vi* to cook; (*en agua*) to boil; (*en horno*) to bake.
coche ['kotʃe] *nm* (*AUTO*) car, automobile (*US*); (*de tren, de caballos*) coach, carriage; (*para niños*) pram (*BRIT*), baby carriage (*US*); ~ **de bomberos** fire engine; ~ **celular** Black Maria, prison van; ~ **(comedor)** (*FERRO*) (dining) car; ~ **fúnebre** hearse.
coche-bomba ['kotʃe'ßomba], *pl* **coches-bomba** *nm* car bomb.
coche-cama ['kotʃe'kama], *pl* **coches-cama** *nm* (*FERRO*) sleeping car, sleeper.
cochera [ko'tʃera] *nf* garage; (*de autobuses, trenes*) depot.
coche-restaurante, *pl* **coches-restaurante** ['kotʃerestau'rante] *nm* (*FERRO*) dining-car, diner.
cochinada [kotʃi'naða] *nf* dirty trick.
cochinillo [kotʃi'niʎo] *nm* piglet, suckling pig.
cochino, a [ko'tʃino, a] *adj* filthy, dirty ♦ *nm/f* pig.
cocido, a [ko'θiðo, a] *adj* boiled; (*fam*) plastered ♦ *nm* stew.
cociente [ko'θjente] *nm* quotient.
cocina [ko'θina] *nf* kitchen; (*aparato*) cooker, stove; (*acto*) cookery; ~ **casera** home cooking; ~ **eléctrica** electric cooker; ~ **francesa** French cuisine; ~ **de gas** gas cooker.
cocinar [koθi'nar] *vt, vi* to cook.
cocinero, a [koθi'nero, a] *nm/f* cook.
coco ['koko] *nm* coconut; (*fantasma*) bogeyman; (*fam: cabeza*) nut; **comer el** ~ **a algn** (*fam*) to brainwash sb.
cocodrilo [koko'ðrilo] *nm* crocodile.
cocotero [koko'tero] *nm* coconut palm.
cóctel ['koktel] *nm* (*bebida*) cocktail; (*reunión*) cocktail party; ~ **Molotov** Molotov cocktail, petrol bomb.
coctelera [kokte'lera] *nf* cocktail shaker.
cod. *abr* (= *código*) code.
codazo [ko'ðaθo] *nm*: **dar un** ~ **a algn** to nudge sb.
codear [koðe'ar] *vi* to elbow, jostle; ~**se** *vr*: ~**se con** to rub shoulders with.
códice ['koðiθe] *nm* manuscript, codex.
codicia [ko'ðiθja] *nf* greed; (*fig*) lust.
codiciar [koði'θjar] *vt* to covet.
codicioso, a [koði'θjoso, a] *adj* covetous.
codificador [koðifika'ðor] *nm* (*INFORM*) encoder; ~ **digital** digitizer.
codificar [koðifi'kar] *vt* (*mensaje*) to (en)code; (*leyes*) to codify.
código ['koðiɣo] *nm* code; ~ **de barras** (*COM*) bar code; ~ **binario** binary code; ~ **de caracteres** (*INFORM*) character code; ~ **de (la) circulación** highway code; ~ **civil** common law; ~ **de control** (*INFORM*) control code; ~ **máquina** (*INFORM*) machine code; ~ **militar** military law; ~ **de operación** (*INFORM*) operational *o* machine code; ~ **penal** penal code; ~ **de práctica** code of practice.
codillo [ko'ðiʎo] *nm* (*ZOOL*) knee; (*TEC*) elbow (joint).
codo ['koðo] *nm* (*ANAT, de tubo*) elbow; (*ZOOL*) knee; **hablar por los** ~**s** to talk nineteen to the dozen.
codorniz [koðor'niθ] *nf* quail.
coeficiente [koefi'θjente] *nm* (*MAT*) coefficient; (*ECON etc*) rate; ~ **intelectual** *o* **de inteligencia** I.Q.
coerción [koer'θjon] *nf* coercion.
coercitivo, a [koerθi'tißo, a] *adj* coercive.
coetáneo, a [koe'taneo, a] *nm/f*: ~**s** contemporaries.
coexistencia [koeksis'tenθja] *nf* coexistence.
coexistir [koeksis'tir] *vi* to coexist.
cofia ['kofja] *nf* (*de enfermera*) (white) cap.

cofradía [kofra'ðia] *nf* brotherhood, fraternity; *V tb* **Semana Santa**.
cofre ['kofre] *nm* (*baúl*) trunk; (*de joyas*) box; (*AM AUTO*) bonnet (*BRIT*), hood (*US*).
cogedor [koxe'ðor] *nm* dustpan.
coger [ko'xer] *vt* (*ESP*) to take (hold of); (*objeto caído*) to pick up; (*frutas*) to pick, harvest; (*resfriado, ladrón, pelota*) to catch; (*AM fam!*) to lay (*!*) ♦ *vi*: ~ **por el buen camino** to take the right road; ~**se** *vr* (*el dedo*) to catch; ~ **a algn desprevenido** to take sb unawares; ~**se a algo** to get hold of sth.
cogida [ko'xiða] *nf* gathering, harvesting; (*de peces*) catch; (*TAUR*) goring.
cogollo [ko'ɣoʎo] *nm* (*de lechuga*) heart; (*fig*) core, nucleus.
cogorza [ko'ɣorθa] *nf* (*fam*): **agarrar una** ~ to get smashed.
cogote [ko'ɣote] *nm* back of the neck.
cohabitar [koaßi'tar] *vi* to live together, cohabit.
cohecho [ko'etʃo] *nm* (*acción*) bribery; (*soborno*) bribe.
coherencia [koe'renθja] *nf* coherence.
coherente [koe'rente] *adj* coherent.
cohesión [koe'sjon] *nm* cohesion.
cohete [ko'ete] *nm* rocket.
cohibido, a [koi'ßiðo, a] *adj* (*PSICO*) inhibited; (*tímido*) shy; **sentirse** ~ to feel embarrassed.
cohibir [koi'ßir] *vt* to restrain, restrict; ~**se** *vr* to feel inhibited.
COI *nm abr* (= *Comité Olímpico Internacional*) IOC.
coima ['koima] *nf* (*AM fam*) bribe.
coincidencia [koinθi'ðenθja] *nf* coincidence.
coincidir [koinθi'ðir] *vi* (*en idea*) to coincide, agree; (*en lugar*) to coincide.
coito ['koito] *nm* intercourse, coitus.
cojear [koxe'ar] *vi* (*persona*) to limp, hobble; (*mueble*) to wobble, rock.
cojera [ko'xera] *nf* lameness; (*andar cojo*) limp.
cojín [ko'xin] *nm* cushion.
cojinete [koxi'nete] *nm* small cushion, pad; (*TEC*) (ball) bearing.
cojo, a ['koxo, a] *etc vb V* **coger** ♦ *adj* (*que no puede andar*) lame, crippled; (*mueble*) wobbly ♦ *nm/f* lame person, cripple.
cojón [ko'xon] *nm* (*fam!*) ball (*!*), testicle; **¡cojones!** shit! (*!*).
cojonudo, a [koxo'nuðo, a] *adj* (*ESP fam*) great, fantastic.
col [kol] *nf* cabbage; ~**es de Bruselas** Brussels sprouts.
col., col.ª *abr* (= *columna*) col.
cola ['kola] *nf* tail; (*de gente*) queue; (*lugar*) end, last place; (*para pegar*) glue, gum; (*de vestido*) train; **hacer** ~ to queue (up).
colaboración [kolaßora'θjon] *nf* collaboration; (*en periódico*) contribution.
colaborador, a [kolaßora'ðor, a] *nm/f* collaborator; contributor.
colaborar [kolaßo'rar] *vi* to collaborate.
colación [kola'θjon] *nf*: **sacar a** ~ to bring up.
colado, a [ko'laðo, a] *adj* (*metal*) cast ♦ *nf*: **hacer la colada** to do the washing.
colador [kola'ðor] *nm* (*de té*) strainer; (*para verduras etc*) colander.
colapsar [kolap'sar] *vt* (*tráfico etc*) to bring to a standstill.
colapso [ko'lapso] *nm* collapse; ~ **nervioso** nervous breakdown.
colar [ko'lar] *vt* (*líquido*) to strain off; (*metal*) to cast ♦ *vi* to ooze, seep (through); ~**se** *vr* to jump the queue; (*en mitin*) to sneak in; (*equivocarse*) to slip up; ~**se en** to get into without paying; (*en una fiesta*) to gatecrash.
colateral [kolate'ral] *nm* collateral.
colcha ['koltʃa] *nf* bedspread.
colchón [kol'tʃon] *nm* mattress; ~ **inflable** inflatable mattress.
colchoneta [koltʃo'neta] *nf* (*en gimnasio*) mattress; ~ **hinchable** airbed.
colear [kole'ar] *vi* (*perro*) to wag its tail.
colección [kolek'θjon] *nf* collection.
coleccionar [kolekθjo'nar] *vt* to collect.
coleccionista [kolekθjo'nista] *nm/f* collector.
colecta [ko'lekta] *nf* collection.
colectivo, a [kolek'tißo, a] *adj* collective, joint ♦ *nm* (*AM*: *autobús*) (small) bus; (: *taxi*) collective taxi.
colector [kolek'tor] *nm* collector; (*sumidero*) sewer.
colega [ko'leɣa] *nm/f* colleague.
colegiado, a [kole'xjaðo, a] *adj* (*profesional*) registered ♦ *nm/f* referee.
colegial, a [kole'xjal, a] *adj* (*ESCOL etc*) school *cpd*, college *cpd* ♦ *nm/f* schoolboy/girl.
colegio [ko'lexjo] *nm* college; (*escuela*) school; (*de abogados etc*) association; ~ **de internos** boarding school; **ir al** ~ to go to school; *see boxed note*.

COLEGIO

A **colegio** *is normally a private school, either primary or secondary. Within the state system, however, the word indicates primary school, although these are also referred to as "escuelas". State secondary* *schools are called "institutos". Extracurricular subjects, such as computing or foreign languages, are taught in private schools called "academias".*

colegir [kole'xir] *vt* (*juntar*) to collect, gather; (*deducir*) to infer, conclude.
cólera ['kolera] *nf* (*ira*) anger; **montar en ~** to get angry ♦ *nm* (*MED*) cholera.
colérico, a [ko'leriko, a] *adj* angry, furious.
colesterol [koleste'rol] *nm* cholesterol.
coleta [ko'leta] *nf* pigtail.
coletazo [kole'taθo] *nm*: **dar un ~** (*animal*) to flap its tail; **los últimos ~s** death throes.
coletilla [kole'tiʎa] *nf* (*en carta*) postscript; (*en conversación*) filler phrase.
colgado, a [kol'ɣaðo, a] *pp de* **colgar** ♦ *adj* hanging; (*ahorcado*) hanged; **dejar ~ a algn** to let sb down.
colgajo [kol'ɣaxo] *nm* tatter.
colgante [kol'ɣante] *adj* hanging; *V* **puente** ♦ *nm* (*joya*) pendant.
colgar [kol'ɣar] *vt* to hang (up); (*tender: ropa*) to hang out ♦ *vi* to hang; (*teléfono*) to hang up.
colgué [kol'ɣe], **colguemos** [kol'ɣemos] *etc vb V* **colgar**.
colibrí [koli'ßri] *nm* hummingbird.
cólico ['koliko] *nm* colic.
coliflor [koli'flor] *nf* cauliflower.
coligiendo [koli'xjenðo] *etc vb V* **colegir**.
colija [ko'lixa] *etc vb V* **colegir**.
colilla [ko'liʎa] *nf* cigarette end, butt.
colina [ko'lina] *nf* hill.
colindante [kolin'dante] *adj* adjacent, neighbouring.
colindar [kolin'dar] *vi* to adjoin, be adjacent.
colisión [koli'sjon] *nf* collision; **~ de frente** head-on crash.
colitis [ko'litis] *nf inv*: **tener ~** to have diarrhoea.
collar [ko'ʎar] *nm* necklace; (*de perro*) collar.
colmado, a [kol'maðo, a] *adj* full ♦ *nm* grocer's (shop) (*BRIT*), grocery store (*US*).
colmar [kol'mar] *vt* to fill to the brim; (*fig*) to fulfil, realize.
colmena [kol'mena] *nf* beehive.
colmillo [kol'miʎo] *nm* (*diente*) eye tooth; (*de elefante*) tusk; (*de perro*) fang.
colmo ['kolmo] *nm* height, summit; **para ~ de desgracias** to cap it all; **¡eso es ya el ~!** that's beyond a joke!
colocación [koloka'θjon] *nf* (*acto*) placing; (*empleo*) job, position; (*situación*) place, position; (*COM*) placement.
colocar [kolo'kar] *vt* to place, put, position; (*poner en empleo*) to find a job for; **~ dinero** to invest money; **~se** *vr* to place o.s.; (*conseguir trabajo*) to find a job.
colofón [kolo'fon] *nm*: **como ~ de las conversaciones** as a sequel to *o* following the talks.
Colombia [ko'lombja] *nf* Colombia.
colombiano, a [kolom'bjano, a] *adj, nm/f* Colombian.
colon ['kolon] *nm* colon.
colón [ko'lon] *nm* (*AM*) *monetary unit of Costa Rica and El Salvador*.
Colonia [ko'lonja] *nf* Cologne.
colonia [ko'lonja] *nf* colony; (*de casas*) housing estate; (*agua de ~*) cologne; **~ escolar** summer camp (for schoolchildren).
colonice [kolo'niθe] *etc vb V* **colonizar**.
colonización [koloniθa'θjon] *nf* colonization.
colonizador, a [koloniθa'ðor, a] *adj* colonizing ♦ *nm/f* colonist, settler.
colonizar [koloni'θar] *vt* to colonize.
colono [ko'lono] *nm* (*POL*) colonist, settler; (*AGR*) tenant farmer.
coloque [ko'loke] *etc vb V* **colocar**.
coloquial [kolo'kjal] *adj* colloquial.
coloquio [ko'lokjo] *nm* conversation; (*congreso*) conference; (*INFORM*) handshake.
color [ko'lor] *nm* colour; **a todo ~** in full colour; **verlo todo ~ de rosa** to see everything through rose-coloured spectacles; **le salieron los ~es** she blushed.
colorado, a [kolo'raðo, a] *adj* (*rojo*) red; (*AM: chiste*) rude, blue; **ponerse ~** to blush.
colorante [kolo'rante] *nm* colouring (matter).
colorar [kolo'rar] *vt* to colour; (*teñir*) to dye.
colorear [kolore'ar] *vt* to colour.
colorete [kolo'rete] *nm* blusher.
colorido [kolo'riðo] *nm* colour(ing).
coloso [ko'loso] *nm* colossus.
columbrar [kolum'brar] *vt* to glimpse, spy.
columna [ko'lumna] *nf* column; (*pilar*) pillar; (*apoyo*) support; **~ blindada** (*MIL*) armoured column; **~ vertebral** spine, spinal column.
columpiar [kolum'pjar] *vt*, **~se** *vr* to swing.
columpio [ko'lumpjo] *nm* swing.
colza ['kolθa] *nf* rape; **aceite de ~** rapeseed oil.
coma ['koma] *nf* comma ♦ *nm* (*MED*) coma.

comadre [ko'maðre] *nf* (*madrina*) godmother; (*vecina*) neighbour; (*chismosa*) gossip.
comadrear [komaðre'ar] *vi* (*esp AM*) to gossip.
comadreja [koma'ðrexa] *nf* weasel.
comadrona [koma'ðrona] *nf* midwife.
comandancia [koman'danθja] *nf* command.
comandante [koman'dante] *nm* commandant; (*grado*) major.
comandar [koman'dar] *vt* to command.
comando [ko'mando] *nm* (*MIL*: *mando*) command; (: *grupo*) commando unit; (*INFORM*) command; ~ **de búsqueda** search command.
comarca [ko'marka] *nf* region; *V tb* **provincia**.
comarcal [komar'kal] *adj* local.
comba ['komba] *nf* (*curva*) curve; (*en viga*) warp; (*cuerda*) skipping rope; **saltar a la ~** to skip.
combar [kom'bar] *vt* to bend, curve.
combate [kom'bate] *nm* fight; (*fig*) battle; **fuera de ~** out of action.
combatiente [komba'tjente] *nm* combatant.
combatir [komba'tir] *vt* to fight, combat.
combatividad [kombatiβi'ðað] *nf* (*actitud*) fighting spirit; (*agresividad*) aggressiveness.
combativo, a [komba'tiβo, a] *adj* full of fight.
combi ['kombi] *nm* fridge-freezer.
combinación [kombina'θjon] *nf* combination; (*QUÍMICA*) compound; (*bebida*) cocktail; (*plan*) scheme, setup; (*prenda*) slip.
combinado, a [kombi'naðo, a] *adj*: **plato ~** *main course served with vegetables.*
combinar [kombi'nar] *vt* to combine; (*colores*) to match.
combustible [kombus'tiβle] *nm* fuel.
combustión [kombus'tjon] *nf* combustion.
comedia [ko'meðja] *nf* comedy; (*TEAT*) play, drama; (*fig*) farce.
comediante [kome'ðjante] *nm/f* (comic) actor/actress.
comedido, a [kome'ðiðo, a] *adj* moderate.
comedirse [kome'ðirse] *vr* to behave moderately; (*ser cortés*) to be courteous.
comedor, a [kome'ðor, a] *nm/f* (*persona*) glutton ♦ *nm* (*habitación*) dining room; (*restaurante*) restaurant; (*cantina*) canteen.
comencé [komen'θe], **comencemos** [komen'θemos] *etc vb V* **comenzar**.
comensal [komen'sal] *nm/f* fellow guest/diner.
comentar [komen'tar] *vt* to comment on; (*fam*) to discuss; **comentó que...** he made the comment that....
comentario [komen'tarjo] *nm* comment, remark; (*LIT*) commentary; **~s** *nmpl* gossip *sg*; **dar lugar a ~s** to cause gossip.
comentarista [komenta'rista] *nm/f* commentator.
comenzar [komen'θar] *vt, vi* to begin, start, commence; ~ **a hacer algo** to begin *o* start doing *o* to do sth.
comer [ko'mer] *vt* to eat; (*DAMAS, AJEDREZ*) to take, capture; (*párrafo etc*) to skip ♦ *vi* to eat; (*almorzar*) to have lunch; **~se** *vr* to eat up; ~ **el coco a** (*fam*) to brainwash; **¡a ~!** food's ready!
comercial [komer'θjal] *adj* commercial; (*relativo al negocio*) business *cpd*.
comerciante [komer'θjante] *nm/f* trader, merchant; (*tendero*) shopkeeper; ~ **exclusivo** (*COM*) sole trader.
comerciar [komer'θjar] *vi* to trade, do business.
comercio [ko'merθjo] *nm* commerce, trade; (*negocio*) business; (*grandes empresas*) big business; (*fig*) dealings *pl*; ~ **autorizado** (*COM*) licensed trade; ~ **electrónico** e-commerce; ~ **exterior** foreign trade.
comestible [komes'tiβle] *adj* eatable, edible ♦ *nm*: **~s** food *sg*, foodstuffs; (*COM*) groceries.
cometa [ko'meta] *nm* comet ♦ *nf* kite.
cometer [kome'ter] *vt* to commit.
cometido [kome'tiðo] *nm* (*misión*) task, assignment; (*deber*) commitment.
comezón [kome'θon] *nf* itch, itching.
cómic, *pl* **cómics** ['komik, 'komiks] *nm* comic.
comicios [ko'miθjos] *nmpl* elections; (*voto*) voting *sg*.
cómico, a ['komiko, a] *adj* comic(al) ♦ *nm/f* comedian; (*de teatro*) (comic) actor/actress.
comida [ko'miða] *etc vb V* **comedirse** ♦ *nf* (*alimento*) food; (*almuerzo, cena*) meal; (*de mediodía*) lunch; (*AM*) dinner.
comidilla [komi'ðiʎa] *nf*: **ser la ~ de la ciudad** to be the talk of the town.
comience [ko'mjenθe] *etc vb V* **comenzar**.
comienzo [ko'mjenθo] *etc vb V* **comenzar** ♦ *nm* beginning, start; **dar ~ a un acto** to begin a ceremony; ~ **del archivo** (*INFORM*) top-of-file.
comillas [ko'miʎas] *nfpl* quotation marks.
comilón, ona [komi'lon, ona] *adj* greedy ♦ *nf* (*fam*) blow-out.
comino [ko'mino] *nm* cumin (seed); **no me**

importa un ~ I don't give a damn.
comisaría [komisa'ria] *nf* police station, precinct (*US*); (*MIL*) commissariat.
comisario [komi'sarjo] *nm* (*MIL etc*) commissary; (*POL*) commissar.
comisión [komi'sjon] *nf* (*COM*: *pago*) commission, rake-off (*fam*); (: *junta*) board; (*encargo*) assignment; ~ **mixta/permanente** joint/standing committee; **Comisiones Obreras** (*ESP*) *formerly Communist Union Confederation.*
comisura [komi'sura] *nf*: ~ **de los labios** corner of the mouth.
comité, *pl* **comités** *nm* [komi'te, komi'tes] committee; ~ **de empresa** works council.
comitiva [komi'tiβa] *nf* suite, retinue.
como ['komo] *adv* as; (*tal* ~) like; (*aproximadamente*) about, approximately ♦ *conj* (*ya que, puesto que*) as, since; (*en seguida que*) as soon as; (*si*: +*subjun*) if; ¡~ **no!** of course!; ~ **no lo haga hoy** unless he does it today; ~ **si** as if; **es tan alto** ~ **ancho** it is as high as it is wide.
cómo ['komo] *adv* how?, why? ♦ *excl* what?, I beg your pardon? ♦ *nm*: **el** ~ **y el porqué** the whys and wherefores; ¿~ **está Ud?** how are you?; ¿~ **no?** why not?; ¡~ **no!** (*esp AM*) of course!; ¿~ **son?** what are they like?
cómoda ['komoða] *nf* chest of drawers.
comodidad [komoði'ðað] *nf* comfort; **venga a su** ~ come at your convenience.
comodín [komo'ðin] *nm* joker; (*INFORM*) wild card; **símbolo** ~ wild-card character.
cómodo, a ['komoðo, a] *adj* comfortable; (*práctico, de fácil uso*) convenient.
comodón, ona [komo'ðon, ona] *adj* comfort-loving ♦ *nm/f*: **ser un(a)** ~ to like one's home comforts.
comoquiera [como'kjera] *conj*: ~ **que** (+ *subjun*) in whatever way; ~ **que sea eso** however that may be.
comp. *abr* (= *compárese*) cp.
compacto, a [kom'pakto, a] *adj* compact.
compadecer [kompaðe'θer] *vt* to pity, be sorry for; ~**se** *vr*: ~**se de** to pity, be sorry for.
compadezca [kompa'ðeθka] *etc vb V* **compadecer**.
compadre [kom'paðre] *nm* (*padrino*) godfather; (*esp AM*: *amigo*) friend, pal.
compaginar [kompaxi'nar] *vt*: ~ **A con B** to bring A into line with B; ~**se** *vr*: ~**se con** to tally with, square with.
compañerismo [kompaɲe'rismo] *nm* comradeship.
compañero, a [kompa'ɲero, a] *nm/f* companion; (*novio*) boyfriend/girlfriend; ~ **de clase** classmate.
compañía [kompa'ɲia] *nf* company; ~ **afiliada** associated company; ~ **concesionadora** franchiser; ~ **(no) cotizable** (un)listed company; ~ **inversionista** investment trust; **hacer** ~ **a algn** to keep sb company.
comparación [kompara'θjon] *nf* comparison; **en** ~ **con** in comparison with.
comparar [kompa'rar] *vt* to compare.
comparativo, a [kompara'tiβo, a] *adj* comparative.
comparecencia [kompare'θenθja] *nf* (*JUR*) appearance (in court); **orden de** ~ summons *sg*.
comparecer [kompare'θer] *vi* to appear (in court).
comparezca [kompa'reθka] *etc vb V* **comparecer**.
comparsa [kom'parsa] *nm/f* extra.
compartimento [komparti'mento], **compartimiento** [komparti'mjento] *nm* (*FERRO*) compartment; (*de mueble, cajón*) section; ~ **estanco** (*fig*) watertight compartment.
compartir [kompar'tir] *vt* to divide (up), share (out).
compás [kom'pas] *nm* (*MUS*) beat, rhythm; (*MAT*) compasses *pl*; (*NAUT etc*) compass; **al** ~ in time.
compasión [kompa'sjon] *nf* compassion, pity.
compasivo, a [kompa'siβo, a] *adj* compassionate.
compatibilidad [kompatiβili'ðað] *nf* (*tb INFORM*) compatibility.
compatible [kompa'tiβle] *adj* compatible.
compatriota [kompa'trjota] *nm/f* compatriot, fellow countryman/woman.
compendiar [kompen'djar] *vt* to summarize; (*libro*) to abridge.
compendio [kom'pendjo] *nm* summary; abridgement.
compenetración [kompenetra'θjon] *nf* (*fig*) mutual understanding.
compenetrarse [kompene'trarse] *vr* (*fig*): ~ **(muy) bien** to get on (very) well together.
compensación [kompensa'θjon] *nf* compensation; (*JUR*) damages *pl*; (*COM*) clearing.
compensar [kompen'sar] *vt* to compensate; (*pérdida*) to make up for.
competencia [kompe'tenθja] *nf* (*incumbencia*) domain, field; (*COM*)

receipt; (*JUR, habilidad*) competence; (*rivalidad*) competition.
competente [kompe'tente] *adj* (*JUR, persona*) competent; (*conveniente*) suitable.
competer [kompe'ter] *vi*: ~ **a** to be the responsibility of, fall to.
competición [kompeti'θjon] *nf* competition.
competidor, a [kompeti'ðor, a] *nm/f* competitor.
competir [kompe'tir] *vi* to compete.
competitivo, a [kompeti'tiβo, a] *adj* competitive.
compilación [kompila'θjon] *nf* compilation; **tiempo de** ~ (*INFORM*) compile time.
compilador [kompila'ðor] *nm* compiler.
compilar [kompi'lar] *vt* to compile.
compinche [kom'pintʃe] *nm/f* (*fam*) crony.
compita [kom'pita] *etc vb V* **competir**.
complacencia [kompla'θenθja] *nf* (*placer*) pleasure; (*satisfacción*) satisfaction; (*buena voluntad*) willingness.
complacer [kompla'θer] *vt* to please; ~**se** *vr* to be pleased.
complaciente [kompla'θjente] *adj* kind, obliging, helpful.
complazca [kom'plaθka] *etc vb V* **complacer**.
complejo, a [kom'plexo, a] *adj, nm* complex.
complementario, a [komplemen'tarjo, a] *adj* complementary.
complemento [komple'mento] *nm* (*de moda, diseño*) accessory; (*LING*) complement.
completar [komple'tar] *vt* to complete.
completo, a [kom'pleto, a] *adj* complete; (*perfecto*) perfect; (*lleno*) full ♦ *nm* full complement.
complexión [komple'ksjon] *nf* constitution.
complicación [komplika'θjon] *nf* complication.
complicado, a [kompli'kaðo, a] *adj* complicated; **estar** ~ **en** to be involved in.
complicar [kompli'kar] *vt* to complicate.
cómplice ['kompliθe] *nm/f* accomplice.
complique [kom'plike] *etc vb V* **complicar**.
complot, *pl* **complots** [kom'plo(t), kom'plos] *nm* plot; (*conspiración*) conspiracy.
compondré [kompon'dre] *etc vb V* **componer**.
componenda [kompo'nenda] *nf* compromise; (*pey*) shady deal.
componente [kompo'nente] *adj, nm* component.
componer [kompo'ner] *vt* to make up, put together; (*MUS, LIT, IMPRENTA*) to compose; (*algo roto*) to mend, repair; (*adornar*) to adorn; (*arreglar*) to arrange; (*reconciliar*) to reconcile; ~**se** *vr*: ~**se de** to consist of; **componérselas para hacer algo** to manage to do sth.
componga [kom'ponga] *etc vb V* **componer**.
comportamiento [komporta'mjento] *nm* behaviour, conduct.
comportarse [kompor'tarse] *vr* to behave.
composición [komposi'θjon] *nf* composition.
compositor, a [komposi'tor, a] *nm/f* composer.
compostelano, a [komposte'lano, a] *adj* of *o* from Santiago de Compostela ♦ *nm/f* native *o* inhabitant of Santiago de Compostela.
compostura [kompos'tura] *nf* (*reparación*) mending, repair; (*composición*) composition; (*acuerdo*) agreement; (*actitud*) composure.
compota [kom'pota] *nf* compote, preserve.
compra ['kompra] *nf* purchase; ~**s** *nfpl* purchases, shopping *sg*; **hacer la** ~**/ir de** ~**s** to do the/go shopping; ~ **a granel** (*COM*) bulk buying; ~ **proteccionista** (*COM*) support buying.
comprador, a [kompra'ðor, a] *nm/f* buyer, purchaser.
comprar [kom'prar] *vt* to buy, purchase; ~ **deudas** (*COM*) to factor.
compraventa [kompra'βenta] *nf* (*JUR*) contract of sale.
comprender [kompren'der] *vt* to understand; (*incluir*) to comprise, include.
comprensible [kompren'siβle] *adj* understandable.
comprensión [kompren'sjon] *nf* understanding; (*totalidad*) comprehensiveness.
comprensivo, a [kompren'siβo, a] *adj* comprehensive; (*actitud*) understanding.
compresa [kom'presa] *nf* compress; ~ **higiénica** sanitary towel (*BRIT*) *o* napkin (*US*).
compresión [kompre'sjon] *nf* compression.
comprimido, a [kompri'miðo] *adj* compressed ♦ *nm* (*MED*) pill, tablet; **en caracteres** ~**s** (*TIP*) condensed.
comprimir [kompri'mir] *vt* to compress;

(*fig*) to control; (*INFORM*) to pack.
comprobación [komproβa'θjon] *nf*: ~ **general de cuentas** (*COM*) general audit.
comprobante [kompro'βante] *nm* proof; (*COM*) voucher; ~ **(de pago)** receipt.
comprobar [kompro'βar] *vt* to check; (*probar*) to prove; (*TEC*) to check, test.
comprometedor, a [komprometе'ðor, a] *adj* compromising.
comprometer [komprome'ter] *vt* to compromise; (*exponer*) to endanger; ~**se** *vr* to compromise o.s.; (*involucrarse*) to get involved.
comprometido, a [komprome'tiðo, a] *a* (*situación*) awkward; (*escritor etc*) committed.
compromiso [kompro'miso] *nm* (*obligación*) obligation; (*cita*) engagement, date; (*cometido*) commitment; (*convenio*) agreement; (*dificultad*) awkward situation; **libre de** ~ (*COM*) without obligation.
comprueba [kom'prweβa] *etc vb V* **comprobar**.
compuerta [kom'pwerta] *nf* (*en canal*) sluice, floodgate; (*INFORM*) gate.
compuesto, a [kom'pwesto, a] *pp de* **componer** ♦ *adj*: ~ **de** composed of, made up of ♦ *nm* compound; (*MED*) preparation.
compulsar [kompul'sar] *vt* (*cotejar*) to collate, compare; (*JUR*) to make an attested copy of.
compulsivo, a [kompul'siβo, a] *adj* compulsive.
compungido, a [kompun'xiðo, a] *adj* remorseful.
compuse [com'puse] *etc vb V* **componer**.
computador [komputa'ðor] *nm*, **computadora** [komputa'ðora] *nf* computer; ~ **central** mainframe computer; ~ **especializado** dedicated computer; ~ **personal** personal computer.
computar [kompu'tar] *vt* to calculate, compute.
cómputo ['komputo] *nm* calculation.
comulgar [komul'ɣar] *vi* to receive communion.
comulgue [ko'mulɣe] *etc vb V* **comulgar**.
común [ko'mun] *adj* (*gen*) common; (*corriente*) ordinary; **por lo** ~ generally ♦ *nm*: **el** ~ the community.
comuna [ko'muna] *nf* commune; (*AM*) district.
comunicación [komunika'θjon] *nf* communication; (*informe*) report.
comunicado [komuni'kaðo] *nm* announcement; ~ **de prensa** press release.
comunicar [komuni'kar] *vt* to communicate; (*ARQ*) to connect ♦ *vi* to communicate; to send a report; ~**se** *vr* to communicate; **está comunicando** (*TELEC*) the line's engaged (*BRIT*) *o* busy (*US*).
comunicativo, a [komunika'tiβo, a] *adj* communicative.
comunidad [komuni'ðað] *nf* community; ~ **autónoma** autonomous region; ~ **de vecinos** residents' association; **C~ Económica Europea (CEE)** European Economic Community (EEC); *see boxed note.*

COMUNIDAD AUTÓNOMA

The 1978 constitution provides for a degree of self-government in the 19 regions of Spain, called **comunidades autónomas** *or "autonomías". Some, such as Catalonia and the Basque Country, which have their own language, history and culture, have long felt separate from the rest of Spain, and this explains why some of the autonomous regions have more devolved powers than others, in all matters except foreign affairs and national defence. The Spanish names of the regions are: Andalucía, Aragón, Asturias, Islas Baleares, Canarias, Cantabria, Castilla y León, Castilla-La Mancha, Cataluña, Extremadura, Galicia, Madrid, Murcia, Navarra, País Vasco, La Rioja, Comunidad Valenciana, Ceuta and Melilla.*

comunión [komu'njon] *nf* communion.
comunique [komu'nike] *etc vb V* **comunicar**.
comunismo [komu'nismo] *nm* communism.
comunista [komu'nista] *adj, nm/f* communist.
comunitario, a [komuni'tarjo, a] *adj* (*de la CE*) Community *cpd*, EC *cpd*.

PALABRA CLAVE

con [kon] *prep* **1** (*medio, compañía, modo*) with; **comer ~ cuchara** to eat with a spoon; **café ~ leche** white coffee; **estoy ~ un catarro** I've got a cold; **pasear ~ algn** to go for a walk with sb; ~ **habilidad** skilfully
2 (*a pesar de*): ~ **todo, merece nuestros respetos** all the same *o* even so, he deserves our respect
3 (*para ~*): **es muy bueno para ~ los niños** he's very good with (the) children
4 (*+infin*): ~ **llegar tan tarde se quedó sin comer** by arriving *o* because he arrived so late he missed out on eating;

~ **estudiar un poco apruebas** with a bit of studying you should pass
5 (*queja*): ¡~ **las ganas que tenía de ir!** and I really wanted to go (too)!
♦ *conj*: ~ **que: será suficiente ~ que le escribas** it will be enough if you write to her.

conato [ko'nato] *nm* attempt; ~ **de robo** attempted robbery.
cóncavo, a ['konkaβo, a] *adj* concave.
concebir [konθe'βir] *vt* to conceive; (*imaginar*) to imagine ♦ *vi* to conceive.
conceder [konθe'ðer] *vt* to concede.
concejal, a [konθe'xal, a] *nm/f* town councillor.
concejo [kon'θexo] *nm* council.
concentración [konθentra'θjon] *nf* concentration.
concentrar [konθen'trar] *vt*, **~se** *vr* to concentrate.
concéntrico, a [kon'θentriko, a] *adj* concéntric.
concepción [konθep'θjon] *nf* conception.
concepto [kon'θepto] *nm* concept; **por ~ de** as, by way of; **tener buen ~ de algn** to think highly of sb; **bajo ningún ~** under no circumstances.
conceptuar [konθep'twar] *vt* to judge.
concernir [konθer'nir] *vi*: **en lo que concierne a** concerning.
concertar [konθer'tar] *vt* (*MUS*) to harmonize; (*acordar: precio*) to agree; (: *tratado*) to conclude; (*trato*) to arrange, fix up; (*combinar: esfuerzos*) to coordinate; (*reconciliar: personas*) to reconcile ♦ *vi* to harmonize, be in tune.
concesión [konθe'sjon] *nf* concession; (*COM: fabricación*) licence.
concesionario, a [konθesjo'narjo, a] *nm/f* (*COM*) (licensed) dealer, agent, concessionaire; (: *de venta*) franchisee; (: *de transportes etc*) contractor.
concha ['kontʃa] *nf* shell; (*AM fam!*) cunt (!)
conchabarse [kontʃa'βarse] *vr*: ~ **contra** to gang up on.
conciencia [kon'θjenθja] *nf* (*moral*) conscience; (*conocimiento*) awareness; **libertad de ~** freedom of worship; **tener/tomar ~ de** to be/become aware of; **tener la ~ limpia** *o* **tranquila** to have a clear conscience; **tener plena ~ de** to be fully aware of.
concienciar [konθjen'θjar] *vt* to make aware; **~se** *vr* to become aware.
concienzudo, a [konθjen'θuðo, a] *adj* conscientious.
concierne [kon'θjerne] *etc vb V* **concernir**.
concierto [kon'θjerto] *etc vb V* **concertar** ♦ *nm* concert; (*obra*) concerto.
conciliación [konθilja'θjon] *nf* conciliation.
conciliar [konθi'ljar] *vt* to reconcile ♦ *adj* (*REL*) of a council; ~ **el sueño** to get to sleep.
concilio [kon'θiljo] *nm* council.
concisión [konθi'sjon] *nf* conciseness.
conciso, a [kon'θiso, a] *adj* concise.
conciudadano, a [konθjuða'ðano, a] *nm/f* fellow citizen.
concluir [konklu'ir] *vt* (*acabar*) to conclude; (*inferir*) to infer, deduce ♦ *vi*, **~se** *vr* to conclude; **todo ha concluido** it's all over.
conclusión [konklu'sjon] *nf* conclusion; **llegar a la ~ de que ...** to come to the conclusion that ....
concluya [kon'kluja] *etc vb V* **concluir**.
concluyente [konklu'jente] *adj* (*prueba, información*) conclusive.
concordancia [konkor'ðanθja] *nf* agreement.
concordar [konkor'ðar] *vt* to reconcile ♦ *vi* to agree, tally.
concordia [kon'korðja] *nf* harmony.
concretamente [konkreta'mente] *adv* specifically, to be exact.
concretar [konkre'tar] *vt* to make concrete, make more specific; (*problema*) to pinpoint; **~se** *vr* to become more definite.
concreto, a [kon'kreto, a] *adj, nm* (*AM*) concrete; **en ~** (*en resumen*) to sum up; (*específicamente*) specifically; **no hay nada en ~** there's nothing definite.
concubina [konku'βina] *nf* concubine.
concuerde [kon'kwerðe] *etc vb V* **concordar**.
concupiscencia [konkupis'θenθja] *nf* (*avancia*) greed; (*lujuria*) lustfulness.
concurrencia [konku'rrenθja] *nf* turnout.
concurrido, a [konku'rriðo, a] *a* (*calle*) busy; (*local, reunión*) crowded.
concurrir [konku'rrir] *vi* (*juntarse: ríos*) to meet, come together; (: *personas*) to gather, meet.
concursante [konkur'sante] *nm* competitor.
concursar [konkur'sar] *vi* to compete.
concurso [kon'kurso] *nm* (*de público*) crowd; (*ESCOL, DEPORTE, competencia*) competition; (*COM*) invitation to tender; (*examen*) open competition; (*TV etc*) quiz; (*ayuda*) help, cooperation.
condado [kon'daðo] *nm* county.
condal [kon'dal] *adj*: **la ciudad ~** Barcelona.

conde ['konde] *nm* count.
condecoración [kondekora'θjon] *nf* (*MIL*) medal, decoration.
condecorar [kondeko'rar] *vt* to decorate.
condena [kon'dena] *nf* sentence; **cumplir una** ~ to serve a sentence.
condenación [kondena'θjon] *nf* condemnation; (*REL*) damnation.
condenado, a [konde'naðo, a] *adj* (*JUR*) condemned; (*fam*: *maldito*) damned ♦ *nm/f* (*JUR*) convicted person.
condenar [konde'nar] *vt* to condemn; (*JUR*) to convict; ~**se** *vr* (*JUR*) to confess (one's guilt); (*REL*) to be damned.
condensar [konden'sar] *vt* to condense.
condesa [kon'desa] *nf* countess.
condescendencia [kondesθen'denθja] *nf* condescension; **aceptar algo por** ~ to accept sth so as not to hurt feelings.
condescender [kondesθen'der] *vi* to acquiesce, comply.
condescienda [kondes'θjenda] *etc vb V* **condescender**.
condición [kondi'θjon] *nf* (*gen*) condition; (*rango*) social class; **condiciones** *nfpl* (*cualidades*) qualities; (*estado*) condition; **a** ~ **de que ...** on condition that ...; **las condiciones del contrato** the terms of the contract; **condiciones de trabajo** working conditions; **condiciones de venta** conditions of sale.
condicional [kondiθjo'nal] *adj* conditional.
condicionamiento [kondiθjona'mjento] *nm* conditioning.
condicionar [kondiθjo'nar] *vt* (*acondicionar*) to condition; ~ **algo a algo** to make sth conditional *o* dependent on sth.
condimento [kondi'mento] *nm* seasoning.
condiscípulo, a [kondis'θipulo, a] *nm/f* fellow student.
condolerse [kondo'lerse] *vr* to sympathize.
condominio [kondo'minjo] *nm* (*COM*) joint ownership; (*AM*) condominium, apartment.
condón [kon'don] *nm* condom.
condonar [kondo'nar] *vt* (*JUR*: *reo*) to reprieve; (*COM*: *deuda*) to cancel.
cóndor ['kondor] *nm* condor.
conducente [kondu'θente] *adj*: ~ **a** conducive to, leading to.
conducir [kondu'θir] *vt* to take, convey; (*ELEC etc*) to carry; (*AUTO*) to drive; (*negocio*) to manage ♦ *vi* to drive; (*fig*) to lead; ~**se** *vr* to behave.
conducta [kon'dukta] *nf* conduct, behaviour.
conducto [kon'dukto] *nm* pipe, tube; (*fig*) channel; (*ELEC*) lead; **por** ~ **de** through.
conductor, a [konduk'tor, a] *adj* leading, guiding ♦ *nm* (*FÍSICA*) conductor; (*de vehículo*) driver.
conduela [kon'dwela] *etc vb V* **condolerse**.
conduje [kon'duxe] *etc vb V* **conducir**.
conduzca [kon'duθka] *etc vb V* **conducir**.
conectado, a [konek'taðo, a] *a* (*ELEC*) connected, plugged in; (*INFORM*) on-line.
conectar [konek'tar] *vt* to connect (up), plug in; (*INFORM*) to toggle on; ~**se** *vr* (*INFORM*) to log in (on).
conejillo [kone'xiʎo] *nm*: ~ **de Indias** guinea pig.
conejo [ko'nexo] *nm* rabbit.
conexión [konek'sjon] *nf* connection; (*INFORM*) logging in (on).
confabularse [konfaβu'larse] *vr*: ~ **(para hacer algo)** to plot, conspire (to do sth).
confección [konfek'θjon] *nf* (*preparación*) preparation, making-up; (*industria*) clothing industry; (*producto*) article; **de** ~ (*ropa*) off-the-peg.
confeccionar [konfe(k)θjo'nar] *vt* to make (up).
confederación [konfeðera'θjon] *nf* confederation.
conferencia [konfe'renθja] *nf* conference; (*lección*) lecture; (*TELEC*) call; ~ **de cobro revertido** (*TELEC*) reversed-charge (*BRIT*) *o* collect (*US*) call; ~ **cumbre** summit (conference).
conferenciante [konferen'θjante] *nm/f* lecturer.
conferir [konfe'rir] *vt* to award.
confesar [konfe'sar] *vt* (*admitir*) to confess, admit; (*error*) to acknowledge; (*crimen*) to own up to.
confesión [konfe'sjon] *nf* confession.
confesionario [konfesjo'narjo] *nm* confessional.
confeso, a [kon'feso, a] *adj* (*JUR etc*) self-confessed.
confeti [kon'feti] *nm* confetti.
confiado, a [kon'fjaðo, a] *adj* (*crédulo*) trusting; (*seguro*) confident; (*presumido*) conceited, vain.
confianza [kon'fjanθa] *nf* trust; (*aliento, confidencia*) confidence; (*familiaridad*) intimacy, familiarity; (*pey*) vanity, conceit; **margen de** ~ credibility gap; **tener** ~ **con algn** to be on close terms with sb.
confiar [kon'fjar] *vt* to entrust ♦ *vi* (*fiarse*) to trust; (*contar con*) to rely; ~**se** *vr* to put one's trust.
confidencia [konfi'ðenθja] *nf* confidence.
confidencial [konfiðen'θjal] *adj*

confidential.
confidente [konfi'ðente] *nm/f* confidant/e; (*policial*) informer.
confiera [kon'fjera] *etc vb V* **conferir**.
confiese [kon'fjese] *etc vb V* **confesar**.
configuración [konfiɣura'θjon] *nf* (*tb INFORM*) configuration; **la ~ del terreno** the lie of the land; **~ de bits** (*INFORM*) bit pattern.
configurar [konfiɣu'rar] *vt* to shape, form.
confín [kon'fin] *nm* limit; **confines** *nmpl* confines, limits.
confinar [konfi'nar] *vi* to confine; (*desterrar*) to banish.
confiriendo [konfi'rjendo] *etc vb V* **conferir**.
confirmación [konfirma'θjon] *nf* confirmation; (*REL*) Confirmation.
confirmar [konfir'mar] *vt* to confirm; (*JUR etc*) to corroborate; **la excepción confirma la regla** the exception proves the rule.
confiscar [konfis'kar] *vt* to confiscate.
confisque [kon'fiske] *etc vb V* **confiscar**.
confitado, a [konfi'taðo, a] *adj*: **fruta confitada** crystallized fruit.
confite [kon'fite] *nm* sweet (*BRIT*), candy (*US*).
confitería [konfite'ria] *nf* confectionery; (*tienda*) confectioner's (shop).
confitura [konfi'tura] *nf* jam.
conflagración [konflaɣra'θjon] *nf* conflagration.
conflictivo, a [konflik'tiβo, a] *adj* (*asunto, propuesta*) controversial; (*país, situación*) troubled.
conflicto [kon'flikto] *nm* conflict; (*fig*) clash; (: *dificultad*): **estar en un ~** to be in a jam; **~ laboral** labour dispute.
confluir [konflu'ir] *vi* (*ríos etc*) to meet; (*gente*) to gather.
confluya [kon'fluja] *etc vb V* **confluir**.
conformar [konfor'mar] *vt* to shape, fashion ♦ *vi* to agree; **~se** *vr* to conform; (*resignarse*) to resign o.s.
conforme [kon'forme] *adj* alike, similar; (*de acuerdo*) agreed, in agreement; (*satisfecho*) satisfied ♦ *adv* as ♦ *excl* agreed! ♦ *nm* agreement ♦ *prep*: **~ a** in accordance with.
conformidad [konformi'ðað] *nf* (*semejanza*) similarity; (*acuerdo*) agreement; (*resignación*) resignation; **de/en ~ con** in accordance with; **dar su ~** to consent.
conformismo [konfor'mismo] *nm* conformism.
conformista [konfor'mista] *nm/f* conformist.
confort, *pl* **conforts** [kon'for, kon'for(t)s] *nm* comfort.
confortable [konfor'taβle] *adj* comfortable.
confortar [konfor'tar] *vt* to comfort.
confraternidad [konfraterni'ðað] *nf* brotherhood; **espíritu de ~** feeling of unity.
confraternizar [konfraterni'θar] *vi* to fraternize.
confrontación [konfronta'θjon] *nf* confrontation.
confrontar [konfron'tar] *vt* to confront; (*dos personas*) to bring face to face; (*cotejar*) to compare ♦ *vi* to border.
confundir [konfun'dir] *vt* (*borrar*) to blur; (*equivocar*) to mistake, confuse; (*mezclar*) to mix; (*turbar*) to confuse; **~se** *vr* (*hacerse borroso*) to become blurred; (*turbarse*) to get confused; (*equivocarse*) to make a mistake; (*mezclarse*) to mix.
confusión [konfu'sjon] *nf* confusion.
confusionismo [konfusjo'nismo] *nm* confusion, uncertainty.
confuso, a [kon'fuso, a] *adj* (*gen*) confused; (*recuerdo*) hazy; (*estilo*) obscure.
congelación [konxela'θjon] *nf* freezing; **~ de créditos** credit freeze.
congelado, a [konxe'laðo, a] *adj* frozen ♦ *nmpl*: **~s** frozen food *sg o* foods.
congelador [konxela'ðor] *nm* freezer, deep freeze.
congelar [konxe'lar] *vt* to freeze; **~se** *vr* (*sangre, grasa*) to congeal.
congénere [kon'xenere] *nm/f*: **sus ~s** his peers.
congeniar [konxe'njar] *vi* to get on (*BRIT*) *o* along (*US*) (well).
congénito, a [kon'xenito, a] *adj* congenital.
congestión [konxes'tjon] *nf* congestion.
congestionado, a [konxestjo'naðo, a] *adj* congested.
congestionar [konxestjo'nar] *vt* to congest; **~se** *vr* to become congested; **se le congestionó la cara** his face became flushed.
conglomerado [konglome'raðo] *nm* conglomerate.
Congo ['kongo] *nm*: **el ~** the Congo.
congoja [kon'goxa] *nf* distress, grief.
congraciarse [kongra'θjarse] *vr* to ingratiate o.s.
congratular [kongratu'lar] *vt* to congratulate.
congregación [kongreɣa'θjon] *nf* congregation.

congregar [kongre'ɣar] *vt*, **~se** *vr* to gather together.
congregue [kon'greɣe] *etc vb V* **congregar**.
congresista [kongre'sista] *nm/f* delegate, congressman/woman.
congreso [kon'greso] *nm* congress; **C~ de los Diputados** (*ESP POL*) ≈ House of Commons (*BRIT*), House of Representatives (*US*); *V tb* **Las Cortes (españolas)**.
congrio ['kongrjo] *nm* conger (eel).
congruente [kon'grwente] *adj* congruent, congruous.
conífera [ko'nifera] *nf* conifer.
conjetura [konxe'tura] *nf* guess; (*COM*) guesstimate.
conjeturar [konxetu'rar] *vt* to guess.
conjugación [konxuɣa'θjon] *nf* conjugation.
conjugar [konxu'ɣar] *vt* to combine, fit together; (*LING*) to conjugate.
conjugue [kon'xuɣe] *etc vb V* **conjugar**.
conjunción [konxun'θjon] *nf* conjunction.
conjuntivitis [konxunti'ßitis] *nf* conjunctivitis.
conjunto, a [kon'xunto, a] *adj* joint, united ♦ *nm* whole; (*MUS*) band; (*vestido*) ensemble; (*INFORM*) set; **en ~** as a whole; **~ integrado de programas** (*INFORM*) integrated software suite.
conjura [kon'xura] *nf* plot, conspiracy.
conjurar [konxu'rar] *vt* (*REL*) to exorcise; (*peligro*) to ward off ♦ *vi* to plot.
conjuro [kon'xuro] *nm* spell.
conllevar [konʎe'ßar] *vt* to bear; (*implicar*) to imply, involve.
conmemoración [konmemora'θjon] *nf* commemoration.
conmemorar [konmemo'rar] *vt* to commemorate.
conmigo [kon'miɣo] *pron* with me.
conminar [konmi'nar] *vt* to threaten.
conmiseración [konmisera'θjon] *nf* pity, commiseration.
conmoción [konmo'θjon] *nf* shock; (*POL*) disturbance; (*fig*) upheaval; **~ cerebral** (*MED*) concussion.
conmovedor, a [konmoße'ðor, a] *adj* touching, moving; (*emocionante*) exciting.
conmover [konmo'ßer] *vt* to shake, disturb; (*fig*) to move; **~se** *vr* (*fig*) to be moved.
conmueva [kon'mweßa] *etc vb V* **conmover**.
conmutación [konmuta'θjon] *nf* (*INFORM*) switching; **~ de mensajes** message switching; **~ por paquetes** packet switching.
conmutador [konmuta'ðor] *nm* switch; (*AM TELEC*) switchboard.
conmutar [konmu'tar] *vt* (*JUR*) to commute.
connivencia [konni'ßenθja] *nf*: **estar en ~ con** to be in collusion with.
connotación [konnota'θjon] *nf* connotation.
cono ['kono] *nm* cone; **C~ Sur** Southern Cone.
conocedor, a [konoθe'ðor, a] *adj* expert, knowledgeable ♦ *nm/f* expert, connoisseur.
conocer [kono'θer] *vt* to know; (*por primera vez*) to meet, get to know; (*entender*) to know about; (*reconocer*) to recognize; **~se** *vr* (*una persona*) to know o.s.; (*dos personas*) to (get to) know each other; **darse a ~** (*presentarse*) to make o.s. known; **se conoce que ...** (*parece*) apparently ....
conocido, a [kono'θiðo, a] *adj* (well-) known ♦ *nm/f* acquaintance.
conocimiento [konoθi'mjento] *nm* knowledge; (*MED*) consciousness; (*NAUT*: *tb*: **~ de embarque**) bill of lading; **~s** *nmpl* (*personas*) acquaintances; (*saber*) knowledge *sg*; **hablar con ~ de causa** to speak from experience; **~ (de embarque) aéreo** (*COM*) air waybill.
conozca [ko'noθka] *etc vb V* **conocer**.
conque ['konke] *conj* and so, so then.
conquense [kon'kense] *adj* of *o* from Cuenca ♦ *nm/f* native *o* inhabitant of Cuenca.
conquista [kon'kista] *nf* conquest.
conquistador, a [konkista'ðor, a] *adj* conquering ♦ *nm* conqueror.
conquistar [konkis'tar] *vt* (*MIL*) to conquer; (*puesto, simpatía*) to win; (*enamorar*) to win the heart of.
consabido, a [konsa'ßiðo, a] *adj* (*frase etc*) old; (*pey*): **las consabidas excusas** the same old excuses.
consagrado, a [konsa'ɣraðo, a] *adj* (*REL*) consecrated; (*actor*) established.
consagrar [konsa'ɣrar] *vt* (*REL*) to consecrate; (*fig*) to devote.
consciente [kons'θjente] *adj* conscious; **ser** *o* **estar ~ de** to be aware of.
consecución [konseku'θjon] *nf* acquisition; (*de fin*) attainment.
consecuencia [konse'kwenθja] *nf* consequence, outcome; (*firmeza*) consistency; **de ~** of importance.
consecuente [konse'kwente] *adj* consistent.

consecutivo, a [konseku'tiβo, a] *adj* consecutive.
conseguir [konse'ɣir] *vt* to get, obtain; (*sus fines*) to attain.
consejería [konsexe'ria] *nf* (*POL*) ministry (*in a regional government*).
consejero, a [konse'xero, a] *nm/f* adviser, consultant; (*POL*) minister (*in a regional government*); (*COM*) director; (*en comisión*) member.
consejo [kon'sexo] *nm* advice; (*POL*) council; (*COM*) board; **un** ~ a piece of advice; ~ **de administración** board of directors; ~ **de guerra** court-martial; **C**~ **de Europa** Council of Europe.
consenso [kon'senso] *nm* consensus.
consentido, a [konsen'tiðo, a] *adj* (*mimado*) spoiled.
consentimiento [konsenti'mjento] *nm* consent.
consentir [konsen'tir] *vt* (*permitir, tolerar*) to consent to; (*mimar*) to pamper, spoil ♦ *vi* to agree, consent; ~ **que algn haga algo** to allow sb to do sth.
conserje [kon'serxe] *nm* caretaker; (*portero*) porter.
conserva [kon'serβa] *nf*: **en** ~ (*alimentos*) tinned (*BRIT*), canned; ~**s** tinned *o* canned foods.
conservación [konserβa'θjon] *nf* conservation; (*de alimentos, vida*) preservation.
conservador, a [konserβa'ðor, a] *adj* (*POL*) conservative ♦ *nm/f* conservative.
conservadurismo [konserβaðu'rismo] *nm* (*POL etc*) conservatism.
conservante [konser'βante] *nm* preservative.
conservar [konser'βar] *vt* (*gen*) to preserve; (*recursos*) to conserve, keep; (*alimentos, vida*) to preserve; ~**se** *vr* to survive.
conservas [kon'serβas] *nfpl*: ~ **(alimenticias)** tinned (*BRIT*) *o* canned goods.
conservatorio [konserβa'torjo] *nm* (*MUS*) conservatoire; (*AM*) greenhouse.
considerable [konsiðe'raβle] *adj* considerable.
consideración [konsiðera'θjon] *nf* consideration; (*estimación*) respect; **de** ~ important; **De mi** *o* **nuestra (mayor)** ~ (*AM*) Dear Sir(s) *o* Madam; **tomar en** ~ to take into account.
considerado, a [konsiðe'raðo, a] *adj* (*atento*) considerate; (*respetado*) respected.
considerar [konsiðe'rar] *vt* (*gen*) to consider; (*meditar*) to think about; (*tener en cuenta*) to take into account.
consienta [kon'sjenta] *etc vb V* **consentir**.
consigna [kon'siɣna] *nf* (*orden*) order, instruction; (*para equipajes*) left-luggage office (*BRIT*), checkroom (*US*).
consignación [konsiɣna'θjon] *nf* consignment; ~ **de créditos** allocation of credits.
consignador [konsiɣna'ðor] *nm* (*COM*) consignor.
consignar [konsiɣ'nar] *vt* (*COM*) to send; (*créditos*) to allocate.
consignatario, a [konsiɣna'tarjo, a] *nm/f* (*COM*) consignee.
consigo [kon'siɣo] *etc vb V* **conseguir** ♦ *pron* (*m*) with him; (*f*) with her; (*usted*) with you; (*reflexivo*) with o.s.
consiguiendo [konsi'ɣjendo] *etc vb V* **conseguir**.
consiguiente [konsi'ɣjente] *adj* consequent; **por** ~ and so, therefore, consequently.
consintiendo [konsin'tjendo] *etc vb V* **consentir**.
consistente [konsis'tente] *adj* consistent; (*sólido*) solid, firm; (*válido*) sound; ~ **en** consisting of.
consistir [konsis'tir] *vi*: ~ **en** (*componerse de*) to consist of; (*ser resultado de*) to be due to.
consola [kon'sola] *nf* console, control panel; (*mueble*) console table; ~ **de juegos** games console; ~ **de mando** (*INFORM*) control console; ~ **de visualización** visual display console.
consolación [konsola'θjon] *nf* consolation.
consolar [konso'lar] *vt* to console.
consolidar [konsoli'ðar] *vt* to consolidate.
consomé, *pl* **consomés** [konso'me, konso'mes] *nm* consommé, clear soup.
consonancia [konso'nanθja] *nf* harmony; **en** ~ **con** in accordance with.
consonante [konso'nante] *adj* consonant, harmonious ♦ *nf* consonant.
consorcio [kon'sorθjo] *nm* (*COM*) consortium, syndicate.
consorte [kon'sorte] *nm/f* consort.
conspicuo, a [kons'pikwo, a] *adj* conspicuous.
conspiración [konspira'θjon] *nf* conspiracy.
conspirador, a [konspira'ðor, a] *nm/f* conspirator.
conspirar [konspi'rar] *vi* to conspire.
constancia [kons'tanθja] *nf* (*gen*) constancy; (*certeza*) certainly; **dejar** ~ **de algo** to put sth on record.

constante [kons'tante] *adj, nf* constant.
constar [kons'tar] *vi* (*evidenciarse*) to be clear *o* evident; ~ **(en)** to appear (in); ~ **de** to consist of; **hacer** ~ to put on record; **me consta que ...** I have evidence that ...; **que conste que lo hice por ti** believe me, I did it for your own good.
constatar [konsta'tar] *vt* (*controlar*) to check; (*observar*) to note.
constelación [konstela'θjon] *nf* constellation.
consternación [konsterna'θjon] *nf* consternation.
constipado, a [konsti'paðo, a] *adj*: **estar** ~ to have a cold ♦ *nm* cold.
constiparse [konsti'parse] *vr* to catch a cold.
constitución [konstitu'θjon] *nf* constitution; **Día de la C**~ (*ESP*) Constitution Day (*6th December*).
constitucional [konstituθjo'nal] *adj* constitutional.
constituir [konstitu'ir] *vt* (*formar, componer*) to constitute, make up; (*fundar, erigir, ordenar*) to constitute, establish; (*ser*) to be; ~**se** *vr* (*POL etc*: *cuerpo*) to be composed; (: *fundarse*) to be established.
constitutivo, a [konstitu'tiβo, a] *adj* constitutive, constituent.
constituya [konsti'tuja] *etc vb V* **constituir**.
constituyente [konstitu'jente] *adj* constituent.
constreñir [konstre'ɲir] *vt* (*obligar*) to compel, oblige; (*restringir*) to restrict.
constriño [kons'triɲo] *etc*, **constriñendo** [konstri'ɲendo] *etc vb V* **constreñir**.
construcción [konstruk'θjon] *nf* construction, building.
constructivo, a [konstruk'tiβo, a] *adj* constructive.
constructor, a [konstruk'tor, a] *nm/f* builder.
construir [konstru'ir] *vt* to build, construct.
construyendo [konstru'jendo] *etc vb V* **construir**.
consuelo [kon'swelo] *etc vb V* **consolar** ♦ *nm* consolation, solace.
consuetudinario, a [konswetuði'narjo, a] *adj* customary; **derecho** ~ common law.
cónsul ['konsul] *nm* consul.
consulado [konsu'laðo] *nm* (*sede*) consulate; (*cargo*) consulship.
consulta [kon'sulta] *nf* consultation; (*MED*: *consultorio*) consulting room; (*INFORM*) enquiry; **horas de** ~ surgery hours; **obra de** ~ reference book.
consultar [konsul'tar] *vt* to consult; ~ **un archivo** (*INFORM*) to interrogate a file.
consultor, a [konsul'tor, a] *nm*: ~ **en dirección de empresas** management consultant.
consultorio [konsul'torjo] *nm* (*MED*) surgery.
consumado, a [konsu'maðo, a] *adj* perfect; (*bribón*) out-and-out.
consumar [konsu'mar] *vt* to complete, carry out; (*crimen*) to commit; (*sentencia*) to carry out.
consumición [konsumi'θjon] *nf* consumption; (*bebida*) drink; (*comida*) food; ~ **mínima** cover charge.
consumido, a [konsu'miðo, a] *adj* (*flaco*) skinny.
consumidor, a [konsumi'ðor, a] *nm/f* consumer.
consumir [konsu'mir] *vt* to consume; ~**se** *vr* to be consumed; (*persona*) to waste away.
consumismo [konsu'mismo] *nm* (*COM*) consumerism.
consumo [kon'sumo] *nm* consumption; **bienes de** ~ consumer goods.
contabilice [kontaβi'liθe] *etc vb V* **contabilizar**.
contabilidad [kontaβili'ðað] *nf* accounting, book-keeping; (*profesión*) accountancy; (*COM*): ~ **analítica** variable costing; ~ **de costos** cost accounting; ~ **de doble partida** double-entry book-keeping; ~ **de gestión** management accounting; ~ **por partida simple** single-entry book-keeping.
contabilizar [kontaβili'θar] *vt* to enter in the accounts.
contable [kon'taβle] *nm/f* bookkeeper; (*licenciado*) accountant; ~ **de costos** (*COM*) cost accountant.
contactar [kontak'tar] *vi*: ~ **con algn** to contact sb.
contacto [kon'takto] *nm* contact; **lentes de** ~ contact lenses; **estar en** ~ **con** to be in touch with.
contado, a [kon'taðo, a] *adj*: ~**s** (*escasos*) numbered, scarce, few ♦ *nm*: **al** ~ for cash; **pagar al** ~ to pay (in) cash; **precio al** ~ cash price.
contador [konta'ðor] *nm* (*aparato*) meter; (*AM*: *contable*) accountant.
contaduría [kontaðu'ria] *nf* accountant's office.
contagiar [konta'xjar] *vt* (*enfermedad*) to pass on, transmit; (*persona*) to infect; ~**se** *vr* to become infected.

contagio [kon'taxjo] *nm* infection.
contagioso, a [konta'xjoso, a] *adj* infectious; (*fig*) catching.
contaminación [kontamina'θjon] *nf* (*gen*) contamination; (*del ambiente etc*) pollution.
contaminar [kontami'nar] *vt* (*gen*) to contaminate; (*aire, agua*) to pollute; (*fig*) to taint.
contante [kon'tante] *adj*: **dinero ~ (y sonante)** hard cash.
contar [kon'tar] *vt* (*páginas, dinero*) to count; (*anécdota etc*) to tell ♦ *vi* to count; **~se** *vr* to be counted, figure; **~ con** to rely on, count on; **sin ~** not to mention; **le cuento entre mis amigos** I reckon him among my friends.
contemplación [kontempla'θjon] *nf* contemplation; **no andarse con contemplaciones** not to stand on ceremony.
contemplar [kontem'plar] *vt* to contemplate; (*mirar*) to look at.
contemporáneo, a [kontempo'raneo, a] *adj, nm/f* contemporary.
contemporizar [kontempori'θar] *vi*: **~ con** to keep in with.
contención [konten'θjon] *nf* (*JUR*) suit; **muro de ~** retaining wall.
contencioso, a [konten'θjoso, a] *adj* (*JUR etc*) contentious ♦ *nm* (*POL*) conflict, dispute.
contender [konten'der] *vi* to contend; (*en un concurso*) to compete.
contendiente [konten'djente] *nm/f* contestant.
contendrá [konten'dra] *etc vb V* **contener**.
contenedor [kontene'ðor] *nm* container; (*de escombros*) skip; **~ de (la) basura** wheelie-bin (*BRIT*); **~ de vidrio** bottle bank.
contener [konte'ner] *vt* to contain, hold; (*risa etc*) to hold back, contain; **~se** *vr* to control *o* restrain o.s.
contenga [kon'tenga] *etc vb V* **contener**.
contenido, a [konte'niðo, a] *adj* (*moderado*) restrained; (*risa etc*) suppressed ♦ *nm* contents *pl*, content.
contentar [konten'tar] *vt* (*satisfacer*) to satisfy; (*complacer*) to please; (*COM*) to endorse; **~se** *vr* to be satisfied.
contento, a [kon'tento, a] *adj* contented, content; (*alegre*) pleased; (*feliz*) happy.
contestación [kontesta'θjon] *nf* answer, reply; **~ a la demanda** (*JUR*) defence plea.
contestador [kontesta'ðor] *nm*: **~ automático** answering machine.
contestar [kontes'tar] *vt* to answer (back), reply; (*JUR*) to corroborate, confirm.
contestatario, a [kontes'tarjo, a] *adj* anti-establishment, nonconformist.
contexto [kon'teksto] *nm* context.
contienda [kon'tjenda] *nf* contest, struggle.
contiene [kon'tjene] *etc vb V* **contener**.
contigo [kon'tiɣo] *pron* with you.
contiguo, a [kon'tiɣwo, a] *adj* (*de al lado*) next; (*vecino*) adjacent, adjoining.
continental [kontinen'tal] *adj* continental.
continente [konti'nente] *adj, nm* continent.
contingencia [kontin'xenθja] *nf* contingency; (*riesgo*) risk; (*posibilidad*) eventuality.
contingente [kontin'xente] *adj* contingent ♦ *nm* contingent; (*COM*) quota.
continuación [kontinwa'θjon] *nf* continuation; **a ~** then, next.
continuamente [kon'tinwamente] *adv* (*sin interrupción*) continuously; (*a todas horas*) constantly.
continuar [konti'nwar] *vt* to continue, go on with; (*reanudar*) to resume ♦ *vi* to continue, go on; **~ hablando** to continue talking *o* to talk.
continuidad [kontinwi'ðað] *nf* continuity.
continuo, a [kon'tinwo, a] *adj* (*sin interrupción*) continuous; (*acción perseverante*) continual.
contonearse [kontone'arse] *vr* (*hombre*) to swagger; (*mujer*) to swing her hips.
contorno [kon'torno] *nm* outline; (*GEO*) contour; **~s** *nmpl* neighbourhood *sg*, surrounding area *sg*.
contorsión [kontor'sjon] *nf* contortion.
contra ['kontra] *prep* against; (*COM*: *giro*) on ♦ *adv* against ♦ *adj, nm/f* (*POL fam*) counter-revolutionary ♦ *nm* con ♦ *nf*: **la C~ (nicaragüense)** the Contras *pl*.
contraalmirante [kontraalmi'rante] *nm* rear admiral.
contraataque [kontraa'take] *nm* counterattack.
contrabajo [kontra'βaxo] *nm* double bass.
contrabandista [kontraβan'dista] *nm/f* smuggler.
contrabando [kontra'βando] *nm* (*acción*) smuggling; (*mercancías*) contraband; **~ de armas** gun-running.
contracción [kontrak'θjon] *nf* contraction.
contrachapado [kontratʃa'paðo] *nm* plywood.
contracorriente [kontrako'rrjente] *nf* cross-current.
contradecir [kontraðe'θir] *vt* to contradict.
contradicción [kontraðik'θjon] *nf*

contradiction; **espíritu de ~** contrariness.
contradicho [kontra'ðitʃo] *pp de* **contradecir.**
contradiciendo [kontraði'θjendo] *etc vb V* **contradecir.**
contradictorio, a [kontraðik'torjo, a] *adj* contradictory.
contradiga [kontra'ðiɣa] *etc,* **contradije** [kontra'ðixe], **contradirá** [kontraði'ra] *etc vb V* **contradecir.**
contraer [kontra'er] *vt* to contract; (*hábito*) to acquire; (*limitar*) to restrict; **~se** *vr* to contract; (*limitarse*) to limit o.s.
contraespionage [kontraespjo'naxe] *nm* counter-espionage.
contrafuerte [kontra'fwerte] *nm* (*ARQ*) buttress.
contragolpe [kontra'ɣolpe] *nm* backlash.
contrahaga [kontra'aɣa] *etc,* **contraharé** [kontraa're] *etc vb V* **contrahacer.**
contrahecho, a [kontra'etʃo, a] *pp de* **contrahacer** ♦ *adj* fake; (*ANAT*) hunchbacked.
contrahice [kontra'iθe] *etc vb V* **contrahacer.**
contraiga [kon'traiɣa] *etc vb V* **contraer.**
contraindicaciones [kontraindika'θjones] *nfpl* (*MED*) contraindications.
contraje [kon'traxe] *etc vb V* **contraer.**
contralor [kontra'lor] *nm* (*AM*) government accounting inspector.
contraluz [kontra'luθ] *nf* (*FOTO etc*) back lighting; **a ~** against the light.
contramaestre [kontrama'estre] *nm* foreman.
contraofensiva [kontraofen'siβa] *nf* counteroffensive.
contraorden [kontra'orðen] *nf* counter-order, countermand.
contrapartida [kontrapar'tiða] *nf* (*COM*) balancing entry; **como ~ (de)** in return (for), as *o* in compensation (for).
contrapelo [kontra'pelo]: **a ~** *adv* the wrong way.
contrapesar [kontrape'sar] *vt* to counterbalance; (*fig*) to offset.
contrapeso [kontra'peso] *nm* counterweight; (*fig*) counterbalance; (*COM*) makeweight.
contrapondré [kontrapon'dre] *etc vb V* **contraponer.**
contraponer [kontrapo'ner] *vt* (*cotejar*) to compare; (*oponer*) to oppose.
contraponga [kontra'ponga] *etc vb V* **contraponer.**
contraportada [kontrapor'taða] *nf* (*de revista*) back page.
contraproducente [kontraproðu'θente] *adj* counterproductive.
contrapuesto [kontra'pwesto] *pp de* **contraponer.**
contrapunto [kontra'punto] *nm* counterpoint.
contrapuse [kontra'puse] *etc vb V* **contraponer.**
contrariar [kontra'rjar] *vt* (*oponerse*) to oppose; (*poner obstáculo*) to impede; (*enfadar*) to vex.
contrariedad [kontrarje'ðað] *nf* (*oposición*) opposition; (*obstáculo*) obstacle, setback; (*disgusto*) vexation, annoyance.
contrario, a [kon'trarjo, a] *adj* contrary; (*persona*) opposed; (*sentido, lado*) opposite ♦ *nm/f* enemy, adversary; (*DEPORTE*) opponent; **al ~, por el ~** on the contrary; **de lo ~** otherwise.
Contrarreforma [kontrarre'forma] *nf* Counter-Reformation.
contrarreloj [kontrarre'lo(x)] *nf* (*tb*: **prueba ~**) time trial.
contrarrestar [kontrarres'tar] *vt* to counteract.
contrarrevolución [kontrarreβolu'θjon] *nf* counter-revolution.
contrasentido [kontrasen'tiðo] *nm* contradiction; **es un ~ que él ...** it doesn't make sense for him to ... .
contraseña [kontra'seɲa] *nf* countersign; (*frase*) password.
contrastar [kontras'tar] *vt* to resist ♦ *vi* to contrast.
contraste [kon'traste] *nm* contrast.
contrata [kon'trata] *nf* (*JUR*) written contract; (*empleo*) hiring.
contratar [kontra'tar] *vt* (*firmar un acuerdo para*) to contract for; (*empleados, obreros*) to hire, engage; (*DEPORTE*) to sign up; **~se** *vr* to sign on.
contratiempo [kontra'tjempo] *nm* (*revés*) setback; (*accidente*) mishap; **a ~** (*MUS*) off-beat.
contratista [kontra'tista] *nm/f* contractor.
contrato [kon'trato] *nm* contract; **~ de compraventa** contract of sale; **~ a precio fijo** fixed-price contract; **~ a término** forward contract; **~ de trabajo** contract of employment *o* service.
contravalor [kontraβa'lor] *nm* exchange value.
contravención [kontraβen'θjon] *nf* contravention, violation.
contravendré [kontraβen'dre] *etc,* **contravenga** [kontra'βenga] *etc vb V* **contravenir.**
contravenir [kontraβe'nir] *vi*: **~ a** to

contravene, violate.
contraventana [kontraßen'tana] *nf* shutter.
contraviene [kontra'ßjene] *etc*, **contraviniendo** [kontraßi'njendo] *etc vb V* **contravenir**.
contrayendo [kontra'jendo] *vb V* **contraer**.
contribución [kontrißu'θjon] *nf* (*municipal etc*) tax; (*ayuda*) contribution; **exento de contribuciones** tax-free.
contribuir [kontrißu'ir] *vt, vi* to contribute; (*COM*) to pay (in taxes).
contribuyendo [kontrißu'jendo] *etc vb V* **contribuir**.
contribuyente [kontrißu'jente] *nm/f* (*COM*) taxpayer; (*que ayuda*) contributor.
contrincante [kontrin'kante] *nm* opponent, rival.
control [kon'trol] *nm* control; (*inspección*) inspection, check; (*COM*): ~ **de calidad** quality control; ~ **de cambios** exchange control; ~ **de costos** cost control; ~ **de créditos** credit control; ~ **de existencias** stock control; ~ **de precios** price control.
controlador, a [kontrola'ðor, a] *nm/f* controller; ~ **aéreo** air-traffic controller.
controlar [kontro'lar] *vt* to control; to inspect, check; (*COM*) to audit.
controversia [kontro'ßersja] *nf* controversy.
contubernio [kontu'ßernjo] *nm* ring, conspiracy.
contumaz [kontu'maθ] *adj* obstinate, stubbornly disobedient.
contundente [kontun'dente] *adj* (*prueba*) conclusive; (*fig: argumento*) convincing; **instrumento** ~ blunt instrument.
contusión [kontu'sjon] *nf* bruise.
contuve [kon'tuße] *etc vb V* **contener**.
convalecencia [kombale'θenθja] *nf* convalescence.
convalecer [kombale'θer] *vi* to convalesce, get better.
convaleciente [kombale'θjente] *adj, nm/f* convalescent.
convalezca [komba'leθka] *etc vb V* **convalecer**.
convalidar [kombali'ðar] *vt* (*título*) to recognize.
convencer [komben'θer] *vt* to convince; (*persuadir*) to persuade.
convencimiento [kombenθi'mjento] *nm* (*acción*) convincing; (*persuasión*) persuasion; (*certidumbre*) conviction; **tener el** ~ **de que** ... to be convinced that ... .
convención [komben'θjon] *nf* convention.
convencional [kombenθjo'nal] *adj* conventional.
convendré [komben'dre] *etc*, **convenga** [kom'benga] *etc vb V* **convenir**.
conveniencia [kombe'njenθja] *nf* suitability; (*conformidad*) agreement; (*utilidad, provecho*) usefulness; ~**s** *nfpl* conventions; (*COM*) property *sg*; **ser de la** ~ **de algn** to suit sb.
conveniente [kombe'njente] *adj* suitable; (*útil*) useful; (*correcto*) fit, proper; (*aconsejable*) advisable.
convenio [kom'benjo] *nm* agreement, treaty; ~ **de nivel crítico** threshold agreement.
convenir [kombe'nir] *vi* (*estar de acuerdo*) to agree; (*ser conveniente*) to suit, be suitable; **"sueldo a ~"** "salary to be agreed"; **conviene recordar que** ... it should be remembered that ....
convento [kom'bento] *nm* monastery; (*de monjas*) convent.
convenza [kom'benθa] *etc vb V* **convencer**.
convergencia [komber'xenθja] *nf* convergence.
converger [komber'xer], **convergir** [komber'xir] *vi* to converge; **sus esfuerzos convergen a un fin común** their efforts are directed towards the same objective.
converja [kom'berxa] *etc vb V* **converger, convergir**.
conversación [kombersa'θjon] *nf* conversation.
conversar [komber'sar] *vi* to talk, converse.
conversión [komber'sjon] *nf* conversion.
converso, a [kom'berso, a] *nm/f* convert.
convertir [komber'tir] *vt* to convert; (*transformar*) to transform, turn; (*COM*) to (ex)change; ~**se** *vr* (*REL*) to convert.
convexo, a [kom'bekso, a] *adj* convex.
convicción [kombik'θjon] *nf* conviction.
convicto , a [kom'bikto, a] *adj* convicted; (*condenado*) condemned.
convidado, a [kombi'ðaðo, a] *nm/f* guest.
convidar [kombi'ðar] *vt* to invite.
conviene [kom'bjene] *etc vb V* **convenir**.
convierta [kom'bjerta] *etc vb V* **convertir**.
convincente [kombin'θente] *adj* convincing.
conviniendo [kombi'njendo] *etc vb V* **convenir**.
convirtiendo [kombir'tjendo] *etc vb V* **convertir**.
convite [kom'bite] *nm* invitation; (*banquete*) banquet.

convivencia [kombi'ßenθja] *nf* coexistence, living together.
convivir [kombi'ßir] *vi* to live together; (*POL*) to coexist.
convocar [kombo'kar] *vt* to summon, call (together).
convocatoria [komboka'torja] *nf* summons *sg*; (*anuncio*) notice of meeting; (*ESCOL*) examination session.
convoque [kom'boke] *etc vb V* **convocar**.
convoy [kom'boj] *nm* (*FERRO*) train.
convulsión [kombul'sjon] *nf* convulsion; (*POL etc*) upheaval.
conyugal [konju'ɣal] *adj* conjugal; **vida** ~ married life.
cónyuge ['konyuxe] *nm/f* spouse, partner.
coña ['koɲa] *nf*: **tomar algo a** ~ (*fam!*) to take sth as a joke.
coñac, *pl* **coñacs** ['koɲa(k), 'koɲas] *nm* cognac, brandy.
coñazo [ko'ɲaθo] *nm* (*fam*) pain; **dar el** ~ to be a real pain.
coño ['koɲo] (*fam!*) *nm* cunt (*!*); (*AM pey*) Spaniard ♦ *excl* (*enfado*) shit (*!*); (*sorpresa*) bloody hell (*!*); **¡qué** ~**!** what a pain in the arse (*!*).
cooperación [koopera'θjon] *nf* cooperation.
cooperar [koope'rar] *vi* to cooperate.
cooperativo, a [koopera'tißo, a] *adj* cooperative ♦ *nf* cooperative.
coordenada [koorðe'naða] *nf* (*MAT*) coordinate; (*fig*): ~**s** *nfpl* guidelines, framework *sg*.
coordinación [koorðina'θjon] *nf* coordination.
coordinador, a [koorðina'ðor, a] *nm/f* coordinator ♦ *nf* coordinating committee.
coordinar [koorði'nar] *vt* to coordinate.
copa ['kopa] *nf* (*tb DEPORTE*) cup; (*vaso*) glass; (*de árbol*) top; (*de sombrero*) crown; ~**s** *nfpl* (*NAIPES*) *one of the suits in the Spanish card deck*; **(tomar una)** ~ (to have a) drink; **ir de** ~**s** to go out for a drink; *V tb* **Baraja Española**.
copar [ko'par] *vt* (*puestos*) to monopolize.
coparticipación [kopartiθipa'θjon] *nf* (*COM*) co-ownership.
COPE *nf abr* (= *Cadena de Ondas Populares Españolas*) *Spanish radio network*.
Copenhague [kope'naɣe] *n* Copenhagen.
copete [ko'pete] *nm* tuft (of hair); **de alto** ~ aristocratic, upper-crust (*fam*).
copia ['kopja] *nf* copy; (*ARTE*) replica; (*COM etc*) duplicate; (*INFORM*): ~ **impresa** hard copy; ~ **de respaldo** *o* **de seguridad** backup copy; **hacer** ~ **de seguridad** to back up; ~ **de trabajo** working copy; ~ **vaciada** dump.
copiadora [kopja'ðora] *nf* photocopier; ~ **al alcohol** spirit duplicator.
copiar [ko'pjar] *vt* to copy; ~ **al pie de la letra** to copy word for word.
copiloto [kopi'loto] *nm* (*AVIAT*) co-pilot; (*AUTO*) co-driver.
copioso, a [ko'pjoso, a] *adj* copious, plentiful.
copita [ko'pita] *nf* (small) glass; (*GOLF*) tee.
copla ['kopla] *nf* verse; (*canción*) (popular) song.
copo ['kopo] *nm*: ~**s de maíz** cornflakes; ~ **de nieve** snowflake.
coprocesador [koproθesa'ðor] *nm* (*INFORM*) co-processor.
coproducción [koproðuk'θjon] *nf* (*CINE etc*) joint production.
copropietarios [kopropje'tarjos] *nmpl* (*COM*) joint owners.
cópula ['kopula] *nf* copulation.
copular [kopu'lar] *vi* to copulate.
coqueta [ko'keta] *adj* flirtatious, coquettish ♦ *nf* (*mujer*) flirt.
coquetear [kokete'ar] *vi* to flirt.
coraje [ko'raxe] *nm* courage; (*ánimo*) spirit; (*ira*) anger.
coral [ko'ral] *adj* choral ♦ *nf* choir ♦ *nm* (*ZOOL*) coral.
Corán [ko'ran] *nm*: **el** ~ the Koran.
coraza [ko'raθa] *nf* (*armadura*) armour; (*blindaje*) armour-plating.
corazón [kora'θon] *nm* heart; (*BOT*) core; **corazones** *nmpl* (*NAIPES*) hearts; **de buen** ~ kind-hearted; **de todo** ~ wholeheartedly; **estar mal del** ~ to have heart trouble.
corazonada [koraθo'naða] *nf* impulse; (*presentimiento*) presentiment, hunch.
corbata [kor'ßata] *nf* tie.
corbeta [kor'ßeta] *nf* corvette.
Córcega ['korθeɣa] *nf* Corsica.
corcel [kor'θel] *nm* steed.
corchea [kor'tʃea] *nf* quaver.
corchete [kor'tʃete] *nm* catch, clasp; ~**s** *nmpl* (*TIP*) square brackets.
corcho ['kortʃo] *nm* cork; (*PESCA*) float.
corcovado, a [korko'ßaðo, a] *adj* hunchbacked ♦ *nm/f* hunchback.
cordel [kor'ðel] *nm* cord, line.
cordero [kor'ðero] *nm* lamb; (*piel*) lambskin.
cordial [kor'ðjal] *adj* cordial ♦ *nm* cordial, tonic.
cordialidad [korðjali'ðað] *nf* warmth, cordiality.

cordillera [korði'ʎera] *nf* range (of mountains).
Córdoba ['korðoβa] *nf* Cordova.
cordobés, esa [korðo'βes, esa] *adj, nm/f* Cordovan.
cordón [kor'ðon] *nm* (*cuerda*) cord, string; (*de zapatos*) lace; (*ELEC*) flex, wire (*US*); (*MIL etc*) cordon.
cordura [kor'ðura] *nf* (*MED*) sanity; (*fig*) good sense.
Corea [ko'rea] *nf* Korea; ~ **del Norte/Sur** North/South Korea.
coreano, a [kore'ano, a] *adj, nm/f* Korean.
corear [kore'ar] *vt* to chorus.
coreografía [koreoɣra'fia] *nf* choreography.
corista [ko'rista] *nf* (*TEAT etc*) chorus girl.
cornada [kor'naða] *nf* (*TAUR etc*) butt, goring.
córner, *pl* **córners** ['korner, 'korners] *nm* corner (kick).
corneta [kor'neta] *nf* bugle.
cornisa [kor'nisa] *nf* cornice.
Cornualles [kor'nwaʎes] *nm* Cornwall.
cornudo, a [kor'nuðo, a] *adj* (*ZOOL*) horned; (*marido*) cuckolded.
coro ['koro] *nm* chorus; (*conjunto de cantores*) choir.
corolario [koro'larjo] *nm* corollary.
corona [ko'rona] *nf* crown; (*de flores*) garland.
coronación [korona'θjon] *nf* coronation.
coronar [koro'nar] *vt* to crown.
coronel [koro'nel] *nm* colonel.
coronilla [koro'niʎa] *nf* (*ANAT*) crown (of the head); **estar hasta la ~ (de)** to be utterly fed up (with).
corpiño [korpiɲo] *nm* bodice; (*AM*: *sostén*) bra.
corporación [korpora'θjon] *nf* corporation.
corporal [korpo'ral] *adj* corporal, bodily.
corporativo, a [korpora'tiβo, a] *adj* corporate.
corpulento, a [korpu'lento, a] *adj* (*persona*) well-built.
corral [ko'rral] *nm* (*patio*) farmyard; (*AGR*: *de aves*) poultry yard; (*redil*) pen.
correa [ko'rrea] *nf* strap; (*cinturón*) belt; (*de perro*) lead, leash; ~ **transportadora** conveyor belt.
correaje [korre'axe] *nm* (*AGR*) harness.
corrección [korrek'θjon] *nf* correction; (*reprensión*) rebuke; (*cortesía*) good manners; (*INFORM*): ~ **por líneas** line editing; ~ **en pantalla** screen editing; ~ **(de pruebas)** (*TIP*) proofreading.
correccional [korrekθjo'nal] *nm* reformatory.
correcto, a [ko'rrekto, a] *adj* correct; (*persona*) well-mannered.
corrector, a [korrek'tor, a] *nm/f*: ~ **de pruebas** proofreader.
corredera [korre'ðera] *nf*: **puerta de ~** sliding door.
corredizo, a [korre'ðiθo, a] *adj* (*puerta etc*) sliding; (*nudo*) running.
corredor, a [korre'ðor, a] *adj* running; (*rápido*) fast ♦ *nm/f* (*DEPORTE*) runner ♦ *nm* (*pasillo*) corridor; (*balcón corrido*) gallery; (*COM*) agent, broker; (*pasillo*) corridor, passage; ~ **de bienes raíces** real-estate broker; ~ **de bolsa** stockbroker; ~ **de seguros** insurance broker.
corregir [korre'xir] *vt* (*error*) to correct; (*amonestar, reprender*) to rebuke, reprimand; **~se** *vr* to reform.
correo [ko'rreo] *nm* post, mail; (*persona*) courier; **C~s** *nmpl* Post Office *sg*; ~ **aéreo** airmail; ~ **certificado** registered mail; ~ **electrónico** E-mail, electronic mail; ~ **urgente** special delivery; **a vuelta de ~** by return (of post).
correr [ko'rrer] *vt* to run; (*viajar*) to cover, travel; (*riesgo*) to run; (*aventura*) to have; (*cortinas*) to draw; (*cerrojo*) to shoot ♦ *vi* to run; (*líquido*) to run, flow; (*rumor*) to go round; **~se** *vr* to slide, move; (*colores*) to run; (*fam*: *tener orgasmo*) to come; **echar a ~** to break into a run; ~ **con los gastos** to pay the expenses; **eso corre de mi cuenta** I'll take care of that.
correspondencia [korrespon'denθja] *nf* correspondence; (*FERRO*) connection; (*reciprocidad*) return; ~ **directa** (*COM*) direct mail.
corresponder [korrespon'der] *vi* to correspond; (*convenir*) to be suitable; (*pertenecer*) to belong; (*tocar*) to concern; (*favor*) to repay; **~se** *vr* (*por escrito*) to correspond; (*amarse*) to love one another; **"a quien corresponda"** "to whom it may concern".
correspondiente [korrespon'djente] *adj* corresponding; (*respectivo*) respective.
corresponsal [korrespon'sal] *nm/f* (newspaper) correspondent; (*COM*) agent.
corretaje [korre'taxe] *nm* (*COM*) brokerage.
corretear [korrete'ar] *vi* to loiter.
corrido, a [ko'rriðo, a] *adj* (*avergonzado*) abashed; (*fluido*) fluent ♦ *nf* run, dash; (*de toros*) bullfight; **de ~** fluently; **3 noches corridas** 3 nights running; **un kilo ~** a good kilo.
corriente [ko'rrjente] *adj* (*agua*) running;

(*fig*) flowing; (*dinero, cuenta etc*) current; (*común*) ordinary, normal ♦ *nf* current; (*fig: tendencia*) course ♦ *nm* current month; ~ *f* **de aire** draught; ~ **eléctrica** electric current; **las ~s modernas del arte** modern trends in art; **estar al ~ de** to be informed about.
corrigiendo [korri'xjendo] *etc vb V* **corregir.**
corrija [ko'rrixa] *etc vb V* **corregir.**
corrillo [ko'rriʎo] *nm* ring, circle (of people); (*fig*) clique.
corro ['korro] *nm* ring, circle (of people); (*baile*) ring-a-ring-a-roses; **la gente hizo ~** the people formed a ring.
corroborar [korroβo'rar] *vt* to corroborate.
corroer [korro'er] *vt* (*tb fig*) to corrode, eat away; (*GEO*) to erode.
corromper [korrom'per] *vt* (*madera*) to rot; (*fig*) to corrupt.
corrompido, a [korrom'piðo, a] *adj* corrupt.
corrosivo, a [korro'siβo, a] *adj* corrosive.
corroyendo [korro'jendo] *etc vb V* **corroer.**
corrupción [korrup'θjon] *nf* rot, decay; (*fig*) corruption.
corrupto, a [ko'rrupto, a] *adj* corrupt.
corsario [kor'sarjo] *nm* privateer, corsair.
corsé [kor'se] *nm* corset.
corso, a ['korso, a] *adj, nm/f* Corsican.
cortacésped [korta'θespeð] *nm* lawn mower.
cortado, a [kor'taðo, a] *adj* (*con cuchillo*) cut; (*leche*) sour; (*confuso*) confused; (*desconcertado*) embarrassed; (*tímido*) shy ♦ *nm* white coffee (with a little milk).
cortadora [korta'ðora] *nf* cutter, slicer.
cortadura [korta'ðura] *nf* cut.
cortante [kor'tante] *adj* (*viento*) biting; (*frío*) bitter.
cortapisa [korta'pisa] *nf* (*restricción*) restriction; (*traba*) snag.
cortar [kor'tar] *vt* to cut; (*suministro*) to cut off; (*un pasaje*) to cut out; (*comunicación, teléfono*) to cut off ♦ *vi* to cut; (*AM TELEC*) to hang up; **~se** *vr* (*turbarse*) to become embarrassed; (*leche*) to turn, curdle; **~ por lo sano** to settle things once and for all; **~se el pelo** to have one's hair cut; **se cortó la línea** *o* **el teléfono** I got cut off.
cortauñas [korta'uɲas] *nm inv* nail clippers *pl*.
corte ['korte] *nm* cut, cutting; (*filo*) edge; (*de tela*) piece, length; (*COSTURA*) tailoring ♦ *nf* (*real*) (royal) court; **~ y confección** dressmaking; **~ de corriente** *o* **luz** power cut; **me da ~ pedírselo** I'm embarrassed to ask him for it; **¡qué ~ le di!** I left him with no comeback!; **C~ Internacional de Justicia** International Court of Justice; **las C~s** the Spanish Parliament *sg*; **hacer la ~ a** to woo, court; *see boxed note*.

> **LAS CORTES**
>
> *The Spanish Parliament,* **las Cortes (Españolas)***, has a lower and an upper chamber, the "Congreso de los Diputados" and the "Senado" respectively. Members of the lower house are called "diputados" and are chosen in general elections by a system of proportional representation. Some Senate members, "senadores", are voted in during general elections, while others are appointed by the regional parliaments.*

cortejar [korte'xar] *vt* to court.
cortejo [kor'texo] *nm* entourage; **~ fúnebre** funeral procession, cortège.
cortés [kor'tes] *adj* courteous, polite.
cortesano, a [korte'sano, a] *adj* courtly.
cortesía [korte'sia] *nf* courtesy.
corteza [kor'teθa] *nf* (*de árbol*) bark; (*de pan*) crust; (*de fruta*) peel, skin; (*de queso*) rind.
cortijo [kor'tixo] *nm* farmhouse.
cortina [kor'tina] *nf* curtain; **~ de humo** smoke screen.
corto, a ['korto, a] *adj* (*breve*) short; (*tímido*) bashful; **~ de luces** not very bright; **~ de oído** hard of hearing; **~ de vista** short-sighted; **estar ~ de fondos** to be short of funds.
cortocircuito [kortoθir'kwito] *nm* short-circuit.
cortometraje [kortome'traxe] *nm* (*CINE*) short.
Coruña [ko'ruɲa] *nf*: **La ~** Corunna.
coruñés, esa [koru'ɲes, esa] *adj* of *o* from Corunna ♦ *nm/f* native *o* inhabitant of Corunna.
corvo, a ['korβo, a] *adj* curved; (*nariz*) hooked ♦ *nf* back of knee.
cosa ['kosa] *nf* thing; (*asunto*) affair; **~ de** about; **eso es ~ mía** that's my business; **es poca ~** it's not important; **¡qué ~ más rara!** how strange.
cosaco, a [ko'sako, a] *adj, nm/f* Cossack.
coscorrón [kosko'rron] *nm* bump on the head.
cosecha [ko'setʃa] *nf* (*AGR*) harvest; (*acto*) harvesting; (*de vino*) vintage; (*producción*) yield.

cosechadora [kosetʃa'ðora] *nf* combine harvester.
cosechar [kose'tʃar] *vt* to harvest, gather (in).
coser [ko'ser] *vt* to sew; (*MED*) to stitch (up).
cosido [ko'siðo] *nm* sewing.
cosmético, a [kos'metiko, a] *adj, nm* cosmetic ♦ *nf* cosmetics *pl*.
cosmopolita [kosmopo'lita] *adj* cosmopolitan.
cosmos ['kosmos] *nm* cosmos.
coso ['koso] *nm* bullring.
cosquillas [kos'kiʎas] *nfpl*: **hacer ~** to tickle; **tener ~** to be ticklish.
cosquilleo [koski'ʎeo] *nm* tickling (sensation).
costa ['kosta] *nf* (*GEO*) coast; **C~ Brava** Costa Brava; **C~ Cantábrica** Cantabrian Coast; **C~ de Marfil** Ivory Coast; **C~ del Sol** Costa del Sol; **a ~** (*COM*) at cost; **a ~ de** at the expense of; **a toda ~** at any price.
costado [kos'taðo] *nm* side; **de ~** (*dormir*) on one's side; **español por los 4 ~s** Spanish through and through.
costal [kos'tal] *nm* sack.
costalada [kosta'laða] *nf* bad fall.
costanera [kosta'nera] *nf* (*AM*) (seaside) promenade.
costar [kos'tar] *vt* (*valer*) to cost; **me cuesta hablarle** I find it hard to talk to him; **¿cuánto cuesta?** how much does it cost?
Costa Rica [kosta'rika] *nf* Costa Rica.
costarricense [kostarri'θense], **costarriqueño, a** [kostarri'keɲo, a] *adj, nm/f* Costa Rican.
coste ['koste] *nm* (*COM*): **~ promedio** average cost; **~s fijos** fixed costs; *V tb* **costo**.
costear [koste'ar] *vt* to pay for; (*COM etc*) to finance; (*NAUT*) to sail along the coast of; **~se** *vr* (*negocio*) to pay for itself, cover its costs.
costeño, a [kos'teɲo, a] *adj* coastal.
costero, a [kos'tero, a] *adj* coastal, coast *cpd*.
costilla [kos'tiʎa] *nf* rib; (*CULIN*) cutlet.
costo ['kosto] *nm* cost, price; **~ directo** direct cost; **~ de expedición** shipping charges; **~ de sustitución** replacement cost; **~ unitario** unit cost; **~ de la vida** cost of living.
costoso, a [kos'toso, a] *adj* costly, expensive.
costra ['kostra] *nf* (*corteza*) crust; (*MED*) scab.
costumbre [kos'tumbre] *nf* custom, habit; **como de ~** as usual.
costura [kos'tura] *nf* sewing, needlework; (*confección*) dressmaking; (*zurcido*) seam.
costurera [kostu'rera] *nf* dressmaker.
costurero [kostu'rero] *nm* sewing box *o* case.
cota ['kota] *nf* (*GEO*) height above sea level; (*fig*) height.
cotarro [ko'tarro] *nm*: **dirigir el ~** (*fam*) to rule the roost.
cotejar [kote'xar] *vt* to compare.
cotejo [ko'texo] *nm* comparison.
cotice [ko'tiθe] *etc vb V* **cotizar**.
cotidiano, a [koti'ðjano, a] *adj* daily, day to day.
cotilla [ko'tiʎa] *nf* busybody, gossip.
cotillear [kotiʎe'ar] *vi* to gossip.
cotilleo [koti'ʎeo] *nm* gossip(ing).
cotización [kotiθa'θjon] *nf* (*COM*) quotation, price; (*de club*) dues *pl*.
cotizado, a [koti'θaðo, a] *adj* (*fig*) highly-prized.
cotizar [koti'θar] *vt* (*COM*) to quote, price; **~se** *vr* (*fig*) to be highly prized; **~se a** to sell at, fetch; (*BOLSA*) to stand at, be quoted at.
coto ['koto] *nm* (*terreno cercado*) enclosure; (*de caza*) reserve; (*COM*) price-fixing agreement; **poner ~ a** to put a stop to.
cotorra [ko'torra] *nf* (*ZOOL*: *loro*) parrot; (*fam*: *persona*) windbag.
COU [kou] *nm abr* (*ESP*: = *Curso de Orientación Universitario*) *one year course leading to final school leaving certificate and university entrance examinations; V tb* **sistema educativo**.
coyote [ko'jote] *nm* coyote, prairie wolf.
coyuntura [kojun'tura] *nf* (*ANAT*) joint; (*fig*) juncture, occasion; **esperar una ~ favorable** to await a favourable moment.
coz [koθ] *nf* kick.
CP *nm abr* (= *computador personal*) PC.
C.P. *abr* (*ESP*) = *Caja Postal*.
C.P.A. *nf abr* (= *Caja Postal de Ahorros*) Post Office Savings Bank.
CP/M *nm abr* (= *Programa de control para microprocesadores*) CP/M.
CPN *nm abr* (*ESP*) = *Cuerpo de la Policía Nacional*.
cps *abr* (= *caracteres por segundo*) c.p.s.
crac [krak] *nm* (*ECON*) crash.
cráneo ['kraneo] *nm* skull, cranium.
crápula ['krapula] *nf* drunkenness.
cráter ['krater] *nm* crater.
creación [krea'θjon] *nf* creation.
creador, a [krea'ðor, a] *adj* creative ♦ *nm/f* creator.

crear [kre'ar] *vt* to create, make; (*originar*) to originate; (*INFORM*: *archivo*) to create; **~se** *vr* (*comité etc*) to be set up.
creativo, a [krea'tiβo, a] *adj* creative.
crecer [kre'θer] *vi* to grow; (*precio*) to rise; **~se** *vr* (*engreírse*) to get cocky.
creces ['kreθes]: **con ~** *adv* amply, fully.
crecido, a [kre'θiðo, a] *adj* (*persona, planta*) full-grown; (*cantidad*) large ♦ *nf* (*de río*) spate, flood.
creciente [kre'θjente] *adj* growing; (*cantidad*) increasing; (*luna*) crescent ♦ *nm* crescent.
crecimiento [kreθi'mjento] *nm* growth; (*aumento*) increase; (*COM*) rise.
credenciales [kreðen'θjales] *nfpl* credentials.
crédito ['kreðito] *nm* credit; **a ~** on credit; **dar ~ a** to believe (in); **~ al consumidor** consumer credit; **~ rotativo** *o* **renovable** revolving credit.
credo ['kreðo] *nm* creed.
crédulo, a ['kreðulo, a] *adj* credulous.
creencia [kre'enθja] *nf* belief.
creer [kre'er] *vt, vi* to think, believe; (*considerar*) to think, consider; **~se** *vr* to believe o.s. (to be); **~ en** to believe in; **¡ya lo creo!** I should think so!
creíble [kre'iβle] *adj* credible, believable.
creído, a [kre'iðo, a] *adj* (*engreído*) conceited.
crema ['krema] *adj inv* cream (coloured) ♦ *nf* cream; (*natillas*) custard; **la ~ de la sociedad** the cream of society.
cremallera [krema'ʎera] *nf* zip (fastener) (*BRIT*), zipper (*US*).
crematorio [krema'torjo] *nm* crematorium (*BRIT*), crematory (*US*).
cremoso, a [kre'moso, a] *adj* creamy.
crepitar [krepi'tar] *vi* (*fuego*) to crackle.
crepúsculo [kre'puskulo] *nm* twilight, dusk.
crespo, a ['krespo, a] *adj* (*pelo*) curly.
crespón [kres'pon] *nm* crêpe.
cresta ['kresta] *nf* (*GEO, ZOOL*) crest.
Creta ['kreta] *nf* Crete.
cretino, a [kre'tino, a] *adj* cretinous ♦ *nm/f* cretin.
creyendo [kre'jendo] *etc vb V* **creer**.
creyente [kre'jente] *nm/f* believer.
crezca ['kreθka] *etc vb V* **crecer**.
cría ['kria] *etc vb V* **criar** ♦ *nf V* **crío, a**.
criada [kri'aða] *nf V* **criado, a**.
criadero [kria'ðero] *nm* nursery; (*ZOOL*) breeding place.
criadillas [kria'ðiʎas] *nfpl* (*CULIN*) bull's (*o* sheep's) testicles.
criado, a [kri'aðo, a] *nm* servant ♦ *nf* servant, maid.
criador [kria'ðor] *nm* breeder.
crianza [kri'anθa] *nf* rearing, breeding; (*fig*) breeding; (*MED*) lactation.
criar [kri'ar] *vt* (*amamantar*) to suckle, feed; (*educar*) to bring up; (*producir*) to grow, produce; (*animales*) to breed; **~se** *vr* to grow (up); **~ cuervos** to nourish a viper in one's bosom; **Dios los cría y ellos se juntan** birds of a feather flock together.
criatura [kria'tura] *nf* creature; (*niño*) baby, (small) child.
criba ['kriβa] *nf* sieve.
cribar [kri'βar] *vt* to sieve.
crimen ['krimen] *nm* crime; **~ pasional** crime of passion.
criminal [krimi'nal] *adj, nm/f* criminal.
crin [krin] *nf* (*tb*: **~es**) mane.
crío, a ['krio, a] *nm/f* (*fam*: *chico*) kid ♦ *nf* (*de animales*) rearing, breeding; (*animal*) young.
criollo, a [kri'oʎo, a] *adj* (*gen*) Creole; (*AM*) native (to America), national ♦ *nm/f* (*gen*) Creole; (*AM*) native American.
cripta ['kripta] *nf* crypt.
crisis ['krisis] *nf inv* crisis; **~ nerviosa** nervous breakdown.
crisma ['krisma] *nf*: **romperle la ~ a algn** (*fam*) to knock sb's block off.
crisol [kri'sol] *nm* (*TEC*) crucible; (*fig*) melting pot.
crispación [krispa'θjon] *nf* tension.
crispar [kris'par] *vt* (*músculo*) to cause to contract; (*nervios*) to set on edge.
cristal [kris'tal] *nm* crystal; (*de ventana*) glass, pane; (*lente*) lens; **de ~** glass *cpd*; **~ ahumado/tallado** smoked/cut glass.
cristalería [kristale'ria] *nf* (*tienda*) glassware shop; (*objetos*) glassware.
cristalice [krista'liθe] *etc vb V* **cristalizar**.
cristalino, a [krista'lino, a] *adj* crystalline; (*fig*) clear ♦ *nm* lens of the eye.
cristalizar [kristali'θar] *vt, vi* to crystallize.
cristiandad [kristjan'dað] *nf*, **cristianismo** [kristja'nismo] *nm* Christianity.
cristiano, a [kris'tjano, a] *adj, nm/f* Christian; **hablar en ~** to speak proper Spanish; (*fig*) to speak clearly.
Cristo ['kristo] *nm* (*dios*) Christ; (*crucifijo*) crucifix.
Cristóbal [kris'toβal] *nm*: **~ Colón** Christopher Columbus.
criterio [kri'terjo] *nm* criterion; (*juicio*) judgement; (*enfoque*) attitude, approach; (*punto de vista*) view, opinion; **~ de clasificación** (*INFORM*) sort criterion.
criticar [kriti'kar] *vt* to criticize.

crítico, a ['kritiko, a] *adj* critical ♦ *nm* critic ♦ *nf* criticism; (*TEAT etc*) review, notice; **la crítica** the critics *pl*.
critique [kri'tike] *etc vb V* **criticar**.
Croacia [kro'aθja] *nf* Croatia.
croar [kro'ar] *vi* to croak.
croata [kro'ata] *adj, nm/f* Croat(ian) ♦ *nm* (*LING*) Croat(ian).
croissan(t) [krwa'san] *nm* croissant.
crol ['krol] *nm* crawl.
cromado [kro'maðo] *nm* chromium plating, chrome.
cromo ['kromo] *nm* chrome; (*TIP*) coloured print.
cromosoma [kromo'soma] *nm* chromosome.
crónico, a ['kroniko, a] *adj* chronic ♦ *nf* chronicle, account; (*de periódico*) feature, article.
cronología [kronolo'xia] *nf* chronology.
cronológico, a [krono'loxiko, a] *adj* chronological.
cronometraje [kronome'traxe] *nm* timing.
cronometrar [kronome'trar] *vt* to time.
cronómetro [kro'nometro] *nm* (*DEPORTE*) stopwatch; (*TEC etc*) chronometer.
croqueta [kro'keta] *nf* croquette, rissole.
croquis ['krokis] *nm inv* sketch.
cruce ['kruθe] *etc vb V* **cruzar** ♦ *nm* crossing; (*de carreteras*) crossroads; (*AUTO etc*) junction, intersection; (*BIO: proceso*) crossbreeding; **luces de ~** dipped headlights.
crucero [kru'θero] *nm* (*NAUT: barco*) cruise ship; (*: viaje*) cruise.
crucial [kru'θjal] *adj* crucial.
crucificar [kruθifi'kar] *vt* to crucify; (*fig*) to torment.
crucifijo [kruθi'fixo] *nm* crucifix.
crucifique [kruθi'fike] *etc vb V* **crucificar**.
crucigrama [kruθi'ɣrama] *nm* crossword (puzzle).
crudeza [kru'ðeθa] *nf* (*rigor*) harshness; (*aspereza*) crudeness.
crudo, a ['kruðo, a] *adj* raw; (*no maduro*) unripe; (*petróleo*) crude; (*rudo, cruel*) cruel; (*agua*) hard; (*clima etc*) harsh ♦ *nm* crude (oil).
cruel [krwel] *adj* cruel.
crueldad [krwel'ðað] *nf* cruelty.
cruento, a ['krwento, a] *adj* bloody.
crujido [kru'xiðo] *nm* (*de madera etc*) creak.
crujiente [kru'xjente] *adj* (*galleta etc*) crunchy.
crujir [kru'xir] *vi* (*madera etc*) to creak; (*dedos*) to crack; (*dientes*) to grind; (*nieve, arena*) to crunch.
cruz [kruθ] *nf* cross; (*de moneda*) tails *sg*; (*fig*) burden; **~ gamada** swastika; **C~ Roja** Red Cross.
cruzado, a [kru'θaðo, a] *adj* crossed ♦ *nm* crusader ♦ *nf* crusade.
cruzar [kru'θar] *vt* to cross; (*palabras*) to exchange; **~se** *vr* (*líneas etc*) to cross, intersect; (*personas*) to pass each other; **~se de brazos** to fold one's arms; (*fig*) not to lift a finger to help; **~se con algn en la calle** to pass sb in the street.
c.s.f. *abr* (= *costo, seguro y flete*) c.i.f.
CSIC [θe'sik] *nm abr* (*ESP ESCOL*) = *Consejo Superior de Investigaciones Científicas*.
cta, c.ta *nf abr* (= *cuenta*) a/c.
cta. cto. *abr* (= *carta de crédito*) L.C.
cte. *abr* (= *corriente, de los corrientes*) inst.
CTNE *nf abr* (*TELEC*) = *Compañía Telefónica Nacional de España*.
c/u *abr* (= *cada uno*) ea.
cuaco ['kwako] *nm* (*AM*) nag.
cuaderno [kwa'ðerno] *nm* notebook; (*de escuela*) exercise book; (*NAUT*) logbook.
cuadra ['kwaðra] *nf* (*caballeriza*) stable; (*AM*) (city) block.
cuadrado, a [kwa'ðraðo, a] *adj* square ♦ *nm* (*MAT*) square.
cuadragésimo, a [kwaðra'xesimo, a] *num* fortieth.
cuadrángulo [kwa'ðrangulo, a] *nm* quadrangle.
cuadrante [kwa'ðrante] *nm* quadrant.
cuadrar [kwa'ðrar] *vt* to square; (*TIP*) to justify ♦ *vi*: **~ con** (*cuenta*) to square with, tally with; **~se** *vr* (*soldado*) to stand to attention; **~ por la derecha/izquierda** to right-/left-justify.
cuadrícula [kwa'ðrikula] *nf* (*TIP etc*) grid, ruled squares.
cuadriculado, a [kwaðriku'laðo, a] *adj*: **papel ~** squared *o* graph paper.
cuadrilátero [kwaðri'latero] *nm* (*DEPORTE*) boxing ring; (*GEOM*) quadrilateral.
cuadrilla [kwa'ðriʎa] *nf* (*amigos*) party, group; (*pandilla*) gang; (*obreros*) team.
cuadro ['kwaðro] *nm* square; (*PINTURA*) painting; (*TEAT*) scene; (*diagrama*: *tb*: **~ sinóptico**) chart, table, diagram; (*DEPORTE, MED*) team; (*POL*) executive; **~ de mandos** control panel; **a ~s** check *cpd*.
cuadruplicarse [kwaðrupli'karse] *vr* to quadruple.
cuádruplo, a ['kwaðruplo, a], **cuádruple** ['kwaðruple] *adj* quadruple.
cuajado, a [kwa'xaðo, a] *adj*: **~ de** (*fig*) full of ♦ *nf* (*de leche*) curd.
cuajar [kwa'xar] *vt* to thicken; (*leche*) to curdle; (*sangre*) to congeal; (*adornar*) to

adorn; (*CULIN*) to set ♦ *vi* (*nieve*) to lie; (*fig*) to become set, become established; (*idea*) to be received, be acceptable; **~se** *vr* to curdle; to congeal; (*llenarse*) to fill up.

cuajo ['kwaxo] *nm*: **arrancar algo de ~** to tear sth out by its roots.

cual [kwal] *adv* like, as ♦ *pron*: **el ~** *etc* which; (*persona: sujeto*) who; (: *objeto*) whom; **lo ~** (*relativo*) which; **allá cada ~** every man to his own taste; **son a ~ más gandul** each is as idle as the other; **cada ~** each one ♦ *adj* such as; **tal ~** just as it is.

cuál [kwal] *pron interrogativo* which (one), what.

cualesquier(a) [kwales'kjer(a)] *pl de* **cualquier(a)**.

cualidad [kwali'ðað] *nf* quality.

cualificado, a [kwalifi'kaðo, a] *adj* (*obrero*) skilled, qualified.

cualquiera [kwal'kjera], **cualquier** [kwal'kjer], *pl* **cualesquier(a)** *adj* any ♦ *pron* anybody, anyone; (*quienquiera*) whoever; **en cualquier momento** any time; **en cualquier parte** anywhere; **cualquiera que sea** whichever it is; (*persona*) whoever it is.

cuán [kwan] *adv* how.

cuando ['kwando] *adv* when; (*aún si*) if, even if ♦ *conj* (*puesto que*) since ♦ *prep*: **yo, ~ niño ...** when I was a child *o* as a child I ...; **~ no sea así** even if it is not so; **~ más** at (the) most; **~ menos** at least; **~ no** if not, otherwise; **de ~ en ~** from time to time; **ven ~ quieras** come when(ever) you like.

cuándo ['kwando] *adv* when; **¿desde ~?, ¿de ~ acá?** since when?

cuantía [kwan'tia] *nf* (*alcance*) extent; (*importancia*) importance.

cuantioso, a [kwan'tjoso, a] *adj* substantial.

PALABRA CLAVE

cuanto, a ['kwanto, a] *adj* **1** (*todo*): **tiene todo ~ desea** he's got everything he wants; **le daremos ~s ejemplares necesite** we'll give him as many copies as *o* all the copies he needs; **~s hombres la ven** all the men who see her

2: **unos ~s**: **había unos ~s periodistas** there were (quite) a few journalists

3 (*+más*): **~ más vino bebas peor te sentirás** the more wine you drink the worse you'll feel; **~s más, mejor** the more the merrier

♦ *pron*: **tiene ~ desea** he has everything he wants; **tome ~/~s quiera** take as much/many as you want

♦ *adv*: **en ~**: **en ~ profesor** as a teacher; **en ~ a mí** as for me; *V tb* **antes**

♦ *conj* **1**: **~ más gana menos gasta** the more he earns the less he spends; **~ más joven se es más se es confiado** the younger you are the more trusting you are

2: **en ~**: **en ~ llegue/llegué** as soon as I arrive/arrived.

cuánto, a ['kwanto, a] *adj* (*exclamación*) what a lot of; (*interrogativo*: *sg*) how much?; (: *pl*) how many? ♦ *pron, adv* how; (*interrogativo*: *sg*) how much?; (: *pl*) how many? ♦ *excl*: **¡~ me alegro!** I'm so glad!; **¡cuánta gente!** what a lot of people!; **¿~ tiempo?** how long?; **¿~ cuesta?** how much does it cost?; **¿a ~s estamos?** what's the date?; **¿~ hay de aquí a Bilbao?** how far is it from here to Bilbao?; **Señor no sé ~s** Mr. So-and-So.

cuarenta [kwa'renta] *num* forty.

cuarentena [kwaren'tena] *nf* (*MED etc*) quarantine; (*conjunto*) forty(-odd).

cuarentón, ona [kwaren'ton, ona] *adj* forty-year-old, fortyish ♦ *nm/f* person of about forty.

cuaresma [kwa'resma] *nf* Lent.

cuarta ['kwarta] *nf V* **cuarto**.

cuartear [kwarte'ar] *vt* to quarter; (*dividir*) to divide up; **~se** *vr* to crack, split.

cuartel [kwar'tel] *nm* (*de ciudad*) quarter, district; (*MIL*) barracks *pl*; **~ general** headquarters *pl*.

cuartelazo [kwarte'laθo] *nm* coup, military uprising.

cuarteto [kwar'teto] *nm* quartet.

cuartilla [kwar'tiʎa] *nf* (*hoja*) sheet (of paper); **~s** *nfpl* (*TIP*) copy *sg*.

cuarto, a ['kwarto, a] *adj* fourth ♦ *nm* (*MAT*) quarter, fourth; (*habitación*) room ♦ *nf* (*MAT*) quarter, fourth; (*palmo*) span; **~ de baño** bathroom; **~ de estar** living room; **~ de hora** quarter (of an) hour; **~ de kilo** quarter kilo; **no tener un ~** to be broke (*fam*).

cuarzo ['kwarθo] *nm* quartz.

cuatrero [kwa'trero] *nm* (*AM*) rustler, stock thief.

cuatrimestre [kwatri'mestre] *nm* four-month period.

cuatro ['kwatro] *num* four; **las ~** four o'clock; **el ~ de octubre** (on) the fourth of October; *V tb* **seis**.

cuatrocientos, as [kwatro'θjentos, as] *num* four hundred; *V tb* **seiscientos**.

Cuba ['kuβa] *nf* Cuba.
cuba ['kuβa] *nf* cask, barrel; **estar como una** ~ (*fam*) to be sloshed.
cubalibre [kuβa'liβre] *nm* (white) rum and coke ®.
cubano, a [ku'βano, a] *adj, nm/f* Cuban.
cubata [ku'βata] *nm* = **cubalibre**.
cubertería [kuβerte'ria] *nf* cutlery.
cúbico, a ['kuβiko, a] *adj* cubic.
cubierto, a [ku'βjerto, a] *pp de* **cubrir** ♦ *adj* covered; (*cielo*) overcast ♦ *nm* cover; (*en la mesa*) place ♦ *nf* cover, covering; (*neumático*) tyre; (*NAUT*) deck; ~**s** *nmpl* cutlery *sg*; **a** ~ **de** covered with *o* in; **precio del** ~ cover charge.
cubil [ku'βil] *nm* den.
cubilete [kuβi'lete] *nm* (*en juegos*) cup.
cubito [ku'βito] *nm*: ~ **de hielo** ice cube.
cubo ['kuβo] *nm* cube; (*balde*) bucket, tub; (*TEC*) drum; ~ **de (la) basura** dustbin.
cubrecama [kuβre'kama] *nm* bedspread.
cubrir [ku'βrir] *vt* to cover; (*vacante*) to fill; (*BIO*) to mate with; (*gastos*) to meet; ~**se** *vr* (*cielo*) to become overcast; (*COM*: *gastos*) to be met *o* paid; (: *deuda*) to be covered; ~ **las formas** to keep up appearances; **lo cubrieron las aguas** the waters closed over it; **el agua casi me cubría** I was almost out of my depth.
cucaracha [kuka'ratʃa] *nf* cockroach.
cuchara [ku'tʃara] *nf* spoon; (*TEC*) scoop.
cucharada [kutʃa'raða] *nf* spoonful; ~ **colmada** heaped spoonful.
cucharadita [kutʃara'ðita] *nf* teaspoonful.
cucharilla [kutʃa'riʎa] *nf* teaspoon.
cucharita [kutʃa'rita] *nf* teaspoon.
cucharón [kutʃa'ron] *nm* ladle.
cuchichear [kutʃitʃe'ar] *vi* to whisper.
cuchicheo [kutʃi'tʃeo] *nm* whispering.
cuchilla [ku'tʃiʎa] *nf* (large) knife; (*de arma blanca*) blade; ~ **de afeitar** razor blade; **pasar a** ~ to put to the sword.
cuchillada [kutʃi'ʎaða] *nf* (*golpe*) stab; (*herida*) knife *o* stab wound.
cuchillo [ku'tʃiʎo] *nm* knife.
cuchitril [kutʃi'tril] *nm* hovel; (*habitación etc*) pigsty.
cuclillas [ku'kliʎas] *nfpl*: **en** ~ squatting.
cuco, a ['kuko, a] *adj* pretty; (*astuto*) sharp ♦ *nm* cuckoo.
cucurucho [kuku'rutʃo] *nm* paper cone, cornet.
cuece ['kweθe] *etc vb V* **cocer**.
cuele ['kwele] *etc vb V* **colar**.
cuelgue ['kwelɣe] *etc vb V* **colgar**.
cuello ['kweʎo] *nm* (*ANAT*) neck; (*de vestido, camisa*) collar.
cuenca ['kwenka] *nf* (*ANAT*) eye socket; (*GEO*: *valle*) bowl, deep valley; (: *fluvial*) basin.
cuenco ['kwenko] *nm* (earthenware) bowl.
cuenta ['kwenta] *etc vb V* **contar** ♦ *nf* (*cálculo*) count, counting; (*en café, restaurante*) bill; (*COM*) account; (*de collar*) bead; (*fig*) account; **a fin de** ~**s** in the end; **en resumidas** ~**s** in short; **caer en la** ~ to catch on; **dar** ~ **a algn de sus actos** to account to sb for one's actions; **darse** ~ **de** to realize; **tener en** ~ to bear in mind; **echar** ~**s** to take stock; ~ **atrás** countdown; ~ **corriente/de ahorros/a plazo (fijo)** current/savings/deposit account; ~ **de asignación** appropriation account; ~ **de caja** cash account; ~ **de capital** capital account; ~ **por cobrar** account receivable; ~ **de crédito** credit *o* loan account; ~ **de gastos e ingresos** income and expenditure account; ~ **por pagar** account payable; **abonar una cantidad en** ~ **a algn** to credit a sum to sb's account; **ajustar** *o* **liquidar una** ~ to settle an account; **pasar la** ~ to send the bill.
cuentagotas [kwenta'ɣotas] *nm inv* (*MED*) dropper; **a** *o* **con** ~ (*fam, fig*) drop by drop, bit by bit.
cuentakilómetros [kwentaki'lometros] *nm inv* (*de distancias*) ≈ milometer, clock; (*velocímetro*) speedometer.
cuentista [kwen'tista] *nm/f* gossip; (*LIT*) short-story writer.
cuento ['kwento] *etc vb V* **contar** ♦ *nm* story; (*LIT*) short story; ~ **de hadas** fairy story; **es el** ~ **de nunca acabar** it's an endless business; **eso no viene a** ~ that's irrelevant.
cuerda ['kwerða] *nf* rope; (*hilo*) string; (*de reloj*) spring; (*MUS*: *de violín etc*) string; (*MAT*) chord; (*ANAT*) cord; ~ **floja** tightrope; ~**s vocales** vocal cords; **dar** ~ **a un reloj** to wind up a clock.
cuerdo, a ['kwerðo, a] *adj* sane; (*prudente*) wise, sensible.
cuerear [kwere'ar] *vt* (*AM*) to skin.
cuerno ['kwerno] *nm* (*ZOOL*: *gen*) horn; (: *de ciervo*) antler; **poner los** ~**s a** (*fam*) to cuckold; **saber a** ~ **quemado** to leave a nasty taste.
cuero ['kwero] *nm* (*ZOOL*) skin, hide; (*TEC*) leather; **en** ~**s** stark naked; ~ **cabelludo** scalp.
cuerpo ['kwerpo] *nm* body; (*cadáver*) corpse; (*fig*) main part; ~ **de bomberos** fire brigade; ~ **diplomático** diplomatic

corps; **luchar ~ a ~** to fight hand-to-hand; **tomar ~** (*plan etc*) to take shape.
cuervo ['kwerßo] *nm* (*ZOOL*) raven, crow; *V* **criar**.
cuesta ['kwesta] *etc vb V* **costar** ♦ *nf* slope; (*en camino etc*) hill; **~ arriba/abajo** uphill/downhill; **a ~s** on one's back.
cuestión [kwes'tjon] *nf* matter, question, issue; (*riña*) quarrel, dispute; **eso es otra ~** that's another matter.
cuestionar [kwestjo'nar] *vt* to question.
cuestionario [kwestjo'narjo] *nm* questionnaire.
cueva ['kweßa] *nf* cave.
cueza ['kweθa] *etc vb V* **cocer**.
cuidado [kwi'ðaðo] *nm* care, carefulness; (*preocupación*) care, worry ♦ *excl* careful!, look out!; **eso me tiene sin ~** I'm not worried about that.
cuidadoso, a [kwiða'ðoso, a] *adj* careful; (*preocupado*) anxious.
cuidar [kwi'ðar] *vt* (*MED*) to care for; (*ocuparse de*) to take care of, look after; (*detalles*) to pay attention to ♦ *vi*: **~ de** to take care of, look after; **~se** *vr* to look after o.s.; **~se de hacer algo** to take care to do something.
cuita ['kwita] *nf* (*preocupación*) worry, trouble; (*pena*) grief.
culata [ku'lata] *nf* (*de fusil*) butt.
culatazo [kula'taθo] *nm* kick, recoil.
culebra [ku'leßra] *nf* snake; **~ de cascabel** rattlesnake.
culebrear [kuleßre'ar] *vi* to wriggle along; (*río*) to meander.
culebrón [kule'ßron] *nm* (*fam*) soap (opera).
culinario, a [kuli'narjo, a] *adj* culinary, cooking *cpd*.
culminación [kulmina'θjon] *nf* culmination.
culminante [kulmi'nante] *adj*: **momento ~** climax, highlight, highspot.
culminar [kulmi'nar] *vi* to culminate.
culo ['kulo] *nm* (*fam: asentaderas*) bottom, backside, bum (*BRIT*); (*: ano*) arse(hole) (*BRIT!*), ass(hole) (*US!*); (*de vaso*) bottom.
culpa ['kulpa] *nf* fault; (*JUR*) guilt; **~s** *nfpl* sins; **por ~ de** through, because of; **tener la ~ (de)** to be to blame (for).
culpabilidad [kulpaßili'ðað] *nf* guilt.
culpable [kul'paßle] *adj* guilty ♦ *nm/f* culprit; **confesarse ~** to plead guilty; **declarar ~ a algn** to find sb guilty.
culpar [kul'par] *vt* to blame; (*acusar*) to accuse.
cultivadora [kultißa'ðora] *nf* cultivator.
cultivar [kulti'ßar] *vt* to cultivate; (*cosecha*) to raise; (*talento*) to develop.
cultivo [kul'tißo] *nm* (*acto*) cultivation; (*plantas*) crop; (*BIO*) culture.
culto, a ['kulto, a] *adj* (*cultivado*) cultivated; (*que tiene cultura*) cultured, educated ♦ *nm* (*homenaje*) worship; (*religión*) cult; (*POL etc*) cult.
cultura [kul'tura] *nf* culture.
cultural [kultu'ral] *adj* cultural.
culturismo [kultu'rismo] *nm* body-building.
cumbre ['kumbre] *nf* summit, top; (*fig*) top, height; **conferencia (en la) ~** summit (conference).
cumpleaños [kumple'aɲos] *nm inv* birthday.
cumplido, a [kum'pliðo, a] *adj* complete, perfect; (*abundante*) plentiful; (*cortés*) courteous ♦ *nm* compliment; **visita de ~** courtesy call.
cumplidor, a [kumpli'ðor, a] *adj* reliable.
cumplimentar [kumplimen'tar] *vt* to congratulate; (*órdenes*) to carry out.
cumplimiento [kumpli'mjento] *nm* (*de un deber*) fulfilment, execution, performance; (*acabamiento*) completion; (*COM*) expiry, end.
cumplir [kum'plir] *vt* (*orden*) to carry out, obey; (*promesa*) to carry out, fulfil; (*condena*) to serve; (*años*) to reach, attain ♦ *vi* (*pago*) to fall due; (*plazo*) to expire; **~se** *vr* (*plazo*) to expire; (*plan etc*) to be fulfilled; (*vaticinio*) to come true; **hoy cumple dieciocho años** he is eighteen today; **~ con** (*deberes*) to carry out, fulfil.
cúmulo ['kumulo] *nm* (*montón*) heap; (*nube*) cumulus.
cuna ['kuna] *nf* cradle, cot; **canción de ~** lullaby.
cundir [kun'dir] *vi* (*noticia, rumor, pánico*) to spread; (*rendir*) to go a long way.
cuneta [ku'neta] *nf* ditch.
cuña ['kuɲa] *nf* (*TEC*) wedge; (*COM*) advertising spot; (*MED*) bedpan; **tener ~s** to have influence.
cuñado, a [ku'ɲaðo, a] *nm/f* brother/sister-in-law.
cuño ['kuɲo] *nm* (*TEC*) die-stamp; (*fig*) stamp.
cuota ['kwota] *nf* (*parte proporcional*) share; (*cotización*) fee, dues *pl*; **~ inicial** (*COM*) down payment.
cupo ['kupo] *etc vb V* **caber** ♦ *nm* quota, share; (*COM*): **~ de importación** import quota; **~ de ventas** sales quota.
cupón [ku'pon] *nm* coupon; **~ de la ONCE** *o* **de los ciegos** ONCE lottery ticket; *V tb*

lotería.
cúpula ['kupula] *nf* (*ARQ*) dome.
cura ['kura] *nf* (*curación*) cure; (*método curativo*) treatment ♦ *nm* priest; ~ **de emergencia** emergency treatment.
curación [kura'θjon] *nf* cure; (*acción*) curing.
curado, a [ku'raðo, a] *adj* (*CULIN*) cured; (*pieles*) tanned.
curandero, a [kuran'dero, a] *nm/f* healer.
curar [ku'rar] *vt* (*MED*: *herida*) to treat, dress; (: *enfermo*) to cure; (*CULIN*) to cure, salt; (*cuero*) to tan ♦ *vi*, **~se** *vr* to get well, recover.
curda ['kurða] (*fam*) *nm* drunk ♦ *nf*: **agarrar una/estar** ~ to get/be sloshed.
curiosear [kurjose'ar] *vt* to glance at, look over ♦ *vi* to look round, wander round; (*explorar*) to poke about.
curiosidad [kurjosi'ðað] *nf* curiosity.
curioso, a [ku'rjoso, a] *adj* curious; (*aseado*) neat ♦ *nm/f* bystander, onlooker; **¡qué ~!** how odd!
curita [ku'rita] *nf* (*AM*) sticking plaster.
currante [ku'rrante] *nm/f* (*fam*) worker.
currar [ku'rrar] *vi* (*fam*), **currelar** [kurre'lar] *vi* (*fam*) to work.
currículo [ku'rrikulo] *nm*, **currículum** [ku'rrikulum] *nm* curriculum vitae.
curro ['kurro] *nm* (*fam*) work, job.
cursar [kur'sar] *vt* (*ESCOL*) to study.
cursi ['kursi] *adj* (*fam*) pretentious; (: *amanerado*) affected.
cursilada [kursi'laða] *nf*: **¡qué ~!** how tacky!
cursilería [kursile'ria] *nf* (*vulgaridad*) bad taste; (*amaneramiento*) affectation.
cursillo [kur'siʎo] *nm* short course.
cursiva [kur'siβa] *nf* italics *pl*.
curso ['kurso] *nm* (*dirección*) course; (*fig*) progress; (*ESCOL*) school year; (*UNIV*) academic year; **en ~** (*año*) current; (*proceso*) going on, under way; **moneda de ~ legal** legal tender.
cursor [kur'sor] *nm* (*INFORM*) cursor; (*TEC*) slide.
curtido, a [kur'tiðo, a] *adj* (*cara etc*) weather-beaten; (*fig*: *persona*) experienced.
curtir [kur'tir] *vt* (*piel*) to tan; (*fig*) to harden.
curvo, a ['kurβo, a] *adj* (*gen*) curved; (*torcido*) bent ♦ *nf* (*gen*) curve, bend; **curva de rentabilidad** (*COM*) break-even chart.
cúspide ['kuspiðe] *nf* (*GEO*) summit, peak; (*fig*) top, pinnacle.
custodia [kus'toðja] *nf* (*cuidado*) safekeeping; (*JUR*) custody.
custodiar [kusto'ðjar] *vt* (*conservar*) to keep, take care of; (*vigilar*) to guard.
custodio [kus'toðjo] *nm* guardian, keeper.
cutáneo, a [ku'taneo, a] *adj* skin *cpd*.
cutícula [ku'tikula] *nf* cuticle.
cutis ['kutis] *nm inv* skin, complexion.
cutre ['kutre] *adj* (*fam*: *lugar*) grotty; (: *persona*) naff.
cuyo, a ['kujo, a] *pron* (*de quien*) whose; (*de que*) whose, of which; **la señora en cuya casa me hospedé** the lady in whose house I stayed; **el asunto cuyos detalles conoces** the affair the details of which you know; **por ~ motivo** for which reason.
C.V. *abr* (= *caballos de vapor*) H.P.
C y F *abr* (= *costo y flete*) C & F.

D d

D, d [de] *nf* (*letre*) D, d; **D de Dolores** D for David (*BRIT*), D for Dog (*US*).
D. *abr* = **Don.**
D.ª *abr* = **Doña.**
dactilar [dakti'lar] *adj*: **huellas ~es** fingerprints.
dactilógrafo, a [dakti'loɣrafo, a] *nm/f* typist.
dádiva ['daðiβa] *nf* (*donación*) donation; (*regalo*) gift.
dadivoso, a [daði'βoso, a] *adj* generous.
dado, a ['daðo, a] *pp de* **dar** ♦ *nm* die; **~s** *nmpl* dice ♦ *adj*: **en un momento ~** at a certain point; **ser ~ a (hacer algo)** to be very fond of (doing sth); **~ que** *conj* given that.
daga ['daɣa] *nf* dagger.
daltónico, a [dal'toniko, a] *adj* colour-blind.
daltonismo [dalto'nismo] *nm* colour blindness.
dama ['dama] *nf* (*gen*) lady; (*AJEDREZ*) queen; **~s** *nfpl* draughts; **primera ~** (*TEAT*) leading lady; (*POL*) president's wife, first lady (*US*); **~ de honor** (*de reina*) lady-in-waiting; (*de novia*) bridesmaid.
damasco [da'masko] *nm* (*tela*) damask; (*AM*: *árbol*) apricot tree; (: *fruta*) apricot.
damnificado, a [damnifi'kaðo, a] *nm/f*: **los**

~**s** the victims.
damnificar [damnifi'kar] *vt* to harm; (*persona*) to injure.
damnifique [damni'fike] *etc vb V* **damnificar.**
dance ['danθe] *etc vb V* **danzar.**
danés, esa [da'nes, esa] *adj* Danish ♦ *nm/f* Dane ♦ *nm* (*LING*) Danish.
Danubio [da'nuβjo] *nm* Danube.
danza ['danθa] *nf* (*gen*) dancing; (*una* ~) dance.
danzar [dan'θar] *vt, vi* to dance.
danzarín, ina [danθa'rin, ina] *nm/f* dancer.
dañar [da'ɲar] *vt* (*objeto*) to damage; (*persona*) to hurt; (*estropear*) to spoil; ~**se** *vr* (*objeto*) to get damaged.
dañino, a [da'ɲino, a] *adj* harmful.
daño ['daɲo] *nm* (*a un objeto*) damage; (*a una persona*) harm, injury; ~**s y perjuicios** (*JUR*) damages; **hacer ~ a** to damage; (*persona*) to hurt, injure; **hacerse ~** to hurt o.s.
DAO *abr* (=*Diseño Asistido por Ordenador*) CAD.

PALABRA CLAVE

dar [dar] *vt* **1** (*gen*) to give; (*obra de teatro*) to put on; (*film*) to show; (*fiesta*) to have; ~ **algo a algn** to give sb sth *o* sth to sb; ~ **una patada a algn/algo** to kick sb/sth, give sb/sth a kick; ~ **un susto a algn** to give sb a fright; ~ **de beber a algn** to give sb a drink

2 (*producir: intereses*) to yield; (*fruta*) to produce

3 (*locuciones* + *n*): **da gusto escucharle** it's a pleasure to listen to him; **me da pena/asco** it frightens/sickens me; *V tb* **paseo** *y otros sustantivos*

4 (*considerar*): ~ **algo por descontado/entendido** to take sth for granted/as read; ~ **algo por concluido** to consider sth finished; **le dieron por desaparecido** they gave him up as lost

5 (*hora*): **el reloj dio las 6** the clock struck 6 (o'clock)

6: **me da lo mismo** it's all the same to me; *V tb* **igual, más**

7: **¡y dale!** (*¡otra vez!*) not again!; **estar/seguir dale que dale** *o* **dale que te pego** *o* (*AM*) **dale y dale** to go/keep on and on

♦ *vi* **1**: ~ **a** (*habitación*) to overlook, look on to; (*accionar: botón etc*) to press, hit

2: ~ **con**: **dimos con él dos horas más tarde** we came across him two hours later; **al final di con la solución** I eventually came up with the answer

3: ~ **en** (*blanco, suelo*) to hit; **el sol me da en la cara** the sun is shining (right) in my face

4: ~ **de sí** (*zapatos etc*) to stretch, give

5: ~ **para** to be enough for; **nuestro presupuesto no da para más** our budget's really tight

6: ~ **por**: **le ha dado por estudiar música** now he's into studying music

7: ~ **que hablar** to set people talking; **una película que da que pensar** a thought-provoking film

♦ ~**se** *vr* **1**: ~**se un baño** to have a bath; ~**se un golpe** to hurt o.s.

2: ~**se por vencido** to give up; **con eso me doy por satisfecho** I'd settle for that

3 (*ocurrir*): **se han dado muchos casos** there have been a lot of cases

4: ~**se a**: **se ha dado a la bebida** he's taken to drinking

5: **se me dan bien/mal las ciencias** I'm good/bad at science

6: **dárselas de**: **se las da de experto** he fancies himself *o* poses as an expert.

dardo ['darðo] *nm* dart.
dársena ['darsena] *nf* (*NAUT*) dock.
datar [da'tar] *vi*: ~ **de** to date from.
dátil ['datil] *nm* date.
dativo [da'tiβo] *nm* (*LING*) dative.
dato ['dato] *nm* fact, piece of information; (*MAT*) datum; ~**s** *nmpl* (*INFORM*) data; ~**s de entrada/salida** input/output data; ~**s personales** personal particulars.
dcha. *abr* (= *derecha*) r.h.
d. de J. C. *abr* (= *después de Jesucristo*) A.D.

PALABRA CLAVE

de [de] *prep* (*de*+*el* = *del*) **1** (*posesión, pertenencia*) of; **la casa ~ Isabel/mis padres** Isabel's/my parents' house; **es ~ ellos/ella** it's theirs/hers; **un libro ~ Unamuno** a book by Unamuno

2 (*origen, distancia, con números*) from; **soy ~ Gijón** I'm from Gijón; ~ **8 a 20** from 8 to 20; **5 metros ~ largo** 5 metres long; **salir del cine** to go out of *o* leave the cinema; ~ **... en ...** from ... to ...; ~ **2 en 2** 2 by 2, 2 at a time; **9 ~ cada 10** 9 out of every 10

3 (*valor descriptivo*): **una copa ~ vino** a glass of wine; **una silla ~ madera** a wooden chair; **la mesa ~ la cocina** the kitchen table; **un viaje ~ dos días** a two-day journey; **un billete ~ 1000 pesetas** a 1000 peseta note; **un niño ~ tres años** a three-year-old (child); **una máquina ~ coser** a sewing machine; **la ciudad ~**

Madrid the city of Madrid; **el tonto ~ Juan** that idiot Juan; **ir vestido ~ gris** to be dressed in grey; **la niña del vestido azul** the girl in the blue dress; **la chica del pelo largo** the girl with long hair; **trabaja ~ profesora** she works as a teacher; **~ lado** sideways; **~ atrás/delante** rear/front

4 (*hora, tiempo*): **a las 8 ~ la mañana** at 8 o'clock in the morning; **~ día/noche** by day/night; **~ hoy en ocho días** a week from now; **~ niño era gordo** as a child he was fat

5 (*comparaciones*): **más/menos ~ cien personas** more/less than a hundred people; **el más caro ~ la tienda** the most expensive in the shop; **menos/más ~ lo pensado** less/more than expected

6 (*causa*): **del calor** from the heat; **~ puro tonto** out of sheer stupidity

7 (*tema*) about; **clases ~ inglés** English classes; **¿sabes algo ~ él?** do you know anything about him?; **un libro ~ física** a physics book

8 (*adj + de + infin*): **fácil ~ entender** easy to understand

9 (*oraciones pasivas*): **fue respetado ~ todos** he was loved by all

10 (*condicional + infin*) if; **~ ser posible** if possible; **~ no terminarlo hoy** if I *etc* don't finish it today.

dé [de] *vb V* **dar**.

deambular [deambu'lar] *vi* to stroll, wander.

debajo [de'ßaxo] *adv* underneath; **~ de** below, under; **por ~ de** beneath.

debate [de'ßate] *nm* debate.

debatir [deßa'tir] *vt* to debate; **~se** *vr* to struggle.

debe ['deße] *nm* (*en cuenta*) debit side; **~ y haber** debit and credit.

deber [de'ßer] *nm* duty ♦ *vt* to owe ♦ *vi*: **debe (de)** it must, it should; **~se** *vr*: **~se a** to be owing *o* due to; **~es** *nmpl* (*ESCOL*) homework *sg*; **debo hacerlo** I must do it; **debe de ir** he should go; **¿qué** *o* **cuánto le debo?** how much is it?

debidamente [deßiða'mente] *adv* properly; (*rellenar: documento, solicitud*) duly.

debido, a [de'ßiðo, a] *adj* proper, due; **~ a** due to, because of; **en debida forma** duly.

débil ['deßil] *adj* weak; (*persona: físicamente*) feeble; (*salud*) poor; (*voz, ruido*) faint; (*luz*) dim.

debilidad [deßili'ðað] *nf* weakness; feebleness; dimness; **tener ~ por algn** to have a soft spot for sb.

debilitar [deßili'tar] *vt* to weaken; **~se** *vr* to grow weak.

débito ['deßito] *nm* debit; (*deuda*) debt.

debutante [deßu'tante] *nm/f* beginner.

debutar [deßu'tar] *vi* to make one's debut.

década ['dekaða] *nf* decade.

decadencia [deka'ðenθja] *nf* (*estado*) decadence; (*proceso*) decline, decay.

decadente [deca'ðente] *adj* decadent.

decaer [deka'er] *vi* (*declinar*) to decline; (*debilitarse*) to weaken; (*salud*) to fail; (*negocio*) to fall off.

decaído, a [deka'iðo, a] *adj*: **estar ~** (*persona*) to be down.

decaiga [de'kaiɣa] *etc vb V* **decaer**.

decaimiento [dekai'mjento] *nm* (*declinación*) decline; (*desaliento*) discouragement; (*MED: depresión*) depression.

decanato [deka'nato] *nm* (*cargo*) deanship; (*despacho*) dean's office.

decano, a [de'kano, a] *nm/f* (*UNIV etc*) dean; (*de grupo*) senior member.

decantar [dekan'tar] *vt* (*vino*) to decant.

decapitar [dekapi'tar] *vt* to behead.

decayendo [deca'jendo] *etc vb V* **decaer**.

decena [de'θena] *nf*: **una ~** ten (or so).

decencia [de'θenθja] *nf* (*modestia*) modesty; (*honestidad*) respectability.

decenio [de'θenjo] *nm* decade.

decente [de'θente] *adj* (*correcto*) proper; (*honesto*) respectable.

decepción [deθep'θjon] *nf* disappointment.

decepcionante [deθepθjo'nante] *adj* disappointing.

decepcionar [deθepθjo'nar] *vt* to disappoint.

decibelio [deθi'ßeljo] *nm* decibel.

decidido, a [deθi'ðiðo, a] *a* decided; (*resuelto*) resolute.

decidir [deθi'ðir] *vt* (*persuadir*) to convince, persuade; (*resolver*) to decide ♦ *vi* to decide; **~se** *vr*: **~se a** to make up one's mind to; **~se por** to decide *o* settle on, choose.

decimal [deθi'mal] *adj, nm* decimal.

décimo, a ['deθimo, a] *num* tenth ♦ *nf* (*MAT*) tenth; **tiene unas ~as de fiebre** he has a slight temperature.

decimoctavo, a [deθimok'taßo, a] *num* eighteenth; *V tb* **sexto**.

decimocuarto, a [deθimo'kwarto, a] *num* fourteenth; *V tb* **sexto**.

decimonoveno, a [deθimono'ßeno, a] *num* nineteenth; *V tb* **sexto**.

decimoquinto, a [deθimo'kinto, a] *num* fifteenth; *V tb* **sexto**.

decimoséptimo, a [deθimo'septimo, a] *num* seventeenth; *V tb* **sexto.**

decimosexto, a [deθimo'seksto, a] *num* sixteenth; *V tb* **sexto.**

decimotercero, a [deθimoter'θero, a] *num* thirteenth; *V tb* **sexto.**

decir [de'θir] *vt* (*expresar*) to say; (*contar*) to tell; (*hablar*) to speak; (*indicar*) to show; (*revelar*) to reveal; (*fam: nombrar*) to call ♦ *nm* saying; **~se** *vr*: **se dice** it is said, they say; (*se cuenta*) the story goes; **¿cómo se dice en inglés "cursi"?** what's the English for "cursi"?; **~ para** *o* **entre sí** to say to o.s.; **~ por ~** to talk for talking's sake; **dar que ~ (a la gente)** to make people talk; **querer ~** to mean; **es ~** that is to say, namely; **ni que ~ tiene que ...** it goes without saying that ...; **como quien dice** so to speak; **¡quién lo diría!** would you believe it!; **el qué dirán** gossip; **¡diga!, ¡dígame!** (*en tienda etc*) can I help you?; (*TELEC*) hello?; **le dije que fuera más tarde** I told her to go later; **es un ~** it's just a phrase.

decisión [deθi'sjon] *nf* decision; (*firmeza*) decisiveness; (*voluntad*) determination.

decisivo, a [deθi'siβo, a] *adj* decisive.

declamar [dekla'mar] *vt, vi* to declaim; (*versos etc*) to recite.

declaración [deklara'θjon] *nf* (*manifestación*) statement; (*explicación*) explanation; (*JUR: testimonio*) evidence; **~ de derechos** (*POL*) bill of rights; **~ de impuestos** (*COM*) tax return; **~ de ingresos** *o* **de la renta** income tax return; **~ jurada** affidavit; **falsa ~** (*JUR*) misrepresentation.

declarar [dekla'rar] *vt* to declare ♦ *vi* to declare; (*JUR*) to testify; **~se** *vr* (*opinión*) to make one's opinion known; (*a una chica*) to propose; (*guerra, incendio*) to break out; **~ culpable/inocente a algn** to find sb guilty/not guilty; **~se culpable/inocente** to plead guilty/not guilty.

declinación [deklina'θjon] *nf* (*decaimiento*) decline; (*LING*) declension.

declinar [dekli'nar] *vt* (*gen, LING*) to decline; (*JUR*) to reject ♦ *vi* (*el día*) to draw to a close.

declive [de'kliβe] *nm* (*cuesta*) slope; (*inclinación*) incline; (*fig*) decline; (*COM: tb:* **~ económico**) slump.

decodificador [dekoðifika'ðor] *nm* (*INFORM*) decoder.

decolorarse [dekolo'rarse] *vr* to become discoloured.

decomisar [dekomi'sar] *vt* to seize, confiscate.

decomiso [deko'miso] *nm* seizure.

decoración [dekora'θjon] *nf* decoration; (*TEAT*) scenery, set; **~ de escaparates** window dressing.

decorado [deko'raðo] *nm* (*CINE, TEAT*) scenery, set.

decorador, a [dekora'ðor, a] *nm/f* (*de interiores*) (interior) decorator; (*TEAT*) stage *o* set designer.

decorar [deko'rar] *vt* to decorate.

decorativo, a [dekora'tiβo, a] *adj* ornamental, decorative.

decoro [de'koro] *nm* (*respeto*) respect; (*dignidad*) decency; (*recato*) propriety.

decoroso, a [deko'roso, a] *adj* (*decente*) decent; (*modesto*) modest; (*digno*) proper.

decrecer [dekre'θer] *vi* to decrease, diminish; (*nivel de agua*) to go down; (*días*) to draw in.

decrépito, a [de'krepito, a] *adj* decrepit.

decretar [dekre'tar] *vt* to decree.

decreto [de'kreto] *nm* decree; (*POL*) act.

decreto-ley [dekreto'lei], *pl* **decretos-leyes** *nm* decree.

decrezca [de'kreθka] *etc vb V* **decrecer.**

decúbito [de'kuβito] *nm* (*MED*): **~ prono/supino** prone/supine position.

dedal [de'ðal] *nm* thimble.

dedalera [deða'lera] *nf* foxglove.

dédalo ['deðalo] *nm* (*laberinto*) labyrinth; (*fig*) tangle, mess.

dedicación [deðika'θjon] *nf* dedication; **con ~ exclusiva** *o* **plena** full-time.

dedicar [deði'kar] *vt* (*libro*) to dedicate; (*tiempo, dinero*) to devote; **~se** *vr*: **~se a** to devote o.s. to (*hacer algo* doing sth); (*carrera, estudio*) to go in for, take up; **¿a qué se dedica usted?** what do you do (for a living)?

dedicatoria [deðika'torja] *nf* (*de libro*) dedication.

dedillo [de'ðiʎo] *nm*: **saber algo al ~** to have sth at one's fingertips.

dedique [de'ðike] *etc vb V* **dedicar.**

dedo ['deðo] *nm* finger; (*de vino etc*) drop; **~ (del pie)** toe; **~ pulgar** thumb; **~ índice** index finger; **~ mayor** *o* **cordial** middle finger; **~ anular** ring finger; **~ meñique** little finger; **contar con los ~s** to count on one's fingers; **comerse los ~s** to get very impatient; **entrar a ~** to get a job by pulling strings; **hacer ~** (*fam*) to hitch (a lift); **poner el ~ en la llaga** to put one's finger on it; **no tiene dos ~s de frente** he's pretty dim.

deducción [deðuk'θjon] *nf* deduction.

deducir [deðu'θir] *vt* (*concluir*) to deduce,

infer; (*COM*) to deduct.
deduje [de'ðuxe] *etc*, **dedujera** [deðu'xera] *etc*, **deduzca** [de'ðuθka] *etc* *vb V* **deducir**.
defección [defek'θjon] *nf* defection, desertion.
defecto [de'fekto] *nm* defect, flaw; (*de cara*) imperfection; ~ **de pronunciación** speech defect; **por** ~ (*INFORM*) default; ~ **latente** (*COM*) latent defect.
defectuoso, a [defek'twoso, a] *adj* defective, faulty.
defender [defen'der] *vt* to defend; (*ideas*) to uphold; (*causa*) to champion; (*amigos*) to stand up for; ~**se** *vr* to defend o.s.; ~**se bien** to give a good account of o.s.; **me defiendo en inglés** (*fig*) I can get by in English.
defendible [defen'diβle] *adj* defensible.
defensa [de'fensa] *nf* defence; (*NAUT*) fender ♦ *nm* (*DEPORTE*) back; **en** ~ **propia** in self-defence.
defensivo, a [defen'siβo, a] *adj* defensive ♦ *nf*: **a la defensiva** on the defensive.
defensor, a [defen'sor, a] *adj* defending ♦ *nm/f* (*abogado* ~) defending counsel; (*protector*) protector; ~ **del pueblo** (*ESP*) ≈ ombudsman.
deferente [defe'rente] *adj* deferential.
deferir [defe'rir] *vt* (*JUR*) to refer, delegate ♦ *vi*: ~ **a** to defer to.
deficiencia [defi'θjenθja] *nf* deficiency.
deficiente [defi'θjente] *adj* (*defectuoso*) defective; ~ **en** lacking *o* deficient in ♦ *nm/f*: **ser un** ~ **mental** to be mentally handicapped.
déficit, ~s ['defiθit] *nm* (*COM*) deficit; (*fig*) lack, shortage; ~ **presupuestario** budget deficit.
deficitario, a [defiθi'tarjo, a] *adj* (*COM*) in deficit; (*empresa*) loss-making.
defienda [de'fjenda] *etc vb V* **defender**.
defiera [de'fjera] *etc vb V* **deferir**.
definición [defini'θjon] *nf* definition; (*INFORM*: *de pantalla*) resolution.
definido, a [defi'niðo, a] *adj* (*tb LING*) definite; **bien** ~ well *o* clearly defined; ~ **por el usuario** (*INFORM*) user-defined.
definir [defi'nir] *vt* (*determinar*) to determine, establish; (*decidir*, *INFORM*) to define; (*aclarar*) to clarify.
definitivo, a [defini'tiβo, a] *adj* (*edición, texto*) definitive; (*fecha*) definite; **en definitiva** definitively; (*en conclusión*) finally; (*en resumen*) in short.
defiriendo [defi'rjendo] *etc vb V* **deferir**.
deflacionario, a [deflaθjo'narjo, a], **deflacionista** [deflaθjo'nista] *adj* deflationary.
deflector [deflek'tor] *nm* (*TEC*) baffle.
deforestación [deforesta'θjon] *nf* deforestation.
deformación [deforma'θjon] *nf* (*alteración*) deformation; (*RADIO etc*) distortion.
deformar [defor'mar] *vt* (*gen*) to deform; ~**se** *vr* to become deformed.
deforme [de'forme] *adj* (*informe*) deformed; (*feo*) ugly; (*mal hecho*) misshapen.
deformidad [deformi'ðað] *nf* (*forma anormal*) deformity; (*fig*: *defecto*) (moral) shortcoming.
defraudar [defrau'ðar] *vt* (*decepcionar*) to disappoint; (*estafar*) to cheat; to defraud; ~ **impuestos** to evade tax.
defunción [defun'θjon] *nf* decease, demise.
degeneración [dexenera'θjon] *nf* (*de las células*) degeneration; (*moral*) degeneracy.
degenerar [dexene'rar] *vi* to degenerate; (*empeorar*) to get worse.
deglutir [deɣlu'tir] *vt, vi* to swallow.
degolladero [deɣoʎa'ðero] *nm* (*ANAT*) throat; (*cadalso*) scaffold; (*matadero*) slaughterhouse.
degollar [deɣo'ʎar] *vt* to slaughter.
degradar [deɣra'ðar] *vt* to debase, degrade; (*INFORM*: *datos*) to corrupt; ~**se** *vr* to demean o.s.
degüelle [de'ɣweʎe] *etc vb V* **degollar**.
degustación [deɣusta'θjon] *nf* sampling, tasting.
deificar [deifi'kar] *vt* (*persona*) to deify.
deifique [dei'fike] *etc vb V* **deificar**.
dejadez [dexa'ðeθ] *nf* (*negligencia*) neglect; (*descuido*) untidiness, carelessness.
dejado, a [de'xaðo, a] *adj* (*desaliñado*) slovenly; (*negligente*) careless; (*indolente*) lazy.
dejar [de'xar] *vt* (*gen*) to leave; (*permitir*) to allow, let; (*abandonar*) to abandon, forsake; (*actividad, empleo*) to give up; (*beneficios*) to produce, yield ♦ *vi*: ~ **de** (*parar*) to stop; ~**se** *vr* (*abandonarse*) to let o.s. go; **no puedo** ~ **de fumar** I can't give up smoking; **no dejes de visitarles** don't fail to visit them; **no dejes de comprar un billete** make sure you buy a ticket; ~ **a un lado** to leave *o* set aside; ~ **caer** to drop; ~ **entrar/salir** to let in/out; ~ **pasar** to let through; **¡déjalo!** (*no te preocupes*) don't worry about it; **te dejo en tu casa** I'll drop you off at your place; **deja mucho que desear** it leaves a lot to be desired; ~**se persuadir** to allow o.s. to *o*

let o.s. be persuaded; **¡déjate de tonterías!** stop messing about!
deje ['dexe] *nm* (trace of) accent.
dejo ['dexo] *nm* (*LING*) accent.
del [del] = **de + el**; *V* **de**.
del. *abr* (*ADMIN*: = *Delegación*) district office.
delantal [delan'tal] *nm* apron.
delante [de'lante] *adv* in front; (*enfrente*) opposite; (*adelante*) ahead ♦ *prep*: ~ **de** in front of, before; **la parte de** ~ the front part; **estando otros** ~ with others present.
delantero, a [delan'tero, a] *adj* front; (*patas de animal*) fore ♦ *nm* (*DEPORTE*) forward ♦ *nf* (*de vestido, casa etc*) front part; (*TEAT*) front row; (*DEPORTE*) forward line; **llevar la delantera (a algn)** to be ahead (of sb).
delatar [dela'tar] *vt* to inform on *o* against, betray; **los delató a la policía** he reported them to the police.
delator, a [dela'tor, a] *nm/f* informer.
delegación [deleɣa'θjon] *nf* (*acción, delegados*) delegation; (*COM*: *oficina*) district office, branch; ~ **de poderes** (*POL*) devolution; ~ **de policía** police station.
delegado, a [dele'ɣaðo, a] *nm/f* delegate; (*COM*) agent.
delegar [dele'ɣar] *vt* to delegate.
delegue [de'leɣe] *etc vb V* **delegar**.
deleitar [delei'tar] *vt* to delight; ~**se** *vr*: ~**se con** *o* **en** to delight in, take pleasure in.
deleite [de'leite] *nm* delight, pleasure.
deletrear [deletre'ar] *vt* (*tb fig*) to spell (out).
deletreo [dele'treo] *nm* spelling; (*fig*) interpretation, decipherment.
deleznable [deleθ'naβle] *adj* (*frágil*) fragile; (*fig*: *malo*) poor; (*excusa*) feeble.
delfín [del'fin] *nm* dolphin.
delgadez [delɣa'ðeθ] *nf* thinness, slimness.
delgado, a [del'ɣaðo, a] *adj* thin; (*persona*) slim, thin; (*tierra*) poor; (*tela etc*) light, delicate ♦ *adv*: **hilar (muy)** ~ (*fig*) to split hairs.
deliberación [deliβera'θjon] *nf* deliberation.
deliberar [deliβe'rar] *vt* to debate, discuss ♦ *vi* to deliberate.
delicadeza [delika'ðeθa] *nf* delicacy; (*refinamiento, sutileza*) refinement.
delicado, a [deli'kaðo, a] *adj* delicate; (*sensible*) sensitive; (*rasgos*) dainty; (*gusto*) refined; (*situación*: *difícil*) tricky; (: *violento*) embarrassing; (*punto, tema*) sore; (*persona*: *difícil de contentar*) hard to please; (: *sensible*) touchy, hypersensitive; (: *atento*) considerate.
delicia [de'liθja] *nf* delight.
delicioso, a [deli'θjoso, a] *adj* (*gracioso*) delightful; (*exquisito*) delicious.
delictivo, a [delik'tiβo, a] *adj* criminal *cpd*.
delimitar [delimi'tar] *vt* to delimit.
delincuencia [delin'kwenθja] *nf*: ~ **juvenil** juvenile delinquency; **cifras de la** ~ crime rate.
delincuente [delin'kwente] *nm/f* delinquent; (*criminal*) criminal; ~ **sin antecedentes** first offender; ~ **habitual** hardened criminal.
delineante [deline'ante] *nm/f* draughtsman.
delinear [deline'ar] *vt* to delineate; (*dibujo*) to draw; (*contornos, fig*) to outline; ~ **un proyecto** to outline a project.
delinquir [delin'kir] *vi* to commit an offence.
delirante [deli'rante] *adj* delirious.
delirar [deli'rar] *vi* to be delirious, rave; (*fig*: *desatinar*) to talk nonsense.
delirio [de'lirjo] *nm* (*MED*) delirium; (*palabras insensatas*) ravings *pl*; ~ **de grandeza** megalomania; ~ **de persecución** persecution mania; **con** ~ (*fam*) madly; **¡fue el** ~**!** (*fam*) it was great!
delito [de'lito] *nm* (*gen*) crime; (*infracción*) offence.
delta ['delta] *nm* delta.
demacrado, a [dema'kraðo, a] *adj* emaciated.
demagogia [dema'ɣoxja] *nf* demagogy, demagoguery.
demagogo [dema'ɣoɣo] *nm* demagogue.
demanda [de'manda] *nf* (*pedido, COM*) demand; (*petición*) request; (*pregunta*) inquiry; (*reivindicación*) claim; (*JUR*) action, lawsuit; (*TEAT*) call; (*ELEC*) load; ~ **de pago** demand for payment; **escribir en** ~ **de ayuda** to write asking for help; **entablar** ~ (*JUR*) to sue; **presentar** ~ **de divorcio** to sue for divorce; ~ **final** final demand; ~ **indirecta** derived demand; ~ **de mercado** market demand.
demandado, a [deman'daðo, a] *nm/f* defendant; (*en divorcio*) respondent.
demandante [deman'dante] *nm/f* claimant; (*JUR*) plaintiff.
demandar [deman'dar] *vt* (*gen*) to demand; (*JUR*) to sue, file a lawsuit against, start proceedings against; ~ **a algn por calumnia/daños y perjuicios** to sue sb for libel/damages.
demarcación [demarka'θjon] *nf* (*de terreno*) demarcation.

demás [de'mas] *adj*: **los ~ niños** the other children, the remaining children ♦ *pron*: **los/las ~** the others, the rest (of them); **lo ~** the rest (of it); **por ~** moreover; (*en vano*) in vain; **y ~** etcetera.
demasía [dema'sia] *nf* (*exceso*) excess, surplus; **comer en ~** to eat to excess.
demasiado, a [dema'sjaðo, a] *adj*: **~ vino** too much wine ♦ *adv* (*antes de adj, adv*) too; **~s libros** too many books; **¡es ~!** it's too much!; **es ~ pesado para levantar** it is too heavy to lift; **~ lo sé** I know it only too well; **hace ~ calor** it's too hot.
demencia [de'menθja] *nf* (*locura*) madness.
demencial [demen'θjal] *adj* crazy.
demente [de'mente] *adj* mad, insane ♦ *nm/f* lunatic.
democracia [demo'kraθja] *nf* democracy.
demócrata [de'mokrata] *nm/f* democrat.
democratacristiano, a [demokrata kris'tjano, a], **democristiano, a** [demokris'tjano, a] *adj, nm/f* Christian Democrat.
democrático, a [demo'kratiko, a] *adj* democratic.
demográfico, a [demo'ɣrafiko, a] *adj* demographic, population *cpd*; **la explosión demográfica** the population explosion.
demoledor, a [demole'ðor, a] *adj* (*fig*: *argumento*) overwhelming; (: *ataque*) shattering.
demoler [demo'ler] *vt* to demolish; (*edificio*) to pull down.
demolición [demoli'θjon] *nf* demolition.
demonio [de'monjo] *nm* devil, demon; **¡~s!** hell!; **¿cómo ~s?** how the hell?; **¿qué ~s será?** what the devil can it be?; **¿dónde ~ lo habré dejado?** where the devil can I have left it?; **tener el ~ en el cuerpo** (*no parar*) to be always on the go.
demora [de'mora] *nf* delay.
demorar [demo'rar] *vt* (*retardar*) to delay, hold back; (*dilatar*) to hold up ♦ *vi* to linger, stay on; **~se** *vr* to linger, stay on; (*retrasarse*) to take a long time; **~se en hacer algo** (*esp AM*) to take time doing sth.
demos ['demos] *vb V* **dar**.
demostración [demostra'θjon] *nf* (*gen*, *MAT*) demonstration; (*de cariño, fuerza*) show; (*de teorema*) proof; (*de amistad*) gesture; (*de cólera, gimnasia*) display; **~ comercial** commercial exhibition.
demostrar [demos'trar] *vt* (*probar*) to prove; (*mostrar*) to show; (*manifestar*) to demonstrate.
demostrativo, a [demostra'tiβo, a] *adj* demonstrative.
demudado, a [demu'ðaðo, a] *adj* (*rostro*) pale; (*fig*) upset; **tener el rostro ~** to look pale.
demudar [demu'ðar] *vt* to change, alter; **~se** *vr* (*expresión*) to alter; (*perder color*) to change colour.
demuela [de'mwela] *etc vb V* **demoler**.
demuestre [de'mwestre] *etc vb V* **demostrar**.
den [den] *vb V* **dar**.
denegación [deneɣa'θjon] *nf* refusal.
denegar [dene'ɣar] *vt* (*rechazar*) to refuse; (*negar*) to deny; (*JUR*) to reject.
denegué [dene'ɣe], **deneguemos** [dene'ɣemos] *etc*, **deniego** [de'njeɣo] *etc*, **deniegue** [de'njeɣe] *etc vb V* **denegar**.
dengue ['denɣe] *nm* dengue *o* breakbone fever.
denigrante [deni'ɣrante] *adj* (*injurioso*) insulting; (*deshonroso*) degrading.
denigrar [deni'ɣrar] *vt* (*desacreditar*) to denigrate; (*injuriar*) to insult.
denodado, a [deno'ðaðo, a] *adj* bold, brave.
denominación [denomina'θjon] *nf* (*acto*) naming; (*clase*) denomination; **~ de origen** *see boxed note.*

DENOMINACIÓN DE ORIGEN

The **denominación de origen**, *often abbreviated to DO, is a prestigious classification awarded to food and wine from designated regions by the Consejo Regulador de la Denominación de Origen. Produce must meet the required standards concerning quality and production methods. It is often associated with "manchego" cheeses and many of the wines from the Rioja and Ribera de Duero regions.*

denominador [denomina'ðor] *nm*: **~ común** common denominator.
denostar [denos'tar] *vt* to insult.
denotar [deno'tar] *vt* (*indicar*) to indicate, denote.
densidad [densi'ðað] *nf* (*FÍSICA*) density; (*fig*) thickness.
denso, a ['denso, a] *adj* (*apretado*) solid; (*espeso, pastoso*) thick; (*fig*) heavy.
dentado, a [den'taðo, a] *adj* (*rueda*) cogged; (*filo*) jagged; (*sello*) perforated; (*BOT*) dentate.
dentadura [denta'ðura] *nf* (set of) teeth *pl*; **~ postiza** false teeth *pl*.
dental [den'tal] *adj* dental.
dentellada [dente'ʎaða] *nf* (*mordisco*) bite, nip; (*señal*) tooth mark; **partir algo a ~s**

to sever sth with one's teeth.
dentera [den'tera] *nf* (*sensación desagradable*) the shivers *pl*.
dentición [denti'θjon] *nf* (*acto*) teething; (*ANAT*) dentition; **estar con la ~** to be teething.
dentífrico, a [den'tifriko, a] *adj* dental, tooth *cpd* ♦ *nm* toothpaste; **pasta dentífrica** toothpaste.
dentista [den'tista] *nm/f* dentist.
dentro ['dentro] *adv* inside ♦ *prep*: **~ de** in, inside, within; **allí ~** in there; **mirar por ~** to look inside; **~ de lo posible** as far as possible; **~ de todo** all in all; **~ de tres meses** within three months.
denuedo [de'nweðo] *nm* boldness, daring.
denuesto [de'nwesto] *nm* insult.
denuncia [de'nunθja] *nf* (*delación*) denunciation; (*acusación*) accusation; (*de accidente*) report; **hacer** *o* **poner una ~** to report an incident to the police.
denunciable [denun'θjaßle] *adj* indictable, punishable.
denunciante [denun'θjante] *nm/f* accuser; (*delator*) informer.
denunciar [denun'θjar] *vt* to report; (*delatar*) to inform on *o* against.
Dep. *abr* (= *Departamento*) Dept.; (= *Depósito*) dep.
deparar [depa'rar] *vt* (*brindar*) to provide *o* furnish with; (*suj*: *futuro, destino*) to have in store for; **los placeres que el viaje nos deparó** the pleasures which the trip afforded us.
departamento [departa'mento] *nm* (*sección administrativa*) department, section; (*AM*: *piso*) flat (*BRIT*), apartment (*US*); (*distrito*) department, province; **~ de envíos** (*COM*) dispatch department; **~ de máquinas** (*NAUT*) engine room.
departir [depar'tir] *vi* to talk, converse.
dependencia [depen'denθja] *nf* dependence; (*POL*) dependency; (*COM*) office, section; (*sucursal*) branch office; (*ARQ*: *cuarto*) room; **~s** *nfpl* outbuildings.
depender [depen'der] *vi*: **~ de** to depend on; (*contar con*) to rely on; (*de autoridad*) to be under, be answerable to; **depende** it (all) depends; **no depende de mí** it's not up to me.
dependienta [depen'djenta] *nf* saleswoman, shop assistant.
dependiente [depen'djente] *adj* dependent ♦ *nm* salesman, shop assistant.
depilación [depila'θjon] *nf* hair removal.
depilar [depi'lar] *vt* (*con cera*: *piernas*) to wax; (*cejas*) to pluck.
depilatorio, a [depila'torjo, a] *adj* depilatory ♦ *nm* hair remover.
deplorable [deplo'raßle] *adj* deplorable.
deplorar [deplo'rar] *vt* to deplore.
depondré [depon'dre] *etc vb V* **deponer**.
deponer [depo'ner] *vt* (*armas*) to lay down; (*rey*) to depose; (*gobernante*) to oust; (*ministro*) to remove from office ♦ *vi* (*JUR*) to give evidence; (*declarar*) to make a statement.
deponga [de'ponga] *etc vb V* **deponer**.
deportación [deporta'θjon] *nf* deportation.
deportar [depor'tar] *vt* to deport.
deporte [de'porte] *nm* sport.
deportista [depor'tista] *adj* sports *cpd* ♦ *nm/f* sportsman/woman.
deportivo, a [depor'tißo, a] *adj* (*club, periódico*) sports *cpd* ♦ *nm* sports car.
deposición [deposi'θjon] *nf* (*de funcionario etc*) removal from office; (*JUR*: *testimonio*) evidence.
depositante [deposi'tante] *nm/f* depositor.
depositar [deposi'tar] *vt* (*dinero*) to deposit; (*mercaderías*) to put away, store; **~se** *vr* to settle; **~ la confianza en algn** to place one's trust in sb.
depositario, a [deposi'tarjo, a] *nm/f* trustee; **~ judicial** official receiver.
depósito [de'posito] *nm* (*gen*) deposit; (*de mercaderías*) warehouse, store; (*de animales, coches*) pound; (*de agua, gasolina etc*) tank; (*en retrete*) cistern; **~ afianzado** bonded warehouse; **~ bancario** bank deposit; **~ de cadáveres** mortuary; **~ de maderas** timber yard; **~ de suministro** feeder bin.
depravar [depra'ßar] *vt* to deprave, corrupt; **~se** *vr* to become depraved.
depreciación [depreθja'θjon] *nf* depreciation.
depreciar [depre'θjar] *vt* to depreciate, reduce the value of; **~se** *vr* to depreciate, lose value.
depredador, a [depreða'ðor, a] (*ZOOL*) *adj* predatory ♦ *nm* predator.
depredar [depre'ðar] *vt* to pillage.
depresión [depre'sjon] *nf* (*gen, MED*) depression; (*hueco*) hollow; (*en horizonte, camino*) dip; (*merma*) drop; (*ECON*) slump, recession; **~ nerviosa** nervous breakdown.
deprimente [depri'mente] *adj* depressing.
deprimido, a [depri'miðo, a] *adj* depressed.
deprimir [depri'mir] *vt* to depress; **~se** *vr* (*persona*) to become depressed.
deprisa [de'prisa] *adv V* **prisa**.
depuesto [de'pwesto] *pp de* **deponer**.

depuración [depura'θjon] *nf* purification; (*POL*) purge; (*INFORM*) debugging.
depurador [depura'ðor] *nm* purifier.
depuradora [depura'ðora] *nf* (*de agua*) water-treatment plant; (*tb*: ~ **de aguas residuales**) sewage farm.
depurar [depu'rar] *vt* to purify; (*purgar*) to purge; (*INFORM*) to debug.
depuse [de'puse] *etc vb V* **deponer**.
der., **der.º** *abr* (= *derecho*) r.
derecha [de'retʃa] *nf V* **derecho, a**.
derechazo [dere'tʃaθo] *nm* (*BOXEO*) right; (*TENIS*) forehand drive; (*TAUR*) *a pass with the cape*.
derechista [dere'tʃista] (*POL*) *adj* right-wing ♦ *nm/f* right-winger.
derecho, a [de'retʃo, a] *adj* right, right-hand ♦ *nm* (*privilegio*) right; (*título*) claim, title; (*lado*) right(-hand) side; (*leyes*) law ♦ *nf* right(-hand) side ♦ *adv* straight, directly; ~**s** *nmpl* dues; (*profesionales*) fees; (*impuestos*) taxes; (*de autor*) royalties; **la(s) derecha(s)** (*pl*) (*POL*) the Right; ~**s civiles** civil rights; ~**s de muelle** (*COM*) dock dues; ~**s de patente** patent rights; ~**s portuarios** (*COM*) harbour dues; ~ **de propiedad literaria** copyright; ~ **de retención** (*COM*) lien; ~ **de timbre** (*COM*) stamp duty; ~ **de votar** right to vote; ~ **a voto** voting right; **Facultad de D~** Faculty of Law; **a derechas** rightly, correctly; **de derechas** (*POL*) right-wing; **"reservados todos los ~s"** "all rights reserved"; **¡no hay ~!** it's not fair!; **tener ~ a** to have a right to; **a la derecha** on the right; (*dirección*) to the right.
deriva [de'riβa] *nf*: **ir** *o* **estar a la ~** to drift, be adrift.
derivación [deriβa'θjon] *nf* derivation.
derivado, a [deri'βaðo, a] *adj* derived ♦ *nm* (*LING*) derivative; (*INDUSTRIA, QUÍMICA*) by-product.
derivar [deri'βar] *vt* to derive; (*desviar*) to direct ♦ *vi*, ~**se** *vr* to derive, be derived; ~**(se) de** (*consecuencia*) to spring from.
dermatólogo, a [derma'toloɣo, a] *nm/f* dermatologist.
dérmico, a ['dermiko, a] *adj* skin *cpd*.
dermoprotector, a [dermoprotek'tor, a] *adj* protective.
derogación [deroɣa'θjon] *nf* repeal.
derogar [dero'ɣar] *vt* (*ley*) to repeal; (*contrato*) to revoke.
derogue [de'roɣe] *etc vb V* **derogar**.
derramamiento [derrama'mjento] *nm* (*dispersión*) spilling; (*fig*) squandering; ~ **de sangre** bloodshed.
derramar [derra'mar] *vt* to spill; (*verter*) to pour out; (*esparcir*) to scatter; ~**se** *vr* to pour out; ~ **lágrimas** to weep.
derrame [de'rrame] *nm* (*de líquido*) spilling; (*de sangre*) shedding; (*de tubo etc*) overflow; (*perdida*) leakage; (*MED*) discharge; (*declive*) slope; ~ **cerebral** brain haemorrhage; ~ **sinovial** water on the knee.
derrapar [derra'par] *vi* to skid.
derredor [derre'ðor] *adv*: **al** *o* **en ~ de** around, about.
derrengado, a [derren'gaðo, a] *adj* (*torcido*) bent; (*cojo*) crippled; **estar ~** (*fig*) to ache all over; **dejar ~ a algn** (*fig*) to wear sb out.
derretido, a [derre'tiðo, a] *adj* melted; (*metal*) molten; **estar ~ por algn** (*fig*) to be crazy about sb.
derretir [derre'tir] *vt* (*gen*) to melt; (*nieve*) to thaw; (*fig*) to squander; ~**se** *vr* to melt.
derribar [derri'βar] *vt* to knock down; (*construcción*) to demolish; (*persona, gobierno, político*) to bring down.
derribo [de'rriβo] *nm* (*de edificio*) demolition; (*LUCHA*) throw; (*AVIAT*) shooting down; (*POL*) overthrow; ~**s** *nmpl* rubble *sg*, debris *sg*.
derrita [de'rrita] *etc vb V* **derretir**.
derrocar [derro'kar] *vt* (*gobierno*) to bring down, overthrow; (*ministro*) to oust.
derrochador, a [derrotʃa'ðor, a] *adj, nm/f* spendthrift.
derrochar [derro'tʃar] *vt* (*dinero, recursos*) to squander; (*energía, salud*) to be bursting with *o* full of.
derroche [de'rrotʃe] *nm* (*despilfarro*) waste, squandering; (*exceso*) extravagance; **con un ~ de buen gusto** with a fine display of good taste.
derroque [de'rroke] *etc vb V* **derrocar**.
derrota [de'rrota] *nf* (*NAUT*) course; (*MIL*) defeat, rout; **sufrir una grave ~** (*fig*) to suffer a grave setback.
derrotar [derro'tar] *vt* (*gen*) to defeat.
derrotero [derro'tero] *nm* (*rumbo*) course; **tomar otro ~** (*fig*) to adopt a different course.
derrotista [derro'tista] *adj, nm/f* defeatist.
derruir [derru'ir] *vt* to demolish, tear down.
derrumbamiento [derrumba'mjento] *nm* (*caída*) plunge; (*demolición*) demolition; (*desplome*) collapse; ~ **de tierra** landslide.
derrumbar [derrum'bar] *vt* to throw down; (*despeñar*) to fling *o* hurl down; (*volcar*) to upset; ~**se** *vr* (*hundirse*) to collapse; (: *techo*) to fall in, cave in; (*fig: esperanzas*)

to collapse.
derrumbe [de'rrumbe] *nm* = **derrumbamiento.**
derruyendo [derru'jendo] *etc vb V* **derruir.**
des [des] *vb V* **dar.**
desabastecido, a [desaßaste'θiðo, a] *adj*: **estar ~ de algo** to be short of *o* out of sth.
desabotonar [desaßoto'nar] *vt* to unbutton, undo ♦ *vi* (*flores*) to blossom; **~se** *vr* to come undone.
desabrido, a [desa'ßriðo, a] *adj* (*comida*) insipid, tasteless; (*persona*: *soso*) dull; (: *antipático*) rude, surly; (*respuesta*) sharp; (*tiempo*) unpleasant.
desabrigado, a [desaßri'ɣaðo, a] *adj* (*sin abrigo*) not sufficiently protected; (*fig*) exposed.
desabrigar [desaßri'ɣar] *vt* (*quitar ropa a*) to remove the clothing of; (*descubrir*) to uncover; (*fig*) to deprive of protection; **~se** *vr*: **me desabrigué en la cama** the bedclothes came off.
desabrigue [desa'ßriɣe] *etc vb V* **desabrigar.**
desabrochar [desaßro'tʃar] *vt* (*botones, broches*) to undo, unfasten; **~se** *vr* (*ropa etc*) to come undone.
desacatar [desaka'tar] *vt* (*ley*) to disobey.
desacato [desa'kato] *nm* (*falta de respeto*) disrespect; (*JUR*) contempt.
desacertado, a [desaθer'taðo, a] *adj* (*equivocado*) mistaken; (*inoportuno*) unwise.
desacierto [desa'θjerto] *nm* (*error*) mistake, error; (*dicho*) unfortunate remark.
desaconsejable [desakonse'xaßle] *adj* inadvisable.
desaconsejado, a [desakonse'xaðo, a] *adj* ill-advised.
desaconsejar [desakonse'xar] *vt*: **~ algo a algn** to advise sb against sth.
desacoplar [desako'plar] *vt* (*ELEC*) to disconnect; (*TEC*) to take apart.
desacorde [desa'korðe] *adj* (*MUS*) discordant; (*fig*: *opiniones*) conflicting; **estar ~ con algo** to disagree with sth.
desacreditar [desakreði'tar] *vt* (*desprestigiar*) to discredit, bring into disrepute; (*denigrar*) to run down.
desactivar [desakti'ßar] *vt* to deactivate; (*bomba*) to defuse.
desacuerdo [desa'kwerðo] *nm* (*conflicto*) disagreement, discord; (*error*) error, blunder; **en ~** out of keeping.
desafiante [desa'fjante] *adj* (*insolente*) defiant; (*retador*) challenging ♦ *nm/f* challenger.
desafiar [desa'fjar] *vt* (*retar*) to challenge; (*enfrentarse a*) to defy.
desafilado, a [desafi'laðo, a] *adj* blunt.
desafinado, a [desafi'naðo, a] *adj*: **estar ~** to be out of tune.
desafinar [desafi'nar] *vi* to be out of tune; **~se** *vr* to go out of tune.
desafío [desa'fio] *nm* (*reto*) challenge; (*combate*) duel; (*resistencia*) defiance.
desaforadamente [desaforaða'mente] *adv*: **gritar ~** to shout one's head off.
desaforado, a [desafo'raðo, a] *adj* (*grito*) ear-splitting; (*comportamiento*) outrageous.
desafortunadamente [desafortunaða'mente] *adv* unfortunately.
desafortunado, a [desafortu'naðo, a] *adj* (*desgraciado*) unfortunate, unlucky.
desagradable [desaɣra'ðaßle] *adj* (*fastidioso, enojoso*) unpleasant; (*irritante*) disagreeable; **ser ~ con algn** to be rude to sb.
desagradar [desaɣra'ðar] *vi* (*disgustar*) to displease; (*molestar*) to bother.
desagradecido, a [desaɣraðe'θiðo, a] *adj* ungrateful.
desagrado [desa'ɣraðo] *nm* (*disgusto*) displeasure; (*contrariedad*) dissatisfaction; **con ~** unwillingly.
desagraviar [desaɣra'ßjar] *vt* to make amends to.
desagravio [desa'ɣraßjo] *nm* (*satisfacción*) amends; (*compensación*) compensation.
desaguadero [desaɣwa'ðero] *nm* drain.
desagüe [de'saɣwe] *nm* (*de un líquido*) drainage; (*cañería*: *tb*: **tubo de ~**) drainpipe; (*salida*) outlet, drain.
desaguisado, a [desaɣi'saðo, a] *adj* illegal ♦ *nm* outrage.
desahogado, a [desao'ɣaðo, a] *adj* (*holgado*) comfortable; (*espacioso*) roomy.
desahogar [desao'ɣar] *vt* (*aliviar*) to ease, relieve; (*ira*) to vent; **~se** *vr* (*distenderse*) to relax; (*desfogarse*) to let off steam (*fam*); (*confesarse*) to confess, get sth off one's chest (*fam*).
desahogo [desa'oɣo] *nm* (*alivio*) relief; (*comodidad*) comfort, ease; **vivir con ~** to be comfortably off.
desahogue [desa'oɣe] *etc vb V* **desahogar.**
desahuciado, a [desau'θjaðo, a] *adj* hopeless.
desahuciar [desau'θjar] *vt* (*enfermo*) to give up hope for; (*inquilino*) to evict.
desahucio [de'sauθjo] *nm* eviction.
desairado, a [desai'raðo, a] *adj*

(*menospreciado*) disregarded; (*desgarbado*) shabby; (*sin éxito*) unsuccessful; **quedar** ~ to come off badly.
desairar [desai'rar] *vt* (*menospreciar*) to slight, snub; (*cosa*) to disregard; (*COM*) to default on.
desaire [des'aire] *nm* (*menosprecio*) slight; (*falta de garbo*) unattractiveness; **dar** *o* **hacer un ~ a algn** to offend sb; **¿me va usted a hacer ese ~?** I won't take no for an answer!
desajustar [desaxus'tar] *vt* (*desarreglar*) to disarrange; (*desconcertar*) to throw off balance; (*fig*: *planes*) to upset; **~se** *vr* to get out of order; (*aflojarse*) to loosen.
desajuste [desa'xuste] *nm* (*de máquina*) disorder; (*avería*) breakdown; (*situación*) imbalance; (*desacuerdo*) disagreement.
desalentador, a [desalenta'ðor, a] *adj* discouraging.
desalentar [desalen'tar] *vt* (*desanimar*) to discourage; **~se** *vr* to get discouraged.
desaliento [desa'ljento] *etc vb V* **desalentar** ♦ *nm* discouragement; (*abatimiento*) depression.
desaliñado, a [desali'ɲaðo, a] *adj* (*descuidado*) slovenly; (*raído*) shabby; (*desordenado*) untidy; (*negligente*) careless.
desaliño [desa'liɲo] *nm* (*descuido*) slovenliness; (*negligencia*) carelessness.
desalmado, a [desal'maðo, a] *adj* (*cruel*) cruel, heartless.
desalojar [desalo'xar] *vt* (*gen*) to remove, expel; (*expulsar, echar*) to eject; (*abandonar*) to move out of ♦ *vi* to move out; **la policía desalojó el local** the police cleared people out of the place.
desalquilar [desalki'lar] *vt* to vacate, move out; **~se** *vr* to become vacant.
desamarrar [desama'rrar] *vt* to untie; (*NAUT*) to cast off.
desamor [desa'mor] *nm* (*frialdad*) indifference; (*odio*) dislike.
desamparado, a [desampa'raðo, a] *adj* (*persona*) helpless; (*lugar*: *expuesto*) exposed; (: *desierto*) deserted.
desamparar [desampa'rar] *vt* (*abandonar*) to desert, abandon; (*JUR*) to leave defenceless; (*barco*) to abandon.
desamparo [desam'paro] *nm* (*acto*) desertion; (*estado*) helplessness.
desamueblado, a [desamwe'ßlaðo, a] *adj* unfurnished.
desandar [desan'dar] *vt*: ~ **lo andado** *o* **el camino** to retrace one's steps.
desanduve [desan'duße] *etc*, **desanduviera** [desandu'ßjera] *etc vb V* **desandar**.
desangelado, a [desanxe'laðo, a] *adj* (*habitación, edificio*) lifeless.
desangrar [desan'grar] *vt* to bleed; (*fig*: *persona*) to bleed dry; (*lago*) to drain; **~se** *vr* to lose a lot of blood; (*morir*) to bleed to death.
desanimado, a [desani'maðo, a] *adj* (*persona*) downhearted; (*espectáculo, fiesta*) dull.
desanimar [desani'mar] *vt* (*desalentar*) to discourage; (*deprimir*) to depress; **~se** *vr* to lose heart.
desánimo [de'sanimo] *nm* despondency; (*abatimiento*) dejection; (*falta de animación*) dullness.
desanudar [desanu'ðar] *vt* to untie; (*fig*) to clear up.
desapacible [desapa'θißle] *adj* unpleasant.
desaparecer [desapare'θer] *vi* to disappear; (*el sol, la luz*) to vanish; (~ *de vista*) to drop out of sight; (*efectos, señales*) to wear off ♦ *vt* (*esp AM POL*) to cause to disappear; (: *eufemismo*) to murder.
desaparecido, a [desapare'θiðo, a] *adj* missing; (*especie*) extinct ♦ *nm/f* (*AM POL*) kidnapped *o* missing person.
desaparezca [desapa'reθka] *etc vb V* **desaparecer**.
desaparición [desapari'θjon] *nf* disappearance; (*de especie etc*) extinction.
desapasionado, a [desapasjo'naðo, a] *adj* dispassionate, impartial.
desapego [desa'peɣo] *nm* (*frialdad*) coolness; (*distancia*) detachment.
desapercibido, a [desaperθi'ßiðo, a] *adj* unnoticed; (*desprevenido*) unprepared; **pasar** ~ to go unnoticed.
desaplicado, a [desapli'kado, a] *adj* slack, lazy.
desaprensivo, a [desapren'sißo, a] *adj* unscrupulous.
desaprobar [desapro'ßar] *vt* (*reprobar*) to disapprove of; (*condenar*) to condemn; (*no consentir*) to reject.
desaprovechado, a [desaproße'tʃaðo, a] *adj* (*oportunidad, tiempo*) wasted; (*estudiante*) slack.
desaprovechar [desaproße'tʃar] *vt* to waste; (*talento*) not to use to the full ♦ *vi* (*perder terreno*) to lose ground.
desapruebe [desa'prweße] *etc vb V* **desaprobar**.
desarmar [desar'mar] *vt* (*MIL, fig*) to disarm; (*TEC*) to take apart, dismantle.

desarme [de'sarme] *nm* disarmament.
desarraigado, a [desarrai'ɣaðo, a] *adj* (*persona*) without roots, rootless.
desarraigar [desarrai'ɣar] *vt* to uproot; (*fig*: *costumbre*) to root out; (: *persona*) to banish.
desarraigo [desa'rraiɣo] *nm* uprooting.
desarraigue [desa'rraiɣe] *etc vb V* **desarraigar**.
desarreglado, a [desarre'ɣlaðo, a] *adj* (*desordenado*) disorderly, untidy; (*hábitos*) irregular.
desarreglar [desarre'ɣlar] *vt* to mess up; (*desordenar*) to disarrange; (*trastocar*) to upset, disturb.
desarreglo [desa'rreɣlo] *nm* (*de casa, persona*) untidiness; (*desorden*) disorder; (*TEC*) trouble; (*MED*) upset; **viven en el mayor ~** they live in complete chaos.
desarrollado, a [desarro'ʎaðo, a] *adj* developed.
desarrollar [desarro'ʎar] *vt* (*gen*) to develop; (*extender*) to unfold; (*teoría*) to explain; **~se** *vr* to develop; (*extenderse*) to open (out); (*film*) to develop; (*fig*) to grow; (*tener lugar*) to take place; **aquí desarrollan un trabajo muy importante** they carry on *o* out very important work here; **la acción se desarrolla en Roma** (*CINE etc*) the scene is set in Rome.
desarrollo [desa'rroʎo] *nm* development; (*de acontecimientos*) unfolding; (*de industria, mercado*) expansion, growth; **país en vías de ~** developing country; **la industria está en pleno ~** industry is expanding steadily.
desarrugar [desarru'ɣar] *vt* (*alisar*) to smooth (out); (*ropa*) to remove the creases from.
desarrugue [desa'rruɣe] *etc vb V* **desarrugar**.
desarticulado, a [desartiku'laðo, a] *adj* disjointed.
desarticular [desartiku'lar] *vt* (*huesos*) to dislocate, put out of joint; (*objeto*) to take apart; (*grupo terrorista etc*) to break up.
desaseado, a [desase'aðo, a] *adj* (*sucio*) dirty; (*desaliñado*) untidy.
desaseo [desa'seo] *nm* (*suciedad*) dirtiness; (*desarreglo*) untidiness.
desasga [de'sasɣa] *etc vb V* **desasir**.
desasir [desa'sir] *vt* to loosen; **~se** *vr* to extricate o.s.; **~se de** to let go, give up.
desasosegar [desasose'ɣar] *vt* (*inquietar*) to disturb, make uneasy; **~se** *vr* to become uneasy.
desasosegué [desasose'ɣe], **desasoseguemos** [desasose'ɣemos] *etc vb V* **desasosegar**.
desasosiego [desaso'sjeɣo] *etc vb V* **desasosegar** ♦ *nm* (*intranquilidad*) uneasiness, restlessness; (*ansiedad*) anxiety; (*POL etc*) unrest.
desasosiegue [desaso'sjeɣue] *etc vb V* **desasosegar**.
desastrado, a [desas'traðo, a] *adj* (*desaliñado*) shabby; (*sucio*) dirty.
desastre [de'sastre] *nm* disaster; **¡un ~!** how awful!; **la función fue un ~** the show was a shambles.
desastroso, a [desas'troso, a] *adj* disastrous.
desatado, a [desa'taðo, a] *adj* (*desligado*) untied; (*violento*) violent, wild.
desatar [desa'tar] *vt* (*nudo*) to untie; (*paquete*) to undo; (*perro, odio*) to unleash; (*misterio*) to solve; (*separar*) to detach; **~se** *vr* (*zapatos*) to come untied; (*tormenta*) to break; (*perder control de sí*) to lose self-control; **~se en injurias** to pour out a stream of insults.
desatascar [desatas'kar] *vt* (*cañería*) to unblock, clear; (*carro*) to pull out of the mud; **~ a algn** (*fig*) to get sb out of a jam.
desatasque [desa'taske] *etc vb V* **desatascar**.
desatención [desaten'θjon] *nf* (*descuido*) inattention; (*distracción*) absent-mindedness.
desatender [desaten'der] *vt* (*no prestar atención a*) to disregard; (*abandonar*) to neglect.
desatento, a [desa'tento, a] *adj* (*distraído*) inattentive; (*descortés*) discourteous.
desatienda [desa'tjenda] *etc vb V* **desatender**.
desatinado, a [desati'naðo, a] *adj* foolish, silly.
desatino [desa'tino] *nm* (*idiotez*) foolishness, folly; (*error*) blunder; **~s** *nmpl* nonsense *sg*; **¡qué ~!** how silly!, what rubbish!
desatornillar [desatorni'ʎar] *vt* to unscrew.
desatrancar [desatran'kar] *vt* (*puerta*) to unbolt; (*cañería*) to unblock.
desatranque [desa'tranke] *etc vb V* **desatrancar**.
desautorice [desauto'riθe] *etc vb V* **desautorizar**.
desautorizado, a [desautori'θaðo, a] *adj* unauthorized.
desautorizar [desautori'θar] *vt* (*oficial*) to

deprive of authority; (*informe*) to deny.
desavendré [desaβen'dre] *etc vb V* **desavenir**.
desavenencia [desaβe'nenθja] *nf* (*desacuerdo*) disagreement; (*discrepancia*) quarrel.
desavenga [desa'βenga] *etc vb V* **desavenir**.
desavenido, a [desaβe'niðo, a] *adj* (*opuesto*) contrary; (*reñidos*) in disagreement; **ellos están ~s** they are at odds.
desavenir [desaβe'nir] *vt* (*enemistar*) to make trouble between; **~se** *vr* to fall out.
desaventajado, a [desaβenta'xaðo, a] *adj* (*inferior*) inferior; (*poco ventajoso*) disadvantageous.
desaviene [desa'βjene] *etc*, **desaviniendo** [desaβi'njendo] *etc vb V* **desavenir**.
desayunar [desaju'nar] *vi*, **~se** *vr* to have breakfast ♦ *vt* to have for breakfast; **~ con café** to have coffee for breakfast; **~ con algo** (*fig*) to get the first news of sth.
desayuno [desa'juno] *nm* breakfast.
desazón [desa'θon] *nf* (*angustia*) anxiety; (*MED*) discomfort; (*fig*) annoyance.
desazonar [desaθo'nar] *vt* (*fig*) to annoy, upset; **~se** *vr* (*enojarse*) to be annoyed; (*preocuparse*) to worry, be anxious.
desbancar [desβan'kar] *vt* (*quitar el puesto a*) to oust; (*suplantar*) to supplant (in sb's affections).
desbandada [desβan'daða] *nf* rush; **~ general** mass exodus; **a la ~** in disorder.
desbandarse [desβan'darse] *vr* (*MIL*) to disband; (*fig*) to flee in disorder.
desbanque [des'βanke] *etc vb V* **desbancar**.
desbarajuste [desβara'xuste] *nm* confusion, disorder; **¡qué ~!** what a mess!
desbaratar [desβara'tar] *vt* (*gen*) to mess up; (*plan*) to spoil; (*deshacer, destruir*) to ruin ♦ *vi* to talk nonsense; **~se** *vr* (*máquina*) to break down; (*persona*: *irritarse*) to fly off the handle (*fam*).
desbarrar [desβa'rrar] *vi* to talk nonsense.
desbloquear [desβloke'ar] *vt* (*negociaciones, tráfico*) to get going again; (*COM*: *cuenta*) to unfreeze.
desbocado, a [desβo'kaðo, a] *adj* (*caballo*) runaway; (*herramienta*) worn.
desbocar [desβo'kar] *vt* (*vasija*) to break the rim of; **~se** *vr* (*caballo*) to bolt; (*persona*: *soltar injurias*) to let out a stream of insults.
desboque [des'βoke] *etc vb V* **desbocar**.
desbordamiento [desβorða'mjento] *nm* (*de río*) overflowing; (*INFORM*) overflow; (*de cólera*) outburst; (*de entusiasmo*) upsurge.
desbordar [desβor'ðar] *vt* (*sobrepasar*) to go beyond; (*exceder*) to exceed ♦ *vi*, **~se** *vr* (*líquido, río*) to overflow; (*entusiasmo*) to erupt; (*persona*: *exaltarse*) to get carried away.
desbravar [desβra'βar] *vt* (*caballo*) to break in; (*animal*) to tame.
descabalgar [deskaβal'ɣar] *vi* to dismount.
descabalgue [deska'βalɣe] *etc vb V* **descabalgar**.
descabellado, a [deskaβe'ʎaðo, a] *adj* (*disparatado*) wild, crazy; (*insensato*) preposterous.
descabellar [deskaβe'ʎar] *vt* to ruffle; (*TAUR*: *toro*) to give the coup de grace to.
descabezado, a [deskaβe'θaðo, a] *adj* (*sin cabeza*) headless; (*insensato*) wild.
descafeinado, a [deskafei'naðo, a] *adj* decaffeinated ♦ *nm* decaffeinated coffee, de-caff.
descalabrar [deskala'βrar] *vt* to smash; (*persona*) to hit; (: *en la cabeza*) to hit on the head; (*NAUT*) to cripple; (*dañar*) to harm, damage; **~se** *vr* to hurt one's head.
descalabro [deska'laβro] *nm* blow; (*desgracia*) misfortune.
descalce [des'kalθe] *etc vb V* **descalzar**.
descalificación [deskalifika'θjon] *nf* disqualification; **descalificaciones** *nfpl* discrediting *sg*.
descalificar [deskalifi'kar] *vt* to disqualify; (*desacreditar*) to discredit.
descalifique [deskali'fike] *etc vb V* **descalificar**.
descalzar [deskal'θar] *vt* (*zapato*) to take off.
descalzo, a [des'kalθo, a] *adj* barefoot(ed); (*fig*) destitute; **estar (con los pies) ~(s)** to be barefooted.
descambiar [deskam'bjar] *vt* to exchange.
descaminado, a [deskami'naðo, a] *adj* (*equivocado*) on the wrong road; (*fig*) misguided; **en eso no anda usted muy ~** you're not far wrong there.
descamisado, a [deskami'saðo, a] *adj* bare-chested.
descampado [deskam'paðo] *nm* open space, piece of empty ground; **comer al ~** to eat in the open air.
descansado, a [deskan'saðo, a] *adj* (*gen*) rested; (*que tranquiliza*) restful.
descansar [deskan'sar] *vt* (*gen*) to rest; (*apoyar*): **~ (sobre)** to lean (on) ♦ *vi* to rest, have a rest; (*echarse*) to lie down;

(*cadáver, restos*) to lie; **¡que usted descanse!** sleep well!; ~ **en** (*argumento*) to be based on.
descansillo [deskan'siʎo] *nm* (*de escalera*) landing.
descanso [des'kanso] *nm* (*reposo*) rest; (*alivio*) relief; (*pausa*) break; (*DEPORTE*) interval, half time; **día de** ~ day off; ~ **de enfermedad/maternidad** sick/ maternity leave; **tomarse unos días de** ~ to take a few days' leave *o* rest.
descapitalizado, a [deskapitali'θaðo, a] *adj* undercapitalized.
descapotable [deskapo'taβle] *nm* (*tb*: **coche** ~) convertible.
descarado, a [deska'raðo, a] *adj* (*sin vergüenza*) shameless; (*insolente*) cheeky.
descarga [des'karɣa] *nf* (*ARQ, ELEC, MIL*) discharge; (*NAUT*) unloading.
descargador [deskarɣa'ðor] *nm* (*de barcos*) docker.
descargar [deskar'ɣar] *vt* to unload; (*golpe*) to let fly; (*arma*) to fire; (*ELEC*) to discharge; (*pila*) to run down; (*conciencia*) to relieve; (*COM*) to take up; (*persona*: *de una obligación*) to release; (: *de una deuda*) to free; (*JUR*) to clear ♦ *vi* (*río*): ~ **(en)** to flow (into); ~**se** *vr* to unburden o.s.; ~**se de algo** to get rid of sth.
descargo [des'karɣo] *nm* (*de obligación*) release; (*COM*: *recibo*) receipt; (: *de deuda*) discharge; (*JUR*) evidence; ~ **de una acusación** acquittal on a charge.
descargue [des'karɣe] *etc vb V* **descargar**.
descarnado, a [deskar'naðo, a] *adj* scrawny; (*fig*) bare; (*estilo*) straightforward.
descaro [des'karo] *nm* nerve.
descarriar [deska'rrjar] *vt* (*descaminar*) to misdirect; (*fig*) to lead astray; ~**se** *vr* (*perderse*) to lose one's way; (*separarse*) to stray; (*pervertirse*) to err, go astray.
descarrilamiento [deskarrila'mjento] *nm* (*de tren*) derailment.
descarrilar [deskarri'lar] *vi* to be derailed.
descartable [deskar'taβle] *adj* (*INFORM*) temporary.
descartar [deskar'tar] *vt* (*rechazar*) to reject; (*eliminar*) to rule out; ~**se** *vr* (*NAIPES*) to discard; ~**se de** to shirk.
descascarar [deskaska'rar] *vt* (*naranja, limón*) to peel; (*nueces, huevo duro*) to shell; ~**se** *vr* to peel (off).
descascarillado, a [deskaskari'ʎaðo, a] *adj* (*paredes*) peeling.
descendencia [desθen'denθja] *nf* (*origen*) origin, descent; (*hijos*) offspring; **morir sin dejar** ~ to die without issue.
descendente [desθen'dente] *adj* (*cantidad*) diminishing; (*INFORM*) top-down.
descender [desθen'der] *vt* (*bajar*: *escalera*) to go down ♦ *vi* to descend; (*temperatura, nivel*) to fall, drop; (*líquido*) to run; (*cortina etc*) to hang; (*fuerzas, persona*) to fail, get weak; ~ **de** to be descended from.
descendiente [desθen'djente] *nm/f* descendant.
descenso [des'θenso] *nm* descent; (*de temperatura*) drop; (*de producción*) downturn; (*de calidad*) decline; (*MINERÍA*) collapse; (*bajada*) slope; (*fig*: *decadencia*) decline; (*de empleado etc*) demotion.
descentrado, a [desθen'traðo, a] *adj* (*pieza de una máquina*) off-centre; (*rueda*) out of true; (*persona*) bewildered; (*desequilibrado*) unbalanced; (*problema*) out of focus; **todavía está algo** ~ he is still somewhat out of touch.
descentralice [desθentra'liθe] *etc vb V* **descentralizar**.
descentralizar [desθentrali'θar] *vt* to decentralize.
descerrajar [desθerra'xar] *vt* (*puerta*) to break open.
descienda [des'θjenda] *etc vb V* **descender**.
descifrable [desθi'fraβle] *adj* (*gen*) decipherable; (*letra*) legible.
descifrar [desθi'frar] *vt* (*escritura*) to decipher; (*mensaje*) to decode; (*problema*) to puzzle out; (*misterio*) to solve.
descocado, a [desko'kaðo, a] *adj* (*descarado*) cheeky; (*desvergonzado*) brazen.
descoco [des'koko] *nm* (*descaro*) cheek; (*atrevimiento*) brazenness.
descodificador [deskoðifika'ðor] *nm* decoder.
descodificar [deskoðifi'kar] *vt* to decode.
descolgar [deskol'ɣar] *vt* (*bajar*) to take down; (*desde una posición alta*) to lower; (*de una pared etc*) to unhook; (*teléfono*) to pick up; ~**se** *vr* to let o.s. down; ~**se por** (*bajar escurriéndose*) to slip down; (*pared*) to climb down; **dejó el teléfono descolgado** he left the phone off the hook.
descolgué [deskol'ɣe], **descolguemos** [deskol'ɣemos] *etc vb V* **descolgar**.
descollar [desko'ʎar] *vi* (*sobresalir*) to stand out; (*montaña etc*) to rise; **la obra que más descuella de las suyas** his most outstanding work.
descolocado, a [deskolo'kaðo, a] *adj*: **estar**

~ (*cosa*) to be out of place; (*criada*) to be unemployed.

descolorido, a [deskolo'riðo, a] *adj* (*color, tela*) faded; (*pálido*) pale; (*fig: estilo*) colourless.

descompaginar [deskompaxi'nar] *vt* (*desordenar*) to disarrange, mess up.

descompasado, a [deskompa'saðo, a] *adj* (*sin proporción*) out of all proportion; (*excesivo*) excessive; (*hora*) unearthly.

descompensar [deskompen'sar] *vt* to unbalance.

descompondré [deskompon'dre] *etc vb V* **descomponer**.

descomponer [deskompo'ner] *vt* (*gen, LING, MAT*) to break down; (*desordenar*) to disarrange, disturb; (*materia orgánica*) to rot, decompose; (*TEC*) to put out of order; (*facciones*) to distort; (*estómago etc*) to upset; (*planes*) to mess up; (*persona: molestar*) to upset; (*: irritar*) to annoy; **~se** *vr* (*corromperse*) to rot, decompose; (*estómago*) to get upset; (*el tiempo*) to change (for the worse); (*TEC*) to break down.

descomponga [deskom'ponga] *etc vb V* **descomponer**.

descomposición [deskomposi'θjon] *nf* (*gen*) breakdown; (*de fruta etc*) decomposition; (*putrefacción*) rotting; (*de cara*) distortion; ~ **de vientre** (*MED*) stomach upset, diarrhoea.

descompostura [deskompos'tura] *nf* (*TEC*) breakdown; (*desorganización*) disorganization; (*desorden*) untidiness.

descompuesto, a [deskom'pwesto, a] *pp de* **descomponer** ♦ *adj* (*corrompido*) decomposed; (*roto*) broken (down).

descompuse [deskom'puse] *etc vb V* **descomponer**.

descomunal [deskomu'nal] *adj* (*enorme*) huge; (*fam: excelente*) fantastic.

desconcertado, a [deskonθer'taðo, a] *adj* disconcerted, bewildered.

desconcertar [deskonθer'tar] *vt* (*confundir*) to baffle; (*incomodar*) to upset, put out; (*orden*) to disturb; **~se** *vr* (*turbarse*) to be upset; (*confundirse*) to be bewildered.

desconchado, a [deskon'tʃaðo, a] *adj* (*pintura*) peeling.

desconchar [deskon'tʃar] *vt* (*pared*) to strip off; (*loza*) to chip off.

desconcierto [deskon'θjerto] *etc vb V* **desconcertar** ♦ *nm* (*gen*) disorder; (*desorientación*) uncertainty; (*inquietud*) uneasiness; (*confusión*) bewilderment.

desconectado, a [deskonek'taðo, a] *adj* (*ELEC*) disconnected, switched off; (*INFORM*) offline; **estar ~ de** (*fig*) to have no contact with.

desconectar [deskonek'tar] *vt* to disconnect; (*desenchufar*) to unplug; (*radio, televisión*) to switch off; (*INFORM*) to toggle off.

desconfiado, a [deskon'fjaðo, a] *adj* suspicious.

desconfianza [deskon'fjanθa] *nf* distrust.

desconfiar [deskon'fjar] *vi* to be distrustful; ~ **de** (*sospechar*) to mistrust, suspect; (*no tener confianza en*) to have no faith *o* confidence in; **desconfío de ello** I doubt it; **desconfíe de las imitaciones** (*COM*) beware of imitations.

desconforme [deskon'forme] *adj* = **disconforme**.

descongelar [deskonxe'lar] *vt* (*nevera*) to defrost; (*comida*) to thaw; (*AUTO*) to de-ice; (*COM, POL*) to unfreeze.

descongestionar [desconxestjo'nar] *vt* (*cabeza, tráfico*) to clear; (*calle, ciudad*) to relieve congestion in; (*fig: despejar*) to clear.

desconocer [deskono'θer] *vt* (*ignorar*) not to know, be ignorant of; (*no aceptar*) to deny; (*repudiar*) to disown.

desconocido, a [deskono'θiðo, a] *adj* unknown; (*que no se conoce*) unfamiliar; (*no reconocido*) unrecognized ♦ *nm/f* stranger; (*recién llegado*) newcomer; **está ~** he is hardly recognizable.

desconocimiento [deskonoθi'mjento] *nm* (*falta de conocimientos*) ignorance; (*repudio*) disregard.

desconozca [desko'noθka] *etc vb V* **desconocer**.

desconsiderado, a [deskonsiðe'raðo, a] *adj* inconsiderate; (*insensible*) thoughtless.

desconsolado, a [deskonso'laðo, a] *adj* (*afligido*) disconsolate; (*cara*) sad; (*desanimado*) dejected.

desconsolar [deskonso'lar] *vt* to distress; **~se** *vr* to despair.

desconsuelo [deskon'swelo] *etc vb V* **desconsolar** ♦ *nm* (*tristeza*) distress; (*desesperación*) despair.

descontado, a [deskon'taðo, a] *adj*: **por ~** of course; **dar por ~ (que)** to take it for granted (that).

descontar [deskon'tar] *vt* (*deducir*) to take away, deduct; (*rebajar*) to discount.

descontento, a [deskon'tento, a] *adj* dissatisfied ♦ *nm* dissatisfaction, discontent.

descontrol [deskon'trol] *nm* (*fam*) lack of control.

descontrolado, a [deskontro'laðo, a] *adj* uncontrolled.
descontrolarse [deskontro'larse] *vr* (*persona*) to lose control.
desconvenir [deskombe'nir] *vi* (*personas*) to disagree; (*no corresponder*) not to fit; (*no convenir*) to be inconvenient.
desconvocar [deskombo'kar] *vt* to call off.
descorazonar [deskoraθo'nar] *vt* to discourage, dishearten; **~se** *vr* to get discouraged, lose heart.
descorchador [deskortʃa'ðor] *nm* corkscrew.
descorchar [deskor'tʃar] *vt* to uncork, open.
descorrer [desko'rrer] *vt* (*cortina, cerrojo*) to draw back; (*velo*) to remove.
descortés [deskor'tes] *adj* (*mal educado*) discourteous; (*grosero*) rude.
descortesía [deskorte'sia] *nf* discourtesy; (*grosería*) rudeness.
descoser [desko'ser] *vt* to unstitch; **~se** *vr* to come apart (at the seams); (*fam: descubrir un secreto*) to blurt out a secret; **~se de risa** to split one's sides laughing.
descosido, a [desko'siðo, a] *adj* (*costura*) unstitched; (*desordenado*) disjointed ♦ *nm*: **como un ~** (*obrar*) wildly; (*beber, comer*) to excess; (*estudiar*) like mad.
descoyuntar [deskojun'tar] *vt* (*ANAT*) to dislocate; (*hechos*) to twist; **~se** *vr*: **~se un hueso** (*ANAT*) to put a bone out of joint; **~se de risa** (*fam*) to split one's sides laughing; **estar descoyuntado** (*persona*) to be double-jointed.
descrédito [des'kreðito] *nm* discredit; **caer en ~** to fall into disrepute; **ir en ~ de** to be to the discredit of.
descreído, a [deskre'iðo, a] *adj* (*incrédulo*) incredulous; (*falto de fe*) unbelieving.
descremado, a [deskre'maðo, a] *adj* skimmed.
descremar [deskre'mar] *vt* (*leche*) to skim.
describir [deskri'βir] *vt* to describe.
descripción [deskrip'θjon] *nf* description.
descrito [des'krito] *pp de* **describir**.
descuajar [deskwa'xar] *vt* (*disolver*) to melt; (*planta*) to pull out by the roots; (*extirpar*) to eradicate, wipe out; (*desanimar*) to dishearten.
descuajaringarse [deskwaxarin'garse] *vr* to fall to bits.
descuajaringue [deskwaxa'ringe] *etc vb V* **descuajaringarse**.
descuartice [deskwar'tiθe] *etc vb V* **descuartizar**.
descuartizar [deskwarti'θar] *vt* (*animal*) to carve up, cut up; (*fig: hacer pedazos*) to tear apart.
descubierto, a [desku'βjerto, a] *pp de* **descubrir** ♦ *adj* uncovered, bare; (*persona*) bare-headed; (*cielo*) clear; (*coche*) open; (*campo*) treeless ♦ *nm* (*lugar*) open space; (*COM: en el presupuesto*) shortage; (*: bancario*) overdraft; **al ~** in the open; **poner al ~** to lay bare; **quedar al ~** to be exposed; **estar en ~** to be overdrawn.
descubridor, a [deskuβri'ðor, a] *nm/f* discoverer.
descubrimiento [deskuβri'mjento] *nm* (*hallazgo*) discovery; (*de criminal, fraude*) detection; (*revelación*) revelation; (*de secreto etc*) disclosure; (*de estatua etc*) unveiling.
descubrir [desku'βrir] *vt* to discover, find; (*petróleo*) to strike; (*inaugurar*) to unveil; (*vislumbrar*) to detect; (*sacar a luz: crimen*) to bring to light; (*revelar*) to reveal, show; (*poner al descubierto*) to expose to view; (*naipes*) to lay down; (*quitar la tapa de*) to uncover; (*cacerola*) to take the lid off; (*enterarse de: causa, solución*) to find out; (*divisar*) to see, make out; (*delatar*) to give away, betray; **~se** *vr* to reveal o.s.; (*quitarse sombrero*) to take off one's hat; (*confesar*) to confess; (*fig: salir a luz*) to come out *o* to light.
descuelga [des'kwelɣa] *etc*, **descuelgue** [des'kwelɣe] *etc vb V* **descolgar**.
descuelle [des'kweʎe] *etc vb V* **descollar**.
descuento [des'kwento] *etc vb V* **descontar** ♦ *nm* discount; **~ del 3%** 3% off; **con ~** at a discount; **~ por pago al contado** (*COM*) cash discount; **~ por volumen de compras** (*COM*) volume discount.
descuidado, a [deskwi'ðaðo, a] *adj* (*sin cuidado*) careless; (*desordenado*) untidy; (*olvidadizo*) forgetful; (*dejado*) neglected; (*desprevenido*) unprepared.
descuidar [deskwi'ðar] *vt* (*dejar*) to neglect; (*olvidar*) to overlook ♦ *vi*, **~se** *vr* (*distraerse*) to be careless; (*estar desaliñado*) to let o.s. go; (*desprevenirse*) to drop one's guard; **¡descuida!** don't worry!
descuido [des'kwiðo] *nm* (*dejadez*) carelessness; (*olvido*) negligence; (*un ~*) oversight; **al ~** casually; (*sin cuidado*) carelessly; **al menor ~** if my *etc* attention wanders for a minute; **con ~** thoughtlessly; **por ~** by an oversight.

PALABRA CLAVE

desde ['desðe] *prep* **1** (*lugar*) from; ~ **Burgos hasta mi casa hay 30 km** it's 30 kms from Burgos to my house; ~ **lejos** from a distance
2 (*posición*): **hablaba ~ el balcón** she was speaking from the balcony
3 (*tiempo*: +*adv, n*): ~ **ahora** from now on; ~ **entonces/la boda** since then/the wedding; ~ **niño** since I *etc* was a child; ~ **3 años atrás** since 3 years ago
4 (*tiempo*: +*vb*) since; for; **nos conocemos ~ 1978/~ hace 20 años** we've known each other since 1978/for 20 years; **no le veo ~ 1983/~ hace 5 años** I haven't seen him since 1983/for 5 years; **¿~ cuándo vives aquí?** how long have you lived here?
5 (*gama*): ~ **los más lujosos hasta los más económicos** from the most luxurious to the most reasonably priced
6: ~ **luego (que no)** of course (not)
♦ *conj*: ~ **que**: ~ **que recuerdo** for as long as I can remember; ~ **que llegó no ha salido** he hasn't been out since he arrived.

desdecir [desðe'θir] *vi*: ~ **de** (*no merecer*) to be unworthy of; (*no corresponder*) to clash with; **~se** *vr*: **~se de** to go back on.
desdén [des'ðen] *nm* scorn.
desdentado, a [desðen'taðo, a] *adj* toothless.
desdeñable [desðe'ɲaßle] *adj* contemptible; **nada ~** far from negligible, considerable.
desdeñar [desðe'ɲar] *vt* (*despreciar*) to scorn.
desdeñoso, a [desðe'ɲoso, a] *adj* scornful.
desdibujar [desðißu'xar] *vt* to blur (the outlines of); **~se** *vr* to get blurred, fade (away); **el recuerdo se ha desdibujado** the memory has become blurred.
desdichado, a [desði'tʃaðo, a] *adj* (*sin suerte*) unlucky; (*infeliz*) unhappy; (*día*) ill-fated ♦ *nm/f* (*pobre desgraciado*) poor devil.
desdicho, a [des'ðitʃo, a] *pp de* **desdecir** ♦ *nf* (*desgracia*) misfortune; (*infelicidad*) unhappiness.
desdiciendo [desði'θjendo] *etc vb V* **desdecir**.
desdiga [des'ðiɣa] *etc*, **desdije** [des'dixe] *etc vb V* **desdecir**.
desdoblado, a [desðo'ßlaðo, a] *adj* (*personalidad*) split.
desdoblar [desðo'ßlar] *vt* (*extender*) to spread out; (*desplegar*) to unfold.
deseable [dese'aßle] *adj* desirable.
desear [dese'ar] *vt* to want, desire, wish for; **¿qué desea la señora?** (*tienda etc*) what can I do for you, madam?; **estoy deseando que esto termine** I'm longing for this to finish.
desecar [dese'kar] *vt*, **desecarse** *vr* to dry up.
desechable [dese'tʃaßle] *adj* (*envase etc*) disposable.
desechar [dese'tʃar] *vt* (*basura*) to throw out *o* away; (*ideas*) to reject, discard; (*miedo*) to cast aside; (*plan*) to drop.
desecho [de'setʃo] *nm* (*desprecio*) contempt; (*lo peor*) dregs *pl*; **~s** *nmpl* rubbish *sg*, waste *sg*; **de ~** (*hierro*) scrap; (*producto*) waste; (*ropa*) cast-off.
desembalar [desemba'lar] *vt* to unpack.
desembarace [desemba'raθe] *etc vb V* **desembarazar**.
desembarazado, a [desembara'θaðo, a] *adj* (*libre*) clear, free; (*desenvuelto*) free and easy.
desembarazar [desembara'θar] *vt* (*desocupar*) to clear; (*desenredar*) to free; **~se** *vr*: **~se de** to free o.s. of, get rid of.
desembarazo [desemba'raθo] *nm* (*acto*) clearing; (*AM*: *parto*) birth; (*desenfado*) ease.
desembarcadero [desembarka'ðero] *nm* quay.
desembarcar [desembar'kar] *vt* (*personas*) to land; (*mercancías etc*) to unload ♦ *vi*, **~se** *vr* (*de barco, avión*) to disembark.
desembarco [desem'barko] *nm* landing.
desembargar [desembar'ɣar] *vt* (*gen*) to free; (*JUR*) to remove the embargo on.
desembargue [desem'ßarɣe] *etc vb V* **desembargar**.
desembarque [desem'barke] *etc vb V* **desembarcar** ♦ *nm* disembarkation; (*de pasajeros*) landing; (*de mercancías*) unloading.
desembocadura [desemboka'ðura] *nf* (*de río*) mouth; (*de calle*) opening.
desembocar [desembo'kar] *vi*: ~ **en** to flow into; (*fig*) to result in.
desemboce [desem'boθe] *etc vb V* **desembozar**.
desembolsar [desembol'sar] *vt* (*pagar*) to pay out; (*gastar*) to lay out.
desembolso [desem'bolso] *nm* payment.
desemboque [desem'boke] *etc vb V* **desembocar**.
desembozar [desembo'θar] *vt* to unmask.
desembragar [desembra'ɣar] *vt* (*TEC*) to disengage; (*embrague*) to release ♦ *vi*

(*AUTO*) to declutch.
desembrague [desem'ßraɣe] *etc vb V* **desembragar.**
desembrollar [desembro'ʎar] *vt* (*madeja*) to unravel; (*asunto, malentendido*) to sort out.
desembuchar [desembu'tʃar] *vt* to disgorge; (*fig*) to come out with ♦ *vi* (*confesar*) to spill the beans (*fam*); **¡desembucha!** out with it!
desemejante [deseme'xante] *adj* dissimilar; ~ **de** different from, unlike.
desemejanza [deseme'xanθa] *nf* dissimilarity.
desempacar [desempa'kar] *vt* (*esp AM*) to unpack.
desempañar [desempa'ɲar] *vt* (*cristal*) to clean, demist.
desempaque [desem'pake] *etc vb V* **desempacar.**
desempaquetar [desempake'tar] *vt* to unpack, unwrap.
desempatar [desempa'tar] *vi* to break a tie; **volvieron a jugar para** ~ they held a play-off.
desempate [desem'pate] *nm* (*FÚTBOL*) play-off; (*TENIS*) tie-break(er).
desempeñar [desempe'ɲar] *vt* (*cargo*) to hold; (*papel*) to play; (*deber, función*) to perform, carry out; (*lo empeñado*) to redeem; ~**se** *vr* to get out of debt; ~ **un papel** (*fig*) to play (a role).
desempeño [desem'peɲo] *nm* occupation; (*de lo empeñado*) redeeming; **de mucho** ~ very capable.
desempleado, a [desemple'aðo, a] *adj* unemployed, out of work ♦ *nm/f* unemployed person.
desempleo [desem'pleo] *nm* unemployment.
desempolvar [desempol'ßar] *vt* (*muebles etc*) to dust; (*lo olvidado*) to revive.
desencadenar [desenkaðe'nar] *vt* to unchain; (*ira*) to unleash; (*provocar*) to cause, set off; ~**se** *vr* to break loose; (*tormenta*) to burst; (*guerra*) to break out; **se desencadenó una lucha violenta** a violent struggle ensued.
desencajar [desenka'xar] *vt* (*hueso*) to put out of joint; (*mandíbula*) to dislocate; (*mecanismo, pieza*) to disconnect, disengage.
desencantar [desenkan'tar] *vt* to disillusion, disenchant.
desencanto [desen'kanto] *nm* disillusionment, disenchantment.
desenchufar [desentʃu'far] *vt* to unplug, disconnect.
desenfadado, a [desenfa'ðaðo, a] *adj* (*desenvuelto*) uninhibited; (*descarado*) forward; (*en el vestir*) casual.
desenfado [desen'faðo] *nm* (*libertad*) freedom; (*comportamiento*) free and easy manner; (*descaro*) forwardness; (*desenvoltura*) self-confidence.
desenfocado, a [desenfo'kaðo, a] *adj* (*FOTO*) out of focus.
desenfrenado, a [desenfre'naðo, a] *adj* (*descontrolado*) uncontrolled; (*inmoderado*) unbridled.
desenfrenarse [desenfre'narse] *vr* (*persona: desmandarse*) to lose all self-control; (*multitud*) to run riot; (*tempestad*) to burst; (*viento*) to rage.
desenfreno [desen'freno] *nm* (*vicio*) wildness; (*falta de control*) lack of self-control; (*de pasiones*) unleashing.
desenganchar [desengan'tʃar] *vt* (*gen*) to unhook; (*FERRO*) to uncouple; (*TEC*) to disengage.
desengañar [desenga'ɲar] *vt* to disillusion; (*abrir los ojos a*) to open the eyes of; ~**se** *vr* to become disillusioned; **¡desengáñate!** don't you believe it!
desengaño [desen'gaɲo] *nm* disillusionment; (*decepción*) disappointment; **sufrir un** ~ **amoroso** to be disappointed in love.
desengrasar [desengra'sar] *vt* to degrease.
desenlace [desen'laθe] *etc vb V* **desenlazar** ♦ *nm* outcome; (*LIT*) ending.
desenlazar [desenla'θar] *vt* (*desatar*) to untie; (*problema*) to solve; (*aclarar: asunto*) to unravel; ~**se** *vr* (*desatarse*) to come undone; (*LIT*) to end.
desenmarañar [desenmara'ɲar] *vt* (*fig*) to unravel.
desenmascarar [desenmaska'rar] *vt* to unmask, expose.
desenredar [desenre'ðar] *vt* to resolve.
desenrollar [desenro'ʎar] *vt* to unroll, unwind.
desenroscar [desenros'kar] *vt* (*tornillo etc*) to unscrew.
desenrosque [desen'roske] *etc vb V* **desenroscar.**
desentenderse [desenten'derse] *vr*: ~ **de** to pretend not to know about; (*apartarse*) to have nothing to do with.
desentendido, a [desenten'diðo, a] *adj*: **hacerse el** ~ to pretend not to notice; **se hizo el** ~ he didn't take the hint.
desenterrar [desente'rrar] *vt* to exhume; (*tesoro, fig*) to unearth, dig up.
desentierre [desen'tjerre] *etc vb V* **desenterrar.**

desentonar [desento'nar] *vi* (*MUS*) to sing (*o* play) out of tune; (*no encajar*) to be out of place; (*color*) to clash.
desentorpecer [desentorpe'θer] *vt* (*miembro*) to stretch; (*fam*: *persona*) to polish up.
desentorpezca [desentor'peθka] *etc vb V* **desentorpecer**.
desentrañar [desentra'ɲar] *vt* (*misterio*) to unravel.
desentrenado, a [desentre'naðo, a] *adj* out of training.
desentumecer [desentume'θer] *vt* (*pierna etc*) to stretch; (*DEPORTE*) to loosen up.
desentumezca [desentu'meθka] *etc vb V* **desentumecer**.
desenvainar [desembai'nar] *vt* (*espada*) to draw, unsheathe.
desenvoltura [desembol'tura] *nf* (*libertad, gracia*) ease; (*descaro*) free and easy manner; (*al hablar*) fluency.
desenvolver [desembol'βer] *vt* (*paquete*) to unwrap; (*fig*) to develop; **~se** *vr* (*desarrollarse*) to unfold, develop; (*suceder*) to go off; (*prosperar*) to prosper; (*arreglárselas*) to cope.
desenvolvimiento [desembolβi'mjento] *nm* (*desarrollo*) development; (*de idea*) exposition.
desenvuelto, a [desem'bwelto, a] *pp de* **desenvolver** ♦ *adj* (*suelto*) easy; (*desenfadado*) confident; (*al hablar*) fluent; (*pey*) forward.
desenvuelva [desem'buelβa] *etc vb V* **desenvolver**.
deseo [de'seo] *nm* desire, wish; **~ de saber** thirst for knowledge; **buen ~** good intentions *pl*; **arder en ~s de algo** to yearn for sth.
deseoso, a [dese'oso, a] *adj*: **estar ~ de hacer** to be anxious to do.
deseque [de'seke] *etc vb V* **desecar**.
desequilibrado, a [desekili'βraðo, a] *adj* unbalanced ♦ *nm/f* unbalanced person; **~ mental** mentally disturbed person.
desequilibrar [desekili'βrar] *vt* (*mente*) to unbalance; (*objeto*) to throw out of balance; (*persona*) to throw off balance.
desequilibrio [deseki'liβrio] *nm* (*de mente*) unbalance; (*entre cantidades*) imbalance; (*MED*) unbalanced mental condition.
desertar [deser'tar] *vt* (*JUR*: *derecho de apelación*) to forfeit ♦ *vi* to desert; **~ de sus deberes** to neglect one's duties.
desértico, a [de'sertiko, a] *adj* desert *cpd*; (*vacío*) deserted.
desertor, a [deser'tor, a] *nm/f* deserter.
desesperación [desespera'θjon] *nf* desperation, despair; (*irritación*) fury; **es una ~** it's maddening; **es una ~ tener que ...** it's infuriating to have to ....
desesperado, a [desespe'raðo, a] *adj* (*persona*: *sin esperanza*) desperate; (*caso, situación*) hopeless; (*esfuerzo*) furious ♦ *nm*: **como un ~** like mad ♦ *nf*: **hacer algo a la desesperada** to do sth as a last resort *o* in desperation.
desesperance [desespe'ranθe] *etc vb V* **desesperanzar**.
desesperante [desespe'rante] *adj* (*exasperante*) infuriating; (*persona*) hopeless.
desesperanzar [desesperan'θar] *vt* to drive to despair; **~se** *vr* to lose hope, despair.
desesperar [desespe'rar] *vt* to drive to despair; (*exasperar*) to drive to distraction ♦ *vi*: **~ de** to despair of; **~se** *vr* to despair, lose hope.
desespero [deses'pero] *nm* (*AM*) despair.
desestabilice [desestaβi'liθe] *etc vb V* **desestabilizar**.
desestabilizar [desestaβili'θar] *vt* to destabilize.
desestimar [desesti'mar] *vt* (*menospreciar*) to have a low opinion of; (*rechazar*) to reject.
desfachatez [desfatʃa'teθ] *nf* (*insolencia*) impudence; (*descaro*) rudeness.
desfalco [des'falko] *nm* embezzlement.
desfallecer [desfaʎe'θer] *vi* (*perder las fuerzas*) to become weak; (*desvanecerse*) to faint.
desfallecido, a [desfaʎe'θiðo, a] *adj* (*débil*) weak.
desfallezca [desfa'ʎeθka] *etc vb V* **desfallecer**.
desfasado, a [desfa'saðo, a] *adj* (*anticuado*) old-fashioned; (*TEC*) out of phase.
desfasar [desfa'sar] *vt* to phase out.
desfase [des'fase] *nm* (*diferencia*) gap.
desfavorable [desfaβo'raβle] *adj* unfavourable.
desfavorecer [desfaβore'θer] *vt* (*sentar mal*) not to suit.
desfavorezca [desfaβo'reθka] *etc vb V* **desfavorecer**.
desfiguración [desfiɣura'θjon] *nf*, **desfiguramiento** [desfiɣura'mjento] *nm* (*de persona*) disfigurement; (*de monumento*) defacement; (*FOTO*) blurring.
desfigurar [desfiɣu'rar] *vt* (*cara*) to disfigure; (*cuerpo*) to deform; (*cuadro, monumento*) to deface; (*FOTO*) to blur; (*sentido*) to twist; (*suceso*) to misrepresent.
desfiladero [desfila'ðero] *nm* gorge, defile.

desfilar [desfi'lar] *vi* to parade; **desfilaron ante el general** they marched past the general.
desfile [des'file] *nm* procession; (*MIL*) parade; ~ **de modelos** fashion show.
desflorar [desflo'rar] *vt* (*mujer*) to deflower; (*arruinar*) to tarnish; (*asunto*) to touch on.
desfogar [desfo'ɣar] *vt* (*fig*) to vent ♦ *vi* (*NAUT*: *tormenta*) to burst; **~se** *vr* (*fig*) to let off steam.
desfogue [des'foɣe] *etc vb V* **desfogar**.
desgajar [desɣa'xar] *vt* (*arrancar*) to tear off; (*romper*) to break off; (*naranja*) to split into segments; **~se** *vr* to come off.
desgana [des'ɣana] *nf* (*falta de apetito*) loss of appetite; (*renuencia*) unwillingness; **hacer algo a** ~ to do sth unwillingly.
desganado, a [desɣa'naðo, a] *adj*: **estar** ~ (*sin apetito*) to have no appetite; (*sin entusiasmo*) to have lost interest.
desgañitarse [desɣaɲi'tarse] *vr* to shout o.s. hoarse.
desgarbado, a [desɣar'ßaðo, a] *adj* (*sin gracia*) clumsy, ungainly.
desgarrador, a [desɣarra'ðor, a] *adj* heartrending.
desgarrar [desɣa'rrar] *vt* to tear (up); (*fig*) to shatter.
desgarro [des'ɣarro] *nm* (*en tela*) tear; (*aflicción*) grief; (*descaro*) impudence.
desgastar [desɣas'tar] *vt* (*deteriorar*) to wear away *o* down; (*estropear*) to spoil; **~se** *vr* to get worn out.
desgaste [des'ɣaste] *nm* wear (and tear); (*de roca*) erosion; (*de cuerda*) fraying; (*de metal*) corrosion; ~ **económico** drain on one's resources.
desglosar [desɣlo'sar] *vt* to detach.
desgobierno [desɣo'ßjerno] *etc vb V* **desgobernar** ♦ *nm* (*POL*) misgovernment, misrule.
desgracia [des'ɣraθja] *nf* misfortune; (*accidente*) accident; (*vergüenza*) disgrace; (*contratiempo*) setback; **por** ~ unfortunately; **en el accidente no hay que lamentar ~s personales** there were no casualties in the accident; **caer en** ~ to fall from grace; **tener la** ~ **de** to be unlucky enough to.
desgraciadamente [desɣraθjaða'mente] *adv* unfortunately.
desgraciado, a [desɣra'θjaðo, a] *adj* (*sin suerte*) unlucky, unfortunate; (*miserable*) wretched; (*infeliz*) miserable ♦ *nm/f* (*malo*) swine; (*infeliz*) poor creature; **¡esa radio desgraciada!** (*esp AM*) that lousy radio!
desgraciar [desɣra'θjar] *vt* (*estropear*) to spoil; (*ofender*) to displease.
desgranar [desɣra'nar] *vt* (*trigo*) to thresh; (*guisantes*) to shell; ~ **un racimo** to pick the grapes from a bunch; ~ **mentiras** to come out with a string of lies.
desgravación [desɣraßa'θjon] *nf* (*COM*): ~ **de impuestos** tax relief; ~ **personal** personal allowance.
desgravar [desɣra'ßar] *vt* (*producto*) to reduce the tax *o* duty on.
desgreñado, a [desɣre'ɲaðo, a] *adj* dishevelled.
desguace [des'ɣwaθe] *nm* (*de coches*) scrapping; (*lugar*) scrapyard.
desguazar [desɣwa'θar] *vt* (*coche*) to scrap.
deshabitado, a [desaßi'taðo, a] *adj* uninhabited.
deshabitar [desaßi'tar] *vt* (*casa*) to leave empty; (*despoblar*) to depopulate.
deshacer [desa'θer] *vt* (*lo hecho*) to undo, unmake; (*proyectos*: *arruinar*) to spoil; (*casa*) to break up; (*TEC*) to take apart; (*enemigo*) to defeat; (*diluir*) to melt; (*contrato*) to break; (*intriga*) to solve; (*cama*) to strip; (*maleta*) to unpack; (*paquete*) to unwrap; (*nudo*) to untie; (*costura*) to unpick; **~se** *vr* (*desatarse*) to come undone; (*estropearse*) to be spoiled; (*descomponerse*) to fall to pieces; (*disolverse*) to melt; (*despedazarse*) to come apart *o* undone; **~se de** to get rid of; (*COM*) to dump, unload; **~se en** (*cumplidos, elogios*) to be lavish with; **~se en lágrimas** to burst into tears; **~se por algo** to be crazy about sth.
deshaga [de'saɣa] *etc*, **desharé** [desa're] *etc vb V* **deshacer**.
des(h)arrapado, a [desarra'paðo, a] *adj* ragged; **(de aspecto)** ~ shabby.
deshecho, a [de'setʃo, a] *pp de* **deshacer** ♦ *adj* (*lazo, nudo*) undone; (*roto*) smashed; (*despedazado*) in pieces; (*cama*) unmade; (*MED*: *persona*) weak, emaciated; (: *salud*) broken; **estoy** ~ I'm shattered.
deshelar [dese'lar] *vt* (*cañería*) to thaw; (*heladera*) to defrost.
desheredar [desere'ðar] *vt* to disinherit.
deshice [de'siθe] *etc vb V* **deshacer**.
deshidratación [desiðrata'θjon] *nf* dehydration.
deshidratar [desiðra'tar] *vt* to dehydrate.
deshielo [des'jelo] *etc vb V* **deshelar** ♦ *nm* thaw.
deshilachar [desila'tʃar] *vt*, **deshilacharse** *vr* to fray.
deshilar [desi'lar] *vt* (*tela*) to unravel.

deshilvanado, a [desilβa'naðo, a] *adj* (*fig*) disjointed, incoherent.
deshinchar [desin'tʃar] *vt* (*neumático*) to let down; (*herida etc*) to reduce (the swelling of); **~se** *vr* (*neumático*) to go flat; (*hinchazón*) to go down.
deshojar [deso'xar] *vt* (*árbol*) to strip the leaves off; (*flor*) to pull the petals off; **~se** *vr* to lose its leaves *etc*.
deshollinar [desoʎi'nar] *vt* (*chimenea*) to sweep.
deshonesto, a [deso'nesto, a] *adj* (*no honrado*) dishonest; (*indecente*) indecent.
deshonor [deso'nor] *nm* dishonour, disgrace; (*un* ~) insult, affront.
deshonra [de'sonra] *nf* (*deshonor*) dishonour; (*vergüenza*) shame.
deshonrar [deson'rar] *vt* to dishonour.
deshonroso, a [deson'roso, a] *adj* dishonourable, disgraceful.
deshora [de'sora]: **a** ~ *adv* at the wrong time; (*llegar*) unexpectedly; (*acostarse*) at some unearthly hour.
deshuesar [deswe'sar] *vt* (*carne*) to bone; (*fruta*) to stone.
desidia [de'siðja] *nf* (*pereza*) idleness.
desierto, a [de'sjerto, a] *adj* (*casa, calle, negocio*) deserted; (*paisaje*) bleak ♦ *nm* desert.
designación [desiɣna'θjon] *nf* (*para un cargo*) appointment; (*nombre*) designation.
designar [desiɣ'nar] *vt* (*nombrar*) to designate; (*indicar*) to fix.
designio [de'siɣnjo] *nm* plan; **con el** ~ **de** with the intention of.
desigual [desi'ɣwal] *adj* (*lucha*) unequal; (*diferente*) different; (*terreno*) uneven; (*tratamiento*) unfair; (*cambiadizo*: *tiempo*) changeable; (: *carácter*) unpredictable.
desigualdad [desiɣwal'ðað] *nf* (*ECON, POL*) inequality; (*de carácter, tiempo*) unpredictability; (*de escritura*) unevenness; (*de terreno*) roughness.
desilusión [desilu'sjon] *nf* disillusionment; (*decepción*) disappointment.
desilusionar [desilusjo'nar] *vt* to disillusion; (*decepcionar*) to disappoint; **~se** *vr* to become disillusioned.
desinencia [desi'nenθja] *nf* (*LING*) ending.
desinfectar [desinfek'tar] *vt* to disinfect.
desinfestar [desinfes'tar] *vt* to decontaminate.
desinflación [desinfla'θjon] *nf* (*COM*) disinflation.
desinflar [desin'flar] *vt* to deflate; **~se** *vr* (*neumático*) to go down *o* flat.
desintegración [desinteɣra'θjon] *nf* disintegration; ~ **nuclear** nuclear fission.
desintegrar [desinte'ɣrar] *vt* (*gen*) to disintegrate; (*átomo*) to split; (*grupo*) to break up; **~se** *vr* to disintegrate; to split; to break up.
desinterés [desinte'res] *nm* (*objetividad*) disinterestedness; (*altruismo*) unselfishness.
desinteresado, a [desintere'saðo, a] *adj* (*imparcial*) disinterested; (*altruista*) unselfish.
desintoxicar [desintoksi'kar] *vt* to detoxify; **~se** *vr* (*drogadicto*) to undergo treatment for drug addiction; **~se de** (*rutina, trabajo*) to get away from.
desintoxique [desintok'sike] *etc vb V* **desintoxicar**.
desistir [desis'tir] *vi* (*renunciar*) to stop, desist; ~ **de** (*empresa*) to give up; (*derecho*) to waive.
deslavazado, a [deslaβa'θaðo, a] *adj* (*lacio*) limp; (*desteñido*) faded; (*insípido*) colourless; (*incoherente*) disjointed.
desleal [desle'al] *adj* (*infiel*) disloyal; (*COM*: *competencia*) unfair.
deslealtad [desleal'tað] *nf* disloyalty.
desleído, a [desle'iðo, a] *adj* weak, woolly.
desleír [desle'ir] *vt* (*líquido*) to dilute; (*sólido*) to dissolve.
deslenguado, a [deslen'gwaðo, a] *adj* (*grosero*) foul-mouthed.
deslía [des'lia] *etc vb V* **desleír**.
desliar [des'ljar] *vt* (*desatar*) to untie; (*paquete*) to open; **~se** *vr* to come undone.
deslice [des'liθe] *etc vb V* **deslizar**.
desliendo [desli'endo] *etc vb V* **desleír**.
desligar [desli'ɣar] *vt* (*desatar*) to untie, undo; (*separar*) to separate; **~se** *vr* (*de un compromiso*) to extricate o.s.
desligue [des'liɣe] *etc vb V* **desligar**.
deslindar [deslin'dar] *vt* (*señalar las lindes de*) to mark out, fix the boundaries of; (*fig*) to define.
desliz [des'liθ] *nm* (*fig*) lapse; ~ **de lengua** slip of the tongue; **cometer un** ~ to slip up.
deslizar [desli'θar] *vt* to slip, slide; **~se** *vr* (*escurrirse*: *persona*) to slip, slide; (: *coche*) to skid; (*aguas mansas*) to flow gently; (*error*) to creep in; (*tiempo*) to pass; (*persona*: *irse*) to slip away; **~se en un cuarto** to slip into a room.
deslomar [deslo'mar] *vt* (*romper el lomo de*) to break the back of; (*fig*) to wear out; **~se** *vr* (*fig fam*) to work one's guts out.
deslucido, a [deslu'θiðo, a] *adj* dull; (*torpe*)

awkward, graceless; (*deslustrado*) tarnished; (*fracasado*) unsuccessful; **quedar** ~ to make a poor impression.
deslucir [deslu'θir] *vt* (*deslustrar*) to tarnish; (*estropear*) to spoil, ruin; (*persona*) to discredit; **la lluvia deslució el acto** the rain ruined the ceremony.
deslumbrar [deslum'brar] *vt* (*con la luz*) to dazzle; (*cegar*) to blind; (*impresionar*) to dazzle; (*dejar perplejo a*) to puzzle, confuse.
deslustrar [deslus'trar] *vt* (*vidrio*) to frost; (*quitar lustre a*) to dull; (*reputación*) to sully.
desluzca [des'luθka] *etc vb V* **deslucir**.
desmadrarse [desma'ðrarse] *vr* (*fam*) to run wild.
desmadre [des'maðre] *nm* (*fam*: *desorganización*) chaos; (: *jaleo*) commotion.
desmán [des'man] *nm* (*exceso*) outrage; (*abuso de poder*) abuse.
desmandarse [desman'darse] *vr* (*portarse mal*) to behave badly; (*excederse*) to get out of hand; (*caballo*) to bolt.
desmano [des'mano]: **a** ~ *adv*: **me coge** *o* **pilla a** ~ it's out of my way.
desmantelar [desmante'lar] *vt* (*deshacer*) to dismantle; (*casa*) to strip; (*organización*) to disband; (*MIL*) to raze; (*andamio*) to take down; (*NAUT*) to unrig.
desmaquillador [desmakiʎa'ðor] *nm* make-up remover.
desmaquillarse [desmaki'ʎarse] *vr* to take off one's make up.
desmarcarse [desmar'karse] *vr*: ~ **de** (*DEPORTE*) to get clear of; (*fig*) to distance o.s. from.
desmayado, a [desma'jaðo, a] *adj* (*sin sentido*) unconscious; (*carácter*) dull; (*débil*) faint, weak; (*color*) pale.
desmayar [desma'jar] *vi* to lose heart; ~**se** *vr* (*MED*) to faint.
desmayo [des'majo] *nm* (*MED*: *acto*) faint; (*estado*) unconsciousness; (*depresión*) dejection; (*de voz*) faltering; **sufrir un** ~ to have a fainting fit.
desmedido, a [desme'ðiðo, a] *adj* excessive; (*ambición*) boundless.
desmejorado, a [desmexo'raðo, a] *adj*: **está muy desmejorada** (*MED*) she's not looking too well.
desmejorar [desmexo'rar] *vt* (*dañar*) to impair, spoil; (*MED*) to weaken.
desmembración [desmembra'θjon] *nf* dismemberment; (*fig*) break-up.
desmembrar [desmem'brar] *vt* (*MED*) to dismember; (*fig*) to separate.
desmemoriado, a [desmemo'rjaðo, a] *adj* forgetful, absent-minded.
desmentir [desmen'tir] *vt* (*contradecir*) to contradict; (*refutar*) to deny; (*rumor*) to scotch ♦ *vi*: ~ **de** to refute; ~**se** *vr* to contradict o.s.
desmenuce [desme'nuθe] *etc vb V* **desmenuzar**.
desmenuzar [desmenu'θar] *vt* (*deshacer*) to crumble; (*carne*) to chop; (*examinar*) to examine closely.
desmerecer [desmere'θer] *vt* to be unworthy of ♦ *vi* (*deteriorarse*) to deteriorate.
desmerezca [desme'reθka] *etc vb V* **desmerecer**.
desmesurado, a [desmesu'raðo, a] *adj* (*desmedido*) disproportionate; (*enorme*) enormous; (*ambición*) boundless; (*descarado*) insolent.
desmiembre [des'mjembre] *etc vb V* **desmembrar**.
desmienta [des'mjenta] *etc vb V* **desmentir**.
desmigajar [desmiɣa'xar], **desmigar** [desmi'ɣar] *vt* to crumble.
desmigue [des'miɣe] *etc vb V* **desmigar**.
desmilitarice [desmilita'riθe] *etc vb V* **desmilitarizar**.
desmilitarizar [desmilitari'θar] *vt* to demilitarize.
desmintiendo [desmin'tjendo] *etc vb V* **desmentir**.
desmochar [desmo'tʃar] *vt* (*árbol*) to lop; (*texto*) to cut, hack about.
desmontable [desmon'taβle] *adj* (*que se quita*) detachable; (*en compartimientos*) sectional; (*que se puede plegar etc*) collapsible.
desmontar [desmon'tar] *vt* (*deshacer*) to dismantle; (*motor*) to strip down; (*máquina*) to take apart; (*escopeta*) to uncock; (*tienda de campaña*) to take down; (*tierra*) to level; (*quitar los árboles a*) to clear; (*jinete*) to throw ♦ *vi* to dismount.
desmonte [des'monte] *nm* (*de tierra*) levelling; (*de árboles*) clearing; (*terreno*) levelled ground; (*FERRO*) cutting.
desmoralice [desmora'liθe] *etc vb V* **desmoralizar**.
desmoralizador, a [desmoraliθa'ðor, a] *adj* demoralizing.
desmoralizar [desmorali'θar] *vt* to demoralize.
desmoronado, a [desmoro'naðo, a] *adj* (*casa, edificio*) dilapidated.
desmoronamiento [desmorona'mjento]

nm (*tb fig*) crumbling.
desmoronar [desmoro'nar] *vt* to wear away, erode; **~se** *vr* (*edificio, dique*) to fall into disrepair; (*economía*) to decline.
desmovilice [desmoßi'liθe] *etc vb V* **desmovilizar**.
desmovilizar [desmoßili'θar] *vt* to demobilize.
desnacionalización [desnaθjonaliθa'θjon] *nf* denationalization.
desnacionalizado, a [desnaθjonali'θaðo, a] *adj* (*industria*) denationalized; (*persona*) stateless.
desnatado, a [desna'taðo, a] *adj* skimmed; (*yogur*) low fat.
desnatar [desna'tar] *vt* (*leche*) to skim; **leche sin ~** whole milk.
desnaturalice [desnatura'liθe] *etc vb V* **desnaturalizar**.
desnaturalizado, a [desnaturali'θaðo, a] *adj* (*persona*) unnatural; **alcohol ~** methylated spirits.
desnaturalizar [desnaturali'θar] *vt* (*QUÍMICA*) to denature; (*corromper*) to pervert; (*sentido de algo*) to distort; **~se** *vr* (*perder la nacionalidad*) to give up one's nationality.
desnivel [desni'ßel] *nm* (*de terreno*) unevenness; (*POL*) inequality; (*diferencia*) difference.
desnivelar [desniße'lar] *vt* (*terreno*) to make uneven; (*fig: desequilibrar*) to unbalance; (*balanza*) to tip.
desnuclearizado, a [desnukleari'θaðo, a] *adj*: **región desnuclearizada** nuclear-free zone.
desnudar [desnu'ðar] *vt* (*desvestir*) to undress; (*despojar*) to strip; **~se** *vr* (*desvestirse*) to get undressed.
desnudez [desnu'ðeθ] *nf* (*de persona*) nudity; (*fig*) bareness.
desnudo, a [des'nuðo, a] *adj* (*cuerpo*) naked; (*árbol, brazo*) bare; (*paisaje*) flat; (*estilo*) unadorned; (*verdad*) plain ♦ *nm/f* nude; **~ de** devoid *o* bereft of; **la retrató al ~** he painted her in the nude; **poner al ~** to lay bare.
desnutrición [desnutri'θjon] *nf* malnutrition.
desnutrido, a [desnu'triðo, a] *adj* undernourished.
desobedecer [desoßeðe'θer] *vt, vi* to disobey.
desobedezca [desoße'ðeθka] *etc vb V* **desobedecer**.
desobediencia [desoße'ðjenθja] *nf* disobedience.
desocupación [desokupa'θjon] *nf* (*AM*) unemployment.
desocupado, a [desoku'paðo, a] *adj* at leisure; (*desempleado*) unemployed; (*deshabitado*) empty, vacant.
desocupar [desoku'par] *vt* to vacate; **~se** *vr* (*quedar libre*) to be free; **se ha desocupado aquella mesa** that table's free now.
desodorante [desoðo'rante] *nm* deodorant.
desoiga [de'soiɣa] *etc vb V* **desoír**.
desoír [deso'ir] *vt* to ignore, disregard.
desolación [desola'θjon] *nf* (*de lugar*) desolation; (*fig*) grief.
desolar [deso'lar] *vt* to ruin, lay waste.
desollar [deso'ʎar] *vt* (*quitar la piel a*) to skin; (*criticar*): **~ vivo a** to criticize unmercifully.
desorbitado, a [desorßi'taðo, a] *adj* (*excesivo*) excessive; (*precio*) exorbitant; **con los ojos ~s** pop-eyed.
desorbitar [desorßi'tar] *vt* (*exagerar*) to exaggerate; (*interpretar mal*) to misinterpret; **~se** *vr* (*persona*) to lose one's sense of proportion; (*asunto*) to get out of hand.
desorden [de'sorðen] *nm* confusion; (*de casa, cuarto*) mess; (*político*) disorder; **desórdenes** *nmpl* (*alborotos*) disturbances; (*excesos*) excesses; **en ~** (*gente*) in confusion.
desordenado, a [desorðe'naðo, a] *adj* (*habitación, persona*) untidy; (*objetos: revueltos*) in a mess, jumbled; (*conducta*) disorderly.
desordenar [desorðe'nar] *vt* (*gen*) to disarrange; (*pelo*) to mess up; (*cuarto*) to make a mess in; (*causar confusión a*) to throw into confusion.
desorganice [desorɣa'niθe] *etc vb V* **desorganizar**.
desorganizar [desorɣani'θar] *vt* to disorganize.
desorientar [desorjen'tar] *vt* (*extraviar*) to mislead; (*confundir, desconcertar*) to confuse; **~se** *vr* (*perderse*) to lose one's way.
desovar [deso'ßar] *vi* (*peces*) to spawn; (*insectos*) to lay eggs.
desoyendo [deso'jendo] *etc vb V* **desoír**.
despabilado, a [despaßi'laðo, a] *adj* (*despierto*) wide-awake; (*fig*) alert, sharp.
despabilar [despaßi'lar] *vt* (*despertar*) to wake up; (*fig: persona*) to liven up; (*trabajo*) to get through quickly ♦ *vi*, **~se** *vr* to wake up; (*fig*) to get a move on.
despachar [despa'tʃar] *vt* (*negocio*) to do, complete; (*resolver: problema*) to settle; (*correspondencia*) to deal with; (*fam:*

comida) to polish off; (: *bebida*) to knock back; (*enviar*) to send, dispatch; (*vender*) to sell, deal in; (COM: *cliente*) to attend to; (*billete*) to issue; (*mandar ir*) to send away ♦ *vi* (*decidirse*) to get things settled; (*apresurarse*) to hurry up; ~**se** *vr* to finish off; (*apresurarse*) to hurry up; ~**se de algo** to get rid of sth; ~**se a su gusto con algn** to give sb a piece of one's mind; **¿quién despacha?** is anybody serving?

despacho [des'patʃo] *nm* (*oficina*) office; (: *en una casa*) study; (*de paquetes*) dispatch; (COM: *venta*) sale (of goods); (*comunicación*) message; ~ **de billetes** *o* **boletos** (AM) booking office; ~ **de localidades** box office; **géneros sin** ~ unsaleable goods; **tener buen** ~ to find a ready sale.

despachurrar [despatʃu'rrar] *vt* (*aplastar*) to crush; (*persona*) to flatten.

despacio [des'paθjo] *adv* (*lentamente*) slowly; (*esp AM*: *en voz baja*) softly; ¡~! take it easy!

despacito [despa'θito] *adv* (*fam*) slowly; (*suavemente*) softly.

despampanante [despampa'nante] *adj* (*fam*: *chica*) stunning.

desparejado, a [despare'xaðo, a] *adj* odd.

desparpajo [despar'paxo] *nm* (*desenvoltura*) self-confidence; (*pey*) nerve.

desparramar [desparra'mar] *vt* (*esparcir*) to scatter; (*líquido*) to spill.

despatarrarse [despata'rrarse] *vr* (*abrir las piernas*) to open one's legs wide; (*caerse*) to tumble; (*fig*) to be flabbergasted.

despavorido, a [despaβo'riðo, a] *adj* terrified.

despecho [des'petʃo] *nm* spite; **a** ~ **de** in spite of; **por** ~ out of (sheer) spite.

despectivo, a [despek'tiβo, a] *adj* (*despreciativo*) derogatory; (LING) pejorative.

despedace [despe'ðaθe] *etc vb V* **despedazar.**

despedazar [despeða'θar] *vt* to tear to pieces.

despedida [despe'ðiða] *nf* (*adiós*) goodbye, farewell; (*antes de viaje*) send-off; (*en carta*) closing formula; (*de obrero*) sacking; (INFORM) logout; **cena/función de** ~ farewell dinner/performance; **regalo de** ~ parting gift; ~ **de soltero/soltera** stag/hen party.

despedir [despe'ðir] *vt* (*visita*) to see off, show out; (*empleado*) to dismiss; (*inquilino*) to evict; (*objeto*) to hurl; (*olor etc*) to give out *o* off; ~**se** *vr* (*dejar un empleo*) to give up one's job; (INFORM) to log out *o* off; ~**se de** to say goodbye to; **se despidieron** they said goodbye to each other.

despegado, a [despe'ɣaðo, a] *adj* (*separado*) detached; (*persona*: *poco afectuoso*) cold, indifferent ♦ *nm/f*: **es un** ~ he has cut himself off from his family.

despegar [despe'ɣar] *vt* to unstick; (*sobre*) to open ♦ *vi* (*avión*) to take off; (*cohete*) to blast off; ~**se** *vr* to come loose, come unstuck; **sin** ~ **los labios** without uttering a word.

despego [des'peɣo] *nm* detachment.

despegue [des'peɣe] *etc vb V* **despegar** ♦ *nm* takeoff; (*de cohete*) blastoff.

despeinado, a [despei'naðo, a] *adj* dishevelled, unkempt.

despeinar [despei'nar] *vt* (*pelo*) to ruffle; **¡me has despeinado todo!** you've completely ruined my hairdo!

despejado, a [despe'xaðo, a] *adj* (*lugar*) clear, free; (*cielo*) clear; (*persona*) wide-awake, bright.

despejar [despe'xar] *vt* (*gen*) to clear; (*misterio*) to clarify, clear up; (MAT: *incógnita*) to find ♦ *vi* (*el tiempo*) to clear; ~**se** *vr* (*tiempo, cielo*) to clear (up); (*misterio*) to become clearer; (*cabeza*) to clear; **¡despejen!** (*moverse*) move along!; (*salirse*) everybody out!

despeje [des'pexe] *nm* (DEPORTE) clearance.

despellejar [despeʎe'xar] *vt* (*animal*) to skin; (*criticar*) to criticize unmercifully; (*fam*: *arruinar*) to fleece.

despelotarse [despelo'tarse] *vr* (*fam*) to strip off; (*fig*) to let one's hair down.

despelote [despe'lote] (*fam*) *nm* (AM: *lío*) mess; **¡qué** *o* **vaya** ~**!** what a riot *o* laugh!

despenalizar [despenali'θar] *vt* to decriminalize.

despensa [des'pensa] *nf* (*armario*) larder; (NAUT) storeroom; (*provisión de comestibles*) stock of food.

despeñadero [despeɲa'ðero] *nm* (GEO) cliff, precipice.

despeñar [despe'ɲar] *vt* (*arrojar*) to fling down; ~**se** *vr* to fling o.s. down; (*caer*) to fall headlong.

desperdiciar [desperði'θjar] *vt* (*comida, tiempo*) to waste; (*oportunidad*) to throw away.

desperdicio [desper'ðiθjo] *nm* (*despilfarro*) squandering; (*residuo*) waste; ~**s** *nmpl* (*basura*) rubbish *sg*, refuse *sg*, garbage *sg*

(*US*); (*residuos*) waste *sg*; **~s de cocina** kitchen scraps; **el libro no tiene ~** the book is excellent from beginning to end.
desperdigar [desperði'ɣar] *vt* (*esparcir*) to scatter; (*energía*) to dissipate; **~se** *vr* to scatter.
desperdigue [desper'ðiɣe] *etc vb V* **desperdigar.**
desperece [despe'reθe] *etc vb V* **desperezarse.**
desperezarse [despere'θarse] *vr* to stretch.
desperfecto [desper'fekto] *nm* (*deterioro*) slight damage; (*defecto*) flaw, imperfection.
despertador [desperta'ðor] *nm* alarm clock; **~ de viaje** travelling clock.
despertar [desper'tar] *vt* (*persona*) to wake up; (*recuerdos*) to revive; (*esperanzas*) to raise; (*sentimiento*) to arouse ♦ *vi*, **~se** *vr* to awaken, wake up ♦ *nm* awakening; **~se a la realidad** to wake up to reality.
despiadado a [despja'ðaðo, a] *adj* (*ataque*) merciless; (*persona*) heartless.
despido [des'piðo] *etc vb V* **despedir** ♦ *nm* dismissal, sacking; **~ improcedente** *o* **injustificado** wrongful dismissal; **~ injusto** unfair dismissal; **~ libre** right to hire and fire; **~ voluntario** voluntary redundancy.
despierto, a [des'pjerto, a] *etc vb V* **despertar** ♦ *adj* awake; (*fig*) sharp, alert.
despilfarrar [despilfa'rrar] *vt* (*gen*) to waste; (*dinero*) to squander.
despilfarro [despil'farro] *nm* (*derroche*) squandering; (*lujo desmedido*) extravagance.
despintar [despin'tar] *vt* (*quitar pintura a*) to take the paint off; (*hechos*) to distort ♦ *vi*: **A no despinta a B** A is in no way inferior to B; **~se** *vr* (*desteñir*) to fade.
despiojar [despjo'xar] *vt* to delouse.
despistado, a [despis'taðo, a] *adj* (*distraído*) vague, absent-minded; (*poco práctico*) unpractical; (*confuso*) confused; (*desorientado*) off the track ♦ *nm/f* (*tipo*: *distraído*) scatterbrain, absent-minded person.
despistar [despis'tar] *vt* to throw off the track *o* scent; (*fig*) to mislead, confuse; **~se** *vr* to take the wrong road; (*fig*) to become confused.
despiste [des'piste] *nm* (*AUTO etc*) swerve; (*error*) slip; (*distracción*) absent-mindedness; **tiene un terrible ~** he's terribly absent-minded.
desplace [des'plaθe] *etc vb V* **desplazar.**
desplante [des'plante] *nm*: **hacer un ~ a algn** to be rude to sb.
desplazado, a [despla'θaðo, a] *adj* (*pieza*) wrongly placed ♦ *nm/f* (*inadaptado*) misfit; **sentirse un poco ~** to feel rather out of place.
desplazamiento [desplaθa'mjento] *nm* displacement; (*viaje*) journey; (*de opinión, votos*) shift, swing; (*INFORM*) scrolling; **~ hacia arriba/abajo** (*INFORM*) scroll up/down.
desplazar [despla'θar] *vt* (*gen*) to move; (*FÍSICA, NAUT, TEC*) to displace; (*tropas*) to transfer; (*suplantar*) to take the place of; (*INFORM*) to scroll; **~se** *vr* (*persona, vehículo*) to travel, go; (*objeto*) to move, shift; (*votos, opinión*) to shift, swing.
desplegar [desple'ɣar] *vt* (*tela, papel*) to unfold, open out; (*bandera*) to unfurl; (*alas*) to spread; (*MIL*) to deploy; (*manifestar*) to display.
desplegué [desple'ɣe], **despleguemos** [desple'ɣemos] *etc vb V* **desplegar.**
despliegue [des'pljeɣe] *etc vb V* **desplegar** ♦ *nm* unfolding, opening; deployment, display.
desplomarse [desplo'marse] *vr* (*edificio, gobierno, persona*) to collapse; (*derrumbarse*) to topple over; (*precios*) to slump; **se ha desplomado el techo** the ceiling has fallen in.
desplumar [desplu'mar] *vt* (*ave*) to pluck; (*fam*: *estafar*) to fleece.
despoblado, a [despo'βlaðo, a] *adj* (*sin habitantes*) uninhabited; (*con pocos habitantes*) depopulated; (*con insuficientes habitantes*) underpopulated ♦ *nm* deserted spot.
despojar [despo'xar] *vt* (*alguien*: *de sus bienes*) to divest of, deprive of; (*casa*) to strip, leave bare; (*de su cargo*) to strip of; **~se** *vr* (*desnudarse*) to undress; **~se de** (*ropa, hojas*) to shed; (*poderes*) to relinquish.
despojo [des'poxo] *nm* (*acto*) plundering; (*objetos*) plunder, loot; **~s** *nmpl* (*de ave, res*) offal *sg*.
desposado, a [despo'saðo, a] *adj, nm/f* newly-wed.
desposar [despo'sar] *vt* (*suj*: *sacerdote*: *pareja*) to marry; **~se** *vr* (*casarse*) to marry, get married.
desposeer [despose'er] *vt* (*despojar*) to dispossess; **~ a algn de su autoridad** to strip sb of his authority.
desposeído, a [despose'iðo, a] *nm/f*: **los ~s** the have-nots.
desposeyendo [despose'jendo] *etc vb V* **desposeer.**
desposorios [despo'sorjos] *nmpl*

(*esponsales*) betrothal *sg*; (*boda*) marriage ceremony *sg*.
déspota ['despota] *nm/f* despot.
despotismo [despo'tismo] *nm* despotism.
despotricar [despotri'kar] *vi*: ~ **contra** to moan *o* complain about.
despotrique [despo'trike] *etc vb V* **despotricar**.
despreciable [despre'θjaβle] *adj* (*moralmente*) despicable; (*objeto*) worthless; (*cantidad*) negligible.
despreciar [despre'θjar] *vt* (*desdeñar*) to despise, scorn; (*afrentar*) to slight.
despreciativo, a [despreθja'tiβo, a] *adj* (*observación, tono*) scornful, contemptuous; (*comentario*) derogatory.
desprecio [des'preθjo] *nm* scorn, contempt; slight.
desprender [despren'der] *vt* (*soltar*) to loosen; (*separar*) to separate; (*desatar*) to unfasten; (*olor*) to give off; ~**se** *vr* (*botón*: *caerse*) to fall off; (: *abrirse*) to unfasten; (*olor, perfume*) to be given off; ~**se de** to follow from; ~**se de algo** (*ceder*) to give sth up; (*desembarazarse*) to get rid of sth; **se desprende que** it transpires that.
desprendido, a [despren'dido, a] *adj* (*pieza*) loose; (*sin abrochar*) unfastened; (*desinteresado*) disinterested; (*generoso*) generous.
desprendimiento [desprendi'mjento] *nm* (*gen*) loosening; (*generosidad*) disinterestedness; (*indiferencia*) detachment; (*de gas*) leak; (*de tierra, rocas*) landslide.
despreocupado, a [despreoku'paðo, a] *adj* (*sin preocupación*) unworried, unconcerned; (*tranquilo*) nonchalant; (*en el vestir*) casual; (*negligente*) careless.
despreocuparse [despreoku'parse] *vr* to be carefree; (*dejar de inquietarse*) to stop worrying; (*ser indiferente*) to be unconcerned; ~ **de** to have no interest in.
desprestigiar [despresti'xjar] *vt* (*criticar*) to run down, disparage; (*desacreditar*) to discredit.
desprestigio [despres'tixjo] *nm* (*denigración*) disparagement; (*impopularidad*) unpopularity.
desprevenido, a [despreβe'niðo, a] *adj* (*no preparado*) unprepared, unready; **coger** (*ESP*) *o* **agarrar** (*AM*) **a algn** ~ to catch sb unawares.
desproporción [despropor'θjon] *nf* disproportion, lack of proportion.
desproporcionado, a [desproporθjo'naðo, a] *adj* disproportionate, out of proportion.
despropósito [despro'posito] *nm* (*salida de tono*) irrelevant remark; (*disparate*) piece of nonsense.
desprovisto, a [despro'βisto, a] *adj*: ~ **de** devoid of; **estar** ~ **de** to lack.
después [des'pwes] *adv* afterwards, later; (*desde entonces*) since (then); (*próximo paso*) next; **poco** ~ soon after; **un año** ~ a year later; ~ **se debatío el tema** next the matter was discussed ♦ *prep*: ~ **de** (*tiempo*) after, since; (*orden*) next (to); ~ **de comer** after lunch; ~ **de corregido el texto** after the text had been corrected; ~ **de esa fecha** (*pasado*) since that date; (*futuro*) from *o* after that date; ~ **de todo** after all; ~ **de verlo** after seeing it, after I *etc* saw it; **mi nombre está** ~ **del tuyo** my name comes next to yours ♦ *conj*: ~ **(de) que** after; ~ **(de) que lo escribí** after *o* since I wrote it, after writing it.
despuntar [despun'tar] *vt* (*lápiz*) to blunt ♦ *vi* (*BOT*: *plantas*) to sprout; (: *flores*) to bud; (*alba*) to break; (*día*) to dawn; (*persona*: *descollar*) to stand out.
desquiciar [deski'θjar] *vt* (*puerta*) to take off its hinges; (*descomponer*) to upset; (*persona*: *turbar*) to disturb; (: *volver loco a*) to unhinge.
desquitarse [deski'tarse] *vr* to obtain satisfaction; (*COM*) to recover a debt; (*fig*: *vengarse de*) to get one's own back; ~ **de una pérdida** to make up for a loss.
desquite [des'kite] *nm* (*satisfacción*) satisfaction; (*venganza*) revenge.
Dest. *abr* = **destinatario**.
destacado, a [desta'kaðo, a] *adj* outstanding.
destacamento [destaka'mento] *nm* (*MIL*) detachment.
destacar [desta'kar] *vt* (*ARTE*: *hacer resaltar*) to make stand out; (*subrayar*) to emphasize, point up; (*MIL*) to detach, detail; (*INFORM*) to highlight ♦ *vi*, ~**se** *vr* (*resaltarse*) to stand out; (*persona*) to be outstanding *o* exceptional; **quiero** ~ **que...** I wish to emphasize that...; ~**(se) contra** *o* **en** *o* **sobre** to stand out *o* be outlined against.
destajo [des'taxo] *nm*: **a** ~ (*por pieza*) by the job; (*con afán*) eagerly; **trabajar a** ~ to do piecework; (*fig*) to work one's fingers to the bone.
destapar [desta'par] *vt* (*botella*) to open; (*cacerola*) to take the lid off; (*descubrir*) to uncover; ~**se** *vr* (*descubrirse*) to get uncovered; (*revelarse*) to reveal one's true character.

destape [des'tape] *nm* nudity; (*fig*) permissiveness; **el ~ español** *the process of liberalization in Spain after Franco's death.*
destaque [des'take] *etc vb V* **destacar.**
destartalado, a [destarta'laðo, a] *adj* (*desordenado*) untidy; (*casa etc: grande*) rambling; (: *ruinoso*) tumbledown.
destellar [deste'ʎar] *vi* (*diamante*) to sparkle; (*metal*) to glint; (*estrella*) to twinkle.
destello [des'teʎo] *nm* (*de diamante*) sparkle; (*de metal*) glint; (*de estrella*) twinkle; (*de faro*) signal light; **no tiene un ~ de verdad** there's not a grain of truth in it.
destemplado, a [destem'plaðo, a] *adj* (*MUS*) out of tune; (*voz*) harsh; (*MED*) out of sorts; (*METEOROLOGÍA*) unpleasant, nasty.
destemplar [destem'plar] *vt* (*MUS*) to put out of tune; (*alterar*) to upset; **~se** *vr* (*MUS*) to lose its pitch; (*descomponerse*) to get out of order; (*persona: irritarse*) to get upset; (*MED*) to get out of sorts.
desteñir [deste'ɲir] *vt* to fade ♦ *vi*, **~se** *vr* to fade; **esta tela no destiñe** this fabric will not run.
desternillarse [desterni'ʎarse] *vr*: **~ de risa** to split one's sides laughing.
desterrado, a [deste'rraðo, a] *nm/f* (*exiliado*) exile.
desterrar [deste'rrar] *vt* (*exilar*) to exile; (*fig*) to banish, dismiss.
destetar [deste'tar] *vt* to wean.
destiempo [des'tjempo]: **a ~** *adv* at the wrong time.
destierro [des'tjerro] *etc vb V* **desterrar** ♦ *nm* exile; **vivir en el ~** to live in exile.
destilar [desti'lar] *vt* to distil; (*pus, sangre*) to ooze; (*fig: rebosar*) to exude; (: *revelar*) to reveal ♦ *vi* (*gotear*) to drip.
destilería [destile'ria] *nf* distillery; **~ de petróleo** oil refinery.
destinar [desti'nar] *vt* (*funcionario*) to appoint, assign; (*fondos*) to set aside; **es un libro destinado a los niños** it is a book (intended *o* meant) for children; **una carta que viene destinada a usted** a letter for you, a letter addressed to you.
destinatario, a [destina'tarjo, a] *nm/f* addressee; (*COM*) payee.
destino [des'tino] *nm* (*suerte*) destiny; (*de viajero*) destination; (*función*) use; (*puesto*) post, placement; **~ público** public appointment; **salir con ~ a** to leave for; **con ~ a Londres** (*avión, barco*) (bound) for London; (*carta*) to London.
destiña [des'tiɲa] *etc*, **destiñendo** [desti'ɲenðo] *etc vb V* **desteñir.**
destitución [destitu'θjon] *nf* dismissal, removal.
destituir [destitu'ir] *vt* (*despedir*) to dismiss; (: *ministro, funcionario*) to remove from office.
destituyendo [destitu'jendo] *etc vb V* **destituir.**
destornillador [destorniʎa'ðor] *nm* screwdriver.
destornillar [destorni'ʎar] *vt*, **~se** *vr* (*tornillo*) to unscrew.
destreza [des'treθa] *nf* (*habilidad*) skill; (*maña*) dexterity.
destripar [destri'par] *vt* (*animal*) to gut; (*reventar*) to mangle.
destroce [de'stroθe] *etc vb V* **destrozar.**
destronar [destro'nar] *vt* (*rey*) to dethrone; (*fig*) to overthrow.
destroncar [destron'kar] *vt* (*árbol*) to chop off, lop; (*proyectos*) to ruin; (*discurso*) to interrupt.
destronque [des'tronke] *etc vb V* **destroncar.**
destrozar [destro'θar] *vt* (*romper*) to smash, break (up); (*estropear*) to ruin; (*nervios*) to shatter; **~ a algn en una discusión** to crush sb in an argument.
destrozo [des'troθo] *nm* (*acción*) destruction; (*desastre*) smashing; **~s** *nmpl* (*pedazos*) pieces; (*daños*) havoc *sg.*
destrucción [destruk'θjon] *nf* destruction.
destructor, a [destruk'tor, a] *adj* destructive ♦ *nm* (*NAUT*) destroyer.
destruir [destru'ir] *vt* to destroy; (*casa*) to demolish; (*equilibrio*) to upset; (*proyecto*) to spoil; (*esperanzas*) to dash; (*argumento*) to demolish.
destruyendo [destru'jendo] *etc vb V* **destruir.**
desuelle [de'sweʎe] *etc vb V* **desollar.**
desueve [de'sweβe] *etc vb V* **desovar.**
desunión [desu'njon] *nf* (*separación*) separation; (*discordia*) disunity.
desunir [desu'nir] *vt* to separate; (*TEC*) to disconnect; (*fig*) to cause a quarrel *o* rift between.
desuso [de'suso] *nm* disuse; **caer en ~** to fall into disuse, become obsolete; **una expresión caída en ~** an obsolete expression.
desvaído, a [desβa'iðo, a] *adj* (*color*) pale; (*contorno*) blurred.
desvalido, a [desβa'liðo, a] *adj* (*desprotegido*) destitute; (*sin fuerzas*) helpless; **niños ~s** waifs and strays.
desvalijar [desβali'xar] *vt* (*persona*) to rob;

(*casa, tienda*) to burgle; (*coche*) to break into.
desvalorice [desβalo'riθe] *etc vb V* **desvalorizar**.
desvalorizar [desβalori'θar] *vt* to devalue.
desván [des'βan] *nm* attic.
desvanecer [desβane'θer] *vt* (*disipar*) to dispel; (*recuerdo, temor*) to banish; (*borrar*) to blur; **~se** *vr* (*humo etc*) to vanish, disappear; (*duda*) to be dispelled; (*color*) to fade; (*recuerdo, sonido*) to fade away; (*MED*) to pass out.
desvanecido, a [desβane'θiðo, a] *adj* (*MED*) faint; **caer ~** to fall in a faint.
desvanecimiento [desβaneθi'mjento] *nm* (*desaparición*) disappearance; (*de dudas*) dispelling; (*de colores*) fading; (*evaporación*) evaporation; (*MED*) fainting fit.
desvanezca [desβa'neθka] *etc vb V* **desvanecer**.
desvariar [desβa'rjar] *vi* (*enfermo*) to be delirious; (*delirar*) to talk nonsense.
desvarío [desβa'rio] *nm* delirium; (*desatino*) absurdity; **~s** *nmpl* ravings.
desvelar [desβe'lar] *vt* to keep awake; **~se** *vr* (*no poder dormir*) to stay awake; (*vigilar*) to be vigilant *o* watchful; **~se por algo** (*inquietarse*) to be anxious about sth; (*poner gran cuidado*) to take great care over sth.
desvelo [des'βelo] *nm* lack of sleep; (*insomnio*) sleeplessness; (*fig*) vigilance; **~s** *nmpl* (*preocupación*) anxiety *sg*, effort *sg*.
desvencijado, a [desβenθi'xaðo, a] *adj* (*silla*) rickety; (*máquina*) broken-down.
desvencijar [desβenθi'xar] *vt* (*romper*) to break; (*soltar*) to loosen; (*persona: agotar*) to exhaust; **~se** *vr* to come apart.
desventaja [desβen'taxa] *nf* disadvantage; (*inconveniente*) drawback.
desventajoso, a [desβenta'xoso, a] *adj* disadvantageous, unfavourable.
desventura [desβen'tura] *nf* misfortune.
desventurado, a [desβentu'raðo, a] *adj* (*desgraciado*) unfortunate; (*de poca suerte*) ill-fated.
desvergonzado, a [desβerɣon'θaðo, a] *adj* (*sin vergüenza*) shameless; (*descarado*) insolent ♦ *nm/f* shameless person.
desvergüenza [desβer'ɣwenθa] *nf* (*descaro*) shamelessness; (*insolencia*) impudence; (*mala conducta*) effrontery; **esto es una ~** this is disgraceful; **¡qué ~!** what a nerve!
desvestir [desβes'tir] *vt*, **desvestirse** *vr* to undress.
desviación [desβja'θjon] *nf* deviation; (*AUTO: rodeo*) diversion, detour; (*: carretera de circunvalación*) ring road (*BRIT*), circular route (*US*); **~ de la circulación** traffic diversion; **es una ~ de sus principios** it is a departure from his usual principles.
desviar [des'βjar] *vt* to turn aside; (*balón, flecha, golpe*) to deflect; (*pregunta*) to parry; (*ojos*) to avert, turn away; (*río*) to alter the course of; (*navío*) to divert, re-route; (*conversación*) to sidetrack; **~se** *vr* (*apartarse del camino*) to turn aside; (*: barco*) to go off course; (*AUTO: dar un rodeo*) to make a detour; **~se de un tema** to get away from the point.
desvincular [desβinku'lar] *vt* to free, release; **~se** *vr* (*aislarse*) to be cut off; (*alejarse*) to cut o.s. off.
desvío [des'βio] *etc vb V* **desviar** ♦ *nm* (*desviación*) detour, diversion; (*fig*) indifference.
desvirgar [desβir'ɣar] *vt* to deflower.
desvirtuar [desβir'twar] *vt* (*estropear*) to spoil; (*argumento, razonamiento*) to detract from; (*efecto*) to counteract; (*sentido*) to distort; **~se** *vr* to spoil.
desvistiendo [desβis'tjendo] *etc vb V* **desvestir**.
desvitalizar [desβitali'θar] *vt* (*nervio*) to numb.
desvivirse [desβi'βirse] *vr*: **~ por** to long for, crave for; **~ por los amigos** to do anything for one's friends.
detalladamente [detaʎaða'mente] *adv* (*con detalles*) in detail; (*extensamente*) at great length.
detallar [deta'ʎar] *vt* to detail; (*asunto por asunto*) to itemize.
detalle [de'taʎe] *nm* detail; (*fig*) gesture, token; **al ~** in detail; (*COM*) retail *cpd*; **comercio al ~** retail trade; **vender al ~** to sell retail; **no pierde ~** he doesn't miss a trick; **me observaba sin perder ~** he watched my every move; **tiene muchos ~s** she is very considerate.
detallista [deta'ʎista] *nm/f* retailer ♦ *adj* (*meticuloso*) meticulous; **comercio ~** retail trade.
detectar [detek'tar] *vt* to detect.
detective [detek'tiβe] *nm/f* detective; **~ privado** private detective.
detector [detek'tor] *nm* (*NAUT, TEC etc*) detector; **~ de mentiras/de minas** lie/mine detector.
detención [deten'θjon] *nf* (*acción*) stopping; (*estancamiento*) stoppage; (*retraso*) holdup, delay; (*JUR: arresto*)

arrest; (*cuidado*) care; ~ **de juego** (*DEPORTE*) stoppage of play; ~ **ilegal** unlawful detention.

detendré [deten'dre] *etc vb V* **detener**.

detener [dete'ner] *vt* (*gen*) to stop; (*JUR*: *arrestar*) to arrest; (: *encarcelar*) to detain; (*objeto*) to keep; (*retrasar*) to hold up, delay; (*aliento*) to hold; **~se** *vr* to stop; **~se en** (*demorarse*) to delay over, linger over.

detenga [de'tenga] *etc vb V* **detener**.

detenidamente [deteniða'mente] *adv* (*minuciosamente*) carefully; (*extensamente*) at great length.

detenido, a [dete'niðo, a] *adj* (*arrestado*) under arrest; (*minucioso*) detailed; (*examen*) thorough; (*tímido*) timid ♦ *nm/f* person under arrest, prisoner.

detenimiento [deteni'mjento] *nm* care; **con** ~ thoroughly.

detentar [deten'tar] *vt* to hold; (*sin derecho*: *título*) to hold unlawfully; (: *puesto*) to occupy unlawfully.

detergente [deter'xente] *adj, nm* detergent.

deteriorado, a [deterjo'raðo, a] *adj* (*estropeado*) damaged; (*desgastado*) worn.

deteriorar [deterjo'rar] *vt* to spoil, damage; **~se** *vr* to deteriorate.

deterioro [dete'rjoro] *nm* deterioration.

determinación [determina'θjon] *nf* (*empeño*) determination; (*decisión*) decision; (*de fecha, precio*) settling, fixing.

determinado, a [determi'naðo, a] *adj* (*preciso*) fixed, set; (*LING*: *artículo*) definite; (*persona*: *resuelto*) determined; **un día** ~ on a certain day; **no hay ningún tema** ~ there is no particular theme.

determinar [determi'nar] *vt* (*plazo*) to fix; (*precio*) to settle; (*daños, impuestos*) to assess; (*pleito*) to decide; (*causar*) to cause; **~se** *vr* to decide; **el reglamento determina que ...** the rule lays it down *o* states that ...; **aquello determinó la caída del gobierno** that brought about the fall of the government; **esto le determinó** this decided him.

detestable [detes'taβle] *adj* (*persona*) hateful; (*acto*) detestable.

detestar [detes'tar] *vt* to detest.

detonación [detona'θjon] *nf* detonation; (*sonido*) explosion.

detonante [deto'nante] *nm* (*fig*) trigger.

detonar [deto'nar] *vi* to detonate.

detractor, a [detrak'tor, a] *adj* disparaging ♦ *nm/f* detractor.

detrás [de'tras] *adv* behind; (*atrás*) at the back ♦ *prep*: ~ **de** behind; **por** ~ **de algn** (*fig*) behind sb's back; **salir de** ~ to come out from behind; **por** ~ behind.

detrasito [detra'sito] *adv* (*AM fam*) behind.

detrimento [detri'mento] *nm*: **en** ~ **de** to the detriment of.

detuve [de'tuβe] *etc vb V* **detener**.

deuda [de'uða] *nf* (*condición*) indebtedness, debt; (*cantidad*) debt; ~ **a largo plazo** long-term debt; ~ **exterior/pública** foreign/national debt; ~ **incobrable** *o* **morosa** bad debt; **~s activas/pasivas** assets/liabilities; **contraer ~s** to get into debt.

deudor, a [deu'ðor, a] *nm/f* debtor; ~ **hipotecario** mortgager; ~ **moroso** slow payer.

devaluación [deβalwa'θjon] *nf* devaluation.

devaluar [deβalu'ar] *vt* to devalue.

devanar [deβa'nar] *vt* (*hilo*) to wind; **~se** *vr*: **~se los sesos** to rack one's brains.

devaneo [deβa'neo] *nm* (*MED*) delirium; (*desatino*) nonsense; (*fruslería*) idle pursuit; (*amorío*) flirtation.

devastar [deβas'tar] *vt* (*destruir*) to devastate.

devendré [deβen'dre] *etc*, **devenga** [de'βenga] *etc vb V* **devenir**.

devengar [deβen'gar] *vt* (*salario*: *ganar*) to earn; (: *tener que cobrar*) to be due; (*intereses*) to bring in, accrue, earn.

devengue [de'βenge] *etc vb V* **devengar**.

devenir [deβe'nir] *vi*: ~ **en** to become, turn into ♦ *nm* (*movimiento progresivo*) process of development; (*transformación*) transformation.

deviene [de'βjene] *etc*, **deviniendo** [deβi'njendo] *etc vb V* **devenir**.

devoción [deβo'θjon] *nf* devotion; (*afición*) strong attachment.

devolución [deβolu'θjon] *nf* (*reenvío*) return, sending back; (*reembolso*) repayment; (*JUR*) devolution.

devolver [deβol'βer] *vt* (*lo extraviado, prestado*) to give back; (*a su sitio*) to put back; (*carta al correo*) to send back; (*COM*) to repay, refund; (*visita, la palabra*) to return; (*salud, vista*) to restore; (*fam*: *vomitar*) to throw up ♦ *vi* (*fam*) to be sick; **~se** *vr* (*AM*) to return; ~ **mal por bien** to return ill for good; ~ **la pelota a algn** to give sb tit for tat.

devorar [deβo'rar] *vt* to devour; (*comer ávidamente*) to gobble up; (*fig*: *fortuna*) to run through; **todo lo devoró el fuego** the

fire consumed everything; **le devoran los celos** he is consumed with jealousy.
devoto, a [de'ßoto, a] *adj* (*REL*: *persona*) devout; (: *obra*) devotional; (*amigo*): ~ **(de algn)** devoted (to sb) ♦ *nm/f* admirer; **los ~s** (*REL*) the faithful; **su muy ~** your devoted servant.
devuelto [de'ßwelto], **devuelva** [de'ßwelßa] *etc vb V* **devolver.**
D.F. *abr* (*México*) = *Distrito Federal.*
dg. *abr* (= *decigramo*) dg.
D.G. *abr* = *Dirección General*; (= *Director General*) D.G.
DGT *nf abr* = *Dirección General de Tráfico*; = *Dirección General de Turismo.*
di [di] *vb V* **dar; decir.**
día ['dia] *nm* day; ~ **de asueto** day off; ~ **feriado** (*AM*) *o* **festivo** (public) holiday; ~ **hábil/inhábil** working/non-working day; ~ **domingo**, ~ **lunes** (*AM*) Sunday, Monday; ~ **lectivo** teaching day; ~ **libre** day off; **D~ de Reyes** Epiphany (*6 January*); **¿qué ~ es?** what's the date?; **estar/poner al ~** to be/keep up to date; **el ~ de hoy/de mañana** today/tomorrow; **el ~ menos pensado** when you least expect it; **al ~ siguiente** on the following day; **todos los ~s** every day; **un ~ sí y otro no** every other day; **vivir al ~** to live from hand to mouth; **de ~** during the day, by day; **es de ~** it's daylight; **del ~** (*estilos*) fashionable; (*menú*) today's; **de un ~ para otro** any day now; **en pleno ~** in full daylight; **en su ~** in due time; **¡hasta otro ~!** so long!
diabetes [dja'betes] *nf* diabetes *sg.*
diabético, a [dja'betiko, a] *adj, nm/f* diabetic.
diablo ['djaßlo] *nm* (*tb fig*) devil; **pobre ~** poor devil; **hace un frío de todos los ~s** it's hellishly cold.
diablura [dja'ßlura] *nf* prank; (*travesura*) mischief.
diabólico, a [dja'ßoliko, a] *adj* diabolical.
diadema [dja'ðema] *nf* (*para el pelo*) Alice band, headband; (*joya*) tiara.
diáfano, a ['djafano, a] *adj* (*tela*) diaphanous; (*agua*) crystal-clear.
diafragma [dja'fraɣma] *nm* diaphragm.
diagnosis [djaɣ'nosis] *nf inv*, **diagnóstico** [diaɣ'nostiko] *nm* diagnosis.
diagnosticar [djaɣnosti'kar] *vt* to diagnose.
diagonal [djaɣo'nal] *adj* diagonal ♦ *nf* (*GEOM*) diagonal; **en ~** diagonally.
diagrama [dja'ɣrama] *nm* diagram; ~ **de barras** (*COM*) bar chart; ~ **de dispersión** (*COM*) scatter diagram; ~ **de flujo** (*INFORM*) flowchart.
dial [di'al] *nm* dial.
dialecto [dja'lekto] *nm* dialect.
dialogar [djalo'ɣar] *vt* to write in dialogue form ♦ *vi* (*conversar*) to have a conversation; ~ **con** (*POL*) to hold talks with.
diálogo ['djaloɣo] *nm* dialogue.
dialogue [dja'loɣe] *etc vb V* **dialogar.**
diamante [dja'mante] *nm* diamond.
diametralmente [djametral'mente] *adv* diametrically; ~ **opuesto a** diametrically opposed to.
diámetro [di'ametro] *nm* diameter; ~ **de giro** (*AUTO*) turning circle; **faros de gran ~** wide-angle headlights.
diana ['djana] *nf* (*MIL*) reveille; (*de blanco*) centre, bull's-eye.
diantre ['djantre] *nm*: **¡~!** (*fam*) oh hell!
diapasón [djapa'son] *nm* (*instrumento*) tuning fork; (*de violín etc*) fingerboard; (*de voz*) tone.
diapositiva [djaposi'tißa] *nf* (*FOTO*) slide, transparency.
diario, a ['djarjo, a] *adj* daily ♦ *nm* newspaper; (*libro diario*) diary; (: *COM*) daybook; (*COM*: *gastos*) daily expenses; ~ **de navegación** (*NAUT*) logbook; ~ **hablado** (*RADIO*) news (bulletin); ~ **de sesiones** parliamentary report; **a ~** daily; **de** *o* **para ~** everyday.
diarrea [dja'rrea] *nf* diarrhoea.
diatriba [dja'trißa] *nf* diatribe, tirade.
dibujante [dißu'xante] *nm/f* (*de bosquejos*) sketcher; (*de dibujos animados*) cartoonist; (*de moda*) designer; ~ **de publicidad** commercial artist.
dibujar [dißu'xar] *vt* to draw, sketch; **~se** *vr* (*emoción*) to show; **~se contra** to be outlined against.
dibujo [di'ßuxo] *nm* drawing; (*TEC*) design; (*en papel, tela*) pattern; (*en periódico*) cartoon; (*fig*) description; **~s animados** cartoons; ~ **del natural** drawing from life.
dic., dic.^e *abr* (= *diciembre*) Dec.
diccionario [dikθjo'narjo] *nm* dictionary.
dicharachero, a [ditʃara'tʃero, a] *adj* talkative ♦ *nm/f* (*ingenioso*) wit; (*parlanchín*) chatterbox.
dicho, a ['ditʃo, a] *pp de* **decir** ♦ *adj* (*susodicho*) aforementioned ♦ *nm* saying; (*proverbio*) proverb; (*ocurrencia*) bright remark ♦ *nf* (*buena suerte*) good luck; **mejor ~** rather; ~ **y hecho** no sooner said than done.
dichoso, a [di'tʃoso, a] *adj* (*feliz*) happy; (*afortunado*) lucky; **¡aquel ~ coche!** (*fam*)

that blessed car!
diciembre [di'θjembre] *nm* December.
diciendo [di'θjendo] *etc vb V* **decir.**
dictado [dik'taðo] *nm* dictation; **escribir al ~** to take dictation; **los ~s de la conciencia** (*fig*) the dictates of conscience.
dictador [dikta'ðor] *nm* dictator.
dictadura [dikta'ðura] *nf* dictatorship.
dictáfono ® [dik'tafono] *nm* Dictaphone ®.
dictamen [dik'tamen] *nm* (*opinión*) opinion; (*informe*) report; ~ **contable** auditor's report; ~ **facultativo** (*MED*) medical report.
dictar [dik'tar] *vt* (*carta*) to dictate; (*JUR: sentencia*) to pass; (*decreto*) to issue; (*AM: clase*) to give; (*: conferencia*) to deliver.
didáctico, a [di'ðaktiko, a] *adj* didactic; (*material*) teaching *cpd*; (*juguete*) educational.
diecinueve [djeθinu'eße] *num* nineteen; (*fecha*) nineteenth; *V tb* **seis.**
dieciochesco, a [djeθio'tʃesko, a] *adj* eighteenth-century.
dieciocho [djeθi'otʃo] *num* eighteen; (*fecha*) eighteenth; *V tb* **seis.**
dieciséis [djeθi'seis] *num* sixteen; (*fecha*) sixteenth; *V tb* **seis.**
diecisiete [djeθi'sjete] *num* seventeen; (*fecha*) seventeenth; *V tb* **seis.**
diente ['djente] *nm* (*ANAT, TEC*) tooth; (*ZOOL*) fang; (*: de elefante*) tusk; (*de ajo*) clove; ~ **de león** dandelion; **~s postizos** false teeth; **enseñar los ~s** (*fig*) to show one's claws; **hablar entre ~s** to mutter, mumble; **hincar el ~ en** (*comida*) to bite into.
diera ['djera] *etc vb V* **dar.**
diéresis [di'eresis] *nf* diaeresis.
dieron ['djeron] *vb V* **dar.**
diesel ['disel] *adj*: **motor ~** diesel engine.
diestro, a ['djestro, a] *adj* (*derecho*) right; (*hábil*) skilful; (*: con las manos*) handy ♦ *nm* (*TAUR*) matador ♦ *nf* right hand; **a ~ y siniestro** (*sin método*) wildly.
dieta ['djeta] *nf* diet; **~s** *nfpl* expenses; **estar a ~** to be on a diet.
dietético, a [dje'tetiko, a] *adj* dietetic ♦ *nm/f* dietician ♦ *nf* dietetics *sg*.
dietista [dje'tista] *nm/f* dietician.
diez [djeθ] *num* ten; (*fecha*) tenth; **hacer las ~ de últimas** (*NAIPES*) to sweep the board; *V tb* **seis.**
diezmar [djeθ'mar] *vt* to decimate.
difamación [difama'θjon] *nf* slander; libel.
difamar [difa'mar] *vt* (*JUR: hablando*) to slander; (*: por escrito*) to libel.
difamatorio, a [difama'torjo, a] *adj* slanderous; libellous.
diferencia [dife'renθja] *nf* difference; **a ~ de** unlike; **hacer ~ entre** to make a distinction between; ~ **salarial** (*COM*) wage differential.
diferencial [diferen'θjal] *nm* (*AUTO*) differential.
diferenciar [diferen'θjar] *vt* to differentiate between ♦ *vi* to differ; **~se** *vr* to differ, be different; (*distinguirse*) to distinguish o.s.
diferente [dife'rente] *adj* different.
diferido [dife'riðo] *nm*: **en ~** (*TV etc*) recorded.
diferir [dife'rir] *vt* to defer.
difícil [di'fiθil] *adj* difficult; (*tiempos, vida*) hard; (*situación*) delicate; **es un hombre ~** he's a difficult man to get on with.
difícilmente [di'fiθilmente] *adv* (*con dificultad*) with difficulty; (*apenas*) hardly.
dificultad [difikul'tað] *nf* difficulty; (*problema*) trouble; (*objeción*) objection.
dificultar [difikul'tar] *vt* (*complicar*) to complicate, make difficult; (*estorbar*) to obstruct; **las restricciones dificultan el comercio** the restrictions hinder trade.
dificultoso, a [difikul'toso, a] *adj* (*difícil*) difficult, hard; (*fam: cara*) odd, ugly; (*persona: exigente*) fussy.
difiera [di'fjera] *etc*, **difiriendo** [difi'rjendo] *etc vb V* **diferir.**
difuminar [difumi'nar] *vt* to blur.
difundir [difun'dir] *vt* (*calor, luz*) to diffuse; (*RADIO*) to broadcast; **~se** *vr* to spread (out); ~ **una noticia** to spread a piece of news.
difunto, a [di'funto, a] *adj* dead, deceased ♦ *nm/f*: **el ~** the deceased.
difusión [difu'sjon] *nf* (*de calor, luz*) diffusion; (*de noticia, teoría*) dissemination; (*de programa*) broadcasting; (*programa*) broadcast.
difuso, a [di'fuso, a] *adj* (*luz*) diffused; (*conocimientos*) widespread; (*estilo, explicación*) wordy.
diga ['diɣa] *etc vb V* **decir.**
digerir [dixe'rir] *vt* to digest; (*fig*) to absorb; (*reflexionar sobre*) to think over.
digestión [dixes'tjon] *nf* digestion; **corte de ~** indigestion.
digestivo, a [dixes'tißo, a] *adj* digestive ♦ *nm* (*bebida*) liqueur, digestif.
digiera [di'xjera] *etc*, **digiriendo** [dixi'rjenðo] *etc vb V* **digerir.**
digital [dixi'tal] *adj* (*INFORM*) digital; (*dactilar*) finger *cpd* ♦ *nf* (*BOT*) foxglove; (*droga*) digitalis.

digitalizador [dixitaliθa'ðor] *nm* (*INFORM*) digitizer.
dignarse [diɣ'narse] *vr* to deign to.
dignidad [diɣni'ðað] *nf* dignity; (*honra*) honour; (*rango*) rank; (*persona*) dignitary; **herir la ~ de algn** to hurt sb's pride.
dignificar [diɣnifi'kar] *vt* to dignify.
dignifique [diɣni'fike] *etc vb V* **dignificar**.
digno, a ['diɣno, a] *adj* worthy; (*persona: honesto*) honourable; **~ de elogio** praiseworthy; **~ de mención** worth mentioning; **es ~ de verse** it is worth seeing; **poco ~** unworthy.
digresión [diɣre'sjon] *nf* digression.
dije ['dixe] *etc*, **dijera** [di'xera] *etc vb V* **decir**.
dilación [dila'θjon] *nf* delay; **sin ~** without delay, immediately.
dilapidar [dilapi'ðar] *vt* to squander, waste.
dilatación [dilata'θjon] *nf* (*expansión*) dilation.
dilatado, a [dila'taðo, a] *adj* dilated; (*período*) long drawn-out; (*extenso*) extensive.
dilatar [dila'tar] *vt* (*gen*) to dilate; (*prolongar*) to prolong; (*aplazar*) to delay; **~se** *vr* (*pupila etc*) to dilate; (*agua*) to expand.
dilema [di'lema] *nm* dilemma.
diligencia [dili'xenθja] *nf* diligence; (*rapidez*) speed; (*ocupación*) errand, job; (*carruaje*) stagecoach; **~s** *nfpl* (*JUR*) formalities; **~s judiciales** judicial proceedings; **~s previas** inquest *sg*.
diligente [dili'xente] *adj* diligent; **poco ~** slack.
dilucidar [diluθi'ðar] *vt* (*aclarar*) to elucidate, clarify; (*misterio*) to clear up.
diluir [dilu'ir] *vt* to dilute; (*aguar, fig*) to water down.
diluviar [dilu'ßjar] *vi* to pour with rain.
diluvio [di'lußjo] *nm* deluge, flood; **un ~ de cartas** (*fig*) a flood of letters.
diluyendo [dilu'jendo] *etc vb V* **diluir**.
dimanar [dima'nar] *vi*: **~ de** to arise *o* spring from.
dimensión [dimen'sjon] *nf* dimension; **dimensiones** *nfpl* size *sg*; **tomar las dimensiones de** to take the measurements of.
dimes ['dimes] *nmpl*: **andar en ~ y diretes con algn** to bicker *o* squabble with sb.
diminutivo [diminu'tißo] *nm* diminutive.
diminuto, a [dimi'nuto, a] *adj* tiny, diminutive.
dimisión [dimi'sjon] *nf* resignation.
dimitir [dimi'tir] *vt* (*cargo*) to give up; (*despedir*) to sack ♦ *vi* to resign.
dimos ['dimos] *vb V* **dar**.
Dinamarca [dina'marka] *nf* Denmark.
dinamarqués, esa [dinamar'kes, esa] *adj* Danish ♦ *nm/f* Dane ♦ *nm* (*LING*) Danish.
dinámico, a [di'namiko, a] *adj* dynamic ♦ *nf* dynamics *sg*.
dinamita [dina'mita] *nf* dynamite.
dinamitar [dinami'tar] *vt* to dynamite.
dinamo [di'namo], **dínamo** ['dinamo] *nf* (*nm en AM*) dynamo.
dinastía [dinas'tia] *nf* dynasty.
dineral [dine'ral] *nm* fortune.
dinero [di'nero] *nm* money; (*~ en circulación*) currency; **~ caro** (*COM*) dear money; **~ contante (y sonante)** hard cash; **~ de curso legal** legal tender; **~ efectivo** cash, ready cash; **es hombre de ~** he is a man of means; **andar mal de ~** to be short of money; **ganar ~ a espuertas** to make money hand over fist.
dinosaurio [dino'saurjo] *nm* dinosaur.
dintel [din'tel] *nm* lintel; (*umbral*) threshold.
diñar [di'ɲar] *vt* (*fam*) to give; **~la** to kick the bucket.
dio [djo] *vb V* **dar**.
diócesis ['djoθesis] *nf inv* diocese.
Dios [djos] *nm* God; **~ mediante** God willing; **a ~ gracias** thank heaven; **a la buena de ~** any old how; **una de ~ es Cristo** an almighty row; **~ los cría y ellos se juntan** birds of a feather flock together; **como ~ manda** as is proper; **¡~ mío!** (oh,) my God!; **¡por ~!** for God's sake!; **¡válgame ~!** bless my soul!
dios [djos] *nm* god.
diosa ['djosa] *nf* goddess.
Dip. *abr* (= *Diputación*) ≈ CC.
diploma [di'ploma] *nm* diploma.
diplomacia [diplo'maθja] *nf* diplomacy; (*fig*) tact.
diplomado, a [diplo'maðo, a] *adj* qualified ♦ *nm/f* holder of a diploma; (*UNIV*) graduate; *V tb* **licenciado**.
diplomático, a [diplo'matiko, a] *adj* (*cuerpo*) diplomatic; (*que tiene tacto*) tactful ♦ *nm/f* diplomat.
diptongo [dip'tongo] *nm* diphthong.
diputación [diputa'θjon] *nf* deputation; **~ permanente** (*POL*) standing committee; **~ provincial** ≈ county council.
diputado, a [dipu'taðo, a] *nm/f* delegate; (*POL*) ≈ member of parliament (*BRIT*), ≈ representative (*US*); *V tb* **Las Cortes (españolas)**.
dique ['dike] *nm* dyke; (*rompeolas*)

breakwater; ~ **de contención** dam.

Dir. *abr* = **dirección**; (= *director*) dir.

diré [di're] *etc vb V* **decir**.

dirección [direk'θjon] *nf* direction; (*fig: tendencia*) trend; (*señas, tb INFORM*) address; (*AUTO*) steering; (*gerencia*) management; (*de periódico*) editorship; (*en escuela*) headship; (*POL*) leadership; (*junta*) board of directors; (*despacho*) director's/manager's/headmaster's/ editor's office; ~ **absoluta** (*INFORM*) absolute address; ~ **administrativa** office management; ~ **asistida** power-assisted steering; **D~ General de Seguridad/Turismo** State Security/ Tourist Office; ~ **relativa** (*INFORM*) relative address; ~ **única** *o* **prohibida** one-way; **tomar la ~ de una empresa** to take over the running of a company.

direccionamiento [direkθjona'mjento] *nm* (*INFORM*) addressing.

directivo, a [direk'tiβo, a] *adj* (*junta*) managing; (*función*) administrative ♦ *nm/f* (*COM*) manager ♦ *nf* (*norma*) directive; (*tb*: **junta directiva**) board of directors.

directo, a [di'rekto, a] *adj* direct; (*línea*) straight; (*inmediato*) immediate; (*tren*) through; (*TV*) live; **en ~** (*INFORM*) on line; **transmitir en ~** to broadcast live.

director, a [direk'tor, a] *adj* leading ♦ *nm/f* director; (*ESCOL*) head (teacher) (*BRIT*), principal (*US*); (*gerente*) manager(ess); (*de compañía*) president; (*jefe*) head; (*PRENSA*) editor; (*de prisión*) governor; (*MUS*) conductor; ~ **adjunto** assistant manager; ~ **de cine** film director; ~ **comercial** marketing manager; ~ **ejecutivo** executive director; ~ **de empresa** company director; ~ **general** general manager; ~ **gerente** managing director; ~ **de sucursal** branch manager.

directorio [direk'torjo] *nm* (*INFORM*) directory.

directrices [direk'triθes] *nfpl* guidelines.

dirigente [diri'xente] *adj* leading ♦ *nm/f* (*POL*) leader; **los ~s del partido** the party leaders.

dirigible [diri'xiβle] *adj* (*AVIAT, NAUT*) steerable ♦ *nm* airship.

dirigir [diri'xir] *vt* to direct; (*acusación*) to level; (*carta*) to address; (*obra de teatro, film*) to produce, direct; (*MUS*) to conduct; (*comercio*) to manage; (*expedición*) to lead; (*sublevación*) to head; (*periódico*) to edit; (*guiar*) to guide; **~se** *vr*: **~se a** to go towards, make one's way towards; (*hablar con*) to speak to; **~se a algn solicitando algo** to apply to sb for sth; **"diríjase a ..."** "apply to ...".

dirigismo [diri'xismo] *nm* management, control; ~ **estatal** state control.

dirija [di'rixa] *etc vb V* **dirigir**.

dirimir [diri'mir] *vt* (*contrato, matrimonio*) to dissolve.

discado [dis'kaðo] *nm*: ~ **automático** autodial.

discernir [disθer'nir] *vt* to discern ♦ *vi* to distinguish.

discierna [dis'θjerna] *etc vb V* **discernir**.

disciplina [disθi'plina] *nf* discipline.

disciplinar [disθipli'nar] *vt* to discipline; (*enseñar*) to school; (*MIL*) to drill; (*azotar*) to whip.

discípulo, a [dis'θipulo, a] *nm/f* disciple; (*seguidor*) follower; (*ESCOL*) pupil.

disco ['disko] *nm* disc (*BRIT*), disk (*US*); (*DEPORTE*) discus; (*TELEC*) dial; (*AUTO: semáforo*) light; (*MUS*) record; (*INFORM*) disk; ~ **de arranque** boot disk; ~ **compacto** compact disc; ~ **de densidad sencilla/doble** single/double density disk; ~ **de larga duración** long-playing record (LP); ~ **flexible** *o* **floppy** floppy disk; ~ **de freno** brake disc; ~ **maestro** master disk; ~ **de reserva** backup disk; ~ **rígido** hard disk; ~ **de una cara/dos caras** single-/double-sided disk; ~ **virtual** ramdisk.

discóbolo [dis'koβolo] *nm* discus thrower.

discográfico, a [disko'ɣrafiko, a] *adj* record *cpd*; **casa discográfica** record company; **sello ~** label.

díscolo, a ['diskolo, a] *adj* (*rebelde*) unruly.

disconforme [diskon'forme] *adj* differing; **estar ~ (con)** to be in disagreement (with).

discontinuo, a [diskon'tinwo, a] *adj* discontinuous; (*AUTO: línea*) broken.

discordar [diskor'ðar] *vi* (*MUS*) to be out of tune; (*estar en desacuerdo*) to disagree; (*colores, opiniones*) to clash.

discorde [dis'korðe] *adj* (*sonido*) discordant; (*opiniones*) clashing.

discordia [dis'korðja] *nf* discord.

discoteca [disko'teka] *nf* disco(theque).

discreción [diskre'θjon] *nf* discretion; (*reserva*) prudence; **¡a ~!** (*MIL*) stand easy!; **añadir azúcar a ~** (*CULIN*) add sugar to taste; **comer a ~** to eat as much as one wishes.

discrecional [diskreθjo'nal] *adj* (*facultativo*) discretionary; **parada ~** request stop.

discrepancia [diskre'panθja] *nf* (*diferencia*) discrepancy; (*desacuerdo*) disagreement.

discrepante [diskre'pante] *adj* divergent; **hubo varias voces ~s** there were some dissenting voices.
discrepar [diskre'par] *vi* to disagree.
discreto, a [dis'kreto, a] *adj* (*diplomático*) discreet; (*sensato*) sensible; (*reservado*) quiet; (*sobrio*) sober; (*mediano*) fair, fairly good; **le daremos un plazo ~** we'll allow him a reasonable time.
discriminación [diskrimina'θjon] *nf* discrimination.
discriminar [diskrimi'nar] *vt* to discriminate against; (*diferenciar*) to discriminate between.
discuerde [dis'kwerðe] *etc vb V* **discordar**.
disculpa [dis'kulpa] *nf* excuse; (*pedir perdón*) apology; **pedir ~s a/por** to apologize to/for.
disculpar [diskul'par] *vt* to excuse, pardon; **~se** *vr* to excuse o.s.; to apologize.
discurrir [disku'rrir] *vt* to contrive, think up ♦ *vi* (*pensar, reflexionar*) to think, meditate; (*recorrer*) to roam, wander; (*río*) to flow; (*el tiempo*) to pass, flow by.
discurso [dis'kurso] *nm* speech; **~ de clausura** closing speech; **pronunciar un ~** to make a speech; **en el ~ del tiempo** with the passage of time.
discusión [disku'sjon] *nf* (*diálogo*) discussion; (*riña*) argument; **tener una ~** to have an argument.
discutible [disku'tiβle] *adj* debatable; **de mérito ~** of dubious worth.
discutido, a [disku'tiðo, a] *adj* controversial.
discutir [disku'tir] *vt* (*debatir*) to discuss; (*pelear*) to argue about; (*contradecir*) to argue against ♦ *vi* to discuss; (*disputar*) to argue; **~ de política** to argue about politics; **¡no discutas!** don't argue!
disecar [dise'kar] *vt* (*para conservar: animal*) to stuff; (*: planta*) to dry.
diseminar [disemi'nar] *vt* to disseminate, spread.
disentir [disen'tir] *vi* to dissent, disagree.
diseñador, a [diseɲa'ðor, a] *nm/f* designer.
diseñar [dise'ɲar] *vt* to design.
diseño [di'seɲo] *nm* (*TEC*) design; (*ARTE*) drawing; (*COSTURA*) pattern; **de ~ italiano** Italian-designed; **~ asistido por ordenador** computer-assisted design, CAD.
diseque [di'seke] *etc vb V* **disecar**.
disertar [diser'tar] *vi* to speak.
disfrace [dis'fraθe] *etc vb V* **disfrazar**.
disfraz [dis'fraθ] *nm* (*máscara*) disguise; (*traje*) fancy dress; (*excusa*) pretext; **bajo el ~ de** under the cloak of.
disfrazado, a [disfra'θaðo, a] *adj* disguised; **ir ~ de** to masquerade as.
disfrazar [disfra'θar] *vt* to disguise; **~se** *vr* to dress (o.s.) up; **~se de** to disguise o.s. as.
disfrutar [disfru'tar] *vt* to enjoy ♦ *vi* to enjoy o.s.; **¡que disfrutes!** have a good time; **~ de** to enjoy, possess; **~ de buena salud** to enjoy good health.
disfrute [dis'frute] *nm* (*goce*) enjoyment; (*aprovechamiento*) use.
disgregar [disɣre'ɣar] *vt* (*desintegrar*) to disintegrate; (*manifestantes*) to disperse; **~se** *vr* to disintegrate, break up.
disgregue [dis'ɣreɣe] *etc vb V* **disgregar**.
disgustar [disɣus'tar] *vt* (*no gustar*) to displease; (*contrariar, enojar*) to annoy; to upset; **~se** *vr* to be annoyed; (*dos personas*) to fall out; **estaba muy disgustado con el asunto** he was very upset about the affair.
disgusto [dis'ɣusto] *nm* (*repugnancia*) disgust; (*contrariedad*) annoyance; (*desagrado*) displeasure; (*tristeza*) grief; (*riña*) quarrel; (*avería*) misfortune; **hacer algo a ~** to do sth unwillingly; **matar a algn a ~s** to drive sb to distraction.
disidente [disi'ðente] *nm* dissident.
disienta [di'sjenta] *etc vb V* **disentir**.
disimulado, a [disimu'laðo, a] *adj* (*solapado*) furtive, underhand; (*oculto*) covert; **hacerse el ~** to pretend not to notice.
disimular [disimu'lar] *vt* (*ocultar*) to hide, conceal ♦ *vi* to dissemble.
disimulo [disi'mulo] *nm* (*fingimiento*) dissimulation; **con ~** cunningly.
disipar [disi'par] *vt* (*duda, temor*) to dispel; (*esperanza*) to destroy; (*fortuna*) to squander; **~se** *vr* (*nubes*) to vanish; (*dudas*) to be dispelled; (*indisciplinarse*) to dissipate.
diskette [dis'ket] *nm* (*INFORM*) diskette, floppy disk.
dislate [dis'late] *nm* (*absurdo*) absurdity; **~s** *nmpl* nonsense *sg*.
dislexia [dis'leksja] *nf* dyslexia.
dislocar [dislo'kar] *vt* (*gen*) to dislocate; (*tobillo*) to sprain.
disloque [dis'loke] *etc vb V* **dislocar** ♦ *nm*: **es el ~** (*fam*) it's the last straw.
disminución [disminu'θjon] *nf* diminution.
disminuido, a [disminu'iðo, a] *nm/f*: **~ mental/físico** mentally/physically-handicapped person.
disminuir [disminu'ir] *vt* to decrease, diminish; (*estrechar*) to lessen; (*temperatura*) to lower; (*gastos, raciones*)

to cut down; (*dolor*) to relieve; (*autoridad, prestigio*) to weaken; (*entusiasmo*) to damp ♦ *vi* (*días*) to grow shorter; (*precios, temperatura*) to drop, fall; (*velocidad*) to slacken; (*población*) to decrease; (*beneficios, número*) to fall off; (*memoria, vista*) to fail.

disminuyendo [disminu'jendo] *etc vb V* **disminuir**.

disociar [diso'θjar] *vt* to disassociate; **~se** *vr* to disassociate o.s.

disoluble [diso'lußle] *adj* soluble.

disolución [disolu'θjon] *nf* (*acto*) dissolution; (*QUÍMICA*) solution; (*COM*) liquidation; (*moral*) dissoluteness.

disoluto, a [diso'luto, a] *adj* dissolute.

disolvente [disol'ßente] *nm* (*solvent*) thinner.

disolver [disol'ßer] *vt* (*gen*) to dissolve; (*manifestación*) to break up; **~se** *vr* to dissolve; (*COM*) to go into liquidation.

dispar [dis'par] *adj* (*distinto*) different; (*irregular*) uneven.

disparado, a [dispa'raðo, a] *adj*: **entrar ~** to shoot in; **salir ~** to shoot out; **ir ~** to go like mad.

disparador [dispara'ðor] *nm* (*de arma*) trigger; (*FOTO, TEC*) release; **~ atómico** aerosol; **~ de bombas** bomb release.

disparar [dispa'rar] *vt, vi* to shoot, fire; **~se** *vr* (*arma de fuego*) to go off; (*persona: marcharse*) to rush off; (*caballo*) to bolt; (*enojarse*) to lose control.

disparatado, a [dispara'taðo, a] *adj* crazy.

disparate [dispa'rate] *nm* (*tontería*) foolish remark; (*error*) blunder; **decir ~s** to talk nonsense; **¡qué ~!** how absurd!; **costar un ~** to cost a hell of a lot.

disparo [dis'paro] *nm* shot; (*acto*) firing; **~s** *nmpl* shooting *sg*, (exchange of) shots (*sg*); **~ inicial** (*de cohete*) blastoff.

dispendio [dis'pendjo] *nm* waste.

dispensar [dispen'sar] *vt* to dispense; (*ayuda*) to give; (*honores*) to grant; (*disculpar*) to excuse; **¡usted dispense!** I beg your pardon!; **~ a algn de hacer algo** to excuse sb from doing sth.

dispensario [dispen'sarjo] *nm* (*clínica*) community clinic; (*de hospital*) outpatients' department.

dispersar [disper'sar] *vt* to disperse; (*manifestación*) to break up; **~se** *vr* to scatter.

disperso, a [dis'perso, a] *adj* scattered.

displicencia [displi'θenθja] *nf* (*mal humor*) peevishness; (*desgana*) lack of enthusiasm.

displicente [displi'θente] *adj* (*malhumorado*) peevish; (*poco entusiasta*) unenthusiastic.

dispondré [dispon'dre] *etc vb V* **disponer**.

disponer [dispo'ner] *vt* (*arreglar*) to arrange; (*ordenar*) to put in order; (*preparar*) to prepare, get ready ♦ *vi*: **~ de** to have, own; **~se** *vr*: **~se para** to prepare to, prepare for; **la ley dispone que ...** the law provides that ...; **no puede ~ de esos bienes** she cannot dispose of those properties.

disponga [dis'ponga] *etc vb V* **disponer**.

disponibilidad [disponißili'ðað] *nf* availability; **~es** *nfpl* (*COM*) resources, financial assets.

disponible [dispo'nißle] *adj* available; (*tiempo*) spare; (*dinero*) on hand.

disposición [disposi'θjon] *nf* arrangement, disposition; (*de casa, INFORM*) layout; (*ley*) order; (*cláusula*) provision; (*aptitud*) aptitude; **~ de ánimo** attitude of mind; **última ~** last will and testament; **a la ~ de** at the disposal of; **a su ~** at your service.

dispositivo [disposi'tißo] *nm* device, mechanism; **~ de alimentación** hopper; **~ de almacenaje** storage device; **~ periférico** peripheral (device); **~ de seguridad** safety catch; (*fig*) security measure.

dispuesto, a [dis'pwesto, a] *pp de* **disponer** ♦ *adj* (*arreglado*) arranged; (*preparado*) disposed; (*persona: dinámico*) bright; **estar ~/poco ~ a hacer algo** to be inclined/reluctant to do sth.

dispuse [dis'puse] *etc vb V* **disponer**.

disputa [dis'puta] *nf* (*discusión*) dispute, argument; (*controversia*) controversy.

disputar [dispu'tar] *vt* (*discutir*) to dispute, question; (*contender*) to contend for ♦ *vi* to argue.

disquete [dis'kete] *nm* (*INFORM*) diskette, floppy disk.

disquetera [diske'tera] *nf* disk drive.

Dist. *abr* (= *distancia, Distrito*) dist.

distancia [dis'tanθja] *nf* distance; (*de tiempo*) interval; **~ de parada** braking distance; **~ del suelo** (*AUTO etc*) height off the ground; **a gran** *o* **a larga ~** long-distance; **mantenerse a ~** to keep one's distance; (*fig*) to remain aloof; **guardar las ~s** to keep one's distance.

distanciado, a [distan'θjaðo, a] *adj* (*remoto*) remote; (*fig: alejado*) far apart; **estamos ~s en ideas** our ideas are poles apart.

distanciamiento [distanθja'mjento] *nm* (*acto*) spacing out; (*estado*) remoteness;

(*fig*) distance.
distanciar [distan'θjar] *vt* to space out; **~se** *vr* to become estranged.
distante [dis'tante] *adj* distant.
distar [dis'tar] *vi*: **dista 5 kms de aquí** it is 5 kms from here; **¿dista mucho?** is it far?; **dista mucho de la verdad** it's very far from the truth.
diste ['diste], **disteis** ['disteis] *vb V* **dar**.
distensión [disten'sjon] *nf* distension; (*POL*) détente; ~ **muscular** (*MED*) muscular strain.
distinción [distin'θjon] *nf* distinction; (*elegancia*) elegance; (*honor*) honour; **a ~ de** unlike; **sin** ~ indiscriminately; **sin ~ de edades** irrespective of age.
distinga [dis'tinga] *etc vb V* **distinguir**.
distinguido, a [distin'giðo, a] *adj* distinguished; (*famoso*) prominent, well-known; (*elegante*) elegant.
distinguir [distin'gir] *vt* to distinguish; (*divisar*) to make out; (*escoger*) to single out; (*caracterizar*) to mark out; **~se** *vr* to be distinguished; (*destacarse*) to distinguish o.s.; **a lo lejos no se distingue** it's not visible from a distance.
distintivo, a [distin'tiβo, a] *adj* distinctive; (*signo*) distinguishing ♦ *nm* (*de policía etc*) badge; (*fig*) characteristic.
distinto, a [dis'tinto, a] *adj* different; (*claro*) clear; **~s** several, various.
distorsión [distor'sjon] *nf* (*ANAT*) twisting; (*RADIO etc*) distortion.
distorsionar [distorsjo'nar] *vt, vi* to distort.
distracción [distrak'θjon] *nf* distraction; (*pasatiempo*) hobby, pastime; (*olvido*) absent-mindedness, distraction.
distraer [distra'er] *vt* (*atención*) to distract; (*divertir*) to amuse; (*fondos*) to embezzle ♦ *vi* to be relaxing; **~se** *vr* (*entretenerse*) to amuse o.s.; (*perder la concentración*) to allow one's attention to wander; **~ a algn de su pensamiento** to divert sb from his train of thought; **el pescar distrae** fishing is a relaxation.
distraído, a [distra'iðo, a] *adj* (*gen*) absent-minded; (*desatento*) inattentive; (*entretenido*) amusing ♦ *nm*: **hacerse el ~** to pretend not to notice; **con aire ~** idly; **me miró distraída** she gave me a casual glance.
distraiga [dis'traiɣa] *etc*, **distraje** [dis'traxe] *etc*, **distrajera** [distra'xera] *etc*, **distrayendo** [distra'jendo] *vb V* **distraer**.
distribución [distriβu'θjon] *nf* distribution; (*entrega*) delivery; (*en estadística*) distribution, incidence; (*ARQ*) layout; **~ de premios** prize giving; **la ~ de los impuestos** the incidence of taxes.
distribuidor, a [distriβui'ðor, a] *nm/f* (*persona*: *gen*) distributor; (: *CORREOS*) sorter; (: *COM*) dealer; **su ~ habitual** your regular dealer.
distribuir [distriβu'ir] *vt* to distribute; (*prospectos*) to hand out; (*cartas*) to deliver; (*trabajo*) to allocate; (*premios*) to award; (*dividendos*) to pay; (*peso*) to distribute; (*ARQ*) to plan.
distribuyendo [distriβu'jendo] *etc vb V* **distribuir**.
distrito [dis'trito] *nm* (*sector, territorio*) region; (*barrio*) district; ~ **electoral** constituency; ~ **postal** postal district.
disturbio [dis'turβjo] *nm* disturbance; (*desorden*) riot; **los ~s** the troubles.
disuadir [diswa'ðir] *vt* to dissuade.
disuasión [diswa'sjon] *nf* dissuasion; (*MIL*) deterrent; ~ **nuclear** nuclear deterrent.
disuasivo, a [diswa'siβo, a] *adj* dissuasive; **arma disuasiva** deterrent.
disuasorio, a [diswa'sorjo, a] *adj* = **disuasivo**.
disuelto [di'swelto] *pp de* **disolver**.
disuelva [di'swelβa] *etc vb V* **disolver**.
disuene [di'swene] *etc vb V* **disonar**.
disyuntiva [disjun'tiβa] *nf* (*dilema*) dilemma.
DIU ['diu] *nm abr* (= *dispositivo intrauterino*) I.U.D.
diurno, a ['djurno, a] *adj* day *cpd*, diurnal.
diva ['diβa] *nf* prima donna.
divagar [diβa'ɣar] *vi* (*desviarse*) to digress.
divague [di'βaɣe] *etc vb V* **divagar**.
diván [di'βan] *nm* divan.
divergencia [diβer'xenθja] *nf* divergence.
divergir [diβer'xir] *vi* (*líneas*) to diverge; (*opiniones*) to differ; (*personas*) to disagree.
diverja [di'βerxa] *etc vb V* **divergir**.
diversidad [diβersi'ðað] *nf* diversity, variety.
diversificación [diβersifika'θjon] *nf* (*COM*) diversification.
diversificar [diβersifi'kar] *vt* to diversify.
diversifique [diβersi'fike] *etc vb V* **diversificar**.
diversión [diβer'sjon] *nf* (*gen*) entertainment; (*actividad*) hobby, pastime.
diverso, a [di'βerso, a] *adj* diverse; (*diferente*) different ♦ *nm*: **~s** (*COM*) sundries; **~s libros** several books.
divertido, a [diβer'tiðo, a] *adj* (*chiste*) amusing, funny; (*fiesta etc*) enjoyable; (*película, libro*) entertaining; **está ~**

(*irónico*) this is going to be fun.
divertir [diβer'tir] *vt* (*entretener, recrear*) to amuse; ~**se** *vr* (*pasarlo bien*) to have a good time; (*distraerse*) to amuse o.s.
dividendo [diβi'ðendo] *nm* (*COM*): ~**s** *nmpl* dividends; ~**s por acción** earnings per share; ~ **definitivo** final dividend.
dividir [diβi'ðir] *vt* (*gen*) to divide; (*separar*) to separate; (*distribuir*) to distribute.
divierta [di'βjerta] *etc vb V* **divertir**.
divinidad [diβini'ðað] *nf* (*esencia divina*) divinity; **la D~** God.
divino, a [di'βino, a] *adj* divine; (*fig*) lovely.
divirtiendo [diβir'tjendo] *etc vb V* **divertir**.
divisa [di'βisa] *nf* (*emblema, moneda*) emblem, badge; ~**s** *nfpl* currency *sg*; (*COM*) foreign exchange *sg*; **control de ~s** exchange control; ~ **de reserva** reserve currency.
divisar [diβi'sar] *vt* to make out.
división [diβi'sjon] *nf* division; (*de partido*) split; (*de país*) partition.
divisorio, a [diβi'sorjo, a] *adj* (*línea*) dividing; **línea divisoria de las aguas** watershed.
divorciado, a [diβor'θjaðo, a] *adj* divorced; (*opinion*) split ♦ *nm/f* divorcé(e).
divorciar [diβor'θjar] *vt* to divorce; ~**se** *vr* to get divorced.
divorcio [di'βorθjo] *nm* divorce; (*fig*) split.
divulgación [diβulɣa'θjon] *nf* (*difusión*) spreading; (*popularización*) popularization.
divulgar [diβul'ɣar] *vt* (*desparramar*) to spread; (*popularizar*) to popularize; (*hacer circular*) to divulge, circulate; ~**se** *vr* (*secreto*) to leak out; (*rumor*) to get about.
divulgue [di'βulɣe] *etc vb V* **divulgar**.
dizque ['diske] *adv* (*AM fam*) apparently.
Dls., dls *abr* (*AM*) = **dólares**.
DM *abr* = **decimal**.
dm. *abr* (= *decímetro*) dm.
DNI *nm abr* (*ESP*) = **Documento Nacional de Identidad**.
Dña. *abr* = **Doña**.
do [do] *nm* (*MUS*) C.
D.O. *abr* = **Denominación de Origen**.
dobladillo [doβla'ðiʎo] *nm* (*de vestido*) hem; (*de pantalón*: *vuelta*) turn-up (*BRIT*), cuff (*US*).
doblaje [do'βlaxe] *nm* (*CINE*) dubbing.
doblar [do'βlar] *vt* to double; (*papel*) to fold; (*caño*) to bend; (*la esquina*) to turn, go round; (*film*) to dub ♦ *vi* to turn; (*campana*) to toll; ~**se** *vr* (*plegarse*) to fold (up), crease; (*encorvarse*) to bend.
doble ['doβle] *adj* (*gen*) double; (*de dos aspectos*) dual; (*cuerda*) thick; (*fig*) two-faced ♦ *nm* double ♦ *nm/f* (*TEAT*) double, stand-in; ~**s** *nmpl* (*DEPORTE*) doubles *sg*; ~ **o nada** double or quits; ~ **página** double-page spread; **con ~ sentido** with a double meaning; **el ~** twice the quantity *o* as much; **su sueldo es el ~ del mío** his salary is twice (as much as) mine; (*INFORM*): ~ **cara** double-sided; ~ **densidad** double density.
doblegar [doβle'ɣar] *vt* to fold, crease; ~**se** *vr* to yield.
doblegue [do'βleɣe] *etc vb V* **doblegar**.
doblez [do'βleθ] *nm* (*pliegue*) fold, hem ♦ *nf* (*falsedad*) duplicity.
doc. *abr* (= *docena*) doz.; (= *documento*) doc.
doce ['doθe] *num* twelve; (*fecha*) twelfth; **las ~** twelve o'clock; *V tb* **seis**.
docena [do'θena] *nf* dozen; **por ~s** by the dozen.
docente [do'θente] *adj*: **centro/personal ~** teaching institution/staff.
dócil ['doθil] *adj* (*pasivo*) docile; (*manso*) gentle; (*obediente*) obedient.
docto, a ['dokto, a] *adj* learned, erudite ♦ *nm/f* scholar.
doctor, a [dok'tor, a] *nm/f* doctor; ~ **en filosofía** Doctor of Philosophy.
doctorado [dokto'raðo] *nm* doctorate.
doctorarse [dokto'rarse] *vr* to get a doctorate.
doctrina [dok'trina] *nf* doctrine, teaching.
documentación [dokumenta'θjon] *nf* documentation; (*de identidad etc*) papers *pl*.
documental [dokumen'tal] *adj, nm* documentary.
documentar [dokumen'tar] *vt* to document; ~**se** *vr* to gather information.
documento [doku'mento] *nm* (*certificado*) document; (*JUR*) exhibit; ~**s** *nmpl* papers; ~ **justificativo** voucher; **D~ Nacional de Identidad** national identity card; *see boxed note*.

DOCUMENTO NACIONAL DE IDENTIDAD

A laminated plastic ID card with the holder's personal details and photograph, the **Documento Nacional de Identidad** *is renewed every ten years. People are required to carry it at all times and to produce it on request for the police. In Spain it is commonly known as a "DNI" or "carnet de identidad". In Spanish America a similar card is called a "cédula (de identidad)".*

dogma ['doɣma] *nm* dogma.
dogmático, a [doɣ'matiko, a] *adj* dogmatic.
dogo ['doɣo] *nm* bulldog.
dólar ['dolar] *nm* dollar.
dolencia [do'lenθja] *nf* (*achaque*) ailment; (*dolor*) ache.
doler [do'ler] *vt, vi* to hurt; (*fig*) to grieve; **~se** *vr* (*de su situación*) to grieve, feel sorry; (*de las desgracias ajenas*) to sympathize; (*quejarse*) to complain; **me duele el brazo** my arm hurts; **no me duele el dinero** I don't mind about the money; **¡ahí le duele!** you've put your finger on it!
doliente [do'ljente] *adj* (*enfermo*) sick; (*dolorido*) aching; (*triste*) sorrowful; **la familia ~** the bereaved family.
dolor [do'lor] *nm* pain; (*fig*) grief, sorrow; **~ de cabeza** headache; **~ de estómago** stomach ache; **~ de oídos** earache; **~ sordo** dull ache.
dolorido, a [dolo'riðo, a] *adj* (*MED*) sore, aching; **la parte dolorida** the part which hurts.
doloroso, a [dolo'roso, a] *adj* (*MED*) painful; (*fig*) distressing.
domar [do'mar] *vt* to tame.
domesticado, a [domesti'kaðo, a] *adj* (*amansado*) tame.
domesticar [domesti'kar] *vt* to tame.
doméstico, a [do'mestiko, a] *adj* domestic ♦ *nm/f* servant; **economía doméstica** home economy; **gastos ~s** household expenses.
domestique [domes'tike] *etc vb V* **domesticar**.
domiciliación [domiθilja'θjon] *nf*: **~ de pagos** (*COM*) standing order, direct debit.
domiciliar [domiθi'ljar] *vt* to domicile; **~se** *vr* to take up (one's) residence.
domiciliario, a [domiθi'ljarjo, a] *adj*: **arresto ~** house arrest.
domicilio [domi'θiljo] *nm* home; **~ particular** private residence; **~ social** (*COM*) head office, registered office; **servicio a ~** delivery service; **sin ~ fijo** of no fixed abode.
dominante [domi'nante] *adj* dominant; (*person*) domineering.
dominar [domi'nar] *vt* (*gen*) to dominate; (*países*) to rule over; (*adversario*) to overpower; (*caballo, nervios, emoción*) to control; (*incendio, epidemia*) to bring under control; (*idiomas*) to be fluent in ♦ *vi* to dominate, prevail; **~se** *vr* to control o.s.
domingo [do'mingo] *nm* Sunday; **D~ de Ramos** Palm Sunday; **D~ de Resurrección** Easter Sunday; *V tb* **sábado**; **Semana Santa**.
dominguero, a [domin'gero, a] *adj* Sunday *cpd*.
dominical [domini'kal] *adj* Sunday *cpd*; **periódico ~** Sunday newspaper.
dominicano, a [domini'kano, a] *adj, nm/f* Dominican.
dominio [do'minjo] *nm* (*tierras*) domain; (*POL*) dominion; (*autoridad*) power, authority; (*supremacía*) supremacy; (*de las pasiones*) grip, hold; (*de idioma*) command; **ser del ~ público** to be widely known.
dominó [domi'no] *nm* (*pieza*) domino; (*juego*) dominoes.
dom.º *abr* (= *domingo*) Sun.
don [don] *nm* (*talento*) gift; **D~ Juan Gómez** Mr Juan Gómez, Juan Gómez Esq. (*BRIT*); **tener ~ de gentes** to known how to handle people; **~ de lenguas** gift for languages; **~ de mando** (qualities of) leadership; **~ de palabra** gift of the gab; *see boxed note*.

> **DON**
>
> *The title* **don** *or* **doña** *is used before a person's first name – for example, Don Diego, Doña Inés – as a mark of respect or politeness to someone of superior social standing or an older person. Its use is dying out but it continues to be found in official documents and correspondence: for example, Sr. D. Pedro Rodríguez Hernández, Sra. Dña Inés Rodríguez Hernández.*

donación [dona'θjon] *nf* donation.
donaire [do'naire] *nm* charm.
donante [do'nante] *nm/f* donor; **~ de sangre** blood donor.
donar [do'nar] *vt* to donate.
donativo [dona'tiβo] *nm* donation.
doncella [don'θeʎa] *nf* (*criada*) maid.
donde ['donde] *adv* where ♦ *prep*: **el coche está allí ~ el farol** the car is over there by the lamppost *o* where the lamppost is; **por ~** through which; **a ~** to where, to which; **en ~** where, in which; **es a ~ vamos nosotros** that's where we're going.
dónde ['donde] *adv interrogativo* where?; **¿a ~ vas?** where are you going (to)?; **¿de ~ vienes?** where have you come from?; **¿en ~?** where?; **¿por ~?** where?,

whereabouts?; **¿por ~ se va al estadio?** how do you get to the stadium?
dondequiera [donde'kjera] *adv* anywhere ♦ *conj*: **~ que** wherever; **por ~** everywhere, all over the place.
donostiarra [donos'tjarra] *adj* of *o* from San Sebastián ♦ *nm/f* native *o* inhabitant of San Sebastián.
doña ['doɲa] *nf*: **D~ Carmen Gómez** Mrs Carmen Gómez; *V tb* **don.**
dopar [do'par] *vt* to dope, drug.
doping ['dopin] *nm* doping, drugging.
doquier [do'kjer] *adv*: **por ~** all over, everywhere.
dorado, a [do'raðo, a] *adj* (*color*) golden; (*TEC*) gilt.
dorar [do'rar] *vt* (*TEC*) to gild; (*CULIN*) to brown, cook lightly; **~ la píldora** to sweeten the pill.
dormilón, ona [dormi'lon, ona] *adj* fond of sleeping ♦ *nm/f* sleepyhead.
dormir [dor'mir] *vt*: **~ la siesta por la tarde** to have an afternoon nap ♦ *vi* to sleep; **~se** *vr* (*persona, brazo, pierna*) to fall asleep; **~la** (*fam*) to sleep it off; **~ la mona** (*fam*) to sleep off a hangover; **~ como un lirón** *o* **tronco** to sleep like a log; **~ a pierna suelta** to sleep soundly.
dormitar [dormi'tar] *vi* to doze.
dormitorio [dormi'torjo] *nm* bedroom; **~ común** dormitory.
dorsal [dor'sal] *adj* dorsal ♦ *nm* (*DEPORTE*) number.
dorso ['dorso] *nm* back; **escribir algo al ~** to write sth on the back; **"vease al ~"** "see other side", "please turn over".
DOS *nm abr* (= *sistema operativo de disco*) DOS.
dos [dos] *num* two; (*fecha*) second; **los ~** the two of them, both of them; **cada ~ por tres** every five minutes; **de ~ en ~** in twos; **estamos a ~** (*TENIS*) the score is deuce; *V tb* **seis.**
doscientos, as [dos'θjentos, as] *num* two hundred.
dosel [do'sel] *nm* canopy.
dosificar [dosifi'kar] *vt* (*CULIN, MED, QUÍMICA*) to measure out; (*no derrochar*) to be sparing with.
dosifique [dosi'fike] *etc vb V* **dosificar.**
dosis ['dosis] *nf inv* dose, dosage.
dossier [do'sjer] *nm* dossier, file.
dotación [dota'θjon] *nf* (*acto, dinero*) endowment; (*plantilla*) staff; (*NAUT*) crew; **la ~ es insuficiente** we are under staffed.
dotado, a [do'taðo, a] *adj* gifted; **~ de** (*persona*) endowed with; (*máquina*) equipped with.
dotar [do'tar] *vt* to endow; (*TEC*) to fit; (*barco*) to man; (*oficina*) to staff.
dote ['dote] *nf* (*de novia*) dowry; **~s** *nfpl* (*talentos*) gifts.
doy [doj] *vb V* **dar.**
Dpto. *abr* (= *Departamento*) dept.
Dr(a). *abr* (= *Doctor, Doctora*) Dr.
draga ['draɣa] *nf* dredge.
dragado [dra'ɣaðo] *nm* dredging.
dragar [dra'ɣar] *vt* to dredge; (*minas*) to sweep.
dragón [dra'ɣon] *nm* dragon.
drague ['draɣe] *etc vb V* **dragar.**
drama ['drama] *nm* drama; (*obra*) play.
dramático, a [dra'matiko, a] *adj* dramatic ♦ *nm/f* dramatist; (*actor*) actor; **obra dramática** play.
dramaturgo, a [drama'turɣo, a] *nm/f* dramatist, playwright.
dramón [dra'mon] *nm* (*TEAT*) melodrama; **¡qué ~!** what a scene!
drástico, a ['drastiko, a] *adj* drastic.
drenaje [dre'naxe] *nm* drainage.
drenar [dre'nar] *vt* to drain.
droga ['droɣa] *nf* drug; (*DEPORTE*) dope; **el problema de la ~** the drug problem.
drogadicto, a [droɣa'ðikto, a] *nm/f* drug addict.
drogar [dro'ɣar] *vt* to drug; (*DEPORTE*) to dope; **~se** *vr* to take drugs.
drogodependencia [droɣoðepen'denθja] *nf* drug addiction.
drogue ['droɣe] *etc vb V* **drogar.**
droguería [droɣe'ria] *nf* ≈ hardware shop (*BRIT*) *o* store (*US*).
dromedario [drome'ðarjo] *nm* dromedary.
Dto., D.to *abr* = **descuento.**
Dtor(a). *abr* (= *Director, Directora*) Dir.
ducado [du'kaðo] *nm* duchy, dukedom.
ducha ['dutʃa] *nf* (*baño*) shower; (*MED*) douche.
ducharse [du'tʃarse] *vr* to take a shower.
ducho, a ['dutʃo, a] *adj*: **~ en** (*experimentado*) experienced in; (*hábil*) skilled at.
dúctil ['duktil] *adj* (*metal*) ductile; (*persona*) easily influenced.
duda ['duða] *nf* doubt; **sin ~** no doubt, doubtless; **¡sin ~!** of course!; **no cabe ~** there is no doubt about it; **no le quepa ~** make no mistake about it; **no quiero poner en ~ su conducta** I don't want to call his behaviour into question; **sacar a algn de la ~** to settle sb's doubts; **tengo una ~** I have a query.
dudar [du'ðar] *vt* to doubt ♦ *vi* to doubt, have doubts; **~ acerca de algo** to be

uncertain about sth; **dudó en comprarlo** he hesitated to buy it; **dudan que sea verdad** they doubt whether *o* if it's true.

dudoso, a [du'ðoso, a] *adj* (*incierto*) hesitant; (*sospechoso*) doubtful; (*conducta*) dubious.

duelo ['dwelo] *etc vb V* **doler** ♦ *nm* (*combate*) duel; (*luto*) mourning; **batirse en ~** to fight a duel.

duende ['dwende] *nm* imp, goblin; **tiene ~** he's got real soul.

dueño, a ['dweɲo, a] *nm/f* (*propietario*) owner; (*de pensión, taberna*) landlord/lady; (*de casa, perro*) master/mistress; (*empresario*) employer; **ser ~ de sí mismo** to have self-control; (*libre*) to be one's own boss; **eres ~ de hacer como te parezca** you're free to do as you think fit; **hacerse ~ de una situación** to take command of a situation.

duerma ['dwerma] *etc vb V* **dormir**.

duermevela [dwerme'ßela] *nf* (*fam*) nap, snooze.

Duero ['dwero] *nm* Douro.

dulce ['dulθe] *adj* sweet; (*carácter, clima*) gentle, mild ♦ *adv* gently, softly ♦ *nm* sweet.

dulcificar [dulθifi'kar] *vt* (*fig*) to soften.

dulcifique [dulθi'fike] *etc vb V* **dulcificar**.

dulzón, ona [dul'θon, ona] *adj* (*alimento*) sickly-sweet, too sweet; (*canción etc*) gooey.

dulzura [dul'θura] *nf* sweetness; (*ternura*) gentleness.

duna ['duna] *nf* dune.

Dunquerque [dun'kerke] *nm* Dunkirk.

dúo ['duo] *nm* duet, duo.

duodécimo, a [duo'deθimo, a] *adj* twelfth; *V tb* **sexto, a**.

dup., dup.do *abr* (= *duplicado*) duplicated.

dúplex ['dupleks] *nm inv* (*piso*) flat on two floors; (*TELEC*) link-up; (*INFORM*): **~ integral** full duplex.

duplicar [dupli'kar] *vt* (*hacer el doble de*) to duplicate; (*cantidad*) to double; **~se** *vr* to double.

duplique [du'plike] *etc vb V* **duplicar**.

duque ['duke] *nm* duke.

duquesa [du'kesa] *nf* duchess.

duración [dura'θjon] *nf* duration, length; (*de máquina*) life; **~ media de la vida** average life expectancy; **de larga ~** (*enfermedad*) lengthy; (*pila*) long-life; (*disco*) long-playing; **de poca ~** short.

duradero, a [dura'ðero, a] *adj* (*tela*) hard-wearing; (*fe, paz*) lasting.

durante [du'rante] *adv* during; **~ toda la noche** all night long; **habló ~ una hora** he spoke for an hour.

durar [du'rar] *vi* (*permanecer*) to last; (*recuerdo*) to remain; (*ropa*) to wear (well).

durazno [du'rasno] *nm* (*AM*: *fruta*) peach; (: *árbol*) peach tree.

durex ['dureks] *nm* (*AM*: *tira adhesiva*) Sellotape ® (*BRIT*), Scotch tape ® (*US*).

dureza [du'reθa] *nf* (*cualidad*) hardness; (*de carácter*) toughness.

durmiendo [dur'mjendo] *etc vb V* **dormir**.

durmiente [dur'mjente] *adj* sleeping ♦ *nm/f* sleeper.

duro, a ['duro, a] *adj* hard; (*carácter*) tough; (*pan*) stale; (*cuello, puerta*) stiff; (*clima, luz*) harsh ♦ *adv* hard ♦ *nm* (*moneda*) five peseta coin; **el sector ~ del partido** the hardliners *pl* in the party; **ser ~ con algn** to be tough with *o* hard on sb; **~ de mollera** (*torpe*) dense; **~ de oído** hard of hearing; **trabajar ~** to work hard; **estar sin un ~** to be broke.

DVD *nm abr* (= *disco de vídeo digital*) DVD.

Ee

E, e [e] *nf* (*letra*) E, e; **E de Enrique** E for Edward (*BRIT*) *o* Easy (*US*).

E *abr* (= *este*) E.

e [e] *conj* (*delante de* **i-** *e* **hi-**, *pero no* **hie-**) and; *V tb* **y**.

e/ *abr* (*COM*: = *envío*) shpt.

ebanista [eßa'nista] *nm/f* cabinetmaker.

ébano ['eßano] *nm* ebony.

ebrio, a ['eßrjo, a] *adj* drunk.

Ebro ['eßro] *nm* Ebro.

ebullición [eßuʎi'θjon] *nf* boiling; **punto de ~** boiling point.

eccema [ek'θema] *nm* (*MED*) eczema.

echar [e'tʃar] *vt* to throw; (*agua, vino*) to pour (out); (*CULIN*) to put in, add; (*dientes*) to cut; (*discurso*) to give; (*empleado*: *despedir*) to fire, sack; (*hojas*) to sprout; (*cartas*) to post; (*humo*) to emit, give out; (*reprimenda*) to deal out; (*cuenta*) to make up; (*freno*) to put on ♦ *vi*: **~ a correr/llorar** to break into a run/burst into tears; **~ a reír** to burst out laughing; **~se** *vr* to lie down; **~ abajo** (*gobierno*) to overthrow; (*edificio*) to demolish; **~ la buenaventura a algn** to tell sb's fortune; **~ la culpa a** to lay the

blame on; ~ **de menos** to miss; ~**se atrás** to throw o.s. back(wards); (*fig*) to go back on what one has said; ~**se una novia** to get o.s. a girlfriend; ~**se una siestecita** to have a nap.
echarpe [e'tʃarpe] *nm* (woman's) stole.
eclesiástico, a [ekle'sjastiko, a] *adj* ecclesiastical; (*autoridades etc*) church *cpd* ♦ *nm* clergyman.
eclipsar [eklip'sar] *vt* to eclipse; (*fig*) to outshine, overshadow.
eclipse [e'klipse] *nm* eclipse.
eco ['eko] *nm* echo; **encontrar un ~ en** to produce a response from; **hacerse ~ de una opinión** to echo an opinion; **tener ~** to catch on.
ecografía [ekoɣra'fia] *nf* ultrasound.
ecología [ekolo'xia] *nf* ecology.
ecológico, a [eko'loxiko, a] *adj* ecological; (*producto, método*) environmentally-friendly; (*agricultura*) organic.
ecologista [ekolo'xista] *adj* environmental, conservation *cpd* ♦ *nm/f* environmentalist.
economato [ekono'mato] *nm* cooperative store.
economía [ekono'mia] *nf* (*sistema*) economy; (*cualidad*) thrift; ~ **dirigida** planned economy; ~ **doméstica** housekeeping; ~ **de mercado** market economy; ~ **mixta** mixed economy; ~ **sumergida** black economy; **hacer ~s** to economize; ~**s de escala** economies of scale.
economice [ekono'miθe] *etc vb V* **economizar**.
económico, a [eko'nomiko, a] *adj* (*barato*) cheap, economical; (*persona*) thrifty; (*COM: año etc*) financial; (: *situación*) economic.
economista [ekono'mista] *nm/f* economist.
economizar [ekonomi'θar] *vt* to economize on ♦ *vi* (*ahorrar*) to save up; (*pey*) to be miserly.
ecosistema [ekosis'tema] *nm* ecosystem.
ecu ['eku] *nm* ecu.
ecuación [ekwa'θjon] *nf* equation.
ecuador [ekwa'ðor] *nm* equator; **(el) E~** Ecuador.
ecuánime [e'kwanime] *adj* (*carácter*) level-headed; (*estado*) calm.
ecuatorial [ekwato'rjal] *adj* equatorial.
ecuatoriano, a [ekwato'rjano, a] *adj, nm/f* Ecuador(i)an.
ecuestre [e'kwestre] *adj* equestrian.
eczema [ek'θema] *nm* = **eccema**.
ed. *abr* (= *edición*) ed.
edad [e'ðað] *nf* age; **¿qué ~ tienes?** how old are you?; **tiene ocho años de ~** he is eight (years old); **de ~ corta** young; **ser de ~ mediana/avanzada** to be middle-aged/getting on; **ser mayor de ~** to be of age; **llegar a mayor ~** to come of age; **ser menor de ~** to be under age; **la E~ Media** the Middle Ages; **la E~ de Oro** the Golden Age.
Edén [e'ðen] *nm* Eden.
edición [eði'θjon] *nf* (*acto*) publication; (*ejemplar*) edition; **"al cerrar la ~"** (*TIP*) "stop press".
edicto [e'ðikto] *nm* edict, proclamation.
edificante [eðifi'kante] *adj* edifying.
edificar [edifi'kar] *vt* (*ARQ*) to build.
edificio [eði'fiθjo] *nm* building; (*fig*) edifice, structure.
edifique [eði'fike] *etc vb V* **edificar**.
Edimburgo [eðim'burɣo] *nm* Edinburgh.
editar [eði'tar] *vt* (*publicar*) to publish; (*preparar textos, tb INFORM*) to edit.
editor, a [eði'tor, a] *nm/f* (*que publica*) publisher; (*redactor*) editor ♦ *adj*: **casa ~a** publishing company.
editorial [eðito'rjal] *adj* editorial ♦ *nm* leading article, editorial ♦ *nf* (*tb*: **casa ~**) publishers.
editorialista [eðitorja'lista] *nm/f* leader-writer.
Edo. *abr* (*AM*) = **Estado**.
edredón [eðre'ðon] *nm* eiderdown, quilt; ~ **nórdico** continental quilt, duvet.
educación [eðuka'θjon] *nf* education; (*crianza*) upbringing; (*modales*) (good) manners *pl*; (*formación*) training; **sin ~** ill-mannered; **¡qué falta de ~!** how rude!
educado, a [eðu'kaðo, a] *adj* well-mannered; **mal ~** ill-mannered.
educar [eðu'kar] *vt* to educate; (*criar*) to bring up; (*voz*) to train.
educativo, a [eðuka'tiβo, a] *adj* educational; (*política*) education *cpd*.
eduque [e'ðuke] *etc vb V* **educar**.
EE.UU. *nmpl abr* (= *Estados Unidos*) USA.
efectista [efek'tista] *adj* sensationalist.
efectivamente [efektiβa'mente] *adv* (*como respuesta*) exactly, precisely; (*verdaderamente*) really; (*de hecho*) in fact.
efectivo, a [efek'tiβo, a] *adj* effective; (*real*) actual, real ♦ *nm*: **pagar en ~** to pay (in) cash; **hacer ~ un cheque** to cash a cheque.
efecto [e'fekto] *nm* effect, result; (*objetivo*) purpose, end; ~**s** *nmpl* (*personales*) effects; (*bienes*) goods; (*COM*) assets; (*ECON*) bills, securities; ~ **2000** millennium bug; ~ **invernadero** greenhouse effect; ~**s de consumo** consumer goods; ~**s a cobrar**

bills receivable; ~**s especiales** special effects; ~**s personales** personal effects; ~**s secundarios** (*COM*) spin-off effects; ~**s sonoros** sound effects; **hacer** *o* **surtir** ~ to have the desired effect; **hacer** ~ (*impresionar*) to make an impression; **llevar algo a** ~ to carry sth out; **en** ~ in fact; (*respuesta*) exactly, indeed.
efectuar [efek'twar] *vt* to carry out; (*viaje*) to make.
efervescente [eferβes'θente] *adj* (*bebida*) fizzy, bubbly.
eficacia [efi'kaθja] *nf* (*de persona*) efficiency; (*de medicamento etc*) effectiveness.
eficaz [efi'kaθ] *adj* (*persona*) efficient; (*acción*) effective.
eficiencia [efi'θjenθja] *nf* efficiency.
eficiente [efi'θjente] *adj* efficient.
efigie [e'fixje] *nf* effigy.
efímero, a [e'fimero, a] *adj* ephemeral.
efusión [efu'sjon] *nf* outpouring; (*en el trato*) warmth; **con** ~ effusively.
efusivo, a [efu'siβo, a] *adj* effusive; **mis más efusivas gracias** my warmest thanks.
EGB *nf abr* (*ESP ESCOL*: = *Educación General Básica*) *primary education for 6-14 year olds; V tb* **sistema educativo**.
Egeo [e'xeo] *nm*: **(Mar)** ~ Aegean (Sea).
egipcio, a [e'xipθjo, a] *adj, nm/f* Egyptian.
Egipto [e'xipto] *nm* Egypt.
egocéntrico, a [eɣo'θentriko, a] *adj* self-centred.
egoísmo [eɣo'ismo] *nm* egoism.
egoísta [eɣo'ista] *adj* egoistical, selfish ♦ *nm/f* egoist.
ególatra [e'ɣolatra] *adj* big-headed.
egregio, a [e'ɣrexjo, a] *adj* eminent, distinguished.
egresado, a [eɣre'saðo, a] *nm/f* (*AM*) graduate.
egresar [eɣre'sar] *vi* (*AM*) to graduate.
eh [e] *excl* hey!, hi!
Eire ['eire] *nm* Eire.
ej. *abr* (= *ejemplo*) ex.
eje ['exe] *nm* (*GEO, MAT*) axis; (*POL, fig*) axis, main line; (*de rueda*) axle; (*de máquina*) shaft, spindle.
ejecución [exeku'θjon] *nf* execution; (*cumplimiento*) fulfilment; (*actuación*) performance; (*JUR*: *embargo de deudor*) attachment.
ejecutar [exeku'tar] *vt* to execute, carry out; (*matar*) to execute; (*cumplir*) to fulfil; (*MUS*) to perform; (*JUR*: *embargar*) to attach, distrain; (*deseos*) to fulfil; (*INFORM*) to run.
ejecutivo, a [exeku'tiβo, a] *adj, nm/f* executive; **el (poder)** ~ the Executive (Power).
ejecutor [exeku'tor] *nm* (*tb*: ~ **testamentario**) executor.
ejecutoria [exeku'torja] *nf* (*JUR*) final judgment.
ejemplar [exem'plar] *adj* exemplary ♦ *nm* example; (*ZOOL*) specimen; (*de libro*) copy; (*de periódico*) number, issue; ~ **de regalo** complimentary copy; **sin** ~ unprecedented.
ejemplificar [exemplifi'kar] *vt* to exemplify, illustrate.
ejemplifique [exempli'fike] *etc vb V* **ejemplificar.**
ejemplo [e'xemplo] *nm* example; (*caso*) instance; **por** ~ for example; **dar** ~ to set an example.
ejercer [exer'θer] *vt* to exercise; (*funciones*) to perform; (*negocio*) to manage; (*influencia*) to exert; (*un oficio*) to practise; (*poder*) to wield ♦ *vi*: ~ **de** to practise as.
ejercicio [exer'θiθjo] *nm* exercise; (*MIL*) drill; (*COM*) fiscal *o* financial year; (*período*) tenure; ~ **acrobático** (*AVIAT*) stunt; ~ **comercial** business year; ~**s espirituales** (*REL*) retreat *sg*; **hacer** ~ to take exercise.
ejercitar [exerθi'tar] *vt* to exercise; (*MIL*) to drill.
ejército [e'xerθito] *nm* army; **E~ del Aire/de Tierra** Air Force/Army; ~ **de ocupación** army of occupation; ~ **permanente** standing army; **entrar en el** ~ to join the army, join up.
ejerza [e'xerθa] *etc vb V* **ejercer.**
ejote [e'xote] *nm* (*AM*) green bean.

PALABRA CLAVE

el [el] (*f* **la**, *pl* **los, las**, *neutro* **lo**) *art def* **1** the; **el libro/la mesa/los estudiantes/las flores** the book/table/students/flowers; **me gusta el fútbol** I like football; **está en la cama** she's in bed
2 (*con n abstracto o propio*: *no se traduce*): **el amor/la juventud** love/youth; ~ **Conde Drácula** Count Dracula
3 (*posesión*: *se traduce a menudo por adj posesivo*): **romperse el brazo** to break one's arm; **levantó la mano** he put his hand up; **se puso el sombrero** she put her hat on
4 (*valor descriptivo*): **tener la boca grande/los ojos azules** to have a big mouth/blue eyes
5 (*con días*) on; **me iré el viernes** I'll leave on Friday; **los domingos suelo ir a**

nadar on Sundays I generally go swimming
6 (*lo + adj*): **lo difícil/caro** what is difficult/expensive; (= *cuán*): **no se da cuenta de lo pesado que es** he doesn't realise how boring he is
♦ *pron demos* **1**: **mi libro y el de usted** my book and yours; **las de Pepe son mejores** Pepe's are better; **no la(s) blanca(s) sino la(s) gris(es)** not the white one(s) but the grey one(s)
2: **lo de**: **lo de ayer** what happened yesterday; **lo de las facturas** that business about the invoices
♦ *pron relativo*: **el que** *etc* **1** (*indef*): **el (los) que quiera(n) que se vaya(n)** anyone who wants to can leave; **llévese el/la que más le guste** take the one you like best
2 (*def*): **el que compré ayer** the one I bought yesterday; **los que se van** those who leave
3: **lo que**: **lo que pienso yo/más me gusta** what I think/like most
♦ *conj*: **el que**: **el que lo diga** the fact that he says so; **el que sea tan vago me molesta** his being so lazy bothers me
♦ *excl*: **¡el susto que me diste!** what a fright you gave me!
♦ *pron personal* **1** (*persona*: *m*) him; (: *f*) her; (: *pl*) them; **lo/las veo** I can see him/them
2 (*animal, cosa*: *sg*) it; (: *pl*) them; **lo** (*o* **la**) **veo** I can see it; **los** (*o* **las**) **veo** I can see them
3: **lo** (*como sustituto de frase*): **no lo sabía** I didn't know; **ya lo entiendo** I understand now.

él [el] *pron* (*persona*) he; (*cosa*) it; (*después de prep*: *persona*) him; (: *cosa*) it; **mis libros y los de ~** my books and his.
elaboración [elaβora'θjon] *nf* (*producción*) manufacture; **~ de presupuestos** (*COM*) budgeting.
elaborar [elaβo'rar] *vt* (*producto*) to make, manufacture; (*preparar*) to prepare; (*madera, metal etc*) to work; (*proyecto etc*) to work on *o* out.
elasticidad [elastiθi'ðað] *nf* elasticity.
elástico, a [e'lastiko, a] *adj* elastic; (*flexible*) flexible ♦ *nm* elastic; (*gomita*) elastic band.
elección [elek'θjon] *nf* election; (*selección*) choice, selection; **elecciones parciales** by-election *sg*; **elecciones generales** general election *sg*.
electo, a [e'lekto, a] *adj* elect; **el presidente ~** the president-elect.
electorado [elekto'raðo] *nm* electorate, voters *pl*.
electoral [elekto'ral] *adj* electoral.
electrice [elek'triθe] *etc vb V* **electrizar**.
electricidad [elektriθi'ðað] *nf* electricity.
electricista [elektri'θista] *nm/f* electrician.
eléctrico, a [e'lektriko, a] *adj* electric.
electrificar [elektrifi'kar] *vt* to electrify.
electrizar [elektri'θar] *vt* (*FERRO, fig*) to electrify.
electro... [elektro] *pref* electro....
electrocardiograma [elektrokarðjo'ɣrama] *nm* electrocardiogram.
electrocución [elektroku'θjon] *nf* electrocution.
electrocutar [elektroku'tar] *vt* to electrocute.
electrodo [elek'troðo] *nm* electrode.
electrodomésticos [elektroðo'mestikos] *nmpl* (electrical) household appliances; (*COM*) white goods.
electroimán [electroi'man] *nm* electromagnet.
electromagnético, a [elektromaɣ'netiko, a] *adj* electromagnetic.
electrón [elek'tron] *nm* electron.
electrónico, a [elek'troniko, a] *adj* electronic ♦ *nf* electronics *sg*; **proceso ~ de datos** (*INFORM*) electronic data processing.
electrotecnia [elektro'teknja] *nf* electrical engineering.
electrotécnico, a [elektro'tekniko, a] *nm/f* electrical engineer.
elefante [ele'fante] *nm* elephant.
elegancia [ele'ɣanθja] *nf* elegance, grace; (*estilo*) stylishness.
elegante [ele'ɣante] *adj* elegant, graceful; (*traje etc*) smart, fashionable; (*decoración*) tasteful.
elegía [ele'xia] *nf* elegy.
elegir [ele'xir] *vt* (*escoger*) to choose, select; (*optar*) to opt for; (*presidente*) to elect.
elemental [elemen'tal] *adj* (*claro, obvio*) elementary; (*fundamental*) elemental, fundamental.
elemento [ele'mento] *nm* element; (*fig*) ingredient; (*AM*) person, individual; (*tipo raro*) odd person; (*de pila*) cell; **~s** *nmpl* elements, rudiments; **estar en su ~** to be in one's element; **vino a verle un ~** someone came to see you.
elenco [e'lenko] *nm* catalogue, list; (*TEAT*) cast; (*AM*: *equipo*) team.
elepé [ele'pe] *nm* LP.
elevación [eleβa'θjon] *nf* elevation; (*acto*) raising, lifting; (*de precios*) rise; (*GEO*

etc) height, altitude.
elevador [eleßa'ðor] *nm* (*AM*) lift (*BRIT*), elevator (*US*).
elevar [ele'ßar] *vt* to raise, lift (up); (*precio*) to put up; (*producción*) to step up; (*informe etc*) to present; **~se** *vr* (*edificio*) to rise; (*precios*) to go up; (*transportarse, enajenarse*) to get carried away; **la cantidad se eleva a ...** the total amounts to ... .
eligiendo [eli'xjenðo] *etc*, **elija** [e'lixa] *etc* *vb V* **elegir**.
eliminar [elimi'nar] *vt* to eliminate, remove; (*olor, persona*) to get rid of; (*DEPORTE*) to eliminate, knock out.
eliminatoria [elimina'torja] *nf* heat, preliminary (round).
elite [e'lite], **élite** ['elite] *nf* elite, élite.
elitista [eli'tista] *adj* elitist.
elixir [elik'sir] *nm* elixir; (*tb*: **~ bucal**) mouthwash.
ella ['eʎa] *pron* (*persona*) she; (*cosa*) it; (*después de prep*: *persona*) her; (: *cosa*) it; **de ~** hers.
ellas ['eʎas] *pron V* **ellos**.
ello ['eʎo] *pron neutro* it; **es por ~ que ...** that's why ....
ellos, as ['eʎos, as] *pron personal pl* they; (*después de prep*) them; **de ~** theirs.
elocuencia [elo'kwenθja] *nf* eloquence.
elocuente [elo'kwente] *adj* eloquent; (*fig*) significant; **un dato ~** a fact which speaks for itself.
elogiar [elo'xjar] *vt* to praise, eulogize.
elogio [e'loxjo] *nm* praise; **queda por encima de todo ~** it's beyond praise; **hacer ~ de** to sing the praises of.
elote [e'lote] *nm* (*AM*) corn on the cob.
El Salvador *nm* El Salvador.
eludir [elu'ðir] *vt* (*evitar*) to avoid, evade; (*escapar*) to escape, elude.
E.M. *abr* (*MIL*: = *Estado Mayor*) G.S.
Em.ª *abr* = **Eminencia**.
emanar [ema'nar] *vi*: **~ de** to emanate from, come from; (*derivar de*) to originate in.
emancipar [emanθi'par] *vt* to emancipate; **~se** *vr* to become emancipated, free o.s.
embadurnar [embaður'nar] *vt* to smear.
embajada [emba'xaða] *nf* embassy.
embajador, a [embaxa'ðor, a] *nm/f* ambassador/ambassadress.
embaladura [embala'ðura] *nf* (*AM*), **embalaje** [emba'laxe] *nm* packing.
embalar [emba'lar] *vt* (*envolver*) to parcel, wrap (up); (*envasar*) to package ♦ *vi* to sprint.
embalsamar [embalsa'mar] *vt* to embalm.
embalsar [embal'sar] *vt* (*río*) to dam (up); (*agua*) to retain.
embalse [em'balse] *nm* (*presa*) dam; (*lago*) reservoir.
embarace [emba'raθe] *etc vb V* **embarazar**.
embarazada [embara'θaða] *adj f* pregnant ♦ *nf* pregnant woman.
embarazar [embara'θar] *vt* to obstruct, hamper; **~se** *vr* (*aturdirse*) to become embarrassed; (*confundirse*) to get into a mess.
embarazo [emba'raθo] *nm* (*de mujer*) pregnancy; (*impedimento*) obstacle, obstruction; (*timidez*) embarrassment.
embarazoso, a [embara'θoso, a] *adj* (*molesto*) awkward; (*violento*) embarrassing.
embarcación [embarka'θjon] *nf* (*barco*) boat, craft; (*acto*) embarkation; **~ de arrastre** trawler; **~ de cabotaje** coasting vessel.
embarcadero [embarka'ðero] *nm* pier, landing stage.
embarcar [embar'kar] *vt* (*cargamento*) to ship, stow; (*persona*) to embark, put on board; (*fig*): **~ a algn en una empresa** to involve sb in an undertaking; **~se** *vr* to embark, go on board; (*marinero*) to sign on; (*AM*: *en tren etc*) to get on, get in.
embargar [embar'ɣar] *vt* (*frenar*) to restrain; (*sentidos*) to overpower; (*JUR*) to seize, impound.
embargo [em'barɣo] *nm* (*JUR*) seizure; (*COM etc*) embargo; **sin ~** still, however, nonetheless.
embargue [em'barɣe] *etc vb V* **embargar**.
embarque [em'barke] *etc vb V* **embarcar** ♦ *nm* shipment, loading.
embarrancar [embarran'kar] *vt, vi* (*NAUT*) to run aground; (*AUTO etc*) to run into a ditch.
embarranque [emba'rranke] *etc vb V* **embarrancar**.
embarullar [embaru'ʎar] *vt* to make a mess of.
embate [em'bate] *nm* (*de mar, viento*) beating, violence.
embaucador, a [embauka'ðor, a] *nm/f* (*estafador*) trickster; (*impostor*) impostor.
embaucar [embau'kar] *vt* to trick, fool.
embauque [em'bauke] *etc vb V* **embaucar**.
embeber [embe'ßer] *vt* (*absorber*) to absorb, soak up; (*empapar*) to saturate ♦ *vi* to shrink; **~se** *vr*: **~se en un libro** to be engrossed *o* absorbed in a book.
embelesado, a [embele'saðo, a] *adj* spellbound.

embelesar [embele'sar] *vt* to enchant; **~se** *vr*: **~se (con)** to be enchanted (by).
embellecer [embeʎe'θer] *vt* to embellish, beautify.
embellezca [embe'ʎeθka] *etc vb V* **embellecer.**
embestida [embes'tiða] *nf* attack, onslaught; (*carga*) charge.
embestir [embes'tir] *vt* to attack, assault; to charge, attack ♦ *vi* to attack.
embistiendo [embis'tjendo] *etc vb V* **embestir.**
emblanquecer [emblanke'θer] *vt* to whiten, bleach; **~se** *vr* to turn white.
emblanquezca [emblan'keθka] *etc vb V* **emblanquecer.**
emblema [em'blema] *nm* emblem.
embobado, a [embo'ßaðo, a] *adj* (*atontado*) stunned, bewildered.
embobar [embo'ßar] *vt* (*asombrar*) to amaze; (*fascinar*) to fascinate; **~se** *vr*: **~se con** *o* **de** *o* **en** to be amazed at; to be fascinated by.
embocadura [emboka'ðura] *nf* narrow entrance; (*de río*) mouth; (*MUS*) mouthpiece.
embolado [embo'laðo] *nm* (*TEAT*) bit part, minor role; (*fam*) trick.
embolia [em'bolja] *nf* (*MED*) embolism; **~ cerebral** clot on the brain.
émbolo ['embolo] *nm* (*AUTO*) piston.
embolsar [embol'sar] *vt* to pocket, put in one's pocket.
emboquillado, a [emboki'ʎaðo, a] *adj* (*cigarrillo*) tipped, filter *cpd.*
emborrachar [emborra'tʃar] *vt* to make drunk; **~se** *vr* to get drunk.
emboscada [embos'kaða] *nf* (*celada*) ambush.
embotar [embo'tar] *vt* to blunt, dull; **~se** *vr* (*adormecerse*) to go numb.
embotellamiento [emboteʎa'mjento] *nm* (*AUTO*) traffic jam.
embotellar [embote'ʎar] *vt* to bottle; **~se** *vr* (*circulación*) to get into a jam.
embozo [em'boθo] *nm* muffler, mask; (*de sábana*) turn over.
embragar [embra'ɣar] *vt* (*AUTO, TEC*) to engage; (*partes*) to connect ♦ *vi* to let in the clutch.
embrague [em'braɣe] *etc vb V* **embragar** ♦ *nm* (*tb*: **pedal de ~**) clutch.
embravecer [embraße'θer] *vt* to enrage, infuriate; **~se** *vr* to become furious; (*mar*) to get rough; (*tormenta*) to rage.
embravecido, a [embraße'θiðo, a] *adj* (*mar*) rough; (*persona*) furious.
embriagador, a [embrjaɣa'ðor, a] *adj* intoxicating.
embriagar [embrja'ɣar] *vt* (*emborrachar*) to make drunk; (*alegrar*) to delight; **~se** *vr* (*emborracharse*) to get drunk.
embriague [em'brjaɣe] *etc vb V* **embriagar.**
embriaguez [embrja'ɣeθ] *nf* (*borrachera*) drunkenness.
embrión [em'brjon] *nm* embryo.
embrionario, a [embrjo'narjo, a] *adj* embryonic.
embrollar [embro'ʎar] *vt* (*asunto*) to confuse, complicate; (*persona*) to involve, embroil; **~se** *vr* (*confundirse*) to get into a muddle *o* mess.
embrollo [em'broʎo] *nm* (*enredo*) muddle, confusion; (*aprieto*) fix, jam.
embromado, a [embro'maðo, a] *adj* (*AM fam*) tricky, difficult.
embromar [embro'mar] *vt* (*burlarse de*) to tease, make fun of; (*AM fam: molestar*) to annoy.
embrujado, a [embru'xaðo, a] *adj* (*persona*) bewitched; **casa embrujada** haunted house.
embrujo [em'bruxo] *nm* (*de mirada etc*) charm, magic.
embrutecer [embrute'θer] *vt* (*atontar*) to stupefy; **~se** *vr* to be stupefied.
embrutezca [embru'teθka] *etc vb V* **embrutecer.**
embudo [em'buðo] *nm* funnel.
embuste [em'buste] *nm* trick; (*mentira*) lie; (*hum*) fib.
embustero, a [embus'tero, a] *adj* lying, deceitful ♦ *nm/f* (*tramposo*) cheat; (*mentiroso*) liar; (*hum*) fibber.
embutido [embu'tiðo] *nm* (*CULIN*) sausage; (*TEC*) inlay.
embutir [embu'tir] *vt* to insert; (*TEC*) to inlay; (*llenar*) to pack tight, cram.
emergencia [emer'xenθja] *nf* emergency; (*surgimiento*) emergence.
emergente [emer'xente] *adj* resultant, consequent; (*nación*) emergent.
emerger [emer'xer] *vi* to emerge, appear.
emeritense [emeri'tense] *adj* of *o* from Mérida ♦ *nm/f* native *o* inhabitant of Mérida.
emerja [e'merxa] *etc vb V* **emerger.**
emigración [emiɣra'θjon] *nf* emigration; (*de pájaros*) migration.
emigrado, a [emi'ɣraðo, a] *nm/f* emigrant; (*POL etc*) émigré(e).
emigrante [emi'ɣrante] *adj, nm/f* emigrant.
emigrar [emi'ɣrar] *vi* (*personas*) to emigrate; (*pájaros*) to migrate.
eminencia [emi'nenθja] *nf* eminence; (*en títulos*): **Su E~** His Eminence; **Vuestra**

E~ Your Eminence.
eminente [emi'nente] *adj* eminent, distinguished; (*elevado*) high.
emisario [emi'sarjo] *nm* emissary.
emisión [emi'sjon] *nf* (*acto*) emission; (*COM etc*) issue; (*RADIO, TV*: *acto*) broadcasting; (: *programa*) broadcast, programme, program (*US*); **~ de acciones** (*COM*) share issue; **~ gratuita de acciones** (*COM*) rights issue; **~ de valores** (*COM*) flotation.
emisor, a [emi'sor, a] *nm* transmitter ♦ *nf* radio *o* broadcasting station.
emitir [emi'tir] *vt* (*olor etc*) to emit, give off; (*moneda etc*) to issue; (*opinión*) to express; (*voto*) to cast; (*señal*) to send out; (*RADIO*) to broadcast; **~ una señal sonora** to beep.
emoción [emo'θjon] *nf* emotion; (*excitación*) excitement; (*sentimiento*) feeling; **¡qué ~!** how exciting!; (*irónico*) what a thrill!
emocionado, a [emoθjo'naðo, a] *adj* deeply moved, stirred.
emocionante [emoθjo'nante] *adj* (*excitante*) exciting, thrilling.
emocionar [emoθjo'nar] *vt* (*excitar*) to excite, thrill; (*conmover*) to move, touch; (*impresionar*) to impress; **~se** *vr* to get excited.
emotivo, a [emo'tiβo, a] *adj* emotional.
empacar [empa'kar] *vt* (*gen*) to pack; (*en caja*) to bale, crate.
empacharse [empa'tʃarse] *vr* (*MED*) to get indigestion.
empacho [em'patʃo] *nm* (*MED*) indigestion; (*fig*) embarrassment.
empadronamiento [empaðrona'mjento] *nm* census; (*de electores*) electoral register.
empadronarse [empaðro'narse] *vr* (*POL*: *como elector*) to register.
empalagar [empala'ɣar] *vt* (*suj*: *comida*) to cloy; (*hartar*) to pall on ♦ *vi* to pall.
empalagoso, a [empala'ɣoso, a] *adj* cloying; (*fig*) tiresome.
empalague [empa'laɣe] *etc vb V* **empalagar**.
empalizada [empali'θaða] *nf* fence; (*MIL*) palisade.
empalmar [empal'mar] *vt* to join, connect ♦ *vi* (*dos caminos*) to meet, join.
empalme [em'palme] *nm* joint, connection; (*de vías*) junction; (*de trenes*) connection.
empanada [empa'naða] *nf* pie, pasty.
empanar [empa'nar] *vt* (*CULIN*) to cook *o* roll in breadcrumbs *o* pastry.
empantanarse [empanta'narse] *vr* to get swamped; (*fig*) to get bogged down.
empañarse [empa'ɲarse] *vr* (*nublarse*) to get misty, steam up.
empapar [empa'par] *vt* (*mojar*) to soak, saturate; (*absorber*) to soak up, absorb; **~se** *vr*: **~se de** to soak up.
empapelar [empape'lar] *vt* (*paredes*) to paper.
empaque [em'pake] *etc vb V* **empacar**.
empaquetar [empake'tar] *vt* to pack, parcel up; (*COM*) to package.
emparedado [empare'ðaðo] *nm* sandwich.
emparejar [empare'xar] *vt* to pair ♦ *vi* to catch up.
emparentar [emparen'tar] *vi*: **~ con** to marry into.
empariente [empa'rjente] *etc vb V* **emparentar**.
empastar [empas'tar] *vt* (*embadurnar*) to paste; (*diente*) to fill.
empaste [em'paste] *nm* (*de diente*) filling.
empatar [empa'tar] *vi* to draw, tie.
empate [em'pate] *nm* draw, tie; **un ~ a cero** a no-score draw.
empecé [empe'θe], **empecemos** [empe'θemos] *etc vb V* **empezar**.
empecinado, a [empeθi'naðo, a] *adj* stubborn.
empedernido, a [empeðer'niðo, a] *adj* hard, heartless; (*fijado*) hardened, inveterate; **un fumador ~** a heavy smoker.
empedrado, a [empe'ðraðo, a] *adj* paved ♦ *nm* paving.
empedrar [empe'ðrar] *vt* to pave.
empeine [em'peine] *nm* (*de pie, zapato*) instep.
empellón [empe'ʎon] *nm* push, shove; **abrirse paso a empellones** to push *o* shove one's way past *o* through.
empeñado, a [empe'ɲaðo, a] *adj* (*persona*) determined; (*objeto*) pawned.
empeñar [empe'ɲar] *vt* (*objeto*) to pawn, pledge; (*persona*) to compel; **~se** *vr* (*obligarse*) to bind o.s., pledge o.s.; (*endeudarse*) to get into debt; **~se en hacer** to be set on doing, be determined to do.
empeño [em'peɲo] *nm* (*determinación*) determination; (*cosa prendada*) pledge; **casa de ~s** pawnshop; **con ~** insistently; (*con celo*) eagerly; **tener ~ en hacer algo** to be bent on doing sth.
empeoramiento [empeora'mjento] *nm* worsening.
empeorar [empeo'rar] *vt* to make worse, worsen ♦ *vi* to get worse, deteriorate.
empequeñecer [empekeɲe'θer] *vt* to

dwarf; (*fig*) to belittle.
empequeñezca [empeke'ɲeθka] *etc vb V* **empequeñecer**.
emperador [empera'ðor] *nm* emperor.
emperatriz [empera'triθ] *nf* empress.
emperrarse [empe'rrarse] *vr* to get stubborn; ~ **en algo** to persist in sth.
empezar [empe'θar] *vt, vi* to begin, start; **empezó a llover** it started to rain; **bueno, para** ~ well, to start with.
empiece [em'pjeθe] *etc vb V* **empezar**.
empiedre [em'pjeðre] *etc vb V* **empedrar**.
empiezo [em'pjeθo] *etc vb V* **empezar**.
empinado, a [empi'naðo, a] *adj* steep.
empinar [empi'nar] *vt* to raise; (*botella*) to tip up; ~**se** *vr* (*persona*) to stand on tiptoe; (*animal*) to rear up; (*camino*) to climb steeply; ~ **el codo** to booze (*fam*).
empingorotado, a [empingoro'taðo, a] *adj* (*fam*) stuck-up.
empírico, a [em'piriko, a] *adj* empirical.
emplace [em'plaθe] *etc vb V* **emplazar**.
emplaste [em'plaste], **emplasto** [em'plasto] *nm* (*MED*) plaster.
emplazamiento [emplaθa'mjento] *nm* site, location; (*JUR*) summons *sg*.
emplazar [empla'θar] *vt* (*ubicar*) to site, place, locate; (*JUR*) to summons; (*convocar*) to summon.
empleado, a [emple'aðo, a] *nm/f* (*gen*) employee; (*de banco etc*) clerk; ~ **público** civil servant.
emplear [emple'ar] *vt* (*usar*) to use, employ; (*dar trabajo a*) to employ; ~**se** *vr* (*conseguir trabajo*) to be employed; (*ocuparse*) to occupy o.s.; ~ **mal el tiempo** to waste time; **¡te está bien empleado!** it serves you right!
empleo [em'pleo] *nm* (*puesto*) job; (*puestos: colectivamente*) employment; (*uso*) use, employment; **"modo de ~"** "instructions for use".
emplumar [emplu'mar] *vt* (*estafar*) to swindle.
empobrecer [empoβre'θer] *vt* to impoverish; ~**se** *vr* to become poor *o* impoverished.
empobrecimiento [empoβreθi'mjento] *nm* impoverishment.
empobrezca [empo'βreθka] *etc vb V* **empobrecer**.
empollar [empo'ʎar] *vt* to incubate; (*ESCOL fam*) to swot (up) ♦ *vi* (*gallina*) to brood; (*ESCOL fam*) to swot.
empollón, ona [empo'ʎon, ona] *nm/f* (*ESCOL fam*) swot.
empolvar [empol'βar] *vt* (*cara*) to powder; ~**se** *vr* to powder one's face; (*superficie*) to get dusty.
emponzoñar [emponθo'ɲar] *vt* (*esp fig*) to poison.
emporio [em'porjo] *nm* emporium, trading centre; (*AM: gran almacén*) department store.
empotrado, a [empo'traðo, a] *adj* (*armario etc*) built-in.
empotrar [empo'trar] *vt* to embed; (*armario etc*) to build in.
emprendedor, a [emprende'ðor, a] *adj* enterprising.
emprender [empren'der] *vt* to undertake; (*empezar*) to begin, embark on; (*acometer*) to tackle, take on; ~ **marcha a** to set out for.
empresa [em'presa] *nf* enterprise; (*COM: sociedad*) firm, company; (*: negocio*) business; (*esp TEAT*) management; ~ **filial** (*COM*) affiliated company; ~ **matriz** (*COM*) parent company.
empresario, a [empre'sarjo, a] *nm/f* (*COM*) businessman/woman, entrepreneur; (*TEC*) manager; (*MUS: de ópera etc*) impresario; ~ **de pompas fúnebres** undertaker (*BRIT*), mortician (*US*).
empréstito [em'prestito] *nm* (public) loan; (*COM*) loan capital.
empujar [empu'xar] *vt* to push, shove.
empuje [em'puxe] *nm* thrust; (*presión*) pressure; (*fig*) vigour, drive.
empujón [empu'xon] *nm* push, shove; **abrirse paso a empujones** to shove one's way through.
empuñadura [empuɲa'ðura] *nf* (*de espada*) hilt; (*de herramienta etc*) handle.
empuñar [empu'ɲar] *vt* (*asir*) to grasp, take (firm) hold of; ~ **las armas** (*fig*) to take up arms.
emulación [emula'θjon] *nf* emulation.
emular [emu'lar] *vt* to emulate; (*rivalizar*) to rival.
émulo, a ['emulo, a] *nm/f* rival, competitor.
emulsión [emul'sjon] *nf* emulsion.

PALABRA CLAVE

en [en] *prep* **1** (*posición*) in; (*: sobre*) on; **está ~ el cajón** it's in the drawer; ~ **Argentina/La Paz** in Argentina/La Paz; ~ **el colegio/la oficina** at school/the office; ~ **casa** at home; **está ~ el suelo/quinto piso** it's on the floor/the fifth floor; ~ **el periódico** in the paper
2 (*dirección*) into; **entró ~ el aula** she went into the classroom; **meter algo ~ el bolso** to put sth into one's bag; **ir de puerta ~ puerta** to go from door to door

3 (*tiempo*) in; on; ~ **1605/3 semanas/invierno** in 1605/3 weeks/winter; ~ **(el mes de) enero** in (the month of) January; ~ **aquella ocasión/época** on that occasion/at that time
4 (*precio*) for; **lo vendió ~ 20 dólares** he sold it for 20 dollars
5 (*diferencia*) by; **reducir/aumentar ~ una tercera parte/un 20 por ciento** to reduce/increase by a third/20 per cent
6 (*manera, forma*): ~ **avión/autobús** by plane/bus; **escrito ~ inglés** written in English; ~ **serio** seriously; ~ **espiral/círculo** in a spiral/circle
7 (*después de vb que indica gastar etc*) on; **han cobrado demasiado ~ dietas** they've charged too much to expenses; **se le va la mitad del sueldo ~ comida** half his salary goes on food
8 (*tema, ocupación*): **experto ~ la materia** expert on the subject; **trabaja ~ la construcción** he works in the building industry
9 (*adj + ~ + infin*): **lento ~ reaccionar** slow to react.

enagua(s) [enaɣwa(s)] *nf(pl)* (*esp AM*) petticoat.
enajenación [enaxena'θjon] *nf*, **enajenamiento** [enaxena'mjento] *nm* alienation; (*fig*: *distracción*) absent-mindedness; (: *embelesamiento*) rapture, trance; ~ **mental** mental derangement.
enajenar [enaxe'nar] *vt* to alienate; (*fig*) to carry away.
enamorado, a [enamo'raðo, a] *adj* in love ♦ *nm/f* lover; **estar ~ (de)** to be in love (with).
enamorar [enamo'rar] *vt* to win the love of; **~se** *vr*: **~se (de)** to fall in love (with).
enano, a [e'nano, a] *adj* tiny, dwarf ♦ *nm/f* dwarf; (*pey*) runt.
enarbolar [enarβo'lar] *vt* (*bandera etc*) to hoist; (*espada etc*) to brandish.
enardecer [enarðe'θer] *vt* (*pasiones*) to fire, inflame; (*persona*) to fill with enthusiasm; **~se** *vr* to get excited; **~se por** to get enthusiastic about.
enardezca [enar'deθka] *etc vb V* **enardecer**.
encabece [enka'βeθe] *etc vb V* **encabezar**.
encabezado [enkaβe'θaðo] *nm* (*COM*) header.
encabezamiento [enkaβeθa'mjento] *nm* (*de carta*) heading; (*COM*) billhead, letterhead; (*de periódico*) headline; (*preámbulo*) foreword, preface; ~ **normal** (*TIP etc*) running head.
encabezar [enkaβe'θar] *vt* (*movimiento, revolución*) to lead, head; (*lista*) to head; (*carta*) to put a heading to; (*libro*) to entitle.
encadenar [enkaðe'nar] *vt* to chain (together); (*poner grilletes a*) to shackle.
encajar [enka'xar] *vt* (*ajustar*): ~ **en** to fit (into); (*meter a la fuerza*) to push in; (*máquina etc*) to house; (*partes*) to join; (*fam*: *golpe*) to give, deal; (*entrometer*) to insert ♦ *vi* to fit (well); (*fig*: *corresponder a*) to match; **~se** *vr*: **~se en un sillón** to squeeze into a chair.
encaje [en'kaxe] *nm* (*labor*) lace.
encajonar [enkaxo'nar] *vt* to box (up), put in a box.
encalar [enka'lar] *vt* (*pared*) to whitewash.
encallar [enka'ʎar] *vi* (*NAUT*) to run aground.
encaminado, a [enkami'naðo, a] *adj*: **medidas encaminadas a ...** measures designed to *o* aimed at ....
encaminar [enkami'nar] *vt* to direct, send; **~se** *vr*: **~se a** to set out for; ~ **por** (*expedición etc*) to route via.
encandilar [enkandi'lar] *vt* to dazzle; (*persona*) to daze, bewilder.
encanecer [enkane'θer] *vi*, **encanecerse** *vr* (*pelo*) to go grey.
encanezca [enka'neθka] *etc vb V* **encanecer**.
encantado, a [enkan'taðo, a] *adj* delighted; ¡~! how do you do!, pleased to meet you.
encantador, a [enkanta'ðor, a] *adj* charming, lovely ♦ *nm/f* magician, enchanter/enchantress.
encantar [enkan'tar] *vt* to charm, delight; (*cautivar*) to fascinate; (*hechizar*) to bewitch, cast a spell on.
encanto [en'kanto] *nm* (*magia*) spell, charm; (*fig*) charm, delight; (*expresión de ternura*) sweetheart; **como por ~** as if by magic.
encapotado, a [enkapo'taðo, a] *adj* (*cielo*) overcast.
encapricharse [enkapri'tʃarse] *vr*: **se ha encaprichado con ir** he's taken it into his head to go; **se ha encaprichado** he's digging his heels in.
encaramar [enkara'mar] *vt* (*subir*) to raise, lift up; **~se** *vr* (*subir*) to perch; **~se a** (*árbol etc*) to climb.
encararse [enka'rarse] *vr*: ~ **a** *o* **con** to confront, come face to face with.
encarcelar [enkarθe'lar] *vt* to imprison, jail.
encarecer [enkare'θer] *vt* to put up the price of ♦ *vi*, **~se** *vr* to get dearer.

encarecidamente [enkareθiða'mente] *adv* earnestly.
encarecimiento [enkareθi'mjento] *nm* price increase.
encarezca [enka'reθka] *etc vb V* **encarecer**.
encargado, a [enkar'ɣaðo, a] *adj* in charge ♦ *nm/f* agent, representative; (*responsable*) person in charge.
encargar [enkar'ɣar] *vt* to entrust; (*COM*) to order; (*recomendar*) to urge, recommend; **~se** *vr*: **~se de** to look after, take charge of; **~ algo a algn** to put sb in charge of sth.
encargo [en'karɣo] *nm* (*pedido*) assignment, job; (*responsabilidad*) responsibility; (*recomendación*) recommendation; (*COM*) order.
encargue [en'karɣe] *etc vb V* **encargar**.
encariñarse [enkari'ɲarse] *vr*: **~ con** to grow fond of, get attached to.
encarnación [enkarna'θjon] *nf* incarnation, embodiment.
encarnado, a [enkar'naðo, a] *adj* (*color*) red; **ponerse ~** to blush.
encarnar [enkar'nar] *vt* to personify; (*TEAT*: *papel*) to play ♦ *vi* (*REL etc*) to become incarnate.
encarnizado, a [enkarni'θaðo, a] *adj* (*lucha*) bloody, fierce.
encarrilar [enkarri'lar] *vt* (*tren*) to put back on the rails; (*fig*) to correct, put on the right track.
encasillar [enkasi'ʎar] *vt* (*TEAT*) to typecast; (*clasificar*: *pey*) to pigeonhole.
encasquetar [enkaske'tar] *vt* (*sombrero*) to pull down *o* on; **~se** *vr*: **~se el sombrero** to pull one's hat down *o* on; **~ algo a algn** to offload sth onto sb.
encauce [en'kauθe] *etc vb V* **encauzar**.
encausar [enkau'sar] *vt* to prosecute, sue.
encauzar [enkau'θar] *vt* to channel; (*fig*) to direct.
encendedor [enθende'ðor] *nm* lighter.
encender [enθen'der] *vt* (*con fuego*) to light; (*incendiar*) to set fire to; (*luz, radio*) to put on, switch on; (*INFORM*) to toggle on, switch on; (*avivar*: *pasiones etc*) to inflame; (*despertar*: *entusiasmo*) to arouse; (*odio*) to awaken; **~se** *vr* to catch fire; (*excitarse*) to get excited; (*de cólera*) to flare up; (*el rostro*) to blush.
encendidamente [enθendiða'mente] *adv* passionately.
encendido, a [enθen'diðo, a] *adj* alight; (*aparato*) (switched) on; (*mejillas*) glowing; (*cara*: *por el vino etc*) flushed; (*mirada*) passionate ♦ *nm* (*AUTO*) ignition; (*de faroles*) lighting.
encerado, a [enθe'raðo, a] *adj* (*suelo*) waxed, polished ♦ *nm* (*ESCOL*) blackboard; (*hule*) oilcloth.
encerar [enθe'rar] *vt* (*suelo*) to wax, polish.
encerrar [enθe'rrar] *vt* (*confinar*) to shut in *o* up; (*con llave*) to lock in *o* up; (*comprender, incluir*) to include, contain; **~se** *vr* to shut *o* lock o.s. up *o* in.
encerrona [enθe'rrona] *nf* trap.
encestar [enθes'tar] *vi* to score a basket.
encharcar [entʃar'kar] *vt* to swamp, flood; **~se** *vr* to become flooded.
encharque [en'tʃarke] *etc vb V* **encharcar**.
enchufar [entʃu'far] *vt* (*ELEC*) to plug in; (*TEC*) to connect, fit together; (*COM*) to merge.
enchufe [en'tʃufe] *nm* (*ELEC*: *clavija*) plug; (: *toma*) socket; (*de dos tubos*) joint, connection; (*fam*: *influencia*) contact, connection; (: *puesto*) cushy job; **~ de clavija** jack plug; **tiene un ~ en el ministerio** he can pull strings at the ministry.
encía [en'θia] *nf* (*ANAT*) gum.
enciclopedia [enθiklo'peðja] *nf* encyclopaedia.
encienda [en'θjenda] *etc vb V* **encender**.
encierro [en'θjerro] *etc vb V* **encerrar** ♦ *nm* shutting in *o* up; (*calabozo*) prison; (*AGR*) pen; (*TAUR*) penning.
encima [en'θima] *adv* (*sobre*) above, over; (*además*) besides; **~ de** (*en*) on, on top of; (*sobre*) above, over; (*además de*) besides, on top of; **por ~ de** over; **¿llevas dinero ~?** have you (got) any money on you?; **se me vino ~** it took me by surprise.
encina [en'θina] *nf* (holm) oak.
encinta [en'θinta] *adj f* pregnant.
enclave [en'klaβe] *nm* enclave.
enclenque [en'klenke] *adj* weak, sickly.
encoger [enko'xer] *vt* (*gen*) to shrink, contract; (*fig*: *asustar*) to scare; (: *desanimar*) to discourage; **~se** *vr* to shrink, contract; (*fig*) to cringe; **~se de hombros** to shrug one's shoulders.
encoja [en'koxa] *etc vb V* **encoger**.
encolar [enko'lar] *vt* (*engomar*) to glue, paste; (*pegar*) to stick down.
encolerice [enkole'riθe] *etc vb V* **encolerizar**.
encolerizar [enkoleri'θar] *vt* to anger, provoke; **~se** *vr* to get angry.
encomendar [enkomen'dar] *vt* to entrust, commend; **~se** *vr*: **~se a** to put one's trust in.
encomiar [enko'mjar] *vt* to praise, pay tribute to.
encomienda [enko'mjenda] *etc vb V*

encomendar ♦ *nf* (*encargo*) charge, commission; (*elogio*) tribute; (*AM*) parcel, package; ~ **postal** (*AM*) parcel post.
encomio [en'komjo] *nm* praise, tribute.
encono [en'kono] *nm* (*rencor*) rancour, spite.
encontrado, a [enkon'traðo, a] *adj* (*contrario*) contrary, conflicting; (*hostil*) hostile.
encontrar [enkon'trar] *vt* (*hallar*) to find; (*inesperadamente*) to meet, run into; ~**se** *vr* to meet (each other); (*situarse*) to be (situated); (*persona*) to find o.s., be; (*entrar en conflicto*) to crash, collide; ~**se con** to meet; ~**se bien (de salud)** to feel well; **no se encuentra aquí en este momento** he's not in at the moment.
encontronazo [enkontro'naθo] *nm* collision, crash.
encorvar [enkor'ßar] *vt* to curve; (*inclinar*) to bend (down); ~**se** *vr* to bend down, bend over.
encrespado, a [enkres'paðo, a] *adj* (*pelo*) curly; (*mar*) rough.
encrespar [enkres'par] *vt* (*cabellos*) to curl; (*fig*) to anger, irritate; ~**se** *vr* (*el mar*) to get rough; (*fig*) to get cross *o* irritated.
encrucijada [enkruθi'xaða] *nf* crossroads *sg*; (*empalme*) junction.
encuadernación [enkwaðerna'θjon] *nf* binding; (*taller*) binder's.
encuadernador, a [enkwaðerna'ðor, a] *nm/f* bookbinder.
encuadrar [enkwa'ðrar] *vt* (*retrato*) to frame; (*ajustar*) to fit, insert; (*encerrar*) to contain.
encubierto [enku'ßjerto] *pp de* **encubrir**.
encubrir [enku'ßrir] *vt* (*ocultar*) to hide, conceal; (*criminal*) to harbour, shelter; (*ayudar*) to be an accomplice in.
encuentro [en'kwentro] *etc vb V* **encontrar** ♦ *nm* (*de personas*) meeting; (*AUTO etc*) collision, crash; (*DEPORTE*) match, game; (*MIL*) encounter.
encuesta [en'kwesta] *nf* inquiry, investigation; (*sondeo*) public opinion poll; ~ **judicial** post mortem.
encumbrado, a [enkum'braðo, a] *adj* eminent, distinguished.
encumbrar [enkum'brar] *vt* (*persona*) to exalt; ~**se** *vr* (*fig*) to become conceited.
endeble [en'deßle] *adj* (*argumento, excusa, persona*) weak.
endémico, a [en'demiko, a] *adj* endemic.
endemoniado, a [endemo'njaðo, a] *adj* possessed (of the devil); (*travieso*) devilish.
enderece [ende'reθe] *etc vb V* **enderezar**.
enderezar [endere'θar] *vt* (*poner derecho*) to straighten (out); (: *verticalmente*) to set upright; (*fig*) to straighten *o* sort out; (*dirigir*) to direct; ~**se** *vr* (*persona sentada*) to sit up straight.
endeudarse [endeu'ðarse] *vr* to get into debt.
endiablado, a [endja'ßlaðo, a] *adj* devilish, diabolical; (*hum*) mischievous.
endibia [en'dißja] *nf* endive.
endilgar [endil'ɣar] *vt* (*fam*): ~ **algo a algn** to lumber sb with sth; ~ **un sermón a algn** to give sb a lecture.
endilgue [en'dilɣe] *etc vb V* **endilgar**.
endiñar [endi'ɲar] *vt*: ~ **algo a algn** to land sth on sb.
endomingarse [endomin'garse] *vr* to dress up, put on one's best clothes.
endomingue [endo'minge] *etc vb V* **endomingarse**.
endosar [endo'sar] *vt* (*cheque etc*) to endorse.
endulce [en'dulθe] *etc vb V* **endulzar**.
endulzar [endul'θar] *vt* to sweeten; (*suavizar*) to soften.
endurecer [endure'θer] *vt* to harden; ~**se** *vr* to harden, grow hard.
endurecido, a [endure'θiðo, a] *adj* (*duro*) hard; (*fig*) hardy, tough; **estar ~ a algo** to be hardened *o* used to sth.
endurezca [endu'reθka] *etc vb V* **endurecer**.
ene. *abr* (= *enero*) Jan.
enemigo, a [ene'miɣo, a] *adj* enemy, hostile ♦ *nm/f* enemy ♦ *nf* enmity, hostility; **ser ~ de** (*persona*) to dislike; (*suj*: *tendencia*) to be inimical to.
enemistad [enemis'tað] *nf* enmity.
enemistar [enemis'tar] *vt* to make enemies of, cause a rift between; ~**se** *vr* to become enemies; (*amigos*) to fall out.
energético, a [ener'xetiko, a] *adj*: **política energética** energy policy.
energía [ener'xia] *nf* (*vigor*) energy, drive; (*TEC, ELEC*) energy, power; ~ **atómica/eléctrica/eólica** atomic/electric/wind power.
enérgico, a [e'nerxiko, a] *adj* (*gen*) energetic; (*ataque*) vigorous; (*ejercicio*) strenuous; (*medida*) bold; (*voz, modales*) forceful.
energúmeno, a [ener'ɣumeno, a] *nm/f* madman/woman; **ponerse como un ~ con algn** to get furious with sb.
enero [e'nero] *nm* January.
enervar [ener'ßar] *vt* (*poner nervioso a*) to get on sb's nerves.
enésimo, a [e'nesimo, a] *adj* (*MAT*) nth; **por enésima vez** (*fig*) for the umpteenth

time.
enfadado, a [enfa'ðaðo, a] *adj* angry, annoyed.
enfadar [enfa'ðar] *vt* to anger, annoy; **~se** *vr* to get angry *o* annoyed.
enfado [en'faðo] *nm* (*enojo*) anger, annoyance; (*disgusto*) trouble, bother.
énfasis ['enfasis] *nm* emphasis, stress; **poner ~ en** to stress.
enfático, a [en'fatiko, a] *adj* emphatic.
enfatizado, a [enfati'θaðo, a] *adj*: **en caracteres ~s** (*INFORM*) emphasized.
enfermar [enfer'mar] *vt* to make ill ♦ *vi* to fall ill, be taken ill; **su actitud me enferma** his attitude makes me sick; **~ del corazón** to develop heart trouble.
enfermedad [enferme'ðað] *nf* illness; **~ venérea** venereal disease.
enfermera [enfer'mera] *nf V* **enfermero**.
enfermería [enferme'ria] *nf* infirmary; (*de colegio etc*) sick bay.
enfermero, a [enfer'mero, a] *nm* (male) nurse ♦ *nf* nurse; **enfermera jefa** matron.
enfermizo, a [enfer'miθo, a] *adj* (*persona*) sickly, unhealthy; (*fig*) unhealthy.
enfermo, a [en'fermo, a] *adj* ill, sick ♦ *nm/f* invalid, sick person; (*en hospital*) patient.
enfilar [enfi'lar] *vt* (*aguja*) to thread; (*calle*) to go down.
enflaquecer [enflake'θer] *vt* (*adelgazar*) to make thin; (*debilitar*) to weaken.
enflaquezca [enfla'keθka] *etc vb V* **enflaquecer**.
enfocar [enfo'kar] *vt* (*foto etc*) to focus; (*problema etc*) to consider, look at.
enfoque [en'foke] *etc vb V* **enfocar** ♦ *nm* focus; (*acto*) focusing; (*óptica*) approach.
enfrascado, a [enfras'kaðo, a] *adj*: **estar ~ en algo** (*fig*) to be wrapped up in sth.
enfrascarse [enfras'karse] *vr*: **~ en un libro** to bury o.s. in a book.
enfrasque [en'fraske] *etc vb V* **enfrascar**.
enfrentamiento [enfrenta'mjento] *nm* confrontation.
enfrentar [enfren'tar] *vt* (*peligro*) to face (up to), confront; (*oponer*) to bring face to face; **~se** *vr* (*dos personas*) to face *o* confront each other; (*DEPORTE: dos equipos*) to meet; **~se a** *o* **con** to face up to, confront.
enfrente [en'frente] *adv* opposite; **~ de** *prep* opposite, facing; **la casa de ~** the house opposite, the house across the street.
enfriamiento [enfria'mjento] *nm* chilling, refrigeration; (*MED*) cold, chill.
enfriar [enfri'ar] *vt* (*alimentos*) to cool, chill; (*algo caliente*) to cool down; (*habitación*) to air, freshen; (*entusiasmo*) to dampen; **~se** *vr* to cool down; (*MED*) to catch a chill; (*amistad*) to cool.
enfurecer [enfure'θer] *vt* to enrage, madden; **~se** *vr* to become furious, fly into a rage; (*mar*) to get rough.
enfurezca [enfu'reθka] *etc vb V* **enfurecer**.
engalanar [engala'nar] *vt* (*adornar*) to adorn; (*ciudad*) to decorate; **~se** *vr* to get dressed up.
enganchar [engan'tʃar] *vt* to hook; (*ropa*) to hang up; (*dos vagones*) to hitch up; (*TEC*) to couple, connect; (*MIL*) to recruit; (*fam: atraer: persona*) to rope into; **~se** *vr* (*MIL*) to enlist, join up; **~se (a)** (*drogas*) to get hooked (on).
enganche [en'gantʃe] *nm* hook; (*TEC*) coupling, connection; (*acto*) hooking (up); (*MIL*) recruitment, enlistment; (*AM: depósito*) deposit.
engañar [enga'ɲar] *vt* to deceive; (*estafar*) to cheat, swindle ♦ *vi*: **las apariencias engañan** appearances are deceptive; **~se** *vr* (*equivocarse*) to be wrong; (*asimismo*) to deceive *o* kid o.s.; **engaña a su mujer** he's unfaithful to *o* cheats on his wife.
engaño [en'gaɲo] *nm* deceit; (*estafa*) trick, swindle; (*error*) mistake, misunderstanding; (*ilusión*) delusion.
engañoso, a [enga'ɲoso, a] *adj* (*tramposo*) crooked; (*mentiroso*) dishonest, deceitful; (*aspecto*) deceptive; (*consejo*) misleading.
engarce [en'garθe] *etc vb V* **engarzar**.
engarzar [engar'θar] *vt* (*joya*) to set, mount; (*fig*) to link, connect.
engatusar [engatu'sar] *vt* (*fam*) to coax.
engendrar [enxen'drar] *vt* to breed; (*procrear*) to beget; (*fig*) to cause, produce.
engendro [en'xendro] *nm* (*BIO*) foetus; (*fig*) monstrosity; (*idea*) brainchild.
englobar [englo'βar] *vt* (*comprender*) to include, comprise; (*incluir*) to lump together.
engomar [engo'mar] *vt* to glue, stick.
engordar [engor'ðar] *vt* to fatten ♦ *vi* to get fat, put on weight.
engorro [en'gorro] *nm* bother, nuisance.
engorroso, a [engo'rroso, a] *adj* bothersome, trying.
engranaje [engra'naxe] *nm* (*AUTO*) gear; (*juego*) gears *pl*.
engrandecer [engrande'θer] *vt* to enlarge, magnify; (*alabar*) to praise, speak highly of; (*exagerar*) to exaggerate.
engrandezca [engran'deθka] *etc vb V*

engrandecer.
engrasar [engra'sar] *vt* (*TEC*: *poner grasa*) to grease; (: *lubricar*) to lubricate, oil; (*manchar*) to make greasy.
engrase [en'grase] *nm* greasing, lubrication.
engreído, a [engre'iðo, a] *adj* vain, conceited.
engrosar [engro'sar] *vt* (*ensanchar*) to enlarge; (*aumentar*) to increase; (*hinchar*) to swell.
engrudo [en'gruðo] *nm* paste.
engruese [en'grwese] *etc vb V* **engrosar**.
engullir [engu'ʎir] *vt* to gobble, gulp (down).
enhebrar [ene'ßrar] *vt* to thread.
enhiesto, a [e'njesto, a] *adj* (*derecho*) erect; (*bandera*) raised; (*edificio*) lofty.
enhorabuena [enora'ßwena] *excl* congratulations.
enigma [e'niɣma] *nm* enigma; (*problema*) puzzle; (*misterio*) mystery.
enigmático, a [eniɣ'matiko, a] *adj* enigmatic.
enjabonar [enxaßo'nar] *vt* to soap; (*barba*) to lather; (*fam*: *adular*) to soft-soap; (: *regañar*) to tick off.
enjalbegar [enxalße'ɣar] *vt* (*pared*) to whitewash.
enjalbegue [enxal'ßeɣe] *etc vb V* **enjalbegar**.
enjambre [en'xamßre] *nm* swarm.
enjaular [enxau'lar] *vt* to (put in a) cage; (*fam*) to jail, lock up.
enjuagar [enxwa'ɣar] *vt* (*ropa*) to rinse (out).
enjuague [en'xwaɣe] *etc vb V* **enjuagar** ♦ *nm* (*MED*) mouthwash; (*de ropa*) rinse, rinsing.
enjugar [enxu'ɣar] *vt* to wipe (off); (*lágrimas*) to dry; (*déficit*) to wipe out.
enjugue [en'xuɣe] *etc vb V* **enjugar**.
enjuiciar [enxwi'θjar] *vt* (*JUR*: *procesar*) to prosecute, try; (*fig*) to judge.
enjuto, a [en'xuto, a] *adj* dry, dried up; (*fig*) lean, skinny.
enlace [en'laθe] *etc vb V* **enlazar** ♦ *nm* link, connection; (*relación*) relationship; (*tb*: **~ matrimonial**) marriage; (*de trenes*) connection; **~ de datos** data link; **~ sindical** shop steward; **~ telefónico** telephone link-up.
enlazar [enla'θar] *vt* (*unir con lazos*) to bind together; (*atar*) to tie; (*conectar*) to link, connect; (*AM*) to lasso.
enlodar [enlo'ðar] *vt* to cover in mud; (*fig*: *manchar*) to stain; (: *rebajar*) to debase.
enloquecer [enloke'θer] *vt* to drive mad ♦ *vi*, **~se** *vr* to go mad.
enloquezca [enlo'keθka] *etc vb V* **enloquecer**.
enlutado, a [enlu'taðo, a] *adj* (*persona*) in mourning.
enlutar [enlu'tar] *vt* to dress in mourning; **~se** *vr* to go into mourning.
enmarañar [enmara'ɲar] *vt* (*enredar*) to tangle up, entangle; (*complicar*) to complicate; (*confundir*) to confuse; **~se** *vr* (*enredarse*) to become entangled; (*confundirse*) to get confused.
enmarcar [enmar'kar] *vt* (*cuadro*) to frame; (*fig*) to provide a setting for.
enmarque [en'marke] *etc vb V* **enmarcar**.
enmascarar [enmaska'rar] *vt* to mask; (*intenciones*) to disguise; **~se** *vr* to put on a mask.
enmendar [enmen'dar] *vt* to emend, correct; (*constitución etc*) to amend; (*comportamiento*) to reform; **~se** *vr* to reform, mend one's ways.
enmienda [en'mjenda] *etc vb V* **enmendar** ♦ *nf* correction; amendment; reform.
enmohecerse [enmoe'θerse] *vr* (*metal*) to rust, go rusty; (*muro, plantas*) to go mouldy.
enmohezca [enmo'eθka] *etc vb V* **enmohecerse**.
enmudecer [enmuðe'θer] *vt* to silence ♦ *vi*, **~se** *vr* (*perder el habla*) to fall silent; (*guardar silencio*) to remain silent; (*por miedo*) to be struck dumb.
enmudezca [enmu'ðeθka] *etc vb V* **enmudecer**.
ennegrecer [enneɣre'θer] *vt* (*poner negro*) to blacken; (*oscurecer*) to darken; **~se** *vr* to turn black; (*oscurecerse*) to get dark, darken.
ennegrezca [enne'ɣreθka] *etc vb V* **ennegrecer**.
ennoblecer [ennoßle'θer] *vt* to ennoble.
ennoblezca [enno'ßleθka] *etc vb V* **ennoblecer**.
en.° *abr* (= *enero*) Jan.
enojadizo, a [enoxa'ðiθo, a] *adj* irritable, short-tempered.
enojar [eno'xar] (*esp AM*) *vt* (*encolerizar*) to anger; (*disgustar*) to annoy, upset; **~se** *vr* to get angry; to get annoyed.
enojo [e'noxo] (*esp AM*) *nm* (*cólera*) anger; (*irritación*) annoyance; **~s** *nmpl* trials, problems.
enojoso, a [eno'xoso, a] *adj* annoying.
enorgullecerse [enorɣuʎe'θerse] *vr* to be proud; **~ de** to pride o.s. on, be proud of.
enorgullezca [enorɣu'ʎeθka] *etc vb V* **enorgullecerse**.

enorme [e'norme] *adj* enormous, huge; (*fig*) monstrous.
enormidad [enormi'ðað] *nf* hugeness, immensity.
enraice [en'raiθe] *etc vb V* **enraizar.**
enraizar [enrai'θar] *vi* to take root.
enrarecido, a [enrare'θiðo, a] *adj* rarefied.
enredadera [enreða'ðera] *nf* (*BOT*) creeper, climbing plant.
enredar [enre'ðar] *vt* (*cables, hilos etc*) to tangle (up), entangle; (*situación*) to complicate, confuse; (*meter cizaña*) to sow discord among *o* between; (*implicar*) to embroil, implicate; ~**se** *vr* to get entangled, get tangled (up); (*situación*) to get complicated; (*persona*) to get embroiled.
enredo [en'reðo] *nm* (*maraña*) tangle; (*confusión*) mix-up, confusion; (*intriga*) intrigue; (*apuro*) jam; (*amorío*) love affair.
enrejado [enre'xaðo] *nm* grating; (*de ventana*) lattice; (*en jardín*) trellis.
enrevesado, a [enreβe'saðo, a] *adj* (*asunto*) complicated, involved.
enriquecer [enrike'θer] *vt* to make rich; (*fig*) to enrich; ~**se** *vr* to get rich.
enriquezca [enri'keθka] *etc vb V* **enriquecer.**
enrojecer [enroxe'θer] *vt* to redden ♦ *vi*, ~**se** *vr* (*persona*) to blush.
enrojezca [enro'xeθka] *etc vb V* **enrojecer.**
enrolar [enro'lar] *vt* (*MIL*) to enlist; (*reclutar*) to recruit; ~**se** *vr* (*MIL*) to join up; (*afiliarse*) to enrol, sign on.
enrollar [enro'ʎar] *vt* to roll (up), wind (up); ~**se** *vr*: ~**se con algn** to get involved with sb.
enroque [en'roke] *nm* (*AJEDREZ*) castling.
enroscar [enros'kar] *vt* (*torcer, doblar*) to twist; (*arrollar*) to coil (round), wind; (*tornillo, rosca*) to screw in; ~**se** *vr* to coil, wind.
enrosque [en'roske] *etc vb V* **enroscar.**
ensalada [ensa'laða] *nf* salad; (*lío*) mix-up.
ensaladilla [ensala'ðiʎa] *nf* (*tb*: ~ **rusa**) ≈ Russian salad.
ensalce [en'salθe] *etc vb V* **ensalzar.**
ensalzar [ensal'θar] *vt* (*alabar*) to praise, extol; (*exaltar*) to exalt.
ensamblador [ensambla'ðor] *nm* (*INFORM*) assembler.
ensambladura [ensambla'ðura] *nf*, **ensamblaje** [ensam'blaxe] *nm* assembly; (*TEC*) joint.
ensamblar [ensam'blar] *vt* (*montar*) to assemble; (*madera etc*) to join.
ensanchar [ensan'tʃar] *vt* (*hacer más ancho*) to widen; (*agrandar*) to enlarge, expand; (*COSTURA*) to let out; ~**se** *vr* to get wider, expand; (*pey*) to give o.s. airs.
ensanche [en'santʃe] *nm* (*de calle*) widening; (*de negocio*) expansion.
ensangrentado, a [ensangren'taðo, a] *adj* bloodstained, covered with blood.
ensangrentar [ensangren'tar] *vt* to stain with blood.
ensangriente [ensan'grjente] *etc vb V* **ensangrentar.**
ensañarse [ensa'ɲarse] *vr*: ~ **con** to treat brutally.
ensartar [ensar'tar] *vt* (*gen*) to string (together); (*carne*) to spit, skewer.
ensayar [ensa'jar] *vt* to test, try (out); (*TEAT*) to rehearse.
ensayista [ensa'jista] *nm/f* essayist.
ensayo [en'sajo] *nm* test, trial; (*QUÍMICA*) experiment; (*TEAT*) rehearsal; (*DEPORTE*) try; (*ESCOL, LITERATURA*) essay; **pedido de** ~ (*COM*) trial order; ~ **general** (*TEAT*) dress rehearsal; (*MUS*) full rehearsal.
enseguida [ense'ɣuiða] *adv* at once, right away; ~ **termino** I've nearly finished, I shan't be long now.
ensenada [ense'naða] *nf* inlet, cove.
enseña [en'seɲa] *nf* ensign, standard.
enseñante [ense'ɲante] *nm/f* teacher.
enseñanza [ense'ɲanθa] *nf* (*educación*) education; (*acción*) teaching; (*doctrina*) teaching, doctrine; ~ **primaria/secundaria/superior** primary/secondary/higher education.
enseñar [ense'ɲar] *vt* (*educar*) to teach; (*instruir*) to teach, instruct; (*mostrar, señalar*) to show.
enseres [en'seres] *nmpl* belongings.
ENSIDESA [ensi'ðesa] *abr* (*ESP COM*) = *Empresa Nacional Siderúrgica, S. A.*
ensillar [ensi'ʎar] *vt* to saddle (up).
ensimismarse [ensimis'marse] *vr* (*abstraerse*) to become lost in thought; (*estar absorto*) to be lost in thought; (*AM*) to become conceited.
ensopar [enso'par] *vt* (*AM*) to soak.
ensordecer [ensorðe'θer] *vt* to deafen ♦ *vi* to go deaf.
ensordezca [ensor'ðeθka] *etc vb V* **ensordecer.**
ensortijado, a [ensorti'xaðo, a] *adj* (*pelo*) curly.
ensuciar [ensu'θjar] *vt* (*manchar*) to dirty, soil; (*fig*) to defile; ~**se** *vr* (*mancharse*) to get dirty; (*niño*) to dirty (*o* wet) o.s.
ensueño [en'sweɲo] *nm* (*sueño*) dream, fantasy; (*ilusión*) illusion; (*soñando despierto*) daydream; **de** ~ dream-like.

entablado [enta'ßlaðo] *nm* (*piso*) floorboards *pl;* (*armazón*) boarding.
entablar [enta'ßlar] *vt* (*recubrir*) to board (up); (*AJEDREZ, DAMAS*) to set up; (*conversación*) to strike up; (*JUR*) to file ♦ *vi* to draw.
entablillar [entaßli'ʎar] *vt* (*MED*) to (put in a) splint.
entallado, a [enta'ʎaðo, a] *adj* waisted.
entallar [enta'ʎar] *vt* (*traje*) to tailor ♦ *vi*: **el traje entalla bien** the suit fits well.
ente ['ente] *nm* (*organización*) body, organization; (*compañía*) company; (*fam: persona*) odd character; (*ser*) being; ~ **público** (*ESP*) state(-owned) body.
entender [enten'der] *vt* (*comprender*) to understand; (*darse cuenta*) to realize; (*querer decir*) to mean ♦ *vi* to understand; (*creer*) to think, believe ♦ *nm*: **a mi** ~ in my opinion; ~ **de** to know all about; ~ **algo de** to know a little about; ~ **en** to deal with, have to do with; ~**se** *vr* (*comprenderse*) to be understood; (*2 personas*) to get on together; (*ponerse de acuerdo*) to agree, reach an agreement; **dar a** ~ **que** ... to lead to believe that ...; ~**se mal** to get on badly; **¿entiendes?** (do you) understand?
entendido, a [enten'diðo, a] *adj* (*comprendido*) understood; (*hábil*) skilled; (*inteligente*) knowledgeable ♦ *nm/f* (*experto*) expert ♦ *excl* agreed!
entendimiento [entendi'mjento] *nm* (*comprensión*) understanding; (*inteligencia*) mind, intellect; (*juicio*) judgement.
enterado, a [ente'raðo, a] *adj* well-informed; **estar** ~ **de** to know about, be aware of; **no darse por** ~ to pretend not to understand.
enteramente [entera'mente] *adv* entirely, completely.
enterarse [ente'rarse] *vr*: ~ **(de)** to find out (about); **para que te enteres** ... (*fam*) for your information ....
entereza [ente'reθa] *nf* (*totalidad*) entirety; (*fig: carácter*) strength of mind; (*honradez*) integrity.
enternecedor, a [enterneθe'ðor, a] *adj* touching.
enternecer [enterne'θer] *vt* (*ablandar*) to soften; (*apiadar*) to touch, move; ~**se** *vr* to be touched, be moved.
enternezca [enter'neθka] *etc vb V* **enternecer**.
entero, a [en'tero, a] *adj* (*total*) whole, entire; (*fig: recto*) honest; (*: firme*) firm, resolute ♦ *nm* (*MAT*) integer; (*COM: punto*) point; (*AM: pago*) payment; **las acciones han subido dos ~s** the shares have gone up two points.
enterrador [enterra'ðor] *nm* gravedigger.
enterrar [ente'rrar] *vt* to bury; (*fig*) to forget.
entibiar [enti'ßjar] *vt* (*enfriar*) to cool; (*calentar*) to warm; ~**se** *vr* (*fig*) to cool.
entidad [enti'ðað] *nf* (*empresa*) firm, company; (*organismo*) body; (*sociedad*) society; (*FILOSOFÍA*) entity.
entienda [en'tjenda] *etc vb V* **entender**.
entierro [en'tjerro] *etc vb V* **enterrar** ♦ *nm* (*acción*) burial; (*funeral*) funeral.
entomología [entomolo'xia] *nf* entomology.
entomólogo, a [ento'moloɣo, a] *nm/f* entomologist.
entonación [entona'θjon] *nf* (*LING*) intonation; (*fig*) conceit.
entonar [ento'nar] *vt* (*canción*) to intone; (*colores*) to tone; (*MED*) to tone up ♦ *vi* to be in tune; ~**se** *vr* (*engreírse*) to give o.s. airs.
entonces [en'tonθes] *adv* then, at that time; **desde** ~ since then; **en aquel** ~ at that time; **(pues)** ~ and so; **el** ~ **embajador de España** the then Spanish ambassador.
entornar [entor'nar] *vt* (*puerta, ventana*) to half close, leave ajar; (*los ojos*) to screw up.
entorno [en'torno] *nm* setting, environment; ~ **de redes** (*INFORM*) network environment.
entorpecer [entorpe'θer] *vt* (*entendimiento*) to dull; (*impedir*) to obstruct, hinder; (*: tránsito*) to slow down, delay.
entorpezca [entor'peθka] *etc vb V* **entorpecer**.
entrado, a [en'traðo, a] *adj*: ~ **en años** elderly; **(una vez)** ~ **el verano** in the summer(time), when summer comes ♦ *nf* (*acción*) entry, access; (*sitio*) entrance, way in; (*principio*) beginning; (*COM*) receipts *pl*, takings *pl*; (*CULIN*) entrée; (*DEPORTE*) innings *sg*; (*TEAT*) house, audience; (*para el cine etc*) ticket; (*INFORM*) input; (*ECON*): **entradas** *nfpl* income *sg*; **entradas brutas** gross receipts; **entradas y salidas** (*COM*) income and expenditure; **entrada de aire** (*TEC*) air intake *o* inlet; **de entrada** right away; **"entrada gratis"** "admission free"; **entrada de datos vocal** (*INFORM*) voice input; **tiene entradas** he's losing his hair.

entrante [en'trante] *adj* next, coming; (*POL*) incoming ♦ *nm* inlet; (*CULIN*) starter; **mes/año** ~ next month/year.
entraña [en'traɲa] *nf* (*fig: centro*) heart, core; (*raíz*) root; ~**s** *nfpl* (*ANAT*) entrails; (*fig*) heart *sg*.
entrañable [entra'ɲaßle] *adj* (*persona, lugar*) dear; (*relación*) close; (*acto*) intimate.
entrañar [entra'ɲar] *vt* to entail.
entrar [en'trar] *vt* (*introducir*) to bring in; (*persona*) to show in; (*INFORM*) to input ♦ *vi* (*meterse*) to go *o* come in, enter; (*comenzar*): ~ **diciendo** to begin by saying; **entré en** *o* **a** (*AM*) **la casa** I went into the house; **le entraron ganas de reír** he felt a sudden urge to laugh; **no me entra** I can't get the hang of it.
entre ['entre] *prep* (*dos*) between; (*en medio de*) among(st); (*por*): **se abrieron paso** ~ **la multitud** they forced their way through the crowd; ~ **una cosa y otra** what with one thing and another; ~ **más estudia más aprende** (*AM*) the more he studies the more he learns.
entreabierto [entrea'ßjerto] *pp de* **entreabrir**.
entreabrir [entrea'ßrir] *vt* to half-open, open halfway.
entreacto [entre'akto] *nm* interval.
entrecano, a [entre'kano, a] *a* greying; **ser** ~ (*persona*) to be going grey.
entrecejo [entre'θexo] *nm*: **fruncir el** ~ to frown.
entrechocar [entretʃo'kar] *vi* (*dientes*) to chatter.
entrechoque [entre'tʃoke] *etc vb V* **entrechocar**.
entrecomillado, a [entrekomi'ʎaðo, a] *adj* in inverted commas.
entrecortado, a [entrekor'taðo, a] *adj* (*respiración*) laboured, difficult; (*habla*) faltering.
entrecot [entre'ko(t)] *nm* (*CULIN*) sirloin steak.
entrecruce [entre'kruθe] *etc vb V* **entrecruzarse**.
entrecruzarse [entrekru'θarse] *vr* (*BIO*) to interbreed.
entredicho [entre'ðitʃo] *nm* (*JUR*) injunction; **poner en** ~ to cast doubt on; **estar en** ~ to be in doubt.
entrega [en'treɣa] *nf* (*de mercancías*) delivery; (*de premios*) presentation; (*de novela etc*) instalment; **"~ a domicilio"** "door-to-door delivery service".
entregar [entre'ɣar] *vt* (*dar*) to hand (over), deliver; (*ejercicios*) to hand in; ~**se** *vr* (*rendirse*) to surrender, give in, submit; ~**se a** (*dedicarse*) to devote o.s. to; **a** ~ (*COM*) to be supplied.
entregue [en'treɣe] *etc vb V* **entregar**.
entrelace [entre'laθe] *etc vb V* **entrelazar**.
entrelazar [entrela'θar] *vt* to entwine.
entremedias [entre'meðjas] *adv* (*en medio*) in between, halfway.
entremeses [entre'meses] *nmpl* hors d'œuvres.
entremeter [entreme'ter] *vt* to insert, put in; ~**se** *vr* to meddle, interfere.
entremetido, a [entreme'tiðo, a] *adj* meddling, interfering.
entremezclar [entremeθ'klar] *vt*, ~**se** *vr* to intermingle.
entrenador, a [entrena'ðor, a] *nm/f* trainer, coach.
entrenamiento [entrena'mjento] *nm* training.
entrenar [entre'nar] *vt* (*DEPORTE*) to train; (*caballo*) to exercise ♦ *vi*, ~**se** *vr* to train.
entrepierna [entre'pjerna] *nf* (*tb*: ~**s**) crotch, crutch.
entresacar [entresa'kar] *vt* to pick out, select.
entresaque [entre'sake] *etc vb V* **entresacar**.
entresuelo [entre'swelo] *nm* mezzanine, entresol; (*TEAT*) dress *o* first circle.
entretanto [entre'tanto] *adv* meanwhile, meantime.
entretejer [entrete'xer] *vt* to interweave.
entretela [entre'tela] *nf* (*de ropa*) interlining; ~**s** *nfpl* heart-strings.
entretención [entreten'sjon] *nf* (*AM*) entertainment.
entretendré [entreten'dre] *etc vb V* **entretener**.
entretener [entrete'ner] *vt* (*divertir*) to entertain, amuse; (*detener*) to hold up, delay; (*mantener*) to maintain; ~**se** *vr* (*divertirse*) to amuse o.s.; (*retrasarse*) to delay, linger; **no le entretengo más** I won't keep you any longer.
entretenga [entrete'tenga] *etc vb V* **entretener**.
entretenido, a [entrete'niðo, a] *adj* entertaining, amusing.
entretenimiento [entreteni'mjento] *nm* entertainment, amusement; (*mantenimiento*) upkeep, maintenance.
entretiempo [entre'tjempo] *nm*: **ropa de** ~ *clothes for spring and autumn*.
entretiene [entre'tjene] *etc*, **entretuve** [entre'tuße] *etc vb V* **entretener**.
entreveía [entreße'ia] *etc vb V* **entrever**.
entrever [entre'ßer] *vt* to glimpse, catch a

glimpse of.
entrevista [entre'ßista] *nf* interview.
entrevistar [entreßis'tar] *vt* to interview; **~se** *vr*: **~se con** to have an interview with, see; **el ministro se entrevistó con el Rey ayer** the minister had an audience with the King yesterday.
entrevisto [entre'ßisto] *pp de* **entrever.**
entristecer [entriste'θer] *vt* to sadden, grieve; **~se** *vr* to grow sad.
entristezca [entris'teθka] *etc vb V* **entristecer.**
entrometerse [entrome'terse] *vr*: **~ (en)** to interfere (in *o* with).
entrometido, a [entrome'tiðo, a] *adj* interfering, meddlesome.
entroncar [entron'kar] *vi* to be connected *o* related.
entronque [en'tronke] *etc vb V* **entroncar.**
entuerto [en'twerto] *nm* wrong, injustice; **~s** *nmpl* (*MED*) afterpains.
entumecer [entume'θer] *vt* to numb, benumb; **~se** *vr* (*por el frío*) to go *o* become numb.
entumecido, a [entume'θiðo, a] *adj* numb, stiff.
entumezca [entu'meθka] *etc vb V* **entumecer.**
enturbiar [entur'ßjar] *vt* (*el agua*) to make cloudy; (*fig*) to confuse; **~se** *vr* (*oscurecerse*) to become cloudy; (*fig*) to get confused, become obscure.
entusiasmar [entusjas'mar] *vt* to excite, fill with enthusiasm; (*gustar mucho*) to delight; **~se** *vr*: **~se con** *o* **por** to get enthusiastic *o* excited about.
entusiasmo [entu'sjasmo] *nm* enthusiasm; (*excitación*) excitement.
entusiasta [entu'sjasta] *adj* enthusiastic ♦ *nm/f* enthusiast.
enumerar [enume'rar] *vt* to enumerate.
enunciación [enunθja'θjon] *nf*, **enunciado** [enun'θjaðo] *nm* enunciation; (*declaración*) declaration, statement.
enunciar [enun'θjar] *vt* to enunciate; to declare, state.
envainar [embai'nar] *vt* to sheathe.
envalentonar [embalento'nar] *vt* to give courage to; **~se** *vr* (*pey: jactarse*) to boast, brag.
envanecer [embane'θer] *vt* to make conceited; **~se** *vr* to grow conceited.
envanezca [emba'neθka] *etc vb V* **envanecer.**
envasar [emba'sar] *vt* (*empaquetar*) to pack, wrap; (*enfrascar*) to bottle; (*enlatar*) to can; (*embolsar*) to pocket.
envase [em'base] *nm* packing, wrapping; bottling; canning; pocketing; (*recipiente*) container; (*paquete*) package; (*botella*) bottle; (*lata*) tin (*BRIT*), can.
envejecer [embexe'θer] *vt* to make old, age ♦ *vi*, **~se** *vr* (*volverse viejo*) to grow old; (*parecer viejo*) to age.
envejecido, a [embexe'θiðo, a] *adj* old, aged; (*de aspecto*) old-looking.
envejezca [embe'xeθka] *etc vb V* **envejecer.**
envenenar [embene'nar] *vt* to poison; (*fig*) to embitter.
envergadura [emberɣa'ðura] *nf* (*expansión*) expanse; (*NAUT*) breadth; (*fig*) scope; **un programa de gran ~** a wide-ranging programme.
envés [em'bes] *nm* (*de tela*) back, wrong side.
enviado, a [em'bjaðo, a] *nm/f* (*POL*) envoy; **~ especial** (*de periódico, TV*) special correspondent.
enviar [em'bjar] *vt* to send.
enviciar [embi'θjar] *vt* to corrupt ♦ *vi* (*trabajo etc*) to be addictive; **~se** *vr*: **~se (con** *o* **en)** to get addicted (to).
envidia [em'biðja] *nf* envy; **tener ~ a** to envy, be jealous of.
envidiar [embi'ðjar] *vt* (*desear*) to envy; (*tener celos de*) to be jealous of.
envidioso, a [embi'ðjoso, a] *adj* envious, jealous.
envío [em'bio] *nm* (*acción*) sending; (*de mercancías*) consignment; (*de dinero*) remittance; (*en barco*) shipment; **gastos de ~** postage and packing; **~ contra reembolso** COD shipment.
enviudar [embju'ðar] *vi* to be widowed.
envoltura [embol'tura] *nf* (*cobertura*) cover; (*embalaje*) wrapper, wrapping.
envolver [embol'ßer] *vt* to wrap (up); (*cubrir*) to cover; (*enemigo*) to surround; (*implicar*) to involve, implicate.
envuelto [em'bwelto], **envuelva** [em'bwelßa] *etc vb V* **envolver.**
enyesar [enje'sar] *vt* (*pared*) to plaster; (*MED*) to put in plaster.
enzarzarse [enθar'θarse] *vr*: **~ en algo** to get mixed up in sth.
epa ['epa], **épale** ['epale] (*AM*) *excl* hey!, wow!
E.P.D. *abr* (= *en paz descanse*) R.I.P.
epicentro [epi'θentro] *nm* epicentre.
épico, a ['epiko, a] *adj* epic ♦ *nf* epic (poetry).
epidemia [epi'ðemja] *nf* epidemic.
epidémico, a [epi'ðemiko, a] *adj* epidemic.
epidermis [epi'ðermis] *nf* epidermis.
epifanía [epifa'nia] *nf* Epiphany.
epilepsia [epi'lepsja] *nf* epilepsy.

epiléptico, a [epi'leptiko, a] *adj, nm/f* epileptic.
epílogo [e'piloɣo] *nm* epilogue.
episcopado [episko'paðo] *nm* (*cargo*) bishopric; (*obispos*) bishops *pl* (*collectively*).
episodio [epi'soðjo] *nm* episode; (*suceso*) incident.
epístola [e'pistola] *nf* epistle.
epitafio [epi'tafjo] *nm* epitaph.
epíteto [e'piteto] *nm* epithet.
época ['epoka] *nf* period, time; (*temporada*) season; (*HISTORIA*) age, epoch; **hacer ~** to be epoch-making.
equidad [eki'ðað] *nf* equity, fairness.
equilibrar [ekili'βrar] *vt* to balance.
equilibrio [eki'liβrjo] *nm* balance, equilibrium; **~ político** balance of power.
equilibrista [ekili'βrista] *nm/f* (*funámbulo*) tightrope walker; (*acróbata*) acrobat.
equinoccio [eki'nokθjo] *nm* equinox.
equipaje [eki'paxe] *nm* luggage (*BRIT*), baggage (*US*); (*avíos*) equipment, kit; **~ de mano** hand luggage; **hacer el ~** to pack.
equipar [eki'par] *vt* (*proveer*) to equip.
equiparar [ekipa'rar] *vt* (*igualar*) to put on the same level; (*comparar*) to compare (*con* with); **~se** *vr*: **~se con** to be on a level with.
equipo [e'kipo] *nm* (*conjunto de cosas*) equipment; (*DEPORTE, grupo*) team; (*de obreros*) shift; (*de máquinas*) plant; (*turbinas etc*) set; **~ de caza** hunting gear; **~ físico** (*INFORM*) hardware; **~ médico** medical team; **~ de música** music centre.
equis ['ekis] *nf* (the letter) X.
equitación [ekita'θjon] *nf* (*acto*) riding; (*arte*) horsemanship.
equitativo, a [ekita'tiβo, a] *adj* equitable, fair.
equivaldré [ekiβal'dre] *etc vb V* **equivaler**.
equivalencia [ekiβa'lenθja] *nf* equivalence.
equivalente [ekiβa'lente] *adj, nm* equivalent.
equivaler [ekiβa'ler] *vi*: **~ a** to be equivalent *o* equal to; (*en rango*) to rank as.
equivalga [eki'βalɣa] *etc vb V* **equivaler**.
equivocación [ekiβoka'θjon] *nf* mistake, error; (*malentendido*) misunderstanding.
equivocado, a [ekiβo'kaðo, a] *adj* wrong, mistaken.
equivocarse [ekiβo'karse] *vr* to be wrong, make a mistake; **~ de camino** to take the wrong road.
equívoco, a [e'kiβoko, a] *adj* (*dudoso*) suspect; (*ambiguo*) ambiguous ♦ *nm* ambiguity; (*malentendido*) misunderstanding.
equivoque [eki'βoke] *etc vb V* **equivocar**.
era ['era] *vb V* **ser** ♦ *nf* era, age; (*AGR*) threshing floor.
erais ['erais], **éramos** ['eramos], **eran** ['eran] *vb V* **ser**.
erario [e'rarjo] *nm* exchequer, treasury.
eras ['eras], **eres** ['eres] *vb V* **ser**.
erección [erek'θjon] *nf* erection.
ergonomía [erɣono'mia] *nf* ergonomics *sg*, human engineering.
erguir [er'ɣir] *vt* to raise, lift; (*poner derecho*) to straighten; **~se** *vr* to straighten up.
erice [e'riθe] *etc vb V* **erizarse**.
erigir [eri'xir] *vt* to erect, build; **~se** *vr*: **~se en** to set o.s. up as.
erija [e'rixa] *etc vb V* **erigir**.
erizado, a [eri'θaðo, a] *adj* bristly.
erizarse [eri'θarse] *vr* (*pelo: de perro*) to bristle; (*: de persona*) to stand on end.
erizo [e'riθo] *nm* hedgehog; **~ de mar** sea urchin.
ermita [er'mita] *nf* hermitage.
ermitaño, a [ermi'taɲo, a] *nm/f* hermit.
erosión [ero'sjon] *nf* erosion.
erosionar [erosjo'nar] *vt* to erode.
erótico, a [e'rotiko, a] *adj* erotic.
erotismo [ero'tismo] *nm* eroticism.
erradicar [erraði'kar] *vt* to eradicate.
erradique [erra'ðike] *etc vb V* **erradicar**.
errado, a [e'rraðo, a] *adj* mistaken, wrong.
errante [e'rrante] *adj* wandering, errant.
errar [e'rrar] *vi* (*vagar*) to wander, roam; (*equivocarse*) to be mistaken ♦ *vt*: **~ el camino** to take the wrong road; **~ el tiro** to miss.
errata [e'rrata] *nf* misprint.
erre ['erre] *nf* (the letter) R; **~ que ~** stubbornly.
erróneo, a [e'rroneo, a] *adj* (*equivocado*) wrong, mistaken; (*falso*) false, untrue.
error [e'rror] *nm* error, mistake; (*INFORM*) bug; **~ de imprenta** misprint; **~ de lectura/escritura** (*INFORM*) read/write error; **~ sintáctico** syntax error; **~ judicial** miscarriage of justice.
Ertzaintza [er'tʃantʃa] *nf* Basque police; *V tb* **policía**.
eructar [eruk'tar] *vt* to belch, burp.
eructo [e'rukto] *nm* belch.
erudición [eruði'θjon] *nf* erudition, learning.
erudito, a [eru'ðito, a] *adj* erudite, learned ♦ *nm/f* scholar; **los ~s en esta materia** the

experts in this field.
erupción [erup'θjon] *nf* eruption; (*MED*) rash; (*de violencia*) outbreak; (*de ira*) outburst.
es [es] *vb V* **ser**.
E/S *abr* (*INFORM*: *entrada/salida*) I/O.
esa ['esa], **esas** ['esas] *adj demostrativo V* **ese**.
ésa ['esa], **ésas** ['esas] *pron V* **ése**.
esbelto, a [es'ßelto, a] *adj* slim, slender.
esbirro [es'ßirro] *nm* henchman.
esbozar [esßo'θar] *vt* to sketch, outline.
esbozo [es'ßoθo] *nm* sketch, outline.
escabeche [eska'ßetʃe] *nm* brine; (*de aceitunas etc*) pickle; **en ~** pickled.
escabechina [eskaße'tʃina] *nf* (*batalla*) massacre; **hacer una ~** (*ESCOL*) to fail a lot of students.
escabroso, a [eska'ßroso, a] *adj* (*accidentado*) rough, uneven; (*fig*) tough, difficult; (: *atrevido*) risqué.
escabullirse [eskaßu'ʎirse] *vr* to slip away; (*largarse*) to clear out.
escacharrar [eskatʃa'rrar] *vt* (*fam*) to break; **~se** *vr* to get broken.
escafandra [eska'fandra] *nf* (*buzo*) diving suit; (*~ espacial*) spacesuit.
escala [es'kala] *nf* (*proporción, MUS*) scale; (*de mano*) ladder; (*AVIAT*) stopover; (*de colores etc*) range; **~ de tiempo** time scale; **~ de sueldos** salary scale; **una investigación a ~ nacional** a nationwide inquiry; **reproducir según ~** to reproduce to scale; **hacer ~ en** to stop off *o* over at.
escalada [eska'laða] *nf* (*de montaña*) climb; (*de pared*) scaling.
escalafón [eskala'fon] *nm* (*escala de salarios*) salary scale, wage scale.
escalar [eska'lar] *vt* to climb, scale ♦ *vi* (*MIL, POL*) to escalate.
escaldar [eskal'dar] *vt* (*quemar*) to scald; (*escarmentar*) to teach a lesson.
escalera [eska'lera] *nf* stairs *pl*, staircase; (*escala*) ladder; (*NAIPES*) run; (*de camión*) tailboard; **~ mecánica** escalator; **~ de caracol** spiral staircase; **~ de incendios** fire escape.
escalerilla [eskale'riʎa] *nf* (*de avión*) steps *pl*.
escalfar [eskal'far] *vt* (*huevos*) to poach.
escalinata [eskali'nata] *nf* staircase.
escalofriante [eskalo'frjante] *adj* chilling.
escalofrío [eskalo'frio] *nm* (*MED*) chill; **~s** *nmpl* (*fig*) shivers.
escalón [eska'lon] *nm* step, stair; (*de escalera*) rung; (*fig*: *paso*) step; (*al éxito*) ladder.
escalonar [eskalo'nar] *vt* to spread out; (*tierra*) to terrace; (*horas de trabajo*) to stagger.
escalope [eska'lope] *nm* (*CULIN*) escalope.
escama [es'kama] *nf* (*de pez, serpiente*) scale; (*de jabón*) flake; (*fig*) resentment.
escamar [eska'mar] *vt* (*pez*) to scale; (*producir recelo*) to make wary.
escamotear [eskamote'ar] *vt* (*fam*: *robar*) to lift, swipe; (*hacer desaparecer*) to make disappear.
escampar [eskam'par] *vb impersonal* to stop raining.
escanciar [eskan'θjar] *vt* (*vino*) to pour (out).
escandalice [eskanda'liθe] *etc vb V* **escandalizar**.
escandalizar [eskandali'θar] *vt* to scandalize, shock; **~se** *vr* to be shocked; (*ofenderse*) to be offended.
escándalo [es'kandalo] *nm* scandal; (*alboroto, tumulto*) row, uproar; **armar un ~** to make a scene; **¡es un ~!** it's outrageous!
escandaloso, a [eskanda'loso, a] *adj* scandalous, shocking; (*risa*) hearty; (*niño*) noisy.
Escandinavia [eskandi'naßja] *nf* Scandinavia.
escandinavo, a [eskandi'naßo, a] *adj, nm/f* Scandinavian.
escáner [es'kaner] *nm* scanner.
escaño [es'kaɲo] *nm* bench; (*POL*) seat.
escapada [eska'paða] *nf* (*huida*) escape, flight; (*deportes*) breakaway; (*viaje*) quick trip.
escapar [eska'par] *vi* (*gen*) to escape, run away; (*DEPORTE*) to break away; **~se** *vr* to escape, get away; (*agua, gas, noticias*) to leak (out); **se me escapa su nombre** his name escapes me.
escaparate [eskapa'rate] *nm* shop window; (*COM*) showcase.
escapatoria [eskapa'torja] *nf*: **no tener ~** (*fig*) to have no way out.
escape [es'kape] *nm* (*huida*) escape; (*de agua, gas*) leak; (*de motor*) exhaust; **salir a ~** to rush out.
escapismo [eska'pismo] *nm* escapism.
escaquearse [eskake'arse] *vr* (*fam*) to duck out.
escarabajo [eskara'ßaxo] *nm* beetle.
escaramuza [eskara'muθa] *nf* skirmish; (*fig*) brush.
escarbar [eskar'ßar] *vt* (*gallina*) to scratch; (*fig*) to inquire into, investigate.
escarceos [eskar'θeos] *nmpl*: **en sus ~ con la política** in his occasional forays into politics; **~ amorosos** flirtations.
escarcha [es'kartʃa] *nf* frost.

escarlata [eskar'lata] *adj inv* scarlet.
escarlatina [eskarla'tina] *nf* scarlet fever.
escarmentar [eskarmen'tar] *vt* to punish severely ♦ *vi* to learn one's lesson; **¡para que escarmientes!** that'll teach you!
escarmiento [eskar'mjento] *etc vb V* **escarmentar** ♦ *nm* (*ejemplo*) lesson; (*castigo*) punishment.
escarnio [es'karnjo] *nm* mockery; (*injuria*) insult.
escarola [eska'rola] *nf* (*BOT*) endive.
escarpado, a [eskar'paðo, a] *adj* (*pendiente*) sheer, steep; (*rocas*) craggy.
escasamente [eskasa'mente] *adv* (*insuficientemente*) scantily; (*apenas*) scarcely.
escasear [eskase'ar] *vi* to be scarce.
escasez [eska'seθ] *nf* (*falta*) shortage, scarcity; (*pobreza*) poverty; **vivir con ~** to live on the breadline.
escaso, a [es'kaso, a] *adj* (*poco*) scarce; (*raro*) rare; (*ralo*) thin, sparse; (*limitado*) limited; (*recursos*) scanty; (*público*) sparse; (*posibilidad*) slim; (*visibilidad*) poor.
escatimar [eskati'mar] *vt* (*limitar*) to skimp (on), be sparing with; **no ~ esfuerzos (para)** to spare no effort (to).
escayola [eska'jola] *nf* plaster.
escayolar [eskajo'lar] *vt* to put in plaster.
escena [es'θena] *nf* scene; (*decorado*) scenery; (*escenario*) stage; **poner en ~** to put on.
escenario [esθe'narjo] *nm* (*TEAT*) stage; (*CINE*) set; (*fig*) scene; **el ~ del crimen** the scene of the crime; **el ~ político** the political scene.
escenografía [esθenoɣra'fia] *nf* set *o* stage design.
escepticismo [esθepti'θismo] *nm* scepticism.
escéptico, a [es'θeptiko, a] *adj* sceptical ♦ *nm/f* sceptic.
escindir [esθin'dir] *vt* to split; **~se** *vr* (*facción*) to split off; **~se en** to split into.
escisión [esθi'sjon] *nf* (*MED*) excision; (*fig, POL*) split; **~ nuclear** nuclear fission.
esclarecer [esklare'θer] *vt* (*iluminar*) to light up, illuminate; (*misterio, problema*) to shed light on.
esclarezca [eskla'reθka] *etc vb V* **esclarecer**.
esclavice [eskla'βiθe] *etc vb V* **esclavizar**.
esclavitud [esklaβi'tuð] *nf* slavery.
esclavizar [esklaβi'θar] *vt* to enslave.
esclavo, a [es'klaβo, a] *nm/f* slave.
esclusa [es'klusa] *nf* (*de canal*) lock; (*compuerta*) floodgate.
escoba [es'koβa] *nf* broom; **pasar la ~** to sweep up.
escobazo [esko'βaθo] *nm* (*golpe*) blow with a broom; **echar a algn a ~s** to kick sb out.
escobilla [esko'βiʎa] *nf* brush.
escocer [esko'θer] *vi* to burn, sting; **~se** *vr* to chafe, get chafed.
escocés, esa [esko'θes, esa] *adj* Scottish; (*whisky*) Scotch ♦ *nm/f* Scotsman/woman, Scot ♦ *nm* (*LING*) Scots *sg*; **tela escocesa** tartan.
Escocia [es'koθja] *nf* Scotland.
escoger [esko'xer] *vt* to choose, pick, select.
escogido, a [esko'xiðo, a] *adj* chosen, selected; (*calidad*) choice, select; (*persona*): **ser muy ~** to be very fussy.
escoja [es'koxa] *etc vb V* **escoger**.
escolar [esko'lar] *adj* school *cpd* ♦ *nm/f* schoolboy/girl, pupil.
escolaridad [eskolari'ðað] *nf* schooling; **libro de ~** school record.
escolarización [eskolariθa'θjon] *nf*: **~ obligatoria** compulsory education.
escolarizado, a [eskolari'θaðo, a] *adj, nm/f*: **los ~s** those in *o* attending school.
escollo [es'koʎo] *nm* (*arrecife*) reef, rock; (*fig*) pitfall.
escolta [es'kolta] *nf* escort.
escoltar [eskol'tar] *vt* to escort; (*proteger*) to guard.
escombros [es'kombros] *nmpl* (*basura*) rubbish *sg*; (*restos*) debris *sg*.
esconder [eskon'der] *vt* to hide, conceal; **~se** *vr* to hide.
escondidas [eskon'diðas] *nfpl* (*AM*) hide-and-seek *sg*; **a ~** secretly; **hacer algo a ~ de algn** to do sth behind sb's back.
escondite [eskon'dite] *nm* hiding place; (*juego*) hide-and-seek.
escondrijo [eskon'drixo] *nm* hiding place, hideout.
escopeta [esko'peta] *nf* shotgun; **~ de aire comprimido** air gun.
escoria [es'korja] *nf* (*desecho mineral*) slag; (*fig*) scum, dregs *pl*.
Escorpio [es'korpjo] *nm* (*ASTRO*) Scorpio.
escorpión [eskor'pjon] *nm* scorpion.
escotado, a [esko'taðo, a] *adj* low-cut.
escotar [esko'tar] *vt* (*vestido*: *ajustar*) to cut to fit; (*cuello*) to cut low.
escote [es'kote] *nm* (*de vestido*) low neck; **pagar a ~** to share the expenses.
escotilla [esko'tiʎa] *nf* (*NAUT*) hatchway.
escotillón [eskoti'ʎon] *nm* trapdoor.
escozor [esko'θor] *nm* (*dolor*) sting(ing).
escribano, a [eskri'βano, a], **escribiente**

[eskri'ßjente] *nm/f* clerk; (*secretario judicial*) court *o* lawyer's clerk.
escribir [eskri'ßir] *vt, vi* to write; ~ **a máquina** to type; **¿cómo se escribe?** how do you spell it?
escrito, a [es'krito, a] *pp de* **escribir** ♦ *adj* written, in writing; (*examen*) written ♦ *nm* (*documento*) document; (*manuscrito*) text, manuscript; **por** ~ in writing.
escritor, a [eskri'tor, a] *nm/f* writer.
escritorio [eskri'torjo] *nm* desk; (*oficina*) office.
escritura [eskri'tura] *nf* (*acción*) writing; (*caligrafía*) (hand)writing; (*JUR: documento*) deed; (*COM*) indenture; ~ **de propiedad** title deed; **Sagrada E~** (Holy) Scripture; ~ **social** articles *pl* of association.
escroto [es'kroto] *nm* scrotum.
escrúpulo [es'krupulo] *nm* scruple; (*minuciosidad*) scrupulousness.
escrupuloso, a [eskrupu'loso, a] *adj* scrupulous.
escrutar [eskru'tar] *vt* to scrutinize, examine; (*votos*) to count.
escrutinio [eskru'tinjo] *nm* (*examen atento*) scrutiny; (*POL: recuento de votos*) count(ing).
escuadra [es'kwaðra] *nf* (*TEC*) square; (*MIL etc*) squad; (*NAUT*) squadron; (*de coches etc*) fleet.
escuadrilla [eskwa'ðriʎa] *nf* (*de aviones*) squadron.
escuadrón [eskwa'ðron] *nm* squadron.
escuálido, a [es'kwaliðo, a] *adj* skinny, scraggy; (*sucio*) squalid.
escucha [es'kutʃa] *nf* (*acción*) listening ♦ *nm* (*TELEC: sistema*) monitor; (*oyente*) listener; **estar a la** ~ to listen in; **estar de** ~ to spy; **~s teléfonicas** (phone) tapping *sg*.
escuchar [esku'tʃar] *vt* to listen to; (*consejo*) to heed; (*esp AM: oír*) to hear ♦ *vi* to listen; **~se** *vr*: **se escucha muy mal** (*TELEC*) it's a very bad line.
escudarse [esku'ðarse] *vr*: ~ **en** (*fig*) to hide behind.
escudería [eskuðe'ria] *nf*: **la** ~ **Ferrari** the Ferrari team.
escudero [esku'ðero] *nm* squire.
escudilla [esku'ðiʎa] *nf* bowl, basin.
escudo [es'kuðo] *nm* shield; ~ **de armas** coat of arms.
escudriñar [eskuðri'ɲar] *vt* (*examinar*) to investigate, scrutinize; (*mirar de lejos*) to scan.
escuece [es'kweθe] *etc vb V* **escocer.**
escuela [es'kwela] *nf* (*tb fig*) school; ~ **normal** teacher training college; ~ **técnica superior** *university offering 5-year courses in engineering and technical subjects*; ~ **universitaria** *university offering 3-year diploma courses;* ~ **de párvulos** kindergarten; *V tb* **colegio.**
escueto, a [es'kweto, a] *adj* plain; (*estilo*) simple; (*explicación*) concise.
escueza [es'kweθa] *etc vb V* **escocer.**
escuincle [es'kwinkle] *nm* (*AM fam*) kid.
esculpir [eskul'pir] *vt* to sculpt; (*grabar*) to engrave; (*tallar*) to carve.
escultor, a [eskul'tor, a] *nm/f* sculptor.
escultura [eskul'tura] *nf* sculpture.
escupidera [eskupi'ðera] *nf* spittoon.
escupir [esku'pir] *vt* to spit (out) ♦ *vi* to spit.
escupitajo [eskupi'taxo] *nm* (*fam*) gob of spit.
escurreplatos [eskurre'platos] *nm inv* plate rack.
escurridizo, a [eskurri'ðiθo, a] *adj* slippery.
escurrir [esku'rrir] *vt* (*ropa*) to wring out; (*verduras, platos*) to drain ♦ *vi* (*los líquidos*) to drip; **~se** *vr* (*secarse*) to drain; (*resbalarse*) to slip, slide; (*escaparse*) to slip away.
ese¹ ['ese] *nf* (the letter) S; **hacer ~s** (*carretera*) to zigzag; (*borracho*) to reel about.
ese² ['ese], **esa** ['esa], **esos** ['esos], **esas** ['esas] *adj demostrativo* (*sg*) that; (*pl*) those.
ése ['ese], **ésa** ['esa], **ésos** ['esos], **ésas** ['esas] *pron* (*sg*) that (one); (*pl*) those (ones); **ése ... éste** ... the former ... the latter ...; **¡no me vengas con ésas!** don't give me any more of that nonsense!
esencia [e'senθja] *nf* essence.
esencial [esen'θjal] *adj* essential; (*principal*) chief; **lo** ~ the main thing.
esfera [es'fera] *nf* sphere; (*de reloj*) face; ~ **de acción** scope; ~ **terrestre** globe.
esférico, a [es'feriko, a] *adj* spherical.
esfinge [es'finxe] *nf* sphinx.
esforcé [esfor'θe], **esforcemos** [esfor'θemos] *etc vb V* **esforzar.**
esforzado, a [esfor'θaðo, a] *adj* (*enérgico*) energetic, vigorous.
esforzarse [esfor'θarse] *vr* to exert o.s., make an effort.
esfuerce [es'fwerθe] *etc vb V* **esforzar.**
esfuerzo [es'fwerθo] *etc vb V* **esforzar** ♦ *nm* effort; **sin** ~ effortlessly.
esfumarse [esfu'marse] *vr* (*apoyo, esperanzas*) to fade away; (*persona*) to vanish.
esgrima [es'ɣrima] *nf* fencing.

esgrimidor [esɤrimi'ðor] *nm* fencer.
esgrimir [esɤri'mir] *vt* (*arma*) to brandish; (*argumento*) to use ♦ *vi* to fence.
esguince [es'ɤinθe] *nm* (*MED*) sprain.
eslabón [esla'ßon] *nm* link; ~ **perdido** (*BIO, fig*) missing link.
eslabonar [eslaßo'nar] *vt* to link, connect.
eslálom [es'lalom] *nm* slalom.
eslavo, a [es'laßo, a] *adj* Slav, Slavonic ♦ *nm/f* Slav ♦ *nm* (*LING*) Slavonic.
eslogan [es'loɤan] *nm, pl* **eslogans** slogan.
eslora [es'lora] *nf* (*NAUT*) length.
eslovaco, a [eslo'ßako, a] *adj, nm/f* Slovak, Slovakian ♦ *nm* (*LING*) Slovak, Slovakian.
Eslovaquia [eslo'ßakja] *nf* Slovakia.
Eslovenia [eslo'ßenja] *nf* Slovenia.
esloveno, a [eslo'ßeno, a] *adj, nm/f* Slovene, Slovenian ♦ *nm* (*LING*) Slovene, Slovenian.
esmaltar [esmal'tar] *vt* to enamel.
esmalte [es'malte] *nm* enamel; ~ **de uñas** nail varnish *o* polish.
esmerado, a [esme'raðo, a] *adj* careful, neat.
esmeralda [esme'ralda] *nf* emerald.
esmerarse [esme'rarse] *vr* (*aplicarse*) to take great pains, exercise great care; (*afanarse*) to work hard; (*hacer lo mejor*) to do one's best.
esmero [es'mero] *nm* (great) care.
esmirriado, a [esmi'rrjaðo, a] *adj* puny.
esmoquin [es'mokin] *nm* dinner jacket (*BRIT*), tuxedo (*US*).
esnob [es'nob] *adj inv* (*persona*) snobbish; (*coche etc*) posh ♦ *nm/f* snob.
esnobismo [esno'ßismo] *nm* snobbery.
eso ['eso] *pron* that, that thing *o* matter; ~ **de su coche** that business about his car; ~ **de ir al cine** all that about going to the cinema; **a ~ de las cinco** at about five o'clock; **en ~** thereupon, at that point; **por ~** therefore; **~ es** that's it; **nada de ~** far from it; **¡~ sí que es vida!** now this is really living!; **por ~ te lo dije** that's why I told you; **y ~ que llovía** in spite of the fact it was raining.
esófago [e'sofaɤo] *nm* (*ANAT*) oesophagus.
esos ['esos] *adj demostrativo V* **ese**.
ésos ['esos] *pron V* **ése**.
esotérico, a [eso'teriko, a] *adj* esoteric.
esp. *abr* (= *español*) Sp., Span.
espabilado, a [espaßi'laðo, a] *adj* quick-witted.
espabilar [espaßi'lar] *vt*, **espabilarse** *vr* = **despabilar(se)**.
espachurrar [espatʃu'rrar] *vt* to squash; **~se** *vr* to get squashed.
espaciado [espa'θjaðo] *nm* (*INFORM*) spacing.
espacial [espa'θjal] *adj* (*del espacio*) space *cpd*.
espaciar [espa'θjar] *vt* to space (out).
espacio [es'paθjo] *nm* space; (*MUS*) interval; (*RADIO, TV*) programme, program (*US*); **el ~** space; **ocupar mucho ~** to take up a lot of room; **a dos ~s, a doble ~** (*TIP*) double-spaced; **por ~ de** during, for.
espacioso, a [espa'θjoso, a] *adj* spacious, roomy.
espada [es'paða] *nf* sword ♦ *nm* swordsman; (*TAUR*) matador; **~s** *nfpl* (*NAIPES*) *one of the suits in the Spanish card deck*; **estar entre la ~ y la pared** to be between the devil and the deep blue sea; *V tb* **baraja española**.
espadachín [espaða'tʃin] *nm* (*esgrimidor*) skilled swordsman.
espaguetis [espa'ɤetis] *nmpl* spaghetti *sg*.
espalda [es'palda] *nf* (*gen*) back; (*NATACIÓN*) backstroke; **~s** *nfpl* (*hombros*) shoulders; **a ~s de algn** behind sb's back; **estar de ~s** to have one's back turned; **tenderse de ~s** to lie (down) on one's back; **volver la ~ a algn** to cold-shoulder sb.
espaldarazo [espalda'raθo] *nm* (*tb fig*) slap on the back.
espaldilla [espal'diʎa] *nf* shoulder blade.
espantadizo, a [espanta'ðiθo, a] *adj* timid, easily frightened.
espantajo [espan'taxo] *nm*, **espantapájaros** [espanta'paxaros] *nm inv* scarecrow.
espantar [espan'tar] *vt* (*asustar*) to frighten, scare; (*ahuyentar*) to frighten off; (*asombrar*) to horrify, appal; **~se** *vr* to get frightened *o* scared; to be appalled.
espanto [es'panto] *nm* (*susto*) fright; (*terror*) terror; (*asombro*) astonishment; **¡qué ~!** how awful!
espantoso, a [espan'toso, a] *adj* frightening, terrifying; (*ruido*) dreadful.
España [es'paɲa] *nf* Spain; **la ~ de pandereta** touristy Spain.
español, a [espa'ɲol, a] *adj* Spanish ♦ *nm/f* Spaniard ♦ *nm* (*LING*) Spanish; *V tb* **castellano**.
españolice [espaɲo'liθe] *etc vb V* **españolizar**.
españolizar [espaɲoli'θar] *vt* to make Spanish, Hispanicize; **~se** *vr* to adopt Spanish ways.
esparadrapo [espara'ðrapo] *nm* (sticking)

plaster, Band-Aid ® (*US*).
esparcido, a [espar'θiðo, a] *adj* scattered.
esparcimiento [esparθi'mjento] *nm* (*dispersión*) spreading; (*derramamiento*) scattering; (*fig*) cheerfulness.
esparcir [espar'θir] *vt* to spread; (*derramar*) to scatter; **~se** *vr* to spread (out); to scatter; (*divertirse*) to enjoy o.s.
espárrago [es'parraɣo] *nm* (*tb*: **~s**) asparagus; **estar hecho un ~** to be as thin as a rake; **¡vete a freír ~s!** (*fam*) go to hell!
esparto [es'parto] *nm* esparto (grass).
esparza [es'parθa] *etc vb V* **esparcir.**
espasmo [es'pasmo] *nm* spasm.
espátula [es'patula] *nf* (*MED*) spatula; (*ARTE*) palette knife; (*CULIN*) fish slice.
especia [es'peθja] *nf* spice.
especial [espe'θjal] *adj* special.
especialidad [espeθjali'ðað] *nf* speciality, specialty (*US*); (*ESCOL*: *ramo*) specialism.
especialista [espeθja'lista] *nm/f* specialist; (*CINE*) stuntman/woman.
especializado, a [espeθjali'θaðo, a] *adj* specialized; (*obrero*) skilled.
especialmente [espeθjal'mente] *adv* particularly, especially.
especie [es'peθje] *nf* (*BIO*) species; (*clase*) kind, sort; **pagar en ~** to pay in kind.
especificar [espeθifi'kar] *vt* to specify.
específico, a [espe'θifiko, a] *adj* specific.
especifique [espeθi'fike] *etc vb V* **especificar.**
espécimen [es'peθimen], *pl* **especímenes** *nm* specimen.
espectáculo [espek'takulo] *nm* (*gen*) spectacle; (*TEAT etc*) show; (*función*) performance; **dar un ~** to make a scene.
espectador, a [espekta'ðor, a] *nm/f* spectator; (*de incidente*) onlooker; **los ~es** (*TEAT*) the audience *sg*.
espectro [es'pektro] *nm* ghost; (*fig*) spectre.
especulación [espekula'θjon] *nf* speculation; **~ bursátil** speculation on the Stock Market.
especular [espeku'lar] *vt, vi* to speculate.
especulativo, a [espekula'tiβo, a] *adj* speculative.
espejismo [espe'xismo] *nm* mirage.
espejo [es'pexo] *nm* mirror; (*fig*) model; **~ retrovisor** rear-view mirror; **mirarse al ~** to look (at o.s.) in the mirror.
espeleología [espeleolo'xia] *nf* potholing.
espeluznante [espeluθ'nante] *adj* horrifying, hair-raising.
espera [es'pera] *nf* (*pausa, intervalo*) wait; (*JUR*: *plazo*) respite; **en ~ de** waiting for; (*con expectativa*) expecting; **en ~ de su contestación** awaiting your reply.
esperance [espe'ranθe] *etc vb V* **esperanzar.**
esperanza [espe'ranθa] *nf* (*confianza*) hope; (*expectativa*) expectation; **hay pocas ~s de que venga** there is little prospect of his coming.
esperanzador, a [esperanθa'ðor, a] *adj* hopeful, encouraging.
esperanzar [esperan'θar] *vt* to give hope to.
esperar [espe'rar] *vt* (*aguardar*) to wait for; (*tener expectativa de*) to expect; (*desear*) to hope for ♦ *vi* to wait; to expect; to hope; **~se** *vr*: **como podía ~se** as was to be expected; **hacer ~ a uno** to keep sb waiting; **ir a ~ a uno** to go and meet sb; **~ un bebé** to be expecting (a baby).
esperma [es'perma] *nf* sperm.
espermatozoide [espermato'θoiðe] *nm* spermatozoid.
esperpento [esper'pento] *nm* (*persona*) sight (*fam*); (*disparate*) (piece of) nonsense.
espesar [espe'sar] *vt* to thicken; **~se** *vr* to thicken, get thicker.
espeso, a [es'peso, a] *adj* thick; (*bosque*) dense; (*nieve*) deep; (*sucio*) dirty.
espesor [espe'sor] *nm* thickness; (*de nieve*) depth.
espesura [espe'sura] *nf* (*bosque*) thicket.
espetar [espe'tar] *vt* (*reto, sermón*) to give.
espía [es'pia] *nm/f* spy.
espiar [espi'ar] *vt* (*observar*) to spy on ♦ *vi*: **~ para** to spy for.
espiga [es'piɣa] *nf* (*BOT*: *de trigo etc*) ear; (: *de flores*) spike.
espigado, a [espi'ɣaðo, a] *adj* (*BOT*) ripe; (*fig*) tall, slender.
espigón [espi'ɣon] *nm* (*BOT*) ear; (*NAUT*) breakwater.
espina [es'pina] *nf* thorn; (*de pez*) bone; **~ dorsal** (*ANAT*) spine; **me da mala ~** I don't like the look of it.
espinaca [espi'naka] *nf* (*tb*: **~s**) spinach.
espinar [espi'nar] *nm* (*matorral*) thicket.
espinazo [espi'naθo] *nm* spine, backbone.
espinilla [espi'niʎa] *nf* (*ANAT*: *tibia*) shin(bone); (: *en la piel*) blackhead.
espino [es'pino] *nm* hawthorn.
espinoso, a [espi'noso, a] *adj* (*planta*) thorny, prickly; (*fig*) bony; (*problema*) knotty.
espionaje [espjo'naxe] *nm* spying, espionage.
espiral [espi'ral] *adj, nf* spiral; **la ~ inflacionista** the inflationary spiral.

espirar [espi'rar] *vt, vi* to breathe out, exhale.
espiritista [espiri'tista] *adj, nm/f* spiritualist.
espíritu [es'piritu] *nm* spirit; (*mente*) mind; (*inteligencia*) intelligence; (*REL*) spirit, soul; **E~ Santo** Holy Ghost; **con ~ amplio** with an open mind.
espiritual [espiri'twal] *adj* spiritual.
espita [es'pita] *nf* tap (*BRIT*), faucet (*US*).
esplendidez [esplendi'ðeθ] *nf* (*abundancia*) lavishness; (*magnificencia*) splendour.
espléndido, a [es'plendiðo, a] *adj* (*magnífico*) magnificent, splendid; (*generoso*) generous, lavish.
esplendor [esplen'dor] *nm* splendour.
espliego [es'pljeɣo] *nm* lavender.
espolear [espole'ar] *vt* to spur on.
espoleta [espo'leta] *nf* (*de bomba*) fuse.
espolvorear [espolβore'ar] *vt* to dust, sprinkle.
esponja [es'ponxa] *nf* sponge; (*fig*) sponger.
esponjoso, a [espon'xoso, a] *adj* spongy.
esponsales [espon'sales] *nmpl* betrothal *sg.*
espontaneidad [espontanei'ðað] *nf* spontaneity.
espontáneo, a [espon'taneo, a] *adj* spontaneous; (*improvisado*) impromptu; (*persona*) natural.
espora [es'pora] *nf* spore.
esporádico, a [espo'raðiko, a] *adj* sporadic.
esposa [es'posa] *nf V* **esposo.**
esposar [espo'sar] *vt* to handcuff.
esposo, a [es'poso, a] *nm* husband ♦ *nf* wife; **esposas** *nfpl* handcuffs.
espuela [es'pwela] *nf* spur; (*fam: trago*) one for the road.
espuerta [es'pwerta] *nf* basket, pannier.
espuma [es'puma] *nf* foam; (*de cerveza*) froth, head; (*de jabón*) lather; (*de olas*) surf.
espumadera [espuma'ðera] *nf* skimmer.
espumarajo [espuma'raxo] *nm* froth, foam; **echar ~s (de rabia)** to splutter with rage.
espumoso, a [espu'moso, a] *adj* frothy, foamy; (*vino*) sparkling.
esputo [es'puto] *nm* (*saliva*) spit; (*MED*) sputum.
esqueje [es'kexe] *nm* (*BOT*) cutting.
esquela [es'kela] *nf*: **~ mortuoria** announcement of death.
esquelético, a [eske'letiko, a] *adj* (*fam*) skinny.
esqueleto [eske'leto] *nm* skeleton; (*lo esencial*) bare bones (of a matter); **en ~** unfinished.
esquema [es'kema] *nm* (*diagrama*) diagram; (*dibujo*) plan; (*plan*) scheme; (*FILOSOFÍA*) schema.
esquemático, a [eske'matiko, a] *adj* schematic; **un resumen ~** a brief outline.
esquí [es'ki], *pl* **esquís** *nm* (*objeto*) ski; (*deporte*) skiing; **~ acuático** water-skiing; **hacer ~** to go skiing.
esquiador, a [eskja'ðor, a] *nm/f* skier.
esquiar [es'kjar] *vi* to ski.
esquila [es'kila] *nf* (*campanilla*) small bell; (*encerro*) cowbell.
esquilar [eski'lar] *vt* to shear.
esquimal [eski'mal] *adj, nm/f* Eskimo.
esquina [es'kina] *nf* corner; **doblar la ~** to turn the corner.
esquinazo [eski'naθo] *nm*: **dar ~ a algn** to give sb the slip.
esquirla [es'kirla] *nf* splinter.
esquirol [eski'rol] *nm* blackleg.
esquivar [eski'βar] *vt* to avoid; (*evadir*) to dodge, elude.
esquivo, a [es'kiβo, a] *adj* (*altanero*) aloof; (*desdeñoso*) scornful, disdainful.
esquizofrenia [eskiθo'frenja] *nf* schizophrenia.
esta ['esta] *adj demostrativo V* **este.**
ésta ['esta] *pron V* **éste.**
está [es'ta] *vb V* **estar.**
estabilice [estaβi'liθe] *etc vb V* **estabilizar.**
estabilidad [estaβili'ðað] *nf* stability.
estabilización [estaβiliθa'θjon] *nf* (*COM*) stabilization.
estabilizar [estaβili'θar] *vt* to stabilize; (*fijar*) to make steady; (*precios*) to peg; **~se** *vr* to become stable.
estable [es'taβle] *adj* stable.
establecer [estaβle'θer] *vt* to establish; (*fundar*) to set up; (*colonos*) to settle; (*récord*) to set (up); **~se** *vr* to establish o.s.; (*echar raíces*) to settle (down); (*COM*) to start up.
establecimiento [estaβleθi'mjento] *nm* establishment; (*fundación*) institution; (*de negocio*) start-up; (*de colonias*) settlement; (*local*) establishment; **~ comercial** business house.
establezca [esta'βleθka] *etc vb V* **establecer.**
establo [es'taβlo] *nm* (*AGR*) stall; (: *esp AM*) barn.
estaca [es'taka] *nf* stake, post; (*de tienda de campaña*) peg.
estacada [esta'kaða] *nf* (*cerca*) fence, fencing; (*palenque*) stockade; **dejar a algn en la ~** to leave sb in the lurch.

estación [esta'θjon] *nf* station; (*del año*) season; ~ **de autobuses/ferrocarril** bus/railway station; ~ **balnearia (de turistas)** seaside resort; ~ **de servicio** service station; ~ **terminal** terminus; ~ **de trabajo** (*COM*) work station; ~ **transmisora** transmitter; ~ **de visualización** display unit.
estacionamiento [estaθjona'mjento] *nm* (*AUTO*) parking; (*MIL*) stationing.
estacionar [estaθjo'nar] *vt* (*AUTO*) to park; (*MIL*) to station.
estacionario, a [estaθjo'narjo, a] *adj* stationary; (*COM*: *mercado*) slack.
estada [es'taða], **estadía** [esta'ðia] *nf* (*AM*) stay.
estadio [es'taðjo] *nm* (*fase*) stage, phase; (*DEPORTE*) stadium.
estadista [esta'ðista] *nm* (*POL*) statesman; (*ESTADÍSTICA*) statistician.
estadística [esta'ðistika] *nf* (*una* ~) figure, statistic; (*ciencia*) statistics *sg*.
estado [es'taðo] *nm* (*POL*: *condición*) state; ~ **civil** marital status; ~ **de cuenta(s)** bank statement, statement of accounts; ~ **de excepción** (*POL*) state of emergency; ~ **financiero** (*COM*) financial statement; ~ **mayor** (*MIL*) staff; ~ **de pérdidas y ganancias** (*COM*) profit and loss statement, operating statement; **E~s Unidos (EE.UU.)** United States (of America) (USA); **estar en** ~ **(de buena esperanza)** to be pregnant.
estadounidense [estaðouni'ðense] *adj* United States *cpd*, American ♦ *nm/f* United States citizen, American.
estafa [es'tafa] *nf* swindle, trick; (*COM etc*) racket.
estafar [esta'far] *vt* to swindle, defraud.
estafeta [esta'feta] *nf* (*oficina de correos*) post office; ~ **diplomática** diplomatic bag.
estalactita [estalak'tita] *nf* stalactite.
estalagmita [estalaɣ'mita] *nf* stalagmite.
estallar [esta'ʎar] *vi* to burst; (*bomba*) to explode, go off; (*volcán*) to erupt; (*vidrio*) to shatter; (*látigo*) to crack; (*epidemia, guerra, rebelión*) to break out; ~ **en llanto** to burst into tears.
estallido [esta'ʎiðo] *nm* explosion; (*de látigo, trueno*) crack; (*fig*) outbreak.
estambre [es'tambre] *nm* (*tela*) worsted; (*BOT*) stamen.
Estambul [estam'bul] *nm* Istanbul.
estamento [esta'mento] *nm* (social) class.
estampa [es'tampa] *nf* (*impresión, imprenta*) print, engraving; (*imagen, figura*: *de persona*) appearance.
estampado, a [estam'paðo, a] *adj* printed ♦ *nm* (*impresión*: *acción*) printing; (: *efecto*) print; (*marca*) stamping.
estampar [estam'par] *vt* (*imprimir*) to print; (*marcar*) to stamp; (*metal*) to engrave; (*poner sello en*) to stamp; (*fig*) to stamp, imprint.
estampida [estam'piða] *nf* stampede.
estampido [estam'piðo] *nm* bang, report.
estampilla [estam'piʎa] *nf* (*sello de goma*) (rubber) stamp; (*AM*) (postage) stamp.
están [es'tan] *vb V* **estar**.
estancado, a [estan'kaðo, a] *adj* (*agua*) stagnant.
estancamiento [estanka'mjento] *nm* stagnation.
estancar [estan'kar] *vt* (*aguas*) to hold up, hold back; (*COM*) to monopolize; (*fig*) to block, hold up; **~se** *vr* to stagnate.
estancia [es'tanθja] *nf* (*permanencia*) stay; (*sala*) room; (*AM*) farm, ranch.
estanciero [estan'sjero] *nm* (*AM*) farmer, rancher.
estanco, a [es'tanko, a] *adj* watertight ♦ *nm* tobacconist's (shop); *see boxed note*.

ESTANCO

Cigarettes, tobacco, postage stamps and official forms are all sold under a state monopoly and are usually purchased at a shop called an **estanco**. *Tobacco products are also sold in "quioscos" and bars but are generally more expensive. The number of* **estanco** *licences is regulated by the state.*

estándar [es'tandar] *adj, nm* standard.
estandarice [estanda'riθe] *etc vb V* **estandarizar**.
estandarizar [estandari'θar] *vt* to standardize.
estandarte [estan'darte] *nm* banner, standard.
estanque [es'tanke] *etc vb V* **estancar** ♦ *nm* (*lago*) pool, pond; (*AGR*) reservoir.
estanquero, a [estan'kero, a] *nm/f* tobacconist.
estante [es'tante] *nm* (*armario*) rack, stand; (*biblioteca*) bookcase; (*anaquel*) shelf; (*AM*) prop.
estantería [estante'ria] *nf* shelving, shelves *pl*.
estaño [es'taɲo] *nm* tin.

PALABRA CLAVE

estar [es'tar] *vi* **1** (*posición*) to be; **está en la plaza** it's in the square; **¿está Juan?** is Juan in?; **estamos a 30 km de Junín** we're 30 kms from Junín
2 (+*adj o adv*: *estado*) to be; ~ **enfermo**

to be ill; **está muy elegante** he's looking very smart; ~ **lejos** to be far (away); **¿cómo estás?** how are you keeping?
3 (+*gerundio*) to be; **estoy leyendo** I'm reading
4 (*uso pasivo*): **está condenado a muerte** he's been condemned to death; **está envasado en ...** it's packed in ...
5: ~ **a**: **¿a cuántos estamos?** what's the date today?; **estamos a 5 de mayo** it's the 5th of May; **las manzanas están a 200 ptas** apples are (selling at) 200 pesetas; **estamos a 25 grados** it's 25 degrees today
6 (*locuciones*): **¿estamos?** (*¿de acuerdo?*) okay?; (*¿listo?*) ready?; **¡ya está bien!** that's enough!; **¿está la comida?** is dinner ready?; **¡ya está!**, (*AM*) **¡ya estuvo!** that's it!
7: ~ **con**: **está con gripe** he's got (the) flu
8: ~ **de**: ~ **de vacaciones/viaje** to be on holiday/away *o* on a trip; **está de camarero** he's working as a waiter
9: ~ **para**: **está para salir** he's about to leave; **no estoy para bromas** I'm not in the mood for jokes
10: ~ **por** (*propuesta etc*) to be in favour of; (*persona etc*) to support, side with; **está por limpiar** it still has to be cleaned; **¡estoy por dejarlo!** I think I'm going to leave this!
11 (+*que*): **está que rabia** (*fam*) he's hopping mad (*fam*); **estoy que me caigo de sueño** I'm terribly sleepy, I can't keep my eyes open
12: ~ **sin**: ~ **sin dinero** to have no money; **está sin terminar** it isn't finished yet
♦ ~**se** *vr*: **se estuvo en la cama toda la tarde** he stayed in bed all afternoon; **¡estáte quieto!** stop fidgeting!

estárter [es'tarter] *nm* (*AUTO*) choke.
estas ['estas] *adj demostrativo V* **este**.
éstas ['estas] *pron V* **éste**.
estás [es'tas] *vb V* **estar**.
estatal [esta'tal] *adj* state *cpd*.
estático, a [es'tatiko, a] *adj* static.
estatua [es'tatwa] *nf* statue.
estatura [esta'tura] *nf* stature, height.
estatus [es'tatus] *nm inv* status.
estatutario, a [estatu'tarjo, a] *adj* statutory.
estatuto [esta'tuto] *nm* (*JUR*) statute; (*de ciudad*) bye-law; (*de comité*) rule; ~**s sociales** (*COM*) articles of association.
este¹ ['este] *adj* (*lado*) east; (*dirección*) easterly ♦ *nm* east; **en la parte del** ~ in the eastern part.
este² ['este], **esta** ['esta], **estos** ['estos], **estas** ['estas] *adj demostrativo* (*sg*) this; (*pl*) these; (*AM*: *como muletilla*) er, um.
éste ['este], **ésta** ['esta], **éstos** ['estos], **éstas** ['estas] *pron* (*sg*) this (one); (*pl*) these (ones); **ése ... éste ...** the former ... the latter ....
esté [es'te] *vb V* **estar**.
estela [es'tela] *nf* wake, wash; (*fig*) trail.
estelar [este'lar] *adj* (*ASTRO*) stellar; (*TEAT*) star *cpd*.
estén [es'ten] *vb V* **estar**.
estenografía [estenoɣra'fia] *nf* shorthand.
estentóreo, a [esten'toreo, a] *adj* (*sonido*) strident; (*voz*) booming.
estepa [es'tepa] *nf* (*GEO*) steppe.
estera [es'tera] *nf* (*alfombra*) mat; (*tejido*) matting.
estercolero [esterko'lero] *nm* manure heap, dunghill.
estéreo [es'tereo] *adj inv, nm* stereo.
estereofónico, a [estereo'foniko, a] *adj* stereophonic.
estereotipar [estereoti'par] *vt* to stereotype.
estereotipo [estereo'tipo] *nm* stereotype.
estéril [es'teril] *adj* sterile, barren; (*fig*) vain, futile.
esterilice [esteri'liθe] *etc vb V* **esterilizar**.
esterilizar [esterili'θar] *vt* to sterilize.
esterilla [este'riʎa] *nf* (*alfombrilla*) small mat.
esterlina [ester'lina] *adj*: **libra** ~ pound sterling.
esternón [ester'non] *nm* breastbone.
estero [es'tero] *nm* (*AM*) swamp.
estertor [ester'tor] *nm* death rattle.
estés [es'tes] *vb V* **estar**.
esteta [es'teta] *nm/f* aesthete.
esteticienne [esteti'θjen] *nf* beautician.
estético, a [es'tetiko, a] *adj* aesthetic ♦ *nf* aesthetics *sg*.
estetoscopio [estetos'kopjo] *nm* stethoscope.
estibador [estiβa'ðor] *nm* stevedore.
estibar [esti'βar] *vt* (*NAUT*) to stow.
estiércol [es'tjerkol] *nm* dung, manure.
estigma [es'tiɣma] *nm* stigma.
estigmatice [estiɣma'tiθe] *etc vb V* **estigmatizar**.
estigmatizar [estiɣmati'θar] *vt* to stigmatize.
estilarse [esti'larse] *vr* (*estar de moda*) to be in fashion; (*usarse*) to be used.
estilice [esti'liθe] *etc vb V* **estilizar**.
estilizar [estili'θar] *vt* to stylize; (*TEC*) to design.

estilo [es'tilo] *nm* style; (*TEC*) stylus; (*NATACIÓN*) stroke; ~ **de vida** lifestyle; **al** ~ **de** in the style of; **algo por el** ~ something along those lines.
estilográfica [estilo'ɤrafika] *nf* fountain pen.
estima [es'tima] *nf* esteem, respect.
estimación [estima'θjon] *nf* (*evaluación*) estimation; (*aprecio, afecto*) esteem, regard.
estimado, a [esti'maðo, a] *adj* esteemed; **"E~ Señor"** "Dear Sir".
estimar [esti'mar] *vt* (*evaluar*) to estimate; (*valorar*) to value; (*apreciar*) to esteem, respect; (*pensar, considerar*) to think, reckon.
estimulante [estimu'lante] *adj* stimulating ♦ *nm* stimulant.
estimular [estimu'lar] *vt* to stimulate; (*excitar*) to excite; (*animar*) to encourage.
estímulo [es'timulo] *nm* stimulus; (*ánimo*) encouragement; (*INFORM*) prompt.
estío [es'tio] *nm* summer.
estipendio [esti'pendjo] *nm* salary; (*COM*) stipend.
estipulación [estipula'θjon] *nf* stipulation, condition.
estipular [estipu'lar] *vt* to stipulate.
estirado, a [esti'raðo, a] *adj* (*tenso*) (stretched *o* drawn) tight; (*fig: persona*) stiff, pompous; (*engreído*) stuck-up.
estirar [esti'rar] *vt* to stretch; (*dinero, suma etc*) to stretch out; (*cuello*) to crane; (*dinero*) to eke out; (*discurso*) to spin out; ~ **la pata** (*fam*) to kick the bucket; **~se** *vr* to stretch.
estirón [esti'ron] *nm* pull, tug; (*crecimiento*) spurt, sudden growth; **dar un** ~ (*niño*) to shoot up.
estirpe [es'tirpe] *nf* stock, lineage.
estival [esti'ßal] *adj* summer *cpd*.
esto ['esto] *pron* this, this thing *o* matter; (*como muletilla*) er, um; ~ **de la boda** this business about the wedding; **en** ~ at this *o* that point; **por** ~ for this reason.
estocada [esto'kaða] *nf* (*acción*) stab; (*TAUR*) death blow.
Estocolmo [esto'kolmo] *nm* Stockholm.
estofa [es'tofa] *nf*: **de baja** ~ poor-quality.
estofado [esto'faðo] *nm* stew.
estofar [esto'far] *vt* (*bordar*) to quilt; (*CULIN*) to stew.
estoico, a [es'toiko, a] *adj* (*FILOSOFÍA*) stoic(al); (*fig*) cold, indifferent.
estomacal [estoma'kal] *adj* stomach *cpd*; **trastorno** ~ stomach upset.
estómago [es'tomaɤo] *nm* stomach; **tener** ~ to be thick-skinned.
Estonia [es'tonja] *nf* Estonia.
estonio, a [es'tonjo, a] *adj, nm/f* Estonian ♦ *nm* (*LING*) Estonian.
estoque [es'toke] *nm* rapier, sword.
estorbar [estor'ßar] *vt* to hinder, obstruct; (*fig*) to bother, disturb ♦ *vi* to be in the way.
estorbo [es'torßo] *nm* (*molestia*) bother, nuisance; (*obstáculo*) hindrance, obstacle.
estornino [estor'nino] *nm* starling.
estornudar [estornu'ðar] *vi* to sneeze.
estornudo [estor'nuðo] *nm* sneeze.
estos ['estos] *adj demostrativo V* **este.**
éstos ['estos] *pron V* **éste.**
estoy [es'toi] *vb V* **estar.**
estrabismo [estra'ßismo] *nm* squint.
estrado [es'traðo] *nm* (*tarima*) platform; (*MUS*) bandstand; **~s** *nmpl* law courts.
estrafalario, a [estrafa'larjo, a] *adj* odd, eccentric; (*desarreglado*) slovenly, sloppy.
estrago [es'traɤo] *nm* ruin, destruction; **hacer ~s en** to wreak havoc among.
estragón [estra'ɤon] *nm* (*CULIN*) tarragon.
estrambótico, a [estram'botiko, a] *adj* odd, eccentric.
estrangulación [estrangula'θjon] *nf* strangulation.
estrangulador, a [estrangula'ðor, a] *nm/f* strangler ♦ *nm* (*TEC*) throttle; (*AUTO*) choke.
estrangulamiento [estrangula'mjento] *nm* (*AUTO*) bottleneck.
estrangular [estrangu'lar] *vt* (*persona*) to strangle; (*MED*) to strangulate.
estraperlista [estraper'lista] *nm/f* black marketeer.
estraperlo [estra'perlo] *nm* black market.
estratagema [estrata'xema] *nf* (*MIL*) stratagem; (*astucia*) cunning.
estratega [estra'teɤa] *nm/f* strategist.
estrategia [estra'texja] *nf* strategy.
estratégico, a [estra'texiko, a] *adj* strategic.
estratificar [estratifi'kar] *vt* to stratify.
estratifique [estrati'fike] *etc vb V* **estratificar.**
estrato [es'trato] *nm* stratum, layer.
estratosfera [estratos'fera] *nf* stratosphere.
estrechar [estre'tʃar] *vt* (*reducir*) to narrow; (*vestido*) to take in; (*persona*) to hug, embrace; **~se** *vr* (*reducirse*) to narrow, grow narrow; (*2 personas*) to embrace; ~ **la mano** to shake hands.
estrechez [estre'tʃeθ] *nf* narrowness; (*de ropa*) tightness; (*intimidad*) intimacy;

(*COM*) want *o* shortage of money; **estrecheces** *nfpl* financial difficulties.
estrecho, a [es'tretʃo, a] *adj* narrow; (*apretado*) tight; (*íntimo*) close, intimate; (*miserable*) mean ♦ *nm* strait; ~ **de miras** narrow-minded; **E~ de Gibraltar** Straits of Gibraltar.
estrella [es'treʎa] *nf* star; ~ **fugaz** shooting star; ~ **de mar** starfish; **tener (buena)/ mala** ~ to be lucky/unlucky.
estrellado, a [estre'ʎaðo, a] *adj* (*forma*) star-shaped; (*cielo*) starry; (*huevos*) fried.
estrellar [estre'ʎar] *vt* (*hacer añicos*) to smash (to pieces); (*huevos*) to fry; ~**se** *vr* to smash; (*chocarse*) to crash; (*fracasar*) to fail.
estrellato [estre'ʎato] *nm* stardom.
estremecer [estreme'θer] *vt* to shake; ~**se** *vr* to shake, tremble; ~ **de** (*horror*) to shudder with; (*frío*) to shiver with.
estremecimiento [estremeθi'mjento] *nm* (*temblor*) trembling, shaking.
estremezca [estre'meθka] *etc vb V* **estremecer**.
estrenar [estre'nar] *vt* (*vestido*) to wear for the first time; (*casa*) to move into; (*película, obra de teatro*) to present for the first time; ~**se** *vr* (*persona*) to make one's début; (*película*) to have its premiere; (*TEAT*) to open.
estreno [es'treno] *nm* (*primer uso*) first use; (*CINE etc*) premiere.
estreñido, a [estre'ɲiðo, a] *adj* constipated.
estreñimiento [estreɲi'mjento] *nm* constipation.
estreñir [estre'ɲir] *vt* to constipate.
estrépito [es'trepito] *nm* noise, racket; (*fig*) fuss.
estrepitoso, a [estrepi'toso, a] *adj* noisy; (*fiesta*) rowdy.
estrés [es'tres] *nm* stress.
estresante [estre'sante] *adj* stressful.
estría [es'tria] *nf* groove; ~**s (en el cutis)** stretchmarks.
estribación [estriβa'θjon] *nf* (*GEO*) spur; **estribaciones** *nfpl* foothills.
estribar [estri'βar] *vi*: ~ **en** to rest on, be supported by; **la dificultad estriba en el texto** the difficulty lies in the text.
estribillo [estri'βiʎo] *nm* (*LITERATURA*) refrain; (*MUS*) chorus.
estribo [es'triβo] *nm* (*de jinete*) stirrup; (*de coche, tren*) step; (*de puente*) support; (*GEO*) spur; **perder los** ~**s** to fly off the handle.
estribor [estri'βor] *nm* (*NAUT*) starboard.
estricnina [estrik'nina] *nf* strychnine.
estricto, a [es'trikto, a] *adj* (*riguroso*) strict; (*severo*) severe.
estridente [estri'ðente] *adj* (*color*) loud; (*voz*) raucous.
estro ['estro] *nm* inspiration.
estrofa [es'trofa] *nf* verse.
estropajo [estro'paxo] *nm* scourer.
estropeado, a [estrope'aðo, a] *adj*: **está** ~ it's not working.
estropear [estrope'ar] *vt* (*arruinar*) to spoil; (*dañar*) to damage; (: *máquina*) to break; ~**se** *vr* (*objeto*) to get damaged; (*coche*) to break down; (*la piel etc*) to be ruined.
estropicio [estro'piθjo] *nm* (*rotura*) breakage; (*efectos*) harmful effects *pl*.
estructura [estruk'tura] *nf* structure.
estruendo [es'trwendo] *nm* (*ruido*) racket, din; (*fig: alboroto*) uproar, turmoil.
estrujar [estru'xar] *vt* (*apretar*) to squeeze; (*aplastar*) to crush; (*fig*) to drain, bleed.
estuario [es'twarjo] *nm* estuary.
estuche [es'tutʃe] *nm* box, case.
estudiante [estu'ðjante] *nm/f* student.
estudiantil [estuðjan'til] *adj inv* student *cpd*.
estudiantina [estuðjan'tina] *nf* student music group.
estudiar [estu'ðjar] *vt* to study; (*propuesta*) to think about *o* over; ~ **para abogado** to study to become a lawyer.
estudio [es'tuðjo] *nm* study; (*encuesta*) research; (*proyecto*) plan; (*piso*) studio flat; (*CINE, ARTE, RADIO*) studio; ~**s** *nmpl* studies; (*erudición*) learning *sg*; **cursar** *o* **hacer** ~**s** to study; ~ **de casos prácticos** case study; ~ **de desplazamientos y tiempos** (*COM*) time and motion study; ~**s de motivación** motivational research *sg*; ~ **del trabajo** (*COM*) work study; ~ **de viabilidad** (*COM*) feasibility study.
estudioso, a [estu'ðjoso, a] *adj* studious.
estufa [es'tufa] *nf* heater, fire.
estulticia [estul'tiθja] *nf* foolishness.
estupefaciente [estupefa'θjente] *adj, nm* narcotic.
estupefacto, a [estupe'fakto, a] *adj* speechless, thunderstruck.
estupendamente [estupenda'mente] *adv* (*fam*): **estoy** ~ I feel great; **le salió** ~ he did it very well.
estupendo, a [estu'pendo, a] *adj* wonderful, terrific; (*fam*) great; ¡~! that's great!, fantastic!
estupidez [estupi'ðeθ] *nf* (*torpeza*) stupidity; (*acto*) stupid thing (to do); **fue una** ~ **mía** that was a silly thing for me to do *o* say.
estúpido, a [es'tupiðo, a] *adj* stupid, silly.

estupor [estu'por] *nm* stupor; (*fig*) astonishment, amazement.
estupro [es'tupro] *nm* rape.
estuve [es'tuße] *etc*, **estuviera** [estu'ßjera] *etc vb V* **estar.**
esvástica [es'ßastika] *nf* swastika.
ET *abr* = *Ejército de Tierra.*
ETA ['eta] *nf abr* (*POL*: = *Euskadi Ta Askatasuna*) ETA.
etapa [e'tapa] *nf* (*de viaje*) stage; (*DEPORTE*) leg; (*parada*) stopping place; (*fig*) stage, phase; **por ~s** gradually *o* in stages.
etarra [e'tarra] *adj* ETA *cpd* ♦ *nm/f* member of ETA.
etc. *abr* (= *etcétera*) etc.
etcétera [et'θetera] *adv* etcetera.
etéreo, a [e'tereo, a] *adj* ethereal.
eternice [eter'niθe] *etc vb V* **eternizar.**
eternidad [eterni'ðað] *nf* eternity.
eternizarse [eterni'θarse] *vr*: ~ **en hacer algo** to take ages to do sth.
eterno, a [e'terno, a] *adj* eternal, everlasting; (*despectivo*) never-ending.
ético, a ['etiko, a] *adj* ethical ♦ *nf* ethics.
etimología [etimolo'xia] *nf* etymology.
etiqueta [eti'keta] *nf* (*modales*) etiquette; (*rótulo*) label, tag; **de ~** formal.
etnia ['etnja] *nf* ethnic group.
étnico, a ['etniko, a] *adj* ethnic.
EU(A) *abr* (*esp AM*) = **Estados Unidos (de América).**
eucalipto [euka'lipto] *nm* eucalyptus.
Eucaristía [eukaris'tia] *nf* Eucharist.
eufemismo [eufe'mismo] *nm* euphemism.
euforia [eu'forja] *nf* euphoria.
eufórico, a [eu'foriko, a] *adj* euphoric.
eunuco [eu'nuko] *nm* eunuch.
euro ['euro] *sm* (*moneda*) euro.
eurodiputado, a [euroðipu'taðo, a] *nm/f* Euro MP, MEP.
Eurolandia [euro'landja] *nf* Euroland.
Europa [eu'ropa] *nf* Europe.
europeice [euro'peiθe] *etc vb V* **europeizar.**
europeizar [europei'θar] *vt* to Europeanize; **~se** *vr* to become Europeanized.
europeo, a [euro'peo, a] *adj, nm/f* European.
Euskadi [eus'kaði] *nm* the Basque Provinces *pl.*
euskera, eusquera [eus'kera] *nm* (*LING*) Basque; *V tb* **lenguas cooficiales.**
eutanasia [euta'nasja] *nf* euthanasia.
evacuación [eßakwa'θjon] *nf* evacuation.
evacuar [eßa'kwar] *vt* to evacuate.
evadir [eßa'ðir] *vt* to evade, avoid; **~se** *vr* to escape.
evaluación [eßalwa'θjon] *nf* evaluation, assessment.
evaluar [eßa'lwar] *vt* to evaluate, assess.
evangélico, a [eßan'xeliko, a] *adj* evangelical.
evangelio [eßan'xeljo] *nm* gospel.
evaporación [eßapora'θjon] *nf* evaporation.
evaporar [eßapo'rar] *vt* to evaporate; **~se** *vr* to vanish.
evasión [eßa'sjon] *nf* escape, flight; (*fig*) evasion; ~ **fiscal** *o* **tributaria** tax evasion.
evasivo, a [eßa'sißo, a] *adj* evasive, non-committal ♦ *nf* (*pretexto*) excuse; **contestar con evasivas** to avoid giving a straight answer.
evento [e'ßento] *nm* event; (*eventualidad*) eventuality.
eventual [eßen'twal] *adj* possible, conditional (upon circumstances); (*trabajador*) casual, temporary.
Everest [eße'rest] *nm*: **el (Monte) ~** (Mount) Everest.
evidencia [eßi'ðenθja] *nf* evidence, proof; **poner en ~** to make clear; **ponerse en ~** (*persona*) to show o.s. up.
evidenciar [eßiðen'θjar] *vt* (*hacer patente*) to make evident; (*probar*) to prove, show; **~se** *vr* to be evident.
evidente [eßi'ðente] *adj* obvious, clear, evident.
evitar [eßi'tar] *vt* (*evadir*) to avoid; (*impedir*) to prevent; (*peligro*) to escape; (*molestia*) to save; (*tentación*) to shun; **si puedo ~lo** if I can help it.
evocador, a [eßoka'ðor, a] *adj* (*sugestivo*) evocative.
evocar [eßo'kar] *vt* to evoke, call forth.
evolución [eßolu'θjon] *nf* (*desarrollo*) evolution, development; (*cambio*) change; (*MIL*) manoeuvre.
evolucionar [eßoluθjo'nar] *vi* to evolve; (*MIL, AVIAT*) to manoeuvre.
evoque [e'ßoke] *etc vb V* **evocar.**
ex [eks] *adj* ex-; **el ~ ministro** the former minister, the ex-minister.
exabrupto [eksa'ßrupto] *nm* interjection.
exacción [eksak'θjon] *nf* (*acto*) exaction; (*de impuestos*) demand.
exacerbar [eksaθer'ßar] *vt* to irritate, annoy.
exactamente [eksakta'mente] *adv* exactly.
exactitud [eksakti'tuð] *nf* exactness; (*precisión*) accuracy; (*puntualidad*) punctuality.
exacto, a [ek'sakto, a] *adj* exact; accurate; punctual; **¡~!** exactly!; **eso no es del todo ~** that's not quite right; **para ser ~** to be precise.
exageración [eksaxera'θjon] *nf* exaggeration.

exagerado, a [eksaxe'raðo, a] *adj* (*relato*) exaggerated; (*precio*) excessive; (*persona*) over-demonstrative; (*gesto*) theatrical.
exagerar [eksaxe'rar] *vt* to exaggerate; (*exceder*) to overdo.
exaltado, a [eksal'taðo, a] *adj* (*apasionado*) over-excited, worked up; (*exagerado*) extreme; (*fanático*) hot-headed; (*discurso*) impassioned ♦ *nm/f* (*fanático*) hothead; (*POL*) extremist.
exaltar [eksal'tar] *vt* to exalt, glorify; **~se** *vr* (*excitarse*) to get excited *o* worked up.
examen [ek'samen] *nm* examination; (*de problema*) consideration; **~ de** (*encuesta*) inquiry into; **~ de ingreso** entrance examination; **~ de conducir** driving test; **~ eliminatorio** qualifying examination.
examinar [eksami'nar] *vt* to examine; (*poner a prueba*) to test; (*inspeccionar*) to inspect; **~se** *vr* to be examined, take an examination.
exánime [ek'sanime] *adj* lifeless; (*fig*) exhausted.
exasperar [eksaspe'rar] *vt* to exasperate; **~se** *vr* to get exasperated, lose patience.
Exc.ª *abr* = **Excelencia.**
excarcelar [ekskarθe'lar] *vt* to release (from prison).
excavador, a [ekskaβa'ðor, a] *nm/f* (*persona*) excavator ♦ *nf* (*TEC*) digger.
excavar [ekska'βar] *vt* to excavate, dig (out).
excedencia [eksθe'ðenθja] *nf* (*MIL*) leave; (*ESCOL*) sabbatical.
excedente [eksθe'ðente] *adj, nm* excess, surplus.
exceder [eksθe'ðer] *vt* to exceed, surpass; **~se** *vr* (*extralimitarse*) to go too far; (*sobrepasarse*) to excel o.s.
excelencia [eksθe'lenθja] *nf* excellence; **E~** Excellency; **por ~** par excellence.
excelente [eksθe'lente] *adj* excellent.
excelso, a [eks'θelso, a] *adj* lofty, sublime.
excentricidad [eksθentriθi'ðað] *nf* eccentricity.
excéntrico, a [eks'θentriko, a] *adj, nm/f* eccentric.
excepción [eksθep'θjon] *nf* exception; **la ~ confirma la regla** the exception proves the rule.
excepcional [eksθepθjo'nal] *adj* exceptional.
excepto [eks'θepto] *adv* excepting, except (for).
exceptuar [eksθep'twar] *vt* to except, exclude.
excesivo, a [eksθe'siβo, a] *adj* excessive.
exceso [eks'θeso] *nm* excess; (*COM*) surplus; **~ de equipaje/peso** excess luggage/weight; **~ de velocidad** speeding; **en *o* por ~** excessively.
excitación [eksθita'θjon] *nf* (*sensación*) excitement; (*acción*) excitation.
excitado, a [eksθi'taðo, a] *adj* excited; (*emociones*) aroused.
excitante [eksθi'tante] *adj* exciting; (*MED*) stimulating ♦ *nm* stimulant.
excitar [eksθi'tar] *vt* to excite; (*incitar*) to urge; (*emoción*) to stir up; (*esperanzas*) to raise; (*pasión*) to arouse; **~se** *vr* to get excited.
exclamación [eksklama'θjon] *nf* exclamation.
exclamar [ekskla'mar] *vi* to exclaim; **~se** *vr*: **~se (contra)** to complain (about).
excluir [eksklu'ir] *vt* to exclude; (*dejar fuera*) to shut out; (*solución*) to reject; (*posibilidad*) to rule out.
exclusión [eksklu'sjon] *nf* exclusion.
exclusiva [eksklu'siβa] *nf V* **exclusivo.**
exclusive [eksklu'siβe] *prep* exclusive of, not counting.
exclusivo, a [eksklu'siβo, a] *adj* exclusive ♦ *nf* (*PRENSA*) exclusive, scoop; (*COM*) sole right *o* agency; **derecho ~** sole *o* exclusive right.
excluyendo [eksklu'jendo] *etc vb V* **excluir.**
Excma., Excmo. *abr* (= *Excelentísima, Excelentísimo*) *courtesy title.*
excombatiente [ekskomba'tjente] *nm* ex-serviceman, war veteran (*US*).
excomulgar [ekskomul'ɣar] *vt* (*REL*) to excommunicate.
excomulgue [eksko'mulɣe] *etc vb V* **excomulgar.**
excomunión [ekskomu'njon] *nf* excommunication.
excoriar [eksko'rjar] *vt* to flay, skin.
excremento [ekskre'mento] *nm* excrement.
exculpar [ekskul'par] *vt* to exonerate; (*JUR*) to acquit; **~se** *vr* to exonerate o.s.
excursión [ekskur'sjon] *nf* excursion, outing; **ir de ~** to go (off) on a trip.
excursionista [ekskursjo'nista] *nm/f* (*turista*) sightseer.
excusa [eks'kusa] *nf* excuse; (*disculpa*) apology; **presentar sus ~s** to excuse o.s.
excusado, a [eksku'saðo, a] *adj* unnecessary; (*disculpado*) excused, forgiven.
excusar [eksku'sar] *vt* to excuse; (*evitar*) to avoid, prevent; **~se** *vr* (*disculparse*) to apologize.
execrable [ekse'kraβle] *adj* appalling.
exención [eksen'θjon] *nf* exemption.

exento, a [ek'sento, a] *pp de* **eximir** ♦ *adj* exempt.
exequias [ek'sekjas] *nfpl* funeral rites.
exfoliar [eksfo'ljar] *vt* to exfoliate.
exhalación [eksala'θjon] *nf* (*del aire*) exhalation; (*vapor*) fumes *pl*, vapour; (*rayo*) shooting star; **salir como una ~** to shoot out.
exhalar [eksa'lar] *vt* to exhale, breathe out; (*olor etc*) to give off; (*suspiro*) to breathe, heave.
exhaustivo, a [eksaus'tiβo, a] *adj* exhaustive.
exhausto, a [ek'sausto, a] *adj* exhausted, worn-out.
exhibición [eksiβi'θjon] *nf* exhibition; (*demostración*) display, show; (*de película*) showing; (*de equipo*) performance.
exhibicionista [eksiβiθjo'nista] *adj, nm/f* exhibitionist.
exhibir [eksi'βir] *vt* to exhibit; to display, show; (*cuadros*) to exhibit; (*artículos*) to display; (*pasaporte*) to show; (*película*) to screen; (*mostrar con orgullo*) to show off; **~se** *vr* (*mostrarse en público*) to show o.s. off; (*fam: indecentemente*) to expose o.s.
exhortación [eksorta'θjon] *nf* exhortation.
exhortar [eksor'tar] *vt*: **~ a** to exhort to.
exhumar [eksu'mar] *vt* to exhume.
exigencia [eksi'xenθja] *nf* demand, requirement.
exigente [eksi'xente] *adj* demanding; (*profesor*) strict; **ser ~ con algn** to be hard on sb.
exigir [eksi'xir] *vt* (*gen*) to demand, require; (*impuestos*) to exact, levy; **~ el pago** to demand payment.
exiguo, a [ek'siɣwo, a] *adj* (*cantidad*) meagre; (*objeto*) tiny.
exija [e'ksixa] *etc vb V* **exigir.**
exiliado, a [eksi'ljaðo, a] *adj* exiled, in exile ♦ *nm/f* exile.
exiliar [eksi'ljar] *vt* to exile; **~se** *vr* to go into exile.
exilio [ek'siljo] *nm* exile.
eximio, a [ek'simjo, a] *adj* (*eminente*) distinguished, eminent.
eximir [eksi'mir] *vt* to exempt.
existencia [eksis'tenθja] *nf* existence; **~s** *nfpl* stock *sg*; **~ de mercancías** (*COM*) stock-in-trade; **tener en ~** to have in stock; **amargar la ~ a algn** to make sb's life a misery.
existir [eksis'tir] *vi* to exist, be.
éxito ['eksito] *nm* (*resultado*) result, outcome; (*triunfo*) success; (*MUS, TEAT*) hit; **~ editorial** bestseller; **~ rotundo** smash hit; **tener ~** to be successful.
exitoso, a [eksi'toso, a] *adj* (*esp AM*) successful.
éxodo ['eksoðo] *nm* exodus; **el ~ rural** the drift from the land.
ex oficio [ekso'fiθjo] *adj, adv* ex officio.
exonerar [eksone'rar] *vt* to exonerate; **~ de una obligación** to free from an obligation.
exorcice [eksor'θiθe] *etc vb V* **exorcizar.**
exorcismo [eksor'θismo] *nm* exorcism.
exorcizar [eksorθi'θar] *vt* to exorcize.
exótico, a [ek'sotiko, a] *adj* exotic.
expandido, a [ekspan'diðo, a] *adj*: **en caracteres ~s** (*INFORM*) double width.
expandir [ekspan'dir] *vt* to expand; (*COM*) to expand, enlarge; **~se** *vr* to expand, spread.
expansión [ekspan'sjon] *nf* expansion; (*recreo*) relaxation; **la ~ económica** economic growth; **economía en ~** expanding economy.
expansionarse [ekspansjo'narse] *vr* (*dilatarse*) to expand; (*recrearse*) to relax.
expansivo, a [ekspan'siβo, a] *adj* expansive; (*efusivo*) communicative.
expatriado, a [ekspa'trjaðo, a] *nm/f* (*emigrado*) expatriate; (*exiliado*) exile.
expatriarse [ekspa'trjarse] *vr* to emigrate; (*POL*) to go into exile.
expectación [ekspekta'θjon] *nf* (*esperanza*) expectation; (*ilusión*) excitement.
expectativa [ekspekta'tiβa] *nf* (*espera*) expectation; (*perspectiva*) prospect; **~ de vida** life expectancy; **estar a la ~** to wait and see (what will happen).
expedición [ekspeði'θjon] *nf* (*excursión*) expedition; **gastos de ~** shipping charges.
expedientar [ekspeðjen'tar] *vt* to open a file on; (*funcionario*) to discipline, start disciplinary proceedings against.
expediente [ekspe'ðjente] *nm* expedient; (*JUR: procedimento*) action, proceedings *pl*; (*: papeles*) dossier, file, record; **~ judicial** court proceedings *pl*; **~ académico** (student's) record.
expedir [ekspe'ðir] *vt* (*despachar*) to send, forward; (*pasaporte*) to issue; (*cheque*) to make out.
expedito, a [ekspe'ðito, a] *adj* (*libre*) clear, free.
expeler [ekspe'ler] *vt* to expel, eject.
expendedor, a [ekspende'ðor, a] *nm/f* (*vendedor*) dealer; (*TEAT*) ticket agent ♦ *nm* (*aparato*) (vending) machine; **~ de cigarrillos** cigarette machine.
expendeduría [ekspendedu'ria] *nf* (*estanco*)

tobacconist's (shop) (*BRIT*), cigar store (*US*).
expendio [eks'pendjo] *nm* (*AM*) small shop (*BRIT*) *o* store (*US*).
expensas [eks'pensas] *nfpl* (*JUR*) costs; **a ~ de** at the expense of.
experiencia [ekspe'rjenθja] *nf* experience.
experimentado, a [eksperimen'taðo, a] *adj* experienced.
experimentar [eksperimen'tar] *vt* (*en laboratorio*) to experiment with; (*probar*) to test, try out; (*notar, observar*) to experience; (*deterioro, pérdida*) to suffer; (*aumento*) to show; (*sensación*) to feel.
experimento [eksperi'mento] *nm* experiment.
experto, a [eks'perto, a] *adj* expert ♦ *nm/f* expert.
expiar [ekspi'ar] *vt* to atone for.
expida [eks'piða] *etc vb V* **expedir**.
expirar [ekspi'rar] *vi* to expire.
explanada [ekspla'naða] *nf* (*paseo*) esplanade; (*a orillas del mar*) promenade.
explayarse [ekspla'jarse] *vr* (*en discurso*) to speak at length; **~ con algn** to confide in sb.
explicación [eksplika'θjon] *nf* explanation.
explicar [ekspli'kar] *vt* to explain; (*teoría*) to expound; (*UNIV*) to lecture in; **~se** *vr* to explain (o.s.); **no me lo explico** I can't understand it.
explícito, a [eks'pliθito, a] *adj* explicit.
explique [eks'plike] *etc vb V* **explicar**.
exploración [eksplora'θjon] *nf* exploration; (*MIL*) reconnaissance.
explorador, a [eksplora'ðor, a] *nm/f* (*pionero*) explorer; (*MIL*) scout ♦ *nm* (*MED*) probe; (*radar*) (radar) scanner.
explorar [eksplo'rar] *vt* to explore; (*MED*) to probe; (*radar*) to scan.
explosión [eksplo'sjon] *nf* explosion.
explosivo, a [eksplo'siβo, a] *adj* explosive.
explotación [eksplota'θjon] *nf* exploitation; (*de planta etc*) running; (*de mina*) working; (*de recurso*) development; **~ minera** mine; **gastos de ~** operating costs.
explotar [eksplo'tar] *vt* to exploit; (*planta*) to run, operate; (*mina*) to work ♦ *vi* (*bomba etc*) to explode, go off.
expondré [ekspon'dre] *etc vb V* **exponer**.
exponer [ekspo'ner] *vt* to expose; (*cuadro*) to display; (*vida*) to risk; (*idea*) to explain; (*teoría*) to expound; (*hechos*) to set out; **~se** *vr*: **~se a (hacer) algo** to run the risk of (doing) sth.
exponga [eks'ponga] *etc vb V* **exponer**.
exportación [eksporta'θjon] *nf* (*acción*) export; (*mercancías*) exports *pl*.
exportador, a [eksporta'ðor, a] *adj* (*país*) exporting ♦ *nm/f* exporter.
exportar [ekspor'tar] *vt* to export.
exposición [eksposi'θjon] *nf* (*gen*) exposure; (*de arte*) show, exhibition; (*COM*) display; (*feria*) show, fair; (*explicación*) explanation; (*de teoría*) exposition; (*narración*) account, statement.
exprés [eks'pres] *adj inv* (*café*) espresso ♦ *nm* (*FERRO*) express (train).
expresamente [ekspresa'mente] *adv* (*concretamente*) expressly; (*a propósito*) on purpose.
expresar [ekspre'sar] *vt* to express; (*redactar*) to phrase, put; (*emoción*) to show; **~se** *vr* to express o.s.; (*dato*) to be stated; **como abajo se expresa** as stated below.
expresión [expre'sjon] *nf* expression; **~ familiar** colloquialism.
expresivo, a [ekspre'siβo, a] *adj* expressive; (*cariñoso*) affectionate.
expreso, a [eks'preso, a] *adj* (*explícito*) express; (*claro*) specific, clear; (*tren*) fast ♦ *nm* (*FERRO*) fast train ♦ *adv*: **mandar ~** to send by express (delivery).
exprimidor [eksprimi'ðor] *nm* (lemon) squeezer.
exprimir [ekspri'mir] *vt* (*fruta*) to squeeze; (*zumo*) to squeeze out.
ex profeso [ekspro'feso] *adv* expressly.
expropiar [ekspro'pjar] *vt* to expropriate.
expuesto, a [eks'pwesto, a] *pp de* **exponer** ♦ *adj* exposed; (*cuadro etc*) on show, on display; **según lo ~ arriba** according to what has been stated above.
expulsar [ekspul'sar] *vt* (*echar*) to eject, throw out; (*alumno*) to expel; (*despedir*) to sack, fire; (*DEPORTE*) to send off.
expulsión [ekspul'sjon] *nf* expulsion; sending-off.
expurgar [ekspur'ɣar] *vt* to expurgate.
expuse [eks'puse] *etc vb V* **exponer**.
exquisito, a [ekski'sito, a] *adj* exquisite; (*comida*) delicious; (*afectado*) affected.
Ext. *abr* (= *Exterior*) ext.; (= *Extensión*) ext.
éxtasis ['ekstasis] *nm* (*tb droga*) ecstasy.
extemporáneo, a [ekstempo'raneo, a] *adj* unseasonal.
extender [eksten'der] *vt* to extend; (*los brazos*) to stretch out, hold out; (*mapa, tela*) to spread (out), open (out); (*mantequilla*) to spread; (*certificado*) to issue; (*cheque, recibo*) to make out; (*documento*) to draw up; **~se** *vr* to extend; (*terreno*) to stretch *o* spread

(out); (*persona: en el suelo*) to stretch out; (*en el tiempo*) to extend, last; (*costumbre, epidemia*) to spread; (*guerra*) to escalate; **~se sobre un tema** to enlarge on a subject.

extendido, a [eksten'diðo, a] *adj* (*abierto*) spread out, open; (*brazos*) outstretched; (*costumbre etc*) widespread.

extensible [eksten'sißle] *adj* extending.

extensión [eksten'sjon] *nf* (*de terreno, mar*) expanse, stretch; (*MUS*) range; (*de conocimientos*) extent; (*de programa*) scope; (*de tiempo*) length, duration; (*TELEC*) extension; **~ de plazo** (*COM*) extension; **en toda la ~ de la palabra** in every sense of the word; **de ~** (*INFORM*) add-on.

extenso, a [eks'tenso, a] *adj* extensive.

extenuar [ekste'nwar] *vt* (*debilitar*) to weaken.

exterior [ekste'rjor] *adj* (*de fuera*) external; (*afuera*) outside, exterior; (*apariencia*) outward; (*deuda, relaciones*) foreign ♦ *nm* exterior, outside; (*aspecto*) outward appearance; (*DEPORTE*) wing(er); (*países extranjeros*) abroad; **asuntos ~es** foreign affairs; **al ~** outwardly, on the outside; **en el ~** abroad; **noticias del ~** foreign *o* overseas news.

exteriorice [eksterjo'riθe] *etc vb V* **exteriorizar**.

exteriorizar [eksterjori'θar] *vt* (*emociones*) to show, reveal.

exteriormente [eksterjor'mente] *adv* outwardly.

exterminar [ekstermi'nar] *vt* to exterminate.

exterminio [ekster'minjo] *nm* extermination.

externo, a [eks'terno, a] *adj* (*exterior*) external, outside; (*superficial*) outward ♦ *nm/f* day pupil.

extienda [eks'tjenda] *etc vb V* **extender**.

extinción [ekstin'θjon] *nf* extinction.

extinga [eks'tinga] *etc vb V* **extinguir**.

extinguido, a [ekstin'giðo, a] *adj* (*animal, volcán*) extinct; (*fuego*) out, extinguished.

extinguir [ekstin'gir] *vt* (*fuego*) to extinguish, put out; (*raza, población*) to wipe out; **~se** *vr* (*fuego*) to go out; (*BIO*) to die out, become extinct.

extinto, a [eks'tinto, a] *adj* extinct.

extintor [ekstin'tor] *nm* (fire) extinguisher.

extirpar [ekstir'par] *vt* (*vicios*) to eradicate, stamp out; (*MED*) to remove (surgically).

extorsión [ekstor'sjon] *nf* blackmail.

extra ['ekstra] *adj inv* (*tiempo*) extra; (*vino*) vintage; (*chocolate*) good-quality; (*gasolina*) high-octane ♦ *nm/f* extra ♦ *nm* (*bono*) bonus; (*periódico*) special edition.

extracción [ekstrak'θjon] *nf* extraction; (*en lotería*) draw; (*de carbón*) mining.

extracto [eks'trakto] *nm* extract.

extractor [ekstrak'tor] *nm* (*tb*: **~ de humos**) extractor fan.

extradición [ekstraði'θjon] *nf* extradition.

extraditar [ekstraði'tar] *vt* to extradite.

extraer [ekstra'er] *vt* to extract, take out.

extrafino, a [ekstra'fino, a] *adj* extra-fine; **azúcar ~** caster sugar.

extraiga [eks'traiɣa] *etc*, **extraje** [eks'traxe] *etc*, **extrajera** [ekstra'xera] *etc vb V* **extraer**.

extralimitarse [ekstralimi'tarse] *vr* to go too far.

extranjerismo [ekstranxe'rismo] *nm* foreign word *o* phrase *etc*.

extranjero, a [ekstran'xero, a] *adj* foreign ♦ *nm/f* foreigner ♦ *nm* foreign lands *pl*; **en el ~** abroad.

extrañamiento [ekstraɲa'mjento] *nm* estrangement.

extrañar [ekstra'ɲar] *vt* (*sorprender*) to find strange *o* odd; (*echar de menos*) to miss; **~se** *vr* (*sorprenderse*) to be amazed, be surprised; (*distanciarse*) to become estranged, grow apart; **me extraña** I'm surprised.

extrañeza [ekstra'ɲeθa] *nf* (*rareza*) strangeness, oddness; (*asombro*) amazement, surprise.

extraño, a [eks'traɲo, a] *adj* (*extranjero*) foreign; (*raro, sorprendente*) strange, odd.

extraoficial [ekstraofi'θjal] *adj* unofficial, informal.

extraordinario, a [ekstraorði'narjo, a] *adj* extraordinary; (*edición, número*) special ♦ *nm* (*de periódico*) special edition; **horas extraordinarias** overtime *sg*.

extrarradio [ekstra'rraðjo] *nm* suburbs *pl*.

extrasensorial [ekstrasenso'rjal] *adj*: **percepción ~** extrasensory perception.

extraterrestre [ekstrate'rrestre] *adj* of *o* from outer space ♦ *nm/f* creature from outer space.

extravagancia [ekstraßa'ɣanθja] *nf* oddness; outlandishness; (*rareza*) peculiarity; **~s** *nfpl* (*tonterías*) nonsense *sg*.

extravagante [ekstraßa'ɣante] *adj* (*excéntrico*) eccentric; (*estrafalario*) outlandish.

extraviado, a [ekstra'ßjaðo, a] *adj* lost, missing.

extraviar [ekstra'ßjar] *vt* to mislead, misdirect; (*perder*) to lose, misplace; **~se** *vr* to lose one's way, get lost; (*objeto*) to go missing, be mislaid.
extravío [ekstra'ßio] *nm* loss; (*fig*) misconduct.
extrayendo [ekstra'jendo] *vb V* **extraer**.
extremado, a [ekstre'maðo, a] *adj* extreme, excessive.
Extremadura [ekstrema'ðura] *nf* Estremadura.
extremar [ekstre'mar] *vt* to carry to extremes; **~se** *vr* to do one's utmost, make every effort.
extremaunción [ekstremaun'θjon] *nf* extreme unction, last rites *pl*.
extremidad [ekstremi'ðað] *nf* (*punta*) extremity; (*fila*) edge; **~es** *nfpl* (*ANAT*) extremities.
extremista [ekstre'mista] *adj, nm/f* extremist.
extremo, a [eks'tremo, a] *adj* extreme; (*más alejado*) furthest; (*último*) last ♦ *nm* end; (*situación*) extreme; **E~ Oriente** Far East; **en último ~** as a last resort; **pasar de un ~ a otro** (*fig*) to go from one extreme to the other; **con ~** in the extreme; **la extrema derecha** (*POL*) the far right; **~ derecho/izquierdo** (*DEPORTE*) outside right/left.
extrínseco, a [eks'trinseko, a] *adj* extrinsic.
extrovertido, a [ekstroßer'tiðo, a] *adj* extrovert, outgoing ♦ *nm/f* extrovert.
exuberancia [eksuße'ranθja] *nf* exuberance.
exuberante [eksuße'rante] *adj* exuberant; (*fig*) luxuriant, lush.
exudar [eksu'ðar] *vt, vi* to exude.
exultar [eksul'tar] *vi*: **~ (en)** to exult (in); (*pey*) to gloat (over).
exvoto [eks'ßoto] *nm* votive offering.
eyaculación [ejakula'θjon] *nf* ejaculation.
eyacular [ejaku'lar] *vt, vi* to ejaculate.

Ff

F, f ['efe] *nf* (*letra*) F, f; **F de Francia** F for Frederick (*BRIT*), F for Fox (*US*).
fa [fa] *nm* (*MUS*) F.
f.ª *abr* (*COM*: = *factura*) Inv.
f.a.b. *abr* (= *franco a bordo*) f.o.b.
fabada [fa'ßaða] *nf* *bean and sausage stew*.
fábrica ['faßrika] *nf* factory; **~ de moneda** mint; **marca de ~** trademark; **precio de ~** factory price.
fabricación [faßrika'θjon] *nf* (*manufactura*) manufacture; (*producción*) production; **de ~ casera** home-made; **de ~ nacional** home produced; **~ en serie** mass production.
fabricante [faßri'kante] *nm/f* manufacturer.
fabricar [faßri'kar] *vt* (*manufacturar*) to manufacture, make; (*construir*) to build; (*cuento*) to fabricate, devise; **~ en serie** to mass-produce.
fabril [fa'ßril] *adj*: **industria ~** manufacturing industry.
fabrique [fa'ßrike] *etc vb V* **fabricar**.
fábula ['faßula] *nf* (*cuento*) fable; (*chisme*) rumour; (*mentira*) fib.
fabuloso, a [faßu'loso, a] *adj* fabulous, fantastic.
FACA ['faka] *nm abr* (*ESP AVIAT*) = *Futuro Avión de Combate y Ataque*.
facción [fak'θjon] *nf* (*POL*) faction; **facciones** *nfpl* (*del rostro*) features.
faceta [fa'θeta] *nf* facet.
facha ['fatʃa] (*fam*) *nm/f* fascist, right-wing extremist ♦ *nf* (*aspecto*) look; (*cara*) face; **¡qué ~ tienes!** you look a sight!
fachada [fa'tʃaða] *nf* (*ARQ*) façade, front; (*TIP*) title page; (*fig*) façade, outward show.
facial [fa'θjal] *adj* facial.
fácil ['faθil] *adj* (*simple*) easy; (*sencillo*) simple, straightforward; (*probable*) likely; (*respuesta*) facile; **~ de usar** (*INFORM*) user-friendly.
facilidad [faθili'ðað] *nf* (*capacidad*) ease; (*sencillez*) simplicity; (*de palabra*) fluency; **~es** *nfpl* facilities; **"~es de pago"** (*COM*) "credit facilities",

"payment terms".

facilitar [faθili'tar] *vt* (*hacer fácil*) to make easy; (*proporcionar*) to provide; (*documento*) to issue; **le agradecería me facilitara ...** I would be grateful if you could let me have ....

fácilmente ['faθilmente] *adv* easily.

facsímil [fak'simil] *nm* (*documento*) facsimile; **enviar por** ~ to fax.

factible [fak'tiβle] *adj* feasible.

factor [fak'tor] *nm* factor; (*COM*) agent; (*FERRO*) freight clerk.

factoría [fakto'ria] *nf* (*COM: agencia*) agency; (*: fábrica*) factory.

factura [fak'tura] *nf* (*cuenta*) bill; (*nota de pago*) invoice; (*hechura*) manufacture; **presentar ~ a** to invoice.

facturación [faktura'θjon] *nf* (*COM*) invoicing; (*: ventas*) turnover; **~ de equipajes** luggage check-in.

facturar [faktu'rar] *vt* (*COM*) to invoice, charge for; (*AVIAT*) to check in; (*equipaje*) to register, check (*US*).

facultad [fakul'tað] *nf* (*aptitud, ESCOL etc*) faculty; (*poder*) power.

facultativo, a [fakulta'tiβo, a] *adj* optional; (*de un oficio*) professional; **prescripción facultativa** medical prescription.

FAD *nm abr* (*ESP*) = *Fondo de Ayuda y Desarrollo.*

faena [fa'ena] *nf* (*trabajo*) work; (*quehacer*) task, job; **~s domésticas** housework *sg.*

faenar [fae'nar] *vi* to fish.

fagot [fa'ɣot] *nm* (*MUS*) bassoon.

faisán [fai'san] *nm* pheasant.

faja ['faxa] *nf* (*para la cintura*) sash; (*de mujer*) corset; (*de tierra*) strip.

fajo ['faxo] *nm* (*de papeles*) bundle; (*de billetes*) role, wad.

falange [fa'lanxe] *nf*: **la F~** (*POL*) the Falange.

falda ['falda] *nf* (*prenda de vestir*) skirt; (*GEO*) foothill; ~ **escocesa** kilt.

fálico, a ['faliko, a] *adj* phallic.

falla ['faʎa] *nf* (*defecto*) fault, flaw.

fallar [fa'ʎar] *vt* (*JUR*) to pronounce sentence on; (*NAIPES*) to trump ♦ *vi* (*memoria*) to fail; (*plan*) to go wrong; (*motor*) to miss; ~ **a algn** to let sb down.

Fallas ['faʎas] *nfpl see boxed note.*

FALLAS

In the week of 19 March (the feast of St Joseph, San José), Valencia honours its patron saint with a spectacular "fiesta" called **las Fallas.** *The Fallas are, more precisely, huge figures made of wood, cardboard, paper and cloth, depicting famous politicians and other prime targets of ridicule. At the end of the festival, these figures are set on fire by the "falleros", members of competing local groups who will have spent months working on them.*

fallecer [faʎe'θer] *vi* to pass away, die.

fallecido, a [faʎe'θiðo, a] *adj* late ♦ *nm/f* deceased.

fallecimiento [faʎeθi'mjento] *nm* decease, demise.

fallero, a [fa'ʎero, a] *nm/f* maker of "Fallas".

fallezca [fa'ʎeθka] *etc vb V* **fallecer**.

fallido, a [fa'ʎiðo, a] *adj* vain; (*intento*) frustrated, unsuccessful.

fallo ['faʎo] *nm* (*JUR*) verdict, ruling; (*decisión*) decision; (*de jurado*) findings; (*fracaso*) failure; (*DEPORTE*) miss; (*INFORM*) bug.

falo ['falo] *nm* phallus.

falsear [false'ar] *vt* to falsify; (*firma etc*) to forge ♦ *vi* (*MUS*) to be out of tune.

falsedad [false'ðað] *nf* falseness; (*hipocresía*) hypocrisy; (*mentira*) falsehood.

falsificación [falsifika'θjon] *nf* (*acto*) falsification; (*objeto*) forgery.

falsificar [falsifi'kar] *vt* (*firma etc*) to forge; (*voto etc*) to rig; (*moneda*) to counterfeit.

falsifique [falsi'fike] *etc vb V* **falsificar**.

falso, a ['falso, a] *adj* false; (*erróneo*) wrong, mistaken; (*firma, documento*) forged; (*documento, moneda etc*) fake; **en ~** falsely; **dar un paso en ~** to trip; (*fig*) to take a false step.

falta ['falta] *nf* (*defecto*) fault, flaw; (*privación*) lack, want; (*ausencia*) absence; (*carencia*) shortage; (*equivocación*) mistake; (*JUR*) default; (*DEPORTE*) foul; (*TENIS*) fault; **~ de ortografía** spelling mistake; **~ de respeto** disrespect; **echar en ~** to miss; **hacer ~ hacer algo** to be necessary to do sth; **me hace ~ una pluma** I need a pen; **sin ~** without fail; **por ~ de** through *o* for lack of.

faltar [fal'tar] *vi* (*escasear*) to be lacking, be wanting; (*ausentarse*) to be absent, be missing; **¿falta algo?** is anything missing?; **falta mucho todavía** there's plenty of time yet; **¿falta mucho?** is there long to go?; **faltan 2 horas para llegar** there are 2 hours to go till arrival; **~ (al respeto) a algn** to be disrespectful to sb; **~ a una cita** to miss an appointment; **~ a la verdad** to lie; **¡no faltaba más!** that's the last straw!

falto, a ['falto, a] *adj* (*desposeído*) deficient,

lacking; (*necesitado*) poor, wretched; **estar ~ de** to be short of.
fama ['fama] *nf* (*renombre*) fame; (*reputación*) reputation.
famélico, a [fa'meliko, a] *adj* starving.
familia [fa'milja] *nf* family; **~ política** in-laws *pl*.
familiar [fami'ljar] *adj* (*relativo a la familia*) family *cpd*; (*conocido, informal*) familiar; (*estilo*) informal; (*LING*) colloquial ♦ *nm/f* relative, relation.
familiarice [familja'riθe] *etc vb V* **familiarizarse**.
familiaridad [familjari'ðað] *nf* familiarity; (*informalidad*) homeliness.
familiarizarse [familjari'θarse] *vr*: **~ con** to familiarize o.s. with.
famoso, a [fa'moso, a] *adj* (*renombrado*) famous.
fan, *pl* **fans** [fan, fans] *nm* fan.
fanático, a [fa'natiko, a] *adj* fanatical ♦ *nm/f* fanatic; (*CINE, DEPORTE etc*) fan.
fanatismo [fana'tismo] *nm* fanaticism.
fanfarrón, ona [fanfa'rron, ona] *adj* boastful; (*pey*) showy.
fanfarronear [fanfarrone'ar] *vi* to boast.
fango ['fango] *nm* mud.
fangoso, a [fan'goso, a] *adj* muddy.
fantasear [fantase'ar] *vi* to fantasize; **~ con una idea** to toy with an idea.
fantasía [fanta'sia] *nf* fantasy, imagination; (*MUS*) fantasia; (*capricho*) whim; **joyas de ~** imitation jewellery *sg*.
fantasma [fan'tasma] *nm* (*espectro*) ghost, apparition; (*presumido*) show-off.
fantástico, a [fan'tastiko, a] *adj* (*irreal, fam*) fantastic.
fanzine [fan'θine] *nm* fanzine.
FAO ['fao] *nf abr* (= *Organización de las Naciones Unidas para la Agricultura y la Alimentación*) FAO.
faquir [fa'kir] *nm* fakir.
faraón [fara'on] *nm* Pharaoh.
faraónico, a [fara'oniko, a] *adj* Pharaonic; (*fig*) grandiose.
fardar [far'ðar] *vi* to show off; **~ de** to boast about.
fardo ['farðo] *nm* bundle; (*fig*) burden.
faringe [fa'rinxe] *nf* pharynx.
faringitis [farin'xitis] *nf* pharyngitis.
farmacéutico, a [farma'θeutiko, a] *adj* pharmaceutical ♦ *nm/f* chemist (*BRIT*), pharmacist.
farmacia [far'maθja] *nf* (*ciencia*) pharmacy; (*tienda*) chemist's (shop) (*BRIT*), pharmacy, drugstore (*US*); **~ de turno** duty chemist.
fármaco ['farmako] *nm* medicine, drug.
faro ['faro] *nm* (*NAUT: torre*) lighthouse; (*señal*) beacon; (*AUTO*) headlamp; **~s antiniebla** fog lamps; **~s delanteros/traseros** headlights/rear lights.
farol [fa'rol] *nm* (*luz*) lantern, lamp; (*FERRO*) headlamp; (*poste*) lamppost; **echarse un ~** (*fam*) to show off.
farola [fa'rola] *nf* street lamp (*BRIT*) *o* light (*US*), lamppost.
farruco, a [fa'rruko, a] *adj* (*fam*): **estar** *o* **ponerse ~** to get aggressive.
farsa ['farsa] *nf* (*gen*) farce.
farsante [far'sante] *nm/f* fraud, fake.
FASA ['fasa] *nf abr* (*ESP AUTO*) = *Fábrica de Automóviles, S.A.*
fascículo [fas'θikulo] *nm* (*gen*) part, instalment (*BRIT*), installment (*US*).
fascinante [fasθi'nante] *adj* fascinating.
fascinar [fasθi'nar] *vt* to fascinate; (*encantar*) to captivate.
fascismo [fas'θismo] *nm* fascism.
fascista [fas'θista] *adj, nm/f* fascist.
fase ['fase] *nf* phase.
fastidiar [fasti'ðjar] *vt* (*disgustar*) to annoy, bother; (*estropear*) to spoil; **~se** *vr* (*disgustarse*) to get annoyed *o* cross; **¡no fastidies!** you're joking!; **¡que se fastidie!** (*fam*) he'll just have to put up with it!
fastidio [fas'tiðjo] *nm* (*disgusto*) annoyance.
fastidioso, a [fasti'ðjoso, a] *adj* (*molesto*) annoying.
fastuoso, a [fas'twoso, a] *adj* (*espléndido*) magnificent; (*banquete etc*) lavish.
fatal [fa'tal] *adj* (*gen*) fatal; (*desgraciado*) ill-fated; (*fam: malo, pésimo*) awful ♦ *adv* terribly; **lo pasó ~** he had a terrible time (of it).
fatalidad [fatali'ðað] *nf* (*destino*) fate; (*mala suerte*) misfortune.
fatídico, a [fa'tiðiko, a] *adj* fateful.
fatiga [fa'tiɣa] *nf* (*cansancio*) fatigue, weariness; **~s** *nfpl* hardships.
fatigar [fati'ɣar] *vt* to tire, weary; **~se** *vr* to get tired.
fatigoso, a [fati'ɣoso, a] *adj* (*cansador*) tiring.
fatigue [fa'tiɣe] *etc vb V* **fatigar**.
fatuo, a ['fatwo, a] *adj* (*vano*) fatuous; (*presuntuoso*) conceited.
fauces ['fauθes] *nfpl* (*ANAT*) gullet *sg*; (*fam*) jaws.
fauna ['fauna] *nf* fauna.
favor [fa'ßor] *nm* favour (*BRIT*), favor (*US*); **haga el ~ de ...** would you be so good as to ..., kindly ...; **por ~** please; **a ~** in favo(u)r; **a ~ de** to be in favo(u)r of;

(*COM*) to the order of.
favorable [faβo'raβle] *adj* favourable (*BRIT*), favorable (*US*); (*condiciones etc*) advantageous.
favorecer [faβore'θer] *vt* to favour (*BRIT*), favor (*US*); (*amparar*) to help; (*vestido etc*) to become, flatter; **este peinado le favorece** this hairstyle suits him.
favorezca [faβo'reθka] *etc vb V* **favorecer**.
favorito, a [faβo'rito, a] *adj, nm/f* favourite (*BRIT*), favorite (*US*).
fax [faks] *nm inv* fax; **mandar por ~** to fax.
faz [faθ] *nf* face; **la ~ de la tierra** the face of the earth.
F.C., f.c. *abr* = **ferrocarril**.
FE *nf abr* = *Falange Española*.
fe [fe] *nf* (*REL*) faith; (*confianza*) belief; (*documento*) certificate; **de buena ~** (*JUR*) bona fide; **prestar ~ a** to believe, credit; **actuar con buena/mala ~** to act in good/bad faith; **dar ~ de** to bear witness to; **~ de erratas** errata.
fealdad [feal'dað] *nf* ugliness.
feb., feb.º *abr* (= *febrero*) Feb.
febrero [fe'βrero] *nm* February.
febril [fe'βril] *adj* feverish; (*movido*) hectic.
fecha ['fetʃa] *nf* date; **~ límite** *o* **tope** closing *o* last date; **~ límite de venta** (*de alimentos*) sell-by date; **~ de caducidad** (*de alimentos*) sell-by date; (*de contrato*) expiry date; **en ~ próxima** soon; **hasta la ~** to date, so far; **~ de vencimiento** (*COM*) due date; **~ de vigencia** (*COM*) effective date.
fechar [fe'tʃar] *vt* to date.
fechoría [fetʃo'ria] *nf* misdeed.
fécula ['fekula] *nf* starch.
fecundación [fekunda'θjon] *nf* fertilization; **~ in vitro** in vitro fertilization, I.V.F.
fecundar [fekun'dar] *vt* (*generar*) to fertilize, make fertile.
fecundidad [fekundi'ðað] *nf* fertility; (*fig*) productiveness.
fecundo, a [fe'kundo, a] *adj* (*fértil*) fertile; (*fig*) prolific; (*productivo*) productive.
FED *nm abr* (= *Fondo Europeo de Desarrollo*) EDF.
FEDER *nm abr* (= *Fondo Europeo de Desarrollo Regional*) ERDF.
federación [feðera'θjon] *nf* federation.
federal [feðe'ral] *adj* federal.
federalismo [feðera'lismo] *nm* federalism.
FEF [fef] *nf abr* = *Federación Española de Fútbol*.
felicidad [feliθi'ðað] *nf* (*satisfacción, contento*) happiness; **~es** *nfpl* best wishes, congratulations.
felicitación [feliθita'θjon] *nf* (*tarjeta*) greetings card; **felicitaciones** *nfpl* (*enhorabuena*) congratulations; **~ navideña** *o* **de Navidad** Christmas Greetings.
felicitar [feliθi'tar] *vt* to congratulate.
feligrés, esa [feli'ɣres, esa] *nm/f* parishioner.
felino, a [fe'lino, a] *adj* cat-like; (*ZOOL*) feline ♦ *nm* feline.
feliz [fe'liθ] *adj* (*contento*) happy; (*afortunado*) lucky.
felonía [felo'nia] *nf* felony, crime.
felpa ['felpa] *nf* (*terciopelo*) plush; (*toalla*) towelling.
felpudo [fel'puðo] *nm* doormat.
femenino, a [feme'nino, a] *adj* feminine; (*ZOOL etc*) female ♦ *nm* (*LING*) feminine.
feminismo [femi'nismo] *nm* feminism.
feminista [femi'nista] *adj, nm/f* feminist.
fenomenal [fenome'nal] *adj* phenomenal; (*fam*) great, terrific.
fenómeno [fe'nomeno] *nm* phenomenon; (*fig*) freak, accident ♦ *adv*: **lo pasamos ~** we had a great time ♦ *excl* great!, marvellous!
feo, a ['feo, a] *adj* (*gen*) ugly; (*desagradable*) bad, nasty ♦ *nm* insult; **hacer un ~ a algn** to offend sb; **más ~ que Picio** as ugly as sin.
féretro ['feretro] *nm* (*ataúd*) coffin; (*sarcófago*) bier.
feria ['ferja] *nf* (*gen*) fair; (*AM: mercado*) market; (*descanso*) holiday, rest day; (*AM: cambio*) small change; **~ comercial** trade fair; **~ de muestras** trade show.
feriado, a [fe'rjaðo, a] (*AM*) *adj*: **día ~** (public) holiday ♦ *nm* (public) holiday.
fermentar [fermen'tar] *vi* to ferment.
fermento [fer'mento] *nm* leaven, leavening.
ferocidad [feroθi'ðað] *nf* fierceness, ferocity.
ferocísimo, a [fero'θisimo, a] *adj superlativo de* **feroz**.
feroz [fe'roθ] *adj* (*cruel*) cruel; (*salvaje*) fierce.
férreo, a ['ferreo, a] *adj* iron *cpd*; (*TEC*) ferrous; (*fig*) (of) iron.
ferretería [ferrete'ria] *nf* (*tienda*) ironmonger's (shop) (*BRIT*), hardware store.
ferrocarril [ferroka'rril] *nm* railway, railroad (*US*); **~ de vía estrecha/única** narrow-gauge/single-track railway *o* line.
ferroviario, a [ferrovja'rjo, a] *adj* rail *cpd*, railway *cpd* (*BRIT*), railroad *cpd* (*US*) ♦ *nm*:

~**s** railway (*BRIT*) *o* railroad (*US*) workers.
fértil ['fertil] *adj* (*productivo*) fertile; (*rico*) rich.
fertilice [ferti'liθe] *etc vb V* **fertilizar**.
fertilidad [fertili'ðað] *nf* (*gen*) fertility; (*productividad*) fruitfulness.
fertilizante [fertili'θante] *nm* fertilizer.
fertilizar [fertili'θar] *vt* to fertilize.
ferviente [fer'ßjente] *adj* fervent.
fervor [fer'ßor] *nm* fervour (*BRIT*), fervor (*US*).
fervoroso, a [ferßo'roso, a] *adj* fervent.
festejar [feste'xar] *vt* (*agasajar*) to wine and dine, fête; (*galantear*) to court; (*celebrar*) to celebrate.
festejo [fes'texo] *nm* (*diversión*) entertainment; (*galanteo*) courtship; (*fiesta*) celebration.
festín [fes'tin] *nm* feast, banquet.
festival [festi'ßal] *nm* festival.
festividad [festißi'ðað] *nf* festivity.
festivo, a [fes'tißo, a] *adj* (*de fiesta*) festive; (*fig*) witty; (*CINE, LIT*) humorous; **día** ~ holiday.
fetiche [fe'titʃe] *nm* fetish.
fetichista [feti'tʃista] *adj* fetishistic ♦ *nm/f* fetishist.
fétido, a ['fetiðo, a] *adj* (*hediondo*) foul-smelling.
feto ['feto] *nm* foetus; (*fam*) monster.
F.E.V.E. *nf abr* (= *Ferrocarriles Españoles de Vía Estrecha*) *Spanish narrow-gauge railways*.
FF.AA. *nfpl abr* (*MIL*) = **Fuerzas Armadas**.
FF.CC. *nmpl abr* = **Ferrocarriles**.
fiable [fi'aßle] *adj* (*persona*) trustworthy; (*máquina*) reliable.
fiado [fi'aðo] *nm*: **comprar al** ~ to buy on credit; **en** ~ on bail.
fiador, a [fia'ðor, a] *nm/f* (*JUR*) surety, guarantor; (*COM*) backer; **salir** ~ **por algn** to stand bail for sb.
fiambre ['fjambre] *adj* (*CULIN*) (served) cold ♦ *nm* (*CULIN*) cold meat (*BRIT*), cold cut (*US*); (*fam*) corpse, stiff.
fiambrera [fjam'brera] *nf* ≈ lunch box, dinner pail (*US*).
fianza ['fjanθa] *nf* surety; (*JUR*): **libertad bajo** ~ release on bail.
fiar [fi'ar] *vt* (*salir garante de*) to guarantee; (*JUR*) to stand bail *o* bond (*US*) for; (*vender a crédito*) to sell on credit; (*secreto*) to confide ♦ *vi*: ~ **(de)** to trust (in); **ser de** ~ to be trustworthy; ~**se** *vr*: ~ **de** to trust (in), rely on.
fiasco ['fjasko] *nm* fiasco.
fibra ['fißra] *nf* fibre (*BRIT*), fiber (*US*); (*fig*) vigour (*BRIT*), vigor (*US*); ~ **óptica** (*INFORM*) optical fibre (*BRIT*) *o* fiber (*US*).
ficción [fik'θjon] *nf* fiction.
ficha ['fitʃa] *nf* (*TELEC*) token; (*en juegos*) counter, marker; (*en casino*) chip; (*COM, ECON*) tally, check (*US*); (*INFORM*) file; (*tarjeta*) (index) card; (*ELEC*) plug; (*en hotel*) registration form; ~ **policíaca** police dossier.
fichaje [fi'tʃaxe] *nm* signing(-up).
fichar [fi'tʃar] *vt* (*archivar*) to file, index; (*DEPORTE*) to sign (up) ♦ *vi* (*deportista*) to sign (up); (*obrero*) to clock in *o* on; **estar fichado** to have a record.
fichero [fi'tʃero] *nm* card index; (*archivo*) filing cabinet; (*COM*) box file; (*INFORM*) file, archive; (*de policía*) criminal records; ~ **activo** (*INFORM*) active file; ~ **archivado** (*INFORM*) archived file; ~ **indexado** (*INFORM*) index file; ~ **de reserva** (*INFORM*) backup file; ~ **de tarjetas** card index; **nombre de** ~ filename.
ficticio, a [fik'tiθjo, a] *adj* (*imaginario*) fictitious; (*falso*) fabricated.
ficus ['fikus] *nm inv* (*BOT*) rubber plant.
fidedigno, a [fiðe'ðiɣno, a] *adj* reliable.
fideicomiso [fiðeiko'miso] *nm* (*COM*) trust.
fidelidad [fiðeli'ðað] *nf* (*lealtad*) fidelity, loyalty; (*exactitud: de dato etc*) accuracy; **alta** ~ high fidelity, hi-fi.
fidelísimo, a [fiðe'lisimo, a] *adj superlativo de* **fiel**.
fideos [fi'ðeos] *nmpl* noodles.
fiduciario, a [fiðu'θjarjo, a] *nm/f* fiduciary.
fiebre ['fjeßre] *nf* (*MED*) fever; (*fig*) fever, excitement; ~ **amarilla/del heno** yellow/hay fever; ~ **palúdica** malaria; **tener** ~ to have a temperature.
fiel [fjel] *adj* (*leal*) faithful, loyal; (*fiable*) reliable; (*exacto*) accurate ♦ *nm* (*aguja*) needle, pointer; **los** ~**es** the faithful.
fieltro ['fjeltro] *nm* felt.
fiera ['fjera] *nf V* **fiero**.
fiereza [fje'reθa] *nf* (*ZOOL*) wildness; (*bravura*) fierceness.
fiero, a ['fjero, a] *adj* (*cruel*) cruel; (*feroz*) fierce; (*duro*) harsh ♦ *nm/f* (*fig*) fiend ♦ *nf* (*animal feroz*) wild animal *o* beast; (*fig*) dragon.
fierro ['fjerro] *nm* (*AM*) iron.
fiesta ['fjesta] *nf* party; (*de pueblo*) festival; **la** ~ **nacional** bullfighting; **(día de)** ~ (public) holiday; **mañana es** ~ it's a holiday tomorrow; ~ **de guardar** (*REL*) day of obligation; see boxed note.

> **FIESTA**
>
> ***Fiestas** can be national public holidays (such as the Día de la Constitución), or special regional ones for each autonomous region, many of which are religious feast days. All over Spain there are also special local **fiestas** in honour of a patron saint or the Virgin Mary. These often last several days and can include religious processions, carnival parades, bullfights, dancing and feasting on local produce.*

FIFA *nf abr* (= *Federación Internacional de Fútbol Asociación*) FIFA.
figura [fi'ɣura] *nf* (*gen*) figure; (*forma, imagen*) shape, form; (*NAIPES*) face card.
figurado, a [fiɣu'raðo, a] *adj* figurative.
figurante [fiɣu'rante] *nm/f* (*TEAT*) walk-on part; (*CINE*) extra.
figurar [fiɣu'rar] *vt* (*representar*) to represent; (*fingir*) to feign ♦ *vi* to figure; **~se** *vr* (*imaginarse*) to imagine; (*suponer*) to suppose; **ya me lo figuraba** I thought as much.
fijador [fixa'ðor] *nm* (*FOTO etc*) fixative; (*de pelo*) gel.
fijar [fi'xar] *vt* (*gen*) to fix; (*cartel*) to post, put up; (*estampilla*) to affix, stick (on); (*pelo*) to set; (*fig*) to settle (on), decide; **~se** *vr*: **~se en** to notice; **¡fíjate!** just imagine!; **¿te fijas?** see what I mean?
fijo, a ['fixo, a] *adj* (*gen*) fixed; (*firme*) firm; (*permanente*) permanent; (*trabajo*) steady; (*color*) fast ♦ *adv*: **mirar ~** to stare.
fila ['fila] *nf* row; (*MIL*) rank; (*cadena*) line; (*MIL*) rank; (*en marcha*) file; **~ india** single file; **ponerse en ~** to line up, get into line; **primera ~** front row.
filántropo, a [fi'lantropo, a] *nm/f* philanthropist.
filarmónico, a [filar'moniko, a] *adj, nf* philharmonic.
filatelia [fila'telja] *nf* philately, stamp collecting.
filatelista [filate'lista] *nm/f* philatelist, stamp collector.
filete [fi'lete] *nm* (*carne*) fillet steak; (*de cerdo*) tenderloin; (*pescado*) fillet; (*MEC: rosca*) thread.
filiación [filja'θjon] *nf* (*POL etc*) affiliation; (*señas*) particulars *pl*; (*MIL, POLICÍA*) records *pl*.
filial [fi'ljal] *adj* filial ♦ *nf* subsidiary; (*sucursal*) branch.
Filipinas [fili'pinas] *nfpl*: **las (Islas) ~** the Philippines.
filipino, a [fili'pino, a] *adj, nm/f* Philippine.
film [film], *pl* **films** *nm* = **filme**.
filmación [filma'θjon] *nf* filming, shooting.
filmar [fil'mar] *vt* to film, shoot.
filme ['filme] *nm* film, movie (*US*).
filmoteca [filmo'teka] *nf* film library.
filo ['filo] *nm* (*gen*) edge; **sacar ~ a** to sharpen; **al ~ del medio día** at about midday; **de doble ~** double-edged.
filología [filolo'xia] *nf* philology.
filólogo, a [fi'loloɣo, a] *nm/f* philologist.
filón [fi'lon] *nm* (*MINERÍA*) vein, lode; (*fig*) gold mine.
filoso, a [fi'loso, a] *adj* (*AM*) sharp.
filosofía [filoso'fia] *nf* philosophy.
filosófico, a [filo'sofiko, a] *adj* philosophic(al).
filósofo, a [fi'losofo, a] *nm/f* philosopher.
filtración [filtra'θjon] *nf* (*TEC*) filtration; (*INFORM*) sorting; (*fig: de fondos*) misappropriation; (*de datos*) leak.
filtrar [fil'trar] *vt, vi* to filter, strain; (*información*) to leak; **~se** *vr* to filter; (*fig: dinero*) to dwindle.
filtro ['filtro] *nm* (*TEC, utensilio*) filter.
filudo, a [fi'luðo, a] *adj* (*AM*) sharp.
fin [fin] *nm* end; (*objetivo*) aim, purpose; **a ~ de cuentas** at the end of the day; **al ~ y al cabo** when all's said and done; **a ~ de** in order to; **por ~** finally; **en ~** (*resumiendo*) in short; **¡en ~!** (*resignación*) oh, well!; **~ de archivo** (*INFORM*) end-of-file; **~ de semana** weekend; **sin ~** endless(ly).
final [fi'nal] *adj* final ♦ *nm* end, conclusion ♦ *nf* (*DEPORTE*) final.
finalice [fina'liθe] *etc vb V* **finalizar**.
finalidad [finali'ðað] *nf* finality; (*propósito*) purpose, aim.
finalista [fina'lista] *nm/f* finalist.
finalizar [finali'θar] *vt* to end, finish ♦ *vi* to end, come to an end; **~ la sesión** (*INFORM*) to log out *o* off.
financiación [finanθja'θjon] *nf* financing.
financiar [finan'θjar] *vt* to finance.
financiero, a [finan'θjero, a] *adj* financial ♦ *nm/f* financier.
financista [finan'sista] *nm/f* (*AM*) financier.
finanzas [fi'nanθas] *nfpl* finances.
finca ['finka] *nf* country estate.
fineza [fi'neθa] *nf* (*cualidad*) fineness; (*modales*) refinement.
fingir [fin'xir] *vt* (*simular*) to simulate, feign; (*pretextar*) to sham, fake ♦ *vi* (*aparentar*) to pretend; **~se** *vr*: **~se dormido** to pretend to be asleep.
finiquitar [finiki'tar] *vt* (*ECON: cuenta*) to settle and close.

Finisterre [finis'terre] *nm*: **el cabo de ~** Cape Finisterre.
finja ['finxa] *etc vb V* **fingir**.
finlandés, esa [finlan'des, esa] *adj* Finnish ♦ *nm/f* Finn ♦ *nm* (*LING*) Finnish.
Finlandia [fin'landja] *nf* Finland.
fino, a ['fino, a] *adj* fine; (*delgado*) slender; (*de buenas maneras*) polite, refined; (*inteligente*) shrewd; (*punta*) sharp; (*gusto*) discriminating; (*oído*) sharp; (*jerez*) fino, dry ♦ *nm* (*jerez*) dry sherry.
finura [fi'nura] *nf* (*calidad*) fineness; (*cortesía*) politeness; (*elegancia*) elegance; (*agudeza*) shrewdness.
FIP [fip] *nf abr* (*ESP*) = *Formación Intensiva Profesional*.
firma ['firma] *nf* signature; (*COM*) firm, company.
firmamento [firma'mento] *nm* firmament.
firmante [fir'mante] *adj, nm/f* signatory; **los abajo ~s** the undersigned.
firmar [fir'mar] *vt* to sign; **~ un contrato** (*COM*: *colocarse*) to sign on; **firmado y sellado** signed and sealed.
firme ['firme] *adj* firm; (*estable*) stable; (*sólido*) solid; (*constante*) steady; (*decidido*) resolute; (*duro*) hard; **¡~s!** (*MIL*) attention!; **oferta en ~** (*COM*) firm offer ♦ *nm* road (surface).
firmemente [firme'mente] *adv* firmly.
firmeza [fir'meθa] *nf* firmness; (*constancia*) steadiness; (*solidez*) solidity.
fiscal [fis'kal] *adj* fiscal ♦ *nm* (*JUR*) ≈ Crown Prosecutor, Procurator Fiscal (*Escocia*), district attorney (*US*).
fiscalice [fiska'liθe] *etc vb V* **fiscalizar**.
fiscalizar [fiskali'θar] *vt* (*controlar*) to control; (*registrar*) to inspect (officially); (*fig*) to criticize.
fisco ['fisko] *nm* (*hacienda*) treasury, exchequer; **declarar algo al ~** to declare sth for tax purposes.
fisgar [fis'ɣar] *vt* to pry into.
fisgón, ona [fis'ɣon, ona] *adj* nosey.
fisgue ['fisɣe] *etc vb V* **fisgar**.
físico, a ['fisiko, a] *adj* physical ♦ *nm* physique; (*aspecto*) appearance, looks ♦ *nm/f* physicist ♦ *nf* physics *sg*.
fisioterapeuta [fisjotera'peuta] *nm/f* physiotherapist.
fisioterapia [fisjote'rapja] *nf* physiotherapy.
fisioterapista [fisjotera'pista] *nm/f* (*AM*) physiotherapist.
fisonomía [fisono'mia] *nf* physiognomy, features *pl*.
fisonomista [fisono'mista] *nm/f*: **ser buen ~** to have a good memory for faces.
flac(c)idez [fla(k)θi'ðeθ] *nf* softness, flabbiness.
flác(c)ido, a ['fla(k)θiðo, a] *adj* flabby.
flaco, a ['flako, a] *adj* (*muy delgado*) skinny, thin; (*débil*) weak, feeble.
flagrante [fla'ɣrante] *adj* flagrant.
flamante [fla'mante] *adj* (*fam*) brilliant; (: *nuevo*) brand-new.
flamear [flame'ar] *vt* (*CULIN*) to flambé.
flamenco, a [fla'menko, a] *adj* (*de Flandes*) Flemish; (*baile, música*) gipsy ♦ *nm/f* Fleming; **los ~s** the Flemish ♦ *nm* (*LING*) Flemish; (*baile, música*) flamenco; (*ZOOL*) flamingo.
flan [flan] *nm* creme caramel.
flanco ['flanko] *nm* side; (*MIL*) flank.
Flandes ['flandes] *nm* Flanders.
flanquear [flanke'ar] *vt* to flank; (*MIL*) to outflank.
flaquear [flake'ar] *vi* (*debilitarse*) to weaken; (*persona*) to slack.
flaqueza [fla'keθa] *nf* (*delgadez*) thinness, leanness; (*fig*) weakness.
flaquísimo, a [fla'kisimo, a] *adj superlativo de* **flaco**.
flash [flas], *pl* **flashes** [flas] *nm* (*FOTO*) flash.
flato ['flato] *nm*: **el** (*o* **un**) **~** the (*o* a) stitch.
flauta ['flauta] (*MUS*) *nf* flute ♦ *nm/f* flautist, flute player; **¡la gran ~!** (*AM*) my God!; **hijo de la gran ~** (*AM fam!*) bastard (!), son of a bitch (*US!*).
flecha ['fletʃa] *nf* arrow.
flechazo [fle'tʃaθo] *nm* (*acción*) bowshot; (*fam*): **fue un ~** it was love at first sight.
fleco ['fleko] *nm* fringe.
flema ['flema] *nm* phlegm.
flemático, a [fle'matiko, a] *adj* phlegmatic; (*tono etc*) matter-of-fact.
flemón [fle'mon] *nm* (*MED*) gumboil.
flequillo [fle'kiʎo] *nm* (*pelo*) fringe.
fletar [fle'tar] *vt* (*COM*) to charter; (*embarcar*) to load; (*AUTO*) to lease (-purchase).
flete ['flete] *nm* (*carga*) freight; (*alquiler*) charter; (*precio*) freightage; **~ debido** (*COM*) freight forward; **~ sobre compras** (*COM*) freight inward.
flexible [flek'sißle] *adj* flexible; (*individuo*) compliant.
flexión [flek'sjon] *nf* (*DEPORTE*) bend; (: *en el suelo*) press-up.
flexo ['flekso] *nm* adjustable table lamp.
flipper ['fliper] *nm* pinball machine.
flirtear [flirte'ar] *vi* to flirt.
FLN *nm abr* (*POL*: *ESP, Perú, Venezuela*) = *Frente de Liberación Nacional*.
flojear [floxe'ar] *vi* (*piernas*: *al andar*) to

give way; (*alumno*) to do badly; (*cosecha, mercado*) to be poor.
flojera [flo'xera] *nf* (*AM*) laziness; **me da ~** I can't be bothered.
flojo, a ['floxo, a] *adj* (*gen*) loose; (*sin fuerzas*) limp; (*débil*) weak; (*viento*) light; (*bebida*) weak; (*trabajo*) poor; (*actitud*) slack; (*precio*) low; (*COM: mercado*) dull, slack; (*AM*) lazy.
flor [flor] *nf* flower; (*piropo*) compliment; **la ~ y nata de la sociedad** (*fig*) the cream of society; **en la ~ de la vida** in the prime of life; **a ~ de** on the surface of.
flora ['flora] *nf* flora.
florecer [flore'θer] *vi* (*BOT*) to flower, bloom; (*fig*) to flourish.
floreciente [flore'θjente] *adj* (*BOT*) in flower, flowering; (*fig*) thriving.
Florencia [flo'renθja] *nf* Florence.
florero [flo'rero] *nm* vase.
florezca [flo'reθka] *etc vb V* **florecer**.
florista [flo'rista] *nm/f* florist.
floristería [floriste'ria] *nf* florist's (shop).
flota ['flota] *nf* fleet.
flotación [flota'θjon] *nf* (*COM*) flotation.
flotador [flota'ðor] *nm* (*gen*) float; (*para nadar*) rubber ring; (*de cisterna*) ballcock.
flotante [flo'tante] *adj* floating; (*INFORM*): **de coma ~** floating-point.
flotar [flo'tar] *vi* to float.
flote ['flote] *nm*: **a ~** afloat; **ponerse a ~** (*fig*) to get back on one's feet.
FLS *nm abr* (*POL: Nicaragua*) = *Frente de Liberación Sandinista*.
fluctuación [fluktwa'θjon] *nf* fluctuation.
fluctuante [fluk'twante] *adj* fluctuating.
fluctuar [fluk'twar] *vi* (*oscilar*) to fluctuate.
fluidez [flui'ðeθ] *nf* fluidity; (*fig*) fluency.
fluido, a ['flwiðo, a] *adj* fluid; (*lenguaje*) fluent; (*estilo*) smooth ♦ *nm* (*líquido*) fluid.
fluir [flu'ir] *vi* to flow.
flujo ['fluxo] *nm* flow; (*POL*) swing; (*NAUT*) rising tide; **~ y reflujo** ebb and flow; **~ de sangre** (*MED*) haemorrhage (*BRIT*), hemorrhage (*US*); **~ positivo/negativo de efectivo** (*COM*) positive/negative cash flow.
flúor ['fluor] *nm* fluorine; (*en dentífrico*) fluoride.
fluorescente [flwores'θente] *adj* fluorescent ♦ *nm* (*tb*: **tubo ~**) fluorescent tube.
fluoruro [flwo'ruro] *nm* fluoride.
fluvial [fluβi'al] *adj* fluvial, river *cpd*.
fluyendo [flu'jendo] *etc vb V* **fluir**.
F.M. *nf abr* (= *Frecuencia Modulada*) F.M.
FMI *nm abr* (= *Fondo Monetario Internacional*) I.M.F.
F.N. *nf abr* (*ESP POL*) = *Fuerza Nueva* ♦ *nm* = *Frente Nacional*.
FNPT *nm abr* (*ESP*) = *Fondo Nacional de Protección del Trabajo*.
f.º *abr* (= *folio*) fo., fol.
foca ['foka] *nf* seal.
foco ['foko] *nm* focus; (*centro*) focal point; (*fuente*) source; (*de incendio*) seat; (*ELEC*) floodlight; (*TEAT*) spotlight; (*AM*) (light) bulb, light.
fofo, a ['fofo, a] *adj* (*esponjoso*) soft, spongy; (*músculo*) flabby.
fogata [fo'ɣata] *nf* (*hoguera*) bonfire.
fogón [fo'ɣon] *nm* (*de cocina*) ring, burner.
fogoso, a [fo'ɣoso, a] *adj* spirited.
foja ['foxa] *nf* (*AM*) sheet (of paper); **~ de servicios** record (file).
fol. *abr* (= *folio*) fo., fol.
folder, fólder ['folder] *nm* (*AM*) folder.
folio ['foljo] *nm* folio; (*hoja*) leaf.
folklore [fol'klore] *nm* folklore.
folklórico, a [fol'kloriko, a] *adj* traditional.
follaje [fo'ʎaxe] *nm* foliage.
follar [fo'ʎar] *vt, vi* (*fam!*) to fuck (*!*).
folletinesco, a [foʎetin'esko, a] *adj* melodramatic.
folleto [fo'ʎeto] *nm* pamphlet; (*COM*) brochure; (*prospecto*) leaflet; (*ESCOL etc*) handout.
follón [fo'ʎon] *nm* (*fam: lío*) mess; (*: conmoción*) fuss, rumpus, shindy; **armar un ~** to kick up a fuss; **se armó un ~** there was a hell of a row.
fomentar [fomen'tar] *vt* (*MED*) to foment; (*fig: promover*) to promote, foster; (*odio etc*) to stir up.
fomento [fo'mento] *nm* (*fig: ayuda*) fostering; (*promoción*) promotion.
fonda ['fonda] *nf* ≈ guest house; *V tb* **hotel**.
fondear [fonde'ar] *vt* (*NAUT: sondear*) to sound; (*barco*) to search.
fondo ['fondo] *nm* (*de caja etc*) bottom; (*medida*) depth; (*de coche, sala*) back; (*ARTE etc*) background; (*reserva*) fund; (*fig: carácter*) nature; **~s** *nmpl* (*COM*) funds, resources; **~ de amortización** (*COM*) sinking fund; **F~ Monetario Internacional** International Monetary Fund; **~ del mar** sea bed *o* floor; **una investigación a ~** a thorough investigation; **en el ~** at bottom, deep down; **tener buen ~** to be good natured.
fonética [fo'netika] *nf* phonetics *sg*.
fono ['fono] *nm* (*AM*) telephone (number).
fonobuzón [fonoβu'θon] *nm* voice mail.
fonógrafo [fo'noɣrafo] *nm* (*esp AM*) gramophone, phonograph (*US*).
fonología [fonolo'xia] *nf* phonology.
fontanería [fontane'ria] *nf* plumbing.

fontanero [fonta'nero] *nm* plumber.
footing ['futin] *nm* jogging; **hacer ~** to jog.
F.O.P. [fop] *nfpl abr* (*ESP*) = **Fuerzas del Orden Público.**
forajido [fora'xiðo] *nm* outlaw.
foráneo, a [fo'raneo, a] *adj* foreign ♦ *nm/f* outsider.
forastero, a [foras'tero, a] *nm/f* stranger.
forcé [for'θe] *vb V* **forzar.**
forcejear [forθexe'ar] *vi* (*luchar*) to struggle.
forcemos [for'θemos] *etc vb V* **forzar.**
fórceps ['forθeps] *nm inv* forceps.
forense [fo'rense] *adj* forensic ♦ *nm/f* pathologist.
forestal [fores'tal] *adj* forest *cpd.*
forjar [for'xar] *vt* to forge; (*formar*) to form.
forma ['forma] *nf* (*figura*) form, shape; (*molde*) mould, pattern; (*MED*) fitness; (*método*) way, means; **estar en ~** to be fit; **~ de pago** (*COM*) method of payment; **las ~s** the conventions; **de ~ que ...** so that ...; **de todas ~s** in any case.
formación [forma'θjon] *nf* (*gen*) formation; (*enseñanza*) training; **~ profesional** vocational training; **~ fuera del trabajo** off-the-job training; **~ en el trabajo** *o* **sobre la práctica** on-the-job training.
formal [for'mal] *adj* (*gen*) formal; (*fig*: *persona*) serious; (: *de fiar*) reliable; (*conducta*) steady.
formalice [forma'liθe] *etc vb V* **formalizar.**
formalidad [formali'ðað] *nf* formality; seriousness; reliability; steadiness.
formalizar [formali'θar] *vt* (*JUR*) to formalize; (*plan*) to draw up; (*situación*) to put in order, regularize; **~se** *vr* (*situación*) to be put in order, be regularized.
formar [for'mar] *vt* (*componer*) to form, shape; (*constituir*) to make up, constitute; (*ESCOL*) to train, educate ♦ *vi* (*MIL*) to fall in; (*DEPORTE*) to line up; **~se** *vr* (*ESCOL*) to be trained (*o* educated); (*cobrar forma*) to form, take form; (*desarrollarse*) to develop.
formatear [formate'ar] *vt* (*INFORM*) to format.
formateo [forma'teo] *nm* (*INFORM*) formatting.
formato [for'mato] *nm* (*INFORM*): **sin ~** (*disco, texto*) unformatted; **~ de registro** record format.
formica ® [for'mika] *nf* Formica ®.
formidable [formi'ðaβle] *adj* (*temible*) formidable; (*asombroso*) tremendous.
fórmula ['formula] *nf* formula.
formular [formu'lar] *vt* (*queja*) to lodge; (*petición*) to draw up; (*pregunta*) to pose, formulate; (*idea*) to formulate.
formulario [formu'larjo] *nm* form; **~ de solicitud/de pedido** (*COM*) application/ order form; **llenar un ~** to fill in a form; **~ contínuo desplegable** (*INFORM*) fanfold paper.
fornicar [forni'kar] *vi* to fornicate.
fornido, a [for'niðo, a] *adj* well-built.
fornique [for'nike] *etc vb V* **fornicar.**
foro ['foro] *nm* (*gen*) forum; (*JUR*) court.
forofo, a [fo'rofo, a] *nm/f* fan.
FORPPA ['forpa] *nm abr* (*ESP*) = *Fondo de Ordenación y Regulación de Productos y Precios Agrarios.*
FORPRONU [for'pronu] *nf abr* (= *Fuerza de Protección de las Naciones Unidas*) UNPROFOR.
forrado, a [fo'rraðo, a] *adj* (*ropa*) lined; (*fam*) well-heeled.
forrar [fo'rrar] *vt* (*abrigo*) to line; (*libro*) to cover; (*coche*) to upholster; **~se** *vr* (*fam*) to line one's pockets.
forro ['forro] *nm* (*de cuaderno*) cover; (*costura*) lining; (*de sillón*) upholstery.
fortalecer [fortale'θer] *vt* to strengthen; **~se** *vr* to fortify o.s.; (*opinión etc*) to become stronger.
fortaleza [forta'leθa] *nf* (*MIL*) fortress, stronghold; (*fuerza*) strength; (*determinación*) resolution.
fortalezca [forta'leθka] *etc vb V* **fortalecer.**
fortificar [fortifi'kar] *vt* to fortify; (*fig*) to strengthen.
fortifique [forti'fike] *etc vb V* **fortificar.**
fortísimo, a [for'tisimo, a] *adj superlativo de* **fuerte.**
fortuito, a [for'twito, a] *adj* accidental, chance *cpd.*
fortuna [for'tuna] *nf* (*suerte*) fortune, (good) luck; (*riqueza*) fortune, wealth.
forzar [for'θar] *vt* (*puerta*) to force (open); (*compeler*) to compel; (*violar*) to rape; (*ojos etc*) to strain.
forzoso, a [for'θoso, a] *adj* necessary; (*inevitable*) inescapable; (*obligatorio*) compulsory.
forzudo, a [for'θuðo, a] *adj* burly.
fosa ['fosa] *nf* (*sepultura*) grave; (*en tierra*) pit; (*MED*) cavity; **~s nasales** nostrils.
fosfato [fos'fato] *nm* phosphate.
fosforescente [fosfores'θente] *adj* phosphorescent.
fósforo ['fosforo] *nm* (*QUÍMICA*) phosphorus; (*esp AM*: *cerilla*) match.
fósil ['fosil] *adj* fossil, fossilized ♦ *nm* fossil.
foso ['foso] *nm* ditch; (*TEAT*) pit; (*AUTO*): ~

de reconocimiento inspection pit.
foto ['foto] *nf* photo, snap(shot); **sacar una ~** to take a photo *o* picture.
fotocopia [foto'kopja] *nf* photocopy.
fotocopiadora [fotokopja'ðora] *nf* photocopier.
fotocopiar [fotoko'pjar] *vt* to photocopy.
fotogénico, a [foto'xeniko, a] *adj* photogenic.
fotografía [fotoɤra'fia] *nf* (*arte*) photography; (*una ~*) photograph.
fotografiar [fotoɤra'fjar] *vt* to photograph.
fotógrafo, a [fo'toɤrafo, a] *nm/f* photographer.
fotomatón [fotoma'ton] *nm* (*cabina*) photo booth.
fotómetro [fo'tometro] *nm* (*FOTO*) light meter.
fotonovela [fotono'ßela] *nf* photo-story.
foulard [fu'lar] *nm* (head)scarf.
FP *nf abr* (*ESP*: *ESCOL, COM*) = *Formación Profesional* ♦ *nm abr* (*POL*) = *Frente Popular.*
FPLP *nm abr* (*POL*: = *Frente Popular para la Liberación de Palestina*) PFLP.
Fr. *abr* (= *Fray, franco*) Fr.
frac [frak], *pl* **fracs** *o* **fraques** ['frakes] *nm* dress coat, tails.
fracasar [fraka'sar] *vi* (*gen*) to fail; (*plan etc*) to fall through.
fracaso [fra'kaso] *nm* (*desgracia, revés*) failure; (*de negociaciones etc*) collapse, breakdown.
fracción [frak'θjon] *nf* fraction; (*POL*) faction, splinter group.
fraccionamiento [fraksjona'mjento] *nm* (*AM*) housing estate.
fractura [frak'tura] *nf* fracture, break.
fragancia [fra'ɤanθja] *nf* (*olor*) fragrance, perfume.
fragante [fra'ɤante] *adj* fragrant, scented.
fraganti [fra'ɤanti]: **in ~** *adv*: **coger a algn in ~** to catch sb red-handed.
fragata [fra'ɤata] *nf* frigate.
frágil ['fraxil] *adj* (*débil*) fragile; (*COM*) breakable; (*fig*) frail, delicate.
fragilidad [fraxili'ðað] *nf* fragility; (*de persona*) frailty.
fragmento [fraɤ'mento] *nm* fragment; (*pedazo*) piece; (*de discurso*) excerpt; (*de canción*) snatch.
fragor [fra'ɤor] *nm* (*ruido intenso*) din.
fragua ['fraɤwa] *nf* forge.
fraguar [fra'ɤwar] *vt* to forge; (*fig*) to concoct ♦ *vi* to harden.
fragüe ['fraɤwe] *etc vb V* **fraguar**.
fraile ['fraile] *nm* (*REL*) friar; (: *monje*) monk.
frambuesa [fram'bwesa] *nf* raspberry.
francés, esa [fran'θes, esa] *adj* French ♦ *nm/f* Frenchman/woman ♦ *nm* (*LING*) French.
Francia ['franθja] *nf* France.
franco, a ['franko, a] *adj* (*cándido*) frank, open; (*COM*: *exento*) free ♦ *nm* (*moneda*) franc; **~ de derechos** duty-free; **~ al costado del buque** (*COM*) free alongside ship; **~ puesto sobre vagón** (*COM*) free on rail; **~ a bordo** free on board.
francotirador, a [frankotira'ðor, a] *nm/f* sniper.
franela [fra'nela] *nf* flannel.
franja ['franxa] *nf* fringe; (*de uniforme*) stripe; (*de tierra etc*) strip.
franquear [franke'ar] *vt* (*camino*) to clear; (*carta, paquete*) to frank, stamp; (*obstáculo*) to overcome; (*COM etc*) to free, exempt.
franqueo [fran'keo] *nm* postage.
franqueza [fran'keθa] *nf* frankness.
franquicia [fran'kiθja] *nf* exemption; **~ aduanera** exemption from customs duties.
franquismo [fran'kismo] *nm*: **el ~** (*sistema*) the Franco system; (*período*) the Franco years; *see boxed note.*

> **FRANQUISMO**
>
> *Both the political reign and style of government of Francisco Franco (from the end of the Spanish Civil War in 1939 until his death in 1975) are commonly called* **franquismo.** *The General was a powerful, authoritarian, right-wing dictator, who promoted traditional Catholic values and self-sufficiency. From the 1960s on, Spain gradually opened its doors to the outside world and this coincided with a period of economic growth and the rise of internal political opposition. On Franco's death Spain became a democratic constitutional monarchy.*

franquista [fran'kista] *adj* pro-Franco ♦ *nm/f* supporter of Franco.
frasco ['frasko] *nm* bottle, flask; **~ al vacío** (vacuum) flask.
frase ['frase] *nf* sentence; (*locución*) phrase, expression; **~ hecha** set phrase.
fraternal [frater'nal] *adj* brotherly, fraternal.
fraude ['frauðe] *nm* (*cualidad*) dishonesty; (*acto*) fraud, swindle.
fraudulento, a [frauðu'lento, a] *adj* fraudulent.
frazada [fra'saða] *nf* (*AM*) blanket.
frecuencia [fre'kwenθja] *nf* frequency; **con ~** frequently, often; **~ de red** (*INFORM*)

mains frequency; ~ **del reloj** (*INFORM*) clock speed; ~ **telefónica** voice frequency.
frecuentar [frekwen'tar] *vt* (*lugar*) to frequent; (*persona*) to see frequently *o* often; ~ **la buena sociedad** to mix in high society.
frecuente [fre'kwente] *adj* frequent; (*costumbre*) common; (*vicio*) rife.
fregadero [freɣa'ðero] *nm* (kitchen) sink.
fregado, a [fre'gaðo, a] *adj* (*AM fam!*) damn, bloody (*!*).
fregar [fre'ɣar] *vt* (*frotar*) to scrub; (*platos*) to wash (up); (*AM*) to annoy.
fregón, ona [fre'ɣon, ona] *adj* = **fregado** ♦ *nf* (*utensilio*) mop; (*pey: sirvienta*) skivvy.
fregué [fre'ɣe], **freguemos** [fre'ɣemos] *etc vb V* **fregar**.
freidora [frei'ðora] *nf* deep-fat fryer.
freír [fre'ir] *vt* to fry.
fréjol ['frexol] *nm* = **fríjol**.
frenar [fre'nar] *vt* to brake; (*fig*) to check.
frenazo [fre'naθo] *nm*: **dar un** ~ to brake sharply.
frenesí [frene'si] *nm* frenzy.
frenético, a [fre'netiko, a] *adj* frantic; **ponerse** ~ to lose one's head.
freno ['freno] *nm* (*TEC, AUTO*) brake; (*de cabalgadura*) bit; (*fig*) check.
frente ['frente] *nm* (*ARQ, MIL, POL*) front; (*de objeto*) front part ♦ *nf* forehead, brow; ~ **de batalla** battle front; **hacer** ~ **común con algn** to make common cause with sb; ~ **a** in front of; (*en situación opuesta de*) opposite; **chocar de** ~ to crash head-on; **hacer** ~ **a** to face up to.
fresa ['fresa] *nf* (*ESP: fruta*) strawberry; (*de dentista*) drill.
fresco, a ['fresko, a] *adj* (*nuevo*) fresh; (*huevo*) newly-laid; (*frío*) cool; (*descarado*) cheeky, bad-mannered ♦ *nm* (*aire*) fresh air; (*ARTE*) fresco; (*AM: bebida*) fruit juice *o* drink ♦ *nm/f* (*fam*) shameless person; (*persona insolente*) impudent person; **tomar el** ~ to get some fresh air; **¡qué** ~**!** what a cheek!
frescor [fres'kor] *nm* freshness.
frescura [fres'kura] *nf* freshness; (*descaro*) cheek, nerve; (*calma*) calmness.
fresno ['fresno] *nm* ash (tree).
fresón [fre'son] *nm* strawberry.
frialdad [frjal'dað] *nf* (*gen*) coldness; (*indiferencia*) indifference.
fricción [frik'θjon] *nf* (*gen*) friction; (*acto*) rub(bing); (*MED*) massage; (*POL, fig etc*) friction, trouble.
friega ['frjeɣa] *etc*, **friegue** ['frjeɣe] *etc vb V* **fregar**.
friendo [fri'endo] *etc vb V* **freír**.
frigidez [frixi'ðeθ] *nf* frigidity.
frígido, a ['frixiðo, a] *adj* frigid.
frigorífico, a [friɣo'rifiko, a] *adj* refrigerating ♦ *nm* refrigerator; (*camión*) freezer lorry *o* truck (*US*); **instalación frigorífica** cold-storage plant.
frijol [fri'xol], **fríjol** ['frixol] *nm* kidney bean.
frió [fri'o] *vb V* **freír**.
frío, a ['frio, a] *etc vb V* **freír** ♦ *adj* cold; (*fig: indiferente*) unmoved, indifferent; (*poco entusiasta*) chilly ♦ *nm* cold(ness); indifference; **¡qué** ~**!** how cold it is!
friolento, a [frjo'lento, a] (*AM*), **friolero, a** [frjo'lero, a] *adj* sensitive to cold.
frito, a ['frito, a] *pp de* **freír** ♦ *adj* fried ♦ *nm* fry; **me trae** ~ **ese hombre** I'm sick and tired of that man; ~**s variados** mixed grill.
frívolo, a ['frißolo, a] *adj* frivolous.
frondoso, a [fron'doso, a] *adj* leafy.
frontal [fron'tal] *nm*: **choque** ~ head-on collision.
frontera [fron'tera] *nf* frontier; (*línea divisoria*) border; (*zona*) frontier area.
fronterizo, a [fronte'riθo, a] *adj* frontier *cpd*; (*contiguo*) bordering.
frontón [fron'ton] *nm* (*DEPORTE: cancha*) pelota court; (*: juego*) pelota.
frotar [fro'tar] *vt* to rub; (*fósforo*) to strike; ~**se** *vr*: ~**se las manos** to rub one's hands.
frs. *abr* (= *francos*) fr.
fructífero, a [fruk'tifero, a] *adj* productive, fruitful.
frugal [fru'ɣal] *adj* frugal.
fruncir [frun'θir] *vt* (*COSTURA*) to gather; (*ceño*) to frown; (*labios*) to purse.
frunza ['frunθa] *etc vb V* **fruncir**.
frustración [frustra'θjon] *nf* frustration.
frustrar [frus'trar] *vt* to frustrate; ~**se** *vr* to be frustrated; (*plan etc*) to fail.
fruta ['fruta] *nf* fruit.
frutal [fru'tal] *adj* fruit-bearing, fruit *cpd* ♦ *nm*: (**árbol**) ~ fruit tree.
frutería [frute'ria] *nf* fruit shop.
frutero, a [fru'tero, a] *adj* fruit *cpd* ♦ *nm/f* fruiterer ♦ *nm* fruit dish *o* bowl.
frutilla [fru'tiʎa] *nf* (*AM*) strawberry.
fruto ['fruto] *nm* (*BOT*) fruit; (*fig: resultado*) result, outcome; ~**s secos** ≈ nuts and raisins.
FSLN *nm abr* (*POL: Nicaragua*) = *Frente Sandinista de Liberación Nacional.*
fue [fwe] *vb V* **ser, ir**.

fuego ['fweɣo] *nm* (*gen*) fire; (*CULIN*: *gas*) burner, ring; (*MIL*) fire; (*fig*: *pasión*) fire, passion; **~s artificiales** *o* **de artificio** fireworks; **prender ~ a** to set fire to; **a ~ lento** on a low flame *o* gas; **¡alto el ~!** cease fire!; **estar entre dos ~s** to be in the crossfire; **¿tienes ~?** have you (got) a light?
fuelle ['fweʎe] *nm* bellows *pl*.
fuel-oil [fuel'oil] *nm* paraffin (*BRIT*), kerosene (*US*).
fuente ['fwente] *nf* fountain; (*manantial, fig*) spring; (*origen*) source; (*plato*) large dish; **~ de alimentación** (*INFORM*) power supply; **de ~ desconocida/fidedigna** from an unknown/reliable source.
fuera ['fwera] *etc vb V* **ser, ir** ♦ *adv* out(side); (*en otra parte*) away; (*excepto, salvo*) except, save ♦ *prep*: **~ de** outside; (*fig*) besides; **~ de alcance** out of reach; **~ de combate** out of action; (*boxeo*) knocked out; **~ de sí** beside o.s.; **por ~** (on the) outside; **los de ~** strangers, newcomers; **estar ~** (*en el extranjero*) to be abroad.
fuera-borda [fwera'βorða] *nm inv* outboard engine *o* motor.
fuerce ['fwerθe] *etc vb V* **forzar**.
fuereño, a [fwe'reɲo, a] *nm/f* (*AM*) outsider.
fuero ['fwero] *nm* (*carta municipal*) municipal charter; (*leyes locales*) local *o* regional law code; (*privilegio*) privilege; (*autoridad*) jurisdiction; (*fig*): **en mi** *etc* **~ interno** in my *etc* heart of hearts ..., deep down ....
fuerte ['fwerte] *adj* strong; (*golpe*) hard; (*ruido*) loud; (*comida*) rich; (*lluvia*) heavy; (*dolor*) intense ♦ *adv* strongly; hard; loud(ly) ♦ *nm* (*MIL*) fort, strongpoint; (*fig*): **el canto no es mi ~** singing is not my strong point.
fuerza ['fwerθa] *etc vb V* **forzar** ♦ *nf* (*fortaleza*) strength; (*TEC, ELEC*) power; (*coacción*) force; (*violencia*) violence; (*MIL*: *tb*: **~s**) forces *pl*; **~ de arrastre** (*TEC*) pulling power; **~ de brazos** manpower; **~ mayor** force majeure; **~ bruta** brute force; **~s armadas (FF.AA.)** armed forces; **~ de Orden Público (F.O.P.)** police (forces); **~ vital** vitality; **a ~ de** by (dint of); **cobrar ~s** to recover one's strength; **tener ~s para** to have the strength to; **hacer algo a la ~** to be forced to do sth; **con ~ legal** (*COM*) legally binding; **a la ~, por ~** of necessity; **~ de voluntad** willpower.
fuete ['fwete] *nm* (*AM*) whip.
fuga ['fuɣa] *nf* (*huida*) flight, escape; (*de enamorados*) elopement; (*de gas etc*) leak; **~ de cerebros** (*fig*) brain drain.
fugarse [fu'ɣarse] *vr* to flee, escape.
fugaz [fu'ɣaθ] *adj* fleeting.
fugitivo, a [fuxi'tiβo, a] *adj* fugitive, fleeing ♦ *nm/f* fugitive.
fugue ['fuɣe] *etc vb V* **fugarse**.
fui [fwi] *etc vb V* **ser, ir**.
fulano, a [fu'lano, a] *nm/f* so-and-so, what's-his-name.
fulgor [ful'ɣor] *nm* brilliance.
fulminante [fulmi'nante] *adj* (*pólvora*) fulminating; (*fig*: *mirada*) withering; (*MED*) fulminant; (*fam*) terrific, tremendous.
fulminar [fulmi'nar] *vt*: **caer fulminado por un rayo** to be struck down by lightning; **~ a algn con la mirada** to look daggers at sb.
fumador, a [fuma'ðor, a] *nm/f* smoker; **no ~** non-smoker.
fumar [fu'mar] *vt, vi* to smoke; **~se** *vr* (*disipar*) to squander; **~ en pipa** to smoke a pipe.
fumigar [fumi'ɣar] *vt* to fumigate.
funámbulo, a [fu'nambulo, a], **funambulista** [funambu'lista] *nm/f* tightrope walker.
función [fun'θjon] *nf* function; (*de puesto*) duties *pl*; (*TEAT etc*) show; **entrar en funciones** to take up one's duties; **~ de tarde/de noche** matinée/evening performance.
funcional [funθjo'nal] *adj* functional.
funcionamiento [funθjona'mjento] *nm* functioning; (*TEC*) working; **en ~** (*COM*) on stream; **entrar en ~** to come into operation.
funcionar [funθjo'nar] *vi* (*gen*) to function; (*máquina*) to work; **"no funciona"** "out of order".
funcionario, a [funθjo'narjo, a] *nm/f* official; (*público*) civil servant.
funda ['funda] *nf* (*gen*) cover; (*de almohada*) pillowcase; **~ protectora del disco** (*INFORM*) disk-jacket.
fundación [funda'θjon] *nf* foundation.
fundado, a [fun'daðo, a] *adj* (*justificado*) well-founded.
fundamental [fundamen'tal] *adj* fundamental, basic.
fundamentalismo [fundamenta'lismo] *nm* fundamentalism.
fundamentalista [fundamenta'lista] *adj, nm/f* fundamentalist.
fundamentar [fundamen'tar] *vt* (*poner base*) to lay the foundations of; (*establecer*) to found; (*fig*) to base.

fundamento [funda'mento] *nm* (*base*) foundation; (*razón*) grounds; **eso carece de ~** that is groundless.
fundar [fun'dar] *vt* to found; (*crear*) to set up; (*fig: basar*): **~ (en)** to base *o* found (on); **~se** *vr*: **~se en** to be founded on.
fundición [fundi'θjon] *nf* (*acción*) smelting; (*fábrica*) foundry; (*TIP*) fount (*BRIT*), font.
fundir [fun'dir] *vt* (*gen*) to fuse; (*metal*) to smelt, melt down; (*COM*) to merge; (*estatua*) to cast; **~se** *vr* (*colores etc*) to merge, blend; (*unirse*) to fuse together; (*ELEC: fusible, lámpara etc*) to blow; (*nieve etc*) to melt.
fúnebre ['funeßre] *adj* funeral *cpd*, funereal.
funeral [fune'ral] *nm* funeral.
funeraria [fune'rarja] *nf* undertaker's (*BRIT*), mortician's (*US*).
funesto, a [fu'nesto, a] *adj* ill-fated; (*desastroso*) fatal.
fungir [fun'xir] *vi*: **~ de** (*AM*) to act as.
furgón [fur'ɣon] *nm* wagon.
furgoneta [furɣo'neta] *nf* (*AUTO, COM*) (transit) van (*BRIT*), pickup (truck) (*US*).
furia ['furja] *nf* (*ira*) fury; (*violencia*) violence.
furibundo, a [furi'ßundo, a] *adj* furious.
furioso, a [fu'rjoso, a] *adj* (*iracundo*) furious; (*violento*) violent.
furor [fu'ror] *nm* (*cólera*) rage; (*pasión*) frenzy, passion; **hacer ~** to be a sensation.
furtivo, a [fur'tißo, a] *adj* furtive ♦ *nm* poacher.
furúnculo [fu'runkulo] *nm* (*MED*) boil.
fuselaje [fuse'laxe] *nm* fuselage.
fusible [fu'sißle] *nm* fuse.
fusil [fu'sil] *nm* rifle.
fusilamiento [fusila'mjento] *nm* (*JUR*) execution by firing squad.
fusilar [fusi'lar] *vt* to shoot.
fusión [fu'sjon] *nf* (*gen*) melting; (*unión*) fusion; (*COM*) merger, amalgamation.
fusionar [fusjo'nar] *vt* to fuse (together); (*COM*) to merge; **~se** *vr* (*COM*) to merge, amalgamate.
fusta ['fusta] *nf* (*látigo*) riding crop.
fútbol ['futßol] *nm* football.
futbolín [futßo'lin] *nm* table football.
futbolista [futßo'lista] *nm/f* footballer.
fútil ['futil] *adj* trifling.
futilidad [futili'ðað], **futileza** [futi'leθa] *nf* triviality.
futón [fu'ton] *nm* futon.
futuro, a [fu'turo, a] *adj* future ♦ *nm* future; (*LING*) future tense; **~s** *nmpl* (*COM*) futures.

Gg

G, g [xe] *nf* (*letra*) G, g; **G de Gerona** G for George.
g/ *abr* = **giro**.
gabacho, a [ga'ßatʃo, a] *adj* Pyrenean; (*fam*) Frenchified ♦ *nm/f* Pyrenean villager; (*fam*) Frenchy.
gabán [ga'ßan] *nm* overcoat.
gabardina [gaßar'ðina] *nf* (*tela*) gabardine; (*prenda*) raincoat.
gabinete [gaßi'nete] *nm* (*POL*) cabinet; (*estudio*) study; (*de abogados etc*) office; **~ de consulta/de lectura** consulting/reading room.
gacela [ga'θela] *nf* gazelle.
gaceta [ga'θeta] *nf* gazette.
gacetilla [gaθe'tiʎa] *nf* (*en periódico*) news in brief; (*de personalidades*) gossip column.
gachas ['gatʃas] *nfpl* porridge *sg*.
gacho, a ['gatʃo, a] *adj* (*encorvado*) bent down; (*orejas*) drooping.
gaditano, a [gaði'tano, a] *adj* of *o* from Cadiz ♦ *nm/f* native *o* inhabitant of Cadiz.
GAE *nm abr* (*ESP MIL*) = *Grupo Aéreo Embarcado*.
gaélico, a [ga'eliko, a] *adj* Gaelic ♦ *nm/f* Gael ♦ *nm* (*LING*) Gaelic.
gafar [ga'far] *vt* (*fam: traer mala suerte*) to put a jinx on.
gafas ['gafas] *nfpl* glasses; **~ oscuras** dark glasses; **~ de sol** sunglasses.
gafe ['gafe] *adj*: **ser ~** to be jinxed ♦ *nm* (*fam*) jinx.
gaita ['gaita] *nf* flute; (*~ gallega*) bagpipes *pl*; (*dificultad*) bother; (*cosa engorrosa*) tough job.
gajes ['gaxes] *nmpl* (*salario*) pay *sg*; **los ~ del oficio** occupational hazards; **~ y emolumentos** perquisites.
gajo ['gaxo] *nm* (*gen*) bunch; (*de árbol*) bough; (*de naranja*) segment.
gala ['gala] *nf* full dress; (*fig: lo mejor*) cream, flower; **~s** *nfpl* finery *sg*; **estar de ~** to be in one's best clothes; **hacer ~ de** to display, show off; **tener algo a ~** to be proud of sth.
galaico, a [ga'laiko, a] *adj* Galician.
galán [ga'lan] *nm* lover, gallant; (*hombre*

atractivo) ladies' man; (*TEAT*): **primer ~** leading man.
galante [ga'lante] *adj* gallant; (*atento*) charming; (*cortés*) polite.
galantear [galante'ar] *vt* (*hacer la corte a*) to court, woo.
galanteo [galan'teo] *nm* (*coqueteo*) flirting; (*de pretendiente*) wooing.
galantería [galante'ria] *nf* (*caballerosidad*) gallantry; (*cumplido*) politeness; (*piropo*) compliment.
galápago [ga'lapaɣo] *nm* (*ZOOL*) freshwater tortoise.
galardón [galar'ðon] *nm* award, prize.
galardonar [galarðo'nar] *vt* (*premiar*) to reward; (*una obra*) to award a prize for.
galaxia [ga'laksja] *nf* galaxy.
galbana [gal'ßana] *nf* (*pereza*) sloth, laziness.
galeote [gale'ote] *nm* galley slave.
galera [ga'lera] *nf* (*nave*) galley; (*carro*) wagon; (*MED*) hospital ward; (*TIP*) galley.
galería [gale'ria] *nf* (*gen*) gallery; (*balcón*) veranda(h); (*de casa*) corridor; (*fam*: *público*) audience; **~ secreta** secret passage.
Gales ['gales] *nm*: **(el País de) ~** Wales.
galés, esa [ga'les, esa] *adj* Welsh ♦ *nm/f* Welshman/woman ♦ *nm* (*LING*) Welsh.
galgo, a ['galɣo, a] *nm/f* greyhound.
Galia ['galja] *nf* Gaul.
Galicia [ga'liθja] *nf* Galicia.
galicismo [gali'θismo] *nm* gallicism.
Galilea [gali'lea] *nf* Galilee.
galimatías [galima'tias] *nm inv* (*asunto*) rigmarole; (*lenguaje*) gibberish, nonsense.
gallardía [gaʎar'ðia] *nf* (*galantería*) dash; (*gracia*) gracefulness; (*valor*) bravery; (*elegancia*) elegance; (*nobleza*) nobleness.
gallego, a [ga'ʎeɣo, a] *adj* Galician; (*AM pey*) Spanish ♦ *nm/f* Galician; (*AM pey*) Spaniard ♦ *nm* (*LING*) Galician; *V tb* **lenguas cooficiales.**
galleta [ga'ʎeta] *nf* biscuit; (*fam*: *bofetada*) whack, slap.
gallina [ga'ʎina] *nf* hen ♦ *nm* (*fam*) coward; **~ ciega** blind man's buff; **~ clueca** broody hen.
gallinazo [gaʎi'naso] *nm* (*AM*) turkey buzzard.
gallinero [gaʎi'nero] *nm* (*criadero*) henhouse; (*TEAT*) gods *sg*, top gallery; (*voces*) hubbub.
gallo ['gaʎo] *nm* cock, rooster; (*MUS*) false *o* wrong note; (*cambio de voz*) break in the voice; **en menos que canta un ~** in an instant.
galo, a ['galo, a] *adj* Gallic; (= *francés*) French ♦ *nm/f* Gaul.
galón [ga'lon] *nm* (*COSTURA*) braid; (*MIL*) stripe; (*medida*) gallon.
galopante [galo'pante] *adj* galloping.
galopar [galo'par] *vi* to gallop.
galope [ga'lope] *nm* gallop; **al ~** (*fig*) in great haste; **a ~ tendido** at full gallop.
galvanice [galßa'niθe] *etc vb V* **galvanizar.**
galvanizar [galßani'θar] *vt* to galvanize.
gama ['gama] *nf* (*MUS*) scale; (*fig*) range; (*ZOOL*) doe.
gamba ['gamba] *nf* prawn.
gamberrada [gambe'rraða] *nf* act of hooliganism.
gamberro, a [gam'berro, a] *nm/f* hooligan, lout.
gamo ['gamo] *nm* (*ZOOL*) buck.
gamuza [ga'muθa] *nf* chamois; (*bayeta*) duster; (*AM*: *piel*) suede.
gana ['gana] *nf* (*deseo*) desire, wish; (*apetito*) appetite; (*voluntad*) will; (*añoranza*) longing; **de buena ~** willingly; **de mala ~** reluctantly; **me dan ~s de** I feel like, I want to; **tener ~s de** to feel like; **no me da la (real) ~** I don't (damned well) want to; **son ~s de molestar** they're just trying to be awkward.
ganadería [ganaðe'ria] *nf* (*ganado*) livestock; (*ganado vacuno*) cattle *pl*; (*cría, comercio*) cattle raising.
ganadero, a [gana'ðero, a] *adj* stock *cpd* ♦ *nm* stockman.
ganado [ga'naðo] *nm* livestock; **~ caballar/cabrío** horses *pl*/goats *pl*; **~ lanar** *u* **ovejuno** sheep *pl*; **~ porcino/vacuno** pigs *pl*/cattle *pl*.
ganador, a [gana'ðor, a] *adj* winning ♦ *nm/f* winner; (*ECON*) earner.
ganancia [ga'nanθja] *nf* (*lo ganado*) gain; (*aumento*) increase; (*beneficio*) profit; **~s** *nfpl* (*ingresos*) earnings; (*beneficios*) profit *sg*, winnings; **~s y pérdidas** profit and loss; **~ bruta/líquida** gross/net profit; **~s de capital** capital gains; **sacar ~ de** to draw profit from.
ganapán [gana'pan] *nm* (*obrero casual*) odd-job man; (*individuo tosco*) lout.
ganar [ga'nar] *vt* (*obtener*) to get, obtain; (*sacar ventaja*) to gain; (*COM*) to earn; (*DEPORTE, premio*) to win; (*derrotar*) to beat; (*alcanzar*) to reach; (*MIL*: *objetivo*) to take; (*apoyo*) to gain, win ♦ *vi* (*DEPORTE*) to win; **~se** *vr*: **~se la vida** to earn one's living; **se lo ha ganado** he deserves it; **~ tiempo** to gain time.
ganchillo [gan'tʃiʎo] *nm* (*para croché*)

crochet hook; (*arte*) crochet work.
gancho ['gantʃo] *nm* (*gen*) hook; (*colgador*) hanger; (*pey: revendedor*) tout; (*fam: atractivo*) sex appeal; (*BOXEO: golpe*) hook.
gandul, a [gan'dul, a] *adj, nm/f* good-for-nothing.
ganga ['ganga] *nf* (*cosa*) bargain; (*buena situación*) cushy job.
Ganges ['ganxes] *nm*: **el (Río)** ~ the Ganges.
ganglio ['gangljo] *nm* (*ANAT*) ganglion; (*MED*) swelling.
gangrena [gan'grena] *nf* gangrene.
gansada [gan'saða] *nf* (*fam*) stupid thing (to do).
ganso, a ['ganso, a] *nm/f* (*ZOOL*) gander/goose; (*fam*) idiot.
Gante ['gante] *nm* Ghent.
ganzúa [gan'θua] *nf* skeleton key ♦ *nm/f* burglar.
gañán [ga'ɲan] *nm* farmhand, farm labourer.
garabatear [garaβate'ar] *vt* to scribble, scrawl.
garabato [gara'βato] *nm* (*gancho*) hook; (*garfio*) grappling iron; (*escritura*) scrawl, scribble; (*fam*) sex appeal.
garaje [ga'raxe] *nm* garage.
garante [ga'rante] *adj* responsible ♦ *nm/f* guarantor.
garantía [garan'tia] *nf* guarantee; (*seguridad*) pledge; (*compromiso*) undertaking; (*JUR: caución*) warranty; **de máxima** ~ absolutely guaranteed; ~ **de trabajo** job security.
garantice [garan'tiθe] *etc vb V* **garantizar**.
garantizar [garanti'θar] *vt* (*hacerse responsable de*) to vouch for; (*asegurar*) to guarantee.
garbanzo [gar'βanθo] *nm* chickpea.
garbeo [gar'βeo] *nm*: **darse un** ~ to go for a walk.
garbo ['garβo] *nm* grace, elegance; (*aire*) jauntiness; (*de mujer*) glamour; **andar con** ~ to walk gracefully.
garboso, a [gar'βoso, a] *adj* graceful, elegant.
garete [ga'rete] *nm*: **irse al** ~ to go to the dogs.
garfio ['garfjo] *nm* grappling iron; (*gancho*) hook; (*ALPINISMO*) climbing iron.
gargajo [gar'ɣaxo] *nm* phlegm, sputum.
garganta [gar'ɣanta] *nf* (*interna*) throat; (*externa, de botella*) neck; (*GEO: barranco*) ravine; (*desfiladero*) narrow pass.
gargantilla [garɣan'tiʎa] *nf* necklace.
gárgara ['garɣara] *nf* gargle, gargling; **hacer** ~**s** to gargle; **¡vete a hacer** ~**s!** (*fam*) go to blazes!
gárgola ['garɣola] *nf* gargoyle.
garita [ga'rita] *nf* cabin, hut; (*MIL*) sentry box; (*puesto de vigilancia*) lookout post.
garito [ga'rito] *nm* (*lugar*) gaming house *o* den.
garra ['garra] *nf* (*de gato, TEC*) claw; (*de ave*) talon; (*fam*) hand, paw; (*fig: de canción etc*) bite; **caer en las** ~**s de algn** to fall into sb's clutches.
garrafa [ga'rrafa] *nf* carafe, decanter.
garrafal [garra'fal] *adj* enormous, terrific; (*error*) terrible.
garrapata [garra'pata] *nf* (*ZOOL*) tick.
garrotazo [garro'taθo] *nm* blow with a stick *o* club.
garrote [ga'rrote] *nm* (*palo*) stick; (*porra*) club, cudgel; (*suplicio*) garrotte.
garza ['garθa] *nf* heron.
gas [gas] *nm* gas; (*vapores*) fumes *pl*; ~**es de escape** exhaust (fumes).
gasa ['gasa] *nf* gauze; (*de pañal*) nappy liner.
gaseoso, a [gase'oso, a] *adj* gassy, fizzy ♦ *nf* lemonade, pop (*fam*).
gasoducto [gaso'ðukto] *nm* gas pipeline.
gasoil [ga'soil], **gasóleo** [ga'soleo] *nm* diesel (oil).
gasolina [gaso'lina] *nf* petrol, gas(oline) (*US*); ~ **sin plomo** unleaded petrol.
gasolinera [gasoli'nera] *nf* petrol (*BRIT*) *o* gas (*US*) station.
gastado, a [gas'taðo, a] *adj* (*ropa*) worn out; (*usado: frase etc*) trite.
gastar [gas'tar] *vt* (*dinero, tiempo*) to spend; (*consumir*) to use (up), consume; (*desperdiciar*) to waste; (*llevar*) to wear; ~**se** *vr* to wear out; (*terminarse*) to run out; (*estropearse*) to waste; ~ **bromas** to crack jokes; **¿qué número gastas?** what size (shoe) do you take?
gasto ['gasto] *nm* (*desembolso*) expenditure, spending; (*cantidad gastada*) outlay, expense; (*consumo, uso*) use; (*desgaste*) waste; ~**s** *nmpl* (*desembolsos*) expenses; (*cargos*) charges, costs; ~ **corriente** (*COM*) revenue expenditure; ~ **fijo** (*COM*) fixed charge; ~**s bancarios** bank charges; ~**s corrientes** running expenses; ~**s de distribución** (*COM*) distribution costs; ~**s generales** overheads; ~**s de mantenimiento** maintenance expenses; ~**s operacionales** operating costs; ~**s de tramitación** (*COM*) handling charge *sg*; ~**s vencidos** (*COM*) accrued charges; **cubrir** ~**s** to cover expenses; **meterse en**

~**s** to incur expense.
gastronomía [gastrono'mia] *nf* gastronomy.
gata ['gata] *nf* (*ZOOL*) she-cat; **andar a** ~**s** to go on all fours.
gatear [gate'ar] *vi* to go on all fours.
gatillo [ga'tiʎo] *nm* (*de arma de fuego*) trigger; (*de dentista*) forceps.
gato ['gato] *nm* (*ZOOL*) cat; (*TEC*) jack; ~ **de Angora** Angora cat; ~ **montés** wildcat; **dar a algn** ~ **por liebre** to take sb in; **aquí hay** ~ **encerrado** there's something fishy here.
gatuno, a [ga'tuno, a] *adj* feline.
gaucho, a ['gautʃo, a] *adj, nm/f* gaucho.
gaveta [ga'ßeta] *nf* drawer.
gavilán [gaßi'lan] *nm* sparrowhawk.
gavilla [ga'ßiʎa] *nf* sheaf.
gaviota [ga'ßjota] *nf* seagull.
gay [ge] *adj, nm* gay, homosexual.
gazapo [ga'θapo] *nm* young rabbit.
gaznate [gaθ'nate] *nm* (*pescuezo*) gullet; (*garganta*) windpipe.
gazpacho [gaθ'patʃo] *nm* gazpacho.
gel [xel] *nm* gel.
gelatina [xela'tina] *nf* jelly; (*polvos etc*) gelatine.
gema ['xema] *nf* gem.
gemelo, a [xe'melo, a] *adj, nm/f* twin; ~**s** *nmpl* (*de camisa*) cufflinks; ~**s de campo** field glasses, binoculars; ~**s de teatro** opera glasses.
gemido [xe'miðo] *nm* (*quejido*) moan, groan; (*lamento*) wail, howl.
Géminis ['xeminis] *nm* (*ASTRO*) Gemini.
gemir [xe'mir] *vi* (*quejarse*) to moan, groan; (*animal*) to whine; (*viento*) to howl.
gen [xen] *nm* gene.
gen. *abr* (*LING*) = **género; genitivo**.
gendarme [xen'darme] *nm* (*AM*) policeman.
genealogía [xenealo'xia] *nf* genealogy.
generación [xenera'θjon] *nf* generation; **primera/segunda/tercera/cuarta** ~ (*INFORM*) first/second/third/fourth generation.
generado, a [xene'raðo, a] *adj* (*INFORM*): ~ **por ordenador** computer generated.
generador [xenera'ðor] *nm* generator; ~ **de programas** (*INFORM*) program generator.
general [xene'ral] *adj* general; (*común*) common; (*pey*: *corriente*) rife; (*frecuente*) usual ♦ *nm* general; ~ **de brigada/de división** brigadier-/major-general; **por lo** *o* **en** ~ in general.
generalice [xenera'liθe] *etc vb V* **generalizar**.
generalidad [xenerali'ðað] *nf* generality.
Generalitat [jenerali'tat] *nf regional government of Catalonia*; ~ **Valenciana** *regional government of Valencia.*
generalización [xeneraliθa'θjon] *nf* generalization.
generalizar [xenerali'θar] *vt* to generalize; ~**se** *vr* to become generalized, spread; (*difundirse*) to become widely known.
generalmente [xeneral'mente] *adv* generally.
generar [xene'rar] *vt* to generate.
genérico, a [xe'neriko, a] *adj* generic.
género ['xenero] *nm* (*clase*) kind, sort; (*tipo*) type; (*BIO*) genus; (*LING*) gender; (*COM*) material; ~**s** *nmpl* (*productos*) goods; ~ **humano** human race; ~ **chico** (*zarzuela*) Spanish operetta; ~**s de punto** knitwear *sg*.
generosidad [xenerosi'ðað] *nf* generosity.
generoso, a [xene'roso, a] *adj* generous.
genético, a [xe'netiko, a] *adj* genetic ♦ *nf* genetics *sg*.
genial [xe'njal] *adj* inspired; (*idea*) brilliant; (*afable*) genial.
genialidad [xenjali'ðað] *nf* (*singularidad*) genius; (*acto genial*) stroke of genius; **es una** ~ **suya** it's one of his brilliant ideas.
genio ['xenjo] *nm* (*carácter*) nature, disposition; (*humor*) temper; (*facultad creadora*) genius; **mal** ~ bad temper; ~ **vivo** quick *o* hot temper; **de mal** ~ bad-tempered.
genital [xeni'tal] *adj* genital ♦ *nm*: ~**es** genitals, genital organs.
genocidio [xeno'θiðjo] *nm* genocide.
Génova ['xenoßa] *nf* Genoa.
genovés, esa [xeno'ßes, esa] *adj, nm/f* Genoese.
gente ['xente] *nf* (*personas*) people *pl*; (*raza*) race; (*nación*) nation; (*parientes*) relatives *pl*; ~ **bien/baja** posh/lower-class people *pl*; ~ **menuda** (*niños*) children *pl*; **es buena** ~ (*fam*: *esp AM*) he's a good sort; **una** ~ **como Vd** (*AM*) a person like you.
gentil [xen'til] *adj* (*elegante*) graceful; (*encantador*) charming; (*REL*) gentile.
gentileza [xenti'leθa] *nf* grace; charm; (*cortesía*) courtesy; **por** ~ **de** by courtesy of.
gentilicio, a [xenti'liθjo, a] *adj* (*familiar*) family *cpd*.
gentío [xen'tio] *nm* crowd, throng.
gentuza [xen'tuθa] *nf* (*pey*: *plebe*) rabble; (: *chusma*) riffraff.
genuflexión [xenuflek'sjon] *nf* genuflexion.

genuino, a [xe'nwino, a] *adj* genuine.
GEO ['xeo] *nmpl abr (ESP: = Grupos Especiales de Operaciones) Special Police Units used in anti-terrorist operations etc.*
geografía [xeoɤra'fia] *nf* geography.
geográfico, a [xeo'ɤrafiko, a] *adj* geographic(al).
geología [xeolo'xia] *nf* geology.
geólogo, a [xe'oloɤo, a] *nm/f* geologist.
geometría [xeome'tria] *nf* geometry.
geométrico, a [xeo'metriko, a] *adj* geometric(al).
Georgia [xe'orxja] *nf* Georgia.
georgiano, a [xeor'xjano, a] *adj, nm/f* Georgian ♦ *nm (LING)* Georgian.
geranio [xe'ranjo] *nm (BOT)* geranium.
gerencia [xe'renθja] *nf* management; *(cargo)* post of manager; *(oficina)* manager's office.
gerente [xe'rente] *nm/f (supervisor)* manager; *(jefe)* director.
geriatría [xerja'tria] *nf (MED)* geriatrics *sg*.
geriátrico, a [xer'jatriko, a] *adj* geriatric.
germano, a [xer'mano, a] *adj* German, Germanic ♦ *nm/f* German.
germen ['xermen] *nm* germ.
germinar [xermi'nar] *vi* to germinate; *(brotar)* to sprout.
gerundense [xerun'dense] *adj* of *o* from Gerona ♦ *nm/f* native *o* inhabitant of Gerona.
gerundio [xe'rundjo] *nm (LING)* gerund.
gestación [xesta'θjon] *nf* gestation.
gesticulación [xestikula'θjon] *nf (ademán)* gesticulation; *(mueca)* grimace.
gesticular [xestiku'lar] *vi (con ademanes)* to gesture; *(con muecas)* to make faces.
gestión [xes'tjon] *nf* management; *(diligencia, acción)* negotiation; **hacer las gestiones preliminares** to do the groundwork; ~ **de cartera** *(COM)* portfolio management; ~ **financiera** *(COM)* financial management; ~ **interna** *(INFORM)* housekeeping; ~ **de personal** personnel management; ~ **de riesgos** *(COM)* risk management.
gestionar [xestjo'nar] *vt (lograr)* to try to arrange; *(llevar)* to manage.
gesto ['xesto] *nm (mueca)* grimace; *(ademán)* gesture; **hacer ~s** to make faces.
gestor, a [xes'tor, a] *adj* managing ♦ *nm/f* manager; *(promotor)* promoter; *(agente)* business agent.
gestoría [xesto'ria] *nf agency undertaking business with government departments, insurance companies etc.*
Gibraltar [xiβral'tar] *nm* Gibraltar.
gibraltareño, a [xiβralta'reɲo, a] *adj* of *o* from Gibraltar ♦ *nm/f* native *o* inhabitant of Gibraltar.
gigante [xi'ɤante] *adj, nm/f* giant.
gijonés [xixo'nes, esa] *adj* of *o* from Gijón ♦ *nm/f* native *o* inhabitant of Gijón.
gilipollas [xili'poʎas] *(fam) adj inv* daft ♦ *nm/f* berk.
gilipollez [xilipo'ʎez] *nf (fam)*: **es una ~** that's a load of crap *(!)*; **decir gilipolleces** to talk crap *(!)*.
gima ['xima] *etc vb V* **gemir**.
gimnasia [xim'nasja] *nf* gymnastics *pl*; **confundir la ~ con la magnesia** to get things mixed up.
gimnasio [xim'nasjo] *nm* gym(nasium).
gimnasta [xim'nasta] *nm/f* gymnast.
gimotear [ximote'ar] *vi* to whine, whimper; *(lloriquear)* to snivel.
Ginebra [xi'neβra] *n* Geneva.
ginebra [xi'neβra] *nf* gin.
ginecología [xinekolo'xia] *nf* gyn(a)ecology.
ginecológico, a [xineko'loxiko, a] *adj* gyn(a)ecological.
ginecólogo, a [xine'koloɤo, a] *nm/f* gyn(a)ecologist.
gira ['xira] *nf* tour, trip.
girar [xi'rar] *vt (dar la vuelta)* to turn (around); *(: rápidamente)* to spin; *(COM: giro postal)* to draw; *(comerciar: letra de cambio)* to issue ♦ *vi* to turn (round); *(dar vueltas)* to rotate; *(rápido)* to spin; **la conversación giraba en torno a las elecciones** the conversation centred on the election; ~ **en descubierto** to overdraw.
giratorio, a [xira'torjo, a] *adj (gen)* revolving; *(puente)* swing *cpd*; *(silla)* swivel *cpd*.
giro ['xiro] *nm (movimiento)* turn, revolution; *(LING)* expression; *(COM)* draft; *(de sucesos)* trend, course; ~ **bancario** money order, bank giro; ~ **de existencias** *(COM)* stock turnover; ~ **postal** postal order; ~ **a la vista** *(COM)* sight draft.
gis [xis] *nm (AM)* chalk.
gitano, a [xi'tano, a] *adj, nm/f* gypsy.
glacial [gla'θjal] *adj* icy, freezing.
glaciar [gla'θjar] *nm* glacier.
glándula ['glandula] *nf (ANAT, BOT)* gland.
glicerina [gliθe'rina] *nf (TEC)* glycerin(e).
global [glo'βal] *adj (en conjunto)* global; *(completo)* total; *(investigación)* full; *(suma)* lump *cpd*.
globo ['gloβo] *nm (esfera)* globe, sphere;

(*aeróstato, juguete*) balloon.
glóbulo ['gloβulo] *nm* globule; (*ANAT*) corpuscle; ~ **blanco/rojo** white/red corpuscle.
gloria ['glorja] *nf* glory; (*fig*) delight; (*delicia*) bliss.
glorieta [glo'rjeta] *nf* (*de jardín*) bower, arbour, (*US*) arbor; (*AUTO*) roundabout (*BRIT*), traffic circle (*US*); (*plaza redonda*) circus; (*cruce*) junction.
glorificar [glorifi'kar] *vt* (*enaltecer*) to glorify, praise.
glorifique [glori'fike] *etc vb V* **glorificar**.
glorioso, a [glo'rjoso, a] *adj* glorious.
glosa ['glosa] *nf* comment; (*explicación*) gloss.
glosar [glo'sar] *vt* (*comentar*) to comment on.
glosario [glo'sarjo] *nm* glossary.
glotón, ona [glo'ton, ona] *adj* gluttonous, greedy ♦ *nm/f* glutton.
glotonería [glotone'ria] *nf* gluttony, greed.
glúteo ['gluteo] *nm* (*fam: nalga*) buttock.
gnomo ['nomo] *nm* gnome.
gobernación [goβerna'θjon] *nf* government, governing; (*POL*) Provincial Governor's office; **Ministro de la G~** Minister of the Interior, Home Secretary (*BRIT*).
gobernador, a [goβerna'ðor, a] *adj* governing ♦ *nm/f* governor.
gobernanta [goβer'nanta] *nf* (*esp AM: niñera*) governess.
gobernante [goβer'nante] *adj* governing ♦ *nm* ruler, governor ♦ *nf* (*en hotel etc*) housekeeper.
gobernar [goβer'nar] *vt* (*dirigir*) to guide, direct; (*POL*) to rule, govern ♦ *vi* to govern; (*NAUT*) to steer; ~ **mal** to misgovern.
gobierno [go'βjerno] *etc vb V* **gobernar** ♦ *nm* (*POL*) government; (*gestión*) management; (*dirección*) guidance, direction; (*NAUT*) steering; (*puesto*) governorship.
goce ['goθe] *etc vb V* **gozar** ♦ *nm* enjoyment.
godo, a ['goðo, a] *nm/f* Goth; (*AM pey*) Spaniard.
gol [gol] *nm* goal.
golear [gole'ar] *vt* (*marcar*) to score a goal against.
golf [golf] *nm* golf.
golfo, a ['golfo, a] *nm/f* (*pilluelo*) street urchin; (*vago*) tramp; (*gorrón*) loafer; (*gamberro*) lout ♦ *nm* (*GEO*) gulf ♦ *nf* (*fam: prostituta*) slut, whore, hooker (*US*).
golondrina [golon'drina] *nf* swallow.
golosina [golo'sina] *nf* titbit; (*dulce*) sweet.
goloso, a [go'loso, a] *adj* sweet-toothed; (*fam: glotón*) greedy.
golpe ['golpe] *nm* blow; (*de puño*) punch; (*de mano*) smack; (*de remo*) stroke; (*FÚTBOL*) kick; (*TENIS etc*) hit, shot; (*mala suerte*) misfortune; (*fam: atraco*) job, heist (*US*); (*fig: choque*) clash; **no dar** ~ to be bone idle; **de un** ~ with one blow; **de** ~ suddenly; ~ **(de estado)** coup (d'état); ~ **de gracia** coup de grâce (*tb fig*); ~ **de fortuna/maestro** stroke of luck/genius; **cerrar una puerta de** ~ to slam a door.
golpear [golpe'ar] *vt, vi* to strike, knock; (*asestar*) to beat; (*de puño*) to punch; (*golpetear*) to tap; (*mesa*) to bang.
golpista [gol'pista] *adj*: **intentona** ~ coup attempt ♦ *nm/f* participant in a coup (d'état).
golpiza [gol'pisa] *nf*: **dar una** ~ **a algn** (*AM*) to beat sb up.
goma ['goma] *nf* (*caucho*) rubber; (*elástico*) elastic; (*tira*) rubber *o* elastic (*BRIT*) band; (*fam: preservativo*) condom; (*droga*) hashish; (*explosivo*) plastic explosive; ~ **(de borrar)** eraser, rubber (*BRIT*); ~ **de mascar** chewing gum; ~ **de pegar** gum, glue.
goma-espuma [gomaes'puma] *nf* foam rubber.
gomina [go'mina] *nf* hair gel.
gomita [go'mita] *nf* rubber *o* elastic (*BRIT*) band.
góndola ['gondola] *nf* (*barco*) gondola; (*de tren*) goods wagon.
gordo, a ['gorðo, a] *adj* (*gen*) fat; (*persona*) plump; (*agua*) hard; (*fam*) enormous ♦ *nm/f* fat man *o* woman; **el (premio)** ~ (*en lotería*) first prize; ¡~! (*fam*) fatty!
gordura [gor'ðura] *nf* fat; (*corpulencia*) fatness, stoutness.
gorgojo [gor'ɣoxo] *nm* (*insecto*) grub.
gorgorito [gorɣ'rito] *nm* (*gorjeo*) trill, warble.
gorila [go'rila] *nm* gorilla; (*fam*) tough, thug; (*guardaespaldas*) bodyguard.
gorjear [gorxe'ar] *vi* to twitter, chirp.
gorjeo [gor'xeo] *nm* twittering, chirping.
gorra ['gorra] *nf* (*gen*) cap; (*de niño*) bonnet; (*militar*) bearskin; ~ **de montar/de paño/de punto/de visera** riding/cloth/knitted/peaked cap; **andar** *o* **ir** *o* **vivir de** ~ to sponge, scrounge; **entrar de** ~ (*fam*) to gatecrash.
gorrión [go'rrjon] *nm* sparrow.
gorro ['gorro] *nm* cap; (*de niño, mujer*) bonnet; **estoy hasta el** ~ I am fed up.
gorrón, ona [go'rron, ona] *nm* pebble;

(*TEC*) pivot ♦ *nm/f* scrounger.
gorronear [gorrone'ar] *vi* (*fam*) to sponge, scrounge.
gota ['gota] *nf* (*gen*) drop; (*de pintura*) blob; (*de sudor*) bead; (*MED*) gout; **~ a ~** drop by drop; **caer a ~s** to drip.
gotear [gote'ar] *vi* to drip; (*escurrir*) to trickle; (*salirse*) to leak; (*cirio*) to gutter; (*lloviznar*) to drizzle.
gotera [go'tera] *nf* leak.
gótico, a ['gotiko, a] *adj* Gothic.
gozar [go'θar] *vi* to enjoy o.s.; **~ de** (*disfrutar*) to enjoy; (*poseer*) to possess; **~ de buena salud** to enjoy good health.
gozne ['goθne] *nm* hinge.
gozo ['goθo] *nm* (*alegría*) joy; (*placer*) pleasure; **¡mi ~ en el pozo!** that's torn it!, just my luck!
g.p. *nm abr* (= *giro postal*) m.o.
gr. *abr* (= *gramo(s)*) g.
grabación [graβa'θjon] *nf* recording.
grabado, a [gra'βaðo, a] *adj* (*MUS*) recorded; (*en cinta*) taped, on tape ♦ *nm* print, engraving; **~ al agua fuerte** etching; **~ al aguatinta** aquatint; **~ en cobre** copperplate; **~ en madera** woodcut; **~ rupestre** rock carving.
grabador, a [graβa'ðor, a] *nm/f* engraver ♦ *nf* tape-recorder; **~a de cassettes** cassette recorder.
grabar [gra'βar] *vt* to engrave; (*discos, cintas*) to record; (*impresionar*) to impress.
gracejo [gra'θexo] *nm* (*humor*) wit, humour; (*elegancia*) grace.
gracia ['graθja] *nf* (*encanto*) grace, gracefulness; (*REL*) grace; (*chiste*) joke; (*humor*) humour, wit; **¡muchas ~s!** thanks very much!; **~s a** thanks to; **tener ~** (*chiste etc*) to be funny; **¡qué ~!** how funny!; (*irónico*) what a nerve!; **no me hace ~** (*broma*) it's not funny; (*plan*) I am not too keen; **con ~s anticipadas/repetidas** thanking you in advance/again; **dar las ~s a algn por algo** to thank sb for sth.
grácil ['graθil] *adj* (*sutil*) graceful; (*delgado*) slender; (*delicado*) delicate.
gracioso, a [gra'θjoso, a] *adj* (*garboso*) graceful; (*chistoso*) funny; (*cómico*) comical; (*agudo*) witty; (*título*) gracious ♦ *nm/f* (*TEAT*) comic character, fool; **su graciosa Majestad** His/Her Gracious Majesty.
grada ['graða] *nf* (*de escalera*) step; (*de anfiteatro*) tier, row; **~s** *nfpl* (*de estadio*) terraces.
gradación [graða'θjon] *nf* gradation; (*serie*) graded series.
gradería [graðe'ria] *nf* (*gradas*) (flight of) steps *pl*; (*de anfiteatro*) tiers *pl*, rows *pl*; **~ cubierta** covered stand.
grado ['graðo] *nm* degree; (*etapa*) stage, step; (*nivel*) rate; (*de parentesco*) order of lineage; (*de aceite, vino*) grade; (*grada*) step; (*ESCOL*) class, year, grade (*US*); (*UNIV*) degree; (*LING*) degree of comparison; (*MIL*) rank; **de buen ~** willingly; **en sumo ~, en ~ superlativo** in the highest degree.
graduación [graðwa'θjon] *nf* (*acto*) gradation; (*clasificación*) rating; (*del alcohol*) proof, strength; (*ESCOL*) graduation; (*MIL*) rank; **de alta ~** high-ranking.
gradual [gra'ðwal] *adj* gradual.
graduar [gra'ðwar] *vt* (*gen*) to graduate; (*medir*) to gauge; (*TEC*) to calibrate; (*UNIV*) to confer a degree on; (*MIL*) to commission; **~se** *vr* to graduate; **~se la vista** to have one's eyes tested.
grafía [gra'fia] *nf* (*escritura*) writing; (*ortografía*) spelling.
gráfico, a ['grafiko, a] *adj* graphic; (*fig: vívido*) vivid, lively ♦ *nm* diagram ♦ *nf* graph; **~ de barras** (*COM*) bar chart; **~ de sectores** *o* **de tarta** (*COM*) pie chart; **~s** *nmpl* (*tb INFORM*) graphics; **~s empresariales** (*COM*) business graphics.
grafito [gra'fito] *nm* (*TEC*) graphite, black lead.
grafología [grafolo'xia] *nf* graphology.
gragea [gra'xea] *nf* (*MED*) pill; (*caramelo*) dragée.
grajo ['graxo] *nm* rook.
Gral. *abr* (*MIL*: = *General*) Gen.
gramático, a [gra'matiko, a] *nm/f* (*persona*) grammarian ♦ *nf* grammar.
gramo ['gramo] *nm* gramme (*BRIT*), gram (*US*).
gran [gran] *adj V* **grande.**
grana ['grana] *nf* (*BOT*) seedling; (*color*) scarlet; **ponerse como la ~** to go as red as a beetroot.
granada [gra'naða] *nf* pomegranate; (*MIL*) grenade; **~ de mano** hand grenade; **~ de metralla** shrapnel shell.
granadilla [grana'ðiʎa] *nf* (*AM*) passion fruit.
granadino, a [grana'ðino, a] *adj* of *o* from Granada ♦ *nm/f* native *o* inhabitant of Granada ♦ *nf* grenadine.
granar [gra'nar] *vi* to seed.
granate [gra'nate] *adj inv* maroon ♦ *nm* garnet; (*color*) maroon.
Gran Bretaña [grambre'taɲa] *nf* Great

Britain.
Gran Canaria [granka'narja] *nf* Grand Canary.
grancanario, a [granka'narjo, a] *adj* of *o* from Grand Canary ♦ *nm/f* native *o* inhabitant of Grand Canary.
grande ['grande], **gran** *adj* (*de tamaño*) big, large; (*alto*) tall; (*distinguido*) great; (*impresionante*) grand ♦ *nm* grandee; **¿cómo es de ~?** how big is it?, what size is it?; **pasarlo en ~** to have a tremendous time.
grandeza [gran'deθa] *nf* greatness; (*tamaño*) bigness; (*esplendidez*) grandness; (*nobleza*) nobility.
grandioso, a [gran'djoso, a] *adj* magnificent, grand.
grandullón, ona [granðu'ʎon, ona] *adj* oversized.
granel [gra'nel] *nm* (*montón*) heap; **a ~** (*COM*) in bulk.
granero [gra'nero] *nm* granary, barn.
granice [gra'niθe] *etc vb V* **granizar**.
granito [gra'nito] *nm* (*AGR*) small grain; (*roca*) granite.
granizada [grani'θaða] *nf* hailstorm; (*fig*) hail; **una ~ de balas** a hail of bullets.
granizado [grani'θaðo] *nm* iced drink; **~ de café** iced coffee.
granizar [grani'θar] *vi* to hail.
granizo [gra'niθo] *nm* hail.
granja ['granxa] *nf* (*gen*) farm; **~ avícola** chicken *o* poultry farm.
granjear [granxe'ar] *vt* (*cobrar*) to earn; (*ganar*) to win; (*avanzar*) to gain; **~se** *vr* (*amistad etc*) to gain for o.s.
granjero, a [gran'xero, a] *nm/f* farmer.
grano ['grano] *nm* grain; (*semilla*) seed; (*baya*) berry; (*MED*) pimple, spot; (*partícula*) particle; (*punto*) speck; **~s** *nmpl* cereals; **~ de café** coffee bean; **ir al ~** to get to the point.
granuja [gra'nuxa] *nm* rogue; (*golfillo*) urchin.
grapa ['grapa] *nf* staple; (*TEC*) clamp; (*sujetador*) clip, fastener; (*ARQ*) cramp.
grapadora [grapa'ðora] *nf* stapler.
GRAPO ['grapo] *nm abr* (*ESP POL*) = *Grupo de Resistencia Antifascista Primero de Octubre*.
grasa ['grasa] *nf V* **graso**.
grasiento, a [gra'sjento, a] *adj* greasy; (*de aceite*) oily; (*mugriento*) filthy.
graso, a ['graso, a] *adj* fatty; (*aceitoso*) greasy, oily ♦ *nf* (*gen*) grease; (*de cocina*) fat, lard; (*sebo*) suet; (*mugre*) filth; (*AUTO*) oil; (*lubricante*) grease; **~ de ballena** blubber; **~ de pescado** fish oil.
grasoso, a [gra'soso, a] *adj* (*AM*) greasy, sticky.
gratificación [gratifika'θjon] *nf* (*propina*) tip; (*aguinaldo*) gratuity; (*bono*) bonus; (*recompensa*) reward.
gratificar [gratifi'kar] *vt* (*dar propina*) to tip; (*premiar*) to reward; **"se gratificará"** "a reward is offered".
gratifique [grati'fike] *etc vb V* **gratificar**.
gratinar [grati'nar] *vt* to cook au gratin.
gratis ['gratis] *adv* free, for nothing.
gratitud [grati'tuð] *nf* gratitude.
grato, a ['grato, a] *adj* (*agradable*) pleasant, agreeable; (*bienvenido*) welcome; **nos es ~ informarle que ...** we are pleased to inform you that ....
gratuito, a [gra'twito, a] *adj* (*gratis*) free; (*sin razón*) gratuitous; (*acusación*) unfounded.
grava ['graβa] *nf* (*guijos*) gravel; (*piedra molida*) crushed stone; (*en carreteras*) road metal.
gravamen [gra'βamen] *nm* (*carga*) burden; (*impuesto*) tax; **libre de ~** (*ECON*) free from encumbrances.
gravar [gra'βar] *vt* to burden; (*COM*) to tax; (*ECON*) to assess for tax; **~ con impuestos** to burden with taxes.
grave ['graβe] *adj* heavy; (*fig, MED*) grave, serious; (*importante*) important; (*herida*) severe; (*MUS*) low, deep; (*LING*: *acento*) grave; **estar ~** to be seriously ill.
gravedad [graβe'ðað] *nf* gravity; (*fig*) seriousness; (*grandeza*) importance; (*dignidad*) dignity; (*MUS*) depth.
grávido, a ['graβiðo, a] *adj* (*preñada*) pregnant.
gravilla [gra'βiʎa] *nf* gravel.
gravitación [graβita'θjon] *nf* gravitation.
gravitar [graβi'tar] *vi* to gravitate; **~ sobre** to rest on.
gravoso, a [gra'βoso, a] *adj* (*pesado*) burdensome; (*costoso*) costly.
graznar [graθ'nar] *vi* (*cuervo*) to squawk; (*pato*) to quack; (*hablar ronco*) to croak.
graznido [graθ'niðo] *nm* squawk; croak.
Grecia ['greθja] *nf* Greece.
gregario, a [gre'ɣarjo, a] *adj* gregarious; **instinto ~** herd instinct.
gremio ['gremjo] *nm* (*asociación*) professional association, guild.
greña ['greɲa] *nf* (*cabellos*) shock of hair; (*maraña*) tangle; **andar a la ~** to bicker, squabble.
greñudo, a [gre'ɲuðo, a] *adj* (*persona*) dishevelled; (*pelo*) tangled.
gresca ['greska] *nf* uproar; (*trifulca*) row.
griego, a ['grjeɣo, a] *adj* Greek, Grecian

♦ *nm/f* Greek ♦ *nm* (*LING*) Greek.
grieta ['grjeta] *nf* crack; (*hendidura*) chink; (*quiebra*) crevice; (*MED*) chap; (*POL*) rift.
grifa ['grifa] *nf* (*fam: droga*) marijuana.
grifo ['grifo] *nm* tap (*BRIT*), faucet (*US*); (*AM*) petrol (*BRIT*) *o* gas (*US*) station.
grilletes [gri'ʎetes] *nmpl* fetters, shackles.
grillo ['griʎo] *nm* (*ZOOL*) cricket; (*BOT*) shoot; **~s** *nmpl* shackles, irons.
grima ['grima] *nf* (*horror*) loathing; (*desagrado*) reluctance; (*desazón*) uneasiness; **me da ~** it makes me sick.
gringo, a ['gringo, a] (*AM*) *adj* (*pey: extranjero*) foreign; (*: norteamericano*) Yankee; (*idioma*) foreign ♦ *nm/f* foreigner; Yank.
gripa ['gripa] *nf* (*AM*) flu, influenza.
gripe ['gripe] *nf* flu, influenza.
gris [gris] *adj* grey.
grisáceo, a [gri'saθeo, a] *adj* greyish.
grisoso, a [gri'soso, a] *adj* (*AM*) greyish, grayish (*esp US*).
gritar [gri'tar] *vt, vi* to shout, yell; **¡no grites!** stop shouting!
grito ['grito] *nm* shout, yell; (*de horror*) scream; **a ~ pelado** at the top of one's voice; **poner el ~ en el cielo** to scream blue murder; **es el último ~** (*de moda*) it's all the rage.
groenlandés, esa [groenlan'des, esa] *adj* Greenland *cpd* ♦ *nm/f* Greenlander.
Groenlandia [groen'landja] *nf* Greenland.
grosella [gro'seʎa] *nf* (red)currant; **~ negra** blackcurrant.
grosería [grose'ria] *nf* (*actitud*) rudeness; (*comentario*) vulgar comment; (*palabrota*) swearword.
grosero, a [gro'sero, a] *adj* (*poco cortés*) rude, bad-mannered; (*ordinario*) vulgar, crude.
grosor [gro'sor] *nm* thickness.
grotesco, a [gro'tesko, a] *adj* grotesque; (*absurdo*) bizarre.
grúa ['grua] *nf* (*TEC*) crane; (*de petróleo*) derrick; **~ corrediza** *o* **móvil/de pescante/puente/de torre** travelling/jib/overhead/tower crane.
grueso, a ['grweso, a] *adj* thick; (*persona*) stout; (*calidad*) coarse ♦ *nm* bulk; (*espesor*) thickness; (*densidad*) density; (*de gente*) main body, mass; **el ~ de** the bulk of.
grulla ['gruʎa] *nf* (*ZOOL*) crane.
grumete [gru'mete] *nm* (*NAUT*) cabin *o* ship's boy.
grumo ['grumo] *nm* (*coágulo*) clot, lump; (*masa*) dollop.
gruñido [gru'ɲiðo] *nm* grunt, growl; (*fig*) grumble.
gruñir [gru'ɲir] *vi* (*animal*) to grunt, growl; (*fam*) to grumble.
gruñón, ona [gru'ɲon, ona] *adj* grumpy ♦ *nm/f* grumbler.
grupa ['grupa] *nf* (*ZOOL*) rump.
grupo ['grupo] *nm* group; (*TEC*) unit, set; (*de árboles*) cluster; **~ sanguíneo** blood group.
gruta ['gruta] *nf* grotto.
Gta. *abr* (*AUTO*) = **Glorieta.**
guaca ['gwaka] *nf* Indian tomb.
guacamole [gwaka'mole] *nm* (*AM*) avocado salad.
guachimán [gwatʃi'man] *nm* (*AM*) night watchman.
guadalajareño, a [gwaðalaxa'reɲo, a] *adj* of *o* from Guadalajara ♦ *nm/f* native *o* inhabitant of Guadalajara.
Guadalquivir [gwaðalki'ßir] *nm*: **el (Río) ~** the Guadalquivir.
guadaña [gwa'ðaɲa] *nf* scythe.
guadañar [gwaða'ɲar] *vt* to scythe, mow.
Guadiana [gwa'ðjana] *nm*: **el (Río) ~** the Guadiana.
guagua ['gwaɣwa] *nf* (*AM, Canarias*) bus; (*AM: criatura*) baby.
guajolote [gwajo'lote] *nm* (*AM*) turkey.
guano ['gwano] *nm* guano.
guantada [gwan'taða] *nf*, **guantazo** [gwan'taθo] *nm* slap.
guante ['gwante] *nm* glove; **se ajusta como un ~** it fits like a glove; **echar el ~ a algn** to catch hold of sb; (*fig: policía*) to catch sb.
guapo, a ['gwapo, a] *adj* good-looking; (*mujer*) pretty, attractive; (*hombre*) handsome; (*elegante*) smart ♦ *nm* lover, gallant; (*AM fam*) tough guy, bully.
guaraní [gwara'ni] *adj, nm/f* Guarani ♦ *nm* (*moneda*) *monetary unit of Paraguay.*
guarapo [gwa'rapo] *nm* (*AM*) fermented cane juice.
guarda ['gwarða] *nm/f* (*persona*) warden, keeper ♦ *nf* (*acto*) guarding; (*custodia*) custody; (*TIP*) flyleaf, endpaper; **~ forestal** game warden.
guarda(a)gujas [gwarda'ɣuxas] *nm inv* (*FERRO*) switchman.
guardabarros [gwarða'ßarros] *nm inv* mudguard (*BRIT*), fender (*US*).
guardabosques [gwarda'ßoskes] *nm inv* gamekeeper.
guardacoches [gwarða'kotʃes] *nm/f inv* (*celador*) parking attendant.
guardacostas [gwarda'kostas] *nm inv* coastguard vessel.
guardador, a [gwarða'ðor, a] *adj* protective; (*tacaño*) mean, stingy ♦ *nm/f*

guardian, protector.
guardaespaldas [gwardaes'paldas] *nm/f inv* bodyguard.
guardameta [gwarða'meta] *nm* goalkeeper.
guardapolvo [gwarda'polβo] *nm* dust cover; (*prenda de vestir*) overalls *pl*.
guardar [gwar'ðar] *vt* (*gen*) to keep; (*vigilar*) to guard, watch over; (*conservar*) to put away; (*dinero: ahorrar*) to save; (*promesa etc*) to keep; (*ley*) to observe; (*rencor*) to bear, harbour; (*INFORM: archivo*) to save; **~se** *vr* (*preservarse*) to protect o.s.; **~se de algo** (*evitar*) to avoid sth; (*abstenerse*) to refrain from sth; **~se de hacer algo** to be careful not to do sth; **guardársela a algn** to have it in for sb.
guardarropa [gwarða'rropa] *nm* (*armario*) wardrobe; (*en establecimiento público*) cloakroom.
guardería [gwarðe'ria] *nf* nursery.
guardia ['gwarðja] *nf* (*MIL*) guard; (*cuidado*) care, custody ♦ *nm/f* guard; (*policía*) policeman/woman; **estar de ~** to be on guard; **montar ~** to mount guard; **la G~ Civil** the Civil Guard; **~ municipal** *o* **urbana** municipal police; **un ~ civil** a Civil Guard(sman); **un(a) ~ nacional** a policeman/woman; **~ urbano** traffic policeman; *see boxed note*.

GUARDIA CIVIL

The **Guardia Civil** *is a branch of the army, or "Ejército de Tierra", and is run along military lines. It has a policing role outside large towns and cities and comes under the joint control of the Spanish Ministry of Defence and the Ministry of the Interior. It is also known as "La Benemérita".*

guardián, ana [gwar'ðjan, ana] *nm/f* (*gen*) guardian, keeper.
guarecer [gware'θer] *vt* (*proteger*) to protect; (*abrigar*) to shelter; **~se** *vr* to take refuge.
guarezca [gwa'reθka] *etc vb V* **guarecer**.
guarida [gwa'riða] *nf* (*de animal*) den, lair; (*de persona*) haunt, hideout; (*refugio*) refuge.
guarnecer [gwarne'θer] *vt* (*equipar*) to provide; (*adornar*) to adorn; (*TEC*) to reinforce.
guarnezca [gwar'neθka] *etc vb V* **guarnecer**.
guarnición [gwarni'θjon] *nf* (*de vestimenta*) trimming; (*de piedra*) mount; (*CULIN*) garnish; (*arneses*) harness; (*MIL*) garrison.
guarrada [gwa'rraða] (*fam*) *nf* (*cosa sucia*) dirty mess; (*acto o dicho obsceno*) obscenity; **hacer una ~ a algn** to do the dirty on sb.
guarrería [gwarre'ria] *nf* = **guarrada**.
guarro, a ['gwarro, a] *nm/f* (*fam*) pig; (*fig*) dirty *o* slovenly person.
guasa ['gwasa] *nf* joke; **con** *o* **de ~** jokingly, in fun.
guasón, ona [gwa'son, ona] *adj* witty; (*bromista*) joking ♦ *nm/f* wit; joker.
Guatemala [gwate'mala] *nf* Guatemala.
guatemalteco, a [gwatemal'teko, a] *adj*, *nm/f* Guatemalan.
guateque [gwa'teke] *nm* (*fiesta*) party.
guay [gwai] *adj* (*fam*) super, great.
guayaba [gwa'jaβa] *nf* (*BOT*) guava.
Guayana [gwa'jana] *nf* Guyana, Guiana.
gubernamental [guβernamen'tal], **gubernativo, a** [guβerna'tiβo, a] *adj* governmental.
guedeja [ge'ðexa] *nf* long hair.
guerra ['gerra] *nf* war; (*arte*) warfare; (*pelea*) struggle; **~ atómica/bacteriológica/nuclear/de guerrillas** atomic/germ/nuclear/guerrilla warfare; **Primera/Segunda G~ Mundial** First/Second World War; **~ de precios** (*COM*) price war; **~ civil/fría** civil/cold war; **~ a muerte** fight to the death; **de ~** military, war *cpd*; **estar en ~** to be at war; **dar ~** to be annoying.
guerrear [gerre'ar] *vi* to wage war.
guerrero, a [ge'rrero, a] *adj* fighting; (*carácter*) warlike ♦ *nm/f* warrior.
guerrilla [ge'rriʎa] *nf* guerrilla warfare; (*tropas*) guerrilla band *o* group.
guerrillero, a [gerri'ʎero, a] *nm/f* guerrilla (fighter); (*contra invasor*) partisan.
gueto ['geto] *nm* ghetto.
guía ['gia] *etc vb V* **guiar** ♦ *nm/f* (*persona*) guide ♦ *nf* (*libro*) guidebook; (*manual*) handbook; (*INFORM*) prompt; **~ de ferrocarriles** railway timetable; **~ telefónica** telephone directory; **~ del turista/del viajero** tourist/traveller's guide.
guiar [gi'ar] *vt* to guide, direct; (*dirigir*) to lead; (*orientar*) to advise; (*AUTO*) to steer; **~se** *vr*: **~se por** to be guided by.
guijarro [gi'xarro] *nm* pebble.
guillotina [giʎo'tina] *nf* guillotine.
guinda ['ginda] *nf* morello cherry; (*licor*) cherry liqueur.
guindar [gin'dar] *vt* to hoist; (*fam: robar*) to nick.
guindilla [gin'diʎa] *nf* chil(l)i pepper.
Guinea [gi'nea] *nf* Guinea.

guineo, a [gi'neo, a] *adj* Guinea *cpd*, Guinean ♦ *nm/f* Guinean.
guiñapo [gi'ɲapo] *nm* (*harapo*) rag; (*persona*) rogue.
guiñar [gi'ɲar] *vi* to wink.
guiño ['giɲo] *nm* (*parpadeo*) wink; (*muecas*) grimace; **hacer ~s a** (*enamorados*) to make eyes at.
guiñol [gi'ɲol] *nm* (*TEAT*) puppet theatre.
guión [gi'on] *nm* (*LING*) hyphen, dash; (*esquema*) summary, outline; (*CINE*) script.
guionista [gjo'nista] *nm/f* scriptwriter.
guipuzcoano, a [gipuθko'ano, a] *adj* of *o* from Guipúzcoa ♦ *nm/f* native *o* inhabitant of Guipúzcoa.
guiri ['giri] *nm/f* (*fam, pey*) foreigner.
guirigay [giri'gai] *nm* (*griterío*) uproar; (*confusión*) chaos.
guirnalda [gir'nalda] *nf* garland.
guisa ['gisa] *nf*: **a ~ de** as, like.
guisado [gi'saðo] *nm* stew.
guisante [gi'sante] *nm* pea.
guisar [gi'sar] *vt, vi* to cook; (*fig*) to arrange.
guiso ['giso] *nm* cooked dish.
guita ['gita] *nf* twine; (*fam*: *dinero*) dough.
guitarra [gi'tarra] *nf* guitar.
guitarrista [gita'rrista] *nm/f* guitarist.
gula ['gula] *nf* gluttony, greed.
gusano [gu'sano] *nm* maggot, worm; (*de mariposa, polilla*) caterpillar; (*fig*) worm; (*ser despreciable*) creep; **~ de seda** silk-worm.
gustar [gus'tar] *vt* to taste, sample ♦ *vi* to please, be pleasing; **~ de algo** to like *o* enjoy sth; **me gustan las uvas** I like grapes; **le gusta nadar** she likes *o* enjoys swimming; **¿gusta Ud?** would you like some?; **como Ud guste** as you wish.
gusto ['gusto] *nm* (*sentido, sabor*) taste; (*agrado*) liking; (*placer*) pleasure; **tiene un ~ amargo** it has a bitter taste; **tener buen ~** to have good taste; **sobre ~s no hay nada escrito** there's no accounting for tastes; **de buen/mal ~** in good/bad taste; **sentirse a ~** to feel at ease; **¡mucho *o* tanto ~ (en conocerle)!** how do you do?, pleased to meet you; **el ~ es mío** the pleasure is mine; **tomar ~ a** to take a liking to; **con ~** willingly, gladly.
gustoso, a [gus'toso, a] *adj* (*sabroso*) tasty; (*agradable*) pleasant; (*con voluntad*) willing, glad; **lo hizo ~** he did it gladly.
gutural [gutu'ral] *adj* guttural.
guyanés, esa [gwaja'nes, esa] *adj, nm/f* Guyanese.

Hh

H, h ['atʃe] *nf* (*letra*) H, h; **H de Historia** H for Harry (*BRIT*) *o* How (*US*).
H. *abr* (*QUÍMICA*: = *Hidrógeno*) H; (= *Hectárea(s)*) ha.; (*COM*: = *Haber*) cr.
h. *abr* (= *hora(s)*) h., hr(s).; (= *hacia*) c. ♦ *nmpl abr* (= *habitantes*) pop.
ha [a] *vb V* **haber**.
Ha. *abr* (= *Hectárea(s)*) ha.
haba ['aβa] *nf* bean; **son ~s contadas** it goes without saying; **en todas partes cuecen ~s** it's the same (story) the whole world over.
Habana [a'βana] *nf*: **la ~** Havana.
habanero, a [aβa'nero, a] *adj* of *o* from Havana ♦ *nm/f* native *o* inhabitant of Havana ♦ *nf* (*MUS*) habanera.
habano [a'βano] *nm* Havana cigar.
habeas corpus [a'βeas'korpus] *nm* (*LAW*) habeas corpus.

PALABRA CLAVE

haber [a'βer] *vb aux* **1** (*tiempos compuestos*) to have; **había comido** I have/had eaten; **antes/después de ~lo visto** before seeing/after seeing *o* having seen it; **si lo hubiera sabido habría ido** if I had known I would have gone
2: **¡~lo dicho antes!** you should have said so before!; **¿habráse visto (cosa igual)?** have you ever seen anything like it?
3: **~ de**: **he de hacerlo** I must do it; **ha de llegar mañana** it should arrive tomorrow
♦ *vb impers* **1** (*existencia*: *sg*) there is; (: *pl*) there are; **hay un hermano/dos hermanos** there is one brother/there are two brothers; **¿cuánto hay de aquí a Sucre?** how far is it from here to Sucre?; **habrá unos 4 grados** it must be about 4 degrees; **no hay quien te entienda** there's no understanding you
2 (*obligación*): **hay que hacer algo** something must be done; **hay que apuntarlo para acordarse** you have to write it down to remember
3: **¡hay que ver!** well I never!
4: **¡no hay de *o* por (*AM*) qué!** don't

mention it!, not at all!
5: **¿qué hay?** (*¿qué pasa?*) what's up?, what's the matter?; (*¿qué tal?*) how's it going?
♦ **~se** *vr*: **habérselas con algn** to have it out with sb
♦ *vt*: **he aquí unas sugerencias** here are some suggestions; **todos los inventos habidos y por ~** all inventions present and future; **en el encuentro habido ayer** in yesterday's game
♦ *nm* (*en cuenta*) credit side; **~es** *nmpl* assets; **¿cuánto tengo en el ~?** how much do I have in my account?; **tiene varias novelas en su ~** he has several novels to his credit.

habichuela [aβi'tʃwela] *nf* kidney bean.
hábil ['aβil] *adj* (*listo*) clever, smart; (*capaz*) fit, capable; (*experto*) expert; **día ~** working day.
habilidad [aβili'ðað] *nf* (*gen*) skill, ability; (*inteligencia*) cleverness; (*destreza*) expertness, expertise; (*JUR*) competence; **~ (para)** fitness (for); **tener ~ manual** to be clever with one's hands.
habilitación [aβilita'θjon] *nf* qualification; (*colocación de muebles*) fitting out; (*financiamiento*) financing; (*oficina*) paymaster's office.
habilitado [aβili'taðo] *nm* paymaster.
habilitar [aβili'tar] *vt* to qualify; (*autorizar*) to authorize; (*capacitar*) to enable; (*dar instrumentos*) to equip; (*financiar*) to finance.
hábilmente [aβil'mente] *adv* skilfully, expertly.
habitable [aβi'taβle] *adj* inhabitable.
habitación [aβita'θjon] *nf* (*cuarto*) room; (*casa*) dwelling, abode; (*BIO*: *morada*) habitat; **~ sencilla** *o* **individual** single room; **~ doble** *o* **de matrimonio** double room.
habitante [aβi'tante] *nm/f* inhabitant.
habitar [aβi'tar] *vt* (*residir en*) to inhabit; (*ocupar*) to occupy ♦ *vi* to live.
hábitat, *pl* **hábitats** ['aβitat, 'aβitats] *nm* habitat.
hábito ['aβito] *nm* habit; **tener el ~ de hacer algo** to be in the habit of doing sth.
habitual [aβi'twal] *adj* habitual.
habituar [aβi'twar] *vt* to accustom; **~se** *vr*: **~se a** to get used to.
habla ['aβla] *nf* (*capacidad de hablar*) speech; (*idioma*) language; (*dialecto*) dialect; **perder el ~** to become speechless; **de ~ francesa** French-speaking; **estar al ~** to be in contact; (*TELEC*) to be on the line; **¡González al ~!** (*TELEC*) Gonzalez speaking!
hablador, a [aβla'ðor, a] *adj* talkative ♦ *nm/f* chatterbox.
habladuría [aβlaðu'ria] *nf* rumour; **~s** *nfpl* gossip *sg*.
hablante [a'βlante] *adj* speaking ♦ *nm/f* speaker.
hablar [a'βlar] *vt* to speak, talk ♦ *vi* to speak; **~se** *vr* to speak to each other; **~ con** to speak to; **¡hable!, ¡puede ~!** (*TELEC*) you're through!; **de eso ni ~** no way, that's not on; **~ alto/bajo/claro** to speak loudly/quietly/plainly *o* bluntly; **~ de** to speak of *o* about; **"se habla inglés"** "English spoken here"; **no se hablan** they are not on speaking terms.
habré [a'βre] *etc vb V* **haber.**
hacedor, a [aθe'ðor, a] *nm/f* maker.
hacendado, a [aθen'daðo, a] *adj* property-owning ♦ *nm* (*terrateniente*) large landowner.
hacendoso, a [aθen'doso, a] *adj* industrious, hard-working.

PALABRA CLAVE

hacer [a'θer] *vt* **1** (*fabricar, producir, conseguir*) to make; (*construir*) to build; **~ una película/un ruido** to make a film/noise; **el guisado lo hice yo** I made *o* cooked the stew; **~ amigos** to make friends
2 (*ejecutar*: *trabajo etc*) to do; **~ la colada** to do the washing; **~ la comida** to do the cooking; **¿qué haces?** what are you doing?; **¡eso está hecho!** you've got it!; **~ el tonto/indio** to act the fool/clown; **~ el malo** *o* **el papel del malo** (*TEAT*) to play the villain
3 (*estudios, algunos deportes*) to do; **~ español/económicas** to do *o* study Spanish/economics; **~ yoga/gimnasia** to do yoga/go to gym
4 (*transformar, incidir en*): **esto lo hará más difícil** this will make it more difficult; **salir te hará sentir mejor** going out will make you feel better; **te hace más joven** it makes you look younger
5 (*cálculo*): **2 y 2 hacen 4** 2 and 2 make 4; **éste hace 100** this one makes 100
6 (*+sub*): **esto hará que ganemos** this will make us win; **harás que no quiera venir** you'll stop him wanting to come
7 (*como sustituto de vb*) to do; **él bebió y yo hice lo mismo** he drank and I did likewise
8: **no hace más que criticar** all he does is

criticize
♦ *vb semi-aux*: ~ *+infin* **1** (*directo*): **les hice venir** I made *o* had them come; ~ **trabajar a los demás** to get others to work
2 (*por intermedio de otros*): ~ **reparar algo** to get sth repaired
♦ *vi* **1**: **haz como que no lo sabes** act as if you don't know; **hiciste bien en decírmelo** you were right to tell me
2 (*ser apropiado*): **si os hace** if it's alright with you
3: ~ **de**: ~ **de madre para uno** to be like a mother to sb; (*TEAT*): ~ **de Otelo** to play Othello; **la tabla hace de mesa** the board does as a table
♦ *vb impers* **1**: **hace calor/frío** it's hot/cold; *V tb* **bueno; sol; tiempo**
2 (*tiempo*): **hace 3 años** 3 years ago; **hace un mes que voy/no voy** I've been going/I haven't been for a month; **no le veo desde hace mucho** I haven't seen him for a long time
3: **¿cómo has hecho para llegar tan rápido?** how did you manage to get here so quickly?
♦ ~**se** *vr* **1** (*volverse*) to become; **se hicieron amigos** they became friends; ~**se viejo** to get *o* grow old; **se hace tarde** it's getting late
2: ~**se algo**: **me hice un traje** I got a suit made
3 (*acostumbrarse*): ~**se a** to get used to; ~**se a la idea** to get used to the idea
4: **se hace con huevos y leche** it's made out of eggs and milk; **eso no se hace** that's not done
5 (*obtener*): ~**se de** *o* **con algo** to get hold of sth
6 (*fingirse*): ~**se el sordo/sueco** to turn a deaf ear/pretend not to notice.

hacha ['atʃa] *nf* axe; (*antorcha*) torch.
hachazo [a'tʃaθo] *nm* axe blow.
hache ['atʃe] *nf* (the letter) H; **llámele usted** ~ call it what you will.
hachís [a'tʃis] *nm* hashish.
hacia ['aθja] *prep* (*en dirección de, actitud*) towards; (*cerca de*) near; ~ **arriba/abajo** up(wards)/down(wards); ~ **mediodía** about noon.
hacienda [a'θjenda] *nf* (*propiedad*) property; (*finca*) farm; (*AM*) ranch; ~ **pública** public finance; **(Ministerio de) H~** Exchequer (*BRIT*), Treasury Department (*US*).
hacinar [aθi'nar] *vt* to pile (up); (*AGR*) to stack; (*fig*) to overcrowd.
hada ['aða] *nf* fairy; ~ **madrina** fairy godmother.
hado ['aðo] *nm* fate, destiny.
haga ['aɣa] *etc vb V* **hacer.**
Haití [ai'ti] *nm* Haiti.
haitiano, a [ai'tjano, a] *adj, nm/f* Haitian.
hala ['ala] *excl* (*vamos*) come on!; (*anda*) get on with it!
halagar [ala'ɣar] *vt* (*lisonjear*) to flatter.
halago [a'laɣo] *nm* (*adulación*) flattery.
halague [a'laɣe] *etc vb V* **halagar.**
halagüeño, a [ala'ɣweɲo, a] *adj* flattering.
halcón [al'kon] *nm* falcon, hawk.
hálito ['alito] *nm* breath.
halitosis [ali'tosis] *nf* halitosis, bad breath.
hallar [a'ʎar] *vt* (*gen*) to find; (*descubrir*) to discover; (*toparse con*) to run into; ~**se** *vr* to be (situated); (*encontrarse*) to find o.s.; **se halla fuera** he is away; **no se halla** he feels out of place.
hallazgo [a'ʎaθɣo] *nm* discovery; (*cosa*) find.
halo ['alo] *nm* halo.
halógeno, a [a'loxeno, a] *adj*: **faro** ~ halogen lamp.
halterofilia [altero'filja] *nf* weightlifting.
hamaca [a'maka] *nf* hammock.
hambre ['ambre] *nf* hunger; (*carencia*) famine; (*inanición*) starvation; (*fig*) longing; **tener** ~ to be hungry.
hambriento, a [am'brjento, a] *adj* hungry, starving ♦ *nm/f* starving person; **los ~s** the hungry; ~ **de** hungry *o* longing for.
hambruna [am'bruna] *nf* famine.
Hamburgo [am'burɣo] *nm* Hamburg.
hamburguesa [ambur'ɣesa] *nf* hamburger, burger.
hampa ['ampa] *nf* underworld.
hampón [am'pon] *nm* thug.
han [an] *vb V* **haber.**
haragán, ana [ara'ɣan, ana] *adj, nm/f* good-for-nothing.
haraganear [araɣane'ar] *vi* to idle, loaf about.
harapiento, a [ara'pjento, a] *adj* tattered, in rags.
harapo [a'rapo] *nm* rag.
hardware ['xardwer] *nm* (*INFORM*) hardware.
haré [a're] *etc vb V* **hacer.**
harén [a'ren] *nm* harem.
harina [a'rina] *nf* flour; **eso es ~ de otro costal** that's another kettle of fish.
harinero, a [ari'nero, a] *nm/f* flour merchant.
harinoso, a [ari'noso, a] *adj* floury.
hartar [ar'tar] *vt* to satiate, glut; (*fig*) to tire, sicken; ~**se** *vr* (*de comida*) to fill o.s.,

gorge o.s.; (*cansarse*) to get fed up (*de* with).
hartazgo [ar'taθɣo] *nm* surfeit, glut.
harto, a ['arto, a] *adj* (*lleno*) full; (*cansado*) fed up ♦ *adv* (*bastante*) enough; (*muy*) very; **estar ~ de** to be fed up with; **¡estoy ~ de decírtelo!** I'm sick and tired of telling you (so)!
hartura [ar'tura] *nf* (*exceso*) surfeit; (*abundancia*) abundance; (*satisfacción*) satisfaction.
has [as] *vb V* **haber.**
Has. *abr* (= *Hectáreas*) ha.
hasta ['asta] *adv* even ♦ *prep* (*alcanzando a*) as far as, up/down to; (*de tiempo*: *a tal hora*) till, until; (: *antes de*) before ♦ *conj*: **~ que** until; **~ luego** *o* **ahora** (*fam*)**/el sábado** see you soon/on Saturday; **~ la fecha** (up) to date; **~ nueva orden** until further notice; **~ en Valencia hiela a veces** even in Valencia it freezes sometimes.
hastiar [as'tjar] *vt* (*gen*) to weary; (*aburrir*) to bore; **~se** *vr*: **~se de** to get fed up with.
hastío [as'tio] *nm* weariness; boredom.
hatajo [a'taxo] *nm*: **un ~ de gamberros** a bunch of hooligans.
hatillo [a'tiʎo] *nm* belongings *pl*, kit; (*montón*) bundle, heap.
Hawai [a'wai] *nm* (*tb*: **las Islas ~**) Hawaii.
hawaianas [awa'janas] *nfpl* (*esp AM*) flip-flops (*BRIT*), thongs.
hawaiano, a [awa'jano, a] *adj, nm/f* Hawaian.
hay [ai] *vb V* **haber.**
Haya ['aja] *nf*: **la ~** The Hague.
haya ['aja] *etc vb V* **haber** ♦ *nf* beech tree.
hayal [a'jal] *nm* beech grove.
haz [aθ] *vb V* **hacer** ♦ *nm* bundle, bunch; (*rayo*: *de luz*) beam ♦ *nf*: **~ de la tierra** face of the earth.
hazaña [a'θaɲa] *nf* feat, exploit; **sería una ~** it would be a great achievement.
hazmerreír [aθmerre'ir] *nm inv* laughing stock.
HB *abr* (= *Herri Batasuna*) *Basque political party.*
he [e] *vb V* **haber** ♦ *adv*: **~ aquí** here is, here are; **~ aquí por qué** ... that is why ....
hebilla [e'βiʎa] *nf* buckle, clasp.
hebra ['eβra] *nf* thread; (*BOT*: *fibra*) fibre, grain.
hebreo, a [e'βreo, a] *adj, nm/f* Hebrew ♦ *nm* (*LING*) Hebrew.
Hébridas ['eβriðas] *nfpl*: **las ~** the Hebrides.
hechice [e'tʃiθe] *etc vb V* **hechizar.**
hechicero, a [etʃi'θero, a] *nm/f* sorcerer/sorceress.
hechizar [etʃi'θar] *vt* to cast a spell on, bewitch.
hechizo [e'tʃiθo] *nm* witchcraft, magic; (*acto de magia*) spell, charm.
hecho, a ['etʃo, a] *pp de* **hacer** ♦ *adj* complete; (*maduro*) mature; (*COSTURA*) ready-to-wear ♦ *nm* deed, act; (*dato*) fact; (*cuestión*) matter; (*suceso*) event ♦ *excl* agreed!, done!; **¡bien ~!** well done!; **de ~** in fact, as a matter of fact; (*POL etc*: *adj, adv*) de facto; **de ~ y de derecho** de facto and de jure; **~ a la medida** made-to-measure; **a lo ~, pecho** it's no use crying over spilt milk.
hechura [e'tʃura] *nf* making, creation; (*producto*) product; (*forma*) form, shape; (*de persona*) build; (*TEC*) craftsmanship.
hectárea [ek'tarea] *nf* hectare.
heder [e'ðer] *vi* to stink, smell; (*fig*) to be unbearable.
hediondez [eðjon'deθ] *nf* stench, stink; (*cosa*) stinking thing.
hediondo, a [e'ðjondo, a] *adj* stinking.
hedor [e'ðor] *nm* stench.
hegemonía [exemo'nia] *nf* hegemony.
helada [e'laða] *nf* frost.
heladera [ela'ðera] *nf* (*AM*: *refrigerador*) refrigerator.
heladería [elaðe'ria] *nf* ice-cream stall (*o* parlour).
helado, a [e'laðo, a] *adj* frozen; (*glacial*) icy; (*fig*) chilly, cold ♦ *nm* ice-cream; **dejar ~ a algn** to dumbfound sb.
helador, a [ela'ðor, a] *adj* (*viento etc*) icy, freezing.
helar [e'lar] *vt* to freeze, ice (up); (*dejar atónito*) to amaze; (*desalentar*) to discourage ♦ *vi*, **~se** *vr* to freeze; (*AVIAT, FERRO etc*) to ice (up), freeze up; (*líquido*) to set.
helecho [e'letʃo] *nm* bracken, fern.
helénico, a [e'leniko, a] *adj* Hellenic, Greek.
heleno, a [e'leno, a] *nm/f* Hellene, Greek.
hélice ['eliθe] *nf* spiral; (*TEC*) propeller; (*MAT*) helix.
helicóptero [eli'koptero] *nm* helicopter.
helio ['eljo] *nm* helium.
helmántico, a [el'mantiko, a] *adj* of *o* from Salamanca.
helvético, a [el'βetiko, a] *adj, nm/f* Swiss.
hematoma [ema'toma] *nm* bruise.
hembra ['embra] *nf* (*BOT, ZOOL*) female; (*mujer*) woman; (*TEC*) nut; **un elefante ~** a she-elephant.
hemeroteca [emero'teka] *nf* newspaper

library.
hemiciclo [emi'θiklo] *nm*: **el** ~ (*POL*) the floor.
hemisferio [emis'ferjo] *nm* hemisphere.
hemofilia [emo'filja] *nf* haemophilia (*BRIT*), hemophilia (*US*).
hemorragia [emo'rraxja] *nf* haemorrhage (*BRIT*), hemorrhage (*US*).
hemorroides [emo'rroiðes] *nfpl* haemorrhoids (*BRIT*), hemorrhoids (*US*).
hemos ['emos] *vb V* **haber.**
henar [e'nar] *nm* meadow, hayfield.
henchir [en'tʃir] *vt* to fill, stuff; ~**se** *vr* (*llenarse de comida*) to stuff o.s. (with food); (*inflarse*) to swell (up).
Hendaya [en'daja] *nf* Hendaye.
hender [en'der] *vt* to cleave, split.
hendidura [endi'ðura] *nf* crack, split; (*GEO*) fissure.
henequén [ene'ken] *nm* (*AM*) henequen.
heno ['eno] *nm* hay.
hepatitis [epa'titis] *nf inv* hepatitis.
herbario, a [er'ßarjo, a] *adj* herbal ♦ *nm* (*colección*) herbarium; (*especialista*) herbalist; (*botánico*) botanist.
herbicida [erßi'θiða] *nm* weedkiller.
herbívoro, a [er'ßißoro, a] *adj* herbivorous.
herboristería [erßoriste'ria] *nf* herbalist's shop.
heredad [ere'ðað] *nf* landed property; (*granja*) farm.
heredar [ere'ðar] *vt* to inherit.
heredero, a [ere'ðero, a] *nm/f* heir(ess); ~ **del trono** heir to the throne.
hereditario, a [ereði'tarjo, a] *adj* hereditary.
hereje [e'rexe] *nm/f* heretic.
herejía [ere'xia] *nf* heresy.
herencia [e'renθja] *nf* inheritance; (*fig*) heritage; (*BIO*) heredity.
herético, a [e'retiko, a] *adj* heretical.
herido, a [e'riðo, a] *adj* injured, wounded; (*fig*) offended ♦ *nm/f* casualty ♦ *nf* wound, injury.
herir [e'rir] *vt* to wound, injure; (*fig*) to offend; (*conmover*) to touch, move.
hermana [er'mana] *nf V* **hermano.**
hermanar [erma'nar] *vt* to match; (*unir*) to join; (*ciudades*) to twin.
hermanastro, a [erma'nastro, a] *nm/f* stepbrother/sister.
hermandad [erman'dað] *nf* brotherhood; (*de mujeres*) sisterhood; (*sindicato etc*) association.
hermano, a [er'mano, a] *adj* similar ♦ *nm* brother ♦ *nf* sister; ~ **gemelo** twin brother; ~ **político** brother-in-law; ~ **primo** first cousin; **mis** ~**s** my brothers, my brothers and sisters; **hermana política** sister-in-law.
hermético, a [er'metiko, a] *adj* hermetic; (*fig*) watertight.
hermoso, a [er'moso, a] *adj* beautiful, lovely; (*estupendo*) splendid; (*guapo*) handsome.
hermosura [ermo'sura] *nf* beauty; (*de hombre*) handsomeness.
hernia ['ernja] *nf* hernia, rupture; ~ **discal** slipped disc.
herniarse [er'njarse] *vr* to rupture o.s.; (*fig*) to break one's back.
héroe ['eroe] *nm* hero.
heroicidad [eroiθi'ðað] *nf* heroism; (*una* ~) heroic deed.
heroico, a [e'roiko, a] *adj* heroic.
heroína [ero'ina] *nf* (*mujer*) heroine; (*droga*) heroin.
heroinómano, a [eroi'nomano, a] *nm/f* heroin addict.
heroísmo [ero'ismo] *nm* heroism.
herpes ['erpes] *nmpl o nfpl* (*MED*: *gen*) herpes *sg*; (: *de la piel*) shingles *sg*.
herradura [erra'ðura] *nf* horseshoe.
herraje [e'rraxe] *nm* (*trabajos*) ironwork.
herramienta [erra'mjenta] *nf* tool.
herrería [erre'ria] *nf* smithy; (*TEC*) forge.
herrero [e'rrero] *nm* blacksmith.
herrumbre [e'rrumbre] *nf* rust.
herrumbroso, a [errum'broso, a] *adj* rusty.
hervidero [erßi'ðero] *nm* (*fig*) swarm; (*POL etc*) hotbed.
hervir [er'ßir] *vi* to boil; (*burbujear*) to bubble; (*fig*): ~ **de** to teem with; ~ **a fuego lento** to simmer.
hervor [er'ßor] *nm* boiling; (*fig*) ardour, fervour.
heterogéneo, a [etero'xeneo, a] *adj* heterogeneous.
heterosexual [eterosek'swal] *adj, nm/f* heterosexual.
hez [eθ] *nf* (*tb*: **heces** *pl*) dregs.
hibernar [ißer'nar] *vi* to hibernate.
híbrido, a ['ißriðo, a] *adj* hybrid.
hice ['iθe] *etc vb V* **hacer.**
hidalgo, a [i'ðalɣo, a] *adj* noble; (*honrado*) honourable (*BRIT*), honorable (*US*) ♦ *nm/f* noble(man/woman).
hidratante [iðra'tante] *adj*: **crema** ~ moisturizing cream, moisturizer.
hidratar [iðra'tar] *vt* to moisturize.
hidrato [i'ðrato] *nm* hydrate; ~ **de carbono** carbohydrate.
hidráulico, a [i'ðrauliko, a] *adj* hydraulic ♦ *nf* hydraulics *sg*.
hidro... [iðro] *pref* hydro..., water-....
hidroavión [iðroa'ßjon] *nm* seaplane.

hidroeléctrico, a [iðroe'lektriko, a] *adj* hydroelectric.
hidrófilo, a [i'ðrofilo, a] *adj* absorbent; **algodón** ~ cotton wool (*BRIT*), absorbent cotton (*US*).
hidrofobia [iðro'foßja] *nf* hydrophobia, rabies.
hidrófugo, a [i'ðrofuɣo, a] *adj* damp-proof.
hidrógeno [i'ðroxeno] *nm* hydrogen.
hieda ['jeða] *etc vb V* **heder.**
hiedra ['jeðra] *nf* ivy.
hiel [jel] *nf* gall, bile; (*fig*) bitterness.
hielo ['jelo] *etc vb V* **helar** ♦ *nm* (*gen*) ice; (*escarcha*) frost; (*fig*) coldness, reserve; **romper el** ~ (*fig*) to break the ice.
hiena ['jena] *nf* (*ZOOL*) hyena.
hiera ['jera] *etc vb V* **herir.**
hierba ['jerßa] *nf* (*pasto*) grass; (*CULIN, MED: planta*) herb; **mala** ~ weed; (*fig*) evil influence.
hierbabuena [jerßa'ßwena] *nf* mint.
hierro ['jerro] *nm* (*metal*) iron; (*objeto*) iron object; ~ **acanalado** corrugated iron; ~ **colado** *o* **fundido** cast iron; **de** ~ iron *cpd.*
hierva ['jerßa] *etc vb V* **hervir.**
hígado ['iɣaðo] *nm* liver; ~**s** *nmpl* (*fig*) guts; **echar los** ~**s** to wear o.s. out.
higiene [i'xjene] *nf* hygiene.
higiénico, a [i'xjeniko, a] *adj* hygienic.
higo ['iɣo] *nm* fig; ~ **seco** dried fig; ~ **chumbo** prickly pear; **de** ~**s a brevas** once in a blue moon.
higuera [i'gera] *nf* fig tree.
hijastro, a [i'xastro, a] *nm/f* stepson/daughter.
hijo, a ['ixo, a] *nm/f* son/daughter, child; (*uso vocativo*) dear; ~**s** *nmpl* children, sons and daughters; **sin** ~**s** childless; ~**/hija político/a** son-/daughter-in-law; ~ **pródigo** prodigal son; ~ **de papá/mamá** daddy's/mummy's boy; ~ **de puta** (*fam!*) bastard (*!*), son of a bitch (*!*); **cada** ~ **de vecino** any Tom, Dick or Harry.
hilacha [i'latʃa] *nf* ravelled thread; ~ **de acero** steel wool.
hilado, a [i'laðo, a] *adj* spun.
hilandero, a [ilan'dero, a] *nm/f* spinner.
hilar [i'lar] *vt* to spin; (*fig*) to reason, infer; ~ **delgado** to split hairs.
hilera [i'lera] *nf* row, file.
hilo ['ilo] *nm* thread; (*BOT*) fibre; (*tela*) linen; (*metal*) wire; (*de agua*) trickle, thin stream; (*de luz*) beam, ray; (*de conversación*) thread, theme; (*de pensamientos*) train; ~ **dental** dental floss; **colgar de un** ~ (*fig*) to hang by a thread; **traje de** ~ linen suit.
hilvanar [ilßa'nar] *vt* (*COSTURA*) to tack (*BRIT*), baste (*US*); (*fig*) to do hurriedly.
Himalaya [ima'laja] *nm*: **el** ~, **los Montes** ~ the Himalayas.
himno ['imno] *nm* hymn; ~ **nacional** national anthem.
hincapié [inka'pje] *nm*: **hacer** ~ **en** to emphasize, stress.
hincar [in'kar] *vt* to drive (in), thrust (in); (*diente*) to sink; ~**se** *vr*: ~**se de rodillas** (*esp AM*) to kneel down.
hincha ['intʃa] *nm/f* (*fam: DEPORTE*) fan.
hinchado, a [in'tʃaðo, a] *adj* (*gen*) swollen; (*persona*) pompous ♦ *nf* (group of) supporters *o* fans.
hinchar [in'tʃar] *vt* (*gen*) to swell; (*inflar*) to blow up, inflate; (*fig*) to exaggerate; ~**se** *vr* (*inflarse*) to swell up; (*fam: llenarse*) to stuff o.s.; (*fig*) to get conceited; ~**se de reír** to have a good laugh.
hinchazón [intʃa'θon] *nf* (*MED*) swelling; (*protuberancia*) bump, lump; (*altivez*) arrogance.
hindú [in'du] *adj, nm/f* Hindu.
hinojo [i'noxo] *nm* fennel.
hinque ['inke] *etc vb V* **hincar.**
hipar [i'par] *vi* to hiccup.
hiper... [iper] *pref* hyper....
hiperactivo, a [iperak'tißo, a] *adj* hyperactive.
hipermercado [ipermer'kaðo] *nm* hypermarket, superstore.
hipersensible [ipersen'sißle] *adj* hypersensitive.
hipertensión [iperten'sjon] *nf* high blood pressure, hypertension.
hípico, a ['ipiko, a] *adj* horse *cpd*, equine; **club** ~ riding club.
hipnosis [ip'nosis] *nf inv* hypnosis.
hipnotice [ipno'tiθe] *etc vb V* **hipnotizar.**
hipnotismo [ipno'tismo] *nm* hypnotism.
hipnotizar [ipnoti'θar] *vt* to hypnotize.
hipo ['ipo] *nm* hiccups *pl*; **quitar el** ~ **a algn** to cure sb's hiccups.
hipocondría [ipokon'dria] *nf* hypochondria.
hipocondríaco, a [ipokon'driako, a] *adj, nm/f* hypochondriac.
hipocresía [ipokre'sia] *nf* hypocrisy.
hipócrita [i'pokrita] *adj* hypocritical ♦ *nm/f* hypocrite.
hipodérmico, a [ipo'ðermiko, a] *adj*: **aguja hipodérmica** hypodermic needle.
hipódromo [i'poðromo] *nm* racetrack.
hipopótamo [ipo'potamo] *nm* hippopotamus.
hipoteca [ipo'teka] *nf* mortgage; **redimir una** ~ to pay off a mortgage.
hipotecar [ipote'kar] *vt* to mortgage; (*fig*)

to jeopardize.
hipotecario, a [ipote'karjo, a] *adj* mortgage *cpd.*
hipótesis [i'potesis] *nf inv* hypothesis; **es una ~ (nada más)** that's just a theory.
hipotético, a [ipo'tetiko, a] *adj* hypothetic(al).
hiriendo [i'rjendo] *etc vb V* **herir.**
hiriente [i'rjente] *adj* offensive, wounding.
hirsuto, a [ir'suto, a] *adj* hairy.
hirviendo [ir'ßjendo] *etc vb V* **hervir.**
hisopo [i'sopo] *nm* (*REL*) sprinkler; (*BOT*) hyssop; (*de algodón*) swab.
hispánico, a [is'paniko, a] *adj* Hispanic, Spanish.
hispanidad [ispani'ðað] *nf* (*cualidad*) Spanishness; (*POL*) Spanish *o* Hispanic world.
hispanista [ispa'nista] *nm/f* (*UNIV etc*) Hispan(ic)ist.
hispano, a [is'pano, a] *adj* Hispanic, Spanish, Hispano- ♦ *nm/f* Spaniard.
Hispanoamérica [ispanoa'merika] *nf* Spanish *o* Latin America.
hispanoamericano, a [ispanoameri'kano, a] *adj, nm/f* Spanish *o* Latin American.
hispanohablante [ispanoa'ßlante], **hispanoparlante** [ispanopar'lante] *adj* Spanish-speaking.
histeria [is'terja] *nf* hysteria.
histérico, a [is'teriko, a] *adj* hysterical.
histerismo [iste'rismo] *nm* (*MED*) hysteria; (*fig*) hysterics.
histograma [isto'ɣrama] *nm* histogram.
historia [is'torja] *nf* history; (*cuento*) story, tale; **~s** *nfpl* (*chismes*) gossip *sg*; **dejarse de ~s** to come to the point; **pasar a la ~** to go down in history.
historiador, a [istorja'ðor, a] *nm/f* historian.
historial [isto'rjal] *nm* record; (*profesional*) curriculum vitae, c.v., résumé (*US*); (*MED*) case history.
histórico, a [is'toriko, a] *adj* historical; (*fig*) historic.
historieta [isto'rjeta] *nf* tale, anecdote; (*dibujos*) comic strip.
histrionismo [istrjo'nismo] *nm* (*TEAT*) acting; (*fig*) histrionics *pl.*
hito ['ito] *nm* (*fig*) landmark; (*objetivo*) goal, target; (*fig*) milestone.
hizo ['iθo] *vb V* **hacer.**
Hna(s). *abr* (= *Hermana(s)*) Sr(s).
Hno(s). *abr* (= *Hermano(s)*) Bro(s).
hocico [o'θiko] *nm* snout; (*fig*) grimace.
hockey ['xoki] *nm* hockey; **~ sobre hielo** ice hockey.
hogar [o'ɣar] *nm* fireplace, hearth; (*casa*) home; (*vida familiar*) home life.
hogareño, a [oɣa'reɲo, a] *adj* home *cpd*; (*persona*) home-loving.
hogaza [o'ɣaθa] *nf* (*pan*) large loaf.
hoguera [o'ɣera] *nf* (*gen*) bonfire; (*para herejes*) stake.
hoja ['oxa] *nf* (*gen*) leaf; (*de flor*) petal; (*de hierba*) blade; (*de papel*) sheet; (*página*) page; (*formulario*) form; (*de puerta*) leaf; **~ de afeitar** razor blade; **~ de cálculo electrónico** spreadsheet; **~ de trabajo** (*INFORM*) worksheet; **de ~ ancha** broad-leaved; **de ~ caduca/perenne** deciduous/evergreen.
hojalata [oxa'lata] *nf* tin(plate).
hojaldre [o'xaldre] *nm* (*CULIN*) puff pastry.
hojarasca [oxa'raska] *nf* (*hojas*) dead *o* fallen leaves *pl*; (*fig*) rubbish.
hojear [oxe'ar] *vt* to leaf through, turn the pages of.
hola ['ola] *excl* hello!
Holanda [o'landa] *nf* Holland.
holandés, esa [olan'des, esa] *adj* Dutch ♦ *nm/f* Dutchman/woman; **los holandeses** the Dutch ♦ *nm* (*LING*) Dutch.
holgado, a [ol'ɣaðo, a] *adj* loose, baggy; (*rico*) well-to-do.
holgar [ol'ɣar] *vi* (*descansar*) to rest; (*sobrar*) to be superfluous; **huelga decir que** it goes without saying that.
holgazán, ana [olɣa'θan, ana] *adj* idle, lazy ♦ *nm/f* loafer.
holgazanear [olɣaθane'ar] *vi* to laze *o* loaf around.
holgura [ol'ɣura] *nf* looseness, bagginess; (*TEC*) play, free movement; (*vida*) comfortable living, luxury.
hollar [o'ʎar] *vt* to tread (on), trample.
hollín [o'ʎin] *nm* soot.
hombre ['ombre] *nm* man; (*raza humana*): **el ~** man(kind) ♦ *excl*: **¡sí ~!** (*claro*) of course!; (*para énfasis*) man, old chap; **~ de negocios** businessman; **~-rana** frogman; **~ de bien** *o* **pro** honest man; **~ de confianza** right-hand man; **~ de estado** statesman; **el ~ medio** the average man.
hombrera [om'brera] *nf* shoulder strap.
hombro ['ombro] *nm* shoulder; **arrimar el ~** to lend a hand; **encogerse de ~s** to shrug one's shoulders.
hombruno, a [om'bruno, a] *adj* mannish.
homenaje [ome'naxe] *nm* (*gen*) homage; (*tributo*) tribute; **un partido ~** a benefit match.
homeopatía [omeopa'tia] *nf* hom(o)eopathy.
homeopático, a [omeo'patiko, a] *adj*

hom(o)eopathic.
homicida [omi'θiða] *adj* homicidal ♦ *nm/f* murderer.
homicidio [omi'θiðjo] *nm* murder, homicide; (*involuntario*) manslaughter.
homologación [omoloɣa'θjon] *nf* (*de sueldo, condiciones*) parity.
homologar [omolo'ɣar] *vt* (*COM*) to standardize; (*ESCOL*) to officially approve; (*DEPORTE*) to officially recognize; (*sueldos*) to equalize.
homólogo, a [o'moloɣo, a] *nm/f* counterpart, opposite number.
homónimo [o'monimo] *nm* (*tocayo*) namesake.
homosexual [omosek'swal] *adj, nm/f* homosexual.
hondo, a ['ondo, a] *adj* deep; **lo** ~ the depth(s) (*pl*), the bottom; **con** ~ **pesar** with deep regret.
hondonada [ondo'naða] *nf* hollow, depression; (*cañón*) ravine; (*GEO*) lowland.
hondura [on'dura] *nf* depth, profundity.
Honduras [on'duras] *nf* Honduras.
hondureño, a [ondu'reɲo, a] *adj, nm/f* Honduran.
honestidad [onesti'ðað] *nf* purity, chastity; (*decencia*) decency.
honesto, a [o'nesto, a] *adj* chaste; decent, honest; (*justo*) just.
hongo ['ongo] *nm* (*BOT: gen*) fungus; (*: comestible*) mushroom; (*: venenoso*) toadstool; (*sombrero*) bowler (hat) (*BRIT*), derby (*US*); ~**s del pie** footrot *sg*, athlete's foot *sg*.
honor [o'nor] *nm* (*gen*) honour (*BRIT*), honor (*US*); (*gloria*) glory; ~ **profesional** professional etiquette; **en** ~ **a la verdad** to be fair.
honorable [ono'raβle] *adj* honourable (*BRIT*), honorable (*US*).
honorario, a [ono'rarjo, a] *adj* honorary ♦ *nm*: ~**s** fees.
honorífico, a [ono'rifiko, a] *adj* honourable (*BRIT*), honorable (*US*); **mención honorífica** hono(u)rable mention.
honra ['onra] *nf* (*gen*) honour; (*renombre*) good name; ~**s fúnebres** funeral rites; **tener algo a mucha** ~ to be proud of sth.
honradez [onra'ðeθ] *nf* honesty; (*de persona*) integrity.
honrado, a [on'raðo, a] *adj* honest, upright.
honrar [on'rar] *vt* to honour; ~**se** *vr*: ~**se con algo/de hacer algo** to be honoured by sth/to do sth.
honroso, a [on'roso, a] *adj* (*honrado*) honourable; (*respetado*) respectable.
hora ['ora] *nf* hour; (*tiempo*) time; **¿qué** ~ **es?** what time is it?; **¿a qué** ~**?** at what time?; **media** ~ half an hour; **a la** ~ **de comer/de recreo** at lunchtime/at playtime; **a primera** ~ first thing (in the morning); **a última** ~ at the last moment; **"última** ~**"** "stop press"; **noticias de última** ~ last-minute news; **a altas** ~**s** in the small hours; **a la** ~ **en punto** on the dot; **¡a buena** ~**!** about time, too!; **en mala** ~ unluckily; **dar la** ~ to strike the hour; **poner el reloj en** ~ to set one's watch; ~**s de oficina/de trabajo** office/working hours; ~**s de visita** visiting times; ~**s extras** *o* **extraordinarias** overtime *sg*; ~**s punta** rush hours; **no ver la** ~ **de** to look forward to; **¡ya era** ~**!** and about time too!
horadar [ora'ðar] *vt* to drill, bore.
horario, a [o'rarjo, a] *adj* hourly, hour *cpd* ♦ *nm* timetable; ~ **comercial** business hours.
horca ['orka] *nf* gallows *sg*; (*AGR*) pitchfork.
horcajadas [orka'xaðas]: **a** ~ *adv* astride.
horchata [or'tʃata] *nf cold drink made from tiger nuts and water*, tiger nut milk.
horda ['orða] *nf* horde.
horizontal [oriθon'tal] *adj* horizontal.
horizonte [ori'θonte] *nm* horizon.
horma ['orma] *nf* mould; ~ **(de calzado)** last; ~ **de sombrero** hat block.
hormiga [or'miɣa] *nf* ant; ~**s** *nfpl* (*MED*) pins and needles.
hormigón [ormi'ɣon] *nm* concrete; ~ **armado/pretensado** reinforced/ prestressed concrete.
hormigueo [ormi'ɣeo] *nm* (*comezón*) itch; (*fig*) uneasiness.
hormiguero [ormi'ɣero] *nm* (*ZOOL*) ant's nest; **era un** ~ it was swarming with people.
hormona [or'mona] *nf* hormone.
hornada [or'naða] *nf* batch of loaves (*etc*).
hornillo [or'niʎo] *nm* (*cocina*) portable stove.
horno ['orno] *nm* (*CULIN*) oven; (*TEC*) furnace; (*para cerámica*) kiln; ~ **microondas** microwave (oven); **alto** ~ blast furnace; ~ **crematorio** crematorium.
horóscopo [o'roskopo] *nm* horoscope.
horquilla [or'kiʎa] *nf* hairpin; (*AGR*) pitchfork.
horrendo, a [o'rrendo, a] *adj* horrendous,

frightful.
horrible [o'rriβle] *adj* horrible, dreadful.
horripilante [orripi'lante] *adj* hair-raising, horrifying.
horripilar [orripi'lar] *vt*: ~ **a algn** to horrify sb; ~**se** *vr* to be horrified.
horror [o'rror] *nm* horror, dread; (*atrocidad*) atrocity; **¡qué ~!** (*fam*) how awful!; **estudia horrores** he studies a hell of a lot.
horrorice [orro'riθe] *etc vb V* **horrorizar.**
horrorizar [orrori'θar] *vt* to horrify, frighten; ~**se** *vr* to be horrified.
horroroso, a [orro'roso, a] *adj* horrifying, ghastly.
hortaliza [orta'liθa] *nf* vegetable.
hortelano, a [orte'lano, a] *nm/f* (market) gardener.
hortera [or'tera] *adj* (*fam*) vulgar, naff.
horterada [orte'raða] *nf* (*fam*): **es una ~** it's really naff.
hortícola [or'tikola] *adj* horticultural.
horticultura [ortikul'tura] *nf* horticulture.
hortofrutícola [ortofru'tikola] *adj* fruit and vegetable *cpd.*
hosco, a ['osko, a] *adj* dark; (*persona*) sullen, gloomy.
hospedaje [ospe'ðaxe] *nm* (cost of) board and lodging.
hospedar [ospe'ðar] *vt* to put up; ~**se** *vr*: ~**se (con/en)** to stay *o* lodge (with/at).
hospedería [ospeðe'ria] *nf* (*edificio*) inn; (*habitación*) guest room.
hospicio [os'piθjo] *nm* (*para niños*) orphanage.
hospital [ospi'tal] *nm* hospital.
hospitalario, a [ospita'larjo, a] *adj* (*acogedor*) hospitable.
hospitalice [ospita'liθe] *etc vb V* **hospitalizar.**
hospitalidad [ospitali'ðað] *nf* hospitality.
hospitalizar [ospitali'θar] *vt* to send *o* take to hospital, hospitalize.
hosquedad [oske'ðað] *nf* sullenness.
hostal [os'tal] *nm* small hotel; *V tb* **hotel.**
hostelería [ostele'ria] *nf* hotel business *o* trade.
hostia ['ostja] *nf* (*REL*) host, consecrated wafer; (*fam: golpe*) whack, punch ♦ *excl*: **¡~(s)!** (*fam!*) damn!
hostigar [osti'ɣar] *vt* to whip; (*fig*) to harass, pester.
hostigue [os'tiɣe] *etc vb V* **hostigar.**
hostil [os'til] *adj* hostile.
hostilidad [ostili'ðað] *nf* hostility.
hotel [o'tel] *nm* hotel; *see boxed note.*

> **HOTEL**
>
> *In Spain you can choose from the following categories of accommodation, in descending order of quality and price:* **hotel** *(from five stars down to one), "hostal", 'pensión", "casa de huéspedes" or "fonda". Standards can vary widely even within these categories. The state also runs luxury hotels called "paradores", which are usually sited in places of particular historical interest and are often architecturally important buildings themselves.*

hotelero, a [ote'lero, a] *adj* hotel *cpd* ♦ *nm/f* hotelier.
hoy [oi] *adv* (*este día*) today; (*en la actualidad*) now(adays) ♦ *nm* present time; **~ (en) día** now(adays); **el día de ~**, **~ día** (*AM*) this very day; **~ por ~** right now; **de ~ en ocho días** a week today; **de ~ en adelante** from now on.
hoya ['oja] *nf* pit; (*sepulcro*) grave; (*GEO*) valley.
hoyo ['ojo] *nm* hole, pit; (*tumba*) grave; (*GOLF*) hole; (*MED*) pockmark.
hoyuelo [oj'welo] *nm* dimple.
hoz [oθ] *nf* sickle.
hube ['uβe] *etc vb V* **haber.**
hucha ['utʃa] *nf* money box.
hueco, a ['weko, a] *adj* (*vacío*) hollow, empty; (*resonante*) booming; (*sonido*) resonant; (*persona*) conceited; (*estilo*) pompous ♦ *nm* hollow, cavity; (*agujero*) hole; (*de escalera*) well; (*de ascensor*) shaft; (*vacante*) vacancy; **~ de la mano** hollow of the hand.
huela ['wela] *etc vb V* **oler.**
huelga ['welɣa] *etc vb V* **holgar** ♦ *nf* strike; **declararse en ~** to go on strike, come out on strike; **~ general** general strike; **~ de hambre** hunger strike; **~ oficial** official strike.
huelgue ['welɣe] *etc vb V* **holgar.**
huelguista [wel'ɣista] *nm/f* striker.
huella ['weʎa] *nf* (*acto de pisar, pisada*) tread(ing); (*marca del paso*) footprint, footstep; (*: de animal, máquina*) track; **~ digital** fingerprint; **sin dejar ~** without leaving a trace.
huérfano, a ['werfano, a] *adj* orphan(ed); (*fig*) unprotected ♦ *nm/f* orphan.
huerta ['werta] *nf* market garden (*BRIT*), truck farm (*US*); (*Murcia, Valencia*) irrigated region.
huerto ['werto] *nm* kitchen garden; (*de*

árboles frutales) orchard.

hueso ['weso] *nm* (*ANAT*) bone; (*de fruta*) stone, pit (*US*); **sin ~** (*carne*) boned; **estar en los ~s** to be nothing but skin and bone; **ser un ~** (*profesor*) to be terribly strict; **un ~ duro de roer** a hard nut to crack.

huesoso, a [we'soso, a] *adj* (*esp AM*) bony.

huésped, a ['wespeð, a] *nm/f* (*invitado*) guest; (*habitante*) resident; (*anfitrión*) host(ess).

huesudo, a [we'suðo, a] *adj* bony, big-boned.

huevas ['weßas] *nfpl* eggs, roe *sg*; (*AM*: *fam!*) balls (*!*).

huevera [we'ßera] *nf* eggcup.

huevo ['weßo] *nm* egg; (*fam!*) ball (*!*), testicle; **~ duro/escalfado/estrellado** *o* **frito/pasado por agua** hard-boiled/poached/fried/soft-boiled egg; **~s revueltos** scrambled eggs; **me costó un ~** (*fam!*) it was hard work; **tener ~s** (*fam!*) to have guts.

huevón, ona [we'ßon, ona] *nm/f* (*AM fam!*) stupid bastard (*!*), stupid idiot.

huida [u'iða] *nf* escape, flight; **~ de capitales** (*COM*) flight of capital.

huidizo, a [ui'ðiθo, a] *adj* (*tímido*) shy; (*pasajero*) fleeting.

huir [u'ir] *vt* (*escapar*) to flee, escape; (*evadir*) to avoid ♦ *vi* to flee, run away; **~se** *vr* (*escaparse*) to escape.

hule ['ule] *nm* (*encerado*) oilskin; (*esp AM*) rubber.

hulla ['uʎa] *nf* bituminous coal.

humanice [uma'niθe] *etc vb V* **humanizar.**

humanidad [umani'ðað] *nf* (*género humano*) man(kind); (*cualidad*) humanity; (*fam*: *gordura*) corpulence.

humanitario, a [umani'tarjo, a] *adj* humanitarian; (*benévolo*) humane.

humanizar [umani'θar] *vt* to humanize; **~se** *vr* to become more human.

humano, a [u'mano, a] *adj* (*gen*) human; (*humanitario*) humane ♦ *nm* human; **ser ~** human being.

humareda [uma'reða] *nf* cloud of smoke.

humeante [ume'ante] *adj* smoking, smoky.

humedad [ume'ðað] *nf* (*del clima*) humidity; (*de pared etc*) dampness; **a prueba de ~** damp-proof.

humedecer [umeðe'θer] *vt* to moisten, wet; **~se** *vr* to get wet.

humedezca [ume'ðeθka] *etc vb V* **humedecer.**

húmedo, a ['umeðo, a] *adj* (*mojado*) damp, wet; (*tiempo etc*) humid.

humildad [umil'dað] *nf* humility, humbleness.

humilde [u'milde] *adj* humble, modest; (*clase etc*) low, modest.

humillación [umiʎa'θjon] *nf* humiliation.

humillante [umi'ʎante] *adj* humiliating.

humillar [umi'ʎar] *vt* to humiliate; **~se** *vr* to humble o.s., grovel.

humo ['umo] *nm* (*de fuego*) smoke; (*gas nocivo*) fumes *pl*; (*vapor*) steam, vapour; **~s** *nmpl* (*fig*) conceit *sg*; **irse todo en ~** (*fig*) to vanish without trace; **bajar los ~s a algn** to take sb down a peg or two.

humor [u'mor] *nm* (*disposición*) mood, temper; (*lo que divierte*) humour; **de buen/mal ~** in a good/bad mood.

humorismo [umo'rismo] *nm* humour.

humorista [umo'rista] *nm/f* comic.

humorístico, a [umo'ristiko, a] *adj* funny, humorous.

hundimiento [undi'mjento] *nm* (*gen*) sinking; (*colapso*) collapse.

hundir [un'dir] *vt* to sink; (*edificio, plan*) to ruin, destroy; **~se** *vr* to sink, collapse; (*fig*: *arruinarse*) to be ruined; (*desaparecer*) to disappear; **se hundió la economía** the economy collapsed; **se hundieron los precios** prices slumped.

húngaro, a ['ungaro, a] *adj, nm/f* Hungarian ♦ *nm* (*LING*) Hungarian, Magyar.

Hungría [un'gria] *nf* Hungary.

huracán [ura'kan] *nm* hurricane.

huraño, a [u'raɲo, a] *adj* shy; (*antisocial*) unsociable.

hurgar [ur'ɣar] *vt* to poke, jab; (*remover*) to stir (up); **~se** *vr*: **~se (las narices)** to pick one's nose.

hurgonear [urɣone'ar] *vt* to poke.

hurgue ['urɣe] *etc vb V* **hurgar.**

hurón [u'ron] *nm* (*ZOOL*) ferret.

hurra ['urra] *excl* hurray!, hurrah!

hurtadillas [urta'ðiʎas]: **a ~** *adv* stealthily, on the sly.

hurtar [ur'tar] *vt* to steal; **~se** *vr* to hide, keep out of the way.

hurto ['urto] *nm* theft, stealing; (*lo robado*) (piece of) stolen property, loot.

husmear [usme'ar] *vt* (*oler*) to sniff out, scent; (*fam*) to pry into ♦ *vi* to smell bad.

huso ['uso] *nm* (*TEC*) spindle; (*de torno*) drum.

huy ['ui] *excl* (*dolor*) ow!, ouch!; (*sorpresa*) well!; (*alivio*) phew!; **¡~, perdona!** oops, sorry!

huyendo [u'jendo] *etc vb V* **huir.**

Ii

I, i [i] *nf* (*letra*) I, i; **I de Inés** I for Isaac (*BRIT*) *o* Item (*US*).
I.A. *abr* = **inteligencia artificial**.
iba ['iβa] *etc vb V* **ir**.
Iberia [i'βerja] *nf* Iberia.
ibérico, a [i'βeriko, a] *adj* Iberian; **la Península ibérica** the Iberian Peninsula.
ibero, a [i'βero, a], **íbero, a** ['iβero, a] *adj, nm/f* Iberian.
iberoamericano, a [iβeroameri'kano, a] *adj, nm/f* Latin American.
íbice ['iβiθe] *nm* ibex.
ibicenco, a [iβi'θenko, a] *adj* of *o* from Ibiza ♦ *nm/f* native *o* inhabitant of Ibiza.
Ibiza [i'βiθa] *nf* Ibiza.
ice ['iθe] *etc vb V* **izar**.
iceberg [iθe'ber] *nm* iceberg.
ICONA [i'kona] *nm abr* (*ESP*) = *Instituto Nacional para la Conservación de la Naturaleza*.
icono [i'kono] *nm* (*tb INFORM*) icon.
iconoclasta [ikono'klasta] *adj* iconoclastic ♦ *nm/f* iconoclast.
ictericia [ikte'riθja] *nf* jaundice.
íd. *abr* = **ídem**.
I+D *abr* (= *Investigación y Desarrollo*) R&D.
ida ['iða] *nf* going, departure; ~ **y vuelta** round trip, return; ~**s y venidas** comings and goings.
IDE [iðe] *nf abr* (= *Iniciativa de Defensa Estratégica*) SDI.
idea [i'ðea] *nf* idea; (*impresión*) opinion; (*propósito*) intention; ~ **genial** brilliant idea; **a mala** ~ out of spite; **no tengo la menor** ~ I haven't a clue.
ideal [iðe'al] *adj, nm* ideal.
idealice [iðea'liθe] *etc vb V* **idealizar**.
idealista [iðea'lista] *adj* idealistic ♦ *nm/f* idealist.
idealizar [iðeali'θar] *vt* to idealize.
idear [iðe'ar] *vt* to think up; (*aparato*) to invent; (*viaje*) to plan.
ídem ['iðem] *pron* ditto.
idéntico, a [i'ðentiko, a] *adj* identical.
identidad [iðenti'ðað] *nf* identity; ~ **corporativa** corporate identity *o* image.
identificación [iðentifika'θjon] *nf* identification.
identificar [iðentifi'kar] *vt* to identify; ~**se** *vr*: ~**se con** to identify with.
identifique [iðenti'fike] *etc vb V* **identificar**.
ideología [iðeolo'xia] *nf* ideology.
ideológico, a [iðeo'loxiko, a] *adj* ideological.
idílico, a [i'ðiliko, a] *adj* idyllic.
idilio [i'ðiljo] *nm* love affair.
idioma [i'ðjoma] *nm* language.
idiomático, a [iðjo'matiko, a] *adj* idiomatic.
idiota [i'ðjota] *adj* idiotic ♦ *nm/f* idiot.
idiotez [iðjo'teθ] *nf* idiocy.
idolatrar [iðola'trar] *vt* (*fig*) to idolize.
ídolo ['iðolo] *nm* (*tb fig*) idol.
idoneidad [iðonei'ðað] *nf* suitability; (*capacidad*) aptitude.
idóneo, a [i'ðoneo, a] *adj* suitable.
iglesia [i'ɣlesja] *nf* church; ~ **parroquial** parish church; **¡con la ~ hemos topado!** now we're really up against it!
iglú [i'ɣlu] *nm* igloo; (*contenedor*) bottle bank.
ignición [iɣni'θjon] *nf* ignition.
ignominia [iɣno'minja] *nf* ignominy.
ignominioso, a [iɣnomi'njoso, a] *adj* ignominious.
ignorado, a [iɣno'raðo, a] *adj* unknown; (*dato*) obscure.
ignorancia [iɣno'ranθja] *nf* ignorance; **por** ~ through ignorance.
ignorante [iɣno'rante] *adj* ignorant, uninformed ♦ *nm/f* ignoramus.
ignorar [iɣno'rar] *vt* not to know, be ignorant of; (*no hacer caso a*) to ignore; **ignoramos su paradero** we don't know his whereabouts.
ignoto, a [iɣ'noto, a] *adj* unknown.
igual [i'ɣwal] *adj* equal; (*similar*) like, similar; (*mismo*) (the) same; (*constante*) constant; (*temperatura*) even ♦ *nm/f* equal; **al ~ que** *prep, conj* like, just like; ~ **que** the same as; **sin** ~ peerless; **me da** *o* **es** ~ I don't care, it makes no difference; **no tener** ~ to be unrivalled; **son ~es** they're the same.
iguala [i'ɣwala] *nf* equalization; (*COM*) agreement.
igualada [iɣwa'laða] *nf* equalizer.
igualar [iɣwa'lar] *vt* (*gen*) to equalize, make equal; (*terreno*) to make even; (*COM*) to agree upon; ~**se** *vr* (*platos de balanza*) to balance out; ~**se (a)** (*equivaler*) to be equal (to).
igualdad [iɣwal'dað] *nf* equality; (*similaridad*) sameness; (*uniformidad*) uniformity; **en ~ de condiciones** on an equal basis.

igualmente [iɣwal'mente] *adv* equally; (*también*) also, likewise ♦ *excl* the same to you!
iguana [i'ɣwana] *nf* iguana.
ikurriña [iku'rriɲa] *nf* Basque flag.
ilegal [ile'ɣal] *adj* illegal.
ilegitimidad [ilexitimi'ðað] *nf* illegitimacy.
ilegítimo, a [ile'xitimo, a] *adj* illegitimate.
ileso, a [i'leso, a] *adj* unhurt, unharmed.
ilícito, a [i'liθito, a] *adj* illicit.
ilimitado, a [ilimi'taðo, a] *adj* unlimited.
Ilma., Ilmo. *abr* (= *Ilustrísima, Ilustrísimo*) *courtesy title*.
ilógico, a [i'loxiko, a] *adj* illogical.
iluminación [ilumina'θjon] *nf* illumination; (*alumbrado*) lighting; (*fig*) enlightenment.
iluminar [ilumi'nar] *vt* to illuminate, light (up); (*fig*) to enlighten.
ilusión [ilu'sjon] *nf* illusion; (*quimera*) delusion; (*esperanza*) hope; (*emoción*) excitement, thrill; **hacerse ilusiones** to build up one's hopes; **no te hagas ilusiones** don't build up your hopes *o* get too excited.
ilusionado, a [ilusjo'naðo, a] *adj* excited.
ilusionar [ilusjo'nar] *vt*: ~ **a algn** (*falsamente*) to build up sb's hopes; ~**se** *vr* (*falsamente*) to build up one's hopes; (*entusiasmarse*) to get excited; **me ilusiona mucho el viaje** I'm really excited about the trip.
ilusionista [ilusjo'nista] *nm/f* conjurer.
iluso, a [i'luso, a] *adj* gullible, easily deceived ♦ *nm/f* dreamer, visionary.
ilusorio, a [ilu'sorjo, a] *adj* (*de ilusión*) illusory, deceptive; (*esperanza*) vain.
ilustración [ilustra'θjon] *nf* illustration; (*saber*) learning, erudition; **la I~** the Enlightenment.
ilustrado, a [ilus'traðo, a] *adj* illustrated; learned.
ilustrar [ilus'trar] *vt* to illustrate; (*instruir*) to instruct; (*explicar*) to explain, make clear; ~**se** *vr* to acquire knowledge.
ilustre [i'lustre] *adj* famous, illustrious.
imagen [i'maxen] *nf* (*gen*) image; (*dibujo, TV*) picture; (*REL*) statue; **ser la viva ~ de** to be the spitting *o* living image of; **a su ~** in one's own image.
imaginación [imaxina'θjon] *nf* imagination; (*fig*) fancy; **ni por ~** on no account; **no se me pasó por la ~ que ...** it never even occurred to me that ....
imaginar [imaxi'nar] *vt* (*gen*) to imagine; (*idear*) to think up; (*suponer*) to suppose; ~**se** *vr* to imagine; **¡imagínate!** just imagine!, just fancy!; **imagínese que ...** suppose that ...; **me imagino que sí** I should think so.
imaginario, a [imaxi'narjo, a] *adj* imaginary.
imaginativo, a [imaxina'tiβo, a] *adj* imaginative ♦ *nf* imagination.
imán [i'man] *nm* magnet.
iman(t)ar [ima'n(t)ar] *vt* to magnetize.
imbécil [im'beθil] *nm/f* imbecile, idiot.
imbecilidad [imbeθili'ðað] *nf* imbecility, stupidity.
imberbe [im'berβe] *adj* beardless.
imborrable [imbo'rraβle] *adj* indelible; (*inolvidable*) unforgettable.
imbuir [imbu'ir] *vi* to imbue.
imbuyendo [imbu'jendo] *etc vb V* **imbuir**.
imitación [imita'θjon] *nf* imitation; (*parodia*) mimicry; **a ~ de** in imitation of; **desconfíe de las imitaciones** (*COM*) beware of copies *o* imitations.
imitador, a [imita'ðor, a] *adj* imitative ♦ *nm/f* imitator; (*TEAT*) mimic.
imitar [imi'tar] *vt* to imitate; (*parodiar, remedar*) to mimic, ape; (*copiar*) to follow.
impaciencia [impa'θjenθja] *nf* impatience.
impacientar [impaθjen'tar] *vt* to make impatient; (*enfadar*) to irritate; ~**se** *vr* to get impatient; (*inquietarse*) to fret.
impaciente [impa'θjente] *adj* impatient; (*nervioso*) anxious.
impacto [im'pakto] *nm* impact; (*esp AM: fig*) shock.
impagado, a [impa'ɣaðo, a] *adj* unpaid, still to be paid.
impar [im'par] *adj* odd ♦ *nm* odd number.
imparable [impa'raβle] *adj* unstoppable.
imparcial [impar'θjal] *adj* impartial, fair.
imparcialidad [imparθjali'ðað] *nf* impartiality, fairness.
impartir [impar'tir] *vt* to impart, give.
impasible [impa'siβle] *adj* impassive.
impávido, a [im'paβiðo, a] *adj* fearless, intrepid.
IMPE ['impe] *nm abr* (*ESP COM*) = *Instituto de la Mediana y Pequeña Empresa*.
impecable [impe'kaβle] *adj* impeccable.
impedido, a [impe'ðiðo, a] *adj*: **estar ~** to be an invalid ♦ *nm/f*: **ser un ~ físico** to be an invalid.
impedimento [impeði'mento] *nm* impediment, obstacle.
impedir [impe'ðir] *vt* (*obstruir*) to impede, obstruct; (*estorbar*) to prevent; **~ el tráfico** to block the traffic.
impeler [impe'ler] *vt* to drive, propel; (*fig*) to impel.
impenetrabilidad [impenetraβili'ðað] *nf*

impenetrability.
impenetrable [impene'traßle] *adj* impenetrable; (*fig*) incomprehensible.
impensable [impen'saßle] *adj* unthinkable.
impepinable [impepi'naßle] *adj* (*fam*) certain, inevitable.
imperante [impe'rante] *adj* prevailing.
imperar [impe'rar] *vi* (*reinar*) to rule, reign; (*fig*) to prevail, reign; (*precio*) to be current.
imperativo, a [impera'tißo, a] *adj* (*persona*) imperious; (*urgente, LING*) imperative.
imperceptible [imperθep'tißle] *adj* imperceptible.
imperdible [imper'ðißle] *nm* safety pin.
imperdonable [imperðo'naßle] *adj* unforgivable, inexcusable.
imperecedero, a [impereθe'ðero, a] *adj* undying.
imperfección [imperfek'θjon] *nf* imperfection; (*falla*) flaw, fault.
imperfecto, a [imper'fekto, a] *adj* faulty, imperfect ♦ *nm* (*LING*) imperfect tense.
imperial [impe'rjal] *adj* imperial.
imperialismo [imperja'lismo] *nm* imperialism.
imperialista [imperja'lista] *adj* imperialist(ic) ♦ *nm/f* imperialist.
impericia [impe'riθja] *nf* (*torpeza*) unskilfulness; (*inexperiencia*) inexperience.
imperio [im'perjo] *nm* empire; (*autoridad*) rule, authority; (*fig*) pride, haughtiness; **vale un** ~ (*fig*) it's worth a fortune.
imperioso, a [impe'rjoso, a] *adj* imperious; (*urgente*) urgent; (*imperativo*) imperative.
impermeable [imperme'aßle] *adj* (*a prueba de agua*) waterproof ♦ *nm* raincoat, mac (*BRIT*).
impersonal [imperso'nal] *adj* impersonal.
impertérrito, a [imper'territo, a] *adj* undaunted.
impertinencia [imperti'nenθja] *nf* impertinence.
impertinente [imperti'nente] *adj* impertinent.
imperturbable [impertur'ßaßle] *adj* imperturbable; (*sereno*) unruffled; (*impasible*) impassive.
ímpetu ['impetu] *nm* (*impulso*) impetus, impulse; (*impetuosidad*) impetuosity; (*violencia*) violence.
impetuosidad [impetwosi'ðað] *nf* impetuousness; (*violencia*) violence.
impetuoso, a [impe'twoso, a] *adj* impetuous; (*río*) rushing; (*acto*) hasty.
impida [im'piða] *etc vb V* **impedir**.
impío, a [im'pio, a] *adj* impious, ungodly; (*cruel*) cruel, pitiless.
implacable [impla'kaßle] *adj* implacable, relentless.
implantación [implanta'θjon] *nf* introduction; (*BIO*) implantation.
implantar [implan'tar] *vt* (*costumbre*) to introduce; (*BIO*) to implant; **~se** *vr* to be introduced.
implicar [impli'kar] *vt* to involve; (*entrañar*) to imply; **esto no implica que** ... this does not mean that ....
implícito, a [im'pliθito, a] *adj* (*tácito*) implicit; (*sobreentendido*) implied.
implique [im'plike] *etc vb V* **implicar**.
implorar [implo'rar] *vt* to beg, implore.
impondré [impon'dre] *etc vb V* **imponer**.
imponente [impo'nente] *adj* (*impresionante*) impressive, imposing; (*solemne*) grand ♦ *nm/f* (*COM*) depositor.
imponer [impo'ner] *vt* (*gen*) to impose; (*tarea*) to set; (*exigir*) to exact; (*miedo*) to inspire; (*COM*) to deposit; **~se** *vr* to assert o.s.; (*prevalecer*) to prevail; (*costumbre*) to grow up; **~se un deber** to assume a duty.
imponga [im'ponga] *etc vb V* **imponer**.
imponible [impo'nißle] *adj* (*COM*) taxable, subject to tax; (*importación*) dutiable, subject to duty; **no** ~ tax-free, tax-exempt (*US*).
impopular [impopu'lar] *adj* unpopular.
importación [importa'θjon] *nf* (*acto*) importing; (*mercancías*) imports *pl*.
importancia [impor'tanθja] *nf* importance; (*valor*) value, significance; (*extensión*) size, magnitude; **no dar ~ a** to consider unimportant; (*fig*) to make light of; **no tiene** ~ it's nothing.
importante [impor'tante] *adj* important; valuable, significant.
importar [impor'tar] *vt* (*del extranjero*) to import; (*costar*) to amount to; (*implicar*) to involve ♦ *vi* to be important, matter; **me importa un bledo** I don't give a damn; **¿le importa que fume?** do you mind if I smoke?; **¿te importa prestármelo?** would you mind lending it to me?; **¿qué importa?** what difference does it make?; **no importa** it doesn't matter; **no le importa** he doesn't care, it doesn't bother him; **"no importa precio"** "cost no object".
importe [im'porte] *nm* (*total*) amount; (*valor*) value.
importunar [importu'nar] *vt* to bother, pester.

importuno, a [impor'tuno, a] *adj* (*inoportuno, molesto*) inopportune; (*indiscreto*) troublesome.
imposibilidad [imposiβili'ðað] *nf* impossibility; **mi ~ para hacerlo** my inability to do it.
imposibilitado, a [imposiβili'taðo, a] *adj*: **verse ~ para hacer algo** to be unable to do sth.
imposibilitar [imposiβili'tar] *vt* to make impossible, prevent.
imposible [impo'siβle] *adj* impossible; (*insoportable*) unbearable, intolerable; **es ~** it's out of the question; **es ~ de predecir** it's impossible to forecast *o* predict.
imposición [imposi'θjon] *nf* imposition; (*COM*) tax; (*inversión*) deposit; **efectuar una ~** to make a deposit.
impostor, a [impos'tor, a] *nm/f* impostor.
impostura [impos'tura] *nf* fraud, imposture.
impotencia [impo'tenθja] *nf* impotence.
impotente [impo'tente] *adj* impotent.
impracticable [imprakti'kaβle] *adj* (*irrealizable*) impracticable; (*intransitable*) impassable.
imprecar [impre'kar] *vi* to curse.
imprecisión [impreθi'sjon] *nf* lack of precision, vagueness.
impreciso, a [impre'θiso, a] *adj* imprecise, vague.
impredecible [impreðe'θiβle], **impredictible** [impreðik'tiβle] *adj* unpredictable.
impregnar [impreɣ'nar] *vt* to impregnate; (*fig*) to pervade; **~se** *vr* to become impregnated.
imprenta [im'prenta] *nf* (*acto*) printing; (*aparato*) press; (*casa*) printer's; (*letra*) print.
impreque [im'preke] *etc vb V* **imprecar**.
imprescindible [impresθin'diβle] *adj* essential, vital.
impresión [impre'sjon] *nf* impression; (*IMPRENTA*) printing; (*edición*) edition; (*FOTO*) print; (*marca*) imprint; **~ digital** fingerprint.
impresionable [impresjo'naβle] *adj* (*sensible*) impressionable.
impresionado, a [impresjo'naðo, a] *adj* impressed; (*FOTO*) exposed.
impresionante [impresjo'nante] *adj* impressive; (*tremendo*) tremendous; (*maravilloso*) great, marvellous.
impresionar [impresjo'nar] *vt* (*conmover*) to move; (*afectar*) to impress, strike; (*película fotográfica*) to expose; **~se** *vr* to be impressed; (*conmoverse*) to be moved.
impresionista [impresjo'nista] *adj* impressionist(ic); (*ARTE*) impressionist ♦ *nm/f* impressionist.
impreso, a [im'preso, a] *pp de* **imprimir** ♦ *adj* printed ♦ *nm* printed paper/book *etc*; **~s** *nmpl* printed matter *sg*; **~ de solicitud** application form.
impresora [impre'sora] *nf* (*INFORM*) printer; **~ de chorro de tinta** ink-jet printer; **~ (por) láser** laser printer; **~ de línea** line printer; **~ de matriz (de agujas)** dot-matrix printer; **~ de rueda** *o* **de margarita** daisy-wheel printer.
imprevisible [impreβi'siβle] *adj* unforeseeable; (*individuo*) unpredictable.
imprevisión [impreβi'sjon] *nf* short-sightedness; (*irreflexión*) thoughtlessness.
imprevisto, a [impre'βisto, a] *adj* unforeseen; (*inesperado*) unexpected ♦ *nm*: **~s** (*dinero*) incidentals, unforeseen expenses.
imprimir [impri'mir] *vt* to stamp; (*textos*) to print; (*INFORM*) to output, print out.
improbabilidad [improβaβili'ðað] *nf* improbability, unlikelihood.
improbable [impro'βaβle] *adj* improbable; (*inverosímil*) unlikely.
improcedente [improθe'ðente] *adj* inappropriate; (*JUR*) inadmissible.
improductivo, a [improðuk'tiβo, a] *adj* unproductive.
impronunciable [impronun'θjaβle] *adj* unpronounceable.
improperio [impro'perjo] *nm* insult; **~s** *nmpl* abuse *sg*.
impropiedad [impropje'ðað] *nf* impropriety (of language).
impropio, a [im'propjo, a] *adj* improper; (*inadecuado*) inappropriate.
improvisación [improβisa'θjon] *nf* improvization.
improvisado, a [improβi'saðo, a] *adj* improvised, impromptu.
improvisar [improβi'sar] *vt* to improvise; (*comida*) to rustle up ♦ *vi* to improvise; (*MUS*) to extemporize; (*TEAT etc*) to ad-lib.
improviso [impro'βiso]: *adv* **de ~** unexpectedly, suddenly; (*MUS etc*) impromptu.
imprudencia [impru'ðenθja] *nf* imprudence; (*indiscreción*) indiscretion; (*descuido*) carelessness.
imprudente [impru'ðente] *adj* imprudent;

indiscreet.
Impte. *abr* (= *Importe*) amt.
impúdico, a [im'puðiko, a] *adj* shameless; (*lujurioso*) lecherous.
impudor [impu'ðor] *nm* shamelessness; (*lujuria*) lechery.
impuesto, a [im'pwesto, a] *pp de* **imponer** ♦ *adj* imposed ♦ *nm* tax; (*derecho*) duty; **anterior al ~** pre-tax; **sujeto a ~** taxable; **~ de lujo** luxury tax; **~ de plusvalía** capital gains tax; **~ sobre la propiedad** property tax; **~ sobre la renta** income tax; **~ sobre la renta de las personas físicas (IRPF)** personal income tax; **~ sobre la riqueza** wealth tax; **~ de transferencia de capital** capital transfer tax; **~ de venta** sales tax; **~ sobre el valor añadido (IVA)** value added tax (VAT).
impugnar [impuɣ'nar] *vt* to oppose, contest; (*refutar*) to refute, impugn.
impulsar [impul'sar] *vt* to promote.
impulsivo, a [impul'siβo, a] *adj* impulsive.
impulso [im'pulso] *nm* impulse; (*fuerza, empuje*) thrust, drive; (*fig: sentimiento*) urge, impulse; **a ~s del miedo** driven on by fear.
impune [im'pune] *adj* unpunished.
impunemente [impune'mente] *adv* with impunity.
impureza [impu'reθa] *nf* impurity; (*fig*) lewdness.
impuro, a [im'puro, a] *adj* impure; lewd.
impuse [im'puse] *etc vb V* **imponer**.
imputación [imputa'θjon] *nf* imputation.
imputar [impu'tar] *vt*: **~ a** to attribute to, to impute to.
inabordable [inaβor'ðaβle] *adj* unapproachable.
inacabable [inaka'βaβle] *adj* (*infinito*) endless; (*interminable*) interminable.
inaccesible [inakθe'siβle] *adj* inaccessible; (*fig: precio*) beyond one's reach, prohibitive; (*individuo*) aloof.
inacción [inak'θjon] *nf* inactivity.
inaceptable [inaθep'taβle] *adj* unacceptable.
inactividad [inaktiβi'ðað] *nf* inactivity; (*COM*) dullness.
inactivo, a [inak'tiβo, a] *adj* inactive; (*COM*) dull; (*población*) non-working.
inadaptación [inaðapta'θjon] *nf* maladjustment.
inadaptado, a [inaðap'taðo, a] *adj* maladjusted ♦ *nm/f* misfit.
inadecuado, a [inaðe'kwaðo, a] *adj* (*insuficiente*) inadequate; (*inapto*) unsuitable.
inadmisible [inaðmi'siβle] *adj* inadmissible.
inadvertido, a [inaðβer'tiðo, a] *adj* (*no visto*) unnoticed.
inagotable [inaɣo'taβle] *adj* inexhaustible.
inaguantable [inaɣwan'taβle] *adj* unbearable.
inalámbrico, a [ina'lambriko, a] *adj* cordless.
inalcanzable [inalkan'θaβle] *adj* unattainable.
inalterable [inalte'raβle] *adj* immutable, unchangeable.
inamovible [inamo'βiβle] *adj* fixed, immovable; (*TEC*) undetachable.
inanición [inani'θjon] *nf* starvation.
inanimado, a [inani'maðo, a] *adj* inanimate.
inapelable [inape'laβle] *adj* (*JUR*) unappealable; (*fig*) irremediable.
inapetencia [inape'tenθja] *nf* lack of appetite.
inaplicable [inapli'kaβle] *adj* not applicable.
inapreciable [inapre'θjaβle] *adj* invaluable.
inarrugable [inarru'ɣaβle] *adj* crease-resistant.
inasequible [inase'kiβle] *adj* unattainable.
inaudito, a [inau'ðito, a] *adj* unheard-of.
inauguración [inauɣura'θjon] *nf* inauguration; (*de exposición*) opening.
inaugurar [inauɣu'rar] *vt* to inaugurate; to open.
I.N.B. *abr* (= *Instituto Nacional de Bachillerato*) ≈ comprehensive school (*BRIT*), high school (*US*).
I.N.B.A. *abr* (*AM*) = *Instituto Nacional de Bellas Artes.*
inca ['inka] *nm/f* Inca.
INCAE [in'kae] *nm abr* = *Instituto Centroamericano de Administración de Empresas.*
incaico, a [in'kaiko, a] *adj* Inca.
incalculable [inkalku'laβle] *adj* incalculable.
incandescente [inkandes'θente] *adj* incandescent.
incansable [inkan'saβle] *adj* tireless, untiring.
incapacidad [inkapaθi'ðað] *nf* incapacity; (*incompetencia*) incompetence; **~ física/mental** physical/mental disability.
incapacitar [inkapaθi'tar] *vt* (*inhabilitar*) to incapacitate, handicap; (*descalificar*) to disqualify.
incapaz [inka'paθ] *adj* incapable; **~ de hacer algo** unable to do sth.
incautación [inkauta'θjon] *nf* seizure,

confiscation.
incautarse [inkau'tarse] *vr*: ~ **de** to seize, confiscate.
incauto, a [in'kauto, a] *adj* (*imprudente*) incautious, unwary.
incendiar [inθen'djar] *vt* to set fire to; (*fig*) to inflame; ~**se** *vr* to catch fire.
incendiario, a [inθen'djarjo, a] *adj* incendiary ♦ *nm/f* fire-raiser, arsonist.
incendio [in'θendjo] *nm* fire; ~ **intencionado** arson.
incentivo [inθen'tiβo] *nm* incentive.
incertidumbre [inθerti'ðumbre] *nf* (*inseguridad*) uncertainty; (*duda*) doubt.
incesante [inθe'sante] *adj* incessant.
incesto [in'θesto] *nm* incest.
incidencia [inθi'ðenθja] *nf* (*MAT*) incidence; (*fig*) effect.
incidente [inθi'ðente] *nm* incident.
incidir [inθi'ðir] *vi*: ~ **en** (*influir*) to influence; (*afectar*) to affect; ~ **en un error** to be mistaken.
incienso [in'θjenso] *nm* incense.
incierto, a [in'θjerto, a] *adj* uncertain.
incineración [inθinera'θjon] *nf* incineration; (*de cadáveres*) cremation.
incinerar [inθine'rar] *vt* to burn; to cremate.
incipiente [inθi'pjente] *adj* incipient.
incisión [inθi'sjon] *nf* incision.
incisivo, a [inθi'siβo, a] *adj* sharp, cutting; (*fig*) incisive.
inciso [in'θiso] *nm* (*LING*) clause, sentence; (*coma*) comma; (*JUR*) subsection.
incitante [inθi'tante] *adj* (*estimulante*) exciting; (*provocativo*) provocative.
incitar [inθi'tar] *vt* to incite, rouse.
incivil [inθi'βil] *adj* rude, uncivil.
inclemencia [inkle'menθja] *nf* (*severidad*) harshness, severity; (*del tiempo*) inclemency.
inclemente [inkle'mente] *adj* harsh, severe; inclement.
inclinación [inklina'θjon] *nf* (*gen*) inclination; (*de tierras*) slope, incline; (*de cabeza*) nod, bow; (*fig*) leaning, bent.
inclinado, a [inkli'naðo, a] *adj* (*objeto*) leaning; (*superficie*) sloping.
inclinar [inkli'nar] *vt* to incline; (*cabeza*) to nod, bow; ~**se** *vr* to lean, slope; (*en reverencia*) to bow; (*encorvarse*) to stoop; ~**se a** (*parecerse*) to take after, resemble; ~**se ante** to bow down to; **me inclino a pensar que ...** I'm inclined to think that ....
incluir [inklu'ir] *vt* to include; (*incorporar*) to incorporate; (*meter*) to enclose; **todo incluido** (*COM*) inclusive, all-in.
inclusive [inklu'siβe] *adv* inclusive ♦ *prep* including.
incluso, a [in'kluso, a] *adj* included ♦ *adv* inclusively; (*hasta*) even.
incluyendo [inklu'jendo] *etc vb V* **incluir.**
incobrable [inko'βraβle] *adj* irrecoverable; (*deuda*) bad.
incógnita [in'koɣnita] *nf* (*fig*) mystery.
incógnito [in'koɣnito]: **de** ~ *adv* incognito.
incoherencia [inkoe'renθja] *nf* incoherence; (*falta de conexión*) disconnectedness.
incoherente [inkoe'rente] *adj* incoherent.
incoloro, a [inko'loro, a] *adj* colourless.
incólume [in'kolume] *adj* safe; (*indemne*) unhurt, unharmed.
incombustible [inkombus'tiβle] *adj* (*gen*) fire-resistant; (*telas*) fireproof.
incomodar [inkomo'ðar] *vt* to inconvenience; (*molestar*) to bother, trouble; (*fastidiar*) to annoy; ~**se** *vr* to put o.s. out; (*fastidiarse*) to get annoyed; **no se incomode** don't bother.
incomodidad [inkomoði'ðað] *nf* inconvenience; (*fastidio, enojo*) annoyance; (*de vivienda*) discomfort.
incómodo, a [in'komoðo, a] *adj* (*inconfortable*) uncomfortable; (*molesto*) annoying; (*inconveniente*) inconvenient; **sentirse** ~ to feel ill at ease.
incomparable [inkompa'raβle] *adj* incomparable.
incomparecencia [inkompare'θenθja] *nf* (*JUR etc*) failure to appear.
incompatible [inkompa'tiβle] *adj* incompatible.
incompetencia [inkompe'tenθja] *nf* incompetence.
incompetente [inkompe'tente] *adj* incompetent.
incompleto, a [inkom'pleto, a] *adj* incomplete, unfinished.
incomprendido, a [inkompren'diðo, a] *adj* misunderstood.
incomprensible [inkompren'siβle] *adj* incomprehensible.
incomunicado, a [inkomuni'kaðo, a] *adj* (*aislado*) cut off, isolated; (*confinado*) in solitary confinement.
incomunicar [inkomuni'kar] *vt* (*gen*) to cut off; (*preso*) to put into solitary confinement; ~**se** *vr* (*fam*) to go into one's shell.
incomunique [inkomu'nike] *etc vb V* **incomunicar.**
inconcebible [inkonθe'βiβle] *adj* inconceivable.
inconcluso, a [inkon'kluso, a] *adj*

(*inacabado*) unfinished.
incondicional [inkondiθjo'nal] *adj* unconditional; (*apoyo*) wholehearted; (*partidario*) staunch.
inconexo, a [inko'nekso, a] *adj* unconnected; (*desunido*) disconnected; (*incoherente*) incoherent.
inconfeso, a [inkon'feso, a] *adj* unconfessed; **un homosexual** ~ a closet homosexual.
inconformista [inkonfor'mista] *adj, nm/f* nonconformist.
inconfundible [inkonfun'dißle] *adj* unmistakable.
incongruente [inkon'grwente] *adj* incongruous.
inconmensurable [inkonmensu'raßle] *adj* immeasurable, vast.
inconsciencia [inkons'θjenθja] *nf* unconsciousness; (*fig*) thoughtlessness.
inconsciente [inkons'θjente] *adj* unconscious; thoughtless; (*ignorante*) unaware; (*involuntario*) unwitting.
inconsecuencia [inkonse'kwenθja] *nf* inconsistency.
inconsecuente [inkonse'kwente] *adj* inconsistent.
inconsiderado, a [inkonsiðe'raðo, a] *adj* inconsiderate.
inconsistente [inkonsis'tente] *adj* inconsistent; (*CULIN*) lumpy; (*endeble*) weak; (*tela*) flimsy.
inconstancia [inkons'tanθja] *nf* inconstancy; (*de tiempo*) changeability; (*capricho*) fickleness.
inconstante [inkons'tante] *adj* inconstant; changeable; fickle.
incontable [inkon'taßle] *adj* countless, innumerable.
incontestable [inkontes'taßle] *adj* unanswerable; (*innegable*) undeniable.
incontinencia [inkonti'nenθja] *nf* incontinence.
incontrolado, a [inkontro'laðo, a] *adj* uncontrolled.
incontrovertible [inkontroßer'tißle] *adj* undeniable, incontrovertible.
inconveniencia [inkombe'njenθja] *nf* unsuitability, inappropriateness; (*descortesía*) impoliteness.
inconveniente [inkombe'njente] *adj* unsuitable; impolite ♦ *nm* obstacle; (*desventaja*) disadvantage; **el ~ es que ...** the trouble is that ...; **no hay ~ en** *o* **para hacer eso** there is no objection to doing that; **no tengo** ~ I don't mind.
incordiar [inkor'ðjar] *vt* (*fam*) to hassle.
incorporación [inkorpora'θjon] *nf* incorporation; (*fig*) inclusion.
incorporado, a [inkorpo'raðo, a] *adj* (*TEC*) built-in.
incorporar [inkorpo'rar] *vt* to incorporate; (*abarcar*) to embody; (*CULIN*) to mix; **~se** *vr* to sit up; **~se a** to join.
incorrección [inkorrek'θjon] *nf* incorrectness, inaccuracy; (*descortesía*) bad-mannered behaviour.
incorrecto, a [inko'rrekto, a] *adj* incorrect, wrong; (*comportamiento*) bad-mannered.
incorregible [inkorre'xißle] *adj* incorrigible.
incorruptible [inkorrup'tißle] *adj* incorruptible.
incorrupto, a [inko'rrupto, a] *adj* uncorrupted; (*fig*) pure.
incredulidad [inkreðuli'ðað] *nf* incredulity; (*escepticismo*) scepticism.
incrédulo, a [in'kreðulo, a] *adj* incredulous, unbelieving; sceptical.
increíble [inkre'ißle] *adj* incredible.
incrementar [inkremen'tar] *vt* (*aumentar*) to increase; (*alzar*) to raise; **~se** *vr* to increase.
incremento [inkre'mento] *nm* increment; (*aumento*) rise, increase; **~ de precio** rise in price.
increpar [inkre'par] *vt* to reprimand.
incriminar [inkrimi'nar] *vt* (*JUR*) to incriminate.
incruento, a [in'krwento, a] *adj* bloodless.
incrustar [inkrus'tar] *vt* to incrust; (*piedras: en joya*) to inlay; (*fig*) to graft; (*TEC*) to set.
incubar [inku'ßar] *vt* to incubate; (*fig*) to hatch.
incuestionable [inkwestjo'naßle] *adj* unchallengeable.
inculcar [inkul'kar] *vt* to inculcate.
inculpar [inkul'par] *vt*: **~ de** (*acusar*) to accuse of; (*achacar, atribuir*) to charge with, blame for.
inculque [in'kulke] *etc vb V* **inculcar**.
inculto, a [in'kulto, a] *adj* (*persona*) uneducated, uncultured; (*fig: grosero*) uncouth ♦ *nm/f* ignoramus.
incumbencia [inkum'benθja] *nf* obligation; **no es de mi** ~ it is not my field.
incumbir [inkum'bir] *vi*: **~ a** to be incumbent upon; **no me incumbe a mí** it is no concern of mine.
incumplimiento [inkumpli'mjento] *nm* non-fulfilment; (*COM*) repudiation; **~ de contrato** breach of contract; **por ~** by default.
incurable [inku'raßle] *adj* (*enfermedad*) incurable; (*paciente*) incurably ill.

incurrir [inku'rrir] *vi*: ~ **en** to incur; (*crimen*) to commit; ~ **en un error** to make a mistake.
indagación [indaɤa'θjon] *nf* investigation; (*búsqueda*) search; (*JUR*) inquest.
indagar [inda'ɤar] *vt* to investigate; to search; (*averiguar*) to ascertain.
indague [in'daɤe] *etc vb V* **indagar**.
indebido, a [inde'βiðo, a] *adj* undue; (*dicho*) improper.
indecencia [inde'θenθja] *nf* indecency; (*dicho*) obscenity.
indecente [inde'θente] *adj* indecent, improper; (*lascivo*) obscene.
indecible [inde'θiβle] *adj* unspeakable; (*indescriptible*) indescribable.
indeciso, a [inde'θiso, a] *adj* (*por decidir*) undecided; (*vacilante*) hesitant.
indefenso, a [inde'fenso, a] *adj* defenceless.
indefinido, a [indefi'niðo, a] *adj* indefinite; (*vago*) vague, undefined.
indeleble [inde'leβle] *adj* indelible.
indemne [in'demne] *adj* (*objeto*) undamaged; (*persona*) unharmed, unhurt.
indemnice [indem'niθe] *etc vb V* **indemnizar**.
indemnización [indemniθa'θjon] *nf* (*acto*) indemnification; (*suma*) indemnity; ~ **de cese** redundancy payment; ~ **de despido** severance pay; **doble** ~ double indemnity.
indemnizar [indemni'θar] *vt* to indemnify; (*compensar*) to compensate.
independencia [indepen'denθja] *nf* independence.
independice [indepen'diθe] *etc vb V* **independizar**.
independiente [indepen'djente] *adj* (*libre*) independent; (*autónomo*) self-sufficient; (*INFORM*) stand-alone.
independizar [independi'θar] *vt* to make independent; ~**se** *vr* to become independent.
indescifrable [indesθi'fraβle] *adj* (*MIL*: *código*) indecipherable; (*fig*: *misterio*) impenetrable.
indeseable [indese'aβle] *adj*, *nm/f* undesirable.
indeterminado, a [indetermi'naðo, a] *adj* (*tb LING*) indefinite; (*desconocido*) indeterminate.
India ['indja] *nf*: **la** ~ India.
indiano, a [in'djano, a] *adj* (Spanish-) American ♦ *nm Spaniard who has made good in America.*
indicación [indika'θjon] *nf* indication; (*dato*) piece of information; (*señal*) sign; (*sugerencia*) suggestion, hint; **indicaciones** *nfpl* (*COM*) instructions.
indicado, a [indi'kaðo, a] *adj* (*apto*) right, appropriate.
indicador [indika'ðor] *nm* indicator; (*TEC*) gauge, meter; (*aguja*) hand, pointer; (*de carretera*) roadsign; ~ **de encendido** (*INFORM*) power-on indicator.
indicar [indi'kar] *vt* (*mostrar*) to indicate, show; (*suj*: *termómetro etc*) to read, register; (*señalar*) to point to.
indicativo, a [indika'tiβo, a] *adj* indicative ♦ *nm* (*RADIO*) call sign; ~ **de nacionalidad** (*AUTO*) national identification plate.
índice ['indiθe] *nm* index; (*catálogo*) catalogue; (*ANAT*) index finger, forefinger; ~ **del coste de (la) vida** cost-of-living index; ~ **de crédito** credit rating; ~ **de materias** table of contents; ~ **de natalidad** birth rate; ~ **de precios al por menor (IPM)** (*COM*) retail price index (RPI).
indicio [in'diθjo] *nm* indication, sign; (*en pesquisa etc*) clue; (*INFORM*) marker, mark.
indiferencia [indife'renθja] *nf* indifference; (*apatía*) apathy.
indiferente [indife'rente] *adj* indifferent; **me es** ~ it makes no difference to me.
indígena [in'dixena] *adj* indigenous, native ♦ *nm/f* native.
indigencia [indi'xenθja] *nf* poverty, need.
indigenista [indixe'nista] (*AM*) *adj* pro-Indian ♦ *nm/f* (*estudiante*) student of Indian cultures; (*POL etc*) promoter of Indian cultures.
indigestar [indixes'tar] *vt* to cause indigestion to; ~**se** *vr* to get indigestion.
indigestión [indixes'tjon] *nf* indigestion.
indigesto, a [indi'xesto, a] *adj* undigested; (*indigestible*) indigestible; (*fig*) turgid.
indignación [indiɤna'θjon] *nf* indignation.
indignante [indiɤ'nante] *adj* outrageous, infuriating.
indignar [indiɤ'nar] *vt* to anger, make indignant; ~**se** *vr*: ~**se por** to get indignant about.
indigno, a [in'diɤno, a] *adj* (*despreciable*) low, contemptible; (*inmerecido*) unworthy.
indio, a ['indjo, a] *adj*, *nm/f* Indian.
indique [in'dike] *etc vb V* **indicar**.
indirecto, a [indi'rekto, a] *adj* indirect ♦ *nf* insinuation, innuendo; (*sugerencia*) hint.
indisciplina [indisθi'plina] *nf* (*gen*) lack of discipline; (*MIL*) insubordination.
indiscreción [indiskre'θjon] *nf*

(*imprudencia*) indiscretion; (*irreflexión*) tactlessness; (*acto*) gaffe, faux pas; ..., **si no es ~** ..., if I may say so.
indiscreto, a [indis'kreto, a] *adj* indiscreet.
indiscriminado, a [indiskrimi'naðo, a] *adj* indiscriminate.
indiscutible [indisku'tißle] *adj* indisputable, unquestionable.
indispensable [indispen'saßle] *adj* indispensable.
indispondré [indispon'dre] *etc vb V* **indisponer**.
indisponer [indispo'ner] *vt* to spoil, upset; (*salud*) to make ill; **~se** *vr* to fall ill; **~se con algn** to fall out with sb.
indisponga [indis'ponga] *etc vb V* **indisponer**.
indisposición [indisposi'θjon] *nf* indisposition; (*desgana*) unwillingness.
indispuesto, a [indis'pwesto, a] *pp de* **indisponer** ♦ *adj* indisposed; **sentirse ~** to feel unwell *o* indisposed.
indispuse [indis'puse] *etc vb V* **indisponer**.
indistinto, a [indis'tinto, a] *adj* indistinct; (*vago*) vague.
individual [indißi'ðwal] *adj* individual; (*habitación*) single ♦ *nm* (*DEPORTE*) singles *sg*.
individuo, a [indi'ßiðwo, a] *adj* individual ♦ *nm* individual.
Indochina [indo'tʃina] *nf* Indochina.
indocumentado, a [indokumen'taðo, a] *adj* without identity papers.
indoeuropeo, a [indoeuro'peo, a] *adj, nm/f* Indo-European.
índole ['indole] *nf* (*naturaleza*) nature; (*clase*) sort, kind.
indolencia [indo'lenθja] *nf* indolence, laziness.
indoloro, a [in'doloro, a] *adj* painless.
indomable [indo'maßle] *adj* (*animal*) untameable; (*espíritu*) indomitable.
indómito, a [in'domito, a] *adj* indomitable.
Indonesia [indo'nesja] *nf* Indonesia.
indonesio, a [indo'nesjo, a] *adj, nm/f* Indonesian.
inducción [induk'θjon] *nf* (*FILOSOFÍA, ELEC*) induction; **por ~** by induction.
inducir [indu'θir] *vt* to induce; (*inferir*) to infer; (*persuadir*) to persuade; **~ a algn en el error** to mislead sb.
indudable [indu'ðaßle] *adj* undoubted; (*incuestionable*) unquestionable; **es ~ que** ... there is no doubt that ....
indulgencia [indul'xenθja] *nf* indulgence; (*JUR etc*) leniency; **proceder sin ~ contra** to proceed ruthlessly against.
indultar [indul'tar] *vt* (*perdonar*) to pardon, reprieve; (*librar de pago*) to exempt.
indulto [in'dulto] *nm* pardon; exemption.
indumentaria [indumen'tarja] *nf* (*ropa*) clothing, dress.
industria [in'dustrja] *nf* industry; (*habilidad*) skill; **~ agropecuaria** farming and fishing; **~ pesada** heavy industry; **~ petrolífera** oil industry.
industrial [indus'trjal] *adj* industrial ♦ *nm* industrialist.
industrializar [industrjali'θar] *vt* to industrialize; **~se** *vr* to become industrialized.
INE ['ine] *nm abr* (*ESP*) = *Instituto Nacional de Estadística*.
inédito, a [i'neðito, a] *adj* (*libro*) unpublished; (*nuevo*) unheard-of.
inefable [ine'faßle] *adj* ineffable, indescribable.
ineficacia [inefi'kaθja] *nf* (*de medida*) ineffectiveness; (*de proceso*) inefficiency.
ineficaz [inefi'kaθ] *adj* (*inútil*) ineffective; (*ineficiente*) inefficient.
ineludible [inelu'ðißle] *adj* inescapable, unavoidable.
INEM, Inem [i'nem] *nm abr* (*ESP*: = *Instituto Nacional de Empleo*) ≈ Department of Employment (*BRIT*).
INEN ['inen] *nm abr* (*México*) = *Instituto Nacional de Energía Nuclear*.
inenarrable [inena'rraßle] *adj* inexpressible.
ineptitud [inepti'tuð] *nf* ineptitude, incompetence.
inepto, a [i'nepto, a] *adj* inept, incompetent.
inequívoco, a [ine'kißoko, a] *adj* unequivocal; (*inconfundible*) unmistakable.
inercia [i'nerθja] *nf* inertia; (*pasividad*) passivity.
inerme [i'nerme] *adj* (*sin armas*) unarmed; (*indefenso*) defenceless.
inerte [i'nerte] *adj* inert; (*inmóvil*) motionless.
inescrutable [ineskru'taßle] *adj* inscrutable.
inesperado, a [inespe'raðo, a] *adj* unexpected, unforeseen.
inestable [ines'taßle] *adj* unstable.
inestimable [inesti'maßle] *adj* inestimable; **de valor ~** invaluable.
inevitable [ineßi'taßle] *adj* inevitable.
inexactitud [ineksakti'tuð] *nf* inaccuracy.
inexacto, a [inek'sakto, a] *adj* inaccurate; (*falso*) untrue.
inexistente [ineksis'tente] *adj* non-

existent.
inexorable [inekso'raßle] *adj* inexorable.
inexperiencia [inekspe'rjenθja] *nf* inexperience, lack of experience.
inexperto, a [ineks'perto, a] *adj* (*novato*) inexperienced.
inexplicable [inekspli'kaßle] *adj* inexplicable.
inexpresable [inekspre'saßle] *adj* inexpressible.
inexpresivo, a [inekspre'sißo, a] *adj* inexpressive; (*ojos*) dull; (*cara*) wooden.
inexpugnable [inekspuɣ'naßle] *adj* (*MIL*) impregnable; (*fig*) firm.
infalible [infa'lißle] *adj* infallible; (*indefectible*) certain, sure; (*plan*) foolproof.
infame [in'fame] *adj* infamous.
infamia [in'famja] *nf* infamy; (*deshonra*) disgrace.
infancia [in'fanθja] *nf* infancy, childhood; **jardín de la ~** nursery school.
infanta [in'fanta] *nf* (*hija del rey*) infanta, princess.
infante [in'fante] *nm* (*hijo del rey*) infante, prince.
infantería [infante'ria] *nf* infantry.
infantil [infan'til] *adj* child's, children's; (*pueril, aniñado*) infantile; (*cándido*) childlike.
infarto [in'farto] *nm* (*tb*: **~ de miocardio**) heart attack.
infatigable [infati'ɣaßle] *adj* tireless, untiring.
infección [infek'θjon] *nf* infection.
infeccioso, a [infek'θjoso, a] *adj* infectious.
infectar [infek'tar] *vt* to infect; **~se** *vr*: **~se (de)** (*tb fig*) to become infected (with).
infecundidad [infekundi'ðað] *nf* (*de tierra*) infertility, barrenness; (*de mujer*) sterility.
infecundo, a [infe'kundo, a] *adj* infertile, barren; sterile.
infeliz [infe'liθ] *adj* (*desgraciado*) unhappy, wretched; (*inocente*) gullible ♦ *nm/f* (*desgraciado*) wretch; (*inocentón*) simpleton.
inferior [infe'rjor] *adj* inferior; (*situación, MAT*) lower ♦ *nm/f* inferior, subordinate; **cualquier número ~ a 9** any number less than *o* under *o* below 9; **una cantidad ~** a lesser quantity.
inferioridad [inferjori'ðað] *nf* inferiority; **estar en ~ de condiciones** to be at a disadvantage.
inferir [infe'rir] *vt* (*deducir*) to infer, deduce; (*causar*) to cause.
infernal [infer'nal] *adj* infernal.
infértil [in'fertil] *adj* infertile.
infestar [infes'tar] *vt* to infest.
infidelidad [infiðeli'ðað] *nf* (*gen*) infidelity, unfaithfulness.
infiel [in'fjel] *adj* unfaithful, disloyal; (*falso*) inaccurate ♦ *nm/f* infidel, unbeliever.
infiera [in'fjera] *etc vb V* **inferir**.
infierno [in'fjerno] *nm* hell; **¡vete al ~!** go to hell; **está en el quinto ~** it's at the back of beyond.
infiltrar [infil'trar] *vt* to infiltrate; **~se** *vr* to infiltrate, filter; (*líquidos*) to percolate.
ínfimo, a ['infimo, a] *adj* (*vil*) vile, mean; (*más bajo*) lowest; (*peor*) worst; (*miserable*) wretched.
infinidad [infini'ðað] *nf* infinity; (*abundancia*) great quantity; **~ de** vast numbers of; **~ de veces** countless times.
infinitivo [infini'tißo] *nm* infinitive.
infinito, a [infi'nito, a] *adj* infinite; (*fig*) boundless ♦ *adv* infinitely ♦ *nm* infinite; (*MAT*) infinity; **hasta lo ~** ad infinitum.
infiriendo [infi'rjendo] *etc vb V* **inferir**.
inflación [infla'θjon] *nf* (*hinchazón*) swelling; (*monetaria*) inflation; (*fig*) conceit.
inflacionario, a [inflaθjo'narjo, a] *adj* inflationary.
inflacionismo [inflaθjo'nismo] *nm* (*ECON*) inflation.
inflacionista [inflaθjo'nista] *adj* inflationary.
inflamar [infla'mar] *vt* to set on fire; (*MED, fig*) to inflame; **~se** *vr* to catch fire; to become inflamed.
inflar [in'flar] *vt* (*hinchar*) to inflate, blow up; (*fig*) to exaggerate; **~se** *vr* to swell (up); (*fig*) to get conceited.
inflexible [inflek'sißle] *adj* inflexible; (*fig*) unbending.
infligir [infli'xir] *vt* to inflict.
inflija [in'flixa] *etc vb V* **infligir**.
influencia [in'flwenθja] *nf* influence.
influenciar [inflwen'θjar] *vt* to influence.
influir [influ'ir] *vt* to influence ♦ *vi* to have influence, carry weight; **~ en** *o* **sobre** to influence, affect; (*contribuir a*) to have a hand in.
influjo [in'fluxo] *nm* influence; **~ de capitales** (*ECON etc*) capital influx.
influyendo [influ'jendo] *etc vb V* **influir**.
influyente [influ'jente] *adj* influential.
información [informa'θjon] *nf* information; (*noticias*) news *sg*; (*informe*) report; (*INFORM*: *datos*) data; (*JUR*) inquiry; **I~** (*oficina*) Information; (*TELEC*)

Directory Enquiries (*BRIT*), Directory Assistance (*US*); (*mostrador*) Information Desk; **una** ~ a piece of information; **abrir una** ~ (*JUR*) to begin proceedings; ~ **deportiva** (*en periódico*) sports section.
informal [infor'mal] *adj* (*gen*) informal.
informante [infor'mante] *nm/f* informant.
informar [infor'mar] *vt* (*gen*) to inform; (*revelar*) to reveal, make known ♦ *vi* (*JUR*) to plead; (*denunciar*) to inform; (*dar cuenta de*) to report on; **~se** *vr* to find out; **~se de** to inquire into.
informática [infor'matika] *nf* V **informático**.
informatice [informa'tiθe] *etc vb* V **informatizar**.
informático, a [infor'matiko, a] *adj* computer *cpd* ♦ *nf* (*TEC*) information technology; computing; (*ESCOL*) computer science *o* studies; ~ **de gestión** commercial computing.
informativo, a [informa'tiβo, a] *adj* (*libro*) informative; (*folleto*) information *cpd*; (*RADIO, TV*) news *cpd* ♦ *nm* (*RADIO, TV*) news programme.
informatización [informatiθa'θjon] *nf* computerization.
informatizar [informati'θar] *vt* to computerize.
informe [in'forme] *adj* shapeless ♦ *nm* report; (*dictamen*) statement; (*MIL*) briefing; (*JUR*) plea; **~s** *nmpl* information *sg*; (*datos*) data; ~ **anual** annual report; ~ **del juez** summing-up.
infortunio [infor'tunjo] *nm* misfortune.
infracción [infrak'θjon] *nf* infraction, infringement; (*AUTO*) offence.
infraestructura [infraestruk'tura] *nf* infrastructure.
in fraganti [infra'ɣanti] *adv*: **pillar a algn** ~ to catch sb red-handed.
infranqueable [infranke'aβle] *adj* impassable; (*fig*) insurmountable.
infrarrojo, a [infra'rroxo, a] *adj* infrared.
infravalorar [infraβalo'rar] *vt* to undervalue; (*FIN*) to underestimate.
infringir [infrin'xir] *vt* to infringe, contravene.
infrinja [in'frinxa] *etc vb* V **infringir**.
infructuoso, a [infruk'twoso, a] *adj* fruitless, unsuccessful.
infundado, a [infun'daðo, a] *adj* groundless, unfounded.
infundir [infun'dir] *vt* to infuse, instil; ~ **ánimo a algn** to encourage sb; ~ **miedo a algn** to intimidate sb.
infusión [infu'sjon] *nf* infusion; ~ **de manzanilla** camomile tea.
Ing. *abr* = **Ingeniero**.
ingeniar [inxe'njar] *vt* to think up, devise; **~se** *vr* to manage; **~se para** to manage to.
ingeniería [inxenje'ria] *nf* engineering; ~ **genética** genetic engineering; ~ **de sistemas** (*INFORM*) systems engineering.
ingeniero, a [inxe'njero, a] *nm/f* engineer; ~ **de sonido** sound engineer; ~ **de caminos** civil engineer.
ingenio [in'xenjo] *nm* (*talento*) talent; (*agudeza*) wit; (*habilidad*) ingenuity, inventiveness; (*TEC*): ~ **azucarero** sugar refinery.
ingenioso, a [inxe'njoso, a] *adj* ingenious, clever; (*divertido*) witty.
ingente [in'xente] *adj* huge, enormous.
ingenuidad [inxenwi'ðað] *nf* ingenuousness; (*sencillez*) simplicity.
ingenuo, a [in'xenwo, a] *adj* ingenuous.
ingerir [inxe'rir] *vt* to ingest; (*tragar*) to swallow; (*consumir*) to consume.
ingiera [in'xjera] *etc*, **ingiriendo** [inxi'rjenðo] *etc vb* V **ingerir**.
Inglaterra [ingla'terra] *nf* England.
ingle ['ingle] *nf* groin.
inglés, esa [in'gles, esa] *adj* English ♦ *nm/f* Englishman/woman ♦ *nm* (*LING*) English; **los ingleses** the English.
ingratitud [ingrati'tuð] *nf* ingratitude.
ingrato, a [in'grato, a] *adj* ungrateful; (*tarea*) thankless.
ingravidez [ingraβi'ðeθ] *nf* weightlessness.
ingrediente [ingre'ðjente] *nm* ingredient; **~s** *nmpl* (*AM*: *tapas*) titbits.
ingresar [ingre'sar] *vt* (*dinero*) to deposit ♦ *vi* to come *o* go in; ~ **a** (*esp AM*) to enter; ~ **en** (*club*) to join; (*MIL, ESCOL*) to enrol in; ~ **en el hospital** to go into hospital.
ingreso [in'greso] *nm* (*entrada*) entry; (: *en hospital etc*) admission; (*MIL, ESCOL*) enrolment; **~s** *nmpl* (*dinero*) income *sg*; (: *COM*) takings *pl*; ~ **gravable** taxable income *sg*; **~s accesorios** fringe benefits; **~s brutos** gross receipts; **~s devengados** earned income *sg*; **~s exentos de impuestos** non-taxable income *sg*; **~s personales disponibles** disposable personal income *sg*.
íngrimo, a ['ingrimo, a] *adj* (*AM*: *tb* ~ **y solo**) all alone.
inhábil [i'naβil] *adj* unskilful, clumsy.
inhabilitar [inaβili'tar] *vt* (*POL, MED*): ~ **a algn (para hacer algo)** to disqualify sb (from doing sth).
inhabitable [inaβi'taβle] *adj* uninhabitable.
inhabituado, a [inaβi'twaðo, a] *adj* unaccustomed.

inhalador [inala'ðor] *nm* (*MED*) inhaler.
inhalar [ina'lar] *vt* to inhale.
inherente [ine'rente] *adj* inherent.
inhibición [iniβi'θjon] *nf* inhibition.
inhibir [ini'βir] *vt* to inhibit; (*REL*) to restrain; ~**se** *vr* to keep out.
inhospitalario, a [inospita'larjo, a], **inhóspito, a** [i'nospito, a] *adj* inhospitable.
inhumación [inuma'θjon] *nf* burial, interment.
inhumano, a [inu'mano, a] *adj* inhuman.
INI ['ini] *nm abr* = **Instituto Nacional de Industria.**
inicial [ini'θjal] *adj, nf* initial.
inicialice [iniθja'liθe] *etc vb V* **inicializar.**
inicializar [iniθjali'θar] *vt* (*INFORM*) to initialize.
iniciar [ini'θjar] *vt* (*persona*) to initiate; (*empezar*) to begin, commence; (*conversación*) to start up; ~ **a algn en un secreto** to let sb into a secret; ~ **la sesión** (*INFORM*) to log in *o* on.
iniciativa [iniθja'tiβa] *nf* initiative; (*liderazgo*) leadership; **la ~ privada** private enterprise.
inicio [i'niθjo] *nm* start, beginning.
inicuo, a [i'nikwo, a] *adj* iniquitous.
inigualado, a [iniɣwa'laðo, a] *adj* unequalled.
ininteligible [ininteli'xiβle] *adj* unintelligible.
ininterrumpido, a [ininterrum'piðo, a] *adj* uninterrupted; (*proceso*) continuous; (*progreso*) steady.
injerencia [inxe'renθja] *nf* interference.
injertar [inxer'tar] *vt* to graft.
injerto [in'xerto] *nm* graft; ~ **de piel** skin graft.
injuria [in'xurja] *nf* (*agravio, ofensa*) offence; (*insulto*) insult; ~**s** *nfpl* abuse *sg*.
injuriar [inxu'rjar] *vt* to insult.
injurioso, a [inxu'rjoso, a] *adj* offensive; insulting.
injusticia [inxus'tiθja] *nf* injustice, unfairness; **con ~** unjustly.
injusto, a [in'xusto, a] *adj* unjust, unfair.
inmaculado, a [inmaku'laðo, a] *adj* immaculate, spotless.
inmadurez [inmaðu'reθ] *nf* immaturity.
inmaduro, a [inma'ðuro, a] *adj* immature; (*fruta*) unripe.
inmediaciones [inmeðja'θjones] *nfpl* neighbourhood *sg*, environs.
inmediatez [inmeðja'teθ] *nf* immediacy.
inmediato, a [inme'ðjato, a] *adj* immediate; (*contiguo*) adjoining; (*rápido*) prompt; (*próximo*) neighbouring, next; **de ~** (*esp AM*) immediately.
inmejorable [inmexo'raβle] *adj* unsurpassable; (*precio*) unbeatable.
inmemorable [inmemo'raβle], **inmemorial** [inmemo'rjal] *adj* immemorial.
inmenso, a [in'menso, a] *adj* immense, huge.
inmerecido, a [inmere'θiðo, a] *adj* undeserved.
inmersión [inmer'sjon] *nf* immersion; (*buzo*) dive.
inmigración [inmiɣra'θjon] *nf* immigration.
inmigrante [inmi'ɣrante] *adj, nm/f* immigrant.
inminente [inmi'nente] *adj* imminent, impending.
inmiscuirse [inmisku'irse] *vr* to interfere, meddle.
inmiscuyendo [inmisku'jendo] *etc vb V* **inmiscuirse.**
inmobiliario, a [inmoβi'ljarjo, a] *adj* real-estate *cpd*, property *cpd* ♦ *nf* estate agency.
inmolar [inmo'lar] *vt* to immolate, sacrifice.
inmoral [inmo'ral] *adj* immoral.
inmortal [inmor'tal] *adj* immortal.
inmortalice [inmorta'liθe] *etc vb V* **inmortalizar.**
inmortalizar [inmortali'θar] *vt* to immortalize.
inmotivado, a [inmoti'βaðo, a] *adj* motiveless; (*sospecha*) groundless.
inmóvil [in'moβil] *adj* immobile.
inmovilizar [inmoβili'θar] *vt* to immobilize; (*paralizar*) to paralyse; ~**se** *vr*: **se le ha inmovilizado la pierna** her leg was paralysed.
inmueble [in'mweβle] *adj*: **bienes ~s** real estate *sg*, landed property *sg* ♦ *nm* property.
inmundicia [inmun'diθja] *nf* filth.
inmundo, a [in'mundo, a] *adj* filthy.
inmune [in'mune] *adj* (*MED*) immune.
inmunidad [inmuni'ðað] *nf* immunity; (*fisco*) exemption; ~ **diplomática/parlamentaria** diplomatic/parliamentary immunity.
inmunitario, a [inmuni'tarjo, a] *adj*: **sistema ~** immune system.
inmunización [inmuniθa'θjon] *nf* immunization.
inmunizar [inmuni'θar] *vt* to immunize.
inmutable [inmu'taβle] *adj* immutable; **permaneció ~** he didn't flinch.
inmutarse [inmu'tarse] *vr*: **siguió sin ~** he

carried on unperturbed.
innato, a [in'nato, a] *adj* innate.
innecesario, a [inneθe'sarjo, a] *adj* unnecessary.
innegable [inne'ɣaβle] *adj* undeniable.
innoble [in'noβle] *adj* ignoble.
innovación [innoβa'θjon] *nf* innovation.
innovador, a [innoβa'ðor, a] *adj* innovatory, innovative ♦ *nm/f* innovator.
innovar [inno'βar] *vt* to introduce.
innumerable [innume'raβle] *adj* countless.
inocencia [ino'θenθja] *nf* innocence.
inocentada [inoθen'taða] *nf* practical joke.
inocente [ino'θente] *adj* (*ingenuo*) naive, innocent; (*inculpable*) innocent; (*sin malicia*) harmless ♦ *nm/f* simpleton; **día de los (Santos) I~s** ≈ April Fool's Day; *see boxed note*.

DÍA DE LOS SANTOS INOCENTES

El día de los (Santos) Inocentes, *28 December, is when the Church commemorates Herod's slaughter of the innocent children of Judea in biblical times. On this day Spaniards play "inocentadas" (practical jokes) on each other, much like British April Fools' Day pranks, perhaps sticking a "monigote" (cut-out paper figure) on someone's back or broadcasting unlikely news stories.*

inocuidad [inokwi'ðað] *nf* harmlessness.
inocular [inoku'lar] *vt* to inoculate.
inocuo, a [i'nokwo, a] *adj* (*sustancia*) harmless.
inodoro, a [ino'ðoro, a] *adj* odourless ♦ *nm* toilet (*BRIT*), lavatory (*BRIT*), washroom (*US*).
inofensivo, a [inofen'siβo, a] *adj* inoffensive.
inolvidable [inolβi'ðaβle] *adj* unforgettable.
inoperante [inope'rante] *adj* ineffective.
inopinado, a [inopi'naðo, a] *adj* unexpected.
inoportuno, a [inopor'tuno, a] *adj* untimely; (*molesto*) inconvenient; (*inapropiado*) inappropriate.
inoxidable [inoksi'ðaβle] *adj* stainless; **acero ~** stainless steel.
inquebrantable [inkeβran'taβle] *adj* unbreakable; (*fig*) unshakeable.
inquiera [in'kjera] *etc vb V* **inquirir**.
inquietante [inkje'tante] *adj* worrying.
inquietar [inkje'tar] *vt* to worry, trouble; **~se** *vr* to worry, get upset.
inquieto, a [in'kjeto, a] *adj* anxious, worried; **estar ~ por** to be worried about.
inquietud [inkje'tuð] *nf* anxiety, worry.
inquilino, a [inki'lino, a] *nm/f* tenant; (*COM*) lessee.
inquiriendo [inki'rjendo] *etc vb V* **inquirir**.
inquirir [inki'rir] *vt* to enquire into, investigate.
insaciable [insa'θjaβle] *adj* insatiable.
insalubre [insa'luβre] *adj* unhealthy; (*condiciones*) insanitary.
INSALUD [insa'luð] *nm abr* (*ESP*) = *Instituto Nacional de la Salud*.
insano, a [in'sano, a] *adj* (*loco*) insane; (*malsano*) unhealthy.
insatisfacción [insatisfak'θjon] *nf* dissatisfaction.
insatisfecho, a [insatis'fetʃo, a] *adj* (*condición*) unsatisfied; (*estado de ánimo*) dissatisfied.
inscribir [inskri'βir] *vt* to inscribe; (*en lista*) to put; (*en censo*) to register; **~se** *vr* to register; (*ESCOL etc*) to enrol.
inscripción [inskrip'θjon] *nf* inscription; (*ESCOL etc*) enrolment; (*en censo*) registration.
inscrito [ins'krito] *pp de* **inscribir**.
insecticida [insekti'θiða] *nm* insecticide.
insecto [in'sekto] *nm* insect.
inseguridad [inseɣuri'ðað] *nf* insecurity.
inseguro, a [inse'ɣuro, a] *adj* insecure; (*inconstante*) unsteady; (*incierto*) uncertain.
inseminación [insemina'θjon] *nf*: **~ artificial** artificial insemination (A.I.).
inseminar [insemi'nar] *vt* to inseminate, fertilize.
insensato, a [insen'sato, a] *adj* foolish, stupid.
insensibilice [insensiβi'liθe] *etc vb V* **insensibilizar**.
insensibilidad [insensiβili'ðað] *nf* (*gen*) insensitivity; (*dureza de corazón*) callousness.
insensibilizar [insensiβili'θar] *vt* to desensitize; (*MED*) to anaesthetize (*BRIT*), anesthetize (*US*); (*eufemismo*) to knock out *o* unconscious.
insensible [insen'siβle] *adj* (*gen*) insensitive; (*movimiento*) imperceptible; (*sin sentido*) numb.
inseparable [insepa'raβle] *adj* inseparable.
INSERSO [in'serso] *nm abr* (= *Instituto Nacional de Servicios Sociales*) *branch of social services*.
insertar [inser'tar] *vt* to insert.
inservible [inser'βiβle] *adj* useless.
insidioso, a [insi'ðjoso, a] *adj* insidious.

insigne [in'siɤne] *adj* distinguished; (*famoso*) notable.
insignia [in'siɤnja] *nf* (*señal distintiva*) badge; (*estandarte*) flag.
insignificante [insiɤnifi'kante] *adj* insignificant.
insinuar [insi'nwar] *vt* to insinuate, imply; ~**se** *vr*: ~**se con algn** to ingratiate o.s. with sb.
insípido, a [in'sipiðo, a] *adj* insipid.
insistencia [insis'tenθja] *nf* insistence.
insistir [insis'tir] *vi* to insist; ~ **en algo** to insist on sth; (*enfatizar*) to stress sth.
in situ [in'situ] *adv* on the spot, in situ.
insobornable [insoβor'naβle] *adj* incorruptible.
insociable [inso'θjaβle] *adj* unsociable.
insolación [insola'θjon] *nf* (*MED*) sunstroke.
insolencia [inso'lenθja] *nf* insolence.
insolente [inso'lente] *adj* insolent.
insólito, a [in'solito, a] *adj* unusual.
insoluble [inso'luβle] *adj* insoluble.
insolvencia [insol'βenθja] *nf* insolvency.
insomne [in'somne] *adj* sleepless ♦ *nm/f* insomniac.
insomnio [in'somnjo] *nm* insomnia.
insondable [inson'daβle] *adj* bottomless.
insonorización [insonoriθa'θjon] *nf* soundproofing.
insonorizado, a [insonori'θaðo, a] *adj* (*cuarto etc*) soundproof.
insoportable [insopor'taβle] *adj* unbearable.
insoslayable [insosla'jaβle] *adj* unavoidable.
insospechado, a [insospe'tʃaðo, a] *adj* (*inesperado*) unexpected.
insostenible [insoste'niβle] *adj* untenable.
inspección [inspek'θjon] *nf* inspection, check; **I**~ inspectorate; ~ **técnica (de vehículos)** ≈ MOT (test) (*BRIT*).
inspeccionar [inspekθjo'nar] *vt* (*examinar*) to inspect, examine; (*controlar*) to check; (*INFORM*) to peek.
inspector, a [inspek'tor, a] *nm/f* inspector.
inspectorado [inspekto'raðo] *nm* inspectorate.
inspiración [inspira'θjon] *nf* inspiration.
inspirador, a [inspira'ðor, a] *adj* inspiring.
inspirar [inspi'rar] *vt* to inspire; (*MED*) to inhale; ~**se** *vr*: ~**se en** to be inspired by.
instalación [instala'θjon] *nf* (*equipo*) fittings *pl*, equipment; ~ **eléctrica** wiring.
instalar [insta'lar] *vt* (*establecer*) to instal; (*erguir*) to set up, erect; ~**se** *vr* to establish o.s.; (*en una vivienda*) to move into.
instancia [ins'tanθja] *nf* (*solicitud*) application; (*ruego*) request; (*JUR*) petition; **a** ~ **de** at the request of; **en última** ~ in the last resort.
instantáneo, a [instan'taneo, a] *adj* instantaneous ♦ *nf* snap(shot); **café** ~ instant coffee.
instante [ins'tante] *nm* instant, moment; **en un** ~ in a flash.
instar [ins'tar] *vt* to press, urge.
instaurar [instau'rar] *vt* (*establecer*) to establish, set up.
instigador, a [instiɤa'ðor, a] *nm/f* instigator; ~ **de un delito** (*JUR*) accessory before the fact.
instigar [insti'ɤar] *vt* to instigate.
instigue [ins'tiɤe] *etc vb V* **instigar**.
instintivo, a [instin'tiβo, a] *adj* instinctive.
instinto [ins'tinto] *nm* instinct; **por** ~ instinctively.
institución [institu'θjon] *nf* institution, establishment; ~ **benéfica** charitable foundation.
instituir [institu'ir] *vt* to establish; (*fundar*) to found.
instituto [insti'tuto] *nm* (*gen*) institute; **I**~ **Nacional de Enseñanza** (*ESP*) ≈ comprehensive (*BRIT*) *o* high (*US*) school; **I**~ **Nacional de Industria (INI)** (*ESP COM*) ≈ National Enterprise Board (*BRIT*).
institutriz [institu'triθ] *nf* governess.
instituyendo [institu'jendo] *etc vb V* **instituir**.
instrucción [instruk'θjon] *nf* instruction; (*enseñanza*) education, teaching; (*JUR*) proceedings *pl*; (*MIL*) training; (*DEPORTE*) coaching; (*conocimientos*) knowledge; (*INFORM*) statement; **instrucciones para el uso** directions for use; **instrucciones de funcionamiento** operating instructions.
instructivo, a [instruk'tiβo, a] *adj* instructive.
instruir [instru'ir] *vt* (*gen*) to instruct; (*enseñar*) to teach, educate; (*JUR*: *proceso*) to prepare, draw up; ~**se** *vr* to learn, teach o.s.
instrumento [instru'mento] *nm* (*gen*, *MUS*) instrument; (*herramienta*) tool, implement; (*COM*) indenture; (*JUR*) legal document; ~ **de percusión/cuerda/viento** percussion/string(ed)/wind instrument.
instruyendo [instru'jendo] *etc vb V* **instruir**.
insubordinarse [insuβorði'narse] *vr* to rebel.
insuficiencia [insufi'θjenθja] *nf* (*carencia*)

lack; (*inadecuación*) inadequacy; ~ **cardíaca/renal** heart/kidney failure.
insuficiente [insufi'θjente] *adj* (*gen*) insufficient; (*ESCOL*: *nota*) unsatisfactory.
insufrible [insu'frißle] *adj* insufferable.
insular [insu'lar] *adj* insular.
insulina [insu'lina] *nf* insulin.
insulso, a [in'sulso, a] *adj* insipid; (*fig*) dull.
insultar [insul'tar] *vt* to insult.
insulto [in'sulto] *nm* insult.
insumisión [insumi'sjon] *nf refusal to do military service or community service.*
insumiso, a [insu'miso, a] *adj* (*rebelde*) rebellious ♦ *nm/f* (*POL*) *person who refuses to do military service or community service*; *V tb* **mili**.
insuperable [insupe'raßle] *adj* (*excelente*) unsurpassable; (*problema etc*) insurmountable.
insurgente [insur'xente] *adj, nm/f* insurgent.
insurrección [insurrek'θjon] *nf* insurrection, rebellion.
insustituible [insusti'twißle] *adj* irreplaceable.
intachable [inta'tʃaßle] *adj* irreproachable.
intacto, a [in'takto, a] *adj* (*sin tocar*) untouched; (*entero*) intact.
integrado, a [inte'ɣraðo, a] *adj* (*INFORM*): **circuito** ~ integrated circuit.
integral [inte'ɣral] *adj* integral; (*completo*) complete; (*TEC*) built-in; **pan** ~ wholemeal bread.
integrante [inte'ɣrante] *adj* integral ♦ *nm/f* member.
integrar [inte'ɣrar] *vt* to make up, compose; (*MAT, fig*) to integrate.
integridad [inteɣri'ðað] *nf* wholeness; (*carácter, tb INFORM*) integrity; **en su** ~ completely.
integrismo [inte'ɣrismo] *nm* fundamentalism.
integrista [inte'ɣrista] *adj, nm/f* fundamentalist.
íntegro, a ['inteɣro, a] *adj* whole, entire; (*texto*) uncut, unabridged; (*honrado*) honest.
intelectual [intelek'twal] *adj, nm/f* intellectual.
intelectualidad [intelektwali'ðað] *nf* intelligentsia, intellectuals *pl*.
inteligencia [inteli'xenθja] *nf* intelligence; (*ingenio*) ability; ~ **artificial** artificial intelligence.
inteligente [inteli'xente] *adj* intelligent.
inteligible [inteli'xißle] *adj* intelligible.
intemperancia [intempe'ranθja] *nf* excess, intemperance.
intemperie [intem'perje] *nf*: **a la** ~ outdoors, in the open air.
intempestivo, a [intempes'tißo, a] *adj* untimely.
intención [inten'θjon] *nf* (*gen*) intention, purpose; **con segundas intenciones** maliciously; **con** ~ deliberately.
intencionado, a [intenθjo'naðo, a] *adj* deliberate; **bien** ~ well-meaning; **mal** ~ ill-disposed, hostile.
intendencia [inten'denθja] *nf* management, administration; (*MIL*: *tb*: **cuerpo de** ~) ≈ service corps.
intensidad [intensi'ðað] *nf* (*gen*) intensity; (*ELEC, TEC*) strength; (*de recuerdo*) vividness; **llover con** ~ to rain hard.
intensificar [intensifi'kar] *vt*, **intensificarse** *vr* to intensify.
intensifique [intensi'fike] *etc vb V* **intensificar**.
intensivo, a [inten'sißo, a] *adj* intensive; **curso** ~ crash course.
intenso, a [in'tenso, a] *adj* intense; (*impresión*) vivid; (*sentimiento*) profound, deep.
intentar [inten'tar] *vt* (*tratar*) to try, attempt.
intento [in'tento] *nm* (*intención*) intention, purpose; (*tentativa*) attempt.
intentona [inten'tona] *nf* (*POL*) attempted coup.
interaccionar [interakθjo'nar] *vi* (*INFORM*) to interact.
interactivo, a [interak'tißo, a] *adj* interactive; (*INFORM*): **computación interactiva** interactive computing.
intercalación [interkala'θjon] *nf* (*INFORM*) merging.
intercalar [interka'lar] *vt* to insert; (*INFORM*: *archivos, texto*) to merge.
intercambiable [interkam'bjaßle] *adj* interchangeable.
intercambio [inter'kambjo] *nm* (*canje*) exchange; (*trueque*) swap.
interceder [interθe'ðer] *vi* to intercede.
interceptar [interθep'tar] *vt* to intercept, cut off; (*AUTO*) to hold up.
interceptor [interθep'tor] *nm* interceptor; (*TEC*) trap.
intercesión [interθe'sjon] *nf* intercession.
interés [inte'res] *nm* (*gen, COM*) interest; (*importancia*) concern; (*parte*) share, part; (*pey*) self-interest; ~ **compuesto** compound interest; ~ **simple** simple interest; **con un** ~ **de 9 por ciento** at an interest of 9%; **dar a** ~ to lend at

interest; **tener ~ en** (*COM*) to hold a share in; **intereses acumulados** accrued interest *sg*; **intereses por cobrar** interest receivable *sg*; **intereses creados** vested interests; **intereses por pagar** interest payable *sg*.

interesado, a [intere'saðo, a] *adj* interested; (*prejuiciado*) prejudiced; (*pey*) mercenary, self-seeking ♦ *nm/f* person concerned; (*firmante*) the undersigned.

interesante [intere'sante] *adj* interesting.

interesar [intere'sar] *vt* to interest, be of interest to ♦ *vi* to interest, be of interest; (*importar*) to be important; **~se** *vr*: **~se en** *o* **por** to take an interest in; **no me interesan los toros** bullfighting does not appeal to me.

interestatal [interesta'tal] *adj* inter-state.

interface [inter'faθe], **interfase** [inter'fase] *nm* (*INFORM*) interface; **~ hombre/máquina/por menús** man/machine/menu interface.

interfaz [inter'faθ] *nm* = **interface**.

interferencia [interfe'renθja] *nf* interference.

interferir [interfe'rir] *vt* to interfere with; (*TELEC*) to jam ♦ *vi* to interfere.

interfiera [inter'fjera] *etc*, **interfiriendo** [interfi'rjendo] *etc vb V* **interferir**.

interfono [inter'fono] *nm* intercom.

ínterin ['interin] *adv* meanwhile ♦ *nm* interim; **en el ~** in the meantime.

interino, a [inte'rino, a] *adj* temporary; (*empleado etc*) provisional ♦ *nm/f* temporary holder of a post; (*MED*) locum; (*ESCOL*) supply teacher; (*TEAT*) stand-in.

interior [inte'rjor] *adj* inner, inside; (*COM*) domestic, internal ♦ *nm* interior, inside; (*fig*) soul, mind; (*DEPORTE*) inside forward; **Ministerio del I~** ≈ Home Office (*BRIT*), Ministry of the Interior; **dije para mí ~** I said to myself.

interjección [interxek'θjon] *nf* interjection.

interlínea [inter'linea] *nf* (*INFORM*) line feed.

interlocutor, a [interloku'tor, a] *nm/f* speaker; (*al teléfono*) person at the other end (of the line); **mi ~** the person I was speaking to.

intermediario, a [interme'ðjarjo, a] *adj* (*mediador*) mediating ♦ *nm/f* intermediary, go-between; (*mediador*) mediator.

intermedio, a [inter'meðjo, a] *adj* intermediate; (*tiempo*) intervening ♦ *nm* interval; (*POL*) recess.

interminable [intermi'naβle] *adj* endless, interminable.

intermitente [intermi'tente] *adj* intermittent ♦ *nm* (*AUTO*) indicator.

internacional [internaθjo'nal] *adj* international.

internado [inter'naðo] *nm* boarding school.

internamiento [interna'mjento] *nm* internment.

internar [inter'nar] *vt* to intern; (*en un manicomio*) to commit; **~se** *vr* (*penetrar*) to penetrate; **~se en** to go into *o* right inside; **~se en un estudio** to study a subject in depth.

internauta [inter'nauta] *nmf* Internet user.

Internet [inter'net] *nm o nf* Internet.

interno, a [in'terno, a] *adj* internal, interior; (*POL etc*) domestic ♦ *nm/f* (*alumno*) boarder.

interpelación [interpela'θjon] *nf* appeal, plea.

interpelar [interpe'lar] *vt* (*rogar*) to implore; (*hablar*) to speak to; (*POL*) to ask for explanations, question formally.

interpondré [interpon'dre] *etc vb V* **interponer**.

interponer [interpo'ner] *vt* to interpose, put in; **~se** *vr* to intervene.

interponga [inter'ponga] *etc vb V* **interponer**.

interposición [interposi'θjon] *nf* insertion.

interpretación [interpreta'θjon] *nf* interpretation; (*MUS, TEAT*) performance; **mala ~** misinterpretation.

interpretar [interpre'tar] *vt* to interpret.

intérprete [in'terprete] *nm/f* (*LING*) interpreter, translator; (*MUS, TEAT*) performer, artist(e).

interpuesto [inter'pwesto], **interpuse** [inter'puse] *etc vb V* **interponer**.

interrogación [interroɤa'θjon] *nf* interrogation; (*LING*: *tb*: **signo de ~**) question mark; (*TELEC*) polling.

interrogante [interro'ɤante] *adj* questioning ♦ *nm* question mark; (*fig*) question mark, query.

interrogar [interro'ɤar] *vt* to interrogate, question.

interrogatorio [interroɤa'torjo] *nm* interrogation; (*MIL*) debriefing; (*JUR*) examination.

interrogue [inte'rroɤe] *etc vb V* **interrogar**.

interrumpir [interrum'pir] *vt* to interrupt; (*vacaciones*) to cut short; (*servicio*) to cut off; (*tráfico*) to block.

interrupción [interrup'θjon] *nf* interruption.

interruptor [interrup'tor] *nm* (*ELEC*) switch.
intersección [intersek'θjon] *nf* intersection; (*AUTO*) junction.
interurbano, a [interur'ßano, a] *adj* inter city; (*TELEC*) long-distance.
intervalo [inter'ßalo] *nm* interval; (*descanso*) break; **a ~s** at intervals, every now and then.
intervención [interßen'θjon] *nf* supervision; (*COM*) audit(ing); (*MED*) operation; (*TELEC*) tapping; (*participación*) intervention; **~ quirúrgica** surgical operation; **la política de no ~** the policy of non-intervention.
intervencionista [interßenθjo'nista] *adj*: **no ~** (*COM*) laissez-faire.
intervendré [interßen'dre] *etc*, **intervenga** [inter'ßenga] *etc vb V* **intervenir**.
intervenir [interße'nir] *vt* (*controlar*) to control, supervise; (*COM*) to audit; (*MED*) to operate on; (*TELEC*) to tap ♦ *vi* (*participar*) to take part, participate; (*mediar*) to intervene.
interventor, a [interßen'tor, a] *nm/f* inspector; (*COM*) auditor.
interviniendo [interßi'njendo] *etc vb V* **intervenir**.
interviú [inter'ßju] *nf* interview.
intestino [intes'tino] *nm* intestine.
inti ['inti] *nm monetary unit of Peru.*
intimar [inti'mar] *vt* to intimate, announce; (*mandar*) to order ♦ *vi*, **~se** *vr* to become friendly.
intimidad [intimi'ðað] *nf* intimacy; (*familiaridad*) familiarity; (*vida privada*) private life; (*JUR*) privacy.
intimidar [intimi'ðar] *vt* to intimidate, scare.
íntimo, a ['intimo, a] *adj* intimate; (*pensamientos*) innermost; (*vida*) personal, private; **una boda íntima** a quiet wedding.
intolerable [intole'raßle] *adj* intolerable, unbearable.
intolerancia [intole'ranθja] *nf* intolerance.
intoxicación [intoksika'θjon] *nf* poisoning; **~ alimenticia** food poisoning.
intraducible [intraðu'θißle] *adj* untranslatable.
intranet [intra'net] *nf* intranet.
intranquilice [intranki'liθe] *etc vb V* **intranquilizarse**.
intranquilizarse [intrankili'θarse] *vr* to get worried *o* anxious.
intranquilo, a [intran'kilo, a] *adj* worried.
intranscendente [intransθen'dente] *adj* unimportant.
intransferible [intransfe'rißle] *adj* not transferable.
intransigente [intransi'xente] *adj* intransigent.
intransitable [intransi'taßle] *adj* impassable.
intransitivo, a [intransi'tißo, a] *adj* intransitive.
intratable [intra'taßle] *adj* (*problema*) intractable; (*dificultad*) awkward; (*individuo*) unsociable.
intrepidez [intrepi'ðeθ] *nf* courage, bravery.
intrépido, a [in'trepiðo, a] *adj* intrepid, fearless.
intriga [in'triɣa] *nf* intrigue; (*plan*) plot.
intrigar [intri'ɣar] *vt, vi* to intrigue.
intrigue [in'triɣe] *etc vb V* **intrigar**.
intrincado, a [intrin'kaðo, a] *adj* intricate.
intrínseco, a [in'trinseko, a] *adj* intrinsic.
introducción [introðuk'θjon] *nf* introduction; (*de libro*) foreword; (*INFORM*) input.
introducir [introðu'θir] *vt* (*gen*) to introduce; (*moneda*) to insert; (*INFORM*) to input, enter.
introduje [intro'ðuxe] *etc*, **introduzca** [intro'ðuθka] *etc vb V* **introducir**.
intromisión [intromi'sjon] *nf* interference, meddling.
introvertido, a [introßer'tiðo, a] *adj, nm/f* introvert.
intruso, a [in'truso, a] *adj* intrusive ♦ *nm/f* intruder.
intuición [intwi'θjon] *nf* intuition.
intuir [intu'ir] *vt* to know by intuition, intuit.
intuyendo [intu'jendo] *etc vb V* **intuir**.
inundación [inunda'θjon] *nf* flood(ing).
inundar [inun'dar] *vt* to flood; (*fig*) to swamp, inundate.
inusitado, a [inusi'taðo, a] *adj* unusual.
inútil [i'nutil] *adj* useless; (*esfuerzo*) vain, fruitless.
inutilice [inuti'liθe] *etc vb V* **inutilizar**.
inutilidad [inutili'ðað] *nf* uselessness.
inutilizar [inutili'θar] *vt* to make unusable, put out of action; (*incapacitar*) to disable; **~se** *vr* to become useless.
invadir [imba'ðir] *vt* to invade.
invalidar [imbali'ðar] *vt* to invalidate.
invalidez [imbali'ðeθ] *nf* (*MED*) disablement; (*JUR*) invalidity.
inválido, a [im'baliðo, a] *adj* invalid; (*JUR*) null and void ♦ *nm/f* invalid.
invariable [imba'rjable] *adj* invariable.
invasión [imba'sjon] *nf* invasion.
invasor, a [imba'sor, a] *adj* invading ♦ *nm/f* invader.

invencible [imben'θiβle] *adj* invincible; (*timidez, miedo*) unsurmountable.
invención [imben'θjon] *nf* invention.
inventar [imben'tar] *vt* to invent.
inventario [imben'tarjo] *nm* inventory; (*COM*) stocktaking.
inventiva [imben'tiβa] *nf* inventiveness.
invento [im'bento] *nm* invention; (*fig*) brainchild; (*pey*) silly idea.
inventor, a [imben'tor, a] *nm/f* inventor.
invernadero [imberna'ðero] *nm* greenhouse.
invernal [imber'nal] *adj* wintry, winter *cpd*.
invernar [imber'nar] *vi* (*ZOOL*) to hibernate.
inverosímil [imbero'simil] *adj* implausible.
inversión [imber'sjon] *nf* (*COM*) investment; ~ **de capitales** capital investment; **inversiones extranjeras** foreign investment *sg*.
inverso, a [im'berso, a] *adj* inverse, opposite; **en el orden** ~ in reverse order; **a la inversa** inversely, the other way round.
inversor, a [imber'sor, a] *nm/f* (*COM*) investor.
invertebrado, a [imberte'βraðo, a] *adj*, *nm* invertebrate.
invertido, a [imber'tiðo, a] *adj* inverted; (*al revés*) reversed; (*homosexual*) homosexual ♦ *nm/f* homosexual.
invertir [imber'tir] *vt* (*COM*) to invest; (*volcar*) to turn upside down; (*tiempo etc*) to spend.
investigación [imbestiɣa'θjon] *nf* investigation; (*indagación*) inquiry; (*UNIV*) research; ~ **y desarrollo** (*COM*) research and development (R & D); ~ **de los medios de publicidad** media research; ~ **del mercado** market research.
investigador, a [imbestiɣa'ðor, a] *nm/f* investigator; (*UNIV*) research fellow.
investigar [imbesti'ɣar] *vt* to investigate; (*estudiar*) to do research into.
investigue [imbes'tiɣe] *etc vb V* **investigar**.
investir [imbes'tir] *vt*: ~ **a algn con algo** to confer sth on sb; **fue investido Doctor Honoris Causa** he was awarded an honorary doctorate.
invicto, a [im'bikto, a] *adj* unconquered.
invidente [imbi'ðente] *adj* sightless ♦ *nm/f* blind person; **los** ~**s** the sightless.
invierno [im'bjerno] *nm* winter.
invierta [im'bjerta] *etc vb V* **invertir**.
inviolabilidad [imbjolaβili'ðað] *nf* inviolability; ~ **parlamentaria** parliamentary immunity.
invirtiendo [imbir'tjendo] *etc vb V* **invertir**.
invisible [imbi'siβle] *adj* invisible; **exportaciones/importaciones** ~**s** invisible exports/imports.
invitación [imbita'θjon] *nf* invitation.
invitado, a [imbi'taðo, a] *nm/f* guest.
invitar [imbi'tar] *vt* to invite; (*incitar*) to entice; ~ **a algn a hacer algo** to invite sb to do sth; ~ **a algo** to pay for sth; **nos invitó a cenar fuera** she took us out for dinner; **invito yo** it's on me.
in vitro [im'bitro] *adv* in vitro.
invocar [imbo'kar] *vt* to invoke, call on; (*INFORM*) to call.
involucrar [imbolu'krar] *vt*: ~ **algo en un discurso** to bring something irrelevant into a discussion; ~ **a algn en algo** to involve sb in sth; ~**se** *vr* (*interesarse*) to get involved.
involuntario, a [imbolun'tarjo, a] *adj* involuntary; (*ofensa etc*) unintentional.
invoque [im'boke] *etc vb V* **invocar**.
inyección [injek'θjon] *nf* injection.
inyectar [injek'tar] *vt* to inject.
ión [i'on] *nm* ion.
IPC *nm abr* (*ESP*: = *índice de precios al consumo*) CPI.
IPM *nm abr* (= *índice de precios al por menor*) RPI.

PALABRA CLAVE

ir [ir] *vi* **1** to go; (*a pie*) to walk; (*viajar*) to travel; ~ **caminando** to walk; **fui en tren** I went *o* travelled by train; **voy a la calle** I'm going out; ~ **en coche/en bicicleta** to drive/cycle; ~ **a pie** to walk, go on foot; ~ **de pesca** to go fishing; **¡(ahora) voy!** (I'm just) coming!
2: ~ **(a) por**: ~ **(a) por el médico** to fetch the doctor
3 (*progresar*: *persona, cosa*) to go; **el trabajo va muy bien** work is going very well; **¿cómo te va?** how are things going?; **me va muy bien** I'm getting on very well; **le fue fatal** it went awfully badly for him
4 (*funcionar*): **el coche no va muy bien** the car isn't running very well
5 (*sentar*): **me va estupendamente** (*ropa, color*) it suits me really well; (*medicamento*) it works really well for me; ~ **bien con algo** to go well with sth
6 (*aspecto*): **iba muy bien vestido** he was very well dressed; ~ **con zapatos negros** to wear black shoes
7 (*locuciones*): **¿vino? – ¡que va!** did he come? – of course not!; **vamos, no llores** come on, don't cry; **¡vaya coche!** (*admiración*) what a car!, that's some

car!; (*desprecio*) that's a terrible car!; **¡vaya!** (*regular*) so so; (*desagrado*) come on!; **¡vamos!** come on!; **¡que le vaya bien!** (*adiós*) take care!
8: **no vaya a ser: tienes que correr, no vaya a ser que pierdas el tren** you'll have to run so as not to miss the train
9: **no me** *etc* **va ni me viene** I *etc* don't care
♦ *vb aux* **1**: ~ **a: voy/iba a hacerlo hoy** I am/was going to do it today
2 (*+gerundio*): **iba anocheciendo** it was getting dark; **todo se me iba aclarando** everything was gradually becoming clearer to me
3 (*+pp = pasivo*): **van vendidos 300 ejemplares** 300 copies have been sold so far
♦ **~se** *vr* **1**: **¿por dónde se va al zoológico?** which is the way to the zoo?
2 (*marcharse*) to leave; **ya se habrán ido** they must already have left *o* gone; **¡vámonos!**, (*AM*) **¡nos fuimos!** let's go!; **¡vete!** go away!; **¡vete a saber!** your guess is as good as mine!, who knows!

ira ['ira] *nf* anger, rage.
iracundo, a [ira'kundo, a] *adj* irascible.
Irak [i'rak] *nm* = **Iraq**.
Irán [i'ran] *nm* Iran.
iraní [ira'ni] *adj, nm/f* Iranian.
Iraq [i'rak] *nm* Iraq.
iraquí [ira'ki] *adj, nm/f* Iraqui.
irascible [iras'θiβle] *adj* irascible.
irguiendo [ir'ɣjendo] *etc vb V* **erguir**.
iris ['iris] *nm inv* (*arco* ~) rainbow; (*ANAT*) iris.
Irlanda [ir'landa] *nf* Ireland; ~ **del Norte** Northern Ireland, Ulster.
irlandés, esa [irlan'des, esa] *adj* Irish ♦ *nm/f* Irishman/woman ♦ *nm* (*LING*) Gaelic, Irish; **los irlandeses** *npl* the Irish.
ironía [iro'nia] *nf* irony.
irónico, a [i'roniko, a] *adj* ironic(al).
IRPF *nm abr* (*ESP*) = *impuesto sobre la renta de las personas físicas*.
irracional [irraθjo'nal] *adj* irrational.
irrazonable [irraθo'naβle] *adj* unreasonable.
irreal [irre'al] *adj* unreal.
irrealizable [irreali'θaβle] *adj* (*gen*) unrealizable; (*meta*) unrealistic.
irrebatible [irreβa'tiβle] *adj* irrefutable.
irreconocible [irrekono'θiβle] *adj* unrecognizable.
irrecuperable [irrekupe'raβle] *adj* irrecoverable, irretrievable.
irreembolsable [irreembol'saβle] *adj* (*COM*) non-returnable.
irreflexión [irreflek'sjon] *nf* thoughtlessness; (*ímpetu*) rashness.
irregular [irreɣu'lar] *adj* irregular; (*situación*) abnormal, anomalous; **margen izquierdo/derecho** ~ (*texto*) ragged left/right (margin).
irregularidad [irreɣulari'ðað] *nf* irregularity.
irremediable [irreme'ðjaβle] *adj* irremediable; (*vicio*) incurable.
irreprochable [irrepro'tʃaβle] *adj* irreproachable.
irresistible [irresis'tiβle] *adj* irresistible.
irresoluto, a [irreso'luto, a] *adj* irresolute, hesitant; (*sin resolver*) unresolved.
irrespetuoso, a [irrespe'twoso, a] *adj* disrespectful.
irresponsable [irrespon'saβle] *adj* irresponsible.
irreverente [irreβe'rente] *adj* disrespectful.
irreversible [irreβer'siβle] *adj* irreversible.
irrevocable [irreβo'kaβle] *adj* irrevocable.
irrigar [irri'ɣar] *vt* to irrigate.
irrigue [i'rriɣe] *etc vb V* **irrigar**.
irrisorio, a [irri'sorjo, a] *adj* derisory, ridiculous; (*precio*) bargain *cpd*.
irritación [irrita'θjon] *nf* irritation.
irritar [irri'tar] *vt* to irritate, annoy; **~se** *vr* to get angry, lose one's temper.
irrompible [irrom'piβle] *adj* unbreakable.
irrumpir [irrum'pir] *vi*: ~ **en** to burst *o* rush into.
irrupción [irrup'θjon] *nf* irruption; (*invasión*) invasion.
IRTP *nm abr* (*ESP*: = *impuesto sobre el rendimiento del trabajo personal*) ≈ PAYE.
isla ['isla] *nf* (*GEO*) island; **I~s Británicas** British Isles; **I~s Filipinas/Malvinas/Canarias** Philippines/Falklands/Canaries.
Islam [is'lam] *nm* Islam.
islámico, a [is'lamiko, a] *adj* Islamic.
islandés, esa [islan'des, esa] *adj* Icelandic ♦ *nm/f* Icelander ♦ *nm* (*LING*) Icelandic.
Islandia [is'landja] *nf* Iceland.
isleño, a [is'leɲo, a] *adj* island *cpd* ♦ *nm/f* islander.
islote [is'lote] *nm* small island.
isotónico, a [iso'toniko, a] *adj* isotonic.
isótopo [i'sotopo] *nm* isotope.
Israel [isra'el] *nm* Israel.
israelí [israe'li] *adj, nm/f* Israeli.
istmo ['istmo] *nm* isthmus; **el I~ de Panamá** the Isthmus of Panama.
Italia [i'talja] *nf* Italy.
italiano, a [ita'ljano, a] *adj, nm/f* Italian

♦ *nm* (*LING*) Italian.
itinerante [itine'rante] *adj* travelling; (*embajador*) roving.
itinerario [itine'rarjo] *nm* itinerary, route.
ITV *nf abr* (= *Inspección Técnica de Vehículos*) ≈ MOT (test) (*BRIT*).
IVA ['iβa] *nm abr* (*ESP COM*: = *Impuesto sobre el Valor Añadido*) VAT.
IVP *nm abr* = *Instituto Venezolano de Petroquímica*.
izada [i'saða] *nf* (*AM*) lifting, raising.
izar [i'θar] *vt* to hoist.
izda, izq.ª *abr* = **izquierda**.
izdo, izq, izq.º *abr* = **izquierdo**.
izquierda [iθ'kjerða] *nf V* **izquierdo**.
izquierdista [iθkjer'ðista] *adj* leftist, left-wing ♦ *nm/f* left-winger, leftist.
izquierdo, a [iθ'kjerðo, a] *adj* left ♦ *nf* left; (*POL*) left (wing); **a la ~** on the left; **es un cero a la ~** (*fam*) he is a nonentity; **conducción por la ~** left-hand drive.

Jj

J, j ['xota] *nf* (*letra*) J, j; **J de José** J for Jack (*BRIT*) *o* Jig (*US*).
jabalí [xaβa'li] *nm* wild boar.
jabalina [xaβa'lina] *nf* javelin.
jabato, a [xa'βato, a] *adj* brave, bold ♦ *nm* young wild boar.
jabón [xa'βon] *nm* soap; (*fam*: *adulación*) flattery; **~ de afeitar** shaving soap; **~ de tocador** toilet soap; **dar ~ a algn** to soft-soap sb.
jabonar [xaβo'nar] *vt* to soap.
jaca ['xaka] *nf* pony.
jacinto [xa'θinto] *nm* hyacinth.
jactancia [xak'tanθja] *nf* boasting, boastfulness.
jactarse [xak'tarse] *vr*: **~ (de)** to boast *o* brag (about *o* of).
jadear [xaðe'ar] *vi* to pant, gasp for breath.
jadeo [xa'ðeo] *nm* panting, gasping.
jaguar [xa'ɣwar] *nm* jaguar.
jalar [xa'lar] *vt* (*AM*) to pull.
jalbegue [xal'βeɣe] *nm* (*pintura*) whitewash.
jalea [xa'lea] *nf* jelly.
jaleo [xa'leo] *nm* racket, uproar; **armar un ~** to kick up a racket.
jalón [xa'lon] *nm* (*AM*) tug.
jalonar [xalo'nar] *vt* to stake out; (*fig*) to mark.
Jamaica [xa'maika] *nf* Jamaica.
jamaicano, a [xamai'kano, a] *adj*, *nm/f* Jamaican.
jamás [xa'mas] *adv* never, not ... ever; (*interrogativo*) ever; **¿~ se vio tal cosa?** did you ever see such a thing?
jamón [xa'mon] *nm* ham; **~ dulce/serrano** boiled/cured ham.
Japón [xa'pon] *nm*: **el ~** Japan.
japonés, esa [xapo'nes, esa] *adj*, *nm/f* Japanese ♦ *nm* (*LING*) Japanese.
jaque ['xake] *nm*: **~ mate** checkmate.
jaqueca [xa'keka] *nf* (very bad) headache, migraine.
jarabe [xa'raβe] *nm* syrup; **~ para la tos** cough syrup *o* mixture.
jarana [xa'rana] *nf* (*juerga*) spree (*fam*); **andar/ir de ~** to be/go on a spree.
jarcia ['xarθja] *nf* (*NAUT*) ropes *pl*, rigging.
jardín [xar'ðin] *nm* garden; **~ botánico** botanical garden; **~ de (la) infancia** (*ESP*) *o* **de niños** (*AM*) *o* **infantil** (*AM*) kindergarten, nursery school.
jardinería [xarðine'ria] *nf* gardening.
jardinero, a [xarði'nero, a] *nm/f* gardener.
jarra ['xarra] *nf* jar; (*jarro*) jug; (*de leche*) churn; (*de cerveza*) mug; **de** *o* **en ~s** with arms akimbo.
jarro ['xarro] *nm* jug.
jarrón [xa'rron] *nm* vase; (*ARQUEOLOGÍA*) urn.
jaspeado, a [xaspe'ado, a] *adj* mottled, speckled.
jaula ['xaula] *nf* cage; (*embalaje*) crate.
jauría [xau'ria] *nf* pack of hounds.
jazmín [xaθ'min] *nm* jasmine.
J. C. *abr* = **Jesucristo**.
jeep, *pl* **jeeps** ® [jip, jips] *nm* jeep ®.
jefa ['xefa] *nf V* **jefe**.
jefatura [xefa'tura] *nf* (*liderato*) leadership; (*sede*) central office; **J~ de la aviación civil** ≈ Civil Aviation Authority; **~ de policía** police headquarters *sg*.
jefazo [xe'faθo] *nm* bigwig.
jefe, a ['xefe, a] *nm/f* (*gen*) chief, head; (*patrón*) boss; (*POL*) leader; (*COM*) manager(ess); **~ de camareros** head waiter; **~ de cocina** chef; **~ ejecutivo** (*COM*) chief executive; **~ de estación** stationmaster; **~ de estado** head of state; **~ de oficina** (*COM*) office manager; **~ de producción** (*COM*) production manager; **~ supremo** commander-in-chief; **ser el ~** (*fig*) to be the boss.
JEN [xen] *nf abr* (*ESP*) = *Junta de Energía*

Nuclear.
jengibre [xen'xißre] *nm* ginger.
jeque ['xeke] *nm* sheik(h).
jerarquía [xerar'kia] *nf* (*orden*) hierarchy; (*rango*) rank.
jerárquico, a [xe'rarkiko, a] *adj* hierarchic(al).
jerez [xe'reθ] *nm* sherry; **J~ de la Frontera** Jerez.
jerezano, a [xere'θano, a] *adj* of *o* from Jerez ♦ *nm/f* native *o* inhabitant of Jerez.
jerga ['xerɣa] *nf* (*tela*) coarse cloth; (*lenguaje*) jargon; ~ **informática** computer jargon.
jerigonza [xeri'ɣonθa] *nf* (*jerga*) jargon, slang; (*galimatías*) nonsense, gibberish.
jeringa [xe'ringa] *nf* syringe; (*AM*) annoyance, bother; ~ **de engrase** grease gun.
jeringar [xerin'gar] *vt* to annoy, bother.
jeringue [xe'ringe] *etc vb V* **jeringar.**
jeringuilla [xerin'guiʎa] *nf* hypodermic (syringe).
jeroglífico [xero'ɣlifiko] *nm* hieroglyphic.
jersey [xer'sei], *pl* **jerseys** *nm* jersey, pullover, jumper.
Jerusalén [xerusa'len] *n* Jerusalem.
Jesucristo [xesu'kristo] *nm* Jesus Christ.
jesuita [xe'swita] *adj, nm* Jesuit.
Jesús [xe'sus] *nm* Jesus; **¡~!** good heavens!; (*al estornudar*) bless you!
jet, *pl* **jets** [jet, jet] *nm* jet (plane) ♦ *nf*: **la ~** the jet set.
jeta ['xeta] *nf* (*ZOOL*) snout; (*fam*: *cara*) mug; **¡que ~ tienes!** (*fam*: *insolencia*) you've got a nerve!
jíbaro, a ['xißaro, a] *adj, nm/f* Jibaro (Indian).
jícara ['xikara] *nf* small cup.
jiennense [xjen'nense] *adj* of *o* from Jaén ♦ *nm/f* native *o* inhabitant of Jaén.
jilguero [xil'ɣero] *nm* goldfinch.
jinete, a [xi'nete, a] *nm/f* horseman/woman.
jipijapa [xipi'xapa] *nm* (*AM*) straw hat.
jira ['xira] *nf* (*de tela*) strip; (*excursión*) picnic.
jirafa [xi'rafa] *nf* giraffe.
jirón [xi'ron] *nm* rag, shred.
JJ.OO. *nmpl abr* = **Juegos Olímpicos.**
jocosidad [xokosi'ðað] *nf* humour; (*chiste*) joke.
jocoso, a [xo'koso, a] *adj* humorous, jocular.
joder [xo'ðer] (*fam!*) *vt* to fuck (*!*), screw (*!*); (*fig*: *fastidiar*) to piss off (*!*), bug; **~se** *vr* (*fracasar*) to fail; **¡~!** damn it!; **se jodió todo** everything was ruined.
jodido, a [xo'ðiðo, a] *adj* (*fam!*: *difícil*) awkward; **estoy ~** I'm knackered.
jofaina [xo'faina] *nf* washbasin.
jojoba [xo'xoßa] *nf* jojoba.
jolgorio [xol'ɣorjo] *nm* (*juerga*) fun, revelry.
jonrón [xon'ron] *nm* home run.
Jordania [xor'ðanja] *nf* Jordan.
jornada [xor'naða] *nf* (*viaje de un día*) day's journey; (*camino o viaje entero*) journey; (*día de trabajo*) working day; ~ **de 8 horas** 8-hour day; **(trabajar a) ~ partida** (to work a) split shift.
jornal [xor'nal] *nm* (day's) wage.
jornalero, a [xorna'lero, a] *nm/f* (day) labourer.
joroba [xo'roßa] *nf* hump.
jorobado, a [xoro'ßaðo, a] *adj* hunchbacked ♦ *nm/f* hunchback.
jorobar [xoro'ßar] *vt* to annoy, pester, bother; **~se** *vr* to get cross; **¡hay que ~se!** to hell with it!; **esto me joroba** I'm fed up with this!
jota ['xota] *nf* letter J; (*danza*) *Aragonese dance*; (*fam*) jot, iota; **no saber ni ~** to have no idea.
joven ['xoßen] *adj* young ♦ *nm* young man, youth ♦ *nf* young woman, girl.
jovencito, a [xoßen'θito, a] *nm/f* youngster.
jovial [xo'ßjal] *adj* cheerful, jolly.
jovialidad [xoßjali'ðað] *nf* cheerfulness.
joya ['xoja] *nf* jewel, gem; (*fig*: *persona*) gem; **~s de fantasía** imitation jewellery *sg*.
joyería [xoje'ria] *nf* (*joyas*) jewellery; (*tienda*) jeweller's (shop).
joyero [xo'jero] *nm* (*persona*) jeweller; (*caja*) jewel case.
Juan [xwan] *nm*: **Noche de San ~** *see boxed note.*

NOCHE DE SAN JUAN

The **Noche de San Juan** *(evening of the Feast of Saint John) on 24 June coincides with the summer solstice; the "fiesta" has in fact replaced other more ancient pagan festivals. Traditionally fire plays a major part in these festivities, which can last for days in certain areas. Celebrations, fireworks and dancing centre around "hogueras" (bonfires) in towns and villages across Spain.*

juanete [xwa'nete] *nm* (*del pie*) bunion.
jubilación [xußila'θjon] *nf* (*retiro*) retirement.
jubilado, a [xußi'lado, a] *adj* retired ♦ *nm/f* retired person, pensioner (*BRIT*), senior citizen.
jubilar [xußi'lar] *vt* to pension off, retire;

(*fam*) to discard; ~**se** *vr* to retire.
jubileo [xuβi'leo] *nm* jubilee.
júbilo ['xuβilo] *nm* joy, rejoicing.
jubiloso, a [xuβi'loso, a] *adj* jubilant.
judaísmo [xuða'ismo] *nm* Judaism.
judía [xu'ðia] *nf V* **judío**.
judicatura [xuðika'tura] *nf* (*cargo de juez*) office of judge; (*cuerpo de jueces*) judiciary.
judicial [xuði'θjal] *adj* judicial.
judío, a [xu'ðio, a] *adj* Jewish ♦ *nm* Jew ♦ *nf* Jewess, Jewish woman; (*CULIN*) bean; **judía blanca** haricot bean; **judía verde** French *o* string bean.
juego ['xweɣo] *etc vb V* **jugar** ♦ *nm* (*gen*) play; (*pasatiempo, partido*) game; (*en casino*) gambling; (*deporte*) sport; (*conjunto*) set; (*herramientas*) kit; ~ **de azar** game of chance; ~ **de café** coffee set; ~ **de caracteres** (*INFORM*) font; ~ **limpio/sucio** fair/foul *o* dirty play; **J~s Olímpicos** Olympic Games; ~ **de programas** (*INFORM*) suite of programs; **fuera de** ~ (*DEPORTE*: *persona*) offside; (: *pelota*) out of play; **por** ~ in fun, for fun.
juegue ['xweɣe] *etc vb V* **jugar**.
juerga ['xwerɣa] *nf* binge; (*fiesta*) party; **ir de** ~ to go out on a binge.
juerguista [xwer'ɣista] *nm/f* reveller.
jueves ['xweβes] *nm inv* Thursday.
juez [xweθ] *nm/f* (*f tb*: **jueza**) judge; (*TENIS*) umpire; ~ **de línea** linesman; ~ **de paz** justice of the peace; ~ **de salida** starter.
jugada [xu'ɣaða] *nf* play; **buena** ~ good move (*o* shot *o* stroke) *etc*.
jugador, a [xuɣa'ðor, a] *nm/f* player; (*en casino*) gambler.
jugar [xu'ɣar] *vt* to play; (*en casino*) to gamble; (*apostar*) to bet ♦ *vi* to play; to gamble; (*COM*) to speculate; ~**se** *vr* to gamble (away); ~**se el todo por el todo** to stake one's all, go for bust; **¿quién juega?** whose move is it?; **¡me la han jugado!** (*fam*) I've been had!
jugarreta [xuɣa'rreta] *nf* (*mala jugada*) bad move; (*trampa*) dirty trick; **hacer una** ~ **a algn** to play a dirty trick on sb.
juglar [xu'ɣlar] *nm* minstrel.
jugo ['xuɣo] *nm* (*BOT, de fruta*) juice; (*fig*) essence, substance; ~ **de naranja** (*esp AM*) orange juice.
jugoso, a [xu'ɣoso, a] *adj* juicy; (*fig*) substantial, important.
jugué [xu'ɣe], **juguemos** [xu'ɣemos] *etc vb V* **jugar**.
juguete [xu'ɣete] *nm* toy.
juguetear [xuɣete'ar] *vi* to play.
juguetería [xuɣete'ria] *nf* toyshop.
juguetón, ona [xuɣe'ton, ona] *adj* playful.
juicio ['xwiθjo] *nm* judgement; (*sana razón*) sanity, reason; (*opinión*) opinion; (*JUR*: *proceso*) trial; **estar fuera de** ~ to be out of one's mind; **a mi** ~ in my opinion.
juicioso, a [xwi'θjoso, a] *adj* wise, sensible.
JUJEM [xu'xem] *nf abr* (*ESP MIL*) = *Junta de Jefes del Estado Mayor.*
jul. *abr* (= *julio*) Jul.
julio ['xuljo] *nm* July.
jumento, a [xu'mento, a] *nm/f* donkey.
jun. *abr* (= *junio*) Jun.
junco ['xunko] *nm* rush, reed.
jungla ['xungla] *nf* jungle.
junio ['xunjo] *nm* June.
junta ['xunta] *nf V* **junto**.
juntar [xun'tar] *vt* to join, unite; (*maquinaria*) to assemble, put together; (*dinero*) to collect; ~**se** *vr* to join, meet; (*reunirse*: *personas*) to meet, assemble; (*arrimarse*) to approach, draw closer; ~**se con algn** to join sb.
junto, a ['xunto, a] *adj* joined; (*unido*) united; (*anexo*) near, close; (*contiguo, próximo*) next, adjacent ♦ *nf* (*asamblea*) meeting, assembly; (*comité, consejo*) board, council, committee; (*MIL, POL*) junta; (*articulación*) joint ♦ *adv*: **todo** ~ all at once ♦ *prep*: ~ **a** near (to), next to; ~**s** together; **junta constitutiva** (*COM*) statutory meeting; **junta directiva** (*COM*) board of management; **junta general extraordinaria** (*COM*) extraordinary general meeting.
juntura [xun'tura] *nf* (*punto de unión*) join, junction; (*articulación*) joint.
jura ['xura] *nf* oath, pledge; ~ **de bandera** (ceremony of taking the) oath of allegiance.
jurado [xu'raðo] *nm* (*JUR*: *individuo*) juror; (: *grupo*) jury; (*de concurso*: *grupo*) panel (of judges); (: *individuo*) member of a panel.
juramentar [xuramen'tar] *vt* to swear in, administer the oath to; ~**se** *vr* to be sworn in, take the oath.
juramento [xura'mento] *nm* oath; (*maldición*) oath, curse; **bajo** ~ on oath; **prestar** ~ to take the oath; **tomar** ~ **a** to swear in, administer the oath to.
jurar [xu'rar] *vt, vi* to swear; ~ **en falso** to commit perjury; **jurárselas a algn** to have it in for sb.
jurídico, a [xu'riðiko, a] *adj* legal, juridical.
jurisdicción [xurisðik'θjon] *nf* (*poder, autoridad*) jurisdiction; (*territorio*)

district.
jurisprudencia [xurispru'ðenθja] *nf* jurisprudence.
jurista [xu'rista] *nm/f* jurist.
justamente [xusta'mente] *adv* justly, fairly; (*precisamente*) just, exactly.
justicia [xus'tiθja] *nf* justice; (*equidad*) fairness, justice; **de ~** deservedly.
justiciero, a [xusti'θjero, a] *adj* just, righteous.
justificable [xustifi'kaβle] *adj* justifiable.
justificación [xustifika'θjon] *nf* justification; ~ **automática** (*INFORM*) automatic justification.
justificado, a [xustifi'kaðo, a] *adj* (*TIP*): **(no)** ~ (un)justified.
justificante [xustifi'kante] *nm* voucher; ~ **médico** sick note.
justificar [xustifi'kar] *vt* (*tb TIP*) to justify; (*probar*) to verify.
justifique [xusti'fike] *etc vb V* **justificar.**
justo, a ['xusto, a] *adj* (*equitativo*) just, fair, right; (*preciso*) exact, correct; (*ajustado*) tight ♦ *adv* (*precisamente*) exactly, precisely; (*apenas a tiempo*) just in time; **¡~!** that's it!, correct!; **llegaste muy ~** you just made it; **vivir muy ~** to be hard up.
juvenil [xuβe'nil] *adj* youthful.
juventud [xuβen'tuð] *nf* (*adolescencia*) youth; (*jóvenes*) young people *pl.*
juzgado [xuθ'ɣaðo] *nm* tribunal; (*JUR*) court.
juzgar [xuθ'ɣar] *vt* to judge; **a ~ por** ... to judge by ..., judging by ...; ~ **mal** to misjudge; **júzguelo usted mismo** see for yourself.

Kk

K, k [ka] *nf* (*letra*) K, k; **K de Kilo** K for King.
K *abr* (= *1.000*) K; (*INFORM*: = *1.024*) K.
Kampuchea [kampu'tʃea] *nf* Kampuchea.
karaoke [kara'oke] *nm* karaoke.
kárate ['karate] *nm*, **karate** [ka'rate] *nm* karate.
KAS *nf abr* (= *Koordinadora Abertzale Sozialista*) *Basque nationalist umbrella group.*
Kazajstán [kaθaxs'tan] *nm* Kazakhstan.
k/c. *abr* (= *kilociclos*) kc.
Kenia ['kenja] *nf* Kenya.
keniata [ke'njata] *adj, nm/f* Kenyan.
kepí, kepis [ke'pi, 'kepis] *nm* (*esp AM*) kepi, military hat.
kerosene [kero'sene] *nm* kerosene.
kg. *abr* (= *kilogramo(s)*) kg.
kilate [ki'late] *nm* = **quilate.**
kilo ['kilo] *nm* kilo.
kilobyte ['kiloβait] *nm* (*INFORM*) kilobyte.
kilogramo [kilo'ɣramo] *nm* kilogramme (*BRIT*), kilogram (*US*).
kilolitro [kilo'litro] *nm* kilolitre (*BRIT*), kiloliter (*US*).
kilometraje [kilome'traxe] *nm* distance in kilometres, ≈ mileage.
kilométrico, a [kilo'metriko, a] *adj* kilometric; (*fam*) very long; **(billete)** ~ (*FERRO*) mileage ticket.
kilómetro [ki'lometro] *nm* kilometre (*BRIT*), kilometer (*US*).
kiloocteto [kilook'teto] *nm* (*INFORM*) kilobyte.
kilovatio [kilo'βatjo] *nm* kilowatt.
kiosco ['kjosko] *nm* = **quiosco.**
Kirguizistán [kirɣiθis'tan] *nm* Kirghizia.
kiwi ['kiwi] *nm* kiwi (fruit).
km *abr* (= *kilómetro(s)*) km.
km/h *abr* (= *kilómetros por hora*) km/h.
knock-out ['nokau], **K.O.** ['kao] *nm* knockout; (*golpe*) knockout blow; **dejar** *o* **poner a algn ~** to knock sb out.
kosovar [koso'βar] *adj* Kosovan.
Kosovo ['kosoβo] *nm* Kosovo.
k.p.h. *abr* (= *kilómetros por hora*) km/h.
k.p.l. *abr* (= *kilómetros por litro*) ≈ m.p.g.
kurdo, a ['kurðo, a] *adj* Kurdish ♦ *nm/f* Kurd ♦ *nm* (*LING*) Kurdish.
kuwaití [kuβai'ti] *adj, nm/f* Kuwaiti.
kv *abr* (= *kilovatio*) kw.
kv/h *abr* (= *kilovatios-hora*) kw-h.

Ll

L, l ['ele] *nf* (*letra*) L, l; **L de Lorenzo** L for Lucy (*BRIT*) *o* Love (*US*).
l. *abr* (= *litro(s)*) l.; (*JUR*) = **ley;** (*LITERATURA*: = *libro*) bk.
L/ *abr* (*COM*) = **letra.**
la [la] *artículo definido fsg* the ♦ *pron* her; (*usted*) you; (*cosa*) it ♦ *nm* (*MUS*) A; **está en ~ cárcel** he's in jail; **~ del sombrero rojo** the woman/girl/one in the red hat.

laberinto [laße'rinto] *nm* labyrinth.
labia ['laßja] *nf* fluency; (*pey*) glibness; **tener mucha ~** to have the gift of the gab.
labial [la'ßjal] *adj* labial.
labio ['laßjo] *nm* lip; (*de vasija etc*) edge, rim; **~ inferior/superior** lower/upper lip.
labor [la'ßor] *nf* labour; (*AGR*) farm work; (*tarea*) job, task; (*COSTURA*) needlework, sewing; (*punto*) knitting; **~ de equipo** teamwork; **~ de ganchillo** crochet.
laborable [laßo'raßle] *adj* (*AGR*) workable; **día ~** working day.
laboral [laßo'ral] *adj* (*accidente, conflictividad*) industrial; (*jornada*) working; (*derecho, relaciones*) labour *cpd*.
laboralista [laßora'lista] *adj*: **abogado ~** labour lawyer.
laborar [laßo'rar] *vi* to work.
laboratorio [laßora'torjo] *nm* laboratory.
laborioso, a [laßo'rjoso, a] *a* (*persona*) hard-working; (*trabajo*) tough.
laborista [laßo'rista] (*BRIT POL*) *adj*: **Partido L~** Labour Party ♦ *nm/f* Labour Party member *o* supporter.
labrado, a [la'ßraðo, a] *adj* worked; (*madera*) carved; (*metal*) wrought ♦ *nm* (*AGR*) cultivated field.
Labrador [laßra'ðor] *nm* Labrador.
labrador, a [laßra'ðor, a] *nm/f* farmer.
labranza [la'ßranθa] *nf* (*AGR*) cultivation.
labrar [la'ßrar] *vt* (*gen*) to work; (*madera etc*) to carve; (*fig*) to cause, bring about.
labriego, a [la'ßrjeɤo, a] *nm/f* peasant.
laca ['laka] *nf* lacquer; (*de pelo*) hairspray; **~ de uñas** nail varnish.
lacayo [la'kajo] *nm* lackey.
lacerar [laθe'rar] *vt* to lacerate.
lacio, a ['laθjo, a] *adj* (*pelo*) lank, straight.
lacón [la'kon] *nm* shoulder of pork.
lacónico, a [la'koniko, a] *adj* laconic.
lacra ['lakra] *nf* (*defecto*) blemish; **~ social** social disgrace.
lacrar [la'krar] *vt* (*cerrar*) to seal (with sealing wax).
lacre ['lakre] *nm* sealing wax.
lacrimógeno, a [lakri'moxeno, a] *adj* (*fig*) sentimental; **gas ~** tear gas.
lacrimoso, a [lakri'moso, a] *adj* tearful.
lactancia [lak'tanθja] *nf* breast-feeding.
lactar [lak'tar] *vt, vi* to suckle, breast-feed.
lácteo, a ['lakteo, a] *adj*: **productos ~s** dairy products.
ladear [laðe'ar] *vt* to tip, tilt ♦ *vi* to tilt; **~se** *vr* to lean; (*DEPORTE*) to swerve; (*AVIAT*) to bank, turn.
ladera [la'ðera] *nf* slope.
ladino, a [la'ðino, a] *adj* cunning.
lado ['laðo] *nm* (*gen*) side; (*fig*) protection; (*MIL*) flank; **~ izquierdo** left(-hand) side; **~ a ~** side by side; **al ~ de** next to, beside; **hacerse a un ~** to stand aside; **poner de ~** to put on its side; **poner a un ~** to put aside; **me da de ~** I don't care; **por un ~ ..., por otro ~ ...** on the one hand ..., on the other (hand), ...; **por todos ~s** on all sides, all round (*BRIT*).
ladrar [la'ðrar] *vi* to bark.
ladrido [la'ðriðo] *nm* bark, barking.
ladrillo [la'ðriʎo] *nm* (*gen*) brick; (*azulejo*) tile.
ladrón, ona [la'ðron, ona] *nm/f* thief.
lagar [la'ɤar] *nm* (wine/oil) press.
lagartija [laɤar'tixa] *nf* (small) lizard, wall lizard.
lagarto [la'ɤarto] *nm* (*ZOOL*) lizard; (*AM*) alligator.
lago ['laɤo] *nm* lake.
Lagos ['laɤos] *nm* Lagos.
lágrima ['laɤrima] *nf* tear.
lagrimal [laɤri'mal] *nm* (inner) corner of the eye.
lagrimear [laɤrime'ar] *vi* to weep; (*ojos*) to water.
laguna [la'ɤuna] *nf* (*lago*) lagoon; (*en escrito, conocimientos*) gap.
laico, a ['laiko, a] *adj* lay ♦ *nm/f* layman/woman.
laja ['laxa] *nf* rock.
lamber [lam'ber] *vt* (*AM*) to lick.
lambiscón, ona [lambis'kon, ona] *adj* flattering ♦ *nm/f* flatterer.
lameculos [lame'kulos] *nm/f inv* (*fam*) arselicker (*!*), crawler.
lamentable [lamen'taßle] *adj* lamentable, regrettable; (*miserable*) pitiful.
lamentación [lamenta'θjon] *nf* lamentation; **ahora no sirven lamentaciones** it's no good crying over spilt milk.
lamentar [lamen'tar] *vt* (*sentir*) to regret; (*deplorar*) to lament; **~se** *vr* to lament; **lo lamento mucho** I'm very sorry.
lamento [la'mento] *nm* lament.
lamer [la'mer] *vt* to lick.
lámina ['lamina] *nf* (*plancha delgada*) sheet; (*para estampar, estampa*) plate; (*grabado*) engraving.
laminar [lami'nar] *vt* (*en libro*) to laminate; (*TEC*) to roll.
lámpara ['lampara] *nf* lamp; **~ de alcohol/gas** spirit/gas lamp; **~ de pie** standard lamp.
lamparilla [lampa'riʎa] *nf* nightlight.
lamparón [lampa'ron] *nm* (*MED*) scrofula; (*mancha*) (large) grease spot.

lampiño, a [lam'piɲo, a] *adj* (*sin pelo*) hairless.
lana ['lana] *nf* wool; (*tela*) woollen (*BRIT*) *o* woolen (*US*) cloth; (*AM fam: dinero*) dough; **(hecho) de ~** wool *cpd*.
lance ['lanθe] *etc vb V* **lanzar** ♦ *nm* (*golpe*) stroke; (*suceso*) event, incident.
lanceta [lan'seta] *nf* (*AM*) sting.
lancha ['lantʃa] *nf* launch; **~ motora** motorboat; **~ de pesca** fishing boat; **~ salvavidas/torpedera** lifeboat/torpedo boat; **~ neumática** rubber dinghy.
lanero, a [la'nero, a] *adj* wool *cpd*.
langosta [lan'gosta] *nf* (*insecto*) locust; (*crustáceo*) lobster (: *de río*) crayfish.
langostino [langos'tino] *nm* prawn; (*de agua dulce*) crayfish.
languidecer [langiðe'θer] *vi* to languish.
languidez [langi'ðeθ] *nf* languor.
languidezca [langi'ðeθka] *etc vb V* **languidecer**.
lánguido, a ['langiðo, a] *adj* (*gen*) languid; (*sin energía*) listless.
lanilla [la'niʎa] *nf* nap; (*tela*) thin flannel cloth.
lanolina [lano'lina] *nf* lanolin(e).
lanudo, a [la'nuðo, a] *adj* woolly, fleecy.
lanza ['lanθa] *nf* (*arma*) lance, spear; **medir ~s** to cross swords.
lanzacohetes [lanθako'etes] *nm inv* rocket launcher.
lanzadera [lanθa'ðera] *nf* shuttle.
lanzado, a [lan'θaðo, a] *adj* (*atrevido*) forward; (*decidido*) determined; **ir ~** (*rápido*) to fly along.
lanzallamas [lanθa'ʎamas] *nm inv* flamethrower.
lanzamiento [lanθa'mjento] *nm* (*gen*) throwing; (*NAUT, COM*) launch, launching; **~ de pesos** putting the shot.
lanzar [lan'θar] *vt* (*gen*) to throw; (*con violencia*) to fling; (*DEPORTE: pelota*) to bowl; (: *US*) to pitch; (*NAUT, COM*) to launch; (*JUR*) to evict; (*grito*) to give, utter; **~se** *vr* to throw o.s.; (*fig*) to take the plunge; **~se a** (*fig*) to embark upon.
Lanzarote [lanθa'rote] *nm* Lanzarote.
lanzatorpedos [lanθator'peðos] *nm inv* torpedo tube.
lapa ['lapa] *nf* limpet.
La Paz *nf* La Paz.
lapicero [lapi'θero] *nm* pencil; (*AM*) propelling (*BRIT*) *o* mechanical (*US*) pencil; (: *bolígrafo*) Biro ®.
lápida ['lapiða] *nf* stone; **~ conmemorativa** memorial stone; **~ mortuoria** headstone.
lapidar [lapi'ðar] *vt* to stone; (*TEC*) to polish, lap.
lapidario, a [lapi'ðarjo, a] *adj, nm* lapidary.
lápiz ['lapiθ] *nm* pencil; **~ de color** coloured pencil; **~ de labios** lipstick; **~ óptico** *o* **luminoso** light pen.
lapón, ona [la'pon, ona] *adj* Lapp ♦ *nm/f* Laplander, Lapp ♦ *nm* (*LING*) Lapp.
Laponia [la'ponja] *nf* Lapland.
lapso ['lapso] *nm* lapse; (*error*) error; **~ de tiempo** interval of time.
lapsus ['lapsus] *nm inv* error, mistake.
LAR [lar] *nf abr* (*ESP JUR*) = *Ley de Arrendamientos Rústicos*.
largamente [larɣa'mente] *adv* for a long time; (*relatar*) at length.
largar [lar'ɣar] *vt* (*soltar*) to release; (*aflojar*) to loosen; (*lanzar*) to launch; (*fam*) to let fly; (*velas*) to unfurl; (*AM*) to throw; **~se** *vr* (*fam*) to beat it; **~se a** (*AM*) to start to.
largo, a ['larɣo, a] *adj* (*longitud*) long; (*tiempo*) lengthy; (*persona: alta*) tall; (: *fig*) generous ♦ *nm* length; (*MUS*) largo; **dos años ~s** two long years; **a ~ plazo** in the long term; **tiene 9 metros de ~** it is 9 metres long; **a lo ~** (*posición*) lengthways; **a lo ~ de** along; (*tiempo*) all through, throughout; **a la larga** in the long run; **me dio largas con una promesa** she put me off with a promise; **¡~ de aquí!** (*fam*) clear off!
largometraje [larɣome'traxe] *nm* full-length *o* feature film.
largue ['larɣe] *etc vb V* **largar**.
larguero [lar'ɣero] *nm* (*ARQ*) main beam, chief support; (*de puerta*) jamb; (*DEPORTE*) crossbar; (*en cama*) bolster.
largueza [lar'ɣeθa] *nf* generosity.
larguirucho, a [larɣi'rutʃo, a] *adj* lanky, gangling.
larguísimo, a [lar'ɣisimo, a] *adj superlativo de* **largo**.
largura [lar'ɣura] *nf* length.
laringe [la'rinxe] *nf* larynx.
laringitis [larin'xitis] *nf* laryngitis.
larva ['larβa] *nf* larva.
las [las] *artículo definido fpl* the ♦ *pron* them; **~ que cantan** the ones/women/girls who sing.
lasaña [la'saɲa] *nf* lasagne, lasagna.
lasca ['laska] *nf* chip of stone.
lascivia [las'θiβja] *nf* lewdness; (*lujuria*) lust; (*fig*) playfulness.
lascivo, a [las'θiβo, a] *adj* lewd.
láser ['laser] *nm* laser.
Las Palmas *nf* Las Palmas.
lástima ['lastima] *nf* (*pena*) pity; **dar ~** to be pitiful; **es una ~ que** it's a pity that;

¡qué ~! what a pity!; **estar hecho una ~** to be a sorry sight.
lastimar [lasti'mar] *vt* (*herir*) to wound; (*ofender*) to offend; **~se** *vr* to hurt o.s.
lastimero, a [lasti'mero, a] *adj* pitiful, pathetic.
lastre ['lastre] *nm* (*TEC, NAUT*) ballast; (*fig*) dead weight.
lata ['lata] *nf* (*metal*) tin; (*envase*) tin, can; (*fam*) nuisance; **en ~** tinned; **dar (la) ~** to be a nuisance.
latente [la'tente] *adj* latent.
lateral [late'ral] *adj* side, lateral ♦ *nm* (*TEAT*) wings *pl*.
latido [la'tiðo] *nm* (*del corazón*) beat; (*de herida*) throb(bing).
latifundio [lati'fundjo] *nm* large estate.
latifundista [latifun'dista] *nm/f* owner of a large estate.
latigazo [lati'ɣaθo] *nm* (*golpe*) lash; (*sonido*) crack; (*fig*: *regaño*) dressing-down.
látigo ['latiɣo] *nm* whip.
latiguillo [lati'ɣiʎo] *nm* (*TEAT*) hamming.
latín [la'tin] *nm* Latin; **saber (mucho) ~** (*fam*) to be pretty sharp.
latinajo [lati'naxo] *nm* dog Latin; **echar ~s** to come out with Latin words.
latino, a [la'tino, a] *adj* Latin.
Latinoamérica [latinoa'merika] *nf* Latin America.
latinoamericano, a [latinoameri'kano, a] *adj, nm/f* Latin American.
latir [la'tir] *vi* (*corazón, pulso*) to beat.
latitud [lati'tuð] *nf* (*GEO*) latitude; (*fig*) breadth, extent.
lato, a ['lato, a] *adj* broad.
latón [la'ton] *nm* brass.
latoso, a [la'toso, a] *adj* (*molesto*) annoying; (*aburrido*) boring.
latrocinio [latro'θinjo] *nm* robbery.
LAU *nf abr* (*ESP JUR*) = *Ley de Arrendamientos Urbanos*.
laúd [la'uð] *nm* lute.
laudatorio, a [lauða'torjo, a] *adj* laudatory.
laudo ['lauðo] *nm* (*JUR*) decision, finding.
laurear [laure'ar] *vt* to honour, reward.
laurel [lau'rel] *nm* (*BOT*) laurel; (*CULIN*) bay.
Lausana [lau'sana] *nf* Lausanne.
lava ['laβa] *nf* lava.
lavable [la'βaβle] *adj* washable.
lavabo [la'βaβo] *nm* (*jofaina*) washbasin; (*retrete*) lavatory (*BRIT*), toilet (*BRIT*), washroom (*US*).
lavadero [laβa'ðero] *nm* laundry.
lavado [la'βaðo] *nm* washing; (*de ropa*) wash, laundry; (*ARTE*) wash; **~ de cerebro** brainwashing.
lavadora [laβa'ðora] *nf* washing machine.
lavanda [la'βanda] *nf* lavender.
lavandería [laβande'ria] *nf* laundry; **~ automática** launderette.
lavaparabrisas [laβapara'βrisas] *nm inv* windscreen washer.
lavaplatos [laβa'platos] *nm inv* dishwasher.
lavar [la'βar] *vt* to wash; (*borrar*) to wipe away; **~se** *vr* to wash o.s.; **~se las manos** to wash one's hands; (*fig*) to wash one's hands of it; **~ y marcar** (*pelo*) to shampoo and set; **~ en seco** to dry-clean.
lavativa [laβa'tiβa] *nf* (*MED*) enema.
lavavajillas [laβaβa'xiʎas] *nm inv* dishwasher.
laxante [lak'sante] *nm* laxative.
laxitud [laksi'tuð] *nf* laxity, slackness.
lazada [la'θaða] *nf* bow.
lazarillo [laθa'riʎo] *nm*: **perro de ~** guide dog.
lazo ['laθo] *nm* knot; (*lazada*) bow; (*para animales*) lasso; (*trampa*) snare; (*vínculo*) tie; **~ corredizo** slipknot.
LBE *nf abr* (*ESP JUR*) = *Ley Básica de Empleo*.
lb(s) *abr* = **libra(s)**.
L/C *abr* (= *Letra de Crédito*) B/E.
Lda., Ldo. *abr* = **Licenciado, a.**
le [le] *pron* (*directo*) him (*o* her); (: *usted*) you; (*indirecto*) to him (*o* her *o* it); (: *usted*) to you.
leal [le'al] *adj* loyal.
lealtad [leal'tað] *nf* loyalty.
lebrel [le'βrel] *nm* greyhound.
lección [lek'θjon] *nf* lesson; **~ práctica** object lesson; **dar lecciones** to teach, give lessons; **dar una ~ a algn** (*fig*) to teach sb a lesson.
leche ['letʃe] *nf* milk; (*fam!*) semen, spunk (*!*); **dar una ~ a algn** (*fam*) to belt sb; **estar de mala ~** (*fam*) to be in a foul mood; **tener mala ~** (*fam*) to be a nasty piece of work; **~ condensada/en polvo** condensed/powdered milk; **~ desnatada** skimmed milk; **~ de magnesia** milk of magnesia; **¡~!** hell!
lechera [le'tʃera] *nf* V **lechero**.
lechería [letʃe'ria] *nf* dairy.
lechero, a [le'tʃero, a] *adj* milk *cpd* ♦ *nm* milkman ♦ *nf* (*vendedora*) milkmaid; (*recipiente*) milk pan; (*para servir*) milk churn.
lecho ['letʃo] *nm* (*cama, de río*) bed; (*GEO*) layer; **~ mortuorio** deathbed.
lechón [le'tʃon] *nm* sucking (*BRIT*) *o* suckling (*US*) pig.
lechoso, a [le'tʃoso, a] *adj* milky.

lechuga [le'tʃuɣa] *nf* lettuce.
lechuza [le'tʃuθa] *nf* (barn) owl.
lectivo, a [lek'tiβo, a] *adj* (*horas*) teaching *cpd*; **año** *o* **curso** ~ (*ESCOL*) school year; (*UNIV*) academic year.
lector, a [lek'tor, a] *nm/f* reader; (*ESCOL, UNIV*) (conversation) assistant ♦ *nm*: ~ **óptico de caracteres** (*INFORM*) optical character reader ♦ *nf*: ~**a de fichas** (*INFORM*) card reader.
lectura [lek'tura] *nf* reading; ~ **de marcas sensibles** (*INFORM*) mark sensing.
leer [le'er] *vt* to read; ~ **entre líneas** to read between the lines.
legación [leɣa'θjon] *nf* legation.
legado [le'ɣaðo] *nm* (*don*) bequest; (*herencia*) legacy; (*enviado*) legate.
legajo [le'ɣaxo] *nm* file, bundle (of papers).
legal [le'ɣal] *adj* legal, lawful; (*persona*) trustworthy.
legalice [leɣa'liθe] *etc vb V* **legalizar**.
legalidad [leɣali'ðað] *nf* legality.
legalizar [leɣali'θar] *vt* to legalize; (*documento*) to authenticate.
legaña [le'ɣaɲa] *nf* sleep (*in eyes*).
legar [le'ɣar] *vt* to bequeath, leave.
legatario, a [leɣa'tarjo, a] *nm/f* legatee.
legendario, a [lexen'darjo, a] *adj* legendary.
legible [le'xiβle] *adj* legible; ~ **por máquina** (*INFORM*) machine-readable.
legión [le'xjon] *nf* legion.
legionario, a [lexjo'narjo, a] *adj* legionary ♦ *nm* legionnaire.
legislación [lexisla'θjon] *nf* legislation; (*leyes*) laws *pl*; ~ **antimonopolio** (*COM*) anti-trust legislation.
legislar [lexis'lar] *vt* to legislate.
legislativo, a [lexisla'tiβo, a] *adj*: **(elecciones) legislativas** ≈ general election.
legislatura [lexisla'tura] *nf* (*POL*) period of office.
legitimar [lexiti'mar] *vt* to legitimize.
legítimo, a [le'xitimo, a] *adj* (*genuino*) authentic; (*legal*) legitimate, rightful.
lego, a ['leɣo, a] *adj* (*REL*) secular; (*ignorante*) ignorant ♦ *nm* layman.
legua ['leɣwa] *nf* league; **se ve** (*o* **nota**) **a la** ~ you can tell (it) a mile off.
legue ['leɣe] *etc vb V* **legar**.
leguleyo [leɣu'lejo] *nm* (*pey*) petty *o* shyster (*US*) lawyer.
legumbres [le'ɣumbres] *nfpl* pulses.
leído, a [le'iðo, a] *adj* well-read.
lejanía [lexa'nia] *nf* distance.
lejano, a [le'xano, a] *adj* far-off; (*en el tiempo*) distant; (*fig*) remote; **L~ Oriente** Far East.
lejía [le'xia] *nf* bleach.
lejísimos [le'xisimos] *adv* a long, long way.
lejos ['lexos] *adv* far, far away; **a lo** ~ in the distance; **de** *o* **desde** ~ from a distance; **está muy** ~ it's a long way (away); **¿está ~?** is it far?; ~ **de** *prep* far from.
lelo, a ['lelo, a] *adj* silly ♦ *nm/f* idiot.
lema ['lema] *nm* motto; (*POL*) slogan.
lencería [lenθe'ria] *nf* (*telas*) linen, drapery; (*ropa interior*) lingerie.
lendakari [lenda'kari] *nm* *head of the Basque Autonomous Government.*
lengua ['lengwa] *nf* tongue; ~ **cooficial** *see boxed note*; ~ **materna** mother tongue; ~ **oficial** official language; ~ **de tierra** (*GEO*) spit *o* tongue of land; **dar a la** ~ to chatter; **morderse la** ~ to hold one's tongue; **sacar la** ~ **a algn** (*fig*) to cock a snook at sb.

LENGUAS COOFICIALES

Under the Spanish constitution **lenguas cooficiales** *or* **oficiales** *enjoy the same status as "castellano" in those regions which have retained their own distinct language: in Galicia, "gallego"; in the Basque Country, "euskera"; in Catalonia and the Balearic Islands, "catalán". The regional governments actively promote their own language through the media and the education system. Of these three regions, Catalonia has the highest number of native speakers.*

lenguado [len'gwaðo] *nm* sole.
lenguaje [len'gwaxe] *nm* language; (*forma de hablar*) (mode of) speech; ~ **comercial** business language; ~ **ensamblador** *o* **de alto nivel** (*INFORM*) high-level language; ~ **máquina** (*INFORM*) machine language; ~ **original** source language; ~ **periodístico** journalese; ~ **de programación** (*INFORM*) programming language; **en** ~ **llano** ≈ in plain English.
lenguaraz [lengwa'raθ] *adj* talkative; (*pey*) foul-mouthed.
lengüeta [len'gweta] *nf* (*ANAT*) epiglottis; (*de zapatos, MUS*) tongue.
lenidad [leni'ðað] *nf* lenience.
Leningrado [lenin'graðo] *nm* Leningrad.
lente ['lente] *nm o nf* lens; (*lupa*) magnifying glass; ~**s** *pl* glasses; ~**s de contacto** contact lenses.
lenteja [len'texa] *nf* lentil.
lentejuela [lente'xwela] *nf* sequin.
lentilla [len'tiʎa] *nf* contact lens.
lentitud [lenti'tuð] *nf* slowness; **con** ~

slowly.
lento, a ['lento, a] *adj* slow.
leña ['leɲa] *nf* firewood; **dar ~ a** to thrash; **echar ~ al fuego** to add fuel to the flames.
leñador, a [leɲa'ðor, a] *nm/f* woodcutter.
leño ['leɲo] *nm* (*trozo de árbol*) log; (*madera*) timber; (*fig*) blockhead.
Leo ['leo] *nm* (*ASTRO*) Leo.
león [le'on] *nm* lion; **~ marino** sea lion.
leonera [leo'nera] *nf* (*jaula*) lion's cage; **parece una ~** it's shockingly dirty.
leonés, esa [leo'nes, esa] *adj, nm/f* Leonese ♦ *nm* (*LING*) Leonese.
leonino, a [leo'nino, a] *adj* leonine.
leopardo [leo'parðo] *nm* leopard.
leotardos [leo'tarðos] *nmpl* tights.
lepra ['lepra] *nf* leprosy.
leprosería [leprose'ria] *nf* leper colony.
leproso, a [le'proso, a] *nm/f* leper.
lerdo, a ['lerðo, a] *adj* (*lento*) slow; (*patoso*) clumsy.
leridano, a [leri'ðano, a] *adj* of *o* from Lérida ♦ *nm/f* native *o* inhabitant of Lérida.
les [les] *pron* (*directo*) them; (: *ustedes*) you; (*indirecto*) to them; (: *ustedes*) to you.
lesbiana [les'ßjana] *nf* lesbian.
lesión [le'sjon] *nf* wound, lesion; (*DEPORTE*) injury.
lesionado, a [lesjo'naðo, a] *adj* injured ♦ *nm/f* injured person.
lesionar [lesjo'nar] *vt* (*dañar*) to hurt; (*herir*) to wound; **~se** *vr* to get hurt.
letal [le'tal] *adj* lethal.
letanía [leta'nia] *nf* litany; (*retahíla*) long list.
letárgico, a [le'tarxiko, a] *adj* lethargic.
letargo [le'tarɣo] *nm* lethargy.
letón, ona [le'ton, ona] *adj, nm/f* Latvian ♦ *nm* (*LING*) Latvian.
Letonia [le'tonja] *nf* Latvia.
letra ['letra] *nf* letter; (*escritura*) handwriting; (*COM*) letter, bill, draft; (*MUS*) lyrics *pl*; **~s** *nfpl* (*UNIV*) arts; **~ bastardilla/negrilla** italics *pl*/bold type; **~ de cambio** bill of exchange; **~ de imprenta** print; **~ inicial/mayúscula/minúscula** initial/capital/small letter; **lo tomó al pie de la ~** he took it literally; **~ bancaria** (*COM*) bank draft; **~ de patente** (*COM*) letters patent *pl*; **escribir 4 ~s a algn** to drop a line to sb.
letrado, a [le'traðo, a] *adj* learned; (*fam*) pedantic ♦ *nm/f* lawyer.
letrero [le'trero] *nm* (*cartel*) sign; (*etiqueta*) label.
letrina [le'trina] *nf* latrine.
leucemia [leu'θemja] *nf* leukaemia.
leucocito [leuko'θito] *nm* white blood cell, leucocyte.
leva ['leßa] *nf* (*NAUT*) weighing anchor; (*MIL*) levy; (*TEC*) lever.
levadizo, a [leßa'ðiθo, a] *adj*: **puente ~** drawbridge.
levadura [leßa'ðura] *nf* yeast, leaven; **~ de cerveza** brewer's yeast.
levantamiento [leßanta'mjento] *nm* raising, lifting; (*rebelión*) revolt, rising; (*GEO*) survey; **~ de pesos** weightlifting.
levantar [leßan'tar] *vt* (*gen*) to raise; (*del suelo*) to pick up; (*hacia arriba*) to lift (up); (*plan*) to make, draw up; (*mesa*) to clear; (*campamento*) to strike; (*fig*) to cheer up, hearten; **~se** *vr* to get up; (*enderezarse*) to straighten up; (*rebelarse*) to rebel; (*sesión*) to be adjourned; (*niebla*) to lift; (*viento*) to rise; **~se (de la cama)** to get up, get out of bed; **~ el ánimo** to cheer up.
levante [le'ßante] *nm* east; (*viento*) east wind; **el L~** *region of Spain extending from Castellón to Murcia.*
levantino, a [leßan'tino, a] *adj* of *o* from the *Levante* ♦ *nm/f*: **los ~s** the people of the *Levante*.
levar [le'ßar] *vi* to weigh anchor.
leve ['leße] *adj* light; (*fig*) trivial; (*mínimo*) slight.
levedad [leße'ðað] *nf* lightness; (*fig*) levity.
levita [le'ßita] *nf* frock coat.
léxico, a ['leksiko, a] *adj* lexical ♦ *nm* (*vocabulario*) vocabulary; (*LING*) lexicon.
ley [lei] *nf* (*gen*) law; (*metal*) standard; **decreto-~** decree law; **de buena ~** (*fig*) genuine; **según la ~** in accordance with the law, by law, in law.
leyenda [le'jenda] *nf* legend; (*TIP*) inscription.
leyendo [le'jendo] *etc vb V* **leer**.
liar [li'ar] *vt* to tie (up); (*unir*) to bind; (*envolver*) to wrap (up); (*enredar*) to confuse; (*cigarrillo*) to roll; **~se** *vr* (*fam*) to get involved; (*confundirse*) to get mixed up; **~se a palos** to get involved in a fight.
lib. *abr* (= *libro*) bk.
libanés, esa [lißa'nes, esa] *adj, nm/f* Lebanese.
Líbano ['lißano] *nm*: **el ~** the Lebanon.
libar [li'ßar] *vt* to suck.
libelo [li'ßelo] *nm* satire, lampoon; (*JUR*) petition.
libélula [li'ßelula] *nf* dragonfly.
liberación [lißera'θjon] *nf* liberation; (*de la cárcel*) release.

liberado, a [liβe'raðo, a] *adj* liberated; (*COM*) paid-up, paid-in (*US*).
liberal [liβe'ral] *adj, nm/f* liberal.
liberar [liβe'rar] *vt* to liberate.
libertad [liβer'tað] *nf* liberty, freedom; ~ **de asociación/de culto/de prensa/de comercio/de palabra** freedom of association/of worship/of the press/of trade/of speech; ~ **condicional** probation; ~ **bajo palabra** parole; ~ **bajo fianza** bail; **estar en** ~ to be free; **poner a algn en** ~ to set sb free.
libertador, a [liβerta'ðor, a] *adj* liberating ♦ *nm/f* liberator; **El L**~ (*AM*) The Liberator.
libertar [liβer'tar] *vt* (*preso*) to set free; (*de una obligación*) to release; (*eximir*) to exempt.
libertinaje [liβerti'naxe] *nm* licentiousness.
libertino, a [liβer'tino, a] *adj* permissive ♦ *nm/f* permissive person.
Libia ['liβja] *nf* Libya.
libidinoso, a [liβiði'noso, a] *adj* lustful; (*viejo*) lecherous.
libido [li'βiðo] *nf* libido.
libio, a ['liβjo, a] *adj, nm/f* Libyan.
libra ['liβra] *nf* pound; **L**~ (*ASTRO*) Libra; ~ **esterlina** pound sterling.
librador, a [liβra'ðor, a] *nm/f* drawer.
libranza [li'βranθa] *nf* (*COM*) draft; (*letra de cambio*) bill of exchange.
librar [li'βrar] *vt* (*de peligro*) to save; (*batalla*) to wage, fight; (*de impuestos*) to exempt; (*cheque*) to make out; (*JUR*) to exempt; ~**se** *vr*: ~**se de** to escape from, free o.s. from; **de buena nos hemos librado** we're well out of that.
libre ['liβre] *adj* (*gen*) free; (*lugar*) unoccupied; (*tiempo*) spare; (*asiento*) vacant; (*COM*): ~ **a bordo** free on board; ~ **de franqueo** post-free; ~ **de impuestos** free of tax; **tiro** ~ free kick; **los 100 metros** ~ the 100 metres freestyle (race); **al aire** ~ in the open air; **¿estás** ~**?** are you free?
librecambio [liβre'kambjo] *nm* free trade.
librecambista [liβrekam'bista] *adj* free-trade *cpd* ♦ *nm* free-trader.
librería [liβre'ria] *nf* (*tienda*) bookshop; (*estante*) bookcase; ~ **de ocasión** secondhand bookshop.
librero, a [li'βrero, a] *nm/f* bookseller.
libreta [li'βreta] *nf* notebook; (*pan*) one-pound loaf; ~ **de ahorros** savings book.
libro ['liβro] *nm* book; ~ **de actas** minute book; ~ **de bolsillo** paperback; ~ **de cabecera** bedside book; ~ **de caja** (*COM*) cashbook; ~ **de caja auxiliar** (*COM*) petty cash book; ~ **de cocina** cookery book (*BRIT*), cookbook (*US*); ~ **de consulta** reference book; ~ **de cuentas** account book; ~ **de cuentos** storybook; ~ **de cheques** cheque (*BRIT*) *o* check (*US*) book; ~ **diario** journal; ~ **de entradas y salidas** (*COM*) daybook; ~ **de honor** visitors' book; ~ **mayor** (*COM*) general ledger; ~ **de reclamaciones** complaints book; ~ **de texto** textbook.
Lic. *abr* = **Licenciado, a.**
licencia [li'θenθja] *nf* (*gen*) licence; (*permiso*) permission; ~ **por enfermedad/con goce de sueldo** sick/paid leave; ~ **de armas/de caza** gun/game licence; ~ **de exportación** (*COM*) export licence; ~ **poética** poetic licence.
licenciado, a [liθen'θjaðo, a] *adj* licensed ♦ *nm/f* graduate; **L**~ **en Filosofía y Letras** ≈ Bachelor of Arts; *see boxed note*.

LICENCIADO

After an average of five years at Spanish universities, successful students are awarded a degree called a **licenciado**. *If they have done a shorter three-year course, such as nursing, or if they choose not to stay on for another two years to specialize, they are awarded a "diplomado" instead. "Cursos de posgrado", postgraduate courses, are becoming increasingly popular, especially one-year specialist courses called "masters".*

licenciar [liθen'θjar] *vt* (*empleado*) to dismiss; (*permitir*) to permit, allow; (*soldado*) to discharge; (*estudiante*) to confer a degree upon; ~**se** *vr*: ~**se en letras** to get an arts degree.
licenciatura [liθenθja'tura] *nf* (*título*) degree; (*estudios*) degree course.
licencioso, a [liθen'θjoso, a] *adj* licentious.
liceo [li'θeo] *nm* (*esp AM*) (high) school.
licitación [liθita'θjon] *nf* bidding; (*oferta*) tender, offer.
licitador [liθita'ðor] *nm* bidder.
licitar [liθi'tar] *vt* to bid for ♦ *vi* to bid.
lícito, a ['liθito, a] *adj* (*legal*) lawful; (*justo*) fair, just; (*permisible*) permissible.
licor [li'kor] *nm* spirits *pl* (*BRIT*), liquor (*US*); (*con hierbas etc*) liqueur.
licra® ['likra] *nf* Lycra®.
licuadora [likwa'ðora] *nf* blender.
licuar [li'kwar] *vt* to liquidize.
lid [lið] *nf* combat; (*fig*) controversy.
líder ['liðer] *nm/f* leader.

liderato [liðe'rato] *nm* = **liderazgo**.
liderazgo [liðe'raθɣo] *nm* leadership.
lidia ['liðja] *nf* bullfighting; (*una* ~) bullfight; **toros de** ~ fighting bulls.
lidiar [li'ðjar] *vt, vi* to fight.
liebre ['ljeβre] *nf* hare; **dar gato por** ~ to con.
Lieja ['ljexa] *nf* Liège.
lienzo ['ljenθo] *nm* linen; (*ARTE*) canvas; (*ARQ*) wall.
lifting ['liftin] *nm* facelift.
liga ['liɣa] *nf* (*de medias*) garter, suspender; (*confederación*) league; (*AM*: *gomita*) rubber band.
ligadura [liɣa'ðura] *nf* bond, tie; (*MED, MUS*) ligature.
ligamento [liɣa'mento] *nm* (*ANAT*) ligament; (*atadura*) tie; (*unión*) bond.
ligar [li'ɣar] *vt* (*atar*) to tie; (*unir*) to join; (*MED*) to bind up; (*MUS*) to slur; (*fam*) to get off with, pick up ♦ *vi* to mix, blend; (*fam*) to get off with sb; (*2 personas*) to get off with one another; ~**se** *vr* (*fig*) to commit o.s.; ~ **con** (*fam*) to get off with, pick up; ~**se a algn** to get off with *o* pick up sb.
ligereza [lixe'reθa] *nf* lightness; (*rapidez*) swiftness; (*agilidad*) agility; (*superficialidad*) flippancy.
ligero, a [li'xero, a] *adj* (*de peso*) light; (*tela*) thin; (*rápido*) swift, quick; (*ágil*) agile, nimble; (*de importancia*) slight; (*de carácter*) flippant, superficial ♦ *adv* quickly, swiftly; **a la ligera** superficially; **juzgar a la ligera** to jump to conclusions.
light ['lait] *adj inv* (*cigarrillo*) low-tar; (*comida*) diet *cpd*.
ligón [li'ɣon] *nm* (*fam*) Romeo.
ligue ['liɣe] *etc vb V* **ligar** ♦ *nm/f* boyfriend/girlfriend ♦ *nm* (*persona*) pick-up.
liguero [li'ɣero] *nm* suspender (*BRIT*) *o* garter (*US*) belt.
lija ['lixa] *nf* (*ZOOL*) dogfish; **(papel de)** ~ sandpaper.
lijar [li'xar] *vt* to sand.
lila ['lila] *adj inv, nf* lilac ♦ *nm* (*fam*) twit.
lima ['lima] *nf* file; (*BOT*) lime; ~ **de uñas** nail file; **comer como una** ~ to eat like a horse.
limar [li'mar] *vt* to file; (*alisar*) to smooth over; (*fig*) to polish up.
limbo ['limbo] *nm* (*REL*) limbo; **estar en el** ~ to be on another planet.
limitación [limita'θjon] *nf* limitation, limit; ~ **de velocidad** speed limit.
limitado, a [limi'taðo, a] *adj* limited; **sociedad limitada** (*COM*) limited company.
limitar [limi'tar] *vt* to limit; (*reducir*) to reduce, cut down ♦ *vi*: ~ **con** to border on; ~**se** *vr*: ~**se a** to limit *o* confine o.s. to.
límite ['limite] *nm* (*gen*) limit; (*fin*) end; (*frontera*) border; **como** ~ at (the) most; (*fecha*) at the latest; **no tener** ~**s** to know no bounds; ~ **de crédito** (*COM*) credit limit; ~ **de página** (*INFORM*) page break; ~ **de velocidad** speed limit.
limítrofe [li'mitrofe] *adj* bordering, neighbouring.
limón [li'mon] *nm* lemon ♦ *adj*: **amarillo** ~ lemon-yellow.
limonada [limo'naða] *nf* lemonade.
limonero [limo'nero] *nm* lemon tree.
limosna [li'mosna] *nf* alms *pl*; **pedir** ~ to beg; **vivir de** ~ to live on charity.
limpiabotas [limpja'βotas] *nm/f inv* bootblack (*BRIT*), shoeshine boy/girl.
limpiacristales [limpjakris'tales] *nm inv* (*detergente*) window cleaner.
limpiador, a [limpja'ðor, a] *adj* cleaning, cleansing ♦ *nm/f* cleaner.
limpiaparabrisas [limpjapara'βrisas] *nm inv* windscreen (*BRIT*) *o* windshield (*US*) wiper.
limpiar [lim'pjar] *vt* to clean; (*con trapo*) to wipe; (*quitar*) to wipe away; (*zapatos*) to shine, polish; (*casa*) to tidy up; (*fig*) to clean up; (: *purificar*) to cleanse, purify; (*MIL*) to mop up; ~ **en seco** to dry-clean.
limpieza [lim'pjeθa] *nf* (*estado*) cleanliness; (*acto*) cleaning; (: *de las calles*) cleansing; (: *de zapatos*) polishing; (*habilidad*) skill; (*fig*: *POLICÍA*) clean-up; (*pureza*) purity; (*MIL*): **operación de** ~ mopping-up operation; ~ **étnica** ethnic cleansing; ~ **en seco** dry cleaning.
limpio, a ['limpjo, a] *adj* clean; (*moralmente*) pure; (*ordenado*) tidy; (*despejado*) clear; (*COM*) clear, net; (*fam*) honest ♦ *adv*: **jugar** ~ to play fair; **pasar a** ~ to make a fair copy; **sacar algo en** ~ to get benefit from sth; ~ **de** free from.
linaje [li'naxe] *nm* lineage, family.
linaza [li'naθa] *nf* linseed; **aceite de** ~ linseed oil.
lince ['linθe] *nm* lynx; **ser un** ~ (*fig*: *observador*) to be very observant; (: *astuto*) to be shrewd.
linchar [lin'tʃar] *vt* to lynch.
lindante [lin'dante] *adj* adjoining; ~ **con** bordering on.
lindar [lin'dar] *vi* to adjoin; ~ **con** to border on; (*ARQ*) to abut on.
linde ['linde] *nm o nf* boundary.
lindero, a [lin'dero, a] *adj* adjoining ♦ *nm*

boundary.
lindo, a ['lindo, a] *adj* pretty, lovely ♦ *adv* (*esp AM*: *fam*) nicely, very well; **canta muy** ~ (*AM*) he sings beautifully; **se divertían de lo** ~ they enjoyed themselves enormously.
línea ['linea] *nf* (*gen, moral, POL etc*) line; (*talle*) figure; (*INFORM*): **en** ~ on line; **fuera de** ~ off line; ~ **de estado** status line; ~ **de formato** format line; ~ **aérea** airline; ~ **de alto el fuego** ceasefire line; ~ **de fuego** firing line; ~ **de meta** goal line; (*de carrera*) finishing line; ~ **de montaje** assembly line; ~ **dura** (*POL*) hard line; ~ **recta** straight line; **la** ~ **de 1995** (*moda*) the 1995 look.
lineal [line'al] *adj* linear; (*INFORM*) on-line.
lingote [lin'gote] *nm* ingot.
lingüista [lin'gwista] *nm/f* linguist.
lingüística [lin'gwistika] *nf* linguistics *sg*.
linimento [lini'mento] *nm* liniment.
lino ['lino] *nm* linen; (*BOT*) flax.
linóleo [li'noleo] *nm* lino, linoleum.
linterna [lin'terna] *nf* lantern, lamp; ~ **eléctrica** *o* **a pilas** torch (*BRIT*), flashlight (*US*).
lío ['lio] *nm* bundle; (*desorden*) muddle, mess; (*fam*: *follón*) fuss; (: *relación amorosa*) affair; **armar un** ~ to make a fuss; **meterse en un** ~ to get into a jam; **tener un** ~ **con algn** to be having an affair with sb.
lipotimia [lipo'timja] *nf* blackout.
liquen ['liken] *nm* lichen.
liquidación [likiða'θjon] *nf* liquidation; (*cuenta*) settlement; **venta de** ~ clearance sale.
liquidar [liki'ðar] *vt* (*QUÍMICA*) to liquefy; (*COM*) to liquidate; (*deudas*) to pay off; (*empresa*) to wind up; ~ **a algn** to bump sb off, rub sb out (*fam*).
liquidez [liki'ðeθ] *nf* liquidity.
líquido, a ['likiðo, a] *adj* liquid; (*ganancia*) net ♦ *nm* liquid; (*COM*: *efectivo*) ready cash *o* money; (: *ganancia*) net amount *o* profit; ~ **imponible** net taxable income.
lira ['lira] *nf* (*MUS*) lyre; (*moneda*) lira.
lírico, a ['liriko, a] *adj* lyrical.
lirio ['lirjo] *nm* (*BOT*) iris.
lirismo [li'rismo] *nm* lyricism; (*sentimentalismo*) sentimentality.
lirón [li'ron] *nm* (*ZOOL*) dormouse; (*fig*) sleepyhead.
Lisboa [lis'ßoa] *nf* Lisbon.
lisboeta [lisßo'eta] *adj* of *o* from Lisbon ♦ *nm/f* native *o* inhabitant of Lisbon.
lisiado, a [li'sjaðo, a] *adj* injured ♦ *nm/f* cripple.
lisiar [li'sjar] *vt* to maim; ~**se** *vr* to injure o.s.
liso, a ['liso, a] *adj* (*terreno*) flat; (*cabello*) straight; (*superficie*) even; (*tela*) plain; **lisa y llanamente** in plain language, plainly.
lisonja [li'sonxa] *nf* flattery.
lisonjear [lisonxe'ar] *vt* to flatter; (*fig*) to please.
lisonjero, a [lison'xero, a] *adj* flattering; (*agradable*) gratifying, pleasing ♦ *nm/f* flatterer.
lista ['lista] *nf* list; (*de alumnos*) school register; (*de libros*) catalogue; (*de correos*) poste restante; (*de platos*) menu; (*de precios*) price list; **pasar** ~ to call the roll; (*ESCOL*) to call the register; ~ **de correos** poste restante; ~ **de direcciones** mailing list; ~ **electoral** electoral roll; ~ **de espera** waiting list; **tela a** ~**s** striped material.
listado, a [lis'taðo, a] *adj* striped ♦ *nm* (*COM, INFORM*) listing; ~ **paginado** (*INFORM*) paged listing.
listar [lis'tar] *vt* (*INFORM*) to list.
listo, a ['listo, a] *adj* (*perspicaz*) smart, clever; (*preparado*) ready; ~ **para usar** ready-to-use; **¿estás** ~**?** are you ready?; **pasarse de** ~ to be too clever by half.
listón [lis'ton] *nm* (*tela*) ribbon; (*de madera, metal*) strip.
litera [li'tera] *nf* (*en barco, tren*) berth; (*en dormitorio*) bunk, bunk bed.
literal [lite'ral] *adj* literal.
literario, a [lite'rarjo, a] *adj* literary.
literato, a [lite'rato, a] *nm/f* writer.
literatura [litera'tura] *nf* literature.
litigante [liti'ɣante] *nm/f* litigant, claimant.
litigar [liti'ɣar] *vt* to fight ♦ *vi* (*JUR*) to go to law; (*fig*) to dispute, argue.
litigio [li'tixjo] *nm* (*JUR*) lawsuit; (*fig*): **en** ~ **con** in dispute with.
litigue [li'tiɣe] *etc vb V* **litigar**.
litografía [litoɣra'fia] *nf* lithography; (*una* ~) lithograph.
litoral [lito'ral] *adj* coastal ♦ *nm* coast, seaboard.
litro ['litro] *nm* litre, liter (*US*).
Lituania [li'twanja] *nf* Lithuania.
lituano, a [li'twano, a] *adj, nm/f* Lithuanian ♦ *nm* (*LING*) Lithuanian.
liturgia [li'turxja] *nf* liturgy.
liviano, a [li'ßjano, a] *adj* (*persona*) fickle; (*cosa, objeto*) trivial; (*AM*) light.
lívido, a ['lißiðo, a] *adj* livid.
living ['lißin], *pl* **livings** *nm* (*esp AM*) sitting room.
Ll, ll ['eʎe] *nf former letter in the Spanish*

alphabet.
llaga ['ʎaɣa] *nf* wound.
llagar [ʎa'ɣar] *vt* to make sore; (*herir*) to wound.
llague ['ʎaɣe] *etc vb V* **llagar**.
llama ['ʎama] *nf* flame; (*fig*) passion; (*ZOOL*) llama; **en ~s** burning, ablaze.
llamada [ʎa'maða] *nf* call; (*a la puerta*) knock; (: *timbre*) ring; **~ a cobro revertido** reverse-charge call; **~ al orden** call to order; **~ a pie de página** reference note; **~ a procedimiento** (*INFORM*) procedure call; **~ interurbana** trunk call.
llamado [ʎa'maðo] *nm* (*AM*) (telephone) call; (*llamamiento*) appeal, call.
llamamiento [ʎama'mjento] *nm* call; **hacer un ~ a algn para que haga algo** to appeal to sb to do sth.
llamar [ʎa'mar] *vt* to call; (*convocar*) to summon; (*invocar*) to invoke; (*atraer con gesto*) to beckon; (*atención*) to attract; (*TELEC*: *tb*: **~ por teléfono**) to call, ring up, telephone; (*MIL*) to call up ♦ *vi* (*por teléfono*) to phone; (*a la puerta*) to knock (*o* ring); (*por señas*) to beckon; **~se** *vr* to be called, be named; **¿cómo se llama usted?** what's your name?; **¿quién llama?** (*TELEC*) who's calling?, who's that?; **no me llama la atención** (*fam*) I don't fancy it.
llamarada [ʎama'raða] *nf* (*llamas*) blaze; (*rubor*) flush; (*fig*) flare-up.
llamativo, a [ʎama'tiβo, a] *adj* showy; (*color*) loud.
llamear [ʎame'ar] *vi* to blaze.
llanamente [ʎana'mente] *adv* (*lisamente*) smoothly; (*sin ostentaciones*) plainly; (*sinceramente*) frankly; *V tb* **liso**.
llaneza [ʎa'neθa] *nf* (*gen*) simplicity; (*honestidad*) straightforwardness, frankness.
llano, a ['ʎano, a] *adj* (*superficie*) flat; (*persona*) straightforward; (*estilo*) clear ♦ *nm* plain, flat ground.
llanta ['ʎanta] *nf* (wheel) rim; (*AM*: *neumático*) tyre; (: *cámara*) (inner) tube.
llanto ['ʎanto] *nm* weeping; (*fig*) lamentation; (*canción*) dirge, lament.
llanura [ʎa'nura] *nf* (*lisura*) flatness, smoothness; (*GEO*) plain.
llave ['ʎaβe] *nf* key; (*de gas, agua*) tap (*BRIT*), faucet (*US*); (*MECÁNICA*) spanner; (*de la luz*) switch; (*MUS*) key; **~ inglesa** monkey wrench; **~ maestra** master key; **~ de contacto** (*AUTO*) ignition key; **~ de paso** stopcock; **echar ~ a** to lock up.
llavero [ʎa'βero] *nm* keyring.
llavín [ʎa'βin] *nm* latchkey.
llegada [ʎe'ɣaða] *nf* arrival.
llegar [ʎe'ɣar] *vt* to bring up, bring over ♦ *vi* to arrive; (*bastar*) to be enough; **~se** *vr*: **~se a** to approach; **~ a** (*alcanzar*) to reach; to manage to, succeed in; **~ a saber** to find out; **~ a ser famoso/el jefe** to become famous/the boss; **~ a las manos** to come to blows; **~ a las manos de** to come into the hands of; **no llegues tarde** don't be late; **esta cuerda no llega** this rope isn't long enough.
llegue ['ʎeɣe] *etc vb V* **llegar**.
llenar [ʎe'nar] *vt* to fill; (*superficie*) to cover; (*espacio, tiempo*) to fill, take up; (*formulario*) to fill in *o* out; (*deber*) to fulfil; (*fig*) to heap; **~se** *vr* to fill (up); **~se de** (*fam*) to stuff o.s. with.
lleno, a ['ʎeno, a] *adj* full, filled; (*repleto*) full up ♦ *nm* (*abundancia*) abundance; (*TEAT*) full house; **dar de ~ contra un muro** to hit a wall head-on.
llevadero, a [ʎeβa'ðero, a] *adj* bearable, tolerable.
llevar [ʎe'βar] *vt* to take; (*ropa*) to wear; (*cargar*) to carry; (*quitar*) to take away; (*en coche*) to drive; (*transportar*) to transport; (*ruta*) to follow, keep to; (*traer*: *dinero*) to carry; (*suj: camino etc*): **~ a** to lead to; (*MAT*) to carry; (*aguantar*) to bear; (*negocio*) to conduct, direct; to manage; **~se** *vr* to carry off, take away; **llevamos dos días aquí** we have been here for two days; **él me lleva 2 años** he's 2 years older than me; **~ adelante** (*fig*) to carry forward; **~ por delante a uno** (*en coche etc*) to run sb over; (*fig*) to ride roughshod over sb; **~ la ventaja** to be winning *o* in the lead; **~ los libros** (*COM*) to keep the books; **llevo las de perder** I'm likely to lose; **no las lleva todas consigo** he's not all there; **nos llevó a cenar fuera** she took us out for a meal; **~se a uno por delante** (*atropellar*) to run sb over; **~se bien** to get on well (together).
llorar [ʎo'rar] *vt* to cry, weep ♦ *vi* to cry, weep; (*ojos*) to water; **~ a moco tendido** to sob one's heart out; **~ de risa** to cry with laughter.
lloriquear [ʎorike'ar] *vi* to snivel, whimper.
lloro ['ʎoro] *nm* crying, weeping.
llorón, ona [ʎo'ron, ona] *adj* tearful ♦ *nm/f* cry-baby.
lloroso, a [ʎo'roso, a] *adj* (*gen*) weeping, tearful; (*triste*) sad, sorrowful.

llover [ʎo'ßer] *vi* to rain; ~ **a cántaros** *o* **a cubos** *o* **a mares** to rain cats and dogs, pour (down); **ser una cosa llovida del cielo** to be a godsend; **llueve sobre mojado** it never rains but it pours.
llovizna [ʎo'ßiθna] *nf* drizzle.
lloviznar [ʎoßiθ'nar] *vi* to drizzle.
llueve ['ʎweße] *etc vb V* **llover**.
lluvia ['ʎußja] *nf* rain; (*cantidad*) rainfall; (*fig*: *balas etc*) hail, shower; ~ **radioactiva** radioactive fallout; **día de** ~ rainy day; **una** ~ **de regalos** a shower of gifts.
lluvioso, a [ʎu'ßjoso, a] *adj* rainy.
lo [lo] *artículo definido neutro*: ~ **bueno** the good ♦ *pron* (*persona*) him; (*cosa*) it; ~ **mío** what is mine; ~ **difícil es que** ... the difficult thing about it is that ...; **no saben** ~ **aburrido que es** they don't know how boring it is; **viste a** ~ **americano** he dresses in the American style; ~ **de** that matter of; ~ **que** what, that which; **toma** ~ **que quieras** take what(ever) you want; ~ **que sea** whatever; **¡toma** ~ **que he dicho!** I stand by what I said!
loa ['loa] *nf* praise.
loable [lo'aßle] *adj* praiseworthy.
LOAPA [lo'apa] *nf abr* (*ESP JUR*) = *Ley Orgánica de Armonización del Proceso Autónomo*.
loar [lo'ar] *vt* to praise.
lobato [lo'ßato] *nm* (*ZOOL*) wolf cub.
lobo ['loßo] *nm* wolf; ~ **de mar** (*fig*) sea dog; ~ **marino** seal.
lóbrego, a ['loßreɣo, a] *adj* dark; (*fig*) gloomy.
lóbulo ['loßulo] *nm* lobe.
LOC *nm abr* (= *lector óptico de caracteres*) OCR.
local [lo'kal] *adj* local ♦ *nm* place, site; (*oficinas*) premises *pl*.
localice [loka'liθe] *etc vb V* **localizar**.
localidad [lokali'ðað] *nf* (*barrio*) locality; (*lugar*) location; (*TEAT*) seat, ticket.
localizar [lokali'θar] *vt* (*ubicar*) to locate, find; (*encontrar*) to find, track down; (*restringir*) to localize; (*situar*) to place.
loción [lo'θjon] *nf* lotion, wash.
loco, a ['loko, a] *adj* mad; (*fig*) wild, mad ♦ *nm/f* lunatic, madman/woman; ~ **de atar**, ~ **de remate**, ~ **rematado** raving mad; **a lo** ~ without rhyme or reason; **ando** ~ **con el examen** the exam is driving me crazy; **estar** ~ **de alegría** to be overjoyed *o* over the moon.
locomoción [lokomo'θjon] *nf* locomotion.
locomotora [lokomo'tora] *nf* engine, locomotive.
locuaz [lo'kwaθ] *adj* loquacious, talkative.
locución [loku'θjon] *nf* expression.
locura [lo'kura] *nf* madness; (*acto*) crazy act.
locutor, a [loku'tor, a] *nm/f* (*RADIO*) announcer; (*comentarista*) commentator; (*TV*) newscaster, newsreader.
locutorio [loku'torjo] *nm* (*TELEC*) telephone box *o* booth.
lodo ['lodo] *nm* mud.
logia ['loxja] *nf* (*MIL, de masones*) lodge; (*ARQ*) loggia.
lógico, a ['loxiko, a] *adj* logical; (*correcto*) natural; (*razonable*) reasonable ♦ *nm* logician ♦ *nf* logic; **es** ~ **que** ... it stands to reason that ...; **ser de una lógica aplastante** to be as clear as day.
logístico, a [lo'xistiko, a] *adj* logistical ♦ *nf* logistics *pl*.
logotipo [loɣo'tipo] *nm* logo.
logrado, a [lo'ɣraðo, a] *adj* accomplished.
lograr [lo'ɣrar] *vt* (*obtener*) to get, obtain; (*conseguir*) to achieve, attain; ~ **hacer** to manage to do; ~ **que algn venga** to manage to get sb to come; ~ **acceso a** (*INFORM*) to access.
logro ['loɣro] *nm* achievement, success; (*COM*) profit.
logroñés, esa [logro'ɲes, esa] *adj* of *o* from Logroño ♦ *nm/f* native *o* inhabitant of Logroño.
LOGSE *nf abr* (= *Ley Orgánica de Ordenación General del Sistema Educativo*) *educational reform act*.
Loira ['loira] *nm* Loire.
loma ['loma] *nf* hillock, low ridge.
Lombardía [lombar'ðia] *nf* Lombardy.
lombriz [lom'briθ] *nf* (earth)worm.
lomo ['lomo] *nm* (*de animal*) back; (*CULIN*: *de cerdo*) pork loin; (: *de vaca*) rib steak; (*de libro*) spine.
lona ['lona] *nf* canvas.
loncha ['lontʃa] *nf* = **lonja**.
lonche ['lontʃe] *nm* (*AM*) lunch.
lonchería [lontʃe'ria] *nf* (*AM*) snack bar, diner (*US*).
londinense [londi'nense] *adj* London *cpd*, of *o* from London ♦ *nm/f* Londoner.
Londres ['londres] *nm* London.
longaniza [longa'niθa] *nf* pork sausage.
longevidad [lonxeßi'ðað] *nf* longevity.
longitud [lonxi'tuð] *nf* length; (*GEO*) longitude; **tener 3 metros de** ~ to be 3 metres long; ~ **de onda** wavelength; **salto de** ~ long jump.
longitudinal [lonxituði'nal] *adj* longitudinal.
lonja ['lonxa] *nf* slice; (*de tocino*) rasher; (*COM*) market, exchange; ~ **de pescado**

fish market.
lontananza [lonta'nanθa] *nf* background; **en ~** far away, in the distance.
Lorena [lo'rena] *nf* Lorraine.
loro ['loro] *nm* parrot.
los [los] *artículo definido mpl* the ♦ *pron* them; (*ustedes*) you; **mis libros y ~ de usted** my books and yours.
losa ['losa] *nf* stone; **~ sepulcral** gravestone.
lote ['lote] *nm* portion, share; (*COM*) lot; (*INFORM*) batch.
lotería [lote'ria] *nf* lottery; (*juego*) lotto; **le tocó la ~** he won a big prize in the lottery; (*fig*) he struck lucky; **~ nacional** national lottery; **~ primitiva** (*ESP*) *type of state-run lottery; see boxed note*.

LOTERÍA

Millions of pounds are spent in Spain every year on **loterías**, *or lotteries. The weekly "Lotería Nacional" is very popular, especially at Christmas. Other weekly lotteries include the Bono Loto and the (Lotería) Primitiva. One of the best known is run by the wealthy and influential society for the blind, "la ONCE"; their form is called "el cupón de la ONCE" or "el cupón de los ciegos".*

lotero, a [lo'tero, a] *nm/f* seller of lottery tickets.
Lovaina [lo'βaina] *nf* Louvain.
loza ['loθa] *nf* crockery; **~ fina** china.
lozanía [loθa'nia] *nf* (*lujo*) luxuriance.
lozano, a [lo'θano, a] *adj* luxuriant; (*animado*) lively.
lubina [lu'βina] *nf* (*ZOOL*) sea bass.
lubricante [luβri'kante] *adj, nm* lubricant.
lubricar [luβri'kar], **lubrificar** [luβrifi'kar] *vt* to lubricate.
lubrifique [luβri'fike] *etc vb V* **lubrificar**.
lubrique [lu'βrike] *etc vb V* **lubricar**.
lucense [lu'θense] *adj* of *o* from Lugo ♦ *nm/f* native *o* inhabitant of Lugo.
Lucerna [lu'θerna] *nf* Lucerne.
lucero [lu'θero] *nm* (*ASTRO*) bright star; (*fig*) brilliance; **~ del alba/de la tarde** morning/evening star.
luces ['luθes] *nfpl de* **luz**.
lucha ['lutʃa] *nf* fight, struggle; **~ de clases** class struggle; **~ libre** wrestling.
luchar [lu'tʃar] *vi* to fight.
lucidez [luθi'ðeθ] *nf* lucidity.
lucido, a [lu'θiðo, a] *adj* (*espléndido*) splendid, brilliant; (*elegante*) elegant; (*exitoso*) successful.
lúcido, a ['luθiðo, a] *adj* lucid.
luciérnaga [lu'θjernaɣa] *nf* glow-worm.
lucimiento [luθi'mjento] *nm* (*brillo*) brilliance; (*éxito*) success.
lucio ['luθjo] *nm* (*ZOOL*) pike.
lucir [lu'θir] *vt* to illuminate, light (up); (*ostentar*) to show off ♦ *vi* (*brillar*) to shine; (*AM: parecer*) to look, seem; **~se** *vr* (*irónico*) to make a fool of o.s.; (*ostentarse*) to show off; **la casa luce limpia** the house looks clean.
lucrativo, a [lukra'tiβo, a] *adj* lucrative, profitable; **institución no lucrativa** non profit-making institution.
lucro ['lukro] *nm* profit, gain; **~s y daños** (*COM*) profit and loss *sg*.
luctuoso, a [luk'twoso, a] *adj* mournful.
lúdico, a ['luðiko, a] *adj* playful; (*actividad*) recreational.
ludopatía [luðopa'tia] *nf* addiction to gambling (*o* videogames).
luego ['lweɣo] *adv* (*después*) next; (*más tarde*) later, afterwards; (*AM fam: en seguida*) at once, immediately; **desde ~** of course; **¡hasta ~!** see you later!, so long!; **¿y ~?** what next?
lugar [lu'ɣar] *nm* place; (*sitio*) spot; (*pueblo*) village, town; **en ~ de** instead of; **en primer ~** in the first place, firstly; **dar ~ a** to give rise to; **hacer ~** to make room; **fuera de ~** out of place; **tener ~** to take place; **~ común** commonplace; **yo en su ~** if I were him; **no hay ~ para preocupaciones** there is no cause for concern.
lugareño, a [luɣa'reɲo, a] *adj* village *cpd* ♦ *nm/f* villager.
lugarteniente [luɣarte'njente] *nm* deputy.
lúgubre ['luɣuβre] *adj* mournful.
lujo ['luxo] *nm* luxury; (*fig*) profusion, abundance; **de ~** luxury *cpd*, de luxe.
lujoso, a [lu'xoso, a] *adj* luxurious.
lujuria [lu'xurja] *nf* lust.
lumbago [lum'baɣo] *nm* lumbago.
lumbre ['lumbre] *nf* (*luz*) light; (*fuego*) fire; **cerca de la ~** near the fire, at the fireside; **¿tienes ~?** (*para cigarro*) have you got a light?
lumbrera [lum'brera] *nf* luminary; (*fig*) leading light.
luminoso, a [lumi'noso, a] *adj* luminous, shining; (*idea*) bright, brilliant.
luna ['luna] *nf* moon; (*vidrio: escaparate*) plate glass; (*: de un espejo*) glass; (*: de gafas*) lens; (*fig*) crescent; **~ creciente/llena/menguante/nueva** crescent/full/waning/new moon; **~ de miel** honeymoon; **estar en la ~** to have one's head in the clouds.

lunar [lu'nar] *adj* lunar ♦ *nm* (*ANAT*) mole; **tela a ~es** spotted material.
lunes ['lunes] *nm inv* Monday.
luneta [lu'neta] *nf* lens.
lupa ['lupa] *nf* magnifying glass.
lusitano, a [lusi'tano, a], **luso, a** ['luso, a] *adj, nm/f* Portuguese.
lustrador [lustra'ðor] *nm* (*AM*) bootblack.
lustrar [lus'trar] *vt* (*esp AM*) (*mueble*) to polish; (*zapatos*) to shine.
lustre ['lustre] *nm* polish; (*fig*) lustre; **dar ~ a** to polish.
lustro ['lustro] *nm* period of five years.
lustroso, a [lus'troso, a] *adj* shining.
luterano, a [lute'rano, a] *adj* Lutheran.
luto ['luto] *nm* mourning; (*congoja*) grief, sorrow; **llevar el** *o* **vestirse de ~** to be in mourning.
luxación [luksa'θjon] *nf* (*MED*) dislocation; **tener una ~ de tobillo** to have a dislocated ankle.
Luxemburgo [luksem'burɣo] *nm* Luxembourg.
luz [luθ], *pl* **luces** *nf* (*tb fig*) light; (*fam*) electricity; **dar a ~ un niño** to give birth to a child; **sacar a la ~** to bring to light; **dar la ~** to switch on the light; **encender** (*ESP*) *o* **prender** (*AM*)**/apagar la ~** to switch the light on/off; **les cortaron la ~** their (electricity) supply was cut off; **a la ~ de** in the light of; **a todas luces** by any reckoning; **hacer la ~ sobre** to shed light on; **tener pocas luces** to be dim *o* stupid; **~ de la luna/del sol** *o* **solar** moonlight/sunlight; **~ eléctrica** electric light; **~ roja/verde** red/green light; **~ de cruce** (*AUTO*) dipped headlight; **~ de freno** brake light; **~ intermitente/trasera** flashing/rear light; **luces de tráfico** traffic lights; **el Siglo de las Luces** the Age of Enlightenment; **traje de luces** bullfighter's costume.

Mm

M, m ['eme] *nf* (*letra*) M, m; **M de Madrid** M for Mike.
M. *abr* (*FERRO*) = **Metro.**
m. *abr* (= *metro(s)*) m; (= *minuto(s)*) min., m; (= *masculino*) m., masc.
M.ª *abr* = **María.**
macabro, [ma'kaβro, a] *adj* macabre.
macaco [ma'kako] *nm* (*ZOOL*) rhesus monkey; (*fam*) runt, squirt.
macana [ma'kana] *nf* (*AM*: *porra*) club; (: *mentira*) lie, fib; (: *tontería*) piece of nonsense.
macanudo, a [maka'nuðo, a] *adj* (*AM fam*) great.
macarra [ma'karra] *nm* (*fam*) thug.
macarrones [maka'rrones] *nmpl* macaroni *sg.*
Macedonia [maθe'ðonja] *nf* Macedonia.
macedonia [maθe'ðonja] *nf*: **~ de frutas** fruit salad.
macedonio [maθe'ðonjo] *adj, nm/f* Macedonian ♦ *nm* (*LING*) Macedonian.
macerar [maθe'rar] *vt* (*CULIN*) to soak, macerate; **~se** *vr* to soak, soften.
maceta [ma'θeta] *nf* (*de flores*) pot of flowers; (*para plantas*) flowerpot.
macetero [maθe'tero] *nm* flowerpot stand *o* holder.
machacar [matʃa'kar] *vt* to crush, pound; (*moler*) to grind (up); (*aplastar*) to mash ♦ *vi* (*insistir*) to go on, keep on.
machacón, ona [matʃa'kon, ona] *adj* (*pesado*) tiresome; (*insistente*) insistent; (*monótono*) monotonous.
machamartillo [matʃamar'tiʎo]: **a ~** *adv*: **creer a ~** (*firmemente*) to believe firmly.
machaque [ma'tʃake] *etc vb V* **machacar.**
machete [ma'tʃete] *nm* machete, (large) knife.
machismo [ma'tʃismo] *nm* sexism; male chauvinism.
machista [ma'tʃista] *adj, nm* sexist; male chauvinist.
macho ['matʃo] *adj* male; (*fig*) virile ♦ *nm* male; (*fig*) he-man, tough guy (*US*); (*TEC*: *perno*) pin, peg; (*ELEC*) pin, plug; (*COSTURA*) hook.

macilento, a [maθi'lento, a] *adj* (*pálido*) pale; (*ojeroso*) haggard.
macizo, a [ma'θiθo, a] *adj* (*grande*) massive; (*fuerte, sólido*) solid ♦ *nm* mass, chunk; (*GEO*) massif.
macramé [makra'me] *nm* macramé.
macrobiótico, a [makro'ßjotiko, a] *adj* macrobiotic.
macro-comando [makroko'mando] *nm* (*INFORM*) macro (command).
macroeconomía [makroekono'mia] *nf* (*COM*) macroeconomics *sg*.
mácula ['makula] *nf* stain, blemish.
macuto [ma'kuto] *nm* (*MIL*) knapsack.
Madagascar [maðaɣas'kar] *nm* Madagascar.
madeja [ma'ðexa] *nf* (*de lana*) skein, hank.
madera [ma'ðera] *nf* wood; (*fig*) nature, character; (*: aptitud*) aptitude; **una ~ a** piece of wood; **~ contrachapada** *o* **laminada** plywood; **tiene buena ~** he's made of solid stuff; **tiene ~ de futbolista** he's got the makings of a footballer.
maderaje [maðe'raxe], **maderamen** [maðe'ramen] *nm* timber; (*trabajo*) woodwork, timbering.
maderero [maðe'rero] *nm* timber merchant.
madero [ma'ðero] *nm* beam; (*fig*) ship.
madrastra [ma'ðrastra] *nf* stepmother.
madre ['maðre] *adj* mother *cpd*; (*AM*) tremendous ♦ *nf* mother; (*de vino etc*) dregs *pl*; **~ adoptiva/política/soltera** foster mother/mother-in-law/unmarried mother; **la M~ Patria** the Mother Country; **sin ~** motherless; **¡~ mía!** oh dear!; **¡tu ~!** (*fam!*) fuck off! (*!*); **salirse de ~** (*río*) to burst its banks; (*persona*) to lose all self-control.
madreperla [maðre'perla] *nf* mother-of-pearl.
madreselva [maðre'selßa] *nf* honeysuckle.
Madrid [ma'ðrið] *n* Madrid.
madriguera [maðri'ɣera] *nf* burrow.
madrileño, a [maðri'leɲo, a] *adj* of *o* from Madrid ♦ *nm/f* native *o* inhabitant of Madrid.
Madriles [ma'ðriles] *nmpl*: **Los ~** (*fam*) Madrid *sg*.
madrina [ma'ðrina] *nf* godmother; (*ARQ*) prop, shore; (*TEC*) brace; **~ de boda** bridesmaid.
madroño [ma'ðroɲo] *nm* (*BOT*) strawberry tree, arbutus.
madrugada [maðru'ɣaða] *nf* early morning, small hours; (*alba*) dawn, daybreak; **a las 4 de la ~** at 4 o'clock in the morning.
madrugador, a [maðruɣa'ðor, a] *adj* early-rising.
madrugar [maðru'ɣar] *vi* to get up early; (*fig*) to get a head start.
madrugue [ma'ðruɣe] *etc vb V* **madrugar**.
madurar [maðu'rar] *vt, vi* (*fruta*) to ripen; (*fig*) to mature.
madurez [maðu'reθ] *nf* ripeness; (*fig*) maturity.
maduro, a [ma'ðuro, a] *adj* ripe; (*fig*) mature; **poco ~** unripe.
MAE *nm abr* (*ESP POL*) = *Ministerio de Asuntos Exteriores.*
maestra [ma'estra] *nf V* **maestro**.
maestría [maes'tria] *nf* mastery; (*habilidad*) skill, expertise; (*AM*) Master's Degree.
maestro, a [ma'estro, a] *adj* masterly; (*perito*) skilled, expert; (*principal*) main; (*educado*) trained ♦ *nm/f* master/mistress; (*profesor*) teacher ♦ *nm* (*autoridad*) authority; (*MUS*) maestro; (*obrero*) skilled workman; **~ albañil** master mason; **~ de obras** foreman.
mafia ['mafja] *nf* mafia; **la M~** the Mafia.
mafioso [ma'fjoso] *nm* gangster.
Magallanes [maɣa'ʎanes] *nm*: **Estrecho de ~** Strait of Magellan.
magia ['maxja] *nf* magic.
mágico, a ['maxiko, a] *adj* magic(al) ♦ *nm/f* magician.
magisterio [maxis'terjo] *nm* (*enseñanza*) teaching; (*profesión*) teaching profession; (*maestros*) teachers *pl*.
magistrado [maxis'traðo] *nm* magistrate; **Primer M~** (*AM*) President, Prime Minister.
magistral [maxis'tral] *adj* magisterial; (*fig*) masterly.
magistratura [maxistra'tura] *nf* magistracy; **M~ del Trabajo** (*ESP*) ≈ Industrial Tribunal.
magnánimo, a [maɣ'nanimo, a] *adj* magnanimous.
magnate [maɣ'nate] *nm* magnate, tycoon; **~ de la prensa** press baron.
magnesio [maɣ'nesjo] *nm* (*QUÍMICA*) magnesium.
magnetice [maɣne'tiθe] *etc vb V* **magnetizar**.
magnético, a [maɣ'netiko, a] *adj* magnetic.
magnetismo [maɣne'tismo] *nm* magnetism.
magnetizar [maɣneti'θar] *vt* to magnetize.
magnetofón [maɣneto'fon], **magnetófono** [maɣne'tofono] *nm* tape recorder.
magnetofónico, a [maɣneto'fonico, a] *adj*:

cinta magnetofónica recording tape.
magnicidio [maɣni'θiðjo] *nm* assassination (*of an important person*).
magnífico, a [maɣ'nifiko, a] *adj* splendid, magnificent.
magnitud [maɣni'tuð] *nf* magnitude.
mago, a ['maɣo, a] *nm/f* magician, wizard; **los Reyes M~s** the Magi, the Three Wise Men; *V tb* **Reyes Magos**.
magrear [maɣre'ar] *vt* (*fam*) to touch up.
magro, a ['maɣro, a] *adj* (*persona*) thin, lean; (*carne*) lean.
maguey [ma'ɣei] *nm* (*BOT*) agave.
magulladura [maɣuʎa'ðura] *nf* bruise.
magullar [maɣu'ʎar] *vt* (*amoratar*) to bruise; (*dañar*) to damage; (*fam*: *golpear*) to bash, beat.
Maguncia [ma'ɣunθja] *nf* Mainz.
mahometano, a [maome'tano, a] *adj* Mohammedan.
mahonesa [mao'nesa] *nf* = **mayonesa**.
maicena [mai'θena] *nf* cornflour, corn starch (*US*).
maillot [ma'jot] *nm* swimming costume; (*DEPORTE*) vest.
maître ['metre] *nm* head waiter.
maíz [ma'iθ] *nm* maize (*BRIT*), corn (*US*); sweet corn.
maizal [mai'θal] *nm* maize field, cornfield.
majadero, a [maxa'ðero, a] *adj* silly, stupid.
majar [ma'xar] *vt* to crush, grind.
majareta [maxa'reta] *adj* (*fam*) cracked, potty.
majestad [maxes'tað] *nf* majesty; **Su M~** His/Her Majesty; **(Vuestra) M~** Your Majesty.
majestuoso, a [maxes'twoso, a] *adj* majestic.
majo, a ['maxo, a] *adj* nice; (*guapo*) attractive, good-looking; (*elegante*) smart.
mal [mal] *adv* badly; (*equivocadamente*) wrongly; (*con dificultad*) with difficulty ♦ *adj* = **malo, a** ♦ *nm* evil; (*desgracia*) misfortune; (*daño*) harm, damage; (*MED*) illness ♦ *conj*: ~ **que le pese** whether he likes it or not; **me entendió** ~ he misunderstood me; **hablar** ~ **de algn** to speak ill of sb; **huele** ~ it smells bad; **ir de** ~ **en peor** to go from bad to worse; **oigo/veo** ~ I can't hear/see very well; **si** ~ **no recuerdo** if my memory serves me right; **¡menos** ~**!** just as well!; ~ **que bien** rightly or wrongly; **no hay** ~ **que por bien no venga** every cloud has a silver lining; ~ **de ojo** evil eye.
malabarismo [malaβa'rismo] *nm* juggling.
malabarista [malaβa'rista] *nm/f* juggler.
malaconsejado, a [malakonse'xaðo, a] *adj* ill-advised.
malacostumbrado, a [malakostum'braðo, a] *adj* (*consentido*) spoiled.
malacostumbrar [malakostum'brar] *vt*: ~ **a algn** to get sb into bad habits.
malagueño, a [mala'ɣeɲo, a] *adj* of *o* from Málaga ♦ *nm/f* native *o* inhabitant of Málaga.
Malaisia [ma'laisja] *nf* Malaysia.
malaria [ma'larja] *nf* malaria.
Malasia [ma'lasja] *nf* Malaysia.
malavenido, a [malaβe'niðo, a] *adj* incompatible.
malayo, a [ma'lajo, a] *adj* Malay(an) ♦ *nm/f* Malay ♦ *nm* (*LING*) Malay.
Malaysia [ma'laisia] *nf* Malaysia.
malcarado, a [malka'raðo, a] *adj* ugly, grim-faced.
malcriado, a [mal'krjaðo, a] *adj* (*consentido*) spoiled.
malcriar [mal'krjar] *vt* to spoil, pamper.
maldad [mal'dað] *nf* evil, wickedness.
maldecir [malde'θir] *vt* to curse ♦ *vi*: ~ **de** to speak ill of.
maldiciendo [maldi'θjendo] *etc vb V* **maldecir**.
maldición [maldi'θjon] *nf* curse; **¡~!** curse it!, damn!
maldiga [mal'diɣa] *etc*, **maldije** [mal'dixe] *etc vb V* **maldecir**.
maldito, a [mal'dito, a] *adj* (*condenado*) damned; (*perverso*) wicked ♦ *nm*: **el** ~ the devil; **¡~ sea!** damn it!; **no le hace** ~ **(el) caso** he doesn't take a blind bit of notice.
maleable [male'aβle] *adj* malleable.
maleante [male'ante] *adj* wicked ♦ *nm/f* criminal, crook.
malecón [male'kon] *nm* pier, jetty.
maledicencia [maleði'θenθja] *nf* slander, scandal.
maleducado, a [maleðu'kaðo, a] *adj* bad-mannered, rude.
maleficio [male'fiθjo] *nm* curse, spell.
malentendido [malenten'diðo] *nm* misunderstanding.
malestar [males'tar] *nm* (*gen*) discomfort; (*enfermedad*) indisposition; (*fig*: *inquietud*) uneasiness; (*POL*) unrest; **siento un** ~ **en el estómago** my stomach is upset.
maleta [ma'leta] *nf* case, suitcase; (*AUTO*) boot (*BRIT*), trunk (*US*); **hacer la** ~ to pack.
maletera [male'tera] *nf* (*AM AUTO*) boot (*BRIT*), trunk (*US*).
maletero [male'tero] *nm* (*AUTO*) boot

(*BRIT*), trunk (*US*); (*persona*) porter.
maletín [male'tin] *nm* small case, bag; (*portafolio*) briefcase.
malevolencia [maleβo'lenθja] *nf* malice, spite.
malévolo, a [ma'leβolo, a] *adj* malicious, spiteful.
maleza [ma'leθa] *nf* (*hierbas malas*) weeds *pl*; (*arbustos*) thicket.
malgache [mal'ɣatʃe] *adj* of *o* from Madagascar ♦ *nm/f* native *o* inhabitant of Madagascar.
malgastar [malɣas'tar] *vt* (*tiempo, dinero*) to waste; (*recursos*) to squander; (*salud*) to ruin.
malhaya [ma'laja] *excl* (*esp AM*: *fam!*) damn (it)! (*!*); **¡~ sea/sean!** damn it/them! (*!*).
malhechor, a [male'tʃor, a] *nm/f* delinquent; (*criminal*) criminal.
malherido, a [male'riðo, a] *adj* badly injured.
malhumorado, a [malumo'raðo, a] *adj* bad-tempered.
malicia [ma'liθja] *nf* (*maldad*) wickedness; (*astucia*) slyness, guile; (*mala intención*) malice, spite; (*carácter travieso*) mischievousness.
malicioso, a [mali'θjoso, a] *adj* wicked, evil; sly, crafty; malicious, spiteful; mischievous.
malignidad [maliɣni'ðað] *nf* (*MED*) malignancy; (*malicia*) malice.
maligno, a [ma'liɣno, a] *adj* evil; (*dañino*) pernicious, harmful; (*malévolo*) malicious; (*MED*) malignant ♦ *nm*: **el ~** the devil.
malintencionado, a [malintenθjo'naðo, a] *adj* (*comentario*) hostile; (*persona*) malicious.
malla ['maʎa] *nf* (*de una red*) mesh; (*red*) network; (*AM*: *de baño*) swimsuit; (*de ballet, gimnasia*) leotard; **~s** *nfpl* tights; **~ de alambre** wire mesh.
Mallorca [ma'ʎorka] *nf* Majorca.
mallorquín, ina [maʎor'kin, ina] *adj, nm/f* Majorcan ♦ *nm* (*LING*) Majorcan.
malnutrido, a [malnu'triðo, a] *adj* undernourished.
malo, a ['malo, a] *adj* (**mal** *before nmsg*) bad; (*calidad*) poor; (*falso*) false; (*espantoso*) dreadful; (*niño*) naughty ♦ *nm/f* villain ♦ *nm* (*CINE fam*) bad guy ♦ *nf* spell of bad luck; **estar ~** to be ill; **andar a malas con algn** to be on bad terms with sb; **estar de malas** (*mal humor*) to be in a bad mood; **lo ~ es que** ... the trouble is that ....
malograr [malo'ɣrar] *vt* to spoil; (*plan*) to upset; (*ocasión*) to waste; **~se** *vr* (*plan etc*) to fail, come to grief; (*persona*) to die before one's time.
maloliente [malo'ljente] *adj* stinking, smelly.
malparado, a [malpa'raðo, a] *adj*: **salir ~** to come off badly.
malpensado, a [malpen'saðo, a] *adj* evil-minded.
malquerencia [malke'renθja] *nf* dislike.
malquistar [malkis'tar] *vt*: **~ a dos personas** to cause a rift between two people; **~se** *vr* to fall out.
malsano, a [mal'sano, a] *adj* unhealthy.
malsonante [malso'nante] *adj* (*palabra*) nasty, rude.
Malta ['malta] *nf* Malta.
malta ['malta] *nf* malt.
malteada [malte'aða] *nf* (*AM*) milk shake.
maltés, esa [mal'tes, esa] *adj, nm/f* Maltese.
maltraer [maltra'er] *vt* (*abusar*) to insult, abuse; (*maltratar*) to ill-treat.
maltratar [maltra'tar] *vt* to ill-treat, mistreat.
maltrecho, a [mal'tretʃo, a] *adj* battered, damaged.
malva ['malβa] *nf* mallow; **~ loca** hollyhock; **(de color de) ~** mauve.
malvado, a [mal'βaðo, a] *adj* evil, villainous.
malvavisco [malβa'βisko] *nm* marshmallow.
malvender [malβen'der] *vt* to sell off cheap *o* at a loss.
malversación [malβersa'θjon] *nf* embezzlement, misappropriation.
malversar [malβer'sar] *vt* to embezzle, misappropriate.
Malvinas [mal'βinas] *nfpl*: **Islas ~** Falkland Islands.
mama ['mama], *pl* **mamás** *nf* (*de animal*) teat; (*de mujer*) breast.
mamá [ma'ma] *nf* (*fam*) mum, mummy.
mamacita [mama'sita] *nf* (*AM fam*) mum, mummy.
mamadera [mama'dera] *nf* (*AM*) baby's bottle.
mamagrande [mama'grande] *nf* (*AM*) grandmother.
mamar [ma'mar] *vt* (*pecho*) to suck; (*fig*) to absorb, assimilate ♦ *vi* to suck; **dar de ~** to (breast-)feed; (*animal*) to suckle.
mamarracho [mama'rratʃo] *nm* sight, mess.
mambo ['mambo] *nf* (*MUS*) mambo.
mamífero, a [ma'mifero, a] *adj* mammalian, mammal *cpd* ♦ *nm* mammal.
mamón, ona [ma'mon, ona] *adj* small,

baby *cpd* ♦ *nm/f* small baby; (*fam!*) wanker (*!*).
mamotreto [mamo'treto] *nm* hefty volume; (*fam*) whacking great thing.
mampara [mam'para] *nf* (*entre habitaciones*) partition; (*biombo*) screen.
mamporro [mam'porro] *nm* (*fam*): **dar un ~ a** to clout.
mampostería [mamposte'ria] *nf* masonry.
mamut [ma'mut] *nm* mammoth.
maná [ma'na] *nm* manna.
manada [ma'naðа] *nf* (*ZOOL*) herd; (: *de leones*) pride; (: *de lobos*) pack; **llegaron en ~s** (*fam*) they came in droves.
Managua [ma'naɣwa] *n* Managua.
manantial [manan'tjal] *nm* spring; (*fuente*) fountain; (*fig*) source.
manar [ma'nar] *vt* to run with, flow with ♦ *vi* to run, flow; (*abundar*) to abound.
manaza [ma'naθa] *nf* big hand ♦ *adj, nm/f inv*: **~s: ser un ~s** to be clumsy.
mancebo [man'θeβo] *nm* (*joven*) young man.
mancha ['mantʃa] *nf* stain, mark; (*de tinta*) blot; (*de vegetación*) patch; (*imperfección*) stain, blemish, blot; (*boceto*) sketch, outline; **la M~** La Mancha.
manchado, a [man'tʃaðo, a] *adj* (*sucio*) dirty; (*animal*) spotted; (*ave*) speckled; (*tinta*) smudged.
manchar [man'tjar] *vt* to stain, mark; (*ZOOL*) to patch; (*ensuciar*) to soil, dirty; **~se** *vr* to get dirty; (*fig*) to dirty one's hands.
manchego, a [man'tʃeɣo, a] *adj* of *o* from La Mancha ♦ *nm/f* native *o* inhabitant of La Mancha.
mancilla [man'θiʎa] *nf* stain, blemish.
mancillar [manθi'ʎar] *vt* to stain, sully.
manco, a ['manko, a] *adj* one-armed; one-handed; (*fig*) defective, faulty; **no ser ~** to be useful *o* active.
mancomunar [mankomu'nar] *vt* to unite, bring together; (*recursos*) to pool; (*JUR*) to make jointly responsible.
mancomunidad [mankomuni'ðað] *nf* union, association; (*comunidad*) community; (*JUR*) joint responsibility.
mandado [man'daðo] *nm* (*orden*) order; (*recado*) commission, errand.
mandamás [manda'mas] *adj, nm/f inv* boss; **ser un ~** to be very bossy.
mandamiento [manda'mjento] *nm* (*orden*) order, command; (*REL*) commandment; **~ judicial** warrant.
mandar [man'dar] *vt* (*ordenar*) to order; (*dirigir*) to lead, command; (*país*) to rule over; (*enviar*) to send; (*pedir*) to order, ask for ♦ *vi* to be in charge; (*pey*) to be bossy; **~se** *vr*: **~se mudar** (*AM fam*) to go away, clear off; **¿mande?** pardon?, excuse me? (*US*); **¿manda usted algo más?** is there anything else?; **~ a algn a paseo** *o* **a la porra** to tell sb to go to hell; **se lo mandaremos por correo** we'll post it to you; **~ hacer un traje** to have a suit made.
mandarín [manda'rin] *nm* petty bureaucrat.
mandarina [manda'rina] *nf* (*fruta*) tangerine, mandarin (orange).
mandatario, a [manda'tarjo, a] *nm/f* (*representante*) agent; **primer ~** (*esp AM*) head of state.
mandato [man'dato] *nm* (*orden*) order; (*POL: período*) term of office; (: *territorio*) mandate; (*INFORM*) command; **~ judicial** (search) warrant.
mandíbula [man'diβula] *nf* jaw.
mandil [man'dil] *nm* (*delantal*) apron.
Mandinga [man'dinɣa] *nm* (*AM*) Devil.
mandioca [man'djoka] *nf* cassava.
mando ['mando] *nm* (*MIL*) command; (*de país*) rule; (*el primer lugar*) lead; (*POL*) term of office; (*TEC*) control; **~ a la izquierda** left-hand drive; **los altos ~s** the high command *sg*; **~ por botón** push-button control; **al ~ de** in charge of; **tomar el ~** to take the lead.
mandolina [mando'lina] *nf* mandolin(e).
mandón, ona [man'don, ona] *adj* bossy, domineering.
manecilla [mane'θiʎa] *nf* (*TEC*) pointer; (*de reloj*) hand.
manejable [mane'xaβle] *adj* manageable; (*fácil de usar*) handy.
manejar [mane'xar] *vt* to manage; (*máquina*) to work, operate; (*caballo etc*) to handle; (*casa*) to run, manage; (*AM AUTO*) to drive ♦ *vi* (*AM AUTO*) to drive; **~se** *vr* (*comportarse*) to act, behave; (*arreglárselas*) to manage; **"~ con cuidado"** "handle with care".
manejo [ma'nexo] *nm* management; handling; running; driving; (*facilidad de trato*) ease, confidence; (*de idioma*) command; **~s** *nmpl* intrigues; **tengo ~ del francés** I have a good command of French.
manera [ma'nera] *nf* way, manner, fashion; (*ARTE, LITERATURA etc: estilo*) manner, style; **~s** *nfpl* (*modales*) manners; **su ~ de ser** the way he is; (*aire*) his manner; **de mala ~** (*fam*) badly, unwillingly; **de ninguna ~** no way, by no means; **de otra ~** otherwise; **de todas ~s**

at any rate; **en gran** ~ to a large extent; **sobre** ~ exceedingly; **a mí** ~ **de ver** in my view; **no hay** ~ **de persuadirle** there's no way of convincing him.
manga ['manga] *nf* (*de camisa*) sleeve; (*de riego*) hose; **de** ~ **corta/larga** short-/long-sleeved; **andar** ~ **por hombro** (*desorden*) to be topsy-turvy; **tener** ~ **ancha** to be easy-going.
mangante [man'gante] *adj* (*descarado*) brazen ♦ *nm* (*mendigo*) beggar.
mangar [man'gar] *vt* (*unir*) to plug in; (*fam: birlar*) to pinch, nick, swipe; (*mendigar*) to beg.
mango ['mango] *nm* handle; (*BOT*) mango; ~ **de escoba** broomstick.
mangonear [mangone'ar] *vt* to boss about ♦ *vi* to be bossy.
mangue ['mange] *etc vb V* **mangar.**
manguera [man'gera] *nf* (*de riego*) hose; (*tubo*) pipe; ~ **de incendios** fire hose.
maní [ma'ni] *nm, pl* **maníes** *o* **manises** (*AM: cacahuete*) peanut; (*: planta*) groundnut plant.
manía [ma'nia] *nf* (*MED*) mania; (*fig: moda*) rage, craze; (*disgusto*) dislike; (*malicia*) spite; **tiene** ~**s** she's a bit fussy; **tener** ~ **a algn** to dislike sb.
maníaco, a [ma'niako, a] *adj* maniac(al) ♦ *nm/f* maniac.
maniatar [manja'tar] *vt* to tie the hands of.
maniático, a [ma'njatiko, a] *adj* maniac(al); (*loco*) crazy; (*tiquismiquis*) fussy ♦ *nm/f* maniac.
manicomio [mani'komjo] *nm* mental hospital (*BRIT*), insane asylum (*US*).
manicuro, a [mani'kuro, a] *nm/f* manicurist ♦ *nf* manicure.
manido, a [ma'niðo, a] *adj* (*tema etc*) trite, stale.
manifestación [manifesta'θjon] *nf* (*declaración*) statement, declaration; (*demostración*) show, display; (*POL*) demonstration.
manifestante [manifes'tante] *nm/f* demonstrator.
manifestar [manifes'tar] *vt* to show, manifest; (*declarar*) to state, declare; ~**se** *vr* to show, become apparent; (*POL: desfilar*) to demonstrate; (*: reunirse*) to hold a mass meeting.
manifiesto, a [mani'fjesto, a] *etc vb V* **manifestar** ♦ *adj* clear, manifest ♦ *nm* manifesto; (*ANAT, NAUT*) manifest; **poner algo de** ~ (*aclarar*) to make sth clear; (*revelar*) to reveal sth; **quedar** ~ to be plain *o* clear.
manija [ma'nixa] *nf* handle.
manilla [ma'niʎa] *nf* (*de reloj*) hand; (*AM*) handle, lever; ~**s (de hierro)** *nfpl* handcuffs.
manillar [mani'ʎar] *nm* handlebars *pl.*
maniobra [ma'njoβra] *nf* manœuvring; (*maneja*) handling; (*fig: movimiento*) manœuvre, move; (*: estratagema*) trick, stratagem; ~**s** *nfpl* manœuvres.
maniobrar [manio'βrar] *vt* to manœuvre; (*manejar*) to handle ♦ *vi* to manœuvre.
manipulación [manipula'θjon] *nf* manipulation; (*COM*) handling.
manipular [manipu'lar] *vt* to manipulate; (*manejar*) to handle.
maniquí [mani'ki] *nm/f* model ♦ *nm* dummy.
manirroto, a [mani'rroto, a] *adj* lavish, extravagant ♦ *nm/f* spendthrift.
manita [ma'nita] *nf* little hand; ~**s de plata** artistic hands.
manitas [ma'nitas] *adj inv* good with one's hands ♦ *nm/f inv*: **ser un** ~ to be very good with one's hands.
manito [ma'nito] *nm* (*AM: en conversación*) mate (*fam*), chum.
manivela [mani'βela] *nf* crank.
manjar [man'xar] *nm* (tasty) dish.
mano¹ ['mano] *nf* hand; (*ZOOL*) foot, paw; (*de pintura*) coat; (*serie*) lot, series; **a** ~ by hand; **a** ~ **derecha/izquierda** on (*o* to) the right(-hand side)/left(-hand side); **hecho a** ~ handmade; **a** ~**s llenas** lavishly, generously; **de primera** ~ (at) first hand; **de segunda** ~ (at) second hand; **robo a** ~ **armada** armed robbery; **Pedro es mi** ~ **derecha** Pedro is my right-hand man; ~ **de obra** labour, manpower; ~ **de santo** sure remedy; **darse la(s)** ~**(s)** to shake hands; **echar una** ~ to lend a hand; **echar una** ~ **a** to lay hands on; **echar** ~ **de** to make use of; **estrechar la** ~ **a algn** to shake sb's hand; **traer** *o* **llevar algo entre** ~**s** to deal *o* be busy with sth; **está en tus** ~**s** it's up to you; **se le fue la** ~ his hand slipped; (*fig*) he went too far; **¡**~**s a la obra!** to work!
mano² ['mano] *nm* (*AM fam*) friend, mate.
manojo [ma'noxo] *nm* handful, bunch; ~ **de llaves** bunch of keys.
manómetro [ma'nometro] *nm* (pressure) gauge.
manopla [ma'nopla] *nf* (*paño*) flannel; ~**s** *nfpl* mittens.
manoseado, a [manose'aðo, a] *adj* well-worn.
manosear [manose'ar] *vt* (*tocar*) to handle, touch; (*desordenar*) to mess up, rumple; (*insistir en*) to overwork; (*acariciar*) to caress, fondle; (*pey: persona*) to feel *o*

touch up.
manotazo [mano'taθo] *nm* slap, smack.
mansalva [man'salβa]: **a ~** *adv* indiscriminately.
mansedumbre [manse'ðumbre] *nf* gentleness, meekness; (*de animal*) tameness.
mansión [man'sjon] *nf* mansion.
manso, a ['manso, a] *adj* gentle, mild; (*animal*) tame.
manta ['manta] *nf* blanket; (*AM*) poncho.
manteca [man'teka] *nf* fat; (*AM*) butter; ~ **de cacahuete/cacao** peanut/cocoa butter; ~ **de cerdo** lard.
mantecado [mante'kaðo] *nm* ice cream.
mantecoso, a [mante'koso, a] *adj* fat, greasy; **queso ~** soft cheese.
mantel [man'tel] *nm* tablecloth.
mantelería [mantele'ria] *nf* table linen.
mantendré [manten'dre] *etc vb V* **mantener.**
mantener [mante'ner] *vt* to support, maintain; (*alimentar*) to sustain; (*conservar*) to keep; (*TEC*) to maintain, service; **~se** *vr* (*seguir de pie*) to be still standing; (*no ceder*) to hold one's ground; (*subsistir*) to sustain o.s., keep going; **~ algo en equilibrio** to keep sth balanced; **~se a distancia** to keep one's distance; **~se firme** to hold one's ground.
mantenga [man'tenga] *etc vb V* **mantener.**
mantenimiento [manteni'mjento] *nm* maintenance; sustenance; (*sustento*) support.
mantequería [manteke'ria] *nf* (*ultramarinos*) grocer's (shop).
mantequilla [mante'kiʎa] *nf* butter.
mantilla [man'tiʎa] *nf* mantilla; **~s** *nfpl* baby clothes; **estar en ~s** (*persona*) to be terribly innocent; (*proyecto*) to be in its infancy.
manto ['manto] *nm* (*capa*) cloak; (*de ceremonia*) robe, gown.
mantón [man'ton] *nm* shawl.
mantuve [man'tuβe] *etc vb V* **mantener.**
manual [ma'nwal] *adj* manual ♦ *nm* manual, handbook; **habilidad ~** manual skill.
manubrio [ma'nuβrio] *nm* (*AM AUTO*) steering wheel.
manufactura [manufak'tura] *nf* manufacture; (*fábrica*) factory.
manufacturado, a [manufaktu'raðo, a] *adj* manufactured.
manuscrito, a [manus'krito, a] *adj* handwritten ♦ *nm* manuscript.
manutención [manuten'θjon] *nf* maintenance; (*sustento*) support.
manzana [man'θana] *nf* apple; (*ARQ*) block; **~ de la discordia** (*fig*) bone of contention.
manzanal [manθa'nal] *nm* apple orchard.
manzanilla [manθa'niʎa] *nf* (*planta*) camomile; (*infusión*) camomile tea; (*vino*) manzanilla.
manzano [man'θano] *nm* apple tree.
maña ['maɲa] *nf* (*gen*) skill, dexterity; (*pey*) guile; (*costumbre*) habit; (*una ~*) trick, knack; **con ~** craftily.
mañana [ma'ɲana] *adv* tomorrow ♦ *nm* future ♦ *nf* morning; **de** *o* **por la ~** in the morning; **¡hasta ~!** see you tomorrow!; **pasado ~** the day after tomorrow; **~ por la ~** tomorrow morning.
mañanero, a [maɲa'nero, a] *adj* early-rising.
maño, a ['maɲo, a] *adj* Aragonese ♦ *nm/f* native *o* inhabitant of Aragon.
mañoso, a [ma'ɲoso, a] *adj* (*hábil*) skilful; (*astuto*) smart, clever.
mapa ['mapa] *nm* map.
mapuche, a [ma'putʃhe, a] *adj, nm/f* Mapuche, Araucanian.
maqueta [ma'keta] *nf* (scale) model.
maquiavélico, a [makja'βeliko, a] *adj* Machiavellian.
maquillador, a [makiʎa'ðor, a] *nm/f* (*TEAT etc*) make-up artist.
maquillaje [maki'ʎaxe] *nm* make-up; (*acto*) making up.
maquillar [maki'ʎar] *vt* to make up; **~se** *vr* to put on (some) make-up.
máquina ['makina] *nf* machine; (*de tren*) locomotive, engine; (*FOTO*) camera; (*AM: coche*) car; (*fig*) machinery; (*: proyecto*) plan, project; **a toda ~** at full speed; **escrito a ~** typewritten; **~ de escribir** typewriter; **~ de coser/lavar** sewing/washing machine; **~ de facsímil** facsimile (machine), fax; **~ de franqueo** franking machine; **~ tragaperras** fruit machine; (*COM*) slot machine.
maquinación [makina'θjon] *nf* machination, plot.
maquinal [maki'nal] *adj* (*fig*) mechanical, automatic.
maquinar [maki'nar] *vt, vi* to plot.
maquinaria [maki'narja] *nf* (*máquinas*) machinery; (*mecanismo*) mechanism, works *pl*.
maquinilla [maki'niʎa] *nf* small machine; (*torno*) winch; **~ de afeitar** razor; **~ eléctrica** electric razor.
maquinista [maki'nista] *nm* (*FERRO*) engine driver (*BRIT*), engineer (*US*); (*TEC*)

operator; (*NAUT*) engineer.
mar [mar] *nm* sea; ~ **de fondo** groundswell; ~ **llena** high tide; ~ **adentro** *o* **afuera** out at sea; **en alta** ~ on the high seas; **por** ~ by sea *o* boat; **hacerse a la** ~ to put to sea; **a ~es** in abundance; **un** ~ **de** lots of; **es la** ~ **de guapa** she is ever so pretty; **el M~ Negro/Báltico** the Black/Baltic Sea; **el M~ Muerto/Rojo** the Dead/Red Sea; **el M~ del Norte** the North Sea.
mar. *abr* (= *marzo*) Mar.
maraca [ma'raka] *nf* maraca.
maraña [ma'raɲa] *nf* (*maleza*) thicket; (*confusión*) tangle.
maravilla [mara'ßiʎa] *nf* marvel, wonder; (*BOT*) marigold; **hacer ~s** to work wonders; **a (las mil) ~s** wonderfully well.
maravillar [maraßi'ʎar] *vt* to astonish, amaze; **~se** *vr* to be astonished, be amazed.
maravilloso, a [maraßi'ʎoso, a] *adj* wonderful, marvellous.
marbellí [marße'ʎi] *adj* of *o* from Marbella ♦ *nm/f* native *o* inhabitant of Marbella.
marca ['marka] *nf* mark; (*sello*) stamp; (*COM*) make, brand; (*de ganado*) brand; (: *acto*) branding; (*NAUT*) seamark; (: *boya*) marker; (*DEPORTE*) record; **de** ~ excellent, outstanding; ~ **de fábrica** trademark; ~ **propia** own brand; ~ **registrada** registered trademark.
marcación [marka'θjon] *nf* (*TELEC*): ~ **automática** autodial.
marcado, a [mar'kaðo, a] *adj* marked, strong.
marcador [marka'ðor] *nm* marker; (*rotulador*) marker (pen); (*de libro*) bookmark; (*DEPORTE*) scoreboard; (: *persona*) scorer.
marcapasos [marka'pasos] *nm inv* pacemaker.
marcar [mar'kar] *vt* to mark; (*número de teléfono*) to dial; (*gol*) to score; (*números*) to record, keep a tally of; (*el pelo*) to set; (*ganado*) to brand; (*suj*: *termómetro*) to read, register; (: *reloj*) to show; (*tarea*) to assign; (*COM*) to put a price on ♦ *vi* (*DEPORTE*) to score; (*TELEC*) to dial; **mi reloj marca las 2** it's 2 o'clock by my watch; ~ **el compás** (*MUS*) to keep time; ~ **el paso** (*MIL*) to mark time.
marcha ['martʃa] *nf* march; (*DEPORTE*) walk; (*TEC*) running, working; (*AUTO*) gear; (*velocidad*) speed; (*fig*) progress; (*dirección*) course; **dar** ~ **atrás** to reverse, put into reverse; **estar en** ~ to be under way, be in motion; **hacer algo sobre la** ~ to do sth as you *etc* go along; **poner en** ~ to put into gear; **ponerse en** ~ to start, get going; **a ~s forzadas** (*fig*) with all speed; **¡en ~!** (*MIL*) forward march!; (*fig*) let's go!; **"~ moderada"** (*AUTO*) "drive slowly"; **que tiene** *o* **de mucha** ~ (*fam*) very lively.
marchante, a [mar'tʃante, a] *nm/f* dealer, merchant.
marchar [mar'tʃar] *vi* (*ir*) to go; (*funcionar*) to work, go; (*fig*) to go, proceed; **~se** *vr* to go (away), leave; **todo marcha bien** everything is going well.
marchitar [martʃi'tar] *vt* to wither, dry up; **~se** *vr* (*BOT*) to wither; (*fig*) to fade away.
marchito, a [mar'tʃito, a] *adj* withered, faded; (*fig*) in decline.
marchoso, a [mar'tʃoso, a] *adj* (*fam*: *animado*) lively; (: *moderno*) modern.
marcial [mar'θjal] *adj* martial, military.
marciano, a [mar'θjano, a] *adj* Martian, of *o* from Mars.
marco ['marko] *nm* frame; (*DEPORTE*) goalposts *pl*; (*moneda*) mark; (*fig*) setting; (*contexto*) framework; ~ **de chimenea** mantelpiece.
marea [ma'rea] *nf* tide; (*llovizna*) drizzle; ~ **alta/baja** high/low tide; ~ **negra** oil slick.
mareado, a [mare'aðo, a] *adj*: **estar** ~ (*con náuseas*) to feel sick; (*aturdido*) to feel dizzy.
marear [mare'ar] *vt* (*fig*: *irritar*) to annoy, upset; (*MED*): ~ **a algn** to make sb feel sick; **~se** *vr* (*tener náuseas*) to feel sick; (*desvanecerse*) to feel faint; (*aturdirse*) to feel dizzy; (*fam*: *emborracharse*) to get tipsy.
marejada [mare'xaða] *nf* (*NAUT*) swell, heavy sea.
maremágnum [mare'maɣnum] *nm* (*fig*) ocean, abundance.
maremoto [mare'moto] *nm* tidal wave.
mareo [ma'reo] *nm* (*náusea*) sick feeling; (*aturdimiento*) dizziness; (*fam*: *lata*) nuisance.
marfil [mar'fil] *nm* ivory.
margarina [marɣa'rina] *nf* margarine.
margarita [marɣa'rita] *nf* (*BOT*) daisy; **(rueda)** ~ (*en máquina impresora*) daisy wheel.
margen ['marxen] *nm* (*borde*) edge, border; (*fig*) margin, space ♦ *nf* (*de río etc*) bank; ~ **de beneficio** *o* **de ganancia** profit margin; ~ **comercial** mark-up; ~ **de confianza** credibility gap; **dar** ~ **para** to give an opportunity for; **dejar a algn al** ~ to leave sb out (in the cold);

mantenerse al ~ to keep out (of things); **al ~ de lo que digas** despite what you say.
marginado, a [marxi'naðo, a] *nm/f* outcast.
marginal [marxi'nal] *adj* (*tema, error*) minor; (*grupo*) fringe *cpd*; (*anotación*) marginal.
marginar [marxi'nar] *vt* to exclude.
maría [ma'ria] *nf* (*fam*: *mujer*) housewife.
mariachi [ma'rjatʃi] *nm* (*música*) mariachi music; (*grupo*) mariachi band; (*persona*) mariachi player.
marica [ma'rika] *nm* (*fam*) sissy; (*homosexual*) queer.
Maricastaña [marikas'taɲa] *nf*: **en los días** *o* **en tiempos de ~** way back, in the good old days.
maricón [mari'kon] *nm* (*fam*) queer.
marido [ma'riðo] *nm* husband.
marihuana [mari'wənə] *nf* marijuana, cannabis.
marimacho [mari'matʃo] *nf* (*fam*) mannish woman.
marimorena [marimo'rena] *nf* fuss, row; **armar una ~** to kick up a row.
marina [ma'rina] *nf* navy; **~ mercante** merchant navy.
marinero, a [mari'nero, a] *adj* sea *cpd*; (*barco*) seaworthy ♦ *nm* sailor, seaman.
marino, a [ma'rino, a] *adj* sea *cpd*, marine ♦ *nm* sailor; **~ de agua dulce/de cubierta/de primera** landlubber/ deckhand/able seaman.
marioneta [marjo'neta] *nf* puppet.
mariposa [mari'posa] *nf* butterfly.
mariposear [maripose'ar] *vi* (*revolotear*) to flutter about; (*ser inconstante*) to be fickle; (*coquetear*) to flirt.
mariquita [mari'kita] *nm* (*fam*) sissy; (*homosexual*) queer ♦ *nf* (*ZOOL*) ladybird (*BRIT*), ladybug (*US*).
marisco [ma'risko] *nm* (*tb*: **~s**) shellfish, seafood.
marisma [ma'risma] *nf* marsh, swamp.
marisquería [mariske'ria] *nf* shellfish bar, seafood restaurant.
marítimo, a [ma'ritimo, a] *adj* sea *cpd*, maritime.
marmita [mar'mita] *nf* pot.
mármol ['marmol] *nm* marble.
marmóreo, a [mar'moreo, a] *adj* marble.
marmota [mar'mota] *nf* (*ZOOL*) marmot; (*fig*) sleepyhead.
maroma [ma'roma] *nf* rope.
marque ['marke] *etc vb V* **marcar**.
marqués, esa [mar'kes, esa] *nm/f* marquis/marchioness.
marquesina [marke'sina] *nf* (*de parada*) bus-shelter.
marquetería [markete'ria] *nf* marquetry, inlaid work.
marranada [marra'naða] *nf* (*fam*): **es una ~** that's disgusting; **hacer una ~ a algn** to do the dirty on sb.
marrano, a [ma'rrano, a] *adj* filthy, dirty ♦ *nm* (*ZOOL*) pig; (*malo*) swine; (*sucio*) dirty pig.
marras ['marras]: **de ~** *adv*: **es el problema de ~** it's the same old problem.
marrón [ma'rron] *adj* brown.
marroquí [marro'ki] *adj, nm/f* Moroccan ♦ *nm* Morocco (leather).
Marruecos [ma'rrwekos] *nm* Morocco.
marta ['marta] *nf* (*animal*) (pine) marten; (*piel*) sable.
Marte ['marte] *nm* Mars.
martes ['martes] *nm inv* Tuesday; **~ de carnaval** Shrove Tuesday; *V tb* **Carnaval**.
martillar [marti'ʎar], **martillear** [martiʎe'ar] *vt* to hammer.
martilleo [marti'ʎeo] *nm* hammering.
martillo [mar'tiʎo] *nm* hammer; (*de presidente de asamblea, comité*) gavel; **~ neumático** pneumatic drill (*BRIT*), jackhammer (*US*).
Martinica [marti'nika] *nf* Martinique.
mártir ['martir] *nm/f* martyr.
martirice [marti'riθe] *etc vb V* **martirizar**.
martirio [mar'tirjo] *nm* martyrdom; (*fig*) torture, torment.
martirizar [martiri'θar] *vt* (*REL*) to martyr; (*fig*) to torture, torment.
maruja [ma'ruxa] *nf* (*fam*) = **maría**.
marxismo [mark'sismo] *nm* Marxism.
marxista [mark'sista] *adj, nm/f* Marxist.
marzo ['marθo] *nm* March.
mas [mas] *conj* but.

PALABRA CLAVE

más [mas] *adj, adv* **1**: **~ (que, de)** (*compar*) more (than), ...+er (than); **~ grande/ inteligente** bigger/more intelligent; **trabaja ~ (que yo)** he works more (than me); **~ de 6** more than 6; **es ~ de medianoche** it's after midnight; **durar ~** to last longer; *V tb* **cada**
2 (*superl*): **el ~** the most, ...+est; **el ~ grande/inteligente (de)** the biggest/most intelligent (in)
3 (*negativo*): **no tengo ~ dinero** I haven't got any more money; **no viene ~ por aquí** he doesn't come round here any more; **no sé ~** I don't know any more, that's all I know
4 (*adicional*): **un kilómetro ~** one more kilometre; **no le veo ~ solución que ...** I

see no other solution than to ...; **¿algo ~?** anything else?; (*en tienda*) will that be all?; **¿quién ~?** anybody else?
5 (*+adj: valor intensivo*): **¡qué perro ~ sucio!** what a filthy dog!; **¡es ~ tonto!** he's so stupid!
6 (*locuciones*): **~ o menos** more or less; **los ~** most people; **es ~** in fact, furthermore; **~ bien** rather; **¡qué ~ da!** what does it matter!; *V tb* **no**
7: **por ~**: **por ~ que lo intento** no matter how much *o* hard I try; **por ~ que quisiera ayudar** much as I should like to help
8: **de ~**: **veo que aquí estoy de ~** I can see I'm not needed here; **tenemos uno de ~** we've got one extra
9: (*AM*): **no ~** only, just; **ayer no ~** just yesterday
♦ *prep*: **2 ~ 2 son 4** 2 and *o* plus 2 are 4
♦ *nm inv*: **este trabajo tiene sus ~ y sus menos** this job's got its good points and its bad points.

masa ['masa] *nf* (*mezcla*) dough; (*volumen*) volume, mass; (*FÍSICA*) mass; **en ~** en masse; **las ~s** (*POL*) the masses.
masacrar [masa'krar] *vt* to massacre.
masacre [ma'sakre] *nf* massacre.
masaje [ma'saxe] *nm* massage; **dar ~ a** to massage.
masajista [masa'xista] *nm/f* masseur/ masseuse.
mascar [mas'kar] *vt, vi* to chew; (*fig*) to mumble, mutter.
máscara ['maskara] *nf* (*tb INFORM*) mask ♦ *nm/f* masked person; **~ antigás** gas mask.
mascarada [maska'raða] *nf* masquerade.
mascarilla [maska'riʎa] *nf* mask; (*vaciado*) deathmask; (*maquillaje*) face pack.
mascarón [maska'ron] *nm* large mask; **~ de proa** figurehead.
mascota [mas'kota] *nf* mascot.
masculino, a [masku'lino, a] *adj* masculine; (*BIO*) male ♦ *nm* (*LING*) masculine.
mascullar [masku'ʎar] *vt* to mumble, mutter.
masificación [masifika'θjon] *nf* overcrowding.
masilla [ma'siʎa] *nf* putty.
masivo, a [ma'sißo, a] *adj* (*en masa*) mass.
masón [ma'son] *nm* (free)mason.
masonería [masone'ria] *nf* (free)masonry.
masoquista [maso'kista] *adj* masochistic ♦ *nm/f* masochist.
masque ['maske] *etc vb V* **mascar**.
mastectomía [mastekto'mia] *nf* mastectomy.
máster, *pl* **masters** ['master, 'masters] *nm* postgraduate degree; *V tb* **licenciado**.
masticar [masti'kar] *vt* to chew; (*fig*) to ponder over.
mástil ['mastil] *nm* (*de navío*) mast; (*de guitarra*) neck.
mastín [mas'tin] *nm* mastiff.
mastique [mas'tike] *etc vb V* **masticar**.
masturbación [masturßa'θjon] *nf* masturbation.
masturbarse [mastur'ßarse] *vr* to masturbate.
Mat. *abr* = **Matemáticas**.
mata ['mata] *nf* (*arbusto*) bush, shrub; (*de hierbas*) tuft; (*campo*) field; (*manojo*) tuft, blade; **~s** *nfpl* scrub *sg*; **~ de pelo** mop of hair; **a salto de ~** (*día a día*) from day to day; (*al azar*) haphazardly.
matadero [mata'ðero] *nm* slaughterhouse, abattoir.
matador, a [mata'ðor, a] *adj* killing ♦ *nm/f* killer ♦ *nm* (*TAUR*) matador, bullfighter.
matamoscas [mata'moskas] *nm inv* (*palo*) fly swat.
matanza [ma'tanθa] *nf* slaughter.
matar [ma'tar] *vt* to kill; (*tiempo, pelota*) to kill ♦ *vi* to kill; **~se** *vr* (*suicidarse*) to kill o.s., commit suicide; (*morir*) to be *o* get killed; (*gastarse*) to wear o.s. out; **~ el hambre** to stave off hunger; **~ a algn a disgustos** to make sb's life a misery; **~las callando** to go about things slyly; **~se trabajando** to kill o.s. with work; **~se por hacer algo** to struggle to do sth.
matarife [mata'rife] *nm* slaughterman.
matasanos [mata'sanos] *nm inv* quack.
matasellos [mata'seʎos] *nm inv* postmark.
mate ['mate] *adj* (*sin brillo: color*) dull, matt ♦ *nm* (*en ajedrez*) (check)mate; (*AM: hierba*) maté; (*: vasija*) gourd.
matemático, a [mate'matiko, a] *adj* mathematical ♦ *nm/f* mathematician ♦ **matemáticas** *nfpl* mathematics *sg*.
materia [ma'terja] *nf* (*gen*) matter; (*TEC*) material; (*ESCOL*) subject; **en ~ de** on the subject of; (*en cuanto a*) as regards; **~ prima** raw material; **entrar en ~** to get down to business.
material [mate'rjal] *adj* material; (*dolor*) physical; (*real*) real; (*literal*) literal ♦ *nm* material; (*TEC*) equipment; **~ de construcción** building material; **~es de derribo** rubble *sg*.
materialismo [materja'lismo] *nm* materialism.
materialista [materja'lista] *adj* materialist(ic).

materialmente [materjal'mente] *adv* materially; (*fig*) absolutely.
maternal [mater'nal] *adj* motherly, maternal.
maternidad [materni'ðað] *nf* motherhood, maternity.
materno, a [ma'terno, a] *adj* maternal; (*lengua*) mother *cpd.*
matice [ma'tiθe] *etc vb V* **matizar.**
matinal [mati'nal] *adj* morning *cpd.*
matiz [ma'tiθ] *nm* shade; (*de sentido*) shade, nuance; (*ironía etc*) touch.
matizar [mati'θar] *vt* (*variar*) to vary; (*ARTE*) to blend; ~ **de** to tinge with.
matón [ma'ton] *nm* bully.
matorral [mato'rral] *nm* thicket.
matraca [ma'traka] *nf* rattle; (*fam*) nuisance.
matraz [ma'traθ] *nm* (*QUÍMICA*) flask.
matriarcado [matrjar'kaðo] *nm* matriarchy.
matrícula [ma'trikula] *nf* (*registro*) register; (*ESCOL*: *inscripción*) registration; (*AUTO*) registration number; (: *placa*) number plate.
matricular [matriku'lar] *vt* to register, enrol.
matrimonial [matrimo'njal] *adj* matrimonial.
matrimonio [matri'monjo] *nm* (*pareja*) (married) couple; (*acto*) marriage; ~ **civil/clandestino** civil/secret marriage; **contraer** ~ **(con)** to marry.
matriz [ma'triθ] *nf* (*ANAT*) womb; (*TEC*) mould; (*MAT*) matrix; **casa** ~ (*COM*) head office.
matrona [ma'trona] *nf* (*persona de edad*) matron.
matutino, a [matu'tino, a] *adj* morning *cpd.*
maula ['maula] *adj* (*persona*) good-for-nothing ♦ *nm/f* (*vago*) idler, slacker ♦ *nf* (*persona*) dead loss (*fam*).
maullar [mau'ʎar] *vi* to mew, miaow.
maullido [mau'ʎiðo] *nm* mew(ing), miaow(ing).
Mauricio [mau'riθjo] *nm* Mauritius.
Mauritania [mauri'tanja] *nf* Mauritania.
mausoleo [mauso'leo] *nm* mausoleum.
maxilar [maksi'lar] *nm* jaw(bone).
máxima ['maksima] *nf V* **máximo.**
máxime ['maksime] *adv* especially.
máximo, a ['maksimo, a] *adj* maximum; (*más alto*) highest; (*más grande*) greatest ♦ *nm* maximum ♦ *nf* maxim; ~ **jefe** *o* **líder** (*AM*) President, leader; **como** ~ at most; **al** ~ to the utmost.
maxisingle [maksi'singel] *nm* twelve-inch (single).
maya ['maja] *adj* Mayan ♦ *nm/f* Maya(n).
mayo ['majo] *nm* May.
mayonesa [majo'nesa] *nf* mayonnaise.
mayor [ma'jor] *adj* main, chief; (*adulto*) grown-up, adult; (*JUR*) of age; (*de edad avanzada*) elderly; (*MUS*) major; (*comparativo*: *de tamaño*) bigger; (: *de edad*) older; (*superlativo*: *de tamaño*) biggest; (*tb*: *fig*) greatest; (: *de edad*) oldest ♦ *nm* chief, boss; (*adulto*) adult; **al por** ~ wholesale; ~ **de edad** adult; *V tb* **mayores.**
mayoral [majo'ral] *nm* foreman.
mayordomo [major'ðomo] *nm* butler.
mayoreo [majo'reo] *nm* (*AM*) wholesale (trade).
mayores [ma'jores] *nmpl* grown-ups; **llegar a** ~**es** to get out of hand.
mayoría [majo'ria] *nf* majority, greater part; **en la** ~ **de los casos** in most cases; **en su** ~ on the whole.
mayorista [majo'rista] *nm/f* wholesaler.
mayoritario, a [majori'tarjo, a] *adj* majority *cpd*; **gobierno** ~ majority government.
mayúsculo, a [ma'juskulo, a] *adj* (*fig*) big, tremendous ♦ *nf* capital (letter); **mayúsculas** *nfpl* capitals; (*TIP*) upper case *sg.*
maza ['maθa] *nf* (*arma*) mace; (*DEPORTE*) bat; (*POLO*) stick.
mazacote [maθa'kote] *nm* hard mass; (*CULIN*) dry doughy food; (*ARTE, LITERATURA etc*) mess, hotchpotch.
mazapán [maθa'pan] *nm* marzipan.
mazmorra [maθ'morra] *nf* dungeon.
mazo ['maθo] *nm* (*martillo*) mallet; (*de mortero*) pestle; (*de flores*) bunch; (*DEPORTE*) bat.
mazorca [ma'θorka] *nf* (*BOT*) spike; (*de maíz*) cob, ear.
MCAC *nm abr* = *Mercado Común de la América Central.*
MCI *nm abr* = *Mercado Común Iberoamericano.*
me [me] *pron* (*directo*) me; (*indirecto*) (to) me; (*reflexivo*) (to) myself; **¡dámelo!** give it to me!; ~ **lo compró** (*de mí*) he bought it from me; (*para mí*) he bought it for me.
meandro [me'andro] *nm* meander.
mear [me'ar] (*fam*) *vt* to piss on (*!*) ♦ *vi* to pee, piss (*!*), have a piss (*!*); ~**se** *vr* to wet o.s.
Meca ['meka] *nf*: **La** ~ Mecca.
mecánica [me'kanika] *nf V* **mecánico.**
mecanice [meka'niθe] *etc vb V* **mecanizar.**
mecánico, a [me'kaniko, a] *adj*

mechanical; (*repetitivo*) repetitive ♦ *nm/f* mechanic ♦ *nf* (*estudio*) mechanics *sg*; (*mecanismo*) mechanism.
mecanismo [meka'nismo] *nm* mechanism; (*engranaje*) gear.
mecanizar [mekani'θar] *vt* to mechanize.
mecanografía [mekanoɣra'fia] *nf* typewriting.
mecanografiado, a [mekanoɣra'fjaðo, a] *adj* typewritten ♦ *nm* typescript.
mecanógrafo, a [meka'noɣrafo, a] *nm/f* (copy) typist.
mecate [me'kate] *nm* (*AM*) rope.
mecedor [mese'ðor] *nm* (*AM*), **mecedora** [meθe'ðora] *nf* rocking chair.
mecenas [me'θenas] *nm inv* patron.
mecenazgo [meθe'naθɣo] *nm* patronage.
mecer [me'θer] *vt* (*cuna*) to rock; **~se** *vr* to rock; (*rama*) to sway.
mecha ['metʃa] *nf* (*de vela*) wick; (*de bomba*) fuse; **a toda ~** at full speed; **ponerse ~s** to streak one's hair.
mechero [me'tʃero] *nm* (cigarette) lighter.
mechón [me'tʃon] *nm* (*gen*) tuft; (*manojo*) bundle; (*de pelo*) lock.
medalla [me'ðaʎa] *nf* medal.
media ['meðja] *nf V* **medio**.
mediación [meða'θjon] *nf* mediation; **por ~ de** through.
mediado, a [me'ðjaðo, a] *adj* half-full; (*trabajo*) half-completed; **a ~s de** in the middle of, halfway through.
medianamente [meðjana'mente] *adv* (*moderadamente*) moderately, fairly; (*regularmente*) moderately well.
mediano, a [me'ðjano, a] *adj* (*regular*) medium, average; (*mediocre*) mediocre ♦ *nf* (*AUT*) central reservation, median (*US*); **(de tamaño)** ~ medium-sized.
medianoche [meðja'notʃe] *nf* midnight.
mediante [me'ðjante] *adv* by (means of), through.
mediar [me'ðjar] *vi* (*tiempo*) to elapse; (*interceder*) to mediate, intervene; (*existir*) to exist; **media el hecho de que** ... there is the fact that ....
medicación [meðika'θjon] *nf* medication, treatment.
medicamento [meðika'mento] *nm* medicine, drug.
medicina [meði'θina] *nf* medicine.
medicinal [meðici'nal] *adj* medicinal.
medición [meði'θjon] *nf* measurement.
médico, a ['meðiko, a] *adj* medical ♦ *nm/f* doctor; **~ de cabecera** family doctor; **~ pediatra** paediatrician; **~ residente** house physician, intern (*US*).
medida [me'ðiða] *nf* measure; (*medición*) measurement; (*de camisa, zapato etc*) size, fitting; (*prudencia*) moderation, prudence; **en cierta/gran ~** up to a point/to a great extent; **un traje a la ~** made-to-measure suit; **~ de cuello** collar size; **a ~ de** in proportion to; (*de acuerdo con*) in keeping with; **con ~** with restraint; **sin ~** immoderately; **a ~ que** ... (at the same time) as ...; **tomar ~s** to take steps.
medieval [meðje'ßal] *adj* medieval.
medio, a ['meðjo, a] *adj* half (a); (*punto*) mid, middle; (*promedio*) average ♦ *adv* half-; (*esp AM*: *un tanto*) rather, quite ♦ *nm* (*centro*) middle, centre; (*promedio*) average; (*método*) means, way; (*ambiente*) environment ♦ *nf* (*prenda de vestir*) stocking, (*AM*) sock; (*promedio*) average; **~s** *nfpl* tights; **media hora** half an hour; **~ litro** half a litre; **las tres y media** half past three; **M~ Oriente** Middle East; **a ~ camino** halfway (there); **~ dormido** half asleep; **~ enojado** (*esp AM*) rather annoyed; **lo dejó a ~s** he left it half-done; **ir a ~s** to go fifty-fifty; **a ~ terminar** half finished; **en ~** in the middle; (*entre*) in between; **por ~ de** by (means of), through; **en los ~s financieros** in financial circles; **encontrarse en su ~** to be in one's element; **~ circulante** (*COM*) money supply; *V tb* **medios**.
medioambiental [meðjoambjen'tal] *adj* environmental.
mediocre [me'ðjokre] *adj* middling, average; (*pey*) mediocre.
mediocridad [meðjokri'ðað] *nf* middling quality; (*pey*) mediocrity.
mediodía [meðjo'ðia] *nm* midday, noon.
mediopensionista [meðjopensjo'nista] *nm/f* day boy/girl.
medios ['meðjos] *nmpl* means, resources; **los ~ de comunicación** the media.
medir [me'ðir] *vt* (*gen*) to measure ♦ *vi* to measure; **~se** *vr* (*moderarse*) to be moderate, act with restraint; **¿cuánto mides? — mido 1.50 m** how tall are you? — I am 1.50 m tall.
meditabundo, a [meðita'ßundo, a] *adj* pensive.
meditar [meði'tar] *vt* to ponder, think over, meditate on; (*planear*) to think out ♦ *vi* to ponder, think, meditate.
mediterráneo, a [meðite'rraneo, a] *adj* Mediterranean ♦ *nm*: **el (mar) M~** the Mediterranean (Sea).
medrar [me'ðrar] *vi* to increase, grow; (*mejorar*) to improve; (*prosperar*) to

prosper, thrive; (*animal, planta etc*) to grow.
medroso, a [me'ðroso, a] *adj* fearful, timid.
médula ['meðula] *nf* (*ANAT*) marrow; (*BOT*) pith; ~ **espinal** spinal cord; **hasta la** ~ (*fig*) to the core.
medusa [me'ðusa] *nf* (*ESP*) jellyfish.
megabyte ['meɣaßait] *nm* (*INFORM*) megabyte.
megafonía [meɣgafo'nia] *nf* PA *o* public address system.
megáfono [me'ɣafono] *nm* public address system.
megalomanía [meɣaloma'nia] *nf* megalomania.
megalómano, a [meɣa'lomano, a] *nm/f* megalomaniac.
megaocteto [meɣaok'teto] *nm* (*INFORM*) megabyte.
mejicano, a [mexi'kano, a] *adj, nm/f* Mexican.
Méjico ['mexiko] *nm* Mexico.
mejilla [me'xiʎa] *nf* cheek.
mejillón [mexi'ʎon] *nm* mussel.
mejor [me'xor] *adj, adv* (*comparativo*) better; (*superlativo*) best; **lo** ~ the best thing; **lo** ~ **de la vida** the prime of life; **a lo** ~ probably; (*quizá*) maybe; ~ **dicho** rather; **tanto** ~ so much the better; **es el** ~ **de todos** he's the best of all.
mejora [me'xora] *nf*, **mejoramiento** [mexora'mjento] *nm* improvement.
mejorar [mexo'rar] *vt* to improve, make better ♦ *vi*, ~**se** *vr* to improve, get better; (*COM*) to do well, prosper; ~ **a** to be better than; **los negocios mejoran** business is picking up.
mejoría [mexo'ria] *nf* improvement; (*restablecimiento*) recovery.
mejunje [me'xunxe] *nm* (*pey*) concoction.
melancolía [melanko'lia] *nf* melancholy.
melancólico, a [melan'koliko, a] *adj* (*triste*) sad, melancholy; (*soñador*) dreamy.
melena [me'lena] *nf* (*de persona*) long hair; (*ZOOL*) mane.
melillense [meli'ʎense] *adj* of *o* from Melilla ♦ *nm/f* native *o* inhabitant of Melilla.
mella ['meʎa] *nf* (*rotura*) notch, nick; **hacer** ~ (*fig*) to make an impression.
mellizo, a [me'ʎiθo, a] *adj, nm/f* twin.
melocotón [meloko'ton] *nm* (*ESP*) peach.
melodía [melo'ðia] *nf* melody; (*aire*) tune.
melodrama [melo'ðrama] *nm* melodrama.
melodramático, a [meloðra'matiko, a] *adj* melodramatic.
melón [me'lon] *nm* melon.
melopea [melo'pea] *nf* (*fam*): **tener una** ~ to be sloshed.
meloso, a [me'loso, a] *adj* honeyed, sweet; (*empalagoso*) sickly, cloying; (*voz*) sweet; (*zalamero*) smooth.
membrana [mem'brana] *nf* membrane.
membrete [mem'brete] *nm* letterhead; **papel con** ~ headed notepaper.
membrillo [mem'briʎo] *nm* quince; **carne de** ~ quince jelly.
memo, a ['memo, a] *adj* silly, stupid ♦ *nm/f* idiot.
memorable [memo'raßle] *adj* memorable.
memorándum [memo'randum] *nm* (*libro*) notebook; (*comunicación*) memorandum.
memoria [me'morja] *nf* (*gen*) memory; (*artículo*) (learned) paper; ~**s** *nfpl* (*de autor*) memoirs; ~ **anual** annual report; **aprender algo de** ~ to learn sth by heart; **si tengo buena** ~ if my memory serves me right; **venir a la** ~ to come to mind; (*INFORM*): ~ **de acceso aleatorio** random access memory, RAM; ~ **auxiliar** backing storage; ~ **fija** read-only memory, ROM; ~ **fija programable** programmable memory; ~ **del teclado** keyboard memory.
memorice [memo'riθe] *etc vb V* **memorizar**.
memorizar [memori'θar] *vt* to memorize.
menaje [me'naxe] *nm* (*muebles*) furniture; (*utensilios domésticos*) household equipment; ~ **de cocina** kitchenware.
mención [men'θjon] *nf* mention; **digno de** ~ noteworthy; **hacer** ~ **de** to mention.
mencionar [menθjo'nar] *vt* to mention; (*nombrar*) to name; **sin** ~ ... let alone ....
mendicidad [mendiθi'ðað] *nf* begging.
mendigar [mendi'ɣar] *vt* to beg (for).
mendigo, a [men'diɣo, a] *nm/f* beggar.
mendigue [men'diɣe] *etc vb V* **mendigar**.
mendrugo [men'druɣo] *nm* crust.
menear [mene'ar] *vt* to move; (*cola*) to wag; (*cadera*) to swing; (*fig*) to handle; ~**se** *vr* to shake; (*balancearse*) to sway; (*moverse*) to move; (*fig*) to get a move on.
menester [menes'ter] *nm* (*necesidad*) necessity; ~**es** *nmpl* (*deberes*) duties; **es** ~ **hacer algo** it is necessary to do sth, sth must be done.
menestra [me'nestra] *nf*: ~ **de verduras** vegetable stew.
mengano, a [men'gano, a] *nm/f* Mr (*o* Mrs *o* Miss) So-and-so.
mengua ['mengwa] *nf* (*disminución*) decrease; (*falta*) lack; (*pobreza*) poverty; (*fig*) discredit; **en** ~ **de** to the detriment of.

menguante [men'gwante] *adj* decreasing, diminishing; (*luna*) waning; (*marea*) ebb *cpd.*

menguar [men'gwar] *vt* to lessen, diminish; (*fig*) to discredit ♦ *vi* to diminish, decrease; (*fig*) to decline.

mengüe ['mengwe] *etc vb V* **menguar.**

menopausia [meno'pausja] *nf* menopause.

menor [me'nor] *adj* (*más pequeño*: *comparativo*) smaller; (*número*) less, lesser; (: *superlativo*) smallest; (*número*) least; (*más joven*: *comparativo*) younger; (: *superlativo*) youngest; (*MUS*) minor ♦ *nm/f* (*joven*) young person, juvenile; **Juanito es ~ que Pepe** Juanito is younger than Pepe; **ella es la ~ de todas** she is the youngest of all; **no tengo la ~ idea** I haven't the faintest idea; **al por ~** retail; **~ de edad** under age.

Menorca [me'norka] *nf* Minorca.

menorquín, ina [menor'kin, ina] *adj, nm/f* Minorcan.

PALABRA CLAVE

menos [menos] *adj* **1**: **~ (que, de)** (*compar*: *cantidad*) less (than); (: *número*) fewer (than); **con ~ entusiasmo** with less enthusiasm; **~ gente** fewer people; *V tb* **cada**

2 (*superl*): **es el que ~ culpa tiene** he is the least to blame; **donde ~ problemas hay** where there are fewest problems

♦ *adv* **1** (*compar*): **~ (que, de)** less (than); **me gusta ~ que el otro** I like it less than the other one; **~ de 5** less than 5; **~ de lo que piensas** less than you think

2 (*superl*): **es el ~ listo (de su clase)** he's the least bright (in his class); **de todas ellas es la que ~ me agrada** out of all of them she's the one I like least; **(por) lo ~** at (the very) least; **es lo ~ que puedo hacer** it's the least I can do; **lo ~ posible** as little as possible

3 (*locuciones*): **no quiero verle y ~ visitarle** I don't want to see him let alone visit him; **tenemos 7 (de) ~** we're 7 short; **eso es lo de ~** that's the least of it; **¡todo ~ eso!** anything but that!; **al/por lo ~** at (the very) least; **si al ~** if only

♦ *prep* except; (*cifras*) minus; **todos ~ él** everyone except (for) him; **5 ~ 2** 5 minus 2; **las 7 ~ 20** (*hora*) 20 to 7

♦ *conj*: **a ~ que**: **a ~ que venga mañana** unless he comes tomorrow.

menoscabar [menoska'βar] *vt* (*estropear*) to damage, harm; (*fig*) to discredit.

menospreciar [menospre'θjar] *vt* to underrate, undervalue; (*despreciar*) to scorn, despise.

menosprecio [menos'preθjo] *nm* underrating, undervaluation; scorn, contempt.

mensaje [men'saxe] *nm* message; **~ de error** (*INFORM*) error message.

mensajero, a [mensa'xero, a] *nm/f* messenger.

menstruación [menstrwa'θjon] *nf* menstruation.

menstruar [mens'trwar] *vi* to menstruate.

mensual [men'swal] *adj* monthly; **100 ptas ~es** 100 ptas. a month.

mensualidad [menswali'ðað] *nf* (*salario*) monthly salary; (*COM*) monthly payment *o* instalment.

menta ['menta] *nf* mint.

mentado, a [men'taðo, a] *adj* (*mencionado*) aforementioned; (*famoso*) well-known ♦ *nf*: **hacerle una mentada a algn** (*AM fam*) to (seriously) insult sb.

mental [men'tal] *adj* mental.

mentalidad [mentali'ðað] *nf* mentality, way of thinking.

mentalizar [mentali'θar] *vt* (*sensibilizar*) to make aware; (*convencer*) to convince; (*preparar mentalmente*) to psych up; **~se** *vr* (*concienciarse*) to become aware; (*prepararse mentalmente*) to get psyched up; **~se de que ...** (*convencerse*) to get it into one's head that ...

mentar [men'tar] *vt* to mention, name; **~ la madre a algn** to swear at sb.

mente ['mente] *nf* mind; (*inteligencia*) intelligence; **no tengo en ~ hacer eso** it is not my intention to do that.

mentecato, a [mente'kato, a] *adj* silly, stupid ♦ *nm/f* fool, idiot.

mentir [men'tir] *vi* to lie; **¡miento!** sorry, I'm wrong!

mentira [men'tira] *nf* (*una ~*) lie; (*acto*) lying; (*invención*) fiction; **~ piadosa** white lie; **una ~ como una casa** a whopping great lie (*fam*); **parece ~ que** ... it seems incredible that ..., I can't believe that ....

mentiroso, a [menti'roso, a] *adj* lying; (*falso*) deceptive ♦ *nm/f* liar.

mentís [men'tis] *nm inv* denial; **dar el ~ a** to deny.

mentón [men'ton] *nm* chin.

menú [me'nu] *nm* (*tb INFORM*) menu; (*en restaurante*) set meal; **guiado por ~** (*INFORM*) menu-driven.

menudear [menuðe'ar] *vt* (*repetir*) to repeat frequently ♦ *vi* (*ser frecuente*) to

be frequent; (*detallar*) to go into great detail.
menudencia [menu'ðenθja] *nf* (*bagatela*) trifle; **~s** *nfpl* odds and ends.
menudeo [menu'ðeo] *nm* retail sales *pl.*
menudillos [menu'ðiʎos] *nmpl* giblets.
menudo, a [me'nuðo, a] *adj* (*pequeño*) small, tiny; (*sin importancia*) petty, insignificant; **¡~ negocio!** (*fam*) some deal!; **a ~** often, frequently.
meñique [me'ɲike] *nm* little finger.
meollo [me'oʎo] *nm* (*fig*) essence, core.
mequetrefe [meke'trefe] *nm* good-for-nothing, whippersnapper.
mercader [merka'ðer] *nm* merchant.
mercadería [merkaðe'ria] *nf* commodity; **~s** *nfpl* goods, merchandise *sg.*
mercado [mer'kaðo] *nm* market; **~ en baja** falling market; **M~ Común** Common Market; **~ de demanda/de oferta** seller's/buyer's market; **~ laboral** labour market; **~ objetivo** target market; **~ de productos básicos** commodity market; **~ de valores** stock market; **~ exterior/interior** *o* **nacional/libre** overseas/home/free market.
mercancía [merkan'θia] *nf* commodity; **~s** *nfpl* goods, merchandise *sg*; **~s en depósito** bonded goods; **~s perecederas** perishable goods.
mercancías [merkan'θias] *nm inv* goods train, freight train (*US*).
mercantil [merkan'til] *adj* mercantile, commercial.
mercenario, a [merθe'narjo, a] *adj, nm* mercenary.
mercería [merθe'ria] *nf* (*artículos*) haberdashery (*BRIT*), notions *pl* (*US*); (*tienda*) haberdasher's shop (*BRIT*), drapery (*BRIT*), notions store (*US*).
Mercosur [merko'sur] *nm abr* = *Mercado Común del Sur.*
mercurio [mer'kurjo] *nm* mercury.
merecedor, a [mereθe'ðor, a] *adj* deserving; **~ de confianza** trustworthy.
merecer [mere'θer] *vt* to deserve, merit ♦ *vi* to be deserving, be worthy; **merece la pena** it's worthwhile.
merecido, a [mere'θiðo, a] *adj* (well) deserved; **llevarse su ~** to get one's deserts.
merendar [meren'dar] *vt* to have for tea ♦ *vi* to have tea; (*en el campo*) to have a picnic.
merendero [meren'dero] *nm* (*café*) tearoom; (*en el campo*) picnic spot.
merengue [me'renge] *nm* meringue.
merezca [me'reθka] *etc vb V* **merecer.**
meridiano [meri'ðjano] *nm* (*ASTRO, GEO*) meridian; **la explicación es de una claridad meridiana** the explanation is as clear as day.
meridional [meriðjo'nal] *adj* Southern ♦ *nm/f* Southerner.
merienda [me'rjenda] *etc vb V* **merendar** ♦ *nf* (light) tea, afternoon snack; (*de campo*) picnic; **~ de negros** free-for-all.
mérito ['merito] *nm* merit; (*valor*) worth, value; **hacer ~s** to make a good impression; **restar ~ a** to detract from.
meritorio, a [meri'torjo, a] *adj* deserving.
merluza [mer'luθa] *nf* hake; **coger una ~** (*fam*) to get sozzled.
merma ['merma] *nf* decrease; (*pérdida*) wastage.
mermar [mer'mar] *vt* to reduce, lessen ♦ *vi* to decrease, dwindle.
mermelada [merme'laða] *nf* jam; **~ de naranja** marmalade.
mero, a ['mero, a] *adj* mere, simple; (*AM fam*) real ♦ *adv* (*AM*) just, right ♦ *nm* (*ZOOL*) grouper; **el ~ ~** (*AM fam*) the boss.
merodear [meroðe'ar] *vi* (*MIL*) to maraud; (*de noche*) to prowl (about); (*curiosear*) to snoop around.
mes [mes] *nm* month; (*salario*) month's pay; **el ~ corriente** this *o* the current month.
mesa ['mesa] *nf* table; (*de trabajo*) desk; (*COM*) counter; (*en mitin*) platform; (*GEO*) plateau; (*ARQ*) landing; **~ de noche/de tijera/de operaciones** *u* **operatoria** bedside/folding/operating table; **~ redonda** (*reunión*) round table; **~ digitalizadora** (*INFORM*) graph pad; **~ directiva** board; **~ y cama** bed and board; **poner/quitar la ~** to lay/clear the table.
mesarse [me'sarse] *vr*: **~ el pelo** *o* **los cabellos** to tear one's hair.
mesera [me'sera] *nf* (*AM*) waitress.
mesero [me'sero] *nm* (*AM*) waiter.
meseta [me'seta] *nf* (*GEO*) meseta, tableland; (*ARQ*) landing.
mesilla [me'siʎa], **mesita** [me'sita] *nf*: **~ de noche** bedside table.
mesón [me'son] *nm* inn.
mestizo, a [mes'tiθo, a] *adj* half-caste, of mixed race; (*ZOOL*) crossbred ♦ *nm/f* half-caste.
mesura [me'sura] *nf* (*calma*) calm; (*moderación*) moderation, restraint; (*cortesía*) courtesy.
mesurar [mesu'rar] *vt* (*contener*) to restrain; **~se** *vr* to restrain o.s.

meta ['meta] *nf* goal; (*de carrera*) finish; (*fig*) goal, aim, objective.
metabolismo [metaβo'lismo] *nm* metabolism.
metafísico, a [meta'fisiko, a] *adj* metaphysical ♦ *nf* metaphysics *sg*.
metáfora [me'tafora] *nf* metaphor.
metafórico, a [meta'foriko, a] *adj* metaphorical.
metal [me'tal] *nm* (*materia*) metal; (*MUS*) brass.
metálico, a [me'taliko, a] *adj* metallic; (*de metal*) metal ♦ *nm* (*dinero contante*) cash.
metalurgia [meta'lurxja] *nf* metallurgy.
metalúrgico, a [meta'lurxiko, a] *adj* metallurgic(al); **industria ~a** engineering industry.
metamorfosear [metamorfose'ar] *vt*: **~ (en)** to metamorphose *o* transform (into).
metamorfosis [metamor'fosis] *nf inv* metamorphosis, transformation.
metedura [mete'ðura] *nf*: **~ de pata** (*fam*) blunder.
meteorito [meteo'rito] *nm* meteorite.
meteoro [mete'oro] *nm* meteor.
meteorología [meteorolo'xia] *nf* meteorology.
meteorólogo, a [meteo'roloɣo, a] *nm/f* meteorologist; (*RADIO, TV*) weather reporter.
meter [me'ter] *vt* (*colocar*) to put, place; (*introducir*) to put in, insert; (*involucrar*) to involve; (*causar*) to make, cause; **~se** *vr*: **~se en** to go into, enter; (*fig*) to interfere in, meddle in; **~se a** to start; **~se a escritor** to become a writer; **~se con algn** to provoke sb, pick a quarrel with sb; **~ prisa a algn** to hurry sb up.
meticuloso, a [metiku'loso, a] *adj* meticulous, thorough.
metido, a [me'tiðo, a] *adj*: **estar muy ~ en un asunto** to be deeply involved in a matter; **~ en años** elderly; **~ en carne** plump.
metódico, a [me'toðiko, a] *adj* methodical.
metodismo [meto'ðismo] *nm* Methodism.
método ['metoðo] *nm* method.
metodología [metoðolo'xia] *nf* methodology.
metomentodo [metomen'toðo] *nm inv* meddler, busybody.
metraje [me'traxe] *nm* (*CINE*) length; **cinta de largo/corto ~** full-length film/short.
metralla [me'traʎa] *nf* shrapnel.
metralleta [metra'ʎeta] *nf* sub-machine-gun.
métrico, a ['metriko, a] *adj* metric ♦ *nf* metrics *pl*; **cinta métrica** tape measure.
metro ['metro] *nm* metre; (*tren*: *tb*: **metropolitano**) underground (*BRIT*), subway (*US*); (*instrumento*) rule; **~ cuadrado/cúbico** square/cubic metre.
metrópoli [me'tropoli], **metrópolis** [me'tropolis] *nf* (*ciudad*) metropolis; (*colonial*) mother country.
mexicano, a [mexi'kano, a] *adj, nm/f* (*AM*) Mexican.
México ['mexiko] *nm* (*AM*) Mexico; **Ciudad de ~** Mexico City.
mezcla ['meθkla] *nf* mixture; (*fig*) blend.
mezclar [meθ'klar] *vt* to mix (up); (*armonizar*) to blend; (*combinar*) to merge; **~se** *vr* to mix, mingle; **~ en** to get mixed up in, get involved in.
mezcolanza [meθko'lanθa] *nf* hotchpotch, jumble.
mezquindad [meθkin'dað] *nf* (*cicatería*) meanness; (*miras estrechas*) pettiness; (*acto*) mean action.
mezquino, a [meθ'kino, a] *adj* (*cicatero*) mean ♦ *nm/f* (*avaro*) mean person; (*miserable*) petty individual.
mezquita [meθ'kita] *nf* mosque.
MF *abr* (= *Modulación de Frecuencia*) FM.
mg. *abr* (= *miligramo(s)*) mg.
mi [mi] *adj posesivo* my ♦ *nm* (*MUS*) E.
mí [mi] *pron* me, myself; **¿y a ~ qué?** so what?
miaja ['mjaxa] *nf* crumb; **ni una ~** (*fig*) not the least little bit.
miau [mjau] *nm* miaow.
michelín [mitʃe'lin] *nm* (*fam*) spare tyre.
mico ['miko] *nm* monkey.
micro ['mikro] *nm* (*RADIO*) mike, microphone; (*AM*: *pequeño*) minibus; (: *grande*) coach, bus.
microbio [mi'kroβjo] *nm* microbe.
microbús [mikro'βus] *nm* minibus.
microchip [mikro'tʃip] *nm* microchip.
microcomputador [mikrokomputa'ðor] *nm*, **microcomputadora** [mikrokomputa'ðora] *nf* micro(computer).
microeconomía [mikroekono'mia] *nf* microeconomics *sg*.
microficha [mikro'fitʃa] *nf* microfiche.
microfilm, *pl* **microfilms** [mikro'film, mikro'films] *nm* microfilm.
micrófono [mi'krofono] *nm* microphone.
microinformática [mikroinfor'matika] *nf* microcomputing.
micrómetro [mi'krometro] *nm* micrometer.
microonda [mikro'onda] *nf* microwave; **(horno) ~s** microwave (oven).
microordenador [mikroordena'ðor] *nm*

microcomputer.
micropastilla [mikropas'tiʎa], **microplaqueta** [mikropla'keta] *nf* (*INFORM*) chip, wafer.
microplaquita [mikropla'kita] *nf*: **~ de silicio** silicon chip.
microprocesador [mikroprocesa'ðor] *nm* microprocessor.
microscópico, a [mikros'kopiko, a] *adj* microscopic.
microscopio [mikros'kopjo] *nm* microscope.
midiendo [mi'ðjendo] *etc vb V* **medir.**
miedo ['mjeðo] *nm* fear; (*nerviosismo*) apprehension, nervousness; **meter ~ a** to scare, frighten; **tener ~** to be afraid; **de ~** wonderful, marvellous; **¡qué ~!** (*fam*) how awful!; **me da ~** it scares me; **hace un frío de ~** (*fam*) it's terribly cold.
miedoso, a [mje'ðoso, a] *adj* fearful, timid.
miel [mjel] *nf* honey; **no hay ~ sin hiel** there's no rose without a thorn.
miembro ['mjembro] *nm* limb; (*socio*) member; (*de institución*) fellow; **~ viril** penis.
mientes ['mjentes] *etc vb V* **mentar; mentir** ♦ *nfpl*: **no parar ~ en** to pay no attention to; **traer a las ~** to recall.
mientras ['mjentras] *conj* while; (*duración*) as long as ♦ *adv* meanwhile; **~ (que)** whereas; **~ tanto** meanwhile; **~ más tiene, más quiere** the more he has, the more he wants.
miérc. *abr* (= *miércoles*) Wed.
miércoles ['mjerkoles] *nm inv* Wednesday; **~ de ceniza** Ash Wednesday; *V tb* **Carnaval.**
mierda ['mjerða] *nf* (*fam!*) shit (*!*), crap (*!*); (*fig*) filth, dirt; **¡vete a la ~!** go to hell!
mies [mjes] *nf* (ripe) corn, wheat, grain.
miga ['miɣa] *nf* crumb; (*fig*: *meollo*) essence; **hacer buenas ~s** (*fam*) to get on well; **esto tiene su ~** there's more to this than meets the eye.
migaja [mi'ɣaxa] *nf*: **una ~ de** (*un poquito*) a little; **~s** *nfpl* crumbs; (*pey*) left-overs.
migración [miɣra'θjon] *nf* migration.
migratorio, a [miɣra'torjo, a] *adj* migratory.
mil [mil] *num* thousand; **dos ~ libras** two thousand pounds.
milagro [mi'laɣro] *nm* miracle; **hacer ~s** (*fig*) to work wonders.
milagroso, a [mila'ɣroso, a] *adj* miraculous.
Milán [mi'lan] *nm* Milan.
milenario, a [mile'narjo, a] *adj* millennial; (*fig*) very ancient.
milenio [mi'lenjo] *nm* millennium.
milésimo, a [mi'lesimo, a] *num* thousandth.
mili ['mili] *nf*: **hacer la ~** (*fam*) to do one's military service; *see boxed note.*

MILI

La mili, *military service, is compulsory in Spain, although the number of months' service has been reduced and recruits are now posted close to their home town. There continues to be strong opposition from conscientious objectors, who are obliged to do "Prestación Social Sustitutoria" instead; this usually involves doing some form of community service and lasts longer. Those who refuse to do either of these, "los insumisos", can be sent to prison.*

milicia [mi'liθja] *nf* (*MIL*) militia; (*servicio militar*) military service.
miligramo [mili'ɣramo] *nm* milligram.
milímetro [mi'limetro] *nm* millimetre (*BRIT*), millimeter (*US*).
militante [mili'tante] *adj* militant.
militar [mili'tar] *adj* military ♦ *nm/f* soldier ♦ *vi* to serve in the army; (*fig*) to militate, fight.
militarismo [milita'rismo] *nm* militarism.
milla ['miʎa] *nf* mile; **~ marina** nautical mile.
millar [mi'ʎar] *num* thousand; **a ~es** in thousands.
millón [mi'ʎon] *num* million.
millonario, a [miʎo'narjo, a] *nm/f* millionaire.
millonésimo, a [miʎo'nesimo, a] *num* millionth.
mimado, a [mi'maðo, a] *adj* spoiled.
mimar [mi'mar] *vt* to spoil, pamper.
mimbre ['mimbre] *nm* wicker; **de ~** wicker *cpd*, wickerwork.
mimetismo [mime'tismo] *nm* mimicry.
mímica ['mimika] *nf* (*para comunicarse*) sign language; (*imitación*) mimicry.
mimo ['mimo] *nm* (*caricia*) caress; (*de niño*) spoiling; (*TEAT*) mime; (*: actor*) mime artist.
mina ['mina] *nf* mine; (*pozo*) shaft; (*de lápiz*) lead refill; **hullera** *o* **~ de carbón** coalmine.
minar [mi'nar] *vt* to mine; (*fig*) to undermine.
mineral [mine'ral] *adj* mineral ♦ *nm* (*GEO*) mineral; (*mena*) ore.
minería [mine'ria] *nf* mining.

minero, a [mi'nero, a] *adj* mining *cpd* ♦ *nm/f* miner.
miniatura [minja'tura] *adj inv, nf* miniature.
minicadena [minika'ðena] *nf* (*MUS*) mini hi-fi.
minicomputador [minikomputa'ðor] *nm* minicomputer.
MiniDisc® [mini'ðisk] *nm* MiniDisc®.
minidisco [mini'ðisko] *nm* diskette.
minifalda [mini'falda] *nf* miniskirt.
minifundio [mini'fundjo] *nm* smallholding, small farm.
minimizar [minimi'θar] *vt* to minimize.
mínimo, a ['minimo, a] *adj* minimum; (*insignificante*) minimal ♦ *nm* minimum; **precio/salario ~** minimum price/wage; **lo ~ que pueden hacer** the least they can do.
minino, a [mi'nino, a] *nm/f* (*fam*) puss, pussy.
ministerio [minis'terjo] *nm* ministry (*BRIT*), department (*US*); **M~ de Asuntos Exteriores** Foreign Office (*BRIT*), State Department (*US*); **M~ del Comercio e Industria** Department of Trade and Industry; **M~ de (la) Gobernación** *o* **del Interior** ≈ Home Office (*BRIT*), Ministry of the Interior; **M~ de Hacienda** Treasury (*BRIT*), Treasury Department (*US*).
ministro, a [mi'nistro, a] *nm/f* minister, secretary (*esp US*); **M~ de Hacienda** Chancellor of the Exchequer, Secretary of the Treasury (*US*); **M~ de (la) Gobernación** *o* **del Interior** ≈ Home Secretary (*BRIT*), Secretary of the Interior (*US*).
minoría [mino'ria] *nf* minority.
minorista [mino'rista] *nm* retailer.
mintiendo [min'tjendo] *etc vb V* **mentir**.
minucia [mi'nuθja] *nf* (*detalle insignificante*) trifle; (*bagatela*) mere nothing.
minuciosidad [minuθjosi'ðað] *nf* (*meticulosidad*) thoroughness, meticulousness.
minucioso, a [minu'θjoso, a] *adj* thorough, meticulous; (*prolijo*) very detailed.
minúsculo, a [mi'nuskulo, a] *adj* tiny, minute ♦ *nf* small letter; **minúsculas** *nfpl* (*TIP*) lower case *sg*.
minusvalía [minusβa'lia] *nf* physical handicap; (*COM*) depreciation, capital loss.
minusválido, a [minus'βaliðo, a] *adj* (physically) handicapped *o* disabled ♦ *nm/f* disabled person.
minuta [mi'nuta] *nf* (*de comida*) menu; (*de abogado etc*) fee.
minutero [minu'tero] *nm* minute hand.
minuto [mi'nuto] *nm* minute.
Miño ['miɲo] *nm*: **el (río) ~** the Miño.
mío, a ['mio, a] *adj, pron*: **el ~** mine; **un amigo ~** a friend of mine; **lo ~** what is mine; **los ~s** my people, my relations.
miope ['mjope] *adj* short-sighted.
miopía [mjo'pia] *nf* near- *o* short-sightedness.
MIR [mir] *nm abr* (*POL*) = *Movimiento de Izquierda Revolucionaria*; (*ESP MED*) = *Médico Interno y Residente*.
mira ['mira] *nf* (*de arma*) sight(s) (*pl*); (*fig*) aim, intention; **de amplias/estrechas ~s** broad-/narrow-minded.
mirada [mi'raða] *nf* look, glance; (*expresión*) look, expression; **~ de soslayo** sidelong glance; **~ fija** stare, gaze; **~ perdida** distant look; **echar una ~ a** to glance at; **levantar/bajar la ~** to look up/down; **resistir la ~ de algn** to stare sb out.
mirado, a [mi'raðo, a] *adj* (*sensato*) sensible; (*considerado*) considerate; **bien/mal ~** well/not well thought of.
mirador [mira'ðor] *nm* viewpoint, vantage point.
miramiento [mira'mjento] *nm* (*consideración*) considerateness; **tratar sin ~s a algn** to ride roughshod over sb.
mirar [mi'rar] *vt* to look at; (*observar*) to watch; (*considerar*) to consider, think over; (*vigilar, cuidar*) to watch, look after ♦ *vi* to look; (*ARQ*) to face; **~se** *vr* (*dos personas*) to look at each other; **~ algo/a algn de reojo** *o* **de través** to look askance at sth/sb; **~ algo/a algn por encima del hombro** to look down on sth/sb; **~ bien/mal** to think highly of/have a poor opinion of; **~ fijamente** to stare *o* gaze at; **~ por** (*fig*) to look after; **~ por la ventana** to look out of the window; **~se al espejo** to look at o.s. in the mirror; **~se a los ojos** to look into each other's eyes.
mirilla [mi'riʎa] *nf* (*agujero*) spyhole, peephole.
mirlo ['mirlo] *nm* blackbird.
misa ['misa] *nf* mass; **~ del gallo** midnight mass (*on Christmas Eve*); **~ de difuntos** requiem mass; **como en ~** in dead silence; **estos datos van a ~** (*fig*) these facts are utterly trustworthy.
misántropo [mi'santropo] *nm* misanthrope, misanthropist.
miscelánea [misθe'lanea] *nf* miscellany.
miserable [mise'raβle] *adj* (*avaro*) mean, stingy; (*nimio*) miserable, paltry; (*lugar*) squalid; (*fam*) vile, despicable ♦ *nm/f* (*malvado*) rogue.

miseria [mi'serja] *nf* misery; (*pobreza*) poverty; (*tacañería*) meanness, stinginess; (*condiciones*) squalor; **una ~** a pittance.
misericordia [miseri'korðja] *nf* (*compasión*) compassion, pity; (*perdón*) forgiveness, mercy.
misil [mi'sil] *nm* missile.
misión [mi'sjon] *nf* mission; (*tarea*) job, duty; (*POL*) assignment; **misiones** *nfpl* (*REL*) overseas missions.
misionero, a [misjo'nero, a] *nm/f* missionary.
mismamente [misma'mente] *adv* (*fam*: *sólo*) only, just.
mismísimo, a [mis'misimo, a] *adj superlativo* selfsame, very (same).
mismo, a ['mismo, a] *adj* (*semejante*) same; (*después de pronombre*) -self; (*para énfasis*) very ♦ *adv*: **aquí/ayer/hoy ~** right here/only yesterday/this very day; **ahora ~** right now ♦ *conj*: **lo ~ que** just like, just as; **por lo ~** for the same reason; **el ~ traje** the same suit; **en ese ~ momento** at that very moment; **vino el ~ Ministro** the Minister himself came; **yo ~ lo vi** I saw it myself; **lo hizo por sí ~** he did it by himself; **lo ~** the same (thing); **da lo ~** it's all the same; **quedamos en las mismas** we're no further forward.
misógino [mi'soxino] *nm* misogynist.
miss [mis] *nf* beauty queen.
misterio [mis'terjo] *nm* mystery; (*lo secreto*) secrecy.
misterioso, a [miste'rjoso, a] *adj* mysterious; (*inexplicable*) puzzling.
misticismo [misti'θismo] *nm* mysticism.
místico, a ['mistiko, a] *adj* mystic(al) ♦ *nm/f* mystic ♦ *nf* mysticism.
mitad [mi'tað] *nf* (*medio*) half; (*centro*) middle; **~ (y) ~** half-and-half; (*fig*) yes and no; **a ~ de precio** (at) half-price; **en** *o* **a ~ del camino** halfway along the road; **cortar por la ~** to cut through the middle.
mítico, a ['mitiko, a] *adj* mythical.
mitigar [miti'ɣar] *vt* to mitigate; (*dolor*) to relieve; (*sed*) to quench; (*ira*) to appease; (*preocupación*) to allay; (*soledad*) to alleviate.
mitigue [mi'tiɣe] *etc vb V* **mitigar.**
mitin ['mitin] *nm* (*esp POL*) meeting.
mito ['mito] *nm* myth.
mitología [mitolo'xia] *nf* mythology.
mitológico, a [mito'loxiko, a] *adj* mythological.
mixto, a ['miksto, a] *adj* mixed; (*comité*) joint.
ml. *abr* (= *mililitro*) ml.
mm. *abr* (= *milímetro*) mm.
m/n *abr* (*ECON*) = *moneda nacional.*
M.º *abr* (*POL*: = *Ministerio*) Min.
m/o *abr* (*COM*) = *mi orden.*
mobiliario [moβi'ljarjo] *nm* furniture.
MOC *nm abr* = *Movimiento de Objeción de Conciencia.*
mocasín [moka'sin] *nm* moccasin.
mocedad [moθe'ðað] *nf* youth.
mochila [mo'tʃila] *nf* rucksack (*BRIT*), backpack.
moción [mo'θjon] *nf* motion; **~ compuesta** (*POL*) composite motion.
moco ['moko] *nm* mucus; **limpiarse los ~s** to blow one's nose; **no es ~ de pavo** it's no trifle.
mocoso, a [mo'koso, a] *adj* snivelling; (*fig*) ill-bred ♦ *nm/f* (*fam*) brat.
moda ['moða] *nf* fashion; (*estilo*) style; **de** *o* **a la ~** in fashion, fashionable; **pasado de ~** out of fashion; **vestido a la última ~** trendily dressed.
modal [mo'ðal] *adj* modal ♦ *nm*: **~es** *nmpl* manners.
modalidad [moðali'ðað] *nf* (*clase*) kind, variety; (*manera*) way; (*INFORM*) mode; **~ de texto** (*INFORM*) text mode.
modelar [moðe'lar] *vt* to model.
modelo [mo'ðelo] *adj inv* model ♦ *nm/f* model ♦ *nm* (*patrón*) pattern; (*norma*) standard.
módem ['moðem] *nm* (*INFORM*) modem.
moderado, a [moðe'raðo, a] *adj* moderate.
moderar [moðe'rar] *vt* to moderate; (*violencia*) to restrain, control; (*velocidad*) to reduce; **~se** *vr* to restrain o.s., control o.s.
modernice [moðer'niθe] *etc vb V* **modernizar.**
modernizar [moðerni'θar] *vt* to modernize; (*INFORM*) to upgrade.
moderno, a [mo'ðerno, a] *adj* modern; (*actual*) present-day; (*equipo etc*) up-to-date.
modestia [mo'ðestja] *nf* modesty.
modesto, a [mo'ðesto, a] *adj* modest.
módico, a ['moðiko, a] *adj* moderate, reasonable.
modificar [moðifi'kar] *vt* to modify.
modifique [moði'fike] *etc vb V* **modificar.**
modismo [mo'ðismo] *nm* idiom.
modisto, a [mo'ðisto, a] *nm/f* dressmaker.
modo ['moðo] *nm* (*manera, forma*) way, manner; (*INFORM, MUS*) mode; (*LING*) mood; **~s** *nmpl* manners; **"~ de empleo"** "instructions for use"; **~ de gobierno**

form of government; **a ~ de** like; **de este ~** in this way; **de ningún ~** in no way; **de todos ~s** at any rate; **de un ~ u otro** (in) one way or another.
modorra [mo'ðorra] *nf* drowsiness.
modoso, a [mo'ðoso, a] *adj* (*educado*) quiet, well-mannered.
modulación [moðula'θjon] *nf* modulation; **~ de frecuencia** (*RADIO*) frequency modulation, FM.
módulo ['moðulo] *nm* module; (*de mueble*) unit.
mofarse [mo'farse] *vr*: **~ de** to mock, scoff at.
moflete [mo'flete] *nm* fat cheek, chubby cheek.
mogollón [moɣo'ʎon] (*fam*) *nm*: **~ de discos** *etc* loads of records *etc* ♦ *adv*: **un ~** a hell of a lot.
mohín [mo'in] *nm* (*mueca*) (wry) face; (*pucheros*) pout.
mohino, a [mo'ino, a] *adj* (*triste*) gloomy, depressed; (*enojado*) sulky.
moho ['moo] *nm* (*BOT*) mould, mildew; (*en metal*) rust.
mohoso, a [mo'oso, a] *adj* mouldy; rusty.
mojado, a [mo'xaðo, a] *adj* wet; (*húmedo*) damp; (*empapado*) drenched.
mojar [mo'xar] *vt* to wet; (*humedecer*) to damp(en), moisten; (*calar*) to soak; **~se** *vr* to get wet; **~ el pan en el café** to dip *o* dunk one's bread in one's coffee.
mojigato, a [moxi'ɣato, a] *adj* (*hipócrita*) hypocritical; (*santurrón*) sanctimonious; (*gazmoño*) prudish ♦ *nm/f* hypocrite; sanctimonious person; prude.
mojón [mo'xon] *nm* (*hito*) landmark; (*en un camino*) signpost; (*~ kilométrico*) milestone.
mol. *abr* (= *molécula*) mol.
molar [mo'lar] *nm* molar ♦ *vt* (*fam*): **lo que más me mola es ...** what I'm really into is ...; **¿te mola un pitillo?** do you fancy a smoke?
Moldavia [mol'ðaβja], **Moldova** [mol'ðoβa] *nf* Moldavia, Moldova.
moldavo, a [mol'ðaβo, a] *adj, nm/f* Moldavian, Moldovan.
molde ['molde] *nm* mould; (*vaciado*) cast; (*de costura*) pattern; (*fig*) model.
moldear [molde'ar] *vt* to mould; (*en yeso etc*) to cast.
mole ['mole] *nf* mass, bulk; (*edificio*) pile.
molécula [mo'lekula] *nf* molecule.
moler [mo'ler] *vt* to grind, crush; (*pulverizar*) to pound; (*trigo etc*) to mill; (*cansar*) to tire out, exhaust; **~ a algn a palos** to give sb a beating.
molestar [moles'tar] *vt* to bother; (*fastidiar*) to annoy; (*incomodar*) to inconvenience, put out; (*perturbar*) to trouble, upset ♦ *vi* to be a nuisance; **~se** *vr* to bother; (*incomodarse*) to go to a lot of trouble; (*ofenderse*) to take offence; **¿le molesta el ruido?** do you mind the noise?; **siento ~le** I'm sorry to trouble you.
molestia [mo'lestja] *nf* bother, trouble; (*incomodidad*) inconvenience; (*MED*) discomfort; **no es ninguna ~** it's no trouble at all.
molesto, a [mo'lesto, a] *adj* (*que fastidia*) annoying; (*incómodo*) inconvenient; (*inquieto*) uncomfortable, ill at ease; (*enfadado*) annoyed; **estar ~** (*MED*) to be in some discomfort; **estar ~ con algn** (*fig*) to be cross with sb; **me sentí ~** I felt embarrassed.
molido, a [mo'liðo, a] *adj* (*machacado*) ground; (*pulverizado*) powdered; **estar ~** (*fig*) to be exhausted *o* dead beat.
molinero [moli'nero] *nm* miller.
molinillo [moli'niʎo] *nm* hand mill; **~ de carne/café** mincer/coffee grinder.
molino [mo'lino] *nm* (*edificio*) mill; (*máquina*) grinder.
mollera [mo'ʎera] *nf* (*ANAT*) crown of the head; (*fam: seso*) brains *pl*; **duro de ~** (*estúpido*) thick.
Molucas [mo'lukas] *nfpl*: **las (Islas) ~** the Moluccas, the Molucca Islands.
molusco [mo'lusko] *nm* mollusc.
momentáneo, a [momen'taneo, a] *adj* momentary.
momento [mo'mento] *nm* (*gen*) moment; (*TEC*) momentum; **de ~** at the moment, for the moment; **en ese ~** at that moment, just then; **por el ~** for the time being.
momia ['momja] *nf* mummy.
mona ['mona] *nf V* **mono**.
Mónaco ['monako] *nm* Monaco.
monada [mo'naða] *nf* (*de niño*) charming habit; (*cosa primorosa*) lovely thing; (*chica*) pretty girl; **¡qué ~!** isn't it cute?
monaguillo [mona'ɣiʎo] *nm* altar boy.
monarca [mo'narka] *nm/f* monarch, ruler.
monarquía [monar'kia] *nf* monarchy.
monárquico, a [mo'narkiko, a] *nm/f* royalist, monarchist.
monasterio [monas'terjo] *nm* monastery.
Moncloa [mon'kloa] *nf*: **la ~** *official residence of the Spanish Prime Minister*.
monda ['monda] *nf* (*poda*) pruning; (*: de árbol*) lopping; (*: de fruta*) peeling; (*cáscara*) skin; **¡es la ~!** (*fam: fantástico*)

it's great!; (: *el colmo*) it's the limit!; (: *persona*: *gracioso*) he's a knockout!
mondadientes [monda'ðjentes] *nm inv* toothpick.
mondar [mon'dar] *vt* (*limpiar*) to clean; (*pelar*) to peel; ~**se** *vr*: ~**se de risa** (*fam*) to split one's sides laughing.
moneda [mo'neða] *nf* (*tipo de dinero*) currency, money; (*pieza*) coin; **una ~ de 5 pesetas** a 5 peseta coin; **~ de curso** legal tender; ~ **extranjera** foreign exchange; ~ **única** single currency; **es ~ corriente** (*fig*) it's common knowledge.
monedero [mone'ðero] *nm* purse.
monegasco, a [mone'ɣasko, a] *adj* of *o* from Monaco, Monegasque ♦ *nm/f* Monegasque.
monetario, a [mone'tarjo, a] *adj* monetary, financial.
monetarista [moneta'rista] *adj, nm/f* monetarist.
mongólico, a [mon'goliko, a] *adj, nm/f* Mongol.
monigote [moni'ɣote] *nm* (*dibujo*) doodle; (*de papel*) cut-out figure; (*pey*) wimp; *V tb* **Día de los (Santos) Inocentes.**
monitor [moni'tor] *nm* (*INFORM*) monitor; ~ **en color** colour monitor; ~ **fósfor verde** green screen.
monja ['monxa] *nf* nun.
monje ['monxe] *nm* monk.
mono, a ['mono, a] *adj* (*bonito*) lovely, pretty; (*gracioso*) nice, charming ♦ *nm/f* monkey, ape ♦ *nm* dungarees *pl*; (*overoles*) overalls *pl*; (*fam*: *de droges*) cold turkey; **una chica muy mona** a very pretty girl; **dormir la** ~ to sleep it off.
monóculo [mo'nokulo] *nm* monocle.
monografía [monoɣra'fia] *nf* monograph.
monolingüe [mono'lingwe] *adj* monolingual.
monólogo [mo'noloɣo] *nm* monologue.
monomando [mono'mando] *nm* (*tb*: **grifo** ~) mixer tap.
monoparental [monoparen'tal] *adj*: **familia** ~ single-parent family.
monopatín [monopa'tin] *nm* skateboard.
monopolice [monopo'liθe] *etc vb V* **monopolizar.**
monopolio [mono'poljo] *nm* monopoly; ~ **total** absolute monopoly.
monopolista [monopo'lista] *adj, nm/f* monopolist.
monopolizar [monopoli'θar] *vt* to monopolize.
monosílabo, a [mono'silaβo, a] *adj* monosyllabic ♦ *nm* monosyllable.
monotonía [monoto'nia] *nf* (*sonido*) monotone; (*fig*) monotony.
monótono, a [mo'notono, a] *adj* monotonous.
mono-usuario, a [monou'swarjo, a] *adj* (*INFORM*) single-user.
monóxido [mo'noksiðo] *nm* monoxide; ~ **de carbono** carbon monoxide.
Mons. *abr* (*REL*) = **Monseñor.**
monseñor [monse'ɲor] *nm* monsignor.
monserga [mon'serɣa] *nf* (*lenguaje confuso*) gibberish; (*tonterías*) drivel.
monstruo ['monstrwo] *nm* monster ♦ *adj inv* fantastic.
monstruoso, a [mons'trwoso, a] *adj* monstrous.
monta ['monta] *nf* total, sum; **de poca** ~ unimportant, of little account.
montacargas [monta'karɣas] *nm inv* service lift (*BRIT*), freight elevator (*US*).
montador [monta'ðor] *nm* (*para montar*) mounting block; (*profesión*) fitter; (*CINE*) film editor.
montaje [mon'taxe] *nm* assembly; (*organización*) fitting up; (*TEAT*) décor; (*CINE*) montage.
montante [mon'tante] *nm* (*poste*) upright; (*soporte*) stanchion; (*ARQ*: *de puerta*) transom; (: *de ventana*) mullion; (*suma*) amount, total.
montaña [mon'taɲa] *nf* (*monte*) mountain; (*sierra*) mountains *pl*, mountainous area; (*AM*: *selva*) forest; ~ **rusa** roller coaster.
montañero, a [monta'ɲero, a] *adj* mountain *cpd* ♦ *nm/f* mountaineer, climber.
montañés, esa [monta'ɲes, esa] *adj* mountain *cpd*; (*de Santander*) of *o* from the Santander region ♦ *nm/f* highlander; native *o* inhabitant of the Santander region.
montañismo [monta'ɲismo] *nm* mountaineering, climbing.
montañoso, a [monta'ɲoso, a] *adj* mountainous.
montar [mon'tar] *vt* (*subir a*) to mount, get on; (*caballo etc*) to ride; (*TEC*) to assemble, put together; (*negocio*) to set up; (*colocar*) to lift on to; (*CINE*: *película*) to edit; (*TEAT*: *obra*) to stage, put on; (*CULIN*: *batir*) to whip, beat ♦ *vi* to mount, get on; (*sobresalir*) to overlap; ~ **en cólera** to get angry; ~ **un número** *o* **numerito** to make a scene; **tanto monta** it makes no odds.
montaraz [monta'raθ] *adj* mountain *cpd*, highland *cpd*; (*pey*) uncivilized.
monte ['monte] *nm* (*montaña*) mountain; (*bosque*) woodland; (*área sin cultivar*) wild

area, wild country; ~ **de piedad** pawnshop; ~ **alto** forest; ~ **bajo** scrub(land).
montera [mon'tera] *nf* (*sombrero*) cloth cap; (*de torero*) bullfighter's hat.
monto ['monto] *nm* total, amount.
montón [mon'ton] *nm* heap, pile; **un ~ de** (*fig*) heaps of, lots of; **a montones** by the score, galore.
montura [mon'tura] *nf* (*cabalgadura*) mount; (*silla*) saddle; (*arreos*) harness; (*de joya*) mounting; (*de gafas*) frame.
monumental [monumen'tal] *adj* (*tb fig*) monumental; **zona ~** area of historical interest.
monumento [monu'mento] *nm* monument; (*de conmemoración*) memorial.
monzón [mon'θon] *nm* monsoon.
moña ['moɲa] *nf* hair ribbon.
moño ['moɲo] *nm* (*de pelo*) bun; **estar hasta el ~** (*fam*) to be fed up to the back teeth.
MOPTMA *nm abr* = *Ministerio de Obras Públicas, Transporte y Medio Ambiente.*
moqueta [mo'keta] *nf* fitted carpet.
moquillo [mo'kiʎo] *nm* (*enfermedad*) distemper.
mora ['mora] *nf* (*BOT*) mulberry; (: *zarzamora*) blackberry; (*COM*): **en ~** in arrears.
morado, a [mo'raðo, a] *adj* purple, violet ♦ *nm* bruise ♦ *nf* (*casa*) dwelling, abode; **pasarlas moradas** to have a tough time of it.
moral [mo'ral] *adj* moral ♦ *nf* (*ética*) ethics *pl*; (*moralidad*) morals *pl*, morality; (*ánimo*) morale; **tener baja la ~** to be in low spirits.
moraleja [mora'lexa] *nf* moral.
moralice [mora'liθe] *etc vb V* **moralizar**.
moralidad [morali'ðað] *nf* morals *pl*, morality.
moralizar [morali'θar] *vt* to moralize.
morar [mo'rar] *vi* to live, dwell.
moratón [mora'ton] *nm* bruise.
moratoria [mora'torja] *nf* moratorium.
morbo ['morβo] *nm* (*fam*) morbid pleasure.
morbosidad [morβosi'ðað] *nf* morbidity.
morboso, a [mor'βoso, a] *adj* morbid.
morcilla [mor'θiʎa] *nf* blood sausage, ≈ black pudding (*BRIT*).
mordaz [mor'ðaθ] *adj* (*crítica*) biting, scathing.
mordaza [mor'ðaθa] *nf* (*para la boca*) gag; (*TEC*) clamp.
morder [mor'ðer] *vt* to bite; (*mordisquear*) to nibble; (*fig*: *consumir*) to eat away, eat into ♦ *vi*, **~se** *vr* to bite; **está que muerde** he's hopping mad; **~se la lengua** to hold one's tongue.
mordida [mor'ðiða] *nf* (*AM fam*) bribe.
mordisco [mor'ðisko] *nm* bite.
mordisquear [morðiske'ar] *vt* to nibble at.
moreno, a [mo'reno, a] *adj* (*color*) (dark) brown; (*de tez*) dark; (*de pelo ~*) dark-haired; (*negro*) black ♦ *nm/f* (*de tez*) dark-skinned man/woman; (*de pelo*) dark-haired man/woman.
morfina [mor'fina] *nf* morphine.
morfinómano, a [morfi'nomano, a] *adj* addicted to hard drugs ♦ *nm/f* drug addict.
morgue ['morgue] *nf* (*AM*) mortuary (*BRIT*), morgue (*US*).
moribundo, a [mori'βundo, a] *adj* dying ♦ *nm/f* dying person.
morir [mo'rir] *vi* to die; (*fuego*) to die down; (*luz*) to go out; **~se** *vr* to die; (*fig*) to be dying; (*FERRO etc*: *vías*) to end; (*calle*) to come out; **fue muerto a tiros/en un accidente** he was shot (dead)/was killed in an accident; **~ de frío/hambre** to die of cold/starve to death; **¡me muero de hambre!** (*fig*) I'm starving!; **~se por algo** to be dying for sth; **~se por algn** to be crazy about sb.
mormón, ona [mor'mon, ona] *nm/f* Mormon.
moro, a ['moro, a] *adj* Moorish ♦ *nm/f* Moor; **¡hay ~s en la costa!** watch out!
moroso, a [mo'roso, a] *adj* (*lento*) slow ♦ *nm* (*COM*) bad debtor, defaulter; **deudor ~** (*COM*) slow payer.
morral [mo'rral] *nm* haversack.
morriña [mo'rriɲa] *nf* homesickness; **tener ~** to be homesick.
morro ['morro] *nm* (*ZOOL*) snout, nose; (*AUTO, AVIAT*) nose; (*fam*: *labio*) (thick) lip; **beber a ~** to drink from the bottle; **caer de ~** to nosedive; **estar de ~s (con algn)** to be in a bad mood (with sb); **tener ~** to have a nerve.
morrocotudo, a [morroko'tuðo, a] *adj* (*fam*) (*fantástico*) smashing; (*riña, golpe*) tremendous; (*fuerte*) strong; (*pesado*) heavy; (*difícil*) awkward.
morsa ['morsa] *nf* walrus.
morse ['morse] *nm* Morse (code).
mortadela [morta'ðela] *nf* mortadella, bologna sausage.
mortaja [mor'taxa] *nf* shroud; (*TEC*) mortise; (*AM*) cigarette paper.
mortal [mor'tal] *adj* mortal; (*golpe*) deadly.
mortalidad [mortali'ðað], **mortandad** [mortan'dað] *nf* mortality.
mortecino, a [morte'θino, a] *adj* (*débil*)

weak; (*luz*) dim; (*color*) dull.
mortero [mor'tero] *nm* mortar.
mortífero, a [mor'tifero, a] *adj* deadly, lethal.
mortificar [mortifi'kar] *vt* to mortify; (*atormentar*) to torment.
mortifique [morti'fike] *etc vb V* **mortificar**.
mortuorio, a [mor'tworjo, a] *adj* mortuary, death *cpd*.
Mosa ['mosa] *nm*: **el (Río)** ~ the Meuse.
mosaico [mo'saiko] *nm* mosaic.
mosca ['moska] *nf* fly; **por si las ~s** just in case; **estar** ~ (*desconfiar*) to smell a rat; **tener la ~ en** *o* **detrás de la oreja** to be wary.
moscovita [mosko'ßita] *adj* Muscovite, Moscow *cpd* ♦ *nm/f* Muscovite.
Moscú [mos'ku] *nm* Moscow.
mosquear [moske'ar] (*fam*) *vt* (*hacer sospechar*) to make suspicious; (*fastidiar*) to annoy; **~se** *vr* (*enfadarse*) to get annoyed; (*ofenderse*) to take offence.
mosquita [mos'kita] *nf*: **parece una ~ muerta** he looks as though butter wouldn't melt in his mouth.
mosquitero [moski'tero] *nm* mosquito net.
mosquito [mos'kito] *nm* mosquito.
Mossos ['mosos] *nmpl*: ~ **d'Esquadra** Catalan police; *V tb* **policía**.
mostaza [mos'taθa] *nf* mustard.
mosto ['mosto] *nm* unfermented grape juice.
mostrador [mostra'ðor] *nm* (*de tienda*) counter; (*de café*) bar.
mostrar [mos'trar] *vt* to show; (*exhibir*) to display, exhibit; (*explicar*) to explain; **~se** *vr*: **~se amable** to be kind; to prove to be kind; **no se muestra muy inteligente** he doesn't seem (to be) very intelligent; ~ **en pantalla** (*INFORM*) to display.
mota ['mota] *nf* speck, tiny piece; (*en diseño*) dot.
mote ['mote] *nm* (*apodo*) nickname.
motín [mo'tin] *nm* (*del pueblo*) revolt, rising; (*del ejército*) mutiny.
motivación [motißa'θjon] *nf* motivation.
motivar [moti'ßar] *vt* (*causar*) to cause, motivate; (*explicar*) to explain, justify.
motivo [mo'tißo] *nm* motive, reason; (*ARTE, MUS*) motif; **con ~ de** (*debido a*) because of; (*en ocasión de*) on the occasion of; (*con el fin de*) in order to; **sin ~** for no reason at all.
moto ['moto] *nf*, **motocicleta** [motoθi'kleta] *nf* motorbike (*BRIT*), motorcycle.
motoneta [moto'neta] *nf* (*AM*) Vespa ®.
motor, a [mo'tor, a] *adj* (*TEC*) motive; (*ANAT*) motor ♦ *nm* motor, engine; ~ **a chorro** *o* **de reacción/de explosión** jet engine/internal combustion engine ♦ *nf* motorboat.
motorismo [moto'rismo] *nm* motorcycling.
motorista [moto'rista] *nm/f* (*esp AM*: *automovilista*) motorist; (: *motociclista*) motorcyclist.
motorizado, a [motori'θaðo, a] *adj* motorized.
motosierra [moto'sjerra] *nf* mechanical saw.
motriz [mo'triz] *adj*: **fuerza ~** motive power; (*fig*) driving force.
movedizo, a [moße'ðiθo, a] *adj* (*inseguro*) unsteady; (*fig*) unsettled, changeable; (*persona*) fickle.
mover [mo'ßer] *vt* to move; (*cambiar de lugar*) to shift; (*cabeza*: *para negar*) to shake; (: *para asentir*) to nod; (*accionar*) to drive; (*fig*) to cause, provoke; **~se** *vr* to move; (*mar*) to get rough; (*viento*) to rise; (*fig*: *apurarse*) to get a move on; (: *transformarse*) to be on the move.
movible [mo'ßißle] *adj* (*no fijo*) movable; (*móvil*) mobile; (*cambiadizo*) changeable.
movido, a [mo'ßiðo, a] *adj* (*FOTO*) blurred; (*persona*: *activo*) active; (*mar*) rough; (*día*) hectic ♦ *nf* move; **la movida madrileña** the Madrid scene.
móvil ['moßil] *adj* mobile; (*pieza de máquina*) moving; (*mueble*) movable ♦ *nm* motive.
movilice [moßi'liθe] *etc vb V* **movilizar**.
movilidad [moßili'ðað] *nf* mobility.
movilizar [moßili'θar] *vt* to mobilize.
movimiento [moßi'mjento] *nm* (*gen, LITERATURA, POL*) movement; (*TEC*) motion; (*actividad*) activity; (*MUS*) tempo; **el M~** the Falangist Movement; ~ **de bloques** (*INFORM*) block move; ~ **de mercancías** (*COM*) turnover, volume of business; ~ **obrero/sindical** workers'/trade union movement; ~ **sísmico** earth tremor.
Mozambique [moθam'bike] *nm* Mozambique.
mozambiqueño, a [moθambi'keɲo, a] *adj, nm/f* Mozambican.
mozo, a ['moθo, a] *adj* (*joven*) young; (*soltero*) single, unmarried ♦ *nm/f* (*joven*) youth, young man/girl; (*camarero*) waiter; (*camarera*) waitress; ~ **de**

estación porter.
MPAIAC [emepa'jak] *nm abr* (*ESP POL*) = *Movimiento para la Autodeterminación y la Independencia del Archipiélago Canario.*
mucama [mu'kama] *nf* (*AM*) maid.
muchacho, a [mu'tʃatʃo, a] *nm/f* (*niño*) boy/girl; (*criado*) servant/servant *o* maid.
muchedumbre [mutʃe'ðumbre] *nf* crowd.
muchísimo, a [mu'tʃisimo, a] *adj* (*superlativo de* **mucho**) lots and lots of, ever so much ♦ *adv* ever so much.

PALABRA CLAVE

mucho, a ['mutʃo, a] *adj* **1** (*cantidad*) a lot of, much; (*número*) lots of, a lot of, many; ~ **dinero** a lot of money; **hace ~ calor** it's very hot; **muchas amigas** lots *o* a lot of *o* many friends
2 (*sg*: *fam*): **ésta es mucha casa para él** this house is much too big for him; **había ~ borracho** there were a lot *o* lots of drunks
♦ *pron*: **tengo ~ que hacer** I've got a lot to do; **~s dicen que ...** a lot of people say that ...; *V tb* **tener**
♦ *adv* **1**: **me gusta ~** I like it a lot *o* very much; **lo siento ~** I'm very sorry; **come ~** he eats a lot; **trabaja ~** he works hard; **¿te vas a quedar ~?** are you going to be staying long?; ~ **más/menos** much *o* a lot more/less
2 (*respuesta*) very; **¿estás cansado? – ¡~!** are you tired? – very!
3 (*locuciones*): **como ~** at (the) most; **el mejor con ~** by far the best; **¡ni ~ menos!** far from it!; **no es rico ni ~ menos** he's far from being rich
4: **por ~ que**: **por ~ que le creas** however much *o* no matter how much you believe him.

muda ['muða] *nf* (*de ropa*) change of clothing; (*ZOOL*) moult; (*de serpiente*) slough.
mudanza [mu'ðanθa] *nf* (*cambio*) change; (*de casa*) move; **estar de ~** to be moving.
mudar [mu'ðar] *vt* to change; (*ZOOL*) to shed ♦ *vi* to change; **~se** *vr* (*la ropa*) to change; **~se de casa** to move house.
mudo, a ['muðo, a] *adj* dumb; (*callado, película*) silent; (*LING*: *letra*) mute; (: *consonante*) voiceless; **quedarse ~ (de)** (*fig*) to be dumb with; **quedarse ~ de asombro** to be speechless.
mueble ['mweßle] *nm* piece of furniture; **~s** *nmpl* furniture *sg*.
mueble-bar [mweßle'ßar] *nm* cocktail cabinet.
mueca ['mweka] *nf* face, grimace; **hacer ~s a** to make faces at.
muela ['mwela] *etc vb V* **moler** ♦ *nf* (*diente*) tooth; (: *de atrás*) molar; (*de molino*) millstone; (*de afilar*) grindstone; ~ **del juicio** wisdom tooth.
muelle ['mweʎe] *adj* (*blando*) soft; (*fig*) soft, easy ♦ *nm* spring; (*NAUT*) wharf; (*malecón*) jetty.
muera ['mwera] *etc vb V* **morir.**
muerda ['mwerða] *etc vb V* **morder.**
muermo ['mwermo] *nm* (*fam*) wimp.
muerte ['mwerte] *nf* death; (*homicidio*) murder; **dar ~ a** to kill; **de mala ~** (*fam*) lousy, rotten; **es la ~** (*fam*) it's deadly boring.
muerto, a ['mwerto, a] *pp de* **morir** ♦ *adj* dead; (*color*) dull ♦ *nm/f* dead man/woman; (*difunto*) deceased; (*cadáver*) corpse; **cargar con el ~** (*fam*) to carry the can; **echar el ~ a algn** to pass the buck; **hacer el ~** (*nadando*) to float; **estar ~ de cansancio** to be dead tired.
muesca ['mweska] *nf* nick.
muestra ['mwestra] *etc vb V* **mostrar** ♦ *nf* (*señal*) indication, sign; (*demostración*) demonstration; (*prueba*) proof; (*estadística*) sample; (*modelo*) model, pattern; (*testimonio*) token; **dar ~s de** to show signs of; ~ **al azar** (*COM*) random sample.
muestrario [mwes'trarjo] *nm* collection of samples; (*exposición*) showcase.
muestreo [mwes'treo] *nm* sample, sampling.
mueva [mweßa] *etc vb V* **mover.**
mugir [mu'xir] *vi* (*vaca*) to moo.
mugre ['muɣre] *nf* dirt, filth, muck.
mugriento, a [mu'ɣrjento, a] *adj* dirty, filthy mucky.
mugroso, a [muɣ'roso, a] *adj* (*AM*) filthy, grubby.
muja ['muxa] *etc vb V* **mugir.**
mujer [mu'xer] *nf* woman; (*esposa*) wife.
mujeriego [muxe'rjeɣo] *nm* womaniser.
mula ['mula] *nf* mule.
muladar [mula'ðar] *nm* dungheap, dunghill.
mulato, a [mu'lato, a] *adj, nm/f* mulatto.
muleta [mu'leta] *nf* (*para andar*) crutch; (*TAUR*) *stick with red cape attached.*
muletilla [mule'tiʎa] *nf* (*palabra*) pet word, tag; (*de cómico*) catch phrase.
mullido, a [mu'ʎiðo, a] *adj* (*cama*) soft; (*hierba*) soft, springy.
multa ['multa] *nf* fine; **echar** *o* **poner una ~**

a to fine.
multar [mul'tar] *vt* to fine; (*DEPORTE*) to penalize.
multiacceso [multjak'θeso] *adj* (*INFORM*) multi-access.
multicine [multi'θine] *nm* multiscreen cinema.
multicolor [multiko'lor] *adj* multicoloured.
multicopista [multiko'pista] *nm* duplicator.
multimillonario, a [multimiʎo'narjo, a] *adj* (*contrato*) multimillion pound *o* dollar *cpd* ♦ *nm/f* multimillionaire/-millionairess.
multinacional [multinaθjo'nal] *adj, nf* multinational.
múltiple ['multiple] *adj* multiple; (*pl*) many, numerous; **de tarea** ~ (*INFORM*) multi-tasking; **de usuario** ~ (*INFORM*) multi-user.
multiplicar [multipli'kar] *vt* (*MAT*) to multiply; (*fig*) to increase; **~se** *vr* (*BIO*) to multiply; (*fig*) to be everywhere at once.
multiplique [multi'plike] *etc vb V* **multiplicar**.
múltiplo ['multiplo] *adj, nm* multiple.
multitud [multi'tuð] *nf* (*muchedumbre*) crowd; ~ **de** lots of.
multitudinario, a [multituði'narjo, a] *adj* (*numeroso*) multitudinous; (*de masa*) mass *cpd*.
mundanal [munda'nal] *adj* worldly; **lejos del ~ ruido** far from the madding crowd.
mundano, a [mun'dano, a] *adj* worldly; (*de moda*) fashionable.
mundial [mun'djal] *adj* world-wide, universal; (*guerra, récord*) world *cpd*.
mundialmente [mundjal'mente] *adv* worldwide; ~ **famoso** world-famous.
mundo ['mundo] *nm* world; (*ámbito*) world, circle; **el otro** ~ the next world; **el ~ del espectáculo** show business; **todo el** ~ everybody; **tener** ~ to be experienced, know one's way around; **el ~ es un pañuelo** it's a small world; **no es nada del otro** ~ it's nothing special; **se le cayó el ~ (encima)** his world fell apart.
Munich ['munitʃ] *nm* Munich.
munición [muni'θjon] *nf* (*MIL: provisiones*) stores *pl*, supplies *pl*; (: *de armas*) ammunition.
municipal [muniθi'pal] *adj* (*elección*) municipal; (*concejo*) town *cpd*, local; (*piscina etc*) public ♦ *nm* (*guardia*) policeman.
municipio [muni'θipjo] *nm* (*ayuntamiento*) town council, corporation; (*territorio administrativo*) town, municipality.
muñeca [mu'ɲeka] *nf* (*ANAT*) wrist; (*juguete*) doll.
muñeco [mu'ɲeko] *nm* (*figura*) figure; (*marioneta*) puppet; (*fig*) puppet, pawn; (*niño*) pretty little boy; ~ **de nieve** snowman.
muñequera [muɲe'kera] *nf* wristband.
muñón [mu'ɲon] *nm* (*ANAT*) stump.
mural [mu'ral] *adj* mural, wall *cpd* ♦ *nm* mural.
muralla [mu'raʎa] *nf* (city) wall(s) (*pl*).
murciano, a [mur'θjano, a] *adj* of *o* from Murcia ♦ *nm/f* native *o* inhabitant of Murcia.
murciélago [mur'θjelaɣo] *nm* bat.
murga ['murɣa] *nf* (*banda*) band of street musicians; **dar la** ~ to be a nuisance.
murmullo [mur'muʎo] *nm* murmur(ing); (*cuchicheo*) whispering; (*de arroyo*) murmur, rippling; (*de hojas, viento*) rustle, rustling; (*ruido confuso*) hum(ming).
murmuración [murmura'θjon] *nf* gossip; (*críticas*) backbiting.
murmurador, a [murmura'ðor, a] *adj* gossiping; (*criticón*) backbiting ♦ *nm/f* gossip; backbiter.
murmurar [murmu'rar] *vi* to murmur, whisper; (*criticar*) to criticize; (*cotillear*) to gossip.
muro ['muro] *nm* wall; ~ **de contención** retaining wall.
mus [mus] *nm card game*.
musaraña [musa'raɲa] *nf* (*ZOOL*) shrew; (*insecto*) creepy-crawly; **pensar en las ~s** to daydream.
muscular [musku'lar] *adj* muscular.
músculo ['muskulo] *nm* muscle.
musculoso, a [musku'loso, a] *adj* muscular.
museo [mu'seo] *nm* museum; ~ **de arte** *o* **de pintura** art gallery; ~ **de cera** waxworks.
musgo ['musɣo] *nm* moss.
musical [musi'kal] *adj, nm* musical.
músico, a ['musiko, a] *adj* musical ♦ *nm/f* musician ♦ *nf* music; **irse con la música a otra parte** to clear off.
musitar [musi'tar] *vt, vi* to mutter, mumble.
muslo ['muslo] *nm* thigh; (*de pollo*) leg, drumstick.
mustio, a ['mustjo, a] *adj* (*persona*) depressed, gloomy; (*planta*) faded, withered.
musulmán, ana [musul'man, ana] *nm/f* Moslem, Muslim.
mutación [muta'θjon] *nf* (*BIO*) mutation;

(: *cambio*) (sudden) change.
mutilar [muti'lar] *vt* to mutilate; (*a una persona*) to maim.
mutis ['mutis] *nm inv* (*TEAT*) exit; **hacer ~** (*TEAT: retirarse*) to exit, go off; (*fig*) to say nothing.
mutismo [mu'tismo] *nm* silence.
mutualidad [mutwali'ðað] *nf* (*reciprocidad*) mutual character; (*asociación*) friendly *o* benefit (*US*) society.
mutuamente [mutwa'mente] *adv* mutually.
mutuo, a ['mutwo, a] *adj* mutual.
muy [mwi] *adv* very; (*demasiado*) too; **M~ Señor mío** Dear Sir; **~ bien** (*de acuerdo*) all right; **~ de noche** very late at night; **eso es ~ de él** that's just like him; **eso es ~ español** that's typically Spanish.

Nn

N, n ['ene] *nf* (*letra*) N, n; **N de Navarra** N for Nellie (*BRIT*) *o* Nan (*US*).
N *abr* (= *norte*) N.
N. *abr* (= *noviembre*) Nov; (*AM*: = *moneda nacional*) local currency; **le entregaron sólo N.$2.000** they only gave him $2000 pesos.
N.º *abr* (= *número*) No.
n. *abr* (*LING*: = *nombre*) n; (= *nacido*) b.
n/ *abr* = **nuestro, a.**
nabo ['naβo] *nm* turnip.
nácar ['nakar] *nm* mother-of-pearl.
nacer [na'θer] *vi* to be born; (*huevo*) to hatch; (*vegetal*) to sprout; (*río*) to rise; (*fig*) to begin, originate, have its origins; **nació para poeta** he was born to be a poet; **nadie nace enseñado** we all have to learn; **nació una sospecha en su mente** a suspicion formed in her mind.
nacido, a [na'θiðo, a] *adj* born; **recién ~** newborn.
naciente [na'θjente] *adj* new, emerging; (*sol*) rising.
nacimiento [naθi'mjento] *nm* birth; (*fig*) birth, origin; (*de Navidad*) Nativity; (*linaje*) descent, family; (*de río*) source; **ciego de ~** blind from birth.
nación [na'θjon] *nf* nation; (*pueblo*) people; **Naciones Unidas** United Nations.
nacional [naθjo'nal] *adj* national; (*COM, ECON*) domestic, home *cpd.*
nacionalice [naθjona'liθe] *etc vb V* **nacionalizar.**
nacionalidad [naθjonali'ðað] *nf* nationality; (*ESP POL*) autonomous region.
nacionalismo [naθjona'lismo] *nm* nationalism.
nacionalista [naθjona'lista] *adj, nm/f* nationalist.
nacionalizar [naθjonali'θar] *vt* to nationalize; **~se** *vr* (*persona*) to become naturalized.
nada ['naða] *pron* nothing ♦ *adv* not at all, in no way ♦ *nf* nothingness; **no decir ~ (más)** to say nothing (else), not to say anything (else); **¡~ más!** that's all; **de ~** don't mention it; **~ de eso** nothing of the kind; **antes de ~** right away; **como si ~** as if it didn't matter; **no ha sido ~** it's nothing; **la ~** the void.
nadador, a [naða'ðor, a] *nm/f* swimmer.
nadar [na'ðar] *vi* to swim; **~ en la abundancia** (*fig*) to be rolling in money.
nadie ['naðje] *pron* nobody, no-one; **~ habló** nobody spoke; **no había ~** there was nobody there, there wasn't anybody there; **es un don ~** he's a nobody *o* nonentity.
nadita [na'ðita] (*esp AM: fam*) = **nada.**
nado ['naðo]: **a ~** *adv*: **pasar a ~** to swim across.
nafta ['nafta] *nf* (*AM*) petrol (*BRIT*), gas(oline) (*US*).
naftalina [nafta'lina] *nf*: **bolas de ~** mothballs.
náhuatl ['nawatl] *adj, nm* Nahuatl.
naipe ['naipe] *nm* (playing) card; **~s** *nmpl* cards.
nal. *abr* (= *nacional*) nat.
nalgas ['nalɣas] *nfpl* buttocks.
Namibia [na'miβja] *nf* Namibia.
nana ['nana] *nf* lullaby.
napias ['napjas] *nfpl* (*fam*) conk *sg.*
Nápoles ['napoles] *nf* Naples.
napolitano, a [napoli'tano, a] *adj* of *o* from Naples, Neapolitan ♦ *nm/f* Neapolitan.
naranja [na'ranxa] *adj inv, nf* orange; **media ~** (*fam*) better half; **¡~s de la China!** nonsense!
naranjada [naran'xaða] *nf* orangeade.
naranjo [na'ranxo] *nm* orange tree.
Narbona [nar'βona] *nf* Narbonne.
narcisista [narθi'sista] *adj* narcissistic.
narciso [nar'θiso] *nm* narcissus.
narcotice [narko'tiθe] *etc vb V* **narcotizar.**
narcótico, a [nar'kotiko, a] *adj, nm* narcotic.

narcotizar [narkoti'θar] *vt* to drug.
narcotraficante [narkotrafi'kante] *nm/f* narcotics *o* drug trafficker.
narcotráfico [narko'trafiko] *nm* narcotics *o* drug trafficking.
nardo ['narðo] *nm* lily.
narices [na'riθes] *nfpl V* **nariz**.
narigón, ona [nari'ɣon, ona], **narigudo, a** [nari'ɣuðo, a] *adj* big-nosed.
nariz [na'riθ] *nf* nose; **narices** *nfpl* nostrils; **¡narices!** (*fam*) rubbish!; **delante de las narices de algn** under one's (very) nose; **estar hasta las narices** to be completely fed up; **meter las narices en algo** to poke one's nose into sth.
narración [narra'θjon] *nf* narration.
narrador, a [narra'ðor, a] *nm/f* narrator.
narrar [na'rrar] *vt* to narrate, recount.
narrativo, a [narra'tiβo, a] *adj* narrative ♦ *nf* narrative, story.
nasal [na'sal] *adj* nasal.
N.ª S.ra *abr* = *Nuestra Señora*.
nata ['nata] *nf* cream (*tb fig*); (*en leche cocida etc*) skin; ~ **batida** whipped cream.
natación [nata'θjon] *nf* swimming.
natal [na'tal] *adj* natal; (*país*) native; **ciudad** ~ home town.
natalicio [nata'liθjo] *nm* birthday.
natalidad [natali'ðað] *nf* birth rate.
natillas [na'tiʎas] *nfpl* (egg) custard *sg*.
natividad [natiβi'ðað] *nf* nativity.
nativo, a [na'tiβo, a] *adj, nm/f* native.
nato, a ['nato, a] *adj* born; **un músico** ~ a born musician.
natural [natu'ral] *adj* natural; (*fruta etc*) fresh ♦ *nm/f* native ♦ *nm* disposition, temperament; **buen** ~ good nature; **fruta al** ~ fruit in its own juice.
naturaleza [natura'leθa] *nf* nature; (*género*) nature, kind; ~ **muerta** still life.
naturalice [natura'liθe] *etc vb V* **naturalizarse**.
naturalidad [naturali'ðað] *nf* naturalness.
naturalización [naturaliθa'θjon] *nf* naturalization.
naturalizarse [naturali'θarse] *vr* to become naturalized; (*aclimatarse*) to become acclimatized.
naturalmente [natural'mente] *adv* naturally; **¡~!** of course!
naturista [natu'rista] *adj* (*MED*) naturopathic ♦ *nm/f* naturopath.
naufragar [naufra'ɣar] *vi* (*barco*) to sink; (*gente*) to be shipwrecked; (*fig*) to fail.
naufragio [nau'fraxjo] *nm* shipwreck.
náufrago, a ['naufraɣo, a] *nm/f* castaway, shipwrecked person.
naufrague [nau'fraɣe] *etc vb V* **naufragar**.
náusea ['nausea] *nf* nausea; **me da ~s** it makes me feel sick.
nauseabundo, a [nausea'βundo, a] *adj* nauseating, sickening.
náutico, a ['nautiko, a] *adj* nautical; **club** ~ sailing *o* yacht club ♦ *nf* navigation, seamanship.
navaja [na'βaxa] *nf* (*cortaplumas*) clasp knife (*BRIT*), penknife; ~ **(de afeitar)** razor.
navajazo [naβa'xaθo] *nm* (*herida*) gash; (*golpe*) slash.
naval [na'βal] *adj* (*MIL*) naval; **construcción** ~ shipbuilding; **sector** ~ shipbuilding industry.
Navarra [na'βarra] *nf* Navarre.
navarro, a [na'βarro, a] *adj* of *o* from Navarre, Navarrese ♦ *nm/f* Navarrese ♦ *nm* (*LING*) Navarrese.
nave ['naβe] *nf* (*barco*) ship, vessel; (*ARQ*) nave; ~ **espacial** spaceship; **quemar las ~s** to burn one's boats.
navegación [naβeɣa'θjon] *nf* navigation; (*viaje*) sea journey; ~ **aérea** air traffic; ~ **costera** coastal shipping; ~ **fluvial** river navigation.
navegador [naβeɣa'ðor] *nm* (*INFORM*) browser.
navegante [naβe'ɣante] *nm/f* navigator.
navegar [naβe'ɣar] *vi* (*barco*) to sail; (*avión*) to fly ♦ *vt* to sail; to fly; (*dirigir el rumbo de*) to navigate.
navegue [na'βeɣe] *etc vb V* **navegar**.
Navidad [naβi'ðað] *nf* Christmas; **~es** *nfpl* Christmas time *sg*; **día de** ~ Christmas Day; **por ~es** at Christmas (time); **¡felices ~es!** Merry Christmas.
navideño, a [naβi'ðeɲo, a] *adj* Christmas *cpd*.
navío [na'βio] *nm* ship.
nazi ['naθi] *adj, nm/f* Nazi.
nazismo [na'θismo] *nm* Nazism.
n/cta *abr* (*COM*) = *nuestra cuenta*.
N. de la R. *abr* (= *nota de la redacción*) editor's note.
N. de la T./del T. *abr* (= *nota de la traductora/del traductor*) translator's note.
NE *abr* (= *nor(d)este*) NE.
neblina [ne'βlina] *nf* mist.
nebuloso, a [neβu'loso, a] *adj* foggy; (*calinoso*) misty; (*indefinido*) nebulous, vague ♦ *nf* nebula.
necedad [neθe'ðað] *nf* foolishness; (*una* ~) foolish act.
necesario, a [neθe'sarjo, a] *adj* necessary; **si fuera** *o* **fuese** ~ if need(s) be.
neceser [neθe'ser] *nm* vanity case; (*bolsa grande*) holdall.
necesidad [neθesi'ðað] *nf* need; (*lo*

inevitable) necessity; (*miseria*) poverty, need; **en caso de** ~ in case of need *o* emergency; **hacer sus ~es** to relieve o.s.
necesitado, a [neθesi'taðo, a] *adj* needy, poor; ~ **de** in need of.
necesitar [neθesi'tar] *vt* to need, require ♦ *vi*: ~ **de** to have need of; **~se** *vr* to be needed; (*anuncios*) **"necesítase coche"** "car wanted".
necio, a ['neθjo, a] *adj* foolish ♦ *nm/f* fool.
necrología [nekrolo'xia] *nf* obituary.
necrópolis [ne'kropolis] *nf inv* cemetery.
néctar ['nektar] *nm* nectar.
nectarina [nekta'rina] *nf* nectarine.
neerlandés, esa [neerlan'des, esa] *adj* Dutch ♦ *nm/f* Dutchman/woman ♦ *nm* (*LING*) Dutch; **los neerlandeses** the Dutch.
nefando, a [ne'fando, a] *adj* unspeakable.
nefasto, a [ne'fasto, a] *adj* ill-fated, unlucky.
negación [neɣa'θjon] *nf* negation; (*LING*) negative; (*rechazo*) refusal, denial.
negado, a [ne'ɣaðo, a] *adj*: ~ **para** inept at, unfitted for.
negar [ne'ɣar] *vt* (*renegar, rechazar*) to refuse; (*prohibir*) to refuse, deny; (*desmentir*) to deny; **~se** *vr*: **~se a hacer algo** to refuse to do sth.
negativo, a [neɣa'tiβo, a] *adj* negative ♦ *nm* (*FOTO*) negative; (*MAT*) minus ♦ *nf* (*gen*) negative; (*rechazo*) refusal, denial; **negativa rotunda** flat refusal.
negligencia [neɣli'xenθja] *nf* negligence.
negligente [neɣli'xente] *adj* negligent.
negociable [neɣo'θjaβle] *adj* (*COM*) negotiable.
negociación [neɣoθja'θjon] *nf* negotiation.
negociado [neɣo'θjaðo] *nm* department, section.
negociante [neɣo'θjante] *nm/f* businessman/woman.
negociar [neɣo'θjar] *vt, vi* to negotiate; ~ **en** to deal in, trade in.
negocio [ne'ɣoθjo] *nm* (*COM*) business; (*asunto*) affair, business; (*operación comercial*) deal, transaction; (*AM*) shop, store; (*lugar*) place of business; **los ~s** business *sg*; **hacer** ~ to do business; **el ~ del libro** the book trade; ~ **autorizado** licensed trade; **hombre de ~s** businessman; ~ **sucio** shady deal; **hacer un buen** ~ to pull off a profitable deal; **¡mal** ~! it looks bad!
negra ['neɣra] *nf V* **negro** ♦ *nf* (*MUS*) crotchet.
negrita [ne'ɣrita] *nf* (*TIP*) bold face; **en** ~ in bold (type).
negro, a ['neɣro, a] *adj* black; (*suerte*) awful, atrocious; (*humor etc*) sad; (*lúgubre*) gloomy ♦ *nm* (*color*) black ♦ *nm/f* Negro/Negress, black ♦ *nf* (*MUS*) crotchet; ~ **como la boca del lobo** pitch-black; **estoy ~ con esto** I'm getting desperate about it; **ponerse** ~ (*fam*) to get cross.
negrura [ne'ɣrura] *nf* blackness.
negué [ne'ɣe], **neguemos** [ne'ɣemos] *etc vb V* **negar**.
nene, a ['nene, a] *nm/f* baby, small child.
nenúfar [ne'nufar] *nm* water lily.
neologismo [neolo'xismo] *nm* neologism.
neón [ne'on] *nm* neon.
neoyorquino, a [neojor'kino, a] *adj* New York *cpd* ♦ *nm/f* New Yorker.
neozelandés, esa [neoθelan'des, esa] *adj* New Zealand *cpd* ♦ *nm/f* New Zealander.
nepotismo [nepo'tismo] *nm* nepotism.
nervio ['nerβjo] *nm* (*ANAT*) nerve; (: *tendón*) tendon; (*fig*) vigour; (*TEC*) rib; **crispar los ~s a algn, poner los ~s de punta a algn** to get on sb's nerves.
nerviosismo [nerβjo'sismo] *nm* nervousness, nerves *pl*.
nervioso, a [ner'βjoso, a] *adj* nervous; (*sensible*) nervy, highly-strung; (*impaciente*) restless; **¡no te pongas ~!** take it easy!
nervudo, a [ner'βuðo, a] *adj* tough; (*mano*) sinewy.
neto, a ['neto, a] *adj* clear; (*limpio*) clean; (*COM*) net.
neumático, a [neu'matiko, a] *adj* pneumatic ♦ *nm* (*ESP*) tyre (*BRIT*), tire (*US*); ~ **de recambio** spare tyre.
neumonía [neumo'nia] *nf* pneumonia.
neura ['neura] (*fam*) *nm/f* (*persona*) neurotic ♦ *nf* (*obsesión*) obsession.
neuralgia [neu'ralxja] *nf* neuralgia.
neurálgico, a [neu'ralxiko, a] *adj* neuralgic; (*fig*: *centro*) nerve *cpd*.
neurastenia [neuras'tenja] *nf* neurasthenia; (*fig*) excitability.
neurasténico, a [neuras'teniko, a] *adj* neurasthenic; excitable.
neurólogo, a [neu'roloɣo, a] *nm/f* neurologist.
neurona [neu'rona] *nf* neuron.
neurosis [neu'rosis] *nf inv* neurosis.
neurótico, a [neu'rotiko, a] *adj, nm/f* neurotic.
neutral [neu'tral] *adj* neutral.
neutralice [neutra'liθe] *etc vb V* **neutralizar**.
neutralizar [neutrali'θar] *vt* to neutralize; (*contrarrestar*) to counteract.
neutro, a ['neutro, a] *adj* (*BIO, LING*) neuter.

neutrón [neu'tron] *nm* neutron.
nevado, a [ne'ßaðo, a] *adj* snow-covered; (*montaña*) snow-capped; (*fig*) snowy, snow-white ♦ *nf* snowstorm; (*caída de nieve*) snowfall.
nevar [ne'ßar] *vi* to snow ♦ *vt* (*fig*) to whiten.
nevera [ne'ßera] *nf* (*ESP*) refrigerator (*BRIT*), icebox (*US*).
nevisca [ne'ßiska] *nf* flurry of snow.
nexo ['nekso] *nm* link, connection.
n/f *abr* (*COM*) = *nuestro favor*.
ni [ni] *conj* nor, neither; (*tb*: ~ **siquiera**) not even; ~ **que** not even if; ~ **blanco** ~ **negro** neither white nor black; ~ **el uno** ~ **el otro** neither one nor the other.
Nicaragua [nika'raɣwa] *nf* Nicaragua.
nicaragüense [nikara'ɣwense] *adj*, *nm/f* Nicaraguan.
nicho ['nitʃo] *nm* niche.
nicotina [niko'tina] *nf* nicotine.
nido ['niðo] *nm* nest; (*fig*) hiding place; ~ **de ladrones** den of thieves.
niebla ['njeßla] *nf* fog; (*neblina*) mist; **hay** ~ it is foggy.
niego ['njeɣo] *etc*, **niegue** ['njeɣe] *etc vb V* **negar**.
nieto, a ['njeto, a] *nm/f* grandson/daughter; ~**s** *nmpl* grandchildren.
nieve ['njeße] *etc vb V* **nevar** ♦ *nf* snow; (*AM*) ice cream; **copo de** ~ snowflake.
N.I.F. *nm abr* (= *Número de Identificación Fiscal*) *ID number used for tax purposes*.
Nigeria [ni'xerja] *nf* Nigeria.
nigeriano, a [nixe'rjano, a] *adj*, *nm/f* Nigerian.
nigromancia [niɣro'manθja] *nf* necromancy, black magic.
nihilista [nii'lista] *adj* nihilistic ♦ *nm* nihilist.
Nilo ['nilo] *nm*: **el (Río)** ~ the Nile.
nimbo ['nimbo] *nm* (*aureola*) halo; (*nube*) nimbus.
nimiedad [nimje'ðað] *nf* small-mindedness; (*trivialidad*) triviality; (*una* ~) trifle, tiny detail.
nimio, a ['nimjo, a] *adj* trivial, insignificant.
ninfa ['ninfa] *nf* nymph.
ninfómana [nin'fomana] *nf* nymphomaniac.
ninguno, a [nin'guno, a] *adj* (**ningún** *delante de nmsg*) no ♦ *pron* (*nadie*) nobody; (*ni uno*) none, not one; (*ni uno ni otro*) neither; **de ninguna manera** by no means, not at all; **no voy a ninguna parte** I'm not going anywhere.
niña ['niɲa] *nf V* **niño**.
niñera [ni'ɲera] *nf* nursemaid, nanny.
niñería [niɲe'ria] *nf* childish act.
niñez [ni'ɲeθ] *nf* childhood; (*infancia*) infancy.
niño, a ['niɲo, a] *adj* (*joven*) young; (*inmaduro*) immature ♦ *nm* (*chico*) boy, child ♦ *nf* girl, child; (*ANAT*) pupil; **los** ~**s** the children; ~ **bien** rich kid; ~ **expósito** foundling; ~ **de pecho** babe-in-arms; ~ **prodigio** child prodigy; **de** ~ as a child; **ser el** ~ **mimado de algn** to be sb's pet; **ser la niña de los ojos de algn** to be the apple of sb's eye.
nipón, ona [ni'pon, ona] *adj*, *nm/f* Japanese; **los nipones** the Japanese.
níquel ['nikel] *nm* nickel.
niquelar [nike'lar] *vt* (*TEC*) to nickel-plate.
níspero ['nispero] *nm* medlar.
nitidez [niti'ðeθ] *nf* (*claridad*) clarity; (: *de atmósfera*) brightness; (: *de imagen*) sharpness.
nítido, a ['nitiðo, a] *adj* bright; (*fig*) pure; (*imagen*) clear, sharp.
nitrato [ni'trato] *nm* nitrate.
nitrógeno [ni'troxeno] *nm* nitrogen.
nitroglicerina [nitroɣliθe'rina] *nf* nitroglycerine.
nivel [ni'ßel] *nm* (*GEO*) level; (*norma*) level, standard; (*altura*) height; ~ **de aceite** oil level; ~ **de aire** spirit level; ~ **de vida** standard of living; **al** ~ **de** on a level with, at the same height as; (*fig*) on a par with; **a 900m sobre el** ~ **del mar** at 900m above sea level.
nivelado, a [niße'laðo, a] *adj* level, flat; (*TEC*) flush.
nivelar [niße'lar] *vt* to level out; (*fig*) to even up; (*COM*) to balance.
Niza ['niθa] *nf* Nice.
n/l. *abr* (*COM*) = *nuestra letra*.
NNE *abr* (= *nornordeste*) NNE.
NNO *abr* (= *nornoroeste*) NNW.
NN. UU. *nfpl abr* (= *Naciones Unidas*) UN *sg*.
NO *abr* (= *noroeste*) NW.
no [no] *adv* no; (*con verbo*) not ♦ *excl* no!; ~ **tengo nada** I don't have anything, I have nothing; ~ **es el mío** it's not mine; **ahora** ~ not now; **¿**~ **lo sabes?** don't you know?; ~ **mucho** not much; ~ **bien termine, lo entregaré** as soon as I finish I'll hand it over; **¡a que** ~ **lo sabes!** I bet you don't know!; **¡cómo** ~**!** of course!; **pacto de** ~ **agresión** non-aggression pact; **los países** ~ **alineados** the non-aligned countries; **el** ~ **va más** the ultimate; **la** ~ **intervención** non-intervention.

n/o *abr* (*COM*) = *nuestra orden.*
noble ['noβle] *adj, nm/f* noble; **los ~s** the nobility *sg*.
nobleza [noβ'leθa] *nf* nobility.
noche ['notʃe] *nf* night, night-time; (*la tarde*) evening; (*fig*) darkness; **de ~, por la ~** at night; **ayer por la ~** last night; **esta ~** tonight; **(en) toda la ~** all night; **hacer ~ en un sitio** to spend the night in a place; **se hace de ~** it's getting dark.
Nochebuena [notʃe'βwena] *nf* Christmas Eve; *see boxed note.*

> **NOCHEBUENA**
>
> *On* **Nochebuena** *in Spanish homes family members normally gather together for a large supper and the more religiously inclined attend "la misa del gallo" at midnight. The tradition of receiving Christmas presents from Santa Claus on Christmas Eve is becoming more and more widespread and is gradually replacing the visit of "los Reyes Magos" (the Three Wise Men) who bring gifts on 6 January.*

Nochevieja [notʃe'βjexa] *nf* New Year's Eve; *V tb* **uvas.**
noción [no'θjon] *nf* notion; **nociones** *nfpl* elements, rudiments.
nocivo, a [no'θiβo, a] *adj* harmful.
noctambulismo [noktambu'lismo] *nm* sleepwalking.
noctámbulo, a [nok'tambulo, a] *nm/f* sleepwalker.
nocturno, a [nok'turno, a] *adj* (*de la noche*) nocturnal, night *cpd*; (*de la tarde*) evening *cpd* ♦ *nm* nocturne.
Noé [no'e] *nm* Noah.
nogal [no'ɣal] *nm* walnut tree; (*madera*) walnut.
nómada ['nomaða] *adj* nomadic ♦ *nm/f* nomad.
nomás [no'mas] *adv*: (*AM*: *gen*) just; (: *tan sólo*) only; **así ~** (*AM fam*) just like that; **ayer ~** only yesterday ♦ *conj* (*AM*: *en cuanto*) **~ se fue se acordó** no sooner had she left than she remembered.
nombramiento [nombra'mjento] *nm* naming; (*a un empleo*) appointment; (*POL etc*) nomination; (*MIL*) commission.
nombrar [nom'brar] *vt* (*gen*) to name; (*mencionar*) to mention; (*designar*) to appoint, nominate; (*MIL*) to commission.
nombre ['nombre] *nm* name; (*sustantivo*) noun; (*fama*) renown; **~ y apellidos** name in full; **~ común/propio** common/proper noun; **~ de pila/de soltera** Christian/maiden name; **~ de fichero** (*INFORM*) file name; **en ~ de** in the name of, on behalf of; **sin ~** nameless; **su conducta no tiene ~** his behaviour is utterly despicable.
nomenclatura [nomenkla'tura] *nf* nomenclature.
nomeolvides [nomeol'βiðes] *nm inv* forget-me-not.
nómina ['nomina] *nf* (*lista*) list; (*COM*: *tb*: **~s**) payroll.
nominal [nomi'nal] *adj* nominal; (*valor*) face *cpd*; (*LING*) noun *cpd*, substantival.
nominar [nomi'nar] *vt* to nominate.
nominativo, a [nomina'tiβo, a] *adj* (*LING*) nominative; (*COM*): **un cheque ~ a X** a cheque made out to X.
non [non] *adj* odd, uneven ♦ *nm* odd number; **pares y ~es** odds and evens.
nonagésimo, a [nona'xesimo, a] *num* ninetieth.
nono, a ['nono, a] *num* ninth.
nordeste [nor'ðeste] *adj* north-east, north-eastern, north-easterly ♦ *nm* north-east; (*viento*) north-east wind, north-easterly.
nórdico, a ['norðiko, a] *adj* (*del norte*) northern, northerly; (*escandinavo*) Nordic, Norse ♦ *nm/f* northerner; (*escandinavo*) Norseman/woman ♦ *nm* (*LING*) Norse.
noreste [no'reste] *adj, nm* = **nordeste.**
noria ['norja] *nf* (*AGR*) waterwheel; (*de carnaval*) big (*BRIT*) *o* Ferris (*US*) wheel.
norma ['norma] *nf* standard, norm, rule; (*patrón*) pattern; (*método*) method.
normal [nor'mal] *adj* (*corriente*) normal; (*habitual*) usual, natural; (*TEC*) standard; **Escuela N~** teacher training college; **(gasolina) ~** two-star petrol.
normalice [norma'liθe] *etc vb V* **normalizar.**
normalidad [normali'ðað] *nf* normality.
normalización [normaliθa'θjon] *nf* (*COM*) standardization.
normalizar [normali'θar] *vt* (*reglamentar*) to normalize; (*COM, TEC*) to standardize; **~se** *vr* to return to normal.
normalmente [normal'mente] *adv* (*con normalidad*) normally; (*habitualmente*) usually.
Normandía [norman'dia] *nf* Normandy.
normando, a [nor'mando, a] *adj, nm/f* Norman.
normativo, a [norma'tiβo, a] *adj*: **es ~ en todos los coches nuevos** it is standard in all new cars ♦ *nf* regulations *pl*.
noroeste [noro'este] *adj* north-west, north-western, north-westerly ♦ *nm*

north-west; (*viento*) north-west wind, north-westerly.
norte ['norte] *adj* north, northern, northerly ♦ *nm* north; (*fig*) guide.
Norteamérica [nortea'merika] *nf* North America.
norteamericano, a [norteameri'kano, a] *adj, nm/f* (North) American.
norteño, a [nor'teɲo, a] *adj* northern ♦ *nm/f* northerner.
Noruega [no'rweɣa] *nf* Norway.
noruego, a [no'rweɣo, a] *adj, nm/f* Norwegian ♦ *nm* (*LING*) Norwegian.
nos [nos] *pron* (*directo*) us; (*indirecto*) (to) us; (*reflexivo*) (to) ourselves; (*recíproco*) (to) each other; ~ **levantamos a las 7** we get up at 7.
nosocomio [noso'komio] *nm* (*AM*) hospital.
nosotros, as [no'sotros, as] *pron* (*sujeto*) we; (*después de prep*) us; ~ **(mismos)** ourselves.
nostalgia [nos'talxja] *nf* nostalgia, homesickness.
nostálgico, a [nos'talxiko, a] *adj* nostalgic, homesick.
nota ['nota] *nf* note; (*ESCOL*) mark; (*de fin de año*) report; (*UNIV etc*) footnote; (*COM*) account; ~ **de aviso** advice note; ~ **de crédito/débito** credit/debit note; ~ **de gastos** expenses claim; ~ **de sociedad** gossip column; **tomar ~s** to take notes.
notable [no'taβle] *adj* noteworthy, notable; (*ESCOL etc*) outstanding ♦ *nm/f* notable.
notar [no'tar] *vt* to notice, note; (*percibir*) to feel; (*ver*) to see; **~se** *vr* to be obvious; **se nota que** ... one observes that ....
notaría [nota'ria] *nf* (*profesión*) profession of notary; (*despacho*) notary's office.
notarial [nota'rjal] *adj* (*estilo*) legal; **acta** ~ affidavit.
notario [no'tarjo] *nm* notary; (*abogado*) solicitor.
noticia [no'tiθja] *nf* (*información*) piece of news; (*TV etc*) news item; **las ~s** the news *sg*; **según nuestras ~s** according to our information; **tener ~s de algn** to hear from sb.
noticiario [noti'θjarjo] *nm* (*CINE*) newsreel; (*TV*) news bulletin.
noticiero [noti'θjero] *nm* newspaper, gazette; (*AM*: *tb*: ~ **telediario**) news bulletin.
notificación [notifika'θjon] *nf* notification.
notificar [notifi'kar] *vt* to notify, inform.
notifique [noti'fike] *etc vb V* **notificar**.
notoriedad [notorje'ðað] *nf* fame, renown.
notorio, a [no'torjo, a] *adj* (*público*) well-known; (*evidente*) obvious.
nov. *abr* (= *noviembre*) Nov.
novatada [noβa'taða] *nf* (*burla*) teasing, hazing (*US*); **pagar la** ~ to learn the hard way.
novato, a [no'βato, a] *adj* inexperienced ♦ *nm/f* beginner, novice.
novecientos, as [noβe'θjentos, as] *num* nine hundred.
novedad [noβe'ðað] *nf* (*calidad de nuevo*) newness, novelty; (*noticia*) piece of news; (*cambio*) change, (new) development; (*sorpresa*) surprise; **~es** *nfpl* (*noticia*) latest (news) *sg*.
novedoso, a [noβe'ðoso, a] *adj* novel.
novel [no'βel] *adj* new; (*inexperto*) inexperienced ♦ *nm/f* beginner.
novela [no'βela] *nf* novel; ~ **policíaca** detective story.
novelero, a [noβe'lero, a] *adj* highly imaginative.
novelesco, a [noβe'lesko, a] *adj* fictional; (*romántico*) romantic; (*fantástico*) fantastic.
novelista [noβe'lista] *nm/f* novelist.
novelística [noβe'listika] *nf*: **la** ~ fiction, the novel.
noveno, a [no'βeno, a] *num* ninth.
noventa [no'βenta] *num* ninety.
novia ['noβja] *nf V* **novio**.
noviazgo [no'βjaθɣo] *nm* engagement.
novicio, a [no'βiθjo, a] *nm/f* novice.
noviembre [no'βjembre] *nm* November.
novilla [no'βiʎa] *nf* heifer.
novillada [noβi'ʎaða] *nf* (*TAUR*) *bullfight with young bulls*.
novillero [noβi'ʎero] *nm* novice bullfighter.
novillo [no'βiʎo] *nm* young bull, bullock; **hacer ~s** (*fam*) to play truant (*BRIT*) *o* hooky (*US*).
novio, a ['noβjo, a] *nm/f* boyfriend/girlfriend; (*prometido*) fiancé/fiancée; (*recién casado*) bridegroom/bride; **los ~s** the newly-weds.
novísimo, a [no'βisimo, a] *adj superlativo de* **nuevo, a**.
NPI *nm abr* (*INFORM*: = *número personal de identificación*) PIN.
N. S. *abr* = *Nuestro Señor*.
ntra., ntro. *abr* = **nuestra, nuestro**.
NU *nfpl abr* (= *Naciones Unidas*) UN *sg*.
nubarrón [nuβa'rron] *nm* storm cloud.
nube ['nuβe] *nf* cloud; (*MED*: *ocular*) cloud, film; (*fig*) mass; **una ~ de críticas** a storm of criticism; **los precios están por las ~s** prices are sky-high; **estar en las ~s** to be away with the fairies.
nublado, a [nu'βlaðo, a] *adj* cloudy ♦ *nm* storm cloud.
nublar [nu'βlar] *vt* (*oscurecer*) to darken;

(*confundir*) to cloud; ~**se** *vr* to cloud over.
nuca ['nuka] *nf* nape of the neck.
nuclear [nukle'ar] *adj* nuclear.
nuclearizado, a [nukleari'θaðo, a] *adj*: **países** ~**s** countries possessing nuclear weapons.
núcleo ['nukleo] *nm* (*centro*) core; (*FÍSICA*) nucleus.
nudillo [nu'ðiʎo] *nm* knuckle.
nudista [nu'dista] *adj, nm/f* nudist.
nudo ['nuðo] *nm* knot; (*unión*) bond; (*de problema*) crux; (*FERRO*) junction; (*fig*) lump; ~ **corredizo** slipknot; **con un** ~ **en la garganta** with a lump in one's throat.
nudoso, a [nu'ðoso, a] *adj* knotty; (*tronco*) gnarled; (*bastón*) knobbly.
nueces ['nweθes] *nfpl de* **nuez**.
nuera ['nwera] *nf* daughter-in-law.
nuestro, a ['nwestro, a] *adj posesivo* our ♦ *pron* ours; ~ **padre** our father; **un amigo** ~ a friend of ours; **es el** ~ it's ours; **los** ~**s** our people; (*DEPORTE*) our *o* the local team *o* side.
nueva ['nweβa] *nf V* **nuevo**.
Nueva Escocia *nf* Nova Scotia.
nuevamente [nweβa'mente] *adv* (*otra vez*) again; (*de nuevo*) anew.
Nueva York [-'jork] *nf* New York.
Nueva Zeland(i)a [-θe'land(j)a] *nf* New Zealand.
nueve ['nweβe] *num* nine.
nuevo, a ['nweβo, a] *adj* (*gen*) new ♦ *nf* piece of news; **¿qué hay de ~?** (*fam*) what's new?; **de** ~ again.
Nuevo Méjico *nm* New Mexico.
nuez [nweθ], *pl* **nueces** *nf* (*del nogal*) walnut; (*fruto*) nut; ~ **de Adán** Adam's apple; ~ **moscada** nutmeg.
nulidad [nuli'ðað] *nf* (*incapacidad*) incompetence; (*abolición*) nullity; (*individuo*) nonentity; **es una** ~ he's a dead loss.
nulo, a ['nulo, a] *adj* (*inepto, torpe*) useless; (*inválido*) (null and) void; (*DEPORTE*) drawn, tied.
núm. *abr* (= *número*) no.
numen ['numen] *nm* inspiration.
numeración [numera'θjon] *nf* (*cifras*) numbers *pl*; (*arábiga, romana etc*) numerals *pl*; ~ **de línea** (*INFORM*) line numbering.
numerador [numera'ðor] *nm* (*MAT*) numerator.
numeral [nume'ral] *nm* numeral.
numerar [nume'rar] *vt* to number; ~**se** *vr* (*MIL etc*) to number off.
numerario, a [nume'rarjo, a] *adj* numerary; **profesor** ~ permanent *o* tenured member of teaching staff ♦ *nm* hard cash.
numérico, a [nu'meriko, a] *adj* numerical.
número ['numero] *nm* (*gen*) number; (*tamaño: de zapato*) size; (*ejemplar: de diario*) number, issue; (*TEAT etc*) turn, act, number; **sin** ~ numberless, unnumbered; ~ **binario** (*INFORM*) binary number; ~ **de matrícula/de teléfono** registration/telephone number; ~ **personal de identificación** (*INFORM etc*) personal identification number; ~ **de serie** (*COM*) serial number; ~ **atrasado** back number.
numeroso, a [nume'roso, a] *adj* numerous; **familia numerosa** large family.
numerus ['numerus] *nm*: ~ **clausus** (*UNIV*) restricted *o* selective entry.
nunca ['nunka] *adv* (*jamás*) never; (*con verbo negativo*) ever; ~ **lo pensé** I never thought it; **no viene** ~ he never comes; ~ **más** never again.
nuncio ['nunθjo] *nm* (*REL*) nuncio.
nupcial [nup'θjal] *adj* wedding *cpd*.
nupcias ['nupθjas] *nfpl* wedding *sg*, nuptials.
nutria ['nutrja] *nf* otter.
nutrición [nutri'θjon] *nf* nutrition.
nutrido, a [nu'triðo, a] *adj* (*alimentado*) nourished; (*fig: grande*) large; (*abundante*) abundant; **mal** ~ undernourished; ~ **de** full of.
nutrir [nu'trir] *vt* to feed, nourish; (*fig*) to feed, strengthen.
nutritivo, a [nutri'tiβo, a] *adj* nourishing, nutritious.
nylon [ni'lon] *nm* nylon.

Ñ ñ

Ñ, ñ ['eɲe] *nf* (*letra*) Ñ, ñ.
ñato, a ['ɲato, a] *adj* (*AM*) snub-nosed.
ñoñería [ɲoɲe'ria], **ñoñez** [ɲo'ɲeθ] *nf* insipidness.
ñoño, a ['ɲoɲo, a] *adj* (*soso*) insipid; (*persona: débil*) spineless.
ñoquis ['ɲokis] *nmpl* (*CULIN*) gnocchi.

Oo

O, o [o] *nf* (*letra*) O, o; **O de Oviedo** O for Oliver (*BRIT*) *o* Oboe (*US*).
O *abr* (= *oeste*) W.
o [o] *conj* or; ~ ... ~ either ... or; ~ **sea** that is.
ó [o] *conj* (*en números para evitar confusión*) or; **5 ~ 6** 5 or 6.
o/ *nm* (*COM*: = *orden*) o.
OACI *nf abr* (= *Organización de la Aviación Civil Internacional*) ICAO.
oasis [o'asis] *nm inv* oasis.
obcecado, a [oβθe'kaðo, a] *adj* blind; (*terco*) stubborn.
obcecarse [oβθe'karse] *vr* to be obstinate; ~ **en hacer** to insist on doing.
obceque [oβ'θeke] *etc vb V* **obcecarse**.
obedecer [oβeðe'θer] *vt* to obey; ~ **a** (*MED etc*) to yield to; (*fig*) ~ **a ...**, ~ **al hecho de que ...** to be due to ..., arise from ....
obedezca [oβe'ðeθka] *etc vb V* **obedecer**.
obediencia [oβe'ðjenθja] *nf* obedience.
obediente [oβe'ðjente] *adj* obedient.
obertura [oβer'tura] *nf* overture.
obesidad [oβesi'ðað] *nf* obesity.
obeso, a [o'βeso, a] *adj* obese.
óbice ['oβiθe] *nm* obstacle, impediment.
obispado [oβis'paðo] *nm* bishopric.
obispo [o'βispo] *nm* bishop.
óbito ['oβito] *nm* demise.
objeción [oβxe'θjon] *nf* objection; **hacer una ~, poner objeciones** to raise objections, object.
objetar [oβxe'tar] *vt, vi* to object.
objetivo, a [oβxe'tiβo, a] *adj* objective ♦ *nm* objective; (*fig*) aim; (*FOTO*) lens.
objeto [oβ'xeto] *nm* (*cosa*) object; (*fin*) aim.
objetor, a [oβxe'tor, a] *nm/f* objector; ~ **de conciencia** conscientious objector; *V tb* **mili**.
oblea [o'βlea] *nf* (*REL, fig*) wafer; (*INFORM*) chip, wafer.
oblicuo, a [o'βlikwo, a] *adj* oblique; (*mirada*) sidelong.
obligación [oβliɣa'θjon] *nf* obligation; (*COM*) bond, debenture.
obligar [oβli'ɣar] *vt* to force; **~se** *vr*: **~se a** to commit o.s. to.
obligatorio, a [oβliɣa'torjo, a] *adj* compulsory, obligatory.
obligue [o'βliɣe] *etc vb V* **obligar**.
oboe [o'βoe] *nm* oboe; (*músico*) oboist.
Ob.po *abr* (= *Obispo*) Bp.
obra ['oβra] *nf* work; (*hechura*) piece of work; (*ARQ*) construction, building; (*libro*) book; (*MUS*) opus; (*TEAT*) play; ~ **de arte** work of art; ~ **maestra** masterpiece; ~ **de consulta** reference book; **~s completas** complete works; ~ **benéfica** charity; **"~s"** (*en carretera*) "men at work"; **~s públicas** public works; **por ~ de** thanks to (the efforts of); **~s son amores y no buenas razones** actions speak louder than words.
obrar [o'βrar] *vt* to work; (*tener efecto*) to have an effect on ♦ *vi* to act, behave; (*tener efecto*) to have an effect; **la carta obra en su poder** the letter is in his/her possession.
obr. cit. *abr* (= *obra citada*) op. cit.
obrero, a [o'βrero, a] *adj* working; (*movimiento*) labour *cpd*; **clase obrera** working class ♦ *nm/f* (*gen*) worker; (*sin oficio*) labourer.
obscenidad [oβsθeni'ðað] *nf* obscenity.
obsceno, a [oβs'θeno, a] *adj* obscene.
obscu... = oscu...
obsequiar [oβse'kjar] *vt* (*ofrecer*) to present; (*agasajar*) to make a fuss of, lavish attention on.
obsequio [oβ'sekjo] *nm* (*regalo*) gift; (*cortesía*) courtesy, attention.
obsequioso, a [oβse'kjoso, a] *adj* attentive.
observación [oβserβa'θjon] *nf* observation; (*reflexión*) remark; (*objeción*) objection.
observador, a [oβserβa'ðor, a] *adj* observant ♦ *nm/f* observer.
observancia [oβser'βanθja] *nf* observance.
observar [oβser'βar] *vt* to observe; (*notar*) to notice; (*leyes*) to observe, respect; (*reglas*) to abide by.
observatorio [oβserβa'torjo] *nm* observatory; ~ **del tiempo** weather station.
obsesión [oβse'sjon] *nf* obsession.
obsesionar [oβsesjo'nar] *vt* to obsess.
obseso, a [oβ'seso, a] *nm/f* (*sexual*) sex maniac.
obsolescencia [oβsoles'θenθja] *nf*: ~ **incorporada** (*COM*) built-in obsolescence.
obsoleto, a [oβso'leto, a] *adj* obsolete.
obstaculice [oβstaku'liθe] *etc vb V* **obstaculizar**.
obstaculizar [oβstakuli'θar] *vt* (*dificultar*) to hinder, hamper.
obstáculo [oβs'takulo] *nm* (*gen*) obstacle;

(*impedimento*) hindrance, drawback.
obstante [oßs'tante]: **no ~** *adv* nevertheless; (*de todos modos*) all the same ♦ *prep* in spite of.
obstetra [oßs'tetra] *nm/f* obstetrician.
obstetricia [oßste'triθja] *nf* obstetrics *sg*.
obstinado, a [oßsti'naðo, a] *adj* (*gen*) obstinate; (*terco*) stubborn.
obstinarse [oßsti'narse] *vr* to dig one's heels in; **~ en** to persist in.
obstrucción [oßstruk'θjon] *nf* obstruction.
obstruir [oßstru'ir] *vt* to obstruct; (*bloquear*) to block; (*estorbar*) to hinder.
obstruyendo [oßstru'jendo] *etc vb V* **obstruir**.
obtención [oßten'θjon] *nf* (*COM*) procurement.
obtendré [oßten'dre] *etc vb V* **obtener**.
obtener [oßte'ner] *vt* (*conseguir*) to obtain; (*ganar*) to gain.
obtenga [oß'tenga] *etc vb V* **obtener**.
obturación [oßtura'θjon] *nf* plugging, stopping; (*FOTO*): **velocidad de ~** shutter speed.
obturador [oßtura'ðor] *nm* (*FOTO*) shutter.
obtuso, a [oß'tuso, a] *adj* (*filo*) blunt; (*MAT, fig*) obtuse.
obtuve [oß'tuße] *etc vb V* **obtener**.
obús [o'ßus] *nm* (*MIL*) shell.
obviar [oß'ßjar] *vt* to obviate, remove.
obvio, a ['oßßjo, a] *adj* obvious.
oca ['oka] *nf* goose; (*tb*: **juego de la ~**) ≈ snakes and ladders.
ocasión [oka'sjon] *nf* (*oportunidad*) opportunity, chance; (*momento*) occasion, time; (*causa*) cause; **de ~** secondhand; **con ~ de** on the occasion of; **en algunas ocasiones** sometimes; **aprovechar la ~** to seize one's opportunity.
ocasionar [okasjo'nar] *vt* to cause.
ocaso [o'kaso] *nm* sunset; (*fig*) decline.
occidental [okθiðen'tal] *adj* western ♦ *nm/f* westerner ♦ *nm* west.
occidente [okθi'ðente] *nm* west; **el O~** the West.
occiso, a [ok'θiso, a] *nm/f*: **el ~** the deceased; (*de asesinato*) the victim.
O.C.D.E. *nf abr* (= *Organización de Cooperación y Desarrollo Económicos*) OECD.
océano [o'θeano] *nm* ocean; **el ~ Índico** the Indian Ocean.
ochenta [o'tʃenta] *num* eighty.
ocho ['otʃo] *num* eight; (*fecha*) eighth; **~ días** a week.
ochocientos, as [otʃo'θjentos, as] *num* eight hundred.
OCI ['oθi] *nf abr* (*POL*: *Venezuela, Perú*) = *Oficina Central de Información*.
ocio ['oθjo] *nm* (*tiempo*) leisure; (*pey*) idleness; **"guía del ~"** "what's on".
ociosidad [oθjosi'ðað] *nf* idleness.
ocioso, a [o'θjoso, a] *adj* (*inactivo*) idle; (*inútil*) useless.
oct. *abr* (= *octubre*) Oct.
octanaje [okta'naxe] *nm*: **de alto ~** high octane.
octano [ok'tano] *nm* octane.
octavilla [okta'ßiʎa] *nm* leaflet, pamphlet.
octavo, a [ok'taßo, a] *num* eighth.
octeto [ok'teto] *nm* (*INFORM*) byte.
octogenario, a [oktoxe'narjo, a] *adj, nm/f* octogenarian.
octubre [ok'tußre] *nm* October.
OCU ['oku] *nf abr* (*ESP*: = *Organización de Consumidores y Usuarios*) ≈ Consumers' Association.
ocular [oku'lar] *adj* ocular, eye *cpd*; **testigo ~** eyewitness.
oculista [oku'lista] *nm/f* oculist.
ocultar [okul'tar] *vt* (*esconder*) to hide; (*callar*) to conceal; (*disfrazar*) to screen; **~se** *vr* to hide (o.s.); **~se a la vista** to keep out of sight.
oculto, a [o'kulto, a] *adj* hidden; (*fig*) secret.
ocupación [okupa'θjon] *nf* occupation; (*tenencia*) occupancy.
ocupado, a [oku'paðo, a] *adj* (*persona*) busy; (*plaza*) occupied, taken; (*teléfono*) engaged; **¿está ocupada la silla?** is that seat taken?
ocupar [oku'par] *vt* (*gen*) to occupy; (*puesto*) to hold, fill; (*individuo*) to engage; (*obreros*) to employ; (*confiscar*) to seize; **~se** *vr*: **~se de** *o* **en** to concern o.s. with; (*cuidar*) to look after; **~se de lo suyo** to mind one's own business.
ocurrencia [oku'rrenθja] *nf* (*ocasión*) occurrence; (*agudeza*) witticism.
ocurrir [oku'rrir] *vi* to happen; **~se** *vr*: **se me ocurrió que ...** it occurred to me that ...; **¿se te ocurre algo?** can you think of *o* come up with anything? **¿qué ocurre?** what's going on?
oda ['oða] *nf* ode.
ODECA [o'ðeka] *nf abr* = *Organización de Estados Centroamericanos*.
odiar [o'ðjar] *vt* to hate.
odio ['oðjo] *nm* (*gen*) hate, hatred; (*disgusto*) dislike.
odioso, a [o'ðjoso, a] *adj* (*gen*) hateful; (*malo*) nasty.
odisea [oði'sea] *nf* odyssey.
odontología [oðontolo'xia] *nf* dentistry,

dental surgery.
odontólogo, a [oðon'toloɣo, a] *nm/f* dentist, dental surgeon.
odre ['oðre] *nm* wineskin.
O.E.A. *nf abr* (= *Organización de Estados Americanos*) O.A.S.
OECE *nf abr* (= *Organización Europea de Cooperación Económica*) OEEC.
OELA [o'ela] *nf abr* = *Organización de Estados Latinoamericanos.*
oeste [o'este] *nm* west; **una película del** ~ a western.
ofender [ofen'der] *vt* (*agraviar*) to offend; (*insultar*) to insult; ~**se** *vr* to take offence.
ofensa [o'fensa] *nf* offence; (*insulto*) slight.
ofensivo, a [ofen'siβo, a] *adj* (*insultante*) insulting; (*MIL*) offensive ♦ *nf* offensive.
oferta [o'ferta] *nf* offer; (*propuesta*) proposal; (*para contrato*) bid, tender; **la ~ y la demanda** supply and demand; **artículos en** ~ goods on offer; ~ **excedentaria** (*COM*) excess supply; ~ **monetaria** money supply; ~ **pública de adquisición (OPA)** (*COM*) takeover bid; ~**s de trabajo** (*en periódicos*) situations vacant column.
offset ['ofset] *nm* offset.
oficial [ofi'θjal] *adj* official ♦ *nm* official; (*MIL*) officer.
oficialista [ofisja'lista] *adj* (*AM*) (pro-) government; **el candidato** ~ the governing party's candidate.
oficiar [ofi'θjar] *vt* to inform officially ♦ *vi* (*REL*) to officiate.
oficina [ofi'θina] *nf* office; ~ **de colocación** employment agency; ~ **de información** information bureau; ~ **de objetos perdidos** lost property office (*BRIT*), lost-and-found department (*US*); ~ **de turismo** tourist office.
oficinista [ofiθi'nista] *nm/f* clerk; **los ~s** white-collar workers.
oficio [o'fiθjo] *nm* (*profesión*) profession; (*puesto*) post; (*REL*) service; (*función*) function; (*comunicado*) official letter; **ser del** ~ to be an old hand; **tener mucho** ~ to have a lot of experience; ~ **de difuntos** funeral service; **de** ~ officially.
oficioso, a [ofi'θjoso, a] *adj* (*pey*) officious; (*no oficial*) unofficial, informal.
ofimática [ofi'matika] *nf* office automation.
ofrecer [ofre'θer] *vt* (*dar*) to offer; (*proponer*) to propose; ~**se** *vr* (*persona*) to offer o.s., volunteer; (*situación*) to present itself; **¿qué se le ofrece?, ¿se le ofrece algo?** what can I do for you?, can I get you anything?
ofrecimiento [ofreθi'mjento] *nm* offer, offering.
ofrendar [ofren'dar] *vt* to offer, contribute.
ofrezca [o'freθka] *etc vb V* **ofrecer**.
oftalmología [oftalmolo'xia] *nf* ophthalmology.
oftalmólogo, a [oftal'moloɣo, a] *nm/f* ophthalmologist.
ofuscación [ofuska'θjon] *nf*, **ofuscamiento** [ofuska'mjento] *nm* (*fig*) bewilderment.
ofuscar [ofus'kar] *vt* (*confundir*) to bewilder; (*enceguecer*) to dazzle, blind.
ofusque [o'fuske] *etc vb V* **ofuscar**.
ogro ['oɣro] *nm* ogre.
OIC *nf abr* = *Organización Interamericana del Café*; (*COM*) = *Organización Internacional del Comercio.*
oída [o'iða] *nf*: **de ~s** by hearsay.
oído [o'iðo] *nm* (*ANAT, MUS*) ear; (*sentido*) hearing; ~ **interno** inner ear; **de** ~ by ear; **apenas pude dar crédito a mis ~s** I could scarcely believe my ears; **hacer ~s sordos a** to turn a deaf ear to.
OIEA *nm abr* (= *Organismo Internacional de Energía Atómica*) IAEA.
oiga ['oiɣa] *etc vb V* **oír**.
OIR [o'ir] *nf abr* (= *Organización Internacional para los Refugiados*) IRO.
oír [o'ir] *vt* (*gen*) to hear; (*esp AM*: *escuchar*) to listen to; **¡oye!** (*sorpresa*) I say!, say! (*US*); **¡oiga!** (*TELEC*) hullo?; ~ **misa** to attend mass; **como quien oye llover** without paying (the slightest) attention.
O.I.T. *nf abr* (= *Organización Internacional del Trabajo*) ILO.
ojal [o'xal] *nm* buttonhole.
ojalá [oxa'la] *excl* if only (it were so)!, some hope! ♦ *conj* if only...!, would that...!; ~ **que venga hoy** I hope he comes today; **¡~ pudiera!** I wish I could!
ojeada [oxe'aða] *nf* glance; **echar una ~ a** to take a quick look at.
ojera [o'xera] *nf*: **tener ~s** to have bags under one's eyes.
ojeriza [oxe'riθa] *nf* ill-will; **tener ~ a** to have a grudge against, have it in for.
ojeroso, a [oxe'roso, a] *adj* haggard.
ojete [o'xete] *nm* eye(let).
ojo ['oxo] *nm* eye; (*de puente*) span; (*de cerradura*) keyhole ♦ *excl* careful!; **tener ~ para** to have an eye for; **~s saltones** bulging *o* goggle eyes; ~ **de buey** porthole; ~ **por** ~ an eye for an eye; **en un abrir y cerrar de ~s** in the twinkling of an eye; **a ~s vistas** openly; (*crecer etc*)

before one's (very) eyes; **a ~ (de buen cubero)** roughly; **~s que no ven, corazón que no siente** out of sight, out of mind; **ser el ~ derecho de algn** (*fig*) to be the apple of sb's eye.
okupa [o'kupa] *nm/f* (*fam*) squatter.
ola ['ola] *nf* wave; **~ de calor/frío** heatwave/cold spell; **la nueva ~** the latest fashion; (*CINE, MUS*) (the) new wave.
OLADE [o'laðe] *nf abr* = *Organización Latinoamericana de Energía.*
olé [o'le] *excl* bravo!, olé!
oleada [ole'aða] *nf* big wave, swell; (*fig*) wave.
oleaje [ole'axe] *nm* swell.
óleo ['oleo] *nm* oil.
oleoducto [oleo'ðukto] *nm* (oil) pipeline.
oler [o'ler] *vt* (*gen*) to smell; (*inquirir*) to pry into; (*fig: sospechar*) to sniff out ♦ *vi* to smell; **~ a** to smell of; **huele mal** it smells bad, it stinks.
olfatear [olfate'ar] *vt* to smell; (*fig: sospechar*) to sniff out; (*inquirir*) to pry into.
olfato [ol'fato] *nm* sense of smell.
oligarquía [oliɣar'kia] *nf* oligarchy.
olimpiada [olim'piaða] *nf*: **la ~** *o* **las ~s** the Olympics.
olímpicamente [o'limpikamente] *adv*: **pasar ~ de algo** to totally ignore sth.
olímpico, a [o'limpiko, a] *adj* Olympian; (*deportes*) Olympic.
oliva [o'liβa] *nf* (*aceituna*) olive; **aceite de ~** olive oil.
olivar [oli'βar] *nm* olive grove *o* plantation.
olivo [o'liβo] *nm* olive tree.
olla ['oʎa] *nf* pan; (*para hervir agua*) kettle; (*comida*) stew; **~ a presión** pressure cooker.
olmo ['olmo] *nm* elm (tree).
olor [o'lor] *nm* smell.
oloroso, a [olo'roso, a] *adj* scented.
OLP *nf abr* (= *Organización para la Liberación de Palestina*) PLO.
olvidadizo, a [olβiða'ðiθo, a] *adj* (*desmemoriado*) forgetful; (*distraído*) absent-minded.
olvidar [olβi'ðar] *vt* to forget; (*omitir*) to omit; (*abandonar*) to leave behind; **~se** *vr* (*fig*) to forget o.s.; **se me olvidó** I forgot.
olvido [ol'βiðo] *nm* oblivion; (*acto*) oversight; (*descuido*) slip; **caer en el ~** to fall into oblivion.
O.M. *abr* (*POL*) = *Orden Ministerial.*
ombligo [om'bliɣo] *nm* navel.
OMI *nf abr*(= *Organización Marítima Internacional*) IMO.
ominoso, a [omi'noso, a] *adj* ominous.
omisión [omi'sjon] *nf* (*abstención*) omission; (*descuido*) neglect.
omiso, a [o'miso, a] *adj*: **hacer caso ~ de** to ignore, pass over.
omitir [omi'tir] *vt* to leave *o* miss out, omit.
ómnibus ['omniβus] *nm* (*AM*) bus.
omnipotente [omnipo'tente] *adj* omnipotent.
omnipresente [omnipre'sente] *adj* omnipresent.
omnívoro, a [om'niβoro, a] *adj* omnivorous.
omoplato [omo'plato], **omóplato** [o'moplato] *nm* shoulder-blade.
OMS *nf abr* (= *Organización Mundial de la Salud*) WHO.
ONCE ['onθe] *nf abr* (= *Organización Nacional de Ciegos Españoles*) *charity for the blind.*
once ['onθe] *num* eleven ♦ *nm* (*AM*): **~s** *nfpl* tea break *sg.*
onda ['onda] *nf* wave; **~ corta/larga/media** short/long/medium wave; **~s acústicas/hertzianas** acoustic/Hertzian waves; **~ sonora** sound wave.
ondear [onde'ar] *vi* to wave; (*tener ondas*) to be wavy; (*agua*) to ripple; **~se** *vr* to swing, sway.
ondulación [ondula'θjon] *nf* undulation.
ondulado, a [ondu'laðo, a] *adj* wavy ♦ *nm* wave.
ondulante [ondu'lante] *adj* undulating.
ondular [ondu'lar] *vt* (*el pelo*) to wave ♦ *vi*, **~se** *vr* to undulate.
oneroso, a [one'roso, a] *adj* onerous.
ONG *nf abr* (= *organización no gubernamental*) NGO.
onomástico, a [ono'mastiko, a] *adj*: **fiesta onomástica** saint's day ♦ *nm* saint's day.
ONU ['onu] *nf abr V* **Organización de las Naciones Unidas.**
onubense [onu'βense] *adj* of *o* from Huelva ♦ *nm/f* native *o* inhabitant of Huelva.
ONUDI [o'nuði] *nf abr* (= *Organización de las Naciones Unidas para el Desarrollo Industrial*) UNIDO (*United Nations Industrial Development Organization*).
onza ['onθa] *nf* ounce.
O.P. *nfpl abr* = **obras públicas**; (*COM*) = *Oficina Principal.*
OPA *nf abr* (= *oferta pública de adquisición*) takeover bid.
opaco, a [o'pako, a] *adj* opaque; (*fig*) dull.
ópalo ['opalo] *nm* opal.
opción [op'θjon] *nf* (*gen*) option; (*derecho*) right, option; **no hay ~** there is no

alternative.
opcional [opθjo'nal] *adj* optional.
O.P.E.P. [o'pep] *nf abr* (= *Organización de Países Exportadores de Petróleo*) OPEC.
ópera ['opera] *nf* opera; ~ **bufa** *o* **cómica** comic opera.
operación [opera'θjon] *nf* (*gen*) operation; (*COM*) transaction, deal; ~ **"llave en manos"** (*INFORM*) turnkey operation; ~ **a plazo** (*COM*) forward transaction; **operaciones accesorias** (*INFORM*) housekeeping; **operaciones a término** (*COM*) futures.
operador, a [opera'ðor, a] *nm/f* operator; (*CINE*: *proyección*) projectionist; (: *rodaje*) cameraman.
operar [ope'rar] *vt* (*producir*) to produce, bring about; (*MED*) to operate on ♦ *vi* (*COM*) to operate, deal; ~**se** *vr* to occur; (*MED*) to have an operation; **se han operado grandes cambios** great changes have been made *o* have taken place.
operario, a [ope'rarjo, a] *nm/f* worker.
opereta [ope'reta] *nf* operetta.
opinar [opi'nar] *vt* (*estimar*) to think ♦ *vi* (*enjuiciar*) to give one's opinion; ~ **bien de** to think well of.
opinión [opi'njon] *nf* (*creencia*) belief; (*criterio*) opinion; **la** ~ **pública** public opinion.
opio ['opjo] *nm* opium.
opíparo, a [o'piparo, a] *adj* sumptuous.
opondré [opon'dre] *etc vb V* **oponer**.
oponente [opo'nente] *nm/f* opponent.
oponer [opo'ner] *vt* (*resistencia*) to put up, offer; (*negativa*) to raise; ~**se** *vr* (*objetar*) to object; (*estar frente a frente*) to be opposed; (*dos personas*) to oppose each other; ~ **A a B** to set A against B; **me opongo a pensar que** ... I refuse to believe *o* think that ....
oponga [o'ponga] *etc vb V* **oponer**.
Oporto [o'porto] *nm* Oporto.
oporto [o'porto] *nm* port.
oportunidad [oportuni'ðað] *nf* (*ocasión*) opportunity; (*posibilidad*) chance.
oportunismo [oportu'nismo] *nm* opportunism.
oportunista [oportu'nista] *nm/f* opportunist; (*infección*) opportunistic.
oportuno, a [opor'tuno, a] *adj* (*en su tiempo*) opportune, timely; (*respuesta*) suitable; **en el momento** ~ at the right moment.
oposición [oposi'θjon] *nf* opposition; **oposiciones** *nfpl* public examinations; **ganar un puesto por oposiciones** to win a post by public competitive examination; **hacer oposiciones a, presentarse a unas oposiciones a** to sit a competitive examination for; *see boxed note.*

> **OPOSICIONES**
>
> **Oposiciones** *are examinations which are held every year in Spain in which candidates compete, both nationally and locally, for posts in the public sector, state education, the judiciary and so on. These posts are permanent and the number of entrants is high, so the examinations are correspondingly tough. The candidates, "opositores", have to study a wide range of subjects relating to their field and must also know and understand the constitution. People can spend years studying for* **oposiciones** *and resitting them if necessary.*

opositar [oposi'tar] *vi* to sit a public entrance examination.
opositor, a [oposi'tor, a] *nm/f* (*ADMIN*) candidate to a public examination; (*adversario*) opponent.
opresión [opre'sjon] *nf* oppression.
opresivo, a [opre'siβo, a] *adj* oppressive.
opresor, a [opre'sor, a] *nm/f* oppressor.
oprimir [opri'mir] *vt* to squeeze; (*asir*) to grasp; (*pulsar*) to press; (*fig*) to oppress.
optar [op'tar] *vi* (*elegir*) to choose; ~ **a** *o* **por** to opt for.
optativo, a [opta'tiβo, a] *adj* optional.
óptico, a ['optiko, a] *adj* optic(al) ♦ *nm/f* optician ♦ *nf* optics *sg*; (*fig*) viewpoint.
optimismo [opti'mismo] *nm* optimism.
optimista [opti'mista] *nm/f* optimist.
óptimo, a ['optimo, a] *adj* (*el mejor*) very best.
opuesto, a [o'pwesto, a] *pp de* **oponer** ♦ *adj* (*contrario*) opposite; (*antagónico*) opposing.
opulencia [opu'lenθja] *nf* opulence.
opulento, a [opu'lento, a] *adj* opulent.
opuse [o'puse] *etc vb V* **oponer**.
ORA ['ora] *nf abr* (*ESP*: = *Operación de Regulación de Aparcamientos*) *parking regulations*.
ora ['ora] *adv*: ~ **tú** ~ **yo** now you, now me.
oración [ora'θjon] *nf* (*discurso*) speech; (*REL*) prayer; (*LING*) sentence.
oráculo [o'rakulo] *nm* oracle.
orador, a [ora'ðor, a] *nm/f* orator; (*conferenciante*) speaker.
oral [o'ral] *adj* oral; **por vía** ~ (*MED*) orally.
orangután [orangu'tan] *nm* orang-utan.
orar [o'rar] *vi* (*REL*) to pray.
oratoria [ora'torja] *nf* oratory.

orbe ['orβe] *nm* orb, sphere; (*fig*) world; **en todo el** ~ all over the globe.
órbita ['orβita] *nf* orbit; (*ANAT: ocular*) (eye-)socket.
orden ['orðen] *nm* (*gen*) order; (*INFORM*) command; ~ **público** public order, law and order; (*números*) **del** ~ **de** about; **de primer** ~ first-rate; **en** ~ **de prioridad** in order of priority ♦ *nf* (*gen*) order; ~ **bancaria** banker's order; ~ **de compra** (*COM*) purchase order; ~ **del día** agenda; **eso ahora está a la** ~ **del día** that is now the order of the day; **a la** ~ **de usted** at your service; **dar la** ~ **de hacer algo** to give the order to do sth.
ordenación [orðena'θjon] *nf* (*estado*) order; (*acto*) ordering; (*REL*) ordination.
ordenado, a [orðe'naðo, a] *adj* (*metódico*) methodical; (*arreglado*) orderly.
ordenador [orðena'ðor] *nm* computer; ~ **central** mainframe computer; ~ **de gestión** business computer; ~ **portátil** laptop (computer); ~ **de sobremesa** desktop computer.
ordenamiento [orðena'mjento] *nm* legislation.
ordenanza [orðe'nanθa] *nf* ordinance; ~**s municipales** by-laws ♦ *nm* (*COM etc*) messenger; (*MIL*) orderly; (*bedel*) porter.
ordenar [orðe'nar] *vt* (*mandar*) to order; (*poner orden*) to put in order, arrange; ~**se** *vr* (*REL*) to be ordained.
ordeñadora [orðeɲa'ðora] *nf* milking machine.
ordeñar [orðe'ɲar] *vt* to milk.
ordinariez [orðina'rjeθ] *nf* (*cualidad*) coarseness, vulgarity; (*una* ~) coarse remark *o* joke *etc*.
ordinario, a [orði'narjo, a] *adj* (*común*) ordinary, usual; (*vulgar*) vulgar, common.
ordinograma [orðino'ɣrama] *nm* flowchart.
orear [ore'ar] *vt* to air; ~**se** *vr* (*ropa*) to air.
orégano [o'reɣano] *nm* oregano.
oreja [o'rexa] *nf* ear; (*MECÁNICA*) lug, flange.
orensano, a [oren'sano, a] *adj* of *o* from Orense ♦ *nm/f* native *o* inhabitant of Orense.
orfanato [orfa'nato] *nm*, **orfanatorio** [orfana'torjo] *nm* orphanage.
orfandad [orfan'dað] *nf* orphanhood.
orfebre [or'feβre] *nm* gold-/silversmith.
orfebrería [orfeβre'ria] *nf* gold/silver work.
orfelinato [orfeli'nato] *nm* orphanage.
orfeón [orfe'on] *nm* (*MUS*) choral society.
organice [orɣa'niθe] *etc vb V* **organizar**.
orgánico, a [or'ɣaniko, a] *adj* organic.
organigrama [orɣani'ɣrama] *nm* flow chart; (*de organización*) organization chart.
organillo [orɣa'niʎo] *nm* barrel organ.
organismo [orɣa'nismo] *nm* (*BIO*) organism; (*POL*) organization; **O~ Internacional de Energía Atómica** International Atomic Energy Agency.
organista [orɣa'nista] *nm/f* organist.
organización [orɣaniθa'θjon] *nf* organization; **O~ de las Naciones Unidas (ONU)** United Nations Organization **O~ del Tratado del Atlántico Norte (OTAN)** North Atlantic Treaty Organization (NATO).
organizador, a [orɣaniθa'ðor, a] *adj* organizing; **el comité** ~ the organizing committee ♦ *nm/f* organizer.
organizar [orɣani'θar] *vt* to organize.
órgano ['orɣano] *nm* organ.
orgasmo [or'ɣasmo] *nm* orgasm.
orgía [or'xia] *nf* orgy.
orgullo [or'ɣuʎo] *nm* (*altanería*) pride; (*autorespeto*) self-respect.
orgulloso, a [orɣu'ʎoso, a] *adj* (*gen*) proud; (*altanero*) haughty.
orientación [orjenta'θjon] *nf* (*posición*) position; (*dirección*) direction; ~ **profesional** occupational guidance.
oriental [orjen'tal] *adj* oriental; (*región etc*) eastern ♦ *nm/f* oriental.
orientar [orjen'tar] *vt* (*situar*) to orientate; (*señalar*) to point; (*dirigir*) to direct; (*guiar*) to guide; ~**se** *vr* to get one's bearings; (*decidirse*) to decide on a course of action.
oriente [o'rjente] *nm* east; **el O~** the East, the Orient; **Cercano/Medio/Lejano O~** Near/ Middle/Far East.
orificio [ori'fiθjo] *nm* orifice.
origen [o'rixen] *nm* origin; (*nacimiento*) lineage, birth; **dar** ~ **a** to cause, give rise to.
original [orixi'nal] *adj* (*nuevo*) original; (*extraño*) odd, strange ♦ *nm* original; (*TIP*) manuscript; (*TEC*) master (copy).
originalidad [orixinali'ðað] *nf* originality.
originar [orixi'nar] *vt* to originate; ~**se** *vr* to originate.
originario, a [orixi'narjo, a] *adj* (*nativo*) native; (*primordial*) original; **ser** ~ **de** to originate from; **país** ~ country of origin.
orilla [o'riʎa] *nf* (*borde*) border; (*de río*) bank; (*de bosque, tela*) edge; (*de mar*) shore; **a** ~**s de** on the banks of.
orillar [ori'ʎar] *vt* (*bordear*) to skirt, go round; (*COSTURA*) to edge; (*resolver*) to

wind up; (*tocar: asunto*) to touch briefly on; (*dificultad*) to avoid.
orín [o'rin] *nm* rust.
orina [o'rina] *nf* urine.
orinal [ori'nal] *nm* (chamber) pot.
orinar [ori'nar] *vi* to urinate; ~**se** *vr* to wet o.s.
orines [o'rines] *nmpl* urine *sg*.
oriundo, a [o'rjundo, a] *adj*: ~ **de** native of.
orla ['orla] *nf* edge, border; (*ESCOL*) graduation photograph.
ornamentar [ornamen'tar] *vt* (*adornar, ataviar*) to adorn; (*revestir*) to bedeck.
ornar [or'nar] *vt* to adorn.
ornitología [ornitolo'xia] *nf* ornithology, bird watching.
ornitólogo, a [orni'toloɣo, a] *nm/f* ornithologist.
oro ['oro] *nm* gold; ~ **en barras** gold ingots; **de** ~ gold, golden; **no es** ~ **todo lo que reluce** all that glitters is not gold; **hacerse de** ~ to make a fortune; *V tb* **oros**.
orondo, a [o'rondo, a] *adj* (*vasija*) rounded; (*individuo*) smug, self-satisfied.
oropel [oro'pel] *nm* tinsel.
oros ['oros] *nmpl* (*NAIPES*) *one of the suits in the Spanish card deck*; *V tb* **Baraja Española**.
orquesta [or'kesta] *nf* orchestra; ~ **de cámara/sinfónica** chamber/symphony orchestra; ~ **de jazz** jazz band.
orquestar [orkes'tar] *vt* to orchestrate.
orquídea [or'kiðea] *nf* orchid.
ortiga [or'tiɣa] *nf* nettle.
ortodoncia [orto'ðonθja] *nf* orthodontics *sg*.
ortodoxo, a [orto'ðokso, a] *adj* orthodox.
ortografía [ortoɣra'fia] *nf* spelling.
ortopedia [orto'peðja] *nf* orthop(a)edics *sg*.
ortopédico, a [orto'peðiko, a] *adj* orthop(a)edic.
oruga [o'ruɣa] *nf* caterpillar.
orujo [o'ruxo] *nm type of strong grape liqueur made from grape pressings*.
orzuelo [or'θwelo] *nm* (*MED*) stye.
os [os] *pron* (*gen*) you; (*a vosotros*) (to) you; (*reflexivo*) (to) yourselves; (*mutuo*) (to) each other; **vosotros** ~ **laváis** you wash yourselves; **¡callar**~! (*fam*) shut up!
osa ['osa] *nf* (she-)bear; **O**~ **Mayor/Menor** Great/Little Bear, Ursa Major/Minor.
osadía [osa'ðia] *nf* daring; (*descaro*) impudence.
osamenta [osa'menta] *nf* skeleton.
osar [o'sar] *vi* to dare.
oscense [os'θense] *adj* of *o* from Huesca ♦ *nm/f* native *o* inhabitant of Huesca.
oscilación [osθila'θjon] *nf* (*movimiento*) oscillation; (*fluctuación*) fluctuation; (*vacilación*) hesitation; (*columpio*) swinging, movement to and fro.
oscilar [osθi'lar] *vi* to oscillate; to fluctuate; to hesitate.
ósculo ['oskulo] *nm* kiss.
oscurecer [oskure'θer] *vt* to darken ♦ *vi* to grow dark; ~**se** *vr* to grow *o* get dark.
oscurezca [osku'reθka] *etc vb V* **oscurecer**.
oscuridad [oskuri'ðað] *nf* obscurity; (*tinieblas*) darkness.
oscuro, a [os'kuro, a] *adj* dark; (*fig*) obscure; (*indefinido*) confused; (*cielo*) overcast, cloudy; (*futuro etc*) uncertain; **a oscuras** in the dark.
óseo, a ['oseo, a] *adj* bony; (*MED etc*) bone *cpd*.
oso ['oso] *nm* bear; ~ **blanco/gris/pardo** polar/grizzly/brown bear; ~ **de peluche** teddy bear; ~ **hormiguero** anteater; **hacer el** ~ to play the fool.
Ostende [os'tende] *nm* Ostend.
ostensible [osten'siβle] *adj* obvious.
ostensiblemente [ostensiβle'mente] *adv* perceptibly, visibly.
ostentación [ostenta'θjon] *nf* (*gen*) ostentation; (*acto*) display.
ostentar [osten'tar] *vt* (*gen*) to show; (*pey*) to flaunt, show off; (*poseer*) to have, possess.
ostentoso, a [osten'toso, a] *adj* ostentatious, showy.
osteópata [oste'opata] *nm/f* osteopath.
ostra ['ostra] *nf* oyster ♦ *excl*: **¡**~**s!** (*fam*) sugar!
ostracismo [ostra'θismo] *nm* ostracism.
OTAN ['otan] *nf abr V* **Organización del Tratado del Atlántico Norte**.
OTASE [o'tase] *nf abr* (= *Organización del Tratado del Sudeste Asiático*) SEATO.
otear [ote'ar] *vt* to observe; (*fig*) to look into.
otero [o'tero] *nm* low hill, hillock.
otitis [o'titis] *nf* earache.
otoñal [oto'ɲal] *adj* autumnal.
otoño [o'toɲo] *nm* autumn, fall (*US*).
otorgamiento [otorɣa'mjento] *nm* conferring, granting; (*JUR*) execution.
otorgar [otor'ɣar] *vt* (*conceder*) to concede; (*dar*) to grant; (*poderes*) to confer; (*premio*) to award.
otorgue [o'torɣe] *etc vb V* **otorgar**.
otorrinolaringólogo, a [otorrinolarin'goloɣo, a] *nm/f* (*MED*: *tb*: **otorrino**) ear, nose and throat specialist.

PALABRA CLAVE

otro, a ['otro, a] *adj* **1** (*distinto*: *sg*) another; (: *pl*) other; **otra cosa/persona** something/someone else; **con ~s amigos** with other *o* different friends; **a/en otra parte** elsewhere, somewhere else
2 (*adicional*): **tráigame ~ café (más), por favor** can I have another coffee please; **~s 10 días más** another 10 days
♦ *pron* **1** (*sg*) another one; **el ~** the other one; **(los) ~s** (the) others; **¡otra!** (*MUS*) more!; **de ~** somebody *o* someone else's; **que lo haga ~** let somebody *o* someone else do it; **ni uno ni ~** neither one nor the other
2 (*recíproco*): **se odian (la) una a (la) otra** they hate one another *o* each other
3: **~ tanto**: **comer ~ tanto** to eat the same *o* as much again; **recibió una decena de telegramas y otras tantas llamadas** he got about ten telegrams and as many calls.

otrora [o'trora] *adv* formerly; **el ~ señor del país** the one-time ruler of the country.
OUA *nf abr* (= *Organización de la Unidad Africana*) OAU.
ovación [oßa'θjon] *nf* ovation.
ovacionar [oßaθjo'nar] *vt* to cheer.
oval [o'ßal], **ovalado, a** [oßa'laðo, a] *adj* oval.
óvalo ['oßalo] *nm* oval.
ovario [o'ßarjo] *nm* ovary.
oveja [o'ßexa] *nf* sheep; **~ negra** (*fig*) black sheep (of the family).
overol [oße'rol] *nm* (*AM*) overalls *pl*.
ovetense [oße'tense] *adj* of *o* from Oviedo ♦ *nm/f* native *o* inhabitant of Oviedo.
ovillo [o'ßiʎo] *nm* (*de lana*) ball; (*fig*) tangle; **hacerse un ~** to curl up (into a ball).
OVNI ['oßni] *nm abr* (= *objeto volante no identificado*) UFO.
ovulación [oßula'θjon] *nf* ovulation.
óvulo ['oßulo] *nm* ovum.
oxidación [oksiða'θjon] *nf* rusting.
oxidar [oksi'ðar] *vt* to rust; **~se** *vr* to go rusty; (*TEC*) to oxidize.
óxido ['oksiðo] *nm* oxide.
oxigenado, a [oksixe'naðo, a] *adj* (*QUÍMICA*) oxygenated; (*pelo*) bleached.
oxigenar [oksixe'nar] *vt* to oxygenate; **~se** *vr* to become oxygenated; (*fam*) to get some fresh air.
oxígeno [ok'sixeno] *nm* oxygen.
oyendo [o'jendo] *etc vb V* **oír**.
oyente [o'jente] *nm/f* listener, hearer; (*ESCOL*) unregistered *o* occasional student.

Pp

P, p [pe] *nf* (*letra*) P, p; **P de París** P for Peter.
P *abr* (*REL*: = *padre*) Fr.; = **papa**.
p. *abr* (= *página*) p.
p.a. *abr* = **por autorización**.
pabellón [paße'ʎon] *nm* bell tent; (*ARQ*) pavilion; (*de hospital etc*) block, section; (*bandera*) flag; **~ de conveniencia** (*COM*) flag of convenience; **~ de la oreja** outer ear.
pábilo ['paßilo] *nm* wick.
pábulo ['paßulo] *nm* food; **dar ~ a** to feed, encourage.
PAC *nf abr* (= *Política Agrícola Común*) CAP.
pacense [pa'θense] *adj* of *o* from Badajoz ♦ *nm/f* native *o* inhabitant of Badajoz.
paceño, a [pa'θeɲo, a] *adj* of *o* from La Paz ♦ *nm/f* native *o* inhabitant of La Paz.
pacer [pa'θer] *vi* to graze ♦ *vt* to graze on.
pachá [pa'tʃa] *nm*: **vivir como un ~** to live like a king.
pachanguero, a [patʃan'gero, a] *adj* (*pey*: *música*) *noisy and catchy*.
pachorra [pa'tʃorra] *nf* (*indolencia*) slowness; (*tranquilidad*) calmness.
pachucho, a [pa'tʃutʃo, a] *adj* (*fruta*) overripe; (*persona*) off-colour, poorly.
paciencia [pa'θjenθja] *nf* patience; **¡~!** be patient!; **¡~ y barajar!** don't give up!; **perder la ~** to lose one's temper.
paciente [pa'θjente] *adj, nm/f* patient.
pacificación [paθifika'θjon] *nf* pacification.
pacificar [paθifi'kar] *vt* to pacify; (*tranquilizar*) to calm.
pacífico, a [pa'θifiko, a] *adj* peaceful; (*persona*) peace-loving; (*existencia*) pacific; **el (Océano) P~** the Pacific (Ocean).
pacifique [paθi'fike] *etc vb V* **pacificar**.
pacifismo [paθi'fismo] *nm* pacifism.
pacifista [paθi'fista] *nm/f* pacifist.
pacotilla [pako'tiʎa] *nf* trash; **de ~** shoddy.
pactar [pak'tar] *vt* to agree to, agree on ♦ *vi* to come to an agreement.
pacto ['pakto] *nm* (*tratado*) pact; (*acuerdo*) agreement.

padecer [paðe'θer] *vt* (*sufrir*) to suffer; (*soportar*) to endure, put up with; (*ser víctima de*) to be a victim of ♦ *vi*: ~ **de** to suffer from.
padecimiento [paðeθi'mjento] *nm* suffering.
padezca [pa'ðeθka] *etc vb V* **padecer**.
padrastro [pa'ðrastro] *nm* stepfather.
padre ['paðre] *nm* father ♦ *adj* (*fam*): **un éxito** ~ a tremendous success; ~**s** *nmpl* parents; ~ **espiritual** confessor; **P**~ **Nuestro** Lord's Prayer; ~ **político** father-in-law; **García** ~ García senior; ¡**tu** ~! (*fam!*) up yours! (*!*).
padrino [pa'ðrino] *nm* godfather; (*fig*) sponsor, patron; ~**s** *nmpl* godparents; ~ **de boda** best man.
padrón [pa'ðron] *nm* (*censo*) census, roll; (*de socios*) register.
paella [pa'eʎa] *nf* paella, *dish of rice with meat, shellfish etc.*
paga ['paɣa] *nf* (*dinero pagado*) payment; (*sueldo*) pay, wages *pl*.
pagadero, a [paɣa'ðero, a] *adj* payable; ~ **a la entrega/a plazos** payable on delivery/in instalments.
pagano, a [pa'ɣano, a] *adj, nm/f* pagan, heathen.
pagar [pa'ɣar] *vt* (*gen*) to pay; (*las compras, crimen*) to pay for; (*deuda*) to pay (off); (*fig*: *favor*) to repay ♦ *vi* to pay; ~**se** *vr*: ~**se con algo** to be content with sth; ¡**me las pagarás**! I'll get you for this!
pagaré [paɣa're] *nm* I.O.U.
página ['paxina] *nf* page; ~ **de inicio** (*INFORM*) home page; ~**s amarillas** Yellow Pages ®.
paginación [paxina'θjon] *nf* (*INFORM, TIP*) pagination.
paginar [paxi'nar] *vt* (*INFORM, TIP*) to paginate.
pago ['paɣo] *nm* (*dinero*) payment; (*fig*) return; ~ **anticipado/a cuenta/a la entrega/en especie/inicial** advance payment/payment on account/cash on delivery/payment in kind/down payment; ~ **a título gracioso** ex gratia payment; **en** ~ **de** in return for.
pág(s). *abr* (= *página(s)*) p(p).
pague ['paɣe] *etc vb V* **pagar**.
paila ['paila] *nf* (*AM*) frying pan.
país [pa'is] *nm* (*gen*) country; (*región*) land; **los Paises Bajos** the Low Countries; **el P**~ **Vasco** the Basque Country.
paisaje [pai'saxe] *nm* countryside, landscape; (*vista*) scenery.
paisano, a [pai'sano, a] *adj* of the same country ♦ *nm/f* (*compatriota*) fellow countryman/woman; **vestir de** ~ (*soldado*) to be in civilian clothes; (*guardia*) to be in plain clothes.
paja ['paxa] *nf* straw; (*fig*) trash, rubbish; (*en libro, ensayo*) padding, waffle; **riñeron por un quítame allá esas** ~**s** they quarrelled over a trifle.
pajar [pa'xar] *nm* hay loft.
pajarita [paxa'rita] *nf* bow tie.
pájaro ['paxaro] *nm* bird; (*fam*: *astuto*) clever fellow; **tener la cabeza a** ~**s** to be featherbrained.
pajita [pa'xita] *nf* (drinking) straw.
pajizo, a [pa'xiθo, a] *adj* (*de paja*) straw *cpd*; (*techo*) thatched; (*color*) straw-coloured.
pakistaní [pakista'ni] *adj, nm/f* Pakistani.
pala ['pala] *nf* (*de mango largo*) spade; (*de mango corto*) shovel; (*raqueta etc*) bat; (: *de tenis*) racquet; (*CULIN*) slice; ~ **matamoscas** fly swat.
palabra [pa'laβra] *nf* (*gen, promesa*) word; (*facultad*) (power of) speech; (*derecho de hablar*) right to speak; **faltar a su** ~ to go back on one's word; **quedarse con la** ~ **en la boca** to stop short; (*en reunión, comité etc*) **tomar la** ~ to speak, take the floor; **pedir la** ~ to ask to be allowed to speak; **tener la** ~ to have the floor; **no encuentro** ~**s para expresarme** words fail me.
palabrería [palaβre'ria] *nf* hot air.
palabrota [pala'βrota] *nf* swearword.
palacio [pa'laθjo] *nm* palace; (*mansión*) mansion, large house; ~ **de justicia** courthouse; ~ **municipal** town/city hall.
palada [pa'laða] *nf* shovelful, spadeful; (*de remo*) stroke.
paladar [pala'ðar] *nm* palate.
paladear [palaðe'ar] *vt* to taste.
palanca [pa'lanka] *nf* lever; (*fig*) pull, influence; ~ **de cambio** (*AUTO*) gear lever, gearshift (*US*); ~ **de freno** (*AUTO*) brake lever; ~ **de gobierno** *o* **de control** (*INFORM*) joystick.
palangana [palan'gana] *nf* washbasin.
palco ['palko] *nm* box.
palenque [pa'lenke] *nm* (*cerca*) stockade, fence; (*área*) arena, enclosure; (*de gallos*) pit.
palentino, a [palen'tino, a] *adj* of *o* from Palencia ♦ *nm/f* native *o* inhabitant of Palencia.
paleolítico, a [paleo'litiko, a] *adj* paleolithic.
paleontología [paleontolo'xia] *nf* paleontology.
Palestina [pales'tina] *nf* Palestine.
palestino, a [pales'tino, a] *adj, nm/f* Palestinian.

palestra [pa'lestra] *nf*: **salir** *o* **saltar a la ~** to come into the spotlight.
paleto, a [pa'leto, a] *nm/f* yokel, hick (*US*) ♦ *nf* (*pala*) small shovel; (*ARTE*) palette; (*ANAT*) shoulder blade; (*AM*) ice lolly.
paliar [pa'ljar] *vt* (*mitigar*) to mitigate; (*disfrazar*) to conceal.
paliativo [palja'tiβo] *nm* palliative.
palidecer [paliðe'θer] *vi* to turn pale.
palidez [pali'ðeθ] *nf* paleness.
palidezca [pali'ðeθka] *etc vb V* **palidecer**.
pálido, a ['paliðo, a] *adj* pale.
palillo [pa'liʎo] *nm* small stick; (*para dientes*) toothpick; **~s (chinos)** chopsticks; **estar hecho un ~** to be as thin as a rake.
palio ['paljo] *nm* canopy.
palique [pa'like] *nm*: **estar de ~** (*fam*) to have a chat.
paliza [pa'liθa] *nf* beating, thrashing; **dar** *o* **propinar** (*fam*) **una ~ a algn** to give sb a thrashing.
palma ['palma] *nf* (*ANAT*) palm; (*árbol*) palm tree; **batir** *o* **dar ~s** to clap, applaud; **llevarse la ~** to triumph, win.
palmada [pal'maða] *nf* slap; **~s** *nfpl* clapping *sg*, applause *sg*.
Palma de Mallorca *nf* Palma.
palmar [pal'mar] *vi* (*tb*: **~la**) to die, kick the bucket.
palmarés [palma'res] *nm* (*lista*) list of winners; (*historial*) track record.
palmear [palme'ar] *vi* to clap.
palmero, a [pal'mero, a] *adj* of the island of Palma ♦ *nm/f* native *o* inhabitant of the island of Palma ♦ *nm* (*AM*), *nf* palm tree.
palmo ['palmo] *nm* (*medida*) span; (*fig*) small amount; **~ a ~** inch by inch.
palmotear [palmote'ar] *vi* to clap, applaud.
palmoteo [palmo'teo] *nm* clapping, applause.
palo ['palo] *nm* stick; (*poste*) post, pole; (*mango*) handle, shaft; (*golpe*) blow, hit; (*de golf*) club; (*de béisbol*) bat; (*NAUT*) mast; (*NAIPES*) suit; **vermut a ~ seco** straight vermouth; **de tal ~ tal astilla** like father like son.
paloma [pa'loma] *nf* dove, pigeon; **~ mensajera** carrier *o* homing pigeon.
palomilla [palo'miʎa] *nf* moth; (*TEC*: *tuerca*) wing nut; (*soporte*) bracket.
palomitas [palo'mitas] *nfpl* popcorn *sg*.
palpable [pal'paβle] *adj* palpable; (*fig*) tangible.
palpar [pal'par] *vt* to touch, feel.
palpitación [palpita'θjon] *nf* palpitation.
palpitante [palpi'tante] *adj* palpitating; (*fig*) burning.
palpitar [palpi'tar] *vi* to palpitate; (*latir*) to beat.
palta ['palta] *nf* (*AM*) avocado.
palúdico, a [pa'luðiko, a] *adj* marshy.
paludismo [palu'ðismo] *nm* malaria.
palurdo, a [pa'lurðo, a] *adj* coarse, uncouth ♦ *nm/f* yokel, hick (*US*).
pamela [pa'mela] *nf* sun hat.
pampa ['pampa] *nf* (*AM*) pampa(s), prairie.
pamplinas [pam'plinas] *nfpl* nonsense *sg*.
pamplonés, esa [pamplo'nes, esa], **pamplonica** [pamplo'nika] *adj* of *o* from Pamplona ♦ *nm/f* native *o* inhabitant of Pamplona.
pan [pan] *nm* bread; (*una barra*) loaf; **~ de molde** sliced loaf; **~ integral** wholemeal bread; **~ rallado** breadcrumbs *pl*; **eso es ~ comido** it's a cinch; **llamar al ~ ~ y al vino vino** to call a spade a spade.
pana ['pana] *nf* corduroy.
panadería [panaðe'ria] *nf* baker's (shop).
panadero, a [pana'ðero, a] *nm/f* baker.
panal [pa'nal] *nm* honeycomb.
Panamá [pana'ma] *nm* Panama.
panameño, a [pana'meɲo, a] *adj* Panamanian.
pancarta [pan'karta] *nf* placard, banner.
pancho, a ['pantʃo, a] *adj*: **estar tan ~** to remain perfectly calm.
pancito [pan'sito] *nm* (*AM*) (bread) roll.
páncreas ['pankreas] *nm* pancreas.
panda ['panda] *nm* panda ♦ *nf* gang.
pandereta [pande'reta] *nf* tambourine.
pandilla [pan'diʎa] *nf* set, group; (*de criminales*) gang; (*pey*) clique.
pando, a ['pando, a] *adj* sagging.
panel [pa'nel] *nm* panel; **~ acústico** acoustic screen.
panera [pa'nera] *nf* bread basket.
panfleto [pan'fleto] *nm* (*POL etc*) pamphlet; lampoon.
pánico ['paniko] *nm* panic.
panificadora [panifika'ðora] *nf* bakery.
panorama [pano'rama] *nm* panorama; (*vista*) view.
panqué [pan'ke] *nm* (*AM*) pancake.
pantaletas [panta'letas] *nfpl* (*AM*) panties.
pantalla [pan'taʎa] *nf* (*de cine*) screen; (*cubreluz*) lampshade; (*INFORM*) screen, display; **servir de ~ a** to be a blind for; **~ de cristal líquido** liquid crystal display; **~ táctil** touch-sensitive screen; **~ de ayuda** help screen; **~ plana** plane screen.
pantalón [panta'lon] *nm*, **pantalones** [panta'lones] *nmpl* trousers *pl*, pants *pl* (*US*); **pantalones vaqueros** jeans *pl*.
pantano [pan'tano] *nm* (*ciénaga*) marsh,

swamp; (*depósito*: *de agua*) reservoir; (*fig*) jam, fix, difficulty.
pantera [pan'tera] *nf* panther.
pantis ['pantis] *nmpl* tights.
pantomima [panto'mima] *nf* pantomime.
pantorrilla [panto'rriʎa] *nf* calf (of the leg).
pantufla [pan'tufla] *nf* slipper.
panty ['panti] *nm* = **pantis**.
panza ['panθa] *nf* belly, paunch.
panzón, ona [pan'θon, ona], **panzudo, a** [pan'θuðo, a] *adj* fat, potbellied.
pañal [pa'ɲal] *nm* nappy, diaper (*US*); **estar todavía en ~es** to be still wet behind the ears.
pañería [paɲe'ria] *nf* (*artículos*) drapery; (*tienda*) draper's (shop), dry-goods store (*US*).
paño ['paɲo] *nm* (*tela*) cloth; (*pedazo de tela*) (piece of) cloth; (*trapo*) duster, rag; **~ de cocina** dishcloth; **~ higiénico** sanitary towel; **~s menores** underclothes; **~s calientes** (*fig*) half-measures; **no andarse con ~s calientes** to pull no punches.
pañuelo [pa'ɲwelo] *nm* handkerchief, hanky (*fam*); (*para la cabeza*) (head)scarf.
papa ['papa] *nf* (*AM*) potato ♦ *nm*: **el P~** the Pope.
papá [pa'pa] *nm, pl* **papás** (*fam*) dad, daddy, pop (*US*); **~s** *nmpl* parents; **hijo de ~** Hooray Henry (*fam*).
papada [pa'paða] *nf* double chin.
papagayo [papa'ɣajo] *nm* parrot.
papanatas [papa'natas] *nm inv* (*fam*) sucker, simpleton.
paparrucha [papa'rrutʃa] *nf* (*tontería*) piece of nonsense.
papaya [pa'paja] *nf* papaya.
papear [pape'ar] *vt, vi* (*fam*) to eat.
papel [pa'pel] *nm* (*gen*) paper; (*hoja de papel*) sheet of paper; (*TEAT*) part, role; **~es** *nmpl* identification papers; **~ de calco/carbón/de cartas** tracing paper/carbon paper/stationery; **~ contínuo** (*INFORM*) continuous stationery; **~ de envolver/de empapelar** brown paper, wrapping paper/wallpaper; **~ de aluminio/higiénico** tinfoil/toilet paper; **~ del** *o* **de pagos al Estado** government bonds *pl*; **~ de lija** sandpaper; **~ moneda** paper money; **~ plegado (en abanico** *o* **en acordeón)** fanfold paper; **~ secante** blotting paper; **~ térmico** thermal paper.
papeleo [pape'leo] *nm* red tape.
papelera [pape'lera] *nf* (*cesto*) wastepaper basket; (*escritorio*) desk.
papelería [papele'ria] *nf* (*tienda*) stationer's (shop).
papeleta [pape'leta] *nf* (*pedazo de papel*) slip *o* bit of paper; (*POL*) ballot paper; (*ESCOL*) report; **¡vaya ~!** this is a tough one!
paperas [pa'peras] *nfpl* mumps *sg*.
papilla [pa'piʎa] *nf* (*de bebé*) baby food; (*pey*) mush; **estar hecho ~** to be dog-tired.
paquete [pa'kete] *nm* (*caja*) packet; (*bulto*) parcel; (*AM fam*) nuisance, bore; (*INFORM*) package (*of software*); (*vacaciones*) package tour; **~ de aplicaciones** (*INFORM*) applications package; **~ integrado** (*INFORM*) integrated package; **~ de gestión integrado** combined management suite; **~s postales** parcel post *sg*.
paquistaní [pakista'ni] = **pakistaní**.
par [par] *adj* (*igual*) like, equal; (*MAT*) even ♦ *nm* equal; (*de guantes*) pair; (*de veces*) couple; (*dignidad*) peer; (*GOLF, COM*) par ♦ *nf* par; **~es o nones** odds or evens; **abrir de ~ en ~** to open wide; **a la ~** par; **sobre/bajo la ~** above/below par.
para ['para] *prep* (*gen*) for; **no es ~ comer** it's not for eating; **decir ~ sí** to say to o.s.; **¿~ qué lo quieres?** what do you want it for?; **se casaron ~ separarse otra vez** they married only to separate again; **~ entonces** by then *o* that time; **lo tendré ~ mañana** I'll have it for tomorrow; **ir ~ casa** to go home, head for home; **~ profesor es muy estúpido** he's very stupid for a teacher; **¿quién es usted ~ gritar así?** who are you to shout like that?; **tengo bastante ~ vivir** I have enough to live on.
parabellum [paraße'lum] *nm* (automatic) pistol.
parabién [para'ßjen] *nm* congratulations *pl*.
parábola [pa'raßola] *nf* parable; (*MAT*) parabola.
parabólica [para'ßolika] *nf* (*tb*: **antena ~**) satellite dish.
parabrisas [para'ßrisas] *nm inv* windscreen, windshield (*US*).
paracaídas [paraka'iðas] *nm inv* parachute.
paracaidista [parakai'ðista] *nm/f* parachutist; (*MIL*) paratrooper.
parachoques [para'tʃokes] *nm inv* bumper, fender (*US*); shock absorber.
parada [pa'raða] *nf* V **parado**.
paradero [para'ðero] *nm* stopping-place; (*situación*) whereabouts.
parado, a [pa'raðo, a] *adj* (*persona*) motionless, standing still; (*fábrica*)

closed, at a standstill; (*coche*) stopped; (*AM: de pie*) standing (up); (*sin empleo*) unemployed, idle; (*confuso*) confused ♦ *nf* (*gen*) stop; (*acto*) stopping; (*de industria*) shutdown, stoppage; (*lugar*) stopping-place; **salir bien** ~ to come off well; **parada de autobús** bus stop; **parada discrecional** request stop; **parada en seco** sudden stop; **parada de taxis** taxi rank.

paradoja [para'ðoxa] *nf* paradox.

paradójico, a [para'ðoxiko, a] *adj* paradoxical.

parador [para'ðor] *nm* (luxury) hotel.

parafrasear [parafrase'ar] *vt* to paraphrase.

paráfrasis [pa'rafrasis] *nf inv* paraphrase.

paraguas [pa'raɣwas] *nm inv* umbrella.

Paraguay [para'ɣwai] *nm*: **el** ~ Paraguay.

paraguayo, a [para'ɣwajo, a] *adj, nm/f* Paraguayan.

paraíso [para'iso] *nm* paradise, heaven; ~ **fiscal** (*COM*) tax haven.

paraje [pa'raxe] *nm* place, spot.

paralelo, a [para'lelo, a] *adj, nm* parallel; **en** ~ (*ELEC, INFORM*) (in) parallel.

paralice [para'liθe] *etc vb V* **paralizar**.

parálisis [pa'ralisis] *nf inv* paralysis; ~ **cerebral** cerebral palsy; ~ **progresiva** creeping paralysis.

paralítico, a [para'litiko, a] *adj, nm/f* paralytic.

paralizar [parali'θar] *vt* to paralyse; ~**se** *vr* to become paralysed; (*fig*) to come to a standstill.

parámetro [pa'rametro] *nm* parameter.

paramilitar [paramili'tar] *adj* paramilitary.

páramo ['paramo] *nm* bleak plateau.

parangón [paran'gon] *nm*: **sin** ~ incomparable.

paraninfo [para'ninfo] *nm* (*ESCOL*) assembly hall.

paranoia [para'noia] *nf* paranoia.

paranoico, a [para'noiko, a] *adj, nm/f* paranoid.

paranormal [paranor'mal] *adj* paranormal.

parapetarse [parape'tarse] *vr* to shelter.

parapléjico, a [para'plexiko, a] *adj, nm/f* paraplegic.

parar [pa'rar] *vt* to stop; (*progreso etc*) to check, halt; (*golpe*) to ward off ♦ *vi* to stop; (*hospedarse*) to stay, put up; ~**se** *vr* to stop; (*AM*) to stand up; **no** ~ **de hacer algo** to keep on doing sth; **ha parado de llover** it has stopped raining; **van a** ~ **en la comisaría** they're going to end up in the police station; **no sabemos en qué va a** ~ **todo esto** we don't know where all this is going to end; ~**se a hacer algo** to stop to do sth; ~**se en** to pay attention to.

pararrayos [para'rrajos] *nm inv* lightning conductor.

parásito, a [pa'rasito, a] *nm/f* parasite.

parasol [para'sol] *nm* parasol, sunshade.

parcela [par'θela] *nf* plot, piece of ground, smallholding.

parche ['partʃe] *nm* patch.

parchís [par'tʃis] *nm* ludo.

parcial [par'θjal] *adj* (*pago*) part-; (*eclipse*) partial; (*juez*) prejudiced, biased.

parcialidad [parθjali'ðað] *nf* (*prejuicio*) prejudice, bias.

parco, a ['parko, a] *adj* (*frugal*) sparing; (*moderado*) moderate.

pardillo, a [par'ðiʎo, a] *adj* (*pey*) provincial ♦ *nm/f* (*pey*) country bumpkin ♦ *nm* (*ZOOL*) linnet.

pardo, a ['parðo, a] *adj* (*color*) brown; (*cielo*) overcast; (*voz*) flat, dull.

parear [pare'ar] *vt* (*juntar, hacer par*) to match, put together; (*calcetines*) to put into pairs; (*BIO*) to mate, pair.

parecer [pare'θer] *nm* (*opinión*) opinion, view; (*aspecto*) looks *pl* ♦ *vi* (*tener apariencia*) to seem, look; (*asemejarse*) to look like, seem like; (*aparecer, llegar*) to appear; ~**se** *vr* to look alike, resemble each other; ~**se a** to look like, resemble; **al** ~ apparently; **me parece que** I think (that), it seems to me that.

parecido, a [pare'θiðo, a] *adj* similar ♦ *nm* similarity, likeness, resemblance; ~ **a** like, similar to; **bien** ~ good-looking, nice-looking.

pared [pa'reð] *nf* wall; ~ **divisoria/ medianera** dividing/party wall; **subirse por las** ~**es** (*fam*) to go up the wall.

paredón [pare'ðon] *nm*: **llevar a algn al** ~ to put sb up against a wall, shoot sb.

parejo, a [pa'rexo, a] *adj* (*igual*) equal; (*liso*) smooth, even ♦ *nf* (*dos*) pair; (: *de personas*) couple; (*el otro: de un par*) other one (of a pair); (: *persona*) partner; (*Guardias*) Civil Guard patrol.

parentela [paren'tela] *nf* relations *pl*.

parentesco [paren'tesko] *nm* relationship.

paréntesis [pa'rentesis] *nm inv* parenthesis; (*digresión*) digression; (*en escrito*) bracket.

parezca [pa'reθka] *etc vb V* **parecer**.

parida [pa'riða] *nf*: ~ **mental** (*fam*) dumb idea.

paridad [pari'ðað] *nf* (*ECON*) parity.

pariente, a [pa'rjente, a] *nm/f* relative, relation.

parihuela [pari'wela] *nf* stretcher.
paripé [pari'pe] *nm*: **hacer el** ~ to put on an act.
parir [pa'rir] *vt* to give birth to ♦ *vi* (*mujer*) to give birth, have a baby; (*yegua*) to foal; (*vaca*) to calve.
París [pa'ris] *nm* Paris.
parisiense [pari'sjense] *adj, nm/f* Parisian.
paritario, a [pari'tarjo, a] *adj* equal.
parking ['parkin] *nm* car park, parking lot (*US*).
parlamentar [parlamen'tar] *vi* (*negociar*) to parley.
parlamentario, a [parlamen'tarjo, a] *adj* parliamentary ♦ *nm/f* member of parliament.
parlamento [parla'mento] *nm* (*POL*) parliament; (*JUR*) speech.
parlanchín, ina [parlan'tʃin, ina] *adj* loose-tongued, indiscreet ♦ *nm/f* chatterbox.
parlante [par'lante] *nm* (*AM*) loudspeaker.
parlar [par'lar] *vi* to chatter (away).
parlotear [parlote'ar] *vi* to chatter, prattle.
parloteo [parlo'teo] *nm* chatter, prattle.
parné [par'ne] *nm* (*fam: dinero*) dough.
paro ['paro] *nm* (*huelga*) stoppage (of work), strike; (*desempleo*) unemployment; ~ **cardiaco** cardiac arrest; **subsidio de** ~ unemployment benefit; **hay** ~ **en la industria** work in the industry is at a standstill; ~ **del sistema** (*INFORM*) system shutdown.
parodia [pa'roðja] *nf* parody.
parodiar [paro'ðjar] *vt* to parody.
parpadear [parpaðe'ar] *vi* (*los ojos*) to blink; (*luz*) to flicker.
parpadeo [parpa'ðeo] *nm* (*de ojos*) blinking, winking; (*de luz*) flickering.
párpado ['parpaðo] *nm* eyelid.
parque ['parke] *nm* (*lugar verde*) park; ~ **de atracciones/de bomberos/zoológico** fairground/fire station/zoo.
parqué, parquet [par'ke] *nm* parquet.
parqueadero [parkea'ðero] *nm* (*AM*) car park, parking lot (*US*).
parquímetro [par'kimetro] *nm* parking meter.
parra ['parra] *nf* grapevine.
párrafo ['parrafo] *nm* paragraph; **echar un** ~ (*fam*) to have a chat.
parranda [pa'rranda] *nf* (*fam*) spree, binge.
parrilla [pa'rriʎa] *nf* (*CULIN*) grill; (*AM AUTO*) roof-rack; ~ (**de salida**) (*AUTO*) starting grid; **carne a la** ~ grilled meat.
parrillada [parri'ʎaða] *nf* barbecue.
párroco ['parroko] *nm* parish priest.
parroquia [pa'rrokja] *nf* parish; (*iglesia*) parish church; (*COM*) clientele, customers *pl*.
parroquiano, a [parro'kjano, a] *nm/f* parishioner; client, customer.
parsimonia [parsi'monja] *nf* (*frugalidad*) sparingness; (*calma*) deliberateness; **con** ~ calmly.
parte ['parte] *nm* message; (*informe*) report; ~ **meteorológico** weather forecast ♦ *nf* part; (*lado, cara*) side; (*de reparto*) share; (*JUR*) party; **en alguna** ~ **de Europa** somewhere in Europe; **en cualquier** ~ anywhere; **por ahí no se va a ninguna** ~ that leads nowhere; (*fig*) this is getting us nowhere; **en gran** ~ to a large extent; **la mayor** ~ **de los españoles** most Spaniards; **de algún tiempo a esta** ~ for some time past; **de** ~ **de algn** on sb's behalf; **¿de** ~ **de quién?** (*TELEC*) who is speaking?; **por** ~ **de** on the part of; **yo por mi** ~ I for my part; **por una** ~ ... **por otra** ~ on the one hand, ... on the other (hand); **dar** ~ **a algn** to report to sb; **tomar** ~ to take part.
partera [par'tera] *nf* midwife.
parterre [par'terre] *nm* (*de flores*) (flower)bed.
partición [parti'θjon] *nf* division, sharing-out; (*POL*) partition.
participación [partiθipa'θjon] *nf* (*acto*) participation, taking part; (*parte*) share; (*COM*) share, stock (*US*); (*de lotería*) shared prize; (*aviso*) notice, notification; ~ **en los beneficios** profit-sharing; ~ **minoritaria** minority interest.
participante [partiθi'pante] *nm/f* participant.
participar [partiθi'par] *vt* to notify, inform ♦ *vi* to take part, participate; ~ **en una empresa** (*COM*) to invest in an enterprise; **le participo que** ... I have to tell you that ....
partícipe [par'tiθipe] *nm/f* participant; **hacer** ~ **a algn de algo** to inform sb of sth.
participio [parti'θipjo] *nm* participle; ~ **de pasado/presente** past/present participle.
partícula [par'tikula] *nf* particle.
particular [partiku'lar] *adj* (*especial*) particular, special; (*individual, personal*) private, personal ♦ *nm* (*punto, asunto*) particular, point; (*individuo*) individual; **tiene coche** ~ he has a car of his own; **no dijo mucho sobre el** ~ he didn't say much about the matter.
particularice [partikula'riθe] *etc vb V* **particularizar**.

particularidad [partikulari'ðað] *nf* peculiarity; **tiene la ~ de que ...** one of its special features is (that) ....
particularizar [partikulari'θar] *vt* to distinguish; (*especificar*) to specify; (*detallar*) to give details about.
partida [par'tiða] *nf* (*salida*) departure; (*COM*) entry, item; (*juego*) game; (*grupo, bando*) band, group; **mala ~** dirty trick; **~ de nacimiento/matrimonio/defunción** birth/marriage/death certificate; **echar una ~** to have a game.
partidario, a [parti'ðarjo, a] *adj* partisan ♦ *nm/f* (*DEPORTE*) supporter; (*POL*) partisan.
partidismo [parti'ðismo] *nm* (*JUR*) partisanship, bias; (*POL*) party politics.
partido [par'tiðo] *nm* (*POL*) party; (*encuentro*) game, match; (*apoyo*) support; (*equipo*) team; **~ amistoso** (*DEPORTE*) friendly (game); **~ de fútbol** football match; **sacar ~ de** to profit from, benefit from; **tomar ~** to take sides.
partir [par'tir] *vt* (*dividir*) to split, divide; (*compartir, distribuir*) to share (out), distribute; (*romper*) to break open, split open; (*rebanada*) to cut (off) ♦ *vi* (*tomar camino*) to set off, set out; (*comenzar*) to start (off *o* out); **~se** *vr* to crack *o* split *o* break (in two *etc*); **a ~ de** (starting) from; **~se de risa** to split one's sides (laughing).
partitura [parti'tura] *nf* score.
parto ['parto] *nm* birth, delivery; (*fig*) product, creation; **estar de ~** to be in labour.
parvulario [parβu'larjo] *nm* nursery school, kindergarten.
párvulo, a ['parβulo, a] *nm/f* infant.
pasa ['pasa] *nf V* **paso**.
pasable [pa'saβle] *adj* passable.
pasada [pa'saða] *nf V* **pasado**.
pasadizo [pasa'ðiθo] *nm* (*pasillo*) passage, corridor; (*callejuela*) alley.
pasado, a [pa'saðo, a] *adj* past; (*malo: comida, fruta*) bad; (*muy cocido*) overdone; (*anticuado*) out of date ♦ *nm* past; (*LING*) past (tense) ♦ *nf* passing, passage; (*acción de pulir*) rub, polish; **~ mañana** the day after tomorrow; **el mes ~** last month; **~s dos días** after two days; **lo ~, ~** let bygones be bygones; **~ de moda** old-fashioned; **~ por agua** (*huevo*) boiled; **de pasada** in passing, incidentally; **una mala pasada** a dirty trick.
pasador [pasa'ðor] *nm* (*gen*) bolt; (*de pelo*) pin, grip, slide; **~es** *nmpl* (*AM: cordones*) shoelaces.
pasaje [pa'saxe] *nm* (*gen*) passage; (*pago de viaje*) fare; (*los pasajeros*) passengers *pl*; (*pasillo*) passageway.
pasajero, a [pasa'xero, a] *adj* passing; (*ave*) migratory ♦ *nm/f* passenger; (*viajero*) traveller.
pasamanos [pasa'manos] *nm inv* rail, handrail; (*de escalera*) banister.
pasamontañas [pasamon'taɲas] *nm inv* balaclava (helmet).
pasaporte [pasa'porte] *nm* passport.
pasar [pa'sar] *vt* (*gen*) to pass; (*tiempo*) to spend; (*durezas*) to suffer, endure; (*noticia*) to give, pass on; (*película*) to show; (*persona*) to take, conduct; (*río*) to cross; (*barrera*) to pass through; (*falta*) to overlook, tolerate; (*contrincante*) to surpass, do better than; (*coche*) to overtake; (*contrabando*) to smuggle (in/out); (*enfermedad*) to give, infect with ♦ *vi* (*gen*) to pass, go; (*terminarse*) to be over; (*ocurrir*) to happen; **~se** *vr* (*efectos*) to pass, be over; (*flores*) to fade; (*comida*) to go bad, go off; (*fig*) to overdo it, go too far *o* over the top; **~ de** to go beyond, exceed; **¡pase!** come in!; **nos hicieron ~** they showed us in; **~ por** to fetch; **~ por alto** to skip; **~ por una crisis** to go through a crisis; **se hace ~ por médico** he passes himself off as a doctor; **~lo bien/bomba** *o* **de maravilla** to have a good/great time; **~se al enemigo** to go over to the enemy; **~se de la raya** to go too far; **¡no te pases!** don't try me!; **se me pasó** I forgot; **se me pasó el turno** I missed my turn; **no se le pasa nada** nothing escapes him, he misses nothing; **ya se te pasará** you'll get over it; **¿qué pasa?** what's happening?, what's going on?, what's up?; **¡cómo pasa el tiempo!** time just flies!; **pase lo que pase** come what may; **el autobús pasa por nuestra casa** the bus goes past our house.
pasarela [pasa'rela] *nf* footbridge; (*en barco*) gangway.
pasatiempo [pasa'tjempo] *nm* pastime, hobby; (*distracción*) amusement.
Pascua, pascua ['paskwa] *nf*: **~ (de Resurrección)** Easter; **~ de Navidad** Christmas; **~s** *nfpl* Christmas time *sg*; **¡felices ~s!** Merry Christmas; **de ~s a Ramos** once in a blue moon; **hacer la ~ a** (*fam*) to annoy, bug.
pase ['pase] *nm* pass; (*CINE*) performance, showing; (*COM*) permit; (*JUR*) licence.
pasear [pase'ar] *vt* to take for a walk;

(*exhibir*) to parade, show off ♦ *vi*, **~se** *vr* to walk, go for a walk; **~ en coche** to go for a drive.
paseo [pa'seo] *nm* (*avenida*) avenue; (*distancia corta*) short walk; **~ marítimo** promenade; **dar un ~** to go for a walk; **mandar a algn a ~** to tell sb to go to blazes; **¡vete a ~!** get lost!
pasillo [pa'siʎo] *nm* passage, corridor.
pasión [pa'sjon] *nf* passion.
pasional [pasjo'nal] *adj* passionate; **crimen ~** crime of passion.
pasivo, a [pa'siβo, a] *adj* passive; (*inactivo*) inactive ♦ *nm* (*COM*) liabilities *pl*, debts *pl*; (*de cuenta*) debit side; **~ circulante** current liabilities.
pasma ['pasma] *nm* (*fam*) cop.
pasmado, a [pas'maðo, a] *adj* (*asombrado*) astonished; (*atontado*) bewildered.
pasmar [pas'mar] *vt* (*asombrar*) to amaze, astonish; **~se** *vr* to be amazed *o* astonished.
pasmo ['pasmo] *nm* amazement, astonishment; (*fig*) wonder, marvel.
pasmoso, a [pas'moso, a] *adj* amazing, astonishing.
paso, a ['paso, a] *adj* dried ♦ *nm* (*gen, de baile*) step; (*modo de andar*) walk; (*huella*) footprint; (*rapidez*) speed, pace, rate; (*camino accesible*) way through, passage; (*cruce*) crossing; (*pasaje*) passing, passage; (*REL*) *religious float or sculpture*; (*GEO*) pass; (*estrecho*) strait; (*fig*) step, measure; (*apuro*) difficulty ♦ *nf* raisin; **pasa de Corinto/de Esmirna** currant/sultana; **~ a ~** step by step; **a ese ~** (*fig*) at that rate; **salir al ~ de** *o* **a** to waylay; **salir del ~** to get out of trouble; **dar un ~ en falso** to trip; (*fig*) to take a false step; **estar de ~** to be passing through; **~ atrás** step backwards; (*fig*) backward step; **~ elevado/subterráneo** flyover/subway, underpass (*US*); **prohibido el ~** no entry; **ceda el ~** give way; *V tb* **Semana Santa**.
pasota [pa'sota] *adj, nm/f* (*fam*) ≈ dropout; **ser un (tipo) ~** to be a bit of a dropout; (*ser indiferente*) not to care about anything.
pasotismo [paso'tismo] *nm* underground *o* alternative culture.
pasta ['pasta] *nf* (*gen*) paste; (*CULIN*: *masa*) dough; (: *de bizcochos etc*) pastry; (*fam*) money, dough; (*encuadernación*) hardback; **~s** *nfpl* (*bizcochos*) pastries, small cakes; (*fideos, espaguetis etc*) noodles, spaghetti *sg etc*; **~ de dientes** *o* **dentífrica** toothpaste; **~ de madera** wood pulp.
pastar [pas'tar] *vt, vi* to graze.
pastel [pas'tel] *nm* (*dulce*) cake; (*de carne*) pie; (*ARTE*) pastel; (*fig*) plot; **~es** *nmpl* pastry *sg*, confectionery *sg*.
pastelería [pastele'ria] *nf* cake shop, pastry shop.
pasteurizado, a [pasteuri'θaðo, a] *adj* pasteurized.
pastilla [pas'tiʎa] *nf* (*de jabón, chocolate*) cake, bar; (*píldora*) tablet, pill.
pastizal [pasti'θal] *nm* pasture.
pasto ['pasto] *nm* (*hierba*) grass; (*lugar*) pasture, field; (*fig*) food, nourishment.
pastor, a [pas'tor, a] *nm/f* shepherd(ess) ♦ *nm* clergyman, pastor; (*ZOOL*) sheepdog; **~ alemán** Alsatian.
pastoso, a [pas'toso, a] *adj* (*material*) doughy, pasty; (*lengua*) furry; (*voz*) mellow.
pat. *abr* (= *patente*) pat.
pata ['pata] *nf* (*pierna*) leg; (*pie*) foot; (*de muebles*) leg; **~s arriba** upside down; **a cuatro ~s** on all fours; **meter la ~** to put one's foot in it; **~ de cabra** (*TEC*) crowbar; **~s de gallo** crow's feet; **tener buena/mala ~** to be lucky/unlucky.
patada [pa'taða] *nf* stamp; (*puntapié*) kick; **a ~s** in abundance; (*trato*) roughly; **echar a algn a ~s** to kick sb out.
patagón, ona [pata'ɣon, ona] *adj, nm/f* Patagonian.
Patagonia [pata'ɣonja] *nf*: **la ~** Patagonia.
patalear [patale'ar] *vi* to stamp one's feet.
pataleo [pata'leo] *nm* stamping.
patán [pa'tan] *nm* rustic, yokel.
patata [pa'tata] *nf* potato; **~s fritas** *o* **a la española** chips, French fries; **~s a la inglesa** crisps; **ni ~** (*fam*) nothing at all; **no entendió ni ~** he didn't understand a single word.
paté [pa'te] *nm* pâté.
patear [pate'ar] *vt* (*pisar*) to stamp on, trample (on); (*pegar con el pie*) to kick ♦ *vi* to stamp (with rage), stamp one's foot.
patentar [paten'tar] *vt* to patent.
patente [pa'tente] *adj* obvious, evident; (*COM*) patent ♦ *nf* patent.
patera [pa'tera] *nf* boat.
paternal [pater'nal] *adj* fatherly, paternal.
paternalista [paterna'lista] *adj* (*tono, actitud etc*) patronizing.
paternidad [paterni'ðað] *nf* fatherhood, parenthood; (*JUR*) paternity.
paterno, a [pa'terno, a] *adj* paternal.
patético, a [pa'tetiko, a] *adj* pathetic, moving.
patíbulo [pa'tiβulo] *nm* scaffold,

gallows *sg*.
patilla [pa'tiʎa] *nf* (*de gafas*) arm; (*de pelo*) sideburn.
patín [pa'tin] *nm* skate; (*de tobogán*) runner; ~ **de hielo** ice skate; ~ **de ruedas** roller skate.
patinaje [pati'naxe] *nm* skating.
patinar [pati'nar] *vi* to skate; (*resbalarse*) to skid, slip; (*fam*) to slip up, blunder.
patinazo [pati'naθo] *nm* (*AUTO*) skid; **dar un** ~ (*fam*) to blunder.
patio ['patjo] *nm* (*de casa*) patio, courtyard; ~ **de recreo** playground.
pato ['pato] *nm* duck; **pagar el** ~ (*fam*) to take the blame, carry the can.
patológico, a [pato'loxiko, a] *adj* pathological.
patoso, a [pa'toso, a] *adj* awkward, clumsy.
patraña [pa'traɲa] *nf* story, fib.
patria ['patrja] *nf* native land, mother country; ~ **chica** home town.
patrimonio [patri'monjo] *nm* inheritance; (*fig*) heritage; (*COM*) net worth.
patriota [pa'trjota] *nm/f* patriot.
patriotero, a [patrjo'tero, a] *adj* chauvinistic.
patriótico, a [pa'trjotiko, a] *adj* patriotic.
patriotismo [patrjo'tismo] *nm* patriotism.
patrocinador, a [patroθina'ðor, a] *nm/f* sponsor.
patrocinar [patroθi'nar] *vt* to sponsor; (*apoyar*) to back, support.
patrocinio [patro'θinjo] *nm* sponsorship; backing, support.
patrón, ona [pa'tron, ona] *nm/f* (*jefe*) boss, chief, master/mistress; (*propietario*) landlord/lady; (*REL*) patron saint ♦ *nm* (*COSTURA*) pattern; (*TEC*) standard; ~ **oro** gold standard.
patronal [patro'nal] *adj*: **la clase** ~ management; **cierre** ~ lockout.
patronato [patro'nato] *nm* sponsorship; (*acto*) patronage; (*COM*) employers' association; (*fundación*) trust; **el** ~ **de turismo** the tourist board.
patrulla [pa'truʎa] *nf* patrol.
patrullar [patru'ʎar] *vi* to patrol.
paulatino, a [paula'tino, a] *adj* gradual, slow.
paupérrimo, a [pau'perrimo, a] *adj* very poor, poverty-stricken.
pausa ['pausa] *nf* pause; (*intervalo*) break; (*interrupción*) interruption; (*TEC: en videograbadora*) hold; **con** ~ slowly.
pausado, a [pau'saðo, a] *adj* slow, deliberate.
pauta ['pauta] *nf* line, guide line.
pavimento [paβi'mento] *nm* (*ARQ*) flooring.
pavo ['paβo] *nm* turkey; (*necio*) silly thing, idiot; ~ **real** peacock; **¡no seas** ~**!** don't be silly!
pavonearse [paβone'arse] *vr* to swagger, show off.
pavor [pa'βor] *nm* dread, terror.
payasada [paja'saða] *nf* ridiculous thing (to do); ~**s** *nfpl* clowning *sg*.
payaso, a [pa'jaso, a] *nm/f* clown.
payo, a ['pajo, a] *adj, nm/f* non-gipsy.
paz [paθ] *nf* peace; (*tranquilidad*) peacefulness, tranquillity; **dejar a algn en** ~ to leave sb alone *o* in peace; **hacer las paces** to make peace; (*fig*) to make up; **¡haya** ~**!** stop it!
pazca ['paθka] *etc vb V* **pacer**.
PC *nm abr* (*POL:* = *Partido Comunista*) CP.
P.C.E. *nm abr* = *Partido Comunista Español*.
PCL *nf abr* (= *pantalla de cristal líquido*) LCD.
PCUS [pe'kus] *nm abr* (= *Partido Comunista de la Unión Soviética*) *Soviet Communist Party*.
P.D. *abr* (= *posdata*) P.S.
pdo. *abr* (= *pasado*) ult.
peaje [pe'axe] *nm* toll; **autopista de** ~ toll motorway, turnpike (*US*).
peatón [pea'ton] *nm* pedestrian; **paso de peatones** pedestrian crossing, crosswalk (*US*).
peca ['peka] *nf* freckle.
pecado [pe'kaðo] *nm* sin.
pecador, a [peka'ðor, a] *adj* sinful ♦ *nm/f* sinner.
pecaminoso, a [pekami'noso, a] *adj* sinful.
pecar [pe'kar] *vi* (*REL*) to sin; (*fig*): ~ **de generoso** to be too generous.
pecera [pe'θera] *nf* goldfish bowl.
pecho ['petʃo] *nm* (*ANAT*) chest; (*de mujer*) breast(s) (*pl*), bosom; (*corazón*) heart, breast; (*valor*) courage, spirit; **dar el** ~ **a** to breast-feed; **tomar algo a** ~ to take sth to heart; **no le cabía en el** ~ he was bursting with happiness.
pechuga [pe'tʃuɣa] *nf* breast (of chicken *etc*).
pecoso, a [pe'koso, a] *adj* freckled.
peculiar [peku'ljar] *adj* special, peculiar; (*característico*) typical, characteristic.
peculiaridad [pekuljari'ðað] *nf* peculiarity; special feature, characteristic.
pedagogía [peðaɣo'xia] *nf* education.
pedagogo [peða'ɣoɣo] *nm* pedagogue, teacher.
pedal [pe'ðal] *nm* pedal; ~ **de embrague** clutch (pedal); ~ **de freno** footbrake.
pedalear [peðale'ar] *vi* to pedal.

pedante [pe'ðante] *adj* pedantic ♦ *nm/f* pedant.
pedantería [peðante'ria] *nf* pedantry.
pedazo [pe'ðaθo] *nm* piece, bit; **hacerse ~s** to fall to pieces; (*romperse*) to smash, shatter; **un ~ de pan** a scrap of bread; (*fig*) a terribly nice person.
pedernal [peðer'nal] *nm* flint.
pedestal [peðes'tal] *nm* base; **tener/poner a algn en un ~** to put sb on a pedestal.
pedestre [pe'ðestre] *adj* pedestrian; **carrera ~** foot race.
pediatra [pe'ðjatra] *nm/f* paediatrician (*BRIT*), pediatrician (*US*).
pediatría [peðja'tria] *nf* paediatrics *sg* (*BRIT*), pediatrics *sg* (*US*).
pedicuro, a [peði'kuro, a] *nm/f* chiropodist (*BRIT*), podiatrist (*US*).
pedido [pe'ðiðo] *nm* (*COM*: *mandado*) order; (*petición*) request; **~s en cartera** (*COM*) backlog *sg*.
pedigrí [peði'ɣri] *nm* pedigree.
pedir [pe'ðir] *vt* to ask for, request; (*comida, COM*: *mandar*) to order; (*exigir*: *precio*) to ask; (*necesitar*) to need, demand, require ♦ *vi* to ask; **~ prestado** to borrow; **~ disculpas** to apologize; **me pidió que cerrara la puerta** he asked me to shut the door; **¿cuánto piden por el coche?** how much are they asking for the car?
pedo ['peðo] (*fam*) *adj inv*: **estar ~** to be pissed (*!*) ♦ *nm* fart (*!*).
pedrada [pe'ðraða] *nf* throw of a stone; (*golpe*) blow from a stone; **herir a algn de una ~** to hit sb with a stone.
pedrea [pe'ðrea] *nf* (*granizada*) hailstorm; (*de lotería*) minor prizes.
pedrisco [pe'ðrisko] *nm* (*granizo*) hail; (*granizada*) hailstorm.
Pedro ['peðro] *nm* Peter; **entrar como ~ por su casa** to come in as if one owned the place.
pega ['peɣa] *nf* (*dificultad*) snag; **de ~** false, dud; **poner ~s** to raise objections.
pegadizo, a [peɣa'ðiθo, a] *adj* (*canción etc*) catchy.
pegajoso, a [peɣa'xoso, a] *adj* sticky, adhesive.
pegamento [peɣa'mento] *nm* gum.
pegar [pe'ɣar] *vt* (*papel, sellos*) to stick (on); (*con cola*) to glue; (*cartel*) to post, stick up; (*coser*) to sew (on); (*unir*: *partes*) to join, fix together; (*MED*) to give, infect with; (*dar*: *golpe*) to give, deal ♦ *vi* (*adherirse*) to stick, adhere; (*ir juntos*: *colores*) to match, go together; (*golpear*) to hit; (*quemar*: *el sol*) to strike hot, burn (*fig*); **~se** *vr* (*gen*) to stick; (*dos personas*) to hit each other, fight; **~le a algo** to be a great one for sth; **~ un grito** to let out a yell; **~ un salto** to jump (with fright); **~ fuego** to catch fire; **~ en** to touch; **~se un tiro** to shoot o.s.; **no pega** that doesn't seem right; **ese sombrero no pega con el abrigo** that hat doesn't go with the coat.
pegatina [peɣa'tina] *nf* (*POL etc*) sticker.
pego ['peɣo] *nm*: **dar el ~** (*pasar por verdadero*) to look like the real thing.
pegote [pe'ɣote] *nm* (*fig*) patch, ugly mend; **tirarse ~s** (*fam*) to come on strong.
pegue ['peɣe] *etc vb V* **pegar**.
peinado [pei'naðo] *nm* (*en peluquería*) hairdo; (*estilo*) hair style.
peinar [pei'nar] *vt* to comb sb's hair; (*hacer estilo*) to style; **~se** *vr* to comb one's hair.
peine ['peine] *nm* comb.
peineta [pei'neta] *nf* ornamental comb.
p.ej. *abr* (= *por ejemplo*) e.g.
Pekín [pe'kin] *n* Peking.
pela ['pela] *nf* (*ESP fam*) peseta; *V tb* **pelas**.
pelado, a [pe'laðo, a] *adj* (*cabeza*) shorn; (*fruta*) peeled; (*campo, fig*) bare; (*fam*: *sin dinero*) broke.
pelaje [pe'laxe] *nm* (*ZOOL*) fur, coat; (*fig*) appearance.
pelambre [pe'lambre] *nm* long hair, mop.
pelar [pe'lar] *vt* (*fruta, patatas*) to peel; (*cortar el pelo a*) to cut the hair of; (*quitar la piel*: *animal*) to skin; (*ave*) to pluck; (*habas etc*) to shell; **~se** *vr* (*la piel*) to peel off; **corre que se las pela** (*fam*) he runs like nobody's business.
pelas ['pelas] *nfpl* (*ESP fam*) dough.
peldaño [pel'daɲo] *nm* step; (*de escalera portátil*) rung.
pelea [pe'lea] *nf* (*lucha*) fight; (*discusión*) quarrel, row.
peleado, a [pele'aðo, a] *adj*: **estar ~ (con algn)** to have fallen out (with sb).
pelear [pele'ar] *vi* to fight; **~se** *vr* to fight; (*reñirse*) to fall out, quarrel.
pelele [pe'lele] *nm* (*figura*) guy, dummy; (*fig*) puppet.
peletería [pelete'ria] *nf* furrier's, fur shop.
peliagudo, a [pelja'ɣuðo, a] *adj* tricky.
pelícano [pe'likano] *nm* pelican.
película [pe'likula] *nf* (*CINE*) film, movie (*US*); (*cobertura ligera*) film, thin covering; (*FOTO*: *rollo*) roll *o* reel of film; **~ de dibujos (animados)** cartoon film; **~ muda** silent film; **de ~** (*fam*) astonishing, out of this world.
peligrar [peli'ɣrar] *vi* to be in danger.
peligro [pe'liɣro] *nm* danger; (*riesgo*) risk;

"~ **de muerte**" "danger"; **correr** ~ **de** to be in danger of; **con** ~ **de la vida** at the risk of one's life.
peligrosidad [peliɣrosi'ðað] *nf* danger, riskiness.
peligroso, a [peli'ɣroso, a] *adj* dangerous; risky.
pelirrojo, a [peli'rroxo, a] *adj* red-haired, red-headed.
pellejo [pe'ʎexo] *nm* (*de animal*) skin, hide; **salvar el** ~ to save one's skin.
pellizcar [peʎiθ'kar] *vt* to pinch, nip.
pellizco [pe'ʎiθko] *nm* (*gen*) pinch.
pellizque [pe'ʎiθke] *etc vb V* **pellizcar**.
pelma ['pelma] *nm/f*, **pelmazo** [pel'maθo] *nm* (*fam*) pest.
pelo ['pelo] *nm* (*cabellos*) hair; (*de barba, bigote*) whisker; (*de animal*: *pellejo*) fur, coat; (*de perro etc*) hair, coat; (*de ave*) down; (*de tejido*) nap; (*TEC*) fibre; **a** ~ bareheaded; (*desnudo*) naked; **al** ~ just right; **venir al** ~ to be exactly what one needs; **por los** ~**s** by the skin of one's teeth; **escaparse por un** ~ to have a close shave; **se me pusieron los** ~**s de punta** my hair stood on end; **no tener** ~**s en la lengua** to be outspoken, not mince words; **tomar el** ~ **a algn** to pull sb's leg.
pelón, ona [pe'lon, ona] *adj* hairless, bald.
pelota [pe'lota] *nf* ball; (*fam*: *cabeza*) nut (*fam*); **en** ~**(s)** stark naked; ~ **vasca** pelota; **devolver la** ~ **a algn** (*fig*) to turn the tables on sb; **hacer la** ~ **(a algn)** to creep (to sb).
pelotera [pelo'tera] *nf* (*fam*) barney.
pelotón [pelo'ton] *nm* (*MIL*) squad, detachment.
peluca [pe'luka] *nf* wig.
peluche [pe'lutʃe] *nm*: **muñeco de** ~ soft toy.
peludo, a [pe'luðo, a] *adj* hairy, shaggy.
peluquería [peluke'ria] *nf* hairdresser's; (*para hombres*) barber's (shop).
peluquero, a [pelu'kero, a] *nm/f* hairdresser; barber.
peluquín [pelu'kin] *nm* toupée.
pelusa [pe'lusa] *nf* (*BOT*) down; (*COSTURA*) fluff.
pelvis ['pelβis] *nf* pelvis.
PEMEX [pe'meks] *nm abr* = *Petróleos Mejicanos*.
PEN [pen] *nm abr* (*ESP*) = *Plan Energético Nacional*.
pena ['pena] *nf* (*congoja*) grief, sadness; (*remordimiento*) regret; (*dificultad*) trouble; (*dolor*) pain; (*AM*: *vergüenza*) shame; (*JUR*) sentence; (*DEPORTE*) penalty; ~ **capital** capital punishment; ~ **de muerte** death penalty; ~ **pecuniaria** fine; **merecer** *o* **valer la** ~ to be worthwhile; **a duras** ~**s** with great difficulty; **so** ~ **de** on pain of; **me dan** ~ I feel sorry for them; **¿no te da** ~ **hacerlo?** (*AM*) aren't you embarrassed doing that?; **¡qué** ~**!** what a shame *o* pity!
penal [pe'nal] *adj* penal ♦ *nm* (*cárcel*) prison.
penalidad [penali'ðað] *nf* (*problema, dificultad*) trouble, hardship; (*JUR*) penalty, punishment.
penalizar [penali'θar] *vt* to penalize.
penalti, penalty [pe'nalti] *nm* (*DEPORTE*) penalty.
penar [pe'nar] *vt* to penalize; (*castigar*) to punish ♦ *vi* to suffer.
pendejo, a [pen'dexo, a] *nm/f* (*AM fam!*) wanker (*BRIT!*), jerk (*US!*).
pender [pen'der] *vi* (*colgar*) to hang; (*JUR*) to be pending.
pendiente [pen'djente] *adj* pending, unsettled ♦ *nm* earring ♦ *nf* hill, slope; **tener una asignatura** ~ to have to resit a subject.
pendón [pen'don] *nm* banner, standard.
péndulo ['pendulo] *nm* pendulum.
pene ['pene] *nm* penis.
penene [pe'nene] *nm/f* = **PNN**.
penetración [penetra'θjon] *nf* (*acto*) penetration; (*agudeza*) sharpness, insight.
penetrante [pene'trante] *adj* (*herida*) deep; (*persona, arma*) sharp; (*sonido*) penetrating, piercing; (*mirada*) searching; (*viento, ironía*) biting.
penetrar [pene'trar] *vt* to penetrate, pierce; (*entender*) to grasp ♦ *vi* to penetrate, go in; (*líquido*) to soak in; (*emoción*) to pierce.
penicilina [peniθi'lina] *nf* penicillin.
península [pe'ninsula] *nf* peninsula; **P**~ **Ibérica** Iberian Peninsula.
peninsular [peninsu'lar] *adj* peninsular.
penique [pe'nike] *nm* penny; ~**s** *nmpl* pence.
penitencia [peni'tenθja] *nf* (*remordimiento*) penitence; (*castigo*) penance; **en** ~ as a penance.
penitencial [peniten'θjal] *adj* penitential.
penitenciaría [penitenθja'ria] *nf* prison, penitentiary.
penitenciario, a [peniten'θjarjo, a] *adj* prison *cpd*.
penoso, a [pe'noso, a] *adj* laborious, difficult.
pensado, a [pen'saðo, a] *adj*: **bien/mal** ~

well intentioned/cynical; **en el momento menos** ~ when least expected.
pensador, a [pensa'ðor, a] *nm/f* thinker.
pensamiento [pensa'mjento] *nm* (*gen*) thought; (*mente*) mind; (*idea*) idea; (*BOT*) pansy; **no se le pasó por el** ~ it never occurred to him.
pensar [pen'sar] *vt* to think; (*considerar*) to think over, think out; (*proponerse*) to intend, plan, propose; (*imaginarse*) to think up, invent ♦ *vi* to think; ~ **en** to think of *o* about; (*anhelar*) to aim at, aspire to; **dar que** ~ **a algn** to give sb food for thought.
pensativo, a [pensa'tiβo, a] *adj* thoughtful, pensive.
pensión [pen'sjon] *nf* (*casa*) ≈ guest house; (*dinero*) pension; (*cama y comida*) board and lodging; ~ **de jubilación** retirement pension; ~ **escalada** graduated pension; ~ **completa** full board; **media** ~ half board.
pensionista [pensjo'nista] *nm/f* (*jubilado*) (old-age) pensioner; (*quien vive en pensión*) lodger; (*ESCOL*) boarder.
pentágono [pen'taɣono] *nm* pentagon: **el P~** (*US*) the Pentagon.
pentagrama [penta'ɣrama] *nm* (*MUS*) stave, staff.
penúltimo, a [pe'nultimo, a] *adj* penultimate, second last.
penumbra [pe'numbra] *nf* half-light, semi-darkness.
penuria [pe'nurja] *nf* shortage, want.
peña ['peɲa] *nf* (*roca*) rock; (*cuesta*) cliff, crag; (*grupo*) group, circle; (*DEPORTE*) supporters' club.
peñasco [pe'ɲasko] *nm* large rock, boulder.
peñón [pe'ɲon] *nm* crag; **el P~** the Rock (of Gibraltar).
peón [pe'on] *nm* labourer; (*AM*) farm labourer, farmhand; (*TEC*) spindle, shaft; (*AJEDREZ*) pawn.
peonza [pe'onθa] *nf* spinning top.
peor [pe'or] *adj* (*comparativo*) worse; (*superlativo*) worst ♦ *adv* worse; worst; **de mal en** ~ from bad to worse; **tanto** ~ so much the worse; **A es** ~ **que B** A is worse than B; **Z es el** ~ **de todos** Z is the worst of all.
pepenar [pepe'nar] *vi* (*AM*) to sift through rubbish *o* garbage.
pepinillo [pepi'niʎo] *nm* gherkin.
pepino [pe'pino] *nm* cucumber; **(no) me importa un** ~ I don't care two hoots.
pepita [pe'pita] *nf* (*BOT*) pip; (*MINERÍA*) nugget.
pepito [pe'pito] *nm* meat sandwich.
peque ['peke] *etc vb V* **pecar**.
pequeñez [peke'ɲeθ] *nf* smallness, littleness; (*trivialidad*) trifle, triviality.
pequeño, a [pe'keɲo, a] *adj* small, little; (*cifra*) small, low; (*bajo*) short; ~ **burgués** lower middle-class.
pequinés, esa [peki'nes, esa] *adj, nm/f* Pekinese.
pera ['pera] *adj inv* classy; **niño** ~ spoiled upper-class brat ♦ *nf* pear; **eso es pedir ~s al olmo** that's asking the impossible.
peral [pe'ral] *nm* pear tree.
percance [per'kanθe] *nm* setback, misfortune.
per cápita [per'kapita] *adj*: **renta** ~ per capita income.
percatarse [perka'tarse] *vr*: ~ **de** to notice, take note of.
percebe [per'θeβe] *nm* (*ZOOL*) barnacle; (*fam*) idiot.
percepción [perθep'θjon] *nf* (*vista*) perception; (*idea*) notion, idea; (*COM*) collection.
perceptible [perθep'tiβle] *adj* perceptible, noticeable; (*COM*) payable, receivable.
percha ['pertʃa] *nf* (*poste*) pole, support; (*gancho*) peg; (*de abrigos*) coat stand; (*colgador*) coat hanger; (*de ave*) perch.
perchero [per'tʃero] *nm* clothes rack.
percibir [perθi'βir] *vt* to perceive, notice; (*ver*) to see; (*peligro etc*) to sense; (*COM*) to earn, receive, get.
percusión [perku'sjon] *nf* percussion.
percusor [perku'sor], **percutor** [perku'tor] *nm* (*TEC*) hammer; (*de arma*) firing pin.
perdedor, a [perðe'ðor, a] *adj* losing ♦ *nm/f* loser.
perder [per'ðer] *vt* to lose; (*tiempo, palabras*) to waste; (*oportunidad*) to lose, miss; (*tren*) to miss ♦ *vi* to lose; **~se** *vr* (*extraviarse*) to get lost; (*desaparecer*) to disappear, be lost to view; (*arruinarse*) to be ruined; **echar a** ~ (*comida*) to spoil, ruin; (*oportunidad*) to waste; **tener buen** ~ to be a good loser; **¡no te lo pierdas!** don't miss it!; **he perdido la costumbre** I have got out of the habit.
perdición [perði'θjon] *nf* perdition; (*fig*) ruin.
pérdida ['perðiða] *nf* loss; (*de tiempo*) waste; (*COM*) net loss; **~s** *nfpl* (*COM*) losses; **¡no tiene ~!** you can't go wrong!; ~ **contable** (*COM*) book loss.
perdido, a [per'ðiðo, a] *adj* lost; **estar** ~ **por** to be crazy about; **es un caso** ~ he is a hopeless case.
perdigón [perði'ɣon] *nm* pellet.

perdiz [per'ðiθ] *nf* partridge.
perdón [per'ðon] *nm* (*disculpa*) pardon, forgiveness; (*clemencia*) mercy; **¡~!** sorry!, I beg your pardon!; **con ~** if I may, if you don't mind.
perdonar [perðo'nar] *vt* to pardon, forgive; (*la vida*) to spare; (*excusar*) to exempt, excuse ♦ *vi* to pardon, forgive; **¡perdone (usted)!** sorry!, I beg your pardon!; **perdone, pero me parece que ...** excuse me, but I think ...
perdurable [perðu'raßle] *adj* lasting; (*eterno*) everlasting.
perdurar [perðu'rar] *vi* (*resistir*) to last, endure; (*seguir existiendo*) to stand, still exist.
perecedero, a [pereθe'ðero, a] *adj* perishable.
perecer [pere'θer] *vi* to perish, die.
peregrinación [pereɣrina'θjon] *nf* (*REL*) pilgrimage.
peregrino, a [pere'ɣrino] *adj* (*extraño*) strange; (*singular*) rare ♦ *nm/f* pilgrim.
perejil [pere'xil] *nm* parsley.
perenne [pe'renne] *adj* everlasting, perennial.
perentorio, a [peren'torjo, a] *adj* (*urgente*) urgent; (*terminante*) peremptory; (*fijo*) set, fixed.
pereza [pe'reθa] *nf* (*flojera*) laziness; (*lentitud*) sloth, slowness.
perezca [pe'reθka] *etc vb V* **perecer**.
perezoso, a [pere'θoso, a] *adj* lazy; slow, sluggish.
perfección [perfek'θjon] *nf* perfection; **a la ~** to perfection.
perfeccionar [perfekθjo'nar] *vt* to perfect; (*acabar*) to complete, finish.
perfecto, a [per'fekto, a] *adj* perfect ♦ *nm* (*LING*) perfect (tense).
perfidia [per'fiðja] *nf* perfidy, treachery.
pérfido, a ['perfiðo, a] *adj* perfidious, treacherous.
perfil [per'fil] *nm* (*parte lateral*) profile; (*silueta*) silhouette, outline; (*TEC*) (cross) section; **~es** *nmpl* features; (*fig*) social graces; **~ del cliente** (*COM*) customer profile; **en ~** from the side, in profile.
perfilado, a [perfi'laðo, a] *adj* (*bien formado*) well-shaped; (*largo*: *cara*) long.
perfilar [perfi'lar] *vt* (*trazar*) to outline; (*dar carácter a*) to shape, give character to; **~se** *vr* to be silhouetted (*en* against); **el proyecto se va perfilando** the project is taking shape.
perforación [perfora'θjon] *nf* perforation; (*con taladro*) drilling.
perforadora [perfora'ðora] *nf* drill; **~ de fichas** card-punch.
perforar [perfo'rar] *vt* to perforate; (*agujero*) to drill, bore; (*papel*) to punch a hole in ♦ *vi* to drill, bore.
perfumado, a [perfu'maðo, a] *adj* scented, perfumed.
perfumar [perfu'mar] *vt* to scent, perfume.
perfume [per'fume] *nm* perfume, scent.
pergamino [perɣa'mino] *nm* parchment.
pericia [pe'riθja] *nf* skill, expertise.
periferia [peri'ferja] *nf* periphery; (*de ciudad*) outskirts *pl*.
periférico, a [peri'feriko, a] *adj* peripheral ♦ *nm* (*INFORM*) peripheral; (*AM*: *AUTO*) ring road; **barrio ~** outlying district.
perilla [pe'riʎa] *nf* goatee.
perímetro [pe'rimetro] *nm* perimeter.
periódico, a [pe'rjoðiko, a] *adj* periodic(al) ♦ *nm* (news)paper; **~ dominical** Sunday (news)paper.
periodismo [perjo'ðismo] *nm* journalism.
periodista [perjo'ðista] *nm/f* journalist.
periodístico, a [perjo'ðistiko, a] *adj* journalistic.
periodo [pe'rjoðo], **período** [pe'rioðo] *nm* period; **~ contable** (*COM*) accounting period.
peripecias [peri'peθjas] *nfpl* adventures.
peripuesto, a [peri'pwesto, a] *adj* dressed up; **tan ~** all dressed up (to the nines).
perito, a [pe'rito, a] *adj* (*experto*) expert; (*diestro*) skilled, skilful ♦ *nm/f* expert; skilled worker; (*técnico*) technician.
perjudicar [perxuði'kar] *vt* (*gen*) to damage, harm; (*fig*) to prejudice.
perjudicial [perxuði'θjal] *adj* damaging, harmful; (*en detrimento*) detrimental.
perjudique [perxu'ðike] *etc vb V* **perjudicar**.
perjuicio [per'xwiθjo] *nm* damage, harm; **en/sin ~ de** to the detriment of/without prejudice to.
perjurar [perxu'rar] *vi* to commit perjury.
perla ['perla] *nf* pearl; **me viene de ~s** it suits me fine.
permanecer [permane'θer] *vi* (*quedarse*) to stay, remain; (*seguir*) to continue to be.
permanencia [perma'nenθja] *nf* (*duración*) permanence; (*estancia*) stay.
permanente [perma'nente] *adj* (*que queda*) permanent; (*constante*) constant; (*comisión etc*) standing ♦ *nf* perm; **hacerse una ~** to have one's hair permed.
permanezca [perma'neθka] *etc vb V* **permanecer**.
permisible [permi'sißle] *adj* permissible, allowable.

permiso [per'miso] *nm* permission; (*licencia*) permit, licence (*BRIT*), license (*US*); **con ~** excuse me; **estar de ~** (*MIL*) to be on leave; **~ de conducir** *o* **conductor** driving licence (*BRIT*), driver's license (*US*); **~ de exportación/importación** export/import licence; **~ por asuntos familiares** compassionate leave.
permitir [permi'tir] *vt* to permit, allow; **~se** *vr*: **~se algo** to allow o.s. sth; **no me puedo ~ ese lujo** I can't afford that; **¿me permite?** may I?; **si lo permite el tiempo** weather permitting.
permuta [per'muta] *nf* exchange.
permutar [permu'tar] *vt* to switch, exchange; **~ destinos con algn** to swap *o* exchange jobs with sb.
pernicioso, a [perni'θjoso, a] *adj* (*maligno, MED*) pernicious; (*persona*) wicked.
perno ['perno] *nm* bolt.
pernoctar [pernok'tar] *vi* to stay for the night.
pero ['pero] *conj* but; (*aún*) yet ♦ *nm* (*defecto*) flaw, defect; (*reparo*) objection; **¡no hay ~ que valga!** there are no buts about it.
perogrullada [peroɣru'ʎaða] *nf* platitude, truism.
perol [pe'rol] *nm*, **perola** [pe'rola] *nf* pan.
peronista [pero'nista] *adj, nm/f* Peronist.
perorata [pero'rata] *nf* long-winded speech.
perpendicular [perpendiku'lar] *adj* perpendicular; **el camino es ~ al río** the road is at right angles to the river.
perpetrar [perpe'trar] *vt* to perpetrate.
perpetuamente [perpetwa'mente] *adv* perpetually.
perpetuar [perpe'twar] *vt* to perpetuate.
perpetuo, a [per'petwo, a] *adj* perpetual; (*JUR etc: condena*) life *cpd*.
Perpiñán [perpi'ɲan] *nm* Perpignan.
perplejo, a [per'plexo, a] *adj* perplexed, bewildered.
perra ['perra] *nf* bitch; (*fam: dinero*) money; (*: manía*) mania, crazy idea; (*: rabieta*) tantrum; **estar sin una ~** to be flat broke.
perrera [pe'rrera] *nf* kennel.
perro ['perro] *nm* dog; **~ caliente** hot dog; **"~ peligroso"** "beware of the dog"; **ser ~ viejo** to be an old hand; **tiempo de ~s** filthy weather; **~ que ladra no muerde** his bark is worse than his bite.
persa ['persa] *adj, nm/f* Persian ♦ *nm* (*LING*) Persian.
persecución [perseku'θjon] *nf* pursuit, hunt, chase; (*REL, POL*) persecution.
perseguir [perse'ɣir] *vt* to pursue, hunt; (*cortejar*) to chase after; (*molestar*) to pester, annoy; (*REL, POL*) to persecute; (*JUR*) to prosecute.
perseverante [perseβe'rante] *adj* persevering, persistent.
perseverar [perseve'rar] *vi* to persevere, persist; **~ en** to persevere in, persist with.
persiana [per'sjana] *nf* (Venetian) blind.
persiga [per'siɣa] *etc vb V* **perseguir**.
persignarse [persiɣ'narse] *vr* to cross o.s.
persiguiendo [persi'ɣjenðo] *etc vb V* **perseguir**.
persistente [persis'tente] *adj* persistent.
persistir [persis'tir] *vi* to persist.
persona [per'sona] *nf* person; **10 ~s** 10 people; **tercera ~** third party; (*LING*) third person; **en ~** in person *o* the flesh; **por ~** a head; **es buena ~** he's a good sort.
personaje [perso'naxe] *nm* important person, celebrity; (*TEAT*) character.
personal [perso'nal] *adj* (*particular*) personal; (*para una persona*) single, for one person ♦ *nm* (*plantilla*) personnel, staff; (*NAUT*) crew; (*fam: gente*) people.
personalidad [personali'ðað] *nf* personality; (*JUR*) status.
personalizar [personali'θar] *vt* to personalize ♦ *vi* (*al hablar*) to name names.
personarse [perso'narse] *vr* to appear in person; **~ en** to present o.s. at, report to.
personero, a [perso'nero, a] *nm/f* (*AM*) (government) official.
personificar [personifi'kar] *vt* to personify.
personifique [personi'fike] *etc vb V* **personificar**.
perspectiva [perspek'tiβa] *nf* perspective; (*vista, panorama*) view, panorama; (*posibilidad futura*) outlook, prospect; **tener algo en ~** to have sth in view.
perspicacia [perspi'kaθja] *nf* discernment, perspicacity.
perspicaz [perspi'kaθ] *adj* shrewd.
persuadir [perswa'ðir] *vt* (*gen*) to persuade; (*convencer*) to convince; **~se** *vr* to become convinced.
persuasión [perswa'sjon] *nf* (*acto*) persuasion; (*convicción*) conviction.
persuasivo, a [perwa'siβo, a] *adj* persuasive; convincing.
pertenecer [pertene'θer] *vi*: **~ a** to belong to; (*fig*) to concern.
perteneciente [pertene'θjente] *adj*: **~ a** belonging to.
pertenencia [perte'nenθja] *nf* ownership;

~**s** *nfpl* possessions, property *sg*.
pertenezca [perte'neθka] *etc vb V* **pertenecer**.
pértiga ['pertiɣa] *nf* pole; **salto de** ~ pole vault.
pertinaz [perti'naθ] *adj* (*persistente*) persistent; (*terco*) obstinate.
pertinente [perti'nente] *adj* relevant, pertinent; (*apropiado*) appropriate; ~ **a** concerning, relevant to.
pertrechar [pertre'tʃar] *vt* (*gen*) to supply; (*MIL*) to supply with ammunition and stores; ~**se** *vr*: ~**se de algo** to provide o.s. with sth.
pertrechos [per'tretʃos] *nmpl* (*gen*) implements; (*MIL*) supplies and stores.
perturbación [perturβa'θjon] *nf* (*POL*) disturbance; (*MED*) upset, disturbance; ~ **del orden público** breach of the peace.
perturbador, a [perturβa'ðor, a] *adj* (*que perturba*) perturbing, disturbing; (*subversivo*) subversive.
perturbar [pertur'βar] *vt* (*el orden*) to disturb; (*MED*) to upset, disturb; (*mentalmente*) to perturb.
Perú [pe'ru] *nm*: **el** ~ Peru.
peruano, a [pe'rwano, a] *adj, nm/f* Peruvian.
perversión [perβer'sjon] *nf* perversion.
perverso, a [perβerso, a] *adj* perverse; (*depravado*) depraved.
pervertido, a [perβer'tiðo, a] *adj* perverted ♦ *nm/f* pervert.
pervertir [perβer'tir] *vt* to pervert, corrupt.
pervierta [per'βjerta] *etc*, **pervirtiendo** [perβir'tjendo] *etc vb V* **pervertir**.
pesa ['pesa] *nf* weight; (*DEPORTE*) shot.
pesadez [pesa'ðeθ] *nf* (*calidad de pesado*) heaviness; (*lentitud*) slowness; (*aburrimiento*) tediousness; **es una** ~ **tener que** ... it's a bind having to ....
pesadilla [pesa'ðiʎa] *nf* nightmare, bad dream; (*fig*) worry, obsession.
pesado, a [pe'saðo, a] *adj* (*gen*) heavy; (*lento*) slow; (*difícil, duro*) tough, hard; (*aburrido*) tedious, boring; (*bochornoso*) sultry ♦ *nm/f* bore; **tener el estómago** ~ to feel bloated; **¡no seas** ~**!** come off it!
pesadumbre [pesa'ðumbre] *nf* grief, sorrow.
pésame ['pesame] *nm* expression of condolence, message of sympathy; **dar el** ~ to express one's condolences.
pesar [pe'sar] *vt* to weigh; (*fig*) to weigh heavily on; (*afligir*) to grieve ♦ *vi* to weigh; (*ser pesado*) to weigh a lot, be heavy; (*fig*: *opinión*) to carry weight ♦ *nm* (*sentimiento*) regret; (*pena*) grief, sorrow; **a** ~ **de (que)** in spite of, despite; **no me pesa haberlo hecho** I'm not sorry I did it.
pesca ['peska] *nf* (*acto*) fishing; (*cantidad de pescado*) catch; ~ **de altura/en bajura** deep sea/coastal fishing; **ir de** ~ to go fishing.
pescadería [peskaðe'ria] *nf* fish shop, fishmonger's.
pescadilla [peska'ðiʎa] *nf* whiting.
pescado [pes'kaðo] *nm* fish.
pescador, a [peska'ðor, a] *nm/f* fisherman/woman.
pescar [pes'kar] *vt* (*coger*) to catch; (*tratar de coger*) to fish for; (*fam*: *lograr*) to get hold of, land; (*conseguir*: *trabajo*) to manage to get; (*sorprender*) to catch unawares ♦ *vi* to fish, go fishing.
pescuezo [pes'kweθo] *nm* neck.
pese ['pese] *prep*: ~ **a** despite, in spite of.
pesebre [pe'seβre] *nm* manger.
peseta [pe'seta] *nf* peseta.
pesetero, a [pese'tero, a] *adj* money-grubbing.
pesimismo [pesi'mismo] *nm* pessimism.
pesimista [pesi'mista] *adj* pessimistic ♦ *nm/f* pessimist.
pésimo, a ['pesimo, a] *adj* abominable, vile.
peso ['peso] *nm* weight; (*balanza*) scales *pl*; (*AM COM*) *monetary unit*; (*moneda*) peso; (*DEPORTE*) shot; ~ **bruto/neto** gross/net weight; ~ **mosca/pesado** fly-/heavyweight; **de poco** ~ light(weight); **levantamiento de** ~**s** weightlifting; **vender a** ~ to sell by weight; **argumento de** ~ weighty argument; **eso cae de su** ~ that goes without saying.
pesque ['peske] *etc vb V* **pescar**.
pesquero, a [pes'kero, a] *adj* fishing *cpd*.
pesquisa [pes'kisa] *nf* inquiry, investigation.
pestaña [pes'taɲa] *nf* (*ANAT*) eyelash; (*borde*) rim.
pestañear [pestaɲe'ar] *vi* to blink.
peste ['peste] *nf* plague; (*fig*) nuisance; (*mal olor*) stink, stench; ~ **negra** Black Death; **echar** ~**s** to swear, fume.
pesticida [pesti'θiða] *nm* pesticide.
pestilencia [pesti'lenθja] *nf* (*mal olor*) stink, stench.
pestillo [pes'tiʎo] *nm* bolt, latch; (*cerrojo*) catch; (*picaporte*) (door) handle.
petaca [pe'taka] *nf* (*de cigarrillos*) cigarette case; (*de pipa*) tobacco pouch; (*AM*: *maleta*) suitcase.
pétalo ['petalo] *nm* petal.
petanca [pe'tanka] *nf a game in which*

metal bowls are thrown at a target bowl.

petardo [pe'tarðo] *nm* firework, firecracker.

petición [peti'θjon] *nf* (*pedido*) request, plea; (*memorial*) petition; (*JUR*) plea; **a ~ de** at the request of; **~ de aumento de salarios** wage demand *o* claim.

petirrojo [peti'rroxo] *nm* robin.

peto ['peto] *nm* (*corpiño*) bodice; (*TAUR*) horse's padding.

pétreo, a ['petreo, a] *adj* stony, rocky.

petrificar [petrifi'kar] *vt* to petrify.

petrifique [petri'fike] *etc vb V* **petrificar**.

petrodólar [petro'ðolar] *nm* petrodollar.

petróleo [pe'troleo] *nm* oil, petroleum.

petrolero, a [petro'lero, a] *adj* petroleum *cpd* ♦ *nm* (*COM*) oil man; (*buque*) (oil) tanker.

petulancia [petu'lanθja] *nf* (*insolencia*) vanity, opinionated nature.

peyorativo, a [pejora'tiβo, a] *adj* pejorative.

pez [peθ] *nm* fish; **~ de colores** goldfish; **~ espada** swordfish; **estar como ~ en el agua** to feel completely at home.

pezón [pe'θon] *nm* teat, nipple.

pezuña [pe'θuɲa] *nf* hoof.

piadoso, a [pja'ðoso, a] *adj* (*devoto*) pious, devout; (*misericordioso*) kind, merciful.

Piamonte [pja'monte] *nm* Piedmont.

pianista [pja'nista] *nm/f* pianist.

piano ['pjano] *nm* piano; **~ de cola** grand piano.

piar [pjar] *vi* to cheep.

piara ['pjara] *nf* (*manada*) herd, drove.

PIB *nm abr* (*ESP COM*: = *Producto Interno Bruto*) GDP.

pibe, a ['piβe, a] *nm/f* (*AM*) boy/girl, kid, child.

pica ['pika] *nf* (*MIL*) pike; (*TAUR*) goad; **poner una ~ en Flandes** to bring off something difficult.

picadero [pika'ðero] *nm* riding school.

picadillo [pika'ðiʎo] *nm* mince, minced meat.

picado, a [pi'kaðo, a] *adj* pricked, punctured; (*mar*) choppy; (*diente*) bad; (*tabaco*) cut; (*enfadado*) cross.

picador [pika'ðor] *nm* (*TAUR*) picador; (*minero*) faceworker.

picadora [pika'ðora] *nf* mincer.

picadura [pika'ðura] *nf* (*pinchazo*) puncture; (*de abeja*) sting; (*de mosquito*) bite; (*tabaco picado*) cut tobacco.

picana [pi'kana] (*AM*) *nf* (*AGR*) cattle prod; (*POL*: *para tortura*) electric prod.

picante [pi'kante] *adj* (*comida, sabor*) hot; (*comentario*) racy, spicy.

picaporte [pika'porte] *nm* (*tirador*) handle; (*pestillo*) latch.

picar [pi'kar] *vt* (*agujerear, perforar*) to prick, puncture; (*billete*) to punch, clip; (*abeja*) to sting; (*mosquito, serpiente*) to bite; (*persona*) to nibble (at); (*incitar*) to incite, goad; (*dañar, irritar*) to annoy, bother; (*quemar*: *lengua*) to burn, sting ♦ *vi* (*pez*) to bite, take the bait; (*el sol*) to burn, scorch; (*abeja, MED*) to sting; (*mosquito*) to bite; **~se** *vr* (*agriarse*) to turn sour, go off; (*mar*) to get choppy; (*ofenderse*) to take offence; **me pican los ojos** my eyes sting; **me pica el brazo** my arm itches.

picardía [pikar'ðia] *nf* villainy; (*astucia*) slyness, craftiness; (*una ~*) dirty trick; (*palabra*) rude/bad word *o* expression.

picaresco, a [pika'resko, a] *adj* (*travieso*) roguish, rascally; (*LIT*) picaresque.

pícaro, a ['pikaro, a] *adj* (*malicioso*) villainous; (*travieso*) mischievous ♦ *nm* (*astuto*) sly sort; (*sinvergüenza*) rascal, scoundrel.

picazón [pika'θon] *nf* (*comezón*) itch; (*ardor*) sting(ing feeling); (*remordimiento*) pang of conscience.

pichón, ona [pi'tʃon, ona] *nm/f* (*paloma*) young pigeon; (*apelativo*) darling, dearest.

pico ['piko] *nm* (*de ave*) beak; (*punto agudo*) peak, sharp point; (*TEC*) pick, pickaxe; (*GEO*) peak, summit; (*labia*) talkativeness; **no abrir el ~** to keep quiet; **~ parásito** (*ELEC*) spike; **y ~** and a bit; **son las 3 y ~** it's just after 3; **tiene 50 libros y ~** he has 50-odd books; **me costó un ~** it cost me quite a bit.

picor [pi'kor] *nm* itch; (*ardor*) sting(ing feeling).

picota [pi'kota] *nf* pillory; **poner a algn en la ~** (*fig*) to ridicule sb.

picotada [piko'taða] *nf*, **picotazo** [piko'taθo] *nm* (*de pájaro*) peck; (*de insecto*) sting, bite.

picotear [pikote'ar] *vt* to peck ♦ *vi* to nibble, pick.

pictórico, a [pik'toriko, a] *adj* pictorial; **tiene dotes pictóricas** she has a talent for painting.

picudo, a [pi'kuðo, a] *adj* pointed, with a point.

pidiendo [pi'ðjendo] *etc vb V* **pedir**.

pie [pje] (*pl* **~s**) *nm* (*gen, MAT*) foot; (*de cama, página, escalera*) foot, bottom; (*TEAT*) cue; (*fig*: *motivo*) motive, basis; (: *fundamento*) foothold; **~s planos** flat feet; **ir a** ~ to go on foot, walk; **estar de** ~ to be standing (up); **ponerse de** ~ to stand up; **al** ~ **de la letra** (*citar*) literally, verbatim; (*copiar*) exactly, word for word; **de ~s a cabeza** from head to foot; **en** ~ **de guerra** on a war footing; **sin ~s ni cabeza** pointless, absurd; **dar** ~ **a** to give cause for; **no dar** ~ **con bola** to be no good at anything; **saber de qué** ~ **cojea algn** to know sb's weak spots.

piedad [pje'ðað] *nf* (*lástima*) pity, compassion; (*clemencia*) mercy; (*devoción*) piety, devotion; **tener** ~ **de** to take pity on.

piedra ['pjeðra] *nf* stone; (*roca*) rock; (*de mechero*) flint; (*METEOROLOGÍA*) hailstone; **primera** ~ foundation stone; ~ **de afilar** grindstone; ~ **arenisca/caliza** sand-/limestone.

piel [pjel] *nf* (*ANAT*) skin; (*ZOOL*) skin, hide; (*de oso*) fur; (*cuero*) leather; (*BOT*) skin, peel ♦ *nm/f*: ~ **roja** redskin.

pienso ['pjenso] *etc vb V* **pensar** ♦ *nm* (*AGR*) feed.

pierda ['pjerða] *etc vb V* **perder**.

pierna ['pjerna] *nf* leg; **en ~s** bare-legged.

pieza ['pjeθa] *nf* piece; (*esp AM*: *habitación*) room; (*MUS*) piece, composition; (*TEAT*) work, play; ~ **de recambio** *o* **repuesto** spare (part), extra (*US*); ~ **de ropa** article of clothing; **quedarse de una** ~ to be dumbfounded.

pigmento [piɣ'mento] *nm* pigment.

pigmeo, a [piɣ'meo, a] *adj, nm/f* pigmy.

pijama [pi'xama] *nm* pyjamas *pl*.

pijo, a ['pixo, a] *nm/f* (*fam*) upper-class twit.

pijotada [pixo'taða] *nf* nuisance.

pila ['pila] *nf* (*ELEC*) battery; (*montón*) heap, pile; (*fuente*) sink; (*REL*: *tb*: ~ **bautismal**) font; **nombre de** ~ Christian *o* first name; **tengo una** ~ **de cosas que hacer** (*fam*) I have heaps *o* stacks of things to do; ~ **de discos** (*INFORM*) disk pack.

pilar [pi'lar] *nm* pillar; (*de puente*) pier; (*fig*) prop, mainstay.

píldora ['pildora] *nf* pill; **la** ~ **(anticonceptiva)** the pill; **tragarse la** ~ to be taken in.

pileta [pi'leta] *nf* basin, bowl; (*AM*: *de cocina*) sink; (: *piscina*) swimming pool.

pillaje [pi'ʎaxe] *nm* pillage, plunder.

pillar [pi'ʎar] *vt* (*fam*: *coger*) to catch; (: *agarrar*) to grasp, seize; (: *entender*) to grasp, catch on to; (*suj*: *coche etc*) to run over; ~ **un resfriado** (*fam*) to catch a cold.

pillo, a ['piʎo, a] *adj* villainous; (*astuto*) sly, crafty ♦ *nm/f* rascal, rogue, scoundrel.

pilón [pi'lon] *nm* pillar, post; (*ELEC*) pylon; (*bebedero*) drinking trough; (*de fuente*) basin.

pilotar [pilo'tar] *vt* (*avión*) to pilot; (*barco*) to steer.

piloto [pi'loto] *nm* pilot; (*AUTO*) rear light, tail light; (*conductor*) driver ♦ *adj inv*: **planta** ~ pilot plant; **luz** ~ side light.

piltrafa [pil'trafa] *nf* (*carne*) poor quality meat; (*fig*) worthless object; (: *individuo*) wretch.

pimentón [pimen'ton] *nm* (*polvo*) paprika.

pimienta [pi'mjenta] *nf* pepper.

pimiento [pi'mjento] *nm* pepper, pimiento.

pimpante [pim'pante] *adj* (*encantador*) charming; (*tb*: **tan** ~) smug, self-satisfied.

PIN *nm abr* (*ESP COM*: = *Producto Interior Neto*) net domestic product.

pin, *pl* **pins** [pin, pins] *nm* badge.

pinacoteca [pinako'teka] *nf* art gallery.

pinar [pi'nar] *nm* pinewood.

pincel [pin'θel] *nm* paintbrush.

pincelada [pinθe'laða] *nf* brushstroke; **última** ~ (*fig*) finishing touch.

pinchadiscos [pintʃa'diskos] *nm/f inv* disc jockey, DJ.

pinchar [pin'tʃar] *vt* (*perforar*) to prick, pierce; (*neumático*) to puncture; (*incitar*) to prod ♦ *vi* (*MUS fam*) to be DJ; **~se** *vr* (*con droga*) to inject o.s.; (*neumático*) to burst, puncture; **no** ~ **ni cortar** (*fam*) to cut no ice; **tener un neumático pinchado** to have a puncture *o* a flat tyre.

pinchazo [pin'tʃaθo] *nm* (*perforación*) prick; (*de llanta*) puncture, flat (*US*).

pinche ['pintʃe] *nm* (*de cocina*) kitchen boy, scullion.

pinchito [pin'tʃito] *nm* shish kebab.

pincho ['pintʃo] *nm* point; (*aguijón*) spike; (*CULIN*) savoury (snack); ~ **moruno** shish kebab; ~ **de tortilla** small slice of omelette.

ping-pong ['pimpon] *nm* table tennis.

pingüe ['pingwe] *adj* (*grasoso*) greasy; (*cosecha*) bumper *cpd*; (*negocio*) lucrative.

pingüino [pin'gwino] *nm* penguin.

pinitos [pi'nitos] *nmpl*: **hacer sus primeros** ~ to take one's first steps.

pino ['pino] *nm* pine (tree); **vivir en el quinto** ~ to live at the back of beyond.

pinta ['pinta] *nf* spot; (*gota*) spot, drop; (*aspecto*) appearance, look(s) (*pl*); (*medida*) pint; **tener buena** ~ to look good, look well; **por la** ~ by the look of it.

pintado, a [pin'taðo, a] *adj* spotted; (*de muchos colores*) colourful ♦ *nf* piece of political graffiti; ~**s** *nfpl* political graffiti *sg*; **me sienta que ni ~, me viene que ni ~** it suits me a treat.
pintar [pin'tar] *vt* to paint ♦ *vi* to paint; (*fam*) to count, be important; ~**se** *vr* to put on make-up; **pintárselas solo para hacer algo** to manage to do sth by o.s.; **no pinta nada** (*fam*) he has no say.
pintor, a [pin'tor, a] *nm/f* painter; ~ **de brocha gorda** house painter; (*fig*) bad painter.
pintoresco, a [pinto'resko, a] *adj* picturesque.
pintura [pin'tura] *nf* painting; ~ **a la acuarela** watercolour; ~ **al óleo** oil painting; ~ **rupestre** cave painting.
pinza ['pinθa] *nf* (*ZOOL*) claw; (*para colgar ropa*) clothes peg, clothespin (*US*); (*TEC*) pincers *pl*; ~**s** *nfpl* (*para depilar*) tweezers.
piña ['piɲa] *nf* (*fruto del pino*) pine cone; (*fruta*) pineapple; (*fig*) group.
piñón [pi'ɲon] *nm* (*BOT*) pine nut; (*TEC*) pinion.
PIO *nm abr* (*ESP*: = *Patronato de Igualdad de Oportunidades*) ≈ Equal Opportunities Board.
pío, a ['pio, a] *adj* (*devoto*) pious, devout; (*misericordioso*) merciful ♦ *nm*: **no decir ni ~** not to breathe a word.
piojo ['pjoxo] *nm* louse.
piojoso, a [pjo'xoso, a] *adj* lousy; (*sucio*) dirty.
piolet [pjo'le], *pl* ~**s** [-s] *nm* ice axe.
pionero, a [pjo'nero, a] *adj* pioneering ♦ *nm/f* pioneer.
pipa ['pipa] *nf* pipe; (*BOT*) seed, pip.
pipí [pi'pi] *nm* (*fam*): **hacer ~** to have a wee(-wee).
pipiolo [pi'pjolo] *nm* youngster; (*novato*) novice, greenhorn.
pique ['pike] *etc vb V* **picar** ♦ *nm* (*resentimiento*) pique, resentment; (*rivalidad*) rivalry, competition; **irse a ~** to sink; (*familia*) to be ruined; **tener un ~ con algn** to have a grudge against sb.
piqueta [pi'keta] *nf* pick(axe).
piquete [pi'kete] *nm* (*agujerito*) small hole; (*MIL*) squad, party; (*de obreros*) picket; ~ **secundario** secondary picket.
pirado, a [pi'raðo, a] *adj* (*fam*) round the bend.
piragua [pi'raɣwa] *nf* canoe.
piragüismo [pira'ɣwismo] *nm* (*DEPORTE*) canoeing.
pirámide [pi'ramiðe] *nf* pyramid.
piraña [pi'raɲa] *nf* piranha.
pirarse [pi'rarse] *vr*: ~**(las)** (*largarse*) to beat it (*fam*); (*ESCOL*) to cut class.
pirata [pi'rata] *adj*: **edición/disco ~** pirate edition/bootleg record ♦ *nm* pirate; (*tb*: ~ **informático**) hacker.
pirenaico, a [pire'naiko, a] *adj* Pyrenean.
Pirineo(s) [piri'neo(s)] *nm(pl)* Pyrenees *pl*.
pirómano, a [pi'romano, a] *nm/f* (*PSICO*) pyromaniac; (*JUR*) arsonist.
piropo [pi'ropo] *nm* compliment, (piece of) flattery; **echar ~s a** to make flirtatious remarks to.
pirueta [pi'rweta] *nf* pirouette.
piruleta [piru'leta] *nf* lollipop.
pirulí [piru'li] *nm* lollipop.
pis [pis] *nm* (*fam*) pee; **hacer ~** to have a pee.
pisada [pi'saða] *nf* (*paso*) footstep; (*huella*) footprint.
pisar [pi'sar] *vt* (*caminar sobre*) to walk on, tread on; (*apretar con el pie*) to press; (*fig*) to trample on, walk all over ♦ *vi* to tread, step, walk; ~ **el acelerador** to step on the accelerator; ~ **fuerte** (*fig*) to act determinedly.
piscifactoría [pisθifakto'ria] *nf* fish farm.
piscina [pis'θina] *nf* swimming pool.
Piscis ['pisθis] *nm* (*ASTRO*) Pisces.
piso ['piso] *nm* (*suelo, de edificio*) floor; (*AM*) ground; (*apartamento*) flat, apartment; **primer ~** (*ESP*) first *o* second (*US*) floor; (*AM*) ground *o* first (*US*) floor.
pisotear [pisote'ar] *vt* to trample (on *o* underfoot); (*fig*: *humillar*) to trample on.
pisotón [piso'ton] *nm* (*con el pie*) stamp.
pista ['pista] *nf* track, trail; (*indicio*) clue; (*INFORM*) track; ~ **de auditoría** (*COM*) audit trail; ~ **de aterrizaje** runway; ~ **de baile** dance floor; ~ **de tenis** tennis court; ~ **de hielo** ice rink; **estar sobre la ~ de algn** to be on sb's trail.
pisto ['pisto] *nm* (*CULIN*) ratatouille; **darse ~** (*fam*) to show off.
pistola [pis'tola] *nf* pistol; (*TEC*) spray-gun.
pistolero, a [pisto'lero, a] *nm/f* gunman, gangster ♦ *nf* holster.
pistón [pis'ton] *nm* (*TEC*) piston; (*MUS*) key.
pitar [pi'tar] *vt* (*hacer sonar*) to blow; (*partido*) to referee; (*rechiflar*) to whistle at, boo; (*actor, obra*) to hiss ♦ *vi* to whistle; (*AUTO*) to sound *o* toot one's horn; (*AM*) to smoke; **salir pitando** to beat it.
pitido [pi'tiðo] *nm* whistle; (*sonido agudo*) beep; (*sonido corto*) pip.
pitillera [piti'ʎera] *nf* cigarette case.
pitillo [pi'tiʎo] *nm* cigarette.
pito ['pito] *nm* whistle; (*de coche*) horn;

(*cigarrillo*) cigarette; (*fam*: *de marijuana*) joint; (*fam!*) prick (*!*); **me importa un** ~ I don't care two hoots.
pitón [pi'ton] *nm* (*ZOOL*) python.
pitonisa [pito'nisa] *nf* fortune-teller.
pitorrearse [pitorre'arse] *vr*: ~ **de** to scoff at, make fun of.
pitorreo [pito'rreo] *nm* joke, laugh; **estar de** ~ to be in a joking mood.
píxel ['piksel] *nm* (*INFORM*) pixel.
piyama [pi'jama] *nm* (*AM*) pyjamas *pl*, pajamas (*US*) *pl*.
pizarra [pi'θarra] *nf* (*piedra*) slate; (*encerado*) blackboard.
pizca ['piθka] *nf* pinch, spot; (*fig*) spot, speck, trace; **ni** ~ not a bit.
pizza ['pitsa] *nf* pizza.
placa ['plaka] *nf* plate; (*MED*) dental plate; (*distintivo*) badge; ~ **de matrícula** number plate; ~ **madre** (*INFORM*) mother board.
placaje [pla'kaxe] *nm* tackle.
placard [pla'kar] *nm* (*AM*) built-in cupboard, (clothes) closet (*US*).
placenta [pla'θenta] *nf* placenta; (*tras el parto*) afterbirth.
placentero, a [plaθen'tero, a] *adj* pleasant, agreeable ♦ *vt* to please.
placer [pla'θer] *nm* pleasure; **a** ~ at one's pleasure.
plácido, a ['plaθiðo, a] *adj* placid.
plafón [pla'fon] *nm* (*AM*) ceiling.
plaga ['plaɣa] *nf* pest; (*MED*) plague; (*fig*) swarm.
plagar [pla'ɣar] *vt* to infest, plague; (*llenar*) to fill; **plagado de** riddled with; **han plagado la ciudad de carteles** they have plastered the town with posters.
plagiar [pla'gjar] *vt* to plagiarize; (*AM*) to kidnap.
plagiario, a [pla'gjario, a] *nm/f* plagiarist; (*AM*) kidnapper.
plagio ['plaxjo] *nm* plagiarism; (*AM*) kidnap.
plague ['plaɣe] *etc vb V* **plagar**.
plan [plan] *nm* (*esquema, proyecto*) plan; (*idea, intento*) idea, intention; (*de curso*) programme; ~ **cotizable de jubilación** contributory pension scheme; ~ **de estudios** curriculum, syllabus; ~ **de incentivos** (*COM*) incentive scheme; **tener** ~ (*fam*) to have a date; **tener un** ~ (*fam*) to have an affair; **en** ~ **de cachondeo** for a laugh; **en** ~ **económico** (*fam*) on the cheap; **vamos en** ~ **de turismo** we're going as tourists; **si te pones en ese** ~ ... if that's your attitude ...
plana ['plana] *nf V* **plano**.
plancha ['plantʃa] *nf* (*para planchar*) iron; (*rótulo*) plate, sheet; (*NAUT*) gangway; (*CULIN*) grill; **pescado a la** ~ grilled fish.
planchado, a [plan'tʃaðo, a] *adj* (*ropa*) ironed; (*traje*) pressed ♦ *nm* ironing.
planchar [plan'tʃar] *vt* to iron ♦ *vi* to do the ironing.
planeador [planea'ðor] *nm* glider.
planear [plane'ar] *vt* to plan ♦ *vi* to glide.
planeta [pla'neta] *nm* planet.
planetario, a [plane'tarjo, a] *adj* planetary ♦ *nm* planetarium.
planicie [pla'niθje] *nf* plain.
planificación [planifika'θjon] *nf* planning; ~ **corporativa** (*COM*) corporate planning; ~ **familiar** family planning; **diagrama de** ~ (*COM*) planner.
planilla [pla'niʎa] *nf* (*AM*) form.
plano, a ['plano, a] *adj* flat, level, even; (*liso*) smooth ♦ *nm* (*MAT, TEC, AVIAT*) plane; (*FOTO*) shot; (*ARQ*) plan; (*GEO*) map; (*de ciudad*) map, street plan ♦ *nf* sheet of paper, page; (*TEC*) trowel **primer** ~ close-up; **caer de** ~ to fall flat; **rechazar algo de** ~ to turn sth down flat; **le daba el sol de** ~ (*fig*) the sun shone directly on it; **en primera plana** on the front page; **plana mayor** staff.
planta ['planta] *nf* (*BOT, TEC*) plant; (*ANAT*) sole of the foot, foot; ~ **baja** ground floor.
plantación [planta'θjon] *nf* (*AGR*) plantation; (*acto*) planting.
plantar [plan'tar] *vt* (*BOT*) to plant; (*puesto*) to put in; (*levantar*) to erect, set up; ~**se** *vr* to stand firm; ~ **a algn en la calle** to chuck sb out; **dejar plantado a algn** (*fam*) to stand sb up; ~**se en** to reach, get to.
plantear [plante'ar] *vt* (*problema*) to pose; (*dificultad*) to raise; **se lo plantearé** I'll put it to him.
plantel [plan'tel] *nm* (*fig*) group, set.
plantilla [plan'tiʎa] *nf* (*de zapato*) insole; (*personal*) personnel; **ser de** ~ to be on the staff.
plantío [plan'tio] *nm* (*acto*) planting; (*lugar*) plot, bed, patch.
plantón [plan'ton] *nm* (*MIL*) guard, sentry; (*fam*) long wait; **dar (un)** ~ **a algn** to stand sb up.
plañir [pla'ɲir] *vi* to mourn.
plasma ['plasma] *nm* plasma.
plasmar [plas'mar] *vt* (*dar forma*) to mould, shape; (*representar*) to represent ♦ *vi*: ~ **en** to take the form of.
plasta ['plasta] *nf* soft mass, lump; (*desastre*) botch, mess.

plasticidad [plastiθi'ðað] *nf* (*fig*) expressiveness.
plástico, a ['plastiko, a] *adj* plastic ♦ *nf* (art of) sculpture, modelling ♦ *nm* plastic.
plastificar [plastifi'kar] *vt* (*documento*) to laminate.
plastifique [plasti'fike] *etc vb V* **plastificar**.
plastilina [plasti'lina] *nf* Plasticine ®.
plata ['plata] *nf* (*metal*) silver; (*cosas hechas de plata*) silverware; (*AM*) cash, dough (*fam*); **hablar en ~** to speak bluntly *o* frankly.
plataforma [plata'forma] *nf* platform; ~ **de lanzamiento/perforación** launch(ing) pad/drilling rig.
plátano ['platano] *nm* (*fruta*) banana; (*árbol*) plane tree.
platea [pla'tea] *nf* (*TEAT*) pit.
plateado, a [plate'aðo, a] *adj* silver; (*TEC*) silver-plated.
platense [pla'tense] (*fam*) = **ríoplatense**.
plática ['platika] *nf* (*AM*) talk, chat; (*REL*) sermon.
platicar [plati'kar] *vi* (*AM*) to talk, chat.
platillo [pla'tiʎo] *nm* saucer; (*de limosnas*) collecting bowl; **~s** *nmpl* cymbals; ~ **volador** *o* **volante** flying saucer; **pasar el ~** to pass the hat round.
platina [pla'tina] *nf* (*MUS*) tape deck.
platino [pla'tino] *nm* platinum; **~s** *nmpl* (*AUTO*) (contact) points.
platique [pla'tike] *etc vb V* **platicar**.
plato ['plato] *nm* plate, dish; (*parte de comida*) course; (*guiso*) dish; ~ **frutero/sopero** fruit/soup dish; **pagar los ~s rotos** (*fam*) to carry the can (*fam*).
plató [pla'to] *nm* set.
platónico, a [pla'toniko, a] *adj* platonic.
playa ['plaja] *nf* beach; (*costa*) seaside; ~ **de estacionamiento** (*AM*) car park.
playero, a [pla'jero, a] *adj* beach *cpd* ♦ *nf* (*AM*: *camiseta*) T-shirt; **~s** *nfpl* canvas shoes; (*TENIS*) tennis shoes.
plaza ['plaθa] *nf* square; (*mercado*) market(place); (*sitio*) room, space; (*en vehículo*) seat, place; (*colocación*) post, job; ~ **de abastos** food market; ~ **mayor** main square; ~ **de toros** bullring; **hacer la ~** to do the daily shopping; **reservar una ~** to reserve a seat; **el hotel tiene 100 ~s** the hotel has 100 beds.
plazca ['plaθka] *etc vb V* **placer**.
plazo ['plaθo] *nm* (*lapso de tiempo*) time, period, term; (*fecha de vencimiento*) expiry date; (*pago parcial*) instalment; **a corto/largo ~** short-/long-term; **comprar a ~s** to buy on hire purchase, pay for in instalments; **nos dan un ~ de 8 días** they allow us a week.
plazoleta [plaθo'leta], **plazuela** [pla'θwela] *nf* small square.
pleamar [plea'mar] *nf* high tide.
plebe ['pleβe] *nf*: **la ~** the common people *pl*, the masses *pl*; (*pey*) the plebs *pl*.
plebeyo, a [ple'βejo, a] *adj* plebeian; (*pey*) coarse, common.
plebiscito [pleβis'θito] *nm* plebiscite.
pleca ['pleka] *nf* (*INFORM*) backslash.
plegable [ple'ɣaβle] *adj* pliable; (*silla*) folding.
plegar [ple'ɣar] *vt* (*doblar*) to fold, bend; (*COSTURA*) to pleat; **~se** *vr* to yield, submit.
plegaria [ple'ɣarja] *nf* (*oración*) prayer.
plegué [ple'ɣe], **pleguemos** [ple'ɣemos] *etc vb V* **plegar**.
pleitear [pleite'ar] *vi* (*JUR*) to plead, conduct a lawsuit; (*litigar*) to go to law.
pleito ['pleito] *nm* (*JUR*) lawsuit, case; (*fig*) dispute, feud; **~s** *nmpl* litigation *sg*; **entablar ~** to bring an action *o* a lawsuit; **poner ~** to sue.
plenario, a [ple'narjo, a] *adj* plenary, full.
plenilunio [pleni'lunjo] *nm* full moon.
plenitud [pleni'tuð] *nf* plenitude, fullness; (*abundancia*) abundance.
pleno, a ['pleno, a] *adj* full; (*completo*) complete ♦ *nm* plenum; **en ~** as a whole; (*por unanimidad*) unanimously; **en ~ día** in broad daylight; **en ~ verano** at the height of summer; **en plena cara** full in the face.
pletina *nf* (*MUS*) tape deck.
pleuresía [pleure'sia] *nf* pleurisy.
plexiglás [pleksi'ɣlas] *nm* acrylic.
pliego ['pljeɣo] *etc vb V* **plegar** ♦ *nm* (*hoja*) sheet (of paper); (*carta*) sealed letter/document; ~ **de condiciones** details *pl*, specifications *pl*.
pliegue ['pljeɣe] *etc vb V* **plegar** ♦ *nm* fold, crease; (*de vestido*) pleat.
plisado [pli'saðo] *nm* pleating.
plomero [plo'mero] *nm* (*AM*) plumber.
plomizo, a [plo'miθo, a] *adj* leaden, lead-coloured.
plomo ['plomo] *nm* (*metal*) lead; (*ELEC*) fuse; **caer a ~** to fall heavily *o* flat.
pluma ['pluma] *nf* (*ZOOL*) feather; ~ **estilográfica,** ~ **fuente** (*AM*) fountain pen.
plumazo [plu'maθo] *nm* (*lit, fig*) stroke of the pen.
plumero [plu'mero] *nm* (*quitapolvos*) feather duster; **ya te veo el ~** I know what you're up to.
plumón [plu'mon] *nm* (*AM*) felt-tip pen.

plural [plu'ral] *adj* plural ♦ *nm*: **en ~** in the plural.
pluralidad [plurali'ðað] *nf* plurality; **una ~ de votos** a majority of votes.
pluriempleo [pluriem'pleo] *nm* moonlighting.
plus [plus] *nm* bonus.
plusmarquista [plusmar'kista] *nm/f* (*DEPORTE*) record holder.
plusvalía [plusβa'lia] *nf* (*mayor valor*) appreciation, added value; (*COM*) goodwill.
plutocracia [pluto'kraθja] *nf* plutocracy.
PM *nf abr* (*MIL*: = *Policía Militar*) MP.
p.m. *abr* (= *post meridiem*) p.m.; (= *por minuto*) per minute.
PMA *nm abr* (= *Programa Mundial de Alimentos*) World Food Programme.
pmo. *abr* (= *próximo*) prox.
PN *nf abr* (*MIL*: = *Policía Naval*) Naval Police.
PNB *nm abr* (*ESP COM*: = *producto nacional bruto*) GNP.
P.N.D. *nm abr* (*ESCOL*: = *personal no docente*) non-teaching staff.
PNN *nm/f abr* (= *profesor no numerario*) untenured teacher; (*ESP COM*: = *producto nacional neto*) net national product.
PNUD *nm abr* (= *Programa de las Naciones Unidas para el Desarrollo*) United Nations Development Programme.
PNV *nm abr* (*ESP POL*) = *Partido Nacional Vasco*.
P.º *abr* (= *Paseo*) Av(e).
p.o. *abr* = **por orden**.
p.º n.º *abr* (= *peso neto*) nt. wt.
población [poβla'θjon] *nf* population; (*pueblo, ciudad*) town, city; **~ activa** working population.
poblado, a [po'βlaðo, a] *adj* inhabited; (*barba*) thick; (*cejas*) bushy ♦ *nm* (*aldea*) village; (*pueblo*) (small) town; **~ de** (*lleno*) filled with; **densamente ~** densely populated.
poblador, a [poβla'ðor, a] *nm/f* settler, colonist.
poblar [po'βlar] *vt* (*colonizar*) to colonize; (*fundar*) to found; (*habitar*) to inhabit; **~se** *vr*: **~se de** to fill up with; (*irse cubriendo*) to become covered with.
pobre ['poβre] *adj* poor ♦ *nm/f* poor person; (*mendigo*) beggar; **los ~s** the poor; **¡~!** poor thing!; **~ diablo** (*fig*) poor wretch *o* devil.
pobreza [po'βreθa] *nf* poverty.
pocho, a ['potʃo, a] *adj* (*flor, color*) faded, discoloured; (*persona*) pale; (*fruta*) overripe; (*deprimido*) depressed.
pocilga [po'θilɣa] *nf* pigsty.
pocillo [po'siʎo] *nm* (*AM*) coffee cup.
pócima ['poθima], **poción** [po'θjon] *nf* potion; (*brebaje*) concoction, nasty drink.

PALABRA CLAVE

poco, a ['poko, a] *adj* **1** (*sg*) little, not much; **~ tiempo** little *o* not much time; **de ~ interés** of little interest, not very interesting; **poca cosa** not much
2 (*pl*) few, not many; **unos ~s** a few, some; **~s niños comen lo que les conviene** few children eat what they should
♦ *adv* **1** little, not much; **cuesta ~** it doesn't cost much; **~ más o menos** more or less
2 (*+adj*: = *negativo, antónimo*): **~ amable/inteligente** not very nice/intelligent
3: **por ~ me caigo** I almost fell
4 (*tiempo*): **~ después** soon after that; **dentro de ~** shortly; **hace ~** a short time ago, not long ago; **a ~ de haberse casado** shortly after getting married
5: **~ a ~** little by little
6 (*AM*): **¿a ~ no está divino?** isn't it just divine?; **de a ~** gradually
♦ *nm* a little, a bit; **un ~ triste/de dinero** a little sad/money.

poda ['poða] *nf* (*acto*) pruning; (*temporada*) pruning season.
podar [po'ðar] *vt* to prune.
podenco [po'ðenko] *nm* hound.

PALABRA CLAVE

poder [po'ðer] *vi* **1** (*capacidad*) can, be able to; **no puedo hacerlo** I can't do it, I'm unable to do it
2 (*permiso*) can, may, be allowed to; **¿se puede?** may I (*o* we)?; **puedes irte ahora** you may go now; **no se puede fumar en este hospital** smoking is not allowed in this hospital
3 (*posibilidad*) may, might, could; **puede llegar mañana** he may *o* might arrive tomorrow; **pudiste haberte hecho daño** you might *o* could have hurt yourself; **¡podías habérmelo dicho antes!** you might have told me before!
4: **puede (ser)** perhaps; **puede que lo sepa Tomás** Tomás may *o* might know
5: **¡no puedo más!** I've had enough!; **no pude menos que dejarlo** I couldn't help but leave it; **es tonto a más no ~** he's as stupid as they come
6: **~ con**: **¿puedes con eso?** can you manage that?; **no puedo con este crío**

this kid's too much for me
7: **él me puede** (*fam*) he's stronger than me
♦ *nm* power; **el** ~ the Government; ~ **adquisitivo** purchasing power; **detentar** *u* **ocupar** *o* **estar en el** ~ to be in power *o* office; **estar** *u* **obrar en** ~ **de** to be in the hands *o* possession of; **por** ~**(es)** by proxy.

poderío [poðe'rio] *nm* power; (*autoridad*) authority.
poderoso, a [poðe'roso, a] *adj* powerful.
podio ['poðjo] *nm* podium.
podólogo, a [po'ðoloɣo, a] *nm/f* chiropodist (*BRIT*), podiatrist (*US*).
podré [po'ðre] *etc vb V* **poder**.
podrido, a [po'ðriðo, a] *adj* rotten, bad; (*fig*) rotten, corrupt.
podrir [po'ðrir] = **pudrir**.
poema [po'ema] *nm* poem.
poesía [poe'sia] *nf* poetry.
poeta [po'eta] *nm* poet.
poético, a [po'etiko, a] *adj* poetic(al).
poetisa [poe'tisa] *nf* (woman) poet.
póker ['poker] *nm* poker.
polaco, a [po'lako, a] *adj* Polish ♦ *nm/f* Pole ♦ *nm* (*LING*) Polish.
polar [po'lar] *adj* polar.
polarice [pola'riθe] *etc vb V* **polarizar**.
polaridad [polari'ðað] *nf* polarity.
polarizar [polari'θar] *vt* to polarize.
polea [po'lea] *nf* pulley.
polémica [po'lemika] *nf* polemics *sg*; (*una* ~) controversy.
polemice [pole'miθe] *etc vb V* **polemizar**.
polémico, a [po'lemiko, a] *adj* polemic(al).
polemizar [polemi'θar] *vi* to argue.
polen ['polen] *nm* pollen.
poleo [po'leo] *nm* pennyroyal.
poli ['poli] *nm* (*fam*) cop (*fam*) ♦ *nf*: **la** ~ the cops *pl* (*fam*).
policía [poli'θia] *nm/f* policeman/woman ♦ *nf* police; ~ **municipal** local police; ~ **nacional** national police; *see boxed note*.

POLICÍA

There are two branches of the Spanish police, both of which are armed. The **policía nacional** *is in charge of national security and public order in general, while the remit of the* **policía municipal** *is mainly to deal with traffic offences, and police the local community. Catalonia and the Basque Country have their own police forces, the "Mossos d'Esquadra" and the "Ertzaintza" respectively.*

policíaco, a [poli'θiako, a] *adj* police *cpd*; **novela policíaca** detective story.
polideportivo [poliðepor'tiβo] *nm* sports centre.
poliéster [poli'ester] *nm* polyester.
polietileno [polieti'leno] *nm* polythene (*BRIT*), polyethylene (*US*).
polifacético, a [polifa'θetiko, a] *adj* (*persona, talento*) many-sided, versatile.
poligamia [poli'ɣamja] *nf* polygamy.
polígamo, a [po'liɣamo, a] *adj* polygamous ♦ *nm* polygamist.
polígono [po'liɣono] *nm* (*MAT*) polygon; (*solar*) building lot; (*zona*) area; (*unidad vecina*) housing estate; ~ **industrial** industrial estate.
polígrafo [po'liɣrafo] *nm* polygraph.
polilla [po'liʎa] *nf* moth.
Polinesia [poli'nesja] *nf* Polynesia.
polinesio, a [poli'nesjo, a] *adj, nm/f* Polynesian.
polio ['poljo] *nf* polio.
Polisario [poli'sarjo] *nm abr* (*POL*: *tb*: **Frente** ~) = *Frente Político de Liberación del Sáhara y Río de Oro*.
politécnico [poli'tekniko] *nm* polytechnic.
político, a [po'litiko, a] *adj* political; (*discreto*) tactful; (*pariente*) in-law ♦ *nm/f* politician ♦ *nf* politics *sg*; (*económica, agraria*) policy; **padre** ~ father-in-law; **política exterior/de ingresos y precios** foreign/prices and incomes policy.
póliza ['poliθa] *nf* certificate, voucher; (*impuesto*) tax *o* fiscal stamp; ~ **de seguro(s)** insurance policy.
polizón [poli'θon] *nm* (*AVIAT, NAUT*) stowaway.
pollera [po'ʎera] *nf* (*criadero*) hencoop; (*AM*) skirt, overskirt.
pollería [poʎe'ria] *nf* poulterer's (shop).
pollo ['poʎo] *nm* chicken; (*joven*) young man; (*señorito*) playboy; ~ **asado** roast chicken.
polo ['polo] *nm* (*GEO, ELEC*) pole; (*helado*) ice lolly; (*DEPORTE*) polo; (*suéter*) polo-neck; **P**~ **Norte/Sur** North/South Pole; **esto es el** ~ **opuesto de lo que dijo antes** this is the exact opposite of what he said before.
Polonia [po'lonja] *nf* Poland.
poltrona [pol'trona] *nf* reclining chair, easy chair.
polución [polu'θjon] *nf* pollution; ~ **ambiental** environmental pollution.
polvera [pol'βera] *nf* powder compact.
polvo ['polβo] *nm* dust; (*QUÍMICA, CULIN, MED*) powder; (*fam!*) screw(*!*); **en** ~ powdered; ~ **de talco** talcum powder;

estar hecho ~ to be worn out *o* exhausted; **hacer algo** ~ to smash sth; **hacer** ~ **a algn** to shatter sb; *V tb* **polvos**.

pólvora ['polβora] *nf* gunpowder; (*fuegos artificiales*) fireworks *pl*; **propagarse como la** ~ (*noticia*) to spread like wildfire.

polvoriento, a [polβo'rjento, a] *adj* (*superficie*) dusty; (*sustancia*) powdery.

polvorín [polβo'rin] *nm* (*fig*) powder keg.

polvorosa [polβo'rosa] *adj* (*fam*): **poner pies en** ~ to beat it.

polvos ['polβos] *nmpl* powder *sg*.

polvoso, a [pol'βoso, a] *adj* (*AM*) dusty.

pomada [po'maða] *nf* pomade.

pomelo [po'melo] *nm* grapefruit.

pómez ['pomeθ] *nf*: **piedra** ~ pumice stone.

pomo ['pomo] *nm* handle.

pompa ['pompa] *nf* (*burbuja*) bubble; (*bomba*) pump; (*esplendor*) pomp, splendour; ~**s fúnebres** funeral *sg*.

pomposo, a [pom'poso, a] *adj* splendid, magnificent; (*pey*) pompous.

pómulo ['pomulo] *nm* cheekbone.

ponche ['pontʃe] *nm* punch.

poncho ['pontʃo] *nm* (*AM*) poncho, cape.

ponderar [ponde'rar] *vt* (*considerar*) to weigh up, consider; (*elogiar*) to praise highly, speak in praise of.

pondré [pon'dre] *etc vb V* **poner**.

ponencia [po'nenθja] *nf* (*exposición*) (learned) paper, communication; (*informe*) report.

PALABRA CLAVE

poner [po'ner] *vt* **1** to put; (*colocar*) to place, set; (*ropa*) to put on; (*problema, la mesa*) to set; (*interés*) to show; (*telegrama*) to send; (*obra de teatro*) to put on; (*película*) to show; **ponlo más alto** turn it up; **¿qué ponen en el Excelsior?** what's on at the Excelsior?; ~ **algo a secar** to put sth (out) to dry; **¡no pongas esa cara!** don't look at me like that!

2 (*tienda*) to open; (*instalar: gas etc*) to put in; (*radio, TV*) to switch *o* turn on

3 (*suponer*): **pongamos que** ... let's suppose that ...

4 (*contribuir*): **el gobierno ha puesto otro millón** the government has contributed another million

5 (*TELEC*): **póngame con el Sr. López** can you put me through to Mr. López?

6 (*estar escrito*) to say; **¿qué pone aquí?** what does it say here?

7: ~ **de**: **le han puesto de director general** they've appointed him general manager

8 (+*adj*) to make; **me estás poniendo nerviosa** you're making me nervous

9 (*dar nombre*): **al hijo le pusieron Diego** they called their son Diego

♦ *vi* (*gallina*) to lay

♦ ~**se** *vr* **1** (*colocarse*): **se puso a mi lado** he came and stood beside me; **tú ponte en esa silla** you go and sit on that chair

2 (*vestido, cosméticos*) to put on; **¿por qué no te pones el vestido nuevo?** why don't you put on *o* wear your new dress?

3 (*sol*) to set

4 (+*adj*) to get, become; to turn; ~**se enfermo/gordo/triste** to get ill/fat/sad; **se puso muy serio** he got very serious; **después de lavarla la tela se puso azul** after washing it the material turned blue; **¡no te pongas así!** don't be like that!; ~**se cómodo** to make o.s. comfortable

5: ~**se a**: **se puso a llorar** he started to cry; **tienes que ~te a estudiar** you must get down to studying

6: ~**se a bien con algn** to make it up with sb; ~**se a mal con algn** to get on the wrong side of sb

7 (*AM*): **se me pone que** ... it seems to me that ..., I think that ....

ponga ['ponga] *etc vb V* **poner**.

poniente [po'njente] *nm* west.

pontevedrés, esa [ponteβe'ðres, esa] *adj* of *o* from Pontevedra ♦ *nm/f* native *o* inhabitant of Pontevedra.

pontificado [pontifi'kaðo] *nm* papacy, pontificate.

pontífice [pon'tifiθe] *nm* pope, pontiff; **el Sumo P**~ His Holiness the Pope.

pontón [pon'ton] *nm* pontoon.

ponzoña [pon'θoɲa] *nf* poison, venom.

ponzoñoso, a [ponθo'ɲoso, a] *adj* poisonous, venomous.

pop [pop] *adj inv, nm* (*MUS*) pop.

popa ['popa] *nf* stern; **a** ~ astern, abaft; **de** ~ **a proa** fore and aft.

popular [popu'lar] *adj* popular; (*del pueblo*) of the people.

popularice [popula'riθe] *etc vb V* **popularizarse**.

popularidad [populari'ðað] *nf* popularity.

popularizarse [populari'θarse] *vr* to become popular.

poquísimo, a [po'kisimo, a] *adj* (*superlativo de* **poco**) very little; (*pl*) very few; (*casi nada*) hardly any.

poquito [po'kito] *nm*: **un** ~ a little bit ♦ *adv* a little, a bit; **a** ~**s** bit by bit.

PALABRA CLAVE

por [por] *prep* **1** (*objetivo*) for; **luchar ~ la patria** to fight for one's country; **hazlo ~ mí** do it for my sake
2 (*+infin*): **~ no llegar tarde** so as not to arrive late; **~ citar unos ejemplos** to give a few examples
3 (*causa*) out of, because of; **no es ~ eso** that's not the reason; **~ escasez de fondos** through *o* for lack of funds
4 (*tiempo*): **~ la mañana/noche** in the morning/at night; **se queda ~ una semana** she's staying (for) a week
5 (*lugar*): **pasar ~ Madrid** to pass through Madrid; **ir a Guayaquil ~ Quito** to go to Guayaquil via Quito; **caminar ~ la calle** to walk along the street; **~ allí** over there; **se va ~ ahí** we have to go that way; **¿~ dónde?** which way?; **está ~ el norte** it's somewhere in the north; **~ todo el país** throughout the country
6 (*cambio, precio*): **te doy uno nuevo ~ el que tienes** I'll give you a new one (in return) for the one you've got; **lo vendí ~ 15 dólares** I sold it for 15 dollars
7 (*valor distributivo*): **550 pesetas ~ hora/cabeza** 550 pesetas an *o* per hour/a *o* per head; **10 ~ ciento** 10 per cent; **80 (kms) ~ hora** 80 (km) an *o* per hour
8 (*modo, medio*) by; **~ correo/avión** by post/air; **día ~ día** day by day; **~ orden** in order; **entrar ~ la entrada principal** to go in through the main entrance
9 (*agente*) by; **hecho ~ él** done by him; **"dirigido ~"** "directed by"
10: **10 ~ 10 son 100** 10 by 10 is 100
11 (*en lugar de*): **vino él ~ su jefe** he came instead of his boss
12: **~ mí que revienten** as far as I'm concerned they can drop dead
13 (*evidencia*): **~ lo que dicen** judging by *o* from what they say
14: **estar/quedar ~ hacer** to be still *o* remain to be done
15: **~ (muy) difícil que sea** however hard it is *o* may be; **~ más que lo intente** no matter how *o* however hard I try
16: **~ qué** why; **¿~ qué?** why?; **¿~?** (*fam*) why (do you ask)?

porcelana [porθe'lana] *nf* porcelain; (*china*) china.
porcentaje [porθen'taxe] *nm* percentage; **~ de actividad** (*INFORM*) hit rate.
porche ['portʃe] *nm* (*de una plaza*) arcade; (*de casa*) porch.
porción [por'θjon] *nf* (*parte*) portion, share; (*cantidad*) quantity, amount.
pordiosero, a [porðjo'sero, a] *nm/f* beggar.
porfía [por'fia] *nf* persistence; (*terquedad*) obstinacy.
porfiado, a [por'fjaðo, a] *adj* persistent; obstinate.
porfiar [por'fjar] *vi* to persist, insist; (*disputar*) to argue stubbornly.
pormenor [porme'nor] *nm* detail, particular.
pormenorice [pormeno'riθe] *etc vb V* **pormenorizar**.
pormenorizar [pormenori'θar] *vt* to (set out in) detail ♦ *vi* to go into detail.
porno ['porno] *adj inv* porno ♦ *nm* porn.
pornografía [pornoɣra'fia] *nf* pornography.
poro ['poro] *nm* pore.
poroso, a [po'roso, a] *adj* porous.
poroto [po'roto] *nm* (*AM*) kidney bean.
porque ['porke] *conj* (*a causa de*) because; (*ya que*) since; **~ sí** because I feel like it.
porqué [por'ke] *nm* reason, cause.
porquería [porke'ria] *nf* (*suciedad*) filth, muck, dirt; (*acción*) dirty trick; (*objeto*) small thing, trifle; (*fig*) rubbish.
porqueriza [porke'riθa] *nf* pigsty.
porra ['porra] *nf* (*arma*) stick, club; (*cachiporra*) truncheon; **¡~s!** oh heck!; **¡vete a la ~!** go to heck!
porrazo [po'rraθo] *nm* (*golpe*) blow; (*caída*) bump; **de un ~** in one go.
porro ['porro] *nm* joint.
porrón [po'rron] *nm glass wine jar with a long spout.*
port [por(t)] *nm* (*INFORM*) port.
portaaviones [port(a)a'ßjones] *nm inv* aircraft carrier.
portada [por'taða] *nf* (*TIP*) title page; (: *de revista*) cover.
portador, a [porta'ðor, a] *nm/f* carrier, bearer; (*COM*) bearer, payee; (*MED*) carrier; **ser ~ del virus del sida** to be HIV-positive.
portaequipajes [portaeki'paxes] *nm inv* boot (*BRIT*), trunk (*US*); (*baca*) luggage rack.
portafolio(s) [porta'foljo(s)] *nm* (*AM*) briefcase; **~ de inversiones** (*COM*) investment portfolio.
portal [por'tal] *nm* (*entrada*) vestibule, hall; (*pórtico*) porch, doorway; (*puerta de entrada*) main door; (*DEPORTE*) goal; **~es** *nmpl* arcade *sg*.
portaligas [porta'liɣas] *nm inv* (*AM*) suspender belt.
portamaletas [portama'letas] *nm inv* roof rack.

portamonedas [portamo'neðas] *nm inv* purse.
portar [por'tar] *vt* to carry, bear; **~se** *vr* to behave, conduct o.s.; **~se mal** to misbehave; **se portó muy bien conmigo** he treated me very well.
portátil [por'tatil] *adj* portable.
portaviones [porta'ßjones] *nm inv* aircraft carrier.
portavoz [porta'ßoθ] *nm/f* spokesman/woman.
portazo [por'taθo] *nm*: **dar un ~** to slam the door.
porte ['porte] *nm* (*COM*) transport; (*precio*) transport charges *pl*; (*CORREOS*) postage; **~ debido** (*COM*) carriage forward; **~ pagado** (*COM*) carriage paid, post-paid.
portento [por'tento] *nm* marvel, wonder.
portentoso, a [porten'toso, a] *adj* marvellous, extraordinary.
porteño, a [por'teɲo, a] *adj* of *o* from Buenos Aires ♦ *nm/f* native *o* inhabitant of Buenos Aires.
portería [porte'ria] *nf* (*oficina*) porter's office; (*gol*) goal.
portero, a [por'tero, a] *nm/f* porter; (*conserje*) caretaker; (*DEPORTE*) goalkeeper.
pórtico ['portiko] *nm* (*porche*) portico, porch; (*fig*) gateway; (*arcada*) arcade.
portilla [por'tiʎa] *nf*, **portillo** [por'tiʎo] *nm* gate.
portón [pro'ton] *nm* proton.
portorriqueño, a [portorri'keɲo, a] *adj, nm/f* Puerto Rican.
portuario, a [por'twarjo] *adj* (*del puerto*) port *cpd*, harbour *cpd*; (*del muelle*) dock *cpd*; **trabajador ~** docker.
Portugal [portu'ɣal] *nm* Portugal.
portugués, esa [portu'ɣes, esa] *adj, nm/f* Portuguese ♦ *nm* (*LING*) Portuguese.
porvenir [porße'nir] *nm* future.
pos [pos]: **en ~ de**: *prep* after, in pursuit of.
posada [po'saða] *nf* (*refugio*) shelter, lodging; (*mesón*) guest house; **dar ~ a** to give shelter to, take in.
posaderas [posa'ðeras] *nfpl* backside *sg*, buttocks.
posar [po'sar] *vt* (*en el suelo*) to lay down, put down; (*la mano*) to place, put gently ♦ *vi* to sit, pose; **~se** *vr* to settle; (*pájaro*) to perch; (*avión*) to land, come down.
posdata [pos'ðata] *nf* postscript.
pose ['pose] *nf* (*ARTE, afectación*) pose.
poseedor, a [posee'ðor, a] *nm/f* owner, possessor; (*de récord, puesto*) holder.
poseer [pose'er] *vt* to have, possess, own; (*ventaja*) to enjoy; (*récord, puesto*) to hold.
poseído, a [pose'iðo, a] *adj* possessed; **estar muy ~ de** to be very vain about.
posesión [pose'sjon] *nf* possession; **tomar ~ (de)** to take over.
posesionarse [posesjo'narse] *vr*: **~ de** to take possession of, take over.
posesivo, a [pose'sißo, a] *adj* possessive.
poseyendo [pose'jendo] *etc vb V* **poseer**.
posgrado [pos'ɣraðo] *nm* = **postgrado**.
posgraduado, a [posɣra'ðwaðo, a] *adj, nm/f* = **postgraduado**.
posibilidad [posißili'ðað] *nf* possibility; (*oportunidad*) chance.
posibilitar [posißili'tar] *vt* to make possible, permit; (*hacer factible*) to make feasible.
posible [po'sißle] *adj* possible; (*factible*) feasible ♦ *nm*: **~s** means; (*bienes*) funds, assets; **de ser ~** if possible; **en** *o* **dentro de lo ~** as far as possible; **lo antes ~** as quickly as possible.
posición [posi'θjon] *nf* (*gen*) position; (*rango social*) status.
positivo, a [posi'tißo, a] *adj* positive ♦ *nf* (*FOTO*) print.
poso ['poso] *nm* sediment.
posoperatorio, a [posopera'torjo, a] *adj, nm* = **postoperatorio**.
posponer [pospo'ner] *vt* to put behind *o* below; (*aplazar*) to postpone.
posponga [pos'ponga] *etc*, **pospuesto** [pos'pwesto], **pospuse** [pos'puse] *etc vb V* **posponer**.
posta ['posta] *nf* (*de caballos*) relay, team; **a ~** on purpose, deliberately.
postal [pos'tal] *adj* postal ♦ *nf* postcard.
poste ['poste] *nm* (*de telégrafos*) post, pole; (*columna*) pillar.
póster ['poster], *pl* **posters** ['posters] *nm* poster.
postergar [poster'ɣar] *vt* (*esp AM*) to put off, postpone, delay.
postergue [pos'terɣe] *etc vb V* **postergar**.
posteridad [posteri'ðað] *nf* posterity.
posterior [poste'rjor] *adj* back, rear; (*siguiente*) following, subsequent; (*más tarde*) later; **ser ~ a** to be later than.
posterioridad [posterjori'ðað] *nf*: **con ~** later, subsequently.
postgrado [post'ɣraðo] *nm*: **curso de ~** postgraduate course.
postgraduado, a [postɣra'ðwaðo, a] *adj, nm/f* postgraduate.
pos(t)guerra [pos(t)'ɣerra] *nf* postwar period; **en la ~** after the war.
postigo [pos'tiɣo] *nm* (*portillo*) postern;

(*contraventana*) shutter.
postín [pos'tin] *nm* (*fam*) elegance; **de ~** posh; **darse ~** to show off.
postizo, a [pos'tiθo, a] *adj* false, artificial; (*sonrisa*) false, phoney ♦ *nm* hairpiece.
postoperatorio, a [postopera'torjo, a] *adj* postoperative ♦ *nm* postoperative period.
postor, a [pos'tor, a] *nm/f* bidder; **mejor ~** highest bidder.
postrado, a [pos'traðo, a] *adj* prostrate.
postrar [pos'trar] *vt* (*derribar*) to cast down, overthrow; (*humillar*) to humble; (*MED*) to weaken, exhaust; **~se** *vr* to prostrate o.s.
postre ['postre] *nm* sweet, dessert ♦ *nf*: **a la ~** in the end, when all is said and done; **para ~** (*fam*) to crown it all; **llegar a los ~s** (*fig*) to come too late.
postrero, a [pos'trero, a] *adj* (*delante de nmsg*: **postrer**: *último*) last; (: *que viene detrás*) rear.
postrimerías [postrime'rias] *nfpl* final stages.
postulado [postu'laðo] *nm* postulate.
postulante [postu'lante] *nm/f* petitioner; (*REL*) postulant.
póstumo, a ['postumo, a] *adj* posthumous.
postura [pos'tura] *nf* (*del cuerpo*) posture, position; (*fig*) attitude, position.
post-venta [pos'ßenta] *adj* (*COM*) after-sales.
potable [po'taßle] *adj* drinkable.
potaje [po'taxe] *nm* thick vegetable soup.
pote ['pote] *nm* pot, jar.
potencia [po'tenθja] *nf* power; (*capacidad*) capacity; **~ (en caballos)** horsepower; **en ~** potential, in the making; **las grandes ~s** the great powers.
potencial [poten'θjal] *adj, nm* potential.
potenciar [poten'θjar] *vt* (*promover*) to promote; (*fortalecer*) to boost.
potente [po'tente] *adj* powerful.
potestad [potes'tað] *nf* authority; **patria ~** paternal authority.
potosí [poto'si] *nm* fortune; **cuesta un ~** it costs the earth.
potra ['potra] *nf* (*ZOOL*) filly; **tener ~** to be lucky.
potro ['potro] *nm* (*ZOOL*) colt; (*DEPORTE*) vaulting horse.
pozo ['poθo] *nm* well; (*de río*) deep pool; (*de mina*) shaft; **~ negro** cesspool; **ser un ~ de ciencia** (*fig*) to be deeply learned.
PP *abr* (= *por poderes*) pp; (= *porte pagado*) carriage paid.
p.p.m. *abr* (= *palabras por minuto*) wpm.
práctica ['praktika] *nf V* **práctico**.
practicable [prakti'kaßle] *adj* practicable; (*camino*) passable, usable.
prácticamente ['praktikamente] *adv* practically.
practicante [prakti'kante] *nm/f* (*MED*: *ayudante de doctor*) medical assistant; (: *enfermero*) nurse; (*quien practica algo*) practitioner ♦ *adj* practising.
practicar [prakti'kar] *vt* to practise; (*deporte*) to go in for, play; (*ejecutar*) to carry out, perform.
práctico, a ['praktiko, a] *adj* (*gen*) practical; (*conveniente*) handy; (*instruído*: *persona*) skilled, expert ♦ *nf* practice; (*método*) method; (*arte, capacidad*) skill; **en la práctica** in practice.
practique [prak'tike] *etc vb V* **practicar**.
pradera [pra'ðera] *nf* meadow; (*de Canadá*) prairie.
prado ['praðo] *nm* (*campo*) meadow, field; (*pastizal*) pasture; (*AM*) lawn.
Praga ['praɣa] *nf* Prague.
pragmático, a [praɣ'matiko, a] *adj* pragmatic.
preámbulo [pre'ambulo] *nm* preamble, introduction; **decir algo sin ~s** to say sth without beating about the bush.
precalentamiento [prekalenta'mjento] *nm* (*DEPORTE*) warm-up.
precalentar [prekalen'tar] *vt* to preheat.
precaliente [preka'ljente] *etc vb V* **precalentar**.
precario, a [pre'karjo, a] *adj* precarious.
precaución [prekau'θjon] *nf* (*medida preventiva*) preventive measure, precaution; (*prudencia*) caution, wariness.
precaver [preka'ßer] *vt* to guard against; (*impedir*) to forestall; **~se** *vr*: **~se de** *o* **contra algo** to (be on one's) guard against sth.
precavido, a [preka'ßiðo, a] *adj* cautious, wary.
precedencia [preθe'ðenθja] *nf* precedence; (*prioridad*) priority; (*superioridad*) greater importance, superiority.
precedente [preθe'ðente] *adj* preceding; (*anterior*) former ♦ *nm* precedent; **sin ~(s)** unprecedented; **establecer** *o* **sentar un ~** to establish *o* set a precedent.
preceder [preθe'ðer] *vt, vi* to precede, go/come before.
precepto [pre'θepto] *nm* precept.
preceptor [preθep'tor] *nm* (*maestro*) teacher; (: *particular*) tutor.
preciado, a [pre'θjaðo, a] *adj* (*estimado*) esteemed, valuable.
preciar [pre'θjar] *vt* to esteem, value; **~se**

vr to boast; ~**se de** to pride o.s. on.
precintar [preθin'tar] *vt* (*local*) to seal off; (*producto*) to seal.
precinto [pre'θinto] *nm* (*COM*: *tb*: ~ **de garantía**) seal.
precio ['preθjo] *nm* (*de mercado*) price; (*costo*) cost; (*valor*) value, worth; (*de viaje*) fare; ~ **de coste** *o* **de cobertura** cost price; ~ **al contado** cash price; ~ **al detalle** *o* **al por menor** retail price; ~ **al detallista** trade price; ~ **de entrega inmediata** spot price; ~ **de oferta** offer price; ~ **de oportunidad** bargain price; ~ **de salida** upset price; ~ **tope** top price; ~ **unitario** unit price; **no tener** ~ (*fig*) to be priceless; **"no importa** ~**"** "cost no object".
preciosidad [preθjosi'ðað] *nf* (*valor*) (high) value, (great) worth; (*encanto*) charm; (*cosa bonita*) beautiful thing; **es una** ~ it's lovely, it's really beautiful.
precioso, a [pre'θjoso, a] *adj* precious; (*de mucho valor*) valuable; (*fam*) lovely, beautiful.
precipicio [preθi'piθjo] *nm* cliff, precipice; (*fig*) abyss.
precipitación [preθipita'θjon] *nf* (*prisa*) haste; (*lluvia*) rainfall; (*QUÍMICA*) precipitation.
precipitado, a [preθipi'taðo, a] *adj* hasty, rash; (*salida*) hasty, sudden ♦ *nm* (*QUÍMICA*) precipitate.
precipitar [preθipi'tar] *vt* (*arrojar*) to hurl, throw; (*apresurar*) to hasten; (*acelerar*) to speed up, accelerate; (*QUÍMICA*) to precipitate; ~**se** *vr* to throw o.s.; (*apresurarse*) to rush; (*actuar sin pensar*) to act rashly; ~**se hacia** to rush towards.
precisado, a [preθi'saðo, a] *adj*: **verse** ~ **a hacer algo** to be obliged to do sth.
precisamente [preθisa'mente] *adv* precisely; (*justo*) precisely, exactly, just; ~ **por eso** for that very reason; ~ **fue él quien lo dijo** as a matter of fact he said it; **no es eso** ~ it's not really that.
precisar [preθi'sar] *vt* (*necesitar*) to need, require; (*fijar*) to determine exactly, fix; (*especificar*) to specify; (*señalar*) to pinpoint.
precisión [preθi'sjon] *nf* (*exactitud*) precision.
preciso, a [pre'θiso, a] *adj* (*exacto*) precise; (*necesario*) necessary, essential; (*estilo, lenguaje*) concise; **es** ~ **que lo hagas** you must do it.
precocidad [prekoθi'ðað] *nf* precociousness, precocity.
preconcebido, a [prekonθe'βiðo, a] *adj* preconceived.
preconice [preko'niθe] *etc vb V* **preconizar**.
preconizar [prekoni'θar] *vt* (*aconsejar*) to advise; (*prever*) to foresee.
precoz [pre'koθ] *adj* (*persona*) precocious; (*calvicie*) premature.
precursor, a [prekur'sor, a] *nm/f* precursor.
predecesor, a [preðeθe'sor, a] *nm/f* predecessor.
predecir [preðe'θir] *vt* to predict, foretell, forecast.
predestinado, a [preðesti'naðo, a] *adj* predestined.
predeterminar [preðetermi'nar] *vt* to predetermine.
predicado [preði'kaðo] *nm* predicate.
predicador, a [preðika'ðor, a] *nm/f* preacher.
predicar [preði'kar] *vt, vi* to preach.
predicción [preðik'θjon] *nf* prediction; (*pronóstico*) forecast; ~ **del tiempo** weather forecast(ing).
predicho [pre'ðitʃo], **prediga** [pre'ðiɣa] *etc*, **predije** [pre'ðixe] *etc vb V* **predecir**.
predilecto, a [preði'lekto, a] *adj* favourite.
predique [pre'ðike] *etc vb V* **predicar**.
prediré [preði're] *etc vb V* **predecir**.
predispondré [preðispon'dre] *etc vb V* **predisponer**.
predisponer [preðispo'ner] *vt* to predispose; (*pey*) to prejudice.
predisponga [preðis'ponga] *etc vb V* **predisponer**.
predisposición [preðisposi'θjon] *nf* predisposition, inclination; prejudice, bias; (*MED*) tendency.
predispuesto [preðis'pwesto], **predispuse** [preðis'puse] *etc vb V* **predisponer**.
predominante [preðomi'nante] *adj* predominant; (*preponderante*) prevailing; (*interés*) controlling.
predominar [preðomi'nar] *vt* to dominate ♦ *vi* to predominate; (*prevalecer*) to prevail.
predominio [preðo'minjo] *nm* predominance; prevalence.
preescolar [preesko'lar] *adj* preschool.
preestreno [prees'treno] *nm* preview, press view.
prefabricado, a [prefaβri'kaðo, a] *adj* prefabricated.
prefacio [pre'faθjo] *nm* preface.
preferencia [prefe'renθja] *nf* preference; **de** ~ preferably, for preference; **localidad de** ~ reserved seat.
preferible [prefe'riβle] *adj* preferable.

preferir [prefe'rir] *vt* to prefer.
prefiera [pre'fjera] *etc vb V* **preferir**.
prefijo [pre'fixo] *nm* prefix.
prefiriendo [prefi'rjendo] *etc vb V* **preferir**.
pregón [pre'ɣon] *nm* proclamation, announcement.
pregonar [preɣo'nar] *vt* to proclaim, announce; (*mercancía*) to hawk.
pregonero [preɣo'nero] *nm* town crier.
pregunta [pre'ɣunta] *nf* question; ~ **capciosa** catch question; **hacer una** ~ to ask a question.
preguntar [preɣun'tar] *vt* to ask; (*cuestionar*) to question ♦ *vi* to ask; ~**se** *vr* to wonder; ~ **por algn** to ask for sb; ~ **por la salud de algn** to ask after sb's health.
preguntón, ona [preɣun'ton, ona] *adj* inquisitive.
prehistórico, a [preis'toriko, a] *adj* prehistoric.
prejuicio [pre'xwiθjo] *nm* prejudgement; (*preconcepción*) preconception; (*pey*) prejudice, bias.
prejuzgar [prexuθ'ɣar] *vt* (*predisponer*) to prejudge.
prejuzgue [pre'xuθɣe] *etc vb V* **prejuzgar**.
preliminar [prelimi'nar] *adj, nm* preliminary.
preludio [pre'luðjo] *nm* (*MUS, fig*) prelude.
premamá [prema'ma] *adj*: **vestido** ~ maternity dress.
prematrimonial [prematrimo'njal] *adj*: **relaciones** ~**es** premarital sex.
prematuro, a [prema'turo, a] *adj* premature.
premeditación [premeðita'θjon] *nf* premeditation.
premeditado, a [premeði'taðo, a] *adj* premeditated, deliberate; (*intencionado*) wilful.
premeditar [premeði'tar] *vt* to premeditate.
premiar [pre'mjar] *vt* to reward; (*en un concurso*) to give a prize to.
premio ['premjo] *nm* reward; prize; (*COM*) premium; ~ **gordo** first prize.
premisa [pre'misa] *nf* premise.
premonición [premoni'θjon] *nf* premonition.
premura [pre'mura] *nf* (*prisa*) haste, urgency.
prenatal [prena'tal] *adj* antenatal, prenatal.
prenda ['prenda] *nf* (*ropa*) garment, article of clothing; (*garantía*) pledge; (*fam*) darling!; ~**s** *nfpl* talents, gifts; **dejar algo en** ~ to pawn sth; **no soltar** ~ to give nothing away; (*fig*) not to say a word.
prendar [pren'dar] *vt* to captivate, enchant; ~**se de algo** to fall in love with sth.
prendedor [prende'ðor] *nm* brooch.
prender [pren'der] *vt* (*captar*) to catch, capture; (*detener*) to arrest; (*coser*) to pin, attach; (*sujetar*) to fasten; (*AM*) to switch on ♦ *vi* to catch; (*arraigar*) to take root; ~**se** *vr* (*encenderse*) to catch fire.
prendido, a [pren'diðo, a] *adj* (*AM: luz etc*) on.
prensa ['prensa] *nf* press; **la P**~ the press; **tener mala** ~ to have *o* get a bad press; **la** ~ **nacional** the national press.
prensar [pren'sar] *vt* to press.
preñado, a [pre'ɲaðo, a] *adj* (*mujer*) pregnant; ~ **de** pregnant with, full of.
preocupación [preokupa'θjon] *nf* worry, concern; (*ansiedad*) anxiety.
preocupado, a [preoku'paðo, a] *adj* worried, concerned; anxious.
preocupar [preoku'par] *vt* to worry; ~**se** *vr* to worry; ~**se de algo** (*hacerse cargo*) to take care of sth; ~**se por algo** to worry about sth.
preparación [prepara'θjon] *nf* (*acto*) preparation; (*estado*) preparedness, readiness; (*entrenamiento*) training.
preparado, a [prepa'raðo, a] *adj* (*dispuesto*) prepared; (*CULIN*) ready (to serve) ♦ *nm* (*MED*) preparation; **¡~s, listos, ya!** ready, steady, go!
preparar [prepa'rar] *vt* (*disponer*) to prepare, get ready; (*TEC: tratar*) to prepare, process, treat; (*entrenar*) to teach, train; ~**se** *vr*: ~**se a** *o* **para hacer algo** to prepare *o* get ready to do sth.
preparativo, a [prepara'tiβo] *adj* preparatory, preliminary ♦ *nm*: ~**s** *nmpl* preparations.
preparatoria [prepara'torja] *nf* (*AM*) sixth form college (*BRIT*), senior high school (*US*).
preposición [preposi'θjon] *nf* preposition.
prepotencia [prepo'tenθja] *nf* abuse of power; (*POL*) high-handedness; (*soberbia*) arrogance.
prepotente [prepo'tente] *adj* (*POL*) high-handed; (*soberbio*) arrogant.
prerrogativa [prerroɣa'tiβa] *nf* prerogative, privilege.
presa ['presa] *nf* (*cosa apresada*) catch; (*víctima*) victim; (*de animal*) prey; (*de agua*) dam; **hacer** ~ **en** to clutch (on to), seize; **ser** ~ **de** (*fig*) to be a prey to.
presagiar [presa'xjar] *vt* to threaten.
presagio [pre'saxjo] *nm* omen.

presbítero [pres'ßitero] *nm* priest.
prescindir [presθin'dir] *vi*: ~ **de** (*privarse de*) to do without, go without; (*descartar*) to dispense with; **no podemos ~ de él** we can't manage without him.
prescribir [preskri'ßir] *vt* to prescribe.
prescripción [preskrip'θjon] *nf* prescription; ~ **facultativa** medical prescription.
prescrito [pres'krito] *pp de* **prescribir**.
preseleccionar [preselekθjo'nar] *vt* (*DEPORTE*) to seed.
presencia [pre'senθja] *nf* presence; **en ~ de** in the presence of.
presencial [presen'θjal] *adj*: **testigo ~** eyewitness.
presenciar [presen'θjar] *vt* to be present at; (*asistir a*) to attend; (*ver*) to see, witness.
presentación [presenta'θjon] *nf* presentation; (*introducción*) introduction.
presentador, a [presenta'ðor, a] *nm/f* compère.
presentar [presen'tar] *vt* to present; (*ofrecer*) to offer; (*mostrar*) to show, display; (*renuncia*) to tender; (*moción*) to propose; (*a una persona*) to introduce; **~se** *vr* (*llegar inesperadamente*) to appear, turn up; (*ofrecerse*: *como candidato*) to run, stand; (*aparecer*) to show, appear; (*solicitar empleo*) to apply; **~ al cobro** (*COM*) to present for payment; **~se a la policía** to report to the police.
presente [pre'sente] *adj* present ♦ *nm* present; (*LING*) present (tense); (*regalo*) gift; **los ~s** those present; **hacer ~** to state, declare; **tener ~** to remember, bear in mind; **la carta ~, la ~** this letter.
presentimiento [presenti'mjento] *nm* premonition, presentiment.
presentir [presen'tir] *vt* to have a premonition of.
preservación [preserßa'θjon] *nf* protection, preservation.
preservar [preser'ßar] *vt* to protect, preserve.
preservativo [preserßa'tißo] *nm* sheath, condom.
presidencia [presi'ðenθja] *nf* presidency; (*de comité*) chairmanship; **ocupar la ~** to preside, be in *o* take the chair.
presidente [presi'ðente] *nm/f* president; chairman/woman; (*en parlamento*) speaker; (*JUR*) presiding magistrate.
presidiario [presi'ðjarjo] *nm* convict.
presidio [pre'siðjo] *nm* prison, penitentiary.
presidir [presi'ðir] *vt* (*dirigir*) to preside at, preside over; (: *comité*) to take the chair at; (*dominar*) to dominate, rule ♦ *vi* to preside; to take the chair.
presienta [pre'sjenta] *etc*, **presintiendo** [presin'tjendo] *etc vb V* **presentir**.
presión [pre'sjon] *nf* pressure; ~ **arterial** *o* **sanguínea** blood pressure; **a ~** under pressure.
presionar [presjo'nar] *vt* to press; (*botón*) to push, press; (*fig*) to press, put pressure on ♦ *vi*: ~ **para** *o* **por** to press for.
preso, a ['preso, a] *adj*: **estar ~ de terror** *o* **pánico** to be panic-stricken ♦ *nm/f* prisoner; **tomar** *o* **llevar ~ a algn** to arrest sb, take sb prisoner.
prestación [presta'θjon] *nf* (*aportación*) lending; (*INFORM*) capability; (*servicio*) service; (*subsidio*) benefit; **prestaciones** *nfpl* (*AUTO*) performance features; ~ **de juramento** oath-taking; ~ **personal** obligatory service; **P~ Social Sustitutoria** community service for conscientious objectors; *V tb* **mili**.
prestado, a [pres'taðo, a] *adj* on loan; **dar algo ~** to lend sth; **pedir ~** to borrow.
prestamista [presta'mista] *nm/f* moneylender.
préstamo ['prestamo] *nm* loan; ~ **con garantía** loan against collateral; ~ **hipotecario** mortgage.
prestar [pres'tar] *vt* to lend, loan; (*atención*) to pay; (*ayuda*) to give; (*servicio*) to do, render; (*juramento*) to take, swear; **~se** *vr* (*ofrecerse*) to offer *o* volunteer.
prestatario, a [presta'tarjo, a] *nm/f* borrower.
presteza [pres'teθa] *nf* speed, promptness.
prestidigitador [prestiðixita'ðor] *nm* conjurer.
prestigio [pres'tixjo] *nm* prestige; (*reputación*) face; (*renombre*) good name.
prestigioso, a [presti'xjoso, a] *adj* (*honorable*) prestigious; (*famoso, renombrado*) renowned, famous.
presto, a ['presto, a] *adj* (*rápido*) quick, prompt; (*dispuesto*) ready ♦ *adv* at once, right away.
presumido, a [presu'miðo, a] *adj* conceited.
presumir [presu'mir] *vt* to presume ♦ *vi* (*tener aires*) to be conceited; **según cabe ~** as may be presumed, presumably; ~ **de listo** to think o.s. very smart.
presunción [presun'θjon] *nf* presumption; (*sospecha*) suspicion; (*vanidad*) conceit.
presunto, a [pre'sunto, a] *adj* (*supuesto*)

supposed, presumed; (*así llamado*) so-called.
presuntuoso, a [presun'twoso, a] *adj* conceited, presumptuous.
presupondré [presupon'dre] *etc vb V* **presuponer**.
presuponer [presupo'ner] *vt* to presuppose.
presuponga [presu'ponga] *etc vb V* **presuponer**.
presupuestar [presupwes'tar] *vi* to budget ♦ *vt*: ~ **algo** to budget for sth.
presupuestario, a [presupwes'tarjo, a] *adj* (*FINANZAS*) budgetary, budget *cpd*.
presupuesto [presu'pwesto] *pp de* **presuponer** ♦ *nm* (*FINANZAS*) budget; (*estimación*: *de costo*) estimate; **asignación de** ~ (*COM*) budget appropriation.
presupuse [presu'puse] *etc vb V* **presuponer**.
presuroso, a [presu'roso, a] *adj* (*rápido*) quick, speedy; (*que tiene prisa*) hasty.
pretencioso, a [preten'θjoso, a] *adj* pretentious.
pretender [preten'der] *vt* (*intentar*) to try to, seek to; (*reivindicar*) to claim; (*buscar*) to seek, try for; (*cortejar*) to woo, court; ~ **que** to expect that; **¿qué pretende usted?** what are you after?
pretendiente [preten'djente] *nm/f* (*candidato*) candidate, applicant; (*amante*) suitor.
pretensión [preten'sjon] *nf* (*aspiración*) aspiration; (*reivindicación*) claim; (*orgullo*) pretension.
pretérito, a [pre'terito, a] *adj* (*LING*) past; (*fig*) past, former.
pretextar [preteks'tar] *vt* to plead, use as an excuse.
pretexto [pre'teksto] *nm* pretext; (*excusa*) excuse; **so** ~ **de** under pretext of.
pretil [pre'til] *nm* (*valla*) parapet; (*baranda*) handrail.
prevalecer [preßale'θer] *vi* to prevail.
prevaleciente [preßale'θjente] *adj* prevailing, prevalent.
prevalezca [preßa'leθka] *etc vb V* **prevalecer**.
prevención [preßen'θjon] *nf* (*preparación*) preparation; (*estado*) preparedness, readiness; (*medida*) prevention; (*previsión*) foresight, forethought; (*precaución*) precaution.
prevendré [preßen'dre] *etc*, **prevenga** [pre'ßenga] *etc vb V* **prevenir**.
prevenido, a [preße'niðo, a] *adj* prepared, ready; (*cauteloso*) cautious; **estar** ~ (*preparado*) to be ready; **ser** ~ (*cuidadoso*) to be cautious; **hombre** ~ **vale por dos** forewarned is forearmed.
prevenir [preße'nir] *vt* (*impedir*) to prevent; (*prever*) to foresee, anticipate; (*predisponer*) to prejudice, bias; (*avisar*) to warn; (*preparar*) to prepare, get ready; ~**se** *vr* to get ready, prepare; ~**se contra** to take precautions against.
preventivo, a [preßen'tißo, a] *adj* preventive, precautionary.
prever [pre'ßer] *vt* to foresee; (*anticipar*) to anticipate.
previniendo [preßi'njendo] *etc vb V* **prevenir**.
previo, a ['preßjo, a] *adj* (*anterior*) previous, prior ♦ *prep*: ~ **acuerdo de los otros** subject to the agreement of the others; ~ **pago de los derechos** on payment of the fees.
previsible [preßi'sißle] *adj* foreseeable.
previsión [preßi'sjon] *nf* (*perspicacia*) foresight; (*predicción*) forecast; (*prudencia*) caution; ~ **de ventas** (*COM*) sales forecast.
previsor, a [preßi'sor, a] *adj* (*precavido*) far-sighted; (*prudente*) thoughtful.
previsto [pre'ßisto] *pp de* **prever**.
P.R.I. *nm abr* (*AM*) = **Partido Revolucionario Institucional**.
prieto, a ['prjeto, a] *adj* (*oscuro*) dark; (*AM*) dark(-skinned); (*fig*) mean; (*comprimido*) tight, compressed.
prima ['prima] *nf V* **primo**.
primacía [prima'θia] *nf* primacy.
primar [pri'mar] *vi* (*tener primacía*) to occupy first place; ~ **sobre** to have priority over.
primario, a [pri'marjo, a] *adj* primary ♦ *nf* primary education; *V tb* **sistema educativo**.
primavera [prima'ßera] *nf* (*temporada*) spring; (*período*) springtime.
primaveral [primaße'ral] *adj* spring *cpd*, springlike.
primero, a [pri'mero, a] *adj* (*delante de nmsg*: **primer**) first; (*fig*) prime; (*anterior*) former; (*básico*) fundamental ♦ *adv* first; (*más bien*) sooner, rather ♦ *nf* (*AUTO*) first gear; (*FERRO*) first class; **de primera** (*fam*) first-class, first-rate; **de buenas a primeras** suddenly; **primera dama** (*TEAT*) leading lady.
primicia [pri'miθja] *nf* (*PRENSA*) scoop; ~**s** *nfpl* (*tb fig*) first fruits.
primitivo, a [primi'tißo, a] *adj* primitive; (*original*) original; (*COM*: *acción*) ordinary ♦ *nf*: **(Lotería) Primitiva** *weekly state-run*

lottery; *V tb* **lotería**.
primo, a ['primo, a] *adj* (*MAT*) prime ♦ *nm/f* cousin; (*fam*) fool, dupe ♦ *nf* (*COM*) bonus; (*seguro*) premium; (*a la exportación*) subsidy; ~ **hermano** first cousin; **materias primas** raw materials; **hacer el** ~ to be taken for a ride.
primogénito, a [primo'xenito, a] *adj* first-born.
primor [pri'mor] *nm* (*cuidado*) care; **es un** ~ it's lovely.
primordial [primor'ðjal] *adj* basic, fundamental.
primoroso, a [primo'roso, a] *adj* exquisite, fine.
princesa [prin'θesa] *nf* princess.
principado [prinθi'paðo] *nm* principality.
principal [prinθi'pal] *adj* principal, main; (*más destacado*) foremost; (*piso*) first, second (*US*); (*INFORM*) foreground ♦ *nm* (*jefe*) chief, principal.
príncipe ['prinθipe] *nm* prince; ~ **heredero** crown prince; **P~ de Asturias** *King's son and heir to the Spanish throne*; ~ **de gales** (*tela*) check.
principiante [prinθi'pjante] *nm/f* beginner; (*novato*) novice.
principio [prin'θipjo] *nm* (*comienzo*) beginning, start; (*origen*) origin; (*base*) rudiment, basic idea; (*moral*) principle; **a ~s de** at the beginning of; **desde el** ~ from the first; **en un** ~ at first.
pringar [prin'gar] *vt* (*CULIN*: *pan*) to dip; (*ensuciar*) to dirty; **~se** *vr* to get splashed *o* soiled; ~ **a algn en un asunto** (*fam*) to involve sb in a matter.
pringoso, a [prin'goso, a] *adj* greasy; (*pegajoso*) sticky.
pringue ['pringe] *etc vb V* **pringar** ♦ *nm* (*grasa*) grease, fat, dripping.
prioridad [priori'ðað] *nf* priority; (*AUTO*) right of way.
prioritario, a [priori'tarjo, a] *adj* (*INFORM*) foreground.
prisa ['prisa] *nf* (*apresuramiento*) hurry, haste; (*rapidez*) speed; (*urgencia*) (sense of) urgency; **correr** ~ to be urgent; **darse** ~ to hurry up; **estar de** *o* **tener** ~ to be in a hurry.
prisión [pri'sjon] *nf* (*cárcel*) prison; (*período de cárcel*) imprisonment.
prisionero, a [prisjo'nero, a] *nm/f* prisoner.
prismáticos [pris'matikos] *nmpl* binoculars.
privación [priβa'θjon] *nf* deprivation; (*falta*) want, privation; **privaciones** *nfpl* hardships, privations.
privado, a [pri'βaðo, a] *adj* (*particular*) private; (*POL*: *favorito*) favourite (*BRIT*), favorite (*US*); **en** ~ privately, in private; "**~ y confidencial**" "private and confidential".
privar [pri'βar] *vt* to deprive; **~se** *vr*: **~se de** (*abstenerse*) to deprive o.s. of; (*renunciar*) to give up.
privativo, a [priβa'tiβo, a] *adj* exclusive.
privatizar [priβati'θar] *vt* to privatize.
privilegiado, a [priβile'xjaðo, a] *adj* privileged; (*memoria*) very good ♦ *nm/f* (*afortunado*) privileged person.
privilegiar [priβile'xjar] *vt* to grant a privilege to; (*favorecer*) to favour.
privilegio [priβi'lexjo] *nm* privilege; (*concesión*) concession.
pro [pro] *nm o nf* profit, advantage ♦ *prep*: **asociación ~ ciegos** association for the blind ♦ *pref*: ~ **soviético/americano** pro-Soviet/-American; **en ~ de** on behalf of, for; **los ~s y los contras** the pros and cons.
proa ['proa] *nf* (*NAUT*) bow, prow.
probabilidad [proβaβili'ðað] *nf* probability, likelihood; (*oportunidad, posibilidad*) chance, prospect.
probable [pro'βaβle] *adj* probable, likely; **es ~ que** + *subjun* it is probable *o* likely that; **es ~ que no venga** he probably won't come.
probador [proβa'ðor] *nm* (*persona*) taster (*of wine etc*); (*en una tienda*) fitting room.
probar [pro'βar] *vt* (*demostrar*) to prove; (*someter a prueba*) to test, try out; (*ropa*) to try on; (*comida*) to taste ♦ *vi* to try; **~se** *vr*: **~se un traje** to try on a suit.
probeta [pro'βeta] *nf* test tube.
problema [pro'βlema] *nm* problem.
procaz [pro'kaθ] *adj* insolent, impudent.
procedencia [proθe'ðenθja] *nf* (*principio*) source, origin; (*lugar de salida*) point of departure.
procedente [proθe'ðente] *adj* (*razonable*) reasonable; (*conforme a derecho*) proper, fitting; ~ **de** coming from, originating in.
proceder [proθe'ðer] *vi* (*avanzar*) to proceed; (*actuar*) to act; (*ser correcto*) to be right (and proper), be fitting ♦ *nm* (*comportamiento*) behaviour, conduct; **no procede obrar así** it is not right to act like that; ~ **de** to come from, originate in.
procedimiento [proθeði'mjento] *nm* procedure; (*proceso*) process; (*método*) means, method; (*trámite*) proceedings *pl*.
prócer ['proθer] *nm* (*persona eminente*) worthy; (*líder*) great man, leader; (*esp*

AM) national hero.
procesado, a [proθe'saðo, a] *nm/f* accused (person).
procesador [proθesa'ðor] *nm*: ~ **de textos** (*INFORM*) word processor.
procesamiento [proθesa'mjento] *nm* (*INFORM*) processing; ~ **de datos** data processing; ~ **por lotes** batch processing; ~ **solapado** multiprogramming; ~ **de textos** word processing.
procesar [proθe'sar] *vt* to try, put on trial; (*INFORM*) to process.
procesión [proθe'sjon] *nf* procession; **la ~ va por dentro** he keeps his troubles to himself.
proceso [pro'θeso] *nm* process; (*JUR*) trial; (*lapso*) course (of time); (*INFORM*): ~ **(automático) de datos** (automatic) data processing; ~ **no prioritario** background process; ~ **por pasadas** batch processing; ~ **en tiempo real** real-time programming.
proclama [pro'klama] *nf* (*acto*) proclamation; (*cartel*) poster.
proclamar [prokla'mar] *vt* to proclaim.
proclive [pro'kliβe] *adj*: ~ **(a)** inclined *o* prone (to).
procreación [prokrea'θjon] *nf* procreation.
procrear [prokre'ar] *vt, vi* to procreate.
procurador, a [prokura'ðor, a] *nm/f* attorney, solicitor.
procurar [proku'rar] *vt* (*intentar*) to try, endeavour; (*conseguir*) to get, obtain; (*asegurar*) to secure; (*producir*) to produce.
prodigar [proði'ɣar] *vt* to lavish; **~se** *vr*: **~se en** to be lavish with.
prodigio [pro'ðixjo] *nm* prodigy; (*milagro*) wonder, marvel; **niño ~** child prodigy.
prodigioso, a [proði'xjoso, a] *adj* prodigious, marvellous.
pródigo, a ['proðiɣo, a] *adj* (*rico*) rich, productive; **hijo ~** prodigal son.
producción [proðuk'θjon] *nf* production; (*suma de productos*) output; (*producto*) product; ~ **en serie** mass production.
producir [proðu'θir] *vt* to produce; (*generar*) to cause, bring about; (*impresión*) to give; (*COM*: *interés*) to bear; **~se** *vr* (*gen*) to come about, happen; (*hacerse*) to be produced, be made; (*estallar*) to break out; (*accidente*) to take place.
productividad [proðuktiβi'ðað] *nf* productivity.
productivo, a [proðuk'tiβo, a] *adj* productive; (*provechoso*) profitable.
producto [pro'ðukto] *nm* (*resultado*) product; *producción*) production; ~ **alimenticio** foodstuff; ~ **(nacional) bruto** gross (national) product; ~ **interno bruto** gross domestic product.
productor, a [proðuk'tor, a] *adj* productive, producing ♦ *nm/f* producer.
produje [pro'ðuxe], **produjera** [proðu'xera], **produzca** [pro'ðuθka] *etc vb V* **producir**.
proeza [pro'eθa] *nf* exploit, feat.
profanar [profa'nar] *vt* to desecrate, profane.
profano, a [pro'fano, a] *adj* profane ♦ *nm/f* (*inexperto*) layman/woman; **soy ~ en música** I don't know anything about music.
profecía [profe'θia] *nf* prophecy.
proferir [profe'rir] *vt* (*palabra, sonido*) to utter; (*injuria*) to hurl, let fly.
profesar [profe'sar] *vt* (*declarar*) to profess; (*practicar*) to practise.
profesión [profe'sjon] *nf* profession; (*confesión*) avowal; **abogado de ~, de ~ abogado** a lawyer by profession.
profesional [profesjo'nal] *adj* professional.
profesor, a [profe'sor, a] *nm/f* teacher; (*instructor*) instructor; (~ *de universidad*) lecturer; ~ **adjunto** assistant lecturer, associate professor (*US*).
profesorado [profeso'raðo] *nm* (*profesión*) teaching profession; (*cuerpo*) teaching staff, faculty (*US*); (*cargo*) professorship.
profeta [pro'feta] *nm/f* prophet.
profetice [profe'tiθe] *etc vb V* **profetizar**.
profetizar [profeti'θar] *vt, vi* to prophesy.
profiera [pro'fjera] *etc*, **profiriendo** [profi'rjendo] *etc vb V* **proferir**.
profilaxis [profi'laksis] *nf inv* prevention.
prófugo, a ['profuɣo, a] *nm/f* fugitive; (*desertor*) deserter.
profundice [profun'diθe] *etc vb V* **profundizar**.
profundidad [profundi'ðað] *nf* depth; **tener una ~ de 30 cm** to be 30 cm deep.
profundizar [profundi'θar] *vt* (*fig*) to go deeply into, study in depth.
profundo, a [pro'fundo, a] *adj* deep; (*misterio, pensador*) profound; **poco ~** shallow.
profusión [profu'sjon] *nf* (*abundancia*) profusion; (*prodigalidad*) wealth.
progenie [pro'xenje] *nf* offspring.
progenitor [proxeni'tor] *nm* ancestor; **~es** *nmpl* (*fam*) parents.
programa [pro'ɣrama] *nm* programme; (*INFORM*) program; ~ **de estudios** curriculum, syllabus; ~ **verificador de**

ortografía (*INFORM*) spelling checker.
programación [proɣrama'θjon] *nf* (*INFORM*) programming; ~ **estructurada** structured programming.
programador, a [proɣrama'ðor, a] *nm/f* (computer) programmer; ~ **de aplicaciones** applications programmer.
programar [proɣra'mar] *vt* (*INFORM*) to programme.
programería [proɣrame'ria] *nf* (*INFORM*): ~ **fija** firmware.
progre ['proɣre] *adj* (*fam*) liberal.
progresar [proɣre'sar] *vi* to progress, make progress.
progresión [proɣres'jon] *nf*: ~ **geométrica/aritmética** geometric/arithmetic progression.
progresista [proɣre'sista] *adj, nm/f* progressive.
progresivo, a [proɣre'siβo, a] *adj* progressive; (*gradual*) gradual; (*continuo*) continuous.
progreso [pro'ɣreso] *nm* (*tb*: ~**s**) progress; **hacer** ~**s** to progress, advance.
prohibición [proiβi'θjon] *nf* prohibition, ban; **levantar la** ~ **de** to remove the ban on.
prohibir [proi'βir] *vt* to prohibit, ban, forbid; **se prohíbe fumar** no smoking.
prohibitivo, a [proiβi'tiβo, a] *adj* prohibitive.
prójimo, a ['proximo, a] *nm* fellow man ♦ *nm/f* (*vecino*) neighbour.
prole ['prole] *nf* (*descendencia*) offspring.
proletariado [proleta'rjaðo] *nm* proletariat.
proletario, a [prole'tarjo, a] *adj, nm/f* proletarian.
proliferación [prolifera'θjon] *nf* proliferation; ~ **de armas nucleares** spread of nuclear arms.
proliferar [prolife'rar] *vi* to proliferate.
prolífico, a [pro'lifiko, a] *adj* prolific.
prolijo, a [pro'lixo, a] *adj* long-winded, tedious; (*AM*) neat.
prólogo ['proloɣo] *nm* prologue; (*preámbulo*) preface, introduction.
prolongación [prolonga'θjon] *nf* extension.
prolongado, a [prolon'gaðo, a] *adj* (*largo*) long; (*alargado*) lengthy.
prolongar [prolon'gar] *vt* (*gen*) to extend; (*en el tiempo*) to prolong; (*calle, tubo*) to make longer, extend; ~**se** *vr* (*alargarse*) to extend, go on.
prolongue [pro'longe] *etc vb V* **prolongar**.
prom. *abr* (= *promedio*) av.
promedio [pro'meðjo] *nm* average; (*de distancia*) middle, mid-point.
promesa [pro'mesa] *nf* promise ♦ *adj*: **jugador** ~ promising player; **faltar a una** ~ to break a promise.
prometer [prome'ter] *vt* to promise ♦ *vi* to show promise; ~**se** *vr* (*dos personas*) to get engaged.
prometido, a [prome'tiðo, a] *adj* promised; engaged ♦ *nm/f* fiancé/fiancée.
prominente [promi'nente] *adj* prominent.
promiscuidad [promiskwi'ðað] *nf* promiscuity.
promiscuo, a [pro'miskwo, a] *adj* promiscuous.
promoción [promo'θjon] *nf* promotion; (*año*) class, year; ~ **por correspondencia directa** (*COM*) direct mailshot; ~ **de ventas** sales promotion *o* drive.
promocionar [promoθjo'nar] *vt* (*COM*: *dar publicidad*) to promote.
promontorio [promon'torjo] *nm* promontory.
promotor [promo'tor] *nm* promoter; (*instigador*) instigator.
promover [promo'βer] *vt* to promote; (*causar*) to cause; (*juicio*) to bring; (*motín*) to instigate, stir up.
promueva [pro'mweβa] *etc vb V* **promover**.
promulgar [promul'ɣar] *vt* to promulgate; (*fig*) to proclaim.
promulgue [pro'mulɣe] *etc vb V* **promulgar**.
pronombre [pro'nombre] *nm* pronoun.
pronosticar [pronosti'kar] *vt* to predict, foretell, forecast.
pronóstico [pro'nostiko] *nm* prediction, forecast; (*profecía*) omen; (*MED*: *diagnóstico*) prognosis; **de** ~ **leve** slight, not serious; ~ **del tiempo** weather forecast.
pronostique [pronos'tike] *etc vb V* **pronosticar**.
prontitud [pronti'tuð] *nf* speed, quickness.
pronto, a ['pronto, a] *adj* (*rápido*) prompt, quick; (*preparado*) ready ♦ *adv* quickly, promptly; (*en seguida*) at once, right away; (*dentro de poco*) soon; (*temprano*) early ♦ *nm* urge, sudden feeling; **tener** ~**s de enojo** to be quick-tempered; **al** ~ at first; **de** ~ suddenly; **¡hasta** ~**!** see you soon!; **lo más** ~ **posible** as soon as possible; **por lo** ~ meanwhile, for the present; **tan** ~ **como** as soon as.
pronunciación [pronunθja'θjon] *nf* pronunciation.
pronunciado, a [pronun'θjaðo, a] *adj* (*marcado*) pronounced; (*curva etc*) sharp; (*facciones*) marked.

pronunciamiento [pronunθja'mjento] *nm* (*rebelión*) insurrection.

pronunciar [pronun'θjar] *vt* to pronounce; (*discurso*) to make, deliver; (*JUR*: *sentencia*) to pass, pronounce; **~se** *vr* to revolt, rise, rebel; (*declararse*) to declare o.s.; **~se sobre** to pronounce on.

propagación [propaɣa'θjon] *nf* propagation; (*difusión*) spread(ing).

propaganda [propa'ɣanda] *nf* (*política*) propaganda; (*comercial*) advertising; **hacer ~ de** (*COM*) to advertise.

propagar [propa'ɣar] *vt* to propagate; (*difundir*) to spread, disseminate; **~se** *vr* (*BIO*) to propagate; (*fig*) to spread.

propague [pro'paɣe] *etc vb V* **propagar**.

propalar [propa'lar] *vt* (*divulgar*) to divulge; (*publicar*) to publish an account of.

propano [pro'pano] *nm* propane.

propasarse [propa'sarse] *vr* (*excederse*) to go too far; (*sexualmente*) to take liberties.

propensión [propen'sjon] *nf* inclination, propensity.

propenso, a [pro'penso, a] *adj*: **~ a** prone *o* inclined to; **ser ~ a hacer algo** to be inclined *o* have a tendency to do sth.

propiamente [propja'mente] *adv* properly; (*realmente*) really, exactly; **~ dicho** real, true.

propicio, a [pro'piθjo, a] *adj* favourable, propitious.

propiedad [propje'ðað] *nf* property; (*posesión*) possession, ownership; (*conveniencia*) suitability; (*exactitud*) accuracy; **~ particular** private property; **~ pública** (*COM*) public ownership; **ceder algo a algn en ~** to transfer to sb the full rights over sth.

propietario, a [propje'tarjo, a] *nm/f* owner, proprietor.

propina [pro'pina] *nf* tip; **dar algo de ~** to give something extra.

propinar [propi'nar] *vt* (*golpe*) to strike; (*azotes*) to give.

propio, a ['propjo, a] *adj* own, of one's own; (*característico*) characteristic, typical; (*conveniente*) proper; (*mismo*) selfsame, very; **el ~ ministro** the minister himself; **¿tienes casa propia?** have you a house of your own?; **eso es muy ~ de él** that's just like him; **tiene un olor muy ~** it has a smell of its own.

propondré [propon'dre] *etc vb V* **proponer**.

proponente [propo'nente] *nm* proposer, mover.

proponer [propo'ner] *vt* to propose, put forward; (*candidato*) to propose, nominate; (*problema*) to pose; **~se** *vr* to propose, plan, intend.

proponga [pro'ponga] *etc vb V* **proponer**.

proporción [propor'θjon] *nf* proportion; (*MAT*) ratio; (*razón, porcentaje*) rate; **proporciones** *nfpl* dimensions; (*fig*) size *sg*; **en ~ con** in proportion to.

proporcionado, a [proporθjo'naðo, a] *adj* proportionate; (*regular*) medium, middling; (*justo*) just right; **bien ~** well-proportioned.

proporcional [proporθjo'nal] *adj* proportional; **~ a** proportional to.

proporcionar [proporθjo'nar] *vt* (*dar*) to give, supply, provide; **esto le proporciona una renta anual de ...** this brings him in a yearly income of ....

proposición [proposi'θjon] *nf* proposition; (*propuesta*) proposal.

propósito [pro'posito] *nm* (*intención*) purpose; (*intento*) aim, intention ♦ *adv*: **a ~** by the way, incidentally; **a ~ de** about, with regard to.

propuesto, a [pro'pwesto, a] *pp de* **proponer** ♦ *nf* proposal.

propugnar [propuɣ'nar] *vt* to uphold.

propulsar [propul'sar] *vt* to drive, propel; (*fig*) to promote, encourage.

propulsión [propul'sjon] *nf* propulsion; **~ a chorro** *o* **por reacción** jet propulsion.

propuse [pro'puse] *etc vb V* **proponer**.

prorrata [pro'rrata] *nf* (*porción*) share, quota, prorate (*US*) ♦ *adv* (*COM*) pro rata.

prorratear [prorrate'ar] *vt* (*dividir*) to share out, prorate (*US*).

prórroga ['prorroɣa] *nf* (*gen*) extension; (*JUR*) stay; (*COM*) deferment.

prorrogable [prorro'ɣaßle] *adj* which can be extended.

prorrogar [prorro'ɣar] *vt* (*período*) to extend; (*decisión*) to defer, postpone.

prorrogue [pro'rroɣe] *etc vb V* **prorrogar**.

prorrumpir [prorrum'pir] *vi* to burst forth, break out; **~ en gritos** to start shouting; **~ en lágrimas** to burst into tears.

prosa ['prosa] *nf* prose.

prosaico, a [pro'saiko, a] *adj* prosaic, dull.

proscribir [proskri'ßir] *vt* to prohibit, ban; (*desterrar*) to exile, banish; (*partido*) to proscribe.

proscripción [proskrip'θjon] *nf* prohibition, ban; banishment; proscription.

proscrito, a [pros'krito, a] *pp de* **proscribir** ♦ *adj* (*prohibido*) banned; (*desterrado*) outlawed ♦ *nm/f* (*exilado*) exile; (*bandido*) outlaw.

prosecución [proseku'θjon] *nf* continuation; (*persecución*) pursuit.
proseguir [prose'ɣir] *vt* to continue, carry on, proceed with; (*investigación, estudio*) to pursue ♦ *vi* to continue, go on.
prosiga [pro'siɣa] *etc*, **prosiguiendo** [prosi'ɣjenðo] *etc vb V* **proseguir**.
prosista [pro'sista] *nm/f* (*escritor*) prose writer.
prospección [prospek'θjon] *nf* exploration; (*del petróleo, del oro*) prospecting.
prospecto [pros'pekto] *nm* prospectus; (*folleto*) leaflet, sheet of instructions.
prosperar [prospe'rar] *vi* to prosper, thrive, flourish.
prosperidad [prosperi'ðað] *nf* prosperity; (*éxito*) success.
próspero, a ['prospero, a] *adj* prosperous; (*que tiene éxito*) successful.
prostíbulo [pros'tiβulo] *nm* brothel.
prostitución [prostitu'θjon] *nf* prostitution.
prostituir [prosti'twir] *vt* to prostitute; **~se** *vr* to prostitute o.s., become a prostitute.
prostituta [prosti'tuta] *nf* prostitute.
prostituyendo [prostitu'jendo] *etc vb V* **prostituir**.
protagonice [protaɣo'niθe] *etc vb V* **protagonizar**.
protagonista [protaɣo'nista] *nm/f* protagonist; (*LIT: personaje*) main character, hero(ine).
protagonizar [protaɣoni'θar] *vt* to head, take the chief role in.
protección [protek'θjon] *nf* protection.
proteccionismo [protekθjo'nismo] *nm* (*COM*) protectionism.
protector, a [protek'tor, a] *adj* protective, protecting; (*tono*) patronizing ♦ *nm/f* protector; (*bienhechor*) patron; (*de la tradición*) guardian.
proteger [prote'xer] *vt* to protect; ~ **contra grabación** *o* **contra escritura** (*INFORM*) to write-protect.
protegido, a [prote'xiðo, a] *nm/f* protégé/ protégée.
proteína [prote'ina] *nf* protein.
proteja [pro'texa] *etc vb V* **proteger**.
prótesis ['protesis] *nf* (*MED*) prosthesis.
protesta [pro'testa] *nf* protest.
protestante [protes'tante] *adj* Protestant.
protestar [protes'tar] *vt* to protest, declare; (*fe*) to protest ♦ *vi* to protest; (*objetar*) to object; **cheque protestado por falta de fondos** cheque referred to drawer.
protocolo [proto'kolo] *nm* protocol; **sin ~s** (*formalismo*) informal(ly).
protón [pro'ton] *nm* proton.
prototipo [proto'tipo] *nm* prototype; (*ideal*) model.
protuberancia [protuβe'ranθja] *nf* protuberance.
prov. *abr* (= *provincia*) prov.
provecho [pro'βetʃo] *nm* advantage, benefit; (*FINANZAS*) profit; **¡buen ~!** bon appétit!; **en ~ de** to the benefit of; **sacar ~ de** to benefit from, profit by.
provechoso, a [proβe'tʃoso, a] *adj* (*ventajoso*) advantageous; (*beneficioso*) beneficial, useful; (*FINANZAS: lucrativo*) profitable.
proveedor, a [proβee'ðor, a] *nm/f* (*abastecedor*) supplier; (*distribuidor*) dealer; **~ de (acceso a) Internet** Internet Service Provider.
proveer [proβe'er] *vt* to provide, supply; (*preparar*) to provide, get ready; (*vacante*) to fill; (*negocio*) to transact, dispatch ♦ *vi*: ~ **a** to provide for; **~se** *vr*: **~se de** to provide o.s. with.
provendré [proβen'dre] *etc*, **provenga** [pro'βenga] *etc vb V* **provenir**.
provenir [proβe'nir] *vi*: ~ **de** to come from.
Provenza [pro'βenθa] *nf* Provence.
proverbial [proβer'βjal] *adj* proverbial; (*fig*) notorious.
proverbio [pro'βerβjo] *nm* proverb.
proveyendo [proβe'jendo] *etc vb V* **proveer**.
providencia [proβi'ðenθja] *nf* providence; (*previsión*) foresight; **~s** *nfpl* measures, steps.
provincia [pro'βinθja] *nf* province; (*ESP: ADMIN*) ≈ county, ≈ region (*Scot*); **un pueblo de ~(s)** a country town; *see boxed note*.

PROVINCIA

Spain is divided up into 55 administrative **provincias**, *including the islands and also the territories in North Africa. Each one has a "capital de provincia", which generally bears the same name. Provinces are grouped together by way of geographical, historical and cultural links into "comunidades autónomas". The term "comarca" (region) normally has purely geographical connotations, but in Catalonia designates administrative boundaries.*

provinciano, a [proβin'θjano, a] *adj* provincial; (*del campo*) country *cpd*.
proviniendo [proβi'njendo] *etc vb V* **provenir**.

provisión [proßi'sjon] *nf* provision; (*abastecimiento*) provision, supply; (*medida*) measure, step.
provisional [proßisjo'nal] *adj* provisional.
provisorio, a [proßi'sorjo, a] *adj* (*esp AM*) provisional.
provisto, a [pro'ßisto, a] *adj*: ~ **de** provided *o* supplied with; (*que tiene*) having, possessing.
provocación [proßoka'θjon] *nf* provocation.
provocador, a [proßoka'ðor, a] *adj* provocative, provoking.
provocar [proßo'kar] *vt* to provoke; (*alentar*) to tempt, invite; (*causar*) to bring about, lead to; (*promover*) to promote; (*estimular*) to rouse, stir, stimulate; (*protesta, explosión*) to cause, spark off; (*AM*): **¿te provoca un café?** would you like a coffee?
provocativo, a [proßoka'tißo, a] *adj* provocative.
provoque [pro'ßoke] *etc vb V* **provocar**.
proxeneta [prokse'neta] *nm/f* go-between; (*de prostitutas*) pimp/procuress.
próximamente [proksima'mente] *adv* shortly, soon.
proximidad [proksimi'ðað] *nf* closeness, proximity.
próximo, a ['proksimo, a] *adj* near, close; (*vecino*) neighbouring; (*el que viene*) next; **en fecha próxima** at an early date; **el mes** ~ next month.
proyección [projek'θjon] *nf* projection; (*CINE*) showing; (*diapositiva*) slide, transparency; (*influencia*) influence; **el tiempo de ~ es de 35 minutos** the film runs for 35 minutes.
proyectar [projek'tar] *vt* (*objeto*) to hurl, throw; (*luz*) to cast, shed; (*CINE*) to screen, show; (*planear*) to plan.
proyectil [projek'til] *nm* projectile, missile; ~ **(tele)dirigido** guided missile.
proyecto [pro'jekto] *nm* plan; (*idea*) project; (*estimación de costo*) detailed estimate; **tener algo en** ~ to be planning sth; ~ **de ley** (*POL*) bill.
proyector [projek'tor] *nm* (*CINE*) projector.
prudencia [pru'ðenθja] *nf* (*sabiduría*) wisdom, prudence; (*cautela*) care.
prudente [pru'ðente] *adj* sensible, wise, prudent; (*cauteloso*) careful.
prueba ['prweßa] *etc vb V* **probar** ♦ *nf* proof; (*ensayo*) test, trial; (*cantidad*) taste, sample; (*saboreo*) testing, sampling; (*de ropa*) fitting; (*DEPORTE*) event; **a** ~ on trial; (*COM*) on approval; **a ~ de** proof against; **a ~ de agua/fuego** waterproof/fireproof; ~ **de capacitación** (*COM*) proficiency test; ~ **de fuego** (*fig*) acid test; ~ **de vallas** hurdles; **someter a** ~ to put to the test; **¿tiene usted ~ de ello?** can you prove it?, do you have proof?
prurito [pru'rito] *nm* itch; (*de bebé*) nappy rash; (*anhelo*) urge.
psico... [siko] *pref* psycho...
psicoanálisis [sikoa'nalisis] *nm* psychoanalysis.
psicoanalista [sikoana'lista] *nm/f* psychoanalyst.
psicología [sikolo'xia] *nf* psychology.
psicológico, a [siko'loxiko, a] *adj* psychological.
psicólogo, a [si'koloɣo, a] *nm/f* psychologist.
psicópata [si'kopata] *nm/f* psychopath.
psicosis [si'kosis] *nf inv* psychosis.
psicosomático, a [sikoso'matiko, a] *adj* psychosomatic.
psicoterapia [sikote'rapja] *nf* psychotherapy.
psiquiatra [si'kjatra] *nm/f* psychiatrist.
psiquiátrico, a [si'kjatriko, a] *adj* psychiatric ♦ *nm* mental hospital.
psíquico, a ['sikiko, a] *adj* psychic(al).
PSOE [pe'soe] *nm abr* = *Partido Socialista Obrero Español*.
PSS *nf abr* (= *Prestación Social Sustitutoria*) *community service for conscientious objectors*.
Pta. *abr* (*GEO*: = *Punta*) Pt.
pta(s). *abr* = **peseta(s)**.
ptmo. *abr* (*COM*) = **préstamo**.
pts. *abr* = **pesetas**.
púa ['pua] *nf* sharp point; (*para guitarra*) plectrum; **alambre de ~s** barbed wire.
pub [puß/paß/paf] *nm* bar.
púber, a ['pußer, a] *adj, nm/f* adolescent.
pubertad [pußer'tað] *nf* puberty.
publicación [pußlika'θjon] *nf* publication.
publicar [pußli'kar] *vt* (*editar*) to publish; (*hacer público*) to publicize; (*divulgar*) to make public, divulge.
publicidad [pußliθi'ðað] *nf* publicity; (*COM*) advertising; **dar ~ a** to publicize, give publicity to; ~ **gráfica** display advertising; ~ **en el punto de venta** point-of-sale advertising.
publicitar [pußliθi'tar] *vt* to publicize.
publicitario, a [pußliθi'tarjo, a] *adj* publicity *cpd*; advertising *cpd*.
público, a ['pußliko, a] *adj* public ♦ *nm* public; (*TEAT etc*) audience; (*DEPORTE*) spectators *pl*, crowd; (*restaurantes etc*) clients *pl*; **el gran** ~ the general public; **hacer** ~ to publish; (*difundir*) to disclose;

~ **objetivo** (*COM*) target audience.
publique [pu'ßlike] *etc vb V* **publicar**.
pucherazo [putʃe'raθo] *nm* (*fraude*) electoral fiddle; **dar** ~ to rig an election.
puchero [pu'tʃero] *nm* (*CULIN*: *olla*) cooking pot; (: *guiso*) stew; **hacer ~s** to pout.
pudibundo, a [puði'ßundo, a] *adj* bashful.
púdico, a ['puðiko, a] *adj* modest; (*pudibundo*) bashful.
pudiendo [pu'ðjendo] *etc vb V* **poder**.
pudiente [pu'ðjente] *adj* (*opulento*) wealthy; (*poderoso*) powerful.
pudín [pu'ðin] *nm* pudding.
pudor [pu'ðor] *nm* modesty; (*vergüenza*) (sense of) shame.
pudoroso, a [puðo'roso, a] *adj* (*modesto*) modest; (*casto*) chaste.
pudrir [pu'ðrir] *vt* to rot; (*fam*) to upset, annoy; **~se** *vr* to rot, decay; (*fig*) to rot, languish.
pueblerino, a [pweßle'rino, a] *adj* (*lugareño*) small-town *cpd*; (*persona*) rustic, provincial ♦ *nm/f* (*aldeano*) country person.
pueblo ['pweßlo] *etc vb V* **poblar** ♦ *nm* people; (*nación*) nation; (*aldea*) village; (*plebe*) common people; (*población pequeña*) small town, country town.
pueda ['pweða] *etc vb V* **poder**.
puente ['pwente] *nm* (*gen*) bridge; (*NAUT*: *tb*: ~ **de mando**) bridge; (: *cubierta*) deck; ~ **aéreo** airlift; ~ **colgante** suspension bridge; ~ **levadizo** drawbridge; **hacer (el)** ~ (*fam*) to take a long weekend.
puenting ['pwentin] *nm* bungee jumping.
puerco, a ['pwerko, a] *adj* (*sucio*) dirty, filthy; (*obsceno*) disgusting ♦ *nm/f* pig/sow.
pueril [pwe'ril] *adj* childish.
puerro ['pwerro] *nm* leek.
puerta ['pwerta] *nf* door; (*de jardín*) gate; (*portal*) doorway; (*fig*) gateway; (*gol*) goal; (*INFORM*) port; **a la** ~ at the door; **a** ~ **cerrada** behind closed doors; ~ **corredera/giratoria** sliding/swing *o* revolving door; ~ **principal/trasera** *o* **de servicio** front/back door; ~ **(de transmisión en) paralelo/serie** (*INFORM*) parallel/serial port; **tomar la** ~ (*fam*) to leave.
puerto ['pwerto] *nm* (*tb INFORM*) port; (*de mar*) seaport; (*paso*) pass; (*fig*) haven, refuge; **llegar a** ~ (*fig*) to get over a difficulty.
Puerto Rico [pwerto'riko] *nm* Puerto Rico.
puertorriqueño, a [pwertorri'keɲo, a] *adj*, *nm/f* Puerto Rican.
pues [pwes] *adv* (*entonces*) then; (*¡entonces!*) well, well then; (*así que*) so ♦ *conj* (*porque*) since; ~ ... **no sé** well ... I don't know.
puesto, a ['pwesto, a] *pp de* **poner** ♦ *adj* dressed ♦ *nm* (*lugar, posición*) place; (*trabajo*) post, job; (*MIL*) post; (*COM*) stall; (*quiosco*) kiosk ♦ *conj*: ~ **que** since, as ♦ *nf* (*apuesta*) bet, stake; ~ **de mercado** market stall; ~ **de policía** police station; ~ **de socorro** first aid post; **puesta en escena** staging; **puesta en marcha** starting; **puesta del sol** sunset; **puesta a cero** (*INFORM*) reset.
pugna ['puɣna] *nf* battle, conflict.
pugnar [puɣ'nar] *vi* (*luchar*) to struggle, fight; (*pelear*) to fight.
puja ['puxa] *nf* (*esfuerzo*) attempt; (*en una subasta*) bid.
pujante [pu'xante] *adj* strong, vigorous.
pujar [pu'xar] *vt* (*precio*) to raise, push up ♦ *vi* (*en licitación*) to bid, bid up; (*fig*: *esforzarse*) to struggle, strain.
pulcro, a ['pulkro, a] *adj* neat, tidy.
pulga ['pulɣa] *nf* flea; **tener malas ~s** to be short-tempered.
pulgada [pul'ɣaða] *nf* inch.
pulgar [pul'ɣar] *nm* thumb.
pulgón [pul'ɣon] *nm* plant louse, greenfly.
pulir [pu'lir] *vt* to polish; (*alisar*) to smooth; (*fig*) to polish up, touch up.
pulla ['puʎa] *nf* cutting remark.
pulmón [pul'mon] *nm* lung; **a pleno** ~ (*respirar*) deeply; (*gritar*) at the top of one's voice; ~ **de acero** iron lung.
pulmonía [pulmo'nia] *nf* pneumonia.
pulpa ['pulpa] *nf* pulp; (*de fruta*) flesh, soft part.
pulpería [pulpe'ria] *nf* (*AM*) small grocery store.
púlpito ['pulpito] *nm* pulpit.
pulpo ['pulpo] *nm* octopus.
pulsación [pulsa'θjon] *nf* beat, pulsation; (*ANAT*) throb(bing); (*en máquina de escribir*) tap; (*de pianista, mecanógrafo*) touch; ~ **(de una tecla)** (*INFORM*) keystroke; ~ **doble** (*INFORM*) strikeover.
pulsador [pulsa'ðor] *nm* button, push button.
pulsar [pul'sar] *vt* (*tecla*) to touch, tap; (*MUS*) to play; (*botón*) to press, push ♦ *vi* to pulsate; (*latir*) to beat, throb.
pulsera [pul'sera] *nf* bracelet; **reloj de** ~ wristwatch.
pulso ['pulso] *nm* (*MED*) pulse; **hacer algo a** ~ to do sth unaided *o* by one's own efforts.
pulular [pulu'lar] *vi* (*estar plagado*): ~ **(de)** to swarm (with).

pulverice [pulβe'riθe] *etc vb V* **pulverizar**.
pulverizador [pulβeriθa'ðor] *nm* spray, spray gun.
pulverizar [pulβeri'θar] *vt* to pulverize; (*líquido*) to spray.
puna ['puna] *nf* (*AM MED*) mountain sickness.
punce ['punθe] *etc vb V* **punzar**.
punción [pun'θjon] *nf* (*MED*) puncture.
pundonor [pundo'nor] *nm* (*dignidad*) self-respect.
punición [puni'θjon] *nf* punishment.
punitivo, a [puni'tiβo, a] *adj* punitive.
punki ['punki] *adj, nm/f* punk.
punta ['punta] *nf* point, tip; (*extremidad*) end; (*promontorio*) headland; (*COSTURA*) corner; (*TEC*) small nail; (*fig*) touch, trace; **horas ~s** peak hours, rush hours; **sacar ~ a** to sharpen; **de ~** on end; **de ~ a ~** from one end to the other; **estar de ~** to be edgy; **ir de ~ en blanco** to be all dressed up to the nines; **tener algo en la ~ de la lengua** to have sth on the tip of one's tongue; **se le pusieron los pelos de ~** her hair stood on end.
puntada [pun'taða] *nf* (*COSTURA*) stitch.
puntal [pun'tal] *nm* prop, support.
puntapié [punta'pje], *pl* **puntapiés** *nm* kick; **echar a algn a ~s** to kick sb out.
punteado, a [punte'aðo, a] *adj* (*moteado*) dotted; (*diseño*) of dots ♦ *nm* (*MUS*) twang.
puntear [punte'ar] *vt* to tick, mark; (*MUS*) to pluck.
puntería [punte'ria] *nf* (*de arma*) aim, aiming; (*destreza*) marksmanship.
puntero, a [pun'tero, a] *adj* leading ♦ *nm* (*señal, INFORM*) pointer; (*dirigente*) leader.
puntiagudo, a [puntja'ɣuðo, a] *adj* sharp, pointed.
puntilla [pun'tiʎa] *nf* (*TEC*) tack, braid; (*COSTURA*) lace edging; **(andar) de ~s** (to walk) on tiptoe.
puntilloso, a [punti'ʎoso, a] *adj* (*pundonoroso*) punctilious; (*susceptible*) touchy.
punto ['punto] *nm* (*gen*) point; (*señal diminuta*) spot, dot; (*lugar*) spot, place; (*momento*) point, moment; (*en un examen*) mark; (*tema*) item; (*COSTURA*) stitch; (*INFORM*: *impresora*) pitch; (: *pantalla*) pixel; **a ~** ready; **estar a ~ de** to be on the point of *o* about to; **llegar a ~** to come just at the right moment; **al ~** at once; **en ~** on the dot; **estar en su ~** (*CULIN*) to be done to a turn; **hasta cierto ~** to some extent; **hacer ~** to knit; **poner un motor en ~** to tune an engine; **~ de partida/de congelación/de fusión** starting/freezing/melting point; **~ de vista** point of view, viewpoint; **~ muerto** dead centre; (*AUTO*) neutral (gear); **~s a tratar** matters to be discussed, agenda *sg*; **~ final** full stop; **dos ~s** colon; **~ y coma** semicolon; **~ acápite** (*AM*) full stop, new paragraph; **~ de interrogación** question mark; **~s suspensivos** suspension points; **~ de equilibrio/de pedido** (*COM*) breakeven/reorder point; **~ inicial** *o* **de partida** (*INFORM*) home; **~ de referencia/de venta** (*COM*) benchmark point/point-of-sale.
puntuación [puntwa'θjon] *nf* punctuation; (*puntos*: *en examen*) mark(s) (*pl*); (: *DEPORTE*) score.
puntual [pun'twal] *adj* (*a tiempo*) punctual; (*cálculo*) exact, accurate; (*informe*) reliable.
puntualice [puntwa'liθe] *etc vb V* **puntualizar**.
puntualidad [puntwali'ðað] *nf* punctuality; exactness, accuracy; reliability.
puntualizar [puntwali'θar] *vt* to fix, specify.
puntuar [pun'twar] *vt* (*LING, TIP*) to punctuate; (*examen*) to mark ♦ *vi* (*DEPORTE*) to score, count.
punzada [pun'θaða] *nf* (*puntura*) prick; (*MED*) stitch; (*dolor*) twinge (of pain).
punzante [pun'θante] *adj* (*dolor*) shooting, sharp; (*herramienta*) sharp; (*comentario*) biting.
punzar [pun'θar] *vt* to prick, pierce ♦ *vi* to shoot, stab.
punzón [pun'θon] *nm* (*TEC*) punch.
puñado [pu'ɲaðo] *nm* handful (*tb fig*); **a ~s** by handfuls.
puñal [pu'ɲal] *nm* dagger.
puñalada [puɲa'laða] *nf* stab.
puñeta [pu'ɲeta] *nf*: **¡~!, ¡qué ~(s)!** (*fam!*) hell!; **mandar a algn a hacer ~s** (*fam*) to tell sb to go to hell.
puñetazo [puɲe'taθo] *nm* punch.
puño ['puɲo] *nm* (*ANAT*) fist; (*cantidad*) fistful, handful; (*COSTURA*) cuff; (*de herramienta*) handle; **como un ~** (*verdad*) obvious; (*palpable*) tangible, visible; **de ~ y letra del poeta** in the poet's own handwriting.
pupila [pu'pila] *nf* (*ANAT*) pupil.
pupitre [pu'pitre] *nm* desk.
puré [pu're], *pl* **purés** *nm* puree; (*sopa*) (thick) soup; **~ de patatas** mashed potatoes; **estar hecho ~** (*fig*) to be knackered.

pureza [pu'reθa] *nf* purity.
purga ['purɣa] *nf* purge.
purgante [pur'ɣante] *adj, nm* purgative.
purgar [pur'ɣar] *vt* to purge; (*POL: depurar*) to purge, liquidate; ~**se** *vr* (*MED*) to take a purge.
purgatorio [purɣa'torjo] *nm* purgatory.
purgue ['purɣe] *etc vb V* **purgar**.
purificar [purifi'kar] *vt* to purify; (*refinar*) to refine.
purifique [puri'fike] *etc vb V* **purificar**.
puritano, a [puri'tano, a] *adj* (*actitud*) puritanical; (*iglesia, tradición*) puritan ♦ *nm/f* puritan.
puro, a ['puro, a] *adj* pure; (*depurado*) unadulterated; (*oro*) solid; (*cielo*) clear; (*verdad*) simple, plain ♦ *adv*: **de ~ cansado** out of sheer tiredness ♦ *nm* cigar; **por pura casualidad** by sheer chance.
púrpura ['purpura] *nf* purple.
purpúreo, a [pur'pureo, a] *adj* purple.
pus [pus] *nm* pus.
puse ['puse] *etc vb V* **poner**.
pústula ['pustula] *nf* pimple, sore.
puta ['puta] *nf* whore, prostitute.
putada [pu'taða] *nf* (*fam!*): **hacer una ~ a algn** to play a dirty trick on sb; **¡qué ~!** what a pain in the arse!(*!*).
putería [pute'ria] *nf* (*prostitución*) prostitution; (*prostíbulo*) brothel.
putrefacción [putrefak'θjon] *nf* rotting, putrefaction.
pútrido, a ['putriðo, a] *adj* rotten.
puzzle ['puθle] *nm* puzzle.
PVP *abr* (*ESP*: = *Precio Venta al Público*) ≈ RRP.
PYME *nf abr* (= *Pequeña y Mediana Empresa*) SME.

Q q

Q, q [ku] *nf* (*letra*) Q, q; **Q de Querido** Q for Queen.
q.e.g.e. *abr* (= *que en gloria esté*) R.I.P.
q.e.p.d. *abr* (= *que en paz descanse*) R.I.P.
q.e.s.m. *abr* (= *que estrecha su mano*) *courtesy formula*.
qm. *abr* = **quintal(es) métrico(s)**.
qts. *abr* = **quilates**.

PALABRA CLAVE

que [ke] *conj* **1** (*con oración subordinada: muchas veces no se traduce*) that; **dijo ~ vendría** he said (that) he would come; **espero ~ lo encuentres** I hope (that) you find it; **dile ~ me llame** ask him to call me; *V tb* **el**
2 (*en oración independiente*): **¡~ entre!** send him in; **¡que se mejore tu padre!** I hope your father gets better; **¡~ lo haga él!** he can do it!; (*orden*) get him to do it!
3 (*enfático*): **¿me quieres? – ¡~ sí!** do you love me? – of course!; **te digo ~ sí** I'm telling you
4 (*consecutivo: muchas veces no se traduce*) that; **es tan grande ~ no lo puedo levantar** it's so big (that) I can't lift it
5 (*comparaciones*) than; **yo ~ tú/él** if I were you/him; *V tb* **más; menos**
6 (*valor disyuntivo*): **~ le guste o no** whether he likes it or not; **~ venga o ~ no venga** whether he comes or not
7 (*porque*): **no puedo, ~ tengo ~ quedarme en casa** I can't, I've got to stay in
8: **siguió toca ~ toca** he kept on playing
♦ *pron* **1** (*cosa*) that, which; (+*prep*) which; **el sombrero ~ te compraste** the hat (that *o* which) you bought; **la cama en ~ dormí** the bed (that *o* which) I slept in; **el día (en) ~ ella nació** the day (when) she was born
2 (*persona: suj*) that, who; (: *objeto*) that, whom; **el amigo ~ me acompañó al museo** the friend that *o* who went to the museum with me: **la chica ~ invité** the girl (that *o* whom) I invited.

qué [ke] *adj* what?, which? ♦ *pron* what?; **¡~ divertido/asco!** how funny/revolting!; **¡~ día más espléndido!** what a glorious day!; **¿~ edad tienes?** how old are you?; **¿de ~ me hablas?** what are you saying to me?; **¿~ tal?** how are you?, how are things?; **¿~ hay (de nuevo)?** what's new?; **¿~ más?** anything else?
quebrada [ke'ßraða] *nf V* **quebrado**.
quebradero [keßra'ðero] *nm*: **~ de cabeza** headache, worry.
quebradizo, a [keßra'ðiθo, a] *adj* fragile; (*persona*) frail.
quebrado, a [ke'ßraðo, a] *adj* (*roto*) broken; (*terreno*) rough, uneven ♦ *nm/f* bankrupt ♦ *nm* (*MAT*) fraction ♦ *nf* ravine; **~ rehabilitado** discharged bankrupt.
quebradura [keßra'ðura] *nf* (*fisura*) fissure;

(*MED*) rupture.

quebrantamiento [keβranta'mjento] *nm* (*acto*) breaking; (*de ley*) violation; (*estado*) exhaustion.

quebrantar [keβran'tar] *vt* (*infringir*) to violate, transgress; **~se** *vr* (*persona*) to fail in health.

quebranto [ke'βranto] *nm* damage, harm; (*decaimiento*) exhaustion; (*dolor*) grief, pain.

quebrar [ke'βrar] *vt* to break, smash ♦ *vi* to go bankrupt; **~se** *vr* to break, get broken; (*MED*) to be ruptured.

quechua ['ketʃua] *adj, nm/f* Quechua.

queda ['keða] *nf*: **(toque de)** ~ curfew.

quedar [ke'ðar] *vi* to stay, remain; (*encontrarse*) to be; (*restar*) to remain, be left; **~se** *vr* to remain, stay (behind); ~ **en** (*acordar*) to agree on/to; (*acabar siendo*) to end up as; ~ **por hacer** to be still to be done; ~ **ciego/mudo** to be left blind/dumb; **no te queda bien ese vestido** that dress doesn't suit you; **quedamos a las seis** we agreed to meet at six; **eso queda muy lejos** that's a long way (away); **nos quedan 12 kms para llegar al pueblo** there are still 12 kms before we get to the village; **no queda otra** there's no alternative; **~se (con) algo** to keep sth; **~se con algn** (*fam*) to swindle sb; **~se en nada** to come to nothing *o* nought; **~se sin** to run out of.

quedo, a ['keðo, a] *adj* still ♦ *adv* softly, gently.

quehacer [kea'θer] *nm* task, job; **~es (domésticos)** household chores.

queja ['kexa] *nf* complaint.

quejarse [ke'xarse] *vr* (*enfermo*) to moan, groan; (*protestar*) to complain; ~ **de que** ... to complain (about the fact) that ....

quejica [ke'xika] *adj* grumpy, complaining ♦ *nm/f* grumbler, whinger.

quejido [ke'xiðo] *nm* moan.

quejoso, a [ke'xoso, a] *adj* complaining.

quema ['kema] *nf* fire; (*combustión*) burning.

quemado, a [ke'maðo, a] *adj* burnt; (*irritado*) annoyed.

quemadura [kema'ðura] *nf* burn, scald; (*de sol*) sunburn; (*de fusible*) blow-out.

quemar [ke'mar] *vt* to burn; (*fig*: *malgastar*) to burn up, squander; (*COM*: *precios*) to slash, cut; (*fastidiar*) to annoy, bug ♦ *vi* to be burning hot; **~se** *vr* (*consumirse*) to burn (up); (*del sol*) to get sunburnt.

quemarropa [kema'rropa]: **a** ~ *adv* point-blank.

quemazón [kema'θon] *nf* burn; (*calor*) intense heat; (*sensación*) itch.

quena ['kena] *nf* (*AM*) Indian flute.

quepo ['kepo] *etc vb V* **caber.**

querella [ke'reʎa] *nf* (*JUR*) charge; (*disputa*) dispute.

querellarse [kere'ʎarse] *vr* to file a complaint.

querencia [ke'renθja] *nf* (*ZOOL*) homing instinct; (*fig*) homesickness.

PALABRA CLAVE

querer [ke'rer] *vt* **1** (*desear*) to want; **quiero más dinero** I want more money; **quisiera** *o* **querría un té** I'd like a tea; **quiero ayudar/que vayas** I want to help/you to go; **como Vd quiera** as you wish, as you please; **ven cuando quieras** come when you like; **lo hizo sin** ~ he didn't mean to do it; **no quiero** I don't want to; **le pedí que me dejara ir pero no quiso** I asked him to let me go but he refused

2 (*preguntas*: *para pedir u ofrecer algo*): **¿quiere abrir la ventana?** could you open the window?; **¿quieres echarme una mano?** can you give me a hand?; **¿quiere un café?** would you like some coffee?

3 (*amar*) to love; (*tener cariño a*) to be fond of; **quiere mucho a sus hijos** he's very fond of his children

4 (*requerir*): **esta planta quiere más luz** this plant needs more light

5: ~ **decir** to mean; **¿qué quieres decir?** what do you mean?

querido, a [ke'riðo, a] *adj* dear ♦ *nm/f* darling; (*amante*) lover; **nuestra querida patria** our beloved country.

querosén [kero'sen], **querosene** [kero'sene] *nm* (*AM*) kerosene, paraffin.

querré [ke'rre] *etc vb V* **querer.**

quesería [kese'ria] *nf* dairy; (*fábrica*) cheese factory.

quesero, a [ke'sero, a] *adj*: **la industria quesera** the cheese industry ♦ *nm/f* cheesemaker ♦ *nf* cheese dish.

queso ['keso] *nm* cheese; ~ **rallado** grated cheese; ~ **crema** cream cheese; **dárselas con** ~ **a algn** (*fam*) to take sb in.

quetzal [ket'sal] *nm monetary unit of Guatemala.*

quicio ['kiθjo] *nm* hinge; **estar fuera de** ~ to be beside o.s.; **sacar a algn de** ~ to drive sb up the wall.

quid [kið] *nm* gist, crux; **dar en el** ~ to hit the nail on the head.

quiebra ['kjeβra] *nf* break, split; (*COM*) bankruptcy; (*ECON*) slump.

quiebro ['kjeβro] *etc vb V* **quebrar** ♦ *nm* (*del*

cuerpo) swerve.
quien [kjen] *pron relativo* (*suj*) who; (*complemento*) whom; (*indefinido*): ~ **dice eso es tonto** whoever says that is a fool; **hay ~ piensa que** there are those who think that; **no hay ~ lo haga** no-one will do it; ~ **más,** ~ **menos tiene sus problemas** everybody has problems.
quién [kjen] *pron interrogativo* who; (*complemento*) whom; **¿~ es?** who is it?, who's there?; (*TELEC*) who's calling?
quienquiera [kjen'kjera] (*pl* **quienesquiera**) *pron* whoever.
quiera ['kjera] *etc vb V* **querer**.
quieto, a ['kjeto, a] *adj* still; (*carácter*) placid; **¡estáte ~!** keep still!
quietud [kje'tuð] *nf* stillness.
quijada [ki'xaða] *nf* jaw, jawbone.
quijote [ki'xote] *nm* dreamer; **Don Q~** Don Quixote.
quil. *abr* = **quilates**.
quilate [ki'late] *nm* carat.
quilla ['kiʎa] *nf* keel.
quilo... ['kilo] = **kilo...**
quimera [ki'mera] *nf* (*sueño*) pipe dream.
quimérico, a [ki'meriko, a] *adj* fantastic.
químico, a ['kimiko, a] *adj* chemical ♦ *nm/f* chemist ♦ *nf* chemistry.
quimioterapia [kimiote'rapia] *nf* chemotherapy.
quina ['kina] *nf* quinine.
quincallería [kinkaʎe'ria] *nf* ironmonger's (shop), hardware store (*US*).
quince ['kinθe] *num* fifteen; ~ **días** a fortnight.
quinceañero, a [kinθea'ɲero, a] *adj* fifteen-year-old; (*adolescente*) teenage ♦ *nm/f* fifteen-year-old; (*adolescente*) teenager.
quincena [kin'θena] *nf* fortnight; (*pago*) fortnightly pay.
quincenal [kinθe'nal] *adj* fortnightly.
quincuagésimo, a [kinkwa'xesimo, a] *num* fiftieth.
quiniela [ki'njela] *nf* football pools *pl*; **~s** *nfpl* pools coupon *sg*.
quinientos, as [ki'njentos, as] *num* five hundred.
quinina [ki'nina] *nf* quinine.
quinqué [kin'ke] *nm* oil lamp.
quinquenal [kinke'nal] *adj* five-year *cpd*.
quinqui ['kinki] *nm* delinquent.
quinta ['kinta] *nf V* **quinto**.
quintaesencia [kintae'senθja] *nf* quintessence.
quintal [kin'tal] *nm* (*Castilla: peso*) = *46kg*; ~ **métrico** = *100kg*.
quinteto [kin'teto] *nm* quintet.
quinto, a ['kinto, a] *adj* fifth ♦ *nm* (*MIL*) conscript, draftee ♦ *nf* country house; (*MIL*) call-up, draft.
quíntuplo, a ['kintuplo, a] *adj* quintuple, five-fold.
quiosco ['kjosko] *nm* (*de música*) bandstand; (*de periódicos*) news stand (*also selling sweets, cigarettes etc*).
quirófano [ki'rofano] *nm* operating theatre.
quiromancia [kiro'manθja] *nf* palmistry.
quirúrgico, a [ki'rurxiko, a] *adj* surgical.
quise ['kise] *etc vb V* **querer**.
quisque ['kiske] *pron* (*fam*): **cada** *o* **todo** ~ (absolutely) everyone.
quisquilloso [kiski'ʎoso, a] *adj* (*susceptible*) touchy; (*meticuloso*) pernickety.
quiste ['kiste] *nm* cyst.
quitaesmalte [kitaes'malte] *nm* nail polish remover.
quitamanchas [kita'mantʃas] *nm inv* stain remover.
quitanieves [kita'njeβes] *nm inv* snowplough (*BRIT*), snowplow (*US*).
quitar [ki'tar] *vt* to remove, take away; (*ropa*) to take off; (*dolor*) to relieve; (*vida*) to take; (*valor*) to reduce; (*hurtar*) to remove, steal ♦ *vi*: **¡quita de ahí!** get away!; **~se** *vr* to withdraw; (*mancha*) to come off *o* out; (*ropa*) to take off; **me quita mucho tiempo** it takes up a lot of my time; **el café me quita el sueño** coffee stops me sleeping; ~ **de en medio a algn** to get rid of sb; **~se algo de encima** to get rid of sth; **~se del tabaco** to give up smoking; **se quitó el sombrero** he took off his hat.
quitasol [kita'sol] *nm* sunshade (*BRIT*), parasol.
quite ['kite] *nm* (*esgrima*) parry; (*evasión*) dodge; **estar al** ~ to be ready to go to sb's aid.
Quito ['kito] *n* Quito.
quizá(s) [ki'θa(s)] *adv* perhaps, maybe.
quórum ['kworum] *pl* **quórums** ['kworum] *nm* quorum.

Rr

R, r ['erre] *nf* (*letra*) R, r; **R de Ramón** R for Robert (*BRIT*) *o* Roger (*US*).
R. *abr* = **Remite, Remitente.**
rabadilla [raβa'ðiʎa] *nf* base of the spine.
rábano ['raβano] *nm* radish; **me importa un ~** I don't give a damn.
rabia ['raβja] *nf* (*MED*) rabies *sg*; (*fig*: *ira*) fury, rage; **¡qué ~!** isn't it infuriating!; **me da ~** it maddens me; **tener ~ a algn** to have a grudge against sb.
rabiar [ra'βjar] *vi* to have rabies; to rage, be furious; **~ por algo** to long for sth.
rabieta [ra'βjeta] *nf* tantrum, fit of temper.
rabino [ra'βino] *nm* rabbi.
rabioso, a [ra'βjoso, a] *adj* rabid; (*fig*) furious.
rabo ['raβo] *nm* tail.
racanear [rakane'ar] *vi* (*fam*) to skive.
rácano ['rakano] *nm* (*fam*) slacker, skiver.
RACE *nm abr* (= *Real Automóvil Club de España*) ≈ RAC.
racha ['ratʃa] *nf* gust of wind; (*serie*) string, series; **buena/mala ~** spell of good/bad luck.
racial [ra'θjal] *adj* racial, race *cpd*.
racimo [ra'θimo] *nm* bunch.
raciocinio [raθjo'θinjo] *nm* reason; (*razonamiento*) reasoning.
ración [ra'θjon] *nf* portion; **raciones** *nfpl* rations.
racional [raθjo'nal] *adj* (*razonable*) reasonable; (*lógico*) rational.
racionalice [raθjona'liθe] *etc vb V* **racionalizar**.
racionalizar [raθjonali'θar] *vt* to rationalize; (*COM*) to streamline.
racionamiento [raθjona'mjento] *nm* (*COM*) rationing.
racionar [raθjo'nar] *vt* to ration (out).
racismo [ra'θismo] *nm* racialism, racism.
racista [ra'θista] *adj, nm/f* racist.
radar [ra'ðar] *nm* radar.
radiación [raðja'θjon] *nf* radiation; (*TELEC*) broadcasting.
radiactividad [raðjaktiβi'ðað] *nf* radioactivity.
radiado, a [ra'ðjaðo, a] *adj* radio *cpd*, broadcast.
radiador [raðja'ðor] *nm* radiator.
radial [ra'ðjal] *adj* (*AM*) radio *cpd*.
radiante [ra'ðjante] *adj* radiant.
radiar [ra'ðjar] *vt* to radiate; (*TELEC*) to broadcast; (*MED*) to give radiotherapy to.
radical [raði'kal] *adj, nm/f* radical ♦ *nm* (*LING*) root; (*MAT*) square-root sign.
radicar [raði'kar] *vi* to take root; **~ en** to lie *o* consist in; **~se** *vr* to establish o.s., put down (one's) roots.
radio ['raðjo] *nf* radio; (*aparato*) radio (set) ♦ *nm* (*MAT*) radius; (*AM*) radio; (*QUÍMICA*) radium; **~ de acción** extent of one's authority, sphere of influence.
radioactivo, a [raðjoak'tiβo, a] *adj* radioactive.
radioaficionado, a [raðjoafiθjo'naðo, a] *nm/f* radio ham.
radiocasete [raðjoka'sete] *nm* radiocassette (player).
radiodifusión [raðjodifu'sjon] *nf* broadcasting.
radioemisora [raðjoemi'sora] *nf* transmitter, radio station.
radiofónico, a [raðjo'foniko, a] *adj* radio *cpd*.
radiografía [raðjoɣra'fia] *nf* X-ray.
radiólogo, a [ra'ðjoloɣo, a] *nm/f* radiologist.
radionovela [raðjono'βela] *nf* radio series.
radiotaxi [raðjo'taksi] *nm* radio taxi.
radioterapia [raðjote'rapja] *nf* radiotherapy.
radioyente [raðjo'jente] *nm/f* listener.
radique [ra'ðike] *etc vb V* **radicar**.
RAE *nf abr* = **Real Academia Española.**
ráfaga ['rafaɣa] *nf* gust; (*de luz*) flash; (*de tiros*) burst.
raído, a [ra'iðo, a] *adj* (*ropa*) threadbare; (*persona*) shabby.
raigambre [rai'ɣambre] *nf* (*BOT*) roots *pl*; (*fig*) tradition.
raíz [ra'iθ] (*pl* **raíces**) *nf* root; **~ cuadrada** square root; **a ~ de** as a result of; (*después de*) immediately after.
raja ['raxa] *nf* (*de melón etc*) slice; (*hendedura*) slit, split; (*grieta*) crack.
rajar [ra'xar] *vt* to split; (*fam*) to slash; **~se** *vr* to split, crack; **~se de** to back out of.
rajatabla [raxa'taβla]: **a ~** *adv* (*estrictamente*) strictly, to the letter.
ralea [ra'lea] *nf* (*pey*) kind, sort.
ralenti [ra'lenti] *nm* (*TV etc*) slow motion; (*AUTO*) neutral; **al ~** in slow motion; (*AUTO*) ticking over.
rallador [raʎa'ðor] *nm* grater.
rallar [ra'ʎar] *vt* to grate.

ralo, a ['ralo, a] *adj* thin, sparse.
RAM [ram] *nf abr* (= *random access memory*) RAM.
rama ['rama] *nf* bough, branch; **andarse por las ~s** (*fig, fam*) to beat about the bush.
ramaje [ra'maje] *nm* branches *pl*, foliage.
ramal [ra'mal] *nm* (*de cuerda*) strand; (*FERRO*) branch line; (*AUTO*) branch (road).
rambla ['rambla] *nf* (*avenida*) avenue.
ramera [ra'mera] *nf* whore, hooker (*US*).
ramificación [ramifika'θjon] *nf* ramification.
ramificarse [ramifi'karse] *vr* to branch out.
ramifique [rami'fike] *etc vb V* **ramificarse**.
ramillete [rami'ʎete] *nm* bouquet; (*fig*) select group.
ramo ['ramo] *nm* branch, twig; (*sección*) department, section; (*sector*) field, sector.
rampa ['rampa] *nf* ramp.
ramplón, ona [ram'plon, ona] *adj* uncouth, coarse.
rana ['rana] *nf* frog; **salto de ~** leapfrog; **cuando las ~s críen pelos** when pigs fly.
ranchero [ran'tʃero] *nm* (*AM*) rancher; (*pequeño propietario*) smallholder.
rancho ['rantʃo] *nm* (*MIL*) food; (*AM*: *grande*) ranch; (: *pequeño*) small farm.
rancio, a ['ranθjo, a] *adj* (*comestibles*) stale, rancid; (*vino*) aged, mellow; (*fig*) ancient.
rango ['rango] *nm* rank; (*prestigio*) standing.
ranura [ra'nura] *nf* groove; (*de teléfono etc*) slot; **~ de expansión** (*INFORM*) expansion slot.
rap [rap] *nm* (*MUS*) rap.
rapacidad [rapaθi'ðað] *nf* rapacity.
rapapolvo [rapa'polβo] *nm*: **echar un ~ a algn** to give sb a ticking off.
rapar [ra'par] *vt* to shave; (*los cabellos*) to crop.
rapaz [ra'paθ] *adj* (*ZOOL*) predatory ♦ *nm/f* (*f*: **rapaza**) young boy/girl.
rape ['rape] *nm* quick shave; (*pez*) angler (fish); **al ~** cropped.
rapé [ra'pe] *nm* snuff.
rapidez [rapi'ðeθ] *nf* speed, rapidity.
rápido, a ['rapiðo, a] *adj* fast, quick ♦ *adv* quickly ♦ *nm* (*FERRO*) express; **~s** *nmpl* rapids.
rapiña [ra'piɲa] *nm* robbery; **ave de ~** bird of prey.
rap(p)el [ra'pel] *nm* (*DEPORTE*) abseiling.
raptar [rap'tar] *vt* to kidnap.
rapto ['rapto] *nm* kidnapping; (*impulso*) sudden impulse; (*éxtasis*) ecstasy, rapture.
raqueta [ra'keta] *nf* racquet.
raquítico, a [ra'kitiko, a] *adj* stunted; (*fig*) poor, inadequate.
raquitismo [raki'tismo] *nm* rickets *sg*.
rareza [ra'reθa] *nf* rarity; (*fig*) eccentricity.
raro, a ['raro, a] *adj* (*poco común*) rare; (*extraño*) odd, strange; (*excepcional*) remarkable; **¡qué ~!** how (very) odd!; **¡(qué) cosa más rara!** how strange!
ras [ras] *nm*: **a ~ de** level with; **a ~ de tierra** at ground level.
rasar [ra'sar] *vt* to level.
rascacielos [raska'θjelos] *nm inv* skyscraper.
rascar [ras'kar] *vt* (*con las uñas etc*) to scratch; (*raspar*) to scrape; **~se** *vr* to scratch (o.s.).
rasgar [ras'ɣar] *vt* to tear, rip (up).
rasgo ['rasɣo] *nm* (*con pluma*) stroke; **~s** *nmpl* features, characteristics; **a grandes ~s** in outline, broadly.
rasgue ['rasɣe] *etc vb V* **rasgar**.
rasguear [rasɣe'ar] *vt* (*MUS*) to strum.
rasguñar [rasɣu'ɲar] *vt* to scratch; (*bosquejar*) to sketch.
rasguño [ras'ɣuɲo] *nm* scratch.
raso, a ['raso, a] *adj* (*liso*) flat, level; (*a baja altura*) very low ♦ *nm* satin; (*campo llano*) flat country; **cielo ~** clear sky; **al ~** in the open.
raspado [ras'paðo] *nm* (*MED*) scrape.
raspador [raspa'ðor] *nm* scraper.
raspadura [raspa'ðura] *nf* (*acto*) scrape, scraping; (*marca*) scratch; **~s** *nfpl* scrapings.
raspar [ras'par] *vt* to scrape; (*arañar*) to scratch; (*limar*) to file ♦ *vi* (*manos*) to be rough; (*vino*) to be sharp, have a rough taste.
rasque ['raske] *etc vb V* **rascar**.
rastra ['rastra] *nf*: **a ~s** by dragging; (*fig*) unwillingly.
rastreador [rastrea'ðor] *nm* tracker; **~ de minas** minesweeper.
rastrear [rastre'ar] *vt* (*seguir*) to track; (*minas*) to sweep.
rastrero, a [ras'trero, a] *adj* (*BOT, ZOOL*) creeping; (*fig*) despicable, mean.
rastrillar [rastri'ʎar] *vt* to rake.
rastrillo [ras'triʎo] *nm* rake; (*AM*) safety razor.
rastro ['rastro] *nm* (*AGR*) rake; (*pista*) track, trail; (*vestigio*) trace; (*mercado*) fleamarket; **el R~** *the Madrid fleamarket*; **perder el ~** to lose the scent; **desaparecer sin ~** to vanish without

trace.
rastrojo [ras'troxo] *nm* stubble.
rasurador [rasura'ðor] *nm*, (*AM*) **rasuradora** [rasura'ðora] *nf* electric shaver *o* razor.
rasurarse [rasu'rarse] *vr* to shave.
rata ['rata] *nf* rat.
ratear [rate'ar] *vt* (*robar*) to steal.
ratero, a [ra'tero, a] *adj* light-fingered ♦ *nm/f* pickpocket; (*AM*: *de casas*) burglar.
ratificar [ratifi'kar] *vt* to ratify.
ratifique [rati'fike] *etc vb V* **ratificar**.
rato ['rato] *nm* while, short time; **a ~s** from time to time; **al poco ~** shortly after, soon afterwards; **~s libres** *o* **de ocio** leisure *sg*, spare *o* free time *sg*; **hay para ~** there's still a long way to go; **pasar el ~** to kill time; **pasar un buen/mal ~** to have a good/rough time.
ratón [ra'ton] *nm* (*tb INFORM*) mouse.
ratonera [rato'nera] *nf* mousetrap.
RAU *nf abr* (= *República Árabe Unida*) UAR.
raudal [rau'ðal] *nm* torrent; **a ~es** in abundance; **entrar a ~es** to pour in.
raya ['raja] *nf* line; (*marca*) scratch; (*en tela*) stripe; (*TIP*) hyphen; (*de pelo*) parting; (*límite*) boundary; (*pez*) ray; **a ~s** striped; **pasarse de la ~** to overstep the mark; **tener a ~** to keep in check.
rayado, a [ra'jaðo, a] *adj* (*papel*) ruled; (*tela, diseño*) striped.
rayar [ra'jar] *vt* to line; to scratch; (*subrayar*) to underline ♦ *vi*: **~ en** *o* **con** to border on; **al ~ el alba** at first light.
rayo ['rajo] *nm* (*del sol*) ray, beam; (*de luz*) shaft; (*en una tormenta*) (flash of) lightning; **~ solar** *o* **de sol** sunbeam; **~s infrarrojos** infrared rays; **~s X** X-rays; **como un ~** like a shot; **la noticia cayó como un ~** the news was a bombshell; **pasar como un ~** to flash past.
raza ['raθa] *nf* race; (*de animal*) breed; **~ humana** human race; **de pura ~** (*caballo*) thoroughbred; (*perro etc*) pedigree.
razón [ra'θon] *nf* reason; (*justicia*) right, justice; (*razonamiento*) reasoning; (*motivo*) reason, motive; (*proporción*) rate; (*MAT*) ratio; **a ~ de 10 cada día** at the rate of 10 a day; "**~: ...**" "inquiries to ..."; **en ~ de** with regard to; **perder la ~** to go out of one's mind; **dar ~ a algn** to agree that sb is right; **dar ~ de** to give an account of, report on; **tener/no tener ~** to be right/wrong; **~ directa/inversa** direct/inverse proportion; **~ de ser** raison d'être.
razonable [raθo'naβle] *adj* reasonable; (*justo, moderado*) fair.
razonamiento [raθona'mjento] *nm* (*juicio*) judgement; (*argumento*) reasoning.
razonar [raθo'nar] *vt, vi* to reason, argue.
RDA *nf* = **República Democrática Alemana**.
Rdo. *abr* (*REL*: = *Reverendo*) Rev.
RDSI *nf abr* (= *Red Digital de Servicios Integrados*) ISDN.
re [re] *nm* (*MUS*) D.
reabierto [rea'βjerto] *pp de* **reabrir**.
reabrir [rea'βrir] *vt*, **~se** *vr* to reopen.
reacción [reak'θjon] *nf* reaction; **avión a ~** jet plane; **~ en cadena** chain reaction.
reaccionar [reakθjo'nar] *vi* to react.
reaccionario, a [reakθjo'narjo, a] *adj* reactionary.
reacio, a [re'aθjo, a] *adj* stubborn; **ser** *o* **estar ~ a** to be opposed to.
reactivar [reakti'βar] *vt* to reactivate; **~se** *vr* (*economía*) to be on the upturn.
reactor [reak'tor] *nm* reactor; (*avión*) jet plane; **~ nuclear** nuclear reactor.
readaptación [reaðapta'θjon] *nf*: **~ profesional** industrial retraining.
readmitir [reaðmi'tir] *vt* to readmit.
reafirmar [reafir'mar] *vt* to reaffirm.
reagrupar [reaɤru'par] *vt* to regroup.
reajustar [reaxus'tar] *vt* (*INFORM*) to reset.
reajuste [rea'xuste] *nm* readjustment; **~ salarial** wage increase; **~ de plantilla** rationalization.
real [re'al] *adj* real; (*del rey, fig*) royal; (*espléndido*) grand ♦ *nm* (*de feria*) fairground; **la R~ Academia Española** *see boxed note*.

REAL ACADEMIA ESPAÑOLA

The **Real Academia Española** *(RAE), dating back to 1713, is the regulatory body for the Spanish language in Spain. It produces its own dictionaries and grammars, and is considered to be the leading authority on the language, although it has been criticized in the past for being too conservative. In 1994, along with the Spanish American "academias", it approved a fundamental change to the Spanish alphabet: "ch" and "ll" are no longer treated as separate letters, although. "ñ" continues to follow "n" as a new letter.*

realce [re'alθe] *etc vb V* **realzar** ♦ *nm* (*TEC*) embossing; **poner de ~** to emphasize.
real-decreto [re'alde'kreto] (*pl* **~es-~s**) *nm* royal decree.
realeza [rea'leθa] *nf* royalty.
realice [rea'liθe] *etc vb V* **realizar**.

realidad [reali'ðað] *nf* reality; (*verdad*) truth; ~ **virtual** virtual reality; **en** ~ in fact.
realismo [rea'lismo] *nm* realism.
realista [rea'lista] *nm/f* realist.
realización [realiθa'θjon] *nf* fulfilment, realization; (*COM*) selling up (*BRIT*), conversion into money (*US*); ~ **de plusvalías** profit-taking.
realizador, a [realiθa'ðor, a] *nm/f* (*TV etc*) producer.
realizar [reali'θar] *vt* (*objetivo*) to achieve; (*plan*) to carry out; (*viaje*) to make, undertake; (*COM*) to realize; ~**se** *vr* to come about, come true; ~**se como persona** to fulfil one's aims in life.
realmente [real'mente] *adv* really.
realojar [realo'xar] *vt* to rehouse.
realquilar [realki'lar] *vt* (*subarrendar*) to sublet; (*alquilar de nuevo*) to relet.
realzar [real'θar] *vt* (*TEC*) to raise; (*embellecer*) to enhance; (*acentuar*) to highlight.
reanimar [reani'mar] *vt* to revive; (*alentar*) to encourage; ~**se** *vr* to revive.
reanudar [reanu'ðar] *vt* (*renovar*) to renew; (*historia, viaje*) to resume.
reaparición [reapari'θjon] *nf* reappearance; (*vuelta*) return.
reapertura [reaper'tura] *nf* reopening.
rearme [re'arme] *nm* rearmament.
reata [re'ata] *nf* (*AM*) lasso.
reavivar [reaßi'ßar] *vt* (*persona*) to revive; (*fig*) to rekindle.
rebaja [re'ßaxa] *nf* reduction, lowering; (*COM*) discount; **"grandes ~s"** "big reductions", "sale".
rebajar [reßa'xar] *vt* (*bajar*) to lower; (*reducir*) to reduce; (*precio*) to cut; (*disminuir*) to lessen; (*humillar*) to humble; ~**se** *vr*: ~**se a hacer algo** to stoop to doing sth.
rebanada [reßa'naða] *nf* slice.
rebañar [reßa'ɲar] *vt* to scrape clean.
rebaño [re'ßaɲo] *nm* herd; (*de ovejas*) flock.
rebasar [reßa'sar] *vt* (*tb*: ~ **de**) to exceed; (*AUTO*) to overtake.
rebatir [reßa'tir] *vt* to refute; (*rebajar*) to reduce; (*ataque*) to repel.
rebato [re'ßato] *nm* alarm; (*ataque*) surprise attack; **llamar** *o* **tocar a** ~ (*fig*) to sound the alarm.
rebeca [re'ßeka] *nf* cardigan.
rebelarse [reße'larse] *vr* to rebel, revolt.
rebelde [re'ßelde] *adj* rebellious; (*niño*) unruly ♦ *nm/f* rebel; **ser** ~ **a** to be in revolt against, rebel against.
rebeldía [reßel'dia] *nf* rebelliousness; (*desobediencia*) disobedience; (*JUR*) default.
rebelión [reße'ljon] *nf* rebellion.
rebenque [re'ßenke] *nm* (*AM*) whip.
reblandecer [reßlande'θer] *vt* to soften.
reblandezca [reßlan'deθka] *etc vb V* **reblandecer**.
rebobinar [reßoßi'nar] *vt* to rewind.
reboce [re'ßoθe] *etc vb V* **rebozar**.
rebosante [reßo'sante] *adj*: ~ **de** (*fig*) brimming *o* overflowing with.
rebosar [reßo'sar] *vi* to overflow; (*abundar*) to abound, be plentiful; ~ **de salud** to be bursting *o* brimming with health.
rebotar [reßo'tar] *vt* to bounce; (*rechazar*) to repel.
rebote [re'ßote] *nm* rebound; **de** ~ on the rebound.
rebozado, a [reßo'θaðo, a] *adj* (*CULIN*) fried in batter *o* breadcrumbs *o* flour.
rebozar [reßo'θar] *vt* to wrap up; (*CULIN*) to fry in batter *etc*.
rebozo [reßo'θo] *nm*: **sin** ~ openly.
rebuscado, a [reßus'kaðo, a] *adj* affected.
rebuscar [reßus'kar] *vi* (*en bolsillo, cajón*) to fish; (*en habitación*) to search high and low.
rebuznar [reßuθ'nar] *vi* to bray.
recabar [reka'ßar] *vt* (*obtener*) to manage to get; ~ **fondos** to collect money.
recadero [reka'ðero] *nm* messenger.
recado [re'kaðo] *nm* message; **dejar/tomar un** ~ (*TELEC*) to leave/take a message.
recaer [reka'er] *vi* to relapse; ~ **en** to fall to *o* on; (*criminal etc*) to fall back into, relapse into; (*premio*) to go to.
recaída [reka'iða] *nf* relapse.
recaiga [re'kaiɣa] *etc vb V* **recaer**.
recalcar [rekal'kar] *vt* (*fig*) to stress, emphasize.
recalcitrante [rekalθi'trante] *adj* recalcitrant.
recalentamiento [rekalenta'mjento] *nm*: ~ **global** global warming.
recalentar [rekalen'tar] *vt* (*comida*) to warm up, reheat; (*demasiado*) to overheat; ~**se** *vr* to overheat, get too hot.
recaliente [reka'ljente] *etc vb V* **recalentar**.
recalque [re'kalke] *etc vb V* **recalcar**.
recámara [re'kamara] *nf* side room; (*AM*) bedroom.
recamarera [rekama'rera] *nf* (*AM*) maid.
recambio [re'kambjo] *nm* spare; (*de pluma*) refill; **piezas de** ~ spares.
recapacitar [rekapaθi'tar] *vi* to reflect.
recapitular [rekapitu'lar] *vt* to recap.
recargable [rekar'ɣaßle] *adj* (*batería, pila*)

rechargeable; (*mechero, pluma*) refillable.
recargado, a [rekar'ɣaðo, a] *adj* overloaded; (*exagerado*) over-elaborate.
recargar [rekar'ɣar] *vt* to overload; (*batería*) to recharge; (*mechero, pluma*) to refill.
recargo [re'karɣo] *nm* surcharge; (*aumento*) increase.
recargue [re'karɣe] *etc vb V* **recargar**.
recatado, a [reka'taðo, a] *adj* (*modesto*) modest, demure; (*prudente*) cautious.
recato [re'kato] *nm* (*modestia*) modesty, demureness; (*cautela*) caution.
recauchutado, a [rekautʃu'taðo, a] *adj* remould *cpd*.
recaudación [rekauða'θjon] *nf* (*acción*) collection; (*cantidad*) takings *pl*; (*en deporte*) gate; (*oficina*) tax office.
recaudador, a [rekauða'ðor, a] *nm/f* tax collector.
recaudar [rekau'ðar] *vt* to collect.
recaudo [re'kauðo] *nm* (*impuestos*) collection; (*JUR*) surety; **estar a buen ~** to be in safekeeping; **poner algo a buen ~** to put sth in a safe place.
recayendo [reka'jendo] *etc vb V* **recaer**.
rece ['reθe] *etc vb V* **rezar**.
recelar [reθe'lar] *vt*: **~ que** (*sospechar*) to suspect that; (*temer*) to fear that ♦ *vi*: **~(se) de** to distrust.
recelo [re'θelo] *nm* distrust, suspicion.
receloso, a [reθe'loso, a] *adj* distrustful, suspicious.
recepción [reθep'θjon] *nf* reception; (*acto de recibir*) receipt.
recepcionista [reθepθjo'nista] *nm/f* receptionist.
receptáculo [reθep'takulo] *nm* receptacle.
receptivo, a [reθep'tiβo, a] *adj* receptive.
receptor, a [reθep'tor, a] *nm/f* recipient ♦ *nm* (*TELEC*) receiver; **descolgar el ~** to pick up the receiver.
recesión [reθe'sjon] *nf* (*COM*) recession.
receta [re'θeta] *nf* (*CULIN*) recipe; (*MED*) prescription.
recetar [reθe'tar] *vt* to prescribe.
rechace [re'tʃaθe] *etc vb V* **rechazar**.
rechazar [retʃa'θar] *vt* to repel, drive back; (*idea*) to reject; (*oferta*) to turn down.
rechazo [re'tʃaθo] *nm* (*de fusil*) recoil; (*rebote*) rebound; (*negación*) rebuff.
rechifla [re'tʃifla] *nf* hissing, booing; (*fig*) derision.
rechinar [retʃi'nar] *vi* to creak; (*dientes*) to grind; (*máquina*) to clank, clatter; (*metal seco*) to grate; (*motor*) to hum.
rechistar [retʃis'tar] *vi*: **sin ~** without complaint.
rechoncho, a [re'tʃontʃo, a] *adj* (*fam*) stocky, thickset (*BRIT*), heavy-set (*US*).
rechupete [retʃu'pete]: **de ~** *adj* (*comida*) delicious.
recibidor [reθiβi'ðor] *nm* entrance hall.
recibimiento [reθiβi'mjento] *nm* reception, welcome.
recibir [reθi'βir] *vt* to receive; (*dar la bienvenida*) to welcome; (*salir al encuentro de*) to go and meet ♦ *vi* to entertain; **~se** *vr*: **~se de** to qualify as.
recibo [re'θiβo] *nm* receipt; **acusar ~ de** to acknowledge receipt of.
reciclaje [reθi'klaxe] *nm* recycling; (*de trabajadores*) retraining; **cursos de ~** refresher courses.
reciclar [reθi'klar] *vt* to recycle; (*trabajador*) to retrain.
recién [re'θjen] *adv* recently, newly; (*AM*) just, recently; **~ casado** newly-wed; **el ~ llegado** the newcomer; **el ~ nacido** the newborn child; **~ a las seis** only at six o'clock.
reciente [re'θjente] *adj* recent; (*fresco*) fresh.
recientemente [reθjente'mente] *adv* recently.
recinto [re'θinto] *nm* enclosure; (*área*) area, place.
recio, a ['reθjo, a] *adj* strong, tough; (*voz*) loud ♦ *adv* hard; loud(ly).
recipiente [reθi'pjente] *nm* (*objeto*) container, receptacle; (*persona*) recipient.
reciprocidad [reθiproθi'ðað] *nf* reciprocity.
recíproco, a [re'θiproco, a] *adj* reciprocal.
recital [reθi'tal] *nm* (*MUS*) recital; (*LIT*) reading.
recitar [reθi'tar] *vt* to recite.
reclamación [reklama'θjon] *nf* claim, demand; (*queja*) complaint; **~ salarial** pay claim.
reclamar [rekla'mar] *vt* to claim, demand ♦ *vi*: **~ contra** to complain about; **~ a algn en justicia** to take sb to court.
reclamo [re'klamo] *nm* (*anuncio*) advertisement; (*tentación*) attraction.
reclinar [rekli'nar] *vt* to recline, lean; **~se** *vr* to lean back.
recluir [reklu'ir] *vt* to intern, confine.
reclusión [reklu'sjon] *nf* (*prisión*) prison; (*refugio*) seclusion; **~ perpetua** life imprisonment.
recluso, a [re'kluso, a] *adj* imprisoned; **población reclusa** prison population ♦ *nm/f* (*solitario*) recluse; (*JUR*) prisoner.
recluta [re'kluta] *nm/f* recruit ♦ *nf*

recruitment.
reclutamiento [rekluta'mjento] *nm* recruitment.
recluyendo [reklu'jendo] *etc vb V* **recluir**.
recobrar [reko'ßrar] *vt* (*recuperar*) to recover; (*rescatar*) to get back; (*ciudad*) to recapture; (*tiempo*) to make up (for); **~se** *vr* to recover.
recochineo [rekotʃi'neo] *nm* (*fam*) mickey-taking.
recodo [re'koðo] *nm* (*de río, camino*) bend.
recogedor, a [rekoxe'ðor, a] *nm/f* picker, harvester.
recoger [reko'xer] *vt* to collect; (*AGR*) to harvest; (*fruta*) to pick; (*levantar*) to pick up; (*juntar*) to gather; (*pasar a buscar*) to come for, get; (*dar asilo*) to give shelter to; (*faldas*) to gather up; (*mangas*) to roll up; (*pelo*) to put up; **~se** *vr* (*retirarse*) to retire; **me recogieron en la estación** they picked me up at the station.
recogido, a [reko'xiðo, a] *adj* (*lugar*) quiet, secluded; (*pequeño*) small ♦ *nf* (*CORREOS*) collection; (*AGR*) harvest; **recogida de datos** (*INFORM*) data capture.
recogimiento [rekoxi'mjento] *nm* collection; (*AGR*) harvesting.
recoja [re'koxa] *etc vb V* **recoger**.
recolección [rekolek'θjon] *nf* (*AGR*) harvesting; (*colecta*) collection.
recomencé [rekomen'θe], **recomencemos** [rekomen'θemos] *etc vb V* **recomenzar**.
recomendable [rekomen'daßle] *adj* recommendable; **poco ~** inadvisable.
recomendación [rekomenda'θjon] *nf* (*sugerencia*) suggestion, recommendation; (*referencia*) reference; **carta de ~ para** letter of introduction to.
recomendar [rekomen'dar] *vt* to suggest, recommend; (*confiar*) to entrust.
recomenzar [rekomen'θar] *vt, vi* to begin again, recommence.
recomience [reko'mjenθe] *etc vb V* **recomenzar**.
recomiende [reko'mjende] *etc vb V* **recomendar**.
recomienzo [reko'mjenθo] *etc vb V* **recomenzar**.
recompensa [rekom'pensa] *nf* reward, recompense; (*compensación*): **~ (de una pérdida)** compensation (for a loss); **como** *o* **en ~ por** in return for.
recompensar [rekompen'sar] *vt* to reward, recompense.
recompondré [rekompon'dre] *etc vb V* **recomponer**.
recomponer [rekompo'ner] *vt* to mend; (*INFORM: texto*) to reformat.
recomponga [rekom'ponga] *etc*, **recompuesto** [rekom'pwesto], **recompuse** [rekom'puse] *etc vb V* **recomponer**.
reconciliación [rekonθilja'θjon] *nf* reconciliation.
reconciliar [rekonθi'ljar] *vt* to reconcile; **~se** *vr* to become reconciled.
recóndito, a [re'kondito, a] *adj* (*lugar*) hidden, secret.
reconfortar [rekonfor'tar] *vt* to comfort.
reconocer [rekono'θer] *vt* to recognize; **~ los hechos** to face the facts.
reconocido, a [rekono'θiðo, a] *adj* recognized; (*agradecido*) grateful.
reconocimiento [rekonoθi'mjento] *nm* recognition; (*registro*) search; (*inspección*) examination; (*gratitud*) gratitude; (*confesión*) admission; **~ óptico de caracteres** (*INFORM*) optical character recognition; **~ de la voz** (*INFORM*) speech recognition.
reconozca [reko'noθka] *etc vb V* **reconocer**.
reconquista [rekon'kista] *nf* reconquest.
reconquistar [rekonkis'tar] *vt* (*MIL*) to reconquer; (*fig*) to recover, win back.
reconstituyente [rekonstitu'jente] *nm* tonic.
reconstruir [rekonstru'ir] *vt* to reconstruct.
reconstruyendo [rekonstru'jendo] *etc vb V* **reconstruir**.
reconversión [recomber'sjon] *nf* restructuring, reorganization; (*tb*: **~ industrial**) rationalization.
recopilación [rekopila'θjon] *nf* (*resumen*) summary; (*compilación*) compilation.
recopilar [rekopi'lar] *vt* to compile.
récord ['rekorð] *adj inv* record; **cifras ~** record figures ♦ *nm, pl* **records, récords** ['rekorð] record; **batir el ~** to break the record.
recordar [rekor'ðar] *vt* (*acordarse de*) to remember; (*traer a la memoria*) to recall; (*acordar a otro*) to remind ♦ *vi* to remember; **recuérdale que me debe 5 dólares** remind him that he owes me 5 dollars; **que yo recuerde** as far as I can remember; **creo ~, si mal no recuerdo** if my memory serves me right.
recordatorio [rekorða'torjo] *nm* (*de fallecimiento*) in memoriam card; (*de bautizo, comunión*) commemorative card.
recorrer [reko'rrer] *vt* (*país*) to cross, travel through; (*distancia*) to cover; (*registrar*) to search; (*repasar*) to look over.
recorrido [reko'rriðo] *nm* run, journey;

tren de largo ~ main-line *o* inter-city (*BRIT*) train.
recortado, a [rekor'taðo, a] *adj* uneven, irregular.
recortar [rekor'tar] *vt* (*papel*) to cut out; (*el pelo*) to trim; (*dibujar*) to draw in outline; ~**se** *vr* to stand out, be silhouetted.
recorte [re'korte] *nm* (*acción, de prensa*) cutting; (*de telas, chapas*) trimming; ~ **presupuestario** budget cut; ~ **salarial** wage cut.
recostado, a [rekos'taðo, a] *adj* leaning; **estar** ~ to be lying down.
recostar [rekos'tar] *vt* to lean; ~**se** *vr* to lie down.
recoveco [reko'ßeko] *nm* (*de camino, río etc*) bend; (*en casa*) cubbyhole.
recreación [rekrea'θjon] *nf* recreation.
recrear [rekre'ar] *vt* (*entretener*) to entertain; (*volver a crear*) to recreate.
recreativo, a [rekrea'tißo, a] *adj* recreational.
recreo [re'kreo] *nm* recreation; (*ESCOL*) break, playtime.
recriminar [rekrimi'nar] *vt* to reproach ♦ *vi* to recriminate; ~**se** *vr* to reproach each other.
recrudecer [rekruðe'θer] *vt, vi*, **recrudecerse** *vr* to worsen.
recrudecimiento [rekruðeθi'mjento] *nm* upsurge.
recrudezca [recru'ðeθka] *etc vb V* **recrudecer**.
recta ['rekta] *nf V* **recto**.
rectangular [rektangu'lar] *adj* rectangular.
rectángulo, a [rek'tangulo, a] *adj* rectangular ♦ *nm* rectangle.
rectificable [rektifi'kaßle] *adj* rectifiable; **fácilmente** ~ easily rectified.
rectificación [rektifika'θjon] *nf* correction.
rectificar [rektifi'kar] *vt* to rectify; (*volverse recto*) to straighten ♦ *vi* to correct o.s.
rectifique [rekti'fike] *etc vb V* **rectificar**.
rectitud [rekti'tuð] *nf* straightness; (*fig*) rectitude.
recto, a ['rekto, a] *adj* straight; (*persona*) honest, upright; (*estricto*) strict; (*juez*) fair; (*juicio*) sound ♦ *nm* rectum; (*ATLETISMO*) straight ♦ *nf* straight line; **en el sentido** ~ **de la palabra** in the proper sense of the word; **recta final** *o* **de llegada** home straight.
rector, a [rek'tor, a] *adj* governing ♦ *nm/f* head, chief; (*ESCOL*) rector, president (*US*).
rectorado [rekto'raðo] *nm* (*cargo*) rectorship, presidency (*US*); (*oficina*) rector's office.
recuadro [re'kwaðro] *nm* box; (*TIP*) inset.
recubrir [reku'ßir] *vt* to cover.
recuento [re'kwento] *nm* inventory; **hacer el** ~ **de** to count *o* reckon up.
recuerdo [re'kwerðo] *etc vb V* **recordar** ♦ *nm* souvenir; ~**s** *nmpl* memories; **¡~s a tu madre!** give my regards to your mother!; **"R~ de Mallorca"** "a present from Majorca"; **contar los ~s** to reminisce.
recueste [re'kweste] *etc vb V* **recostar**.
recular [reku'lar] *vi* to back down.
recuperable [rekupe'raßle] *adj* recoverable.
recuperación [rekupera'θjon] *nf* recovery; ~ **de datos** (*INFORM*) data retrieval.
recuperar [rekupe'rar] *vt* to recover; (*tiempo*) to make up; (*INFORM*) to retrieve; ~**se** *vr* to recuperate.
recurrir [reku'rrir] *vi* (*JUR*) to appeal; ~ **a** to resort to; (*persona*) to turn to.
recurso [re'kurso] *nm* resort; (*medio*) means *pl*, resource; (*JUR*) appeal; **como último** ~ as a last resort; ~**s económicos** economic resources; ~**s naturales** natural resources.
recusar [reku'sar] *vt* to reject, refuse.
red [reð] *nf* net, mesh; (*FERRO, INFORM*) network; (*ELEC, de agua*) mains, supply system; (*de tiendas*) chain; (*trampa*) trap; **la R~** (*Internet*) the Net; **estar conectado con la** ~ to be connected to the mains; ~ **local** (*INFORM*) local area network; ~ **de transmisión** (*INFORM*) data network.
redacción [reðak'θjon] *nf* (*acción*) writing; (*ESCOL*) essay, composition; (*limpieza de texto*) editing; (*personal*) editorial staff.
redactar [reðak'tar] *vt* to draw up, draft; (*periódico, INFORM*) to edit.
redactor, a [reðak'tor, a] *nm/f* writer; (*en periódico*) editor.
redada [re'ðaða] *nf* (*PESCA*) cast, throw; (*fig*) catch; ~ **policial** police raid, round-up.
redención [reðen'θjon] *nf* redemption.
redentor, a [reðen'tor, a] *adj* redeeming ♦ *nm/f* (*COM*) redeemer.
redescubierto [reðesku'ßjerto] *pp de* **redescubrir**.
redescubrir [reðesku'ßrir] *vt* to rediscover.
redesignar [reðesiɣ'nar] *vt* (*INFORM*) to rename.
redicho, a [re'ðitʃo, a] *adj* affected.
redil [re'ðil] *nm* sheepfold.
redimir [reði'mir] *vt* to redeem; (*rehén*) to ransom.
redistribución [reðistrißu'θjon] *nf* (*COM*)

redeployment.
rédito ['reðito] *nm* interest, yield.
redoblar [reðo'ßlar] *vt* to redouble ♦ *vi* (*tambor*) to play a roll on the drums.
redoble [re'ðoßle] *nm* (*MUS*) drumroll, drumbeat; (*de trueno*) roll.
redomado, a [reðo'maðo, a] *adj* (*astuto*) sly, crafty; (*perfecto*) utter.
redonda [re'ðonda] *nf V* **redondo**.
redondear [reðonde'ar] *vt* to round, round off; (*cifra*) to round up.
redondel [reðon'del] *nm* (*círculo*) circle; (*TAUR*) bullring, arena; (*AUTO*) roundabout.
redondo, a [re'ðondo, a] *adj* (*circular*) round; (*completo*) complete ♦ *nf*: **a la redonda** around, round about; **en muchas millas a la redonda** for many miles around; **rehusar en** ~ to give a flat refusal.
reducción [reðuk'θjon] *nf* reduction; ~ **del activo** (*COM*) divestment; ~ **de precios** (*COM*) price-cutting.
reducido, a [reðu'θiðo, a] *adj* reduced; (*limitado*) limited; (*pequeño*) small; **quedar** ~ **a** to be reduced to.
reducir [reðu'θir] *vt* to reduce, limit; (*someter*) to bring under control; ~**se** *vr* to diminish; (*MAT*): ~ **(a)** to reduce (to), convert (into); ~ **las millas a kilómetros** to convert miles into kilometres; ~**se a** (*fig*) to come *o* boil down to.
reducto [re'ðukto] *nm* redoubt.
reduje [re'ðuxe] *etc vb V* **reducir**.
redundancia [reðun'danθja] *nf* redundancy.
reduzca [re'ðuθka] *etc vb V* **reducir**.
reedición [re(e)ði'θjon] *nf* reissue.
reeditar [re(e)ði'tar] *vt* to reissue.
reelección [re(e)lek'θjon] *nf* re-election.
reelegir [re(e)le'xir] *vt* to re-elect.
reembolsable [re(e)mbol'saßle] *adj* (*COM*) redeemable, refundable.
reembolsar [re(e)mbol'sar] *vt* (*persona*) to reimburse; (*dinero*) to repay, pay back; (*depósito*) to refund.
reembolso [re(e)m'bolso] *nm* reimbursement; refund; **enviar algo contra** ~ to send sth cash on delivery; **contra** ~ **del flete** freight forward; ~ **fiscal** tax rebate.
reemplace [re(e)m'plaθe] *etc vb V* **reemplazar**.
reemplazar [re(e)mpla'θar] *vt* to replace.
reemplazo [re(e)m'plaθo] *nm* replacement; **de** ~ (*MIL*) reserve.
reencuentro [re(e)n'kwentro] *nm* reunion.
reengancharse [re(e)ngan'tʃarse] *vr* (*MIL*) to re-enlist.
reestreno [re(e)s'treno] *nm* rerun.
reestructurar [re(e)struktu'rar] *vt* to restructure.
reexportación [re(e)ksporta'θjon] *nf* (*COM*) re-export.
reexportar [re(e)kspor'tar] *vt* (*COM*) to re-export.
REF *nm abr* (*ESP ECON*) = *Régimen Económico Fiscal.*
Ref.ª *abr* (= *referencia*) ref.
refacción [refak'θjon] *nf* (*AM*) repair(s); **refacciones** *nfpl* (*piezas de repuesto*) spare parts.
referencia [refe'renθja] *nf* reference; **con** ~ **a** with reference to; **hacer** ~ **a** to refer *o* allude to; ~ **comercial** (*COM*) trade reference.
referéndum [refe'rendum], *pl* **referéndums** *nm* referendum.
referente [refe'rente] *adj*: ~ **a** concerning, relating to.
referir [refe'rir] *vt* (*contar*) to tell, recount; (*relacionar*) to refer, relate; ~**se** *vr*: ~**se a** to refer to; ~ **al lector a un apéndice** to refer the reader to an appendix; ~ **a** (*COM*) to convert into; **por lo que se refiere a eso** as for that, as regards that.
refiera [re'fjera] *etc vb V* **referir**.
refilón [refi'lon]: **de** ~ *adv* obliquely; **mirar a algn de** ~ to look out of the corner of one's eye at sb.
refinado, a [refi'naðo, a] *adj* refined.
refinamiento [refina'mjento] *nm* refinement; ~ **por pasos** (*INFORM*) stepwise refinement.
refinar [refi'nar] *vt* to refine.
refinería [refine'ria] *nf* refinery.
refiriendo [refi'rjendo] *etc vb V* **referir**.
reflector [reflek'tor] *nm* reflector; (*ELEC*) spotlight; (*AVIAT, MIL*) searchlight.
reflejar [refle'xar] *vt* to reflect; ~**se** *vr* to be reflected.
reflejo, a [re'flexo, a] *adj* reflected; (*movimiento*) reflex ♦ *nm* reflection; (*ANAT*) reflex; (*en el pelo*): ~**s** *nmpl* highlights; **tiene el pelo castaño con** ~**s rubios** she has chestnut hair with blond streaks.
reflexión [reflek'sjon] *nf* reflection.
reflexionar [refleksjo'nar] *vt* to reflect on ♦ *vi* to reflect; (*detenerse*) to pause (to think); **¡reflexione!** you think it over!
reflexivo, a [reflek'sißo, a] *adj* thoughtful; (*LING*) reflexive.
refluir [reflu'ir] *vi* to flow back.
reflujo [re'fluxo] *nm* ebb.
refluyendo [reflu'jendo] *etc vb V* **refluir**.

reforcé [refor'θe], **reforcemos** [refor'θemos] *etc vb V* **reforzar**.
reforma [re'forma] *nf* reform; (*ARQ etc*) repair; ~ **agraria** agrarian reform.
reformar [refor'mar] *vt* to reform; (*modificar*) to change, alter; (*texto*) to revise; (*ARQ*) to repair; ~**se** *vr* to mend one's ways.
reformatear [reformate'ar] *vt* (*INFORM*: *disco*) to reformat.
reformatorio [reforma'torjo] *nm* reformatory; ~ **de menores** remand home.
reformista [refor'mista] *adj, nm/f* reformist.
reforzamiento [reforθa'mjento] *nm* reinforcement.
reforzar [refor'θar] *vt* to strengthen; (*ARQ*) to reinforce; (*fig*) to encourage.
refractario, a [refrak'tarjo, a] *adj* (*TEC*) heat-resistant; **ser ~ a una reforma** to resist *o* be opposed to a reform.
refrán [re'fran] *nm* proverb, saying.
refregar [refre'ɣar] *vt* to scrub.
refrenar [refre'nar] *vt* to check, restrain.
refrendar [refren'dar] *vt* (*firma*) to endorse, countersign; (*ley*) to approve.
refrescante [refres'kante] *adj* refreshing, cooling.
refrescar [refres'kar] *vt* to refresh ♦ *vi* to cool down; ~**se** *vr* to get cooler; (*tomar aire fresco*) to go out for a breath of fresh air; (*beber*) to have a drink.
refresco [re'fresko] *nm* soft drink, cool drink; "~**s**" "refreshments".
refresque [re'freske] *etc vb V* **refrescar**.
refriega [re'frjeɣa] *etc vb V* **refregar** ♦ *nf* scuffle, brawl.
refriegue [re'frjeɣe] *etc vb V* **refregar**.
refrigeración [refrixera'θjon] *nf* refrigeration; (*de casa*) air-conditioning.
refrigerado, a [refrixe'raðo, a] *adj* cooled; (*sala*) air-conditioned.
refrigerador [refrixera'ðor] *nm*, (*AM*) **refrigeradora** [refrixera'ðora] *nf* refrigerator, icebox (*US*).
refrigerar [refrixe'rar] *vt* to refrigerate; (*sala*) to air-condition.
refrito [re'frito] *nm* (*CULIN*): **un ~ de cebolla y tomate** sautéed onions and tomatoes; **un** ~ (*fig*) a rehash.
refuerce [re'fwerθe] *etc vb V* **reforzar**.
refuerzo [re'fwerθo] *etc vb V* **reforzar** ♦ *nm* reinforcement; (*TEC*) support.
refugiado, a [refu'xjaðo, a] *nm/f* refugee.
refugiarse [refu'xjarse] *vr* to take refuge, shelter.
refugio [re'fuxjo] *nm* refuge; (*protección*) shelter; (*AUTO*) street *o* traffic island; ~ **alpino** *o* **de montaña** mountain hut; ~ **subterráneo** (*MIL*) underground shelter.
refulgencia [reful'xenθja] *nf* brilliance.
refulgir [reful'xir] *vi* to shine, be dazzling.
refulja [re'fulxa] *etc vb V* **refulgir**.
refundir [refun'dir] *vt* to recast; (*escrito etc*) to adapt, rewrite.
refunfuñar [refunfu'ɲar] *vi* to grunt, growl; (*quejarse*) to grumble.
refunfuñón, ona [refunfu'ɲon, ona] (*fam*) *adj* grumpy ♦ *nm/f* grouch.
refutación [refuta'θjon] *nf* refutation.
refutar [refu'tar] *vt* to refute.
regadera [reɣa'ðera] *nf* watering can; (*AM*) shower; **estar como una** ~ (*fam*) to be as mad as a hatter.
regadío [rega'ðio] *nm* irrigated land.
regalado, a [reɣa'laðo, a] *adj* comfortable, luxurious; (*gratis*) free, for nothing; **lo tuvo** ~ it was handed to him on a plate.
regalar [reɣa'lar] *vt* (*dar*) to give (as a present); (*entregar*) to give away; (*mimar*) to pamper, make a fuss of; ~**se** *vr* to treat o.s. to.
regalía [reɣa'lia] *nf* privilege, prerogative; (*COM*) bonus; (*de autor*) royalty.
regaliz [reɣa'liθ] *nm* liquorice.
regalo [re'ɣalo] *nm* (*obsequio*) gift, present; (*gusto*) pleasure; (*comodidad*) comfort.
regañadientes [reɣaɲa'ðjentes]: **a** ~ *adv* reluctantly.
regañar [reɣa'ɲar] *vt* to scold ♦ *vi* to grumble; (*dos personas*) to fall out, quarrel.
regañón, ona [reɣa'ɲon, ona] *adj* nagging.
regar [re'ɣar] *vt* to water, irrigate; (*fig*) to scatter, sprinkle.
regata [re'ɣata] *nf* (*NAUT*) race.
regatear [reɣate'ar] *vt* (*COM*) to bargain over; (*escatimar*) to be mean with ♦ *vi* to bargain, haggle; (*DEPORTE*) to dribble; **no ~ esfuerzo** to spare no effort.
regateo [reɣa'teo] *nm* bargaining; (*DEPORTE*) dribbling; (*del cuerpo*) swerve, dodge.
regazo [re'ɣaθo] *nm* lap.
regencia [re'xenθja] *nf* regency.
regeneración [rexenera'θjon] *nf* regeneration.
regenerar [rexene'rar] *vt* to regenerate.
regentar [rexen'tar] *vt* to direct, manage; (*puesto*) to hold in an acting capacity; (*negocio*) to be in charge of.
regente, a [re'xente, a] *adj* (*príncipe*) regent; (*director*) managing ♦ *nm* (*COM*) manager; (*POL*) regent.
régimen ['reximen], *pl* **regímenes**

[re'ximenes] *nm* regime; (*reinado*) rule; (*MED*) diet; (*reglas*) (set of) rules *pl*; (*manera de vivir*) lifestyle; **estar a** ~ to be on a diet.
regimiento [rexi'mjento] *nm* regiment.
regio, a ['rexjo, a] *adj* royal, regal; (*fig: suntuoso*) splendid; (*AM fam*) great, terrific.
región [re'xjon] *nf* region; (*área*) area.
regional [rexjo'nal] *adj* regional.
regir [re'xir] *vt* to govern, rule; (*dirigir*) to manage, run; (*ECON, JUR, LING*) to govern ♦ *vi* to apply, be in force.
registrador [rexistra'ðor] *nm* registrar, recorder.
registrar [rexis'trar] *vt* (*buscar*) to search; (*en cajón*) to look through; (*inspeccionar*) to inspect; (*anotar*) to register, record; (*INFORM, MUS*) to record; ~**se** *vr* to register; (*ocurrir*) to happen.
registro [re'xistro] *nm* (*acto*) registration; (*MUS, libro*) register; (*lista*) list, record; (*INFORM*) record; (*inspección*) inspection, search; ~ **civil** registry office; ~ **electoral** voting register; ~ **de la propiedad** land registry (office).
regla ['reɣla] *nf* (*ley*) rule, regulation; (*de medir*) ruler, rule; (*MED: período*) period; (~ *científica*) law, principle; **no hay ~ sin excepción** every rule has its exception.
reglamentación [reɣlamenta'θjon] *nf* (*acto*) regulation; (*lista*) rules *pl*.
reglamentar [reɣlamen'tar] *vt* to regulate.
reglamentario, a [reɣlamen'tarjo, a] *adj* statutory; **en la forma reglamentaria** in the properly established way.
reglamento [reɣla'mento] *nm* rules *pl*, regulations *pl*; ~ **del tráfico** highway code.
reglar [re'ɣlar] *vt* (*acciones*) to regulate; ~**se** *vr*: ~**se por** to be guided by.
regocijarse [reɣoθi'xarse] *vr*: ~ **de** *o* **por** to rejoice at, be glad about.
regocijo [reɣo'θixo] *nm* joy, happiness.
regodearse [reɣoðe'arse] *vr* to be glad, be delighted; (*pey*): ~ **con** *o* **en** to gloat over.
regodeo [reɣo'ðeo] *nm* delight; (*pey*) perverse pleasure.
regresar [reɣre'sar] *vi* to come/go back, return; ~**se** *vr* (*AM*) to return.
regresivo, a [reɣre'siβo, a] *adj* backward; (*fig*) regressive.
regreso [re'ɣreso] *nm* return; **estar de** ~ to be back, be home.
regué [re'ɣe], **reguemos** [re'ɣemos] *etc vb V* **regar**.
reguero [re'ɣero] *nm* (*de sangre*) trickle; (*de humo*) trail.
regulación [reɣula'θjon] *nf* regulation; (*TEC*) adjustment; (*control*) control; ~ **de empleo** redundancies *pl*; ~ **del tráfico** traffic control.
regulador [reɣula'ðor] *nm* (*TEC*) regulator; (*de radio etc*) knob, control.
regular [reɣu'lar] *adj* regular; (*normal*) normal, usual; (*común*) ordinary; (*organizado*) regular, orderly; (*mediano*) average; (*fam*) not bad, so-so ♦ *adv*: **estar** ~ to be so-so *o* alright ♦ *vt* (*controlar*) to control, regulate; (*TEC*) to adjust; **por lo** ~ as a rule.
regularice [reɣula'riθe] *etc vb V* **regularizar**.
regularidad [reɣulari'ðað] *nf* regularity; **con** ~ regularly.
regularizar [reɣulari'θar] *vt* to regularize.
regusto [re'ɣusto] *nm* aftertaste.
rehabilitación [reaβilita'θjon] *nf* rehabilitation; (*ARQ*) restoration.
rehabilitar [reaβili'tar] *vt* to rehabilitate; (*ARQ*) to restore; (*reintegrar*) to reinstate.
rehacer [rea'θer] *vt* (*reparar*) to mend, repair; (*volver a hacer*) to redo, repeat; ~**se** *vr* (*MED*) to recover.
rehaga [re'aɣa] *etc*, **reharé** [rea're] *etc*, **rehaz** [re'aθ], **rehecho** [re'etʃo] *vb V* **rehacer**.
rehén [re'en] *nm/f* hostage.
rehice [re'iθe] *etc*, **rehizo** [re'iθo] *vb V* **rehacer**.
rehogar [reo'ɣar] *vt* to sauté, toss in oil.
rehuir [reu'ir] *vt* to avoid, shun.
rehusar [reu'sar] *vt, vi* to refuse.
rehuyendo [reu'jendo] *etc vb V* **rehuir**.
reina ['reina] *nf* queen.
reinado [rei'naðo] *nm* reign.
reinante [rei'nante] *adj* (*fig*) prevailing.
reinar [rei'nar] *vi* to reign; (*fig: prevalecer*) to prevail, be general.
reincidir [reinθi'ðir] *vi* to relapse; (*criminal*) to repeat an offence.
reincorporarse [reinkorpo'rarse] *vr*: ~ **a** to rejoin.
reinicializar [reiniθjali'θar] *vt* (*INFORM*) to reset.
reino ['reino] *nm* kingdom; **el R~ Unido** the United Kingdom.
reinserción [reinser'θjon] *nf* rehabilitation.
reinsertar [reinser'tar] *vt* to rehabilitate.
reintegración [reinteɣra'θjon] *nf* (*COM*) reinstatement.
reintegrar [reinte'ɣrar] *vt* (*reconstituir*) to reconstruct; (*persona*) to reinstate; (*dinero*) to refund, pay back; ~**se** *vr*: ~**se a** to return to.
reintegro [rein'teɣro] *nm* refund,

reimbursement; (*en banco*) withdrawal.
reír [re'ir] *vi*, **reírse** *vr* to laugh; ~**se de** to laugh at.
reiterado, a [reite'raðo, a] *adj* repeated.
reiterar [reite'rar] *vt* to reiterate; (*repetir*) to repeat.
reivindicación [reißindika'θjon] *nf* (*demanda*) claim, demand; (*justificación*) vindication.
reivindicar [reißindi'kar] *vt* to claim.
reivindique [reißin'dike] *etc vb V* **reivindicar**.
reja ['rexa] *nf* (*de ventana*) grille, bars *pl*; (*en la calle*) grating.
rejamos [re'xamos] *etc vb V* **regir**.
rejilla [re'xiʎa] *nf* grating, grille; (*muebles*) wickerwork; (*de ventilación*) vent; (*de coche etc*) luggage rack.
rejuvenecer [rexußene'θer] *vt, vi* to rejuvenate.
rejuvenezca [rexuße'neθka] *etc vb V* **rejuvenecer**.
relación [rela'θjon] *nf* relation, relationship; (*MAT*) ratio; (*lista*) list; (*narración*) report; ~ **costo-efectivo** *o* **costo-rendimiento** (*COM*) cost-effectiveness; **relaciones** *nfpl* (*enchufes*) influential friends, connections; **relaciones carnales** sexual relations; **relaciones comerciales** business connections; **relaciones empresariales/humanas** industrial/human relations; **relaciones laborales/públicas** labour/public relations; **con** ~ **a, en** ~ **con** in relation to; **estar en** *o* **tener buenas relaciones con** to be on good terms with.
relacionar [relaθjo'nar] *vt* to relate, connect; ~**se** *vr* to be connected *o* linked.
relajación [relaxa'θjon] *nf* relaxation.
relajado, a [rela'xaðo, a] *adj* (*disoluto*) loose; (*cómodo*) relaxed; (*MED*) ruptured.
relajante [rela'xante] *adj* relaxing; (*MED*) sedative.
relajar [rela'xar] *vt*, **relajarse** *vr* to relax.
relamerse [rela'merse] *vr* to lick one's lips.
relamido, a [rela'miðo, a] *adj* (*pulcro*) overdressed; (*afectado*) affected.
relámpago [re'lampaɣo] *nm* flash of lightning ♦ *adj* lightning *cpd*; **como un** ~ as quick as lightning, in a flash; **visita/huelga** ~ lightning visit/strike.
relampaguear [relampaɣe'ar] *vi* to flash.
relanzar [relan'θar] *vt* to relaunch.
relatar [rela'tar] *vt* to tell, relate.
relatividad [relatißi'ðað] *nf* relativity.
relativo, a [rela'tißo, a] *adj* relative; **en lo** ~ **a** concerning.
relato [re'lato] *nm* (*narración*) story, tale.
relax [re'las] *nm* rest; **"R~"** (*en anuncio*) "Personal services".
relegar [rele'ɣar] *vt* to relegate; ~ **algo al olvido** to banish sth from one's mind.
relegue [re'leɣe] *etc vb V* **relegar**.
relevante [rele'ßante] *adj* eminent, outstanding.
relevar [rele'ßar] *vt* (*sustituir*) to relieve; ~**se** *vr* to relay; ~ **a algn de un cargo** to relieve sb of his post.
relevo [re'leßo] *nm* relief; **carrera de** ~**s** relay race; ~ **con cinta** (*INFORM*) tape relay; **coger** *o* **tomar el** ~ to take over, stand in.
relieve [re'ljeße] *nm* (*ARTE, TEC*) relief; (*fig*) prominence, importance; **bajo** ~ bas-relief; **un personaje de** ~ an important man; **dar** ~ **a** to highlight.
religión [reli'xjon] *nf* religion.
religioso, a [reli'xjoso, a] *adj* religious ♦ *nm/f* monk/nun.
relinchar [relin'tʃar] *vi* to neigh.
relincho [re'lintʃo] *nm* neigh; (*acto*) neighing.
reliquia [re'likja] *nf* relic; ~ **de familia** heirloom.
rellano [re'ʎano] *nm* (*ARQ*) landing.
rellenar [reʎe'nar] *vt* (*llenar*) to fill up; (*CULIN*) to stuff; (*COSTURA*) to pad; (*formulario etc*) to fill in *o* out.
relleno, a [re'ʎeno, a] *adj* full up; (*CULIN*) stuffed ♦ *nm* stuffing; (*de tapicería*) padding.
reloj [re'lo(x)] *nm* clock; ~ **de pie** grandfather clock; ~ **(de pulsera)** wristwatch; ~ **de sol** sundial; ~ **despertador** alarm (clock); **como un** ~ like clockwork; **contra (el)** ~ against the clock.
relojería [reloxe'ria] *nf* (*tienda*) watchmaker's (shop); **aparato de** ~ clockwork; **bomba de** ~ time bomb.
relojero, a [relo'xero, a] *nm/f* clockmaker; watchmaker.
reluciente [relu'θjente] *adj* brilliant, shining.
relucir [relu'θir] *vi* to shine; (*fig*) to excel; **sacar algo a** ~ to show sth off.
relumbrante [relum'brante] *adj* dazzling.
relumbrar [relum'brar] *vi* to dazzle, shine brilliantly.
reluzca [re'luθka] *etc vb V* **relucir**.
remachar [rema'tʃar] *vt* to rivet; (*fig*) to hammer home, drive home.
remache [re'matʃe] *nm* rivet.
remanente [rema'nente] *nm* remainder; (*COM*) balance; (*de producto*) surplus.
remangarse [reman'garse] *vr* to roll one's

sleeves up.
remanso [re'manso] *nm* pool.
remar [re'mar] *vi* to row.
rematado, a [rema'taðo, a] *adj* complete, utter; **es un loco** ~ he's a raving lunatic.
rematar [rema'tar] *vt* to finish off; (*animal*) to put out of its misery; (*COM*) to sell off cheap ♦ *vi* to end, finish off; (*DEPORTE*) to shoot.
remate [re'mate] *nm* end, finish; (*punta*) tip; (*DEPORTE*) shot; (*ARQ*) top; (*COM*) auction sale; **de** *o* **para** ~ to crown it all (*BRIT*), to top it off.
remediable [reme'ðjaβle] *adj*: **fácilmente** ~ easily remedied.
remediar [reme'ðjar] *vt* (*gen*) to remedy; (*subsanar*) to make good, repair; (*evitar*) to avoid; **sin poder ~lo** without being able to prevent it.
remedio [re'meðjo] *nm* remedy; (*JUR*) recourse, remedy; **poner** ~ **a** to correct, stop; **no tener más** ~ to have no alternative; **¡qué ~!** there's no other way; **como último** ~ as a last resort; **sin** ~ inevitable; (*MED*) hopeless.
remedo [re'meðo] *nm* imitation; (*pey*) parody.
remendar [remen'dar] *vt* to repair; (*con parche*) to patch; (*fig*) to correct.
remesa [re'mesa] *nf* remittance; (*COM*) shipment.
remiendo [re'mjendo] *etc vb V* **remendar** ♦ *nm* mend; (*con parche*) patch; (*cosido*) darn; (*fig*) correction.
remilgado, a [remil'ɣaðo, a] *adj* prim; (*afectado*) affected.
remilgo [re'milɣo] *nm* primness; (*afectación*) affectation.
reminiscencia [reminis'θenθja] *nf* reminiscence.
remirar [remi'rar] *vt* (*volver a mirar*) to look at again; (*examinar*) to look hard at.
remisión [remi'sjon] *nf* (*acto*) sending, shipment; (*REL*) forgiveness, remission; **sin** ~ hopelessly.
remiso, a [re'miso, a] *adj* remiss.
remite [re'mite] *nm* (*en sobre*) name and address of sender.
remitente [remi'tente] *nm/f* (*CORREOS*) sender.
remitir [remi'tir] *vt* to remit, send ♦ *vi* to slacken.
remo ['remo] *nm* (*de barco*) oar; (*DEPORTE*) rowing; **cruzar un río a** ~ to row across a river.
remoce [re'moθe] *etc vb V* **remozar**.
remodelación [remodela'θjon] *nf* (*POL*): ~ **del gobierno** cabinet reshuffle.
remojar [remo'xar] *vt* to steep, soak; (*galleta etc*) to dip, dunk; (*fam*) to celebrate with a drink.
remojo [re'moxo] *nm* steeping, soaking; (*por la lluvia*) drenching, soaking; **dejar la ropa en** ~ to leave clothes to soak.
remojón [remo'xon] *nm* soaking; **darse un** ~ (*fam*) to go (in) for a dip.
remolacha [remo'latʃa] *nf* beet, beetroot (*BRIT*).
remolcador [remolka'ðor] *nm* (*NAUT*) tug; (*AUTO*) breakdown lorry.
remolcar [remol'kar] *vt* to tow.
remolino [remo'lino] *nm* eddy; (*de agua*) whirlpool; (*de viento*) whirlwind; (*de gente*) crowd.
remolón, ona [remo'lon, ona] *adj* lazy ♦ *nm/f* slacker, shirker.
remolque [re'molke] *etc vb V* **remolcar** ♦ *nm* tow, towing; (*cuerda*) towrope; **llevar a** ~ to tow.
remontar [remon'tar] *vt* to mend; (*obstáculo*) to negotiate, get over; **~se** *vr* to soar; **~se a** (*COM*) to amount to; (*en tiempo*) to go back to, date from; ~ **el vuelo** to soar.
rémora ['remora] *nf* hindrance.
remorder [remor'ðer] *vt* to distress, disturb.
remordimiento [remorði'mjento] *nm* remorse.
remotamente [remota'mente] *adv* vaguely.
remoto, a [re'moto, a] *adj* remote.
remover [remo'βer] *vt* to stir; (*tierra*) to turn over; (*objetos*) to move round.
remozar [remo'θar] *vt* (*ARQ*) to refurbish; (*fig*) to brighten *o* polish up.
remuerda [re'mwerða] *etc vb V* **remorder**.
remueva [re'mweβa] *etc vb V* **remover**.
remuneración [remunera'θjon] *nf* remuneration.
remunerado, a [remune'raðo, a] *adj*: **trabajo bien/mal** ~ well-/badly-paid job.
remunerar [remune'rar] *vt* to remunerate; (*premiar*) to reward.
renacer [rena'θer] *vi* to be reborn; (*fig*) to revive.
renacimiento [renaθi'mjento] *nm* rebirth; **el R~** the Renaissance.
renacuajo [rena'kwaxo] *nm* (*ZOOL*) tadpole.
renal [re'nal] *adj* renal, kidney *cpd*.
Renania [re'nanja] *nf* Rhineland.
renazca [re'naθka] *etc vb V* **renacer**.
rencilla [ren'θiʎa] *nf* quarrel; **~s** *nfpl* bickering *sg*.
rencor [ren'kor] *nm* rancour, bitterness; (*resentimiento*) ill feeling, resentment;

guardar ~ a to have a grudge against.
rencoroso, a [renko'roso, a] *adj* spiteful.
rendición [rendi'θjon] *nf* surrender.
rendido, a [ren'diðo, a] *adj* (*sumiso*) submissive; (*agotado*) worn-out, exhausted; (*enamorado*) devoted.
rendija [ren'dixa] *nf* (*hendedura*) crack; (*abertura*) aperture; (*fig*) rift, split; (*JUR*) loophole.
rendimiento [rendi'mjento] *nm* (*producción*) output; (*COM*) yield, profit(s) (*pl*); (*TEC, COM*) efficiency; **~ de capital** (*COM*) return on capital.
rendir [ren'dir] *vt* (*vencer*) to defeat; (*producir*) to produce; (*dar beneficio*) to yield; (*agotar*) to exhaust ♦ *vi* to pay; (*COM*) to yield, produce; **~se** *vr* (*someterse*) to surrender; (*ceder*) to yield; (*cansarse*) to wear o.s. out; **~ homenaje** *o* **culto a** to pay homage to; **el negocio no rinde** the business doesn't pay.
renegado, a [rene'ɣaðo, a] *adj, nm/f* renegade.
renegar [rene'ɣar] *vt* (*negar*) to deny vigorously ♦ *vi* (*blasfemar*) to blaspheme; **~ de** (*renunciar*) to renounce; (*quejarse*) to complain about.
renegué [rene'ɣe], **reneguemos** [rene'ɣemos] *etc vb V* **renegar**.
RENFE ['renfe] *nf abr ESP*: = *Red Nacional de Ferrocarriles Españoles*.
renglón [ren'glon] *nm* (*línea*) line; (*COM*) item, article; **a ~ seguido** immediately after.
rengo, a ['rengo, a] *adj* (*AM*) lame.
reniego [re'njeɣo] *etc*, **reniegue** [re'njeɣe] *etc vb V* **renegar**.
reno ['reno] *nm* reindeer.
renombrado, a [renom'braðo, a] *adj* renowned.
renombre [re'nombre] *nm* renown.
renovable [reno'βaβle] *adj* renewable.
renovación [renoβa'θjon] *nf* (*de contrato*) renewal; (*ARQ*) renovation.
renovar [reno'βar] *vt* to renew; (*ARQ*) to renovate; (*sala*) to redecorate.
renquear [renke'ar] *vi* to limp; (*fam*) to get along, scrape by.
renta ['renta] *nf* (*ingresos*) income; (*beneficio*) profit; (*alquiler*) rent; **~ gravable** *o* **imponible** taxable income; **~ nacional (bruta)** (gross) national income; **~ no salarial** unearned income; **~ sobre el terreno** (*COM*) ground rent; **~ vitalicia** annuity; **política de ~s** incomes policy; **vivir de sus ~s** to live on one's private income.
rentabilizar [rentaβili'θar] *vt* to make profitable.
rentable [ren'taβle] *adj* profitable; **no ~** unprofitable.
rentar [ren'tar] *vt* to produce, yield; (*AM*) to rent.
rentista [ren'tista] *nm/f* (*accionista*) shareholder (*BRIT*), stockholder (*US*).
renuencia [re'nwenθja] *nf* reluctance.
renuente [re'nwente] *adj* reluctant.
renueve [re'nweβe] *etc vb V* **renovar**.
renuncia [re'nunθja] *nf* resignation.
renunciar [renun'θjar] *vt* to renounce, give up ♦ *vi* to resign; **~ a hacer algo** to give up doing sth.
reñido, a [re'ɲiðo, a] *adj* (*batalla*) bitter, hard-fought; **estar ~ con algn** to be on bad terms with sb; **está ~ con su familia** he has fallen out with his family.
reñir [re'ɲir] *vt* (*regañar*) to scold ♦ *vi* (*estar peleado*) to quarrel, fall out; (*combatir*) to fight.
reo ['reo] *nm/f* culprit, offender; (*JUR*) accused.
reojo [re'oxo]: **de ~** *adv* out of the corner of one's eye.
reorganice [reorɣa'niθe] *etc vb V* **reorganizar**.
reorganizar [reorɣani'θar] *vt* to reorganize.
Rep *abr* = **República**.
reparación [repara'θjon] *nf* (*acto*) mending, repairing; (*TEC*) repair; (*fig*) amends, reparation; **"reparaciones en el acto"** "repairs while you wait".
reparar [repa'rar] *vt* to repair; (*fig*) to make amends for; (*suerte*) to retrieve; (*observar*) to observe ♦ *vi*: **~ en** (*darse cuenta de*) to notice; (*poner atención en*) to pay attention to; **sin ~ en los gastos** regardless of the cost.
reparo [re'paro] *nm* (*advertencia*) observation; (*duda*) doubt; (*dificultad*) difficulty; (*escrúpulo*) scruple, qualm; **poner ~s (a)** to raise objections (to); (*criticar*) to criticize; **no tuvo ~ en hacerlo** he did not hesitate to do it.
repartición [reparti'θjon] *nf* distribution; (*división*) division.
repartidor, a [reparti'ðor, a] *nm/f* distributor; **~ de leche** milkman.
repartir [repar'tir] *vt* to distribute, share out; (*COM, CORREOS*) to deliver; (*MIL*) to partition; (*libros*) to give out; (*comida*) to serve out; (*NAIPES*) to deal.
reparto [re'parto] *nm* distribution; (*COM, CORREOS*) delivery; (*TEAT, CINE*) cast; (*AM*: *urbanización*) housing estate (*BRIT*),

real estate development (*US*); "~ **a domicilio**" "home delivery service".
repasar [repa'sar] *vt* (*ESCOL*) to revise; (*MECÁNICA*) to check, overhaul; (*COSTURA*) to mend.
repaso [re'paso] *nm* revision; (*MECÁNICA*) overhaul, checkup; (*COSTURA*) mending; ~ **general** servicing, general overhaul; **curso de** ~ refresher course.
repatriar [repa'trjar] *vt* to repatriate; ~**se** *vr* to return home.
repelente [repe'lente] *adj* repellent, repulsive.
repeler [repe'ler] *vt* to repel; (*idea, oferta*) to reject.
repensar [repen'sar] *vt* to reconsider.
repente [re'pente] *nm* sudden movement; (*fig*) impulse; **de** ~ suddenly; ~ **de ira** fit of anger.
repentice [repen'tiθe] *etc vb V* **repentizar**.
repentino, a [repen'tino, a] *adj* sudden; (*imprevisto*) unexpected.
repentizar [repenti'θar] *vi* (*MUS*) to sight-read.
repercusión [reperku'sjon] *nf* repercussion; **de amplia** *o* **ancha** ~ far-reaching.
repercutir [reperku'tir] *vi* (*objeto*) to rebound; (*sonido*) to echo; ~ **en** (*fig*) to have repercussions *o* effects on.
repertorio [reper'torjo] *nm* list; (*TEAT*) repertoire.
repesca [re'peska] *nf* (*ESCOL fam*) resit.
repetición [repeti'θjon] *nf* repetition.
repetido, a [repe'tiðo, a] *adj* repeated; **repetidas veces** repeatedly.
repetir [repe'tir] *vt* to repeat; (*plato*) to have a second helping of; (*TEAT*) to give as an encore, sing *etc* again ♦ *vi* to repeat; (*sabor*) to come back; ~**se** *vr* to repeat o.s.; (*suceso*) to recur.
repetitivo, a [repeti'tiβo, a] *adj* repetitive, repetitious.
repicar [repi'kar] *vi* (*campanas*) to ring (out).
repiense [re'pjense] *etc vb V* **repensar**.
repipi [re'pipi] *adj* la-di-da ♦ *nf*: **es una** ~ she's a little madam.
repique [re'pike] *etc vb V* **repicar** ♦ *nm* pealing, ringing.
repiqueteo [repike'teo] *nm* pealing; (*de tambor*) drumming.
repisa [re'pisa] *nf* ledge, shelf; ~ **de chimenea** mantelpiece; ~ **de ventana** windowsill.
repitiendo [repi'tjendo] *etc vb V* **repetir**.
replantear [replante'ar] *vt* (*cuestión pública*) to readdress; (*problema personal*) to reconsider; (*en reunión*) to raise again; ~**se** *vr*: ~**se algo** to reconsider sth.
replegarse [reple'ɣarse] *vr* to fall back, retreat.
replegué [reple'ɣe], **repleguemos** [reple'ɣemos] *etc vb V* **replegarse**.
repleto, a [re'pleto, a] *adj* replete, full up; ~ **de** filled *o* crammed with.
réplica ['replika] *nf* answer; (*ARTE*) replica; **derecho de** ~ right of *o* to reply.
replicar [repli'kar] *vi* to answer; (*objetar*) to argue, answer back.
repliego [re'pljeɣo] *etc vb V* **replegarse**.
repliegue [re'pljeɣe] *etc vb V* **replegarse** ♦ *nm* (*MIL*) withdrawal.
replique [re'plike] *etc vb V* **replicar**.
repoblación [repoβla'θjon] *nf* repopulation; (*de río*) restocking; ~ **forestal** reafforestation.
repoblar [repo'βlar] *vt* to repopulate; to restock.
repollo [re'poʎo] *nm* cabbage.
repondré [repon'dre] *etc vb V* **reponer**.
reponer [repo'ner] *vt* to replace, put back; (*máquina*) to re-set; (*TEAT*) to revive; ~**se** *vr* to recover; ~ **que** to reply that.
reponga [re'ponga] *etc vb V* **reponer**.
reportaje [repor'taxe] *nm* report, article; ~ **gráfico** illustrated report.
reportar [repor'tar] *vt* (*traer*) to bring, carry; (*conseguir*) to obtain; (*fig*) to check; ~**se** *vr* (*contenerse*) to control o.s.; (*calmarse*) to calm down; **la cosa no le reportó sino disgustos** the affair brought him nothing but trouble.
reportero, a [repor'tero, a] *nm/f* reporter; ~ **gráfico/a** news photographer.
reposacabezas [reposaka'βeθas] *nm inv* headrest.
reposado, a [repo'saðo, a] *adj* (*descansado*) restful; (*tranquilo*) calm.
reposar [repo'sar] *vi* to rest, repose; (*muerto*) to lie, rest.
reposición [reposi'θjon] *nf* replacement; (*CINE*) second showing; (*TEAT*) revival.
reposo [re'poso] *nm* rest.
repostar [repos'tar] *vt* to replenish; (*AUTO*) to fill up (with petrol *o* gasoline).
repostería [reposte'ria] *nf* (*arte*) confectionery, pastry-making; (*tienda*) confectioner's (shop).
repostero, a [repos'tero, a] *nm/f* confectioner.
reprender [repren'der] *vt* to reprimand; (*niño*) to scold.
reprensión [repren'sjon] *nf* rebuke, reprimand; (*de niño*) telling-off,

scolding.
represa [re'presa] *nf* dam; (*lago artificial*) lake, pool.
represalia [repre'salja] *nf* reprisal; **tomar ~s** to take reprisals, retaliate.
representación [representa'θjon] *nf* representation; (*TEAT*) performance; **en ~ de** representing; **por ~** by proxy; **~ visual** (*INFORM*) display.
representante [represen'tante] *nm/f* (*POL, COM*) representative; (*TEAT*) performer.
representar [represen'tar] *vt* to represent; (*significar*) to mean; (*TEAT*) to perform; (*edad*) to look; **~se** *vr* to imagine; **tal acto representaría la guerra** such an act would mean war.
representativo, a [representa'tiβo, a] *adj* representative.
represión [repre'sjon] *nf* repression.
represivo, a [repre'siβo, a] *adj* repressive.
reprimenda [repri'menda] *nf* reprimand, rebuke.
reprimir [repri'mir] *vt* to repress; **~se** *vr*: **~se de hacer algo** to stop o.s. from doing sth.
reprobación [reproβa'θjon] *nf* reproval; (*culpa*) blame.
reprobar [repro'βar] *vt* to censure, reprove.
réprobo, a ['reproβo, a] *nm/f* reprobate.
reprochar [repro'tʃar] *vt* to reproach; (*censurar*) to condemn, censure.
reproche [re'protʃe] *nm* reproach.
reproducción [reproðuk'θjon] *nf* reproduction.
reproducir [reproðu'θir] *vt* to reproduce; **~se** *vr* to breed; (*situación*) to recur.
reproductor, a [reproðuk'tor, a] *adj* reproductive ♦ *nm*: **~ de discos compactos** CD player.
reproduje [repro'ðuxe], **reprodujera** [reproðu'xera] *etc*, **reproduzca** [repro'duθka] *etc vb V* **reproducir**.
repruebe [re'prweβe] *etc vb V* **reprobar**.
reptar [rep'tar] *vi* to creep, crawl.
reptil [rep'til] *nm* reptile.
república [re'puβlika] *nf* republic; **R~ Dominicana** Dominican Republic; **R~ Democrática Alemana (RDA)** German Democratic Republic; **R~ Federal Alemana (RFA)** Federal Republic of Germany; **R~ Árabe Unida** United Arab Republic.
republicano, a [repuβli'kano, a] *adj, nm/f* republican.
repudiar [repu'ðjar] *vt* to repudiate; (*fe*) to renounce.
repudio [re'puðjo] *nm* repudiation.
repueble [re'pweβle] *etc vb V* **repoblar**.
repuesto [re'pwesto] *pp de* **reponer** ♦ *nm* (*pieza de recambio*) spare (part); (*abastecimiento*) supply; **rueda de ~** spare wheel; **y llevamos otro de ~** and we have another as a spare *o* in reserve.
repugnancia [repuɣ'nanθja] *nf* repugnance.
repugnante [repuɣ'nante] *adj* repugnant, repulsive.
repugnar [repuɣ'nar] *vt* to disgust ♦ *vi*, **~se** *vr* (*contradecirse*) to contradict each other; (*dar asco*) to be disgusting.
repujar [repu'xar] *vt* to emboss.
repulsa [re'pulsa] *nf* rebuff.
repulsión [repul'sjon] *nf* repulsion, aversion.
repulsivo, a [repul'siβo, a] *adj* repulsive.
repuse [re'puse] *etc vb V* **reponer**.
reputación [reputa'θjon] *nf* reputation.
reputar [repu'tar] *vt* to consider, deem.
requemado, a [reke'maðo, a] *adj* (*quemado*) scorched; (*bronceado*) tanned.
requemar [reke'mar] *vt* (*quemar*) to scorch; (*secar*) to parch; (*CULIN*) to overdo, burn; (*la lengua*) to burn, sting.
requerimiento [rekeri'mjento] *nm* request; (*demanda*) demand; (*JUR*) summons.
requerir [reke'rir] *vt* (*pedir*) to ask, request; (*exigir*) to require; (*ordenar*) to call for; (*llamar*) to send for, summon.
requesón [reke'son] *nm* cottage cheese.
requete... [rekete] *pref* extremely.
requiebro [re'kjeβro] *nm* (*piropo*) compliment, flirtatious remark.
réquiem ['rekjem] *nm* requiem.
requiera [re'kjera] *etc*, **requiriendo** [reki'rjendo] *etc vb V* **requerir**.
requisa [re'kisa] *nf* (*inspección*) survey, inspection; (*MIL*) requisition.
requisar [reki'sar] *vt* (*MIL*) to requisition; (*confiscar*) to seize, confiscate.
requisito [reki'sito] *nm* requirement, requisite; **~ previo** prerequisite; **tener los ~s para un cargo** to have the essential qualifications for a post.
res [res] *nf* beast, animal.
resabio [re'saβjo] *nm* (*maña*) vice, bad habit; (*dejo*) (unpleasant) aftertaste.
resaca [re'saka] *nf* (*en el mar*) undertow, undercurrent; (*fig*) backlash; (*fam*) hangover.
resaltar [resal'tar] *vi* to project, stick out; (*fig*) to stand out.
resarcir [resar'θir] *vt* to compensate; (*pagar*) to repay; **~se** *vr* to make up for; **~ a algn de una pérdida** to compensate sb for a loss; **~ a algn de una cantidad** to

repay sb a sum.
resarza [re'sarθa] *etc vb V* **resarcir**.
resbalada [resβa'laðа] *nf (AM)* slip.
resbaladizo, a [resβala'ðiθo, a] *adj* slippery.
resbalar [resβa'lar] *vi*, **resbalarse** *vr* to slip, slide; (*fig*) to slip (up); **le resbalaban las lágrimas por las mejillas** tears were trickling down his cheeks.
resbalón [resβa'lon] *nm* (*acción*) slip; (*deslizamiento*) slide; (*fig*) slip.
rescatar [reska'tar] *vt* (*salvar*) to save, rescue; (*objeto*) to get back, recover; (*cautivos*) to ransom.
rescate [res'kate] *nm* rescue; (*objeto*) recovery; **pagar un** ~ to pay a ransom.
rescindir [resθin'dir] *vt* (*contrato*) to annul, rescind.
rescisión [resθi'sjon] *nf* cancellation.
rescoldo [res'koldo] *nm* embers *pl*.
resecar [rese'kar] *vt* to dry off, dry thoroughly; (*MED*) to cut out, remove; **~se** *vr* to dry up.
reseco, a [re'seko, a] *adj* very dry; (*fig*) skinny.
resentido, a [resen'tiðo, a] *adj* resentful; **es un** ~ he's bitter.
resentimiento [resenti'mjento] *nm* resentment, bitterness.
resentirse [resen'tirse] *vr* (*debilitarse*: *persona*) to suffer; ~ **con** to resent; ~ **de** (*consecuencias*) to feel the effects of.
reseña [re'seɲa] *nf* (*cuenta*) account; (*informe*) report; (*LIT*) review.
reseñar [rese'ɲar] *vt* to describe; (*LIT*) to review.
reseque [re'seke] *etc vb V* **resecar**.
reserva [re'serβa] *nf* reserve; (*reservación*) reservation; **a ~ de que** ... unless ...; **con toda** ~ in strictest confidence; **de** ~ spare; **tener algo de** ~ to have sth in reserve; ~ **de indios** Indian reservation; (*COM*): ~ **para amortización** depreciation allowance; ~ **de caja** *o* **en efectivo** cash reserves; **~s del Estado** government stock; **~s en oro** gold reserves.
reservado, a [reser'βaðo, a] *adj* reserved; (*retraído*) cold, distant ♦ *nm* private room; (*FERRO*) reserved compartment.
reservar [reser'βar] *vt* (*guardar*) to keep; (*FERRO, TEAT etc*) to reserve, book; **~se** *vr* to save o.s.; (*callar*) to keep to o.s.; ~ **con exceso** to overbook.
resfriado [res'friaðo] *nm* cold.
resfriarse [res'friarse] *vr* to cool off; (*MED*) to catch (a) cold.
resfrío [resf'rio] *nm* (*esp AM*) cold.
resguardar [resɣwar'ðar] *vt* to protect, shield; **~se** *vr*: **~se de** to guard against.
resguardo [res'ɣwarðo] *nm* defence; (*vale*) voucher; (*recibo*) receipt, slip.
residencia [resi'ðenθja] *nf* residence; (*UNIV*) hall of residence; ~ **para ancianos** *o* **jubilados** rest home.
residencial [resiðen'θjal] *adj* residential ♦ *nf* (*urbanización*) housing estate (*BRIT*), real estate development (*US*).
residente [resi'ðente] *adj, nm/f* resident.
residir [resi'ðir] *vi* to reside, live; ~ **en** to reside *o* lie in; (*consistir en*) to consist of.
residual [resi'ðwal] *adj* residual; **aguas ~es** sewage.
residuo [re'siðwo] *nm* residue; **~s atmosféricos** *o* **radiactivos** fallout *sg*.
resienta [re'sjenta] *etc vb V* **resentir**.
resignación [resiɣna'θjon] *nf* resignation.
resignarse [resiɣ'narse] *vr*: ~ **a** *o* **con** to resign o.s. to, be resigned to.
resina [re'sina] *nf* resin.
resintiendo [resin'tjendo] *etc vb V* **resentir**.
resistencia [resis'tenθja] *nf* (*dureza*) endurance, strength; (*oposición, ELEC*) resistance; **la R~** (*MIL*) the Resistance.
resistente [resis'tente] *adj* strong, hardy; (*TEC*) resistant; ~ **al calor** heat-resistant.
resistir [resis'tir] *vt* (*soportar*) to bear; (*oponerse a*) to resist, oppose; (*aguantar*) to put up with ♦ *vi* to resist; (*aguantar*) to last, endure; **~se** *vr*: **~se a** to refuse to, resist; **no puedo ~ este frío** I can't bear *o* stand this cold; **me resisto a creerlo** I refuse to believe it; **se le resiste la química** chemistry escapes her.
resol [re'sol] *nm* glare of the sun.
resollar [reso'ʎar] *vi* to breathe noisily, wheeze.
resolución [resolu'θjon] *nf* resolution; (*decisión*) decision; (*moción*) motion; ~ **judicial** legal ruling; **tomar una** ~ to take a decision.
resoluto, a [reso'luto, a] *adj* resolute.
resolver [resol'βer] *vt* to resolve; (*solucionar*) to solve, resolve; (*decidir*) to decide, settle; **~se** *vr* to make up one's mind.
resonancia [reso'nanθja] *nf* (*del sonido*) resonance; (*repercusión*) repercussion; (*fig*) wide effect, impact.
resonante [reso'nante] *adj* resonant, resounding; (*fig*) tremendous.
resonar [reso'nar] *vi* to ring, echo.
resoplar [reso'plar] *vi* to snort; (*por cansancio*) to puff.
resoplido [reso'pliðo] *nm* heavy breathing.
resorte [re'sorte] *nm* spring; (*fig*) lever.
respaldar [respal'dar] *vt* to back (up),

support; (*INFORM*) to back up; ~**se** *vr* to lean back; ~**se con** *o* **en** (*fig*) to take one's stand on.
respaldo [res'paldo] *nm* (*de sillón*) back; (*fig*) support, backing.
respectivo, a [respek'tiβo, a] *adj* respective; **en lo ~ a** with regard to.
respecto [res'pekto] *nm*: **al ~** on this matter; **con ~ a, ~ de** with regard to, in relation to.
respetable [respe'taβle] *adj* respectable.
respetar [respe'tar] *vt* to respect.
respeto [res'peto] *nm* respect; (*acatamiento*) deference; ~**s** *nmpl* respects; **por ~ a** out of consideration for; **presentar sus ~s a** to pay one's respects to.
respetuoso, a [respe'twoso, a] *adj* respectful.
respingo [res'pingo] *nm* start, jump.
respiración [respira'θjon] *nf* breathing; (*MED*) respiration; (*ventilación*) ventilation.
respirar [respi'rar] *vt, vi* to breathe; **no dejar ~ a algn** to keep on at sb; **estuvo escuchándole sin ~** he listened to him in complete silence.
respiratorio, a [respira'torjo, a] *adj* respiratory.
respiro [res'piro] *nm* breathing; (*fig: descanso*) respite, rest; (*COM*) period of grace.
resplandecer [resplande'θer] *vi* to shine.
resplandeciente [resplande'θjente] *adj* resplendent, shining.
resplandezca [resplan'deθka] *etc vb V* **resplandecer**.
resplandor [resplan'dor] *nm* brilliance, brightness; (*del fuego*) blaze.
responder [respon'der] *vt* to answer ♦ *vi* to answer; (*fig*) to respond; (*pey*) to answer back; (*corresponder*) to correspond; ~ **a** (*situación etc*) to respond to; ~ **a una pregunta** to answer a question; ~ **a una descripción** to fit a description; ~ **de** *o* **por** to answer for.
respondón, ona [respon'don, ona] *adj* cheeky.
responsabilice [responsaβi'liθe] *etc vb V* **responsabilizarse**.
responsabilidad [responsaβili'ðað] *nf* responsibility; **bajo mi ~** on my authority; ~ **ilimitada** (*COM*) unlimited liability.
responsabilizarse [responsaβili'θarse] *vr* to make o.s. responsible, take charge.
responsable [respon'sable] *adj* responsible; **la persona ~** the person in charge; **hacerse ~ de algo** to assume responsibility for sth.
respuesta [res'pwesta] *nf* answer, reply; (*reacción*) response.
resquebrajar [reskeβra'xar] *vt*, **resquebrajarse** *vr* to crack, split.
resquemor [reske'mor] *nm* resentment.
resquicio [res'kiθjo] *nm* chink; (*hendedura*) crack.
resta ['resta] *nf* (*MAT*) remainder.
restablecer [restaβle'θer] *vt* to re-establish, restore; ~**se** *vr* to recover.
restablecimiento [restaβleθi'mjento] *nm* re-establishment; (*restauración*) restoration; (*MED*) recovery.
restablezca [resta'βleθka] *etc vb V* **restablecer**.
restallar [resta'ʎar] *vi* to crack.
restante [res'tante] *adj* remaining; **lo ~** the remainder; **los ~s** the rest, those left (over).
restar [res'tar] *vt* (*MAT*) to subtract; (*descontar*) to deduct; (*fig*) to take away ♦ *vi* to remain, be left.
restauración [restaura'θjon] *nf* restoration.
restaurador, a [restaura'ðor, a] *nm/f* (*persona*) restorer.
restaurante [restau'rante] *nm* restaurant.
restaurar [restau'rar] *vt* to restore.
restitución [restitu'θjon] *nf* return, restitution.
restituir [restitu'ir] *vt* (*devolver*) to return, give back; (*rehabilitar*) to restore.
restituyendo [restitu'jendo] *etc vb V* **restituir**.
resto ['resto] *nm* (*residuo*) rest, remainder; (*apuesta*) stake; ~**s** *nmpl* remains; (*CULIN*) leftovers, scraps; ~**s mortales** mortal remains.
restregar [restre'ɣar] *vt* to scrub, rub.
restregué [restre'ɣe], **restreguemos** [restre'ɣemos] *etc vb V* **restregar**.
restricción [restrik'θjon] *nf* restriction; **sin ~ de** without restrictions on *o* as to; **hablar sin restricciones** to talk freely.
restrictivo, a [restrik'tiβo, a] *adj* restrictive.
restriego [res'trjeɣo] *etc*, **restriegue** [res'trjeɣe] *etc vb V* **restregar**.
restringir [restrin'xir] *vt* to restrict, limit.
restrinja [res'trinxa] *etc vb V* **restringir**.
resucitar [resuθi'tar] *vt, vi* to resuscitate, revive.
resuello [re'sweʎo] *etc vb V* **resollar** ♦ *nm* (*aliento*) breath.
resuelto, a [re'swelto, a] *pp de* **resolver** ♦ *adj* resolute, determined; **estar ~ a**

algo to be set on sth; **estar ~ a hacer algo** to be determined to do sth.
resuelva [re'swelβa] *etc vb V* **resolver.**
resuene [re'swene] *etc vb V* **resonar.**
resulta [re'sulta] *nf* result; **de ~s de** as a result of.
resultado [resul'taðo] *nm* result; (*conclusión*) outcome; **~s** *nmpl* (*INFORM*) output *sg*; **dar ~** to produce results.
resultante [resul'tante] *adj* resulting, resultant.
resultar [resul'tar] *vi* (*ser*) to be; (*llegar a ser*) to turn out to be; (*salir bien*) to turn out well; (*seguir*) to ensue; **~ a** (*COM*) to amount to; **~ de** to stem from; **~ en** to result in, produce; **resulta que ...** (*por consecuencia*) it follows that ...; (*parece que*) it seems that ...; **el conductor resultó muerto** the driver was killed; **no resultó** it didn't work *o* come off; **me resulta difícil hacerlo** it's difficult for me to do it.
resumen [re'sumen] *nm* summary, résumé; **en ~** in short.
resumir [resu'mir] *vt* to sum up; (*condensar*) to summarize; (*cortar*) to abridge, cut down; (*condensar*) to summarize; **~se** *vr*: **la situación se resume en pocas palabras** the situation can be summed up in a few words.
resurgir [resur'xir] *vi* (*reaparecer*) to reappear.
resurrección [resurrek'θjon] *nf* resurrection.
retablo [re'taβlo] *nm* altarpiece.
retaguardia [reta'ɣwarðja] *nf* rearguard.
retahíla [reta'ila] *nf* series, string; (*de injurias*) volley, stream.
retal [re'tal] *nm* remnant.
retar [re'tar] *vt* (*gen*) to challenge; (*desafiar*) to defy, dare.
retardar [retar'ðar] *vt* (*demorar*) to delay; (*hacer más lento*) to slow down; (*retener*) to hold back.
retardo [re'tarðo] *nm* delay.
retazo [re'taθo] *nm* snippet (*BRIT*), fragment.
RETD *nf abr* (*ESP TELEC*) = *Red Especial de Transmisión de Datos.*
rete... ['rete] *pref* very, extremely.
retén [re'ten] *nm* (*AM*) roadblock, checkpoint.
retención [reten'θjon] *nf* retention; (*de pago*) deduction; **~ de llamadas** (*TELEC*) hold facility.
retendré [reten'dre] *etc vb V* **retener.**
retener [rete'ner] *vt* (*guardar*) to retain, keep; (*intereses*) to withhold.
retenga [re'tenga] *etc vb V* **retener.**
reticencia [reti'θenθja] *nf* (*sugerencia*) insinuation, (malevolent) suggestion; (*engaño*) half-truth.
reticente [reti'θente] *adj* (*insinuador*) insinuating; (*engañoso*) deceptive.
retiene [re'tjene] *etc vb V* **retener.**
retina [re'tina] *nf* retina.
retintín [retin'tin] *nm* jangle, jingle; **decir algo con ~** to say sth sarcastically.
retirado, a [reti'raðo, a] *adj* (*lugar*) remote; (*vida*) quiet; (*jubilado*) retired ♦ *nf* (*MIL*) retreat; (*de dinero*) withdrawal; (*de embajador*) recall; (*refugio*) safe place; **batirse en retirada** to retreat.
retirar [reti'rar] *vt* to withdraw; (*la mano*) to draw back; (*quitar*) to remove; (*dinero*) to take out, withdraw; (*jubilar*) to retire, pension off; **~se** *vr* to retreat, withdraw; (*jubilarse*) to retire; (*acostarse*) to retire, go to bed.
retiro [re'tiro] *nm* retreat; (*jubilación, tb DEPORTE*) retirement; (*pago*) pension; (*lugar*) quiet place.
reto ['reto] *nm* dare, challenge.
retocar [reto'kar] *vt* to touch up, retouch.
retoce [re'toθe] *etc vb V* **retozar.**
retoño [re'toɲo] *nm* sprout, shoot; (*fig*) offspring, child.
retoque [re'toke] *etc vb V* **retocar** ♦ *nm* retouching.
retorcer [retor'θer] *vt* to twist; (*argumento*) to turn, twist; (*manos, lavado*) to wring; **~se** *vr* to become twisted; (*persona*) to writhe; **~se de dolor** to writhe in *o* squirm with pain.
retorcido, a [retor'θiðo, a] *adj* (*tb fig*) twisted.
retorcimiento [retorθi'mjento] *nm* twist, twisting; (*fig*) deviousness.
retórico, a [re'toriko, a] *adj* rhetorical; (*pey*) affected, windy ♦ *nf* rhetoric; (*pey*) affectedness.
retornable [retor'naβle] *adj* returnable.
retornar [retor'nar] *vt* to return, give back ♦ *vi* to return, go/come back.
retorno [re'torno] *nm* return; **~ del carro** (*INFORM, TIP*) carriage return; **~ del carro automático** (*INFORM*) wordwrap, word wraparound.
retortero [retor'tero] *nm*: **andar al ~** to bustle about, have heaps of things to do; **andar al ~ por algn** to be madly in love with sb.
retortijón [retorti'xon] *nm* twist, twisting; **~ de tripas** stomach cramp.
retorzamos [retor'θamos] *etc vb V* **retorcer.**

retozar [reto'θar] *vi* (*juguetear*) to frolic, romp; (*saltar*) to gambol.
retozón, ona [reto'θon, ona] *adj* playful.
retracción [retrak'θjon] *nf* retraction.
retractarse [retrak'tarse] *vr* to retract; **me retracto** I take that back.
retraerse [retra'erse] *vr* to retreat, withdraw.
retraído, a [retra'iðo, a] *adj* shy, retiring.
retraiga [re'traiɣa] *etc vb V* **retraerse**.
retraimiento [retrai'mjento] *nm* retirement; (*timidez*) shyness.
retraje [re'traxe] *etc*, **retrajera** [retra'xera] *etc vb V* **retraerse**.
retransmisión [retransmi'sjon] *nf* repeat (broadcast).
retransmitir [retransmi'tir] *vt* (*mensaje*) to relay; (*TV etc*) to repeat, retransmit; (: *en vivo*) to broadcast live.
retrasado, a [retra'saðo, a] *adj* late; (*MED*) mentally retarded; (*país etc*) backward, underdeveloped; **estar ~** (*reloj*) to be slow; (*persona, industria*) to be *o* lag behind.
retrasar [retra'sar] *vt* (*demorar*) to postpone, put off; (*retardar*) to slow down ♦ *vi*, **~se** *vr* (*atrasarse*) to be late; (*reloj*) to be slow; (*producción*) to fall (away); (*quedarse atrás*) to lag behind.
retraso [re'traso] *nm* (*demora*) delay; (*lentitud*) slowness; (*tardanza*) lateness; (*atraso*) backwardness; **~s** *nmpl* (*COM*) arrears; (*deudas*) deficit *sg*, debts; **llegar con ~** to arrive late; **llegar con 25 minutos de ~** to be 25 minutes late; **llevo un ~ de 6 semanas** I'm 6 weeks behind (with my work *etc*); **~ mental** mental deficiency.
retratar [retra'tar] *vt* (*ARTE*) to paint the portrait of; (*fotografiar*) to photograph; (*fig*) to depict, describe; **~se** *vr* to have one's portrait painted; to have one's photograph taken.
retratista [retra'tista] *nm/f* (*pintura*) (portrait) painter; (*FOTO*) photographer.
retrato [re'trato] *nm* portrait; (*FOTO*) photograph; (*descripción*) portrayal, depiction; (*fig*) likeness; **ser el vivo ~ de** to be the spitting image of.
retrato-robot [re'tratoro'βo(t)], *pl* **retratos-robot** *nm* identikit picture.
retrayendo [retra'jendo] *etc vb V* **retraerse**.
retreta [re'treta] *nf* retreat.
retrete [re'trete] *nm* toilet.
retribución [retriβu'θjon] *nf* (*recompensa*) reward; (*pago*) pay, payment.
retribuir [retriβu'ir] *vt* (*recompensar*) to reward; (*pagar*) to pay.
retribuyendo [retriβu'jendo] *etc vb V* **retribuir**.
retro... [retro] *pref* retro....
retroactivo, a [retroak'tiβo, a] *adj* retroactive, retrospective; **dar efecto ~ a un pago** to backdate a payment.
retroalimentación [retroalimenta'θjon] *nf* (*INFORM*) feedback.
retroceder [retroθe'ðer] *vi* (*echarse atrás*) to move back(wards); (*fig*) to back down; **no ~** to stand firm; **la policía hizo ~ a la multitud** the police forced the crowd back.
retroceso [retro'θeso] *nm* backward movement; (*MED*) relapse; (*COM*) recession, depression; (*fig*) backing down.
retrógrado, a [re'troɣraðo, a] *adj* retrograde, retrogressive; (*POL*) reactionary.
retropropulsión [retropropul'sjon] *nf* jet propulsion.
retrospectivo, a [retrospek'tiβo, a] *adj* retrospective; **mirada retrospectiva** backward glance.
retrovisor [retroβi'sor] *nm* rear-view mirror.
retuerce [re'twerθe] *etc*, **retuerza** [re'twerθa] *etc vb V* **retorcer**.
retumbante [retum'bante] *adj* resounding.
retumbar [retum'bar] *vi* to echo, resound; (*continuamente*) to reverberate.
retuve [re'tuβe] *etc vb V* **retener**.
reuma ['reuma] *nm* rheumatism.
reumático, a [reu'matiko, a] *adj* rheumatic.
reumatismo [reuma'tismo] *nm* rheumatism.
reunificar [reunifi'kar] *vt* to reunify.
reunifique [reuni'fike] *etc vb V* **reunificar**.
reunión [reu'njon] *nf* (*asamblea*) meeting; (*fiesta*) party; **~ en la cumbre** summit meeting; **~ de ventas** (*COM*) sales meeting.
reunir [reu'nir] *vt* (*juntar*) to reunite, join (together); (*recoger*) to gather (together); (*personas*) to bring *o* get together; (*cualidades*) to combine; **~se** *vr* (*personas*: *en asamblea*) to meet, gather; **reunió a sus amigos para discutirlo** he got his friends together to talk it over.
reválida [re'βaliða] *nf* (*ESCOL*) final examination.
revalidar [reβali'ðar] *vt* (*ratificar*) to confirm, ratify.
revalorar [reβalo'rar] *vt* to revalue, reassess.
revalor(iz)ación [reβalor(iθ)a'θjon] *nf*

revaluation; (*ECON*) reassessment.
revancha [re'ßantʃa] *nf* revenge; (*DEPORTE*) return match; (*BOXEO*) return fight.
revelación [reßela'θjon] *nf* revelation.
revelado [reße'laðo] *nm* developing.
revelador, a [reßela'ðor, a] *adj* revealing.
revelar [reße'lar] *vt* to reveal; (*secreto*) to disclose; (*mostrar*) to show; (*FOTO*) to develop.
revendedor, a [reßende'ðor, a] *nm/f* retailer; (*pey*) ticket tout.
revendré [reßen'dre] *etc*, **revenga** [re'ßenga] *etc vb V* **revenirse.**
revenirse [reße'nirse] *vr* to shrink; (*comida*) to go bad *o* off; (*vino*) to sour; (*CULIN*) to get tough.
reventa [re'ßenta] *nf* resale; (*especulación*) speculation; (*de entradas*) touting.
reventar [reßen'tar] *vt* to burst, explode; (*molestar*) to annoy, rile ♦ *vi*, **~se** *vr* (*estallar*) to burst, explode; **me revienta tener que ponérmelo** I hate having to wear it; **~ de** (*fig*) to be bursting with; **~ por** to be bursting to.
reventón [reßen'ton] *nm* (*AUTO*) blow-out (*BRIT*), flat (*US*).
reverberación [reßerßera'θjon] *nf* reverberation.
reverberar [reßerße'rar] *vi* (*luz*) to play, be reflected; (*superficie*) to shimmer; (*nieve*) to glare; (*sonido*) to reverberate.
reverbero [reßer'ßero] *nm* play; shimmer, shine; glare; reverberation.
reverencia [reße'renθja] *nf* reverence; (*inclinación*) bow.
reverenciar [reßeren'θjar] *vt* to revere.
reverendo, a [reße'rendo, a] *adj* reverend; (*fam*) big, awful; **un ~ imbécil** an awful idiot.
reverente [reße'rente] *adj* reverent.
reversible [reßer'sißle] *adj* reversible.
reverso [re'ßerso] *nm* back, other side; (*de moneda*) reverse.
revertir [reßer'tir] *vi* to revert; **~ en beneficio de** to be to the advantage of; **~ en perjuicio de** to be to the detriment of.
revés [re'ßes] *nm* back, wrong side; (*fig*) reverse, setback; (*DEPORTE*) backhand; **al ~** the wrong way round; (*de arriba abajo*) upside down; (*ropa*) inside out; **y al ~** and vice versa; **volver algo al ~** to turn sth round; (*ropa*) to turn sth inside out; **los reveses de la fortuna** the blows of fate.
revestir [reßes'tir] *vt* (*poner*) to put on; (*cubrir*) to cover, coat; (*cualidad*) to have, possess; **~se** *vr* (*REL*) to put on one's vestments; (*ponerse*) to put on; **~ con** *o* **de** to arm o.s. with; **el acto revestía gran solemnidad** the ceremony had great dignity.
reviejo, a [re'ßjexo, a] *adj* very old, ancient.
reviene [re'ßjene] *etc vb V* **revenirse.**
reviente [re'ßjente] *etc vb V* **reventar.**
revierta [re'ßjerta] *etc vb V* **revertir.**
reviniendo [reßi'njendo] *etc vb V* **revenirse.**
revirtiendo [reßir'tjendo] *etc vb V* **revertir.**
revisar [reßi'sar] *vt* (*examinar*) to check; (*texto etc*) to revise; (*JUR*) to review.
revisión [reßi'sjon] *nf* revision; **~ aduanera** customs inspection; **~ de cuentas** audit.
revisor, a [reßi'sor, a] *nm/f* inspector; (*FERRO*) ticket collector; **~ de cuentas** auditor.
revista [re'ßista] *etc vb V* **revestir** ♦ *nf* magazine, review; (*sección*) section, page; (*TEAT*) revue; (*inspección*) inspection; **~ literaria** literary review; **~ de libros** book reviews (page); **pasar ~ a** to review, inspect.
revivir [reßi'ßir] *vt* (*recordar*) to revive memories of ♦ *vi* to revive.
revocación [reßoka'θjon] *nf* repeal.
revocar [reßo'kar] *vt* (*decisión*) to revoke; (*ARQ*) to plaster.
revolcar [reßol'kar] *vt* to knock down, send flying; **~se** *vr* to roll about.
revolcón [reßol'kon] *nm* tumble.
revolotear [reßolote'ar] *vi* to flutter.
revoloteo [reßolo'teo] *nm* fluttering.
revolqué [reßol'ke], **revolquemos** [reßol'kemos] *etc vb V* **revolcar.**
revoltijo [reßol'tixo] *nm* mess, jumble.
revoltoso, a [reßol'toso, a] *adj* (*travieso*) naughty, unruly.
revolución [reßolu'θjon] *nf* revolution.
revolucionar [reßoluθjo'nar] *vt* to revolutionize.
revolucionario, a [reßoluθjo'narjo, a] *adj, nm/f* revolutionary.
revolver [reßol'ßer] *vt* (*desordenar*) to disturb, mess up; (*agitar*) to shake; (*líquido*) to stir; (*mover*) to move about; (*POL*) to stir up ♦ *vi*: **~ en** to go through, rummage (about) in; **~se** *vr* (*en cama*) to toss and turn; (*METEOROLOGÍA*) to break, turn stormy; **~se contra** to turn on *o* against; **han revuelto toda la casa** they've turned the whole house upside down.
revólver [re'ßolßer] *nm* revolver.
revoque [re'ßoke] *etc vb V* **revocar.**
revuelco [re'ßwelko] *etc vb V* **revolcar.**
revuelo [re'ßwelo] *nm* fluttering; (*fig*) commotion; **armar** *o* **levantar un gran ~**

to cause a great stir.
revuelque [re'ßwelke] *etc vb V* **revolcar**.
revuelto, a [re'ßwelto, a] *pp de* **revolver** ♦ *adj* (*mezclado*) mixed-up, in disorder; (*mar*) rough; (*tiempo*) unsettled ♦ *nf* (*motín*) revolt; (*agitación*) commotion; **todo estaba ~** everything was in disorder *o* was topsy-turvy.
revuelva [re'ßwelßa] *etc vb V* **revolver**.
revulsivo [reßul'sißo] *nm*: **servir de ~** to have a salutary effect.
rey [rei] *nm* king; **los R~es** the King and Queen; **los R~es Magos** the Magi; *see boxed note*.

REYES MAGOS

On the night before 6 January (Epiphany), a holiday in Spain, children go to bed expecting **los Reyes Magos**, *the Three Wise Men, to bring them presents. Twelfth Night processions, known as "cabalgatas", take place that evening too; three people dressed as* **los Reyes Magos** *arrive in town by land or sea to the delight of the local children.*

reyerta [re'jerta] *nf* quarrel, brawl.
rezagado, a [reθa'ɣaðo, a] *adj*: **quedar ~** to be left behind; (*estar retrasado*) to be late, be behind ♦ *nm/f* straggler.
rezagar [reθa'ɣar] *vt* (*dejar atrás*) to leave behind; (*retrasar*) to delay, postpone; **~se** *vr* (*atrasarse*) to fall behind.
rezague [re'θaɣe] *etc vb V* **rezagar**.
rezar [re'θar] *vi* to pray; **~ con** (*fam*) to concern, have to do with.
rezo ['reθo] *nm* prayer.
rezongar [reθon'gar] *vi* to grumble; (*murmurar*) to mutter; (*refunfuñar*) to growl.
rezongue [re'θonge] *etc vb V* **rezongar**.
rezumar [reθu'mar] *vt* to ooze ♦ *vi* to leak; **~se** *vr* to leak out.
RFA *nf abr* = **República Federal Alemana**.
ría ['ria] *nf* estuary.
riachuelo [rja'tʃwelo] *nm* stream.
riada [ri'aða] *nf* flood.
ribera [ri'ßera] *nf* (*de río*) bank; (: *área*) riverside.
ribete [ri'ßete] *nm* (*de vestido*) border; (*fig*) addition.
ribetear [rißete'ar] *vt* to edge, border.
rice ['riθe] *etc vb V* **rizar**.
ricino [ri'θino] *nm*: **aceite de ~** castor oil.
rico, a ['riko, a] *adj* (*adinerado*) rich, wealthy; (*lujoso*) luxurious; (*comida*) delicious; (*niño*) lovely, cute ♦ *nm/f* rich person; **nuevo ~** nouveau riche.
rictus ['riktus] *nm* (*mueca*) sneer, grin; **~ de amargura** bitter smile.
ridiculez [riðiku'leθ] *nf* absurdity.
ridiculice [riðiku'liθe] *etc vb V* **ridiculizar**.
ridiculizar [riðikuli'θar] *vt* to ridicule.
ridículo, a [ri'ðikulo, a] *adj* ridiculous; **hacer el ~** to make a fool of o.s.; **poner a algn en ~** to make a fool of sb; **ponerse en ~** to make a fool of o.s.
riego ['rjeɣo] *etc vb V* **regar** ♦ *nm* (*aspersión*) watering; (*irrigación*) irrigation.
riegue ['rjeɣe] *etc vb V* **regar**.
riel [rjel] *nm* rail.
rienda ['rjenda] *nf* rein; (*fig*) restraint, moderating influence; **dar ~ suelta a** to give free rein to; **llevar las ~s** to be in charge.
riendo ['rjendo] *vb V* **reír**.
riesgo ['rjesɣo] *nm* risk; **seguro a** *o* **contra todo ~** comprehensive insurance; **~ para la salud** health hazard; **correr el ~ de** to run the risk of.
Rif [rif] *nm* Rif(f).
rifa ['rifa] *nf* (*lotería*) raffle.
rifar [ri'far] *vt* to raffle.
rifeño, a [ri'feɲo, a] *adj* of the Rif(f), Rif(f)ian ♦ *nm/f* Rif(f)ian, Rif(f).
rifle ['rifle] *nm* rifle.
rigidez [rixi'ðeθ] *nf* rigidity, stiffness; (*fig*) strictness.
rígido, a ['rixiðo, a] *adj* rigid, stiff; (*moralmente*) strict, inflexible; (*cara*) wooden, expressionless.
rigiendo [ri'xjendo] *etc vb V* **regir**.
rigor [ri'ɣor] *nm* strictness, rigour; (*dureza*) toughness; (*inclemencia*) harshness; (*meticulosidad*) accuracy; **el ~ del verano** the hottest part of the summer; **con todo ~ científico** with scientific precision; **de ~** de rigueur, essential; **después de los saludos de ~** after the inevitable greetings.
riguroso, a [riɣu'roso, a] *adj* rigorous; (*METEOROLOGÍA*) harsh; (*severo*) severe.
rija ['rixa] *etc vb V* **regir** ♦ *nf* quarrel.
rima ['rima] *nf* rhyme; **~s** *nfpl* verse *sg*; **~ imperfecta** assonance; **~ rimando** (*fam*) merrily.
rimar [ri'mar] *vi* to rhyme.
rimbombante [rimbom'bante] *adj* (*fig*) pompous.
rímel, rímmel ['rimel] *nm* mascara.
rimero [ri'mero] *nm* stack, pile.
Rin [rin] *nm* Rhine.
rincón [rin'kon] *nm* corner (*inside*).
rindiendo [rin'djendo] *etc vb V* **rendir**.
ring [riŋ] *nm* (*BOXEO*) ring.

rinoceronte [rinoθe'ronte] *nm* rhinoceros.
riña ['riɲa] *nf* (*disputa*) argument; (*pelea*) brawl.
riñendo [ri'ɲendo] *etc vb V* **reñir.**
riñón [ri'ɲon] *nm* kidney; **me costó un ~** (*fam*) it cost me an arm and a leg; **tener riñones** to have guts.
río ['rio] *etc vb V* **reír** ♦ *nm* river; (*fig*) torrent, stream; **~ abajo/arriba** downstream/upstream; **cuando el ~ suena, agua lleva** there's no smoke without fire.
rió [ri'o] *vb V* **reír.**
Río de Janeiro ['rioðexa'neiro] *nm* Rio de Janeiro.
Río de la Plata ['rioðela'plata] *nm* Rio de la Plata, River Plate.
Rioja [ri'oxa] *nf*: **La ~** La Rioja ♦ *nm*: **r~** rioja wine.
riojano, a [rjo'xano, a] *adj, nm/f* Riojan.
rioplatense [riopla'tense] *adj* of *o* from the River Plate region ♦ *nm/f* native *o* inhabitant of the River Plate region.
riqueza [ri'keθa] *nf* wealth, riches *pl*; (*cualidad*) richness.
risa ['risa] *nf* laughter; (*una* ~) laugh; **¡qué ~!** what a laugh!; **caerse** *o* **morirse de ~** to split one's sides laughing, die laughing; **tomar algo a ~** to laugh sth off.
risco ['risko] *nm* crag, cliff.
risible [ri'siβle] *adj* ludicrous, laughable.
risotada [riso'taða] *nf* guffaw, loud laugh.
ristra ['ristra] *nf* string.
ristre ['ristre] *nm*: **en ~** at the ready.
risueño, a [ri'sweɲo, a] *adj* (*sonriente*) smiling; (*contento*) cheerful.
ritmo ['ritmo] *nm* rhythm; **a ~ lento** slowly; **trabajar a ~ lento** to go slow.
rito ['rito] *nm* rite.
ritual [ri'twal] *adj, nm* ritual.
rival [ri'βal] *adj, nm/f* rival.
rivalice [riβa'liθe] *etc vb V* **rivalizar.**
rivalidad [riβali'ðað] *nf* rivalry, competition.
rivalizar [riβali'θar] *vi*: **~ con** to rival, compete with.
rizado, a [ri'θaðo, a] *adj* (*pelo*) curly; (*superficie*) ridged; (*terreno*) undulating; (*mar*) choppy ♦ *nm* curls *pl*.
rizar [ri'θar] *vt* to curl; **~se** *vr* (*el pelo*) to curl; (*agua*) to ripple; (*el mar*) to become choppy.
rizo ['riθo] *nm* curl; (*agua*) ripple.
Rma. *abr* (= *Reverendísima*) *courtesy title.*
Rmo. *abr* (= *Reverendísimo*) Rt. Rev.
RNE *nf abr* = *Radio Nacional de España.*
R. O. *abr* (=*Real Orden*) royal order.
robar [ro'βar] *vt* to rob; (*objeto*) to steal; (*casa etc*) to break into; (*NAIPES*) to draw; (*atención*) to steal, capture; (*paciencia*) to exhaust.
roble ['roβle] *nm* oak.
robledal [roβle'ðal], **robledo** [ro'βleðo] *nm* oakwood.
robo ['roβo] *nm* robbery, theft; (*objeto robado*) stolen article *o* goods *pl*; **¡esto es un ~!** this is daylight robbery!
robot [ro'βo(t)], *pl* **robots** *adj, nm* robot ♦ *nm* (*tb*: **~ de cocina**) food processor.
robótica [ro'βotika] *nf* robotics *sg*.
robustecer [roβuste'θer] *vt* to strengthen.
robustezca [roβus'teθka] *etc vb V* **robustecer.**
robusto, a [ro'βusto, a] *adj* robust, strong.
ROC *abr* (*INFORM*: = *reconocimiento óptico de caracteres*) OCR.
roca ['roka] *nf* rock; **la R~** the Rock (of Gibraltar).
roce ['roθe] *etc vb V* **rozar** ♦ *nm* rub, rubbing; (*caricia*) brush; (*TEC*) friction; (*en la piel*) graze; **tener ~ con** to have a brush with.
rociar [ro'θjar] *vt* to sprinkle, spray.
rocín [ro'θin] *nm* nag, hack.
rocío [ro'θio] *nm* dew.
rock [rok] *adj inv, nm* (*MUS*) rock (*cpd*).
rockero, a [ro'kero, a] *adj* rock *cpd* ♦ *nm/f* rocker.
rocoso, a [ro'koso, a] *adj* rocky.
rodado, a [ro'ðaðo, a] *adj* (*con ruedas*) wheeled ♦ *nf* rut.
rodaja [ro'ðaxa] *nf* (*raja*) slice.
rodaje [ro'ðaxe] *nm* (*CINE*) shooting, filming; (*AUTO*): **en ~** running in.
rodamiento [roða'mjento] *nm* (*AUTO*) tread.
Ródano ['roðano] *nm* Rhône.
rodar [ro'ðar] *vt* (*vehículo*) to wheel (along); (*escalera*) to roll down; (*viajar por*) to travel (over) ♦ *vi* to roll; (*coche*) to go, run; (*CINE*) to shoot, film; (*persona*) to move about (from place to place), drift; **echarlo todo a ~** (*fig*) to mess it all up.
Rodas ['roðas] *nf* Rhodes.
rodear [roðe'ar] *vt* to surround ♦ *vi* to go round; **~se** *vr*: **~se de amigos** to surround o.s. with friends.
rodeo [ro'ðeo] *nm* (*ruta indirecta*) long way round, roundabout way; (*desvío*) detour; (*evasión*) evasion; (*AM*) rodeo; **dejarse de ~s** to talk straight; **hablar sin ~s** to come to the point, speak plainly.
rodilla [ro'ðiʎa] *nf* knee; **de ~s** kneeling.
rodillo [ro'ðiʎo] *nm* roller; (*CULIN*) rolling-pin; (*en máquina de escribir, impresora*)

platen.
rododendro [roðo'ðendro] *nm* rhododendron.
roedor, a [roe'ðor, a] *adj* gnawing ♦ *nm* rodent.
roer [ro'er] *vt* (*masticar*) to gnaw; (*corroer, fig*) to corrode.
rogar [ro'ɣar] *vt* (*pedir*) to beg, ask for ♦ *vi* (*suplicar*) to beg, plead; **~se** *vr*: **se ruega no fumar** please do not smoke; ~ **que** + *subjun* to ask to ...; **ruegue a este señor que nos deje en paz** please ask this gentleman to leave us alone; **no se hace de** ~ he doesn't have to be asked twice.
rogué [ro'ɣe], **roguemos** [ro'ɣemos] *etc vb V* **rogar**.
rojizo, a [ro'xiθo, a] *adj* reddish.
rojo, a ['roxo, a] *adj* red ♦ *nm* red (colour); (*POL*) red; **ponerse** ~ to turn red, blush; **al ~ vivo** red-hot.
rol [rol] *nm* list, roll; (*esp AM: papel*) role.
rollizo, a [ro'ʎiθo, a] *adj* (*objeto*) cylindrical; (*persona*) plump.
rollo, a ['roʎo, a] *adj* (*fam*) boring, tedious ♦ *nm* roll; (*de cuerda*) coil; (*madera*) log; (*fam*) bore; (*discurso*) boring speech; **¡qué ~!** what a carry-on!; **la conferencia fue un** ~ the lecture was a big drag.
ROM [rom] *nf abr* (= *memoria de sólo lectura*) ROM.
Roma ['roma] *nf* Rome; **por todas partes se va a** ~ all roads lead to Rome.
romance [ro'manθe] *nm* (*LING*) Romance language; (*LIT*) ballad; **hablar en** ~ to speak plainly.
románico, a [ro'maniko, a] *adj, nm* Romanesque.
romano, a [ro'mano, a] *adj* Roman, of Rome ♦ *nm/f* Roman.
romanticismo [romanti'θismo] *nm* romanticism.
romántico, a [ro'mantiko, a] *adj* romantic.
rombo ['rombo] *nm* (*GEOM*) rhombus; (*diseño*) diamond; (*TIP*) lozenge.
romería [rome'ria] *nf* (*REL*) pilgrimage; (*excursión*) trip, outing; *see boxed note.*

ROMERÍA

Originally a pilgrimage to a shrine or church to express devotion to the Virgin Mary or a local saint, the term **romería** *has been extended to describe the rural "fiesta" which accompanies the pilgrimage. People come from all over the country to spend the day in celebration, bringing copious amounts of food and drink with them.*

romero, a [ro'mero, a] *nm/f* pilgrim ♦ *nm* rosemary.
romo, a ['romo, a] *adj* blunt; (*fig*) dull.
rompecabezas [rompeka'ßeθas] *nm inv* riddle, puzzle; (*juego*) jigsaw (puzzle).
rompehielos [rompe'jelos] *nm inv* icebreaker.
rompeolas [rompe'olas] *nm inv* breakwater.
romper [rom'per] *vt* to break; (*hacer pedazos*) to smash; (*papel, tela etc*) to tear, rip; (*relaciones*) to break off ♦ *vi* (*olas*) to break; (*sol, diente*) to break through; ~ **un contrato** to break a contract; ~ **a** to start (suddenly) to; ~ **a llorar** to burst into tears; ~ **con algn** to fall out with sb; **ha roto con su novio** she has broken up with her fiancé.
rompimiento [rompi'mjento] *nm* (*acto*) breaking; (*fig*) break; (*quiebra*) crack; ~ **de relaciones** breaking off of relations.
ron [ron] *nm* rum.
roncar [ron'kar] *vi* (*al dormir*) to snore; (*animal*) to roar.
roncha ['rontʃa] *nf* (*cardenal*) bruise; (*hinchazón*) swelling.
ronco, a ['ronko, a] *adj* (*afónico*) hoarse; (*áspero*) raucous.
ronda ['ronda] *nf* (*de bebidas etc*) round; (*patrulla*) patrol; (*de naipes*) hand, game; **ir de** ~ to do one's round.
rondar [ron'dar] *vt* to patrol; (*a una persona*) to hang round; (*molestar*) to harass; (*a una chica*) to court ♦ *vi* to patrol; (*fig*) to prowl round; (*MUS*) to go serenading.
rondeño, a [ron'deɲo, a] *adj* of *o* from Ronda ♦ *nm/f* native *o* inhabitant of Ronda.
ronque ['ronke] *etc vb V* **roncar**.
ronquido [ron'kiðo] *nm* snore, snoring.
ronronear [ronrone'ar] *vi* to purr.
ronroneo [ronro'neo] *nm* purr.
roña ['roɲa] *nf* (*veterinaria*) mange; (*mugre*) dirt, grime; (*óxido*) rust.
roñica [ro'ɲika] *nm/f* (*fam*) skinflint.
roñoso, a [ro'ɲoso, a] *adj* (*mugriento*) filthy; (*tacaño*) mean.
ropa ['ropa] *nf* clothes *pl*, clothing; ~ **blanca** linen; ~ **de cama** bed linen; ~ **interior** underwear; ~ **lavada** *o* **para lavar** washing; ~ **planchada** ironing; ~ **sucia** dirty clothes *pl*, washing; ~ **usada** secondhand clothes.
ropaje [ro'paxe] *nm* gown, robes *pl*.
ropero [ro'pero] *nm* linen cupboard; (*guardarropa*) wardrobe.
rosa ['rosa] *adj inv* pink ♦ *nf* rose; (*ANAT*)

red birthmark; ~ **de los vientos** the compass; **estar como una** ~ to feel as fresh as a daisy; **(color) de** ~ pink.
rosado, a [ro'saðo, a] *adj* pink ♦ *nm* rosé.
rosal [ro'sal] *nm* rosebush.
rosaleda [rosa'leða] *nf* rose bed *o* garden.
rosario [ro'sarjo] *nm* (*REL*) rosary; (*fig: serie*) string; **rezar el** ~ to say the rosary.
rosbif [ros'ßif] *nm* roast beef.
rosca ['roska] *nf* (*de tornillo*) thread; (*de humo*) coil, spiral; (*pan, postre*) ring-shaped roll/pastry; **hacer la** ~ **a algn** (*fam*) to suck up to sb; **pasarse de** ~ (*fig*) to go too far.
Rosellón [rose'ʎon] *nm* Roussillon.
rosetón [rose'ton] *nm* rosette; (*ARQ*) rose window.
rosquilla [ros'kiʎa] *nf small ring-shaped cake*; (*de humo*) ring.
rosticería [rostise'ria] *nf* (*AM*) *roast chicken shop*.
rostro ['rostro] *nm* (*cara*) face; (*fig*) cheek.
rotación [rota'θjon] *nf* rotation; ~ **de cultivos** crop rotation.
rotativo, a [rota'tißo, a] *adj* rotary ♦ *nm* newspaper.
roto, a ['roto, a] *pp de* **romper** ♦ *adj* broken; (*en pedazos*) smashed; (*tela, papel*) torn; (*vida*) shattered ♦ *nm* (*en vestido*) hole, tear.
rótula ['rotula] *nf* kneecap; (*TEC*) ball-and-socket joint.
rotulador [rotula'ðor] *nm* felt-tip pen.
rotular [rotu'lar] *vt* (*carta, documento*) to head, entitle; (*objeto*) to label.
rótulo ['rotulo] *nm* (*título*) heading, title; (*etiqueta*) label; (*letrero*) sign.
rotundo, a [ro'tundo, a] *adj* round; (*enfático*) emphatic.
rotura [ro'tura] *nf* (*rompimiento*) breaking; (*MED*) fracture.
roturar [rotu'rar] *vt* to plough.
roulote [ru'lote] *nf* caravan (*BRIT*), trailer (*US*).
rozado, a [ro'θaðo, a] *adj* worn.
rozadura [roθa'ðura] *nf* abrasion, graze.
rozar [ro'θar] *vt* (*frotar*) to rub; (*ensuciar*) to dirty; (*MED*) to graze; (*tocar ligeramente*) to shave, skim; (*fig*) to touch *o* border on; ~**se** *vr* to rub (together); ~ **con** (*fam*) to rub shoulders with.
Rte. *abr* = **remite, remitente**.
RTVE *nf abr* (*TV*) = *Radiotelevisión Española*.
Ruán [ru'an] *nm* Rouen.
rubéola [ru'ßeola] *nf* German measles, rubella.
rubí [ru'ßi] *nm* ruby; (*de reloj*) jewel.
rubio, a ['rußjo, a] *adj* fair-haired, blond(e) ♦ *nm/f* blond/blonde; **tabaco** ~ Virginia tobacco; **(cerveza) rubia** lager.
rubor [ru'ßor] *nm* (*sonrojo*) blush; (*timidez*) bashfulness.
ruborice [rußo'riθe] *etc vb V* **ruborizarse**.
ruborizarse [rußori'θarse] *vr* to blush.
ruboroso, a [rußo'roso, a] *adj* blushing.
rúbrica ['rußrika] *nf* (*título*) title, heading; (*de la firma*) flourish; **bajo la** ~ **de** under the heading of.
rubricar [rußri'kar] *vt* (*firmar*) to sign with a flourish; (*concluir*) to sign and seal.
rubrique [ru'ßrike] *etc vb V* **rubricar**.
rudeza [ru'ðeθa] *nf* (*tosquedad*) coarseness; (*sencillez*) simplicity.
rudimentario, a [ruðimen'tarjo, a] *adj* rudimentary, basic.
rudo, a ['ruðo, a] *adj* (*sin pulir*) unpolished; (*grosero*) coarse; (*violento*) violent; (*sencillo*) simple.
rueda ['rweða] *nf* wheel; (*círculo*) ring, circle; (*rodaja*) slice, round; (*en impresora etc*) sprocket; ~ **delantera/trasera/de repuesto** front/back/spare wheel; ~ **impresora** (*INFORM*) print wheel; ~ **de prensa** press conference.
ruedo ['rweðo] *etc vb V* **rodar** ♦ *nm* (*contorno*) edge, border; (*de vestido*) hem; (*círculo*) circle; (*TAUR*) arena, bullring; (*esterilla*) (round) mat.
ruego ['rweɣo] *etc vb V* **rogar** ♦ *nm* request; **a** ~ **de** at the request of; **"~s y preguntas"** "question and answer session".
ruegue ['rweɣe] *etc vb V* **rogar**.
rufián [ru'fjan] *nm* scoundrel.
rugby ['ruɣßi] *nm* rugby.
rugido [ru'xiðo] *nm* roar.
rugir [ru'xir] *vi* to roar; (*toro*) to bellow; (*estómago*) to rumble.
rugoso, a [ru'ɣoso, a] *adj* (*arrugado*) wrinkled; (*áspero*) rough; (*desigual*) ridged.
ruibarbo [rwi'ßarßo] *nm* rhubarb.
ruido ['rwiðo] *nm* noise; (*sonido*) sound; (*alboroto*) racket, row; (*escándalo*) commotion, rumpus; ~ **de fondo** background noise; **hacer** *o* **meter** ~ to cause a stir.
ruidoso, a [rwi'ðoso, a] *adj* noisy, loud; (*fig*) sensational.
ruin [rwin] *adj* contemptible, mean.
ruina ['rwina] *nf* ruin; (*colapso*) collapse; (*de persona*) ruin, downfall; **estar hecho una** ~ to be a wreck; **la empresa le llevó a la** ~ the venture ruined him (financially).
ruindad [rwin'dað] *nf* lowness, meanness;

(*acto*) low *o* mean act.
ruinoso, a [rwi'noso, a] *adj* ruinous; (*destartalado*) dilapidated, tumbledown; (*COM*) disastrous.
ruiseñor [rwise'ɲor] *nm* nightingale.
ruja ['ruxa] *etc vb V* **rugir**.
ruleta [ru'leta] *nf* roulette.
rulo ['rulo] *nm* (*para el pelo*) curler.
rulot(e) [ru'lot(e)] *nf* caravan (*BRIT*), trailer (*US*).
Rumanía [ru'manja] *nf* Rumania.
rumano, a [ru'mano, a] *adj, nm/f* Rumanian.
rumba ['rumba] *nf* rumba.
rumbo ['rumbo] *nm* (*ruta*) route, direction; (*ángulo de dirección*) course, bearing; (*fig*) course of events; **con ~ a** in the direction of; **ir con ~ a** to be heading for; (*NAUT*) to be bound for.
rumboso, a [rum'boso, a] *adj* (*generoso*) generous.
rumiante [ru'mjante] *nm* ruminant.
rumiar [ru'mjar] *vt* to chew; (*fig*) to chew over ♦ *vi* to chew the cud.
rumor [ru'mor] *nm* (*ruido sordo*) low sound; (*murmuración*) murmur, buzz.
rumorearse [rumore'arse] *vr*: **se rumorea que** it is rumoured that.
rumoroso, a [rumo'roso, a] *adj* full of sounds; (*arroyo*) murmuring.
runrún [run'run] *nm* (*voces*) murmur, sound of voices; (*fig*) rumour; (*de una máquina*) whirr.
rupestre [ru'pestre] *adj* rock *cpd*; **pintura ~** cave painting.
ruptura [rup'tura] *nf* (*gen*) rupture; (*disputa*) split; (*de contrato*) breach; (*de relaciones*) breaking-off.
rural [ru'ral] *adj* rural.
Rusia ['rusja] *nf* Russia.
ruso, a ['ruso, a] *adj, nm/f* Russian ♦ *nm* (*LING*) Russian.
rústico, a ['rustiko, a] *adj* rustic; (*ordinario*) coarse, uncouth ♦ *nm/f* yokel ♦ *nf*: **libro en rústica** paperback (book).
ruta ['ruta] *nf* route.
rutina [ru'tina] *nf* routine; **~ diaria** daily routine; **por ~** as a matter of course.
rutinario, a [ruti'narjo, a] *adj* routine.

S s

S, s ['ese] *nf* S, s; **S de Sábado** S for Sugar.
S *abr* (= *san, santo, a*) St.; (= *sur*) S.
s. *abr* (= *siglo*) c.; (= *siguiente*) foll.
s/ *abr* (*COM*) = **su(s)**.
S.ª *abr* (= *Sierra*) Mts.
S.A. *abr* (= *Sociedad Anónima*) Ltd., Inc. (*US*); (= *Su Alteza*) H.H.
sáb. *abr* (= *sábado*) Sat.
sábado ['saβaðo] *nm* Saturday; (*de los judíos*) Sabbath; **del ~ en ocho días** a week on Saturday; **un ~ sí y otro no, cada dos ~s** every other Saturday; **S~ Santo** Holy Saturday; *V tb* **Semana Santa**.
sabana [sa'βana] *nf* savannah.
sábana ['saβana] *nf* sheet; **se le pegan las ~s** he can't get up in the morning.
sabandija [saβan'dixa] *nf* (*bicho*) bug; (*fig*) louse.
sabañón [saβa'ɲon] *nm* chilblain.
sabático, a [sa'βatiko, a] *adj* (*REL, UNIV*) sabbatical.
sabelotodo [saβelo'toðo] *nm/f inv* know-all.
saber [sa'βer] *vt* to know; (*llegar a conocer*) to find out, learn; (*tener capacidad de*) to know how to ♦ *vi*: **~ a** to taste of, taste like ♦ *nm* knowledge, learning; **~se** *vr*: **se sabe que ...** it is known that ...; **no se sabe** nobody knows; **a ~** namely; **¿sabes conducir/nadar?** can you drive/swim?; **¿sabes francés?** do you *o* can you speak French?; **~ de memoria** to know by heart; **lo sé** I know; **hacer ~** to inform, let know; **que yo sepa** as far as I know; **vete *o* anda a ~** your guess is as good as mine, who knows!; **¿sabe?** (*fam*) you know (what I mean)?; **le sabe mal que otro la saque a bailar** it upsets him that anybody else should ask her to dance.
sabido, a [sa'βiðo, a] *adj* (*consabido*) well-known; **como es ~** as we all know.
sabiduría [saβiðu'ria] *nf* (*conocimientos*) wisdom; (*instrucción*) learning; **~ popular** folklore.
sabiendas [sa'βjendas]: **a ~** *adv* knowingly; **a ~ de que ...** knowing full well that ....
sabihondo, a [sa'βjondo, a] *adj, nm/f*

know-all, know-it-all (*US*).
sabio, a ['saβjo,a] *adj* (*docto*) learned; (*prudente*) wise, sensible.
sablazo [sa'βlaθo] *nm* (*herida*) sword wound; (*fam*) sponging; **dar un ~ a algn** to tap sb for money.
sable [sa'βle] *nm* sabre.
sabor [sa'βor] *nm* taste, flavour; (*fig*) flavour; **sin ~** flavourless.
saborear [saβore'ar] *vt* to taste, savour; (*fig*) to relish.
sabotaje [saβo'taxe] *nm* sabotage.
saboteador, a [saβotea'ðor, a] *nm/f* saboteur.
sabotear [saβote'ar] *vt* to sabotage.
Saboya [sa'βoja] *nf* Savoy.
sabré [sa'βre] *etc vb V* **saber**.
sabroso, a [sa'βroso, a] *adj* tasty; (*fig fam*) racy, salty.
saca ['saka] *nf* big sack; **~ de correo(s)** mailbag; (*COM*) withdrawal.
sacacorchos [saka'kortʃos] *nm inv* corkscrew.
sacapuntas [saka'puntas] *nm inv* pencil sharpener.
sacar [sa'kar] *vt* to take out; (*fig: extraer*) to get (out); (*quitar*) to remove, get out; (*hacer salir*) to bring out; (*fondos: de cuenta*) to draw out, withdraw; (*obtener: legado etc*) to get; (*demostrar*) to show; (*conclusión*) to draw; (*novela etc*) to publish, bring out; (*ropa*) to take off; (*obra*) to make; (*premio*) to receive; (*entradas*) to get; (*TENIS*) to serve; (*FÚTBOL*) to put into play; **~ adelante** (*niño*) to bring up; **~ a algn a bailar** to dance with sb; **~ a algn de sí** to infuriate sb; **~ una foto** to take a photo; **~ la lengua** to stick out one's tongue; **~ buenas/malas notas** to get good/bad marks.
sacarina [saka'rina] *nf* saccharin(e).
sacerdote [saθer'ðote] *nm* priest.
saciar [sa'θjar] *vt* (*hartar*) to satiate; (*fig*) to satisfy; **~se** *vr* (*fig*) to be satisfied.
saciedad [saθje'ðað] *nf* satiety; **hasta la ~** (*comer*) one's fill; (*repetir*) ad nauseam.
saco ['sako] *nm* bag; (*grande*) sack; (*su contenido*) bagful; (*AM: chaqueta*) jacket; **~ de dormir** sleeping bag.
sacramento [sakra'mento] *nm* sacrament.
sacrificar [sakrifi'kar] *vt* to sacrifice; (*animal*) to slaughter; (*perro etc*) to put to sleep; **~se** *vr* to sacrifice o.s.
sacrificio [sakri'fiθjo] *nm* sacrifice.
sacrifique [sakri'fike] *etc vb V* **sacrificar**.
sacrilegio [sakri'lexjo] *nm* sacrilege.
sacrílego, a [sa'krileɣo, a] *adj* sacrilegious.
sacristán [sakris'tan] *nm* verger.
sacristía [sakris'tia] *nf* sacristy.
sacro, a ['sakro, a] *adj* sacred.
sacudida [saku'ðiða] *nf* (*agitación*) shake, shaking; (*sacudimiento*) jolt, bump; (*fig*) violent change; (*POL etc*) upheaval; **~ eléctrica** electric shock.
sacudir [saku'ðir] *vt* to shake; (*golpear*) to hit; (*ala*) to flap; (*alfombra*) to beat; **~ a algn** (*fam*) to belt sb.
sádico, a ['saðiko, a] *adj* sadistic ♦ *nm/f* sadist.
sadismo [sa'ðismo] *nm* sadism.
sadomasoquismo [saðomaso'kismo] *nm* sadomasochism, S & M.
sadomasoquista [saðomaso'kista] *adj* sadomasochistic ♦ *nm/f* sadomasochist.
saeta [sa'eta] *nf* (*flecha*) arrow; (*MUS*) *sacred song in flamenco style*.
safari [sa'fari] *nm* safari.
sagacidad [saɣaθi'ðað] *nf* shrewdness, cleverness.
sagaz [sa'ɣaθ] *adj* shrewd, clever.
Sagitario [saxi'tarjo] *nm* (*ASTRO*) Sagittarius.
sagrado, a [sa'ɣraðo, a] *adj* sacred, holy.
Sáhara ['saara] *nm*: **el ~** the Sahara (desert).
saharaui [saxa'rawi] *adj* Saharan ♦ *nm/f* native *o* inhabitant of the Sahara.
sajón, ona [sa'xon, 'xona] *adj, nm/f* Saxon.
Sajonia [sa'xonja] *nf* Saxony.
sal [sal] *vb ver* **salir** ♦ *nf* salt; (*gracia*) wit; (*encanto*) charm; **~es de baño** bath salts; **~ gorda** *o* **de cocina** kitchen *o* cooking salt.
sala ['sala] *nf* (*cuarto grande*) large room; (*~ de estar*) living room; (*TEAT*) house, auditorium; (*de hospital*) ward; **~ de apelación** court; **~ de conferencias** lecture hall; **~ de espera** waiting room; **~ de embarque** departure lounge; **~ de estar** living room; **~ de fiestas** function room; **~ de juntas** (*COM*) boardroom.
salado, a [sa'laðo, a] *adj* salty; (*fig*) witty, amusing; **agua salada** salt water.
salar [sa'lar] *vt* to salt, add salt to.
salarial [sala'rjal] *adj* (*aumento, revisión*) wage *cpd*, salary *cpd*, pay *cpd*.
salario [sa'larjo] *nm* wage, pay.
salchicha [sal'tʃitʃa] *nf* (pork) sausage.
salchichón [saltʃi'tʃon] *nm* (salami-type) sausage.
saldar [sal'dar] *vt* to pay; (*vender*) to sell off; (*fig*) to settle, resolve.
saldo ['saldo] *nm* (*pago*) settlement; (*de una cuenta*) balance; (*lo restante*) remnant(s) (*pl*), remainder; (*liquidación*)

sale; (*COM*): ~ **anterior** balance brought forward; ~ **acreedor/deudor** *o* **pasivo** credit/debit balance; ~ **final** final balance.

saldré [sal'dre] *etc vb V* **salir.**

salero [sa'lero] *nm* salt cellar; (*ingenio*) wit; (*encanto*) charm.

salga ['salɣa] *etc vb V* **salir.**

salida [sa'liða] *nf* (*puerta etc*) exit, way out; (*acto*) leaving, going out; (*de tren, AVIAT*) departure; (*COM, TEC*) output, production; (*fig*) way out; (*resultado*) outcome; (*COM: oportunidad*) opening; (*GEO, válvula*) outlet; (*de gas*) escape; (*ocurrencia*) joke; **calle sin** ~ cul-de-sac; **a la** ~ **del teatro** after the theatre; **dar la** ~ (*DEPORTE*) to give the starting signal; ~ **de incendios** fire escape; ~ **impresa** (*INFORM*) hard copy; **no hay** ~ there's no way out of it; **no tenemos otra** ~ we have no option; **tener** ~**s** to be witty.

salido, a [sa'liðo, a] *adj* (*fam*) randy.

saliente [sa'ljente] *adj* (*ARQ*) projecting; (*sol*) rising; (*fig*) outstanding.

salina [sa'lina] *nf* salt mine; ~**s** *nfpl* saltworks *sg*.

PALABRA CLAVE

salir [sa'lir] *vi* **1** (*persona*) to come *o* go out; (*tren, avión*) to leave; **Juan ha salido** Juan has gone out; **salió de la cocina** he came out of the kitchen; **salimos de Madrid a las 8** we left Madrid at 8 (o'clock); **salió corriendo (del cuarto)** he ran out (of the room); ~ **de un apuro** to get out of a jam

2 (*pelo*) to grow; (*diente*) to come through; (*disco, libro*) to come out; (*planta, número de lotería*) to come up; ~ **a la superficie** to come to the surface; **anoche salió en la tele** she appeared *o* was on TV last night; **salió en todos los periódicos** it was in all the papers; **le salió un trabajo** he got a job

3 (*resultar*): **la muchacha nos salió muy trabajadora** the girl turned out to be a very hard worker; **la comida te ha salido exquisita** the food was delicious; **sale muy caro** it's very expensive; **la entrevista que hice me salió bien/mal** the interview I did turned out *o* went well/badly; **nos salió a 5.000 ptas cada uno** it worked out at 5,000 pesetas each; **no salen las cuentas** it doesn't work out *o* add up; ~ **ganando** to come out on top; ~ **perdiendo** to lose out

4 (*DEPORTE*) to start; (*NAIPES*) to lead

5: ~ **con algn** to go out with sb

6: ~ **adelante: no sé como haré para** ~ **adelante** I don't know how I'll get by

♦ ~**se** *vr* **1** (*líquido*) to spill; (*animal*) to escape

2 (*desviarse*): ~**se de la carretera** to leave *o* go off the road; ~**se de lo normal** to be unusual; ~**se del tema** to get off the point

3: ~**se con la suya** to get one's own way

saliva [sa'liβa] *nf* saliva.

salivadera [saliβa'ðera] *nf* (*AM*) spittoon.

salmantino, a [salman'tino, a] *adj* of *o* from Salamanca ♦ *nm/f* native *o* inhabitant of Salamanca.

salmo ['salmo] *nm* psalm.

salmón [sal'mon] *nm* salmon.

salmonete [salmo'nete] *nm* red mullet.

salmuera [sal'mwera] *nf* pickle, brine.

salón [sa'lon] *nm* (*de casa*) living-room, lounge; (*muebles*) lounge suite; ~ **de belleza** beauty parlour; ~ **de baile** dance hall; ~ **de sesiones** assembly hall.

salpicadero [salpika'ðero] *nm* (*AUTO*) dashboard.

salpicar [salpi'kar] *vt* (*de barro, pintura*) to splash; (*rociar*) to sprinkle, spatter; (*esparcir*) to scatter.

salpicón [salpi'kon] *nm* (*acto*) splashing; (*CULIN*) meat *o* fish salad.

salpimentar [salpimen'tar] *vt* (*CULIN*) to season.

salpique [sal'pike] *etc vb V* **salpicar.**

salsa ['salsa] *nf* sauce; (*con carne asada*) gravy; (*fig*) spice; ~ **mayonesa** mayonnaise; **estar en su** ~ (*fam*) to be in one's element.

saltamontes [salta'montes] *nm inv* grasshopper.

saltar [sal'tar] *vt* to jump (over), leap (over); (*dejar de lado*) to skip, miss out ♦ *vi* to jump, leap; (*pelota*) to bounce; (*al aire*) to fly up; (*quebrarse*) to break; (*al agua*) to dive; (*fig*) to explode, blow up; (*botón*) to come off; (*corcho*) to pop out; ~**se** *vr* (*omitir*) to skip, miss; **salta a la vista** it's obvious; ~**se todas las reglas** to break all the rules.

salteado, a [salte'aðo, a] *adj* (*CULIN*) sauté(ed).

salteador [saltea'ðor] *nm* (*tb:* ~ **de caminos**) highwayman.

saltear [salte'ar] *vt* (*robar*) to rob (in a holdup); (*asaltar*) to assault, attack; (*CULIN*) to sauté.

saltimbanqui [saltim'banki] *nm/f* acrobat.

salto ['salto] *nm* jump, leap; (*al agua*) dive; **a** ~**s** by jumping; ~ **de agua** waterfall; ~ **de altura** high jump; ~ **de cama**

negligee; ~ **mortal** somersault; (*INFORM*): ~ **de línea** line feed; ~ **de línea automático** wordwrap; ~ **de página** formfeed.
saltón, ona [sal'ton, ona] *adj* (*ojos*) bulging, popping; (*dientes*) protruding.
salubre [sa'lußre] *adj* healthy, salubrious.
salud [sa'luð] *nf* health; **estar bien/mal de ~** to be in good/poor health; **¡(a su) ~!** cheers!, good health!; **beber a la ~ de** to drink (to) the health of.
saludable [salu'ðaßle] *adj* (*de buena salud*) healthy; (*provechoso*) good, beneficial.
saludar [salu'ðar] *vt* to greet; (*MIL*) to salute; **ir a ~ a algn** to drop in to see sb; **salude de mi parte a X** give my regards to X; **le saluda atentamente** (*en carta*) yours faithfully.
saludo [sa'luðo] *nm* greeting; **~s** (*en carta*) best wishes, regards; **un ~ afectuoso** *o* **cordial** yours sincerely.
salva ['salßa] *nf* (*MIL*) salvo; **una ~ de aplausos** thunderous applause.
salvación [salßa'θjon] *nf* salvation; (*rescate*) rescue.
salvado [sal'ßaðo] *nm* bran.
salvador [salßa'ðor] *nm* rescuer, saviour; **el S~** the Saviour; **El S~** El Salvador; **San S~** San Salvador.
salvadoreño, a [salßaðo'reɲo, a] *adj, nm/f* Salvadoran, Salvadorian.
salvaguardar [salßaɣwar'ðar] *vt* to safeguard; (*INFORM*) to back up, make a backup copy of.
salvajada [salßa'xaða] *nf* savage deed, atrocity.
salvaje [sal'ßaxe] *adj* wild; (*tribu*) savage.
salvajismo [salßa'xismo] *nm* savagery.
salvamento [salßa'mento] *nm* (*acción*) rescue; (*de naufragio*) salvage; **~ y socorrismo** life-saving.
salvapantallas [salßapan'taʎas] *nm inv* screen saver.
salvar [sal'ßar] *vt* (*rescatar*) to save, rescue; (*resolver*) to overcome, resolve; (*cubrir distancias*) to cover, travel; (*hacer excepción*) to except, exclude; (*un barco*) to salvage; **~se** *vr* to save o.s., escape; **¡sálvese el que pueda!** every man for himself!
salvavidas [salßa'ßiðas] *adj inv*: **bote/chaleco/cinturón ~** lifeboat/lifejacket/lifebelt.
salvedad [salße'ðað] *nf* reservation, qualification; **con la ~ de que** ... with the proviso that ....
salvia ['salßja] *nf* sage.
salvo, a ['salßo, a] *adj* safe ♦ *prep* except (for), save; **~ error u omisión** (*COM*) errors and omissions excepted; **a ~** out of danger; **~ que** unless.
salvoconducto [salßokon'dukto] *nm* safe-conduct.
samba ['samba] *nf* samba.
san [san] *nm* (*apócope de* **santo**) saint; **~ Juan** St. John; *V tb* **Juan**.
sanar [sa'nar] *vt* (*herida*) to heal; (*persona*) to cure ♦ *vi* (*persona*) to get well, recover; (*herida*) to heal.
sanatorio [sana'torjo] *nm* sanatorium.
sanción [san'θjon] *nf* sanction.
sancionar [sanθjo'nar] *vt* to sanction.
sancocho [san'kotʃo] *nm* (*AM*) stew.
sandalia [san'dalja] *nf* sandal.
sándalo ['sandalo] *nm* sandal(wood).
sandez [san'deθ] *nf* (*cualidad*) foolishness; (*acción*) stupid thing; **decir sandeces** to talk nonsense.
sandía [san'dia] *nf* watermelon.
sandinista [sanði'nista] *adj, nm/f* Sandinist(a).
sandwich ['sandwitʃ], *pl* **sandwichs** *o* **sandwiches** *nm* sandwich.
saneamiento [sanea'mjento] *nm* sanitation.
sanear [sane'ar] *vt* to drain; (*indemnizar*) to compensate; (*ECON*) to reorganize.
sanfermines [sanfer'mines] *nmpl see boxed note.*

SANFERMINES

The **sanfermines** *are week-long "fiestas" which take place in Pamplona, the capital of Navarre. They were made famous by the American writer Ernest Hemingway. From 7 July, the feast of San Fermín, onwards, crowds of mainly young people take to the streets, drinking, singing and dancing. Early in the morning bulls are released along the narrow streets which lead to the bullring, and people risk serious injury by running in front of them, a custom which is also typical of many Spanish villages.*

sangrar [san'grar] *vt, vi* to bleed; (*texto*) to indent.
sangre ['sangre] *nf* blood; **~ fría** sangfroid; **a ~ fría** in cold blood.
sangría [san'gria] *nf* (*MED*) bleeding; (*CULIN*) sangria, *sweetened drink of red wine with fruit*, ≈ fruit cup.
sangriento, a [san'grjento, a] *adj* bloody.
sanguijuela [sangi'xwela] *nf* (*ZOOL, fig*) leech.
sanguinario, a [sangi'narjo, a] *adj* bloodthirsty.
sanguíneo, a [san'gineo, a] *adj* blood *cpd.*

sanidad [sani'ðað] *nf* sanitation; (*calidad de sano*) health, healthiness; ~ **pública** public health (department).
sanitario, a [sani'tarjo, a] *adj* sanitary; (*de la salud*) health *cpd* ♦ *nm*: ~**s** *nmpl* toilets (*BRIT*), restroom *sg* (*US*).
San Marino [sanma'rino] *nm*: **(La República de)** ~ San Marino.
sano, a ['sano, a] *adj* healthy; (*sin daños*) sound; (*comida*) wholesome; (*entero*) whole, intact; ~ **y salvo** safe and sound.
santanderino, a [santande'rino, a] *adj* of *o* from Santander ♦ *nm/f* native *o* inhabitant of Santander.
Santiago [san'tjaɣo] *nm*: ~ **(de Chile)** Santiago.
santiamén [santja'men] *nm*: **en un** ~ in no time at all.
santidad [santi'ðað] *nf* holiness, sanctity.
santificar [santifi'kar] *vt* to sanctify.
santifique [santi'fike] *etc vb V* **santificar**.
santiguarse [santi'ɣwarse] *vr* to make the sign of the cross.
santigüe [san'tiɣwe] *etc vb V* **santiguarse**.
santo, a ['santo, a] *adj* holy; (*fig*) wonderful, miraculous ♦ *nm/f* saint ♦ *nm* saint's day; **hacer su santa voluntad** to do as one jolly well pleases; **¿a ~ de qué ...?** why on earth ...?; **se le fue el ~ al cielo** he forgot what he was about to say; ~ **y seña** password; *see boxed note*.

SANTO

As well as having a birthday, Spaniards have traditionally celebrated **el santo**, *their saint's day, when the saint they were called after — San Pedro or la Virgen de los Dolores, for example — is honoured in the Christian calendar. The custom is gradually dying out.*

santuario [san'twarjo] *nm* sanctuary, shrine.
saña ['saɲa] *nf* rage, fury.
sapo ['sapo] *nm* toad.
saque ['sake] *etc vb V* **sacar** ♦ *nm* (*TENIS*) service, serve; (*FÚTBOL*) throw-in; ~ **inicial** kick-off; ~ **de esquina** corner (kick); **tener buen** ~ to eat heartily.
saquear [sake'ar] *vt* (*MIL*) to sack; (*robar*) to loot, plunder; (*fig*) to ransack.
saqueo [sa'keo] *nm* sacking; looting, plundering; ransacking.
S.A.R. *abr* (= *Su Alteza Real*) HRH.
sarampión [saram'pjon] *nm* measles *sg*.
sarape [sa'rape] *nm* (*AM*) blanket.
sarcasmo [sar'kasmo] *nm* sarcasm.
sarcástico, a [sar'kastiko, a] *adj* sarcastic.
sarcófago [sar'kofaɣo] *nm* sarcophagus.
sardina [sar'ðina] *nf* sardine.
sardo, a ['sarðo, a] *adj, nm/f* Sardinian.
sardónico, a [sar'ðoniko, a] *adj* sardonic; (*irónico*) ironical, sarcastic.
sargento [sar'xento] *nm* sergeant.
sarmiento [sar'mjento] *nm* vine shoot.
sarna ['sarna] *nf* itch; (*MED*) scabies.
sarpullido [sarpu'ʎiðo] *nm* (*MED*) rash.
sarro ['sarro] *nm* deposit; (*en dientes*) tartar.
sarta ['sarta] *nf* (*fig*): **una ~ de mentiras** a pack of lies.
sartén [sar'ten] *nf* frying pan; **tener la ~ por el mango** to rule the roost.
sastre ['sastre] *nm* tailor.
sastrería [sastre'ria] *nf* (*arte*) tailoring; (*tienda*) tailor's (shop).
Satanás [sata'nas] *nm* Satan.
satélite [sa'telite] *nm* satellite.
satinado, a [sati'naðo, a] *adj* glossy ♦ *nm* gloss, shine.
sátira ['satira] *nf* satire.
satírico, a [sa'tiriko, a] *adj* satiric(al).
sátiro ['satiro] *nm* (*MITOLOGÍA*) satyr; (*fig*) sex maniac.
satisfacción [satisfak'θjon] *nf* satisfaction.
satisfacer [satisfa'θer] *vt* to satisfy; (*gastos*) to meet; (*deuda*) to pay; (*COM: letra de cambio*) to honour (*BRIT*), honor (*US*); (*pérdida*) to make good; ~**se** *vr* to satisfy o.s., be satisfied; (*vengarse*) to take revenge.
satisfaga [satis'faɣa] *etc*, **satisfaré** [satisfa're] *etc vb V* **satisfacer**.
satisfecho, a [satis'fetʃo, a] *pp de* **satisfacer** ♦ *adj* satisfied; (*contento*) content(ed), happy; (*tb*: ~ **de sí mismo**) self-satisfied, smug.
satisfice [satis'fiθe] *etc vb V* **satisfacer**.
saturación [satura'θjon] *nf* saturation; **llegar a la** ~ to reach saturation point.
saturar [satu'rar] *vt* to saturate; ~**se** *vr* (*mercado, aeropuerto*) to reach saturation point; **¡estoy saturado de tanta televisión!** I can't take any more television!
sauce ['sauθe] *nm* willow; ~ **llorón** weeping willow.
saúco [sa'uko] *nm* (*BOT*) elder.
saudí [sau'ði] *adj, nm/f* Saudi.
sauna ['sauna] *nf* sauna.
savia ['saβja] *nf* sap.
saxo ['sakso] *nm* sax.
saxofón [sakso'fon] *nm* saxophone.
saya ['saja] *nf* (*falda*) skirt; (*enagua*) petticoat.
sayo ['sajo] *nm* smock.

sazón [sa'θon] *nf* (*de fruta*) ripeness; **a la ~** then, at that time.
sazonado, a [saθo'naðo, a] *adj* (*fruta*) ripe; (*CULIN*) flavoured, seasoned.
sazonar [saθo'nar] *vt* to ripen; (*CULIN*) to flavour, season.
s/c *abr* (*COM*: = *su casa*) your firm; (: = *su cuenta*) your account.
Sdo. *abr* (*COM*: = *Saldo*) bal.
SE *abr* (= *sudeste*) SE.

PALABRA CLAVE

se [se] *pron* **1** (*reflexivo*: *sg*: *m*) himself; (: *f*) herself; (: *pl*) themselves; (: *cosa*) itself; (: *de Vd*) yourself; (: *de Vds*) yourselves; (*indefinido*) oneself; **~ mira en el espejo** he looks at himself in the mirror; **¡siénte~!** sit down!; **~ durmió** he fell asleep; **~ está preparando** she's getting (herself) ready; *para usos léxicos del pron ver el vb en cuestión, p.ej.* **arrepentirse**
2 (*como complemento indirecto*) to him; to her; to them; to it; to you; **~ lo dije ayer** (*a Vd*) I told you yesterday; **~ compró un sombrero** he bought himself a hat; **~ rompió la pierna** he broke his leg; **cortar~ el pelo** to get one's hair cut; (*uno mismo*) to cut one's hair; **~ comió un pastel** he ate a cake
3 (*uso recíproco*) each other, one another; **~ miraron (el uno al otro)** they looked at each other *o* one another
4 (*en oraciones pasivas*): **se han vendido muchos libros** a lot of books have been sold; **"~ vende coche"** "car for sale"
5 (*impers*): **~ dice que** people say that, it is said that; **allí ~ come muy bien** the food there is very good, you can eat very well there.

sé [se] *vb V* **saber, ser.**
sea ['sea] *etc vb V* **ser.**
SEAT ['seat] *nf abr* = *Sociedad Española de Automóviles de Turismo.*
sebo ['seβo] *nm* fat, grease.
Sec. *abr* (= *Secretario*) Sec.
seca ['seka] *nf V* **seco.**
secado [se'kaðo] *nm* drying; **~ a mano** blow-dry.
secador [seka'ðor] *nm*: **~ para el pelo** hairdryer.
secadora [seka'ðora] *nf* tumble dryer; **~ centrífuga** spin-dryer.
secano [se'kano] *nm* (*AGR*: *tb*: **tierra de ~**) dry land *o* region; **cultivo de ~** dry farming.
secante [se'kante] *adj* (*viento*) drying ♦ *nm* blotting paper.
secar [se'kar] *vt* to dry; (*superficie*) to wipe dry; (*frente, suelo*) to mop; (*líquido*) to mop up; (*tinta*) to blot; **~se** *vr* to dry (off); (*río, planta*) to dry up.
sección [sek'θjon] *nf* section; (*COM*) department; **~ deportiva** (*en periódico*) sports page(s).
seco, a ['seko, a] *adj* dry; (*fruta*) dried; (*persona*: *magro*) thin, skinny; (*carácter*) cold; (*antipático*) disagreeable; (*respuesta*) sharp, curt ♦ *nf* dry season; **habrá pan a secas** there will be just bread; **decir algo a secas** to say sth curtly; **parar en ~** to stop dead.
secreción [sekre'θjon] *nf* secretion.
secretaría [sekreta'ria] *nf* secretariat; (*oficina*) secretary's office.
secretariado [sekreta'rjaðo] *nm* (*oficina*) secretariat; (*cargo*) secretaryship; (*curso*) secretarial course.
secretario, a [sekre'tarjo, a] *nm/f* secretary; **~ adjunto** (*COM*) assistant secretary.
secreto, a [se'kreto, a] *adj* secret; (*información*) confidential; (*persona*) secretive ♦ *nm* secret; (*calidad*) secrecy.
secta ['sekta] *nf* sect.
sectario, a [sek'tarjo, a] *adj* sectarian.
sector [sek'tor] *nm* sector (*tb INFORM*); (*de opinión*) section; (*fig*: *campo*) area, field; **~ privado/público** (*COM, ECON*) private/public sector.
secuela [se'kwela] *nf* consequence.
secuencia [se'kwenθja] *nf* sequence.
secuestrar [sekwes'trar] *vt* to kidnap; (*avión*) to hijack; (*bienes*) to seize, confiscate.
secuestro [se'kwestro] *nm* kidnapping; hijack; seizure, confiscation.
secular [seku'lar] *adj* secular.
secundar [sekun'dar] *vt* to second, support.
secundario, a [sekun'darjo, a] *adj* secondary; (*carretera*) side *cpd*; (*INFORM*) background *cpd* ♦ *nf* secondary education; *V tb* **sistema educativo.**
sed [seð] *nf* thirst; (*fig*) thirst, craving; **tener ~** to be thirsty.
seda ['seða] *nf* silk; **~ dental** dental floss.
sedal [se'ðal] *nm* fishing line.
sedante [se'ðante] *nm* sedative.
sede ['seðe] *nf* (*de gobierno*) seat; (*de compañía*) headquarters *pl*, head office; **Santa S~** Holy See.
sedentario, a [seðen'tarjo, a] *adj* sedentary.
SEDIC [se'ðik] *nf abr* = *Sociedad Española de*

Documentación e Información Científica.
sedición [seði'θjon] *nf* sedition.
sediento, a [se'ðjento, a] *adj* thirsty.
sedimentar [seðimen'tar] *vt* to deposit; **~se** *vr* to settle.
sedimento [seði'mento] *nm* sediment.
sedoso, a [se'ðoso, a] *adj* silky, silken.
seducción [seðuk'θjon] *nf* seduction.
seducir [seðu'θir] *vt* to seduce; (*sobornar*) to bribe; (*cautivar*) to charm, fascinate; (*atraer*) to attract.
seductor, a [seðuk'tor, a] *adj* seductive; charming, fascinating; attractive; (*engañoso*) deceptive, misleading ♦ *nm/f* seducer.
seduje [se'ðuxe] *etc*, **seduzca** [se'ðuθka] *etc vb V* **seducir**.
sefardí [sefar'ði], **sefardita** [sefar'ðita] *adj* Sephardi(c) ♦ *nm/f* Sephardi.
segador, a [seɣa'ðor, a] *nm/f* (*persona*) harvester ♦ *nf* (*TEC*) mower, reaper.
segadora-trilladora [seɣa'ðoratriʎa'ðora] *nf* combine harvester.
segar [se'ɣar] *vt* (*mies*) to reap, cut; (*hierba*) to mow, cut; (*esperanzas*) to ruin.
seglar [se'ɣlar] *adj* secular, lay.
segoviano, a [seɣo'ßjano, a] *adj* of *o* from Segovia ♦ *nm/f* native *o* inhabitant of Segovia.
segregación [seɣreɣa'θjon] *nf* segregation; ~ **racial** racial segregation.
segregar [seɣre'ɣar] *vt* to segregate, separate.
segregue [se'ɣreɣe] *etc vb V* **segregar**.
segué [se'ɣe], **seguemos** [se'ɣemos] *etc vb V* **segar**.
seguidamente [seɣiða'mente] *adv* (*sin parar*) without a break; (*inmediatamente después*) immediately after.
seguido, a [se'ɣiðo, a] *adj* (*continuo*) continuous, unbroken; (*recto*) straight ♦ *adv* (*directo*) straight (on); (*después*) after; (*AM*: *a menudo*) often ♦ *nf*: **en seguida** at once, right away; **5 días ~s** 5 days running, 5 days in a row; **en seguida termino** I've nearly finished, I shan't be long now.
seguimiento [seɣi'mjento] *nm* chase, pursuit; (*continuación*) continuation.
seguir [se'ɣir] *vt* to follow; (*venir después*) to follow on, come after; (*proseguir*) to continue; (*perseguir*) to chase, pursue; (*indicio*) to follow up; (*mujer*) to court ♦ *vi* (*gen*) to follow; (*continuar*) to continue, carry *o* go on; **~se** *vr* to follow; **a ~** to be continued; **sigo sin comprender** I still don't understand; **sigue lloviendo** it's still raining; **sigue** (*en carta*) P.T.O.; (*en libro, TV*) continued; **"hágase ~"** "please forward"; **¡siga!** (*AM*: *pase*) come in!
según [se'ɣun] *prep* according to ♦ *adv*: ~ **(y conforme)** it all depends ♦ *conj* as; ~ **esté el tiempo** depending on the weather; ~ **me consta** as far as I know; **está ~ lo dejaste** it is just as you left it.
segundo, a [se'ɣundo, a] *adj* second; (*en discurso*) secondly ♦ *nm* (*gen, medida de tiempo*) second; (*piso*) second floor ♦ *nf* (*sentido*) second meaning; ~ **(de a bordo)** (*NAUT*) first mate; **segunda (clase)** (*FERRO*) second class; **segunda (marcha)** (*AUTO*) second (gear); **de segunda mano** second hand.
seguramente [seɣura'mente] *adv* surely; (*con certeza*) for sure, with certainty; (*probablemente*) probably; **¿lo va a comprar? — ~** is he going to buy it? — I should think so.
seguridad [seɣuri'ðað] *nf* safety; (*del estado, de casa etc*) security; (*certidumbre*) certainty; (*confianza*) confidence; (*estabilidad*) stability; ~ **social** social security; ~ **contra incendios** fire precautions *pl*; ~ **en sí mismo** (self-) confidence.
seguro, a [se'ɣuro, a] *adj* (*cierto*) sure, certain; (*fiel*) trustworthy; (*libre de peligro*) safe; (*bien defendido, firme*) secure; (*datos etc*) reliable; (*fecha*) firm ♦ *adv* for sure, certainly ♦ *nm* (*dispositivo*) safety device; (*de cerradura*) tumbler; (*de arma*) safety catch; (*COM*) insurance; ~ **contra accidentes/incendios** fire/accident insurance; ~ **contra terceros/a todo riesgo** third party/comprehensive insurance; ~ **dotal con beneficios** with-profits endowment assurance; **S~ de Enfermedad** ≈ National Insurance; ~ **marítimo** marine insurance; ~ **mixto** endowment assurance; ~ **temporal** term insurance; ~ **de vida** life insurance.
seis [seis] *num* six; ~ **mil** six thousand; **tiene ~ años** she is six (years old); **unos ~** about six; **hoy es el ~** today is the sixth.
seiscientos, as [seis'θjentos, as] *num* six hundred.
seísmo [se'ismo] *nm* tremor, earthquake.
selección [selek'θjon] *nf* selection; ~ **múltiple** multiple choice; ~ **nacional** (*DEPORTE*) national team.
seleccionador, a [selekθjona'ðor, a] *nm/f* (*DEPORTE*) selector.
seleccionar [selekθjo'nar] *vt* to pick, choose, select.

selectividad [selektiβi'ðað] *nf* (*UNIV*) entrance examination; *see boxed note.*

> **SELECTIVIDAD**
>
> *School-leavers wishing to go on to university sit the dreaded entrance examination, the* **selectividad**, *in June, with resits in September. When student numbers are too high for a particular course, only the best candidates get through. The others must wait a year to sit the examination again.*

selecto, a [se'lekto, a] *adj* select, choice; (*escogido*) selected.
sellado, a [se'ʎaðo, a] *adj* (*documento oficial*) sealed; (*pasaporte*) stamped.
sellar [se'ʎar] *vt* (*documento oficial*) to seal; (*pasaporte, visado*) to stamp; (*marcar*) to brand; (*pacto, labios*) to seal.
sello ['seʎo] *nm* stamp; (*precinto*) seal; (*fig*: *tb*: ~ **distintivo**) hallmark; ~ **fiscal** revenue stamp; ~**s de prima** (*COM*) trading stamps.
selva ['selβa] *nf* (*bosque*) forest, woods *pl*; (*jungla*) jungle; **la S~ Negra** the Black Forest.
semáforo [se'maforo] *nm* (*AUTO*) traffic lights *pl*; (*FERRO*) signal.
semana [se'mana] *nf* week; ~ **inglesa** 5-day (working) week; ~ **laboral** working week; **S~ Santa** Holy Week; **entre** ~ during the week; *see boxed note.*

> **SEMANA**
>
> **Semana Santa** *is an important national holiday in Spain. The whole country takes "Viernes Santo" (Good Friday) "Sábado Santo", (Holy Saturday), and "Domingo de Resurrección" (Easter Sunday) off, while other days around this time of year vary according to region. There are spectacular processions all over the country, with members of "cofradías" (brotherhoods) dressing in hooded robes and parading their "pasos" (religious floats or sculptures) through the streets. Holy Week in Seville is very famous, on account of the religious fervour shown by the locals.*

semanal [sema'nal] *adj* weekly.
semanario [sema'narjo] *nm* weekly (magazine).
semántica [se'mantika] *nf* semantics *sg*.
semblante [sem'blante] *nm* face; (*fig*) look.
sembrar [sem'brar] *vt* to sow; (*objetos*) to sprinkle, scatter about; (*noticias etc*) to spread.
semejante [seme'xante] *adj* (*parecido*) similar; (*tal*) such; ~**s** alike, similar ♦ *nm* fellow man, fellow creature; **son muy** ~**s** they are very much alike; **nunca hizo cosa** ~ he never did such a thing.
semejanza [seme'xanθa] *nf* similarity, resemblance; **a** ~ **de** like, as.
semejar [seme'xar] *vi* to seem like, resemble; ~**se** *vr* to look alike, be similar.
semen ['semen] *nm* semen.
semental [semen'tal] *nm* (*macho*) stud.
sementera [semen'tera] *nf* (*acto*) sowing; (*temporada*) seedtime; (*tierra*) sown land.
semestral [semes'tral] *adj* half-yearly, bi-annual.
semestre [se'mestre] *nm* period of six months; (*US UNIV*) semester; (*COM*) half-yearly payment.
semicírculo [semi'θirkulo] *nm* semicircle.
semiconductor [semikonduk'tor] *nm* semiconductor.
semiconsciente [semikons'θjente] *adj* semiconscious.
semidesnatado, a [semiðesna'taðo, a] *adj* semi-skimmed.
semifinal [semifi'nal] *nf* semifinal.
semiinconsciente [semi(i)nkons'θjente] *adj* semiconscious.
semilla [se'miʎa] *nf* seed.
semillero [semi'ʎero] *nm* (*AGR etc*) seedbed; (*fig*) hotbed.
seminario [semi'narjo] *nm* (*REL*) seminary; (*ESCOL*) seminar.
semiseco [semi'seko] *nm* medium-dry.
semita [se'mita] *adj* Semitic ♦ *nm/f* Semite.
sémola ['semola] *nf* semolina.
sempiterno, a [sempi'terno, a] *adj* everlasting.
Sena ['sena] *nm*: **el** ~ the (river) Seine.
senado [se'naðo] *nm* senate; *V tb* **Las Cortes (españolas)**.
senador, a [sena'ðor, a] *nm/f* senator.
sencillez [senθi'ʎeθ] *nf* simplicity; (*de persona*) naturalness.
sencillo, a [sen'θiʎo, a] *adj* simple; (*carácter*) natural, unaffected; (*billete*) single ♦ *nm* (*disco*) single; (*AM*) small change.
senda ['senda] *nf*, **sendero** [sen'dero] *nm* path, track; **Sendero Luminoso** the Shining Path (guerrilla movement).
senderismo [sende'rismo] *nm* trekking.
sendos, as ['sendos, as] *adj pl*: **les dio** ~ **golpes** he hit both of them.
senil [se'nil] *adj* senile.
seno ['seno] *nm* (*ANAT*) bosom, bust; (*fig*)

bosom; ~**s** *nmpl* breasts; ~ **materno** womb.
sensación [sensa'θjon] *nf* sensation; (*sentido*) sense; (*sentimiento*) feeling; **causar** *o* **hacer** ~ to cause a sensation.
sensacional [sensaθjo'nal] *adj* sensational.
sensatez [sensa'teθ] *nf* common sense.
sensato, a [sen'sato, a] *adj* sensible.
sensibilidad [sensiβili'ðað] *nf* sensitivity; (*para el arte*) feel.
sensibilizar [sensiβili'θar] *vt*: ~ **a la población/opinión pública** to raise public awareness.
sensible [sen'sible] *adj* sensitive; (*apreciable*) perceptible, appreciable; (*pérdida*) considerable.
sensiblero, a [sensi'βlero, a] *adj* sentimental, slushy.
sensitivo, a [sensi'tiβo, a], **sensorial** [senso'rjal] *adj* sense *cpd*.
sensor [sen'sor] *nm*: ~ **de fin de papel** paper out sensor.
sensual [sen'swal] *adj* sensual.
sentado, a [sen'taðo, a] *adj* (*establecido*) settled; (*carácter*) sensible ♦ *nf* sitting; (*POL*) sit-in, sit-down protest; **dar por** ~ to take for granted, assume; **dejar algo** ~ to establish sth firmly; **estar** ~ to sit, be sitting (down); **de una sentada** at one sitting.
sentar [sen'tar] *vt* to sit, seat; (*fig*) to establish ♦ *vi* (*vestido*) to suit; (*alimento*): ~ **bien/mal a** to agree/disagree with; ~**se** *vr* (*persona*) to sit, sit down; (*el tiempo*) to settle (down); (*los depósitos*) to settle; **¡siéntese!** (do) sit down, take a seat.
sentencia [sen'tenθja] *nf* (*máxima*) maxim, saying; (*JUR*) sentence; (*INFORM*) statement; ~ **de muerte** death sentence.
sentenciar [senten'θjar] *vt* to sentence.
sentido, a [sen'tiðo, a] *adj* (*pérdida*) regrettable; (*carácter*) sensitive ♦ *nm* sense; (*sentimiento*) feeling; (*significado*) sense, meaning; (*dirección*) direction; **mi más** ~ **pésame** my deepest sympathy; ~ **del humor** sense of humour; ~ **común** common sense; **en el buen** ~ **de la palabra** in the best sense of the word; **sin** ~ meaningless; **tener** ~ to make sense; ~ **único** one-way (street).
sentimental [sentimen'tal] *adj* sentimental; **vida** ~ love life.
sentimiento [senti'mjento] *nm* (*emoción*) feeling, emotion; (*sentido*) sense; (*pesar*) regret, sorrow.
sentir [sen'tir] *vt* to feel; (*percibir*) to perceive, sense; (*esp AM*: *oír*) to hear; (*lamentar*) to regret, be sorry for; (*música etc*) to have a feeling for ♦ *vi* to feel; (*lamentarse*) to feel sorry ♦ *nm* opinion, judgement; ~**se** *vr* to feel; **lo siento** I'm sorry; ~**se mejor/mal** to feel better/ill; ~**se como en su casa** to feel at home.
seña ['seɲa] *nf* sign; (*MIL*) password; ~**s** *nfpl* address *sg*; ~**s personales** personal description *sg*; **por más** ~**s** moreover; **dar** ~**s de** to show signs of.
señal [se'ɲal] *nf* sign; (*síntoma*) symptom; (*indicio*) indication; (*FERRO, TELEC*) signal; (*marca*) mark; (*COM*) deposit; (*INFORM*) marker, mark; **en** ~ **de** as a token of, as a sign of; **dar** ~**es de** to show signs of; ~ **de auxilio/de peligro** distress/danger signal; ~ **de llamada** ringing tone; ~ **para marcar** dialling tone.
señalado, a [seɲa'laðo, a] *adj* (*persona*) distinguished; (*pey*) notorious.
señalar [seɲa'lar] *vt* to mark; (*indicar*) to point out, indicate; (*significar*) to denote; (*referirse a*) to allude to; (*fijar*) to fix, settle; (*pey*) to criticize.
señalice [seɲa'liθe] *etc vb V* **señalizar**.
señalización [seɲaliθa'θjon] *nf* signposting; signals *pl*.
señalizar [seɲali'θar] *vt* (*AUTO*) to put up road signs on; (*FERRO*) to put signals on; (*AUTO*: *ruta*): **está bien señalizada** it's well signposted.
señas ['seɲas] *nfpl V* **seña**.
señor, a [se'ɲor, a] *adj* (*fam*) lordly ♦ *nm* (*hombre*) man; (*caballero*) gentleman; (*dueño*) owner, master; (*trato*: *antes de nombre propio*) Mr; (: *hablando directamente*) sir ♦ *nf* (*dama*) lady; (*trato*: *antes de nombre propio*) Mrs; (: *hablando directamente*) madam; (*esposa*) wife; **los** ~**es González** Mr and Mrs González; **S**~ **Don Jacinto Benavente** (*en sobre*) Mr J. Benavente, J. Benavente Esq.; **S**~ **Director ...** (*de periódico*) Dear Sir ...; ~ **juez** my lord, your worship (*US*); ~ **Presidente** Mr Chairman *o* President; **Muy** ~ **mío** Dear Sir; **Muy** ~**es nuestros** Dear Sirs; **Nuestro S**~ (*REL*) Our Lord; **¿está la señora?** is the lady of the house in?; **la señora de Smith** Mrs Smith; **Nuestra Señora** (*REL*) Our Lady.
señoría [seɲo'ria] *nf* rule; **su** *o* **vuestra S**~ your *o* his/her lordship/ladyship.
señorío [seɲo'rio] *nm* manor; (*fig*) rule.
señorita [seɲo'rita] *nf* (*gen*) Miss; (*mujer joven*) young lady; (*maestra*) schoolteacher.
señorito [seɲo'rito] *nm* young gentleman;

(*lenguaje de criados*) master; (*pey*) toff.
señuelo [se'ɲwelo] *nm* decoy.
Sep. *abr* (= *septiembre*) Sept.
sepa ['sepa] *etc vb V* **saber.**
separable [sepa'raßle] *adj* separable; (*TEC*) detachable.
separación [separa'θjon] *nf* separation; (*división*) division; (*distancia*) gap, distance; ~ **de bienes** division of property.
separado, a [sepa'raðo, a] *adj* separate; (*TEC*) detached; **vive ~ de su mujer** he is separated from his wife; **por ~** separately.
separador [separa'ðor] *nm* (*INFORM*) delimiter.
separadora [separa'ðora] *nf*: ~ **de hojas** burster.
separar [sepa'rar] *vt* to separate; (*silla de la mesa*) to move away; (*TEC: pieza*) to detach; (*persona: de un cargo*) to remove, dismiss; (*dividir*) to divide; **~se** *vr* (*parte*) to come away; (*partes*) to come apart; (*persona*) to leave, go away; (*matrimonio*) to separate.
separata [sepa'rata] *nf* offprint.
separatismo [separa'tismo] *nm* (*POL*) separatism.
sepelio [se'peljo] *nm* burial, interment.
sepia ['sepja] *nf* cuttlefish.
Sept. *abr* (= *septiembre*) Sept.
septentrional [septentrjo'nal] *adj* north *cpd*, northern.
septiembre [sep'tjembre] *nm* September.
séptimo, a ['septimo, a] *adj, nm* seventh.
septuagésimo, a [septwa'xesimo, a] *adj* seventieth.
sepulcral [sepul'kral] *adj* sepulchral; (*fig*) gloomy, dismal.
sepulcro [se'pulkro] *nm* tomb, grave, sepulchre.
sepultar [sepul'tar] *vt* to bury; (*en accidente*) to trap; **quedaban sepultados en la caverna** they were trapped in the cave.
sepultura [sepul'tura] *nf* (*acto*) burial; (*tumba*) grave, tomb; **dar ~ a** to bury; **recibir ~** to be buried.
sepulturero, a [sepultu'rero, a] *nm/f* gravedigger.
seque ['seke] *etc vb V* **secar.**
sequedad [seke'ðað] *nf* dryness; (*fig*) brusqueness, curtness.
sequía [se'kia] *nf* drought.
séquito ['sekito] *nm* (*de rey etc*) retinue; (*POL*) followers *pl.*
SER *nf abr* (= *Sociedad Española de Radiodifusión*) *Spanish radio network.*

PALABRA CLAVE

ser [ser] *vi* **1** (*descripción, identidad*) to be; **es médica/muy alta** she's a doctor/very tall; **la familia es de Cuzco** his (*o* her *etc*) family is from Cuzco; ~ **de madera** to be made of wood; **soy Ana** it's Ana
2 (*propiedad*): **es de Joaquín** it's Joaquín's, it belongs to Joaquín
3 (*horas, fechas, números*): **es la una** it's one o'clock; **son las seis y media** it's half-past six; **es el 1 de junio** it's the first of June; **somos/son seis** there are six of us/them; **2 y 2 son 4** 2 and 2 are *o* make 4
4 (*suceso*): **¿qué ha sido eso?** what was that?; **la fiesta es en mi casa** the party's at my house; **¿qué será de mí?** what will become of me?; **"érase una vez ..."** "once upon a time ..."
5 (*en oraciones pasivas*): **ha sido descubierto ya** it's already been discovered
6: **es de esperar que** ... it is to be hoped *o* I *etc* hope that ...
7 (*locuciones con sub*): **o sea** that is to say; **sea él sea su hermana** either him or his sister; **tengo que irme, no sea que mis hijos estén esperándome** I have to go in case my children are waiting for me
8: **a** *o* **de no ~ por él** ... but for him ...
9: **a no ~ que: a no ~ que tenga uno ya** unless he's got one already
♦ *nm* being; ~ **humano** human being; ~ **vivo** living creature.

Serbia ['serßja] *nf* Serbia.
serbio, a ['serßjo, a] *adj* Serbian ♦ *nm/f* Serb.
serenarse [sere'narse] *vr* to calm down; (*mar*) to grow calm; (*tiempo*) to clear up.
serenidad [sereni'ðað] *nf* calmness.
sereno, a [se'reno, a] *adj* (*persona*) calm, unruffled; (*el tiempo*) fine, settled; (*ambiente*) calm, peaceful ♦ *nm* night watchman.
serial [se'rjal] *nm* serial.
serie ['serje] *nf* series; (*cadena*) sequence, succession; (*TV etc*) serial; (*de inyecciones*) course; **fuera de ~** out of order; (*fig*) special, out of the ordinary; **fabricación en ~** mass production; (*INFORM*): **interface/impresora en ~** serial interface/printer.
seriedad [serje'ðað] *nf* seriousness; (*formalidad*) reliability; (*de crisis*) gravity, seriousness.

serigrafía [seriɣra'fia] *nf* silk screen printing.
serio, a ['serjo, a] *adj* serious; reliable, dependable; grave, serious; **poco ~** (*actitud*) undignified; (*carácter*) unreliable; **en ~** seriously.
sermón [ser'mon] *nm* (*REL*) sermon.
sermonear [sermone'ar] *vt* (*fam*) to lecture ♦ *vi* to sermonize.
seropositivo, a [seroposi'tiβo, a] *adj* HIV-positive.
serpentear [serpente'ar] *vi* to wriggle; (*camino, río*) to wind, snake.
serpentina [serpen'tina] *nf* streamer.
serpiente [ser'pjente] *nf* snake; **~ boa** boa constrictor; **~ de cascabel** rattlesnake.
serranía [serra'nia] *nf* mountainous area.
serrano, a [se'rrano, a] *adj* highland *cpd*, hill *cpd* ♦ *nm/f* highlander.
serrar [se'rrar] *vt* to saw.
serrín [se'rrin] *nm* sawdust.
serrucho [se'rrutʃo] *nm* handsaw.
Servia ['serβja] *nf* Serbia.
servicial [serβi'θjal] *adj* helpful, obliging.
servicio [ser'βiθjo] *nm* service; (*CULIN etc*) set; **~s** *nmpl* toilet(s) (*pl*); **estar de ~** to be on duty; **~ aduanero** *o* **de aduana** customs service; **~ a domicilio** home delivery service; **~ incluido** (*en hotel etc*) service charge included; **~ militar** military service; **~ público** (*COM*) public utility.
servidor, a [serβi'ðor, a] *nm/f* servant ♦ *nm* (*INFORM*) server; **su seguro ~ (s.s.s.)** yours faithfully; **un ~** (*el que habla o escribe*) your humble servant.
servidumbre [serβi'ðumbre] *nf* (*sujeción*) servitude; (*criados*) servants *pl*, staff.
servil [ser'βil] *adj* servile.
servilleta [serβi'ʎeta] *nf* serviette, napkin.
servilletero [serβiʎe'tero] *nm* napkin ring.
servir [ser'βir] *vt* to serve; (*comida*) to serve out *o* up; (*TENIS etc*) to serve ♦ *vi* to serve; (*camarero*) to serve, wait; (*tener utilidad*) to be of use, be useful; **~se** *vr* to serve *o* help o.s.; **¿en qué puedo ~le?** how can I help you?; **~ vino a algn** to pour out wine for sb; **~ de guía** to act *o* serve as a guide; **no sirve para nada** it's no use at all; **~se de algo** to make use of sth, use sth; **sírvase pasar** please come in.
sesantía [θesan'tia] *nf*(*AM*) unemployment.
sesenta [se'senta] *num* sixty.
sesentón, ona [sesen'ton, ona] *adj, nm/f* sixty-year-old.
sesgado, a [ses'ɣaðo, a] *adj* slanted, slanting.
sesgo ['sesɣo] *nm* slant; (*fig*) slant, twist.
sesión [se'sjon] *nf* (*POL*) session, sitting; (*CINE*) showing; (*TEAT*) performance; **abrir/levantar la ~** to open/close *o* adjourn the meeting; **la segunda ~** the second house.
seso ['seso] *nm* brain; (*fig*) intelligence; **~s** *nmpl* (*CULIN*) brains; **devanarse los ~s** to rack one's brains.
sesudo, a [se'suðo, a] *adj* sensible, wise.
set, *pl* **sets** [set, sets] *nm* (*TENIS*) set.
Set. *abr* (= *setiembre*) Sept.
seta ['seta] *nf* mushroom; **~ venenosa** toadstool.
setecientos, as [sete'θjentos, as] *num* seven hundred.
setenta [se'tenta] *num* seventy.
setiembre [se'tjembre] *nm* = **septiembre**.
seto ['seto] *nm* fence; **~ vivo** hedge.
seudo... [seuðo] *pref* pseudo....
seudónimo [seu'ðonimo] *nm* pseudonym.
Seúl [se'ul] *nm* Seoul.
s.e.u.o. *abr* (= *salvo error u omisión*) E & O E.
severidad [seβeri'ðað] *nf* severity.
severo, a [se'βero, a] *adj* severe; (*disciplina*) strict; (*frío*) bitter.
Sevilla [se'βiʎa] *nf* Seville.
sevillano, a [seβi'ʎano, a] *adj* of *o* from Seville ♦ *nm/f* native *o* inhabitant of Seville.
sexagenario, a [seksaxe'narjo, a] *adj* sixty-year-old ♦ *nm/f* person in his/her sixties.
sexagésimo, a [seksa'xesimo, a] *num* sixtieth.
sexo ['sekso] *nm* sex; **el ~ femenino/masculino** the female/male sex.
sexto, a ['seksto, a] *num* sixth; **Juan S~** John the Sixth.
sexual [sek'swal] *adj* sexual; **vida ~** sex life.
sexualidad [sekswali'ðað] *nf* sexuality.
s.f. *abr* (= *sin fecha*) no date.
s/f *abr* (*COM*: = *su favor*) your favour.
sgte(s). *abr* (= *siguiente(s)*) foll.
si [si] *conj* if; (*en pregunta indirecta*) if, whether ♦ *nm* (*MUS*) B; **~ ... ~ ...** whether ... or ...; **me pregunto ~ ...** I wonder if *o* whether ...; **~ no** if not, otherwise; **¡~ fuera verdad!** if only it were true!; **por ~ viene** in case he comes.
sí [si] *adv* yes ♦ *nm* consent ♦ *pron* (*uso impersonal*) oneself; (*sg*: *m*) himself; (: *f*) herself; (: *de cosa*) itself; (: *de usted*) yourself; (*pl*) themselves; (: *de ustedes*) yourselves; (: *recíproco*) each other; **él no**

quiere pero yo ~ he doesn't want to but I do; **ella ~ vendrá** she will certainly come, she is sure to come; **claro que ~** of course; **creo que ~** I think so; **porque ~** because that's the way it is; (*porque lo digo yo*) because I say so; **¡~ que lo es!** I'll say it is!; **¡eso ~ que no!** never; **se ríe de ~ misma** she laughs at herself; **cambiaron una mirada entre ~** they gave each other a look; **de por ~** in itself.

siamés, esa [sja'mes, esa] *adj, nm/f* Siamese.

sibarita [siβa'rita] *adj* sybaritic ♦ *nm/f* sybarite.

sicario [si'karjo] *nm* hired killer.

Sicilia [si'θilja] *nf* Sicily.

siciliano, a [siθi'ljano, a] *adj, nm/f* Sicilian ♦ *nm* (*LING*) Sicilian.

SIDA ['siða] *nm abr* (= *síndrome de inmunodeficiencia adquirida*) AIDS.

sida ['siða] *nm* AIDS.

siderurgia [siðe'rurxja] *nf* iron and steel industry.

siderúrgico, a [siðe'rurxico, a] *adj* iron and steel *cpd*.

sidra ['siðra] *nf* cider.

siega ['sjeɣa] *etc vb V* **segar** ♦ *nf* (*cosechar*) reaping; (*segar*) mowing; (*época*) harvest (time).

siegue ['sjeɣe] *etc vb V* **segar**.

siembra ['sjembra] *etc vb V* **sembrar** ♦ *nf* sowing.

siempre ['sjempre] *adv* always; (*todo el tiempo*) all the time; (*AM*: *así y todo*) still ♦ *conj*: **~ que ...** (+ *indic*) whenever ...; (+ *subjun*) provided that ...; **es lo de ~** it's the same old story; **como ~** as usual; **para ~** forever; **~ me voy mañana** (*AM*) I'm still leaving tomorrow.

sien [sjen] *nf* (*ANAT*) temple.

siento ['sjento] *etc vb V* **sentar, sentir**.

sierra ['sjerra] *etc vb V* **serrar** ♦ *nf* (*TEC*) saw; (*GEO*) mountain range; **S~ Leona** Sierra Leone.

siervo, a ['sjerβo, a] *nm/f* slave.

siesta ['sjesta] *nf* siesta, nap; **dormir la** *o* **echarse una** *o* **tomar una ~** to have an afternoon nap *o* a doze.

siete ['sjete] *num* seven ♦ *excl* (*AM fam*): **¡la gran ~!** wow!, hell!; **hijo de la gran ~** (*fam!*) bastard(*!*), son of a bitch (*US!*).

sífilis ['sifilis] *nf* syphilis.

sifón [si'fon] *nm* syphon; **whisky con ~** whisky and soda.

siga ['siɣa] *etc vb V* **seguir**.

sigilo [si'xilo] *nm* secrecy; (*discreción*) discretion.

sigla ['siɣla] *nf* initial, abbreviation.

siglo ['siɣlo] *nm* century; (*fig*) age; **S~ de las Luces** Age of Enlightenment; **S~ de Oro** Golden Age.

significación [siɣnifika'θjon] *nf* significance.

significado [siɣnifi'kaðo] *nm* significance; (*de palabra etc*) meaning.

significar [siɣnifi'kar] *vt* to mean, signify; (*notificar*) to make known, express.

significativo, a [siɣnifika'tiβo, a] *adj* significant.

signifique [siɣni'fike] *etc vb V* **significar**.

signo ['siɣno] *nm* sign; **~ de admiración** *o* **exclamación** exclamation mark; **~ igual** equals sign; **~ de interrogación** question mark; **~ de más/de menos** plus/minus sign; **~s de puntuación** punctuation marks.

siguiendo [si'ɣjendo] *etc vb V* **seguir**.

siguiente [si'ɣjente] *adj* following; (*próximo*) next.

silbar [sil'βar] *vt, vi* to whistle; (*silbato*) to blow; (*TEAT etc*) to hiss.

silbato [sil'βato] *nm* (*instrumento*) whistle.

silbido [sil'βiðo] *nm* whistle, whistling; (*abucheo*) hiss.

silenciador [silenθja'ðor] *nm* silencer.

silenciar [silen'θjar] *vt* (*persona*) to silence; (*escándalo*) to hush up.

silencio [si'lenθjo] *nm* silence, quiet; **en el ~ más absoluto** in dead silence; **guardar ~** to keep silent.

silencioso, a [silen'θjoso, a] *adj* silent, quiet.

sílfide ['silfiðe] *nf* sylph.

silicio [si'liθjo] *nm* silicon.

silla ['siʎa] *nf* (*asiento*) chair; (*tb*: **~ de montar**) saddle; **~ de ruedas** wheelchair.

sillería [siʎe'ria] *nf* (*asientos*) chairs *pl*, set of chairs; (*REL*) choir stalls *pl*; (*taller*) chairmaker's workshop.

sillín [si'ʎin] *nm* saddle, seat.

sillón [si'ʎon] *nm* armchair, easy chair.

silueta [si'lweta] *nf* silhouette; (*de edificio*) outline; (*figura*) figure.

silvestre [sil'βestre] *adj* (*BOT*) wild; (*fig*) rustic, rural.

sima ['sima] *nf* abyss, chasm.

simbolice [simbo'liθe] *etc vb V* **simbolizar**.

simbólico, a [sim'boliko, a] *adj* symbolic(al).

simbolizar [simboli'θar] *vt* to symbolize.

símbolo ['simbolo] *nm* symbol; **~ gráfico** (*INFORM*) icon.

simetría [sime'tria] *nf* symmetry.

simétrico, a [si'metriko, a] *adj* symmetrical.

simiente [si'mjente] *nf* seed.

similar [simi'lar] *adj* similar.
similitud [simili'tuð] *nf* similarity, resemblance.
simio ['simjo] *nm* ape.
simpatía [simpa'tia] *nf* liking; (*afecto*) affection; (*amabilidad*) kindness; (*de ambiente*) friendliness; (*de persona, lugar*) charm, attractiveness; (*solidaridad*) mutual support, solidarity; **tener ~ a** to like; **la famosa ~ andaluza** that well-known Andalusian charm.
simpatice [simpa'tiθe] *etc vb V* **simpatizar**.
simpático, a [sim'patiko, a] *adj* nice, pleasant; (*bondadoso*) kind; **no le hemos caído muy ~s** she didn't much take to us.
simpatiquísimo, a [simpati'kisimo, a] *adj* (*superl de* **simpático**) ever so nice; ever so kind.
simpatizante [simpati'θante] *nm/f* sympathizer.
simpatizar [simpati'θar] *vi*: **~ con** to get on well with.
simple ['simple] *adj* simple; (*elemental*) simple, easy; (*mero*) mere; (*puro*) pure, sheer ♦ *nm/f* simpleton; **un ~ soldado** an ordinary soldier.
simpleza [sim'pleθa] *nf* simpleness; (*necedad*) silly thing.
simplicidad [simpliθi'ðað] *nf* simplicity.
simplificar [simplifi'kar] *vt* to simplify.
simplifique [simpli'fike] *etc vb V* **simplificar**.
simplón, ona [sim'plon, ona] *adj* simple, gullible ♦ *nm/f* simple soul.
simposio [sim'posjo] *nm* symposium.
simulacro [simu'lakro] *nm* (*apariencia*) semblance; (*fingimiento*) sham.
simular [simu'lar] *vt* to simulate; (*fingir*) to feign, sham.
simultanear [simultane'ar] *vt*: **~ dos cosas** to do two things simultaneously.
simultáneo, a [simul'taneo, a] *adj* simultaneous.
sin [sin] *prep* without; (*a no ser por*) but for ♦ *conj*: **~ que** (*+ subjun*) without; **~ decir nada** without a word; **~ verlo yo** without my seeing it; **platos ~ lavar** unwashed *o* dirty dishes; **la ropa está ~ lavar** the clothes are unwashed; **~ que lo sepa él** without his knowing; **~ embargo** however.
sinagoga [sina'ɣoɣa] *nf* synagogue.
Sinaí [sina'i] *nm*: **El ~** Sinai, the Sinai Peninsula; **el Monte ~** Mount Sinai.
sinceridad [sinθeri'ðað] *nf* sincerity.
sincero, a [sin'θero, a] *adj* sincere; (*persona*) genuine; (*opinión*) frank; (*felicitaciones*) heartfelt.
síncope ['sinkope] *nm* (*desmayo*) blackout; **~ cardíaco** (*MED*) heart failure.
sincronice [sinkro'niθe] *etc vb V* **sincronizar**.
sincronizar [sinkroni'θar] *vt* to synchronize.
sindical [sindi'kal] *adj* union *cpd*, trade-union *cpd*.
sindicalista [sindika'lista] *adj* trade-union *cpd* ♦ *nm/f* trade unionist.
sindicar [sindi'kar] *vt* (*obreros*) to organize, unionize; **~se** *vr* (*obrero*) to join a union.
sindicato [sindi'kato] *nm* (*de trabajadores*) trade(s) *o* labor (*US*) union; (*de negociantes*) syndicate.
sindique [sin'dike] *etc vb V* **sindicar**.
síndrome ['sindrome] *nm* syndrome; **~ de abstinencia** withdrawal symptoms.
sine qua non [sine'kwanon] *adj*: **condición ~** sine qua non.
sinfín [sin'fin] *nm*: **un ~ de** a great many, no end of.
sinfonía [sinfo'nia] *nf* symphony.
sinfónico, a [sin'foniko, a] *adj* (*música*) symphonic; **orquesta sinfónica** symphony orchestra.
Singapur [singa'pur] *nm* Singapore.
singular [singu'lar] *adj* singular; (*fig*) outstanding, exceptional; (*pey*) peculiar, odd ♦ *nm* (*LING*) singular; **en ~** in the singular.
singularice [singula'riθe] *etc vb V* **singularizar**.
singularidad [singulari'ðað] *nf* singularity, peculiarity.
singularizar [singulari'θar] *vt* to single out; **~se** *vr* to distinguish o.s., stand out.
siniestro, a [si'njestro, a] *adj* left; (*fig*) sinister ♦ *nm* (*accidente*) accident; (*desastre*) natural disaster.
sinnúmero [sin'numero] *nm* = **sinfín**.
sino ['sino] *nm* fate, destiny ♦ *conj* (*pero*) but; (*salvo*) except, save; **no son 8 ~ 9** there are not 8 but 9; **todos ~ él** all except him.
sinónimo, a [si'nonimo, a] *adj* synonymous ♦ *nm* synonym.
sinrazón [sinra'θon] *nf* wrong, injustice.
sinsabor [sinsa'βor] *nm* (*molestia*) trouble; (*dolor*) sorrow; (*preocupación*) uneasiness.
sintaxis [sin'taksis] *nf* syntax.
síntesis ['sintesis] *nf inv* synthesis.
sintetice [sinte'tiθe] *etc vb V* **sintetizar**.
sintético, a [sin'tetiko, a] *adj* synthetic.
sintetizador [sintetiθa'ðor] *nm* synthesizer.
sintetizar [sinteti'θar] *vt* to synthesize.
sintiendo [sin'tjendo] *etc vb V* **sentir**.
síntoma ['sintoma] *nm* symptom.
sintomático, a [sinto'matiko, a] *adj*

symptomatic.
sintonía [sinto'nia] *nf* (*RADIO*) tuning; (*melodía*) signature tune.
sintonice [sinto'niθe] *etc vb V* **sintonizar**.
sintonizador [sintoniθa'ðor] *nm* (*RADIO*) tuner.
sintonizar [sintoni'θar] *vt* (*RADIO*) to tune (in) to, pick up.
sinuoso, a [si'nwoso, a] *adj* (*camino*) winding; (*rumbo*) devious.
sinvergüenza [simber'ɣwenθa] *nm/f* rogue, scoundrel.
sionismo [sjo'nismo] *nm* Zionism.
siquiera [si'kjera] *conj* even if, even though ♦ *adv* (*esp AM*) at least; **ni ~** not even; **~ bebe algo** at least drink something.
sirena [si'rena] *nf* siren, mermaid; (*bocina*) siren, hooter.
Siria ['sirja] *nf* Syria.
sirio, a ['sirjo, a] *adj, nm/f* Syrian.
sirviendo [sir'ßjendo] *etc vb V* **servir**.
sirviente, a [sir'ßjente, a] *nm/f* servant.
sisa ['sisa] *nf* petty theft; (*COSTURA*) dart; (*sobaquera*) armhole.
sisar [si'sar] *vt* (*robar*) to thieve; (*COSTURA*) to take in.
sisear [sise'ar] *vt, vi* to hiss.
sísmico, a ['sismiko, a] *adj*: **movimiento ~** earthquake.
sismógrafo [sis'moɣrafo] *nm* seismograph.
sistema [sis'tema] *nm* system; (*método*) method; **~ educativo** education system; **~ impositivo** *o* **tributario** taxation, tax system; **~ pedagógico** educational system; **~ de alerta inmediata** early-warning system; **~ binario** (*INFORM*) binary system; **~ experto** expert system; **~ de facturación** (*COM*) invoicing system; **~ de fondo fijo** (*COM*) imprest system; **~ de lógica compartida** (*INFORM*) shared logic system; **~ métrico** metric system; **~ operativo (en disco)** (*INFORM*) (disk-based) operating system; *see boxed note.*

SISTEMA EDUCATIVO

The reform of the Spanish **sistema educativo** (*education system*) *begun in the early 1990s, has replaced the old EGB, BUP and COU courses with the following: six years of compulsory primary education ("primaria"); four years of compulsory secondary education ("secundaria"); and a two-year "bachillerato", which is optional but a prerequisite for entry into higher education.*

sistemático, a [siste'matiko, a] *adj* systematic.
sitiar [si'tjar] *vt* to besiege, lay siege to.
sitio ['sitjo] *nm* (*lugar*) place; (*espacio*) room, space; (*MIL*) siege; **~ Web** (*INFORM*) website; **¿hay ~?** is there any room?; **hay ~ de sobra** there's plenty of room.
situación [sitwa'θjon] *nf* situation, position; (*estatus*) position, standing.
situado, a [si'twaðo, a] *adj* situated, placed; **estar ~** (*COM*) to be financially secure.
situar [si'twar] *vt* to place, put; (*edificio*) to locate, situate.
S.L. *abr* (*COM*: = *Sociedad Limitada*) Ltd.
slip [es'lip], *pl* **slips** *nm* pants *pl*, briefs *pl*.
slot [es'lot], *pl* **slots** *nm*: **~ de expansión** expansion slot.
S.M. *abr* (= *Su Majestad*) HM.
SME *nm abr* (= *Sistema Monetario Europeo*) EMS; **(mecanismo de cambios del) ~** ERM.
smoking [(e)'smokin] (*pl* **~s**) *nm* dinner jacket (*BRIT*), tuxedo (*US*).
s/n *abr* (= *sin número*) no number.
snob [es'nob] = **esnob**.
SO *abr* (= *suroeste*) SW.
so [so] *excl* whoa!; **¡~ burro!** you idiot! ♦ *prep* under.
s/o *abr* (*COM*: = *su orden*) your order.
sobaco [so'ßako] *nm* armpit.
sobado, a [so'ßaðo, a] *adj* (*ropa*) worn; (*arrugado*) crumpled; (*libro*) well-thumbed; (*CULIN*: *masa*) short.
sobar [so'ßar] *vt* (*tela*) to finger; (*ropa*) to rumple, mess up; (*músculos*) to rub, massage.
soberanía [soßera'nia] *nf* sovereignty.
soberano, a [soße'rano, a] *adj* sovereign; (*fig*) supreme ♦ *nm/f* sovereign; **los ~s** the king and queen.
soberbio, a [so'ßerßjo, a] *adj* (*orgulloso*) proud; (*altivo*) haughty, arrogant; (*fig*) magnificent, superb ♦ *nf* pride; haughtiness, arrogance; magnificence.
sobornar [soßor'nar] *vt* to bribe.
soborno [so'ßorno] *nm* (*un ~*) bribe; (*el ~*) bribery.
sobra ['soßra] *nf* excess, surplus; **~s** *nfpl* left-overs, scraps; **de ~** surplus, extra; **lo sé de ~** I'm only too aware of it; **tengo de ~** I've more than enough.
sobradamente [soßraða'mente] *adv* amply; (*saber*) only too well.
sobrado, a [so'ßraðo, a] *adj* (*más que suficiente*) more than enough; (*superfluo*) excessive ♦ *adv* too, exceedingly;

sobradas veces repeatedly.
sobrante [so'ßrante] *adj* remaining, extra ♦ *nm* surplus, remainder.
sobrar [so'ßrar] *vt* to exceed, surpass ♦ *vi* (*tener de más*) to be more than enough; (*quedar*) to remain, be left (over).
sobrasada [soßra'saða] *nf* ≈ sausage spread.
sobre ['soßre] *prep* (*gen*) on; (*encima*) on (top of); (*por encima de, arriba de*) over, above; (*más que*) more than; (*además*) in addition to, besides; (*alrededor de*) about; (*porcentaje*) in, out of; (*tema*) about, on ♦ *nm* envelope; **~ todo** above all; **3 ~ 100** 3 in a 100, 3 out of every 100; **un libro ~ Tirso** a book about Tirso; **~ de ventanilla** window envelope.
sobrecama [soßre'kama] *nf* bedspread.
sobrecapitalice [soßrekapita'liθe] *etc vb V* **sobrecapitalizar**.
sobrecapitalizar [soßrekapitali'θar] *vi* to overcapitalize.
sobrecargar [soßrekar'ɣar] *vt* (*camión*) to overload; (*COM*) to surcharge.
sobrecargue [soßre'karɣe] *etc vb V* **sobrecargar**.
sobrecoger [soßreko'xer] *vt* (*sobresaltar*) to startle; (*asustar*) to scare; **~se** *vr* (*sobresaltarse*) to be startled; (*asustarse*) to get scared; (*quedar impresionado*): **~se (de)** to be overawed (by).
sobrecoja [soßre'koxa] *etc vb V* **sobrecoger**.
sobredosis [soßre'ðosis] *nf inv* overdose.
sobre(e)ntender [soßre(e)nten'der] *vt* to understand; (*adivinar*) to deduce, infer; **~se** *vr*: **se sobre(e)ntiende que ...** it is implied that ....
sobreescribir [soßreeskri'ßir] *vt* (*INFORM*) to overwrite.
sobre(e)stimar [soßre(e)sti'mar] *vt* to overestimate.
sobregiro [soßre'xiro] *nm* (*COM*) overdraft.
sobrehumano, a [soßreu'mano, a] *adj* superhuman.
sobreimprimir [soßreimpri'mir] *vt* (*COM*) to merge.
sobrellevar [soßreʎe'ßar] *vt* (*fig*) to bear, endure.
sobremesa [soßre'mesa] *nf* (*después de comer*) sitting on after a meal; (*INFORM*) desktop; **conversación de ~** table talk.
sobremodo [soßre'moðo] *adv* very much, enormously.
sobrenatural [soßrenatu'ral] *adj* supernatural.
sobrenombre [soßre'nombre] *nm* nickname.
sobrepasar [soßrepa'sar] *vt* to exceed, surpass.
sobrepondré [soßrepon'dre] *etc vb V* **sobreponer**.
sobreponer [soßrepo'ner] *vt* (*poner encima*) to put on top; (*añadir*) to add; **~se** *vr*: **~se a** to overcome.
sobreponga [soßre'ponga] *etc vb V* **sobreponer**.
sobreprima [soßre'prima] *nf* (*COM*) loading.
sobreproducción [soßreproðuk'θjon] *nf* overproduction.
sobrepuesto [soßre'pwesto], **sobrepuse** [soßre'puse] *etc vb V* **sobreponer**.
sobresaldré [soßresal'dre] *etc*, **sobresalga** [soßre'salɣa] *etc vb V* **sobresalir**.
sobresaliente [soßresa'ljente] *adj* projecting; (*fig*) outstanding, excellent; (*UNIV etc*) first class ♦ *nm* (*UNIV etc*) first class (mark), distinction.
sobresalir [soßresa'lir] *vi* to project, jut out; (*fig*) to stand out, excel.
sobresaltar [soßresal'tar] *vt* (*asustar*) to scare, frighten; (*sobrecoger*) to startle.
sobresalto [soßre'salto] *nm* (*movimiento*) start; (*susto*) scare; (*turbación*) sudden shock.
sobreseer [soßrese'er] *vt*: **~ una causa** (*JUR*) to stop a case.
sobrestadía [soßresta'ðia] *nf* (*COM*) demurrage.
sobretensión [soßreten'sjon] *nf* (*ELEC*): **~ transitoria** surge.
sobretiempo [soßre'tjempo] *nm* (*AM*) overtime.
sobretodo [soßre'toðo] *nm* overcoat.
sobrevendré [soßreßen'dre] *etc*, **sobrevenga** [soßre'ßenga] *etc vb V* **sobrevenir**.
sobrevenir [soßreße'nir] *vi* (*ocurrir*) to happen (unexpectedly); (*resultar*) to follow, ensue.
sobreviene [soßre'ßjene] *etc*, **sobrevine** [soßre'ßine] *etc vb V* **sobrevenir**.
sobreviviente [soßreßi'ßjente] *adj* surviving ♦ *nm/f* survivor.
sobrevivir [soßreßi'ßir] *vi* to survive; (*persona*) to outlive; (*objeto etc*) to outlast.
sobrevolar [soßreßo'lar] *vt* to fly over.
sobrevuele [soßre'ßwele] *etc vb V* **sobrevolar**.
sobriedad [soßrje'ðað] *nf* sobriety, soberness; (*moderación*) moderation, restraint.
sobrino, a [so'ßrino, a] *nm/f* nephew/niece.

sobrio, a ['soβrjo, a] *adj* (*moderado*) moderate, restrained.
socarrón, ona [soka'rron, ona] *adj* (*sarcástico*) sarcastic, ironic(al).
socavar [soka'βar] *vt* to undermine; (*excavar*) to dig underneath *o* below.
socavón [soka'βon] *nm* (*en mina*) gallery; (*hueco*) hollow; (*en la calle*) hole.
sociable [so'θjaβle] *adj* (*persona*) sociable, friendly; (*animal*) social.
social [so'θjal] *adj* social; (*COM*) company *cpd*.
socialdemócrata [soθjalde'mokrata] *adj* social-democratic ♦ *nm/f* social democrat.
socialice [soθja'liθe] *etc vb V* **socializar**.
socialista [soθja'lista] *adj, nm/f* socialist.
socializar [soθjali'θar] *vt* to socialize.
sociedad [soθje'ðað] *nf* society; (*COM*) company; ~ **de ahorro y préstamo** savings and loan society; ~ **anónima (S.A.)** limited company (Ltd) (*BRIT*), incorporated company (Inc) (*US*); ~ **de beneficiencia** friendly society (*BRIT*), benefit association (*US*); ~ **de cartera** investment trust; ~ **comanditaria** (*COM*) co-ownership; ~ **conjunta** (*COM*) joint venture; ~ **inmobiliaria** building society (*BRIT*), savings and loan (society) (*US*); ~ **de responsabilidad limitada** (*COM*) private limited company.
socio, a ['soθjo, a] *nm/f* (*miembro*) member; (*COM*) partner; ~ **activo** active partner; ~ **capitalista** *o* **comanditario** sleeping *o* silent (*US*) partner.
socioeconómico, a [soθjoeko'nomiko, a] *adj* socio-economic.
sociología [soθjolo'xia] *nf* sociology.
sociólogo, a [so'θjoloɣo, a] *nm/f* sociologist.
socorrer [soko'rrer] *vt* to help.
socorrido, a [soko'rriðo, a] *adj* (*tienda*) well-stocked; (*útil*) handy; (*persona*) helpful.
socorrismo [soko'rrismo] *nm* life-saving.
socorrista [soko'rrista] *nm/f* first aider; (*en piscina, playa*) lifeguard.
socorro [so'korro] *nm* (*ayuda*) help, aid; (*MIL*) relief; ¡~! help!
soda ['soða] *nf* (*sosa*) soda; (*bebida*) soda (water).
sódico, a ['soðiko, a] *adj* sodium *cpd*.
soez [so'eθ] *adj* dirty, obscene.
sofá [so'fa] *nm* sofa, settee.
sofá-cama [so'fakama] *nm* studio couch, sofa bed.
Sofia ['sofja] *nf* Sofia.
sofisticación [sofistika'θjon] *nf* sophistication.
sofisticado, a [sofisti'kaðo, a] *adj* sophisticated.
sofocado, a [sofo'kaðo, a] *adj*: **estar** ~ (*fig*) to be out of breath; (*ahogarse*) to feel stifled.
sofocar [sofo'kar] *vt* to suffocate; (*apagar*) to smother, put out; ~**se** *vr* to suffocate; (*fig*) to blush, feel embarrassed.
sofoco [so'foko] *nm* suffocation; (*azoro*) embarrassment.
sofocón [sofo'kon] *nm*: **llevarse** *o* **pasar un** ~ to have a sudden shock.
sofreír [sofre'ir] *vt* to fry lightly.
sofría [so'fria] *etc*, **sofriendo** [so'frjendo] *etc*, **sofrito** [so'frito] *vb V* **sofreír**.
soft(ware) ['sof(wer)] *nm* (*INFORM*) software.
soga ['soɣa] *nf* rope.
sois [sois] *vb V* **ser**.
soja ['soxa] *nf* soya.
sojuzgar [soxuθ'ɣar] *vt* to subdue, rule despotically.
sojuzgue [so'xuθɣe] *etc vb V* **sojuzgar**.
sol [sol] *nm* sun; (*luz*) sunshine, sunlight; (*MUS*) G; ~ **naciente/poniente** rising/setting sun; **tomar el** ~ to sunbathe; **hace** ~ it is sunny.
solace [so'laθe] *etc vb V* **solazar**.
solamente [sola'mente] *adv* only, just.
solapa [so'lapa] *nf* (*de chaqueta*) lapel; (*de libro*) jacket.
solapado, a [sola'paðo, a] *adj* sly, underhand.
solar [so'lar] *adj* solar, sun *cpd* ♦ *nm* (*terreno*) plot (of ground); (*local*) undeveloped site.
solaz [so'laθ] *nm* recreation, relaxation.
solazar [sola'θar] *vt* (*divertir*) to amuse; ~**se** *vr* to enjoy o.s., relax.
soldada [sol'daða] *nf* pay.
soldado [sol'daðo] *nm* soldier; ~ **raso** private.
soldador [solda'ðor] *nm* soldering iron; (*persona*) welder.
soldar [sol'dar] *vt* to solder, weld; (*unir*) to join, unite.
soleado, a [sole'aðo, a] *adj* sunny.
soledad [sole'ðað] *nf* solitude; (*estado infeliz*) loneliness.
solemne [so'lemne] *adj* solemn; (*tontería*) utter; (*error*) complete.
solemnidad [solemni'ðað] *nf* solemnity.
soler [so'ler] *vi* to be in the habit of, be accustomed to; **suele salir a las ocho** she usually goes out at 8 o'clock; **solíamos ir todos los años** we used to go every year.

solera [so'lera] *nf* (*tradición*) tradition; **vino de ~** vintage wine.
solfeo [sol'feo] *nm* singing of scales; **ir a clases de ~** to take singing lessons.
solicitar [soliθi'tar] *vt* (*permiso*) to ask for, seek; (*puesto*) to apply for; (*votos*) to canvass for; (*atención*) to attract; (*persona*) to pursue, chase after.
solícito, a [so'liθito, a] *adj* (*diligente*) diligent; (*cuidadoso*) careful.
solicitud [soliθi'tuð] *nf* (*calidad*) great care; (*petición*) request; (*a un puesto*) application.
solidaridad [soliðari'ðað] *nf* solidarity; **por ~ con** (*POL etc*) out of *o* in solidarity with.
solidario, a [soli'ðarjo, a] *adj* (*participación*) joint, common; (*compromiso*) mutually binding; **hacerse ~ de** to declare one's solidarity with.
solidarizarse [soliðari'θarse] *vr*: **~ con algn** to support sb, sympathize with sb.
solidez [soli'ðeθ] *nf* solidity.
sólido, a ['soliðo, a] *adj* solid; (*TEC*) solidly made; (*bien construido*) well built.
soliloquio [soli'lokjo] *nm* soliloquy.
solista [so'lista] *nm/f* soloist.
solitario, a [soli'tarjo, a] *adj* (*persona*) lonely, solitary; (*lugar*) lonely, desolate ♦ *nm/f* (*reclusa*) recluse; (*en la sociedad*) loner ♦ *nm* solitaire ♦ *nf* tapeworm.
soliviantar [solißjan'tar] *vt* to stir up, rouse (to revolt); (*enojar*) to anger; (*sacar de quicio*) to exasperate.
solloce [so'ʎoθe] *etc vb V* **sollozar**.
sollozar [soʎo'θar] *vi* to sob.
sollozo [so'ʎoθo] *nm* sob.
solo, a ['solo, a] *adj* (*único*) single, sole; (*sin compañía*) alone; (*MUS*) solo; (*solitario*) lonely; **hay una sola dificultad** there is just one difficulty; **a solas** alone, by o.s.
sólo ['solo] *adv* only, just; (*exclusivamente*) solely; **tan ~** only just.
solomillo [solo'miʎo] *nm* sirloin.
solsticio [sols'tiθjo] *nm* solstice.
soltar [sol'tar] *vt* (*dejar ir*) to let go of; (*desprender*) to unfasten, loosen; (*librar*) to release, set free; (*amarras*) to cast off; (*AUTO: freno etc*) to release; (*suspiro*) to heave; (*risa etc*) to let out; **~se** *vr* (*desanudarse*) to come undone; (*desprenderse*) to come off; (*adquirir destreza*) to become expert; (*en idioma*) to become fluent.
soltero, a [sol'tero, a] *adj* single, unmarried ♦ *nm* bachelor ♦ *nf* single woman, spinster.
solterón [solte'ron] *nm* confirmed bachelor.
solterona [solte'rona] *nf* spinster, maiden lady; (*pey*) old maid.
soltura [sol'tura] *nf* looseness, slackness; (*de los miembros*) agility, ease of movement; (*en el hablar*) fluency, ease.
soluble [so'lußle] *adj* (*QUÍMICA*) soluble; (*problema*) solvable; **~ en agua** soluble in water.
solución [solu'θjon] *nf* solution; **~ de continuidad** break in continuity.
solucionar [soluθjo'nar] *vt* (*problema*) to solve; (*asunto*) to settle, resolve.
solvencia [sol'ßenθja] *nf* (*COM: estado*) solvency; (*: acción*) settlement, payment.
solventar [solßen'tar] *vt* (*pagar*) to settle, pay; (*resolver*) to resolve.
solvente [sol'ßente] *adj* solvent, free of debt.
Somalia [so'malja] *nf* Somalia.
sombra ['sombra] *nf* shadow; (*como protección*) shade; **~s** *nfpl* darkness *sg*, shadows; **sin ~ de duda** without a shadow of doubt; **tener buena/mala ~** (*suerte*) to be lucky/unlucky; (*carácter*) to be likeable/disagreeable.
sombrero [som'brero] *nm* hat; **~ hongo** bowler (hat), derby (*US*); **~ de copa** *o* **de pelo** (*AM*) top hat.
sombrilla [som'briʎa] *nf* parasol, sunshade.
sombrío, a [som'brio, a] *adj* (*oscuro*) shady; (*fig*) sombre, sad; (*persona*) gloomy.
somero, a [so'mero, a] *adj* superficial.
someter [some'ter] *vt* (*país*) to conquer; (*persona*) to subject to one's will; (*informe*) to present, submit; **~se** *vr* to give in, yield, submit; **~se a** to submit to; **~se a una operación** to undergo an operation.
sometimiento [someti'mjento] *nm* (*estado*) submission; (*acción*) presentation.
somier [so'mjer], *pl* **somiers** *nm* spring mattress.
somnífero [som'nifero] *nm* sleeping pill *o* tablet.
somnolencia [somno'lenθja] *nf* sleepiness, drowsiness.
somos ['somos] *vb V* **ser**.
son [son] *vb V* **ser** ♦ *nm* sound; **en ~ de broma** as a joke.
sonado, a [so'naðo, a] *adj* (*comentado*) talked-of; (*famoso*) famous; (*COM: pey*) hyped(-up).
sonajero [sona'xero] *nm* (baby's) rattle.
sonambulismo [sonambu'lismo] *nm*

sleepwalking.
sonámbulo, a [so'nambulo, a] *nm/f* sleepwalker.
sonar [so'nar] *vt* (*campana*) to ring; (*trompeta, sirena*) to blow ♦ *vi* to sound; (*hacer ruido*) to make a noise; (*LING*) to be sounded, be pronounced; (*ser conocido*) to sound familiar; (*campana*) to ring; (*reloj*) to strike, chime; **~se** *vr*: **~se (la nariz)** to blow one's nose; **es un nombre que suena** it's a name that's in the news; **me suena ese nombre** that name rings a bell.
sonda ['sonda] *nf* (*NAUT*) sounding; (*TEC*) bore, drill; (*MED*) probe.
sondear [sonde'ar] *vt* to sound; to bore (into), drill; to probe, sound; (*fig*) to sound out.
sondeo [son'deo] *nm* sounding; boring, drilling; (*encuesta*) poll, enquiry; **~ de la opinión pública** public opinion poll.
sónico, a ['soniko, a] *adj* sonic, sound *cpd*.
sonido [so'niðo] *nm* sound.
sonoro, a [so'noro, a] *adj* sonorous; (*resonante*) loud, resonant; (*LING*) voiced; **efectos ~s** sound effects.
sonreír [sonre'ir] *vi*, **sonreírse** *vr* to smile.
sonría [son'ria] *etc*, **sonriendo** [son'rjendo] *etc vb V* **sonreír**.
sonriente [son'rjente] *adj* smiling.
sonrisa [son'risa] *nf* smile.
sonrojar [sonro'xar] *vt*: **~ a algn** to make sb blush; **~se** *vr*: **~se (de)** to blush (at).
sonrojo [son'roxo] *nm* blush.
sonsacar [sonsa'kar] *vt* to wheedle, coax; **~ a algn** to pump sb for information.
sonsaque [son'sake] *etc vb V* **sonsacar**.
sonsonete [sonso'nete] *nm* (*golpecitos*) tap(ping); (*voz monótona*) monotonous delivery, singsong (voice).
soñador, a [soɲa'ðor, a] *nm/f* dreamer.
soñar [so'ɲar] *vt, vi* to dream; **~ con** to dream about *o* of; **soñé contigo anoche** I dreamed about you last night.
soñoliento, a [soɲo'ljento, a] *adj* sleepy, drowsy.
sopa ['sopa] *nf* soup; **~ de fideos** noodle soup.
sopero, a [so'pero, a] *adj* (*plato, cuchara*) soup *cpd* ♦ *nm* soup plate ♦ *nf* soup tureen.
sopesar [sope'sar] *vt* to try the weight of; (*fig*) to weigh up.
sopetón [sope'ton] *nm*: **de ~** suddenly, unexpectedly.
soplar [so'plar] *vt* (*polvo*) to blow away, blow off; (*inflar*) to blow up; (*vela*) to blow out; (*ayudar a recordar*) to prompt; (*birlar*) to nick; (*delatar*) to split on ♦ *vi* to blow; (*delatar*) to squeal; (*beber*) to booze, bend the elbow.
soplete [so'plete] *nm* blowlamp; **~ soldador** welding torch.
soplo ['soplo] *nm* blow, puff; (*de viento*) puff, gust.
soplón, ona [so'plon, ona] *nm/f* (*fam*: *chismoso*) telltale; (: *de policía*) informer, grass.
soponcio [so'ponθjo] *nm* dizzy spell.
sopor [so'por] *nm* drowsiness.
soporífero, a [sopo'rifero, a] *adj* sleep-inducing; (*fig*) soporific ♦ *nm* sleeping pill.
soportable [sopor'taβle] *adj* bearable.
soportal [sopor'tal] *nm* porch; **~es** *nmpl* arcade *sg*.
soportar [sopor'tar] *vt* to bear, carry; (*fig*) to bear, put up with.
soporte [so'porte] *nm* support; (*fig*) pillar, support; (*INFORM*) medium; **~ de entrada/salida** input/output medium.
soprano [so'prano] *nf* soprano.
sor [sor] *nf*: **S~ María** Sister Mary.
sorber [sor'βer] *vt* (*chupar*) to sip; (*inhalar*) to sniff, inhale; (*absorber*) to soak up, absorb.
sorbete [sor'βete] *nm* sherbet.
sorbo ['sorβo] *nm* (*trago*) gulp, swallow; (*chupada*) sip; **beber a ~s** to sip.
sordera [sor'ðera] *nf* deafness.
sórdido, a ['sorðiðo, a] *adj* dirty, squalid.
sordo, a ['sorðo, a] *adj* (*persona*) deaf; (*ruido*) dull; (*LING*) voiceless ♦ *nm/f* deaf person; **quedarse ~** to go deaf.
sordomudo, a [sorðo'muðo, a] *adj* deaf and dumb ♦ *nm/f* deaf-mute.
soriano, a [so'rjano, a] *adj* of *o* from Soria ♦ *nm/f* native *o* inhabitant of Soria.
sorna ['sorna] *nf* (*malicia*) slyness; (*tono burlón*) sarcastic tone.
soroche [so'rotʃe] *nm* (*AM MED*) mountain sickness.
sorprendente [sorpren'dente] *adj* surprising.
sorprender [sorpren'der] *vt* to surprise; (*asombrar*) to amaze; (*sobresaltar*) to startle; (*coger desprevenido*) to catch unawares; **~se** *vr*: **~se (de)** to be surprised *o* amazed (at).
sorpresa [sor'presa] *nf* surprise.
sorpresivo, a [sorpre'siβo, a] *adj* (*AM*) surprising; (*imprevisto*) sudden.
sortear [sorte'ar] *vt* to draw lots for; (*rifar*) to raffle; (*dificultad*) to dodge, avoid.
sorteo [sor'teo] *nm* (*en lotería*) draw; (*rifa*) raffle.
sortija [sor'tixa] *nf* ring; (*rizo*) ringlet, curl.

sortilegio [sorti'lexjo] *nm* (*hechicería*) sorcery; (*hechizo*) spell.
sosegado, a [sose'ɣaðo, a] *adj* quiet, calm.
sosegar [sose'ɣar] *vt* to quieten, calm; (*el ánimo*) to reassure ♦ *vi* to rest.
sosegué [sose'ɣe], **soseguemos** [sose'ɣemos] *etc vb V* **sosegar**.
sosiego [so'sjeɣo] *etc vb V* **sosegar** ♦ *nm* quiet(ness), calm(ness).
sosiegue [so'sjeɣe] *etc vb V* **sosegar**.
soslayar [sosla'jar] *vt* (*preguntas*) to get round.
soslayo [sos'lajo]: **de** ~ *adv* obliquely, sideways; **mirar de** ~ to look out of the corner of one's eye (at).
soso, a ['soso, a] *adj* (*CULIN*) tasteless; (*fig*) dull, uninteresting.
sospecha [sos'petʃa] *nf* suspicion.
sospechar [sospe'tʃar] *vt* to suspect ♦ *vi*: ~ **de** to be suspicious of.
sospechoso, a [sospe'tʃoso, a] *adj* suspicious; (*testimonio, opinión*) suspect ♦ *nm/f* suspect.
sostén [sos'ten] *nm* (*apoyo*) support; (*sujetador*) bra; (*alimentación*) sustenance, food.
sostendré [sosten'dre] *etc vb V* **sostener**.
sostener [soste'ner] *vt* to support; (*mantener*) to keep up, maintain; (*alimentar*) to sustain, keep going; ~**se** *vr* to support o.s.; (*seguir*) to continue, remain.
sostenga [sos'tenga] *etc vb V* **sostener**.
sostenido, adj [soste'niðo, a] *adj* continuous, sustained; (*prolongado*) prolonged; (*MUS*) sharp ♦ *nm* (*MUS*) sharp.
sostuve [sos'tuβe] *etc vb V* **sostener**.
sota ['sota] *nf* (*NAIPES*) ≈ jack; *V tb* **baraja española**.
sotana [so'tana] *nf* (*REL*) cassock.
sótano ['sotano] *nm* basement.
sotavento [sota'βento] *nm* (*NAUT*) lee, leeward.
soterrar [sote'rrar] *vt* to bury; (*esconder*) to hide away.
sotierre [so'tjerre] *etc vb V* **soterrar**.
soviético, a [so'βjetiko, a] *adj, nm/f* Soviet; **los** ~**s** the Soviets, the Russians.
soy [soi] *vb V* **ser**.
soya ['soja] *nf* (*AM*) soya (bean).
SP *abr* (*AUTO*) = **servicio público**.
SPM *nm abr* (= *síndrome premenstrual*) PMS.
spooling [es'pulin] *nm* (*INFORM*) spooling.
sport [es'por(t)] *nm* sport.
spot [es'pot], *pl* **spot** *nm* (*publicitario*) ad.
squash [es'kwas] *nm* (*DEPORTE*) squash.
Sr. *abr* (= *Señor*) Mr.
Sra. *abr* (= *Señora*) Mrs.
S.R.C. *abr* (= *se ruega contestación*) R.S.V.P.
Sres., Srs. *abr* (= *Señores*) Messrs.
Sri Lanka [sri'lanka] *nm* Sri Lanka.
Srta. *abr* = **Señorita**.
SS *abr* (= *Santos, Santas*) SS.
ss. *abr* (= *siguientes*) foll.
S.S. *abr* (*REL*: = *Su Santidad*) H.H.
SS.MM. *abr* (= *Sus Majestades*) Their Royal Highnesses.
Sta. *abr* (= *Santa*) St; (= *Señorita*) Miss.
stand, *pl* **stands** [es'tan, es'tan(s)] *nm* (*COM*) stand.
stárter [es'tarter] *nm* (*AUTO*) self-starter, starting motor.
status ['status, es'tatus] *nm inv* status.
statu(s) quo [es'tatu(s)'kuo] *nm* status quo.
Sto. *abr* (= *Santo*) St.
stop, *pl* **stops** [es'top, es'top(s)] *nm* (*AUTO*) stop sign.
su [su] *pron* (*de él*) his; (*de ella*) her; (*de una cosa*) its; (*de ellos, ellas*) their; (*de usted, ustedes*) your.
suave ['swaβe] *adj* gentle; (*superficie*) smooth; (*trabajo*) easy; (*música, voz*) soft, sweet; (*clima, sabor*) mild.
suavice [swa'βiθe] *etc vb V* **suavizar**.
suavidad [swaβi'ðað] *nf* gentleness; (*de superficie*) smoothness; (*de música*) softness, sweetness.
suavizante [swaβi'θante] *nm* conditioner.
suavizar [swaβi'θar] *vt* to soften; (*quitar la aspereza*) to smooth (out); (*pendiente*) to ease; (*colores*) to tone down; (*carácter*) to mellow; (*dureza*) to temper.
subalimentado, a [suβalimen'taðo, a] *adj* undernourished.
subalterno, a [suβal'terno, a] *adj* (*importancia*) secondary; (*personal*) minor, auxiliary ♦ *nm* subordinate.
subarrendar [suβarren'dar] *vt* (*COM*) to lease back.
subarriendo [suβa'rrjendo] *nm* (*COM*) leaseback.
subasta [su'βasta] *nf* auction; **poner en** *o* **sacar a pública** ~ to put up for public auction; ~ **a la rebaja** Dutch auction.
subastador, a [suβasta'ðor, a] *nm/f* auctioneer.
subastar [suβas'tar] *vt* to auction (off).
subcampeón, ona [suβkampe'on, ona] *nm/f* runner-up.
subconsciente [suβkons'θjente] *adj* subconscious.
subcontratar [suβkontra'tar] *vt* (*COM*) to

subcontract.
subcontrato [sußkon'trato] *nm* (*COM*) subcontract.
subdesarrollado, a [sußðesarro'ʎaðo, a] *adj* underdeveloped.
subdesarrollo [sußðesa'rroʎo] *nm* underdevelopment.
subdirector, a [sußðirek'tor, a] *nm/f* assistant *o* deputy manager.
subdirectorio [sußðirek'torjo] *nm* (*INFORM*) subdirectory.
súbdito, a ['sußðito, a] *nm/f* subject.
subdividir [sußðißi'ðir] *vt* to subdivide.
subempleo [sußem'pleo] *nm* underemployment.
subestimar [sußesti'mar] *vt* to underestimate, underrate.
subido, a [su'ßiðo, a] *adj* (*color*) bright, strong; (*precio*) high ♦ *nf* (*de montaña etc*) ascent, climb; (*de precio*) rise, increase; (*pendiente*) slope, hill.
subíndice [su'ßindiθe] *nm* (*INFORM, TIP*) subscript.
subir [su'ßir] *vt* (*objeto*) to raise, lift up; (*cuesta, calle*) to go up; (*colina, montaña*) to climb; (*precio*) to raise, put up; (*empleado etc*) to promote ♦ *vi* to go/come up; (*a un coche*) to get in; (*a un autobús, tren*) to get on; (*precio*) to rise, go up; (*en el empleo*) to be promoted; (*río, marea*) to rise; **~se** *vr* to get up, climb; **~se a un coche** to get in(to) a car.
súbito, a ['sußito, a] *adj* (*repentino*) sudden; (*imprevisto*) unexpected.
subjetivo, a [sußxe'tißo, a] *adj* subjective.
subjuntivo [sußxun'tißo] *nm* subjunctive (mood).
sublevación [sußleßa'θjon] *nf* revolt, rising.
sublevar [sußle'ßar] *vt* to rouse to revolt; **~se** *vr* to revolt, rise.
sublimar [sußli'mar] *vt* (*persona*) to exalt; (*deseos etc*) to sublimate.
sublime [su'ßlime] *adj* sublime.
subliminal [sußlimi'nal] *adj* subliminal.
submarinista [sußmari'nista] *nm/f* underwater explorer.
submarino, a [sußma'rino, a] *adj* underwater ♦ *nm* submarine.
subnormal [sußnor'mal] *adj* subnormal ♦ *nm/f* subnormal person.
suboficial [sußofi'θjal] *nm* non-commissioned officer.
subordinado, a [sußorði'naðo, a] *adj, nm/f* subordinate.
subproducto [sußpro'ðukto] *nm* by-product.
subrayado [sußra'jaðo] *nm* underlining.
subrayar [sußra'jar] *vt* to underline; (*recalcar*) to underline, emphasize.
subrepticio, a [sußrep'tiθjo, a] *adj* surreptitious.
subrutina [sußru'tina] *nf* (*INFORM*) subroutine.
subsanar [sußsa'nar] *vt* (*reparar*) to make good; (*perdonar*) to excuse; (*sobreponerse a*) to overcome.
subscribir [sußskri'ßir] *vt* = **suscribir**.
subscrito [sußs'krito] *pp de* **subscribir**.
subsecretario, a [sußsekre'tarjo, a] *nm/f* undersecretary, assistant secretary.
subsidiariedad [sußsiðjarie'ðað] *nf* (*POL*) subsidiarity.
subsidiario, a [sußsi'ðjarjo, a] *adj* subsidiary.
subsidio [suß'siðjo] *nm* (*ayuda*) aid, financial help; (*subvención*) subsidy, grant; (*de enfermedad, paro etc*) benefit, allowance.
subsistencia [sußsis'tenθja] *nf* subsistence.
subsistir [sußsis'tir] *vi* to subsist; (*vivir*) to live; (*sobrevivir*) to survive, endure.
subsuelo [suß'swelo] *nm* subsoil.
subterfugio [sußter'fuxjo] *nm* subterfuge.
subterráneo, a [sußte'rraneo, a] *adj* underground, subterranean ♦ *nm* underpass, underground passage; (*AM*) underground railway, subway (*US*).
subtítulo [suß'titulo] *nm* subtitle, subheading.
suburbano, a [sußur'ßano, a] *adj* suburban.
suburbio [su'ßurßjo] *nm* (*barrio*) slum quarter; (*afueras*) suburbs *pl*.
subvención [sußßen'θjon] *nf* subsidy, subvention, grant; ~ **estatal** state subsidy *o* support; ~ **para la inversión** (*COM*) investment grant.
subvencionar [sußßenθjo'nar] *vt* to subsidize.
subversión [sußßer'sjon] *nf* subversion.
subversivo, a [sußßer'sißo, a] *adj* subversive.
subyacente [sußja'θente] *adj* underlying.
subyugar [sußju'ɣar] *vt* (*país*) to subjugate, subdue; (*enemigo*) to overpower; (*voluntad*) to dominate.
subyugue [sub'juɣe] *etc vb V* **subyugar**.
succión [suk'θjon] *nf* suction.
succionar [sukθjo'nar] *vt* (*sorber*) to suck; (*TEC*) to absorb, soak up.
sucedáneo, a [suθe'ðaneo, a] *adj* substitute ♦ *nm* substitute (food).
suceder [suθe'ðer] *vi* to happen; ~ **a** (*seguir*) to succeed, follow; **lo que sucede**

es que ... the fact is that ...; ~ **al trono** to succeed to the throne.
sucesión [suθe'sjon] *nf* succession; (*serie*) sequence, series; (*hijos*) issue, offspring.
sucesivamente [suθesiβa'mente] *adv*: **y así** ~ and so on.
sucesivo, a [suθe'siβo, a] *adj* successive, following; **en lo** ~ in future, from now on.
suceso [su'θeso] *nm* (*hecho*) event, happening; (*incidente*) incident.
sucesor, a [suθe'sor, a] *nm/f* successor; (*heredero*) heir/heiress.
suciedad [suθje'ðað] *nf* (*estado*) dirtiness; (*mugre*) dirt, filth.
sucinto, a [su'θinto, a] *adj* (*conciso*) succinct, concise.
sucio, a ['suθjo, a] *adj* dirty; (*mugriento*) grimy; (*manchado*) grubby; (*borroso*) smudged; (*conciencia*) bad; (*conducta*) vile; (*táctica*) dirty, unfair.
Sucre ['sukre] *n* Sucre.
sucre ['sukre] *nm* *Ecuadorean monetary unit*.
suculento, a [suku'lento, a] *adj* (*sabroso*) tasty; (*jugoso*) succulent.
sucumbir [sukum'bir] *vi* to succumb.
sucursal [sukur'sal] *nf* branch (office); (*filial*) subsidiary.
Sudáfrica [su'ðafrika] *nf* South Africa.
sudafricano, a [suðafri'kano, a] *adj, nm/f* South African.
Sudamérica [suða'merika] *nf* South America.
sudamericano, a [suðameri'kano, a] *adj, nm/f* South American.
sudanés, esa [suða'nes, esa] *adj, nm/f* Sudanese.
sudar [su'ðar] *vt, vi* to sweat; (*BOT*) to ooze, give out *o* off.
sudeste [su'ðeste] *adj* south-east(ern); (*rumbo, viento*) south-easterly ♦ *nm* south-east; (*viento*) south-east wind.
sudoeste [suðo'este] *adj* south-west(ern); (*rumbo, viento*) south-westerly ♦ *nm* south-west; (*viento*) south-west wind.
sudor [su'ðor] *nm* sweat.
sudoroso, a [suðo'roso, a] *adj* sweaty, sweating.
Suecia ['sweθja] *nf* Sweden.
sueco, a ['sweko, a] *adj* Swedish ♦ *nm/f* Swede ♦ *nm* (*LING*) Swedish; **hacerse el** ~ to pretend not to hear *o* understand.
suegro, a ['sweɣro, a] *nm/f* father-/mother-in-law; **los ~s** one's in-laws.
suela ['swela] *nf* (*de zapato, tb pescado*) sole.
sueldo ['sweldo] *etc vb V* **soldar** ♦ *nm* pay, wage(s) (*pl*).
suelo ['swelo] *etc vb V* **soler** ♦ *nm* (*tierra*) ground; (*de casa*) floor.
suelto, a ['swelto, a] *etc vb V* **soltar** ♦ *adj* loose; (*libre*) free; (*separado*) detached; (*ágil*) quick, agile; (*corriente*) fluent, flowing ♦ *nm* (loose) change, small change; **está muy** ~ **en inglés** he is very good at *o* fluent in English.
suene ['swene] *etc vb V* **sonar**.
sueño ['sweɲo] *etc vb V* **soñar** ♦ *nm* sleep; (*somnolencia*) sleepiness, drowsiness; (*lo soñado, fig*) dream; ~ **pesado** *o* **profundo** deep *o* heavy sleep; **tener** ~ to be sleepy.
suero ['swero] *nm* (*MED*) serum; (*de leche*) whey.
suerte ['swerte] *nf* (*fortuna*) luck; (*azar*) chance; (*destino*) fate, destiny; (*condición*) lot; (*género*) sort, kind; **lo echaron a ~s** they drew lots *o* tossed up for it; **tener** ~ to be lucky; **de otra** ~ otherwise, if not; **de** ~ **que** so that, in such a way that.
suéter ['sweter], *pl* **suéters** *nm* sweater.
suficiencia [sufi'θjenθja] *nf* (*cabida*) sufficiency; (*idoneidad*) suitability; (*aptitud*) adequacy.
suficiente [sufi'θjente] *adj* enough, sufficient.
sufijo [su'fixo] *nm* suffix.
sufragar [sufra'ɣar] *vt* (*ayudar*) to help; (*gastos*) to meet; (*proyecto*) to pay for.
sufragio [su'fraxjo] *nm* (*voto*) vote; (*derecho de voto*) suffrage.
sufrague [su'fraɣe] *etc vb V* **sufragar**.
sufrido, a [su'friðo, a] *adj* (*de carácter fuerte*) tough; (*paciente*) long-suffering; (*tela*) hard-wearing; (*color*) that does not show the dirt; (*marido*) complaisant.
sufrimiento [sufri'mjento] *nm* suffering.
sufrir [su'frir] *vt* (*padecer*) to suffer; (*soportar*) to bear, stand, put up with; (*apoyar*) to hold up, support ♦ *vi* to suffer.
sugerencia [suxe'renθja] *nf* suggestion.
sugerir [suxe'rir] *vt* to suggest; (*sutilmente*) to hint; (*idea*: *incitar*) to prompt.
sugestión [suxes'tjon] *nf* suggestion; (*sutil*) hint; (*poder*) hypnotic power.
sugestionar [suxestjo'nar] *vt* to influence.
sugestivo, a [suxes'tiβo, a] *adj* stimulating; (*atractivo*) attractive; (*fascinante*) fascinating.
sugiera [su'xjera] *etc*, **sugiriendo** [suxi'rjendo] *etc vb V* **sugerir**.
suicida [sui'θiða] *adj* suicidal ♦ *nm/f*

suicidal person; (*muerto*) suicide, person who has committed suicide.

suicidarse [suiθi'ðarse] *vr* to commit suicide, kill o.s.

suicidio [sui'θiðjo] *nm* suicide.

Suiza ['swiθa] *nf* Switzerland.

suizo, a ['swiθo, a] *adj, nm/f* Swiss ♦ *nm* sugared bun.

sujeción [suxe'θjon] *nf* subjection.

sujetador [suxeta'ðor] *nm* fastener, clip; (*prenda femenina*) bra, brassiere.

sujetapapeles [suxetapa'peles] *nm inv* paper clip.

sujetar [suxe'tar] *vt* (*fijar*) to fasten; (*detener*) to hold down; (*fig*) to subject, subjugate; (*pelo etc*) to keep *o* hold in place; (*papeles*) to fasten together; **~se** *vr* to subject o.s.

sujeto, a [su'xeto, a] *adj* fastened, secure ♦ *nm* subject; (*individuo*) individual; (*fam*: *tipo*) fellow, character, type, guy (*US*); **~ a** subject to.

sulfurar [sulfu'rar] *vt* (*TEC*) to sulphurate; (*sacar de quicio*) to annoy; **~se** *vr* (*enojarse*) to get riled, see red, blow up.

sulfuro [sul'furo] *nm* sulphide.

suma ['suma] *nf* (*cantidad*) total, sum; (*de dinero*) sum; (*acto*) adding (up), addition; **en ~** in short; **~ y sigue** (*COM*) carry forward.

sumador [suma'ðor] *nm* (*INFORM*) adder.

sumamente [suma'mente] *adv* extremely, exceedingly.

sumar [su'mar] *vt* to add (up); (*reunir*) to collect, gather ♦ *vi* to add up.

sumario, a [su'marjo, a] *adj* brief, concise ♦ *nm* summary.

sumergir [sumer'xir] *vt* to submerge; (*hundir*) to sink; (*bañar*) to immerse, dip; **~se** *vr* (*hundirse*) to sink beneath the surface.

sumerja [su'merxa] *etc vb V* **sumergir**.

sumidero [sumi'ðero] *nm* drain, sewer; (*TEC*) sump.

suministrador, a [suministra'ðor, a] *nm/f* supplier.

suministrar [suminis'trar] *vt* to supply, provide.

suministro [sumi'nistro] *nm* supply; (*acto*) supplying, providing.

sumir [su'mir] *vt* to sink, submerge; (*fig*) to plunge; **~se** *vr* (*objeto*) to sink; **~se en el estudio** to become absorbed in one's studies.

sumisión [sumi'sjon] *nf* (*acto*) submission; (*calidad*) submissiveness, docility.

sumiso, a [su'miso, a] *adj* submissive, docile.

súmmum ['sumum] *nm inv* (*fig*) height.

sumo, a ['sumo, a] *adj* great, extreme; (*mayor*) highest, supreme ♦ *nm* sumo (wrestling); **a lo ~** at most.

suntuoso, a [sun'twoso, a] *adj* sumptuous, magnificent; (*lujoso*) lavish.

sup. *abr* (= *superior*) sup.

supe ['supe] *etc vb V* **saber**.

supeditar [supeði'tar] *vt* to subordinate; (*sojuzgar*) to subdue; (*oprimir*) to oppress; **~se** *vr*: **~se a** to subject o.s. to.

super... [super] *pref* super..., over....

súper ['super] *adj* (*fam*) super, great.

superable [supe'raβle] *adj* (*dificultad*) surmountable; (*tarea*) that can be performed.

superación [supera'θjon] *nf* (*tb*: **~ personal**) self-improvement.

superar [supe'rar] *vt* (*sobreponerse a*) to overcome; (*rebasar*) to surpass, do better than; (*pasar*) to go beyond; (*marca, récord*) to break; (*etapa*: *dejar atrás*) to get past; **~se** *vr* to excel o.s.

superávit [supe'raβit], *pl* **superávits** *nm* surplus.

superchería [supertʃe'ria] *nf* fraud, trick, swindle.

superficial [superfi'θjal] *adj* superficial; (*medida*) surface *cpd*.

superficie [super'fiθje] *nf* surface; (*área*) area; **grandes ~s** (*COM*) superstores.

superfluo, a [su'perflwo, a] *adj* superfluous.

superíndice [supe'rindiθe] *nm* (*INFORM, TIP*) superscript.

superintendente [superinten'dente] *nm/f* supervisor, superintendent.

superior [supe'rjor] *adj* (*piso, clase*) upper; (*temperatura, número, nivel*) higher; (*mejor*: *calidad, producto*) superior, better ♦ *nm/f* superior.

superiora [supe'rjora] *nf* (*REL*) mother superior.

superioridad [superjori'ðað] *nf* superiority.

superlativo, a [superla'tiβo, a] *adj, nm* superlative.

supermercado [supermer'kaðo] *nm* supermarket.

superpoblación [superpoβla'θjon] *nf* overpopulation; (*congestionamiento*) overcrowding.

superponer [superpo'ner] *vt* (*INFORM*) to overstrike.

superposición [superposi'θjon] *nf* (*en impresora*) overstrike.

superpotencia [superpo'tenθja] *nf* superpower, great power.

superproducción [superproðuk'θjon] *nf* overproduction.
supersónico, a [super'soniko, a] *adj* supersonic.
superstición [supersti'θjon] *nf* superstition.
supersticioso, a [supersti'θjoso, a] *adj* superstitious.
supervisar [superβi'sar] *vt* to supervise; (*COM*) to superintend.
supervisor, a [superβi'sor, a] *nm/f* supervisor.
supervivencia [superβi'βenθja] *nf* survival.
superviviente [superβi'βjente] *adj* surviving ♦ *nm/f* survivor.
suplantar [suplan'tar] *vt* (*persona*) to supplant; (*hacerse pasar por otro*) to take the place of.
suplementario, a [suplemen'tarjo, a] *adj* supplementary.
suplemento [suple'mento] *nm* supplement.
suplencia [su'plenθja] *nf* substitution, replacement; (*etapa*) period during which one deputizes *etc*.
suplente [su'plente] *adj* substitute; (*disponible*) reserve ♦ *nm/f* substitute.
supletorio, a [suple'torjo, a] *adj* supplementary; (*adicional*) extra ♦ *nm* supplement; **mesa supletoria** spare table.
súplica ['suplika] *nf* request; (*REL*) supplication; (*JUR*: *instancia*) petition; **~s** *nfpl* entreaties.
suplicar [supli'kar] *vt* (*cosa*) to beg (for), plead for; (*persona*) to beg, plead with; (*JUR*) to appeal to, petition.
suplicio [su'pliθjo] *nm* torture; (*tormento*) torment; (*emoción*) anguish; (*experiencia penosa*) ordeal.
suplique [su'plike] *etc vb V* **suplicar**.
suplir [su'plir] *vt* (*compensar*) to make good, make up for; (*reemplazar*) to replace, substitute ♦ *vi*: **~ a** to take the place of, substitute for.
supo ['supo] *etc vb V* **saber**.
supondré [supon'dre] *etc vb V* **suponer**.
suponer [supo'ner] *vt* to suppose; (*significar*) to mean; (*acarrear*) to involve ♦ *vi* to count, have authority; **era de ~ que ...** it was to be expected that ....
suponga [su'ponga] *etc vb V* **suponer**.
suposición [suposi'θjon] *nf* supposition.
supositorio [suposi'torjo] *nm* suppository.
supremacía [suprema'θia] *nf* supremacy.
supremo, a [su'premo, a] *adj* supreme.
supresión [supre'sjon] *nf* suppression; (*de derecho*) abolition; (*de dificultad*) removal; (*de palabra etc*) deletion; (*de restricción*) cancellation, lifting.
suprimir [supri'mir] *vt* to suppress; (*derecho, costumbre*) to abolish; (*dificultad*) to remove; (*palabra etc, INFORM*) to delete; (*restricción*) to cancel, lift.
supuestamente [supwesta'mente] *adv* supposedly.
supuesto, a [su'pwesto, a] *pp de* **suponer** ♦ *adj* (*hipotético*) supposed; (*falso*) false ♦ *nm* assumption, hypothesis ♦ *conj*: **~ que** since; **dar por ~ algo** to take sth for granted; **por ~** of course.
supurar [supu'rar] *vi* to fester, suppurate.
supuse [su'puse] *etc vb V* **suponer**.
sur [sur] *adj* southern; (*rumbo*) southerly ♦ *nm* south; (*viento*) south wind.
Suráfrica [su'rafrika] *etc* = **Sudáfrica** *etc*.
Suramérica [sura'merika] *etc* = **Sudamérica** *etc*.
surcar [sur'kar] *vt* to plough; (*superficie*) to cut, score.
surco ['surko] *nm* (*en metal, disco*) groove; (*AGR*) furrow.
surcoreano, a [surkore'ano, a] *adj, nm/f* South Korean.
sureño, a [su'reɲo, a] *adj* southern ♦ *nm/f* southerner.
sureste [su'reste] = **sudeste**.
surf [surf] *nm* surfing.
surgir [sur'xir] *vi* to arise, emerge; (*dificultad*) to come up, crop up.
surja ['surxa] *etc vb V* **surgir**.
suroeste [suro'este] = **sudoeste**.
surque ['surke] *etc vb V* **surcar**.
surrealismo [surrea'lismo] *nm* surrealism.
surrealista [surrea'lista] *adj, nm/f* surrealist.
surtido, a [sur'tiðo, a] *adj* mixed, assorted ♦ *nm* (*selección*) selection, assortment; (*abastecimiento*) supply, stock.
surtidor [surti'ðor] *nm* (*chorro*) jet, spout; (*fuente*) fountain; **~ de gasolina** petrol (*BRIT*) *o* gas (*US*) pump.
surtir [sur'tir] *vt* to supply, provide; (*efecto*) to have, produce ♦ *vi* to spout, spurt; **~se** *vr*: **~se de** to provide o.s. with.
susceptible [susθep'tiβle] *adj* susceptible; (*sensible*) sensitive; **~ de** capable of.
suscitar [susθi'tar] *vt* to cause, provoke; (*discusión*) to start; (*duda, problema*) to raise; (*interés, sospechas*) to arouse.
suscribir [suskri'βir] *vt* (*firmar*) to sign; (*respaldar*) to subscribe to, endorse; (*COM*: *acciones*) to take out an option on; **~se** *vr* to subscribe; **~ a algn a una revista** to take out a subscription to a

journal for sb.
suscripción [suskrip'θjon] *nf* subscription.
suscrito, a [sus'krito, a] *pp de* **suscribir** ♦ *adj*: ~ **en exceso** oversubscribed.
susodicho, a [suso'ditʃo, a] *adj* above-mentioned.
suspender [suspen'der] *vt* (*objeto*) to hang (up), suspend; (*trabajo*) to stop, suspend; (*ESCOL*) to fail.
suspense [sus'pense] *nm* suspense.
suspensión [suspen'sjon] *nf* suspension; (*fig*) stoppage, suspension; (*JUR*) stay; ~ **de fuego** *o* **de hostilidades** ceasefire, cessation of hostilities; ~ **de pagos** suspension of payments.
suspensivo, a [suspen'siβo, a] *adj*: **puntos ~s** dots, suspension points.
suspenso, a [sus'penso, a] *adj* hanging, suspended; (*ESCOL*) failed ♦ *nm* (*ESCOL*) fail(ure); **quedar** *o* **estar en** ~ to be pending.
suspicacia [suspi'kaθja] *nf* suspicion, mistrust.
suspicaz [suspi'kaθ] *adj* suspicious, distrustful.
suspirar [suspi'rar] *vi* to sigh.
suspiro [sus'piro] *nm* sigh.
sustancia [sus'tanθja] *nf* substance; ~ **gris** (*ANAT*) grey matter; **sin** ~ lacking in substance, shallow.
sustancial [sustan'θjal] *adj* substantial.
sustancioso, a [sustan'θjoso, a] *adj* substantial; (*discurso*) solid.
sustantivo, a [sustan'tiβo, a] *adj* substantive; (*LING*) substantival, noun *cpd* ♦ *nm* noun, substantive.
sustentar [susten'tar] *vt* (*alimentar*) to sustain, nourish; (*objeto*) to hold up, support; (*idea, teoría*) to maintain, uphold; (*fig*) to sustain, keep going.
sustento [sus'tento] *nm* support; (*alimento*) sustenance, food.
sustituir [sustitu'ir] *vt* to substitute, replace.
sustituto, a [susti'tuto, a] *nm/f* substitute, replacement.
sustituyendo [sustitu'jendo] *etc vb V* **sustituir**.
susto ['susto] *nm* fright, scare; **dar un ~ a algn** to give sb a fright; **darse** *o* **pegarse un** ~ (*fam*) to get a fright.
sustraer [sustra'er] *vt* to remove, take away; (*MAT*) to subtract.
sustraiga [sus'traiɣa] *etc*, **sustraje** [sus'traxe] *etc*, **sustrajera** [sustra'xera] *etc vb V* **sustraer**.
sustrato [sus'trato] *nm* substratum.
sustrayendo [sustra'jendo] *etc vb V* **sustraer**.
susurrar [susu'rrar] *vi* to whisper.
susurro [su'surro] *nm* whisper.
sutil [su'til] *adj* (*aroma*) subtle; (*tenue*) thin; (*hilo, hebra*) fine; (*olor*) delicate; (*brisa*) gentle; (*diferencia*) fine, subtle; (*inteligencia*) sharp, keen.
sutileza [suti'leθa] *nf* subtlety; (*delgadez*) thinness; (*delicadeza*) delicacy; (*agudeza*) keenness.
sutura [su'tura] *nf* suture.
suturar [sutu'rar] *vt* to suture; (*juntar con puntos*) to stitch.
suyo, a ['sujo, a] *adj* (*con artículo o después del verbo* ser: *de él*) his; (: *de ella*) hers; (: *de ellos, ellas*) theirs; (: *de usted, ustedes*) yours; (*después de un nombre*: *de él*) of his; (: *de ella*) of hers; (: *de ellos, ellas*) of theirs; (: *de usted, ustedes*) of yours; **lo** ~ (what is) his; (*su parte*) his share, what he deserves; **los ~s** (*familia*) one's family *o* relations; (*partidarios*) one's own people *o* supporters; ~ **afectísimo** (*en carta*) yours faithfully *o* sincerely; **de** ~ in itself; **eso es muy** ~ that's just like him; **hacer de las suyas** to get up to one's old tricks; **ir a la suya, ir a lo** ~ to go one's own way; **salirse con la suya** to get one's way.

Tt

T, t [te] *nf* (*letra*) T, t; **T de Tarragona** T for Tommy.
t *abr* = **tonelada**.
T. *abr* (= *Telefón, Telégrafo*) tel.; (*COM*) = **Tarifa**; **Tasa**.
t. *abr* (= *tomo(s)*) vol(s).
Tabacalera [taβaka'lera] *nf Spanish state tobacco monopoly*.
tabaco [ta'βako] *nm* tobacco; (*fam*) cigarettes *pl*.
tábano ['taβano] *nm* horsefly.
tabaquería [tabake'ria] *nf* tobacconist's (*BRIT*), cigar store (*US*).
tabarra [ta'βarra] *nf* (*fam*) nuisance; **dar la** ~ to be a pain in the neck.
taberna [ta'βerna] *nf* bar.
tabernero, a [taβer'nero, a] *nm/f* (*encargado*) publican; (*camarero*) barman/barmaid.

tabique [ta'ßike] *nm* (*pared*) thin wall; (*para dividir*) partition.
tabla ['taßla] *nf* (*de madera*) plank; (*estante*) shelf; (*de anuncios*) board; (*lista, catálogo*) list; (*mostrador*) counter; (*de vestido*) pleat; (*ARTE*) panel; **~s** *nfpl* (*TAUR, TEAT*) boards; **hacer ~s** to draw; **~ de consulta** (*INFORM*) lookup table.
tablado [ta'ßlaðo] *nm* (*plataforma*) platform; (*suelo*) plank floor; (*TEAT*) stage.
tablao [ta'ßlao] *nm* (*tb*: **~ flamenco**) flamenco show.
tablero [ta'ßlero] *nm* (*de madera*) plank, board; (*pizarra*) blackboard; (*de ajedrez, damas*) board; (*AUTO*) dashboard; **~ de gráficos** (*INFORM*) graph pad.
tableta [ta'ßleta] *nf* (*MED*) tablet; (*de chocolate*) bar.
tablilla [ta'ßliʎa] *nf* small board; (*MED*) splint.
tablón [ta'ßlon] *nm* (*de suelo*) plank; (*de techo*) beam; (*de anuncios*) notice board.
tabú [ta'ßu] *nm* taboo.
tabulación [taßula'θjon] *nf* (*INFORM*) tab(bing).
tabulador [taßula'ðor] *nm* (*INFORM, TIP*) tab.
tabuladora [taßula'ðora] *nf*: **~ eléctrica** electric accounting machine.
tabular [taßu'lar] *vt* to tabulate; (*INFORM*) to tab.
taburete [taßu'rete] *nm* stool.
tacaño, a [ta'kaɲo, a] *adj* (*avaro*) mean; (*astuto*) crafty.
tacha ['tatʃa] *nf* (*defecto*) flaw, defect; (*TEC*) stud; **poner ~ a** to find fault with; **sin ~** flawless.
tachar [ta'tʃar] *vt* (*borrar*) to cross out; (*corregir*) to correct; (*criticar*) to criticize; **~ de** to accuse of.
tacho ['tatʃo] *nm* (*AM*) bucket, pail.
tachón [ta'tʃon] *nm* erasure; (*tachadura*) crossing-out; (*TEC*) ornamental stud; (*COSTURA*) trimming.
tachuela [ta'tʃwela] *nf* (*clavo*) tack.
tácito, a ['taθito, a] *adj* tacit; (*acuerdo*) unspoken; (*LING*) understood; (*ley*) unwritten.
taciturno, a [taθi'turno, a] *adj* (*callado*) silent; (*malhumorado*) sullen.
taco ['tako] *nm* (*BILLAR*) cue; (*libro de billetes*) book; (*manojo de billetes*) wad; (*AM*) heel; (*tarugo*) peg; (*fam*: *bocado*) snack; (: *palabrota*) swear word; (: *trago de vino*) swig; (*Méjico*) filled tortilla; **armarse** *o* **hacerse un ~** to get into a mess.
tacógrafo [ta'koɣrafo] *nm* (*COM*) tachograph.
tacón [ta'kon] *nm* heel; **de ~ alto** high-heeled.
taconear [takone'ar] *vi* (*dar golpecitos*) to tap with one's heels; (*MIL etc*) to click one's heels.
taconeo [tako'neo] *nm* (heel) tapping *o* clicking.
táctico, a ['taktiko, a] *adj* tactical ♦ *nf* tactics *pl*.
tacto ['takto] *nm* touch; (*acción*) touching; (*fig*) tact.
TAE *nf abr* (= *tasa anual equivalente*) APR.
tafetán [tafe'tan] *nm* taffeta; **tafetanes** *nmpl* (*fam*) frills; **~ adhesivo** *o* **inglés** sticking plaster.
tafilete [tafi'lete] *nm* morocco leather.
tahona [ta'ona] *nf* (*panadería*) bakery; (*molino*) flourmill.
tahúr [ta'ur] *nm* gambler; (*pey*) cheat.
tailandés, esa [tailan'des, esa] *adj, nm/f* Thai ♦ *nm* (*LING*) Thai.
Tailandia [tai'landja] *nf* Thailand.
taimado, a [tai'maðo, a] *adj* (*astuto*) sly; (*resentido*) sullen.
taita ['taita] *nm* dad, daddy.
tajada [ta'xaða] *nf* slice; (*fam*) rake-off; **sacar ~** to get one's share.
tajante [ta'xante] *adj* sharp; (*negativa*) emphatic; **es una persona ~** he's an emphatic person.
tajar [ta'xar] *vt* to cut, slice.
Tajo ['taxo] *nm* Tagus.
tajo ['taxo] *nm* (*corte*) cut; (*filo*) cutting edge; (*GEO*) cleft.
tal [tal] *adj* such; **un ~ García** a man called García; **~ vez** perhaps ♦ *pron* (*persona*) someone, such a one; (*cosa*) something, such a thing; **~ como** such as; **~ para cual** tit for tat; (*dos iguales*) two of a kind; **hablábamos de que si ~ si cual** we were talking about this, that and the other ♦ *adv*: **~ como** (*igual*) just as; **~ cual** (*como es*) just as it is; **~ el padre, cual el hijo** like father, like son; **¿qué ~?** how are things?; **¿qué ~ te gusta?** how do you like it? ♦ *conj*: **con ~ (de) que** provided that.
tala ['tala] *nf* (*de árboles*) tree felling.
taladradora [talaðra'ðora] *nf* drill; **~ neumática** pneumatic drill.
taladrar [tala'ðrar] *vt* to drill; (*fig*: *suj*: *ruido*) to pierce.
taladro [ta'laðro] *nm* (*gen*) drill; (*hoyo*) drill hole; **~ neumático** pneumatic drill.
talante [ta'lante] *nm* (*humor*) mood; (*voluntad*) will, willingness.
talar [ta'lar] *vt* to fell, cut down; (*fig*) to devastate.

talco ['talko] *nm* (*polvos*) talcum powder; (*MINERALOGÍA*) talc.
talega [ta'leɣa] *nf* sack.
talego [ta'leɣo] *nm* sack; **tener ~** (*fam*) to have money.
talento [ta'lento] *nm* talent; (*capacidad*) ability; (*don*) gift.
Talgo ['talgo] *nm abr* (*FERRO = tren articulado ligero Goicoechea-Oriol*) high-speed train.
talidomida [taliðo'miða] *nm* thalidomide.
talismán [talis'man] *nm* talisman.
talla ['taʎa] *nf* (*estatura, fig, MED*) height, stature; (*de ropa*) size, fitting; (*palo*) measuring rod; (*ARTE: de madera*)) carving; (*de piedra*) sculpture.
tallado, a [ta'ʎaðo, a] *adj* carved ♦ *nm* (*de madera*) carving; (*de piedra*) sculpture.
tallar [ta'ʎar] *vt* (*trabajar*) to work, carve; (*grabar*) to engrave; (*medir*) to measure; (*repartir*) to deal ♦ *vi* to deal.
tallarín [taʎa'rin] *nm* noodle.
talle ['taʎe] *nm* (*ANAT*) waist; (*medida*) size; (*física*) build; (*: de mujer*) figure; (*fig*) appearance; **de ~ esbelto** with a slim figure.
taller [ta'ʎer] *nm* (*TEC*) workshop; (*fábrica*) factory; (*AUTO*) garage; (*de artista*) studio.
tallo ['taʎo] *nm* (*de planta*) stem; (*de hierba*) blade; (*brote*) shoot; (*col*) cabbage; (*CULIN*) candied peel.
talmente [tal'mente] *adv* (*de esta forma*) in such a way; (*hasta tal punto*) to such an extent; (*exactamente*) exactly.
talón [ta'lon] *nm* (*gen*) heel; (*COM*) counterfoil; (*TEC*) rim; **~ de Aquiles** Achilles heel.
talonario [talo'narjo] *nm* (*de cheques*) cheque book; (*de billetes*) book of tickets; (*de recibos*) receipt book.
tamaño, a [ta'maɲo, a] *adj* (*tan grande*) such a big; (*tan pequeño*) such a small ♦ *nm* size; **de ~ natural** full-size; **¿de qué ~ es?** what size is it?
tamarindo [tama'rindo] *nm* tamarind.
tambaleante [tambale'ante] *adj* (*persona*) staggering; (*mueble*) wobbly; (*vehículo*) swaying.
tambalearse [tambale'arse] *vr* (*persona*) to stagger; (*mueble*) to wobble; (*vehículo*) to sway.
también [tam'bjen] *adv* (*igualmente*) also, too, as well; (*además*) besides; **estoy cansado — yo ~** I'm tired — so am I *o* me too.
tambor [tam'bor] *nm* drum; (*ANAT*) eardrum; **~ del freno** brake drum; **~ magnético** (*INFORM*) magnetic drum.
tamboril [tambo'ril] *nm* small drum.
tamborilear [tamborile'ar] *vi* (*MUS*) to drum; (*con los dedos*) to drum with one's fingers.
tamborilero [tambori'lero] *nm* drummer.
Támesis ['tamesis] *nm* Thames.
tamice [ta'miθe] *etc vb V* **tamizar**.
tamiz [ta'miθ] *nm* sieve.
tamizar [tami'θar] *vt* to sieve.
tampoco [tam'poko] *adv* nor, neither; **yo ~ lo compré** I didn't buy it either.
tampón [tam'pon] *nm* plug; (*MED*) tampon.
tan [tan] *adv* so; **~ es así que** so much so that; **¡qué cosa ~ rara!** how strange!; **no es una idea ~ buena** it is not such a good idea.
tanatorio [tana'torjo] *nm* (*privado*) funeral home *o* parlour; (*público*) mortuary.
tanda ['tanda] *nf* (*gen*) series; (*de inyecciones*) course; (*juego*) set; (*turno*) shift; (*grupo*) gang.
tándem ['tandem] *nm* tandem; (*POL*) duo.
tanga ['tanga] *nm* (*bikini*) tanga; (*ropa interior*) tanga briefs.
tangente [tan'xente] *nf* tangent; **salirse por la ~** to go off at a tangent.
Tánger ['tanxer] *n* Tangier.
tangerino, a [tanxe'rino, a] *adj* of *o* from Tangier ♦ *nm/f* native *o* inhabitant of Tangier.
tangible [tan'xiβle] *adj* tangible.
tango ['tango] *nm* tango.
tanino [ta'nino] *nm* tannin.
tanque ['tanke] *nm* (*gen*) tank; (*AUTO, NAUT*) tanker.
tanqueta [tan'keta] *nf* (*MIL*) small tank, armoured vehicle.
tantear [tante'ar] *vt* (*calcular*) to reckon (up); (*medir*) to take the measure of; (*probar*) to test, try out; (*tomar la medida: persona*) to take the measurements of; (*considerar*) to weigh up ♦ *vi* (*DEPORTE*) to score.
tanteo [tan'teo] *nm* (*cálculo*) (rough) calculation; (*prueba*) test, trial; (*DEPORTE*) scoring; (*adivinanzas*) guesswork; **al ~** by trial and error.
tantísimo, a [tan'tisimo, a] *adj* so much; **~s** so many.
tanto, a ['tanto, a] *adj* (*cantidad*) so much, as much; **~s** so many, as many; **20 y ~s** 20-odd ♦ *adv* (*cantidad*) so much, as much; (*tiempo*) so long, as long; **~ tú como yo** both you and I; **~ como eso** it's not as bad as that; **~ más ... cuanto que** it's all the more ... because; **~ mejor/peor** so much the better/the worse; **~ si**

viene como si va whether he comes or whether he goes; ~ **es así que** so much so that; **por ~, por lo ~** therefore; **me he vuelto ronco de** *o* **con ~ hablar** I have become hoarse with so much talking ♦ *conj*: **con ~ que** provided (that); **en ~ que** while; **hasta ~ (que)** until such time as ♦ *nm* (*suma*) certain amount; (*proporción*) so much; (*punto*) point; (*gol*) goal; ~ **alzado** agreed price; ~ **por ciento** percentage; **al ~** up to date; **estar al ~ de los acontecimientos** to be fully abreast of events; **un ~ perezoso** somewhat lazy; **al ~ de que** because of the fact that ♦ *pron*: **cado uno paga ~** each one pays so much; **uno de ~s** one of many; **a ~s de agosto** on such and such a day in August; **entre ~** meanwhile.

tañer [ta'ɲer] *vt* (*MUS*) to play; (*campana*) to ring.

T/año *abr* = *toneladas por año.*

TAO *nf abr* (= *traducción asistida por ordenador*) MAT.

tapa ['tapa] *nf* (*de caja, olla*) lid; (*de botella*) top; (*de libro*) cover; (*comida*) snack.

tapacubos [tapa'kuβos] *nm inv* hub cap.

tapadera [tapa'ðera] *nf* lid, cover.

tapado [ta'paðo] *nm* (*AM*: *abrigo*) coat.

tapar [ta'par] *vt* (*cubrir*) to cover; (*envolver*) to wrap *o* cover up; (*la vista*) to obstruct; (*persona, falta*) to conceal; (*AM*) to fill; **~se** *vr* to wrap o.s. up.

tapete [ta'pete] *nm* table cover; **estar sobre el ~** (*fig*) to be under discussion.

tapia ['tapja] *nf* (garden) wall.

tapiar [ta'pjar] *vt* to wall in.

tapice [ta'piθe] *etc vb V* **tapizar.**

tapicería [tapiθe'ria] *nf* tapestry; (*para muebles*) upholstery; (*tienda*) upholsterer's (shop).

tapicero, a [tapi'θero, a] *nm/f* (*de muebles*) upholsterer.

tapiz [ta'piθ] *nm* (*alfombra*) carpet; (*tela tejida*) tapestry.

tapizar [tapi'θar] *vt* (*pared*) to wallpaper; (*suelo*) to carpet; (*muebles*) to upholster.

tapón [ta'pon] *nm* (*corcho*) stopper; (*TEC*) plug; (*MED*) tampon; ~ **de rosca** *o* **de tuerca** screw-top.

taponar [tapo'nar] *vt* (*botella*) to cork; (*tubería*) to block.

taponazo [tapo'naθo] *nm* (*de tapón*) pop.

tapujo [ta'puxo] *nm* (*embozo*) muffler; (*engaño*) deceit; **sin ~s** honestly.

taquigrafía [takiɣra'fia] *nf* shorthand.

taquígrafo, a [ta'kiɣrafo, a] *nm/f* shorthand writer.

taquilla [ta'kiʎa] *nf* (*de estación etc*) booking office; (*de teatro*) box office; (*suma recogida*) takings *pl*; (*archivador*) filing cabinet.

taquillero, a [taki'ʎero, a] *adj*: **función taquillera** box office success ♦ *nm/f* ticket clerk.

taquimecanografía [takimekanoɣra'fia] *nf* shorthand and typing.

taquímetro [ta'kimetro] *nm* speedometer; (*de control*) tachymeter.

tara ['tara] *nf* (*defecto*) defect; (*COM*) tare.

tarado, a [ta'raðo, a] *adj* (*COM*) defective, imperfect; (*idiota*) stupid; (*loco*) crazy, nuts ♦ *nm/f* idiot, cretin.

tarántula [ta'rantula] *nf* tarantula.

tararear [tarare'ar] *vi* to hum.

tardanza [tar'ðanθa] *nf* (*demora*) delay; (*lentitud*) slowness.

tardar [tar'ðar] *vi* (*tomar tiempo*) to take a long time; (*llegar tarde*) to be late; (*demorar*) to delay; **¿tarda mucho el tren?** does the train take long?; **a más ~** at the (very) latest; ~ **en hacer algo** to be slow *o* take a long time to do sth; **no tardes en venir** come soon, come before long.

tarde ['tarðe] *adv* (*hora*) late; (*fuera de tiempo*) too late ♦ *nf* (*de día*) afternoon; (*de noche*) evening; ~ **o temprano** sooner or later; **de ~ en ~** from time to time; **¡buenas ~s!** (*de día*) good afternoon!; (*de noche*) good evening!; **a** *o* **por la ~** in the afternoon; in the evening.

tardío, a [tar'ðio, a] *adj* (*retrasado*) late; (*lento*) slow (to arrive).

tardo, a ['tarðo, a] *adj* (*lento*) slow; (*torpe*) dull; ~ **de oído** hard of hearing.

tarea [ta'rea] *nf* task; **~s** *nfpl* (*ESCOL*) homework *sg*; ~ **de ocasión** chore.

tarifa [ta'rifa] *nf* (*lista de precios*) price list; (*COM*) tariff; ~ **básica** basic rate; ~ **completa** all-in cost; ~ **a destajo** piece rate; ~ **doble** double time.

tarima [ta'rima] *nf* (*plataforma*) platform; (*taburete*) stool; (*litera*) bunk.

tarjeta [tar'xeta] *nf* card; ~ **postal/de crédito/de Navidad** postcard/credit card/Christmas card; ~ **de circuitos** (*INFORM*) circuit board; ~ **cliente** loyalty card; ~ **comercial** (*COM*) calling card; ~ **dinero** cash card; ~ **gráficos** (*INFORM*) graphics card; ~ **de multifunción** (*INFORM*) multiplication card.

tarot [ta'rot] *nm* tarot.

tarraconense [tarrako'nense] *adj* of *o* from Tarragona ♦ *nm/f* native *o* inhabitant of Tarragona.

tarro ['tarro] *nm* jar, pot.
tarta ['tarta] *nf* (*pastel*) cake; (*torta*) tart.
tartajear [tartaxe'ar] *vi* to stammer.
tartamudear [tartamuðe'ar] *vi* to stutter, stammer.
tartamudo, a [tarta'muðo, a] *adj* stuttering, stammering ♦ *nm/f* stutterer, stammerer.
tartárico, a [tar'tariko, a] *adj*: **ácido** ~ tartaric acid.
tártaro ['tartaro] *adj, nm* Tartar ♦ *nm* (*QUIMICA*) tartar.
tarugo, a [ta'ruɣo, a] *adj* stupid ♦ *nm* (*de madera*) lump.
tarumba [ta'rumba] *adj* (*confuso*) confused.
tasa ['tasa] *nf* (*precio*) (fixed) price, rate; (*valoración*) valuation; (*medida, norma*) measure, standard; ~ **básica** (*COM*) basic rate; ~ **de cambio** exchange rate; **de** ~ **cero** (*COM*) zero-rated; ~ **de crecimiento** growth rate; ~ **de interés/de nacimiento** rate of interest/birth rate; ~ **de rendimiento** (*COM*) rate of return; ~**s universitarias** university fees.
tasación [tasa'θjon] *nf* assessment, valuation; (*fig*) appraisal.
tasador, a [tasa'ðor, a] *nm/f* valuer; (*COM*: *de impuestos*) assessor.
tasar [ta'sar] *vt* (*arreglar el precio*) to fix a price for; (*valorar*) to value, assess; (*limitar*) to limit.
tasca ['taska] *nf* (*fam*) pub.
tata ['tata] *nm* (*fam*) dad(dy) ♦ *nf* (*niñera*) nanny, maid.
tatarabuelo, a [tatara'ßwelo, a] *nm/f* great-great-grandfather/mother; **los** ~**s** one's great-great-grandparents.
tatuaje [ta'twaxe] *nm* (*dibujo*) tattoo; (*acto*) tattooing.
tatuar [ta'twar] *vt* to tattoo.
taumaturgo [tauma'turɣo] *nm* miracle-worker.
taurino, a [tau'rino, a] *adj* bullfighting *cpd*.
Tauro ['tauro] *nm* Taurus.
tauromaquia [tauro'makja] *nf* (art of) bullfighting.
tautología [tautolo'xia] *nf* tautology.
taxativo, a [taksa'tißo, a] *adj* (*restringido*) limited; (*sentido*) specific.
taxi ['taksi] *nm* taxi.
taxidermia [taksi'ðermja] *nf* taxidermy.
taxímetro [tak'simetro] *nm* taximeter.
taxista [tak'sista] *nm/f* taxi driver.
Tayikistán [tajikis'tan] *nm* Tajikistan.
taza ['taθa] *nf* cup; (*de retrete*) bowl; ~ **para café** coffee cup.
tazón [ta'θon] *nm* mug, large cup; (*escudilla*) basin.
TCI *nf abr* (= *tarjeta de circuito impreso*) PCB.
te [te] *pron* (*complemento de objeto*) you; (*complemento indirecto*) (to) you; (*reflexivo*) (to) yourself; **¿~ duele mucho el brazo?** does your arm hurt a lot?; ~ **equivocas** you're wrong; **¡cálma~!** calm yourself!
té [te], *pl* **tés** *nm* tea; (*reunión*) tea party.
tea ['tea] *nf* (*antorcha*) torch.
teatral [tea'tral] *adj* theatre *cpd*; (*fig*) theatrical.
teatro [te'atro] *nm* theatre; (*LITERATURA*) plays *pl*, drama; **el** ~ (*carrera*) the theatre, acting; ~ **de aficionados/de variedades** amateur/variety theatre, vaudeville theater (*US*); **hacer** ~ (*fig*) to make a fuss.
tebeo [te'ßeo] *nm* children's comic.
techado [te'tʃaðo] *nm* (*techo*) roof; **bajo** ~ under cover.
techo ['tetʃo] *nm* (*externo*) roof; (*interno*) ceiling.
techumbre [te'tʃumbre] *nf* roof.
tecla ['tekla] *nf* (*INFORM, MUS, TIP*) key; (*INFORM*): ~ **de anulación/de borrar** cancel/delete key; ~ **de control/de edición** control/edit key; ~ **con flecha** arrow key; ~ **programable** user-defined key; ~ **de retorno/de tabulación** return/tab key; ~ **del cursor** cursor key; ~**s de control direccional del cursor** cursor control keys.
teclado [te'klaðo] *nm* keyboard (*tb INFORM*); ~ **numérico** (*INFORM*) numeric keypad.
teclear [tekle'ar] *vi* to strum; (*fam*) to drum ♦ *vt* (*INFORM*) to key (in), type in, keyboard.
tecleo [te'kleo] *nm* (*MUS*: *sonido*) strumming; (: *forma de tocar*) fingering; (*fam*) drumming.
tecnicismo [tekni'θismo] *nm* (*carácter técnico*) technical nature; (*LING*) technical term.
técnico, a ['tekniko, a] *adj* technical ♦ *nm* technician; (*experto*) expert ♦ *nf* (*procedimientos*) technique; (*arte, oficio*) craft.
tecnicolor [tekniko'lor] *nm* Technicolor ®.
tecnócrata [tek'nokrata] *nm/f* technocrat.
tecnología [teknolo'xia] *nf* technology; ~ **de estado sólido** (*INFORM*) solid-state technology; ~ **de la información** information technology.
tecnológico, a [tekno'loxiko, a] *adj* technological.

tecnólogo, a [tek'noloɣo, a] *nm/f* technologist.
tedio ['teðjo] *nm* (*aburrimiento*) boredom; (*apatía*) apathy; (*fastidio*) depression.
tedioso, a [te'ðjoso, a] *adj* boring; (*cansado*) wearisome, tedious.
Teherán [tee'ran] *nm* Teheran.
teja ['texa] *nf* (*azulejo*) tile; (*BOT*) lime (tree).
tejado [te'xaðo] *nm* (tiled) roof.
tejano, a [te'xano, a] *adj, nm/f* Texan ♦ *nmpl*: ~**s** (*vaqueros*) jeans.
Tejas ['texas] *nm* Texas.
tejemaneje [texema'nexe] *nm* (*actividad*) bustle; (*lío*) fuss, to-do; (*intriga*) intrigue.
tejer [te'xer] *vt* to weave; (*tela de araña*) to spin; (*AM*) to knit; (*fig*) to fabricate ♦ *vi*: ~ **y destejer** to chop and change.
tejido [te'xiðo] *nm* fabric; (*estofa, tela*) (knitted) material; (*ANAT*) tissue; (*textura*) texture.
tejo ['texo] *nm* (*BOT*) yew (tree).
tel. *abr* (= *teléfono*) tel.
tela ['tela] *nf* (*material*) material; (*de fruta, en líquido*) skin; (*del ojo*) film; **hay ~ para rato** there's lots to talk about; **poner en ~ de juicio** to (call in) question; ~ **de araña** cobweb, spider's web.
telar [te'lar] *nm* (*máquina*) loom; (*de teatro*) gridiron; ~**es** *nmpl* textile mill *sg*.
telaraña [tela'raɲa] *nf* cobweb, spider's web.
tele... [tele] *pref* tele...
tele ['tele] *nf* (*fam*) TV.
telecargar [telekar'ɣar] *vt* (*INFORM*) to download.
telecomunicación [telekomunika'θjon] *nf* telecommunication.
teleconferencia [telekonfe'renθja] *nf* (*reunión*) teleconference; (*sistema*) teleconferencing.
telecontrol [telekon'trol] *nm* remote control.
telecopiadora [telekopja'ðora] *nf*: ~ **facsímil** fax copier.
telediario [tele'ðjarjo] *nm* television news.
teledifusión [teleðifu'sjon] *nf* (television) broadcast.
teledirigido, a [teleðiri'xiðo, a] *adj* remote-controlled.
teléf. *abr* (= *teléfono*) tel.
teleférico [tele'feriko] *nm* (*tren*) cable-railway; (*de esquí*) ski-lift.
telefilm [tele'film], **telefilme** [tele'filme] *nm* TV film.
telefonazo [telefo'naθo] *nm* (*fam*) telephone call; **te daré un** ~ I'll give you a ring.
telefonear [telefone'ar] *vi* to telephone.
telefónicamente [tele'fonikamente] *adv* by (tele)phone.
telefónico, a [tele'foniko, a] *adj* telephone *cpd* ♦ *nf*: **Telefónica** (*ESP*) *Spanish national telephone company*, ≈ British Telecom.
telefonista [telefo'nista] *nm/f* telephonist.
teléfono [te'lefono] *nm* (tele)phone; ~ **móvil** mobile phone; **está hablando por** ~ he's on the phone.
telefoto [tele'foto] *nf* telephoto.
telegrafía [teleɣra'fia] *nf* telegraphy.
telégrafo [te'leɣrafo] *nm* telegraph; (*fam: persona*) telegraph boy.
telegrama [tele'ɣrama] *nm* telegram.
teleimpresor [teleimpre'sor] *nm* teleprinter.
telemática [tele'matika] *nf* telematics *sg*.
telémetro [te'lemetro] *nm* rangefinder.
telenovela [teleno'βela] *nf* soap (opera).
teleobjetivo [teleobxe'tiβo] *nm* telephoto lens.
telepatía [telepa'tia] *nf* telepathy.
telepático, a [tele'patiko, a] *adj* telepathic.
teleproceso [telepro'θeso] *nm* teleprocessing.
telescópico, a [tele'skopiko, a] *adj* telescopic.
telescopio [tele'skopjo] *nm* telescope.
telesilla [tele'siʎa] *nm* chairlift.
telespectador, a [telespekta'ðor, a] *nm/f* viewer.
telesquí [teles'ki] *nm* ski-lift.
teletex(to) [tele'teks(to)] *nm* teletext.
teletipista [teleti'pista] *nm/f* teletypist.
teletipo [tele'tipo] *nm* teletype(writer).
teletrabajo [teletra'βaxo] *nm* teleworking.
televentas [tele'βentas] *nfpl* telesales.
televidente [teleβi'ðente] *nm/f* viewer.
televisar [teleβi'sar] *vt* to televise.
televisión [teleβi'sjon] *nf* television; ~ **en color/por satélite** colour/satellite television; ~ **digital** digital television.
televisivo,a [teleβi'siβo, a] *adj* television *cpd*.
televisor [teleβi'sor] *nm* television set.
télex ['teleks] *nm* telex; **máquina** ~ telex (machine); **enviar por** ~ to telex.
telón [te'lon] *nm* curtain; ~ **de boca/seguridad** front/safety curtain; ~ **de acero** (*POL*) iron curtain; ~ **de fondo** backcloth, background.
telonero, a [telo'nero, a] *nm/f* support act; **los ~s** (*MUS*) the support band.
tema ['tema] *nm* (*asunto*) subject, topic; (*MUS*) theme; ~**s de actualidad** current affairs ♦ *nf* (*obsesión*) obsession; (*manía*) ill-will; **tener ~ a algn** to have a grudge against sb.
temario [te'marjo] *nm* (*ESCOL*) set of topics; (*de una conferencia*) agenda.

temático, a [te'matiko, a] *adj* thematic ♦ *nf* subject matter.
tembladera [tembla'ðera] *nf* shaking; (*AM*) quagmire.
temblar [tem'blar] *vi* to shake, tremble; (*de frío*) to shiver.
tembleque [tem'bleke] *adj* shaking ♦ *nm* shaking.
temblón, ona [tem'blon, ona] *adj* shaking.
temblor [tem'blor] *nm* trembling; (*AM*: *de tierra*) earthquake.
tembloroso, a [temblo'roso, a] *adj* trembling.
temer [te'mer] *vt* to fear ♦ *vi* to be afraid; **temo que Juan llegue tarde** I am afraid Juan may be late.
temerario, a [teme'rarjo, a] *adj* (*imprudente*) rash; (*descuidado*) reckless; (*arbitrario*) hasty.
temeridad [temeri'ðað] *nf* (*imprudencia*) rashness; (*audacia*) boldness.
temeroso, a [teme'roso, a] *adj* (*miedoso*) fearful; (*que inspira temor*) frightful.
temible [te'mißle] *adj* fearsome.
temor [te'mor] *nm* (*miedo*) fear; (*duda*) suspicion.
témpano ['tempano] *nm* (*MUS*) kettledrum; ~ **de hielo** ice floe.
temperamento [tempera'mento] *nm* temperament; **tener** ~ to be temperamental.
temperar [tempe'rar] *vt* to temper, moderate.
temperatura [tempera'tura] *nf* temperature.
tempestad [tempes'tað] *nf* storm; ~ **en un vaso de agua** (*fig*) storm in a teacup.
tempestuoso, a [tempes'twoso, a] *adj* stormy.
templado, a [tem'plaðo, a] *adj* (*moderado*) moderate; (: *en el comer*) frugal; (: *en el beber*) abstemious; (*agua*) lukewarm; (*clima*) mild; (*MUS*) in tune, well-tuned.
templanza [tem'planθa] *nf* moderation; (*en el beber*) abstemiousness; (*del clima*) mildness.
templar [tem'plar] *vt* (*moderar*) to moderate; (*furia*) to restrain; (*calor*) to reduce; (*solución*) to dilute; (*afinar*) to tune (up); (*acero*) to temper ♦ *vi* to moderate; ~**se** *vr* to be restrained.
temple ['temple] *nm* (*humor*) mood; (*coraje*) courage; (*ajuste*) tempering; (*afinación*) tuning; (*pintura*) tempera.
templo ['templo] *nm* (*iglesia*) church; (*pagano etc*) temple; ~ **metodista** Methodist chapel.
temporada [tempo'raða] *nf* time, period; (*estación, social, DEPORTE*) season; **en plena** ~ at the height of the season.
temporal [tempo'ral] *adj* (*no permanente*) temporary; (*REL*) temporal ♦ *nm* storm.
temporario, a [tempo'rarjo, a] *adj* (*AM*) temporary.
tempranero, a [tempra'nero, a] *adj* (*BOT*) early; (*persona*) early-rising.
temprano, a [tem'prano, a] *adj* early ♦ *adv* early; (*demasiado pronto*) too soon, too early; **lo más** ~ **posible** as soon as possible.
ten [ten] *vb V* **tener**.
tenacidad [tenaθi'ðað] *nf* (*gen*) tenacity; (*dureza*) toughness; (*terquedad*) stubbornness.
tenacillas [tena'θiʎas] *nfpl* (*gen*) tongs; (*para el pelo*) curling tongs; (*MED*) forceps.
tenaz [te'naθ] *adj* (*material*) tough; (*persona*) tenacious; (*pegajoso*) sticky; (*terco*) stubborn.
tenaza(s) [te'naθa(s)] *nf(pl)* (*MED*) forceps; (*TEC*) pliers; (*ZOOL*) pincers.
tendal [ten'dal] *nm* awning.
tendedero [tende'ðero] *nm* (*para ropa*) drying-place; (*cuerda*) clothes line.
tendencia [ten'denθja] *nf* tendency; (*proceso*) trend; ~ **imperante** prevailing tendency; ~ **del mercado** run of the market; **tener** ~ **a** to tend *o* have a tendency to.
tendenciosidad [tendenθjosi'ðað] *nf* tendentiousness.
tendencioso, a [tenden'θjoso, a] *adj* tendentious.
tender [ten'der] *vt* (*extender*) to spread out; (*ropa*) to hang out; (*vía férrea, cable*) to lay; (*cuerda*) to stretch; (*trampa*) to set ♦ *vi* to tend; ~**se** *vr* to lie down; (*fig*: *dejarse llevar*) to let o.s. go; (: *dejar ir*) to let things go; ~ **la cama/la mesa** (*AM*) to make the bed/lay the table.
ténder ['tender] *nm* (*FERRO*) tender.
tenderete [tende'rete] *nm* (*puesto*) stall; (*carretilla*) barrow; (*exposición*) display of goods.
tendero, a [ten'dero, a] *nm/f* shopkeeper.
tendido, a [ten'diðo, a] *adj* (*acostado*) lying down, flat; (*colgado*) hanging ♦ *nm* (*ropa*) washing; (*TAUR*) front rows *pl* of seats; (*colocación*) laying; (*ARQ*: *enyesado*) coat of plaster; **a galope** ~ flat out.
tendón [ten'don] *nm* tendon.
tendré [ten'dre] *etc vb V* **tener**.
tenducho [ten'dutʃo] *nm* small dirty shop.
tenebroso, a [tene'ßroso, a] *adj* (*oscuro*) dark; (*fig*) gloomy; (*siniestro*) sinister.

tenedor [tene'ðor] *nm* (*CULIN*) fork; (*poseedor*) holder; ~ **de libros** book-keeper; ~ **de acciones** shareholder; ~ **de póliza** policyholder.

teneduría [teneðu'ria] *nf* keeping; ~ **de libros** book-keeping.

tenencia [te'nenθja] *nf* (*de casa*) tenancy; (*de oficio*) tenure; (*de propiedad*) possession; ~ **asegurada** security of tenure; ~ **ilícita de armas** illegal possession of weapons.

PALABRA CLAVE

tener [te'ner] *vt* **1** (*poseer, gen*) to have; (*en la mano*) to hold; **¿tienes un boli?** have you got a pen?; **va a ~ un niño** she's going to have a baby; **tiene los ojos azules** he's got blue eyes; **¡ten** (*o* **tenga**)!, **¡aquí tienes** (*o* **tiene**)! here you are!
2 (*edad, medidas*) to be; **tiene 7 años** she's 7 (years old); **tiene 15 cm de largo** it's 15 cm long
3 (*sentimientos, sensaciones*): ~ **sed/hambre/frío/calor** to be thirsty/hungry/cold/hot; ~ **celos** to be jealous; ~ **cuidado** to be careful; ~ **razón** to be right; ~ **suerte** to be lucky
4 (*considerar*): **lo tengo por brillante** I consider him to be brilliant; ~ **en mucho a algn** to think very highly of sb
5 (+*pp*, +*adj*, +*gerundio*): **tengo terminada ya la mitad del trabajo** I've done half the work already; **tenía el sombrero puesto** he had his hat on; **tenía pensado llamarte** I had been thinking of phoning you; **nos tiene hartos** we're fed up with him; **me ha tenido tres horas esperando** he kept me waiting three hours
6: ~ **que hacer algo** to have to do sth; **tengo que acabar este trabajo hoy** I have to finish this job today
7: **¿qué tienes, estás enfermo?** what's the matter with you, are you ill?
8 (*locuciones*): **¿conque ésas tenemos?** so it's like that, then?; **no las tengo todas conmigo** I'm a bit unsure (about it); **lo tiene difícil** he'll have a hard job
♦ **~se** *vr* **1**: **~se en pie** to stand up
2: **~se por** to think o.s.; **se tiene por un gran cantante** he thinks himself a great singer.

tenga ['tenga] *etc vb V* **tener**.

tenia ['tenja] *nf* tapeworm.

teniente [te'njente] *nm* lieutenant; ~ **coronel** lieutenant colonel.

tenis ['tenis] *nm* tennis; ~ **de mesa** table tennis.

tenista [te'nista] *nm/f* tennis player.

tenor [te'nor] *nm* (*tono*) tone; (*sentido*) meaning; (*MUS*) tenor; **a ~ de** on the lines of.

tenorio [te'norjo] *nm* (*fam*) ladykiller, Don Juan.

tensar [ten'sar] *vt* to tauten; (*arco*) to draw.

tensión [ten'sjon] *nf* tension; (*TEC*) stress; (*MED*): ~ **arterial** blood pressure; ~ **nerviosa** nervous strain; **tener la ~ alta** to have high blood pressure.

tenso, a ['tenso, a] *adj* tense; (*relaciones*) strained.

tentación [tenta'θjon] *nf* temptation.

tentáculo [ten'takulo] *nm* tentacle.

tentador, a [tenta'ðor, a] *adj* tempting ♦ *nm/f* tempter/temptress.

tentar [ten'tar] *vt* (*tocar*) to touch, feel; (*seducir*) to tempt; (*atraer*) to attract; (*probar*) to try (out); (*MED*) to probe; ~ **hacer algo** to try to do sth.

tentativa [tenta'tiβa] *nf* attempt; ~ **de asesinato** attempted murder.

tentempié [tentem'pje] *nm* (*fam*) snack.

tenue ['tenwe] *adj* (*delgado*) thin, slender; (*alambre*) fine; (*insustancial*) tenuous; (*sonido*) faint; (*neblina*) light; (*lazo, vínculo*) slight.

teñir [te'ɲir] *vt* to dye; (*fig*) to tinge; **~se el pelo** to dye one's hair.

teología [teolo'xia] *nf* theology.

teólogo, a [te'oloɣo, a] *nm/f* theologist, theologian.

teorema [teo'rema] *nm* theorem.

teoría [teo'ria] *nf* theory; **en ~** in theory.

teóricamente [te'orikamente] *adv* theoretically.

teorice [teo'riθe] *etc vb V* **teorizar**.

teórico, a [te'oriko, a] *adj* theoretic(al) ♦ *nm/f* theoretician, theorist.

teorizar [teori'θar] *vi* to theorize.

tequila [te'kila] *nm o f* tequila.

TER [ter] *nm abr* (*FERRO*) = *tren español rápido*.

terapeuta [tera'peuta] *nm/f* therapist.

terapéutico, a [tera'peutiko, a] *adj* therapeutic(al) ♦ *nf* therapeutics *sg*.

terapia [te'rapja] *nf* therapy; ~ **laboral** occupational therapy.

tercer [ter'θer] *adj V* **tercero**.

tercermundista [terθermun'dista] *adj* Third World *cpd*.

tercero, a [ter'θero, a] *adj* third (*delante de nmsg*: **tercer**) ♦ *nm* (*árbitro*) mediator; (*JUR*) third party.

terceto [ter'θeto] *nm* trio.

terciado, a [ter'θjaðo, a] *adj* slanting;

azúcar ~ brown sugar.
terciar [ter'θjar] *vt* (*MAT*) to divide into three; (*inclinarse*) to slope; (*llevar*) to wear across one's chest ♦ *vi* (*participar*) to take part; (*hacer de árbitro*) to mediate; **~se** *vr* to arise.
terciario, a [ter'θjarjo, a] *adj* tertiary.
tercio ['terθjo] *nm* third.
terciopelo [terθjo'pelo] *nm* velvet.
terco, a ['terko, a] *adj* obstinate, stubborn; (*material*) tough.
tergal ® [ter'ɣal] *nm* Terylene ®.
tergiversación [terxiβersa'θjon] *nf* (*deformación*) distortion; (*evasivas*) prevarication.
tergiversar [terxiβer'sar] *vt* to distort ♦ *vi* to prevaricate.
termal [ter'mal] *adj* thermal.
termas ['termas] *nfpl* hot springs.
térmico, a ['termiko, a] *adj* thermic, thermal, heat *cpd*.
terminación [termina'θjon] *nf* (*final*) end; (*conclusión*) conclusion, ending.
terminal [termi'nal] *adj* terminal ♦ *nm* (*ELEC, INFORM*) terminal; ~ **conversacional** interactive terminal; ~ **de pantalla** visual display unit ♦ *nf* (*AVIAT, FERRO*) terminal.
terminante [termi'nante] *adj* (*final*) final, definitive; (*tajante*) categorical.
terminar [termi'nar] *vt* (*completar*) to complete, finish; (*concluir*) to end ♦ *vi* (*llegar a su fin*) to end; (*parar*) to stop; (*acabar*) to finish; **~se** *vr* to come to an end; ~ **por hacer algo** to end up (by) doing sth.
término ['termino] *nm* end, conclusion; (*parada*) terminus; (*límite*) boundary; (*en discusión*) point; (*LING, COM*) term; ~ **medio** average; (*fig*) middle way; **en otros ~s** in other words; **en último** ~ (*a fin de cuentas*) in the last analysis; (*como último recurso*) as a last resort; **en ~s de** in terms of; **según los ~s del contrato** according to the terms of the contract.
terminología [terminolo'xia] *nf* terminology.
termita [ter'mita] *nf* termite.
termo ['termo] *nm* Thermos ® (flask).
termodinámico, a [termoði'namiko, a] *adj* thermodynamic ♦ *nf* thermodynamics *sg*.
termoimpresora [termoimpre'sora] *nf* thermal printer.
termómetro [ter'mometro] *nm* thermometer.
termonuclear [termonukle'ar] *adj* thermonuclear.
termostato [termos'tato] *nm* thermostat.
ternero, a [ter'nero, a] *nm/f* (*animal*) calf ♦ *nf* (*carne*) veal.
terneza [ter'neθa] *nf* tenderness.
ternilla [ter'niʎa] *nf* gristle; (*cartílago*) cartilage.
terno ['terno] *nm* (*traje*) three-piece suit; (*conjunto*) set of three.
ternura [ter'nura] *nf* (*trato*) tenderness; (*palabra*) endearment; (*cariño*) fondness.
terquedad [terke'ðað] *nf* obstinacy; (*dureza*) harshness.
terrado [te'rraðo] *nm* terrace.
Terranova [terra'noβa] *nf* Newfoundland.
terraplén [terra'plen] *nm* (*AGR*) terrace; (*FERRO*) embankment; (*MIL*) rampart; (*cuesta*) slope.
terráqueo, a [te'rrakeo, a] *adj*: **globo** ~ globe.
terrateniente [terrate'njente] *nm* landowner.
terraza [te'rraθa] *nf* (*balcón*) balcony; (*techo*) flat roof; (*AGR*) terrace.
terremoto [terre'moto] *nm* earthquake.
terrenal [terre'nal] *adj* earthly.
terreno, a [te'rreno, a] *adj* (*de la tierra*) earthly, worldly ♦ *nm* (*tierra*) land; (*parcela*) plot; (*suelo*) soil; (*fig*) field; **un** ~ a piece of land; **sobre el** ~ on the spot; **ceder/perder** ~ to give/lose ground; **preparar el** ~ **(a)** (*fig*) to pave the way (for).
terrestre [te'rrestre] *adj* terrestrial; (*ruta*) land *cpd*.
terrible [te'rriβle] *adj* (*espantoso*) terrible; (*aterrador*) dreadful; (*tremendo*) awful.
territorial [territo'rjal] *adj* territorial.
territorio [terri'torjo] *nm* territory; ~ **bajo mandato** mandated territory.
terrón [te'rron] *nm* (*de azúcar*) lump; (*de tierra*) clod, lump; **terrones** *nmpl* land *sg*.
terror [te'rror] *nm* terror.
terrorífico, a [terro'rifiko, a] *adj* terrifying.
terrorismo [terro'rismo] *nm* terrorism.
terrorista [terro'rista] *adj, nm/f* terrorist.
terroso, a [te'rroso, a] *adj* earthy.
terruño [te'rruɲo] *nm* (*pedazo*) clod; (*parcela*) plot; (*fig*) native soil; **apego al** ~ attachment to one's native soil.
terso, a ['terso, a] *adj* (*liso*) smooth; (*pulido*) polished; (*fig: estilo*) flowing.
tersura [ter'sura] *nf* smoothness; (*brillo*) shine.
tertulia [ter'tulja] *nf* (*reunión informal*) social gathering; (*grupo*) group, circle; (*sala*) clubroom; ~ **literaria** literary circle.
tesina [te'sina] *nf* dissertation.

tesis ['tesis] *nf inv* thesis.
tesón [te'son] *nm* (*firmeza*) firmness; (*tenacidad*) tenacity.
tesorería [tesore'ria] *nf* treasurership.
tesorero, a [teso'rero, a] *nm/f* treasurer.
tesoro [te'soro] *nm* treasure; **T~ público** (*POL*) Exchequer.
test, *pl* **tests** [tes(t), tes(t)] *nm* test.
testaferro [testa'ferro] *nm* figurehead.
testamentaría [testamenta'ria] *nf* execution of a will.
testamentario, a [testamen'tarjo, a] *adj* testamentary ♦ *nm/f* executor/executrix.
testamento [testa'mento] *nm* will.
testar [tes'tar] *vi* to make a will.
testarada [testa'raða] *nf*, **testarazo** [testa'raθo] *nm*: **darse un(a) ~** (*fam*) to bump one's head.
testarudo, a [testa'ruðo, a] *adj* stubborn.
testículo [tes'tikulo] *nm* testicle.
testificar [testifi'kar] *vt* to testify; (*fig*) to attest ♦ *vi* to give evidence.
testifique [testi'fike] *etc vb V* **testificar**.
testigo [tes'tiɤo] *nm/f* witness; **~ de cargo/descargo** witness for the prosecution/defence; **~ ocular** eye witness; **poner a algn por ~** to cite sb as a witness.
testimonial [testimo'njal] *adj* (*prueba*) testimonial; (*gesto*) token.
testimoniar [testimo'njar] *vt* to testify to; (*fig*) to show.
testimonio [testi'monjo] *nm* testimony; **en ~ de** as a token *o* mark of; **falso ~** perjured evidence, false witness.
teta ['teta] *nf* (*de biberón*) teat; (*ANAT*) nipple; (*fam*) breast; (*fam!*) tit (*!*).
tétanos ['tetanos] *nm* tetanus.
tetera [te'tera] *nf* teapot; **~ eléctrica** (electric) kettle.
tetilla [te'tiʎa] *nf* (*ANAT*) nipple; (*de biberón*) teat.
tétrico, a ['tetriko, a] *adj* gloomy, dismal.
textil [teks'til] *adj* textile.
texto ['teksto] *nm* text.
textual [teks'twal] *adj* textual; **palabras ~es** exact words.
textura [teks'tura] *nf* (*de tejido*) texture; (*de mineral*) structure.
tez [teθ] *nf* (*cutis*) complexion; (*color*) colouring.
tfno. *abr* (= *teléfono*) tel.
ti [ti] *pron* you; (*reflexivo*) yourself.
tía ['tia] *nf* (*pariente*) aunt; (*mujer cualquiera*) girl, bird (*col*); (*fam: pej: vieja*) old bag; (*: prostituta*) whore.
Tibet [ti'ßet] *nm*: **El ~** Tibet.
tibetano, a [tiße'tano, a] *adj, nm/f* Tibetan ♦ *nm* (*LING*) Tibetan.
tibia ['tißja] *nf* tibia.
tibieza [ti'ßjeθa] *nf* (*temperatura*) tepidness; (*fig*) coolness.
tibio, a ['tißjo, a] *adj* lukewarm, tepid.
tiburón [tißu'ron] *nm* shark.
tic [tik] *nm* (*ruido*) click; (*de reloj*) tick; **~ nervioso** (*MED*) nervous tic.
tico, a ['tiko, a] *adj, nm/f* (*AM fam*) Costa Rican.
tictac [tik'tak] *nm* (*de reloj*) tick tock.
tiemble ['tjemble] *etc vb V* **temblar**.
tiempo ['tjempo] *nm* (*gen*) time; (*época, período*) age, period; (*METEOROLOGÍA*) weather; (*LING*) tense; (*edad*) age; (*de juego*) half; **a ~** in time; **a un** *o* **al mismo ~** at the same time; **al poco ~** very soon (after); **andando el ~** in due course; **cada cierto ~** every so often; **con ~** in time; **con el ~** eventually; **de ~ en ~** from time to time; **en mis ~s** in my time; **en los buenos ~s** in the good old days; **hace buen/mal ~** the weather is fine/bad; **estar a ~** to be in time; **hace ~** some time ago; **hacer ~** to while away the time; **¿qué ~ tiene?** how old is he?; **motor de 2 ~s** two-stroke engine; **~ compartido** (*INFORM*) time sharing; **~ de ejecución** (*INFORM*) run time; **~ inactivo** (*COM*) downtime; **~ libre** spare time; **~ de paro** (*COM*) idle time; **a ~ partido** (*trabajar*) part-time; **~ preferencial** (*COM*) prime time; **en ~ real** (*INFORM*) real time.
tienda ['tjenda] *etc vb V* **tender** ♦ *nf* shop; (*más grande*) store; (*NAUT*) awning; **~ de campaña** tent.
tiene ['tjene] *etc vb V* **tener**.
tienta ['tjenta] *nf* (*MED*) probe; (*fig*) tact; **andar a ~s** to grope one's way along.
tiento ['tjento] *etc vb V* **tentar** ♦ *nm* (*tacto*) touch; (*precaución*) wariness; (*pulso*) steady hand; (*ZOOL*) feeler, tentacle.
tierno, a ['tjerno, a] *adj* (*blando, dulce*) tender; (*fresco*) fresh.
tierra ['tjerra] *nf* earth; (*suelo*) soil; (*mundo*) world; (*país*) country, land; (*ELEC*) earth, ground (*US*); **~ adentro** inland; **~ natal** native land; **echar ~ a un asunto** to hush an affair up; **no es de estas ~s** he's not from these parts; **la T~ Santa** the Holy Land.
tieso, a ['tjeso, a] *adj* (*rígido*) rigid; (*duro*) stiff; (*fig: testarudo*) stubborn; (*fam: orgulloso*) conceited ♦ *adv* strongly.
tiesto ['tjesto] *nm* flowerpot; (*pedazo*)

piece of pottery.
tifoidea [tifoi'ðea] *nf* typhoid.
tifón [ti'fon] *nm* (*huracán*) typhoon; (*de mar*) tidal wave.
tifus ['tifus] *nm* typhus; ~ **icteroides** yellow fever.
tigre ['tiɣre] *nm* tiger; (*AM*) jaguar.
tijera [ti'xera] *nf* (*una* ~) (pair of) scissors *pl*; (*ZOOL*) claw; (*persona*) gossip; **de** ~ folding; ~**s** *nfpl* scissors; (*para plantas*) shears; **unas** ~**s** a pair of scissors.
tijeretear [tixerete'ar] *vt* to snip ♦ *vi* (*fig*) to meddle.
tila ['tila] *nf* (*BOT*) lime tree; (*CULIN*) lime flower tea.
tildar [til'dar] *vt*: ~ **de** to brand as.
tilde ['tilde] *nf* (*defecto*) defect; (*trivialidad*) triviality; (*TIP*) tilde.
tilín [ti'lin] *nm* tinkle.
tilo ['tilo] *nm* lime tree.
timador, a [tima'ðor, a] *nm/f* swindler.
timar [ti'mar] *vt* (*robar*) to steal; (*estafar*) to swindle; (*persona*) to con; ~**se** *vr* (*fam*) to make eyes (*con algn* at sb).
timbal [tim'bal] *nm* small drum.
timbrar [tim'brar] *vt* to stamp; (*sellar*) to seal; (*carta*) to postmark.
timbrazo [tim'braθo] *nm* ring; **dar un** ~ to ring the bell.
timbre ['timbre] *nm* (*sello*) stamp; (*campanilla*) bell; (*tono*) timbre; (*COM*) stamp duty.
timidez [timi'ðeθ] *nf* shyness.
tímido, a ['timiðo, a] *adj* shy, timid.
timo ['timo] *nm* swindle; **dar un** ~ **a algn** to swindle sb.
timón [ti'mon] *nm* helm, rudder; (*AM*) steering wheel; **coger el** ~ (*fig*) to take charge.
timonel [timo'nel] *nm* helmsman.
timorato, a [timo'rato, a] *adj* God-fearing; (*mojigato*) sanctimonious.
tímpano ['timpano] *nm* (*ANAT*) eardrum; (*MUS*) small drum.
tina ['tina] *nf* tub; (*AM*: *baño*) bath(tub).
tinaja [ti'naxa] *nf* large earthen jar.
tinerfeño, a [tiner'feɲo, a] *adj* of *o* from Tenerife ♦ *nm/f* native *o* inhabitant of Tenerife.
tinglado [tin'glaðo] *nm* (*cobertizo*) shed; (*fig*: *truco*) trick; (*intriga*) intrigue; **armar un** ~ to lay a plot.
tinieblas [ti'njeβlas] *nfpl* darkness *sg*; (*sombras*) shadows; **estamos en** ~ **sobre sus proyectos** (*fig*) we are in the dark about his plans.
tino ['tino] *nm* (*habilidad*) skill; (*MIL*) marksmanship; (*juicio*) insight; (*moderación*) moderation; **sin** ~ immoderately; **coger el** ~ to get the feel *o* hang of it.
tinta ['tinta] *nf* ink; (*TEC*) dye; (*ARTE*) colour; ~ **china** Indian ink; ~**s** *nfpl* (*fig*) shades; **medias** ~**s** (*fig*) half measures; **saber algo de buena** ~ to have sth on good authority.
tinte ['tinte] *nm* (*acto*) dyeing; (*fig*) tinge; (*barniz*) veneer.
tintero [tin'tero] *nm* inkwell; **se le quedó en el** ~ he clean forgot about it.
tintinear [tintine'ar] *vt* to tinkle.
tinto, a ['tinto, a] *adj* (*teñido*) dyed; (*manchado*) stained ♦ *nm* red wine.
tintorera [tinto'rera] *nf* shark.
tintorería [tintore'ria] *nf* dry cleaner's.
tintorero [tinto'rero] *nm* dry cleaner('s).
tintura [tin'tura] *nf* (*acto*) dyeing; (*QUÍMICA*) dye; (*farmacéutico*) tincture.
tiña ['tiɲa] *etc vb V* **teñir** ♦ *nf* (*MED*) ringworm.
tío ['tio] *nm* (*pariente*) uncle; (*fam*: *viejo*) old fellow; (: *individuo*) bloke, chap, guy (*US*).
tiovivo [tio'βiβo] *nm* roundabout.
típico, a ['tipiko, a] *adj* typical; (*pintoresco*) picturesque.
tiple ['tiple] *nm* soprano (voice) ♦ *nf* soprano.
tipo ['tipo] *nm* (*clase*) type, kind; (*norma*) norm; (*patrón*) pattern; (*fam*: *hombre*) fellow, bloke, guy (*US*); (*ANAT*) build; (: *de mujer*) figure; (*IMPRENTA*) type; ~ **bancario/de descuento** bank/discount rate; ~ **de interés** interest rate; ~ **de interés vigente** (*COM*) standard rate; ~ **de cambio** exchange rate; ~ **base** (*COM*) base rate; ~ **a término** (*COM*) forward rate; **dos** ~**s sospechosos** two suspicious characters; ~ **de letra** (*INFORM, TIP*) typeface; ~ **de datos** (*INFORM*) data type.
tipografía [tipoɣra'fia] *nf* (*tipo*) printing; (*lugar*) printing press.
tipográfico, a [tipo'ɣrafiko, a] *adj* printing.
tipógrafo, a [ti'poɣrafo, a] *nm/f* printer.
tíque(t) ['tike], *pl* **tíque(t)s** ['tikes] *nm* ticket; (*en tienda*) cash slip.
tiquismiquis [tikis'mikis] *nm* fussy person ♦ *nmpl* (*querellas*) squabbling *sg*; (*escrúpulos*) silly scruples.
tira ['tira] *nf* strip; (*fig*) abundance ♦ *nm*: ~ **y afloja** give and take; (*cautela*) caution; **la** ~ **de ...** (*fam*) lots of ....
tirabuzón [tiraβu'θon] *nm* corkscrew; (*rizo*) curl.
tiradero [tira'ðero] *nm* (*AM*) rubbish dump.

tirado, a [ti'raðo, a] *adj* (*barato*) dirt-cheap; (*fam: fácil*) very easy ♦ *nf* (*acto*) cast, throw; (*distancia*) distance; (*serie*) series; (*TIP*) printing, edition; **de una tirada** at one go; **está** ~ (*fam*) it's a cinch.

tirador, a [tira'ðor, a] *nm/f* (*persona*) shooter ♦ *nm* (*mango*) handle; (*ELEC*) flex; ~ **certero** sniper.

tiralíneas [tira'lineas] *nm inv* ruling-pen.

tiranía [tira'nia] *nf* tyranny.

tiránico, a [ti'raniko, a] *adj* tyrannical.

tiranizar [tirani'θar] *vt* (*pueblo, empleado*) to tyrannize.

tirano, a [ti'rano, a] *adj* tyrannical ♦ *nm/f* tyrant.

tirante [ti'rante] *adj* (*cuerda*) tight, taut; (*relaciones*) strained ♦ *nm* (*ARQ*) brace; (*TEC*) stay; (*correa*) shoulder strap; ~**s** *nmpl* braces, suspenders (*US*).

tirantez [tiran'teθ] *nf* tightness; (*fig*) tension.

tirar [ti'rar] *vt* to throw; (*volcar*) to upset; (*derribar*) to knock down *o* over; (*tiro*) to fire; (*cohete*) to launch; (*bomba*) to drop; (*edificio*) to pull down; (*desechar*) to throw out *o* away; (*disipar*) to squander; (*imprimir*) to print; (*dar: golpe*) to deal ♦ *vi* (*disparar*) to shoot; (*jalar*) to pull; (*fig*) to draw; (*interesar*) to appeal; (*fam: andar*) to go; (*tender a, buscar realizar*) to tend to; (*DEPORTE*) to shoot; ~**se** *vr* to throw o.s.; (*fig*) to demean o.s.; (*fam !*) to screw (*!*); ~ **abajo** to bring down, destroy; **tira más a su padre** he takes more after his father; ~ **de algo** to pull *o* tug (on) sth; **ir tirando** to manage; ~ **a la derecha** to turn *o* go right; **a todo** ~ at the most.

tirita [ti'rita] *nf* (sticking) plaster, bandaid (*US*).

tiritar [tiri'tar] *vi* to shiver.

tiritona [tiri'tona] *nf* shivering (fit).

tiro ['tiro] *nm* (*lanzamiento*) throw; (*disparo*) shot; (*tiroteo*) shooting; (*DEPORTE*) shot; (*TENIS, GOLF*) drive; (*alcance*) range; (*de escalera*) flight (of stairs); (*golpe*) blow; (*engaño*) hoax; ~ **al blanco** target practice; **caballo de** ~ cart-horse; **andar de** ~**s largos** to be all dressed up; **al** ~ (*AM*) at once; **de a** ~ (*AM fam*) completely; **se pegó un** ~ he shot himself; **le salió el** ~ **por la culata** it backfired on him.

tiroides [ti'roiðes] *nm inv* thyroid.

Tirol [ti'rol] *nm*: **El** ~ the Tyrol.

tirolés, esa [tiro'les, esa] *adj, nm/f* Tyrolean.

tirón [ti'ron] *nm* (*sacudida*) pull, tug; **de un** ~ in one go; **dar un** ~ **a** to pull at, tug at.

tirotear [tirote'ar] *vt* to shoot at; ~**se** *vr* to exchange shots.

tiroteo [tiro'teo] *nm* exchange of shots, shooting; (*escaramuza*) skirmish.

tirria ['tirrja] *nf*: **tener una** ~ **a algn** to have a grudge against sb.

tísico, a ['tisiko, a] *adj, nm/f* consumptive.

tisis ['tisis] *nf* consumption, tuberculosis.

tít. *abr* = **título.**

titánico, a [ti'taniko, a] *adj* titanic.

títere ['titere] *nm* puppet; **no dejar** ~ **con cabeza** to turn everything upside-down.

titilar [titi'lar] *vi* (*luz, estrella*) to twinkle; (*parpado*) to flutter.

titiritero, a [titiri'tero, a] *nm/f* (*acróbata*) acrobat; (*malabarista*) juggler.

titubeante [tituβe'ante] *adj* (*inestable*) shaky, tottering; (*farfullante*) stammering; (*dudoso*) hesitant.

titubear [tituβe'ar] *vi* to stagger; (*tartamudear*) to stammer; (*vacilar*) to hesitate.

titubeo [titu'βeo] *nm* staggering; stammering; hesitation.

titulado, a [titu'laðo, a] *adj* (*libro*) entitled; (*persona*) titled.

titular [titu'lar] *adj* titular ♦ *nm/f* (*de oficina*) occupant; (*de pasaporte*) holder ♦ *nm* headline ♦ *vt* to title; ~**se** *vr* to be entitled.

título ['titulo] *nm* (*gen*) title; (*de diario*) headline; (*certificado*) professional qualification; (*universitario*) university degree; (*COM*) bond; (*fig*) right; ~**s** *nmpl* qualifications; **a** ~ **de** by way of; (*en calidad de*) in the capacity of; **a** ~ **de curiosidad** as a matter of interest; ~ **de propiedad** title deed; ~**s convertibles de interés fijo** (*COM*) convertible loan stock *sg*.

tiza ['tiθa] *nf* chalk; **una** ~ a piece of chalk.

tizna ['tiθna] *nf* grime.

tiznar [tiθ'nar] *vt* to blacken; (*manchar*) to smudge, stain; (*fig*) to tarnish.

tizón [ti'θon], **tizo** ['tiθo] *nm* brand; (*fig*) stain.

TLC *nm abr* (= *Tratado de Libre Comercio*) NAFTA.

Tm. *abr* = **tonelada(s) métrica(s).**

toalla [to'aʎa] *nf* towel.

tobillo [to'βiʎo] *nm* ankle.

tobogán [toβo'ɣan] *nm* toboggan; (*montaña rusa*) switchback; (*resbaladilla*) chute, slide.

toca ['toka] *nf* headdress.

tocadiscos [toka'ðiskos] *nm inv* record player.

tocado, a [to'kaðo, a] *adj* (*fruta etc*) rotten; ♦ *nm* headdress; **estar ~ de la cabeza** (*fam*) to be weak in the head.
tocador [toka'ðor] *nm* (*mueble*) dressing table; (*cuarto*) boudoir; (*neceser*) toilet case; (*fam*) ladies' room.
tocante [to'kante]: **~ a** *prep* with regard to; **en lo ~ a** as for, so far as concerns.
tocar [to'kar] *vt* to touch; (*sentir*) to feel; (*con la mano*) to handle; (*MUS*) to play; (*campana*) to ring; (*tambor*) to beat; (*trompeta*) to blow; (*topar con*) to run into, strike; (*referirse a*) to allude to; (*ser emparentado con*) to be related to ♦ *vi* (*a la puerta*) to knock (on *o* at the door); (*ser de turno*) to fall to, be the turn of; (*ser hora*) to be due; (*atañer*) to concern; **~se** *vr* (*cubrirse la cabeza*) to cover one's head; (*tener contacto*) to touch (each other); **~le a algn** to fall to sb's lot; **~ en** (*NAUT*) to call at; **por lo que a mí me toca** as far as I am concerned; **esto toca en la locura** this verges on madness.
tocateja [toka'texa] (*fam*): **a ~** *adv* in readies.
tocayo, a [to'kajo, a] *nm/f* namesake.
tocino [to'θino] *nm* (bacon) fat; **~ de panceta** bacon.
todavía [toða'βia] *adv* (*aun*) even; (*aún*) still, yet; **~ más** yet *o* still more; **~ no** not yet; **~ en 1970** as late as 1970; **está lloviendo ~** it's still raining.
toditito, a [toði'tito, a], **todito, a** [to'ðito, a] *adj* (*AM fam*) (absolutely) all.

PALABRA CLAVE

todo, a ['toðo, a] *adj* **1** (*sg*) all; **toda la carne** all the meat; **toda la noche** all night, the whole night; **~ el libro** the whole book; **toda una botella** a whole bottle; **~ lo contrario** quite the opposite; **está toda sucia** she's all dirty; **a toda velocidad** at full speed; **por ~ el país** throughout the whole country; **es ~ un hombre** he's every inch a man; **soy ~ oídos** I'm all ears
2 (*pl*) all; every; **~s los libros** all the books; **todas las noches** every night; **~s los que quieran salir** all those who want to leave; **~s vosotros** all of you
♦ *pron* **1** everything, all; **~s** everyone, everybody; **lo sabemos ~** we know everything; **~s querían más tiempo** everybody *o* everyone wanted more time; **nos marchamos ~s** all of us left; **corriendo y ~, no llegaron a tiempo** even though they ran, they still didn't arrive in time
2 (*con preposición*): **a pesar de ~** even so, in spite of everything; **con ~ él me sigue gustando** even so I still like him; **le llamaron de todo** they called him all the names under the sun; **no me agrada del ~** I don't entirely like it
♦ *adv* all; **vaya ~ seguido** keep straight on *o* ahead
♦ *nm*: **como un ~** as a whole; **arriba del ~** at the very top.

todopoderoso, a [toðopoðe'roso, a] *adj* all powerful; (*REL*) almighty.
todoterreno [toðote'rreno] *nm* (*tb*: **vehículo ~**) four-by-four.
toga ['toɣa] *nf* toga; (*ESCOL*) gown.
Tokio ['tokjo] *n* Tokyo.
toldo ['toldo] *nm* (*para el sol*) sunshade; (*tienda*) marquee; (*fig*) pride.
tole ['tole] *nm* (*fam*) commotion.
toledano, a [tole'ðano, a] *adj* of *o* from Toledo ♦ *nm/f* native *o* inhabitant of Toledo.
tolerable [tole'raβle] *adj* tolerable.
tolerancia [tole'ranθja] *nf* tolerance.
tolerante [tole'rante] *adj* tolerant; (*fig*) open-minded.
tolerar [tole'rar] *vt* to tolerate; (*resistir*) to endure.
Tolón [to'lon] *nm* Toulon.
toma ['toma] *nf* (*gen*) taking; (*MED*) dose; (*ELEC*: *tb*: **~ de corriente**) socket; (*MEC*) inlet; **~ de posesión** (*por presidente*) taking up office; **~ de tierra** (*AVIAT*) landing.
tomadura [toma'ðura] *nf*: **~ de pelo** hoax.
tomar [to'mar] *vt* (*gen, CINE, FOTO, TV*) to take; (*actitud*) to adopt; (*aspecto*) to take on; (*notas*) to take down; (*beber*) to drink ♦ *vi* to take; (*AM*) to drink; **~se** *vr* to take; **~se por** to consider o.s. to be; **¡toma!** here you are!; **~ asiento** to sit down; **~ a algn por loco** to think sb mad; **~ a bien/a mal** to take well/badly; **~ en serio** to take seriously; **~ el pelo a algn** to pull sb's leg; **~la con algn** to pick a quarrel with sb; **~ por escrito** to write down; **toma y daca** give and take.
tomate [to'mate] *nm* tomato.
tomatera [toma'tera] *nf* tomato plant.
tomavistas [toma'βistas] *nm inv* movie camera.
tomillo [to'miʎo] *nm* thyme.
tomo ['tomo] *nm* (*libro*) volume; (*fig*) importance.
ton [ton] *abr* = **tonelada** ♦ *nm*: **sin ~ ni son** without rhyme or reason.
tonada [to'naða] *nf* tune.

tonalidad [tonali'ðað] *nf* tone.
tonel [to'nel] *nm* barrel.
tonelada [tone'laða] *nf* ton; ~ **métrica** metric ton.
tonelaje [tone'laxe] *nm* tonnage.
tonelero [tone'lero] *nm* cooper.
tongo ['tongo] *nm* (*DEPORTE*) fix.
tónico, a ['toniko, a] *adj* tonic ♦ *nm* (*MED*) tonic ♦ *nf* (*MUS*) tonic; (*fig*) keynote.
tonificador, a [tonifika'ðor, a], **tonificante** [tonifi'kante] *adj* invigorating, stimulating.
tonificar [tonifi'kar] *vt* to tone up.
tonifique [toni'fike] *etc vb V* **tonificar**.
tonillo [to'niʎo] *nm* monotonous voice.
tono ['tono] *nm* (*MUS*) tone; (*altura*) pitch; (*color*) shade; **fuera de** ~ inappropriate; ~ **de marcar** (*TELEC*) dialling tone; **darse** ~ to put on airs.
tontear [tonte'ar] *vi* (*fam*) to fool about; (*enamorados*) to flirt.
tontería [tonte'ria] *nf* (*estupidez*) foolishness; (*una* ~) silly thing; ~**s** *nfpl* rubbish *sg*, nonsense *sg*.
tonto, a ['tonto, a] *adj* stupid; (*ridículo*) silly ♦ *nm/f* fool; (*payaso*) clown; **a tontas y a locas** anyhow; **hacer(se) el** ~ to act the fool.
topacio [to'paθjo] *nm* topaz.
topar [to'par] *vt* (*tropezar*) to bump into; (*encontrar*) to find, come across; (*cabra etc*) to butt ♦ *vi*: ~ **contra** *o* **en** to run into; ~ **con** to run up against; **el problema topa en eso** that's where the problem lies.
tope ['tope] *adj* maximum ♦ *nm* (*fin*) end; (*límite*) limit; (*riña*) quarrel; (*FERRO*) buffer; (*AUTO*) bumper; **al** ~ end to end; **fecha** ~ closing date; **precio** ~ top price; **sueldo** ~ maximum salary; ~ **de tabulación** tab stop.
tópico, a ['topiko, a] *adj* topical; (*MED*) local ♦ *nm* platitude, cliché; **de uso** ~ for external application.
topo ['topo] *nm* (*ZOOL*) mole; (*fig*) blunderer.
topografía [topoɣra'fia] *nf* topography.
topógrafo, a [to'poɣrafo, a] *nm/f* topographer; (*agrimensor*) surveyor.
toponimia [topo'nimja] *nf* place names *pl*; (*estudio*) study of place names.
toque ['toke] *etc vb V* **tocar** ♦ *nm* touch; (*MUS*) beat; (*de campana*) ring, chime; (*MIL*) bugle call; (*fig*) crux; **dar un** ~ **a** to test; **dar el último** ~ **a** to put the final touch to; ~ **de queda** curfew.
toquetear [tokete'ar] *vt* to handle; (*fam!*) to touch up.
toquilla [to'kiʎa] *nf* (*chal*) shawl.
tórax ['toraks] *nm inv* thorax.
torbellino [torbe'ʎino] *nm* whirlwind; (*fig*) whirl.
torcedura [torθe'ðura] *nf* twist; (*MED*) sprain.
torcer [tor'θer] *vt* to twist; (*la esquina*) to turn; (*MED*) to sprain; (*cuerda*) to plait; (*ropa, manos*) to wring; (*persona*) to corrupt; (*sentido*) to distort ♦ *vi* (*cambiar de dirección*) to turn; ~**se** *vr* to twist; (*doblar*) to bend; (*desviarse*) to go astray; (*fracasar*) to go wrong; ~ **el gesto** to scowl; ~**se un pie** to twist one's foot; **el coche torció a la derecha** the car turned right.
torcido, a [tor'θiðo, a] *adj* twisted; (*fig*) crooked ♦ *nm* curl.
tordo, a ['torðo, a] *adj* dappled ♦ *nm* thrush.
torear [tore'ar] *vt* (*fig*: *evadir*) to dodge; (*toro*) to fight ♦ *vi* to fight bulls.
toreo [to'reo] *nm* bullfighting.
torero, a [to'rero, a] *nm/f* bullfighter.
toril [to'ril] *nm* bullpen.
tormenta [tor'menta] *nf* storm; (*fig*: *confusión*) turmoil.
tormento [tor'mento] *nm* torture; (*fig*) anguish.
tormentoso, a [tormen'toso, a] *adj* stormy.
tornar [tor'nar] *vt* (*devolver*) to return, give back; (*transformar*) to transform ♦ *vi* to go back; ~**se** *vr* (*ponerse*) to become; (*volver*) to return.
tornasol [torna'sol] *nm* (*BOT*) sunflower; **papel de** ~ litmus paper.
tornasolado, a [tornaso'laðo, a] *adj* (*brillante*) iridescent; (*reluciente*) shimmering.
torneo [tor'neo] *nm* tournament.
tornero, a [tor'nero, a] *nm/f* machinist.
tornillo [tor'niʎo] *nm* screw; **apretar los** ~**s a algn** to apply pressure on sb; **le falta un** ~ (*fam*) he's got a screw loose.
torniquete [torni'kete] *nm* (*puerta*) turnstile; (*MED*) tourniquet.
torno ['torno] *nm* (*TEC*: *grúa*) winch; (: *de carpintero*) lathe; (*tambor*) drum; ~ **de banco** vice, vise (*US*); **en** ~ **(a)** round, about.
toro ['toro] *nm* bull; (*fam*) he-man; **los** ~**s** bullfighting *sg*.
toronja [to'ronxa] *nf* grapefruit.
torpe ['torpe] *adj* (*poco hábil*) clumsy, awkward; (*movimiento*) sluggish; (*necio*) dim; (*lento*) slow; (*indecente*) crude; (*no honrado*) dishonest.

torpedo [tor'peðo] *nm* torpedo.
torpemente [torpe'mente] *adv* (*sin destreza*) clumsily; (*lentamente*) slowly.
torpeza [tor'peθa] *nf* (*falta de agilidad*) clumsiness; (*lentitud*) slowness; (*rigidez*) stiffness; (*error*) mistake; (*crudeza*) obscenity.
torre ['torre] *nf* tower; (*de petróleo*) derrick; (*de electricidad*) pylon; (*AJEDREZ*) rook; (*AVIAT, MIL, NAUT*) turret.
torrefacto, a [torre'fakto, a] *adj*: **café ~** high roast coffee.
torrencial [torren'θjal] *adj* torrential.
torrente [to'rrente] *nm* torrent.
tórrido, a ['torriðo, a] *adj* torrid.
torrija [to'rrixa] *nf* fried bread; **~s** French toast *sg*.
torsión [tor'sjon] *nf* twisting.
torso ['torso] *nm* torso.
torta ['torta] *nf* cake; (*fam*) slap; **~ de huevos** (*AM*) omelette; **no entendió ni ~** he didn't understand a word of it.
tortazo [tor'taθo] *nm* (*bofetada*) slap; (*de coche*) crash.
tortícolis [tor'tikolis] *nm inv* stiff neck.
tortilla [tor'tiʎa] *nf* omelette; (*AM*) maize pancake; **~ francesa/española** plain/ potato omelette; **cambiar** *o* **volver la ~ a algn** to turn the tables on sb.
tortillera [torti'ʎera] *nf* (*fam!*) lesbian.
tórtola ['tortola] *nf* turtledove.
tortuga [tor'tuɣa] *nf* tortoise; **~ marina** turtle.
tortuoso, a [tor'twoso, a] *adj* winding.
tortura [tor'tura] *nf* torture.
torturar [tortu'rar] *vt* to torture.
torvo, a ['torβo, a] *adj* grim, fierce.
torzamos [tor'θamos] *etc vb V* **torcer**.
tos [tos] *nf inv* cough; **~ ferina** whooping cough.
Toscana [tos'kana] *nf*: **La ~** Tuscany.
tosco, a ['tosko, a] *adj* coarse.
toser [to'ser] *vi* to cough; **no hay quien le tosa** he's in a class by himself.
tostado, a [tos'taðo, a] *adj* toasted; (*por el sol*) dark brown; (*piel*) tanned ♦ *nf* tan; (*pan*) piece of toast; **tostadas** *nfpl* toast *sg*.
tostador [tosta'ðor] *nm* toaster.
tostar [tos'tar] *vt* to toast; (*café*) to roast; (*al sol*) to tan; **~se** *vr* to get brown.
tostón [tos'ton] *nm*: **ser un ~** to be a drag.
total [to'tal] *adj* total ♦ *adv* in short; (*al fin y al cabo*) when all is said and done ♦ *nm* total; **en ~** in all; **~ que** to cut a long story short; **~ de comprobación** (*INFORM*) hash total; **~ debe/haber** (*COM*) debit/assets total.
totalidad [totali'ðað] *nf* whole.
totalitario, a [totali'tarjo, a] *adj* totalitarian.
totalmente [to'talmente] *adv* totally.
tóxico, a ['toksiko, a] *adj* toxic ♦ *nm* poison.
toxicómano, a [toksi'komano, a] *adj* addicted to drugs ♦ *nm/f* drug addict.
toxina [to'ksina] *nf* toxin.
tozudo, a [to'θuðo, a] *adj* obstinate.
traba ['traβa] *nf* bond, tie; (*cadena*) fetter; **poner ~s a** to restrain.
trabajador, a [traβaxa'ðor, a] *nm/f* worker ♦ *adj* hard-working.
trabajar [traβa'xar] *vt* to work; (*arar*) to till; (*empeñarse en*) to work at; (*empujar: persona*) to push; (*convencer*) to persuade ♦ *vi* to work; (*esforzarse*) to strive; **¡a ~!** let's get to work!; **~ por hacer algo** to strive to do sth.
trabajo [tra'βaxo] *nm* work; (*tarea*) task; (*POL*) labour; (*fig*) effort; **tomarse el ~ de** to take the trouble to; **~ por turno/a destajo** shift work/piecework; **~ en proceso** (*COM*) work-in-progress.
trabajoso, a [traβa'xoso, a] *adj* hard; (*MED*) pale.
trabalenguas [traβa'lengwas] *nm inv* tongue twister.
trabar [tra'βar] *vt* (*juntar*) to join, unite; (*atar*) to tie down, fetter; (*agarrar*) to seize; (*amistad*) to strike up; **~se** *vr* to become entangled; (*reñir*) to squabble; **se le traba la lengua** he gets tongue-tied.
trabazón [traβa'θon] *nf* (*TEC*) joining, assembly; (*fig*) bond, link.
trabucar [traβu'kar] *vt* (*confundir*) to confuse, mix up; (*palabras*) to misplace.
trabuque [tra'βuke] *etc vb V* **trabucar**.
tracción [trak'θjon] *nf* traction; **~ delantera/trasera** front-wheel/rear-wheel drive.
trace ['traθe] *etc vb V* **trazar**.
tractor [trak'tor] *nm* tractor.
trad. *abr* (= *traducido*) trans.
tradición [traði'θjon] *nf* tradition.
tradicional [traðiθjo'nal] *adj* traditional.
traducción [traðuk'θjon] *nf* translation; **~ asistida por ordenador** computer-assisted translation.
traducible [traðu'θiβle] *adj* translatable.
traducir [traðu'θir] *vt* to translate; **~se** *vr*: **~se en** (*fig*) to entail, result in.
traductor, a [traðuk'tor, a] *nm/f* translator.
traduzca [tra'ðuθka] *etc vb V* **traducir**.
traer [tra'er] *vt* to bring; (*llevar*) to carry; (*ropa*) to wear; (*incluir*) to carry; (*fig*) to cause; **~se** *vr*: **~se algo** to be up to sth; **~se bien/mal** to dress well/badly; **traérselas** to be annoying; **~ consigo** to involve, entail; **es un problema que se**

las trae it's a difficult problem.
traficante [trafi'kante] *nm/f* trader, dealer.
traficar [trafi'kar] *vi* to trade; ~ **con** (*pey*) to deal illegally in.
tráfico ['trafiko] *nm* (*COM*) trade; (*AUTO*) traffic.
trafique [tra'fike] *etc vb V* **traficar**.
tragaderas [traɣa'ðeras] *nfpl* (*garganta*) throat *sg*, gullet *sg*; (*credulidad*) gullibility *sg*.
tragaluz [traɣa'luθ] *nm* skylight.
tragamonedas [traɣamo'neðas] *nm inv*, **tragaperras** [traɣa'perras] *nm inv* slot machine.
tragar [tra'ɣar] *vt* to swallow; (*devorar*) to devour, bolt down; ~**se** *vr* to swallow; (*tierra*) to absorb, soak up; **no le puedo** ~ (*persona*) I can't stand him.
tragedia [tra'xeðja] *nf* tragedy.
trágico, a ['traxiko, a] *adj* tragic.
trago ['traɣo] *nm* (*líquido*) drink; (*comido de golpe*) gulp; (*fam*: *de bebida*) swig; (*desgracia*) blow; ~ **amargo** (*fig*) hard time.
trague ['traɣe] *etc vb V* **tragar**.
traición [trai'θjon] *nf* treachery; (*JUR*) treason; (*una* ~) act of treachery.
traicionar [traiθjo'nar] *vt* to betray.
traicionero, a [traiθjo'nero, a] = **traidor, a**.
traída [tra'iða] *nf* carrying; ~ **de aguas** water supply.
traidor, a [trai'ðor, a] *adj* treacherous ♦ *nm/f* traitor.
traiga ['traiɣa] *etc vb V* **traer**.
trailer, *pl* **trailers** ['trailer, 'trailer(s)] *nm* trailer.
traje ['traxe] *etc vb V* **traer** ♦ *nm* (*gen*) dress; (*de hombre*) suit; (~ *típico*) costume; (*fig*) garb; ~ **de baño** swimsuit; ~ **de luces** bullfighter's costume; ~ **hecho a la medida** made-to-measure suit.
trajera [tra'xera] *etc vb V* **traer**.
trajín [tra'xin] *nm* haulage; (*fam*: *movimiento*) bustle; **trajines** *nmpl* goings-on.
trajinar [traxi'nar] *vt* (*llevar*) to carry, transport ♦ *vi* (*moverse*) to bustle about; (*viajar*) to travel around.
trama ['trama] *nf* (*fig*) link; (: *intriga*) plot; (*de tejido*) weft.
tramar [tra'mar] *vt* to plot; (*TEC*) to weave; ~**se** *vr* (*fig*): **algo se está tramando** there's something going on.
tramitar [trami'tar] *vt* (*asunto*) to transact; (*negociar*) to negotiate; (*manejar*) to handle.
trámite ['tramite] *nm* (*paso*) step; (*JUR*) transaction; ~**s** *nmpl* (*burocracia*) paperwork *sg*, procedures; (*JUR*) proceedings.
tramo ['tramo] *nm* (*de tierra*) plot; (*de escalera*) flight; (*de vía*) section.
tramoya [tra'moja] *nf* (*TEAT*) piece of stage machinery; (*fig*) trick.
tramoyista [tramo'jista] *nm/f* scene shifter; (*fig*) trickster.
trampa ['trampa] *nf* trap; (*en el suelo*) trapdoor; (*prestidigitación*) conjuring trick; (*engaño*) trick; (*fam*) fiddle; (*de pantalón*) fly; **caer en la** ~ to fall into the trap; **hacer** ~**s** (*hacer juegos de manos*) to juggle, conjure; (*trampear*) to cheat.
trampear [trampe'ar] *vt, vi* to cheat.
trampilla [tram'piʎa] *nf* trap, hatchway.
trampolín [trampo'lin] *nm* trampoline; (*de piscina etc*) diving board.
tramposo, a [tram'poso, a] *adj* crooked, cheating ♦ *nm/f* crook, cheat.
tranca ['tranka] *nf* (*palo*) stick; (*viga*) beam; (*de puerta, ventana*) bar; (*borrachera*) binge; **a** ~**s y barrancas** with great difficulty.
trancar [tran'kar] *vt* to bar ♦ *vi* to stride along.
trancazo [tran'kaθo] *nm* (*golpe*) blow.
trance ['tranθe] *nm* (*momento difícil*) difficult moment; (*situación crítica*) critical situation; (*estado hipnotizado*) trance; **estar en** ~ **de muerte** to be at death's door.
tranco ['tranko] *nm* stride.
tranque ['tranke] *etc vb V* **trancar**.
tranquilamente [tran'kilamente] *adv* (*sin preocupaciones*: *leer, trabajar*) peacefully; (*sin enfadarse*: *hablar, discutir*) calmly.
tranquilice [tranki'liθe] *etc vb V* **tranquilizar**.
tranquilidad [trankili'ðað] *nf* (*calma*) calmness, stillness; (*paz*) peacefulness.
tranquilizador, a [trankiliθa'ðor, a] *adj* (*música*) soothing; (*hecho*) reassuring.
tranquilizante [trankili'θante] *nm* tranquillizer.
tranquilizar [trankili'θar] *vt* (*calmar*) to calm (down); (*asegurar*) to reassure.
tranquilo, a [tran'kilo, a] *adj* (*calmado*) calm; (*apacible*) peaceful; (*mar*) calm; (*mente*) untroubled.
Trans. *abr* (*COM*) = **transferencia**.
transacción [transak'θjon] *nf* transaction.
transar [tran'sar] *vi* (*AM*) = **transigir**.
transatlántico, a [transat'lantiko, a] *adj* transatlantic ♦ *nm* (ocean) liner.
transbordador [transβorða'ðor] *nm* ferry.
transbordar [transβor'ðar] *vt* to transfer;

~**se** *vr* to change.
transbordo [trans'ßorðo] *nm* transfer; **hacer ~** to change (trains).
transcender [transθen'der] *vt* = **trascender**.
transcribir [transkri'ßir] *vt* to transcribe.
transcurrir [transku'rrir] *vi* (*tiempo*) to pass; (*hecho*) to turn out.
transcurso [trans'kurso] *nm* passing, lapse; **en el ~ de 8 días** in the course of a week.
transeúnte [transe'unte] *adj* transient ♦ *nm/f* passer-by.
transexual [transe'kswal] *adj, nm/f* transsexual.
transferencia [transfe'renθja] *nf* transference; (*COM*) transfer; **~ bancaria** banker's order; **~ de crédito** (*COM*) credit transfer; **~ electrónica de fondos** (*COM*) electronic funds transfer.
transferir [transfe'rir] *vt* to transfer; (*aplazar*) to postpone.
transfiera [trans'fjera] *etc vb V* **transferir**.
transfigurar [transfiɣu'rar] *vt* to transfigure.
transfiriendo [transfi'rjendo] *etc vb V* **transferir**.
transformación [transforma'θjon] *nf* transformation.
transformador [transforma'ðor] *nm* transformer.
transformar [transfor'mar] *vt* to transform; (*convertir*) to convert.
tránsfuga ['transfuɣa] *nm/f* (*MIL*) deserter; (*POL*) turncoat.
transfusión [transfu'sjon] *nf* (*tb*: **~ de sangre**) (blood) transfusion.
transgénico, a [trans'xeniko, a] *adj* genetically modified.
transgredir [transɣre'dir] *vt* to transgress.
transgresión [transɣre'sjon] *nf* transgression.
transición [transi'θjon] *nf* transition; **período de ~** transitional period.
transido, a [tran'siðo, a] *adj* overcome; **~ de angustia** beset with anxiety; **~ de dolor** racked with pain.
transigir [transi'xir] *vi* to compromise; (*ceder*) to make concessions.
transija [tran'sixa] *etc vb V* **transigir**.
Transilvania [transil'ßanja] *nf* Transylvania.
transistor [transis'tor] *nm* transistor.
transitable [transi'taßle] *adj* (*camino*) passable.
transitar [transi'tar] *vi* to go (from place to place).
transitivo, a [transi'tißo, a] *adj* transitive.
tránsito ['transito] *nm* transit; (*AUTO*) traffic; (*parada*) stop; **horas de máximo ~** rush hours; **"se prohíbe el ~"** "no thoroughfare."
transitorio, a [transi'torjo, a] *adj* transitory.
transmisión [transmi'sjon] *nf* (*RADIO, TV*) transmission, broadcast(ing); (*transferencia*) transfer; **~ en circuito** hookup; **~ en directo/exterior** live/outside broadcast; **~ de datos (en paralelo/en serie)** (*INFORM*) (parallel/serial) data transfer *o* transmission; **plena/media ~ bidireccional** (*INFORM*) full/half duplex.
transmitir [transmi'tir] *vt* to transmit; (*RADIO, TV*) to broadcast; (*enfermedad*) to give, pass on.
transparencia [transpa'renθja] *nf* transparency; (*claridad*) clearness, clarity; (*foto*) slide.
transparentar [transparen'tar] *vt* to reveal ♦ *vi* to be transparent.
transparente [transpa'rente] *adj* transparent; (*aire*) clear; (*ligero*) diaphanous ♦ *nm* curtain.
transpirar [transpi'rar] *vi* to perspire; (*fig*) to transpire.
transpondré [transpon'dre] *etc vb V* **transponer**.
transponer [transpo'ner] *vt* to transpose; (*cambiar de sitio*) to move about ♦ *vi* (*desaparecer*) to disappear; (*ir más allá*) to go beyond; ~**se** *vr* to change places; (*ocultarse*) to hide; (*sol*) to go down.
transponga [trans'ponga] *etc vb V* **transponer**.
transportador [transporta'ðor] *nm* (*MECÁNICA*): **~ de correa** belt conveyor.
transportar [transpor'tar] *vt* to transport; (*llevar*) to carry.
transporte [trans'porte] *nm* transport; (*COM*) haulage; **Ministerio de T~s** Ministry of Transport.
transpuesto [trans'pwesto], **transpuse** [trans'puse] *etc vb V* **transponer**.
transversal [transßer'sal] *adj* transverse, cross ♦ *nf* (*tb*: **calle ~**) cross street.
transversalmente [transßersal'mente] *adv* obliquely.
tranvía [tram'bia] *nm* tram, streetcar (*US*).
trapecio [tra'peθjo] *nm* trapeze.
trapecista [trape'θista] *nm/f* trapeze artist.
trapero, a [tra'pero, a] *nm/f* ragman.
trapicheos [trapi'tʃeos] *nmpl* (*fam*) schemes, fiddles.
trapisonda [trapi'sonda] *nf* (*jaleo*) row; (*estafa*) swindle.
trapo ['trapo] *nm* (*tela*) rag; (*de cocina*) cloth; ~**s** *nmpl* (*fam*: *de mujer*) clothes,

dresses; **a todo** ~ under full sail; **soltar el** ~ (*llorar*) to burst into tears.
tráquea ['trakea] *nf* trachea, windpipe.
traqueteo [trake'teo] *nm* (*crujido*) crack; (*golpeteo*) rattling.
tras [tras] *prep* (*detrás*) behind; (*después*) after; ~ **de** besides; **día** ~ **día** day after day; **uno** ~ **otro** one after the other.
trascendencia [trasθen'denθja] *nf* (*importancia*) importance; (*filosofía*) transcendence.
trascendental [trasθenden'tal] *adj* important; transcendental.
trascender [trasθen'der] *vi* (*oler*) to smell; (*noticias*) to come out, leak out; (*eventos, sentimientos*) to spread, have a wide effect; ~ **a** (*afectar*) to reach, have an effect on; (*oler a*) to smack of; **en su novela todo trasciende a romanticismo** everything in his novel smacks of romanticism.
trascienda [tras'θjenda] *etc vb V* **trascender**.
trasegar [trase'ɣar] *vt* (*mover*) to move about; (*vino*) to decant.
trasegué [trase'ɣe], **traseguemos** [trase'ɣemos] *etc vb V* **trasegar**.
trasero, a [tra'sero, a] *adj* back, rear ♦ *nm* (*ANAT*) bottom; ~**s** *nmpl* ancestors.
trasfondo [tras'fondo] *nm* background.
trasgo ['trasɣo] *nm* (*duende*) goblin.
trasgredir [trasɣre'ðir] *vt* to contravene.
trashumante [trasu'mante] *adj* migrating.
trasiego [tra'sjeɣo] *etc vb V* **trasegar** ♦ *nm* (*cambiar de sitio*) move, switch; (*de vino*) decanting; (*trastorno*) upset.
trasiegue [tra'sjeɣe] *etc vb V* **trasegar**.
trasladar [trasla'ðar] *vt* to move; (*persona*) to transfer; (*postergar*) to postpone; (*copiar*) to copy; (*interpretar*) to interpret; ~**se** *vr* (*irse*) to go; (*mudarse*) to move; ~**se a otro puesto** to move to a new job.
traslado [tras'laðo] *nm* move; (*mudanza*) move, removal; (*de persona*) transfer; (*copia*) copy; ~ **de bloque** (*INFORM*) block move, cut-and-paste.
traslucir [traslu'θir] *vt* to show; ~**se** *vr* to be translucent; (*fig*) to be revealed.
trasluz [tras'luθ] *nm* reflected light; **al** ~ against *o* up to the light.
trasluzca [tras'luθka] *etc vb V* **traslucir**.
trasmano [tras'mano]: **a** ~ *adv* (*fuera de alcance*) out of reach; (*apartado*) out of the way.
trasnochado, a [trasno'tʃaðo, a] *adj* dated.
trasnochador, a [trasnotʃa'ðor, a] *adj* given to staying up late ♦ *nm/f* (*fig*) night bird.
trasnochar [trasno'tʃar] *vi* (*acostarse tarde*) to stay up late; (*no dormir*) to have a sleepless night; (*pasar la noche*) to stay the night.
traspasar [traspa'sar] *vt* (*bala*) to pierce, go through; (*propiedad*) to sell, transfer; (*calle*) to cross over; (*límites*) to go beyond; (*ley*) to break; **"traspaso negocio"** "business for sale".
traspaso [tras'paso] *nm* transfer; (*fig*) anguish.
traspié [tras'pje], *pl* **traspiés** *nm* (*caída*) stumble; (*tropezón*) trip; (*fig*) blunder.
trasplantar [trasplan'tar] *vt* to transplant.
trasplante [tras'plante] *nm* transplant.
traspuesto, a [tras'pwesto, a] *adj*: **quedarse** ~ to doze off.
trastada [tras'taða] *nf* (*fam*) prank.
trastazo [tras'taθo] *nm* (*fam*) bump; **darse un** ~ (*persona*) to bump o.s.; (*en coche*) to have a bump.
traste ['traste] *nm* (*MUS*) fret; **dar al** ~ **con algo** to ruin sth; **ir al** ~ to fall through.
trastero [tras'tero] *nm* lumber room.
trastienda [tras'tjenda] *nf* backshop; **obtener algo por la** ~ to get sth by underhand means.
trasto ['trasto] *nm* (*mueble*) piece of furniture; (*tarro viejo*) old pot; (*pey: cosa*) piece of junk; (*: persona*) dead loss; ~**s** *nmpl* (*TEAT*) scenery *sg*; **tirar los** ~**s a la cabeza** to have a blazing row.
trastocar [trasto'kar] *vt* (*papeles*) to mix up.
trastornado, a [trastor'naðo, a] *adj* (*loco*) mad; (*agitado*) crazy.
trastornar [trastor'nar] *vt* to overturn, upset; (*fig: ideas*) to confuse; (*: nervios*) to shatter; (*: persona*) to drive crazy; ~**se** *vr* (*plan*) to fall through.
trastorno [tras'torno] *nm* (*acto*) overturning; (*confusión*) confusion; (*POL*) disturbance, upheaval; (*MED*) upset; ~ **estomacal** stomach upset; ~ **mental** mental disorder, breakdown.
trasunto [tra'sunto] *nm* copy.
trasvase [tras'βase] *nm* (*de río*) diversion.
tratable [tra'taβle] *adj* friendly.
tratado [tra'taðo] *nm* (*POL*) treaty; (*COM*) agreement; (*LITERATURA*) treatise.
tratamiento [trata'mjento] *nm* treatment; (*TEC*) processing; (*de problema*) handling; ~ **de datos** (*INFORM*) data processing; ~ **de gráficos** (*INFORM*) graphics; ~ **de márgenes** margin settings; ~ **de textos** (*INFORM*) word processing; ~ **por lotes** (*INFORM*) batch processing; ~ **de tú** familiar address.

tratante [tra'tante] *nm/f* dealer, merchandizer.

tratar [tra'tar] *vt* (*ocuparse de*) to treat; (*manejar, TEC*) to handle; (*INFORM*) to process; (*MED*) to treat; (*dirigirse a: persona*) to address ♦ *vi*: ~ **de** (*hablar sobre*) to deal with, be about; (*intentar*) to try to; ~ **con** (*COM*) to trade in; (*negociar*) to negotiate with; (*tener contactos*) to have dealings with; ~**se** *vr* to treat each other; **se trata de la nueva piscina** it's about the new pool; **¿de qué se trata?** what's it about?

trato ['trato] *nm* dealings *pl*; (*relaciones*) relationship; (*comportamiento*) manner; (*COM, JUR*) agreement, contract; (*título*) (form of) address; **de ~ agradable** pleasant; **de fácil** ~ easy to get on with; ~ **equitativo** fair deal; **¡~ hecho!** it's a deal!; **malos ~s** ill-treatment *sg*.

trauma ['trauma] *nm* trauma.

traumático, a [trau'matiko, a] *adj* traumatic.

través [tra'ßes] *nm* (*contratiempo*) reverse; **al** ~ across, crossways; **a ~ de** across; (*sobre*) over; (*por*) through; **de** ~ across; (*de lado*) sideways.

travesaño [traße'saɲo] *nm* (*ARQ*) crossbeam; (*DEPORTE*) crossbar.

travesía [traße'sia] *nf* (*calle*) cross-street; (*NAUT*) crossing.

travesti [tra'ßesti] *nm/f* transvestite.

travesura [traße'sura] *nf* (*broma*) prank; (*ingenio*) wit.

travieso, a [tra'ßjeso, a] *adj* (*niño*) naughty; (*adulto*) restless; (*ingenioso*) witty ♦ *nf* crossing; (*ARQ*) crossbeam; (*FERRO*) sleeper.

trayecto [tra'jekto] *nm* (*ruta*) road, way; (*viaje*) journey; (*tramo*) stretch; (*curso*) course; **final del** ~ end of the line.

trayectoria [trajek'torja] *nf* trajectory; (*desarrollo*) development, path; **la ~ actual del partido** the party's present line.

trayendo [tra'jendo] *etc vb V* **traer**.

traza ['traθa] *nf* (*ARQ*) plan, design; (*aspecto*) looks *pl*; (*señal*) sign; (*engaño*) trick; (*habilidad*) skill; (*INFORM*) trace.

trazado, a [tra'θaðo, a] *adj*: **bien** ~ shapely, well-formed ♦ *nm* (*ARQ*) plan, design; (*fig*) outline; (*de carretera etc*) line, route.

trazador [traθa'ðor] *nm* plotter; ~ **plano** flatbed plotter.

trazar [tra'θar] *vt* (*ARQ*) to plan; (*ARTE*) to sketch; (*fig*) to trace; (*itinerario: hacer*) to plot; (*plan*) to follow.

trazo ['traθo] *nm* (*línea*) line; (*bosquejo*) sketch; ~**s** *nmpl* (*de cara*) lines, features.

TRB *abr* = *toneladas de registro bruto.*

trébol ['treßol] *nm* (*BOT*) clover; ~**es** *nmpl* (*NAIPES*) clubs.

trece ['treθe] *num* thirteen; **estar en sus** ~ to stand firm.

trecho ['tretʃo] *nm* (*distancia*) distance; (*de tiempo*) while; (*fam*) piece; **de ~ en ~** at intervals.

tregua ['treɣwa] *nf* (*MIL*) truce; (*fig*) lull; **sin** ~ without respite.

treinta ['treinta] *num* thirty.

treintena [trein'tena] *nf* (about) thirty.

tremendo, a [tre'mendo, a] *adj* (*terrible*) terrible; (*imponente: cosa*) imposing; (*fam: fabuloso*) tremendous; (*divertido*) entertaining.

trémulo, a ['tremulo, a] *adj* quivering; (*luz*) flickering.

tren [tren] *nm* (*FERRO*) train; ~ **de aterrizaje** undercarriage; ~ **directo/expreso/(de) mercancías/de pasajeros/suplementario** through/fast/goods *o* freight/passenger/relief train; ~ **de vida** way of life.

trenca ['trenka] *nf* duffel coat.

trence ['trenθe] *etc vb V* **trenzar**.

trenza ['trenθa] *nf* (*de pelo*) plait.

trenzar [tren'θar] *vt* (*el pelo*) to plait ♦ *vi* (*en baile*) to weave in and out; ~**se** *vr* (*AM*) to become involved.

trepa ['trepa] *nf* (*subida*) climb; (*ardid*) trick.

trepador(a) [trepa'ðor(a)] *nm/f* (*fam*): **ser un(a)** ~ to be on the make ♦ *nf* (*BOT*) climber.

trepar [tre'par] *vt, vi* to climb; (*TEC*) to drill.

trepidación [trepiða'θjon] *nf* shaking, vibration.

trepidar [trepi'ðar] *vi* to shake, vibrate.

tres [tres] *num* three; (*fecha*) third; **las** ~ three o'clock.

trescientos, as [tres'θjentos, as] *num* three hundred.

tresillo [tre'siʎo] *nm* three-piece suite; (*MUS*) triplet.

treta ['treta] *nf* (*COM etc*) gimmick; (*fig*) trick.

tri... [tri] *pref* tri..., three-....

tríada ['triaða] *nf* triad.

triangular [trjangu'lar] *adj* triangular.

triángulo [tri'angulo] *nm* triangle.

tribal [tri'ßal] *adj* tribal.

tribu ['trißu] *nf* tribe.

tribuna [tri'ßuna] *nf* (*plataforma*) platform; (*DEPORTE*) stand; (*fig*) public speaking; ~ **de la prensa** press box; ~ **del acusado** (*JUR*) dock; ~ **del jurado** jury box.

tribunal [triβu'nal] *nm* (*juicio*) court; (*comisión, fig*) tribunal; (*ESCOL: examinadores*) board of examiners; **T~ Supremo** High Court, (*US*) Supreme Court; **T~ de Justicia de las Comunidades Europeas** European Court of Justice.
tributar [triβu'tar] *vt* to pay; (*las gracias*) to give; (*cariño*) to show.
tributario, a [triβu'tarjo, a] *adj* (*GEO, POL*) tributary *cpd*; (*ECON*) tax *cpd*, taxation *cpd* ♦ *nm* (*GEO*) tributary ♦ *nm/f* (*COM*) taxpayer; **sistema** ~ tax system.
tributo [tri'βuto] *nm* (*COM*) tax.
trice ['triθe] *etc vb V* **trizar**.
triciclo [tri'θiklo] *nm* tricycle.
tricornio [tri'kornjo] *nm* three-cornered hat.
tricota [tri'kota] *nf* (*AM*) knitted sweater.
tricotar [triko'tar] *vi* to knit.
tridimensional [triðimensjo'nal] *adj* three-dimensional.
trienal [trje'nal] *adj* three-year.
trifulca [tri'fulka] *nf* (*fam*) row, shindy.
trigal [tri'ɣal] *nm* wheat field.
trigésimo, a [tri'xesimo, a] *num* thirtieth.
trigo ['triɣo] *nm* wheat; **~s** *nmpl* wheat field(s) (*pl*).
trigueño, a [tri'ɣeɲo, a] *adj* (*pelo*) corn-coloured; (*piel*) olive-skinned.
trillado, a [tri'ʎaðo, a] *adj* threshed; (*fig*) trite, hackneyed.
trilladora [triʎa'ðora] *nf* threshing machine.
trillar [tri'ʎar] *vt* (*AGR*) to thresh; (*fig*) to frequent.
trillizos, as [tri'ʎiθos, as] *nmpl/nfpl* triplets.
trilogía [trilo'xia] *nf* triology.
trimestral [trimes'tral] *adj* quarterly; (*ESCOL*) termly.
trimestre [tri'mestre] *nm* (*ESCOL*) term; (*COM*) quarter, financial period; (: *pago*) quarterly payment.
trinar [tri'nar] *vi* (*MUS*) to trill; (*ave*) to sing, warble; **está que trina** he's hopping mad.
trincar [trin'kar] *vt* (*atar*) to tie up; (*NAUT*) to lash; (*agarrar*) to pinion.
trinchante [trin'tʃante] *nm* (*para cortar carne*) carving knife; (*tenedor*) meat fork.
trinchar [trin'tʃar] *vt* to carve.
trinchera [trin'tʃera] *nf* (*fosa*) trench; (*para vía*) cutting; (*impermeable*) trench-coat.
trineo [tri'neo] *nm* sledge.
trinidad [trini'ðað] *nf* trio; (*REL*): **la T~** the Trinity.
trino ['trino] *nm* trill.
trinque ['trinke] *etc vb V* **trincar**.
trinquete [trin'kete] *nm* (*TEC*) pawl; (*NAUT*) foremast.
trío ['trio] *nm* trio.
tripa ['tripa] *nf* (*ANAT*) intestine; (*fig, fam*) belly; **~s** *nfpl* (*ANAT*) insides; (*CULIN*) tripe *sg*; **tener mucha ~** to be fat; **me duelen las ~s** I have a stomach ache.
tripartito, a [tripar'tito, a] *adj* tripartite.
triple ['triple] *adj* triple; (*tres veces*) threefold.
triplicado, a [tripli'kaðo, a] *adj*: **por ~** in triplicate.
triplicar [tripli'kar] *vt* to treble.
triplo ['triplo] *adj* = **triple**.
trípode ['tripoðe] *nm* tripod.
Trípoli ['tripoli] *nm* Tripoli.
tríptico ['triptiko] *nm* (*ARTE*) triptych; (*documento*) three-part document.
tripulación [tripula'θjon] *nf* crew.
tripulante [tripu'lante] *nm/f* crewman/woman.
tripular [tripu'lar] *vt* (*barco*) to man; (*AUTO*) to drive.
triquiñuela [triki'ɲwela] *nf* trick.
tris [tris] *nm* crack; **en un ~** in an instant; **estar en un ~ de hacer algo** to be within an inch of doing sth.
triste ['triste] *adj* (*afligido*) sad; (*sombrío*) melancholy, gloomy; (*desolado*) desolate; (*lamentable*) sorry, miserable; (*viejo*) old; (*único*) single; **no queda sino un ~ penique** there's just one miserable penny left.
tristeza [tris'teθa] *nf* (*aflicción*) sadness; (*melancolía*) melancholy; (*de lugar*) desolation; (*pena*) misery.
tristón, ona [tris'ton, ona] *adj* sad, downhearted.
trituradora [tritura'ðora] *nf* shredder.
triturar [tritu'rar] *vt* (*moler*) to grind; (*mascar*) to chew; (*documentos*) to shred.
triunfador, a [triunfa'ðor, a] *adj* triumphant; (*ganador*) winning ♦ *nm/f* winner.
triunfal [triun'fal] *adj* triumphant; (*arco*) triumphal.
triunfante [triun'fante] *adj* triumphant; (*ganador*) winning.
triunfar [triun'far] *vi* (*tener éxito*) to triumph; (*ganar*) to win; (*NAIPES*) to be trumps; **triunfan corazones** hearts are trumps; **~ en la vida** to succeed in life.
triunfo [tri'unfo] *nm* triumph; (*NAIPES*) trump.
trivial [tri'βjal] *adj* trivial.
trivialice [triβja'liθe] *etc vb V* **trivializar**.
trivializar [triβjali'θar] *vt* to minimize, play

down.

triza ['triθa] *nf* bit, piece; **hacer algo ~s** to smash sth to bits; (*papel*) to tear sth to shreds.

trocar [tro'kar] *vt* (*COM*) to exchange; (*dinero, de lugar*) to change; (*palabras*) to exchange; (*confundir*) to confuse; (*vomitar*) to vomit; **~se** *vr* (*confundirse*) to get mixed up; (*transformarse*): **~se (en)** to change (into).

trocear [troθe'ar] *vt* to cut up.

trocha ['trotʃa] *nf* (*sendero*) by-path; (*atajo*) short cut.

troche ['trotʃe]: **a ~ y moche** *adv* helter-skelter, pell-mell.

trofeo [tro'feo] *nm* (*premio*) trophy; (*éxito*) success.

trola ['trola] *nf* (*fam*) fib.

tromba ['tromba] *nf* whirlwind; **~ de agua** cloudburst.

trombón [trom'bon] *nm* trombone.

trombosis [trom'bosis] *nf inv* thrombosis.

trompa ['trompa] *nf* (*MUS*) horn; (*de elefante*) trunk; (*trompo*) humming top; (*hocico*) snout; (*ANAT*) tube, duct ♦ *nm* (*MUS*) horn player; **~ de Falopio** Fallopian tube; **cogerse una ~** (*fam*) to get tight.

trompada [trom'paða] *nf*, **trompazo** [trom'paθo] *nm* (*choque*) bump, bang; (*puñetazo*) punch.

trompeta [trom'peta] *nf* trumpet; (*clarín*) bugle ♦ *nm* trumpeter.

trompetilla [trompe'tiʎa] *nf* ear trumpet.

trompicón [trompi'kon]: **a trompicones** *adv* in fits and starts.

trompo ['trompo] *nm* spinning top.

trompón [trom'pon] *nm* bump.

tronado, a [tro'naðo, a] *adj* broken-down.

tronar [tro'nar] *vt* (*AM*) to shoot, execute ♦ *vi* to thunder; (*fig*) to rage; (*fam*) to go broke.

tronchar [tron'tʃar] *vt* (*árbol*) to chop down; (*fig: vida*) to cut short; (*esperanza*) to shatter; (*persona*) to tire out; **~se** *vr* to fall down; **~se de risa** to split one's sides with laughter.

tronco ['tronko] *nm* (*de árbol, ANAT*) trunk; (*de planta*) stem; **estar hecho un ~** to be sound asleep.

tronera [tro'nera] *nf* (*MIL*) loophole; (*ARQ*) small window.

trono ['trono] *nm* throne.

tropa ['tropa] *nf* (*MIL*) troop; (*soldados*) soldiers *pl*; (*soldados rasos*) ranks *pl*; (*gentío*) mob.

tropecé [trope'θe], **tropecemos** [trope'θemos] *etc vb V* **tropezar**.

tropel [tro'pel] *nm* (*muchedumbre*) crowd; (*prisa*) rush; (*montón*) throng; **acudir** *etc* **en ~** to come *etc* in a mad rush.

tropelía [trope'lia] *nm* outrage.

tropezar [trope'θar] *vi* to trip, stumble; (*fig*) to slip up; **~se** *vr* (*dos personas*) to run into each other; **~ con** (*encontrar*) to run into; (*topar con*) to bump into.

tropezón [trope'θon] *nm* trip; (*fig*) blunder; (*traspié*): **dar un ~** to trip.

tropical [tropi'kal] *adj* tropical.

trópico ['tropiko] *nm* tropic.

tropiece [tro'pjeθe] *etc vb V* **tropezar**.

tropiezo [tro'pjeθo] *etc vb V* **tropezar** ♦ *nm* (*error*) slip, blunder; (*desgracia*) misfortune; (*revés*) setback; (*obstáculo*) snag; (*discusión*) quarrel.

troqué [tro'ke], **troquemos** [tro'kemos] *etc vb V* **trocar**.

trotamundos [trota'mundos] *nm inv* globetrotter.

trotar [tro'tar] *vi* to trot; (*viajar*) to travel about.

trote ['trote] *nm* trot; (*fam*) travelling; **de mucho ~** hard-wearing.

Troya ['troja] *nf* Troy; **aquí fue ~** now there's nothing but ruins.

trozo ['troθo] *nm* bit, piece; (*LITERATURA, MUS*) passage; **a ~s** in bits.

trucha ['trutʃa] *nf* (*pez*) trout; (*TEC*) crane.

truco ['truko] *nm* (*habilidad*) knack; (*engaño*) trick; (*CINE*) trick effect *o* photography; **~s** *nmpl* billiards *sg*; **~ publicitario** advertising gimmick.

trueco ['trweko] *etc vb V* **trocar**.

trueno ['trweno] *etc vb V* **tronar** ♦ *nm* (*gen*) thunder; (*estampido*) boom; (*de arma*) bang.

trueque ['trweke] *etc vb V* **trocar** ♦ *nm* exchange; (*COM*) barter.

trufa ['trufa] *nf* (*BOT*) truffle; (*fig: fam*) fib.

truhán, ana [tru'an, ana] *nm/f* rogue.

truncado, a [trun'kaðo, a] *adj* truncated.

truncar [trun'kar] *vt* (*cortar*) to truncate; (*la vida etc*) to cut short; (*el desarrollo*) to stunt.

trunque ['trunke] *etc vb V* **truncar**.

tu [tu] *adj* your.

tú [tu] *pron* you.

tubérculo [tu'ßerkulo] *nm* (*BOT*) tuber.

tuberculosis [tußerku'losis] *nf inv* tuberculosis.

tubería [tuße'ria] *nf* pipes *pl*, piping; (*conducto*) pipeline.

tubo ['tußo] *nm* tube, pipe; **~ de desagüe** drainpipe; **~ de ensayo** test-tube; **~ de escape** exhaust (pipe); **~ digestivo** alimentary canal.

tuerca ['twerka] *nf* (*TEC*) nut.
tuerce ['twerθe] *etc vb V* **torcer**.
tuerto, a ['twerto, a] *adj* (*torcido*) twisted; (*ciego*) blind in one eye ♦ *nm/f* one-eyed person ♦ *nm* (*ofensa*) wrong; **a tuertas** upside-down.
tuerza ['twerθa] *etc vb V* **torcer**.
tueste ['tweste] *etc vb V* **tostar**.
tuétano ['twetano] *nm* (*ANAT: médula*) marrow; (*BOT*) pith; **hasta los ~s** through and through, utterly.
tufo ['tufo] *nm* vapour; (*fig: pey*) stench.
tugurio [tu'ɣurjo] *nm* slum.
tul [tul] *nm* tulle.
tulipán [tuli'pan] *nm* tulip.
tullido, a [tu'ʎiðo, a] *adj* crippled; (*cansado*) exhausted.
tumba ['tumba] *nf* (*sepultura*) tomb; (*sacudida*) shake; (*voltereta*) somersault; **ser (como) una ~** to keep one's mouth shut.
tumbar [tum'bar] *vt* to knock down; (*doblar*) to knock over; (*fam: suj: olor*) to overpower ♦ *vi* to fall down; **~se** *vr* (*echarse*) to lie down; (*extenderse*) to stretch out.
tumbo ['tumbo] *nm* (*caída*) fall; (*de vehículo*) jolt; (*momento crítico*) critical moment.
tumbona [tum'bona] *nf* lounger.
tumor [tu'mor] *nm* tumour.
tumulto [tu'multo] *nm* turmoil; (*POL: motín*) riot.
tuna ['tuna] *nf* (*MUS*) student music group; *V tb* **tuno**; *see boxed note.*

TUNA

*A **tuna** is a musical group made up of university students, or quite often former students, who dress up in costumes from the "Edad de Oro", the Spanish Golden Age. These musical troupes wander through town, playing guitars, lutes and tambourines and serenading young women in the halls of residence. Sometimes they make impromptu appearances at weddings or parties, singing traditional songs for a few "pesetas".*

tunante [tu'nante] *adj* rascally ♦ *nm* rogue, villain; ¡~! you villain!
tunda ['tunda] *nf* (*de tela*) shearing; (*golpeo*) beating.
tundir [tun'dir] *vt* (*tela*) to shear; (*hierba*) to mow; (*fig*) to exhaust; (*fam: golpear*) to beat.
tunecino, a [tune'θino, a] *adj, nm/f* Tunisian.
túnel ['tunel] *nm* tunnel.
Túnez ['tuneθ] *nm* Tunis.
túnica ['tunika] *nf* tunic; (*vestido largo*) long dress; (*ANAT, BOT*) tunic.
Tunicia [tu'niθja] *nf* Tunisia.
tuno, a ['tuno, a] *nm/f* (*fam*) rogue ♦ *nm* (*MUS*) *member of a "tuna".*
tuntún [tun'tun]: **al ~** *adv* thoughtlessly.
tupamaro, a [tupa'maro, a] *adj, nm/f* (*AM*) urban guerrilla.
tupé [tu'pe] *nm* quiff.
tupí [tu'pi], **tupí-guaraní** [tupigwara'ni] *adj, nm/f* Tupi-Guarani.
tupido, a [tu'piðo, a] *adj* (*denso*) dense; (*fig: torpe*) dim; (*tela*) close-woven.
turba ['turβa] *nf* (*combustible*) turf; (*muchedumbre*) crowd.
turbación [turβa'θjon] *nf* (*molestia*) disturbance; (~~*preocupación*~~) worry.
turbado, a [tur'βaðo, a] *adj* (*molesto*) disturbed; (*preocupado*) worried.
turbante [tur'βante] *nm* turban.
turbar [tur'βar] *vt* (*molestar*) to disturb; (*incomodar*) to upset; **~se** *vr* to be disturbed.
turbina [tur'βina] *nf* turbine.
turbio, a ['turβjo, a] *adj* (*agua etc*) cloudy; (*vista*) dim, blurred; (*tema*) unclear, confused; (*negocio*) shady ♦ *adv* indistinctly.
turbión [tur'βjon] *nf* downpour; (*fig*) shower, hail.
turbo ['turβo] *adj inv* turbo(-charged) ♦ *nm* (*tb coche*) turbo.
turbulencia [turβu'lenθja] *nf* turbulence; (*fig*) restlessness.
turbulento, a [turβu'lento, a] *adj* turbulent; (*fig: intranquilo*) restless; (: *ruidoso*) noisy.
turco, a ['turko, a] *adj* Turkish ♦ *nm/f* Turk ♦ *nm* (*LING*) Turkish.
Turena [tu'rena] *nf* Touraine.
turgente [tur'xente], **túrgido, a** ['turxiðo, a] *adj* (*hinchado*) turgid, swollen.
Turín [tu'rin] *nm* Turin.
turismo [tu'rismo] *nm* tourism; (*coche*) saloon car; **hacer ~** to go travelling (abroad).
turista [tu'rista] *nm/f* tourist; (*vacacionista*) holidaymaker (*BRIT*), vacationer (*US*).
turístico, a [tu'ristiko, a] *adj* tourist *cpd.*
Turkmenistán [turkmeni'stan] *nm* Turkmenistan.
turnar [tur'nar] *vi*, **turnarse** *vr* to take (it in) turns.
turno ['turno] *nm* (*oportunidad, orden de prioridad*) opportunity; (*DEPORTE etc*) turn; **es su ~** it's his turn (next); **~ de**

día/de noche (*INDUSTRIA*) day/night shift.
turolense [turo'lense] *adj* of *o* from Teruel ♦ *nm/f* native *o* inhabitant of Teruel.
turquesa [tur'kesa] *nf* turquoise.
Turquía [tur'kia] *nf* Turkey.
turrón [tu'rron] *nm* (*dulce*) nougat; (*fam*) sinecure, cushy job *o* number.
tute ['tute] *nm* (*NAIPES*) *card game*; **darse un** ~ to break one's back.
tutear [tute'ar] *vt* to address as familiar "tú"; ~**se** *vr* to be on familiar terms.
tutela [tu'tela] *nf* (*legal*) guardianship; (*instrucción*) guidance; **estar bajo la** ~ **de** (*fig*) to be under the protection of.
tutelar [tute'lar] *adj* tutelary ♦ *vt* to protect.
tutor, a [tu'tor, a] *nm/f* (*legal*) guardian; (*ESCOL*) tutor; ~ **de curso** form master/mistress.
tuve ['tuβe] *etc vb V* **tener**.
tuyo, a ['tujo, a] *adj* yours, of yours ♦ *pron* yours; **los** ~**s** (*fam*) your relations, your family.
TVE *nf abr* = *Televisión Española*.

Uu

U, u [u] *nf* (*letra*) U, u; **viraje en U** U-turn; **U de Ulises** U for Uncle.
u [u] *conj* or.
UAR [war] *nfpl abr* (*ESP*) = *Unidades Antiterroristas Rurales*.
ubérrimo, a [u'βerrimo, a] *adj* very rich, fertile.
ubicación [uβika'θjon] *nf* (*esp AM*) place, position, location.
ubicado, a [uβi'kaðo, a] *adj* (*esp AM*) situated.
ubicar [uβi'kar] *vt* (*esp AM*) to place, situate; (: *fig*) to install in a post; (: *encontrar*) to find; ~**se** *vr* to be situated, be located.
ubicuo, a [u'βikwo, a] *adj* ubiquitous.
ubique [u'βike] *etc vb V* **ubicar**.
ubre ['uβre] *nf* udder.
Ucrania [u'kranja] *nf* Ukraine.
ucraniano, a [ukra'njano, a] *adj, nm/f* Ukrainian ♦ *nm* (*LING*) Ukrainian.
ucranio [u'kranjo] *nm* (*LING*) Ukrainian.
Ud(s) *abr* = **usted(es)**.
UE *nf abr* (= *Unión Europea*) EU.
UEFA *nf abr* (= *Unión de Asociaciones de Fútbol Europeo*) UEFA.
UEO *nf abr* (= *Unión Europea Occidental*) WEU.
UEP *nf abr* = *Unión Europea de Pagos*.
uf [uf] *excl* (*cansancio*) phew!; (*repugnancia*) ugh!
ufanarse [ufa'narse] *vr* to boast; ~ **de** to pride o.s. on.
ufano, a [u'fano, a] *adj* (*arrogante*) arrogant; (*presumido*) conceited.
UGT *nf abr V* **Unión General de Trabajadores**.
ujier [u'xjer] *nm* usher; (*portero*) doorkeeper.
úlcera ['ulθera] *nf* ulcer.
ulcerar [ulθe'rar] *vt* to make sore; ~**se** *vr* to ulcerate.
ulterior [ulte'rjor] *adj* (*más allá*) farther, further; (*subsecuente, siguiente*) subsequent.
ulteriormente [ulterjor'mente] *adv* later, subsequently.
últimamente ['ultimamente] *adv* (*recientemente*) lately, recently; (*finalmente*) finally; (*como último recurso*) as a last resort.
ultimar [ulti'mar] *vt* to finish; (*finalizar*) to finalize; (*AM*: *rematar*) to finish off, murder.
ultimátum [ulti'matum] *nm, pl* **ultimátums** ultimatum.
último, a ['ultimo, a] *adj* last; (*más reciente*) latest, most recent; (*más bajo*) bottom; (*más alto*) top; (*fig*) final, extreme; **en las últimas** on one's last legs; **por** ~ finally.
ultra ['ultra] *adj* ultra ♦ *nm/f* extreme right-winger.
ultracongelar [ultrakonxe'lar] *vt* to deep-freeze.
ultraderecha [ultraðe'retʃa] *nf* extreme right (wing).
ultrajar [ultra'xar] *vt* (*escandalizar*) to outrage; (*insultar*) to insult, abuse.
ultraje [ul'traxe] *nm* outrage; insult.
ultraligero [ultrali'xero] *nm* microlight (*BRIT*), microlite (*US*).
ultramar [ultra'mar] *nm*: **de** *o* **en** ~ abroad, overseas; **los países de** ~ the overseas countries.
ultramarino, a [ultrama'rino, a] *adj* overseas, foreign ♦ *nmpl*: ~**s** groceries; **tienda de** ~**s** grocer's (shop).
ultranza [ul'tranθa]: **a** ~ *adv* to the death; (*a todo trance*) at all costs; (*completo*) outright; (*POL etc*) out-and-out, extreme; **un nacionalista a** ~ a rabid nationalist.
ultrarrojo, a [ultra'rroxo, a] *adj*

= **infrarrojo, a.**
ultrasónico, a [ultra'soniko, a] *adj* ultrasonic.
ultratumba [ultra'tumba] *nf*: **la vida de ~** the next life; **una voz de ~** a ghostly voice.
ultravioleta [ultraßjo'leta] *adj inv* ultraviolet.
ulular [ulu'lar] *vi* to howl; (*búho*) to hoot.
umbilical [umbili'kal] *adj*: **cordón ~** umbilical cord.
umbral [um'bral] *nm* (*gen*) threshold; **~ de rentabilidad** (*COM*) break-even point.
umbrío, a [um'brio, a] *adj* shady.
UME *nf abr* (= *Unión Monetaria y Económica*) EMU.

PALABRA CLAVE

un, una [un, 'una] *art indef* a; (*antes de vocal*) an; **una mujer/naranja** a woman/an orange
♦ *adj* **1**: **unos** (*o* **unas**): **hay unos regalos para ti** there are some presents for you; **hay unas cervezas en la nevera** there are some beers in the fridge
2 (*enfático*): **¡hace un frío!** it's so cold!; **¡tiene una casa!** he's got some house!

U.N.A.M. ['unam] *nf abr* = *Universidad Nacional Autónoma de México*.
unánime [u'nanime] *adj* unanimous.
unanimidad [unanimi'ðað] *nf* unanimity; **por ~** unanimously.
unción [un'θjon] *nf* anointing.
uncir [un'θir] *vt* to yoke.
undécimo, a [un'deθimo, a] *adj, nm/f* eleventh.
UNED [u'ned] *nf abr* (*ESP UNIV*: = *Universidad Nacional de Enseñanza a Distancia*) ≈ Open University (*BRIT*).
ungir [un'xir] *vt* to rub with ointment; (*REL*) to anoint.
ungüento [un'gwento] *nm* ointment; (*fig*) salve, balm.
únicamente ['unikamente] *adv* solely; (*solamente*) only.
unicidad [uniθi'ðað] *nf* uniqueness.
único, a ['uniko, a] *adj* only; (*solo*) sole, single; (*sin par*) unique; **hijo ~** only child.
unidad [uni'ðað] *nf* unity; (*TEC*) unit; **~ móvil** (*TV*) mobile unit; (*INFORM*): **~ central** system unit, central processing unit; **~ de control** control unit; **~ de disco** disk drive; **~ de entrada/salida** input/output device; **~ de información** data item; **~ periférica** peripheral device; **~ de presentación visual** *o* **de visualización** visual display unit; **~ procesadora central** central processing unit.
unido, a [u'niðo, a] *adj* joined, linked; (*fig*) united.
unifamiliar [unifamil'jar] *adj*: **vivienda ~** single-family home.
unificar [unifi'kar] *vt* to unite, unify.
unifique [uni'fike] *etc vb V* **unificar.**
uniformado, a [unifor'maðo, a] *adj* uniformed, in uniform.
uniformar [unifor'mar] *vt* to make uniform; (*TEC*) to standardize.
uniforme [uni'forme] *adj* uniform, equal; (*superficie*) even ♦ *nm* uniform.
uniformidad [uniformi'ðað] *nf* uniformity; (*llaneza*) levelness, evenness.
unilateral [unilate'ral] *adj* unilateral.
unión [u'njon] *nf* (*gen*) union; (*acto*) uniting, joining; (*calidad*) unity; (*TEC*) joint; (*fig*) closeness, togetherness; **en ~ con** (together) with, accompanied by; **~ aduanera** customs union; **U~ General de Trabajadores (UGT)** (*ESP*) *Socialist Union Confederation;* **U~ Europea** European Union; **la U~ Soviética** the Soviet Union; **punto de ~** (*TEC*) junction.
unir [u'nir] *vt* (*juntar*) to join, unite; (*atar*) to tie, fasten; (*combinar*) to combine ♦ *vi* (*ingredientes*) to mix well; **~se** *vr* to join together, unite; (*empresas*) to merge; **les une una fuerte simpatía** they are bound by (a) strong affection; **~se en matrimonio** to marry.
unisex [uni'seks] *adj inv* unisex.
unísono [u'nisono] *nm*: **al ~** in unison.
unitario, a [uni'tarjo, a] *adj* unitary; (*REL*) Unitarian ♦ *nm/f* (*REL*) Unitarian.
universal [unißer'sal] *adj* universal; (*mundial*) world *cpd*; **historia ~** world history.
universidad [unißersi'ðað] *nf* university; **~ laboral** polytechnic, poly.
universitario, a [unißersi'tarjo, a] *adj* university *cpd* ♦ *nm/f* (*profesor*) lecturer; (*estudiante*) (university) student.
universo [uni'ßerso] *nm* universe.
unja ['unxa] *etc vb V* **ungir.**

PALABRA CLAVE

uno, a ['uno, a] *adj* one; **es todo ~** it's all one and the same; **~s pocos** a few; **~s cien** about a hundred
♦ *pron* **1** one; **quiero sólo uno** I only want one; **~ de ellos** one of them; **una de dos** either one or the other; **no doy una hoy** I can't do anything right today
2 (*alguien*) somebody, someone; **conozco a ~ que se te parece** I know somebody *o* someone who looks like you; **~s querían quedarse** some (people) wanted to stay

3 (*impersonal*) one; ~ **mismo** oneself; ~ **nunca sabe qué hacer** one never knows what to do

4: ~**s ... otros ...** some ... others; **una y otra son muy agradables** they're both very nice; **(los) ~(s) a (los) otro(s)** each other, one another

♦ *nf* one; **es la una** it's one o'clock

♦ *num* (number) one; **el día ~** the first.

untar [un'tar] *vt* (*gen*) to rub; (*engrasar*) to grease, oil; (*MED*) to rub (with ointment); (*fig*) to bribe; ~**se** *vr* (*fig*) to be crooked; ~ **el pan con mantequilla** to spread butter on one's bread.

unto ['unto] *nm* animal fat; (*MED*) ointment.

unza ['unθa] *etc vb V* **uncir.**

uña ['uɲa] *nf* (*ANAT*) nail; (*del pie*) toenail; (*garra*) claw; (*casco*) hoof; (*arrancaclavos*) claw; **ser ~ y carne** to be as thick as thieves; **enseñar** *o* **mostrar** *o* **sacar las ~s** to show one's claws.

UOE *nf abr* (*ESP MIL*) = *Unidad de Operaciones Especiales.*

UPA *nf abr* = *Unión Panamericana.*

UPC *nf abr* (= *unidad procesadora central*) CPU.

uperizado, a [uperi'θaðo, a] *adj*: **leche uperizada** UHT milk.

Urales [u'rales] *nmpl* (*tb*: **Montes** ~) Urals.

uralita® [ura'lita] *nf* corrugated asbestos cement.

uranio [u'ranjo] *nm* uranium.

urbanidad [urβani'ðað] *nf* courtesy, politeness.

urbanismo [urβa'nismo] *nm* town planning.

urbanista [urβa'nista] *nm/f* town planner.

urbanización [urβaniθa'θjon] *nf* (*colonia, barrio*) estate, housing scheme.

urbanizar [urβani'θar] *vt* to develop.

urbano, a [ur'βano, a] *adj* (*de ciudad*) urban, town *cpd*; (*cortés*) courteous, polite.

urbe ['urβe] *nf* large city, metropolis.

urdimbre [ur'ðimbre] *nf* (*de tejido*) warp; (*intriga*) intrigue.

urdir [ur'ðir] *vt* to warp; (*fig*) to plot, contrive.

urgencia [ur'xenθja] *nf* urgency; (*prisa*) haste, rush; **salida de ~** emergency exit; **servicios de ~** emergency services.

urgente [ur'xente] *adj* urgent; (*insistente*) insistent; **carta ~** registered (*BRIT*) *o* special delivery (*US*) letter.

urgir [ur'xir] *vi* to be urgent; **me urge** I'm in a hurry for it; **me urge terminarlo** I must finish it as soon as I can.

urinario, a [uri'narjo, a] *adj* urinary ♦ *nm* urinal, public lavatory, comfort station (*US*).

urja ['urxa] *etc vb V* **urgir.**

urna ['urna] *nf* urn; (*POL*) ballot box; **acudir a las ~s** (*fig*: *persona*) to (go and) vote; (: *gobierno*) to go to the country.

urología [urolo'xia] *nf* urology.

urólogo, a [u'roloɣo, a] *nm/f* urologist.

urraca [u'rraka] *nf* magpie.

URSS *nf abr* (= *Unión de Repúblicas Socialistas Soviéticas*) USSR.

Uruguay [uru'ɣwai] *nm*: **El ~** Uruguay.

uruguayo, a [uru'ɣwajo, a] *adj, nm/f* Uruguayan.

usado, a [u'saðo, a] *adj* (*gen*) used; (*ropa etc*) worn; **muy ~** worn out.

usanza [u'sanθa] *nf* custom, usage.

usar [u'sar] *vt* to use; (*ropa*) to wear; (*tener costumbre*) to be in the habit of ♦ *vi*: ~ **de** to make use of; ~**se** *vr* to be used; (*ropa*) to be worn *o* in fashion.

USO *nf abr* (*ESP*: = *Unión Sindical Obrera*) workers' union.

uso ['uso] *nm* use; (*MECÁNICA etc*) wear; (*costumbre*) usage, custom; (*moda*) fashion; **al ~** in keeping with custom; **al ~ de** in the style of; **de ~ externo** (*MED*) for external application; **estar en el ~ de la palabra** to be speaking, have the floor; **~ y desgaste** (*COM*) wear and tear.

usted [us'teð] *pron* (*sg*: *abr* **Ud** *o* **Vd**: *formal*) you *sg*; ~**es** (*pl*: *abr* **Uds** *o* **Vds**: *formal*) you *pl*; (*AM*: *formal y fam*) you *pl.*

usual [u'swal] *adj* usual.

usuario, a [usw'arjo, a] *nm/f* user; ~ **final** (*COM*) end user.

usufructo [usu'frukto] *nm* use; ~ **vitalicio (de)** life interest (in).

usura [u'sura] *nf* usury.

usurero, a [usu'rero, a] *nm/f* usurer.

usurpar [usur'par] *vt* to usurp.

utensilio [uten'siljo] *nm* tool; (*CULIN*) utensil.

útero ['utero] *nm* uterus, womb.

útil ['util] *adj* useful; (*servible*) usable, serviceable ♦ *nm* tool; **día ~** working day, weekday; **es muy ~ tenerlo aquí cerca** it's very handy having it here close by.

utilice [uti'liθe] *etc vb V* **utilizar.**

utilidad [utili'ðað] *nf* usefulness, utility; (*COM*) profit; ~**es líquidas** net profit *sg.*

utilitario [utili'tarjo] *nm* (*INFORM*) utility.

utilizar [utili'θar] *vt* to use, utilize; (*explotar*) to harness.

utopía [uto'pia] *nf* Utopia.

utópico, a [u'topiko, a] *adj* Utopian.
uva ['ußa] *nf* grape; ~ **pasa** raisin; ~ **de Corinto** currant; **estar de mala** ~ to be in a bad mood; **las (doce)** ~**s** *see boxed note.*

LAS UVAS

Las uvas *play an important part in the New Years' Eve ("Nochevieja") celebrations; on the stroke of midnight people from every part of Spain, at home, in restaurants or in the "plaza mayor", eat a grape for each stroke of the clock at the Puerta del Sol in Madrid. It is said to bring luck for the coming year.*

uve ['uße] *nf name of the letter V*; **en forma de** ~ V-shaped; ~ **doble** *name of the letter W.*
UVI ['ußi] *nf abr* (*ESP MED*: = *unidad de vigilancia intensiva*) ICU.

V v

V, v [(*ESP*) 'uße, (*AM*) be'lkorta, betʃika] *nf* (*letra*) V, v; **V de Valencia** V for Victor.
V. *abr* (= *visto*) approved, passed.
v. *abr* (= *voltio*) v.; (= *véase*) v.; (= *verso*) v.
va [ba] *vb V* **ir.**
V.A. *abr* = *Vuestra Alteza.*
vaca ['baka] *nf* (*animal*) cow; (*carne*) beef; (*cuero*) cowhide; ~**s flacas/gordas** (*fig*) bad/good times.
vacaciones [baka'θjones] *nfpl* holiday(s); **estar/irse** *o* **marcharse de** ~ to be/go (away) on holiday.
vacante [ba'kante] *adj* vacant, empty ♦ *nf* vacancy.
vaciado, a [ba'θjaðo, a] *adj* (*hecho en molde*) cast in a mould; (*hueco*) hollow ♦ *nm* cast, mould(ing).
vaciar [ba'θjar] *vt* to empty (out); (*ahuecar*) to hollow out; (*moldear*) to cast; (*INFORM*) to dump ♦ *vi* (*río*) to flow (*en* into); ~**se** *vr* to empty; (*fig*) to blab, spill the beans.
vaciedad [baθje'ðað] *nf* emptiness.
vacilación [baθila'θjon] *nf* hesitation.
vacilante [baθi'lante] *adj* unsteady; (*habla*) faltering; (*luz*) flickering; (*fig*) hesitant.
vacilar [baθi'lar] *vi* to be unsteady; to falter; to flicker; to hesitate, waver; (*persona*) to stagger, stumble; (*memoria*) to fail; (*esp AM*: *divertirse*) to have a great time.
vacilón [baθi'lon] *nm* (*esp AM*): **estar** *o* **ir de** ~ to have a great time.
vacío, a [ba'θio, a] *adj* empty; (*puesto*) vacant; (*desocupado*) idle; (*vano*) vain; (*charla etc*) light, superficial ♦ *nm* emptiness; (*FÍSICA*) vacuum; (*un* ~) (empty) space; **hacer el** ~ **a algn** to send sb to Coventry.
vacuna [ba'kuna] *nf* vaccine.
vacunar [baku'nar] *vt* to vaccinate; ~**se** *vr* to get vaccinated.
vacuno, a [ba'kuno, a] *adj* bovine.
vacuo, a ['bakwo, a] *adj* empty.
vadear [baðe'ar] *vt* (*río*) to ford; (*problema*) to overcome; (*persona*) to sound out.
vado ['baðo] *nm* ford; (*solución*) solution; (*descanso*) respite.
vagabundo, a [baɣa'ßundo, a] *adj* wandering; (*pey*) vagrant ♦ *nm/f* (*errante*) wanderer; (*vago*) tramp, bum (*US*).
vagamente [baɣa'mente] *adv* vaguely.
vagancia [ba'ɣanθja] *nf* vagrancy.
vagar [ba'ɣar] *vi* to wander; (*pasear*) to saunter up and down; (*no hacer nada*) to idle ♦ *nm* leisure.
vagido [ba'xiðo] *nm* wail.
vagina [ba'xina] *nf* vagina.
vago, a ['baɣo, a] *adj* vague; (*perezoso*) lazy; (*ambulante*) wandering ♦ *nm/f* (*vagabundo*) tramp, bum (*US*); (*flojo*) lazybones *sg*, idler.
vagón [ba'ɣon] *nm* (*de pasajeros*) carriage; (*de mercancías*) wagon; ~ **cama/restaurante** sleeping/dining car.
vague ['baɣe] *etc vb V* **vagar.**
vaguear [baɣe'ar] *vi* to laze around.
vaguedad [baɣe'ðað] *nf* vagueness.
vahído [ba'iðo] *nm* dizzy spell.
vaho ['bao] *nm* (*vapor*) vapour, steam; (*olor*) smell; (*respiración*) breath; ~**s** *nmpl* (*MED*) inhalation *sg.*
vaina ['baina] *nf* sheath ♦ *nm* (*AM*) nuisance.
vainilla [bai'niʎa] *nf* vanilla.
vainita [bai'nita] *nf* (*AM*) green *o* French bean.
vais [bais] *vb V* **ir.**
vaivén [bai'ßen] *nm* to-and-fro movement; (*de tránsito*) coming and going; **vaivenes** *nmpl* (*fig*) ups and downs.
vajilla [ba'xiʎa] *nf* crockery, dishes *pl*; (*una* ~) service; ~ **de porcelana** chinaware.
val [bal], **valdré** [bal'dre] *etc vb V* **valer.**
vale ['bale] *nm* voucher; (*recibo*) receipt; (*pagaré*) I.O.U.; ~ **de regalo** gift voucher

o token.
valedero, a [bale'ðero, a] *adj* valid.
valenciano, a [balen'θjano, a] *adj, nm/f* Valencian ♦ *nm* (*LING*) Valencian.
valentía [balen'tia] *nf* courage, bravery; (*pey*) boastfulness; (*acción*) heroic deed.
valentísimo, a [balen'tisimo, a] *adj* (*superl de* **valiente**) very brave, courageous.
valentón, ona [balen'ton, ona] *adj* blustering.
valer [ba'ler] *vt* to be worth; (*MAT*) to equal; (*costar*) to cost; (*amparar*) to aid, protect ♦ *vi* (*ser útil*) to be useful; (*ser válido*) to be valid; **~se** *vr* to defend o.s. ♦ *nm* worth, value; **~ la pena** to be worthwhile; **¿vale?** O.K.?; **¡vale!** (*¡basta!*) that'll do!; **¡eso no vale!** that doesn't count!; **no vale nada** it's no good; (*mercancía*) it's worthless; (*argumento*) it's no use; **no vale para nada** he's no good at all; **más vale tarde que nunca** better late than never; **más vale que nos vayamos** we'd better go; **~se de** to make use of, take advantage of; **~se por sí mismo** to help *o* manage by o.s.
valga ['balɤa] *etc vb V* **valer**.
valía [ba'lia] *nf* worth; **de gran ~** (*objeto*) very valuable.
validar [bali'ðar] *vt* to validate; (*POL*) to ratify.
validez [bali'ðeθ] *nf* validity; **dar ~ a** to validate.
válido, a ['baliðo, a] *adj* valid.
valiente [ba'ljente] *adj* brave, valiant; (*audaz*) bold; (*pey*) boastful; (*con ironía*) fine, wonderful ♦ *nm/f* brave man/woman.
valija [ba'lixa] *nf* case; (*AM*) suitcase; (*mochila*) satchel; (*CORREOS*) mailbag; **~ diplomática** diplomatic bag.
valioso, a [ba'ljoso, a] *adj* valuable; (*rico*) wealthy.
valla ['baʎa] *nf* fence; (*DEPORTE*) hurdle; (*fig*) barrier; **~ publicitaria** billboard.
vallar [ba'ʎar] *vt* to fence in.
valle ['baʎe] *nm* valley, vale.
vallisoletano, a [baʎisole'tano, a] *adj* of *o* from Valladolid ♦ *nm/f* native *o* inhabitant of Valladolid.
valor [ba'lor] *nm* value, worth; (*precio*) price; (*valentía*) valour, courage; (*importancia*) importance; (*cara*) nerve, cheek (*fam*); **sin ~** worthless; **~ adquisitivo** *o* **de compra** purchasing power; **dar ~ a** to attach importance to; **quitar ~ a** to minimize the importance of; (*COM*): **~ según balance** book value; **~ comercial** *o* **de mercado** market value; **~ contable/desglosado** asset/break-up value; **~ de escasez** scarcity value; **~ intrínseco** intrinsic value; **~ a la par** par value; **~ neto** net worth; **~ de rescate/de sustitución** surrender/replacement value; *V tb* **valores**.
valoración [balora'θjon] *nf* valuation.
valorar [balo'rar] *vt* to value; (*tasar*) to price; (*fig*) to assess.
valores [ba'lores] *nmpl* (*COM*) securities; **~ en cartera** *o* **habidos** investments.
vals [bals] *nm* waltz.
válvula ['balßula] *nf* valve.
vamos ['bamos] *vb V* **ir**.
vampiro, iresa [bam'piro, i'resa] *nm/f* vampire ♦ *nf* (*CINE*) vamp, femme fatale.
van [ban] *vb V* **ir**.
vanagloriarse [banaɤlo'rjarse] *vr* to boast.
vandalismo [banda'lismo] *nm* vandalism.
vándalo, a ['bandalo, a] *nm/f* vandal.
vanguardia [ban'gwardja] *nf* vanguard; **de ~** (*ARTE*) avant-garde; **estar en** *o* **ir a la ~ de** (*fig*) to be in the forefront of.
vanguardista [bangwar'ðista] *adj* avant-garde.
vanidad [bani'ðað] *nf* vanity; (*inutilidad*) futility; (*irrealidad*) unreality.
vanidoso, a [bani'ðoso, a] *adj* vain, conceited.
vano, a ['bano, a] *adj* (*irreal*) unreal; (*irracional*) unreasonable; (*inútil*) vain, useless; (*persona*) vain, conceited; (*frívolo*) frivolous.
vapor [ba'por] *nm* vapour; (*vaho*) steam; (*de gas*) fumes *pl*; (*neblina*) mist; **~es** *nmpl* (*MED*) hysterics; **al ~** (*CULIN*) steamed.
vaporice [bapo'riθe] *etc vb V* **vaporizar**.
vaporizador [baporiθa'ðor] *nm* (*perfume etc*) spray.
vaporizar [bapori'θar] *vt* to vaporize; (*perfume*) to spray.
vaporoso, a [bapo'roso, a] *adj* vaporous; (*vahoso*) steamy; (*tela*) light, airy.
vapulear [bapule'ar] *vt* to thrash; (*fig*) to slate.
vaque ['bake] *etc vb V* **vacar**.
vaquería [bake'ria] *nf* dairy.
vaquero, a [ba'kero, a] *adj* cattle *cpd* ♦ *nm* cowboy; **~s** *nmpl* jeans.
vaquilla [ba'kiʎa] *nf* heifer.
vara ['bara] *nf* stick, pole; (*TEC*) rod; **~ mágica** magic wand.
varado, a [ba'raðo, a] *adj* (*NAUT*) stranded; **estar ~** to be aground.
varar [ba'rar] *vt* to beach ♦ *vi*, **~se** *vr* to be beached.
varear [bare'ar] *vt* to hit, beat; (*frutas*) to

knock down (with poles).
variable [ba'rjaβle] *adj, nf* variable (*tb INFORM*).
variación [barja'θjon] *nf* variation; **sin ~** unchanged.
variado, a [ba'rjaðo, a] *adj* varied; (*dulces, galletas*) assorted; **entremeses ~s** a selection of starters.
variante [ba'rjante] *adj* variant ♦ *nf* (*alternativa*) alternative; (*AUTO*) bypass.
variar [ba'rjar] *vt* (*cambiar*) to change; (*poner variedad*) to vary; (*modificar*) to modify; (*cambiar de posición*) to switch around ♦ *vi* to vary; **~ de** to differ from; **~ de opinión** to change one's mind; **para ~** just for a change.
varicela [bari'θela] *nf* chicken pox.
varices [ba'riθes] *nfpl* varicose veins.
variedad [barje'ðað] *nf* variety.
varilla [ba'riʎa] *nf* stick; (*BOT*) twig; (*TEC*) rod; (*de rueda*) spoke; **~ mágica** magic wand.
vario, a ['barjo, a] *adj* (*variado*) varied; (*multicolor*) motley; (*cambiable*) changeable; **~s** various, several.
variopinto, a [barjo'pinto, a] *adj* diverse; **un público ~** a mixed audience.
varita [ba'rita] *nf*: **~ mágica** magic wand.
varón [ba'ron] *nm* male, man.
varonil [baro'nil] *adj* manly.
Varsovia [bar'soβja] *nf* Warsaw.
vas [bas] *vb V* **ir.**
vasco, a ['basko, a], **vascongado, a** [baskon'gaðo, a] *adj, nm/f* Basque ♦ *nm* (*LING*) Basque ♦ *nfpl*: **las Vascongadas** the Basque Country *sg o* Provinces.
vascuence [bas'kwenθe] *nm* (*LING*) Basque.
vasectomía [basekto'mia] *nf* vasectomy.
vaselina [base'lina] *nf* Vaseline ®.
vasija [ba'sixa] *nf* (earthenware) vessel.
vaso ['baso] *nm* glass, tumbler; (*ANAT*) vessel; (*cantidad*) glass(ful); **~ de vino** glass of wine; **~ para vino** wineglass.
vástago ['bastaɣo] *nm* (*BOT*) shoot; (*TEC*) rod; (*fig*) offspring.
vasto, a ['basto, a] *adj* vast, huge.
váter ['bater] *nm* lavatory, W.C.
Vaticano [bati'kano] *nm*: **el ~** the Vatican; **la Ciudad del ~** the Vatican City.
vaticinar [batiθi'nar] *vt* to prophesy, predict.
vaticinio [bati'θinjo] *nm* prophecy.
vatio ['batjo] *nm* (*ELEC*) watt.
vaya ['baja] *etc vb V* **ir.**
Vda. *abr* = **viuda.**
Vd(s) *abr* = **usted(es).**
ve [be] *vb V* **ir, ver.**
vea ['bea] *etc vb V* **ver.**
vecinal [beθi'nal] *adj* (*camino, impuesto etc*) local.
vecindad [beθin'dað] *nf*, **vecindario** [beθin'darjo] *nm* neighbourhood; (*habitantes*) residents *pl*.
vecino, a [be'θino, a] *adj* neighbouring ♦ *nm/f* neighbour; (*residente*) resident; **somos ~s** we live next door to one another.
vector [bek'tor] *nm* vector.
veda ['beða] *nf* prohibition; (*temporada*) close season.
vedado [be'ðaðo] *nm* preserve.
vedar [be'ðar] *vt* (*prohibir*) to ban, prohibit; (*idea, plan*) to veto; (*impedir*) to stop, prevent.
vedette [be'ðet] *nf* (*TEAT, CINE*) star(let).
vega ['beɣa] *nf* fertile plain *o* valley.
vegetación [bexeta'θjon] *nf* vegetation.
vegetal [bexe'tal] *adj, nm* vegetable.
vegetar [bexe'tar] *vi* to vegetate.
vegetariano, a [bexeta'rjano, a] *adj, nm/f* vegetarian.
vegetativo, a [bexeta'tiβo, a] *adj* vegetative.
vehemencia [bee'menθja] *nf* (*insistencia*) vehemence; (*pasión*) passion; (*fervor*) fervour; (*violencia*) violence.
vehemente [bee'mente] *adj* vehement; passionate; fervent; violent.
vehículo [be'ikulo] *nm* vehicle; (*MED*) carrier; **~ de servicio público** public service vehicle; **~ espacial** spacecraft.
veinte ['beinte] *num* twenty; (*orden, fecha*) twentieth; **el siglo ~** the twentieth century.
veintena [bein'tena] *nf*: **una ~** (about) twenty, a score.
vejación [bexa'θjon] *nf* vexation; (*humillación*) humiliation.
vejamen [be'xamen] *nm* satire.
vejar [be'xar] *vt* (*irritar*) to annoy, vex; (*humillar*) to humiliate.
vejatorio, a [bexa'torjo, a] *adj* humiliating, degrading.
vejez [be'xeθ] *nf* old age.
vejiga [be'xiɣa] *nf* (*ANAT*) bladder.
vela ['bela] *nf* (*de cera*) candle; (*NAUT*) sail; (*insomnio*) sleeplessness; (*vigilia*) vigil; (*MIL*) sentry duty; (*fam*) snot; **a toda ~** (*NAUT*) under full sail; **estar a dos ~s** (*fam*) to be skint; **pasar la noche en ~** to have a sleepless night.
velado, a [be'laðo, a] *adj* veiled; (*sonido*) muffled; (*FOTO*) blurred ♦ *nf* soirée.
velador [bela'ðor] *nm* watchman; (*candelero*) candlestick; (*AM*) bedside table.

velar [be'lar] *vt* (*vigilar*) to keep watch over; (*cubrir*) to veil ♦ *vi* to stay awake; ~ **por** to watch over, look after.
velatorio [bela'torjo] *nm* (funeral) wake.
veleidad [belei'ðað] *nf* (*ligereza*) fickleness; (*capricho*) whim.
velero [be'lero] *nm* (*NAUT*) sailing ship; (*AVIAT*) glider.
veleta [be'leta] *nm/f* fickle person ♦ *nf* weather vane.
veliz [be'lis] *nm* (*AM*) suitcase.
vello ['beʎo] *nm* down, fuzz.
vellón [be'ʎon] *nm* fleece.
velloso, a [be'ʎoso, a] *adj* fuzzy.
velludo, a [be'ʎuðo, a] *adj* shaggy ♦ *nm* plush, velvet.
velo ['belo] *nm* veil; ~ **de paladar** (*ANAT*) soft palate.
velocidad [beloθi'ðað] *nf* speed; (*TEC*) rate, pace, velocity; (*MECÁNICA, AUTO*) gear; **¿a qué ~?** how fast?; **de alta ~** high-speed; **cobrar ~** to pick up *o* gather speed; **meter la segunda ~** to change into second gear; ~ **máxima de impresión** (*INFORM*) maximum print speed.
velocímetro [belo'θimetro] *nm* speedometer.
velódromo [be'loðromo] *nm* cycle track.
veloz [be'loθ] *adj* fast, swift.
ven [ben] *vb V* **venir**.
vena ['bena] *nf* vein; (*fig*) vein, disposition; (*GEO*) seam, vein.
venablo [be'naßlo] *nm* javelin.
venado [be'naðo] *nm* deer; (*CULIN*) venison.
venal [be'nal] *adj* (*ANAT*) venous; (*pey*) venal.
venalidad [benali'ðað] *nf* venality.
vencedor, a [benθe'ðor, a] *adj* victorious ♦ *nm/f* victor, winner.
vencer [ben'θer] *vt* (*dominar*) to defeat, beat; (*derrotar*) to vanquish; (*superar, controlar*) to overcome, master ♦ *vi* (*triunfar*) to win (through), triumph; (*pago*) to fall due; (*plazo*) to expire; **dejarse ~** to yield, give in.
vencido, a [ben'θiðo, a] *adj* (*derrotado*) defeated, beaten; (*COM*) payable, due ♦ *adv*: **pagar ~** to pay in arrears; **le pagan por meses ~s** he is paid at the end of the month; **darse por ~** to give up.
vencimiento [benθi'mjento] *nm* collapse; (*COM: plazo*) expiration; **a su ~** when it falls due.
venda ['benda] *nf* bandage.
vendaje [ben'daxe] *nm* bandage, dressing.
vendar [ben'dar] *vt* to bandage; ~ **los ojos** to blindfold.
vendaval [benda'ßal] *nm* (*viento*) gale; (*huracán*) hurricane.
vendedor, a [bende'ðor, a] *nm/f* seller; ~ **ambulante** hawker, pedlar (*BRIT*), peddler (*US*).
vender [ben'der] *vt* to sell; (*comerciar*) to market; (*traicionar*) to sell out, betray; **~se** *vr* to be sold; ~ **al contado/al por mayor/al por menor/a plazos** to sell for cash/wholesale/retail/on credit; **"se vende"** "for sale"; **"véndese coche"** "car for sale"; ~ **al descubierto** to sell short.
vendimia [ben'dimja] *nf* grape harvest; **la ~ de 1973** the 1973 vintage.
vendimiar [bendi'mjar] *vi* to pick grapes.
vendré [ben'dre] *etc vb V* **venir**.
Venecia [be'neθja] *nf* Venice.
veneciano, a [bene'θjano, a] *adj, nm/f* Venetian.
veneno [be'neno] *nm* poison, venom.
venenoso, a [bene'noso, a] *adj* poisonous.
venerable [bene'raßle] *adj* venerable.
veneración [benera'θjon] *nf* veneration.
venerar [bene'rar] *vt* (*reconocer*) to venerate; (*adorar*) to worship.
venéreo, a [be'nereo, a] *adj* venereal.
venezolano, a [beneθo'lano, a] *adj, nm/f* Venezuelan.
Venezuela [bene'θwela] *nf* Venezuela.
venga ['benga] *etc vb V* **venir**.
vengador, a [benga'ðor, a] *adj* avenging ♦ *nm/f* avenger.
venganza [ben'ganθa] *nf* vengeance, revenge.
vengar [ben'gar] *vt* to avenge; **~se** *vr* to take revenge.
vengativo, a [benga'tißo, a] *adj* (*persona*) vindictive.
vengue ['benge] *etc vb V* **vengar**.
venia ['benja] *nf* (*perdón*) pardon; (*permiso*) consent; **con su ~** by your leave.
venial [be'njal] *adj* venial.
venida [be'niða] *nf* (*llegada*) arrival; (*regreso*) return; (*fig*) rashness.
venidero, a [beni'ðero, a] *adj* coming, future; **en lo ~** in (the) future.
venir [be'nir] *vi* to come; (*llegar*) to arrive; (*ocurrir*) to happen; **~se** *vr*: **~se abajo** to collapse; ~ **a menos** (*persona*) to lose status; (*empresa*) to go downhill; ~ **bien** to be suitable, come just right; (*ropa, gusto*) to suit; ~ **mal** to be unsuitable *o* inconvenient, come awkwardly; **el año que viene** next year; **¡ven acá!** come (over) here!; **¡venga!** (*fam*) come on!
venta ['benta] *nf* (*COM*) sale; (*posada*) inn; ~ **a plazos** hire purchase; ~ **al contado/**

al por mayor/al por menor *o* **al detalle** cash sale/wholesale/retail; ~ **a domicilio** door-to-door selling; ~ **y arrendamiento al vendedor** sale and lease back; ~ **de liquidación** clearance sale; **estar de** *o* **en** ~ to be (up) for sale *o* on the market; ~**s brutas** gross sales; ~**s a término** forward sales.

ventaja [ben'taxa] *nf* advantage; **llevar la** ~ (*en carrera*) to be leading *o* ahead.

ventajoso, a [benta'xoso, a] *adj* advantageous.

ventana [ben'tana] *nf* window; ~ **de guillotina/galería** sash/bay window; ~ **de la nariz** nostril.

ventanilla [venta'niʎa] *nf* (*de taquilla, tb* INFORM) window.

ventearse [bente'arse] *vr* (*romperse*) to crack; (ANAT) to break wind.

ventilación [bentila'θjon] *nf* ventilation; (*corriente*) draught; (*fig*) airing.

ventilador [bentila'ðor] *nm* ventilator; (*eléctrico*) fan.

ventilar [benti'lar] *vt* to ventilate; (*a secar*) to put out to dry; (*fig*) to air, discuss.

ventisca [ben'tiska] *nf* blizzard.

ventisquero [bentis'kero] *nm* snowdrift.

ventolera [bento'lera] *nf* (*ráfaga*) gust of wind; (*idea*) whim, wild idea; **le dio la** ~ **de comprarlo** he had a sudden notion to buy it.

ventosear [bentose'ar] *vi* to break wind.

ventosidad [bentosi'ðað] *nf* flatulence.

ventoso, a [ben'toso, a] *adj* windy ♦ *nf* (ZOOL) sucker; (*instrumento*) suction pad.

ventrículo [ben'trikulo] *nm* ventricle.

ventrílocuo, a [ben'trilokwo, a] *nm/f* ventriloquist.

ventriloquia [bentri'lokja] *nf* ventriloquism.

ventura [ben'tura] *nf* (*felicidad*) happiness; (*buena suerte*) luck; (*destino*) fortune; **a la (buena)** ~ at random.

venturoso, a [bentu'roso, a] *adj* happy; (*afortunado*) lucky, fortunate.

venza ['benθa] *etc vb V* **vencer.**

ver [ber] *vt, vi* to see; (*mirar*) to look at, watch; (*investigar*) to look into; (*entender*) to see, understand; ~**se** *vr* (*encontrarse*) to meet; (*dejarse* ~) to be seen; (*hallarse: en un apuro*) to find o.s., be ♦ *nm* looks *pl*, appearance; **a** ~ let's see; **a** ~ **si** ... I wonder if ...; **por lo que veo** apparently; **dejarse** ~ to become apparent; **no tener nada que** ~ **con** to have nothing to do with; **a mi modo de** ~ as I see it; **merece** ~**se** it's worth seeing; **no lo veo** I can't see it; **¡nos vemos!** see you (later)!; **¡habráse visto!** did you ever! (*fam*); **¡viera(n)** *o* **hubiera(n) visto qué casa!** (*AM fam*) if only you'd seen the house!, what a house!; **ya se ve que** ... it is obvious that ...; **si te vi no me acuerdo** they *etc* just don't want to know.

vera ['bera] *nf* edge, verge; (*de río*) bank; **a la** ~ **de** near, next to.

veracidad [beraθi'ðað] *nf* truthfulness.

veraneante [berane'ante] *nm/f* holidaymaker, (summer) vacationer (US).

veranear [berane'ar] *vi* to spend the summer.

veraneo [bera'neo] *nm*: **estar de** ~ to be away on (one's summer) holiday; **lugar de** ~ holiday resort.

veraniego, a [bera'njeɣo, a] *adj* summer *cpd*.

verano [be'rano] *nm* summer.

veras ['beras] *nfpl* truth *sg*; **de** ~ really, truly; **esto va de** ~ this is serious.

veraz [be'raθ] *adj* truthful.

verbal [ber'ßal] *adj* verbal; (*mensaje etc*) oral.

verbena [ber'ßena] *nf* street party.

verbigracia [berßi'ɣraθja] *adv* for example.

verbo ['berßo] *nm* verb.

verborrea [berßo'rrea] *nf* verbosity, verbal diarrhoea.

verboso, a [ber'ßoso, a] *adj* verbose.

verdad [ber'ðað] *nf* (*lo verídico*) truth; (*fiabilidad*) reliability ♦ *adv* really; **¿**~**?, ¿no es** ~**?** isn't it?, aren't you?, don't you? *etc*; **de** ~ *adj* real, proper; **a decir** ~**, no quiero** to tell (you) the truth, I don't want to; **la pura** ~ the plain truth.

verdaderamente [berðaðera'mente] *adv* really, indeed, truly.

verdadero, a [berða'ðero, a] *adj* (*veraz*) true, truthful; (*fiable*) reliable; (*fig*) real.

verde ['berðe] *adj* green; (*fruta etc*) green, unripe; (*chiste etc*) blue, smutty, dirty ♦ *nm* green; **viejo** ~ dirty old man; **poner** ~ **a algn** to give sb a dressing-down.

verdear [berðe'ar], **verdecer** [berðe'θer] *vi* to turn green.

verdezca [ber'ðeθka] *etc vb V* **verdecer.**

verdor [ber'ðor] *nm* (*lo verde*) greenness; (BOT) verdure; (*fig*) youthful vigour.

verdugo [ber'ðuɣo] *nm* executioner; (BOT) shoot; (*cardenal*) weal.

verdulero, a [berðu'lero, a] *nm/f* greengrocer.

verdura [ber'ðura] *nf* greenness; ~**s** *nfpl* (CULIN) greens.

vereda [be'reða] *nf* path; (AM) pavement, sidewalk (US); **meter a algn en** ~ to

bring sb into line.
veredicto [bere'ðikto] *nm* verdict.
vergel [ber'xel] *nm* lush garden.
vergonzoso, a [berɣon'θoso, a] *adj* shameful; (*tímido*) timid, bashful.
vergüenza [ber'ɣwenθa] *nf* shame, sense of shame; (*timidez*) bashfulness; (*pudor*) modesty; **tener ~** to be ashamed; **me da ~ decírselo** I feel too shy *o* it embarrasses me to tell him; **¡qué ~!** (*de situación*) what a disgrace!; (*a persona*) shame on you!
vericueto [beri'kweto] *nm* rough track.
verídico, a [be'riðiko, a] *adj* true, truthful.
verificar [berifi'kar] *vt* to check; (*corroborar*) to verify (*tb INFORM*); (*testamento*) to prove; (*llevar a cabo*) to carry out; **~se** *vr* to occur, happen; (*mitin etc*) to be held; (*profecía etc*) to come *o* prove true.
verifique [beri'fike] *etc vb V* **verificar**.
verja ['berxa] *nf* iron gate; (*cerca*) railing(s) (*pl*); (*rejado*) grating.
vermut [ber'mu], *pl* **vermuts** *nm* vermouth ♦ *nf* (*esp AM*) matinée.
verosímil [bero'simil] *adj* likely, probable; (*relato*) credible.
verosimilitud [berosimili'tuð] *nf* likeliness, probability.
verruga [be'rruɣa] *nf* wart.
versado, a [ber'saðo, a] *adj*: **~ en** versed in.
Versalles [ber'saʎes] *nm* Versailles.
versar [ber'sar] *vi* to go round, turn; **~ sobre** to deal with, be about.
versátil [ber'satil] *adj* versatile.
versículo [ber'sikulo] *nm* (*REL*) verse.
versión [ber'sjon] *nf* version; (*traducción*) translation.
verso ['berso] *nm* (*gen*) verse; **un ~** a line of poetry; **~ libre/suelto** free/blank verse.
vértebra ['berteßra] *nf* vertebra.
vertebrado, a [berte'ßraðo, a] *adj, nm/f* vertebrate.
vertebral [berte'ßral] *adj* vertebral; **columna ~** spine.
vertedero [berte'ðero] *nm* rubbish dump, tip.
verter [ber'ter] *vt* (*vaciar*) to empty, pour (out); (*tirar*) to dump ♦ *vi* to flow.
vertical [berti'kal] *adj* vertical; (*postura, piano etc*) upright ♦ *nf* vertical.
vértice ['bertiθe] *nm* vertex, apex.
vertiente [ber'tjente] *nf* slope.
vertiginoso, a [bertixi'noso, a] *adj* giddy, dizzy.
vértigo ['bertiɣo] *nm* vertigo; (*mareo*) dizziness; (*actividad*) intense activity; **de ~** (*fam: velocidad*) giddy; (*: ruido*) tremendous; (*: talento*) fantastic.
vesícula [be'sikula] *nf* blister; **~ biliar** gall bladder.
vespa ® ['bespa] *nf* (motor) scooter.
vespertino, a [besper'tino, a] *adj* evening *cpd*.
vespino ® [bes'pino] *nm o f* ≈ moped.
vestíbulo [bes'tißulo] *nm* hall; (*de teatro*) foyer.
vestido [bes'tiðo] *nm* (*ropa*) clothes *pl*, clothing; (*de mujer*) dress, frock.
vestigio [bes'tixjo] *nm* (*trazo*) trace; (*señal*) sign; **~s** *nmpl* remains.
vestimenta [besti'menta] *nf* clothing.
vestir [bes'tir] *vt* (*poner: ropa*) to put on; (*llevar: ropa*) to wear; (*cubrir*) to clothe, cover; (*pagar: la ropa*) to clothe, pay for the clothing of; (*sastre*) to make clothes for ♦ *vi* (*ponerse: ropa*) to dress; (*verse bien*) to look good; **~se** *vr* to get dressed, dress o.s.; **traje de ~** (*formal*) formal suit; **estar vestido de** to be dressed *o* clad in; (*como disfraz*) to be dressed as.
vestuario [bes'twarjo] *nm* clothes *pl*, wardrobe; (*TEAT: para actores*) dressing room; (*: para público*) cloakroom; (*DEPORTE*) changing room.
Vesubio [be'sußjo] *nm* Vesuvius.
veta ['beta] *nf* (*vena*) vein, seam; (*raya*) streak; (*de madera*) grain.
vetar [be'tar] *vt* to veto.
veterano, a [bete'rano, a] *adj, nm/f* veteran.
veterinario, a [beteri'narjo, a] *nm/f* vet(erinary surgeon) ♦ *nf* veterinary science.
veto ['beto] *nm* veto.
vetusto, a [be'tusto, a] *adj* ancient.
vez [beθ] *nf* time; (*turno*) turn; **a la ~ que** at the same time as; **a su ~** in its turn; **cada ~ más/menos** more and more/less and less; **una ~** once; **dos veces** twice; **de una ~** in one go; **de una ~ para siempre** once and for all; **en ~ de** instead of; **a veces** sometimes; **otra ~** again; **una y otra ~** repeatedly; **pocas veces** seldom; **de ~ en cuando** from time to time; **7 veces 9** 7 times 9; **hacer las veces de** to stand in for; **tal ~** perhaps; **¿lo viste alguna ~?** did you ever see it?; **¿cuántas veces?** how often?; **érase una ~** once upon a time (there was).
v. g., v. gr. *abr* (= *verbigracia*) viz.
vía ['bia] *nf* (*calle*) road; (*ruta*) track, route; (*FERRO*) line; (*fig*) way; (*ANAT*) passage, tube ♦ *prep* via, by way of; **por ~ bucal** orally; **por ~ judicial** by legal means; **por**

~ **oficial** through official channels; **por ~ de** by way of; **en ~s de** in the process of; **un país en ~s de desarrollo** a developing country; ~ **aérea** airway; **V~ Láctea** Milky Way; ~ **pública** public highway *o* thoroughfare; ~ **única** one-way street; **el tren está en la ~ 8** the train is (standing) at platform 8.
viable ['bjaβle] *adj* (*COM*) viable; (*plan etc*) feasible.
viaducto [bja'ðukto] *nm* viaduct.
viajante [bja'xante] *nm* commercial traveller, traveling salesman (*US*).
viajar [bja'xar] *vi* to travel, journey.
viaje ['bjaxe] *nm* journey; (*gira*) tour; (*NAUT*) voyage; (*COM*: *carga*) load; **los ~s** travel *sg*; **estar de ~** to be on a journey; ~ **de ida y vuelta** round trip; ~ **de novios** honeymoon.
viajero, a [bja'xero, a] *adj* travelling (*BRIT*), traveling (*US*); (*ZOOL*) migratory ♦ *nm/f* (*quien viaja*) traveller; (*pasajero*) passenger.
vial [bjal] *adj* road *cpd*, traffic *cpd*.
vianda ['bjanda] *nf* (*tb*: **~s**) food.
viáticos ['bjatikos] *nmpl* (*COM*) travelling (*BRIT*) *o* traveling (*US*) expenses.
víbora ['biβora] *nf* viper.
vibración [biβra'θjon] *nf* vibration.
vibrador [biβra'ðor] *nm* vibrator.
vibrante [bi'βrante] *adj* vibrant, vibrating.
vibrar [bi'βrar] *vt* to vibrate ♦ *vi* to vibrate; (*pulsar*) to throb, beat, pulsate.
vicario [bi'karjo] *nm* curate.
vicecónsul [biθe'konsul] *nm* vice-consul.
vicegerente [biθexe'rente] *nm/f* assistant manager.
vicepresidente [biθepresi'ðente] *nm/f* vice president; (*de comité etc*) vice-chairman.
viceversa [biθe'βersa] *adv* vice versa.
viciado, a [bi'θjaðo, a] *adj* (*corrompido*) corrupt; (*contaminado*) foul, contaminated.
viciar [bi'θjar] *vt* (*pervertir*) to pervert; (*adulterar*) to adulterate; (*falsificar*) to falsify; (*JUR*) to nullify; (*estropear*) to spoil; (*sentido*) to twist; **~se** *vr* to become corrupted; (*aire, agua*) to be(come) polluted.
vicio ['biθjo] *nm* (*libertinaje*) vice; (*mala costumbre*) bad habit; (*mimo*) spoiling; (*alabeo*) warp, warping; **de** *o* **por ~** out of sheer habit.
vicioso, a [bi'θjoso, a] *adj* (*muy malo*) vicious; (*corrompido*) depraved; (*mimado*) spoiled ♦ *nm/f* depraved person; (*adicto*) addict.
vicisitud [biθisi'tuð] *nf* vicissitude.
víctima ['biktima] *nf* victim; (*de accidente etc*) casualty.
victimario [bikti'marjo] *nm* (*AM*) killer, murderer.
victoria [bik'torja] *nf* victory.
victorioso, a [bikto'rjoso, a] *adj* victorious.
vicuña [bi'kuɲa] *nf* vicuna.
vid [bið] *nf* vine.
vida ['biða] *nf* life; (*duración*) lifetime; (*modo de vivir*) way of life; **¡~!, ¡~ mía!** (*saludo cariñoso*) my love!; **de por ~** for life; **de ~ airada** *o* **libre** loose-living; **en la/mi ~** never; **estar con ~** to be still alive; **ganarse la ~** to earn one's living; **¡esto es ~!** this is the life!; **le va la ~ en esto** his life depends on it.
vidente [bi'ðente] *nm/f* (*adivino*) clairvoyant; (*no ciego*) sighted person.
vídeo ['biðeo] *nm* video; (*aparato*) video (recorder); **cinta de ~** videotape; **película de ~** videofilm; **grabar en ~** to record, (video)tape; ~ **compuesto/inverso** (*INFORM*) composite/reverse video.
videocámara [biðeo'kamara] *nf* video camera; (*pequeña*) camcorder.
videocassette [biðeoka'set] *nm* video cassette.
videoclip [biðeo'klip] *nm* (music) video.
videoclub [biðeo'klub] *nm* video club; (*tienda*) video shop.
videodatos [biðeo'ðatos] *nmpl* (*COM*) viewdata.
videojuego [biðeo'xweɣo] *nm* video game.
videotex(o) [biðeo'teks(o)] *nm* Videotex ®.
vidriero, a [bi'ðrjero, a] *nm/f* glazier ♦ *nf* (*ventana*) stained-glass window; (*AM*: *de tienda*) shop window; (*puerta*) glass door.
vidrio ['biðrjo] *nm* glass; (*AM*) window; ~ **cilindrado/inastillable** plate/splinter-proof glass.
vidrioso, a [bi'ðrjoso, a] *adj* glassy; (*frágil*) fragile, brittle; (*resbaladizo*) slippery.
viejo, a ['bjexo, a] *adj* old ♦ *nm/f* old man/woman; **mi ~/vieja** (*fam*) my old man/woman; **hacerse** *o* **ponerse ~** to grow *o* get old.
Viena ['bjena] *nf* Vienna.
viene ['bjene] *etc vb V* **venir**.
vienés, esa [bje'nes, esa] *adj, nm/f* Viennese.
viento ['bjento] *nm* wind; (*olfato*) scent; **contra ~ y marea** at all costs; **ir ~ en popa** to go splendidly; (*negocio*) to prosper.
vientre ['bjentre] *nm* belly; (*matriz*) womb; **~s** *nmpl* bowels; **hacer de ~** to have a

movement of the bowels.
vier. *abr* (= *viernes*) Fri.
viernes ['bjernes] *nm inv* Friday; **V~ Santo** Good Friday; *V tb* **Semana Santa**.
vierta ['bjerta] *etc vb V* **verter**.
Vietnam [bjet'nam] *nm*: **el** ~ Vietnam.
vietnamita [bjetna'mita] *adj, nm/f* Vietnamese.
viga ['biɣa] *nf* beam, rafter; (*de metal*) girder.
vigencia [bi'xenθja] *nf* validity; (*de contrato etc*) term, life; **estar/entrar en** ~ to be in/come into effect *o* force.
vigente [bi'xente] *adj* valid, in force; (*imperante*) prevailing.
vigésimo, a [bi'xesimo, a] *num* twentieth.
vigía [bi'xia] *nm* look-out ♦ *nf* (*atalaya*) watchtower; (*acción*) watching.
vigilancia [bixi'lanθja] *nf* vigilance.
vigilante [bixi'lante] *adj* vigilant ♦ *nm* caretaker; (*en cárcel*) warder; (*en almacén*) shopwalker (*BRIT*), floor-walker (*US*); ~ **jurado** security guard (*licensed to carry a gun*); ~ **nocturno** night watchman.
vigilar [bixi'lar] *vt* to watch over; (*cuidar*) to look after, keep an eye on ♦ *vi* to be vigilant; (*hacer guardia*) to keep watch.
vigilia [vi'xilja] *nf* wakefulness; (*REL*) fast; **comer de** ~ to fast.
vigor [bi'ɣor] *nm* vigour, vitality; **en** ~ in force; **entrar/poner en** ~ to take/put into effect.
vigoroso, a [biɣo'roso, a] *adj* vigorous.
VIH *nm abr* (= *virus de inmunodeficiencia humana*) HIV.
vil [bil] *adj* vile, low.
vileza [bi'leθa] *nf* vileness; (*acto*) base deed.
vilipendiar [bilipen'djar] *vt* to vilify, revile.
villa ['biʎa] *nf* (*pueblo*) small town; (*municipalidad*) municipality; **la V~** (*ESP*) Madrid; ~ **miseria** shanty town.
villancico [biʎan'θiko] *nm* (Christmas) carol.
villorrio [bi'ʎorrjo] *nm* one-horse town, dump; (*AM*: *barrio pobre*) shanty town.
vilo ['bilo]: **en** ~ *adv* in the air, suspended; (*fig*) on tenterhooks, in suspense; **estar** *o* **quedar en** ~ to be left in suspense.
vinagre [bi'naɣre] *nm* vinegar.
vinagrera [bina'ɣrera] *nf* vinegar bottle; ~**s** *nfpl* cruet stand *sg*.
vinagreta [bina'ɣreta] *nf* French dressing.
vinatería [binate'ria] *nf* wine shop.
vinatero, a [bina'tero, a] *adj* wine *cpd* ♦ *nm* wine merchant.
vinculación [binkula'θjon] *nf* (*lazo*) link, bond; (*acción*) linking.
vincular [binku'lar] *vt* to link, bind.
vínculo ['binkulo] *nm* link, bond.
vindicar [bindi'kar] *vt* to vindicate; (*vengar*) to avenge; (*JUR*) to claim.
vinícola [bi'nikola] *adj* (*industria*) wine *cpd*; (*región*) wine-growing *cpd*.
vinicultura [binikul'tura] *nf* wine growing.
vino ['bino] *etc vb V* **venir** ♦ *nm* wine; ~ **de solera/seco/tinto** vintage/dry/red wine; ~ **de Jerez** sherry; ~ **de Oporto** port (wine).
viña ['biɲa] *nf*, **viñedo** [bi'ɲeðo] *nm* vineyard.
viñeta [bi'ɲeta] *nf* (*en historieta*) cartoon.
viola ['bjola] *nf* viola.
violación [bjola'θjon] *nf* violation; (*JUR*) offence, infringement; (*estupro*): ~ **(sexual)** rape; ~ **de contrato** (*COM*) breach of contract.
violar [bjo'lar] *vt* to violate; (*JUR*) to infringe; (*cometer estupro*) to rape.
violencia [bjo'lenθja] *nf* (*fuerza*) violence, force; (*embarazo*) embarrassment; (*acto injusto*) unjust act.
violentar [bjolen'tar] *vt* to force; (*casa*) to break into; (*agredir*) to assault; (*violar*) to violate.
violento, a [bjo'lento, a] *adj* violent; (*furioso*) furious; (*situación*) embarrassing; (*acto*) forced, unnatural; (*difícil*) awkward; **me es muy** ~ it goes against the grain with me.
violeta [bjo'leta] *nf* violet.
violín [bjo'lin] *nm* violin.
violón [bjo'lon] *nm* double bass.
violoncelo [bjolon'θelo] *nm* cello.
virador [bira'ðor] *nm* (*para fotocopiadora*) toner.
viraje [bi'raxe] *nm* turn; (*de vehículo*) swerve; (*de carretera*) bend; (*fig*) change of direction.
virar [bi'rar] *vi* to turn; to swerve; to change direction.
virgen ['birxen] *adj* virgin; (*cinta*) blank ♦ *nm/f* virgin; **la Santísima V~** (*REL*) the Blessed Virgin.
virginidad [birxini'ðað] *nf* virginity.
Virgo ['birɣo] *nm* Virgo.
viril [bi'ril] *adj* virile.
virilidad [birili'ðað] *nf* virility.
virrey [bi'rrei] *nm* viceroy.
virtual [bir'twal] *adj* (*real*) virtual; (*en potencia*) potential.
virtud [bir'tuð] *nf* virtue; **en** ~ **de** by virtue of.
virtuoso, a [bir'twoso, a] *adj* virtuous

♦ *nm/f* virtuoso.
viruela [bi'rwela] *nf* smallpox; **~s** *nfpl* pockmarks; **~s locas** chickenpox *sg.*
virulento, a [biru'lento, a] *adj* virulent.
virus ['birus] *nm inv* virus.
viruta [bi'ruta] *nf* wood *o* metal shaving.
vis [bis] *nf*: ~ **cómica** sense of humour.
visa ['bisa] *nf* (*AM*), **visado** [bi'saðo] *nm* visa; ~ **de permanencia** residence permit.
visar [bi'sar] *vt* (*pasaporte*) to visa; (*documento*) to endorse.
víscera ['bisθera] *nf* internal organ; **~s** *nfpl* entrails.
visceral [bisθe'ral] *adj* (*odio*) deep-rooted; **reacción** ~ gut reaction.
viscoso, a [bis'koso, a] *adj* viscous.
visera [bi'sera] *nf* visor.
visibilidad [bisiβili'ðað] *nf* visibility.
visible [bi'siβle] *adj* visible; (*fig*) obvious; **exportaciones/importaciones ~s** (*COM*) visible exports/imports.
visillo [bi'siʎo] *nm* lace curtain.
visión [bi'sjon] *nf* (*ANAT*) vision, (eye)sight; (*fantasía*) vision, fantasy; (*panorama*) view; **ver visiones** to see *o* be seeing things.
visionario, a [bisjo'narjo, a] *adj* (*que prevé*) visionary; (*alucinado*) deluded ♦ *nm/f* visionary; (*chalado*) lunatic.
visita [bi'sita] *nf* call, visit; (*persona*) visitor; **horas/tarjeta de** ~ visiting hours/card; ~ **de cortesía/de cumplido/de despedida** courtesy/formal/farewell visit; **hacer una** ~ to pay a visit; **ir de** ~ to go visiting.
visitar [bisi'tar] *vt* to visit, call on; (*inspeccionar*) to inspect.
vislumbrar [bislum'brar] *vt* to glimpse, catch a glimpse of.
vislumbre [bis'lumbre] *nf* glimpse; (*centelleo*) gleam; (*idea vaga*) glimmer.
viso ['biso] *nm* (*de metal*) glint, gleam; (*de tela*) sheen; (*aspecto*) appearance; **hay un ~ de verdad en esto** there is an element of truth in this.
visón [bi'son] *nm* mink.
visor [bi'sor] *nm* (*FOTO*) viewfinder.
víspera ['bispera] *nf* eve, day before; **la** ~ *o* **en ~s de** on the eve of.
vista ['bista] *nf* sight, vision; (*capacidad de ver*) (eye)sight; (*mirada*) look(s) (*pl*); (*FOTO etc*) view; (*JUR*) hearing ♦ *nm* customs officer; **a primera** ~ at first glance; ~ **general** overview; **fijar** *o* **clavar la ~ en** to stare at; **hacer la ~ gorda** to turn a blind eye; **volver la** ~ to look back; **está a la ~ que** it's obvious that; **a la** ~ (*COM*) at sight; **en ~ de** in view of; **en ~ de que** in view of the fact that; **¡hasta la ~!** so long!, see you!; **con ~s a** with a view to; *V tb* **visto, a.**
vistazo [bis'taθo] *nm* glance; **dar** *o* **echar un ~ a** to glance at.
visto, a ['bisto, a] *etc vb V* **vestir** ♦ *pp de* **ver** ♦ *adj* seen; (*considerado*) considered ♦ *nm*: ~ **bueno** approval; **"~ bueno"** "approved"; **por lo** ~ evidently; **dar el ~ bueno a algo** to give sth the go-ahead; **está ~ que** it's clear that; **está bien/mal** ~ it's acceptable/unacceptable; **está muy** ~ it is very common; **estaba** ~ it had to be; ~ **que** *conj* since, considering that.
vistoso, a [bis'toso, a] *adj* colourful; (*alegre*) gay; (*pey*) gaudy.
visual [bi'swal] *adj* visual.
visualice [biswa'liθe] *etc vb V* **visualizar.**
visualizador [biswaliθa'ðor] *nm* (*INFORM*) display screen, VDU.
visualizar [biswali'θar] *vt* (*imaginarse*) to visualize; (*INFORM*) to display.
vital [bi'tal] *adj* life *cpd*, living *cpd*; (*fig*) vital; (*persona*) lively, vivacious.
vitalicio, a [bita'liθjo, a] *adj* for life.
vitalidad [bitali'ðað] *nf* vitality.
vitamina [bita'mina] *nf* vitamin.
vitaminado, a [bitami'naðo, a] *adj* with added vitamins.
vitamínico, a [bita'miniko, a] *adj* vitamin *cpd*; **complejos ~s** vitamin compounds.
viticultor, a [bitikul'tor, a] *nm/f* vine grower.
viticultura [bitikul'tura] *nf* vine growing.
vitorear [bitore'ar] *vt* to cheer, acclaim.
vítores ['bitores] *nmpl* cheers.
vitoriano, a [bito'rjano, a] *adj* of *o* from Vitoria ♦ *nm/f* native *o* inhabitant of Vitoria.
vítreo, a ['bitreo, a] *adj* vitreous.
vitrina [bi'trina] *nf* glass case; (*en casa*) display cabinet; (*AM*) shop window.
vituperar [bitupe'rar] *vt* to condemn.
vituperio [bitu'perjo] *nm* (*condena*) condemnation; (*censura*) censure; (*insulto*) insult.
viudez [bju'ðeθ] *nf* widowhood.
viudo, a ['bjuðo, a] *adj* widowed ♦ *nm* widower ♦ *nf* widow.
viva ['biβa] *excl* hurrah! ♦ *nm* cheer; **¡~ el rey!** long live the King!
vivacidad [biβaθi'ðað] *nf* (*vigor*) vigour; (*vida*) vivacity.
vivamente [biβa'mente] *adv* in lively fashion; (*descripción etc*) vividly; (*protesta*) sharply; (*emoción*) acutely.

vivaracho, a [biβa'ratʃo, a] *adj* jaunty, lively; (*ojos*) bright, twinkling.
vivaz [bi'βaθ] *adj* (*que dura*) enduring; (*vigoroso*) vigorous; (*vivo*) lively.
vivencia [bi'βenθja] *nf* experience.
víveres ['biβeres] *nmpl* provisions.
vivero [bi'βero] *nm* (*HORTICULTURA*) nursery; (*para peces*) fishpond; (: *COM*) fish farm.
viveza [bi'βeθa] *nf* liveliness; (*agudeza*) sharpness.
vividor, a [biβi'ðor, a] *adj* (*pey*) opportunistic ♦ *nm* (*aprovechado*) hustler.
vivienda [bi'βjenda] *nf* (*alojamiento*) housing; (*morada*) dwelling; **~s protegidas** *o* **sociales** council housing *sg* (*BRIT*), public housing *sg* (*US*).
viviente [bi'βjente] *adj* living.
vivificar [biβifi'kar] *vt* to give life to.
vivifique [biβi'fike] *etc vb V* **vivificar**.
vivir [bi'βir] *vt* (*experimentar*) to live *o* go through ♦ *vi* (*gen, COM*): **~ (de)** to live (by, off, on) ♦ *nm* life, living; **¡viva!** hurray!; **¡viva el rey!** long live the king!
vivo, a ['biβo, a] *adj* living, live, alive; (*fig*) vivid; (*movimiento*) quick; (*color*) bright; (*protesta etc*) strong; (*astuto*) smart, clever; **en ~** (*TV etc*) live; **llegar a lo ~** to cut to the quick.
vizcaíno, a [biθka'ino, a] *adj, nm/f* Biscayan.
Vizcaya [biθ'kaja] *nf* Biscay; **el Golfo de ~** the Bay of Biscay.
V.M. *abr* = **Vuestra Majestad.**
V.O. *abr* = *versión original.*
V.°B.° *abr* = **visto bueno.**
vocablo [bo'kaβlo] *nm* (*palabra*) word; (*término*) term.
vocabulario [bokaβu'larjo] *nm* vocabulary, word list.
vocación [boka'θjon] *nf* vocation.
vocacional [bokasjo'nal] *nf* (*AM*) ≈ technical college.
vocal [bo'kal] *adj* vocal ♦ *nm/f* member (of a committee *etc*) ♦ *nm* non-executive director ♦ *nf* vowel.
vocalice [boka'liθe] *etc vb V* **vocalizar**.
vocalizar [bokali'θar] *vt* to vocalize.
voceador [bosea'ðor] *nm* (*AM*): **~ de periódicos** newspaper vendor *o* seller.
vocear [boθe'ar] *vt* (*para vender*) to cry; (*aclamar*) to acclaim; (*fig*) to proclaim ♦ *vi* to yell.
vocerío [boθe'rio] *nm* shouting; (*escándalo*) hullabaloo.
vocero, a [bo'sero, a] *nm/f* (*AM*) spokesman/woman.
vociferar [boθife'rar] *vt* to shout; (*jactarse*) to proclaim boastfully ♦ *vi* to yell.
vocinglero, a [boθin'glero, a] *adj* vociferous; (*gárrulo*) garrulous; (*fig*) blatant.
vodevil [boðe'βil] *nm* music hall, variety, (*US*) vaudeville.
vodka ['boðka] *nm* vodka.
vodú [bo'ðu] *nm* voodoo.
vol *abr* = **volumen**.
volado, a [bo'laðo, a] *adj*: **estar ~** (*fam*: *inquieto*) to be worried; (: *loco*) to be crazy.
volador, a [bola'ðor, a] *adj* flying.
voladura [bola'ðura] *nf* blowing up, demolition; (*MINERÍA*) blasting.
volandas [bo'landas]: **en ~** *adv* in *o* through the air; (*fig*) swiftly.
volante [bo'lante] *adj* flying ♦ *nm* (*de máquina, coche*) steering wheel; (*de reloj*) balance; (*nota*) note; **ir al ~** to be at the wheel, be driving.
volar [bo'lar] *vt* (*demolir*) to blow up, demolish ♦ *vi* to fly; (*fig*: *correr*) to rush, hurry; (*fam*: *desaparecer*) to disappear; **voy volando** I must dash; **¡cómo vuela el tiempo!** how time flies!
volátil [bo'latil] *adj* volatile; (*fig*) changeable.
volcán [bol'kan] *nm* volcano.
volcánico, a [bol'kaniko, a] *adj* volcanic.
volcar [bol'kar] *vt* to upset, overturn; (*tumbar, derribar*) to knock over; (*vaciar*) to empty out ♦ *vi* to overturn; **~se** *vr* to tip over; (*barco*) to capsize.
voleibol [bolei'βol] *nm* volleyball.
voleo [bo'leo] *nm* volley; **a(l) ~** haphazardly; **de un ~** quickly.
Volga ['bolɣa] *nm* Volga.
volición [boli'θjon] *nf* volition.
volqué [bol'ke], **volquemos** [bol'kemos] *etc vb V* **volcar**.
volquete [bol'kete] *nm* dumper, dump truck (*US*).
voltaje [bol'taxe] *nm* voltage.
voltear [bolte'ar] *vt* to turn over; (*volcar*) to knock over; (*doblar*) to peal ♦ *vi* to roll over; **~se** *vr* (*AM*) to turn round; **~ a hacer algo** (*AM*) to do sth again.
voltereta [bolte'reta] *nf* somersault; **~ sobre las manos** handspring; **~ lateral** cartwheel.
voltio ['boltjo] *nm* volt.
voluble [bo'luβle] *adj* fickle.
volumen [bo'lumen] *nm* volume; **~ monetario** money supply; **~ de negocios** turnover; **bajar el ~** to turn down the volume; **poner la radio a todo ~** to turn the radio up full.

voluminoso, a [bolumi'noso, a] *adj* voluminous; (*enorme*) massive.
voluntad [bolun'tað] *nf* will, willpower; (*deseo*) desire, wish; (*afecto*) fondness; **a ~** at will; (*cantidad*) as much as one likes; **buena ~** goodwill; **mala ~** ill will, malice; **por causas ajenas a mi ~** for reasons beyond my control.
voluntario, a [bolun'tarjo, a] *adj* voluntary ♦ *nm/f* volunteer.
voluntarioso, a [bolunta'rjoso, a] *adj* headstrong.
voluptuoso, a [bolup'twoso, a] *adj* voluptuous.
volver [bol'βer] *vt* to turn; (*boca abajo*) to turn (over); (*voltear*) to turn round, turn upside down; (*poner al revés*) to turn inside out; (*devolver*) to return; (*transformar*) to change, transform; (*manga*) to roll up ♦ *vi* to return, go/come back; **~se** *vr* to turn round; (*llegar a ser*) to become; **~ la espalda** to turn one's back; **~ bien por mal** to return good for evil; **~ a hacer** to do again; **~ en sí** to come to *o* round, regain consciousness; **~ la vista atrás** to look back; **~ loco a algn** to drive sb mad; **~se loco** to go mad.
vomitar [bomi'tar] *vt, vi* to vomit.
vómito ['bomito] *nm* (*acto*) vomiting; (*resultado*) vomit.
voracidad [boraθi'ðað] *nf* voracity.
vorágine [bo'raxine] *nf* whirlpool; (*fig*) maelstrom.
voraz [bo'raθ] *adj* voracious; (*fig*) fierce.
vórtice ['bortiθe] *nm* whirlpool; (*de aire*) whirlwind.
vos [bos] *pron* (*AM*) you.
voseo [bo'seo] *nm* (*AM*) addressing a person as "vos", *familiar usage*.
Vosgos ['bosɣos] *nmpl* Vosges.
vosotros, as [bo'sotros, as] *pron* you *pl*; (*reflexivo*) yourselves; **entre ~** among yourselves.
votación [bota'θjon] *nf* (*acto*) voting; (*voto*) vote; **~ a mano alzada** show of hands; **someter algo a ~** to put sth to the vote.
votar [bo'tar] *vt* (*POL*: *partido etc*) to vote for; (*proyecto*: *aprobar*) to pass; (*REL*) to vow ♦ *vi* to vote.
voto ['boto] *nm* vote; (*promesa*) vow; (*maldición*) oath, curse; **~s** *nmpl* (good) wishes; **~ de bloque/de grupo** block/card vote; **~ de censura/de (des)confianza/de gracias** vote of censure/(no) confidence/thanks; **dar su ~** to cast one's vote.
voy [boi] *vb V* **ir**.
voz [boθ] *nf* voice; (*grito*) shout; (*chisme*) rumour; (*LING*: *palabra*) word; (: *forma*) voice; **dar voces** to shout, yell; **llamar a algn a voces** to shout to sb; **llevar la ~ cantante** (*fig*) to be the boss; **tener la ~ tomada** to be hoarse; **tener ~ y voto** to have the right to speak; **a media ~** in a low voice; **a ~ en cuello** *o* **en grito** at the top of one's voice; **de viva ~** verbally; **en ~ alta** aloud; **~ de mando** command.
vozarrón [boθa'rron] *nm* booming voice.
vra., vro. *abr* = **vuestra, vuestro.**
Vto. *abr* (*COM*) = **vencimiento.**
vudú [bu'ðu] *nm* voodoo.
vuelco ['bwelko] *etc vb V* **volcar** ♦ *nm* spill, overturning; (*fig*) collapse; **mi corazón dio un ~** my heart missed a beat.
vuelo ['bwelo] *etc vb V* **volar** ♦ *nm* flight; (*encaje*) lace, frill; (*de falda etc*) loose part; (*fig*) importance; **de altos ~s** (*fig*: *plan*) grandiose; (: *persona*) ambitious; **alzar el ~** to take flight; (*fig*) to dash off; **coger al ~** to catch in flight; **~ en picado** dive; **~ libre** hang-gliding; **~ regular** scheduled flight; **falda de mucho ~** full *o* wide skirt.
vuelque ['bwelke] *etc vb V* **volcar.**
vuelta ['bwelta] *nf* turn; (*curva*) bend, curve; (*regreso*) return; (*revolución*) revolution; (*paseo*) stroll; (*circuito*) lap; (*de papel, tela*) reverse; (*de pantalón*) turn-up (*BRIT*), cuff (*US*); (*dinero*) change; **~ a empezar** back to square one; **~ al mundo** world trip; **V~ de Francia** Tour de France; **~ cerrada** hairpin bend; **a la ~** (*ESP*) on one's return; **a la ~ de la esquina, a la ~** (*AM*) round the corner; **a ~ de correo** by return of post; **dar ~s** to turn, revolve; **dar ~s a una idea** to turn over an idea (in one's mind); **dar una ~** to go for a walk; **dar media ~** (*AUTO*) to do a U-turn; (*fam*) to beat it; **estar de ~** (*fam*) to be back; **poner a algn de ~ y media** to heap abuse on sb; **no tiene ~ de hoja** there's no alternative.
vueltita [bwel'tita] *nf* (*esp AM fam*) (little) walk; (: *en coche*) (little) drive.
vuelto ['bwelto] *pp de* **volver** ♦ *nm* (*AM*: *moneda*) change.
vuelva ['bwelβa] *etc vb V* **volver.**
vuestro, a ['bwestro, a] *adj* your; (*después de n*) of yours ♦ *pron*: **el ~/la vuestra/los ~s/las vuestras** yours; **lo ~** (what is) yours; **un amigo ~** a friend of yours; **una idea vuestra** an idea of yours.
vulgar [bul'ɣar] *adj* (*ordinario*) vulgar; (*común*) common.
vulgarice [bulɣa'riθe] *etc vb V* **vulgarizar.**

vulgaridad [bulɣari'ðað] *nf* commonness; (*acto*) vulgarity; (*expresión*) coarse expression; **~es** *nfpl* banalities.
vulgarismo [bulɣa'rismo] *nm* popular form of a word.
vulgarizar [bulɣari'θar] *vt* to popularize.
vulgo ['bulɣo] *nm* common people.
vulnerable [bulne'raβle] *adj* vulnerable.
vulnerar [bulne'rar] *vt* to harm, damage; (*derechos*) to interfere with; (*JUR, COM*) to violate.
vulva ['bulβa] *nf* vulva.

W w

W, w ['uβe'doβle, (*AM*) 'doβleβe] *nf* (*letra*) W, w; **W de Washington** W for William.
walkie-talkie [walki'talki] *nm* walkie-talkie.
walkman ® ['wal(k)man] *nm* Walkman ®.
wáter ['bater] *nm* lavatory.
waterpolo [water'polo] *nm* waterpolo.
wátman ['watman] *adj inv* (*fam*) cool.
whisky ['wiski] *nm* whisky.
Winchester ['wintʃester] *nm* (*INFORM*): **disco ~** Winchester disk.
windsurf ['winsurf] *nm* windsurfing.
WWW *nm o nf abr* (*INFORM*: = *World Wide Web*) WWW.

X x

X, x ['ekis] *nf* (*letra*) X, x; **X de Xiquena** X for Xmas.
xenofobia [seno'foβja] *nf* xenophobia.
xenófobo, a [se'nofoβo, a] *adj* xenophobic ♦ *nm/f* xenophobe.
xerografía [seroɣra'fia] *nf* xerography.
xilófono [si'lofono] *nm* xylophone.
Xunta ['shunta] *nf* (*tb* **~ de Galicia**) *regional government of Galicia.*

Y y

Y, y [i'ɣrjeɣa] *nf* (*letra*) Y, y; **Y de Yegua** Y for Yellow (*BRIT*) *o* Yoke (*US*).
y [i] *conj* and; (*AM fam*: *pues*) well; **¿~ eso?** why?, how so?; **¡~ los demás?** what about the others?; **~ bueno, ...** (*AM*) well ...
ya [ja] *adv* (*gen*) already; (*ahora*) now; (*en seguida*) at once; (*pronto*) soon ♦ *excl* all right!; (*por supuesto*) of course! ♦ *conj* (*ahora que*) now that; **~ no** not any more, no longer; **~ lo sé** I know; **~ dice que sí, ~ dice que no** first he says yes, then he says no; **¡~, ~!** yes, yes!; (*con impaciencia*) all right!, O.K.!; **¡~ voy!** (*enfático*: *no se suele traducir*) coming!; **~ que** since.
yacer [ja'θer] *vi* to lie.
yacimiento [jaθi'mjento] *nm* bed, deposit; **~ petrolífero** oilfield.
Yakarta [ja'karta] *nf* Jakarta.
yanqui ['janki] *adj* Yankee ♦ *nm/f* Yank, Yankee.
yate ['jate] *nm* yacht.
yazca ['jaθka] *etc vb V* **yacer**.
yedra ['jeðra] *nf* ivy.
yegua ['jeɣwa] *nf* mare.
yema ['jema] *nf* (*del huevo*) yolk; (*BOT*) leaf bud; (*fig*) best part; **~ del dedo** fingertip.
Yemen ['jemen] *nm*: **el ~ del Norte** Yemen; **el ~ del Sur** Southern Yemen.
yemení [jeme'ni] *adj, nm/f* Yemeni.
yendo ['jendo] *vb V* **ir**.
yerba ['jerβa] *nf* = **hierba**.
yerbatero, a [jerβa'tero, a] *adj* (*AM*) maté ♦ *nm/f* (*AM*) herbal healer.
yerga ['jerɣa] *etc*, **yergue** ['jerɣe] *etc vb V* **erguir**.
yermo, a ['jermo, a] *adj* barren; (*de gente*) uninhabited ♦ *nm* waste land.
yerno ['jerno] *nm* son-in-law.
yerre ['jerre] *etc vb V* **errar**.
yerto, a ['jerto, a] *adj* stiff.
yesca ['jeska] *nf* tinder.
yeso ['jeso] *nm* (*GEO*) gypsum; (*ARQ*) plaster.
yo ['jo] *pron personal* I; **soy ~** it's me, it is I; **~ que tú/usted** if I were you.

yodo ['joðo] *nm* iodine.
yoga ['joɣa] *nm* yoga.
yogur(t) [jo'ɣur(t)] *nm* yogurt.
yogurtera [joɣur'tera] *nf* yogurt maker.
yuca ['juka] *nf* yucca.
yudo ['juðo] *nm* judo.
yugo ['juɣo] *nm* yoke.
Yugoslavia [juɣos'laβja] *nf* Yugoslavia.
yugoslavo, a [juɣos'laβo, a] *adj* Yugoslavian ♦ *nm/f* Yugoslav.
yugular [juɣu'lar] *adj* jugular.
yunque ['junke] *nm* anvil.
yunta ['junta] *nf* yoke.
yuntero [jun'tero] *nm* ploughman.
yute ['jute] *nm* jute.
yuxtapondré [jukstapond're] *etc vb V* **yuxtaponer.**
yuxtaponer [jukstapo'ner] *vt* to juxtapose.
yuxtaponga [juksta'ponga] *etc vb V* **yuxtaponer.**
yuxtaposición [jukstaposi'θjon] *nf* juxtaposition.
yuxtapuesto [juksta'pwesto], **yuxtapuse** [juksta'puse] *etc vb V* **yuxtaponer.**

Z z

Z, z ['θeta, (*esp AM*) 'seta] *nf* (*letra*) Z, z; **Z de Zaragoza** Z for Zebra.
zafar [θa'far] *vt* (*soltar*) to untie; (*superficie*) to clear; ~**se** *vr* (*escaparse*) to escape; (*ocultarse*) to hide o.s. away; (*TEC*) to slip off; ~**se de** (*persona*) to get away from.
zafio, a ['θafjo, a] *adj* coarse.
zafiro [θa'firo] *nm* sapphire.
zaga ['θaɣa] *nf* rear; **a la** ~ behind, in the rear.
zagal [θa'ɣal] *nm* boy, lad.
zagala [θa'ɣala] *nf* girl, lass.
zaguán [θa'ɣwan] *nm* hallway.
zaherir [θae'rir] *vt* (*criticar*) to criticize; (*fig: herir*) to wound.
zahiera *etc*, **zahiriendo** [θa'jera, θai'rjendo] *etc vb V* **zaherir.**
zahorí [θao'ri] *nm* clairvoyant.
zaino, a ['θaino, a] *adj* (*color de caballo*) chestnut; (*pérfido*) treacherous; (*animal*) vicious.
zalamería [θalame'ria] *nf* flattery.
zalamero, a [θala'mero, a] *adj* flattering; (*relamido*) suave.
zamarra [θa'marra] *nf* (*piel*) sheepskin; (*saco*) sheepskin jacket.
Zambeze [θam'beθe] *nm* Zambezi.
zambo, a ['θambo, a] *adj* knock-kneed ♦ *nm/f* (*AM*) half-breed (*of Negro and Indian parentage*); (*mulato*) mulatto ♦ *nf* samba.
zambullida [θambu'ʎiða] *nf* dive, plunge.
zambullirse [θambu'ʎirse] *vr* to dive; (*ocultarse*) to hide o.s.
zamorano, a [θamo'rano, a] *adj* of *o* from Zamora ♦ *nm/f* native *o* inhabitant of Zamora.
zampar [θam'par] *vt* (*esconder*) to hide *o* put away (hurriedly); (*comer*) to gobble; (*arrojar*) to hurl ♦ *vi* to eat voraciously; ~**se** *vr* (*chocar*) to bump; (*fig*) to gatecrash.
zanahoria [θana'orja] *nf* carrot.
zancada [θan'kaða] *nf* stride.
zancadilla [θanka'ðiʎa] *nf* trip; (*fig*) stratagem; **echar la ~ a algn** to trip sb up.
zancajo [θan'kaxo] *nm* (*ANAT*) heel; (*fig*) dwarf.
zanco ['θanko] *nm* stilt.
zancudo, a [θan'kuðo, a] *adj* long-legged ♦ *nm* (*AM*) mosquito.
zángano ['θangano] *nm* drone; (*holgazán*) idler, slacker.
zanja ['θanxa] *nf* (*fosa*) ditch; (*tumba*) grave.
zanjar [θan'xar] *vt* (*fosa*) to ditch, trench; (*problema*) to surmount; (*conflicto*) to resolve.
zapapico [θapa'piko] *nm* pick, pickaxe.
zapata [θa'pata] *nf* half-boot; (*MECÁNICA*) shoe.
zapateado [θapate'aðo] *nm* (flamenco) tap dance.
zapatear [θapate'ar] *vt* (*tocar*) to tap with one's foot; (*patear*) to kick; (*fam*) to ill-treat ♦ *vi* to tap with one's feet.
zapatería [θapate'ria] *nf* (*oficio*) shoemaking; (*tienda*) shoe-shop; (*fábrica*) shoe factory.
zapatero, a [θapa'tero, a] *nm/f* shoemaker; ~ **remendón** cobbler.
zapatilla [θapa'tiʎa] *nf* slipper; (*TEC*) washer; (*para deporte*) training shoe.
zapato [θa'pato] *nm* shoe.
zapear [θape'ar] *vi* to flick through the channels.
zapping ['θapin] *nm* channel-hopping; **hacer** ~ to channel-hop.
zar [θar] *nm* tsar, czar.
zarabanda [θara'βanda] *nf* saraband; (*fig*) whirl.
Zaragoza [θara'ɣoθa] *nf* Saragossa.

zaragozano, a [θaraɣo'θano, a] *adj* of *o* from Saragossa ♦ *nm/f* native *o* inhabitant of Saragossa.
zaranda [θa'randa] *nf* sieve.
zarandear [θarande'ar] *vt* to sieve; (*fam*) to shake vigorously.
zarpa ['θarpa] *nf* (*garra*) claw, paw; **echar la ~ a** to claw at; (*fam*) to grab.
zarpar [θar'par] *vi* to weigh anchor.
zarpazo [θar'paθo] *nm*: **dar un ~** to claw.
zarza ['θarθa] *nf* (*BOT*) bramble.
zarzal [θar'θal] *nm* (*matorral*) bramble patch.
zarzamora [θarθa'mora] *nf* blackberry.
zarzuela [θar'θwela] *nf* Spanish light opera; **la Z~** *home of the Spanish Royal Family*.
zigzag [θiɣ'θaɣ] *adj* zigzag.
zigzaguear [θiɣθaɣe'ar] *vi* to zigzag.
zinc [θink] *nm* zinc.
zíper ['siper] *nm* (*AM*) zip, zipper (*US*).
zócalo ['θokalo] *nm* (*ARQ*) plinth, base; (*de pared*) skirting board.
zoco ['θoko] *nm* (Arab) market, souk.
zodíaco [θo'ðiako] *nm* zodiac; **signo del ~** star sign.
zona ['θona] *nf* zone; **~ fronteriza** border area; **~ del dólar** (*COM*) dollar area; **~ de fomento** *o* **de desarrollo** development area.
zonzo, a ['sonso, a] *adj* (*AM*) silly.
zoología [θoolo'xia] *nf* zoology.
zoológico, a [θoo'loxiko, a] *adj* zoological ♦ *nm* (*tb*: **parque ~**) zoo.
zoólogo, a [θo'oloɣo, a] *nm/f* zoologist.
zoom [θum] *nm* zoom lens.
zopenco, a [θo'penko, a] (*fam*) *adj* dull, stupid ♦ *nm/f* clot, nitwit.
zopilote [sopi'lote] *nm* (*AM*) buzzard.
zoquete [θo'kete] *nm* (*madera*) block; (*pan*) crust; (*fam*) blockhead.
zorro, a ['θorro, a] *adj* crafty ♦ *nm/f* fox/vixen ♦ *nf* (*fam*) whore, tart, hooker (*US*).
zote ['θote] (*fam*) *adj* dim, stupid ♦ *nm/f* dimwit.
zozobra [θo'θoβra] *nf* (*fig*) anxiety.
zozobrar [θoθo'βrar] *vi* (*hundirse*) to capsize; (*fig*) to fail.
zueco ['θweko] *nm* clog.
zulo ['θulo] *nm* (*de armas*) cache.
zumbar [θum'bar] *vt* (*burlar*) to tease; (*golpear*) to hit ♦ *vi* to buzz; (*fam*) to be very close; **~se** *vr*: **~se de** to tease; **me zumban los oídos** I have a buzzing *o* ringing in my ears.
zumbido [θum'biðo] *nm* buzzing; (*fam*) punch; **~ de oídos** buzzing *o* ringing in the ears.
zumo ['θumo] *nm* juice; (*ganancia*) profit; **~ de naranja** (fresh) orange juice.
zurcir [θur'θir] *vt* (*coser*) to darn; (*fig*) to put together; **¡que las zurzan!** to blazes with them!
zurdo, a ['θurðo, a] *adj* (*mano*) left; (*persona*) left-handed.
zurrar [θu'rrar] *vt* (*TEC*) to dress; (*fam*: *pegar duro*) to wallop; (: *aplastar*) to flatten; (: *criticar*) to criticize harshly.
zurriagazo [θurrja'ɣaθo] *nm* lash, stroke; (*desgracia*) stroke of bad luck.
zurrón [θu'rron] *nm* pouch.
zurza ['θurθa] *etc vb V* **zurcir**.
zutano, a [θu'tano, a] *nm/f* so-and-so.

English-Spanish
Inglés-Español

A a

A, a [eɪ] *n* (*letter*) A, a; (*SCOL*: *mark*) ≈ sobresaliente; (*MUS*): **A** la *m*; **A for Andrew,** (*US*) **A for Able** A de Antonio; **A road** *n* (*BRIT AUT*) ≈ carretera nacional; **A shares** *npl* (*BRIT STOCK EXCHANGE*) acciones *fpl* de clase A.

KEYWORD

a [ə] *indef art* (*before vowel or silent h*: **an**) **1** un(a); ~ **book** un libro; **an apple** una manzana; **she's ~ nurse** (ella) es enfermera; **I haven't got ~ car** no tengo coche
2 (*instead of the number "one"*) un(a); ~ **year ago** hace un año; ~ **hundred/thousand pounds** cien/mil libras
3 (*in expressing ratios, prices etc*): **3 ~ day/week** 3 al día/a la semana; **10 km an hour** 10 km por hora; **£5 ~ person** £5 por persona; **30p ~ kilo** 30p el kilo; **3 times ~ month** 3 veces al mes.

a. *abbr* = **acre.**
AA *n abbr* (*BRIT*: = *Automobile Association*) ≈ RACE *m* (*SP*); = *Alcoholics Anonymous*; (*US*: = *Associate in/of Arts*) *título universitario*; (= *anti-aircraft*) A.A.
AAA *n abbr* (= *American Automobile Association*) ≈ RACE *m* (*SP*); ['θriː'eɪz] (*BRIT*: = *Amateur Athletics Association*) *asociación de atletismo amateur*.
A & R *n abbr* (*MUS*) (= *artists and repertoire*) *nuevos artistas y canciones*; ~ **man** *descubridor de jóvenes talentos*.
AAUP *n abbr* (= *American Association of University Professors*) *asociación de profesores universitarios*.
AB *abbr* (*BRIT*) = **able-bodied seaman;** (*Canada*) = *Alberta*.
aback [ə'bæk] *adv*: **to be taken ~** quedar(se) desconcertado.
abandon [ə'bændən] *vt* abandonar; (*renounce*) renunciar a ♦ *n* abandono; (*wild behaviour*): **with ~** con desenfreno; **to ~ ship** abandonar el barco.
abandoned [ə'bændənd] *adj* (*child, house etc*) abandonado; (*unrestrained*: *manner*) desinhibido.
abase [ə'beɪs] *vt*: **to ~ o.s. (so far as to do ...)** rebajarse (hasta el punto de hacer ...).
abashed [ə'bæʃt] *adj* avergonzado.
abate [ə'beɪt] *vi* moderarse; (*lessen*) disminuir; (*calm down*) calmarse.
abatement [ə'beɪtmənt] *n* (*of pollution, noise*) disminución *f*.
abattoir ['æbətwɑː*] *n* (*BRIT*) matadero.
abbey ['æbɪ] *n* abadía.
abbot ['æbət] *n* abad *m*.
abbreviate [ə'briːvɪeɪt] *vt* abreviar.
abbreviation [əbriːvɪ'eɪʃən] *n* (*short form*) abreviatura; (*act*) abreviación *f*.
ABC *n abbr* (= *American Broadcasting Company*) *cadena de televisión*.
abdicate ['æbdɪkeɪt] *vt, vi* abdicar.
abdication [æbdɪ'keɪʃən] *n* abdicación *f*.
abdomen ['æbdəmən] *n* abdomen *m*.
abdominal [æb'dɔmɪnl] *adj* abdominal.
abduct [æb'dʌkt] *vt* raptar, secuestrar.
abductor [æb'dʌktə*] *n* raptor(a) *m/f*, secuestrador(a) *m/f*.
abduction [æb'dʌkʃən] *n* rapto, secuestro.
Aberdonian [æbə'dəunɪən] *adj* de Aberdeen ♦ *n* nativo/a *or* habitante *m/f* de Aberdeen.
aberration [æbə'reɪʃən] *n* aberración *f*; **in a moment of mental ~** en un momento de enajenación mental.

abet [ə'bɛt] *vt see* **aid**.
abeyance [ə'beɪəns] *n*: **in** ~ (*law*) en desuso; (*matter*) en suspenso.
abhor [əb'hɔː*] *vt* aborrecer, abominar (de).
abhorrent [əb'hɔrənt] *adj* aborrecible, detestable.
abide [ə'baɪd] *vt*: **I can't** ~ **it/him** no lo/le puedo ver *or* aguantar; **to** ~ **by** *vt fus* atenerse a.
abiding [ə'baɪdɪŋ] *adj* (*memory etc*) perdurable.
ability [ə'bɪlɪtɪ] *n* habilidad *f*, capacidad *f*; (*talent*) talento; **to the best of my** ~ lo mejor que pueda *etc*.
abject ['æbdʒɛkt] *adj* (*poverty*) sórdido; (*apology*) rastrero; (*coward*) vil.
ablaze [ə'bleɪz] *adj* en llamas, ardiendo.
able ['eɪbl] *adj* capaz; (*skilled*) hábil; **to be** ~ **to do sth** poder hacer algo.
able-bodied ['eɪbl'bɔdɪd] *adj* sano; ~ **seaman** marinero de primera.
ably ['eɪblɪ] *adv* hábilmente.
ABM *n abbr* = *anti-ballistic missile*.
abnormal [æb'nɔːməl] *adj* anormal.
abnormality [æbnɔː'mælɪtɪ] *n* (*condition*) anormalidad *f*; (*instance*) anomalía.
aboard [ə'bɔːd] *adv* a bordo ♦ *prep* a bordo de; ~ **the train** en el tren.
abode [ə'bəud] *n* (*old*) morada; (*LAW*) domicilio; **of no fixed** ~ sin domicilio fijo.
abolish [ə'bɔlɪʃ] *vt* suprimir, abolir.
abolition [æbəu'lɪʃən] *n* supresión *f*, abolición *f*.
abominable [ə'bɔmɪnəbl] *adj* abominable.
aborigine [æbə'rɪdʒɪnɪ] *n* aborigen *m/f*.
abort [ə'bɔːt] *vt* abortar; (*COMPUT*) interrumpir ♦ *vi* (*COMPUT*) interrumpir el programa.
abortion [ə'bɔːʃən] *n* aborto (provocado); **to have an** ~ abortar.
abortionist [ə'bɔːʃənɪst] *n* persona que practica abortos.
abortive [ə'bɔːtɪv] *adj* fracasado.
abound [ə'baund] *vi*: **to** ~ **(in** *or* **with)** abundar (de *or* en).

KEYWORD

about [ə'baut] *adv* **1** (*approximately*) más o menos, aproximadamente; ~ **a hundred/thousand** *etc* unos(unas) *or* como cien/mil *etc*; **it takes** ~ **10 hours** se tarda unas *or* más o menos 10 horas; **at** ~ **2 o'clock** sobre las dos; **I've just** ~ **finished** casi he terminado
2 (*referring to place*) por todas partes; **to leave things lying** ~ dejar las cosas (tiradas) por ahí; **to run** ~ correr por todas partes; **to walk** ~ pasearse, ir y venir; **is Paul** ~**?** ¿está por aquí Paul?; **it's the other way** ~ es al revés
3: **to be** ~ **to do sth** estar a punto de hacer algo; **I'm not** ~ **to do all that for nothing** no pienso hacer todo eso para nada
♦ *prep* **1** (*relating to*) de, sobre, acerca de; **a book** ~ **London** un libro sobre *or* acerca de Londres; **what is it** ~**?** (*book, film*) ¿de qué se trata?; **we talked** ~ **it** hablamos de eso *or* ello; **what** *or* **how** ~ **doing this?** ¿qué tal si hacemos esto?
2 (*referring to place*) por; **to walk** ~ **the town** caminar por la ciudad.

about face, about turn *n* (*MIL*) media vuelta; (*fig*) cambio radical.
above [ə'bʌv] *adv* encima, por encima, arriba ♦ *prep* encima de; **mentioned** ~ susodicho; ~ **all** sobre todo; **he's not** ~ **a bit of blackmail** es capaz hasta de hacer chantaje.
above board *adj* legítimo.
above-mentioned [əbʌv'mɛnʃnd] *adj* susodicho.
abrasion [ə'breɪʒən] *n* (*on skin*) abrasión *f*.
abrasive [ə'breɪzɪv] *adj* abrasivo.
abreast [ə'brɛst] *adv* uno al lado de otro; **to keep** ~ **of** mantenerse al corriente de.
abridge [ə'brɪdʒ] *vt* abreviar.
abroad [ə'brɔːd] *adv* (*to be*) en el extranjero; (*to go*) al extranjero; **there is a rumour** ~ **that ...** corre el rumor de que ...
abrupt [ə'brʌpt] *adj* (*sudden*: *departure*) repentino; (*manner*) brusco.
abruptly [ə'brʌptlɪ] *adv* (*leave*) repentinamente; (*speak*) bruscamente.
abscess ['æbsɪs] *n* absceso.
abscond [əb'skɔnd] *vi* fugarse.
absence ['æbsəns] *n* ausencia; **in the** ~ **of** (*person*) en ausencia de; (*thing*) a falta de.
absent ['æbsənt] *adj* ausente; ~ **without leave (AWOL)** ausente sin permiso.
absentee [æbsən'tiː] *n* ausente *m/f*.
absenteeism [æbsən'tiːɪzəm] *n* absentismo.
absent-minded [æbsənt'maɪndɪd] *adj* distraído.
absolute ['æbsəluːt] *adj* absoluto; ~ **monopoly** monopolio total.
absolutely [æbsə'luːtlɪ] *adv* totalmente; **oh yes,** ~**!** ¡claro *or* por supuesto que sí!
absolution [æbsə'luːʃən] *n* (*REL*) absolución *f*.
absolve [əb'zɔlv] *vt*: **to** ~ **sb (from)** absolver a alguien (de).
absorb [əb'zɔːb] *vt* absorber; **to be** ~**ed in a**

book estar enfrascado en un libro.
absorbent [əb'zɔːbənt] *adj* absorbente.
absorbent cotton *n* (*US*) algodón *m* hidrófilo.
absorbing [əb'zɔːbɪŋ] *adj* absorbente; (*book etc*) interesantísimo.
absorption [əb'zɔːpʃən] *n* absorción *f*.
abstain [əb'steɪn] *vi*: **to ~ (from)** abstenerse (de).
abstemious [əb'stiːmɪəs] *adj* abstemio.
abstention [əb'stɛnʃən] *n* abstención *f*.
abstinence ['æbstɪnəns] *n* abstinencia.
abstract ['æbstrækt] *adj* abstracto.
abstruse [æb'struːs] *adj* abstruso, oscuro.
absurd [əb'səːd] *adj* absurdo.
absurdity [əb'səːdɪtɪ] *n* absurdo.
ABTA ['æbtə] *n abbr* = *Association of British Travel Agents*.
abundance [ə'bʌndəns] *n* abundancia.
abundant [ə'bʌndənt] *adj* abundante.
abuse [ə'bjuːs] *n* (*insults*) insultos *mpl*, improperios *mpl*; (*misuse*) abuso ♦ *vt* [ə'bjuːz] (*ill-treat*) maltratar; (*take advantage of*) abusar de; **open to ~** sujeto al abuso.
abusive [ə'bjuːsɪv] *adj* ofensivo.
abysmal [ə'bɪzməl] *adj* pésimo; (*ignorance*) supino.
abyss [ə'bɪs] *n* abismo.
AC *abbr* (= *alternating current*) corriente *f* alterna ♦ *n abbr* (*US*) = *athletic club*.
a/c *abbr* (*BANKING etc*) = *account, account current*.
academic [ækə'dɛmɪk] *adj* académico, universitario; (*pej*: *issue*) puramente teórico ♦ *n* estudioso/a; (*lecturer*) profesor(a) *m/f* universitario/a; **~ year** (*UNIV*) año académico.
academy [ə'kædəmɪ] *n* (*learned body*) academia; (*school*) instituto, colegio; **~ of music** conservatorio.
ACAS ['eɪkæs] *n abbr* (*BRIT*: = *Advisory, Conciliation and Arbitration Service*) ≈ Instituto de Mediación, Arbitraje y Conciliación.
accede [æk'siːd] *vi*: **to ~ to** acceder a.
accelerate [æk'sɛləreɪt] *vt* acelerar ♦ *vi* acelerarse.
acceleration [æksɛlə'reɪʃən] *n* aceleración *f*.
accelerator [æk'sɛləreɪtə*] *n* (*BRIT*) acelerador *m*.
accent ['æksɛnt] *n* acento.
accentuate [æk'sɛntjueɪt] *vt* (*syllable*) acentuar; (*need, difference etc*) recalcar, subrayar.
accept [ək'sɛpt] *vt* aceptar; (*approve*) aprobar; (*concede*) admitir.
acceptable [ək'sɛptəbl] *adj* aceptable; admisible.
acceptance [ək'sɛptəns] *n* aceptación *f*; aprobación *f*; **to meet with general ~** recibir la aprobación general.
access ['æksɛs] *n* acceso ♦ *vt* (*COMPUT*) acceder a; **the burglars gained ~ through a window** los ladrones lograron entrar por una ventana; **to have ~ to** tener acceso a.
accessible [æk'sɛsəbl] *adj* accesible.
accession [æk'sɛʃən] (*of monarch*) subida, ascenso; (*addition*) adquisición *f*.
accessory [æk'sɛsərɪ] *n* accesorio; **toilet accessories** artículos *mpl* de tocador.
access road *n* carretera de acceso; (*to motorway*) carril *m* de acceso.
access time *n* (*COMPUT*) tiempo de acceso.
accident ['æksɪdənt] *n* accidente *m*; (*chance*) casualidad *f*; **by ~** (*unintentionally*) sin querer; (*by coincidence*) por casualidad; **~s at work** accidentes *mpl* de trabajo; **to meet with** *or* **to have an ~** tener *or* sufrir un accidente.
accidental [æksɪ'dɛntl] *adj* accidental, fortuito.
accidentally [æksɪ'dɛntəlɪ] *adv* sin querer; por casualidad.
accident insurance *n* seguro contra accidentes.
accident-prone ['æksɪdənt'prəun] *adj* propenso a los accidentes.
acclaim [ə'kleɪm] *vt* aclamar, aplaudir ♦ *n* aclamación *f*, aplausos *mpl*.
acclamation [æklə'meɪʃən] *n* (*approval*) aclamación *f*; (*applause*) aplausos *mpl*; **by ~** por aclamación.
acclimatize [ə'klaɪmətaɪz], (*US*) **acclimate** [ə'klaɪmət] *vt*: **to become ~d** aclimatarse.
accolade ['ækəuleɪd] *n* (*prize*) premio; (*praise*) alabanzas *fpl*, homenaje *m*.
accommodate [ə'kɔmədeɪt] *vt* alojar, hospedar; (*oblige, help*) complacer; **this car ~s 4 people comfortably** en este coche caben 4 personas cómodamente.
accommodating [ə'kɔmədeɪtɪŋ] *adj* servicial, complaciente.
accommodation *n*, (*US*) **accommodations** *npl* [əkɔmə'deɪʃən(z)] alojamiento; **"~ to let"** "se alquilan habitaciones"; **seating ~** asientos *mpl*.
accompaniment [ə'kʌmpənɪmənt] *n* acompañamiento.
accompanist [ə'kʌmpənɪst] *n* (*MUS*) acompañante *m/f*.
accompany [ə'kʌmpənɪ] *vt* acompañar.
accomplice [ə'kʌmplɪs] *n* cómplice *m/f*.
accomplish [ə'kʌmplɪʃ] *vt* (*finish*) acabar;

(*aim*) realizar; (*task*) llevar a cabo.
accomplished [ə'kʌmplɪʃt] *adj* experto, hábil.
accomplishment [ə'kʌmplɪʃmənt] *n* (*ending*) conclusión *f*; (*bringing about*) realización *f*; (*skill*) talento.
accord [ə'kɔːd] *n* acuerdo ♦ *vt* conceder; **of his own ~** espontáneamente; **with one ~** de *or* por común acuerdo.
accordance [ə'kɔːdəns] *n*: **in ~ with** de acuerdo con.
according [ə'kɔːdɪŋ]: **~ to** *prep* según; (*in accordance with*) conforme a; **it went ~ to plan** salió según lo previsto.
accordingly [ə'kɔːdɪŋlɪ] *adv* (*thus*) por consiguiente.
accordion [ə'kɔːdɪən] *n* acordeón *m*.
accordionist [ə'kɔːdɪənɪst] *n* acordeonista *m/f*.
accost [ə'kɔst] *vt* abordar, dirigirse a.
account [ə'kaunt] *n* (*COMM*) cuenta, factura; (*report*) informe *m*; **~s** *npl* (*COMM*) cuentas *fpl*; **"~ payee only"** "únicamente en cuenta del beneficiario"; **your ~ is still outstanding** su cuenta está todavía pendiente; **of little ~** de poca importancia; **on ~** a crédito; **to buy sth on ~** comprar algo a crédito; **on no ~** bajo ningún concepto; **on ~ of** a causa de, por motivo de; **to take into ~, take ~ of** tener en cuenta; **to keep an ~ of** llevar la cuenta de; **to bring sb to ~ for sth/for having done sth** pedirle cuentas a algn por algo/por haber hecho algo.
▶**account for** *vt fus* (*explain*) explicar; **all the children were ~ed for** no faltaba ningún niño.
accountability [əkauntə'bɪlɪtɪ] *n* responsabilidad *f*.
accountable [ə'kauntəbl] *adj*: **~ (for)** responsable (de).
accountancy [ə'kauntənsɪ] *n* contabilidad *f*.
accountant [ə'kauntənt] *n* contable *m/f*, contador(a) *m/f* (*LAM*).
accounting [ə'kauntɪŋ] *n* contabilidad *f*.
accounting period *n* período contable, ejercicio financiero.
account number *n* (*at bank etc*) número de cuenta.
account payable *n* cuenta por pagar.
account receivable *n* cuenta por cobrar.
accoutrements [ə'kuːtrəmənts] *npl* equipo, pertrechos *mpl*.
accredited [ə'krɛdɪtɪd] *adj* (*agent etc*) autorizado, acreditado.
accretion [ə'kriːʃən] *n* acumulación *f*.
accrue [ə'kruː] *vi* (*mount up*) aumentar, incrementarse; (*interest*) acumularse; **to ~ to** corresponder a; **~d charges** gastos *mpl* vencidos; **~d interest** interés *m* acumulado.
accumulate [ə'kjuːmjuleɪt] *vt* acumular ♦ *vi* acumularse.
accumulation [əkjuːmju'leɪʃən] *n* acumulación *f*.
accuracy ['ækjurəsɪ] *n* exactitud *f*, precisión *f*.
accurate ['ækjurɪt] *adj* (*number*) exacto; (*answer*) acertado; (*shot*) certero.
accurately ['ækjurɪtlɪ] *adv* (*count, shoot, answer*) con precisión.
accursed [ə'kəːst] *adj* maldito.
accusation [ækju'zeɪʃən] *n* acusación *f*.
accusative [ə'kjuːzətɪv] *n* acusativo.
accuse [ə'kjuːz] *vt* acusar; (*blame*) echar la culpa a.
accused [ə'kjuːzd] *n* acusado/a.
accuser [ə'kjuːzə*] *n* acusador(a) *m/f*.
accustom [ə'kʌstəm] *vt* acostumbrar; **to ~ o.s. to sth** acostumbrarse a algo.
accustomed [ə'kʌstəmd] *adj*: **~ to** acostumbrado a.
AC/DC *abbr* = *alternating current/direct current*.
ACE [eɪs] *n abbr* = *American Council on Education*.
ace [eɪs] *n* as *m*.
acerbic [ə'səːbɪk] *adj* acerbo; (*fig*) mordaz.
acetate ['æsɪteɪt] *n* acetato.
ache [eɪk] *n* dolor *m* ♦ *vi* doler; (*yearn*): **to ~ to do sth** ansiar hacer algo; **I've got stomach ~** *or* (*US*) **a stomach ~** tengo dolor de estómago, me duele el estómago; **my head ~s** me duele la cabeza.
achieve [ə'tʃiːv] *vt* (*reach*) alcanzar; (*realize*) realizar; (*victory, success*) lograr, conseguir.
achievement [ə'tʃiːvmənt] *n* (*completion*) realización *f*; (*success*) éxito.
Achilles heel [ə'kɪliːz-] *n* talón *m* de Aquiles.
acid ['æsɪd] *adj* ácido; (*bitter*) agrio ♦ *n* ácido.
acidity [ə'sɪdɪtɪ] *n* acidez *f*; (*MED*) acedía.
acid rain *n* lluvia ácida.
acid test *n* (*fig*) prueba de fuego.
acknowledge [ək'nɔlɪdʒ] *vt* (*letter: also*: **~ receipt of**) acusar recibo de; (*fact*) reconocer.
acknowledgement [ək'nɔlɪdʒmənt] *n* acuse *m* de recibo; reconocimiento; **~s** (*in book*) agradecimientos *mpl*.
ACLU *n abbr* (= *American Civil Liberties Union*) *unión americana por libertades civiles*.

acme ['ækmɪ] *n* súmmum *m.*
acne ['æknɪ] *n* acné *m.*
acorn ['eɪkɔːn] *n* bellota.
acoustic [ə'kuːstɪk] *adj* acústico.
acoustic coupler [-'kʌplə*] *n* (*COMPUT*) acoplador *m* acústico.
acoustics [ə'kuːstɪks] *n, npl* acústica *sg.*
acquaint [ə'kweɪnt] *vt*: **to ~ sb with sth** (*inform*) poner a algn al corriente de algo; **to be ~ed with** (*person*) conocer; (*fact*) estar al corriente de.
acquaintance [ə'kweɪntəns] *n* conocimiento; (*person*) conocido/a; **to make sb's ~** conocer a algn.
acquiesce [ækwɪ'ɛs] *vi* (*agree*): **to ~ (in)** consentir (en), conformarse (con).
acquire [ə'kwaɪə*] *vt* adquirir.
acquired [ə'kwaɪəd] *adj* adquirido; **it's an ~ taste** es algo a lo que uno se aficiona poco a poco.
acquisition [ækwɪ'zɪʃən] *n* adquisición *f.*
acquisitive [ə'kwɪzɪtɪv] *adj* codicioso.
acquit [ə'kwɪt] *vt* absolver, exculpar; **to ~ o.s. well** defenderse bien.
acquittal [ə'kwɪtl] *n* absolución *f,* exculpación *f.*
acre ['eɪkə*] *n* acre *m.*
acreage ['eɪkərɪdʒ] *n* extensión *f.*
acrid ['ækrɪd] *adj* (*smell*) acre; (*fig*) mordaz, sarcástico.
acrimonious [ækrɪ'məunɪəs] *adj* (*remark*) mordaz; (*argument*) reñido.
acrobat ['ækrəbæt] *n* acróbata *m/f.*
acrobatic [ækrə'bætɪk] *adj* acrobático.
acrobatics [ækrə'bætɪks] *npl* acrobacias *fpl.*
acronym ['ækrənɪm] *n* siglas *fpl.*
across [ə'krɔs] *prep* (*on the other side of*) al otro lado de; (*crosswise*) a través de ♦ *adv* de un lado a otro, de una parte a otra; a través, al través; **to run/swim ~** atravesar corriendo/nadando; **~ from** enfrente de; **the lake is 12 km ~** el lago tiene 12 km de ancho; **to get sth ~ to sb** (*fig*) hacer comprender algo a algn.
acrylic [ə'krɪlɪk] *adj* acrílico.
act [ækt] *n* acto, acción *f*; (*THEAT*) acto; (*in music-hall etc*) número; (*LAW*) decreto, ley *f* ♦ *vi* (*behave*) comportarse; (*THEAT*) actuar; (*pretend*) fingir; (*take action*) tomar medidas ♦ *vt* (*part*) hacer, representar; **~ of God** fuerza mayor; **it's only an ~** es cuento; **to catch sb in the ~** coger a algn in fraganti *or* con las manos en la masa; **to ~ Hamlet** hacer el papel de Hamlet; **to ~ as** actuar *or* hacer de; **~ing in my capacity as chairman, I ...** en mi calidad de presidente, yo ...; **it ~s as a deterrent** sirve para disuadir; **he's only ~ing** está fingiendo nada más.
▸**act on** *vt*: **to ~ on sth** actuar *or* obrar sobre algo.
▸**act out** *vt* (*event*) representar; (*fantasies*) realizar.
acting ['æktɪŋ] *adj* suplente ♦ *n*: **to do some ~** hacer algo de teatro; **he is the ~ manager** es el gerente en funciones.
action ['ækʃən] *n* acción *f,* acto; (*MIL*) acción *f*; (*LAW*) proceso, demanda; **to put a plan into ~** poner un plan en acción *or* en marcha; **killed in ~** (*MIL*) muerto en acto de servicio *or* en combate; **out of ~** (*person*) fuera de combate; (*thing*) averiado, descompuesto; **to take ~** tomar medidas; **to bring an ~ against sb** entablar *or* presentar demanda contra algn.
action replay *n* (*TV*) repetición *f.*
activate ['æktɪveɪt] *vt* activar.
active ['æktɪv] *adj* activo, enérgico; (*volcano*) en actividad; **to play an ~ part in** colaborar activamente en; **~ file** (*COMPUT*) fichero activo.
active duty (AD) *n* (*US MIL*) servicio activo.
actively ['æktɪvlɪ] *adv* (*participate*) activamente; (*discourage, dislike*) enérgicamente.
active partner *n* (*COMM*) socio activo.
activist ['æktɪvɪst] *n* activista *m/f.*
activity [æk'tɪvɪtɪ] *n* actividad *f.*
actor ['æktə*] *n* actor *m.*
actress ['aektrɪs] *n* actriz *f.*
ACTT *n abbr* (*BRIT*: = *Association of Cinematographic, Television and Allied Technicians*) *sindicato de técnicos de cine y televisión.*
actual ['æktjuəl] *adj* verdadero, real.
actually ['æktjuəlɪ] *adv* realmente, en realidad.
actuary ['æktjuərɪ] *n* (*COMM*) actuario/a (de seguros).
actuate ['æktjueɪt] *vt* mover, impulsar.
acumen ['ækjumən] *n* perspicacia; **business ~** talento para los negocios.
acupuncture ['ækjupʌŋktʃə*] *n* acupuntura.
acute [ə'kjuːt] *adj* agudo.
acutely [ə'kjuːtlɪ] *adv* profundamente, extremadamente.
AD *adv abbr* (= *Anno Domini*) A.C. ♦ *n abbr* (*US MIL*) *see* **active duty**.
ad [æd] *n abbr* = **advertisement.**
adage ['ædɪdʒ] *n* refrán *m,* adagio.
Adam ['ædəm] *n* Adán; **~'s apple** *n* nuez *f* (de la garganta).
adamant ['ædəmənt] *adj* firme, inflexible.

adapt [ə'dæpt] *vt* adaptar; (*reconcile*) acomodar ♦ *vi*: **to ~ (to)** adaptarse (a), ajustarse (a).
adaptability [ədæptə'bılıtı] *n* (*of person, device etc*) adaptabilidad *f*.
adaptable [ə'dæptəbl] *adj* (*device*) adaptable; (*person*) acomodadizo, que se adapta.
adaptation [ædæp'teıʃən] *n* adaptación *f*.
adapter, adaptor [ə'dæptə*] *n* (*ELEC*) adaptador *m*.
ADC *n abbr* (*MIL*) = *aide-de-camp*; (*US*: = *Aid to Dependent Children*) *ayuda para niños dependientes*.
add [æd] *vt* añadir, agregar (*esp LAM*); (*figures*: *also*: ~ **up**) sumar ♦ *vi*: **to ~ to** (*increase*) aumentar, acrecentar.
▸**add on** *vt* añadir.
▸**add up** *vt* (*figures*) sumar ♦ *vi* (*fig*): **it doesn't ~ up** no tiene sentido; **it doesn't ~ up to much** es poca cosa, no tiene gran *or* mucha importancia.
addendum [ə'dɛndəm] *n* ad(d)enda *m or f*.
adder ['ædə*] *n* víbora.
addict ['ædıkt] *n* (*to drugs etc*) adicto/a; (*enthusiast*) aficionado/a, entusiasta *m/f*; **heroin ~** heroinómano/a.
addicted [ə'dıktıd] *adj*: **to be ~ to** ser adicto a; ser aficionado a.
addiction [ə'dıkʃən] *n* (*dependence*) hábito morboso; (*enthusiasm*) afición *f*.
addictive [ə'dıktıv] *adj* que causa adicción.
adding machine ['ædıŋ-] *n* calculadora.
Addis Ababa ['ædıs'æbəbə] *n* Addis Abeba *m*.
addition [ə'dıʃən] *n* (*adding up*) adición *f*; (*thing added*) añadidura, añadido; **in ~** además, por añadidura; **in ~ to** además de.
additional [ə'dıʃənl] *adj* adicional.
additive ['ædıtıv] *n* aditivo.
addled ['ædld] *adj* (*BRIT*: *rotten*) podrido; (: *fig*) confuso.
address [ə'drɛs] *n* dirección *f*, señas *fpl*; (*speech*) discurso; (*COMPUT*) dirección *f* ♦ *vt* (*letter*) dirigir; (*speak to*) dirigirse a, dirigir la palabra a; **form of ~** tratamiento; **absolute/relative ~** (*COMPUT*) dirección *f* absoluta/relativa; **to ~ o.s. to sth** (*issue, problem*) abordar.
address book *n* agenda (de direcciones).
addressee [ædrɛ'si:] *n* destinatario/a.
Aden ['eıdn] *n* Adén *m*.
adenoids ['ædınɔıdz] *npl* vegetaciones *fpl* (adenoideas).
adept ['ædɛpt] *adj*: **~ at** experto *or* ducho en.
adequacy ['ædıkwəsı] *n* idoneidad *f*.
adequate ['ædıkwıt] *adj* (*satisfactory*) adecuado; (*enough*) suficiente; **to feel ~ to a task** sentirse con fuerzas para una tarea.
adequately ['ædıkwıtlı] *adv* adecuadamente.
adhere [əd'hıə*] *vi*: **to ~ to** adherirse a; (*fig*: *abide by*) observar.
adherent [əd'hıərənt] *n* partidario/a.
adhesion [əd'hi:ʒən] *n* adherencia.
adhesive [əd'hi:zıv] *adj, n* adhesivo.
adhesive tape *n* (*BRIT*) cinta adhesiva; (*US*: *MED*) esparadrapo.
ad hoc [æd'hɔk] *adj* (*decision*) ad hoc; (*committee*) formado con fines específicos ♦ *adv* ad hoc.
adieu [ə'dju:] *excl* ¡vaya con Dios!
ad inf ['æd'ınf] *adv* hasta el infinito.
adjacent [ə'dʒeısənt] *adj*: **~ to** contiguo a, inmediato a.
adjective ['ædʒɛktıv] *n* adjetivo.
adjoin [ə'dʒɔın] *vt* estar contiguo a; (*land*) lindar con.
adjoining [ə'dʒɔınıŋ] *adj* contiguo, vecino.
adjourn [ə'dʒə:n] *vt* aplazar; (*session*) suspender, levantar; (*US*: *end*) terminar ♦ *vi* suspenderse; **the meeting has been ~ed till next week** se ha levantado la sesión hasta la semana que viene; **they ~ed to the pub** (*col*) se trasladaron al bar.
adjournment [ə'dʒə:nmənt] *n* (*period*) suspensión *f*; (*postponement*) aplazamiento.
Adjt. *abbr* = **adjutant**.
adjudicate [ə'dʒu:dıkeıt] *vi* sentenciar; (*contest*) hacer de árbitro en, juzgar; (*claim*) decidir.
adjudication [ədʒu:dı'keıʃən] *n* fallo.
adjudicator [ə'dʒu:dıkeıtə*] *n* juez *m*, árbitro.
adjust [ə'dʒʌst] *vt* (*change*) modificar; (*arrange*) arreglar; (*machine*) ajustar ♦ *vi*: **to ~ (to)** adaptarse (a).
adjustable [ə'dʒʌstəbl] *adj* ajustable.
adjuster [ə'dʒʌstə*] *n see* **loss adjuster**.
adjustment [ə'dʒʌstmənt] *n* modificación *f*; arreglo; (*of prices, wages*) ajuste *m*.
adjutant ['ædʒətənt] *n* ayudante *m*.
ad-lib [æd'lıb] *vt, vi* improvisar ♦ *adv*: **ad lib** a voluntad, a discreción.
adman ['ædmæn] *n* (*col*) publicista *m*.
admin ['ædmin] *n abbr* (*col*) = **administration**.
administer [əd'mınıstə*] *vt* proporcionar; (*justice*) administrar.
administration [ədmını'streıʃən] *n* administración *f*; (*government*) gobierno;

the A~ (*US*) la Administración.
administrative [əd'mɪnɪstrətɪv] *adj* administrativo.
administrator [əd'mɪnɪstreɪtə*] *n* administrador(a) *m/f.*
admirable ['ædmərəbl] *adj* admirable.
admiral ['ædmərəl] *n* almirante *m.*
Admiralty ['ædmərəltɪ] *n* (*BRIT*) Ministerio de Marina, Almirantazgo.
admiration [ædmə'reɪʃən] *n* admiración *f.*
admire [əd'maɪə*] *vt* admirar.
admirer [əd'maɪərə*] *n* admirador(a) *m/f;* (*suitor*) pretendiente *m.*
admiring [əd'maɪərɪŋ] *adj* (*expression*) de admiración.
admissible [əd'mɪsəbl] *adj* admisible.
admission [əd'mɪʃən] *n* (*exhibition, nightclub*) entrada; (*enrolment*) ingreso; (*confession*) confesión *f;* **"~ free"** "entrada gratis *or* libre"; **by his own ~** él mismo reconoce que.
admit [əd'mɪt] *vt* dejar entrar, dar entrada a; (*permit*) admitir; (*acknowledge*) reconocer; **"this ticket ~s two"** "entrada para 2 personas"; **children not ~ted** se prohíbe la entrada a (los) menores de edad; **I must ~ that** ... debo reconocer que ...
►**admit of** *vt fus* admitir, permitir.
►**admit to** *vt fus* confesarse culpable de.
admittance [əd'mɪtəns] *n* entrada; **"no ~"** "se prohíbe la entrada", "prohibida la entrada".
admittedly [əd'mɪtədlɪ] *adv* de acuerdo que.
admonish [əd'mɔnɪʃ] *vt* amonestar; (*advise*) aconsejar.
ad nauseam [æd'nɔːsɪæm] *adv* hasta la saciedad.
ado [ə'duː] *n*: **without (any) more ~** sin más (ni más).
adolescence [ædəu'lɛsns] *n* adolescencia.
adolescent [ædəu'lɛsnt] *adj, n* adolescente *m/f.*
adopt [ə'dɔpt] *vt* adoptar.
adopted [ə'dɔptɪd] *adj* adoptivo.
adoption [ə'dɔpʃən] *n* adopción *f.*
adoptive [ə'dɔptɪv] *adj* adoptivo.
adorable [ə'dɔːrəbl] *adj* adorable.
adoration [ædə'reɪʃən] *n* adoración *f.*
adore [ə'dɔː*] *vt* adorar.
adoring [ə'dɔːrɪŋ] *adj*: **to his ~ public** a un público que le adora *or* le adoraba *etc.*
adorn [ə'dɔːn] *vt* adornar.
adornment [ə'dɔːnmənt] *n* adorno.
ADP *n abbr see* **automatic data processing**.
adrenalin [ə'drɛnəlɪn] *n* adrenalina.
Adriatic [eɪdrɪ'ætɪk] *n*: **the ~ (Sea)** el (Mar) Adriático.
adrift [ə'drɪft] *adv* a la deriva; **to come ~** (*boat*) ir a la deriva, soltarse; (*wire, rope etc*) soltarse.
adroit [ə'drɔɪt] *adj* diestro, hábil.
ADT *abbr* (*US*: = *Atlantic Daylight Time*) *hora de verano de Nueva York.*
adulation [ædju'leɪʃən] *n* adulación *f.*
adult ['ædʌlt] *n* adulto/a ♦ *adj*: **~ education** educación *f* para adultos.
adulterate [ə'dʌltəreɪt] *vt* adulterar.
adulterer [ə'dʌltərə*] *n* adúltero.
adulteress [ə'dʌltrɪs] *n* adúltera.
adultery [ə'dʌltərɪ] *n* adulterio.
adulthood ['ædʌlthud] *n* edad *f* adulta.
advance [əd'vɑːns] *n* adelanto, progreso; (*money*) anticipo; (*MIL*) avance *m* ♦ *vt* avanzar, adelantar; (*money*) anticipar ♦ *vi* avanzar, adelantarse; **in ~** por adelantado; (*book*) con antelación; **to make ~s to sb** (*gen*) ponerse en contacto con algn; (*amorously*) insinuarse a algn.
advanced *adj* avanzado; (*SCOL: studies*) adelantado; **~ in years** entrado en años.
advancement [əd'vɑːnsmənt] *n* progreso; (*in rank*) ascenso.
advance notice *n* previo aviso.
advance payment *n* (*part sum*) anticipo.
advantage [əd'vɑːntɪdʒ] *n* (*also TENNIS*) ventaja; **to take ~ of** aprovecharse de; **it's to our ~** es ventajoso para nosotros.
advantageous [ædvən'teɪdʒəs] *adj* ventajoso, provechoso.
advent ['ædvənt] *n* advenimiento; **A~** Adviento.
adventure [əd'vɛntʃə*] *n* aventura.
adventure playground *n* parque *m* infantil.
adventurous [əd'vɛntʃərəs] *adj* aventurero; (*bold*) arriesgado.
adverb ['ædvəːb] *n* adverbio.
adversary ['ædvəsərɪ] *n* adversario, contrario.
adverse ['ædvəːs] *adj* adverso, contrario; **~ to** adverso a.
adversity [əd'vəːsɪtɪ] *n* infortunio.
advert ['ædvəːt] *n abbr* (*BRIT*) = **advertisement**.
advertise ['ædvətaɪz] *vi* hacer propaganda; (*in newspaper etc*) poner un anuncio, anunciarse; **to ~ for** (*staff*) buscar por medio de anuncios ♦ *vt* anunciar.
advertisement [əd'vəːtɪsmənt] *n* (*COMM*) anuncio.
advertiser ['ædvətaɪzə*] *n* anunciante *m/f.*
advertising ['ædvətaɪzɪŋ] *n* publicidad *f,* propaganda; anuncios *mpl.*
advertising agency *n* agencia de

publicidad.
advertising campaign *n* campaña de publicidad.
advice [əd'vaɪs] *n* consejo, consejos *mpl*; (*notification*) aviso; **a piece of** ~ un consejo; **to take legal** ~ consultar a un abogado; **to ask (sb) for** ~ pedir consejo (a algn).
advice note *n* (*BRIT*) nota de aviso.
advisable [əd'vaɪzəbl] *adj* aconsejable, conveniente.
advise [əd'vaɪz] *vt* aconsejar; **to** ~ **sb of sth** (*inform*) informar a algn de algo; **to** ~ **sb against sth/doing sth** desaconsejar algo a algn/aconsejar a algn que no haga algo; **you will be well/ill** ~**d to go** deberías/no deberías ir.
advisedly [əd'vaɪzɪdlɪ] *adv* (*deliberately*) deliberadamente.
adviser [əd'vaɪzə*] *n* consejero/a; (*business adviser*) asesor(a) *m/f*.
advisory [ad'vaɪzərɪ] *adj* consultivo; **in an** ~ **capacity** como asesor.
advocate ['ædvəkeɪt] *vt* (*argue for*) abogar por; (*give support to*) ser partidario de ♦ *n* ['ædvəkɪt] abogado/a.
advt. *abbr* = **advertisement**.
AEA *n abbr* (*BRIT*: = *Atomic Energy Authority*) *consejo de energía nuclear*.
AEC *n abbr* (*US*: = *Atomic Energy Commission*) AEC *f*.
AEEU *n abbr* (*BRIT*: = *Amalgamated Engineering and Electrical Union*) *sindicato mixto de ingenieros y electricistas*.
Aegean [iː'dʒiːən] *n*: **the** ~ **(Sea)** el (Mar) Egeo.
aegis ['iːdʒɪs] *n*: **under the** ~ **of** bajo la tutela de.
aeon ['iːən] *n* eón *m*.
aerial ['ɛərɪəl] *n* antena ♦ *adj* aéreo.
aerie ['ɛərɪ] *n* (*US*) aguilera.
aero- ['ɛərəu] *pref* aero-.
aerobatics [ɛərəu'bætɪks] *npl* acrobacia aérea.
aerobics [ɛə'rəubɪks] *nsg* aerobic *m*, aerobismo (*LAM*).
aerodrome ['ɛərədrəum] *n* (*BRIT*) aeródromo.
aerodynamic [ɛərəudaɪ'næmɪk] *adj* aerodinámico.
aeronautics [ɛərəu'nɔːtɪks] *nsg* aeronáutica.
aeroplane ['ɛərəpleɪn] *n* (*BRIT*) avión *m*.
aerosol ['ɛərəsɔl] *n* aerosol *m*.
aerospace industry ['ɛərəuspeɪs-] *n* industria aerospacial.
aesthetic [iːs'θɛtɪk] *adj* estético.
aesthetics [iːs'θɛtɪks] *npl* estética.
a.f. *abbr* = *audiofrequency*.
afar [ə'fɑː*] *adv* lejos; **from** ~ desde lejos.
AFB *n abbr* (*US*) = *Air Force Base*.
AFDC *n abbr* (*US*: = *Aid to Families with Dependent Children*) *ayuda a familias con hijos menores*.
affable ['æfəbl] *adj* afable.
affair [ə'fɛə*] *n* asunto; (*also*: **love** ~) aventura *f* amorosa; ~**s** (*business*) asuntos *mpl*; **the Watergate** ~ el asunto (de) Watergate.
affect [ə'fɛkt] *vt* afectar, influir en; (*move*) conmover.
affectation [æfɛk'teɪʃən] *n* afectación *f*.
affected [ə'fɛktɪd] *adj* afectado.
affection [ə'fɛkʃən] *n* afecto, cariño.
affectionate [ə'fɛkʃənɪt] *adj* afectuoso, cariñoso.
affectionately [ə'fɛkʃənɪtlɪ] *adv* afectuosamente.
affidavit [æfɪ'deɪvɪt] *n* (*LAW*) declaración *f* jurada.
affiliated [ə'fɪlɪeɪtɪd] *adj* afiliado; ~ **company** empresa *or* compañía filial *or* subsidiaria.
affinity [ə'fɪnɪtɪ] *n* afinidad *f*.
affirm [ə'fəːm] *vt* afirmar.
affirmation [æfə'meɪʃən] *n* afirmación *f*.
affirmative [ə'fəːmətɪv] *adj* afirmativo.
affix [ə'fɪks] *vt* (*signature*) estampar; (*stamp*) pegar.
afflict [ə'flɪkt] *vt* afligir.
affliction [ə'flɪkʃən] *n* enfermedad *f*, aflicción *f*.
affluence ['æfluəns] *n* opulencia, riqueza.
affluent ['aefluənt] *adj* adinerado, acaudalado; **the** ~ **society** la sociedad opulenta.
afford [ə'fɔːd] *vt* poder permitirse; (*provide*) proporcionar; **can we** ~ **a car?** ¿podemos permitirnos el gasto de comprar un coche?
affordable [ə'fɔːdəbl] *adj* asequible.
affray [ə'freɪ] *n* refriega, reyerta.
affront [ə'frʌnt] *n* afrenta, ofensa.
affronted [ə'frʌntɪd] *adj* ofendido.
Afghan ['æfgæn] *adj*, *n* afgano/a *m/f*.
Afghanistan [æf'gænɪstæn] *n* Afganistán *m*.
afield [ə'fiːld] *adv*: **far** ~ muy lejos.
AFL-CIO *n abbr* (*US*: = *American Federation of Labor and Congress of Industrial Organizations*) *confederación sindicalista*.
afloat [ə'fləut] *adv* (*floating*) a flote; (*at sea*) en el mar.
afoot [ə'fut] *adv*: **there is something** ~ algo se está tramando.
aforesaid [ə'fɔːsɛd] *adj* susodicho; (*COMM*) mencionado anteriormente.

afraid [ə'freɪd] *adj*: **to be ~ of** (*person*) tener miedo a; (*thing*) tener miedo de; **to be ~ to** tener miedo de, temer; **I am ~ that** me temo que; **I'm ~ so** ¡me temo que sí!, ¡lo siento, pero es así!; **I'm ~ not** me temo que no.
afresh [ə'frɛʃ] *adv* de nuevo, otra vez.
Africa ['æfrɪkə] *n* África.
African ['æfrɪkən] *adj, n* africano/a *m/f.*
Afrikaans [æfrɪ'kɑːns] *n* africaans *m.*
Afrikaner [æfrɪ'kɑːnə*] *n* africánder *m/f.*
Afro-American ['æfrəuə'mɛrɪkən] *adj, n* afroamericano/a *m/f.*
AFT *n abbr* (= *American Federation of Teachers*) *sindicato de profesores.*
aft [ɑːft] *adv* (*to be*) en popa; (*to go*) a popa.
after ['ɑːftə*] *prep* (*time*) después de; (*place, order*) detrás de, tras ♦ *adv* después ♦ *conj* después (de) que; **what/who are you ~?** ¿qué/a quién buscas?; **the police are ~ him** la policía le está buscando; **~ having done/he left** después de haber hecho/ después de que se marchó; **~ dinner** después de cenar *or* comer; **the day ~ tomorrow** pasado mañana; **to ask ~ sb** preguntar por algn; **~ all** después de todo, al fin y al cabo; **~ you!** ¡Vd primero!; **quarter ~ two** (*US*) las 2 y cuarto.
afterbirth ['ɑːftəbəːθ] *n* placenta.
aftercare ['ɑːftəkɛə*] *n* (*MED*) asistencia postoperatoria.
after-effects ['ɑːftərɪfɛkts] *npl* secuelas *fpl*, efectos *mpl.*
afterlife ['ɑːftəlaɪf] *n* vida después de la muerte.
aftermath ['ɑːftəmɑːθ] *n* consecuencias *fpl*, resultados *mpl.*
afternoon [ɑːftə'nuːn] *n* tarde *f*; **good ~!** ¡buenas tardes!
afters ['ɑːftəz] *n* (*col: dessert*) postre *m.*
after-sales service [ɑːftə'seɪlz-] *n* (*BRIT COMM: for car, washing machine etc*) servicio de asistencia pos-venta.
after-shave (lotion) ['ɑːftəʃeɪv-] *n* loción *f* para después del afeitado, aftershave *m.*
aftershock ['ɑːftəʃɔk] *n* (*of earthquake*) pequeño temblor *m* posterior.
aftertaste ['ɑːftəteɪst] *n* regusto.
afterthought ['ɑːftəθɔːt] *n* ocurrencia (tardía).
afterwards ['ɑːftəwədz] *adv* después, más tarde.
again [ə'gɛn] *adv* otra vez, de nuevo; **to do sth ~** volver a hacer algo; **~ and ~** una y otra vez; **now and ~** de vez en cuando.
against [ə'gɛnst] *prep* (*opposed*) en contra de; (*close to*) contra, junto a; **I was leaning ~ the desk** estaba apoyado en el escritorio; **(as) ~** frente a.
age [eɪdʒ] *n* edad *f*; (*old ~*) vejez *f*; (*period*) época ♦ *vi* envejecer(se) ♦ *vt* envejecer; **what ~ is he?** ¿qué edad *or* cuántos años tiene?; **he is 20 years of ~** tiene 20 años; **under ~** menor de edad; **to come of ~** llegar a la mayoría de edad; **it's been ~s since I saw you** hace siglos que no te veo.
aged [eɪdʒd] *adj*: **~ 10** de 10 años de edad ♦ *npl* ['eɪdʒɪd]: **the ~** los ancianos.
age group *n*: **to be in the same ~** tener la misma edad; **the 40 to 50 ~** las personas de 40 a 50 años.
ageing ['eɪdʒɪŋ] *adj* que envejece; (*pej*) en declive ♦ *n* envejecimiento.
ageless ['eɪdʒlɪs] *adj* (*eternal*) eterno; (*ever young*) siempre joven.
age limit *n* límite *m* de edad, edad *f* tope.
agency ['eɪdʒənsɪ] *n* agencia; **through** *or* **by the ~ of** por medio de.
agenda [ə'dʒɛndə] *n* orden *m* del día; **on the ~** (*COMM*) en el orden del día.
agent ['eɪdʒənt] *n* (*gen*) agente *m/f*; (*representative*) representante *m/f*, delegado/a.
aggravate ['ægrəveɪt] *vt* agravar; (*annoy*) irritar, exasperar.
aggravating ['ægrəveɪtɪŋ] *adj* irritante, molesto.
aggravation [ægrə'veɪʃən] *n* agravamiento.
aggregate ['ægrɪgeɪt] *n* conjunto.
aggression [ə'grɛʃən] *n* agresión *f.*
aggressive [ə'grɛsɪv] *adj* agresivo; (*vigorous*) enérgico.
aggressiveness [ə'grɛsɪvnɪs] *n* agresividad *f.*
aggressor [ə'grɛsə*] *n* agresor(a) *m/f.*
aggrieved [ə'griːvd] *adj* ofendido, agraviado.
aggro ['ægrəu] *n* (*col*) (*physical violence*) bronca; (*bad feeling*) mal rollo; (*hassle*) rollo, movida.
aghast [ə'gɑːst] *adj* horrorizado.
agile ['ædʒaɪl] *adj* ágil.
agility [ə'dʒɪlɪtɪ] *n* agilidad *f.*
agitate ['ædʒɪteɪt] *vt* (*shake*) agitar; (*trouble*) inquietar; **to ~ for** hacer campaña en pro de *or* en favor de.
agitated ['ædʒɪteɪtɪd] *adj* agitado.
agitator ['ædʒɪteɪtə*] *n* agitador(a) *m/f.*
AGM *n abbr see* **annual general meeting**.
agnostic [æg'nɔstɪk] *adj, n* agnóstico/a *m/f.*
ago [ə'gəu] *adv*: **2 days ~** hace 2 días; **not long ~** hace poco; **how long ~?** ¿hace cuánto tiempo?; **as long ~ as 1960** ya en 1960.
agog [ə'gɔg] *adj* (*anxious*) ansioso; (*excited*):

(all) ~ (for) (todo) emocionado (por).
agonize ['ægənaɪz] *vi*: **to ~ (over)** atormentarse (por).
agonized ['ægənaɪzd] *adj* angustioso.
agonizing ['ægənaɪzɪŋ] *adj* (*pain*) atroz; (*suspense*) angustioso.
agony ['ægənɪ] *n* (*pain*) dolor *m* atroz; (*distress*) angustia; **to be in ~** retorcerse de dolor.
agony aunt *n* (*BRIT col*) consejera sentimental.
agony column *n* consultorio sentimental.
agree [ə'gri:] *vt* (*price*) acordar, quedar en ♦ *vi* (*statements etc*) coincidir, concordar; **to ~ (with)** (*person*) estar de acuerdo (con), ponerse de acuerdo (con); **to ~ to do** aceptar hacer; **to ~ to sth** consentir en algo; **to ~ that** (*admit*) estar de acuerdo en que; **it was ~d that ...** se acordó que ...; **garlic doesn't ~ with me** el ajo no me sienta bien.
agreeable [ə'gri:əbl] *adj* agradable; (*person*) simpático; (*willing*) de acuerdo, conforme.
agreeably [ə'gri:əblɪ] *adv* agradablemente.
agreed [ə'gri:d] *adj* (*time, place*) convenido.
agreement [ə'gri:mənt] *n* acuerdo; (*COMM*) contrato; **in ~** de acuerdo, conforme; **by mutual ~** de común acuerdo.
agricultural [ægrɪ'kʌltʃərəl] *adj* agrícola.
agriculture ['ægrɪkʌltʃə*] *n* agricultura.
aground [ə'graund] *adv*: **to run ~** encallar, embarrancar.
ahead [ə'hɛd] *adv* delante; **~ of** delante de; (*fig*: *schedule etc*) antes de; **~ of time** antes de la hora; **to be ~ of sb** (*fig*) llevar ventaja *or* la delantera a algn; **go right** *or* **straight ~** siga adelante; **they were (right) ~ of us** iban (justo) delante de nosotros.
ahoy [ə'hɔɪ] *excl* ¡oiga!
AI *n abbr* = *Amnesty International*; (*COMPUT*) = **artificial intelligence**.
AIB *n abbr* (*BRIT*: = *Accident Investigation Bureau*) *oficina de investigación de accidentes*.
AID *n abbr* (= *artificial insemination by donor*) inseminación artificial por donante; (*US*: = *Agency for International Development*) Agencia Internacional para el Desarrollo.
aid [eɪd] *n* ayuda, auxilio ♦ *vt* ayudar, auxiliar; **in ~ of** a beneficio de; **with the ~ of** con la ayuda de; **to ~ and abet** (*LAW*) ser cómplice.
aide [eɪd] *n* (*POL*) ayudante *m/f*.
AIDS [eɪdz] *n abbr* (= *acquired immune* (*or immuno-*)*deficiency syndrome*) SIDA *m*, sida *m*.
AIH *abbr* (= *artificial insemination by husband*) *inseminación artificial por esposo*.
ailing ['eɪlɪŋ] *adj* (*person, economy*) enfermizo.
ailment ['eɪlmənt] *n* enfermedad *f*, achaque *m*.
aim [eɪm] *vt* (*gun*) apuntar; (*missile, remark*) dirigir; (*blow*) asestar ♦ *vi* (*also*: **take ~**) apuntar ♦ *n* puntería; (*objective*) propósito, meta; **to ~ at** (*objective*) aspirar a, pretender; **to ~ to do** tener como objetivo hacer, aspirar a hacer.
aimless ['eɪmlɪs] *adj* sin propósito, sin objeto.
aimlessly ['eɪmlɪslɪ] *adv* sin rumbo fijo.
ain't [eɪnt] (*col*) = **am not; aren't; isn't**.
air [ɛə*] *n* aire *m*; (*appearance*) aspecto ♦ *vt* (*room*) ventilar; (*clothes, bed, grievances, ideas*) airear; (*views*) hacer público ♦ *cpd* aéreo; **to throw sth into the ~** (*ball etc*) lanzar algo al aire; **by ~** (*travel*) en avión; **to be on the ~** (*RADIO, TV*: *programme*) estarse emitiendo; (: *station*) estar emitiendo.
airbag ['ɛəbæg] *n* airbag *m inv*.
air base *n* (*MIL*) base *f* aérea.
air bed *n* (*BRIT*) colcheta inflable *or* neumática.
airborne ['ɛəbɔ:n] *adj* (*in the air*) en el aire; (*MIL*) aerotransportado; **as soon as the plane was ~** tan pronto como el avión estuvo en el aire.
air cargo *n* carga aérea.
air-conditioned ['ɛəkən'dɪʃənd] *adj* climatizado.
air conditioning [-kən'dɪʃənɪŋ] *n* aire *m* acondicionado.
air-cooled ['ɛəku:ld] *adj* refrigerado por aire.
aircraft ['ɛəkrɑ:ft] *n, pl inv* avión *m*.
aircraft carrier *n* porta(a)viones *m inv*.
air cushion *n* cojín *m* de aire; (*AVIAT*) colchón *m* de aire.
airdrome ['ɛədrəum] *n* (*US*) aeródromo.
airfield ['ɛəfɪ:ld] *n* campo de aviación.
Air Force *n* fuerzas aéreas *fpl*, aviación *f*.
air freight *n* flete *m* por avión.
air freshener *n* ambientador *m*.
air gun *n* escopeta de aire comprimido.
air hostess (*BRIT*) *n* azafata, aeromoza (*LAM*).
airily ['ɛərɪlɪ] *adv* muy a la ligera.
airing ['ɛərɪŋ] *n*: **to give an ~ to** (*linen*) airear; (*room*) ventilar; (*fig*: *ideas etc*) airear, someter a discusión.
air letter *n* (*BRIT*) carta aérea.
airlift ['ɛəlɪft] *n* puente *m* aéreo.

airline ['ɛəlaɪn] *n* línea aérea.
airliner ['ɛəlaɪnə*] *n* avión *m* de pasajeros.
airlock ['ɛəlɔk] *n* (*in pipe*) esclusa de aire.
airmail ['ɛəmeɪl] *n*: **by** ~ por avión.
air mattress *n* colchón *m* inflable.
airplane ['ɛəpleɪn] *n* (*US*) avión *m*.
air pocket *n* bolsa de aire.
airport ['ɛəpɔːt] *n* aeropuerto.
air rage *n* *conducta agresiva de pasajeros a bordo de un avión.*
air raid *n* ataque *m* aéreo.
air rifle *n* escopeta de aire comprimido.
airsick ['ɛəsɪk] *adj*: **to be** ~ marearse (en avión).
airspeed ['ɛəspiːd] *n* velocidad *f* de vuelo.
airstrip ['ɛəstrɪp] *n* pista de aterrizaje.
air terminal *n* terminal *f*.
airtight ['ɛətaɪt] *adj* hermético.
air time *n* (*RADIO, TV*) tiempo en antena.
air traffic control *n* control *m* de tráfico aéreo.
air traffic controller *n* controlador(a) *m/f* aéreo/a.
airway ['ɛəweɪ] *n* (*AVIAT*) vía aérea; (*ANAT*) vía respiratoria.
airy ['ɛərɪ] *adj* (*room*) bien ventilado; (*manners*) despreocupado.
aisle [aɪl] *n* (*of church*) nave *f* lateral; (*of theatre, plane*) pasillo.
ajar [ə'dʒɑː*] *adj* entreabierto.
AK *abbr* (*US*) = *Alaska*.
aka *abbr* (= *also known as*) alias.
akin [ə'kɪn] *adj*: ~ **to** semejante a.
AL *abbr* (*US*) = *Alabama*.
ALA *n abbr* = *American Library Association*.
Ala. *abbr* (*US*) = *Alabama*.
alabaster ['æləbɑːstə*] *n* alabastro.
à la carte [ælæ'kɑːt] *adv* a la carta.
alacrity [ə'lækrɪtɪ] *n*: **with** ~ con la mayor prontitud.
alarm [ə'lɑːm] *n* alarma; (*anxiety*) inquietud *f* ♦ *vt* asustar, alarmar.
alarm clock *n* despertador *m*.
alarmed [ə'lɑːmd] *adj* (*person*) alarmado, asustado; (*house, car etc*) con alarma.
alarming [ə'lɑːmɪŋ] *adj* alarmante.
alarmingly [ə'lɑːmɪŋlɪ] *adv* de forma alarmante; ~ **quickly** a una velocidad alarmante.
alarmist [ə'lɑːmɪst] *n* alarmista *m/f*.
alas [ə'læs] *adv* desgraciadamente ♦ *excl* ¡ay!
Alas. *abbr* (*US*) = *Alaska*.
Alaska [ə'læskə] *n* Alaska.
Albania [æl'beɪnɪə] *n* Albania.
Albanian [æl'beɪnɪən] *adj* albanés/esa ♦ *n* albanés/esa *m/f*; (*LING*) albanés *m*.
albatross ['ælbətrɔs] *n* albatros *m*.
albeit [ɔːl'biːɪt] *conj* (*although*) aunque.
album ['ælbəm] *n* álbum *m*; (*L.P.*) elepé *m*.
albumen ['ælbjumɪn] *n* albúmina *f*.
alchemy ['ælkɪmɪ] *n* alquimia.
alcohol ['ælkəhɔl] *n* alcohol *m*.
alcohol-free *adj* sin alcohol.
alcoholic [ælkə'hɔlɪk] *adj, n* alcohólico/a *m/f*.
alcoholism ['ælkəhɔlɪzəm] *n* alcoholismo.
alcove ['ælkəuv] *n* nicho, hueco.
Ald. *abbr* = **alderman**.
alderman ['ɔːldəmən] *n* concejal *m*.
ale [eɪl] *n* cerveza.
alert [ə'ləːt] *adj* alerta *inv*; (*sharp*) despierto, despabilado ♦ *n* alerta *m*, alarma ♦ *vt* poner sobre aviso; **to** ~ **sb (to sth)** poner sobre aviso *or* alertar a algn (de algo); **to** ~ **sb to the dangers of sth** poner sobre aviso *or* alertar a algn de los peligros de algo; **to be on the** ~ estar alerta *or* sobre aviso.
alertness [ə'ləːtnɪs] *n* vigilancia.
Aleutian Islands [ə'luːʃən-] *npl* Islas *fpl* Aleutianas.
Alexandria [ælɪg'zɑːndrɪə] *n* Alejandría.
alfresco [æl'frɛskəu] *adj, adv* al aire libre.
algebra ['ældʒɪbrə] *n* álgebra.
Algeria [æl'dʒɪərɪə] *n* Argelia.
Algerian [æl'dʒɪərɪən] *adj, n* argelino/a *m/f*.
Algiers [æl'dʒɪəz] *n* Argel *m*.
algorithm ['ælgərɪðəm] *n* algoritmo.
alias ['eɪlɪəs] *adv* alias, conocido por ♦ *n* alias *m*.
alibi ['ælɪbaɪ] *n* coartada.
alien ['eɪlɪən] *n* (*foreigner*) extranjero/a ♦ *adj*: ~ **to** ajeno a.
alienate ['eɪlɪəneɪt] *vt* enajenar, alejar.
alienation [eɪlɪə'neɪʃən] *n* alejamiento *m*.
alight [ə'laɪt] *adj* ardiendo ♦ *vi* apearse.
align [ə'laɪn] *vt* alinear.
alignment [ə'laɪnmənt] *n* alineación *f*; **the desks are out of** ~ los pupitres no están bien alineados.
alike [ə'laɪk] *adj* semejantes, iguales ♦ *adv* igualmente, del mismo modo; **to look** ~ parecerse.
alimony ['ælɪmənɪ] *n* (*LAW*) pensión *f* alimenticia.
alive [ə'laɪv] *adj* (*gen*) vivo; (*lively*) activo.
alkali ['ælkəlaɪ] *n* álcali *m*.

KEYWORD

all [ɔːl] *adj* (*sg*) todo/a; (*pl*) todos/as; ~ **day** todo el día; ~ **night** toda la noche; ~ **men** todos los hombres; ~ **five came** vinieron los cinco; ~ **the books** todos los libros; ~ **the time/his life** todo el tiempo/toda su vida; **for** ~ **their efforts** a pesar de todos sus esfuerzos

♦ *pron* **1** todo; **I ate it ~, I ate ~ of it** me lo comí todo; **~ of them** todos (ellos); **~ of us went** fuimos todos; **~ the boys went** fueron todos los chicos; **is that ~?** ¿eso es todo?, ¿algo más?; (*in shop*) ¿algo más?, ¿alguna cosa más?
2 (*in phrases*): **above ~** sobre todo; por encima de todo; **after ~** después de todo; **at ~: anything at ~** lo que sea; **not at ~** (*in answer to question*) en absoluto; (*in answer to thanks*) ¡de nada!, ¡no hay de qué!; **I'm not at ~ tired** no estoy nada cansado/a; **anything at ~ will do** cualquier cosa viene bien; **~ in ~** a fin de cuentas
♦ *adv*: **~ alone** completamente solo/a; **to be/feel ~ in** estar rendido; **it's not as hard as ~ that** no es tan difícil como lo pintas; **~ the more/the better** tanto más/mejor; **~ but** casi; **the score is 2 ~** están empatados a 2.

all-around ['ɔːlə'raund] *adj* (*US*) = **all-round**.
allay [ə'leɪ] *vt* (*fears*) aquietar; (*pain*) aliviar.
all clear *n* (*after attack etc*) fin *m* de la alerta; (*fig*) luz *f* verde.
allegation [ælɪ'geɪʃən] *n* alegato.
allege [ə'lɛdʒ] *vt* pretender; **he is ~d to have said** ... se afirma que él dijo ....
alleged [ə'lɛdʒd] *adj* supuesto, presunto.
allegedly [ə'lɛdʒɪdlɪ] *adv* supuestamente, según se afirma.
allegiance [ə'liːdʒəns] *n* lealtad *f*.
allegory ['ælɪgərɪ] *n* alegoría.
all-embracing ['ɔːləm'breɪsɪŋ] *adj* universal.
allergic [ə'ləːdʒɪk] *adj*: **~ to** alérgico a.
allergy ['ælədʒɪ] *n* alergia.
alleviate [ə'liːvɪeɪt] *vt* aliviar.
alleviation [əliːvɪ'eɪʃən] *n* alivio.
alley ['ælɪ] *n* (*street*) callejuela; (*in garden*) paseo.
alleyway ['ælɪweɪ] *n* callejón *m*.
alliance [ə'laɪəns] *n* alianza.
allied ['ælaɪd] *adj* aliado; (*related*) relacionado.
alligator ['ælɪgeɪtə*] *n* caimán *m*.
all-important ['ɔːlɪm'pɔːtənt] *adj* de suma importancia.
all-in ['ɔːlɪn] *adj* (*BRIT*) (*also adv*: *charge*) todo incluido.
all-in wrestling *n* lucha libre.
alliteration [əlɪtə'reɪʃən] *n* aliteración *f*.
all-night ['ɔːl'naɪt] *adj* (*café*) abierto toda la noche; (*party*) que dura toda la noche.
allocate ['æləkeɪt] *vt* (*share out*) repartir; (*devote*) asignar.
allocation [ælə'keɪʃən] *n* (*of money*) ración *f*, cuota; (*distribution*) reparto.
allot [ə'lɔt] *vt* asignar; **in the ~ted time** en el tiempo asignado.
allotment [ə'lɔtmənt] *n* porción *f*; (*garden*) parcela.
all-out ['ɔːlaut] *adj* (*effort etc*) supremo ♦ *adv*: **all out** con todas las fuerzas, a fondo.
allow [ə'lau] *vt* (*permit*) permitir, dejar; (*a claim*) admitir; (*sum to spend, time estimated*) dar, conceder; (*concede*): **to ~ that** reconocer que; **to ~ sb to do** permitir a alguien hacer; **smoking is not ~ed** prohibido *or* se prohíbe fumar; **he is ~ed to** ... se le permite ...; **we must ~ 3 days for the journey** debemos dejar 3 días para el viaje.
►**allow for** *vt fus* tener en cuenta.
allowance [ə'lauəns] *n* concesión *f*; (*payment*) subvención *f*, pensión *f*; (*discount*) descuento, rebaja; **to make ~s for** (*person*) disculpar a; (*thing*: *take into account*) tener en cuenta.
alloy ['ælɔɪ] *n* aleación *f*.
all right *adv* (*feel, work*) bien; (*as answer*) ¡de acuerdo!, ¡está bien!
all-round ['ɔːl'raund] *adj* completo; (*view*) amplio.
all-rounder ['ɔːl'raundə*] *n*: **to be a good ~** ser una persona que hace de todo.
allspice ['ɔːlspaɪs] *n* pimienta inglesa *or* de Jamaica.
all-time ['ɔːl'taɪm] *adj* (*record*) de todos los tiempos.
allude [ə'luːd] *vi*: **to ~ to** aludir a.
alluring [ə'ljuərɪŋ] *adj* seductor(a), atractivo.
allusion [ə'luːʒən] *n* referencia, alusión *f*.
ally *n* ['ælaɪ] aliado/a ♦ *vt* [ə'laɪ]: **to ~ o.s. with** aliarse con.
almanac ['ɔːlmənæk] *n* almanaque *m*.
almighty [ɔːl'maɪtɪ] *adj* todopoderoso.
almond ['ɑːmənd] *n* (*fruit*) almendra; (*tree*) almendro.
almost ['ɔːlməust] *adv* casi; **he ~ fell** casi *or* por poco se cae.
alms [ɑːmz] *npl* limosna *sg*.
aloft [ə'lɔft] *adv* arriba.
alone [ə'ləun] *adj* solo ♦ *adv* sólo, solamente; **to leave sb ~** dejar a algn en paz; **to leave sth ~** no tocar algo; **let ~** ... y mucho menos, y no digamos ...
along [ə'lɔŋ] *prep* a lo largo de, por ♦ *adv*: **is he coming ~ with us?** ¿viene con nosotros?; **he was limping ~** iba cojeando; **~ with** junto con; **all ~** (*all the time*) desde el principio.
alongside [ə'lɔŋ'saɪd] *prep* al lado de ♦ *adv* (*NAUT*) de costado; **we brought our boat**

~ atracamos nuestro barco.
aloof [ə'lu:f] *adj* distante ♦ *adv*: **to stand ~** mantenerse a distancia.
aloud [ə'laud] *adv* en voz alta.
alphabet ['ælfəbɛt] *n* alfabeto.
alphabetical [ælfə'bɛtɪkəl] *adj* alfabético; **in ~ order** por orden alfabético.
alphanumeric [ælfənju:'mɛrɪk] *adj* alfanumérico.
alpine ['ælpaɪn] *adj* alpino, alpestre.
Alps [ælps] *npl*: **the ~** los Alpes.
already [ɔ:l'rɛdɪ] *adv* ya.
alright ['ɔ:l'raɪt] *adv* (*BRIT*) = **all right.**
Alsatian [æl'seɪʃən] *n* (*dog*) pastor *m* alemán.
also ['ɔ:lsəu] *adv* también, además.
Alta. *abbr* (*Canada*) = *Alberta.*
altar ['ɔltə*] *n* altar *m.*
alter ['ɔltə*] *vt* cambiar, modificar ♦ *vi* cambiarse, modificarse.
alteration [ɔltə'reɪʃən] *n* cambio, modificación *f*; **~s** *npl* (*ARCH*) reformas *fpl*; (*SEWING*) arreglos *mpl*; **timetable subject to ~** el horario puede cambiar.
altercation [ɔltə'keɪʃən] *n* altercado.
alternate [ɔl'tə:nɪt] *adj* alterno ♦ *vi* ['ɔltəneɪt]: **to ~ (with)** alternar (con); **on ~ days** en días alternos.
alternately [ɔl'tə:nɪtlɪ] *adv* alternativamente, por turno.
alternating ['ɔltəneɪtɪŋ] *adj* (*current*) alterno.
alternative [ɔl'tə:nətɪv] *adj* alternativo ♦ *n* alternativa.
alternatively [ɔl'tə:nətɪvlɪ] *adv*: **~ one could ...** por otra parte se podría....
alternative medicine *n* medicina alternativa.
alternator ['ɔltəneɪtə*] *n* (*AUT*) alternador *m.*
although [ɔ:l'ðəu] *conj* aunque, si bien.
altitude ['æltɪtju:d] *n* altitud *f*, altura.
altitude sickness *n* mal *m* de altura, soroche *m* (*LAM*).
alto ['æltəu] *n* (*female*) contralto *f*; (*male*) alto.
altogether [ɔ:ltə'gɛðə*] *adv* completamente, del todo; (*on the whole, in all*) en total, en conjunto; **how much is that ~?** ¿cuánto es todo *or* en total?
altruism ['æltruɪzəm] *n* altruismo.
altruistic [æltru'ɪstɪk] *adj* altruista.
aluminium [ælju'mɪnɪəm], (*US*) **aluminum** [ə'lu:mɪnəm] *n* aluminio.
always ['ɔ:lweɪz] *adv* siempre.
Alzheimer's ['æltshaɪməz] (*also*: **~ disease**) enfermedad *f* de Alzheimer.
AM *abbr* (= *amplitude modulation*) A.M. *f*; (*POL*) = **Assembly Member**.
am [æm] *vb see* **be.**
a.m. *adv abbr* (= *ante meridiem*) de la mañana.
AMA *n abbr* = *American Medical Association.*
amalgam [ə'mælgəm] *n* amalgama.
amalgamate [ə'mælgəmeɪt] *vi* amalgamarse ♦ *vt* amalgamar.
amalgamation [əmælgə'meɪʃən] *n* (*COMM*) fusión *f*.
amass [ə'mæs] *vt* amontonar, acumular.
amateur ['æmətə*] *n* aficionado/a, amateur *m/f*; **~ dramatics** dramas *mpl* presentados por aficionados.
amateurish ['æmətərɪʃ] *adj* (*pej*) torpe, inexperto.
amaze [ə'meɪz] *vt* asombrar, pasmar; **to be ~d (at)** asombrarse (de).
amazement [ə'meɪzmənt] *n* asombro, sorpresa; **to my ~** para mi sorpresa.
amazing [ə'meɪzɪŋ] *adj* extraordinario, asombroso; (*bargain, offer*) increíble.
amazingly [ə'meɪzɪŋlɪ] *adv* extraordinariamente.
Amazon ['æməzən] *n* (*GEO*) Amazonas *m*; (*MYTHOLOGY*) amazona ♦ *cpd*: **the ~ basin/jungle** la cuenca/selva del Amazonas.
Amazonian [æmə'zəunɪən] *adj* amazónico.
ambassador [æm'bæsədə*] *n* embajador(a) *m/f.*
amber ['æmbə*] *n* ámbar *m*; **at ~** (*BRIT AUT*) en amarillo.
ambidextrous [æmbɪ'dɛkstrəs] *adj* ambidextro.
ambience ['æmbɪəns] *n* ambiente *m.*
ambiguity [æmbɪ'gjuɪtɪ] *n* ambigüedad *f*; (*of meaning*) doble sentido.
ambiguous [æm'bɪgjuəs] *adj* ambiguo.
ambition [æm'bɪʃən] *n* ambición *f*; **to achieve one's ~** realizar su ambición.
ambitious [æm'bɪʃəs] *adj* ambicioso; (*plan*) grandioso.
ambivalent [æm'bɪvələnt] *adj* ambivalente; (*pej*) equívoco.
amble ['æmbl] *vi* (*gen*: **~ along**) deambular, andar sin prisa.
ambulance ['æmbjuləns] *n* ambulancia.
ambulanceman/woman ['æmbjulənsmən/wumən] *n* ambulanciero/a.
ambush ['æmbuʃ] *n* emboscada ♦ *vt* tender una emboscada a; (*fig*) coger (*SP*) *or* agarrar (*LAM*) por sorpresa.
ameba [ə'mi:bə] *n* (*US*) = **amoeba**.
ameliorate [ə'mi:lɪəreɪt] *vt* mejorar.
amelioration [əmi:lɪə'reɪʃən] *n* mejora.
amen [ɑ:'mɛn] *excl* amén.
amenable [ə'mi:nəbl] *adj*: **~ to** (*advice etc*)

sensible a.
amend [ə'mɛnd] *vt* (*law, text*) enmendar; **to make ~s** (*apologize*) enmendarlo, dar cumplida satisfacción.
amendment [ə'mɛndmənt] *n* enmienda.
amenities [ə'mi:nɪtɪz] *npl* comodidades *fpl.*
amenity [ə'mi:nɪtɪ] *n* servicio.
America [ə'mɛrɪkə] *n* América (del Norte).
American [ə'mɛrɪkən] *adj, n* (norte)americano/a *m/f*, estadounidense *m/f.*
Americanism [ə'mɛrɪkənɪzəm] *n* americanismo.
americanize [ə'mɛrɪkənaɪz] *vt* americanizar.
Amerindian [æmər'ɪndɪən] *adj, n* amerindio/a.
amethyst ['æmɪθɪst] *n* amatista.
Amex ['æmɛks] *n abbr* = *American Stock Exchange.*
amiable ['eɪmɪəbl] *adj* (*kind*) amable, simpático.
amicable ['æmɪkəbl] *adj* amistoso, amigable.
amicably ['æmɪkəblɪ] *adv* amigablemente, amistosamente; **to part** ~ separarse amistosamente.
amid(st) [ə'mɪd(st)] *prep* entre, en medio de.
amiss [ə'mɪs] *adv*: **to take sth** ~ tomar algo a mal; **there's something** ~ pasa algo.
ammo ['æməu] *n abbr* (*col*) = **ammunition.**
ammonia [ə'məunɪə] *n* amoníaco.
ammunition [æmju'nɪʃən] *n* municiones *fpl*; (*fig*) argumentos *mpl.*
ammunition dump *n* depósito de municiones.
amnesia [æm'ni:zɪə] *n* amnesia.
amnesty ['æmnɪstɪ] *n* amnistía; **to grant an ~ to** amnistiar (a); **A~ International** Amnistía Internacional.
amoeba, (*US*) **ameba** [ə'mi:bə] *n* amiba.
amok [ə'mɔk] *adv*: **to run** ~ enloquecerse, desbocarse.
among(st) [ə'mʌŋ(st)] *prep* entre, en medio de.
amoral [æ'mɔrəl] *adj* amoral.
amorous ['æmərəs] *adj* cariñoso.
amorphous [ə'mɔ:fəs] *adj* amorfo.
amortization [əmɔ:taɪ'zeɪʃən] *n* amortización *f.*
amount [ə'maunt] *n* (*gen*) cantidad *f*; (*of bill etc*) suma, importe *m* ♦ *vi*: **to ~ to** (*total*) sumar; (*be same as*) equivaler a, significar; **this ~s to a refusal** esto equivale a una negativa; **the total** ~ (*of money*) la suma total.
amp(ère) ['æmp(ɛə*)] *n* amperio; **a 13 amp plug** un enchufe de 13 amperios.
ampersand ['æmpəsænd] *n* signo &, "y" comercial.
amphetamine [æm'fɛtəmi:n] *n* anfetamina.
amphibian [æm'fɪbɪən] *n* anfibio.
amphibious [æm'fɪbɪəs] *adj* anfibio.
amphitheatre, (*US*) **amphitheater** ['æmfɪθɪətə*] *n* anfiteatro.
ample ['æmpl] *adj* (*spacious*) amplio; (*abundant*) abundante; **to have ~ time** tener tiempo de sobra.
amplifier ['æmplɪfaɪə*] *n* amplificador *m.*
amplify ['æmplɪfaɪ] *vt* amplificar, aumentar; (*explain*) explicar.
amply ['æmplɪ] *adv* ampliamente.
ampoule, (*US*) **ampule** ['æmpu:l] *n* (*MED*) ampolla.
amputate ['æmpjuteɪt] *vt* amputar.
amputee [æmpju'ti:] *n* persona que ha sufrido una amputación.
Amsterdam ['æmstədæm] *n* Amsterdam *m.*
amt *abbr* = **amount.**
amuck [ə'mʌk] *adv* = **amok.**
amuse [ə'mju:z] *vt* divertir; (*distract*) distraer, entretener; **to ~ o.s. with sth/ by doing sth** distraerse con algo/ haciendo algo; **he was ~d at the joke** le divirtió el chiste.
amusement [ə'mju:zmənt] *n* diversión *f*; (*pastime*) pasatiempo; (*laughter*) risa; **much to my** ~ con gran regocijo mío.
amusement arcade *n* salón *m* de juegos.
amusement park *n* parque *m* de atracciones.
amusing [ə'mju:zɪŋ] *adj* divertido.
an [æn, ən, n] *indef art see* **a.**
ANA *n abbr* = *American Newspaper Association; American Nurses Association.*
anachronism [ə'nækrənɪzəm] *n* anacronismo.
anaemia [ə'ni:mɪə] *n* anemia.
anaemic [ə'ni:mɪk] *adj* anémico; (*fig*) flojo.
anaesthetic [ænɪs'θɛtɪk] *n* anestesia; **local/ general** ~ anestesia local/general.
anaesthetist [æ'ni:sθɪtɪst] *n* anestesista *m/f.*
anagram ['ænəgræm] *n* anagrama *m.*
anal ['eɪnl] *adj* anal.
analgesic [ænæl'dʒi:sɪk] *adj, n* analgésico.
analogous [ə'næləgəs] *adj*: ~ **to** *or* **with** análogo a.
analog(ue) ['ænəlɔg] *adj* (*computer, watch*) analógico.
analogy [ə'nælədʒɪ] *n* analogía; **to draw an ~ between** señalar la analogía entre.
analyse ['ænəlaɪz] *vt* (*BRIT*) analizar.
analysis, *pl* **analyses** [ə'næləsɪs, -si:z] *n* análisis *m inv.*
analyst ['ænəlɪst] *n* (*political* ~) analista *m/f,*

(*psycho~*) psicoanalista *m/f*.
analytic(al) [ænə'lɪtɪk(əl)] *adj* analítico.
analyze ['ænəlaɪz] *vt* (*US*) = **analyse**.
anarchic [æ'nɑːkɪk] *adj* anárquico.
anarchist ['ænəkɪst] *adj, n* anarquista *m/f*.
anarchy ['ænəkɪ] *n* anarquía, desorden *m*.
anathema [ə'næθɪmə] *n*: **that is ~ to him** eso es pecado para él.
anatomical [ænə'tɔmɪkəl] *adj* anatómico.
anatomy [ə'nætəmɪ] *n* anatomía.
ANC *n abbr* = *African National Congress*.
ancestor ['ænsɪstə*] *n* antepasado.
ancestral [æn'sɛstrəl] *adj* ancestral.
ancestry ['ænsɪstrɪ] *n* ascendencia, abolengo.
anchor ['æŋkə*] *n* ancla, áncora ♦ *vi* (*also*: **to drop ~**) anclar, echar el ancla ♦ *vt* (*fig*) sujetar, afianzar; **to weigh ~** levar anclas.
anchorage ['æŋkərɪdʒ] *n* ancladero.
anchor man, anchor woman *n* (*RADIO, TV*) presentador(a) *m/f*.
anchovy ['æntʃəvɪ] *n* anchoa.
ancient ['eɪnʃənt] *adj* antiguo; **~ monument** monumento histórico.
ancillary [æn'sɪlərɪ] *adj* (*worker, staff*) auxiliar.
and [ænd] *conj* y; (*before i, hi*) e; **~ so on** etcétera; **try ~ come** procure *or* intente venir; **better ~ better** cada vez mejor.
Andalusia [ændə'luːzɪə] *n* Andalucía.
Andean ['ændɪən] *adj* andino/a; **~ high plateau** altiplanicie *f*, altiplano (*LAM*).
Andes ['ændiːz] *npl*: **the ~** los Andes.
anecdote ['ænɪkdəut] *n* anécdota.
anemia [ə'niːmɪə] *n* (*US*) = **anaemia**.
anemic [ə'niːmɪk] *adj* (*US*) = **anaemic**.
anemone [ə'nɛmənɪ] *n* (*BOT*) anémone *f*; **sea ~** anémona.
anesthetic [ænɪs'θɛtɪk] *adj, n* (*US*) = **anaesthetic**.
anesthetist [æ'niːsθɪtɪst] *n* (*US*) = **anaesthetist**.
anew [ə'njuː] *adv* de nuevo, otra vez.
angel ['eɪndʒəl] *n* ángel *m*.
angel dust *n* polvo de ángel.
angelic [æn'dʒɛlɪk] *adj* angélico.
anger ['æŋgə*] *n* ira, cólera, enojo (*LAM*) ♦ *vt* enojar, enfurecer.
angina [æn'dʒaɪnə] *n* angina (del pecho).
angle ['æŋgl] *n* ángulo; **from their ~** desde su punto de vista.
angler ['æŋglə*] *n* pescador(a) *m/f* (de caña).
Anglican ['æŋglɪkən] *adj, n* anglicano/a.
anglicize ['æŋglɪsaɪz] *vt* anglicanizar.
angling ['æŋglɪŋ] *n* pesca con caña.
Anglo- [æŋgləu] *pref* anglo... .
Angola [æŋ'gəulə] *n* Angola.
Angolan [æŋ'gəulən] *adj, n* angoleño/a *m/f*.
angrily ['æŋgrɪlɪ] *adv* enojado, enfadado.
angry ['æŋgrɪ] *adj* enfadado, enojado (*esp LAM*); **to be ~ with sb/at sth** estar enfadado con algn/por algo; **to get ~** enfadarse, enojarse (*esp LAM*).
anguish ['æŋgwɪʃ] *n* (*physical*) tormentos *mpl*; (*mental*) angustia.
anguished ['æŋgwɪʃt] *adj* angustioso.
angular ['æŋgjulə*] *adj* (*shape*) angular; (*features*) anguloso.
animal ['ænɪməl] *adj, n* animal *m*.
animal rights [-raɪts] *npl* derechos *mpl* de los animales.
animate ['ænɪmeɪt] *vt* (*enliven*) animar; (*encourage*) estimular, alentar ♦ ['ænɪmɪt] *adj* vivo, animado.
animated ['ænɪmeɪtɪd] *adj* vivo, animado.
animation [ænɪ'meɪʃən] *n* animación *f*.
animosity [ænɪ'mɔsɪtɪ] *n* animosidad *f*, rencor *m*.
aniseed ['ænɪsiːd] *n* anís *m*.
Ankara ['æŋkərə] *n* Ankara.
ankle ['æŋkl] *n* tobillo *m*.
ankle sock *n* calcetín *m*.
annex ['ænɛks] *n* (*also*: *Brit*: **annexe**) (*building*) edificio anexo ♦ *vt* [æ'nɛks] (*territory*) anexar.
annihilate [ə'naɪəleɪt] *vt* aniquilar.
annihilation [ənaɪə'leɪʃən] *n* aniquilación *f*.
anniversary [ænɪ'vəːsərɪ] *n* aniversario.
annotate ['ænəuteɪt] *vt* anotar.
announce [ə'nauns] *vt* (*gen*) anunciar; (*inform*) comunicar; **he ~d that he wasn't going** declaró que no iba.
announcement [ə'naunsmənt] *n* (*gen*) anuncio; (*declaration*) declaración *f*; **I'd like to make an ~** quisiera anunciar algo.
announcer [ə'naunsə*] *n* (*RADIO, TV*) locutor(a) *m/f*.
annoy [ə'nɔɪ] *vt* molestar, fastidiar, fregar (*LAM*), embromar (*LAM*); **to be ~ed (at sth/with sb)** estar enfadado *or* molesto (por algo/con algn); **don't get ~ed!** ¡no se enfade!
annoyance [ə'nɔɪəns] *n* enojo; (*thing*) molestia.
annoying [ə'nɔɪɪŋ] *adj* molesto, fastidioso, fregado (*LAM*), embromado (*LAM*); (*person*) pesado.
annual ['ænjuəl] *adj* anual ♦ *n* (*BOT*) anual *m*; (*book*) anuario.
annual general meeting (AGM) *n* junta general anual.
annually ['ænjuəlɪ] *adv* anualmente, cada año.
annual report *n* informe *m or* memoria

anual.
annuity [ə'nju:ɪtɪ] *n* renta *or* pensión *f* vitalicia.
annul [ə'nʌl] *vt* anular; (*law*) revocar.
annulment [ə'nʌlmənt] *n* anulación *f*.
annum ['ænəm] *n see* **per annum.**
Annunciation [ənʌnsɪ'eɪʃən] *n* Anunciación *f*.
anode ['ænəud] *n* ánodo.
anoint [ə'nɔɪnt] *vt* untar.
anomalous [ə'nɔmələs] *adj* anómalo.
anomaly [ə'nɔməlɪ] *n* anomalía.
anon. [ə'nɔn] *abbr* = **anonymous.**
anonymity [ænə'nɪmɪtɪ] *n* anonimato.
anonymous [ə'nɔnɪməs] *adj* anónimo; **to remain ~** quedar en el anonimato.
anorak ['ænəræk] *n* anorak *m*.
anorexia [ænə'rɛksɪə] *n* (*MED*) anorexia.
anorexic [ænə'rɛksɪk] *adj, n* anoréxico/a *m/f*.
another [ə'nʌðə*] *adj*: **~ book** otro libro; **~ beer?** ¿(quieres) otra cerveza?; **in ~ 5 years** en cinco años más ♦ *pron* otro; *see also* **one.**
ANSI *n abbr* (= *American National Standards Institution*) *oficina de normalización de EEUU*.
answer ['ɑ:nsə*] *n* respuesta, contestación *f*; (*to problem*) solución *f* ♦ *vi* contestar, responder ♦ *vt* (*reply to*) contestar a, responder a; (*problem*) resolver; **to ~ the phone** contestar el teléfono; **in ~ to your letter** contestando *or* en contestación a su carta; **to ~ the door** abrir la puerta.
▸**answer back** *vi* replicar, ser respondón/ona.
▸**answer for** *vt fus* responder de *or* por.
▸**answer to** *vt fus* (*description*) corresponder a.
answerable ['ɑ:nsərəbl] *adj*: **~ to sb for sth** responsable ante algn de algo.
answering machine ['ɑ:nsərɪŋ-] *n* contestador *m* automático.
ant [ænt] *n* hormiga.
ANTA *n abbr* = *American National Theater and Academy*.
antagonism [æn'tægənɪzəm] *n* antagonismo *m*.
antagonist [æn'tægənɪst] *n* antagonista *m/f*, adversario/a.
antagonistic [æntægə'nɪstɪk] *adj* antagónico; (*opposed*) contrario, opuesto.
antagonize [æn'tægənaɪz] *vt* provocar la enemistad de.
Antarctic [ænt'ɑ:ktɪk] *adj* antártico ♦ *n*: **the ~** el Antártico.
Antarctica [æn'tɑ:ktɪkə] *n* Antártida.
Antarctic Circle *n* Círculo Polar Antártico.
Antarctic Ocean *n* Océano Antártico.
ante ['æntɪ] *n*: **to up the ~** subir la apuesta.
ante... ['æntɪ] *pref* ante....
anteater ['ænti:tə*] *n* oso hormiguero.
antecedent [æntɪ'si:dənt] *n* antecedente *m*.
antechamber ['æntɪtʃeɪmbə*] *n* antecámara.
antelope ['æntɪləup] *n* antílope *m*.
antenatal [æntɪ'neɪtl] *adj* prenatal.
antenatal clinic *n* clínica prenatal.
antenna [æn'tɛnə], *pl* **~e** [-ni:] *n* antena.
anteroom ['æntɪrum] *n* antesala.
anthem ['ænθəm] *n*: **national ~** himno nacional.
anthology [æn'θɔlədʒɪ] *n* antología.
anthropologist [ænθrə'pɔlədʒɪst] *n* antropólogo/a.
anthropology [ænθrə'pɔlədʒɪ] *n* antropología.
anti... [æntɪ] *pref* anti....
anti-aircraft ['æntɪ'ɛəkrɑ:ft] *adj* antiaéreo.
antiballistic [æntɪbə'lɪstɪk] *adj* antibalístico.
antibiotic [æntɪbaɪ'ɔtɪk] *adj, n* antibiótico.
antibody ['æntɪbɔdɪ] *n* anticuerpo.
anticipate [æn'tɪsɪpeɪt] *vt* (*foresee*) prever; (*expect*) esperar, contar con; (*forestall*) anticiparse a, adelantarse a; **this is worse than I ~d** esto es peor de lo que esperaba; **as ~d** según se esperaba.
anticipation [æntɪsɪ'peɪʃən] *n* previsión *f*; esperanza; anticipación *f*.
anticlimax [æntɪ'klaɪmæks] *n* decepción *f*.
anticlockwise [æntɪ'klɔkwaɪz] *adv* en dirección contraria a la de las agujas del reloj.
antics ['æntɪks] *npl* payasadas *fpl*.
anticyclone [æntɪ'saɪkləun] *n* anticiclón *m*.
antidepressant ['æntɪdɪ'prɛsnt] *n* antidepresivo.
antidote ['æntɪdəut] *n* antídoto.
antifreeze ['æntɪfri:z] *n* anticongelante *m*.
antihistamine [æntɪ'hɪstəmi:n] *n* antihistamínico.
Antilles [æn'tɪli:z] *npl*: **the ~** las Antillas.
antipathy [æn'tɪpəθɪ] *n* (*between people*) antipatía; (*to person, thing*) aversión *f*.
antiperspirant ['æntɪpə:spɪrənt] *n* antitranspirante *m*.
Antipodean [æntɪpə'di:ən] *adj* antípoda.
Antipodes [æn'tɪpədi:z] *npl*: **the ~** las Antípodas.
antiquarian [æntɪ'kwɛərɪən] *n* anticuario/a.
antiquated ['æntɪkweɪtɪd] *adj* anticuado.
antique [æn'ti:k] *n* antigüedad *f* ♦ *adj* antiguo.
antique dealer *n* anticuario/a.
antique shop *n* tienda de antigüedades.
antiquity [æn'tɪkwɪtɪ] *n* antigüedad *f*.
anti-Semitic ['æntɪsɪ'mɪtɪk] *adj* antisemita.

anti-Semitism [æntɪ'sɛmɪtɪzəm] *n* antisemitismo.
antiseptic [æntɪ'sɛptɪk] *adj, n* antiséptico.
antisocial [æntɪ'səuʃəl] *adj* antisocial.
antitank [æntɪ'tæŋk] *adj* antitanque.
antithesis, *pl* **antitheses** [æn'tɪθɪsɪs, -siːz] *n* antítesis *f inv*.
antitrust [æntɪ'trʌst] *adj*: ~ **legislation** legislación *f* antimonopolio.
antlers ['æntləz] *npl* cornamenta.
anus ['eɪnəs] *n* ano.
anvil ['ænvɪl] *n* yunque *m*.
anxiety [æŋ'zaɪətɪ] *n* (*worry*) inquietud *f*; (*eagerness*) ansia, anhelo.
anxious ['æŋkʃəs] *adj* (*worried*) inquieto; (*keen*) deseoso; **I'm very ~ about you** me tienes muy preocupado.
anxiously ['æŋkʃəslɪ] *adv* con inquietud, de manera angustiada.

KEYWORD

any ['ɛnɪ] *adj* **1** (*in questions etc*) algún/alguna; **have you ~ butter/children?** ¿tienes mantequilla/hijos?; **if there are ~ tickets left** si quedan billetes, si queda algún billete
2 (*with negative*): **I haven't ~ money/books** no tengo dinero/libros
3 (*no matter which*) cualquier; **~ excuse will do** valdrá *or* servirá cualquier excusa; **choose ~ book you like** escoge el libro que quieras; **~ teacher you ask will tell you** cualquier profesor al que preguntes te lo dirá
4 (*in phrases*): **in ~ case** de todas formas, en cualquier caso; **~ day now** cualquier día (de estos); **at ~ moment** en cualquier momento, de un momento a otro; **at ~ rate** en todo caso; **~ time: come (at) ~ time** ven cuando quieras; **he might come (at) ~ time** podría llegar de un momento a otro
♦ *pron* **1** (*in questions etc*): **have you got ~?** ¿tienes alguno/a?; **can ~ of you sing?** ¿sabe cantar alguno de vosotros/ustedes?
2 (*with negative*): **I haven't ~ (of them)** no tengo ninguno
3 (*no matter which one(s)*): **take ~ of those books (you like)** toma el libro que quieras de ésos
♦ *adv* **1** (*in questions etc*): **do you want ~ more soup/sandwiches?** ¿quieres más sopa/bocadillos?; **are you feeling ~ better?** ¿te sientes algo mejor?
2 (*with negative*): **I can't hear him ~ more** ya no le oigo; **don't wait ~ longer** no esperes más.

anybody ['ɛnɪbɔdɪ] *pron* cualquiera, cualquier persona; (*in interrogative sentences*) alguien; (*in negative sentences*): **I don't see ~** no veo a nadie.
anyhow ['ɛnɪhau] *adv* de todos modos, de todas maneras; (*carelessly*) de cualquier manera; (*haphazardly*) de cualquier modo; **I shall go ~** iré de todas maneras.
anyone ['ɛnɪwʌn] = **anybody**.
anyplace ['ɛnɪpleɪs] *adv* (*US*) = **anywhere**.
anything ['ɛnɪθɪŋ] *pron* (*see* **anybody**) cualquier cosa; (*in interrogative sentences*) algo; (*in negative sentences*) nada; (*everything*) todo; **~ else?** ¿algo más?; **it can cost ~ between £15 and £20** puede costar entre 15 y 20 libras.
anytime ['ɛnɪtaɪm] *adv* (*at any moment*) en cualquier momento, de un momento a otro; (*whenever*) no importa cuándo, cuando quiera.
anyway ['ɛnɪweɪ] *adv* de todas maneras; de cualquier modo.
anywhere ['ɛnɪwɛə*] *adv* (*see* **anybody**) dondequiera; (*interrogative*) en algún sitio; (*negative sense*) en ningún sitio; (*everywhere*) en *or* por todas partes; **I don't see him ~** no le veo en ningún sitio; **~ in the world** en cualquier parte del mundo.
Anzac ['ænzæk] *n abbr* (= *Australia-New Zealand Army Corps*).
apace [ə'peɪs] *adv* aprisa.
apart [ə'pɑːt] *adv* aparte, separadamente; **10 miles ~** separados por 10 millas; **to take ~** desmontar; **~ from** *prep* aparte de.
apartheid [ə'pɑːteɪt] *n* apartheid *m*.
apartment [ə'pɑːtmənt] *n* (*US*) piso, departamento (*LAM*), apartamento; (*room*) cuarto.
apartment block *or* **building** (*US*) bloque *m* de pisos.
apathetic [æpə'θɛtɪk] *adj* apático, indiferente.
apathy ['æpəθɪ] *n* apatía, indiferencia.
APB *n abbr* (*US*: = *all points bulletin*) *expresión usada por la policía que significa "descubrir y aprehender al sospechoso"*.
ape [eɪp] *n* mono ♦ *vt* imitar, remedar.
Apennines ['æpənaɪnz] *npl*: **the ~** los Apeninos *mpl*.
aperitif [ə'pɛrɪtiːf] *n* aperitivo.
aperture ['æpətʃjuə*] *n* rendija, resquicio; (*PHOT*) abertura.
APEX ['eɪpɛks] *n abbr* (*AVIAT* = *advance purchase excursion*) APEX *m*.
apex ['eɪpɛks] *n* ápice *m*; (*fig*) cumbre *f*.
aphid ['eɪfɪd] *n* pulgón *m*.

aphorism ['æfərɪzəm] *n* aforismo.
aphrodisiac [æfrəu'dɪzɪæk] *adj, n* afrodisíaco.
API *n abbr* = *American Press Institute.*
apiece [ə'piːs] *adv* cada uno.
aplomb [ə'plɔm] *n* aplomo, confianza.
APO *n abbr* (*US*: = *Army Post Office*) *servicio postal del ejército.*
Apocalypse [ə'pɔkəlɪps] *n* Apocalipsis *m.*
apocryphal [ə'pɔkrɪfəl] *adj* apócrifo.
apolitical [eɪpə'lɪtɪkl] *adj* apolítico.
apologetic [əpɔlə'dʒɛtɪk] *adj* (*look, remark*) de disculpa.
apologetically [əpɔlə'dʒɛtɪkəlɪ] *adv* con aire de disculpa, excusándose, disculpándose.
apologize [ə'pɔlədʒaɪz] *vi*: **to ~ (for sth to sb)** disculparse (con algn por algo).
apology [ə'pɔlədʒɪ] *n* disculpa, excusa; **please accept my apologies** le ruego me disculpe.
apoplectic [æpə'plɛktɪk] *adj* (*MED*) apoplético; (*col*): ~ **with rage** furioso.
apoplexy ['æpəplɛksɪ] *n* apoplegía.
apostle [ə'pɔsl] *n* apóstol *m/f.*
apostrophe [ə'pɔstrəfɪ] *n* apóstrofo *m.*
appal [ə'pɔːl] *vt* horrorizar, espantar.
Appalachian Mountains [æpə'leɪʃən-] *npl*: **the** ~ los (Montes) Apalaches.
appalling [ə'pɔːlɪŋ] *adj* espantoso; (*awful*) pésimo; **she's an ~ cook** es una cocinera malísima.
apparatus [æpə'reɪtəs] *n* aparato; (*in gymnasium*) aparatos *mpl.*
apparel [ə'pærl] *n* (*US*) indumentaria.
apparent [ə'pærənt] *adj* aparente; (*obvious*) manifiesto, evidente; **it is ~ that** está claro que.
apparently [ə'pærəntlɪ] *adv* por lo visto, al parecer, dizque (*LAM*).
apparition [æpə'rɪʃən] *n* aparición *f.*
appeal [ə'piːl] *vi* (*LAW*) apelar ♦ *n* (*LAW*) apelación *f*; (*request*) llamamiento, llamado (*LAM*); (*plea*) súplica; (*charm*) atractivo, encanto; **to ~ for** solicitar; **to ~ to** (*subj: person*) rogar a, suplicar a; (: *thing*) atraer, interesar; **to ~ to sb for mercy** rogarle misericordia a alguien; **it doesn't ~ to me** no me atrae, no me llama la atención; **right of ~** derecho de apelación.
appealing [ə'piːlɪŋ] *adj* (*nice*) atractivo; (*touching*) conmovedor(a), emocionante.
appear [ə'pɪə*] *vi* aparecer, presentarse; (*LAW*) comparecer; (*publication*) salir (a luz), publicarse; (*seem*) parecer; **it would ~ that** parecería que.
appearance [ə'pɪərəns] *n* aparición *f*; (*look, aspect*) apariencia, aspecto; **to keep up ~s** salvar las apariencias; **to all ~s** al parecer.
appease [ə'piːz] *vt* (*pacify*) apaciguar; (*satisfy*) satisfacer.
appeasement [ə'piːzmənt] *n* (*POL*) apaciguamiento.
append [ə'pɛnd] *vt* (*COMPUT*) añadir (al final).
appendage [ə'pɛndɪdʒ] *n* añadidura.
appendicitis [əpɛndɪ'saɪtɪs] *n* apendicitis *f.*
appendix, *pl* **appendices** [ə'pɛndɪks, -dɪsiːz] *n* apéndice *m*; **to have one's ~ out** operarse de apendicitis.
appetite ['æpɪtaɪt] *n* apetito; (*fig*) deseo, anhelo; **that walk has given me an ~** ese paseo me ha abierto el apetito.
appetizer ['æpɪtaɪzə*] *n* (*drink*) aperitivo; (*food*) tapas *fpl* (*SP*).
appetizing ['æpɪtaɪzɪŋ] *adj* apetitoso.
applaud [ə'plɔːd] *vt, vi* aplaudir.
applause [ə'plɔːz] *n* aplausos *mpl.*
apple ['æpl] *n* manzana.
apple tree *n* manzano.
appliance [ə'plaɪəns] *n* aparato; **electrical ~s** electrodomésticos *mpl.*
applicable [ə'plɪkəbl] *adj* aplicable, pertinente; **the law is ~ from January** la ley es aplicable *or* se pone en vigor a partir de enero; **to be ~ to** referirse a.
applicant ['æplɪkənt] *n* candidato/a; solicitante *m/f.*
application [æplɪ'keɪʃən] *n* aplicación *f*; (*for a job, a grant etc*) solicitud *f.*
application form *n* solicitud *f.*
applications package *n* (*COMPUT*) paquete *m* de programas de aplicación.
applied [ə'plaɪd] *adj* (*science, art*) aplicado.
apply [ə'plaɪ] *vt*: **to ~ (to)** aplicar (a); (*fig*) emplear (para) ♦ *vi*: **to ~ to** (*ask*) dirigirse a; (*be suitable for*) ser aplicable a; (*be relevant to*) tener que ver con; **to ~ for** (*permit, grant, job*) solicitar; **to ~ the brakes** echar el freno; **to ~ o.s. to** aplicarse a, dedicarse a.
appoint [ə'pɔɪnt] *vt* (*to post*) nombrar; (*date, place*) fijar, señalar.
appointee [əpɔɪn'tiː] *n* persona nombrada.
appointment [ə'pɔɪntmənt] *n* (*engagement*) cita; (*date*) compromiso; (*act*) nombramiento; (*post*) puesto; **to make an ~ (with)** (*doctor*) pedir hora (con); (*friend*) citarse (con); **"~s (vacant)"** "ofertas de trabajo"; **by ~** mediante cita.
apportion [ə'pɔːʃən] *vt* repartir.
appraisal [ə'preɪzl] *n* evaluación *f.*
appraise [ə'preɪz] *vt* (*value*) tasar, valorar; (*situation etc*) evaluar.
appreciable [ə'priːʃəbl] *adj* sensible.

appreciably [ə'priːʃəblɪ] *adv* sensiblemente, de manera apreciable.
appreciate [ə'priːʃɪeɪt] *vt* (*like*) apreciar, tener en mucho; (*be grateful for*) agradecer; (*be aware of*) comprender ♦ *vi* (*COMM*) aumentar en valor; **I ~d your help** agradecí tu ayuda.
appreciation [əpriːʃɪ'eɪʃən] *n* aprecio; reconocimiento, agradecimiento; aumento en valor.
appreciative [ə'priːʃɪətɪv] *adj* agradecido.
apprehend [æprɪ'hɛnd] *vt* percibir; (*arrest*) detener.
apprehension [æprɪ'hɛnʃən] *n* (*fear*) aprensión *f*.
apprehensive [æprɪ'hɛnsɪv] *adj* aprensivo.
apprentice [ə'prɛntɪs] *n* aprendiz(a) *m/f*.
apprenticeship [ə'prɛntɪsʃɪp] *n* aprendizaje *m*; **to serve one's ~** hacer el aprendizaje.
appro. ['æprəu] *abbr* (*BRIT COMM*: *col*) = **approval.**
approach [ə'prəutʃ] *vi* acercarse ♦ *vt* acercarse a; (*be approximate*) aproximarse a; (*ask, apply to*) dirigirse a; (*problem*) abordar ♦ *n* acercamiento; aproximación *f*; (*access*) acceso; (*proposal*) proposición *f*; (*to problem etc*) enfoque *m*; **to ~ sb about sth** hablar con algn sobre algo.
approachable [ə'prəutʃəbl] *adj* (*person*) abordable; (*place*) accesible.
approach road *n* vía de acceso.
approbation [æprə'beɪʃən] *n* aprobación *f*.
appropriate [ə'prəuprɪɪt] *adj* apropiado, conveniente ♦ *vt* [-rɪeɪt] (*take*) apropiarse de; (*allot*): **to ~ sth for** destinar algo a; **~ for** *or* **to** apropiado para; **it would not be ~ for me to comment** no estaría bien *or* sería pertinente que yo diera mi opinión.
appropriation [əprəuprɪ'eɪʃən] *n* asignación *f*.
approval [ə'pruːvəl] *n* aprobación *f*, visto bueno; **on ~** (*COMM*) a prueba; **to meet with sb's ~** obtener la aprobación de algn.
approve [ə'pruːv] *vt* aprobar.
►**approve of** *vt fus* aprobar.
approved school *n* (*BRIT*) correccional *m*.
approx. *abbr* (= *approximately*) aprox.
approximate [ə'prɔksɪmɪt] *adj* aproximado.
approximately [ə'prɔksɪmɪtlɪ] *adv* aproximadamente, más o menos.
approximation [əprɔksɪ'meɪʃən] *n* aproximación *f*.
Apr. *abbr* (= *April*) abr.
apr *n abbr* (= *annual percentage rate*) tasa de interés anual.
apricot ['eɪprɪkɔt] *n* albaricoque *m* (*SP*), damasco (*LAM*).
April ['eɪprəl] *n* abril *m*; **~ Fools' Day** *n* ≈ día *m* de los (Santos) Inocentes; *ver recuadro.*

> **APRIL FOOLS' DAY**
>
> *El 1 de abril es* **April Fools' Day** *en la tradición anglosajona. Tal día se les gastan bromas a los más desprevenidos, quienes reciben la denominación de "April Fool" (≈ inocente), y tanto la prensa escrita como la televisión difunden alguna historia falsa con la que sumarse al espíritu del día.*

apron ['eɪprən] *n* delantal *m*; (*AVIAT*) pista.
apse [æps] *n* (*ARCH*) ábside *m*.
APT *n abbr* (*BRIT*) = *advanced passenger train.*
Apt. *abbr* = **apartment.**
apt [æpt] *adj* (*to the point*) acertado, oportuno; (*appropriate*) apropiado; **~ to do** (*likely*) propenso a hacer.
aptitude ['æptɪtjuːd] *n* aptitud *f*, capacidad *f*.
aptitude test *n* prueba de aptitud.
aptly ['æptlɪ] *adj* acertadamente.
aqualung ['ækwəlʌŋ] *n* escafandra autónoma.
aquarium [ə'kwɛərɪəm] *n* acuario.
Aquarius [ə'kwɛərɪəs] *n* Acuario.
aquatic [ə'kwætɪk] *adj* acuático.
aqueduct ['ækwɪdʌkt] *n* acueducto.
AR *abbr* (*US*) = *Arkansas.*
ARA *n abbr* (*BRIT*)= *Associate of the Royal Academy.*
Arab ['ærəb] *adj, n* árabe *m/f*.
Arabia [ə'reɪbɪə] *n* Arabia.
Arabian [ə'reɪbɪən] *adj* árabe, arábigo.
Arabian Desert *n* Desierto de Arabia.
Arabian Sea *n* Mar *m* de Omán.
Arabic ['ærəbɪk] *adj* (*language, manuscripts*) árabe, arábigo ♦ *n* árabe *m*; **~ numerals** numeración *f* arábiga.
arable ['ærəbl] *adj* cultivable.
Aragon ['ærəgən] *n* Aragón *m*.
ARAM *n abbr* (*BRIT*) = *Associate of the Royal Academy of Music.*
arbitrary ['ɑːbɪtrərɪ] *adj* arbitrario.
arbitrate ['ɑːbɪtreɪt] *vi* arbitrar.
arbitration [ɑːbɪ'treɪʃən] *n* arbitraje *m*; **the dispute went to ~** el conflicto laboral fue sometido al arbitraje.
arbitrator ['ɑːbɪtreɪtə*] *n* árbitro.
ARC *n abbr* = *American Red Cross.*
arc [ɑːk] *n* arco.
arcade [ɑː'keɪd] *n* (*ARCH*) arcada; (*round a square*) soportales *mpl*; (*shopping ~*) galería comercial.

arch [ɑːtʃ] *n* arco; (*vault*) bóveda; (*of foot*) empeine *m* ♦ *vt* arquear.
archaeological [ɑːkɪə'lɔdʒɪkl] *adj* arqueológico.
archaeologist [ɑːkɪ'ɔlədʒɪst] *n* arqueólogo/a.
archaeology [ɑːkɪ'ɔlədʒɪ] *n* arqueología.
archaic [ɑː'keɪɪk] *adj* arcaico.
archangel ['ɑːkeɪndʒəl] *n* arcángel *m*.
archbishop [ɑːtʃ'bɪʃəp] *n* arzobispo.
arched [ɑːtʃt] *adj* abovedado.
archenemy ['ɑːtʃ'ɛnəmɪ] *n* enemigo jurado.
archeology [ɑːkɪ'ɔlədʒɪ] *etc* (*US*) = **archaeology** *etc*.
archer ['ɑːtʃə*] *n* arquero/a.
archery ['ɑːtʃərɪ] *n* tiro al arco.
archetypal ['ɑːkɪtaɪpəl] *adj* arquetípico.
archetype ['ɑːkɪtaɪp] *n* arquetipo.
archipelago [ɑːkɪ'pɛlɪgəu] *n* archipiélago.
architect ['ɑːkɪtɛkt] *n* arquitecto/a.
architectural [ɑːkɪ'tɛktʃərəl] *adj* arquitectónico.
architecture ['ɑːkɪtɛktʃə*] *n* arquitectura.
archive ['ɑːkaɪv] *n* (*often pl*: *also COMPUT*) archivo.
archive file *n* (*COMPUT*) fichero archivado.
archives ['ɑːkaɪvz] *npl* archivo *sg*.
archivist ['ɑːkɪvɪst] *n* archivero/a.
archway ['ɑːtʃweɪ] *n* arco, arcada.
ARCM *n abbr* (*BRIT*) = *Associate of the Royal College of Music*.
Arctic ['ɑːktɪk] *adj* ártico ♦ *n*: **the ~** el Ártico.
Arctic Circle *n* Círculo Polar Ártico.
Arctic Ocean *n* Océano (Glacial) Ártico.
ARD *n abbr* (*US MED*) = *acute respiratory disease*.
ardent ['ɑːdənt] *adj* (*desire*) ardiente; (*supporter, lover*) apasionado.
ardour, (*US*) **ardor** ['ɑːdə*] *n* ardor *m*, pasión *f*.
arduous ['ɑːdjuəs] *adj* (*gen*) arduo; (*journey*) penoso.
are [ɑː*] *vb see* **be**.
area ['ɛərɪə] *n* área; (*MATH etc*) superficie *f*, extensión *f*; (*zone*) región *f*, zona; **the London ~** la zona de Londres.
area code *n* (*US TEL*) prefijo.
arena [ə'riːnə] *n* arena; (*of circus*) pista; (*for bullfight*) plaza, ruedo.
aren't [ɑːnt] = **are not**.
Argentina [ɑːdʒən'tiːnə] *n* Argentina.
Argentinian [ɑːdʒən'tɪnɪən] *adj, n* argentino/a *m/f*.
arguable ['ɑːgjuəbl] *adj*: **it is ~ whether ...** es dudoso que + *subjun*.
arguably ['ɑːgjuəblɪ] *adv*: **it is ~ ...** es discutiblemente ....
argue ['ɑːgjuː] *vt* (*debate*: *case, matter*) mantener, argüir ♦ *vi* (*quarrel*) discutir; (*reason*) razonar, argumentar; **to ~ that** sostener que; **to ~ about sth (with sb)** pelearse (con algn) por algo.
argument ['ɑːgjumənt] *n* (*reasons*) argumento; (*quarrel*) discusión *f*; (*debate*) debate *m*; **~ for/against** argumento en pro/contra de.
argumentative [ɑːgju'mɛntətɪv] *adj* discutidor(a).
aria ['ɑːrɪə] *n* (*MUS*) aria.
ARIBA *n abbr* (*BRIT*) = *Associate of the Royal Institute of British Architects*.
arid ['ærɪd] *adj* árido.
aridity [ə'rɪdɪtɪ] *n* aridez *f*.
Aries ['ɛərɪz] *n* Aries *m*.
arise [ə'raɪz], *pt* **arose,** *pp* **arisen** [ə'rɪzn] *vi* (*rise up*) levantarse, alzarse; (*emerge*) surgir, presentarse; **to ~ from** derivar de; **should the need ~** si fuera necesario.
aristocracy [ærɪs'tɔkrəsɪ] *n* aristocracia.
aristocrat ['ærɪstəkræt] *n* aristócrata *m/f*.
aristocratic [ərɪstə'krætɪk] *adj* aristocrático.
arithmetic [ə'rɪθmətɪk] *n* aritmética.
arithmetical [ærɪθ'mɛtɪkl] *adj* aritmético.
Ariz. *abbr* (*US*) = *Arizona*.
Ark [ɑːk] *n*: **Noah's ~** el Arca *f* de Noé.
Ark. *abbr* (*US*) = *Arkansas*.
arm [ɑːm] *n* (*ANAT*) brazo ♦ *vt* armar; **~ in ~** cogidos del brazo; *see also* **arms**.
armaments ['ɑːməmənts] *npl* (*weapons*) armamentos *mpl*.
armchair ['ɑːmtʃɛə*] *n* sillón *m*, butaca.
armed [ɑːmd] *adj* armado; **the ~ forces** las fuerzas armadas.
armed robbery *n* robo a mano armada.
Armenia [ɑː'miːnɪə] *n* Armenia.
Armenian [ɑː'miːnɪən] *adj* armenio ♦ *n* armenio/a; (*LING*) armenio.
armful ['ɑːmful] *n* brazada.
armistice ['ɑːmɪstɪs] *n* armisticio.
armour, (*US*) **armor** ['ɑːmə*] *n* armadura.
armo(u)red car *n* coche *m or* carro (*LAM*) blindado.
armo(u)ry ['ɑːmərɪ] *n* arsenal *m*.
armpit ['ɑːmpɪt] *n* sobaco, axila.
armrest ['ɑːmrɛst] *n* reposabrazos *m inv*, brazo.
arms [ɑːmz] *npl* (*weapons*) armas *fpl*; (*HERALDRY*) escudo *sg*.
arms control *n* control *m* de armamentos.
arms race *n* carrera de armamentos.
army ['ɑːmɪ] *n* ejército.
aroma [ə'rəumə] *n* aroma *m*, fragancia.
aromatherapy [ərəumə'θɛrəpɪ] *n* aromaterapia.

aromatic [ærə'mætɪk] *adj* aromático, fragante.
arose [ə'rəuz] *pt of* **arise.**
around [ə'raund] *adv* alrededor; (*in the area*) a la redonda ♦ *prep* alrededor de.
arousal [ə'rauzəl] *n* (*sexual*) excitación *f*; (*of feelings, interest*) despertar *m*.
arouse [ə'rauz] *vt* despertar.
arrange [ə'reɪndʒ] *vt* arreglar, ordenar; (*programme*) organizar ♦ *vi*: **we have ~d for a taxi to pick you up** hemos organizado todo para que le recoja un taxi; **to ~ to do sth** quedar en hacer algo; **it was ~d that** ... se quedó en que ....
arrangement [ə'reɪndʒmənt] *n* arreglo; (*agreement*) acuerdo; **~s** *npl* (*plans*) planes *mpl*, medidas *fpl*; (*preparations*) preparativos *mpl*; **to come to an ~ (with sb)** llegar a un acuerdo (con algn); **by ~** a convenir; **I'll make ~s for you to be met** haré los preparativos para que le estén esperando.
arrant ['ærənt] *adj*: **~ nonsense** una verdadera tontería.
array [ə'reɪ] *n* (*COMPUT*) matriz *f*; **~ of** (*things*) serie *f or* colección *f* de; (*people*) conjunto de.
arrears [ə'rɪəz] *npl* atrasos *mpl*; **in ~** (*COMM*) en mora; **to be in ~ with one's rent** estar retrasado en el pago del alquiler.
arrest [ə'rɛst] *vt* detener; (*sb's attention*) llamar ♦ *n* detención *f*; **under ~** detenido.
arresting [ə'rɛstɪŋ] *adj* (*fig*) llamativo.
arrival [ə'raɪvəl] *n* llegada, arribo (*LAM*); **new ~** recién llegado/a.
arrive [ə'raɪv] *vi* llegar, arribar (*LAM*).
arrogance ['ærəgəns] *n* arrogancia, prepotencia (*LAM*).
arrogant ['ærəgənt] *adj* arrogante, prepotente (*LAM*).
arrow ['ærəu] *n* flecha.
arse [ɑːs] *n* (*BRIT col!*) culo, trasero.
arsenal ['ɑːsɪnl] *n* arsenal *m*.
arsenic ['ɑːsnɪk] *n* arsénico.
arson ['ɑːsn] *n* incendio provocado.
art [ɑːt] *n* arte *m*; (*skill*) destreza; (*technique*) técnica; **A~s** *npl* (*SCOL*) Letras *fpl*; **work of ~** obra de arte.
artefact ['ɑːtɪfækt] *n* artefacto.
arterial [ɑː'tɪərɪəl] *adj* (*ANAT*) arterial; (*road etc*) principal.
artery ['ɑːtərɪ] *n* (*MED, road etc*) arteria.
artful ['ɑːtful] *adj* (*cunning: person, trick*) mañoso.
art gallery *n* pinacoteca, museo de pintura; (*COMM*) galería de arte.
arthritis [ɑː'θraɪtɪs] *n* artritis *f*.
artichoke ['ɑːtɪtʃəuk] *n* alcachofa; **Jerusalem ~** aguaturma.
article ['ɑːtɪkl] *n* artículo, objeto, cosa; (*in newspaper*) artículo; (*BRIT LAW: training*): **~s** *npl* contrato *sg* de aprendizaje; **~s of clothing** prendas *fpl* de vestir.
articles of association *npl* (*COMM*) estatutos *mpl* sociales, escritura social.
articulate *adj* [ɑː'tɪkjulɪt] (*speech*) claro; (*person*) que se expresa bien ♦ *vi* [ɑː'tɪkjuleɪt] articular.
articulated lorry *n* (*BRIT*) trailer *m*.
artifice ['ɑːtɪfɪs] *n* artificio, truco.
artificial [ɑːtɪ'fɪʃəl] *adj* artificial; (*teeth etc*) postizo.
artificial insemination *n* inseminación *f* artificial.
artificial intelligence (A.I.) *n* inteligencia artificial (I.A.).
artificial respiration *n* respiración *f* artificial.
artillery [ɑː'tɪlərɪ] *n* artillería.
artisan ['ɑːtɪzæn] *n* artesano/a.
artist ['ɑːtɪst] *n* artista *m/f*; (*MUS*) intérprete *m/f*.
artistic [ɑː'tɪstɪk] *adj* artístico.
artistry ['ɑːtɪstrɪ] *n* arte *m*, habilidad *f* (artística).
artless ['ɑːtlɪs] *adj* (*innocent*) natural, sencillo; (*clumsy*) torpe.
art school *n* escuela de bellas artes.
artwork ['ɑːtwəːk] *n* material *m* gráfico.
arty ['ɑːtɪ] *adj* artistoide.
ARV *n abbr* (= *American Revised Version*) *traducción americana de la Biblia.*
AS *n abbr* (*US UNIV:* = *Associate in/of Science*) *título universitario* ♦ *abbr* (*US*) = *American Samoa.*

KEYWORD

as [æz] *conj* **1** (*referring to time: while*) mientras; (: *when*) cuando; **she wept ~ she told her story** lloraba mientras contaba lo que le ocurrió; **~ the years go by** a medida que pasan los años, con el paso de los años; **he came in ~ I was leaving** entró cuando me marchaba; **~ from tomorrow** a partir de *or* desde mañana

2 (*in comparisons*): **~ big ~** tan grande como; **twice ~ big ~** el doble de grande que; **~ much money/many books ~** tanto dinero/tantos libros como; **~ soon ~** en cuanto, no bien (*LAM*)

3 (*since, because*) como, ya que; **~ I don't**

speak German I can't understand him como no hablo alemán no le entiendo, no le entiendo ya que no hablo alemán
4 (*although*): **much ~ I like them, ...** aunque me gustan, ...
5 (*referring to manner, way*): **do ~ you wish** haz lo que quieras; **~ she said** como dijo; **he gave it to me ~ a present** me lo dio de regalo; **it's on the left ~ you go in** según se entra, a la izquierda
6 (*concerning*): **~ for** *or* **to that** por *or* en lo que respecta a eso
7: **~ if** *or* **though** como si; **he looked ~ if he was ill** parecía como si estuviera enfermo, tenía aspecto de enfermo; *see also* **long**; **such**; **well**
♦ *prep* (*in the capacity of*): **he works ~ a barman** trabaja de barman; **~ chairman of the company, he ...** como presidente de la compañía, ...

ASA *n abbr* (= *American Standards Association*) *instituto de normalización*; (*BRIT*: = *Advertising Standards Authority*) *departamento de control de la publicidad*; (: = *Amateur Swimming Association*) *federación amateur de natación*.
a.s.a.p. *abbr* (= *as soon as possible*) cuanto antes, lo más pronto posible.
asbestos [æz'bɛstəs] *n* asbesto, amianto.
ascend [ə'sɛnd] *vt* subir, ascender.
ascendancy [ə'sɛndənsɪ] *n* ascendiente *m*, dominio.
ascendant [ə'sɛndənt] *n*: **to be in the ~** estar en auge, ir ganando predominio.
Ascension [ə'sɛnʃən] *n*: **the ~** la Ascensión.
Ascension Island *n* Isla Ascensión.
ascent [ə'sɛnt] *n* subida; (*slope*) cuesta, pendiente *f*; (*of plane*) ascenso.
ascertain [æsə'teɪn] *vt* averiguar.
ascetic [ə'sɛtɪk] *adj* ascético.
asceticism [ə'sɛtɪsɪzəm] *n* ascetismo.
ASCII ['æskiː] *n abbr* (= *American Standard Code for Information Interchange*) ASCII.
ascribe [ə'skraɪb] *vt*: **to ~ sth to** atribuir algo a.
ASCU *n abbr* (*US*) = *Association of State Colleges and Universities*.
ASE *n abbr* = *American Stock Exchange*.
ASH [æʃ] *n abbr* (*BRIT*: = *Action on Smoking and Health*) *organización anti-tabaco*.
ash [æʃ] *n* ceniza; (*tree*) fresno.
ashamed [ə'ʃeɪmd] *adj* avergonzado; **to be ~ of** avergonzarse de.
ashcan ['æʃkæn] *n* (*US*) cubo *or* bote *m* (*LAM*) de la basura.
ashen ['æʃn] *adj* pálido.
ashore [ə'ʃɔː*] *adv* en tierra.
ashtray ['æʃtreɪ] *n* cenicero.
Ash Wednesday *n* miércoles *m* de ceniza.
Asia ['eɪʃə] *n* Asia.
Asian ['eɪʃən], **Asiatic** [eɪsɪ'ætɪk] *adj, n* asiático/a *m/f*.
aside [ə'saɪd] *adv* a un lado ♦ *n* aparte *m*; **~ from** *prep* (*as well as*) aparte *or* además de.
ask [ɑːsk] *vt* (*question*) preguntar; (*demand*) pedir; (*invite*) invitar ♦ *vi*: **to ~ about sth** preguntar acerca de algo; **to ~ sb sth/to do sth** preguntar algo a algn/pedir a algn que haga algo; **to ~ sb about sth** preguntar algo a algn; **to ~ (sb) a question** hacer una pregunta (a algn); **to ~ sb the time** preguntar la hora a algn; **to ~ sb out to dinner** invitar a cenar a algn.
▸**ask after** *vt fus* preguntar por.
▸**ask for** *vt fus* pedir; **it's just ~ing for trouble** *or* **for it** es buscarse problemas.
askance [ə'skɑːns] *adv*: **to look ~ at sb** mirar con recelo a algn.
askew [ə'skjuː] *adv* sesgado, ladeado.
asking price *n* (*COMM*) precio inicial.
asleep [ə'sliːp] *adj* dormido; **to fall ~** dormirse, quedarse dormido.
ASLEF ['æzlɛf] *n abbr* (*BRIT*: = *Associated Society of Locomotive Engineers and Firemen*) *sindicato de ferroviarios*.
asp [æsp] *n* áspid *m*.
asparagus [əs'pærəgəs] *n* espárragos *mpl*.
ASPCA *n abbr* = *American Society for the Prevention of Cruelty to Animals*.
aspect ['æspɛkt] *n* aspecto, apariencia; (*direction in which a building etc faces*) orientación *f*.
aspersions [əs'pəːʃənz] *npl*: **to cast ~ on** difamar a, calumniar a.
asphalt ['æsfælt] *n* asfalto.
asphyxiate [æs'fɪksɪeɪt] *vt* asfixiar.
asphyxiation [aesfɪksɪ'eɪʃən] *n* asfixia.
aspirate ['æspəreɪt] *vt* aspirar ♦ *adj* ['æspərɪt] aspirado.
aspirations [æspə'reɪʃənz] *npl* aspiraciones *fpl*; (*ambition*) ambición *f*.
aspire [əs'paɪə*] *vi*: **to ~ to** aspirar a, ambicionar.
aspirin ['æsprɪn] *n* aspirina.
aspiring [əs'paɪərɪŋ] *adj*: **an ~ actor** un aspirante a actor.
ass [æs] *n* asno, burro; (*col*) imbécil *m/f*; (*US col!*) culo, trasero.
assailant [ə'seɪlənt] *n* agresor(a) *m/f*.
assassin [ə'sæsɪn] *n* asesino/a.
assassinate [ə'sæsɪneɪt] *vt* asesinar.
assassination [əsæsɪ'neɪʃən] *n* asesinato.
assault [ə'sɔːlt] *n* (*gen*: *attack*) asalto,

agresión *f* ♦ *vt* asaltar, agredir; (*sexually*) violar.
assemble [ə'sɛmbl] *vt* reunir, juntar; (*TECH*) montar ♦ *vi* reunirse, juntarse.
assembler [ə'sɛmblə*] *n* (*COMPUT*) ensamblador *m*.
assembly [ə'sɛmblɪ] *n* (*meeting*) reunión *f*, asamblea; (*construction*) montaje *m*.
assembly language *n* (*COMPUT*) lenguaje *m* ensamblador.
assembly line *n* cadena de montaje.
assent [ə'sɛnt] *n* asentimiento, aprobación *f* ♦ *vi* consentir, asentir; **to ~ (to sth)** consentir (en algo).
assert [ə'səːt] *vt* afirmar; (*insist on*) hacer valer; **to ~ o.s.** imponerse.
assertion [ə'səːʃən] *n* afirmación *f*.
assertive [ə'səːtɪv] *adj* enérgico, agresivo, perentorio.
assess [ə'sɛs] *vt* valorar, calcular; (*tax, damages*) fijar; (*property etc: for tax*) gravar.
assessment [ə'sɛsmənt] *n* valoración *f*; gravamen *m*; (*judgment*): **~ (of)** juicio (sobre).
assessor [ə'sɛsə*] *n* asesor(a) *m/f*; (*of tax*) tasador(a) *m/f*.
asset ['æsɛt] *n* posesión *f*; (*quality*) ventaja; **~s** *npl* (*funds*) activo *sg*, fondos *mpl*.
asset-stripping ['æsɛt'strɪpɪŋ] *n* (*COMM*) acaparamiento de activos.
assiduous [ə'sɪdjuəs] *adj* asiduo.
assign [ə'saɪn] *vt* (*date*) fijar; (*task*) asignar; (*resources*) destinar; (*property*) traspasar.
assignment [ə'saɪnmənt] *n* asignación *f*; (*task*) tarea.
assimilate [ə'sɪmɪleɪt] *vt* asimilar.
assimilation [əsɪmɪ'leɪʃən] *n* asimilación *f*.
assist [ə'sɪst] *vt* ayudar.
assistance [ə'sɪstəns] *n* ayuda, auxilio.
assistant [ə'sɪstənt] *n* ayudante *m/f*; (*BRIT: also:* **shop ~**) dependiente/a *m/f*.
assistant manager *n* subdirector(a) *m/f*.
assizes [ə'saɪzɪz] *npl* sesión *f* de un tribunal.
associate [ə'səuʃɪɪt] *adj* asociado ♦ *n* socio/a, colega *m/f*; (*in crime*) cómplice *m/f*; (*member*) miembro/a ♦ *vb* [ə'səuʃɪeɪt] *vt* asociar; (*ideas*) relacionar ♦ *vi*: **to ~ with sb** tratar con alguien; **~ director** subdirector/a *m/f*; **~d company** compañía afiliada.
association [əsəusɪ'eɪʃən] *n* asociación *f*; (*COMM*) sociedad *f*; **in ~ with** en asociación con.
association football *n* (*BRIT*) fútbol *m*.
assorted [ə'sɔːtɪd] *adj* surtido, variado; **in ~ sizes** en distintos tamaños.
assortment [ə'sɔːtmənt] *n* surtido.
Asst. *abbr* = **Assistant.**
assuage [ə'sweɪdʒ] *vt* mitigar.
assume [ə'sjuːm] *vt* (*suppose*) suponer; (*responsibilities etc*) asumir; (*attitude, name*) adoptar, tomar.
assumed name *n* nombre *m* falso.
assumption [ə'sʌmpʃən] *n* (*supposition*) suposición *f*, presunción *f*; (*act*) asunción *f*; **on the ~ that** suponiendo que.
assurance [ə'ʃuərəns] *n* garantía, promesa; (*confidence*) confianza, aplomo; (*BRIT: insurance*) seguro; **I can give you no ~s** no puedo hacerle ninguna promesa.
assure [ə'ʃuə*] *vt* asegurar.
assured [ə'ʃuəd] *adj* seguro.
assuredly [ə'ʃuərɪdlɪ] *adv* indudablemente.
AST *n abbr* (= *Atlantic Standard Time*) *hora oficial del este del Canadá.*
asterisk ['æstərɪsk] *n* asterisco.
astern [ə'stəːn] *adv* a popa.
asteroid ['æstərɔɪd] *n* asteroide *m*.
asthma ['æsmə] *n* asma.
asthmatic [æs'mætɪk] *adj, n* asmático/a *m/f*.
astigmatism [ə'stɪgmətɪzəm] *n* astigmatismo.
astir [ə'stəː*] *adv* en acción.
astonish [ə'stɔnɪʃ] *vt* asombrar, pasmar.
astonishing [ə'stɔnɪʃɪŋ] *adj* asombroso, pasmoso; **I find it ~ that** ... me asombra *or* pasma que ....
astonishingly [ə'stɔnɪʃɪŋlɪ] *adv* increíblemente, asombrosamente.
astonishment [ə'stɔnɪʃmənt] *n* asombro, sorpresa; **to my ~** con gran sorpresa mía.
astound [ə'staund] *vt* asombrar, pasmar.
astounding [ə'staundɪŋ] *adj* asombroso.
astray [ə'streɪ] *adv*: **to go ~** extraviarse; **to lead ~** llevar por mal camino; **to go ~ in one's calculations** equivocarse en sus cálculos.
astride [ə'straɪd] *prep* a caballo *or* horcajadas sobre.
astringent [əs'trɪndʒənt] *adj, n* astringente *m*.
astrologer [əs'trɔlədʒə*] *n* astrólogo/a.
astrology [əs'trɔlədʒɪ] *n* astrología.
astronaut ['æstrənɔːt] *n* astronauta *m/f*.
astronomer [əs'trɔnəmə*] *n* astrónomo/a.
astronomical [æstrə'nɔmɪkəl] *adj* astronómico.
astronomy [aes'trɔnəmɪ] *n* astronomía.
astrophysics ['æstrəu'fɪzɪks] *n* astrofísica.
astute [əs'tjuːt] *adj* astuto.
asunder [ə'sʌndə*] *adv*: **to tear ~** hacer pedazos.
ASV *n abbr* (= *American Standard Version*) *traducción americana de la Biblia.*

asylum [ə'saɪləm] *n* (*refuge*) asilo; (*hospital*) manicomio; **to seek political ~** pedir asilo político.
asymmetric(al) [eɪsɪ'metrɪk(l)] *adj* asimétrico.

KEYWORD

at [æt] *prep* **1** (*referring to position*) en; (*direction*) a; **~ the top** en lo alto; **~ home/school** en casa/la escuela; **to look ~ sth/sb** mirar algo/a algn
2 (*referring to time*): **~ 4 o'clock** a las 4; **~ night** por la noche; **~ Christmas** en Navidad; **~ times** a veces
3 (*referring to rates, speed etc*): **~ £1 a kilo** a una libra el kilo; **two ~ a time** de dos en dos; **~ 50 km/h** a 50 km/h
4 (*referring to manner*): **~ a stroke** de un golpe; **~ peace** en paz
5 (*referring to activity*): **to be ~ work** estar trabajando; (*in the office etc*) estar en el trabajo; **to play ~ cowboys** jugar a los vaqueros; **to be good ~ sth** ser bueno en algo
6 (*referring to cause*): **shocked/surprised/annoyed ~ sth** asombrado/sorprendido/fastidiado por algo; **I went ~ his suggestion** fui a instancias suyas.

ate [ɛt, eɪt] *pt of* **eat**.
atheism ['eɪθɪɪzəm] *n* ateísmo.
atheist ['eɪθɪɪst] *n* ateo/a.
Athenian [ə'θi:nɪən] *adj, n* ateniense *m/f*.
Athens ['æθɪnz] *n* Atenas *f*.
athlete ['æθli:t] *n* atleta *m/f*.
athletic [æθ'lɛtɪk] *adj* atlético.
athletics [æθ'lɛtɪks] *n* atletismo.
Atlantic [ət'læntɪk] *adj* atlántico ♦ *n*: **the ~ (Ocean)** el (Océano) Atlántico.
atlas ['ætləs] *n* atlas *m*.
Atlas Mountains *npl*: **the ~** el Atlas.
A.T.M. *n abbr* (= *Automated Telling Machine*) *cajero automático*.
atmosphere ['ætməsfɪə*] *n* (*air*) atmósfera; (*fig*) ambiente *m*.
atom ['ætəm] *n* átomo.
atomic [ə'tɔmɪk] *adj* atómico.
atom(ic) bomb *n* bomba atómica.
atomic power *n* energía atómica.
atomizer ['ætəmaɪzə*] *n* atomizador *m*.
atone [ə'təun] *vi*: **to ~ for** expiar.
atonement [ə'təunmənt] *n* expiación *f*.
A to Z ® *n* guía alfabética; (*map*) callejero.
ATP *n abbr* (= *Association of Tennis Professionals*) *sindicato de jugadores de tenis profesionales*.
atrocious [ə'trəuʃəs] *adj* atroz; (*fig*) horrible, infame.
atrocity [ə'trɔsɪtɪ] *n* atrocidad *f*.
atrophy ['ætrəfɪ] *n* atrofia ♦ *vi* atrofiarse.
attach [ə'tætʃ] *vt* sujetar; (*stick*) pegar; (*document, letter*) adjuntar; **to be ~ed to sb/sth** (*to like*) tener cariño a algn/algo; **the ~ed letter** la carta adjunta.
attaché [ə'tæʃeɪ] *n* agregado/a.
attaché case *n* (*BRIT*) maletín *m*.
attachment [ə'tætʃmənt] *n* (*tool*) accesorio; (*love*): **~ (to)** apego (a), cariño (a).
attack [ə'tæk] *vt* (*MIL*) atacar; (*criminal*) agredir, asaltar; (*task etc*) emprender ♦ *n* ataque *m*, asalto; (*on sb's life*) atentado; **heart ~** infarto (de miocardio).
attacker [ə'tækə*] *n* agresor(a) *m/f*, asaltante *m/f*.
attain [ə'teɪn] *vt* (*also*: **~ to**) alcanzar; (*achieve*) lograr, conseguir.
attainments [ə'teɪnmənts] *npl* (*skill*) talento *sg*.
attempt [ə'tɛmpt] *n* tentativa, intento; (*attack*) atentado ♦ *vt* intentar, tratar de; **he made no ~ to help** ni siquiera intentó ayudar.
attempted [ə'tɛmptɪd] *adj*: **~ murder/burglary/suicide** tentativa *or* intento de asesinato/robo/suicidio.
attend [ə'tɛnd] *vt* asistir a; (*patient*) atender.
▸**attend to** *vt fus* (*needs, affairs etc*) ocuparse de; (*speech etc*) prestar atención a; (*customer*) atender a.
attendance [ə'tɛndəns] *n* asistencia, presencia; (*people present*) concurrencia.
attendant [ə'tɛndənt] *n* sirviente/a *m/f*, mozo/a; (*THEAT*) acomodador(a) *m/f* ♦ *adj* concomitante.
attention [ə'tɛnʃən] *n* atención *f* ♦ *excl* (*MIL*) ¡firme(s)!; **for the ~ of...** (*ADMIN*) a la atención de...; **it has come to my ~ that ...** me he enterado de que ....
attentive [ə'tɛntɪv] *adj* atento; (*polite*) cortés.
attenuate [ə'tɛnjueɪt] *vt* atenuar.
attest [ə'tɛst] *vi*: **to ~ to** dar fe de.
attic ['ætɪk] *n* desván *m*, altillo (*LAM*), entretecho (*LAM*).
attitude ['ætɪtju:d] *n* (*gen*) actitud *f*; (*disposition*) disposición *f*.
attorney [ə'tə:nɪ] *n* (*US: lawyer*) abogado/a; (*having proxy*) apoderado.
Attorney General *n* (*BRIT*) ≈ Presidente *m* del Consejo del Poder Judicial (*SP*); (*US*) ≈ ministro de justicia.
attract [ə'trækt] *vt* atraer; (*attention*) llamar.
attraction [ə'trækʃən] *n* (*gen*) encanto, atractivo; (*PHYSICS, towards sth*)

atracción *f*.
attractive [ə'træktɪv] *adj* atractivo.
attribute ['ætrɪbjuːt] *n* atributo ♦ *vt* [ə'trɪbjuːt]: **to ~ sth to** atribuir algo a; (*accuse*) achacar algo a.
attrition [ə'trɪʃən] *n*: **war of ~** guerra de agotamiento *or* desgaste.
Atty. Gen. *abbr* = **Attorney General.**
ATV *n abbr* (= *all terrain vehicle*) vehículo todo terreno.
atypical [eɪ'tɪpɪkl] *adj* atípico.
aubergine ['əubəʒiːn] *n* (*BRIT*) berenjena.
auburn ['ɔːbən] *adj* color castaño rojizo.
auction ['ɔːkʃən] *n* (*also*: **sale by ~**) subasta ♦ *vt* subastar.
auctioneer [ɔːkʃə'nɪə*] *n* subastador(a) *m/f*.
auction room *n* sala de subastas.
audacious [ɔː'deɪʃəs] *adj* (*bold*) audaz, osado; (*impudent*) atrevido, descarado.
audacity [ɔː'dæsɪtɪ] *n* audacia, atrevimiento; (*pej*) descaro.
audible ['ɔːdɪbl] *adj* audible, que se puede oír.
audience ['ɔːdɪəns] *n* auditorio; (*gathering*) público; (*interview*) audiencia.
audio-typist ['ɔːdɪəu'taɪpɪst] *n* mecanógrafo/a de dictáfono.
audiovisual [ɔːdɪəu'vɪzjuəl] *adj* audiovisual.
audiovisual aid *n* ayuda *or* medio audiovisual.
audit ['ɔːdɪt] *vt* revisar, intervenir.
audition [ɔː'dɪʃən] *n* audición *f* ♦ *vi*: **to ~ for the part of** hacer una audición para el papel de.
auditor ['ɔːdɪtə*] *n* interventor(a) *m/f*, censor(a) *m/f* de cuentas.
auditorium [ɔːdɪ'tɔːrɪəm] *n* auditorio.
Aug. *abbr* (= *August*) ag.
augment [ɔːg'mɛnt] *vt, vi* aumentar.
augur ['ɔːgə*] *vi*: **it ~s well** es de buen agüero.
August ['ɔːgəst] *n* agosto.
august [ɔː'gʌst] *adj* augusto.
aunt [ɑːnt] *n* tía.
auntie, aunty ['ɑːntɪ] *n diminutive of* **aunt.**
au pair ['əu'pɛə*] *n* (*also*: **~ girl**) chica *f* au pair.
aura ['ɔːrə] *n* aura; (*atmosphere*) ambiente *m*.
auspices ['ɔːspɪsɪz] *npl*: **under the ~ of** bajo los auspicios de.
auspicious [ɔːs'pɪʃəs] *adj* propicio, de buen augurio.
austere [ɔs'tɪə*] *adj* austero; (*manner*) adusto.
austerity [ɔ'stɛrɪtɪ] *n* austeridad *f*.
Australasia [ɔːstrə'leɪzɪə] *n* Australasia.
Australia [ɔs'treɪlɪə] *n* Australia.
Australian [ɔs'treɪlɪən] *adj, n* australiano/a *m/f*.
Austria ['ɔstrɪə] *n* Austria.
Austrian ['ɔstrɪən] *adj, n* austríaco/a *m/f*.
AUT *n abbr* (*BRIT*: = *Association of University Teachers*) *sindicato de profesores de universidad*.
authentic [ɔː'θɛntɪk] *adj* auténtico.
authenticate [ɔː'θɛntɪkeɪt] *vt* autentificar.
authenticity [ɔːθɛn'tɪsɪtɪ] *n* autenticidad *f*.
author ['ɔːθə*] *n* autor(a) *m/f*.
authoritarian [ɔːθɔrɪ'tɛərɪən] *adj* autoritario.
authoritative [ɔː'θɔrɪtətɪv] *adj* autorizado; (*manner*) autoritario.
authority [ɔː'θɔrɪtɪ] *n* autoridad *f*; **the authorities** *npl* las autoridades; **to have ~ to do sth** tener autoridad para hacer algo.
authorization [ɔːθəraɪ'zeɪʃən] *n* autorización *f*.
authorize ['ɔːθəraɪz] *vt* autorizar.
authorized capital *n* (*COMM*) capital *m* autorizado *or* social.
autistic [ɔː'tɪstɪk] *adj* autista.
auto ['ɔːtəu] *n* (*US*) coche *m*, carro (*LAM*), auto (*LAM*), automóvil *m*.
autobiographical [ɔːtəbaɪə'græfɪkəl] *adj* autobiográfico.
autobiography [ɔːtəbaɪ'ɔgrəfɪ] *n* autobiografía.
autocratic [ɔːtə'krætɪk] *adj* autocrático.
Autocue ® ['ɔːtəukjuː] *n* autocue *m*, teleapuntador *m*.
autograph ['ɔːtəgrɑːf] *n* autógrafo ♦ *vt* firmar; (*photo etc*) dedicar.
autoimmune [ɔːtəuɪ'mjuːn] *adj* autoinmune.
automat ['ɔːtəmæt] *n* (*US*) restaurante *m* de autoservicio.
automate ['ɔːtəmeɪt] *vt* automatizar.
automated ['ɔːtəmeɪtɪd] *adj* automatizado.
automatic [ɔːtə'mætɪk] *adj* automático ♦ *n* (*gun*) pistola automática; (*washing machine*) lavadora.
automatically [ɔːtə'mætɪklɪ] *adv* automáticamente.
automatic data processing (ADP) *n* proceso automático de datos.
automation [ɔːtə'meɪʃən] *n* automatización *f*.
automaton, *pl* **automata** [ɔː'tɔmətən, -tə] *n* autómata.
automobile ['ɔːtəməbiːl] *n* (*US*) coche *m*, carro (*LAM*), automóvil *m*.
autonomous [ɔː'tɔnəməs] *adj* autónomo.
autonomy [ɔː'tɔnəmɪ] *n* autonomía.
autopsy ['ɔːtɔpsɪ] *n* autopsia.
autumn ['ɔːtəm] *n* otoño.
auxiliary [ɔːg'zɪlɪərɪ] *adj* auxiliar.

AV *n abbr* (= *Authorized Version*) *traducción inglesa de la Biblia* ♦ *abbr* = **audiovisual**.
Av. *abbr* (= *avenue*) Av., Avda.
avail [ə'veɪl] *vt*: **to ~ o.s. of** aprovechar(se) de, valerse de ♦ *n*: **to no ~** en vano, sin resultado.
availability [əveɪlə'bɪlɪtɪ] *n* disponibilidad *f*.
available [ə'veɪləbl] *adj* disponible; (*obtainable*) asequible; **to make sth ~ to sb** poner algo a la disposición de algn; **is the manager ~?** ¿está libre el gerente?
avalanche ['ævəlɑːnʃ] *n* alud *m*, avalancha.
avant-garde ['ævɑ̃ŋ'gɑːd] *adj* de vanguardia.
avarice ['ævərɪs] *n* avaricia.
avaricious [ævə'rɪʃəs] *adj* avaricioso.
avdp. *abbr* = *avoirdupois*.
Ave. *abbr* (= *avenue*) Av., Avda.
avenge [ə'vɛndʒ] *vt* vengar.
avenue ['ævənjuː] *n* avenida; (*fig*) camino, vía.
average ['ævərɪdʒ] *n* promedio, media ♦ *adj* (*mean*) medio; (*ordinary*) regular, corriente ♦ *vt* calcular el promedio de; **on ~** por término medio.
▸**average out** *vi*: **to ~ out at** salir a un promedio de.
averse [ə'vəːs] *adj*: **to be ~ to sth/doing** sentir aversión *or* antipatía por algo/por hacer.
aversion [ə'vəːʃən] *n* aversión *f*, repugnancia.
avert [ə'vəːt] *vt* prevenir; (*blow*) desviar; (*one's eyes*) apartar.
aviary ['eɪvɪərɪ] *n* pajarera.
aviation [eɪvɪ'eɪʃən] *n* aviación *f*.
aviator ['eɪvɪeɪtə*] *n* aviador(a) *m/f*.
avid ['ævɪd] *adj* ávido, ansioso.
avidly ['ævɪdlɪ] *adv* ávidamente, con avidez.
avocado [ævə'kɑːdəu] *n* (*also*: *Brit*: **~ pear**) aguacate *m*, palta (*LAM*).
avoid [ə'vɔɪd] *vt* evitar, eludir.
avoidable [ə'vɔɪdəbl] *adj* evitable, eludible.
avoidance [ə'vɔɪdəns] *n* evasión *f*.
avow [ə'vau] *vt* prometer.
avowal [ə'vauəl] *n* promesa, voto.
avowed [ə'vaud] *adj* declarado.
AVP *n abbr* (*US*) = *assistant vice-president*.
avuncular [ə'vʌŋkjulə*] *adj* paternal.
AWACS ['eɪwæks] *n abbr* (= *airborne warning and control system*) AWACS *m*.
await [ə'weɪt] *vt* esperar, aguardar; **long ~ed** largamente esperado.
awake [ə'weɪk] *adj* despierto ♦ (*vb*: *pt* **awoke**, *pp* **awoken** *or* **awaked**) *vt* despertar ♦ *vi* despertarse; **to be ~** estar despierto.
awakening [ə'weɪknɪŋ] *n* despertar *m*.
award [ə'wɔːd] *n* (*prize*) premio; (*medal*) condecoración *f*; (*LAW*) fallo, sentencia; (*act*) concesión *f* ♦ *vt* (*prize*) otorgar, conceder; (*LAW*: *damages*) adjudicar.
aware [ə'wɛə*] *adj* consciente; (*awake*) despierto; (*informed*) enterado; **to become ~ of** darse cuenta de, enterarse de; **I am fully ~ that** sé muy bien que.
awareness [ə'wɛənɪs] *n* conciencia, conocimiento.
awash [ə'wɔʃ] *adj* inundado.
away [ə'weɪ] *adv* (*gen*) fuera; (*far ~*) lejos; **two kilometres ~** a dos kilómetros (de distancia); **two hours ~ by car** a dos horas en coche; **the holiday was two weeks ~** faltaban dos semanas para las vacaciones; **~ from** lejos de, fuera de; **he's ~ for a week** estará ausente una semana; **he's ~ in Barcelona** está en Barcelona; **to take ~** llevar(se); **to work/pedal ~** seguir trabajando/pedaleando; **to fade ~** desvanecerse; (*sound*) apagarse.
away game *n* (*SPORT*) partido de fuera.
awe [ɔː] *n* respeto, temor *m* reverencial.
awe-inspiring ['ɔːɪnspaɪərɪŋ], **awesome** ['ɔːsəm] *adj* imponente, pasmoso.
awestruck ['ɔːstrʌk] *adj* pasmado.
awful ['ɔːfəl] *adj* terrible; **an ~ lot of** (*people, cars, dogs*) la mar de, muchísimos.
awfully ['ɔːfəlɪ] *adv* (*very*) terriblemente.
awhile [ə'waɪl] *adv* (durante) un rato, algún tiempo.
awkward ['ɔːkwəd] *adj* (*clumsy*) desmañado, torpe; (*shape, situation*) incómodo; (*difficult*: *question*) difícil; (*problem*) complicado.
awkwardness ['ɔːkwədnɪs] *n* (*clumsiness*) torpeza; (*of situation*) incomodidad *f*.
awl [ɔːl] *n* lezna, subilla.
awning ['ɔːnɪŋ] *n* (*of shop*) toldo; (*of window etc*) marquesina.
awoke [ə'wəuk], **awoken** [ə'wəukən] *pt, pp of* **awake**.
AWOL ['eɪwɔl] *abbr* (*MIL*) *see* **absent without leave**.
awry [ə'raɪ] *adv*: **to be ~** estar descolocado *or* atravesado; **to go ~** salir mal, fracasar.
axe, (*US*) **ax** [æks] *n* hacha ♦ *vt* (*employee*) despedir; (*project etc*) cortar; (*jobs*) reducir; **to have an ~ to grind** (*fig*) tener un interés creado *or* algún fin interesado.
axes ['æksiːz] *npl of* **axis**.
axiom ['æksɪəm] *n* axioma *m*.
axiomatic [æksɪə'mætɪk] *adj* axiomático.
axis, *pl* **axes** ['æksɪs, -siːz] *n* eje *m*.

axle ['æksl] *n* eje *m*, árbol *m*.
ay(e) [aɪ] *excl* (*yes*) sí; **the ayes** *npl* los que votan a favor.
AYH *n abbr* = *American Youth Hostels*.
AZ *abbr* (*US*) = *Arizona*.
Azerbaijan [æzəbaɪ'dʒɑːn] *n* Azerbaiyán *m*.
Azerbaijani [æzəbaɪ'dʒɑːnɪ], **Azeri** [ə'zɛərɪ] *adj, n* azerbaiyano/a, azerí *m/f*.
Azores [ə'zɔːz] *npl*: **the** ~ las (Islas) Azores.
Aztec ['æztɛk] *adj, n* azteca *m/f*.
azure ['eɪʒə*] *adj* celeste.

B b

B, b [biː] *n* (*letter*) B, b *f*; (*SCOL: mark*) N; (*MUS*) si *m*; **B for Benjamin, (***US***) B for Baker** B de Barcelona; **B road** (*BRIT AUT*) ≈ carretera secundaria.
BA *n abbr* = *British Academy*; (*SCOL*) = **Bachelor of Arts**; *see also* **bachelor's degree**.
babble ['bæbl] *vi* farfullar.
baboon [bə'buːn] *n* mandril *m*.
baby ['beɪbɪ] *n* bebé *m/f*.
baby carriage *n* (*US*) cochecito.
babyish ['beɪbɪɪʃ] *adj* infantil.
baby-sit ['beɪbɪsɪt] *vi* hacer de canguro.
baby-sitter ['beɪbɪsɪtə*] *n* canguro *m/f*.
bachelor ['bætʃələ*] *n* soltero; **B~ of Arts/Science (BA/BSc)** licenciado/a en Filosofía y Letras/Ciencias.
bachelor's degree *n* licenciatura; *ver recuadro*.

BACHELOR'S DEGREE

Se denomina **bachelor's degree** *a la titulación que se recibe al finalizar el primer ciclo universitario, normalmente después de un período de estudio de tres o cuatro años. Las titulaciones más frecuentes son las de Letras, "BA (Bachelor of Arts)", Ciencias, "BSc (Bachelor of Science)", Educación, "BEd (Bachelor of Education)" y Derecho, "LLB (Bachelor of Laws)".*

back [bæk] *n* (*of person*) espalda; (*of animal*) lomo; (*of hand, page*) dorso; (*as opposed to front*) parte *f* de atrás; (*of room*) fondo; (*of chair*) respaldo; (*FOOTBALL*) defensa *m*; **to have one's ~ to the wall** (*fig*) estar entre la espada y la pared; **to break the ~ of a job** hacer lo más difícil de un trabajo; **~ to front** al revés; **at the ~ of my mind was the thought that ...** en el fondo tenía la idea de que ... ♦ *vt* (*candidate*: *also*: **~ up**) respaldar, apoyar; (*horse*: *at races*) apostar a; (*car*) dar marcha atrás a *or* con ♦ *vi* (*car etc*) dar marcha atrás ♦ *adj* (*in compounds*) de atrás; **~ seats/wheels** (*AUT*) asientos *mpl*/ruedas *fpl* traseros/as; **~ garden/room** jardín *m*/habitación *f* de atrás; **~ payments** pagos *mpl* con efecto retroactivo; **~ rent** renta atrasada; **to take a ~ seat** (*fig*) pasar a segundo plano ♦ *adv* (*not forward*) (hacia) atrás; **he's ~** (*returned*) ha vuelto; **he ran ~** volvió corriendo; **throw the ball ~** (*restitution*) devuelve la pelota; **can I have it ~?** ¿me lo devuelve?; **he called ~** (*again*) volvió a llamar; **~ and forth** de acá para allá; **as far ~ as the 13th century** ya en el siglo XIII; **when will you be ~?** ¿cuándo volverá?
▸**back down** *vi* echarse atrás.
▸**back on to** *vt fus*: **the house ~s on to the golf course** por atrás la casa da al campo de golf.
▸**back out** *vi* (*of promise*) volverse atrás.
▸**back up** *vt* (*support*: *person*) apoyar, respaldar; (: *theory*) defender; (*car*) dar marcha atrás a; (*COMPUT*) hacer una copia de reserva de.
backache ['bækeɪk] *n* dolor *m* de espalda.
backbencher ['bæk'bɛntʃə*] *n* (*BRIT*) *diputado sin cargo oficial en el gobierno o la oposición*.
back benches *npl* (*BRIT*) *ver recuadro*.

BACK BENCHES

Reciben el nombre genérico de **the back benches** *los escaños más alejados del pasillo central en la Cámara de los Comunes del Parlamento británico, que son ocupados por los "backbenchers", los miembros de la cámara que no tienen cargo en el gobierno o en la oposición.*

backbiting ['bækbaɪtɪŋ] *n* murmuración *f*.
backbone ['bækbəun] *n* columna vertebral; **the ~ of the organization** el pilar de la organización.
backchat ['bæktʃæt] *n* réplicas *fpl*.
backcloth ['bækklɔθ] *n* telón *m* de fondo.
backcomb ['bækkəum] *vt* cardar.
backdate [bæk'deɪt] *vt* (*letter*) poner fecha atrasada a; **~d pay rise** aumento de sueldo con efecto retroactivo.
backdrop ['bækdrɔp] *n* = **backcloth**.
backer ['bækə*] *n* partidario/a; (*COMM*)

promotor(a) *m/f*.
backfire [bæk'faɪə*] *vi* (*AUT*) petardear; (*plans*) fallar, salir mal.
backgammon ['bækgæmən] *n* backgammon *m*.
background ['bækgraund] *n* fondo; (*of events*) antecedentes *mpl*; (*basic knowledge*) bases *fpl*; (*experience*) conocimientos *mpl*, educación *f* ♦ *cpd* (*noise, music*) de fondo; (*COMPUT*) secundario; ~ **reading** lectura de preparación; **family** ~ origen *m*, antecedentes *mpl* familiares.
backhand ['bækhænd] *n* (*TENNIS*: *also*: ~ **stroke**) revés *m*.
backhanded ['bæk'hændɪd] *adj* (*fig*) ambiguo, equívoco.
backhander ['bæk'hændə*] *n* (*BRIT*: *bribe*) soborno.
backing ['bækɪŋ] *n* (*fig*) apoyo, respaldo; (*COMM*) respaldo financiero; (*MUS*) acompañamiento.
backlash ['bæklæʃ] *n* reacción *f* (en contra).
backlog ['bæklɔg] *n*: ~ **of work** trabajo atrasado.
back number *n* (*of magazine etc*) número atrasado.
backpack ['bækpæk] *n* mochila.
backpacker ['bækpækə*] *n* mochilero/a.
back pay *n* atrasos *mpl*.
backpedal ['bækpɛdl] *vi* (*fig*) volverse/echarse atrás.
backseat driver ['bæksiːt-] *n pasajero que se empeña en aconsejar al conductor*.
backside ['bæksaɪd] *n* (*col*) trasero.
backslash ['bækslæʃ] *n* pleca, barra inversa.
backslide ['bækslaɪd] *vi* reincidir, recaer.
backspace ['bækspeɪs] *vi* (*in typing*) retroceder.
backstage [bæk'steɪdʒ] *adv* entre bastidores.
back-street ['bækstriːt] *adj* de barrio; ~ **abortionist** persona que practica abortos clandestinos.
backstroke ['bækstrəuk] *n* espalda.
backtrack ['bæktræk] *vi* (*fig*) = **backpedal**.
backup ['bækʌp] *adj* (*train, plane*) suplementario; (*COMPUT*: *disk, file*) de reserva ♦ *n* (*support*) apoyo; (*also*: ~ **file**) copia de reserva; (*US*: *congestion*) embotellamiento, retención *f*.
back-up lights *npl* (*US*) luces *fpl* de marcha atrás.
backward ['bækwəd] *adj* (*movement*) hacia atrás; (*person, country*) atrasado; (*shy*) tímido.
backwardness ['bækwədnɪs] *n* atraso.
backwards ['bækwədz] *adv* (*move, go*) hacia atrás; (*read a list*) al revés; (*fall*) de espaldas; **to know sth** ~ *or* (*US*) ~ **and forwards** (*col*) saberse algo al dedillo.
backwater ['bækwɔːtə*] *n* (*fig*) lugar *m* atrasado *or* apartado.
backyard [bæk'jɑːd] *n* patio trasero.
bacon ['beɪkən] *n* tocino, bacon *m*, beicon *m*.
bacteria [bæk'tɪərɪə] *npl* bacterias *fpl*.
bacteriology [bæktɪərɪ'ɔlədʒɪ] *n* bacteriología.
bad [bæd] *adj* malo; (*serious*) grave; (*meat, food*) podrido, pasado; **to go** ~ pasarse; **to have a** ~ **time of it** pasarlo mal; **I feel** ~ **about it** (*guilty*) me siento culpable; ~ **debt** (*COMM*) cuenta incobrable; **in** ~ **faith** de mala fe.
baddie, baddy ['bædɪ] *n* (*col*: *CINE etc*) malo/a.
bade [bæd, beɪd] *pt of* **bid**.
badge [bædʒ] *n* insignia; (*metal* ~) chapa; (*of policeman*) placa; (*stick-on*) pegatina.
badger ['bædʒə*] *n* tejón *m*.
badly ['bædlɪ] *adv* (*work, dress etc*) mal; ~ **wounded** gravemente herido; **he needs it** ~ le hace mucha falta; **to be** ~ **off (for money)** andar mal de dinero; **things are going** ~ las cosas van muy mal.
bad-mannered ['bæd'mænəd] *adj* mal educado.
badminton ['bædmɪntən] *n* bádminton *m*.
bad-tempered ['bæd'tɛmpəd] *adj* de mal genio *or* carácter; (*temporary*) de mal humor.
baffle ['bæfl] *vt* desconcertar, confundir.
baffling ['bæflɪŋ] *adj* incomprensible.
bag [bæg] *n* bolsa; (*handbag*) bolso; (*satchel*) mochila; (*case*) maleta; (*of hunter*) caza ♦ *vt* (*col*: *take*) coger (*SP*), agarrar (*LAM*), pescar; ~**s of** (*col*: *lots of*) un montón de; **to pack one's** ~**s** hacer las maletas.
bagful ['bægful] *n* saco (lleno).
baggage ['bægɪdʒ] *n* equipaje *m*.
baggage claim *n* recogida de equipajes.
baggy ['bægɪ] *adj* (*trousers*) ancho, holgado.
Baghdad [bæg'dæd] *n* Bagdad *m*.
bag lady *n* (*col*) *mujer sin hogar cargada de bolsas*.
bagpipes ['bægpaɪps] *npl* gaita *sg*.
bag-snatcher ['bægsnætʃə*] *n* (*BRIT*) ladrón/ona *m/f* de bolsos.
bag-snatching ['bægsnætʃɪŋ] *n* (*BRIT*) tirón *m* (de bolsos).
Bahamas [bə'hɑːməz] *npl*: **the** ~ las (Islas) Bahama.
Bahrain [bɑː'reɪn] *n* Bahrein *m*.
bail [beɪl] *n* fianza ♦ *vt* (*prisoner*: *also*: **grant**

~ **to**) poner en libertad bajo fianza; (*boat*: *also*: ~ **out**) achicar; **on** ~ (*prisoner*) bajo fianza; **to be released on** ~ ser puesto en libertad bajo fianza; **to** ~ **sb out** pagar la fianza de algn; *see also* **bale**.
bailiff ['beɪlɪf] *n* alguacil *m*.
bait [beɪt] *n* cebo ♦ *vt* poner el cebo en.
bake [beɪk] *vt* cocer (al horno) ♦ *vi* (*cook*) cocerse; (*be hot*) hacer un calor terrible.
baked beans *npl* judías *fpl* en salsa de tomate.
baker ['beɪkə*] *n* panadero/a.
baker's dozen *n* docena del fraile.
bakery ['beɪkərɪ] *n* (*for bread*) panadería; (*for cakes*) pastelería.
baking ['beɪkɪŋ] *n* (*act*) cocción *f*; (*batch*) hornada.
baking powder *n* levadura (en polvo).
baking tin *n* molde *m* (para horno).
balaclava [bælə'klɑːvə] *n* (*also*: ~ **helmet**) pasamontañas *m inv*.
balance ['bæləns] *n* equilibrio; (*COMM*: *sum*) balance *m*; (*remainder*) resto; (*scales*) balanza ♦ *vt* equilibrar; (*budget*) nivelar; (*account*) saldar; (*compensate*) compensar; ~ **of trade/payments** balanza de comercio/pagos; ~ **carried forward** balance *m* pasado a cuenta nueva; ~ **brought forward** saldo de hoja anterior; **to** ~ **the books** hacer el balance.
balanced ['bælənst] *adj* (*personality, diet*) equilibrado.
balance sheet *n* balance *m*.
balcony ['bælkənɪ] *n* (*open*) balcón *m*; (*closed*) galería.
bald [bɔːld] *adj* calvo; (*tyre*) liso.
baldness ['bɔːldnɪs] *n* calvicie *f*.
bale [beɪl] *n* (*AGR*) paca, fardo.
►**bale out** *vi* (*of a plane*) lanzarse en paracaídas ♦ *vt* (*NAUT*) achicar; **to** ~ **sb out of a difficulty** sacar a algn de un apuro.
Balearic Islands [bælɪ'ærɪk-] *npl*: **the** ~ las (Islas) Baleares.
baleful ['beɪlful] *adj* (*look*) triste; (*sinister*) funesto, siniestro.
balk [bɔːk] *vi*: **to** ~ **(at)** resistirse (a); (*horse*) plantarse (ante).
Balkan ['bɔːlkən] *adj* balcánico ♦ *n*: **the** ~**s** los Balcanes.
ball [bɔːl] *n* (*sphere*) bola; (*football*) balón *m*; (*for tennis, golf etc*) pelota; (*dance*) baile *m*; **to be on the** ~ (*fig*: *competent*) ser un enterado; (: *alert*) estar al tanto; **to play** ~ **(with sb)** jugar a la pelota (con algn); (*fig*) cooperar; **to start the** ~ **rolling** (*fig*) empezar; **the** ~ **is in your court** (*fig*) le toca a usted.
ballad ['bæləd] *n* balada, romance *m*.
ballast ['bæləst] *n* lastre *m*.
ball bearing *n* cojinete *m* de bolas.
ballcock ['bɔːlkɔk] *n* llave *f* de bola *or* de flotador.
ballerina [bælə'riːnə] *n* bailarina.
ballet ['bæleɪ] *n* ballet *m*.
ballet dancer *n* bailarín/ina *m/f* (de ballet).
ballistic [bə'lɪstɪk] *adj* balístico; **intercontinental** ~ **missile** misil *m* balístico intercontinental.
ballistics [bə'lɪstɪks] *n* balística.
balloon [bə'luːn] *n* globo; (*in comic strip*) bocadillo ♦ *vi* dispararse.
balloonist [bə'luːnɪst] *n* aeróstata *m/f*.
ballot ['bælət] *n* votación *f*.
ballot box *n* urna (electoral).
ballot paper *n* papeleta.
ballpark ['bɔːlpɑːk] *n* (*US*) estadio de béisbol.
ball-point pen ['bɔːlpɔɪnt-] *n* bolígrafo.
ballroom ['bɔːlrum] *n* salón *m* de baile.
balm [bɑːm] *n* (*also fig*) bálsamo.
balmy ['bɑːmɪ] *adj* (*breeze, air*) suave; (*col*) = **barmy**.
BALPA ['bælpə] *n abbr* (= *British Airline Pilots' Association*) *sindicato de pilotos de líneas aéreas.*
balsa (wood) ['bɔːlsə-] *n* (madera de) balsa.
Baltic ['bɔːltɪk] *adj* báltico ♦ *n*: **the** ~ **(Sea)** el (Mar) Báltico.
balustrade ['bæləstreɪd] *n* barandilla.
bamboo [bæm'buː] *n* bambú *m*.
bamboozle [bæm'buːzl] *vt* (*col*) embaucar, engatusar.
ban [bæn] *n* prohibición *f* ♦ *vt* prohibir; (*exclude*) excluir; **he was ~ned from driving** le retiraron el carnet de conducir.
banal [bə'nɑːl] *adj* banal, vulgar.
banana [bə'nɑːnə] *n* plátano, banana (*LAM*).
band [bænd] *n* (*group*) banda; (*gang*) pandilla; (*strip*) faja, tira; (*at a dance*) orquesta; (*MIL*) banda; (*rock* ~) grupo.
►**band together** *vi* juntarse, asociarse.
bandage ['bændɪdʒ] *n* venda, vendaje *m* ♦ *vt* vendar.
Band-Aid ® ['bændeɪd] *n* (*US*) tirita, curita (*LAM*).
bandit ['bændɪt] *n* bandido; **one-armed** ~ máquina tragaperras.
bandstand ['bændstænd] *n* quiosco de música.
bandwagon ['bændwægən] *n*: **to jump on the** ~ (*fig*) subirse al carro.
bandy ['bændɪ] *vt* (*jokes, insults*) intercambiar.

bandy-legged ['bændɪ'lɛgd] *adj* patizambo.
bane [beɪn] *n*: **it** (*or* **he** *etc*) **is the ~ of my life** me amarga la vida.
bang [bæŋ] *n* estallido; (*of door*) portazo; (*blow*) golpe *m* ♦ *vt* golpear ♦ *vi* estallar ♦ *adv*: **to be ~ on time** (*col*) llegar en punto; **to ~ the door** dar un portazo; **to ~ into sth** chocar con algo, golpearse contra algo; *see also* **bangs**.
banger ['bæŋə*] *n* (*BRIT*: *car*: *also*: **old** ~) armatoste *m*, cacharro; (*BRIT col*: *sausage*) salchicha; (*firework*) petardo.
Bangkok [bæŋ'kɔk] *n* Bangkok *m*.
Bangladesh [bæŋglə'dɛʃ] *n* Bangladesh *f*.
bangle ['bæŋgl] *n* brazalete *m*, ajorca.
bangs [bæŋz] *npl* (*US*) flequillo *sg*.
banish ['bænɪʃ] *vt* desterrar.
banister(s) ['bænɪstə(z)] *n(pl)* barandilla *f*, pasamanos *m inv*.
banjo, *pl* **~es** *or* **~s** ['bændʒəu] *n* banjo.
bank [bæŋk] *n* (*COMM*) banco; (*of river, lake*) ribera, orilla; (*of earth*) terraplén *m*.
▸**bank on** *vt fus* contar con.
bank account *n* cuenta bancaria.
bank balance *n* saldo.
bank card *n* = **banker's card**.
bank charges *npl* comisión *fsg*.
bank draft *n* letra de cambio.
banker ['bæŋkə*] *n* banquero; **~'s card** (*BRIT*) tarjeta bancaria; **~'s order** orden *f* bancaria.
bank giro *n* giro bancario.
bank holiday *n* (*BRIT*) día *m* festivo *or* de fiesta; *ver recuadro*.

BANK HOLIDAY

El término **bank holiday** *se aplica en el Reino Unido a todo día festivo oficial en el que cierran bancos y comercios. Los más destacados coinciden con Navidad, Semana Santa, finales de mayo y finales de agosto. Al contrario que en los países de tradición católica, no se celebran las festividades dedicadas a los santos.*

banking ['bæŋkɪŋ] *n* banca.
bank loan *n* préstamo bancario.
bank manager *n* director(a) *m/f* (de sucursal) de banco.
banknote ['bæŋknəut] *n* billete *m* de banco.
bank rate *n* tipo de interés bancario.
bankrupt ['bæŋkrʌpt] *n* quebrado/a ♦ *adj* quebrado, insolvente; **to go ~** quebrar, hacer bancarrota; **to be ~** estar en quiebra.
bankruptcy ['bæŋkrʌptsɪ] *n* quiebra, bancarrota.
bank statement *n* extracto de cuenta.
banner ['bænə*] *n* bandera; (*in demonstration*) pancarta.
banns [bænz] *npl* amonestaciones *fpl*.
banquet ['bæŋkwɪt] *n* banquete *m*.
banter ['bæntə*] *n* guasa, bromas *fpl*.
BAOR *n abbr* (= *British Army of the Rhine*) *fuerzas británicas en Alemania*.
baptism ['bæptɪzəm] *n* bautismo; (*act*) bautizo.
baptize [bæp'taɪz] *vt* bautizar.
bar [bɑː*] *n* barra; (*on door*) tranca; (*of window, cage*) reja; (*of soap*) pastilla; (*fig*: *hindrance*) obstáculo; (*prohibition*) prohibición *f*; (*pub*) bar *m*, cantina (*esp LAM*); (*counter*: *in pub*) barra, mostrador *m*; (*MUS*) barra ♦ *vt* (*road*) obstruir; (*window, door*) atrancar; (*person*) excluir; (*activity*) prohibir; **behind ~s** entre rejas; **the B~** (*LAW*: *profession*) la abogacía; (: *people*) el cuerpo de abogados; **~ none** sin excepción.
Barbados [bɑː'beɪdɔs] *n* Barbados *m*.
barbarian [bɑː'bɛərɪən] *n* bárbaro/a.
barbaric [bɑː'bærɪk] *adj* bárbaro.
barbarity [bɑː'bærɪtɪ] *n* barbaridad *f*.
barbarous ['bɑːbərəs] *adj* bárbaro.
barbecue ['bɑːbɪkjuː] *n* barbacoa, asado (*LAM*).
barbed wire ['bɑːbd-] *n* alambre *m* de espino.
barber ['bɑːbə*] *n* peluquero, barbero.
barbiturate [bɑː'bɪtjurɪt] *n* barbitúrico.
Barcelona [bɑːsɪ'ləunə] *n* Barcelona.
bar chart *n* gráfico de barras.
bar code *n* código de barras.
bare [bɛə*] *adj* desnudo; (*head*) descubierto ♦ *vt* desnudar; **to ~ one's teeth** enseñar los dientes.
bareback ['bɛəbæk] *adv* a pelo.
barefaced ['bɛəfeɪst] *adj* descarado.
barefoot ['bɛəfut] *adj*, *adv* descalzo.
bareheaded [bɛə'hɛdɪd] *adj* descubierto, sin sombrero.
barely ['bɛəlɪ] *adv* apenas.
bareness ['bɛənɪs] *n* desnudez *f*.
Barents Sea ['bærənts-] *n*: **the ~** el Mar de Barents.
bargain ['bɑːgɪn] *n* pacto; (*transaction*) negocio; (*good buy*) ganga ♦ *vi* negociar; (*haggle*) regatear; **into the ~** además, por añadidura.
▸**bargain for** *vt fus* (*col*): **he got more than he ~ed for** le resultó peor de lo que esperaba.
bargaining ['bɑːgənɪŋ] *n* negociación *f*; regateo; **~ table** mesa de negociaciones.
bargaining position *n*: **to be in a strong/**

weak ~ estar/no estar en una posición de fuerza para negociar.
barge [bɑːdʒ] *n* barcaza.
▸**barge in** *vi* irrumpir; (*conversation*) entrometerse.
▸**barge into** *vt fus* dar contra.
baritone ['bærɪtəun] *n* barítono.
barium meal ['bɛərɪəm-] *n* (*MED*) sulfato de bario.
bark [bɑːk] *n* (*of tree*) corteza; (*of dog*) ladrido ♦ *vi* ladrar.
barley ['bɑːlɪ] *n* cebada.
barley sugar *n* azúcar *m* cande.
barmaid ['bɑːmeɪd] *n* camarera.
barman ['bɑːmən] *n* camarero, barman *m*.
barmy ['bɑːmɪ] *adj* (*col*) chiflado, chalado.
barn [bɑːn] *n* granero; (*for animals*) cuadra.
barnacle ['bɑːnəkl] *n* percebe *m*.
barn owl *n* lechuza.
barometer [bə'rɔmɪtə*] *n* barómetro.
baron ['bærən] *n* barón *m*; (*fig*) magnate *m*; **the press ~s** los magnates de la prensa.
baroness ['bærənɪs] *n* baronesa.
baroque [bə'rɔk] *adj* barroco.
barrack ['bærək] *vt* (*BRIT*) abuchear.
barracks ['bærəks] *npl* cuartel *msg*.
barrage ['bærɑːʒ] *n* (*MIL*) cortina de fuego; (*dam*) presa; (*fig*: *of criticism etc*) lluvia, aluvión *m*; **a ~ of questions** una lluvia de preguntas.
barrel ['bærəl] *n* barril *m*; (*of wine*) tonel *m*, cuba; (*of gun*) cañón *m*.
barren ['bærən] *adj* estéril.
barricade [bærɪ'keɪd] *n* barricada ♦ *vt* cerrar con barricadas.
barrier ['bærɪə*] *n* barrera; (*crash ~*) barrera.
barrier cream *n* crema protectora.
barring ['bɑːrɪŋ] *prep* excepto, salvo.
barrister ['bærɪstə*] *n* (*BRIT*) abogado/a; *ver recuadro*.

BARRISTER

En el sistema legal inglés **barrister** *es el abogado que se ocupa de defender los casos de sus clientes en los tribunales superiores. El equivalente escocés es "advocate". Normalmente actúan según instrucciones de un "solicitor", abogado de despacho que no toma parte activa en los juicios de dichos tribunales. El título de* **barrister** *lo otorga el órgano colegiado correspondiente, "the Inns of Court".*

barrow ['bærəu] *n* (*cart*) carretilla.
barstool ['bɑːstuːl] *n* taburete *m* (de bar).
Bart. *abbr* (*BRIT*) = *baronet*.
bartender ['bɑːtɛndə*] *n* (*US*) camarero, barman *m*.
barter ['bɑːtə*] *vt*: **to ~ sth for sth** trocar algo por algo.
base [beɪs] *n* base *f* ♦ *vt*: **to ~ sth on** basar *or* fundar algo en ♦ *adj* bajo, infame; **to ~ at** (*troops*) estacionar en; **I'm ~d in London** (*work*) trabajo en Londres.
baseball ['beɪsbɔːl] *n* béisbol *m*.
base camp *n* campamento base.
Basel ['bɑːzəl] *n* Basilea.
baseless ['beɪslɪs] *adj* infundado.
baseline ['beɪslaɪn] *n* (*TENNIS*) línea de fondo.
basement ['beɪsmənt] *n* sótano.
base rate *n* tipo base.
bases ['beɪsiːz] *npl of* **basis**; ['beɪsɪz] *npl of* **base**.
bash [bæʃ] *n*: **I'll have a ~ (at it)** lo intentaré ♦ *vt* (*col*) golpear.
▸**bash up** *vt* (*col*: *car*) destrozar; (: *person*) aporrear, vapulear.
bashful ['bæʃful] *adj* tímido, vergonzoso.
bashing ['bæʃɪŋ] *n* (*col*) paliza.
BASIC ['beɪsɪk] *n* BASIC *m*.
basic ['beɪsɪk] *adj* (*salary etc*) básico; (*elementary*: *principles*) fundamental.
basically ['beɪsɪklɪ] *adv* fundamentalmente, en el fondo.
basic rate *n* (*of tax*) base *f* mínima imponible.
basil ['bæzl] *n* albahaca.
basin ['beɪsn] *n* (*vessel*) cuenco, tazón *m*; (*GEO*) cuenca; (*also*: **wash~**) palangana, jofaina; (*in bathroom*) lavabo.
basis ['beɪsɪs], *pl* **-ses** [-siːz] *n* base *f*; **on the ~ of what you've said** en base a lo que has dicho.
bask [bɑːsk] *vi*: **to ~ in the sun** tomar el sol.
basket ['bɑːskɪt] *n* cesta, cesto.
basketball ['bɑːskɪtbɔːl] *n* baloncesto.
basketball player *n* jugador(a) *m/f* de baloncesto.
basketwork ['bɑːskɪtwəːk] *n* cestería.
Basle [bɑːl] *n* Basilea.
basmati rice [bəz'mætɪ-] *n* arroz *m* basmati.
Basque [bæsk] *adj, n* vasco/a *m/f*.
Basque Country *n* Euskadi *m*, País *m* Vasco.
bass [beɪs] *n* (*MUS*) bajo.
bass clef *n* clave *f* de fa.
bassoon [bə'suːn] *n* fagot *m*.
bastard ['bɑːstəd] *n* bastardo/a; (*col!*) cabrón *m*, hijo de puta (*!*).
baste [beɪst] *vt* (*CULIN*) rociar (con su salsa).

bastion ['bæstɪən] *n* bastión *m*, baluarte *m*.
bat [bæt] *n* (*ZOOL*) murciélago; (*for ball games*) palo; (*for cricket, baseball*) bate *m*; (*BRIT: for table tennis*) pala; **he didn't ~ an eyelid** ni pestañeó, ni se inmutó.
batch [bætʃ] *n* lote *m*, remesa; (*of bread*) hornada.
batch processing *n* (*COMPUT*) proceso por lotes.
bated ['beɪtɪd] *adj*: **with ~ breath** sin respirar.
bath [bɑːθ, *pl* bɑːðz] *n* (*action*) baño; (*~tub*) bañera, tina (*esp LAM*) ♦ *vt* bañar; **to have a ~** bañarse, darse un baño; *see also* **baths**.
bathchair ['bɑːθtʃɛə*] *n* silla de ruedas.
bathe [beɪð] *vi* bañarse; (*US*) darse un baño, bañarse ♦ *vt* (*wound etc*) lavar; (*US*) bañar, dar un baño a.
bather ['beɪðə*] *n* bañista *m/f*.
bathing ['beɪðɪŋ] *n* baño.
bathing cap *n* gorro de baño.
bathing costume, (*US*) **bathing suit** *n* bañador *m*, traje *m* de baño.
bathing trunks *npl* bañador *msg*.
bathmat ['bɑːθmæt] *n* alfombrilla de baño.
bathrobe ['bɑːθrəub] *n* albornoz *m*.
bathroom ['bɑːθrum] *n* (cuarto de) baño.
baths [bɑːðz] *npl* piscina *sg*.
bath towel *n* toalla de baño.
bathtub ['bɑːθtʌb] *n* bañera.
batman ['bætmən] *n* (*BRIT*) ordenanza *m*.
baton ['bætən] *n* (*MUS*) batuta.
battalion [bə'tælɪən] *n* batallón *m*.
batten ['bætn] *n* (*CARPENTRY*) listón *m*; (*NAUT*) junquillo, sable *m*.
►**batten down** *vt* (*NAUT*): **to ~ down the hatches** atrancar las escotillas.
batter ['bætə*] *vt* maltratar, apalear; (*subj: wind, rain*) azotar ♦ *n* batido.
battered ['bætəd] *adj* (*hat, pan*) estropeado.
battery ['bætərɪ] *n* batería; (*of torch*) pila.
battery charger *n* cargador *m* de baterías.
battery farming *n* cría intensiva.
battle ['bætl] *n* batalla; (*fig*) lucha ♦ *vi* luchar; **that's half the ~** (*col*) ya hay medio camino andado; **to fight a losing ~** (*fig*) luchar por una causa perdida.
battlefield ['bætlfiːld] *n* campo *m* de batalla.
battlements ['bætlmənts] *npl* almenas *fpl*.
battleship ['bætlʃɪp] *n* acorazado.
batty ['bætɪ] *adj* (*col: person*) chiflado; (*: idea*) de chiflado.
bauble ['bɔːbl] *n* chuchería.
baud [bɔːd] *n* (*COMPUT*) baudio.
baud rate *n* (*COMPUT*) velocidad *f* (de transmisión) en baudios.
bauxite ['bɔːksaɪt] *n* bauxita.
Bavaria [bə'vɛərɪə] *n* Baviera.
Bavarian [bə'vɛərɪən] *adj, n* bávaro/a *m/f*.
bawdy ['bɔːdɪ] *adj* indecente; (*joke*) verde.
bawl [bɔːl] *vi* chillar, gritar.
bay [beɪ] *n* (*GEO*) bahía; (*for parking*) parking *m*, estacionamiento; (*loading ~*) patio de carga; (*BOT*) laurel *m* ♦ *vi* aullar; **to hold sb at ~** mantener a alguien a raya.
bay leaf *n* (hoja de) laurel *m*.
bayonet ['beɪənɪt] *n* bayoneta.
bay window *n* ventana salediza.
bazaar [bə'zɑː*] *n* bazar *m*.
bazooka [bə'zuːkə] *n* bazuca.
BB *n abbr* (*BRIT: = Boys' Brigade*) *organización juvenil para chicos.*
B. & B. *n abbr* = **bed and breakfast**.
BBB *n abbr* (*US: = Better Business Bureau*) *organismo para la defensa del consumidor.*
BBC *n abbr* (*= British Broadcasting Corporation*) BBC *f*; *ver recuadro.*

BBC

La **BBC** *es el organismo público británico de radio y televisión, autónomo en cuanto a su política de programas pero regulado por un estatuto ("BBC charter") que ha de aprobar el Parlamento. Además de cadenas nacionales de televisión y de radio, transmite también un servicio informativo mundial ("BBC World Service"). A no tener publicidad, se financia a través de operaciones comerciales paralelas y del cobro de una licencia anual obligatoria ("TV licence") para los que tienen aparato de televisión.*

BC *ad abbr* (*= before Christ*) a. de J.C. ♦ *abbr* (*Canada*) *= British Columbia.*
BCG *n abbr* (*= Bacillus Calmette-Guérin*) *vacuna de la tuberculosis.*
BD *n abbr* (*= Bachelor of Divinity*) *Licenciado/a en Teología.*
B/D *abbr* = **bank draft**.
BDS *n abbr* (*= Bachelor of Dental Surgery*) *título universitario.*

KEYWORD

be [biː] (*pt* **was, were,** *pp* **been**) *aux vb* **1** (*with present participle: forming continuous tenses*): **what are you doing?** ¿qué estás haciendo?, ¿qué haces?; **they're coming tomorrow** vienen mañana; **I've been waiting for you for hours** llevo horas esperándote
2 (*with pp: forming passives*) ser (*but often*

replaced by active or reflexive constructions); **to ~ murdered** ser asesinado; **the box had been opened** habían abierto la caja; **the thief was nowhere to ~ seen** no se veía al ladrón por ninguna parte
3 (*in tag questions*): **it was fun, wasn't it?** fue divertido, ¿no? *or* ¿verdad?; **he's good-looking, isn't he?** es guapo, ¿no te parece?; **she's back again, is she?** entonces, ¿ha vuelto?
4 (*+to +infin*): **the house is to ~ sold** (*necessity*) hay que vender la casa; (*future*) van a vender la casa; **he's not to open it** no tiene que abrirlo; **he was to have come yesterday** debía de haber venido ayer; **am I to understand that ...?** ¿debo entender que ...?
⧫ *vb +complement* **1** (*with n or num complement*) ser; **he's a doctor** es médico; **2 and 2 are 4** 2 y 2 son 4
2 (*with adj complement: expressing permanent or inherent quality*) ser; (: *expressing state seen as temporary or reversible*) estar; **I'm English** soy inglés/esa; **she's tall/pretty** es alta/bonita; **he's young** es joven; **~ careful/good/quiet** ten cuidado/pórtate bien/cállate; **I'm tired** estoy cansado/a; **I'm warm** tengo calor; **it's dirty** está sucio/a
3 (*of health*) estar; **how are you?** ¿cómo estás?; **he's very ill** está muy enfermo; **I'm better now** ya estoy mejor
4 (*of age*) tener; **how old are you?** ¿cuántos años tienes?; **I'm sixteen (years old)** tengo dieciséis años
5 (*cost*) costar; ser; **how much was the meal?** ¿cuánto fue *or* costó la comida?; **that'll ~ £5.75, please** son £5.75, por favor; **this shirt is £17** esta camisa cuesta £17
⧫ *vi* **1** (*exist, occur etc*) existir, haber; **the best singer that ever was** el mejor cantante que existió jamás; **is there a God?** ¿hay un Dios?, ¿existe Dios?; **~ that as it may** sea como sea; **so ~ it** así sea
2 (*referring to place*) estar; **I won't ~ here tomorrow** no estaré aquí mañana
3 (*referring to movement*): **where have you been?** ¿dónde has estado?
⧫ *impers vb* **1** (*referring to time*): **it's 5 o'clock** son las 5; **it's the 28th of April** estamos a 28 de abril
2 (*referring to distance*): **it's 10 km to the village** el pueblo está a 10 km
3 (*referring to the weather*): **it's too hot/cold** hace demasiado calor/frío; **it's windy today** hace viento hoy
4 (*emphatic*): **it's me** soy yo; **it was Maria who paid the bill** fue María la que pagó la cuenta.

B/E *abbr* = **bill of exchange**.
beach [biːtʃ] *n* playa ⧫ *vt* varar.
beach buggy [-bʌgɪ] *n* buggy *m*.
beachcomber ['biːtʃkəumə*] *n* raquero/a.
beachwear ['biːtʃwɛə*] *n* ropa de playa.
beacon ['biːkən] *n* (*lighthouse*) faro; (*marker*) guía; (*radio ~*) radiofaro.
bead [biːd] *n* cuenta, abalorio; (*of dew, sweat*) gota; **~s** *npl* (*necklace*) collar *m*.
beady ['biːdɪ] *adj* (*eyes*) pequeño y brillante.
beagle ['biːgl] *n* sabueso pequeño, beagle *m*.
beak [biːk] *n* pico.
beaker ['biːkə*] *n* vaso.
beam [biːm] *n* (*ARCH*) viga; (*of light*) rayo, haz *m* de luz; (*RADIO*) rayo ⧫ *vi* brillar; (*smile*) sonreír; **to drive on full** *or* **main ~** conducir con las luces largas.
beaming ['biːmɪŋ] *adj* (*sun, smile*) radiante.
bean [biːn] *n* judía, fríjol/frijol *m* (*esp LAM*); **runner/broad ~** habichuela/haba; **coffee ~** grano de café.
beanpole ['biːnpəul] *n* (*col*) espárrago.
beansprouts ['biːnsprauts] *npl* brotes *mpl* de soja.
bear [bɛə*] *n* oso; (*STOCK EXCHANGE*) bajista *m* ⧫ (*vb*: *pt* **bore**, *pp* **borne**) *vt* (*weight etc*) llevar; (*cost*) pagar; (*responsibility*) tener; (*traces, signs*) mostrar; (*produce: fruit*) dar; (*COMM: interest*) devengar; (*endure*) soportar, aguantar; (*stand up to*) resistir a; (*children*) tener, dar a luz ⧫ *vi*: **to ~ right/left** torcer a la derecha/izquierda; **I can't ~ him** no le puedo ver, no lo soporto; **to bring pressure to ~ on sb** ejercer presión sobre algn.
▸**bear on** *vt fus* tener que ver con, referirse a.
▸**bear out** *vt fus* (*suspicions*) corroborar, confirmar; (*person*) confirmar lo dicho por.
▸**bear up** *vi* (*cheer up*) animarse; **he bore up well under the strain** resistió bien la presión.
▸**bear with** *vt fus* (*sb's moods, temper*) tener paciencia con.
bearable ['bɛərəbl] *adj* soportable, aguantable.
beard [bɪəd] *n* barba.
bearded ['bɪədɪd] *adj* con barba.
bearer ['bɛərə*] *n* (*of news, cheque*) portador(a) *m/f*; (*of passport*) titular *m/f*.
bearing ['bɛərɪŋ] *n* porte *m*; (*connection*)

relación *f*; **(ball) ~s** *npl* cojinetes *mpl* a bolas; **to take a ~** marcarse; **to find one's ~s** orientarse.
bearskin ['bɛəskɪn] *n* (*MIL*) gorro militar (*de piel de oso*).
beast [biːst] *n* bestia; (*col*) bruto, salvaje *m*.
beastly ['biːstlɪ] *adj* bestial; (*awful*) horrible.
beat [biːt] *n* (*of heart*) latido; (*MUS*) ritmo, compás *m*; (*of policeman*) ronda ♦ (*vb*: *pt* **beat**, *pp* **beaten**) *vt* (*hit*) golpear; (*eggs*) batir; (*defeat*) vencer, derrotar; (*better*) sobrepasar; (*drum*) tocar; (*rhythm*) marcar ♦ *vi* (*heart*) latir; **off the ~en track** aislado; **to ~ about the bush** andarse con rodeos; **to ~ it** largarse; **that ~s everything!** (*col*) ¡eso es el colmo!; **to ~ on a door** dar golpes en una puerta.
▸**beat down** *vt* (*door*) derribar a golpes; (*price*) conseguir rebajar, regatear; (*seller*) hacer rebajar el precio ♦ *vi* (*rain*) llover a cántaros; (*sun*) caer de plomo.
▸**beat off** *vt* rechazar.
▸**beat up** *vt* (*col: person*) dar una paliza a.
beater ['biːtə*] *n* (*for eggs, cream*) batidora.
beating ['biːtɪŋ] *n* paliza, golpiza (*LAM*); **to take a ~** recibir una paliza.
beat-up ['biːt'ʌp] *adj* (*col*) destartalado.
beautiful ['bjuːtɪful] *adj* hermoso, bello, lindo (*esp LAM*).
beautifully ['bjuːtɪfəlɪ] *adv* de maravilla.
beautify ['bjuːtɪfaɪ] *vt* embellecer.
beauty ['bjuːtɪ] *n* belleza, hermosura; (*concept, person*) belleza; **the ~ of it is that ...** lo mejor de esto es que ....
beauty contest *n* concurso de belleza.
beauty queen *n* reina de la belleza.
beauty salon *n* salón *m* de belleza.
beauty sleep *n*: **to get one's ~** *no perder horas de sueño*.
beauty spot *n* lunar *m* postizo; (*BRIT: TOURISM*) lugar *m* pintoresco.
beaver ['biːvə*] *n* castor *m*.
becalmed [bɪ'kɑːmd] *adj* encalmado.
became [bɪ'keɪm] *pt of* **become**.
because [bɪ'kɔz] *conj* porque; **~ of** *prep* debido a, a causa de.
beck [bɛk] *n*: **to be at the ~ and call of** estar a disposición de.
beckon ['bɛkən] *vt* (*also*: **~ to**) llamar con señas.
become [bɪ'kʌm] (*irreg*: *like* **come**) *vi* (+ *noun*) hacerse, llegar a ser; (+ *adj*) ponerse, volverse ♦ *vt* (*suit*) favorecer, sentar bien a; **to ~ fat** engordar; **to ~ angry** enfadarse; **it became known that ...** se descubrió que ....
becoming [bɪ'kʌmɪŋ] *adj* (*behaviour*) decoroso; (*clothes*) favorecedor(a).
becquerel [bɛkə'rɛl] *n* becquerelio.
BEd *n abbr* (= *Bachelor of Education*) *título universitario*; *see also* **Bachelor's Degree**.
bed [bɛd] *n* cama; (*of flowers*) macizo; (*of sea, lake*) fondo; (*of coal, clay*) capa; **to go to ~** acostarse.
▸**bed down** *vi* acostarse.
bed and breakfast (B & B) *n* ≈ pensión *f*; *ver recuadro*.

BED AND BREAKFAST

Se llama **bed and breakfast** *a la casa de hospedaje particular, o granja si es en el campo, que ofrece cama y desayuno a tarifas inferiores a las de un hotel. El servicio se suele anunciar con carteles colocados en las ventanas del establecimiento, en el jardín o en la carretera y en ellos aparece a menudo únicamente el símbolo "B & B".*

bedbug ['bɛdbʌg] *n* chinche *f*.
bedclothes ['bɛdkləuðz] *npl* ropa de cama.
bedding ['bɛdɪŋ] *n* ropa de cama.
bedeck [bɪ'dɛk] *vt* engalanar, adornar.
bedevil [bɪ'dɛvl] *vt* (*dog*) acosar; (*trouble*) fastidiar.
bedfellow ['bɛdfɛləu] *n*: **they are strange ~s** (*fig*) hacen una pareja rara.
bedlam ['bɛdləm] *n* confusión *f*.
bedpan ['bɛdpæn] *n* cuña.
bedraggled [bɪ'drægld] *adj* desastrado.
bedridden ['bɛdrɪdn] *adj* postrado (en cama).
bedrock ['bɛdrɔk] *n* (*GEO*) roca firme; (*fig*) pilar *m*.
bedroom ['bɛdrum] *n* dormitorio, alcoba.
Beds *abbr* (*BRIT*) = *Bedfordshire*.
bed settee *n* sofá-cama *m*.
bedside ['bɛdsaɪd] *n*: **at sb's ~** a la cabecera de alguien.
bedside lamp *n* lámpara de noche.
bedsit(ter) ['bɛdsɪt(ə*)] *n* (*BRIT*) estudio.
bedspread ['bɛdsprɛd] *n* cubrecama *m*, colcha.
bedtime ['bɛdtaɪm] *n* hora de acostarse; **it's ~** es hora de acostarse *or* de irse a la cama.
bee [biː] *n* abeja; **to have a ~ in one's bonnet (about sth)** tener una idea fija (de algo).
beech [biːtʃ] *n* haya.
beef [biːf] *n* carne *f* de vaca; **roast ~** rosbif *m*.
▸**beef up** *vt* (*col*) reforzar.
beefburger ['biːfbəːgə*] *n* hamburguesa.

beefeater ['bi:fi:tə*] *n alabardero de la Torre de Londres.*
beehive ['bi:haɪv] *n* colmena.
bee-keeping ['bi:ki:pɪŋ] *n* apicultura.
beeline ['bi:laɪn] *n*: **to make a ~ for** ir derecho a.
been [bi:n] *pp of* **be.**
beep [bi:p] *n* pitido ⧫ *vi* pitar.
beeper ['bi:pə*] *n* (*of doctor etc*) busca *m inv.*
beer [bɪə*] *n* cerveza.
beer belly *n* (*col*) barriga (*de bebedor de cerveza*).
beer can *n* bote *m or* lata de cerveza.
beet [bi:t] *n* (*US*) remolacha.
beetle ['bi:tl] *n* escarabajo.
beetroot ['bi:tru:t] *n* (*BRIT*) remolacha.
befall [bɪ'fɔ:l] *vi* (*vt*) (*irreg: like* **fall**) acontecer (a).
befit [bɪ'fɪt] *vt* convenir a, corresponder a.
before [bɪ'fɔ:*] *prep* (*of time*) antes de; (*of space*) delante de ⧫ *conj* antes (de) que ⧫ *adv* (*time*) antes; (*space*) delante, adelante; **~ going** antes de marcharse; **~ she goes** antes de que se vaya; **the week ~** la semana anterior; **I've never seen it ~** no lo he visto nunca.
beforehand [bɪ'fɔ:hænd] *adv* de antemano, con anticipación.
befriend [bɪ'frɛnd] *vt* ofrecer amistad a.
befuddled [bɪ'fʌdld] *adj* aturdido, atontado.
beg [bɛg] *vi* pedir limosna, mendigar ⧫ *vt* pedir, rogar; (*entreat*) suplicar; **I ~ your pardon** (*apologising*) perdóneme; (*not hearing*) ¿perdón?
began [bɪ'gæn] *pt of* **begin.**
beggar ['bɛgə*] *n* mendigo/a.
begin, *pt* **began**, *pp* **begun** [bɪ'gɪn, -gæn, -gʌn] *vt, vi* empezar, comenzar; **to ~ doing** *or* **to do sth** empezar a hacer algo; **I can't ~ to thank you** no encuentro palabras para agradecerle; **to ~ with, I'd like to know** ... en primer lugar, quisiera saber ...; **~ning from Monday** a partir del lunes.
beginner [bɪ'gɪnə*] *n* principiante *m/f.*
beginning [bɪ'gɪnɪŋ] *n* principio, comienzo; **right from the ~** desde el principio.
begrudge [bɪ'grʌdʒ] *vt*: **to ~ sb sth** tenerle envidia a alguien por algo.
beguile [bɪ'gaɪl] *vt* (*enchant*) seducir.
beguiling [bɪ'gaɪlɪŋ] *adj* seductor(a), atractivo.
begun [bɪ'gʌn] *pp of* **begin.**
behalf [bɪ'hɑ:f] *n*: **on ~ of,** (*US*) **in ~ of** en nombre de; (*for benefit of*) por.
behave [bɪ'heɪv] *vi* (*person*) portarse, comportarse; (*thing*) funcionar; (*well: also:* **~ o.s.**) portarse bien.
behaviour, (*US*) **behavior** [bɪ'heɪvjə*] *n* comportamiento, conducta.
behead [bɪ'hɛd] *vt* decapitar.
beheld [bɪ'hɛld] *pt, pp of* **behold.**
behind [bɪ'haɪnd] *prep* detrás de ⧫ *adv* detrás, por detrás, atrás ⧫ *n* trasero; **to be ~ (schedule)** ir retrasado; **~ the scenes** (*fig*) entre bastidores; **we're ~ them in technology** (*fig*) nos dejan atrás en tecnología; **to leave sth ~** olvidar *or* dejarse algo; **to be ~ with sth** estar atrasado en algo; **to be ~ with payments (on sth)** estar atrasado en el pago (de algo).
behold [bɪ'həuld] (*irreg: like* **hold**) *vt* contemplar.
beige [beɪʒ] *adj* (color) beige.
being ['bi:ɪŋ] *n* ser *m*; **to come into ~** nacer, aparecer.
Beirut [beɪ'ru:t] *n* Beirut *m.*
Belarus [bɛlə'rus] *n* Bielorrusia.
Belarussian [bɛlə'rʌʃən] *adj, n* bielorruso/a ⧫ *n* (*LING*) bielorruso.
belated [bɪ'leɪtɪd] *adj* atrasado, tardío.
belch [bɛltʃ] *vi* eructar ⧫ *vt* (*also:* **~ out:** *smoke etc*) vomitar, arrojar.
beleaguered [bɪ'li:gəd] *adj* asediado.
Belfast ['bɛlfɑ:st] *n* Belfast *m.*
belfry ['bɛlfrɪ] *n* campanario.
Belgian ['bɛldʒən] *adj, n* belga *m/f.*
Belgium ['bɛldʒəm] *n* Bélgica.
Belgrade [bel'greɪd] *n* Belgrado.
belie [bɪ'laɪ] *vt* (*give false impression of*) desmentir, contradecir.
belief [bɪ'li:f] *n* (*opinion*) opinión *f*; (*trust, faith*) fe *f*; (*acceptance as true*) creencia; **it's beyond ~** es increíble; **in the ~ that** creyendo que.
believable [bɪ'li:vəbl] *adj* creíble.
believe [bɪ'li:v] *vt, vi* creer; **to ~ (that)** creer (que); **to ~ in** (*God, ghosts*) creer en; (*method*) ser partidario de; **he is ~d to be abroad** se cree que está en el extranjero; **I don't ~ in corporal punishment** no soy partidario del castigo corporal.
believer [bɪ'li:və*] *n* (*in idea, activity*) partidario/a; (*REL*) creyente *m/f*, fiel *m/f.*
belittle [bɪ'lɪtl] *vt* despreciar.
Belize [bɛ'li:z] *n* Belice *f.*
bell [bɛl] *n* campana; (*small*) campanilla; (*on door*) timbre *m*; (*animal's*) cencerro; (*on toy etc*) cascabel *m*; **that rings a ~** (*fig*) eso me suena.
bellboy ['bɛlbɔɪ] *n*, (*US*) **bellhop** ['bɛlhɔp] *n* botones *m inv.*
belligerent [bɪ'lɪdʒərənt] *adj* (*at war*) beligerante; (*fig*) agresivo.

bellow ['bɛləu] *vi* bramar; (*person*) rugir ♦ *vt* (*orders*) gritar.
bellows ['bɛləuz] *npl* fuelle *msg*.
bell push *n* pulsador *m* de timbre.
belly ['bɛlɪ] *n* barriga, panza.
bellyache ['bɛlɪeɪk] *n* dolor *m* de barriga *or* de tripa ♦ *vi* (*col*) gruñir.
bellyful ['bɛlɪful] *n*: **to have had a ~ of** (*col*) estar más que harto de ....
belong [bɪ'lɔŋ] *vi*: **to ~ to** pertenecer a; (*club etc*) ser socio de; **this book ~s here** este libro va aquí.
belongings [bɪ'lɔŋɪŋz] *npl*: **personal ~** pertenencias *fpl*.
Belorussia [bɛləu'rʌʃə] *n* Bielorrusia.
Belorussian [bɛləu'rʌʃən] *adj, n* = **Belarussian**.
beloved [bɪ'lʌvɪd] *adj, n* querido/a *m/f*, amado/a *m/f*.
below [bɪ'ləu] *prep* bajo, debajo de ♦ *adv* abajo, (por) debajo; **see ~** véase más abajo.
belt [bɛlt] *n* cinturón *m*; (*TECH*) correa, cinta ♦ *vt* (*thrash*) golpear con correa; **industrial ~** cinturón industrial.
▸**belt out** *vt* (*song*) cantar a voz en grito *or* a grito pelado.
▸**belt up** *vi* (*AUT*) ponerse el cinturón de seguridad; (*fig, col*) cerrar el pico.
beltway ['bɛltweɪ] *n* (*US AUT*) carretera de circunvalación.
bemoan [bɪ'məun] *vt* lamentar.
bemused [bɪ'mju:zd] *adj* perplejo.
bench [bɛntʃ] *n* banco; **the B~** (*LAW*) el tribunal; (*people*) la judicatura.
bench mark *n* punto de referencia.
bend [bɛnd] *vb* (*pt, pp* **bent** [bɛnt]) *vt* doblar; (*body, head*) inclinar ♦ *vi* inclinarse; (*road*) curvarse ♦ *n* (*BRIT*: *in road, river*) recodo; (*in pipe*) codo; *see also* **bends**.
▸**bend down** *vi* inclinarse, doblarse.
▸**bend over** *vi* inclinarse.
bends [bɛndz] *npl* (*MED*) *apoplejía por cambios bruscos de presión*.
beneath [bɪ'ni:θ] *prep* bajo, debajo de; (*unworthy of*) indigno de ♦ *adv* abajo, (por) debajo.
benefactor ['bɛnɪfæktə*] *n* bienhechor *m*.
benefactress ['bɛnɪfæktrɪs] *n* bienhechora.
beneficial [bɛnɪ'fɪʃəl] *adj*: **~ to** beneficioso para.
beneficiary [bɛnɪ'fɪʃərɪ] *n* (*LAW*) beneficiario/a.
benefit ['bɛnɪfɪt] *n* beneficio, provecho; (*allowance of money*) subsidio ♦ *vt* beneficiar ♦ *vi*: **he'll ~ from it** le sacará provecho; **unemployment ~** subsidio de desempleo.
Benelux ['bɛnɪlʌks] *n* Benelux *m*.
benevolence [bɪ'nɛvələns] *n* benevolencia.
benevolent [bɪ'nɛvələnt] *adj* benévolo.
BEng *n abbr* (= *Bachelor of Engineering*) *título universitario*.
benign [bɪ'naɪn] *adj* (*person, MED*) benigno; (*smile*) afable.
bent [bɛnt] *pt, pp of* **bend** ♦ *n* inclinación *f* ♦ *adj* (*wire, pipe*) doblado, torcido; **to be ~ on** estar empeñado en.
bequeath [bɪ'kwi:ð] *vt* legar.
bequest [bɪ'kwɛst] *n* legado.
bereaved [bɪ'ri:vd] *adj* afligido ♦ *n*: **the ~** los afligidos *mpl*.
bereavement [bɪ'ri:vmənt] *n* aflicción *f*.
beret ['bɛreɪ] *n* boina.
Bering Sea ['bɛərɪŋ-] *n*: **the ~** el Mar de Bering.
berk [bə:k] *n* (*BRIT col*) capullo/a (*!*).
Berks *abbr* (*BRIT*) = *Berkshire*.
Berlin [bə:'lɪn] *n* Berlín *m*; **East/West ~** Berlín del Este/Oeste.
berm [bə:m] *n* (*US AUT*) arcén *m*.
Bermuda [bə:'mju:də] *n* las (Islas) Bermudas.
Bermuda shorts *npl* bermudas *mpl or fpl*.
Bern [bə:n] *n* Berna.
berry ['bɛrɪ] *n* baya.
berserk [bə'sə:k] *adj*: **to go ~** perder los estribos.
berth [bə:θ] *n* (*bed*) litera; (*cabin*) camarote *m*; (*for ship*) amarradero ♦ *vi* atracar, amarrar; **to give sb a wide ~** (*fig*) evitar encontrarse con algn.
beseech, *pt, pp* **besought** [bɪ'si:tʃ, -'sɔ:t] *vt* suplicar.
beset, *pt, pp* **beset** [bɪ'sɛt] *vt* (*person*) acosar ♦ *adj*: **a policy ~ with dangers** una política rodeada de peligros.
besetting [bɪ'sɛtɪŋ] *adj*: **his ~ sin** su principal falta.
beside [bɪ'saɪd] *prep* junto a, al lado de; (*compared with*) comparado con; **to be ~ o.s. with anger** estar fuera de sí; **that's ~ the point** eso no tiene nada que ver con el asunto.
besides [bɪ'saɪdz] *adv* además ♦ *prep* (*as well as*) además de; (*except*) excepto.
besiege [bɪ'si:dʒ] *vt* (*town*) sitiar; (*fig*) asediar.
besmirch [bɪ'smə:tʃ] *vt* (*fig*) manchar, mancillar.
besotted [bɪ'sɔtɪd] *adj*: **~ with** chiflado por.
bespoke [bɪ'spəuk] *adj* (*garment*) hecho a la medida; **~ tailor** sastre *m* que confecciona a la medida.
best [bɛst] *adj* (el/la) mejor ♦ *adv* (lo) mejor; **the ~ part of** (*quantity*) la mayor parte de;

at ~ en el mejor de los casos; **to make the** ~ **of sth** sacar el mejor partido de algo; **to do one's** ~ hacer todo lo posible; **to the** ~ **of my knowledge** que yo sepa; **to the** ~ **of my ability** como mejor puedo; **the** ~ **thing to do is** ... lo mejor (que se puede hacer) es ...; **he's not exactly patient at the** ~ **of times** no es que tenga mucha paciencia precisamente.
bestial ['bɛstɪəl] *adj* bestial.
best man *n* padrino de boda.
bestow [bɪ'stəu] *vt* otorgar; (*honour, praise*) dispensar; **to** ~ **sth on sb** conceder *or* dar algo a algn.
bestseller ['bɛst'sɛlə*] *n* éxito de ventas, best-seller *m.*
bet [bɛt] *n* apuesta ♦ *vt, vi* (*pt, pp* **bet** *or* **betted**) apostar (*on* a); **it's a safe** ~ (*fig*) es cosa segura.
Bethlehem ['bɛθlɪhɛm] *n* Belén *m.*
betray [bɪ'treɪ] *vt* traicionar; (*inform on*) delatar.
betrayal [bɪ'treɪəl] *n* traición *f.*
better ['bɛtə*] *adj* mejor ♦ *adv* mejor ♦ *vt* mejorar; (*record etc*) superar ♦ *n*: **to get the** ~ **of sb** quedar por encima de algn; **you had** ~ **do it** más vale que lo hagas; **he thought** ~ **of it** cambió de parecer; **to get** ~ mejorar(se); (*MED*) reponerse; **that's** ~! ¡eso es!; **I had** ~ **go** tengo que irme; **a change for the** ~ una mejora; ~ **off** *adj* más acomodado.
betting ['bɛtɪŋ] *n* juego, apuestas *fpl.*
betting shop *n* (*BRIT*) casa de apuestas.
between [bɪ'twiːn] *prep* entre ♦ *adv* (*also* **in** ~: *time*) mientras tanto; (: *place*) en medio; **the road** ~ **here and London** la carretera de aquí a Londres; **we only had 5** ~ **us** teníamos sólo 5 entre todos.
bevel ['bɛvəl] *n* (*also*: ~ **edge**) bisel *m*, chaflán *m.*
beverage ['bɛvərɪdʒ] *n* bebida.
bevy ['bɛvɪ] *n*: **a** ~ **of** una bandada de.
bewail [bɪ'weɪl] *vt* lamentar.
beware [bɪ'wɛə*] *vi*: **to** ~ **(of)** tener cuidado (con) ♦ *excl* ¡cuidado!
bewildered [bɪ'wɪldəd] *adj* aturdido, perplejo.
bewildering [bɪ'wɪldərɪŋ] *adj* desconcertante.
bewitching [bɪ'wɪtʃɪŋ] *adj* hechicero, encantador(a).
beyond [bɪ'jɔnd] *prep* más allá de; (*exceeding*) además de, fuera de; (*above*) superior a ♦ *adv* más allá, más lejos; ~ **doubt** fuera de toda duda; ~ **repair** irreparable.
b/f *abbr* (= *brought forward*) saldo previo.
BFPO *n abbr* (= *British Forces Post Office*) *servicio postal del ejército.*
bhp *n abbr* (= *brake horsepower*) potencia al freno.
bi ... [baɪ] *pref* bi ....
biannual [baɪ'ænjuəl] *adj* semestral.
bias ['baɪəs] *n* (*prejudice*) prejuicio; (*preference*) predisposición *f.*
bias(s)ed ['baɪəst] *adj* parcial; **to be** ~ **against** tener perjuicios contra.
biathlon [baɪ'æθlən] *n* biatlón *m.*
bib [bɪb] *n* babero.
Bible ['baɪbl] *n* Biblia.
biblical ['bɪblɪkəl] *adj* bíblico.
bibliography [bɪblɪ'ɔgrəfɪ] *n* bibliografía.
bicarbonate of soda [baɪ'kɑːbənɪt-] *n* bicarbonato de soda.
bicentenary [baɪsɛn'tiːnərɪ], (*US*) **bicentennial** [baɪsɛn'tɛnɪəl] *n* bicentenario.
biceps ['baɪsɛps] *n* bíceps *m.*
bicker ['bɪkə*] *vi* reñir.
bickering ['bɪkərɪŋ] *n* riñas *fpl*, altercados *mpl.*
bicycle ['baɪsɪkl] *n* bicicleta.
bicycle path *n* camino para ciclistas.
bicycle pump *n* bomba de bicicleta.
bid [bɪd] *n* (*at auction*) oferta, puja, postura; (*attempt*) tentativa, conato ♦ *vi* (*pt, pp* **bid**) hacer una oferta ♦ *vt* (*pt* **bade** [bæd], *pp* **bidden** ['bɪdn]) mandar, ordenar; **to** ~ **sb good day** dar a algn los buenos días.
bidder ['bɪdə*] *n*: **the highest** ~ el mejor postor.
bidding ['bɪdɪŋ] *n* (*at auction*) ofertas *fpl*, puja; (*order*) orden *f*, mandato.
bide [baɪd] *vt*: **to** ~ **one's time** esperar el momento adecuado.
bidet ['biːdeɪ] *n* bidet *m.*
bidirectional ['baɪdɪ'rɛkʃənl] *adj* bidireccional.
biennial [baɪ'ɛnɪəl] *adj, n* bienal *f.*
bier [bɪə*] *n* féretro.
bifocals [baɪ'fəuklz] *npl* gafas *fpl or* anteojos *mpl* (*LAM*) bifocales.
big [bɪg] *adj* grande; ~ **business** gran negocio; **to do things in a** ~ **way** hacer las cosas en grande.
bigamy ['bɪgəmɪ] *n* bigamia.
big dipper [-'dɪpə*] *n* montaña rusa.
big end *n* (*AUT*) cabeza de biela.
biggish ['bɪgɪʃ] *adj* más bien grande; (*man*) más bien alto.
bigheaded ['bɪg'hɛdɪd] *adj* engreído.
bigot ['bɪgət] *n* fanático/a, intolerante *m/f.*
bigoted ['bɪgətɪd] *adj* fanático, intolerante.
bigotry ['bɪgətrɪ] *n* fanatismo, intolerancia.
big toe *n* dedo gordo (del pie).

big top *n* (*circus*) circo; (*main tent*) carpa principal.
big wheel *n* (*at fair*) noria.
bigwig ['bɪgwɪg] *n* (*col*) pez *m* gordo.
bike [baɪk] *n* bici *f*.
bikini [bɪ'kiːnɪ] *n* bikini *m*.
bilateral [baɪ'lætərl] *adj* (*agreement*) bilateral.
bile [baɪl] *n* bilis *f*.
bilge [bɪldʒ] *n* (*water*) agua de sentina.
bilingual [baɪ'lɪŋgwəl] *adj* bilingüe.
bilious ['bɪlɪəs] *adj* bilioso (*also fig*).
bill [bɪl] *n* (*gen*) cuenta; (*invoice*) factura; (*POL*) proyecto de ley; (*US*: *banknote*) billete *m*; (*of bird*) pico; (*notice*) cartel *m*; (*THEAT*) programa *m* ♦ *vt* extender *or* pasar la factura a; **may I have the ~ please?** ¿puede traerme la cuenta, por favor?; ~ **of exchange** letra de cambio; ~ **of lading** conocimiento de embarque; ~ **of sale** escritura de venta; **"post no ~s"** "prohibido fijar carteles".
billboard ['bɪlbɔːd] *n* (*US*) valla publicitaria.
billet ['bɪlɪt] *n* alojamiento ♦ *vt*: **to ~ sb (on sb)** alojar a algn (con algn).
billfold ['bɪlfəuld] *n* (*US*) cartera.
billiards ['bɪljədz] *n* billar *m*.
billion ['bɪljən] *n* (*BRIT*) billón *m*; (*US*) mil millones *mpl*.
billow ['bɪləu] *n* (*of smoke*) nube *f*; (*of sail*) ondulación *f* ♦ *vi* (*smoke*) salir en nubes; (*sail*) ondear, ondular.
billowy ['bɪləuɪ] *adj* ondulante.
billy ['bɪlɪ] *n* (*US*) porra.
billy goat *n* macho cabrío.
bimbo ['bɪmbəu] *n* (*col*) tía buena sin seso.
bin [bɪn] *n* (*gen*) cubo *or* bote *m* (*LAM*) de la basura; **litter~** *n* (*BRIT*) papelera.
binary ['baɪnərɪ] *adj* (*MATH*) binario; ~ **code** código binario; ~ **system** sistema *m* binario.
bind, *pt, pp* **bound** [baɪnd, baund] *vt* atar, liar; (*wound*) vendar; (*book*) encuadernar; (*oblige*) obligar.
▸**bind over** *vt* (*LAW*) obligar por vía legal.
▸**bind up** *vt* (*wound*) vendar; **to be bound up in** (*work, research etc*) estar absorto en; **to be bound up with** (*person*) estar estrechamente ligado a.
binder ['baɪndə*] *n* (*file*) archivador *m*.
binding ['baɪndɪŋ] *adj* (*contract*) vinculante.
binge [bɪndʒ] *n* borrachera, juerga; **to go on a ~** ir de juerga.
bingo ['bɪŋgəu] *n* bingo *m*.
bin-liner ['bɪnlaɪnə*] *n* bolsa de la basura.
binoculars [bɪ'nɔkjuləz] *npl* prismáticos *mpl*, gemelos *mpl*.
biochemistry [baɪə'kɛmɪstrɪ] *n* bioquímica.
biodegradable ['baɪəudɪ'greɪdəbl] *adj* biodegradable.
biodiversity ['baɪəudaɪ'vəːsɪtɪ] *n* biodiversidad *f*.
biofuel ['baɪəufjuəl] *n* biocarburante *m*.
biographer [baɪ'ɔgrəfə*] *n* biógrafo/a.
biographical [baɪə'græfɪkəl] *adj* biográfico.
biography [baɪ'ɔgrəfɪ] *n* biografía.
biological [baɪə'lɔdʒɪkəl] *adj* biológico.
biological clock *n* reloj *m* biológico.
biologist [baɪ'ɔlədʒɪst] *n* biólogo/a.
biology [baɪ'ɔlədʒɪ] *n* biología.
biophysics ['baɪəu'fɪzɪks] *nsg* biofísica.
biopic ['baɪəupɪk] *n* filme *m* biográfico.
biopsy ['baɪɔpsɪ] *n* biopsia.
biosphere ['baɪəsfɪə*] *n* biosfera.
biotechnology ['baɪəutɛk'nɔlədʒɪ] *n* biotecnología.
biped ['baɪpɛd] *n* bípedo.
birch [bəːtʃ] *n* abedul *m*; (*cane*) vara.
bird [bəːd] *n* ave *f*, pájaro; (*BRIT col*: *girl*) chica.
birdcage ['bəːdkeɪdʒ] *n* jaula.
bird of prey *n* ave *f* de presa.
bird's-eye view ['bəːdzaɪ-] *n* vista de pájaro.
bird watcher *n* ornitólogo/a.
Biro ® ['baɪrəu] *n* bolígrafo.
birth [bəːθ] *n* nacimiento; (*MED*) parto; **to give ~ to** parir, dar a luz a; (*fig*) dar origen a.
birth certificate *n* partida de nacimiento.
birth control *n* control *m* de natalidad; (*methods*) métodos *mpl* anticonceptivos.
birthday ['bəːθdeɪ] *n* cumpleaños *m inv*.
birthplace ['bəːθpleɪs] *n* lugar *m* de nacimiento.
birth rate *n* (tasa de) natalidad *f*.
Biscay ['bɪskeɪ] *n*: **the Bay of ~** el Mar Cantábrico, el golfo de Vizcaya.
biscuit ['bɪskɪt] *n* (*BRIT*) galleta.
bisect [baɪ'sɛkt] *vt* (*also MATH*) bisecar.
bisexual ['baɪ'sɛksjuəl] *adj, n* bisexual *m/f*.
bishop ['bɪʃəp] *n* obispo; (*CHESS*) alfil *m*.
bistro ['biːstrəu] *n* café-bar *m*.
bit [bɪt] *pt of* **bite** ♦ *n* trozo, pedazo, pedacito; (*COMPUT*) bit *m*; (*for horse*) freno, bocado; **a ~ of** un poco de; **a ~ mad** algo loco; **~ by ~** poco a poco; **to come to ~s** (*break*) hacerse pedazos; **to do one's ~** aportar su granito de arena; **bring all your ~s and pieces** trae todas tus cosas.
bitch [bɪtʃ] *n* (*dog*) perra; (*col!*) zorra (*!*).
bite [baɪt] *vt, vi* (*pt* **bit** [bɪt], *pp* **bitten** ['bɪtn]) morder; (*insect etc*) picar ♦ *n* (*wound*: *of dog, snake etc*) mordedura; (*of insect*)

picadura; (*mouthful*) bocado; **to ~ one's nails** morderse las uñas; **let's have a ~ (to eat)** comamos algo.
biting ['baɪtɪŋ] *adj* (*wind*) que traspasa los huesos; (*criticism*) mordaz.
bit part *n* (*THEAT*) papel *m* sin importancia, papelito.
bitten ['bɪtn] *pp of* **bite.**
bitter ['bɪtə*] *adj* amargo; (*wind, criticism*) cortante, penetrante; (*icy: weather*) glacial; (*battle*) encarnizado ♦ *n* (*BRIT: beer*) *cerveza típica británica a base de lúpulos*.
bitterly ['bɪtəlɪ] *adv* (*disappoint, complain, weep*) desconsoladamente; (*oppose, criticise*) implacablemente; (*jealous*) agriamente; **it's ~ cold** hace un frío glacial.
bitterness ['bɪtənɪs] *n* amargura; (*anger*) rencor *m*.
bitty ['bɪtɪ] *adj* deshilvanado.
bitumen ['bɪtjumɪn] *n* betún *m*.
bivouac ['bɪvuæk] *n* vivac *m*, vivaque *m*.
bizarre [bɪ'zɑː*] *adj* raro, estrafalario.
bk *abbr* = **bank, book.**
BL *n abbr* (= *Bachelor of Law(s), Bachelor of Letters*) *título universitario*; (*US*: = *Bachelor of Literature*) *título universitario*.
bl *abbr* = **bill of lading.**
blab [blæb] *vi* cantar ♦ *vt* (*also*: ~ **out**) soltar, contar.
black [blæk] *adj* (*colour*) negro; (*dark*) oscuro ♦ *n* (*colour*) color *m* negro; (*person*): **B~** negro/a ♦ *vt* (*shoes*) lustrar; (*BRIT: INDUSTRY*) boicotear; **to give sb a ~ eye** ponerle a algn el ojo morado; **~ coffee** café *m* solo; **there it is in ~ and white** (*fig*) ahí está bien claro; **to be in the ~** (*in credit*) tener saldo positivo; **~ and blue** *adj* amoratado.
▸**black out** *vi* (*faint*) desmayarse.
black belt *n* (*SPORT*) cinturón *m* negro; (*US: area*) zona negra.
blackberry ['blækbərɪ] *n* zarzamora.
blackbird ['blækbəːd] *n* mirlo.
blackboard ['blækbɔːd] *n* pizarra.
black box *n* (*AVIAT*) caja negra.
Black Country *n* (*BRIT*): **the ~** *región industrial del centro de Inglaterra*.
blackcurrant ['blæk'kʌrənt] *n* grosella negra.
black economy *n* economía sumergida.
blacken ['blækən] *vt* ennegrecer; (*fig*) denigrar.
Black Forest *n*: **the ~** la Selva Negra.
blackguard ['blægɑːd] *n* canalla *m*, pillo.
black hole *n* (*ASTRO*) agujero negro.
black ice *n* hielo invisible en la carretera.
blackjack ['blækdʒæk] *n* (*US*) veintiuna.
blackleg ['blækleg] *n* (*BRIT*) esquirol *m/f*.
blacklist ['blæklɪst] *n* lista negra ♦ *vt* poner en la lista negra.
blackmail ['blækmeɪl] *n* chantaje *m* ♦ *vt* chantajear.
blackmailer ['blækmeɪlə*] *n* chantajista *m/f*.
black market *n* mercado negro, estraperlo.
blackness ['blæknɪs] *n* negrura.
blackout ['blækaut] *n* (*TV, ELEC*) apagón *m*; (*fainting*) desmayo, pérdida de conocimiento.
black pepper *n* pimienta negra.
Black Sea *n*: **the ~** el Mar Negro.
black sheep *n* oveja negra.
blacksmith ['blæksmɪθ] *n* herrero.
black spot *n* (*AUT*) punto negro.
bladder ['blædə*] *n* vejiga.
blade [bleɪd] *n* hoja; (*cutting edge*) filo; **a ~ of grass** una brizna de hierba.
blame [bleɪm] *n* culpa ♦ *vt*: **to ~ sb for sth** echar a algn la culpa de algo; **to be to ~ (for)** tener la culpa (de); **I'm not to ~** yo no tengo la culpa; **and I don't ~ him** y lo comprendo perfectamente.
blameless ['bleɪmlɪs] *adj* (*person*) inocente.
blanch [blɑːntʃ] *vi* (*person*) palidecer; (*CULIN*) escaldar.
bland [blænd] *adj* suave; (*taste*) soso.
blank [blæŋk] *adj* en blanco; (*shot*) de fogueo; (*look*) sin expresión ♦ *n* blanco, espacio en blanco; cartucho de fogueo; **to draw a ~** (*fig*) no conseguir nada.
blank cheque, (*US*) **blank check** *n* cheque *m* en blanco.
blanket ['blæŋkɪt] *n* manta, frazada (*LAM*), cobija (*LAM*) ♦ *adj* (*statement, agreement*) comprensivo, general; **to give ~ cover** (*subj: insurance policy*) dar póliza a todo riesgo.
blankly ['blæŋklɪ] *adv*: **she looked at me ~** me miró sin comprender.
blare [bleə*] *vi* (*brass band, horns, radio*) resonar.
blasé ['blɑːzeɪ] *adj* de vuelta de todo.
blaspheme [blæs'fiːm] *vi* blasfemar.
blasphemous ['blæsfɪməs] *adj* blasfemo.
blasphemy ['blæsfɪmɪ] *n* blasfemia.
blast [blɑːst] *n* (*of wind*) ráfaga, soplo; (*of whistle*) toque *m*; (*of explosive*) carga explosiva; (*force*) choque *m* ♦ *vt* (*blow up*) volar; (*blow open*) abrir con carga explosiva ♦ *excl* (*BRIT col*) ¡maldito sea!; **(at) full ~** (*also fig*) a toda marcha.
▸**blast off** *vi* (*spacecraft etc*) despegar.
blast furnace *n* alto horno.
blast-off ['blɑːstɔf] *n* (*SPACE*) lanzamiento.

blatant ['bleɪtənt] *adj* descarado.
blatantly ['bleɪtəntlɪ] *adv*: **it's ~ obvious** está clarísimo.
blather ['blæðə*] *vi* decir tonterías.
blaze [bleɪz] *n* (*fire*) fuego; (*flames*) llamarada; (*glow: of fire, sun etc*) resplandor *m*; (*fig*) arranque *m* ♦ *vi* (*fire*) arder con llamaradas; (*fig*) brillar ♦ *vt*: **to ~ a trail** (*fig*) abrir (un) camino; **in a ~ of publicity** bajo los focos de la publicidad.
blazer ['bleɪzə*] *n chaqueta de uniforme de colegial o de socio de club.*
bleach [bli:tʃ] *n* (*also*: **household ~**) lejía ♦ *vt* (*linen*) blanquear.
bleached [bli:tʃt] *adj* (*hair*) de colorado; (*clothes*) blanqueado.
bleachers ['bli:tʃəz] *npl* (*US SPORT*) gradas *fpl*.
bleak [bli:k] *adj* (*countryside*) desierto; (*landscape*) desolado, desierto; (*weather*) desapacible; (*smile*) triste; (*prospect, future*) poco prometedor(a).
bleary-eyed ['blɪərɪ'aɪd] *adj*: **to be ~** tener ojos de cansado.
bleat [bli:t] *vi* balar.
bleed, *pt, pp* **bled** [bli:d, blɛd] *vt* sangrar; (*brakes, radiator*) desaguar ♦ *vi* sangrar.
bleeding ['bli:dɪŋ] *adj* sangrante.
bleep [bli:p] *n* pitido ♦ *vi* pitar ♦ *vt* llamar por el busca.
bleeper ['bli:pə*] *n* (*of doctor etc*) busca *m*.
blemish ['blɛmɪʃ] *n* mancha, tacha.
blench [blɛntʃ] *vi* (*shrink back*) acobardarse; (*grow pale*) palidecer.
blend [blɛnd] *n* mezcla ♦ *vt* mezclar ♦ *vi* (*colours etc*) combinarse, mezclarse.
blender ['blɛndə*] *n* (*CULIN*) batidora.
bless, *pt, pp* **blessed** *or* **blest** [blɛs, blɛst] *vt* bendecir.
blessed ['blɛsɪd] *adj* (*REL: holy*) santo, bendito; (*: happy*) dichoso; **every ~ day** cada santo día.
blessing ['blɛsɪŋ] *n* bendición *f*; (*advantage*) beneficio, ventaja; **to count one's ~s** agradecer lo que se tiene; **it was a ~ in disguise** no hay mal que por bien no venga.
blew [blu:] *pt of* **blow**.
blight [blaɪt] *vt* (*hopes etc*) frustrar, arruinar.
blimey ['blaɪmɪ] *excl* (*BRIT col*) ¡caray!
blind [blaɪnd] *adj* ciego ♦ *n* (*for window*) persiana ♦ *vt* cegar; (*dazzle*) deslumbrar.
blind alley *n* callejón *m* sin salida.
blind corner *n* (*BRIT*) esquina *or* curva sin visibilidad.
blind date *n* cita a ciegas.
blinders ['blaɪndəz] *npl* (*US*) anteojeras *fpl*.
blindfold ['blaɪndfəuld] *n* venda ♦ *adj, adv* con los ojos vendados ♦ *vt* vendar los ojos a.
blinding ['blaɪndɪŋ] *adj* (*flash, light*) cegador; (*pain*) intenso.
blindingly ['blaɪndɪŋlɪ] *adv*: **it's ~ obvious** salta a la vista.
blindly ['blaɪndlɪ] *adv* a ciegas, ciegamente.
blindness ['blaɪndnɪs] *n* ceguera.
blind spot *n* (*AUT*) ángulo muerto; **to have a ~ about sth** estar ciego para algo.
blink [blɪŋk] *vi* parpadear, pestañear; (*light*) oscilar; **to be on the ~** (*col*) estar estropeado.
blinkers ['blɪŋkəz] *npl* (*esp Brit*) anteojeras *fpl*.
blinking ['blɪŋkɪŋ] *adj* (*col*): **this ~...** este condenado....
blip [blɪp] *n* señal *f* luminosa; (*on graph*) pequeña desviación *f*; (*fig*) pequeña anomalía.
bliss [blɪs] *n* felicidad *f*.
blissful ['blɪsful] *adj* dichoso; **in ~ ignorance** feliz en la ignorancia.
blissfully ['blɪsfulɪ] *adv* (*sigh, smile*) con felicidad; **~ happy** sumamente feliz.
blister ['blɪstə*] *n* (*on skin, paint*) ampolla ♦ *vi* ampollarse.
blistering ['blɪstərɪŋ] *adj* (*heat*) abrasador(a).
blithely ['blaɪðlɪ] *adv* alegremente, despreocupadamente.
blithering ['blɪðərɪŋ] *adj* (*col*): **this ~ idiot** este tonto perdido.
BLit(t) *n abbr* (= *Bachelor of Literature*) *título universitario.*
blitz [blɪts] *n* bombardeo aéreo; **to have a ~ on sth** (*fig*) emprenderla con algo.
blizzard ['blɪzəd] *n* ventisca.
BLM *n abbr* (*US*) = *Bureau of Land Management.*
bloated ['bləutɪd] *adj* hinchado.
blob [blɔb] *n* (*drop*) gota; (*stain, spot*) mancha.
bloc [blɔk] *n* (*POL*) bloque *m*.
block [blɔk] *n* bloque *m* (*also COMPUT*); (*in pipes*) obstáculo; (*of buildings*) manzana ♦ *vt* (*gen*) obstruir, cerrar; (*progress*) estorbar; (*COMPUT*) agrupar; **~ of flats** (*BRIT*) bloque *m* de pisos; **mental ~** amnesia temporal; **~ and tackle** (*TECH*) aparejo de polea; **3 ~s from here** a 3 manzanas *or* cuadras (*LAM*) de aquí.
►**block up** *vt* tapar, obstruir; (*pipe*) atascar.
blockade [blɔ'keɪd] *n* bloqueo ♦ *vt* bloquear.
blockage ['blɔkɪdʒ] *n* estorbo, obstrucción *f*.

block booking *n* reserva en grupo.
blockbuster ['blɔkbʌstə*] *n* (*book*) best-seller *m*; (*film*) éxito de público.
block capitals *npl* mayúsculas *fpl*.
block letters *npl* letras *fpl* de molde.
block release *n* (*BRIT*) exención *f* por estudios.
block vote *n* (*BRIT*) voto por delegación.
bloke [bləuk] *n* (*BRIT col*) tipo, tío.
blond(e) [blɔnd] *adj, n* rubio/a *m/f*.
blood [blʌd] *n* sangre *f*; **new** ~ (*fig*) gente *f* nueva.
blood bank *n* banco de sangre.
blood count *n* recuento de glóbulos rojos y blancos.
blood donor *n* donante *m/f* de sangre.
blood group *n* grupo sanguíneo.
bloodhound ['blʌdhaund] *n* sabueso.
bloodless ['blʌdlɪs] *adj* (*pale*) exangüe; (*revolt etc*) sin derramamiento de sangre, incruento.
bloodletting ['blʌdlɛtɪŋ] *n* (*MED*) sangría; (*fig*) sangría, carnicería.
blood poisoning *n* septicemia de la sangre.
blood pressure *n* tensión *f* sanguínea; **to have high/low** ~ tener la tensión alta/baja.
bloodshed ['blʌdʃɛd] *n* baño de sangre.
bloodshot ['blʌdʃɔt] *adj* inyectado en sangre.
bloodstained ['blʌdsteɪnd] *adj* manchado de sangre.
bloodstream ['blʌdstriːm] *n* corriente *f* sanguínea.
blood test *n* análisis *m* de sangre.
bloodthirsty ['blʌdθəːstɪ] *adj* sanguinario.
blood transfusion *n* transfusión *f* de sangre.
blood type *n* grupo sanguíneo.
blood vessel *n* vaso sanguíneo.
bloody ['blʌdɪ] *adj* sangriento; (*BRIT col!*): **this** ~... este condenado *or* puñetero *or* fregado (*LAM*) ... (*!*) ♦ *adv* (*BRIT col!*): ~ **strong/good** terriblemente fuerte/bueno.
bloody-minded ['blʌdɪ'maɪndɪd] *adj* (*BRIT col*) con malas pulgas.
bloom [bluːm] *n* floración *f*; **in** ~ en flor ♦ *vi* florecer.
blooming ['bluːmɪŋ] *adj* (*col*): **this** ~... este condenado....
blossom ['blɔsəm] *n* flor *f* ♦ *vi* florecer; (*fig*) desarrollarse; **to** ~ **into** (*fig*) convertirse en.
blot [blɔt] *n* borrón *m* ♦ *vt* (*dry*) secar; (*stain*) manchar; **to** ~ **out** *vt* (*view*) tapar; (*memories*) borrar; **to be a** ~ **on the landscape** estropear el paisaje; **to** ~ **one's copy book** (*fig*) manchar su reputación.
blotchy ['blɔtʃɪ] *adj* (*complexion*) lleno de manchas.
blotter ['blɔtə*] *n* secante *m*.
blotting paper ['blɔtɪŋ-] *n* papel *m* secante.
blotto ['blɔtəu] *adj* (*col*) mamado.
blouse [blauz] *n* blusa.
blow [bləu] *n* golpe *m* ♦ *vb* (*pt* **blew**, *pp* **blown** [bluː, bləun]) *vi* soplar; (*fuse*) fundirse ♦ *vt* (*glass*) soplar; (*fuse*) quemar; (*instrument*) tocar; **to come to** ~**s** llegar a golpes; **to** ~ **one's nose** sonarse.
▸**blow away** *vt* llevarse, arrancar.
▸**blow down** *vt* derribar.
▸**blow off** *vt* arrebatar.
▸**blow out** *vt* apagar ♦ *vi* apagarse; (*tyre*) reventar.
▸**blow over** *vi* amainar.
▸**blow up** *vi* estallar ♦ *vt* volar; (*tyre*) inflar; (*PHOT*) ampliar.
blow-dry ['bləudraɪ] *n* secado con secador de mano ♦ *vt* secar con secador de mano.
blowlamp ['bləulæmp] *n* (*BRIT*) soplete *m*, lámpara de soldar.
blow-out ['bləuaut] *n* (*of tyre*) pinchazo; (*col: big meal*) banquete *m*, festín *m*.
blowtorch ['bləutɔːtʃ] *n* = **blowlamp**.
blow-up ['bləuʌp] *n* (*PHOT*) ampliación *f*.
blowzy ['blauzɪ] *adj* (*BRIT*) dejado, desaliñado.
BLS *n abbr* (*US*) = *Bureau of Labor Statistics*.
blubber ['blʌbə*] *n* grasa de ballena ♦ *vi* (*pej*) lloriquear.
bludgeon ['blʌdʒən] *vt*: **to** ~ **sb into doing sth** coaccionar a algn a hacer algo.
blue [bluː] *adj* azul; ~ **film** película porno; ~ **joke** chiste verde; **once in a** ~ **moon** de higos a brevas; **to come out of the** ~ (*fig*) ser completamente inesperado; *see also* **blues**.
blue baby *n* niño azul *or* cianótico.
bluebell ['bluːbɛl] *n* campanilla, campánula azul.
blue-blooded [bluː'blʌdɪd] *adj* de sangre azul.
bluebottle ['bluːbɔtl] *n* moscarda, mosca azul.
blue cheese *n* queso azul.
blue-chip ['bluːtʃɪp] *n*: ~ **investment** inversión *f* asegurada.
blue-collar worker ['bluːkɔlə*-] *n* obrero/a.
blue jeans *npl* tejanos *mpl*, vaqueros *mpl*.
blueprint ['bluːprɪnt] *n* proyecto; ~ **(for)** (*fig*) anteproyecto (de).
blues [bluːz] *npl*: **the** ~ (*MUS*) el blues; **to have the** ~ estar triste.
bluff [blʌf] *vi* tirarse un farol, farolear ♦ *n*

bluff *m*, farol *m*; (*GEO*) precipicio, despeñadero; **to call sb's ~** coger a algn en un renuncio.
bluish ['blu:ɪʃ] *adj* azulado.
blunder ['blʌndə*] *n* patinazo, metedura de pata ♦ *vi* cometer un error, meter la pata; **to ~ into sb/sth** tropezar con algn/algo.
blunt [blʌnt] *adj* (*knife*) desafilado; (*person*) franco, directo ♦ *vt* embotar, desafilar; **this pencil is ~** este lápiz está despuntado; **~ instrument** (*LAW*) instrumento contundente.
bluntly ['blʌntlɪ] *adv* (*speak*) francamente, de modo terminante.
bluntness ['blʌntnɪs] *n* (*of person*) franqueza, brusquedad *f*.
blur [blə:*] *n* aspecto borroso ♦ *vt* (*vision*) enturbiar; (*memory*) empañar.
blurb [blə:b] *n* propaganda.
blurred [blə:d] *adj* borroso.
blurt [blə:t]: **to ~ out** *vt* (*say*) descolgarse con, dejar escapar.
blush [blʌʃ] *vi* ruborizarse, ponerse colorado ♦ *n* rubor *m*.
blusher ['blʌʃə*] *n* colorete *m*.
bluster ['blʌstə*] *n* fanfarronada, bravata ♦ *vi* fanfarronear, echar bravatas.
blustering ['blʌstərɪŋ] *adj* (*person*) fanfarrón/ona.
blustery ['blʌstərɪ] *adj* (*weather*) tempestuoso, tormentoso.
Blvd *abbr* = *boulevard*.
BM *n abbr* = *British Museum*; (*UNIV*: = *Bachelor of Medicine*) *título universitario*.
BMA *n abbr* = *British Medical Association*.
BMJ *n abbr* = *British Medical Journal*.
BMus *n abbr* (= *Bachelor of Music*) *título universitario*.
BMX *n abbr* (= *bicycle motocross*) BMX *f*; **~ bike** bici(cleta) *f* BMX.
BO *n abbr* (*col*: = *body odour*) olor *m* a sudor; (*US*) = **box office**.
boa ['bəuə] *n* boa.
boar [bɔ:*] *n* verraco, cerdo.
board [bɔ:d] *n* tabla, tablero; (*on wall*) tablón *m*; (*for chess etc*) tablero; (*committee*) junta, consejo; (*in firm*) mesa *or* junta directiva; (*NAUT, AVIAT*): **on ~** a bordo ♦ *vt* (*ship*) embarcarse en; (*train*) subir a; **full ~** (*BRIT*) pensión *f* completa; **half ~** (*BRIT*) media pensión; **~ and lodging** alojamiento y comida; **to go by the ~** (*fig*) irse por la borda; **above ~** (*fig*) sin tapujos; **across the ~** (*fig*: *adv*) en todos los niveles; (: *adj*) general.
▸**board up** *vt* (*door*) tapar, cegar.
boarder ['bɔ:də*] *n* huésped(a) *m/f*; (*SCOL*) interno/a.
board game *n* juego de tablero.
boarding card ['bɔ:dɪŋ-] *n* (*BRIT*: *AVIAT, NAUT*) tarjeta de embarque.
boarding house ['bɔ:dɪŋ-] *n* casa de huéspedes.
boarding party ['bɔ:dɪŋ-] *n* brigada de inspección.
boarding pass ['bɔ:dɪŋ-] *n* (*US*) = **boarding card**.
boarding school ['bɔ:dɪŋ-] *n* internado.
board meeting *n* reunión *f* de la junta directiva.
board room *n* sala de juntas.
boardwalk ['bɔ:dwɔ:k] *n* (*US*) paseo entablado.
boast [bəust] *vi*: **to ~ (about** *or* **of)** alardear (de) ♦ *vt* ostentar ♦ *n* alarde *m*, baladronada.
boastful ['bəustfəl] *adj* presumido, jactancioso.
boastfulness ['bəustfulnɪs] *n* fanfarronería, jactancia.
boat [bəut] *n* barco, buque *m*; (*small*) barca, bote *m*; **to go by ~** ir en barco.
boater ['bəutə*] *n* (*hat*) canotié *m*.
boating ['bəutɪŋ] *n* canotaje *m*.
boatman ['bəutmən] *n* barquero.
boat people *npl refugiados que huyen en barca*.
boatswain ['bəusn] *n* contramaestre *m*.
bob [bɔb] *vi* (*boat, cork on water*: *also*: **~ up and down**) menearse, balancearse ♦ *n* (*BRIT col*) = **shilling**.
▸**bob up** *vi* (re)aparecer de repente.
bobbin ['bɔbɪn] *n* (*of sewing machine*) carrete *m*, bobina.
bobby ['bɔbɪ] *n* (*BRIT col*) poli *m/f*.
bobsleigh ['bɔbsleɪ] *n* bob *m*, trineo de competición *f*.
bode [bəud] *vi*: **to ~ well/ill (for)** ser de buen/mal agüero (para).
bodice ['bɔdɪs] *n* corpiño.
-bodied ['bɔdɪd] *adj suff* de cuerpo ....
bodily ['bɔdɪlɪ] *adj* (*comfort, needs*) corporal; (*pain*) corpóreo ♦ *adv* (*in person*) en persona; (*carry*) corporalmente; (*lift*) en peso.
body ['bɔdɪ] *n* cuerpo; (*corpse*) cadáver *m*; (*of car*) caja, carrocería; (*also*: **~ stocking**) body *m*; (*fig*: *organization*) organización *f*; (: *public ~*) organismo; (: *quantity*) masa; (: *of speech, document*) parte *f* principal; **ruling ~** directiva; **in a ~** todos juntos, en masa.
body blow *n* (*fig*) palo.
body-building ['bɔdɪ'bɪldɪŋ] *n* culturismo.
bodyguard ['bɔdɪgɑ:d] *n* guardaespaldas *m inv*.

body language *n* lenguaje *m* gestual.
body search *n* cacheo; **to carry out a ~ on sb** registrar a algn; **to submit to** *or* **undergo a ~** ser registrado.
bodywork ['bɔdɪwəːk] *n* carrocería.
boffin ['bɔfɪn] *n* (*BRIT*) científico/a.
bog [bɔg] *n* pantano, ciénaga ♦ *vt*: **to get ~ged down** (*fig*) empantanarse, atascarse.
boggle ['bɔgl] *vi*: **the mind ~s!** ¡no puedo creerlo!
Bogotá [bəugə'tɑː] *n* Bogotá.
bogus ['bəugəs] *adj* falso, fraudulento; (*person*) fingido.
Bohemia [bə'hiːmɪə] *n* Bohemia.
Bohemian [bə'hiːmɪən] *adj, n* bohemio/a *m/f*.
boil [bɔɪl] *vt* cocer; (*eggs*) pasar por agua ♦ *vi* hervir ♦ *n* (*MED*) furúnculo, divieso; **to bring to the ~** calentar hasta que hierva; **to come to the** (*BRIT*) *or* **a** (*US*) **~** comenzar a hervir; **~ed egg** huevo pasado por agua; **~ed potatoes** patatas *fpl* *or* papas *fpl* (*LAM*) cocidas.
▸**boil down** *vi* (*fig*): **to ~ down to** reducirse a.
▸**boil over** *vi* (*liquid*) rebosar; (*anger, resentment*) llegar al colmo.
boiler ['bɔɪlə*] *n* caldera.
boiler suit *n* (*BRIT*) mono, overol *m* (*LAM*).
boiling ['bɔɪlɪŋ] *adj*: **I'm ~ (hot)** (*col*) estoy asado.
boiling point *n* punto de ebullición *f*.
boil-in-the-bag [bɔɪlɪnðə'bæg] *adj*: **~ meals** platos que se cuecen en su misma bolsa.
boisterous ['bɔɪstərəs] *adj* (*noisy*) bullicioso; (*excitable*) exuberante; (*crowd*) tumultuoso.
bold [bəuld] *adj* (*brave*) valiente, audaz; (*pej*) descarado; (*outline*) grueso; (*colour*) vivo; **~ type** (*TYP*) negrita.
boldly ['bəuldlɪ] *adv* audazmente.
boldness ['bəuldnɪs] *n* valor *m*, audacia; (*cheek*) descaro.
Bolivia [bə'lɪvɪə] *n* Bolivia.
Bolivian [bə'lɪvɪən] *adj, n* boliviano/a *m/f*.
bollard ['bɔləd] *n* (*BRIT AUT*) poste *m*.
bolshy ['bɔlʃɪ] *adj* (*BRIT col*) protestón/ona; **to be in a ~ mood** tener el día protestón.
bolster ['bəulstə*] *n* travesero, cabezal *m*.
▸**bolster up** *vt* reforzar; (*fig*) alentar.
bolt [bəult] *n* (*lock*) cerrojo; (*with nut*) perno, tornillo ♦ *adv*: **~ upright** rígido, erguido ♦ *vt* (*door*) echar el cerrojo a; (*food*) engullir ♦ *vi* fugarse; (*horse*) desbocarse.
bomb [bɔm] *n* bomba ♦ *vt* bombardear.
bombard [bɔm'bɑːd] *vt* bombardear; (*fig*) asediar.
bombardment [bɔm'bɑːdmənt] *n* bombardeo.
bombastic [bɔm'bæstɪk] *adj* rimbombante; (*person*) pomposo.
bomb disposal *n* desactivación *f* de explosivos.
bomb disposal expert *n* artificiero/a.
bomber ['bɔmə*] *n* (*AVIAT*) bombardero; (*terrorist*) persona que pone bombas.
bombing ['bɔmɪŋ] *n* bombardeo.
bomb scare *n* amenaza de bomba.
bombshell ['bɔmʃɛl] *n* obús *m*, granada; (*fig*) bomba.
bomb site *n* lugar *m* donde estalló una bomba.
bona fide ['bəunə'faɪdɪ] *adj* genuino, auténtico.
bonanza [bə'nænzə] *n* bonanza.
bond [bɔnd] *n* (*binding promise*) fianza; (*FINANCE*) bono; (*link*) vínculo, lazo; **in ~** (*COMM*) en depósito bajo fianza.
bondage ['bɔndɪdʒ] *n* esclavitud *f*.
bonded goods ['bɔndɪd-] *npl* mercancías *fpl* en depósito de aduanas.
bonded warehouse ['bɔndɪd-] *n* depósito de aduanas.
bone [bəun] *n* hueso; (*of fish*) espina ♦ *vt* deshuesar; quitar las espinas a; **~ of contention** manzana de la discordia.
bone china *n* porcelana fina.
bone-dry ['bəun'draɪ] *adj* completamente seco.
bone idle *adj* gandul.
bone marrow *n* médula; **~ transplant** transplante *m* de médula.
boner ['bəunə*] *n* (*US col*) plancha, patochada.
bonfire ['bɔnfaɪə*] *n* hoguera, fogata.
bonk [bɔŋk] *vt, vi* (*hum, col*) chingar (*!*).
bonkers ['bɔŋkəz] *adj* (*BRIT col*) majareta.
Bonn [bɔn] *n* Bonn *m*.
bonnet ['bɔnɪt] *n* gorra; (*BRIT: of car*) capó *m*.
bonny ['bɔnɪ] *adj* (*esp Scottish*) bonito, hermoso, lindo.
bonus ['bəunəs] *n* (*at Christmas etc*) paga extraordinaria; (*merit award*) sobrepaga, prima.
bony ['bəunɪ] *adj* (*arm, face, MED: tissue*) huesudo; (*meat*) lleno de huesos; (*fish*) lleno de espinas; (*thin: person*) flaco, delgado.
boo [buː] *vt* abuchear.
boob [buːb] *n* (*col: mistake*) disparate *m*, sandez *f*; (*: breast*) teta.
booby prize ['buːbɪ-] *n* premio de consolación (*al último*).
booby trap ['buːbɪ-] *n* (*MIL etc*) trampa

explosiva.
book [buk] *n* libro; (*notebook*) libreta; (*of stamps etc*) librillo; **~s** (*COMM*) cuentas *fpl*, contabilidad *f* ♦ *vt* (*ticket, seat, room*) reservar; (*driver*) fichar; (*FOOTBALL*) amonestar; **to keep the ~s** llevar las cuentas *or* los libros; **by the ~** según las reglas; **to throw the ~ at sb** echar un rapapolvo a algn.
▸**book in** *vi* (*at hotel*) registrarse.
▸**book up** *vt*: **all seats are ~ed up** todas las plazas están reservadas; **the hotel is ~ed up** el hotel está lleno.
bookable ['bukəbl] *adj*: **seats are ~** los asientos se pueden reservar (de antemano).
bookcase ['bukkeɪs] *n* librería, estante *m* para libros.
booking office ['bukɪŋ-] *n* (*BRIT: RAIL*) despacho de billetes *or* boletos (*LAM*); (: *THEAT*) taquilla, boletería (*LAM*).
book-keeping ['buk'kiːpɪŋ] *n* contabilidad *f*.
booklet ['buklɪt] *n* folleto.
bookmaker ['bukmeɪkə*] *n* corredor *m* de apuestas.
bookseller ['buksɛlə*] *n* librero/a.
bookshelf ['bukʃɛlf] *n* estante *m*.
bookshop ['bukʃɔp] *n* librería.
bookstall ['bukstɔːl] *n* quiosco de libros.
book store *n* = **bookshop**.
book token *n* vale *m* para libros.
book value *n* (*COMM*) valor *m* contable.
bookworm ['bukwəːm] *n* (*fig*) ratón *m* de biblioteca.
boom [buːm] *n* (*noise*) trueno, estampido; (*in prices etc*) alza rápida; (*ECON*) boom *m*, auge *m* ♦ *vi* (*cannon*) hacer gran estruendo, retumbar; (*ECON*) estar en alza.
boomerang ['buːməræŋ] *n* bumerang *m* (*also fig*) ♦ *vi*: **to ~ on sb** (*fig*) ser contraproducente para algn.
boom town *n* ciudad *f* de crecimiento rápido.
boon [buːn] *n* favor *m*, beneficio.
boorish ['buərɪʃ] *adj* grosero.
boost [buːst] *n* estímulo, empuje *m* ♦ *vt* estimular, empujar; (*increase: sales, production*) aumentar; **to give a ~ to** (*morale*) levantar; **it gave a ~ to his confidence** le dio confianza en sí mismo.
booster ['buːstə*] *n* (*MED*) reinyección *f*; (*TV*) repetidor *m*; (*ELEC*) elevador *m* de tensión; (*also*: **~ rocket**) cohete *m*.
boot [buːt] *n* bota; (*ankle ~*) botín *m*, borceguí *m*; (*BRIT: of car*) maleta, maletero, baúl *m* (*LAM*) ♦ *vt* dar un puntapié a; (*COMPUT*) arrancar; **to ~** (*in addition*) además, por añadidura; **to give sb the ~** (*col*) despedir a algn, poner a algn en la calle.
booth [buːð] *n* (*at fair*) barraca; (*telephone ~, voting ~*) cabina.
bootleg ['buːtlɛg] *adj* de contrabando; **~ record** disco pirata.
booty ['buːtɪ] *n* botín *m*.
booze [buːz] (*col*) *n* bebida ♦ *vi* emborracharse.
boozer ['buːzə*] *n* (*col: person*) bebedor(a) *m/f*; (: *BRIT: pub*) bar *m*.
border ['bɔːdə*] *n* borde *m*, margen *m*; (*of a country*) frontera ♦ *adj* fronterizo; **the B~s** *región fronteriza entre Escocia e Inglaterra.*
▸**border on** *vt fus* lindar con; (*fig*) rayar en.
borderline ['bɔːdəlaɪn] *n* (*fig*) frontera.
bore [bɔː*] *pt of* **bear** ♦ *vt* (*hole*) taladrar; (*person*) aburrir ♦ *n* (*person*) pelmazo, pesado; (*of gun*) calibre *m*.
bored [bɔːd] *adj* aburrido; **he's ~ to tears** *or* **to death** *or* **stiff** está aburrido como una ostra, está muerto de aburrimiento.
boredom ['bɔːdəm] *n* aburrimiento.
boring ['bɔːrɪŋ] *adj* aburrido, pesado.
born [bɔːn] *adj*: **to be ~** nacer; **I was ~ in 1960** nací en 1960.
born-again [bɔːnə'gɛn] *adj*: **~ Christian** evangelista *m/f*.
borne [bɔːn] *pp of* **bear**.
Borneo ['bɔːnɪəu] *n* Borneo.
borough ['bʌrə] *n* municipio.
borrow ['bɔrəu] *vt*: **to ~ sth (from sb)** tomar algo prestado (a alguien); **may I ~ your car?** ¿me prestas tu coche?
borrower ['bɔrəuə*] *n* prestatario/a.
borrowing ['bɔrəuɪŋ] *n* préstamos *mpl*.
borstal ['bɔːstl] *n* (*BRIT*) reformatorio (de menores).
Bosnia ['bɔznɪə] *n* Bosnia.
Bosnia-Herzegovina, Bosnia-Hercegovina ['bɔːsnɪəhɛrzə'gəuviːnə] *n* Bosnia-Herzegovina.
Bosnian ['bɔznɪən] *adj*, *n* bosnio/a.
bosom ['buzəm] *n* pecho; (*fig*) seno; **~ friend** *n* amigo/a íntimo/a *or* del alma.
boss [bɔs] *n* jefe/a *m/f*; (*employer*) patrón/ona *m/f*; (*political etc*) cacique *m* ♦ *vt* (*also*: **~ about** *or* **around**) mangonear; **stop ~ing everyone about!** ¡deja de dar órdenes *or* de mangonear a todos!
bossy ['bɔsɪ] *adj* mandón/ona.
bosun ['bəusn] *n* contramaestre *m*.
botanical [bə'tænɪkl] *adj* botánico.
botanist ['bɔtənɪst] *n* botanista *m/f*.
botany ['bɔtənɪ] *n* botánica.

botch [bɔtʃ] *vt* (*also*: ~ **up**) arruinar, estropear.
both [bəuθ] *adj, pron* ambos/as, los/las dos; ~ **of us went, we ~ went** fuimos los dos, ambos fuimos ♦ *adv*: ~ **A and B** tanto A como B.
bother ['bɔðə*] *vt* (*worry*) preocupar; (*disturb*) molestar, fastidiar, fregar (*LAM*), embromar (*LAM*) ♦ *vi* (*gen*: ~ **o.s.**) molestarse ♦ *n*: **what a ~!** ¡qué lata! ♦ *excl* ¡maldita sea!, ¡caramba!; **I'm sorry to ~ you** perdona que te moleste; **to ~ doing** tomarse la molestia de hacer; **please don't ~** no te molestes.
Botswana [bɔt'swɑːnə] *n* Botswana.
bottle ['bɔtl] *n* botella; (*small*) frasco; (*baby's*) biberón *m* ♦ *vt* embotellar; ~ **of wine/milk** botella de vino/de leche; **wine/milk ~** botella de vino/de leche.
►**bottle up** *vt* (*fig*) contener, reprimir.
bottle bank *n* contenedor *m* de vidrio, iglú *m*.
bottleneck ['bɔtlnɛk] *n* embotellamiento.
bottle-opener ['bɔtləupnə*] *n* abrebotellas *m inv*.
bottom ['bɔtəm] *n* (*of box, sea*) fondo; (*buttocks*) trasero, culo; (*of page, mountain, tree*) pie *m*; (*of list*) final *m* ♦ *adj* (*lowest*) más bajo; (*last*) último; **to get to the ~ of sth** (*fig*) llegar al fondo de algo.
bottomless ['bɔtəmlɪs] *adj* sin fondo, insondable.
bottom line *n*: **the ~** lo fundamental; **the ~ is he has to go** el caso es que tenemos que despedirle.
bough [bau] *n* rama.
bought [bɔːt] *pt, pp of* **buy**.
bouillon cube ['buːjɔn-] *n* (*US*) cubito de caldo.
boulder ['bəuldə*] *n* canto rodado.
bounce [bauns] *vi* (*ball*) (re)botar; (*cheque*) ser rechazado ♦ *vt* hacer (re)botar ♦ *n* (*rebound*) (re)bote *m*; **he's got plenty of ~** (*fig*) tiene mucha energía.
bouncer ['baunsə*] *n* (*col*) forzudo, gorila *m*.
bouncy castle ® ['baunsɪ-] *n* castillo inflable.
bound [baund] *pt, pp of* **bind** ♦ *n* (*leap*) salto; (*gen pl*: *limit*) límite *m* ♦ *vi* (*leap*) saltar ♦ *adj*: ~ **by** rodeado de; **to be ~ to do sth** (*obliged*) tener el deber de hacer algo; **he's ~ to come** es seguro que vendrá; **"out of ~s to the public"** "prohibido el paso"; ~ **for** con destino a.
boundary ['baundrɪ] *n* límite *m*, lindero.
boundless ['baundlɪs] *adj* ilimitado.
bountiful ['bauntɪful] *adj* (*person*) liberal, generoso; (*God*) bondadoso; (*supply*) abundante.
bouquet ['bukeɪ] *n* (*of flowers*) ramo, ramillete *m*; (*of wine*) aroma *m*.
bourbon ['buəbən] *n* (*US*: *also*: ~ **whiskey**) whisky *m* americano, bourbon *m*.
bourgeois ['bueʒwɑː] *adj, n* burgués/esa *m/f*.
bout [baut] *n* (*of malaria etc*) ataque *m*; (*BOXING etc*) combate *m*, encuentro.
boutique [buː'tiːk] *n* boutique *f*, tienda de ropa.
bow [bəu] *n* (*knot*) lazo; (*weapon, MUS*) arco; [bau] (*of the head*) reverencia; (*NAUT*: *also*: **~s**) proa ♦ *vi* [bau] inclinarse, hacer una reverencia; (*yield*): **to ~ to** *or* **before** ceder ante, someterse a; **to ~ to the inevitable** resignarse a lo inevitable.
bowels ['bauəlz] *npl* intestinos *mpl*, vientre *m*.
bowl [bəul] *n* tazón *m*, cuenco; (*for washing*) palangana, jofaina; (*ball*) bola; (*US*: *stadium*) estadio ♦ *vi* (*CRICKET*) arrojar la pelota; *see also* **bowls**.
bow-legged ['bəu'lɛgɪd] *adj* estevado.
bowler ['bəulə*] *n* (*CRICKET*) lanzador *m* (de la pelota); (*BRIT*: *also*: ~ **hat**) hongo, bombín *m*.
bowling ['bəulɪŋ] *n* (*game*) bolos *mpl*, bochas *fpl*.
bowling alley *n* bolera.
bowling green *n* pista para bochas.
bowls [bəulz] *n* juego de los bolos, bochas *fpl*.
bow tie ['bəu-] *n* corbata de lazo, pajarita.
box [bɔks] *n* (*also*: **cardboard ~**) caja, cajón *m*; (*for jewels*) estuche *m*; (*for money*) cofre *m*; (*crate*) cofre *m*, arca; (*THEAT*) palco ♦ *vt* encajonar ♦ *vi* (*SPORT*) boxear.
boxer ['bɔksə*] *n* (*person*) boxeador *m*; (*dog*) bóxer *m*.
box file *n* fichero.
boxing ['bɔksɪŋ] *n* (*SPORT*) boxeo, box *m* (*LAM*).
Boxing Day *n* (*BRIT*) día *m* de San Esteban; *ver recuadro*.

BOXING DAY

El día después de Navidad es **Boxing Day**, *fiesta en todo el Reino Unido, aunque si el 26 de diciembre cae en domingo el día de descanso se traslada al lunes. En dicho día solía ser tradición entregar "Christmas boxes" (aguinaldos) a empleados, proveedores a domicilio, carteros etc.*

boxing gloves *npl* guantes *mpl* de boxeo.
boxing ring *n* ring *m*, cuadrilátero.

box number *n* (*for advertisements*) apartado.
box office *n* taquilla, boletería (*LAM*).
boxroom ['bɔksrum] *n* trastero.
boy [bɔɪ] *n* (*young*) niño; (*older*) muchacho.
boycott ['bɔɪkɔt] *n* boicot *m* ♦ *vt* boicotear.
boyfriend ['bɔɪfrɛnd] *n* novio.
boyish ['bɔɪɪʃ] *adj* de muchacho, inmaduro.
boy scout *n* boy scout *m.*
Bp *abbr* = **bishop**.
BPOE *n abbr* (*US*: = *Benevolent and Protective Order of Elks*) *organización benéfica.*
BR *abbr see* **British Rail.**
bra [brɑː] *n* sostén *m*, sujetador *m*, corpiño (*LAM*).
brace [breɪs] *n* refuerzo, abrazadera; (*BRIT: on teeth*) corrector *m*; (*tool*) berbiquí *m* ♦ *vt* asegurar, reforzar; **to ~ o.s. (for)** (*fig*) prepararse (para); *see also* **braces.**
bracelet ['breɪslɪt] *n* pulsera, brazalete *m*, pulso (*LAM*).
braces ['breɪsɪz] *npl* (*BRIT*) tirantes *mpl*, suspensores *mpl* (*LAM*); (*US: on teeth*) corrector *m.*
bracing ['breɪsɪŋ] *adj* vigorizante, tónico.
bracken ['brækən] *n* helecho.
bracket ['brækɪt] *n* (*TECH*) soporte *m*, puntal *m*; (*group*) clase *f*, categoría; (*also*: **brace** ~) soporte *m*, abrazadera; (*also*: **round** ~) paréntesis *m inv*; (*gen*: **square** ~) corchete *m* ♦ *vt* (*fig*: *also*: ~ **together**) agrupar; **income** ~ nivel *m* económico; **in ~s** entre paréntesis.
brackish ['brækɪʃ] *adj* (*water*) salobre.
brag [bræg] *vi* jactarse.
braid [breɪd] *n* (*trimming*) galón *m*; (*of hair*) trenza.
Braille [breɪl] *n* Braille *m.*
brain [breɪn] *n* cerebro; **~s** *npl* sesos *mpl*; **she's got ~s** es muy lista.
brainchild ['breɪntʃaɪld] *n* invención *f.*
braindead ['breɪndɛd] *adj* (*MED*) clínicamente muerto; (*col*) subnormal, tarado.
brainless ['breɪnlɪs] *adj* estúpido, insensato.
brainstorm ['breɪnstɔːm] *n* (*fig*) ataque *m* de locura, frenesí *m*; (*US*: *brainwave*) idea luminosa *or* genial, inspiración *f.*
brainstorming ['breɪnstɔːmɪŋ] *n discusión intensa para solucionar problemas.*
brainwash ['breɪnwɔʃ] *vt* lavar el cerebro a.
brainwave ['breɪnweɪv] *n* idea luminosa *or* genial, inspiración *f.*
brainy ['breɪnɪ] *adj* muy listo *or* inteligente.
braise [breɪz] *vt* cocer a fuego lento.
brake [breɪk] *n* (*on vehicle*) freno ♦ *vt, vi* frenar.
brake drum *n* tambor *m* de freno.
brake fluid *n* líquido de frenos.
brake light *n* luz *f* de frenado.
brake pedal *n* pedal *m* de freno.
bramble ['bræmbl] *n* (*fruit*) zarza.
bran [bræn] *n* salvado.
branch [brɑːntʃ] *n* rama; (*fig*) ramo; (*COMM*) sucursal *f* ♦ *vi* ramificarse; (*fig*) extenderse.
►**branch out** *vi* ramificarse.
branch line *n* (*RAIL*) ramal *m*, línea secundaria.
branch manager *n* director(a) *m/f* de sucursal.
brand [brænd] *n* marca; (*iron*) hierro de marcar ♦ *vt* (*cattle*) marcar con hierro candente.
brandish ['brændɪʃ] *vt* blandir.
brand name *n* marca.
brand-new ['brænd'njuː] *adj* flamante, completamente nuevo.
brandy ['brændɪ] *n* coñac *m*, brandy *m.*
brash [bræʃ] *adj* (*rough*) tosco; (*cheeky*) descarado.
Brasilia [brə'zɪlɪə] *n* Brasilia.
brass [brɑːs] *n* latón *m*; **the** ~ (*MUS*) los cobres.
brass band *n* banda de metal.
brassière ['bræsɪə*] *n* sostén *m*, sujetador *m.*
brass tacks *npl*: **to get down to** ~ ir al grano.
brat [bræt] *n* (*pej*) mocoso/a.
bravado [brə'vɑːdəu] *n* fanfarronería.
brave [breɪv] *adj* valiente, valeroso ♦ *n* guerrero indio ♦ *vt* (*challenge*) desafiar; (*resist*) aguantar.
bravely ['breɪvlɪ] *adv* valientemente, con valor.
bravery ['breɪvərɪ] *n* valor *m*, valentía.
bravo [brɑː'vəu] *excl* ¡bravo!, ¡olé!
brawl [brɔːl] *n* pendencia, reyerta ♦ *vi* pelearse.
brawn [brɔːn] *n* fuerza muscular; (*meat*) carne *f* en gelatina.
brawny ['brɔːnɪ] *adj* fornido, musculoso.
bray [breɪ] *n* rebuzno ♦ *vi* rebuznar.
brazen ['breɪzn] *adj* descarado, cínico ♦ *vt*: **to ~ it out** echarle cara al asunto.
brazier ['breɪzɪə*] *n* brasero.
Brazil [brə'zɪl] *n* (el) Brasil.
Brazilian [brə'zɪlɪən] *adj, n* brasileño/a *m/f.*
breach [briːtʃ] *vt* abrir brecha en ♦ *n* (*gap*) brecha; (*estrangement*) ruptura; (*breaking*): ~ **of confidence** abuso de confianza; ~ **of contract** infracción *f* de contrato; ~ **of the peace** perturbación *f* del órden público; **in ~ of** por

incumplimiento *or* infracción de.
bread [brɛd] *n* pan *m*; (*col*: *money*) pasta, lana (*LAM*); ~ **and butter** *n* pan con mantequilla; (*fig*) pan (de cada día) ♦ *adj* común y corriente; **to earn one's daily** ~ ganarse el pan; **to know which side one's** ~ **is buttered (on)** saber dónde aprieta el zapato.
breadbin ['brɛdbɪn] *n* panera.
breadboard ['brɛdbɔːd] *n* (*COMPUT*) circuito experimental.
breadbox ['brɛdbɔks] *n* (*US*) panera.
breadcrumbs ['brɛdkrʌmz] *npl* migajas *fpl*; (*CULIN*) pan *msg* rallado.
breadline ['brɛdlaɪn] *n*: **on the** ~ en la miseria.
breadth [brɛtθ] *n* anchura; (*fig*) amplitud *f*.
breadwinner ['brɛdwɪnə*] *n* sostén *m* de la familia.
break [breɪk] *vb* (*pt* **broke** [brəuk], *pp* **broken** ['brəukən]) *vt* (*gen*) romper; (*promise*) no cumplir; (*fall*) amortiguar; (*journey*) interrumpir; (*law*) violar, infringir; (*record*) batir; (*news*) comunicar ♦ *vi* romperse, quebrarse; (*storm*) estallar; (*weather*) cambiar ♦ *n* (*gap*) abertura; (*crack*) grieta; (*fracture*) fractura; (*in relations*) ruptura; (*rest*) descanso; (*time*) intervalo; (: *at school*) (período de) recreo; (*holiday*) vacaciones *fpl*; (*chance*) oportunidad *f*; (*escape*) evasión *f*, fuga; **to** ~ **with sb** (*fig*) romper con algn; **to** ~ **even** *vi* cubrir los gastos; **to** ~ **free** *or* **loose** *vi* escaparse; **lucky** ~ (*col*) chiripa, racha de buena suerte; **to have** *or* **take a** ~ (*few minutes*) descansar; **without a** ~ sin descanso *or* descansar.
▸**break down** *vt* (*door etc*) echar abajo, derribar; (*resistance*) vencer, acabar con; (*figures, data*) analizar, descomponer; (*undermine*) acabar con ♦ *vi* estropearse; (*MED*) sufrir un colapso; (*AUT*) averiarse, descomponerse (*LAM*); (*person*) romper a llorar.
▸**break in** *vt* (*horse etc*) domar ♦ *vi* (*burglar*) forzar una entrada.
▸**break into** *vt fus* (*house*) forzar.
▸**break off** *vi* (*speaker*) pararse, detenerse; (*branch*) partir ♦ *vt* (*talks*) suspender; (*engagement*) romper.
▸**break open** *vt* (*door etc*) abrir por la fuerza, forzar.
▸**break out** *vi* estallar; **to** ~ **out in spots** salir a algn granos.
▸**break through** *vi*: **the sun broke through** asomó el sol ♦ *vt fus* (*defences, barrier*) abrirse paso por; (*crowd*) abrirse paso por.
▸**break up** *vi* (*partnership*) disolverse; (*friends*) romper ♦ *vt* (*rocks, ice etc*) partir; (*crowd*) disolver.
breakable ['breɪkəbl] *adj* quebradizo ♦ *n*: ~**s** cosas *fpl* frágiles.
breakage ['breɪkɪdʒ] *n* rotura; **to pay for** ~**s** pagar por los objetos rotos.
breakaway ['breɪkəweɪ] *adj* (*group etc*) disidente.
break-dancing ['breɪkdɑːnsɪŋ] *n* break *m*.
breakdown ['breɪkdaun] *n* (*AUT*) avería; (*in communications*) interrupción *f*; (*MED*: *also*: **nervous** ~) colapso, crisis *f* nerviosa; (*of figures*) desglose *m*.
breakdown van *n* (*BRIT*) (camión *m*) grúa.
breaker ['breɪkə*] *n* rompiente *m*, ola grande.
breakeven ['breɪk'iːvn] *cpd*: ~ **chart** gráfico del punto de equilibrio; ~ **point** punto de break-even *or* de equilibrio.
breakfast ['brɛkfəst] *n* desayuno.
breakfast cereal *n* cereales *mpl* para el desayuno.
break-in ['breɪkɪn] *n* robo con allanamiento de morada.
breaking and entering ['breɪkɪŋənd 'ɛntərɪŋ] *n* (*LAW*) violación *f* de domicilio, allanamiento de morada.
breaking point ['breɪkɪŋ-] *n* punto de ruptura.
breakthrough ['breɪkθruː] *n* ruptura; (*fig*) avance *m*, adelanto.
break-up ['breɪkʌp] *n* (*of partnership, marriage*) disolución *f*.
break-up value *n* (*COMM*) valor *m* de liquidación.
breakwater ['breɪkwɔːtə*] *n* rompeolas *m inv*.
breast [brɛst] *n* (*of woman*) pecho, seno; (*chest*) pecho; (*of bird*) pechuga.
breast-feed ['brɛstfiːd] *vt, vi* (*irreg*: *like* **feed**) amamantar, dar el pecho.
breaststroke ['brɛststrəuk] *n* braza de pecho.
breath [brɛθ] *n* aliento, respiración *f*; **out of** ~ sin aliento, sofocado; **to go out for a** ~ **of air** salir a tomar el fresco.
Breathalyser ® ['brɛθəlaɪzə*] *n* (*BRIT*) alcoholímetro *m*; ~ **test** *n* prueba de alcoholemia.
breathe [briːð] *vt, vi* respirar; (*noisily*) resollar; **I won't** ~ **a word about it** no diré ni una palabra de ello.
▸**breathe in** *vt, vi* aspirar.
▸**breathe out** *vt, vi* espirar.
breather ['briːðə*] *n* respiro, descanso.
breathing ['briːðɪŋ] *n* respiración *f*.
breathing space *n* (*fig*) respiro, pausa.

breathless ['brɛθlɪs] *adj* sin aliento, jadeante; (*with excitement*) pasmado.
breathtaking ['brɛθteɪkɪŋ] *adj* imponente, pasmoso.
breath test *n* prueba de la alcoholemia.
-bred [brɛd] *suff*: **to be well/ill~** estar bien/mal criado.
breed [bri:d] *vb* (*pt, pp* **bred** [brɛd]) *vt* criar; (*fig*: *hate, suspicion*) crear, engendrar ♦ *vi* reproducirse, procrear ♦ *n* raza, casta.
breeder ['bri:də*] *n* (*person*) criador(a) *m/f*; (*PHYSICS*: *also*: ~ **reactor**) reactor *m*.
breeding ['bri:dɪŋ] *n* (*of person*) educación *f*.
breeze [bri:z] *n* brisa.
breezeblock ['bri:zblɔk] *n* (*BRIT*) bovedilla.
breezy ['bri:zɪ] *adj* de mucho viento, ventoso; (*person*) despreocupado.
Breton ['brɛtən] *adj* bretón/ona ♦ *n* bretón/ona *m/f*; (*LING*) bretón *m*.
brevity ['brɛvɪtɪ] *n* brevedad *f*.
brew [bru:] *vt* (*tea*) hacer; (*beer*) elaborar; (*plot*) tramar ♦ *vi* hacerse; elaborarse; tramarse; (*storm*) amenazar.
brewer ['bru:ə*] *n* cervecero, fabricante *m* de cerveza.
brewery ['bru:ərɪ] *n* fábrica de cerveza.
briar ['braɪə*] *n* (*thorny bush*) zarza; (*wild rose*) escaramujo, rosa silvestre.
bribe [braɪb] *n* soborno ♦ *vt* sobornar, cohechar; **to ~ sb to do sth** sobornar a algn para que haga algo.
bribery ['braɪbərɪ] *n* soborno, cohecho.
bric-a-brac ['brɪkəbræk] *n inv* baratijas *fpl*.
brick [brɪk] *n* ladrillo.
bricklayer ['brɪkleɪə*] *n* albañil *m*.
brickwork ['brɪkwə:k] *n* enladrillado.
brickworks ['brɪkwə:ks] *n* ladrillar *m*.
bridal ['braɪdl] *adj* nupcial.
bride [braɪd] *n* novia.
bridegroom ['braɪdgru:m] *n* novio.
bridesmaid ['braɪdzmeɪd] *n* dama de honor.
bridge [brɪdʒ] *n* puente *m*; (*NAUT*) puente *m* de mando; (*of nose*) caballete *m*; (*CARDS*) bridge *m* ♦ *vt* (*river*) tender un puente sobre.
bridgehead ['brɪdʒhɛd] *n* cabeza de puente.
bridging loan ['brɪdʒɪŋ-] *n* crédito provisional.
bridle ['braɪdl] *n* brida, freno ♦ *vt* poner la brida a; (*fig*) reprimir, refrenar ♦ *vi* (*in anger etc*) picarse.
bridle path *n* camino de herradura.
brief [bri:f] *adj* breve, corto ♦ *n* (*LAW*) escrito ♦ *vt* (*inform*) informar; (*instruct*) dar instrucciones a; **in ~** ... en resumen ...; **to ~ sb (about sth)** informar a algn (sobre algo).
briefcase ['bri:fkeɪs] *n* cartera, portafolio(s) *m inv* (*LAM*).
briefing ['bri:fɪŋ] *n* (*PRESS*) informe *m*.
briefly *adv* (*smile, glance*) brevemente; (*explain, say*) brevemente, en pocas palabras.
briefs [bri:fs] *npl* (*for men*) calzoncillos *mpl*; (*for women*) bragas *fpl*.
Brig. *abbr* = **brigadier**.
brigade [brɪ'geɪd] *n* (*MIL*) brigada.
brigadier [brɪgə'dɪə*] *n* general *m* de brigada.
bright [braɪt] *adj* claro; (*room*) luminoso; (*day*) de sol; (*person*: *clever*) listo, inteligente; (: *lively*) alegre, animado; (*colour*) vivo; **to look on the ~ side** mirar el lado bueno.
brighten ['braɪtn] (*also*: ~ **up**) *vt* (*room*) hacer más alegre ♦ *vi* (*weather*) despejarse; (*person*) animarse, alegrarse.
brill [brɪl] *adj* (*BRIT col*) guay.
brilliance ['brɪljəns] *n* brillo, brillantez *f*; (*fig*: *of person*) inteligencia.
brilliant ['brɪljənt] *adj* (*light, idea, person, success*) brillante; (*clever*) genial.
brilliantly ['brɪljəntlɪ] *adv* brillantemente.
brim [brɪm] *n* borde *m*; (*of hat*) ala.
brimful ['brɪm'ful] *adj* lleno hasta el borde; (*fig*) rebosante.
brine [braɪn] *n* (*CULIN*) salmuera.
bring, *pt, pp* **brought** [brɪŋ, brɔ:t] *vt* (*thing*) traer; (*person*) conducir; **to ~ sth to an end** terminar con algo; **I can't ~ myself to sack him** no soy capaz de echarle.
▸**bring about** *vt* ocasionar, producir.
▸**bring back** *vt* volver a traer; (*return*) devolver.
▸**bring down** *vt* bajar; (*price*) rebajar.
▸**bring forward** *vt* adelantar; (*BOOKKEEPING*) sumar y seguir.
▸**bring in** *vt* (*harvest*) recoger; (*person*) hacer entrar *or* pasar; (*object*) traer; (*POL*: *bill, law*) presentar; (*LAW*: *verdict*) pronunciar; (*produce*: *income*) producir, rendir.
▸**bring off** *vt* (*task, plan*) lograr, conseguir; (*deal*) cerrar.
▸**bring out** *vt* (*object*) sacar; (*new product*) sacar; (*book*) publicar.
▸**bring round** *vt* (*unconscious person*) hacer volver en sí; (*convince*) convencer.
▸**bring up** *vt* (*person*) educar, criar; (*carry up*) subir; (*question*) sacar a colación; (*food*: *vomit*) devolver, vomitar.
brink [brɪŋk] *n* borde *m*; **on the ~ of doing sth** a punto de hacer algo; **she was on the ~ of tears** estaba al borde de las lágrimas.

brisk [brɪsk] *adj* (*walk*) enérgico, vigoroso; (*speedy*) rápido; (*wind*) fresco; (*trade*) activo, animado; (*abrupt*) brusco; **business is** ~ el negocio va bien.
brisket ['brɪskɪt] *n* falda de vaca.
bristle ['brɪsl] *n* cerda ♦ *vi* erizarse.
bristly ['brɪslɪ] *adj* (*beard, hair*) erizado; **to have a** ~ **chin** tener la barba crecida.
Brit [brɪt] *n abbr* (*col*: = *British person*) británico/a.
Britain ['brɪtən] *n* (*also*: **Great** ~) Gran Bretaña.
British ['brɪtɪʃ] *adj* británico; **the** ~ *npl* los británicos; **the** ~ **Isles** *npl* las Islas Británicas.
British Rail (BR) *n* ≈ RENFE *f* (*SP*).
British Summer Time *n hora de verano británica*.
Briton ['brɪtən] *n* británico/a.
brittle ['brɪtl] *adj* quebradizo, frágil.
Br(o). *abbr* (*REL*) = **brother**.
broach [brəutʃ] *vt* (*subject*) abordar.
broad [brɔːd] *adj* ancho, amplio; (*accent*) cerrado ♦ *n* (*US col*) tía; **in** ~ **daylight** en pleno día; **the** ~ **outlines** las líneas generales.
broad bean *n* haba.
broadcast ['brɔːdkɑːst] *n* emisión *f* ♦ *vb* (*pt, pp* **broadcast**) *vt* (*RADIO*) emitir; (*TV*) transmitir ♦ *vi* emitir; transmitir.
broadcaster ['brɔːdkɑːstə*] *n* locutor(a) *m/f*.
broadcasting ['brɔːdkɑːstɪŋ] *n* radiodifusión *f*, difusión *f*.
broadcasting station *n* emisora.
broaden ['brɔːdn] *vt* ensanchar ♦ *vi* ensancharse.
broadly ['brɔːdlɪ] *adv* en general.
broad-minded ['brɔːd'maɪndɪd] *adj* tolerante, liberal.
broadsheet ['brɔːdʃiːt] *n* (*BRIT*) periódico de gran formato (*no sensacionalista*); *see also* **quality press**.
brocade [brə'keɪd] *n* brocado.
broccoli ['brɔkəlɪ] *n* brécol *m*, bróculi *m*.
brochure ['brəuʃjuə*] *n* folleto.
brogue [brəug] *n* (*accent*) acento regional; (*shoe*) (*tipo de*) *zapato de cuero grueso*.
broil [brɔɪl] *vt* (*US*) asar a la parrilla.
broiler ['brɔɪlə*] *n* (*fowl*) pollo (para asar).
broke [brəuk] *pt of* **break** ♦ *adj* (*col*) pelado, sin una perra; **to go** ~ quebrar.
broken ['brəukən] *pp of* **break** ♦ *adj* (*stick*) roto; (*fig*: *marriage*) deshecho; (: *promise, vow*) violado; ~ **leg** pierna rota; **in** ~ **English** en un inglés chapurreado.
broken-down ['brəukn'daun] *adj* (*car*) averiado; (*machine*) estropeado; (*house*) destartalado.
broken-hearted ['brəukn'hɑːtɪd] *adj* con el corazón destrozado.
broker ['brəukə*] *n* corredor(a) *m/f* de bolsa.
brokerage ['brəukərɪdʒ] *n* corretaje *m*.
brolly ['brɔlɪ] *n* (*BRIT col*) paraguas *m inv*.
bronchitis [brɔŋ'kaɪtɪs] *n* bronquitis *f*.
bronze [brɔnz] *n* bronce *m*.
bronzed [brɔnzd] *adj* bronceado.
brooch [brəutʃ] *n* broche *m*.
brood [bruːd] *n* camada, cría; (*children*) progenie *f* ♦ *vi* (*hen*) empollar; **to** ~ **over** dar vueltas a, rumiar.
broody ['bruːdɪ] *adj* (*fig*) triste, melancólico.
brook [bruk] *n* arroyo.
broom [brum] *n* escoba; (*BOT*) retama.
broomstick ['brumstɪk] *n* palo de escoba.
Bros. *abbr* (*COMM*: = *Brothers*) Hnos.
broth [brɔθ] *n* caldo.
brothel ['brɔθl] *n* burdel *m*.
brother ['brʌðə*] *n* hermano.
brotherhood ['brʌðəhud] *n* hermandad *f*.
brother-in-law ['brʌðərɪn'lɔː] *n* cuñado.
brotherly ['brʌðəlɪ] *adj* fraternal.
brought [brɔːt] *pt, pp of* **bring**.
brow [brau] *n* (*forehead*) frente *f*; (*of hill*) cumbre *f*.
browbeat ['braubiːt] *vt* (*irreg*: *like* **beat**) intimidar.
brown [braun] *adj* marrón; (*hair*) castaño; (*tanned*) moreno ♦ *n* (*colour*) marrón *m* ♦ *vt* (*tan*) poner moreno; (*CULIN*) dorar; **to go** ~ (*person*) ponerse moreno; (*leaves*) dorarse.
brown bread *n* pan *m* moreno.
brownie ['braunɪ] *n* niña exploradora.
brown paper *n* papel *m* de estraza.
brown rice *n* arroz *m* integral.
brown sugar *n* azúcar *m* moreno.
browse [brauz] *vi* (*animal*) pacer; (*among books*) hojear libros; **to** ~ **through a book** hojear un libro.
browser ['brauzə*] *n* (*COMPUT*) navegador *m*.
bruise [bruːz] *n* (*on person*) cardenal *m*, hematoma *m* ♦ *vt* (*leg etc*) magullar; (*fig*: *feelings*) herir.
Brum [brʌm] *n abbr*, **Brummagem** ['brʌmədʒəm] *n* (*col*) = *Birmingham*.
Brummie ['brʌmɪ] *n* (*col*) habitante *m/f* de Birmingham.
brunch [brʌntʃ] *n desayuno-almuerzo*.
brunette [bruː'nɛt] *n* morena, morocha (*LAM*).
brunt [brʌnt] *n*: **to bear the** ~ **of** llevar el peso de.
brush [brʌʃ] *n* cepillo, escobilla (*LAM*); (*large*) escoba; (*for painting, shaving etc*)

brocha; (*artist's*) pincel *m*; (*BOT*) maleza ♦ *vt* cepillar; (*gen*: ~ **past**, ~ **against**) rozar al pasar; **to have a ~ with the police** tener un roce con la policía.

►**brush aside** *vt* rechazar, no hacer caso a.

►**brush up** *vt* (*knowledge*) repasar, refrescar.

brushed [brʌʃt] *adj* (*nylon, denim etc*) afelpado; (*TECH*: *steel, chrome etc*) cepillado.

brushwood ['brʌʃwud] *n* (*bushes*) maleza; (*sticks*) leña.

brusque [bruːsk] *adj* (*person, manner*) brusco; (*tone*) áspero.

Brussels ['brʌslz] *n* Bruselas.

Brussels sprout *n* col *f* de Bruselas.

brutal ['bruːtl] *adj* brutal.

brutality [bruː'tælɪtɪ] *n* brutalidad *f*.

brutalize ['bruːtəlaɪz] *vt* (*harden*) embrutecer; (*ill-treat*) tratar brutalmente a.

brute [bruːt] *n* bruto; (*person*) bestia ♦ *adj*: **by ~ force** por la fuerza bruta.

BS *n abbr* (*US*: = *Bachelor of Science*) *título universitario*.

bs *abbr* = **bill of sale**.

BSA *n abbr* = *Boy Scouts of America*.

BSc *abbr* = **Bachelor of Science**; *see also* **Bachelor's Degree**.

BSE *n abbr* (= *bovine spongiform encephalopathy*) encefalopatía espongiforme bovina.

BSI *n abbr* (= *British Standards Institution*) *institución británica de normalización*.

BST *n abbr* (= *British Summer Time*) *hora de verano británica*.

Bt. *abbr* (*BRIT*) = *baronet*.

btu *n abbr* (= *British thermal unit*) ≈ *1054.2 julios*.

bubble ['bʌbl] *n* burbuja; (*in paint*) ampolla ♦ *vi* burbujear, borbotar.

bubble bath *n* espuma para el baño.

bubble gum *n* chicle *m*.

bubblejet printer ['bʌbldʒɛt-] *n* impresora de injección por burbujas.

bubbly ['bʌblɪ] *adj* (*person*) vivaracho; (*liquid*) con burbujas ♦ *n* (*col*) champán *m*.

Bucharest [buːkə'rɛst] *n* Bucarest *m*.

buck [bʌk] *n* macho; (*US col*) dólar *m* ♦ *vi* corcovear; **to pass the ~ (to sb)** echar (a algn) el muerto.

►**buck up** *vi* (*cheer up*) animarse, cobrar ánimo ♦ *vt*: **to ~ one's ideas up** poner más empeño.

bucket ['bʌkɪt] *n* cubo, balde *m* (*esp LAM*) ♦ *vi*: **the rain is ~ing (down)** (*col*) está lloviendo a cántaros.

Buckingham Palace ['bʌkɪŋəm-] *n* el Palacio de Buckingham; *ver recuadro*.

BUCKINGHAM PALACE

Buckingham Palace *es la residencia oficial del monarca británico en Londres. Data de 1703 y fue en principio el palacio del Duque de Buckingham, para pasar a manos de Jorge III en 1762. Fue reconstruido el siglo pasado y reformado después a principios de este siglo. Hoy en día parte del palacio está abierto al público.*

buckle ['bʌkl] *n* hebilla ♦ *vt* abrochar con hebilla ♦ *vi* torcerse, combarse.

►**buckle down** *vi* poner empeño.

Bucks [bʌks] *abbr* (*BRIT*) = *Buckinghamshire*.

bud [bʌd] *n* brote *m*, yema; (*of flower*) capullo ♦ *vi* brotar, echar brotes.

Budapest [bjuːdə'pɛst] *n* Budapest *m*.

Buddhism ['budɪzm] *n* Budismo.

Buddhist ['budɪst] *adj, n* budista *m/f*.

budding ['bʌdɪŋ] *adj* en ciernes, en embrión.

buddy ['bʌdɪ] *n* (*US*) compañero, compinche *m*.

budge [bʌdʒ] *vt* mover; (*fig*) hacer ceder ♦ *vi* moverse.

budgerigar ['bʌdʒərɪgɑː*] *n* periquito.

budget ['bʌdʒɪt] *n* presupuesto ♦ *vi*: **to ~ for sth** presupuestar algo; **I'm on a tight ~** no puedo gastar mucho; **she works out her ~ every month** planea su presupuesto todos los meses.

budgie ['bʌdʒɪ] *n* = **budgerigar**.

Buenos Aires ['bweɪnɔs'aɪrɪz] *n* Buenos Aires *m* ♦ *adj* bonaerense, porteño (*LAM*).

buff [bʌf] *adj* (*colour*) color *m* de ante ♦ *n* (*enthusiast*) entusiasta *m/f*.

buffalo ['bʌfələu], *pl* ~ *or* **buffaloes** *n* (*BRIT*) búfalo; (*US*: *bison*) bisonte *m*.

buffer ['bʌfə*] *n* amortiguador *m*; (*COMPUT*) memoria intermedia, buffer *m*.

buffer zone *n* zona (que sirve de) colchón.

buffet ['bufeɪ] *n* (*BRIT*: *bar*) bar *m*, cafetería; (*food*) buffet *m* ♦ *vt* ['bʌfɪt] (*strike*) abofetear; (*wind etc*) golpear.

buffet car *n* (*BRIT RAIL*) coche-restaurante *m*.

buffet lunch *n* buffet *m* (almuerzo).

buffoon [bə'fuːn] *n* bufón *m*.

bug [bʌg] *n* (*insect*) chinche *m*; (: *gen*) bicho, sabandija; (*germ*) microbio, bacilo; (*spy device*) micrófono oculto; (*COMPUT*) fallo, error *m* ♦ *vt* (*annoy*) fastidiar; (*room*) poner un micrófono oculto en; (*phone*) pinchar; **I've got the travel ~** (*fig*) me encanta viajar; **it really ~s me** me

fastidia *or* molesta mucho.
bugbear ['bʌgbɛə*] *n* pesadilla.
bugle ['bju:gl] *n* corneta, clarín *m*.
build [bɪld] *n* (*of person*) talle *m*, tipo ♦ *vt* (*pt, pp* **built** [bɪlt]) construir, edificar.
▸**build on** *vt fus* (*fig*) basar en.
▸**build up** *vt* (*MED*) fortalecer; (*stocks*) acumular; (*establish*: *business*) fomentar, desarrollar; (: *reputation*) crear(se); (*increase*: *production*) aumentar; **don't ~ your hopes up too soon** no te hagas demasiadas ilusiones.
builder ['bɪldə*] *n* constructor(a) *m/f*; (*contractor*) contratista *m/f*.
building ['bɪldɪŋ] *n* (*act of*) construcción *f*; (*habitation, offices*) edificio.
building contractor *n* contratista *m/f* de obras.
building industry *n* construcción *f*.
building site *n* solar *m* (*SP*), obra (*LAM*).
building society *n* (*BRIT*) sociedad *f* de préstamo inmobiliario; *ver recuadro*.

BUILDING SOCIETY

En el Reino Unido existe un tipo de entidad financiera llamada **building society** *de la que sus clientes son también propietarios y cuyos servicios son similares a los de los bancos, aunque se centran fundamentalmente en créditos hipotecarios y cuentas de ahorro. Son la entidad más utilizada por el público en general a la hora de pedir créditos para la compra de la vivienda.*

building trade *n* = **building industry**.
build-up ['bɪldʌp] *n* (*publicity*): **to give sb/sth a good ~** hacer mucha propaganda de algn/algo.
built [bɪlt] *pt, pp of* **build**.
built-in ['bɪlt'ɪn] *adj* (*cupboard*) empotrado; (*device*) interior, incorporado; **~ obsolescence** caducidad *f* programada.
built-up ['bɪltʌp] *adj* (*area*) urbanizado.
bulb [bʌlb] *n* (*BOT*) bulbo; (*ELEC*) bombilla, bombillo (*LAM*), foco (*LAM*).
Bulgaria [bʌl'gɛərɪə] *n* Bulgaria.
Bulgarian [bʌl'gɛərɪən] *adj* búlgaro ♦ *n* búlgaro/a; (*LING*) búlgaro.
bulge [bʌldʒ] *n* bombeo, pandeo; (*in birth rate, sales*) alza, aumento ♦ *vi* bombearse, pandearse; (*pocket etc*) hacer bulto.
bulimia [bə'lɪmɪə] *n* bulimia.
bulk [bʌlk] *n* (*mass*) bulto, volumen *m*; (*major part*) grueso; **in ~** (*COMM*) a granel; **the ~ of** la mayor parte de; **to buy in ~** comprar en grandes cantidades.
bulk buying *n* compra a granel.
bulk carrier *n* (buque *m*) granelero.
bulkhead ['bʌlkhɛd] *n* mamparo.
bulky ['bʌlkɪ] *adj* voluminoso, abultado.
bull [bul] *n* toro; (*STOCK EXCHANGE*) alcista *m/f* de bolsa; (*REL*) bula.
bulldog ['buldɔg] *n* dogo.
bulldoze ['buldəuz] *vt* mover con excavadora; **I was ~d into doing it** (*fig col*) me obligaron a hacerlo.
bulldozer ['buldəuzə*] *n* buldozer *m*, excavadora.
bullet ['bulɪt] *n* bala; **~ wound** balazo.
bulletin ['bulɪtɪn] *n* comunicado, parte *m*; (*journal*) boletín *m*.
bulletin board *n* (*US*) tablón *m* de anuncios; (*COMPUT*) tablero de noticias.
bulletproof ['bulɪtpru:f] *adj* a prueba de balas; **~ vest** chaleco anti-balas.
bullfight ['bulfaɪt] *n* corrida de toros.
bullfighter ['bulfaɪtə*] *n* torero.
bullfighting ['bulfaɪtɪŋ] *n* los toros *mpl*, el toreo; (*art of ~*) tauromaquia.
bullion ['buljən] *n* oro *or* plata en barras.
bullock ['bulək] *n* novillo.
bullring ['bulrɪŋ] *n* plaza de toros.
bull's-eye ['bulzaɪ] *n* blanco, diana.
bullshit ['bulʃɪt] (*col!*) *excl* chorradas ♦ *n* chorradas *fpl* ♦ *vi* decir chorradas ♦ *vt*: **to ~ sb** quedarse con algn.
bully ['bulɪ] *n* valentón *m*, matón *m* ♦ *vt* intimidar, tiranizar.
bum [bʌm] *n* (*BRIT*: *col*: *backside*) culo; (: *tramp*) vagabundo; (*col*: *esp US*: *idler*) holgazán/ana *m/f*, flojo/a.
bumble ['bʌmbl] *vi* (*walk unsteadily*) andar de forma vacilante; (*fig*) farfullar, trastabillar.
bumblebee ['bʌmblbi:] *n* abejorro.
bumbling ['bʌmblɪŋ] *n* divagación *f*.
bumf [bʌmf] *n* (*col*: *forms etc*) papeleo.
bump [bʌmp] *n* (*blow*) tope *m*, choque *m*; (*jolt*) sacudida; (*noise*) choque *m*, topetón *m*; (*on road etc*) bache *m*; (*on head*) chichón *m* ♦ *vt* (*strike*) chocar contra, topetar ♦ *vi* dar sacudidas.
▸**bump into** *vt fus* chocar contra, tropezar con; (*person*) topar con; (*col*: *meet*) tropezar con, toparse con.
bumper ['bʌmpə*] *n* (*BRIT*) parachoques *m inv* ♦ *adj*: **~ crop/harvest** cosecha abundante.
bumper cars *npl* (*US*) autos *or* coches *mpl* de choque.
bumph [bʌmf] *n* = **bumf**.
bumptious ['bʌmpʃəs] *adj* engreído, presuntuoso.
bumpy ['bʌmpɪ] *adj* (*road*) lleno de baches; (*journey, flight*) agitado.

bun [bʌn] *n* (*BRIT*: *cake*) pastel *m*; (*US*: *bread*) bollo; (*of hair*) moño.
bunch [bʌntʃ] *n* (*of flowers*) ramo; (*of keys*) manojo; (*of bananas*) piña; (*of people*) grupo; (*pej*) pandilla.
bundle ['bʌndl] *n* (*gen*) bulto, fardo; (*of sticks*) haz *m*; (*of papers*) legajo ♦ *vt* (*also*: ~ **up**) atar, envolver; **to ~ sth/sb into** meter algo/a algn precipitadamente en.
bun fight *n* (*BRIT col*: *tea party*) merienda; (: *function*) fiesta oficial.
bung [bʌŋ] *n* tapón *m*, bitoque *m* ♦ *vt* (*throw*: *also*: ~ **into**) arrojar; (*also*: ~ **up**: *pipe, hole*) tapar; **my nose is ~ed up** (*col*) tengo la nariz atascada *or* taponada.
bungalow ['bʌŋgələu] *n* bungalow *m*, chalé *m*.
bungee jumping ['bʌndʒiː'dʒʌmpɪŋ] *n* puenting *m*, banyi *m*.
bungle ['bʌŋgl] *vt* chapucear.
bunion ['bʌnjən] *n* juanete *m*.
bunk [bʌŋk] *n* litera; ~ **beds** *npl* literas *fpl*.
bunker ['bʌŋkə*] *n* (*coal store*) carbonera; (*MIL*) refugio; (*GOLF*) bunker *m*.
bunk off *vi*: **to ~ school** (*BRIT col*) pirarse las clases; **I'll ~ at 3 this afternoon** me voy a pirar a las 3 esta tarde.
bunny ['bʌnɪ] *n* (*also*: ~ **rabbit**) conejito.
Bunsen burner ['bʌnsn-] *n* mechero Bunsen.
bunting ['bʌntɪŋ] *n* empavesada, banderas *fpl*.
buoy [bɔɪ] *n* boya.
▶**buoy up** *vt* mantener a flote; (*fig*) animar.
buoyancy ['bɔɪənsɪ] *n* (*of ship*) flotabilidad *f*.
buoyant ['bɔɪənt] *adj* (*carefree*) boyante, optimista; (*COMM*: *market, prices etc*) sostenido.
BUPA ['buːpə] *n abbr* (= *British United Provident Association*) *seguro médico privado*.
burden ['bəːdn] *n* carga ♦ *vt* cargar; **to be a ~ to sb** ser una carga para algn.
bureau, *pl* **~x** ['bjuərəu, -z] *n* (*BRIT*: *writing desk*) escritorio, buró *m*; (*US*: *chest of drawers*) cómoda; (*office*) oficina, agencia.
bureaucracy [bjuə'rɔkrəsɪ] *n* burocracia.
bureaucrat ['bjuərəkræt] *n* burócrata *m/f*.
bureaucratic [bjuərə'krætɪk] *adj* burocrático.
burgeon ['bəːdʒən] *vi* (*develop rapidly*) crecer, incrementarse; (*trade etc*) florecer.
burger ['bəːgə*] *n* hamburguesa.
burglar ['bəːglə*] *n* ladrón/ona *m/f*.
burglar alarm *n* alarma *f* contra robo.
burglarize ['bəːgləraɪz] *vt* (*US*) robar (con allanamiento).
burglary ['bəːglərɪ] *n* robo con allanamiento *or* fractura, robo de una casa.
burgle ['bəːgl] *vt* robar (con allanamiento).
burial ['bɛrɪəl] *n* entierro.
burial ground *n* cementerio.
burlesque [bəː'lɛsk] *n* parodia.
burly ['bəːlɪ] *adj* fornido, membrudo.
Burma ['bəːmə] *n* Birmania; *see also* **Myanmar**.
Burmese [bəː'miːz] *adj* birmano ♦ *n* (*pl inv*) birmano/a; (*LING*) birmano.
burn [bəːn] *vb* (*pt, pp* **burned** *or* **burnt** [bəːnt]) *vt* quemar; (*house*) incendiar ♦ *vi* quemarse, arder; incendiarse; (*sting*) escocer ♦ *n* (*MED*) quemadura; **the cigarette ~t a hole in her dress** se ha quemado el vestido con el cigarrillo; **I've ~t myself!** ¡me he quemado!
▶**burn down** *vt* incendiar.
▶**burn out** *vt* (*subj*: *writer etc*): **to ~ o.s. out** agotarse.
burner ['bəːnə*] *n* (*gas*) quemador *m*.
burning ['bəːnɪŋ] *adj* ardiente; (*building, forest*) en llamas.
Burns' Night [bəːnz-] *n ver recuadro*.

BURNS' NIGHT

Cada veinticinco de enero los escoceses celebran la llamada **Burns' Night** *(noche de Burns), en honor al poeta escocés Robert Burns (1759-1796). Es tradición hacer una cena en la que, al son de la música de la gaita escocesa, se sirve "haggis", plato tradicional de asadura de cordero cocida en el estómago del animal, acompañado de nabos y puré de patatas. Durante la misma se recitan poemas del autor y varios discursos conmemorativos de carácter festivo.*

burp [bəːp] (*col*) *n* eructo ♦ *vi* eructar.
burrow ['bʌrəu] *n* madriguera ♦ *vt* hacer una madriguera.
bursar ['bəːsə*] *n* tesorero; (*BRIT*: *student*) becario/a.
bursary ['bəːsərɪ] *n* (*BRIT*) beca.
burst [bəːst] *vb* (*pt, pp* **burst**) *vt* (*balloon, pipe*) reventar; (*banks etc*) romper ♦ *vi* reventarse; romperse; (*tyre*) pincharse; (*bomb*) estallar ♦ *n* (*explosion*) estallido; (*also*: ~ **pipe**) reventón *m*; **the river has ~ its banks** el río se ha desbordado; **to ~ into flames** estallar en llamas; **to ~ out laughing** soltar la carcajada; **to ~ into tears** deshacerse en lágrimas; **to be ~ing with** reventar de; **a ~ of energy** una

explosión de energía; **a ~ of applause** una salva de aplausos; **a ~ of speed** una escapada; **to ~ open** *vi* abrirse de golpe.
▸**burst into** *vt fus* (*room etc*) irrumpir en.
bury ['bɛrɪ] *vt* enterrar; (*body*) enterrar, sepultar; **to ~ the hatchet** enterrar el hacha (de guerra), echar pelillos a la mar.
bus [bʌs] *n* autobús *m*, camión *m* (*LAM*).
bus boy *n* (*US*) ayudante *m/f* de camarero.
bush [buʃ] *n* arbusto; (*scrub land*) monte *m* bajo; **to beat about the ~** andar(se) con rodeos.
bushed [buʃt] *adj* (*col*) molido.
bushel ['buʃl] *n* (*measure*: *Brit*) = *36,36 litros*; (: *US*) = *35,24 litros*.
bush fire *n* incendio en el monte.
bushy ['buʃɪ] *adj* (*beard, eyebrows*) poblado; (*hair*) espeso; (*fur*) tupido.
busily ['bɪzɪlɪ] *adv* afanosamente.
business ['bɪznɪs] *n* (*matter, affair*) asunto; (*trading*) comercio, negocios *mpl*; (*firm*) empresa, casa; (*occupation*) oficio; **to be away on ~** estar en viaje de negocios; **it's my ~ to...** me toca *or* corresponde...; **it's none of my ~** no es asunto mío; **he means ~** habla en serio; **he's in the insurance ~** se dedica a los seguros; **I'm here on ~** estoy aquí por mi trabajo; **to do ~ with sb** hacer negocios con algn.
business address *n* dirección *f* comercial.
business card *n* tarjeta de visita.
businesslike ['bɪznɪslaɪk] *adj* (*company*) serio; (*person*) eficiente.
businessman ['bɪznɪsmən] *n* hombre *m* de negocios.
business trip *n* viaje *m* de negocios.
businesswoman ['bɪznɪswumən] *n* mujer *f* de negocios.
busker ['bʌskə*] *n* (*BRIT*) músico/a ambulante.
bus route *n* recorrido del autobús.
bus station *n* estación *f or* terminal *f* de autobuses.
bus-stop ['bʌsstɔp] *n* parada de autobús, paradero (*LAM*).
bust [bʌst] *n* (*ANAT*) pecho ♦ *adj* (*col*: *broken*) roto, estropeado ♦ *vt* (*col*: *POLICE*: *arrest*) detener; **to go ~** quebrar.
bustle ['bʌsl] *n* bullicio, movimiento ♦ *vi* menearse, apresurarse.
bustling ['bʌslɪŋ] *adj* (*town*) animado, bullicioso.
bust-up ['bʌstʌp] *n* (*col*) riña.
busty ['bʌstɪ] *adj* (*col*) pechugona, con buena delantera.
busy ['bɪzɪ] *adj* ocupado, atareado; (*shop, street*) concurrido, animado ♦ *vt*: **to ~ o.s. with** ocuparse en; **he's a ~ man** (*normally*) es un hombre muy ocupado; (*temporarily*) está muy ocupado; **the line's ~** (*esp US*) está comunicando.
busybody ['bɪzɪbɔdɪ] *n* entrometido/a.
busy signal *n* (*US TEL*) señal *f* de comunicando.

KEYWORD

but [bʌt] *conj* **1** pero; **he's not very bright, ~ he's hard-working** no es muy inteligente, pero es trabajador
2 (*in direct contradiction*) sino; **he's not English ~ French** no es inglés sino francés; **he didn't sing ~ he shouted** no cantó sino que gritó
3 (*showing disagreement, surprise etc*): **~ that's far too expensive!** ¡pero eso es carísimo!; **~ it does work!** ¡(pero) sí que funciona!
♦ *prep* (*apart from, except*) menos, salvo; **we've had nothing ~ trouble** no hemos tenido más que problemas; **no-one ~ him can do it** nadie más que él puede hacerlo; **the last ~ one** el penúltimo; **who ~ a lunatic would do such a thing?** ¡sólo un loco haría una cosa así!; **~ for you/your help** si no fuera por ti/tu ayuda; **anything ~ that** cualquier cosa menos eso
♦ *adv* (*just, only*): **she's ~ a child** no es más que una niña; **had I ~ known** si lo hubiera sabido; **I can ~ try** al menos lo puedo intentar; **it's all ~ finished** está casi acabado.

butane ['bjuːteɪn] *n* (*also*: **~ gas**) (gas *m*) butano.
butch [butʃ] *adj* (*pej*: *woman*) machirula, marimacho; (*col*: *man*) muy macho.
butcher ['butʃə*] *n* carnicero/a ♦ *vt* hacer una carnicería con; (*cattle etc for meat*) matar; **~'s (shop)** carnicería.
butler ['bʌtlə*] *n* mayordomo.
butt [bʌt] *n* (*cask*) tonel *m*; (*for rain*) tina; (*thick end*) cabo, extremo; (*of gun*) culata; (*of cigarette*) colilla; (*BRIT fig*: *target*) blanco ♦ *vt* dar cabezadas contra, topetar.
▸**butt in** *vi* (*interrupt*) interrumpir.
butter ['bʌtə*] *n* mantequilla, manteca (*LAM*) ♦ *vt* untar con mantequilla.
butter bean *n* judía blanca.
buttercup ['bʌtəkʌp] *n* ranúnculo.
butterfingers ['bʌtəfɪŋgəz] *n* (*col*) torpe *m/f*.
butterfly ['bʌtəflaɪ] *n* mariposa; (*SWIMMING*: *also*: **~ stroke**) (braza de) mariposa.
buttocks ['bʌtəks] *npl* nalgas *fpl*.
button ['bʌtn] *n* botón *m* ♦ *vt* (*also*: **~ up**)

abotonar, abrochar ♦ *vi* abrocharse.
buttonhole ['bʌtnhəul] *n* ojal *m*; (*flower*) flor *f* que se lleva en el ojal.
buttress ['bʌtrɪs] *n* contrafuerte *m*; (*fig*) apoyo, sostén *m*.
buy [baɪ] *vb* (*pt, pp* **bought** [bɔːt]) *vt* comprar ♦ *n* compra; **to ~ sb sth/sth from sb** comprarle algo a algn; **to ~ sb a drink** invitar a algn a una copa; **a good/bad ~** una buena/mala compra.
▸**buy back** *vt* volver a comprar.
▸**buy in** *vt* proveerse *or* abastecerse de.
▸**buy into** *vt fus* comprar acciones en.
▸**buy off** *vt* (*col: bribe*) sobornar.
▸**buy out** *vt* (*partner*) comprar la parte de.
buyer ['baɪə*] *n* comprador(a) *m/f*; **~'s market** mercado favorable al comprador.
buy-out ['baɪaut] *n* (*COMM*) adquisición *f* de (la totalidad de) las acciones.
buzz [bʌz] *n* zumbido; (*col: phone call*) llamada (telefónica) ♦ *vt* (*call on intercom*) llamar; (*with buzzer*) hacer sonar; (*AVIAT: plane, building*) pasar rozando ♦ *vi* zumbar; **my head is ~ing** me zumba la cabeza.
▸**buzz off** *vi* (*BRIT col*) largarse.
buzzard ['bʌzəd] *n* (*BRIT*) águila ratonera; (*US*) buitre *m*, gallinazo (*LAM*).
buzzer ['bʌzə*] *n* timbre *m*.
buzz word *n* palabra que está de moda.

KEYWORD

by [baɪ] *prep* **1** (*referring to cause, agent*) por; de; **abandoned ~ his mother** abandonado por su madre; **surrounded ~ enemies** rodeado de enemigos; **a painting ~ Picasso** un cuadro de Picasso
2 (*referring to method, manner, means*): **~ bus/car/train** en autobús/coche/tren; **to pay ~ cheque** pagar con cheque(s); **~ moonlight/candlelight** a la luz de la luna/una vela; **~ saving hard, he ...** ahorrando, ...
3 (*via, through*) por; **we came ~ Dover** vinimos por Dover
4 (*close to, past*): **the house ~ the river** la casa junto al río; **she rushed ~ me** pasó a mi lado como una exhalación; **I go ~ the post office every day** paso por delante de Correos todos los días
5 (*time: not later than*) para; (*: during*): **~ daylight** de día; **~ 4 o'clock** para las cuatro; **~ this time tomorrow** mañana a estas horas; **~ the time I got here it was too late** cuando llegué ya era demasiado tarde
6 (*amount*): **~ the metre/kilo** por metro/kilo; **paid ~ the hour** pagado por hora
7 (*MATH, measure*): **to divide/multiply ~ 3** dividir/multiplicar por 3; **a room 3 metres ~ 4** una habitación de 3 metros por 4; **it's broader ~ a metre** es un metro más ancho; **the bus missed me ~ inches** no me pilló el autobús por un pelo
8 (*according to*) según, de acuerdo con; **it's 3 o'clock ~ my watch** según mi reloj, son las tres; **it's all right ~ me** por mí, está bien
9: **(all) ~ oneself** *etc* todo solo; **he did it (all) ~ himself** lo hizo él solo; **he was standing (all) ~ himself in a corner** estaba de pie solo en un rincón
10: **~ the way** a propósito, por cierto; **this wasn't my idea, ~ the way** pues, no fue idea mía
♦ *adv* **1** *see* **go**; **pass** *etc*
2: **~ and ~** finalmente; **they'll come back ~ and ~** acabarán volviendo; **~ and large** en líneas generales, en general.

bye(-bye) ['baɪ('baɪ)] *excl* adiós, hasta luego, chao (*esp LAM*).
by(e)-law ['baɪlɔː] *n* ordenanza municipal.
by-election ['baɪɪlɛkʃən] *n* (*BRIT*) elección *f* parcial; *ver recuadro*.

BY-ELECTION

Se celebra una **by-election** *en el Reino Unido y otros países de la "Commonwealth" cuando es necesario reemplazar a un parlamentario ("Member of Parliament") cesado o fallecido durante una legislatura. Dichas elecciones tienen lugar únicamente en el área electoral representada por el citado parlamentario, su "constituency".*

bygone ['baɪgɔn] *adj* pasado, del pasado ♦ *n*: **let ~s be ~s** lo pasado, pasado está.
Byelorussia [bjɛləu'rʌʃə] *n* Bielorrusia.
Byelorussian [bjɛləu'rʌʃən] *adj, n* = **Belorussian**.
bypass ['baɪpɑːs] *n* carretera de circunvalación; (*MED*) (operación *f* de) by-pass *m* ♦ *vt* evitar.
by-product ['baɪprɔdʌkt] *n* subproducto, derivado.
bystander ['baɪstændə*] *n* espectador(a) *m/f*.
byte [baɪt] *n* (*COMPUT*) byte *m*, octeto.
byway ['baɪweɪ] *n* camino poco frecuentado.
byword ['baɪwəːd] *n*: **to be a ~ for** ser sinónimo de.
by-your-leave ['baɪjɔː'liːv] *n*: **without so**

much as a ~ sin decir nada, sin dar ningún tipo de explicación.

C c

C, c [siː] *n* (*letter*) C, c *f*; (*MUS*): **C** do *m*; **C for Charlie** C de Carmen.
C *abbr* (= *Celsius, centigrade*) C.
c *abbr* (= *century*) S.; (= *circa*) hacia; (*US etc*) = **cent(s)**.
CA *n abbr* = **Central America**; (*BRIT*) = **chartered accountant**; (*US*) = *California*.
ca. *abbr* (= *circa*) c.
c/a *abbr* = **capital account, credit account, current account**.
CAA *n abbr* (*BRIT*: = *Civil Aviation Authority*) *organismo de control y desarrollo de la aviación civil*.
CAB *n abbr* (*BRIT*: = *Citizens' Advice Bureau*) ≈ Servicio de Información Ciudadana.
cab [kæb] *n* taxi *m*; (*of truck*) cabina.
cabaret ['kæbəreɪ] *n* cabaret *m*.
cabbage ['kæbɪdʒ] *n* col *f*, berza.
cabbie, cabby ['kæbɪ] *n* (*col*) taxista *m/f*.
cab driver *n* taxista *m/f*.
cabin ['kæbɪn] *n* cabaña; (*on ship*) camarote *m*.
cabin cruiser *n* yate *m* de motor.
cabinet ['kæbɪnɪt] *n* (*POL*) consejo de ministros; (*furniture*) armario; (*also*: **display** ~) vitrina.
cabinet-maker ['kæbɪnɪt'meɪkə*] *n* ebanista *m*.
cabinet minister *n* ministro/a (del gabinete).
cable ['keɪbl] *n* cable *m* ♦ *vt* cablegrafiar.
cable-car ['keɪblkɑː*] *n* teleférico.
cablegram ['keɪblgræm] *n* cablegrama *m*.
cable television *n* televisión *f* por cable.
cache [kæʃ] *n* (*drugs*) alijo; (*arms*) zulo.
cackle ['kækl] *vi* cacarear.
cactus, *pl* **cacti** ['kæktəs, -taɪ] *n* cacto.
CAD *n abbr* (= *computer-aided design*) DAO *m*.
caddie, caddy ['kædɪ] *n* (*GOLF*) cadi *m*.
cadence ['keɪdəns] *n* ritmo; (*MUS*) cadencia.
cadet [kə'dɛt] *n* (*MIL*) cadete *m*; **police** ~ cadete *m* de policía.
cadge [kædʒ] *vt* gorronear.
cadger ['kædʒə*] *n* gorrón/ona *m/f*.
cadre ['kædrɪ] *n* cuadro.
Caesarean, (*US*) **Cesarean** [siː'zɛərɪən] *adj*: ~ **(section)** cesárea.
CAF *abbr* (*BRIT*: = *cost and freight*) C y F.
café ['kæfeɪ] *n* café *m*.
cafeteria [kæfɪ'tɪərɪə] *n* cafetería (*con autoservicio para comer*).
caffein(e) ['kæfiːn] *n* cafeína.
cage [keɪdʒ] *n* jaula ♦ *vt* enjaular.
cagey ['keɪdʒɪ] *adj* (*col*) cauteloso, reservado.
cagoule [kə'guːl] *n* canguro.
cahoots [kə'huːts] *n*: **to be in** ~ **(with sb)** estar conchabado (con algn).
CAI *n abbr* (= *computer-aided instruction*) enseñanza asistida por ordenador.
Cairo ['kaɪərəu] *n* El Cairo.
cajole [kə'dʒəul] *vt* engatusar.
cake [keɪk] *n* pastel *m*; (*of soap*) pastilla; **he wants to have his** ~ **and eat it** (*fig*) quiere estar en misa y repicando; **it's a piece of** ~ (*col*) es pan comido.
caked [keɪkt] *adj*: ~ **with** cubierto de.
cake shop *n* pastelería.
Cal. *abbr* (*US*) = *California*.
calamine ['kæləmaɪn] *n* calamina.
calamitous [kə'læmɪtəs] *adj* calamitoso.
calamity [kə'læmɪtɪ] *n* calamidad *f*.
calcium ['kælsɪəm] *n* calcio.
calculate ['kælkjuleɪt] *vt* (*estimate*: *chances, effect*) calcular.
▸**calculate on** *vt fus*: **to** ~ **on sth/on doing sth** contar con algo/con hacer algo.
calculated ['kælkjuleɪtɪd] *adj*: **we took a** ~ **risk** calculamos el riesgo.
calculating ['kælkjuleɪtɪŋ] *adj* (*scheming*) calculador(a).
calculation [kælkju'leɪʃən] *n* cálculo, cómputo.
calculator ['kælkjuleɪtə*] *n* calculadora.
calculus ['kælkjuləs] *n* cálculo.
calendar ['kæləndə*] *n* calendario; ~ **month/year** *n* mes *m*/año civil.
calf, *pl* **calves** [kɑːf, kɑːvz] *n* (*of cow*) ternero, becerro; (*of other animals*) cría; (*also*: ~**skin**) piel *f* de becerro; (*ANAT*) pantorrilla, canilla (*LAM*).
caliber ['kælɪbə*] *n* (*US*) = **calibre**.
calibrate ['kælɪbreɪt] *vt* (*gun etc*) calibrar; (*scale of measuring instrument*) graduar.
calibre, (*US*) **caliber** ['kælɪbə*] *n* calibre *m*.
calico ['kælɪkəu] *n* calicó *m*.
Calif. *abbr* (*US*) = *California*.
California [kælɪ'fɔːnɪə] *n* California.
calipers ['kælɪpəz] *npl* (*US*) = **callipers**.
call [kɔːl] *vt* (*gen, also TEL*) llamar; (*announce*: *flight*) anunciar; (*meeting, strike*) convocar ♦ *vi* (*shout*) llamar;

(*telephone*) llamar (por teléfono), telefonear; (*visit*: *also*: ~ **in,** ~ **round**) hacer una visita ♦ *n* (*shout, TEL*) llamada, llamado (*LAM*); (*of bird*) canto; (*appeal*) llamamiento, llamado (*LAM*); (*summons*: *for flight etc*) llamada; (*fig*: *lure*) llamada; **to be ~ed** (*person, object*) llamarse; **to ~ sb names** poner verde a algn; **let's ~ it a day** (*col*) ¡dejémoslo!, ¡ya está bien!; **who is ~ing?** ¿de parte de quién?; **London ~ing** (*RADIO*) aquí Londres; **on ~** (*nurse, doctor etc*) de guardia; **please give me a ~ at 7** llámeme a las 7, por favor; **long-distance ~** conferencia (interurbana); **to make a ~** llamar por teléfono; **port of ~** puerto de escala; **to pay a ~ on sb** pasarse a ver a algn; **there's not much ~ for these items** estos artículos no tienen mucha demanda.

►**call at** *vt fus* (*ship*) hacer escala en, tocar en; (*train*) parar en.

►**call back** *vi* (*return*) volver; (*TEL*) volver a llamar.

►**call for** *vt fus* (*demand*) pedir, exigir; (*fetch*) venir por.

►**call in** *vt* (*doctor, expert, police*) llamar.

►**call off** *vt* suspender; **the strike was ~ed off** se desconvocó la huelga.

►**call on** *vt fus* (*visit*) ir a ver; (*turn to*) acudir a.

►**call out** *vi* gritar, dar voces ♦ *vt* (*doctor*) llamar; (*police, troops*) hacer intervenir.

►**call up** *vt* (*MIL*) llamar a filas.

Callanetics ® [kælə'nɛtɪks] *nsg gimnasia de repetición de pequeños ejercicios musculares.*

callbox ['kɔːlbɔks] *n* (*BRIT*) cabina telefónica.

call centre *n* (*BRIT*) centro de llamadas.

caller ['kɔːlə*] *n* visita *f*; (*TEL*) usuario/a; **hold the line, ~!** ¡no cuelgue!

call girl *n* prostituta.

call-in ['kɔːlɪn] *n* (*US*) *programa de línea abierta al público.*

calling ['kɔːlɪŋ] *n* vocación *f*; (*profession*) profesión *f*.

calling card *n* tarjeta de visita.

callipers, (*US*) **calipers** ['kælɪpəz] *npl* (*MED*) aparato ortopédico; (*MATH*) calibrador *m*.

callous ['kæləs] *adj* insensible, cruel.

callousness ['kæləsnɪs] *n* insensibilidad, crueldad *f*.

callow ['kæləu] *adj* inexperto, novato.

calm [kɑːm] *adj* tranquilo; (*sea*) tranquilo, en calma ♦ *n* calma, tranquilidad *f* ♦ *vt* calmar, tranquilizar.

►**calm down** *vi* calmarse, tranquilizarse ♦ *vt* calmar, tranquilizar.

calmly ['kɑːmlɪ] *adv* tranquilamente, con calma.

calmness ['kɑːmnɪs] *n* calma.

Calor gas ® ['kælə*-] *n* butano.

calorie ['kælərɪ] *n* caloría; **low-~ product** producto bajo en calorías.

calve [kɑːv] *vi* parir.

calves [kɑːvz] *npl of* **calf.**

CAM *n abbr* (= *computer-aided manufacturing*) producción *f* asistida por ordenador.

camber ['kæmbə*] *n* (*of road*) combadura.

Cambodia [kæm'bəudjə] *n* Camboya.

Cambodian [kæm'bəudjən] *adj, n* camboyano/a *m/f*.

Cambs *abbr* (*BRIT*) = *Cambridgeshire.*

camcorder ['kæmkɔːdə*] *n* videocámara.

came [keɪm] *pt of* **come.**

camel ['kæməl] *n* camello.

cameo ['kæmɪəu] *n* camafeo.

camera ['kæmərə] *n* cámara *or* máquina fotográfica; (*CINE, TV*) cámara; (*movie ~*) cámara, tomavistas *m inv*; **in ~** a puerta cerrada.

cameraman ['kæmərəmən] *n* cámara *m*.

Cameroon, Cameroun [kæme'ruːn] *n* Camerún *m*.

camomile tea ['kæməmaɪl-] *n* manzanilla.

camouflage ['kæməflɑːʒ] *n* camuflaje *m* ♦ *vt* camuflar.

camp [kæmp] *n* campo, campamento ♦ *vi* acampar ♦ *adj* afectado, afeminado; **to go ~ing** ir de *or* hacer camping.

campaign [kæm'peɪn] *n* (*MIL, POL etc*) campaña ♦ *vi*: **to ~ (for/against)** hacer campaña (a favor de/en contra de).

campaigner [kæm'peɪnə*] *n*: **~ for** defensor(a) *m/f* de; **~ against** persona que hace campaña contra.

campbed ['kæmpbɛd] *n* (*BRIT*) cama plegable.

camper ['kæmpə*] *n* campista *m/f*; (*vehicle*) caravana.

camping ['kæmpɪŋ] *n* camping *m*.

campsite ['kæmpsaɪt] *n* camping *m*.

campus ['kæmpəs] *n* campus *m*.

camshaft ['kæmʃɑːft] *n* árbol *m* de levas.

can [kæn] *aux vb see next headword* ♦ *n* (*of oil, water*) bidón *m*; (*tin*) lata, bote *m* ♦ *vt* enlatar; (*preserve*) conservar en lata; **a ~ of beer** una lata *or* un bote de cerveza; **to carry the ~** (*col*) pagar el pato.

KEYWORD

can (*negative* **cannot, can't**; *conditional and pt* **could**) *aux vb* **1** (*be able to*) poder; **you ~ do it if you try** puedes hacerlo si lo intentas; **I ~'t see you** no te veo; **~ you hear me?**

(*not translated*) ¿me oyes?
2 (*know how to*) saber; **I ~ swim/play tennis/drive** sé nadar/jugar al tenis/conducir; **~ you speak French?** ¿hablas *or* sabes hablar francés?
3 (*may*) poder; **~ I use your phone?** ¿me dejas *or* puedo usar tu teléfono?; **could I have a word with you?** ¿podría hablar contigo un momento?
4 (*expressing disbelief, puzzlement etc*): **it ~'t be true!** ¡no puede ser (verdad)!; **what** *CAN* **he want?** ¿qué querrá?
5 (*expressing possibility, suggestion etc*): **he could be in the library** podría estar en la biblioteca; **she could have been delayed** puede que se haya retrasado.

Canada ['kænədə] *n* Canadá *m.*
Canadian [kə'neɪdɪən] *adj, n* canadiense *m/f.*
canal [kə'næl] *n* canal *m.*
canary [kə'nɛərɪ] *n* canario.
Canary Islands, Canaries [kə'nɛərɪz] *npl* las (Islas) Canarias.
Canberra ['kænbərə] *n* Canberra.
cancel ['kænsəl] *vt* cancelar; (*train*) suprimir; (*appointment, cheque*) anular; (*cross out*) tachar.
►**cancel out** *vt* (*MATH*) anular; (*fig*) contrarrestar; **they ~ each other out** se anulan mutuamente.
cancellation [kænsə'leɪʃən] *n* cancelación *f*; supresión *f.*
cancer ['kænsə*] *n* cáncer *m*; **C~** (*ASTRO*) Cáncer *m.*
cancerous ['kænsərəs] *adj* canceroso.
cancer patient *n* enfermo/a *m/f* de cáncer.
cancer research *n* investigación *f* del cáncer.
C and F *abbr* (= *cost and freight*) C y F.
candid ['kændɪd] *adj* franco, abierto.
candidacy ['kændɪdəsɪ] *n* candidatura.
candidate ['kændɪdeɪt] *n* candidato/a.
candidature ['kændɪdətʃə*] *n* (*BRIT*) = **candidacy.**
candidly ['kændɪdlɪ] *adv* francamente, con franqueza.
candle ['kændl] *n* vela; (*in church*) cirio.
candle holder *n see* **candlestick.**
candlelight ['kændllaɪt] *n*: **by ~** a la luz de una vela.
candlestick ['kændlstɪk] *n* (*also*: **candle holder**: *single*) candelero; (: *low*) palmatoria; (*bigger, ornate*) candelabro.
candour, (*US*) **candor** ['kændə*] *n* franqueza.
candy ['kændɪ] *n* azúcar *m* cande; (*US*) caramelo ♦ *vt* (*fruit*) escarchar.
candy-floss ['kændɪflɔs] *n* (*BRIT*) algodón *m* (azucarado).
cane [keɪn] *n* (*BOT*) caña; (*for baskets, chairs etc*) mimbre *m*; (*stick*) vara, palmeta; (: *for walking*) bastón *m* ♦ *vt* (*BRIT SCOL*) castigar (con palmeta); **~ liquor** caña.
canine ['kænaɪn] *adj* canino.
canister ['kænɪstə*] *n* bote *m.*
cannabis ['kænəbɪs] *n* canabis *m.*
canned [kænd] *adj* en lata, de lata; (*col*: *music*) grabado; (: *drunk*) mamado.
cannibal ['kænɪbəl] *n* caníbal *m/f*, antropófago/a.
cannibalism ['kænɪbəlɪzəm] *n* canibalismo.
cannon, *pl* **~** *or* **~s** ['kænən] *n* cañón *m.*
cannonball ['kænənbɔːl] *n* bala (de cañón).
cannon fodder *n* carne *f* de cañón.
cannot ['kænɔt] = **can not.**
canny ['kænɪ] *adj* avispado.
canoe [kə'nuː] *n* canoa; (*SPORT*) piragua.
canoeing [kə'nuːɪŋ] *n* (*SPORT*) piragüismo.
canoeist [kə'nuːɪst] *n* piragüista *m/f.*
canon ['kænən] *n* (*clergyman*) canónigo; (*standard*) canon *m.*
canonize ['kænənaɪz] *vt* canonizar.
can opener *n* abrelatas *m inv.*
canopy ['kænəpɪ] *n* dosel *m*, toldo.
can't [kænt] = **can not.**
Cantab. *abbr* (*BRIT*: = *cantabrigiensis*) = *of Cambridge.*
cantankerous [kæn'tæŋkərəs] *adj* arisco, malhumorado.
canteen [kæn'tiːn] *n* (*eating place*) comedor *m*; (*BRIT*: *of cutlery*) juego.
canter ['kæntə*] *n* medio galope ♦ *vi* ir a medio galope.
cantilever ['kæntɪliːvə*] *n* viga voladiza.
canvas ['kænvəs] *n* (*material*) lona; (*painting*) lienzo; (*NAUT*) velamen *m*; **under ~** (*camping*) en tienda de campaña.
canvass ['kænvəs] *vt* (*POL*: *district*) hacer campaña (puerta a puerta) en; (: *person*) hacer campaña (puerta a puerta) a favor de; (*COMM*: *district*) sondear el mercado en; (: *citizens, opinions*) sondear.
canvasser ['kænvəsə*] *n* (*POL*) representante *m/f* electoral; (*COMM*) corredor(a) *m/f.*
canyon ['kænjən] *n* cañón *m.*
CAP *n abbr* (= *Common Agricultural Policy*) PAC *f.*
cap [kæp] *n* (*hat*) gorra; (*for swimming*) gorro; (*of pen*) capuchón *m*; (*of bottle*) tapón *m*; (: *metal*) chapa; (*contraceptive*) diafragma *m* ♦ *vt* (*outdo*) superar; (*BRIT SPORT*) seleccionar (para el equipo nacional); **and to ~ it all, he ...** y para colmo, él ....
capability [keɪpə'bɪlɪtɪ] *n* capacidad *f.*

capable ['keɪpəbl] *adj* capaz.
capacity [kə'pæsɪtɪ] *n* capacidad *f*; (*position*) calidad *f*; **filled to** ~ lleno a reventar; **this work is beyond my** ~ este trabajo es superior a mí; **in an advisory** ~ como asesor.
cape [keɪp] *n* capa; (*GEO*) cabo.
Cape of Good Hope *n* Cabo de Buena Esperanza.
caper ['keɪpə*] *n* (*CULIN*: *also*: ~**s**) alcaparra; (*prank*) travesura.
Cape Town *n* Ciudad *f* del Cabo.
capital ['kæpɪtl] *n* (*also*: ~ **city**) capital *f*; (*money*) capital *m*; (*also*: ~ **letter**) mayúscula.
capital account *n* cuenta de capital.
capital allowance *n* desgravación *f* sobre bienes del capital.
capital assets *n* activo fijo.
capital expenditure *n* inversión *f* de capital.
capital gains tax *n* impuesto sobre la plusvalía.
capital goods *npl* bienes *mpl* de capital.
capital-intensive [kæpɪtlɪn'tɛnsɪv] *adj* de utilización intensiva de capital.
capital investment *n* inversión *f* de capital.
capitalism ['kæpɪtəlɪzəm] *n* capitalismo.
capitalist ['kæpɪtəlɪst] *adj*, *n* capitalista *m/f*.
capitalize ['kæpɪtəlaɪz] *vt* (*COMM*: *provide with capital*) capitalizar.
►**capitalize on** *vt fus* (*fig*) sacar provecho de, aprovechar.
capital punishment *n* pena de muerte.
capital transfer tax *n* impuesto sobre plusvalía de cesión.
Capitol ['kæpɪtl] *n*: **the** ~ el Capitolio; *ver recuadro*.

> **CAPITOL**
>
> *El Capitolio* (**Capitol**) *es el edificio en el que se reúne el Congreso de los Estados Unidos ("Congress"), situado en la ciudad de Washington. Por extensión, también se suele llamar así al edificio en el que tienen lugar las sesiones parlamentarias de la cámara de representantes de muchos de los estados.*

capitulate [kə'pɪtjuleɪt] *vi* capitular, rendirse.
capitulation [kəpɪtju'leɪʃən] *n* capitulación *f*, rendición *f*.
capricious [kə'prɪʃəs] *adj* caprichoso.
Capricorn ['kæprɪkɔːn] *n* Capricornio.
caps [kæps] *abbr* (= *capital letters*) may.
capsize [kæp'saɪz] *vt* volcar, hacer zozobrar ♦ *vi* volcarse, zozobrar.
capstan ['kæpstən] *n* cabrestante *m*.
capsule ['kæpsjuːl] *n* cápsula.
Capt. *abbr* = **Captain.**
captain ['kæptɪn] *n* capitán *m* ♦ *vt* capitanear, ser el capitán de.
caption ['kæpʃən] *n* (*heading*) título; (*to picture*) leyenda, pie *m*.
captivate ['kæptɪveɪt] *vt* cautivar, encantar.
captive ['kæptɪv] *adj*, *n* cautivo/a *m/f*.
captivity [kæp'tɪvɪtɪ] *n* cautiverio.
captor ['kæptə*] *n* captor(a) *m/f*.
capture ['kæptʃə*] *vt* capturar; (*place*) tomar; (*attention*) captar, llamar ♦ *n* captura; toma; (*data* ~) formulación *f* de datos.
car [kɑː*] *n* coche *m*, carro (*LAM*), automóvil *m*, auto (*LAM*); (*US RAIL*) vagón *m*; **by** ~ en coche.
Caracas [kə'rækəs] *n* Caracas *m*.
carafe [kə'ræf] *n* garrafa.
caramel ['kærəməl] *n* caramelo.
carat ['kærət] *n* quilate *m*; **18-~ gold** oro de 18 quilates.
caravan ['kærəvæn] *n* (*BRIT*) caravana, remolque *m*; (*of camels*) caravana.
caravan site *n* (*BRIT*) camping *m* para caravanas.
caraway ['kærəweɪ] *n*: ~ **seed** carvi *m*.
carbohydrates [kɑːbəu'haɪdreɪts] *npl* (*foods*) hidratos *mpl* de carbono.
car bomb *n* coche-bomba *m*.
carbon ['kɑːbən] *n* carbono.
carbonated ['kɑːbəneɪtɪd] *adj* (*drink*) con gas.
carbon copy *n* copia al carbón.
carbon dioxide *n* dióxido de carbono, anhídrido carbónico.
carbon monoxide *n* monóxido de carbono.
carbon paper *n* papel *m* carbón.
carbon ribbon *n* cinta de carbón.
car boot sale *n* mercadillo (*de objetos usados expuestos en el maletero del coche*).
carburettor, (*US*) **carburetor** [kɑːbju'rɛtə*] *n* carburador *m*.
carcass ['kɑːkəs] *n* (*animal*) res *f* muerta; (*dead body*) cadáver *m*.
carcinogenic [kɑːsɪnə'dʒɛnɪk] *adj* cancerígeno.
card [kɑːd] *n* (*thin cardboard*) cartulina; (*playing* ~) carta, naipe *m*; (*visiting* ~, *greetings* ~ *etc*) tarjeta; (*index* ~) ficha; **membership** ~ carnet *m*; **to play ~s** jugar a las cartas *or* los naipes.
cardamom ['kɑːdəməm] *n* cardamomo.

cardboard ['kɑːdbɔːd] *n* cartón *m*, cartulina.
cardboard box *n* caja de cartón.
cardboard city *n* zona de marginados sin hogar (*que se refugian entre cartones*).
card-carrying member ['kɑːdkærɪɪŋ-] *n* miembro con carnet.
card game *n* juego de naipes *or* cartas.
cardiac ['kɑːdɪæk] *adj* cardíaco.
cardigan ['kɑːdɪgən] *n* chaqueta (de punto), rebeca.
cardinal ['kɑːdɪnl] *adj* cardinal ♦ *n* cardenal *m*.
cardinal number *n* número cardinal.
card index *n* fichero.
cardphone ['kɑːdfəun] *n cabina que funciona con tarjetas telefónicas.*
cardsharp ['kɑːdʃɑːp] *n* fullero/a.
card vote *n* voto por delegación.
CARE [kɛə*] *n abbr* (= *Cooperative for American Relief Everywhere*) *sociedad benéfica.*
care [kɛə*] *n* cuidado; (*worry*) preocupación *f*; (*charge*) cargo, custodia ♦ *vi*: **to ~ about** preocuparse por; **~ of (c/o)** en casa de, al cuidado de; (: *on letter*) para (entregar a); **in sb's ~** a cargo de algn; **the child has been taken into ~** pusieron al niño bajo custodia del gobierno; **"with ~"** "¡frágil!"; **to take ~ to** cuidarse de, tener cuidado de; **to take ~ of** *vt* cuidar; (*details, arrangements*) encargarse de; **I don't ~** no me importa; **I couldn't ~ less** me trae sin cuidado.
►**care for** *vt fus* cuidar; (*like*) querer.
careen [kə'riːn] *vi* (*ship*) inclinarse, escorar ♦ *vt* carenar.
career [kə'rɪə*] *n* carrera (profesional); (*occupation*) profesión *f* ♦ *vi* (*also*: **~ along**) correr a toda velocidad.
career girl *n* mujer *f* dedicada a su profesión.
careers officer *n* consejero/a de orientación profesional.
carefree ['kɛəfriː] *adj* despreocupado.
careful ['kɛəful] *adj* cuidadoso; (*cautious*) cauteloso; **(be) ~!** ¡ten cuidado!; **he's very ~ with his money** mira mucho el dinero; (*pej*) es muy tacaño.
carefully ['kɛəfəlɪ] *adv* con cuidado, cuidadosamente.
careless ['kɛəlɪs] *adj* descuidado; (*heedless*) poco atento.
carelessly ['kɛəlɪslɪ] *adv* sin cuidado, a la ligera.
carelessness ['kɛəlɪsnɪs] *n* descuido, falta de atención.
carer ['kɛərə*] *n persona que cuida de enfermos, ancianos o disminuidos.*
caress [kə'rɛs] *n* caricia ♦ *vt* acariciar.
caretaker ['kɛəteɪkə*] *n* portero/a, conserje *m/f*.
caretaker government *n* gobierno provisional.
car-ferry ['kɑːfɛrɪ] *n* transbordador *m* para coches.
cargo, *pl* **~es** ['kɑːgəu] *n* cargamento, carga.
cargo boat *n* buque *m* de carga, carguero.
cargo plane *n* avión *m* de carga.
car hire *n* alquiler *m* de coches.
Caribbean [kærɪ'biːən] *adj* caribe, caribeño; **the ~ (Sea)** el (Mar) Caribe.
caricature ['kærɪkətjuə*] *n* caricatura.
caring ['kɛərɪŋ] *adj* humanitario.
carnage ['kɑːnɪdʒ] *n* matanza, carnicería.
carnal ['kɑːnl] *adj* carnal.
carnation [kɑː'neɪʃən] *n* clavel *m*.
carnival ['kɑːnɪvəl] *n* carnaval *m*; (*US*) parque *m* de atracciones.
carnivore ['kɑːnɪvɔː*] *n* carnívoro/a.
carnivorous [kɑː'nɪvrəs] *adj* carnívoro.
carol ['kærəl] *n*: **(Christmas) ~** villancico.
carouse [kə'rauz] *vi* estar de juerga.
carousel [kærə'sɛl] *n* (*US*) tiovivo, caballitos *mpl*.
carp [kɑːp] *n* (*fish*) carpa.
►**carp at** *or* **about** *vt fus* sacar faltas de.
car park *n* (*BRIT*) aparcamiento, parking *m*, playa de estacionamiento (*LAM*).
carpenter ['kɑːpɪntə*] *n* carpintero.
carpentry ['kɑːpɪntrɪ] *n* carpintería.
carpet ['kɑːpɪt] *n* alfombra ♦ *vt* alfombrar; **fitted ~** moqueta.
carpet bombing *n* bombardeo de arrasamiento.
carpet slippers *npl* zapatillas *fpl*.
carpet sweeper [-'swiːpə*] *n* cepillo mecánico.
car phone *n* teléfono de coche.
carping ['kɑːpɪŋ] *adj* (*critical*) criticón/ona.
carriage ['kærɪdʒ] *n* coche *m*; (*BRIT RAIL*) vagón *m*; (*for goods*) transporte *m*; (*of typewriter*) carro; (*bearing*) porte *m*; **~ forward** porte *m* debido; **~ free** franco de porte; **~ paid** porte pagado; **~ inwards/ outwards** gastos *mpl* de transporte a cargo del comprador/vendedor.
carriage return *n* (*on typewriter etc*) tecla de regreso.
carriageway ['kærɪdʒweɪ] *n* (*BRIT*: *part of road*) calzada; **dual ~** autovía.
carrier ['kærɪə*] *n* transportista *m/f*; (*company*) empresa de transportes; (*MED*) portador(a) *m/f*.
carrier bag *n* (*BRIT*) bolsa de papel *or*

plástico.
carrier pigeon *n* paloma mensajera.
carrion ['kærıən] *n* carroña.
carrot ['kærət] *n* zanahoria.
carry ['kærı] *vt* (*subj*: *person*) llevar; (*transport*) transportar; (*a motion, bill*) aprobar; (*involve*: *responsibilities etc*) entrañar, conllevar; (*COMM*: *stock*) tener en existencia; (: *interest*) llevar; (*MATH*: *figure*) llevarse ♦ *vi* (*sound*) oírse; **to get carried away** (*fig*) entusiasmarse; **this loan carries 10% interest** este empréstito devenga un interés del 10 por ciento.
►**carry forward** *vt* (*MATH, COMM*) pasar a la página/columna siguiente.
►**carry on** *vi* (*continue*) seguir (adelante), continuar; (*fam*: *complain*) montar el número ♦ *vt* seguir, continuar.
►**carry out** *vt* (*orders*) cumplir; (*investigation*) llevar a cabo, realizar.
carrycot ['kærıkɔt] *n* (*BRIT*) cuna portátil, capazo.
carry-on ['kærı'ɔn] *n* (*col*) follón *m*.
cart [kɑːt] *n* carro, carreta ♦ *vt* cargar con.
carte blanche ['kɑːt'blɔnʃ] *n*: **to give sb ~** dar carta blanca a algn.
cartel [kɑː'tɛl] *n* (*COMM*) cartel *m*.
cartilage ['kɑːtılıdʒ] *n* cartílago.
cartographer [kɑː'tɔgrəfə*] *n* cartógrafo/a.
carton ['kɑːtən] *n* caja (de cartón); (*of cigarettes*) cartón *m*.
cartoon [kɑː'tuːn] *n* (*PRESS*) chiste *m*; (*comic strip*) historieta, tira cómica; (*film*) dibujos *mpl* animados.
cartoonist [kɑː'tuːnıst] *n* humorista *m/f* gráfico.
cartridge ['kɑːtrıdʒ] *n* cartucho.
cartwheel ['kɑːtwiːl] *n*: **to turn a ~** dar una voltereta lateral.
carve [kɑːv] *vt* (*meat*) trinchar; (*wood*) tallar; (*stone*) cincelar, esculpir; (*on tree*) grabar.
►**carve up** *vt* dividir, repartir; (*meat*) trinchar.
carving ['kɑːvıŋ] *n* (*in wood etc*) escultura, talla.
carving knife *n* trinchante *m*.
car wash *n* túnel *m* de lavado.
Casablanca [kæsə'blæŋkə] *n* Casablanca.
cascade [kæs'keıd] *n* salto de agua, cascada; (*fig*) chorro ♦ *vi* caer a chorros.
case [keıs] *n* (*container*) caja; (*MED*) caso; (*for jewels etc*) estuche *m*; (*LAW*) causa, proceso; (*BRIT*: *also*: **suit~**) maleta; **lower/upper ~** (*TYP*) caja baja/alta; **in ~ of** en caso de; **in any ~** en todo caso; **just in ~** por si acaso; **to have a good ~** tener buenas razones; **there's a strong ~ for reform** hay razones sólidas para exigir una reforma.
case history *n* (*MED*) historial *m* médico, historia clínica.
case study *n* estudio de casos prácticos.
cash [kæʃ] *n* (dinero) efectivo; (*col*: *money*) dinero ♦ *vt* cobrar, hacer efectivo; **to pay (in) ~** pagar al contado; **~ on delivery (COD)** entrega contra reembolso; **~ with order** paga al hacer el pedido; **to be short of ~** estar pelado, estar sin blanca.
►**cash in** *vt* (*insurance policy etc*) cobrar ♦ *vi*: **to ~ in on sth** sacar partido *or* aprovecharse de algo.
cash account *n* cuenta de caja.
cash and carry *n* cash and carry *m*, autoservicio mayorista.
cashbook ['kæʃbuk] *n* libro de caja.
cash box *n* hucha.
cash card *n* tarjeta *f* de(l) cajero (automático).
cash desk *n* (*BRIT*) caja.
cash discount *n* descuento por pago al contado.
cash dispenser *n* cajero automático.
cashew [kæ'ʃuː] *n* (*also*: **~ nut**) anacardo.
cash flow *n* flujo de fondos, cash-flow *m*, movimiento de efectivo.
cashier [kæ'ʃıə*] *n* cajero/a ♦ *vt* (*MIL*) destituir, expulsar.
cashmere ['kæʃmıə*] *n* cachemir *m*, cachemira.
cash payment *n* pago al contado.
cash price *n* precio al contado.
cash register *n* caja.
cash reserves *npl* reserva en efectivo.
cash sale *n* venta al contado.
casing ['keısıŋ] *n* revestimiento.
casino [kə'siːnəu] *n* casino.
cask [kɑːsk] *n* tonel *m*, barril *m*.
casket ['kɑːskıt] *n* cofre *m*, estuche *m*; (*US*: *coffin*) ataúd *m*.
Caspian Sea ['kæspıən-] *n*: **the ~** el Mar Caspio.
cassava [kə'sɑːvə] *n* mandioca.
casserole ['kæsərəul] *n* (*food, pot*) cazuela.
cassette [kæ'sɛt] *n* cas(s)et(t)e *m or f*.
cassette deck *n* platina.
cassette player, cassette recorder *n* cas(s)et(t)e *m*.
cassock ['kæsək] *n* sotana.
cast [kɑːst] *vb* (*pt, pp* **cast**) *vt* (*throw*) echar, arrojar, lanzar; (*skin*) mudar, perder; (*metal*) fundir; (*THEAT*): **to ~ sb as Othello** dar a algn el papel de Otelo ♦ *n* (*THEAT*) reparto; (*mould*) forma, molde *m*; (*also*: **plaster ~**) vaciado; **to ~ loose** soltar; **to ~ one's vote** votar.

►**cast aside** *vt* (*reject*) descartar, desechar.
►**cast away** *vt* desechar.
►**cast down** *vt* derribar.
►**cast off** *vi* (*NAUT*) soltar amarras; (*KNITTING*) cerrar los puntos ♦ *vt* (*KNITTING*) cerrar; **to ~ sb off** abandonar a algn, desentenderse de algn.
►**cast on** *vt* (*KNITTING*) montar.
castanets [kæstə'nɛts] *npl* castañuelas *fpl*.
castaway ['kɑːstəwəɪ] *n* náufrago/a.
caste [kɑːst] *n* casta.
caster sugar ['kɑːstə*-] *n* (*BRIT*) azúcar *m* en polvo.
Castile [kæs'tiːl] *n* Castilla.
Castilian [kæs'tɪlɪən] *adj, n* castellano/a ♦ *n* (*LING*) castellano.
casting vote ['kɑːstɪŋ-] *n* (*BRIT*) voto decisivo.
cast iron *n* hierro fundido *or* colado ♦ *adj* (*fig*: *alibi*) irrebatible; (*will*) férreo.
castle ['kɑːsl] *n* castillo; (*CHESS*) torre *f*.
castor ['kɑːstə*] *n* (*wheel*) ruedecilla.
castor oil *n* aceite *m* de ricino.
castrate [kæs'treɪt] *vt* castrar.
casual ['kæʒjul] *adj* (*by chance*) fortuito; (*irregular*: *work etc*) eventual, temporero; (*unconcerned*) despreocupado; (*informal*: *clothes*) de sport.
casually ['kæʒjulɪ] *adv* por casualidad; de manera despreocupada.
casualty ['kæʒjultɪ] *n* víctima, herido; (*dead*) muerto; (*MIL*) baja; **heavy casualties** numerosas bajas *fpl*.
casualty ward *n* urgencias *fpl*.
cat [kæt] *n* gato.
catacombs ['kætəkuːmz] *npl* catacumbas *fpl*.
Catalan ['kætəlæn] *adj, n* catalán/ana *m/f*.
catalogue, (*US*) **catalog** ['kætəlɔg] *n* catálogo ♦ *vt* catalogar.
Catalonia [kætə'ləunɪə] *n* Cataluña.
catalyst ['kætəlɪst] *n* catalizador *m*.
catalytic converter [kætə'lɪtɪkkən'vəːtə*] *n* catalizador *m*.
catapult ['kætəpʌlt] *n* tirachinas *m inv*.
cataract ['kætərækt] *n* (*MED*) cataratas *fpl*.
catarrh [kə'tɑː*] *n* catarro.
catastrophe [kə'tæstrəfɪ] *n* catástrofe *f*.
catastrophic [kætə'strɔfɪk] *adj* catastrófico.
catcall ['kætkɔːl] *n* (*at meeting etc*) rechifla, silbido.
catch [kætʃ] *vb* (*pt, pp* **caught** [kɔːt]) *vt* coger (*SP*), agarrar (*LAM*); (*arrest*) atrapar, coger (*SP*); (*grasp*) asir; (*breath*) recobrar; (*person*: *by surprise*) pillar; (*attract*: *attention*) captar; (*MED*) pillar, coger; (*also*: **~ up**) alcanzar ♦ *vi* (*fire*) encenderse; (*in branches etc*) engancharse ♦ *n* (*fish etc*) captura; (*act of catching*) cogida; (*trick*) trampa; (*of lock*) pestillo, cerradura; **to ~ fire** prenderse; (*house*) incendiarse; **to ~ sight of** divisar.
►**catch on** *vi* (*understand*) caer en la cuenta; (*grow popular*) tener éxito, cuajar.
►**catch out** *vt* (*fig*: *with trick question*) hundir.
►**catch up** *vi* (*fig*) ponerse al día.
catching ['kætʃɪŋ] *adj* (*MED*) contagioso.
catchment area ['kætʃmənt-] *n* (*BRIT*) zona de captación.
catch phrase *n* frase *f* de moda.
catch-22 ['kætʃtwɛntɪ'tuː] *n*: **it's a ~ situation** es un callejón sin salida, es un círculo vicioso.
catchy ['kætʃɪ] *adj* (*tune*) pegadizo.
catechism ['kætɪkɪzəm] *n* (*REL*) catecismo.
categoric(al) [kætɪ'gɔrɪk(əl)] *adj* categórico, terminante.
categorically [kætɪ'gɔrɪkəlɪ] *adv* categóricamente, terminantemente.
categorize ['kætɪgəraɪz] *vt* clasificar.
category ['kætɪgərɪ] *n* categoría.
cater ['keɪtə*] *vi*: **to ~ for** (*BRIT*) abastecer a; (*needs*) atender a; (*consumers*) proveer a.
caterer ['keɪtərə*] *n* abastecedor(a) *m/f*, proveedor(a) *m/f*.
catering ['keɪtərɪŋ] *n* (*trade*) hostelería.
caterpillar ['kætəpɪlə*] *n* oruga.
caterpillar track *n* rodado de oruga.
cat flap *n* gatera.
cathedral [kə'θiːdrəl] *n* catedral *f*.
cathode-ray tube ['kæθəudreɪ'tjuːb] *n* tubo de rayos catódicos.
catholic ['kæθəlɪk] *adj* católico; **C~** *adj, n* (*REL*) católico/a *m/f*.
CAT scanner [kæt-] (*MED*) *n abbr* (= *computerized axial tomography scanner*) escáner *m* TAC.
cat's-eye ['kætsaɪ] *n* (*BRIT AUT*) catafaro.
catsup ['kætsəp] *n* (*US*) ketchup, catsup *m*.
cattle ['kætl] *npl* ganado *sg*.
catty ['kætɪ] *adj* malicioso.
catwalk ['kætwɔːk] *n* pasarela.
Caucasian [kɔː'keɪzɪən] *adj, n* caucásico/a *m/f*.
Caucasus ['kɔːkəsəs] *n* Cáucaso.
caucus ['kɔːkəs] *n* (*POL*: *local committee*) comité *m* local; (: *US*: *to elect candidates*) comité *m* electoral; (: *group*) camarilla política.
caught [kɔːt] *pt, pp of* **catch**.
cauliflower ['kɔlɪflauə*] *n* coliflor *f*.
cause [kɔːz] *n* causa; (*reason*) motivo,

razón *f* ♦ *vt* causar; (*provoke*) provocar; **to ~ sb to do sth** hacer que algn haga algo.
causeway ['kɔːzweɪ] *n* (*road*) carretera elevada; (*embankment*) terraplén *m*.
caustic ['kɔːstɪk] *adj* cáustico; (*fig*) mordaz.
cauterize ['kɔːtəraɪz] *vt* cauterizar.
caution ['kɔːʃən] *n* cautela, prudencia; (*warning*) advertencia, amonestación *f* ♦ *vt* amonestar.
cautious ['kɔːʃəs] *adj* cauteloso, prudente, precavido.
cautiously ['kɔːʃəslɪ] *adv* con cautela.
cautiousness ['kɔːʃəsnɪs] *n* cautela.
cavalcade [kævəl'keɪd] *n* cabalgata.
cavalier [kævə'lɪə*] *n* (*knight*) caballero ♦ *adj* (*pej*: *offhand*: *person, attitude*) arrogante, desdeñoso.
cavalry ['kævəlrɪ] *n* caballería.
cave [keɪv] *n* cueva, caverna ♦ *vi*: **to go caving** ir en una expedición espeleológica.
▶**cave in** *vi* (*roof etc*) derrumbarse, hundirse.
caveman ['keɪvmæn] *n* cavernícola *m*.
cavern ['kævən] *n* caverna.
cavernous ['kævənəs] *adj* (*cheeks, eyes*) hundido.
caviar(e) ['kævɪɑː*] *n* caviar *m*.
cavity ['kævɪtɪ] *n* hueco, cavidad *f*.
cavity wall insulation *n* aislamiento térmico.
cavort [kə'vɔːt] *vi* hacer cabrioladas.
cayenne [keɪ'ɛn] *n*: **~ pepper** pimentón *m* picante.
CB *n abbr* (= *Citizens' Band (Radio)*) *frecuencias de radio usadas para la comunicación privada*; (*BRIT*: = *Companion of (the Order of) the Bath*) *título de nobleza*.
CBC *n abbr* (= *Canadian Broadcasting Corporation*) *cadena de radio y televisión*.
CBE *n abbr* (= *Companion of (the Order of) the British Empire*) *título de nobleza*.
CBI *n abbr* (= *Confederation of British Industry*) ≈ C.E.O.E. *f* (*SP*).
CBS *n abbr* (*US*: = *Columbia Broadcasting System*) *cadena de radio y televisión*.
CC *abbr* (*BRIT*) = *County Council*.
cc *abbr* (= *cubic centimetres*) cc, cm^3; (*on letter etc*) = **carbon copy**.
CCA *n abbr* (*US*: = *Circuit Court of Appeals*) *tribunal de apelación itinerante*.
CCTV *n abbr* = **closed-circuit television**.
CCU *n abbr* (*US*: = *coronary care unit*) unidad *f* de cuidados cardiológicos.
CD *n abbr* (= *compact disc*) CD *m*; **~ player** reproductor *m* de compact disc; (*MIL*) = *Civil Defence (Corps)* (*BRIT*), *Civil Defense* (*US*) ♦ *abbr* (*BRIT*: = *Corps Diplomatique*) CD.
CDC *n abbr* (*US*) = *center for disease control*.
CD-I ® *n* (= *Compact Disc Interactive*) CD-I *m*, disco *m* compacto interactivo.
Cdr. *abbr* = **Commander**.
CD-ROM *n abbr* (= *compact disc read-only memory*) CD-ROM *m*.
CDT *n abbr* (*US*: = *Central Daylight Time*) *hora de verano del centro*.
cease [siːs] *vt* cesar.
ceasefire ['siːsfaɪə*] *n* alto *m* el fuego.
ceaseless ['siːslɪs] *adj* incesante.
ceaselessly ['siːslɪslɪ] *adv* sin cesar.
CED *n abbr* (*US*) = *Committee for Economic Development*.
cedar ['siːdə*] *n* cedro.
cede [siːd] *vt* ceder.
CEEB *n abbr* (*US*: = *College Entrance Examination Board*) *tribunal para las pruebas de acceso a la universidad*.
ceilidh ['keɪlɪ] *n baile con música y danzas tradicionales escocesas o irlandesas*.
ceiling ['siːlɪŋ] *n* techo; (*fig*: *upper limit*) límite *m*, tope *m*.
celebrate ['sɛlɪbreɪt] *vt* celebrar; (*have a party*) festejar ♦ *vi*: **let's ~!** ¡vamos a celebrarlo!
celebrated ['sɛlɪbreɪtɪd] *adj* célebre.
celebration [sɛlɪ'breɪʃən] *n* celebración *f*.
celebrity [sɪ'lɛbrɪtɪ] *n* celebridad *f*.
celeriac [sə'lɛrɪæk] *n* apio-nabo.
celery ['sɛlərɪ] *n* apio.
celestial [sɪ'lɛstɪəl] *adj* (*of sky*) celeste; (*divine*) celestial.
celibacy ['sɛlɪbəsɪ] *n* celibato.
cell [sɛl] *n* celda; (*BIOL*) célula; (*ELEC*) elemento.
cellar ['sɛlə*] *n* sótano; (*for wine*) bodega.
cellist ['tʃɛlɪst] *n* violoncelista *m/f*.
cello ['tʃɛləu] *n* violoncelo.
cellophane ['sɛləfeɪn] *n* celofán *m*.
cellphone ['sɛlfəun] *n* teléfono celular.
cellular ['sɛljulə*] *adj* celular.
celluloid ['sɛljulɔɪd] *n* celuloide *m*.
cellulose ['sɛljuləus] *n* celulosa.
Celsius ['sɛlsɪəs] *adj* centígrado.
Celt [kɛlt, sɛlt] *n* celta *m/f*.
Celtic ['kɛltɪk, 'sɛltɪk] *adj* celta, céltico ♦ *n* (*LING*) celta *m*.
cement [sə'mɛnt] *n* cemento ♦ *vt* cementar; (*fig*) cimentar.
cement mixer *n* hormigonera.
cemetery ['sɛmɪtrɪ] *n* cementerio.
cenotaph ['sɛnətɑːf] *n* cenotafio.
censor ['sɛnsə*] *n* censor(a) *m/f* ♦ *vt* (*cut*) censurar.
censorship ['sɛnsəʃɪp] *n* censura.

censure ['sɛnʃə*] *vt* censurar.
census ['sɛnsəs] *n* censo.
cent [sɛnt] *n* (*unit of dollar*) centavo; (*unit of euro*) céntimo; *see also* **per**.
centenary [sɛn'tiːnəri], (*US*) **centennial** [sɛn'tɛnɪəl] *n* centenario.
center ['sɛntə*] *n* (*US*) = **centre**.
centigrade ['sɛntɪgreɪd] *adj* centígrado.
centilitre, (*US*) **centiliter** ['sɛntɪliːtə*] *n* centilitro.
centimetre, (*US*) **centimeter** ['sɛntɪmiːtə*] *n* centímetro.
centipede ['sɛntɪpiːd] *n* ciempiés *m inv*.
central ['sɛntrəl] *adj* central; (*of house etc*) céntrico.
Central African Republic *n* República Centroafricana.
Central America *n* Centroamérica.
Central American *adj, n* centroamericano/a *m/f*.
central heating *n* calefacción *f* central.
centralize ['sɛntrəlaɪz] *vt* centralizar.
central processing unit (CPU) *n* (*COMPUT*) unidad *f* procesadora central, unidad *f* central de proceso.
central reservation *n* (*BRIT AUT*) mediana.
centre, (*US*) **center** ['sɛntə*] *n* centro ♦ *vt* centrar; **to ~ (on)** (*concentrate*) concentrar (en).
centrefold, (*US*) **centerfold** ['sɛntəfəuld] *n* página central plegable.
centre-forward ['sɛntə'fɔːwəd] *n* (*SPORT*) delantero centro.
centre-half ['sɛntə'hɑːf] *n* (*SPORT*) medio centro.
centrepiece, (*US*) **centerpiece** ['sɛntəpiːs] *n* punto central.
centre spread *n* (*BRIT*) páginas *fpl* centrales.
centre-stage *n*: **to take ~** pasar a primer plano.
centrifuge ['sɛntrɪfjuːdʒ] *n* centrifugadora.
century ['sɛntjurɪ] *n* siglo; **in the twentieth ~** en el siglo veinte.
CEO *n abbr* (*US*) = **chief executive officer**.
ceramic [sɪ'ræmɪk] *adj* de cerámica.
ceramics [sɪ'ræmɪks] *n* cerámica.
cereal ['siːrɪəl] *n* cereal *m*.
cerebral ['sɛrɪbrəl] *adj* cerebral.
ceremonial [sɛrɪ'məunɪəl] *n* ceremonial.
ceremony ['sɛrɪmənɪ] *n* ceremonia; **to stand on ~** hacer ceremonias, andarse con cumplidos.
cert [səːt] *n* (*BRIT col*): **it's a dead ~** ¡es cosa segura!
certain ['səːtən] *adj* seguro; (*correct*) cierto; (*particular*) cierto; **for ~** a ciencia cierta.
certainly ['səːtənlɪ] *adv* desde luego, por supuesto.
certainty ['səːtəntɪ] *n* certeza, certidumbre *f*, seguridad *f*.
certificate [sə'tɪfɪkɪt] *n* certificado.
certified ['səːtɪfaɪd] *adj*: **~ mail** (*US*) correo certificado.
certified public accountant (CPA) *n* (*US*) contable *m/f* diplomado/a.
certify ['səːtɪfaɪ] *vt* certificar.
cervical ['səːvɪkl] *adj*: **~ cancer** cáncer *m* cervical; **~ smear** citología.
cervix ['səːvɪks] *n* cerviz *f*, cuello del útero.
Cesarean [sɪ'zɛərɪən] *adj, n* (*US*) = **Caesarean**.
cessation [sə'seɪʃən] *n* cese *m*, suspensión *f*.
cesspit ['sɛspɪt] *n* pozo negro.
CET *n abbr* (= *Central European Time*) *hora de Europa central*.
Ceylon [sɪ'lɔn] *n* Ceilán *m*.
cf. *abbr* (= *compare*) cfr.
CFC *n abbr* (= *chlorofluorocarbon*) CFC *m*.
c/f *abbr* (*COMM*) = *carried forward*.
CG *n abbr* (*US*) = **coastguard**.
cg *abbr* (= *centigram*) cg.
CH *n abbr* (*BRIT*: = *Companion of Honour*) *título de nobleza*.
ch *abbr* (*BRIT*: = *central heating*) cal. cen.
ch. *abbr* (= *chapter*) cap.
Chad [tʃæd] *n* Chad *m*.
chafe [tʃeɪf] *vt* (*rub*) rozar; (*irritate*) irritar; **to ~ (against)** (*fig*) irritarse *or* enojarse (con).
chaffinch ['tʃæfɪntʃ] *n* pinzón *m* (vulgar).
chagrin ['ʃægrɪn] *n* (*annoyance*) disgusto; (*disappointment*) desazón *f*.
chain [tʃeɪn] *n* cadena ♦ *vt* (*also*: **~ up**) encadenar.
chain reaction *n* reacción *f* en cadena.
chain-smoke ['tʃeɪnsməuk] *vi* fumar un cigarrillo tras otro.
chain store *n* tienda de una cadena, ≈ grandes almacenes *mpl*.
chair [tʃɛə*] *n* silla; (*armchair*) sillón *m*; (*of university*) cátedra ♦ *vt* (*meeting*) presidir; **the ~** (*US*: *electric* ~) la silla eléctrica; **please take a ~** siéntese *or* tome asiento, por favor.
chairlift ['tʃɛəlɪft] *n* telesilla *m*.
chairman ['tʃɛəmən] *n* presidente *m*.
chairperson ['tʃɛəpəːsn] *n* presidente/a *m/f*.
chairwoman ['tʃɛəwumən] *n* presidenta.
chalet ['ʃæleɪ] *n* chalet *m* (de madera).
chalice ['tʃælɪs] *n* cáliz *m*.
chalk [tʃɔːk] *n* (*GEO*) creta; (*for writing*) tiza, gis *m* (*LAM*).
►**chalk up** *vt* apuntar; (*fig*: *success, victory*) apuntarse.
challenge ['tʃælɪndʒ] *n* desafío, reto ♦ *vt*

desafiar, retar; (*statement, right*) poner en duda; **to ~ sb to do sth** retar a algn a que haga algo.
challenger ['tʃælɪndʒə*] *n* (*SPORT*) contrincante *m/f*.
challenging ['tʃælɪndʒɪŋ] *adj* que supone un reto; (*tone*) de desafío.
chamber ['tʃeɪmbə*] *n* cámara, sala; **~ of commerce** cámara de comercio.
chambermaid ['tʃeɪmbəmeɪd] *n* camarera.
chamber music *n* música de cámara.
chamberpot ['tʃeɪmbəpɔt] *n* orinal *m*.
chameleon [kə'miːlɪən] *n* camaleón *m*.
chamois ['ʃæmwɑː] *n* gamuza.
champagne [ʃæm'peɪn] *n* champaña *m*, champán *m*.
champers ['ʃæmpəz] *nsg* (*col*) champán *m*.
champion ['tʃæmpɪən] *n* campeón/ona *m/f*; (*of cause*) defensor(a) *m/f*, paladín *m/f* ♦ *vt* defender, apoyar.
championship ['tʃæmpɪənʃɪp] *n* campeonato.
chance [tʃɑːns] *n* (*coincidence*) casualidad *f*; (*luck*) suerte *f*; (*fate*) azar *m*; (*opportunity*) ocasión *f*, oportunidad *f*, chance *m or f* (*LAM*); (*likelihood*) posibilidad *f*; (*risk*) riesgo ♦ *vt* arriesgar, probar ♦ *adj* fortuito, casual; **to ~ it** arriesgarse, intentarlo; **to take a ~** arriesgarse; **by ~** por casualidad; **it's the ~ of a lifetime** es la oportunidad de su vida; **the ~s are that** ... lo más probable es que ...; **to ~ to do sth** (*happen*) hacer algo por casualidad.
▶**chance (up)on** *vt fus* tropezar(se) con.
chancel ['tʃɑːnsəl] *n* coro y presbiterio.
chancellor ['tʃɑːnsələ*] *n* canciller *m*; **C~ of the Exchequer** (*BRIT*) Ministro de Economía y Hacienda; *see also* **Downing Street**.
chancy ['tʃɑːnsɪ] *adj* (*col*) arriesgado.
chandelier [ʃændə'lɪə*] *n* araña (de luces).
change [tʃeɪndʒ] *vt* cambiar; (*clothes, house*) cambiarse de, mudarse de; (*transform*) transformar ♦ *vi* cambiar(se); (*trains*) hacer transbordo; (*be transformed*): **to ~ into** transformarse en ♦ *n* cambio; (*alteration*) modificación *f*, transformación *f*; (*coins*) suelto; (*money returned*) vuelta, vuelto (*LAM*); **to ~ one's mind** cambiar de opinión *or* idea; **to ~ gear** (*AUT*) cambiar de marcha; **she ~d into an old skirt** se puso una falda vieja; **for a ~** para variar; **can you give me ~ for £1?** ¿tiene cambio de una libra?; **keep the ~** quédese con la vuelta.
changeable ['tʃeɪndʒəbl] *adj* (*weather*) cambiable; (*person*) variable.
changeless ['tʃeɪndʒlɪs] *adj* inmutable.
change machine *n* máquina de cambio.
changeover ['tʃeɪndʒəuvə*] *n* (*to new system*) cambio.
changing ['tʃeɪndʒɪŋ] *adj* cambiante.
changing room *n* (*BRIT*) vestuario.
channel ['tʃænl] *n* (*TV*) canal *m*; (*of river*) cauce *m*; (*of sea*) estrecho; (*groove, fig: medium*) conducto, medio ♦ *vt* (*river etc*) encauzar; **to ~ into** (*fig: interest, energies*) encauzar a, dirigir a; **the (English) C~** el Canal (de la Mancha); **the C~ Islands** las Islas Anglonormandas; **~s of communication** canales *mpl* de comunicación; **green/red ~** (*CUSTOMS*) pasillo verde/rojo.
Channel Tunnel *n*: **the ~** el túnel del Canal de la Mancha, el Eurotúnel.
chant [tʃɑːnt] *n* canto; (*of crowd*) gritos *mpl* ♦ *vt* cantar; **the demonstrators ~ed their disapproval** los manifestantes corearon su desaprobación.
chaos ['keɪɔs] *n* caos *m*.
chaos theory *n* teoría del caos.
chaotic [keɪ'ɔtɪk] *adj* caótico.
chap [tʃæp] *n* (*BRIT col: man*) tío, tipo; **old ~** amigo (mío).
chapel ['tʃæpəl] *n* capilla.
chaperone ['ʃæpərəun] *n* carabina.
chaplain ['tʃæplɪn] *n* capellán *m*.
chapped [tʃæpt] *adj* agrietado.
chapter ['tʃæptə*] *n* capítulo.
char [tʃɑː*] *vt* (*burn*) carbonizar, chamuscar ♦ *n* (*BRIT*) = **charlady**.
character ['kærɪktə*] *n* carácter *m*, naturaleza, índole *f*; (*in novel, film*) personaje *m*; (*role*) papel *m*; (*individuality, COMPUT*) carácter *m*; **a person of good ~** una persona de buena reputación.
character code *n* código de caracteres.
characteristic [kærɪktə'rɪstɪk] *adj* característico ♦ *n* característica.
characterize ['kærɪktəraɪz] *vt* caracterizar.
charade [ʃə'rɑːd] *n* farsa, comedia; **~s** (*game*) charadas *fpl*.
charcoal ['tʃɑːkəul] *n* carbón *m* vegetal; (*ART*) carboncillo.
charge [tʃɑːdʒ] *n* carga; (*LAW*) cargo, acusación *f*; (*cost*) precio, coste *m*; (*responsibility*) cargo; (*task*) encargo ♦ *vt* (*LAW*) acusar (*with* de); (*gun, battery, MIL: enemy*) cargar; (*price*) pedir; (*customer*) cobrar; (*sb with task*) encargar ♦ *vi* precipitarse; (*make pay*) cobrar; **~s** *npl*: **bank ~s** comisiones *fpl* bancarias; **extra ~** recargo, suplemento; **free of ~** gratis; **to reverse the ~s** (*BRIT TEL*) llamar a cobro revertido; **to take ~ of** hacerse cargo de, encargarse de; **to be in ~ of** estar

encargado de; **how much do you ~?** ¿cuánto cobra usted?; **to ~ an expense (up) to sb's account** cargar algo a cuenta de algn; **~ it to my account** póngalo *or* cárguelo a mi cuenta.
charge account *n* (*US*) cuenta abierta *or* a crédito.
charge card *n* tarjeta de cuenta.
chargé d'affaires ['ʃɑːʒeɪdæ'fɛə*] *n* encargado de negocios.
chargehand ['tʃɑːdʒhænd] *n* capataz *m*.
charger ['tʃɑːdʒə*] *n* (*also*: **battery ~**) cargador *m* (de baterías); (*old*: *warhorse*) caballo de batalla.
chariot ['tʃærɪət] *n* carro.
charisma [kæ'rɪzmə] *n* carisma *m*.
charitable ['tʃærɪtəbl] *adj* caritativo.
charity ['tʃærɪtɪ] *n* (*gen*) caridad *f*; (*organization*) organización *f* benéfica.
charlady ['tʃɑːleɪdɪ] *n* (*BRIT*) mujer *f* de la limpieza.
charlatan ['ʃɑːlətən] *n* charlatán *m*.
charm [tʃɑːm] *n* encanto, atractivo; (*spell*) hechizo; (*object*) amuleto ♦ *vt* encantar; hechizar.
charm bracelet *n* pulsera amuleto.
charming ['tʃɑːmɪŋ] *adj* encantador(a); (*person*) simpático.
chart [tʃɑːt] *n* (*table*) cuadro; (*graph*) gráfica; (*map*) carta de navegación; (*weather ~*) mapa *m* meteorológico ♦ *vt* (*course*) trazar; (*sales, progress*) hacer una gráfica de; **to be in the ~s** (*record, pop group*) estar en la lista de éxitos.
charter ['tʃɑːtə*] *vt* (*bus*) alquilar; (*plane, ship*) fletar ♦ *n* (*document*) estatuto, carta; **on ~** en alquiler, alquilado.
chartered accountant (CA) *n* (*BRIT*) contable *m/f* diplomado/a.
charter flight *n* vuelo chárter.
charwoman ['tʃɑːwumən] *n* = **charlady**.
chase [tʃeɪs] *vt* (*pursue*) perseguir; (*hunt*) cazar ♦ *n* persecución *f*; caza; **to ~ after** correr tras.
▸**chase up** *vt* (*information*) tratar de conseguir; **to ~ sb up about sth** recordar algo a algn.
chasm ['kæzəm] *n* abismo.
chassis ['ʃæsɪ] *n* chasis *m*.
chaste [tʃeɪst] *adj* casto.
chastened ['tʃeɪsənd] *adj* escarmentado.
chastening ['tʃeɪsnɪŋ] *adj* aleccionador(a).
chastity ['tʃæstɪtɪ] *n* castidad *f*.
chat [tʃæt] *vi* (*also*: **have a ~**) charlar ♦ *n* charla.
▸**chat up** *vt* (*col*: *girl*) ligar con, enrollarse con.
chatline ['tʃætlaɪn] *n* línea (telefónica) múltiple, party line *f*.
chat show *n* (*BRIT*) programa *m* de entrevistas.
chattel ['tʃætl] *n* bien *m* mueble.
chatter ['tʃætə*] *vi* (*person*) charlar; (*teeth*) castañetear ♦ *n* (*of birds*) parloteo; (*of people*) charla, cháchara.
chatterbox ['tʃætəbɔks] *n* parlanchín/ina *m/f*.
chattering classes ['tʃætərɪŋ'klɑːsɪz] *npl*: **the ~** (*col: pej*) los intelectualillos.
chatty ['tʃætɪ] *adj* (*style*) informal; (*person*) hablador(a).
chauffeur ['ʃəufə*] *n* chófer *m*.
chauvinist ['ʃəuvɪnɪst] *n* (*male ~*) machista *m*; (*nationalist*) chovinista *m/f*, patriotero/a *m/f*.
ChE *abbr* = *chemical engineer*.
cheap [tʃiːp] *adj* barato; (*joke*) de mal gusto, chabacano; (*poor quality*) malo; (*reduced*: *ticket*) económico, (: *fare*) barato ♦ *adv* barato.
cheapen ['tʃiːpn] *vt* rebajar el precio de, abaratar.
cheaply ['tʃiːplɪ] *adv* barato, a bajo precio.
cheat [tʃiːt] *vi* hacer trampa; (*in exam*) copiar ♦ *vt* estafar, timar ♦ *n* trampa; estafa; (*person*) tramposo/a; **he's been ~ing on his wife** ha estado engañando a su esposa.
cheating ['tʃiːtɪŋ] *n* trampa.
check [tʃɛk] *vt* comprobar; (*count*) contar; (*halt*) frenar; (*restrain*) refrenar, restringir ♦ *vi*: **to ~ with sb** consultar con algn; (*official etc*) informarse por ♦ *n* (*inspection*) control *m*, inspección *f*; (*curb*) freno; (*bill*) nota, cuenta; (*US*) = **cheque**; (*pattern*: *gen pl*) cuadro ♦ *adj* (*also*: **~ed**: *pattern, cloth*) a cuadros; **to keep a ~ on sth/sb** controlar algo/a algn.
▸**check in** *vi* (*in hotel*) registrarse; (*at airport*) facturar ♦ *vt* (*luggage*) facturar.
▸**check out** *vi* (*of hotel*) desocupar la habitación ♦ *vt* (*investigate*: *story*) comprobar; (: *person*) informarse sobre.
▸**check up** *vi*: **to ~ up on sth** comprobar algo; **to ~ up on sb** investigar a algn.
checkbook ['tʃɛkbuk] *n* (*US*) = **chequebook**.
checkered ['tʃɛkəd] *adj* (*US*) = **chequered**.
checkers ['tʃɛkəz] *n* (*US*) damas *fpl*.
check-in ['tʃɛkɪn] *n* (*also*: **~ desk**: *at airport*) mostrador *m* de facturación.
checking account ['tʃɛkɪŋ-] *n* (*US*) cuenta corriente.
checklist ['tʃɛklɪst] *n* lista.
checkmate ['tʃɛkmeɪt] *n* jaque *m* mate.
checkout ['tʃɛkaut] *n* (*in supermarket*) caja.

checkpoint ['tʃɛkpɔɪnt] *n* (punto de) control *m*, retén *m* (*LAM*).
checkroom ['tʃɛkrum] *n* (*US*) consigna.
checkup ['tʃɛkʌp] *n* (*MED*) reconocimiento general; (*of machine*) revisión *f*.
cheek [tʃiːk] *n* mejilla; (*impudence*) descaro.
cheekbone ['tʃiːkbəun] *n* pómulo.
cheeky ['tʃiːkɪ] *adj* fresco, descarado.
cheep [tʃiːp] *n* (*of bird*) pío ♦ *vi* piar.
cheer [tʃɪə*] *vt* vitorear, ovacionar; (*gladden*) alegrar, animar ♦ *vi* dar vivas ♦ *n* viva *m*; **~s** *npl* vítores *mpl*; **~s!** ¡salud!
►**cheer on** *vt* (*person etc*) animar con aplausos *or* gritos.
►**cheer up** *vi* animarse ♦ *vt* alegrar, animar.
cheerful ['tʃɪəful] *adj* alegre.
cheerfulness ['tʃɪəfulnɪs] *n* alegría.
cheering ['tʃɪərɪŋ] *n* ovaciones *fpl*, vítores *mpl*.
cheerio [tʃɪərɪ'əu] *excl* (*BRIT*) ¡hasta luego!
cheerleader ['tʃɪəliːdə*] *n* animador(a) *m/f*.
cheerless ['tʃɪəlɪs] *adj* triste, sombrío.
cheese [tʃiːz] *n* queso.
cheeseboard ['tʃiːzbɔːd] *n* tabla de quesos.
cheeseburger ['tʃiːzbəːgə*] *n* hamburguesa con queso.
cheesecake ['tʃiːzkeɪk] *n* pastel *m* de queso.
cheetah ['tʃiːtə] *n* guepardo.
chef [ʃɛf] *n* jefe/a *m/f* de cocina.
chemical ['kɛmɪkəl] *adj* químico ♦ *n* producto químico.
chemist ['kɛmɪst] *n* (*BRIT*: *pharmacist*) farmacéutico/a; (*scientist*) químico/a; **~'s (shop)** *n* (*BRIT*) farmacia.
chemistry ['kɛmɪstrɪ] *n* química.
chemotherapy [kiːməu'θɛrəpɪ] *n* quimioterapia.
cheque, (*US*) **check** [tʃɛk] *n* (*BRIT*) cheque *m*; **to pay by ~** pagar con cheque.
chequebook, (*US*) **checkbook** ['tʃɛkbuk] *n* talonario (de cheques), chequera (*LAM*).
cheque card *n* (*BRIT*) tarjeta de identificación bancaria.
chequered, (*US*) **checkered** ['tʃɛkəd] *adj* (*fig*) accidentado; (*pattern*) de cuadros.
cherish ['tʃɛrɪʃ] *vt* (*love*) querer, apreciar; (*protect*) cuidar; (*hope etc*) abrigar.
cheroot [ʃə'ruːt] *n* puro (*cortado en los dos extremos*).
cherry ['tʃɛrɪ] *n* cereza.
Ches *abbr* (*BRIT*) = *Cheshire*.
chess [tʃɛs] *n* ajedrez *m*.
chessboard ['tʃɛsbɔːd] *n* tablero (de ajedrez).
chessman ['tʃɛsmən] *n* pieza (de ajedrez).
chest [tʃɛst] *n* (*ANAT*) pecho; (*box*) cofre *m*; **to get sth off one's ~** (*col*) desahogarse; **~ of drawers** *n* cómoda.
chest measurement *n* talla (*de chaqueta etc*).
chestnut ['tʃɛsnʌt] *n* castaña; (*also*: **~ tree**) castaño; (*colour*) castaño ♦ *adj* (color) castaño *inv*.
chesty ['tʃɛstɪ] *adj* (*cough*) de bronquios, de pecho.
chew [tʃuː] *vt* mascar, masticar.
chewing gum ['tʃuːɪŋ-] *n* chicle *m*.
chic [ʃiːk] *adj* elegante.
chicanery [ʃɪ'keɪnərɪ] *n* embustes *mpl*, sofismas *mpl*.
Chicano [tʃɪ'kɑːnəu] *adj*, *n* chicano/a.
chick [tʃɪk] *n* pollito, polluelo; (*US col*) chica.
chicken ['tʃɪkɪn] *n* gallina, pollo; (*food*) pollo; (*col*: *coward*) gallina *m/f*.
►**chicken out** *vi* (*col*) rajarse; **to ~ out of doing sth** rajarse y no hacer algo.
chickenpox ['tʃɪkɪnpɔks] *n* varicela.
chickpea ['tʃɪkpiː] *n* garbanzo.
chicory ['tʃɪkərɪ] *n* (*for coffee*) achicoria; (*salad*) escarola.
chide [tʃaɪd] *vt*: **to ~ sb for sth** reprender a algn por algo.
chief [tʃiːf] *n* jefe/a *m/f* ♦ *adj* principal, máximo (*esp LAM*); **C~ of Staff** (*MIL*) Jefe *m* del Estado mayor.
chief executive, (*US*) **chief executive officer** *n* director *m* general.
chiefly ['tʃiːflɪ] *adv* principalmente.
chieftain ['tʃiːftən] *n* jefe *m*, cacique *m*.
chiffon ['ʃɪfɔn] *n* gasa.
chilblain ['tʃɪlbleɪn] *n* sabañón *m*.
child, *pl* **~ren** [tʃaɪld, 'tʃɪldrən] *n* niño/a; (*offspring*) hijo/a.
child benefit *n* (*BRIT*) *subsidio por cada hijo pequeño*.
childbirth ['tʃaɪldbəːθ] *n* parto.
childhood ['tʃaɪldhud] *n* niñez *f*, infancia.
childish ['tʃaɪldɪʃ] *adj* pueril, infantil.
childless ['tʃaɪldlɪs] *adj* sin hijos.
childlike ['tʃaɪldlaɪk] *adj* de niño, infantil.
child minder *n* (*BRIT*) niñera, madre *f* de día.
child prodigy *n* niño/a prodigio *inv*.
children's home *n* centro de acogida para niños.
child's play *n* (*fig*): **this is ~** esto es coser y cantar.
Chile ['tʃɪlɪ] *n* Chile *m*.
Chilean ['tʃɪlɪən] *adj*, *n* chileno/a *m/f*.
chill [tʃɪl] *n* frío; (*MED*) resfriado ♦ *adj* frío ♦ *vt* enfriar; (*CULIN*) refrigerar.
►**chill out** *vi* (*esp US col*) tranquilizarse.

chil(l)i ['tʃɪlɪ] *n* (*BRIT*) chile *m*, ají *m* (*LAM*).
chilling ['tʃɪlɪŋ] *adj* escalofriante.
chilly ['tʃɪlɪ] *adj* frío.
chime [tʃaɪm] *n* repique *m*, campanada ♦ *vi* repicar, sonar.
chimney ['tʃɪmnɪ] *n* chimenea.
chimney sweep *n* deshollinador *m*.
chimpanzee [tʃɪmpæn'ziː] *n* chimpancé *m*.
chin [tʃɪn] *n* mentón *m*, barbilla.
China ['tʃaɪnə] *n* China.
china ['tʃaɪnə] *n* porcelana; (*crockery*) loza.
Chinese [tʃaɪ'niːz] *adj* chino ♦ *n* (*pl inv*) chino/a; (*LING*) chino.
chink [tʃɪŋk] *n* (*opening*) rendija, hendedura; (*noise*) tintineo.
chintz [tʃɪnts] *n* cretona.
chip [tʃɪp] *n* (*gen pl*: *CULIN*: *BRIT*) patata *or* papa (*LAM*) frita; (: *US*: *also*: **potato ~**) patata *or* papa (*LAM*) frita; (*of wood*) astilla; (*stone*) lasca; (*in gambling*) ficha; (*COMPUT*) chip *m* ♦ *vt* (*cup, plate*) desconchar; **when the ~s are down** (*fig*) a la hora de la verdad.
▸**chip in** *vi* (*col*: *interrupt*) interrumpir, meterse; (: *contribute*) contribuir.
chipboard ['tʃɪpbɔːd] *n* madera aglomerada.
chipmunk ['tʃɪpmʌŋk] *n* ardilla listada.
chip shop *n ver recuadro*.

> **CHIP SHOP**
>
> *Se denomina* **chip shop** *o "fish-and-chip shop" a un tipo de tienda popular de comida rápida en la que se despachan platos tradicionales británicos, principalmente filetes de pescado rebozado frito y patatas fritas.*

chiropodist [kɪ'rɔpədɪst] *n* (*BRIT*) podólogo/a.
chiropody [kɪ'rɔpədɪ] *n* podología.
chirp [tʃəːp] *vi* gorjear; (*cricket*) cantar ♦ *n* (*of cricket*) canto.
chirpy ['tʃəːpɪ] *adj* alegre, animado.
chisel ['tʃɪzl] *n* (*for wood*) escoplo; (*for stone*) cincel *m*.
chit [tʃɪt] *n* nota.
chitchat ['tʃɪttʃæt] *n* chismes *mpl*, habladurías *fpl*.
chivalrous ['ʃɪvəlrəs] *adj* caballeroso.
chivalry ['ʃɪvəlrɪ] *n* caballerosidad *f*.
chives [tʃaɪvz] *npl* cebollinos *mpl*.
chloride ['klɔːraɪd] *n* cloruro.
chlorine ['klɔːriːn] *n* cloro.
chock-a-block ['tʃɔkə'blɔk], **chock-full** [tʃɔk'ful] *adj* atestado.
chocolate ['tʃɔklɪt] *n* chocolate *m*.
choice [tʃɔɪs] *n* elección *f*; (*preference*) preferencia ♦ *adj* escogido; **I did it by** *or* **from ~** lo hice de buena gana; **a wide ~** un gran surtido, una gran variedad.
choir ['kwaɪə*] *n* coro.
choirboy ['kwaɪəbɔɪ] *n* niño de coro.
choke [tʃəuk] *vi* ahogarse; (*on food*) atragantarse ♦ *vt* ahogar; (*block*) atascar ♦ *n* (*AUT*) estárter *m*.
choker ['tʃəukə*] *n* (*necklace*) gargantilla.
cholera ['kɔlərə] *n* cólera *m*.
cholesterol [kɔ'lɛstərəl] *n* colesterol *m*.
choose, *pt* **chose**, *pp* **chosen** [tʃuːz, tʃəuz, 'tʃəuzn] *vt* escoger, elegir; (*team*) seleccionar; **to ~ between** elegir *or* escoger entre; **to ~ from** escoger entre.
choosy ['tʃuːzɪ] *adj* remilgado.
chop [tʃɔp] *vt* (*wood*) cortar, talar; (*CULIN*: *also*: **~ up**) picar ♦ *n* tajo, golpe *m* cortante; (*CULIN*) chuleta; **~s** *npl* (*jaws*) boca *sg*; **to get the ~** (*col*: *project*) ser suprimido; (: *person*: *be sacked*) ser despedido.
chopper ['tʃɔpə*] *n* (*helicopter*) helicóptero.
choppy ['tʃɔpɪ] *adj* (*sea*) picado, agitado.
chopsticks ['tʃɔpstɪks] *npl* palillos *mpl*.
choral ['kɔːrəl] *adj* coral.
chord [kɔːd] *n* (*MUS*) acorde *m*.
chore [tʃɔː*] *n* faena, tarea; (*routine task*) trabajo rutinario.
choreographer [kɔrɪ'ɔgrəfə*] *n* coreógrafo/a.
choreography [kɔrɪ'ɔgrəfɪ] *n* coreografía.
chorister ['kɔrɪstə*] *n* corista *m/f*; (*US*) director(a) *m/f* de un coro.
chortle ['tʃɔːtl] *vi* reírse satisfecho.
chorus ['kɔːrəs] *n* coro; (*repeated part of song*) estribillo.
chose [tʃəuz] *pt of* **choose**.
chosen ['tʃəuzn] *pp of* **choose**.
chow [tʃau] *n* (*dog*) perro chino.
chowder ['tʃaudə*] *n* (*esp US*) sopa de pescado.
Christ [kraɪst] *n* Cristo.
christen ['krɪsn] *vt* bautizar.
christening ['krɪsnɪŋ] *n* bautizo.
Christian ['krɪstɪən] *adj*, *n* cristiano/a *m/f*.
Christianity [krɪstɪ'ænɪtɪ] *n* cristianismo.
Christian name *n* nombre *m* de pila.
Christmas ['krɪsməs] *n* Navidad *f*; **Merry ~!** ¡Felices Navidades!, ¡Felices Pascuas!
Christmas card *n* crismas *m inv*, tarjeta de Navidad.
Christmas Day *n* día *m* de Navidad.
Christmas Eve *n* Nochebuena.
Christmas Island *n* Isla Christmas.
Christmas tree *n* árbol *m* de Navidad.
chrome [krəum] *n* = **chromium plating.**

chromium ['krəumɪəm] *n* cromo; (*also*: ~ **plating**) cromado.
chromosome ['krəuməsəum] *n* cromosoma *m*.
chronic ['krɔnɪk] *adj* crónico; (*fig*: *liar, smoker*) empedernido.
chronicle ['krɔnɪkl] *n* crónica.
chronological [krɔnə'lɔdʒɪkəl] *adj* cronológico.
chrysalis ['krɪsəlɪs] *n* (*BIO*) crisálida.
chrysanthemum [krɪ'sænθəməm] *n* crisantemo.
chubby ['tʃʌbɪ] *adj* rechoncho.
chuck [tʃʌk] *vt* tirar; **to ~ (up** *or* **in)** *vt* (*BRIT*) dejar, mandar a paseo.
chuckle ['tʃʌkl] *vi* reírse entre dientes.
chuffed [tʃʌft] *adj* (*col*): **to be ~ (about sth)** estar encantado (con algo).
chug [tʃʌg] *vi* (*also*: ~ **along**: *train*) ir despacio; (: *fig*) ir tirando.
chum [tʃʌm] *n* amiguete/a *m/f*, coleguilla *m/f*.
chump [tʃʌmp] *n* (*col*) tonto/a, estúpido/a.
chunk [tʃʌŋk] *n* pedazo, trozo.
chunky ['tʃʌŋkɪ] *adj* (*furniture etc*) achaparrado; (*person*) fornido; (*knitwear*) de lana gorda, grueso.
Chunnel [tʃʌnl] *n* = **Channel Tunnel**.
church [tʃə:tʃ] *n* iglesia; **the C~ of England** la Iglesia Anglicana.
churchyard ['tʃə:tʃjɑ:d] *n* cementerio, camposanto.
churlish ['tʃə:lɪʃ] *adj* grosero; (*mean*) arisco.
churn [tʃə:n] *n* (*for butter*) mantequera; (*for milk*) lechera.
▶**churn out** *vt* producir en serie.
chute [ʃu:t] *n* (*also*: **rubbish ~**) vertedero; (*BRIT*: *children's slide*) tobogán *m*.
chutney ['tʃʌtnɪ] *n salsa picante de frutas y especias*.
CIA *n abbr* (*US*: = *Central Intelligence Agency*) CIA *f*, Agencia Central de Inteligencia.
cicada [sɪ'kɑ:də] *n* cigarra.
CID *n abbr* (*BRIT*: = *Criminal Investigation Department*) ≈ B.I.C. *f* (*SP*).
cider ['saɪdə*] *n* sidra.
C.I.F. *abbr* (= *cost, insurance and freight*) c.s.f.
cigar [sɪ'gɑ:*] *n* puro.
cigarette [sɪgə'rɛt] *n* cigarrillo, pitillo.
cigarette case *n* pitillera.
cigarette end *n* colilla.
cigarette holder *n* boquilla.
C-in-C *abbr* = **commander-in-chief**.
cinch [sɪntʃ] *n*: **it's a ~** está tirado.
Cinderella [sɪndə'rɛlə] *n* Cenicienta.
cinders ['sɪndəz] *npl* cenizas *fpl*.
cine-camera ['sɪnɪ'kæmərə] *n* (*BRIT*) cámara cinematográfica.
cine-film ['sɪnɪfɪlm] *n* (*BRIT*) película de cine.
cinema ['sɪnəmə] *n* cine *m*.
cinnamon ['sɪnəmən] *n* canela.
cipher ['saɪfə*] *n* clave *f*; (*fig*) cero; **in ~** en clave.
circle ['sə:kl] *n* círculo; (*in theatre*) anfiteatro ♦ *vi* dar vueltas ♦ *vt* (*surround*) rodear, cercar; (*move round*) dar la vuelta a.
circuit ['sə:kɪt] *n* circuito; (*track*) pista; (*lap*) vuelta.
circuit board *n* tarjeta de circuitos.
circuitous [sə:'kjuɪtəs] *adj* indirecto.
circular ['sə:kjulə*] *adj* circular ♦ *n* circular *f*; (*as advertisement*) panfleto.
circulate ['sə:kjuleɪt] *vi* circular; (*person*: *socially*) alternar, circular ♦ *vt* poner en circulación.
circulation [sə:kju'leɪʃən] *n* circulación *f*; (*of newspaper etc*) tirada.
circumcise ['sə:kəmsaɪz] *vt* circuncidar.
circumference [sə'kʌmfərəns] *n* circunferencia.
circumscribe ['sə:kəmskraɪb] *vt* circunscribir.
circumspect ['sə:kəmspɛkt] *adj* circunspecto, prudente.
circumstances ['sə:kəmstənsɪz] *npl* circunstancias *fpl*; (*financial condition*) situación *f* económica; **in the ~** en *or* dadas las circunstancias; **under no ~** de ninguna manera, bajo ningún concepto.
circumstantial [sə:kəm'stænʃəl] *adj* detallado; ~ **evidence** prueba indiciaria.
circumvent ['sə:kəmvɛnt] *vt* (*rule etc*) burlar.
circus ['sə:kəs] *n* circo; (*also*: **C~**: *in place names*) Plaza.
cirrhosis [sɪ'rəusɪs] *n* (*also*: ~ **of the liver**) cirrosis *f inv*.
CIS *n abbr* (= *Commonwealth of Independent States*) CEI *f*.
cissy ['sɪsɪ] *n* = **sissy**.
cistern ['sɪstən] *n* tanque *m*, depósito; (*in toilet*) cisterna.
citation [saɪ'teɪʃən] *n* cita; (*LAW*) citación *f*; (*MIL*) mención *f*.
cite [saɪt] *vt* citar.
citizen ['sɪtɪzn] *n* (*POL*) ciudadano/a; (*of city*) habitante *m/f*.
Citizens' Advice Bureau *n* (*BRIT*) *organización voluntaria británica que aconseja especialmente en temas legales o financieros*.
citizenship ['sɪtɪznʃɪp] *n* ciudadanía.

citric ['sɪtrɪk] *adj*: ~ **acid** ácido cítrico.
citrus fruits ['sɪtrəs-] *npl* cítricos *mpl*.
city ['sɪtɪ] *n* ciudad *f*; **the C~** *centro financiero de Londres*.
city centre *n* centro de la ciudad.
City Hall *n* (*US*) ayuntamiento.
City Technology College *n* (*BRIT*) ≈ Centro de formación profesional.
civic ['sɪvɪk] *adj* cívico; (*authorities*) municipal.
civic centre *n* (*BRIT*) centro de administración municipal.
civil ['sɪvɪl] *adj* civil; (*polite*) atento, cortés; (*well-bred*) educado.
civil defence *n* protección *f* civil.
civil engineer *n* ingeniero/a de caminos.
civil engineering *n* ingeniería de caminos.
civilian [sɪ'vɪlɪən] *adj* civil; (*clothes*) de paisano ♦ *n* civil *m/f*.
civilization [sɪvɪlaɪ'zeɪʃən] *n* civilización *f*.
civilized ['sɪvɪlaɪzd] *adj* civilizado.
civil law *n* derecho civil.
civil liberties *npl* libertades *fpl* civiles.
civil rights *npl* derechos *mpl* civiles.
civil servant *n* funcionario/a (del Estado).
Civil Service *n* administración *f* pública.
civil war *n* guerra civil.
civvies ['sɪvɪz] *npl*: **in** ~ (*col*) de paisano.
cl *abbr* (= *centilitre*) cl.
clad [klæd] *adj*: ~ **(in)** vestido (de).
claim [kleɪm] *vt* exigir, reclamar; (*rights etc*) reivindicar; (*assert*) pretender ♦ *vi* (*for insurance*) reclamar ♦ *n* (*for expenses*) reclamación *f*; (*LAW*) demanda; (*pretension*) pretensión *f*; **to put in a ~ for sth** presentar una demanda por algo.
claimant ['kleɪmənt] *n* (*ADMIN, LAW*) demandante *m/f*.
claim form *n* solicitud *f*.
clairvoyant [klɛə'vɔɪənt] *n* clarividente *m/f*.
clam [klæm] *n* almeja.
▸**clam up** *vi* (*col*) cerrar el pico.
clamber ['klæmbə*] *vi* trepar.
clammy ['klæmɪ] *adj* (*cold*) frío y húmedo; (*sticky*) pegajoso.
clamour, (*US*) **clamor** ['klæmə*] *n* (*noise*) clamor *m*; (*protest*) protesta ♦ *vi*: **to ~ for sth** clamar por algo, pedir algo a voces.
clamp [klæmp] *n* abrazadera; (*laboratory* ~) grapa; (*wheel* ~) cepo ♦ *vt* afianzar (con abrazadera).
▸**clamp down on** *vt fus* (*subj: government, police*) poner coto a.
clampdown ['klæmpdaun] *n* restricción *f*; **there has been a ~ on terrorism** se ha puesto coto al terrorismo.
clan [klæn] *n* clan *m*.
clandestine [klæn'dɛstɪn] *adj* clandestino.
clang [klæŋ] *n* estruendo ♦ *vi* sonar con estruendo.
clanger [klæŋə*] *n*: **to drop a** ~ (*BRIT col*) meter la pata.
clansman ['klænzmən] *n* miembro del clan.
clap [klæp] *vi* aplaudir ♦ *vt* (*hands*) batir ♦ *n* (*of hands*) palmada; **to ~ one's hands** dar palmadas, batir las palmas; **a ~ of thunder** un trueno.
clapping ['klæpɪŋ] *n* aplausos *mpl*.
claptrap ['klæptræp] *n* (*col*) gilipolleces *fpl*.
claret ['klærət] *n* burdeos *m inv*.
clarification [klærɪfɪ'keɪʃən] *n* aclaración *f*.
clarify ['klærɪfaɪ] *vt* aclarar.
clarinet [klærɪ'nɛt] *n* clarinete *m*.
clarity ['klærɪtɪ] *n* claridad *f*.
clash [klæʃ] *n* estruendo; (*fig*) choque *m* ♦ *vi* enfrentarse; (*personalities, interests*) oponerse, chocar; (*colours*) desentonar; (*dates, events*) coincidir.
clasp [klɑːsp] *n* broche *m*; (*on jewels*) cierre *m* ♦ *vt* abrochar; (*hand*) apretar; (*embrace*) abrazar.
class [klɑːs] *n* (*gen*) clase *f*; (*group, category*) clase *f*, categoría ♦ *cpd* de clase ♦ *vt* clasificar.
class-conscious ['klɑːs'kɔnʃəs] *adj* clasista, con conciencia de clase.
classic ['klæsɪk] *adj* clásico ♦ *n* (*work*) obra clásica, clásico; **~s** *npl* (*UNIV*) clásicas *fpl*.
classical ['klæsɪkəl] *adj* clásico; ~ **music** música clásica.
classification [klæsɪfɪ'keɪʃən] *n* clasificación *f*.
classified ['klæsɪfaɪd] *adj* (*information*) reservado.
classified advertisement *n* anuncio por palabras.
classify ['klæsɪfaɪ] *vt* clasificar.
classless ['klɑːslɪs] *adj*: ~ **society** sociedad *f* sin clases.
classmate ['klɑːsmeɪt] *n* compañero/a de clase.
classroom ['klɑːsrum] *n* aula.
classy ['klɑːsɪ] *adj* (*col*) elegante, con estilo.
clatter ['klætə*] *n* ruido, estruendo; (*of hooves*) trápala ♦ *vi* hacer ruido *or* estruendo.
clause [klɔːz] *n* cláusula; (*LING*) oración *f*.
claustrophobia [klɔːstrə'fəubɪə] *n* claustrofobia.
claustrophobic [klɔːstrə'fəubɪk] *adj* claustrofóbico; **I feel** ~ me entra claustrofobia.
claw [klɔː] *n* (*of cat*) uña; (*of bird of prey*) garra; (*of lobster*) pinza; (*TECH*) garfio ♦ *vi*: **to ~ at** arañar; (*tear*) desgarrar.

clay [kleɪ] *n* arcilla.
clean [kliːn] *adj* limpio; (*copy*) en limpio; (*lines*) bien definido ♦ *vt* limpiar ♦ *adv*: **he ~ forgot** lo olvidó por completo; **to come ~** (*col*: *admit guilt*) confesarlo todo; **to have a ~ driving licence** tener el carnet de conducir sin sanciones; **to ~ one's teeth** lavarse los dientes.
▸**clean off** *vt* limpiar.
▸**clean out** *vt* limpiar (a fondo).
▸**clean up** *vt* limpiar, asear ♦ *vi* (*fig*: *make profit*): **to ~ up on** sacar provecho de.
clean-cut ['kliːn'kʌt] *adj* bien definido; (*outline*) nítido; (*person*) de buen parecer.
cleaner ['kliːnə*] *n* encargado/a *m/f* de la limpieza; (*also*: **dry ~**) tintorero/a.
cleaning ['kliːnɪŋ] *n* limpieza.
cleaning lady *n* señora de la limpieza, asistenta.
cleanliness ['klɛnlɪnɪs] *n* limpieza.
cleanse [klɛnz] *vt* limpiar.
cleanser ['klɛnzə*] *n* detergente *m*; (*cosmetic*) loción *f or* crema limpiadora.
clean-shaven ['kliːn'ʃeɪvn] *adj* bien afeitado.
cleansing department ['klɛnzɪŋ-] *n* (*BRIT*) servicio municipal de limpieza.
clean sweep *n*: **to make a ~** (*SPORT*) arrasar, barrer.
clear [klɪə*] *adj* claro; (*road, way*) libre; (*profit*) neto; (*majority*) absoluto ♦ *vt* (*space*) despejar, limpiar; (*LAW*: *suspect*) absolver; (*obstacle*) salvar, saltar por encima de; (*debt*) liquidar; (*cheque*) aceptar; (*site, woodland*) desmontar ♦ *vi* (*fog etc*) despejarse ♦ *n*: **to be in the ~** (*out of debt*) estar libre de deudas; (*out of suspicion*) estar fuera de toda sospecha; (*out of danger*) estar fuera de peligro ♦ *adv*: **~ of** a distancia de; **to make o.s. ~** explicarse claramente; **to make it ~ to sb that ...** hacer entender a algn que ...; **I have a ~ day tomorrow** mañana tengo el día libre; **to keep ~ of sth/sb** evitar algo/ a algn; **to ~ a profit of ...** sacar una ganancia de ...; **to ~ the table** recoger *or* quitar la mesa.
▸**clear off** *vi* (*col*: *leave*) marcharse, mandarse mudar (*LAM*).
▸**clear up** *vt* limpiar; (*mystery*) aclarar, resolver.
clearance ['klɪərəns] *n* (*removal*) despeje *m*; (*permission*) acreditación *f*.
clear-cut ['klɪə'kʌt] *adj* bien definido, claro.
clearing ['klɪərɪŋ] *n* (*in wood*) claro.
clearing bank *n* (*BRIT*) banco central.
clearing house *n* (*COMM*) cámara de compensación.
clearly ['klɪəlɪ] *adv* claramente.
clearway ['klɪəweɪ] *n* (*BRIT*) *carretera en la que no se puede estacionar*.
cleaver ['kliːvə] *n* cuchilla (de carnicero).
clef [klɛf] *n* (*MUS*) clave *f*.
cleft [klɛft] *n* (*in rock*) grieta, hendedura.
clemency ['klɛmənsɪ] *n* clemencia.
clement ['klɛmənt] *adj* (*weather*) clemente.
clench [klɛntʃ] *vt* apretar, cerrar.
clergy ['kləːdʒɪ] *n* clero.
clergyman ['kləːdʒɪmən] *n* clérigo.
clerical ['klɛrɪkəl] *adj* de oficina; (*REL*) clerical; (*error*) de copia.
clerk [klɑːk, (*US*) kləːrk] *n* oficinista *m/f*; (*US*) dependiente/a *m/f*, vendedor(a) *m/f*; **C~ of the Court** secretario/a de juzgado.
clever ['klɛvə*] *adj* (*mentally*) inteligente, listo; (*skilful*) hábil; (*device, arrangement*) ingenioso.
cleverly ['klɛvəlɪ] *adv* ingeniosamente.
clew [kluː] *n* (*US*) = **clue**.
cliché ['kliːʃeɪ] *n* cliché *m*, frase *f* hecha.
click [klɪk] *vt* (*tongue*) chasquear ♦ *vi* (*COMPUT*) hacer clic; **to ~ one's heels** taconear.
client ['klaɪənt] *n* cliente *m/f*.
clientele [kliːɑ̃ːn'tɛl] *n* clientela.
cliff [klɪf] *n* acantilado.
cliffhanger ['klɪfhæŋə*] *n*: **it was a ~** estuvimos *etc* en ascuas hasta el final.
climactic [klaɪ'mæktɪk] *adj* culminante.
climate ['klaɪmɪt] *n* clima *m*; (*fig*) clima *m*, ambiente *m*.
climax ['klaɪmæks] *n* punto culminante; (*of play etc*) clímax *m*; (*sexual ~*) orgasmo.
climb [klaɪm] *vi* subir, trepar; (*plane*) elevarse, remontar el vuelo ♦ *vt* (*stairs*) subir; (*tree*) trepar a; (*mountain*) escalar ♦ *n* subida, ascenso; **to ~ over a wall** saltar una tapia.
▸**climb down** *vi* (*fig*) volverse atrás.
climbdown ['klaɪmdaun] *n* vuelta atrás.
climber ['klaɪmə*] *n* escalador(a) *m/f*.
climbing ['klaɪmɪŋ] *n* escalada.
clinch [klɪntʃ] *vt* (*deal*) cerrar; (*argument*) rematar.
clincher ['klɪntʃə*] *n* (*col*): **that was the ~ for me** eso me hizo decidir.
cling, *pt, pp* **clung** [klɪŋ, klʌŋ] *vi*: **to ~ (to)** agarrarse (a); (*clothes*) pegarse (a).
clingfilm ['klɪŋfɪlm] *n* plástico adherente.
clinic ['klɪnɪk] *n* clínica.
clinical ['klɪnɪkl] *adj* clínico; (*fig*) frío, impasible.
clink [klɪŋk] *vi* tintinear.
clip [klɪp] *n* (*for hair*) horquilla; (*also*: **paper ~**) sujetapapeles *m inv*, clip *m*; (*clamp*) grapa ♦ *vt* (*cut*) cortar; (*hedge*) podar;

(*also*: ~ **together**) unir.
clippers ['klɪpəz] *npl* (*for gardening*) tijeras *fpl* de podar; (*for hair*) maquinilla *sg*; (*for nails*) cortauñas *m inv*.
clipping ['klɪpɪŋ] *n* (*from newspaper*) recorte *m*.
clique [kli:k] *n* camarilla.
cloak [kləuk] *n* capa, manto ♦ *vt* (*fig*) encubrir, disimular.
cloakroom ['kləukrum] *n* guardarropa *m*; (*BRIT*: *WC*) lavabo, aseos *mpl*, baño (*esp LAM*).
clobber ['klɔbə*] *n* (*col*) bártulos *mpl*, trastos *mpl* ♦ *vt* dar una paliza a.
clock [klɔk] *n* reloj *m*; (*in taxi*) taxímetro; **to work against the** ~ trabajar contra reloj; **around the** ~ las veinticuatro horas; **to sleep round the** ~ dormir un día entero; **30,000 on the** ~ (*AUT*) treinta mil millas en el cuentakilómetros.
▸**clock in, clock on** *vi* fichar, picar.
▸**clock off, clock out** *vi* fichar *or* picar la salida.
▸**clock up** *vt* hacer.
clockwise ['klɔkwaɪz] *adv* en el sentido de las agujas del reloj.
clockwork ['klɔkwə:k] *n* aparato de relojería ♦ *adj* (*toy, train*) de cuerda.
clog [klɔg] *n* zueco, chanclo ♦ *vt* atascar ♦ *vi* atascarse.
cloister ['klɔɪstə*] *n* claustro.
clone [kləun] *n* clon *m*.
close *adj, adv and derivatives* [kləus] *adj* cercano, próximo; (*near*): ~ **(to)** cerca (de); (*print, weave*) tupido, compacto; (*friend*) íntimo; (*connection*) estrecho; (*examination*) detallado, minucioso; (*weather*) bochornoso; (*atmosphere*) sofocante; (*room*) mal ventilado ♦ *adv* cerca; ~ **by,** ~ **at hand** *adj, adv* muy cerca; ~ **to** *prep* cerca de; **to have a** ~ **shave** (*fig*) escaparse por un pelo; **how** ~ **is Edinburgh to Glasgow?** ¿qué distancia hay de Edimburgo a Glasgow?; **at** ~ **quarters** de cerca ♦ *vb and derivatives* [kləuz] *vt* cerrar; (*end*) concluir, terminar ♦ *vi* (*shop etc*) cerrar; (*end*) concluir(se), terminar(se) ♦ *n* (*end*) fin *m*, final *m*, conclusión *f*; **to bring sth to a** ~ terminar algo.
▸**close down** *vi* cerrar definitivamente.
▸**close in** *vi* (*hunters*) acercarse rodeando, rodear; (*evening, night*) caer; (*fog*) cerrarse; **to** ~ **in on sb** rodear *or* cercar a algn; **the days are closing in** los días son cada vez más cortos.
▸**close off** *vt* (*area*) cerrar al tráfico *or* al público.
closed [kləuzd] *adj* (*shop etc*) cerrado.
closed-circuit ['kləuzd'sə:kɪt] *adj*: ~ **television** televisión *f* por circuito cerrado.
closed shop *n empresa en la que todo el personal está afiliado a un sindicato.*
close-knit ['kləus'nɪt] *adj* (*fig*) muy unido.
closely ['kləuslɪ] *adv* (*study*) con detalle; (*listen*) con atención; (*watch*: *person, events*) de cerca; **we are** ~ **related** somos parientes cercanos; **a** ~ **guarded secret** un secreto rigurosamente guardado.
close season [kləuz-] *n* (*FOOTBALL*) temporada de descanso; (*HUNTING*) veda.
closet ['klɔzɪt] *n* (*cupboard*) armario, placar(d) *m* (*LAM*).
close-up ['kləusʌp] *n* primer plano.
closing ['kləuzɪŋ] *adj* (*stages, remarks*) último, final; ~ **price** (*STOCK EXCHANGE*) cotización *f* de cierre.
closing time *n* hora de cierre.
closure ['kləuʒə*] *n* cierre *m*.
clot [klɔt] *n* (*gen*: **blood** ~) embolia; (*col*: *idiot*) imbécil *m/f* ♦ *vi* (*blood*) coagularse.
cloth [klɔθ] *n* (*material*) tela, paño; (*table* ~) mantel *m*; (*rag*) trapo.
clothe [kləuð] *vt* vestir; (*fig*) revestir.
clothes [kləuðz] *npl* ropa *sg*; **to put one's** ~ **on** vestirse, ponerse la ropa; **to take one's** ~ **off** desvestirse, desnudarse.
clothes brush *n* cepillo (para la ropa).
clothes line *n* cuerda (para tender la ropa).
clothes peg, (*US*) **clothes pin** *n* pinza.
clothing ['kləuðɪŋ] *n* = **clothes.**
clotted cream ['klɔtɪd-] *n nata muy espesa.*
cloud [klaud] *n* nube *f*; (*storm* ~) nubarrón *m* ♦ *vt* (*liquid*) enturbiar; **every** ~ **has a silver lining** no hay mal que por bien no venga; **to** ~ **the issue** empañar el problema.
▸**cloud over** *vi* (*also fig*) nublarse.
cloudburst ['klaudbə:st] *n* chaparrón *m*.
cloud-cuckoo-land ['klaud'kuku:'lænd] *n* Babia.
cloudy ['klaudɪ] *adj* nublado; (*liquid*) turbio.
clout [klaut] *n* (*fig*) influencia, peso ♦ *vt* dar un tortazo a.
clove [kləuv] *n* clavo; ~ **of garlic** diente *m* de ajo.
clover ['kləuvə*] *n* trébol *m*.
clown [klaun] *n* payaso ♦ *vi* (*also*: ~ **about,** ~ **around**) hacer el payaso.
cloying ['klɔɪɪŋ] *adj* (*taste*) empalagoso.
club [klʌb] *n* (*society*) club *m*; (*weapon*) porra, cachiporra; (*also*: **golf** ~) palo ♦ *vt* aporrear ♦ *vi*: **to** ~ **together** (*join forces*)

unir fuerzas; ~**s** *npl* (*CARDS*) tréboles *mpl*.
club car *n* (*US RAIL*) coche *m* salón.
club class *n* (*AVIAT*) clase *f* preferente.
clubhouse ['klʌbhaus] *n local social, sobre todo en clubs deportivos.*
club soda *n* (*US*) soda.
cluck [klʌk] *vi* cloquear.
clue [klu:] *n* pista; (*in crosswords*) indicación *f*; **I haven't a** ~ no tengo ni idea.
clued up, (*US*) **clued in** [klu:d-] *adj* (*col*) al tanto, al corriente.
clueless ['klu:lɪs] *adj* (*col*) desorientado.
clump [klʌmp] *n* (*of trees*) grupo.
clumsy ['klʌmzɪ] *adj* (*person*) torpe; (*tool*) difícil de manejar.
clung [klʌŋ] *pt, pp of* **cling.**
cluster ['klʌstə*] *n* grupo; (*BOT*) racimo ♦ *vi* agruparse, apiñarse.
clutch [klʌtʃ] *n* (*AUT*) embrague *m*; (*pedal*) (pedal *m* de) embrague *m*; **to fall into sb's ~es** caer en las garras de algn ♦ *vt* agarrar.
clutter ['klʌtə*] *vt* (*also*: ~ **up**) atestar, llenar desordenadamente ♦ *n* desorden *m*, confusión *f*.
CM *abbr* (*US*) = *North Mariana Islands.*
cm *abbr* (= *centimetre*) cm.
CNAA *n abbr* (*BRIT*: = *Council for National Academic Awards*) *organismo no universitario que otorga diplomas.*
CND *n abbr* (= *Campaign for Nuclear Disarmament*) *plataforma pro desarme nuclear.*
CO *n abbr* = **commanding officer**; (*BRIT*) = *Commonwealth Office* ♦ *abbr* (*US*) = *Colorado.*
Co. *abbr* = **county**; = **company.**
c/o *abbr* (= *care of*) c/a, a/c.
coach [kəutʃ] *n* (*bus*) autocar *m* (*SP*), autobús *m*; (*horse-drawn*) coche *m*; (*ceremonial*) carroza; (*of train*) vagón *m*, coche *m*; (*SPORT*) entrenador(a) *m/f*, instructor(a) *m/f* ♦ *vt* (*SPORT*) entrenar; (*student*) preparar, enseñar.
coach trip *n* excursión *f* en autocar.
coagulate [kəu'ægjuleɪt] *vi* coagularse.
coal [kəul] *n* carbón *m*.
coal face *n* frente *m* de carbón.
coalfield ['kəulfi:ld] *n* yacimiento de carbón.
coalition [kəuə'lɪʃən] *n* coalición *f*.
coal man *n* carbonero.
coalmine ['kəulmaɪn] *n* mina de carbón.
coalminer ['kəulmaɪnə*] *n* minero (de carbón).
coalmining ['keulmaɪnɪŋ] *n* minería (de carbón).
coarse [kɔ:s] *adj* basto, burdo; (*vulgar*) grosero, ordinario.
coast [kəust] *n* costa, litoral *m* ♦ *vi* (*AUT*) ir en punto muerto.
coastal ['kəustl] *adj* costero.
coaster ['kəustə*] *n* buque *m* costero, barco de cabotaje.
coastguard ['kəustgɑ:d] *n* guardacostas *m inv*.
coastline ['kəustlaɪn] *n* litoral *m*.
coat [kəut] *n* (*jacket*) chaqueta, saco (*LAM*); (*overcoat*) abrigo; (*of animal*) pelo, lana; (*of paint*) mano *f*, capa ♦ *vt* cubrir, revestir.
coat hanger *n* percha, gancha (*LAM*).
coating ['kəutɪŋ] *n* capa, baño.
coat of arms *n* escudo de armas.
co-author ['kəu'ɔ:θə*] *n* coautor(a) *m/f*.
coax [kəuks] *vt* engatusar.
cob [kɔb] *n see* **corn.**
cobbler ['kɔblə*] *n* zapatero (remendón).
cobbles ['kɔblz], **cobblestones** ['kɔblstəunz] *npl* adoquines *mpl*.
COBOL ['kəubɔl] *n* COBOL *m*.
cobra ['kəubrə] *n* cobra.
cobweb ['kɔbwɛb] *n* telaraña.
cocaine [kə'keɪn] *n* cocaína.
cock [kɔk] *n* (*rooster*) gallo; (*male bird*) macho ♦ *vt* (*gun*) amartillar.
cock-a-hoop [kɔkə'hu:p] *adj*: **to be** ~ estar más contento que unas pascuas.
cockatoo [kɔkə'tu:] *n* cacatúa.
cockerel ['kɔkərl] *n* gallito, gallo joven.
cock-eyed ['kɔkaɪd] *adj* bizco; (*fig*: *crooked*) torcido; (: *idea*) disparatado.
cockle ['kɔkl] *n* berberecho.
cockney ['kɔknɪ] *n habitante de ciertos barrios de Londres.*
cockpit ['kɔkpɪt] *n* (*in aircraft*) cabina.
cockroach ['kɔkrəutʃ] *n* cucaracha.
cocktail ['kɔkteɪl] *n* combinado, cóctel *m*; **prawn** ~ cóctel *m* de gambas.
cocktail cabinet *n* mueble-bar *m*.
cocktail party *n* cóctel *m*.
cocktail shaker [-ʃeɪkə*] *n* coctelera.
cocky ['kɔkɪ] *adj* farruco, flamenco.
cocoa ['kəukəu] *n* cacao; (*drink*) chocolate *m*.
coconut ['kəukənʌt] *n* coco.
cocoon [kə'ku:n] *n* capullo.
cod [kɔd] *n* bacalao.
COD *abbr see* **cash on delivery, collect on delivery** (*US*).
code [kəud] *n* código; (*cipher*) clave *f*; (*TEL*) prefijo; ~ **of behaviour** código de conducta; ~ **of practice** código profesional.
codeine ['kəudi:n] *n* codeína.

codger [kɔdʒə*] *n* (*BRIT col*): **an old ~** un abuelo.
codicil ['kɔdɪsɪl] *n* codicilo.
codify ['kəudɪfaɪ] *vt* codificar.
cod-liver oil ['kɔdlɪvə*-] *n* aceite *m* de hígado de bacalao.
co-driver ['kəu'draɪvə*] *n* (*in race*) copiloto *m/f*; (*of lorry*) segundo conductor *m*.
co-ed ['kəuɛd] *adj abbr* = **coeducational** ♦ *n abbr* (*US*: = *female student*) *alumna de una universidad mixta*; (*BRIT*: *school*) colegio mixto.
coeducational [kəuɛdju'keɪʃənl] *adj* mixto.
coerce [kəu'ə:s] *vt* forzar, coaccionar.
coercion [kəu'ə:ʃən] *n* coacción *f*.
coexistence ['kəuɪg'zɪstəns] *n* coexistencia.
C. of C. *n abbr* = **chamber of commerce**.
C of E *abbr* = **Church of England**.
coffee ['kɔfɪ] *n* café *m*; **white ~**, (*US*) **~ with cream** café con leche.
coffee bar *n* (*BRIT*) cafetería.
coffee bean *n* grano de café.
coffee break *n* descanso (para tomar café).
coffee cup *n* taza de café, pocillo (*LAM*).
coffeepot ['kɔfɪpɔt] *n* cafetera.
coffee table *n* mesita baja.
coffin ['kɔfɪn] *n* ataúd *m*.
C of I *abbr* = *Church of Ireland*.
C of S *abbr* = *Church of Scotland*.
cog [kɔg] *n* diente *m*.
cogent ['kəudʒənt] *adj* lógico, convincente.
cognac ['kɔnjæk] *n* coñac *m*.
cogwheel ['kɔgwi:l] *n* rueda dentada.
cohabit [kəu'hæbɪt] *vi* (*formal*): **to ~ (with sb)** cohabitar (con algn).
coherent [kəu'hɪərənt] *adj* coherente.
cohesion [kəu'hi:ʒen] *n* cohesión *f*.
cohesive [kəu'hi:sɪv] *adj* (*fig*) cohesivo, unido.
COI *n abbr* (*BRIT*: = *Central Office of Information*) *servicio de información gubernamental*.
coil [kɔɪl] *n* rollo; (*of rope*) vuelta; (*of smoke*) espiral *f*; (*AUT, ELEC*) bobina, carrete *m*; (*contraceptive*) DIU *m* ♦ *vt* enrollar.
coin [kɔɪn] *n* moneda ♦ *vt* acuñar; (*word*) inventar, acuñar.
coinage ['kɔɪnɪdʒ] *n* moneda.
coin-box ['kɔɪnbɔks] *n* (*BRIT*) caja recaudadora.
coincide [kəuɪn'saɪd] *vi* coincidir.
coincidence [kəu'ɪnsɪdəns] *n* casualidad *f*, coincidencia.
coin-operated ['kɔɪn'ɔpəreɪtɪd] *adj* (*machine*) que funciona con monedas.
Coke ® [kəuk] *n* Coca Cola ® *f*.
coke [kəuk] *n* (*coal*) coque *m*.
Col. *abbr* (= *colonel*) col; (*US*) = *Colorado*.
COLA *n abbr* (*US*: = *cost-of-living adjustment*) *reajuste salarial de acuerdo con el coste de la vida*.
colander ['kɔləndə*] *n* escurridor *m*.
cold [kəuld] *adj* frío ♦ *n* frío; (*MED*) resfriado; **it's ~** hace frío; **to be ~** tener frío; **to catch a ~** coger un catarro, resfriarse, acatarrarse; **in ~ blood** a sangre fría; **the room's getting ~** está empezando a hacer frío en la habitación; **to give sb the ~ shoulder** tratar a algn con frialdad.
cold-blooded ['kəuld'blʌdɪd] *adj* (*ZOOL*) de sangre fría.
cold cream *n* crema.
coldly ['kəuldlɪ] *adj* fríamente.
cold sore *n* calentura, herpes *m* labial.
cold sweat *n*: **to be in a ~ (about sth)** tener sudores fríos (por algo).
cold turkey *n* (*col*) mono.
Cold War *n*: **the ~** la guerra fría.
coleslaw ['kəulslɔ:] *n* ensalada de col con zanahoria.
colic ['kɔlɪk] *n* cólico.
colicky ['kɔlɪkɪ] *adj*: **to be ~** tener un cólico.
collaborate [kə'læbəreɪt] *vi* colaborar.
collaboration [kəlæbə'reɪʃən] *n* colaboración *f*; (*POL*) colaboracionismo.
collaborator [kə'læbəreɪtə*] *n* colaborador(a) *m/f*; (*POL*) colaboracionista *m/f*.
collage [kɔ'lɑ:ʒ] *n* collage *m*.
collagen ['kɔlədʒən] *n* colágeno.
collapse [kə'læps] *vi* (*gen*) hundirse, derrumbarse; (*MED*) sufrir un colapso ♦ *n* (*gen*) hundimiento; (*MED*) colapso; (*of government*) caída; (*of plans, scheme*) fracaso; (*of business*) ruina.
collapsible [kə'læpsəbl] *adj* plegable.
collar ['kɔlə*] *n* (*of coat, shirt*) cuello; (*for dog, TECH*) collar *m* ♦ *vt* (*col*: *person*) agarrar; (: *object*) birlar.
collarbone ['kɔləbəun] *n* clavícula.
collate [kɔ'leɪt] *vt* cotejar.
collateral [kɔ'lætərəl] *n* (*COMM*) garantía subsidiaria.
collation [kə'leɪʃən] *n* colación *f*.
colleague ['kɔli:g] *n* colega *m/f*, compañero/a *m/f*.
collect [kə'lɛkt] *vt* reunir; (*as a hobby*) coleccionar; (*BRIT*: *call and pick up*) recoger; (*wages*) cobrar; (*debts*) recaudar; (*donations, subscriptions*) colectar ♦ *vi* (*crowd*) reunirse ♦ *adv*: **to call ~** (*US TEL*) llamar a cobro revertido; **to ~ one's thoughts** reponerse, recobrar el dominio de sí mismo; **~ on delivery (COD)** (*US*) entrega contra reembolso.

collection [kəˈlɛkʃən] *n* colección *f*; (*of fares, wages*) cobro; (*of post*) recogida.
collective [kəˈlɛktɪv] *adj* colectivo.
collective bargaining *n* negociación *f* del convenio colectivo.
collector [kəˈlɛktə*] *n* coleccionista *m/f*; (*of taxes etc*) recaudador(a) *m/f*; **~'s item** *or* **piece** pieza de coleccionista.
college [ˈkɔlɪdʒ] *n* colegio; (*of technology, agriculture etc*) escuela.
collide [kəˈlaɪd] *vi* chocar.
collie [ˈkɔlɪ] *n* (*dog*) collie *m*, perro pastor escocés.
colliery [ˈkɔlɪərɪ] *n* (*BRIT*) mina de carbón.
collision [kəˈlɪʒən] *n* choque *m*, colisión *f*; **to be on a ~ course** (*also fig*) ir rumbo al desastre.
colloquial [kəˈləukwɪəl] *adj* coloquial.
collusion [kəˈlu:ʒən] *n* confabulación *f*, connivencia; **in ~ with** en connivencia con.
Colo. *abbr* (*US*) = *Colorado*.
cologne [kəˈləun] *n* (*also*: **eau de ~**) (agua de) colonia.
Colombia [kəˈlɔmbɪə] *n* Colombia.
Colombian [kəˈlɔmbɪən] *adj, n* colombiano/a *m/f*.
colon [ˈkəulən] *n* (*sign*) dos puntos; (*MED*) colon *m*.
colonel [ˈkə:nl] *n* coronel *m*.
colonial [kəˈləunɪəl] *adj* colonial.
colonize [ˈkɔlənaɪz] *vt* colonizar.
colonnade [kɔləˈneɪd] *n* columnata.
colony [ˈkɔlənɪ] *n* colonia.
color [ˈkʌlə*] *etc* (*US*) = **colour**.
Colorado beetle [kɔləˈrɑ:dəu-] *n* escarabajo de la patata.
colossal [kəˈlɔsl] *adj* colosal.
colour, (*US*) **color** [ˈkʌlə*] *n* color *m* ♦ *vt* colorear, pintar; (*dye*) teñir ♦ *vi* (*blush*) sonrojarse; **~s** *npl* (*of party, club*) colores *mpl*.
colo(u)r bar *n* segregación *f* racial.
colo(u)r-blind [ˈkʌləblaɪnd] *adj* daltónico.
colo(u)red [ˈkʌləd] *adj* de color; (*photo*) en color; (*of race*) de color.
colo(u)r film *n* película en color.
colo(u)rful [ˈkʌləful] *adj* lleno de color; (*person*) pintoresco.
colo(u)ring [ˈkʌlərɪŋ] *n* colorido, color; (*substance*) colorante *m*.
colo(u)rless [ˈkʌləlɪs] *adj* incoloro, sin color.
colo(u)r scheme *n* combinación *f* de colores.
colour supplement *n* (*BRIT PRESS*) suplemento semanal *or* dominical.
colo(u)r television *n* televisión *f* en color.
colt [kəult] *n* potro.
column [ˈkɔləm] *n* columna; (*fashion ~, sports ~ etc*) sección *f*, columna; **the editorial ~** el editorial.
columnist [ˈkɔləmnɪst] *n* columnista *m/f*.
coma [ˈkəumə] *n* coma *m*.
comb [kəum] *n* peine *m*; (*ornamental*) peineta ♦ *vt* (*hair*) peinar; (*area*) registrar a fondo, peinar.
combat [ˈkɔmbæt] *n* combate *m* ♦ *vt* combatir.
combination [kɔmbɪˈneɪʃən] *n* (*gen*) combinación *f*.
combination lock *n* cerradura de combinación.
combine [kəmˈbaɪn] *vt* combinar; (*qualities*) reunir ♦ *vi* combinarse ♦ *n* [ˈkɔmbaɪn] (*ECON*) cartel *m*; **a ~d effort** un esfuerzo conjunto.
combine (harvester) *n* cosechadora.
combo [ˈkɔmbəu] *n* (*JAZZ etc*) conjunto.
combustion [kəmˈbʌstʃən] *n* combustión *f*.

KEYWORD

come [kʌm] (*pt* **came**, *pp* **come**) *vi* **1** (*movement towards*) venir; **to ~ running** venir corriendo; **~ with me** ven conmigo
2 (*arrive*) llegar; **he's ~ here to work** ha venido aquí para trabajar; **to ~ home** volver a casa; **we've just ~ from Seville** acabamos de llegar de Sevilla; **coming!** ¡voy!
3 (*reach*): **to ~ to** llegar a; **the bill came to £40** la cuenta ascendía a cuarenta libras
4 (*occur*): **an idea came to me** se me ocurrió una idea; **if it ~s to it** llegado el caso
5 (*be, become*): **to ~ loose/undone** *etc* aflojarse/desabrocharse, desatarse *etc*; **I've ~ to like him** por fin ha llegado a gustarme
►**come about** *vi* suceder, ocurrir
►**come across** *vt fus* (*person*) encontrarse con; (*thing*) encontrar ♦ *vi*: **to ~ across well/badly** causar buena/mala impresión
►**come away** *vi* (*leave*) marcharse; (*become detached*) desprenderse
►**come back** *vi* (*return*) volver; (*reply*): **can I ~ back to you on that one?** volvamos sobre ese punto
►**come by** *vt fus* (*acquire*) conseguir
►**come down** *vi* (*price*) bajar; (*building*) derrumbarse; (*: be demolished*) ser derribado
►**come forward** *vi* presentarse
►**come from** *vt fus* (*place, source*) ser de
►**come in** *vi* (*visitor*) entrar; (*train, report*)

llegar; (*fashion*) ponerse de moda; (*on deal etc*) entrar
►**come in for** *vt fus* (*criticism etc*) recibir
►**come into** *vt fus* (*money*) heredar; (*be involved*) tener que ver con; **to ~ into fashion** ponerse de moda
►**come off** *vi* (*button*) soltarse, desprenderse; (*attempt*) salir bien
►**come on** *vi* (*pupil, work, project*) marchar; (*lights*) encenderse; (*electricity*) volver; **~ on!** ¡vamos!
►**come out** *vi* (*fact*) salir a la luz; (*book, sun*) salir; (*stain*) quitarse; **to ~ out (on strike)** declararse en huelga; **to ~ out for/against** declararse a favor/en contra de
►**come over** *vt fus*: **I don't know what's ~ over him!** ¡no sé lo que le pasa!
►**come round** *vi* (*after faint, operation*) volver en sí
►**come through** *vi* (*survive*) sobrevivir; (*telephone call*): **the call came through** recibimos la llamada
►**come to** *vi* (*wake*) volver en sí; (*total*) sumar; **how much does it ~ to?** ¿cuánto es en total?, ¿a cuánto asciende?
►**come under** *vt fus* (*heading*) entrar dentro de; (*influence*) estar bajo
►**come up** *vi* (*sun*) salir; (*problem*) surgir; (*event*) aproximarse; (*in conversation*) mencionarse
►**come up against** *vt fus* (*resistance etc*) tropezar con
►**come up to** *vt fus* llegar hasta; **the film didn't ~ up to our expectations** la película no fue tan buena como esperábamos
►**come up with** *vt fus* (*idea*) sugerir; (*money*) conseguir
►**come upon** *vt fus* (*find*) dar con.

comeback ['kʌmbæk] *n* (*reaction*) reacción *f*; (*response*) réplica; **to make a ~** (*THEAT*) volver a las tablas.
Comecon ['kɔmɪkɔn] *n abbr* (= *Council for Mutual Economic Aid*) COMECON *m*.
comedian [kə'miːdɪən] *n* humorista *m*.
comedienne [kəmiːdɪ'ɛn] *n* humorista.
comedown ['kʌmdaun] *n* revés *m*.
comedy ['kɔmɪdɪ] *n* comedia.
comet ['kɔmɪt] *n* cometa *m*.
comeuppance [kʌm'ʌpəns] *n*: **to get one's ~** llevar su merecido.
comfort ['kʌmfət] *n* comodidad *f*, confort *m*; (*well-being*) bienestar *m*; (*solace*) consuelo; (*relief*) alivio ♦ *vt* consolar; *see also* **comforts**.
comfortable ['kʌmfətəbl] *adj* cómodo; (*income*) adecuado; (*majority*) suficiente; **I don't feel very ~ about it** la cosa me tiene algo preocupado.
comfortably ['kʌmfətəblɪ] *adv* (*sit*) cómodamente; (*live*) holgadamente.
comforter ['kʌmfətə*] *n* (*US*: *pacifier*) chupete *m*; (: *bed cover*) colcha.
comforts ['kʌmfəts] *npl* comodidades *fpl*.
comfort station *n* (*US*) servicios *mpl*.
comic ['kɔmɪk] *adj* (*also*: **~al**) cómico, gracioso ♦ *n* (*magazine*) tebeo; (*for adults*) cómic *m*.
comic strip *n* tira cómica.
coming ['kʌmɪŋ] *n* venida, llegada ♦ *adj* que viene; (*next*) próximo; (*future*) venidero; **~(s) and going(s)** *n(pl)* ir y venir *m*, ajetreo; **in the ~ weeks** en las próximas semanas.
Comintern ['kɔmɪntəːn] *n* Comintern *m*.
comma ['kɔmə] *n* coma.
command [kə'mɑːnd] *n* orden *f*, mandato; (*MIL*: *authority*) mando; (*mastery*) dominio; (*COMPUT*) orden *f*, comando ♦ *vt* (*troops*) mandar; (*give orders to*) mandar, ordenar; (*be able to get*) disponer de; (*deserve*) merecer; **to have at one's ~** (*money, resources etc*) disponer de; **to have/take ~ of** estar al/asumir el mando de.
command economy *n* economía dirigida.
commandeer [kɔmən'dɪə*] *vt* requisar.
commander [kə'mɑːndə*] *n* (*MIL*) comandante *m/f*, jefe/a *m/f*.
commanding [kə'mɑːndɪŋ] *adj* (*appearance*) imponente; (*voice, tone*) imperativo; (*lead*) abrumador(a); (*position*) dominante.
commanding officer *n* comandante *m*.
commandment [kə'mɑːndmənt] *n* (*REL*) mandamiento.
command module *n* módulo de mando.
commando [kə'mɑːndəu] *n* comando.
commemorate [kə'mɛməreɪt] *vt* conmemorar.
commemoration [kəmɛmə'reɪʃən] *n* conmemoración *f*.
commemorative [kə'mɛmərətɪv] *adj* conmemorativo.
commence [kə'mɛns] *vt, vi* comenzar.
commend [kə'mɛnd] *vt* (*praise*) elogiar, alabar; (*recommend*) recomendar; (*entrust*) encomendar.
commendable [kə'mɛndəbl] *adj* encomiable.
commendation [kɔmɛn'deɪʃən] *n* (*for bravery etc*) elogio, encomio.
commensurate [kə'mɛnʃərɪt] *adj*: **~ with** en proporción a.
comment ['kɔmɛnt] *n* comentario ♦ *vt*: **to ~**

that comentar *or* observar que ♦ *vi*: **to ~ (on)** comentar, hacer comentarios (sobre); **"no ~"** "no tengo nada que decir", "sin comentarios".
commentary ['kɔməntərɪ] *n* comentario.
commentator ['kɔmənteɪtə*] *n* comentarista *m/f*.
commerce ['kɔməːs] *n* comercio.
commercial [kə'məːʃəl] *adj* comercial ♦ *n* (*TV*) anuncio.
commercial bank *n* banco comercial.
commercial break *n* intermedio para publicidad.
commercialism [kə'məːʃəlɪzəm] *n* comercialismo.
commercial television *n* televisión *f* comercial.
commercial vehicle *n* vehículo comercial.
commiserate [kə'mɪzəreɪt] *vi*: **to ~ with** compadecerse de, condolerse de.
commission [kə'mɪʃən] *n* (*committee, fee, order for work of art etc*) comisión *f*; (*act*) perpetración *f* ♦ *vt* (*MIL*) nombrar; (*work of art*) encargar; **out of ~** (*machine*) fuera de servicio; **~ of inquiry** comisión *f* investigadora; **I get 10% ~** me dan el diez por ciento de comisión; **to ~ sb to do sth** encargar a algn que haga algo; **to ~ sth from sb** (*painting etc*) encargar algo a algn.
commissionaire [kəmɪʃə'nɛə*] *n* (*BRIT*) portero, conserje *m*.
commissioner [kə'mɪʃənə*] *n* comisario; (*POLICE*) comisario *m* de policía.
commit [kə'mɪt] *vt* (*act*) cometer; (*to sb's care*) entregar; **to ~ o.s. (to do)** comprometerse (a hacer); **to ~ suicide** suicidarse; **to ~ sb for trial** remitir a algn al tribunal.
commitment [kə'mɪtmənt] *n* compromiso.
committed [kə'mɪtɪd] *adj* (*writer, politician etc*) comprometido.
committee [kə'mɪtɪ] *n* comité *m*; **to be on a ~** ser miembro/a de un comité.
committee meeting *n* reunión *f* del comité.
commodious [kə'məudɪəs] *adj* grande, espacioso.
commodity [kə'mɔdɪtɪ] *n* mercancía.
commodity exchange *n* bolsa de productos *or* de mercancías.
commodity market *n* mercado de productos básicos.
commodore ['kɔmədɔː*] *n* comodoro.
common ['kɔmən] *adj* (*gen*) común; (*pej*) ordinario ♦ *n* campo común; **in ~** en común; **in ~ use** de uso corriente.
common cold *n*: **the ~** el resfriado.
common denominator *n* común denominador *m*.
commoner ['kɔmənə*] *n* plebeyo/a.
common land *n* campo comunal, ejido.
common law *n* ley *f* consuetudinaria.
common-law ['kɔmənlɔː] *adj*: **~ wife** esposa de hecho.
commonly ['kɔmənlɪ] *adv* comúnmente.
Common Market *n* Mercado Común.
commonplace ['kɔmənpleɪs] *adj* corriente.
commonroom ['kɔmənrum] *n* sala de reunión.
Commons ['kɔmənz] *npl* (*BRIT POL*): **the ~** (la Cámara de) los Comunes.
common sense *n* sentido común.
Commonwealth ['kɔmənwɛlθ] *n*: **the ~** la Comunidad (Británica) de Naciones, la Commonwealth; *ver recuadro*.

COMMONWEALTH

La **Commonwealth** *es la asociación de estados soberanos independientes y territorios asociados que formaban parte del antiguo Imperio Británico. Éste pasó a llamarse así después de la Segunda Guerra Mundial, aunque ya desde 1931 se le conocía como "British Commonwealth of Nations". Todos los estados miembros reconocen al monarca británico como "Head of the Commonwealth".*

commotion [kə'məuʃən] *n* tumulto, confusión *f*.
communal ['kɔmjuːnl] *adj* comunal; (*kitchen*) común.
commune ['kɔmjuːn] *n* (*group*) comuna ♦ *vi* [kə'mjuːn]: **to ~ with** comunicarse con.
communicate [kə'mjuːnɪkeɪt] *vt* comunicar ♦ *vi*: **to ~ (with)** comunicarse (con).
communication [kəmjuːnɪ'keɪʃən] *n* comunicación *f*.
communications network *n* red *f* de comunicaciones.
communications satellite *n* satélite *m* de comunicaciones.
communicative [kə'mjuːnɪkətɪv] *adj* comunicativo.
communion [kə'mjuːnɪən] *n* (*also*: **Holy C~**) comunión *f*.
communiqué [kə'mjuːnɪkeɪ] *n* comunicado, parte *m*.
communism ['kɔmjunɪzəm] *n* comunismo.
communist ['kɔmjunɪst] *adj, n* comunista *m/f*.
community [kə'mjuːnɪtɪ] *n* comunidad *f*; (*large group*) colectividad *f*; (*local*)

vecindario.
community centre *n* centro social.
community chest *n* (*US*) fondo social.
community health centre *n* centro médico, casa de salud.
community spirit *n* civismo.
commutation ticket [kɔmju'teɪʃən-] *n* (*US*) billete *m* de abono.
commute [kə'mjuːt] *vi viajar a diario de casa al trabajo* ♦ *vt* conmutar.
commuter [kə'mjuːtə*] *n persona que viaja a diario de casa al trabajo.*
compact [kəm'pækt] *adj* compacto; (*style*) conciso; (*packed*) apretado ♦ *n* ['kɔmpækt] (*pact*) pacto; (*also*: **powder ~**) polvera.
compact disc *n* compact disc *m*, disco compacto.
compact disc player *n* lector *m or* reproductor *m* de discos compactos.
companion [kəm'pænɪən] *n* compañero/a.
companionship [kəm'pænjənʃɪp] *n* compañerismo.
companionway [kəm'pænjənweɪ] *n* (*NAUT*) escalerilla.
company ['kʌmpənɪ] *n* (*gen*) compañía; (*COMM*) empresa, compañía; **to keep sb ~** acompañar a algn; **Smith and C~** Smith y Compañía.
company car *n* coche *m* de la empresa.
company director *n* director(a) *m/f* de empresa.
company secretary *n* (*BRIT*) administrador(a) *m/f* de empresa.
comparable ['kɔmpərəbl] *adj* comparable.
comparative [kəm'pærətɪv] *adj* (*freedom, luxury, cost*) relativo; (*study, linguistics*) comparado.
comparatively [kəm'pærətɪvlɪ] *adv* (*relatively*) relativamente.
compare [kəm'pɛə*] *vt* comparar ♦ *vi*: **to ~ (with)** poder compararse (con); **~d with** *or* **to** comparado con *or* a; **how do the prices ~?** ¿cómo son los precios en comparación?
comparison [kəm'pærɪsn] *n* comparación *f*; **in ~ (with)** en comparación (con).
compartment [kəm'pɑːtmənt] *n* compartim(i)ento; (*RAIL*) departamento, compartimento.
compass ['kʌmpəs] *n* brújula; **~es** *npl* compás *m*; **within the ~ of** al alcance de.
compassion [kəm'pæʃən] *n* compasión *f*.
compassionate [kəm'pæʃənɪt] *adj* compasivo; **on ~ grounds** por compasión.
compassionate leave *n* permiso por asuntos familiares.
compatibility [kəmpætɪ'bɪlɪtɪ] *n* compatibilidad *f*.
compatible [kəm'pætɪbl] *adj* compatible.
compel [kəm'pɛl] *vt* obligar.
compelling [kəm'pɛlɪŋ] *adj* (*fig: argument*) convincente.
compendium [kəm'pɛndɪəm] *n* compendio.
compensate ['kɔmpənseɪt] *vt* compensar ♦ *vi*: **to ~ for** compensar.
compensation [kɔmpən'seɪʃən] *n* (*for loss*) indemnización *f*.
compère ['kɔmpɛə*] *n* presentador(a) *m/f*.
compete [kəm'piːt] *vi* (*take part*) competir; (*vie with*) competir, hacer la competencia.
competence ['kɔmpɪtəns] *n* capacidad *f*, aptitud *f*.
competent ['kɔmpɪtənt] *adj* competente, capaz.
competing [kəm'piːtɪŋ] *adj* (*rival*) competidor(a); (*ideas*) contrapuesto.
competition [kɔmpɪ'tɪʃən] *n* (*contest*) concurso; (*SPORT*) competición *f*; (*ECON, rivalry*) competencia; **in ~ with** en competencia con.
competitive [kəm'pɛtɪtɪv] *adj* (*ECON, SPORT*) competitivo; (*spirit*) competidor(a), de competencia; (*selection*) por concurso.
competitor [kəm'pɛtɪtə*] *n* (*rival*) competidor(a) *m/f*; (*participant*) concursante *m/f*.
compile [kəm'paɪl] *vt* recopilar.
complacency [kəm'pleɪsnsɪ] *n* autosatisfacción *f*.
complacent [kəm'pleɪsənt] *adj* autocomplaciente.
complain [kəm'pleɪn] *vi* (*gen*) quejarse; (*COMM*) reclamar.
complaint [kəm'pleɪnt] *n* (*gen*) queja; (*COMM*) reclamación *f*; (*LAW*) demanda, querella; (*MED*) enfermedad *f*.
complement ['kɔmplɪmənt] *n* complemento; (*esp ship's crew*) dotación *f* ♦ *vt* ['kɔmplɪmɛnt] (*enhance*) complementar.
complementary [kɔmplɪ'mɛntərɪ] *adj* complementario.
complete [kəm'pliːt] *adj* (*full*) completo; (*finished*) acabado ♦ *vt* (*fulfil*) completar; (*finish*) acabar; (*a form*) rellenar; **it's a ~ disaster** es un desastre total.
completely [kəm'pliːtlɪ] *adv* completamente.
completion [kəm'pliːʃən] *n* (*gen*) conclusión *f*, terminación *f*; **to be nearing ~** estar a punto de terminarse; **on ~ of contract** cuando se realice el contrato.
complex ['kɔmplɛks] *adj* complejo ♦ *n* (*gen*) complejo.
complexion [kəm'plɛkʃən] *n* (*of face*) tez *f*,

cutis *m*; (*fig*) aspecto.

complexity [kəm'plɛksɪtɪ] *n* complejidad *f*.

compliance [kəm'plaɪəns] *n* (*submission*) sumisión *f*; (*agreement*) conformidad *f*; **in ~ with** de acuerdo con.

compliant [kəm'plaɪənt] *adj* sumiso; conforme.

complicate ['kɔmplɪkeɪt] *vt* complicar.

complicated ['kɔmplɪkeɪtɪd] *adj* complicado.

complication [kɔmplɪ'keɪʃən] *n* complicación *f*.

complicity [kəm'plɪsɪtɪ] *n* complicidad *f*.

compliment ['kɔmplɪmənt] *n* (*formal*) cumplido; (*flirtation*) piropo ♦ *vt* felicitar; **~s** *npl* saludos *mpl*; **to pay sb a ~** (*formal*) hacer cumplidos a algn; (*flirt*) piropear, echar piropos a algn; **to ~ sb (on sth/on doing sth)** felicitar a algn (por algo/por haber hecho algo).

complimentary [kɔmplɪ'mɛntərɪ] *adj* elogioso; (*copy*) de regalo; **~ ticket** invitación *f*.

compliments slip *n* saluda *m*.

comply [kəm'plaɪ] *vi*: **to ~ with** acatar.

component [kəm'pəunənt] *adj* componente ♦ *n* (*TECH*) pieza, componente *m*.

compose [kəm'pəuz] *vt* componer; **to be ~d of** componerse de, constar de; **to ~ o.s.** tranquilizarse.

composed [kəm'pəuzd] *adj* sosegado.

composer [kəm'pəuzə*] *n* (*MUS*) compositor(a) *m/f*.

composite ['kɔmpəzɪt] *adj* compuesto; **~ motion** (*COMM*) moción *f* compuesta.

composition [kɔmpə'zɪʃən] *n* composición *f*.

compos mentis ['kɔmpəs'mɛntɪs] *adj*: **to be ~** estar en su sano juicio.

compost ['kɔmpɔst] *n* abono.

compost heap *n montón de basura orgánica para abono.*

composure [kəm'pəuʒə*] *n* serenidad *f*, calma.

compound ['kɔmpaund] *n* (*CHEM*) compuesto; (*LING*) término compuesto; (*enclosure*) recinto ♦ *adj* (*gen*) compuesto; (*fracture*) complicado ♦ *vt* [kəm'paund] (*fig: problem, difficulty*) agravar.

comprehend [kɔmprɪ'hɛnd] *vt* comprender.

comprehension [kɔmprɪ'hɛnʃən] *n* comprensión *f*.

comprehensive [kɔmprɪ'hɛnsɪv] *adj* (*broad*) extenso; (*general*) de conjunto; **~ (school)** *n centro estatal de enseñanza secundaria*, ≈ Instituto Nacional de Bachillerato (*SP*); *ver recuadro*.

> **COMPREHENSIVE SCHOOL**
>
> *En los años 60 se creó un nuevo tipo de centro educativo de enseñanza secundaria (aproximadamente de los once años en adelante) denominado* **comprehensive school**, *abierto a todos los alumnos independientemente de sus capacidades, con el que se intentó poner fin a la división tradicional entre centros de enseñanzas teóricas para acceder a la educación superior ("grammar schools") y otros de enseñanzas básicamente profesionales ("secondary modern schools").*

comprehensive insurance policy *n* seguro a todo riesgo.

compress [kəm'prɛs] *vt* comprimir ♦ *n* ['kɔmprɛs] (*MED*) compresa.

comprise [kəm'praɪz] *vt* (*also*: **be ~d of**) comprender, constar de.

compromise ['kɔmprəmaɪz] *n* solución *f* intermedia; (*agreement*) arreglo ♦ *vt* comprometer ♦ *vi* transigir, transar (*LAM*) ♦ *cpd* (*decision, solution*) de término medio.

compulsion [kəm'pʌlʃən] *n* obligación *f*; **under ~** a la fuerza, por obligación.

compulsive [kəm'pʌlsɪv] *adj* compulsivo.

compulsory [kəm'pʌlsərɪ] *adj* obligatorio.

compulsory purchase *n* expropiación *f*.

compunction [kəm'pʌŋkʃən] *n* escrúpulo; **to have no ~ about doing sth** no tener escrúpulos en hacer algo.

computer [kəm'pju:tə*] *n* ordenador *m*, computador *m*, computadora.

computer game *n* juego de ordenador.

computerize [kəm'pju:təraɪz] *vt* (*data*) computerizar; (*system*) informatizar.

computer language *n* lenguaje *m* de ordenador *or* computadora.

computer literate *adj*: **to be ~** tener conocimientos de informática a nivel de usuario.

computer peripheral *n* periférico.

computer program *n* programa *m* informático *or* de ordenador.

computer programmer *n* programador(a) *m/f*.

computer programming *n* programación *f*.

computer science *n* informática.

computing [kəm'pju:tɪŋ] *n* (*activity*) informática.

comrade ['kɔmrɪd] *n* compañero/a.

comradeship ['kɔmrɪdʃɪp] *n* camaradería, compañerismo.

comsat ® ['kɔmsæt] *n abbr*

= **communications satellite**.
con [kɔn] *vt* timar, estafar ♦ *n* timo, estafa; **to ~ sb into doing sth** (*col*) engañar a algn para que haga algo.
concave ['kɔn'keɪv] *adj* cóncavo.
conceal [kən'si:l] *vt* ocultar; (*thoughts etc*) disimular.
concede [kən'si:d] *vt* reconocer; (*game*) darse por vencido en; (*territory*) ceder ♦ *vi* darse por vencido.
conceit [kən'si:t] *n* orgullo, presunción *f*.
conceited [kən'si:tɪd] *adj* orgulloso.
conceivable [kən'si:vəbl] *adj* concebible; **it is ~ that ...** es posible que ....
conceivably [kən'si:vəblɪ] *adv*: **he may ~ be right** es posible que tenga razón.
conceive [kən'si:v] *vt, vi* concebir; **to ~ of sth/of doing sth** imaginar algo/ imaginarse haciendo algo.
concentrate ['kɔnsəntreɪt] *vi* concentrarse ♦ *vt* concentrar.
concentration [kɔnsən'treɪʃən] *n* concentración *f*.
concentration camp *n* campo de concentración.
concentric [kən'sɛntrɪk] *adj* concéntrico.
concept ['kɔnsɛpt] *n* concepto.
conception [kən'sɛpʃən] *n* (*idea*) concepto, idea; (*BIOL*) concepción *f*.
concern [kən'sə:n] *n* (*matter*) asunto; (*COMM*) empresa; (*anxiety*) preocupación *f* ♦ *vt* tener que ver con; (*affect*) atañer, concernir; **to be ~ed (about)** interesarse (por), preocuparse (por); **to be ~ed with** tratar de; **"to whom it may ~"** "a quien corresponda"; **the department ~ed** (*under discussion*) el departamento en cuestión; (*relevant*) el departamento competente; **as far as I am ~ed** en cuanto a mí, por lo que a mí se refiere.
concerning [kən'sə:nɪŋ] *prep* sobre, acerca de.
concert ['kɔnsət] *n* concierto.
concerted [kən'sə:təd] *adj* (*efforts etc*) concertado.
concert hall *n* sala de conciertos.
concertina [kɔnsə'ti:nə] *n* concertina.
concerto [kən'tʃə:təu] *n* concierto.
concession [kən'sɛʃən] *n* concesión *f*; (*price ~*) descuento; **tax ~** privilegio fiscal.
concessionaire [kənsɛʃə'nɛə*] *n* concesionario/a.
concessionary [kən'sɛʃənərɪ] *adj* (*ticket, fare*) con descuento, a precio reducido.
conciliation [kənsɪlɪ'eɪʃən] *n* conciliación *f*.
conciliatory [kən'sɪlɪətrɪ] *adj* conciliador(a).
concise [kən'saɪs] *adj* conciso.
conclave ['kɔnkleɪv] *n* cónclave *m*.
conclude [kən'klu:d] *vt* (*finish*) concluir; (*treaty etc*) firmar; (*agreement*) llegar a; (*decide*): **to ~ that ...** llegar a la conclusión de que ... ♦ *vi* (*events*) concluir, terminar.
concluding [kən'klu:dɪŋ] *adj* (*remarks etc*) final.
conclusion [kən'klu:ʒən] *n* conclusión *f*; **to come to the ~ that** llegar a la conclusión de que.
conclusive [kən'klu:sɪv] *adj* decisivo, concluyente.
conclusively [kən'klu:sɪvlɪ] *adv* concluyentemente.
concoct [kən'kɔkt] *vt* (*food, drink*) preparar; (*story*) inventar; (*plot*) tramar.
concoction [kən'kɔkʃən] *n* (*food*) mezcla; (*drink*) brebaje *m*.
concord ['kɔŋkɔ:d] *n* (*harmony*) concordia; (*treaty*) acuerdo.
concourse ['kɔŋkɔ:s] *n* (*hall*) vestíbulo.
concrete ['kɔnkri:t] *n* hormigón *m* ♦ *adj* concreto.
concrete mixer *n* hormigonera.
concur [kən'kə:*] *vi* estar de acuerdo.
concurrently [kən'kʌrntlɪ] *adv* al mismo tiempo.
concussion [kən'kʌʃən] *n* conmoción *f* cerebral.
condemn [kən'dɛm] *vt* condenar.
condemnation [kɔndɛm'neɪʃən] *n* (*gen*) condena; (*blame*) censura.
condensation [kɔndɛn'seɪʃən] *n* condensación *f*.
condense [kən'dɛns] *vi* condensarse ♦ *vt* condensar; (*text*) abreviar.
condensed milk *n* leche *f* condensada.
condescend [kɔndɪ'sɛnd] *vi* condescender; **to ~ to sb** tratar a algn con condescendencia; **to ~ to do sth** dignarse hacer algo.
condescending [kɔndɪ'sɛndɪŋ] *adj* superior.
condition [kən'dɪʃən] *n* condición *f*; (*of health*) estado; (*disease*) enfermedad *f* ♦ *vt* condicionar; **on ~ that** a condición (de) que; **weather ~s** condiciones atmosféricas; **in good/poor ~** en buenas/ malas condiciones, en buen/mal estado; **~s of sale** condiciones de venta.
conditional [kən'dɪʃənl] *adj* condicional.
conditioned reflex [kən'dɪʃənd-] *n* reflejo condicionado.
conditioner [kən'dɪʃənə*] *n* (*for hair*) suavizante *m*, acondicionador *m*.
condo ['kɔndəu] *n* (*US col*) = **condominium**.

condolences [kən'dəulənsız] *npl* pésame *msg.*
condom ['kɔndəm] *n* condón *m.*
condominium [kɔndə'mınıəm] *n* (*US*: *building*) bloque *m* de pisos *or* apartamentos (*propiedad de quienes lo habitan*), condominio (*LAM*); (: *apartment*) piso *or* apartamento (en propiedad), condominio (*LAM*).
condone [kən'dəun] *vt* condonar.
conducive [kən'dju:sıv] *adj*: ~ **to** conducente a.
conduct ['kɔndʌkt] *n* conducta, comportamiento ♦ *vt* [kən'dʌkt] (*lead*) conducir; (*manage*) llevar, dirigir; (*MUS*) dirigir ♦ *vi* (*MUS*) llevar la batuta; **to ~ o.s.** comportarse.
conducted tour *n* (*BRIT*) visita con guía.
conductor [kən'dʌktə*] *n* (*of orchestra*) director(a) *m/f*; (*US*: *on train*) revisor(a) *m/f*; (*on bus*) cobrador *m*; (*ELEC*) conductor *m.*
conductress [kən'dʌktrıs] *n* (*on bus*) cobradora.
cone [kəun] *n* cono; (*pine ~*) piña; (*for ice cream*) cucurucho.
confectioner [kən'fɛkʃənə*] *n* (*of cakes*) pastelero/a; (*of sweets*) confitero/a; **~'s (shop)** *n* pastelería; confitería.
confectionery [kən'fɛkʃənrı] *n* pasteles *mpl*; dulces *mpl.*
confederate [kən'fɛdrıt] *adj* confederado ♦ *n* (*pej*) cómplice *m/f*; (*US*: *HISTORY*) confederado/a.
confederation [kənfɛdə'reıʃən] *n* confederación *f.*
confer [kən'fə:*] *vt* otorgar (*on* a) ♦ *vi* conferenciar; **to ~ (with sb about sth)** consultar (con algn sobre algo).
conference ['kɔnfərns] *n* (*meeting*) reunión *f*; (*convention*) congreso; **to be in ~** estar en una reunión.
conference room *n* sala de conferencias.
confess [kən'fɛs] *vt* confesar ♦ *vi* confesar; (*REL*) confesarse.
confession [kən'fɛʃən] *n* confesión *f.*
confessional [kən'fɛʃənl] *n* confesionario.
confessor [kən'fɛsə*] *n* confesor *m.*
confetti [kən'fɛtı] *n* confeti *m.*
confide [kən'faıd] *vi*: **to ~ in** confiar en.
confidence ['kɔnfıdns] *n* (*gen*, *also*: **self-~**) confianza; (*secret*) confidencia; **in ~** (*speak*, *write*) en confianza; **to have (every) ~ that** estar seguro *or* confiado de que; **motion of no ~** moción *f* de censura; **to tell sb sth in strict ~** decir algo a algn de manera confidencial.
confidence trick *n* timo.
confident ['kɔnfıdənt] *adj* seguro de sí mismo.
confidential [kɔnfı'dɛnʃəl] *adj* confidencial; (*secretary*) de confianza.
confidentiality [kɔnfıdɛnʃı'ælıtı] *n* confidencialidad *f.*
configuration [kənfıgju'reıʃən] *n* (*also COMPUT*) configuración *f.*
confine [kən'faın] *vt* (*limit*) limitar; (*shut up*) encerrar; **to ~ o.s. to doing sth** limitarse a hacer algo.
confined [kən'faınd] *adj* (*space*) reducido.
confinement [kən'faınmənt] *n* (*prison*) reclusión *f*; (*MED*) parto; **in solitary ~** incomunicado.
confines ['kɔnfaınz] *npl* confines *mpl.*
confirm [kən'fə:m] *vt* confirmar.
confirmation [kɔnfə'meıʃən] *n* confirmación *f.*
confirmed [kən'fə:md] *adj* empedernido.
confiscate ['kɔnfıskeıt] *vt* confiscar.
confiscation [kɔnfıs'keıʃən] *n* incautación *f.*
conflagration [kɔnflə'greıʃən] *n* conflagración *f.*
conflict ['kɔnflıkt] *n* conflicto ♦ *vi* [kən'flıkt] (*opinions*) estar reñido; (*reports*, *evidence*) contradecirse.
conflicting [kən'flıktıŋ] *adj* (*reports*, *evidence*, *opinions*) contradictorio.
conform [kən'fɔ:m] *vi*: **to ~ to** (*laws*) someterse a; (*usages*, *mores*) amoldarse a; (*standards*) ajustarse a.
conformist [kən'fɔ:mıst] *n* conformista *m/f.*
confound [kən'faund] *vt* confundir; (*amaze*) pasmar.
confounded [kən'faundıd] *adj* condenado.
confront [kən'frʌnt] *vt* (*problems*) hacer frente a; (*enemy*, *danger*) enfrentarse con.
confrontation [kɔnfrən'teıʃən] *n* enfrentamiento, confrontación *f.*
confrontational [kɔnfrən'teıʃənəl] *adj* conflictivo.
confuse [kən'fju:z] *vt* (*perplex*) desconcertar; (*mix up*) confundir.
confused [kən'fju:zd] *adj* confuso; (*person*) desconcertado; **to get ~** desconcertarse; (*muddled up*) hacerse un lío.
confusing [kən'fju:zıŋ] *adj* confuso.
confusion [kən'fju:ʒən] *n* confusión *f.*
congeal [kən'dʒi:l] *vi* coagularse.
congenial [kən'dʒi:nıəl] *adj* agradable.
congenital [kən'dʒɛnıtl] *adj* congénito.
congested [kən'dʒɛstıd] *adj* (*gen*) atestado; (*telephone lines*) saturado.
congestion [kən'dʒɛstʃən] *n* congestión *f.*
conglomerate [kən'glɔmərət] *n* (*COMM*, *GEO*) conglomerado.

conglomeration [kənglɔmə'reɪʃən] *n* conglomeración *f*.
Congo ['kɔŋgəu] *n* (*state*) Congo.
congratulate [kən'grætjuleɪt] *vt* felicitar.
congratulations [kəngrætju'leɪʃənz] *npl*: ~ **(on)** felicitaciones *fpl* (por); ~! ¡enhorabuena!, ¡felicidades!
congregate ['kɔŋgrɪgeɪt] *vi* congregarse.
congregation [kɔŋgrɪ'geɪʃən] *n* (*in church*) fieles *mpl*.
congress ['kɔŋgrɛs] *n* congreso; (*US POL*): **C~** el Congreso (de los Estados Unidos); *ver recuadro*.

> **CONGRESS**
>
> *En el Congreso de los Estados Unidos (**Congress**) se elaboran y aprueban las leyes federales. Consta de dos cámaras: la Cámara de Representantes ("House of Representatives"), cuyos 435 miembros son elegidos cada dos años por voto popular directo y en número proporcional a los habitantes de cada estado, y el Senado ("Senate"), con 100 senadores ("senators"), 2 por estado, de los que un tercio se elige cada dos años y el resto cada seis.*

congressman ['kɔŋgrɛsmən] *n* (*US*) diputado, miembro del Congreso.
congresswoman ['kɔŋgrɛswumən] *n* (*US*) diputada, miembro *f* del Congreso.
conical ['kɔnɪkl] *adj* cónico.
conifer ['kɔnɪfə*] *n* conífera.
coniferous [kə'nɪfərəs] *adj* (*forest*) conífero.
conjecture [kən'dʒɛktʃə*] *n* conjetura.
conjugal ['kɔndʒugl] *adj* conyugal.
conjugate ['kɔndʒugeɪt] *vt* conjugar.
conjunction [kən'dʒʌŋkʃən] *n* conjunción *f*; **in ~ with** junto con.
conjunctivitis [kəndʒʌŋktɪ'vaɪtɪs] *n* conjuntivitis *f*.
conjure ['kʌndʒə*] *vi* hacer juegos de manos.
▸**conjure up** *vt* (*ghost, spirit*) hacer aparecer; (*memories*) evocar.
conjurer ['kʌndʒərə*] *n* ilusionista *m/f*.
conjuring trick ['kʌndʒərɪŋ-] *n* juego de manos.
conker ['kɔŋkə*] *n* (*BRIT*) castaño de Indias.
conk out [kɔŋk-] *vi* (*col*) estropearse, fastidiarse, descomponerse (*LAM*).
con man *n* timador *m*.
Conn. *abbr* (*US*) = *Connecticut*.
connect [kə'nɛkt] *vt* juntar, unir; (*ELEC*) conectar; (*pipes*) empalmar; (*fig*) relacionar, asociar ♦ *vi*: **to ~ with** (*train*) enlazar con; **to be ~ed with** (*associated*) estar relacionado con; (*related*) estar emparentado con; **I am trying to ~ you** (*TEL*) estoy intentando ponerle al habla.
connection [kə'nɛkʃən] *n* juntura, unión *f*; (*ELEC*) conexión *f*; (*TECH*) empalme *m*; (*RAIL*) enlace *m*; (*TEL*) comunicación *f*; (*fig*) relación *f*; **what is the ~ between them?** ¿qué relación hay entre ellos?; **in ~ with** con respecto a, en relación a; **she has many business ~s** tiene muchos contactos profesionales; **to miss/make a ~** perder/coger el enlace.
connoisseur [kɔnɪ'səː*] *n* experto/a, entendido/a.
connotation [kɔnə'teɪʃən] *n* connotación *f*.
conquer ['kɔŋkə*] *vt* (*territory*) conquistar; (*enemy, feelings*) vencer.
conqueror ['kɔŋkərə*] *n* conquistador(a) *m/f*.
conquest ['kɔŋkwɛst] *n* conquista.
cons [kɔnz] *npl see* **convenience, pro.**
conscience ['kɔnʃəns] *n* conciencia; **in all ~** en conciencia.
conscientious [kɔnʃɪ'ɛnʃəs] *adj* concienzudo; (*objection*) de conciencia.
conscientious objector *n* objetor *m* de conciencia.
conscious ['kɔnʃəs] *adj* consciente; (*deliberate: insult, error*) premeditado, intencionado; **to become ~ of sth/that** darse cuenta de algo/de que.
consciousness ['kɔnʃəsnɪs] *n* conciencia; (*MED*) conocimiento.
conscript ['kɔnskrɪpt] *n* recluta *m/f*.
conscription [kən'skrɪpʃən] *n* servicio militar (obligatorio).
consecrate ['kɔnsɪkreɪt] *vt* consagrar.
consecutive [kən'sɛkjutɪv] *adj* consecutivo; **on 3 ~ occasions** en 3 ocasiones consecutivas.
consensus [kən'sɛnsəs] *n* consenso; **the ~ of opinion** el consenso general.
consent [kən'sɛnt] *n* consentimiento ♦ *vi*: **to ~ to** consentir en; **by common ~** de común acuerdo.
consequence ['kɔnsɪkwəns] *n* consecuencia; **in ~** por consiguiente.
consequently ['kɔnsɪkwəntlɪ] *adv* por consiguiente.
conservation [kɔnsə'veɪʃən] *n* conservación *f*; (*of nature*) conservación, protección *f*.
conservationist [kɔnsə'veɪʃnɪst] *n* conservacionista *m/f*.
conservative [kən'səːvətɪv] *adj* conservador(a); (*cautious*) moderado; **C~** *adj*, *n* (*BRIT POL*) conservador(a) *m/f*; **the**

C~ Party el partido conservador (británico).
conservatory [kən'sə:vətrɪ] *n* (*greenhouse*) invernadero.
conserve [kən'sə:v] *vt* conservar ♦ *n* conserva.
consider [kən'sɪdə*] *vt* considerar; (*take into account*) tomar en cuenta; (*study*) estudiar, examinar; **to ~ doing sth** pensar en (la posibilidad de) hacer algo; **all things ~ed** pensándolo bien; **~ yourself lucky** ¡date por satisfecho!
considerable [kən'sɪdərəbl] *adj* considerable.
considerably [kən'sɪdərəblɪ] *adv* bastante, considerablemente.
considerate [kən'sɪdərɪt] *adj* considerado.
consideration [kənsɪdə'reɪʃən] *n* consideración *f*; (*reward*) retribución *f*; **to be under ~** estar estudiándose; **my first ~ is my family** mi primera consideración es mi familia.
considered [kən'sɪdəd] *adj*: **it's my ~ opinion that ...** depués de haber reflexionado mucho, pienso que ....
considering [kən'sɪdərɪŋ] *prep*: **~ (that)** teniendo en cuenta (que).
consign [kən'saɪn] *vt* consignar.
consignee [kɔnsaɪ'ni:] *n* consignatario/a.
consignment [kən'saɪnmənt] *n* envío.
consignment note *n* (*COMM*) talón *m* de expedición.
consist [kən'sɪst] *vi*: **to ~ of** consistir en.
consistency [kən'sɪstənsɪ] *n* (*of person etc*) consecuencia, coherencia; (*thickness*) consistencia.
consistent [kən'sɪstənt] *adj* (*person, argument*) consecuente, coherente; (*results*) constante.
consolation [kɔnsə'leɪʃən] *n* consuelo.
console [kən'səul] *vt* consolar ♦ *n* ['kɔnsəul] (*control panel*) consola.
consolidate [kən'sɔlɪdeɪt] *vt* consolidar.
consols ['kɔnsɔlz] *npl* (*BRIT STOCK EXCHANGE*) valores *mpl* consolidados.
consommé [kən'sɔmeɪ] *n* consomé *m*, caldo.
consonant ['kɔnsənənt] *n* consonante *f*.
consort ['kɔnsɔ:t] *n* consorte *m/f* ♦ *vi* [kən'sɔ:t]: **to ~ with sb** (*often pej*) asociarse con algn; **prince ~** príncipe *m* consorte.
consortium [kən'sɔ:tɪəm] *n* consorcio.
conspicuous [kən'spɪkjuəs] *adj* (*visible*) visible; (*garish etc*) llamativo; (*outstanding*) notable; **to make o.s. ~** llamar la atención.
conspiracy [kən'spɪrəsɪ] *n* conjura, complot *m*.
conspire [kən'spaɪə*] *vi* conspirar.
constable ['kʌnstəbl] *n* (*BRIT*) agente *m/f* (de policía); **chief ~** ≈ jefe *m/f* de policía.
constabulary [kən'stæbjulərɪ] *n* ≈ policía.
constancy ['kɔnstənsɪ] *n* constancia; fidelidad *f*.
constant ['kɔnstənt] *adj* (*gen*) constante; (*loyal*) leal, fiel.
constantly ['kɔnstəntlɪ] *adv* constantemente.
constellation [kɔnstə'leɪʃən] *n* constelación *f*.
consternation [kɔnstə'neɪʃən] *n* consternación *f*.
constipated ['kɔnstɪpeɪtəd] *adj* estreñido.
constipation [kɔnstɪ'peɪʃən] *n* estreñimiento.
constituency [kən'stɪtjuənsɪ] *n* (*POL*) distrito electoral; (*people*) electorado; *ver recuadro*.

CONSTITUENCY

***Constituency** es la denominación que recibe un distrito o circunscripción electoral y el grupo de electores registrados en ella en el sistema electoral británico. Cada circunscripción elige a un diputado ("Member of Parliament"), el cual se halla disponible semanalmente para las consultas y peticiones de sus electores durante ciertas horas a la semana, tiempo al que se llama "surgery".*

constituency party *n* partido local.
constituent [kən'stɪtjuənt] *n* (*POL*) elector(a) *m/f*; (*part*) componente *m*.
constitute ['kɔnstɪtju:t] *vt* constituir.
constitution [kɔnstɪ'tju:ʃən] *n* constitución *f*.
constitutional [kɔnstɪ'tju:ʃənl] *adj* constitucional; **~ monarchy** monarquía constitucional.
constrain [kən'streɪn] *vt* obligar.
constrained [kən'streɪnd] *adj*: **to feel ~ to ...** sentirse obligado a ....
constraint [kən'streɪnt] *n* (*force*) fuerza; (*limit*) restricción *f*; (*restraint*) reserva; (*embarrassment*) cohibición *f*.
constrict [kən'strɪkt] *vt* oprimir.
constriction [kən'strɪkʃən] *n* constricción *f*, opresión *f*.
construct [kən'strʌkt] *vt* construir.
construction [kən'strʌkʃən] *n* construcción *f*; (*fig: interpretation*) interpretación *f*; **under ~** en construcción.
construction industry *n* industria de la

construcción.
constructive [kən'strʌktɪv] *adj* constructivo.
construe [kən'struː] *vt* interpretar.
consul ['kɔnsl] *n* cónsul *m/f*.
consulate ['kɔnsjulɪt] *n* consulado.
consult [kən'sʌlt] *vt, vi* consultar; **to ~ sb (about sth)** consultar a algn (sobre algo).
consultancy [kən'sʌltənsɪ] *n* (*COMM*) consultoría; (*MED*) puesto de especialista.
consultant [kən'sʌltənt] *n* (*BRIT MED*) especialista *m/f*; (*other specialist*) asesor(a) *m/f*, consultor(a) *m/f*.
consultation [kɔnsəl'teɪʃən] *n* consulta; **in ~ with** en consulta con.
consultative [kən'sʌltətɪv] *adj* consultivo.
consulting room *n* (*BRIT*) consulta, consultorio.
consume [kən'sjuːm] *vt* (*eat*) comerse; (*drink*) beberse; (*fire etc, COMM*) consumir.
consumer [kən'sjuːmə*] *n* (*of electricity, gas etc*) consumidor(a) *m/f*.
consumer association *n* asociación *f* de consumidores.
consumer credit *n* crédito al consumidor.
consumer durables *npl* bienes *mpl* de consumo duraderos.
consumer goods *npl* bienes *mpl* de consumo.
consumerism [kən'sjuːmərɪzəm] *n* consumismo.
consumer society *n* sociedad *f* de consumo.
consumer watchdog *n* organización *f* protectora del consumidor.
consummate ['kɔnsʌmeɪt] *vt* consumar.
consumption [kən'sʌmpʃən] *n* consumo; (*MED*) tisis *f*; **not fit for human ~** no apto para el consumo humano.
cont. *abbr* (= *continued*) sigue.
contact ['kɔntækt] *n* contacto; (*person: pej*) enchufe *m* ♦ *vt* ponerse en contacto con; **~ lenses** *npl* lentes *fpl* de contacto; **to be in ~ with sb/sth** estar en contacto con algn/algo; **business ~s** relaciones *fpl* comerciales.
contagious [kən'teɪdʒəs] *adj* contagioso.
contain [kən'teɪn] *vt* contener; **to ~ o.s.** contenerse.
container [kən'teɪnə*] *n* recipiente *m*; (*for shipping etc*) contenedor *m*.
containerize [kən'teɪnəraɪz] *vt* transportar en contenedores.
container ship *n* buque *m* contenedor, portacontenedores *m inv*.
contaminate [kən'tæmɪneɪt] *vt* contaminar.
contamination [kəntæmɪ'neɪʃən] *n* contaminación *f*.
cont'd *abbr* (= *continued*) sigue.
contemplate ['kɔntəmpleɪt] *vt* (*gen*) contemplar; (*reflect upon*) considerar; (*intend*) pensar.
contemplation [kɔntəm'pleɪʃən] *n* contemplación *f*.
contemporary [kən'tɛmpərərɪ] *adj, n* (*of the same age*) contemporáneo/a *m/f*.
contempt [kən'tɛmpt] *n* desprecio; **~ of court** (*LAW*) desacato (a los tribunales *or* a la justicia).
contemptible [kən'tɛmptɪbl] *adj* despreciable, desdeñable.
contemptuous [kən'tɛmptjuəs] *adj* desdeñoso.
contend [kən'tɛnd] *vt* (*argue*) afirmar ♦ *vi* (*struggle*) luchar; **he has a lot to ~ with** tiene que hacer frente a muchos problemas.
contender [kən'tɛndə*] *n* (*SPORT*) contendiente *m/f*.
content [kən'tɛnt] *adj* (*happy*) contento; (*satisfied*) satisfecho ♦ *vt* contentar; satisfacer ♦ *n* ['kɔntɛnt] contenido; **~s** *npl* contenido *msg*; **(table of) ~s** índice *m* de materias; (*in magazine*) sumario; **to be ~ with** conformarse con; **to ~ o.s. with sth/with doing sth** conformarse con algo/con hacer algo.
contented [kən'tɛntɪd] *adj* contento; satisfecho.
contentedly [kən'tɛntɪdlɪ] *adv* con aire satisfecho.
contention [kən'tɛnʃən] *n* discusión *f*; (*belief*) argumento; **bone of ~** manzana de la discordia.
contentious [kən'tɛnʃəs] *adj* discutible.
contentment [kən'tɛntmənt] *n* satisfacción *f*.
contest ['kɔntɛst] *n* contienda; (*competition*) concurso ♦ *vt* [kən'tɛst] (*dispute*) impugnar; (*LAW*) disputar, litigar; (*POL: election, seat*) presentarse como candidato/a a.
contestant [kən'tɛstənt] *n* concursante *m/f*; (*in fight*) contendiente *m/f*.
context ['kɔntɛkst] *n* contexto; **in/out of ~** en/fuera de contexto.
continent ['kɔntɪnənt] *n* continente *m*; **the C~** (*BRIT*) el continente europeo, Europa; **on the C~** en el continente europeo, en Europa.
continental [kɔntɪ'nɛntl] *adj* continental; (*BRIT: European*) europeo.
continental breakfast *n* desayuno estilo europeo.
continental quilt *n* (*BRIT*) edredón *m*.
contingency [kən'tɪndʒənsɪ] *n*

contingencia.
contingent [kən'tɪndʒənt] *n* (*group*) representación *f*.
continual [kən'tɪnjuəl] *adj* continuo.
continually [kən'tɪnjuəlɪ] *adv* continuamente.
continuation [kəntɪnju'eɪʃən] *n* prolongación *f*; (*after interruption*) reanudación *f*; (*story, episode*) continuación *f*.
continue [kən'tɪnjuː] *vi, vt* seguir, continuar; **~d on page 10** sigue en la página 10.
continuing education [kən'tɪnjuɪŋ] *n* educación *f* continua de adultos.
continuity [kɔntɪ'njuɪtɪ] *n* (*also CINE*) continuidad *f*.
continuity girl *n* (*CINE*) secretaria de continuidad.
continuous [kən'tɪnjuəs] *adj* continuo; **~ performance** (*CINE*) sesión *f* continua; **~ stationery** papel *m* continuo.
continuously [kən'tɪnjuəslɪ] *adv* continuamente.
contort [kən'tɔːt] *vt* retorcer.
contortion [kən'tɔːʃən] *n* (*movement*) contorsión *f*.
contortionist [kən'tɔːʃənɪst] *n* contorsionista *m/f*.
contour ['kɔntuə*] *n* contorno; (*also*: **~ line**) curva de nivel.
contraband ['kɔntrəbænd] *n* contrabando ♦ *adj* de contrabando.
contraception [kɔntrə'sɛpʃən] *n* contracepción *f*.
contraceptive [kɔntrə'sɛptɪv] *adj, n* anticonceptivo.
contract ['kɔntrækt] *n* contrato ♦ *cpd* ['kɔntrækt] (*price, date*) contratado, de contrato; (*work*) bajo contrato ♦ *vb* [kən'trækt] *vi* (*COMM*): **to ~ to do sth** comprometerse por contrato a hacer algo; (*become smaller*) contraerse, encogerse ♦ *vt* contraer; **to be under ~ to do sth** estar bajo contrato para hacer algo; **~ of employment** *or* **of service** contrato de trabajo.
►**contract in** *vi* tomar parte.
►**contract out** *vi*: **to ~ out (of)** optar por no tomar part (en); **to ~ out of a pension scheme** dejar de cotizar en un plan de jubilación.
contraction [kən'trækʃən] *n* contracción *f*.
contractor [kən'træktə*] *n* contratista *m/f*.
contractual [kən'træktjuəl] *adj* contractual.
contradict [kɔntrə'dɪkt] *vt* (*declare to be wrong*) desmentir; (*be contrary to*) contradecir.
contradiction [kɔntrə'dɪkʃən] *n* contradicción *f*; **to be in ~ with** contradecir.
contradictory [kɔntrə'dɪktərɪ] *adj* (*statements*) contradictorio; **to be ~ to** contradecir.
contralto [kən'træltəu] *n* contralto *f*.
contraption [kən'træpʃən] *n* (*pej*) artilugio *m*.
contrary ['kɔntrərɪ] *adj* (*opposite, different*) contrario; [kən'trɛərɪ] (*perverse*) terco ♦ *n*: **on the ~** al contrario; **unless you hear to the ~** a no ser que le digan lo contrario; **~ to what we thought** al contrario de lo que pensábamos.
contrast ['kɔntrɑːst] *n* contraste *m* ♦ *vt* [kən'trɑːst] contrastar; **in ~ to** *or* **with** a diferencia de.
contrasting [kən'trɑːstɪŋ] *adj* (*opinion*) opuesto; (*colour*) que hace contraste.
contravene [kɔntrə'viːn] *vt* contravenir.
contravention [kɔntrə'vɛnʃən] *n*: **~ (of)** contravención *f* (de).
contribute [kən'trɪbjuːt] *vi* contribuir ♦ *vt*: **to ~ to** (*gen*) contribuir a; (*newspaper*) colaborar en; (*discussion*) intervenir en.
contribution [kɔntrɪ'bjuːʃən] *n* (*money*) contribución *f*; (*to debate*) intervención *f*; (*to journal*) colaboración *f*.
contributor [kən'trɪbjutə*] *n* (*to newspaper*) colaborador(a) *m/f*.
contributory [kən'trɪbjutərɪ] *adj* (*cause*) contribuyente; **it was a ~ factor in ...** fue un factor que contribuyó en ....
contributory pension scheme *n* plan *m* cotizable de jubilación.
contrivance [kən'traɪvəns] *n* (*machine, device*) aparato, dispositivo.
contrive [kən'traɪv] *vt* (*invent*) idear ♦ *vi*: **to ~ to do** lograr hacer; (*try*) procurar hacer.
control [kən'trəul] *vt* controlar; (*traffic etc*) dirigir; (*machinery*) manejar; (*temper*) dominar; (*disease, fire*) dominar, controlar ♦ *n* (*command*) control *m*; (*of car*) conducción *f*; (*check*) freno; **~s** *npl* mandos *mpl*; **to ~ o.s.** controlarse, dominarse; **everything is under ~** todo está bajo control; **to be in ~ of** estar al mando de; **the car went out of ~** el coche se descontroló.
control group *n* (*MED, PSYCH etc*) grupo de control.
control key *n* (*COMPUT*) tecla de control.
controlled economy *n* economía dirigida.
controller [kən'trəulə*] *n* controlador(a) *m/f*.
controlling interest [kən'trəulɪŋ-] *n*

participación *f* mayoritaria.
control panel *n* (*on aircraft, ship, TV etc*) tablero de instrumentos.
control point *n* (puesto de) control *m*.
control room *n* (*NAUT, MIL*) sala de mandos; (*RADIO, TV*) sala de control.
control tower *n* (*AVIAT*) torre *f* de control.
control unit *n* (*COMPUT*) unidad *f* de control.
controversial [kɔntrəˈvəːʃl] *adj* polémico.
controversy [ˈkɔntrəvəːsɪ] *n* polémica.
conurbation [kɔnəːˈbeɪʃən] *n* conurbación *f*.
convalesce [kɔnvəˈlɛs] *vi* convalecer.
convalescence [kɔnvəˈlɛsns] *n* convalecencia.
convalescent [kɔnvəˈlɛsnt] *adj, n* convaleciente *m/f*.
convector [kənˈvɛktə*] *n* calentador *m* de convección.
convene [kənˈviːn] *vt* (*meeting*) convocar ♦ *vi* reunirse.
convenience [kənˈviːnɪəns] *n* (*comfort*) comodidad *f*; (*advantage*) ventaja; **at your earliest ~** (*COMM*) tan pronto como le sea posible; **all modern ~s**, (*BRIT*) **all mod cons** todo confort.
convenience foods *npl* platos *mpl* preparados.
convenient [kənˈviːnɪənt] *adj* (*useful*) útil; (*place*) conveniente; (*time*) oportuno; **if it is ~ for you** si le viene bien.
conveniently [kənˈviːnɪəntlɪ] *adv* (*happen*) oportunamente; (*situated*) convenientemente.
convent [ˈkɔnvənt] *n* convento.
convent school *n* colegio de monjas.
convention [kənˈvɛnʃən] *n* convención *f*; (*meeting*) asamblea.
conventional [kənˈvɛnʃənl] *adj* convencional.
converge [kənˈvəːdʒ] *vi* converger.
conversant [kənˈvəːsnt] *adj*: **to be ~ with** estar familiarizado con.
conversation [kɔnvəˈseɪʃən] *n* conversación *f*.
conversational [kɔnvəˈseɪʃənl] *adj* (*familiar*) familiar; (*talkative*) locuaz; **~ mode** (*COMPUT*) modo de conversación.
converse [ˈkɔnvəːs] *n* inversa ♦ *vi* [kənˈvəːs] conversar; **to ~ (with sb about sth)** conversar *or* platicar (*LAM*) (con algn de algo).
conversely [kɔnˈvəːslɪ] *adv* a la inversa.
conversion [kənˈvəːʃən] *n* conversión *f*; (*house ~*) reforma, remodelación *f*.
conversion table *n* tabla de equivalencias.
convert [kənˈvəːt] *vt* (*REL, COMM*) convertir; (*alter*) transformar ♦ *n* [ˈkɔnvəːt] converso/a.
convertible [kənˈvəːtəbl] *adj* convertible ♦ *n* descapotable *m*; **~ loan stock** obligaciones *fpl* convertibles.
convex [ˈkɔnˈvɛks] *adj* convexo.
convey [kənˈveɪ] *vt* transportar; (*thanks*) comunicar; (*idea*) expresar.
conveyance [kənˈveɪəns] *n* (*of goods*) transporte *m*; (*vehicle*) vehículo, medio de transporte.
conveyancing [kənˈveɪənsɪŋ] *n* (*LAW*) preparación *f* de escrituras de traspaso.
conveyor belt [kənˈveɪə*-] *n* cinta transportadora.
convict [kənˈvɪkt] *vt* (*gen*) condenar; (*find guilty*) declarar culpable a ♦ *n* [ˈkɔnvɪkt] presidiario/a.
conviction [kənˈvɪkʃən] *n* condena; (*belief*) creencia, convicción *f*.
convince [kənˈvɪns] *vt* convencer; **to ~ sb (of sth/that)** convencer a algn (de algo/de que).
convinced [kənˈvɪnst] *adj*: **~ of/that** convencido de/de que.
convincing [kənˈvɪnsɪŋ] *adj* convincente.
convincingly [kənˈvɪnsɪŋlɪ] *adv* de modo convincente, convincentemente.
convivial [kənˈvɪvɪəl] *adj* (*person*) sociable; (*atmosphere*) alegre.
convoluted [ˈkɔnvəluːtɪd] *adj* (*argument etc*) enrevesado; (*shape*) enrollado, enroscado.
convoy [ˈkɔnvɔɪ] *n* convoy *m*.
convulse [kənˈvʌls] *vt* convulsionar; **to be ~d with laughter** dislocarse de risa.
convulsion [kənˈvʌlʃən] *n* convulsión *f*.
coo [kuː] *vi* arrullar.
cook [kuk] *vt* cocinar; (*stew etc*) guisar; (*meal*) preparar ♦ *vi* hacerse; (*person*) cocinar ♦ *n* cocinero/a.
►**cook up** *vt* (*col*: *excuse, story*) inventar.
cookbook [ˈkukbuk] *n* libro de cocina.
cooker [ˈkukə*] *n* cocina.
cookery [ˈkukərɪ] *n* cocina.
cookery book *n* (*BRIT*) = **cookbook**.
cookie [ˈkukɪ] *n* (*US*) galleta.
cooking [ˈkukɪŋ] *n* cocina ♦ *cpd* (*apples*) para cocinar; (*utensils, salt, foil*) de cocina.
cooking chocolate *n* chocolate *m* fondant *or* de hacer.
cookout [ˈkukaut] *n* (*US*) comida al aire libre.
cool [kuːl] *adj* fresco; (*not hot*) tibio; (*not afraid*) tranquilo; (*unfriendly*) frío ♦ *vt* enfriar ♦ *vi* enfriarse; **it is ~** (*weather*) hace fresco; **to keep sth ~** *or* **in a ~ place** conservar algo fresco *or* en un sitio

fresco.
►**cool down** *vi* enfriarse; (*fig*: *person, situation*) calmarse.
coolant ['ku:lənt] *n* refrigerante *m*.
cool box, (*US*) **cooler** ['ku:lə*] *n* nevera portátil.
cooling ['ku:lɪŋ] *adj* refrescante.
cooling-off period [ku:lɪŋ'ɔf-] *n* (*INDUSTRY*) plazo de negociaciones.
cooling tower *n* torre *f* de refrigeración.
coolly ['ku:lɪ] *adv* (*calmly*) con tranquilidad; (*audaciously*) descaradamente; (*unenthusiastically*) fríamente, con frialdad.
coolness ['ku:lnɪs] *n* frescura; tranquilidad *f*; (*hostility*) frialdad *f*; (*indifference*) falta de entusiasmo.
coop [ku:p] *n* gallinero ♦ *vt*: **to ~ up** (*fig*) encerrar.
co-op ['kəuɔp] *n abbr* (= *Cooperative* (*Society*)) cooperativa.
cooperate [kəu'ɔpəreɪt] *vi* cooperar, colaborar; **will he ~?** ¿querrá cooperar?
cooperation [kəuɔpə'reɪʃən] *n* cooperación *f*, colaboración *f*.
cooperative [kəu'ɔpərətɪv] *adj* cooperativo; (*person*) dispuesto a colaborar ♦ *n* cooperativa.
co-opt [kəu'ɔpt] *vt*: **to ~ sb into sth** nombrar a algn para algo.
coordinate [kəu'ɔ:dɪneɪt] *vt* coordinar ♦ *n* [kəu'ɔ:dɪnət] (*MATH*) coordenada; **~s** *npl* (*clothes*) coordinados *mpl*.
coordination [kəuɔ:dɪ'neɪʃən] *n* coordinación *f*.
coot [ku:t] *n* focha *f* (común).
co-ownership [kəu'əunəʃɪp] *n* copropiedad *f*.
cop [kɔp] *n* (*col*) poli *m*.
cope [kəup] *vi*: **to ~ with** poder con; (*problem*) hacer frente a.
Copenhagen [kəupən'heɪgən] *n* Copenhague *m*.
copier ['kɔpɪə*] *n* (*photo~*) (foto)copiadora.
co-pilot ['kəu'paɪlət] *n* copiloto *m/f*.
copious ['kəupɪəs] *adj* copioso, abundante.
copper ['kɔpə*] *n* (*metal*) cobre *m*; (*col*: *policeman*) poli *m*; **~s** *npl* perras *fpl*; (*small change*) calderilla.
coppice ['kɔpɪs], **copse** [kɔps] *n* bosquecillo.
copulate ['kɔpjuleɪt] *vi* copular.
copulation [kɔpju'leɪʃən] *n* cópula.
copy ['kɔpɪ] *n* copia; (*of book*) ejemplar *m*; (*of magazine*) número; (*material*: *for printing*) original *m* ♦ *vt* copiar (*also COMPUT*); (*imitate*) copiar, imitar; **to make good ~** (*fig*) ser una noticia de interés; **rough ~** borrador *m*; **fair ~** copia en limpio.
►**copy out** *vt* copiar.
copycat ['kɔpɪkæt] *n* (*pej*) imitador(a) *m/f*.
copyright ['kɔpɪraɪt] *n* derechos *mpl* de autor.
copy typist *n* mecanógrafo/a.
coral ['kɔrəl] *n* coral *m*.
coral reef *n* arrecife *m* (de coral).
Coral Sea *n*: **the ~** el Mar del Coral.
cord [kɔ:d] *n* cuerda; (*ELEC*) cable *m*; (*fabric*) pana; **~s** *npl* (*trousers*) pantalones *mpl* de pana.
cordial ['kɔ:dɪəl] *adj* cordial ♦ *n* cordial *m*.
cordless ['kɔ:dlɪs] *adj* sin hilos.
cordon ['kɔ:dn] *n* cordón *m*.
►**cordon off** *vt* acordonar.
Cordova ['kɔ:dəvə] *n* Córdoba.
corduroy ['kɔ:dərɔɪ] *n* pana.
CORE [kɔ:*] *n abbr* (*US*) = *Congress of Racial Equality*.
core [kɔ:*] *n* (*of earth, nuclear reactor*) centro, núcleo; (*of fruit*) corazón *m*; (*of problem etc*) esencia, meollo ♦ *vt* quitar el corazón de.
Corfu [kɔ:'fu] *n* Corfú *m*.
coriander [kɔrɪ'ændə*] *n* culantro, cilantro.
cork [kɔ:k] *n* corcho; (*tree*) alcornoque *m*.
corkage ['kɔ:kɪdʒ] *n* *precio que se cobra en un restaurante por una botella de vino traída de fuera*.
corked [kɔ:kt] *adj* (*wine*) con sabor a corcho.
corkscrew ['kɔ:kskru:] *n* sacacorchos *m inv*.
cormorant ['kɔ:mərnt] *n* cormorán *m*.
Corn *abbr* (*BRIT*) = *Cornwall*.
corn [kɔ:n] *n* (*BRIT*: *wheat*) trigo; (*US*: *maize*) maíz *m*, choclo (*LAM*); (*on foot*) callo; **~ on the cob** (*CULIN*) maíz en la mazorca.
cornea ['kɔ:nɪə] *n* córnea.
corned beef ['kɔ:nd-] *n* carne *f* de vaca acecinada.
corner ['kɔ:nə*] *n* (*outside*) esquina; (*inside*) rincón *m*; (*in road*) curva; (*FOOTBALL*) córner *m*, saque *m* de esquina ♦ *vt* (*trap*) arrinconar; (*COMM*) acaparar ♦ *vi* (*in car*) tomar las curvas; **to cut ~s** atajar.
corner flag *n* (*FOOTBALL*) banderola de esquina.
corner kick *n* (*FOOTBALL*) córner *m*, saque *m* de esquina.
cornerstone ['kɔ:nəstəun] *n* piedra angular.
cornet ['kɔ:nɪt] *n* (*MUS*) corneta; (*BRIT*: *of ice cream*) cucurucho.
cornflakes ['kɔ:nfleɪks] *npl* copos *mpl* de maíz, cornflakes *mpl*.
cornflour ['kɔ:nflauə*] *n* (*BRIT*) harina de

maíz.
cornice ['kɔːnɪs] *n* cornisa.
Cornish ['kɔːnɪʃ] *adj* de Cornualles.
corn oil *n* aceite *m* de maíz.
cornstarch ['kɔːnstɑːtʃ] *n* (*US*) = **cornflour.**
cornucopia [kɔːnju'kəupɪə] *n* cornucopia.
Cornwall ['kɔːnwəl] *n* Cornualles *m.*
corny ['kɔːnɪ] *adj* (*col*) gastado.
corollary [kə'rɔlərɪ] *n* corolario.
coronary ['kɔrənərɪ] *n*: ~ **(thrombosis)** infarto.
coronation [kɔrə'neɪʃən] *n* coronación *f.*
coroner ['kɔrənə*] *n* juez *m/f* de instrucción.
coronet ['kɔrənɪt] *n* corona.
Corp. *abbr* = **corporation.**
corporal ['kɔːpərl] *n* cabo ♦ *adj*: ~ **punishment** castigo corporal.
corporate ['kɔːpərɪt] *adj* corporativo.
corporate hospitality *n obsequios a los clientes por cortesía de la empresa.*
corporate identity, corporate image *n* (*of organization*) identidad *f* corporativa.
corporation [kɔːpə'reɪʃən] *n* (*of town*) ayuntamiento; (*COMM*) corporación *f.*
corps [kɔː*], *pl* **corps** [kɔːz] *n* cuerpo; **press** ~ gabinete *m* de prensa.
corpse [kɔːps] *n* cadáver *m.*
corpulent ['kɔːpjulənt] *adj* corpulento/a.
Corpus Christi ['kɔːpəs'krɪstɪ] *n* Corpus *m* (Christi).
corpuscle ['kɔːpʌsl] *n* corpúsculo.
corral [kə'rɑːl] *n* corral *m.*
correct [kə'rɛkt] *adj* correcto, (*accurate*) exacto ♦ *vt* corregir; **you are** ~ tiene razón.
correction [kə'rɛkʃən] *n* rectificación *f*; (*erasure*) tachadura.
correlate ['kɔrɪleɪt] *vi*: **to** ~ **with** tener correlación con.
correlation [kɔrɪ'leɪʃən] *n* correlación *f.*
correspond [kɔrɪs'pɔnd] *vi* (*write*) escribirse; (*be equal to*) corresponder.
correspondence [kɔrɪs'pɔndəns] *n* correspondencia.
correspondence course *n* curso por correspondencia.
correspondent [kɔrɪs'pɔndənt] *n* corresponsal *m/f.*
corresponding [kɔrɪs'pɔndɪŋ] *adj* correspondiente.
corridor ['kɔrɪdɔː*] *n* pasillo.
corroborate [kə'rɔbəreɪt] *vt* corroborar.
corroboration [kərɔbə'reɪʃən] *n* corroboración *f*, confirmación *f.*
corrode [kə'rəud] *vt* corroer ♦ *vi* corroerse.
corrosion [kə'rəuʒən] *n* corrosión *f.*
corrosive [kə'rəusɪv] *adj* corrosivo.
corrugated ['kɔrəgeɪtɪd] *adj* ondulado.
corrugated cardboard *n* cartón *m* ondulado.
corrugated iron *n* chapa ondulada.
corrupt [kə'rʌpt] *adj* corrompido; (*person*) corrupto ♦ *vt* corromper; (*bribe*) sobornar; (*data*) degradar; ~ **practices** (*dishonesty, bribery*) corrupción *f.*
corruption [kə'rʌpʃən] *n* corrupción *f*; (*of data*) alteración *f.*
corset ['kɔːsɪt] *n* faja; (*old-style*) corsé *m.*
Corsica ['kɔːsɪkə] *n* Córcega.
Corsican ['kɔːsɪkən] *adj, n* corso/a *m/f.*
cortège [kɔː'teɪʒ] *n* cortejo, comitiva.
cortisone ['kɔːtɪzəun] *n* cortisona.
c.o.s. *abbr* (= *cash on shipment*) pago al embarcar.
cosh [kɔʃ] *n* (*BRIT*) cachiporra.
cosignatory ['kəu'sɪgnətərɪ] *n* cosignatario/a.
cosine ['kəusaɪn] *n* coseno.
cosiness ['kəuzɪnɪs] *n* comodidad *f*; (*atmosphere*) lo acogedor.
cos lettuce [kɔs-] *n* lechuga romana.
cosmetic [kɔz'mɛtɪk] *n* cosmético ♦ *adj* (*also fig*) cosmético; (*surgery*) estético.
cosmic ['kɔzmɪk] *adj* cósmico.
cosmonaut ['kɔzmənɔːt] *n* cosmonauta *m/f.*
cosmopolitan [kɔzmə'pɔlɪtn] *adj* cosmopolita.
cosmos ['kɔzmɔs] *n* cosmos *m.*
cosset ['kɔsɪt] *vt* mimar.
cost [kɔst] *n* (*gen*) coste *m*, costo; (*price*) precio; ~**s** *npl* (*LAW*) costas *fpl* ♦ *vb* (*pt, pp* **cost**) *vi* costar, valer ♦ *vt* preparar el presupuesto de; **how much does it** ~? ¿cuánto cuesta?, ¿cuánto vale?; **what will it** ~ **to have it repaired?** ¿cuánto costará repararlo?; **the** ~ **of living** el coste *or* costo de la vida; **at all** ~**s** cueste lo que cueste.
cost accountant *n* contable *m* de costos.
co-star ['kəustɑː*] *n* coprotagonista *m/f.*
Costa Rica ['kɔstə'riːkə] *n* Costa Rica.
Costa Rican ['kɔstə'riːkən] *adj, n* costarriqueño/a *m/f*, costarricense *m/f.*
cost centre *n* centro (de determinación) de coste.
cost control *n* control *m* de costes.
cost-effective [kɔstɪ'fɛktɪv] *adj* (*COMM*) rentable.
cost-effectiveness ['kɔstɪ'fɛktɪvnɪs] *n* relación *f* coste-rendimiento.
costing ['kɔstɪŋ] *n* cálculo del coste.
costly ['kɔstlɪ] *adj* (*expensive*) costoso.
cost-of-living [kɔstəv'lɪvɪŋ] *adj*: ~ **allowance** *n* plus *m* de carestía de vida; ~ **index** *n* índice *m* del coste de vida.
cost price *n* (*BRIT*) precio de coste.

costume ['kɔstjuːm] *n* traje *m*; (*BRIT: also:* **swimming ~**) traje de baño.
costume jewellery *n* bisutería.
cosy, (*US*) **cozy** ['kəuzɪ] *adj* cómodo, a gusto; (*room, atmosphere*) acogedor(a).
cot [kɔt] *n* (*BRIT: child's*) cuna; (*US: folding bed*) cama plegable.
cot death *n* muerte *f* en la cuna.
Cotswolds ['kɔtswəuldz] *npl región de colinas del suroeste inglés.*
cottage ['kɔtɪdʒ] *n* casita de campo.
cottage cheese *n* requesón *m*.
cottage industry *n* industria artesanal.
cottage pie *n pastel de carne cubierta de puré de patatas.*
cotton ['kɔtn] *n* algodón *m*; (*thread*) hilo.
▶**cotton on** *vi* (*col*): **to ~ on (to sth)** caer en la cuenta (de algo).
cotton candy *n* (*US*) algodón *m* (azucarado).
cotton wool *n* (*BRIT*) algodón *m* (hidrófilo).
couch [kautʃ] *n* sofá *m*; (*in doctor's surgery*) camilla.
couchette [kuː'ʃɛt] *n* litera.
couch potato *n* (*col*) *persona comodona que no se mueve en todo el día.*
cough [kɔf] *vi* toser ♦ *n* tos *f*.
▶**cough up** *vt* escupir.
cough drop *n* pastilla para la tos.
cough mixture *n* jarabe *m* para la tos.
could [kud] *pt of* **can**.
couldn't ['kudnt] = **could not.**
council ['kaunsl] *n* consejo; **city** *or* **town ~** ayuntamiento; **C~ of Europe** Consejo de Europa.
council estate *n* (*BRIT*) barriada de viviendas sociales de alquiler.
council house *n* (*BRIT*) vivienda social de alquiler.
councillor ['kaunslə*] *n* concejal *m/f*.
council tax *n* (*BRIT*) contribución *f* municipal (*dependiente del valor de la vivienda*).
counsel ['kaunsl] *n* (*advice*) consejo; (*lawyer*) abogado/a ♦ *vt* aconsejar; **~ for the defence/the prosecution** abogado/a defensor(a)/fiscal; **to ~ sth/sb to do sth** aconsejar algo/a algn que haga algo.
counsellor, (*US*) **counselor** ['kaunslə*] *n* consejero/a; (*US LAW*) abogado/a.
count [kaunt] *vt* (*gen*) contar; (*include*) incluir ♦ *vi* contar ♦ *n* cuenta; (*of votes*) escrutinio; (*nobleman*) conde *m*; (*sum*) total *m*, suma; **to ~ the cost of** calcular el coste de; **not ~ing the children** niños aparte; **10 ~ing him** diez incluyéndolo a él, diez con él; **~ yourself lucky** date por satisfecho; **that doesn't ~!** ¡eso no vale!; **to ~ (up) to 10** contar hasta diez; **it ~s for very little** cuenta poco; **to keep ~ of sth** llevar la cuenta de algo.
▶**count on** *vt fus* contar con; **to ~ on doing sth** contar con hacer algo.
▶**count up** *vt* contar.
countdown ['kauntdaun] *n* cuenta atrás.
countenance ['kauntɪnəns] *n* semblante *m*, rostro ♦ *vt* (*tolerate*) aprobar, consentir.
counter ['kauntə*] *n* (*in shop*) mostrador *m*; (*position: in post office, bank*) ventanilla; (*in games*) ficha; (*TECH*) contador *m* ♦ *vt* contrarrestar; (*blow*) parar; (*attack*) contestar a ♦ *adv*: **~ to** contrario a; **to buy under the ~** (*fig*) comprar de estraperlo *or* bajo mano; **to ~ sth with sth/by doing sth** contestar algo con algo/haciendo algo.
counteract ['kauntər'ækt] *vt* contrarrestar.
counterattack ['kauntərə'tæk] *n* contraataque *m* ♦ *vi* contraatacar.
counterbalance ['kauntə'bæləns] *n* contrapeso.
counter-clockwise ['kauntə'klɔkwaɪz] *adv* en sentido contrario al de las agujas del reloj.
counter-espionage ['kauntər'ɛspɪənɑːʒ] *n* contraespionaje *m*.
counterfeit ['kauntəfɪt] *n* falsificación *f* ♦ *vt* falsificar ♦ *adj* falso, falsificado.
counterfoil ['kauntəfɔɪl] *n* (*BRIT*) matriz *f*, talón *m*.
counterintelligence ['kauntərɪn'tɛlɪdʒəns] *n* contraespionaje *m*.
countermand ['kauntəmɑːnd] *vt* revocar.
counter-measure ['kauntəmɛʒə*] *n* contramedida.
counteroffensive ['kauntərə'fɛnsɪv] *n* contraofensiva.
counterpane ['kauntəpeɪn] *n* colcha.
counterpart ['kauntəpɑːt] *n* (*of person*) homólogo/a.
counter-productive [kauntəprə'dʌktɪv] *adj* contraproducente.
counterproposal ['kauntəprə'pəuzl] *n* contrapropuesta.
countersign ['kauntəsaɪn] *vt* ratificar, refrendar.
countess ['kauntɪs] *n* condesa.
countless ['kauntlɪs] *adj* innumerable.
countrified ['kʌntrɪfaɪd] *adj* rústico.
country ['kʌntrɪ] *n* país *m*; (*native land*) patria; (*as opposed to town*) campo; (*region*) región *f*, tierra; **in the ~** en el campo; **mountainous ~** región *f* montañosa.
country and western (music) *n* música country.

country dancing *n* (*BRIT*) baile *m* regional.
country house *n* casa de campo.
countryman ['kʌntrɪmən] *n* (*national*) compatriota *m*; (*rural*) hombre *m* del campo.
countryside ['kʌntrɪsaɪd] *n* campo.
countrywide ['kʌntrɪ'waɪd] *adj* nacional ♦ *adv* por todo el país.
county ['kauntɪ] *n* condado; *see also* **district council**.
county council *n* (*BRIT*) ≈ diputación *f* provincial.
county town *n* cabeza de partido.
coup, ~s [ku:, -z] *n* golpe *m*; (*triumph*) éxito; (*also*: ~ **d'état**) golpe de estado.
coupé ['ku:peɪ] *n* cupé *m*.
couple ['kʌpl] *n* (*of things*) par *m*; (*of people*) pareja; (*married* ~) matrimonio ♦ *vt* (*ideas, names*) unir, juntar; (*machinery*) acoplar; **a ~ of** un par de.
couplet ['kʌplɪt] *n* pareado.
coupling ['kʌplɪŋ] *n* (*RAIL*) enganche *m*.
coupon ['ku:pɔn] *n* cupón *m*; (*pools* ~) boleto (de quiniela).
courage ['kʌrɪdʒ] *n* valor *m*, valentía.
courageous [kə'reɪdʒəs] *adj* valiente.
courgette [kuə'ʒɛt] *n* (*BRIT*) calabacín *m*.
courier ['kurɪə*] *n* mensajero/a; (*diplomatic*) correo; (*for tourists*) guía *m/f* (de turismo).
course [kɔ:s] *n* (*direction*) dirección *f*; (*of river, SCOL*) curso; (*of ship*) rumbo; (*fig*) proceder *m*; (*GOLF*) campo; (*part of meal*) plato; **of ~** *adv* desde luego, naturalmente; **of ~!** ¡claro!, ¡cómo no! (*LAM*); **(no) of ~ not!** ¡claro que no!, ¡por supuesto que no!; **in due ~** a su debido tiempo; **in the ~ of the next few days** durante los próximos días; **we have no other ~ but to ...** no tenemos más remedio que ...; **there are 2 ~s open to us** se nos ofrecen dos posibilidades; **the best ~ would be to ...** lo mejor sería ...; **~ of treatment** (*MED*) tratamiento.
court [kɔ:t] *n* (*royal*) corte *f*; (*LAW*) tribunal *m*, juzgado; (*TENNIS*) pista, cancha (*LAM*) ♦ *vt* (*woman*) cortejar; (*fig*: *favour, popularity*) solicitar, buscar; (: *death, disaster, danger etc*) buscar; **to take to ~** demandar; **~ of appeal** tribunal *m* de apelación.
courteous ['kə:tɪəs] *adj* cortés.
courtesan [kɔ:tɪ'zæn] *n* cortesana.
courtesy ['kə:təsɪ] *n* cortesía; **by ~ of** (por) cortesía de.
courtesy light *n* (*AUT*) luz *f* interior.
court-house ['kɔ:thaus] *n* (*US*) palacio de justicia.
courtier ['kɔ:tɪə*] *n* cortesano.
court martial, *pl* **courts martial** ['kɔ:t'mɑ:ʃəl] *n* consejo de guerra ♦ *vt* someter a consejo de guerra.
courtroom ['kɔ:trum] *n* sala de justicia.
court shoe *n* *zapato de mujer de estilo clásico.*
courtyard ['kɔ:tjɑ:d] *n* patio.
cousin ['kʌzn] *n* primo/a; **first ~** primo/a carnal.
cove [kəuv] *n* cala, ensenada.
covenant ['kʌvənənt] *n* convenio ♦ *vt*: **to ~ £20 per year to a charity** concertar el pago de veinte libras anuales a una sociedad benéfica.
Coventry ['kɔvəntrɪ] *n*: **to send sb to ~** (*fig*) hacer el vacío a algn.
cover ['kʌvə*] *vt* cubrir; (*with lid*) tapar; (*chairs etc*) revestir; (*distance*) cubrir, recorrer; (*include*) abarcar; (*protect*) abrigar; (*journalist*) investigar; (*issues*) tratar ♦ *n* cubierta; (*lid*) tapa; (*for chair etc*) funda; (*for bed*) cobertor *m*; (*envelope*) sobre *m*; (*of magazine*) portada; (*shelter*) abrigo; (*insurance*) cobertura; **to take ~** (*shelter*) protegerse, resguardarse; **under ~** (*indoors*) bajo techo; **under ~ of darkness** al amparo de la oscuridad; **under separate ~** (*COMM*) por separado; **£10 will ~ everything** con diez libras cubriremos todos los gastos.
▸**cover up** *vt* (*child, object*) cubrir completamente, tapar; (*fig*: *hide*: *truth, facts*) ocultar; **to ~ up for sb** (*fig*) encubrir a algn.
coverage ['kʌvərɪdʒ] *n* alcance *m*; (*in media*) reportaje *m*; (*INSURANCE*) cobertura.
coveralls ['kʌvərɔ:lz] *npl* (*US*) mono *sg*.
cover charge *n* precio del cubierto.
covering ['kʌvərɪŋ] *n* cubierta, envoltura.
covering letter, (*US*) **cover letter** *n* carta de explicación.
cover note *n* (*INSURANCE*) póliza provisional.
cover price *n* precio de cubierta.
covert ['kəuvət] *adj* (*secret*) secreto, encubierto; (*dissembled*) furtivo.
cover-up ['kʌvərʌp] *n* encubrimiento.
covet ['kʌvɪt] *vt* codiciar.
covetous ['kʌvɪtəs] *adj* codicioso.
cow [kau] *n* vaca ♦ *vt* intimidar.
coward ['kauəd] *n* cobarde *m/f*.
cowardice ['kauədɪs] *n* cobardía.
cowardly ['kauədlɪ] *adj* cobarde.
cowboy ['kaubɔɪ] *n* vaquero.
cower ['kauə*] *vi* encogerse (de miedo).
co-worker ['kəuwə:kə*] *n* colaborador(a) *m/f*.

cowshed ['kaufɛd] *n* establo.
cowslip ['kauslɪp] *n* (*BOT*) primavera, prímula.
coxswain ['kɔksn] *n* (*abbr*: **cox**) timonel *m*.
coy [kɔɪ] *adj* tímido.
coyote [kɔɪ'əutɪ] *n* coyote *m*.
cozy ['kəuzɪ] *adj* (*US*) = **cosy**.
CP *n abbr* (= *Communist Party*) PC *m*.
cp. *abbr* (= *compare*) cfr.
c/p *abbr* (*BRIT*) = **carriage paid**.
CPA *n abbr* (*US*) = **certified public accountant**.
CPI *n abbr* (= *Consumer Price Index*) IPC *m*.
Cpl. *abbr* (*MIL*) = **corporal**.
CP/M *n abbr* (= *Central Program for Microprocessors*) CP/M *m*.
c.p.s. *abbr* (= *characters per second*) c.p.s.
CPSA *n abbr* (*BRIT*: = *Civil and Public Services Association*) *sindicato de funcionarios*.
CPU *n abbr* = **central processing unit**.
cr. *abbr* = **credit, creditor**.
crab [kræb] *n* cangrejo.
crab apple *n* manzana silvestre.
crack [kræk] *n* grieta; (*noise*) crujido; (: *of whip*) chasquido; (*joke*) chiste *m*; (*col*: *drug*) crack *m*; (*attempt*): **to have a ~ at sth** intentar algo ♦ *vt* agrietar, romper; (*nut*) cascar; (*safe*) forzar; (*whip etc*) chasquear; (*knuckles*) crujir; (*joke*) contar; (*case*: *solve*) resolver; (*code*) descifrar ♦ *adj* (*athlete*) de primera clase; **to ~ jokes** (*col*) bromear.
▸**crack down on** *vt fus* reprimir fuertemente, adoptar medidas severas contra.
▸**crack up** *vi* sufrir una crisis nerviosa.
crackdown ['krækdaun] *n*: **~ (on)** (*on crime*) campaña (contra); (*on spending*) reducción *f* (en).
cracker ['krækə*] *n* (*biscuit*) galleta salada, cráker *m*; (*Christmas* ~) sorpresa (navideña).
crackle ['krækl] *vi* crepitar.
crackling ['kræklɪŋ] *n* (*on radio, telephone*) interferencia; (*of fire*) chisporroteo, crepitación *f*; (*of leaves etc*) crujido; (*of pork*) chicharrón *m*.
crackpot ['krækpɔt] (*col*) *n* pirado/a ♦ *adj* de pirado.
cradle ['kreɪdl] *n* cuna ♦ *vt* (*child*) mecer, acunar; (*object*) abrazar.
craft [krɑːft] *n* (*skill*) arte *m*; (*trade*) oficio; (*cunning*) astucia; (*boat*) embarcación *f*.
craftsman ['krɑːftsmən] *n* artesano.
craftsmanship ['krɑːftsmənʃɪp] *n* artesanía.
crafty ['krɑːftɪ] *adj* astuto.
crag [kræg] *n* peñasco.
craggy ['krægɪ] *adj* escarpado.
cram [kræm] *vt* (*fill*): **to ~ sth with** llenar algo (a reventar) de; (*put*): **to ~ sth into** meter algo a la fuerza en ♦ *vi* (*for exams*) empollar.
crammed [kræmd] *adj* atestado.
cramp [kræmp] *n* (*MED*) calambre *m*; (*TECH*) grapa ♦ *vt* (*limit*) poner trabas a.
cramped [kræmpt] *adj* apretado; (*room*) minúsculo.
crampon ['kræmpən] *n* crampón *m*.
cranberry ['krænbərɪ] *n* arándano.
crane [kreɪn] *n* (*TECH*) grúa; (*bird*) grulla ♦ *vt, vi*: **to ~ forward, to ~ one's neck** estirar el cuello.
cranium ['kreɪnɪəm] *n* cráneo.
crank [kræŋk] *n* manivela; (*person*) chiflado/a.
crankshaft ['kræŋkʃɑːft] *n* cigüeñal *m*.
cranky ['kræŋkɪ] *adj* (*eccentric*) maniático; (*bad-tempered*) de mal genio.
cranny ['krænɪ] *n see* **nook**.
crap [kræp] *n* (*col!*) mierda (*!*).
crappy ['kræpɪ] *adj* (*col*) chungo.
craps [kræps] *n* (*US*) dados *mpl*.
crash [kræʃ] *n* (*noise*) estrépito; (*of cars, plane*) accidente *m*; (*of business*) quiebra; (*STOCK EXCHANGE*) crac *m* ♦ *vt* (*plane*) estrellar ♦ *vi* (*plane*) estrellarse; (*two cars*) chocar; (*fall noisily*) caer con estrépito; **he ~ed the car into a wall** estrelló el coche contra una pared *or* tapia.
crash barrier *n* (*AUT*) barrera de protección.
crash course *n* curso acelerado.
crash helmet *n* casco (protector).
crash landing *n* aterrizaje *m* forzoso.
crass [kræs] *adj* grosero, maleducado.
crate [kreɪt] *n* caja, cajón *m* de embalaje; (*col*) armatoste *m*.
crater ['kreɪtə*] *n* cráter *m*.
cravat(e) [krə'væt] *n* pañuelo.
crave [kreɪv] *vt, vi*: **to ~ (for)** ansiar, anhelar.
craving ['kreɪvɪŋ] *n* (*for food, cigarettes, etc*) ansias *fpl*; (*during pregnancy*) antojo.
crawl [krɔːl] *vi* (*drag o.s.*) arrastrarse; (*child*) andar a gatas, gatear; (*vehicle*) avanzar (lentamente); (*col*): **to ~ to sb** dar coba a algn, hacerle la pelota a algn ♦ *n* (*SWIMMING*) crol *m*.
crawler lane [krɔːlə-] *n* (*BRIT AUT*) carril *m* para tráfico lento.
crayfish ['kreɪfɪʃ] *n, pl inv* (*freshwater*) cangrejo (de río); (*saltwater*) cigala.
crayon ['kreɪən] *n* lápiz *m* de color.
craze [kreɪz] *n* manía; (*fashion*) moda.
crazed [kreɪzd] *adj* (*look, person*) loco,

demente; (*pottery, glaze*) agrietado, cuarteado.
crazy ['kreɪzɪ] *adj* (*person*) loco; (*idea*) disparatado; **to go** ~ volverse loco; **to be ~ about sb/sth** (*col*) estar loco por algn/ algo.
crazy paving *n pavimento de baldosas irregulares.*
creak [kriːk] *vi* crujir; (*hinge etc*) chirriar, rechinar.
cream [kriːm] *n* (*of milk*) nata, crema; (*lotion*) crema; (*fig*) flor *f* y nata ♦ *adj* (*colour*) color *m* crema; **whipped** ~ nata batida.
▶**cream off** *vt* (*fig*) (*best talents, part of profits*) separar lo mejor de.
cream cake *n* pastel *m* de nata.
cream cheese *n* queso fresco cremoso.
creamery ['kriːmərɪ] *n* (*shop*) quesería; (*factory*) central *f* lechera.
creamy ['kriːmɪ] *adj* cremoso.
crease [kriːs] *n* (*fold*) pliegue *m*; (*in trousers*) raya; (*wrinkle*) arruga ♦ *vt* (*fold*) doblar, plegar; (*wrinkle*) arrugar ♦ *vi* (*wrinkle up*) arrugarse.
crease-resistant ['kriːsrɪzɪstənt] *adj* inarrugable.
create [kriː'eɪt] *vt* (*also COMPUT*) crear; (*impression*) dar; (*fuss, noise*) hacer.
creation [kriː'eɪʃən] *n* creación *f*.
creative [kriː'eɪtɪv] *adj* creativo.
creativity [kriːeɪ'tɪvɪtɪ] *n* creatividad *f*.
creator [kriː'eɪtə*] *n* creador(a) *m/f*.
creature ['kriːtʃə*] *n* (*living thing*) criatura; (*animal*) animal *m*; (*insect*) bicho.
creature comforts *npl* comodidades *fpl* materiales.
crèche, creche [krɛʃ] *n* (*BRIT*) guardería (infantil).
credence ['kriːdəns] *n*: **to lend** *or* **give ~ to** creer en, dar crédito a.
credentials [krɪ'dɛnʃlz] *npl* credenciales *fpl*; (*letters of reference*) referencias *fpl*.
credibility [krɛdɪ'bɪlɪtɪ] *n* credibilidad *f*.
credible ['krɛdɪbl] *adj* creíble; (*witness, source*) fidedigno.
credit ['krɛdɪt] *n* (*gen*) crédito; (*merit*) honor *m*, mérito ♦ *vt* (*COMM*) abonar; (*believe*) creer, dar crédito a ♦ *adj* crediticio; **to be in** ~ (*person, bank account*) tener saldo a favor; **on** ~ a crédito; (*col*) al fiado; **he's a ~ to his family** hace honor a su familia; **to ~ sb with** (*fig*) reconocer a algn el mérito de; *see also* **credits.**
creditable ['krɛdɪtəbl] *adj* estimable, digno de elogio.
credit account *n* cuenta de crédito.
credit agency *n* agencia de informes comerciales.
credit balance *n* saldo acreedor.
credit card *n* tarjeta de crédito.
credit control *n* control *m* de créditos.
credit facilities *npl* facilidades *fpl* de crédito.
credit limit *n* límite *m* de crédito.
credit note *n* nota de crédito.
creditor ['krɛdɪtə*] *n* acreedor(a) *m/f*.
credits ['krɛdɪts] *npl* (*CINE*) títulos *mpl or* rótulos *mpl* de crédito, créditos *mpl*.
credit transfer *n* transferencia de crédito.
creditworthy ['krɛdɪtwəːðɪ] *adj* solvente.
credulity [krɪ'djuːlɪtɪ] *n* credulidad *f*.
creed [kriːd] *n* credo.
creek [kriːk] *n* cala, ensenada; (*US*) riachuelo.
creel [kriːl] *n* nasa.
creep, *pt, pp* **crept** [kriːp, krɛpt] *vi* (*animal*) deslizarse; (*plant*) trepar; **to ~ up on sb** acercarse sigilosamente a algn; (*fig: old age etc*) acercarse ♦ *n* (*col*): **he's a ~** ¡qué lameculos es!; **it gives me the ~s** me da escalofríos.
creeper ['kriːpə*] *n* enredadera.
creepers ['kriːpəz] *npl* (*US: for baby*) pelele *msg*.
creepy ['kriːpɪ] *adj* (*frightening*) horripilante.
creepy-crawly ['kriːpɪ'krɔːlɪ] *n* (*col*) bicho.
cremate [krɪ'meɪt] *vt* incinerar.
cremation [krɪ'meɪʃən] *n* incineración *f*, cremación *f*.
crematorium, *pl* **crematoria** [krɛmə'tɔːrɪəm, -'tɔːrɪə] *n* crematorio.
creosote ['krɪəsəut] *n* creosota.
crêpe [kreɪp] *n* (*fabric*) crespón *m*; (*also*: **~ rubber**) crep(é) *m*.
crêpe bandage *n* (*BRIT*) venda elástica.
crêpe paper *n* papel *m* crep(é).
crêpe sole *n* (*on shoes*) suela de crep(é).
crept [krɛpt] *pt, pp of* **creep.**
crescent ['krɛsnt] *n* media luna; (*street*) calle *f* (*en forma de semicírculo*).
cress [krɛs] *n* berro.
crest [krɛst] *n* (*of bird*) cresta; (*of hill*) cima, cumbre *f*; (*of helmet*) cimera; (*of coat of arms*) blasón *m*.
crestfallen ['krɛstfɔːlən] *adj* alicaído.
Crete [kriːt] *n* Creta.
cretin ['krɛtɪn] *n* cretino/a.
crevasse [krɪ'væs] *n* grieta.
crevice ['krɛvɪs] *n* grieta, hendedura.
crew [kruː] *n* (*of ship etc*) tripulación *f*; (*CINE etc*) equipo; (*gang*) pandilla, banda; (*MIL*) dotación *f*.
crew-cut ['kruːkʌt] *n* corte *m* al rape.

crew-neck ['kru:nɛk] *n* cuello de caja.
crib [krɪb] *n* pesebre *m* ♦ *vt* (*col*) plagiar; (*SCOL*) copiar.
crick [krɪk] *n*: ~ **in the neck** tortícolis *f inv*.
cricket ['krɪkɪt] *n* (*insect*) grillo; (*game*) críquet *m*.
cricketer ['krɪkɪtə*] *n* jugador(a) *m/f* de críquet.
crime [kraɪm] *n* crimen *m*; (*less serious*) delito.
crime wave *n* ola de crímenes *or* delitos.
criminal ['krɪmɪnl] *n* criminal *m/f*, delincuente *m/f* ♦ *adj* criminal; (*law*) penal.
Criminal Investigation Department (CID) *n* ≈ Brigada de Investigación Criminal (B.I.C. *f*) (*SP*).
crimp [krɪmp] *vt* (*hair*) rizar.
crimson ['krɪmzn] *adj* carmesí.
cringe [krɪndʒ] *vi* encogerse.
crinkle ['krɪŋkl] *vt* arrugar.
crinkly ['krɪŋklɪ] *adj* (*hair*) rizado, crespo.
cripple ['krɪpl] *n* lisiado/a, cojo/a ♦ *vt* lisiar, mutilar; (*ship, plane*) inutilizar; (*production, exports*) paralizar; ~**d with arthritis** paralizado por la artritis.
crippling ['krɪplɪŋ] *adj* (*injury etc*) debilitador(a); (*prices, taxes*) devastador(a).
crisis, *pl* **crises** ['kraɪsɪs, -si:z] *n* crisis *f*.
crisp [krɪsp] *adj* fresco; (*toast, snow*) crujiente; (*manner*) seco.
crisps [krɪsps] *npl* (*BRIT*) patatas *fpl* fritas.
crisscross ['krɪskrɔs] *adj* entrelazado, entrecruzado ♦ *vt* entrecruzar(se).
criterion, *pl* **criteria** [kraɪ'tɪərɪən, -'tɪərɪə] *n* criterio.
critic ['krɪtɪk] *n* crítico/a.
critical ['krɪtɪkl] *adj* (*gen*) crítico; (*illness*) grave; **to be ~ of sb/sth** criticar a algn/algo.
critically ['krɪtɪklɪ] *adv* (*speak etc*) en tono crítico; (*ill*) gravemente.
criticism ['krɪtɪsɪzm] *n* crítica.
criticize ['krɪtɪsaɪz] *vt* criticar.
critique [krɪ'ti:k] *n* crítica.
croak [krəuk] *vi* (*frog*) croar; (*raven*) graznar ♦ *n* (*of raven*) graznido.
Croat ['krəuæt] *adj, n* = **Croatian**.
Croatia [krəu'eɪʃə] *n* Croacia.
Croatian [krəu'eɪʃən] *adj, n* croata *m/f* ♦ *n* (*LING*) croata *m*.
crochet ['krəuʃeɪ] *n* ganchillo.
crock [krɔk] *n* cántaro; (*col*: *person*: *also*: **old** ~) carcamal *m/f*, vejestorio; (: *car etc*) cacharro.
crockery ['krɔkərɪ] *n* (*plates, cups etc*) loza, vajilla.
crocodile ['krɔkədaɪl] *n* cocodrilo.
crocus ['krəukəs] *n* azafrán *m*.
croft [krɔft] *n* granja pequeña.
crofter ['krɔftə*] *n* pequeño granjero.
croissant ['krwasã] *n* croissant *m*, medialuna (*esp LAM*).
crone [krəun] *n* arpía, bruja.
crony ['krəunɪ] *n* compinche *m/f*.
crook [kruk] *n* (*fam*) ladrón/ona *m/f*; (*of shepherd*) cayado; (*of arm*) pliegue *m*.
crooked ['krukɪd] *adj* torcido; (*path*) tortuoso; (*fam*) sucio.
crop [krɔp] *n* (*produce*) cultivo; (*amount produced*) cosecha; (*riding* ~) látigo de montar; (*of bird*) buche *m* ♦ *vt* cortar, recortar; (*subj*: *animals*: *grass*) pacer.
►**crop up** *vi* surgir, presentarse.
crop spraying [-'spreɪɪŋ] *n* fumigación *f* de los cultivos.
croquet ['krəukeɪ] *n* croquet *m*.
croquette [krə'kɛt] *n* croqueta (*de patata*).
cross [krɔs] *n* cruz *f* ♦ *vt* (*street etc*) cruzar, atravesar; (*thwart*: *person*) contrariar, ir contra ♦ *vi*: **the boat ~es from Santander to Plymouth** el barco hace la travesía de Santander a Plymouth ♦ *adj* de mal humor, enojado; **it's a ~ between geography and sociology** es una mezcla de geografía y sociología; **to ~ o.s.** santiguarse; **they've got their lines ~ed** (*fig*) hay un malentendido entre ellos; **to be/get ~ with sb (about sth)** estar enfadado/enfadarse con algn (por algo).
►**cross out** *vt* tachar.
►**cross over** *vi* cruzar.
crossbar ['krɔsbɑ:*] *n* travesaño; (*of bicycle*) barra.
crossbow ['krɔsbəu] *n* ballesta.
cross-Channel ferry ['krɔs'tʃænl-] *n* transbordador *m* que cruza el Canal de la Mancha.
cross-check ['krɔstʃɛk] *n* verificación *f* ♦ *vt* verificar.
cross-country (race) ['krɔs'kʌntrɪ-] *n* carrera a campo traviesa, cross *m*.
cross-dressing [krɔs'drɛsɪŋ] *n* travestismo.
cross-examination ['krɔsɪgzæmɪ'neɪʃən] *n* interrogatorio.
cross-examine ['krɔsɪg'zæmɪn] *vt* interrogar.
cross-eyed ['krɔsaɪd] *adj* bizco.
crossfire ['krɔsfaɪə*] *n* fuego cruzado.
crossing ['krɔsɪŋ] *n* (*road*) cruce *m*; (*rail*) paso a nivel; (*sea passage*) travesía; (*also*: **pedestrian** ~) paso de peatones.
crossing guard *n* (*US*) *persona encargada de ayudar a los niños a cruzar la calle*.
crossing point *n* paso; (*at border*) paso fronterizo.

cross purposes *npl*: **to be at ~ with sb** tener un malentendido con algn.
cross-question ['krɔs'kwɛstʃən] *vt* interrogar.
cross-reference ['krɔs'rɛfrəns] *n* remisión *f*.
crossroads ['krɔsrəudz] *nsg* cruce *m*; (*fig*) encrucijada.
cross section *n* corte *m* transversal; (*of population*) muestra (representativa).
crosswalk ['krɔswɔːk] *n* (*US*) paso de peatones.
crosswind ['krɔswɪnd] *n* viento de costado.
crossword ['krɔswəːd] *n* crucigrama *m*.
crotch [krɔtʃ] *n* (*of garment*) entrepierna.
crotchet ['krɔtʃɪt] *n* (*BRIT MUS*) negra.
crotchety ['krɔtʃɪtɪ] *adj* (*person*) arisco.
crouch [krautʃ] *vi* agacharse.
crouton ['kruːtɔn] *n* cubito de pan frito.
crow [krəu] *n* (*bird*) cuervo; (*of cock*) canto, cacareo ♦ *vi* (*cock*) cantar; (*fig*) jactarse.
crowbar ['krəubɑː*] *n* palanca.
crowd [kraud] *n* muchedumbre *f*; (*SPORT*) público; (*common herd*) vulgo ♦ *vt* (*gather*) amontonar; (*fill*) llenar ♦ *vi* (*gather*) reunirse; (*pile up*) amontonarse; **~s of people** gran cantidad de gente.
crowded ['kraudɪd] *adj* (*full*) atestado; (*well-attended*) concurrido.
crowd scene *n* (*CINE, THEAT*) escena con muchos comparsas.
crown [kraun] *n* corona; (*of head*) coronilla; (*of hat*) copa; (*of hill*) cumbre *f* ♦ *vt* (*also tooth*) coronar; **and to ~ it all ...** (*fig*) y para colmo *or* remate ....
crown court *n* (*LAW*) tribunal *m* superior; *ver recuadro*.

CROWN COURT

En el sistema legal inglés los delitos graves como asesinato, violación o atraco son juzgados por un jurado en un tribunal superior llamado **crown court** *con sede en noventa ciudades. Los jueces de paz ("Justice of the Peace") juzgan delitos menores e infracciones de la ley en juzgados llamados "Magistrates' Courts". Es el juez de paz quien decide remitir los casos pertinentes a la* **crown court**, *que en caso de recursos se remite al tribunal de apelación, "Court of Appeal".*

crowning ['kraunɪŋ] *adj* (*achievement, glory*) máximo.
crown jewels *npl* joyas *fpl* reales.
crown prince *n* príncipe *m* heredero.
crow's feet ['krəuzfiːt] *npl* patas *fpl* de gallo.
crucial ['kruːʃl] *adj* crucial, decisivo; **his approval is ~ to the success of the project** su aprobación es crucial para el éxito del proyecto.
crucifix ['kruːsɪfɪks] *n* crucifijo.
crucifixion [kruːsɪ'fɪkʃən] *n* crucifixión *f*.
crucify ['kruːsɪfaɪ] *vt* crucificar; (*fig*) martirizar.
crude [kruːd] *adj* (*materials*) bruto; (*fig: basic*) tosco; (*: vulgar*) ordinario.
crude (oil) *n* (petróleo) crudo.
cruel ['kruəl] *adj* cruel.
cruelty ['kruəltɪ] *n* crueldad *f*.
cruet ['kruːɪt] *n* vinagreras *fpl*.
cruise [kruːz] *n* crucero ♦ *vi* (*ship*) navegar; (*holidaymakers*) hacer un crucero; (*car*) ir a velocidad constante.
cruise missile *n* misil *m* de crucero.
cruiser ['kruːzə*] *n* crucero.
cruising speed ['kruːzɪŋ-] *n* velocidad *f* de crucero.
crumb [krʌm] *n* miga, migaja.
crumble ['krʌmbl] *vt* desmenuzar ♦ *vi* (*gen*) desmenuzarse; (*building*) desmoronarse.
crumbly ['krʌmblɪ] *adj* desmenuzable.
crummy ['krʌmɪ] *adj* (*col: poor quality*) pésimo, cutre (*SP*); (*: unwell*) fatal.
crumpet ['krʌmpɪt] *n* ≈ bollo para tostar.
crumple ['krʌmpl] *vt* (*paper*) estrujar; (*material*) arrugar.
crunch [krʌntʃ] *vt* (*with teeth*) ronzar; (*underfoot*) hacer crujir ♦ *n* (*fig*) hora de la verdad.
crunchy ['krʌntʃɪ] *adj* crujiente.
crusade [kruː'seɪd] *n* cruzada ♦ *vi*: **to ~ for/against** (*fig*) hacer una campaña en pro de/en contra de.
crusader [kruː'seɪdə*] *n* (*fig*) paladín *m/f*.
crush [krʌʃ] *n* (*crowd*) aglomeración *f* ♦ *vt* (*gen*) aplastar; (*paper*) estrujar; (*cloth*) arrugar; (*grind, break up: garlic, ice*) picar; (*fruit*) exprimir; (*grapes*) exprimir, prensar; **to have a ~ on sb** estar enamorado de algn.
crushing ['krʌʃɪŋ] *adj* aplastante; (*burden*) agobiante.
crust [krʌst] *n* corteza.
crustacean [krʌs'teɪʃən] *n* crustáceo.
crusty ['krʌstɪ] *adj* (*bread*) crujiente; (*person*) de mal carácter; (*remark*) brusco.
crutch [krʌtʃ] *n* (*MED*) muleta; (*support*) apoyo.
crux [krʌks] *n*: **the ~** lo esencial, el quid.
cry [kraɪ] *vi* llorar; (*shout: also*: **~ out**) gritar ♦ *n* grito; (*of animal*) aullido; (*weep*): **she had a good ~** lloró a lágrima viva; **what are you ~ing about?** ¿por qué lloras?; **to ~ for help** pedir socorro a voces; **it's a far**

~ **from** ... (*fig*) dista mucho de ....
►**cry off** *vi* retirarse.
crypt [krɪpt] *n* cripta.
cryptic ['krɪptɪk] *adj* enigmático.
crystal ['krɪstl] *n* cristal *m*.
crystal-clear ['krɪstl'klɪə*] *adj* claro como el agua; (*fig*) cristalino.
crystallize ['krɪstəlaɪz] *vt* (*fig*) cristalizar ♦ *vi* cristalizarse; ~**d fruits** frutas *fpl* escarchadas.
CSA *n abbr* = *Confederate States of America*; (= *Child Support Agency*) *organismo que supervisa el pago de la pensión a hijos de padres separados*.
CSC *n abbr* (= *Civil Service Commission*) *comisión para la contratación de funcionarios*.
CSE *n abbr* (*BRIT*: = *Certificate of Secondary Education*) ≈ título de BUP.
CS gas *n* (*BRIT*) gas *m* lacrimógeno.
CST *n abbr* (*US*: = *Central Standard Time*) *huso horario*.
CT, Ct. *abbr* (*US*) = *Connecticut*.
ct *abbr* = **carat**.
CTC *n abbr* (*BRIT*: *city technology college*) ≈ centro de formación profesional.
cu. *abbr* = **cubic**.
cub [kʌb] *n* cachorro; (*also*: ~ **scout**) niño explorador.
Cuba ['kju:bə] *n* Cuba.
Cuban ['kju:bən] *adj*, *n* cubano/a *m/f*.
cubbyhole ['kʌbɪhəul] *n* cuchitril *m*.
cube [kju:b] *n* cubo; (*of sugar*) terrón *m* ♦ *vt* (*MATH*) elevar al cubo.
cube root *n* raíz *f* cúbica.
cubic ['kju:bɪk] *adj* cúbico; ~ **capacity** (*AUT*) capacidad *f* cúbica.
cubicle ['kju:bɪkl] *n* (*at pool*) caseta; (*for bed*) cubículo.
cubism ['kju:bɪzəm] *n* cubismo.
cuckoo ['kuku:] *n* cuco.
cuckoo clock *n* reloj *m* de cuco.
cucumber ['kju:kʌmbə*] *n* pepino.
cuddle ['kʌdl] *vt* abrazar ♦ *vi* abrazarse.
cuddly ['kʌdlɪ] *adj* mimoso; (*toy*) de peluche.
cudgel ['kʌdʒəl] *vt*: **to ~ one's brains** devanarse los sesos.
cue [kju:] *n* (*snooker* ~) taco; (*THEAT etc*) entrada.
cuff [kʌf] *n* (*BRIT*: *of shirt, coat etc*) puño; (*US*: *of trousers*) vuelta; (*blow*) bofetada ♦ *vt* bofetear; **off the** ~ *adv* improvisado.
cufflinks ['kʌflɪŋks] *npl* gemelos *mpl*.
cu. in. *abbr* = *cubic inches*.
cuisine [kwɪ'zi:n] *n* cocina.
cul-de-sac ['kʌldəsæk] *n* callejón *m* sin salida.
culinary ['kʌlɪnərɪ] *adj* culinario.
cull [kʌl] *vt* (*select*) entresacar; (*kill selectively*: *animals*) matar selectivamente ♦ *n* matanza selectiva; **seal** ~ matanza selectiva de focas.
culminate ['kʌlmɪneɪt] *vi*: **to ~ in** culminar en.
culmination [kʌlmɪ'neɪʃən] *n* culminación *f*, colmo.
culottes [ku:'lɔts] *npl* falda *f* pantalón.
culpable ['kʌlpəbl] *adj* culpable.
culprit ['kʌlprɪt] *n* culpable *m/f*.
cult [kʌlt] *n* culto; **a ~ figure** un ídolo.
cultivate ['kʌltɪveɪt] *vt* (*also fig*) cultivar.
cultivated ['kʌltɪveɪtɪd] *adj* culto.
cultivation [kʌltɪ'veɪʃən] *n* cultivo; (*fig*) cultura.
cultural ['kʌltʃərəl] *adj* cultural.
culture ['kʌltʃə*] *n* (*also fig*) cultura.
cultured ['kʌltʃəd] *adj* culto.
cumbersome ['kʌmbəsəm] *adj* voluminoso.
cumin ['kʌmɪn] *n* (*spice*) comino.
cummerbund ['kʌməbʌnd] *n* faja, fajín *m*.
cumulative ['kju:mjulətɪv] *adj* cumulativo.
cunning ['kʌnɪŋ] *n* astucia ♦ *adj* astuto; (*clever*: *device, idea*) ingenioso.
cunt [kʌnt] *n* (*col!*) *n* coño (*!*); (*insult*) mamonazo/a (*!*).
cup [kʌp] *n* taza; (*prize, event*) copa; **a ~ of tea** una taza de té.
cupboard ['kʌbəd] *n* armario, placar(d) *m* (*LAM*).
cup final *n* (*FOOTBALL*) final *f* de copa.
cupful ['kʌpful] *n* taza.
Cupid ['kju:pɪd] *n* Cupido.
cupola ['kju:pələ] *n* cúpula.
cuppa ['kʌpa] *n* (*BRIT col*) (taza de) té *m*.
cup-tie ['kʌptaɪ] *n* (*BRIT*) partido de copa.
cur [kə:*] *n* perro de mala raza; (*person*) canalla *m*.
curable ['kjuərəbl] *adj* curable.
curate ['kjuərɪt] *n* coadjutor *m*.
curator [kjuə'reɪtə*] *n* director(a) *m/f*.
curb [kə:b] *vt* refrenar; (*powers, spending*) limitar ♦ *n* freno; (*US*: *kerb*) bordillo.
curd cheese [kə:d-] *n* requesón *m*.
curdle ['kə:dl] *vi* cuajarse.
curds [kə:dz] *npl* requesón *msg*.
cure [kjuə*] *vt* curar ♦ *n* cura, curación *f*; **to be ~d of sth** curarse de algo; **to take a** ~ tomar un remedio.
cure-all ['kjuərɔ:l] *n* (*also fig*) panacea.
curfew ['kə:fju:] *n* toque *m* de queda.
curio ['kjuərɪəu] *n* curiosidad *f*.
curiosity [kjuərɪ'ɔsɪtɪ] *n* curiosidad *f*.
curious ['kjuərɪəs] *adj* curioso; **I'm ~ about him** me intriga.
curiously ['kjuərɪəslɪ] *adv* curiosamente; ~

enough, ... aunque parezca extraño ....
curl [kəːl] *n* rizo; (*of smoke etc*) espiral *f*, voluta ♦ *vt* (*hair*) rizar; (*paper*) arrollar; (*lip*) fruncir ♦ *vi* rizarse; arrollarse.
▸**curl up** *vi* arrollarse; (*person*) hacerse un ovillo; (*fam*) morirse de risa.
curler [ˈkəːlə*] *n* bigudí *m*.
curlew [ˈkəːluː] *n* zarapito.
curling tongs, (*US*) **curling irons** [ˈkəːlɪŋ-] *npl* tenacillas *fpl*.
curly [ˈkəːlɪ] *adj* rizado.
currant [ˈkʌrnt] *n* pasa; (*black, red*) grosella.
currency [ˈkʌrnsɪ] *n* moneda; **to gain** ~ (*fig*) difundirse.
current [ˈkʌrnt] *n* corriente *f* ♦ *adj* actual; **direct/alternating** ~ corriente directa/alterna; **the** ~ **issue of a magazine** el último número de una revista; **in** ~ **use** de uso corriente.
current account *n* (*BRIT*) cuenta corriente.
current affairs *npl* (noticias *fpl* de) actualidad *f*.
current assets *npl* (*COMM*) activo disponible.
current liabilities *npl* (*COMM*) pasivo circulante.
currently [ˈkʌrntlɪ] *adv* actualmente.
curriculum, *pl* ~**s** *or* **curricula** [kəˈrɪkjuləm, -lə] *n* plan *m* de estudios.
curriculum vitae (CV) [-ˈviːtaɪ] *n* currículum *m* (vitae).
curry [ˈkʌrɪ] *n* curry *m* ♦ *vt*: **to** ~ **favour with** buscar el favor de.
curry powder *n* curry *m* en polvo.
curse [kəːs] *vi* echar pestes ♦ *vt* maldecir ♦ *n* maldición *f*; (*swearword*) palabrota.
cursor [ˈkəːsə*] *n* (*COMPUT*) cursor *m*.
cursory [ˈkəːsərɪ] *adj* rápido, superficial.
curt [kəːt] *adj* seco.
curtail [kəːˈteɪl] *vt* (*cut short*) acortar; (*restrict*) restringir.
curtain [ˈkəːtn] *n* cortina; (*THEAT*) telón *m*; **to draw the** ~**s** (*together*) cerrar las cortinas; (*apart*) abrir las cortinas.
curtain call *n* (*THEAT*) llamada a escena.
curtain ring *n* anilla.
curts(e)y [ˈkəːtsɪ] *n* reverencia ♦ *vi* hacer una reverencia.
curvature [ˈkəːvətʃə*] *n* curvatura.
curve [kəːv] *n* curva ♦ *vt, vi* torcer.
curved [kəːvd] *adj* curvo.
cushion [ˈkuʃən] *n* cojín *m*; (*SNOOKER*) banda ♦ *vt* (*seat*) acolchar; (*shock*) amortiguar.
cushy [ˈkuʃɪ] *adj* (*col*): **a** ~ **job** un chollo; **to have a** ~ **time** tener la vida arreglada.
custard [ˈkʌstəd] *n* (*for pouring*) natillas *fpl*.
custard powder *n* polvos *mpl* para natillas.
custodial sentence [kʌsˈtəudɪəl-] *n* pena de prisión.
custodian [kʌsˈtəudɪən] *n* guardián/ana *m/f*; (*of museum etc*) conservador(a) *m/f*.
custody [ˈkʌstədɪ] *n* custodia; **to take sb into** ~ detener a algn; **in the** ~ **of** al cuidado *or* cargo de.
custom [ˈkʌstəm] *n* costumbre *f*; (*COMM*) clientela; *see also* **customs.**
customary [ˈkʌstəmərɪ] *adj* acostumbrado; **it is** ~ **to do** ... es la costumbre hacer ....
custom-built [ˈkʌstəmˈbɪlt] *adj* = **custom-made.**
customer [ˈkʌstəmə*] *n* cliente *m/f*; **he's an awkward** ~ (*col*) es un tipo difícil.
customer profile *n* perfil *m* del cliente.
customized [ˈkʌstəmaɪzd] *adj* (*car etc*) hecho a encargo.
custom-made [ˈkʌstəmˈmeɪd] *adj* hecho a la medida.
customs [ˈkʌstəmz] *npl* aduana *sg*; **to go through (the)** ~ pasar la aduana.
Customs and Excise *n* (*BRIT*) Aduanas *fpl* y Arbitrios.
customs officer *n* aduanero/a, funcionario/a de aduanas.
cut [kʌt] *vb* (*pt, pp* **cut**) *vt* cortar; (*price*) rebajar; (*record*) grabar; (*reduce*) reducir; (*col: avoid: class, lecture*) fumarse, faltar a ♦ *vi* cortar; (*intersect*) cruzarse ♦ *n* corte *m*; (*in skin*) corte, cortadura; (*with sword*) tajo; (*of knife*) cuchillada; (*in salary etc*) recorte *m*; (*slice of meat*) tajada; **to** ~ **one's finger** cortarse un dedo; **to get one's hair** ~ cortarse el pelo; **to** ~ **sb dead** negarle el saludo *or* cortarle (*LAM*) a algn; **it** ~**s both ways** (*fig*) tiene doble filo; **to** ~ **a tooth** echar un diente; **power** ~ (*BRIT*) apagón *m*.
▸**cut back** *vt* (*plants*) podar; (*production, expenditure*) reducir.
▸**cut down** *vt* (*tree*) cortar, derribar; (*consumption, expenses*) reducir; **to** ~ **sb down to size** (*fig*) bajarle los humos a algn.
▸**cut in** *vi*: **to** ~ **in (on)** (*interrupt: conversation*) interrumpir, intervenir (en); (*AUT*) cerrar el paso (a).
▸**cut off** *vt* cortar; (*fig*) aislar; (*troops*) cercar; **we've been** ~ **off** (*TEL*) nos han cortado la comunicación.
▸**cut out** *vt* (*shape*) recortar; (*delete*) suprimir.
▸**cut up** *vt* cortar (en pedazos); (*chop: food*) trinchar, cortar.
cut-and-dried [ˈkʌtənˈdraɪd] *adj* (*also*: **cut-and-dry**) arreglado de antemano, seguro.

cutback ['kʌtbæk] *n* reducción *f.*
cute [kjuːt] *adj* lindo, mono; (*shrewd*) listo.
cuticle ['kjuːtɪkl] *n* cutícula.
cutlery ['kʌtlərɪ] *n* cubiertos *mpl.*
cutlet ['kʌtlɪt] *n* chuleta.
cutoff ['kʌtɔf] *n* (*also*: ~ **point**) límite *m.*
cutout ['kʌtaut] *n* (*shape*) recortable *m.*
cut-price ['kʌt'praɪs], (*US*) **cut-rate** ['kʌt'reɪt] *adj* a precio reducido.
cutthroat ['kʌtθrəut] *n* asesino/a ♦ *adj* feroz; ~ **competition** competencia encarnizada *or* despiadada.
cutting ['kʌtɪŋ] *adj* (*gen*) cortante; (*remark*) mordaz ♦ *n* (*BRIT*: *from newspaper*) recorte *m*; (: *RAIL*) desmonte *m*; (*CINE*) montaje *m.*
cutting edge *n* (*of knife*) filo; (*fig*) vanguardia; **a country on** *or* **at the** ~ **of space technology** un país puntero en tecnología del espacio.
CV *n abbr see* **curriculum vitae.**
C & W *n abbr* = **country and western (music).**
cwo *abbr* (*COMM*) = **cash with order.**
cwt. *abbr* = **hundredweight(s).**
cyanide ['saɪənaɪd] *n* cianuro.
cybercafé ['saɪbəˌkæfeɪ] *n* cibercafé *m.*
cybernetics [saɪbə'nɛtɪks] *nsg* cibernética.
cyberspace ['saɪbəspeɪs] *n* ciberespacio.
cyclamen ['sɪkləmən] *n* ciclamen *m.*
cycle ['saɪkl] *n* ciclo; (*bicycle*) bicicleta ♦ *vi* ir en bicicleta.
cycle race *n* carrera ciclista.
cycle rack *n* soporte *m* para bicicletas.
cycling ['saɪklɪŋ] *n* ciclismo.
cycling holiday *n* vacaciones *fpl* en bicicleta.
cyclist ['saɪklɪst] *n* ciclista *m/f.*
cyclone ['saɪkləun] *n* ciclón *m.*
cygnet ['sɪgnɪt] *n* pollo de cisne.
cylinder ['sɪlɪndə*] *n* cilindro.
cylinder block *n* bloque *m* de cilindros.
cylinder capacity *n* cilindrada.
cylinder head *n* culata de cilindro.
cylinder-head gasket *n* junta de culata.
cymbals ['sɪmblz] *npl* platillos *mpl*, címbalos *mpl.*
cynic ['sɪnɪk] *n* cínico/a.
cynical ['sɪnɪkl] *adj* cínico.
cynicism ['sɪnɪsɪzəm] *n* cinismo.
CYO *n abbr* (*US*) = *Catholic Youth Organization.*
cypress ['saɪprɪs] *n* ciprés *m.*
Cypriot ['sɪprɪət] *adj, n* chipriota *m/f.*
Cyprus ['saɪprəs] *n* Chipre *f.*
cyst [sɪst] *n* quiste *m.*
cystitis [sɪs'taɪtɪs] *n* cistitis *f.*
CZ *n abbr* (*US*: = *Central Zone*) *zona del Canal de Panamá.*
czar [zɑː*] *n* zar *m.*
czarina [zɑː'riːnə] *n* zarina.
Czech [tʃɛk] *adj* checo ♦ *n* checo/a; (*LING*) checo; **the** ~ **Republic** la República Checa.
Czechoslovak [tʃɛkə'sləuvæk] *adj, n* = **Czechoslovakian.**
Czechoslovakia [tʃɛkəslə'vækɪə] *n* Checoslovaquia.
Czechoslovakian [tʃɛkəslə'vækɪən] *adj, n* checoslovaco/a *m/f.*

D d

D, d [diː] *n* (*letter*) D, d; (*MUS*): **D** re *m*; **D for David,** (*US*) **D for Dog** D de Dolores.
D *abbr* (*US POL*) = **democrat(ic).**
d *abbr* (*BRIT*: *old*) = **penny.**
d. *abbr* = *died.*
DA *n abbr* (*US*) = **district attorney.**
dab [dæb] *v*: **to** ~ **ointment onto a wound** aplicar pomada sobre una herida; **to** ~ **with paint** dar unos toques de pintura ♦ *n* (*light stroke*) toque *m*; (*small amount*) pizca.
dabble ['dæbl] *vi*: **to** ~ **in** hacer por afición.
Dacca ['dækə] *n* Dacca.
dachshund ['dækshund] *n* perro tejonero.
Dacron ® ['deɪkrɔn] *n* (*US*) terylene *m.*
dad [dæd], **daddy** ['dædɪ] *n* papá *m.*
daddy-long-legs [dædɪ'lɔŋlɛgz] *n* típula.
daffodil ['dæfədɪl] *n* narciso.
daft [dɑːft] *adj* chiflado.
dagger ['dægə*] *n* puñal *m*, daga; **to look ~s at sb** fulminar a algn con la mirada.
dahlia ['deɪljə] *n* dalia.
daily ['deɪlɪ] *adj* diario, cotidiano ♦ *n* (*paper*) diario; (*domestic help*) asistenta ♦ *adv* todos los días, cada día; **twice** ~ dos veces al día.
dainty ['deɪntɪ] *adj* delicado.
dairy ['dɛərɪ] *n* (*shop*) lechería; (*on farm*) vaquería ♦ *adj* (*cow etc*) lechero.
dairy cow *n* vaca lechera.
dairy farm *n* vaquería.
dairy produce *n* productos *mpl* lácteos.
dais ['deɪɪs] *n* estrado.
daisy ['deɪzɪ] *n* margarita.
daisy wheel *n* (*on printer*) (rueda) margarita.
daisy-wheel printer *n* impresora de

margarita.
Dakar ['dækə*] *n* Dakar *m*.
dale [deɪl] *n* valle *m*.
dally ['dælɪ] *vi* entretenerse.
dalmatian [dæl'meɪʃən] *n* (*dog*) (perro) dálmata *m*.
dam [dæm] *n* presa; (*reservoir*) embalse ♦ *vt* embalsar.
damage ['dæmɪdʒ] *n* daño; (*fig*) perjuicio; (*to machine*) avería ♦ *vt* dañar; perjudicar; averiar; ~ **to property** daños materiales.
damages ['dæmɪdʒɪz] *npl* (*LAW*) daños y perjuicios; **to pay £5000 in** ~ pagar £5000 por daños y perjuicios.
damaging ['dæmɪdʒɪŋ] *adj*: ~ **(to)** perjudicial (a).
Damascus [də'mɑːskəs] *n* Damasco.
dame [deɪm] *n* (*title*) dama; (*US col*) tía; (*THEAT*) vieja; *see also* **pantomime**.
damn [dæm] *vt* condenar; (*curse*) maldecir ♦ *n* (*col*): **I don't give a** ~ me importa un pito ♦ *adj* (*col*: *also*: ~**ed**) maldito, fregado (*LAM*); ~ **(it)**! ¡maldito sea!
damnable ['dæmnəbl] *adj* (*col*: *behaviour*) detestable; (: *weather*) horrible.
damnation [dæm'neɪʃən] *n* (*REL*) condenación *f* ♦ *excl* (*col*) ¡maldición!, ¡maldito sea!
damning ['dæmɪŋ] *adj* (*evidence*) irrecusable.
damp [dæmp] *adj* húmedo, mojado ♦ *n* humedad *f* ♦ *vt* (*also*: ~**en**) (*cloth, rag*) mojar; (*enthusiasm*) enfriar.
dampcourse ['dæmpkɔːs] *n* aislante *m* hidrófugo.
damper ['dæmpə*] *n* (*MUS*) sordina; (*of fire*) regulador *m* de tiro; **to put a** ~ **on things** ser un jarro de agua fría.
dampness ['dæmpnɪs] *n* humedad *f*.
damson ['dæmzən] *n* ciruela damascena.
dance [dɑːns] *n* baile *m* ♦ *vi* bailar; **to** ~ **about** saltar.
dance hall *n* salón *m* de baile.
dancer ['dɑːnsə*] *n* bailador(a) *m/f*; (*professional*) bailarín/ina *m/f*.
dancing ['dɑːnsɪŋ] *n* baile *m*.
D and C *n abbr* (*MED*: = *dilation and curettage*) raspado.
dandelion ['dændɪlaɪən] *n* diente *m* de león.
dandruff ['dændrəf] *n* caspa.
dandy ['dændɪ] *n* dandi *m* ♦ *adj* (*US col*) estupendo.
Dane [deɪn] *n* danés/esa *m/f*.
danger ['deɪndʒə*] *n* peligro; (*risk*) riesgo; ~! (*on sign*) ¡peligro!; **to be in** ~ **of** correr riesgo de; **out of** ~ fuera de peligro.
danger list *n* (*MED*): **to be on the** ~ estar grave.
dangerous ['deɪndʒərəs] *adj* peligroso.
dangerously ['deɪndʒərəslɪ] *adv* peligrosamente; ~ **ill** gravemente enfermo.
danger zone *n* área *or* zona de peligro.
dangle ['dæŋgl] *vt* colgar ♦ *vi* pender, estar colgado.
Danish ['deɪnɪʃ] *adj* danés/esa ♦ *n* (*LING*) danés *m*.
Danish pastry *n* pastel *m* de almendra.
dank [dæŋk] *adj* húmedo y malsano.
Danube ['dænjuːb] *n* Danubio.
dapper ['dæpə*] *adj* pulcro, apuesto.
Dardanelles [dɑːdə'nɛlz] *npl* Dardanelos *mpl*.
dare [dɛə*] *vt*: **to** ~ **sb to do** desafiar a algn a hacer ♦ *vi*: **to** ~ **(to) do sth** atreverse a hacer algo; **I** ~ **say** (*I suppose*) puede ser, a lo mejor; **I** ~ **say he'll turn up** puede ser que *or* quizás venga; **I** ~**n't tell him** no me atrevo a decírselo.
daredevil ['dɛədɛvl] *n* temerario/a, atrevido/a.
Dar-es-Salaam ['dɑːrɛssə'lɑːm] *n* Dar es Salaam *m*.
daring ['dɛərɪŋ] *adj* (*person*) osado; (*plan, escape*) atrevido ♦ *n* atrevimiento, osadía.
dark [dɑːk] *adj* oscuro; (*hair, complexion*) moreno; (*fig*: *cheerless*) triste, sombrío ♦ *n* (*gen*) oscuridad *f*; (*night*) tinieblas *fpl*; ~ **chocolate** chocolate *m* amargo; **it is/is getting** ~ es de noche/está oscureciendo; **in the** ~ **about** (*fig*) ignorante de; **after** ~ después del anochecer.
darken ['dɑːkn] *vt* oscurecer; (*colour*) hacer más oscuro ♦ *vi* oscurecerse; (*cloud over*) nublarse.
dark glasses *npl* gafas *fpl* oscuras.
dark horse *n* (*fig*) incógnita.
darkly ['dɑːklɪ] *adv* (*gloomily*) tristemente; (*sinisterly*) siniestramente.
darkness ['dɑːknɪs] *n* (*in room*) oscuridad *f*; (*night*) tinieblas *fpl*.
darkroom ['dɑːkrum] *n* cuarto oscuro.
darling ['dɑːlɪŋ] *adj, n* querido/a *m/f*.
darn [dɑːn] *vt* zurcir.
dart [dɑːt] *n* dardo; (*in sewing*) pinza ♦ *vi* precipitarse; **to** ~ **away/along** *vi* salir/marchar disparado.
dartboard ['dɑːtbɔːd] *n* diana.
darts [dɑːts] *n* dardos *mpl*.
dash [dæʃ] *n* (*small quantity*: *of liquid*) gota, chorrito; (: *of solid*) pizca; (*sign*) guión *m*; (: *long*) raya ♦ *vt* (*break*) romper, estrellar; (*hopes*) defraudar ♦ *vi* precipitarse, ir de prisa; **a** ~ **of soda** un poco *or* chorrito de sifón *or* soda.
►**dash away, dash off** *vi* marcharse

apresuradamente.
dashboard ['dæʃbɔːd] *n* (*AUT*) salpicadero.
dashing ['dæʃɪŋ] *adj* gallardo.
dastardly ['dæstədlɪ] *adj* ruin, vil.
DAT *n abbr* (= *digital audio tape*) cas(s)et(t)e *m or f* digital.
data ['deɪtə] *npl* datos *mpl*.
database ['deɪtəbeɪs] *n* base *f* de datos.
data capture *n* recogida de datos.
data link *n* enlace *m* de datos.
data processing *n* proceso *or* procesamiento de datos.
data transmission *n* transmisión *f* de datos.
date [deɪt] *n* (*day*) fecha; (*with friend*) cita; (*fruit*) dátil *m* ♦ *vt* fechar; (*col*: *girl etc*) salir con; **what's the ~ today?** ¿qué fecha es hoy?; **~ of birth** fecha de nacimiento; **closing ~** fecha tope; **to ~** *adv* hasta la fecha; **out of ~** pasado de moda; **up to ~** moderno; puesto al día; **to bring up to ~** (*correspondence, information*) poner al día; (*method*) actualizar; **to bring sb up to ~** poner a algn al corriente; **letter ~d 5th July** *or* (*US*) **July 5th** carta fechada el 5 de julio.
dated ['deɪtɪd] *adj* anticuado.
date rape *n violación ocurrida durante una cita con un conocido.*
date stamp *n* matasellos *m inv*; (*on fresh foods*) sello de fecha.
dative ['deɪtɪv] *n* dativo.
daub [dɔːb] *vt* embadurnar.
daughter ['dɔːtə*] *n* hija.
daughter-in-law ['dɔːtərɪnlɔː] *n* nuera, hija política.
daunting ['dɔːntɪŋ] *adj* desalentador(a).
davenport ['dævnpɔːt] *n* escritorio; (*US*: *sofa*) sofá *m*.
dawdle ['dɔːdl] *vi* (*waste time*) perder el tiempo; (*go slowly*) andar muy despacio; **to ~ over one's work** trabajar muy despacio.
dawn [dɔːn] *n* alba, amanecer *m* ♦ *vi* amanecer; (*fig*): **it ~ed on him that ...** cayó en la cuenta de que ...; **at ~** al amanecer; **from ~ to dusk** de sol a sol.
dawn chorus *n* canto de los pájaros al amanecer.
day [deɪ] *n* día *m*; (*working ~*) jornada; **the ~ before** el día anterior; **the ~ after tomorrow** pasado mañana; **the ~ before yesterday** anteayer, antes de ayer; **the ~ after, the following ~** el día siguiente; **by ~** de día; **~ by ~** día a día; **(on) the ~ that ...** el día que ...; **to work an 8-hour ~** trabajar 8 horas diarias *or* al día; **he works 8 hours a ~** trabaja 8 horas al día; **paid by the ~** pagado por día; **these ~s, in the present ~** hoy en día.
daybook ['deɪbuk] *n* (*BRIT*) diario *or* libro de entradas y salidas.
daybreak ['deɪbreɪk] *n* amanecer *m*.
day-care centre ['deɪkɛə-] *n* centro de día; (*for children*) guardería infantil.
daydream ['deɪdriːm] *n* ensueño ♦ *vi* soñar despierto.
daylight ['deɪlaɪt] *n* luz *f* (del día).
daylight robbery *n*: **it's ~!** (*fig, col*) ¡es un robo descarado!
Daylight Saving Time *n* (*US*) hora de verano.
day-release course [deɪrɪ'liːs-] *n* curso de formación de un día a la semana.
day return (ticket) *n* (*BRIT*) billete *m* de ida y vuelta (en un día).
day shift *n* turno de día.
daytime ['deɪtaɪm] *n* día *m*.
day-to-day ['deɪtə'deɪ] *adj* cotidiano, diario; (*expenses*) diario; **on a ~ basis** día por día.
day trip *n* excursión *f* (de un día).
day tripper *n* excursionista *m/f*.
daze [deɪz] *vt* (*stun*) aturdir ♦ *n*: **in a ~** aturdido.
dazed [deɪzd] *adj* aturdido.
dazzle ['dæzl] *vt* deslumbrar.
dazzling ['dæzlɪŋ] *adj* (*light, smile*) deslumbrante; (*colour*) fuerte.
DBS *n abbr* (= *direct broadcasting by satellite*) transmisión vía satélite.
DC *abbr* (*ELEC*) = **direct current**; (*US*) = *District of Columbia*.
DCC ® *n abbr* (= *digital compact cassette*) cas(s)et(t)e *m* digital compacto.
DD *n abbr* (= *Doctor of Divinity*) *título universitario*.
dd. *abbr* (*COMM*) = *delivered*.
D/D *abbr* = *direct debit*.
D-day ['diːdeɪ] *n* (*fig*) día *m* clave.
DDS *n abbr* (*US*: = *Doctor of Dental Science*; *Doctor of Dental Surgery*) *títulos universitarios*.
DDT *n abbr* (= *dichlorodiphenyltrichloroethane*) DDT *m*.
DE *abbr* (*US*) = *Delaware*.
DEA *n abbr* (*US*: = *Drug Enforcement Administration*) *brigada especial dedicada a la lucha contra el tráfico de estupefacientes*.
deacon ['diːkən] *n* diácono.
dead [dɛd] *adj* muerto; (*limb*) dormido; (*battery*) agotado ♦ *adv* totalmente; (*exactly*) justo; **he was ~ on arrival** ingresó cadáver; **to shoot sb ~** matar a algn a tiros; **~ tired** muerto (de

cansancio); **to stop** ~ parar en seco; **the line has gone** ~ (*TEL*) se ha cortado la línea; **the** ~ *npl* los muertos.
dead beat *adj*: **to be** ~ (*col*) estar hecho polvo.
deaden ['dɛdn] *vt* (*blow, sound*) amortiguar; (*pain*) calmar, aliviar.
dead end *n* callejón *m* sin salida.
dead-end ['dɛdɛnd] *adj*: **a** ~ **job** un trabajo sin porvenir.
dead heat *n* (*SPORT*) empate *m*.
deadline ['dɛdlaɪn] *n* fecha tope; **to work to a** ~ trabajar con una fecha tope.
deadlock ['dɛdlɔk] *n* punto muerto.
dead loss *n* (*col*): **to be a** ~ (*person*) ser un inútil; (*thing*) ser una birria.
deadly ['dɛdlɪ] *adj* mortal, fatal; ~ **dull** aburridísimo.
deadly nightshade [-'naɪtʃeɪd] *n* belladona.
deadpan ['dɛdpæn] *adj* sin expresión.
Dead Sea *n*: **the** ~ el Mar Muerto.
dead season *n* (*TOURISM*) temporada baja.
deaf [dɛf] *adj* sordo; **to turn a** ~ **ear to sth** hacer oídos sordos a algo.
deaf-aid ['dɛfeɪd] *n* audífono.
deaf-and-dumb ['dɛfən'dʌm] *adj* (*person*) sordomudo; (*alphabet*) para sordomudos.
deafen ['dɛfn] *vt* ensordecer.
deafening ['dɛfnɪŋ] *adj* ensordecedor(a).
deaf-mute ['dɛfmjuːt] *n* sordomudo/a.
deafness ['dɛfnɪs] *n* sordera.
deal [diːl] *n* (*agreement*) pacto, convenio; (*business*) negocio, transacción *f*; (*CARDS*) reparto ♦ *vt* (*pt, pp* **dealt**) (*gen*) dar; **a great** ~ **(of)** bastante, mucho; **it's a** ~! (*col*) ¡trato hecho!, ¡de acuerdo!; **to do a** ~ **with sb** hacer un trato con algn; **he got a bad/fair** ~ **from them** le trataron mal/bien.
▸**deal in** *vt fus* tratar en, comerciar en.
▸**deal with** *vt fus* (*people*) tratar con; (*problem*) ocuparse de; (*subject*) tratar de.
dealer ['diːlə*] *n* comerciante *m/f*; (*CARDS*) mano *f*.
dealership ['diːləʃɪp] *n* concesionario.
dealings ['diːlɪŋz] *npl* (*COMM*) transacciones *fpl*; (*relations*) relaciones *fpl*.
dealt [dɛlt] *pt, pp of* **deal**.
dean [diːn] *n* (*REL*) deán *m*; (*SCOL*) decano/a.
dear [dɪə*] *adj* querido; (*expensive*) caro ♦ *n*: **my** ~ querido/a; ~ **me!** ¡Dios mío!; **D**~ **Sir/Madam** (*in letter*) Muy señor mío, Estimado señor/Estimada señora, De mi/nuestra (mayor) consideración (*esp LAM*); **D**~ **Mr/Mrs X** Estimado/a señor(a) X.
dearly ['dɪəlɪ] *adv* (*love*) mucho; (*pay*) caro.
dearth [dəːθ] *n* (*of food, resources, money*) escasez *f*.
death [dɛθ] *n* muerte *f*.
deathbed ['dɛθbɛd] *n* lecho de muerte.
death certificate *n* partida de defunción.
death duties *npl* (*BRIT*) derechos *mpl* de sucesión.
deathly ['dɛθlɪ] *adj* mortal; (*silence*) profundo.
death penalty *n* pena de muerte.
death rate *n* tasa de mortalidad.
death row *n*: **to be on** ~ (*US*) estar condenado a muerte.
death sentence *n* condena a muerte.
death squad *n* escuadrón *m* de la muerte.
deathtrap ['dɛθtræp] *n* lugar *m* (*or* vehículo *etc*) muy peligroso.
deb [dɛb] *n abbr* (*col*) = **debutante**.
debacle [deɪ'bɑːkl] *n* desastre *m*, catástrofe *f*.
debar [dɪ'bɑː*] *vt*: **to** ~ **sb from doing** prohibir a algn hacer.
debase [dɪ'beɪs] *vt* degradar.
debatable [dɪ'beɪtəbl] *adj* discutible; **it is** ~ **whether** ... es discutible si ....
debate [dɪ'beɪt] *n* debate *m* ♦ *vt* discutir.
debauched [dɪ'bɔːtʃt] *adj* vicioso.
debauchery [dɪ'bɔːtʃərɪ] *n* libertinaje *m*.
debenture [dɪ'bɛntʃə*] *n* (*COMM*) bono, obligación *f*.
debenture capital *n* capital *m* hipotecario.
debilitate [dɪ'bɪlɪteɪt] *vt* debilitar.
debilitating [dɪ'bɪlɪteɪtɪŋ] *adj* (*illness etc*) debilitante.
debit ['dɛbɪt] *n* debe *m* ♦ *vt*: **to** ~ **a sum to sb** *or* **to sb's account** cargar una suma en cuenta a algn.
debit balance *n* saldo deudor *or* pasivo.
debit note *n* nota de débito *or* cargo.
debonair [dɛbə'nɛə*] *adj* jovial, cortés/esa.
debrief [diː'briːf] *vt* hacer dar parte.
debriefing [diː'briːfɪŋ] *n* relación *f* (de un informe).
debris ['dɛbriː] *n* escombros *mpl*.
debt [dɛt] *n* deuda; **to be in** ~ tener deudas; ~**s of £5000** deudas de cinco mil libras; **bad** ~ deuda incobrable.
debt collector *n* cobrador(a) *m/f* de deudas.
debtor ['dɛtə*] *n* deudor(a) *m/f*.
debug ['diː'bʌg] *vt* (*COMPUT*) depurar.
debunk [diː'bʌŋk] *vt* (*col*: *theory*) desprestigiar, desacreditar; (: *claim*) desacreditar; (: *person, institution*) desenmascarar.
début ['deɪbjuː] *n* presentación *f*.
debutante ['dɛbjutænt] *n* debutante *f*.
Dec. *abbr* (= *December*) dic.

decade ['dɛkeɪd] *n* década, decenio.
decadence ['dɛkədəns] *n* decadencia.
decadent ['dɛkədənt] *adj* decadente.
de-caff ['di:kæf] *n* (*col*) descafeinado.
decaffeinated [dɪ'kæfɪneɪtɪd] *adj* descafeinado.
decamp [dɪ'kæmp] *vi* (*col*) escaparse, largarse, rajarse (*LAM*).
decant [dɪ'kænt] *vt* decantar.
decanter [dɪ'kæntə*] *n* jarra, decantador *m*.
decathlon [dɪ'kæθlən] *n* decatlón *m*.
decay [dɪ'keɪ] *n* (*fig*) decadencia; (*of building*) desmoronamiento; (*of tooth*) caries *f inv* ♦ *vi* (*rot*) pudrirse; (*fig*) decaer.
decease [dɪ'si:s] *n* fallecimiento ♦ *vi* fallecer.
deceased [dɪ'si:st] *adj* difunto.
deceit [dɪ'si:t] *n* engaño.
deceitful [dɪ'si:tful] *adj* engañoso.
deceive [dɪ'si:v] *vt* engañar.
decelerate [di:'sɛləreɪt] *vt* moderar la marcha de ♦ *vi* decelerar.
December [dɪ'sɛmbə*] *n* diciembre *m*.
decency ['di:sənsɪ] *n* decencia.
decent ['di:sənt] *adj* (*proper*) decente; (*person*) amable, bueno.
decently ['di:səntlɪ] *adv* (*respectably*) decentemente; (*kindly*) amablemente.
decentralization [di:sɛntrəlaɪ'zeɪʃən] *n* descentralización *f*.
decentralize [di:'sɛntrəlaɪz] *vt* descentralizar.
deception [dɪ'sɛpʃən] *n* engaño.
deceptive [dɪ'sɛptɪv] *adj* engañoso.
decibel ['dɛsɪbɛl] *n* decibel(io) *m*.
decide [dɪ'saɪd] *vt* (*person*) decidir; (*question, argument*) resolver ♦ *vi*: **to ~ to do/that** decidir hacer/que; **to ~ on sth** tomar una decisión sobre algo; **to ~ against doing sth** decidir en contra de hacer algo.
decided [dɪ'saɪdɪd] *adj* (*resolute*) decidido; (*clear, definite*) indudable.
decidedly [dɪ'saɪdɪdlɪ] *adv* decididamente.
deciding [dɪ'saɪdɪŋ] *adj* decisivo.
deciduous [dɪ'sɪdjuəs] *adj* de hoja caduca.
decimal ['dɛsɪməl] *adj* decimal ♦ *n* decimal *f*; **to 3 ~ places** con 3 cifras decimales.
decimalize ['dɛsɪməlaɪz] *vt* convertir al sistema decimal.
decimal point *n* coma decimal.
decimal system *n* sistema *m* métrico decimal.
decimate ['dɛsɪmeɪt] *vt* diezmar.
decipher [dɪ'saɪfə*] *vt* descifrar.
decision [dɪ'sɪʒən] *n* decisión *f*; **to make a ~** tomar una decisión.
decisive [dɪ'saɪsɪv] *adj* (*influence*) decisivo; (*manner, person*) decidido; (*reply*) tajante.
deck [dɛk] *n* (*NAUT*) cubierta; (*of bus*) piso; (*of cards*) baraja; **cassette ~** platina; **to go up on ~** subir a (la) cubierta; **below ~** en la bodega.
deckchair ['dɛktʃɛə*] *n* tumbona.
deckhand ['dɛkhænd] *n* marinero de cubierta.
declaration [dɛklə'reɪʃən] *n* declaración *f*.
declare [dɪ'klɛə*] *vt* (*gen*) declarar.
declassify [di:'klæsɪfaɪ] *vt* permitir que salga a la luz.
decline [dɪ'klaɪn] *n* decaimiento, decadencia; (*lessening*) disminución *f* ♦ *vt* rehusar ♦ *vi* decaer; disminuir; **~ in living standards** disminución *f* del nivel de vida; **to ~ to do sth** rehusar hacer algo.
declutch ['di:'klʌtʃ] *vi* desembragar.
decode [di:'kəud] *vt* descifrar.
decoder [di:'kəudə*] *n* (*COMPUT*, *TV*) de(s)codificador *m*.
decompose [di:kəm'pəuz] *vi* descomponerse.
decomposition [di:kɔmpə'zɪʃən] *n* descomposición *f*.
decompression [di:kəm'prɛʃən] *n* descompresión *f*.
decompression chamber *n* cámara de descompresión.
decongestant [di:kən'dʒɛstənt] *n* descongestionante.
decontaminate [di:kən'tæmɪneɪt] *vt* descontaminar.
decontrol [di:kən'trəul] *vt* (*trade*) quitar controles a; (*prices*) descongelar.
décor ['deɪkɔ:*] *n* decoración *f*; (*THEAT*) decorado.
decorate ['dɛkəreɪt] *vt* (*paint*) pintar; (*paper*) empapelar; (*adorn*): **to ~ (with)** adornar (de), decorar (de).
decoration [dɛkə'reɪʃən] *n* adorno; (*act*) decoración *f*; (*medal*) condecoración *f*.
decorative ['dɛkərətɪv] *adj* decorativo.
decorator ['dɛkəreɪtə*] *n* (*workman*) pintor *m* decorador.
decorum [dɪ'kɔ:rəm] *n* decoro.
decoy ['di:kɔɪ] *n* señuelo; **police ~** trampa *or* señuelo policial.
decrease ['di:kri:s] *n* disminución *f* ♦ (*vb*: [dɪ'kri:s]) *vt* disminuir, reducir ♦ *vi* reducirse; **to be on the ~** ir disminuyendo.
decreasing [dɪ'kri:sɪŋ] *adj* decreciente.
decree [dɪ'kri:] *n* decreto ♦ *vt*: **to ~ (that)** decretar (que); **~ absolute/nisi** sentencia absoluta/provisional de divorcio.
decrepit [dɪ'krɛpɪt] *adj* (*person*) decrépito; (*building*) ruinoso.

decry [dɪ'kraɪ] *vt* criticar, censurar.
dedicate ['dɛdɪkeɪt] *vt* dedicar.
dedicated ['dɛdɪkeɪtɪd] *adj* dedicado; (*COMPUT*) especializado; ~ **word processor** procesador *m* de textos especializado *or* dedicado.
dedication [dɛdɪ'keɪʃən] *n* (*devotion*) dedicación *f*; (*in book*) dedicatoria.
deduce [dɪ'dju:s] *vt* deducir.
deduct [dɪ'dʌkt] *vt* restar; (*from wage etc*) descontar, deducir.
deduction [dɪ'dʌkʃən] *n* (*amount deducted*) descuento; (*conclusion*) deducción *f*, conclusión *f*.
deed [di:d] *n* hecho, acto; (*feat*) hazaña; (*LAW*) escritura; ~ **of covenant** escritura de contrato.
deem [di:m] *vt* (*formal*) juzgar, considerar; **to ~ it wise to do** considerar prudente hacer.
deep [di:p] *adj* profundo; (*voice*) bajo; (*breath*) profundo, a pleno pulmón ♦ *adv*: **the spectators stood 20 ~** los espectadores se formaron de 20 en fondo; **to be 4 metres ~** tener 4 metros de profundidad.
deepen ['di:pn] *vt* ahondar, profundizar ♦ *vi* (*darkness*) intensificarse.
deep-freeze ['di:p'fri:z] *n* arcón *m* congelador.
deep-fry ['di:p'fraɪ] *vt* freír en aceite abundante.
deeply ['di:plɪ] *adv* (*breathe*) profundamente, a pleno pulmón; (*interested, moved, grateful*) profundamente, hondamente; **to regret sth ~** sentir algo profundamente.
deep-rooted ['di:p'ru:tɪd] *adj* (*prejudice, habit*) profundamente arraigado; (*affection*) profundo.
deep-sea ['di:p'si:] *adj*: ~ **diver** buzo; ~ **diving** buceo de altura.
deep-seated ['di:p'si:tɪd] *adj* (*beliefs*) (profundamente) arraigado.
deep-set ['di:psɛt] *adj* (*eyes*) hundido.
deer [dɪə*] *n, pl inv* ciervo.
deerstalker ['dɪəstɔ:kə*] *n* (*hat*) gorro de cazador.
deface [dɪ'feɪs] *vt* desfigurar, mutilar.
defamation [dɛfə'meɪʃən] *n* difamación *f*.
defamatory [dɪ'fæmətrɪ] *adj* difamatorio.
default [dɪ'fɔ:lt] *vi* faltar al pago; (*SPORT*) no presentarse, no comparecer ♦ *n* (*COMPUT*) defecto; **by ~** (*LAW*) en rebeldía; (*SPORT*) por incomparecencia; **to ~ on a debt** dejar de pagar una deuda.
defaulter [dɪ'fɔ:ltə*] *n* (*in debt*) moroso/a.
default option *n* (*COMPUT*) opción *f* por defecto.
defeat [dɪ'fi:t] *n* derrota ♦ *vt* derrotar, vencer; (*fig*: *efforts*) frustrar.
defeatism [dɪ'fi:tɪzəm] *n* derrotismo.
defeatist [dɪ'fi:tɪst] *adj, n* derrotista *m/f*.
defecate ['dɛfəkeɪt] *vi* defecar.
defect ['di:fɛkt] *n* defecto ♦ *vi* [dɪ'fɛkt]: **to ~ to the enemy** pasarse al enemigo; **physical ~** defecto físico; **mental ~** deficiencia mental.
defective [dɪ'fɛktɪv] *adj* (*gen*) defectuoso; (*person*) anormal.
defector [dɪ'fɛktə*] *n* tránsfuga *m/f*.
defence, (*US*) defense [dɪ'fɛns] *n* defensa; **the Ministry of D~** el Ministerio de Defensa; **witness for the ~** testigo de descargo.
defenceless [dɪ'fɛnslɪs] *adj* indefenso.
defence spending *n* gasto militar.
defend [dɪ'fɛnd] *vt* defender; (*decision, action*) defender; (*opinion*) mantener.
defendant [dɪ'fɛndənt] *n* acusado/a; (*in civil case*) demandado/a.
defender [dɪ'fɛndə*] *n* defensor(a) *m/f*.
defending champion [dɪ'fɛndɪŋ-] *n* (*SPORT*) defensor(a) *m/f* del título.
defending counsel *n* (*LAW*) abogado defensor.
defense [dɪ'fɛns] *n* (*US*) = **defence**.
defensive [dɪ'fɛnsɪv] *adj* defensivo ♦ *n* defensiva; **on the ~** a la defensiva.
defer [dɪ'fə:*] *vt* (*postpone*) aplazar; **to ~ to** diferir a; (*submit*): **to ~ to sb/sb's opinion** someterse a algn/a la opinión de algn.
deference ['dɛfərəns] *n* deferencia, respeto; **out of** *or* **in ~ to** por respeto a.
deferential [dɛfə'rɛnʃəl] *adj* respetuoso.
deferred [dɪ'fə:d] *adj*: ~ **creditor** acreedor *m* diferido.
defiance [dɪ'faɪəns] *n* desafío; **in ~ of** en contra de.
defiant [dɪ'faɪənt] *adj* (*insolent*) insolente; (*challenging*) retador(a).
defiantly [dɪ'faɪəntlɪ] *adv* con aire de desafío.
deficiency [dɪ'fɪʃənsɪ] *n* (*lack*) falta; (*COMM*) déficit *m*; (*defect*) defecto.
deficient [dɪ'fɪʃənt] *adj* (*lacking*) insuficiente; (*incomplete*) incompleto; (*defective*) defectuoso; (*mentally*) anormal; **~ in** deficiente en.
deficit ['dɛfɪsɪt] *n* déficit *m*.
defile [dɪ'faɪl] *vt* manchar; (*violate*) violar.
define [dɪ'faɪn] *vt* (*also COMPUT*) definir.
definite ['dɛfɪnɪt] *adj* (*fixed*) determinado; (*clear, obvious*) claro; **he was ~ about it** no dejó lugar a dudas (sobre ello).
definitely ['dɛfɪnɪtlɪ] *adv*: **he's ~ mad** no

cabe duda de que está loco.
definition [dɛfɪ'nɪʃən] *n* definición *f.*
definitive [dɪ'fɪnɪtɪv] *adj* definitivo.
deflate [diː'fleɪt] *vt* (*gen*) desinflar; (*pompous person*) quitar *or* rebajar los humos a; (*ECON*) deflacionar.
deflation [diː'fleɪʃən] *n* (*ECON*) deflación *f.*
deflationary [diː'fleɪʃənrɪ] *adj* (*ECON*) deflacionario.
deflect [dɪ'flɛkt] *vt* desviar.
defog [diː'fɔg] *vt* desempañar.
defogger [diːfɔgə*] *n* (*US AUT*) dispositivo antivaho.
deform [dɪ'fɔːm] *vt* deformar.
deformed [dɪ'fɔːmd] *adj* deformado.
deformity [dɪ'fɔːmɪtɪ] *n* deformación *f.*
defraud [dɪ'frɔːd] *vt* estafar; **to ~ sb of sth** estafar algo a algn.
defray [dɪ'freɪ] *vt*: **to ~ sb's expenses** reembolsar a algn los gastos.
defrost [diː'frɔst] *vt* (*frozen food, fridge*) descongelar.
defroster [diː'frɔstə*] *n* (*US*) eliminador *m* de vaho.
deft [dɛft] *adj* diestro, hábil.
defunct [dɪ'fʌŋkt] *adj* difunto; (*organization etc*) ya desaparecido.
defuse [diː'fjuːz] *vt* desarmar; (*situation*) calmar, apaciguar.
defy [dɪ'faɪ] *vt* (*resist*) oponerse a; (*challenge*) desafiar; (*order*) contravenir.
degenerate [dɪ'dʒɛnəreɪt] *vi* degenerar ♦ *adj* [dɪ'dʒɛnərɪt] degenerado.
degradation [dɛgrə'deɪʃən] *n* degradación *f.*
degrade [dɪ'greɪd] *vt* degradar.
degrading [dɪ'greɪdɪŋ] *adj* degradante.
degree [dɪ'griː] *n* grado; (*SCOL*) título; **10 ~s below freezing** 10 grados bajo cero; **to have a ~ in maths** ser licenciado/a en matemáticas; **by ~s** (*gradually*) poco a poco, por etapas; **to some ~, to a certain ~** hasta cierto punto; **a considerable ~ of risk** un gran índice de riesgo.
dehydrated [diːhaɪ'dreɪtɪd] *adj* deshidratado; (*milk*) en polvo.
dehydration [dɪːhaɪ'dreɪʃən] *n* deshidratación *f.*
de-ice [diː'aɪs] *vt* (*windscreen*) deshelar.
de-icer [diː'aɪsə*] *n* descongelador *m.*
deign [deɪn] *vi*: **to ~ to do** dignarse hacer.
deity ['diːɪtɪ] *n* deidad *f*, divinidad *f.*
déjà vu [deɪʒɑː'vuː] *n*: **I had a sense of ~** sentía como si ya lo hubiera vivido.
dejected [dɪ'dʒɛktɪd] *adj* abatido, desanimado.
dejection [dɪ'dʒɛkʃən] *n* abatimiento.
Del. *abbr* (*US*) = *Delaware.*
del. *abbr* = **delete.**
delay [dɪ'leɪ] *vt* demorar, aplazar; (*person*) entretener; (*train*) retrasar; (*payment*) aplazar ♦ *vi* tardar ♦ *n* demora, retraso; **without ~** en seguida, sin tardar.
delayed-action [dɪleɪd'ækʃən] *adj* (*bomb etc*) de acción retardada.
delectable [dɪ'lɛktəbl] *adj* (*person*) encantador(a); (*food*) delicioso.
delegate ['dɛlɪgɪt] *n* delegado/a ♦ *vt* ['dɛlɪgeɪt] delegar; **to ~ sth to sb/sb to do sth** delegar algo en algn/en algn para hacer algo.
delegation [dɛlɪ'geɪʃən] *n* (*of work etc*) delegación *f.*
delete [dɪ'liːt] *vt* suprimir, tachar; (*COMPUT*) suprimir, borrar.
Delhi ['dɛlɪ] *n* Delhi *m.*
deli ['dɛlɪ] *n* = **delicatessen.**
deliberate [dɪ'lɪbərɪt] *adj* (*intentional*) intencionado; (*slow*) pausado, lento ♦ *vi* [dɪ'lɪbəreɪt] deliberar.
deliberately [dɪ'lɪbərɪtlɪ] *adv* (*on purpose*) a propósito; (*slowly*) pausadamente.
deliberation [dɪlɪbə'reɪʃən] *n* (*consideration*) reflexión *f*; (*discussion*) deliberación *f*, discusión *f.*
delicacy ['dɛlɪkəsɪ] *n* delicadeza; (*choice food*) manjar *m.*
delicate ['dɛlɪkɪt] *adj* (*gen*) delicado; (*fragile*) frágil.
delicately ['dɛlɪkɪtlɪ] *adv* con delicadeza, delicadamente; (*act, express*) con discreción.
delicatessen [dɛlɪkə'tɛsn] *n tienda especializada en comida exótica.*
delicious [dɪ'lɪʃəs] *adj* delicioso, rico.
delight [dɪ'laɪt] *n* (*feeling*) placer *m*, deleite *m*; (*object*) encanto, delicia ♦ *vt* encantar, deleitar; **to take ~ in** deleitarse en.
delighted [dɪ'laɪtɪd] *adj*: **~ (at *or* with/to do)** encantado (con/de hacer); **to be ~ that** estar encantado de que; **I'd be ~** con mucho *or* todo gusto.
delightful [dɪ'laɪtful] *adj* encantador(a), delicioso.
delimit [diː'lɪmɪt] *vt* delimitar.
delineate [dɪ'lɪnɪeɪt] *vt* delinear.
delinquency [dɪ'lɪŋkwənsɪ] *n* delincuencia.
delinquent [dɪ'lɪŋkwənt] *adj, n* delincuente *m/f.*
delirious [dɪ'lɪrɪəs] *adj* (*MED, fig*) delirante; **to be ~** delirar, desvariar.
delirium [dɪ'lɪrɪəm] *n* delirio.
deliver [dɪ'lɪvə*] *vt* (*distribute*) repartir; (*hand over*) entregar; (*message*) comunicar; (*speech*) pronunciar; (*blow*) lanzar, dar; (*MED*) asistir al parto de.

deliverance [dɪ'lɪvrəns] *n* liberación *f.*
delivery [dɪ'lɪvərɪ] *n* reparto; entrega; (*of speaker*) modo de expresarse; (*MED*) parto, alumbramiento; **to take ~ of** recibir.
delivery note *n* nota de entrega.
delivery van *n* furgoneta de reparto.
delta ['dɛltə] *n* delta *m.*
delude [dɪ'lu:d] *vt* engañar.
deluge ['dɛlju:dʒ] *n* diluvio ♦ *vt* (*fig*): **to ~ (with)** inundar (de).
delusion [dɪ'lu:ʒən] *n* ilusión *f*, engaño.
de luxe [də'lʌks] *adj* de lujo.
delve [dɛlv] *vi*: **to ~ into** hurgar en.
Dem. *abbr* (*US POL*) = **democrat(ic)**.
demand [dɪ'mɑ:nd] *vt* (*gen*) exigir; (*rights*) reclamar; (*need*) requerir ♦ *n* (*gen*) exigencia; (*claim*) reclamación *f*; (*ECON*) demanda; **to ~ sth (from** *or* **of sb)** exigir algo (a algn); **to be in ~** ser muy solicitado; **on ~** a solicitud.
demanding [dɪ'mɑ:ndɪŋ] *adj* (*boss*) exigente; (*work*) absorbente.
demarcation [di:mɑ:'keɪʃən] *n* demarcación *f.*
demarcation dispute *n* conflicto de definición *or* demarcación del trabajo.
demean [dɪ'mi:n] *vt*: **to ~ o.s.** rebajarse.
demeanour, (*US*) **demeanor** [dɪ'mi:nə*] *n* porte *m*, conducta, comportamiento.
demented [dɪ'mɛntɪd] *adj* demente.
demi- ['dɛmɪ] *pref* semi..., medio....
demilitarize [di:'mɪlɪtəraɪz] *vt* desmilitarizar; **~d zone** zona desmilitarizada.
demise [dɪ'maɪz] *n* (*death*) fallecimiento.
demist [di:'mɪst] *vt* (*AUT*) eliminar el vaho de.
demister [di:'mɪstə*] *n* (*AUT*) eliminador *m* de vaho.
demo ['dɛməu] *n abbr* (*col*: = *demonstration*) manifestación *f.*
demobilization [di:'məubɪlaɪ'zeɪʃən] *n* desmovilización *f.*
democracy [dɪ'mɔkrəsɪ] *n* democracia.
democrat ['dɛməkræt] *n* demócrata *m/f.*
democratic [dɛmə'krætɪk] *adj* democrático; **the D~ Party** el partido demócrata (estadounidense).
demography [dɪ'mɔgrəfɪ] *n* demografía.
demolish [dɪ'mɔlɪʃ] *vt* derribar, demoler.
demolition [dɛmə'lɪʃən] *n* derribo, demolición *f.*
demon ['di:mən] *n* (*evil spirit*) demonio ♦ *cpd* temible.
demonstrate ['dɛmənstreɪt] *vt* demostrar ♦ *vi* manifestarse; **to ~ (for/against)** manifestarse (a favor de/en contra de).
demonstration [dɛmən'streɪʃən] *n* (*POL*) manifestación *f*; (*proof*) prueba, demostración *f*; **to hold a ~** (*POL*) hacer una manifestación.
demonstrative [dɪ'mɔnstrətɪv] *adj* (*person*) expresivo; (*LING*) demostrativo.
demonstrator ['dɛmənstreɪtə*] *n* (*POL*) manifestante *m/f.*
demoralize [dɪ'mɔrəlaɪz] *vt* desmoralizar.
demote [dɪ'məut] *vt* degradar.
demotion [dɪ'məuʃən] *n* degradación *f*; (*COMM*) descenso.
demur [dɪ'mə:*] *vi*: **to ~ (at)** hacer objeciones (a), vacilar (ante) ♦ *n*: **without ~** sin objeción.
demure [dɪ'mjuə*] *adj* recatado.
demurrage [dɪ'mʌrɪdʒ] *n* sobrestadía.
den [dɛn] *n* (*of animal*) guarida; (*study*) estudio.
denationalization [di:næʃnəlaɪ'zeɪʃən] *n* desnacionalización *f.*
denationalize [di:'næʃnəlaɪz] *vt* desnacionalizar.
denatured alcohol [di:'neɪtʃəd-] *n* (*US*) alcohol *m* desnaturalizado.
denial [dɪ'naɪəl] *n* (*refusal*) negativa; (*of report etc*) denegación *f.*
denier ['dɛnɪə*] *n* denier *m.*
denim ['dɛnɪm] *n* tela vaquera; *see also* **denims**.
denim jacket *n* chaqueta vaquera, saco vaquero (*LAM*).
denims ['dɛnɪms] *npl* vaqueros *mpl.*
denizen ['dɛnɪzn] *n* (*inhabitant*) habitante *m/f*; (*foreigner*) residente *m/f* extranjero/a.
Denmark ['dɛnmɑ:k] *n* Dinamarca.
denomination [dɪnɔmɪ'neɪʃən] *n* valor *m*; (*REL*) confesión *f.*
denominator [dɪ'nɔmɪneɪtə*] *n* denominador *m.*
denote [dɪ'nəut] *vt* indicar, significar.
denounce [dɪ'nauns] *vt* denunciar.
dense [dɛns] *adj* (*thick*) espeso; (: *foliage etc*) tupido; (*stupid*) torpe.
densely [dɛnslɪ] *adv*: **~ populated** con una alta densidad de población.
density ['dɛnsɪtɪ] *n* densidad *f*; **single/double-~ disk** *n* disco de densidad sencilla/de doble densidad.
dent [dɛnt] *n* abolladura ♦ *vt* (*also*: **make a ~ in**) abollar.
dental ['dɛntl] *adj* dental.
dental floss [-flɔs] *n* seda dental.
dental surgeon *n* odontólogo/a.
dentifrice ['dɛntɪfrɪs] *n* dentífrico.
dentist ['dɛntɪst] *n* dentista *m/f*; **~'s surgery** (*BRIT*) consultorio dental.
dentistry ['dɛntɪstrɪ] *n* odontología.

dentures ['dɛntʃəz] *npl* dentadura *sg* (postiza).
denude [dɪ'njuːd] *vt*: **to ~ of** despojar de.
denunciation [dɪnʌnsɪ'eɪʃən] *n* denuncia, denunciación *f*.
deny [dɪ'naɪ] *vt* negar; (*charge*) rechazar; (*report*) desmentir; **to ~ o.s.** privarse (de); **he denies having said it** niega haberlo dicho.
deodorant [diː'əudərənt] *n* desodorante *m*.
depart [dɪ'pɑːt] *vi* irse, marcharse; (*train*) salir; **to ~ from** (*fig*: *differ from*) apartarse de.
departed [dɪ'pɑːtɪd] *adj* (*bygone*: *days, glory*) pasado; (*dead*) difunto ♦ *n*: **the (dear) ~** el/la/los/las difunto/a/os/as.
department [dɪ'pɑːtmənt] *n* (*COMM*) sección *f*; (*SCOL*) departamento; (*POL*) ministerio; **that's not my ~** (*fig*) no tiene que ver conmigo; **D~ of State** (*US*) Ministerio de Asuntos Exteriores.
departmental [diːpɑːt'mɛntl] *adj* (*dispute*) departamental; (*meeting*) departamental, de departamento; **~ manager** jefe/a *m/f* de sección *or* de departamento *or* de servicio.
department store *n* gran almacén *m*.
departure [dɪ'pɑːtʃə*] *n* partida, ida; (*of train*) salida; **a new ~** un nuevo rumbo.
departure lounge *n* (*at airport*) sala de embarque.
depend [dɪ'pɛnd] *vi*: **to ~ (up)on** (*be dependent upon*) depender de; (*rely on*) contar con; **it ~s** depende, según; **~ing on the result** según el resultado.
dependable [dɪ'pɛndəbl] *adj* (*person*) formal, serio.
dependant [dɪ'pɛndənt] *n* dependiente *m/f*.
dependence [dɪ'pɛndəns] *n* dependencia.
dependent [dɪ'pɛndənt] *adj*: **to be ~ (on)** depender (de) ♦ *n* = **dependant**.
depict [dɪ'pɪkt] *vt* (*in picture*) pintar; (*describe*) representar.
depilatory [dɪ'pɪlətrɪ] *n* (*also*: **~ cream**) depilatorio.
depleted [dɪ'pliːtɪd] *adj* reducido.
deplorable [dɪ'plɔːrəbl] *adj* deplorable.
deplore [dɪ'plɔː*] *vt* deplorar.
deploy [dɪ'plɔɪ] *vt* desplegar.
depopulate [diː'pɔpjuleɪt] *vt* despoblar.
depopulation ['diːpɔpju'leɪʃən] *n* despoblación *f*.
deport [dɪ'pɔːt] *vt* deportar.
deportation [diːpɔː'teɪʃən] *n* deportación *f*.
deportation order *n* orden *f* de expulsión *or* deportación.
deportee [diːpɔː'tiː] *n* deportado/a.
deportment [dɪ'pɔːtmənt] *n* comportamiento.
depose [dɪ'pəuz] *vt* deponer.
deposit [dɪ'pɔzɪt] *n* depósito; (*CHEM*) sedimento; (*of ore, oil*) yacimiento ♦ *vt* (*gen*) depositar; **to put down a ~ of £50** dejar un depósito de 50 libras.
deposit account *n* (*BRIT*) cuenta de ahorros.
depositor [dɪ'pɔzɪtə*] *n* depositante *m/f*, cuentacorrentista *m/f*.
depository [dɪ'pɔzɪtərɪ] *n* almacén *m* depositario.
depot ['dɛpəu] *n* (*storehouse*) depósito; (*for vehicles*) parque *m*.
deprave [dɪ'preɪv] *vt* depravar.
depraved [dɪ'preɪvd] *adj* depravado, vicioso.
depravity [dɪ'prævɪtɪ] *n* depravación *f*, vicio.
deprecate ['dɛprɪkeɪt] *vt* desaprobar, lamentar.
deprecating ['dɛprɪkeɪtɪŋ] *adj* (*disapproving*) de desaprobación; (*apologetic*): **a ~ smile** una sonrisa de disculpa.
depreciate [dɪ'priːʃɪeɪt] *vi* depreciarse, perder valor.
depreciation [dɪpriːʃɪ'eɪʃən] *n* depreciación *f*.
depress [dɪ'prɛs] *vt* deprimir; (*press down*) apretar.
depressant [dɪ'prɛsnt] *n* (*MED*) calmante *m*, sedante *m*.
depressed [dɪ'prɛst] *adj* deprimido; (*COMM*: *market, economy*) deprimido; (*area*) deprimido (económicamente); **to get ~** deprimirse.
depressing [dɪ'prɛsɪŋ] *adj* deprimente.
depression [dɪ'prɛʃən] *n* depresión *f*; **the economy is in a state of ~** la economía está deprimida.
deprivation [dɛprɪ'veɪʃən] *n* privación *f*; (*loss*) pérdida.
deprive [dɪ'praɪv] *vt*: **to ~ sb of** privar a algn de.
deprived [dɪ'praɪvd] *adj* necesitado.
dept. *abbr* (= *department*) dto.
depth [dɛpθ] *n* profundidad *f*; **at a ~ of 3 metres** a 3 metros de profundidad; **to be out of one's ~** (*swimmer*) perder pie; (*fig*) estar perdido; **to study sth in ~** estudiar algo a fondo; **in the ~s of** en lo más hondo de.
depth charge *n* carga de profundidad.
deputation [dɛpju'teɪʃən] *n* delegación *f*.
deputize ['dɛpjutaɪz] *vi*: **to ~ for sb** sustituir a algn.
deputy ['dɛpjutɪ] *adj*: **~ head**

subdirector(a) *m/f* ♦ *n* sustituto/a, suplente *m/f*; (*POL*) diputado/a; (*agent*) representante *m/f*.

deputy leader *n* (*POL*) vicepresidente/a *m/f*.

derail [dɪ'reɪl] *vt*: **to be ~ed** descarrilarse.

derailment [dɪ'reɪlmənt] *n* descarrilamiento.

deranged [dɪ'reɪndʒd] *adj* trastornado.

derby ['də:bɪ] *n* (*US*) hongo.

Derbys *abbr* (*BRIT*) = *Derbyshire*.

deregulate [di:'rɛgjuleɪt] *vt* desreglamentar.

deregulation [di:rɛgju'leɪʃən] *n* desreglamentación *f*.

derelict ['dɛrɪlɪkt] *adj* abandonado.

deride [dɪ'raɪd] *vt* ridiculizar, mofarse de.

derision [dɪ'rɪʒən] *n* irrisión *f*, mofas *fpl*.

derisive [dɪ'raɪsɪv] *adj* burlón/ona.

derisory [dɪ'raɪzərɪ] *adj* (*sum*) irrisorio; (*laughter, person*) burlón/ona, irónico.

derivation [dɛrɪ'veɪʃən] *n* derivación *f*.

derivative [dɪ'rɪvətɪv] *n* derivado ♦ *adj* (*work*) poco original.

derive [dɪ'raɪv] *vt* derivar ♦ *vi*: **to ~ from** derivarse de.

derived [dɪ'raɪvd] *adj* derivado.

dermatitis [də:mə'taɪtɪs] *n* dermatitis *f*.

dermatology [də:mə'tɔlədʒɪ] *n* dermatología.

derogatory [dɪ'rɔgətərɪ] *adj* despectivo.

derrick ['dɛrɪk] *n* torre *f* de perforación.

derv [də:v] *n* (*BRIT*) gasoil *m*.

DES *n abbr* (*BRIT*: = *Department of Education and Science*) *ministerio de educación y ciencia*.

descend [dɪ'sɛnd] *vt, vi* descender, bajar; **to ~ from** descender de; **in ~ing order of importance** de mayor a menor importancia.

▸**descend on** *vt fus* (*subj*: *enemy, angry person*) caer sobre; (: *misfortune*) sobrevenir; (*fig*: *gloom, silence*) invadir; **visitors ~ed (up)on us** las visitas nos invadieron.

descendant [dɪ'sɛndənt] *n* descendiente *m/f*.

descent [dɪ'sɛnt] *n* descenso; (*GEO*) pendiente *f*, declive *m*; (*origin*) descendencia.

describe [dɪs'kraɪb] *vt* describir.

description [dɪs'krɪpʃən] *n* descripción *f*; (*sort*) clase *f*, género; **of every ~** de toda clase.

descriptive [dɪs'krɪptɪv] *adj* descriptivo.

desecrate ['dɛsɪkreɪt] *vt* profanar.

desegregation [di:sɛgrɪ'geɪʃən] *n* desegregación *f*.

desert ['dɛzət] *n* desierto ♦ *vb* [dɪ'zə:t] *vt* abandonar, desamparar ♦ *vi* (*MIL*) desertar; *see also* **deserts**.

deserter [dɪ'zə:tə*] *n* desertor(a) *m/f*.

desertion [dɪ'zə:ʃən] *n* deserción *f*.

desert island *n* isla desierta.

deserts [dɪ'zə:ts] *npl*: **to get one's just ~** llevarse su merecido.

deserve [dɪ'zə:v] *vt* merecer, ser digno de, ameritar (*LAM*).

deservedly [dɪ'zə:vɪdlɪ] *adv* con razón.

deserving [dɪ'zə:vɪŋ] *adj* (*person*) digno; (*action, cause*) meritorio.

desiccated ['dɛsɪkeɪtɪd] *adj* desecado.

design [dɪ'zaɪn] *n* (*sketch*) bosquejo; (*of dress, car*) diseño; (*pattern*) dibujo ♦ *vt* (*gen*) diseñar; **industrial ~** diseño industrial; **to have ~s on sb** tener la(s) mira(s) puesta(s) en algn; **to be ~ed for sb/sth** estar hecho para algn/algo.

designate ['dɛzɪgneɪt] *vt* (*appoint*) nombrar; (*destine*) designar ♦ *adj* ['dɛzɪgnɪt] designado.

designation [dɛzɪg'neɪʃən] *n* (*appointment*) nombramiento; (*name*) denominación *f*.

designer [dɪ'zaɪnə*] *n* diseñador(a) *m/f*; (*fashion ~*) modisto/a.

desirability [dɪzaɪərə'bɪlɪtɪ] *n* ventaja, atractivo.

desirable [dɪ'zaɪərəbl] *adj* (*proper*) deseable; (*attractive*) atractivo; **it is ~ that** es conveniente que.

desire [dɪ'zaɪə*] *n* deseo ♦ *vt* desear; **to ~ sth/to do sth/that** desear algo/hacer algo/que.

desirous [dɪ'zaɪərəs] *adj* deseoso.

desist [dɪ'zɪst] *vi*: **to ~ (from)** desistir (de).

desk [dɛsk] *n* (*in office*) escritorio; (*for pupil*) pupitre *m*; (*in hotel, at airport*) recepción *f*; (*BRIT*: *in shop, restaurant*) caja.

desktop computer ['dɛsktɔp-] *n* ordenador *m* de sobremesa.

desktop publishing ['dɛsktɔp-] *n* autoedición *f*.

desolate ['dɛsəlɪt] *adj* (*place*) desierto; (*person*) afligido.

desolation [dɛsə'leɪʃən] *n* (*of place*) desolación *f*; (*of person*) aflicción *f*.

despair [dɪs'pɛə*] *n* desesperación *f* ♦ *vi*: **to ~ of** desesperar de; **in ~** desesperado.

despatch [dɪs'pætʃ] *n, vt* = **dispatch**.

desperate ['dɛspərɪt] *adj* desesperado; (*fugitive*) peligroso; (*measures*) extremo; **we are getting ~** estamos al borde de desesperación.

desperately ['dɛspərɪtlɪ] *adv* desesperadamente; (*very*) terriblemente, gravemente; **~ ill** gravemente enfermo.

desperation [dɛspə'reɪʃən] *n* desesperación *f*; **in ~** desesperado.
despicable [dɪs'pɪkəbl] *adj* vil, despreciable.
despise [dɪs'paɪz] *vt* despreciar.
despite [dɪs'paɪt] *prep* a pesar de, pese a.
despondent [dɪs'pɔndənt] *adj* deprimido, abatido.
despot ['dɛspɔt] *n* déspota *m/f*.
dessert [dɪ'zəːt] *n* postre *m*.
dessertspoon [dɪ'zəːtspuːn] *n* cuchara (de postre).
destabilize [diː'steɪbɪlaɪz] *vt* desestabilizar.
destination [dɛstɪ'neɪʃən] *n* destino.
destine ['dɛstɪn] *vt* destinar.
destined ['dɛstɪnd] *adj*: **~ for London** con destino a Londres.
destiny ['dɛstɪnɪ] *n* destino.
destitute ['dɛstɪtjuːt] *adj* desamparado, indigente.
destitution [dɛstɪ'tjuːʃən] *n* indigencia, miseria.
destroy [dɪs'trɔɪ] *vt* destruir; (*finish*) acabar con.
destroyer [dɪs'trɔɪə*] *n* (*NAUT*) destructor *m*.
destruction [dɪs'trʌkʃən] *n* destrucción *f*; (*fig*) ruina.
destructive [dɪs'trʌktɪv] *adj* destructivo, destructor(a).
desultory ['dɛsəltərɪ] *adj* (*reading*) poco metódico; (*conversation*) inconexo; (*contact*) intermitente.
detach [dɪ'tætʃ] *vt* separar; (*unstick*) despegar.
detachable [dɪ'tætʃəbl] *adj* separable; (*TECH*) desmontable.
detached [dɪ'tætʃt] *adj* (*attitude*) objetivo, imparcial.
detached house *n* chalé *m*, chalet *m*.
detachment [dɪ'tætʃmənt] *n* separación *f*; (*MIL*) destacamento; (*fig*) objetividad *f*, imparcialidad *f*.
detail ['diːteɪl] *n* detalle *m*; (*MIL*) destacamento ♦ *vt* detallar; (*MIL*) destacar; **in ~** detalladamente; **to go into ~(s)** entrar en detalles.
detailed ['diːteɪld] *adj* detallado.
detain [dɪ'teɪn] *vt* retener; (*in captivity*) detener.
detainee [diːteɪ'niː] *n* detenido/a.
detect [dɪ'tɛkt] *vt* (*discover*) descubrir; (*MED, POLICE*) identificar; (*MIL, RADAR, TECH*) detectar; (*notice*) percibir.
detection [dɪ'tɛkʃən] *n* descubrimiento; identificación *f*; **crime ~** investigación *f*; **to escape ~** (*criminal*) escaparse sin ser descubierto; (*mistake*) pasar inadvertido.
detective [dɪ'tɛktɪv] *n* detective *m*.
detective story *n* novela policíaca.
detector [dɪ'tɛktə*] *n* detector *m*.
détente [deɪ'tɑːnt] *n* distensión *f*, detente *f*.
detention [dɪ'tɛnʃən] *n* detención *f*, arresto.
deter [dɪ'təː*] *vt* (*dissuade*) disuadir; (*prevent*) impedir; **to ~ sb from doing sth** disuadir a algn de que haga algo.
detergent [dɪ'təːdʒənt] *n* detergente *m*.
deteriorate [dɪ'tɪərɪəreɪt] *vi* deteriorarse.
deterioration [dɪtɪərɪə'reɪʃən] *n* deterioro.
determination [dɪtəːmɪ'neɪʃən] *n* resolución *f*.
determine [dɪ'təːmɪn] *vt* determinar; **to ~ to do sth** decidir hacer algo.
determined [dɪ'təːmɪnd] *adj*: **to be ~ to do sth** estar decidido *or* resuelto a hacer algo; **a ~ effort** un esfuerzo enérgico.
deterrence [dɪ'tɛrns] *n* disuasión *f*.
deterrent [dɪ'tɛrənt] *n* fuerza de disuasión; **to act as a ~** servir para prevenir.
detest [dɪ'tɛst] *vt* aborrecer.
detestable [dɪ'tɛstəbl] *adj* aborrecible.
dethrone [diː'θrəun] *vt* destronar.
detonate ['dɛtəneɪt] *vi* estallar ♦ *vt* hacer detonar.
detonator ['dɛtəneɪtə*] *n* detonador *m*, fulminante *m*.
detour ['diːtuə*] *n* (*gen, US AUT: diversion*) desvío ♦ *vt* (*US: traffic*) desviar; **to make a ~** dar un rodeo.
detract [dɪ'trækt] *vt*: **to ~ from** quitar mérito a, restar valor a.
detractor [dɪ'træktə*] *n* detractor(a) *m/f*.
detriment ['dɛtrɪmənt] *n*: **to the ~ of** en perjuicio de; **without ~ to** sin detrimento de, sin perjuicio para.
detrimental [dɛtrɪ'mɛntl] *adj* perjudicial.
deuce [djuːs] *n* (*TENNIS*) cuarenta iguales.
devaluation [dɪvælju'eɪʃən] *n* devaluación *f*.
devalue [dɪ'væljuː] *vt* devaluar.
devastate ['dɛvəsteɪt] *vt* devastar; **he was ~d by the news** las noticias le dejaron desolado.
devastating ['dɛvəsteɪtɪŋ] *adj* devastador(a); (*fig*) arrollador(a).
devastation [dɛvəs'teɪʃən] *n* devastación *f*, ruina.
develop [dɪ'vɛləp] *vt* desarrollar; (*PHOT*) revelar; (*disease*) contraer; (*habit*) adquirir ♦ *vi* desarrollarse; (*advance*) progresar; **this land is to be ~ed** se va a construir en este terreno; **to ~ a taste for sth** tomar gusto a algo; **to ~ into** transformarse *or* convertirse en.
developer [dɪ'vɛləpə*] *n* (*property ~*)

promotor(a) *m/f*.
developing country *n* país *m* en (vías de) desarrollo.
development [dɪ'vɛləpmənt] *n* desarrollo; (*advance*) progreso; (*of affair, case*) desenvolvimiento; (*of land*) urbanización *f*.
development area *n* zona de fomento *or* desarrollo.
deviant ['diːvɪənt] *adj* anómalo, pervertido.
deviate ['diːvɪeɪt] *vi*: **to ~ (from)** desviarse (de).
deviation [diːvɪ'eɪʃən] *n* desviación *f*.
device [dɪ'vaɪs] *n* (*scheme*) estratagema, recurso; (*apparatus*) aparato, mecanismo; (*explosive* ~) artefacto explosivo.
devil ['dɛvl] *n* diablo, demonio.
devilish ['dɛvlɪʃ] *adj* diabólico.
devil-may-care ['dɛvlmeɪ'kɛə*] *adj* despreocupado.
devil's advocate *n*: **to play (the) ~** hacer de abogado del diablo.
devious ['diːvɪəs] *adj* intricado, enrevesado; (*person*) taimado.
devise [dɪ'vaɪz] *vt* idear, inventar.
devoid [dɪ'vɔɪd] *adj*: **~ of** desprovisto de.
devolution [diːvə'luːʃən] *n* (*POL*) descentralización *f*.
devolve [dɪ'vɔlv] *vi*: **to ~ (up)on** recaer sobre.
devote [dɪ'vəut] *vt*: **to ~ sth to** dedicar algo a.
devoted [dɪ'vəutɪd] *adj* (*loyal*) leal, fiel; **the book is ~ to politics** el libro trata de política.
devotee [dɛvəu'tiː] *n* devoto/a.
devotion [dɪ'vəuʃən] *n* dedicación *f*; (*REL*) devoción *f*.
devour [dɪ'vauə*] *vt* devorar.
devout [dɪ'vaut] *adj* devoto.
dew [djuː] *n* rocío.
dexterity [dɛks'tɛrɪtɪ] *n* destreza.
dext(e)rous ['dɛkstrəs] *adj* (*skilful*) diestro, hábil; (*movement*) ágil.
dg *abbr* (= *decigram*) dg.
diabetes [daɪə'biːtiːz] *n* diabetes *f*.
diabetic [daɪə'bɛtɪk] *n* diabético/a ♦ *adj* diabético; (*chocolate, jam*) para diabéticos.
diabolical [daɪə'bɔlɪkəl] *adj* diabólico; (*col*: *dreadful*) horrendo, horroroso.
diagnose ['daɪəgnəuz] *vt* diagnosticar.
diagnosis, *pl* **diagnoses** [daɪəg'nəusɪs, -siːz] *n* diagnóstico.
diagonal [daɪ'ægənl] *adj* diagonal ♦ *n* diagonal *f*.
diagram ['daɪəgræm] *n* diagrama *m*, esquema *m*.
dial ['daɪəl] *n* esfera; (*of radio*) dial *m*; (: *tuner*) sintonizador *m*; (*of phone*) disco ♦ *vt* (*number*) marcar, discar (*LAM*); **to ~ a wrong number** equivocarse de número; **can I ~ London direct?** ¿puedo marcar un número de Londres directamente?
dial. *abbr* = **dialect**.
dial code *n* (*US*) prefijo.
dialect ['daɪəlɛkt] *n* dialecto.
dialling code ['daɪəlɪŋ-] *n* (*BRIT*) prefijo.
dialling tone *n* (*BRIT*) señal *f or* tono de marcar.
dialogue, (*US*) **dialog** ['daɪəlɔg] *n* diálogo.
dial tone *n* (*US*) señal *f or* tono de marcar.
dialysis [daɪ'ælɪsɪs] *n* diálisis *f*.
diameter [daɪ'æmɪtə*] *n* diámetro.
diametrically [daɪə'mɛtrɪklɪ] *adv*: **~ opposed (to)** diametralmente opuesto (a).
diamond ['daɪəmənd] *n* diamante *m*; **~s** *npl* (*CARDS*) diamantes *mpl*.
diamond ring *n* anillo *or* sortija de diamantes.
diaper ['daɪəpə*] *n* (*US*) pañal *m*.
diaphragm ['daɪəfræm] *n* diafragma *m*.
diarrhoea, (*US*) **diarrhea** [daɪə'riːə] *n* diarrea.
diary ['daɪərɪ] *n* (*daily account*) diario; (*book*) agenda; **to keep a ~** escribir un diario.
diatribe ['daɪətraɪb] *n*: **~ (against)** diatriba (contra).
dice [daɪs] *n, pl inv* dados *mpl* ♦ *vt* (*CULIN*) cortar en cuadritos.
dicey ['daɪsɪ] *adj* (*col*): **it's a bit ~** (*risky*) es un poco arriesgado; (*doubtful*) es un poco dudoso.
dichotomy [daɪ'kɔtəmɪ] *n* dicotomía.
dickhead ['dɪkhɛd] *n* (*BRIT col!*) gilipollas *m inv*.
Dictaphone® ['dɪktəfəun] *n* dictáfono®.
dictate [dɪk'teɪt] *vt* dictar ♦ *n* ['dɪkteɪt] dictado.
▸**dictate to** *vt fus* (*person*) dar órdenes a; **I won't be ~d to** no recibo órdenes de nadie.
dictation [dɪk'teɪʃən] *n* (*to secretary etc*) dictado; **at ~ speed** para tomar al dictado.
dictator [dɪk'teɪtə*] *n* dictador *m*.
dictatorship [dɪk'teɪtəʃɪp] *n* dictadura.
diction ['dɪkʃən] *n* dicción *f*.
dictionary ['dɪkʃənrɪ] *n* diccionario.
did [dɪd] *pt of* **do**.
didactic [daɪ'dæktɪk] *adj* didáctico.
diddle ['dɪdl] *vt* estafar, timar.
didn't ['dɪdənt] = **did not**.
die [daɪ] *vi* morir; **to ~ (of *or* from)** morirse (de); **to be dying** morirse, estar muriéndose; **to be dying for sth/to do sth**

morirse por algo/de ganas de hacer algo.
▸**die away** *vi* (*sound, light*) desvanecerse.
▸**die down** *vi* (*gen*) apagarse; (*wind*) amainar.
▸**die out** *vi* desaparecer, extinguirse.
diehard ['daɪhɑːd] *n* intransigente *m/f*.
diesel ['diːzl] *n* diesel *m*.
diesel engine *n* motor *m* diesel.
diesel fuel, diesel oil *n* gas-oil *m*.
diet ['daɪət] *n* dieta; (*restricted food*) régimen *m* ♦ *vi* (*also*: **be on a ~**) estar a dieta, hacer régimen; **to live on a ~ of** alimentarse de.
dietician [daɪə'tɪʃən] *n* dietista *mf*.
differ ['dɪfə*] *vi* (*be different*) ser distinto, diferenciarse; (*disagree*) discrepar.
difference ['dɪfrəns] *n* diferencia; (*quarrel*) desacuerdo; **it makes no ~ to me** me da igual *or* lo mismo; **to settle one's ~s** arreglarse.
different ['dɪfrənt] *adj* diferente, distinto.
differential [dɪfə'rɛnʃəl] *n* diferencial *f*.
differentiate [dɪfə'rɛnʃɪeɪt] *vt* distinguir ♦ *vi* diferenciarse; **to ~ between** distinguir entre.
differently ['dɪfrəntlɪ] *adv* de otro modo, en forma distinta.
difficult ['dɪfɪkəlt] *adj* difícil; **~ to understand** difícil de entender.
difficulty ['dɪfɪkəltɪ] *n* dificultad *f*; **to have difficulties with** (*police, landlord etc*) tener problemas con; **to be in ~** estar en apuros.
diffidence ['dɪfɪdəns] *n* timidez *f*, falta de confianza en sí mismo.
diffident ['dɪfɪdənt] *adj* tímido.
diffuse [dɪ'fjuːs] *adj* difuso ♦ *vt* [dɪ'fjuːz] difundir.
dig [dɪg] *vt* (*pt, pp* **dug** [dʌg]) (*hole*) cavar; (*ground*) remover; (*coal*) extraer; (*nails etc*) hincar ♦ *n* (*prod*) empujón *m*; (*archaeological*) excavación *f*; (*remark*) indirecta; **to ~ into** (*savings*) consumir; **to ~ into one's pockets for sth** hurgar en el bolsillo buscando algo; **to ~ one's nails into** clavar las uñas en; *see also* **digs**.
▸**dig in** *vi* (*also*: **~ o.s. in**: *MIL*) atrincherarse; (*col*: *eat*) hincar los dientes ♦ *vt* (*compost*) añadir al suelo; (*knife, claw*) clavar; **to ~ in one's heels** (*fig*) mantenerse en sus trece.
▸**dig out** *vt* (*hole*) excavar; (*survivors, car from snow*) sacar.
▸**dig up** *vt* desenterrar; (*plant*) desarraigar.
digest [daɪ'dʒɛst] *vt* (*food*) digerir; (*facts*) asimilar ♦ *n* ['daɪdʒɛst] resumen *m*.
digestible [daɪ'dʒɛstəbl] *adj* digerible.
digestion [dɪ'dʒɛstʃən] *n* digestión *f*.
digestive [daɪ'dʒɛstɪv] *adj* (*juices, system*) digestivo.
digit ['dɪdʒɪt] *n* (*number*) dígito; (*finger*) dedo.
digital ['dɪdʒɪtl] *adj* digital.
digital camera *n* cámara digital.
digital compact cassette *n* cas(s)et(t)e *m or f* digital compacto.
digital TV *n* televisión *f* digital.
dignified ['dɪgnɪfaɪd] *adj* grave, solemne; (*action*) decoroso.
dignify ['dɪgnɪfaɪ] *vt* dignificar.
dignitary ['dɪgnɪtərɪ] *n* dignatario/a.
dignity ['dɪgnɪtɪ] *n* dignidad *f*.
digress [daɪ'grɛs] *vi*: **to ~ from** apartarse de.
digression [daɪ'grɛʃən] *n* digresión *f*.
digs [dɪgz] *npl* (*BRIT*: *col*) alojamiento.
dike [daɪk] *n* = **dyke**.
dilapidated [dɪ'læpɪdeɪtɪd] *adj* desmoronado, ruinoso.
dilate [daɪ'leɪt] *vt* dilatar ♦ *vi* dilatarse.
dilatory ['dɪlətərɪ] *adj* (*person*) lento; (*action*) dilatorio.
dilemma [daɪ'lɛmə] *n* dilema *m*; **to be in a ~** estar en un dilema.
dilettante [dɪlɪ'tæntɪ] *n* diletante *m/f*.
diligence ['dɪlɪdʒəns] *n* diligencia.
diligent ['dɪlɪdʒənt] *adj* diligente.
dill [dɪl] *n* eneldo.
dilly-dally ['dɪlɪ'dælɪ] *vi* (*hesitate*) vacilar; (*dawdle*) entretenerse.
dilute [daɪ'luːt] *vt* diluir.
dim [dɪm] *adj* (*light*) débil; (*sight*) turbio; (*outline*) borroso; (*stupid*) lerdo; (*room*) oscuro ♦ *vt* (*light*) bajar; **to take a ~ view of sth** tener una pobre opinión de algo.
dime [daɪm] *n* (*US*) *moneda de diez centavos*.
dimension [dɪ'mɛnʃən] *n* dimensión *f*.
-dimensional [dɪ'mɛnʃənl] *adj suff*: **two~** de dos dimensiones.
dimensions [dɪ'mɛnʃənz] *npl* dimensiones *fpl*.
diminish [dɪ'mɪnɪʃ] *vt, vi* disminuir.
diminished [dɪ'mɪnɪʃt] *adj*: **~ responsibility** (*LAW*) responsabilidad *f* disminuida.
diminutive [dɪ'mɪnjutɪv] *adj* diminuto ♦ *n* (*LING*) diminutivo.
dimly ['dɪmlɪ] *adv* débilmente; (*not clearly*) vagamente.
dimmer ['dɪmə*] *n* (*also*: **~ switch**) regulador *m* (de intensidad); (*US AUT*) interruptor *m*.
dimple ['dɪmpl] *n* hoyuelo.
dimwitted ['dɪm'wɪtɪd] *adj* (*col*) lerdo, de pocas luces.

din [dɪn] *n* estruendo, estrépito ♦ *vt*: **to ~ sth into sb** (*col*) meter algo en la cabeza a algn.
dine [daɪn] *vi* cenar.
diner ['daɪnə*] *n* (*person*: *in restaurant*) comensal *m/f*; (*BRIT RAIL*) = **dining car**; (*US*) restaurante económico.
dinghy ['dɪŋgɪ] *n* bote *m*; (*also*: **rubber ~**) lancha (neumática).
dingy ['dɪndʒɪ] *adj* (*room*) sombrío; (*dirty*) sucio; (*dull*) deslucido.
dining car ['daɪnɪŋ-] *n* (*BRIT*) coche-restaurante *m*.
dining room ['daɪnɪŋ-] *n* comedor *m*.
dinner ['dɪnə*] *n* (*evening meal*) cena, comida (*LAM*); (*lunch*) comida; (*public*) cena, banquete *m*; **~'s ready!** ¡la cena está servida!
dinner jacket *n* smoking *m*.
dinner party *n* cena.
dinner time *n* hora de cenar *or* comer.
dinosaur ['daɪnəsɔː*] *n* dinosaurio.
dint [dɪnt] *n*: **by ~ of (doing) sth** a fuerza de (hacer) algo.
diocese ['daɪəsɪs] *n* diócesis *f*.
dioxide [daɪ'ɔksaɪd] *n* bióxido; **carbon ~** bióxido de carbono.
Dip. *abbr* (*BRIT*) = **diploma**.
dip [dɪp] *n* (*slope*) pendiente *f*; (*in sea*) chapuzón *m* ♦ *vt* (*in water*) mojar; (*ladle etc*) meter; (*BRIT AUT*): **to ~ one's lights** poner la luz de cruce ♦ *vi* inclinarse hacia abajo.
diphtheria [dɪf'θɪərɪə] *n* difteria.
diphthong ['dɪfθɔŋ] *n* diptongo.
diploma [dɪ'pləumə] *n* diploma *m*.
diplomacy [dɪ'pləuməsɪ] *n* diplomacia.
diplomat ['dɪpləmæt] *n* diplomático/a *m/f*.
diplomatic [dɪplə'mætɪk] *adj* diplomático; **to break off ~ relations** romper las relaciones diplomáticas.
diplomatic corps *n* cuerpo diplomático.
diplomatic immunity *n* inmunidad *f* diplomática.
dipstick ['dɪpstɪk] *n* (*AUT*) varilla de nivel (del aceite).
dipswitch ['dɪpswɪtʃ] *n* (*BRIT AUT*) interruptor *m*.
dire [daɪə*] *adj* calamitoso.
direct [daɪ'rɛkt] *adj* (*gen*) directo; (*manner, person*) franco ♦ *vt* dirigir; **can you ~ me to...?** ¿puede indicarme dónde está...?; **to ~ sb to do sth** mandar a algn hacer algo.
direct access *n* (*COMPUT*) acceso directo.
direct cost *n* costo directo.
direct current *n* corriente *f* continua.
direct debit *n* domiciliación *f* bancaria de recibos; **to pay by ~** domiciliar el pago.
direct dialling *n* servicio automático de llamadas.
direction [dɪ'rɛkʃən] *n* dirección *f*; **sense of ~** sentido de la orientación; **~s** *npl* (*advice*) órdenes *fpl*, instrucciones *fpl*; (*to a place*) señas *fpl*; **in the ~ of** hacia, en dirección a; **~s for use** modo de empleo; **to ask for ~s** preguntar el camino.
directional [dɪ'rɛkʃənl] *adj* direccional.
directive [daɪ'rɛktɪv] *n* orden *f*, instrucción *f*; **a government ~** una orden del gobierno.
direct labour *n* mano *f* de obra directa.
directly [dɪ'rɛktlɪ] *adv* (*in straight line*) directamente; (*at once*) en seguida.
direct mail *n* correspondencia personalizada.
direct mailshot *n* (*BRIT*) promoción *f* por correspondencia personalizada.
directness [dɪ'rɛktnɪs] *n* (*of person, speech*) franqueza.
director [dɪ'rɛktə*] *n* director(a) *m/f*; **managing ~** director(a) *m/f* gerente.
Director of Public Prosecutions *n* ≈ fiscal *m/f* general del Estado.
directory [dɪ'rɛktərɪ] *n* (*TEL*) guía (telefónica); (*street ~*) callejero; (*trade ~*) directorio de comercio; (*COMPUT*) directorio.
directory enquiries, (*US*) **directory assistance** *n* (*service*) (servicio de) información *f*.
dirt [dəːt] *n* suciedad *f*.
dirt-cheap ['dəːt'tʃiːp] *adj* baratísimo.
dirt road *n* (*US*) camino sin firme.
dirty ['dəːtɪ] *adj* sucio; (*joke*) verde, colorado (*LAM*) ♦ *vt* ensuciar; (*stain*) manchar.
dirty trick *n* mala jugada, truco sucio.
disability [dɪsə'bɪlɪtɪ] *n* incapacidad *f*.
disability allowance *n* pensión *f* de invalidez.
disable [dɪs'eɪbl] *vt* (*subj*: *illness, accident*) dejar incapacitado *or* inválido; (*tank, gun*) inutilizar; (*LAW*: *disqualify*) incapacitar.
disabled [dɪs'eɪbld] *adj* minusválido.
disabuse [dɪsə'bjuːz] *vt* desengañar.
disadvantage [dɪsəd'vɑːntɪdʒ] *n* desventaja, inconveniente *m*.
disadvantaged [dɪsəd'vɑːntɪdʒd] *adj* (*person*) desventajado.
disadvantageous [dɪsædvən'teɪdʒəs] *adj* desventajoso.
disaffected [dɪsə'fɛktɪd] *adj* descontento; **to be ~ (to *or* towards)** estar descontento (de).
disaffection [dɪsə'fɛkʃən] *n* desafecto, descontento.

disagree [dɪsə'griː] *vi* (*differ*) discrepar; **to ~ (with)** no estar de acuerdo (con); **I ~ with you** no estoy de acuerdo contigo.
disagreeable [dɪsə'grɪəbl] *adj* desagradable.
disagreement [dɪsə'griːmənt] *n* (*gen*) desacuerdo; (*quarrel*) riña; **to have a ~ with sb** estar en desacuerdo con algn.
disallow ['dɪsə'lau] *vt* (*goal*) anular; (*claim*) rechazar.
disappear [dɪsə'pɪə*] *vi* desaparecer.
disappearance [dɪsə'pɪərəns] *n* desaparición *f*.
disappoint [dɪsə'pɔɪnt] *vt* decepcionar; (*hopes*) defraudar.
disappointed [dɪsə'pɔɪntɪd] *adj* decepcionado.
disappointing [dɪsə'pɔɪntɪŋ] *adj* decepcionante.
disappointment [dɪsə'pɔɪntmənt] *n* decepción *f*.
disapproval [dɪsə'pruːvəl] *n* desaprobación *f*.
disapprove [dɪsə'pruːv] *vi*: **to ~ of** desaprobar.
disapproving [dɪsə'pruːvɪŋ] *adj* de desaprobación, desaprobador(a).
disarm [dɪs'ɑːm] *vt* desarmar.
disarmament [dɪs'ɑːməmənt] *n* desarme *m*.
disarmament talks *npl* conversaciones *fpl* de *or* sobre desarme.
disarming [dɪs'ɑːmɪŋ] *adj* (*smile*) que desarma, encantador(a).
disarray [dɪsə'reɪ] *n*: **in ~** (*troops*) desorganizado; (*thoughts*) confuso; (*hair, clothes*) desarreglado; **to throw into ~** provocar el caos.
disaster [dɪ'zɑːstə*] *n* desastre *m*.
disaster area *n* zona catastrófica.
disastrous [dɪ'zɑːstrəs] *adj* desastroso.
disband [dɪs'bænd] *vt* disolver ♦ *vi* desbandarse.
disbelief [dɪsbə'liːf] *n* incredulidad *f*; **in ~** con incredulidad.
disbelieve ['dɪsbə'liːv] *vt* (*person, story*) poner en duda, no creer.
disc [dɪsk] *n* disco; (*COMPUT*) = **disk.**
disc. *abbr* (*COMM*) = **discount.**
discard [dɪs'kɑːd] *vt* (*old things*) tirar; (*fig*) descartar.
discern [dɪ'səːn] *vt* percibir, discernir; (*understand*) comprender.
discernible [dɪ'səːnəbl] *adj* perceptible.
discerning [dɪ'səːnɪŋ] *adj* perspicaz.
discharge [dɪs'tʃɑːdʒ] *vt* (*task, duty*) cumplir; (*ship etc*) descargar; (*patient*) dar de alta; (*employee*) despedir; (*soldier*) licenciar; (*defendant*) poner en libertad; (*settle*: *debt*) saldar ♦ *n* ['dɪstʃɑːdʒ] (*ELEC*) descarga; (*vaginal ~*) emisión *f* vaginal; (*dismissal*) despedida; (*of duty*) desempeño; (*of debt*) pago, descargo; (*of gas, chemicals*) escape *m*; **~d bankrupt** quebrado/a rehabilitado/a.
disciple [dɪ'saɪpl] *n* discípulo/a.
disciplinary ['dɪsɪplɪnərɪ] *adj*: **to take ~ action against sb** disciplinar a algn.
discipline ['dɪsɪplɪn] *n* disciplina ♦ *vt* disciplinar; **to ~ o.s. to do sth** obligarse a hacer algo.
disc jockey (DJ) *n* pinchadiscos *m/f inv*.
disclaim [dɪs'kleɪm] *vt* negar tener.
disclaimer [dɪs'kleɪmə*] *n* rectificación *f*; **to issue a ~** hacer una rectificación.
disclose [dɪs'kləuz] *vt* revelar.
disclosure [dɪs'kləuʒə*] *n* revelación *f*.
disco ['dɪskəu] *n abbr* = **discothèque.**
discolouration, (*US*) **discoloration** [dɪskʌlə'reɪʃən] *n* descoloramiento, decoloración *f*.
discolo(u)red [dɪs'kʌləd] *adj* descolorido.
discomfort [dɪs'kʌmfət] *n* incomodidad *f*; (*unease*) inquietud *f*; (*physical*) malestar *m*.
disconcert [dɪskən'səːt] *vt* desconcertar.
disconnect [dɪskə'nɛkt] *vt* (*gen*) separar; (*ELEC etc*) desconectar; (*supply*) cortar (el suministro) a.
disconsolate [dɪs'kɔnsəlɪt] *adj* desconsolado.
discontent [dɪskən'tɛnt] *n* descontento.
discontented [dɪskən'tɛntɪd] *adj* descontento.
discontinue [dɪskən'tɪnjuː] *vt* interrumpir; (*payments*) suspender.
discord ['dɪskɔːd] *n* discordia; (*MUS*) disonancia.
discordant [dɪs'kɔːdənt] *adj* disonante.
discothèque ['dɪskəutɛk] *n* discoteca.
discount ['dɪskaunt] *n* descuento ♦ *vt* [dɪs'kaunt] descontar; (*report etc*) descartar; **at a ~** con descuento; **~ for cash** descuento por pago en efectivo; **to give sb a ~ on sth** hacer un descuento a algn en algo.
discount house *n* (*FINANCE*) banco de descuento; (*COMM*: *also*: **discount store**) ≈ tienda de saldos.
discount rate *n* (*COMM*) tipo de descuento.
discount store *n* ≈ tienda de saldos.
discourage [dɪs'kʌrɪdʒ] *vt* desalentar; (*oppose*) oponerse a; (*dissuade, deter*) desanimar, disuadir.
discouragement [dɪs'kʌrɪdʒmənt] *n* (*dissuasion*) disuasión *f*; (*depression*) desánimo, desaliento; **to act as a ~ to**

servir para disuadir.
discouraging [dɪs'kʌrɪdʒɪŋ] *adj* desalentador(a).
discourteous [dɪs'kəːtɪəs] *adj* descortés.
discover [dɪs'kʌvə*] *vt* descubrir.
discovery [dɪs'kʌvərɪ] *n* descubrimiento.
discredit [dɪs'krɛdɪt] *vt* desacreditar.
discreet [dɪ'skriːt] *adj* (*tactful*) discreto; (*careful*) circunspecto, prudente.
discreetly [dɪ'skriːtlɪ] *adv* discretamente.
discrepancy [dɪ'skrɛpənsɪ] *n* (*difference*) diferencia; (*disagreement*) discrepancia.
discretion [dɪ'skrɛʃən] *n* (*tact*) discreción *f*; (*care*) prudencia, circunspección *f*; **use your own** ~ haz lo que creas oportuno.
discretionary [dɪ'skrɛʃənrɪ] *adj* (*powers*) discrecional.
discriminate [dɪ'skrɪmɪneɪt] *vi*: **to** ~ **between** distinguir entre; **to** ~ **against** discriminar contra.
discriminating [dɪ'skrɪmɪneɪtɪŋ] *adj* entendido.
discrimination [dɪskrɪmɪ'neɪʃən] *n* (*discernment*) perspicacia; (*bias*) discriminación *f*; **racial/sexual** ~ discriminación racial/sexual.
discus ['dɪskəs] *n* disco.
discuss [dɪ'skʌs] *vt* (*gen*) discutir; (*a theme*) tratar.
discussion [dɪ'skʌʃən] *n* discusión *f*; **under** ~ en discusión.
disdain [dɪs'deɪn] *n* desdén *m* ♦ *vt* desdeñar.
disease [dɪ'ziːz] *n* enfermedad *f*.
diseased [dɪ'ziːzd] *adj* enfermo.
disembark [dɪsɪm'bɑːk] *vt, vi* desembarcar.
disembarkation [dɪsɛmbɑː'keɪʃən] *n* desembarque *m*.
disenchanted [dɪsɪn'tʃɑːntɪd] *adj*: ~ **(with)** desilusionado (con).
disenfranchise ['dɪsɪn'fræntʃaɪz] *vt* privar del derecho al voto; (*COMM*) privar de franquicias.
disengage [dɪsɪn'geɪdʒ] *vt* soltar; **to** ~ **the clutch** (*AUT*) desembragar.
disentangle [dɪsɪn'tæŋgl] *vt* desenredar.
disfavour, (*US*) **disfavor** [dɪs'feɪvə*] *n* desaprobación *f*.
disfigure [dɪs'fɪgə*] *vt* desfigurar.
disgorge [dɪs'gɔːdʒ] *vt* verter.
disgrace [dɪs'greɪs] *n* ignominia; (*downfall*) caída; (*shame*) vergüenza, escándalo ♦ *vt* deshonrar.
disgraceful [dɪs'greɪsful] *adj* vergonzoso; (*behaviour*) escandaloso.
disgruntled [dɪs'grʌntld] *adj* disgustado, descontento.
disguise [dɪs'gaɪz] *n* disfraz *m* ♦ *vt* disfrazar; (*voice*) disimular; (*feelings etc*) ocultar; **in** ~ disfrazado; **to** ~ **o.s. as** disfrazarse de; **there's no disguising the fact that** ... no puede ocultarse el hecho de que ....
disgust [dɪs'gʌst] *n* repugnancia ♦ *vt* repugnar, dar asco a.
disgusting [dɪs'gʌstɪŋ] *adj* repugnante, asqueroso.
dish [dɪʃ] *n* (*gen*) plato; **to do** *or* **wash the** ~**es** fregar los platos.
▸**dish out** *vt* (*money, exam papers*) repartir; (*food*) servir; (*advice*) dar.
▸**dish up** *vt* servir.
dishcloth ['dɪʃklɔθ] *n* paño de cocina, bayeta.
dishearten [dɪs'hɑːtn] *vt* desalentar.
dishevelled, (*US*) **disheveled** [dɪ'ʃɛvəld] *adj* (*hair*) despeinado; (*clothes, appearance*) desarreglado.
dishonest [dɪs'ɔnɪst] *adj* (*person*) poco honrado, tramposo; (*means*) fraudulento.
dishonesty [dɪs'ɔnɪstɪ] *n* falta de honradez.
dishonour, (*US*) **dishonor** [dɪs'ɔnə*] *n* deshonra.
dishono(u)rable [dɪs'ɔnərəbl] *adj* deshonroso.
dish soap *n* (*US*) lavavajillas *m inv*.
dishtowel ['dɪʃtauəl] *n* (*US*) trapo de fregar.
dishwasher ['dɪʃwɔʃə*] *n* lavaplatos *m inv*; (*person*) friegaplatos *m/f inv*.
dishy ['dɪʃɪ] *adj* (*BRIT col*) buenón/ona.
disillusion [dɪsɪ'luːʒən] *vt* desilusionar; **to become** ~**ed (with)** quedar desilusionado (con).
disillusionment [dɪsɪ'luːʒənmənt] *n* desilusión *f*.
disincentive [dɪsɪn'sɛntɪv] *n* freno; **to act as a** ~ **(to)** actuar de freno (a); **to be a** ~ **to** ser un freno a.
disinclined ['dɪsɪn'klaɪnd] *adj*: **to be** ~ **to do sth** estar poco dispuesto a hacer algo.
disinfect [dɪsɪn'fɛkt] *vt* desinfectar.
disinfectant [dɪsɪn'fɛktənt] *n* desinfectante *m*.
disinflation [dɪsɪn'fleɪʃən] *n* desinflación *f*.
disinformation [dɪsɪnfə'meɪʃən] *n* desinformación *f*.
disingenuous [dɪsɪn'dʒɛnjuəs] *adj* poco sincero, falso.
disinherit [dɪsɪn'hɛrɪt] *vt* desheredar.
disintegrate [dɪs'ɪntɪgreɪt] *vi* disgregarse, desintegrarse.
disinterested [dɪs'ɪntrəstɪd] *adj* desinteresado.
disjointed [dɪs'dʒɔɪntɪd] *adj* inconexo.
disk [dɪsk] *n* (*COMPUT*) disco, disquete *m*; **single-/double-sided** ~ disco de una

cara/dos caras.
disk drive *n* disc drive *m*.
diskette [dɪs'kɛt] *n* diskette *m*, disquete *m*, disco flexible.
disk operating system (DOS) *n* sistema *m* operativo de discos (DOS).
dislike [dɪs'laɪk] *n* antipatía, aversión *f* ♦ *vt* tener antipatía a; **to take a ~ to sb/sth** cogerle *or* agarrarle (*LAM*) antipatía a algn/algo; **I ~ the idea** no me gusta la idea.
dislocate ['dɪsləkeɪt] *vt* dislocar; **he ~d his shoulder** se dislocó el hombro.
dislodge [dɪs'lɔdʒ] *vt* sacar; (*enemy*) desalojar.
disloyal [dɪs'lɔɪəl] *adj* desleal.
dismal ['dɪzml] *adj* (*dark*) sombrío; (*depressing*) triste; (*very bad*) fatal.
dismantle [dɪs'mæntl] *vt* desmontar, desarmar.
dismay [dɪs'meɪ] *n* consternación *f* ♦ *vt* consternar; **much to my ~** para gran consternación mía.
dismiss [dɪs'mɪs] *vt* (*worker*) despedir; (*official*) destituir; (*idea*, *LAW*) rechazar; (*possibility*) descartar ♦ *vi* (*MIL*) romper filas.
dismissal [dɪs'mɪsl] *n* despedida; destitución *f*.
dismount [dɪs'maunt] *vi* apearse; (*rider*) desmontar.
disobedience [dɪsə'bi:dɪəns] *n* desobediencia.
disobedient [dɪsə'bi:dɪənt] *adj* desobediente.
disobey [dɪsə'beɪ] *vt* desobedecer; (*rule*) infringir.
disorder [dɪs'ɔ:də*] *n* desorden *m*; (*rioting*) disturbio; (*MED*) trastorno; (*disease*) enfermedad *f*; **civil ~** desorden *m* civil.
disorderly [dɪs'ɔ:dəlɪ] *adj* (*untidy*) desordenado; (*meeting*) alborotado; **~ conduct** (*LAW*) conducta escandalosa.
disorganized [dɪs'ɔ:gənaɪzd] *adj* desorganizado.
disorientated [dɪs'ɔ:rɪenteɪtəd] *adj* desorientado.
disown [dɪs'əun] *vt* renegar de.
disparaging [dɪs'pærɪdʒɪŋ] *adj* despreciativo; **to be ~ about sth/sb** menospreciar algo/a algn.
disparate ['dɪspərɪt] *adj* dispar.
disparity [dɪs'pærɪtɪ] *n* disparidad *f*.
dispassionate [dɪs'pæʃənɪt] *adj* (*unbiased*) imparcial; (*unemotional*) desapasionado.
dispatch [dɪs'pætʃ] *vt* enviar; (*kill*) despachar; (*deal with*: *business*) despachar ♦ *n* (*sending*) envío; (*speed*) prontitud *f*; (*PRESS*) informe *m*; (*MIL*) parte *m*.
dispatch department *n* (*COMM*) departamento de envíos.
dispatch rider *n* (*MIL*) correo.
dispel [dɪs'pɛl] *vt* disipar, dispersar.
dispensary [dɪs'pɛnsərɪ] *n* dispensario.
dispensation [dɪspɛn'seɪʃən] *n* (*REL*) dispensa.
dispense [dɪs'pɛns] *vt* dispensar, repartir; (*medicine*) preparar.
▶**dispense with** *vt fus* (*make unnecessary*) prescindir de.
dispenser [dɪs'pɛnsə*] *n* (*container*) distribuidor *m* automático.
dispensing chemist [dɪs'pɛnsɪŋ-] *n* (*BRIT*) farmacia.
dispersal [dɪs'pə:sl] *n* dispersión *f*.
disperse [dɪs'pə:s] *vt* dispersar ♦ *vi* dispersarse.
dispirited [dɪ'spɪrɪtɪd] *adj* desanimado, desalentado.
displace [dɪs'pleɪs] *vt* (*person*) desplazar; (*replace*) reemplazar.
displaced person *n* (*POL*) desplazado/a.
displacement [dɪs'pleɪsmənt] *n* cambio de sitio.
display [dɪs'pleɪ] *n* (*exhibition*) exposición *f*; (*COMPUT*) visualización *f*; (*MIL*) desfile *m*; (*of feeling*) manifestación *f*; (*pej*) aparato, pompa ♦ *vt* exponer; manifestar; (*ostentatiously*) lucir; **on ~** (*exhibits*) expuesto, exhibido; (*goods*) en el escaparate.
display advertising *n* publicidad *f* gráfica.
displease [dɪs'pli:z] *vt* (*offend*) ofender; (*annoy*) fastidiar; **~d with** disgustado con.
displeasure [dɪs'plɛʒə*] *n* disgusto.
disposable [dɪs'pəuzəbl] *adj* (*not reusable*) desechable; **~ personal income** ingresos *mpl* personales disponibles.
disposable nappy *n* pañal *m* desechable.
disposal [dɪs'pəuzl] *n* (*sale*) venta; (*of house*) traspaso; (*by giving away*) donación *f*; (*arrangement*) colocación *f*; (*of rubbish*) destrucción *f*; **at one's ~** a la disposición de algn; **to put sth at sb's ~** poner algo a disposición de algn.
disposed [dɪs'pəuzd] *adj*: **~ to do** dispuesto a hacer.
dispose of [dɪs'pəuz] *vt fus* (*time, money*) disponer de; (*unwanted goods*) deshacerse de; (*COMM*: *sell*) traspasar, vender; (*throw away*) tirar.
disposition [dɪspə'zɪʃən] *n* disposición *f*; (*temperament*) carácter *m*.
dispossess ['dɪspə'zɛs] *vt*: **to ~ sb (of)**

desposeer a algn (de).
disproportion [dɪsprəˈpɔːʃən] *n* desproporción *f*.
disproportionate [dɪsprəˈpɔːʃənət] *adj* desproporcionado.
disprove [dɪsˈpruːv] *vt* refutar.
dispute [dɪsˈpjuːt] *n* disputa; (*verbal*) discusión *f*; (*also*: **industrial** ~) conflicto (laboral) ♦ *vt* (*argue*) disputar; (*question*) cuestionar; **to be in** *or* **under** ~ (*matter*) discutirse; (*territory*) estar en disputa; (*JUR*) estar en litigio.
disqualification [dɪskwɔlɪfɪˈkeɪʃən] *n* inhabilitación *f*; (*SPORT, from driving*) descalificación *f*.
disqualify [dɪsˈkwɔlɪfaɪ] *vt* (*SPORT*) desclasificar; **to ~ sb for sth/from doing sth** incapacitar a algn para algo/hacer algo.
disquiet [dɪsˈkwaɪət] *n* preocupación *f*, inquietud *f*.
disquieting [dɪsˈkwaɪətɪŋ] *adj* inquietante.
disregard [dɪsrɪˈgɑːd] *vt* desatender; (*ignore*) no hacer caso de ♦ *n* (*indifference*: *to feelings, danger, money*): ~ **(for)** indiferencia (a); ~ **(of)** (*non-observance*: *of law, rules*) violación *f* (de).
disrepair [dɪsrɪˈpɛə*] *n*: **to fall into** ~ (*building*) desmoronarse; (*street*) deteriorarse.
disreputable [dɪsˈrɛpjutəbl] *adj* (*person, area*) de mala fama; (*behaviour*) vergonzoso.
disrepute [ˈdɪsrɪˈpjuːt] *n* descrédito, ignominia; **to bring into** ~ desacreditar.
disrespectful [dɪsrɪˈspɛktful] *adj* irrespetuoso.
disrupt [dɪsˈrʌpt] *vt* (*meeting, public transport, conversation*) interrumpir; (*plans*) desbaratar, alternar, trastornar.
disruption [dɪsˈrʌpʃən] *n* trastorno; desbaratamiento; interrupción *f*.
disruptive [dɪsˈrʌptɪv] *adj* (*influence*) disruptivo; (*strike action*) perjudicial.
dissatisfaction [dɪssætɪsˈfækʃən] *n* disgusto, descontento.
dissatisfied [dɪsˈsætɪsfaɪd] *adj* insatisfecho.
dissect [dɪˈsɛkt] *vt* (*also fig*) disecar.
disseminate [dɪˈsɛmɪneɪt] *vt* divulgar, difundir.
dissent [dɪˈsɛnt] *n* disensión *f*.
dissenter [dɪˈsɛntə*] *n* (*REL, POL etc*) disidente *m/f*.
dissertation [dɪsəˈteɪʃən] *n* (*UNIV*) tesina; *see also* **master's degree**.
disservice [dɪsˈsəːvɪs] *n*: **to do sb a** ~ perjudicar a alguien.
dissident [ˈdɪsɪdnt] *adj*, *n* disidente *m/f*.
dissimilar [dɪˈsɪmɪlə*] *adj* distinto.
dissipate [ˈdɪsɪpeɪt] *vt* disipar; (*waste*) desperdiciar.
dissipated [ˈdɪsɪpeɪtɪd] *adj* disoluto.
dissipation [dɪsɪˈpeɪʃən] *n* disipación *f*; (*moral*) libertinaje *m*, vicio; (*waste*) derroche *m*.
dissociate [dɪˈsəuʃɪeɪt] *vt* disociar; **to ~ o.s. from** disociarse de.
dissolute [ˈdɪsəluːt] *adj* disoluto.
dissolution [dɪsəˈluːʃən] *n* (*of organization, marriage, POL*) disolución *f*.
dissolve [dɪˈzɔlv] *vt* (*gen, COMM*) disolver ♦ *vi* disolverse.
dissuade [dɪˈsweɪd] *vt*: **to ~ sb (from)** disuadir a algn (de).
distaff [ˈdɪstæf] *n*: ~ **side** rama femenina.
distance [ˈdɪstns] *n* distancia; **in the** ~ a lo lejos; **what ~ is it to London?** ¿qué distancia hay de aquí a Londres?; **it's within walking** ~ se puede ir andando.
distant [ˈdɪstnt] *adj* lejano; (*manner*) reservado, frío.
distaste [dɪsˈteɪst] *n* repugnancia.
distasteful [dɪsˈteɪstful] *adj* repugnante, desagradable.
Dist. Atty. *abbr* (*US*) = **district attorney**.
distemper [dɪsˈtɛmpə*] *n* (*of dogs*) moquillo.
distend [dɪˈstɛnd] *vt* dilatar, hinchar ♦ *vi* dilatarse, hincharse.
distended [dɪˈstɛndɪd] *adj* (*stomach*) hinchado.
distil, (*US*) **distill** [dɪsˈtɪl] *vt* destilar.
distillery [dɪsˈtɪlərɪ] *n* destilería.
distinct [dɪsˈtɪŋkt] *adj* (*different*) distinto; (*clear*) claro; (*unmistakeable*) inequívoco; **as ~ from** a diferencia de.
distinction [dɪsˈtɪŋkʃən] *n* distinción *f*; (*in exam*) sobresaliente *m*; **a writer of** ~ un escritor destacado; **to draw a ~ between** hacer una distinción entre.
distinctive [dɪsˈtɪŋktɪv] *adj* distintivo.
distinctly [dɪsˈtɪŋktlɪ] *adv* claramente.
distinguish [dɪsˈtɪŋgwɪʃ] *vt* distinguir ♦ *vi*: **to ~ (between)** distinguir (entre).
distinguished [dɪsˈtɪŋgwɪʃt] *adj* (*eminent*) distinguido; (*career*) eminente; (*refined*) distinguido, de categoría.
distinguishing [dɪsˈtɪŋgwɪʃɪŋ] *adj* (*feature*) distintivo.
distort [dɪsˈtɔːt] *vt* torcer, retorcer; (*account, news*) desvirtuar, deformar.
distortion [dɪsˈtɔːʃən] *n* deformación *f*; (*of sound*) distorsión *f*; (*of truth etc*) tergiversación *f*; (*of facts*) falseamiento.
distract [dɪsˈtrækt] *vt* distraer.
distracted [dɪsˈtræktɪd] *adj* distraído.

distracting [dɪs'træktɪŋ] *adj* que distrae la atención, molesto.
distraction [dɪs'trækʃən] *n* distracción *f*; (*confusion*) aturdimiento; (*amusement*) diversión *f*; **to drive sb to ~** (*distress, anxiety*) volver loco a algn.
distraught [dɪs'trɔːt] *adj* turbado, enloquecido.
distress [dɪs'trɛs] *n* (*anguish*) angustia; (*want*) miseria; (*pain*) dolor *m*; (*danger*) peligro ♦ *vt* afligir; (*pain*) doler; **in ~** (*ship etc*) en peligro.
distressing [dɪs'trɛsɪŋ] *adj* angustioso; doloroso.
distress signal *n* señal *f* de socorro.
distribute [dɪs'trɪbjuːt] *vt* (*gen*) distribuir; (*share out*) repartir.
distribution [dɪstrɪ'bjuːʃən] *n* distribución *f*.
distribution cost *n* gastos *mpl* de distribución.
distributor [dɪs'trɪbjutə*] *n* (*AUT*) distribuidor *m*; (*COMM*) distribuidora.
district ['dɪstrɪkt] *n* (*of country*) zona, región *f*; (*of town*) barrio; (*ADMIN*) distrito.
district attorney *n* (*US*) fiscal *m/f*.
district council *n* ≈ municipio; *ver recuadro*.

DISTRICT COUNCIL

En Inglaterra y Gales, con la excepción de Londres, la administración local corre a cargo del **district council**, *responsable de los servicios municipales como vivienda, urbanismo, recolección de basuras, salud medioambiental etc. La mayoría de sus miembros son elegidos a nivel local cada cuatro años. Hay un total de 369 "districts" (distritos), repartidos en 53 "counties" (condados), que se financian a través de los impuestos municipales y partidas presupuestarias del Estado. Éste controla sus gastos a través de una comisión independiente.*

district manager *n* representante *m/f* regional.
district nurse *n* (*BRIT*) *enfermera que atiende a pacientes a domicilio*.
distrust [dɪs'trʌst] *n* desconfianza ♦ *vt* desconfiar de.
distrustful [dɪs'trʌstful] *adj* desconfiado.
disturb [dɪs'təːb] *vt* (*person*: *bother, interrupt*) molestar; (*meeting*) interrumpir; (*disorganize*) desordenar; **sorry to ~ you** perdone la molestia.
disturbance [dɪs'təːbəns] *n* (*political etc*) disturbio; (*violence*) alboroto; (*of mind*) trastorno; **to cause a ~** causar alboroto; **~ of the peace** alteración *f* del orden público.
disturbed [dɪs'təːbd] *adj* (*worried, upset*) preocupado, angustiado; **to be emotionally/mentally ~** tener problemas emocionales/ser un trastornado mental.
disturbing [dɪs'təːbɪŋ] *adj* inquietante, perturbador(a).
disuse [dɪs'juːs] *n*: **to fall into ~** caer en desuso.
disused [dɪs'juːzd] *adj* abandonado.
ditch [dɪtʃ] *n* zanja; (*irrigation ~*) acequia ♦ *vt* (*col*) deshacerse de.
dither ['dɪðə*] *vi* vacilar.
ditto ['dɪtəu] *adv* ídem, lo mismo.
divan [dɪ'væn] *n* diván *m*.
divan bed *n* cama turca.
dive [daɪv] *n* (*from board*) salto; (*underwater*) buceo; (*of submarine*) inmersión *f*; (*AVIAT*) picada ♦ *vi* saltar; bucear; sumergirse; picar.
diver ['daɪvə*] *n* (*SPORT*) saltador(a) *m/f*; (*underwater*) buzo.
diverge [daɪ'vəːdʒ] *vi* divergir.
divergent [daɪ'vəːdʒənt] *adj* divergente.
diverse [daɪ'vəːs] *adj* diversos/as, varios/as.
diversification [daɪvəːsɪfɪ'keɪʃən] *n* diversificación *f*.
diversify [daɪ'vəːsɪfaɪ] *vt* diversificar.
diversion [daɪ'vəːʃən] *n* (*BRIT AUT*) desviación *f*; (*distraction, MIL*) diversión *f*.
diversity [daɪ'vəːsɪtɪ] *n* diversidad *f*.
divert [daɪ'vəːt] *vt* (*BRIT*: *train, plane, traffic*) desviar; (*amuse*) divertir.
divest [daɪ'vɛst] *vt*: **to ~ sb of sth** despojar a alguien de algo.
divide [dɪ'vaɪd] *vt* dividir; (*separate*) separar ♦ *vi* dividirse; (*road*) bifurcarse; **to ~ (between, among)** repartir *or* dividir (entre); **40 ~d by 5** 40 dividido por 5.
▸**divide out** *vt*: **to ~ out (between, among)** (*sweets, tasks etc*) repartir (entre).
divided [dɪ'vaɪdɪd] *adj* (*country, couple*) dividido, separado; (*opinions*) en desacuerdo.
divided highway *n* (*US*) carretera de doble calzada.
dividend ['dɪvɪdɛnd] *n* dividendo; (*fig*) beneficio.
dividend cover *n* cobertura de dividendo.
dividers [dɪ'vaɪdəz] *npl* compás *m* de puntas.
divine [dɪ'vaɪn] *adj* divino ♦ *vt* (*future*) vaticinar; (*truth*) alumbrar; (*water, metal*) descubrir, detectar.
diving ['daɪvɪŋ] *n* (*SPORT*) salto; (*underwater*) buceo.

diving board *n* trampolín *m*.
diving suit *n* escafandra.
divinity [dɪ'vɪnɪtɪ] *n* divinidad *f*; (*SCOL*) teología.
divisible [dɪ'vɪzɪbl] *adj* divisible.
division [dɪ'vɪʒən] *n* (*also BRIT FOOTBALL*) división *f*; (*sharing out*) repartimiento; (*BRIT POL*) votación *f*; ~ **of labour** división *f* del trabajo.
divisive [dɪ'vaɪsɪv] *adj* divisivo.
divorce [dɪ'vɔːs] *n* divorcio ♦ *vt* divorciarse de.
divorced [dɪ'vɔːst] *adj* divorciado.
divorcee [dɪvɔː'siː] *n* divorciado/a.
divot ['dɪvət] *n* (*GOLF*) chuleta.
divulge [daɪ'vʌldʒ] *vt* divulgar, revelar.
D.I.Y. *adj, n abbr* (*BRIT*) = **do-it-yourself**.
dizziness ['dɪzɪnɪs] *n* vértigo.
dizzy ['dɪzɪ] *adj* (*person*) mareado; (*height*) vertiginoso; **to feel** ~ marearse; **I feel** ~ estoy mareado.
DJ *n abbr see* **disc jockey**.
d.j. *n abbr* = **dinner jacket**.
Djakarta [dʒə'kɑːtə] *n* Yakarta.
DJIA *n abbr* (*US STOCK EXCHANGE*) = *Dow Jones Industrial Average*.
dl *abbr* (= *decilitre(s)*) dl.
DLit(t) *abbr* (= *Doctor of Literature, Doctor of Letters*) *título universitario*.
DLO *n abbr* (= *dead-letter office*) *oficina de Correos que se encarga de las cartas que no llegan a su destino*.
dm *abbr* (= *decimetre(s)*) dm.
DMus *abbr* (= *Doctor of Music*) *título universitario*.
DMZ *n abbr* (= *demilitarized zone*) zona desmilitarizada.
DNA *n abbr* = (*deoxyribonucleic acid*) ADN *m*.

KEYWORD

do [duː] (*pt* **did**, *pp* **done**) *n* **1** (*inf: party etc*): **we're having a little ~ on Saturday** damos una fiestecita el sábado; **it was rather a grand ~** fue un acontecimiento a lo grande
2: **the ~s and don'ts** lo que se debe y no se debe hacer
♦ *aux vb* **1** (*in negative constructions: not translated*) **I don't understand** no entiendo
2 (*to form questions: not translated*) **~ you speak English?** ¿habla (usted) inglés?; **didn't you know?** ¿no lo sabías?; **what ~ you think?** ¿qué opinas?
3 (*for emphasis, in polite expressions*): **people ~ make mistakes sometimes** a veces sí se cometen errores; **she does seem rather late** a mí también me parece que se ha retrasado; **~ sit down/help yourself** siéntate/sírvete por favor; **~ take care!** ¡ten cuidado! ¿eh?; **I *DO* wish I could ...** ojalá (que) pudiera ...; **but I *DO* like it** pero, sí (que) me gusta
4 (*used to avoid repeating vb*): **she sings better than I ~** canta mejor que yo; **~ you agree? — yes, I ~/no, I don't** ¿estás de acuerdo? — sí (lo estoy)/no (lo estoy); **she lives in Glasgow — so ~ I** vive en Glasgow — yo también; **he didn't like it and neither did we** no le gustó y a nosotros tampoco; **who made this mess? — I did** ¿quién hizo esta chapuza? — yo; **he asked me to help him and I did** me pidió que le ayudara y lo hice
5 (*in question tags*): **you like him, don't you?** te gusta, ¿verdad? *or* ¿no?; **I don't know him, ~ I?** creo que no le conozco; **he laughed, didn't he?** se rió ¿no?
♦ *vt* **1** (*gen, carry out, perform etc*): **what are you ~ing tonight?** ¿qué haces esta noche?; **what can I ~ for you?** (*in shop*) ¿en qué puedo servirle?; **what does he ~ for a living?** ¿a qué se dedica?; **I'll ~ all I can** haré todo lo que pueda; **what have you done with my slippers?** ¿qué has hecho con mis zapatillas?; **to ~ the washing-up/cooking** fregar los platos/cocinar; **to ~ one's teeth/hair/nails** lavarse los dientes/arreglarse el pelo/arreglarse las uñas
2 (*AUT etc*): **the car was ~ing 100** el coche iba a 100; **we've done 200 km already** ya hemos hecho 200 km; **he can ~ 100 in that car** puede ir a 100 en ese coche
3 (*visit: city, museum*) visitar, recorrer
4 (*cook*): **a steak – well done please** un filete bien hecho, por favor
♦ *vi* **1** (*act, behave*) hacer; **~ as I ~** haz como yo
2 (*get on, fare*): **he's ~ing well/badly at school** va bien/mal en la escuela; **the firm is ~ing well** la empresa anda *or* va bien; **how ~ you ~?** mucho gusto; (*less formal*) ¿qué tal?
3 (*suit*): **will it ~?** ¿sirve?, ¿está *or* va bien?; **it doesn't ~ to upset her** cuidado en ofenderla
4 (*be sufficient*) bastar; **will £10 ~?** ¿será bastante con £10?; **that'll ~** así está bien; **that'll ~!** (*in annoyance*) ¡ya está bien!, ¡basta ya!; **to make ~ (with)** arreglárselas (con)
▸**do away with** *vt fus* (*kill, disease*) eliminar; (*abolish: law etc*) abolir; (*withdraw*) retirar
▸**do out of** *vt fus*: **to ~ sb out of sth** pisar

algo a algn
▸**do up** *vt* (*laces*) atar; (*zip, dress, shirt*) abrochar; (*renovate*: *room, house*) renovar
▸**do with** *vt fus* (*need*): **I could ~ with a drink/some help** no me vendría mal un trago/un poco de ayuda; (*be connected*) tener que ver con; **what has it got to ~ with you?** ¿qué tiene que ver contigo?
▸**do without** *vi*: **if you're late for dinner then you'll ~ without** si llegas tarde tendrás que quedarte sin cenar ♦ *vt fus* pasar sin; **I can ~ without a car** puedo pasar sin coche.

do. *abbr* = **ditto.**
DOA *abbr* = *dead on arrival.*
d.o.b. *abbr* = **date of birth.**
doc [dɔk] *n* (*col*) médico/a.
docile ['dəusaɪl] *adj* dócil.
dock [dɔk] *n* (*NAUT*: *wharf*) dársena, muelle *m*; (*LAW*) banquillo (de los acusados); **~s** *npl* muelles *mpl*, puerto *sg* ♦ *vi* (*enter~*) atracar (en el muelle) ♦ *vt* (*pay etc*) descontar.
dock dues *npl* derechos *mpl* de muelle.
docker ['dɔkə*] *n* trabajador *m* portuario, estibador *m*.
docket ['dɔkɪt] *n* (*on parcel etc*) etiqueta.
dockyard ['dɔkjɑːd] *n* astillero.
doctor ['dɔktə*] *n* médico; (*Ph.D. etc*) doctor(a) *m/f* ♦ *vt* (*fig*) arreglar, falsificar; (*drink etc*) adulterar.
doctorate ['dɔktərɪt] *n* doctorado; *ver recuadro.*

DOCTORATE

*El grado más alto que conceden las universidades es el doctorado (**doctorate**), tras un período de estudio e investigación original no inferior a tres años que culmina con la presentación de una tesis ("thesis") en la que se exponen los resultados. El título más frecuente es el de "PhD" ("Doctor of Philosophy"), que se obtiene en Letras, Ciencias e Ingeniería, aunque también existen otros doctorados específicos en Música, Derecho etc.*

Doctor of Philosophy (Ph.D.) *n* Doctor *m* (en Filosofía y Letras).
doctrinaire [dɔktrɪ'nɛə*] *adj* doctrinario.
doctrine ['dɔktrɪn] *n* doctrina.
docudrama [dɔkju'drɑːmə] *n* (*TV*) docudrama *m*.
document ['dɔkjumənt] *n* documento ♦ *vt* documentar.
documentary [dɔkju'mɛntərɪ] *adj* documental ♦ *n* documental *m*.
documentation [dɔkjumɛn'teɪʃən] *n* documentación *f*.
DOD *n abbr* (*US*: = *Department of Defense*) Ministerio de Defensa.
doddering ['dɔdərɪŋ] *adj*, **doddery** ['dɔdərɪ] *adj* vacilante.
doddle ['dɔdl] *n*: **it's a ~** (*BRIT col*) es pan comido.
dodge [dɔdʒ] *n* (*of body*) regate *m*; (*fig*) truco ♦ *vt* (*gen*) evadir; (*blow*) esquivar ♦ *vi* escabullirse; (*SPORT*) hacer una finta; **to ~ out of the way** echarse a un lado; **to ~ through the traffic** esquivar el tráfico.
dodgems ['dɔdʒəmz] *npl* (*BRIT*) autos *or* coches *mpl* de choque.
dodgy ['dɔdʒɪ] (*col*) *adj* (*uncertain*) dudoso; (*shady*) sospechoso; (*risky*) arriesgado.
DOE *n abbr* (*BRIT*) = **Department of the Environment**; (*US*) = *Department of Energy.*
doe [dəu] *n* (*deer*) cierva, gama; (*rabbit*) coneja.
does [dʌz] *vb see* **do.**
doesn't ['dʌznt] = **does not.**
dog [dɔg] *n* perro ♦ *vt* seguir (de cerca); (*fig*: *memory etc*) perseguir; **to go to the ~s** (*person*) echarse a perder; (*nation etc*) ir a la ruina.
dog biscuit *n* galleta de perro.
dog collar *n* collar *m* de perro; (*fig*) alzacuello(s) *msg*.
dog-eared ['dɔgɪəd] *adj* sobado; (*page*) con la esquina doblada.
dogfish ['dɔgfɪʃ] *n* cazón *m*, perro marino.
dog food *n* comida para perros.
dogged ['dɔgɪd] *adj* tenaz, obstinado.
doggy ['dɔgɪ] *n* (*col*) perrito.
doggy bag *n bolsa para llevarse las sobras de la comida.*
dogma ['dɔgmə] *n* dogma *m*.
dogmatic [dɔg'mætɪk] *adj* dogmático.
do-gooder [duː'gudə*] *n* (*col pej*): **to be a ~** ser una persona bien intencionada *or* un filantropista.
dogsbody ['dɔgzbɔdɪ] *n* (*BRIT*) burro de carga.
doily ['dɔɪlɪ] *n* pañito de adorno.
doing ['duɪŋ] *n*: **this is your ~** esto es obra tuya.
doings ['duɪŋz] *npl* (*events*) sucesos *mpl*; (*acts*) hechos *mpl*.
do-it-yourself [duːɪtjɔː'sɛlf] *n* bricolaje *m*.
doldrums ['dɔldrəmz] *npl*: **to be in the ~** (*person*) estar abatido; (*business*) estar estancado.
dole [dəul] *n* (*BRIT*: *payment*) subsidio de paro; **on the ~** parado.
▸**dole out** *vt* repartir.
doleful ['dəulful] *adj* triste, lúgubre.

doll [dɔl] *n* muñeca.
▸**doll up** *vt*: **to ~ o.s. up** ataviarse.
dollar ['dɔlə*] *n* dólar *m*.
dollop ['dɔləp] *n* buena cucharada.
dolly ['dɔlɪ] *n* muñeca.
dolphin ['dɔlfɪn] *n* delfín *m*.
domain [də'meɪn] *n* (*fig*) campo, competencia; (*land*) dominios *mpl*.
dome [dəum] *n* (*ARCH*) cúpula; (*shape*) bóveda.
domestic [də'mɛstɪk] *adj* (*animal, duty*) doméstico; (*flight, news, policy*) nacional.
domesticated [də'mɛstɪkeɪtɪd] *adj* domesticado; (*person*: *home-loving*) casero, hogareño.
domesticity [dəumɛs'tɪsɪtɪ] *n* vida casera.
domestic servant *n* sirviente/a *m/f*.
domicile ['dɔmɪsaɪl] *n* domicilio.
dominant ['dɔmɪnənt] *adj* dominante.
dominate ['dɔmɪneɪt] *vt* dominar.
domination [dɔmɪ'neɪʃən] *n* dominación *f*.
domineering [dɔmɪ'nɪərɪŋ] *adj* dominante.
Dominican Republic [də'mɪnɪkən-] *n* República Dominicana.
dominion [də'mɪnɪən] *n* dominio.
domino, *pl* **~es** ['dɔmɪnəu] *n* ficha de dominó.
dominoes ['dɔmɪnəuz] *n* (*game*) dominó.
don [dɔn] *n* (*BRIT*) profesor(a) *m/f* de universidad.
donate [də'neɪt] *vt* donar.
donation [də'neɪʃən] *n* donativo.
done [dʌn] *pp of* **do.**
donkey ['dɔŋkɪ] *n* burro.
donkey-work ['dɔŋkɪwəːk] *n* (*BRIT col*) trabajo pesado.
donor ['dəunə*] *n* donante *m/f*.
donor card *n* carnet *m* de donante de órganos.
don't [dəunt] = **do not.**
donut ['dəunʌt] *n* (*US*) = **doughnut.**
doodle ['duːdl] *n* garabato ♦ *vi* pintar dibujitos *or* garabatos.
doom [duːm] *n* (*fate*) suerte *f*; (*death*) muerte *f* ♦ *vt*: **to be ~ed to failure** estar condenado al fracaso.
doomsday ['duːmzdeɪ] *n* día *m* del juicio final.
door [dɔː*] *n* puerta; (*of car*) portezuela; (*entry*) entrada; **from ~ to ~** de puerta en puerta.
doorbell ['dɔːbɛl] *n* timbre *m*.
door handle *n* tirador *m*; (*of car*) manija.
door knocker *n* aldaba.
doorman ['dɔːmən] *n* (*in hotel*) portero.
doormat ['dɔːmæt] *n* felpudo, estera.
doorstep ['dɔːstɛp] *n* peldaño; **on your ~** en la puerta de casa; (*fig*) al lado de casa.
door-to-door ['dɔːtə'dɔː*] *adj*: **~ selling** venta a domicilio.
doorway ['dɔːweɪ] *n* entrada, puerta; **in the ~** en la puerta.
dope [dəup] *n* (*col*: *person*) imbécil *m/f*; (: *information*) información *f*, informes *mpl* ♦ *vt* (*horse etc*) drogar.
dopey ['dəupɪ] *adj* atontado.
dormant ['dɔːmənt] *adj* inactivo; (*latent*) latente.
dormer ['dɔːmə*] *n* (*also*: **~ window**) buhardilla.
dormitory ['dɔːmɪtrɪ] *n* (*BRIT*) dormitorio; (*US*: *hall of residence*) residencia, colegio mayor.
dormouse, *pl* **dormice** ['dɔːmaus, -maɪs] *n* lirón *m*.
Dors *abbr* (*BRIT*) = *Dorset*.
DOS *n abbr see* **disk operating system.**
dosage ['dəusɪdʒ] *n* (*on medicine bottle*) dosis *f inv*, dosificación *f*.
dose [dəus] *n* (*of medicine*) dosis *f inv*; **a ~ of flu** un ataque de gripe ♦ *vt*: **to ~ o.s. with** automedicarse con.
dosser ['dɔsə*] *n* (*BRIT col*) mendigo/a; (*lazy person*) vago/a.
doss house ['dɔs-] *n* (*BRIT*) pensión *f* de mala muerte.
dossier ['dɔsɪeɪ] *n*: **~ (on)** expediente *m* (sobre).
DOT *n abbr* (*US*: = *Department of Transportation*) *ministerio de transporte*.
dot [dɔt] *n* punto; **~ted with** salpicado de; **on the ~** en punto.
dot command *n* (*COMPUT*) instrucción *f* (precedida) de punto.
dote [dəut]: **to ~ on** *vt fus* adorar, idolatrar.
dot-matrix printer [dɔt'meɪtrɪks-] *n* impresora matricial *or* de matriz.
dotted line ['dɔtɪd-] *n* línea de puntos; **to sign on the ~** firmar.
dotty ['dɔtɪ] *adj* (*col*) disparatado, chiflado.
double ['dʌbl] *adj* doble ♦ *adv* (*twice*): **to cost ~** costar el doble ♦ *n* (*gen*) doble *m* ♦ *vt* doblar; (*efforts*) redoblar ♦ *vi* doblarse; (*have two uses etc*): **to ~ as** hacer las veces de; **~ five two six (5526)** (*TELEC*) cinco cinco dos seis; **spelt with a ~ "s"** escrito con dos "eses"; **on the ~,** (*BRIT*) **at the ~** corriendo.
▸**double back** *vi* (*person*) volver sobre sus pasos.
▸**double up** *vi* (*bend over*) doblarse; (*share bedroom*) compartir.
double bass *n* contrabajo.
double bed *n* cama matrimonial.
double-breasted ['dʌbl'brɛstɪd] *adj* cruzado.

double-check ['dʌbltʃɛk] *vt* volver a revisar ♦ *vi*: **I'll** ~ voy a revisarlo otra vez.
double-click ['dʌbl,klɪk] *vi* (*COMPUT*) hacer doble clic.
double cream *n* nata enriquecida.
doublecross ['dʌbl'krɔs] *vt* (*trick*) engañar; (*betray*) traicionar.
doubledecker ['dʌbl'dɛkə*] *n* autobús *m* de dos pisos.
double glazing *n* (*BRIT*) doble acristalamiento.
double indemnity *n* doble indemnización *f*.
double-page ['dʌblpeɪdʒ] *adj*: ~ **spread** doble página.
double room *n* cuarto para dos.
doubles ['dʌblz] *n* (*TENNIS*) juego de dobles.
double time *n* tarifa doble.
double whammy [-'wæmɪ] *n* (*col*) palo doble.
doubly ['dʌblɪ] *adv* doblemente.
doubt [daut] *n* duda ♦ *vt* dudar; (*suspect*) dudar de; **to** ~ **that** dudar que; **there is no** ~ **that** no cabe duda de que; **without (a)** ~ sin duda (alguna); **beyond** ~ fuera de duda; **I** ~ **it very much** lo dudo mucho.
doubtful ['dautful] *adj* dudoso; (*person*) sospechoso; **to be** ~ **about sth** tener dudas sobre algo; **I'm a bit** ~ no estoy convencido.
doubtless ['dautlɪs] *adv* sin duda.
dough [dəu] *n* masa, pasta; (*col*: *money*) pasta, lana (*LAM*).
doughnut ['dəunʌt] *n* buñuelo.
douse [daus] *vt* (*drench*: *with water*) mojar; (*extinguish*: *flames*) apagar.
dove [dʌv] *n* paloma.
dovetail ['dʌvteɪl] *vi* (*fig*) encajar.
dowager ['dauɪdʒə*] *n*: ~ **duchess** duquesa viuda.
dowdy ['daudɪ] *adj* desaliñado; (*inelegant*) poco elegante.
Dow-Jones average ['daudʒəunz-] *n* (*US*) índice *m* Dow-Jones.
down [daun] *n* (*fluff*) pelusa; (*feathers*) plumón *m*, flojel *m*; (*hill*) loma ♦ *adv* (~*wards*) abajo, hacia abajo; (*on the ground*) por/en tierra ♦ *prep* abajo ♦ *vt* (*col*: *drink*) beberse, tragar(se); ~ **with X!** ¡abajo X!; ~ **there** allí abajo; ~ **here** aquí abajo; **I'll be** ~ **in a minute** ahora bajo; **England is two goals** ~ Inglaterra está perdiendo por dos tantos; **I've been** ~ **with flu** he estado con gripe; **the price of meat is** ~ ha bajado el precio de la carne; **I've got it** ~ **in my diary** lo he apuntado en mi agenda; **to pay £2** ~ dejar £2 de depósito; **he went** ~ **the hill** fue cuesta abajo; ~ **under** (*in Australia etc*) en Australia/Nueva Zelanda; **to** ~ **tools** (*fig*) declararse en huelga.
down-and-out ['daunəndaut] *n* (*tramp*) vagabundo/a.
down-at-heel ['daunət'hi:l] *adj* venido a menos; (*appearance*) desaliñado.
downbeat ['daunbi:t] *n* (*MUS*) compás *m* ♦ *adj* (*gloomy*) pesimista.
downcast ['daunkɑ:st] *adj* abatido.
downfall ['daunfɔ:l] *n* caída, ruina.
downgrade [daun'greɪd] *vt* (*job*) degradar; (*hotel*) bajar de categoría a.
downhearted [daun'hɑ:tɪd] *adj* desanimado.
downhill [daun'hɪl] *adv*: **to go** ~ ir cuesta abajo; (*business*) estar en declive.
Downing Street ['daunɪŋ-] *n* (*BRIT*) Downing Street *f*; *ver recuadro*.

> **DOWNING STREET**
>
> **Downing Street** *es la calle de Londres en la que tienen su residencia oficial tanto el Primer Ministro ("Prime Minister") como el Ministro de Economía ("Chancellor of the Exchequer"). El primero vive en el nº10 y el segundo en el nº11. Es una calle cerrada al público que se encuentra en el barrio de Westminster, en el centro de Londres.* **Downing Street** *se usa también en lenguaje periodístico para referirse al jefe del gobierno británico.*

download ['daunləud] *vt* (*COMPUT*) transferir, telecargar.
down-market ['daun'mɑ:kɪt] *adj* de escasa calidad.
down payment *n* entrada, pago al contado.
downplay ['daunpleɪ] *vt* (*US*) quitar importancia a.
downpour ['daunpɔ:*] *n* aguacero.
downright ['daunraɪt] *adj* (*nonsense, lie*) manifiesto; (*refusal*) terminante.
downsize [daun'saɪz] *vt* reducir la plantilla de.
Down's syndrome [daunz-] *n* síndrome *m* de Down.
downstairs [daun'stɛəz] *adv* (*below*) (en el piso de) abajo; (*motion*) escaleras abajo; **to come** (*or* **go**) ~ bajar la escalera.
downstream [daun'stri:m] *adv* aguas *or* río abajo.
downtime ['dauntaɪm] *n* (*COMM*) tiempo inactivo.

down-to-earth [dauntu'ə:θ] *adj* práctico.
downtown [daun'taun] *adv* en el centro de la ciudad.
downtrodden ['dauntrɔdn] *adj* oprimido.
downward ['daunwəd] *adv* hacia abajo ♦ *adj*: **a ~ trend** una tendencia descendente.
downward(s) ['daunwəd(z)] *adv* hacia abajo; **face ~s** (*person*) boca abajo; (*object*) cara abajo.
dowry ['daurɪ] *n* dote *f*.
doz. *abbr* = **dozen**.
doze [dəuz] *vi* dormitar.
▸**doze off** *vi* echar una cabezada.
dozen ['dʌzn] *n* docena; **a ~ books** una docena de libros; **~s of** cantidad de; **~s of times** cantidad de veces; **80p a ~** 80 peniques la docena.
DPh., D. Phil. *n abbr* (= *Doctor of Philosophy*) *título universitario*.
DPP *n abbr* (*BRIT*) = **Director of Public Prosecutions**.
DPT *n abbr* (= *diphtheria, pertussis, tetanus*) vacuna trivalente.
DPW *n abbr* (*US*: = *Department of Public Works*) *ministerio de obras públicas*.
Dr, Dr. *abbr* (= *doctor*) Dr.
Dr. *abbr* (*in street names*) = **Drive**.
dr *abbr* (*COMM*) = **debtor**.
drab [dræb] *adj* gris, monótono.
draft [drɑ:ft] *n* (*first copy*: *of document, report*) borrador *m*; (*COMM*) giro; (*US*: *call-up*) quinta ♦ *vt* (*write roughly*) hacer un borrador de; *see also* **draught**.
draftsman ['drɑ:ftsmən] *etc* (*US*) = **draughtsman** *etc*.
drag [dræg] *vt* arrastrar; (*river*) dragar, rastrear ♦ *vi* arrastrarse por el suelo ♦ *n* (*AVIAT*: *resistance*) resistencia aerodinámica; (*col*) lata; (*women's clothing*): **in ~** travestido.
▸**drag away** *vt*: **to ~ away (from)** separar a rastras (de).
▸**drag on** *vi* ser interminable.
dragnet ['drægnɛt] *n* (*NAUT*) rastra; (*fig*) emboscada.
dragon ['drægən] *n* dragón *m*.
dragonfly ['drægənflaɪ] *n* libélula.
dragoon [drə'gu:n] *n* (*cavalryman*) dragón *m* ♦ *vt*: **to ~ sb into doing sth** forzar a algn a hacer algo.
drain [dreɪn] *n* desaguadero; (*in street*) sumidero; (*~ cover*) rejilla del sumidero ♦ *vt* (*land, marshes*) desecar; (*MED*) drenar; (*reservoir*) desecar; (*fig*) agotar ♦ *vi* escurrirse; **to be a ~ on** consumir, agotar; **to feel ~ed (of energy)** (*fig*) sentirse agotado.
drainage ['dreɪnɪdʒ] *n* (*act*) desagüe *m*; (*MED, AGR*) drenaje *m*; (*sewage*) alcantarillado.
draining board ['dreɪnɪŋ-], (*US*) **drainboard** ['dreɪnbɔ:d] *n* escurridero, escurridor *m*.
drainpipe ['dreɪnpaɪp] *n* tubo de desagüe.
drake [dreɪk] *n* pato (macho).
dram [dræm] *n* (*drink*) traguito, copita.
drama ['drɑ:mə] *n* (*art*) teatro; (*play*) drama *m*.
dramatic [drə'mætɪk] *adj* dramático.
dramatist ['dræmətɪst] *n* dramaturgo/a.
dramatize ['dræmətaɪz] *vt* (*events etc*) dramatizar; (*adapt*: *novel*: *for TV, cinema*) adaptar.
drank [dræŋk] *pt of* **drink**.
drape [dreɪp] *vt* cubrir.
draper ['dreɪpə*] *n* (*BRIT*) pañero, mercero.
drapes [dreɪps] *npl* (*US*) cortinas *fpl*.
drastic ['dræstɪk] *adj* (*measure, reduction*) severo; (*change*) radical.
draught, (*US*) **draft** [drɑ:ft] *n* (*of air*) corriente *f* de aire; (*drink*) trago; (*NAUT*) calado; **on ~** (*beer*) de barril.
draught beer *n* cerveza de barril.
draughtboard ['drɑ:ftbɔ:d] (*BRIT*) *n* tablero de damas.
draughts [drɑ:fts] *n* (*BRIT*) juego de damas.
draughtsman, (*US*) **draftsman** ['drɑ:ftsmən] *n* proyectista *m*, delineante *m*.
draughtsmanship, (*US*) **draftsmanship** ['drɑ:ftsmənʃɪp] *n* (*drawing*) dibujo lineal; (*skill*) habilidad *f* para el dibujo.
draw [drɔ:] *vb* (*pt* **drew**, *pp* **drawn** [dru:, drɔ:n]) *vt* (*pull*) tirar; (*take out*) sacar; (*attract*) atraer; (*picture*) dibujar; (*money*) retirar; (*formulate*: *conclusion*): **to ~ (from)** sacar (de); (*comparison, distinction*): **to ~ (between)** hacer (entre) ♦ *vi* (*SPORT*) empatar ♦ *n* (*SPORT*) empate *m*; (*lottery*) sorteo; (*attraction*) atracción *f*; **to ~ near** *vi* acercarse.
▸**draw back** *vi*: **to ~ back (from)** echarse atrás (de).
▸**draw in** *vi* (*car*) aparcar; (*train*) entrar en la estación.
▸**draw on** *vt* (*resources*) utilizar, servirse de; (*imagination, person*) recurrir a.
▸**draw out** *vi* (*lengthen*) alargarse.
▸**draw up** *vi* (*stop*) pararse ♦ *vt* (*document*) redactar; (*plans*) trazar.
drawback ['drɔ:bæk] *n* inconveniente *m*, desventaja.
drawbridge ['drɔ:brɪdʒ] *n* puente *m* levadizo.
drawee [drɔ:'i:] *n* girado, librado.
drawer [drɔ:*] *n* cajón *m*; (*of cheque*)

librador(a) *m/f*.
drawing ['drɔːɪŋ] *n* dibujo.
drawing board *n* tablero (de dibujante).
drawing pin *n* (*BRIT*) chincheta *m*.
drawing room *n* salón *m*.
drawl [drɔːl] *n* habla lenta y cansina.
drawn [drɔːn] *pp of* **draw** ♦ *adj* (*haggard: with tiredness*) ojeroso; (*: with pain*) macilento.
drawstring ['drɔːstrɪŋ] *n* cordón *m*.
dread [drɛd] *n* pavor *m*, terror *m* ♦ *vt* temer, tener miedo *or* pavor a.
dreadful ['drɛdful] *adj* espantoso; **I feel ~!** (*ill*) ¡me siento fatal *or* malísimo!; (*ashamed*) ¡qué vergüenza!
dream [driːm] *n* sueño ♦ *vt, vi* (*pt, pp* **dreamed** *or* **dreamt** [drɛmt]) soñar; **to have a ~ about sb/sth** soñar con algn/algo; **sweet ~s!** ¡que sueñes con los angelitos!
▸**dream up** *vt* (*reason, excuse*) inventar; (*plan, idea*) idear.
dreamer ['driːmə*] *n* soñador(a) *m/f*.
dream world *n* mundo imaginario *or* de ensueño.
dreamy ['driːmɪ] *adj* (*person*) soñador(a), distraído; (*music*) de sueño.
dreary ['drɪərɪ] *adj* monótono, aburrido.
dredge [drɛdʒ] *vt* dragar.
▸**dredge up** *vt* sacar con draga; (*fig: unpleasant facts*) pescar, sacar a luz.
dredger ['drɛdʒə*] *n* (*ship, machine*) draga; (*CULIN*) tamiz *m*.
dregs [drɛgz] *npl* heces *fpl*.
drench [drɛntʃ] *vt* empapar; **~ed to the skin** calado hasta los huesos.
dress [drɛs] *n* vestido; (*clothing*) ropa ♦ *vt* vestir; (*wound*) vendar; (*CULIN*) aliñar; (*shop window*) decorar, arreglar ♦ *vi* vestirse; **to ~ o.s., get ~ed** vestirse; **she ~es very well** se viste muy bien.
▸**dress up** *vi* vestirse de etiqueta; (*in fancy dress*) disfrazarse.
dress circle *n* (*BRIT*) principal *m*.
dress designer *n* modisto/a.
dresser ['drɛsə*] *n* (*furniture*) aparador *m*; (*: US*) tocador *m*; (*THEAT*) camarero/a.
dressing ['drɛsɪŋ] *n* (*MED*) vendaje *m*; (*CULIN*) aliño.
dressing gown *n* (*BRIT*) bata.
dressing room *n* (*THEAT*) camarín *m*; (*SPORT*) vestidor *m*.
dressing table *n* tocador *m*.
dressmaker ['drɛsmeɪkə*] *n* modista, costurera.
dressmaking ['drɛsmeɪkɪŋ] *n* costura.
dress rehearsal *n* ensayo general.
dress shirt *n* camisa de frac.
dressy ['drɛsɪ] *adj* (*col*) elegante.
drew [druː] *pt of* **draw**.
dribble ['drɪbl] *vi* gotear, caer gota a gota; (*baby*) babear ♦ *vt* (*ball*) driblar, regatear.
dried [draɪd] *adj* (*gen*) seco; (*fruit*) paso; (*milk*) en polvo.
drier ['draɪə*] *n* = **dryer**.
drift [drɪft] *n* (*of current etc*) velocidad *f*; (*of sand*) montón *m*; (*of snow*) ventisquero; (*meaning*) significado ♦ *vi* (*boat*) ir a la deriva; (*sand, snow*) amontonarse; **to catch sb's ~** cogerle el hilo a algn; **to let things ~** dejar las cosas como están; **to ~ apart** (*friends*) seguir su camino; (*lovers*) disgustarse, romper.
drifter ['drɪftə*] *n* vagabundo/a.
driftwood ['drɪftwud] *n* madera flotante.
drill [drɪl] *n* taladro; (*bit*) broca; (*of dentist*) fresa; (*for mining etc*) perforadora, barrena; (*MIL*) instrucción *f* ♦ *vt* perforar, taladrar; (*soldiers*) ejercitar; (*pupils: in grammar*) hacer ejercicios con ♦ *vi* (*for oil*) perforar.
drilling ['drɪlɪŋ] *n* (*for oil*) perforación *f*.
drilling rig *n* (*on land*) torre *f* de perforación; (*at sea*) plataforma de perforación.
drily ['draɪlɪ] *adv* secamente.
drink [drɪŋk] *n* bebida ♦ *vt, vi* (*pt* **drank**, *pp* **drunk**) beber, tomar (*LAM*); **to have a ~** tomar algo; tomar una copa *or* un trago; **a ~ of water** un trago de agua; **to invite sb for ~s** invitar a algn a tomar unas copas; **there's food and ~ in the kitchen** hay de comer y de beber en la cocina; **would you like something to ~?** ¿quieres beber *or* tomar algo?
▸**drink in** *vt* (*subj: person: fresh air*) respirar; (*story, sight*) beberse.
drinkable ['drɪŋkəbl] *adj* (*not poisonous*) potable; (*palatable*) aguantable.
drink-driving [drɪŋk'draɪvɪŋ] *n*: **to be charged with ~** ser acusado de conducir borracho *or* en estado de embriaguez.
drinker ['drɪŋkə*] *n* bebedor(a) *m/f*.
drinking ['drɪŋkɪŋ] *n* (*drunkenness*) beber *m*.
drinking fountain *n* fuente *f* de agua potable.
drinking water *n* agua potable.
drip [drɪp] *n* (*act*) goteo; (*one ~*) gota; (*MED*) gota a gota *m*; (*sound: of water etc*) goteo; (*col: spineless person*) soso/a ♦ *vi* gotear, caer gota a gota.
drip-dry ['drɪp'draɪ] *adj* (*shirt*) de lava y pon.
dripping ['drɪpɪŋ] *n* (*animal fat*) pringue *m* ♦ *adj*: **~ wet** calado.
drive [draɪv] *n* paseo (en coche); (*journey*) viaje *m* (en coche); (*also*: **~way**) entrada; (*street*) calle; (*energy*) energía, vigor *m*;

(*PSYCH*) impulso; (*SPORT*) ataque *m*; (*COMPUT*: *also*: **disk ~**) disc drive *m* ♦ *vb* (*pt* **drove,** *pp* **driven** [drəuv, 'drɪvn]) *vt* (*car*) conducir, manejar (*LAM*); (*nail*) clavar; (*push*) empujar; (*TECH*: *motor*) impulsar ♦ *vi* (*AUT*: *at controls*) conducir; (: *travel*) pasearse en coche; **to go for a ~** dar una vuelta en coche; **it's 3 hours' ~ from London** es un viaje de 3 horas en coche desde Londres; **left-/right-hand ~** conducción *f* a la izquierda/derecha; **front-/rear-wheel ~** tracción *f* delantera/trasera; **sales ~** promoción *f* de ventas; **to ~ sb mad** volverle loco a algn; **to ~ sb to (do) sth** empujar a algn a (hacer) algo; **he ~s a taxi** es taxista; **he ~s a Mercedes** tiene un Mercedes; **can you ~?** ¿sabes conducir *or* (*LAM*) manejar?; **to ~ at 50 km an hour** ir a 50km por hora.

▶**drive at** *vt fus* (*fig*: *intend, mean*) querer decir, insinuar.

▶**drive on** *vi* no parar, seguir adelante ♦ *vt* (*incite, encourage*) empujar.

drive-by ['draɪvbaɪ] *n*: **~ shooting** tiroteo desde el coche.

drive-in ['draɪvɪn] *adj* (*esp US*): **~ cinema** autocine *m*.

drivel ['drɪvl] *n* (*col*) tonterías *fpl*.

driven ['drɪvn] *pp of* **drive.**

driver ['draɪvə*] *n* conductor(a) *m/f*, chofer *m* (*LAM*); (*of taxi*) taxista *m/f*.

driver's license *n* (*US*) carnet *m or* permiso de conducir.

driveway ['draɪvweɪ] *n* camino de entrada.

driving ['draɪvɪŋ] *n* conducir *m*, manejar *m* (*LAM*) ♦ *adj* (*force*) impulsor(a).

driving instructor *n* instructor(a) *m/f* de autoescuela.

driving lesson *n* clase *f* de conducir.

driving licence *n* (*BRIT*) carnet *m or* permiso de conducir.

driving school *n* autoescuela.

driving test *n* examen *m* de conducir.

drizzle ['drɪzl] *n* llovizna, garúa (*LAM*) ♦ *vi* lloviznar.

droll [drəul] *adj* gracioso.

dromedary ['drɔmɪdərɪ] *n* dromedario.

drone [drəun] *vi* (*bee, aircraft, engine*) zumbar; (*also*: **~ on**) murmurar sin interrupción ♦ *n* zumbido; (*male bee*) zángano.

drool [dru:l] *vi* babear; **to ~ over sb/sth** caérsele la baba por algn/algo.

droop [dru:p] *vi* (*fig*) decaer, desanimarse.

drop [drɔp] *n* (*of water*) gota; (*fall*: *in price*) bajada; (: *in salary*) disminución *f* ♦ *vt* (*allow to fall*) dejar caer; (*voice, eyes, price*) bajar; (*set down from car*) dejar ♦ *vi* (*price, temperature*) bajar; (*wind*) calmarse, amainar; (*numbers, attendance*) disminuir; **~s** *npl* (*MED*) gotas *fpl*; **cough ~s** pastillas *fpl* para la tos; **a ~ of 10%** una bajada del 10 por ciento; **to ~ anchor** echar el ancla; **to ~ sb a line** mandar unas líneas a algn.

▶**drop in** *vi* (*col*: *visit*): **to ~ in (on)** pasar por casa (de).

▶**drop off** *vi* (*sleep*) dormirse ♦ *vt* (*passenger*) bajar, dejar.

▶**drop out** *vi* (*withdraw*) retirarse.

droplet ['drɔplɪt] *n* gotita.

dropout ['drɔpaut] *n* (*from society*) marginado/a; (*from university*) estudiante *m/f* que ha abandonado los estudios.

dropper ['drɔpə*] *n* (*MED*) cuentagotas *m inv*.

droppings ['drɔpɪŋz] *npl* excremento *sg*.

dross [drɔs] *n* (*coal, fig*) escoria.

drought [draut] *n* sequía.

drove [drəuv] *pt of* **drive.**

drown [draun] *vt* (*also*: **~ out**: *sound*) ahogar ♦ *vi* ahogarse.

drowse [drauz] *vi* estar medio dormido.

drowsy ['drauzɪ] *adj* soñoliento; **to be ~** tener sueño.

drudge [drʌdʒ] *n* esclavo del trabajo.

drudgery ['drʌdʒərɪ] *n* trabajo pesado *or* monótono.

drug [drʌg] *n* (*MED*) medicamento, droga; (*narcotic*) droga ♦ *vt* drogar; **to be on ~s** drogarse; **he's on ~s** se droga.

drug addict *n* drogadicto/a.

druggist ['drʌgɪst] *n* (*US*) farmacéutico/a.

drug peddler *n* traficante *m/f* de drogas.

drugstore ['drʌgstɔ:*] *n* (*US*) tienda (*de comestibles, periódicos y medicamentos*).

drug trafficker *n* narcotraficante *m/f*.

drum [drʌm] *n* tambor *m*; (*large*) bombo; (*for oil, petrol*) bidón *m* ♦ *vi* tocar el tambor; (*with fingers*) tamborilear ♦ *vt*: **to ~ one's fingers on the table** tamborilear con los dedos sobre la mesa; **~s** *npl* batería *sg*.

▶**drum up** *vt* (*enthusiasm, support*) movilizar, fomentar.

drummer ['drʌmə*] *n* (*in military band*) tambor *m/f*; (*in jazz/pop group*) batería *m/f*.

drumstick ['drʌmstɪk] *n* (*MUS*) palillo, baqueta; (*chicken leg*) muslo (de pollo).

drunk [drʌŋk] *pp of* **drink** ♦ *adj* borracho ♦ *n* (*also*: **~ard**) borracho/a; **to get ~** emborracharse.

drunken ['drʌŋkən] *adj* borracho.

drunkenness ['drʌŋkənnɪs] *n* embriaguez *f*.

dry [draɪ] *adj* seco; (*day*) sin lluvia; (*climate*) árido, seco; (*humour*) agudo; (*uninteresting*: *lecture*) aburrido, pesado

♦ *vt* secar; (*tears*) enjugarse ♦ *vi* secarse; **on ~ land** en tierra firme; **to ~ one's hands/hair/eyes** secarse las manos/el pelo/las lágrimas.
▸**dry up** *vi* (*supply, imagination etc*) agotarse; (*in speech*) atascarse.
dry-clean ['draɪ'kli:n] *vt* limpiar *or* lavar en seco; "**~ only**" (*on label*) "limpieza *or* lavado en seco".
dry-cleaner's ['draɪ'kli:nəz] *n* tintorería.
dry-cleaning ['draɪ'kli:nɪŋ] *n* lavado en seco.
dry dock *n* (*NAUT*) dique *m* seco.
dryer ['draɪə*] *n* (*for hair*) secador *m*; (*for clothes*) secadora.
dry goods *npl* (*COMM*) mercería *sg*.
dry goods store *n* (*US*) mercería.
dry ice *n* nieve *f* carbónica, hielo seco.
dryness ['draɪnɪs] *n* sequedad *f*.
dry rot *n* putrefacción *f*.
dry run *n* (*fig*) ensayo.
dry ski slope *n* pista artificial de esquí.
DSc *n abbr* (= *Doctor of Science*) *título universitario*.
DST *n abbr* (*US*: = *Daylight Saving Time*) *hora de verano*.
DT *n abbr* (*COMPUT*) = **data transmission.**
DTI *n abbr* (*BRIT*) = *Department of Trade and Industry*.
DTP *n abbr* = **desktop publishing**.
DT's *n abbr* (*col*: = *delirium tremens*) delirium *m* tremens.
dual ['djuəl] *adj* doble.
dual carriageway *n* (*BRIT*) ≈ autovía.
dual-control ['djuəlkən'trəul] *adj* de doble mando.
dual nationality *n* doble nacionalidad *f*.
dual-purpose ['djuəl'pə:pəs] *adj* de doble uso.
dubbed [dʌbd] *adj* (*CINE*) doblado.
dubious ['dju:bɪəs] *adj* indeciso; (*reputation, company*) dudoso; (*character*) sospechoso; **I'm very ~ about it** tengo mis dudas sobre ello.
Dublin ['dʌblɪn] *n* Dublín.
Dubliner ['dʌblɪnə*] *n* dublinés/esa *m/f*.
duchess ['dʌtʃɪs] *n* duquesa.
duck [dʌk] *n* pato ♦ *vi* agacharse ♦ *vt* (*plunge in water*) zambullir.
duckling ['dʌklɪŋ] *n* patito.
duct [dʌkt] *n* conducto, canal *m*.
dud [dʌd] *n* (*shell*) obús *m* que no estalla; (*object, tool*): **it's a ~** es una filfa ♦ *adj*: **~ cheque** (*BRIT*) cheque *m* sin fondos.
due [dju:] *adj* (*proper*) debido; (*fitting*) conveniente, oportuno ♦ *adv*: **~ north** derecho al norte; **~s** *npl* (*for club, union*) cuota *sg*; (*in harbour*) derechos *mpl*; **in ~ course** a su debido tiempo; **~ to** debido a; **to be ~ to** deberse a; **the train is ~ to arrive at 8.00** el tren tiene (prevista) la llegada a las ocho; **the rent's ~ on the 30th** hay que pagar el alquiler el día 30; **I am ~ 6 days' leave** me deben 6 días de vacaciones; **she is ~ back tomorrow** ella debe volver mañana.
due date *n* fecha de vencimiento.
duel ['djuəl] *n* duelo.
duet [dju:'ɛt] *n* dúo.
duff [dʌf] *adj* sin valor.
duffel bag ['dʌfl-] *n* macuto.
duffel coat ['dʌfl-] *n* trenca.
dug [dʌg] *pt, pp of* **dig.**
dugout ['dʌgaut] *n* (*canoe*) piragua (*hecha de un solo tronco*); (*SPORT*) banquillo; (*MIL*) refugio subterráneo.
duke [dju:k] *n* duque *m*.
dull [dʌl] *adj* (*light*) apagado; (*stupid*) torpe; (*boring*) pesado; (*sound, pain*) sordo; (*weather, day*) gris ♦ *vt* (*pain, grief*) aliviar; (*mind, senses*) entorpecer.
duly ['dju:lɪ] *adv* debidamente; (*on time*) a su debido tiempo.
dumb [dʌm] *adj* mudo; (*stupid*) estúpido; **to be struck ~** (*fig*) quedar boquiabierto.
dumbbell ['dʌmbɛl] *n* (*SPORT*) pesa.
dumbfounded [dʌm'faundɪd] *adj* pasmado.
dummy ['dʌmɪ] *n* (*tailor's model*) maniquí *m*; (*BRIT*: *for baby*) chupete *m* ♦ *adj* falso, postizo; **~ run** ensayo.
dump [dʌmp] *n* (*heap*) montón *m* de basura; (*place*) basurero, vertedero; (*col*) tugurio; (*MIL*) depósito; (*COMPUT*) copia vaciada ♦ *vt* (*put down*) dejar; (*get rid of*) deshacerse de; (*COMPUT*) vaciar; (*COMM*: *goods*) inundar el mercado de; **to be (down) in the ~s** (*col*) tener murria, estar deprimido.
dumping ['dʌmpɪŋ] *n* (*ECON*) dumping *m*; (*of rubbish*): **"no ~"** "prohibido verter basura".
dumpling ['dʌmplɪŋ] *n bola de masa hervida*.
dumpy ['dʌmpɪ] *adj* regordete/a.
dunce [dʌns] *n* zopenco.
dune [dju:n] *n* duna.
dung [dʌŋ] *n* estiércol *m*.
dungarees [dʌŋgə'ri:z] *npl* mono *sg*, overol *msg* (*LAM*).
dungeon ['dʌndʒən] *n* calabozo.
dunk [dʌŋk] *vt* mojar.
duo ['dju:əu] *n* (*gen, MUS*) dúo.
duodenal [dju:ə'di:nl] *adj* (*ulcer*) de duodeno.
duodenum [dju:ə'di:nəm] *n* duodeno.
dupe [dju:p] *n* (*victim*) víctima ♦ *vt* engañar.

duplex ['dju:plɛks] *n* (*US*: *also*: ~ **apartment**) dúplex *m*.
duplicate ['dju:plɪkət] *n* duplicado; (*copy of letter etc*) copia ♦ *adj* (*copy*) duplicado ♦ *vt* ['dju:plɪkeɪt] duplicar; (*on machine*) multicopiar; **in** ~ por duplicado.
duplicate key *n* duplicado de una llave.
duplicating machine ['dju:plɪkeɪtɪŋ-], **duplicator** ['dju:plɪkeɪtə*] *n* multicopista *m*.
duplicity [dju:'plɪsɪtɪ] *n* doblez *f*.
Dur *abbr* (*BRIT*) = *Durham*.
durability [djuərə'bɪlɪtɪ] *n* durabilidad *f*.
durable ['djuərəbl] *adj* duradero.
duration [djuə'reɪʃən] *n* duración *f*.
duress [djuə'rɛs] *n*: **under** ~ por coacción.
Durex ® ['djuərɛks] *n* (*BRIT*) preservativo.
during ['djuərɪŋ] *prep* durante.
dusk [dʌsk] *n* crepúsculo, anochecer *m*.
dusky ['dʌskɪ] *adj* oscuro; (*complexion*) moreno.
dust [dʌst] *n* polvo ♦ *vt* (*furniture*) desempolvar; (*cake etc*): **to** ~ **with** espolvorear de.
►**dust off** *vt* (*also fig*) desempolvar, quitar el polvo de.
dustbin ['dʌstbɪn] *n* (*BRIT*) cubo de la basura, balde *m* (*LAM*).
dustbin liner *n* bolsa de basura.
duster ['dʌstə*] *n* paño, trapo; (*feather* ~) plumero.
dust jacket *n* sobrecubierta.
dustman ['dʌstmən] *n* (*BRIT*) basurero.
dustpan ['dʌstpæn] *n* cogedor *m*.
dust storm *n* vendaval *m* de polvo.
dusty ['dʌstɪ] *adj* polvoriento.
Dutch [dʌtʃ] *adj* holandés/esa ♦ *n* (*LING*) holandés *m* ♦ *adv*: **to go** ~ pagar a escote; **the** ~ *npl* los holandeses.
Dutch auction *n* subasta a la rebaja.
Dutchman ['dʌtʃmən], **Dutchwoman** ['dʌtʃwumən] *n* holandés/esa *m/f*.
dutiful ['dju:tɪful] *adj* (*child*) obediente; (*husband*) sumiso; (*employee*) cumplido.
duty ['dju:tɪ] *n* deber *m*; (*tax*) derechos *mpl* de aduana; **on** ~ de servicio; (*at night etc*) de guardia; **off** ~ libre (de servicio); **to make it one's** ~ **to do sth** encargarse de hacer algo sin falta; **to pay** ~ **on sth** pagar los derechos sobre algo.
duty-free [dju:tɪ'fri:] *adj* libre de derechos de aduana; ~ **shop** tienda libre de impuestos.
duty officer *n* (*MIL etc*) oficial *m/f* de guardia.
duvet ['du:veɪ] *n* (*BRIT*) edredón *m* (nórdico).
DV *abbr* (= *Deo volente*) Dios mediante.
DVD *n abbr* (= *digital versatile or video disc*) DVD *m*.
DVLA *n abbr* (*BRIT*: = *Driver and Vehicle Licensing Agency*) *organismo encargado de la expedición de permisos de conducir y matriculación de vehículos*.
DVM *n abbr* (*US*: = *Doctor of Veterinary Medicine*) *título universitario*.
dwarf [dwɔ:f], *pl* **dwarves** [dwɔ:vz] *n* enano ♦ *vt* empequeñecer.
dwell [dwɛl], *pt, pp* **dwelt** [dwɛlt] *vi* morar.
►**dwell on** *vt fus* explayarse en.
dweller ['dwɛlə*] *n* habitante *m*; **city** ~ habitante *m* de la ciudad.
dwelling ['dwɛlɪŋ] *n* vivienda.
dwelt [dwɛlt] *pt, pp of* **dwell**.
dwindle ['dwɪndl] *vi* menguar, disminuir.
dwindling ['dwɪndlɪŋ] *adj* (*strength, interest*) menguante; (*resources, supplies*) en disminución.
dye [daɪ] *n* tinte *m* ♦ *vt* teñir; **hair** ~ tinte *m* para el pelo.
dying ['daɪɪŋ] *adj* moribundo, agonizante; (*moments*) final; (*words*) último.
dyke [daɪk] *n* (*BRIT*) dique *m*; (*channel*) arroyo, acequia; (*causeway*) calzada.
dynamic [daɪ'næmɪk] *adj* dinámico.
dynamics [daɪ'næmɪks] *n or npl* dinámica *sg*.
dynamite ['daɪnəmaɪt] *n* dinamita ♦ *vt* dinamitar.
dynamo ['daɪnəməu] *n* dinamo *f or m* (*LAM*).
dynasty ['dɪnəstɪ] *n* dinastía.
dysentery ['dɪsɪntrɪ] *n* disentería.
dyslexia [dɪs'lɛksɪə] *n* dislexia.
dyslexic [dɪs'lɛksɪk] *adj, n* disléxico/a *m/f*.
dyspepsia [dɪs'pɛpsɪə] *n* dispepsia.
dystrophy ['dɪstrəfɪ] *n* distrofia; **muscular** ~ distrofia muscular.

E e

E, e [i:] *n* (*letter*) E, e *f*; (*MUS*) mi *m*; **E for Edward**, (*US*) **E for Easy** E de Enrique.
E *abbr* (= *east*) E ♦ *n abbr* (= *Ecstasy*) éxtasis *m*.
E111 *n abbr* (*also*: **form** ~) impreso E111.
ea. *abbr* = **each**.
E.A. *abbr* (*US*: = *educational age*) *nivel escolar*.
each [i:tʃ] *adj* cada *inv* ♦ *pron* cada uno; ~ **other** el uno al otro; **they hate** ~ **other** se

odian (entre ellos *or* mutuamente); ~ **day** cada día; **they have 2 books** ~ tienen 2 libros cada uno; **they cost £5** ~ cuestan cinco libras cada uno; ~ **of us** cada uno de nosotros.

eager ['iːgə*] *adj* (*gen*) impaciente; (*hopeful*) ilusionado; (*keen*) entusiasmado; (: *pupil*) apasionado; **to be ~ to do sth** estar deseoso de hacer algo; **to be ~ for** ansiar, anhelar.

eagerly ['iːgəlɪ] *adv* con impaciencia; con ilusión; con entusiasmo.

eagerness ['iːgənɪs] *n* impaciencia; ilusión *f*; entusiasmo.

eagle ['iːgl] *n* águila.

E and OE *abbr* = **errors and omissions excepted.**

ear [ɪə*] *n* oreja; (*sense of hearing*) oído; (*of corn*) espiga; **up to the ~s in debt** abrumado de deudas.

earache ['ɪəreɪk] *n* dolor *m* de oídos.

eardrum ['ɪədrʌm] *n* tímpano.

earful ['ɪəful] *n*: **to give sb an** ~ (*col*) echar una bronca a algn.

earl [əːl] *n* conde *m*.

early ['əːlɪ] *adv* (*gen*) temprano; (*ahead of time*) con tiempo, con anticipación ♦ *adj* (*gen*) temprano; (*reply*) pronto; (*man*) primitivo; (*first*: *Christians, settlers*) primero; **to have an ~ night** acostarse temprano; **in the** ~ *or* ~ **in the spring/ 19th century** a principios de primavera/ del siglo diecinueve; **you're ~!** ¡has llegado temprano *or* pronto!; ~ **in the morning/afternoon** a primeras horas de la mañana/tarde; **she's in her ~ forties** tiene poco más de cuarenta años; **at your earliest convenience** (*COMM*) con la mayor brevedad posible; **I can't come any earlier** no puedo llegar antes.

early retirement *n* jubilación *f* anticipada.

early warning system *n* sistema *m* de alerta inmediata.

earmark ['ɪəmɑːk] *vt*: **to ~ for** reservar para, destinar a.

earn [əːn] *vt* (*gen*) ganar; (*interest*) devengar; (*praise*) ganarse; **to ~ one's living** ganarse la vida.

earned income *n* renta del trabajo.

earnest ['əːnɪst] *adj* serio, formal ♦ *n* (*also*: ~ **money**) anticipo, señal *f*; **in ~** *adv* en serio.

earnings ['əːnɪŋz] *npl* (*personal*) ingresos *mpl*; (*of company etc*) ganancias *fpl*.

earphones ['ɪəfəunz] *npl* auriculares *mpl*.

earplugs ['ɪəplʌgz] *npl* tapones *mpl* para los oídos.

earring ['ɪərɪŋ] *n* pendiente *m*, arete *m* (*esp LAM*).

earshot ['ɪəʃɔt] *n*: **out of/within ~** fuera del/al alcance del oído.

earth [əːθ] *n* (*gen*) tierra; (*BRIT*: *ELEC*) toma de tierra ♦ *vt* (*BRIT*: *ELEC*) conectar a tierra.

earthenware ['əːθnwɛə*] *n* loza (de barro).

earthly ['əːθlɪ] *adj* terrenal, mundano; ~ **paradise** paraíso terrenal; **there is no ~ reason to think ...** no existe razón para pensar ....

earthquake ['əːθkweɪk] *n* terremoto.

earth-shattering ['əːθʃætərɪŋ] *adj* trascendental.

earthworm ['əːθwəːm] *n* lombriz *f*.

earthy ['əːθɪ] *adj* (*fig*: *uncomplicated*) sencillo; (: *coarse*) grosero.

earwig ['ɪəwɪg] *n* tijereta.

ease [iːz] *n* facilidad *f*; (*comfort*) comodidad *f* ♦ *vt* (*task*) facilitar; (*pain*) aliviar; (*loosen*) soltar; (*relieve*: *pressure, tension*) aflojar; (*weight*) aligerar; (*help pass*): **to ~ sth in/ out** meter/sacar algo con cuidado ♦ *vi* (*situation*) relajarse; **with** ~ con facilidad; **to feel at ~/ill at** ~ sentirse a gusto/a disgusto; **at ~!** (*MIL*) ¡descansen!

►**ease off, ease up** *vi* (*work, business*) aflojar; (*person*) relajarse.

easel ['iːzl] *n* caballete *m*.

easily ['iːzɪlɪ] *adv* fácilmente.

easiness ['iːzɪnɪs] *n* facilidad *f*; (*of manners*) soltura.

east [iːst] *n* este *m*, oriente *m* ♦ *adj* del este, oriental ♦ *adv* al este, hacia el este; **the E~** el Oriente; (*POL*) el Este.

Easter ['iːstə*] *n* Pascua (de Resurrección).

Easter egg *n* huevo de Pascua.

Easter holidays *npl* Semana Santa *sg*.

Easter Island *n* Isla de Pascua.

easterly ['iːstəlɪ] *adj* (*to the east*) al este; (*from the east*) del este.

Easter Monday *n* lunes *m* de Pascua.

eastern ['iːstən] *adj* del este, oriental; **E~ Europe** Europa del Este; **the E~ bloc** (*POL*) los países del Este.

Easter Sunday *n* Domingo de Resurrección.

East Germany *n* (*formerly*) Alemania Oriental *or* del Este.

eastward(s) ['iːstwəd(z)] *adv* hacia el este.

easy ['iːzɪ] *adj* fácil; (*life*) holgado, cómodo; (*relaxed*) natural ♦ *adv*: **to take it** *or* **things** ~ (*not worry*) no preocuparse; (*go slowly*) tomarlo con calma; (*rest*) descansar; **payment on ~ terms** (*COMM*) facilidades de pago; **I'm** ~ (*col*) me da igual, no me importa; **easier said than done** del dicho al hecho hay buen trecho.

easy chair *n* butaca.
easy-going ['iːzɪ'gəuɪŋ] *adj* acomodadizo.
easy touch [iːzɪ'tʌtʃ] *n*: **he's an** ~ (*col*) es fácil de convencer.
eat, *pt* **ate**, *pp* **eaten** [iːt, eɪt, 'iːtn] *vt* comer.
▸**eat away** *vt* (*subj*: *sea*) desgastar; (: *acid*) corroer.
▸**eat into, eat away at** *vt fus* corroer.
▸**eat out** *vi* comer fuera.
▸**eat up** *vt* (*meal etc*) comerse; **it** ~**s up electricity** devora la electricidad.
eatable ['iːtəbl] *adj* comestible.
eau de Cologne [əudəkə'ləun] *n* (agua de) colonia.
eaves [iːvz] *npl* alero *sg*.
eavesdrop ['iːvzdrɔp] *vi*: **to** ~ **(on sb)** escuchar a escondidas (a algn).
ebb [ɛb] *n* reflujo ♦ *vi* bajar; (*fig*: *also*: ~ **away**) decaer; ~ **and flow** el flujo y reflujo; **to be at a low** ~ (*fig*: *person*) estar de capa caída.
ebb tide *n* marea menguante.
ebony ['ɛbənɪ] *n* ébano.
ebullient [ɪ'bʌlɪənt] *adj* entusiasta, animado.
EC *n abbr* (= *European Community*) CE *f*.
ECB *n abbr* (= *European Central Bank*) BCE *m*.
eccentric [ɪk'sɛntrɪk] *adj, n* excéntrico/a.
ecclesiastical [ɪkliːzɪ'æstɪkəl] *adj* eclesiástico.
ECG *n abbr* (= *electrocardiogram*) E.C. *m*.
ECGD *n abbr* (= *Export Credits Guarantee Department*) *servicio de garantía financiera a la exportación*.
echo, ~**es** ['ɛkəu] *n* eco *m* ♦ *vt* (*sound*) repetir ♦ *vi* resonar, hacer eco.
ECLA *n abbr* (= *Economic Commission for Latin America*) CEPAL *f*.
éclair ['eɪklɛə*] *n* petisú *m*.
eclipse [ɪ'klɪps] *n* eclipse *m* ♦ *vt* eclipsar.
ECM *n abbr* (*US*: = *European Common Market*) MCE *m*.
eco- ['iːkəu] *pref* eco-.
eco-friendly ['iːkəufrɛndlɪ] *adj* ecológico.
ecological [iːkə'lɔdʒɪkl] *adj* ecológico.
ecologist [ɪ'kɔlədʒɪst] *n* ecologista *m/f*; (*scientist*) ecólogo/a *m/f*.
ecology [ɪ'kɔlədʒɪ] *n* ecología.
e-commerce *n abbr* (= *electronic commerce*) comercio electrónico.
economic [iːkə'nɔmɪk] *adj* (*profitable*: *price*) económico; (: *business etc*) rentable.
economical [iːkə'nɔmɪkl] *adj* económico.
economically [iːkə'nɔmɪklɪ] *adv* económicamente.
economics [iːkə'nɔmɪks] *n* economía ♦ *npl* (*financial aspects*) finanzas *fpl*.
economist [ɪ'kɔnəmɪst] *n* economista *m/f*.
economize [ɪ'kɔnəmaɪz] *vi* economizar, ahorrar.
economy [ɪ'kɔnəmɪ] *n* economía; **economies of scale** economías *fpl* de escala.
economy class *n* (*AVIAT etc*) clase *f* turista.
economy size *n* tamaño familiar.
ecosystem ['iːkəusɪstəm] *n* ecosistema *m*.
eco-tourism [iːkəu'tuərɪzm] *n* turismo verde *or* ecológico.
ECSC *n abbr* (= *European Coal and Steel Community*) CECA *f*.
ecstasy ['ɛkstəsɪ] *n* éxtasis *m inv*.
ecstatic [ɛks'tætɪk] *adj* extático, extasiado.
ECT *n abbr see* **electroconvulsive therapy**.
ECU, ecu *n abbr* (= *European Currency Unit*) ECU, ecu *m*.
Ecuador ['ɛkwədɔː*] *n* Ecuador *m*.
Ecuador(i)an [ɛkwə'dɔːr(ɪ)ən] *adj, n* ecuatoriano/a *m/f*.
ecumenical [iːkju'mɛnɪkl] *adj* ecuménico.
eczema ['ɛksɪmə] *n* eczema *m*.
eddy ['ɛdɪ] *n* remolino.
Eden ['iːdn] *n* Edén *m*.
edge [ɛdʒ] *n* (*of knife etc*) filo; (*of object*) borde *m*; (*of lake etc*) orilla ♦ *vt* (*SEWING*) ribetear ♦ *vi*: **to** ~ **past** pasar con dificultad; **on** ~ (*fig*) = **edgy**; **to** ~ **away from** alejarse poco a poco de; **to** ~ **forward** avanzar poco a poco.
edgeways ['ɛdʒweɪz] *adv*: **he couldn't get a word in** ~ no pudo meter baza.
edging ['ɛdʒɪŋ] *n* (*SEWING*) ribete *m*; (*of path*) borde *m*.
edgy ['ɛdʒɪ] *adj* nervioso, inquieto.
edible ['ɛdɪbl] *adj* comestible.
edict ['iːdɪkt] *n* edicto.
edifice ['ɛdɪfɪs] *n* edificio.
edifying ['ɛdɪfaɪɪŋ] *adj* edificante.
Edinburgh ['ɛdɪnbərə] *n* Edimburgo.
edit ['ɛdɪt] *vt* (*be editor of*) dirigir; (*re-write*) redactar; (*cut*) cortar; (*COMPUT*) editar.
edition [ɪ'dɪʃən] *n* (*gen*) edición *f*; (*number printed*) tirada.
editor ['ɛdɪtə*] *n* (*of newspaper*) director(a) *m/f*; (*of book*) redactor(a) *m/f*; (*film* ~) montador(a) *m/f*.
editorial [ɛdɪ'tɔːrɪəl] *adj* editorial ♦ *n* editorial *m*; ~ **staff** redacción *f*.
EDP *n abbr* (= *electronic data processing*) PED *m*.
EDT *n abbr* (*US*: = *Eastern Daylight Time*) *hora de verano de Nueva York*.
educate ['ɛdjukeɪt] *vt* (*gen*) educar; (*instruct*) instruir.
educated guess ['ɛdjukeɪtɪd-] *n* hipótesis *f* sólida.
education [ɛdju'keɪʃən] *n* educación *f*;

(*schooling*) enseñanza; (*SCOL: subject etc*) pedagogía; **primary/secondary** ~ enseñanza primaria/secundaria.
educational [ɛdju'keɪʃənl] *adj* (*policy etc*) de educación, educativo; (*teaching*) docente; (*instructive*) educativo; ~ **technology** tecnología educacional.
Edwardian [ɛd'wɔːdɪən] *adj* eduardiano.
E.E. *abbr* = **electrical engineer.**
EEC *n abbr* (= *European Economic Community*) CEE *f.*
EEG *n abbr see* **electroencephalogram.**
eel [iːl] *n* anguila.
EENT *n abbr* (*US MED*) = *eye, ear, nose and throat.*
EEOC *n abbr* (*US*: = *Equal Employment Opportunities Commission*) *comisión que investiga discriminación racial o sexual en el empleo.*
eerie ['ɪərɪ] *adj* (*sound, experience*) espeluznante.
EET *n abbr* (= *Eastern European Time*) *hora de Europa oriental.*
efface [ɪ'feɪs] *vt* borrar.
effect [ɪ'fɛkt] *n* efecto ♦ *vt* efectuar, llevar a cabo; ~**s** *npl* (*property*) efectos *mpl*; **to take** ~ (*law*) entrar en vigor *or* vigencia; (*drug*) surtir efecto; **in** ~ en realidad; **to have an** ~ **on sb/sth** hacerle efecto a algn/afectar algo; **to put into** ~ (*plan*) llevar a la práctica; **his letter is to the** ~ **that...** su carta viene a decir que....
effective [ɪ'fɛktɪv] *adj* (*gen*) eficaz; (*striking: display, outfit*) impresionante; (*real*) efectivo; **to become** ~ (*LAW*) entrar en vigor; ~ **date** fecha de vigencia.
effectively [ɪ'fɛktɪvlɪ] *adv* (*efficiently*) eficazmente; (*strikingly*) de manera impresionante; (*in reality*) en efecto.
effectiveness [ɪ'fɛktɪvnɪs] *n* eficacia.
effeminate [ɪ'fɛmɪnɪt] *adj* afeminado.
effervescent [ɛfə'vɛsnt] *adj* efervescente.
efficacy ['ɛfɪkəsɪ] *n* eficacia.
efficiency [ɪ'fɪʃənsɪ] *n* (*gen*) eficiencia; (*of machine*) rendimiento.
efficient [ɪ'fɪʃənt] *adj* eficiente; (*remedy, product, system*) eficaz; (*machine, car*) de buen rendimiento.
effigy ['ɛfɪdʒɪ] *n* efigie *f.*
effluent ['ɛfluənt] *n* vertidos *mpl.*
effort ['ɛfət] *n* esfuerzo; **to make an** ~ **to do sth** estar deseoso de hacer algo.
effortless ['ɛfətlɪs] *adj* sin ningún esfuerzo.
effrontery [ɪ'frʌntərɪ] *n* descaro.
effusive [ɪ'fjuːsɪv] *adj* efusivo.
EFL *n abbr* (*SCOL*) = *English as a foreign language.*
EFTA ['ɛftə] *n abbr* (= *European Free Trade Association*) EFTA *f.*
e.g. *adv abbr* (= *exempli gratia*) p.ej.
egg [ɛg] *n* huevo; **hard-boiled/soft-boiled/poached** ~ huevo duro *or* a la copa (*LAM*) *or* tibio (*LAM*)/pasado por agua/escalfado; **scrambled** ~**s** huevos revueltos.
►**egg on** *vt* incitar.
eggcup ['ɛgkʌp] *n* huevera.
eggnog [ɛg'nɔg] *n* ponche *m* de huevo.
eggplant ['ɛgplɑːnt] *n* (*esp US*) berenjena.
eggshell ['ɛgʃɛl] *n* cáscara de huevo.
egg-timer ['ɛgtaɪmə*] *n* reloj *m* de arena (*para cocer huevos*).
egg white *n* clara de huevo.
egg yolk *n* yema de huevo.
ego ['iːgəu] *n* ego.
egotism ['ɛgəutɪzəm] *n* egoísmo.
egotist ['ɛgəutɪst] *n* egoísta *m/f.*
ego trip *n*: **to be on an** ~ creerse el centro del mundo.
Egypt ['iːdʒɪpt] *n* Egipto.
Egyptian [ɪ'dʒɪpʃən] *adj, n* egipcio/a *m/f.*
eiderdown ['aɪdədaun] *n* edredón *m.*
eight [eɪt] *num* ocho.
eighteen [eɪ'tiːn] *num* dieciocho.
eighth [eɪtθ] *num* octavo.
eighty ['eɪtɪ] *num* ochenta.
Eire ['ɛərə] *n* Eire *m.*
EIS *n abbr* (= *Educational Institute of Scotland*) *sindicato de profesores escoceses.*
either ['aɪðə*] *adj* cualquiera de los dos ...; (*both, each*) cada ♦ *pron*: ~ **(of them)** cualquiera (de los dos) ♦ *adv* tampoco ♦ *conj*: ~ **yes or no** o sí o no; **on** ~ **side** en ambos lados; **I don't like** ~ no me gusta ninguno de los dos; **no, I don't** ~ no, yo tampoco.
eject [ɪ'dʒɛkt] *vt* echar; (*tenant*) desahuciar ♦ *vi* eyectarse.
ejector seat [ɪ'dʒɛktə-] *n* asiento proyectable.
eke out [iːk-] *vt fus* (*money*) hacer que llegue.
EKG *n abbr* (*US*) *see* **electrocardiogram.**
el [ɛl] *n abbr* (*US col*) = **elevated railroad.**
elaborate *adj* [ɪ'læbərɪt] (*design, pattern*) complicado ♦ *vb* [ɪ'læbəreɪt] *vt* elaborar ♦ *vi* explicarse con muchos detalles.
elaborately [ɪ'læbərɪtlɪ] *adv* de manera complicada; (*decorated*) profusamente.
elaboration [ɪlæbə'reɪʃən] *n* elaboración *f.*
elapse [ɪ'læps] *vi* transcurrir.
elastic [ɪ'læstɪk] *adj, n* elástico.
elastic band *n* (*BRIT*) gomita.
elated [ɪ'leɪtɪd] *adj*: **to be** ~ estar eufórico.
elation [ɪ'leɪʃən] *n* euforia.
elbow ['ɛlbəu] *n* codo ♦ *vt*: **to** ~ **one's way through the crowd** abrirse paso a

codazos por la muchedumbre.
elbow grease *n* (*col*): **to use some** *or* **a bit of ~** menearse.
elder ['ɛldə*] *adj* mayor ♦ *n* (*tree*) saúco; (*person*) mayor; (*of tribe*) anciano.
elderly ['ɛldəlɪ] *adj* de edad, mayor ♦ *npl*: **the ~** la gente mayor, los ancianos.
eldest ['ɛldɪst] *adj, n* el/la mayor.
elect [ɪ'lɛkt] *vt* elegir; (*choose*): **to ~ to do** optar por hacer.
election [ɪ'lɛkʃən] *n* elección *f*; **to hold an ~** convocar elecciones.
election campaign *n* campaña electoral.
electioneering [ɪlɛkʃə'nɪərɪŋ] *n* campaña electoral.
elector [ɪ'lɛktə*] *n* elector(a) *m/f*.
electoral [ɪ'lɛktərəl] *adj* electoral.
electoral college *n* colegio electoral.
electoral roll *n* censo electoral.
electorate [ɪ'lɛktərɪt] *n* electorado.
electric [ɪ'lɛktrɪk] *adj* eléctrico.
electrical [ɪ'lɛktrɪkl] *adj* eléctrico.
electrical engineer *n* ingeniero/a electricista.
electrical failure *n* fallo eléctrico. .
electric blanket *n* manta eléctrica.
electric chair *n* silla eléctrica.
electric cooker *n* cocina eléctrica.
electric current *n* corriente *f* eléctrica.
electric fire *n* estufa eléctrica.
electrician [ɪlɛk'trɪʃən] *n* electricista *m/f*.
electricity [ɪlɛk'trɪsɪtɪ] *n* electricidad *f*; **to switch on/off the ~** conectar/desconectar la electricidad.
electricity board *n* (*BRIT*) compañía eléctrica (estatal).
electric light *n* luz *f* eléctrica.
electric shock *n* electrochoque *m*.
electrify [ɪ'lɛktrɪfaɪ] *vt* (*RAIL*) electrificar; (*fig: audience*) electrizar.
electro... [ɪ'lɛktrəu] *pref* electro....
electrocardiogram (ECG, (*US*) **EKG)** [ɪ'lɛktrə'kɑːdɪəgræm] *n* electrocardiograma *m*.
electrocardiograph [ɪ'lɛktrəu'kɑːdɪəgræf] *n* electrocardiógrafo.
electro-convulsive therapy (ECT) [ɪ'lɛktrəkən'vʌlsɪv-] *n* electroterapia.
electrocute [ɪ'lɛktrəukjuːt] *vt* electrocutar.
electrode [ɪ'lɛktrəud] *n* electrodo.
electroencephalogram (EEG) [ɪ'lɛktrəuɛn'sɛfələgræm] *n* electroencefalograma *m*.
electrolysis [ɪlɛk'trɔlɪsɪs] *n* electrólisis *f inv*.
electromagnetic [ɪ'lɛktrəmæg'nɛtɪk] *adj* electromagnético.
electron [ɪ'lɛktrɔn] *n* electrón *m*.
electronic [ɪlɛk'trɔnɪk] *adj* electrónico.
electronic data processing (EDP) *n* tratamiento *or* proceso electrónico de datos.
electronic mail *n* correo electrónico.
electronics [ɪlɛk'trɔnɪks] *n* electrónica.
electron microscope *n* microscopio electrónico.
electroplated [ɪ'lɛktrə'pleɪtɪd] *adj* galvanizado.
electrotherapy [ɪ'lɛktrə'θɛrəpɪ] *n* electroterapia.
elegance ['ɛlɪgəns] *n* elegancia.
elegant ['ɛlɪgənt] *adj* elegante.
elegy ['ɛlɪdʒɪ] *n* elegía.
element ['ɛlɪmənt] *n* (*gen*) elemento; (*of heater, kettle etc*) resistencia.
elementary [ɛlɪ'mɛntərɪ] *adj* elemental; (*primitive*) rudimentario; (*school, education*) primario.
elementary school *n* (*US*) escuela de enseñanza primaria; *ver recuadro*.

> **ELEMENTARY SCHOOL**
>
> *En Estados Unidos y Canadá se llama* **elementary school** *al centro estatal en el que los niños reciben los primeros seis u ocho años de su educación, también llamado "grade school" o "grammar school".*

elephant ['ɛlɪfənt] *n* elefante *m*.
elevate ['ɛlɪveɪt] *vt* (*gen*) elevar; (*in rank*) ascender.
elevated railroad *n* (*US*) *ferrocarril m urbano elevado*.
elevation [ɛlɪ'veɪʃən] *n* elevación *f*; (*rank*) ascenso; (*height*) altitud *f*.
elevator ['ɛlɪveɪtə*] *n* (*US*) ascensor *m*, elevador *m* (*LAM*).
eleven [ɪ'lɛvn] *num* once.
elevenses [ɪ'lɛvnzɪz] *npl* (*BRIT*) ≈ café *m* de media mañana.
eleventh [ɪ'lɛvnθ] *adj* undécimo; **at the ~ hour** (*fig*) a última hora.
elf, *pl* **elves** [ɛlf, ɛlvz] *n* duende *m*.
elicit [ɪ'lɪsɪt] *vt*: **to ~ sth (from sb)** obtener algo (de algn).
eligible ['ɛlɪdʒəbl] *adj* cotizado; **to be ~ for a pension** tener derecho a una pensión.
eliminate [ɪ'lɪmɪneɪt] *vt* eliminar; (*score out*) suprimir; (*a suspect, possibility*) descartar.
elimination [ɪlɪmɪ'neɪʃən] *n* eliminación *f*; supresión *f*; **by process of ~** por eliminación.
elite [eɪ'liːt] *n* élite *f*.
elitist [eɪ'liːtɪst] *adj* (*pej*) elitista.

elixir [ɪ'lɪksɪə*] *n* elixir *m.*
Elizabethan [ɪlɪzə'bi:θən] *adj* isabelino.
elm [ɛlm] *n* olmo.
elocution [ɛlə'kju:ʃən] *n* elocución *f.*
elongated ['i:lɔŋgeɪtɪd] *adj* alargado.
elope [ɪ'ləup] *vi* fugarse.
elopement [ɪ'ləupmənt] *n* fuga.
eloquence ['ɛləkwəns] *n* elocuencia.
eloquent ['ɛləkwənt] *adj* elocuente.
else [ɛls] *adv*: **or** ~ si no; **something** ~ otra cosa *or* algo más; **somewhere** ~ en otra parte; **everywhere** ~ en los demás sitios; **everyone** ~ todos los demás; **nothing** ~ nada más; **is there anything** ~ **I can do?** ¿puedo hacer algo más?; **where** ~**?** ¿dónde más?, ¿en qué otra parte?; **there was little** ~ **to do** apenas quedaba otra cosa que hacer; **nobody** ~ **spoke** no habló nadie más.
elsewhere [ɛls'wɛə*] *adv* (*be*) en otra parte; (*go*) a otra parte.
ELT *n abbr* (*SCOL*) = *English Language Teaching.*
elucidate [ɪ'lu:sɪdeɪt] *vt* esclarecer, elucidar.
elude [ɪ'lu:d] *vt* eludir; (*blow, pursuer*) esquivar.
elusive [ɪ'lu:sɪv] *adj* escurridizo; (*answer*) difícil de encontrar; **he is very** ~ no es fácil encontrarlo.
elves [ɛlvz] *npl of* **elf**.
emaciated [ɪ'meɪsɪeɪtɪd] *adj* escuálido.
E-Mail, e-mail ['i:meɪl] *n abbr* (= *electronic mail*) correo electrónico ♦ *vt*: **to** ~ **sb** mandar un mensaje por correo electrónico a algn.
emanate ['ɛməneɪt] *vi* emanar, provenir.
emancipate [ɪ'mænsɪpeɪt] *vt* emancipar.
emancipated [ɪ'mænsɪpeɪtɪd] *adj* liberado.
emancipation [ɪmænsɪ'peɪʃən] *n* emancipación *f*, liberación *f.*
emasculate [ɪ'mæskjuleɪt] *vt* castrar; (*fig*) debilitar.
embalm [ɪm'bɑ:m] *vt* embalsamar.
embankment [ɪm'bæŋkmənt] *n* (*of railway*) terraplén *m*; (*riverside*) dique *m.*
embargo, *pl* ~**es** [ɪm'bɑ:gəu] *n* prohibición *f*; (*COMM, NAUT*) embargo; **to put an** ~ **on sth** poner un embargo en algo.
embark [ɪm'bɑ:k] *vi* embarcarse ♦ *vt* embarcar; **to** ~ **on** (*journey*) comenzar, iniciar; (*fig*) emprender.
embarkation [ɛmbɑ:'keɪʃən] *n* (*people*) embarco; (*goods*) embarque *m.*
embarkation card *n* tarjeta de embarque.
embarrass [ɪm'bærəs] *vt* avergonzar, dar vergüenza a; (*financially etc*) poner en un aprieto.
embarrassed [ɪm'baerəst] *adj* azorado, violento; **to be** ~ sentirse azorado *or* violento.
embarrassing [ɪm'bærəsɪŋ] *adj* (*situation*) violento; (*question*) embarazoso.
embarrassment [ɪm'bærəsmənt] *n* vergüenza, azoramiento; (*financial*) apuros *mpl.*
embassy ['ɛmbəsɪ] *n* embajada; **the Spanish E**~ la embajada española.
embed [ɪm'bɛd] *vt* (*jewel*) empotrar; (*teeth etc*) clavar.
embellish [ɪm'bɛlɪʃ] *vt* embellecer; (*fig: story, truth*) adornar.
embers ['ɛmbəz] *npl* rescoldo *sg*, ascuas.
embezzle [ɪm'bɛzl] *vt* desfalcar, malversar.
embezzlement [ɪm'bɛzlmənt] *n* desfalco, malversación *f.*
embezzler [ɪm'bɛzlə*] *n* malversador(a) *m/f.*
embitter [ɪm'bɪtə*] *vt* (*person*) amargar; (*relationship*) envenenar.
embittered [ɪm'bɪtəd] *adj* resentido, amargado.
emblem ['ɛmbləm] *n* emblema *m.*
embody [ɪm'bɔdɪ] *vt* (*spirit*) encarnar; (*ideas*) expresar.
embolden [ɪm'bəuldən] *vt* envalentonar; (*TYP*) poner en negrita.
embolism ['ɛmbəlɪzəm] *n* embolia.
emboss [ɪm'bɔs] *vt* estampar en relieve; (*metal, leather*) repujar.
embossed [ɪm'bɔst] *adj* realzado; ~ **with ...** con ... en relieve.
embrace [ɪm'breɪs] *vt* abrazar, dar un abrazo a; (*include*) abarcar; (*adopt: idea*) adherirse a ♦ *vi* abrazarse ♦ *n* abrazo.
embroider [ɪm'brɔɪdə*] *vt* bordar; (*fig: story*) adornar, embellecer.
embroidery [ɪm'brɔɪdərɪ] *n* bordado.
embroil [ɪm'brɔɪl] *vt*: **to become** ~**ed (in sth)** enredarse (en algo).
embryo ['ɛmbrɪəu] *n* (*also fig*) embrión *m.*
emcee [ɛm'si:] *n* (*US*) presentador(a) *m/f.*
emend [ɪ'mɛnd] *vt* (*text*) enmendar.
emerald ['ɛmərəld] *n* esmeralda.
emerge [ɪ'mə:dʒ] *vi* (*gen*) salir; (*arise*) surgir; **it** ~**s that** resulta que.
emergence [ɪ'mə:dʒəns] *n* (*of nation*) surgimiento.
emergency [ɪ'mə:dʒənsɪ] *n* (*event*) emergencia; (*crisis*) crisis *f inv*; **in an** ~ en caso de urgencia; **(to declare a) state of** ~ (declarar) estado de emergencia *or* de excepción.
emergency cord *n* (*US*) timbre *m* de alarma.

emergency exit *n* salida de emergencia.
emergency landing *n* aterrizaje *m* forzoso.
emergency lane *n* (*US*) arcén *m*.
emergency meeting *n* reunión *f* extraordinaria.
emergency service *n* servicio de urgencia.
emergency stop *n* (*AUT*) parada en seco.
emergent [ɪ'məːdʒənt] *adj* (*nation*) recientemente independizado.
emery board ['ɛmərɪ-] *n* lima de uñas.
emetic [ɪ'mɛtɪk] *n* vomitivo, emético.
emigrant ['ɛmɪgrənt] *n* emigrante *m/f*.
emigrate ['ɛmɪgreɪt] *vi* emigrar.
emigration [ɛmɪ'greɪʃən] *n* emigración *f*.
émigré ['ɛmɪgreɪ] *n* emigrado/a.
eminence ['ɛmɪnəns] *n* eminencia; **to gain** *or* **win** ~ ganarse fama.
eminent ['ɛmɪnənt] *adj* eminente.
eminently ['ɛmɪnəntlɪ] *adv* eminentemente.
emirate ['ɛmɪrɪt] *n* emirato.
emission [ɪ'mɪʃən] *n* emisión *f*.
emit [ɪ'mɪt] *vt* emitir; (*smell, smoke*) despedir.
emolument [ɪ'mɔljumənt] *n* (*often pl*: *formal*) honorario, emolumento.
emotion [ɪ'məuʃən] *n* emoción *f*.
emotional [ɪ'məuʃənl] *adj* (*person*) sentimental; (*scene*) conmovedor(a), emocionante.
emotionally [ɪ'məuʃnəlɪ] *adv* (*behave, speak*) con emoción; (*be involved*) sentimentalmente.
emotive [ɪ'məutɪv] *adj* emotivo.
empathy ['ɛmpəθɪ] *n* empatía; **to feel ~ with sb** sentirse identificado con algn.
emperor ['ɛmpərə*] *n* emperador *m*.
emphasis, *pl* **emphases** ['ɛmfəsɪs, -siːz] *n* énfasis *m inv*; **to lay** *or* **place ~ on sth** (*fig*) hacer hincapié en algo; **the ~ is on sport** se da mayor importancia al deporte.
emphasize ['ɛmfəsaɪz] *vt* (*word, point*) subrayar, recalcar; (*feature*) hacer resaltar.
emphatic [ɛm'fætɪk] *adj* (*condemnation*) enérgico; (*denial*) rotundo.
emphatically [ɛm'fætɪklɪ] *adv* con énfasis.
emphysema [ɛmfɪ'siːmə] *n* (*MED*) enfisema *m*.
empire ['ɛmpaɪə*] *n* imperio.
empirical [ɛm'pɪrɪkl] *adj* empírico.
employ [ɪm'plɔɪ] *vt* (*give job to*) emplear; (*make use of*: *thing, method*) emplear, usar; **he's ~ed in a bank** está empleado en un banco.
employee [ɪmplɔɪ'iː] *n* empleado/a.
employer [ɪm'plɔɪə*] *n* patrón/ona *m/f*; (*businessman*) empresario/a.
employment [ɪm'plɔɪmənt] *n* empleo; **full ~** pleno empleo; **without ~** sin empleo; **to find ~** encontrar trabajo; **place of ~** lugar *m* de trabajo.
employment agency *n* agencia de colocaciones *or* empleo.
employment exchange *n* bolsa de trabajo.
empower [ɪm'pauə*] *vt*: **to ~ sb to do sth** autorizar a algn para hacer algo.
empress ['ɛmprɪs] *n* emperatriz *f*.
emptiness ['ɛmptɪnɪs] *n* vacío.
empty ['ɛmptɪ] *adj* vacío; (*street, area*) desierto; (*threat*) vano ♦ *n* (*bottle*) envase *m* ♦ *vt* vaciar; (*place*) dejar vacío ♦ *vi* vaciarse; (*house*) quedar(se) vacío *or* desocupado; (*place*) quedar(se) desierto; **to ~ into** (*river*) desembocar en.
empty-handed ['ɛmptɪ'hændɪd] *adj* con las manos vacías.
empty-headed ['ɛmptɪ'hɛdɪd] *adj* casquivano.
EMS *n abbr* (= *European Monetary System*) SME *m*.
EMT *n abbr* = *emergency medical technician*.
EMU *n abbr* (= *Economic and Monetary Union*) UME *f*.
emulate ['ɛmjuleɪt] *vt* emular.
emulsion [ɪ'mʌlʃən] *n* emulsión *f*.
enable [ɪ'neɪbl] *vt*: **to ~ sb to do sth** (*allow*) permitir a algn hacer algo; (*prepare*) capacitar a algn para hacer algo.
enact [ɪn'ækt] *vt* (*law*) promulgar; (*play, scene, role*) representar.
enamel [ɪ'næməl] *n* esmalte *m*.
enamel paint *n* esmalte *m*.
enamoured [ɪ'næməd] *adj*: **to be ~ of** (*person*) estar enamorado de; (*activity etc*) tener gran afición a; (*idea*) aferrarse a.
encampment [ɪn'kæmpmənt] *n* campamento.
encase [ɪn'keɪs] *vt*: **to ~ in** (*contain*) encajar; (*cover*) cubrir.
encased [ɪn'keɪst] *adj*: **~ in** (*covered*) revestido de.
enchant [ɪn'tʃɑːnt] *vt* encantar.
enchanting [ɪn'tʃɑːntɪŋ] *adj* encantador(a).
encircle [ɪn'səːkl] *vt* (*gen*) rodear; (*waist*) ceñir.
encl. *abbr* (= *enclosed*) adj.
enclave ['ɛnkleɪv] *n* enclave *m*.
enclose [ɪn'kləuz] *vt* (*land*) cercar; (*with letter etc*) adjuntar; (*in receptacle*): **to ~ (with)** encerrar (con); **please find ~d** le mandamos adjunto.
enclosure [ɪn'kləuʒə*] *n* cercado, recinto; (*COMM*) carta adjunta.

encoder [ɪn'kəudə*] *n* (*COMPUT*) codificador *m*.
encompass [ɪn'kʌmpəs] *vt* abarcar.
encore [ɔŋ'kɔː*] *excl* ¡otra!, ¡bis! ♦ *n* bis *m*.
encounter [ɪn'kauntə*] *n* encuentro ♦ *vt* encontrar, encontrarse con; (*difficulty*) tropezar con.
encourage [ɪn'kʌrɪdʒ] *vt* alentar, animar; (*growth*) estimular; **to ~ sb (to do sth)** animar a algn (a hacer algo).
encouragement [ɪn'kʌrɪdʒmənt] *n* estímulo; (*of industry*) fomento.
encouraging [ɪn'kʌrɪdʒɪŋ] *adj* alentador(a).
encroach [ɪn'krəutʃ] *vi*: **to ~ (up)on** (*gen*) invadir; (*time*) adueñarse de.
encrust [ɪn'krʌst] *vt* incrustar.
encrusted [ɪn'krʌstəd] *adj*: **~ with** recubierto de.
encumber [ɪn'kʌmbə*] *vt*: **to be ~ed with** (*carry*) estar cargado de; (*debts*) estar gravado de.
encyclop(a)edia [ɛnsaɪkləu'piːdɪə] *n* enciclopedia.
end [ɛnd] *n* (*gen, also aim*) fin *m*; (*of table*) extremo; (*of line, rope etc*) cabo; (*of pointed object*) punta; (*of town*) barrio; (*of street*) final *m*; (*SPORT*) lado ♦ *vt* terminar, acabar; (*also*: **bring to an ~, put an ~ to**) acabar con ♦ *vi* terminar, acabar; **to ~ (with)** terminar (con); **in the ~** al final; **to be at an ~** llegar a su fin; **at the ~ of the day** (*fig*) al fin y al cabo, a fin de cuentas; **to this ~, with this ~ in view** con este propósito; **from ~ to ~** de punta a punta; **on ~** (*object*) de punta, de cabeza; **to stand on ~** (*hair*) erizarse, ponerse de punta; **for hours on ~** hora tras hora.
▸**end up** *vi*: **to ~ up in** terminar en; (*place*) ir a parar a.
endanger [ɪn'deɪndʒə*] *vt* poner en peligro; **an ~ed species** (*of animal*) una especie en peligro de extinción.
endear [ɪn'dɪə*] *vt*: **to ~ o.s. to sb** ganarse la simpatía de algn.
endearing [ɪn'dɪərɪŋ] *adj* entrañable.
endearment [ɪn'dɪərmənt] *n* cariño, palabra cariñosa; **to whisper ~s** decir unas palabras cariñosas al oído; **term of ~** nombre *m* cariñoso.
endeavour, (*US*) **endeavor** [ɪn'dɛvə*] *n* esfuerzo; (*attempt*) tentativa ♦ *vi*: **to ~ to do** esforzarse por hacer; (*try*) procurar hacer.
endemic [ɛn'dɛmɪk] *adj* (*poverty, disease*) endémico.
ending ['ɛndɪŋ] *n* fin *m*, final *m*; (*of book*) desenlace *m*; (*LING*) terminación *f*.
endive ['ɛndaɪv] *n* (*curly*) escarola; (*smooth, flat*) endibia.
endless ['ɛndlɪs] *adj* interminable, inacabable; (*possibilities*) infinito.
endorse [ɪn'dɔːs] *vt* (*cheque*) endosar; (*approve*) aprobar.
endorsee [ɪndɔː'siː] *n* endorsatario/a.
endorsement [ɪn'dɔːsmənt] *n* (*approval*) aprobación *f*; (*signature*) endoso; (*BRIT*: *on driving licence*) nota de sanción.
endorser [ɪn'dɔːsə*] *n* avalista *m/f*.
endow [ɪn'dau] *vt* (*provide with money*) dotar; (*found*) fundar; **to be ~ed with** (*fig*) estar dotado de.
endowment [ɪn'daumənt] *adj* (*amount*) donación *f*.
endowment mortgage *n* hipoteca dotal.
endowment policy *n* póliza dotal.
end product *n* (*INDUSTRY*) producto final; (*fig*) resultado.
end result *n* resultado.
endurable [ɪn'djuərəbl] *adj* soportable, tolerable.
endurance [ɪn'djuərəns] *n* resistencia.
endurance test *n* prueba de resistencia.
endure [ɪn'djuə*] *vt* (*bear*) aguantar, soportar; (*resist*) resistir ♦ *vi* (*last*) perdurar; (*resist*) resistir.
enduring [ɪn'djuərɪŋ] *adj* duradero.
end user *n* (*COMPUT*) usuario final.
enema ['ɛnɪmə] *n* (*MED*) enema *m*.
enemy ['ɛnəmɪ] *adj, n* enemigo/a *m/f*; **to make an ~ of sb** enemistarse con algn.
energetic [ɛnə'dʒɛtɪk] *adj* enérgico.
energy ['ɛnədʒɪ] *n* energía.
energy crisis *n* crisis *f* energética.
energy-saving ['ɛnədʒɪseɪvɪŋ] *adj* (*policy*) para ahorrar energía; (*device*) que ahorra energía ♦ *n* ahorro de energía.
enervating ['ɛnəveɪtɪŋ] *adj* deprimente.
enforce [ɪn'fɔːs] *vt* (*LAW*) hacer cumplir.
enforced [ɪn'fɔːst] *adj* forzoso, forzado.
enfranchise [ɪn'fræntʃaɪz] *vt* (*give vote to*) conceder el derecho de voto a; (*set free*) emancipar.
engage [ɪn'geɪdʒ] *vt* (*attention*) captar; (*in conversation*) abordar; (*worker, lawyer*) contratar ♦ *vi* (*TECH*) engranar; **to ~ in** dedicarse a, ocuparse en; **to ~ sb in conversation** entablar conversación con algn; **to ~ the clutch** embragar.
engaged [ɪn'geɪdʒd] *adj* (*BRIT*: *busy, in use*) ocupado; (*betrothed*) prometido; **to get ~** prometerse; **he is ~ in research** se dedica a la investigación.
engaged tone *n* (*BRIT TEL*) señal *f* de comunicando.
engagement [ɪn'geɪdʒmənt] *n*

(*appointment*) compromiso, cita; (*battle*) combate *m*; (*to marry*) compromiso; (*period*) noviazgo; **I have a previous** ~ ya tengo un compromiso.

engagement ring *n* anillo de pedida.

engaging [ɪn'geɪdʒɪŋ] *adj* atractivo, simpático.

engender [ɪn'dʒɛndə*] *vt* engendrar.

engine ['ɛndʒɪn] *n* (*AUT*) motor *m*; (*RAIL*) locomotora.

engine driver *n* (*BRIT*: *of train*) maquinista *m/f*.

engineer [ɛndʒɪ'nɪə*] *n* ingeniero/a; (*BRIT*: *for repairs*) técnico/a; (*US RAIL*) maquinista *m/f*; **civil/mechanical** ~ ingeniero/a de caminos, canales y puertos/industrial.

engineering [ɛndʒɪ'nɪərɪŋ] *n* ingeniería ♦ *cpd* (*works, factory*) de componentes mecánicos.

engine failure, engine trouble *n* avería del motor.

England ['ɪŋglənd] *n* Inglaterra.

English ['ɪŋglɪʃ] *adj* inglés/esa ♦ *n* (*LING*) el inglés; **the** ~ *npl* los ingleses.

English Channel *n*: **the** ~ el Canal de la Mancha.

Englishman ['ɪŋglɪʃmən], **Englishwoman** ['ɪŋglɪʃwumən] *n* inglés/esa *m/f*.

English-speaker ['ɪŋglɪʃspiːkə*] *n* persona de habla inglesa.

English-speaking ['ɪŋglɪʃspiːkɪŋ] *adj* de habla inglesa.

engraving [ɪn'greɪvɪŋ] *n* grabado.

engrossed [ɪn'grəust] *adj*: ~ **in** absorto en.

engulf [ɪn'gʌlf] *vt* sumergir, hundir; (*subj*: *fire*) devorar.

enhance [ɪn'hɑːns] *vt* (*gen*) aumentar; (*beauty*) realzar; (*position, reputation*) mejorar.

enigma [ɪ'nɪgmə] *n* enigma *m*.

enigmatic [ɛnɪg'mætɪk] *adj* enigmático.

enjoy [ɪn'dʒɔɪ] *vt* (*have*: *health, fortune*) disfrutar de, gozar de; (*food*) comer con gusto; **I** ~ **doing...** me gusta hacer...; **to** ~ **o.s.** divertirse, pasarlo bien.

enjoyable [ɪn'dʒɔɪəbl] *adj* (*pleasant*) agradable; (*amusing*) divertido.

enjoyment [ɪn'dʒɔɪmənt] *n* (*use*) disfrute *m*; (*joy*) placer *m*.

enlarge [ɪn'lɑːdʒ] *vt* aumentar; (*broaden*) extender; (*PHOT*) ampliar ♦ *vi*: **to** ~ **on** (*subject*) tratar con más detalles.

enlarged [ɪn'lɑːdʒd] *adj* (*edition*) aumentado; (*MED*: *organ, gland*) dilatado.

enlargement [ɪn'lɑːdʒmənt] *n* (*PHOT*) ampliación *f*.

enlighten [ɪn'laɪtn] *vt* informar, instruir.

enlightened [ɪn'laɪtnd] *adj* iluminado; (*tolerant*) comprensivo.

enlightening [ɪn'laɪtnɪŋ] *adj* informativo, instructivo.

Enlightenment [ɪn'laɪtnmənt] *n* (*HISTORY*): **the** ~ la Ilustración, el Siglo de las Luces.

enlist [ɪn'lɪst] *vt* alistar; (*support*) conseguir ♦ *vi* alistarse; ~**ed man** (*US*: *MIL*) soldado raso.

enliven [ɪn'laɪvn] *vt* (*people*) animar; (*events*) avivar, animar.

enmity ['ɛnmɪtɪ] *n* enemistad *f*.

ennoble [ɪ'nəubl] *vt* ennoblecer.

enormity [ɪ'nɔːmɪtɪ] *n* enormidad *f*.

enormous [ɪ'nɔːməs] *adj* enorme.

enough [ɪ'nʌf] *adj*: ~ **time/books** bastante tiempo/bastantes libros ♦ *n*: **have you got** ~? ¿tiene usted bastante? ♦ *adv*: **big** ~ bastante grande; **he has not worked** ~ no ha trabajado bastante; **(that's)** ~! ¡basta ya!, ¡ya está bien!; **that's** ~**, thanks** con eso basta, gracias; **will 5 be** ~**?** ¿bastará con 5?; **I've had** ~ estoy harto; **he was kind** ~ **to lend me the money** tuvo la bondad *or* amabilidad de prestarme el dinero; **... which, funnily** ~ **...** ... lo que, por extraño que parezca ... .

enquire [ɪn'kwaɪə*] *vt, vi* = **inquire**.

enrage [ɪn'reɪdʒ] *vt* enfurecer.

enrich [ɪn'rɪtʃ] *vt* enriquecer.

enrol, (*US*) **enroll** [ɪn'rəul] *vt* (*members*) inscribir; (*SCOL*) matricular ♦ *vi* inscribirse; (*SCOL*) matricularse.

enrol(l)ment [ɪn'rəulmənt] *n* inscripción *f*; matriculación *f*.

en route [ɔn'ruːt] *adv* durante el viaje; ~ **for/from/to** camino de/de/a.

ensconce [ɪn'skɔns] *vt*: **to** ~ **o.s.** instalarse cómodamente, acomodarse.

ensemble [ɔn'sɔmbl] *n* (*MUS*) conjunto.

enshrine [ɪn'ʃraɪn] *vt* recoger.

ensign ['ɛnsaɪn] *n* (*flag*) bandera; (*NAUT*) alférez *m*.

enslave [ɪn'sleɪv] *vt* esclavizar.

ensue [ɪn'sjuː] *vi* seguirse; (*result*) resultar.

ensuing [ɪn'sjuːɪŋ] *adj* subsiguiente.

ensure [ɪn'ʃuə*] *vt* asegurar.

ENT *n abbr* (= *Ear, Nose and Throat*) otorrinolaringología.

entail [ɪn'teɪl] *vt* (*imply*) suponer; (*result in*) acarrear.

entangle [ɪn'tæŋgl] *vt* (*thread etc*) enredar, enmarañar; **to become** ~**d in sth** (*fig*) enredarse en algo.

entanglement [ɪn'tæŋglmənt] *n* enredo.

enter ['ɛntə*] *vt* (*room, profession*) entrar en; (*club*) hacerse socio de; (*army*) alistarse en; (*sb for a competition*) inscribir; (*write down*) anotar, apuntar; (*COMPUT*) introducir ♦ *vi* entrar; **to ~ for** *vt fus* presentarse a; **to ~ into** *vt fus* (*relations*) establecer; (*plans*) formar parte de; (*debate*) tomar parte en; (*negotiations*) entablar; (*agreement*) llegar a, firmar; **to ~ (up)on** *vt fus* (*career*) emprender.

enteritis [ɛntəˈraɪtɪs] *n* enteritis *f.*

enterprise [ˈɛntəpraɪz] *n* empresa; (*spirit*) iniciativa; **free ~** la libre empresa; **private ~** la iniciativa privada.

enterprising [ˈɛntəpraɪzɪŋ] *adj* emprendedor(a).

entertain [ɛntəˈteɪn] *vt* (*amuse*) divertir; (*receive: guest*) recibir (en casa); (*idea*) abrigar.

entertainer [ɛntəˈteɪnə*] *n* artista *m/f.*

entertaining [ɛntəˈteɪnɪŋ] *adj* divertido, entretenido ♦ *n*: **to do a lot of ~** dar muchas fiestas, tener muchos invitados.

entertainment [ɛntəˈteɪnmənt] *n* (*amusement*) diversión *f*; (*show*) espectáculo; (*party*) fiesta.

entertainment allowance *n* (*COMM*) gastos *mpl* de representación.

enthral [ɪnˈθrɔːl] *vt* embelesar, cautivar.

enthralled [ɪnˈθrɔːld] *adj* cautivado.

enthralling [ɪnˈθrɔːlɪŋ] *adj* cautivador(a).

enthuse [ɪnˈθuːz] *vi*: **to ~ about** *or* **over** entusiasmarse por.

enthusiasm [ɪnˈθuːzɪæzəm] *n* entusiasmo.

enthusiast [ɪnˈθuːzɪæst] *n* entusiasta *m/f.*

enthusiastic [ɪnθuːzɪˈæstɪk] *adj* entusiasta; **to be ~ about sb/sth** estar entusiasmado con algn/algo.

entice [ɪnˈtaɪs] *vt* tentar; (*seduce*) seducir.

entire [ɪnˈtaɪə*] *adj* entero, todo.

entirely [ɪnˈtaɪəlɪ] *adv* totalmente.

entirety [ɪnˈtaɪərətɪ] *n*: **in its ~** en su totalidad.

entitle [ɪnˈtaɪtl] *vt*: **to ~ sb to sth** dar a algn derecho a algo.

entitled [ɪnˈtaɪtld] *adj* (*book*) titulado; **to be ~ to sth/to do sth** tener derecho a algo/a hacer algo.

entity [ˈɛntɪtɪ] *n* entidad *f.*

entourage [ɔntuˈrɑːʒ] *n* séquito.

entrails [ˈɛntreɪlz] *npl* entrañas *fpl*; (*US*) asadura *sg*, menudos *mpl.*

entrance [ˈɛntrəns] *n* entrada ♦ *vt* [ɪnˈtrɑːns] encantar, hechizar; **to gain ~ to** (*university etc*) ingresar en.

entrance examination *n* (*to school*) examen *m* de ingreso.

entrance fee *n* entrada.

entrance ramp *n* (*US AUT*) rampa de acceso.

entrancing [ɪnˈtrɑːnsɪŋ] *adj* encantador(a).

entrant [ˈɛntrənt] *n* (*in race, competition*) participante *m/f*; (*in exam*) candidato/a.

entreat [ɛnˈtriːt] *vt* rogar, suplicar.

entrenched [ɛnˈtrɛntʃd] *adj*: **~ interests** intereses *mpl* creados.

entrepreneur [ɔntrəprəˈnəː*] *n* empresario/a, capitalista *m/f.*

entrepreneurial [ɔntrəprəˈnəːrɪəl] *adj* empresarial.

entrust [ɪnˈtrʌst] *vt*: **to ~ sth to sb** confiar algo a algn.

entry [ˈɛntrɪ] *n* entrada; (*permission to enter*) acceso; (*in register, diary, ship's log*) apunte *m*; (*in account book, ledger, list*) partida; **no ~** prohibido el paso; (*AUT*) dirección prohibida; **single/double ~ book-keeping** contabilidad *f* simple/por partida doble.

entry form *n* boletín *m* de inscripción.

entry phone *n* (*BRIT*) portero automático.

E-number [ˈiːnʌmbə*] *n* número E.

enumerate [ɪˈnjuːməreɪt] *vt* enumerar.

enunciate [ɪˈnʌnsɪeɪt] *vt* pronunciar; (*principle etc*) enunciar.

envelop [ɪnˈvɛləp] *vt* envolver.

envelope [ˈɛnvələup] *n* sobre *m.*

enviable [ˈɛnvɪəbl] *adj* envidiable.

envious [ˈɛnvɪəs] *adj* envidioso; (*look*) de envidia.

environment [ɪnˈvaɪərnmənt] *n* medio ambiente; (*surroundings*) entorno; **Department of the E~** ministerio del medio ambiente.

environmental [ɪnvaɪərnˈmɛntl] *adj* (medio) ambiental; **~ studies** (*in school etc*) ecología *sg.*

environmentalist [ɪnvaɪərnˈmɛntlɪst] *n* ecologista *m/f.*

environmentally [ɪnvaɪərnˈmɛntlɪ] *adv*: **~ sound/friendly** ecológico.

envisage [ɪnˈvɪzɪdʒ] *vt* (*foresee*) prever; (*imagine*) concebir.

envision [ɪnˈvɪʒən] *vt* imaginar.

envoy [ˈɛnvɔɪ] *n* enviado/a.

envy [ˈɛnvɪ] *n* envidia ♦ *vt* tener envidia a; **to ~ sb sth** envidiar algo a algn.

enzyme [ˈɛnzaɪm] *n* enzima *m or f.*

EPA *n abbr* (*US*: = *Environmental Protection Agency*) *Agencia del Medio Ambiente.*

ephemeral [ɪˈfɛmərl] *adj* efímero.

epic [ˈɛpɪk] *n* epopeya ♦ *adj* épico.

epicentre, (*US*) **epicenter** [ˈɛpɪsɛntə*] *n* epicentro.

epidemic [ɛpɪˈdɛmɪk] *n* epidemia.

epigram [ˈɛpɪgræm] *n* epigrama *m.*

epilepsy [ˈɛpɪlɛpsɪ] *n* epilepsia.

epileptic [ɛpɪˈlɛptɪk] *adj, n* epiléptico/a *m/f.*

epilogue [ˈɛpɪlɔg] *n* epílogo.

episcopal [ɪ'pɪskəpl] *adj* episcopal.
episode ['ɛpɪsəud] *n* episodio.
epistle [ɪ'pɪsl] *n* epístola.
epitaph ['ɛpɪtɑːf] *n* epitafio.
epithet ['ɛpɪθɛt] *n* epíteto.
epitome [ɪ'pɪtəmɪ] *n* arquetipo.
epitomize [ɪ'pɪtəmaɪz] *vt* representar.
epoch ['iːpɔk] *n* época.
eponymous [ɪ'pɔnɪməs] *adj* epónimo.
equable ['ɛkwəbl] *adj* (*climate*) estable; (*character*) ecuánime.
equal ['iːkwl] *adj* (*gen*) igual; (*treatment*) equitativo ♦ *n* igual *m/f* ♦ *vt* ser igual a; (*fig*) igualar; **to be ~ to** (*task*) estar a la altura de; **the E~ Opportunities Commission** (*BRIT*) *comisión para la igualdad de la mujer en el trabajo.*
equality [iː'kwɔlɪtɪ] *n* igualdad *f.*
equalize ['iːkwəlaɪz] *vt, vi* igualar; (*SPORT*) empatar.
equalizer ['iːkwəlaɪzə*] *n* igualada.
equally ['iːkwəlɪ] *adv* igualmente; (*share etc*) a partes iguales; **they are ~ clever** son tan listos uno como otro.
equals sign *n* signo igual.
equanimity [ɛkwə'nɪmɪtɪ] *n* ecuanimidad *f.*
equate [ɪ'kweɪt] *vt*: **to ~ sth with** equiparar algo con.
equation [ɪ'kweɪʒən] *n* (*MATH*) ecuación *f.*
equator [ɪ'kweɪtə*] *n* ecuador *m.*
equatorial [ɛkwə'tɔːrɪəl] *adj* ecuatorial.
Equatorial Guinea *n* Guinea Ecuatorial.
equestrian [ɪ'kwɛstrɪən] *adj* ecuestre ♦ *n* jinete *m/f.*
equilibrium [iːkwɪ'lɪbrɪəm] *n* equilibrio.
equinox ['iːkwɪnɔks] *n* equinoccio.
equip [ɪ'kwɪp] *vt* (*gen*) equipar; (*person*) proveer; **~ped with** (*machinery etc*) provisto de; **to be well ~ped** estar bien equipado; **he is well ~ped for the job** está bien preparado para este puesto.
equipment [ɪ'kwɪpmənt] *n* equipo.
equitable ['ɛkwɪtəbl] *adj* equitativo.
equities ['ɛkwɪtɪz] *npl* (*BRIT COMM*) acciones *fpl* ordinarias.
equity ['ɛkwɪtɪ] *n* (*fairness*) equidad *f*; (*ECON*: *of debtor*) valor *m* líquido.
equity capital *n* capital *m* propio, patrimonio neto.
equivalent [ɪ'kwɪvəlnt] *adj, n* equivalente *m*; **to be ~ to** equivaler a.
equivocal [ɪ'kwɪvəkl] *adj* equívoco.
equivocate [ɪ'kwɪvəkeɪt] *vi* andarse con ambigüedades.
equivocation [ɪkwɪvə'keɪʃən] *n* ambigüedad *f.*
ER *abbr* (*BRIT*: = *Elizabeth Regina*) *la reina Isabel.*
er [əː] *interj* (*col*: *in hesitation*) esto, este (*LAM*).
ERA *n abbr* (*US POL*: = *Equal Rights Amendment*) *enmienda sobre la igualdad de derechos de la mujer.*
era ['ɪərə] *n* era, época.
eradicate [ɪ'rædɪkeɪt] *vt* erradicar, extirpar.
erase [ɪ'reɪz] *vt* (*also COMPUT*) borrar.
eraser [ɪ'reɪzə*] *n* goma de borrar.
erect [ɪ'rɛkt] *adj* erguido ♦ *vt* erigir, levantar; (*assemble*) montar.
erection [ɪ'rɛkʃən] *n* (*of building*) construcción *f*; (*of machinery*) montaje *m*; (*structure*) edificio; (*MED*) erección *f.*
ergonomics [əːgə'nɔmɪks] *n* ergonomía.
ERISA *n abbr* (*US*: = *Employee Retirement Income Security Act*) *ley que regula las pensiones de jubilados.*
Eritrea [ɛrɪ'treɪə] *n* Eritrea.
ERM *n abbr* (= *Exchange Rate Mechanism*) (mecanismo de cambios del) SME *m.*
ermine ['əːmɪn] *n* armiño.
ERNIE ['əːnɪ] *n abbr* (*BRIT*: = *Electronic Random Number Indicating Equipment*) *ordenador que elige al azar los números ganadores de los bonos del Estado.*
erode [ɪ'rəud] *vt* (*GEO*) erosionar; (*metal*) corroer, desgastar.
erogenous zone [ɪ'rɔdʒənəs-] *n* zona erógena.
erosion [ɪ'rəuʒən] *n* erosión *f*, desgaste *m.*
erotic [ɪ'rɔtɪk] *adj* erótico.
eroticism [ɪ'rɔtɪsɪzm] *n* erotismo.
err [əː*] *vi* errar; (*REL*) pecar.
errand ['ɛrnd] *n* recado, mandado; **to run ~s** hacer recados; **~ of mercy** misión *f* de caridad.
errand boy *n* recadero.
erratic [ɪ'rætɪk] *adj* variable; (*results etc*) desigual, poco uniforme.
erroneous [ɪ'rəunɪəs] *adj* erróneo.
error ['ɛrə*] *n* error *m*, equivocación *f*; **typing/spelling ~** error *m* de mecanografía/ortografía; **in ~** por equivocación; **~s and omissions excepted** salvo error u omisión.
error message *n* (*COMPUT*) mensaje *m* de error.
erstwhile ['əːstwaɪl] *adj* antiguo, previo.
erudite ['ɛrudaɪt] *adj* erudito.
erudition [ɛru'dɪʃən] *n* erudición *f.*
erupt [ɪ'rʌpt] *vi* entrar en erupción; (*MED*) hacer erupción; (*fig*) estallar.
eruption [ɪ'rʌpʃən] *n* erupción *f*; (*fig*: *of anger, violence*) explosión *f*, estallido.
ESA *n abbr* (= *European Space Agency*) Agencia Espacial Europea.

escalate ['ɛskəleɪt] *vi* extenderse, intensificarse; (*costs*) aumentar vertiginosamente.
escalation clause [ɛskə'leɪʃən-] *n* cláusula de reajuste de los precios.
escalator ['ɛskəleɪtə*] *n* escalera mecánica.
escapade [ɛskə'peɪd] *n* aventura.
escape [ɪ'skeɪp] *n* (*gen*) fuga; (*TECH*) escape *m*; (*from duties*) escapatoria; (*from chase*) evasión *f* ♦ *vi* (*gen*) escaparse; (*flee*) huir, evadirse ♦ *vt* evitar, eludir; (*consequences*) escapar a; **to ~ from** (*place*) escaparse de; (*person*) huir de; (*clutches*) librarse de; **to ~ to** (*another place, freedom, safety*) huir a; **to ~ notice** pasar desapercibido.
escape artist *n* artista *m/f* de la evasión.
escape clause *n* (*fig: in agreement*) cláusula de excepción.
escapee [ɪskeɪ'piː] *n* fugado/a.
escape hatch *n* (*in submarine, space rocket*) escotilla de salvamento.
escape key *n* (*COMPUT*) tecla de escape.
escape route *n* (*from fire*) vía de escape.
escapism [ɪ'skeɪpɪzəm] *n* escapismo, evasión *f*.
escapist [ɪ'skeɪpɪst] *adj* escapista, de evasión ♦ *n* escapista *m/f*.
escapologist [ɛskə'pɔlədʒɪst] *n* (*BRIT*) = **escape artist**.
escarpment [ɪ'skɑːpmənt] *n* escarpa.
eschew [ɪs'tʃuː] *vt* evitar, abstenerse de.
escort ['ɛskɔːt] *n* acompañante *m/f*; (*MIL*) escolta; (*NAUT*) convoy *m* ♦ *vt* [ɪ'skɔːt] acompañar; (*MIL, NAUT*) escoltar.
escort agency *n* agencia de acompañantes.
Eskimo ['ɛskɪməu] *adj* esquimal ♦ *n* esquimal *m/f*; (*LING*) esquimal *m*.
ESL *n abbr* (*SCOL*) = *English as a Second Language*.
esophagus [iː'sɔfəgəs] *n* (*US*) = **oesophagus**.
esoteric [ɛsəu'tɛrɪk] *adj* esotérico.
ESP *n abbr* = **extrasensory perception**; (*SCOL: = English for Special Purposes*) *inglés especializado*.
esp. *abbr* = **especially**.
especially [ɪ'spɛʃlɪ] *adv* (*gen*) especialmente; (*above all*) sobre todo; (*particularly*) en especial.
espionage ['ɛspɪənɑːʒ] *n* espionaje *m*.
esplanade [ɛsplə'neɪd] *n* (*by sea*) paseo marítimo.
espouse [ɪ'spauz] *vt* adherirse a.
Esq. *abbr* (= *Esquire*) D.
Esquire [ɪ'skwaɪə*] *n*: **J. Brown, ~** Sr. D. J. Brown.
essay ['ɛseɪ] *n* (*SCOL*) redacción *f*; (: *longer*) trabajo.
essayist ['ɛseɪɪst] *n* ensayista *m/f*.
essence ['ɛsns] *n* esencia; **in ~** esencialmente; **speed is of the ~** es esencial hacerlo con la mayor prontitud.
essential [ɪ'sɛnʃl] *adj* (*necessary*) imprescindible; (*basic*) esencial ♦ *n* (*often pl*) lo esencial; **it is ~ that** es imprescindible que.
essentially [ɪ'sɛnʃlɪ] *adv* esencialmente.
EST *n abbr* (*US: = Eastern Standard Time*) *hora de invierno de Nueva York*.
est. *abbr* (= *established*) fundado; (= *estimated*) aprox.
establish [ɪ'stæblɪʃ] *vt* establecer; (*prove: fact, identity*) comprobar, verificar; (*prove*) demostrar; (*relations*) entablar.
established [ɪ'stæblɪʃt] *adj* (*business*) de buena reputación; (*staff*) de plantilla.
establishment [ɪ'stæblɪʃmənt] *n* (*also business*) establecimiento; **the E~** la clase dirigente; **a teaching ~** un centro de enseñanza.
estate [ɪ'steɪt] *n* (*land*) finca, hacienda; (*property*) propiedad *f*; (*inheritance*) herencia; (*POL*) estado; **housing ~** (*BRIT*) urbanización *f*; **industrial ~** polígono industrial.
estate agency *n* (*BRIT*) agencia inmobiliaria.
estate agent *n* (*BRIT*) agente *m/f* inmobiliario/a.
estate car *n* (*BRIT*) ranchera.
esteem [ɪ'stiːm] *n*: **to hold sb in high ~** estimar en mucho a algn ♦ *vt* estimar.
esthetic [iːs'θɛtɪk] *adj* (*US*) = **aesthetic**.
estimate ['ɛstɪmət] *n* estimación *f*; (*assessment*) tasa, cálculo; (*COMM*) presupuesto ♦ *vt* ['ɛstɪmeɪt] estimar; tasar, calcular; **to give sb an ~ of** presentar a algn un presupuesto de; **at a rough ~** haciendo un cálculo aproximado; **to ~ for** (*COMM*) hacer un presupuesto de, presupuestar.
estimation [ɛstɪ'meɪʃən] *n* opinión *f*, juicio; (*esteem*) aprecio; **in my ~** a mi juicio.
Estonia [ɛ'stəunɪə] *n* Estonia.
Estonian [ɛ'stəunɪən] *adj* estonio ♦ *n* estonio/a; (*LING*) estonio.
estranged [ɪ'streɪndʒd] *adj* separado.
estrangement [ɪ'streɪndʒmənt] *n* alejamiento, distanciamiento.
estrogen ['iːstrəudʒən] *n* (*US*) = **oestrogen**.
estuary ['ɛstjuərɪ] *n* estuario, ría.
ET *n abbr* (*BRIT: = Employment Training*) *plan estatal de formación para los*

desempleados ♦ *abbr* (*US*) = *Eastern Time*.
et al. *abbr* (= *et alii: and others*) et al.
etc *abbr* (= *et cetera*) etc.
etch [ɛtʃ] *vt* grabar al aguafuerte.
etching ['ɛtʃɪŋ] *n* aguafuerte *m or f*.
ETD *n abbr* = *estimated time of departure*.
eternal [ɪ'tə:nl] *adj* eterno.
eternity [ɪ'tə:nɪtɪ] *n* eternidad *f*.
ether ['i:θə*] *n* éter *m*.
ethereal [ɪ'θɪərɪəl] *adj* etéreo.
ethical ['ɛθɪkl] *adj* ético; (*honest*) honrado.
ethics ['ɛθɪks] *n* ética ♦ *npl* moralidad *f*.
Ethiopia [i:θɪ'əupɪə] *n* Etiopía.
Ethiopian [i:θɪ'əupɪən] *adj, n* etíope *m/f*.
ethnic ['ɛθnɪk] *adj* étnico.
ethnic cleansing [-klɛnzɪŋ] *n* limpieza étnica.
ethos ['i:θɔs] *n* (*of culture, group*) sistema *m* de valores.
etiquette ['ɛtɪkɛt] *n* etiqueta.
ETV *n abbr* (*US*: = *Educational Television*) *televisión f escolar*.
etymology [ɛtɪ'mɔlədʒɪ] *n* etimología.
EU *n abbr* (= *European Union*) UE *f*.
eucalyptus [ju:kə'lɪptəs] *n* eucalipto.
Eucharist ['ju:kərɪst] *n* Eucaristía.
eulogy ['ju:lədʒɪ] *n* elogio, encomio.
euphemism ['ju:fəmɪzm] *n* eufemismo.
euphemistic [ju:fə'mɪstɪk] *adj* eufemístico.
euphoria [ju:'fɔ:rɪə] *n* euforia.
Eurasia [juə'reɪʃə] *n* Eurasia.
Eurasian [juə'reɪʃən] *adj, n* eurasiático/a *m/f*.
Euratom [juə'rætəm] *n abbr* (= *European Atomic Energy Commission*) Euratom *m*.
Euro- *pref* euro-.
euro ['juərəu] *n* (*currency*) euro.
Eurocheque ['juərəutʃɛk] *n* Eurocheque *m*.
Eurocrat ['juərəukræt] *n* eurócrata *m/f*.
Eurodollar ['juərəudɔlə*] *n* eurodólar *m*.
Euroland ['juərəulænd] *n* Eurolandia.
Europe ['juərəp] *n* Europa.
European [juərə'pi:ən] *adj, n* europeo/a *m/f*.
European Court of Justice *n* Tribunal *m* de Justicia de las Comunidades Europeas.
European Economic Community *n* Comunidad *f* Económica Europea.
Euro-sceptic [juərəu'skɛptɪk] *n* euroescéptico/a.
euthanasia [ju:θə'neɪzɪə] *n* eutanasia.
evacuate [ɪ'vækjueɪt] *vt* evacuar; (*place*) desocupar.
evacuation [ɪvækju'eɪʃən] *n* evacuación *f*.
evacuee [ɪvækju'i:] *n* evacuado/a.
evade [ɪ'veɪd] *vt* evadir, eludir.
evaluate [ɪ'væljueɪt] *vt* evaluar; (*value*) tasar; (*evidence*) interpretar.
evangelical [i:væn'dʒɛlɪkəl] *adj* evangélico.
evangelist [ɪ'vændʒəlɪst] *n* evangelista *m*; (*preacher*) evangelizador(a) *m/f*.
evaporate [ɪ'væpəreɪt] *vi* evaporarse; (*fig*) desvanecerse ♦ *vt* evaporar.
evaporated milk [ɪ'væpəreɪtɪd-] *n* leche *f* evaporada.
evaporation [ɪvæpə'reɪʃən] *n* evaporación *f*.
evasion [ɪ'veɪʒən] *n* evasión *f*.
evasive [ɪ'veɪsɪv] *adj* evasivo.
eve [i:v] *n*: **on the ~ of** en vísperas de.
even ['i:vn] *adj* (*level*) llano; (*smooth*) liso; (*speed, temperature*) uniforme; (*number*) par; (*SPORT*) igual(es) ♦ *adv* hasta, incluso; **~ if, ~ though** aunque + *subjun*, así + *subjun* (*LAM*); **~ more** aun más; **~ so** aun así; **not ~** ni siquiera; **~ he was there** hasta él estaba allí; **~ on Sundays** incluso los domingos; **~ faster** aún más rápido; **to break ~** cubrir los gastos; **to get ~ with sb** ajustar cuentas con algn; **to ~ out** *vi* nivelarse.
even-handed [i:vn'hændɪd] *adj* imparcial.
evening ['i:vnɪŋ] *n* tarde *f*; (*dusk*) atardecer *m*; (*night*) noche *f*; **in the ~** por la tarde; **this ~** esta tarde *or* noche; **tomorrow/yesterday ~** mañana/ayer por la tarde *or* noche.
evening class *n* clase *f* nocturna.
evening dress *n* (*man's*) traje *m* de etiqueta; (*woman's*) traje *m* de noche.
evenly ['i:vnlɪ] *adv* de modo uniforme; (*divide*) equitativamente.
evensong ['i:vnsɔŋ] *n* vísperas *fpl*.
event [ɪ'vɛnt] *n* suceso, acontecimiento; (*SPORT*) prueba; **in the ~ of** en caso de; **in the ~** en realidad; **in the course of ~s** en el curso de los acontecimientos; **at all ~s, in any ~** en cualquier caso.
eventful [ɪ'vɛntful] *adj* azaroso; (*game etc*) lleno de emoción.
eventing [ɪ'vɛntɪŋ] *n* (*HORSERIDING*) competición *f*.
eventual [ɪ'vɛntʃuəl] *adj* final.
eventuality [ɪvɛntʃu'ælɪtɪ] *n* eventualidad *f*.
eventually [ɪ'vɛntʃuəlɪ] *adv* (*finally*) por fin; (*in time*) con el tiempo.
ever ['ɛvə*] *adv* nunca, jamás; (*at all times*) siempre; **for ~** (para) siempre; **the best ~** lo nunca visto; **did you ~ meet him?** ¿llegaste a conocerle?; **have you ~ been there?** ¿has estado allí alguna vez?; **have you ~ seen it?** ¿lo has visto alguna vez?; **better than ~** mejor que nunca; **thank you ~ so much** muchísimas gracias; **yours ~** (*in letters*) un abrazo de; **~ since** *adv* desde entonces ♦ *conj* después de que.
Everest ['ɛvərɪst] *n* (*also*: **Mount ~**) el Everest *m*.

evergreen ['ɛvəgri:n] *n* árbol *m* de hoja perenne.
everlasting [ɛvə'lɑ:stɪŋ] *adj* eterno, perpetuo.

KEYWORD

every ['ɛvrɪ] *adj* **1** (*each*) cada; **~ one of them** (*persons*) todos ellos/as; (*objects*) cada uno de ellos/as; **~ shop in the town was closed** todas las tiendas de la ciudad estaban cerradas
2 (*all possible*) todo/a; **I gave you ~ assistance** te di toda la ayuda posible; **I have ~ confidence in him** tiene toda mi confianza; **we wish you ~ success** te deseamos toda suerte de éxitos
3 (*showing recurrence*) todo/a; **~ day/week** todos los días/todas las semanas; **~ other car had been broken into** habían forzado uno de cada dos coches; **she visits me ~ other/third day** me visita cada dos/tres días; **~ now and then** de vez en cuando.

everybody ['ɛvrɪbɔdɪ] *pron* todos *pl*, todo el mundo; **~ knows about it** todo el mundo lo sabe; **~ else** todos los demás.
everyday ['ɛvrɪdeɪ] *adj* (*daily*: *use, occurrence, experience*) diario, cotidiano; (*usual*: *expression*) corriente; (*common*) vulgar; (*routine*) rutinario.
everyone ['ɛvrɪwʌn] = **everybody**.
everything ['ɛvrɪθɪŋ] *pron* todo; **~ is ready** todo está dispuesto; **he did ~ possible** hizo todo lo posible.
everywhere ['ɛvrɪwɛə*] *adv* (*be*) en todas partes; (*go*) a *or* por todas partes; **~ you go you meet...** en todas partes encontrarás....
evict [ɪ'vɪkt] *vt* desahuciar.
eviction [ɪ'vɪkʃən] *n* desahucio.
eviction notice *n* orden *f* de desahucio *or* desalojo (*LAM*).
evidence ['ɛvɪdəns] *n* (*proof*) prueba; (*of witness*) testimonio; (*facts*) datos *mpl*, hechos *mpl*; **to give ~** prestar declaración, dar testimonio.
evident ['ɛvɪdənt] *adj* evidente, manifiesto.
evidently ['ɛvɪdəntlɪ] *adv* (*obviously*) obviamente, evidentemente; (*apparently*) por lo visto.
evil ['i:vl] *adj* malo; (*influence*) funesto; (*smell*) horrible ♦ *n* mal *m*.
evildoer ['i:vldu:ə*] *n* malhechor(a) *m/f*.
evince [ɪ'vɪns] *vt* mostrar, dar señales de.
evocative [ɪ'vɔkətɪv] *adj* sugestivo, evocador(a).
evoke [ɪ'vəuk] *vt* evocar; (*admiration*) provocar.
evolution [i:və'lu:ʃən] *n* evolución *f*, desarrollo.
evolve [ɪ'vɔlv] *vt* desarrollar ♦ *vi* evolucionar, desarrollarse.
ewe [ju:] *n* oveja.
ex- [ɛks] *pref* (*former*: *husband, president etc*) ex-; (*out of*): **the price ~ works** precio de fábrica.
exacerbate [ɛk'sæsəbeɪt] *vt* exacerbar.
exact [ɪg'zækt] *adj* exacto ♦ *vt*: **to ~ sth (from)** exigir algo (de).
exacting [ɪg'zæktɪŋ] *adj* exigente; (*conditions*) arduo.
exactitude [ɪg'zæktɪtju:d] *n* exactitud *f*.
exactly [ɪg'zæktlɪ] *adv* exactamente; (*time*) en punto; **~!** ¡exacto!
exactness [ɪg'zæktnɪs] *n* exactitud *f*.
exaggerate [ɪg'zædʒəreɪt] *vt, vi* exagerar.
exaggerated [ɪg'zædʒəreɪtɪd] *adj* exagerado.
exaggeration [ɪgzædʒə'reɪʃən] *n* exageración *f*.
exalt [ɪg'zɔ:lt] *vt* (*praise*) ensalzar; (*elevate*) elevar.
exalted [ɪg'zɔ:ltɪd] *adj* (*position*) elevado; (*elated*) enardecido.
exam [ɪg'zæm] *n abbr* (*SCOL*) = **examination**.
examination [ɪgzæmɪ'neɪʃən] *n* (*gen*) examen *m*; (*LAW*) interrogación *f*; (*inquiry*) investigación *f*; **to take** *or* **sit an ~** hacer un examen; **the matter is under ~** se está examinando el asunto.
examine [ɪg'zæmɪn] *vt* (*gen*) examinar; (*inspect*: *machine, premises*) inspeccionar; (*SCOL, LAW*: *person*) interrogar; (*at customs*: *luggage, passport*) registrar; (*MED*) hacer un reconocimiento médico de, examinar.
examiner [ɪg'zæmɪnə*] *n* examinador(a) *m/f*.
example [ɪg'zɑ:mpl] *n* ejemplo; **for ~** por ejemplo; **to set a good/bad ~** dar buen/mal ejemplo.
exasperate [ɪg'zɑ:spəreɪt] *vt* exasperar, irritar; **~d by** *or* **at** *or* **with** exasperado por *or* con.
exasperating [ɪg'zɑ:spəreɪtɪŋ] *adj* irritante.
exasperation [ɪgzɑ:spə'reɪʃən] *n* exasperación *f*, irritación *f*.
excavate ['ɛkskəveɪt] *vt* excavar.
excavation [ɛkskə'veɪʃən] *n* excavación *f*.
excavator ['ɛkskəveɪtə*] *n* excavadora.
exceed [ɪk'si:d] *vt* exceder; (*number*) pasar de; (*speed limit*) sobrepasar; (*limits*) rebasar; (*powers*) excederse en; (*hopes*) superar.
exceedingly [ɪk'si:dɪŋlɪ] *adv* sumamente,

sobremanera.
excel [ɪk'sɛl] *vi* sobresalir; **to ~ o.s.** lucirse.
excellence ['ɛksələns] *n* excelencia.
Excellency ['ɛksələnsɪ] *n*: **His ~** Su Excelencia.
excellent ['ɛksələnt] *adj* excelente.
except [ɪk'sɛpt] *prep* (*also*: **~ for, ~ing**) excepto, salvo ♦ *vt* exceptuar, excluir; **~ if/when** excepto si/cuando; **~ that** salvo que.
exception [ɪk'sɛpʃən] *n* excepción *f*; **to take ~ to** ofenderse por; **with the ~ of** a excepción de; **to make an ~** hacer una excepción.
exceptional [ɪk'sɛpʃənl] *adj* excepcional.
excerpt ['ɛksə:pt] *n* extracto.
excess [ɪk'sɛs] *n* exceso; **in ~ of** superior a; *see also* **excesses.**
excess baggage *n* exceso de equipaje.
excesses *npl* excesos *mpl*.
excess fare *n* suplemento.
excessive [ɪk'sɛsɪv] *adj* excesivo.
excess supply *n* exceso de oferta.
excess weight *n* exceso de peso.
exchange [ɪks'tʃeɪndʒ] *n* cambio; (*of prisoners*) canje *m*; (*of ideas*) intercambio; (*also*: **telephone ~**) central *f* (telefónica) ♦ *vt* intercambiar; **to ~ (for)** cambiar (por); **in ~ for** a cambio de; **foreign ~** (*COMM*) divisas *fpl*.
exchange control *n* control *m* de divisas.
exchange rate *n* tipo de cambio.
exchequer [ɪks'tʃɛkə*] *n*: **the ~** (*BRIT*) Hacienda.
excisable [ɛk'saɪzəbl] *adj* sujeto al pago de impuestos sobre el consumo.
excise ['ɛksaɪz] *n* impuestos *mpl* sobre el consumo interior.
excitable [ɪk'saɪtəbl] *adj* excitable.
excite [ɪk'saɪt] *vt* (*stimulate*) entusiasmar; (*anger*) suscitar, provocar; (*move*) emocionar; **to get ~d** emocionarse.
excitement [ɪk'saɪtmənt] *n* emoción *f*.
exciting [ɪk'saɪtɪŋ] *adj* emocionante.
excl. *abbr* = **excluding; exclusive (of).**
exclaim [ɪk'skleɪm] *vi* exclamar.
exclamation [ɛksklə'meɪʃən] *n* exclamación *f*.
exclamation mark *n* signo de admiración.
exclude [ɪk'sklu:d] *vt* excluir; (*except*) exceptuar.
excluding [ɪks'klu:dɪŋ] *prep*: **~ VAT** IVA no incluido.
exclusion [ɪk'sklu:ʒən] *n* exclusión *f*; **to the ~ of** con exclusión de.
exclusion clause *n* cláusula de exclusión.
exclusion zone *n* zona de exclusión.
exclusive [ɪk'sklu:sɪv] *adj* exclusivo; (*club, district*) selecto; **~ of tax** excluyendo impuestos; **~ of postage/service** franqueo/servicio no incluido; **from 1st to 13th March ~** del 1 al 13 de marzo exclusive.
exclusively [ɪk'sklu:sɪvlɪ] *adv* únicamente.
excommunicate [ɛkskə'mju:nɪkeɪt] *vt* excomulgar.
excrement ['ɛkskrəmənt] *n* excremento.
excrete [ɪk'skri:t] *vi* excretar.
excruciating [ɪk'skru:ʃɪeɪtɪŋ] *adj* (*pain*) agudísimo, atroz.
excursion [ɪk'skə:ʃən] *n* excursión *f*.
excursion ticket *n* billete *m* (especial) de excursión.
excusable [ɪk'skju:səbl] *adj* perdonable.
excuse *n* [ɪk'skju:s] disculpa, excusa; (*evasion*) pretexto ♦ *vt* [ɪk'skju:z] disculpar, perdonar; (*justify*) justificar; **to make ~s for sb** presentar disculpas por algn; **to ~ sb from doing sth** dispensar a algn de hacer algo; **to ~ o.s. (for (doing) sth)** pedir disculpas a algn (por (hacer) algo); **~ me!** ¡perdone!; (*attracting attention*) ¡oiga(, por favor)!; **if you will ~ me** con su permiso.
ex-directory ['ɛksdɪ'rɛktərɪ] *adj* (*BRIT*): **~ (phone) number** número que no figura en la guía (telefónica).
execrable ['ɛksɪkrəbl] *adj* execrable, abominable; (*manners*) detestable.
execute ['ɛksɪkju:t] *vt* (*plan*) realizar; (*order*) cumplir; (*person*) ajusticiar, ejecutar.
execution [ɛksɪ'kju:ʃən] *n* realización *f*; cumplimiento; ejecución *f*.
executioner [ɛksɪ'kju:ʃənə*] *n* verdugo.
executive [ɪg'zɛkjutɪv] *n* (*COMM*) ejecutivo/a; (*POL*) poder *m* ejecutivo ♦ *adj* ejecutivo; (*car, plane, position*) de ejecutivo; (*offices, suite*) de la dirección; (*secretary*) de dirección.
executive director *n* director(a) *m/f* ejecutivo/a.
executor [ɪg'zɛkjutə*] *n* albacea *m*, testamentario.
exemplary [ɪg'zɛmplərɪ] *adj* ejemplar.
exemplify [ɪg'zɛmplɪfaɪ] *vt* ejemplificar.
exempt [ɪg'zɛmpt] *adj*: **~ from** exento de ♦ *vt*: **to ~ sb from** eximir a algn de.
exemption [ɪg'zɛmpʃən] *n* exención *f*; (*immunity*) inmunidad *f*.
exercise ['ɛksəsaɪz] *n* ejercicio ♦ *vt* ejercer; (*patience etc*) proceder con; (*dog*) sacar de paseo ♦ *vi* hacer ejercicio.
exercise bike *n* bicicleta estática.
exercise book *n* cuaderno de ejercicios.
exert [ɪg'zə:t] *vt* ejercer; (*strength, force*)

emplear; **to ~ o.s.** esforzarse.
exertion [ɪg'zəːʃən] *n* esfuerzo.
exfoliant [ɛks'fəulɪənt] *n* exfoliante *m.*
ex gratia ['ɛks'greɪʃə] *adj*: **~ payment** pago a título voluntario.
exhale [ɛks'heɪl] *vt* despedir, exhalar ♦ *vi* espirar.
exhaust [ɪg'zɔːst] *n* (*pipe*) (tubo de) escape *m*; (*fumes*) gases *mpl* de escape ♦ *vt* agotar; **to ~ o.s.** agotarse.
exhausted [ɪg'zɔːstɪd] *adj* agotado.
exhausting [ɪg'zɔːstɪŋ] *adj*: **an ~ journey/day** un viaje/día agotador.
exhaustion [ɪg'zɔːstʃən] *n* agotamiento; **nervous ~** agotamiento nervioso.
exhaustive [ɪg'zɔːstɪv] *adj* exhaustivo.
exhibit [ɪg'zɪbɪt] *n* (*ART*) obra expuesta; (*LAW*) objeto expuesto ♦ *vt* (*show*: *emotions*) manifestar; (: *courage, skill*) demostrar; (*paintings*) exponer.
exhibition [ɛksɪ'bɪʃən] *n* exposición *f.*
exhibitionist [ɛksɪ'bɪʃənɪst] *n* exhibicionista *m/f.*
exhibitor [ɪg'zɪbɪtə*] *n* expositor(a) *m/f.*
exhilarating [ɪg'zɪləreɪtɪŋ] *adj* estimulante, tónico.
exhilaration [ɪgzɪlə'reɪʃən] *n* júbilo.
exhort [ɪg'zɔːt] *vt* exhortar.
exile ['ɛksaɪl] *n* exilio; (*person*) exiliado/a ♦ *vt* desterrar, exiliar.
exist [ɪg'zɪst] *vi* existir.
existence [ɪg'zɪstəns] *n* existencia.
existentialism [ɛgzɪs'tɛnʃəlɪzəm] *n* existencialismo.
existing [ɪg'zɪstɪŋ] *adj* existente, actual.
exit ['ɛksɪt] *n* salida ♦ *vi* (*THEAT*) hacer mutis; (*COMPUT*) salir (del sistema).
exit poll *n encuesta a la salida de los colegios electorales.*
exit ramp *n* (*US AUT*) vía de acceso.
exit visa *n* visado de salida.
exodus ['ɛksədəs] *n* éxodo.
ex officio ['ɛksə'fɪʃɪəu] *adj* de pleno derecho ♦ *adv* ex oficio.
exonerate [ɪg'zɔnəreɪt] *vt*: **to ~ from** exculpar de.
exorbitant [ɪg'zɔːbɪtənt] *adj* (*price, demands*) exorbitante, excesivo.
exorcize ['ɛksɔːsaɪz] *vt* exorcizar.
exotic [ɪg'zɔtɪk] *adj* exótico.
expand [ɪk'spænd] *vt* ampliar, extender; (*number*) aumentar ♦ *vi* (*trade etc*) ampliarse, expandirse; (*gas, metal*) dilatarse; **to ~ on** (*notes, story etc*) ampliar.
expanse [ɪk'spæns] *n* extensión *f.*
expansion [ɪk'spænʃən] *n* ampliación *f*; aumento; (*of trade*) expansión *f.*
expansionism [ɪk'spænʃənɪzəm] *n* expansionismo.
expansionist [ɪk'spænʃənɪst] *adj* expansionista.
expatriate [ɛks'pætrɪət] *n* expatriado/a.
expect [ɪk'spɛkt] *vt* (*gen*) esperar; (*count on*) contar con; (*suppose*) suponer ♦ *vi*: **to be ~ing** estar encinta; **to ~ to do sth** esperar hacer algo; **as ~ed** como era de esperar; **I ~ so** supongo que sí.
expectancy [ɪk'spɛktənsɪ] *n* (*anticipation*) expectación *f*; **life ~** esperanza de vida.
expectantly [ɪk'spɛktəntlɪ] *adv* (*look, listen*) con expectación.
expectant mother [ɪk'spɛktənt-] *n* futura madre *f.*
expectation [ɛkspɛk'teɪʃən] *n* esperanza, expectativa; **in ~ of** esperando; **against** *or* **contrary to all ~(s)** en contra de todas las previsiones; **to come** *or* **live up to sb's ~s** resultar tan bueno como se esperaba; **to fall short of sb's ~s** no cumplir las esperanzas de algn, decepcionar a algn.
expedience [ɪk'spiːdɪəns], **expediency** [ɪk'spiːdɪənsɪ] *n* conveniencia.
expedient [ɪk'spiːdɪənt] *adj* conveniente, oportuno ♦ *n* recurso, expediente *m.*
expedite ['ɛkspɪdaɪt] *vt* (*speed up*) acelerar; (: *progress*) facilitar.
expedition [ɛkspə'dɪʃən] *n* expedición *f.*
expeditionary force [ɛkspə'dɪʃnrɪ-] *n* cuerpo expedicionario.
expel [ɪk'spɛl] *vt* expulsar.
expend [ɪk'spɛnd] *vt* gastar; (*use up*) consumir.
expendable [ɪk'spɛndəbl] *adj* prescindible.
expenditure [ɪk'spɛndɪtʃə*] *n* gastos *mpl*, desembolso; (*of time, effort*) gasto.
expense [ɪk'spɛns] *n* gasto, gastos *mpl*; (*high cost*) coste *m*; **~s** *npl* (*COMM*) gastos *mpl*; **at the ~ of** a costa de; **to meet the ~ of** hacer frente a los gastos de.
expense account *n* cuenta de gastos (de representación).
expensive [ɪk'spɛnsɪv] *adj* caro, costoso.
experience [ɪk'spɪərɪəns] *n* experiencia ♦ *vt* experimentar; (*suffer*) sufrir; **to learn by ~** aprender con la experiencia.
experienced [ɪk'spɪərɪənst] *adj* experimentado.
experiment [ɪk'spɛrɪmənt] *n* experimento ♦ *vi* hacer experimentos, experimentar; **to perform** *or* **carry out an ~** realizar un experimento; **as an ~** como experimento; **to ~ with a new vaccine** experimentar con una vacuna nueva.
experimental [ɪkspɛrɪ'mɛntl] *adj* experimental; **the process is still at the ~**

stage el proceso está todavía en prueba.
expert ['ɛkspəːt] *adj* experto, perito ♦ *n* experto/a, perito/a; (*specialist*) especialista *m/f*; ~ **witness** (*LAW*) testigo pericial; ~ **in** *or* **at doing sth** experto *or* perito en hacer algo; **an** ~ **on sth** un experto en algo.
expertise [ɛkspəː'tiːz] *n* pericia.
expiration [ɛkspɪ'reɪʃən] *n* (*gen*) expiración *f*, vencimiento.
expire [ɪk'spaɪə*] *vi* (*gen*) caducar, vencerse.
expiry [ɪk'spaɪərɪ] *n* caducidad *f*, vencimiento.
explain [ɪk'spleɪn] *vt* explicar; (*mystery*) aclarar.
►**explain away** *vt* justificar.
explanation [ɛksplə'neɪʃən] *n* explicación *f*; aclaración *f*; **to find an** ~ **for sth** encontrarle una explicación a algo.
explanatory [ɪk'splænətrɪ] *adj* explicativo; aclaratorio.
expletive [ɪk'spliːtɪv] *n* imprecación *f*.
explicable [ɪk'splɪkəbl] *adj* explicable.
explicit [ɪk'splɪsɪt] *adj* explícito.
explicitly [ɪk'splɪsɪtlɪ] *adv* explícitamente.
explode [ɪk'spləud] *vi* estallar, explotar; (*with anger*) reventar ♦ *vt* hacer explotar; (*fig*: *theory, myth*) demoler.
exploit ['ɛksplɔɪt] *n* hazaña ♦ *vt* [ɪk'splɔɪt] explotar.
exploitation [ɛksplɔɪ'teɪʃən] *n* explotación *f*.
exploration [ɛksplə'reɪʃən] *n* exploración *f*.
exploratory [ɪk'splɔrətrɪ] *adj* (*fig*: *talks*) exploratorio, preliminar.
explore [ɪk'splɔː*] *vt* explorar; (*fig*) examinar, sondear.
explorer [ɪk'splɔːrə*] *n* explorador(a) *m/f*.
explosion [ɪk'spləuʒən] *n* explosión *f*.
explosive [ɪk'spləusɪv] *adj*, *n* explosivo.
exponent [ɪk'spəunənt] *n* partidario/a; (*of skill, activity*) exponente *m/f*.
export *vt* [ɛk'spɔːt] exportar ♦ *n* ['ɛkspɔːt] exportación *f* ♦ *cpd* de exportación.
exportation [ɛkspɔː'teɪʃən] *n* exportación *f*.
export drive *n* campaña de exportación.
exporter [ɛk'spɔːtə*] *n* exportador(a) *m/f*.
export licence *n* licencia de exportación.
export manager *n* gerente *m/f* de exportación.
export trade *n* comercio exterior.
expose [ɪk'spəuz] *vt* exponer; (*unmask*) desenmascarar.
exposé [ɪk'spəuzeɪ] *n* relevación *f*.
exposed [ɪk'spəuzd] *adj* expuesto; (*land, house*) desprotegido; (*ELEC*: *wire*) al aire; (*pipe, beam*) al descubierto.
exposition [ɛkspə'zɪʃən] *n* exposición *f*.
exposure [ɪk'spəuʒə*] *n* exposición *f*; (*PHOT*: *speed*) (tiempo *m* de) exposición *f*; (: *shot*) fotografía; **to die from** ~ (*MED*) morir de frío.
exposure meter *n* fotómetro.
expound [ɪk'spaund] *vt* exponer; (*theory, text*) comentar; (*one's views*) explicar.
express [ɪk'sprɛs] *adj* (*definite*) expreso, explícito; (*BRIT*: *letter etc*) urgente ♦ *n* (*train*) rápido ♦ *adv* (*send*) por correo extraordinario ♦ *vt* expresar; (*squeeze*) exprimir; **to send sth** ~ enviar algo por correo urgente; **to** ~ **o.s.** expresarse.
expression [ɪk'sprɛʃən] *n* expresión *f*.
expressionism [ɪk'sprɛʃənɪzm] *n* expresionismo.
expressive [ɪk'sprɛsɪv] *adj* expresivo.
expressly [ɪk'sprɛslɪ] *adv* expresamente.
expressway [ɪk'sprɛsweɪ] *n* (*US*: *urban motorway*) autopista.
expropriate [ɛks'prəuprɪeɪt] *vt* expropiar.
expulsion [ɪk'spʌlʃən] *n* expulsión *f*.
expurgate ['ɛkspəgeɪt] *vt* expurgar.
exquisite [ɛk'skwɪzɪt] *adj* exquisito.
exquisitely [ɛk'skwɪzɪtlɪ] *adv* exquisitamente.
ex-serviceman ['ɛks'səːvɪsmən] *n* ex-combatiente *m*.
ext. *abbr* (*TEL*) = **extension.**
extemporize [ɪk'stɛmpəraɪz] *vi* improvisar.
extend [ɪk'stɛnd] *vt* (*visit, street*) prolongar; (*building*) ampliar; (*thanks, friendship etc*) extender; (*COMM*: *credit*) conceder; (*deadline*) prorrogar ♦ *vi* (*land*) extenderse; **the contract ~s to/for ...** el contrato se prolonga hasta/por ....
extension [ɪk'stɛnʃən] *n* extensión *f*; (*building*) ampliación *f*; (*TEL*: *line*) extensión *f*; (: *telephone*) supletorio *m*; (*of deadline*) prórroga; ~ **3718** extensión 3718.
extension cable *n* (*ELEC*) alargador *m*.
extensive [ɪk'stɛnsɪv] *adj* (*gen*) extenso; (*damage*) importante; (*knowledge*) amplio.
extensively [ɪk'stɛnsɪvlɪ] *adv* (*altered, damaged etc*) extensamente; **he's travelled** ~ ha viajado por muchos países.
extent [ɪk'stɛnt] *n* (*breadth*) extensión *f*; (*scope*: *of knowledge, activities*) alcance *m*; (*degree*: *of damage, loss*) grado; **to some** ~ hasta cierto punto; **to a certain** ~ hasta cierto punto; **to a large** ~ en gran parte; **to the** ~ **of...** hasta el punto de...; **to such an** ~ **that...** hasta tal punto que...; **to what** ~? ¿hasta qué punto?; **debts to the** ~ **of £5000** deudas por la cantidad de £5000.
extenuating [ɪk'stɛnjueɪtɪŋ] *adj*: ~

circumstances circunstancias *fpl* atenuantes.
exterior [ɛk'stɪərɪə*] *adj* exterior, externo ♦ *n* exterior *m.*
exterminate [ɪk'stəːmɪneɪt] *vt* exterminar.
extermination [ɪkstəːmɪ'neɪʃən] *n* exterminio.
external [ɛk'stəːnl] *adj* externo, exterior ♦ *n*: **the ~s** la apariencia exterior; **~ affairs** asuntos *mpl* exteriores; **for ~ use only** (*MED*) para uso tópico.
externally [ɛk'stəːnəlɪ] *adv* por fuera.
extinct [ɪk'stɪŋkt] *adj* (*volcano*) extinguido, apagado; (*race*) extinguido.
extinction [ɪk'stɪŋkʃən] *n* extinción *f.*
extinguish [ɪk'stɪŋgwɪʃ] *vt* extinguir, apagar.
extinguisher [ɪk'stɪŋgwɪʃə*] *n* extintor *m.*
extol, (*US*) extoll [ɪk'stəul] *vt* (*merits, virtues*) ensalzar, alabar; (*person*) alabar, elogiar.
extort [ɪk'stɔːt] *vt* sacar a la fuerza; (*confession*) arrancar.
extortion [ɪk'stɔːʃən] *n* extorsión *f.*
extortionate [ɪk'stɔːʃnət] *adj* excesivo, exorbitante.
extra ['ɛkstrə] *adj* adicional ♦ *adv* (*in addition*) más ♦ *n* (*addition*) extra *m*, suplemento; (*THEAT*) extra *m/f*, comparsa *m/f*; (*newspaper*) edición *f* extraordinaria; **wine will cost ~** el vino se paga aparte; **~ large sizes** tallas extragrandes; *see also* **extras.**
extra... ['ɛkstrə] *pref* extra... .
extract *vt* [ɪk'strækt] sacar; (*tooth*) extraer; (*confession*) arrancar ♦ *n* ['ɛkstrækt] fragmento; (*CULIN*) extracto.
extraction [ɪk'strækʃən] *n* extracción *f*; (*origin*) origen *m.*
extractor fan [ɪk'stræktə-] *n* extractor *m* de humos.
extracurricular [ɛkstrəkə'rɪkjulə*] *adj* (*SCOL*) extraescolar.
extradite ['ɛkstrədaɪt] *vt* extraditar.
extradition [ɛkstrə'dɪʃən] *n* extradición *f.*
extramarital [ɛkstrə'mærɪtl] *adj* extramatrimonial.
extramural [ɛkstrə'mjuərl] *adj* extra-académico.
extraneous [ɪk'streɪnɪəs] *adj* extraño, ajeno.
extraordinary [ɪk'strɔːdnrɪ] *adj* extraordinario; (*odd*) raro; **the ~ thing is that ...** lo más extraordinario es que ....
extraordinary general meeting *n* junta general extraordinaria.
extrapolation [ɪkstræpə'leɪʃən] *n* extrapolación *f.*
extras *npl* (*additional expense*) extras *mpl.*
extrasensory perception (ESP) ['ɛkstrə'sɛnsərɪ-] *n* percepción *f* extrasensorial.
extra time *n* (*FOOTBALL*) prórroga.
extravagance [ɪk'strævəgəns] *n* (*excessive spending*) derroche *m*; (*thing bought*) extravagancia.
extravagant [ɪk'strævəgənt] *adj* (*wasteful*) derrochador(a); (*taste, gift*) excesivamente caro; (*price*) exorbitante; (*praise*) excesivo.
extreme [ɪk'striːm] *adj* extremo; (*poverty etc*) extremado; (*case*) excepcional ♦ *n* extremo; **the ~ left/right** (*POL*) la extrema izquierda/derecha; **~s of temperature** temperaturas extremas.
extremely [ɪk'striːmlɪ] *adv* sumamente, extremadamente.
extremist [ɪk'striːmɪst] *adj, n* extremista *m/f.*
extremity [ɪk'strɛmətɪ] *n* extremidad *f*, punta; (*need*) apuro, necesidad *f*; **extremities** *npl* (*hands and feet*) extremidades *fpl.*
extricate ['ɛkstrɪkeɪt] *vt*: **to ~ o.s. from** librarse de.
extrovert ['ɛkstrəvəːt] *n* extrovertido/a.
exuberance [ɪg'zjuːbərns] *n* exuberancia.
exuberant [ɪg'zjuːbərnt] *adj* (*person*) eufórico; (*style*) exuberante.
exude [ɪg'zjuːd] *vt* rezumar.
exult [ɪg'zʌlt] *vi* regocijarse.
exultant [ɪg'zʌltənt] *adj* (*person*) regocijado, jubiloso; (*shout, expression, smile*) de júbilo.
exultation [ɛgzʌl'teɪʃən] *n* regocijo, júbilo.
eye [aɪ] *n* ojo ♦ *vt* mirar; **to keep an ~ on** vigilar; **as far as the ~ can see** hasta donde alcanza la vista; **with an ~ to doing sth** con vistas *or* miras a hacer algo; **to have an ~ for sth** tener mucha vista *or* buen ojo para algo; **there's more to this than meets the ~** esto tiene su miga.
eyeball ['aɪbɔːl] *n* globo ocular.
eyebath ['aɪbɑːθ] *n* baño ocular, lavaojos *m inv.*
eyebrow ['aɪbrau] *n* ceja.
eyebrow pencil *n* lápiz *m* de cejas.
eye-catching ['aɪkætʃɪŋ] *adj* llamativo.
eye cup *n* (*US*) = **eyebath.**
eyedrops ['aɪdrɔps] *npl* gotas *fpl* para los ojos.
eyeful ['aɪful] *n* (*col*): **to get an ~ of sth** ver bien algo.
eyelash ['aɪlæʃ] *n* pestaña.
eyelet ['aɪlɪt] *n* ojete *m.*
eye-level ['aɪlɛvl] *adj* a la altura de los ojos.

eyelid ['aɪlɪd] *n* párpado.
eyeliner ['aɪlaɪnə*] *n* lápiz *m* de ojos.
eye-opener ['aɪəupnə*] *n* revelación *f*, gran sorpresa.
eyeshadow ['aɪʃædəu] *n* sombra de ojos.
eyesight ['aɪsaɪt] *n* vista.
eyesore ['aɪsɔː*] *n* monstruosidad *f*.
eyestrain ['aɪstreɪn] *n*: **to get** ~ cansar la vista *or* los ojos.
eyetooth, *pl* **eyeteeth** ['aɪtuːθ, -tiːθ] *n* colmillo; **to give one's eyeteeth for sth/to do sth** (*col, fig*) dar un ojo de la cara por algo/por hacer algo.
eyewash ['aɪwɔʃ] *n* (*fig*) disparates *mpl*, tonterías *fpl*.
eye witness *n* testigo *m/f* ocular.
eyrie ['ɪərɪ] *n* aguilera.

Ff

F, f [ɛf] *n* (*letter*) F, f *f*; (*MUS*) fa *m*; **F for Frederick,** (*US*) **F for Fox** F de Francia.
F. *abbr* = **Fahrenheit.**
FA *n abbr* (*BRIT*: = *Football Association*) ≈ AFE *f* (*SP*).
FAA *n abbr* (*US*) = *Federal Aviation Administration.*
fable ['feɪbl] *n* fábula.
fabric ['fæbrɪk] *n* tejido, tela.
fabricate ['fæbrɪkeɪt] *vt* fabricar; (*fig*) inventar.
fabrication [fæbrɪ'keɪʃən] *n* fabricación *f*; (*fig*) invención *f*.
fabric ribbon *n* (*for typewriter*) cinta de tela.
fabulous ['fæbjuləs] *adj* fabuloso.
façade [fə'sɑːd] *n* fachada.
face [feɪs] *n* (*ANAT*) cara, rostro; (*of clock*) esfera, cara; (*side*) cara; (*surface*) superficie *f* ♦ *vt* mirar a; (*fig*) enfrentarse a; ~ **down** (*person, card*) boca abajo; **to lose** ~ desprestigiarse; **to save** ~ salvar las apariencias; **to make** *or* **pull a** ~ hacer muecas; **in the** ~ **of** (*difficulties etc*) en vista de, ante; **on the** ~ **of it** a primera vista; ~ **to** ~ cara a cara; **to** ~ **the fact that** ... reconocer que ....
▸**face up to** *vt fus* hacer frente a, enfrentarse a.
face cloth *n* (*BRIT*) toallita.
face cream *n* crema (de belleza).
faceless ['feɪslɪs] *adj* (*fig*) anónimo.
face lift *n* lifting *m*, estirado facial.
face powder *n* polvos *mpl* para la cara.
face-saving ['feɪsseɪvɪŋ] *adj* para salvar las apariencias.
facet ['fæsɪt] *n* faceta.
facetious [fə'siːʃəs] *adj* chistoso.
facetiously [fə'siːʃəslɪ] *adv* chistosamente.
face value *n* (*of stamp*) valor *m* nominal; **to take sth at** ~ (*fig*) tomar algo en sentido literal, aceptar las apariencias de algo.
facial ['feɪʃəl] *adj* de la cara ♦ *n* (*also*: **beauty** ~) tratamiento facial, limpieza.
facile ['fæsaɪl] *adj* superficial.
facilitate [fə'sɪlɪteɪt] *vt* facilitar.
facility [fə'sɪlɪtɪ] *n* facilidad *f*; **facilities** *npl* instalaciones *fpl*; **credit** ~ facilidades de crédito.
facing ['feɪsɪŋ] *prep* frente a ♦ *adj* de enfrente.
facsimile [fæk'sɪmɪlɪ] *n* facsímil(e) *m*.
fact [fækt] *n* hecho; **in** ~ en realidad; **to know for a** ~ **that** ... saber a ciencia cierta que ....
fact-finding ['fæktfaɪndɪŋ] *adj*: **a** ~ **tour/mission** un viaje/una misión de reconocimiento.
faction ['fækʃən] *n* facción *f*.
factional ['fækʃənl] *adj* (*fighting*) entre distintas facciones.
factor ['fæktə*] *n* factor *m*; (*COMM*: *person*) agente *m/f* comisionado/a ♦ *vi* (*COMM*) comprar deudas; **safety** ~ factor de seguridad.
factory ['fæktərɪ] *n* fábrica.
factory farming *n* cría industrial.
factory floor *n* (*workers*) trabajadores *mpl*, mano *f* de obra directa; (*area*) talleres *mpl*.
factory ship *n* buque *m* factoría.
factual ['fæktjuəl] *adj* basado en los hechos.
faculty ['fækəltɪ] *n* facultad *f*; (*US*: *teaching staff*) personal *m* docente.
fad [fæd] *n* novedad *f*, moda.
fade [feɪd] *vi* descolorarse, desteñirse; (*sound, hope*) desvanecerse; (*light*) apagarse; (*flower*) marchitarse.
▸**fade away** *vi* (*sound*) apagarse.
▸**fade in** *vt* (*TV, CINE*) fundir; (*RADIO*: *sound*) mezclar ♦ *vi* (*TV, CINE*) fundirse; (*RADIO*) oírse por encima.
▸**fade out** *vt* (*TV, CINE*) fundir; (*RADIO*) apagar, disminuir el volumen de ♦ *vi* (*TV, CINE*) desvanecerse; (*RADIO*) apagarse, dejarse de oír.
faded ['feɪdɪd] *adj* (*clothes, colour*) descolorido; (*flower*) marchito.
faeces, (*US*) **feces** ['fiːsiːz] *npl* excremento

sg, heces *fpl*.
fag [fæg] *n* (*BRIT col*: *cigarette*) pitillo (*SP*), cigarro; (*US col*: *homosexual*) maricón *m*.
fag end *n* (*BRIT col*) colilla.
fagged [fægd] *adj* (*BRIT col*: *exhausted*) rendido, agotado.
Fahrenheit ['fɑːrənhaɪt] *n* Fahrenheit *m*.
fail [feɪl] *vt* suspender; (*subj*: *memory etc*) fallar a ♦ *vi* suspender; (*be unsuccessful*) fracasar; (*strength, brakes, engine*) fallar; **to ~ to do sth** (*neglect*) dejar de hacer algo; (*be unable*) no poder hacer algo; **without** ~ sin falta; **words ~ me!** ¡no sé qué decir!
failing ['feɪlɪŋ] *n* falta, defecto ♦ *prep* a falta de; ~ **that** de no ser posible eso.
failsafe ['feɪlseɪf] *adj* (*device etc*) de seguridad.
failure ['feɪljə*] *n* fracaso; (*person*) fracasado/a; (*mechanical etc*) fallo; (*in exam*) suspenso; (*of crops*) pérdida, destrucción *f*; **it was a complete** ~ fue un fracaso total.
faint [feɪnt] *adj* débil; (*smell, breeze, trace*) leve; (*recollection*) vago; (*mark*) apenas visible ♦ *n* desmayo ♦ *vi* desmayarse; **to feel** ~ estar mareado, marearse.
faintest ['feɪntɪst] *adj*: **I haven't the ~ idea** no tengo la más remota idea.
faint-hearted ['feɪnt'hɑːtɪd] *adj* apocado.
faintly ['feɪntlɪ] *adv* débilmente; (*vaguely*) vagamente.
faintness ['feɪntnɪs] *n* debilidad *f*; vaguedad *f*.
fair [fɛə*] *adj* justo; (*hair, person*) rubio; (*weather*) bueno; (*good enough*) suficiente; (*sizeable*) considerable ♦ *adv*: **to play** ~ jugar limpio ♦ *n* feria; (*BRIT*: *funfair*) parque *m* de atracciones; **it's not ~!** ¡no es justo!, ¡no hay derecho!; ~ **copy** copia en limpio; ~ **play** juego limpio; **a ~ amount of** bastante; ~ **wear and tear** desgaste *m* natural; **trade** ~ feria de muestras.
fair game *n*: **to be** ~ ser presa fácil.
fairground ['fɛəgraund] *n* recinto ferial.
fair-haired [fɛə'hɛəd] *adj* (*person*) rubio.
fairly ['fɛəlɪ] *adv* (*justly*) con justicia; (*equally*) equitativamente; (*quite*) bastante; **I'm ~ sure** estoy bastante seguro.
fairness ['fɛənɪs] *n* justicia; (*impartiality*) imparcialidad *f*; **in all** ~ a decir verdad.
fairy ['fɛərɪ] *n* hada.
fairy godmother *n* hada madrina.
fairyland ['fɛərɪlænd] *n* el país de ensueño.
fairy lights *npl* bombillas *fpl* de colores.
fairy tale *n* cuento de hadas.
faith [feɪθ] *n* fe *f*; (*trust*) confianza; (*sect*) religión *f*; **to have ~ in sb/sth** confiar en algn/algo.
faithful ['feɪθful] *adj* fiel.
faithfully ['feɪθfulɪ] *adv* fielmente; **yours** ~ (*BRIT*: *in letters*) le saluda atentamente.
faith healer *n* curador(a) *m/f* por fe.
fake [feɪk] *n* (*painting etc*) falsificación *f*; (*person*) impostor(a) *m/f* ♦ *adj* falso ♦ *vt* fingir; (*painting etc*) falsificar.
falcon ['fɔːlkən] *n* halcón *m*.
Falkland Islands ['fɔːlklənd-] *npl* Islas *fpl* Malvinas.
fall [fɔːl] *n* caída; (*US*) otoño; (*decrease*) disminución *f* ♦ *vi*, *pt* **fell**, *pp* **fallen** ['fɔːlən] caer; (*accidentally*) caerse; (*price*) bajar; **~s** *npl* (*waterfall*) cataratas *fpl*, salto *sg* de agua; **a ~ of earth** un desprendimiento de tierra; **a ~ of snow** una nevada; **to ~ flat** *vi* (*on one's face*) caerse de bruces; (*joke, story*) no hacer gracia; **to ~ short of sb's expectations** decepcionar a algn; **to ~ in love (with sb/sth)** enamorarse (de algn/algo).
►**fall apart** *vi* deshacerse.
►**fall back** *vi* retroceder.
►**fall back on** *vt fus* (*remedy etc*) recurrir a; **to have sth to ~ back on** tener algo a que recurrir.
►**fall behind** *vi* quedarse atrás; (*fig*: *with payments*) retrasarse.
►**fall down** *vi* (*person*) caerse; (*building, hopes*) derrumbarse.
►**fall for** *vt fus* (*trick*) tragar; (*person*) enamorarse de.
►**fall in** *vi* (*roof*) hundirse; (*MIL*) alinearse.
►**fall in with** *vt fus*: **to ~ in with sb's plans** acomodarse con los planes de algn.
►**fall off** *vi* caerse; (*diminish*) disminuir.
►**fall out** *vi* (*friends etc*) reñir; (*MIL*) romper filas.
►**fall over** *vi* caer(se).
►**fall through** *vi* (*plan, project*) fracasar.
fallacy ['fæləsɪ] *n* error *m*.
fallback position ['fɔːlbæk-] *n* posición *f* de repliegue.
fallen ['fɔːlən] *pp of* **fall**.
fallible ['fæləbl] *adj* falible.
falling ['fɔːlɪŋ] *adj*: ~ **market** mercado en baja.
falling-off ['fɔːlɪŋ'ɔf] *n* (*reduction*) disminución *f*.
Fallopian tube [fə'ləupɪən-] *n* (*ANAT*) trompa de Falopio.
fallout ['fɔːlaut] *n* lluvia radioactiva.
fallout shelter *n* refugio antinuclear.
fallow ['fæləu] *adj* (*land, field*) en barbecho.
false [fɔːls] *adj* (*gen*) falso; (*teeth etc*)

postizo; (*disloyal*) desleal, traidor(a); **under ~ pretences** con engaños.
false alarm *n* falsa alarma.
falsehood ['fɔːlshud] *n* falsedad *f*.
falsely ['fɔːlslɪ] *adv* falsamente.
false teeth *npl* (*BRIT*) dentadura *sg* postiza.
falsify ['fɔːlsɪfaɪ] *vt* falsificar.
falter ['fɔːltə*] *vi* vacilar.
fame [feɪm] *n* fama.
familiar [fə'mɪlɪə*] *adj* familiar; (*well-known*) conocido; (*tone*) de confianza; **to be ~ with** (*subject*) estar enterado de; **to make o.s. ~ with** familiarizarse con; **to be on ~ terms with sb** tener confianza con algn.
familiarity [fəmɪlɪ'ærɪtɪ] *n* familiaridad *f*.
familiarize [fə'mɪlɪəraɪz] *vt*: **to ~ o.s. with** familiarizarse con.
family ['fæmɪlɪ] *n* familia.
family allowance *n subsidio que se recibe por cada hijo.*
family business *n* negocio familiar.
family credit *n* (*BRIT*) ≃ ayuda familiar.
family doctor *n* médico/a de cabecera.
family life *n* vida doméstica *or* familiar.
family man *n* (*home-loving*) hombre *m* casero; (*having family*) padre *m* de familia.
family planning *n* planificación *f* familiar.
family planning clinic *n* clínica de planificación familiar.
family tree *n* árbol *m* genealógico.
famine ['fæmɪn] *n* hambre *f*, hambruna.
famished ['fæmɪʃt] *adj* hambriento; **I'm ~!** (*col*) ¡estoy muerto de hambre!, ¡tengo un hambre canina!
famous ['feɪməs] *adj* famoso, célebre.
famously ['feɪməslɪ] *adv* (*get on*) estupendamente.
fan [fæn] *n* abanico; (*ELEC*) ventilador *m*; (*person*) aficionado/a; (*SPORT*) hincha *m/f*; (*of pop star*) fan *m/f* ♦ *vt* abanicar; (*fire, quarrel*) atizar.
▸**fan out** *vi* desplegarse.
fanatic [fə'nætɪk] *n* fanático/a.
fanatical [fə'nætɪkəl] *adj* fanático.
fan belt *n* correa de ventilador.
fancied ['fænsɪd] *adj* imaginario.
fanciful ['fænsɪful] *adj* (*gen*) fantástico; (*imaginary*) fantasioso; (*design*) rebuscado.
fan club *n* club *m* de fans.
fancy ['fænsɪ] *n* (*whim*) capricho, antojo; (*imagination*) imaginación *f* ♦ *adj* (*luxury*) de lujo; (*price*) exorbitado ♦ *vt* (*feel like, want*) tener ganas de; (*imagine*) imaginarse, figurarse; **to take a ~ to sb** tomar cariño a algn; **when the ~ takes him** cuando se le antoja; **it took** *or* **caught my ~** me cayó en gracia; **to ~ that ...** imaginarse que ...; **he fancies her** le gusta (ella) mucho.
fancy dress *n* disfraz *m*.
fancy-dress ball ['fænsɪdrɛs-] *n* baile *m* de disfraces.
fancy goods *n* artículos *mpl* de fantasía.
fanfare ['fænfɛə*] *n* fanfarria (de trompeta).
fanfold paper ['fænfəuld-] *n* papel *m* plegado en abanico *or* en acordeón.
fang [fæŋ] *n* colmillo.
fan heater *n* calefactor *m* de aire.
fanlight ['fænlaɪt] *n* (montante *m* en) abanico.
fanny ['fænɪ] *n* (*BRIT col!*) chocho (*!*); (*US col*) pompis *m*, culo.
fantasize ['fæntəsaɪz] *vi* fantasear, hacerse ilusiones.
fantastic [fæn'tæstɪk] *adj* fantástico.
fantasy ['fæntəzɪ] *n* fantasía.
fanzine ['fænziːn] *n* fanzine *m*.
FAO *n abbr* (= *Food and Agriculture Organization*) FAO *f*, OAA *f*.
FAQ *abbr* (= *free alongside quay*) franco sobre muelle.
far [fɑː*] *adj* (*distant*) lejano ♦ *adv* lejos; **the ~ left/right** (*POL*) la extrema izquierda/derecha; **~ away, ~ off** (a lo) lejos; **~ better** mucho mejor; **~ from** lejos de; **by ~** con mucho; **it's by ~ the best** es con mucho el mejor; **go as ~ as the farm** vaya hasta la granja; **is it ~ to London?** ¿a cuánto está Londres?; **it's not ~ (from here)** no está lejos (de aquí); **as ~ as I know** que yo sepa; **how ~ have you got with your work?** ¿hasta dónde has llegado en tu trabajo?
faraway ['fɑːrəweɪ] *adj* remoto; (*look*) ausente, perdido.
farce [fɑːs] *n* farsa.
farcical ['fɑːsɪkəl] *adj* absurdo.
fare [fɛə*] *n* (*on trains, buses*) precio (del billete); (*in taxi: cost*) tarifa; (*: passenger*) pasajero; (*food*) comida; **half/full ~** medio billete *m*/billete *m* completo.
Far East *n*: **the ~** el Extremo *or* Lejano Oriente.
farewell [fɛə'wɛl] *excl, n* adiós *m*.
far-fetched [fɑː'fɛtʃt] *adj* inverosímil.
farm [fɑːm] *n* granja, finca, estancia (*LAM*), chacra (*LAM*), rancho (*LAM*) ♦ *vt* cultivar.
▸**farm out** *vt* (*work*): **to ~ out (to sb)** mandar hacer fuera (a algn).
farmer ['fɑːmə*] *n* granjero/a, estanciero/a (*LAM*).
farmhand ['fɑːmhænd] *n* peón *m*.
farmhouse ['fɑːmhaus] *n* granja, casa de

hacienda (*LAM*).
farming ['fɑːmɪŋ] *n* (*gen*) agricultura; (*tilling*) cultivo; **sheep ~** cría de ovejas.
farm labourer *n* = **farmhand.**
farmland ['fɑːmlænd] *n* tierra de cultivo.
farm produce *n* productos *mpl* agrícolas.
farm worker *n* = **farmhand.**
farmyard ['fɑːmjɑːd] *n* corral *m.*
Faroe Islands ['fɛərəu-], **Faroes** ['fɛərəuz] *npl*: **the ~** las Islas Feroe.
far-reaching [fɑː'riːtʃɪŋ] *adj* (*reform, effect*) de gran alcance.
far-sighted [fɑː'saɪtɪd] *adj* previsor(a).
fart [fɑːt] (*col!*) *n* pedo (*!*) ♦ *vi* tirarse un pedo (*!*).
farther ['fɑːðə*] *adv* más lejos, más allá ♦ *adj* más lejano.
farthest ['fɑːðɪst] *superlative of* **far.**
FAS *abbr* (= *free alongside ship*) franco al costado del buque.
fascinate ['fæsɪneɪt] *vt* fascinar.
fascinating ['fæsɪneɪtɪŋ] *adj* fascinante.
fascination [fæsɪ'neɪʃən] *n* fascinación *f.*
fascism ['fæʃɪzəm] *n* fascismo.
fascist ['fæʃɪst] *adj, n* fascista *m/f.*
fashion ['fæʃən] *n* moda; (*manner*) manera ♦ *vt* formar; **in ~** a la moda; **out of ~** pasado de moda; **in the Greek ~** a la griega, al estilo griego; **after a ~** (*finish, manage etc*) en cierto modo.
fashionable ['fæʃnəbl] *adj* de moda; (*writer*) de moda, popular; **it is ~ to do ...** está de moda hacer ....
fashion designer *n* diseñador(a) *m/f* de modas, modisto/a.
fashion show *n* desfile *m* de modelos.
fast [fɑːst] *adj* (*also PHOT*: *film*) rápido; (*dye, colour*) sólido; (*clock*): **to be ~** estar adelantado ♦ *adv* rápidamente, de prisa; (*stuck, held*) firmemente ♦ *n* ayuno ♦ *vi* ayunar; **~ asleep** profundamente dormido; **in the ~ lane** (*AUT*) en el carril de adelantamiento; **my watch is 5 minutes ~** mi reloj está adelantado 5 minutos; **as ~ as I** *etc* **can** lo más rápido posible; **to make a boat ~** amarrar una barca.
fasten ['fɑːsn] *vt* asegurar, sujetar; (*coat, belt*) abrochar ♦ *vi* cerrarse.
▸**fasten (up)on** *vt fus* (*idea*) aferrarse a.
fastener ['fɑːsnə*] *n* cierre *m*; (*of door etc*) cerrojo; (*BRIT*: *zip ~*) cremallera.
fastening ['fɑːsnɪŋ] *n* = **fastener.**
fast food *n* comida rápida, platos *mpl* preparados.
fastidious [fæs'tɪdɪəs] *adj* (*fussy*) delicado; (*demanding*) exigente.
fat [fæt] *adj* gordo; (*meat*) con mucha grasa; (*greasy*) grasiento ♦ *n* grasa; (*on person*) carnes *fpl*; (*lard*) manteca; **to live off the ~ of the land** vivir a cuerpo de rey.
fatal ['feɪtl] *adj* (*mistake*) fatal; (*injury*) mortal; (*consequence*) funesto.
fatalism ['feɪtəlɪzəm] *n* fatalismo.
fatality [fə'tælɪtɪ] *n* (*road death etc*) víctima *f* mortal.
fatally ['feɪtəlɪ] *adv*: **~ injured** herido de muerte.
fate [feɪt] *n* destino, sino.
fated ['feɪtɪd] *adj* predestinado.
fateful ['feɪtful] *adj* fatídico.
fat-free ['fætfriː] *adj* sin grasa.
father ['fɑːðə*] *n* padre *m.*
Father Christmas *n* Papá *m* Noel.
fatherhood ['fɑːðəhud] *n* paternidad *f.*
father-in-law ['fɑːðərɪnlɔː] *n* suegro.
fatherland ['fɑːðəlænd] *n* patria.
fatherly ['fɑːðəlɪ] *adj* paternal.
fathom ['fæðəm] *n* braza ♦ *vt* (*unravel*) desentrañar; (*understand*) explicarse.
fatigue [fə'tiːg] *n* fatiga, cansancio; **metal ~** fatiga del metal.
fatness ['fætnɪs] *n* gordura.
fatten ['fætn] *vt, vi* engordar; **chocolate is ~ing** el chocolate engorda.
fatty ['fætɪ] *adj* (*food*) graso ♦ *n* (*fam*) gordito/a, gordinflón/ona *m/f.*
fatuous ['fætjuəs] *adj* fatuo, necio.
faucet ['fɔːsɪt] *n* (*US*) grifo, llave *f*, canilla (*LAM*).
fault [fɔːlt] *n* (*blame*) culpa; (*defect*: *in character*) defecto; (*in manufacture*) desperfecto; (*GEO*) falla ♦ *vt* criticar; **it's my ~** es culpa mía; **to find ~ with** criticar, poner peros a; **at ~** culpable.
faultless ['fɔːltlɪs] *adj* (*action*) intachable; (*person*) sin defectos.
faulty ['fɔːltɪ] *adj* defectuoso.
fauna ['fɔːnə] *n* fauna.
faux pas ['fəu'pɑː] *n* desacierto.
favour, (*US*) **favor** ['feɪvə*] *n* favor *m*; (*approval*) aprobación *f* ♦ *vt* (*proposition*) estar a favor de, aprobar; (*person etc*) preferir; (*assist*) favorecer; **to ask a ~ of** pedir un favor a; **to do sb a ~** hacer un favor a algn; **to find ~ with sb** (*subj*: *person*) caerle bien a algn; (: *suggestion*) tener buena acogida por parte de algn; **in ~ of** a favor de; **to be in ~ of sth/of doing sth** ser partidario *or* estar a favor de algo/de hacer algo.
favo(u)rable ['feɪvərəbl] *adj* favorable.
favo(u)rably ['feɪvərəblɪ] *adv* favorablemente.
favo(u)rite ['feɪvərɪt] *adj, n* favorito/a *m/f*, preferido/a *m/f.*

favo(u)ritism ['feɪvərɪtɪzəm] *n* favoritismo.
fawn [fɔːn] *n* cervato ♦ *adj* (*also*: **~-coloured**) de color cervato, leonado ♦ *vi*: **to ~ (up)on** adular.
fax [fæks] *n* fax *m* ♦ *vt* mandar *or* enviar por fax.
FBI *n abbr* (*US*: =*Federal Bureau of Investigation*) FBI *m*.
FCC *n abbr* (*US*) = *Federal Communications Commission*.
FCO *n abbr* (*BRIT*: = *Foreign and Commonwealth Office*) ≈ Min. de AA. EE.
FD *n abbr* (*US*) = **fire department**.
FDA *n abbr* (*US*: = *Food and Drug Administration*) *oficina que se ocupa del control de los productos alimentarios y farmacéuticos*.
FE *n abbr* = **further education**.
fear [fɪə*] *n* miedo, temor *m* ♦ *vt* temer; **for ~ of** por temor a; **~ of heights** vértigo; **to ~ for/that** temer por/que.
fearful ['fɪəful] *adj* temeroso; (*awful*) espantoso; **to be ~ of** (*frightened*) tener miedo de.
fearfully ['fɪəfulɪ] *adv* (*timidly*) con miedo; (*col*: *very*) terriblemente.
fearless ['fɪəlɪs] *adj* (*gen*) sin miedo *or* temor; (*bold*) audaz.
fearlessly ['fɪəlɪslɪ] *adv* temerariamente.
fearlessness ['fɪəlɪsnɪs] *n* temeridad *f*.
fearsome ['fɪəsəm] *adj* (*opponent*) temible; (*sight*) espantoso.
feasibility [fiːzə'bɪlɪtɪ] *n* factibilidad *f*, viabilidad *f*.
feasibility study *n* estudio de viabilidad.
feasible ['fiːzəbl] *adj* factible, viable.
feast [fiːst] *n* banquete *m*; (*REL*: *also*: **~ day**) fiesta ♦ *vi* banquetear.
feat [fiːt] *n* hazaña.
feather ['fɛðə*] *n* pluma ♦ *vt*: **to ~ one's nest** (*fig*) hacer su agosto, sacar tajada ♦ *cpd* (*mattress, bed, pillow*) de plumas.
feather-weight ['fɛðəweɪt] *n* (*BOXING*) peso pluma.
feature ['fiːtʃə*] *n* (*gen*) característica; (*ANAT*) rasgo; (*article*) reportaje *m* ♦ *vt* (*subj*: *film*) presentar ♦ *vi* figurar; **~s** *npl* (*of face*) facciones *fpl*; **a (special) ~ on sth/sb** un reportaje (especial) sobre algo/algn; **it ~d prominently in** ... tuvo un papel destacado en ....
feature film *n* largometraje *m*.
Feb. *abbr* (= *February*) feb.
February ['fɛbruərɪ] *n* febrero.
feces ['fiːsiːz] *npl* (*US*) = **faeces**.
feckless ['fɛklɪs] *adj* irresponsable, irreflexivo.
Fed *abbr* (*US*) = **federal, federation**.
fed [fɛd] *pt, pp of* **feed**.
Fed. [fɛd] *n abbr* (*US col*) = *Federal Reserve Board*.
federal ['fɛdərəl] *adj* federal.
Federal Republic of Germany *n* República Federal de Alemania.
federation [fɛdə'reɪʃən] *n* federación *f*.
fed-up [fɛd'ʌp] *adj*: **to be ~ (with)** estar harto (de).
fee [fiː] *n* (*professional*) honorarios *mpl*; (*for examination*) derechos *mpl*; (*of school*) matrícula; (*membership ~*) cuota; (*entrance ~*) entrada; **for a small ~** por poco dinero.
feeble ['fiːbl] *adj* débil.
feeble-minded [fiːbl'maɪndɪd] *adj* imbécil.
feed [fiːd] *n* (*gen, of baby*) comida; (*of animal*) pienso; (*on printer*) dispositivo de alimentación ♦ *vt* (*pt, pp* **fed**) (*gen*) alimentar; (*BRIT*: *breastfeed*) dar el pecho a; (*animal, baby*) dar de comer a ♦ *vi* (*baby, animal*) comer.
▶**feed back** *vt* (*results*) pasar.
▶**feed in** *vt* (*COMPUT*) introducir.
▶**feed into** *vt* (*data, information*) suministrar a; **to ~ sth into a machine** introducir algo en una máquina.
▶**feed on** *vt fus* alimentarse de.
feedback ['fiːdbæk] *n* (*from person*) reacción *f*; (*TECH*) realimentación *f*, feedback *m*.
feeder ['fiːdə*] *n* (*bib*) babero.
feeding bottle ['fiːdɪŋ-] *n* (*BRIT*) biberón *m*.
feel [fiːl] *n* (*sensation*) sensación *f*; (*sense of touch*) tacto ♦ *vt* (*pt, pp* **felt**) tocar; (*cold, pain etc*) sentir; (*think, believe*) creer; **to get the ~ of sth** (*fig*) acostumbrarse a algo; **to ~ hungry/cold** tener hambre/frío; **to ~ lonely/better** sentirse solo/mejor; **I don't ~ well** no me siento bien; **it ~s soft** es suave al tacto; **it ~s colder out here** se siente más frío aquí fuera; **to ~ like** (*want*) tener ganas de; **I'm still ~ing my way** (*fig*) todavía me estoy orientando; **I ~ that you ought to do it** creo que debes hacerlo; **to ~ about** *or* **around** *vi* tantear.
feeler ['fiːlə*] *n* (*of insect*) antena; **to put out ~s** (*fig*) tantear el terreno.
feeling ['fiːlɪŋ] *n* (*physical*) sensación *f*; (*foreboding*) presentimiento; (*impression*) impresión *f*; (*emotion*) sentimiento; **what are your ~s about the matter?** ¿qué opinas tú del asunto?; **to hurt sb's ~s** herir los sentimientos de algn; **~s ran high about it** causó mucha controversia; **I got the ~ that** ... me dio la impresión de que ...; **there was a general ~ that** ... la

opinión general fue que ....
fee-paying school ['fiːpeɪɪŋ-] *n* colegio de pago.
feet [fiːt] *npl of* **foot**.
feign [feɪn] *vt* fingir.
feigned [feɪnd] *adj* fingido.
feline ['fiːlaɪn] *adj* felino.
fell [fɛl] *pt of* **fall** ♦ *vt* (*tree*) talar ♦ *adj*: **with one ~ blow** con un golpe feroz; **at one ~ swoop** de un solo golpe ♦ *n* (*BRIT*: *mountain*) montaña; (: *moorland*): **the ~s** los páramos.
fellow ['fɛləu] *n* tipo, tío (*SP*); (*of learned society*) socio/a; (*UNIV*) *miembro de la junta de gobierno de un colegio* ♦ *cpd*: **~ students** compañeros/as *m/fpl* de curso, condiscípulos/as *m/fpl*.
fellow citizen *n* conciudadano/a.
fellow countryman *n* compatriota *m*.
fellow feeling *n* compañerismo.
fellow men *npl* semejantes *mpl*.
fellowship ['fɛləuʃɪp] *n* compañerismo; (*grant*) beca.
fellow traveller *n* compañero/a de viaje; (*POL*: *with communists*) simpatizante *m/f*.
fellow worker *n* colega *m/f*.
felon ['fɛlən] *n* criminal *m/f*.
felony ['fɛlənɪ] *n* crimen *m*, delito mayor.
felt [fɛlt] *pt, pp of* **feel** ♦ *n* fieltro.
felt-tip pen ['fɛlttɪp-] *n* rotulador *m*.
female ['fiːmeɪl] *n* (*woman*) mujer *f*; (*ZOOL*) hembra ♦ *adj* femenino.
feminine ['fɛmɪnɪn] *adj* femenino.
femininity [fɛmɪ'nɪnɪtɪ] *n* feminidad *f*.
feminism ['fɛmɪnɪzəm] *n* feminismo.
feminist ['fɛmɪnɪst] *n* feminista *m/f*.
fence [fɛns] *n* valla, cerca; (*RACING*) valla ♦ *vt* (*also*: **~ in**) cercar ♦ *vi* hacer esgrima; **to sit on the ~** (*fig*) nadar entre dos aguas.
▸**fence in** *vt* cercar.
▸**fence off** *vt* separar con cerca.
fencing ['fɛnsɪŋ] *n* esgrima.
fend [fɛnd] *vi*: **to ~ for o.s.** valerse por sí mismo.
▸**fend off** *vt* (*attack, attacker*) rechazar, repeler; (*blow*) desviar; (*awkward question*) esquivar.
fender ['fɛndə*] *n* pantalla; (*US*: *AUT*) parachoques *m inv*; (: *RAIL*) trompa.
fennel ['fɛnl] *n* hinojo.
Fens [fɛnz] *npl* (*BRIT*): **the ~** *las tierras bajas de Norfolk (antiguamente zona de marismas)*.
ferment *vi* [fə'mɛnt] fermentar ♦ *n* ['fəːmɛnt] (*fig*) agitación *f*.
fermentation [fəːmɛn'teɪʃən] *n* fermentación *f*.
fern [fəːn] *n* helecho.
ferocious [fə'rəuʃəs] *adj* feroz.
ferociously [fə'rəuʃəslɪ] *adv* ferozmente, con ferocidad.
ferocity [fə'rɔsɪtɪ] *n* ferocidad *f*.
ferret ['fɛrɪt] *n* hurón *m*.
▸**ferret about, ferret around** *vi* rebuscar.
▸**ferret out** *vt* (*secret, truth*) desentrañar.
ferry ['fɛrɪ] *n* (*small*) barca (de pasaje), balsa; (*large*: *also*: **~boat**) transbordador *m*, ferry *m* ♦ *vt* transportar; **to ~ sth/sb across** *or* **over** transportar algo/a algn a la otra orilla; **to ~ sb to and fro** llevar a algn de un lado para otro.
ferryman ['fɛrɪmən] *n* barquero.
fertile ['fəːtaɪl] *adj* fértil; (*BIOL*) fecundo.
fertility [fə'tɪlɪtɪ] *n* fertilidad *f*; fecundidad *f*.
fertility drug *n* medicamento contra la infertilidad.
fertilization [fəːtɪlaɪ'zeɪʃən] *n* fertilización *f*; (*BIOL*) fecundación *f*.
fertilize ['fəːtɪlaɪz] *vt* fertilizar; (*BIOL*) fecundar; (*AGR*) abonar.
fertilizer ['fəːtɪlaɪzə*] *n* abono, fertilizante *m*.
fervent ['fəːvənt] *adj* ferviente.
fervour, (*US*) **fervor** ['fəːvə*] *n* fervor *m*, ardor *m*.
fester ['fɛstə*] *vi* supurar.
festival ['fɛstɪvəl] *n* (*REL*) fiesta; (*ART, MUS*) festival *m*.
festive ['fɛstɪv] *adj* festivo; **the ~ season** (*BRIT*: *Christmas*) las Navidades.
festivities [fɛs'tɪvɪtɪz] *npl* festejos *mpl*.
festoon [fɛs'tuːn] *vt*: **to ~ with** festonear *or* engalanar de.
fetch [fɛtʃ] *vt* ir a buscar; (*BRIT*: *sell for*) venderse por; **how much did it ~?** ¿por cuánto se vendió?
▸**fetch up** *vi* ir a parar.
fetching ['fɛtʃɪŋ] *adj* atractivo.
fête [feɪt] *n* fiesta.
fetid ['fɛtɪd] *adj* fétido.
fetish ['fɛtɪʃ] *n* fetiche *m*.
fetter ['fɛtə*] *vt* (*person*) encadenar, poner grillos a; (*horse*) trabar; (*fig*) poner trabas a.
fetters ['fɛtəz] *npl* grillos *mpl*.
fettle ['fɛtl] *n*: **in fine ~** en buenas condiciones.
fetus ['fiːtəs] *n* (*US*) = **foetus**.
feud [fjuːd] *n* (*hostility*) enemistad *f*; (*quarrel*) disputa; **a family ~** una pelea familiar.
feudal ['fjuːdl] *adj* feudal.
feudalism ['fjuːdəlɪzəm] *n* feudalismo.
fever ['fiːvə*] *n* fiebre *f*; **he has a ~** tiene

fiebre.
feverish ['fiːvərɪʃ] *adj* febril.
feverishly ['fiːvərɪʃlɪ] *adv* febrilmente.
few [fjuː] *adj* (*not many*) pocos; (*some*) algunos, unos ♦ *pron* algunos; **a** ~ *adj* unos pocos; ~ **people** poca gente; **a good** ~, **quite a** ~ bastantes; **in** *or* **over the next** ~ **days** en los próximos días; **every** ~ **weeks** cada 2 o 3 semanas; **a** ~ **more days** unos días más.
fewer ['fjuːə*] *adj* menos.
fewest ['fjuːɪst] *adj* los/las menos.
FFA *n abbr* = *Future Farmers of America.*
FH *abbr* (*BRIT*) = **fire hydrant.**
FHA *n abbr* (*US*: = *Federal Housing Association*) *oficina federal de la vivienda.*
fiancé [fɪ'ɑ̃ːŋseɪ] *n* novio, prometido.
fiancée [fɪ'ɑ̃ːŋseɪ] *n* novia, prometida.
fiasco [fɪ'æskəu] *n* fiasco.
fib [fɪb] *n* mentirijilla ♦ *vi* decir mentirijillas.
fibre, (*US*) **fiber** ['faɪbə*] *n* fibra.
fibreboard, (*US*) **fiberboard** ['faɪbəbɔːd] *n* fibra vulcanizada.
fibreglass, (*US*) **fiberglass** ['faɪbəglɑːs] *n* fibra de vidrio.
fibrositis [faɪbrə'saɪtɪs] *n* fibrositis *f inv*.
FICA *n abbr* (*US*) = *Federal Insurance Contributions Act.*
fickle ['fɪkl] *adj* inconstante.
fiction ['fɪkʃən] *n* (*gen*) ficción *f*.
fictional ['fɪkʃənl] *adj* novelesco.
fictionalize ['fɪkʃənəlaɪz] *vt* novelar.
fictitious [fɪk'tɪʃəs] *adj* ficticio.
fiddle ['fɪdl] *n* (*MUS*) violín *m*; (*cheating*) trampa ♦ *vt* (*BRIT*: *accounts*) falsificar; **tax** ~ evasión *f* fiscal; **to work a** ~ hacer trampa.
▸**fiddle with** *vt fus* juguetear con.
fiddler ['fɪdlə*] *n* violinista *m/f*.
fiddly ['fɪdlɪ] *adj* (*task*) delicado, mañoso; (*object*) enrevesado.
fidelity [fɪ'delɪtɪ] *n* fidelidad *f*.
fidget ['fɪdʒɪt] *vi* moverse (nerviosamente).
fidgety ['fɪdʒɪtɪ] *adj* nervioso.
fiduciary [fɪ'duːʃɪərɪ] *n* fiduciario/a.
field [fiːld] *n* (*gen*, *COMPUT*) campo; (*fig*) campo, esfera; (*SPORT*) campo, cancha (*LAM*); (*competitors*) competidores *mpl* ♦ *cpd*: **to have a** ~ **day** (*fig*) ponerse las botas; **to lead the** ~ (*SPORT*, *COMM*) llevar la delantera; **to give sth a year's trial in the** ~ (*fig*) sacar algo al mercado a prueba por un año; **my particular** ~ mi especialidad.
field glasses *npl* gemelos *mpl*.
field hospital *n* hospital *m* de campaña.
field marshal *n* mariscal *m*.
fieldwork ['fiːldwəːk] *n* (*ARCHAEOLOGY*, *GEO*) trabajo de campo.
fiend [fiːnd] *n* demonio.
fiendish ['fiːndɪʃ] *adj* diabólico.
fierce [fɪəs] *adj* feroz; (*wind*, *attack*) violento; (*heat*) intenso; (*fighting*, *enemy*) encarnizado.
fiercely ['fɪəslɪ] *adv* con ferocidad; violentamente; intensamente; encarnizadamente.
fierceness ['fɪəsnɪs] *n* ferocidad *f*; violencia; intensidad *f*; encarnizamiento.
fiery ['faɪərɪ] *adj* (*burning*) ardiente; (*temperament*) apasionado.
FIFA ['fiːfə] *n abbr* (= *Fédération Internationale de Football Association*) FIFA *f*.
fifteen [fɪf'tiːn] *num* quince.
fifth [fɪfθ] *num* quinto.
fiftieth ['fɪftɪɪθ] *num* quincuagésimo.
fifty ['fɪftɪ] *num* cincuenta; **the fifties** los años cincuenta; **to be in one's fifties** andar por los cincuenta.
fifty-fifty ['fɪftɪ'fɪftɪ] *adv*: **to go** ~ **with sb** ir a medias con algn ♦ *adj*: **we have a** ~ **chance of success** tenemos un cincuenta por ciento de posibilidades de tener éxito.
fig [fɪg] *n* higo.
fight [faɪt] *n* (*gen*) pelea; (*MIL*) combate *m*; (*struggle*) lucha ♦ *vb* (*pt*, *pp* **fought**) *vt* luchar contra; (*cancer*, *alcoholism*) combatir; (*LAW*): **to** ~ **a case** defenderse; (*quarrel*): **to** ~ **(with sb)** pelear (con algn) ♦ *vi* pelear, luchar; (*fig*): **to** ~ **(for/against)** luchar por/contra.
▸**fight back** *vi* defenderse; (*after illness*) recuperarse ♦ *vt* (*tears*) contener.
▸**fight down** *vt* (*anger*, *anxiety*, *urge*) reprimir.
▸**fight off** *vt* (*attack*, *attacker*) rechazar; (*disease*, *sleep*, *urge*) luchar contra.
▸**fight out** *vt*: **to** ~ **it out** decidirlo en una pelea.
fighter ['faɪtə*] *n* combatiente *m/f*; (*fig*) luchador(a) *m/f*; (*plane*) caza *m*.
fighter-bomber ['faɪtəbɔmə*] *n* cazabombardero.
fighter pilot *n* piloto de caza.
fighting ['faɪtɪŋ] *n* (*gen*) el luchar; (*battle*) combate *m*; (*in streets*) disturbios *mpl*.
figment ['fɪgmənt] *n*: **a** ~ **of the imagination** un producto de la imaginación.
figurative ['fɪgjurətɪv] *adj* (*meaning*) figurado; (*ART*) figurativo.
figure ['fɪgə*] *n* (*DRAWING*, *GEOM*) figura,

dibujo; (*number, cipher*) cifra; (*person, outline*) figura; (*body shape*) línea; (: *attractive*) tipo ♦ *vt* (*esp US*: *think, calculate*) calcular, imaginarse ♦ *vi* (*appear*) figurar; (*esp US*: *make sense*) ser lógico; ~ **of speech** (*LING*) figura retórica; **public** ~ personaje *m*.
▸**figure on** *vt fus* (*US*) contar con.
▸**figure out** *vt* (*understand*) comprender.
figurehead ['fɪgəhɛd] *n* (*fig*) figura decorativa.
figure skating *n* patinaje *m* artístico.
Fiji (Islands) ['fiːdʒiː-] *n(pl)* (Islas *fpl*) Fiji *fpl*.
filament ['fɪləmənt] *n* (*ELEC*) filamento.
filch [fɪltʃ] *vt* (*col*: *steal*) birlar.
file [faɪl] *n* (*tool*) lima; (*for nails*) lima de uñas; (*dossier*) expediente *m*; (*folder*) carpeta; (*in cabinet*) archivo; (*COMPUT*) fichero; (*row*) fila ♦ *vt* limar; (*papers*) clasificar; (*LAW*: *claim*) presentar; (*store*) archivar; **to open/close a** ~ (*COMPUT*) abrir/cerrar un fichero; **to** ~ **in/out** *vi* entrar/salir en fila; **to** ~ **a suit against sb** entablar pleito contra algn; **to** ~ **past** desfilar ante.
file name *n* (*COMPUT*) nombre *m* de fichero.
filibuster ['fɪlɪbʌstə*] (*esp US*: *POL*) *n* obstruccionista *m/f*, filibustero/a ♦ *vi* usar maniobras obstruccionistas.
filing ['faɪlɪŋ] *n*: **to do the** ~ llevar los archivos.
filing cabinet *n* fichero, archivo.
filing clerk *n* oficinista *m/f*.
fill [fɪl] *vt* llenar; (*tooth*) empastar; (*vacancy*) cubrir ♦ *n*: **to eat one's** ~ comer hasta hartarse; **we've already** ~**ed that vacancy** ya hemos cubierto esa vacante; ~**ed with admiration (for)** lleno de admiración (por).
▸**fill in** *vt* rellenar; (*details, report*) completar; **to** ~ **sb in on sth** (*col*) poner a algn al corriente *or* al día sobre algo.
▸**fill out** *vt* (*form, receipt*) rellenar.
▸**fill up** *vt* llenar (hasta el borde) ♦ *vi* (*AUT*) echar gasolina.
fillet ['fɪlɪt] *n* filete *m*.
fillet steak *n* filete *m* de ternera.
filling ['fɪlɪŋ] *n* (*CULIN*) relleno; (*for tooth*) empaste *m*.
filling station *n* estación *f* de servicio.
fillip ['fɪlɪp] *n* estímulo.
filly ['fɪlɪ] *n* potra.
film [fɪlm] *n* película ♦ *vt* (*scene*) filmar ♦ *vi* rodar.
film script *n* guión *m*.
film star *n* estrella de cine.
filmstrip ['fɪlmstrɪp] *n* tira de diapositivas.
film studio *n* estudio de cine.
Filofax ® ['faɪləufæks] *n* agenda (profesional).
filter ['fɪltə*] *n* filtro ♦ *vt* filtrar.
▸**filter in, filter through** *vi* filtrarse.
filter coffee *n* café *m* (molido) para filtrar.
filter lane *n* (*BRIT*) carril *m* de selección.
filter-tipped ['fɪltətɪpt] *adj* con filtro.
filth [fɪlθ] *n* suciedad *f*.
filthy ['fɪlθɪ] *adj* sucio; (*language*) obsceno.
fin [fɪn] *n* (*gen*) aleta.
final ['faɪnl] *adj* (*last*) final, último; (*definitive*) definitivo ♦ *n* (*SPORT*) final *f*; ~**s** *npl* (*SCOL*) exámenes *mpl* finales; ~ **demand** (*on invoice etc*) último aviso; ~ **dividend** dividendo final.
finale [fɪ'nɑːlɪ] *n* final *m*.
finalist ['faɪnəlɪst] *n* (*SPORT*) finalista *m/f*.
finality [faɪ'nælɪtɪ] *n* finalidad *f*; **with an air of** ~ en tono resuelto, de modo terminante.
finalize ['faɪnəlaɪz] *vt* ultimar.
finally ['faɪnəlɪ] *adv* (*lastly*) por último, finalmente; (*eventually*) por fin; (*irrevocably*) de modo definitivo; (*once and for all*) definitivamente.
finance [faɪ'næns] *n* (*money, funds*) fondos *mpl*; ~**s** *npl* finanzas *fpl* ♦ *cpd* (*page, section, company*) financiero ♦ *vt* financiar.
financial [faɪ'nænʃəl] *adj* financiero.
financially [faɪ'nænʃəlɪ] *adv* económicamente.
financial management *n* gestión *f* financiera.
financial statement *n* estado financiero.
financial year *n* ejercicio (financiero).
financier [faɪ'nænsɪə*] *n* financiero/a.
find [faɪnd] *vt* (*pt, pp* **found** [faund]) (*gen*) encontrar, hallar; (*come upon*) descubrir ♦ *n* hallazgo; descubrimiento; **to** ~ **sb guilty** (*LAW*) declarar culpable a algn; **I** ~ **it easy** me resulta fácil.
▸**find out** *vt* averiguar; (*truth, secret*) descubrir ♦ *vi*: **to** ~ **out about** enterarse de.
findings ['faɪndɪŋz] *npl* (*LAW*) veredicto *sg*, fallo *sg*; (*of report*) recomendaciones *fpl*.
fine [faɪn] *adj* (*delicate*) fino; (*beautiful*) hermoso ♦ *adv* (*well*) bien ♦ *n* (*LAW*) multa ♦ *vt* (*LAW*) multar; **the weather is** ~ hace buen tiempo; **he's** ~ está muy bien; **you're doing** ~ lo estás haciendo muy bien; **to cut it** ~ (*of time, money*) calcular muy justo; **to get a** ~ **for (doing) sth** recibir una multa por (hacer) algo.
fine arts *npl* bellas artes *fpl*.
finely ['faɪnlɪ] *adv* (*splendidly*) con elegancia; (*chop*) en trozos pequeños,

fino; (*adjust*) con precisión.
fineness ['faɪnnɪs] *n* (*of cloth*) finura; (*of idea*) sutilidad *f*.
fine print *n*: **the** ~ la letra pequeña *or* menuda.
finery ['faɪnərɪ] *n* galas *fpl*.
finesse [fɪ'nɛs] *n* sutileza.
fine-tooth comb ['faɪntu:θ-] *n*: **to go through sth with a** ~ revisar algo a fondo.
finger ['fɪŋgə*] *n* dedo ♦ *vt* (*touch*) manosear; (*MUS*) puntear; **little/index** ~ (dedo) meñique *m*/índice *m*.
fingernail ['fɪŋgəneɪl] *n* uña.
fingerprint ['fɪŋgəprɪnt] *n* huella dactilar ♦ *vt* tomar las huellas dactilares de.
fingertip ['fɪŋgətɪp] *n* yema del dedo; **to have sth at one's** ~**s** saberse algo al dedillo.
finicky ['fɪnɪkɪ] *adj* (*fussy*) delicado.
finish ['fɪnɪʃ] *n* (*end*) fin *m*; (*SPORT*) meta; (*polish etc*) acabado ♦ *vt, vi* acabar, terminar; **to** ~ **doing sth** acabar de hacer algo; **to** ~ **first/second/third** (*SPORT*) llegar el primero/segundo/tercero; **I've** ~**ed with the paper** he terminado con el periódico; **she's** ~**ed with him** ha roto *or* acabado con él.
▸**finish off** *vt* acabar, terminar; (*kill*) rematar.
▸**finish up** *vt* acabar, terminar ♦ *vi* ir a parar, terminar.
finished ['fɪnɪʃt] *adj* (*product*) acabado; (*performance*) pulido; (*col*: *tired*) rendido, hecho polvo.
finishing ['fɪnɪʃɪŋ] *adj*: ~ **touches** toque *m* final.
finishing line *n* línea de llegada *or* meta.
finishing school *n colegio para la educación social de señoritas*.
finite ['faɪnaɪt] *adj* finito.
Finland ['fɪnlənd] *n* Finlandia.
Finn [fɪn] *n* finlandés/esa *m/f*.
Finnish ['fɪnɪʃ] *adj* finlandés/esa ♦ *n* (*LING*) finlandés *m*.
fiord [fjɔ:d] *n* fiordo.
fir [fə:*] *n* abeto.
fire ['faɪə*] *n* fuego; (*accidental, damaging*) incendio ♦ *vt* (*gun*) disparar; (*set fire to*) incendiar; (*excite*) exaltar; (*interest*) despertar; (*dismiss*) despedir ♦ *vi* encenderse; (*AUT*: *subj*: *engine*) encender; **electric/gas** ~ estufa eléctrica/de gas; **on** ~ ardiendo, en llamas; **to be on** ~ estar ardiendo; **to catch** ~ prenderse fuego; **to set** ~ **to sth, set sth on** ~ prender fuego a algo; **insured against** ~ asegurado contra incendios; **to be/come under** ~ estar/caer bajo el fuego enemigo.
fire alarm *n* alarma de incendios.
firearm ['faɪərɑ:m] *n* arma de fuego.
fire brigade, (*US*) **fire department** *n* (cuerpo de) bomberos *mpl*.
fire door *n* puerta contra incendios.
fire drill *n* (ejercicio de) simulacro de incendio.
fire engine *n* coche *m* de bomberos.
fire escape *n* escalera de incendios.
fire extinguisher *n* extintor *m*.
fireguard ['faɪəgɑ:d] *n* pantalla (guardallama).
fire hazard *n* = **fire risk**.
fire hydrant *n* boca de incendios.
fire insurance *n* seguro contra incendios.
fireman ['faɪəmən] *n* bombero.
fireplace ['faɪəpleɪs] *n* chimenea.
fireplug ['faɪəplʌg] *n* (*US*) boca de incendios.
fire practice *n* = **fire drill**.
fireproof ['faɪəpru:f] *adj* a prueba de fuego; (*material*) incombustible.
fire regulations *npl* reglamentos *mpl* contra incendios.
fire risk *n* peligro de incendio.
firescreen ['faɪəskri:n] *n* pantalla refractaria.
fireside ['faɪəsaɪd] *n*: **by the** ~ al lado de la chimenea.
fire station *n* parque *m* de bomberos.
firewood ['faɪəwud] *n* leña.
fireworks ['faɪəwə:ks] *npl* fuegos *mpl* artificiales.
firing ['faɪərɪŋ] *n* (*MIL*) disparos *mpl*, tiroteo.
firing line *n* línea de fuego; **to be in the** ~ (*fig*: *liable to be criticised*) estar en la línea de fuego.
firing squad *n* pelotón *m* de ejecución.
firm [fə:m] *adj* firme; (*offer, decision*) en firme ♦ *n* empresa; **to be a** ~ **believer in sth** ser un partidario convencido de algo; **to stand** ~ *or* **take a** ~ **stand on sth** (*fig*) mantenerse firme ante algo.
firmly ['fə:mlɪ] *adv* firmemente.
firmness ['fə:mnɪs] *n* firmeza.
first [fə:st] *adj* primero ♦ *adv* (*before others*) primero; (*when listing reasons etc*) en primer lugar, primeramente ♦ *n* (*person*: *in race*) primero/a; (*AUT*: *also*: ~ **gear**) primera; **at** ~ al principio; ~ **of all** ante todo; **the** ~ **of January** el uno *or* primero de enero; **in the** ~ **instance** en primer lugar; **I'll do it** ~ **thing tomorrow** lo haré mañana a primera hora; **for the** ~ **time** por primera vez; **head** ~ de cabeza; **from the (very)** ~ desde el principio.
first aid *n* primeros auxilios *mpl*.

first aid kit *n* botiquín *m*.
first aid post, (*US*) **first aid station** *n* puesto de auxilio.
first-class ['fə:stklɑ:s] *adj* de primera clase; ~ **ticket** (*RAIL etc*) billete *m or* boleto (*LAM*) de primera clase; ~ **mail** correo de primera clase.
first-hand [fə:st'hænd] *adj* de primera mano.
first lady *n* (*esp US*) primera dama.
firstly ['fə:stlɪ] *adv* en primer lugar.
first name *n* nombre *m* de pila.
first night *n* estreno.
first-rate [fə:st'reɪt] *adj* de primera (clase).
first-time buyer [fə:sttaɪm-] *n persona que compra su primera vivienda*.
fir tree *n* abeto.
FIS *n abbr* (*BRIT*: = *Family Income Supplement*) *ayuda estatal familiar*.
fiscal ['fɪskəl] *adj* fiscal; ~ **year** año fiscal, ejercicio.
fish [fɪʃ] *n, pl inv* pez *m*; (*food*) pescado ♦ *vt* pescar en ♦ *vi* pescar; **to go ~ing** ir de pesca.
▸**fish out** *vt* (*from water, box etc*) sacar.
fish-and-chip shop *n* = **chip shop**.
fishbone ['fɪʃbəun] *n* espina.
fisherman ['fɪʃəmən] *n* pescador *m*.
fishery ['fɪʃərɪ] *n* pesquería.
fish factory *n* fábrica de elaboración de pescado.
fish farm *n* piscifactoría.
fish fingers *npl* (*BRIT*) palitos *mpl* de pescado (empanado).
fishing boat ['fɪʃɪŋ-] *n* barca de pesca.
fishing industry *n* industria pesquera.
fishing line *n* sedal *m*.
fishing net *n* red *f* de pesca.
fishing rod *n* caña (de pescar).
fishing tackle *n* aparejo (de pescar).
fish market *n* mercado de pescado.
fishmonger ['fɪʃmʌŋgə*] *n* (*BRIT*) pescadero/a.
fishmonger's (shop) *n* (*BRIT*) pescadería.
fishseller ['fɪʃsɛlə*] *n* (*US*) = **fishmonger**.
fish slice *n* paleta para pescado.
fish sticks *npl* (*US*) = **fish fingers**.
fishstore ['fɪʃstɔ:*] *n* (*US*) = **fishmonger's (shop)**.
fishy ['fɪʃɪ] *adj* (*fig*) sospechoso.
fission ['fɪʃən] *n* fisión *f*; **atomic/nuclear ~** fisión *f* atómica/nuclear.
fissure ['fɪʃə*] *n* fisura.
fist [fɪst] *n* puño.
fistfight ['fɪstfaɪt] *n* lucha a puñetazos.
fit [fɪt] *adj* (*MED, SPORT*) en (buena) forma; (*proper*) adecuado, apropiado ♦ *vt* (*subj*: *clothes*) quedar bien a; (*try on*: *clothes*) probar; (*match*: *facts*) cuadrar *or* corresponder *or* coincidir con; (*description*) estar de acuerdo con; (*accommodate*) ajustar, adaptar ♦ *vi* (*clothes*) quedar bien; (*in space, gap*) caber; (*facts*) coincidir ♦ *n* (*MED*) ataque *m*; (*outburst*) arranque *m*; ~ **to** apto para; ~ **for** apropiado para; **do as you think** *or* **see** ~ haz lo que te parezca mejor; **to keep** ~ mantenerse en forma; **to be ~ for work** (*after illness*) estar en condiciones para trabajar; ~ **of coughing** acceso de tos; ~ **of anger/enthusiasm** arranque de cólera/entusiasmo; **to have** *or* **suffer a** ~ tener un ataque *or* acceso; **this dress is a good** ~ este vestido me queda bien; **by ~s and starts** a rachas.
▸**fit in** *vi* encajar ♦ *vt* (*object*) acomodar; (*fig*: *appointment, visitor*) encontrar un hueco para; **to ~ in with sb's plans** acomodarse a los planes de algn.
▸**fit out** *vt* (*BRIT*: *also*: **fit up**) equipar.
fitful ['fɪtful] *adj* espasmódico, intermitente.
fitfully ['fɪtfəlɪ] *adv* irregularmente; **to sleep** ~ dormir a rachas.
fitment ['fɪtmənt] *n* mueble *m*.
fitness ['fɪtnɪs] *n* (*MED*) forma física; (*of remark*) conveniencia.
fitted carpet ['fɪtɪd-] *n* moqueta.
fitted cupboards ['fɪtɪd-] *npl* armarios *mpl* empotrados.
fitted kitchen ['fɪtɪd-] *n* cocina amueblada.
fitter ['fɪtə*] *n* ajustador(a) *m/f*.
fitting ['fɪtɪŋ] *adj* apropiado ♦ *n* (*of dress*) prueba; *see also* **fittings**.
fitting room *n* (*in shop*) probador *m*.
fittings ['fɪtɪŋz] *npl* instalaciones *fpl*.
five [faɪv] *num* cinco; **she is ~ (years old)** tiene cinco años (de edad); **it costs ~ pounds** cuesta cinco libras; **it's ~ (o'clock)** son las cinco.
five-day week ['faɪvdeɪ] *n* semana inglesa.
fiver ['faɪvə*] *n* (*col*: *BRIT*) billete *m* de cinco libras; (: *US*) billete *m* de cinco dólares.
fix [fɪks] *vt* (*secure*) fijar, asegurar; (*mend*) arreglar; (*make ready*: *meal, drink*) preparar ♦ *n*: **to be in a** ~ estar en un aprieto; **to ~ sth in one's mind** fijar algo en la memoria; **the fight was a** ~ (*col*) la pelea estaba amañada.
▸**fix on** *vt* (*decide on*) fijar.
▸**fix up** *vt* (*arrange*: *date, meeting*) arreglar; **to ~ sb up with sth** conseguirle algo a algn.
fixation [fɪk'seɪʃən] *n* (*PSYCH, fig*) fijación *f*.
fixative ['fiksətɪv] *n* fijador *m*.
fixed [fɪkst] *adj* (*prices etc*) fijo; **how are you**

~ **for money?** (*col*) ¿qué tal andas de dinero?
fixed assets *npl* activo *sg* fijo.
fixed charge *n* gasto fijo.
fixed-price contract ['fɪkstpraɪs-] *n* contrato a precio fijo.
fixture ['fɪkstʃə*] *n* (*SPORT*) encuentro; **~s** *npl* instalaciones *fpl* fijas.
fizz [fɪz] *vi* burbujear.
fizzle out ['fɪzl-] *vi* apagarse; (*enthusiasm, interest*) decaer; (*plan*) quedar en agua de borrajas.
fizzy ['fɪzɪ] *adj* (*drink*) gaseoso.
fjord [fjɔːd] *n* = **fiord.**
FL *abbr* (*US*) = *Florida.*
Fla. *abbr* (*US*) = *Florida.*
flabbergasted ['flæbəgɑːstɪd] *adj* pasmado.
flabby ['flæbɪ] *adj* flojo (de carnes); (*skin*) fofo.
flag [flæg] *n* bandera; (*stone*) losa ♦ *vi* decaer; ~ **of convenience** pabellón *m* de conveniencia.
▸**flag down** *vt*: **to ~ sb down** hacer señas a algn para que se pare.
flagpole ['flægpəul] *n* asta de bandera.
flagrant ['fleɪgrənt] *adj* flagrante.
flagship ['flægʃɪp] *n* buque *m* insignia *or* almirante.
flagstone ['flægstəun] *n* losa.
flag stop *n* (*US*) parada discrecional.
flair [flɛə*] *n* aptitud *f* especial.
flak [flæk] *n* (*MIL*) fuego antiaéreo; (*col: criticism*) lluvia de críticas.
flake [fleɪk] *n* (*of rust, paint*) desconchón *m*; (*of snow*) copo; (*of soap powder*) escama ♦ *vi* (*also*: ~ **off**) (*paint*) desconcharse; (*skin*) descamarse.
flaky ['fleɪkɪ] *adj* (*paintwork*) desconchado; (*skin*) escamoso.
flaky pastry *n* (*CULIN*) hojaldre *m.*
flamboyant [flæm'bɔɪənt] *adj* (*dress*) vistoso; (*person*) extravagante.
flame [fleɪm] *n* llama; **to burst into ~s** incendiarse; **old** ~ (*col*) antiguo amor *m/f.*
flamingo [flə'mɪŋgəu] *n* flamenco.
flammable ['flæməbl] *adj* inflamable.
flan [flæn] *n* (*BRIT*) tarta.
flank [flæŋk] *n* flanco; (*of person*) costado ♦ *vt* flanquear.
flannel ['flænl] *n* (*BRIT*: *also*: **face** ~) toallita; (*fabric*) franela; **~s** *npl* pantalones *mpl* de franela.
flannelette [flænə'lɛt] *n* franela de algodón.
flap [flæp] *n* (*of pocket, envelope*) solapa; (*of table*) hoja (plegadiza); (*wing movement*) aletazo; (*AVIAT*) flap *m* ♦ *vt* (*wings*) batir ♦ *vi* (*sail, flag*) ondear.
flapjack ['flæpdʒæk] *n* (*US*: *pancake*) torta, panqueque *m* (*LAM*).
flare [flɛə*] *n* llamarada; (*MIL*) bengala; (*in skirt etc*) vuelo.
▸**flare up** *vi* encenderse; (*fig*: *person*) encolerizarse; (: *revolt*) estallar.
flash [flæʃ] *n* relámpago; (*also*: **news** ~) noticias *fpl* de última hora; (*PHOT*) flash *m*; (*US*: *torch*) linterna ♦ *vt* (*light, headlights*) lanzar destellos con; (*torch*) encender ♦ *vi* destellar; **in a** ~ en un santiamén; ~ **of inspiration** ráfaga de inspiración; **to ~ sth about** (*fig, col*: *flaunt*) ostentar algo, presumir con algo; **he ~ed by** *or* **past** pasó como un rayo.
flashback ['flæʃbæk] *n* flashback *m*, escena retrospectiva.
flashbulb ['flæʃbʌlb] *n* bombilla de flash.
flash card *n* (*SCOL*) tarjeta.
flash cube *n* cubo *m* de flash.
flasher ['flæʃə*] *n* exhibicionista *m.*
flashlight ['flæʃlaɪt] *n* (*US*: *torch*) linterna.
flashpoint ['flæʃpɔɪnt] *n* punto de inflamación; (*fig*) punto de explosión.
flashy ['flæʃɪ] *adj* (*pej*) ostentoso.
flask [flɑːsk] *n* petaca; (*also*: **vacuum** ~) termo.
flat [flæt] *adj* llano; (*smooth*) liso; (*tyre*) desinflado; (*battery*) descargado; (*beer*) sin gas; (*MUS*: *instrument*) desafinado ♦ *n* (*BRIT*: *apartment*) piso (*SP*), departamento (*LAM*), apartamento; (*AUT*) pinchazo; (*MUS*) bemol *m*; **(to work)** ~ **out** (trabajar) a tope; ~ **rate of pay** sueldo fijo.
flatfooted [flæt'futɪd] *adj* de pies planos.
flatly ['flætlɪ] *adv* rotundamente, de plano.
flatmate ['flætmeɪt] *n* compañero/a de piso.
flatness ['flætnɪs] *n* (*of land*) llanura, lo llano.
flat-screen ['flætskriːn] *adj* de pantalla plana.
flatten ['flætn] *vt* (*also*: ~ **out**) allanar; (*smooth out*) alisar; (*house, city*) arrasar.
flatter ['flætə*] *vt* adular, halagar; (*show to advantage*) favorecer.
flatterer ['flætərə*] *n* adulador(a) *m/f.*
flattering ['flætərɪŋ] *adj* halagador(a); (*clothes etc*) que favorece, favorecedor(a).
flattery ['flætərɪ] *n* adulación *f.*
flatulence ['flætjuləns] *n* flatulencia.
flaunt [flɔːnt] *vt* ostentar, lucir.
flavour, (*US*) **flavor** ['fleɪvə*] *n* sabor *m*, gusto ♦ *vt* sazonar, condimentar; **strawberry ~ed** con sabor a fresa.
flavo(u)ring ['fleɪvərɪŋ] *n* (*in product*) aromatizante *m.*

flaw [flɔː] *n* defecto.
flawless ['flɔːlɪs] *adj* intachable.
flax [flæks] *n* lino.
flaxen ['flæksən] *adj* muy rubio.
flea [fliː] *n* pulga.
flea market *n* rastro, mercadillo.
fleck [flɛk] *n* mota ♦ *vt* (*with blood, mud etc*) salpicar; **brown ~ed with white** marrón con motas blancas.
fledg(e)ling ['flɛdʒlɪŋ] *n* (*fig*) novato/a, principiante *m/f*.
flee [fliː], *pt, pp* **fled** [flɛd] *vt* huir de, abandonar ♦ *vi* huir.
fleece [fliːs] *n* vellón *m*; (*wool*) lana ♦ *vt* (*col*) desplumar.
fleecy ['fliːsɪ] *adj* (*blanket*) lanoso, lanudo; (*cloud*) aborregado.
fleet [fliːt] *n* flota; (*of cars, lorries etc*) parque *m*.
fleeting ['fliːtɪŋ] *adj* fugaz.
Flemish ['flɛmɪʃ] *adj* flamenco ♦ *n* (*LING*) flamenco; **the ~** los flamencos.
flesh [flɛʃ] *n* carne *f*; (*of fruit*) pulpa; **of ~ and blood** de carne y hueso.
flesh wound *n* herida superficial.
flew [fluː] *pt of* **fly**.
flex [flɛks] *n* cable *m* ♦ *vt* (*muscles*) tensar.
flexibility [flɛksɪ'bɪlɪtɪ] *n* flexibilidad *f*.
flexible ['flɛksəbl] *adj* (*gen, disk*) flexible; **~ working hours** horario *sg* flexible.
flexitime ['flɛksɪtaɪm] *n* horario flexible.
flick [flɪk] *n* golpecito; (*with finger*) capirotazo; (*BRIT: col: film*) película ♦ *vt* dar un golpecito a.
►**flick off** *vt* quitar con el dedo.
►**flick through** *vt fus* hojear.
flicker ['flɪkə*] *vi* (*light*) parpadear; (*flame*) vacilar ♦ *n* parpadeo.
flick knife *n* navaja de muelle.
flier ['flaɪə*] *n* aviador(a) *m/f*.
flies [flaɪz] *npl of* **fly**.
flight [flaɪt] *n* vuelo; (*escape*) huida, fuga; (*also*: **~ of steps**) tramo (de escaleras); **to take ~** huir, darse a la fuga; **to put to ~** ahuyentar; **how long does the ~ take?** ¿cuánto dura el vuelo?
flight attendant *n* (*US*) auxiliar *m/f* de vuelo.
flight deck *n* (*AVIAT*) cabina de mandos.
flight path *n* trayectoria de vuelo.
flight recorder *n* registrador *m* de vuelo.
flighty ['flaɪtɪ] *adj* caprichoso.
flimsy ['flɪmzɪ] *adj* (*thin*) muy ligero; (*excuse*) flojo.
flinch [flɪntʃ] *vi* encogerse.
fling [flɪŋ] *vt* (*pt, pp* **flung** [flʌŋ]) arrojar ♦ *n* (*love affair*) aventura amorosa.
flint [flɪnt] *n* pedernal *m*; (*in lighter*) piedra.
flip [flɪp] *vt*: **to ~ a coin** echar a cara o cruz.
►**flip over** *vt* dar la vuelta a.
►**flip through** *vt fus* (*book*) hojear; (*records*) ver de pasada.
flippancy ['flɪpənsɪ] *n* ligereza.
flippant ['flɪpənt] *adj* poco serio.
flipper ['flɪpə*] *n* (*of seal etc, for swimming*) aleta.
flip side *n* (*of record*) cara B.
flirt [fləːt] *vi* coquetear, flirtear ♦ *n* coqueta *f*.
flirtation [fləː'teɪʃən] *n* coqueteo, flirteo.
flit [flɪt] *vi* revolotear.
float [fləut] *n* flotador *m*; (*in procession*) carroza; (*sum of money*) (dinero suelto para) cambio ♦ *vi* (*also COMM: currency*) flotar ♦ *vt* (*gen*) hacer flotar; (*company*) lanzar; **to ~ an idea** plantear una idea.
floating ['fləutɪŋ] *adj*: **~ vote** voto indeciso; **~ voter** votante *m/f* indeciso/a.
flock [flɔk] *n* (*of sheep*) rebaño; (*of birds*) bandada; (*of people*) multitud *f*.
floe [fləu] *n*: **ice ~** témpano de hielo.
flog [flɔg] *vt* azotar; (*col*) vender.
flood [flʌd] *n* inundación *f*; (*of words, tears etc*) torrente *m* ♦ *vt* (*also AUT: carburettor*) inundar; **to ~ the market** (*COMM*) inundar el mercado.
flooding ['flʌdɪŋ] *n* inundación *f*.
floodlight ['flʌdlaɪt] *n* foco ♦ *vt* (*irreg: like* **light**) iluminar con focos.
floodlit ['flʌdlɪt] *pt, pp of* **floodlight** ♦ *adj* iluminado.
flood tide *n* pleamar *f*.
floodwater ['flʌdwɔːtə*] *n* aguas *fpl* (*de la inundación*).
floor [flɔː*] *n* suelo, piso (*LAM*); (*storey*) piso; (*of sea, valley*) fondo; (*dance ~*) pista ♦ *vt* (*fig: baffle*) dejar anonadado; **ground ~**, (*US*) **first ~** planta baja; **first ~**, (*US*) **second ~** primer piso; **top ~** último piso; **to have the ~** (*speaker*) tener la palabra.
floorboard ['flɔːbɔːd] *n* tabla.
flooring ['flɔːrɪŋ] *n* suelo; (*material*) solería.
floor lamp *n* (*US*) lámpara de pie.
floor show *n* cabaret *m*.
floorwalker ['flɔːwɔːkə*] *n* (*US COMM*) supervisor(a) *m/f*.
flop [flɔp] *n* fracaso ♦ *vi* (*fail*) fracasar.
floppy ['flɔpɪ] *adj* flojo ♦ *n* = **floppy disk**.
floppy disk *n* (*COMPUT*) floppy *m*, floppy-disk *m*, disco flexible.
flora ['flɔːrə] *n* flora.
floral ['flɔːrl] *adj* floral; (*dress, wallpaper*) de flores.
Florence ['flɔrəns] *n* Florencia.
Florentine ['flɔrəntaɪn] *adj, n* florentino/a *m/f*.

florid ['flɔrɪd] *adj* (*style*) florido.
florist ['flɔrɪst] *n* florista *m/f*; **~'s (shop)** *n* floristería.
flotation [fləu'teɪʃən] *n* (*of shares*) emisión *f*; (*of company*) lanzamiento.
flounce [flauns] *n* volante *m*.
▸**flounce in** *vi* entrar con gesto exagerado.
▸**flounce out** *vi* salir con gesto airado.
flounder ['flaundə*] *vi* tropezar ♦ *n* (*ZOOL*) platija.
flour ['flauə*] *n* harina.
flourish ['flʌrɪʃ] *vi* florecer ♦ *n* ademán *m*, movimiento (ostentoso).
flourishing ['flʌrɪʃɪŋ] *adj* floreciente.
flout [flaut] *vt* burlarse de; (*order*) no hacer caso de, hacer caso omiso de.
flow [fləu] *n* (*movement*) flujo; (*direction*) curso; (*of river, also ELEC*) corriente *f* ♦ *vi* correr, fluir.
flow chart *n* organigrama *m*.
flow diagram *n* organigrama *m*.
flower ['flauə*] *n* flor *f* ♦ *vi* florecer; **in ~** en flor.
flower bed *n* macizo.
flowerpot ['flauəpɔt] *n* tiesto.
flowery ['flauərɪ] *adj* florido; (*perfume, pattern*) de flores.
flowing ['fləuɪŋ] *adj* (*hair, clothes*) suelto; (*style*) fluido.
flown [fləun] *pp of* **fly**.
flu [flu:] *n* gripe *f*.
fluctuate ['flʌktjueɪt] *vi* fluctuar.
fluctuation [flʌktju'eɪʃən] *n* fluctuación *f*.
flue [flu:] *n* cañón *m*.
fluency ['flu:ənsɪ] *n* fluidez *f*, soltura.
fluent ['flu:ənt] *adj* (*speech*) elocuente; **he speaks ~ French, he's ~ in French** domina el francés.
fluently ['flu:əntlɪ] *adv* con soltura.
fluff [flʌf] *n* pelusa.
fluffy ['flʌfɪ] *adj* lanoso.
fluid ['flu:ɪd] *adj, n* fluido, líquido; (*in diet*) líquido.
fluke [flu:k] *n* (*col*) chiripa.
flummox ['flʌməks] *vt* desconcertar.
flung [flʌŋ] *pt, pp of* **fling**.
flunky ['flʌŋkɪ] *n* lacayo.
fluorescent [fluə'rɛsnt] *adj* fluorescente.
fluoride ['fluəraɪd] *n* fluoruro.
fluoride toothpaste *n* pasta de dientes con flúor.
flurry ['flʌrɪ] *n* (*of snow*) ventisca; (*haste*) agitación *f*; **~ of activity** frenesí *m* de actividad.
flush [flʌʃ] *n* (*on face*) rubor *m*; (*fig: of youth, beauty*) resplandor *m* ♦ *vt* limpiar con agua; (*also:* **~ out**) (*game, birds*) levantar; (*fig: criminal*) poner al descubierto ♦ *vi* ruborizarse ♦ *adj:* **~ with** a ras de; **to ~ the toilet** tirar de la cadena (del wáter); **hot ~es** (*MED*) sofocos *mpl*.
flushed [flʌʃt] *adj* ruborizado.
fluster ['flʌstə*] *n* aturdimiento ♦ *vt* aturdir.
flustered ['flʌstəd] *adj* aturdido.
flute [flu:t] *n* flauta travesera.
flutter ['flʌtə*] *n* (*of wings*) revoloteo, aleteo; (*fam: bet*) apuesta ♦ *vi* revolotear; **to be in a ~** estar nervioso.
flux [flʌks] *n* flujo; **in a state of ~** cambiando continuamente.
fly [flaɪ] *n* (*insect*) mosca; (*on trousers: also:* **flies**) bragueta ♦ *vb* (*pt* **flew**, *pp* **flown**) *vt* (*plane*) pilotar; (*cargo*) transportar (en avión); (*distances*) recorrer (en avión) ♦ *vi* volar; (*passengers*) ir en avión; (*escape*) evadirse; (*flag*) ondear.
▸**fly away** *vi* (*bird, insect*) irse volando.
▸**fly in** *vi* (*person*) llegar en avión; (*plane*) aterrizar; **he flew in from Bilbao** llegó en avión desde Bilbao.
▸**fly off** *vi* irse volando.
▸**fly out** *vi* irse en avión.
fly-fishing ['flaɪfɪʃɪŋ] *n* pesca con mosca.
flying ['flaɪɪŋ] *n* (*activity*) (el) volar ♦ *adj:* **~ visit** visita relámpago; **with ~ colours** con lucimiento.
flying buttress *n* arbotante *m*.
flying picket *n* piquete *m* volante.
flying saucer *n* platillo volante.
flying squad *n* (*POLICE*) brigada móvil.
flying start *n*: **to get off to a ~** empezar con buen pie.
flyleaf, *pl* **flyleaves** ['flaɪli:f, -li:vz] *n* (hoja de) guarda.
flyover ['flaɪəuvə*] *n* (*BRIT: bridge*) paso elevado *or* a desnivel (*LAM*).
flypast ['flaɪpɑ:st] *n* desfile *m* aéreo.
flysheet ['flaɪʃi:t] *n* (*for tent*) doble techo.
flyswatter ['flaɪswɔtə*] *n* matamoscas *m inv*.
flyweight ['flaɪweɪt] *adj* de peso mosca ♦ *n* peso mosca.
flywheel ['flaɪwi:l] *n* volante *m* (de motor).
FM *abbr* (*BRIT MIL*) = **field marshal**; (*RADIO:* = *frequency modulation*) FM.
FMB *n abbr* (*US*) = *Federal Maritime Board*.
FMCS *n abbr* (*US:* = *Federal Mediation and Conciliation Services*) *organismo de conciliación en conflictos laborales*.
FO *n abbr* (*BRIT:* = *Foreign Office*) ≈ Min. de AA. EE.
foal [fəul] *n* potro.
foam [fəum] *n* espuma ♦ *vi* hacer espuma.
foam rubber *n* goma espuma.

FOB *abbr* (= *free on board*) f.a.b.
fob [fɔb] *n* (*also*: **watch ~**) leontina ♦ *vt*: **to ~ sb off with sth** deshacerse de algn con algo.
foc *abbr* (*BRIT*: = *free of charge*) gratis.
focal ['fəukəl] *adj* focal; **~ point** punto focal; (*fig*) centro de atención.
focus ['fəukəs] (*pl*: **~es**) *n* foco ♦ *vt* (*field glasses etc*) enfocar ♦ *vi*: **to ~ (on)** enfocar (a); (*issue etc*) centrarse en; **in/out of ~** enfocado/desenfocado.
fodder ['fɔdə*] *n* pienso.
FOE *n abbr* (= *Friends of the Earth*) Amigos *mpl* de la Tierra; (*US*: = *Fraternal Order of Eagles*) *organización benéfica*.
foe [fəu] *n* enemigo.
foetus, (*US*) **fetus** ['fi:təs] *n* feto.
fog [fɔg] *n* niebla.
fogbound ['fɔgbaund] *adj* inmovilizado por la niebla.
foggy ['fɔgɪ] *adj*: **it's ~** hay niebla.
fog lamp, (*US*) **fog light** *n* (*AUT*) faro antiniebla.
foible ['fɔɪbl] *n* manía.
foil [fɔɪl] *vt* frustrar ♦ *n* hoja; (*kitchen ~*) papel *m* (de) aluminio; (*FENCING*) florete *m*.
foist [fɔɪst] *vt*: **to ~ sth on sb** endilgarle algo a algn.
fold [fəuld] *n* (*bend, crease*) pliegue *m*; (*AGR*) redil *m* ♦ *vt* doblar; (*map etc*) plegar; **to ~ one's arms** cruzarse de brazos.
►**fold up** *vi* plegarse, doblarse; (*business*) quebrar.
folder ['fəuldə*] *n* (*for papers*) carpeta; (*binder*) carpeta de anillas; (*brochure*) folleto.
folding ['fəuldɪŋ] *adj* (*chair, bed*) plegable.
foliage ['fəulɪɪdʒ] *n* follaje *m*.
folio ['fəulɪəu] *n* folio.
folk [fəuk] *npl* gente *f* ♦ *adj* popular, folklórico; **~s** *npl* familia, parientes *mpl*.
folklore ['fəuklɔ:*] *n* folklore *m*.
folk music *n* música folk.
folk singer *n* cantante *m/f* de música folk.
folk song *n* canción *f* popular *or* folk.
follow ['fɔləu] *vt* seguir ♦ *vi* seguir; (*result*) resultar; **he ~ed suit** hizo lo mismo; **to ~ sb's advice** seguir el consejo de algn; **I don't quite ~ you** no te comprendo muy bien; **to ~ in sb's footsteps** seguir los pasos de algn; **it doesn't ~ that ...** no se deduce que ....
►**follow on** *vi* seguir; (*continue*): **to ~ on from** ser la consecuencia lógica de.
►**follow out** *vt* (*implement*: *idea, plan*) realizar, llevar a cabo.
►**follow through** *vt* llevar hasta el fin ♦ *vi* (*SPORT*) dar el remate.
►**follow up** *vt* (*letter, offer*) responder a; (*case*) investigar.
follower ['fɔləuə*] *n* seguidor(a) *m/f*; (*POL*) partidario/a.
following ['fɔləuɪŋ] *adj* siguiente ♦ *n* seguidores *mpl*.
follow-up ['fɔləuʌp] *n* continuación *f*.
follow-up letter *n* carta recordatoria.
folly ['fɔlɪ] *n* locura.
fond [fɔnd] *adj* (*loving*) cariñoso; **to be ~ of sb** tener cariño a algn; **she's ~ of swimming** tiene afición a la natación, le gusta nadar.
fondle ['fɔndl] *vt* acariciar.
fondly ['fɔndlɪ] *adv* (*lovingly*) con cariño; **he ~ believed that ...** creía ingenuamente que ....
fondness ['fɔndnɪs] *n* (*for things*) afición *f*; (*for people*) cariño.
font [fɔnt] *n* pila bautismal.
food [fu:d] *n* comida.
food chain *n* cadena alimenticia.
food mixer *n* batidora.
food poisoning *n* intoxicación *f* alimentaria.
food processor *n* robot *m* de cocina.
food stamp *n* (*US*) vale *m* para comida.
foodstuffs ['fu:dstʌfs] *npl* comestibles *mpl*.
fool [fu:l] *n* tonto/a; (*CULIN*) mousse *m* de frutas ♦ *vt* engañar; **to make a ~ of o.s.** ponerse en ridículo; **you can't ~ me** a mí no me engañas; *see also* **April Fool's Day**.
►**fool about, fool around** *vi* hacer el tonto.
foolhardy ['fu:lhɑ:dɪ] *adj* temerario.
foolish ['fu:lɪʃ] *adj* tonto; (*careless*) imprudente.
foolishly ['fu:lɪʃlɪ] *adv* tontamente, neciamente.
foolproof ['fu:lpru:f] *adj* (*plan etc*) infalible.
foolscap ['fu:lskæp] *n* ≈ papel *m* tamaño folio.
foot [fut], *pl* **feet** *n* (*gen, also*: *of page, stairs etc*) pie *m*; (*measure*) pie (= *304 mm*); (*of animal, table*) pata ♦ *vt* (*bill*) pagar; **on ~** a pie; **to find one's feet** acostumbrarse; **to put one's ~ down** (*say no*) plantarse; (*AUT*) pisar el acelerador.
footage ['futɪdʒ] *n* (*CINE*) imágenes *fpl*.
foot-and-mouth (disease) [futənd'mauθ-] *n* fiebre *f* aftosa.
football ['futbɔ:l] *n* balón *m*; (*game*: *BRIT*) fútbol *m*; (: *US*) fútbol *m* americano.
footballer ['futbɔ:lə*] *n* (*BRIT*) = **football player**.
football match *n* partido de fútbol.
football player *n* futbolista *m/f*, jugador(a)

m/f de fútbol.

footbrake ['futbreɪk] *n* freno de pie.

footbridge ['futbrɪdʒ] *n* pasarela, puente *m* para peatones.

foothills ['futhɪlz] *npl* estribaciones *fpl*.

foothold ['futhəuld] *n* pie *m* firme.

footing ['futɪŋ] *n* (*fig*) nivel *m*; **to lose one's ~** perder el equilibrio; **on an equal ~** en pie de igualdad.

footlights ['futlaɪts] *npl* candilejas *fpl*.

footman ['futmən] *n* lacayo.

footnote ['futnəut] *n* nota (de pie de página).

footpath ['futpɑːθ] *n* sendero.

footprint ['futprɪnt] *n* huella, pisada.

footrest ['futrɛst] *n* apoyapiés *m inv*.

footsie ['futsɪ] *n*: **to play ~ with sb** (*col*) juguetear con los pies de algn.

footsore ['futsɔː*] *adj* con los pies doloridos.

footstep ['futstɛp] *n* paso.

footwear ['futwɛə*] *n* calzado.

FOR *abbr* (= *free on rail*) franco (puesto sobre) vagón.

KEYWORD

for [fɔː] *prep* **1** (*indicating destination, intention*) para; **the train ~ London** el tren para Londres; (*in announcements*) el tren con destino a Londres; **he left ~ Rome** marchó para Roma; **he went ~ the paper** fue por el periódico; **is this ~ me?** ¿es esto para mí?; **it's time ~ lunch** es la hora de comer

2 (*indicating purpose*) para; **what('s it) ~?** ¿para qué (es)?; **what's this button ~?** ¿para qué sirve este botón?; **to pray ~ peace** rezar por la paz

3 (*on behalf of, representing*): **the MP ~ Hove** el diputado por Hove; **he works ~ the government/a local firm** trabaja para el gobierno/en una empresa local; **I'll ask him ~ you** se lo pediré por ti; **G ~ George** G de Gerona

4 (*because of*) por esta razón; **~ fear of being criticized** por temor a ser criticado

5 (*with regard to*) para; **it's cold ~ July** hace frío para julio; **he has a gift ~ languages** tiene don de lenguas

6 (*in exchange for*) por; **I sold it ~ £5** lo vendí por £5; **to pay 50 pence ~ a ticket** pagar 50 peniques por un billete

7 (*in favour of*): **are you ~ or against us?** ¿estás con nosotros o contra nosotros?; **I'm all ~ it** estoy totalmente a favor; **vote ~ X** vote (a) X

8 (*referring to distance*): **there are roadworks ~ 5 km** hay obras en 5 km; **we walked ~ miles** caminamos kilómetros y kilómetros

9 (*referring to time*): **he was away ~ 2 years** estuvo fuera (durante) dos años; **it hasn't rained ~ 3 weeks** no ha llovido durante *or* en 3 semanas; **I have known her ~ years** la conozco desde hace años; **can you do it ~ tomorrow?** ¿lo podrás hacer para mañana?

10 (*with infinitive clauses*): **it is not ~ me to decide** la decisión no es cosa mía; **it would be best ~ you to leave** sería mejor que te fueras; **there is still time ~ you to do it** todavía te queda tiempo para hacerlo; **~ this to be possible ...** para que esto sea posible ...

11 (*in spite of*) a pesar de; **~ all his complaints** a pesar de sus quejas

♦ *conj* (*since, as*: *rather formal*) puesto que.

forage ['fɔrɪdʒ] *n* forraje *m*.

foray ['fɔreɪ] *n* incursión *f*.

forbid, *pt* **forbad(e)**, *pp* **forbidden** [fə'bɪd, -'bæd, -'bɪdn] *vt* prohibir; **to ~ sb to do sth** prohibir a algn hacer algo.

forbidding [fə'bɪdɪŋ] *adj* (*landscape*) inhóspito; (*severe*) severo.

force [fɔːs] *n* fuerza ♦ *vt* obligar, forzar; **to ~ o.s. to do** hacer un esfuerzo por hacer; **the F~s** *npl* (*BRIT*) las Fuerzas Armadas; **sales ~** (*COMM*) personal *m* de ventas; **a ~ 5 wind** un viento fuerza 5; **to join ~s** unir fuerzas; **in ~** (*law etc*) en vigor; **to ~ sb to do sth** obligar a algn a hacer algo.

▶**force back** *vt* (*crowd, enemy*) hacer retroceder; (*tears*) reprimir.

▶**force down** *vt* (*food*) tragar con esfuerzo.

forced [fɔːst] *adj* (*smile*) forzado; (*landing*) forzoso.

force-feed ['fɔːsfiːd] *vt* (*animal, prisoner*) alimentar a la fuerza.

forceful ['fɔːsful] *adj* enérgico.

forcemeat ['fɔːsmiːt] *n* (*CULIN*) relleno.

forceps ['fɔːsɛps] *npl* fórceps *m inv*.

forcible ['fɔːsəbl] *adj* (*violent*) a la fuerza; (*telling*) convincente.

forcibly ['fɔːsəblɪ] *adv* a la fuerza.

ford [fɔːd] *n* vado ♦ *vt* vadear.

fore [fɔː*] *n*: **to bring to the ~** sacar a la luz pública; **to come to the ~** empezar a destacar.

forearm ['fɔːrɑːm] *n* antebrazo.

forebear ['fɔːbɛə*] *n* antepasado.

foreboding [fɔː'bəudɪŋ] *n* presentimiento.

forecast ['fɔːkɑːst] *n* pronóstico ♦ *vt* (*irreg*: *like* **cast**) pronosticar; **weather ~** previsión *f* meteorológica.

foreclose [fɔː'kləuz] *vt* (*LAW*: *also*: ~ **on**) extinguir el derecho de redimir.
foreclosure [fɔː'kləuʒə*] *n* apertura de un juicio hipotecario.
forecourt ['fɔːkɔːt] *n* (*of garage*) área de entrada.
forefathers ['fɔːfɑːðəz] *npl* antepasados *mpl*.
forefinger ['fɔːfɪŋgə*] *n* (dedo) índice *m*.
forefront ['fɔːfrʌnt] *n*: **in the** ~ **of** en la vanguardia de.
forego, *pt* **forewent**, *pp* **foregone** [fɔː'gəu, -'wɛnt, -'gɔn] *vt* = **forgo**.
foregoing ['fɔːgəuɪŋ] *adj* anterior, precedente.
foregone ['fɔːgɔn] *pp of* **forego** ♦ *adj*: **it's a** ~ **conclusion** es una conclusión inevitable.
foreground ['fɔːgraund] *n* primer plano.
forehand ['fɔːhænd] *n* (*TENNIS*) derechazo directo.
forehead ['fɔrɪd] *n* frente *f*.
foreign ['fɔrɪn] *adj* extranjero; (*trade*) exterior.
foreign currency *n* divisas *fpl*.
foreigner ['fɔrɪnə*] *n* extranjero/a.
foreign exchange *n* (*system*) cambio de divisas; (*money*) divisas *fpl*, moneda extranjera.
foreign investment *n* inversión *f* en el extranjero; (*money, stock*) inversiones *fpl* extranjeras.
Foreign Minister *n* Ministro/a de Asuntos Exteriores, Canciller *m* (*LAM*).
Foreign Office *n* Ministerio de Asuntos Exteriores.
Foreign Secretary *n* (*BRIT*) Ministro/a de Asuntos Exteriores, Canciller *m* (*LAM*).
foreleg ['fɔːlɛg] *n* pata delantera.
foreman ['fɔːmən] *n* capataz *m*; (*LAW*: *of jury*) presidente *m/f*.
foremost ['fɔːməust] *adj* principal ♦ *adv*: **first and** ~ ante todo, antes que nada.
forename ['fɔːneɪm] *n* nombre *m* (de pila).
forensic [fə'rɛnsɪk] *adj* forense; ~ **scientist** forense *m/f*.
foreplay ['fɔːpleɪ] *n* preámbulos *mpl* (*de estimulación sexual*).
forerunner ['fɔːrʌnə*] *n* precursor(a) *m/f*.
foresee, *pt* **foresaw**, *pp* **foreseen** [fɔː'siː, -'sɔː, -'siːn] *vt* prever.
foreseeable [fɔː'siːəbl] *adj* previsible.
foreshadow [fɔː'ʃædəu] *vt* prefigurar, anunciar.
foreshore ['fɔːʃɔː*] *n* playa.
foreshorten [fɔː'ʃɔːtn] *vt* (*figure, scene*) escorzar.
foresight ['fɔːsaɪt] *n* previsión *f*.
foreskin ['fɔːskɪn] *n* (*ANAT*) prepucio.
forest ['fɔrɪst] *n* bosque *m*.
forestall [fɔː'stɔːl] *vt* anticiparse a.
forestry ['fɔrɪstrɪ] *n* silvicultura.
foretaste ['fɔːteɪst] *n* anticipo.
foretell, *pt, pp* **foretold** [fɔː'tɛl, -'təuld] *vt* predecir, pronosticar.
forethought ['fɔːθɔːt] *n* previsión *f*.
forever [fə'rɛvə*] *adv* siempre; (*for good*) para siempre.
forewarn [fɔː'wɔːn] *vt* avisar, advertir.
forewent [fɔː'wɛnt] *pt of* **forego**.
foreword ['fɔːwəːd] *n* prefacio.
forfeit ['fɔːfɪt] *n* (*in game*) prenda ♦ *vt* perder (derecho a).
forgave [fə'geɪv] *pt of* **forgive**.
forge [fɔːdʒ] *n* fragua; (*smithy*) herrería ♦ *vt* (*signature*: *BRIT*: *money*) falsificar; (*metal*) forjar.
▸**forge ahead** *vi* avanzar mucho.
forger ['fɔːdʒə*] *n* falsificador(a) *m/f*.
forgery ['fɔːdʒərɪ] *n* falsificación *f*.
forget, *pt* **forgot**, *pp* **forgotten** [fə'gɛt, -'gɔt, -'gɔtn] *vt* olvidar, olvidarse de ♦ *vi* olvidarse.
forgetful [fə'gɛtful] *adj* olvidadizo.
forget-me-not [fə'gɛtmɪnɔt] *n* nomeolvides *f inv*.
forgive, *pt* **forgave**, *pp* **forgiven** [fə'gɪv, -'geɪv, -'gɪvn] *vt* perdonar; **to** ~ **sb for sth/for doing sth** perdonar algo a algn/a algn por haber hecho algo.
forgiveness [fə'gɪvnɪs] *n* perdón *m*.
forgiving [fə'gɪvɪŋ] *adj* compasivo.
forgo, *pt* **forwent**, *pp* **forgone** [fɔː'gəu, -'wɛnt, -'gɔn] *vt* (*give up*) renunciar a; (*go without*) privarse de.
forgot [fə'gɔt] *pt of* **forget**.
forgotten [fə'gɔtn] *pp of* **forget**.
fork [fɔːk] *n* (*for eating*) tenedor *m*; (*for gardening*) horca; (*of roads*) bifurcación *f*; (*in tree*) horcadura ♦ *vi* (*road*) bifurcarse.
▸**fork out** *vt* (*col*: *pay*) soltar.
forked [fɔːkt] *adj* (*lightning*) en zigzag.
fork-lift truck ['fɔːklɪft-] *n* máquina elevadora.
forlorn [fə'lɔːn] *adj* (*person*) triste, melancólico; (*deserted*: *cottage*) abandonado; (*desperate*: *attempt*) desesperado.
form [fɔːm] *n* forma; (*BRIT SCOL*) curso; (*document*) formulario, planilla (*LAM*) ♦ *vt* formar; **in the** ~ **of** en forma de; **in top** ~ en plena forma; **to be in good** ~ (*SPORT, fig*) estar en plena forma; **to** ~ **part of sth** formar parte de algo; **to** ~ **a circle/a queue** hacer una curva/una cola.
formal ['fɔːməl] *adj* (*offer, receipt*) por escrito; (*person etc*) correcto; (*occasion, dinner*) ceremonioso; ~ **dress** traje *m* de

vestir; (*evening dress*) traje *m* de etiqueta.
formalities [fɔːˈmælɪtɪz] *npl* formalidades *fpl*.
formality [fɔːˈmælɪtɪ] *n* ceremonia.
formalize [ˈfɔːməlaɪz] *vt* formalizar.
formally [ˈfɔːməlɪ] *adv* oficialmente.
format [ˈfɔːmæt] *n* formato ♦ *vt* (*COMPUT*) formatear.
formation [fɔːˈmeɪʃən] *n* formación *f*.
formative [ˈfɔːmətɪv] *adj* (*years*) de formación.
format line *n* (*COMPUT*) línea de formato.
former [ˈfɔːmə*] *adj* anterior; (*earlier*) antiguo; (*ex*) ex; **the ~ ... the latter ...** aquél ... éste ...; **the ~ president** el antiguo *or* ex presidente; **the ~ Yugoslavia/Soviet Union** la antigua *or* ex Yugoslavia/Unión Soviética.
formerly [ˈfɔːməlɪ] *adv* antiguamente.
form feed *n* (*on printer*) salto de página.
Formica ® [fɔːˈmaɪkə] *n* formica ®.
formidable [ˈfɔːmɪdəbl] *adj* formidable.
formula [ˈfɔːmjulə] *n* fórmula; **F~ One** (*AUT*) Fórmula Uno.
formulate [ˈfɔːmjuleɪt] *vt* formular.
fornicate [ˈfɔːnɪkeɪt] *vi* fornicar.
forsake, *pt* **forsook**, *pp* **forsaken** [fəˈseɪk, -ˈsuk, -ˈseɪkən] *vt* (*gen*) abandonar; (*plan*) renunciar a.
fort [fɔːt] *n* fuerte *m*; **to hold the ~** (*fig*) quedarse a cargo.
forte [ˈfɔːtɪ] *n* fuerte *m*.
forth [fɔːθ] *adv*: **back and ~** de acá para allá; **and so ~** y así sucesivamente.
forthcoming [fɔːθˈkʌmɪŋ] *adj* próximo, venidero; (*character*) comunicativo.
forthright [ˈfɔːθraɪt] *adj* franco.
forthwith [ˈfɔːθˈwɪθ] *adv* en el acto, acto seguido.
fortification [fɔːtɪfɪˈkeɪʃən] *n* fortificación *f*.
fortified wine [ˈfɔːtɪfaɪd-] *n* vino encabezado.
fortify [ˈfɔːtɪfaɪ] *vt* fortalecer.
fortitude [ˈfɔːtɪtjuːd] *n* fortaleza.
fortnight [ˈfɔːtnaɪt] *n* (*BRIT*) quincena; **it's a ~ since** ... hace quince días que ....
fortnightly [ˈfɔːtnaɪtlɪ] *adj* quincenal ♦ *adv* quincenalmente.
FORTRAN [ˈfɔːtræn] *n* FORTRAN *m*.
fortress [ˈfɔːtrɪs] *n* fortaleza.
fortuitous [fɔːˈtjuːɪtəs] *adj* fortuito.
fortunate [ˈfɔːtʃənɪt] *adj*: **it is ~ that** ... (es una) suerte que ....
fortunately [ˈfɔːtʃənɪtlɪ] *adv* afortunadamente.
fortune [ˈfɔːtʃən] *n* suerte *f*; (*wealth*) fortuna; **to make a ~** hacer un dineral.
fortuneteller [ˈfɔːtʃəntɛlə*] *n* adivino/a.
forty [ˈfɔːtɪ] *num* cuarenta.
forum [ˈfɔːrəm] *n* (*also fig*) foro.
forward [ˈfɔːwəd] *adj* (*position*) avanzado; (*movement*) hacia delante; (*front*) delantero; (*not shy*) atrevido ♦ *n* (*SPORT*) delantero ♦ *vt* (*letter*) remitir; (*career*) promocionar; **to move ~** avanzar; **"please ~"** "remítase al destinatario".
forward contract *n* contrato a término.
forward exchange *n* cambio a término.
forward planning *n* planificación *f* por anticipado.
forward rate *n* tipo a término.
forward(s) [ˈfɔːwəd(z)] *adv* (hacia) adelante.
forward sales *npl* ventas *fpl* a término.
forwent [fɔːˈwɛnt] *pt of* **forgo**.
fossil [ˈfɔsl] *n* fósil *m*; **~ fuel** combustible *m* fósil.
foster [ˈfɔstə*] *vt* (*child*) acoger en familia; (*idea*) fomentar.
foster brother *n* hermano de leche.
foster child *n* hijo/a adoptivo/a.
foster mother *n* madre *f* adoptiva.
fought [fɔːt] *pt, pp of* **fight**.
foul [faul] *adj* (*gen*) sucio, puerco; (*weather, smell etc*) asqueroso ♦ *n* (*FOOTBALL*) falta ♦ *vt* (*dirty*) ensuciar; (*block*) atascar; (*entangle*: *anchor, propeller*) atascar, enredarse en; (*football player*) cometer una falta contra.
foul play *n* (*SPORT*) mala jugada; (*LAW*) muerte *f* violenta.
found [faund] *pt, pp of* **find** ♦ *vt* (*establish*) fundar.
foundation [faunˈdeɪʃən] *n* (*act*) fundación *f*; (*basis*) base *f*; (*also*: **~ cream**) base *f* de maquillaje.
foundations [faunˈdeɪʃənz] *npl* (*of building*) cimientos *mpl*; **to lay the ~** poner los cimientos.
foundation stone *n*: **to lay the ~** poner la primera piedra.
founder [ˈfaundə*] *n* fundador(a) *m/f* ♦ *vi* irse a pique.
founding [ˈfaundɪŋ] *adj*: **~ fathers** (*esp US*) fundadores *mpl*, próceres *mpl*; **~ member** miembro fundador.
foundry [ˈfaundrɪ] *n* fundición *f*.
fountain [ˈfauntɪn] *n* fuente *f*.
fountain pen *n* (pluma) estilográfica, (*LAM*) plumafuente *f*.
four [fɔː*] *num* cuatro; **on all ~s** a gatas.
four-footed [fɔːˈfutɪd] *adj* cuadrúpedo.
four-letter word [ˈfɔːlɛtə-] *n* taco.
four-poster [ˈfɔːˈpəustə*] *n* (*also*: **~ bed**) cama de columnas.
foursome [ˈfɔːsəm] *n* grupo de cuatro

personas.
fourteen ['fɔː'tiːn] *num* catorce.
fourteenth [fɔː'tiːnθ] *num* decimocuarto.
fourth [fɔːθ] *num* cuarto ♦ *n* (*AUT: also*: ~ **gear**) cuarta (velocidad).
four-wheel drive ['fɔːwiːl-] *n* tracción *f* a las cuatro ruedas.
fowl [faul] *n* ave *f* (de corral).
fox [fɔks] *n* zorro ♦ *vt* confundir.
fox fur *n* piel *f* de zorro.
foxglove ['fɔksglʌv] *n* (*BOT*) dedalera.
fox-hunting ['fɔkshʌntɪŋ] *n* caza de zorros.
foxtrot ['fɔkstrɔt] *n* fox(trot) *m*.
foyer ['fɔɪeɪ] *n* vestíbulo.
FP *n abbr* (*BRIT*) = *former pupil*; (*US*) = **fireplug**.
FPA *n abbr* (*BRIT*: = *Family Planning Association*) *asociación de planificación familiar*.
Fr. *abbr* (*REL*) (= *Father*) P.; (= *friar*) Fr.
fr. *abbr* (= *franc*) f.
fracas ['frækɑː] *n* gresca, refriega.
fraction ['frækʃən] *n* fracción *f*.
fractionally ['frækʃnəlɪ] *adv* ligeramente.
fractious ['frækʃəs] *adj* (*person, mood*) irascible.
fracture ['fræktʃə*] *n* fractura ♦ *vt* fracturar.
fragile ['frædʒaɪl] *adj* frágil.
fragment ['frægmənt] *n* fragmento.
fragmentary [fræg'mɛntərɪ] *adj* fragmentario.
fragrance ['freɪgrəns] *n* fragancia.
fragrant ['freɪgrənt] *adj* fragante, oloroso.
frail [freɪl] *adj* (*fragile*) frágil, quebradizo; (*weak*) delicado.
frame [freɪm] *n* (*TECH*) armazón *f*; (*of picture, door etc*) marco; (*of spectacles: also*: ~**s**) montura ♦ *vt* encuadrar; (*picture*) enmarcar; (*reply*) formular; **to ~ sb** (*col*) inculpar por engaños a algn.
frame of mind *n* estado de ánimo.
framework ['freɪmwəːk] *n* marco.
France [frɑːns] *n* Francia.
franchise ['fræntʃaɪz] *n* (*POL*) derecho al voto, sufragio; (*COMM*) licencia, concesión *f*.
franchisee [fræntʃaɪ'ziː] *n* concesionario/a.
franchiser ['fræntʃaɪzə*] *n* compañía concesionaria.
frank [fræŋk] *adj* franco ♦ *vt* (*BRIT: letter*) franquear.
frankfurter ['fræŋkfəːtə*] *n* salchicha de Frankfurt.
frankincense ['fræŋkɪnsɛns] *n* incienso.
franking machine ['fræŋkɪŋ-] *n* máquina de franqueo.
frankly ['fræŋklɪ] *adv* francamente.
frankness ['fræŋknɪs] *n* franqueza.
frantic ['fræntɪk] *adj* (*desperate: need, desire*) desesperado; (*: search*) frenético; (*: person*) desquiciado.
fraternal [frə'təːnl] *adj* fraterno.
fraternity [frə'təːnɪtɪ] *n* (*club*) fraternidad *f*; (*US*) club *m* de estudiantes; (*guild*) gremio.
fraternization [frætənaɪ'zeɪʃən] *n* fraternización *f*.
fraternize ['frætənaɪz] *vi* confraternizar.
fraud [frɔːd] *n* fraude *m*; (*person*) impostor(a) *m/f*.
fraudulent ['frɔːdjulənt] *adj* fraudulento.
fraught [frɔːt] *adj* (*tense*) tenso; **~ with** cargado de.
fray [freɪ] *n* combate *m*, lucha, refriega ♦ *vi* deshilacharse; **tempers were ~ed** el ambiente se ponía tenso.
FRB *n abbr* (*US*) = *Federal Reserve Board*.
FRCM *n abbr* (*BRIT*) = *Fellow of the Royal College of Music*.
FRCO *n abbr* (*BRIT*) = *Fellow of the Royal College of Organists*.
FRCP *n abbr* (*BRIT*) = *Fellow of the Royal College of Physicians*.
FRCS *n abbr* (*BRIT*) = *Fellow of the Royal College of Surgeons*.
freak [friːk] *n* (*person*) fenómeno; (*event*) suceso anormal; (*col: enthusiast*) adicto/a ♦ *adj* (*storm, conditions*) anormal; **health ~** (*col*) maniático/a en cuestión de salud.
▶**freak out** *vi* (*col: on drugs*) flipar.
freakish ['friːkɪʃ] *adj* (*result*) inesperado; (*appearance*) estrambótico; (*weather*) cambiadizo.
freckle ['frɛkl] *n* peca.
freckled ['frɛkld] *adj* pecoso, lleno de pecas.
free [friː] *adj* (*person: at liberty*) libre; (*not fixed*) suelto; (*gratis*) gratuito; (*unoccupied*) desocupado; (*liberal*) generoso ♦ *vt* (*prisoner etc*) poner en libertad; (*jammed object*) soltar; **to give sb a ~ hand** dar carta blanca a algn; **~ and easy** despreocupado; **is this seat ~?** ¿está libre este asiento?; **~ of tax** libre de impuestos; **admission ~** entrada libre; **~ (of charge), for ~** *adv* gratis.
freebie ['friːbɪ] *n* (*col*): **it's a ~** es gratis.
freedom ['friːdəm] *n* libertad *f*; **~ of association** libertad *f* de asociación.
freedom fighter *n* luchador(a) *m/f* por la libertad.
free enterprise *n* libre empresa.
Freefone ® ['friːfəun] *n* (*BRIT*) número gratuito.
free-for-all ['friːfərɔːl] *n* riña general.

free gift *n* regalo.
freehold ['friːhəuld] *n* propiedad *f* absoluta.
free kick *n* tiro libre.
freelance ['friːlɑːns] *adj, adv* por cuenta propia; **to do ~ work** trabajar por su cuenta.
freely ['friːlɪ] *adv* libremente; (*liberally*) generosamente.
free-market economy ['friː'mɑːkɪt-] *n* economía de libre mercado.
freemason ['friːmeɪsn] *n* francmasón *m.*
freemasonry ['friːmeɪsnrɪ] *n* (franc)masonería.
freepost ['friːpəust] *n* porte *m* pagado.
free-range ['friː'reɪndʒ] *adj* (*hen, eggs*) de granja.
free sample *n* muestra gratuita.
freesia ['friːʒə] *n* fresia.
free speech *n* libertad *f* de expresión.
free trade *n* libre comercio.
freeway ['friːweɪ] *n* (*US*) autopista.
freewheel [friː'wiːl] *vi* ir en punto muerto.
freewheeling [friː'wiːlɪŋ] *adj* libre, espontáneo; (*careless*) irresponsable.
free will *n* libre albedrío; **of one's own ~** por su propia voluntad.
freeze [friːz] *vb* (*pt* **froze**, *pp* **frozen** [frəuz, frəuzn]) *vi* helarse, congelarse ♦ *vt* helar; (*prices, food, salaries*) congelar ♦ *n* helada; congelación *f.*
▸**freeze over** *vi* (*lake, river*) helarse, congelarse; (*window, windscreen*) cubrirse de escarcha.
▸**freeze up** *vi* helarse, congelarse.
freeze-dried ['friːzdraɪd] *adj* liofilizado.
freezer ['friːzə*] *n* congelador *m*, congeladora.
freezing ['friːzɪŋ] *adj* helado.
freezing point *n* punto de congelación; **3 degrees below ~** tres grados bajo cero.
freight [freɪt] *n* (*goods*) carga; (*money charged*) flete *m*; **~ forward** contra reembolso del flete, flete por pagar; **~ inward** flete sobre compras.
freight car *n* vagón *m* de mercancías.
freighter ['freɪtə*] *n* buque *m* de carga; (*AVIAT*) avión *m* de transporte de mercancías.
freight forwarder [-'fɔːwədə*] *n* agente *m* expedidor.
freight train *n* (*US*) tren *m* de mercancías.
French [frɛntʃ] *adj* francés/esa ♦ *n* (*LING*) francés *m*; **the ~** *npl* los franceses.
French bean *n* judía verde.
French bread *n* pan *m* francés.
French Canadian *adj, n* francocanadiense *m/f.*
French dressing *n* (*CULIN*) vinagreta.
French fried potatoes, (*US*) **French fries** *npl* patatas *fpl* or papas *fpl* (*LAM*) fritas.
French Guiana [-gaɪ'ænə] *n* la Guayana Francesa.
French loaf *n* barra de pan.
Frenchman ['frɛntʃmən] *n* francés *m.*
French Riviera *n*: **the ~** la Riviera, la Costa Azul.
French stick *n* barra de pan.
French window *n* puertaventana.
Frenchwoman ['frɛntʃwumən] *n* francesa.
frenetic [frə'nɛtɪk] *adj* frenético.
frenzy ['frɛnzɪ] *n* frenesí *m.*
frequency ['friːkwənsɪ] *n* frecuencia.
frequency modulation (FM) *n* frecuencia modulada.
frequent *adj* ['friːkwənt] frecuente ♦ *vt* [frɪ'kwɛnt] frecuentar.
frequently ['friːkwəntlɪ] *adv* frecuentemente, a menudo.
fresco ['frɛskəu] *n* fresco.
fresh [frɛʃ] *adj* (*gen*) fresco; (*new*) nuevo; (*water*) dulce; **to make a ~ start** empezar de nuevo.
freshen ['frɛʃən] *vi* (*wind*) arreciar; (*air*) refrescar.
▸**freshen up** *vi* (*person*) refrescarse.
freshener ['frɛʃnə*] *n*: **air ~** ambientador *m*; **skin ~** tónico.
fresher ['frɛʃə*] *n* (*BRIT SCOL*: *col*) estudiante *m/f* de primer año.
freshly ['frɛʃlɪ] *adv*: **~ painted/arrived** recién pintado/llegado.
freshman ['frɛʃmən] *n* (*US*: *SCOL*) = **fresher**.
freshness ['frɛʃnɪs] *n* frescura.
freshwater ['frɛʃwɔːtə*] *adj* (*fish*) de agua dulce.
fret [frɛt] *vi* inquietarse.
fretful ['frɛtful] *adj* (*child*) quejumbroso.
Freudian ['frɔɪdɪən] *adj* freudiano; **~ slip** lapsus *m* (freudiano).
FRG *n abbr* (= *Federal Republic of Germany*) RFA *f.*
Fri. *abbr* (= *Friday*) vier.
friar ['fraɪə*] *n* fraile *m*; (*before name*) fray.
friction ['frɪkʃən] *n* fricción *f.*
friction feed *n* (*on printer*) avance *m* por fricción.
Friday ['fraɪdɪ] *n* viernes *m inv.*
fridge [frɪdʒ] *n* (*BRIT*) nevera, frigo, refrigeradora (*LAM*), heladera (*LAM*).
fridge-freezer ['frɪdʒ'friːzə*] *n* frigorífico-congelador *m*, combi *m.*
fried [fraɪd] *pt, pp of* **fry** ♦ *adj*: **~ egg** huevo frito, huevo estrellado.
friend [frɛnd] *n* amigo/a.
friendliness ['frɛndlɪnɪs] *n* simpatía.
friendly ['frɛndlɪ] *adj* simpático.

friendly fire *n* fuego amigo, disparos *mpl* del propio bando.
friendship ['frɛndʃɪp] *n* amistad *f*.
frieze [fri:z] *n* friso.
frigate ['frɪgɪt] *n* fragata.
fright [fraɪt] *n* susto; **to take ~** asustarse.
frighten ['fraɪtn] *vt* asustar.
▸**frighten away, frighten off** *vt* (*birds, children etc*) espantar, ahuyentar.
frightened ['fraɪtnd] *adj* asustado.
frightening ['fraɪtnɪŋ] *adj*: **it's ~** da miedo.
frightful ['fraɪtful] *adj* espantoso, horrible.
frightfully ['fraɪtfulɪ] *adv* terriblemente; **I'm ~ sorry** lo siento muchísimo.
frigid ['frɪdʒɪd] *adj* (*MED*) frígido.
frigidity [frɪ'dʒɪdɪtɪ] *n* (*MED*) frigidez *f*.
frill [frɪl] *n* volante *m*; **without ~s** (*fig*) sin adornos.
frilly ['frɪlɪ] *adj* con volantes.
fringe [frɪndʒ] *n* (*BRIT*: *of hair*) flequillo; (*edge*: *of forest etc*) borde *m*, margen *m*.
fringe benefits *npl* ventajas *fpl* complementarias.
fringe theatre *n* teatro experimental.
Frisbee ® ['frɪzbɪ] *n* frisbee ® *m*.
frisk [frɪsk] *vt* cachear, registrar.
frisky ['frɪskɪ] *adj* juguetón/ona.
fritter ['frɪtə*] *n* buñuelo.
▸**fritter away** *vt* desperdiciar.
frivolity [frɪ'vɔlɪtɪ] *n* frivolidad *f*.
frivolous ['frɪvələs] *adj* frívolo.
frizzy ['frɪzɪ] *adj* crespo.
fro [frəu] *see* **to**.
frock [frɔk] *n* vestido.
frog [frɔg] *n* rana; **to have a ~ in one's throat** tener carraspera.
frogman ['frɔgmən] *n* hombre-rana *m*.
frogmarch ['frɔgmɑ:tʃ] *vt*: **to ~ sb in/out** meter/sacar a algn a rastras.
frolic ['frɔlɪk] *vi* juguetear.

KEYWORD

from [frɔm] *prep* **1** (*indicating starting place*) de, desde; **where do you come ~?, where are you ~?** ¿de dónde eres?; **where has he come ~?** ¿de dónde ha venido?; **~ London to Glasgow** de Londres a Glasgow; **to escape ~ sth/sb** escaparse de algo/algn
2 (*indicating origin etc*) de; **a letter/telephone call ~ my sister** una carta/llamada de mi hermana; **tell him ~ me that ...** dígale de mi parte que ...
3 (*indicating time*): **~ one o'clock to** *or* **until** *or* **till nine** de la una a las nueve, desde la una hasta las nueve; **~ January (on)** a partir de enero; **(as) ~ Friday** a partir del viernes
4 (*indicating distance*) de; **the hotel is 1 km from the beach** el hotel está a 1 km de la playa
5 (*indicating price, number etc*) de; **prices range ~ £10 to £50** los precios van desde £10 a *or* hasta £50; **the interest rate was increased ~ 9% to 10%** el tipo de interés fue incrementado de un 9% a un 10%
6 (*indicating difference*) de; **he can't tell red ~ green** no sabe distinguir el rojo del verde; **to be different ~ sb/sth** ser diferente a algn/algo
7 (*because of, on the basis of*): **~ what he says** por lo que dice; **weak ~ hunger** debilitado por el hambre.

frond [frɔnd] *n* fronda.
front [frʌnt] *n* (*foremost part*) parte *f* delantera; (*of house*) fachada; (*promenade*: *also*: **sea ~**) paseo marítimo; (*MIL, POL, METEOROLOGY*) frente *m*; (*fig*: *appearances*) apariencia ♦ *adj* (*wheel, leg*) delantero; (*row, line*) primero ♦ *vi*: **to ~ onto sth** dar a algo; **in ~ (of)** delante (de).
frontage ['frʌntɪdʒ] *n* (*of building*) fachada.
front bench *n* (*BRIT POL*) ver recuadro.

FRONT BENCH

El término genérico **front bench** *se usa para referirse a los escaños situados en primera fila a ambos lados del Presidente ("Speaker") de la Cámara de los Comunes ("House of Commons") del Parlamento británico. Dichos escaños son ocupados por los miembros del gobierno a un lado y los del gobierno en la oposición ("shadow cabinet") al otro. Por esta razón a todos ellos se les denomina "frontbenchers".*

frontbencher ['frʌnt'bɛntʃə*] *n* (*BRIT*) *see* **front bench**.
front desk *n* (*US*) recepción *f*.
front door *n* puerta principal.
frontier ['frʌntɪə*] *n* frontera.
front page *n* primera plana.
front room *n* (*BRIT*) salón *m*, sala.
front runner *n* favorito/a.
front-wheel drive ['frʌntwi:l-] *n* tracción *f* delantera.
frost [frɔst] *n* (*gen*) helada; (*also*: **hoar~**) escarcha ♦ *vt* (*US CULIN*) escarchar.
frostbite ['frɔstbaɪt] *n* congelación *f*.
frosted ['frɔstɪd] *adj* (*glass*) esmerilado; (*esp US*: *cake*) glaseado.
frosting ['frɔstɪŋ] *n* (*esp US*: *icing*) glaseado.
frosty ['frɔstɪ] *adj* (*surface*) cubierto de

escarcha; (*welcome etc*) glacial.
froth [frɔθ] *n* espuma.
frothy ['frɔθɪ] *adj* espumoso.
frown [fraun] *vi* fruncir el ceño ♦ *n*: **with a ~** frunciendo el entrecejo.
▸**frown on** *vt fus* desaprobar.
froze [frəuz] *pt of* **freeze**.
frozen ['frəuzn] *pp of* **freeze** ♦ *adj* (*food*) congelado; (*COMM*): **~ assets** activos *mpl* congelados *or* bloqueados.
FRS *n* (*BRIT*: = *Fellow of the Royal Society*) *miembro de la principal asociación de investigación científica*; (*US*: = *Federal Reserve System*) *banco central de los EE. UU.*
frugal ['fru:gəl] *adj* (*person*) frugal.
fruit [fru:t] *n* (*pl inv*) fruta.
fruiterer ['fru:tərə*] *n* frutero/a; **~'s (shop)** frutería.
fruit fly *n* mosca de la fruta.
fruitful ['fru:tful] *adj* provechoso.
fruition [fru:'ɪʃən] *n*: **to come to ~** realizarse.
fruit juice *n* jugo *or* zumo (*SP*) de fruta.
fruitless ['fru:tlɪs] *adj* (*fig*) infructuoso, inútil.
fruit machine *n* (*BRIT*) máquina tragaperras.
fruit salad *n* macedonia *or* ensalada (*LAM*) de frutas.
frump [frʌmp] *n* espantajo, adefesio.
frustrate [frʌs'treɪt] *vt* frustrar.
frustrated [frʌs'treɪtɪd] *adj* frustrado.
frustrating [frʌs'treɪtɪŋ] *adj* (*job, day*) frustrante.
frustration [frʌs'treɪʃən] *n* frustración *f*.
fry, *pt, pp* **fried** [fraɪ, -d] *vt* freír ♦ *n*: **small ~** gente *f* menuda.
frying pan ['fraɪɪŋ-] *n* sartén *f or m* (*LAM*).
FT *n abbr* (*BRIT*: = *Financial Times*) *periódico financiero*; **the ~ index** *el índice de valores del Financial Times*.
ft. *abbr* = **foot, feet**.
FTC *n abbr* (*US*) = *Federal Trade Commission*.
FTSE 100 Index *n abbr* (= *Financial Times Stock Exchange 100 Index*) *índice bursátil del Financial Times*.
fuchsia ['fju:ʃə] *n* fucsia.
fuck [fʌk] (*col!*) *vt* joder (*SP!*), coger (*LAM!*) ♦ *vi* joder (*SP!*), coger (*LAM!*); **~ off!** ¡vete a tomar por culo! (*!*).
fuddled ['fʌdld] *adj* (*muddled*) confuso, aturdido; (*col*: *tipsy*) borracho.
fuddy-duddy ['fʌdɪdʌdɪ] (*pej*) *n* carcamal *m*, carroza *m/f* ♦ *adj* chapado a la antigua.
fudge [fʌdʒ] *n* (*CULIN*) *caramelo blando* ♦ *vt* (*issue, problem*) rehuir, esquivar.
fuel [fjuəl] *n* (*for heating*) combustible *m*; (*coal*) carbón *m*; (*wood*) leña; (*for engine*) carburante *m* ♦ *vt* (*furnace etc*) alimentar; (*aircraft, ship etc*) aprovisionar de combustible.
fuel oil *n* fuel oil *m*.
fuel pump *n* (*AUT*) surtidor *m* de gasolina.
fuel tank *n* depósito de combustible.
fug [fʌg] *n* aire *m* viciado.
fugitive ['fju:dʒɪtɪv] *n* (*from prison*) fugitivo/a.
fulfil, (*US*) **fulfill** [ful'fɪl] *vt* (*function*) desempeñar; (*condition*) cumplir; (*wish, desire*) realizar.
fulfilled [ful'fɪld] *adj* (*person*) realizado.
fulfil(l)ment [ful'fɪlmənt] *n* realización *f*; (*of promise*) cumplimiento.
full [ful] *adj* lleno; (*fig*) pleno; (*complete*) completo; (*information*) detallado; (*price*) íntegro, sin descuento ♦ *adv*: **~ well** perfectamente; **we're ~ up for July** estamos completos para julio; **I'm ~ (up)** estoy lleno; **~ employment** pleno empleo; **~ name** nombre *m* completo; **a ~ two hours** dos horas enteras; **at ~ speed** a toda velocidad; **in ~** (*reproduce, quote*) íntegramente; **to write sth in ~** escribir algo por extenso; **to pay in ~** pagar la deuda entera.
fullback ['fulbæk] *n* (*FOOTBALL*) defensa *m*; (*RUGBY*) zaguero.
full-blooded ['ful'blʌdɪd] *adj* (*vigorous*: *attack*) vigoroso; (*pure*) puro.
full-cream ['ful'kri:m] *adj*: **~ milk** leche *f* entera.
full driving licence *n* (*BRIT AUT*) carnet *m* de conducir (*definitivo*); *see also* **L-plates**.
full-fledged ['fulflɛdʒd] *adj* (*US*) = **fully-fledged**.
full-grown ['ful'grəun] *adj* maduro.
full-length ['ful'lɛŋθ] *adj* (*portrait*) de cuerpo entero; (*film*) de largometraje.
full moon *n* luna llena, plenilunio.
fullness ['fulnɪs] *n* plenitud *f*, amplitud *f*.
full-scale ['fulskeɪl] *adj* (*attack, war, search, retreat*) en gran escala; (*plan, model*) de tamaño natural.
full stop *n* punto.
full-time ['fultaɪm] *adj* (*work*) de tiempo completo ♦ *adv*: **to work ~** trabajar a tiempo completo.
fully ['fulɪ] *adv* completamente; (*at least*) al menos.
fully-fledged ['fulɪ'flɛdʒd], (*US*) **full-fledged** *adj* (*teacher, barrister*) diplomado; (*bird*) con todas sus plumas, capaz de volar; (*fig*) de pleno derecho.
fully-paid ['fulɪpeɪd] *adj*: **~ share** acción *f* liberada.

fulsome ['fulsəm] *adj (pej: praise, gratitude)* excesivo, exagerado; (: *manner*) obsequioso.
fumble with ['fʌmbl-] *vt fus* manosear.
fume [fju:m] *vi* humear, echar humo.
fumes [fju:mz] *npl* humo *sg*, gases *mpl*.
fumigate ['fju:mɪgeɪt] *vt* fumigar.
fun [fʌn] *n (amusement)* diversión *f*; *(joy)* alegría; **to have ~** divertirse; **for ~** por gusto; **to make ~ of** reírse de.
function ['fʌŋkʃən] *n* función *f* ♦ *vi* funcionar; **to ~ as** hacer (las veces) de, fungir de (*LAM*).
functional ['fʌŋkʃənl] *adj* funcional.
function key *n (COMPUT)* tecla de función.
fund [fʌnd] *n* fondo; *(reserve)* reserva; **~s** *npl* fondos *mpl*.
fundamental [fʌndə'mɛntl] *adj* fundamental ♦ *n*: **~s** fundamentos *mpl*.
fundamentalism [fʌndə'mɛntəlɪzəm] *n* fundamentalismo, integrismo.
fundamentalist [fʌndə'mɛntəlɪst] *n* fundamentalista *m/f*, integrista *m/f*.
fundamentally [fʌndə'mɛntəlɪ] *adv* fundamentalmente.
funding ['fʌndɪŋ] *n* financiación *f*.
fund-raising ['fʌndreɪzɪŋ] *n* recaudación *f* de fondos.
funeral ['fju:nərəl] *n (burial)* entierro; *(ceremony)* funerales *mpl*.
funeral director *n* director(a) *m/f* de pompas fúnebres.
funeral parlour *n (BRIT)* funeraria.
funeral service *n* misa de cuerpo presente.
funereal [fju:'nɪərɪəl] *adj* fúnebre.
funfair ['fʌnfɛə*] *n (BRIT)* parque *m* de atracciones; *(travelling)* feria.
fungus, *pl* **fungi** ['fʌŋgəs, -gaɪ] *n* hongo.
funicular [fju:'nɪkjulə*] *n (also:* **~ railway***)* funicular *m*.
funky ['fʌŋkɪ] *adj (music)* funky; *(col: good)* guay.
funnel ['fʌnl] *n* embudo; *(of ship)* chimenea.
funnily ['fʌnɪlɪ] *adv* de modo divertido, graciosamente; *(oddly)* de una manera rara; **~ enough** aunque parezca extraño.
funny ['fʌnɪ] *adj* gracioso, divertido; *(strange)* curioso, raro.
funny bone *n* hueso de la alegría.
fun run *n* maratón *m* popular.
fur [fə:*] *n* piel *f*; *(BRIT: on tongue etc)* sarro.
fur coat *n* abrigo de pieles.
furious ['fjuərɪəs] *adj* furioso; *(effort, argument)* violento; **to be ~ with sb** estar furioso con algn.
furiously ['fjuərɪəslɪ] *adv* con furia.
furl [fə:l] *vt (sail)* recoger.
furlong ['fə:lɔŋ] *n octava parte de una milla.*
furlough ['fə:ləu] *n (MIL, US)* permiso.
furnace ['fə:nɪs] *n* horno.
furnish ['fə:nɪʃ] *vt* amueblar; *(supply)* proporcionar; *(information)* facilitar.
furnished ['fə:nɪʃt] *adj*: **~ flat** *or (US)* **apartment** piso amueblado.
furnishings ['fə:nɪʃɪŋz] *npl* mobiliario *sg*.
furniture ['fə:nɪtʃə*] *n* muebles *mpl*; **piece of ~** mueble *m*.
furniture polish *n* cera para muebles.
furore [fjuə'rɔ:rɪ] *n (protests)* escándalo.
furrier ['fʌrɪə*] *n* peletero/a.
furrow ['fʌrəu] *n* surco ♦ *vt (forehead)* arrugar.
furry ['fə:rɪ] *adj* peludo; *(toy)* de peluche.
further ['fə:ðə*] *adj (new)* nuevo; *(place)* más lejano ♦ *adv* más lejos; *(more)* más; *(moreover)* además ♦ *vt* hacer avanzar; **how much ~ is it?** ¿a qué distancia queda?; **~ to your letter of ...** *(COMM)* con referencia a su carta de ...; **to ~ one's interests** fomentar sus intereses.
further education *n* educación *f* postescolar.
furthermore [fə:ðə'mɔ:*] *adv* además.
furthermost ['fə:ðəməust] *adj* más lejano.
furthest ['fə:ðɪst] *superlative of* **far**.
furtive ['fə:tɪv] *adj* furtivo.
furtively ['fə:tɪvlɪ] *adv* furtivamente, a escondidas.
fury ['fjuərɪ] *n* furia.
fuse, *(US)* **fuze** [fju:z] *n* fusible *m*; *(for bomb etc)* mecha ♦ *vt (metal)* fundir; *(fig)* fusionar ♦ *vi* fundirse; fusionarse; *(BRIT: ELEC)*: **to ~ the lights** fundir los plomos; **a ~ has blown** se ha fundido un fusible.
fuse box *n* caja de fusibles.
fuselage ['fju:zəlɑ:ʒ] *n* fuselaje *m*.
fuse wire *n* hilo fusible.
fusillade [fju:zɪ'leɪd] *n* descarga cerrada; *(fig)* lluvia.
fusion ['fju:ʒən] *n* fusión *f*.
fuss [fʌs] *n (noise)* bulla; *(dispute)* lío, jaleo; *(complaining)* protesta ♦ *vi* preocuparse (por pequeñeces) ♦ *vt (person)* molestar; **to make a ~** armar jaleo.
▸**fuss over** *vt fus (person)* contemplar, mimar.
fusspot ['fʌspɔt] *n (col)* quisquilloso/a.
fussy ['fʌsɪ] *adj (person)* quisquilloso; **I'm not ~** *(col)* me da igual.
fusty ['fʌstɪ] *adj (pej)* rancio; **to smell ~** oler a cerrado.
futile ['fju:taɪl] *adj* vano.
futility [fju:'tɪlɪtɪ] *n* inutilidad *f*.
futon ['fu:tɔn] *n* futón *m*.

future ['fju:tʃə*] *adj (gen)* futuro; *(coming)* venidero ♦ *n* futuro, porvenir; **in ~** de ahora en adelante.
futures ['fju:tʃəz] *npl (COMM)* operaciones *fpl* a término, futuros *mpl*.
futuristic [fju:tʃə'rɪstɪk] *adj* futurista.
fuze [fju:z] *(US)* = **fuse.**
fuzzy ['fʌzɪ] *adj (PHOT)* borroso; *(hair)* muy rizado.
fwd. *abbr* = **forward.**
fwy *abbr (US)* = **freeway.**
FY *abbr* = **fiscal year.**
FYI *abbr* = *for your information.*

Gg

G, g [dʒi:] *n (letter)* G, g *f*; **G** *(MUS)* sol *m*; **G for George** G de Gerona.
G *n abbr (BRIT SCOL: = good)* N; *(US CINE: = general audience)* todos los públicos.
g. *abbr (= gram(s), gravity)* g.
G7 *n abbr (POL = Group of Seven)* G7 *m*.
GA *abbr (US) = Georgia.*
gab [gæb] *n*: **to have the gift of the ~** *(col)* tener mucha labia.
gabble ['gæbl] *vi* hablar atropelladamente; *(gossip)* cotorrear.
gaberdine [gæbə'di:n] *n* gabardina.
gable ['geɪbl] *n* aguilón *m*.
Gabon [gə'bɔn] *n* Gabón *m*.
gad about [gæd-] *vi (col)* moverse mucho.
gadget ['gædʒɪt] *n* aparato.
gadgetry ['gædʒɪtrɪ] *n* chismes *mpl*.
Gaelic ['geɪlɪk] *adj, n (LING)* gaélico.
gaffe [gæf] *n* plancha, patinazo, metedura de pata.
gaffer ['gæfə*] *n (BRIT col)* jefe *m*; *((old) man)* vejete *m*.
gag [gæg] *n (on mouth)* mordaza; *(joke)* chiste *m* ♦ *vt (prisoner etc)* amordazar ♦ *vi (choke)* tener arcadas.
gaga ['gɑ:gɑ:] *adj*: **to go ~** *(senile)* chochear; *(ecstatic)* caérsele a algn la baba.
gage [geɪdʒ] *n, vt (US)* = **gauge.**
gaiety ['geɪɪtɪ] *n* alegría.
gaily ['geɪlɪ] *adv* alegremente.
gain [geɪn] *n* ganancia ♦ *vt* ganar ♦ *vi (watch)* adelantarse; **to ~ by sth** ganar con algo; **to ~ ground** ganar terreno; **to ~ 3 lbs (in weight)** engordar 3 libras.
▸**gain (up)on** *vt fus* alcanzar.
gainful ['geɪnful] *adj (employment)* remunerado.
gainfully ['geɪnfulɪ] *adv*: **to be ~ employed** tener un trabajo remunerado.
gait [geɪt] *n* forma de andar, andares *mpl*.
gala ['gɑ:lə] *n* gala; **swimming ~** certamen *m* de natación.
Galapagos Islands [gə'læpəgəs-] *npl*: **the ~** las Islas Galápagos.
galaxy ['gæləksɪ] *n* galaxia.
gale [geɪl] *n (wind)* vendaval *m*; **~ force 10** vendaval de fuerza 10.
gall [gɔ:l] *n (ANAT)* bilis *f*, hiel *f*; *(fig: impudence)* descaro, caradura ♦ *vt* molestar.
gal(l). *abbr* = **gallon(s).**
gallant ['gælənt] *adj* valeroso; *(towards ladies)* galante.
gallantry ['gæləntrɪ] *n* valentía; *(courtesy)* galantería.
gall bladder *n* vesícula biliar.
galleon ['gælɪən] *n* galeón *m*.
gallery ['gælərɪ] *n (also THEAT)* galería; *(for spectators)* tribuna; *(also:* **art ~**: *state-owned)* pinacoteca *or* museo de arte; *(: private)* galería de arte.
galley ['gælɪ] *n (ship's kitchen)* cocina; *(ship)* galera.
galley proof *n (TYP)* prueba de galera, galerada.
Gallic ['gælɪk] *adj* galo.
gallon ['gæln] *n* galón *m (= 8 pints; BRIT = 4,546 litros, US = 3,785 litros)*.
gallop ['gæləp] *n* galope *m* ♦ *vi* galopar; **~ing inflation** inflación *f* galopante.
gallows ['gæləuz] *n* horca.
gallstone ['gɔ:lstəun] *n* cálculo biliar.
Gallup poll ['gæləp-] *n* sondeo de opinión.
galore [gə'lɔ:*] *adv* en cantidad, en abundancia.
galvanize ['gælvənaɪz] *vt (metal)* galvanizar; *(fig)*: **to ~ sb into action** mover *or* impulsar a algn a actuar.
Gambia ['gæmbɪə] *n* Gambia.
gambit ['gæmbɪt] *n (fig)*: **opening ~** táctica inicial.
gamble ['gæmbl] *n (risk)* jugada arriesgada; *(bet)* apuesta ♦ *vt*: **to ~ on** apostar a; *(fig)* confiar en que ♦ *vi* jugar; *(COMM)* especular; **to ~ on the Stock Exchange** jugar a la bolsa.
gambler ['gæmblə*] *n* jugador(a) *m/f*.
gambling ['gæmblɪŋ] *n* juego.
gambol ['gæmbl] *vi* brincar, juguetear.
game [geɪm] *n (gen)* juego; *(match)* partido; *(of cards)* partida; *(HUNTING)* caza ♦ *adj* valiente; *(ready)*: **to be ~ for anything**

estar dispuesto a todo; **~s** (*SCOL*) deportes *mpl*; **big ~** caza mayor.
game bird *n* ave *f* de caza.
gamekeeper ['geɪmki:pə*] *n* guardabosque *m/f*.
gamely ['geɪmlɪ] *adv* con decisión.
game reserve *n* coto de caza.
games console [geɪmz-] *n* consola de juegos.
game show *n* programa *m* concurso *inv*, concurso.
gamesmanship ['geɪmzmənʃɪp] *n* (uso de) artimañas *fpl* para ganar.
gaming ['geɪmɪŋ] *n* juego.
gammon ['gæmən] *n* (*bacon*) tocino ahumado; (*ham*) jamón *m* ahumado.
gamut ['gæmət] *n* (*MUS*) gama; **to run the (whole) ~ of emotions** (*fig*) recorrer toda la gama de emociones.
gander ['gændə*] *n* ganso.
gang [gæŋ] *n* pandilla; (*of criminals etc*) banda; (*of kids*) pandilla; (*of colleagues*) peña; (*of workmen*) brigada ♦ *vi*: **to ~ up on sb** conchabarse contra algn.
Ganges ['gændʒi:z] *n*: **the ~** el Ganges.
gangland ['gæŋglænd] *adj*: **~ bosses** cabecillas mafiosos; **~ killings** asesinatos entre bandas.
gangling ['gæŋglɪŋ] *adj* larguirucho.
gangly ['gæŋglɪ] *adj* desgarbado.
gangplank ['gæŋplæŋk] *n* pasarela, plancha.
gangrene ['gæŋgri:n] *n* gangrena.
gangster ['gæŋstə*] *n* gángster *m*.
gang warfare *n* guerra entre bandas.
gangway ['gæŋweɪ] *n* (*BRIT*: *in theatre, bus etc*) pasillo; (*on ship*) pasarela.
gantry ['gæntrɪ] *n* (*for crane, railway signal*) pórtico; (*for rocket*) torre *f* de lanzamiento.
GAO *n abbr* (*US*: = *General Accounting Office*) *tribunal de cuentas*.
gaol [dʒeɪl] *n, vt* (*BRIT*) = **jail**.
gap [gæp] *n* hueco; (*in trees, traffic*) claro; (*in market, records*) laguna; (*in time*) intervalo.
gape [geɪp] *vi* mirar boquiabierto.
gaping ['geɪpɪŋ] *adj* (*hole*) muy abierto.
garage ['gærɑ:ʒ] *n* garaje *m*.
garb [gɑ:b] *n* atuendo.
garbage ['gɑ:bɪdʒ] *n* (*US*) basura; (*nonsense*) bobadas *fpl*; (*fig*: *film, book etc*) basura.
garbage can *n* (*US*) cubo *or* balde *m* (*LAM*) *or* bote *m* (*LAM*) de la basura.
garbage collector *n* (*US*) basurero/a.
garbage disposal unit *n* triturador *m* (de basura).
garbage man *n* basurero.
garbage truck *n* (*US*) camión *m* de la basura.
garbled ['gɑ:bld] *adj* (*account, explanation*) confuso.
garden ['gɑ:dn] *n* jardín *m*; **~s** *npl* (*public*) parque *m*, jardines *mpl*; (*private*) huertos *mpl*.
garden centre *n* centro de jardinería.
garden city *n* (*BRIT*) ciudad *f* jardín.
gardener ['gɑ:dnə*] *n* jardinero/a.
gardening ['gɑ:dnɪŋ] *n* jardinería.
garden party *n* recepción *f* al aire libre.
gargle ['gɑ:gl] *vi* hacer gárgaras, gargarear (*LAM*).
gargoyle ['gɑ:gɔɪl] *n* gárgola.
garish ['gɛərɪʃ] *adj* chillón/ona.
garland ['gɑ:lənd] *n* guirnalda.
garlic ['gɑ:lɪk] *n* ajo.
garment ['gɑ:mənt] *n* prenda (de vestir).
garner ['gɑ:nə*] *vt* hacer acopio de.
garnish ['gɑ:nɪʃ] *vt* adornar; (*CULIN*) aderezar.
garret ['gærɪt] *n* desván *m*, buhardilla.
garrison ['gærɪsn] *n* guarnición *f* ♦ *vt* guarnecer.
garrulous ['gærjuləs] *adj* charlatán/ana.
garter ['gɑ:tə*] *n* (*US*) liga.
garter belt *n* (*US*) liguero, portaligas *m inv*.
gas [gæs] *n* gas *m*; (*US*: *gasoline*) gasolina ♦ *vt* asfixiar con gas; **Calor ~** ® (gas *m*) butano.
gas chamber *n* cámara de gas.
Gascony ['gæskənɪ] *n* Gascuña.
gas cooker *n* (*BRIT*) cocina de gas.
gas cylinder *n* bombona de gas.
gaseous ['gæsɪəs] *adj* gaseoso.
gas fire *n* estufa de gas.
gas-fired ['gæsfaɪəd] *adj* de gas.
gash [gæʃ] *n* brecha, raja; (*from knife*) cuchillada ♦ *vt* rajar; (*with knife*) acuchillar.
gasket ['gæskɪt] *n* (*AUT*) junta.
gas mask *n* careta antigás.
gas meter *n* contador *m* de gas.
gasoline ['gæsəli:n] *n* (*US*) gasolina.
gasp [gɑ:sp] *n* grito sofocado ♦ *vi* (*pant*) jadear.
▸**gasp out** *vt* (*say*) decir jadeando.
gas pedal *n* (*esp US*) acelerador *m*.
gas ring *n* hornillo de gas.
gas station *n* (*US*) gasolinera.
gas stove *n* cocina de gas.
gassy ['gæsɪ] *adj* con mucho gas.
gas tank *n* (*US AUT*) depósito (de gasolina).
gas tap *n* llave *f* del gas.
gastric ['gæstrɪk] *adj* gástrico.
gastric ulcer *n* úlcera gástrica.

gastroenteritis ['gæstrəuɛntə'raɪtɪs] *n* gastroenteritis *f.*
gasworks ['gæswəːks] *nsg or npl* fábrica de gas.
gate [geɪt] *n* (*also at airport*) puerta; (*RAIL: at level crossing*) barrera; (*metal*) verja.
gâteau, *pl* **~x** ['gætəu, z] *n* tarta.
gatecrash ['geɪtkræʃ] *vt* colarse en.
gatecrasher ['geɪtkræʃə*] *n* intruso/a.
gatehouse ['geɪthaus] *n* casa del guarda.
gateway ['geɪtweɪ] *n* puerta.
gather ['gæðə*] *vt* (*flowers, fruit*) coger (*SP*), recoger (*LAM*); (*assemble*) reunir; (*pick up*) recoger; (*SEWING*) fruncir; (*understand*) sacar en consecuencia ♦ *vi* (*assemble*) reunirse; (*dust*) acumularse; (*clouds*) cerrarse; **to ~ speed** ganar velocidad; **to ~ (from/that)** deducir (por/que); **as far as I can ~** por lo que tengo entendido.
gathering ['gæðərɪŋ] *n* reunión *f*, asamblea.
GATT [gæt] *n abbr* (= *General Agreement on Tariffs and Trade*) GATT *m.*
gauche [gəuʃ] *adj* torpe.
gaudy ['gɔːdɪ] *adj* chillón/ona.
gauge, (*US*) **gage** [geɪdʒ] *n* calibre *m*; (*RAIL*) ancho de vía, entrevía; (*instrument*) indicador *m* ♦ *vt* medir; (*fig: sb's capabilities, character*) juzgar, calibrar; **petrol ~** indicador *m* (del nivel) de gasolina; **to ~ the right moment** elegir el momento (oportuno).
Gaul [gɔːl] *n* Galia.
gaunt [gɔːnt] *adj* descarnado; (*fig*) adusto.
gauntlet ['gɔːntlɪt] *n* (*fig*): **to run the ~ of sth** exponerse a algo; **to throw down the ~** arrojar el guante.
gauze [gɔːz] *n* gasa.
gave [geɪv] *pt of* **give.**
gawk [gɔːk] *vi* mirar pasmado.
gawky ['gɔːkɪ] *adj* desgarbado.
gay [geɪ] *adj* (*colour, person*) alegre; (*homosexual*) gay.
gaze [geɪz] *n* mirada fija ♦ *vi*: **to ~ at sth** mirar algo fijamente.
gazelle [gə'zɛl] *n* gacela.
gazette [gə'zɛt] *n* (*newspaper*) gaceta; (*official publication*) boletín *m* oficial.
gazetteer [gæzə'tɪə*] *n* índice geográfico.
gazump [gə'zʌmp] *vti* (*BRIT*) *echarse atrás en la venta ya acordada de una casa por haber una oferta más alta.*
GB *abbr* (= *Great Britain*) G.B.
GBH *n abbr* (*BRIT LAW: col*) = **grievous bodily harm.**
GC *n abbr* (*BRIT:* = *George Cross*) *distinción honorífica.*
GCE *n abbr* (*BRIT:* = *General Certificate of Education*) ≈ certificado de bachillerato.
GCHQ *n abbr* (*BRIT:* = *Government Communications Headquarters*) *centro de intercepción de las telecomunicaciones internacionales.*
GCSE *n abbr* (*BRIT:* = *General Certificate of Secondary Education*) ≈ certificado de bachillerato.
Gdns. *abbr* (= *gardens*) jdns.
GDP *n abbr* (= *gross domestic product*) PIB *m.*
GDR *n abbr* (= *German Democratic Republic*) RDA *f.*
gear [gɪə*] *n* equipo; (*TECH*) engranaje *m*; (*AUT*) velocidad *f*, marcha ♦ *vt* (*fig: adapt*): **to ~ sth to** adaptar *or* ajustar algo a; **top** *or* (*US*) **high/low ~** cuarta/primera; **in ~** con la marcha metida; **our service is ~ed to meet the needs of the disabled** nuestro servicio va enfocado a responder a las necesidades de los minusválidos.
▸**gear up** *vi* prepararse.
gear box *n* caja de cambios.
gear lever, (*US*) **gear shift** *n* palanca de cambio.
gear wheel *n* rueda dentada.
GED *n abbr* (*US SCOL*) = *general educational development.*
geese [giːs] *npl of* **goose.**
geezer ['giːzə*] *n* (*BRIT col*) tipo, maromo (*SP*).
Geiger counter ['gaɪgə-] *n* contador *m* Geiger.
gel [dʒɛl] *n* gel *m.*
gelatin(e) ['dʒɛləti:n] *n* gelatina.
gelignite ['dʒɛlɪgnaɪt] *n* gelignita.
gem [dʒɛm] *n* gema, piedra preciosa; (*fig*) joya.
Gemini ['dʒɛmɪnaɪ] *n* Géminis *m.*
gen [dʒɛn] *n* (*BRIT col*): **to give sb the ~ on sth** poner a algn al tanto de algo.
Gen. *abbr* (*MIL:* = *General*) Gen., Gral.
gen. *abbr* (= *general*) grl.; = **generally.**
gender ['dʒɛndə*] *n* género.
gene [dʒiːn] *n* gen(e) *m.*
genealogy [dʒiːnɪ'ælədʒɪ] *n* genealogía.
general ['dʒɛnərl] *n* general *m* ♦ *adj* general; **in ~** en general; **~ audit** auditoría general; **the ~ public** el gran público.
general anaesthetic, (*US*) **general anesthetic** *n* anestesia general.
general delivery *n* (*US*) lista de correos.
general election *n* elecciones *fpl* generales.
generalization [dʒɛnrəlaɪ'zeɪʃən] *n* generalización *f.*
generalize ['dʒɛnrəlaɪz] *vi* generalizar.
generally ['dʒɛnrəlɪ] *adv* generalmente, en

general.
general manager *n* director(a) *m/f* general.
general practitioner (GP) *n* médico/a de medicina general.
general strike *n* huelga general.
generate ['dʒɛnəreɪt] *vt* generar.
generation [dʒɛnə'reɪʃən] *n* (*of electricity etc*) generación *f*; **first/second/third/fourth ~** (*of computer*) primera/segunda/tercera/cuarta generación.
generator ['dʒɛnəreɪtə*] *n* generador *m*.
generic [dʒɪ'nɛrɪk] *adj* genérico.
generosity [dʒɛnə'rɔsɪtɪ] *n* generosidad *f*.
generous ['dʒɛnərəs] *adj* generoso; (*copious*) abundante.
generously ['dʒɛnərəslɪ] *adv* generosamente; abundantemente.
genesis ['dʒɛnɪsɪs] *n* génesis *f*.
genetic [dʒɪ'nɛtɪk] *adj* genético.
genetic engineering *n* ingeniería genética.
genetic fingerprinting [-'fɪŋgəprɪntɪŋ] *n* identificación *f* genética.
genetics [dʒɪ'nɛtɪks] *n* genética.
Geneva [dʒɪ'ni:və] *n* Ginebra.
genial ['dʒi:nɪəl] *adj* afable.
genitals ['dʒɛnɪtlz] *npl* (órganos *mpl*) genitales *mpl*.
genitive ['dʒɛnɪtɪv] *n* genitivo.
genius ['dʒi:nɪəs] *n* genio.
Genoa ['dʒɛnəuə] *n* Génova.
genocide ['dʒɛnəusaɪd] *n* genocidio.
gent [dʒɛnt] *n abbr* (*BRIT col*) = **gentleman**.
genteel [dʒɛn'ti:l] *adj* fino, distinguido.
Gentile ['dʒɛntaɪl] *n* gentil *m/f*.
gentle ['dʒɛntl] *adj* (*sweet*) dulce; (*touch etc*) ligero, suave.
gentleman ['dʒɛntlmən] *n* señor *m*; (*well-bred man*) caballero; **~'s agreement** acuerdo entre caballeros.
gentlemanly ['dʒɛntlmənlɪ] *adj* caballeroso.
gentleness ['dʒɛntlnɪs] *n* dulzura; (*of touch*) suavidad *f*.
gently ['dʒɛntlɪ] *adv* suavemente.
gentrification [dʒɛntrɪfɪ'keɪʃən] *n* aburguesamiento.
gentry ['dʒɛntrɪ] *npl* pequeña nobleza *sg*.
gents [dʒɛnts] *n* servicios *mpl* (de caballeros).
genuine ['dʒɛnjuɪn] *adj* auténtico; (*person*) sincero.
genuinely ['dʒɛnjuɪnlɪ] *adv* sinceramente.
geographer [dʒɪ'ɔgrəfə*] *n* geográfo/a.
geographic(al) [dʒɪə'græfɪk(l)] *adj* geográfico.
geography [dʒɪ'ɔgrəfɪ] *n* geografía.
geological [dʒɪə'lɔdʒɪkl] *adj* geológico.
geologist [dʒɪ'ɔlədʒɪst] *n* geólogo/a.
geology [dʒɪ'ɔlədʒɪ] *n* geología.
geometric(al) [dʒɪə'mɛtrɪk(l)] *adj* geométrico.
geometry [dʒɪ'ɔmətrɪ] *n* geometría.
Geordie ['dʒɔ:dɪ] *n* habitante *m/f* de Tyneside.
Georgia ['dʒɔ:dʒə] *n* Georgia.
Georgian ['dʒɔ:dʒən] *adj* georgiano ♦ *n* georgiano/a; (*LING*) georgiano.
geranium [dʒɪ'reɪnjəm] *n* geranio.
geriatric [dʒɛrɪ'ætrɪk] *adj*, *n* geriátrico/a *m/f*.
germ [dʒə:m] *n* (*microbe*) microbio, bacteria; (*seed*, *fig*) germen *m*.
German ['dʒə:mən] *adj* alemán/ana ♦ *n* alemán/ana *m/f*; (*LING*) alemán *m*.
German Democratic Republic *n* República Democrática Alemana.
germane [dʒə:'meɪn] *adj*: **~ (to)** pertinente (a).
German measles *n* rubeola, rubéola.
German Shepherd *n* (*dog*) pastor *m* alemán.
Germany ['dʒə:mənɪ] *n* Alemania; **East/West ~** Alemania Oriental *or* Democrática/Occidental *or* Federal.
germination [dʒə:mɪ'neɪʃən] *n* germinación *f*.
germ warfare *n* guerra bacteriológica.
gesticulate [dʒɛs'tɪkjuleɪt] *vi* gesticular.
gesticulation [dʒɛstɪkju'leɪʃən] *n* gesticulación *f*.
gesture ['dʒɛstjə*] *n* gesto; **as a ~ of friendship** en señal de amistad.

KEYWORD

get [gɛt] (*pt, pp* **got**, *pp* **gotten** (*US*)) *vi* **1** (*become, be*) ponerse, volverse; **to ~ old/tired** envejecer/cansarse; **to ~ drunk** emborracharse; **to ~ dirty** ensuciarse; **to ~ ready/washed** prepararse/lavarse; **to ~ married** casarse; **when do I ~ paid?** ¿cuándo me pagan *or* se me paga?; **it's ~ting late** se está haciendo tarde
2 (*go*): **to ~ to/from** llegar a/de; **to ~ home** llegar a casa; **he got under the fence** pasó por debajo de la barrera
3 (*begin*) empezar a; **to ~ to know sb** (llegar a) conocer a algn; **I'm ~ting to like him** me está empezando a gustar; **let's ~ going** *or* **started** ¡vamos (a empezar)!
4 (*modal aux vb*): **you've got to do it** tienes que hacerlo
♦ *vt* **1**: **to ~ sth done** (*finish*) hacer algo; (*have done*) mandar hacer algo; **to ~ one's hair cut** cortarse el pelo; **to ~ the car going** *or* **to go** arrancar el coche; **to ~**

sb to do sth conseguir *or* hacer que algn haga algo; **to ~ sth/sb ready** preparar algo/a algn

2 (*obtain*: *money, permission, results*) conseguir; (*find*: *job, flat*) encontrar; (*fetch*: *person, doctor*) buscar; (*object*) ir a buscar, traer; **to ~ sth for sb** conseguir algo para algn; **~ me Mr Jones, please** (*TEL*) póngame *or* comuníqueme (*LAM*) con el Sr. Jones, por favor; **can I ~ you a drink?** ¿quieres algo de beber?

3 (*receive*: *present, letter*) recibir; (*acquire*: *reputation*) alcanzar; (: *prize*) ganar; **what did you ~ for your birthday?** ¿qué te regalaron por tu cumpleaños?; **how much did you ~ for the painting?** ¿cuánto sacaste por el cuadro?

4 (*catch*) coger (*SP*), agarrar (*LAM*); (*hit*: *target etc*) dar en; **to ~ sb by the arm/throat** coger *or* agarrar a algn por el brazo/cuello; **~ him!** ¡cógelo! (*SP*), ¡atrápalo! (*LAM*); **the bullet got him in the leg** la bala le dio en la pierna

5 (*take, move*) llevar; **to ~ sth to sb** hacer llegar algo a algn; **do you think we'll ~ it through the door?** ¿crees que lo podremos meter por la puerta?

6 (*catch, take*: *plane, bus etc*) coger (*SP*), tomar (*LAM*); **where do I ~ the train for Birmingham?** ¿dónde se coge *or* se toma el tren para Birmingham?

7 (*understand*) entender; (*hear*) oír; **I've got it!** ¡ya lo tengo!, ¡eureka!; **I don't ~ your meaning** no te entiendo; **I'm sorry, I didn't ~ your name** lo siento, no me he enterado de tu nombre

8 (*have, possess*): **to have got** tener

9 (*col*: *annoy*) molestar; (: *thrill*) chiflar

▶**get about** *vi* salir mucho; (*news*) divulgarse

▶**get across** *vt* (*message, meaning*) lograr comunicar ♦ *vi*: **to ~ across to sb** hacer que algn comprenda

▶**get along** *vi* (*agree*) llevarse bien; (*depart*) marcharse; (*manage*) = **get by**

▶**get at** *vt fus* (*attack*) meterse con; (*reach*) alcanzar; (*the truth*) descubrir; **what are you ~ting at?** ¿qué insinúas?

▶**get away** *vi* marcharse; (*escape*) escaparse

▶**get away with** *vt fus* hacer impunemente

▶**get back** *vi* (*return*) volver ♦ *vt* recobrar

▶**get back at** *vt fus* (*col*): **to ~ back at sb (for sth)** vengarse de algn (por algo)

▶**get by** *vi* (*pass*) (lograr) pasar; (*manage*) arreglárselas; **I can ~ by in Dutch** me defiendo en holandés

▶**get down** *vi* bajar(se) ♦ *vt fus* bajar ♦ *vt* bajar; (*depress*) deprimir

▶**get down to** *vt fus* (*work*) ponerse a

▶**get in** *vi* entrar; (*train*) llegar; (*arrive home*) volver a casa, regresar; (*political party*) salir ♦ *vt* (*bring in*: *harvest*) recoger; (: *coal, shopping, supplies*) comprar, traer; (*insert*) meter

▶**get into** *vt fus* entrar en; (*vehicle*) subir a; **to ~ into a rage** enfadarse

▶**get off** *vi* (*from train etc*) bajar(se); (*depart*: *person, car*) marcharse ♦ *vt* (*remove*) quitar; (*send off*) mandar; (*have as leave*: *day, time*) tener libre ♦ *vt fus* (*train, bus*) bajar(se) de; **to ~ off to a good start** (*fig*) empezar muy bien *or* con buen pie

▶**get on** *vi* (*at exam etc*): **how are you ~ting on?** ¿cómo te va?; (*agree*): **to ~ on (with)** llevarse bien (con) ♦ *vt fus* subir(se) a

▶**get on to** *vt fus* (*deal with*) ocuparse de; (*col*: *contact*: *on phone etc*) hablar con

▶**get out** *vi* salir; (*of vehicle*) bajar(se); (*news*) saberse ♦ *vt* sacar

▶**get out of** *vt fus* salir de; (*duty etc*) escaparse de; (*gain from*: *pleasure, benefit*) sacar de

▶**get over** *vt fus* (*illness*) recobrarse de

▶**get round** *vt fus* rodear; (*fig*: *person*) engatusar a ♦ *vi*: **to ~ round to doing sth** encontrar tiempo para hacer algo

▶**get through** *vt fus* (*finish*) acabar ♦ *vi* (*TEL*) (lograr) comunicar

▶**get through to** *vt fus* (*TEL*) comunicar con

▶**get together** *vi* reunirse ♦ *vt* reunir, juntar

▶**get up** *vi* (*rise*) levantarse ♦ *vt fus* subir; **to ~ up enthusiasm for sth** cobrar entusiasmo por algo

▶**get up to** *vt fus* (*reach*) llegar a; (*prank*) hacer.

getaway ['gɛtəweɪ] *n* fuga.

getaway car *n*: **the thieves' ~** el coche en que huyeron los ladrones.

get-together ['gɛttəgɛðə*] *n* reunión *f*; (*party*) fiesta.

get-up ['gɛtʌp] *n* (*BRIT col*: *outfit*) atavío, atuendo.

get-well card [gɛt'wɛl-] *n* *tarjeta en la que se desea a un enfermo que se mejore.*

geyser ['giːzə*] *n* (*water heater*) calentador *m* de agua; (*GEO*) géiser *m*.

Ghana ['gɑːnə] *n* Ghana.

Ghanaian [gɑː'neɪən] *adj, n* ghanés/esa *m/f*.

ghastly ['gɑːstlɪ] *adj* horrible; (*pale*) pálido.

gherkin ['gəːkɪn] *n* pepinillo.

ghetto ['gɛtəu] *n* gueto.

ghetto blaster [-'blɑːstə*] *n* radiocas(s)et(t)e *m* portátil (*de gran tamaño*).
ghost [gəust] *n* fantasma *m* ♦ *vt* (*book*) escribir por otro.
ghostly ['gəustlɪ] *adj* fantasmal.
ghost story *n* cuento de fantasmas.
ghostwriter ['gəustraɪtə*] *n* negro/a.
ghoul [guːl] *n* espíritu *m* necrófago.
GHQ *n abbr* (*MIL*: = *general headquarters*) E.M.
GI *n abbr* (*US col*: = *government issue*) *soldado del ejército norteamericano.*
giant ['dʒaɪənt] *n* gigante *m/f* ♦ *adj* gigantesco, gigante; ~ **(size) packet** paquete *m* (de tamaño) gigante *or* familiar.
giant killer *n* (*SPORT*) matagigantes *m inv*.
gibber ['dʒɪbə*] *vi* farfullar.
gibberish ['dʒɪbərɪʃ] *n* galimatías *m*.
gibe [dʒaɪb] *n* pulla.
giblets ['dʒɪblɪts] *npl* menudillos *mpl*.
Gibraltar [dʒɪ'brɔːltə*] *n* Gibraltar *m*.
giddiness ['gɪdɪnɪs] *n* mareo.
giddy ['gɪdɪ] *adj* (*dizzy*) mareado; (*height, speed*) vertiginoso; **it makes me** ~ me marea; **I feel** ~ me siento mareado.
gift [gɪft] *n* (*gen*) regalo; (*COMM*: *also*: **free** ~) obsequio; (*ability*) don *m*; **to have a** ~ **for sth** tener dotes para algo.
gifted ['gɪftɪd] *adj* dotado.
gift token, gift voucher *n* vale-regalo *m*.
gig [gɪg] *n* (*col*: *concert*) actuación *f*.
gigabyte ['dʒɪgəbaɪt] *n* gigabyte *m*.
gigantic [dʒaɪ'gæntɪk] *adj* gigantesco.
giggle ['gɪgl] *vi* reírse tontamente ♦ *n* risilla.
GIGO ['gaɪgəu] *abbr* (*COMPUT*: *col*) = *garbage in, garbage out.*
gill [dʒɪl] *n* (*measure*) = *0.25 pints* (*BRIT* = *0.148 l*, *US* = *0.118 l*).
gills [gɪlz] *npl* (*of fish*) branquias *fpl*, agallas *fpl*.
gilt [gɪlt] *adj, n* dorado.
gilt-edged ['gɪltɛdʒd] *adj* (*COMM*: *stocks, securities*) de máxima garantía.
gimlet ['gɪmlɪt] *n* barrena de mano.
gimmick ['gɪmɪk] *n* reclamo; **sales** ~ reclamo promocional.
gimmicky ['gɪmɪkɪ] *adj* de reclamo.
gin [dʒɪn] *n* (*liquor*) ginebra.
ginger ['dʒɪndʒə*] *n* jengibre *m*.
ginger ale *n* ginger ale *m*.
ginger beer *n* refresco *m* de jengibre.
gingerbread ['dʒɪndʒəbrɛd] *n* pan *m* de jengibre.
ginger-haired [dʒɪndʒə'hɛəd] *adj* pelirrojo.
gingerly ['dʒɪndʒəlɪ] *adv* con pies de plomo.
ginseng ['dʒɪnsɛŋ] *n* ginseng *m*.
gipsy ['dʒɪpsɪ] *n* gitano/a.
giraffe [dʒɪ'rɑːf] *n* jirafa.
girder ['gəːdə*] *n* viga.
girdle ['gəːdl] *n* (*corset*) faja ♦ *vt* ceñir.
girl [gəːl] *n* (*small*) niña; (*young woman*) chica, joven *f*, muchacha; **an English** ~ una (chica) inglesa.
girlfriend ['gəːlfrɛnd] *n* (*of girl*) amiga; (*of boy*) novia.
Girl Guide *n* exploradora.
girlish ['gəːlɪʃ] *adj* de niña.
Girl Scout *n* (*US*) = **Girl Guide**.
giro ['dʒaɪrəu] *n* (*BRIT*: *bank* ~) giro bancario; (*post office* ~) giro postal.
girth [gəːθ] *n* circunferencia; (*of saddle*) cincha.
gist [dʒɪst] *n* lo esencial.
give [gɪv] *vb* (*pt* **gave**, *pp* **given** [geɪv, 'gɪvn]) *vt* dar; (*deliver*) entregar; (*as gift*) regalar ♦ *vi* (*break*) romperse; (*stretch*: *fabric*) dar de sí; **to** ~ **sb sth,** ~ **sth to sb** dar algo a algn; **how much did you** ~ **for it?** ¿cuánto pagaste por él?; **12 o'clock,** ~ **or take a few minutes** más o menos las doce; ~ **them my regards** dales recuerdos de mi parte; **I can** ~ **you 10 minutes** le puedo conceder 10 minutos; **to** ~ **way** (*BRIT AUT*) ceder el paso; **to** ~ **way to despair** ceder a la desesperación.
▶**give away** *vt* (*give free*) regalar; (*betray*) traicionar; (*disclose*) revelar.
▶**give back** *vt* devolver.
▶**give in** *vi* ceder ♦ *vt* entregar.
▶**give off** *vt* despedir.
▶**give out** *vt* distribuir ♦ *vi* (*be exhausted*: *supplies*) agotarse; (*fail*: *engine*) averiarse; (*strength*) fallar.
▶**give up** *vi* rendirse, darse por vencido ♦ *vt* renunciar a; **to** ~ **up smoking** dejar de fumar; **to** ~ **o.s. up** entregarse.
give-and-take ['gɪvənd'teɪk] *n* (*col*) toma y daca *m*.
giveaway ['gɪvəweɪ] *n* (*col*): **her expression was a** ~ su expresión la delataba; **the exam was a** ~! ¡el examen estaba tirado! ♦ *cpd*: ~ **prices** precios *mpl* de regalo.
given ['gɪvn] *pp of* **give** ♦ *adj* (*fixed*: *time, amount*) determinado ♦ *conj*: ~ **(that) ...** dado (que) ...; ~ **the circumstances ...** dadas las circunstancias ....
glacial ['gleɪsɪəl] *adj* glacial.
glacier ['glæsɪə*] *n* glaciar *m*.
glad [glæd] *adj* contento; **to be** ~ **about sth/that** alegrarse de algo/de que; **I was** ~ **of his help** agradecí su ayuda.
gladden ['glædn] *vt* alegrar.
glade [gleɪd] *n* claro.

gladiator ['glædɪeɪtə*] *n* gladiador *m*.
gladioli [glædɪ'əulaɪ] *npl* gladiolos *mpl*.
gladly ['glædlɪ] *adv* con mucho gusto.
glamorous ['glæmərəs] *adj* con encanto, atractivo.
glamour ['glæmə*] *n* encanto, atractivo.
glance [glɑːns] *n* ojeada, mirada ♦ *vi*: **to ~ at** echar una ojeada a.
▸**glance off** *vt fus* (*bullet*) rebotar en.
glancing ['glɑːnsɪŋ] *adj* (*blow*) oblicuo.
gland [glænd] *n* glándula.
glandular ['glændjulə*] *adj*: **~ fever** mononucleosis *f* infecciosa.
glare [glɛə*] *n* deslumbramiento, brillo ♦ *vi* deslumbrar; **to ~ at** mirar con odio.
glaring ['glɛərɪŋ] *adj* (*mistake*) manifiesto.
glasnost ['glæznɔst] *n* glasnost *f*.
glass [glɑːs] *n* vidrio, cristal *m*; (*for drinking*) vaso; (: *with stem*) copa; (*also*: **looking ~**) espejo.
glass-blowing ['glɑːsbləuɪŋ] *n* soplado de vidrio.
glass ceiling *n* (*fig*) techo *or* barrera invisible (*que impide ascender profesionalmente a las mujeres o miembros de minorías étnicas*).
glasses ['glɑːsəs] *npl* gafas *fpl*, anteojos *mpl* (*LAM*).
glass fibre, (*US*) **glass fiber** *n* fibra de vidrio.
glasshouse ['glɑːshaus] *n* invernadero.
glassware ['glɑːswɛə*] *n* cristalería.
glassy ['glɑːsɪ] *adj* (*eyes*) vidrioso.
Glaswegian [glæs'wiːdʒən] *adj* de Glasgow ♦ *n* nativo/a (*or* habitante *m/f*) de Glasgow.
glaze [gleɪz] *vt* (*window*) acristalar; (*pottery*) vidriar; (*CULIN*) glasear ♦ *n* barniz *m*; (*CULIN*) vidriado.
glazed [gleɪzd] *adj* (*eye*) vidrioso; (*pottery*) vidriado.
glazier ['gleɪzɪə*] *n* vidriero/a.
gleam [gliːm] *n* destello ♦ *vi* relucir; **a ~ of hope** un rayo de esperanza.
gleaming ['gliːmɪŋ] *adj* reluciente.
glean [gliːn] *vt* (*gather*: *information*) recoger.
glee [gliː] *n* alegría, regocijo.
gleeful ['gliːful] *adj* alegre.
glen [glɛn] *n* cañada.
glib [glɪb] *adj* (*person*) de mucha labia; (*comment*) fácil.
glibly ['glɪblɪ] *adv* (*explain*) con mucha labia.
glide [glaɪd] *vi* deslizarse; (*AVIAT*, *birds*) planear.
glider ['glaɪdə*] *n* (*AVIAT*) planeador *m*.
gliding ['glaɪdɪŋ] *n* (*AVIAT*) vuelo sin motor.
glimmer ['glɪmə*] *n* luz *f* tenue.
glimpse [glɪmps] *n* vislumbre *m* ♦ *vt* vislumbrar, entrever; **to catch a ~ of** vislumbrar.
glint [glɪnt] *n* destello; (*in the eye*) chispa ♦ *vi* centellear.
glisten ['glɪsn] *vi* relucir, brillar.
glitter ['glɪtə*] *vi* relucir, brillar ♦ *n* brillo.
glittering ['glɪtərɪŋ] *adj* reluciente, brillante.
glitz [glɪts] *n* (*col*) vistosidad *f*.
gloat [gləut] *vi*: **to ~ over** regodearse con.
global ['gləubl] *adj* (*world-wide*) mundial; (*comprehensive*) global.
global warming [-'wɔːmɪŋ] *n* (re)calentamiento global *or* de la tierra.
globe [gləub] *n* globo, esfera; (*model*) bola del mundo; globo terráqueo.
globetrotter ['gləubtrɔtə*] *n* trotamundos *m inv*.
globule ['glɔbjuːl] *n* glóbulo.
gloom [gluːm] *n* penumbra; (*sadness*) desaliento, melancolía.
gloomily ['gluːmɪlɪ] *adv* tristemente; de modo pesimista.
gloomy ['gluːmɪ] *adj* (*dark*) oscuro; (*sad*) triste; (*pessimistic*) pesimista; **to feel ~** sentirse pesimista.
glorification [glɔːrɪfɪ'keɪʃən] *n* glorificación *f*.
glorify ['glɔːrɪfaɪ] *vt* glorificar.
glorious ['glɔːrɪəs] *adj* glorioso; (*weather, sunshine*) espléndido.
glory ['glɔːrɪ] *n* gloria.
glory hole *n* (*col*) trastero.
Glos *abbr* (*BRIT*) = *Gloucestershire*.
gloss [glɔs] *n* (*shine*) brillo; (*also*: **~ paint**) (pintura) esmalte *m*.
▸**gloss over** *vt fus* restar importancia a; (*omit*) pasar por alto.
glossary ['glɔsərɪ] *n* glosario.
glossy ['glɔsɪ] *adj* (*hair*) brillante; (*photograph*) con brillo; (*magazine*) de papel satinado *or* cuché.
glove [glʌv] *n* guante *m*.
glove compartment *n* (*AUT*) guantera.
glow [gləu] *vi* (*shine*) brillar ♦ *n* brillo.
glower ['glauə*] *vi*: **to ~ at** mirar con ceño.
glowing ['gləuɪŋ] *adj* (*fire*) vivo; (*complexion*) encendido; (*fig*: *report, description*) entusiasta.
glow-worm ['gləuwəːm] *n* luciérnaga.
glucose ['gluːkəus] *n* glucosa.
glue [gluː] *n* pegamento, cemento (*LAM*) ♦ *vt* pegar.
glue-sniffing ['gluːsnɪfɪŋ] *n* inhalación *f* de pegamento *or* cemento (*LAM*).
glum [glʌm] *adj* (*mood*) abatido; (*person, tone*) melancólico.
glut [glʌt] *n* superabundancia.
glutinous ['gluːtɪnəs] *adj* glutinoso,

pegajoso.

glutton ['glʌtn] *n* glotón/ona *m/f*; ~ **for punishment** masoquista *m/f*.

gluttony ['glʌtənɪ] *n* gula, glotonería.

glycerin(e) ['glɪsəri:n] *n* glicerina.

GM *adj abbr* (= *genetically modified*) transgénico.

gm *abbr* (= *gram*) g.

GMAT *n abbr* (*US*: = *Graduate Management Admissions Test*) *examen de admisión al segundo ciclo de la enseñanza superior*.

GMB *n abbr* (*BRIT*: = *General Municipal and Boilermakers (Union)*) *sindicato obrero*.

GMT *abbr* (= *Greenwich Mean Time*) GMT.

gnarled [nɑ:ld] *adj* nudoso.

gnash [næʃ] *vt*: **to ~ one's teeth** hacer rechinar los dientes.

gnat [næt] *n* mosquito.

gnaw [nɔ:] *vt* roer.

gnome [nəum] *n* gnomo.

GNP *n abbr* (= *gross national product*) PNB *m*.

go [gəu] *vb* (*pt* **went**, *pp* **gone** [wɛnt, gɔn]) *vi* ir; (*travel*) viajar; (*depart*) irse, marcharse; (*work*) funcionar, marchar; (*be sold*) venderse; (*time*) pasar; (*become*) ponerse; (*break etc*) estropearse, romperse; (*fit, suit*): **to ~ with** hacer juego con ♦ *n* (*pl* ~**es**): **to have a ~ (at)** probar suerte (con); **to be on the ~** no parar; **whose ~ is it?** ¿a quién le toca?; **to ~ by car/on foot** ir en coche/a pie; **he's ~ing to do it** va a hacerlo; **to ~ for a walk** ir a dar un paseo; **to ~ dancing** ir a bailar; **to ~ looking for sth/sb** ir a buscar algo/a algn; **to make sth ~, get sth ~ing** poner algo en marcha; **my voice has gone** he perdido la voz; **the cake is all gone** se acabó la tarta; **the money will ~ towards our holiday** el dinero es para (ayuda de) nuestras vacaciones; **how did it ~?** ¿qué tal salió *or* resultó?, ¿cómo ha ido?; **the meeting went well** la reunión salió bien; **to ~ and see sb, ~ to see sb** ir a ver a algn; **to ~ to sleep** dormirse; **I'll take whatever is ~ing** acepto lo que haya; ... **to ~** (*US*: *food*) ... para llevar; **to ~ round the back** pasar por detrás.

▸**go about** *vi* (*rumour*) propagarse; (*also*: ~ **round**: *wander about*) andar (de un sitio para otro) ♦ *vt fus*: **how do I ~ about this?** ¿cómo me las arreglo para hacer esto?; **to ~ about one's business** ocuparse de sus asuntos.

▸**go after** *vt fus* (*pursue*) perseguir; (*job, record etc*) andar tras.

▸**go against** *vt fus* (*be unfavourable to*: *results*) ir en contra de; (*be contrary to*: *principles*) ser contrario a.

▸**go ahead** *vi* seguir adelante.

▸**go along** *vi* ir; **as you ~ along** sobre la marcha ♦ *vt fus* bordear.

▸**go along with** *vt fus* (*accompany*) acompañar; (*agree with*: *idea*) estar de acuerdo con.

▸**go around** *vi* = **go round**.

▸**go away** *vi* irse, marcharse.

▸**go back** *vi* volver.

▸**go back on** *vt fus* (*promise*) faltar a.

▸**go by** *vi* (*time*) pasar ♦ *vt fus* guiarse por.

▸**go down** *vi* bajar; (*ship*) hundirse; (*sun*) ponerse ♦ *vt fus* bajar por; **that should ~ down well with him** eso le va a gustar; **she's gone down with the flu** ha cogido la gripe.

▸**go for** *vt fus* (*fetch*) ir por; (*like*) gustar; (*attack*) atacar.

▸**go in** *vi* entrar.

▸**go in for** *vt fus* (*competition*) presentarse a.

▸**go into** *vt fus* entrar en; (*investigate*) investigar; (*embark on*) dedicarse a.

▸**go off** *vi* irse, marcharse; (*food*) pasarse; (*lights etc*) apagarse; (*explode*) estallar; (*event*) realizarse ♦ *vt fus* perder el interés por; **the party went off well** la fiesta salió bien.

▸**go on** *vi* (*continue*) seguir, continuar; (*lights*) encenderse; (*happen*) pasar, ocurrir; (*be guided by*) partir de; **to ~ on doing sth** seguir haciendo algo; **what's ~ing on here?** ¿qué pasa aquí?

▸**go on at** *vt fus* (*nag*) soltarle el rollo a.

▸**go out** *vi* salir; (*fire, light*) apagarse; (*ebb*: *tide*) bajar, menguar; **to ~ out with sb** salir con algn.

▸**go over** *vi* (*ship*) zozobrar ♦ *vt fus* (*check*) revisar; **to ~ over sth in one's mind** repasar algo mentalmente.

▸**go round** *vi* (*circulate*: *news, rumour*) correr; (*suffice*) alcanzar, bastar; (*revolve*) girar, dar vueltas; (*visit*): **to ~ round (to sb's)** pasar a ver (a algn); **to ~ round (by)** (*make a detour*) dar la vuelta (por).

▸**go through** *vt fus* (*town etc*) atravesar; (*search through*) revisar; (*perform*: *ceremony*) realizar; (*examine*: *list, book*) repasar.

▸**go through with** *vt fus* (*plan, crime*) llevar a cabo; **I couldn't ~ through with it** no pude llevarlo a cabo.

▸**go together** *vi* (*harmonize*: *people etc*) entenderse.

▸**go under** *vi* (*sink*: *ship, person*) hundirse; (*fig*: *business, firm*) quebrar.

▸**go up** *vi* subir; **to ~ up in flames** estallar

en llamas.
▸**go without** *vt fus* pasarse sin.
goad [gəud] *vt* aguijonear.
go-ahead ['gəuəhɛd] *adj* emprendedor(a) ♦ *n* luz *f* verde; **to give sth/sb the ~** dar luz verde a algo/algn.
goal [gəul] *n* meta, arco (*LAM*); (*score*) gol *m*.
goal difference *n* diferencia por goles.
goalie ['gəulɪ] *n* (*col*) portero, guardameta *m/f*, arquero (*LAM*).
goalkeeper ['gəulkiːpə*] *n* portero, guardameta *m/f*, arquero (*LAM*).
goal post *n* poste *m* (de la portería).
goat [gəut] *n* cabra *f*.
gobble ['gɔbl] *vt* (*also*: **~ down, ~ up**) engullir.
go-between ['gəubɪtwiːn] *n* intermediario/a.
Gobi Desert ['gəubɪ-] *n* Desierto de Gobi.
goblet ['gɔblɪt] *n* copa.
goblin ['gɔblɪn] *n* duende *m*.
go-cart ['gəukɑːt] *n* = **go-kart**.
god [gɔd] *n* dios *m*; **G~** Dios *m*.
god-awful [gɔd'ɔːfəl] *adj* (*col*) de puta pena.
godchild ['gɔdtʃaɪld] *n* ahijado/a.
goddamn ['gɔddæm] *adj* (*col*: *also*: **goddamned**) maldito, puñetero ♦ *excl*: **~!** ¡cagüen diez!
goddess ['gɔdɪs] *n* diosa.
godfather ['gɔdfɑːðə*] *n* padrino.
god-fearing ['gɔdfɪərɪŋ] *adj* temeroso de Dios.
god-forsaken ['gɔdfəseɪkən] *adj* dejado de la mano de Dios.
godmother ['gɔdmʌðə*] *n* madrina.
godparents ['gɔdpɛərənts] *npl*: **the ~** los padrinos.
godsend ['gɔdsɛnd] *n*: **to be a ~** venir como llovido del cielo.
godson ['gɔdsʌn] *n* ahijado.
goes [gəuz] *vb see* **go**.
gofer ['gəufə*] *n* (*col*) chico/a para todo.
go-getter ['gəugɛtə*] *n* ambicioso/a.
goggle ['gɔgl] *vi*: **to ~ (at)** mirar con ojos desorbitados.
goggles ['gɔglz] *npl* (*AUT*) gafas *fpl*, anteojos *mpl* (*LAM*); (*diver's*) gafas *fpl* submarinas.
going ['gəuɪŋ] *n* (*conditions*) cosas *fpl* ♦ *adj*: **the ~ rate** la tarifa corriente *or* en vigor; **it was slow ~** las cosas iban lentas.
going-over [gəuɪŋ'əuvə*] *n* revisión *f*, (*col*: *beating*) paliza.
goings-on ['gəuɪŋz'ɔn] *npl* (*col*) tejemanejes *mpl*.
go-kart ['gəukɑːt] *n* kart *m*.
gold [gəuld] *n* oro ♦ *adj* (*reserves*) de oro.
golden ['gəuldn] *adj* (*made of gold*) de oro; (*~ in colour*) dorado.
Golden Age *n* Siglo de Oro.
golden handshake *n cuantiosa gratificación por los servicios prestados.*
golden rule *n* regla de oro.
goldfish ['gəuldfɪʃ] *n* pez *m* de colores.
gold leaf *n* pan *m* de oro.
gold medal *n* (*SPORT*) medalla de oro.
goldmine ['gəuldmaɪn] *n* mina de oro.
gold-plated ['gəuld'pleɪtɪd] *adj* chapado en oro.
goldsmith ['gəuldsmɪθ] *n* orfebre *m/f*.
gold standard *n* patrón *m* oro.
golf [gɔlf] *n* golf *m*.
golf ball *n* (*for game*) pelota de golf; (*on typewriter*) esfera impresora.
golf club *n* club *m* de golf; (*stick*) palo (de golf).
golf course *n* campo de golf.
golfer ['gɔlfə*] *n* jugador(a) *m/f* de golf, golfista *m/f*.
golfing ['gɔlfɪŋ] *n*: **to go ~** jugar al golf.
gondola ['gɔndələ] *n* góndola.
gondolier [gɔndə'lɪə*] *n* gondolero.
gone [gɔn] *pp of* **go**.
goner ['gɔnə*] *n* (*col*): **to be a ~** estar en las últimas.
gong [gɔŋ] *n* gong *m*.
gonorrhea [gɔnə'rɪə] *n* gonorrea.
good [gud] *adj* bueno, (*before m sing n* buen); (*well-behaved*) educado ♦ *n* bien *m*; **~!** ¡qué bien!; **he's ~ at it** se le da bien; **to be ~ for** servir para; **it's ~ for you** te hace bien; **would you be ~ enough to...?** ¿podría hacerme el favor de...?, ¿sería tan amable de...?; **that's very ~ of you** es usted muy amable; **to feel ~** sentirse bien; **it's ~ to see you** me alegro de verte; **a ~ deal (of)** mucho; **a ~ many** muchos; **to make ~** reparar; **it's no ~ complaining** no sirve de nada quejarse; **is this any ~?** (*will it do?*) ¿sirve esto?; (*what's it like?*) ¿qué tal es esto?; **it's a ~ thing you were there** menos mal que estabas allí; **for ~** (*for ever*) para siempre, definitivamente; **~ morning/afternoon** ¡buenos días/buenas tardes!; **~ evening!** ¡buenas noches!; **~ night!** ¡buenas noches!; **he's up to no ~** está tramando algo; **for the common ~** para el bien común; *see also* **goods**.
goodbye [gud'baɪ] *excl* ¡adiós!; **to say ~ (to)** (*person*) despedirse (de).
good faith *n* buena fe *f*.
good-for-nothing ['gudfənʌθɪŋ] *n* inútil *m/f*.
Good Friday *n* Viernes *m* Santo.

good-humoured ['gud'hju:məd] *adj* (*person*) afable, de buen humor; (*remark, joke*) bien intencionado.
good-looking ['gud'lukɪŋ] *adj* guapo.
good-natured ['gud'neɪtʃəd] *adj* (*person*) de buen carácter; (*discussion*) cordial.
goodness ['gudnɪs] *n* (*of person*) bondad *f*; **for ~ sake!** ¡por Dios!; **~ gracious!** ¡madre mía!
goods [gudz] *npl* bienes *mpl*; (*COMM etc*) géneros *mpl*, mercancías *fpl*, artículos *mpl*; **all his ~ and chattels** todos sus bienes.
goods train *n* (*BRIT*) tren *m* de mercancías.
goodwill [gud'wɪl] *n* buena voluntad *f*; (*COMM*) fondo de comercio; (*customer connections*) clientela.
goody-goody ['gudɪgudɪ] *n* (*pej*) santurrón/ona *m/f*.
gooey ['gu:ɪ] *adj* (*BRIT col*) pegajoso; (*cake, behaviour*) empalagoso.
goose, *pl* **geese** [gu:s, gi:s] *n* ganso, oca.
gooseberry ['guzbərɪ] *n* grosella espinosa *or* silvestre.
gooseflesh ['gu:sflɛʃ] *n*, **goosepimples** ['gu:spɪmplz] *npl* carne *f* de gallina.
goose step *n* (*MIL*) paso de la oca.
GOP *n abbr* (*US POL: col = Grand Old Party*) *Partido Republicano.*
gopher ['gəufə*] *n* = **gofer**.
gore [gɔ:*] *vt* dar una cornada a, cornear ♦ *n* sangre *f*.
gorge [gɔ:dʒ] *n* garganta ♦ *vr*: **to ~ o.s. (on)** atracarse (de).
gorgeous ['gɔ:dʒəs] *adj* precioso; (*weather*) estupendo; (*person*) guapísimo.
gorilla [gə'rɪlə] *n* gorila *m*.
gormless ['gɔ:mlɪs] *adj* (*col*) ceporro, zoquete.
gorse [gɔ:s] *n* tojo.
gory ['gɔ:rɪ] *adj* sangriento.
go-slow ['gəu'sləu] *n* (*BRIT*) huelga de celo.
gospel ['gɔspl] *n* evangelio.
gossamer ['gɔsəmə*] *n* gasa.
gossip ['gɔsɪp] *n* cotilleo; (*person*) cotilla *m/f* ♦ *vi* cotillear, comadrear (*LAM*); **a piece of ~** un cotilleo.
gossip column *n* ecos *mpl* de sociedad.
got [gɔt] *pt, pp of* **get**.
Gothic ['gɔθɪk] *adj* gótico.
gotten ['gɔtn] (*US*) *pp of* **get**.
gouge [gaudʒ] *vt* (*also*: **~ out**: *hole etc*) excavar; (*: initials*) grabar; **to ~ sb's eyes out** sacar los ojos a algn.
goulash ['gu:læʃ] *n* g(o)ulash *m*.
gourd [guəd] *n* calabaza.
gourmet ['guəmeɪ] *n* gastrónomo/a *m/f*.
gout [gaut] *n* gota.
govern ['gʌvən] *vt* (*gen*) gobernar; (*event, conduct*) regir.
governess ['gʌvənɪs] *n* institutriz *f*.
governing ['gʌvənɪŋ] *adj* (*POL*) de gobierno, gubernamental; **~ body** organismo de gobierno.
government ['gʌvnmənt] *n* gobierno; **local ~** administración *f* municipal.
governmental [gʌvn'mɛntl] *adj* gubernamental.
government stock *n* papel *m* del Estado.
governor ['gʌvənə*] *n* gobernador(a) *m/f*; (*of jail*) director(a) *m/f*.
Govt. *abbr* (= *Government*) gobno.
gown [gaun] *n* vestido; (*of teacher; BRIT: of judge*) toga.
GP *n abbr see* **general practitioner**.
GPMU *n abbr* (*BRIT: = Graphical, Paper and Media Union*) *sindicato de trabajadores del sector editorial.*
GPO *n abbr* (*BRIT: old*) = *General Post Office*; (*US*) = *Government Printing Office*.
gr. *abbr* (*COMM: = gross*) bto.
grab [græb] *vt* coger (*SP*) *or* agarrar; **to ~ at** intentar agarrar.
grace [greɪs] *n* (*REL*) gracia; (*gracefulness*) elegancia, gracia; (*graciousness*) cortesía, gracia ♦ *vt* (*favour*) honrar; (*adorn*) adornar; **5 days' ~** un plazo de 5 días; **to say ~** bendecir la mesa; **his sense of humour is his saving ~** lo que le salva es su sentido del humor.
graceful ['greɪsful] *adj* elegante.
gracious ['greɪʃəs] *adj* amable ♦ *excl*: **good ~!** ¡Dios mío!
grade [greɪd] *n* (*quality*) clase *f*, calidad *f*; (*in hierarchy*) grado; (*US: SCOL*) curso (*: gradient*) pendiente *f*, cuesta ♦ *vt* clasificar; **to make the ~** (*fig*) dar el nivel; *see also* **high school**.
grade crossing *n* (*US*) paso a nivel.
grade school *n* (*US*) escuela primaria; *see also* **elementary school**.
gradient ['greɪdɪənt] *n* pendiente *f*.
gradual ['grædjuəl] *adj* gradual.
gradually ['grædjuəlɪ] *adv* gradualmente.
graduate *n* ['grædjuɪt] licenciado/a, graduado/a, egresado/a (*LAM*); (*US: SCOL*) bachiller *m/f* ♦ *vi* ['grædjueɪt] licenciarse, graduarse, recibirse (*LAM*); (*US*) obtener el título de bachillerato.
graduated pension ['grædjueɪtɪd-] *n* pensión *f* escalonada.
graduation [grædju'eɪʃən] *n* graduación *f*; (*US SCOL*) entrega de los títulos de bachillerato.
graffiti [grə'fi:tɪ] *npl* pintadas *fpl*.
graft [grɑ:ft] *n* (*AGR, MED*) injerto; (*bribery*) corrupción *f* ♦ *vt* injertar; **hard ~** (*col*)

trabajo duro.
grain [greɪn] *n* (*single particle*) grano; (*no pl: cereals*) cereales *mpl*; (*US: corn*) trigo; (*in wood*) veta.
gram [græm] *n* (*US*) gramo.
grammar ['græmə*] *n* gramática.
grammar school *n* (*BRIT*) ≈ instituto (de segunda enseñanza); (*US*) escuela primaria; *see also* **comprehensive school**.
grammatical [grə'mætɪkl] *adj* gramatical.
gramme [græm] *n* = **gram**.
gramophone ['græməfəun] *n* (*BRIT*) gramófono.
granary ['grænərɪ] *n* granero.
grand [grænd] *adj* grandioso ♦ *n* (*US: col*) mil dólares *mpl*.
grandchildren ['græntʃɪldrən] *npl* nietos *mpl*.
granddad ['grændæd] *n* yayo, abuelito.
granddaughter ['grændɔːtə*] *n* nieta.
grandeur ['grændjə*] *n* grandiosidad *f*.
grandfather ['grænfɑːðə*] *n* abuelo.
grandiose ['grændɪəuz] *adj* grandioso; (*pej*) pomposo.
grand jury *n* (*US*) jurado de acusación.
grandma ['grænmɑː] *n* yaya, abuelita.
grandmother ['grænmʌðə*] *n* abuela.
grandpa ['grænpɑː] *n* = **granddad**.
grandparents ['grændpɛərənts] *npl* abuelos *mpl*.
grand piano *n* piano de cola.
Grand Prix ['grɑ̃ː'priː] *n* (*AUT*) gran premio, Grand Prix *m*.
grandson ['grænsʌn] *n* nieto.
grandstand ['grændstænd] *n* (*SPORT*) tribuna.
grand total *n* suma total, total *m*.
granite ['grænɪt] *n* granito.
granny ['grænɪ] *n* abuelita, yaya.
grant [grɑːnt] *vt* (*concede*) conceder; (*admit*): **to ~ (that)** reconocer (que) ♦ *n* (*SCOL*) beca; **to take sth for ~ed** dar algo por sentado.
granulated sugar ['grænjuleɪtɪd-] *n* (*BRIT*) azúcar *m* granulado.
granule ['grænjuːl] *n* gránulo.
grape [greɪp] *n* uva; **sour ~s** (*fig*) envidia *sg*; **a bunch of ~s** un racimo de uvas.
grapefruit ['greɪpfruːt] *n* pomelo, toronja.
grape juice *n* jugo *or* zumo (*SP*) de uva.
grapevine ['greɪpvaɪn] *n* vid *f*, parra; **I heard it on the ~** (*fig*) me enteré, me lo contaron.
graph [grɑːf] *n* gráfica.
graphic ['græfɪk] *adj* gráfico.
graphic designer *n* diseñador(a) *m/f* gráfico/a.
graphic equalizer *n* ecualizador *m* gráfico.
graphics ['græfɪks] *n* (*art, process*) artes *fpl* gráficas ♦ *npl* (*drawings: also COMPUT*) gráficos *mpl*.
graphite ['græfaɪt] *n* grafito.
graph paper *n* papel *m* cuadriculado.
grapple ['græpl] *vi*: **to ~ with a problem** enfrentarse a un problema.
grappling iron ['græplɪŋ-] *n* (*NAUT*) rezón *m*.
grasp [grɑːsp] *vt* agarrar, asir; (*understand*) comprender ♦ *n* (*grip*) asimiento; (*reach*) alcance *m*; (*understanding*) comprensión *f*; **to have a good ~ of** (*subject*) dominar.
▸**grasp at** *vt fus* (*rope etc*) tratar de agarrar; (*fig: opportunity*) aprovechar.
grasping ['grɑːspɪŋ] *adj* avaro.
grass [grɑːs] *n* hierba, grama (*LAM*); (*lawn*) césped *m*; (*pasture*) pasto; (*col: informer*) soplón/ona *m/f*.
grasshopper ['grɑːshɔpə*] *n* saltamontes *m inv*.
grassland ['grɑːslænd] *n* pradera, pampa (*LAM*).
grass roots *adj* de base ♦ *npl* (*POL*) bases *fpl*.
grass snake *n* culebra.
grassy ['grɑːsɪ] *adj* cubierto de hierba.
grate [greɪt] *n* parrilla ♦ *vi* chirriar, rechinar ♦ *vt* (*CULIN*) rallar.
grateful ['greɪtful] *adj* agradecido.
gratefully ['greɪtfəlɪ] *adv* con agradecimiento.
grater ['greɪtə*] *n* rallador *m*.
gratification [grætɪfɪ'keɪʃən] *n* satisfacción *f*.
gratify ['grætɪfaɪ] *vt* complacer; (*whim*) satisfacer.
gratifying ['grætɪfaɪɪŋ] *adj* gratificante.
grating ['greɪtɪŋ] *n* (*iron bars*) rejilla ♦ *adj* (*noise*) chirriante.
gratitude ['grætɪtjuːd] *n* agradecimiento.
gratuitous [grə'tjuːɪtəs] *adj* gratuito.
gratuity [grə'tjuːɪtɪ] *n* gratificación *f*.
grave [greɪv] *n* tumba ♦ *adj* serio, grave.
gravedigger ['greɪvdɪgə*] *n* sepulturero/a.
gravel ['grævl] *n* grava.
gravely ['greɪvlɪ] *adv* seriamente; **~ ill** muy grave.
gravestone ['greɪvstəun] *n* lápida.
graveyard ['greɪvjɑːd] *n* cementerio, camposanto.
gravitate ['grævɪteɪt] *vi* gravitar.
gravitation [grævɪ'teɪʃən] *n* gravitación *f*.
gravity ['grævɪtɪ] *n* gravedad *f*; (*seriousness*) seriedad *f*.
gravy ['greɪvɪ] *n* salsa de carne.
gravy boat *n* salsera.
gravy train *n* (*esp US: col*): **to get on the ~** coger un chollo.

gray [greɪ] *adj* (*US*) = **grey**.
graze [greɪz] *vi* pacer ♦ *vt* (*touch lightly, scrape*) rozar ♦ *n* (*MED*) rozadura.
grazing ['greɪzɪŋ] *n* (*for livestock*) pastoreo.
grease [gri:s] *n* (*fat*) grasa; (*lubricant*) lubricante *m* ♦ *vt* engrasar; **to ~ the skids** (*US*: *fig*) engrasar el mecanismo.
grease gun *n* pistola engrasadora.
greasepaint ['gri:speɪnt] *n* maquillaje *m*.
greaseproof ['gri:spru:f] *adj* a prueba de grasa; (*BRIT*: *paper*) de grasa.
greasy ['gri:sɪ] *adj* (*hands, clothes*) grasiento; (*road, surface*) resbaladizo.
great [greɪt] *adj* grande, (*before n sing*) gran; (*col*) estupendo, macanudo (*LAM*), regio (*LAM*), chévere (*LAM*); (*pain, heat*) intenso; **we had a ~ time** nos lo pasamos muy bien; **they're ~ friends** son íntimos *or* muy amigos; **the ~ thing is that ...** lo bueno es que ...; **it was ~!** ¡fue estupendo!
Great Barrier Reef *n* Gran Barrera de Coral.
Great Britain *n* Gran Bretaña.
greater ['greɪtə*] *adj* mayor; **G~ London** el área metropolitana de Londres.
greatest ['greɪtɪst] *adj* (el/la) mayor.
great-grandchild, *pl* **-children** [greɪt'grændtʃaɪld, 'tʃɪldrən] *n* bisnieto/a.
great-grandfather [greɪt'grændfɑ:ðə*] *n* bisabuelo.
great-grandmother [greɪt'grændmʌðə*] *n* bisabuela.
Great Lakes *npl*: **the ~** los Grandes Lagos.
greatly ['greɪtlɪ] *adv* sumamente, muy.
greatness ['greɪtnɪs] *n* grandeza.
Greece [gri:s] *n* Grecia.
greed [gri:d] *n* (*also*: **~iness**) codicia; (*for food*) gula.
greedily ['gri:dɪlɪ] *adv* con avidez.
greedy ['gri:dɪ] *adj* codicioso; (*for food*) glotón/ona.
Greek [gri:k] *adj* griego ♦ *n* griego/a; (*LING*) griego; **ancient/modern ~** griego antiguo/moderno.
green [gri:n] *adj* verde; (*inexperienced*) novato ♦ *n* verde *m*; (*stretch of grass*) césped *m*; (*of golf course*) campo, "green" *m*; **the G~ party** (*POL*) el partido verde; **~s** *npl* verduras *fpl*; **to have ~ fingers** (*fig*) tener buena mano para las plantas.
green belt *n* cinturón *m* verde.
green card *n* (*AUT*) carta verde.
greenery ['gri:nərɪ] *n* vegetación *f*.
greenfly ['gri:nflaɪ] *n* pulgón *m*.
greengage ['gri:ngeɪdʒ] *n* (ciruela) claudia.
greengrocer ['gri:ngrəusə*] *n* (*BRIT*) frutero/a, verdulero/a.
greenhouse ['gri:nhaus] *n* invernadero.
greenhouse effect *n*: **the ~** el efecto invernadero.
greenhouse gas *n* gas *m* que produce el efecto invernadero.
greenish ['gri:nɪʃ] *adj* verdoso.
Greenland ['gri:nlənd] *n* Groenlandia.
Greenlander ['gri:nləndə*] *n* groenlandés/esa *m/f*.
green light *n* luz *f* verde.
green pepper *n* pimiento verde.
greet [gri:t] *vt* saludar; (*news*) recibir.
greeting ['gri:tɪŋ] *n* (*gen*) saludo; (*welcome*) bienvenida; **~s** saludos *mpl*; **season's ~s** Felices Pascuas.
greeting(s) card *n* tarjeta de felicitación.
gregarious [grə'gɛərɪəs] *adj* gregario.
grenade [grə'neɪd] *n* (*also*: **hand ~**) granada.
grew [gru:] *pt of* **grow**.
grey [greɪ] *adj* gris; **to go ~** salirle canas.
grey-haired [greɪ'hɛəd] *adj* canoso.
greyhound ['greɪhaund] *n* galgo.
grid [grɪd] *n* rejilla; (*ELEC*) red *f*.
griddle ['grɪdl] *n* (*esp US*) plancha.
gridiron ['grɪdaɪən] *n* (*CULIN*) parrilla.
gridlock ['grɪdlɔk] *n* (*esp US*) retención *f*.
grief [gri:f] *n* dolor *m*, pena; **to come to ~** (*plan*) fracasar, ir al traste; (*person*) acabar mal, desgraciarse.
grievance ['gri:vəns] *n* (*cause for complaint*) motivo de queja, agravio.
grieve [gri:v] *vi* afligirse, acongojarse ♦ *vt* afligir, apenar; **to ~ for** llorar por; **to ~ for sb** (*dead person*) llorar la pérdida de algn.
grievous ['gri:vəs] *adj* grave; (*loss*) cruel; **~ bodily harm** (*LAW*) daños *mpl* corporales graves.
grill [grɪl] *n* (*on cooker*) parrilla ♦ *vt* (*BRIT*) asar a la parrilla; (*question*) interrogar; **~ed meat** carne *f* (asada) a la parrilla *or* plancha.
grille [grɪl] *n* rejilla.
grim [grɪm] *adj* (*place*) lúgubre; (*person*) adusto.
grimace [grɪ'meɪs] *n* mueca ♦ *vi* hacer muecas.
grime [graɪm] *n* mugre *f*.
grimly ['grɪmlɪ] *adv* (*say*) sombríamente.
grimy ['graɪmɪ] *adj* mugriento.
grin [grɪn] *n* sonrisa abierta ♦ *vi*: **to ~ (at)** sonreír abiertamente (a).
grind [graɪnd] *vb* (*pt, pp* **ground** [graund]) *vt* (*coffee, pepper etc*) moler; (*US*: *meat*) picar; (*make sharp*) afilar; (*polish*: *gem, lens*) esmerilar ♦ *vi* (*car gears*) rechinar

♦ *n*: **the daily ~** (*col*) la rutina diaria; **to ~ one's teeth** hacer rechinar los dientes; **to ~ to a halt** (*vehicle*) pararse con gran estruendo de frenos; (*fig*: *talks, scheme*) interrumpirse; (*work, production*) paralizarse.

grinder ['graɪndə*] *n* (*machine*: *for coffee*) molinillo.

grindstone ['graɪndstəun] *n*: **to keep one's nose to the ~** trabajar sin descanso.

grip [grɪp] *n* (*hold*) asimiento; (*of hands*) apretón *m*; (*handle*) asidero; (*of racquet etc*) mango; (*understanding*) comprensión *f* ♦ *vt* agarrar; **to get to ~s with** enfrentarse con; **to lose one's ~** (*fig*) perder el control; **he lost his ~ of the situation** la situación se le fue de las manos.

gripe [graɪp] *n* (*col*: *complaint*) queja ♦ *vi* (*col*: *complain*): **to ~ (about)** quejarse (de); **~s** *npl* retortijones *mpl*.

gripping ['grɪpɪŋ] *adj* absorbente.

grisly ['grɪzlɪ] *adj* horripilante, horrible.

gristle ['grɪsl] *n* cartílago.

grit [grɪt] *n* gravilla; (*courage*) valor *m* ♦ *vt* (*road*) poner gravilla en; **I've got a piece of ~ in my eye** tengo una arenilla en el ojo; **to ~ one's teeth** apretar los dientes.

grits [grɪts] *npl* (*US*) maíz *msg* a medio moler.

grizzle ['grɪzl] *vi* (*cry*) lloriquear.

grizzly ['grɪzlɪ] *n* (*also*: **~ bear**) oso pardo.

groan [grəun] *n* gemido, quejido ♦ *vi* gemir, quejarse.

grocer ['grəusə*] *n* tendero (de ultramarinos); **~'s (shop)** *n* tienda de ultramarinos *or* de abarrotes (*LAM*).

groceries ['grəusərɪz] *npl* comestibles *mpl*.

grocery ['grəusərɪ] *n* (*shop*) tienda de ultramarinos.

grog [grɔg] *n* (*BRIT*) grog *m*.

groggy ['grɔgɪ] *adj* atontado.

groin [grɔɪn] *n* ingle *f*.

groom [gru:m] *n* mozo/a de cuadra; (*also*: **bride~**) novio ♦ *vt* (*horse*) almohazar; **well-~ed** acicalado.

groove [gru:v] *n* ranura; (*of record*) surco.

grope [grəup] *vi* ir a tientas; **to ~ for** buscar a tientas.

gross [grəus] *adj* grueso; (*COMM*) bruto ♦ *vt* (*COMM*) recaudar en bruto.

gross domestic product (GDP) *n* producto interior bruto (PIB).

gross income *n* ingresos *mpl* brutos.

grossly ['grəuslɪ] *adv* (*greatly*) enormemente.

gross national product (GNP) *n* producto nacional bruto (PNB).

gross profit *n* beneficios *mpl* brutos.

gross sales *npl* ventas *fpl* brutas.

grotesque [grə'tɛsk] *adj* grotesco.

grotto ['grɔtəu] *n* gruta.

grotty ['grɔtɪ] *adj* asqueroso.

grouch [grautʃ] *vi* (*col*) refunfuñar ♦ *n* (*col*: *person*) refunfuñón/ona *m/f*.

ground [graund] *pt, pp of* **grind** ♦ *n* suelo, tierra; (*SPORT*) campo, terreno; (*reason*: *gen pl*) motivo, razón *f*; (*US*: *also*: **~ wire**) tierra ♦ *vt* (*plane*) mantener en tierra; (*US*: *ELEC*) conectar con tierra ♦ *vi* (*ship*) varar, encallar ♦ *adj* (*coffee etc*) molido; **~s** *npl* (*of coffee etc*) poso *sg*; (*gardens etc*) jardines *mpl*, parque *m*; **on the ~** en el suelo; **common ~** terreno común; **to gain/lose ~** ganar/perder terreno; **to the ~** al suelo; **below ~** bajo tierra; **he covered a lot of ~ in his lecture** abarcó mucho en la clase.

ground cloth *n* (*US*) = **groundsheet**.

ground control *n* (*AVIAT, SPACE*) control *m* desde tierra.

ground floor *n* (*BRIT*) planta baja.

grounding ['graundɪŋ] *n* (*in education*) conocimientos *mpl* básicos.

groundkeeper ['graundki:pə*] *n* = **groundsman**.

groundless ['graundlɪs] *adj* infundado, sin fundamento.

groundnut ['graundnʌt] *n* cacahuete *m*.

ground rent *n* alquiler *m* del terreno.

ground rules *npl* normas básicas.

groundsheet ['graundʃi:t] (*BRIT*) *n* tela impermeable.

groundsman ['graundzmən], (*US*) **groundskeeper** ['graundzki:pə*] *n* (*SPORT*) encargado de pista de deportes.

ground staff *n* personal *m* de tierra.

ground swell *n* mar *m or f* de fondo; (*fig*) ola.

ground-to-air ['grauntə'ɛə] *adj* tierra-aire.

ground-to-ground ['grauntə'graund] *adj* tierra-tierra.

groundwork ['graundwə:k] *n* trabajo preliminar.

group [gru:p] *n* grupo; (*MUS*: *pop ~*) conjunto, grupo ♦ (*vb*: *also*: **~ together**) *vt* agrupar ♦ *vi* agruparse.

groupie ['gru:pɪ] *n* groupie *f*.

group therapy *n* terapia de grupo.

grouse [graus] *n* (*pl inv*) (*bird*) urogallo ♦ *vi* (*complain*) quejarse.

grove [grəuv] *n* arboleda.

grovel ['grɔvl] *vi* (*fig*) arrastrarse.

grow, *pt* **grew**, *pp* **grown** [grəu, gru:, grəun] *vi* crecer; (*increase*) aumentar; (*expand*) desarrollarse; (*become*) volverse ♦ *vt*

cultivar; (*hair, beard*) dejar crecer; **to ~ rich/weak** enriquecerse/debilitarse; **to ~ tired of waiting** cansarse de esperar.
▶**grow apart** *vi* (*fig*) alejarse uno del otro.
▶**grow away from** *vt fus* (*fig*) alejarse de.
▶**grow on** *vt fus*: **that painting is ~ing on me** ese cuadro me gusta cada vez más.
▶**grow out of** *vt fus* (*clothes*): **I've grown out of this shirt** esta camisa se me ha quedado pequeña; (*habit*) perder.
▶**grow up** *vi* crecer, hacerse hombre/mujer.
grower ['grəuə*] *n* (*AGR*) cultivador(a) *m/f*, productor(a) *m/f*.
growing ['grəuɪŋ] *adj* creciente; **~ pains** (*also fig*) problemas *mpl* de crecimiento.
growl [graul] *vi* gruñir.
grown [grəun] *pp of* **grow**.
grown-up [grəun'ʌp] *n* adulto/a, mayor *m/f*.
growth [grəuθ] *n* crecimiento, desarrollo; (*what has grown*) brote *m*; (*MED*) tumor *m*.
growth rate *n* tasa de crecimiento.
GRSM *n abbr* (*BRIT*) = *Graduate of the Royal Schools of Music.*
grub [grʌb] *n* gusano; (*col: food*) comida.
grubby ['grʌbɪ] *adj* sucio, mugriento, mugroso (*LAM*).
grudge [grʌdʒ] *n* rencor ♦ *vt*: **to ~ sb sth** dar algo a algn de mala gana; **to bear sb a ~** guardar rencor a algn; **he ~s (giving) the money** da el dinero de mala gana.
grudgingly ['grʌdʒɪŋlɪ] *adv* de mala gana.
gruelling, (*US*) **grueling** ['gruəlɪŋ] *adj* agotador.
gruesome ['gru:səm] *adj* horrible.
gruff [grʌf] *adj* (*voice*) ronco; (*manner*) brusco.
grumble ['grʌmbl] *vi* refunfuñar, quejarse.
grumpy ['grʌmpɪ] *adj* gruñón/ona.
grunge [grʌndʒ] *n* (*MUS, fashion*) grunge *m*.
grunt [grʌnt] *vi* gruñir ♦ *n* gruñido.
G-string ['dʒi:strɪŋ] *n* tanga *m*.
GSUSA *n abbr* = *Girl Scouts of the United States of America.*
GT *abbr* (*AUT:* = *gran turismo*) GT.
GU *abbr* (*US*) = *Guam.*
guarantee [gærən'ti:] *n* garantía ♦ *vt* garantizar; **he can't ~ (that) he'll come** no está seguro de poder venir.
guarantor [gærən'tɔ:*] *n* garante *m/f*, fiador(a) *m/f*.
guard [gɑ:d] *n* guardia; (*person*) guarda *m/f*; (*BRIT RAIL*) jefe *m* de tren; (*safety device: on machine*) cubierta de protección; (*protection*) protección *f*; (*fire~*) pantalla; (*mud~*) guardabarros *m inv* ♦ *vt* guardar; **to ~ (against** *or* **from)** proteger (de); **to be on one's ~** (*fig*) estar en guardia.
▶**guard against** *vi*: **to ~ against doing sth** guardarse de hacer algo.
guard dog *n* perro guardián.
guarded ['gɑ:dɪd] *adj* (*fig*) cauteloso.
guardian ['gɑ:dɪən] *n* guardián/ana *m/f*; (*of minor*) tutor(a) *m/f*.
guardrail ['gɑ:dreɪl] *n* pretil *m*.
guard's van *n* (*BRIT RAIL*) furgón *m* del jefe de tren.
Guatemala [gwɑ:tə'mɑ:lə] *n* Guatemala.
Guatemalan [gwɑ:tə'mɑ:lən] *adj, n* guatemalteco/a *m/f*.
Guernsey ['gə:nzɪ] *n* Guernsey *m*.
guerrilla [gə'rɪlə] *n* guerrillero/a.
guerrilla warfare *n* guerra de guerrillas.
guess [gɛs] *vi, vt* (*gen*) adivinar; (*suppose*) suponer ♦ *n* suposición *f*, conjetura; **I ~ you're right** (*esp US*) supongo que tienes razón; **to keep sb ~ing** mantener a algn a la expectativa; **to take** *or* **have a ~** tratar de adivinar; **my ~ is that ...** yo creo que ....
guesstimate ['gɛstɪmɪt] *n* cálculo aproximado.
guesswork ['gɛswə:k] *n* conjeturas *fpl*; **I got the answer by ~** acerté a ojo de buen cubero.
guest [gɛst] *n* invitado/a; (*in hotel*) huésped(a) *m/f*; **be my ~** (*col*) estás en tu casa.
guest-house ['gɛsthaus] *n* casa de huéspedes, pensión *f*.
guest room *n* cuarto de huéspedes.
guff [gʌf] *n* (*col*) bobadas *fpl*.
guffaw [gʌ'fɔ:] *n* carcajada ♦ *vi* reírse a carcajadas.
guidance ['gaɪdəns] *n* (*gen*) dirección *f*; (*advice*) consejos *mpl*; **marriage/vocational ~** orientación *f* matrimonial/profesional.
guide [gaɪd] *n* (*person*) guía *m/f*; (*book, fig*) guía *f*; (*also:* **girl ~**) exploradora ♦ *vt* guiar; **to be ~d by sb/sth** dejarse guiar por algn/algo.
guidebook ['gaɪdbuk] *n* guía.
guided missile ['gaɪdɪd-] *n* misil *m* teledirigido.
guide dog *n* perro guía.
guidelines ['gaɪdlaɪnz] *npl* (*fig*) directrices *fpl*.
guild [gɪld] *n* gremio.
guildhall ['gɪldhɔ:l] *n* (*BRIT: town hall*) ayuntamiento.
guile [gaɪl] *n* astucia.
guileless ['gaɪllɪs] *adj* cándido.
guillotine ['gɪləti:n] *n* guillotina.
guilt [gɪlt] *n* culpabilidad *f*.
guilty ['gɪltɪ] *adj* culpable; **to feel ~ (about)** sentirse culpable (de); **to plead ~/not ~**

declararse culpable/inocente.
Guinea ['gɪnɪ] *n*: **Republic of** ~ República de Guinea.
guinea ['gɪnɪ] *n* (*BRIT*: *old*) guinea (= *21 chelines*: *en la actualidad ya no se usa esta moneda*).
guinea pig *n* cobaya; (*fig*) conejillo de Indias.
guise [gaɪz] *n*: **in** *or* **under the** ~ **of** bajo la apariencia de.
guitar [gɪ'tɑː*] *n* guitarra.
guitarist [gɪ'tɑːrɪst] *n* guitarrista *m/f*.
gulch [gʌltʃ] *n* (*US*) barranco.
gulf [gʌlf] *n* golfo; (*abyss*) abismo; **the G~** el Golfo (Pérsico).
Gulf States *npl*: **the** ~ los países del Golfo.
Gulf Stream *n*: **the** ~ la Corriente del Golfo.
gull [gʌl] *n* gaviota.
gullet ['gʌlɪt] *n* esófago.
gullibility [gʌlɪ'bɪlɪtɪ] *n* credulidad *f*.
gullible ['gʌlɪbl] *adj* crédulo.
gully ['gʌlɪ] *n* barranco.
gulp [gʌlp] *vi* tragar saliva ♦ *vt* (*also*: ~ **down**) tragarse ♦ *n* (*of liquid*) trago; (*of food*) bocado; **in** *or* **at one** ~ de un trago.
gum [gʌm] *n* (*ANAT*) encía; (*glue*) goma, cemento (*LAM*); (*sweet*) gominola; (*also*: **chewing-~**) chicle *m* ♦ *vt* pegar con goma.
▸**gum up** *vt*: **to** ~ **up the works** (*col*) entorpecerlo todo.
gumboots ['gʌmbuːts] *npl* (*BRIT*) botas *fpl* de goma.
gum tree *n* árbol *m* gomero.
gun [gʌn] *n* (*small*) pistola; (*shotgun*) escopeta; (*rifle*) fusil *m*; (*cannon*) cañón *m* ♦ *vt* (*also*: ~ **down**) abatir a tiros; **to stick to one's ~s** (*fig*) mantenerse firme *or* en sus trece.
gunboat ['gʌnbəut] *n* cañonero.
gun dog *n* perro de caza.
gunfire ['gʌnfaɪə*] *n* disparos *mpl*.
gung-ho [gʌŋ'həu] *adj* (*col*) patriotero.
gunk [gʌŋk] *n* (*col*) masa viscosa.
gunman ['gʌnmən] *n* pistolero.
gunner ['gʌnə*] *n* artillero.
gunpoint ['gʌnpɔɪnt] *n*: **at** ~ a mano armada.
gunpowder ['gʌnpaudə*] *n* pólvora.
gunrunning ['gʌnrʌnɪŋ] *n* tráfico de armas.
gunshot ['gʌnʃɔt] *n* disparo.
gunsmith ['gʌnsmɪθ] *n* armero.
gurgle ['gəːgl] *vi* gorgotear.
guru ['guːruː] *n* guru *m*.
gush [gʌʃ] *vi* chorrear; (*fig*) deshacerse en efusiones.
gushing ['gʌʃɪŋ] *adj* efusivo.
gusset ['gʌsɪt] *n* (*in tights, pants*) escudete *m*.
gust [gʌst] *n* (*of wind*) ráfaga.
gusto ['gʌstəu] *n* entusiasmo.
gusty ['gʌstɪ] *adj* racheado.
gut [gʌt] *n* intestino; (*MUS etc*) cuerda de tripa ♦ *vt* (*poultry, fish*) destripar; (*building*): **the blaze ~ted the entire building** el fuego destruyó el edificio entero.
gut reaction *n* reacción *f* instintiva.
guts [gʌts] *npl* (*courage*) agallas *fpl*, valor *m*; (*col*: *innards*: *of people, animals*) tripas *fpl*; **to hate sb's** ~ odiar a algn (a muerte).
gutsy ['gʌtsɪ] *adj*: **to be** ~ (*col*) tener agallas.
gutted ['gʌtɪd] *adj* (*col*: *disappointed*): **I was** ~ me quedé hecho polvo.
gutter ['gʌtə*] *n* (*of roof*) canalón *m*; (*in street*) cuneta; **the** ~ (*fig*) el arroyo.
gutter press *n* (*col*): **the** ~ la prensa sensacionalista *or* amarilla; *see also* **tabloid press**.
guttural ['gʌtərl] *adj* gutural.
guy [gaɪ] *n* (*also*: **~rope**) viento, cuerda; (*col*: *man*) tío (*SP*), tipo.
Guyana [gaɪ'ænə] *n* Guayana.
Guy Fawkes' Night [gaɪ'fɔːks-] *n ver recuadro*.

GUY FAWKES' NIGHT

La noche del cinco de noviembre, **Guy Fawkes' Night**, *se celebra el fracaso de la conspiración de la pólvora ("Gunpowder Plot"), el intento fallido de volar el parlamento de Jaime 1 en 1605. Esa noche se lanzan fuegos artificiales y se queman en muchas hogueras muñecos de trapo que representan a "Guy Fawkes", uno de los cabecillas. Días antes los niños tienen por costumbre pedir a los viandantes "a penny for the guy", dinero para comprar los cohetes.*

guzzle ['gʌzl] *vi* tragar ♦ *vt* engullir.
gym [dʒɪm] *n* (*also*: **gymnasium**) gimnasio; (*also*: **gymnastics**) gimnasia.
gymkhana [dʒɪm'kɑːnə] *n* gincana.
gymnast ['dʒɪmnæst] *n* gimnasta *m/f*.
gymnastics [dʒɪm'næstɪks] *n* gimnasia.
gym shoes *npl* zapatillas *fpl* de gimnasia.
gym slip *n* (*BRIT*) pichi *m*.
gynaecologist, (*US*) **gynecologist** [gaɪnɪ'kɔlədʒɪst] *n* ginecólogo/a.
gynaecology, (*US*) **gynecology** [gaɪnə'kɔlədʒɪ] *n* ginecología.
gypsy ['dʒɪpsɪ] *n* = **gipsy**.
gyrate [dʒaɪ'reɪt] *vi* girar.
gyroscope ['dʒaɪrəskəup] *n* giroscopio.

Hh

H, h [eɪtʃ] *n* (*letter*) H, h *f*; **H for Harry,** (*US*) **H for How** H de Historia.
habeas corpus ['heɪbɪəs'kɔːpəs] *n* (*LAW*) hábeas corpus *m*.
haberdashery ['hæbə'dæʃərɪ] *n* (*BRIT*) mercería; (*US*: *men's clothing*) prendas *fpl* de caballero.
habit ['hæbɪt] *n* hábito, costumbre *f*; **to get out of/into the ~ of doing sth** perder la costumbre de/acostumbrarse a hacer algo.
habitable ['hæbɪtəbl] *adj* habitable.
habitat ['hæbɪtæt] *n* hábitat *m*.
habitation [hæbɪ'teɪʃən] *n* habitación *f*.
habitual [hə'bɪtjuəl] *adj* acostumbrado, habitual; (*drinker, liar*) empedernido.
habitually [hə'bɪtjuəlɪ] *adv* por costumbre.
hack [hæk] *vt* (*cut*) cortar; (*slice*) tajar ♦ *n* corte *m*; (*axe blow*) hachazo; (*pej*: *writer*) escritor(a) *m/f* a sueldo; (*old horse*) jamelgo.
hacker ['hækə*] *n* (*COMPUT*) pirata *m* informático.
hackles ['hæklz] *npl*: **to make sb's ~ rise** (*fig*) poner furioso a algn.
hackney cab ['hæknɪ-] *n* coche *m* de alquiler.
hackneyed ['hæknɪd] *adj* trillado, gastado.
hacksaw ['hæksɔː] *n* sierra para metales.
had [hæd] *pt, pp of* **have.**
haddock, *pl* ~ *or* ~**s** ['hædək] *n especie de merluza.*
hadn't ['hædnt] = **had not.**
haematology, (*US*) **hematology** ['hiːmə'tɔlədʒɪ] *n* hematología.
haemoglobin, (*US*) **hemoglobin** ['hiːmə'gləubɪn] *n* hemoglobina.
haemophilia, (*US*) **hemophilia** ['hiːmə'fɪlɪə] *n* hemofilia.
haemorrhage, (*US*) **hemorrhage** ['hɛmərɪdʒ] *n* hemorragia.
haemorrhoids, (*US*) **hemorrhoids** ['hɛmərɔɪdz] *npl* hemorroides *fpl*, almorranas *fpl*.
hag [hæg] *n* (*ugly*) vieja fea, tarasca; (*nasty*) bruja; (*witch*) hechicera.
haggard ['hægəd] *adj* ojeroso.
haggis ['hægɪs] *n* (*Scottish*) *asadura de cordero cocida*; *see also* **Burns' Night**.
haggle ['hægl] *vi* (*argue*) discutir; (*bargain*) regatear.
haggling ['hæglɪŋ] *n* regateo.
Hague [heɪg] *n*: **The** ~ La Haya.
hail [heɪl] *n* (*weather*) granizo ♦ *vt* saludar; (*call*) llamar a ♦ *vi* granizar; **to ~ (as)** aclamar (como), celebrar (como); **he ~s from Scotland** es natural de Escocia.
hailstone ['heɪlstəun] *n* (piedra de) granizo.
hailstorm ['heɪlstɔːm] *n* granizada.
hair [hɛə*] *n* (*gen*) pelo, cabellos *mpl*; (*one* ~) pelo, cabello; (*head of* ~) pelo, cabellera; (*on legs etc*) vello; **to do one's** ~ arreglarse el pelo; **grey** ~ canas *fpl*.
hairbrush ['hɛəbrʌʃ] *n* cepillo (para el pelo).
haircut ['hɛəkʌt] *n* corte *m* de pelo.
hairdo ['hɛəduː] *n* peinado.
hairdresser ['hɛədrɛsə*] *n* peluquero/a; **~'s** peluquería.
hair-dryer ['hɛədraɪə*] *n* secador *m* (de pelo).
-haired [hɛəd] *adj suff*: **fair/long~** (de pelo) rubio *or* güero (*LAM*)/de pelo largo.
hairgrip ['hɛəgrɪp] *n* horquilla.
hairline ['hɛəlaɪn] *n* nacimiento del pelo.
hairline fracture *n* fractura muy fina.
hairnet ['hɛənɛt] *n* redecilla.
hair oil *n* brillantina.
hairpiece ['hɛəpiːs] *n* trenza postiza.
hairpin ['hɛəpɪn] *n* horquilla.
hairpin bend, (*US*) **hairpin curve** *n* curva muy cerrada.
hair-raising ['hɛəreɪzɪŋ] *adj* espeluznante.
hair remover *n* depilatorio.
hair's breadth *n*: **by a** ~ por un pelo.
hair spray *n* laca.
hairstyle ['hɛəstaɪl] *n* peinado.
hairy ['hɛərɪ] *adj* peludo, velludo.
Haiti ['heɪtɪ] *n* Haití *m*.
hake [heɪk] *n* merluza.
halcyon ['hælsɪən] *adj* feliz.
hale [heɪl] *adj*: ~ **and hearty** sano y fuerte.
half [hɑːf] *n* (*pl* **halves** [hɑːvz]) mitad *f*; (*SPORT*: *of match*) tiempo, parte *f*; (: *of ground*) campo ♦ *adj* medio ♦ *adv* medio, a medias; **~-an-hour** media hora; **two and a** ~ dos y media; ~ **a dozen** media docena; ~ **a pound** media libra, ≈ 250 gr.; **to cut sth in** ~ cortar algo por la mitad; **to go halves (with sb)** ir a medias (con algn); **~empty/closed** medio vacío/entreabierto; ~ **asleep** medio dormido; ~ **past 3** las 3 y media.
half-back ['hɑːfbæk] *n* (*SPORT*) medio.
half-baked ['hɑːf'beɪkt] *adj* (*col*: *idea,*

scheme) mal concebido *or* pensado.
half-breed ['hɑːfbriːd] *n* = **half-caste.**
half-brother ['hɑːfbrʌðə*] *n* hermanastro.
half-caste ['hɑːfkɑːst] *n* mestizo/a.
half-hearted ['hɑːf'hɑːtɪd] *adj* indiferente, poco entusiasta.
half-hour [hɑːf'auə*] *n* media hora.
half-mast ['hɑːf'mɑːst] *n*: **at** ~ (*flag*) a media asta.
halfpenny ['heɪpnɪ] *n* medio penique *m.*
half-price ['hɑːf'praɪs] *adj* a mitad de precio.
half term *n* (*BRIT SCOL*) *vacaciones de mediados del trimestre.*
half-time [hɑːf'taɪm] *n* descanso.
halfway ['hɑːf'weɪ] *adv* a medio camino; **to meet sb** ~ (*fig*) llegar a un acuerdo con algn.
halfway house *n centro de readaptación de antiguos presos*; (*fig*) solución *f* intermedia.
half-wit ['hɑːfwɪt] *n* (*col*) zoquete *m.*
half-yearly [hɑːf'jɪəlɪ] *adv* semestralmente ♦ *adj* semestral.
halibut ['hælɪbət] *n, pl inv* halibut *m.*
halitosis [hælɪ'təusɪs] *n* halitosis *f.*
hall [hɔːl] *n* (*for concerts*) sala; (*entrance way*) entrada, vestíbulo.
hallmark ['hɔːlmɑːk] *n* (*mark*) rasgo distintivo; (*seal*) sello.
hallo [hə'ləu] *excl* = **hello.**
hall of residence *n* (*BRIT*) colegio mayor, residencia universitaria.
Hallowe'en [hæləu'iːn] *n* víspera de Todos los Santos; *ver recuadro.*

> **HALLOWE'EN**
>
> *La tradición anglosajona dice que en la noche del 31 de octubre,* **Hallowe'en,** *víspera de Todos los Santos, es fácil ver a brujas y fantasmas. Es una ocasión festiva en la que los niños se disfrazan y van de puerta en puerta llevando un farol hecho con una calabaza en forma de cabeza humana. Cuando se les abre la puerta gritan "trick or treat" para indicar que gastarán una broma a quien no les dé un pequeño regalo (como golosinas o dinero).*

hallucination [həluːsɪ'neɪʃən] *n* alucinación *f.*
hallway ['hɔːlweɪ] *n* vestíbulo.
halo ['heɪləu] *n* (*of saint*) aureola.
halt [hɔːlt] *n* (*stop*) alto, parada; (*RAIL*) apeadero ♦ *vt* parar ♦ *vi* pararse; (*process*) interrumpirse; **to call a** ~ **(to sth)** (*fig*) poner fin (a algo).
halter ['hɔːltə*] *n* (*for horse*) cabestro.
halterneck ['hɔːltənɛk] *adj* de espalda escotada.
halve [hɑːv] *vt* partir por la mitad.
halves [hɑːvz] *pl of* **half.**
ham [hæm] *n* jamón *m* (cocido); (*col*: *also*: **radio** ~) radioaficionado/a *m/f*; (: *also*: ~ **actor**) comicastro.
hamburger ['hæmbəːgə*] *n* hamburguesa.
ham-fisted ['hæm'fɪstɪd] *adj* torpe, desmañado.
hamlet ['hæmlɪt] *n* aldea.
hammer ['hæmə*] *n* martillo ♦ *vt* (*nail*) clavar; **to** ~ **a point home to sb** remacharle un punto a algn.
▸**hammer out** *vt* (*metal*) forjar a martillo; (*fig*: *solution, agreement*) elaborar (trabajosamente).
hammock ['hæmək] *n* hamaca.
hamper ['hæmpə*] *vt* estorbar ♦ *n* cesto.
hamster ['hæmstə*] *n* hámster *m.*
hand [hænd] *n* mano *f*; (*of clock*) aguja, manecilla; (*writing*) letra; (*worker*) obrero; (*measurement*: *of horse*) palmo ♦ *vt* (*give*) dar, pasar; (*deliver*) entregar; **to give sb a** ~ echar una mano a algn, ayudar a algn; **to force sb's** ~ forzarle la mano a algn; **at** ~ a mano; **in** ~ entre manos; **we have the matter in** ~ tenemos el asunto entre manos; **to have in one's** ~ (*knife, victory*) tener en la mano; **to have a free** ~ tener carta blanca; **on** ~ (*person, services*) a mano, al alcance; **to** ~ (*information etc*) a mano; **on the one** ~ **..., on the other** ~ **...** por una parte ... por otra (parte) ....
▸**hand down** *vt* pasar, bajar; (*tradition*) transmitir; (*heirloom*) dejar en herencia; (*US*: *sentence, verdict*) imponer.
▸**hand in** *vt* entregar.
▸**hand out** *vt* (*leaflets, advice*) repartir, distribuir.
▸**hand over** *vt* (*deliver*) entregar; (*surrender*) ceder.
▸**hand round** *vt* (*BRIT*: *information, papers*) pasar (de mano en mano); (: *chocolates etc*) ofrecer.
handbag ['hændbæg] *n* bolso, cartera (*LAM*).
hand baggage *n* = **hand luggage.**
handball ['hændbɔːl] *n* balonmano.
handbasin ['hændbeɪsn] *n* lavabo.
handbook ['hændbuk] *n* manual *m.*
handbrake ['hændbreɪk] *n* freno de mano.
hand cream *n* crema para las manos.
handcuffs ['hændkʌfs] *npl* esposas *fpl.*
handful ['hændful] *n* puñado.
hand-held ['hænd'hɛld] *adj* de mano.
handicap ['hændɪkæp] *n* desventaja;

(*SPORT*) hándicap *m* ♦ *vt* estorbar.
handicapped ['hændɪkæpt] *adj*: **to be mentally** ~ ser deficiente *m/f* mental; **to be physically** ~ ser minusválido/a.
handicraft ['hændɪkrɑːft] *n* artesanía.
handiwork ['hændɪwəːk] *n* manualidad(es) *f(pl)*; (*fig*) obra; **this looks like his** ~ (*pej*) es obra de él, parece.
handkerchief ['hæŋkətʃɪf] *n* pañuelo.
handle ['hændl] *n* (*of door etc*) pomo; (*of cup etc*) asa; (*of knife etc*) mango; (*for winding*) manivela ♦ *vt* (*touch*) tocar; (*deal with*) encargarse de; (*treat*: *people*) manejar; "~ **with care**" "(manéjese) con cuidado"; **to fly off the** ~ perder los estribos.
handlebar(s) ['hændlbɑː(z)] *n(pl)* manillar *msg*.
handling ['hændlɪŋ] *n* (*AUT*) conducción *f*; **his** ~ **of the matter** su forma de llevar el asunto.
handling charges *npl* gastos *mpl* de tramitación.
hand luggage *n* equipaje *m* de mano.
handmade ['hændmeɪd] *adj* hecho a mano.
handout ['hændaut] *n* (*distribution*) repartición *f*; (*charity*) limosna; (*leaflet*) folleto, octavilla; (*press* ~) nota.
hand-picked ['hænd'pɪkt] *adj* (*produce*) escogido a mano; (*staff etc*) seleccionado cuidadosamente.
handrail ['hændreɪl] *n* (*on staircase etc*) pasamanos *m inv*, barandilla.
handset ['hændsɛt] *n* (*TEL*) auricular *m*.
handshake ['hændʃeɪk] *n* apretón *m* de manos; (*COMPUT*) coloquio.
handsome ['hænsəm] *adj* guapo.
hands-on ['hændz'ɔn] *adj* práctico; **she has a very** ~ **approach** le gusta tomar parte activa; ~ **experience** (*COMPUT*) experiencia práctica.
handstand ['hændstænd] *n* voltereta, salto mortal.
hand-to-mouth ['hændtə'mauθ] *adj* (*existence*) precario.
handwriting ['hændraɪtɪŋ] *n* letra.
handwritten ['hændrɪtn] *adj* escrito a mano, manuscrito.
handy ['hændɪ] *adj* (*close at hand*) a mano; (*useful*: *machine, tool etc*) práctico; (*skilful*) hábil, diestro; **to come in** ~ venir bien.
handyman ['hændɪmæn] *n* manitas *m inv*.
hang, *pt, pp* **hung** [hæŋ, hʌŋ] *vt* colgar; (*head*) bajar; (*criminal*: *pt, pp* **hanged**) ahorcar; **to get the** ~ **of sth** (*col*) coger el tranquillo a algo.
►**hang about** *vi* haraganear.
►**hang back** *vi* (*hesitate*): **to** ~ **back (from doing)** vacilar (en hacer).
►**hang on** *vi* (*wait*) esperar ♦ *vt fus* (*depend on*: *decision etc*) depender de; **to** ~ **on to** (*keep hold of*) agarrarse *or* aferrarse a; (*keep*) guardar, quedarse con.
►**hang out** *vt* (*washing*) tender, colgar ♦ *vi* (*col*: *live*) vivir; (: *often be found*) moverse; **to** ~ **out of sth** colgar fuera de algo.
►**hang together** *vi* (*cohere*: *argument etc*) sostenerse.
►**hang up** *vt* (*coat*) colgar ♦ *vi* (*TEL*) colgar; **to** ~ **up on sb** colgarle a algn.
hangar ['hæŋə*] *n* hangar *m*.
hangdog ['hæŋdɔg] *adj* (*guilty*: *look, expression*) avergonzado.
hanger ['hæŋə*] *n* percha.
hanger-on [hæŋər'ɔn] *n* parásito.
hang-glider ['hæŋglaɪdə*] *n* ala delta.
hang-gliding ['hæŋglaɪdɪŋ] *n* vuelo con ala delta.
hanging ['hæŋɪŋ] *n* (*execution*) ejecución *f* (en la horca).
hangman ['hæŋmən] *n* verdugo.
hangover ['hæŋəuvə*] *n* (*after drinking*) resaca.
hang-up ['hæŋʌp] *n* complejo.
hanker ['hæŋkə*] *vi*: **to** ~ **after** (*miss*) echar de menos; (*long for*) añorar.
hankie, hanky ['hæŋkɪ] *n abbr* = **handkerchief**.
Hansard ['hænsɑːd] *n actas oficiales de las sesiones del parlamento británico*.
Hants *abbr* (*BRIT*) = *Hampshire*.
haphazard [hæp'hæzəd] *adj* fortuito.
hapless ['hæplɪs] *adj* desventurado.
happen ['hæpən] *vi* suceder, ocurrir; (*take place*) tener lugar, realizarse; **as it** ~**s** da la casualidad de que; **what's** ~**ing?** ¿qué pasa?
►**happen (up)on** *vt fus* tropezar *or* dar con.
happening ['hæpnɪŋ] *n* suceso, acontecimiento.
happily ['hæpɪlɪ] *adv* (*luckily*) afortunadamente; (*cheerfully*) alegremente.
happiness ['hæpɪnɪs] *n* (*contentment*) felicidad *f*; (*joy*) alegría.
happy ['hæpɪ] *adj* feliz; (*cheerful*) alegre; **to be** ~ **(with)** estar contento (con); **yes, I'd be** ~ **to** sí, con mucho gusto; **H**~ **Christmas/New Year!** ¡Feliz Navidad!/¡Feliz Año Nuevo!; ~ **birthday!** ¡felicidades!, ¡feliz cumpleaños!
happy-go-lucky ['hæpɪgəu'lʌkɪ] *adj* despreocupado.
happy hour *n horas en las que la bebida es más barata en un bar*.
harangue [hə'ræŋ] *vt* arengar.

harass ['hærəs] *vt* acosar, hostigar.
harassed ['hærəst] *adj* agobiado, presionado.
harassment ['hærəsmənt] *n* persecución *f*, acoso; (*worry*) preocupación *f*.
harbour, (*US*) **harbor** ['hɑːbə*] *n* puerto ♦ *vt* (*hope etc*) abrigar; (*hide*) dar abrigo a; (*retain: grudge etc*) guardar.
harbo(u)r dues *npl* derechos *mpl* portuarios.
hard [hɑːd] *adj* duro; (*difficult*) difícil; (*person*) severo ♦ *adv* (*work*) mucho, duro; (*think*) profundamente; **to look ~ at sb/sth** clavar los ojos en algn/algo; **to try ~** esforzarse; **no ~ feelings!** ¡sin rencor(es)!; **to be ~ of hearing** ser duro de oído; **to be ~ done by** ser tratado injustamente; **to be ~ on sb** ser muy duro con algn; **I find it ~ to believe that ...** me cuesta trabajo creer que ....
hard-and-fast ['hɑːdən'fɑːst] *adj* rígido, definitivo.
hardback ['hɑːdbæk] *n* libro de tapas duras.
hard cash *n* dinero en efectivo.
hard copy *n* (*COMPUT*) copia impresa.
hard-core ['hɑːd'kɔː*] *adj* (*pornography*) duro; (*supporters*) incondicional.
hard court *n* (*TENNIS*) pista *or* cancha (de tenis) de cemento.
hard disk *n* (*COMPUT*) disco duro.
harden ['hɑːdn] *vt* endurecer; (*steel*) templar; (*fig*) curtir; (*: determination*) fortalecer ♦ *vi* (*substance*) endurecerse.
hardened ['hɑːdnd] *adj* (*criminal*) habitual; **to be ~ to sth** estar acostumbrado a algo.
hard-headed ['hɑːd'hɛdɪd] *adj* poco sentimental, realista.
hard-hearted ['hɑːd'hɑːtɪd] *adj* insensible.
hard-hitting ['hɑːd'hɪtɪŋ] *adj* (*speech, article*) contundente.
hard labour *n* trabajos *mpl* forzados.
hardliner [hɑːd'laɪnə*] *n* partidario/a de la línea dura.
hard-luck story ['hɑːdlʌk-] *n* dramón *m*.
hardly ['hɑːdlɪ] *adv* (*scarcely*) apenas; **that can ~ be true** eso difícilmente puede ser cierto; **~ ever** casi nunca; **I can ~ believe it** apenas me lo puedo creer.
hardness ['hɑːdnɪs] *n* dureza.
hard-nosed ['hɑːd'nəuzd] *adj* duro, sin contemplaciones.
hard-pressed ['hɑːd'prɛst] *adj* en apuros.
hard sell *n* publicidad *f* agresiva; **~ techniques** técnicas *fpl* agresivas de venta.
hardship ['hɑːdʃɪp] *n* (*troubles*) penas *fpl*; (*financial*) apuro.
hard shoulder *n* (*AUT*) arcén *m*.
hard-up [hɑːd'ʌp] *adj* (*col*) sin un duro (*SP*) *or* plata (*LAM*).
hardware ['hɑːdwɛə*] *n* ferretería; (*COMPUT*) hardware *m*.
hardware shop *n* ferretería.
hard-wearing [hɑːd'wɛərɪŋ] *adj* resistente, duradero; (*shoes*) resistente.
hard-won ['hɑːd'wʌn] *adj* ganado con esfuerzo.
hard-working [hɑːd'wəːkɪŋ] *adj* trabajador(a).
hardy ['hɑːdɪ] *adj* fuerte; (*plant*) resistente.
hare [hɛə*] *n* liebre *f*.
hare-brained ['hɛəbreɪnd] *adj* atolondrado.
harelip ['hɛəlɪp] *n* labio leporino.
harem [hɑː'riːm] *n* harén *m*.
haricot (bean) ['hærɪkəu-] *n* alubia.
hark back [hɑːk-] *vi*: **to ~ back to** (*former days, earlier occasion*) recordar.
harm [hɑːm] *n* daño, mal *m* ♦ *vt* (*person*) hacer daño a; (*health, interests*) perjudicar; (*thing*) dañar; **out of ~'s way** a salvo; **there's no ~ in trying** no se pierde nada con intentar.
harmful ['hɑːmful] *adj* (*gen*) dañino; (*reputation*) perjudicial.
harmless ['hɑːmlɪs] *adj* (*person*) inofensivo; (*drugs*) inocuo.
harmonica [hɑː'mɔnɪkə] *n* armónica.
harmonious [hɑː'məunɪəs] *adj* armonioso.
harmonize ['hɑːmənaɪz] *vt, vi* armonizar.
harmony ['hɑːmənɪ] *n* armonía.
harness ['hɑːnɪs] *n* arreos *mpl* ♦ *vt* (*horse*) enjaezar; (*resources*) aprovechar.
harp [hɑːp] *n* arpa ♦ *vi*: **to ~ on (about)** machacar (con).
harpoon [hɑː'puːn] *n* arpón *m*.
harrow ['hærəu] *n* grada ♦ *vt* gradar.
harrowing ['hærəuɪŋ] *adj* angustioso.
harry ['hærɪ] *vt* (*MIL*) acosar; (*person*) hostigar.
harsh [hɑːʃ] *adj* (*cruel*) duro, cruel; (*severe*) severo; (*words*) hosco; (*colour*) chillón/ona; (*contrast*) violento.
harshly ['hɑːʃlɪ] *adv* (*say*) con aspereza; (*treat*) con mucha dureza.
harshness ['hɑːʃnɪs] *n* dureza.
harvest ['hɑːvɪst] *n* cosecha; (*of grapes*) vendimia ♦ *vt, vi* cosechar.
harvester ['hɑːvɪstə*] *n* (*machine*) cosechadora; (*person*) segador(a) *m/f*; **combine ~** segadora trilladora.
has [hæz] *vb see* **have**.
has-been ['hæzbiːn] *n* (*col: person*) persona acabada; (*: thing*) vieja gloria.
hash [hæʃ] *n* (*CULIN*) picadillo; (*fig: mess*) lío.

hashish ['hæʃɪʃ] *n* hachís *m*.
hasn't ['hæznt] = **has not.**
hassle ['hæsl] *n* (*col*) lío, rollo ♦ *vt* incordiar.
haste [heɪst] *n* prisa.
hasten ['heɪsn] *vt* acelerar ♦ *vi* darse prisa; **I ~ to add that...** me apresuro a añadir que ....
hastily ['heɪstɪlɪ] *adv* de prisa.
hasty ['heɪstɪ] *adj* apresurado.
hat [hæt] *n* sombrero.
hatbox ['hætbɔks] *n* sombrerera.
hatch [hætʃ] *n* (*NAUT*: *also*: **~way**) escotilla ♦ *vi* salir del cascarón ♦ *vt* incubar; (*fig*: *scheme, plot*) idear, tramar.
hatchback ['hætʃbæk] *n* (*AUT*) tres *or* cinco puertas *m*.
hatchet ['hætʃɪt] *n* hacha.
hatchet job *n* (*col*) varapalo.
hatchet man *n* (*col*) ejecutor *m* de faenas desagradables por cuenta de otro.
hate [heɪt] *vt* odiar, aborrecer ♦ *n* odio; **I ~ to trouble you, but ...** siento *or* lamento molestarle, pero ....
hateful ['heɪtful] *adj* odioso.
hatred ['heɪtrɪd] *n* odio.
hat trick *n*: **to score a ~** (*BRIT SPORT*) marcar tres tantos (*or* triunfos) seguidos.
haughtily ['hɔːtɪlɪ] *adv* con arrogancia.
haughty ['hɔːtɪ] *adj* altanero, arrogante.
haul [hɔːl] *vt* tirar, jalar (*LAM*); (*by lorry*) transportar ♦ *n* (*of fish*) redada; (*of stolen goods etc*) botín *m*.
haulage ['hɔːlɪdʒ] *n* (*BRIT*) transporte *m*; (*costs*) gastos *mpl* de transporte.
haulage contractor *n* (*firm*) empresa de transportes; (*person*) transportista *m/f*.
haulier ['hɔːlɪə*], (*US*) **hauler** ['hɔːlə*] *n* transportista *m/f*.
haunch [hɔːntʃ] *n* anca; (*of meat*) pierna.
haunt [hɔːnt] *vt* (*subj*: *ghost*) aparecer en; (*frequent*) frecuentar; (*obsess*) obsesionar ♦ *n* guarida.
haunted ['hɔːntɪd] *adj* (*castle etc*) embrujado; (*look*) de angustia.
haunting ['hɔːntɪŋ] *adj* (*sight, music*) evocativo.
Havana [hə'vɑːnə] *n* La Habana.

KEYWORD

have [haev] (*pt, pp* **had**) *aux vb* **1** (*gen*) haber; **to ~ arrived/eaten** haber llegado/comido; **having finished** *or* **when he had finished, he left** cuando hubo acabado, se fue
2 (*in tag questions*): **you've done it, ~n't you?** lo has hecho, ¿verdad? *or* ¿no?
3 (*in short answers and questions*): **I ~n't** no; **so I ~** pues, es verdad; **we ~n't paid — yes we ~!** no hemos pagado — ¡sí que hemos pagado!; **I've been there before, ~ you?** he estado allí antes, ¿y tú?
♦ *modal aux vb* (*be obliged*): **to ~ (got) to do sth** tener que hacer algo; **you ~n't to tell her** no hay que *or* no debes decírselo
♦ *vt* **1** (*possess*) tener; **he has (got) blue eyes/dark hair** tiene los ojos azules/el pelo negro
2 (*referring to meals etc*): **to ~ breakfast/lunch/dinner** desayunar/comer/cenar; **to ~ a drink/a cigarette** tomar algo/fumar un cigarrillo
3 (*receive*) recibir; (*obtain*) obtener; **may I ~ your address?** ¿puedes darme tu dirección?; **you can ~ it for £5** te lo puedes quedar por £5; **I must ~ it by tomorrow** lo necesito para mañana; **to ~ a baby** tener un niño *or* bebé
4 (*maintain, allow*): **I won't ~ it/this nonsense!** ¡no lo permitiré!/¡no permitiré estas tonterías!; **we can't ~ that** no podemos permitir eso
5: **to ~ sth done** hacer *or* mandar hacer algo; **to ~ one's hair cut** cortarse el pelo; **to ~ sb do sth** hacer que algn haga algo
6 (*experience, suffer*): **to ~ a cold/flu** tener un resfriado/la gripe; **she had her bag stolen/her arm broken** le robaron el bolso/se rompió un brazo; **to ~ an operation** operarse
7 (*+noun*): **to ~ a swim/walk/bath/rest** nadar/dar un paseo/darse un baño/descansar; **let's ~ a look** vamos a ver; **to ~ a meeting/party** celebrar una reunión/una fiesta; **let me ~ a try** déjame intentarlo
►**have in** *vt*: **to ~ it in for sb** (*col*) tenerla tomada con algn
►**have on** *vt*: **~ you anything on tomorrow?** ¿vas a hacer algo mañana?; **I don't ~ any money on me** no llevo dinero (encima); **to ~ sb on** (*BRIT col*) tomarle el pelo a algn
►**have out** *vt*: **to ~ it out with sb** (*settle a problem etc*) dejar las cosas en claro con algn.

haven ['heɪvn] *n* puerto; (*fig*) refugio.
haven't ['hævnt] = **have not.**
haversack ['hævəsæk] *n* macuto.
haves [hævz] *npl*: **the ~ and the have-nots** los ricos y los pobres.
havoc ['hævək] *n* estragos *mpl*; **to play ~**

with sth hacer estragos en algo.
Hawaii [hə'waii:] *n* (Islas *fpl*) Hawai *m*.
Hawaiian [hə'waɪjən] *adj, n* hawaiano/a *m/f*.
hawk [hɔ:k] *n* halcón *m* ♦ *vt* (*goods for sale*) pregonar.
hawkish ['hɔ:kɪʃ] *adj* beligerante.
hawthorn ['hɔ:θɔ:n] *n* espino.
hay [heɪ] *n* heno.
hay fever *n* fiebre *f* del heno.
haystack ['heɪstæk] *n* almiar *m*.
haywire ['heɪwaɪə*] *adj* (*col*): **to go** ~ (*person*) volverse loco; (*plan*) irse al garete.
hazard ['hæzəd] *n* riesgo; (*danger*) peligro ♦ *vt* (*remark*) aventurar; (*one's life*) arriesgar; **to be a health** ~ ser un peligro para la salud; **to** ~ **a guess** aventurar una respuesta *or* hipótesis.
hazardous ['hæzədəs] *adj* (*dangerous*) peligroso; (*risky*) arriesgado.
hazard warning lights *npl* (*AUT*) señales *fpl* de emergencia.
haze [heɪz] *n* neblina.
hazel ['heɪzl] *n* (*tree*) avellano ♦ *adj* (*eyes*) color *m* de avellano.
hazelnut ['heɪzlnʌt] *n* avellana.
hazy ['heɪzɪ] *adj* brumoso; (*idea*) vago.
H-bomb ['eɪtʃbɔm] *n* bomba H.
h & c *abbr* (*BRIT*) = *hot and cold (water)*.
HE *abbr* = **high explosive**; (*REL, DIPLOMACY*: = *His (or Her) Excellency*) S. Exc^{a}.
he [hi:] *pron* él; ~ **who**... aquél que..., quien....
head [hɛd] *n* cabeza; (*leader*) jefe/a *m/f*; (*COMPUT*) cabeza (grabadora) ♦ *vt* (*list*) encabezar; (*group*) capitanear; ~**s (or tails)** cara (o cruz); ~ **first** de cabeza; ~ **over heels** patas arriba; ~ **over heels in love** perdidamente enamorado; **on your** ~ **be it!** ¡allá tú!; **they went over my** ~ **to the manager** fueron directamente al gerente sin hacerme caso; **it was above** *or* **over their** ~**s** no alcanzaron a entenderlo; **to come to a** ~ (*fig*: *situation etc*) llegar a un punto crítico; **to have a** ~ **for business** tener talento para los negocios; **to have no** ~ **for heights** no resistir las alturas; **to lose/keep one's** ~ perder la cabeza/mantener la calma; **to sit at the** ~ **of the table** sentarse a la cabecera de la mesa; **to** ~ **the ball** cabecear (el balón).
▸**head for** *vt fus* dirigirse a.
▸**head off** *vt* (*threat, danger*) evitar.
headache ['hɛdeɪk] *n* dolor *m* de cabeza; **to have a** ~ tener dolor de cabeza.
headband ['hɛdbænd] *n* cinta (para la cabeza), vincha (*LAM*).
headboard ['hɛdbɔ:d] *n* cabecera.
headdress ['hɛddrɛs] *n* (*of bride, Indian*) tocado.
headed notepaper ['hɛdɪd-] *n* papel *m* con membrete.
header ['hɛdə*] *n* (*BRIT col*: *FOOTBALL*) cabezazo; (: *fall*) caída de cabeza.
headfirst [hɛd'fə:st] *adv* de cabeza.
headhunt ['hɛdhʌnt] *vt*: **to be** ~**ed** ser seleccionado por un cazatalentos.
headhunter ['hɛdhʌntə*] *n* (*fig*) cazaejecutivos *m inv*.
heading ['hɛdɪŋ] *n* título.
headlamp ['hɛdlæmp] *n* (*BRIT*) = **headlight**.
headland ['hɛdlənd] *n* promontorio.
headlight ['hɛdlaɪt] *n* faro.
headline ['hɛdlaɪn] *n* titular *m*.
headlong ['hɛdlɔŋ] *adv* (*fall*) de cabeza; (*rush*) precipitadamente.
headmaster/mistress [hɛd'mɑ:stə*/mɪstrɪs] *n* director(a) *m/f* (de escuela).
head office *n* oficina central, central *f*.
head-on [hɛd'ɔn] *adj* (*collision*) de frente.
headphones ['hɛdfəunz] *npl* auriculares *mpl*.
headquarters (HQ) ['hɛdkwɔ:təz] *npl* sede *f* central; (*MIL*) cuartel *m* general.
head-rest ['hɛdrɛst] *n* reposa-cabezas *m inv*.
headroom ['hɛdrum] *n* (*in car*) altura interior; (*under bridge*) (límite *m* de) altura.
headscarf ['hɛdskɑ:f] *n* pañuelo.
headset ['hɛdsɛt] *n* cascos *mpl*.
headstone ['hɛdstəun] *n* lápida.
headstrong ['hɛdstrɔŋ] *adj* testarudo.
head waiter *n* maître *m*.
headway ['hɛdweɪ] *n*: **to make** ~ (*fig*) hacer progresos.
headwind ['hɛdwɪnd] *n* viento contrario.
heady ['hɛdɪ] *adj* (*experience, period*) apasionante; (*wine*) fuerte.
heal [hi:l] *vt* curar ♦ *vi* cicatrizar.
health [hɛlθ] *n* salud *f*.
health care *n* asistencia sanitaria.
health centre *n* ambulatorio, centro médico.
health food(s) *n(pl)* alimentos *mpl* orgánicos.
health hazard *n* riesgo para la salud.
Health Service *n* (*BRIT*) servicio de salud pública, ≈ Insalud *m* (*SP*).
healthy ['hɛlθɪ] *adj* (*gen*) sano; (*economy, bank balance*) saludable.
heap [hi:p] *n* montón *m* ♦ *vt* amontonar; (*plate*) colmar; ~**s (of)** (*col*: *lots*) montones (de); **to** ~ **favours/praise/gifts** *etc* **on sb** colmar a algn de favores/elogios/regalos *etc*.

hear, *pt, pp* **heard** [hɪə*, hə:d] *vt* oír; (*perceive*) sentir; (*listen to*) escuchar; (*lecture*) asistir a; (*LAW*: *case*) ver ♦ *vi* oír; **to ~ about** oír hablar de; **to ~ from sb** tener noticias de alguien; **I've never heard of that book** nunca he oído hablar de ese libro.
►**hear out** *vt*: **to ~ sb out** dejar que algn termine de hablar.
hearing ['hɪərɪŋ] *n* (*sense*) oído; (*LAW*) vista; **to give sb a ~** dar a algn la oportunidad de hablar, escuchar a algn.
hearing aid *n* audífono.
hearsay ['hɪəseɪ] *n* rumores *mpl*, habladurías *fpl*.
hearse [hə:s] *n* coche *m* fúnebre.
heart [hɑ:t] *n* corazón *m*; **~s** *npl* (*CARDS*) corazones *mpl*; **at ~** en el fondo; **by ~** (*learn, know*) de memoria; **to have a weak ~** tener el corazón débil; **to set one's ~ on sth/on doing sth** anhelar algo/hacer algo; **I did not have the ~ to tell her** no tuve valor para decírselo; **to take ~** cobrar ánimos; **the ~ of the matter** lo esencial *or* el meollo del asunto.
heartache ['hɑ:teɪk] *n* angustia.
heart attack *n* infarto (de miocardio).
heartbeat ['hɑ:tbi:t] *n* latido (del corazón).
heartbreak ['hɑ:tbreɪk] *n* angustia, congoja.
heartbreaking ['hɑ:tbreɪkɪŋ] *adj* desgarrador(a).
heartbroken ['hɑ:tbrəukən] *adj*: **she was ~ about it** le partió el corazón.
heartburn ['hɑ:tbə:n] *n* acedía.
-hearted ['hɑ:tɪd] *adj suff*: **a kind~ person** una persona bondadosa.
heartening ['hɑ:tnɪŋ] *adj* alentador(a).
heart failure *n* (*MED*) paro cardíaco.
heartfelt ['hɑ:tfɛlt] *adj* (*cordial*) cordial; (*deeply felt*) sincero.
hearth [hɑ:θ] *n* (*gen*) hogar *m*; (*fireplace*) chimenea.
heartily ['hɑ:tɪlɪ] *adv* sinceramente, cordialmente; (*laugh*) a carcajadas; (*eat*) con buen apetito; **to be ~ sick of** estar completamente harto de.
heartland ['hɑ:tlænd] *n* zona interior *or* central; (*fig*) corazón *m*.
heartless ['hɑ:tlɪs] *adj* despiadado.
heartstrings ['hɑ:tstrɪŋz] *npl*: **to tug (at) sb's ~** tocar la fibra sensible de algn.
heart-throb ['hɑ:tθrɔb] *n* ídolo.
heart-to-heart ['hɑ:ttə'hɑ:t] *n* (*also*: **~ talk**) conversación *f* íntima.
heart transplant *n* transplante *m* de corazón.
hearty ['hɑ:tɪ] *adj* cordial.
heat [hi:t] *n* (*gen*) calor *m*; (*SPORT*: *also*: **qualifying ~**) prueba eliminatoria; (*ZOOL*): **in** *or* **on ~** en celo ♦ *vt* calentar.
►**heat up** *vi* (*gen*) calentarse.
heated ['hi:tɪd] *adj* caliente; (*fig*) acalorado.
heater ['hi:tə*] *n* calentador *m*.
heath [hi:θ] *n* (*BRIT*) brezal *m*.
heathen ['hi:ðn] *adj, n* pagano/a *m/f*.
heather ['hɛðə*] *n* brezo.
heating ['hi:tɪŋ] *n* calefacción *f*.
heat-resistant ['hi:trɪzɪstənt] *adj* refractario.
heat-seeking ['hi:tsi:kɪŋ-] *adj* guiado por infrarrojos, termoguiado.
heatstroke ['hi:tstrəuk] *n* insolación *f*.
heatwave ['hi:tweɪv] *n* ola de calor.
heave [hi:v] *vt* (*pull*) tirar; (*push*) empujar con esfuerzo; (*lift*) levantar (con esfuerzo) ♦ *vi* (*water*) subir y bajar ♦ *n* tirón *m*; empujón *m*; (*effort*) esfuerzo; (*throw*) echada; **to ~ a sigh** dar *or* echar un suspiro, suspirar.
►**heave to** *vi* (*NAUT*) ponerse al pairo.
heaven ['hɛvn] *n* cielo; (*REL*) paraíso; **thank ~!** ¡gracias a Dios!; **for ~'s sake!** (*pleading*) ¡por el amor de Dios!, ¡por lo que más quiera!; (*protesting*) ¡por Dios!
heavenly ['hɛvnlɪ] *adj* celestial; (*REL*) divino.
heavenly body *n* cuerpo celeste.
heavily ['hɛvɪlɪ] *adv* pesadamente; (*drink, smoke*) en exceso; (*sleep, sigh*) profundamente.
heavy ['hɛvɪ] *adj* pesado; (*work*) duro; (*sea, rain, meal*) fuerte; (*drinker, smoker*) empedernido; (*eater*) comilón/ona.
heavy-duty ['hɛvɪ'dju:tɪ] *adj* resistente.
heavy goods vehicle (HGV) *n* (*BRIT*) vehículo pesado.
heavy-handed ['hɛvɪ'hændɪd] *adj* (*clumsy, tactless*) torpe.
heavy industry *n* industria pesada.
heavy metal *n* (*MUS*) heavy *m* (metal).
heavy-set [hevɪ'sɛt] *adj* (*esp US*) corpulento, fornido.
heavy user *n* consumidor *m* intensivo.
heavyweight ['hɛvɪweɪt] *n* (*SPORT*) peso pesado.
Hebrew ['hi:bru:] *adj, n* (*LING*) hebreo.
Hebrides ['hɛbrɪdi:z] *npl*: **the ~** las Hébridas.
heck [hɛk] *n* (*col*): **why the ~ ...?** ¿por qué porras ...?; **a ~ of a lot of** cantidad de.
heckle ['hɛkl] *vt* interrumpir.
heckler ['hɛklə*] *n* el/la que interrumpe a un orador.
hectare ['hɛktɑ:*] *n* (*BRIT*) hectárea.
hectic ['hɛktɪk] *adj* agitado; (*busy*) ocupado.

hector ['hɛktə*] *vt* intimidar con bravatas.
he'd [hi:d] = **he would; he had.**
hedge [hɛdʒ] *n* seto ♦ *vt* cercar (con un seto) ♦ *vi* contestar con evasivas; **as a ~ against inflation** como protección contra la inflación; **to ~ one's bets** (*fig*) cubrirse.
hedgehog ['hɛdʒhɔg] *n* erizo.
hedgerow ['hɛdʒrəu] *n* seto vivo.
hedonism ['hi:dənɪzəm] *n* hedonismo.
heed [hi:d] *vt* (*also*: **take ~ of**) (*pay attention*) hacer caso de; (*bear in mind*) tener en cuenta; **to pay (no) ~ to, take (no) ~ of** (no) hacer caso a, (no) tener en cuenta.
heedless ['hi:dlɪs] *adj* desatento.
heel [hi:l] *n* talón *m* ♦ *vt* (*shoe*) poner tacón a; **to take to one's ~s** (*col*) poner pies en polvorosa; **to bring to ~** meter en cintura.
hefty ['hɛftɪ] *adj* (*person*) fornido; (*piece*) grande; (*price*) alto.
heifer ['hɛfə*] *n* novilla, ternera.
height [haɪt] *n* (*of person*) talla *f*; (*of building*) altura; (*high ground*) cerro; (*altitude*) altitud *f*; **what ~ are you?** ¿cuánto mides?; **of average ~** de estatura mediana; **to be afraid of ~s** tener miedo a las alturas; **it's the ~ of fashion** es el último grito en moda.
heighten ['haɪtn] *vt* elevar; (*fig*) aumentar.
heinous ['heɪnəs] *adj* atroz, nefasto.
heir [ɛə*] *n* heredero.
heir apparent *n* presunto heredero.
heiress ['ɛərɛs] *n* heredera.
heirloom ['ɛəlu:m] *n* reliquia de familia.
heist [haɪst] *n* (*col*: *hold-up*) atraco a mano armada.
held [hɛld] *pt, pp of* **hold.**
helicopter ['hɛlɪkɔptə*] *n* helicóptero.
heliport ['hɛlɪpɔ:t] *n* (*AVIAT*) helipuerto.
helium ['hi:lɪəm] *n* helio.
hell [hɛl] *n* infierno; **oh ~!** (*col*) ¡demonios!, ¡caramba!
he'll [hi:l] = **he will, he shall.**
hellbent [hɛl'bɛnt] *adj* (*col*): **he was ~ on going** se le metió entre ceja y ceja ir.
hellish ['hɛlɪʃ] *adj* infernal; (*col*) horrible.
hello [hə'ləu] *excl* ¡hola!; (*surprise*) ¡caramba!; (*TEL*) ¡dígame! (*esp SP*), ¡aló! (*LAM*).
helm [hɛlm] *n* (*NAUT*) timón *m*.
helmet ['hɛlmɪt] *n* casco.
helmsman ['hɛlmzmən] *n* timonel *m*.
help [hɛlp] *n* ayuda; (*charwoman*) criada, asistenta ♦ *vt* ayudar; **~!** ¡socorro!; **with the ~ of** con la ayuda de; **can I ~ you?** (*in shop*) ¿qué desea?; **to be of ~ to sb** servir a algn; **to ~ sb (to) do sth** echarle una mano *or* ayudar a algn a hacer algo; **~ yourself** sírvete; **he can't ~ it** no lo puede evitar.
helper ['hɛlpə*] *n* ayudante *m/f*.
helpful ['hɛlpful] *adj* útil; (*person*) servicial.
helping ['hɛlpɪŋ] *n* ración *f*.
helping hand *n*: **to give sb a ~** echar una mano a algn.
helpless ['hɛlplɪs] *adj* (*incapable*) incapaz; (*defenceless*) indefenso.
helpline ['hɛlplaɪn] *n* teléfono de asistencia al público.
Helsinki ['hɛlsɪŋkɪ] *n* Helsinki *m*.
helter-skelter ['hɛltə'skɛltə*] *n* (*in funfair*) tobogán *m*.
hem [hɛm] *n* dobladillo ♦ *vt* poner *or* coser el dobladillo a.
▸**hem in** *vt* cercar; **to feel ~med in** (*fig*) sentirse acosado.
he-man ['hi:mæn] *n* macho.
hematology [hi:mə'tɔlədʒɪ] *n* (*US*) = **haematology.**
hemisphere ['hɛmɪsfɪə*] *n* hemisferio.
hemline ['hɛmlaɪn] *n* bajo (del vestido).
hemlock ['hɛmlɔk] *n* cicuta.
hemoglobin [hi:mə'gləubɪn] *n* (*US*) = **haemoglobin.**
hemophilia [hi:mə'fɪlɪə] *n* (*US*) = **haemophilia.**
hemorrhage ['hɛmərɪdʒ] *n* (*US*) = **haemorrhage.**
hemorrhoids ['hɛmərɔɪdz] *npl* (*US*) = **haemorrhoids.**
hemp [hɛmp] *n* cáñamo.
hen [hɛn] *n* gallina; (*female bird*) hembra.
hence [hɛns] *adv* (*therefore*) por lo tanto; **2 years ~** de aquí a 2 años.
henceforth [hɛns'fɔ:θ] *adv* de hoy en adelante.
henchman ['hɛntʃmən] *n* (*pej*) secuaz *m*.
henna ['hɛnə] *n* alheña.
hen night *n* (*col*) despedida de soltera.
hen party *n* (*col*) reunión *f* de mujeres.
henpecked ['hɛnpɛkt] *adj*: **to be ~** ser un calzonazos.
hepatitis [hɛpə'taɪtɪs] *n* hepatitis *f inv*.
her [hə:*] *pron* (*direct*) la; (*indirect*) le; (*stressed, after prep*) ella ♦ *adj* su; *see also* **me; my.**
herald ['hɛrəld] *n* (*forerunner*) precursor(a) *m/f* ♦ *vt* anunciar.
heraldic [hɛ'rældɪk] *adj* heráldico.
heraldry ['hɛrəldrɪ] *n* heráldica.
herb [hə:b] *n* hierba.
herbaceous [hə:'beɪʃəs] *adj* herbáceo.
herbal ['hə:bl] *adj* de hierbas.
herbicide ['hə:bɪsaɪd] *n* herbicida *m*.
herd [hə:d] *n* rebaño; (*of wild animals, swine*) piara ♦ *vt* (*drive, gather*: *animals*) llevar en

manada; (: *people*) reunir.
►**herd together** *vt* agrupar, reunir ♦ *vi* apiñarse, agruparse.
here [hɪə*] *adv* aquí; ~! (*present*) ¡presente!; ~ **is/are** aquí está/están; ~ **she is** aquí está; **come** ~! ¡ven aquí *or* acá!; ~ **and there** aquí y allá.
hereabouts ['hɪərə'bauts] *adv* por aquí (cerca).
hereafter [hɪər'ɑːftə*] *adv* en el futuro ♦ *n*: **the** ~ el más allá.
hereby [hɪə'baɪ] *adv* (*in letter*) por la presente.
hereditary [hɪ'rɛdɪtrɪ] *adj* hereditario.
heredity [hɪ'rɛdɪtɪ] *n* herencia.
heresy ['hɛrəsɪ] *n* herejía.
heretic ['hɛrətɪk] *n* hereje *m/f*.
heretical [hɪ'rɛtɪkəl] *adj* herético.
herewith [hɪə'wɪð] *adv*: **I send you** ~ ... le mando adjunto ....
heritage ['hɛrɪtɪdʒ] *n* (*gen*) herencia; (*fig*) patrimonio; **our national** ~ nuestro patrimonio nacional.
hermetically [həː'mɛtɪkəlɪ] *adv*: ~ **sealed** herméticamente cerrado.
hermit ['həːmɪt] *n* ermitaño/a.
hernia ['həːnɪə] *n* hernia.
hero, *pl* ~**es** ['hɪərəu] *n* héroe *m*; (*in book, film*) protagonista *m*.
heroic [hɪ'rəuɪk] *adj* heroico.
heroin ['hɛrəuɪn] *n* heroína.
heroin addict *n* heroinómano/a, adicto/a a la heroína.
heroine ['hɛrəuɪn] *n* heroína; (*in book, film*) protagonista.
heroism ['hɛrəuɪzm] *n* heroísmo.
heron ['hɛrən] *n* garza.
hero worship *n* veneración *f*.
herring ['hɛrɪŋ] *n* arenque *m*.
hers [həːz] *pron* (el) suyo/(la) suya *etc*; **a friend of** ~ un amigo suyo; **this is** ~ esto es suyo *or* de ella; *see also* **mine**.
herself [həː'sɛlf] *pron* (*reflexive*) se; (*emphatic*) ella misma; (*after prep*) sí (misma); *see also* **oneself**.
Herts *abbr* (*BRIT*) = *Hertfordshire*.
he's [hiːz] = **he is; he has.**
hesitant ['hɛzɪtənt] *adj* indeciso; **to be** ~ **about doing sth** no decidirse a hacer algo.
hesitate ['hɛzɪteɪt] *vi* dudar, vacilar; **don't** ~ **to ask (me)** no dudes en pedírmelo.
hesitation [hɛzɪ'teɪʃən] *n* indecisión *f*; **I have no** ~ **in saying (that)** ... no tengo el menor reparo en afirmar que ....
hessian ['hɛsɪən] *n* arpillera.
heterogeneous ['hɛtərə'dʒiːnɪəs] *adj* heterogéneo.
heterosexual [hɛtərəu'sɛksjuəl] *adj, n* heterosexual *m/f*.
het up [hɛt'ʌp] *adj* (*col*) agitado, nervioso.
HEW *n abbr* (*US*: = *Department of Health, Education and Welfare*) *ministerio de sanidad, educación y bienestar público*.
hew [hjuː] *vt* cortar.
hex [hɛks] (*US*) *n* maleficio, mal *m* de ojo ♦ *vt* embrujar.
hexagon ['hɛksəgən] *n* hexágono.
hexagonal [hɛk'sægənl] *adj* hexagonal.
hey [heɪ] *excl* ¡oye!, ¡oiga!
heyday ['heɪdeɪ] *n*: **the** ~ **of** el apogeo de.
HF *n abbr* = *high frequency*.
HGV *n abbr see* **heavy goods vehicle**.
HI *abbr* (*US*) = *Hawaii*.
hi [haɪ] *excl* ¡hola!
hiatus [haɪ'eɪtəs] *n* vacío, interrupción *f*; (*LING*) hiato.
hibernate ['haɪbəneɪt] *vi* invernar.
hibernation [haɪbə'neɪʃən] *n* hibernación *f*.
hiccough, hiccup ['hɪkʌp] *vi* hipar; ~**s** *npl* hipo *sg*.
hid [hɪd] *pt of* **hide**.
hick [hɪk] *n* (*US col*) paleto/a.
hidden ['hɪdn] *pp of* **hide** ♦ *adj*: **there are no** ~ **extras** no hay suplementos ocultos; ~ **agenda** plan *m* encubierto.
hide [haɪd] *n* (*skin*) piel *f* ♦ *vb* (*pt* **hid**, *pp* **hidden** [hɪd, 'hɪdn]) *vt* esconder, ocultar; (*feelings, truth*) encubrir, ocultar ♦ *vi*: **to** ~ **(from sb)** esconderse *or* ocultarse (de algn).
hide-and-seek ['haɪdən'siːk] *n* escondite *m*.
hideaway ['haɪdəweɪ] *n* escondite *m*.
hideous ['hɪdɪəs] *adj* horrible.
hideously ['hɪdɪəslɪ] *adv* horriblemente.
hide-out ['haɪdaut] *n* escondite *m*, refugio.
hiding ['haɪdɪŋ] *n* (*beating*) paliza; **to be in** ~ (*concealed*) estar escondido.
hiding place *n* escondrijo.
hierarchy ['haɪərɑːkɪ] *n* jerarquía.
hieroglyphic [haɪərə'glɪfɪk] *adj* jeroglífico ♦ *n*: ~**s** jeroglíficos *mpl*.
hi-fi ['haɪfaɪ] *abbr* (= *high fidelity*) *n* estéreo, hifi *m* ♦ *adj* de alta fidelidad.
higgledy-piggledy ['hɪgldɪ'pɪgldɪ] *adv* en desorden, de cualquier modo.
high [haɪ] *adj* alto; (*speed, number*) grande, alto; (*price*) elevado; (*wind*) fuerte; (*voice*) agudo; (*col*: *on drugs*) colocado; (: *on drink*) borracho; (*CULIN*: *meat, game*) pasado; (: *spoilt*) estropeado ♦ *adv* alto, a gran altura ♦ *n*: **exports have reached a new** ~ las exportaciones han alcanzado niveles inusitados; **it is 20 m** ~ tiene 20 m de altura; ~ **in the air** en las alturas; **to pay a** ~ **price for sth** pagar algo muy caro.

highball [ˈhaɪbɔːl] *n* (*US*: *drink*) whisky *m* soda, highball *m* (*LAM*), jaibol *m* (*LAM*).
highboy [ˈhaɪbɔɪ] *n* (*US*) cómoda alta.
highbrow [ˈhaɪbrau] *adj* culto.
highchair [ˈhaɪtʃɛə*] *n* silla alta (para niños).
high-class [ˈhaɪˈklɑːs] *adj* (*neighbourhood*) de alta sociedad; (*hotel*) de lujo; (*person*) distinguido; (*food*) de alta categoría.
High Court *n* (*LAW*) tribunal *m* supremo; *ver recuadro*.

HIGH COURT

En el sistema legal de Inglaterra y Gales **High Court** *es la forma abreviada de "High Court of Justice", tribunal superior que junto con el de apelación ("Court of Appeal") forma el Tribunal Supremo ("Supreme Court of Judicature").*
En el sistema legal escocés es la forma abreviada de "High Court of Justiciary" tribunal con jurado que juzga los delitos más serios, que pueden dar lugar a una pena de gran severidad.

higher [ˈhaɪə*] *adj* (*form of life, study etc*) superior ♦ *adv* más alto.
higher education *n* educación *f* or enseñanza superior.
high explosive *n* explosivo de gran potencia.
highfalutin [haɪfəˈluːtɪn] *adj* (*col*) de altos vuelos, encopetado.
high finance *n* altas finanzas *fpl*.
high-flier, high-flyer [haɪˈflaɪə*] *n* ambicioso/a.
high-handed [haɪˈhændɪd] *adj* despótico.
high-heeled [haɪˈhiːld] *adj* de tacón alto.
highjack [ˈhaɪdʒæk] = **hijack**.
high jump *n* (*SPORT*) salto de altura.
highlands [ˈhaɪləndz] *npl* tierras *fpl* altas; **the H~** (*in Scotland*) las Tierras Altas de Escocia.
high-level [ˈhaɪlɛvl] *adj* (*talks etc*) de alto nivel; ~ **language** (*COMPUT*) lenguaje *m* de alto nivel.
highlight [ˈhaɪlaɪt] *n* (*fig*: *of event*) punto culminante ♦ *vt* subrayar.
highly [ˈhaɪlɪ] *adv* sumamente; ~ **paid** muy bien pagado; **to speak ~ of** hablar muy bien de.
highly-strung [ˈhaɪlɪˈstrʌŋ] *adj* muy excitable.
highness [ˈhaɪnɪs] *n* altura; **Her** *or* **His H~** Su Alteza.
high-pitched [haɪˈpɪtʃt] *adj* agudo.
high point *n*: **the ~** el punto culminante.
high-powered [ˈhaɪˈpauəd] *adj* (*engine*) de gran potencia; (*fig*: *person*) importante.
high-pressure [ˈhaɪprɛʃə*] *adj* de alta presión; (*fig*: *salesman etc*) enérgico.
high-rise [ˈhaɪraɪz] *n* (*also*: ~ **block,** ~ **building**) torre *f* de pisos.
high school *n* centro de enseñanza secundaria, ≈ Instituto Nacional de Bachillerato (*SP*), liceo (*LAM*); *ver recuadro*.

HIGH SCHOOL

El término **high school** *se aplica en Estados Unidos a dos tipos de centros de educación secundaria: "Junior High Schools", en los que se imparten normalmente del 7º al 9º curso* (llamado *"grade"*) *y "Senior High Schools", que abarcan los cursos 10º, 11º y 12º y en ocasiones el 9º. Aquí pueden estudiarse asignaturas tanto de contenido académico como profesional. En Gran Bretaña también se llaman* **high school** *algunos centros de enseñanza secundaria.*

high season *n* (*BRIT*) temporada alta.
high-speed [ˈhaɪspiːd] *adj* de alta velocidad.
high-spirited [haɪˈspɪrɪtɪd] *adj* animado.
high spirits *npl* ánimos *mpl*.
high street *n* (*BRIT*) calle *f* mayor.
high tide *n* marea alta.
highway [ˈhaɪweɪ] *n* carretera; (*US*) autopista; **the information ~** la autopista de la información.
Highway Code *n* (*BRIT*) código de la circulación.
hijack [ˈhaɪdʒæk] *vt* secuestrar ♦ *n* (*also*: **~ing**) secuestro.
hijacker [ˈhaɪdʒækə*] *n* secuestrador(a) *m/f*.
hike [haɪk] *vi* (*go walking*) ir de excursión (a pie); (*tramp*) caminar ♦ *n* caminata; (*col*: *in prices etc*) aumento.
▸**hike up** *vt* (*raise*) aumentar.
hiker [ˈhaɪkə*] *n* excursionista *m/f*.
hilarious [hɪˈlɛərɪəs] *adj* divertidísimo.
hilarity [hɪˈlærɪtɪ] *n* (*laughter*) risas *fpl*, carcajadas *fpl*.
hill [hɪl] *n* colina; (*high*) montaña; (*slope*) cuesta.
hillbilly [ˈhɪlbɪlɪ] *n* (*US*) rústico/a montañés/esa; (*pej*) palurdo/a.
hillside [ˈhɪlsaɪd] *n* ladera.
hilltop [ˈhɪltɔp] *n* cumbre *f*.
hilly [ˈhɪlɪ] *adj* montañoso; (*uneven*) accidentado.
hilt [hɪlt] *n* (*of sword*) empuñadura; **to the ~** (*fig*: *support*) incondicionalmente; **to be in debt up to the ~** estar hasta el cuello de

deudas.

him [hɪm] *pron* (*direct*) le, lo; (*indirect*) le; (*stressed, after prep*) él; *see also* **me.**

Himalayas [hɪmə'leɪəz] *npl*: **the ~** el Himalaya.

himself [hɪm'sɛlf] *pron* (*reflexive*) se; (*emphatic*) él mismo; (*after prep*) sí (mismo); *see also* **oneself.**

hind [haɪnd] *adj* posterior ♦ *n* cierva.

hinder ['hɪndə*] *vt* estorbar, impedir.

hindquarters ['haɪndkwɔːtəz] *npl* (ZOOL) cuartos *mpl* traseros.

hindrance ['hɪndrəns] *n* estorbo, obstáculo.

hindsight ['haɪndsaɪt] *n* percepción *f* tardía *or* retrospectiva; **with the benefit of ~** con la perspectiva del tiempo transcurrido.

Hindu ['hɪnduː] *n* hindú *m/f.*

hinge [hɪndʒ] *n* bisagra, gozne *m* ♦ *vi* (*fig*): **to ~ on** depender de.

hint [hɪnt] *n* indirecta; (*advice*) consejo ♦ *vt*: **to ~ that** insinuar que ♦ *vi*: **to ~ at** aludir a; **to drop a ~** soltar *or* tirar una indirecta; **give me a ~** dame una pista.

hip [hɪp] *n* cadera; (BOT) escaramujo.

hip flask *n* petaca.

hip-hop ['hɪphɔp] *n* hip hop *m.*

hippie ['hɪpɪ] *n* hippie *m/f*, jipi *m/f.*

hip pocket *n* bolsillo de atrás.

hippopotamus, *pl* **~es** *or* **hippopotami** [hɪpə'pɔtəməs, -'pɔtəmaɪ] hipopótamo.

hippy ['hɪpɪ] *n* = **hippie.**

hire ['haɪə*] *vt* (BRIT: *car, equipment*) alquilar; (*worker*) contratar ♦ *n* alquiler *m*; **for ~** se alquila; (*taxi*) libre; **on ~** de alquiler.

▸**hire out** *vt* alquilar, arrendar.

hire(d) car *n* (BRIT) coche *m* de alquiler.

hire purchase (H.P.) *n* (BRIT) compra a plazos; **to buy sth on ~** comprar algo a plazos.

his [hɪz] *pron* (el) suyo/(la) suya *etc* ♦ *adj* su; **this is ~** esto es suyo *or* de él; *see also* **my, mine.**

Hispanic [hɪs'pænɪk] *adj* hispánico.

hiss [hɪs] *vi* sisear; (*in protest*) silbar ♦ *n* siseo; silbido.

histogram ['hɪstəgræm] *n* histograma *m.*

historian [hɪ'stɔːrɪən] *n* historiador(a) *m/f.*

historic(al) [hɪ'stɔrɪk(l)] *adj* histórico.

history ['hɪstərɪ] *n* historia; **there's a long ~ of that illness in his family** esa enfermedad corre en su familia.

histrionics [hɪstrɪ'ɔnɪks] *npl* histrionismo.

hit [hɪt] *vt* (*pt, pp* **hit**) (*strike*) golpear, pegar; (*reach*: *target*) alcanzar; (*collide with*: *car*) chocar contra; (*fig*: *affect*) afectar ♦ *n* golpe *m*; (*success*) éxito; **to ~ the headlines** salir en primera plana; **to ~ the road** (*col*) largarse; **to ~ it off with sb** llevarse bien con algn.

▸**hit back** *vi* defenderse; (*fig*) devolver golpe por golpe.

▸**hit out at** *vt fus* asestar un golpe a; (*fig*) atacar.

▸**hit (up)on** *vt fus* (*answer*) dar con; (*solution*) hallar, encontrar.

hit and miss *adj*: **it's very ~, it's a ~ affair** es cuestión de suerte.

hit-and-run driver ['hɪtən'rʌn-] *n* *conductor(a) que tras atropellar a algn se da a la fuga.*

hitch [hɪtʃ] *vt* (*fasten*) atar, amarrar; (*also*: **~ up**) arremangarse ♦ *n* (*difficulty*) problema, pega; **to ~ a lift** hacer autostop; **technical ~** problema *m* técnico.

▸**hitch up** *vt* (*horse, cart*) enganchar, uncir.

hitch-hike ['hɪtʃhaɪk] *vi* hacer autostop.

hitch-hiker ['hɪtʃhaɪkə*] *n* autostopista *m/f.*

hi-tech [haɪ'tɛk] *adj* de alta tecnología.

hitherto ['hɪðə'tuː] *adv* hasta ahora, hasta aquí.

hit list *n* lista negra.

hitman ['hɪtmæn] *n* asesino a sueldo.

hit or miss ['hɪtə'mɪs] *adj* = **hit and miss.**

hit parade *n*: **the ~** los cuarenta principales.

HIV *n abbr* (= *human immunodeficiency virus*) VIH *m*; **~-negative** no portador(a) del virus del sida, no seropositivo; **~-positive** portador(a) del virus del sida, seropositivo.

hive [haɪv] *n* colmena; **the shop was a ~ of activity** (*fig*) la tienda era una colmena humana.

▸**hive off** *vt* (*col*: *separate*) separar; (: *privatize*) privatizar.

hl *abbr* (= *hectolitre*) hl.

HM *abbr* (= *His (or Her) Majesty*) S.M.

HMG *abbr* = *His (or Her) Majesty's Government.*

HMI *n abbr* (BRIT SCOL) = *His (or Her) Majesty's Inspector.*

HMO *n abbr* (US: = *health maintenance organization*) *seguro médico global.*

HMS *abbr* = *His (or Her) Majesty's Ship.*

HMSO *n abbr* (BRIT = *His (or Her) Majesty's Stationery Office*) *distribuidor oficial de las publicaciones del gobierno del Reino Unido.*

HNC *n abbr* (BRIT: = *Higher National Certificate*) *título académico.*

HND *n abbr* (BRIT: = *Higher National Diploma*) *título académico.*

hoard [hɔːd] *n* (*treasure*) tesoro; (*stockpile*) provisión *f* ♦ *vt* acumular.

hoarding ['hɔːdɪŋ] *n* (*for posters*) valla publicitaria.
hoarfrost ['hɔːfrɔst] *n* escarcha.
hoarse [hɔːs] *adj* ronco.
hoax [həuks] *n* engaño.
hob [hɔb] *n* quemador *m*.
hobble ['hɔbl] *vi* cojear.
hobby ['hɔbɪ] *n* pasatiempo, afición *f*.
hobby-horse ['hɔbɪhɔːs] *n* (*fig*) tema preferido.
hobnob ['hɔbnɔb] *vi*: **to ~ (with)** alternar (con).
hobo ['həubəu] *n* (*US*) vagabundo.
hock [hɔk] *n* (*of animal, CULIN*) corvejón *m*; (*col*): **to be in ~** (*person*) estar empeñado *or* endeudado; (*object*) estar empeñado.
hockey ['hɔkɪ] *n* hockey *m*.
hocus-pocus [həukəs'pəukəs] *n* (*trickery*) engañifa; (*words*: *of magician*) abracadabra *m*.
hod [hɔd] *n* capacho.
hodge-podge ['hɔdʒpɔdʒ] *n* (*US*) = **hotchpotch**.
hoe [həu] *n* azadón *m* ♦ *vt* azadonar.
hog [hɔg] *n* cerdo, puerco ♦ *vt* (*fig*) acaparar; **to go the whole ~** echar el todo por el todo.
Hogmanay [hɔgmə'neɪ] *n* (*Scottish*) Nochevieja.
hoist [hɔɪst] *n* (*crane*) grúa ♦ *vt* levantar, alzar.
hoity-toity [hɔɪtɪ'tɔɪtɪ] *adj* (*col*): **to be ~** darse humos.
hold [həuld] *vb* (*pt, pp* **held** [hɛld]) *vt* tener; (*contain*) contener; (*keep back*) retener; (*believe*) sostener; (*take ~ of*) coger (*SP*), agarrar (*LAM*); (*take weight*) soportar; (*meeting*) celebrar ♦ *vi* (*withstand pressure*) resistir; (*be valid*) ser válido; (*stick*) pegarse ♦ *n* (*grasp*) asimiento; (*fig*) dominio; (*WRESTLING*) presa; (*NAUT*) bodega; **~ the line!** (*TEL*) ¡no cuelgue!; **to ~ one's own** (*fig*) defenderse; **to ~ office** (*POL*) ocupar un cargo; **to ~ firm** *or* **fast** mantenerse firme; **he ~s the view that ...** opina *or* es su opinión que ...; **to ~ sb responsible for sth** culpar *or* echarle la culpa a algn de algo; **where can I get ~ of ...?** ¿dónde puedo encontrar (a) ...?; **to catch** *or* **get (a) ~ of** agarrarse *or* asirse de.
▸**hold back** *vt* retener; (*secret*) ocultar; **to ~ sb back from doing sth** impedir a algn hacer algo, impedir que algn haga algo.
▸**hold down** *vt* (*person*) sujetar; (*job*) mantener.
▸**hold forth** *vi* perorar.
▸**hold off** *vt* (*enemy*) rechazar ♦ *vi*: **if the rain ~s off** si no llueve.
▸**hold on** *vi* agarrarse bien; (*wait*) esperar.
▸**hold on to** *vt fus* agarrarse a; (*keep*) guardar.
▸**hold out** *vt* ofrecer ♦ *vi* (*resist*) resistir; **to ~ out (against)** resistir (a), sobrevivir.
▸**hold over** *vt* (*meeting etc*) aplazar.
▸**hold up** *vt* (*raise*) levantar; (*support*) apoyar; (*delay*) retrasar; (: *traffic*) demorar; (*rob*: *bank*) asaltar, atracar.
holdall ['həuldɔːl] *n* (*BRIT*) bolsa.
holder ['həuldə*] *n* (*of ticket, record*) poseedor(a) *m/f*; (*of passport, post, office, title etc*) titular *m/f*.
holding ['həuldɪŋ] *n* (*share*) participación *f*.
holding company *n* holding *m*.
holdup ['həuldʌp] *n* (*robbery*) atraco; (*delay*) retraso; (*BRIT*: *in traffic*) embotellamiento.
hole [həul] *n* agujero ♦ *vt* agujerear; **~ in the heart** (*MED*) boquete *m* en el corazón; **to pick ~s in** (*fig*) encontrar defectos en; **the ship was ~d** se abrió una vía de agua en el barco.
▸**hole up** *vi* esconderse.
holiday ['hɔlədɪ] *n* vacaciones *fpl*; (*day off*) (día *m* de) fiesta, día *m* festivo *or* feriado (*LAM*); **on ~** de vacaciones; **to be on ~** estar de vacaciones.
holiday camp *n* colonia *or* centro vacacional; (*for children*) colonia veraniega infantil.
holidaymaker ['hɔlədɪmeɪkə*] *n* (*BRIT*) turista *m/f*.
holiday pay *n* paga de las vacaciones.
holiday resort *n* centro turístico.
holiday season *n* temporada de vacaciones.
holiness ['həulɪnɪs] *n* santidad *f*.
holistic [həu'lɪstɪk] *adj* holístico.
Holland ['hɔlənd] *n* Holanda.
holler ['hɔlə*] *vi* (*col*) gritar, vocear.
hollow ['hɔləu] *adj* hueco; (*fig*) vacío; (*eyes*) hundido; (*sound*) sordo ♦ *n* (*gen*) hueco; (*in ground*) hoyo ♦ *vt*: **to ~ out** ahuecar.
holly ['hɔlɪ] *n* acebo.
hollyhock ['hɔlɪhɔk] *n* malva loca.
holocaust ['hɔləkɔːst] *n* holocausto.
hologram ['hɔləgræm] *n* holograma *m*.
hols [hɔlz] *npl* (*col*): **the ~** las vacaciones.
holster ['həulstə*] *n* pistolera.
holy ['həulɪ] *adj* (*gen*) santo, sagrado; (*water*) bendito; **the H~ Father** el Santo Padre.
Holy Communion *n* Sagrada Comunión *f*.
Holy Ghost, Holy Spirit *n* Espíritu *m* Santo.
homage ['hɔmɪdʒ] *n* homenaje *m*; **to pay ~ to** rendir homenaje a.

home [həum] *n* casa; (*country*) patria; (*institution*) asilo; (*COMPUT*) punto inicial ♦ *adj* (*domestic*) casero, de casa; (*ECON, POL*) nacional; (*SPORT: team*) de casa; (: *match, win*) en casa ♦ *adv* (*direction*) a casa; **at** ~ en casa; **to go/come** ~ ir/volver a casa; **make yourself at** ~ ¡estás en tu casa!; **it's near my** ~ está cerca de mi casa.
▸**home in on** *vt fus* (*missiles*) dirigirse hacia.
home address *n* domicilio.
home-brew [həum'bruː] *n* cerveza *etc* casera.
homecoming ['həumkʌmɪŋ] *n* regreso (al hogar).
home computer *n* ordenador *m* doméstico.
Home Counties *npl condados que rodean Londres.*
home economics *n* economía doméstica.
home ground *n*: **to be on** ~ estar en su *etc* terreno.
home-grown ['həumgrəun] *adj* de cosecha propia.
home help *n* (*BRIT*) trabajador(a) *m/f* del servicio de atención domiciliaria.
homeland ['həumlænd] *n* tierra natal.
homeless ['həumlɪs] *adj* sin hogar, sin casa ♦ *npl*: **the** ~ las personas sin hogar.
home loan *n* préstamo para la vivienda.
homely ['həumlɪ] *adj* (*domestic*) casero; (*simple*) sencillo.
home-made [həum'meɪd] *adj* hecho en casa.
Home Office *n* (*BRIT*) Ministerio del Interior.
homeopathy [həumɪ'ɔpəθɪ] *etc* (*US*) = **homoeopathy** *etc*.
home page *n* (*COMPUT*) página de inicio.
home rule *n* autonomía.
Home Secretary *n* (*BRIT*) Ministro del Interior.
homesick ['həumsɪk] *adj*: **to be** ~ tener morriña *or* nostalgia.
home town *n* ciudad *f* natal.
home truth *n*: **to tell sb a few** ~**s** decir cuatro verdades a algn.
homeward ['həumwəd] *adj* (*journey*) de vuelta.
homeward(s) ['həumwəd(z)] *adv* hacia casa.
homework ['həumwəːk] *n* deberes *mpl*.
homicidal [hɔmɪ'saɪdl] *adj* homicida.
homicide ['hɔmɪsaɪd] *n* (*US*) homicidio.
homing ['həumɪŋ] *adj* (*device, missile*) buscador(a); ~ **pigeon** paloma mensajera.
homoeopath, (*US*) **homeopath** ['həumɪəupæθ] *n* homeópata *m/f*.
homoeopathic, (*US*) **homeopathic** [həumɪəu'pæθɪk] *adj* homeopático.
homoeopathy, (*US*) **homeopathy** [həumɪ'ɔpəθɪ] *n* homeopatía.
homogeneous [hɔmə'dʒiːnɪəs] *adj* homogéneo.
homogenize [hə'mɔdʒənaɪz] *vt* homogeneizar.
homosexual [hɔməu'sɛksjuəl] *adj, n* homosexual *m/f*.
Hon. *abbr* (= *honourable, honorary*) *en títulos.*
Honduras [hɔn'djuərəs] *n* Honduras *fpl*.
hone [həun] *vt* (*sharpen*) afilar; (*fig*) perfeccionar.
honest ['ɔnɪst] *adj* honrado; (*sincere*) franco, sincero; **to be quite** ~ **with you ...** para serte franco ....
honestly ['ɔnɪstlɪ] *adv* honradamente; francamente, de verdad.
honesty ['ɔnɪstɪ] *n* honradez *f*.
honey ['hʌnɪ] *n* miel *f*; (*US col*) cariño; (: *to strangers*) guapo, linda.
honeycomb ['hʌnɪkəum] *n* panal *m*; (*fig*) laberinto.
honeymoon ['hʌnɪmuːn] *n* luna de miel.
honeysuckle ['hʌnɪsʌkl] *n* madreselva.
Hong Kong ['hɔŋ'kɔŋ] *n* Hong-Kong *m*.
honk [hɔŋk] *vi* (*AUT*) tocar la bocina.
Honolulu [hɔnə'luːluː] *n* Honolulú *m*.
honorary ['ɔnərərɪ] *adj* no remunerado; (*duty, title*) honorario.
honour, (*US*) **honor** ['ɔnə*] *vt* honrar ♦ *n* honor *m*, honra; **in** ~ **of** en honor de; **it's a great** ~ es un gran honor.
hono(u)rable ['ɔnərəbl] *adj* honrado, honorable.
hono(u)r-bound ['ɔnə'baund] *adj* moralmente obligado.
honours degree *n* (*UNIV*) *licenciatura superior; ver recuadro.*

HONOURS DEGREE

Tras un período de estudios de tres años normalmente (cuatro en Escocia), los universitarios obtienen una licenciatura llamada **honours degree**. *La calificación global que se recibe, en una escala de mayor a menor es la siguiente: "first class" (I), "upper-second class" (II:1), "lower-second class" (II:2) y "third class" (III). El licenciado puede añadir las letras "Hons" al título obtenido tras su nombre y apellidos, por ejemplo "BA Hons"; ver también "ordinary degree".*

honours list *n* (*BRIT*) *lista de distinciones honoríficas que entrega la reina*; *ver recuadro.*

HONOURS LIST

A la lista con los títulos honoríficos y condecoraciones que el monarca británico otorga en Año Nuevo y en el día de su cumpleaños se la conoce con el nombre de **honours list**. *Las personas que reciben dichas distinciones suelen ser miembros destacados de la vida pública (ámbito empresarial, ejército, deportes, espectáculos), aunque últimamente también se reconoce con ellas el trabajo abnegado y anónimo de la gente de la calle.*

Hons. *abbr* (*UNIV*) = **hono(u)rs degree.**

hood [hud] *n* capucha; (*BRIT AUT*) capota; (*US AUT*) capó *m*; (*US col*) matón *m*.

hooded ['hudɪd] *adj* (*robber*) encapuchado.

hoodlum ['hu:dləm] *n* matón *m*.

hoodwink ['hudwɪŋk] *vt* (*BRIT*) timar.

hoof, *pl* **~s** *or* **hooves** [hu:f, hu:vz] *n* pezuña.

hook [huk] *n* gancho; (*on dress*) corchete *m*, broche *m*; (*for fishing*) anzuelo ♦ *vt* enganchar; **~s and eyes** corchetes *mpl*, macho y hembra *m*; **by ~ or by crook** por las buenas o por las malas, cueste lo que cueste; **to be ~ed on** (*col*) estar enganchado a.

►**hook up** *vt* (*RADIO, TV*) transmitir en cadena.

hooligan ['hu:lɪgən] *n* gamberro.

hooliganism ['hu:lɪgənɪzəm] *n* gamberrismo.

hoop [hu:p] *n* aro.

hoot [hu:t] *vi* (*BRIT AUT*) tocar la bocina; (*siren*) sonar la sirena; (*owl*) ulular ♦ *n* bocinazo, toque *m* de sirena; **to ~ with laughter** morirse de risa.

hooter ['hu:tə*] *n* (*BRIT AUT*) bocina; (*of ship, factory*) sirena.

hoover ® ['hu:və*] (*BRIT*) *n* aspiradora ♦ *vt* pasar la aspiradora por.

hooves [hu:vz] *pl of* **hoof.**

hop [hɔp] *vi* saltar, brincar; (*on one foot*) saltar con un pie ♦ *n* salto, brinco; *see also* **hops.**

hope [həup] *vt, vi* esperar ♦ *n* esperanza; **I ~ so/not** espero que sí/no.

hopeful ['həupful] *adj* (*person*) optimista; (*situation*) prometedor(a); **I'm ~ that she'll manage to come** confío en que podrá venir.

hopefully ['həupfulɪ] *adv* con optimismo, con esperanza.

hopeless ['həuplɪs] *adj* desesperado.

hopelessly ['həuplɪslɪ] *adv* (*live etc*) sin esperanzas; **I'm ~ confused/lost** estoy totalmente despistado/perdido.

hopper ['hɔpə*] *n* (*chute*) tolva.

hops [hɔps] *npl* lúpulo *sg*.

horde [hɔ:d] *n* horda.

horizon [hə'raɪzn] *n* horizonte *m*.

horizontal [hɔrɪ'zɔntl] *adj* horizontal.

hormone ['hɔ:məun] *n* hormona.

hormone replacement therapy *n* terapia hormonal sustitutiva.

horn [hɔ:n] *n* cuerno, cacho (*LAM*); (*MUS*: *also*: **French ~**) trompa; (*AUT*) bocina, claxon *m*.

horned [hɔ:nd] *adj* con cuernos.

hornet ['hɔ:nɪt] *n* avispón *m*.

horny ['hɔ:nɪ] *adj* (*material*) córneo; (*hands*) calloso; (*US col*) cachondo.

horoscope ['hɔrəskəup] *n* horóscopo.

horrendous [hɔ'rɛndəs] *adj* horrendo.

horrible ['hɔrɪbl] *adj* horrible.

horribly ['hɔrɪblɪ] *adv* horriblemente.

horrid ['hɔrɪd] *adj* horrible, horroroso.

horridly ['hɔrɪdlɪ] *adv* (*behave*) tremendamente mal.

horrific [hɔ'rɪfɪk] *adj* (*accident*) horroroso; (*film*) horripilante.

horrify ['hɔrɪfaɪ] *vt* horrorizar.

horrifying ['hɔrɪfaɪɪŋ] *adj* horroroso.

horror ['hɔrə*] *n* horror *m*.

horror film *n* película de terror *or* miedo.

horror-struck ['hɔrəstrʌk], **horror-stricken** ['hɔrəstrɪkn] *adj* horrorizado.

hors d'œuvre [ɔ:'də:vrə] *n* entremeses *mpl*.

horse [hɔ:s] *n* caballo.

horseback ['hɔ:sbæk] *n*: **on ~** a caballo.

horsebox ['hɔ:sbɔks] *n* remolque *m* para transportar caballos.

horse chestnut *n* (*tree*) castaño de Indias.

horsedrawn ['hɔ:sdrɔ:n] *adj* de tracción animal.

horsefly ['hɔ:sflaɪ] *n* tábano.

horseman ['hɔ:smən] *n* jinete *m*.

horseplay ['hɔ:spleɪ] *n* pelea amistosa.

horsepower (hp) ['hɔ:spauə*] *n* caballo (de fuerza), potencia en caballos.

horse-racing ['hɔ:sreɪsɪŋ] *n* carreras *fpl* de caballos.

horseradish ['hɔ:srædɪʃ] *n* rábano picante.

horseshoe ['hɔ:sʃu:] *n* herradura.

horse show *n* concurso hípico.

horse-trader ['hɔ:streɪdə*] *n* chalán/ana *m/f*.

horse trials *npl* = **horse show.**

horsewhip ['hɔ:swɪp] *vt* azotar.

horsewoman ['hɔ:swumən] *n* amazona.

horsey ['hɔ:sɪ] *adj* (*col*: *person*) aficionado a los caballos.

horticulture ['hɔːtɪkʌltʃə*] *n* horticultura.
hose [həuz] *n* (*also*: ~**pipe**) manguera.
▸**hose down** *vt* limpiar con manguera.
hosiery ['həuzɪərɪ] *n* calcetería.
hospice ['hɔspɪs] *n* hospicio.
hospitable ['hɔspɪtəbl] *adj* hospitalario.
hospital ['hɔspɪtl] *n* hospital *m*.
hospitality [hɔspɪ'tælɪtɪ] *n* hospitalidad *f*.
hospitalize ['hɔspɪtəlaɪz] *vt* hospitalizar.
host [həust] *n* anfitrión *m*; (*TV, RADIO*) presentador(a) *m/f*; (*of inn etc*) mesonero; (*REL*) hostia; (*large number*): **a ~ of** multitud de.
hostage ['hɔstɪdʒ] *n* rehén *m*.
hostel ['hɔstl] *n* hostal *m*; (*for students, nurses etc*) residencia; (*also*: **youth ~**) albergue *m* juvenil; (*for homeless people*) hospicio.
hostelling ['hɔstlɪŋ] *n*: **to go (youth) ~** hospedarse en albergues.
hostess ['həustɪs] *n* anfitriona; (*BRIT*: *air ~*) azafata; (*in night-club*) señorita de compañía.
hostile ['hɔstaɪl] *adj* hostil.
hostility [hɔ'stɪlɪtɪ] *n* hostilidad *f*.
hot [hɔt] *adj* caliente; (*weather*) caluroso, de calor; (*as opposed to only warm*) muy caliente; (*spicy*) picante; (*fig*) ardiente, acalorado; **to be ~** (*person*) tener calor; (*object*) estar caliente; (*weather*) hacer calor.
▸**hot up** *vi* (*col*: *situation*) ponerse difícil *or* apurado; (: *party*) animarse ♦ *vt* (*col*: *pace*) apretar; (: *engine*) aumentar la potencia de.
hot air *n* (*col*) palabras *fpl* huecas.
hot-air balloon [hɔt'ɛə-] *n* (*AVIAT*) globo aerostático *or* de aire caliente.
hotbed ['hɔtbɛd] *n* (*fig*) semillero.
hot-blooded [hɔt'blʌdɪd] *adj* impetuoso.
hotchpotch ['hɔtʃpɔtʃ] *n* mezcolanza, baturrillo.
hot dog *n* perrito caliente.
hotel [həu'tɛl] *n* hotel *m*.
hotelier [həu'tɛlɪə*] *n* hotelero.
hotel industry *n* industria hotelera.
hotel room *n* habitación *f* de hotel.
hot flush *n* (*BRIT*) sofoco.
hotfoot ['hɔtfut] *adv* a toda prisa.
hothead ['hɔthɛd] *n* (*fig*) exaltado/a.
hotheaded [hɔt'hɛdɪd] *adj* exaltado.
hothouse ['hɔthaus] *n* invernadero.
hot line *n* (*POL*) teléfono rojo, línea directa.
hotly ['hɔtlɪ] *adv* con pasión, apasionadamente.
hotplate ['hɔtpleɪt] *n* (*on cooker*) hornillo.
hotpot ['hɔtpɔt] *n* (*BRIT CULIN*) estofado.
hot potato *n* (*BRIT col*) asunto espinoso; **to drop sth/sb like a ~** no querer saber ya nada de algo/algn.
hot seat *n* primera fila.
hot spot *n* (*trouble spot*) punto caliente; (*night club etc*) lugar *m* popular.
hot spring *n* terma, fuente *f* de aguas termales.
hot-tempered ['hɔt'tɛmpəd] *adj* de mal genio *or* carácter.
hot-water bottle [hɔt'wɔːtə-] *n* bolsa de agua caliente.
hot-wire ['hɔtwaɪə*] *vt* (*col*: *car*) hacer el puente en.
hound [haund] *vt* acosar ♦ *n* perro de caza.
hour ['auə*] *n* hora; **at 30 miles an ~** a 30 millas por hora; **lunch ~** la hora del almuerzo *or* de comer; **to pay sb by the ~** pagar a algn por horas.
hourly ['auəlɪ] *adj* (de) cada hora; (*rate*) por hora ♦ *adv* cada hora.
house *n* [haus] (*pl* **~s** ['hauzɪz]) (*also firm*) casa; (*POL*) cámara; (*THEAT*) sala ♦ *vt* [hauz] (*person*) alojar; **at/to my ~** en/a mi casa; **the H~ (of Commons/Lords)** (*BRIT*) la Cámara de los Comunes/Lores; **the H~ (of Representatives)** (*US*) la Cámara de Representantes; **on the ~** (*fig*) la casa invita.
house arrest *n* arresto domiciliario.
houseboat ['hausbəut] *n* casa flotante.
housebound ['hausbaund] *adj* confinado en casa.
housebreaking ['hausbreɪkɪŋ] *n* allanamiento de morada.
house-broken ['hausbrəukən] *adj* (*US*) = **house-trained.**
housecoat ['hauskəut] *n* bata.
household ['haushəuld] *n* familia.
householder ['haushəuldə*] *n* propietario/a; (*head of house*) cabeza de familia.
househunting ['haushʌntɪŋ] *n*: **to go ~** ir en busca de vivienda.
housekeeper ['hauskiːpə*] *n* ama de llaves.
housekeeping ['hauskiːpɪŋ] *n* (*work*) trabajos *mpl* domésticos; (*COMPUT*) gestión *f* interna; (*also*: **~ money**) dinero para gastos domésticos.
houseman ['hausmən] *n* (*BRIT MED*) médico residente.
house-owner ['hausəunə*] *n* propietario/a de una vivienda.
house plant *n* planta de interior.
house-proud ['hauspraud] *adj* preocupado por el embellecimiento de la casa.
house-to-house ['haustə'haus] *adj* (*collection*) de casa en casa; (*search*) casa por casa.

house-train ['haustreɪn] *vt* (*pet*) enseñar (*a hacer sus necesidades en el sitio apropiado*).
house-trained ['haustreɪnd] *adj* (*BRIT*: *animal*) enseñado.
house-warming ['hauswɔːmɪŋ] *n* (*also*: ~ **party**) fiesta de estreno de una casa.
housewife ['hauswaɪf] *n* ama de casa.
housework ['hauswəːk] *n* faenas *fpl* (de la casa).
housing ['hauzɪŋ] *n* (*act*) alojamiento; (*houses*) viviendas *fpl* ♦ *cpd* (*problem, shortage*) de (la) vivienda.
housing association *n* asociación *f* de la vivienda.
housing benefit *n* (*BRIT*) subsidio por alojamiento.
housing conditions *npl* condiciones *fpl* de habitabilidad.
housing development, (*BRIT*) **housing estate** *n* urbanización *f*.
hovel ['hɔvl] *n* casucha.
hover ['hɔvə*] *vi* flotar (en el aire); (*helicopter*) cernerse; **to ~ on the brink of disaster** estar al borde mismo del desastre.
hovercraft ['hɔvəkrɑːft] *n* aerodeslizador *m*, hovercraft *m*.
hoverport ['hɔvəpɔːt] *n* puerto de aerodeslizadores.
how [hau] *adv* cómo; ~ **are you?** ¿cómo está usted?, ¿cómo estás?; ~ **do you do?** encantado, mucho gusto; ~ **far is it to ...?** ¿qué distancia hay de aquí a ...?; ~ **long have you been here?** ¿cuánto (tiempo) hace que estás aquí?, ¿cuánto (tiempo) llevas aquí?; ~ **lovely!** ¡qué bonito!; ~ **many/much?** ¿cuántos/cuánto?; ~ **old are you?** ¿cuántos años tienes?; ~ **is school?** ¿qué tal la escuela?; ~ **about a drink?** ¿te gustaría algo de beber?, ¿qué te parece una copa?
however [hau'ɛvə*] *adv* de cualquier manera; (+ *adjective*) por muy ... que; (*in questions*) cómo ♦ *conj* sin embargo, no obstante.
howitzer ['hauɪtsə*] *n* (*MIL*) obús *m*.
howl [haul] *n* aullido ♦ *vi* aullar.
howler ['haulə*] *n* plancha, falta garrafal.
howling ['haulɪŋ] *adj* (*wind*) huracanado.
HP *n abbr see* **hire purchase**.
hp *abbr see* **horsepower**.
HQ *n abbr see* **headquarters**.
HR *n abbr* (*US*) = *House of Representatives*.
HRH *abbr* (= *His (or Her) Royal Highness*) S.A.R.
hr(s) *abbr* (= *hour(s)*) h.
HRT *n abbr see* **hormone replacement therapy**.
HS *abbr* (*US*) = **high school**.
HST *abbr* (*US*: = *Hawaiian Standard Time*) *hora de Hawai*.
HTML *n abbr* (= *Hypertext Mark-up Language*) HTML *m*.
hub [hʌb] *n* (*of wheel*) cubo; (*fig*) centro.
hubbub ['hʌbʌb] *n* barahúnda, barullo.
hubcap ['hʌbkæp] *n* tapacubos *m inv*.
HUD *n abbr* (*US*: = *Department of Housing and Urban Development*) *ministerio de la vivienda y urbanismo*.
huddle ['hʌdl] *vi*: **to ~ together** amontonarse.
hue [hjuː] *n* color *m*, matiz *m*; ~ **and cry** *n* protesta.
huff [hʌf] *n*: **in a ~** enojado.
huffy ['hʌfɪ] *adj* (*col*) mosqueado.
hug [hʌg] *vt* abrazar ♦ *n* abrazo.
huge [hjuːdʒ] *adj* enorme.
hulk [hʌlk] *n* (*ship*) barco viejo; (*person, building etc*) mole *f*.
hulking ['hʌlkɪŋ] *adj* pesado.
hull [hʌl] *n* (*of ship*) casco.
hullabaloo ['hʌləbə'luː] *n* (*col*: *noise*) algarabía, jaleo.
hullo [hə'ləu] *excl* = **hello**.
hum [hʌm] *vt* tararear, canturrear ♦ *vi* tararear, canturrear; (*insect*) zumbar ♦ *n* (*also ELEC*) zumbido; (*of traffic, machines*) zumbido, ronroneo; (*of voices etc*) murmullo.
human ['hjuːmən] *adj* humano ♦ *n* (*also*: ~ **being**) ser *m* humano.
humane [hjuː'meɪn] *adj* humano, humanitario.
humanism ['hjuːmənɪzəm] *n* humanismo.
humanitarian [hjuːmænɪ'tɛərɪən] *adj* humanitario.
humanity [hjuː'mænɪtɪ] *n* humanidad *f*.
humanly ['hjuːmənlɪ] *adv* humanamente.
human relations *npl* relaciones *fpl* humanas.
human rights *npl* derechos *mpl* humanos.
humble ['hʌmbl] *adj* humilde ♦ *vt* humillar.
humbly ['hʌmblɪ] *adv* humildemente.
humbug ['hʌmbʌg] *n* patrañas *fpl*; (*BRIT*: *sweet*) caramelo de menta.
humdrum ['hʌmdrʌm] *adj* (*boring*) monótono, aburrido; (*routine*) rutinario.
humid ['hjuːmɪd] *adj* húmedo.
humidifier [hjuː'mɪdɪfaɪə*] *n* humectador *m*.
humidity [hju'mɪdɪtɪ] *n* humedad *f*.
humiliate [hjuː'mɪlɪeɪt] *vt* humillar.
humiliation [hjuːmɪlɪ'eɪʃən] *n* humillación *f*.
humility [hjuː'mɪlɪtɪ] *n* humildad *f*.
humorist ['hjuːmərɪst] *n* humorista *m/f*.
humorous ['hjuːmərəs] *adj* gracioso,

divertido.
humour, (*US*) **humor** ['hju:mə*] *n* humorismo, sentido del humor; (*mood*) humor *m* ♦ *vt* (*person*) complacer; **sense of ~** sentido del humor; **to be in a good/bad ~** estar de buen/mal humor.
humo(u)rless ['hju:məlıs] *adj* serio.
hump [hʌmp] *n* (*in ground*) montículo; (*camel's*) giba.
humus ['hju:məs] *n* (*BIO*) humus *m.*
hunch [hʌntʃ] *n* (*premonition*) presentimiento; **I have a ~ that** tengo la corazonada *or* el presentimiento de que.
hunchback ['hʌntʃbæk] *n* jorobado/a.
hunched [hʌntʃt] *adj* jorobado.
hundred ['hʌndrəd] *num* ciento; (*before n*) cien; **about a ~ people** unas cien personas, alrededor de cien personas; **~s of** centenares de; **~s of people** centenares de personas; **I'm a ~ per cent sure** estoy completamente seguro.
hundredweight ['hʌndrədweıt] *n* (*BRIT*) *= 50.8 kg; 112 lb*; (*US*) *= 45.3 kg; 100 lb.*
hung [hʌŋ] *pt, pp of* **hang.**
Hungarian [hʌŋ'gɛərıən] *adj* húngaro ♦ *n* húngaro/a *m/f*; (*LING*) húngaro.
Hungary ['hʌŋgərı] *n* Hungría.
hunger ['hʌŋgə*] *n* hambre *f* ♦ *vi*: **to ~ for** (*fig*) tener hambre de, anhelar.
hunger strike *n* huelga de hambre.
hungover [hʌŋ'əuvə*] *adj* (*col*): **to be ~** tener resaca.
hungrily ['hʌŋgrəlı] *adv* ávidamente, con ganas.
hungry ['hʌŋgrı] *adj* hambriento; **to be ~** tener hambre; **~ for** (*fig*) sediento de.
hunk [hʌŋk] *n* (*of bread etc*) trozo, pedazo.
hunt [hʌnt] *vt* (*seek*) buscar; (*SPORT*) cazar ♦ *vi* cazar ♦ *n* caza, cacería.
▸**hunt down** *vt* acorralar, seguir la pista a.
hunter ['hʌntə*] *n* cazador(a) *m/f*; (*horse*) caballo de caza.
hunting ['hʌntıŋ] *n* caza.
hurdle ['hə:dl] *n* (*SPORT*) valla; (*fig*) obstáculo.
hurl [hə:l] *vt* lanzar, arrojar.
hurling ['hə:lıŋ] *n* (*SPORT*) *juego irlandés semejante al hockey.*
hurly-burly ['hə:lı'bə:lı] *n* jaleo, follón *m.*
hurrah [hu'rɑ:], **hurray** [hu'reı] *n* ¡viva!, ¡hurra!
hurricane ['hʌrıkən] *n* huracán *m.*
hurried ['hʌrıd] *adj* (*fast*) apresurado; (*rushed*) hecho de prisa.
hurriedly ['hʌrıdlı] *adv* con prisa, apresuradamente.
hurry ['hʌrı] *n* prisa ♦ *vb* (*also*: **~ up**) *vi* apresurarse, darse prisa, apurarse (*LAM*) ♦ *vt* (*person*) dar prisa a; (*work*) apresurar, hacer de prisa; **to be in a ~** tener prisa, tener apuro (*LAM*), estar apurado (*LAM*); **to ~ back/home** darse prisa en volver/volver a casa.
▸**hurry along** *vi* pasar de prisa.
▸**hurry away, hurry off** *vi* irse corriendo.
▸**hurry on** *vi*: **to ~ on to say** apresurarse a decir.
▸**hurry up** *vi* darse prisa, apurarse (*esp LAM*).
hurt [hə:t] *vb* (*pt, pp* **hurt**) *vt* hacer daño a; (*business, interests etc*) perjudicar ♦ *vi* doler ♦ *adj* lastimado; **I ~ my arm** me lastimé el brazo; **where does it ~?** ¿dónde te duele?
hurtful ['hə:tful] *adj* (*remark etc*) hiriente, dañino.
hurtle ['hə:tl] *vi*: **to ~ past** pasar como un rayo.
husband ['hʌzbənd] *n* marido.
hush [hʌʃ] *n* silencio ♦ *vt* hacer callar; (*cover up*) encubrir; **~!** ¡chitón!, ¡cállate!
▸**hush up** *vt* (*fact*) encubrir, callar.
hushed [hʌʃt] *adj* (*voice*) bajo.
hush-hush [hʌʃ'hʌʃ] *adj* (*col*) muy secreto.
husk [hʌsk] *n* (*of wheat*) cáscara.
husky ['hʌskı] *adj* ronco; (*burly*) fornido ♦ *n* perro esquimal.
hustings ['hʌstıŋz] *npl* (*POL*) mítin *msg* preelectoral.
hustle ['hʌsl] *vt* (*push*) empujar; (*hurry*) dar prisa a ♦ *n* bullicio, actividad *f* febril; **~ and bustle** ajetreo.
hut [hʌt] *n* cabaña; (*shed*) cobertizo.
hutch [hʌtʃ] *n* conejera.
hyacinth ['haıəsınθ] *n* jacinto.
hybrid ['haıbrıd] *adj, n* híbrido.
hydrant ['haıdrənt] *n* (*also*: **fire ~**) boca de incendios.
hydraulic [haı'drɔ:lık] *adj* hidráulico.
hydraulics [haı'drɔ:lıks] *n* hidráulica.
hydrochloric ['haıdrəu'klɔrık] *adj*: **~ acid** ácido clorhídrico.
hydroelectric [haıdrəuı'lɛktrık] *adj* hidroeléctrico.
hydrofoil ['haıdrəfɔıl] *n* aerodeslizador *m.*
hydrogen ['haıdrədʒən] *n* hidrógeno.
hydrogen bomb *n* bomba de hidrógeno.
hydrophobia [haıdrə'fəubıə] *n* hidrofobia.
hydroplane ['haıdrəpleın] *n* hidroavión *m*, hidroavioneta.
hyena [haı'i:nə] *n* hiena.
hygiene ['haıdʒi:n] *n* higiene *f.*
hygienic [haı'dʒi:nık] *adj* higiénico.
hymn [hım] *n* himno.
hype [haıp] *n* (*col*) bombo.

hyperactive [haɪpər'æktɪv] *adj* hiperactivo.
hypermarket ['haɪpəmɑːkɪt] *n* hipermercado.
hypertension ['haɪpə'tɛnʃən] *n* hipertensión *f*.
hyphen ['haɪfn] *n* guión *m*.
hypnosis [hɪp'nəusɪs] *n* hipnosis *f*.
hypnotic [hɪp'nɔtɪk] *adj* hipnótico.
hypnotism ['hɪpnətɪzəm] *n* hipnotismo.
hypnotist ['hɪpnətɪst] hipnotista *m/f*.
hypnotize ['hɪpnətaɪz] *vt* hipnotizar.
hypoallergenic ['haɪpəuælə'dʒɛnɪk] *adj* hipoalérgeno.
hypochondriac [haɪpəu'kɔndrɪæk] *n* hipocondríaco/a.
hypocrisy [hɪ'pɔkrɪsɪ] *n* hipocresía.
hypocrite ['hɪpəkrɪt] *n* hipócrita *m/f*.
hypocritical [hɪpə'krɪtɪkl] *adj* hipócrita.
hypodermic [haɪpə'dəːmɪk] *adj* hipodérmico ♦ *n* (*syringe*) aguja hipodérmica.
hypotenuse [haɪ'pɔtɪnjuːz] *n* hipotenusa.
hypothermia [haɪpəu'θəːmɪə] *n* hipotermia.
hypothesis, *pl* **hypotheses** [haɪ'pɔθɪsɪs, -siːz] *n* hipótesis *f inv*.
hypothetical [haɪpə'θɛtɪkl] *adj* hipotético.
hysterectomy [hɪstə'rɛktəmɪ] *n* histerectomía.
hysteria [hɪ'stɪərɪə] *n* histeria.
hysterical [hɪ'stɛrɪkl] *adj* histérico.
hysterics [hɪ'stɛrɪks] *npl* histeria *sg*, histerismo *sg*; **to have** ~ ponerse histérico.
Hz *abbr* (= *Hertz*) Hz.

I i

I, i [aɪ] *n* (*letter*) I, i *f*; **I for Isaac**, (*US*) **I for Item** I de Inés, I de Israel.
I [aɪ] *pron* yo ♦ *abbr* = **island; isle.**
IA, Ia. *abbr* (*US*) = *Iowa.*
IAEA *n abbr see* **International Atomic Energy Agency.**
IBA *n abbr* (*BRIT*) = **Independent Broadcasting Authority**; *see* **ITV**.
Iberian [aɪ'bɪərɪən] *adj* ibero, ibérico.
Iberian Peninsula *n*: **the** ~ la Península Ibérica.
IBEW *n abbr* (*US*: = *International Brotherhood of Electrical Workers*) *sindicato internacional de electricistas.*
ib(id). *abbr* (= *ibidem*: *from the same source*) ibídem.
i/c *abbr* (*BRIT*) = *in charge.*
ICBM *n abbr* (= *intercontinental ballistic missile*) misil *m* balístico intercontinental.
ICC *n abbr* (= *International Chamber of Commerce*) CCI *f*; (*US*) = *Interstate Commerce Commission.*
ice [aɪs] *n* hielo ♦ *vt* (*cake*) alcorzar ♦ *vi* (*also*: ~ **over,** ~ **up**) helarse; **to keep sth on** ~ (*fig*: *plan, project*) tener algo en reserva.
ice age *n* período glaciar.
ice axe *n* piqueta (de alpinista).
iceberg ['aɪsbəːg] *n* iceberg *m*; **the tip of the** ~ la punta del iceberg.
icebox ['aɪsbɔks] *n* (*BRIT*) congelador *m*; (*US*) nevera, refrigeradora (*LAM*).
icebreaker ['aɪsbreɪkə*] *n* rompehielos *m inv*.
ice bucket *n* cubo para el hielo.
icecap ['aɪskæp] *n* casquete *m* polar.
ice-cold [aɪs'kəuld] *adj* helado.
ice cream *n* helado.
ice-cream soda *n* soda mezclada con helado.
ice cube *n* cubito de hielo.
iced [aɪst] *adj* (*drink*) con hielo; (*cake*) escarchado.
ice hockey *n* hockey *m* sobre hielo.
Iceland ['aɪslənd] *n* Islandia.
Icelander ['aɪsləndə*] *n* islandés/esa *m/f*.
Icelandic [aɪs'lændɪk] *adj* islandés/esa ♦ *n* (*LING*) islandés *m*.
ice lolly *n* (*BRIT*) polo.
ice pick *n* piolet *m*.
ice rink *n* pista de hielo.
ice-skate ['aɪsskeɪt] *n* patín *m* de hielo ♦ *vi* patinar sobre hielo.
ice-skating ['aɪsskeɪtɪŋ] *n* patinaje *m* sobre hielo.
icicle ['aɪsɪkl] *n* carámbano.
icing ['aɪsɪŋ] *n* (*CULIN*) alcorza; (*AVIAT etc*) formación *f* de hielo.
icing sugar *n* (*BRIT*) azúcar *m* glas(eado).
ICJ *n abbr see* **International Court of Justice.**
icon ['aɪkɔn] *n* (*gen, COMPUT*) icono.
ICR *n abbr* (*US*) = *Institute for Cancer Research.*
ICRC *n abbr* (= *International Committee of the Red Cross*) CICR.
ICU *n abbr* (= *intensive care unit*) UVI *f*.
icy ['aɪsɪ] *adj* (*road*) helado; (*fig*) glacial.
ID *abbr* (*US*) = *Idaho.*
I'd [aɪd] = **I would; I had.**
Ida. *abbr* (*US*) = *Idaho.*
ID card *n* (= *identity card*) DNI *m*.
IDD *n abbr* (*BRIT TEL*: = *international direct dialling*) *servicio automático*

internacional.
idea [aɪ'dɪə] *n* idea; **good ~!** ¡buena idea!; **to have an ~ that ...** tener la impresión de que ...; **I haven't the least ~** no tengo ni (la más remota) idea.
ideal [aɪ'dɪəl] *n* ideal *m* ♦ *adj* ideal.
idealism [aɪ'dɪəlɪzəm] *n* idealismo.
idealist [aɪ'dɪəlɪst] *n* idealista *m/f*.
ideally [aɪ'dɪəlɪ] *adv* perfectamente; **~, the book should have ...** idealmente, el libro debería tener ....
identical [aɪ'dɛntɪkl] *adj* idéntico.
identification [aɪdɛntɪfɪ'keɪʃən] *n* identificación *f*; **means of ~** documentos *mpl* personales.
identify [aɪ'dɛntɪfaɪ] *vt* identificar ♦ *vi*: **to ~ with** identificarse con.
Identikit ® [aɪ'dɛntɪkɪt] *n*: **~ (picture)** retrato-robot *m*.
identity [aɪ'dɛntɪtɪ] *n* identidad *f*.
identity card *n* carnet *m* de identidad, cédula (de identidad) (*LAM*).
identity papers *npl* documentos *mpl* (de identidad), documentación *fsg*.
identity parade *n* identificación *f* de acusados.
ideological [aɪdɪə'lɔdʒɪkəl] *adj* ideológico.
ideology [aɪdɪ'ɔlədʒɪ] *n* ideología.
idiocy ['ɪdɪəsɪ] *n* idiotez *f*; (*stupid act*) estupidez *f*.
idiom ['ɪdɪəm] *n* modismo; (*style of speaking*) lenguaje *m*.
idiomatic [ɪdɪə'mætɪk] *adj* idiomático.
idiosyncrasy [ɪdɪəu'sɪŋkrəsɪ] *n* idiosincrasia.
idiot ['ɪdɪət] *n* (*gen*) idiota *m/f*; (*fool*) tonto/a.
idiotic [ɪdɪ'ɔtɪk] *adj* idiota; tonto.
idle ['aɪdl] *adj* (*lazy*) holgazán/ana; (*unemployed*) parado, desocupado; (*talk*) frívolo ♦ *vi* (*machine*) funcionar *or* marchar en vacío; **~ capacity** (*COMM*) capacidad *f* sin utilizar; **~ money** (*COMM*) capital *m* improductivo; **~ time** (*COMM*) tiempo de paro.
▸**idle away** *vt*: **to ~ away one's time** malgastar *or* desperdiciar el tiempo.
idleness ['aɪdlnɪs] *n* holgazanería; paro, desocupación *f*.
idler ['aɪdlə*] *n* holgazán/ana *m/f*, vago/a.
idol ['aɪdl] *n* ídolo.
idolize ['aɪdəlaɪz] *vt* idolatrar.
idyllic [ɪ'dɪlɪk] *adj* idílico.
i.e. *abbr* (= *id est*: *that is*) es decir.
if [ɪf] *conj* si ♦ *n*: **there are a lot of ~s and buts** hay muchas dudas sin resolver; **(even) ~** aunque, si bien; **I'd be pleased ~ you could do it** yo estaría contento si pudieras hacerlo; **~ necessary** si resultase necesario; **~ only** si solamente; **as ~** como si.
iffy ['ɪfɪ] *adj* (*col*) dudoso.
igloo ['ɪglu:] *n* iglú *m*.
ignite [ɪg'naɪt] *vt* (*set fire to*) encender ♦ *vi* encenderse.
ignition [ɪg'nɪʃən] *n* (*AUT*) encendido; **to switch on/off the ~** arrancar/apagar el motor.
ignition key *n* (*AUT*) llave *f* de contacto.
ignoble [ɪg'nəubl] *adj* innoble, vil.
ignominious [ɪgnə'mɪnɪəs] *adj* ignominioso, vergonzoso.
ignoramus [ɪgnə'reɪməs] *n* ignorante *m/f*, inculto/a.
ignorance ['ɪgnərəns] *n* ignorancia; **to keep sb in ~ of sth** ocultarle algo a algn.
ignorant ['ɪgnərənt] *adj* ignorante; **to be ~ of** (*subject*) desconocer; (*events*) ignorar.
ignore [ɪg'nɔ:*] *vt* (*person*) no hacer caso de; (*fact*) pasar por alto.
ikon ['aɪkɔn] *n* = **icon**.
IL *abbr* (*US*) = *Illinois*.
ILA *n abbr* (*US*: = *International Longshoremen's Association*) *sindicato internacional de trabajadores portuarios*.
ill [ɪl] *adj* enfermo, malo ♦ *n* mal *m*; (*fig*) infortunio ♦ *adv* mal; **to take *or* be taken ~** caer *or* ponerse enfermo; **to feel ~ (with)** encontrarse mal (de); **to speak/ think ~ of sb** hablar/pensar mal de algn; *see also* **ills**.
Ill. *abbr* (*US*) = *Illinois*.
I'll [aɪl] = **I will, I shall**.
ill-advised [ɪləd'vaɪzd] *adj* poco recomendable; **he was ~ to go** se equivocaba al ir.
ill-at-ease [ɪlət'i:z] *adj* incómodo.
ill-considered [ɪlkən'sɪdəd] *adj* (*plan*) poco pensado.
ill-disposed [ɪldɪs'pəuzd] *adj*: **to be ~ towards sb/sth** estar maldispuesto hacia algn/algo.
illegal [ɪ'li:gl] *adj* ilegal.
illegible [ɪ'lɛdʒɪbl] *adj* ilegible.
illegitimate [ɪlɪ'dʒɪtɪmət] *adj* ilegítimo.
ill-fated [ɪl'feɪtɪd] *adj* malogrado.
ill-favoured, (*US*) **ill-favored** [ɪl'feɪvəd] *adj* poco agraciado.
ill feeling *n* rencor *m*.
ill-gotten ['ɪlgɔtn] *adj* (*gains etc*) mal adquirido.
ill health *n* mala salud *f*; **to be in ~** estar mal de salud.
illicit [ɪ'lɪsɪt] *adj* ilícito.
ill-informed [ɪlɪn'fɔ:md] *adj* (*judgement*) erróneo; (*person*) mal informado.

illiterate [ɪ'lɪtərət] *adj* analfabeto.
ill-mannered [ɪl'mænəd] *adj* mal educado.
illness ['ɪlnɪs] *n* enfermedad *f.*
illogical [ɪ'lɔdʒɪkl] *adj* ilógico.
ills [ɪlz] *npl* males *mpl.*
ill-suited [ɪl'su:tɪd] *adj* (*couple*) incompatible; **he is ~ to the job** no es la persona indicada para el trabajo.
ill-timed [ɪl'taɪmd] *adj* inoportuno.
ill-treat [ɪl'tri:t] *vt* maltratar.
ill-treatment [ɪl'tri:tmənt] *n* malos tratos *mpl.*
illuminate [ɪ'lu:mɪneɪt] *vt* (*room, street*) iluminar, alumbrar; (*subject*) aclarar; **~d sign** letrero luminoso.
illuminating [ɪ'lu:mɪneɪtɪŋ] *adj* revelador(a).
illumination [ɪlu:mɪ'neɪʃən] *n* alumbrado; **~s** *npl* luminarias *fpl*, luces *fpl.*
illusion [ɪ'lu:ʒən] *n* ilusión *f*; **to be under the ~ that...** estar convencido de que ....
illusive [ɪ'lu:sɪv], **illusory** [ɪ'lu:sərɪ] *adj* ilusorio.
illustrate ['ɪləstreɪt] *vt* ilustrar.
illustration [ɪlə'streɪʃən] *n* (*example*) ejemplo, ilustración *f*; (*in book*) lámina, ilustración *f.*
illustrator ['ɪləstreɪtə*] *n* ilustrador(a) *m/f.*
illustrious [ɪ'lʌstrɪəs] *adj* ilustre.
ill will *n* rencor *m.*
ILO *n abbr* (= *International Labour Organization*) OIT *f.*
ILWU *n abbr* (*US*: = *International Longshoremen's and Warehousemen's Union*) *sindicato internacional de trabajadores portuarios y almacenistas.*
I'm [aɪm] = **I am.**
image ['ɪmɪdʒ] *n* imagen *f.*
imagery ['ɪmɪdʒərɪ] *n* imágenes *fpl.*
imaginable [ɪ'mædʒɪnəbl] *adj* imaginable.
imaginary [ɪ'mædʒɪnərɪ] *adj* imaginario.
imagination [ɪmædʒɪ'neɪʃən] *n* imaginación *f*; (*inventiveness*) inventiva; (*illusion*) fantasía.
imaginative [ɪ'mædʒɪnətɪv] *adj* imaginativo.
imagine [ɪ'mædʒɪn] *vt* imaginarse; (*suppose*) suponer.
imbalance [ɪm'bæləns] *n* desequilibrio.
imbecile ['ɪmbəsi:l] *n* imbécil *m/f.*
imbue [ɪm'bju:] *vt*: **to ~ sth with** imbuir algo de.
IMF *n abbr see* **International Monetary Fund.**
imitate ['ɪmɪteɪt] *vt* imitar.
imitation [ɪmɪ'teɪʃən] *n* imitación *f*; (*copy*) copia; (*pej*) remedo.
imitator ['ɪmɪteɪtə*] *n* imitador(a) *m/f.*
immaculate [ɪ'mækjulət] *adj* limpísimo, inmaculado; (*REL*) inmaculado.
immaterial [ɪmə'tɪərɪəl] *adj* incorpóreo; **it is ~ whether...** no importa si... .
immature [ɪmə'tjuə*] *adj* (*person*) inmaduro; (*of one's youth*) joven.
immaturity [ɪmə'tjuərɪtɪ] *n* inmadurez *f.*
immeasurable [ɪ'mɛʒrəbl] *adj* inconmensurable.
immediacy [ɪ'mi:dɪəsɪ] *n* urgencia, proximidad *f.*
immediate [ɪ'mi:dɪət] *adj* inmediato; (*pressing*) urgente, apremiante; **in the ~ future** en un futuro próximo.
immediately [ɪ'mi:dɪətlɪ] *adv* (*at once*) en seguida; **~ next to** justo al lado de.
immense [ɪ'mɛns] *adj* inmenso, enorme.
immensely [ɪ'mɛnslɪ] *adv* enormemente.
immensity [ɪ'mɛnsɪtɪ] *n* (*of size, difference*) inmensidad *f*; (*of problem*) enormidad *f.*
immerse [ɪ'mə:s] *vt* (*submerge*) sumergir; **to be ~d in** (*fig*) estar absorto en.
immersion heater [ɪ'mə:ʃən-] *n* (*BRIT*) calentador *m* de inmersión.
immigrant ['ɪmɪgrənt] *n* inmigrante *m/f.*
immigrate ['ɪmɪgreɪt] *vi* inmigrar.
immigration [ɪmɪ'greɪʃən] *n* inmigración *f.*
immigration authorities *npl* servicio *sg* de inmigración.
immigration laws *npl* leyes *fpl* de inmigración.
imminent ['ɪmɪnənt] *adj* inminente.
immobile [ɪ'məubaɪl] *adj* inmóvil.
immobilize [ɪ'məubɪlaɪz] *vt* inmovilizar.
immoderate [ɪ'mɔdərɪt] *adj* (*person*) desmesurado; (*opinion, reaction, demand*) excesivo.
immodest [ɪ'mɔdɪst] *adj* (*indecent*) desvergonzado, impúdico; (*boasting*) jactancioso.
immoral [ɪ'mɔrl] *adj* inmoral.
immorality [ɪmɔ'rælɪtɪ] *n* inmoralidad *f.*
immortal [ɪ'mɔ:tl] *adj* inmortal.
immortality [ɪmɔ:'tælɪtɪ] *n* inmortalidad *f.*
immortalize [ɪ'mɔ:tlaɪz] *vt* inmortalizar.
immovable [ɪ'mu:vəbl] *adj* (*object*) imposible de mover; (*person*) inconmovible.
immune [ɪ'mju:n] *adj*: **~ (to)** inmune (a).
immune system *n* sistema *m* inmunitario.
immunity [ɪ'mju:nɪtɪ] *n* (*MED, of diplomat*) inmunidad *f*; (*COMM*) exención *f.*
immunization [ɪmjunaɪ'zeɪʃən] *n* inmunización *f.*
immunize ['ɪmjunaɪz] *vt* inmunizar.
imp [ɪmp] *n* (*small devil, also fig: child*) diablillo.
impact ['ɪmpækt] *n* (*gen*) impacto.
impair [ɪm'pɛə*] *vt* perjudicar.

-impaired [ɪm'pɛəd] *suff*: **visually~** con defectos de visión.
impale [ɪm'peɪl] *vt* (*with sword*) atravesar.
impart [ɪm'pɑːt] *vt* comunicar; (*make known*) participar; (*bestow*) otorgar.
impartial [ɪm'pɑːʃl] *adj* imparcial.
impartiality [ɪmpɑːʃɪ'ælɪtɪ] *n* imparcialidad *f*.
impassable [ɪm'pɑːsəbl] *adj* (*barrier*) infranqueable; (*road*) intransitable.
impasse [ɪm'pɑːs] *n* callejón *m* sin salida; **to reach an ~** llegar a un punto muerto.
impassioned [ɪm'pæʃənd] *adj* apasionado, exaltado.
impassive [ɪm'pæsɪv] *adj* impasible.
impatience [ɪm'peɪʃəns] *n* impaciencia.
impatient [ɪm'peɪʃənt] *adj* impaciente; **to get** *or* **grow ~** impacientarse.
impatiently [ɪm'peɪʃəntlɪ] *adv* con impaciencia.
impeachment [ɪm'piːtʃmənt] *n* denuncia, acusación *f*.
impeccable [ɪm'pɛkəbl] *adj* impecable.
impecunious [ɪmpɪ'kjuːnɪəs] *adj* sin dinero.
impede [ɪm'piːd] *vt* estorbar, dificultar.
impediment [ɪm'pɛdɪmənt] *n* obstáculo, estorbo; (*also*: **speech ~**) defecto (del habla).
impel [ɪm'pɛl] *vt* (*force*): **to ~ sb (to do sth)** obligar a algn (a hacer algo).
impending [ɪm'pɛndɪŋ] *adj* inminente.
impenetrable [ɪm'pɛnɪtrəbl] *adj* (*jungle, fortress*) impenetrable; (*unfathomable*) insondable.
imperative [ɪm'pɛrətɪv] *adj* (*tone*) imperioso; (*necessary*) imprescindible ♦ *n* (*LING*) imperativo.
imperceptible [ɪmpə'sɛptɪbl] *adj* imperceptible.
imperfect [ɪm'pəːfɪkt] *adj* imperfecto; (*goods etc*) defectuoso.
imperfection [ɪmpəː'fɛkʃən] *n* (*blemish*) desperfecto; (*fault, flaw*) defecto.
imperial [ɪm'pɪərɪəl] *adj* imperial.
imperialism [ɪm'pɪərɪəlɪzəm] *n* imperialismo.
imperil [ɪm'pɛrɪl] *vt* poner en peligro.
imperious [ɪm'pɪərɪəs] *adj* señorial, apremiante.
impersonal [ɪm'pəːsənl] *adj* impersonal.
impersonate [ɪm'pəːsəneɪt] *vt* hacerse pasar por.
impersonation [ɪmpəːsə'neɪʃən] *n* imitación *f*.
impersonator [ɪm'pəːsəneɪtə*] *n* (*THEAT etc*) imitador(a) *m/f*.
impertinence [ɪm'pəːtɪnəns] *n* impertinencia, insolencia.
impertinent [ɪm'pəːtɪnənt] *adj* impertinente, insolente.
imperturbable [ɪmpə'təːbəbl] *adj* imperturbable, impasible.
impervious [ɪm'pəːvɪəs] *adj* impermeable; (*fig*): **~ to** insensible a.
impetuous [ɪm'pɛtjuəs] *adj* impetuoso.
impetus ['ɪmpətəs] *n* ímpetu *m*; (*fig*) impulso.
impinge [ɪm'pɪndʒ]: **to ~ on** *vt fus* (*affect*) afectar a.
impish ['ɪmpɪʃ] *adj* travieso.
implacable [ɪm'plækəbl] *adj* implacable.
implant [ɪm'plɑːnt] *vt* (*MED*) injertar, implantar; (*fig*: *idea, principle*) inculcar.
implausible [ɪm'plɔːzɪbl] *adj* implausible.
implement *n* ['ɪmplɪmənt] instrumento, herramienta ♦ *vt* ['ɪmplɪmɛnt] hacer efectivo; (*carry out*) realizar.
implicate ['ɪmplɪkeɪt] *vt* (*compromise*) comprometer; (*involve*) enredar; **to ~ sb in sth** comprometer a algn en algo.
implication [ɪmplɪ'keɪʃən] *n* consecuencia; **by ~** indirectamente.
implicit [ɪm'plɪsɪt] *adj* (*gen*) implícito; (*complete*) absoluto.
implicitly [ɪm'plɪsɪtlɪ] *adv* implícitamente.
implore [ɪm'plɔː*] *vt* (*person*) suplicar.
imploring [ɪm'plɔːrɪŋ] *adj* de súplica.
imply [ɪm'plaɪ] *vt* (*involve*) implicar, suponer; (*hint*) insinuar.
impolite [ɪmpə'laɪt] *adj* mal educado.
impolitic [ɪm'pɔlɪtɪk] *adj* poco diplomático.
imponderable [ɪm'pɔndərəbl] *adj* imponderable.
import *vt* [ɪm'pɔːt] importar ♦ *n* ['ɪmpɔːt] (*COMM*) importación *f*; (*meaning*) significado, sentido ♦ *cpd* (*duty, licence etc*) de importación.
importance [ɪm'pɔːtəns] *n* importancia; **to be of great/little ~** tener mucha/poca importancia.
important [ɪm'pɔːtənt] *adj* importante; **it's not ~** no importa, no tiene importancia; **it is ~ that** es importante que.
importantly [ɪm'pɔːtəntlɪ] *adv* (*pej*) dándose importancia; **but, more ~ ...** pero, lo que es aún más importante ....
import duty *n* derechos *mpl* de importación.
imported [ɪm'pɔːtɪd] *adj* importado.
importer [ɪm'pɔːtə*] *n* importador(a) *m/f*.
import licence, (*US*) **import license** *n* licencia de importación.
impose [ɪm'pəuz] *vt* imponer ♦ *vi*: **to ~ on sb** abusar de algn.
imposing [ɪm'pəuzɪŋ] *adj* imponente, impresionante.

imposition [ɪmpə'zɪʃn] *n* (*of tax etc*) imposición *f*; **to be an ~** (*on person*) molestar.
impossibility [ɪmpɔsə'bɪlɪtɪ] *n* imposibilidad *f*.
impossible [ɪm'pɔsɪbl] *adj* imposible; (*person*) insoportable; **it is ~ for me to leave now** me es imposible salir ahora.
impossibly [ɪm'pɔsɪblɪ] *adv* imposiblemente.
impostor [ɪm'pɔstə*] *n* impostor(a) *m/f*.
impotence ['ɪmpətəns] *n* impotencia.
impotent ['ɪmpətənt] *adj* impotente.
impound [ɪm'paund] *vt* embargar.
impoverished [ɪm'pɔvərɪʃt] *adj* necesitado; (*land*) agotado.
impracticable [ɪm'præktɪkəbl] *adj* no factible, irrealizable.
impractical [ɪm'præktɪkl] *adj* (*person*) poco práctico.
imprecise [ɪmprɪ'saɪs] *adj* impreciso.
impregnable [ɪm'prɛgnəbl] *adj* invulnerable; (*castle*) inexpugnable.
impregnate ['ɪmprɛgneɪt] *vt* (*gen*) impregnar; (*soak*) empapar; (*fertilize*) fecundar.
impresario [ɪmprɪ'sɑːrɪəu] *n* empresario/a.
impress [ɪm'prɛs] *vt* impresionar; (*mark*) estampar ♦ *vi* causar buena impresión; **to ~ sth on sb** convencer a algn de la importancia de algo.
impression [ɪm'prɛʃən] *n* impresión *f*; (*footprint etc*) huella; (*print run*) edición *f*; **to be under the ~ that** tener la idea de que; **to make a good/bad ~ on sb** causar buena/mala impresión a algn.
impressionable [ɪm'prɛʃnəbl] *adj* impresionable.
impressionist [ɪm'prɛʃənɪst] *n* impresionista *m/f*.
impressive [ɪm'prɛsɪv] *adj* impresionante.
imprint ['ɪmprɪnt] *n* (*PUBLISHING*) pie *m* de imprenta; (*fig*) sello.
imprison [ɪm'prɪzn] *vt* encarcelar.
imprisonment [ɪm'prɪznmənt] *n* encarcelamiento; (*term of ~*) cárcel *f*; **life ~** cadena perpetua.
improbable [ɪm'prɔbəbl] *adj* improbable, inverosímil.
impromptu [ɪm'prɔmptjuː] *adj* improvisado ♦ *adv* de improviso.
improper [ɪm'prɔpə*] *adj* (*incorrect*) impropio; (*unseemly*) indecoroso; (*indecent*) indecente.
impropriety [ɪmprə'praɪətɪ] *n* falta de decoro; (*indecency*) indecencia; (*of language*) impropiedad *f*.
improve [ɪm'pruːv] *vt* mejorar; (*foreign language*) perfeccionar ♦ *vi* mejorar.
▸**improve (up)on** *vt fus* (*offer*) mejorar.
improvement [ɪm'pruːvmənt] *n* mejora; perfeccionamiento; **to make ~s to** mejorar.
improvise ['ɪmprəvaɪz] *vt, vi* improvisar.
imprudence [ɪm'pruːdns] *n* imprudencia.
imprudent [ɪm'pruːdnt] *adj* imprudente.
impudent ['ɪmpjudnt] *adj* descarado, insolente.
impugn [ɪm'pjuːn] *vt* impugnar.
impulse ['ɪmpʌls] *n* impulso; **to act on ~** sin reflexión dejarse llevar por el impulso.
impulse buying *n* compra impulsiva.
impulsive [ɪm'pʌlsɪv] *adj* irreflexivo, impulsivo.
impunity [ɪm'pjuːnɪtɪ] *n*: **with ~** impunemente.
impure [ɪm'pjuə*] *adj* (*adulterated*) adulterado; (*morally*) impuro.
impurity [ɪm'pjuərɪtɪ] *n* impureza.
IN *abbr* (*US*) = *Indiana*.

KEYWORD

in [ɪn] *prep* **1** (*indicating place, position, with place names*) en; **~ the house/garden** en (la) casa/el jardín; **~ here/there** aquí/ahí *or* allí dentro; **~ London/England** en Londres/Inglaterra; **~ town** en el centro (de la ciudad)
2 (*indicating time*) en; **~ spring** en (la) primavera; **in 1888/May** en 1888/mayo; **~ the afternoon** por la tarde; **at 4 o'clock ~ the afternoon** a las 4 de la tarde; **I did it ~ 3 hours/days** lo hice en 3 horas/días; **I'll see you ~ 2 weeks** *or* **~ 2 weeks' time** te veré dentro de 2 semanas; **once ~ a hundred years** una vez cada cien años
3 (*indicating manner etc*) en; **~ a loud/soft voice** en voz alta/baja; **~ pencil/ink** a lápiz/bolígrafo; **the boy ~ the blue shirt** el chico de la camisa azul; **~ writing** por escrito; **to pay ~ dollars** pagar en dólares
4 (*indicating circumstances*): **~ the sun/shade** al sol/a la sombra; **~ the rain** bajo la lluvia; **a change ~ policy** un cambio de política; **a rise ~ prices** un aumento de precios
5 (*indicating mood, state*): **~ tears** llorando; **~ anger/despair** enfadado/desesperado; **to live ~ luxury** vivir lujosamente
6 (*with ratios, numbers*): **1 ~ 10 households, 1 household ~ 10** una de cada 10 familias; **20 pence ~ the pound** 20 peniques por libra; **they lined up ~ twos** se alinearon de dos en dos; **~**

hundreds a *or* por centenares
7 (*referring to people, works*) en; entre; **the disease is common ~ children** la enfermedad es común entre los niños; ~ **(the works of) Dickens** en (las obras de) Dickens
8 (*indicating profession etc*): **to be ~ teaching** dedicarse a la enseñanza
9 (*after superlative*) de; **the best pupil ~ the class** el/la mejor alumno/a de la clase
10 (*with present participle*): ~ **saying this** al decir esto
♦ *adv*: **to be** ~ (*person*: *at home*) estar en casa; (: *work*) estar; (*train, ship, plane*) haber llegado; (*in fashion*) estar de moda; **she'll be ~ later today** llegará más tarde hoy; **to ask sb** ~ hacer pasar a algn; **to run/limp** *etc* ~ entrar corriendo/ cojeando *etc*
♦ ~ **that** *conj* ya que
♦ *npl*: **the ~s and outs** (*of proposal, situation etc*) los detalles.

in., ins *abbr* = **inch(es)**.
inability [ɪnə'bɪlɪtɪ] *n* incapacidad *f*; ~ **to pay** insolvencia en el pago.
inaccessible [ɪnək'sɛsɪbl] *adj* inaccesible.
inaccuracy [ɪn'ækjurəsɪ] *n* inexactitud *f*.
inaccurate [ɪn'ækjurət] *adj* inexacto, incorrecto.
inaction [ɪn'ækʃən] *n* inacción *f*.
inactive [ɪn'æktɪv] *adj* inactivo.
inactivity [ɪnæk'tɪvɪtɪ] *n* inactividad *f*.
inadequacy [ɪn'ædɪkwəsɪ] *n* insuficiencia; incapacidad *f*.
inadequate [ɪn'ædɪkwət] *adj* (*insufficient*) insuficiente; (*unsuitable*) inadecuado; (*person*) incapaz.
inadmissible [ɪnəd'mɪsəbl] *adj* improcedente, inadmisible.
inadvertent [ɪnəd'vəːtənt] *adj* descuidado, involuntario.
inadvertently [ɪnəd'vəːtntlɪ] *adv* por descuido.
inadvisable [ɪnəd'vaɪzəbl] *adj* poco aconsejable.
inane [ɪ'neɪn] *adj* necio, fatuo.
inanimate [ɪn'ænɪmət] *adj* inanimado.
inapplicable [ɪn'æplɪkəbl] *adj* inaplicable.
inappropriate [ɪnə'prəuprɪət] *adj* inadecuado.
inapt [ɪn'æpt] *adj* impropio.
inaptitude [ɪn'æptɪtjuːd] *n* incapacidad *f*.
inarticulate [ɪnɑː'tɪkjulət] *adj* (*person*) incapaz de expresarse; (*speech*) mal pronunciado.
inartistic [ɪnɑː'tɪstɪk] *adj* antiestético.
inasmuch as [ɪnəz'mʌtʃ-] *adv* en la medida en que.
inattention [ɪnə'tɛnʃən] *n* desatención *f*.
inattentive [ɪnə'tɛntɪv] *adj* distraído.
inaudible [ɪn'ɔːdɪbl] *adj* inaudible.
inaugural [ɪ'nɔːgjurəl] *adj* inaugural; (*speech*) de apertura.
inaugurate [ɪ'nɔːgjureɪt] *vt* inaugurar; (*president, official*) investir.
inauguration [ɪnɔːgju'reɪʃən] *n* inauguración *f*; (*of official*) investidura; (*of event*) ceremonia de apertura.
inauspicious [ɪnɔːs'pɪʃəs] *adj* poco propicio, inoportuno.
in-between [ɪnbɪ'twiːn] *adj* intermedio.
inborn [ɪn'bɔːn] *adj* (*feeling*) innato.
inbred [ɪn'brɛd] *adj* innato; (*family*) consanguíneo.
inbreeding [ɪn'briːdɪŋ] *n* endogamia.
Inc. *abbr* = **incorporated**.
Inca ['ɪŋkə] *adj* (*also*: **~n**) inca, de los incas ♦ *n* inca *m/f*.
incalculable [ɪn'kælkjuləbl] *adj* incalculable.
incapability [ɪnkeɪpə'bɪlɪtɪ] *n* incapacidad *f*.
incapable [ɪn'keɪpəbl] *adj*: ~ **(of doing sth)** incapaz (de hacer algo).
incapacitate [ɪnkə'pæsɪteɪt] *vt*: **to ~ sb** incapacitar a algn.
incapacitated [ɪnkə'pæsɪteɪtɪd] *adj* incapacitado.
incapacity [ɪnkə'pæsɪtɪ] *n* (*inability*) incapacidad *f*.
incarcerate [ɪn'kɑːsəreɪt] *vt* encarcelar.
incarnate *adj* [ɪn'kɑːnɪt] en persona ♦ *vt* ['ɪnkɑːneɪt] encarnar.
incarnation [ɪnkɑː'neɪʃən] *n* encarnación *f*.
incendiary [ɪn'sɛndɪərɪ] *adj* incendiario ♦ *n* (*bomb*) bomba incendiaria.
incense *n* ['ɪnsɛns] incienso ♦ *vt* [ɪn'sɛns] (*anger*) indignar, encolerizar.
incentive [ɪn'sɛntɪv] *n* incentivo, estímulo.
incentive bonus *n* prima.
incentive scheme *n* plan *m* de incentivos.
inception [ɪn'sɛpʃən] *n* comienzo, principio.
incessant [ɪn'sɛsnt] *adj* incesante, continuo.
incessantly [ɪn'sɛsəntlɪ] *adv* constantemente.
incest ['ɪnsɛst] *n* incesto.
inch [ɪntʃ] *n* pulgada; **to be within an ~ of** estar a dos dedos de; **he didn't give an** ~ no hizo la más mínima concesión; **a few ~es** unas pulgadas.
►**inch forward** *vi* avanzar palmo a palmo.
incidence ['ɪnsɪdns] *n* (*of crime, disease*) incidencia.
incident ['ɪnsɪdnt] *n* incidente *m*; (*in book*)

episodio.
incidental [ɪnsɪ'dɛntl] *adj* circunstancial, accesorio; (*unplanned*) fortuito; ~ **to** relacionado con; ~ **expenses** (gastos *mpl*) imprevistos *mpl*.
incidentally [ɪnsɪ'dɛntəlɪ] *adv* (*by the way*) por cierto.
incidental music *n* música de fondo.
incident room *n* (*POLICE*) centro de coordinación.
incinerate [ɪn'sɪnəreɪt] *vt* incinerar, quemar.
incinerator [ɪn'sɪnəreɪtə*] *n* incinerador *m*, incineradora.
incipient [ɪn'sɪpɪənt] *adj* incipiente.
incision [ɪn'sɪʒən] *n* incisión *f*.
incisive [ɪn'saɪsɪv] *adj* (*mind*) penetrante; (*remark etc*) incisivo.
incisor [ɪn'saɪzə*] *n* incisivo.
incite [ɪn'saɪt] *vt* provocar, incitar.
incl. *abbr* = **including; inclusive (of)**.
inclement [ɪn'klɛmənt] *adj* inclemente.
inclination [ɪnklɪ'neɪʃən] *n* (*tendency*) tendencia, inclinación *f*.
incline *n* ['ɪnklaɪn] pendiente *f*, cuesta ♦ *vb* [ɪn'klaɪn] *vt* (*slope*) inclinar; (*head*) poner de lado ♦ *vi* inclinarse; **to be ~d to** (*tend*) ser propenso a; (*be willing*) estar dispuesto a.
include [ɪn'klu:d] *vt* incluir, comprender; (*in letter*) adjuntar; **the tip is/is not ~d** la propina está/no está incluida.
including [ɪn'klu:dɪŋ] *prep* incluso, inclusive; ~ **tip** propina incluida.
inclusion [ɪn'klu:ʒən] *n* inclusión *f*.
inclusive [ɪn'klu:sɪv] *adj* inclusivo ♦ *adv* inclusive; ~ **of tax** incluidos los impuestos; **$50, ~ of all surcharges** 50 dólares, incluidos todos los recargos.
incognito [ɪnkɔg'ni:təu] *adv* de incógnito.
incoherent [ɪnkəu'hɪərənt] *adj* incoherente.
income ['ɪnkʌm] *n* (*personal*) ingresos *mpl*; (*from property etc*) renta; (*profit*) rédito; **gross/net** ~ ingresos *mpl* brutos/netos; ~ **and expenditure account** cuenta de gastos e ingresos.
income bracket *n* categoría económica.
income support *n* (*BRIT*) ≈ ayuda familiar.
income tax *n* impuesto sobre la renta.
income tax inspector *n* inspector(a) *m/f* de Hacienda.
income tax return *n* declaración *f* de ingresos.
incoming ['ɪnkʌmɪŋ] *adj* (*passengers, flight*) de llegada; (*government*) entrante; (*tenant*) nuevo.
incommunicado ['ɪnkəmjunɪ'kɑ:dəu] *adj*: **to hold sb** ~ mantener incomunicado a algn.
incomparable [ɪn'kɔmpərəbl] *adj* incomparable, sin par.
incompatible [ɪnkəm'pætɪbl] *adj* incompatible.
incompetence [ɪn'kɔmpɪtəns] *n* incompetencia.
incompetent [ɪn'kɔmpɪtənt] *adj* incompetente.
incomplete [ɪnkəm'pli:t] *adj* incompleto; (*unfinished*) sin terminar.
incomprehensible [ɪnkɔmprɪ'hɛnsɪbl] *adj* incomprensible.
inconceivable [ɪnkən'si:vəbl] *adj* inconcebible.
inconclusive [ɪnkən'klu:sɪv] *adj* sin resultado (definitivo); (*argument*) poco convincente.
incongruity [ɪnkɔŋ'gru:ɪtɪ] *n* incongruencia.
incongruous [ɪn'kɔŋgruəs] *adj* discordante.
inconsequential [ɪnkɔnsɪ'kwɛnʃl] *adj* intranscendente.
inconsiderable [ɪnkən'sɪdərəbl] *adj* insignificante.
inconsiderate [ɪnkən'sɪdərət] *adj* desconsiderado; **how ~ of him!** ¡qué falta de consideración (de su parte)!
inconsistency [ɪnkən'sɪstənsɪ] *n* inconsecuencia; (*of actions etc*) falta de lógica; (*of work*) carácter *m* desigual, inconsistencia; (*of statement etc*) contradicción *f*.
inconsistent [ɪnkən'sɪstnt] *adj* inconsecuente; ~ **with** que no concuerda con.
inconsolable [ɪnkən'səuləbl] *adj* inconsolable.
inconspicuous [ɪnkən'spɪkjuəs] *adj* (*discreet*) discreto; (*person*) que llama poco la atención.
inconstancy [ɪn'kɔnstənsɪ] *n* inconstancia.
inconstant [ɪn'kɔnstənt] *adj* inconstante.
incontinence [ɪn'kɔntɪnəns] *n* incontinencia.
incontinent [ɪn'kɔntɪnənt] *adj* incontinente.
incontrovertible [ɪnkɔntrə'və:təbl] *adj* incontrovertible.
inconvenience [ɪnkən'vi:njəns] *n* (*gen*) inconvenientes *mpl*; (*trouble*) molestia ♦ *vt* incomodar; **to put sb to great** ~ causar mucha molestia a algn; **don't ~ yourself** no se moleste.
inconvenient [ɪnkən'vi:njənt] *adj* incómodo, poco práctico; (*time, place*) inoportuno; **that time is very ~ for me** esa hora me es muy inconveniente.

incorporate [ɪn'kɔːpəreɪt] *vt* incorporar; (*contain*) comprender; (*add*) agregar.
incorporated [ɪn'kɔːpəreɪtɪd] *adj*: ~ **company** (*US*: *abbr* **Inc.**) ≈ Sociedad *f* Anónima (S.A.).
incorrect [ɪnkə'rɛkt] *adj* incorrecto.
incorrigible [ɪn'kɔrɪdʒəbl] *adj* incorregible.
incorruptible [ɪnkə'rʌptɪbl] *adj* incorruptible.
increase *n* ['ɪnkriːs] aumento ♦ *vb* [ɪn'kriːs] *vi* aumentar; (*grow*) crecer; (*price*) subir ♦ *vt* aumentar; **an ~ of 5%** un aumento de 5%; **to be on the ~** ir en aumento.
increasing [ɪn'kriːsɪŋ] *adj* (*number*) creciente, que va en aumento.
increasingly [ɪn'kriːsɪŋlɪ] *adv* cada vez más.
incredible [ɪn'krɛdɪbl] *adj* increíble.
incredibly [ɪn'krɛdɪblɪ] *adv* increíblemente.
incredulous [ɪn'krɛdjuləs] *adj* incrédulo.
increment ['ɪnkrɪmənt] *n* aumento, incremento.
incriminate [ɪn'krɪmɪneɪt] *vt* incriminar.
incriminating [ɪn'krɪmɪneɪtɪŋ] *adj* incriminatorio.
incrust [ɪn'krʌst] *vt* = **encrust.**
incubate ['ɪnkjubeɪt] *vt* (*eggs*) incubar, empollar ♦ *vi* (*egg, disease*) incubar.
incubation [ɪnkju'beɪʃən] *n* incubación *f.*
incubation period *n* período de incubación.
incubator ['ɪnkjubeɪtə*] *n* incubadora.
inculcate ['ɪnkʌlkeɪt] *vt*: **to ~ sth in sb** inculcar algo en algn.
incumbent [ɪn'kʌmbənt] *n* ocupante *m/f* ♦ *adj*: **it is ~ on him to...** le incumbe....
incur [ɪn'kəː*] *vt* (*expenses*) incurrir en; (*loss*) sufrir.
incurable [ɪn'kjuərəbl] *adj* incurable.
incursion [ɪn'kəːʃən] *n* incursión *f.*
Ind. *abbr* (*US*) = *Indiana.*
indebted [ɪn'dɛtɪd] *adj*: **to be ~ to sb** estar agradecido a algn.
indecency [ɪn'diːsnsɪ] *n* indecencia.
indecent [ɪn'diːsnt] *adj* indecente.
indecent assault *n* (*BRIT*) atentado contra el pudor.
indecent exposure *n* exhibicionismo.
indecipherable [ɪndɪ'saɪfərəbl] *adj* indescifrable.
indecision [ɪndɪ'sɪʒən] *n* indecisión *f.*
indecisive [ɪndɪ'saɪsɪv] *adj* indeciso; (*discussion*) no resuelto, inconcluyente.
indeed [ɪn'diːd] *adv* efectivamente, en realidad; **yes ~!** ¡claro que sí!
indefatigable [ɪndɪ'fætɪgəbl] *adj* incansable, infatigable.
indefensible [ɪndɪ'fɛnsəbl] *adj* (*conduct*) injustificable.
indefinable [ɪndɪ'faɪnəbl] *adj* indefinible.
indefinite [ɪn'dɛfɪnɪt] *adj* indefinido; (*uncertain*) incierto.
indefinitely [ɪn'dɛfɪnɪtlɪ] *adv* (*wait*) indefinidamente.
indelible [ɪn'dɛlɪbl] *adj* imborrable.
indelicate [ɪn'dɛlɪkɪt] *adj* (*tactless*) indiscreto, inoportuno; (*not polite*) poco delicado.
indemnify [ɪn'dɛmnɪfaɪ] *vt* indemnizar, resarcir.
indemnity [ɪn'dɛmnɪtɪ] *n* (*insurance*) indemnidad *f*; (*compensation*) indemnización *f.*
indent [ɪn'dɛnt] *vt* (*text*) sangrar.
indentation [ɪndɛn'teɪʃən] *n* mella; (*TYP*) sangría.
independence [ɪndɪ'pɛndns] *n* independencia.
Independence Day *n* Día *m* de la Independencia; *ver recuadro.*

> **INDEPENDENCE DAY**
>
> *El cuatro de julio es la fiesta nacional de los Estados Unidos,* **Independence Day**, *en conmemoración de la Declaración de Independencia escrita por Thomas Jefferson y adoptada en 1776. En ella se proclamaba la ruptura total con Gran Bretaña de las trece colonias americanas que fueron el origen de los Estados Unidos de América.*

independent [ɪndɪ'pɛndənt] *adj* independiente; **to become ~** independizarse.
in-depth ['ɪndɛpθ] *adj* en profundidad, a fondo.
indescribable [ɪndɪ'skraɪbəbl] *adj* indescriptible.
indestructible [ɪndɪs'trʌktəbl] *adj* indestructible.
indeterminate [ɪndɪ'təːmɪnɪt] *adj* indeterminado.
index ['ɪndɛks] *n* (*pl*: **~es**: *in book*) índice *m*; (: *in library etc*) catálogo; (*pl*: **indices** ['ɪndɪsiːz]: *ratio, sign*) exponente *m.*
index card *n* ficha.
index finger *n* índice *m.*
index-linked ['ɪndɛks'lɪŋkt], (*US*) **indexed** ['ɪndɛkst] *adj* indexado.
India ['ɪndɪə] *n* la India.
Indian ['ɪndɪən] *adj, n* indio/a *m/f*; (*American ~*) indio/a *m/f* de América, amerindio/a *m/f*; **Red ~** piel roja *m/f.*
Indian Ocean *n*: **the ~** el Océano Índico, el Mar de las Indias.
Indian summer *n* (*fig*) veranillo de San

Martín.
india rubber *n* caucho.
indicate ['ɪndɪkeɪt] *vt* indicar ♦ *vi* (*BRIT AUT*): **to ~ left/right** indicar a la izquierda/a la derecha.
indication [ɪndɪ'keɪʃən] *n* indicio, señal *f.*
indicative [ɪn'dɪkətɪv] *adj*: **to be ~ of sth** indicar algo ♦ *n* (*LING*) indicativo.
indicator ['ɪndɪkeɪtə*] *n* (*gen*) indicador *m*; (*AUT*) intermitente *m*, direccional *m* (*LAM*).
indices ['ɪndɪsi:z] *npl of* **index.**
indict [ɪn'daɪt] *vt* acusar.
indictable [ɪn'daɪtəbl] *adj*: **~ offence** delito procesable.
indictment [ɪn'daɪtmənt] *n* acusación *f.*
indifference [ɪn'dɪfrəns] *n* indiferencia.
indifferent [ɪn'dɪfrənt] *adj* indiferente; (*poor*) regular.
indigenous [ɪn'dɪdʒɪnəs] *adj* indígena.
indigestible [ɪndɪ'dʒɛstɪbl] *adj* indigesto.
indigestion [ɪndɪ'dʒɛstʃən] *n* indigestión *f.*
indignant [ɪn'dɪgnənt] *adj*: **to be ~ about sth** indignarse por algo.
indignation [ɪndɪg'neɪʃən] *n* indignación *f.*
indignity [ɪn'dɪgnɪtɪ] *n* indignidad *f.*
indigo ['ɪndɪgəu] *adj* (*colour*) (de color) añil ♦ *n* añil *m.*
indirect [ɪndɪ'rɛkt] *adj* indirecto.
indirectly [ɪndɪ'rɛktlɪ] *adv* indirectamente.
indiscernible [ɪndɪ'sə:nəbl] *adj* imperceptible.
indiscreet [ɪndɪ'skri:t] *adj* indiscreto, imprudente.
indiscretion [ɪndɪ'skrɛʃən] *n* indiscreción *f*, imprudencia.
indiscriminate [ɪndɪ'skrɪmɪnət] *adj* indiscriminado.
indispensable [ɪndɪ'spɛnsəbl] *adj* indispensable, imprescindible.
indisposed [ɪndɪ'spəuzd] *adj* (*unwell*) indispuesto.
indisposition [ɪndɪspə'zɪʃən] *n* indisposición *f.*
indisputable [ɪndɪ'spju:təbl] *adj* incontestable.
indistinct [ɪndɪ'stɪŋkt] *adj* indistinto.
indistinguishable [ɪndɪ'stɪŋgwɪʃəbl] *adj* indistinguible.
individual [ɪndɪ'vɪdjuəl] *n* individuo ♦ *adj* individual; (*personal*) personal; (*for/of one only*) particular.
individualist [ɪndɪ'vɪdjuəlɪst] *n* individualista *m/f.*
individuality [ɪndɪvɪdju'ælɪtɪ] *n* individualidad *f.*
individually [ɪndɪ'vɪdjuəlɪ] *adv* individualmente; particularmente.
indivisible [ɪndɪ'vɪzəbl] *adj* indivisible.
Indo-China ['ɪndəu'tʃaɪnə] *n* Indochina.
indoctrinate [ɪn'dɔktrɪneɪt] *vt* adoctrinar.
indoctrination [ɪndɔktrɪ'neɪʃən] *n* adoctrinamiento.
indolence ['ɪndələns] *n* indolencia.
indolent ['ɪndələnt] *adj* indolente, perezoso.
Indonesia [ɪndə'ni:zɪə] *n* Indonesia.
Indonesian [ɪndə'ni:zɪən] *adj* indonesio ♦ *n* indonesio/a; (*LING*) indonesio.
indoor ['ɪndɔ:*] *adj* (*swimming pool*) cubierto; (*plant*) de interior; (*sport*) bajo cubierta.
indoors [ɪn'dɔ:z] *adv* dentro; (*at home*) en casa.
indubitable [ɪn'dju:bɪtəbl] *adj* indudable.
indubitably [ɪn'dju:bɪtəblɪ] *adv* indudablemente.
induce [ɪn'dju:s] *vt* inducir, persuadir; (*bring about*) producir; **to ~ sb to do sth** persuadir a algn a que haga algo.
inducement [ɪn'dju:smənt] *n* (*incentive*) incentivo, aliciente *m.*
induct [ɪn'dʌkt] *vt* iniciar; (*in job, rank, position*) instalar.
induction [ɪn'dʌkʃən] *n* (*MED: of birth*) inducción *f.*
induction course *n* (*BRIT*) cursillo introductorio *or* de iniciación.
indulge [ɪn'dʌldʒ] *vt* (*whim*) satisfacer; (*person*) complacer; (*child*) mimar ♦ *vi*: **to ~ in** darse el gusto de.
indulgence [ɪn'dʌldʒəns] *n* vicio.
indulgent [ɪn'dʌldʒənt] *adj* indulgente.
industrial [ɪn'dʌstrɪəl] *adj* industrial.
industrial action *n* huelga.
industrial estate *n* (*BRIT*) polígono *or* zona (*LAM*) industrial.
industrial goods *npl* bienes *mpl* de producción.
industrialist [ɪn'dʌstrɪəlɪst] *n* industrial *m/f.*
industrialize [ɪn'dʌstrɪəlaɪz] *vt* industrializar.
industrial park *n* (*US*) = **industrial estate.**
industrial relations *npl* relaciones *fpl* empresariales.
industrial tribunal *n* magistratura de trabajo, tribunal *m* laboral.
industrial unrest *n* (*BRIT*) agitación *f* obrera.
industrious [ɪn'dʌstrɪəs] *adj* (*gen*) trabajador(a); (*student*) aplicado.
industry ['ɪndəstrɪ] *n* industria; (*diligence*) aplicación *f.*
inebriated [ɪ'ni:brɪeɪtɪd] *adj* borracho.
inedible [ɪn'ɛdɪbl] *adj* incomible; (*plant etc*) no comestible.
ineffective [ɪnɪ'fɛktɪv], **ineffectual**

[ɪnɪ'fɛktʃuəl] *adj* ineficaz, inútil.
inefficiency [ɪnɪ'fɪʃənsɪ] *n* ineficacia.
inefficient [ɪnɪ'fɪʃənt] *adj* ineficaz, ineficiente.
inelegant [ɪn'ɛlɪgənt] *adj* poco elegante.
ineligible [ɪn'ɛlɪdʒɪbl] *adj* inelegible.
inept [ɪ'nɛpt] *adj* incompetente, incapaz.
ineptitude [ɪ'nɛptɪtju:d] *n* incapacidad *f*, ineptitud *f*.
inequality [ɪnɪ'kwɔlɪtɪ] *n* desigualdad *f*.
inequitable [ɪn'ɛkwɪtəbl] *adj* injusto.
ineradicable [ɪnɪ'rædɪkəbl] *adj* inextirpable.
inert [ɪ'nə:t] *adj* inerte, inactivo; (*immobile*) inmóvil.
inertia [ɪ'nə:ʃə] *n* inercia; (*laziness*) pereza.
inertia-reel seat-belt [ɪ'nə:ʃə'ri:l-] *n* cinturón *m* de seguridad retráctil.
inescapable [ɪnɪ'skeɪpəbl] *adj* ineludible, inevitable.
inessential [ɪnɪ'sɛnʃl] *adj* no esencial.
inestimable [ɪn'ɛstɪməbl] *adj* inestimable.
inevitability [ɪnɛvɪtə'bɪlɪtɪ] *n* inevitabilidad *f*.
inevitable [ɪn'ɛvɪtəbl] *adj* inevitable; (*necessary*) forzoso.
inevitably [ɪn'ɛvɪtəblɪ] *adv* inevitablemente; **as ~ happens ...** como siempre pasa ....
inexact [ɪnɪg'zaekt] *adj* inexacto.
inexcusable [ɪnɪks'kju:zəbl] *adj* imperdonable.
inexhaustible [ɪnɪg'zɔ:stɪbl] *adj* inagotable.
inexorable [ɪn'ɛksərəbl] *adj* inexorable, implacable.
inexpensive [ɪnɪk'spɛnsɪv] *adj* económico.
inexperience [ɪnɪk'spɪərɪəns] *n* falta de experiencia.
inexperienced [ɪnɪk'spɪərɪənst] *adj* inexperto; **to be ~ in sth** no tener experiencia en algo.
inexplicable [ɪnɪk'splɪkəbl] *adj* inexplicable.
inexpressible [ɪnɪk'sprɛsəbl] *adj* inexpresable.
inextricable [ɪnɪks'trɪkəbl] *adj* inseparable.
inextricably [ɪnɪks'trɪkəblɪ] *adv* indisolublemente.
infallibility [ɪnfælə'bɪlɪtɪ] *n* infalibilidad *f*.
infallible [ɪn'fælɪbl] *adj* infalible.
infamous ['ɪnfəməs] *adj* infame.
infamy ['ɪnfəmɪ] *n* infamia.
infancy ['ɪnfənsɪ] *n* infancia.
infant ['ɪnfənt] *n* niño/a.
infantile ['ɪnfəntaɪl] *adj* infantil; (*pej*) aniñado.
infant mortality *n* mortalidad *f* infantil.
infantry ['ɪnfəntrɪ] *n* infantería.
infantryman ['ɪnfəntrɪmən] *n* soldado de infantería.
infant school *n* (*BRIT*) escuela de párvulos; *see also* **primary school**.
infatuated [ɪn'fætjueɪtɪd] *adj*: **~ with** (*in love*) loco por; **to become ~ (with sb)** enamoriscarse (de algn), encapricharse (con algn).
infatuation [ɪnfætju'eɪʃən] *n* enamoramiento.
infect [ɪn'fɛkt] *vt* (*wound*) infectar; (*person*) contagiar; (*fig*: *pej*) corromper; **~ed with** (*illness*) contagiado de; **to become ~ed** (*wound*) infectarse.
infection [ɪn'fɛkʃən] *n* infección *f*; (*fig*) contagio.
infectious [ɪn'fɛkʃəs] *adj* contagioso; (*also fig*) infeccioso.
infer [ɪn'fə:*] *vt* deducir, inferir; **to ~ (from)** inferir (de), deducir (de).
inference ['ɪnfərəns] *n* deducción *f*, inferencia.
inferior [ɪn'fɪərɪə*] *adj, n* inferior *m/f*; **to feel ~** sentirse inferior.
inferiority [ɪnfɪərɪ'ɔrətɪ] *n* inferioridad *f*.
inferiority complex *n* complejo de inferioridad.
infernal [ɪn'fə:nl] *adj* infernal.
inferno [ɪn'fə:nəu] *n* infierno; (*fig*) hoguera.
infertile [ɪn'fə:taɪl] *adj* estéril; (*person*) infecundo.
infertility [ɪnfə:'tɪlɪtɪ] *n* esterilidad *f*; infecundidad *f*.
infest [ɪn'fɛst] *vt* infestar.
infested [ɪn'fɛstɪd] *adj*: **~ (with)** plagado (de).
infidel ['ɪnfɪdəl] *n* infiel *m/f*.
infidelity [ɪnfɪ'dɛlɪtɪ] *n* infidelidad *f*.
in-fighting ['ɪnfaɪtɪŋ] *n* (*fig*) lucha(s) *f*(*pl*) interna(s).
infiltrate ['ɪnfɪltreɪt] *vt* (*troops etc*) infiltrarse en ♦ *vi* infiltrarse.
infinite ['ɪnfɪnɪt] *adj* infinito; **an ~ amount of money/time** un sinfín de dinero/ tiempo.
infinitely ['ɪnfɪnɪtlɪ] *adv* infinitamente.
infinitesimal [ɪnfɪnɪ'tɛsɪməl] *adj* infinitésimo.
infinitive [ɪn'fɪnɪtɪv] *n* infinitivo.
infinity [ɪn'fɪnɪtɪ] *n* (*also MATH*) infinito; (*an ~*) infinidad *f*.
infirm [ɪn'fə:m] *adj* enfermizo, débil.
infirmary [ɪn'fə:mərɪ] *n* hospital *m*.
infirmity [ɪn'fə:mɪtɪ] *n* debilidad *f*; (*illness*) enfermedad *f*, achaque *m*.
inflame [ɪn'fleɪm] inflamar.
inflamed [ɪn'fleɪmd] *adj*: **to become ~** inflamarse.
inflammable [ɪn'flæməbl] *adj* (*BRIT*)

inflamable; (*situation etc*) explosivo.

inflammation [ɪnflə'meɪʃən] *n* inflamación *f*.

inflammatory [ɪn'flæmətərɪ] *adj* (*speech*) incendiario.

inflatable [ɪn'fleɪtəbl] *adj* inflable.

inflate [ɪn'fleɪt] *vt* (*tyre, balloon*) inflar; (*fig*) hinchar.

inflated [ɪn'fleɪtɪd] *adj* (*tyre etc*) inflado; (*price, self-esteem etc*) exagerado.

inflation [ɪn'fleɪʃən] *n* (*ECON*) inflación *f*.

inflationary [ɪn'fleɪʃnərɪ] *adj* inflacionario.

inflationary spiral *n* espiral *f* inflacionista.

inflexible [ɪn'flɛksɪbl] *adj* inflexible.

inflict [ɪn'flɪkt] *vt*: **to ~ on** infligir en; (*tax etc*) imponer a.

infliction [ɪn'flɪkʃən] *n* imposición *f*.

in-flight ['ɪnflaɪt] *adj* durante el vuelo.

inflow ['ɪnfləu] *n* afluencia.

influence ['ɪnfluəns] *n* influencia ♦ *vt* influir en, influenciar; **under the ~ of alcohol** en estado de embriaguez.

influential [ɪnflu'ɛnʃl] *adj* influyente.

influenza [ɪnflu'ɛnzə] *n* gripe *f*.

influx ['ɪnflʌks] *n* afluencia.

inform [ɪn'fɔːm] *vt*: **to ~ sb of sth** informar a algn sobre *or* de algo; (*warn*) avisar a algn de algo; (*communicate*) comunicar algo a algn ♦ *vi* : **to ~ on sb** delatar a algn.

informal [ɪn'fɔːml] *adj* (*manner, tone*) desenfadado; (*dress, interview, occasion*) informal.

informality [ɪnfɔː'mælɪtɪ] *n* falta de ceremonia; (*intimacy*) intimidad *f*; (*familiarity*) familiaridad *f*; (*ease*) afabilidad *f*.

informally [ɪn'fɔːməlɪ] *adv* sin ceremonia; (*invite*) informalmente.

informant [ɪn'fɔːmənt] *n* informante *m/f*.

informatics [ɪnfɔː'mætɪks] *n* informática.

information [ɪnfə'meɪʃən] *n* información *f*; (*news*) noticias *fpl*; (*knowledge*) conocimientos *mpl*; (*LAW*) delación *f*; **a piece of ~** un dato; **for your ~** para su información.

information bureau *n* oficina de información.

information processing *n* procesamiento de datos.

information retrieval *n* recuperación *f* de información.

information science *n* gestión *f* de la información.

information technology (IT) *n* informática.

informative [ɪn'fɔːmətɪv] *adj* informativo.

informed [ɪn'fɔːmd] *adj* (*observer*) informado, al corriente; **an ~ guess** una opinión bien fundamentada.

informer [ɪn'fɔːmə*] *n* delator(a) *m/f*; (*also*: **police ~**) soplón/ona *m/f*.

infra dig ['ɪnfrə'dɪg] *adj abbr* (*col*: = *infra dignitatem*) denigrante.

infra-red [ɪnfrə'rɛd] *adj* infrarrojo.

infrastructure ['ɪnfrəstrʌktʃə*] *n* (*of system etc, ECON*) infraestructura.

infrequent [ɪn'friːkwənt] *adj* infrecuente.

infringe [ɪn'frɪndʒ] *vt* infringir, violar ♦ *vi*: **to ~ on** invadir.

infringement [ɪn'frɪndʒmənt] *n* infracción *f*; (*of rights*) usurpación *f*; (*SPORT*) falta.

infuriate [ɪn'fjuərɪeɪt] *vt*: **to become ~d** ponerse furioso.

infuriating [ɪn'fjuərɪeɪtɪŋ] *adj*: **I find it ~** me saca de quicio.

infuse [ɪn'fjuːz] *vt* (*with courage, enthusiasm*): **to ~ sb with sth** infundir algo a algn.

infusion [ɪn'fjuːʒən] *n* (*tea etc*) infusión *f*.

ingenious [ɪn'dʒiːnjəs] *adj* ingenioso.

ingenuity [ɪndʒɪ'njuːɪtɪ] *n* ingeniosidad *f*.

ingenuous [ɪn'dʒɛnjuəs] *adj* ingenuo.

ingot ['ɪŋgət] *n* lingote *m*, barra.

ingrained [ɪn'greɪnd] *adj* arraigado.

ingratiate [ɪn'greɪʃɪeɪt] *vt*: **to ~ o.s. with** congraciarse con.

ingratiating [ɪn'greɪʃɪeɪtɪŋ] *adj* (*smile, speech*) insinuante; (*person*) zalamero, congraciador(a).

ingratitude [ɪn'grætɪtjuːd] *n* ingratitud *f*.

ingredient [ɪn'griːdɪənt] *n* ingrediente *m*.

ingrowing ['ɪngrəuɪŋ] *adj*: **~ (toe)nail** uña encarnada.

inhabit [ɪn'hæbɪt] *vt* vivir en; (*occupy*) ocupar.

inhabitable [ɪn'hæbɪtəbl] *adj* habitable.

inhabitant [ɪn'hæbɪtənt] *n* habitante *m/f*.

inhale [ɪn'heɪl] *vt* inhalar ♦ *vi* (*in smoking*) tragar.

inhaler [ɪn'heɪlə*] *n* inhalador *m*.

inherent [ɪn'hɪərənt] *adj*: **~ in** *or* **to** inherente a.

inherently [ɪn'hɪərəntlɪ] *adv* intrínsecamente.

inherit [ɪn'hɛrɪt] *vt* heredar.

inheritance [ɪn'hɛrɪtəns] *n* herencia; (*fig*) patrimonio.

inhibit [ɪn'hɪbɪt] *vt* inhibir, impedir; **to ~ sb from doing sth** impedir a algn hacer algo.

inhibited [ɪn'hɪbɪtɪd] *adj* (*person*) cohibido.

inhibition [ɪnhɪ'bɪʃən] *n* cohibición *f*.

inhospitable [ɪnhɔs'pɪtəbl] *adj* (*person*) inhospitalario; (*place*) inhóspito.

in-house ['ɪnhaus] *adj* dentro de la empresa.

inhuman [ɪn'hjuːmən] *adj* inhumano.

inhumane [ɪnhju:'meɪn] *adj* inhumano.
inimitable [ɪ'nɪmɪtəbl] *adj* inimitable.
iniquity [ɪ'nɪkwɪtɪ] *n* iniquidad *f*; (*injustice*) injusticia.
initial [ɪ'nɪʃl] *adj* inicial; (*first*) primero ♦ *n* inicial *f* ♦ *vt* firmar con las iniciales; **~s** *npl* iniciales *fpl*; (*abbreviation*) siglas *fpl*.
initialize [ɪ'nɪʃəlaɪz] *vt* (*COMPUT*) inicializar.
initially [ɪ'nɪʃəlɪ] *adv* en un principio.
initiate [ɪ'nɪʃɪeɪt] *vt* (*start*) iniciar; **to ~ sb into a secret** iniciar a algn en un secreto; **to ~ proceedings against sb** (*LAW*) poner una demanda contra algn.
initiation [ɪnɪʃɪ'eɪʃən] *n* (*into secret etc*) iniciación *f*; (*beginning*) comienzo.
initiative [ɪ'nɪʃətɪv] *n* iniciativa; **to take the ~** tomar la iniciativa.
inject [ɪn'dʒɛkt] *vt* inyectar; (*money, enthusiasm*) aportar.
injection [ɪn'dʒɛkʃən] *n* inyección *f*; **to have an ~** ponerse una inyección.
injudicious [ɪndʒu'dɪʃəs] *adj* imprudente, indiscreto.
injunction [ɪn'dʒʌŋkʃən] *n* entredicho, interdicto.
injure ['ɪndʒə*] *vt* herir; (*hurt*) lastimar; (*fig: reputation etc*) perjudicar; (*feelings*) herir; **to ~ o.s** hacerse daño, lastimarse.
injured ['ɪndʒəd] *adj* (*also fig*) herido; **~ party** (*LAW*) parte *f* perjudicada.
injurious [ɪn'dʒuərɪəs] *adj*: **~ (to)** perjudicial (para).
injury ['ɪndʒərɪ] *n* herida, lesión *f*; (*wrong*) perjuicio, daño; **to escape without ~** salir ileso.
injury time *n* (*SPORT*) descuento.
injustice [ɪn'dʒʌstɪs] *n* injusticia; **you do me an ~** usted es injusto conmigo.
ink [ɪŋk] *n* tinta.
ink-jet printer ['ɪŋkdʒɛt-] *n* impresora de chorro de tinta.
inkling ['ɪŋklɪŋ] *n* sospecha; (*idea*) idea.
inkpad ['ɪŋkpæd] *n* almohadilla.
inlaid ['ɪnleɪd] *adj* (*wood*) taraceado; (*tiles*) entarimado.
inland *adj* ['ɪnlənd] interior; (*town*) del interior ♦ *adv* [ɪn'lænd] tierra adentro.
Inland Revenue *n* (*BRIT*) Hacienda.
in-laws ['ɪnlɔ:z] *npl* suegros *mpl*.
inlet ['ɪnlɛt] *n* (*GEO*) ensenada, cala; (*TECH*) admisión *f*, entrada.
inmate ['ɪnmeɪt] *n* (*in prison*) preso/a, presidiario/a; (*in asylum*) internado/a.
inmost ['ɪnməust] *adj* más íntimo, más secreto.
inn [ɪn] *n* posada, mesón *m*; **the I~s of Court** *see* **barrister**.
innards ['ɪnədz] *npl* (*col*) tripas *fpl*.
innate [ɪ'neɪt] *adj* innato.
inner ['ɪnə*] *adj* interior, interno.
inner city *n barrios deprimidos del centro de una ciudad.*
innermost ['ɪnəməust] *adj* más íntimo, más secreto.
inner tube *n* (*of tyre*) cámara, llanta (*LAM*).
innings ['ɪnɪŋz] *n* (*CRICKET*) entrada, turno.
innocence ['ɪnəsns] *n* inocencia.
innocent ['ɪnəsnt] *adj* inocente.
innocuous [ɪ'nɔkjuəs] *adj* inocuo.
innovation [ɪnəu'veɪʃən] *n* novedad *f*.
innuendo, ~es [ɪnju'ɛndəu] *n* indirecta.
innumerable [ɪ'nju:mrəbl] *adj* innumerable.
inoculate [ɪ'nɔkjuleɪt] *vt*: **to ~ sb with sth/against sth** inocular *or* vacunar a algn con algo/contra algo.
inoculation [ɪnɔkju'leɪʃən] *n* inoculación *f*.
inoffensive [ɪnə'fɛnsɪv] *adj* inofensivo.
inopportune [ɪn'ɔpətju:n] *adj* inoportuno.
inordinate [ɪ'nɔ:dɪnət] *adj* excesivo, desmesurado.
inordinately [ɪ'nɔ:dɪnətlɪ] *adv* excesivamente, desmesuradamente.
inorganic [ɪnɔ:'gaenɪk] *adj* inorgánico.
in-patient ['ɪnpeɪʃənt] *n* (paciente *m/f*) interno/a.
input ['ɪnput] *n* (*ELEC*) entrada; (*COMPUT*) entrada de datos ♦ *vt* (*COMPUT*) introducir, entrar.
inquest ['ɪnkwɛst] *n* (*coroner's*) investigación *f* post-mortem.
inquire [ɪn'kwaɪə*] *vi* preguntar ♦ *vt*: **to ~ when/where/whether** preguntar cuándo/dónde/si; **to ~ about** (*person*) preguntar por; (*fact*) informarse de.
▸**inquire into** *vt fus*: **to ~ into sth** investigar *or* indagar algo.
inquiring [ɪn'kwaɪərɪŋ] *adj* (*mind*) inquieto; (*look*) interrogante.
inquiry [ɪn'kwaɪərɪ] *n* pregunta; (*LAW*) investigación *f*, pesquisa; (*commission*) comisión *f* investigadora; **to hold an ~ into sth** emprender una investigación sobre algo.
inquiry desk *n* mesa de información.
inquiry office *n* (*BRIT*) oficina de información.
inquisition [ɪnkwɪ'zɪʃən] *n* inquisición *f*.
inquisitive [ɪn'kwɪzɪtɪv] *adj* (*mind*) inquisitivo; (*person*) fisgón/ona.
inroad ['ɪnrəud] *n* incursión *f*; (*fig*) invasión *f*; **to make ~s into** (*time*) ocupar parte de; (*savings, supplies*) agotar parte de.
insane [ɪn'seɪn] *adj* loco; (*MED*) demente.
insanitary [ɪn'sænɪtərɪ] *adj* insalubre.
insanity [ɪn'sænɪtɪ] *n* demencia, locura.

insatiable [ɪn'seɪʃəbl] *adj* insaciable.
inscribe [ɪn'skraɪb] *vt* inscribir; (*book etc*): **to ~ (to sb)** dedicar (a algn).
inscription [ɪn'skrɪpʃən] *n* (*gen*) inscripción *f*; (*in book*) dedicatoria.
inscrutable [ɪn'skruːtəbl] *adj* inescrutable, insondable.
inseam measurement ['ɪnsiːm-] *n* (*US*) = **inside leg measurement.**
insect ['ɪnsɛkt] *n* insecto.
insect bite *n* picadura.
insecticide [ɪn'sɛktɪsaɪd] *n* insecticida *m.*
insect repellent *n* loción *f* contra los insectos.
insecure [ɪnsɪ'kjuə*] *adj* inseguro.
insecurity [ɪnsɪ'kjuərɪtɪ] *n* inseguridad *f.*
insemination [ɪnsɛmɪ'neɪʃn] *n*: **artificial ~** inseminación *f* artificial.
insensible [ɪn'sɛnsɪbl] *adj* inconsciente; (*unconscious*) sin conocimiento.
insensitive [ɪn'sɛnsɪtɪv] *adj* insensible.
insensitivity [ɪnsɛnsɪ'tɪvɪtɪ] *n* insensibilidad *f.*
inseparable [ɪn'sɛprəbl] *adj* inseparable; **they were ~ friends** los unía una estrecha amistad.
insert *vt* [ɪn'səːt] (*into sth*) introducir; (*COMPUT*) insertar ♦ *n* ['ɪnsəːt] encarte *m.*
insertion [ɪn'səːʃən] *n* inserción *f.*
in-service [ɪn'səːvɪs] *adj* (*training, course*) en el trabajo, a cargo de la empresa.
inshore [ɪn'ʃɔː*] *adj*: **~ fishing** pesca *f* costera ♦ *adv* (*fish*) a lo largo de la costa; (*move*) hacia la orilla.
inside ['ɪn'saɪd] *n* interior *m*; (*lining*) forro; (*of road*: *BRIT*) izquierdo; (: *US, Europe etc*) derecho ♦ *adj* interior, interno; (*information*) confidencial ♦ *adv* (*within*) (por) dentro, adentro (*esp LAM*); (*with movement*) hacia dentro; (*fam*: *in prison*) en chirona ♦ *prep* dentro de; (*of time*): **~ 10 minutes** en menos de 10 minutos; **~s** *npl* (*col*) tripas *fpl*; **~ out** *adv* (*turn*) al revés; (*know*) a fondo.
inside forward *n* (*SPORT*) interior *m.*
inside information *n* información *f* confidencial.
inside lane *n* (*AUT*: *in Britain*) carril *m* izquierdo; (: *in US, Europe*) carril *m* derecho.
inside leg measurement *n* medida de pernera.
insider [ɪn'saɪdə*] *n* enterado/a.
insider dealing, insider trading *n* (*STOCK EXCHANGE*) abuso de información privilegiada.
inside story *n* historia íntima.
insidious [ɪn'sɪdɪəs] *adj* insidioso.
insight ['ɪnsaɪt] *n* perspicacia, percepción *f*; **to gain** *or* **get an ~ into sth** comprender algo mejor.
insignia [ɪn'sɪgnɪə] *npl* insignias *fpl.*
insignificant [ɪnsɪg'nɪfɪknt] *adj* insignificante.
insincere [ɪnsɪn'sɪə*] *adj* poco sincero.
insincerity [ɪnsɪn'sɛrɪtɪ] *n* falta de sinceridad, doblez *f.*
insinuate [ɪn'sɪnjueɪt] *vt* insinuar.
insinuation [ɪnsɪnju'eɪʃən] *n* insinuación *f.*
insipid [ɪn'sɪpɪd] *adj* soso, insulso.
insist [ɪn'sɪst] *vi* insistir; **to ~ on doing** empeñarse en hacer; **to ~ that** insistir en que; (*claim*) exigir que.
insistence [ɪn'sɪstəns] *n* insistencia; (*stubbornness*) empeño.
insistent [ɪn'sɪstənt] *adj* insistente; empeñado.
insofar as [ɪnsəu'fɑː-] *conj* en la medida en que, en tanto que.
insole ['ɪnsəul] *n* plantilla.
insolence ['ɪnsələns] *n* insolencia, descaro.
insolent ['ɪnsələnt] *adj* insolente, descarado.
insoluble [ɪn'sɔljubl] *adj* insoluble.
insolvency [ɪn'sɔlvənsɪ] *n* insolvencia.
insolvent [ɪn'sɔlvənt] *adj* insolvente.
insomnia [ɪn'sɔmnɪə] *n* insomnio.
insomniac [ɪn'sɔmnɪæk] *n* insomne *m/f.*
inspect [ɪn'spɛkt] *vt* inspeccionar, examinar; (*troops*) pasar revista a.
inspection [ɪn'spɛkʃən] *n* inspección *f*, examen *m.*
inspector [ɪn'spɛktə*] *n* inspector(a) *m/f*; (*BRIT*: *on buses, trains*) revisor(a) *m/f.*
inspiration [ɪnspə'reɪʃən] *n* inspiración *f.*
inspire [ɪn'spaɪə*] *vt* inspirar; **to ~ sb (to do sth)** alentar a algn (a hacer algo).
inspired [ɪn'spaɪəd] *adj* (*writer, book etc*) inspirado, genial, iluminado; **in an ~ moment** en un momento de inspiración.
inspiring [ɪn'spaɪərɪŋ] *adj* inspirador(a).
inst. *abbr* (*BRIT COMM*: = *instant, of the present month*) cte.
instability [ɪnstə'bɪlɪtɪ] *n* inestabilidad *f.*
install [ɪn'stɔːl] *vt* instalar.
installation [ɪnstə'leɪʃən] *n* instalación *f.*
installment plan *n* (*US*) compra a plazos.
instalment, (*US*) **installment** [ɪn'stɔːlmənt] *n* plazo; (*of story*) entrega; (*of TV serial etc*) capítulo; **in ~s** (*pay, receive*) a plazos; **to pay in ~s** pagar a plazos *or* por abonos.
instance ['ɪnstəns] *n* ejemplo, caso; **for ~** por ejemplo; **in the first ~** en primer lugar; **in that ~** en ese caso.
instant ['ɪnstənt] *n* instante *m*, momento

♦ *adj* inmediato; (*coffee*) instantáneo.
instantaneous [ɪnstən'teɪnɪəs] *adj* instantáneo.
instantly ['ɪnstəntlɪ] *adv* en seguida, al instante.
instant replay *n* (*US TV*) repetición *f* de la jugada.
instead [ɪn'stɛd] *adv* en cambio; ~ **of** en lugar de, en vez de.
instep ['ɪnstɛp] *n* empeine *m*.
instigate ['ɪnstɪgeɪt] *vt* (*rebellion, strike, crime*) instigar; (*new ideas etc*) fomentar.
instigation [ɪnstɪ'geɪʃən] *n* instigación *f*; **at sb's ~** a instigación de algn.
instil [ɪn'stɪl] *vt*: **to ~ into** inculcar a.
instinct ['ɪnstɪŋkt] *n* instinto.
instinctive [ɪn'stɪŋktɪv] *adj* instintivo.
instinctively [ɪn'stɪŋktɪvlɪ] *adv* por instinto.
institute ['ɪnstɪtjuːt] *n* instituto; (*professional body*) colegio ♦ *vt* (*begin*) iniciar, empezar; (*proceedings*) entablar.
institution [ɪnstɪ'tjuːʃən] *n* institución *f*; (*beginning*) iniciación *f*; (*MED: home*) asilo; (*asylum*) manicomio; (*custom*) costumbre *f* arraigada.
institutional [ɪnstɪ'tjuːʃənl] *adj* institucional.
instruct [ɪn'strʌkt] *vt*: **to ~ sb in sth** instruir a algn en *or* sobre algo; **to ~ sb to do sth** dar instrucciones a algn de *or* mandar a algn hacer algo.
instruction [ɪn'strʌkʃən] *n* (*teaching*) instrucción *f*; **~s** *npl* órdenes *fpl*; **~s (for use)** modo *sg* de empleo.
instruction book *n* manual *m*.
instructive [ɪn'strʌktɪv] *adj* instructivo.
instructor [ɪn'strʌktə*] *n* instructor(a) *m/f*.
instrument ['ɪnstrəmənt] *n* instrumento.
instrumental [ɪnstrə'mɛntl] *adj* (*MUS*) instrumental; **to be ~ in** ser el artífice de; **to be ~ in sth/in doing sth** ser responsable de algo/de hacer algo.
instrumentalist [ɪnstrə'mɛntəlɪst] *n* instrumentista *m/f*.
instrument panel *n* tablero (de instrumentos).
insubordinate [ɪnsə'bɔːdənɪt] *adj* insubordinado.
insubordination [ɪnsəbɔːdə'neɪʃən] *n* insubordinación *f*.
insufferable [ɪn'sʌfrəbl] *adj* insoportable.
insufficient [ɪnsə'fɪʃənt] *adj* insuficiente.
insufficiently [ɪnsə'fɪʃəntlɪ] *adv* insuficientemente.
insular ['ɪnsjulə*] *adj* insular; (*outlook*) estrecho de miras.
insularity [ɪnsju'lærɪtɪ] *n* insularidad *f*.
insulate ['ɪnsjuleɪt] *vt* aislar.
insulating tape ['ɪnsjuleɪtɪŋ-] *n* cinta aislante.
insulation [ɪnsju'leɪʃən] *n* aislamiento.
insulator ['ɪnsjuleɪtə*] *n* aislante *m*.
insulin ['ɪnsjulɪn] *n* insulina.
insult *n* ['ɪnsʌlt] insulto; (*offence*) ofensa ♦ *vt* [ɪn'sʌlt] insultar; ofender.
insulting [ɪn'sʌltɪŋ] *adj* insultante; ofensivo.
insuperable [ɪn'sjuːprəbl] *adj* insuperable.
insurance [ɪn'ʃuərəns] *n* seguro; **fire/life ~** seguro de incendios/vida; **to take out ~ (against)** hacerse un seguro (contra).
insurance agent *n* agente *m/f* de seguros.
insurance broker *n* corredor(a) *m/f or* agente *m/f* de seguros.
insurance policy *n* póliza (de seguros).
insurance premium *n* prima de seguros.
insure [ɪn'ʃuə*] *vt* asegurar; **to ~ sb** *or* **sb's life** hacer un seguro de vida a algn; **to ~ (against)** asegurar (contra); **to be ~d for £5000** tener un seguro de 5000 libras.
insured [ɪn'ʃuəd] *n*: **the ~** el/la asegurado/a.
insurer [ɪn'ʃuərə*] *n* asegurador(a).
insurgent [ɪn'səːdʒənt] *adj, n* insurgente *m/f*, insurrecto/a *m/f*.
insurmountable [ɪnsə'mauntəbl] *adj* insuperable.
insurrection [ɪnsə'rɛkʃən] *n* insurrección *f*.
intact [ɪn'tækt] *adj* íntegro; (*untouched*) intacto.
intake ['ɪnteɪk] *n* (*TECH*) entrada, toma; (*: pipe*) tubo de admisión; (*of food*) ingestión *f*; (*BRIT SCOL*): **an ~ of 200 a year** 200 matriculados al año.
intangible [ɪn'tændʒɪbl] *adj* intangible.
integer ['ɪntɪdʒə*] *n* (número) entero.
integral ['ɪntɪgrəl] *adj* (*whole*) íntegro; (*part*) integrante.
integrate ['ɪntɪgreɪt] *vt* integrar ♦ *vi* integrarse.
integrated circuit ['ɪntɪgreɪtɪd-] *n* (*COMPUT*) circuito integrado.
integration [ɪntɪ'greɪʃən] *n* integración *f*; **racial ~** integración de razas.
integrity [ɪn'tɛgrɪtɪ] *n* honradez *f*, rectitud *f*; (*COMPUT*) integridad *f*.
intellect ['ɪntəlɛkt] *n* intelecto.
intellectual [ɪntə'lɛktjuəl] *adj, n* intelectual *m/f*.
intelligence [ɪn'tɛlɪdʒəns] *n* inteligencia.
intelligence quotient (IQ) *n* coeficiente *m* intelectual.
Intelligence Service *n* Servicio de Inteligencia.
intelligence test *n* prueba de inteligencia.
intelligent [ɪn'tɛlɪdʒənt] *adj* inteligente.
intelligently [ɪn'tɛlɪdʒəntlɪ] *adv*

inteligentemente.
intelligentsia [ɪntɛlɪ'dʒɛntsɪə] *n* intelectualidad *f*.
intelligible [ɪn'tɛlɪdʒɪbl] *adj* inteligible, comprensible.
intemperate [ɪn'tɛmpərət] *adj* inmoderado.
intend [ɪn'tɛnd] *vt* (*gift etc*): **to ~ sth for** destinar algo a; **to ~ to do sth** tener intención de *or* pensar hacer algo.
intended [ɪn'tɛndɪd] *adj* (*effect*) deseado.
intense [ɪn'tɛns] *adj* intenso; **to be ~** (*person*) tomárselo todo muy en serio.
intensely [ɪn'tɛnslɪ] *adv* intensamente; (*very*) sumamente.
intensify [ɪn'tɛnsɪfaɪ] *vt* intensificar; (*increase*) aumentar.
intensity [ɪn'tɛnsɪtɪ] *n* (*gen*) intensidad *f*.
intensive [ɪn'tɛnsɪv] *adj* intensivo.
intensive care *n*: **to be in ~** estar bajo cuidados intensivos; **~ unit** *n* unidad *f* de vigilancia intensiva.
intensively [ɪn'tɛnsɪvlɪ] *adv* intensivamente.
intent [ɪn'tɛnt] *n* propósito ♦ *adj* (*absorbed*) absorto; (*attentive*) atento; **to all ~s and purposes** a efectos prácticos; **to be ~ on doing sth** estar resuelto *or* decidido a hacer algo.
intention [ɪn'tɛnʃən] *n* intención *f*, propósito.
intentional [ɪn'tɛnʃənl] *adj* deliberado.
intentionally [ɪn'tɛnʃnəlɪ] *adv* a propósito.
intently [ɪn'tɛntlɪ] *adv* atentamente, fijamente.
inter [ɪn'tə:*] *vt* enterrar, sepultar.
inter- ['ɪntə*] *pref* inter-.
interact [ɪntər'ækt] *vi* (*substances*) influirse mutuamente; (*people*) relacionarse.
interaction [ɪntər'ækʃən] *n* interacción *f*, acción *f* recíproca.
interactive [ɪntər'æktɪv] *adj* (*also* COMPUT) interactivo.
intercede [ɪntə'si:d] *vi*: **to ~ (with)** interceder (con); **to ~ with sb/on behalf of sb** interceder con algn/en nombre de algn.
intercept [ɪntə'sɛpt] *vt* interceptar; (*stop*) detener.
interception [ɪntə'sɛpʃən] *n* interceptación *f*; detención *f*.
interchange *n* ['ɪntətʃeɪndʒ] intercambio; (*on motorway*) intersección *f* ♦ *vt* [ɪntə'tʃeɪndʒ] intercambiar.
interchangeable [ɪntə'tʃeɪndʒəbl] *adj* intercambiable.
intercity [ɪntə'sɪtɪ] *adj*: **~ (train)** (tren *m*) intercity *m*.
intercom ['ɪntəkɔm] *n* interfono.
interconnect [ɪntəkə'nɛkt] *vi* (*rooms*) comunicar(se).
intercontinental ['ɪntəkɔntɪ'nɛntl] *adj* intercontinental.
intercourse ['ɪntəkɔ:s] *n* (*sexual ~*) relaciones *fpl* sexuales, contacto sexual; (*social*) trato.
interdependence [ɪntədɪ'pɛndəns] *n* interdependencia.
interdependent [ɪntədɪ'pɛndənt] *adj* interdependiente.
interest ['ɪntrɪst] *n* (*also* COMM) interés *m* ♦ *vt* interesar; **compound/simple ~** interés compuesto/simple; **business ~s** negocios *mpl*; **British ~s in the Middle East** los intereses británicos en el Medio Oriente.
interested ['ɪntrɪstɪd] *adj* interesado; **to be ~ in** interesarse por.
interest-free ['ɪntrɪst'fri:] *adj* libre de interés.
interesting ['ɪntrɪstɪŋ] *adj* interesante.
interest rate *n* tipo de interés.
interface ['ɪntəfeɪs] *n* (COMPUT) junción *f*, interface *m*.
interfere [ɪntə'fɪə*] *vi*: **to ~ in** (*quarrel, other people's business*) entrometerse en; **to ~ with** (*hinder*) estorbar; (*damage*) estropear; (*radio*) interferir con.
interference [ɪntə'fɪərəns] *n* (*gen*) intromisión *f*; (RADIO, TV) interferencia.
interfering [ɪntə'fɪərɪŋ] *adj* entrometido.
interim ['ɪntərɪm] *adj*: **~ dividend** dividendo parcial ♦ *n*: **in the ~** en el ínterin.
interior [ɪn'tɪərɪə*] *n* interior *m* ♦ *adj* interior.
interior decorator, interior designer *n* interiorista *m/f*, diseñador(a) *m/f* de interiores.
interjection [ɪntə'dʒɛkʃən] *n* interrupción *f*.
interlock [ɪntə'lɔk] *vi* entrelazarse; (*wheels etc*) endentarse.
interloper ['ɪntələupə*] *n* intruso/a.
interlude ['ɪntəlu:d] *n* intervalo; (*rest*) descanso; (THEAT) intermedio.
intermarriage [ɪntə'mærɪdʒ] *n* endogamia.
intermarry [ɪntə'mærɪ] *vi* casarse (entre parientes).
intermediary [ɪntə'mi:dɪərɪ] *n* intermediario/a.
intermediate [ɪntə'mi:dɪət] *adj* intermedio.
interminable [ɪn'tə:mɪnəbl] *adj* inacabable.
intermission [ɪntə'mɪʃən] *n* (THEAT) descanso.
intermittent [ɪntə'mɪtnt] *adj* intermitente.
intermittently [ɪntə'mɪtntlɪ] *adv* intermitentemente.
intern *vt* [ɪn'tə:n] internar; (*enclose*) encerrar ♦ *n* ['ɪntə:n] (US) médico/a *m/f*

interno/a.
internal [ɪn'təːnl] *adj* interno, interior; ~ **injuries** heridas *fpl or* lesiones *fpl* internas.
internally [ɪn'təːnəlɪ] *adv* interiormente; **"not to be taken ~"** "uso externo".
Internal Revenue Service (IRS) *n* (*US*) Hacienda.
international [ɪntə'næʃənl] *adj* internacional; ~ **(game)** partido internacional; ~ **(player)** jugador(a) *m/f* internacional.
International Atomic Energy Agency (IAEA) *n* Organismo Internacional de Energía Atómica.
International Chamber of Commerce (ICC) *n* Cámara de Comercio Internacional (CCI *f*).
International Court of Justice (ICJ) *n* Corte *f* Internacional de Justicia (CIJ *f*).
international date line *n* línea de cambio de fecha.
internationally [ɪntə'næʃnəlɪ] *adv* internacionalmente.
International Monetary Fund (IMF) *n* Fondo Monetario Internacional (FMI *m*).
internee [ɪntəː'niː] *n* interno/a, recluso/a.
Internet ['ɪntənet] *n*: **the** ~ (el *or* la) Internet.
Internet café *n* cibercafé *m*.
Internet Service Provider *n* proveedor *m* de (acceso a) Internet.
internment [ɪn'təːnmənt] *n* internamiento.
interplanetary [ɪntə'plænɪtərɪ] *adj* interplanetario.
interplay ['ɪntəpleɪ] *n* interacción *f*.
Interpol ['ɪntəpɔl] *n* Interpol *f*.
interpret [ɪn'təːprɪt] *vt* interpretar; (*translate*) traducir; (*understand*) entender ♦ *vi* hacer de intérprete.
interpretation [ɪntəːprɪ'teɪʃən] *n* interpretación *f*; traducción *f*.
interpreter [ɪn'təːprɪtə*] *n* intérprete *m/f*.
interrelated [ɪntərɪ'leɪtɪd] *adj* interrelacionado.
interrogate [ɪn'tɛrəugeɪt] *vt* interrogar.
interrogation [ɪntɛrəu'geɪʃən] *n* interrogatorio.
interrogative [ɪntə'rɔgətɪv] *adj* interrogativo.
interrupt [ɪntə'rʌpt] *vt, vi* interrumpir.
interruption [ɪntə'rʌpʃən] *n* interrupción *f*.
intersect [ɪntə'sɛkt] *vt* cruzar ♦ *vi* (*roads*) cruzarse.
intersection [ɪntə'sɛkʃən] *n* intersección *f*; (*of roads*) cruce *m*.
intersperse [ɪntə'spəːs] *vt*: **to ~ with** salpicar de.
intertwine [ɪntə'twaɪn] *vt* entrelazar ♦ *vi* entrelazarse.
interval ['ɪntəvl] *n* intervalo; (*BRIT: THEAT, SPORT*) descanso; **at ~s** a ratos, de vez en cuando; **sunny ~s** (*in weather*) claros *mpl*.
intervene [ɪntə'viːn] *vi* intervenir; (*take part*) participar; (*occur*) sobrevenir.
intervening [ɪntə'viːnɪŋ] *adj* intermedio.
intervention [ɪntə'vɛnʃən] *n* intervención *f*.
interview ['ɪntəvjuː] *n* (*RADIO, TV etc*) entrevista ♦ *vt* entrevistar a.
interviewee [ɪntəvjuː'iː] *n* entrevistado/a.
interviewer ['ɪntəvjuːə*] *n* entrevistador(a) *m/f*.
intestate [ɪn'tɛstɛɪt] *adj* intestado.
intestinal [ɪn'tɛstɪnl] *adj* intestinal.
intestine [ɪn'tɛstɪn] *n*: **large/small ~** intestino grueso/delgado.
intimacy ['ɪntɪməsɪ] *n* intimidad *f*; (*relations*) relaciones *fpl* íntimas.
intimate *adj* ['ɪntɪmət] íntimo; (*friendship*) estrecho; (*knowledge*) profundo ♦ *vt* ['ɪntɪmeɪt] (*announce*) dar a entender.
intimately ['ɪntɪmətlɪ] *adv* íntimamente.
intimidate [ɪn'tɪmɪdeɪt] *vt* intimidar.
intimidation [ɪntɪmɪ'deɪʃən] *n* intimidación *f*.
into ['ɪntuː] *prep* (*gen*) en; (*towards*) a; (*inside*) hacia el interior de; ~ **3 pieces/French** en 3 pedazos/al francés; **to change pounds ~ dollars** cambiar libras por dólares.
intolerable [ɪn'tɔlərəbl] *adj* intolerable, insoportable.
intolerance [ɪn'tɔlərəns] *n* intolerancia.
intolerant [ɪn'tɔlərənt] *adj*: ~ **(of)** intolerante (con).
intonation [ɪntəu'neɪʃən] *n* entonación *f*.
intoxicate [ɪn'tɔksɪkeɪt] *vt* embriagar.
intoxicated [ɪn'tɔksɪkeɪtɪd] *adj* embriagado.
intoxication [ɪntɔksɪ'keɪʃən] *n* embriaguez *f*.
intractable [ɪn'træktəbl] *adj* (*person*) intratable; (*problem*) irresoluble; (*illness*) incurable.
intranet ['ɪntrənɛt] *n* intranet *f*.
intransigence [ɪn'trænsɪdʒəns] *n* intransigencia.
intransigent [ɪn'trænsɪdʒənt] *adj* intransigente.
intransitive [ɪn'trænsɪtɪv] *adj* intransitivo.
intravenous [ɪntrə'viːnəs] *adj* intravenoso.
in-tray ['ɪntreɪ] *n* bandeja de entrada.
intrepid [ɪn'trɛpɪd] *adj* intrépido.
intricacy ['ɪntrɪkəsɪ] *n* complejidad *f*.
intricate ['ɪntrɪkət] *adj* intrincado; (*plot, problem*) complejo.
intrigue [ɪn'triːg] *n* intriga ♦ *vt* fascinar ♦ *vi* andar en intrigas.
intriguing [ɪn'triːgɪŋ] *adj* fascinante.
intrinsic [ɪn'trɪnsɪk] *adj* intrínseco.

introduce [ɪntrə'djuːs] *vt* introducir, meter; **to ~ sb (to sb)** presentar algn (a otro); **to ~ sb to** (*pastime, technique*) introducir a algn a; **may I ~ ...?** permítame presentarle a ....
introduction [ɪntrə'dʌkʃən] *n* introducción *f*; (*of person*) presentación *f*; **a letter of ~** una carta de recomendación.
introductory [ɪntrə'dʌktərɪ] *adj* introductorio; **an ~ offer** una oferta introductoria; **~ remarks** comentarios *mpl* preliminares.
introspection [ɪntrəu'spɛkʃən] *n* introspección *f*.
introspective [ɪntrəu'spɛktɪv] *adj* introspectivo.
introvert ['ɪntrəuvəːt] *adj, n* introvertido/a *m/f*.
intrude [ɪn'truːd] *vi* (*person*) entrometerse; **to ~ on** estorbar.
intruder [ɪn'truːdə*] *n* intruso/a.
intrusion [ɪn'truːʒən] *n* invasión *f*.
intrusive [ɪn'truːsɪv] *adj* intruso.
intuition [ɪntjuː'ɪʃən] *n* intuición *f*.
intuitive [ɪn'tjuːɪtɪv] *adj* intuitivo.
intuitively [ɪn'tjuːɪtɪvlɪ] *adv* por intuición, intuitivamente.
inundate ['ɪnʌndeɪt] *vt*: **to ~ with** inundar de.
inure [ɪn'juə*] *vt*: **to ~ (to)** acostumbrar *or* habituar (a).
invade [ɪn'veɪd] *vt* invadir.
invader [ɪn'veɪdə*] *n* invasor(a) *m/f*.
invalid *n* ['ɪnvəlɪd] minusválido/a ♦ *adj* [ɪn'vælɪd] (*not valid*) inválido, nulo.
invalidate [ɪn'vælɪdeɪt] *vt* invalidar, anular.
invalid chair *n* silla de ruedas.
invaluable [ɪn'væljuəbl] *adj* inestimable.
invariable [ɪn'vɛərɪəbl] *adj* invariable.
invariably [ɪn'vɛərɪəblɪ] *adv* sin excepción, siempre; **she is ~ late** siempre llega tarde.
invasion [ɪn'veɪʒən] *n* invasión *f*.
invective [ɪn'vɛktɪv] *n* invectiva.
inveigle [ɪn'viːgl] *vt*: **to ~ sb into (doing) sth** embaucar *or* engatusar a algn para (que haga) algo.
invent [ɪn'vɛnt] *vt* inventar.
invention [ɪn'vɛnʃən] *n* invento; (*inventiveness*) inventiva; (*lie*) invención *f*.
inventive [ɪn'vɛntɪv] *adj* inventivo.
inventiveness [ɪn'vɛntɪvnɪs] *n* ingenio, inventiva.
inventor [ɪn'vɛntə*] *n* inventor(a) *m/f*.
inventory ['ɪnvəntrɪ] *n* inventario.
inventory control *n* control *m* de existencias.
inverse [ɪn'vəːs] *adj, n* inverso; **in ~ proportion (to)** en proporción inversa (a).
inversely [ɪn'vəːslɪ] *adv* a la inversa.
invert [ɪn'vəːt] *vt* invertir.
invertebrate [ɪn'vəːtɪbrət] *n* invertebrado.
inverted commas [ɪn'vəːtɪd] *npl* (*BRIT*) comillas *fpl*.
invest [ɪn'vɛst] *vt* invertir; (*fig: time, effort*) dedicar ♦ *vi* invertir; **to ~ sb with sth** conferir algo a algn.
investigate [ɪn'vɛstɪgeɪt] *vt* investigar; (*study*) estudiar, examinar.
investigation [ɪnvɛstɪ'geɪʃən] *n* investigación *f*, pesquisa; examen *m*.
investigative journalism [ɪn'vɛstɪgətɪv-] *n* periodismo de investigación.
investigator [ɪn'vɛstɪgeɪtə*] *n* investigador(a) *m/f*; **private ~** investigador(a) *m/f* privado/a.
investiture [ɪn'vɛstɪtʃə*] *n* investidura.
investment [ɪn'vɛstmənt] *n* inversión *f*.
investment grant *n* subvención *f* para la inversión.
investment income *n* ingresos *mpl* procedentes de inversiones.
investment portfolio *n* cartera de inversiones.
investment trust *n* compañía inversionista, sociedad *f* de cartera.
investor [ɪn'vɛstə*] *n* inversor(a) *m/f*.
inveterate [ɪn'vɛtərət] *adj* empedernido.
invidious [ɪn'vɪdɪəs] *adj* odioso.
invigilate [ɪn'vɪdʒɪleɪt] *vt, vi* (*in exam*) vigilar.
invigilator [ɪn'vɪdʒɪleɪtə*] *n* celador(a) *m/f*.
invigorating [ɪn'vɪgəreɪtɪŋ] *adj* vigorizante.
invincible [ɪn'vɪnsɪbl] *adj* invencible.
inviolate [ɪn'vaɪələt] *adj* inviolado.
invisible [ɪn'vɪzɪbl] *adj* invisible.
invisible assets *npl* activo invisible.
invisible ink *n* tinta simpática.
invisible mending *n* puntada invisible.
invitation [ɪnvɪ'teɪʃən] *n* invitación *f*; **at sb's ~** a invitación de algn; **by ~ only** solamente por invitación.
invite [ɪn'vaɪt] *vt* invitar; (*opinions etc*) solicitar, pedir; (*trouble*) buscarse; **to ~ sb (to do)** invitar a algn (a hacer); **to ~ sb to dinner** invitar a algn a cenar.
►**invite out** *vt* invitar a salir.
►**invite over** *vt* invitar a casa.
inviting [ɪn'vaɪtɪŋ] *adj* atractivo; (*look*) provocativo; (*food*) apetitoso.
invoice ['ɪnvɔɪs] *n* factura ♦ *vt* facturar; **to ~ sb for goods** facturar a algn las mercancías.
invoicing ['ɪnvɔɪsɪŋ] *n* facturación *f*.
invoke [ɪn'vəuk] *vt* invocar; (*aid*) pedir; (*law*) recurrir a.

involuntary [ɪn'vɔləntrɪ] *adj* involuntario.
involve [ɪn'vɔlv] *vt (entail)* suponer, implicar; **to ~ sb (in)** involucrar a algn (en).
involved [ɪn'vɔlvd] *adj* complicado; **to be/ become ~ in sth** estar involucrado/ involucrarse en algo.
involvement [ɪn'vɔlvmənt] *n (gen)* enredo; *(obligation)* compromiso; *(difficulty)* apuro.
invulnerable [ɪn'vʌlnərəbl] *adj* invulnerable.
inward ['ɪnwəd] *adj (movement)* interior, interno; *(thought, feeling)* íntimo.
inwardly ['ɪnwədlɪ] *adv (feel, think etc)* para sí, para dentro.
inward(s) ['ɪnwəd(z)] *adv* hacia dentro.
I/O *abbr (COMPUT = input/output)* E/S; **~ error** error *m* de E/S.
IOC *n abbr (= International Olympic Committee)* COI *m.*
iodine ['aɪəudiːn] *n* yodo.
ion ['aɪən] *n* ion *m.*
Ionian Sea [aɪ'əunɪən-] *n*: **the ~** el Mar Jónico.
ioniser ['aɪənaɪzə*] *n* ionizador *m.*
iota [aɪ'əutə] *n (fig)* jota, ápice *m.*
IOU *n abbr (= I owe you)* pagaré *m.*
IOW *abbr (BRIT) = Isle of Wight.*
IPA *n abbr (= International Phonetic Alphabet)* AFI *m.*
IQ *n abbr (= intelligence quotient)* C.I. *m.*
IRA *n abbr (= Irish Republican Army)* IRA *m*; *(US) = individual retirement account.*
Iran [ɪ'rɑːn] *n* Irán *m.*
Iranian [ɪ'reɪnɪən] *adj* iraní ♦ *n* iraní *m/f*; *(LING)* iraní *m.*
Iraq [ɪ'rɑːk] *n* Irak *m.*
Iraqi [ɪ'rɑːkɪ] *adj, n* irakí *m/f.*
irascible [ɪ'ræsɪbl] *adj* irascible.
irate [aɪ'reɪt] *adj* enojado, airado.
Ireland ['aɪələnd] *n* Irlanda; **Republic of ~** República de Irlanda.
iris, ~es ['aɪrɪs, -ɪz] *n (ANAT)* iris *m*; *(BOT)* lirio.
Irish ['aɪrɪʃ] *adj* irlandés/esa ♦ *n (LING)* irlandés *m*; **the ~** *npl* los irlandeses.
Irishman ['aɪrɪʃmən] *n* irlandés *m.*
Irish Sea *n*: **the ~** el Mar de Irlanda.
Irishwoman ['aɪrɪʃwumən] *n* irlandesa.
irk [əːk] *vt* fastidiar.
irksome ['əːksəm] *adj* fastidioso.
IRN *n abbr (= Independent Radio News) servicio de noticias en las cadenas de radio privadas.*
IRO *n abbr (US) = International Refugee Organization.*
iron ['aɪən] *n* hierro; *(for clothes)* plancha ♦ *adj* de hierro ♦ *vt (clothes)* planchar; **~s** *npl (chains)* grilletes *mpl.*
►**iron out** *vt (crease)* quitar; *(fig)* allanar, resolver.
Iron Curtain *n*: **the ~** el Telón de Acero.
iron foundry *n* fundición *f*, fundidora.
ironic(al) [aɪ'rɔnɪk(l)] *adj* irónico.
ironically [aɪ'rɔnɪklɪ] *adv* irónicamente.
ironing ['aɪənɪŋ] *n (act)* planchado; *(ironed clothes)* ropa planchada; *(to be ironed)* ropa por planchar.
ironing board *n* tabla de planchar.
iron lung *n (MED)* pulmón *m* de acero.
ironmonger ['aɪənmʌŋgə*] *n (BRIT)* ferretero/a; **~'s (shop)** ferretería.
iron ore *n* mineral *m* de hierro.
ironworks ['aɪənwəːks] *n* fundición *f.*
irony ['aɪrənɪ] *n* ironía; **the ~ of it is that ...** lo irónico del caso es que ....
irrational [ɪ'ræʃənl] *adj* irracional.
irreconcilable [ɪrɛkən'saɪləbl] *adj* inconciliable; *(enemies)* irreconciliable.
irredeemable [ɪrɪ'diːməbl] *adj* irredimible.
irrefutable [ɪrɪ'fjuːtəbl] *adj* irrefutable.
irregular [ɪ'rɛgjulə*] *adj* irregular; *(surface)* desigual.
irregularity [ɪrɛgju'lærɪtɪ] *n* irregularidad *f*; desigualdad *f.*
irrelevance [ɪ'rɛləvəns] *n* irrelevancia.
irrelevant [ɪ'rɛləvənt] *adj* irrelevante; **to be ~** estar fuera de lugar, no venir al caso.
irreligious [ɪrɪ'lɪdʒəs] *adj* irreligioso.
irreparable [ɪ'rɛprəbl] *adj* irreparable.
irreplaceable [ɪrɪ'pleɪsəbl] *adj* irremplazable.
irrepressible [ɪrɪ'prɛsəbl] *adj* incontenible.
irreproachable [ɪrɪ'prəutʃəbl] *adj* irreprochable.
irresistible [ɪrɪ'zɪstɪbl] *adj* irresistible.
irresolute [ɪ'rɛzəluːt] *adj* indeciso.
irrespective [ɪrɪ'spɛktɪv]: **~ of** *prep* sin tener en cuenta, no importa.
irresponsibility [ɪrɪspɔnsɪ'bɪlɪtɪ] *n* irresponsabilidad *f.*
irresponsible [ɪrɪ'spɔnsɪbl] *adj (act)* irresponsable; *(person)* poco serio.
irretrievable [ɪrɪ'triːvəbl] *adj (object)* irrecuperable; *(loss, damage)* irremediable, irreparable.
irretrievably [ɪrɪ'triːvəblɪ] *adv* irremisiblemente.
irreverence [ɪ'rɛvərns] *n* irreverencia.
irreverent [ɪ'rɛvərnt] *adj* irreverente, irrespetuoso.
irrevocable [ɪ'rɛvəkəbl] *adj* irrevocable.
irrigate ['ɪrɪgeɪt] *vt* regar.
irrigation [ɪrɪ'geɪʃən] *n* riego.
irritability [ɪrɪtə'bɪlɪtɪ] *n* irritabilidad *f.*
irritable ['ɪrɪtəbl] *adj (person: temperament)* irritable; *(: mood)* de mal humor.

irritant ['ɪrɪtənt] *n* agente *m* irritante.
irritate ['ɪrɪteɪt] *vt* fastidiar; (*MED*) picar.
irritating ['ɪrɪteɪtɪŋ] *adj* fastidioso.
irritation [ɪrɪ'teɪʃən] *n* fastidio; picazón *f*.
IRS *n abbr* (*US*) *see* **Internal Revenue Service.**
is [ɪz] *vb see* **be.**
ISA ['aɪsə] *n abbr* (*BRIT COMM = Individual Savings Account*) *plan de ahorro personal para pequeños inversores con fiscalidad cero.*
ISBN *n abbr* (= *International Standard Book Number*) ISBN *m*.
ISDN *n abbr* (= *Integrated Services Digital Network*) RDSI *f*.
Islam ['ɪzlɑːm] *n* Islam *m*.
island ['aɪlənd] *n* isla; (*also*: **traffic ~**) isleta.
islander ['aɪləndə*] *n* isleño/a.
isle [aɪl] *n* isla.
isn't ['ɪznt] = **is not.**
isobar ['aɪsəubɑː*] *n* isobara.
isolate ['aɪsəleɪt] *vt* aislar.
isolated ['aɪsəleɪtɪd] *adj* aislado.
isolation [aɪsə'leɪʃən] *n* aislamiento.
isolation ward *n* pabellón *m* de aislamiento.
isotope ['aɪsəutəup] *n* isótopo.
Israel ['ɪzreɪl] *n* Israel *m*.
Israeli [ɪz'reɪlɪ] *adj, n* israelí *m/f*.
issue ['ɪsjuː] *n* cuestión *f*, asunto; (*outcome*) resultado; (*of banknotes etc*) emisión *f*; (*of newspaper etc*) número; (*offspring*) sucesión *f*, descendencia ♦ *vt* (*rations, equipment*) distribuir, repartir; (*orders*) dar; (*certificate, passport*) expedir; (*decree*) promulgar; (*magazine*) publicar; (*cheques*) extender; (*banknotes, stamps*) emitir ♦ *vi*: **to ~ (from)** derivar (de), brotar (de); **at ~** en cuestión; **to take ~ with sb (over)** disentir con algn (en); **to avoid the ~** andarse con rodeos; **to make an ~ of sth** dar a algo más importancia de lo necesario; **to ~ sth to sb, ~ sb with sth** entregar algo a algn.
Istanbul [ɪstæn'buːl] *n* Estambul *m*.
isthmus ['ɪsməs] *n* istmo.
IT *n abbr* = **information technology.**

KEYWORD

it [ɪt] *pron* **1** (*specific: subject: not generally translated*) él/ella; (*: direct object*) lo, la; (*: indirect object*) le; (*after prep*) él/ella; (*abstract concept*) ello; **~'s on the table** está en la mesa; **I can't find ~** no lo (*or* la) encuentro; **give ~ to me** dámelo (*or* dámela); **I spoke to him about ~** le hablé del asunto; **what did you learn from ~?** ¿qué aprendiste de él (*or* ella)?; **did you go to ~?** (*party, concert*) ¿fuiste?

2 (*impersonal*): **~'s raining** llueve, está lloviendo; **~'s 6 o'clock/the 10th of August** son las 6/es el 10 de agosto; **how far is ~? — ~'s 10 miles/2 hours on the train** ¿a qué distancia está? — a 10 millas/2 horas en tren; **who is ~? — ~'s me** ¿quién es? — soy yo.

Italian [ɪ'tæljən] *adj* italiano ♦ *n* italiano/a; (*LING*) italiano.
italic [ɪ'tælɪk] *adj* cursivo; **~s** *npl* cursiva *sg*.
Italy ['ɪtəlɪ] *n* Italia.
itch [ɪtʃ] *n* picazón *f*; (*fig*) prurito ♦ *vi* (*person*) sentir *or* tener comezón; (*part of body*) picar; **to be ~ing to do sth** rabiar por *or* morirse de ganas de hacer algo.
itching ['ɪtʃɪŋ] *n* picazón *f*, comezón *f*.
itchy ['ɪtʃɪ] *adj*: **to be ~** picar.
it'd ['ɪtd] = **it would; it had.**
item ['aɪtəm] *n* artículo; (*on agenda*) asunto (a tratar); (*in programme*) número; (*also*: **news ~**) noticia; **~s of clothing** prendas *fpl* de vestir.
itemize ['aɪtəmaɪz] *vt* detallar.
itemized bill ['aɪtəmaɪzd-] *n* recibo detallado.
itinerant [ɪ'tɪnərənt] *adj* ambulante.
itinerary [aɪ'tɪnərərɪ] *n* itinerario.
it'll ['ɪtl] = **it will, it shall.**
ITN *n abbr see* **ITV.**
its [ɪts] *adj* su.
it's [ɪts] = **it is; it has.**
itself [ɪt'sɛlf] *pron* (*reflexive*) sí mismo/a; (*emphatic*) él mismo/ella misma.
ITV *n abbr* (*BRIT: = Independent Television*) *ver recuadro.*

ITV

En el Reino Unido la **ITV** (*"Independent Television*) *es una cadena de emisoras comerciales regionales con licencia exclusiva para emitir en su región. Suelen producir sus propios programas, se financian con publicidad y están bajo el control del organismo oficial independiente "Independent Broadcasting Authority" ("IBA"). El servicio de noticias nacionales e internacionales, "ITN" ("Independent Television News"), funciona como una compañía productora para toda la cadena.*

IUD *n abbr* (= *intra-uterine device*) DIU *m*.
I've [aɪv] = **I have.**
ivory ['aɪvərɪ] *n* marfil *m*.
Ivory Coast *n*: **the ~** la Costa de Marfil.
ivory tower *n* (*fig*) torre *f* de marfil.
ivy ['aɪvɪ] *n* hiedra.

Ivy League *n* (*US*) *ver recuadro.*

> **IVY LEAGUE**
>
> *Las ocho universidades más prestigiosas del nordeste de los Estados Unidos reciben el nombre colectivo de* **Ivy League**, *por sus muros cubiertos de hiedra. Son: Brown, Columbia, Cornell, Dartmouth College, Harvard, Princeton, la universidad de Pennsylvania y Yale. También se llaman así las competiciones deportivas que celebran entre ellas.*

J j

J, j [dʒeɪ] *n* (*letter*) J, j *f*; **J for Jack,** (*US*) **J for Jig** J de José.
JA *n abbr* = **judge advocate.**
J/A *abbr* = **joint account.**
jab [dʒæb] *vt* (*elbow*) dar un codazo a; (*punch*) dar un golpe rápido a ♦ *vi*: **to ~ at** intentar golpear a; **to ~ sth into sth** clavar algo en algo ♦ *n* codazo; golpe *m* (rápido); (*MED col*) pinchazo.
jabber ['dʒæbə*] *vt, vi* farfullar.
jack [dʒæk] *n* (*AUT*) gato; (*BOWLS*) boliche *m*; (*CARDS*) sota.
▸**jack in** *vt* (*col*) dejar.
▸**jack up** *vt* (*AUT*) levantar con el gato.
jackal ['dʒækl] *n* (*ZOOL*) chacal *m*.
jackass ['dʒækæs] *n* (*also fig*) asno, burro.
jackdaw ['dʒækdɔː] *n* grajo/a, chova.
jacket ['dʒækɪt] *n* chaqueta, americana, saco (*LAM*); (*of boiler etc*) camisa; (*of book*) sobrecubierta.
jacket potato *n* patata asada (con piel).
jack-in-the-box ['dʒækɪnðəbɔks] *n* caja sorpresa, caja de resorte.
jack-knife ['dʒæknaɪf] *vi* colear.
jack-of-all-trades ['dʒækəv'ɔːltreɪdz] *n* aprendiz *m* de todo.
jack plug *n* (*ELEC*) enchufe *m* de clavija.
jackpot ['dʒækpɔt] *n* premio gordo.
Jacuzzi ® [dʒə'kuːzɪ] *n* jacuzzi ® *m*.
jade [dʒeɪd] *n* (*stone*) jade *m*.
jaded ['dʒeɪdɪd] *adj* (*tired*) cansado; (*fed up*) hastiado.
jagged ['dʒægɪd] *adj* dentado.
jaguar ['dʒægjuə*] *n* jaguar *m*.
jail [dʒeɪl] *n* cárcel *f* ♦ *vt* encarcelar.
jailbird ['dʒeɪlbəːd] *n* preso/a reincidente.
jailbreak ['dʒeɪlbreɪk] *n* fuga *or* evasión *f* (de la cárcel).
jailer ['dʒeɪlə*] *n* carcelero/a.
jam [dʒæm] *n* mermelada; (*also*: **traffic ~**) atasco, embotellamiento; (*difficulty*) apuro ♦ *vt* (*passage etc*) obstruir; (*mechanism, drawer etc*) atascar; (*RADIO*) interferir ♦ *vi* atascarse, trabarse; **to get sb out of a ~** sacar a algn del paso *or* de un apuro; **to ~ sth into sth** meter algo a la fuerza en algo; **the telephone lines are ~med** las líneas están saturadas.
Jamaica [dʒə'meɪkə] *n* Jamaica.
Jamaican [dʒə'meɪkən] *adj, n* jamaicano/a *m/f*.
jamb [dʒæm] *n* jamba.
jamboree [dʒæmbə'riː] *n* congreso de niños exploradores.
jam-packed [dʒæm'pækt] *adj*: **~ (with)** atestado (de).
jam session *n* concierto improvisado de jazz/rock *etc*.
Jan. *abbr* (= *January*) ene.
jangle ['dʒæŋgl] *vi* sonar (de manera) discordante.
janitor ['dʒænɪtə*] *n* (*caretaker*) portero, conserje *m*.
January ['dʒænjuərɪ] *n* enero.
Japan [dʒə'pæn] *n* (el) Japón.
Japanese [dʒæpə'niːz] *adj* japonés/esa ♦ *n* (*pl inv*) japonés/esa *m/f*; (*LING*) japonés *m*.
jar [dʒɑː*] *n* (*glass: large*) jarra; (*: small*) tarro ♦ *vi* (*sound*) chirriar; (*colours*) desentonar.
jargon ['dʒɑːgən] *n* jerga.
jarring ['dʒɑːrɪŋ] *adj* (*sound*) discordante, desafinado; (*colour*) chocante.
Jas. *abbr* = *James*.
jasmin(e) ['dʒæzmɪn] *n* jazmín *m*.
jaundice ['dʒɔːndɪs] *n* ictericia.
jaundiced ['dʒɔːndɪst] *adj* (*fig: embittered*) amargado; (*: disillusioned*) desilusionado.
jaunt [dʒɔːnt] *n* excursión *f*.
jaunty ['dʒɔːntɪ] *adj* alegre; (*relaxed*) desenvuelto.
javelin ['dʒævlɪn] *n* jabalina.
jaw [dʒɔː] *n* mandíbula; **~s** *npl* (*TECH: of vice etc*) mordaza *sg*.
jawbone ['dʒɔːbəun] *n* mandíbula, quijada.
jay [dʒeɪ] *n* (*ZOOL*) arrendajo.
jaywalker ['dʒeɪwɔːkə*] *n* peatón/ona *m/f* imprudente.
jazz [dʒæz] *n* jazz *m*.
▸**jazz up** *vt* (*liven up*) animar.
jazz band *n* orquesta de jazz.
jazzy ['dʒæzɪ] *adj* de colores llamativos.

JCB ® *n abbr* excavadora.
JCS *n abbr (US) = Joint Chiefs of Staff.*
JD *n abbr (US: = Doctor of Laws) título universitario*; (: = *Justice Department*) Ministerio de Justicia.
jealous ['dʒɛləs] *adj* (*gen*) celoso; (*envious*) envidioso; **to be** ~ tener celos.
jealously ['dʒɛləslɪ] *adv* (*enviously*) envidiosamente; (*watchfully*) celosamente.
jealousy ['dʒɛləsɪ] *n* celos *mpl*; envidia.
jeans [dʒiːnz] *npl* (pantalones *mpl*) vaqueros *mpl or* tejanos *mpl*, bluejean *m inv* (*LAM*).
Jeep ® [dʒiːp] *n* jeep *m*.
jeer [dʒɪə*] *vi*: **to** ~ **(at)** (*boo*) abuchear; (*mock*) mofarse (de).
jeering ['dʒɪərɪŋ] *adj* (*crowd*) insolente, ofensivo ♦ *n* protestas *fpl*; (*mockery*) burlas *fpl*.
jelly ['dʒɛlɪ] *n* gelatina, jalea.
jellyfish ['dʒɛlɪfɪʃ] *n* medusa.
jemmy ['dʒɛmɪ] *n* palanqueta.
jeopardize ['dʒɛpədaɪz] *vt* arriesgar, poner en peligro.
jeopardy ['dʒɛpədɪ] *n*: **to be in** ~ estar en peligro.
jerk [dʒəːk] *n* (*jolt*) sacudida; (*wrench*) tirón *m*; (*US col*) imbécil *m/f*, pendejo/a (*LAM*) ♦ *vt* dar una sacudida a; tirar bruscamente de ♦ *vi* (*vehicle*) dar una sacudida.
jerkin ['dʒəːkɪn] *n* chaleco.
jerky ['dʒəːkɪ] *adj* espasmódico.
jerry-built ['dʒɛrɪbɪlt] *adj* mal construido.
jerry can ['dʒɛrɪ-] *n* bidón *m*.
Jersey ['dʒəːzɪ] *n* Jersey *m*.
jersey ['dʒəːzɪ] *n* jersey *m*; (*fabric*) tejido de punto.
Jerusalem [dʒə'ruːsləm] *n* Jerusalén *m*.
jest [dʒɛst] *n* broma.
jester ['dʒɛstə*] *n* bufón *m*.
Jesus ['dʒiːzəs] *n* Jesús *m*; ~ **Christ** Jesucristo.
jet [dʒɛt] *n* (*of gas, liquid*) chorro; (*AVIAT*) avión *m* a reacción.
jet-black ['dʒɛt'blæk] *adj* negro como el azabache.
jet engine *n* motor *m* a reacción.
jet lag *n* desorientación *f* por desfase horario.
jetsam ['dʒɛtsəm] *n* echazón *f*.
jet-setter ['dʒɛtsɛtə*] *n* personaje *m* de la jet.
jettison ['dʒɛtɪsn] *vt* desechar.
jetty ['dʒɛtɪ] *n* muelle *m*, embarcadero.
Jew [dʒuː] *n* judío.
jewel ['dʒuːəl] *n* joya; (*in watch*) rubí *m*.
jeweller, (*US*) **jeweler** ['dʒuːələ*] *n* joyero/a; ~**'s (shop)** joyería.
jewellery, (*US*) **jewelry** ['dʒuːəlrɪ] *n* joyas *fpl*, alhajas *fpl*.
Jewess ['dʒuːɪs] *n* judía.
Jewish ['dʒuːɪʃ] *adj* judío.
JFK *n abbr (US) = John Fitzgerald Kennedy International Airport.*
jib [dʒɪb] *vi* (*horse*) plantarse; **to** ~ **at doing sth** resistirse a hacer algo.
jibe [dʒaɪb] *n* mofa.
jiffy ['dʒɪfɪ] *n* (*col*): **in a** ~ en un santiamén.
jig [dʒɪg] *n* (*dance, tune*) giga.
jigsaw ['dʒɪgsɔː] *n* (*also*: ~ **puzzle**) rompecabezas *m inv*; (*tool*) sierra de vaivén.
jilt [dʒɪlt] *vt* dejar plantado a.
jingle ['dʒɪŋgl] *n* (*advert*) musiquilla ♦ *vi* tintinear.
jingoism ['dʒɪŋgəuɪzəm] *n* patriotería, jingoísmo.
jinx [dʒɪŋks] *n*: **there's a** ~ **on it** está gafado.
jitters ['dʒɪtəz] *npl* (*col*): **to get the** ~ ponerse nervioso.
jittery ['dʒɪtərɪ] *adj* (*col*) agitado.
jiujitsu [dʒuː'dʒɪtsuː] *n* ju-jitsu *m*.
job [dʒɔb] *n* trabajo; (*task*) tarea; (*duty*) deber *m*; (*post*) empleo; (*fam: difficulty*) dificultad *f*; **it's a good** ~ **that...** menos mal que...; **just the** ~! ¡justo lo que necesito!; **a part-time/full-time** ~ un trabajo a tiempo parcial/tiempo completo; **that's not my** ~ eso no me incumbe *or* toca a mí; **he's only doing his** ~ está cumpliendo nada más.
job centre *n* (*BRIT*) oficina de empleo.
job creation scheme *n* plan *m* de creación de puestos de trabajo.
job description *n* descripción *f* del puesto de trabajo.
jobless ['dʒɔblɪs] *adj* sin trabajo ♦ *n*: **the** ~ los parados.
job lot *n* lote *m* de mercancías, saldo.
job satisfaction *n* satisfacción *f* en el trabajo.
job security *n* garantía de trabajo.
job specification *n* especificación *f* del trabajo, profesiograma *m*.
Jock *n* (*col: Scotsman*) escocés *m*.
jockey ['dʒɔkɪ] *n* jockey *m/f* ♦ *vi*: **to** ~ **for position** maniobrar para sacar delantera.
jockey box *n* (*US AUT*) guantera.
jockstrap ['dʒɔkstræp] *n* suspensorio.
jocular ['dʒɔkjulə*] *adj* (*humorous*) gracioso; (*merry*) alegre.
jodhpurs ['dʒɔdpəːz] *npl* pantalón *msg* de montar.
jog [dʒɔg] *vt* empujar (ligeramente) ♦ *vi* (*run*) hacer footing; **to** ~ **along** (*fig*) ir tirando; **to** ~ **sb's memory** refrescar la

memoria a algn.

jogger ['dʒɔgə*] *n* corredor(a) *m/f.*

jogging ['dʒɔgɪŋ] *n* footing *m.*

john [dʒɔn] *n* (*US col*) wáter *m.*

join [dʒɔɪn] *vt* (*things*) unir, juntar; (*become member of: club*) hacerse socio de; (*POL: party*) afiliarse a; (*meet: people*) reunirse con; (*fig*) unirse a ♦ *vi* (*roads*) empalmar; (*rivers*) confluir ♦ *n* juntura; **will you ~ us for dinner?** ¿quieres cenar con nosotros?; **I'll ~ you later** me reuniré contigo luego; **to ~ forces (with)** aliarse (con).

▸**join in** *vi* tomar parte, participar ♦ *vt fus* tomar parte *or* participar en.

▸**join up** *vi* unirse; (*MIL*) alistarse.

joiner ['dʒɔɪnə*] *n* carpintero/a.

joinery ['dʒɔɪnərɪ] *n* carpintería.

joint [dʒɔɪnt] *n* (*TECH*) juntura, unión *f*; (*ANAT*) articulación *f*; (*BRIT CULIN*) pieza de carne (para asar); (*col: place*) garito ♦ *adj* (*common*) común; (*combined*) conjunto; (*responsibility*) compartido; (*committee*) mixto.

joint account (J/A) *n* (*with bank etc*) cuenta común.

jointly ['dʒɔɪntlɪ] *adv* (*gen*) en común; (*together*) conjuntamente.

joint owners *npl* copropietarios *mpl.*

joint ownership *n* copropiedad *f*, propiedad *f* común.

joint-stock bank ['dʒɔɪntstɔk-] *n* banco por acciones.

joint-stock company ['dʒɔɪntstɔk-] *n* sociedad *f* anónima.

joint venture *n* empresa conjunta.

joist [dʒɔɪst] *n* viga.

joke [dʒəuk] *n* chiste *m*; (*also*: **practical ~**) broma ♦ *vi* bromear; **to play a ~ on** gastar una broma a.

joker ['dʒəukə*] *n* chistoso/a, bromista *m/f*; (*CARDS*) comodín *m.*

joking ['dʒəukɪŋ] *n* bromas *fpl.*

jokingly ['dʒəukɪŋlɪ] *adv* en broma.

jollity ['dʒɔlɪtɪ] *n* alegría.

jolly ['dʒɔlɪ] *adj* (*merry*) alegre; (*enjoyable*) divertido ♦ *adv* (*col*) muy, la mar de ♦ *vt*: **to ~ sb along** animar *or* darle ánimos a algn; **~ good!** ¡estupendo!

jolt [dʒəult] *n* (*shake*) sacudida; (*blow*) golpe *m*; (*shock*) susto ♦ *vt* sacudir.

Jordan ['dʒɔːdən] *n* (*country*) Jordania; (*river*) Jordán *m.*

joss stick [dʒɔs-] *n* barrita de incienso, pebete *m.*

jostle ['dʒɔsl] *vt* dar empujones *or* empellones a.

jot [dʒɔt] *n*: **not one ~** ni pizca, ni un ápice.

▸**jot down** *vt* apuntar.

jotter ['dʒɔtə*] *n* (*BRIT*) bloc *m.*

journal ['dʒəːnl] *n* (*paper*) periódico; (*magazine*) revista; (*diary*) diario.

journalese [dʒəːnə'liːz] *n* (*pej*) lenguaje *m* periodístico.

journalism ['dʒəːnəlɪzəm] *n* periodismo.

journalist ['dʒəːnəlɪst] *n* periodista *m/f.*

journey ['dʒəːnɪ] *n* viaje *m*; (*distance covered*) trayecto ♦ *vi* viajar; **return ~** viaje de regreso; **a 5-hour ~** un viaje de 5 horas.

jovial ['dʒəuvɪəl] *adj* risueño, alegre.

jowl [dʒaul] *n* quijada.

joy [dʒɔɪ] *n* alegría.

joyful ['dʒɔɪful] *adj* alegre.

joyfully ['dʒɔɪfulɪ] *adv* alegremente.

joyous ['dʒɔɪəs] *adj* alegre.

joyride ['dʒɔɪraɪd] *n*: **to go for a ~** darse una vuelta en un coche robado.

joyrider ['dʒɔɪraɪdə*] *n* *persona que se da una vuelta en un coche robado.*

joystick ['dʒɔɪstɪk] *n* (*AVIAT*) palanca de mando; (*COMPUT*) palanca de control.

JP *n abbr see* **Justice of the Peace.**

Jr. *abbr* = **junior.**

JTPA *n abbr* (*US*: = *Job Training Partnership Act*) *programa gubernamental de formación profesional.*

jubilant ['dʒuːbɪlnt] *adj* jubiloso.

jubilation [dʒuːbɪ'leɪʃən] *n* júbilo.

jubilee ['dʒuːbɪliː] *n* aniversario; **silver ~** vigésimo quinto aniversario.

judge [dʒʌdʒ] *n* juez *m/f* ♦ *vt* juzgar; (*competition*) actuar de *or* ser juez en; (*estimate*) considerar; (*: weight, size etc*) calcular ♦ *vi*: **judging** *or* **to ~ by his expression** a juzgar por su expresión; **as far as I can ~** por lo que puedo entender, a mi entender; **I ~d it necessary to inform him** consideré necesario informarle.

judge advocate *n* (*MIL*) auditor *m* de guerra.

judg(e)ment ['dʒʌdʒmənt] *n* juicio; (*punishment*) sentencia, fallo; **to pass ~ (on)** (*LAW*) pronunciar *or* dictar sentencia (sobre); (*fig*) emitir un juicio crítico *or* dictaminar (sobre); **in my ~** a mi juicio.

judicial [dʒuː'dɪʃl] *adj* judicial.

judiciary [dʒuː'dɪʃɪərɪ] *n* poder *m* judicial, magistratura.

judicious [dʒuː'dɪʃəs] *adj* juicioso.

judo ['dʒuːdəu] *n* judo.

jug [dʒʌg] *n* jarro.

jugged hare [dʒʌgd-] *n* (*BRIT*) estofado de liebre.

juggernaut ['dʒʌgənɔːt] *n* (*BRIT: huge truck*) camión *m* de carga pesada.

juggle ['dʒʌgl] *vi* hacer juegos malabares.

juggler ['dʒʌglə*] *n* malabarista *m/f*.
Jugoslav ['juːgəuslɑːv] *etc* = **Yugoslav** *etc*.
jugular ['dʒʌgjulə*] *adj*: ~ **vein** (vena) yugular *f*.
juice [dʒuːs] *n* jugo, zumo (*SP*); (*of meat*) jugo; (*col*: *petrol*): **we've run out of** ~ se nos acabó la gasolina.
juicy ['dʒuːsɪ] *adj* jugoso.
jujitsu [dʒuː'dʒɪtsuː] *n* = **juijitsu**.
jukebox ['dʒuːkbɔks] *n* máquina de discos.
Jul. *abbr* (= *July*) jul.
July [dʒuː'laɪ] *n* julio; **the first of** ~ el uno *or* primero de julio; **during** ~ en el mes de julio; **in** ~ **of next year** en julio del año que viene.
jumble ['dʒʌmbl] *n* revoltijo ♦ *vt* (*also*: ~ **together**, ~ **up**: *mix up*) revolver; (: *disarrange*) mezclar.
jumble sale *n* (*BRIT*) mercadillo; *ver recuadro*.

JUMBLE SALE

En cada **jumble sale** *pueden comprarse todo tipo de objetos baratos de segunda mano, especialmente ropa, juguetes, libros, vajillas y muebles. Suelen organizarse en los locales de un colegio, iglesia, ayuntamiento o similar, con fines benéficos, bien en ayuda de una organización benéfica conocida o para solucionar problemas más concretos de la comunidad.*

jumbo (jet) ['dʒʌmbəu-] *n* jumbo.
jump [dʒʌmp] *vi* saltar, dar saltos; (*start*) sobresaltarse; (*increase*) aumentar ♦ *vt* saltar ♦ *n* salto; (*fence*) obstáculo; (*increase*) aumento; **to** ~ **the queue** (*BRIT*) colarse.
▸**jump about** *vi* dar saltos, brincar.
▸**jump at** *vt fus* (*fig*) apresurarse a aprovechar; **he** ~**ed at the offer** se apresuró a aceptar la oferta.
▸**jump down** *vi* bajar de un salto, saltar a tierra.
▸**jump up** *vi* levantarse de un salto.
jumped-up ['dʒʌmptʌp] *adj* (*pej*) engreído.
jumper ['dʒʌmpə*] *n* (*BRIT*: *pullover*) jersey *m*, suéter *m*; (*US*: *pinafore dress*) pichi *m*; (*SPORT*) saltador(a) *m/f*.
jump leads, (*US*) **jumper cables** *npl* cables *mpl* puente de batería.
jump-start ['djʌmpstɑːt] *vt* (*car*) arrancar con ayuda de otra batería *or* empujando; (*fig*: *economy*) reactivar.
jump suit *n* mono.
jumpy ['dʒʌmpɪ] *adj* nervioso.
Jun. *abbr* = **junior**; (= *June*) jun.
junction ['dʒʌŋkʃən] *n* (*BRIT*: *of roads*) cruce *m*; (*RAIL*) empalme *m*.
juncture ['dʒʌŋktʃə*] *n*: **at this** ~ en este momento, en esta coyuntura.
June [dʒuːn] *n* junio.
jungle ['dʒʌŋgl] *n* selva, jungla.
junior ['dʒuːnɪə*] *adj* (*in age*) menor, más joven; (*competition*) juvenil; (*position*) subalterno ♦ *n* menor *m/f*, joven *m/f*; **he's** ~ **to me** es menor que yo.
junior high school *n* (*US*) *centro de educación secundaria*; *see also* **high school**.
junior school *n* (*BRIT*) escuela primaria; *see also* **primary school**.
junk [dʒʌŋk] *n* (*cheap goods*) baratijas *fpl*; (*lumber*) trastos *mpl* viejos; (*rubbish*) basura; (*ship*) junco ♦ *vt* (*esp US*) deshacerse de.
junk bond *n* (*COMM*) obligación *f* basura *inv*.
junk dealer *n* vendedor(a) *m/f* de objetos usados.
junket ['dʒʌŋkɪt] *n* (*CULIN*) *dulce de leche cuajada*; (*BRIT col*): **to go on a** ~, **go** ~**ing** viajar a costa ajena *or* del erario público.
junk food *n* comida basura *or* de plástico.
junkie ['dʒʌŋkɪ] *n* (*col*) yonqui *m/f*, heroinómano/a.
junk mail *n* propaganda (buzoneada).
junk room *n* trastero.
junk shop *n* tienda de objetos usados.
junta ['dʒʌntə] *n* junta militar.
Jupiter ['dʒuːpɪtə*] *n* (*MYTHOLOGY*, *ASTRO*) Júpiter *m*.
jurisdiction [dʒuərɪs'dɪkʃən] *n* jurisdicción *f*; **it falls** *or* **comes within/outside our** ~ es/no es de nuestra competencia.
jurisprudence [dʒuərɪs'pruːdəns] *n* jurisprudencia.
juror ['dʒuərə*] *n* jurado.
jury ['dʒuərɪ] *n* jurado.
jury box *n* tribuna del jurado.
juryman ['dʒuərɪmən] *n* miembro del jurado.
just [dʒʌst] *adj* justo ♦ *adv* (*exactly*) exactamente; (*only*) sólo, solamente, no más (*LAM*); **he's** ~ **done it/left** acaba de hacerlo/irse; **I've** ~ **seen him** acabo de verle; ~ **right** perfecto; ~ **two o'clock** las dos en punto; **she's** ~ **as clever as you** es tan lista como tú; ~ **as well that...** menos mal que...; **it's** ~ **as well you didn't go** menos mal que no fuiste; **it's** ~ **as good (as)** es igual (que), es tan bueno (como); ~ **as he was leaving** en el momento en que se marchaba; **we were** ~ **going** ya nos íbamos; **I was** ~ **about to phone**

estaba a punto de llamar; ~ **before/enough** justo antes/lo suficiente; ~ **here** aquí mismo; **he** ~ **missed** falló por poco; ~ **listen to this** escucha esto un momento; ~ **ask someone the way** simplemente pregúntale a algn por dónde se va; **not** ~ **now** ahora no.

justice ['dʒʌstɪs] *n* justicia; **this photo doesn't do you** ~ esta foto no te favorece.

Justice of the Peace (JP) *n* juez *m/f* de paz; *see also* **Crown Court**.

justifiable [dʒʌstɪ'faɪəbl] *adj* justificable, justificado.

justifiably [dʒʌstɪ'faɪəblɪ] *adv* justificadamente, con razón.

justification [dʒʌstɪfɪ'keɪʃən] *n* justificación *f*.

justify ['dʒʌstɪfaɪ] *vt* justificar; (*text*) alinear, justificar; **to be justified in doing sth** tener motivo para *or* razón al hacer algo.

justly ['dʒʌstlɪ] *adv* (*gen*) justamente; (*with reason*) con razón.

justness ['dʒʌstnɪs] *n* justicia.

jut [dʒʌt] *vi* (*also*: ~ **out**) sobresalir.

jute [dʒu:t] *n* yute *m*.

juvenile ['dʒu:vənaɪl] *adj* juvenil; (*court*) de menores ♦ *n* joven *m/f*, menor *m/f* de edad.

juvenile delinquency *n* delincuencia juvenil.

juvenile delinquent *n* delincuente *m/f* juvenil.

juxtapose ['dʒʌkstəpəuz] *vt* yuxtaponer.

juxtaposition ['dʒʌkstəpə'zɪʃən] *n* yuxtaposición *f*.

Kk

K, k [keɪ] *n* (*letter*) K, k *f*; **K for King** K de Kilo.

K *abbr* (= *one thousand*) K; = **kilobyte**; (*BRIT*: = *Knight*) *caballero de una orden*.

kaftan ['kæftæn] *n* caftán *m*.

Kalahari Desert [kælə'hɑ:rɪ-] *n* desierto de Kalahari.

kale [keɪl] *n* col *f* rizada.

kaleidoscope [kə'laɪdəskəup] *n* calidoscopio.

kamikaze [kæmɪ'kɑ:zɪ] *adj* kamikaze.

Kampala [kæm'pɑ:lə] *n* Kampala.

Kampuchea [kæmpu'tʃɪə] *n* Kampuchea.

kangaroo [kæŋgə'ru:] *n* canguro.

Kans. *abbr* (*US*) = *Kansas*.

kaput [kə'put] *adj* (*col*) roto, estropeado.

karaoke [kɑ:rə'əukɪ] *n* karaoke.

karate [kə'rɑ:tɪ] *n* karate *m*.

Kashmir [kæʃ'mɪə*] *n* Cachemira.

kayak ['kaɪæk] *n* kayak *m*.

Kazakhstan [kɑ:zɑ:k'stæn] *n* Kazajstán *m*.

KC *n abbr* (*BRIT LAW*: = *King's Counsel*) *título concedido a determinados abogados*.

kd *abbr* (*US*: = *knocked down*) desmontado.

kebab [kə'bæb] *n* pincho moruno, brocheta.

keel [ki:l] *n* quilla; **on an even** ~ (*fig*) en equilibrio.

▸**keel over** *vi* (*NAUT*) zozobrar, volcarse; (*person*) desplomarse.

keen [ki:n] *adj* (*interest, desire*) grande, vivo; (*eye, intelligence*) agudo; (*competition*) intenso; (*edge*) afilado; (*BRIT*: *eager*) entusiasta; **to be** ~ **to do** *or* **on doing sth** tener muchas ganas de hacer algo; **to be** ~ **on sth/sb** interesarse por algo/uno; **I'm not** ~ **on going** no tengo ganas de ir.

keenly ['ki:nlɪ] *adv* (*enthusiastically*) con entusiasmo; (*acutely*) vivamente; (*intensely*) intensamente.

keenness ['ki:nnɪs] *n* (*eagerness*) entusiasmo, interés *m*.

keep [ki:p] *vb* (*pt, pp* **kept** [kɛpt]) *vt* (*retain, preserve*) guardar; (*hold back*) quedarse con; (*shop*) ser propietario de; (*feed*: *family etc*) mantener; (*promise*) cumplir; (*chickens, bees etc*) criar ♦ *vi* (*food*) conservarse; (*remain*) seguir, continuar ♦ *n* (*of castle*) torreón *m*; (*food etc*) comida, sustento; **to** ~ **doing sth** seguir haciendo algo; **to** ~ **sb from doing sth** impedir a algn hacer algo; **to** ~ **sth from happening** impedir que algo ocurra; **to** ~ **sb happy** tener a algn contento; **to** ~ **sb waiting** hacer esperar a algn; **to** ~ **a place tidy** mantener un lugar limpio; **to** ~ **sth to o.s.** no decirle algo a nadie; **to** ~ **time** (*clock*) mantener la hora exacta; ~ **the change** quédese con la vuelta; **to** ~ **an appointment** acudir a una cita; **to** ~ **a record** *or* **note of sth** tomar nota de *or* apuntar algo; *see also* **keeps**.

▸**keep away** *vt*: **to** ~ **sth/sb away from sb** mantener algo/a algn apartado de algn ♦ *vi*: **to** ~ **away (from)** mantenerse apartado (de).

▸**keep back** *vt* (*crowd, tears*) contener; (*money*) quedarse con; (*conceal*: *information*): **to** ~ **sth back from sb** ocultar algo a algn ♦ *vi* hacerse a un lado.

▸**keep down** *vt* (*control*: *prices, spending*)

controlar; (*retain: food*) retener ♦ *vi* seguir agachado, no levantar la cabeza.
▸**keep in** *vt* (*invalid, child*) impedir que salga, no dejar salir; (*SCOL*) castigar (a quedarse en el colegio) ♦ *vi* (*col*): **to ~ in with sb** mantener la relación con algn.
▸**keep off** *vt* (*dog, person*) mantener a distancia ♦ *vi* evitar; ~ **your hands off!** ¡no toques!; "~ **off the grass**" "prohibido pisar el césped".
▸**keep on** *vi* seguir, continuar.
▸**keep out** *vi* (*stay out*) permanecer fuera; "~ **out**" "prohibida la entrada".
▸**keep up** *vt* mantener, conservar ♦ *vi* no rezagarse; (*fig: in comprehension*) seguir (el hilo); **to ~ up with** (*pace*) ir al paso de; (*level*) mantenerse a la altura de; **to ~ up with sb** seguir el ritmo a algn; (*fig*) seguir a algn.
keeper ['ki:pə*] *n* guarda *m/f*.
keep-fit [ki:p'fɪt] *n* gimnasia (de mantenimiento).
keeping ['ki:pɪŋ] *n* (*care*) cuidado; **in ~ with** de acuerdo con.
keeps [ki:ps] *n*: **for ~** (*col*) para siempre.
keepsake ['ki:pseɪk] *n* recuerdo.
keg [kɛg] *n* barrilete *m*, barril *m*.
Ken. *abbr* (*US*) = *Kentucky*.
kennel ['kɛnl] *n* perrera; **~s** *npl* perrera.
Kenya ['ki:njə] *n* Kenia.
Kenyan ['ki:njən] *adj, n* keniata *m/f*, keniano/a *m/f*.
kept [kɛpt] *pt, pp of* **keep**.
kerb [kə:b] *n* (*BRIT*) bordillo.
kerb crawler [-krɔ:lə*] *n conductor en busca de prostitutas desde su coche*.
kernel ['kə:nl] *n* (*nut*) fruta; (*fig*) meollo.
kerosene ['kɛrəsi:n] *n* keroseno.
kestrel ['kɛstrəl] *n* cernícalo.
ketchup ['kɛtʃəp] *n* salsa de tomate, ketchup *m*.
kettle ['kɛtl] *n* hervidor *m*.
kettle drum *n* (*MUS*) timbal *m*.
key [ki:] *n* (*gen*) llave *f*; (*MUS*) tono; (*of piano, typewriter*) tecla; (*on map*) clave *f* ♦ *cpd* (*vital: position, industry etc*) clave ♦ *vt* (*also*: ~ **in**) teclear.
keyboard ['ki:bɔ:d] *n* teclado ♦ *vt* (*text*) teclear.
keyboarder ['ki:bɔ:də*] *n* teclista *m/f*.
keyed up [ki:d-] *adj* (*person*) nervioso; **to be (all)** ~ estar nervioso *or* emocionado.
keyhole ['ki:həul] *n* ojo (de la cerradura).
keyhole surgery *n* cirugía cerrada *or* no invasiva.
key man *n* hombre *m* clave.
keynote ['ki:nəut] *n* (*MUS*) tónica; (*fig*) idea fundamental.
keynote speech *n* discurso de apertura.
keypad ['ki:pæd] *n* teclado numérico.
keyring ['ki:rɪŋ] *n* llavero.
keystone ['ki:stəun] *n* piedra clave.
keystroke ['ki:strəuk] *n* pulsación *f* (de una tecla).
kg *abbr* (= *kilogram*) kg.
KGB *n abbr* KGB *m*.
khaki ['kɑ:kɪ] *n* caqui.
kibbutz, ~im [kɪ'buts, -ɪm] *n* kibutz *m*.
kick [kɪk] *vt* (*person*) dar una patada a; (*ball*) dar un puntapié a ♦ *vi* (*horse*) dar coces ♦ *n* patada; puntapié *m*, tiro; (*of rifle*) culetazo; (*col: thrill*): **he does it for ~s** lo hace por pura diversión.
▸**kick around** *vt* (*idea*) dar vueltas a; (*person*) tratar a patadas a.
▸**kick off** *vi* (*SPORT*) hacer el saque inicial.
kick-start ['kɪkstɑ:t] *n* (*also*: **~er**) (pedal *m* de) arranque *m*.
kid [kɪd] *n* (*col: child*) niño/a, chiquillo/a; (*animal*) cabrito; (*leather*) cabritilla ♦ *vi* (*col*) bromear.
kid gloves *npl*: **to treat sb with ~** andarse con pies de plomo con algn.
kidnap ['kɪdnæp] *vt* secuestrar.
kidnapper ['kɪdnæpə*] *n* secuestrador(a) *m/f*.
kidnapping ['kɪdnæpɪŋ] *n* secuestro.
kidney ['kɪdnɪ] *n* riñón *m*.
kidney bean *n* judía, alubia.
kidney machine *n* riñón *m* artificial.
Kilimanjaro [kɪlɪmæn'dʒɑ:rəu] *n* Kilimanjaro.
kill [kɪl] *vt* matar; (*murder*) asesinar; (*fig: rumour, conversation*) acabar con ♦ *n* matanza; **to ~ time** matar el tiempo.
▸**kill off** *vt* exterminar, terminar con; (*fig*) echar por tierra.
killer ['kɪlə*] *n* asesino/a.
killer instinct *n*: **to have the ~** ir a por todas.
killing ['kɪlɪŋ] *n* (*one*) asesinato; (*several*) matanza; (*COMM*): **to make a ~** tener un gran éxito financiero.
killjoy ['kɪldʒɔɪ] *n* (*BRIT*) aguafiestas *m/f inv*.
kiln [kɪln] *n* horno.
kilo ['ki:ləu] *n* (*abbr*. = *kilogram(me)*) kilo.
kilobyte ['kɪləubaɪt] *n* (*COMPUT*) kilobyte *m*, kiloocteto.
kilogram(me) ['kɪləugræm] *n* kilogramo.
kilometre, (*US*) **kilometer** ['kɪləmi:tə*] *n* kilómetro.
kilowatt ['kɪləuwɔt] *n* kilovatio.
kilt [kɪlt] *n* falda escocesa.
kilter ['kɪltə*] *n*: **out of ~** desbaratado.
kimono [kɪ'məunəu] *n* quimono.
kin [kɪn] *n* parientes *mpl*.

kind [kaɪnd] *adj* (*treatment*) bueno, cariñoso; (*person, act, word*) amable, atento ♦ *n* clase *f*, especie *f*; (*species*) género; **in ~** (*COMM*) en especie; **a ~ of** una especie de; **to be two of a ~** ser tal para cual; **would you be ~ enough to ...?, would you be so ~ as to ...?** ¿me hace el favor de ...?; **it's very ~ of you (to do)** le agradezco mucho (el que haya hecho).
kindergarten ['kɪndəgɑːtn] *n* jardín *m* de infancia.
kind-hearted [kaɪnd'hɑːtɪd] *adj* bondadoso, de buen corazón.
kindle ['kɪndl] *vt* encender.
kindliness ['kaɪndlɪnəs] *n* bondad *f*, amabilidad *f*.
kindling ['kɪndlɪŋ] *n* leña (menuda).
kindly ['kaɪndlɪ] *adj* bondadoso; (*gentle*) cariñoso ♦ *adv* bondadosamente, amablemente; **will you ~ ...** sería usted tan amable de ....
kindness ['kaɪndnɪs] *n* bondad *f*, amabilidad *f*.
kindred ['kɪndrɪd] *n* familia, parientes *mpl* ♦ *adj*: **~ spirits** almas *fpl* gemelas.
kinetic [kɪ'nɛtɪk] *adj* cinético.
king [kɪŋ] *n* rey *m*.
kingdom ['kɪŋdəm] *n* reino.
kingfisher ['kɪŋfɪʃə*] *n* martín *m* pescador.
kingpin ['kɪŋpɪn] *n* (*TECH*) perno real *or* pinzote; (*fig*) persona clave.
king-size(d) ['kɪŋsaɪz(d)] *adj* de tamaño gigante; (*cigarette*) extra largo.
kink [kɪŋk] *n* (*in rope etc*) enroscadura; (*in hair*) rizo; (*fig: emotional, psychological*) manía.
kinky ['kɪŋkɪ] *adj* (*pej*) perverso.
kinship ['kɪnʃɪp] *n* parentesco; (*fig*) afinidad *f*.
kinsman ['kɪnzmən] *n* pariente *m*.
kinswoman ['kɪnzwumən] *n* parienta.
kiosk ['kiːɔsk] *n* quiosco; (*BRIT TEL*) cabina; **newspaper ~** quiosco, kiosco.
kipper ['kɪpə*] *n* arenque *m* ahumado.
Kirghizia [kəː'gɪzɪə] *n* Kirguizistán *m*.
kiss [kɪs] *n* beso ♦ *vt* besar; **~ of life** (*artificial respiration*) respiración *f* artificial; **to ~ sb goodbye** dar un beso de despedida a algn; **to ~ (each other)** besarse.
kissogram ['kɪsəgræm] *n servicio de felicitaciones mediante el que se envía a una persona vestida de manera sugerente para besar a algn.*
kit [kɪt] *n* equipo; (*set of tools etc*) (caja de) herramientas *fpl*; (*assembly ~*) juego de armar; **tool ~** juego *or* estuche *m* de herramientas.
▸**kit out** *vt* equipar.
kitbag ['kɪtbæg] *n* (*MIL*) macuto.
kitchen ['kɪtʃɪn] *n* cocina.
kitchen garden *n* huerto.
kitchen sink *n* fregadero.
kitchen unit *n* módulo de cocina.
kitchenware ['kɪtʃɪnwɛə*] *n* batería de cocina.
kite [kaɪt] *n* (*toy*) cometa.
kith [kɪθ] *n*: **~ and kin** parientes *mpl* y allegados.
kitten ['kɪtn] *n* gatito/a.
kitty ['kɪtɪ] *n* (*pool of money*) fondo común; (*CARDS*) bote *m*.
kiwi ['kiːwiː] *n* (*col: New Zealander*) neozelandés/esa *m/f*; (*also*: **~ fruit**) kiwi *m*.
KKK *n abbr* (*US*) = *Ku Klux Klan.*
kleptomaniac [klɛptəu'meɪnɪæk] *n* cleptómano/a.
km *abbr* (= *kilometre*) km.
km/h *abbr* (= *kilometres per hour*) km/h.
knack [næk] *n*: **to have the ~ of doing sth** tener facilidad para hacer algo.
knackered ['nækəd] *adj* (*col*) hecho polvo.
knapsack ['næpsæk] *n* mochila.
knead [niːd] *vt* amasar.
knee [niː] *n* rodilla.
kneecap ['niːkæp] *vt* destrozar a tiros la rótula de ♦ *n* rótula.
knee-deep ['niː'diːp] *adj*: **the water was ~** el agua llegaba hasta la rodilla.
kneel, *pt, pp* **knelt** [niːl, nɛlt] *vi* (*also*: **~ down**) arrodillarse.
kneepad ['niːpæd] *n* rodillera.
knell [nɛl] *n* toque *m* de difuntos.
knelt [nɛlt] *pt, pp of* **kneel**.
knew [njuː] *pt of* **know**.
knickers ['nɪkəz] *npl* (*BRIT*) bragas *fpl*, calzones *mpl* (*LAM*).
knick-knack ['nɪknæk] *n* chuchería, baratija.
knife [naɪf] (*pl* **knives**) *n* cuchillo ♦ *vt* acuchillar; **~, fork and spoon** cubiertos *mpl*.
knife edge *n*: **to be on a ~** estar en la cuerda floja.
knight [naɪt] *n* caballero; (*CHESS*) caballo.
knighthood ['naɪthud] *n* (*title*): **to get a ~** recibir el título de *Sir*.
knit [nɪt] *vt* tejer, tricotar; (*brows*) fruncir; (*fig*): **to ~ together** unir, juntar ♦ *vi* hacer punto, tejer, tricotar; (*bones*) soldarse.
knitted ['nɪtɪd] *adj* de punto.
knitting ['nɪtɪŋ] *n* labor *f* de punto.
knitting machine *n* máquina de tricotar.
knitting needle, (*US*) **knit pin** *n* aguja de hacer punto *or* tejer.
knitting pattern *n* patrón *m* para tricotar.
knitwear ['nɪtwɛə*] *n* prendas *fpl* de punto.

knives [naɪvz] *pl of* **knife.**
knob [nɔb] *n* (*of door*) pomo; (*of stick*) puño; (*lump*) bulto; (*fig*): **a ~ of butter** (*BRIT*) un pedazo de mantequilla.
knobbly ['nɔblɪ], (*US*) **knobby** ['nɔbɪ] *adj* (*wood, surface*) nudoso; (*knee*) huesudo.
knock [nɔk] *vt* (*strike*) golpear; (*bump into*) chocar contra; (*fig: col*) criticar ♦ *vi* (*at door etc*): **to ~ at/on** llamar a ♦ *n* golpe *m*; (*on door*) llamada; **he ~ed at the door** llamó a la puerta.
▶**knock down** *vt* (*pedestrian*) atropellar; (*price*) rebajar.
▶**knock off** *vi* (*col: finish*) salir del trabajo ♦ *vt* (*col: steal*) birlar; (*strike off*) quitar; (*fig: from price, record*): **to ~ off £10** rebajar en £10.
▶**knock out** *vt* dejar sin sentido; (*BOXING*) poner fuera de combate, dejar K.O.; (*stop*) estropear, dejar fuera de servicio.
▶**knock over** *vt* (*object*) derribar, tirar; (*pedestrian*) atropellar.
knockdown ['nɔkdaun] *adj* (*price*) de saldo.
knocker ['nɔkə*] *n* (*on door*) aldaba.
knocking ['nɔkɪŋ] *n* golpes *mpl*, golpeteo.
knock-kneed [nɔk'ni:d] *adj* patizambo.
knockout ['nɔkaut] *n* (*BOXING*) K.O. *m*, knockout *m*.
knock-up ['nɔkʌp] *n* (*TENNIS*) peloteo.
knot [nɔt] *n* (*gen*) nudo ♦ *vt* anudar; **to tie a ~** hacer un nudo.
knotted ['nɔtɪd] *adj* anudado.
knotty ['nɔtɪ] *adj* (*fig*) complicado.
know [nəu] *vb* (*pt* **knew**, *pp* **known** [nju:, nəun]) *vt* (*gen*) saber; (*person, author, place*) conocer ♦ *vi*: **as far as I ~** ... que yo sepa ...; **yes, I ~** sí, ya lo sé; **I don't ~** no lo sé; **to ~ how to do** saber hacer; **to ~ how to swim** saber nadar; **to ~ about** *or* **of sb/sth** saber de algn/algo; **to get to ~ sth** enterarse de algo; **I ~ nothing about it** no sé nada de eso; **I don't ~ him** no lo *or* le conozco; **to ~ right from wrong** saber distinguir el bien del mal.
know-all ['nəuɔ:l] *n* (*BRIT pej*) sabelotodo *m/f inv*, sabihondo/a.
know-how ['nəuhau] *n* conocimientos *mpl*.
knowing ['nəuɪŋ] *adj* (*look*) de complicidad.
knowingly ['nəuɪŋlɪ] *adv* (*purposely*) a sabiendas; (*smile, look*) con complicidad.
know-it-all ['nəuɪtɔ:l] *n* (*US*) = **know-all.**
knowledge ['nɔlɪdʒ] *n* (*gen*) conocimiento; (*learning*) saber *m*, conocimientos *mpl*; **to have no ~ of** no saber nada de; **with my ~** con mis conocimientos, sabiéndolo; **to (the best of) my ~** a mi entender, que yo sepa; **not to my ~** que yo sepa, no; **it is common ~ that** ... es del dominio público que ...; **it has come to my ~ that** ... me he enterado de que ...; **to have a working ~ of Spanish** defenderse con el español.
knowledgeable ['nɔlɪdʒəbl] *adj* entendido.
known [nəun] *pp of* **know** ♦ *adj* (*thief, facts*) conocido; (*expert*) reconocido.
knuckle ['nʌkl] *n* nudillo.
▶**knuckle down** *vi* (*col*) ponerse a trabajar en serio.
▶**knuckle under** *vi* someterse.
knuckleduster ['nʌkldʌstə*] *n* puño de hierro.
KO *abbr n* (= *knockout*) K.O. *m* ♦ *vt* (= *knock out*) dejar K.O.
kook [ku:k] *n* (*US col*) chiflado/a *m/f*, majareta *m/f*.
Koran [kɔ'rɑ:n] *n* Corán *m*.
Korea [kə'rɪə] *n* Corea; **North/South ~** Corea del Norte/Sur.
Korean [kə'rɪən] *adj, n* coreano/a *m/f*.
kosher ['kəuʃə*] *adj* autorizado por la ley judía.
Kosovan ['kɒsəvən], **Kosovar** ['kɒsəvɑ:*] *adj* Kosovar.
Kosovo ['kɒsəvəu] *n* Kosovo *m*.
kowtow ['kau'tau] *vi*: **to ~ to sb** humillarse ante algn.
KS *abbr* (*US*) = *Kansas*.
Kt *abbr* (*BRIT*: = *Knight*) *caballero de una orden.*
Kuala Lumpur ['kwɑ:lə'lumpuə*] *n* Kuala Lumpur *m*.
kudos ['kju:dɔs] *n* gloria, prestigio.
Kurd [kə:d] *n* kurdo/a.
Kuwait [ku'weɪt] *n* Kuwait *m*.
Kuwaiti [ku'weɪtɪ] *adj, n* Kuwaití *m/f*.
kW *abbr* (= *kilowatt*) Kv.
KY, Ky. *abbr* (*US*) = *Kentucky*.

L l

L, l [ɛl] *n* (*letter*) L, l *f*; **L for Lucy**, (*US*) **L for Love** L de Lorenzo.
L *abbr* (*on maps etc*) = **lake; large**; (= *left*) izq.; (*BRIT AUT*: = *learner*) L.
l. *abbr* = **litre.**
LA *n abbr* (*US*) = *Los Angeles* ♦ *abbr* (*US*) = *Louisiana*.
La. *abbr* (*US*) = *Louisiana*.
lab [læb] *n abbr* = **laboratory.**
Lab. *abbr* (*Canada*) = *Labrador*.

label ['leɪbl] *n* etiqueta; (*brand: of record*) sello (discográfico) ♦ *vt* poner una etiqueta a, etiquetar.
labor *etc* ['leɪbə*] (*US*) = **labour**.
laboratory [lə'bɔrətərɪ] *n* laboratorio.
Labor Day *n* (*US*) día *m* de los trabajadores (*primer lunes de septiembre*).
laborious [lə'bɔːrɪəs] *adj* penoso.
laboriously [lə'bɔːrɪəslɪ] *adv* penosamente.
labor union *n* (*US*) sindicato.
labor unrest *n* (*US*) conflictividad *f* laboral.
Labour ['leɪbə*] *n* (*BRIT POL*: *also*: **the ~ Party**) el partido laborista, los laboristas.
labour, (*US*) **labor** ['leɪbə*] *n* (*task*) trabajo; (*~ force*) mano *f* de obra; (*workers*) trabajadores *mpl*; (*MED*) (dolores *mpl* de) parto ♦ *vi*: **to ~ (at)** trabajar (en) ♦ *vt* insistir en; **hard ~** trabajos *mpl* forzados; **to be in ~** estar de parto.
labo(u)r cost *n* costo de la mano de obra.
labo(u)r dispute *n* conflicto laboral.
labo(u)red ['leɪbəd] *adj* (*breathing*) fatigoso; (*style*) forzado, pesado.
labo(u)rer ['leɪbərə*] *n* peón *m*; (*on farm*) peón *m*, obrero; (*day ~*) jornalero.
labo(u)r force *n* mano *f* de obra.
labo(u)r-intensive [leɪbərɪn'tɛnsɪv] *adj* que necesita mucha mano de obra.
labo(u)r relations *npl* relaciones *fpl* laborales.
labo(u)r-saving ['leɪbəseɪvɪŋ] *adj* que ahorra trabajo.
laburnum [lə'bəːnəm] *n* codeso.
labyrinth ['læbɪrɪnθ] *n* laberinto.
lace [leɪs] *n* encaje *m*; (*of shoe etc*) cordón *m* ♦ *vt* (*shoes*: *also*: **~ up**) atarse; (*drink*: *fortify with spirits*) echar licor a.
lacemaking ['leɪsmeɪkɪŋ] *n* obra de encaje.
lacerate ['læsəreɪt] *vt* lacerar.
laceration [læsə'reɪʃən] *n* laceración *f*.
lace-up ['leɪsʌp] *adj* (*shoes etc*) con cordones.
lack [læk] *n* (*absence*) falta, carencia; (*scarcity*) escasez *f* ♦ *vt* faltarle a algn, carecer de; **through** *or* **for ~ of** por falta de; **to be ~ing** faltar, no haber.
lackadaisical [lækə'deɪzɪkl] *adj* (*careless*) descuidado; (*indifferent*) indiferente.
lackey ['lækɪ] *n* (*also fig*) lacayo.
lacklustre, (*US*) **lackluster** ['læklʌstə*] *adj* (*surface*) deslustrado, deslucido; (*style*) inexpresivo; (*eyes*) apagado.
laconic [lə'kɔnɪk] *adj* lacónico.
lacquer ['lækə*] *n* laca; **hair ~** laca para el pelo.
lacrosse [lə'krɔs] *n* lacrosse *f*.
lacy ['leɪsɪ] *adj* (*like lace*) parecido al encaje.
lad [læd] *n* muchacho, chico; (*in stable etc*) mozo.
ladder ['lædə*] *n* escalera (de mano); (*BRIT*: *in tights*) carrera ♦ *vt* (*BRIT*: *tights*) hacer una carrera en.
laden ['leɪdn] *adj*: **~ (with)** cargado (de); **fully ~** (*truck, ship*) cargado hasta el tope.
ladle ['leɪdl] *n* cucharón *m*.
lady ['leɪdɪ] *n* señora; (*distinguished, noble*) dama; **young ~** señorita; **the ladies' (room)** los servicios de señoras.
ladybird ['leɪdɪbəːd], (*US*) **ladybug** ['leɪdɪbʌg] *n* mariquita.
lady doctor *n* médica, doctora.
lady-in-waiting ['leɪdɪɪn'weɪtɪŋ] *n* dama de honor.
ladykiller ['leɪdɪkɪlə*] *n* robacorazones *m inv*.
ladylike ['leɪdɪlaɪk] *adj* fino.
Ladyship ['leɪdɪʃɪp] *n*: **your ~** su Señoría.
LAFTA *n abbr* (= *Latin American Free Trade Association*) ALALC *f*.
lag [læg] *vi* (*also*: **~ behind**) retrasarse, quedarse atrás ♦ *vt* (*pipes*) revestir.
lager ['lɑːgə*] *n* cerveza (rubia).
lager lout *n* (*BRIT col*) gamberro borracho.
lagging ['lægɪŋ] *n* revestimiento.
lagoon [lə'guːn] *n* laguna.
Lagos ['leɪgɔs] *n* Lagos *m*.
laid [leɪd] *pt, pp of* **lay**.
laid-back [leɪd'bæk] *adj* (*col*) tranquilo, relajado.
laid up *adj*: **to be ~** (*person*) tener que guardar cama.
lain [leɪn] *pp of* **lie**.
lair [lɛə*] *n* guarida.
laissez-faire [lɛseɪ'fɛə*] *n* laissez-faire *m*.
laity ['leɪtɪ] *n* laicado.
lake [leɪk] *n* lago.
Lake District *n* (*BRIT*): **the ~** la Región de los Lagos.
lamb [læm] *n* cordero; (*meat*) carne *f* de cordero.
lamb chop *n* chuleta de cordero.
lambswool ['læmzwul] *n* lana de cordero.
lame [leɪm] *adj* cojo, rengo (*LAM*); (*weak*) débil, poco convincente; **~ duck** (*fig*: *person*) inútil *m/f*; (*: firm*) empresa en quiebra.
lamely ['leɪmlɪ] *adv* (*fig*) sin convicción.
lament [lə'mɛnt] *n* lamento ♦ *vt* lamentarse de.
lamentable ['læməntəbl] *adj* lamentable.
lamentation [læmən'teɪʃən] *n* lamento.
laminated ['læmɪneɪtɪd] *adj* laminado.
lamp [læmp] *n* lámpara.
lamplight ['læmplaɪt] *n*: **by ~** a la luz de la lámpara.

lampoon [læm'pu:n] *vt* satirizar.
lamppost ['læmppəust] *n* (*BRIT*) farola.
lampshade ['læmpʃeɪd] *n* pantalla.
lance [lɑ:ns] *n* lanza ♦ *vt* (*MED*) abrir con lanceta.
lance corporal *n* (*BRIT*) soldado de primera clase.
lancet ['lɑ:nsɪt] *n* (*MED*) lanceta.
Lancs [læŋks] *abbr* (*BRIT*) = *Lancashire.*
land [lænd] *n* tierra; (*country*) país *m*; (*piece of* ~) terreno; (*estate*) tierras *fpl*, finca; (*AGR*) campo ♦ *vi* (*from ship*) desembarcar; (*AVIAT*) aterrizar; (*fig*: *fall*) caer ♦ *vt* (*obtain*) conseguir; (*passengers, goods*) desembarcar; **to go/travel by** ~ ir/viajar por tierra; **to own** ~ ser dueño de tierras; **to** ~ **on one's feet** caer de pie; (*fig*: *to be lucky*) salir bien parado.
►**land up** *vi*: **to** ~ **up in/at** ir a parar a/en.
landed ['lændɪd] *adj*: ~ **gentry** terratenientes *mpl*.
landfill site ['lændfɪl-] *n* vertedero.
landing ['lændɪŋ] *n* desembarco; aterrizaje *m*; (*of staircase*) rellano.
landing card *n* tarjeta de desembarque.
landing craft *n* lancha de desembarco.
landing gear *n* (*AVIAT*) tren *m* de aterrizaje.
landing stage *n* (*BRIT*) desembarcadero.
landing strip *n* pista de aterrizaje.
landlady ['lændleɪdɪ] *n* (*of boarding house*) patrona; (*owner*) dueña.
landlocked ['lændlɔkt] *adj* cercado de tierra.
landlord ['lændlɔ:d] *n* propietario; (*of pub etc*) patrón *m*.
landlubber ['lændlʌbə*] *n* marinero de agua dulce.
landmark ['lændmɑ:k] *n* lugar *m* conocido; **to be a** ~ (*fig*) hacer época.
landowner ['lændəunə*] *n* terrateniente *m/f*.
landscape ['lænskeɪp] *n* paisaje *m*.
landscape architecture *n* arquitectura paisajista.
landscaped ['lænskeɪpt] *adj* reformado artísticamente.
landscape gardener *n* diseñador(a) *m/f* de paisajes.
landscape gardening *n* jardinería paisajista.
landscape painting *n* (*ART*) paisaje *m*.
landslide ['lændslaɪd] *n* (*GEO*) corrimiento de tierras; (*fig*: *POL*) victoria arrolladora.
lane [leɪn] *n* (*in country*) camino; (*in town*) callejón *m*; (*AUT*) carril *m*; (*in race*) calle *f*; (*for air or sea traffic*) ruta; **shipping** ~ ruta marina.
language ['læŋgwɪdʒ] *n* lenguaje *m*; (*national tongue*) idioma *m*, lengua; **bad** ~ palabrotas *fpl*.
language laboratory *n* laboratorio de idiomas.
language studies *npl* estudios *mpl* filológicos.
languid ['læŋgwɪd] *adj* lánguido.
languish ['læŋgwɪʃ] *vi* languidecer.
languor ['læŋgə*] *n* languidez *f*.
languorous ['læŋgərəs] *adj* lánguido.
lank [læŋk] *adj* (*hair*) lacio.
lanky ['læŋkɪ] *adj* larguirucho.
lanolin(e) ['lænəlɪn] *n* lanolina.
lantern ['læntn] *n* linterna, farol *m*.
lanyard ['lænjed] *n* acollador *m*.
Laos [laus] *n* Laos *m*.
lap [læp] *n* (*of track*) vuelta; (*of body*): **to sit on sb's** ~ sentarse en las rodillas de algn ♦ *vt* (*also*: ~ **up**) beber a lengüetadas *or* con la lengua ♦ *vi* (*waves*) chapotear.
►**lap up** *vt* beber a lengüetadas *or* con la lengua; (*fig*: *compliments, attention*) disfrutar; (*lies etc*) tragarse.
La Paz [læ'pæz] *n* La Paz.
lapdog ['læpdɔg] *n* perro faldero.
lapel [lə'pɛl] *n* solapa.
Lapland ['læplænd] *n* Laponia.
Laplander ['læplændə*] *n* lapón/ona *m/f*.
lapse [læps] *n* (*fault*) error *m*, fallo; (*moral*) desliz *m* ♦ *vi* (*expire*) caducar; (*morally*) cometer un desliz; (*time*) pasar, transcurrir; **to** ~ **into bad habits** volver a las andadas; ~ **of time** lapso, período; **a** ~ **of memory** un lapsus de memoria.
laptop ['læptɔp] *n* (*also*: ~ **computer**) (ordenador *m*) portátil *m*.
larceny ['lɑ:sənɪ] *n* latrocinio.
lard [lɑ:d] *n* manteca (de cerdo).
larder ['lɑ:də*] *n* despensa.
large [lɑ:dʒ] *adj* grande ♦ *adv*: **by and** ~ en general, en términos generales; **at** ~ (*free*) en libertad; (*generally*) en general; **to make** ~**(r)** hacer mayor *or* más extenso; **a** ~ **number of people** una gran cantidad de personas; **on a** ~ **scale** a gran escala.
largely ['lɑ:dʒlɪ] *adv* en gran parte.
large-scale ['lɑ:dʒ'skeɪl] *adj* (*map, drawing*) a gran escala; (*reforms, business activities*) importante.
largesse [lɑ:'ʒɛs] *n* generosidad *f*.
lark [lɑ:k] *n* (*bird*) alondra; (*joke*) broma.
►**lark about** *vi* bromear, hacer el tonto.
larva, *pl* **larvae** ['lɑ:və, -i:] *n* larva.
laryngitis [lærɪn'dʒaɪtɪs] *n* laringitis *f*.
larynx ['lærɪŋks] *n* laringe *f*.
lasagne [lə'zænjə] *n* lasaña.

lascivious [lə'sɪvɪəs] *adj* lascivo.
laser ['leɪzə*] *n* láser *m*.
laser beam *n* rayo láser.
laser printer *n* impresora láser.
lash [læʃ] *n* latigazo; (*punishment*) azote *m*; (*also*: **eye~**) pestaña ♦ *vt* azotar; (*tie*) atar.
▸**lash down** *vt* sujetar con cuerdas ♦ *vi* (*rain*) caer a trombas.
▸**lash out** *vi* (*col*: *spend*) gastar a la loca; **to ~ out at** *or* **against sb** lanzar invectivas contra algn.
lashing ['læʃɪŋ] *n* (*beating*) azotaina, flagelación *f*; **~s of** (*col*) montones *mpl* de.
lass [læs] *n* chica.
lassitude ['læsɪtju:d] *n* lasitud *f*.
lasso [læ'su:] *n* lazo ♦ *vt* coger con lazo.
last [lɑ:st] *adj* (*gen*) último; (*final*) último, final ♦ *adv* por último ♦ *vi* (*endure*) durar; (*continue*) continuar, seguir; **~ night** anoche; **~ week** la semana pasada; **at ~** por fin; **~ but one** penúltimo; **~ time** la última vez; **it ~s (for) 2 hours** dura dos horas.
last-ditch ['lɑ:st'dɪtʃ] *adj* (*attempt*) de último recurso, último, desesperado.
lasting ['lɑ:stɪŋ] *adj* duradero.
lastly ['lɑ:stlɪ] *adv* por último, finalmente.
last-minute ['lɑ:stmɪnɪt] *adj* de última hora.
latch [lætʃ] *n* picaporte *m*, pestillo.
▸**latch on to** *vt fus* (*cling to*: *person*) pegarse a; (: *idea*) agarrarse de.
latchkey ['lætʃki:] *n* llavín *m*.
latchkey child *n* niño cuyos padres trabajan.
late [leɪt] *adj* (*not on time*) tarde, atrasado; (*towards end of period, life*) tardío; (*hour*) avanzado; (*dead*) fallecido ♦ *adv* tarde; (*behind time, schedule*) con retraso; **to be (10 minutes) ~** llegar con (diez minutos de) retraso; **to be ~ with** estar atrasado con; **~ delivery** entrega tardía; **~ in life** a una edad avanzada; **of ~** últimamente; **in ~ May** hacia fines de mayo; **the ~ Mr X** el difunto Sr X; **to work ~** trabajar hasta tarde.
latecomer ['leɪtkʌmə*] *n* recién llegado/a.
lately ['leɪtlɪ] *adv* últimamente.
lateness ['leɪtnɪs] *n* (*of person*) demora; (*of event*) tardanza.
latent ['leɪtnt] *adj* latente; **~ defect** defecto latente.
later ['leɪtə*] *adj* (*date etc*) posterior; (*version etc*) más reciente ♦ *adv* más tarde, después; **~ on today** hoy más tarde.
lateral ['lætərl] *adj* lateral.
latest ['leɪtɪst] *adj* último; **at the ~** a más tardar.
latex ['leɪtɛks] *n* látex *m*.
lathe [leɪð] *n* torno.
lather ['lɑ:ðə*] *n* espuma (de jabón) ♦ *vt* enjabonar.
Latin ['lætɪn] *n* latín *m* ♦ *adj* latino.
Latin America *n* América Latina, Latinoamérica.
Latin American *adj, n* latinoamericano/a *m/f*.
Latino [læ'ti:nəu] *adj, n* latino/a *m/f*.
latitude ['lætɪtju:d] *n* latitud *f*; (*fig*: *freedom*) libertad *f*.
latrine [lə'tri:n] *n* letrina.
latter ['lætə*] *adj* último; (*of two*) segundo ♦ *n*: **the ~** el último, éste.
latter-day ['lætədeɪ] *adj* moderno.
latterly ['lætəlɪ] *adv* últimamente.
lattice ['lætɪs] *n* enrejado.
lattice window *n* ventana enrejada *or* de celosía.
lattice work *n* enrejado.
Latvia ['lætvɪə] *n* Letonia.
Latvian ['lætvɪən] *adj* letón/ona ♦ *n* letón/ona *m/f*; (*LING*) letón *m*.
laudable ['lɔ:dəbl] *adj* loable.
laugh [lɑ:f] *n* risa; (*loud*) carcajada ♦ *vi* reírse, reír; reírse a carcajadas.
▸**laugh at** *vt fus* reírse de.
▸**laugh off** *vt* tomar a risa.
laughable ['lɑ:fəbl] *adj* ridículo.
laughing ['lɑ:fɪŋ] *adj* risueño ♦ *n*: **it's no ~ matter** no es cosa de risa.
laughing gas *n* gas *m* hilarante.
laughing stock *n*: **to be the ~ of the town** ser el hazmerreír de la ciudad.
laughter ['lɑ:ftə*] *n* risa.
launch [lɔ:ntʃ] *n* (*boat*) lancha; *see also* **launching** ♦ *vt* (*ship*) botar; (*rocket, plan*) lanzar.
▸**launch forth** *vi*: **to ~ forth (into)** lanzarse a *or* en, emprender.
▸**launch out** *vi* = **launch forth.**
launching ['lɔ:ntʃɪŋ] *n* (*of rocket etc*) lanzamiento; (*inauguration*) estreno.
launch(ing) pad *n* plataforma de lanzamiento.
launder ['lɔ:ndə*] *vt* lavar.
Launderette ® [lɔ:n'drɛt], (*US*) **Laundromat** ® ['lɔ:ndrəmæt] *n* lavandería (automática).
laundry ['lɔ:ndrɪ] *n* lavandería; (*clothes*) ropa sucia; **to do the ~** hacer la colada.
laureate ['lɔ:rɪət] *adj see* **poet.**
laurel ['lɔrl] *n* laurel *m*; **to rest on one's ~s** dormirse en *or* sobre los laureles.
lava ['lɑ:və] *n* lava.
lavatory ['lævətərɪ] *n* wáter *m*; **lavatories** *npl* servicios *mpl*, aseos *mpl*, sanitarios *mpl*

(*LAM*).
lavatory paper *n* papel *m* higiénico.
lavender ['lævəndə*] *n* lavanda.
lavish ['lævɪʃ] *adj* abundante; (*giving freely*): ~ **with** pródigo en ♦ *vt*: **to ~ sth on sb** colmar a algn de algo.
lavishly ['lævɪʃlɪ] *adv* (*give, spend*) generosamente; (*furnished*) lujosamente.
law [lɔː] *n* ley *f*; (*study*) derecho; (*of game*) regla; **against the ~** contra la ley; **to study ~** estudiar derecho; **to go to ~** recurrir a la justicia.
law-abiding ['lɔːəbaɪdɪŋ] *adj* respetuoso con la ley.
law and order *n* orden *m* público.
lawbreaker ['lɔːbreɪkə*] *n* infractor(a) *m/f* de la ley.
law court *n* tribunal *m* (de justicia).
lawful ['lɔːful] *adj* legítimo, lícito.
lawfully ['lɔːfulɪ] *adv* legalmente.
lawless ['lɔːlɪs] *adj* (*act*) ilegal; (*person*) rebelde; (*country*) ingobernable.
Law Lord *n* (*BRIT*) *miembro de la Cámara de los Lores y del más alto tribunal de apelación.*
lawmaker ['lɔːmeɪkə*] *n* legislador(a) *m/f*.
lawn [lɔːn] *n* césped *m*.
lawnmower ['lɔːnməuə*] *n* cortacésped *m*.
lawn tennis *n* tenis *m* sobre hierba.
law school *n* (*US*) facultad *f* de derecho.
law student *n* estudiante *m/f* de derecho.
lawsuit ['lɔːsuːt] *n* pleito; **to bring a ~ against** entablar un pleito contra.
lawyer ['lɔːjə*] *n* abogado/a; (*for sales, wills etc*) notario/a.
lax [læks] *adj* (*discipline*) relajado; (*person*) negligente.
laxative ['læksətɪv] *n* laxante *m*.
laxity ['læksɪtɪ] *n* flojedad *f*; (*moral*) relajamiento; (*negligence*) negligencia.
lay [leɪ] *pt of* **lie** ♦ *adj* laico; (*not expert*) lego ♦ *vt* (*pt, pp* **laid** [leɪd]) (*place*) colocar; (*eggs, table*) poner; (*trap*) tender; **to ~ the facts/ one's proposals before sb** presentar los hechos/sus propuestas a algn.
►**lay aside, lay by** *vt* dejar a un lado.
►**lay down** *vt* (*pen etc*) dejar; (*arms*) rendir; (*policy*) trazar; **to ~ down the law** imponer las normas.
►**lay in** *vt* abastecerse de.
►**lay into** *vt fus* (*col: attack, scold*) arremeter contra.
►**lay off** *vt* (*workers*) despedir.
►**lay on** *vt* (*water, gas*) instalar; (*meal, facilities*) proveer.
►**lay out** *vt* (*plan*) trazar; (*display*) exponer; (*spend*) gastar.
►**lay up** *vt* (*store*) guardar; (*ship*) desarmar; (*subj: illness*) obligar a guardar cama.
layabout ['leɪəbaut] *n* vago/a.
lay-by ['leɪbaɪ] *n* (*BRIT AUT*) apartadero.
lay days *npl* días *mpl* de inactividad.
layer ['leɪə*] *n* capa.
layette [leɪ'ɛt] *n* ajuar *m* (de niño).
layman ['leɪmən] *n* lego.
lay-off ['leɪɔf] *n* despido, paro forzoso.
layout ['leɪaut] *n* (*design*) plan *m*, trazado; (*disposition*) disposición *f*; (*PRESS*) composición *f*.
laze [leɪz] *vi* no hacer nada; (*pej*) holgazanear.
lazily ['leɪzɪlɪ] *adv* perezosamente.
laziness ['leɪzɪnɪs] *n* pereza.
lazy ['leɪzɪ] *adj* perezoso, vago, flojo (*LAM*).
LB *abbr* (*Canada*) = *Labrador.*
lb. *abbr* = **pound** (*weight*).
lbw *abr* (*CRICKET*) = *leg before wicket.*
LC *n abbr* (*US*) = *Library of Congress.*
lc *abbr* (*TYP*: = *lower case*) min.
L/C *abbr* = **letter of credit**.
LCD *n abbr see* **liquid crystal display**.
Ld *abbr* (= *Lord*) *título de nobleza.*
LDS *n abbr* (= *Licentiate in Dental Surgery*) *diploma universitario*; (= *Latter-day Saints*) Iglesia de Jesucristo de los Santos del último día.
LEA *n abbr* (*BRIT*: = *local education authority*) *organismos locales encargados de la enseñanza.*
lead [liːd] *n* (*front position*) delantera; (*distance, time ahead*) ventaja; (*clue*) pista; (*ELEC*) cable *m*; (*for dog*) correa; (*THEAT*) papel *m* principal; [lɛd] (*metal*) plomo; (*in pencil*) mina ♦ *vb* (*pt, pp* **led** [lɛd]) *vt* conducir; (*life*) llevar; (*be leader of*) dirigir; (*SPORT*) ir en cabeza de; (*orchestra*: *BRIT*) ser el primer violín en; (: *US*) dirigir ♦ *vi* ir primero; **to be in the ~** (*SPORT*) llevar la delantera; (*fig*) ir a la cabeza; **to take the ~** (*SPORT*) tomar la delantera; (*fig*) tomar la iniciativa; **to ~ sb to believe that ...** hacer creer a algn que ...; **to ~ sb to do sth** llevar a algn a hacer algo.
►**lead astray** *vt* llevar por mal camino.
►**lead away** *vt* llevar.
►**lead back** *vt* hacer volver.
►**lead off** *vt* llevar ♦ *vi* (*in game*) abrir.
►**lead on** *vt* (*tease*) engañar; **to ~ sb on to** (*induce*) incitar a algn a.
►**lead to** *vt fus* producir, provocar.
►**lead up to** *vt fus* conducir a.
leaded ['lɛdɪd] *adj*: **~ windows** ventanas *fpl* emplomadas.
leaden ['lɛdn] *adj* (*sky, sea*) plomizo; (*heavy*:

footsteps) pesado.
leader ['li:də*] *n* jefe/a *m/f*, líder *m*; (*of union etc*) dirigente *m/f*; (*guide*) guía *m/f*; (*of newspaper*) editorial *m*; **they are ~s in their field** (*fig*) llevan la delantera en su especialidad.
leadership ['li:dəʃɪp] *n* dirección *f*; **qualities of ~** iniciativa *sg*; **under the ~ of ...** bajo la dirección de ..., al mando de ....
lead-free ['lɛdfri:] *adj* sin plomo.
leading ['li:dɪŋ] *adj* (*main*) principal; (*outstanding*) destacado; (*first*) primero; (*front*) delantero; **a ~ question** una pregunta tendenciosa.
leading lady *n* (*THEAT*) primera actriz *f*.
leading light *n* (*fig*: *person*) figura principal.
leading man *n* (*THEAT*) primer actor *m*.
leading role *n* papel *m* principal.
lead pencil *n* lápiz *m*.
lead poisoning *n* envenenamiento plúmbico.
lead time *n* (*COMM*) plazo de entrega.
lead-up ['li:dʌp] *n*: **in the ~ to the election** cuando falta *etc* poco para las elecciones.
lead weight *n* peso de plomo.
leaf, *pl* **leaves** [li:f, li:vz] *n* hoja; **to turn over a new ~** (*fig*) volver la hoja, hacer borrón y cuenta nueva; **to take a ~ out of sb's book** (*fig*) seguir el ejemplo de algn.
►**leaf through** *vt fus* (*book*) hojear.
leaflet ['li:flɪt] *n* folleto.
leafy ['li:fɪ] *adj* frondoso.
league [li:g] *n* sociedad *f*; (*FOOTBALL*) liga; **to be in ~ with** estar confabulado con.
league table *n* clasificación *f*.
leak [li:k] *n* (*of liquid, gas*) escape *m*, fuga; (*in pipe*) agujero; (*in roof*) gotera; (*fig*: *of information, in security*) filtración *f* ♦ *vi* (*ship*) hacer agua; (*shoes*) tener un agujero; (*pipe*) tener un escape; (*roof*) tener goteras; (*also*: **~ out**: *liquid, gas*) escaparse, salirse; (*fig*: *news*) trascender, divulgarse ♦ *vt* (*gen*) dejar escapar; (*fig*: *information*) filtrar.
leakage ['li:kɪdʒ] *n* (*of water, gas etc*) escape *m*, fuga.
leaky ['li:kɪ] *adj* (*roof*) con goteras; (*bucket, shoe*) con agujeros; (*pipe*) con un escape; (*boat*) que hace agua.
lean [li:n] *adj* (*thin*) flaco; (*meat*) magro ♦ *vb* (*pt, pp* **leaned** *or* **leant** [lɛnt]) *vt*: **to ~ sth on sth** apoyar algo en algo ♦ *vi* (*slope*) inclinarse; (*rest*): **to ~ against** apoyarse contra; **to ~ on** apoyarse en.
►**lean back** *vi* inclinarse hacia atrás.
►**lean forward** *vi* inclinarse hacia adelante.
►**lean out** *vi*: **to ~ out (of)** asomarse (a).
►**lean over** *vi* inclinarse.
leaning ['li:nɪŋ] *adj* inclinado ♦ *n*: **~ (towards)** inclinación *f* (hacia); **the L~ Tower of Pisa** la Torre Inclinada de Pisa.
leant [lɛnt] *pt, pp of* **lean**.
lean-to ['li:ntu:] *n* (*roof*) tejado de una sola agua; (*building*) cobertizo.
leap [li:p] *n* salto ♦ *vi* (*pt, pp* **leaped** *or* **leapt** [lɛpt]) saltar; **to ~ at an offer** apresurarse a aceptar una oferta.
►**leap up** *vi* (*person*) saltar.
leapfrog ['li:pfrɔg] *n* pídola ♦ *vi*: **to ~ over sb/sth** saltar por encima de algn/algo.
leapt [lɛpt] *pt, pp of* **leap**.
leap year *n* año bisiesto.
learn, *pt, pp* **learned** *or* **learnt** [lə:n, -t] *vt* (*gen*) aprender; (*come to know of*) enterarse de ♦ *vi* aprender; **to ~ how to do sth** aprender a hacer algo; **to ~ that ...** enterarse *or* informarse de que ...; **to ~ about sth** (*SCOL*) aprender algo; (*hear*) enterarse *or* informarse de algo; **we were sorry to ~ that ...** nos dio tristeza saber que ....
learned ['lə:nɪd] *adj* erudito.
learner ['lə:nə*] *n* principiante *m/f*; (*BRIT*: *also*: **~ driver**) conductor(a) *m/f* en prácticas; *see also* **L-plates**.
learning ['lə:nɪŋ] *n* saber *m*, conocimientos *mpl*.
learnt [lə:nt] *pp of* **learn**.
lease [li:s] *n* arriendo ♦ *vt* arrendar; **on ~** en arriendo.
►**lease back** *vt* subarrendar.
leaseback ['li:sbæk] *n* subarriendo.
leasehold ['li:shəuld] *n* (*contract*) derechos *mpl* de arrendamiento ♦ *adj* arrendado.
leash [li:ʃ] *n* correa.
least [li:st] *adj* (*slightest*) menor, más pequeño; (*smallest amount of*) mínimo ♦ *adv* menos ♦ *n*: **the ~** lo menos; **the ~ expensive car** el coche menos caro; **at ~** por lo menos, al menos; **not in the ~** en absoluto.
leather ['lɛðə*] *n* cuero ♦ *cpd*: **~ goods** artículos *mpl* de cuero *or* piel.
leathery ['lɛðərɪ] *adj* (*skin*) curtido.
leave [li:v] *vb* (*pt, pp* **left** [lɛft]) *vt* dejar; (*go away from*) abandonar ♦ *vi* irse; (*train*) salir ♦ *n* permiso; **to ~ school** dejar la escuela *or* el colegio; **~ it to me!** ¡yo me encargo!; **he's already left for the airport** ya se ha marchado al aeropuerto; **to be left** quedar, sobrar; **there's some milk left over** sobra *or* queda algo de leche; **on ~**

de permiso; **to take one's ~ of** despedirse de.
▸**leave behind** *vt* (*on purpose*) dejar (atrás); (*accidentally*) olvidar.
▸**leave off** *vt* (*lid*) no poner; (*switch*) no encender; (*col*: *stop*): **to ~ off doing sth** dejar de hacer algo.
▸**leave on** *vt* (*lid*) dejar puesto; (*light, fire, cooker*) dejar encendido.
▸**leave out** *vt* omitir.
▸**leave over** *vt* (*postpone*) dejar, aplazar.
leave of absence *n* excedencia.
leaves [liːvz] *pl of* **leaf**.
leavetaking ['liːvteɪkɪŋ] *n* despedida.
Lebanon ['lɛbənən] *n*: **the ~** el Líbano.
lecherous ['lɛtʃərəs] *adj* lascivo.
lectern ['lɛktəːn] *n* atril *m*.
lecture ['lɛktʃə*] *n* conferencia; (*SCOL*) clase *f* ♦ *vi* dar clase(s) ♦ *vt* (*scold*) sermonear; (*reprove*) echar una reprimenda a; **to give a ~ on** dar una conferencia sobre.
lecture hall *n* sala de conferencias; (*UNIV*) aula.
lecturer ['lɛktʃərə*] *n* conferenciante *m/f*; (*BRIT*: *at university*) profesor(a) *m/f*.
lecture theatre *n* = **lecture hall**.
LED *n abbr* (= *light-emitting diode*) LED *m*.
led [lɛd] *pt, pp of* **lead**.
ledge [lɛdʒ] *n* (*of window, on wall*) repisa, reborde *m*; (*of mountain*) saliente *m*.
ledger ['lɛdʒə*] *n* libro mayor.
lee [liː] *n* sotavento; **in the ~ of** al abrigo de.
leech [liːtʃ] *n* sanguijuela.
leek [liːk] *n* puerro.
leer [lɪə*] *vi*: **to ~ at sb** mirar de manera lasciva a algn.
leeward ['liːwəd] *adj* (*NAUT*) de sotavento ♦ *n* (*NAUT*) sotavento; **to ~** a sotavento.
leeway ['liːweɪ] *n* (*fig*): **to have some ~** tener cierta libertad de acción.
left [lɛft] *pt, pp of* **leave** ♦ *adj* izquierdo ♦ *n* izquierda ♦ *adv* a la izquierda; **on** *or* **to the ~** a la izquierda; **the L~** (*POL*) la izquierda.
left-hand drive ['lɛfthænd-] *n* conducción *f* por la izquierda.
left-handed [lɛft'hændɪd] *adj* zurdo; **~ scissors** tijeras *fpl* zurdas *or* para zurdos.
left-hand side ['lɛfthænd-] *n* izquierda.
leftie ['lɛftɪ] *n* = **lefty**.
leftist ['lɛftɪst] *adj* (*POL*) izquierdista.
left-luggage (office) [lɛft'lʌgɪdʒ(-)] *n* (*BRIT*) consigna.
left-overs ['lɛftəuvəz] *npl* sobras *fpl*.
left-wing [lɛft'wɪŋ] *adj* (*POL*) de izquierda(s), izquierdista.
left-winger ['lɛft'wɪŋə*] *n* (*POL*) izquierdista *m/f*.
lefty ['lɛftɪ] *n* (*col*: *POL*) rojillo/a.
leg [lɛg] *n* pierna; (*of animal, chair*) pata; (*CULIN*: *of meat*) pierna; (*of journey*) etapa; **1st/2nd ~** (*SPORT*) partido de ida/de vuelta; **to pull sb's ~** tomar el pelo a algn; **to stretch one's ~s** dar una vuelta.
legacy ['lɛgəsɪ] *n* herencia; (*fig*) herencia, legado.
legal ['liːgl] *adj* (*permitted by law*) lícito; (*of law*) legal; (*inquiry etc*) jurídico; **to take ~ action** *or* **proceedings against sb** entablar *or* levantar un pleito contra algn.
legal adviser *n* asesor(a) *m/f* jurídico/a.
legal holiday *n* (*US*) fiesta oficial.
legality [lɪ'gælɪtɪ] *n* legalidad *f*.
legalize ['liːgəlaɪz] *vt* legalizar.
legally ['liːgəlɪ] *adv* legalmente; **~ binding** con fuerza legal.
legal tender *n* moneda de curso legal.
legatee [lɛgə'tiː] *n* legatario/a.
legation [lɪ'geɪʃən] *n* legación *f*.
legend ['lɛdʒənd] *n* leyenda.
legendary ['lɛdʒəndərɪ] *adj* legendario.
-legged ['legɪd] *suff*: **two-~** (*table etc*) de dos patas.
leggings ['legɪŋz] *npl* mallas *fpl*, leggins *mpl*.
leggy ['lɛgɪ] *adj* de piernas largas.
legibility [lɛdʒɪ'bɪlɪtɪ] *n* legibilidad *f*.
legible ['lɛdʒəbl] *adj* legible.
legibly ['lɛdʒəblɪ] *adv* legiblemente.
legion ['liːdʒən] *n* legión *f*.
legionnaire [liːdʒə'nɛə*] *n* legionario.
legionnaire's disease *n* enfermedad *f* del legionario.
legislation [lɛdʒɪs'leɪʃən] *n* legislación *f*; **a piece of ~** (*bill*) un proyecto de ley; (*act*) una ley.
legislative ['lɛdʒɪslətɪv] *adj* legislativo.
legislator ['lɛdʒɪsleɪtə*] *n* legislador(a) *m/f*.
legislature ['lɛdʒɪslətʃə*] *n* cuerpo legislativo.
legitimacy [lɪ'dʒɪtɪməsɪ] *n* legitimidad *f*.
legitimate [lɪ'dʒɪtɪmət] *adj* legítimo.
legitimize [lɪ'dʒɪtɪmaɪz] *vt* legitimar.
legless ['lɛglɪs] *adj* (*BRIT col*) mamado.
leg-room ['lɛgruːm] *n* espacio para las piernas.
Leics *abbr* (*BRIT*) = *Leicestershire*.
leisure ['lɛʒə*] *n* ocio, tiempo libre; **at ~** con tranquilidad.
leisure centre *n* centro recreativo.
leisurely ['lɛʒəlɪ] *adj* sin prisa; lento.
leisure suit *n* conjunto tipo chandal.
lemon ['lɛmən] *n* limón *m*.
lemonade [lɛmə'neɪd] *n* (*fruit juice*) limonada; (*fizzy*) gaseosa.

lemon cheese, lemon curd *n* queso de limón.
lemon juice *n* zumo de limón.
lemon tea *n* té *m* con limón.
lend, *pt, pp* **lent** [lɛnd, lɛnt] *vt*: **to ~ sth to sb** prestar algo a algn.
lender ['lɛndə*] *n* prestamista *m/f*.
lending library ['lɛndɪŋ-] *n* biblioteca de préstamo.
length [lɛŋθ] *n* (*size*) largo, longitud *f*; (*section: of road, pipe*) tramo; (*: of rope etc*) largo; **at ~** (*at last*) por fin, finalmente; (*lengthily*) largamente; **it is 2 metres in ~** tiene dos metros de largo; **what ~ is it?** ¿cuánto tiene de largo?; **to fall full ~** caer de bruces; **to go to any ~(s) to do sth** ser capaz de hacer cualquier cosa para hacer algo.
lengthen ['lɛŋθn] *vt* alargar ♦ *vi* alargarse.
lengthways ['lɛŋθweɪz] *adv* a lo largo.
lengthy ['lɛŋθɪ] *adj* largo, extenso; (*meeting*) prolongado.
lenient ['liːnɪənt] *adj* indulgente.
lens [lɛnz] *n* (*of spectacles*) lente *f*; (*of camera*) objetivo.
Lent [lɛnt] *n* Cuaresma.
lent [lɛnt] *pt, pp of* **lend**.
lentil ['lɛntl] *n* lenteja.
Leo ['liːəu] *n* Leo.
leopard ['lɛpəd] *n* leopardo.
leotard ['liːətɑːd] *n* leotardo.
leper ['lɛpə*] *n* leproso/a.
leper colony *n* colonia de leprosos.
leprosy ['lɛprəsɪ] *n* lepra.
lesbian ['lɛzbɪən] *adj* lesbiano ♦ *n* lesbiana.
lesion ['liːʒən] *n* (MED) lesión *f*.
Lesotho [lɪ'suːtuː] *n* Lesotho.
less [lɛs] *adj* (*in size, degree etc*) menor; (*in quantity*) menos ♦ *pron, adv* menos; **~ than half** menos de la mitad; **~ than £1/a kilo/3 metres** menos de una libra/un kilo/tres metros; **~ than ever** menos que nunca; **~ 5%** menos el cinco por ciento; **~ and ~** cada vez menos; **the ~ he works...** cuanto menos trabaja ....
lessee [lɛ'siː] *n* inquilino/a, arrendatario/a.
lessen ['lɛsn] *vi* disminuir, reducirse ♦ *vt* disminuir, reducir.
lesser ['lɛsə*] *adj* menor; **to a ~ extent** *or* **degree** en menor grado.
lesson ['lɛsn] *n* clase *f*; **a maths ~** una clase de matemáticas; **to give ~s in** dar clases de; **it taught him a ~** (*fig*) le sirvió de lección.
lessor ['lɛsɔː* *or* lɛ'sɔː*] *n* arrendador(a) *m/f*.
lest [lɛst] *conj*: **~ it happen** para que no pase.
let, *pt, pp* **let** [lɛt] *vt* (*allow*) dejar, permitir; (BRIT: *lease*) alquilar; **to ~ sb do sth** dejar que algn haga algo; **to ~ sb have sth** dar algo a algn; **to ~ sb know sth** comunicar algo a algn; **~'s go** ¡vamos!; **~ him come** que venga; **"to ~"** "se alquila".
▸**let down** *vt* (*lower*) bajar; (*dress*) alargar; (*tyre*) desinflar; (*hair*) soltar; (*disappoint*) defraudar.
▸**let go** *vi* soltar; (*fig*) dejarse ir ♦ *vt* soltar.
▸**let in** *vt* dejar entrar; (*visitor etc*) hacer pasar; **what have you ~ yourself in for?** ¿en qué te has metido?
▸**let off** *vt* dejar escapar; (*firework etc*) disparar; (*bomb*) accionar; (*passenger*) dejar, bajar; **to ~ off steam** (*fig, col*) desahogarse, desfogarse.
▸**let on** *vi*: **to ~ on that ...** revelar que ...
▸**let out** *vt* dejar salir; (*dress*) ensanchar; (*rent out*) alquilar.
▸**let up** *vi* disminuir; (*rain etc*) amainar.
let-down ['lɛtdaun] *n* (*disappointment*) decepción *f*.
lethal ['liːθl] *adj* (*weapon*) mortífero; (*poison, wound*) mortal.
lethargic [lɛ'θɑːdʒɪk] *adj* aletargado.
lethargy ['lɛθədʒɪ] *n* letargo.
letter ['lɛtə*] *n* (*of alphabet*) letra; (*correspondence*) carta; **~s** *npl* (*literature, learning*) letras *fpl*; **small/capital ~** minúscula/mayúscula; **covering ~** carta adjunta.
letter bomb *n* carta-bomba.
letterbox ['lɛtəbɔks] *n* (BRIT) buzón *m*.
letterhead ['lɛtəhɛd] *n* membrete *m*, encabezamiento.
lettering ['lɛtərɪŋ] *n* letras *fpl*.
letter of credit *n* carta de crédito; **documentary ~** carta de crédito documentaria; **irrevocable ~** carta de crédito irrevocable.
letter-opener ['lɛtərəupnə*] *n* abrecartas *m inv*.
letterpress ['lɛtəprɛs] *n* (*method*) prensa de copiar; (*printed page*) impresión *f* tipográfica.
letter quality *n* calidad *f* de correspondencia.
letters patent *npl* letra *sg* de patente.
lettuce ['lɛtɪs] *n* lechuga.
let-up ['lɛtʌp] *n* descanso, tregua.
leukaemia, (US) **leukemia** [luː'kiːmɪə] *n* leucemia.
level ['lɛvl] *adj* (*flat*) llano; (*flattened*) nivelado; (*uniform*) igual ♦ *adv* a nivel ♦ *n* nivel *m* ♦ *vt* nivelar, allanar; (*gun*) apuntar; (*accusation*): **to ~ (against)** levantar (contra) ♦ *vi* (*col*): **to ~ with sb** ser franco con algn; **to be ~ with** estar a

nivel de; **a ~ spoonful** (*CULIN*) una cucharada rasa; **to draw ~ with** (*team*) igualar; (*runner, car*) alcanzar a; **"A" ~s** *npl* (*BRIT*) ≈ Bachillerato Superior *sg*, B.U.P. *msg*; **"O" ~s** *npl* (*BRIT*) ≈ bachillerato *sg* elemental, octavo *sg* de Básica; **on the ~** (*fig: honest*) en serio; **talks at ministerial ~** charlas *fpl* a nivel ministerial.

▸**level off** *or* **out** *vi* (*prices etc*) estabilizarse; (*ground*) nivelarse; (*aircraft*) ponerse en una trayectoria horizontal.

level crossing *n* (*BRIT*) paso a nivel.

level-headed [lɛvl'hɛdɪd] *adj* sensato.

levelling, (*US*) **leveling** ['lɛvlɪŋ] *adj* (*process, effect*) de nivelación ♦ *n* igualación *f*, allanamiento.

level playing field *n* situación *f* de igualdad; **to compete on a ~** competir en igualdad de condiciones.

lever ['liːvə*] *n* palanca ♦ *vt*: **to ~ up** levantar con palanca.

leverage ['liːvərɪdʒ] *n* (*fig: influence*) influencia.

levity ['lɛvɪtɪ] *n* frivolidad *f*, informalidad *f*.

levy ['lɛvɪ] *n* impuesto ♦ *vt* exigir, recaudar.

lewd [luːd] *adj* lascivo; obsceno, colorado (*LAM*).

lexicographer [lɛksɪ'kɔgrəfə*] *n* lexicógrafo/a *m/f*.

lexicography [lɛksɪ'kɔgrəfɪ] *n* lexicografía.

LGV *n abbr* (= *Large Goods Vehicle*) vehículo pesado.

LI *abbr* (*US*) = *Long Island*.

liabilities [laɪə'bɪlətɪz] *npl* obligaciones *fpl*; pasivo *sg*.

liability [laɪə'bɪlətɪ] *n* responsabilidad *f*; (*handicap*) desventaja.

liable ['laɪəbl] *adj* (*subject*): **~ to** sujeto a; (*responsible*): **~ for** responsable de; (*likely*): **~ to do** propenso a hacer; **to be ~ to a fine** exponerse a una multa.

liaise [liː'eɪz] *vi*: **to ~ (with)** colaborar (con); **to ~ with sb** mantener informado a algn.

liaison [liː'eɪzɔn] *n* (*coordination*) enlace *m*; (*affair*) relación *f*.

liar ['laɪə*] *n* mentiroso/a.

libel ['laɪbl] *n* calumnia ♦ *vt* calumniar.

libellous ['ləɪbləs] *adj* difamatorio, calumnioso.

liberal ['lɪbərl] *adj* (*gen*) liberal; (*generous*): **~ with** generoso con ♦ *n*: **L~** (*POL*) liberal *m/f*.

Liberal Democrat *n* (*BRIT*) demócrata *m/f* liberal.

liberality [lɪbə'rælɪtɪ] *n* (*generosity*) liberalidad *f*, generosidad *f*.

liberalize ['lɪbərəlaɪz] *vt* liberalizar.

liberally ['lɪbərəlɪ] *adv* liberalmente.

liberal-minded ['lɪbərl'maɪndɪd] *adj* de miras anchas, liberal.

liberate ['lɪbəreɪt] *vt* liberar.

liberation [lɪbə'reɪʃən] *n* liberación *f*.

liberation theology *n* teología de la liberación.

Liberia [laɪ'bɪərɪə] *n* Liberia.

Liberian [laɪ'bɪərɪən] *adj, n* liberiano/a *m/f*.

liberty ['lɪbətɪ] *n* libertad *f*; **to be at ~ to do** estar libre para hacer; **to take the ~ of doing sth** tomarse la libertad de hacer algo.

libido [lɪ'biːdəu] *n* libido.

Libra ['liːbrə] *n* Libra.

librarian [laɪ'brɛərɪən] *n* bibliotecario/a.

library ['laɪbrərɪ] *n* biblioteca.

library book *n* libro de la biblioteca.

libretto [lɪ'brɛtəu] *n* libreto.

Libya ['lɪbɪə] *n* Libia.

Libyan ['lɪbɪən] *adj, n* libio/a *m/f*.

lice [laɪs] *pl of* **louse**.

licence, (*US*) **license** ['laɪsns] *n* licencia; (*permit*) permiso; (*also*: **driving licence**, (*US*) **driver's license**) carnet *m* de conducir; (*excessive freedom*) libertad *f*; **import ~** licencia *or* permiso de importación; **produced under ~** elaborado bajo licencia.

licence number *n* (número de) matrícula.

licence plate *n* (placa de) matrícula.

license ['laɪsns] (*US*) = **licence** ♦ *vt* autorizar, dar permiso a; (*car*) sacar la matrícula de *or* la patente (*LAM*) de.

licensed ['laɪsnst] *adj* (*for alcohol*) autorizado para vender bebidas alcohólicas.

licensed trade *n* comercio *or* negocio autorizado.

licensee [laɪsən'siː] *n* (*in a pub*) concesionario/a, dueño/a de un bar.

licentious [laɪ'sɛnʃəs] *adj* licencioso.

lichen ['laɪkən] *n* liquen *m*.

lick [lɪk] *vt* lamer; (*col: defeat*) dar una paliza a ♦ *n* lamedura; **a ~ of paint** una mano de pintura.

licorice ['lɪkərɪs] *n* = **liquorice**.

lid [lɪd] *n* (*of box, case*) tapa; (*of pan*) cobertera; **to take the ~ off sth** (*fig*) exponer algo a la luz pública.

lido ['laɪdəu] *n* (*BRIT*) piscina, alberca (*LAM*).

lie [laɪ] *n* mentira ♦ *vi* mentir; (*pt* **lay**, *pp* **lain** [leɪ, leɪn]) (*rest*) estar echado, estar acostado; (*of object: be situated*) estar, encontrarse; **to tell ~s** mentir; **to ~ low** (*fig*) mantenerse a escondidas.

▸**lie about, lie around** *vi* (*things*) estar

tirado; (*BRIT*: *people*) estar acostado *or* tumbado.
▸**lie back** *vi* recostarse.
▸**lie down** *vi* echarse, tumbarse.
▸**lie up** *vi* (*hide*) esconderse.
Liechtenstein ['lɪktənstaɪn] *n* Liechtenstein *m*.
lie detector *n* detector *m* de mentiras.
lie-down ['laɪdaun] *n* (*BRIT*): **to have a ~** echarse (una siesta).
lie-in ['laɪɪn] *n* (*BRIT*): **to have a ~** quedarse en la cama.
lieu [lu:]: **in ~ of** *prep* en lugar de.
Lieut *abbr* = **lieutenant.**
lieutenant [lɛf'tɛnənt, (*US*) lu:'tɛnənt] *n* (*MIL*) teniente *m*.
lieutenant colonel *n* teniente *m* coronel.
life, *pl* **lives** [laɪf, laɪvz] *n* vida; (*of licence etc*) vigencia; **to be sent to prison for ~** ser condenado a cadena perpetua; **country/city ~** la vida en el campo/en la ciudad; **true to ~** fiel a la realidad; **to paint from ~** pintar del natural; **to put** *or* **breathe new ~ into** (*person*) reanimar; (*project, area etc*) infundir nueva vida a.
life annuity *n* pensión *f* anual vitalicia.
life assurance *n* (*BRIT*) seguro de vida.
lifebelt ['laɪfbɛlt] *n* (*BRIT*) salvavidas *m inv*.
lifeblood ['laɪfblʌd] *n* (*fig*) alma, nervio.
lifeboat ['laɪfbəut] *n* lancha de socorro.
life-buoy ['laɪfbɔɪ] *n* boya *or* guindola salvavidas.
life expectancy *n* esperanza de vida.
lifeguard ['laɪfgɑ:d] *n* vigilante *m/f*.
life imprisonment *n* cadena perpetua.
life insurance *n* = **life assurance.**
life jacket *n* chaleco salvavidas.
lifeless ['laɪflɪs] *adj* sin vida; (*dull*) soso.
lifelike ['laɪflaɪk] *adj* natural.
lifeline ['laɪflaɪn] *n* (*fig*) cordón *m* umbilical.
lifelong ['laɪflɔŋ] *adj* de toda la vida.
life preserver *n* (*US*) = **lifebelt.**
lifer ['laɪfə*] *n* (*col*) condenado/a *m/f* a cadena perpetua.
life-saver ['laɪfseɪvə*] *n* socorrista *m/f*.
life sentence *n* cadena perpetua.
life-sized ['laɪfsaɪzd] *adj* de tamaño natural.
life span *n* vida.
lifestyle ['laɪfstaɪl] *n* estilo de vida.
life support system *n* (*MED*) sistema *m* de respiración asistida.
lifetime ['laɪftaɪm] *n*: **in his ~** durante su vida; **once in a ~** una vez en la vida; **the chance of a ~** una oportunidad única.
lift [lɪft] *vt* levantar; (*copy*) plagiar ♦ *vi* (*fog*) disiparse ♦ *n* (*BRIT*: *elevator*) ascensor *m*, elevador *m* (*LAM*); **to give sb a ~** (*BRIT*) llevar a algn en coche.
▸**lift off** *vt* levantar, quitar ♦ *vi* (*rocket, helicopter*) despegar.
▸**lift out** *vt* sacar; (*troops, evacuees etc*) evacuar.
▸**lift up** *vt* levantar.
lift-off ['lɪftɔf] *n* despegue *m*.
ligament ['lɪgəmənt] *n* ligamento.
light [laɪt] *n* luz *f*; (*flame*) lumbre *f*; (*lamp*) luz *f*, lámpara; (*daylight*) luz *f* del día; (*headlight*) faro; (*rear ~*) luz *f* trasera; (*for cigarette etc*): **have you got a ~?** ¿tienes fuego? ♦ *vt* (*pt, pp* **lighted** *or* **lit** [lɪt]) (*candle, cigarette, fire*) encender; (*room*) alumbrar ♦ *adj* (*colour*) claro; (*not heavy, also fig*) ligero, liviano (*esp LAM*); (*room*) alumbrado ♦ *adv* (*travel*) con poco equipaje; **to turn the ~ on/off** encender/apagar la luz; **in the ~ of** a la luz de; **to come to ~** salir a la luz; **to cast** *or* **shed** *or* **throw ~ on** arrojar luz sobre; **to make ~ of sth** (*fig*) no dar importancia a algo.
▸**light up** *vi* (*smoke*) encender un cigarrillo; (*face*) iluminarse ♦ *vt* (*illuminate*) iluminar, alumbrar.
light bulb *n* bombilla, bombillo (*LAM*), foco (*LAM*).
lighten ['laɪtn] *vi* (*grow light*) clarear ♦ *vt* (*give light to*) iluminar; (*make lighter*) aclarar; (*make less heavy*) aligerar.
lighter ['laɪtə*] *n* (*also*: **cigarette ~**) encendedor *m* (*esp LAM*), mechero.
light-fingered [laɪt'fɪŋgəd] *adj* de manos largas.
light-headed [laɪt'hɛdɪd] *adj* (*dizzy*) mareado; (*excited*) exaltado; (*by nature*) atolondrado.
light-hearted [laɪt'hɑ:tɪd] *adj* alegre.
lighthouse ['laɪthaus] *n* faro.
lighting ['laɪtɪŋ] *n* (*act*) iluminación *f*; (*system*) alumbrado.
lighting-up time [laɪtɪŋ'ʌp-] *n* (*BRIT*) hora de encendido del alumbrado.
lightly ['laɪtlɪ] *adv* ligeramente; (*not seriously*) con poca seriedad; **to get off ~** ser castigado con poca severidad.
light meter *n* (*PHOT*) fotómetro.
lightness ['laɪtnɪs] *n* claridad *f*; (*in weight*) ligereza.
lightning ['laɪtnɪŋ] *n* relámpago, rayo.
lightning conductor, (*US*) **lightning rod** *n* pararrayos *m inv*.
lightning strike *n* huelga relámpago.
light pen *n* lápiz *m* óptico.
lightweight ['laɪtweɪt] *adj* (*suit*) ligero ♦ *n* (*BOXING*) peso ligero.
light year *n* año luz.
like [laɪk] *vt* (*person*) querer a; (*thing*): **I ~**

swimming/apples me gusta nadar/me gustan las manzanas ♦ *prep* como ♦ *adj* parecido, semejante ♦ *n*: **did you ever see the ~ (of it)?** ¿has visto cosa igual?; **his ~s and dislikes** sus gustos y aversiones; **the ~s of him** personas como él; **I would ~, I'd ~** me gustaría; (*for purchase*) quisiera; **would you ~ a coffee?** ¿te apetece un café?; **to be** *or* **look ~ sb/sth** parecerse a algn/algo; **that's just ~ him** es muy de él, es típico de él; **do it ~ this** hazlo así; **it is nothing ~...** no tiene parecido alguno con...; **what's he ~?** ¿cómo es (él)?; **what's the weather ~?** ¿qué tiempo hace?; **something ~ that** algo así *or* por el estilo; **I feel ~ a drink** me apetece algo de beber; **if you ~** si quieres.

likeable ['laɪkəbl] *adj* simpático, agradable.

likelihood ['laɪklɪhud] *n* probabilidad *f*; **in all ~** según todas las probabilidades.

likely ['laɪklɪ] *adj* probable, capaz (*LAM*); **he's ~ to leave** es probable *or* capaz (*LAM*) que se vaya; **not ~!** ¡ni hablar!

like-minded [laɪk'maɪndɪd] *adj* de la misma opinión.

liken ['laɪkən] *vt*: **to ~ to** comparar con.

likeness ['laɪknɪs] *n* (*similarity*) semejanza, parecido.

likewise ['laɪkwaɪz] *adv* igualmente.

liking ['laɪkɪŋ] *n*: **~ (for)** (*person*) cariño (a); (*thing*) afición (a); **to take a ~ to sb** tomar cariño a algn; **to be to sb's ~** ser del gusto de algn.

lilac ['laɪlək] *n* lila ♦ *adj* (*colour*) de color lila.

Lilo ® ['laɪləu] *n* colchoneta inflable.

lilt [lɪlt] *n* deje *m*.

lilting ['lɪltɪŋ] *adj* melodioso.

lily ['lɪlɪ] *n* lirio, azucena.

lily of the valley *n* lirio de los valles.

Lima ['li:mə] *n* Lima.

limb [lɪm] *n* miembro; (*of tree*) rama; **to be out on a ~** (*fig*) estar aislado.

limber up ['lɪmbə*-] *vi* (*fig*) entrenarse; (*SPORT*) hacer (ejercicios de) precalentamiento.

limbo ['lɪmbəu] *n*: **to be in ~** (*fig*) quedar a la expectativa.

lime [laɪm] *n* (*tree*) limero; (*fruit*) lima; (*GEO*) cal *f*.

lime juice *n* zumo (*SP*) *or* jugo de lima.

limelight ['laɪmlaɪt] *n*: **to be in the ~** (*fig*) ser el centro de atención.

limerick ['lɪmərɪk] *n* quintilla humorística.

limestone ['laɪmstəun] *n* piedra caliza.

limit ['lɪmɪt] *n* límite *m* ♦ *vt* limitar; **weight/speed ~** peso máximo/velocidad *f* máxima; **within ~s** entre límites.

limitation [lɪmɪ'teɪʃən] *n* limitación *f*.

limited ['lɪmɪtɪd] *adj* limitado; **to be ~ to** limitarse a; **~ edition** edición limitada.

limited (liability) company (Ltd) *n* (*BRIT*) sociedad *f* anónima (SA).

limitless ['lɪmɪtlɪs] *adj* sin límites.

limousine ['lɪməzi:n] *n* limusina.

limp [lɪmp] *n*: **to have a ~** tener cojera ♦ *vi* cojear, renguear (*LAM*) ♦ *adj* flojo.

limpet ['lɪmpɪt] *n* lapa.

limpid ['lɪmpɪd] *adj* (*poetic*) límpido, cristalino.

limply ['lɪmplɪ] *adv* desmayadamente; **to say ~** decir débilmente.

linchpin ['lɪntʃpɪn] *n* pezonera; (*fig*) eje *m*.

Lincs [lɪŋks] *abbr* (*BRIT*) = *Lincolnshire*.

line [laɪn] *n* (*also COMM*) línea; (*straight ~*) raya; (*rope*) cuerda; (*for fishing*) sedal *m*; (*wire*) hilo; (*row, series*) fila, hilera; (*of writing*) renglón *m*; (*on face*) arruga; (*speciality*) rama ♦ *vt* (*SEWING*): **to ~ (with)** forrar (de); **to ~ the streets** ocupar las aceras; **in ~ with** de acuerdo con; **she's in ~ for promotion** (*fig*) tiene muchas posibilidades de que la asciendan; **to bring sth into ~ with sth** poner algo de acuerdo con algo; **~ of research/business** campo de investigación/comercio; **to take the ~ that ...** ser de la opinión que ...; **hold the ~ please** (*TEL*) no cuelgue usted, por favor; **to draw the ~ at doing sth** negarse a hacer algo; no permitir que se haga algo; **on the right ~s** por buen camino; **a new ~ in cosmetics** una nueva línea en cosméticos; *see also* **lines**.

►**line up** *vi* hacer cola ♦ *vt* alinear, poner en fila; **to have sth ~d up** tener algo arreglado.

linear ['lɪnɪə*] *adj* lineal.

lined [laɪnd] *adj* (*face*) arrugado; (*paper*) rayado; (*clothes*) forrado.

line editing *n* (*COMPUT*) corrección *f* por líneas.

line feed *n* (*COMPUT*) avance *m* de línea.

lineman ['laɪnmən] *n* (*US*) técnico de las líneas; (*FOOTBALL*) delantero.

linen ['lɪnɪn] *n* ropa blanca; (*cloth*) lino.

line printer *n* impresora de línea.

liner ['laɪnə*] *n* vapor *m* de línea, transatlántico; **dustbin ~** bolsa de la basura.

lines [laɪnz] *npl* (*RAIL*) vía *sg*, raíles *mpl*.

linesman ['laɪnzmən] *n* (*SPORT*) juez *m* de línea.

line-up ['laɪnʌp] *n* alineación *f*.

linger ['lɪŋgə*] *vi* retrasarse, tardar en marcharse; (*smell, tradition*) persistir.

lingerie ['lænʒəri:] *n* ropa interior *or* íntima

(de mujer).
lingering [ˈlɪŋgərɪŋ] *adj* persistente; (*death*) lento.
lingo, ~es [ˈlɪŋgəu] *n* (*pej*) jerga.
linguist [ˈlɪŋgwɪst] *n* lingüista *m/f*.
linguistic [lɪŋˈgwɪstɪk] *adj* lingüístico.
linguistics [lɪŋˈgwɪstɪks] *n* lingüística.
liniment [ˈlɪnɪmənt] *n* linimento.
lining [ˈlaɪnɪŋ] *n* forro; (*TECH*) revestimiento; (*of brake*) guarnición *f*.
link [lɪŋk] *n* (*of a chain*) eslabón *m*; (*connection*) conexión *f*; (*bond*) vínculo, lazo ♦ *vt* vincular, unir; **rail ~** línea de ferrocarril, servicio de trenes.
▸**link up** *vt* acoplar ♦ *vi* unirse.
links [lɪŋks] *npl* (*GOLF*) campo *sg* de golf.
link-up [ˈlɪŋkʌp] *n* (*gen*) unión *f*; (*meeting*) encuentro, reunión *f*; (*of roads*) empalme *m*; (*of spaceships*) acoplamiento; (*RADIO, TV*) enlace *m*.
lino [ˈlaɪnəu] (*BRIT*), **linoleum** [lɪˈnəulɪəm] *n* linóleo.
linseed oil [ˈlɪnsiːd-] *n* aceite *m* de linaza.
lint [lɪnt] *n* gasa.
lintel [ˈlɪntl] *n* dintel *m*.
lion [ˈlaɪən] *n* león *m*.
lioness [ˈlaɪənɪs] *n* leona.
lip [lɪp] *n* labio; (*of jug*) pico; (*of cup etc*) borde *m*.
liposuction [ˈlɪpəusʌkʃən] *n* liposucción *f*.
lipread [ˈlɪpriːd] *vi* leer los labios.
lip salve *n* crema protectora para labios.
lip service *n*: **to pay ~ to sth** alabar algo pero sin hacer nada.
lipstick [ˈlɪpstɪk] *n* lápiz *m or* barra de labios, carmín *m*.
liquefy [ˈlɪkwɪfaɪ] *vt* licuar ♦ *vi* licuarse.
liqueur [lɪˈkjuə*] *n* licor *m*.
liquid [ˈlɪkwɪd] *adj, n* líquido.
liquidate [ˈlɪkwɪdeɪt] *vt* liquidar.
liquidation [lɪkwɪˈdeɪʃən] *n* liquidación *f*; **to go into ~** entrar en liquidación.
liquid crystal display (LCD) *n* pantalla de cristal líquido.
liquidity [lɪˈkwɪdɪtɪ] *n* (*COMM*) liquidez *f*.
liquidize [ˈlɪkwɪdaɪz] *vt* (*CULIN*) licuar.
liquidizer [ˈlɪkwɪdaɪzə*] *n* (*CULIN*) licuadora.
liquor [ˈlɪkə*] *n* licor *m*, bebidas *fpl* alcohólicas.
liquorice [ˈlɪkərɪs] *n* regaliz *m*.
liquor store *n* (*US*) bodega, *tienda de vinos y bebidas alcohólicas*.
Lisbon [ˈlɪzbən] *n* Lisboa.
lisp [lɪsp] *n* ceceo.
lissom [ˈlɪsəm] *adj* ágil.
list [lɪst] *n* lista; (*of ship*) inclinación *f* ♦ *vt* (*write down*) hacer una lista de; (*enumerate*) catalogar; (*COMPUT*) hacer un listado de ♦ *vi* (*ship*) inclinarse; **shopping ~** lista de las compras; *see also* **lists**.
listed building [ˈlɪstɪd-] *n* (*ARCHIT*) edificio de interés histórico-artístico.
listed company [ˈlɪstɪd-] *n* compañía cotizable.
listen [ˈlɪsn] *vi* escuchar, oír; (*pay attention*) atender.
listener [ˈlɪsnə*] *n* oyente *m/f*.
listeria [lɪsˈtɪərɪə] *n* listeria.
listing [ˈlɪstɪŋ] *n* (*COMPUT*) listado.
listless [ˈlɪstlɪs] *adj* apático, indiferente.
listlessly [ˈlɪstlɪslɪ] *adv* con indiferencia.
listlessness [ˈlɪstlɪsnɪs] *n* indiferencia, apatía.
list price *n* precio de catálogo.
lists [lɪsts] *npl* (*HISTORY*) liza *sg*; **to enter the ~ (against sb/sth)** salir a la palestra (contra algn/algo).
lit [lɪt] *pt, pp of* **light**.
litany [ˈlɪtənɪ] *n* letanía.
liter [ˈliːtə*] *n* (*US*) = **litre**.
literacy [ˈlɪtərəsɪ] *n* capacidad *f* de leer y escribir; **~ campaign** campaña de alfabetización.
literal [ˈlɪtərl] *adj* literal.
literally [ˈlɪtrəlɪ] *adv* literalmente.
literary [ˈlɪtərərɪ] *adj* literario.
literate [ˈlɪtərət] *adj* que sabe leer y escribir; (*fig*) culto.
literature [ˈlɪtərɪtʃə*] *n* literatura; (*brochures etc*) folletos *mpl*.
lithe [laɪð] *adj* ágil.
litho(graph) [ˈlɪθəu(grɑːf)] *n* litografía.
lithography [lɪˈθɔgrəfɪ] *n* litografía.
Lithuania [lɪθjuˈeɪnɪə] *n* Lituania.
Lithuanian [lɪθjuˈeɪnɪən] *adj* lituano ♦ *n* lituano/a; (*LING*) lituano.
litigate [ˈlɪtɪgeɪt] *vi* litigar.
litigation [lɪtɪˈgeɪʃən] *n* litigio.
litmus paper [ˈlɪtməs-] *n* papel *m* de tornasol.
litre, (*US*) **liter** [ˈliːtə*] *n* litro.
litter [ˈlɪtə*] *n* (*rubbish*) basura; (*paper*) papeles *mpl* (tirados); (*young animals*) camada, cría.
litter bin *n* (*BRIT*) papelera.
littered [ˈlɪtəd] *adj*: **~ with** lleno de.
litter lout, (*US*) **litterbug** [ˈlɪtəbʌg] *n* *persona que tira papeles usados en la vía pública*.
little [ˈlɪtl] *adj* (*small*) pequeño, chico (*esp LAM*); (*not much*) poco; (*often translated by suffix, eg*): **~ house** casita ♦ *adv* poco; **a ~** un poco (de); **~ by ~** poco a poco; **~ finger** (dedo) meñique *m*; **for a ~ while** (durante) un rato; **with ~ difficulty** sin problema *or* dificultad; **as ~ as possible**

lo menos posible.
little-known ['lɪtl'nəun] *adj* poco conocido.
liturgy ['lɪtədʒɪ] *n* liturgia.
live *vb* [lɪv] *vi* vivir ♦ *vt* (*a life*) llevar; (*experience*) vivir ♦ *adj* [laɪv] (*animal*) vivo; (*wire*) conectado; (*broadcast*) en directo; (*issue*) de actualidad; (*unexploded*) sin explotar; **to ~ in London** vivir en Londres; **to ~ together** vivir juntos.
▸**live down** *vt* hacer olvidar.
▸**live off** *vt fus* (*land, fish etc*) vivir de; (*pej: parents etc*) vivir a costa de.
▸**live on** *vt fus* (*food*) vivir de, alimentarse de; **to ~ on £50 a week** vivir con 50 libras semanales *or* a la semana.
▸**live out** *vi* (*students*) ser externo ♦ *vt*: **to ~ out one's days** *or* **life** pasar el resto de la vida.
▸**live up** *vt*: **to ~ it up** (*col*) tirarse la gran vida.
▸**live up to** *vt fus* (*fulfil*) cumplir con; (*justify*) justificar.
live-in ['lɪvɪn] *adj*: **~ partner** pareja, compañero/a sentimental; **~ maid** asistenta interna.
livelihood ['laɪvlɪhud] *n* sustento.
liveliness ['laɪvlɪnɪs] *n* viveza.
lively ['laɪvlɪ] *adj* (*gen*) vivo; (*talk*) animado; (*pace*) rápido; (*party, tune*) alegre.
liven up ['laɪvn-] *vt* (*discussion, evening*) animar.
liver ['lɪvə*] *n* hígado.
liverish ['lɪvərɪʃ] *adj*: **to feel ~** sentirse *or* encontrarse mal, no estar muy católico.
Liverpudlian [lɪvə'pʌdlɪən] *adj* de Liverpool ♦ *n* nativo/a (*or* habitante *m/f*) de Liverpool.
livery ['lɪvərɪ] *n* librea.
lives [laɪvz] *npl of* **life.**
livestock ['laɪvstɔk] *n* ganado.
live wire [laɪv-] *n* (*fig, col*): **he's a real ~!** ¡tiene una marcha!
livid ['lɪvɪd] *adj* lívido; (*furious*) furioso.
living ['lɪvɪŋ] *adj* (*alive*) vivo ♦ *n*: **to earn** *or* **make a ~** ganarse la vida; **cost of ~** coste *m* de la vida; **in ~ memory** que se recuerde *or* recuerda.
living conditions *npl* condiciones *fpl* de vida.
living expenses *npl* gastos *mpl* de mantenimiento.
living room *n* sala (de estar), living *m* (*LAM*).
living standards *npl* nivel *msg* de vida.
living wage *n* sueldo suficiente para vivir.
lizard ['lɪzəd] *n* lagartija.
llama ['lɑːmə] *n* llama.
LLB *n abbr* (= *Bachelor of Laws*) Ldo./a. en Dcho; *see also* **Bachelor's Degree.**
LLD *n abbr* (= *Doctor of Laws*) Dr(a). en Dcho.
LMT *n abbr* (*US*: = *Local Mean Time*) *hora local.*
load [ləud] *n* (*gen*) carga; (*weight*) peso ♦ *vt* (*COMPUT*) cargar; (*also*: **~ up**): **to ~ (with)** cargar (con *or* de); **a ~ of, ~s of** (*fig*) (gran) cantidad de, montones de.
loaded ['ləudɪd] *adj* (*dice*) cargado; (*question*) intencionado; (*col: rich*) forrado (de dinero).
loading ['ləudɪŋ] *n* (*COMM*) sobreprima.
loading bay *n* área de carga y descarga.
loaf, *pl* **loaves** [ləuf, ləuvz] *n* (barra de) pan *m* ♦ *vi* (*also*: **~ about, ~ around**) holgazanear.
loam [ləum] *n* marga.
loan [ləun] *n* préstamo; (*COMM*) empréstito ♦ *vt* prestar; **on ~** (*book, painting*) prestado; **to raise a ~** (*money*) procurar un empréstito.
loan account *n* cuenta de crédito.
loan capital *n* empréstito.
loan shark *n* (*col: pej*) prestamista *m/f* sin escrúpulos.
loath [ləuθ] *adj*: **to be ~ to do sth** ser reacio a hacer algo.
loathe [ləuð] *vt* aborrecer; (*person*) odiar.
loathing ['ləuðɪŋ] *n* aversión *f*; odio.
loathsome ['ləuðsəm] *adj* asqueroso, repugnante; (*person*) odioso.
loaves [ləuvz] *pl of* **loaf.**
lob [lɔb] *vt* (*ball*) volear por alto.
lobby ['lɔbɪ] *n* vestíbulo, sala de espera; (*POL: pressure group*) grupo de presión ♦ *vt* presionar.
lobbyist ['lɔbɪɪst] *n* cabildero/a.
lobe [ləub] *n* lóbulo.
lobster ['lɔbstə*] *n* langosta.
lobster pot *n* nasa, langostera.
local ['ləukl] *adj* local ♦ *n* (*pub*) bar *m*; **the ~s** *npl* los vecinos, los del lugar.
local anaesthetic *n* (*MED*) anestesia local.
local authority *n* municipio, ayuntamiento (*SP*).
local call *n* (*TEL*) llamada local.
local government *n* gobierno municipal.
locality [ləu'kælɪtɪ] *n* localidad *f*.
localize ['ləukəlaɪz] *vt* localizar.
locally ['ləukəlɪ] *adv* en la vecindad.
locate [ləu'keɪt] *vt* (*find*) localizar; (*situate*) situar, ubicar (*LAM*).
location [ləu'keɪʃən] *n* situación *f*; **on ~** (*CINE*) en exteriores, fuera del estudio.
loch [lɔx] *n* lago.
lock [lɔk] *n* (*of door, box*) cerradura, chapa (*LAM*); (*of canal*) esclusa; (*of hair*) mechón

m ♦ *vt* (*with key*) cerrar con llave; (*immobilize*) inmovilizar ♦ *vi* (*door etc*) cerrarse con llave; (*wheels*) trabarse; ~ **stock and barrel** (*fig*) por completo *or* entero; **on full** ~ (*AUT*) con el volante girado al máximo.
►**lock away** *vt* (*valuables*) guardar bajo llave; (*criminal*) encerrar.
►**lock out** *vt*: **the workers were ~ed out** los trabajadores tuvieron que enfrentarse con un cierre patronal.
►**lock up** *vi* echar la llave.
locker ['lɔkə*] *n* casillero.
locker-room ['lɔkərum] *n* (*US SPORT*) vestuario.
locket ['lɔkɪt] *n* medallón *m*.
lockout ['lɔkaut] *n* (*INDUSTRY*) paro *or* cierre *m* patronal, lockout *m*.
locksmith ['lɔksmɪθ] *n* cerrajero/a.
lock-up ['lɔkʌp] *n* (*prison*) cárcel *f*; (*cell*) jaula; (~ *garage*) jaula, cochera.
locomotive [ləukə'məutɪv] *n* locomotora.
locum ['ləukəm] *n* (*MED*) (médico/a) suplente *m/f*.
locust ['ləukəst] *n* langosta.
lodge [lɔdʒ] *n* casa del guarda; (*porter's*) portería; (*FREEMASONRY*) logia ♦ *vi* (*person*): **to ~ (with)** alojarse (en casa de) ♦ *vt* (*complaint*) presentar.
lodger ['lɔdʒə*] *n* huésped(a) *m/f*.
lodgings ['lɔdʒɪŋz] *npl* alojamiento *sg*; (*house*) casa *sg* de huéspedes.
loft [lɔft] *n* desván *m*.
lofty ['lɔftɪ] *adj* alto; (*haughty*) altivo, arrogante; (*sentiments, aims*) elevado, noble.
log [lɔg] *n* (*of wood*) leño, tronco; (*book*) = **logbook** ♦ *n abbr* (= *logarithm*) log. ♦ *vt* anotar, registrar.
►**log in, log on** *vi* (*COMPUT*) iniciar la (*or* una) sesión.
►**log off, log out** *vi* (*COMPUT*) finalizar la sesión.
logarithm ['lɔgərɪðəm] *n* logaritmo.
logbook ['lɔgbuk] *n* (*NAUT*) diario de a bordo; (*AVIAT*) libro de vuelo; (*of car*) documentación *f* (del coche).
log cabin *n* cabaña de troncos.
log fire *n* fuego de leña.
logger ['lɔgə*] *n* leñador(a) *m/f*.
loggerheads ['lɔgəhɛdz] *npl*: **at ~ (with)** de pique (con).
logic ['lɔdʒɪk] *n* lógica.
logical ['lɔdʒɪkl] *adj* lógico.
logically ['lɔdʒɪkəlɪ] *adv* lógicamente.
logistics [lɔ'dʒɪstɪks] *n* logística.
log jam *n*: **to break the ~** poner fin al estancamiento.
logo ['ləugəu] *n* logotipo.
loin [lɔɪn] *n* (*CULIN*) lomo, solomillo; **~s** *npl* lomos *mpl*.
loin cloth *n* taparrabos *m inv*.
loiter ['lɔɪtə*] *vi* vagar; (*pej*) merodear.
loll [lɔl] *vi* (*also*: **~ about**) repantigarse.
lollipop ['lɔlɪpɔp] *n* pirulí *m*, chupachup(s) ® *m inv*; (*iced*) polo.
lollipop lady *n* (*BRIT*) ver recuadro.
lollipop man *n* (*BRIT*) ver recuadro.

LOLLIPOP LADY, LOLLIPOP MAN

Se llama **lollipop lady** *o* **lollipop man** *a la persona encargada de parar el tráfico en las carreteras cercanas a los colegios británicos para que los niños las crucen sin peligro. Suelen ser personas ya jubiladas, vestidas con un abrigo de color luminoso y llevando una señal de stop en un poste portátil, la cual recuerda por su forma a un chupachups, de ahí su nombre.*

lolly ['lɔlɪ] *n* (*col*: *ice cream*) polo; (: *lollipop*) piruleta; (: *money*) guita.
Lombardy ['lɔmbədɪ] *n* Lombardía.
London ['lʌndən] *n* Londres *m*.
Londoner ['lʌndənə*] *n* londinense *m/f*.
lone [ləun] *adj* solitario.
loneliness ['ləunlɪnɪs] *n* soledad *f*, aislamiento.
lonely ['ləunlɪ] *adj* solitario, solo.
lonely hearts *adj*: **~ ad** anuncio de la sección de contactos; **~ column** sección *f* de contactos.
lone parent family *n* familia monoparental.
loner ['ləunə*] *n* solitario/a.
lonesome ['ləunsəm] *adj* (*esp US*) = **lonely**.
long [lɔŋ] *adj* largo ♦ *adv* mucho tiempo, largamente ♦ *vi*: **to ~ for sth** anhelar algo ♦ *n*: **the ~ and the short of it is that ...** (*fig*) en resumidas cuentas ...; **in the ~ run** a la larga; **so** *or* **as ~ as** mientras, con tal de que; **don't be ~!** ¡no tardes!, ¡vuelve pronto!; **how ~ is the street?** ¿cuánto tiene la calle de largo?; **how ~ is the lesson?** ¿cuánto dura la clase?; **6 metres ~** que mide 6 metros, de 6 metros de largo; **6 months ~** que dura 6 meses, de 6 meses de duración; **all night ~** toda la noche; **~ ago** hace mucho (tiempo); **he no ~er comes** ya no viene; **~ before** mucho antes; **before ~** (+ *future*) dentro de poco; (+ *past*) poco tiempo después; **at ~ last** al fin, por fin; **I shan't be ~** termino pronto.
long-distance [lɔŋ'dɪstəns] *adj* (*race*) de

larga distancia; (*call*) interurbano.
longevity [lɔn'dʒɛvɪtɪ] *n* longevidad *f.*
long-haired ['lɔŋ'hɛəd] *adj* de pelo largo.
longhand ['lɔŋhænd] *n* escritura (corriente).
longing ['lɔŋɪŋ] *n* anhelo, ansia; (*nostalgia*) nostalgia ♦ *adj* anhelante.
longingly ['lɔŋɪŋlɪ] *adv* con ansia.
longitude ['lɔŋgɪtjuːd] *n* longitud *f.*
long jump *n* salto de longitud.
long-lost ['lɔŋlɔst] *adj* desaparecido hace mucho tiempo.
long-playing record (LP) ['lɔŋpleɪɪŋ-] *n* elepé *m*, disco de larga duración.
long-range ['lɔŋ'reɪndʒ] *adj* de gran alcance; (*weather forecast*) a largo plazo.
longshoreman ['lɔŋʃɔːmən] *n* (*US*) estibador *m.*
long-sighted ['lɔŋ'saɪtɪd] *adj* (*BRIT*) présbita.
long-standing ['lɔŋ'stændɪŋ] *adj* de mucho tiempo.
long-suffering [lɔŋ'sʌfərɪŋ] *adj* sufrido.
long-term ['lɔŋtəːm] *adj* a largo plazo.
long wave *n* onda larga.
long-winded [lɔŋ'wɪndɪd] *adj* prolijo.
loo [luː] *n* (*BRIT*: *col*) wáter *m.*
loofah ['luːfə] *n* esponja de lufa.
look [luk] *vi* mirar; (*seem*) parecer; (*building etc*): **to ~ south/on to the sea** dar al sur/al mar ♦ *n* mirada; (*glance*) vistazo; (*appearance*) aire *m*, aspecto; **~s** *npl* físico *sg*, belleza *sg*; **to ~ ahead** mirar hacia delante; **it ~s about 4 metres long** yo calculo que tiene unos 4 metros de largo; **it ~s all right to me** a mí me parece que está bien; **to have a ~ at sth** echar un vistazo a algo; **to have a ~ for sth** buscar algo.
►**look after** *vt fus* cuidar.
►**look around** *vi* echar una mirada alrededor.
►**look at** *vt fus* mirar; (*consider*) considerar.
►**look back** *vi* mirar hacia atrás; **to ~ back at sb/sth** mirar hacia atrás algo/a algn; **to ~ back on** (*event, period*) recordar.
►**look down on** *vt fus* (*fig*) despreciar, mirar con desprecio.
►**look for** *vt fus* buscar.
►**look forward to** *vt fus* esperar con ilusión; (*in letters*): **we ~ forward to hearing from you** quedamos a la espera de su respuesta *or* contestación; **I'm not ~ing forward to it** no tengo ganas de eso, no me hace ilusión.
►**look in** *vi*: **to ~ in on sb** (*visit*) pasar por casa de algn.
►**look into** *vt fus* investigar.
►**look on** *vi* mirar (como espectador).
►**look out** *vi* (*beware*): **to ~ out (for)** tener cuidado (de).
►**look out for** *vt fus* (*seek*) buscar; (*await*) esperar.
►**look over** *vt* (*essay*) revisar; (*town, building*) inspeccionar, registrar; (*person*) examinar.
►**look round** *vi* (*turn*) volver la cabeza; **to ~ round for sth** buscar algo.
►**look through** *vt fus* (*papers, book*) hojear; (*briefly*) echar un vistazo a; (*telescope*) mirar por.
►**look to** *vt fus* ocuparse de; (*rely on*) contar con.
►**look up** *vi* mirar hacia arriba; (*improve*) mejorar ♦ *vt* (*word*) buscar; (*friend*) visitar.
►**look up to** *vt fus* admirar.
look-out ['lukaut] *n* (*tower etc*) puesto de observación; (*person*) vigía *m/f*; **to be on the ~ for sth** estar al acecho de algo.
look-up table ['lukʌp-] *n* (*COMPUT*) tabla de consulta.
LOOM *n abbr* (*US*: = *Loyal Order of Moose*) *asociación benéfica.*
loom [luːm] *n* telar *m* ♦ *vi* (*threaten*) amenazar.
loony ['luːnɪ] *adj*, *n* (*col*) loco/a *m/f.*
loop [luːp] *n* lazo; (*bend*) vuelta, recodo; (*COMPUT*) bucle *m.*
loophole ['luːphəul] *n* laguna.
loose [luːs] *adj* (*gen*) suelto; (*not tight*) flojo; (*wobbly etc*) movedizo; (*clothes*) ancho; (*morals, discipline*) relajado ♦ *vt* (*free*) soltar; (*slacken*) aflojar; (*also*: **~ off**: *arrow*) disparar, soltar; **~ connection** (*ELEC*) hilo desempalmado; **to be at a ~ end** *or* (*US*) **at ~ ends** no saber qué hacer; **to tie up ~ ends** (*fig*) no dejar ningún cabo suelto, atar cabos.
loose change *n* cambio.
loose chippings [-'tʃɪpɪŋz] *npl* (*on road*) gravilla *sg* suelta.
loose-fitting ['luːsfɪtɪŋ] *adj* suelto.
loose-leaf ['luːsliːf] *adj*: **~ binder** *or* **folder** carpeta de anillas.
loose-limbed ['luːslɪmd] *adj* ágil, suelto.
loosely ['luːslɪ] *adv* libremente, aproximadamente.
loosely-knit [-nɪt] *adj* de estructura abierta.
loosen ['luːsn] *vt* (*free*) soltar; (*untie*) desatar; (*slacken*) aflojar.
►**loosen up** *vi* (*before game*) hacer (ejercicios de) precalentamiento; (*col*: *relax*) soltarse, relajarse.
looseness ['luːsnɪs] *n* soltura; flojedad *f.*

loot [luːt] *n* botín *m* ♦ *vt* saquear.
looter ['luːtə*] *n* saqueador(a) *m/f.*
looting ['luːtɪŋ] *n* pillaje *m.*
lop [lɔp]: **to ~ off** *vt* cortar; (*branches*) podar.
lop-sided ['lɔp'saɪdɪd] *adj* desequilibrado.
lord [lɔːd] *n* señor *m*; **L~ Smith** Lord Smith; **the L~** el Señor; **the (House of) L~s** (*BRIT*) la Cámara de los Lores.
lordly ['lɔːdlɪ] *adj* señorial.
Lordship ['lɔːdʃɪp] *n*: **your ~** su Señoría.
lore [lɔː*] *n* saber *m* popular, tradiciones *fpl.*
lorry ['lɔrɪ] *n* (*BRIT*) camión *m.*
lorry driver *n* camionero/a.
lorry load *n* carga.
lose, *pt, pp* **lost** [luːz, lɔst] *vt* perder ♦ *vi* perder, ser vencido; **to ~ (time)** (*clock*) atrasarse; **to ~ no time (in doing sth)** no tardar (en hacer algo); **to get lost** (*object*) extraviarse; (*person*) perderse.
▸**lose out** *vi* salir perdiendo.
loser ['luːzə*] *n* perdedor(a) *m/f*; **to be a bad ~** no saber perder.
losing ['luːzɪŋ] *adj* (*team etc*) vencido, perdedor(a).
loss [lɔs] *n* pérdida; **heavy ~es** (*MIL*) grandes pérdidas *fpl*; **to be at a ~** no saber qué hacer; **to be a dead ~** ser completamente inútil; **to cut one's ~es** reducir las pérdidas; **to sell sth at a ~** vender algo perdiendo dinero.
loss adjuster *n* (*INSURANCE*) perito/a *m/f* or tasador(a) *m/f* de pérdidas.
loss leader *n* (*COMM*) artículo de promoción.
lost [lɔst] *pt, pp of* **lose** ♦ *adj* perdido; **~ in thought** absorto, ensimismado.
lost and found *n* (*US*) = **lost property, lost property office** *or* **department**.
lost cause *n* causa perdida.
lost property *n* (*BRIT*) objetos *mpl* perdidos.
lost property office *or* **department** *n* (*BRIT*) departamento de objetos perdidos.
lot [lɔt] *n* (*at auctions*) lote *m*; (*destiny*) suerte *f*; **the ~** el todo, todos *mpl*, todas *fpl*; **a ~** mucho, bastante; **a ~ of, ~s of** mucho(s)/a(s) (*pl*); **I read a ~** leo bastante; **to draw ~s (for sth)** echar suertes (para decidir algo).
lotion ['ləuʃən] *n* loción *f.*
lottery ['lɔtərɪ] *n* lotería.
loud [laud] *adj* (*voice, sound*) fuerte; (*laugh, shout*) estrepitoso; (*gaudy*) chillón/ona ♦ *adv* (*speak etc*) fuerte; **out ~** en voz alta.
loudhailer [laud'heɪlə*] *n* (*BRIT*) megáfono.
loudly ['laudlɪ] *adv* (*noisily*) fuerte; (*aloud*) en alta voz.
loudness ['laudnɪs] *n* (*of sound etc*) fuerza.
loudspeaker [laud'spiːkə*] *n* altavoz *m.*
lounge [laundʒ] *n* salón *m*, sala de estar; (*of hotel*) salón *m*; (*of airport*) sala de embarque ♦ *vi* (*also*: **~ about, ~ around**) holgazanear, no hacer nada; *see also* **pub**.
lounge bar *n* salón *m.*
lounge suit *n* (*BRIT*) traje *m* de calle.
louse, *pl* **lice** [laus, laɪs] *n* piojo.
▸**louse up** *vt* (*col*) echar a perder.
lousy ['lauzɪ] *adj* (*fig*) vil, asqueroso.
lout [laut] *n* gamberro/a.
louvre, (*US*) **louver** ['luːvə*] *adj*: **~ door** puerta de rejilla; **~ window** ventana de libro.
lovable ['lʌvəbl] *adj* amable, simpático.
love [lʌv] *n* amor *m* ♦ *vt* amar, querer; **to send one's ~ to sb** dar sus recuerdos a algn; **~ from Anne** (*in letter*) con cariño de Anne; **I ~ to read** me encanta leer; **to be in ~ with** estar enamorado de; **to make ~** hacer el amor; **for the ~ of** por amor a; **"15 ~"** (*TENNIS*) "15 a cero"; **I ~ paella** me encanta la paella; **I'd ~ to come** me gustaría muchísimo venir.
love affair *n* aventura sentimental *or* amorosa.
love child *n* hijo/a natural.
loved ones ['lʌvdwʌnz] *npl* seres *mpl* queridos.
love-hate relationship ['lʌvheɪt-] *n* relación *f* de amor y odio.
love letter *n* carta de amor.
love life *n* vida sentimental.
lovely ['lʌvlɪ] *adj* (*delightful*) precioso, encantador(a), lindo (*esp LAM*); (*beautiful*) hermoso, lindo (*esp LAM*); **we had a ~ time** lo pasamos estupendo.
lovemaking ['lʌvmeɪkɪŋ] *n* relaciones *fpl* sexuales.
lover ['lʌvə*] *n* amante *m/f*; (*amateur*): **a ~ of** un(a) aficionado/a *or* un(a) amante de.
lovesick ['lʌvsɪk] *adj* enfermo de amor, amartelado.
lovesong ['lʌvsɔŋ] *n* canción *f* de amor.
loving ['lʌvɪŋ] *adj* amoroso, cariñoso.
lovingly ['lʌvɪŋlɪ] *adv* amorosamente, cariñosamente.
low [ləu] *adj, adv* bajo ♦ *n* (*METEOROLOGY*) área de baja presión ♦ *vi* (*cow*) mugir; **to feel ~** sentirse deprimido; **to turn (down) ~** bajar; **to reach a new** *or* **an all-time ~** llegar a su punto más bajo.
low-alcohol [ləu'ælkəhɔl] *adj* bajo en alcohol.
lowbrow ['ləubrau] *adj* (*person*) de poca cultura.
low-calorie ['ləu'kælərɪ] *adj* bajo en

calorías.
low-cut ['ləukʌt] *adj* (*dress*) escotado.
low-down ['ləudaun] *n* (*col*): **he gave me the ~ on it** me puso al corriente ♦ *adj* (*mean*) vil, bajo.
lower ['ləuə*] *vt* bajar; (*reduce*: *price*) reducir, rebajar; (: *resistance*) debilitar: **to ~ o.s. to** (*fig*) rebajarse a ♦ *vi* ['lauə*]: **to ~ (at sb)** fulminar (a algn) con la mirada.
lower case *n* (*TYP*) minúscula.
Lower House *n* (*POL*): **the ~** la Cámara baja.
lowering ['lauərıŋ] *adj* (*sky*) amenazador(a).
low-fat ['ləu'fæt] *adj* (*milk, yoghurt*) desnatado; (*diet*) bajo en calorías.
low-key ['ləu'kiː] *adj* de mínima intensidad; (*operation*) de poco perfil.
lowland ['ləulənd] *n* tierra baja.
low-level ['ləulɛvl] *adj* de bajo nivel; (*flying*) a poca altura.
low-loader ['ləuləudə*] *n* camión *m* de caja a bajo nivel.
lowly ['ləulı] *adj* humilde.
low-lying [ləu'laııŋ] *adj* bajo.
low-rise ['ləuraız] *adj* bajo.
low-tech ['ləutɛk] *adj* de baja tecnología.
loyal ['lɔıəl] *adj* leal.
loyalist ['lɔıəlıst] *n* legitimista *m/f*.
loyally ['lɔıəlı] *adv* lealmente.
loyalty ['lɔıəltı] *n* lealtad *f*.
loyalty card *n* (*BRIT*) tarjeta cliente.
lozenge ['lɔzındʒ] *n* (*MED*) pastilla.
LP *n abbr see* **long-playing record**.
L-plates ['ɛlpleıts] *npl* (*BRIT*) (placas *fpl* de) la L; *ver recuadro*.

L-PLATES

En el Reino Unido las personas que están aprendiendo a conducir han de llevar indicativos blancos con una L en rojo llamados normalmente **L-plates** *(de "learner") en la parte delantera y trasera de los automóviles que conducen. No tienen que ir a clases teóricas, sino que desde el principio se les entrega un carnet de conducir provisional ("provisional driving licence") para que realicen sus prácticas, que han de estar supervisadas por un conductor con carnet definitivo ("full driving licence"). Tampoco se les permite hacer prácticas en autopistas aunque vayan acompañados.*

LPN *n abbr* (*US*: = *Licensed Practical Nurse*) enfermero/a practicante.
LRAM *n abbr* (*BRIT*) = *Licentiate of the Royal Academy of Music*.
LSD *n abbr* (= *lysergic acid diethylamide*) LSD *m*; (*BRIT*: = *pounds, shillings and pence*) *sistema monetario usado en Gran Bretaña hasta 1971.*
LSE *n abbr* = *London School of Economics*.
Ltd *abbr* (= *limited company*) S.A.
lubricant ['luːbrıkənt] *n* lubricante *m*.
lubricate ['luːbrıkeıt] *vt* lubricar, engrasar.
lubrication [luːbrı'keıʃən] *n* lubricación *f*.
lucid ['luːsıd] *adj* lúcido.
lucidity [luː'sıdıtı] *n* lucidez *f*.
lucidly ['luːsıdlı] *adv* lúcidamente.
luck [lʌk] *n* suerte *f*; **good/bad ~** buena/mala suerte; **good ~!** ¡(que tengas) suerte!; **to be in ~** estar de suerte; **to be out of ~** tener mala suerte.
luckily ['lʌkılı] *adv* afortunadamente.
lucky ['lʌkı] *adj* afortunado.
lucrative ['luːkrətıv] *adj* lucrativo.
ludicrous ['luːdıkrəs] *adj* absurdo.
ludo ['luːdəu] *n* parchís *m*.
lug [lʌg] *vt* (*drag*) arrastrar.
luggage ['lʌgıdʒ] *n* equipaje *m*.
luggage rack *n* (*in train*) rejilla, redecilla; (*on car*) baca, portaequipajes *m inv*.
luggage van *n* furgón *m or* vagón *m* de equipaje.
lugubrious [lu'guːbrıəs] *adj* lúgubre.
lukewarm ['luːkwɔːm] *adj* tibio, templado.
lull [lʌl] *n* tregua ♦ *vt* (*child*) acunar; (*person, fear*) calmar.
lullaby ['lʌləbaı] *n* nana.
lumbago [lʌm'beıgəu] *n* lumbago.
lumber ['lʌmbə*] *n* (*junk*) trastos *mpl* viejos; (*wood*) maderos *mpl* ♦ *vt* (*BRIT col*): **to ~ sb with sth/sb** hacer que algn cargue con algo/algn ♦ *vi* (*also*: **~ about, ~ along**) moverse pesadamente.
lumberjack ['lʌmbədʒæk] *n* maderero.
lumber room *n* (*BRIT*) cuarto trastero.
lumber yard *n* (*US*) almacén *m* de madera.
luminous ['luːmınəs] *adj* luminoso.
lump [lʌmp] *n* terrón *m*; (*fragment*) trozo; (*in sauce*) grumo; (*in throat*) nudo; (*swelling*) bulto ♦ *vt* (*also*: **~ together**) juntar; (*persons*) poner juntos.
lump sum *n* suma global.
lumpy ['lʌmpı] *adj* (*sauce*) lleno de grumos.
lunacy ['luːnəsı] *n* locura.
lunar ['luːnə*] *adj* lunar.
lunatic ['luːnətık] *adj, n* loco/a *m/f*.
lunatic asylum *n* manicomio.
lunch [lʌntʃ] *n* almuerzo, comida ♦ *vi* almorzar; **to invite sb to** *or* **for ~** invitar a algn a almorzar.
lunch break, lunch hour *n* hora del almuerzo.

luncheon ['lʌntʃən] *n* almuerzo.
luncheon meat *n tipo de fiambre.*
luncheon voucher *n* vale *m* de comida.
lunchtime ['lʌntʃtaɪm] *n* hora del almuerzo *or* de comer.
lung [lʌŋ] *n* pulmón *m.*
lung cancer *n* cáncer *m* del pulmón.
lunge [lʌndʒ] *vi* (*also*: ~ **forward**) abalanzarse; **to ~ at** arremeter contra.
lupin ['lu:pɪn] *n* altramuz *m.*
lurch [lə:tʃ] *vi* dar sacudidas ♦ *n* sacudida; **to leave sb in the ~** dejar a algn plantado.
lure [luə*] *n* (*bait*) cebo; (*decoy*) señuelo ♦ *vt* convencer con engaños.
lurid ['luərɪd] *adj* (*colour*) chillón/ona; (*account*) sensacional; (*detail*) horripilante.
lurk [lə:k] *vi* (*hide*) esconderse; (*wait*) estar al acecho.
luscious ['lʌʃəs] *adj* delicioso.
lush [lʌʃ] *adj* exuberante.
lust [lʌst] *n* lujuria; (*greed*) codicia.
▸**lust after** *vt fus* codiciar.
lustful ['lʌstful] *adj* lascivo, lujurioso.
lustre, (*US*) **luster** ['lʌstə*] *n* lustre *m,* brillo.
lustrous ['lʌstrəs] *adj* brillante.
lusty ['lʌstɪ] *adj* robusto, fuerte.
lute [lu:t] *n* laúd *m.*
Luxembourg ['lʌksəmbə:g] *n* Luxemburgo.
luxuriant [lʌg'zjuərɪənt] *adj* exuberante.
luxurious [lʌg'zjuərɪəs] *adj* lujoso.
luxury ['lʌkʃərɪ] *n* lujo ♦ *cpd* de lujo.
luxury tax *n* impuesto de lujo.
LV *n abbr* (*BRIT*) = **luncheon voucher**.
LW *abbr* (*RADIO*) = **long wave**.
Lycra ® ['laɪkrə] *n* licra ®.
lying ['laɪɪŋ] *n* mentiras *fpl* ♦ *adj* (*statement, story*) falso; (*person*) mentiroso.
lynch [lɪntʃ] *vt* linchar.
lynx [lɪnks] *n* lince *m.*
Lyons ['laɪənz] *n* Lyón *m.*
lyre ['laɪə*] *n* lira.
lyric ['lɪrɪk] *adj* lírico; **~s** *npl* (*of song*) letra *sg.*
lyrical ['lɪrɪkl] *adj* lírico.

M m

M, m [ɛm] *n* (*letter*) M, m *f*; **M for Mary**, (*US*) **M for Mike** M de Madrid.
M *n abbr* = **million(s)**; (= *medium*) M; (*BRIT*: = *motorway*): **the M8** ≈ la A8.
m *abbr* (= *metre*) m.; = **mile(s)**.
MA *n abbr* (*US*) = *Military Academy*; *see* **Master of Arts** ♦ *abbr* (*US*) = *Massachusetts.*
mac [mæk] *n* (*BRIT*) impermeable *m.*
macabre [mə'kɑ:brə] *adj* macabro.
macaroni [mækə'rəunɪ] *n* macarrones *mpl.*
macaroon [mækə'ru:n] *n* macarŕon *m,* mostachón *m.*
mace [meɪs] *n* (*weapon, ceremonial*) maza; (*spice*) macis *f.*
Macedonia [mæsɪ'dəunɪə] *n* Macedonia.
Macedonian [mæsɪ'dəunɪən] *adj* macedonio ♦ *n* macedonio/a; (*LING*) macedonio.
machinations [mæʃɪ'neɪʃənz] *npl* intrigas *fpl,* maquinaciones *fpl.*
machine [mə'ʃi:n] *n* máquina ♦ *vt* (*dress etc*) coser a máquina; (*TECH*) trabajar a máquina.
machine code *n* (*COMPUT*) código máquina.
machine gun *n* ametralladora.
machine language *n* (*COMPUT*) lenguaje *m* máquina.
machine readable *adj* (*COMPUT*) legible por máquina.
machinery [mə'ʃi:nərɪ] *n* maquinaria; (*fig*) mecanismo.
machine shop *n* taller *m* de máquinas.
machine tool *n* máquina herramienta.
machine translation *n* traducción *f* automática.
machine washable *adj* lavable a máquina.
machinist [mə'ʃi:nɪst] *n* operario/a *m/f* (de máquina).
macho ['mætʃəu] *adj* macho.
mackerel ['mækrl] *n, pl inv* caballa.
mackintosh ['mækɪntɔʃ] *n* (*BRIT*) impermeable *m.*
macro ... ['mækrəu] *pref* macro....
macro-economics ['mækrəui:kə'nɔmɪks] *n* macroeconomía.
mad [mæd] *adj* loco; (*idea*) disparatado;

(*angry*) furioso, enojado (*LAM*); ~ **(at** *or* **with sb)** furioso con algn; **to be ~ (keen) about** *or* **on sth** estar loco por algo; **to go ~** volverse loco, enloquecer(se).
madam ['mædəm] *n* señora; **can I help you ~?** ¿le puedo ayudar, señora?; **M~ Chairman** señora presidenta.
madcap ['mædkæp] *adj* (*col*) alocado, disparatado.
mad cow disease *n* encefalopatía espongiforme bovina.
madden ['mædn] *vt* volver loco.
maddening ['mædnɪŋ] *adj* enloquecedor(a).
made [meɪd] *pt, pp of* **make.**
Madeira [mə'dɪərə] *n* (*GEO*) Madeira; (*wine*) madeira *m.*
made-to-measure ['meɪdtəmɛʒə*] *adj* (*BRIT*) hecho a la medida.
made-up ['meɪdʌp] *adj* (*story*) ficticio.
madhouse ['mædhaus] *n* (*also fig*) manicomio.
madly ['mædlɪ] *adv* locamente.
madman ['mædmən] *n* loco.
madness ['mædnɪs] *n* locura.
Madonna [mə'dɔnə] *n* Virgen *f.*
Madrid [mə'drɪd] *n* Madrid *m.*
madrigal ['mædrɪgəl] *n* madrigal *m.*
Mafia ['mæfɪə] *n* Mafia.
mag [mæg] *n abbr* (*BRIT col*) = **magazine.**
magazine [mægə'zi:n] *n* revista; (*MIL: store*) almacén *m*; (*of firearm*) recámara.
maggot ['mægət] *n* gusano.
magic ['mædʒɪk] *n* magia ♦ *adj* mágico.
magical ['mædʒɪkəl] *adj* mágico.
magician [mə'dʒɪʃən] *n* mago/a.
magistrate ['mædʒɪstreɪt] *n* juez *m/f* (municipal); **M~s' Courts** *see* **crown court**.
magnanimity [mægnə'nɪmɪtɪ] *n* magnanimidad *f.*
magnanimous [mæg'nænɪməs] *adj* magnánimo.
magnate ['mægneɪt] *n* magnate *m/f.*
magnesium [mæg'ni:zɪəm] *n* magnesio.
magnet ['mægnɪt] *n* imán *m.*
magnetic [mæg'nɛtɪk] *adj* magnético.
magnetic disk *n* (*COMPUT*) disco magnético.
magnetic tape *n* cinta magnética.
magnetism ['mægnɪtɪzəm] *n* magnetismo.
magnification [mægnɪfɪ'keɪʃən] *n* aumento.
magnificence [mæg'nɪfɪsns] *n* magnificencia.
magnificent [mæg'nɪfɪsnt] *adj* magnífico.
magnificently [mæg'nɪfɪsntlɪ] *adv* magníficamente.
magnify ['mægnɪfaɪ] *vt* aumentar; (*fig*) exagerar.
magnifying glass ['mægnɪfaɪɪŋ-] *n* lupa.
magnitude ['mægnɪtju:d] *n* magnitud *f.*
magnolia [mæg'nəulɪə] *n* magnolia.
magpie ['mægpaɪ] *n* urraca.
maharajah [mɑ:hə'rɑ:dʒə] *n* maharajá *m.*
mahogany [mə'hɔgənɪ] *n* caoba ♦ *cpd* de caoba.
maid [meɪd] *n* criada; **old ~** (*pej*) solterona.
maiden ['meɪdn] *n* doncella ♦ *adj* (*aunt etc*) solterona; (*speech, voyage*) inaugural.
maiden name *n* apellido de soltera.
mail [meɪl] *n* correo; (*letters*) cartas *fpl* ♦ *vt* (*post*) echar al correo; (*send*) mandar por correo; **by ~** por correo.
mailbox ['meɪlbɔks] *n* (*US: for letters etc; COMPUT*) buzón *m.*
mailing list ['meɪlɪŋ-] *n* lista de direcciones.
mailman ['meɪlmæn] *n* (*US*) cartero.
mail-order ['meɪlɔ:də*] *n* pedido postal; (*business*) venta por correo ♦ *adj*: **~ firm** *or* **house** casa de venta por correo.
mailshot ['meɪlʃɔt] *n* mailing *m inv.*
mailtrain ['meɪltreɪn] *n* tren *m* correo.
mail van, (*US*) **mail truck** *n* (*AUT*) camioneta de correos *or* de reparto.
maim [meɪm] *vt* mutilar, lisiar.
main [meɪn] *adj* principal, mayor ♦ *n* (*pipe*) cañería principal *or* maestra; (*US*) red *f* eléctrica; **the ~s** (*BRIT ELEC*) la red eléctrica; **in the ~** en general.
main course *n* (*CULIN*) plato principal.
mainframe ['meɪnfreɪm] *n* (*also*: **~ computer**) ordenador *m or* computadora central.
mainland ['meɪnlənd] *n* continente *m.*
main line *n* línea principal.
mainly ['meɪnlɪ] *adv* principalmente, en su mayoría.
main road *n* carretera principal.
mainstay ['meɪnsteɪ] *n* (*fig*) pilar *m.*
mainstream ['meɪnstri:m] *n* (*fig*) corriente *f* principal.
main street *n* calle *f* mayor.
maintain [meɪn'teɪn] *vt* mantener; (*affirm*) sostener; **to ~ that ...** mantener *or* sostener que ... .
maintenance ['meɪntənəns] *n* mantenimiento; (*alimony*) pensión *f* alimenticia.
maintenance contract *n* contrato de mantenimiento.
maintenance order *n* (*LAW*) obligación *f* de pagar una pensión alimenticia al cónyuge.
maisonette [meɪzə'nɛt] *n* dúplex *m.*
maize [meɪz] *n* (*BRIT*) maíz *m*, choclo (*LAM*).
Maj. *abbr* (*MIL*) = **major.**
majestic [mə'dʒɛstɪk] *adj* majestuoso.

majesty ['mædʒɪstɪ] *n* majestad *f*.
major ['meɪdʒə*] *n* (*MIL*) comandante *m* ♦ *adj* principal; (*MUS*) mayor ♦ *vi* (*US UNIV*): **to ~ (in)** especializarse en; **a ~ operation** una operación *or* intervención de gran importancia.
Majorca [mə'jɔːkə] *n* Mallorca.
major general *n* (*MIL*) general *m* de división.
majority [mə'dʒɔrɪtɪ] *n* mayoría ♦ *cpd* (*verdict*) mayoritario.
majority holding *n* (*COMM*): **to have a ~** tener un interés mayoritario.
make [meɪk] *vt* (*pt, pp* **made** [meɪd]) hacer; (*manufacture*) hacer, fabricar; (*cause to be*): **to ~ sb sad** poner triste *or* entristecer a algn; (*force*): **to ~ sb do sth** obligar a algn a hacer algo; (*equal*): **2 and 2 ~ 4** 2 y 2 son 4 ♦ *n* marca; **to ~ a fool of sb** poner a algn en ridículo; **to ~ a profit/loss** obtener ganancias/sufrir pérdidas; **to ~ a profit of £500** sacar una ganancia de 500 libras; **to ~ it** (*arrive*) llegar; (*achieve sth*) tener éxito; **what time do you ~ it?** ¿qué hora tienes?; **to ~ do with** contentarse con.
▸**make for** *vt fus* (*place*) dirigirse a.
▸**make off** *vi* largarse.
▸**make out** *vt* (*decipher*) descifrar; (*understand*) entender; (*see*) distinguir; (*write: cheque*) extender; **to ~ out (that)** (*claim, imply*) dar a entender (que); **to ~ out a case for sth** dar buenas razones en favor de algo.
▸**make over** *vt* (*assign*): **to ~ over (to)** ceder *or* traspasar (a).
▸**make up** *vt* (*invent*) inventar; (*parcel*) hacer ♦ *vi* reconciliarse; (*with cosmetics*) maquillarse; **to be made up of** estar compuesto de.
▸**make up for** *vt fus* compensar.
make-believe ['meɪkbɪliːv] *n* ficción *f*, fantasía.
maker ['meɪkə*] *n* fabricante *m/f*.
makeshift ['meɪkʃɪft] *adj* improvisado.
make-up ['meɪkʌp] *n* maquillaje *m*.
make-up bag *n* bolsita del maquillaje *or* de los cosméticos.
make-up remover *n* desmaquillador *m*.
making ['meɪkɪŋ] *n* (*fig*): **in the ~** en vías de formación; **to have the ~s of** (*person*) tener madera de.
maladjusted [mælə'dʒʌstɪd] *adj* inadaptado.
maladroit [maelə'drɔɪt] *adj* torpe.
malaise [mæ'leɪz] *n* malestar *m*.
malaria [mə'lɛərɪə] *n* malaria.
Malawi [mə'lɑːwɪ] *n* Malawi *m*.
Malay [mə'leɪ] *adj* malayo ♦ *n* malayo/a; (*LING*) malayo.
Malaya [mə'leɪə] *n* Malaya, Malaca.
Malayan [mə'leɪən] *adj, n* = **Malay**.
Malaysia [mə'leɪzɪə] *n* Malaisia, Malaysia.
Malaysian [mə'leɪzɪən] *adj, n* malaisio/a *m/f*, malaysio/a *m/f*.
Maldive Islands ['mɔːldaɪv-], **Maldives** ['mɔːldaɪvz] *npl*: **the ~** las Maldivas.
male [meɪl] *n* (*BIOL, ELEC*) macho ♦ *adj* (*sex, attitude*) masculino; (*child etc*) varón.
male chauvinist (pig) *n* machista *m*.
male nurse *n* enfermero.
malevolence [mə'lɛvələns] *n* malevolencia.
malevolent [mə'lɛvələnt] *adj* malévolo.
malfunction [mæl'fʌŋkʃən] *n* mal funcionamiento.
malice ['mælɪs] *n* (*ill will*) malicia; (*rancour*) rencor *m*.
malicious [mə'lɪʃəs] *adj* malicioso; rencoroso.
maliciously [mə'lɪʃəslɪ] *adv* con malevolencia, con malicia; rencorosamente.
malign [mə'laɪn] *vt* difamar, calumniar ♦ *adj* maligno.
malignant [mə'lɪgnənt] *adj* (*MED*) maligno.
malinger [mə'lɪŋgə*] *vi* fingirse enfermo.
malingerer [mə'lɪŋgərə*] *n* enfermo/a fingido/a.
mall [mɔːl] *n* (*US: also:* **shopping ~**) centro comercial.
malleable ['mælɪəbl] *adj* maleable.
mallet ['mælɪt] *n* mazo.
malnutrition [mælnjuː'trɪʃən] *n* desnutrición *f*.
malpractice [mæl'præktɪs] *n* negligencia profesional.
malt [mɔːlt] *n* malta.
Malta ['mɔːltə] *n* Malta.
Maltese [mɔːl'tiːz] *adj* maltés/esa ♦ *n, pl inv* maltés/esa *m/f*; (*LING*) maltés *m*.
maltreat [mæl'triːt] *vt* maltratar.
mammal ['mæml] *n* mamífero.
mammoth ['mæməθ] *n* mamut *m* ♦ *adj* gigantesco.
man, *pl* **men** [mæn, mɛn] *n* hombre *m*; (*CHESS*) pieza ♦ *vt* (*NAUT*) tripular; (*MIL*) defender; **an old ~** un viejo; **~ and wife** marido y mujer.
Man. *abbr* (*Canada*) = *Manitoba*.
manacle ['mænəkl] *n* esposa, manilla; **~s** *npl* grillos *mpl*.
manage ['mænɪdʒ] *vi* arreglárselas ♦ *vt* (*be in charge of*) dirigir; (*person etc*) manejar; **to ~ to do sth** conseguir hacer algo; **to ~ without sth/sb** poder prescindir de algo/algn.

manageable ['mænɪdʒəbl] *adj* manejable.
management ['mænɪdʒmənt] *n* dirección *f*, administración *f*; **"under new ~"** "bajo nueva dirección".
management accounting *n* contabilidad *f* de gestión.
management consultant *n* consultor(a) *m/f* en dirección de empresas.
manager ['mænɪdʒə*] *n* director *m*; (*SPORT*) entrenador *m*; **sales ~** jefe/a *m/f* de ventas.
manageress ['mænɪdʒərɛs] *n* directora; (*SPORT*) entrenadora.
managerial [mænə'dʒɪerɪəl] *adj* directivo.
managing director (MD) ['mænɪdʒɪŋ-] *n* director(a) *m/f* general.
Mancunian [mæŋ'kju:nɪən] *adj* de Manchester ♦ *n* nativo/a (*or* habitante *m/f*) de Manchester.
mandarin ['mændərɪn] *n* (*also*: **~ orange**) mandarina; (*person*) mandarín *m*.
mandate ['mændeɪt] *n* mandato.
mandatory ['mændətərɪ] *adj* obligatorio.
mandolin(e) ['mændəlɪn] *n* mandolina.
mane [meɪn] *n* (*of horse*) crin *f*; (*of lion*) melena.
maneuver [mə'nu:və*] (*US*) = **manoeuvre**.
manful ['mænful] *adj* resuelto.
manfully ['mænfəlɪ] *adv* resueltamente.
mangetout [mɔnʒ'tu:] *n* tirabeque *m*.
mangle ['mæŋgl] *vt* mutilar, destrozar ♦ *n* escurridor *m*.
mango, **~es** ['mæŋgəu] *n* mango.
mangrove ['mæŋgrəuv] *n* mangle *m*.
mangy ['meɪndʒɪ] *adj* roñoso; (*MED*) sarnoso.
manhandle ['mænhændl] *vt* maltratar; (*move by hand*: *goods*) manipular.
manhole ['mænhəul] *n* boca de acceso.
manhood ['mænhud] *n* edad *f* viril; (*manliness*) virilidad *f*.
man-hour ['mæn'auə*] *n* hora-hombre *f*.
manhunt ['mænhʌnt] *n* caza de hombre.
mania ['meɪnɪə] *n* manía.
maniac ['meɪnɪæk] *n* maníaco/a; (*fig*) maniático.
manic ['mænɪk] *adj* (*behaviour, activity*) frenético.
manic-depressive ['mænɪkdɪ'prɛsɪv] *adj, n* maniacodepresivo/a *m/f*.
manicure ['mænɪkjuə*] *n* manicura.
manicure set *n* estuche *m* de manicura.
manifest ['mænɪfɛst] *vt* manifestar, mostrar ♦ *adj* manifiesto ♦ *n* manifiesto.
manifestation [mænɪfɛs'teɪʃən] *n* manifestación *f*.
manifestly ['mænɪfɛstlɪ] *adv* evidentemente.
manifesto [mænɪ'fɛstəu] *n* manifiesto.
manifold ['mænɪfəuld] *adj* múltiples ♦ *n* (*AUT etc*): **exhaust ~** colector *m* de escape.
Manila [mə'nɪlə] *n* Manila.
manil(l)a [mə'nɪlə] *n* (*paper, envelope*) manila.
manipulate [mə'nɪpjuleɪt] *vt* manipular.
manipulation [mənɪpju'leɪʃən] *n* manipulación *f*, manejo.
mankind [mæn'kaɪnd] *n* humanidad *f*, género humano.
manliness ['mænlɪnɪs] *n* virilidad *f*, hombría.
manly ['mænlɪ] *adj* varonil.
man-made ['mæn'meɪd] *adj* artificial.
manna ['mænə] *n* maná *m*.
mannequin ['maenɪkɪn] *n* (*dummy*) maniquí *m*; (*fashion model*) maniquí *m/f*.
manner ['mænə*] *n* manera, modo; (*behaviour*) conducta, manera de ser; (*type*) clase *f*; **~s** *npl* modales *mpl*, educación *fsg*; **(good) ~s** (buena) educación *fsg*, (buenos) modales *mpl*; **bad ~s** falta *sg* de educación, pocos modales *mpl*; **all ~ of** toda clase *or* suerte de.
mannerism ['mænərɪzəm] *n* gesto típico.
mannerly ['mænəlɪ] *adj* bien educado, formal.
man(o)euvrable [mə'nu:vrəbl] *adj* (*car etc*) manejable.
manoeuvre, (*US*) **maneuver** [mə'nu:və*] *vt, vi* maniobrar ♦ *n* maniobra; **to ~ sb into doing sth** manipular a algn para que haga algo.
manor ['mænə*] *n* (*also*: **~ house**) casa solariega.
manpower ['mænpauə*] *n* mano *f* de obra.
Manpower Services Commission (MSC) *n* (*BRIT*) *comisión para el aprovechamiento de los recursos humanos.*
manservant ['mænsə:vənt] *n* criado.
mansion ['mænʃən] *n* mansión *f*.
manslaughter ['mænslɔ:tə*] *n* homicidio involuntario.
mantelpiece ['mæntlpi:s] *n* repisa de la chimenea.
mantle ['mæntl] *n* manto.
man-to-man ['mæntə'mæn] *adj* de hombre a hombre.
manual ['mænjuəl] *adj* manual ♦ *n* manual *m*; **~ worker** obrero, trabajador *m* manual.
manufacture [mænju'fæktʃə*] *vt* fabricar ♦ *n* fabricación *f*.
manufactured goods [mænju'fæktʃəd-] *npl* manufacturas *fpl*, bienes *mpl* manufacturados.

manufacturer [mænju'fæktʃərə*] *n* fabricante *m/f*.
manufacturing industries [mænju'fæktʃərɪŋ-] *npl* industrias *fpl* manufactureras.
manure [mə'njuə*] *n* estiércol *m*, abono.
manuscript ['mænjuskrɪpt] *n* manuscrito.
Manx [mæŋks] *adj* de la Isla de Man.
many ['mɛnɪ] *adj* muchos/as ♦ *pron* muchos/as; **a great** ~ muchísimos, un buen número de; ~ **a time** muchas veces; **too** ~ **difficulties** demasiadas dificultades; **twice as** ~ el doble; **how** ~**?** ¿cuántos?
Maori ['maurɪ] *adj, n* maorí *m/f*.
map [mæp] *n* mapa *m* ♦ *vt* trazar el mapa de.
▸**map out** *vt* (*fig*: *career, holiday, essay*) proyectar, planear.
maple ['meɪpl] *n* arce *m*, maple *m* (*LAM*).
mar [mɑː*] *vt* estropear.
Mar. *abbr* (= *March*) mar.
marathon ['mærəθən] *n* maratón *m* ♦ *adj*: **a** ~ **session** una sesión maratoniana.
marathon runner *n* corredor(a) *m/f* de maratones.
marauder [mə'rɔːdə*] *n* merodeador(a) *m/f*.
marble ['mɑːbl] *n* mármol *m*; (*toy*) canica.
March [mɑːtʃ] *n* marzo.
march [mɑːtʃ] *vi* (*MIL*) marchar; (*fig*) caminar con resolución ♦ *n* marcha; (*demonstration*) manifestación *f*.
marcher ['mɑːtʃə*] *n* manifestante *m/f*.
marching ['mɑːtʃɪŋ] *n*: **to give sb his** ~ **orders** (*fig*) mandar a paseo a algn; (*employee*) poner de patitas en la calle a algn.
march-past ['mɑːtʃpɑːst] *n* desfile *m*.
mare [mɛə*] *n* yegua.
margarine [mɑːdʒə'riːn] *n* margarina.
marg(e) [mɑːdʒ] *n abbr* = **margarine**.
margin ['mɑːdʒɪn] *n* margen *m*.
marginal ['mɑːdʒɪnl] *adj* marginal.
marginally ['mɑːdʒɪnəlɪ] *adv* ligeramente.
marginal seat *n* (*POL*) circunscripción *f* políticamente no definida.
marigold ['mærɪgəuld] *n* caléndula.
marijuana [mærɪ'wɑːnə] *n* marihuana.
marina [mə'riːnə] *n* marina.
marinade [mærɪ'neɪd] *n* adobo.
marinate ['mærɪneɪt] *vt* adobar.
marine [mə'riːn] *adj* marino ♦ *n* soldado de infantería de marina.
marine insurance *n* seguro marítimo.
mariner ['mærɪnə*] *n* marinero, marino.
marionette [mærɪə'nɛt] *n* marioneta, títere *m*.
marital ['mærɪtl] *adj* matrimonial; ~ **status** estado civil.
maritime ['mærɪtaɪm] *adj* marítimo.
marjoram ['mɑːdʒərəm] *n* mejorana.
mark [mɑːk] *n* marca, señal *f*; (*imprint*) huella; (*stain*) mancha; (*BRIT SCOL*) nota; (*currency*) marco ♦ *vt* (*also SPORT*: *player*) marcar; (*stain*) manchar; (*BRIT SCOL*) calificar, corregir; **punctuation** ~**s** signos *mpl* de puntuación; **to be quick off the** ~ (*fig*) ser listo; **up to the** ~ (*in efficiency*) a la altura de las circunstancias; **to** ~ **time** marcar el paso.
▸**mark down** *vt* (*reduce*: *prices, goods*) rebajar.
▸**mark off** *vt* (*tick*) indicar, señalar.
▸**mark out** *vt* trazar.
▸**mark up** *vt* (*price*) aumentar.
marked [mɑːkt] *adj* marcado, acusado.
markedly ['mɑːkɪdlɪ] *adv* marcadamente, apreciablemente.
marker ['mɑːkə*] *n* (*sign*) marcador *m*; (*bookmark*) registro.
market ['mɑːkɪt] *n* mercado ♦ *vt* (*COMM*) comercializar; (*promote*) publicitar; **open** ~ mercado libre; **to be on the** ~ estar en venta; **to play the** ~ jugar a la bolsa.
marketable ['mɑːkɪtəbl] *adj* comerciable.
market analysis *n* análisis *m* del mercado.
market day *n* día *m* de mercado.
market demand *n* demanda de mercado.
market economy *n* economía de mercado.
market forces *npl* tendencias *fpl* del mercado.
market garden *n* (*BRIT*) huerto.
marketing ['mɑːkɪtɪŋ] *n* marketing *m*, mercadotecnia.
marketing manager *n* director *m* de marketing.
market leader *n* líder *m* de ventas.
marketplace ['mɑːkɪtpleɪs] *n* mercado.
market price *n* precio de mercado.
market research *n* (*COMM*) estudios *mpl* de mercado.
market value *n* valor *m* en el mercado.
marking ['mɑːkɪŋ] *n* (*on animal*) pinta; (*on road*) señal *f*.
marking ink *n* tinta indeleble *or* de marcar.
marksman ['mɑːksmən] *n* tirador *m*.
marksmanship ['mɑːksmənʃɪp] *n* puntería.
mark-up ['mɑːkʌp] *n* (*COMM*: *margin*) margen *m* de beneficio; (: *increase*) aumento.
marmalade ['mɑːməleɪd] *n* mermelada de naranja.
maroon [mə'ruːn] *vt*: **to be** ~**ed** (*shipwrecked*) naufragar; (*fig*) quedar abandonado ♦ *adj* granate *inv*.
marquee [mɑː'kiː] *n* carpa, entoldado.

marquess, marquis ['mɑːkwɪs] *n* marqués *m.*
Marrakech, Marrakesh [mærə'kɛʃ] *n* Marrakech *m.*
marriage ['mærɪdʒ] *n* (*state*) matrimonio; (*wedding*) boda; (*act*) casamiento.
marriage bureau *n* agencia matrimonial.
marriage certificate *n* partida de casamiento.
marriage guidance, (*US*) **marriage counseling** *n* orientación *f* matrimonial.
marriage of convenience *n* matrimonio de conveniencia.
married ['mærɪd] *adj* casado; (*life, love*) conyugal.
marrow ['mærəu] *n* médula; (*vegetable*) calabacín *m.*
marry ['mærɪ] *vt* casarse con; (*subj: father, priest etc*) casar ♦ *vi* (*also*: **get married**) casarse.
Mars [mɑːz] *n* Marte *m.*
Marseilles [mɑː'seɪ] *n* Marsella.
marsh [mɑːʃ] *n* pantano; (*salt* ~) marisma.
marshal ['mɑːʃl] *n* (*MIL*) mariscal *m*; (*at sports meeting, demonstration etc*) oficial *m*; (*US*: *of police, fire department*) jefe/a *m/f* ♦ *vt* (*facts*) ordenar; (*soldiers*) formar.
marshalling yard ['mɑːʃəlɪŋ-] *n* (*RAIL*) estación *f* clasificadora.
marshmallow ['mɑːʃmæləu] *n* (*BOT*) malvavisco; (*sweet*) esponja, dulce *m* de merengue blando.
marshy ['mɑːʃɪ] *adj* pantanoso.
marsupial [mɑː'suːpɪəl] *adj, n* marsupial *m.*
martial ['mɑːʃl] *adj* marcial.
martial arts *npl* artes *fpl* marciales.
martial law *n* ley *f* marcial.
martin ['mɑːtɪn] *n* (*also*: **house** ~) avión *m.*
martyr ['mɑːtə*] *n* mártir *m/f* ♦ *vt* martirizar.
martyrdom ['mɑːtədəm] *n* martirio.
marvel ['mɑːvl] *n* maravilla, prodigio ♦ *vi*: **to** ~ **(at)** maravillarse (de).
marvellous, (*US*) **marvelous** ['mɑːvləs] *adj* maravilloso.
marvel(l)ously ['mɑːvləslɪ] *adv* maravillosamente.
Marxism ['mɑːksɪzəm] *n* marxismo.
Marxist ['mɑːksɪst] *adj, n* marxista *m/f.*
marzipan ['mɑːzɪpæn] *n* mazapán *m.*
mascara [mæs'kɑːrə] *n* rimel *m.*
mascot ['mæskət] *n* mascota.
masculine ['mæskjulɪn] *adj* masculino.
masculinity [mæskju'lɪnɪtɪ] *n* masculinidad *f.*
MASH [mæʃ] *n abbr* (*US*) = *mobile army surgical hospital.*
mash [mæʃ] *n* (*mix*) mezcla; (*CULIN*) puré *m*; (*pulp*) amasijo.
mashed potatoes [mæʃt-] *npl* puré *m* de patatas *or* papas (*LAM*).
mask [mɑːsk] *n* (*also ELEC*) máscara ♦ *vt* enmascarar.
masochism ['mæsəkɪzəm] *n* masoquismo.
masochist ['mæsəukɪst] *n* masoquista *m/f.*
mason ['meɪsn] *n* (*also*: **stone**~) albañil *m*; (*also*: **free**~) masón *m.*
masonic [mə'sɔnɪk] *adj* masónico.
masonry ['meɪsnrɪ] *n* masonería; (*building*) mampostería.
masquerade [mæskə'reɪd] *n* baile *m* de máscaras; (*fig*) mascarada ♦ *vi*: **to** ~ **as** disfrazarse de, hacerse pasar por.
mass [mæs] *n* (*people*) muchedumbre *f*; (*PHYSICS*) masa; (*REL*) misa; (*great quantity*) montón *m* ♦ *vi* reunirse; (*MIL*) concentrarse; **the** ~**es** las masas; **to go to** ~ ir a *or* oír misa.
Mass. *abbr* (*US*) = *Massachusetts.*
massacre ['mæsəkə*] *n* masacre *f* ♦ *vt* masacrar.
massage ['mæsɑːʒ] *n* masaje *m* ♦ *vt* dar masajes *or* un masaje a.
masseur [mæ'səː*] *n* masajista *m.*
masseuse [mæ'səːz] *n* masajista *f.*
massive ['mæsɪv] *adj* enorme; (*support, intervention*) masivo.
mass media *npl* medios *mpl* de comunicación de masas.
mass meeting *n* (*of everyone concerned*) reunión *f* en masa; (*huge*) mitin *m.*
mass-produce ['mæsprə'djuːs] *vt* fabricar en serie.
mass-production ['mæsprə'dʌkʃən] *n* fabricación *f or* producción *f* en serie.
mast [mɑːst] *n* (*NAUT*) mástil *m*; (*RADIO etc*) torre *f*, antena.
mastectomy [mæs'tɛktəmɪ] *n* mastectomía.
master ['mɑːstə*] *n* (*of servant, animal*) amo; (*fig*: *of situation*) dueño; (*ART, MUS*) maestro; (*in secondary school*) profesor *m*; (*title for boys*): **M**~ **X** Señorito X ♦ *vt* dominar.
master disk *n* (*COMPUT*) disco maestro.
masterful ['mɑːstəful] *adj* magistral, dominante.
master key *n* llave *f* maestra.
masterly ['mɑːstəlɪ] *adj* magistral.
mastermind ['mɑːstəmaɪnd] *n* inteligencia superior ♦ *vt* dirigir, planear.
Master of Arts (MA) *n* licenciatura superior en Letras; *see also* **master's degree.**
Master of Ceremonies *n* encargado de protocolo.

Master of Science (MSc) *n* licenciatura superior en Ciencias; *see also* **master's degree**.
masterpiece ['mɑːstəpiːs] *n* obra maestra.
master plan *n* plan *m* rector.
master's degree *n* máster *m*; *ver recuadro.*

MASTER'S DEGREE

Los estudios de postgrado británicos que llevan a la obtención de un **master's degree** *consisten generalmente en una combinación de curso(s) académico(s) y tesina ("dissertation") sobre un tema original, o bien únicamente la redacción de una tesina. El primer caso es el más frecuente para los títulos de "MA" ("Master of Arts") y "MSc" ("Master of Science"), mientras que los de "MLitt" ("Master of Letters") o "MPhil" ("Master of Philosophy") se obtienen normalmente mediante tesina. En algunas universidades, como las escocesas, el título de* **master's degree** *no es de postgrado, sino que corresponde a la licenciatura.*

master stroke *n* golpe *m* maestro.
mastiff ['mæstɪf] *n* mastín *m.*
masturbate ['mæstəbeɪt] *vi* masturbarse.
masturbation [mæstə'beɪʃən] *n* masturbación *f.*
mat [mæt] *n* alfombrilla; (*also*: **door**~) felpudo ♦ *adj* = **matt**.
MAT *n abbr* (= *machine-assisted translation*) TAO.
match [mætʃ] *n* cerilla, fósforo; (*game*) partido; (*fig*) igual *m/f* ♦ *vt* emparejar; (*go well with*) hacer juego con; (*equal*) igualar ♦ *vi* hacer juego; **to be a good** ~ hacer buena pareja.
matchbox ['mætʃbɔks] *n* caja de cerillas.
matching ['mætʃɪŋ] *adj* que hace juego.
matchless ['mætʃlɪs] *adj* sin par.
matchmaker ['mætʃmeɪkə*] *n* casamentero.
mate [meɪt] *n* (*work*~) compañero/a, colega *m/f*; (*col*: *friend*) amigo/a, compadre *m/f* (*LAM*); (*animal*) macho/hembra; (*in merchant navy*) primer oficial *m* ♦ *vi* acoplarse, parearse ♦ *vt* acoplar, parear.
material [mə'tɪərɪəl] *n* (*substance*) materia; (*equipment*) material *m*; (*cloth*) tela, tejido ♦ *adj* material; (*important*) esencial; ~**s** *npl* materiales *mpl*; (*equipment etc*) artículos *mpl.*
materialistic [mətɪərɪə'lɪstɪk] *adj* materialista.
materialize [mə'tɪərɪəlaɪz] *vi* materializarse.
materially [mə'tɪərɪəlɪ] *adv* materialmente.
maternal [mə'təːnl] *adj* maternal; ~ **grandmother** abuela materna.
maternity [mə'təːnɪtɪ] *n* maternidad *f.*
maternity benefit *n* subsidio por maternidad.
maternity dress *n* vestido premamá.
maternity hospital *n* hospital *m* de maternidad.
maternity leave *n* baja por maternidad.
math [mæθ] *n abbr* (*US*: = *mathematics*) matemáticas *fpl.*
mathematical [mæθə'mætɪkl] *adj* matemático.
mathematically [mæθɪ'mætɪklɪ] *adv* matemáticamente.
mathematician [mæθəmə'tɪʃən] *n* matemático.
mathematics [mæθə'mætɪks] *n* matemáticas *fpl.*
maths [mæθs] *n abbr* (*BRIT*: = *mathematics*) matemáticas *fpl.*
matinée ['mætɪneɪ] *n* función *f* de la tarde, vermú(t) *m* (*LAM*).
mating ['meɪtɪŋ] *n* aparejamiento.
mating call *n* llamada del macho.
mating season *n* época de celo.
matins ['mætɪnz] *n* maitines *mpl.*
matriarchal [meɪtrɪ'ɑːkl] *adj* matriarcal.
matrices ['meɪtrɪsiːz] *pl of* **matrix**.
matriculation [mətrɪkju'leɪʃən] *n* matriculación *f*, matrícula.
matrimonial [mætrɪ'məunɪəl] *adj* matrimonial.
matrimony ['mætrɪmənɪ] *n* matrimonio.
matrix, *pl* **matrices** ['meɪtrɪks, 'meɪtrɪsiːz] *n* matriz *f.*
matron ['meɪtrən] *n* (*in hospital*) enfermera jefe; (*in school*) ama de llaves.
matronly ['meɪtrənlɪ] *adj* de matrona; (*fig*: *figure*) corpulento.
matt [mæt] *adj* mate.
matted ['mætɪd] *adj* enmarañado.
matter ['mætə*] *n* cuestión *f*, asunto; (*PHYSICS*) sustancia, materia; (*content*) contenido; (*MED*: *pus*) pus *m* ♦ *vi* importar; **it doesn't** ~ no importa; **what's the** ~**?** ¿qué pasa?; **no** ~ **what** pase lo que pase; **as a** ~ **of course** por rutina; **as a** ~ **of fact** en realidad; **printed** ~ impresos *mpl*; **reading** ~ material *m* de lectura, lecturas *fpl.*
matter-of-fact ['mætərəv'fækt] *adj* (*style*) prosaico; (*person*) práctico; (*voice*) neutro.
mattress ['mætrɪs] *n* colchón *m.*

mature [mə'tjuə*] *adj* maduro ♦ *vi* madurar.
mature student *n estudiante de más de 21 años.*
maturity [mə'tjuərɪtɪ] *n* madurez *f*.
maudlin ['mɔːdlɪn] *adj* llorón/ona.
maul [mɔːl] *vt* magullar.
Mauritania [mɔːrɪ'teɪnɪə] *n* Mauritania.
Mauritius [mə'rɪʃəs] *n* Mauricio.
mausoleum [mɔːsə'lɪəm] *n* mausoleo.
mauve [məuv] *adj* de color malva.
maverick ['mævrɪk] *n* (*fig*) inconformista *m/f*, persona independiente.
mawkish ['mɔːkɪʃ] *adj* sensiblero, empalagoso.
max. *abbr* = **maximum.**
maxim ['mæksɪm] *n* máxima.
maxima ['maeksɪmə] *pl of* **maximum.**
maximize ['mæksɪmaɪz] *vt* (*profits etc*) llevar al máximo; (*chances*) maximizar.
maximum ['mæksɪməm] *adj* máximo ♦ *n* (*pl* **maxima** ['mæksɪmə]) máximo.
May [meɪ] *n* mayo.
may [meɪ] *vi* (*conditional*: **might**) (*indicating possibility*): **he ~ come** puede que venga; (*be allowed to*): **~ I smoke?** ¿puedo fumar?; (*wishes*): **~ God bless you!** ¡que Dios le bendiga!; **~ I sit here?** ¿me puedo sentar aquí?
maybe ['meɪbiː] *adv* quizá(s); **~ not** quizá(s) no.
May Day *n* el primero de Mayo.
mayday ['meɪdeɪ] *n* señal *f* de socorro.
mayhem ['meɪhɛm] *n* caos *m* total.
mayonnaise [meɪə'neɪz] *n* mayonesa.
mayor [mɛə*] *n* alcalde *m*.
mayoress ['mɛərɛs] *n* alcaldesa.
maypole ['meɪpəul] *n* mayo.
maze [meɪz] *n* laberinto.
MB *abbr* (*COMPUT*) = **megabyte**; (*Canada*) = *Manitoba.*
MBA *n abbr* (= *Master of Business Administration*) *título universitario.*
MBBS, MBChB *n abbr* (*BRIT*: = *Bachelor of Medicine and Surgery*) *título universitario.*
MBE *n abbr* (*BRIT*: = *Member of the Order of the British Empire*) *título ceremonial.*
MC *n abbr* (= *master of ceremonies*) e.p.; (*US*: = *Member of Congress*) *diputado del Congreso de los Estados Unidos.*
MCAT *n abbr* (*US*) = *Medical College Admissions Test.*
MCP *n abbr* (*BRIT col*) = **male chauvinist pig.**
MD *n abbr* (= *Doctor of Medicine*) *título universitario*; (*COMM*) = **managing director** ♦ *abbr* (*US*) = *Maryland.*
Md. *abbr* (*US*) = *Maryland.*
MDT *n abbr* (*US*: = *mountain daylight time*) *hora de verano de las Montañas Rocosas.*
ME *abbr* (*US POST*) = *Maine* ♦ *n abbr* (*US MED*) = *medical examiner*; (*MED* = *myalgic encephalomyelitis*) encefalomielitis *f* miálgica.
me [miː] *pron* (*direct*) me; (*stressed, after pronoun*) mí; **can you hear ~?** ¿me oyes?; **he heard ME!** me oyó a mí; **it's ~** soy yo; **give them to ~** dámelos; **with/without ~** conmigo/sin mí; **it's for ~** es para mí.
meadow ['mɛdəu] *n* prado, pradera.
meagre, (*US*) **meager** ['miːgə*] *adj* escaso, pobre.
meal [miːl] *n* comida; (*flour*) harina; **to go out for a ~** salir a comer.
meals on wheels *nsg* (*BRIT*) *servicio de alimentación a domicilio para necesitados y tercera edad.*
mealtime ['miːltaɪm] *n* hora de comer.
mealy-mouthed ['miːlɪmauðd] *adj*: **to be ~** no decir nunca las cosas claras.
mean [miːn] *adj* (*with money*) tacaño; (*unkind*) mezquino, malo; (*average*) medio; (*US*: *vicious*: *animal*) resabiado; (: *person*) malicioso ♦ *vt* (*pt, pp* **meant** [mɛnt]) (*signify*) querer decir, significar; (*intend*): **to ~ to do sth** tener la intención de *or* pensar hacer algo ♦ *n* medio, término medio; **do you ~ it?** ¿lo dices en serio?; **what do you ~?** ¿qué quiere decir?; **to be meant for sb/sth** ser para algn/algo; *see also* **means.**
meander [mɪ'ændə*] *vi* (*river*) serpentear; (*person*) vagar.
meaning ['miːnɪŋ] *n* significado, sentido.
meaningful ['miːnɪŋful] *adj* significativo.
meaningless ['miːnɪŋlɪs] *adj* sin sentido.
meanness ['miːnnɪs] *n* (*with money*) tacañería; (*unkindness*) maldad *f*, mezquindad *f*.
means [miːnz] *npl* medio *sg*, manera *sg*; (*resource*) recursos *mpl*, medios *mpl*; **by ~ of** mediante, por medio de; **by all ~!** ¡naturalmente!, ¡claro que sí!
means test *n* control *m* de los recursos económicos.
meant [mɛnt] *pt, pp of* **mean.**
meantime ['miːntaɪm], **meanwhile** ['miːnwaɪl] *adv* (*also*: **in the meantime**) mientras tanto.
measles ['miːzlz] *n* sarampión *m*.
measly ['miːzlɪ] *adj* (*col*) miserable.
measurable ['mɛʒərəbl] *adj* mensurable, que se puede medir.
measure ['mɛʒə*] *vt* medir; (*for clothes etc*) tomar las medidas a ♦ *vi* medir ♦ *n* medida; (*ruler*) cinta métrica, metro; **a litre ~** una medida de un litro; **some ~ of**

success cierto éxito; **to take ~s to do sth** tomar medidas para hacer algo.
►**measure up** *vi*: **to ~ up (to)** estar a la altura (de).
measured ['mɛʒəd] *adj* moderado; (*tone*) mesurado.
measurement ['mɛʒəmənt] *n* (*measure*) medida; (*act*) medición *f*; **to take sb's ~s** tomar las medidas a algn.
meat [mi:t] *n* carne *f*; **cold ~s** fiambres *mpl*; **crab ~** carne *f* de cangrejo.
meatball ['mi:tbɔ:l] *n* albóndiga.
meat pie *n* pastel *m* de carne.
meaty ['mi:tɪ] *adj* (*person*) fuerte, corpulento; (*role*) sustancioso; **a ~ meal** una comida con bastante carne.
Mecca ['mɛkə] *n* (*city*) la Meca; (*fig*) meca.
mechanic [mɪ'kænɪk] *n* mecánico/a.
mechanical [mɪ'kænɪkl] *adj* mecánico.
mechanical engineering *n* (*science*) ingeniería mecánica; (*industry*) construcción *f* mecánica.
mechanics [mə'kænɪks] *n* mecánica ♦ *npl* mecanismo *sg*.
mechanism ['mɛkənɪzəm] *n* mecanismo.
mechanization [mɛkənaɪ'zeɪʃən] *n* mecanización *f*.
mechanize ['mɛkənaɪz] *vt* mecanizar; (*factory etc*) automatizar.
MEd *n abbr* (= *Master of Education*) *título universitario*.
medal ['mɛdl] *n* medalla.
medallion [mɪ'dælɪən] *n* medallón *m*.
medallist, (*US*) **medalist** ['mɛdlɪst] *n* (*SPORT*) medallista *m/f*.
meddle ['mɛdl] *vi*: **to ~ in** entrometerse en; **to ~ with sth** manosear algo.
meddlesome ['mɛdlsəm], **meddling** ['mɛdlɪŋ] *adj* (*interfering*) entrometido; (*touching things*) curioso.
media ['mi:dɪə] *npl* medios *mpl* de comunicación.
media circus *n excesivo despliegue informativo*.
mediaeval [mɛdɪ'i:vl] *adj* = **medieval**.
median ['mi:dɪən] *n* (*US*: *also*: **~ strip**) mediana.
media research *n* estudio de los medios de publicidad.
mediate ['mi:dɪeɪt] *vi* mediar.
mediation [mi:dɪ'eɪʃən] *n* mediación *f*.
mediator ['mi:dɪeɪtə*] *n* mediador(a) *m/f*.
Medicaid ['mɛdɪkeɪd] *n* (*US*) *programa de ayuda médica*.
medical ['mɛdɪkl] *adj* médico ♦ *n* (*also*: **~ examination**) reconocimiento médico.
medical certificate *n* certificado *m* médico.
Medicare ['mɛdɪkɛə*] *n* (*US*) *seguro médico del Estado*.
medicated ['mɛdɪkeɪtɪd] *adj* medicinal.
medication [mɛdɪ'keɪʃən] *n* (*drugs etc*) medicación *f*.
medicinal [mɛ'dɪsɪnl] *adj* medicinal.
medicine ['mɛdsɪn] *n* medicina; (*drug*) medicamento.
medicine chest *n* botiquín *m*.
medicine man *n* hechicero.
medieval, mediaeval [mɛdɪ'i:vl] *adj* medieval.
mediocre [mi:dɪ'əukə*] *adj* mediocre.
mediocrity [mi:dɪ'ɔkrɪtɪ] *n* mediocridad *f*.
meditate ['mɛdɪteɪt] *vi* meditar.
meditation [mɛdɪ'teɪʃən] *n* meditación *f*.
Mediterranean [mɛdɪtə'reɪnɪən] *adj* mediterráneo; **the ~ (Sea)** el (Mar *m*) Mediterráneo.
medium ['mi:dɪəm] *adj* mediano; (*level, height*) medio ♦ *n* (*pl* **media**: *means*) medio; (*pl* **mediums**: *person*) médium *m/f*; **happy ~** punto justo.
medium-dry ['mi:dɪəm'draɪ] *adj* semiseco.
medium-sized ['mi:dɪəm'saɪzd] *adj* de tamaño mediano; (*clothes*) de (la) talla mediana.
medium wave *n* onda media.
medley ['mɛdlɪ] *n* mezcla; (*MUS*) popurrí *m*.
meek [mi:k] *adj* manso, sumiso.
meekly ['mi:klɪ] *adv* mansamente, dócilmente.
meet [mi:t] *vb* (*pt, pp* **met** [mɛt]) *vt* encontrar; (*accidentally*) encontrarse con; (*by arrangement*) reunirse con; (*for the first time*) conocer; (*go and fetch*) ir a buscar; (*opponent*) enfrentarse con; (*obligations*) cumplir; (*bill, expenses*) pagar, costear ♦ *vi* encontrarse; (*in session*) reunirse; (*join: objects*) unirse; (*get to know*) conocerse ♦ *n* (*BRIT*: *HUNTING*) cacería; (*US*: *SPORT*) encuentro; **pleased to ~ you!** ¡encantado (de conocerle)!, ¡mucho gusto!
►**meet up** *vi*: **to ~ up with sb** reunirse con algn.
►**meet with** *vt fus* reunirse con; (*difficulty*) tropezar con.
meeting ['mi:tɪŋ] *n* (*also SPORT*: *rally*) encuentro; (*arranged*) cita, compromiso (*LAM*); (*formal session, business meet*) reunión *f*; (*POL*) mitin *m*; **to call a ~** convocar una reunión.
meeting place *n* lugar *m* de reunión *or* encuentro.
megabyte ['mɛgə'baɪt] *n* (*COMPUT*) megabyte *m*, megaocteto.
megalomaniac [mɛgələu'meɪnɪæk] *adj, n* megalómano/a *m/f*.

megaphone ['mɛgəfəun] *n* megáfono.
megawatt ['mɛgəwɔt] *n* megavatio.
melancholy ['mɛlənkəlɪ] *n* melancolía ♦ *adj* melancólico.
melee ['mɛleɪ] *n* refriega.
mellow ['mɛləu] *adj* (*wine*) añejo; (*sound, colour*) suave; (*fruit*) maduro ♦ *vi* (*person*) madurar.
melodious [mɪ'ləudɪəs] *adj* melodioso.
melodrama ['mɛləudrɑːmə] *n* melodrama *m*.
melodramatic [mɛləudrə'mætɪk] *adj* melodramático.
melody ['mɛlədɪ] *n* melodía.
melon ['mɛlən] *n* melón *m*.
melt [mɛlt] *vi* (*metal*) fundirse; (*snow*) derretirse; (*fig*) ablandarse ♦ *vt* (*also*: ~ **down**) fundir; ~**ed butter** mantequilla derretida.
▶**melt away** *vi* desvanecerse.
meltdown ['mɛltdaun] *n* (*in nuclear reactor*) fusión *f* (de un reactor nuclear).
melting point ['mɛltɪŋ-] *n* punto de fusión.
melting pot ['mɛltɪŋ-] *n* (*fig*) crisol *m*; **to be in the** ~ estar sobre el tapete.
member ['mɛmbə*] *n* (*of political party*) miembro; (*of club*) socio/a; **M~ of Parliament (MP)** (*BRIT*) diputado/a; **M~ of the European Parliament (MEP)** (*BRIT*) eurodiputado/a; **M~ of the House of Representatives (MHR)** (*US*) diputado/a del Congreso de los Estados Unidos; **M~ of the Scottish Parliament (MSP)** (*BRIT*) diputado/a del Parlamento escocés.
membership ['mɛmbəʃɪp] *n* (*members*) miembros *mpl*; socios *mpl*; (*numbers*) número de miembros *or* socios; **to seek ~ of** pedir el ingreso a.
membership card *n* carnet *m* de socio.
membrane ['mɛmbreɪn] *n* membrana.
memento [mə'mɛntəu] *n* recuerdo.
memo ['mɛməu] *n* nota (de servicio).
memoirs ['mɛmwɑːz] *npl* memorias *fpl*.
memo pad *n* bloc *m* de notas.
memorable ['mɛmərəbl] *adj* memorable.
memorandum, *pl* **memoranda** [mɛmə'rændəm, -də] *n* nota (de servicio); (*POL*) memorándum *m*.
memorial [mɪ'mɔːrɪəl] *n* monumento conmemorativo ♦ *adj* conmemorativo.
Memorial Day *n* (*US*) *día de conmemoración de los caídos en la guerra*.
memorize ['mɛməraɪz] *vt* aprender de memoria.
memory ['mɛmərɪ] *n* memoria; (*recollection*) recuerdo; **to have a good/bad** ~ tener buena/mala memoria; **loss of** ~ pérdida de memoria.
men [mɛn] *pl of* **man**.
menace ['mɛnəs] *n* amenaza; (*col*: *nuisance*) lata ♦ *vt* amenazar; **a public** ~ un peligro público.
menacing ['mɛnɪsɪŋ] *adj* amenazador(a).
menacingly ['mɛnɪsɪŋlɪ] *adv* amenazadoramente.
menagerie [mɪ'nædʒərɪ] *n* casa de fieras.
mend [mɛnd] *vt* reparar, arreglar; (*darn*) zurcir ♦ *vi* reponerse ♦ *n* (*gen*) remiendo; (*darn*) zurcido; **to be on the** ~ ir mejorando.
mending ['mɛndɪŋ] *n* arreglo, reparación *f*; (*clothes*) ropa por remendar.
menial ['miːnɪəl] *adj* (*pej*) bajo, servil.
meningitis [mɛnɪn'dʒaɪtɪs] *n* meningitis *f*.
menopause ['mɛnəupɔːz] *n* menopausia.
men's room *n* (*US*): **the** ~ el servicio de caballeros.
menstrual ['mɛnstruəl] *adj* menstrual.
menstruate ['mɛnstrueɪt] *vi* menstruar.
menstruation [mɛnstru'eɪʃən] *n* menstruación *f*.
menswear ['mɛnzwɛə*] *n* confección *f* de caballero.
mental ['mɛntl] *adj* mental; ~ **illness** enfermedad *f* mental.
mental hospital *n* (hospital *m*) psiquiátrico.
mentality [mɛn'tælɪtɪ] *n* mentalidad *f*.
mentally ['mɛntlɪ] *adv*: **to be ~ handicapped** ser un disminuido mental.
menthol ['mɛnθɔl] *n* mentol *m*.
mention ['mɛnʃən] *n* mención *f* ♦ *vt* mencionar; (*speak of*) hablar de; **don't ~ it!** ¡de nada!; **I need hardly ~ that ...** huelga decir que ...; **not to ~, without ~ing** sin contar.
mentor ['mɛntɔː*] *n* mentor *m*.
menu ['mɛnjuː] *n* (*set* ~) menú *m*; (*printed*) carta; (*COMPUT*) menú *m*.
menu-driven ['mɛnjuːdrɪvn] *adj* (*COMPUT*) guiado por menú.
MEP *n abbr see* **Member of the European Parliament**.
mercantile ['məːkəntaɪl] *adj* mercantil.
mercenary ['məːsɪnərɪ] *adj, n* mercenario.
merchandise ['məːtʃəndaɪz] *n* mercancías *fpl*.
merchandiser ['məːtʃəndaɪzə*] *n* comerciante *m/f*, tratante *m*.
merchant ['məːtʃənt] *n* comerciante *m/f*.
merchant bank *n* (*BRIT*) banco comercial.
merchantman ['məːtʃəntmən] *n* buque *m* mercante.
merchant navy, (*US*) **merchant marine** *n* marina mercante.

merciful ['mə:sɪful] *adj* compasivo.
mercifully ['mə:sɪfulɪ] *adv* con compasión; (*fortunately*) afortunadamente.
merciless ['mə:sɪlɪs] *adj* despiadado.
mercilessly ['mə:sɪlɪslɪ] *adv* despiadadamente, sin piedad.
mercurial [mə:'kjuərɪəl] *adj* veleidoso, voluble.
mercury ['mə:kjurɪ] *n* mercurio.
mercy ['mə:sɪ] *n* compasión *f*; (*REL*) misericordia; **at the ~ of** a la merced de.
mercy killing *n* eutanasia.
mere [mɪə*] *adj* simple, mero.
merely ['mɪəlɪ] *adv* simplemente, sólo.
merge [mə:dʒ] *vt* (*join*) unir; (*mix*) mezclar; (*fuse*) fundir; (*COMPUT*: *files, text*) intercalar ♦ *vi* unirse; (*COMM*) fusionarse.
merger ['mə:dʒə*] *n* (*COMM*) fusión *f*.
meridian [mə'rɪdɪən] *n* meridiano.
meringue [mə'ræŋ] *n* merengue *m*.
merit ['merɪt] *n* mérito ♦ *vt* merecer.
meritocracy [merɪ'tɔkrəsɪ] *n* meritocracia.
mermaid ['mə:meɪd] *n* sirena.
merrily ['merɪlɪ] *adv* alegremente.
merriment ['merɪmənt] *n* alegría.
merry ['merɪ] *adj* alegre; **M~ Christmas!** ¡Felices Pascuas!
merry-go-round ['merɪgəuraund] *n* tiovivo.
mesh [meʃ] *n* malla; (*TECH*) engranaje *m* ♦ *vi* (*gears*) engranar; **wire ~** tela metálica.
mesmerize ['mezməraɪz] *vt* hipnotizar.
mess [mes] *n* confusión *f*; (*of objects*) revoltijo; (*tangle*) lío; (*MIL*) comedor *m*; **to be (in) a ~** (*room*) estar revuelto; **to be/get o.s. in a ~** estar/meterse en un lío.
▸**mess about, mess around** *vi* (*col*) perder el tiempo; (*pass the time*) pasar el rato.
▸**mess about** *or* **around with** *vt fus* (*col*: *play with*) divertirse con; (: *handle*) manosear.
▸**mess up** *vt* (*disarrange*) desordenar; (*spoil*) estropear; (*dirty*) ensuciar.
message ['mesɪdʒ] *n* recado, mensaje *m*; **to get the ~** (*fig, col*) enterarse.
message switching *n* (*COMPUT*) conmutación *f* de mensajes.
messenger ['mesɪndʒə*] *n* mensajero/a.
Messiah [mɪ'saɪə] *n* Mesías *m*.
Messrs *abbr* (*on letters*: = *Messieurs*) Sres.
messy ['mesɪ] *adj* (*dirty*) sucio; (*untidy*) desordenado; (*confused*: *situation etc*) confuso.
Met [met] *n abbr* (*US*) = *Metropolitan Opera*.
met [met] *pt, pp of* **meet** ♦ *adj abbr* = **meteorological**.
metabolism [me'tæbəlɪzəm] *n* metabolismo.
metal ['metl] *n* metal *m*.
metallic [me'tælɪk] *adj* metálico.
metallurgy [me'tælədʒɪ] *n* metalurgia.
metalwork ['metlwə:k] *n* (*craft*) metalistería.
metamorphosis, *pl* **metamorphoses** [metə'mɔ:fəsɪs, -si:z] *n* metamorfosis *f inv*.
metaphor ['metəfə*] *n* metáfora.
metaphorical [metə'fɔrɪkl] *adj* metafórico.
metaphysics [metə'fɪzɪks] *n* metafísica.
mete [mi:t]: **to ~ out** *vt fus* (*punishment*) imponer.
meteor ['mi:tɪə*] *n* meteoro.
meteoric [mi:tɪ'ɔrɪk] *adj* (*fig*) meteórico.
meteorite ['mi:tɪəraɪt] *n* meteorito.
meteorological [mi:tɪərə'lɔdʒɪkl] *adj* meteorológico.
meteorology [mi:tɪə'rɔlədʒɪ] *n* meteorología.
meter ['mi:tə*] *n* (*instrument*) contador *m*; (*US*: *unit*) = **metre** ♦ *vt* (*US POST*) franquear; **parking ~** parquímetro.
methane ['mi:θeɪn] *n* metano.
method ['meθəd] *n* método; **~ of payment** método de pago.
methodical [mɪ'θɔdɪkl] *adj* metódico.
Methodist ['meθədɪst] *adj, n* metodista *m/f*.
methodology [meθə'dɔlədʒɪ] *n* metodología.
meths [meθs], **methylated spirit(s)** ['meθɪleɪtɪd-] *n* (*BRIT*) alcohol *m* metilado *or* desnaturalizado.
meticulous [me'tɪkjuləs] *adj* meticuloso.
metre, (*US*) **meter** ['mi:tə*] *n* metro.
metric ['metrɪk] *adj* métrico; **to go ~** pasar al sistema métrico.
metrication [metrɪ'keɪʃən] *n* conversión *f* al sistema métrico.
metric system *n* sistema *m* métrico.
metric ton *n* tonelada métrica.
metronome ['metrənəum] *n* metrónomo.
metropolis [mɪ'trɔpəlɪs] *n* metrópoli(s) *f*.
metropolitan [metrə'pɔlɪtən] *adj* metropolitano.
Metropolitan Police *n* (*BRIT*): **the ~** la policía londinense.
mettle ['metl] *n* valor *m*, ánimo.
mew [mju:] *vi* (*cat*) maullar.
mews [mju:z] (*BRIT*) *n*: **~ cottage** *casa acondicionada en antiguos establos o cocheras*; **~ flat** *piso en antiguos establos o cocheras*.
Mexican ['meksɪkən] *adj, n* mejicano/a *m/f*, mexicano/a *m/f* (*LAM*).
Mexico ['meksɪkəu] *n* Méjico, México (*LAM*).
Mexico City *n* Ciudad *f* de Méjico *or* México (*LAM*).

mezzanine ['mɛtsəni:n] *n* entresuelo.
MFA *n abbr* (*US*: = *Master of Fine Arts*) *título universitario.*
mfr *abbr* (= *manufacturer*) fab.
mg *abbr* (= *milligram*) mg.
Mgr *abbr* (= *Monseigneur, Monsignor*) Mons.
mgr *abbr* = **manager.**
MHR *n abbr* (*US*) *see* **Member of the House of Representatives.**
MHz *abbr* (= *megahertz*) MHz.
MI *abbr* (*US*) = *Michigan.*
MI5 *n abbr* (*BRIT*: = *Military Intelligence 5*) *servicio de contraespionaje del gobierno británico.*
MI6 *n abbr* (*BRIT*: = *Military Intelligence 6*) *servicio de inteligencia del gobierno británico.*
MIA *abbr* (= *missing in action*) desaparecido.
miaow [mi:'au] *vi* maullar.
mice [maɪs] *pl of* **mouse.**
Mich. *abbr* (*US*) = *Michigan.*
mickey ['mɪkɪ] *n*: **to take the ~ out of sb** tomar el pelo a algn.
micro... [maɪkrəu] *pref* micro....
microbe ['maɪkrəub] *n* microbio.
microbiology [maɪkrəubaɪ'ɔlədʒɪ] *n* microbiología.
microchip ['maɪkrəutʃɪp] *n* microchip *m*, microplaqueta.
micro(computer) ['maɪkrəu(kəm'pju:tə*)] *n* microordenador *m*, microcomputador *m*.
microcosm ['maɪkrəukɔzəm] *n* microcosmo.
microeconomics ['maɪkrəui:kə'nɔmɪks] *n* microeconomía.
microfiche ['maɪkrəufi:ʃ] *n* microficha.
microfilm ['maɪkrəufɪlm] *n* microfilm *m*.
microlight ['maɪkrəulaɪt] *n* ultraligero.
micrometer [maɪ'krɔmɪtə*] *n* micrómetro.
microphone ['maɪkrəfəun] *n* micrófono.
microprocessor ['maɪkrəu'prəusɛsə*] *n* microprocesador *m*.
microscope ['maɪkrəskəup] *n* microscopio; **under the ~** al microscopio.
microscopic [maɪkrə'skɔpɪk] *adj* microscópico.
microwave ['maɪkrəuweɪv] *n* (*also*: **~ oven**) horno microondas.
mid [mɪd] *adj*: **in ~ May** a mediados de mayo; **in ~ afternoon** a media tarde; **in ~ air** en el aire; **he's in his ~ thirties** tiene unos treinta y cinco años.
midday [mɪd'deɪ] *n* mediodía *m*.
middle ['mɪdl] *n* medio, centro; (*waist*) cintura ♦ *adj* de en medio; **in the ~ of the night** en plena noche; **I'm in the ~ of reading it** lo estoy leyendo ahora mismo.
middle-aged [mɪdl'eɪdʒd] *adj* de mediana edad.
Middle Ages *npl*: **the ~** la Edad *sg* Media.
middle class *n*: **the ~(es)** la clase media ♦ *adj* (*also*: **middle-class**) de clase media.
Middle East *n* Oriente *m* Medio.
middleman ['mɪdlmæn] *n* intermediario.
middle management *n* dirección *f* de nivel medio.
middle name *n* segundo nombre *m*.
middle-of-the-road ['mɪdləvðə'rəud] *adj* moderado.
middleweight ['mɪdlweɪt] *n* (*BOXING*) peso medio.
middling ['mɪdlɪŋ] *adj* mediano.
Middx *abbr* (*BRIT*) = *Middlesex.*
midge [mɪdʒ] *n* mosquito.
midget ['mɪdʒɪt] *n* enano/a.
midi system *n* cadena midi.
Midlands ['mɪdləndz] *npl región central de Inglaterra.*
midnight ['mɪdnaɪt] *n* medianoche *f*; **at ~** a medianoche.
midriff ['mɪdrɪf] *n* diafragma *m*.
midst [mɪdst] *n*: **in the ~ of** entre, en medio de.
midsummer [mɪd'sʌmə*] *n*: **a ~ day** un día de pleno verano.
Midsummer's Day *n* Día *m* de San Juan.
midway [mɪd'weɪ] *adj, adv*: **~ (between)** a mitad de camino *or* a medio camino (entre).
midweek [mɪd'wi:k] *adv* entre semana.
midwife, *pl* **midwives** ['mɪdwaɪf, -waɪvz] *n* comadrona.
midwifery ['mɪdwɪfərɪ] *n* tocología.
midwinter [mɪd'wɪntə*] *n*: **in ~** en pleno invierno.
miffed [mɪft] *adj* (*col*) mosqueado.
might [maɪt] *vb see* **may** ♦ *n* fuerza, poder *m*; **he ~ be there** puede que esté allí, a lo mejor está allí; **I ~ as well go** más vale que vaya; **you ~ like to try** podría intentar.
mightily ['maɪtɪlɪ] *adv* fuertemente, poderosamente; **I was ~ surprised** me sorprendí enormemente.
mightn't ['maɪtnt] = **might not.**
mighty ['maɪtɪ] *adj* fuerte, poderoso.
migraine ['mi:greɪn] *n* jaqueca.
migrant ['maɪgrənt] *adj* migratorio ♦ *n* (*bird*) ave *f* migratoria; (*worker*) emigrante *m/f*.
migrate [maɪ'greɪt] *vi* emigrar.
migration [maɪ'greɪʃən] *n* emigración *f*.
mike [maɪk] *n abbr* (= *microphone*) micro.
Milan [mɪ'læn] *n* Milán *m*.
mild [maɪld] *adj* (*person*) apacible; (*climate*) templado; (*slight*) ligero; (*taste*) suave;

(*illness*) leve.
mildew ['mɪldjuː] *n* moho.
mildly ['maɪldlɪ] *adv* ligeramente; suavemente; **to put it ~** por no decir algo peor.
mildness ['maɪldnɪs] *n* suavidad *f*; (*of illness*) levedad *f*.
mile [maɪl] *n* milla; **to do 20 ~s per gallon** hacer 20 millas por galón.
mileage ['maɪlɪdʒ] *n* número de millas; (*AUT*) kilometraje *m*.
mileage allowance *n* ≈ asignación *f* por kilometraje.
mileometer [maɪ'lɔmɪtə*] *n* (*BRIT*) = **milometer**.
milestone ['maɪlstəun] *n* mojón *m*; (*fig*) hito.
milieu ['miːljəː] *n* (medio) ambiente *m*, entorno.
militant ['mɪlɪtnt] *adj, n* militante *m/f*.
militarism ['mɪlɪtərɪzəm] *n* militarismo.
militaristic [mɪlɪtə'rɪstɪk] *adj* militarista.
military ['mɪlɪtərɪ] *adj* militar.
military service *n* servicio militar.
militate ['mɪlɪteɪt] *vi*: **to ~ against** militar en contra de.
militia [mɪ'lɪʃə] *n* milicia.
milk [mɪlk] *n* leche *f* ♦ *vt* (*cow*) ordeñar; (*fig*) chupar.
milk chocolate *n* chocolate *m* con leche.
milk float *n* (*BRIT*) furgoneta de la leche.
milking ['mɪlkɪŋ] *n* ordeño.
milkman ['mɪlkmən] *n* lechero.
milk shake *n* batido, malteada (*LAM*).
milk tooth *n* diente *m* de leche.
milk truck *n* (*US*) = **milk float**.
milky ['mɪlkɪ] *adj* lechoso.
Milky Way *n* Vía Láctea.
mill [mɪl] *n* (*windmill etc*) molino; (*coffee ~*) molinillo; (*factory*) fábrica; (*spinning ~*) hilandería ♦ *vt* moler ♦ *vi* (*also*: **~ about**) arremolinarse.
milled [mɪld] (*grain*) molido; (*coin, edge*) acordonado.
millennium, *pl* **~s** *or* **millennia** [mɪ'lɛnɪəm, 'lɛnɪə] *n* milenio, milenario.
millennium bug *n* (*COMPUT*): **the ~** el (problema del) efecto 2000.
miller ['mɪlə*] *n* molinero.
millet ['mɪlɪt] *n* mijo.
milli... ['mɪlɪ] *pref* mili....
milligram(me) ['mɪlɪgraem] *n* miligramo.
millilitre, (*US*) **milliliter** ['mɪlɪliːtə*] *n* mililitro.
millimetre, (*US*) **millimeter** ['mɪlɪmiːtə*] *n* milímetro.
milliner ['mɪlɪnə*] *n* sombrerero/a.
millinery ['mɪlɪnərɪ] *n* sombrerería.
million ['mɪljən] *n* millón *m*; **a ~ times** un millón de veces.
millionaire [mɪljə'nɛə*] *n* millonario/a.
millipede ['mɪlɪpiːd] *n* milpiés *m inv*.
millstone ['mɪlstəun] *n* piedra de molino.
millwheel ['mɪlwiːl] *n* rueda de molino.
milometer [maɪ'lɔmɪtə*] *n* (*BRIT*) cuentakilómetros *m inv*.
mime [maɪm] *n* mímica; (*actor*) mimo/a ♦ *vt* remedar ♦ *vi* actuar de mimo.
mimic ['mɪmɪk] *n* imitador(a) *m/f* ♦ *adj* mímico ♦ *vt* remedar, imitar.
mimicry ['mɪmɪkrɪ] *n* imitación *f*.
Min. *abbr* (*BRIT POL*: = *Ministry*) Min.
min. *abbr* (= *minute(s)*) m.; = **minimum**.
minaret [mɪnə'rɛt] *n* alminar *m*.
mince [mɪns] *vt* picar ♦ *vi* (*in walking*) andar con pasos menudos ♦ *n* (*BRIT CULIN*) carne *f* picada, picadillo.
mincemeat ['mɪnsmiːt] *n conserva de fruta picada*.
mince pie *n pastelillo relleno de fruta picada*.
mincer ['mɪnsə*] *n* picadora de carne.
mincing ['mɪnsɪŋ] *adj* afectado.
mind [maɪnd] *n* (*gen*) mente *f*; (*contrasted with matter*) espíritu *m* ♦ *vt* (*attend to, look after*) ocuparse de, cuidar; (*be careful of*) tener cuidado con; (*object to*): **I don't ~ the noise** no me molesta el ruido; **it is on my ~** me preocupa; **to my ~** a mi parecer *or* juicio; **to change one's ~** cambiar de idea *or* de parecer; **to bring** *or* **call sth to ~** recordar algo; **to have sth/sb in ~** tener algo/a algn en mente; **to be out of one's ~** haber perdido el juicio; **to bear sth in ~** tomar *or* tener algo en cuenta; **to make up one's ~** decidirse; **it went right out of my ~** se me fue por completo (de la cabeza); **to be in two ~s about sth** estar indeciso *or* dudar ante algo; **I don't ~** me es igual; **~ you, ...** te advierto que ...; **never ~!** ¡es igual!, ¡no importa!; (*don't worry*) ¡no te preocupes!; **'~ the step'** 'cuidado con el escalón'.
mind-boggling ['maɪndbɔglɪŋ] *adj* (*col*) alucinante, increíble.
-minded [-maɪndɪd] *adj*: **fair~** imparcial; **an industrially~ nation** una nación orientada a la industria.
minder ['maɪndə*] *n* guardaespaldas *m inv*.
mindful ['maɪndful] *adj*: **~ of** consciente de.
mindless ['maɪndlɪs] *adj* (*violence, crime*) sin sentido; (*work*) de autómata.
mine [maɪn] *pron* (el) mío/(la) mía *etc*; **a friend of ~** un(a) amigo/a mío/mía ♦ *adj*: **this book is ~** este libro es mío ♦ *n* mina ♦ *vt* (*coal*) extraer; (*ship, beach*) minar.

mine detector *n* detector *m* de minas.
minefield ['maɪnfi:ld] *n* campo de minas.
miner ['maɪnə*] *n* minero/a.
mineral ['mɪnərəl] *adj* mineral ♦ *n* mineral *m*; **~s** *npl* (*BRIT: soft drinks*) refrescos *mpl* con gas.
mineral water *n* agua mineral.
minesweeper ['maɪnswi:pə*] *n* dragaminas *m inv*.
mingle ['mɪŋgl] *vi*: **to ~ with** mezclarse con.
mingy ['mɪndʒɪ] *adj* (*col*) tacaño.
mini ... [mɪnɪ] *pref* mini..., micro....
miniature ['mɪnətʃə*] *adj* (en) miniatura ♦ *n* miniatura.
minibus ['mɪnɪbʌs] *n* microbús *m*.
minicab ['mɪnɪkæb] *n* taxi *m* (*que sólo puede pedirse por teléfono*).
minicomputer ['mɪnɪkəm'pju:tə*] *n* miniordenador *m*.
MiniDisc® ['mɪnɪdɪsk] *n* MiniDisc® *m*.
minim ['mɪnɪm] *n* (*BRIT MUS*) blanca.
minimal ['mɪnɪml] *adj* mínimo.
minimalist ['mɪnɪməlɪst] *adj, n* minimalista *m/f*.
minimize ['mɪnɪmaɪz] *vt* minimizar.
minimum ['mɪnɪməm] *n* (*pl* **minima** ['mɪnɪmə]) mínimo ♦ *adj* mínimo; **to reduce to a ~** reducir algo al mínimo; **~ wage** salario mínimo.
minimum lending rate (MLR) *n* tipo de interés mínimo.
mining ['maɪnɪŋ] *n* minería ♦ *adj* minero.
minion ['mɪnjən] *n* secuaz *m*.
mini-series ['mɪnɪsɪəri:z] *n* serie *f* de pocos capítulos, miniserie *f*.
miniskirt ['mɪnɪskə:t] *n* minifalda.
minister ['mɪnɪstə*] *n* (*BRIT POL*) ministro/a; (*REL*) pastor *m* ♦ *vi*: **to ~ to** atender a.
ministerial [mɪnɪs'tɪərɪəl] *adj* (*BRIT POL*) ministerial.
ministry ['mɪnɪstrɪ] *n* (*BRIT POL*) ministerio; (*REL*) sacerdocio; **M~ of Defence** Ministerio de Defensa.
mink [mɪŋk] *n* visón *m*.
mink coat *n* abrigo de visón.
Minn. *abbr* (*US*) = *Minnesota*.
minnow ['mɪnəu] *n* pececillo (de agua dulce).
minor ['maɪnə*] *adj* (*unimportant*) secundario; (*MUS*) menor ♦ *n* (*LAW*) menor *m/f* de edad.
Minorca [mɪ'nɔ:kə] *n* Menorca.
minority [maɪ'nɔrɪtɪ] *n* minoría; **to be in a ~** estar en *or* ser minoría.
minority interest *n* participación *f* minoritaria.
minster ['mɪnstə*] *n* catedral *f*.
minstrel ['mɪnstrəl] *n* juglar *m*.
mint [mɪnt] *n* (*plant*) menta, hierbabuena; (*sweet*) caramelo de menta ♦ *vt* (*coins*) acuñar; **the (Royal) M~**, (*US*) **the (US) M~** la Casa de la Moneda; **in ~ condition** en perfecto estado.
mint sauce *n* salsa de menta.
minuet [mɪnju'ɛt] *n* minué *m*.
minus ['maɪnəs] *n* (*also*: **~ sign**) signo menos ♦ *prep* menos.
minuscule ['mɪnəskju:l] *adj* minúsculo.
minute *n* ['mɪnɪt] minuto; (*fig*) momento; **~s** *npl* actas *fpl* ♦ *adj* [maɪ'nju:t] diminuto; (*search*) minucioso; **it is 5 ~s past 3** son las 3 y 5 (minutos); **at the last ~** a última hora; **wait a ~!** ¡espera un momento!; **up to the ~** de última hora; **in ~ detail** con todo detalle.
minute book *n* libro de actas.
minute hand *n* minutero.
minutely [maɪ'nju:tlɪ] *adv* (*by a small amount*) por muy poco; (*in detail*) detalladamente, minuciosamente.
minutiae [mɪ'nju:ʃɪi:] *npl* minucias *fpl*.
miracle ['mɪrəkl] *n* milagro.
miracle play *n* auto, milagro.
miraculous [mɪ'rækjuləs] *adj* milagroso.
miraculously [mɪ'rækjuləslɪ] *adv* milagrosamente.
mirage ['mɪrɑ:ʒ] *n* espejismo.
mire [maɪə*] *n* fango, lodo.
mirror ['mɪrə*] *n* espejo; (*in car*) retrovisor *m* ♦ *vt* reflejar.
mirror image *n* reflejo inverso.
mirth [mə:θ] *n* alegría; (*laughter*) risa, risas.
misadventure [mɪsəd'vɛntʃə*] *n* desventura; **death by ~** muerte *f* accidental.
misanthropist [mɪ'zænθrəpɪst] *n* misántropo/a.
misapply [mɪsə'plaɪ] *vt* emplear mal.
misapprehension ['mɪsæprɪ'hɛnʃən] *n* equivocación *f*.
misappropriate [mɪsə'prəuprɪeɪt] *vt* (*funds*) malversar.
misappropriation ['mɪsəprəuprɪ'eɪʃən] *n* malversación *f*, desfalco.
misbehave [mɪsbɪ'heɪv] *vi* portarse mal.
misbehaviour, (*US*) **misbehavior** [mɪsbɪ'heɪvjə*] *n* mala conducta.
misc. *abbr* = **miscellaneous**.
miscalculate [mɪs'kælkjuleɪt] *vt* calcular mal.
miscalculation [mɪskælkju'leɪʃən] *n* error *m* (de cálculo).
miscarriage ['mɪskærɪdʒ] *n* (*MED*) aborto (no provocado); **~ of justice** error *m* judicial.

miscarry [mɪs'kærɪ] *vi* (*MED*) abortar (de forma natural); (*fail: plans*) fracasar, malograrse.
miscellaneous [mɪsɪ'leɪnɪəs] *adj* varios/as, diversos/as; ~ **expenses** gastos diversos.
miscellany [mɪ'sɛlənɪ] *n* miscelánea.
mischance [mɪs'tʃɑːns] *n* desgracia, mala suerte *f*; **by (some)** ~ por (alguna) desgracia.
mischief ['mɪstʃɪf] *n* (*naughtiness*) travesura; (*harm*) mal *m*, daño; (*maliciousness*) malicia.
mischievous ['mɪstʃɪvəs] *adj* travieso; dañino; (*playful*) malicioso.
mischievously ['mɪstʃɪvəslɪ] *adv* por travesura; maliciosamente.
misconception ['mɪskən'sɛpʃən] *n* concepto erróneo; equivocación *f*.
misconduct [mɪs'kɔndʌkt] *n* mala conducta; **professional** ~ falta profesional.
miscount [mɪs'kaunt] *vt, vi* contar mal.
misconstrue [mɪskən'struː] *vt* interpretar mal.
misdeed [mɪs'diːd] *n* (*old*) fechoría, delito.
misdemeanour, (*US*) **misdemeanor** [mɪsdɪ'miːnə*] *n* delito, ofensa.
misdirect [mɪsdɪ'rɛkt] *vt* (*person*) informar mal; (*letter*) poner señas incorrectas en.
miser ['maɪzə*] *n* avaro/a.
miserable ['mɪzərəbl] *adj* (*unhappy*) triste, desgraciado; (*wretched*) miserable; **to feel** ~ sentirse triste.
miserably ['mɪzərəblɪ] *adv* (*smile, answer*) tristemente; (*fail*) rotundamente; **to pay** ~ pagar una miseria.
miserly ['maɪzəlɪ] *adj* avariento, tacaño.
misery ['mɪzərɪ] *n* (*unhappiness*) tristeza; (*wretchedness*) miseria, desdicha.
misfire [mɪs'faɪə*] *vi* fallar.
misfit ['mɪsfɪt] *n* (*person*) inadaptado/a.
misfortune [mɪs'fɔːtʃən] *n* desgracia.
misgiving(s) [mɪs'gɪvɪŋ(z)] *n(pl)* (*mistrust*) recelo; (*apprehension*) presentimiento; **to have ~s about sth** tener dudas sobre algo.
misguided [mɪs'gaɪdɪd] *adj* equivocado.
mishandle [mɪs'hændl] *vt* (*treat roughly*) maltratar; (*mismanage*) manejar mal.
mishap ['mɪshæp] *n* desgracia, contratiempo.
mishear [mɪs'hɪə*] *vt, vi* (*irreg: like* **hear**) oír mal.
mishmash ['mɪʃmæʃ] *n* (*col*) revoltijo.
misinform [mɪsɪn'fɔːm] *vt* informar mal.
misinterpret [mɪsɪn'təːprɪt] *vt* interpretar mal.
misinterpretation ['mɪsɪntəːprɪ'teɪʃən] *n* mala interpretación *f*.
misjudge [mɪs'dʒʌdʒ] *vt* juzgar mal.
mislay [mɪs'leɪ] *vt* (*irreg: like* **lay**) extraviar, perder.
mislead [mɪs'liːd] *vt* (*irreg: like* **lead**) llevar a conclusiones erróneas; (*deliberately*) engañar.
misleading [mɪs'liːdɪŋ] *adj* engañoso.
misled [mɪs'lɛd] *pt, pp of* **mislead**.
mismanage [mɪs'mænɪdʒ] *vt* administrar mal.
mismanagement [mɪs'mænɪdʒmənt] *n* mala administración *f*.
misnomer [mɪs'nəumə*] *n* término inapropiado *or* equivocado.
misogynist [mɪ'sɔdʒɪnɪst] *n* misógino.
misplace [mɪs'pleɪs] *vt* (*lose*) extraviar; **~d** (*trust etc*) inmerecido.
misprint ['mɪsprɪnt] *n* errata, error *m* de imprenta.
mispronounce [mɪsprə'nauns] *vt* pronunciar mal.
misquote ['mɪs'kwəut] *vt* citar incorrectamente.
misread [mɪs'riːd] *vt* (*irreg: like* **read**) leer mal.
misrepresent [mɪsrɛprɪ'zɛnt] *vt* falsificar.
misrepresentation [mɪsrɛprɪzɛn'teɪʃən] *n* (*LAW*) falsa declaración *f*.
Miss [mɪs] *n* Señorita; **Dear ~ Smith** Estimada Señorita Smith.
miss [mɪs] *vt* (*train etc*) perder; (*shot*) errar, fallar; (*appointment, class*) faltar a; (*escape, avoid*) evitar; (*notice loss of: money etc*) notar la falta de, echar en falta; (*regret the absence of*): **I ~ him** le echo de menos ♦ *vi* fallar ♦ *n* (*shot*) tiro fallido; **the bus just ~ed the wall** faltó poco para que el autobús se estrella contra el muro; **you're ~ing the point** no has entendido la idea.
▸**miss out** *vt* (*BRIT*) omitir.
▸**miss out on** *vt fus* (*fun, party, opportunity*) perderse.
Miss. *abbr* (*US*) = *Mississippi*.
missal ['mɪsl] *n* misal *m*.
misshapen [mɪs'ʃeɪpən] *adj* deforme.
missile ['mɪsaɪl] *n* (*AVIAT*) misil *m*; (*object thrown*) proyectil *m*.
missile base *n* base *f* de misiles.
missile launcher *n* lanzamisiles *m inv*.
missing ['mɪsɪŋ] *adj* (*pupil*) ausente, que falta; (*thing*) perdido; (*MIL*) desaparecido; **to be** ~ faltar; ~ **person** desaparecido/a.
mission ['mɪʃən] *n* misión *f*; **on a ~ for sb** en una misión para algn.
missionary ['mɪʃənrɪ] *n* misionero/a.
misspell [mɪs'spɛl] *vt* (*irreg: like* **spell**)

escribir mal.

misspent ['mɪs'spɛnt] *adj*: **his ~ youth** su juventud disipada.

mist [mɪst] *n* (*light*) neblina; (*heavy*) niebla; (*at sea*) bruma ♦ *vi* (*also*: **~ over, ~ up**: *weather*) nublarse; (: *BRIT*: *windows*) empañarse.

mistake [mɪs'teɪk] *n* error *m* ♦ *vt* (*irreg*: *like* **take**) entender mal; **by ~** por equivocación; **to make a ~** (*about sb/sth*) equivocarse; (*in writing, calculating etc*) cometer un error; **to ~ A for B** confundir A con B.

mistaken [mɪs'teɪkən] *pp of* **mistake** ♦ *adj* (*idea etc*) equivocado; **to be ~** equivocarse, engañarse; **~ identity** identificación *f* errónea.

mistakenly [mɪs'teɪkənlɪ] *adv* erróneamente.

mister ['mɪstə*] *n* (*col*) señor *m*; *see* **Mr**.

mistletoe ['mɪsltəu] *n* muérdago.

mistook [mɪs'tuk] *pt of* **mistake**.

mistranslation [mɪstræns'leɪʃən] *n* mala traducción *f*.

mistreat [mɪs'triːt] *vt* maltratar, tratar mal.

mistress ['mɪstrɪs] *n* (*lover*) amante *f*; (*of house*) señora (de la casa); (*BRIT*: *in primary school*) maestra; (*in secondary school*) profesora; *see* **Mrs**.

mistrust [mɪs'trʌst] *vt* desconfiar de ♦ *n*: **~ (of)** desconfianza (de).

mistrustful [mɪs'trʌstful] *adj*: **~ (of)** desconfiado (de), receloso (de).

misty ['mɪstɪ] *adj* nebuloso, brumoso; (*day*) de niebla; (*glasses*) empañado.

misty-eyed ['mɪstɪ'aɪd] *adj* sentimental.

misunderstand [mɪsʌndə'stænd] *vt, vi* (*irreg*: *like* **understand**) entender mal.

misunderstanding [mɪsʌndə'stændɪŋ] *n* malentendido.

misunderstood [mɪsʌndə'stud] *pt, pp of* **misunderstand** ♦ *adj* (*person*) incomprendido.

misuse *n* [mɪs'juːs] mal uso; (*of power*) abuso ♦ *vt* [mɪs'juːz] abusar de; (*funds*) malversar.

MIT *n abbr* (*US*) = *Massachusetts Institute of Technology*.

mite [maɪt] *n* (*small quantity*) pizca; **poor ~!** ¡pobrecito!

mitigate ['mɪtɪgeɪt] *vt* mitigar; **mitigating circumstances** circunstancias *fpl* atenuantes.

mitigation [mɪtɪ'geɪʃən] *n* mitigación *f*, alivio.

mitre, (*US*) **miter** ['maɪtə*] *n* mitra.

mitt(en) ['mɪt(n)] *n* manopla.

mix [mɪks] *vt* (*gen*) mezclar; (*combine*) unir ♦ *vi* mezclarse; (*people*) llevarse bien ♦ *n* mezcla; **to ~ sth with sth** mezclar algo con algo; **to ~ business with pleasure** combinar los negocios con el placer; **cake ~** preparado para pastel.

►**mix in** *vt* (*eggs etc*) añadir.

►**mix up** *vt* mezclar; (*confuse*) confundir; **to be ~ed up in sth** estar metido en algo.

mixed [mɪkst] *adj* (*assorted*) variado, surtido; (*school, marriage etc*) mixto.

mixed-ability ['mɪkstə'bɪlɪtɪ] *adj* (*class etc*) de alumnos de distintas capacidades.

mixed bag *n*: **these results are a bit of a ~** en estos resultados hay un poco de todo.

mixed blessing *n*: **it's a ~** tiene su lado bueno y su lado malo.

mixed doubles *n* (*SPORT*) mixtos *mpl*.

mixed economy *n* economía mixta.

mixed grill *n* (*BRIT*) parrillada mixta.

mixed-up [mɪkst'ʌp] *adj* (*confused*) confuso, revuelto.

mixer ['mɪksə*] *n* (*for food*) batidora; (*person*): **he's a good ~** tiene don de gentes.

mixer tap *n* (grifo) monomando.

mixture ['mɪkstʃə*] *n* mezcla.

mix-up ['mɪksʌp] *n* confusión *f*.

Mk *abbr* (*BRIT TECH*: = *mark*) Mk.

mk *abbr* = **mark** (*currency*).

mkt *abbr* = **market**.

MLitt *n abbr* (= *Master of Literature, Master of Letters*) *título universitario de postgrado*; *see also* **master's degree**.

MLR *n abbr* (*BRIT*) = **minimum lending rate**.

mm *abbr* (= *millimetre*) mm.

MN *abbr* (*BRIT*) = **Merchant Navy**; (*US*) = *Minnesota*.

MO *n abbr* (*MED*) = *medical officer*; (*US col*) = **modus operandi** ♦ *abbr* (*US*) = *Missouri*.

Mo. *abbr* (*US*) = *Missouri*.

m.o. *abbr* (= *money order*) g/.

moan [məun] *n* gemido ♦ *vi* gemir; (*col*: *complain*): **to ~ (about)** quejarse (de).

moaning ['məunɪŋ] *n* gemidos *mpl*; quejas *fpl*.

moat [məut] *n* foso.

mob [mɔb] *n* multitud *f*; (*pej*): **the ~** el populacho ♦ *vt* acosar.

mobile ['məubaɪl] *adj* móvil ♦ *n* móvil *m*.

mobile home *n* caravana.

mobile phone *n* teléfono móvil.

mobility [məu'bɪlɪtɪ] *n* movilidad *f*; **~ of labour** *or* (*US*) **labor** movilidad *f* de la mano de obra.

mobilize ['məubɪlaɪz] *vt* movilizar.

moccasin ['mɔkəsɪn] *n* mocasín *m*.

mock [mɔk] *vt* (*make ridiculous*) ridiculizar;

(*laugh at*) burlarse de ♦ *adj* fingido.
mockery ['mɔkərı] *n* burla; **to make a ~ of** desprestigiar.
mocking ['mɔkıŋ] *adj* (*tone*) burlón/ona.
mockingbird ['mɔkıŋbəːd] *n* sinsonte *m* (*LAM*), zenzontle (*LAM*).
mock-up ['mɔkʌp] *n* maqueta.
mod cons ['mɔd'kɔnz] *npl abbr* (= *modern conveniences*) *see* **convenience**.
mode [məud] *n* modo; (*of transport*) medio; (*COMPUT*) modo, modalidad *f*.
model ['mɔdl] *n* (*gen*) modelo; (*ARCH*) maqueta; (*person*: *for fashion, ART*) modelo *m/f* ♦ *adj* modelo *inv* ♦ *vt* modelar ♦ *vi* ser modelo; **~ railway** ferrocarril *m* de juguete; **to ~ clothes** pasar modelos, ser modelo; **to ~ on** crear a imitación de.
modelling, (*US*) **modeling** ['mɔdlıŋ] *n* (*modelmaking*) modelado.
modem ['məudəm] *n* módem *m*.
moderate *adj, n* ['mɔdərət] moderado/a *m/f* ♦ (*vb*: ['mɔdəreıt]) *vi* moderarse, calmarse ♦ *vt* moderar.
moderately ['mɔdərətlı] *adv* (*act*) con moderación; (*expensive, difficult*) medianamente; (*pleased, happy*) bastante.
moderation [mɔdə'reıʃən] *n* moderación *f*; **in ~** con moderación.
moderator ['mɔdəreıtə*] *n* (*mediator*) moderador(a) *m/f*.
modern ['mɔdən] *adj* moderno; **~ languages** lenguas *fpl* modernas.
modernity [mə'dəːnıtı] *n* modernidad *f*.
modernization [mɔdənaı'zeıʃən] *n* modernización *f*.
modernize ['mɔdənaız] *vt* modernizar.
modest ['mɔdıst] *adj* modesto.
modestly ['mɔdıstlı] *adv* modestamente.
modesty ['mɔdıstı] *n* modestia.
modicum ['mɔdıkəm] *n*: **a ~ of** un mínimo de.
modification [mɔdıfı'keıʃən] *n* modificación *f*; **to make ~s** hacer cambios *or* modificaciones.
modify ['mɔdıfaı] *vt* modificar.
modish ['məudıʃ] *adj* de moda.
Mods [mɔdz] *n abbr* (*BRIT*: = *(Honour) Moderations*) *examen de licenciatura de la universidad de Oxford*.
modular ['mɔdjulə*] *adj* (*filing, unit*) modular.
modulate ['mɔdjuleıt] *vt* modular.
modulation [mɔdju'leıʃən] *n* modulación *f*.
module ['mɔdjuːl] *n* (*unit, component, SPACE*) módulo.
modus operandi ['məudəsɔpə'rændiː] *n* manera de actuar.
Mogadishu [mɔgə'dıʃuː] *n* Mogadiscio.
mogul ['məugəl] *n* (*fig*) magnate *m*.
MOH *n abbr* (*BRIT*) = *Medical Officer of Health*.
mohair ['məuhɛə*] *n* mohair *m*.
Mohammed [mə'hæmɛd] *n* Mahoma *m*.
moist [mɔıst] *adj* húmedo.
moisten ['mɔısn] *vt* humedecer.
moisture ['mɔıstʃə*] *n* humedad *f*.
moisturize ['mɔıstʃəraız] *vt* (*skin*) hidratar.
moisturizer ['mɔıstʃəraızə*] *n* crema hidratante.
molar ['məulə*] *n* muela.
molasses [məu'læsız] *n* melaza.
mold [məuld] *n, vt* (*US*) = **mould**.
Moldavia [mɔl'deıvıə], **Moldova** [mɔl'dəuvə] *n* Moldavia, Moldova.
Moldavian [mɔl'deıvıən], **Moldovan** [mɔl'dəuvən] *adj, n* moldavo/a *m/f*.
mole [məul] *n* (*animal*) topo; (*spot*) lunar *m*.
molecular [mə'lɛkjulə*] *adj* molecular.
molecule ['mɔlıkjuːl] *n* molécula.
molest [məu'lɛst] *vt* importunar; (*sexually*) abordar con propósitos deshonestos.
moll [mɔl] *n* (*slang*) amiga.
mollusc, (*US*) **mollusk** ['mɔləsk] *n* molusco.
mollycoddle ['mɔlıkɔdl] *vt* mimar.
Molotov cocktail ['mɔlətɔf-] *n* cóctel *m* Molotov.
molt [məult] *vi* (*US*) = **moult**.
molten ['məultən] *adj* fundido; (*lava*) líquido.
mom [mɔm] *n* (*US*) = **mum**.
moment ['məumənt] *n* momento; **at** *or* **for the ~** de momento, por el momento, por ahora; **in a ~** dentro de un momento.
momentarily ['məuməntrılı] *adv* momentáneamente; (*US*: *very soon*) de un momento a otro.
momentary ['məuməntərı] *adj* momentáneo.
momentous [məu'mɛntəs] *adj* trascendental, importante.
momentum [məu'mɛntəm] *n* momento; (*fig*) ímpetu *m*; **to gather ~** cobrar velocidad; (*fig*) cobrar fuerza.
mommy ['mɔmı] *n* (*US*) = **mummy**.
Mon. *abbr* (= *Monday*) lun.
Monaco ['mɔnəkəu] *n* Mónaco.
monarch ['mɔnək] *n* monarca *m/f*.
monarchist ['mɔnəkıst] *n* monárquico/a.
monarchy ['mɔnəkı] *n* monarquía.
monastery ['mɔnəstərı] *n* monasterio.
monastic [mə'næstık] *adj* monástico.
Monday ['mʌndı] *n* lunes *m inv*.
Monegasque [mɔnı'gæsk] *adj, n* monegasco/a *m/f*.
monetarist ['mʌnıtərıst] *n* monetarista *m*.

monetary ['mʌnɪtərɪ] *adj* monetario.
monetary policy *n* política monetaria.
money ['mʌnɪ] *n* dinero, plata (*LAM*); **to make ~** ganar dinero; **I've got no ~ left** no me queda dinero.
moneyed ['mʌnɪd] *adj* adinerado.
moneylender ['mʌnɪlɛndə*] *n* prestamista *m/f*.
moneymaker ['mʌnɪmeɪkə*] *n* (*BRIT col*: *business*) filón *m*.
moneymaking ['mʌnɪmeɪkɪŋ] *adj* rentable.
money market *n* mercado monetario.
money order *n* giro.
money-spinner ['mʌnɪspɪnə*] *n* (*col*: *person, idea, business*) filón *m*.
money supply *n* oferta monetaria, medio circulante, volumen *m* monetario.
Mongol ['mɔŋgəl] *n* mongol(a) *m/f*; (*LING*) mongol *m*.
mongol ['mɔŋgəl] *adj, n* (*MED*) mongólico.
Mongolia [mɔŋ'gəulɪə] *n* Mongolia.
Mongolian [mɔŋ'gəulɪən] *adj* mongol(a) ♦ *n* mongol(a) *m/f*; (*LING*) mongol *m*.
mongoose ['mɔŋguːs] *n* mangosta.
mongrel ['mʌŋgrəl] *n* (*dog*) perro cruzado.
monitor ['mɔnɪtə*] *n* monitor *m* ♦ *vt* controlar; (*foreign station*) escuchar.
monk [mʌŋk] *n* monje *m*.
monkey ['mʌŋkɪ] *n* mono.
monkey business *n*, **monkey tricks** *npl* tejemanejes *mpl*.
monkey nut *n* (*BRIT*) cacahuete *m*, maní (*LAM*).
monkey wrench *n* llave *f* inglesa.
mono ['mɔnəu] *adj* (*broadcast etc*) mono *inv*.
mono... [mɔnəu] *pref* mono ... .
monochrome ['mɔnəukrəum] *adj* monocromo.
monocle ['mɔnəkl] *n* monóculo.
monogamous [mə'nɔgəməs] *adj* monógamo.
monogram ['mɔnəgræm] *n* monograma *m*.
monolith ['mɔnəlɪθ] *n* monolito.
monolithic [mɔnə'lɪθɪk] *adj* monolítico.
monologue ['mɔnəlɔg] *n* monólogo.
monoplane ['mɔnəpleɪn] *n* monoplano.
monopolist [mə'nɔpəlɪst] *n* monopolista *m/f*.
monopolize [mə'nɔpəlaɪz] *vt* monopolizar.
monopoly [mə'nɔpəlɪ] *n* monopolio; **Monopolies and Mergers Commission** (*BRIT*) *comisión reguladora de monopolios y fusiones*.
monorail ['mɔnəureɪl] *n* monocarril *m*, monorraíl *m*.
monosodium glutamate [mɔnə'səudɪəm 'gluːtəmeɪt] *n* glutamato monosódico.
monosyllabic [mɔnəsɪ'læbɪk] *adj* monosílabo.
monosyllable ['mɔnəsɪləbl] *n* monosílabo.
monotone ['mɔnətəun] *n* voz *f* (*or* tono) monocorde.
monotonous [mə'nɔtənəs] *adj* monótono.
monotony [mə'nɔtənɪ] *n* monotonía.
monoxide [mə'nɔksaɪd] *n*: **carbon ~** monóxido de carbono.
monseigneur [mɔnsɛn'jəː*], **monsignor** [mɔn'siːnjə*] *n* monseñor *m*.
monsoon [mɔn'suːn] *n* monzón *m*.
monster ['mɔnstə*] *n* monstruo.
monstrosity [mɔns'trɔsɪtɪ] *n* monstruosidad *f*.
monstrous ['mɔnstrəs] *adj* (*huge*) enorme; (*atrocious*) monstruoso.
Mont. *abbr* (*US*) = *Montana*.
montage [mɔn'tɑːʒ] *n* montaje *m*.
Mont Blanc [mɔ̃'blɑ̃] *n* Mont Blanc *m*.
month [mʌnθ] *n* mes *m*; **300 dollars a ~** 300 dólares al mes; **every ~** cada mes.
monthly ['mʌnθlɪ] *adj* mensual ♦ *adv* mensualmente ♦ *n* (*magazine*) revista mensual; **twice ~** dos veces al mes; **~ instalment** mensualidad *f*.
monument ['mɔnjumənt] *n* monumento.
monumental [mɔnju'mɛntl] *adj* monumental.
moo [muː] *vi* mugir.
mood [muːd] *n* humor *m*; **to be in a good/bad ~** estar de buen/mal humor.
moodily ['muːdɪlɪ] *adv* malhumoradamente.
moodiness ['muːdɪnɪs] *n* humor *m* cambiante; (*bad mood*) mal humor *m*.
moody ['muːdɪ] *adj* (*variable*) de humor variable; (*sullen*) malhumorado.
moon [muːn] *n* luna.
moonbeam ['muːnbiːm] *n* rayo de luna.
moon landing *n* alunizaje *m*.
moonless ['muːnlɪs] *adj* sin luna.
moonlight ['muːnlaɪt] *n* luz *f* de la luna ♦ *vi* hacer pluriempleo.
moonlighting ['muːnlaɪtɪŋ] *n* pluriempleo.
moonlit ['muːnlɪt] *adj*: **a ~ night** una noche de luna.
moonshot ['muːnʃɔt] *n* lanzamiento de una astronave a la luna.
moonstruck ['muːnstrʌk] *adj* chiflado.
moony ['muːnɪ] *adj*: **to have ~ eyes** estar soñando despierto, estar pensando en las musarañas.
Moor [muə*] *n* moro/a.
moor [muə*] *n* páramo ♦ *vt* (*ship*) amarrar ♦ *vi* echar las amarras.
moorings ['muərɪŋz] *npl* (*chains*) amarras *fpl*; (*place*) amarradero *sg*.
Moorish ['muərɪʃ] *adj* moro; (*architecture*) árabe.
moorland ['muələnd] *n* páramo, brezal *m*.

moose [muːs] *n, pl inv* alce *m.*
moot [muːt] *vt* proponer para la discusión, sugerir ♦ *adj*: ~ **point** punto discutible.
mop [mɔp] *n* fregona; (*of hair*) greñas *fpl* ♦ *vt* fregar.
▸**mop up** *vt* limpiar.
mope [məup] *vi* estar deprimido.
▸**mope about, mope around** *vi* andar abatido.
moped ['məupɛd] *n* ciclomotor *m.*
moquette [mɔ'kɛt] *n* moqueta.
MOR *adj abbr* (*MUS*: = *middle-of-the-road*) para el gran público.
moral ['mɔrl] *adj* moral ♦ *n* moraleja; ~**s** *npl* moralidad *f*, moral *f.*
morale [mɔ'rɑːl] *n* moral *f.*
morality [mə'rælɪtɪ] *n* moralidad *f.*
moralize ['mɔrəlaɪz] *vi*: **to** ~ **(about)** moralizar (sobre).
morally ['mɔrəlɪ] *adv* moralmente.
moral victory *n* victoria moral.
morass [mə'ræs] *n* pantano.
moratorium [mɔrə'tɔːrɪəm] *n* moratoria.
morbid ['mɔːbɪd] *adj* (*interest*) morboso; (*MED*) mórbido.

KEYWORD

more [mɔː*] *adj* **1** (*greater in number etc*) más; ~ **people/work than before** más gente/trabajo que antes
2 (*additional*) más; **do you want (some)** ~ **tea?** ¿quieres más té?; **is there any** ~ **wine?** ¿queda vino?; **it'll take a few** ~ **weeks** tardará unas semanas más; **it's 2 kms** ~ **to the house** faltan 2 kms para la casa; ~ **time/letters than we expected** más tiempo del que/más cartas de las que esperábamos; **I have no** ~ **money, I don't have any** ~ **money** (ya) no tengo más dinero
♦ *pron* (*greater amount, additional amount*) más; ~ **than 10** más de 10; **it cost** ~ **than the other one/than we expected** costó más que el otro/más de lo que esperábamos; **is there any** ~**?** ¿hay más?; **I want** ~ quiero más; **and what's** ~ **...** y además ...; **many/much** ~ muchos(as)/ mucho(a) más
♦ *adv* más; ~ **dangerous/easily (than)** más peligroso/fácilmente (que); ~ **and** ~ **expensive** cada vez más caro; ~ **or less** más o menos; ~ **than ever** más que nunca; **she doesn't live here any** ~ ya no vive aquí.

moreover [mɔː'rəuvə*] *adv* además, por otra parte.
morgue [mɔːg] *n* depósito de cadáveres.
MORI ['mɔːrɪ] *n abbr* (*BRIT*) = *Market and Opinion Research Institute.*
moribund ['mɔrɪbʌnd] *adj* moribundo.
Mormon ['mɔːmən] *n* mormón/ona *m/f.*
morning ['mɔːnɪŋ] *n* (*gen*) mañana; (*early* ~) madrugada; **in the** ~ por la mañana; **7 o'clock in the** ~ las 7 de la mañana; **this** ~ esta mañana.
morning-after pill ['mɔːnɪŋ'ɑːftə-] *n* píldora del día después.
morning sickness *n* (*MED*) náuseas *fpl* del embarazo.
Moroccan [mə'rɔkən] *adj, n* marroquí *m/f.*
Morocco [mə'rɔkəu] *n* Marruecos *m.*
moron ['mɔːrɔn] *n* imbécil *m/f.*
morose [mə'rəus] *adj* hosco, malhumorado.
morphine ['mɔːfiːn] *n* morfina.
morris dancing ['mɔrɪs] *n* (*BRIT*) *baile tradicional inglés en el que se llevan cascabeles en la ropa.*
Morse [mɔːs] *n* (*also*: ~ **code**) (alfabeto) morse *m.*
morsel ['mɔːsl] *n* (*of food*) bocado.
mortal ['mɔːtl] *adj, n* mortal *m.*
mortality [mɔː'tælɪtɪ] *n* mortalidad *f.*
mortality rate *n* tasa de mortalidad.
mortally ['mɔːtəlɪ] *adv* mortalmente.
mortar ['mɔːtə*] *n* argamasa; (*implement*) mortero.
mortgage ['mɔːgɪdʒ] *n* hipoteca ♦ *vt* hipotecar; **to take out a** ~ sacar una hipoteca.
mortgage company *n* (*US*) ≈ banco hipotecario.
mortgagee [mɔːgə'dʒiː] *n* acreedor(a) *m/f* hipotecario/a.
mortgager ['mɔːgədʒə*] *n* deudor(a) *m/f* hipotecario/a.
mortice ['mɔːtɪs] = **mortise.**
mortician [mɔː'tɪʃən] *n* (*US*) director(a) *m/f* de pompas fúnebres.
mortification ['mɔːtɪfɪ'keɪʃən] *n* mortificación *f*, humillación *f.*
mortified ['mɔːtɪfaɪd] *adj*: **I was** ~ me dio muchísima vergüenza.
mortise (lock) ['mɔːtɪs-] *n* cerradura de muesca.
mortuary ['mɔːtjuərɪ] *n* depósito de cadáveres.
mosaic [məu'zeɪɪk] *n* mosaico.
Moscow ['mɔskəu] *n* Moscú *m.*
Moslem ['mɔzləm] *adj, n* = **Muslim.**
mosque [mɔsk] *n* mezquita.
mosquito, ~**es** [mɔs'kiːtəu] *n* mosquito.
moss [mɔs] *n* musgo.
mossy ['mɔsɪ] *adj* musgoso, cubierto de musgo.
most [məust] *adj* la mayor parte de, la

mayoría de ♦ *pron* la mayor parte, la mayoría ♦ *adv* el más; (*very*) muy; **the** ~ (*also*: + *adjective*) el más; ~ **of them** la mayor parte de ellos; **I saw the** ~ yo fui el que más vi; **at the (very)** ~ a lo sumo, todo lo más; **to make the** ~ **of** aprovechar (al máximo); **a** ~ **interesting book** un libro interesantísimo.

mostly ['məustlɪ] *adv* en su mayor parte, principalmente.

MOT *n abbr* (*BRIT* = *Ministry of Transport*): **the** ~ **(test)** ≈ la ITV.

motel [məu'tɛl] *n* motel *m*.

moth [mɔθ] *n* mariposa nocturna; (*clothes* ~) polilla.

mothball ['mɔθbɔːl] *n* bola de naftalina.

moth-eaten ['mɔθiːtn] *adj* apolillado.

mother ['mʌðə*] *n* madre *f* ♦ *adj* materno ♦ *vt* (*care for*) cuidar (como una madre).

mother board *n* (*COMPUT*) placa madre.

motherhood ['mʌðəhud] *n* maternidad *f*.

mother-in-law ['mʌðərɪnlɔː] *n* suegra.

motherly ['mʌðəlɪ] *adj* maternal.

mother-of-pearl ['mʌðərəv'pəːl] *n* nácar *m*.

mother's help *n* niñera.

mother-to-be ['mʌðətə'biː] *n* futura madre.

mother tongue *n* lengua materna.

mothproof ['mɔθpruːf] *adj* a prueba de polillas.

motif [məu'tiːf] *n* motivo; (*theme*) tema *m*.

motion ['məuʃən] *n* movimiento; (*gesture*) ademán *m*, señal *f*; (*at meeting*) moción *f*; (*BRIT*: *also*: **bowel** ~) evacuación *f* intestinal ♦ *vt*, *vi*: **to** ~ **(to) sb to do sth** hacer señas a algn para que haga algo; **to be in** ~ (*vehicle*) estar en movimiento; **to set in** ~ poner en marcha; **to go through the** ~**s of doing sth** (*fig*) hacer algo mecánicamente *or* sin convicción.

motionless ['məuʃənlɪs] *adj* inmóvil.

motion picture *n* película.

motivate ['məutɪveɪt] *vt* motivar.

motivated ['məutɪveɪtɪd] *adj* motivado.

motivation [məutɪ'veɪʃən] *n* motivación *f*.

motivational research [məutɪ'veɪʃənl-] *n* estudios *mpl* de motivación.

motive ['məutɪv] *n* motivo; **from the best** ~**s** con las mejores intenciones.

motley ['mɔtlɪ] *adj* variopinto.

motor ['məutə*] *n* motor *m*; (*BRIT*: *col*: *vehicle*) coche *m*, carro (*LAM*), automóvil *m*, auto *m* (*esp LAM*) ♦ *adj* motor (*f*: motora, motriz).

motorbike ['məutəbaɪk] *n* moto *f*.

motorboat ['məutəbəut] *n* lancha motora.

motorcade ['məutəkeɪd] *n* desfile *m* de automóviles.

motorcar ['məutəkɑː*] *n* (*BRIT*) coche *m*, carro (*LAM*), automóvil *m*, auto *m* (*esp LAM*).

motorcoach ['məutəkəutʃ] *n* autocar *m*, autobús *m*, camión *m* (*LAM*).

motorcycle ['məutəsaɪkl] *n* motocicleta.

motorcycle racing *n* motociclismo.

motorcyclist ['məutəsaɪklɪst] *n* motociclista *m/f*.

motoring ['məutərɪŋ] *n* (*BRIT*) automovilismo ♦ *adj* (*accident, offence*) de tráfico *or* tránsito.

motorist ['məutərɪst] *n* conductor(a) *m/f*, automovilista *m/f*.

motorize ['məutəraɪz] *vt* motorizar.

motor oil *n* aceite *m* para motores.

motor racing *n* (*BRIT*) carreras *fpl* de coches, automovilismo.

motor scooter *n* vespa ®.

motor vehicle *n* automóvil *m*.

motorway ['məutəweɪ] *n* (*BRIT*) autopista.

mottled ['mɔtld] *adj* moteado.

motto, ~es ['mɔtəu] *n* lema *m*; (*watchword*) consigna.

mould, (*US*) **mold** [məuld] *n* molde *m*; (*mildew*) moho ♦ *vt* moldear; (*fig*) formar.

mo(u)lder ['məuldə*] *vi* (*decay*) decaer.

mo(u)lding ['məuldɪŋ] *n* (*ARCH*) moldura.

mo(u)ldy ['məuldɪ] *adj* enmohecido.

moult, (*US*) **molt** [məult] *vi* mudar la piel; (*bird*) mudar las plumas.

mound [maund] *n* montón *m*, montículo.

mount [maunt] *n* monte *m*; (*horse*) montura; (*for jewel etc*) engarce *m*; (*for picture*) marco ♦ *vt* montar en, subir a; (*stairs*) subir; (*exhibition*) montar; (*attack*) lanzar; (*stamp*) pegar, fijar; (*picture*) enmarcar ♦ *vi* (*also*: ~ **up**) subirse, montarse.

mountain ['mauntɪn] *n* montaña ♦ *cpd* de montaña; **to make a** ~ **out of a molehill** hacer una montaña de un grano de arena.

mountain bike *n* bicicleta de montaña.

mountaineer [mauntɪ'nɪə*] *n* montañero/a, alpinista *m/f*, andinista *m/f* (*LAM*).

mountaineering [mauntɪ'nɪərɪŋ] *n* montañismo, alpinismo, andinismo (*LAM*).

mountainous ['mauntɪnəs] *adj* montañoso.

mountain range *n* sierra.

mountain rescue team *n* equipo de rescate de montaña.

mountainside ['mauntɪnsaɪd] *n* ladera de la montaña.

mounted ['mauntɪd] *adj* montado.

Mount Everest *n* Monte *m* Everest.

mourn [mɔːn] *vt* llorar, lamentar ♦ *vi*: **to** ~

for llorar la muerte de, lamentarse por.
mourner ['mɔːnə*] *n* doliente *m/f*.
mournful ['mɔːnful] *adj* triste, lúgubre.
mourning ['mɔːnɪŋ] *n* luto ♦ *cpd* (*dress*) de luto; **in** ~ de luto.
mouse, *pl* **mice** [maus, maɪs] *n* (*also* COMPUT) ratón *m*.
mouse mat, mouse pad *n* (COMPUT) alfombrilla, almohadilla.
mousetrap ['maustræp] *n* ratonera.
moussaka [mu'sɑːkə] *n* moussaka.
mousse [muːs] *n* (CULIN) mousse *f*; (*for hair*) espuma (moldeadora).
moustache [məs'tɑːʃ], (US) **mustache** ['mʌstæʃ] *n* bigote *m*.
mousy ['mausɪ] *adj* (*person*) tímido; (*hair*) pardusco.
mouth, *pl* **mouths** [mauθ, -ðz] *n* boca; (*of river*) desembocadura.
mouthful ['mauθful] *n* bocado.
mouth organ *n* armónica.
mouthpiece ['mauθpiːs] *n* (MUS) boquilla; (TEL) micrófono; (*person*) portavoz *m/f*.
mouth-to-mouth ['mauθtə'mauθ] *adj*: ~ **resuscitation** boca a boca *m*.
mouthwash ['mauθwɔʃ] *n* enjuague *m* bucal.
mouth-watering ['mauθwɔːtərɪŋ] *adj* apetitoso.
movable ['muːvəbl] *adj* movible.
move [muːv] *n* (*movement*) movimiento; (*in game*) jugada; (: *turn to play*) turno; (*change of house*) mudanza ♦ *vt* mover; (*emotionally*) conmover; (POL: *resolution etc*) proponer ♦ *vi* (*gen*) moverse; (*traffic*) circular; (*also*: BRIT: ~ **house**) trasladarse, mudarse; **to** ~ **sb to do sth** mover a algn a hacer algo; **to be** ~**d** estar conmovido; **to get a** ~ **on** darse prisa.
►**move about** *or* **around** *vi* moverse; (*travel*) viajar.
►**move along** *vi* (*stop loitering*) circular; (*along seat etc*) correrse.
►**move away** *vi* (*leave*) marcharse.
►**move back** *vi* (*return*) volver.
►**move down** *vt* (*demote*) degradar.
►**move forward** *vi* avanzar ♦ *vt* adelantar.
►**move in** *vi* (*to a house*) instalarse.
►**move off** *vi* ponerse en camino.
►**move on** *vi* seguir viaje ♦ *vt* (*onlookers*) hacer circular.
►**move out** *vi* (*of house*) mudarse.
►**move over** *vi* hacerse a un lado.
►**move up** *vi* subir; (*employee*) ascender.
movement ['muːvmənt] *n* movimiento; (TECH) mecanismo; ~ **(of the bowels)** (MED) evacuación *f*.
mover ['muːvə*] *n* proponente *m/f*.
movie ['muːvɪ] *n* película; **the** ~**s** el cine.
movie camera *n* cámara cinematográfica.
moviegoer ['muːvɪgəuə*] *n* (US) aficionado/a al cine.
moving ['muːvɪŋ] *adj* (*emotional*) conmovedor(a); (*that moves*) móvil; (*instigating*) motor(a).
mow, *pt* **mowed**, *pp* **mowed** *or* **mown** [məu, -n] *vt* (*grass*) cortar; (*corn*: *also*: ~ **down**) segar; (*shoot*) acribillar.
mower ['məuə*] *n* (*also*: **lawn**~) cortacésped *m*.
Mozambique [məuzæm'biːk] *n* Mozambique *m*.
MP *n abbr* (= *Military Police*) PM; BRIT: = **Member of Parliament**; (*Canada*) = *Mounted Police*.
mpg *n abbr* (= *miles per gallon*) millas por galón.
mph *abbr* = *miles per hour*.
MPhil *n abbr* (= *Master of Philosophy*) *título universitario de postgrado*; see also **master's degree**.
MPS *n abbr* (BRIT) = *Member of the Pharmaceutical Society*.
Mr, Mr. ['mɪstə*] *n*: ~ **Smith** (el) Sr. Smith.
MRC *n abbr* (BRIT: = *Medical Research Council*) *departamento estatal que controla la investigación médica*.
MRCP *n abbr* (BRIT) = *Member of the Royal College of Physicians*.
MRCS *n abbr* (BRIT) = *Member of the Royal College of Surgeons*.
MRCVS *n abbr* (BRIT) = *Member of the Royal College of Veterinary Surgeons*.
Mrs, Mrs. ['mɪsɪz] *n*: ~ **Smith** (la) Sra. de Smith.
MS *n abbr* (= *manuscript*) MS; = **multiple sclerosis**; (US: = *Master of Science*) *título universitario* ♦ *abbr* (US) = *Mississippi*.
Ms, Ms. [mɪz] *n* (= *Miss or Mrs*) *abreviatura con la que se evita hacer expreso el estado civil de una mujer*.
MSA *n abbr* (US: = *Master of Science in Agriculture*) *título universitario*.
MSc *abbr see* **Master of Science**.
MSG *n abbr* = **monosodium glutamate**.
MSP *n abbr* (BRIT) = **Member of the Scottish Parliament**.
MSS *n abbr* (= *manuscripts*) MSS.
MST *abbr* (US: = *Mountain Standard Time*) *hora de invierno de las Montañas Rocosas*.
MSW *n abbr* (US: = *Master of Social Work*) *título universitario*.
MT *abbr* (US) = *Montana*.
Mt *abbr* (GEO: = *mount*) m.
MTV *n abbr* = *music television*.

mth *abbr* (= *month*) m.
much [mʌtʃ] *adj* mucho ♦ *adv, n, pron* mucho; (*before pp*) muy; **how ~ is it?** ¿cuánto es?, ¿cuánto cuesta?; **too ~** demasiado; **so ~** tanto; **it's not ~** no es mucho; **as ~ as** tanto como; **however ~ he tries** por mucho que se esfuerce; **I like it very/so ~** me gusta mucho/tanto; **thank you very ~** muchas gracias, muy agradecido.
muck [mʌk] *n* (*dirt*) suciedad *f*; (*fig*) porquería.
▸**muck about** *or* **around** *vi* (*col*) perder el tiempo; (*enjoy o.s.*) entretenerse; (*tinker*) manosear.
▸**muck in** *vi* (*col*) arrimar el hombro.
▸**muck out** *vt* (*stable*) limpiar.
▸**muck up** *vt* (*col: dirty*) ensuciar; (*: spoil*) echar a perder; (*: ruin*) estropear.
muckraking ['mʌkreɪkɪŋ] (*fig col*) *n* amarillismo ♦ *adj* especializado en escándalos.
mucky ['mʌkɪ] *adj* (*dirty*) sucio.
mucus ['mju:kəs] *n* mucosidad *f*, moco.
mud [mʌd] *n* barro, lodo.
muddle ['mʌdl] *n* desorden *m*, confusión *f*; (*mix-up*) embrollo, lío ♦ *vt* (*also*: **~ up**) embrollar, confundir.
▸**muddle along, muddle on** *vi* arreglárselas de alguna manera.
▸**muddle through** *vi* salir del paso.
muddle-headed [mʌdl'hɛdɪd] *adj* (*person*) despistado, confuso.
muddy ['mʌdɪ] *adj* fangoso, cubierto de lodo.
mudguard ['mʌdgɑ:d] *n* guardabarros *m inv*.
mudpack ['mʌdpæk] *n* mascarilla.
mud-slinging ['mʌdslɪŋɪŋ] *n* injurias *fpl*, difamación *f*.
muesli ['mju:zlɪ] *n* muesli *m*.
muff [mʌf] *n* manguito ♦ *vt* (*chance*) desperdiciar; (*lines*) estropear; (*shot, catch etc*) fallar; **to ~ it** fracasar.
muffin ['mʌfɪn] *n* bollo.
muffle ['mʌfl] *vt* (*sound*) amortiguar; (*against cold*) abrigar.
muffled ['mʌfld] *adj* sordo, apagado.
muffler ['mʌflə*] *n* (*scarf*) bufanda; (*US AUT*) silenciador *m*; (*on motorbike*) silenciador *m*, mofle *m*.
mufti ['mʌftɪ] *n*: **in ~** (vestido) de paisano.
mug [mʌg] *n* (*cup*) taza alta; (*for beer*) jarra; (*col: face*) jeta; (*: fool*) bobo ♦ *vt* (*assault*) atracar; **it's a ~'s game** es cosa de bobos.
▸**mug up** *vt* (*col: also*: **~ up on**) empollar.
mugger ['mʌgə*] *n* atracador(a) *m/f*.
mugging ['mʌgɪŋ] *n* atraco callejero.
muggins ['mʌgɪnz] *nsg* (*col*) tonto/a el bote.
muggy ['mʌgɪ] *adj* bochornoso.
mug shot *n* (*col*) foto *f* (para la ficha policial).
mulatto, ~es [mju:'lætəu] *n* mulato/a.
mulberry ['mulbrɪ] *n* (*fruit*) mora; (*tree*) morera, moral *m*.
mule [mju:l] *n* mula.
mull [mʌl]: **to ~ over** *vt* meditar sobre.
mulled [mʌld] *adj*: **~ wine** vino caliente (*con especias*).
mullioned ['mʌlɪənd] *adj* (*windows*) dividido por parteluces.
multi... [mʌltɪ] *pref* multi....
multi-access ['mʌltɪ'æksɛs] *adj* (*COMPUT*) multiacceso, de acceso múltiple.
multicoloured, (*US*) **multicolored** ['mʌltɪkʌləd] *adj* multicolor.
multifarious [mʌltɪ'fɛərɪəs] *adj* múltiple, vario.
multilateral [mʌltɪ'lætərl] *adj* (*POL*) multilateral.
multi-level [mʌltɪ'lɛvl] *adj* (*US*) = **multi-storey**.
multimillionaire [mʌltɪmɪljə'nɛə*] *n* multimillonario/a.
multinational [mʌltɪ'næʃənl] *n* multinacional *f* ♦ *adj* multinacional.
multiple ['mʌltɪpl] *adj* múltiple ♦ *n* múltiplo; (*BRIT: also*: **~ store**) (cadena de) grandes almacenes *mpl*.
multiple choice *n* examen *m* de tipo test.
multiple crash *n* colisión *f* en cadena.
multiple sclerosis [-sklɪ'rəusɪs] *n* esclerosis *f* múltiple.
multiplex ['mʌltɪplɛks] *n* (*also*: **~ cinema**) multicines *m inv*.
multiplication [mʌltɪplɪ'keɪʃən] *n* multiplicación *f*.
multiplication table *n* tabla de multiplicar.
multiplicity [mʌltɪ'plɪsɪtɪ] *n* multiplicidad *f*.
multiply ['mʌltɪplaɪ] *vt* multiplicar ♦ *vi* multiplicarse.
multiracial [mʌltɪ'reɪʃl] *adj* multirracial.
multistorey [mʌltɪ'stɔ:rɪ] *adj* (*BRIT: building, car park*) de muchos pisos.
multistrike ribbon ['mʌltɪstraɪk-] *n* (*COMPUT: on printer*) cinta de múltiples impactos.
multi-tasking ['mʌltɪtɑ:skɪŋ] *n* (*COMPUT*) ejecución *f* de tareas múltiples, multitarea.
multitude ['mʌltɪtju:d] *n* multitud *f*.
mum [mʌm] *n* (*BRIT*) mamá ♦ *adj*: **to keep ~ (about sth)** no decir ni mu (de algo).
mumble ['mʌmbl] *vt* decir entre dientes ♦ *vi* hablar entre dientes, musitar.
mumbo jumbo ['mʌmbəu-] *n* (*col*)

galimatías *m inv*.
mummify ['mʌmɪfaɪ] *vt* momificar.
mummy ['mʌmɪ] *n* (*BRIT: mother*) mamá; (*embalmed*) momia.
mumps [mʌmps] *n* paperas *fpl*.
munch [mʌntʃ] *vt, vi* mascar.
mundane [mʌn'deɪn] *adj* mundano.
municipal [mjuː'nɪsɪpl] *adj* municipal.
municipality [mjuːnɪsɪ'pælɪtɪ] *n* municipio.
munificence [muː'nɪfɪsns] *n* munificencia.
munitions [mjuː'nɪʃənz] *npl* municiones *fpl*.
mural ['mjuərl] *n* (pintura) mural *m*.
murder ['məːdə*] *n* asesinato; (*in law*) homicidio ♦ *vt* asesinar, matar; **to commit ~** cometer un asesinato *or* homicidio.
murderer ['məːdərə*] *n* asesino.
murderess ['məːdərɪs] *n* asesina.
murderous ['məːdərəs] *adj* homicida.
murk [məːk] *n* oscuridad *f*, tinieblas *fpl*.
murky ['məːkɪ] *adj* (*water, past*) turbio; (*room*) sombrío.
murmur ['məːmə*] *n* murmullo ♦ *vt, vi* murmurar; **heart ~** soplo cardíaco.
MusB(ac) *n abbr* (= *Bachelor of Music*) *título universitario*.
muscle ['mʌsl] *n* músculo.
▸**muscle in** *vi* entrometerse.
muscular ['mʌskjulə*] *adj* muscular; (*person*) musculoso.
muscular dystrophy *n* distrofia muscular.
MusD(oc) *n abbr* (= *Doctor of Music*) *título universitario*.
muse [mjuːz] *vi* meditar ♦ *n* musa.
museum [mjuː'zɪəm] *n* museo.
mush [mʌʃ] *n* gachas *fpl*.
mushroom ['mʌʃrum] *n* (*gen*) seta, hongo; (*small*) champiñón *m* ♦ *vi* (*fig*) crecer de la noche a la mañana.
mushy ['mʌʃɪ] *adj* (*vegetables*) casi hecho puré; (*story*) sentimentaloide.
music ['mjuːzɪk] *n* música.
musical ['mjuːzɪkl] *adj* melodioso; (*person*) musical ♦ *n* (*show*) (comedia) musical *m*.
music(al) box *n* caja de música.
musical chairs *n* juego de las sillas; (*fig*) **to play ~** cambiar de puesto continuamente.
musical instrument *n* instrumento musical.
musically ['mjuːzɪklɪ] *adv* melodiosamente, armoniosamente.
music centre *n* equipo de música.
music hall *n* teatro de variedades.
musician [mjuː'zɪʃən] *n* músico/a.
music stand *n* atril *m*.
musk [mʌsk] *n* (perfume *m* de) almizcle *m*.
musket ['mʌskɪt] *n* mosquete *m*.
musk rat *n* ratón *m* almizclero.
musk rose *n* (*BOT*) rosa almizcleña.
Muslim ['mʌzlɪm] *adj, n* musulmán/ana *m/f*.
muslin ['mʌzlɪn] *n* muselina.
musquash ['mʌskwɔʃ] *n* (*fur*) piel *f* del ratón almizclero.
muss [mʌs] *vt* (*col: hair*) despeinar; (*: dress*) arrugar.
mussel ['mʌsl] *n* mejillón *m*.
must [mʌst] *aux vb* (*obligation*): **I ~ do it** debo hacerlo, tengo que hacerlo; (*probability*): **he ~ be there by now** ya debe (de) estar allí ♦ *n*: **it's a ~** es imprescindible.
mustache ['mʌstæʃ] *n* (*US*) = **moustache**.
mustard ['mʌstəd] *n* mostaza.
mustard gas *n* gas *m* mostaza.
muster ['mʌstə*] *vt* juntar, reunir; (*also*: **~ up**) reunir; (*: courage*) armarse de.
mustiness ['mʌstɪnɪs] *n* olor *m* a cerrado.
mustn't ['mʌsnt] = **must not**.
musty ['mʌstɪ] *adj* mohoso, que huele a humedad.
mutant ['mjuːtənt] *adj, n* mutante *m*.
mutate [mjuː'teɪt] *vi* sufrir mutación, transformarse.
mutation [mjuː'teɪʃən] *n* mutación *f*.
mute [mjuːt] *adj, n* mudo/a *m/f*.
muted ['mjuːtɪd] *adj* (*noise*) sordo; (*criticism*) callado.
mutilate ['mjuːtɪleɪt] *vt* mutilar.
mutilation [mjuːtɪ'leɪʃən] *n* mutilación *f*.
mutinous ['mjuːtɪnəs] *adj* (*troops*) amotinado; (*attitude*) rebelde.
mutiny ['mjuːtɪnɪ] *n* motín *m* ♦ *vi* amotinarse.
mutter ['mʌtə*] *vt, vi* murmurar.
mutton ['mʌtn] *n* (carne *f* de) cordero.
mutual ['mjuːtʃuəl] *adj* mutuo; (*friend*) común.
mutually ['mjuːtʃuəlɪ] *adv* mutuamente.
Muzak ® ['mjuːzæk] *n* hilo musical.
muzzle ['mʌzl] *n* hocico; (*protective device*) bozal *m*; (*of gun*) boca ♦ *vt* amordazar; (*dog*) poner un bozal a.
MVP *n abbr* (*US SPORT*) = *most valuable player*.
MW *abbr* (= *medium wave*) onda media.
my [maɪ] *adj* mi(s); **~ house/brother/sisters** mi casa/hermano/mis hermanas; **I've washed ~ hair/cut ~ finger** me he lavado el pelo/cortado un dedo; **is this ~ pen or yours?** ¿este bolígrafo es mío o tuyo?
Myanmar ['maɪænmɑː*] *n* Myanmar.
myopic [maɪ'ɔpɪk] *adj* miope.
myriad ['mɪrɪəd] *n* (*of people, things*) miríada.
myrrh [məː*] *n* mirra.

myself [maɪ'sɛlf] *pron* (*reflexive*) me; (*emphatic*) yo mismo; (*after prep*) mí (mismo); *see also* **oneself.**
mysterious [mɪs'tɪərɪəs] *adj* misterioso.
mysteriously [mɪs'tɪərɪəslɪ] *adv* misteriosamente.
mystery ['mɪstərɪ] *n* misterio.
mystery play *n* auto, misterio.
mystic ['mɪstɪk] *adj, n* místico/a *m/f.*
mystical ['mɪstɪkl] *adj* místico.
mysticism ['mɪstɪsɪzəm] *n* misticismo.
mystification [mɪstɪfɪ'keɪʃən] *n* perplejidad *f*; desconcierto.
mystify ['mɪstɪfaɪ] *vt* (*perplex*) dejar perplejo; (*disconcert*) desconcertar.
mystique [mɪs'ti:k] *n* misterio.
myth [mɪθ] *n* mito.
mythical ['mɪθɪkl] *adj* mítico.
mythological [mɪθə'lɔdʒɪkl] *adj* mitológico.
mythology [mɪ'θɔlədʒɪ] *n* mitología.

Nn

N, n [ɛn] *n* (*letter*) N, n *f*; **N for Nellie,** (*US*) **N for Nan** N de Navarra.
N *abbr* (= *North*) N.
NA *n abbr* (*US*: = *Narcotics Anonymous*) *organización de ayuda a los drogadictos*; (*US*) = *National Academy.*
n/a *abbr* (= *not applicable*) no interesa; (*COMM etc*) = *no account.*
NAACP *n abbr* (*US*) = *National Association for the Advancement of Colored People.*
NAAFI ['næfɪ] *n abbr* (*BRIT*: = *Navy, Army & Air Force Institute*) *servicio de cantinas etc para las fuerzas armadas.*
nab [næb] *vt* (*col*: *grab*) coger (*SP*), agarrar (*LAM*); (: *catch out*) pillar.
NACU *n abbr* (*US*) = *National Association of Colleges and Universities.*
nadir ['neɪdɪə*] *n* (*ASTRO*) nadir *m*; (*fig*) punto más bajo.
NAFTA ['næftə] *n abbr* (= *North Atlantic Free Trade Agreement*) TLC *m.*
nag [næg] *n* (*pej*: *horse*) rocín *m* ♦ *vt* (*scold*) regañar; (*annoy*) fastidiar.
nagging ['nægɪŋ] *adj* (*doubt*) persistente; (*pain*) continuo ♦ *n* quejas *fpl.*
nail [neɪl] *n* (*human*) uña; (*metal*) clavo ♦ *vt* clavar; (*fig*: *catch*) coger (*SP*), pillar; **to pay cash on the ~** pagar a tocateja; **to ~ sb down to a date/price** hacer que algn se comprometa a una fecha/un precio.
nailbrush ['neɪlbrʌʃ] *n* cepillo para las uñas.
nailfile ['neɪlfaɪl] *n* lima para las uñas.
nail polish *n* esmalte *m or* laca para las uñas.
nail polish remover *n* quitaesmalte *m.*
nail scissors *npl* tijeras *fpl* para las uñas.
nail varnish *n* (*BRIT*) = **nail polish.**
Nairobi [naɪ'rəubɪ] *n* Nairobi *m.*
naïve [naɪ'i:v] *adj* ingenuo.
naïvely [naɪ'i:vlɪ] *adv* ingenuamente.
naïveté [nɑ:'i:vteɪ], **naivety** [naɪ'i:vɪtɪ] *n* ingenuidad *f*, candidez *f.*
naked ['neɪkɪd] *adj* (*nude*) desnudo; (*flame*) expuesto al aire; **with the ~ eye** a simple vista.
NAM *n abbr* (*US*) = *National Association of Manufacturers.*
name [neɪm] *n* (*gen*) nombre *m*; (*surname*) apellido; (*reputation*) fama, renombre *m* ♦ *vt* (*child*) poner nombre a; (*appoint*) nombrar; **by ~** de nombre; **in the ~ of** en nombre de; **what's your ~?** ¿cómo se llama usted?; **my ~ is Peter** me llamo Pedro; **to give one's ~ and address** dar sus señas; **to take sb's ~ and address** apuntar las señas de algn; **to make a ~ for o.s.** hacerse famoso; **to get (o.s.) a bad ~** forjarse una mala reputación.
name-drop ['neɪmdrɔp] *vi*: **he's always ~ping** siempre está presumiendo de la gente que conoce.
nameless ['neɪmlɪs] *adj* anónimo, sin nombre.
namely ['neɪmlɪ] *adv* a saber.
nameplate ['neɪmpleɪt] *n* (*on door etc*) placa.
namesake ['neɪmseɪk] *n* tocayo/a.
nan bread [nɑ:n-] *n pan indio sin apenas levadura.*
nanny ['nænɪ] *n* niñera.
nap [næp] *n* (*sleep*) sueñecito, siesta; **they were caught ~ping** les pilló desprevenidos.
NAPA *n abbr* (*US*: = *National Association of Performing Artists*) *sindicato de trabajadores del espectáculo.*
napalm ['neɪpɑ:m] *n* napalm *m.*
nape [neɪp] *n*: **~ of the neck** nuca, cogote *m.*
napkin ['næpkɪn] *n* (*also*: **table ~**) servilleta.
Naples ['neɪplz] *n* Nápoles.
nappy ['næpɪ] *n* (*BRIT*) pañal *m.*
nappy liner *n* gasa.
nappy rash *n* prurito.
narcissism [nɑ:'sɪsɪzəm] *n* narcisismo.

narcissus, *pl* **narcissi** [nɑːˈsɪsəs, -saɪ] *n* narciso.
narcotic [nɑːˈkɔtɪk] *adj, n* narcótico.
narrate [nəˈreɪt] *vt* narrar, contar.
narration [nəˈreɪʃən] *n* narración *f*, relato.
narrative [ˈnærətɪv] *n* narrativa ♦ *adj* narrativo.
narrator [nəˈreɪtə*] *n* narrador(a) *m/f*.
narrow [ˈnærəu] *adj* estrecho; (*resources, means*) escaso ♦ *vi* estrecharse; (*diminish*) reducirse; **to have a ~ escape** escaparse por los pelos; **to ~ sth down** reducir algo.
narrow gauge *adj* (*RAIL*) de vía estrecha.
narrowly [ˈnærəlɪ] *adv* (*miss*) por poco.
narrow-minded [nærəuˈmaɪndɪd] *adj* de miras estrechas.
narrow-mindedness [ˈnærəuˈmaɪndɪdnɪs] *n* estrechez *f* de miras.
NAS *n abbr* (*US*) = *National Academy of Sciences.*
NASA *n abbr* (*US*: = *National Aeronautics and Space Administration*) NASA *f*.
nasal [ˈneɪzl] *adj* nasal.
Nassau [ˈnæsɔː] *n* (*in Bahamas*) Nassau *m*.
nastily [ˈnɑːstɪlɪ] *adv* (*unpleasantly*) de mala manera; (*spitefully*) con rencor.
nastiness [ˈnɑːstɪnɪs] *n* (*malice*) malevolencia; (*rudeness*) grosería; (*of person, remark*) maldad *f*; (*spitefulness*) rencor *m*.
nasturtium [nəsˈtəːʃəm] *n* capuchina.
nasty [ˈnɑːstɪ] *adj* (*remark*) feo; (*person*) antipático; (*revolting: taste, smell*) asqueroso; (*wound, disease etc*) peligroso, grave; **to turn ~** (*situation*) ponerse feo; (*weather*) empeorar; (*person*) ponerse negro.
NAS/UWT *n abbr* (*BRIT*: = *National Association of Schoolmasters/Union of Women Teachers*) *sindicato de profesores*.
nation [ˈneɪʃən] *n* nación *f*.
national [ˈnæʃənl] *adj* nacional ♦ *n* súbdito/a.
national anthem *n* himno nacional.
National Curriculum *n* (*BRIT*) plan *m* general de estudios (*en Inglaterra y Gales*).
national debt *n* deuda pública.
national dress *n* traje *m* típico del país.
National Guard *n* (*US*) Guardia Nacional.
National Health Service (NHS) *n* (*BRIT*) servicio nacional de sanidad, ≈ INSALUD *m* (*SP*).
National Insurance *n* (*BRIT*) seguro social nacional, ≈ Seguridad *f* Social.
nationalism [ˈnæʃnəlɪzəm] *n* nacionalismo.
nationalist [ˈnæʃnəlɪst] *adj, n* nacionalista *m/f*.
nationality [næʃəˈnælɪtɪ] *n* nacionalidad *f*.
nationalization [næʃnəlaɪˈzeɪʃən] *n* nacionalización *f*.
nationalize [ˈnæʃnəlaɪz] *vt* nacionalizar; **~d industry** industria nacionalizada.
nationally [ˈnæʃnəlɪ] *adv* (*nationwide*) a escala nacional; (*as a nation*) como nación.
national press *n* prensa nacional.
national service *n* (*MIL*) servicio militar.
National Trust *n* (*BRIT*) *organización encargada de preservar el patrimonio histórico británico*.
nationwide [ˈneɪʃənwaɪd] *adj* a escala nacional.
native [ˈneɪtɪv] *n* (*local inhabitant*) natural *m/f*; (*in colonies*) indígena *m/f*, nativo/a ♦ *adj* (*indigenous*) indígena; (*country*) natal; (*innate*) natural, innato; **a ~ of Russia** un(a) natural de Rusia; **~ language** lengua materna; **a ~ speaker of French** un hablante nativo de francés.
Native American *adj, n* americano/a indígena *m/f*, amerindio/a *m/f*.
Nativity [nəˈtɪvɪtɪ] *n*: **the ~** Navidad *f*.
nativity play *n* auto del nacimiento.
NATO [ˈneɪtəu] *n abbr* (= *North Atlantic Treaty Organization*) OTAN *f*.
natter [ˈnætə*] *vi* (*BRIT*) charlar ♦ *n*: **to have a ~** charlar.
natural [ˈnætʃrəl] *adj* natural; **death from ~ causes** (*LAW*) muerte *f* por causas naturales.
natural childbirth *n* parto natural.
natural gas *n* gas *m* natural.
natural history *n* historia natural.
naturalist [ˈnætʃrəlɪst] *n* naturalista *m/f*.
naturalization [nætʃrəlaɪˈzeɪʃən] *n* naturalización *f*.
naturalize [ˈnætʃrəlaɪz] *vt*: **to become ~d** (*person*) naturalizarse; (*plant*) aclimatarse.
naturally [ˈnætʃrəlɪ] *adv* (*speak etc*) naturalmente; (*of course*) desde luego, por supuesto, ¡cómo no! (*esp LAM*); (*instinctively*) por naturaleza.
naturalness [ˈnætʃrəlnɪs] *n* naturalidad *f*.
natural resources *npl* recursos *mpl* naturales.
natural selection *n* selección *f* natural.
natural wastage *n* (*INDUSTRY*) desgaste *m* natural.
nature [ˈneɪtʃə*] *n* naturaleza; (*group, sort*) género, clase *f*; (*character*) modo de ser, carácter *m*; **by ~** por naturaleza; **documents of a confidential ~** documentos *mpl* de tipo confidencial.
-natured [ˈneɪtʃəd] *suff*: **ill~** malhumorado.

nature reserve *n* reserva natural.
nature trail *n* camino forestal educativo.
naturist ['neɪtʃərɪst] *n* naturista *m/f*.
naught [nɔːt] = **nought**.
naughtily ['nɔːtɪlɪ] *adv* (*behave*) mal; (*say*) con malicia.
naughtiness ['nɔːtɪnɪs] *n* travesuras *fpl*.
naughty ['nɔːtɪ] *adj* (*child*) travieso; (*story, film*) picante, escabroso, colorado (*LAM*).
nausea ['nɔːsɪə] *n* náusea.
nauseate ['nɔːsɪeɪt] *vt* dar náuseas a; (*fig*) dar asco a.
nauseating ['nɔːsɪeɪtɪŋ] *adj* nauseabundo; (*fig*) asqueroso, repugnante.
nauseous ['nɔːsɪəs] *adj* nauseabundo; **to feel** ~ sentir náuseas.
nautical ['nɔːtɪkl] *adj* náutico, marítimo; ~ **mile** milla marina.
naval ['neɪvl] *adj* naval, de marina.
naval officer *n* oficial *m/f* de marina.
nave [neɪv] *n* nave *f*.
navel ['neɪvl] *n* ombligo.
navigable ['nævɪgəbl] *adj* navegable.
navigate ['nævɪgeɪt] *vt* (*ship*) gobernar; (*river etc*) navegar por ♦ *vi* navegar; (*AUT*) hacer de copiloto.
navigation [nævɪ'geɪʃən] *n* (*action*) navegación *f*; (*science*) náutica.
navigator ['nævɪgeɪtə*] *n* navegante *m/f*.
navvy ['nævɪ] *n* (*BRIT*) peón *m* caminero.
navy ['neɪvɪ] *n* marina de guerra; (*ships*) armada, flota.
navy(-blue) ['neɪvɪ('bluː)] *adj* azul marino.
Nazareth ['næzərɪθ] *n* Nazaret *m*.
Nazi ['nɑːtsɪ] *adj, n* nazi *m/f*.
NB *abbr* (= *nota bene*) nótese; (*Canada*) = *New Brunswick*.
NBA *n abbr* (*US*) = *National Basketball Association, National Boxing Association*.
NBC *n abbr* (*US*: = *National Broadcasting Company*) *cadena de televisión*.
NBS *n abbr* (*US*: = *National Bureau of Standards*) ≈ Oficina Nacional de Normalización.
NC *abbr* (*COMM etc*) = *no charge*; (*US*) = *North Carolina*.
NCC *n abbr* (*BRIT*: = *Nature Conservancy Council*) ≈ ICONA *m*; (*US*) = *National Council of Churches*.
NCCL *n abbr* (*BRIT*: = *National Council for Civil Liberties*) *asociación para la defensa de las libertades públicas*.
NCO *n abbr* = **non-commissioned officer**.
ND *abbr* (*US*) = *North Dakota*.
N. Dak. *abbr* (*US*) = *North Dakota*.
NE *abbr* (*US*) = *Nebraska, New England*.
NEA *n abbr* (*US*) = *National Education Association*.
Neapolitan [nɪə'pɔlɪtən] *adj, n* napolitano/a *m/f*.
neap tide [niːp-] *n* marea muerta.
near [nɪə*] *adj* (*place, relation*) cercano; (*time*) próximo ♦ *adv* cerca ♦ *prep* (*also*: ~ **to**: *space*) cerca de, junto a; (: *time*) cerca de ♦ *vt* acercarse a, aproximarse a; ~ **here/there** cerca de aquí/de allí; **£25,000 or ~est offer** 25,000 libras o precio a discutir; **in the ~ future** en fecha próxima; **the building is ~ing completion** el edificio está casi terminado.
nearby [nɪə'baɪ] *adj* cercano, próximo ♦ *adv* cerca.
nearly ['nɪəlɪ] *adv* casi, por poco; **I ~ fell** por poco me caigo; **not** ~ ni mucho menos, ni con mucho.
near miss *n* (*shot*) tiro casi en el blanco; (*AVIAT*) *accidente evitado por muy poco*.
nearness ['nɪənɪs] *n* cercanía, proximidad *f*.
nearside ['nɪəsaɪd] *n* (*AUT*: *right-hand drive*) lado izquierdo (: *left-hand drive*) lado derecho.
near-sighted [nɪə'saɪtɪd] *adj* miope, corto de vista.
neat [niːt] *adj* (*place*) ordenado, bien cuidado; (*person*) pulcro; (*plan*) ingenioso; (*spirits*) solo.
neatly ['niːtlɪ] *adv* (*tidily*) con esmero; (*skilfully*) ingeniosamente.
neatness ['niːtnɪs] *n* (*tidiness*) orden *m*; (*skilfulness*) destreza, habilidad *f*.
Nebr. *abbr* (*US*) = *Nebraska*.
nebulous ['nɛbjuləs] *adj* (*fig*) vago, confuso.
necessarily ['nɛsɪsrɪlɪ] *adv* necesariamente; **not** ~ no necesariamente.
necessary ['nɛsɪsrɪ] *adj* necesario, preciso; **he did all that was** ~ hizo todo lo necesario; **if** ~ si es necesario.
necessitate [nɪ'sɛsɪteɪt] *vt* necesitar, precisar.
necessity [nɪ'sɛsɪtɪ] *n* necesidad *f*; **necessities** *npl* artículos *mpl* de primera necesidad; **in case of** ~ en caso de urgencia.
neck [nɛk] *n* (*ANAT*) cuello; (*of animal*) pescuezo ♦ *vi* besuquearse; ~ **and** ~ parejos; **to stick one's ~ out** (*col*) arriesgarse.
necklace ['nɛklɪs] *n* collar *m*.
neckline ['nɛklaɪn] *n* escote *m*.
necktie ['nɛktaɪ] *n* (*US*) corbata.
nectar ['nɛktə*] *n* néctar *m*.
nectarine ['nɛktərɪn] *n* nectarina.
NEDC *n abbr* (*BRIT*: = *National Economic Development Council*) ≈ Consejo Económico y Social.

Neddy ['nɛdɪ] *n abbr* (*BRIT col*) = **NEDC.**
née [neɪ] *adj*: ~ **Scott** de soltera Scott.
need [ni:d] *n* (*lack*) escasez *f*, falta; (*necessity*) necesidad *f* ♦ *vt* (*require*) necesitar; **in case of** ~ en caso de necesidad; **there's no** ~ **for** ... no hace(n) falta ...; **to be in** ~ **of, have** ~ **of** necesitar; **10 will meet my immediate** ~**s** 10 satisfacerán mis necesidades más apremiantes; **the** ~**s of industry** las necesidades de la industria; **I** ~ **it** lo necesito; **a signature is** ~**ed** se requiere una firma; **I** ~ **to do it** tengo que hacerlo; **you don't** ~ **to go** no hace falta que vayas.
needle ['ni:dl] *n* aguja ♦ *vt* (*fig: col*) picar, fastidiar.
needless ['ni:dlɪs] *adj* innecesario, inútil; ~ **to say** huelga decir que.
needlessly ['ni:dlɪslɪ] *adv* innecesariamente, inútilmente.
needlework ['ni:dlwə:k] *n* (*activity*) costura, labor *f* de aguja.
needn't ['ni:dnt] = **need not.**
needy ['ni:dɪ] *adj* necesitado.
negation [nɪ'geɪʃən] *n* negación *f*.
negative ['nɛgətɪv] *n* (*PHOT*) negativo; (*answer*) negativa; (*LING*) negación *f* ♦ *adj* negativo.
negative cash flow *n* flujo negativo de efectivo.
negative equity *n situación en la que el valor de la vivienda es menor que el de la hipoteca que pesa sobre ella.*
neglect [nɪ'glɛkt] *vt* (*one's duty*) faltar a, no cumplir con; (*child*) descuidar, desatender ♦ *n* (*state*) abandono; (*personal*) dejadez *f*; (*of duty*) incumplimiento; **to** ~ **to do sth** olvidarse de hacer algo.
neglected [nɪ'glɛktɪd] *adj* abandonado.
neglectful [nɪ'glɛktful] *adj* negligente; **to be** ~ **of sth/sb** desatender algo/a algn.
negligee ['nɛglɪʒeɪ] *n* (*nightdress*) salto de cama.
negligence ['nɛglɪdʒəns] *n* negligencia.
negligent ['nɛglɪdʒənt] *adj* negligente; (*casual*) descuidado.
negligently ['nɛglɪdʒəntlɪ] *adv* negligentemente; (*casually*) con descuido.
negligible ['nɛglɪdʒɪbl] *adj* insignificante, despreciable.
negotiable [nɪ'gəuʃɪəbl] *adj* (*cheque*) negociable; **not** ~ (*cheque*) no trasferible.
negotiate [nɪ'gəuʃɪeɪt] *vt* (*treaty, loan*) negociar; (*obstacle*) franquear; (*bend in road*) tomar ♦ *vi*: **to** ~ **(with)** negociar (con); **to** ~ **with sb for sth** tratar *or* negociar con algn por algo.
negotiating table [nɪ'gəuʃɪeɪtɪŋ-] *n* mesa de negociaciones.
negotiation [nɪgəuʃɪ'eɪʃən] *n* negociación *f*, gestión *f*; **to enter into** ~**s with sb** entrar en negociaciones con algn.
negotiator [nɪ'gəuʃɪeɪtə*] *n* negociador(a) *m/f*.
Negress ['ni:grɪs] *n* negra.
Negro ['ni:grəu] *adj, n* negro.
neigh [neɪ] *n* relincho ♦ *vi* relinchar.
neighbour, (*US*) **neighbor** ['neɪbə*] *n* vecino/a.
neighbo(u)rhood ['neɪbəhud] *n* (*place*) vecindad *f*, barrio; (*people*) vecindario.
neighbourhood watch *n* (*BRIT: also*: ~ **scheme**) *vigilancia del barrio por los propios vecinos.*
neighbo(u)ring ['neɪbərɪŋ] *adj* vecino.
neighbo(u)rly ['neɪbəlɪ] *adj* amigable, sociable.
neither ['naɪðə*] *adj* ni ♦ *conj*: **I didn't move and** ~ **did John** no me he movido, ni Juan tampoco ♦ *pron* ninguno; ~ **is true** ninguno/a de los/las dos es cierto/a ♦ *adv*: ~ **good nor bad** ni bueno ni malo.
neo ... [ni:əu] *pref* neo....
neolithic [ni:əu'lɪθɪk] *adj* neolítico.
neologism [nɪ'ɔlədʒɪzəm] *n* neologismo.
neon ['ni:ɔn] *n* neón *m*.
neon light *n* lámpara de neón.
Nepal [nɪ'pɔ:l] *n* Nepal *m*.
nephew ['nɛvju:] *n* sobrino.
nepotism ['nɛpətɪzəm] *n* nepotismo.
nerd [nə:d] *n* (*col*) primo/a.
nerve [nə:v] *n* (*ANAT*) nervio; (*courage*) valor *m*; (*impudence*) descaro, frescura; **a fit of** ~**s** un ataque de nervios; **to lose one's** ~ (*self-confidence*) perder el valor.
nerve centre *n* (*ANAT*) centro nervioso; (*fig*) punto neurálgico.
nerve gas *n* gas *m* nervioso.
nerve-racking ['nə:vrækɪŋ] *adj* angustioso.
nervous ['nə:vəs] *adj* (*anxious, ANAT*) nervioso; (*timid*) tímido, miedoso.
nervous breakdown *n* crisis *f* nerviosa.
nervously ['nə:vəslɪ] *adv* nerviosamente; tímidamente.
nervousness ['nə:vəsnɪs] *n* nerviosismo; timidez *f*.
nervous wreck *n* (*col*): **to be a** ~ estar de los nervios.
nervy ['nə:vɪ] *adj*: **to be** ~ estar nervioso.
nest [nɛst] *n* (*of bird*) nido ♦ *vi* anidar.
nest egg *n* (*fig*) ahorros *mpl*.
nestle ['nɛsl] *vi*: **to** ~ **down** acurrucarse.
nestling ['nɛstlɪŋ] *n* pajarito.
net [nɛt] *n* (*gen*) red *f*; (*fabric*) tul *m* ♦ *adj*

(*COMM*) neto, líquido; (*weight, price, salary*) neto ♦ *vt* coger (*SP*) *or* agarrar (*LAM*) con red; (*money: subj: person*) cobrar; (: *deal, sale*) conseguir; (*SPORT*) marcar; **~ of tax** neto; **he earns £10,000 ~ per year** gana 10,000 libras netas por año; **the N~** (*Internet*) la Red.

netball ['nɛtbɔːl] *n* básquet *m*.

net curtain *n* visillo.

Netherlands ['nɛðələndz] *npl*: **the ~** los Países Bajos.

net income *n* renta neta.

net loss *n* pérdida neta.

net profit *n* beneficio neto.

nett [nɛt] *adj* = **net**.

netting ['nɛtɪŋ] *n* red *f*, redes *fpl*.

nettle ['nɛtl] *n* ortiga.

network ['nɛtwəːk] *n* red *f* ♦ *vt* (*RADIO, TV*) difundir por la red de emisores; **local area ~** red local.

neuralgia [njuə'rældʒə] *n* neuralgia.

neurological [njuərə'lɔdʒɪkl] *adj* neurológico.

neurosis, *pl* **-ses** [njuə'rəusɪs, -siːz] *n* neurosis *f inv*.

neurotic [njuə'rɔtɪk] *adj, n* neurótico/a *m/f*.

neuter ['njuːtə*] *adj* (*LING*) neutro ♦ *vt* castrar, capar.

neutral ['njuːtrəl] *adj* (*person*) neutral; (*colour etc, ELEC*) neutro ♦ *n* (*AUT*) punto muerto.

neutrality [njuː'trælɪtɪ] *n* neutralidad *f*.

neutralize ['njuːtrəlaɪz] *vt* neutralizar.

neutron ['njuːtrɔn] *n* neutrón *m*.

neutron bomb *n* bomba de neutrones.

Nev. *abbr* (*US*) = *Nevada*.

never ['nɛvə*] *adv* nunca, jamás; **I ~ went** no fui nunca; **~ in my life** jamás en la vida; *see also* **mind**.

never-ending [nɛvər'ɛndɪŋ] *adj* interminable, sin fin.

nevertheless [nɛvəðə'lɛs] *adv* sin embargo, no obstante.

new [njuː] *adj* nuevo; (*recent*) reciente; **as good as ~** como nuevo.

New Age *n* Nueva era.

newborn ['njuːbɔːn] *adj* recién nacido.

newcomer ['njuːkʌmə*] *n* recién venido *or* llegado.

new-fangled ['njuːfæŋgld] *adj* (*pej*) modernísimo.

new-found ['njuːfaund] *adj* (*friend*) nuevo; (*enthusiasm*) recién adquirido.

New Guinea *n* Nueva Guinea.

newly ['njuːlɪ] *adv* recién.

newly-weds ['njuːlɪwɛdz] *npl* recién casados.

new moon *n* luna nueva.

newness ['njuːnɪs] *n* novedad *f*.

news [njuːz] *n* noticias *fpl*; **a piece of ~** una noticia; **the ~** (*RADIO, TV*) las noticias *fpl*, el telediario; **good/bad ~** buenas/malas noticias *fpl*; **financial ~** noticias *fpl* financieras.

news agency *n* agencia de noticias.

newsagent ['njuːzeɪdʒənt] *n* (*BRIT*) vendedor(a) *m/f* de periódicos.

news bulletin *n* (*RADIO, TV*) noticiario.

newscaster ['njuːzkɑːstə*] *n* presentador(a) *m/f*, locutor(a) *m/f*.

news dealer *n* (*US*) = **newsagent**.

news flash *n* noticia de última hora.

newsletter ['njuːzlɛtə*] *n* hoja informativa, boletín *m*.

newspaper ['njuːzpeɪpə*] *n* periódico, diario; **daily ~** diario; **weekly ~** periódico semanal.

newsprint ['njuːzprɪnt] *n* papel *m* de periódico.

newsreader ['njuːzriːdə*] *n* = **newscaster**.

newsreel ['njuːzriːl] *n* noticiario.

newsroom ['njuːzruːm] *n* (*PRESS, RADIO, TV*) sala de redacción.

news stand *n* quiosco *or* puesto de periódicos.

newsworthy ['njuːzwəːðɪ] *adj*: **to be ~** ser de interés periodístico.

newt [njuːt] *n* tritón *m*.

new town *n* (*BRIT*) ciudad *f* nueva (*construida con subsidios estatales*).

New Year *n* Año Nuevo; **Happy ~!** ¡Feliz Año Nuevo!; **to wish sb a happy ~** desear a algn un feliz año nuevo.

New Year's Day *n* Día *m* de Año Nuevo.

New Year's Eve *n* Nochevieja.

New York [-'jɔːk] *n* Nueva York.

New Zealand [-'ziːlənd] *n* Nueva Zelanda (*SP*), Nueva Zelandia (*LAM*) ♦ *adj* neozelandés/esa.

New Zealander [-'ziːləndə*] *n* neozelandés/esa *m/f*.

next [nɛkst] *adj* (*house, room*) vecino, de al lado; (*meeting*) próximo; (*page*) siguiente ♦ *adv* después; **the ~ day** el día siguiente; **~ time** la próxima vez; **~ year** el año próximo *or* que viene; **~ month** el mes que viene *or* entrante; **the week after ~** no la semana que viene sino la otra; **"turn to the ~ page"** "vuelva a la página siguiente"; **you're ~** le toca; **~ to** *prep* junto a, al lado de; **~ to nothing** casi nada.

next door *adv* en la casa de al lado ♦ *adj* vecino, de al lado.

next-of-kin ['nɛkstəv'kɪn] *n* pariente(s) *m(pl)* más cercano(s).

NF *n abbr* (*BRIT POL*: = *National Front*) *partido político de la extrema derecha* ♦ *abbr* (*Canada*) = *Newfoundland*.
NFL *n abbr* (*US*) = *National Football League*.
Nfld. *abbr* (*Canada*) = *Newfoundland*.
NG *abbr* (*US*) = **National Guard**.
NGO *n abbr* (= *non-governmental organization*) ONG *f*.
NH *abbr* (*US*) = *New Hampshire*.
NHL *n abbr* (*US*) = *National Hockey League*.
NHS *n abbr see* **National Health Service**.
NI *abbr* = **Northern Ireland**; (*BRIT*) = **National Insurance**.
nib [nɪb] *n* plumilla.
nibble ['nɪbl] *vt* mordisquear.
Nicaragua [nɪkə'rægjuə] *n* Nicaragua.
Nicaraguan [nɪkə'rægjuən] *adj, n* nicaragüense *m/f*, nicaragüeño/a *m/f*.
Nice [ni:s] *n* Niza.
nice [naɪs] *adj* (*likeable*) simpático, majo; (*kind*) amable; (*pleasant*) agradable; (*attractive*) bonito, mono; (*distinction*) fino; (*taste, smell, meal*) rico.
nice-looking ['naɪslukɪŋ] *adj* guapo.
nicely ['naɪslɪ] *adv* amablemente; (*of health etc*) bien; **that will do** ~ perfecto.
niceties ['naɪsɪtɪz] *npl* detalles *mpl*.
niche [ni:ʃ] *n* (*ARCH*) nicho, hornacina.
nick [nɪk] *n* (*wound*) rasguño; (*cut, indentation*) mella, muesca ♦ *vt* (*cut*) cortar; (*col*) birlar, mangar; (*: arrest*) pillar; **in the ~ of time** justo a tiempo; **in good** ~ en buen estado; **to ~ o.s.** cortarse.
nickel ['nɪkl] *n* níquel *m*; (*US*) *moneda de 5 centavos*.
nickname ['nɪkneɪm] *n* apodo, mote *m* ♦ *vt* apodar.
Nicosia [nɪkə'si:ə] *n* Nicosía.
nicotine ['nɪkəti:n] *n* nicotina.
nicotine patch *n* parche *m* de nicotina.
niece [ni:s] *n* sobrina.
nifty ['nɪftɪ] *adj* (*col*: *car, jacket*) elegante, chulo; (*: gadget, tool*) ingenioso.
Niger ['naɪdʒə*] *n* (*country, river*) Níger *m*.
Nigeria [naɪ'dʒɪərɪə] *n* Nigeria.
Nigerian [naɪ'dʒɪərɪən] *adj, n* nigeriano/a *m/f*.
niggardly ['nɪgədlɪ] *adj* (*person*) avaro, tacaño, avariento; (*allowance, amount*) miserable.
nigger ['nɪgə*] *n* (*col!*: *highly offensive*) negro/a.
niggle ['nɪgl] *vt* preocupar ♦ *vi* (*complain*) quejarse; (*fuss*) preocuparse por minucias.
niggling ['nɪglɪŋ] *adj* (*detail*: *trifling*) nimio, insignificante; (*annoying*) molesto; (*doubt, pain*) constante.
night [naɪt] *n* (*gen*) noche *f*; (*evening*) tarde *f*; **last** ~ anoche; **the ~ before last** anteanoche, antes de ayer por la noche; **at ~, by** ~ de noche, por la noche; **in the ~, during the** ~ durante la noche, por la noche.
night-bird ['naɪtbə:d] *n* pájaro nocturno; (*fig*) trasnochador(a) *m/f*, madrugador(a) *m/f* (*LAM*).
nightcap ['naɪtkæp] *n* (*drink*) *bebida que se toma antes de acostarse*.
night club *n* club nocturno, discoteca.
nightdress ['naɪtdrɛs] *n* (*BRIT*) camisón *m*.
nightfall ['naɪtfɔ:l] *n* anochecer *m*.
nightgown ['naɪtgaun], **nightie** ['naɪtɪ] (*BRIT*) *n* = **nightdress**.
nightingale ['naɪtɪŋgeɪl] *n* ruiseñor *m*.
night life *n* vida nocturna.
nightly ['naɪtlɪ] *adj* de todas las noches ♦ *adv* todas las noches, cada noche.
nightmare ['naɪtmɛə*] *n* pesadilla.
night porter *n* guardián *m* nocturno.
night safe *n* caja fuerte.
night school *n* clase(s) *f(pl)* nocturna(s).
nightshade ['naɪtʃeɪd] *n*: **deadly** ~ (*BOT*) belladona.
night shift *n* turno nocturno *or* de noche.
night-time ['naɪttaɪm] *n* noche *f*.
night watchman *n* vigilante *m* nocturno, sereno.
nihilism ['naɪɪlɪzəm] *n* nihilismo.
nil [nɪl] *n* (*BRIT SPORT*) cero, nada.
Nile [naɪl] *n*: **the** ~ el Nilo.
nimble ['nɪmbl] *adj* (*agile*) ágil, ligero; (*skilful*) diestro.
nimbly ['nɪmblɪ] *adv* ágilmente; con destreza.
nine [naɪn] *num* nueve.
nineteen ['naɪn'ti:n] *num* diecinueve.
nineteenth [naɪn'ti:nθ] *num* decimonoveno, decimonono.
ninety ['naɪntɪ] *num* noventa.
ninth [naɪnθ] *num* noveno.
nip [nɪp] *vt* (*pinch*) pellizcar; (*bite*) morder ♦ *vi* (*BRIT col*): **to ~ out/down/up** salir/bajar/subir un momento ♦ *n* (*drink*) trago.
nipple ['nɪpl] *n* (*ANAT*) pezón *m*; (*of bottle*) tetilla; (*TECH*) boquilla, manguito.
nippy ['nɪpɪ] *adj* (*BRIT*: *person*) rápido; (*taste*) picante; **it's a very ~ car** es un coche muy potente para el tamaño que tiene.
nit [nɪt] *n* (*of louse*) liendre *f*; (*col*: *idiot*) imbécil *m/f*.
nit-pick ['nɪtpɪk] *vi* (*col*) sacar punta a todo.
nitrogen ['naɪtrədʒən] *n* nitrógeno.
nitroglycerin(e) ['naɪtrəu'glɪsəri:n] *n* nitroglicerina.
nitty-gritty ['nɪtɪ'grɪtɪ] *n* (*col*): **to get down**

to the ~ ir al grano.
nitwit ['nɪtwɪt] *n* cretino/a.
NJ *abbr (US) = New Jersey.*
NLF *n abbr (= National Liberation Front)* FLN *m.*
NLQ *abbr (= near letter quality)* calidad *f* casi de correspondencia.
NLRB *n abbr (US: = National Labor Relations Board) organismo de protección al trabajador.*
NM, N. Mex. *abbr (US) = New Mexico.*

KEYWORD

no [nəu] (*pl* **~es**) *adv (opposite of "yes")* no; **are you coming? — ~ (I'm not)** ¿vienes? — no; **would you like some more? — ~ thank you** ¿quieres más? — no gracias
♦ *adj (not any)*: **I have ~ money/time/books** no tengo dinero/tiempo/libros; **~ other man would have done it** ningún otro lo hubiera hecho; **"~ entry"** "prohibido el paso"; **"~ smoking"** "prohibido fumar"
♦ *n* no *m.*

no. *abbr (= number)* nº., núm.
nobble ['nɔbl] *vt (BRIT col: bribe)* sobornar; (*: catch*) pescar; (*: RACING*) drogar.
Nobel prize [nəu'bɛl-] *n* premio Nobel.
nobility [nəu'bɪlɪtɪ] *n* nobleza.
noble ['nəubl] *adj (person)* noble; (*title*) de nobleza.
nobleman ['nəublmən] *n* noble *m.*
nobly ['nəublɪ] *adv (selflessly)* noblemente.
nobody ['nəubədɪ] *pron* nadie.
no-claims bonus ['nəukleɪmz-] *n* bonificación *f* por carencia de reclamaciones.
nocturnal [nɔk'tə:nl] *adj* nocturno.
nod [nɔd] *vi* saludar con la cabeza; (*in agreement*) asentir con la cabeza ♦ *vt*: **to ~ one's head** inclinar la cabeza ♦ *n* inclinación *f* de cabeza; **they ~ded their agreement** asintieron con la cabeza.
►**nod off** *vi* cabecear.
no-fly zone [nəu'flaɪ-] *n* zona de exclusión aérea.
noise [nɔɪz] *n* ruido; (*din*) escándalo, estrépito.
noisily ['nɔɪzɪlɪ] *adv* ruidosamente, estrepitosamente.
noisy ['nɔɪzɪ] *adj (gen)* ruidoso; (*child*) escandaloso.
nomad ['nəumæd] *n* nómada *m/f.*
nomadic [nəu'mædɪk] *adj* nómada.
no man's land *n* tierra de nadie.
nominal ['nɔmɪnl] *adj* nominal.
nominate ['nɔmɪneɪt] *vt (propose)* proponer; (*appoint*) nombrar.
nomination [nɔmɪ'neɪʃən] *n* propuesta; nombramiento.
nominee [nɔmɪ'ni:] *n* candidato/a.
non... [nɔn] *pref* no, des..., in....
nonalcoholic [nɔnælkə'hɔlɪk] *adj* sin alcohol.
nonaligned [nɔnə'laɪnd] *adj* no alineado.
nonarrival [nɔnə'raɪvl] *n* falta de llegada.
nonce word [nɔns-] *n* hápax *m.*
nonchalant ['nɔnʃələnt] *adj* indiferente.
noncommissioned [nɔnkə'mɪʃənd] *adj*: **~ officer** suboficial *m/f.*
noncommittal ['nɔnkə'mɪtl] *adj (reserved)* reservado; (*uncommitted*) evasivo.
nonconformist [nɔnkən'fɔ:mɪst] *adj* inconformista ♦ *n* inconformista *m/f*; (*BRIT REL*) no conformista *m/f.*
noncontributory [nɔnkən'trɪbjutərɪ] *adj*: **~ pension scheme** *or* (*US*) **plan** fondo de pensiones no contributivo.
noncooperation ['nɔnkəuɔpə'reɪʃən] *n* no cooperación *f.*
nondescript ['nɔndɪskrɪpt] *adj* anodino, soso.
none [nʌn] *pron* ninguno/a ♦ *adv* de ninguna manera; **~ of you** ninguno de vosotros; **I've ~ left** no me queda ninguno/a; **he's ~ the worse for it** no le ha perjudicado; **I have ~** no tengo ninguno; **~ at all** (*not one*) ni uno.
nonentity [nɔ'nɛntɪtɪ] *n* cero a la izquierda, nulidad *f.*
nonessential [nɔnɪ'sɛnʃl] *adj* no esencial ♦ *n*: **~s** cosas *fpl* secundarias *or* sin importancia.
nonetheless [nʌnðə'lɛs] *adv* sin embargo, no obstante, aún así.
non-event [nɔnɪ'vɛnt] *n* acontecimiento sin importancia; **it was a ~** no pasó absolutamente nada.
nonexecutive [nɔnɪg'zɛkjutɪv] *adj*: **~ director** director *m* no ejecutivo.
nonexistent [nɔnɪg'zɪstənt] *adj* inexistente.
nonfiction [nɔn'fɪkʃən] *n* no ficción *f.*
nonintervention [nɔnɪntə'vɛnʃən] *n* no intervención *f.*
no-no ['nəunəu] *n (col)*: **it's a ~** de eso ni hablar.
non obst. *abbr (= non obstante: notwithstanding)* no obstante.
no-nonsense [nəu'nɔnsəns] *adj* sensato.
nonpayment [nɔn'peɪmənt] *n* falta de pago.
nonplussed [nɔn'plʌst] *adj* perplejo.
non-profit-making [nɔn'prɔfɪtmeɪkɪŋ] *adj* no lucrativo.
nonsense ['nɔnsəns] *n* tonterías *fpl*,

disparates *fpl*; ~! ¡qué tonterías!; **it is ~ to say that ...** es absurdo decir que ....
nonsensical [nɔn'sɛnsɪkl] *adj* disparatado, absurdo.
nonshrink [nɔn'ʃrɪŋk] *adj* que no encoge.
nonskid [nɔn'skɪd] *adj* antideslizante.
nonsmoker ['nɔn'sməukə*] *n* no fumador(a) *m/f*.
nonstarter [nɔn'stɑːtə*] *n*: **it's a ~** no tiene futuro.
nonstick ['nɔn'stɪk] *adj* (*pan, surface*) antiadherente.
nonstop ['nɔn'stɔp] *adj* continuo; (*RAIL*) directo ♦ *adv* sin parar.
nontaxable [nɔn'tæksəbl] *adj*: **~ income** renta no imponible.
non-U ['nɔnjuː] *adj abbr* (*BRIT col*: = *non-upper class*) *que no pertenece a la clase alta*.
nonvolatile [nɔn'vɔlətaɪl] *adj*: **~ memory** (*COMPUT*) memoria permanente.
nonvoting [nɔn'vəutɪŋ] *adj*: **~ shares** acciones *fpl* sin derecho a voto.
nonwhite ['nɔn'waɪt] *adj* de color ♦ *n* (*person*) persona de color.
noodles ['nuːdlz] *npl* tallarines *mpl*.
nook [nuk] *n* rincón *m*; **~s and crannies** escondrijos *mpl*.
noon [nuːn] *n* mediodía *m*.
no-one ['nəuwʌn] *pron* = **nobody**.
noose [nuːs] *n* lazo corredizo.
nor [nɔː*] *conj* = **neither** ♦ *adv see* **neither**.
Norf *abbr* (*BRIT*) = *Norfolk*.
norm [nɔːm] *n* norma.
normal ['nɔːml] *adj* normal; **to return to ~** volver a la normalidad.
normality [nɔː'mælɪtɪ] *n* normalidad *f*.
normally ['nɔːməlɪ] *adv* normalmente.
Normandy ['nɔːməndɪ] *n* Normandía.
north [nɔːθ] *n* norte *m* ♦ *adj* del norte ♦ *adv* al *or* hacia el norte.
North Africa *n* África del Norte.
North African *adj, n* norteafricano/a *m/f*.
North America *n* América del Norte.
North American *adj, n* norteamericano/a *m/f*.
Northants *abbr* (*BRIT*) = *Northamptonshire*.
northbound ['nɔːθbaund] *adj* (*traffic*) que se dirige al norte; (*carriageway*) de dirección norte.
Northd *abbr* (*BRIT*) = *Northumberland*.
north-east [nɔːθ'iːst] *n* nor(d)este *m*.
northerly ['nɔːðəlɪ] *adj* (*point, direction*) hacia el norte, septentrional; (*wind*) del norte.
northern ['nɔːðən] *adj* norteño, del norte.
Northern Ireland *n* Irlanda del Norte.
North Korea *n* Corea del Norte.
North Pole *n*: **the ~** el Polo Norte.
North Sea *n*: **the ~** el Mar del Norte.
North Sea oil *n* petróleo del Mar del Norte.
northward(s) ['nɔːθwəd(z)] *adv* hacia el norte.
north-west [nɔːθ'wɛst] *n* noroeste *m*.
Norway ['nɔːweɪ] *n* Noruega.
Norwegian [nɔː'wiːdʒən] *adj* noruego ♦ *n* noruego/a; (*LING*) noruego.
nos. *abbr* (= *numbers*) núms.
nose [nəuz] *n* (*ANAT*) nariz *f*; (*ZOOL*) hocico; (*sense of smell*) olfato ♦ *vi* (*also*: **~ one's way**) avanzar con cautela; **to pay through the ~ (for sth)** (*col*) pagar un dineral (por algo).
▸**nose about, nose around** *vi* curiosear.
nosebleed ['nəuzbliːd] *n* hemorragia nasal.
nose-dive ['nəuzdaɪv] *n* picado vertical.
nose drops *npl* gotas *fpl* para la nariz.
nosey ['nəuzɪ] *adj* curioso, fisgón(ona).
nostalgia [nɔs'tældʒɪə] *n* nostalgia.
nostalgic [nɔs'tældʒɪk] *adj* nostálgico.
nostril ['nɔstrɪl] *n* ventana *or* orificio de la nariz.
nosy ['nəuzɪ] *adj* = **nosey**.
not [nɔt] *adv* no; **~ at all** no ... en absoluto; **~ that...** no es que...; **it's too late, isn't it?** es demasiado tarde, ¿verdad?; **~ yet** todavía no; **~ now** ahora no; **why ~?** ¿por qué no?; **I hope ~** espero que no; **~ at all** no ... nada; (*after thanks*) de nada.
notable ['nəutəbl] *adj* notable.
notably ['nəutəblɪ] *adv* especialmente; (*in particular*) sobre todo.
notary ['nəutərɪ] *n* (*also*: **~ public**) notario/a.
notation [nəu'teɪʃən] *n* notación *f*.
notch [nɔtʃ] *n* muesca, corte *m*.
▸**notch up** *vt* (*score, victory*) apuntarse.
note [nəut] *n* (*MUS, record, letter*) nota; (*banknote*) billete *m*; (*tone*) tono ♦ *vt* (*observe*) notar, observar; (*write down*) apuntar, anotar; **delivery ~** nota de entrega; **to compare ~s** (*fig*) cambiar impresiones; **of ~** conocido, destacado; **to take ~** prestar atención a; **just a quick ~ to let you know that ...** sólo unas líneas para informarte que ....
notebook ['nəutbuk] *n* libreta, cuaderno; (*for shorthand*) libreta.
notecase ['nəutkeɪs] *n* (*BRIT*) cartera, billetero.
noted ['nəutɪd] *adj* célebre, conocido.
notepad ['nəutpæd] *n* bloc *m*.
notepaper ['nəutpeɪpə*] *n* papel *m* para cartas.

noteworthy ['nəutwəːðɪ] *adj* notable, digno de atención.
nothing ['nʌθɪŋ] *n* nada; (*zero*) cero; **he does** ~ no hace nada; ~ **new** nada nuevo; **for** ~ (*free*) gratis; (*in vain*) en balde; ~ **at all** nada en absoluto.
notice ['nəutɪs] *n* (*announcement*) anuncio; (*dismissal*) despido; (*resignation*) dimisión *f*; (*review: of play etc*) reseña ♦ *vt* (*observe*) notar, observar; **to take** ~ **of** hacer caso de, prestar atención a; **at short** ~ con poca antelación; **without** ~ sin previo aviso; **advance** ~ previo aviso; **until further** ~ hasta nuevo aviso; **to give sb** ~ **of sth** avisar a algn de algo; **to give** ~, **hand in one's** ~ dimitir, renunciar; **it has come to my** ~ **that** ... he llegado a saber que ...; **to escape** *or* **avoid** ~ pasar inadvertido.
noticeable ['nəutɪsəbl] *adj* evidente, obvio.
notice board *n* (*BRIT*) tablón *m* de anuncios.
notification [nəutɪfɪ'keɪʃən] *n* aviso; (*announcement*) anuncio.
notify ['nəutɪfaɪ] *vt*: **to** ~ **sb (of sth)** comunicar (algo) a algn.
notion ['nəuʃən] *n* noción *f*, concepto; (*opinion*) opinión *f*.
notions ['nəuʃənz] *npl* (*US*) mercería.
notoriety [nəutə'raɪətɪ] *n* notoriedad *f*, mala fama.
notorious [nəu'tɔːrɪəs] *adj* notorio, tristemente célebre.
notoriously [nəu'tɔːrɪəslɪ] *adv* notoriamente.
Notts *abbr* (*BRIT*) = *Nottinghamshire.*
notwithstanding [nɔtwɪθ'stændɪŋ] *adv* no obstante, sin embargo; ~ **this** a pesar de esto.
nougat ['nuːgɑː] *n* turrón *m*.
nought [nɔːt] *n* cero.
noun [naun] *n* nombre *m*, sustantivo.
nourish ['nʌrɪʃ] *vt* nutrir, alimentar; (*fig*) fomentar, nutrir.
nourishing ['nʌrɪʃɪŋ] *adj* nutritivo, rico.
nourishment ['nʌrɪʃmənt] *n* alimento, sustento.
Nov. *abbr* (= *November*) nov.
novel ['nɔvl] *n* novela ♦ *adj* (*new*) nuevo, original; (*unexpected*) insólito.
novelist ['nɔvəlɪst] *n* novelista *m/f*.
novelty ['nɔvəltɪ] *n* novedad *f*.
November [nəu'vɛmbə*] *n* noviembre *m*.
novice ['nɔvɪs] *n* principiante *m/f*, novato/a; (*REL*) novicio/a.
NOW [nau] *n abbr* (*US*) = *National Organization for Women.*
now [nau] *adv* (*at the present time*) ahora; (*these days*) actualmente, hoy día ♦ *conj*: ~ **(that)** ya que, ahora que; **right** ~ ahora mismo; **by** ~ ya; **just** ~: **I'll do it just** ~ ahora mismo lo hago; ~ **and then,** ~ **and again** de vez en cuando; **from** ~ **on** de ahora en adelante; **between** ~ **and Monday** entre hoy y el lunes; **in 3 days from** ~ de hoy en 3 días; **that's all for** ~ eso es todo por ahora.
nowadays ['nauədeɪz] *adv* hoy (en) día, actualmente.
nowhere ['nəuwɛə*] *adv* (*direction*) a ninguna parte; (*location*) en ninguna parte; ~ **else** en *or* a ninguna otra parte.
no-win situation [nəu'wɪn-] *n*: **I'm in a** ~ haga lo que haga, llevo las de perder.
noxious ['nɔkʃəs] *adj* nocivo.
nozzle ['nɔzl] *n* boquilla.
NP *n abbr* = **notary public.**
NS *abbr* (*Canada*) = *Nova Scotia.*
NSC *n abbr* (*US*) = *National Security Council.*
NSF *n abbr* (*US*) = *National Science Foundation.*
NSPCC *n abbr* (*BRIT*) = *National Society for the Prevention of Cruelty to Children.*
NSW *abbr* (*Australia*) = *New South Wales.*
NT *n abbr* = *New Testament* ♦ *abbr* (*Canada*) = *Northwest Territories.*
nth [ɛnθ] *adj*: **for the** ~ **time** (*col*) por enésima vez.
nuance ['njuːɑːns] *n* matiz *m*.
nubile ['njuːbaɪl] *adj* núbil.
nuclear ['njuːklɪə*] *adj* nuclear.
nuclear disarmament *n* desarme *m* nuclear.
nuclear family *n* familia nuclear.
nuclear-free zone ['njuːklə'friː-] *n* zona desnuclearizada.
nucleus, *pl* **nuclei** ['njuːklɪəs, 'njuːklɪaɪ] *n* núcleo.
NUCPS *n abbr* (*BRIT* = *National Union of Civil and Public Servants*) *sindicato de funcionarios.*
nude [njuːd] *adj, n* desnudo/a *m/f*; **in the** ~ desnudo.
nudge [nʌdʒ] *vt* dar un codazo a.
nudist ['njuːdɪst] *n* nudista *m/f*.
nudist colony *n* colonia de desnudistas.
nudity ['njuːdɪtɪ] *n* desnudez *f*.
nugget ['nʌgɪt] *n* pepita.
nuisance ['njuːsns] *n* molestia, fastidio; (*person*) pesado, latoso; **what a** ~! ¡qué lata!
NUJ *n abbr* (*BRIT*: = *National Union of Journalists*) *sindicato de periodistas.*
nuke [njuːk] (*col*) *n* bomba atómica ♦ *vt* atacar con arma nuclear.
null [nʌl] *adj*: ~ **and void** nulo y sin efecto.

nullify ['nʌlɪfaɪ] *vt* anular, invalidar.
NUM *n abbr* (*BRIT*: = *National Union of Mineworkers*) *sindicato de mineros.*
numb [nʌm] *adj* entumecido; (*fig*) insensible ♦ *vt* quitar la sensación a, entumecer, entorpecer; **to be ~ with cold** estar entumecido de frío; **~ with fear** paralizado de miedo; **~ with grief** paralizado de dolor.
number ['nʌmbə*] *n* número; (*numeral*) número, cifra ♦ *vt* (*pages etc*) numerar, poner número a; (*amount to*) sumar, ascender a; **reference ~** número de referencia; **telephone ~** número de teléfono; **wrong ~** (*TEL*) número equivocado; **opposite ~** (*person*) homólogo/a; **to be ~ed among** figurar entre; **a ~ of** varios, algunos; **they were ten in ~** eran diez.
numbered account *n* (*in bank*) cuenta numerada.
number plate *n* (*BRIT*) matrícula, placa.
Number Ten *n* (*BRIT*: *10 Downing Street*) *residencia del primer ministro.*
numbness ['nʌmnɪs] *n* insensibilidad *f*, parálisis *f inv*; (*due to cold*) entumecimiento.
numbskull ['nʌmskʌl] *n* (*col*) papanatas *m/f inv*.
numeral ['nju:mərəl] *n* número, cifra.
numerate ['nju:mərɪt] *adj* competente en aritmética.
numerical [nju:'mɛrɪkl] *adj* numérico.
numerous ['nju:mərəs] *adj* numeroso, muchos.
nun [nʌn] *n* monja, religiosa.
nunnery ['nʌnərɪ] *n* convento de monjas.
nuptial ['nʌpʃəl] *adj* nupcial.
nurse [nə:s] *n* enfermero/a; (*nanny*) niñera ♦ *vt* (*patient*) cuidar, atender; (*baby*: *Brit*) mecer; (: *US*) criar, amamantar; **male ~** enfermero.
nursery ['nə:sərɪ] *n* (*institution*) guardería infantil; (*room*) cuarto de los niños; (*for plants*) criadero, semillero.
nursery rhyme *n* canción *f* infantil.
nursery school *n* escuela de preescolar.
nursery slope *n* (*BRIT SKI*) cuesta para principiantes.
nursing ['nə:sɪŋ] *n* (*profession*) profesión *f* de enfermera; (*care*) asistencia, cuidado ♦ *adj* (*mother*) lactante.
nursing home *n* clínica de reposo.
nurture ['nə:tʃə*] *vt* (*child, plant*) alimentar, nutrir.
NUS *n abbr* (*BRIT*: = *National Union of Students*) *sindicato de estudiantes.*
NUT *n abbr* (*BRIT*: = *National Union of Teachers*) *sindicato de profesores.*
nut [nʌt] *n* (*TECH*) tuerca; (*BOT*) nuez *f* ♦ *adj* (*chocolate etc*) con nueces; **~s** (*CULIN*) frutos secos.
nutcrackers ['nʌtkrækəz] *npl* cascanueces *m inv*.
nutmeg ['nʌtmɛg] *n* nuez *f* moscada.
nutrient ['nju:trɪənt] *adj* nutritivo ♦ *n* elemento nutritivo.
nutrition [nju:'trɪʃən] *n* nutrición *f*, alimentación *f*.
nutritionist [nju:'trɪʃənɪst] *n* dietista *m/f*.
nutritious [nju:'trɪʃəs] *adj* nutritivo.
nuts [nʌts] *adj* (*col*) chiflado.
nutshell ['nʌtʃɛl] *n* cáscara de nuez; **in a ~** en resumidas cuentas.
nutty ['nʌtɪ] *adj* (*flavour*) a frutos secos; (*col*: *foolish*) chalado.
nuzzle ['nʌzl] *vi*: **to ~ up to** arrimarse a.
NV *abbr* (*US*) = *Nevada.*
NWT *abbr* (*Canada*) = *Northwest Territories.*
NY *abbr* (*US*) = *New York.*
NYC *abbr* (*US*) = *New York City.*
nylon ['naɪlɔn] *n* nylon *m*, nilón *m* ♦ *adj* de nylon *or* nilón.
nymph [nɪmf] *n* ninfa.
nymphomaniac ['nɪmfəu'meɪnɪæk] *adj, n* ninfómana.
NYSE *n abbr* (*US*) = *New York Stock Exchange.*

O o

O, o [əu] (*letter*) O, o *f*; **O for Oliver**, (*US*) **O for Oboe** O de Oviedo.
oaf [əuf] *n* zoquete *m/f*.
oak [əuk] *n* roble *m* ♦ *adj* de roble.
OAP *abbr see* **old-age pensioner.**
oar [ɔ:*] *n* remo; **to put** *or* **shove one's ~ in** (*fig*: *col*) entrometerse.
oarsman ['ɔ:zmən] *n* remero.
OAS *n abbr* (= *Organization of American States*) OEA *f*.
oasis, *pl* **oases** [əu'eɪsɪs, əu'eɪsi:z] *n* oasis *m inv*.
oath [əuθ] *n* juramento; (*swear word*) palabrota; **on** (*BRIT*) *or* **under ~** bajo juramento.
oatmeal ['əutmi:l] *n* harina de avena.
oats [əuts] *n* avena.
OAU *n abbr* (= *Organization of African Unity*)

OUA *f.*
obdurate ['ɔbdjurɪt] *adj* (*stubborn*) terco, obstinado; (*sinner*) empedernido; (*unyielding*) inflexible, firme.
OBE *n abbr* (*BRIT*: = *Order of the British Empire*) *título ceremonial.*
obedience [ə'biːdɪəns] *n* obediencia; **in ~ to** de acuerdo con.
obedient [ə'biːdɪənt] *adj* obediente.
obelisk ['ɔbɪlɪsk] *n* obelisco.
obese [əu'biːs] *adj* obeso.
obesity [əu'biːsɪtɪ] *n* obesidad *f.*
obey [ə'beɪ] *vt* obedecer; (*instructions, regulations*) cumplir.
obituary [ə'bɪtjuərɪ] *n* necrología.
object ['ɔbdʒɪkt] *n* (*gen*) objeto; (*purpose*) objeto, propósito; (*LING*) objeto, complemento ♦ *vi* [əb'dʒɛkt]: **to ~ to** (*attitude*) protestar contra; (*proposal*) oponerse a; **expense is no ~** no importan los gastos; **I ~!** ¡protesto!; **to ~ that** objetar que.
objection [əb'dʒɛkʃən] *n* objeción *f*; **I have no ~ to ...** no tengo inconveniente en que ....
objectionable [əb'dʒɛkʃənəbl] *adj* (*gen*) desagradable; (*conduct*) censurable.
objective [əb'dʒɛktɪv] *adj, n* objetivo.
objectively [əb'dʒɛktɪvlɪ] *adv* objetivamente.
objectivity [ɔbdʒɪk'tɪvɪtɪ] *n* objetividad *f.*
object lesson *n* (*fig*) (buen) ejemplo.
objector [əb'dʒɛktə*] *n* objetor(a) *m/f.*
obligation [ɔblɪ'geɪʃən] *n* obligación *f*; (*debt*) deber *m*; **"without ~"** "sin compromiso"; **to be under an ~ to sb/to do sth** estar comprometido con algn/a hacer algo.
obligatory [ə'blɪgətərɪ] *adj* obligatorio.
oblige [ə'blaɪdʒ] *vt* (*do a favour for*) complacer, hacer un favor a; **to ~ sb to do sth** obligar a algn a hacer algo; **to be ~d to sb for sth** estarle agradecido a algn por algo; **anything to ~!** (*col*) todo sea por complacerte.
obliging [ə'blaɪdʒɪŋ] *adj* servicial, atento.
oblique [ə'bliːk] *adj* oblicuo; (*allusion*) indirecto ♦ *n* (*TYP*) barra.
obliterate [ə'blɪtəreɪt] *vt* arrasar; (*memory*) borrar.
oblivion [ə'blɪvɪən] *n* olvido.
oblivious [ə'blɪvɪəs] *adj*: **~ of** inconsciente de.
oblong ['ɔblɔŋ] *adj* rectangular ♦ *n* rectángulo.
obnoxious [əb'nɔkʃəs] *adj* odioso, detestable; (*smell*) nauseabundo.
o.b.o. *abbr* (*US*: = *or best offer. in classified ads*) abierto ofertas.
oboe ['əubəu] *n* oboe *m.*
obscene [əb'siːn] *adj* obsceno.
obscenity [əb'sɛnɪtɪ] *n* obscenidad *f.*
obscure [əb'skjuə*] *adj* oscuro ♦ *vt* oscurecer; (*hide*: *sun*) ocultar.
obscurity [əb'skjuərɪtɪ] *n* oscuridad *f*; (*obscure point*) punto oscuro; **to rise from ~** salir de la nada.
obsequious [əb'siːkwɪəs] *adj* servil.
observable [əb'zəːvəbl] *adj* observable, perceptible.
observance [əb'zəːvns] *n* observancia, cumplimiento; (*ritual*) práctica; **religious ~s** prácticas *fpl* religiosas.
observant [əb'zəːvnt] *adj* observador(a).
observation [ɔbzə'veɪʃən] *n* (*also MED*) observación *f*; (*by police etc*) vigilancia.
observation post *n* (*MIL*) puesto de observación.
observatory [əb'zəːvətrɪ] *n* observatorio.
observe [əb'zəːv] *vt* (*gen*) observar; (*rule*) cumplir.
observer [əb'zəːvə*] *n* observador(a) *m/f.*
obsess [əb'sɛs] *vt* obsesionar; **to be ~ed by** *or* **with sb/sth** estar obsesionado con algn/algo.
obsession [əb'sɛʃən] *n* obsesión *f.*
obsessive [əb'sɛsɪv] *adj* obsesivo.
obsolescence [ɔbsə'lɛsns] *n* obsolescencia.
obsolescent [ɔbsə'lɛsnt] *adj* que está cayendo en desuso.
obsolete ['ɔbsəliːt] *adj* obsoleto.
obstacle ['ɔbstəkl] *n* obstáculo; (*nuisance*) estorbo.
obstacle race *n* carrera de obstáculos.
obstetrician [ɔbstə'trɪʃən] *n* obstetra *m/f.*
obstetrics [ɔb'stɛtrɪks] *n* obstetricia.
obstinacy ['ɔbstɪnəsɪ] *n* terquedad *f*, obstinación *f*; tenacidad *f.*
obstinate ['ɔbstɪnɪt] *adj* terco, obstinado; (*determined*) tenaz.
obstinately ['ɔbstɪnɪtlɪ] *adv* tercamente, obstinadamente.
obstreperous [əb'strɛpərəs] *adj* ruidoso; (*unruly*) revoltoso.
obstruct [əb'strʌkt] *vt* (*block*) obstruir; (*hinder*) estorbar, obstaculizar.
obstruction [əb'strʌkʃən] *n* obstrucción *f*; estorbo, obstáculo.
obstructive [əb'strʌktɪv] *adj* obstruccionista; **stop being ~!** ¡deja de poner peros!
obtain [əb'teɪn] *vt* (*get*) obtener; (*achieve*) conseguir; **to ~ sth (for o.s.)** conseguir *or* adquirir algo.
obtainable [əb'teɪnəbl] *adj* asequible.
obtrusive [əb'truːsɪv] *adj* (*person*)

importuno; (: *interfering*) entrometido; (*building etc*) demasiado visible.
obtuse [əb'tjuːs] *adj* obtuso.
obverse ['ɔbvəːs] *n* (*of medal*) anverso; (*fig*) complemento.
obviate ['ɔbvɪeɪt] *vt* obviar, evitar.
obvious ['ɔbvɪəs] *adj* (*clear*) obvio, evidente; (*unsubtle*) poco sutil; **it's ~ that** ... está claro que ..., es evidente que ....
obviously ['ɔbvɪəslɪ] *adv* obviamente, evidentemente; **~ not!** ¡por supuesto que no!; **he was ~ not drunk** era evidente que no estaba borracho; **he was not ~ drunk** no se le notaba que estaba borracho.
OCAS *n abbr* (= *Organization of Central American States*) ODECA *f*.
occasion [ə'keɪʒən] *n* oportunidad *f*, ocasión *f*; (*event*) acontecimiento ♦ *vt* ocasionar, causar; **on that ~** esa vez, en aquella ocasión; **to rise to the ~** ponerse a la altura de las circunstancias.
occasional [ə'keɪʒənl] *adj* poco frecuente, ocasional.
occasionally [ə'keɪʒənlɪ] *adv* de vez en cuando; **very ~** muy de tarde en tarde, en muy contadas ocasiones.
occasional table *n* mesita.
occult [ɔ'kʌlt] *adj* (*gen*) oculto.
occupancy ['ɔkjupənsɪ] *n* ocupación *f*.
occupant ['ɔkjupənt] *n* (*of house*) inquilino/a; (*of boat, car*) ocupante *m/f*.
occupation [ɔkju'peɪʃən] *n* (*of house*) tenencia; (*job*) trabajo; (: *calling*) oficio.
occupational accident [ɔkju'peɪʃənl] *n* accidente *m* laboral.
occupational guidance *n* orientación *f* profesional.
occupational hazard *n* gajes *mpl* del oficio.
occupational pension scheme *n* plan *m* profesional de jubilación.
occupational therapy *n* terapia ocupacional.
occupier ['ɔkjupaɪə*] *n* inquilino/a.
occupy ['ɔkjupaɪ] *vt* (*seat, post, time*) ocupar; (*house*) habitar; **to ~ o.s. with** *or* **by doing** (*as job*) dedicarse a hacer; (*to pass time*) entretenerse haciendo; **to be occupied with sth/in doing sth** estar ocupado con algo/haciendo algo.
occur [ə'kəː*] *vi* ocurrir, suceder; **to ~ to sb** ocurrírsele a algn.
occurrence [ə'kʌrəns] *n* suceso.
ocean ['əuʃən] *n* océano; **~s of** (*col*) la mar de.
ocean bed *n* fondo del océano.
ocean-going ['əuʃəngəuɪŋ] *adj* de alta mar.
Oceania [əuʃɪ'eɪnɪə] *n* Oceanía.
ocean liner *n* buque *m* transoceánico.
ochre, (*US*) **ocher** ['əukə*] *n* ocre *m*.
o'clock [ə'klɔk] *adv*: **it is 5 ~** son las 5.
OCR *n abbr see* **optical character recognition/reader.**
Oct. *abbr* (= *October*) oct.
octagonal [ɔk'tægənl] *adj* octagonal.
octane ['ɔkteɪn] *n* octano; **high ~ petrol** *or* (*US*) **gas** gasolina de alto octanaje.
octave ['ɔktɪv] *n* octava.
October [ɔk'təubə*] *n* octubre *m*.
octogenarian ['ɔktəudʒɪ'nɛərɪən] *n* octogenario/a.
octopus ['ɔktəpəs] *n* pulpo.
oculist ['ɔkjulɪst] *n* oculista *m/f*.
odd [ɔd] *adj* (*strange*) extraño, raro; (*number*) impar; (*left over*) sobrante, suelto; **60-~** 60 y pico; **at ~ times** de vez en cuando; **to be the ~ one out** estar de más; **if you have the ~ minute** si tienes unos minutos libres; *see also* **odds.**
oddball ['ɔdbɔːl] *n* (*col*) bicho raro.
oddity ['ɔdɪtɪ] *n* rareza; (*person*) excéntrico/a.
odd-job man [ɔd'dʒɔb-] *n* hombre *m* que hace chapuzas.
odd jobs *npl* chapuzas *fpl*.
oddly ['ɔdlɪ] *adv* extrañamente.
oddments ['ɔdmənts] *npl* (*BRIT COMM*) restos *mpl*.
odds [ɔdz] *npl* (*in betting*) puntos *mpl* de ventaja; **it makes no ~** da lo mismo; **at ~** reñidos/as; **to succeed against all the ~** tener éxito contra todo pronóstico; **~ and ends** cachivaches *mpl*.
odds-on [ɔdz'ɔn] *adj* (*col*): **the ~ favourite** el máximo favorito; **it's ~ he'll come** seguro que viene.
ode [əud] *n* oda.
odious ['əudɪəs] *adj* odioso.
odometer [ɔ'dɔmɪtə*] *n* (*US*) cuentakilómetros *m inv*.
odour, (*US*) **odor** ['əudə*] *n* olor *m*; (*perfume*) perfume *m*.
odo(u)rless ['əudəlɪs] *adj* sin olor.
OECD *n abbr* (= *Organization for Economic Co-operation and Development*) OCDE *f*.
oesophagus, (*US*) **esophagus** [iː'sɔfəgəs] *n* esófago.
oestrogen, (*US*) **estrogen** ['iːstrədʒən] *n* estrógeno.

KEYWORD

of [ɔv, əv] *prep* **1** (*gen*) de; **a friend ~ ours** un amigo nuestro; **a boy ~ 10** un chico de 10 años; **that was kind ~ you** eso fue muy amable de tu parte

2 (*expressing quantity, amount, dates etc*) de; **a kilo ~ flour** un kilo de harina; **there were 3 ~ them** había tres; **3 ~ us went** tres de nosotros fuimos; **the 5th ~ July** el 5 de julio; **a quarter ~ 4** (*US*) las 4 menos cuarto
3 (*from, out of*) de; **made ~ wood** (hecho) de madera.

off [ɔf] *adj, adv* (*engine, light*) apagado; (*tap*) cerrado; (*BRIT: food: bad*) pasado, malo; (*: milk*) cortado; (*cancelled*) suspendido; (*removed*): **the lid was ~** no estaba puesta la tapadera ♦ *prep* de; **to be ~** (*to leave*) irse, marcharse; **to be ~ sick** estar enfermo *or* de baja; **a day ~** un día libre; **to have an ~ day** tener un mal día; **he had his coat ~** se había quitado el abrigo; **10% ~** (*COMM*) (con el) 10% de descuento; **it's a long way ~** está muy lejos; **5 km ~ (the road)** a 5 km (de la carretera); **~ the coast** frente a la costa; **I'm ~ meat** (*no longer eat/like it*) paso de la carne; **on the ~ chance** por si acaso; **~ and on, on and ~** de vez en cuando; **I must be ~** tengo que irme; **to be well/badly ~** andar bien/mal de dinero; **I'm afraid the chicken is ~** desgraciadamente ya no queda pollo; **that's a bit ~, isn't it!** (*fig, col*) ¡eso no se hace!
offal ['ɔfl] *n* (*BRIT CULIN*) menudillos *mpl*, asaduras *fpl*.
off-centre, (*US*) **off-center** [ɔf'sɛntə*] *adj* descentrado, ladeado.
off-colour ['ɔf'kʌlə*] *adj* (*BRIT: ill*) indispuesto; **to feel ~** sentirse *or* estar mal.
offence, (*US*) **offense** [ə'fɛns] *n* (*crime*) delito; (*insult*) ofensa; **to take ~ at** ofenderse por; **to commit an ~** cometer un delito.
offend [ə'fɛnd] *vt* (*person*) ofender ♦ *vi*: **to ~ against** (*law, rule*) infringir.
offender [ə'fɛndə*] *n* delincuente *m/f*; (*against regulations*) infractor(a) *m/f*.
offending [ə'fɛndɪŋ] *adj* culpable; (*object*) molesto; (*word*) problemático.
offense [ə'fɛns] *n* (*US*) = **offence.**
offensive [ə'fɛnsɪv] *adj* ofensivo; (*smell etc*) repugnante ♦ *n* (*MIL*) ofensiva.
offer ['ɔfə*] *n* (*gen*) oferta, ofrecimiento; (*proposal*) propuesta ♦ *vt* ofrecer; **"on ~"** (*COMM*) "en oferta"; **to make an ~ for sth** hacer una oferta por algo; **to ~ sth to sb, ~ sb sth** ofrecer algo a algn; **to ~ to do sth** ofrecerse a hacer algo.
offering ['ɔfərɪŋ] *n* (*REL*) ofrenda.
offer price *n* precio de oferta.
offertory ['ɔfətrɪ] *n* (*REL*) ofertorio.
offhand [ɔf'hænd] *adj* informal; (*brusque*) desconsiderado ♦ *adv* de improviso, sin pensarlo; **I can't tell you ~** no te lo puedo decir así de improviso *or* así nomás (*LAM*).
office ['ɔfɪs] *n* (*place*) oficina; (*room*) despacho; (*position*) cargo, oficio; **doctor's ~** (*US*) consultorio; **to take ~** entrar en funciones; **through his good ~s** gracias a sus buenos oficios; **O~ of Fair Trading** (*BRIT*) *oficina que regula normas comerciales.*
office automation *n* ofimática, buromática.
office bearer *n* (*of club etc*) titular *m/f* (de una cartera).
office block, (*US*) **office building** *n* bloque *m* de oficinas.
office boy *n* ordenanza *m.*
office hours *npl* horas *fpl* de oficina; (*US MED*) horas *fpl* de consulta.
office manager *n* jefe/a *m/f* de oficina.
officer ['ɔfɪsə*] *n* (*MIL etc*) oficial *m/f*; (*of organization*) director(a) *m/f*; (*also*: **police ~**) agente *m/f* de policía.
office work *n* trabajo de oficina.
office worker *n* oficinista *m/f.*
official [ə'fɪʃl] *adj* (*authorized*) oficial, autorizado; (*strike*) oficial ♦ *n* funcionario/a.
officialdom [ə'fɪʃldəm] *n* burocracia.
officially [ə'fɪʃəlɪ] *adv* oficialmente.
official receiver *n* síndico.
officiate [ə'fɪʃɪeɪt] *vi* (*also REL*) oficiar; **to ~ as Mayor** ejercer las funciones de alcalde; **to ~ at a marriage** celebrar una boda.
officious [ə'fɪʃəs] *adj* oficioso.
offing ['ɔfɪŋ] *n*: **in the ~** (*fig*) en perspectiva.
off-key [ɔf'kiː] *adj* desafinado ♦ *adv* desafinadamente.
off-licence ['ɔflaɪsns] *n* (*BRIT: shop*) *tienda de bebidas alcohólicas*; *ver recuadro.*

OFF-LICENCE

En el Reino Unido una **off-licence** *es una tienda especializada en la venta de bebidas alcohólicas para el consumo fuera del establecimiento. De ahí su nombre, pues se necesita un permiso especial para tal venta, que está estrictamente regulada. Suelen vender además bebidas sin alcohol, tabaco, chocolate, patatas fritas etc y a menudo son parte de grandes cadenas nacionales.*

off-limits [ɔf'lɪmɪts] *adj* (*US MIL*) prohibido al personal militar.

off line *adj, adv* (*COMPUT*) fuera de línea; (*switched off*) desconectado.
off-load ['ɔfləud] *vt* descargar, desembarcar.
off-peak ['ɔf'piːk] *adj* (*holiday*) de temporada baja; (*electricity*) de banda económica.
off-putting ['ɔfputɪŋ] *adj* (*BRIT*: *person*) poco amable, difícil; (*behaviour*) chocante.
off-season ['ɔf'siːzn] *adj, adv* fuera de temporada.
offset ['ɔfsɛt] *vt* (*irreg*: *like* **set**) (*counteract*) contrarrestar, compensar ♦ *n* (*also*: ~ **printing**) offset *m*.
offshoot ['ɔfʃuːt] *n* (*BOT*) vástago; (*fig*) ramificación *f*.
offshore [ɔf'ʃɔː*] *adj* (*breeze, island*) costero; (*fishing*) de bajura; ~ **oilfield** campo petrolífero submarino.
offside ['ɔf'saɪd] *n* (*AUT*: *with right-hand drive*) lado derecho; (: *with left-hand drive*) lado izquierdo ♦ *adj* (*SPORT*) fuera de juego; (*AUT*) del lado derecho; del lado izquierdo.
offspring ['ɔfsprɪŋ] *n* descendencia.
offstage [ɔf'steɪdʒ] *adv* entre bastidores.
off-the-cuff [ɔfðə'kʌf] *adj* espontáneo.
off-the-job [ɔfðə'dʒɔb] *adj*: ~ **training** formación *f* fuera del trabajo.
off-the-peg [ɔfðə'pɛg], (*US*) **off-the-rack** [ɔfðə'ræk] *adv* confeccionado.
off-the-record ['ɔfðə'rɛkɔːd] *adj* extraoficial, confidencial ♦ *adv* extraoficialmente, confidencialmente.
off-white ['ɔfwaɪt] *adj* blanco grisáceo.
Ofgas ['ɔfgæs] *n* (*BRIT*: = *Office of Gas Supply*) *organismo que controla a las empresas del gas en Gran Bretaña.*
Oftel ['ɔftɛl] *n* (*BRIT*: = *Office of Telecommunications*) *organismo que controla las telecomunicaciones británicas.*
often ['ɔfn] *adv* a menudo, con frecuencia, seguido (*LAM*); **how ~ do you go?** ¿cada cuánto vas?
Ofwat ['ɔfwɔt] *n* (*BRIT*: = *Office of Water Services*) *organismo que controla a las empresas suministradoras del agua en Inglaterra y Gales.*
ogle ['əugl] *vt* comerse con los ojos a.
ogre ['əugə*] *n* ogro.
OH *abbr* (*US*) = *Ohio.*
oh [əu] *excl* ¡ah!
OHMS *abbr* (*BRIT*) *On His* (*or Her*) *Majesty's Service.*
oil [ɔɪl] *n* aceite *m*; (*petroleum*) petróleo ♦ *vt* (*machine*) engrasar; **fried in ~** frito en aceite.
oilcan ['ɔɪlkæn] *n* lata de aceite.
oilfield ['ɔɪlfiːld] *n* campo petrolífero.
oil filter *n* (*AUT*) filtro de aceite.
oil-fired ['ɔɪlfaɪəd] *adj* de fuel-oil.
oil gauge *n* indicador *m* del aceite.
oil industry *n* industria petrolífera.
oil level *n* nivel *m* del aceite.
oil painting *n* pintura al óleo.
oil refinery *n* refinería de petróleo.
oil rig *n* torre *f* de perforación.
oilskins ['ɔɪlskɪnz] *npl* impermeable *msg*, chubasquero *sg*.
oil tanker *n* petrolero.
oil well *n* pozo (de petróleo).
oily ['ɔɪlɪ] *adj* aceitoso; (*food*) grasiento.
ointment ['ɔɪntmənt] *n* ungüento.
OK *abbr* (*US*) = *Oklahoma.*
O.K., okay ['əu'keɪ] *excl* O.K., ¡está bien!, ¡vale! ♦ *adj* bien ♦ *n*: **to give sth one's ~** dar el visto bueno a *or* aprobar algo ♦ *vt* dar el visto bueno a; **it's ~ with** *or* **by me** estoy de acuerdo, me parece bien; **are you ~ for money?** ¿andas *or* vas bien de dinero?
Okla. *abbr* (*US*) = *Oklahoma.*
old [əuld] *adj* viejo; (*former*) antiguo; **how ~ are you?** ¿cuántos años tienes?, ¿qué edad tienes?; **he's 10 years ~** tiene 10 años; **~er brother** hermano mayor; **any ~ thing will do** sirve cualquier cosa.
old age *n* vejez *f*.
old-age pension ['əuldeɪdʒ-] *n* (*BRIT*) jubilación *f*, pensión *f*.
old-age pensioner (OAP) ['əuldeɪdʒ-] *n* (*BRIT*) jubilado/a.
olden ['əuldən] *adj* antiguo.
old-fashioned ['əuld'fæʃənd] *adj* anticuado, pasado de moda.
old maid *n* solterona.
old-style ['əuldstaɪl] *adj* tradicional, chapado a la antigua.
old-time ['əuld'taɪm] *adj* antiguo, de antaño.
old-timer [əuld'taɪmə*] *n* veterano/a; (*old person*) anciano/a.
old wives' tale *n* cuento de viejas, patraña.
olive ['ɔlɪv] *n* (*fruit*) aceituna; (*tree*) olivo ♦ *adj* (*also*: **~-green**) verde oliva *inv*.
olive branch *n* (*fig*): **to offer an ~ to sb** ofrecer hacer las paces con algn.
olive oil *n* aceite *m* de oliva.
Olympic [əu'lɪmpɪk] *adj* olímpico; **the ~ Games, the ~s** *npl* las Olimpíadas.
OM *n abbr* (*BRIT*: = *Order of Merit*) *título ceremonial.*
O & M *n abbr* = *organization and method.*
Oman [əu'mɑːn] *n* Omán *m*.
OMB *n abbr* (*US*: = *Office of Management and*

Budget) servicio que asesora al presidente en materia presupuestaria.

omelet(te) ['ɔmlɪt] *n* tortilla, tortilla de huevo (*LAM*).

omen ['əumən] *n* presagio.

ominous ['ɔmɪnəs] *adj* de mal agüero, amenazador(a).

omission [əu'mɪʃən] *n* omisión *f*; (*error*) descuido.

omit [əu'mɪt] *vt* omitir; (*by mistake*) olvidar, descuidar; **to ~ to do sth** olvidarse *or* dejar de hacer algo.

omnivorous [ɔm'nɪvərəs] *adj* omnívoro.

ON *abbr* (*Canada*) = *Ontario.*

KEYWORD

on [ɔn] *prep* **1** (*indicating position*) en; sobre; **~ the wall** en la pared; **it's ~ the table** está sobre *or* en la mesa; **~ the left** a la izquierda; **I haven't got any money ~ me** no llevo dinero encima

2 (*indicating means, method, condition etc*): **~ foot** a pie; **~ the train/plane** (*go*) en tren/avión; (*be*) en el tren/el avión; **~ the radio/television** por *or* en la radio/ televisión; **~ the telephone** al teléfono; **to be ~ drugs** drogarse; (*MED*) estar a tratamiento; **to be ~ holiday/business** estar de vacaciones/en viaje de negocios; **we're ~ irregular verbs** estamos con los verbos irregulares

3 (*referring to time*): **~ Friday** el viernes; **~ Fridays** los viernes; **~ June 20th** el 20 de junio; **a week ~ Friday** del viernes en una semana; **~ arrival** al llegar; **~ seeing this** al ver esto

4 (*about, concerning*) sobre, acerca de; **a book ~ physics** un libro de *or* sobre física

5 (*at the expense of*): **this round's ~ me** esta ronda la pago yo, invito yo (a esta ronda); (*earning*): **he's ~ £16,000 a year** gana dieciséis mil libras al año

♦ *adv* **1** (*referring to dress*): **to have one's coat ~** tener *or* llevar el abrigo puesto; **she put her gloves ~** se puso los guantes

2 (*referring to covering*): **"screw the lid ~ tightly"** "cerrar bien la tapa"

3 (*further, continuously*): **to walk/run** *etc* **~** seguir caminando/corriendo *etc*; **from that day ~** desde aquel día; **it was well ~ in the evening** estaba ya entrada la tarde

4 (*in phrases*): **I'm ~ to sth** creo haber encontrado algo; **my father's always ~ at me to get a job** (*col*) mi padre siempre me está dando la lata para que me ponga a trabajar

♦ *adj* **1** (*functioning, in operation: machine, radio, TV, light*) encendido/a (*SP*), prendido/a (*LAM*); (*: tap*) abierto/a; (*: brakes*) echado/a, puesto/a; **is the meeting still ~?** (*in progress*) ¿todavía continúa la reunión?; (*not cancelled*) ¿va a haber reunión al fin?; **there's a good film ~ at the cinema** ponen una buena película en el cine

2: **that's not ~!** (*inf: not possible*) ¡eso ni hablar!; (*: not acceptable*) ¡eso no se hace!

ONC *n abbr* (*BRIT: = Ordinary National Certificate*) *título escolar.*

once [wʌns] *adv* una vez; (*formerly*) antiguamente ♦ *conj* una vez que; **~ he had left/it was done** una vez que se había marchado/se hizo; **at ~** en seguida, inmediatamente; (*simultaneously*) a la vez; **~ a week** una vez a la semana; **~ more** otra vez; **~ and for all** de una vez por todas; **~ upon a time** érase una vez; **I knew him ~** le conocía hace tiempo.

oncoming ['ɔnkʌmɪŋ] *adj* (*traffic*) que viene de frente.

OND *n abbr* (*BRIT: = Ordinary National Diploma*) *título escolar.*

KEYWORD

one [wʌn] *num* un(o)/una; **~ hundred and fifty** ciento cincuenta; **~ by ~** uno a uno; **it's ~ (o'clock)** es la una

♦ *adj* **1** (*sole*) único; **the ~ book which** el único libro que; **the ~ man who** el único que

2 (*same*) mismo/a; **they came in the ~ car** vinieron en un solo coche

♦ *pron* **1**: **this ~** éste/ésta; **that ~** ése/ésa; (*more remote*) aquél/aquélla; **I've already got (a red) ~** ya tengo uno/a (rojo/a); **~ by ~** uno/a por uno/a; **to be ~ up on sb** llevar ventaja a algn; **to be at ~ (with sb)** estar completamente de acuerdo (con algn)

2: **~ another** (*US*) nos; (*you*) os (*SP*); (*you: polite, them*) se; **do you two ever see ~ another?** ¿os veis alguna vez? (*SP*), ¿se ven alguna vez?; **the two boys didn't dare look at ~ another** los dos chicos no se atrevieron a mirarse (el uno al otro); **they all kissed ~ another** se besaron unos a otros

3 (*impers*): **~ never knows** nunca se sabe; **to cut ~'s finger** cortarse el dedo; **~ needs to eat** hay que comer.

one-armed bandit ['wʌnɑːmd-] *n* máquina tragaperras.

one-day excursion ['wʌndeɪ-] *n* (*US*)

billete *m* de ida y vuelta en un día.
One-hundred share index ['wʌnhʌndrəd-] *n* índice *m* bursátil (*del Financial Times*).
one-man ['wʌn'mæn] *adj* (*business*) individual.
one-man band *n* hombre-orquesta *m*.
one-off [wʌn'ɔf] *n* (*BRIT col: object*) artículo único; (: *event*) caso especial.
one-parent family ['wʌnpɛərənt-] *n* familia monoparental.
one-piece ['wʌnpi:s] *adj* (*bathing suit*) de una pieza.
onerous ['ɔnərəs] *adj* (*task, duty*) pesado; (*responsibility*) oneroso.
oneself [wʌn'sɛlf] *pron* uno mismo; (*after prep, also emphatic*) sí (mismo/a); **to do sth by ~** hacer algo solo *or* por sí solo.
one-shot [wʌn'ʃɔt] *n* (*US*) = **one-off.**
one-sided [wʌn'saɪdɪd] *adj* (*argument*) parcial; (*decision, view*) unilateral; (*game, contest*) desigual.
one-time ['wʌntaɪm] *adj* antiguo, ex-.
one-to-one ['wʌntəwʌn] *adj* (*relationship*) individualizado.
one-upmanship [wʌn'ʌpmənʃɪp] *n*: **the art of ~** el arte de quedar siempre por encima.
one-way ['wʌnweɪ] *adj* (*street, traffic*) de dirección única; (*ticket*) sencillo.
ongoing ['ɔngəuɪŋ] *adj* continuo.
onion ['ʌnjən] *n* cebolla.
on line *adj, adv* (*COMPUT*) en línea; (*switched on*) conectado.
onlooker ['ɔnlukə*] *n* espectador(a) *m/f*.
only ['əunlɪ] *adv* solamente, sólo, nomás (*LAM*) ♦ *adj* único, solo ♦ *conj* solamente que, pero; **an ~ child** un hijo único; **not ~ ... but also...** no sólo ... sino también...; **I'd be ~ too pleased to help** encantado de ayudarles; **I saw her ~ yesterday** le vi ayer mismo; **I would come, ~ I'm very busy** iría, sólo que estoy muy atareado.
ono *abbr* (= *or nearest offer: in classified ads*) abierto ofertas.
onset ['ɔnsɛt] *n* comienzo.
onshore ['ɔnʃɔ:*] *adj* (*wind*) que sopla del mar hacia la tierra.
onslaught ['ɔnslɔ:t] *n* ataque *m*, embestida.
Ont. *abbr* (*Canada*) = *Ontario.*
on-the-job ['ɔnðə'dʒɔb] *adj*: **~ training** formación *f* en el trabajo *or* sobre la práctica.
onto ['ɔntu] *prep* = **on to.**
onus ['əunəs] *n* responsabilidad *f*; **the ~ is upon him to prove it** le incumbe a él demostrarlo.
onward(s) ['ɔnwəd(z)] *adv* (*move*) (hacia) adelante.
onyx ['ɔnɪks] *n* ónice *m*, onyx *m*.
oops [ups] *excl* (*also*: **~-a-daisy!**) ¡huy!
ooze [u:z] *vi* rezumar.
opal ['əupl] *n* ópalo.
opaque [əu'peɪk] *adj* opaco.
OPEC ['əupɛk] *n abbr* (= *Organization of Petroleum-Exporting Countries*) OPEP *f*.
open ['əupn] *adj* abierto; (*car*) descubierto; (*road, view*) despejado; (*meeting*) público; (*admiration*) manifiesto ♦ *vt* abrir ♦ *vi* (*flower, eyes, door, debate*) abrirse; (*book etc: commence*) comenzar; **in the ~ (air)** al aire libre; **~ verdict** veredicto inconcluso; **~ ticket** billete *m* sin fecha; **~ ground** (*among trees*) claro; (*waste ground*) solar *m*; **to have an ~ mind (on sth)** estar sin decidirse aún (sobre algo); **to ~ a bank account** abrir una cuenta en el banco.
►**open on to** *vt fus* (*subj: room, door*) dar a.
►**open out** *vt* abrir ♦ *vi* (*person*) abrirse.
►**open up** *vt* abrir; (*blocked road*) despejar ♦ *vi* abrirse.
open-and-shut ['əupənən'ʃʌt] *adj*: **~ case** caso claro *or* evidente.
open day *n* (*BRIT*) jornada de puertas abiertas *or* acceso público.
open-ended [əupn'ɛndɪd] *adj* (*fig*) indefinido, sin definir.
opener ['əupnə*] *n* (*also*: **can ~, tin ~**) abrelatas *m inv*.
open-heart surgery [əupn'hɑ:t-] *n* cirugía a corazón abierto.
opening ['əupnɪŋ] *n* abertura; (*beginning*) comienzo; (*opportunity*) oportunidad *f*; (*job*) puesto vacante, vacante *f*.
opening night *n* estreno.
open learning *n enseñanza flexible a tiempo parcial.*
openly ['əupnlɪ] *adv* abiertamente.
open-minded [əupn'maɪndɪd] *adj* de amplias miras, sin prejuicios.
open-necked ['əupnnɛkt] *adj* sin corbata.
openness ['əupnnɪs] *n* (*frankness*) franqueza.
open-plan ['əupn'plæn] *adj* sin tabiques, de plan abierto.
open prison *n* centro penitenciario de régimen abierto.
open return *n* vuelta con fecha abierta.
open shop *n empresa que contrata a mano de obra no afiliada a ningún sindicato.*
Open University *n* (*BRIT*) ≈ Universidad *f* Nacional de Enseñanza a Distancia, UNED *f*; *ver recuadro.*

OPEN UNIVERSITY

La **Open University**, *fundada en 1969, está especializada en impartir cursos a distancia y a tiempo parcial con sus propios materiales de apoyo diseñados para tal fin, entre ellos programas de radio y televisión emitidos por la "BBC". Los trabajos se envían por correo y se complementan con la asistencia obligatoria a cursos de verano. Para obtener la licenciatura es necesario estudiar un mínimo de módulos y alcanzar un determinado número de créditos.*

opera ['ɔpərə] *n* ópera.
opera glasses *npl* gemelos *mpl*.
opera house *n* teatro de la ópera.
opera singer *n* cantante *m/f* de ópera.
operate ['ɔpəreɪt] *vt* (*machine*) hacer funcionar; (*company*) dirigir ♦ *vi* funcionar; (*drug*) hacer efecto; **to ~ on sb** (*MED*) operar a algn.
operatic [ɔpə'rætɪk] *adj* de ópera.
operating costs ['ɔpəreɪtɪŋ-] *npl* gastos *mpl* operacionales.
operating profit *n* beneficio de explotación.
operating room *n* (*US*) quirófano, sala de operaciones.
operating table *n* mesa de operaciones.
operating theatre *n* quirófano, sala de operaciones.
operation [ɔpə'reɪʃən] *n* (*gen*) operación *f*; (*of machine*) funcionamiento; **to be in ~** estar funcionando *or* en funcionamiento; **to have an ~** (*MED*) ser operado; **to have an ~ for** operarse de; **the company's ~s during the year** las actividades de la compañía durante el año.
operational [ɔpə'reɪʃənl] *adj* operacional, en buen estado; (*COMM*) en condiciones de servicio; (*ready for use or action*) en condiciones de funcionar.
operative ['ɔpərətɪv] *adj* (*measure*) en vigor; **the ~ word** la palabra clave.
operator ['ɔpəreɪtə*] *n* (*of machine*) operario/a; (*TEL*) operador(a) *m/f*, telefonista *m/f*.
operetta [ɔpə'rɛtə] *n* opereta.
ophthalmic [ɔf'θælmɪk] *adj* oftálmico.
ophthalmologist [ɔfθæl'mɔlədʒɪst] *n* oftalmólogo/a.
opinion [ə'pɪnjən] *n* (*gen*) opinión *f*; **in my ~** en mi opinión, a mi juicio; **to seek a second ~** pedir una segunda opinión.
opinionated [ə'pɪnjəneɪtɪd] *adj* testarudo.
opinion poll *n* encuesta, sondeo.
opium ['əupɪəm] *n* opio.
opponent [ə'pəunənt] *n* adversario/a, contrincante *m/f*.
opportune ['ɔpətjuːn] *adj* oportuno.
opportunism [ɔpə'tjuːnɪzm] *n* oportunismo.
opportunist [ɔpə'tjuːnɪst] *n* oportunista *m/f*.
opportunity [ɔpə'tjuːnɪtɪ] *n* oportunidad *f*, chance *m or f* (*LAM*); **to take the ~ to do** *or* **of doing** aprovechar la ocasión para hacer.
oppose [ə'pəuz] *vt* oponerse a; **to be ~d to sth** oponerse a algo; **as ~d to** en vez de; (*unlike*) a diferencia de.
opposing [ə'pəuzɪŋ] *adj* (*side*) opuesto, contrario.
opposite ['ɔpəzɪt] *adj* opuesto, contrario; (*house etc*) de enfrente ♦ *adv* en frente ♦ *prep* en frente de, frente a ♦ *n* lo contrario; **the ~ sex** el otro sexo, el sexo opuesto.
opposite number *n* (*BRIT*) homólogo/a.
opposition [ɔpə'zɪʃən] *n* oposición *f*.
oppress [ə'prɛs] *vt* oprimir.
oppression [ə'prɛʃən] *n* opresión *f*.
oppressive [ə'prɛsɪv] *adj* opresivo.
opprobrium [ə'prəubrɪəm] *n* (*formal*) oprobio.
opt [ɔpt] *vi*: **to ~ for** optar por; **to ~ to do** optar por hacer; **to ~ out** (*of NHS etc*) salirse.
optical ['ɔptɪkl] *adj* óptico.
optical character recognition/reader (OCR) *n* reconocimiento/lector *m* óptico de caracteres.
optical fibre *n* fibra óptica.
optician [ɔp'tɪʃən] *n* óptico *m/f*.
optics ['ɔptɪks] *n* óptica.
optimism ['ɔptɪmɪzəm] *n* optimismo.
optimist ['ɔptɪmɪst] *n* optimista *m/f*.
optimistic [ɔptɪ'mɪstɪk] *adj* optimista.
optimum ['ɔptɪməm] *adj* óptimo.
option ['ɔpʃən] *n* opción *f*; **to keep one's ~s open** (*fig*) mantener las opciones abiertas; **I have no ~** no tengo más *or* otro remedio.
optional ['ɔpʃənl] *adj* opcional; (*course*) optativo; **~ extras** opciones *fpl* extras.
opulence ['ɔpjuləns] *n* opulencia.
opulent ['ɔpjulənt] *adj* opulento.
OR *abbr* (*US*) = *Oregon*.
or [ɔː*] *conj* o; (*before o, ho*) u; (*with negative*): **he hasn't seen ~ heard anything** no ha visto ni oído nada; **~ else** si no; **let me go ~ I'll scream!** ¡suélteme, o me pongo a gritar!
oracle ['ɔrəkl] *n* oráculo.
oral ['ɔːrəl] *adj* oral ♦ *n* examen *m* oral.

orange ['ɔrɪndʒ] *n* (*fruit*) naranja ♦ *adj* (de color) naranja.
orangeade [ɔrɪndʒ'eɪd] *n* naranjada, refresco de naranja.
orange squash *n* zumo (*SP*) *or* jugo de naranja.
orang-outang, orang-utan [ɔ'ræŋuː'tæn] *n* orangután *m.*
oration [ɔː'reɪʃən] *n* discurso solemne; **funeral** ~ oración *f* fúnebre.
orator ['ɔrətə*] *n* orador(a) *m/f.*
orbit ['ɔːbɪt] *n* órbita ♦ *vt, vi* orbitar; **to be in/go into** ~ **(round)** estar en/entrar en órbita (alrededor de).
orbital ['ɔːbɪtl] *n* (*also*: ~ **motorway**) autopista de circunvalación.
orchard ['ɔːtʃəd] *n* huerto; **apple** ~ manzanar *m*, manzanal *m.*
orchestra ['ɔːkɪstrə] *n* orquesta; (*US*: *seating*) platea.
orchestral [ɔː'kɛstrəl] *adj* de orquesta.
orchestrate ['ɔːkɪstreɪt] *vt* (*MUS*, *fig*) orquestar.
orchid ['ɔːkɪd] *n* orquídea.
ordain [ɔː'deɪn] *vt* (*also REL*) ordenar.
ordeal [ɔː'diːl] *n* experiencia terrible.
order ['ɔːdə*] *n* orden *m*; (*command*) orden *f*; (*type, kind*) clase *f*; (*state*) estado; (*COMM*) pedido, encargo ♦ *vt* (*also*: **put in** ~) ordenar, poner en orden; (*COMM*) encargar, pedir; (*command*) mandar, ordenar; **in** ~ (*gen*) en orden; (*of document*) en regla; **in (working)** ~ en funcionamiento; **to be out of** ~ (*machine, toilets*) estar estropeado *or* descompuesto (*LAM*); **in** ~ **to do** para hacer; **in** ~ **that** para que + *subj*; **on** ~ (*COMM*) pedido; **to be on** ~ estar pedido; **we are under** ~**s to do it** tenemos orden de hacerlo; **a point of** ~ una cuestión de procedimiento; **to place an** ~ **for sth with sb** hacer un pedido de algo a algn; **made to** ~ hecho a la medida; **his income is of the** ~ **of £24,000 per year** sus ingresos son del orden de 24 mil libras al año; **to the** ~ **of** (*BANKING*) a la orden de; **to** ~ **sb to do sth** mandar a algn hacer algo.
order book *n* cartera de pedidos.
order form *n* hoja de pedido.
orderly ['ɔːdəlɪ] *n* (*MIL*) ordenanza *m*; (*MED*) auxiliar *m/f* (de hospital) ♦ *adj* ordenado.
orderly officer *m* (*MIL*) oficial *m* del día.
order number *n* número de pedido.
ordinal ['ɔːdɪnl] *adj* ordinal.
ordinarily ['ɔːdnrɪlɪ] *adv* por lo común.
ordinary ['ɔːdnrɪ] *adj* corriente, normal; (*pej*) común y corriente; **out of the** ~ fuera de lo común, extraordinario.
ordinary degree *n* (*BRIT*) diploma *m*; *ver recuadro.*

ORDINARY DEGREE

Después de tres años de estudios, algunos universitarios obtienen la titulación de **ordinary degree**. *Esto ocurre en el caso poco frecuente de que no aprueben los exámenes que conducen al título de "honours degree" pero sus examinadores consideren que a lo largo de la carrera han logrado unos resultados mínimos satisfactorios. También es una opción que tienen los estudiantes de las universidades escocesas no interesados en estudiar en la universidad más de tres años.*

ordinary shares *npl* acciones *fpl* ordinarias.
ordination [ɔːdɪ'neɪʃən] *n* ordenación *f.*
ordnance ['ɔːdnəns] *n* (*MIL*: *unit*) artillería.
ordnance factory *n* fábrica de artillería.
Ordnance Survey *n* (*BRIT*) *servicio oficial de topografía y cartografía.*
ore [ɔː*] *n* mineral *m.*
Ore(g). *abbr* (*US*) = *Oregon.*
organ ['ɔːgən] *n* órgano.
organic [ɔː'gænɪk] *adj* orgánico; (*vegetables, produce*) biológico.
organism ['ɔːgənɪzəm] *n* organismo.
organist ['ɔːgənɪst] *n* organista *m/f.*
organization [ɔːgənaɪ'zeɪʃən] *n* organización *f.*
organize ['ɔːgənaɪz] *vt* organizar; **to get** ~**d** organizarse.
organized crime *n* crimen organizado.
organizer ['ɔːgənaɪzə*] *n* organizador(a) *m/f.*
orgasm ['ɔːgæzəm] *n* orgasmo.
orgy ['ɔːdʒɪ] *n* orgía.
Orient ['ɔːrɪənt] *n* Oriente *m.*
oriental [ɔːrɪ'ɛntl] *adj* oriental.
orientate ['ɔːrɪənteɪt] *vt* orientar.
origin ['ɔrɪdʒɪn] *n* origen *m*; (*point of departure*) procedencia.
original [ə'rɪdʒɪnl] *adj* original; (*first*) primero; (*earlier*) primitivo ♦ *n* original *m.*
originality [ərɪdʒɪ'nælɪtɪ] *n* originalidad *f.*
originally [ə'rɪdʒɪnəlɪ] *adv* (*at first*) al principio; (*with originality*) con originalidad.
originate [ə'rɪdʒɪneɪt] *vi*: **to** ~ **from, to** ~ **in** surgir de, tener su origen en.
originator [ə'rɪdʒɪneɪtə*] *n* inventor(a) *m/f*, autor(a) *m/f.*
Orkneys ['ɔːknɪz] *npl*: **the** ~ (*also*: **the Orkney Islands**) las Orcadas.

ornament ['ɔːnəmənt] *n* adorno.
ornamental [ɔːnə'mɛntl] *adj* decorativo, de adorno.
ornamentation [ɔːnəmɛn'teɪʃən] *n* ornamentación *f.*
ornate [ɔː'neɪt] *adj* recargado.
ornithologist [ɔːnɪ'θɔlədʒɪst] *n* ornitólogo/a.
ornithology [ɔːnɪ'θɔlədʒɪ] *n* ornitología.
orphan ['ɔːfn] *n* huérfano/a ♦ *vt*: **to be ~ed** quedar huérfano/a.
orphanage ['ɔːfənɪdʒ] *n* orfanato.
orthodox ['ɔːθədɔks] *adj* ortodoxo.
orthodoxy ['ɔːθədɔksɪ] *n* ortodoxia.
orthopaedic, (*US*) **orthopedic** [ɔːθə'piːdɪk] *adj* ortopédico.
orthop(a)edics [ɔːθə'piːdɪks] *n* ortopedia.
OS *abbr* (*BRIT*: = *Ordnance Survey*) *servicio oficial de topografía y cartografía*; (: *NAUT*) = **ordinary seaman;** (: *DRESS*) = **outsize.**
O/S *abbr* = **out of stock.**
Oscar ['ɔskə*] *n* óscar *m.*
oscillate ['ɔsɪleɪt] *vi* oscilar; (*person*) vacilar.
oscillation [ɔsɪ'leɪʃən] *n* oscilación *f*; (*of prices*) fluctuación *f.*
OSHA *n abbr* (*US*: = *Occupational Safety and Health Administration*) *oficina de la higiene y la seguridad en el trabajo.*
Oslo ['ɔzləu] *n* Oslo.
ostensible [ɔs'tɛnsɪbl] *adj* aparente.
ostensibly [ɔs'tɛnsɪblɪ] *adv* aparentemente.
ostentatious [ɔstɛn'teɪʃəs] *adj* pretencioso, aparatoso; (*person*) ostentativo.
osteopath ['ɔstɪəpæθ] *n* osteópata *m/f.*
ostracize ['ɔstrəsaɪz] *vt* hacer el vacio a.
ostrich ['ɔstrɪtʃ] *n* avestruz *m.*
OT *n abbr* (= *Old Testament*) A.T. *m.*
OTB *n abbr* (*US*: = *off-track betting*) *apuestas hechas fuera del hipódromo.*
O.T.E. *abbr* (= *on-target earnings*) *beneficios según objetivos.*
other ['ʌðə*] *adj* otro ♦ *pron*: **the ~** (*one*) el/la otro/a; **~s** (**~** *people*) otros; **~ than** (*apart from*) aparte de; **the ~ day** el otro día; **some ~ people have still to arrive** quedan por llegar otros; **some actor or ~** un actor cualquiera; **somebody or ~** alguien, alguno; **it was no ~ than the bishop** no era otro que el obispo.
otherwise ['ʌðəwaɪz] *adv, conj* de otra manera; (*if not*) si no; **an ~ good piece of work** un trabajo que, quitando eso, es bueno.
OTT *abbr* (*col*) = **over the top;** *see* **top.**
otter ['ɔtə*] *n* nutria.
OU *n abbr* (*BRIT*) = **Open University.**
ouch [autʃ] *excl* ¡ay!
ought, *pt* **ought** [ɔːt] *aux vb*: **I ~ to do it** debería hacerlo; **this ~ to have been corrected** esto debiera de haberse corregido; **he ~ to win** (*probability*) debiera ganar; **you ~ to go and see it** vale la pena ir a verlo.
ounce [auns] *n* onza (*28.35g; 16 in a pound*).
our ['auə*] *adj* nuestro; *see also* **my.**
ours ['auəz] *pron* (el) nuestro/(la) nuestra *etc*; *see also* **mine.**
ourselves [auə'sɛlvz] *pron pl* (*reflexive, after prep*) nosotros; (*emphatic*) nosotros mismos; **we did it (all) by ~** lo hicimos nosotros solos; *see also* **oneself.**
oust [aust] *vt* desalojar.
out [aut] *adv* fuera, afuera; (*not at home*) fuera (de casa); (*light, fire*) apagado; (*on strike*) en huelga ♦ *vt*: **to ~ sb** revelar públicamente la homosexualidad de algn; **~ there** allí (fuera); **he's ~** (*absent*) no está, ha salido; **to be ~ in one's calculations** equivocarse (en sus cálculos); **to run ~** salir corriendo; **~ loud** en alta voz; **~ of** *prep* (*outside*) fuera de; (*because of*: *anger etc*) por; **to look ~ of the window** mirar por la ventana; **to drink ~ of a cup** beber de una taza; **made ~ of wood** de madera; **~ of petrol** sin gasolina; **"~ of order"** "no funciona"; **it's ~ of stock** (*COMM*) está agotado; **to be ~ and about again** estar repuesto y levantado; **the journey ~** el viaje de ida; **the boat was 10 km ~** el barco estaba a diez kilómetros de la costa; **before the week was ~** antes del fin de la semana; **he's ~ for all he can get** busca sus propios fines, anda detrás de lo suyo.
out-and-out ['autəndaut] *adj* (*liar, thief etc*) redomado, empedernido.
outback ['autbæk] *n* interior *m.*
outbid [aut'bɪd] *vt* pujar más alto que, sobrepujar.
outboard ['autbɔːd] *adj*: **~ motor** (motor *m*) fuera borda *m.*
outbound ['autbaund] *adj*: **~ from/for** con salida de/hacia.
outbreak ['autbreɪk] *n* (*of war*) comienzo; (*of disease*) epidemia; (*of violence etc*) ola.
outbuilding ['autbɪldɪŋ] *n* dependencia; (*shed*) cobertizo.
outburst ['autbəːst] *n* explosión *f*, arranque *m.*
outcast ['autkɑːst] *n* paria *m/f.*
outclass [aut'klɑːs] *vt* aventajar, superar.
outcome ['autkʌm] *n* resultado.
outcrop ['autkrɔp] *n* (*of rock*) afloramiento.
outcry ['autkraɪ] *n* protestas *fpl.*

outdated [aut'deɪtɪd] *adj* anticuado.
outdistance [aut'dɪstəns] *vt* dejar atrás.
outdo [aut'du:] *vt* (*irreg*: *like* **do**) superar.
outdoor [aut'dɔ:*] *adj* al aire libre.
outdoors [aut'dɔ:z] *adv* al aire libre.
outer ['autə*] *adj* exterior, externo.
outer space *n* espacio exterior.
outfit ['autfɪt] *n* equipo; (*clothes*) traje *m*; (*col*: *organization*) grupo, organización *f*.
outfitter's ['autfɪtəz] *n* (*BRIT*) sastrería.
outgoing ['autgəuɪŋ] *adj* (*president, tenant*) saliente; (*means of transport*) que sale; (*character*) extrovertido.
outgoings ['autgəuɪŋz] *npl* (*BRIT*) gastos *mpl*.
outgrow [aut'grəu] *vt*: (*irreg*: *like* **grow**) **he has ~n his clothes** su ropa le queda pequeña ya.
outhouse ['authaus] *n* dependencia.
outing ['autɪŋ] *n* excursión *f*, paseo.
outlandish [aut'lændɪʃ] *adj* estrafalario.
outlast [aut'lɑ:st] *vt* durar más tiempo que, sobrevivir a.
outlaw ['autlɔ:] *n* proscrito/a ♦ *vt* (*person*) declarar fuera de la ley; (*practice*) declarar ilegal.
outlay ['autleɪ] *n* inversión *f*.
outlet ['autlɛt] *n* salida; (*of pipe*) desagüe *m*; (*US ELEC*) toma de corriente; (*for emotion*) desahogo; (*also*: **retail** ~) punto de venta.
outline ['autlaɪn] *n* (*shape*) contorno, perfil *m*; **in** ~ (*fig*) a grandes rasgos.
outlive [aut'lɪv] *vt* sobrevivir a.
outlook ['autluk] *n* perspectiva; (*opinion*) punto de vista.
outlying ['autlaɪɪŋ] *adj* remoto, aislado.
outmanoeuvre, (*US*) **outmaneuver** [autmə'nu:və*] *vt* (*MIL, fig*) superar en la estrategia.
outmoded [aut'məudɪd] *adj* anticuado, pasado de moda.
outnumber [aut'nʌmbə*] *vt* exceder *or* superar en número.
out of bounds [autəv'baundz] *adj*: **it's** ~ está prohibido el paso.
out-of-court [autəv'kɔ:t] *adj, adv* sin ir a juicio.
out-of-date [autəv'deɪt] *adj* (*passport*) caducado, vencido; (*theory, idea*) anticuado; (*clothes, customs*) pasado de moda.
out-of-doors [autəv'dɔ:z] *adv* al aire libre.
out-of-the-way [autəvðə'weɪ] *adj* (*remote*) apartado; (*unusual*) poco común *or* corriente.
out-of-touch [autəv'tʌtʃ] *adj*: **to be** ~ estar desconectado.
outpatient ['autpeɪʃənt] *n* paciente *m/f* externo/a.
outpost ['autpəust] *n* puesto avanzado.
outpouring ['autpɔ:rɪŋ] *n* (*fig*) efusión *f*.
output ['autput] *n* (volumen *m* de) producción *f*, rendimiento; (*COMPUT*) salida ♦ *vt* (*COMPUT*: *to power*) imprimir.
outrage ['autreɪdʒ] *n* (*scandal*) escándalo; (*atrocity*) atrocidad *f* ♦ *vt* ultrajar.
outrageous [aut'reɪdʒəs] *adj* (*clothes*) extravagante; (*behaviour*) escandaloso.
outright [aut'raɪt] *adv* (*win*) de manera absoluta; (*be killed*) en el acto; (*ask*) abiertamente; (*completely*) completamente ♦ *adj* ['autraɪt] completo; (*winner*) absoluto; (*refusal*) rotundo.
outrun [aut'rʌn] *vt* (*irreg*: *like* **run**) correr más que, dejar atrás.
outset ['autsɛt] *n* principio.
outshine [aut'ʃaɪn] *vt* (irreg: *like* **shine**) (*fig*) eclipsar, brillar más que.
outside [aut'saɪd] *n* exterior *m* ♦ *adj* exterior, externo ♦ *adv* fuera, afuera (*esp LAM*) ♦ *prep* fuera de; (*beyond*) más allá de; **at the** ~ (*fig*) a lo sumo; **an** ~ **chance** una posibilidad remota; ~ **left/right** (*FOOTBALL*) extremo izquierdo/derecho.
outside broadcast *n* (*RADIO, TV*) emisión *f* exterior.
outside contractor *n* contratista *m/f* independiente.
outside lane *n* (*AUT*) carril *m* de adelantamiento.
outside line *n* (*TEL*) línea (exterior).
outsider [aut'saɪdə*] *n* (*stranger*) forastero.
outsize ['autsaɪz] *adj* (*clothes*) de talla grande.
outskirts ['autskə:ts] *npl* alrededores *mpl*, afueras *fpl*.
outsmart [aut'smɑ:t] *vt* ser más listo que.
outspoken [aut'spəukən] *adj* muy franco.
outspread [aut'sprɛd] *adj* extendido; (*wings*) desplegado.
outstanding [aut'stændɪŋ] *adj* excepcional, destacado; (*unfinished*) pendiente.
outstay [aut'steɪ] *vt*: **to ~ one's welcome** quedarse más de la cuenta.
outstretched [aut'strɛtʃt] *adj* (*arm*) extendido.
outstrip [aut'strɪp] *vt* (*competitors, demand, also fig*) dejar atrás, aventajar.
out-tray ['auttreɪ] *n* bandeja de salida.
outvote [aut'vəut] *vt*: **it was ~d (by ...)** fue rechazado en el voto (por ...).
outward ['autwəd] *adj* (*sign, appearances*) externo; (*journey*) de ida.
outwardly ['autwədlɪ] *adv* por fuera.
outweigh [aut'weɪ] *vt* pesar más que.
outwit [aut'wɪt] *vt* ser más listo que.

outworn [aut'wɔːn] *adj* (*expression*) cansado.
oval ['əuvl] *adj* ovalado ♦ *n* óvalo.
ovarian [əu'vɛərɪən] *adj* ovárico; (*cancer*) de ovario.
ovary ['əuvərɪ] *n* ovario.
ovation [əu'veɪʃən] *n* ovación *f*.
oven ['ʌvn] *n* horno.
ovenproof ['ʌvnpruːf] *adj* refractario, resistente al horno.
oven-ready ['ʌvnrɛdɪ] *adj* listo para el horno.
ovenware ['ʌvnwɛə*] *n* artículos *mpl* para el horno.
over ['əuvə*] *adv* encima, por encima ♦ *adj* (*or adv*) (*finished*) terminado; (*surplus*) de sobra; (*excessively*) demasiado ♦ *prep* (por) encima de; (*above*) sobre; (*on the other side of*) al otro lado de; (*more than*) más de; (*during*) durante; (*about, concerning*): **they fell out ~ money** riñeron por una cuestión de dinero; ~ **here** (por) aquí; ~ **there** (por) allí *or* allá; **all ~** (*everywhere*) por todas partes; ~ **and ~ (again)** una y otra vez; ~ **and above** además de; **to ask sb ~** invitar a algn a casa; **to bend ~** inclinarse; **now ~ to our Paris correspondent** damos la palabra a nuestro corresponsal de París; **the world ~** en todo el mundo, en el mundo entero; **she's not ~ intelligent** no es muy lista que digamos.
over ... [əuvə*] *pref* sobre..., super....
overact [əuvər'ækt] *vi* (*THEAT*) exagerar el papel.
overall ['əuvərɔːl] *adj* (*length*) total; (*study*) de conjunto ♦ *adv* [əuvər'ɔːl] en conjunto ♦ *n* (*BRIT*) guardapolvo; **~s** *npl* mono *sg*, overol *msg* (*LAM*).
overall majority *n* mayoría absoluta.
overanxious [əuvər'æŋkʃəs] *adj* demasiado preocupado *or* ansioso.
overawe [əuvər'ɔː] *vt* intimidar.
overbalance [əuvə'bæləns] *vi* perder el equilibrio.
overbearing [əuvə'bɛərɪŋ] *adj* autoritario, imperioso.
overboard ['əuvəbɔːd] *adv* (*NAUT*) por la borda; **to go ~ for sth** (*fig*) enloquecer por algo.
overbook [əuvə'buk] *vt* sobrereservar, reservar con exceso.
overcapitalize [əuvə'kæpɪtəlaɪz] *vi* sobrecapitalizar.
overcast ['əuvəkɑːst] *adj* encapotado.
overcharge [əuvə'tʃɑːdʒ] *vt*: **to ~ sb** cobrar un precio excesivo a algn.
overcoat ['əuvəkəut] *n* abrigo.
overcome [əuvə'kʌm] *vt* (*irreg*: *like* **come**) (*gen*) vencer; (*difficulty*) superar; **she was quite ~ by the occasion** la ocasión le conmovió mucho.
overconfident [əuvə'kɔnfɪdənt] *adj* demasiado confiado.
overcrowded [əuvə'kraudɪd] *adj* atestado de gente; (*city, country*) superpoblado.
overcrowding [əuvə'kraudɪŋ] *n* (*in town, country*) superpoblación *f*; (*in bus etc*) hacinamiento, apiñamiento.
overdo [əuvə'duː] *vt* (*irreg*: *like* **do**) exagerar; (*overcook*) cocer demasiado; **to ~ it, to ~ things** (*work too hard*) trabajar demasiado.
overdose ['əuvədəus] *n* sobredosis *f inv*.
overdraft ['əuvədrɑːft] *n* saldo deudor.
overdrawn [əuvə'drɔːn] *adj* (*account*) en descubierto.
overdrive ['əuvədraɪv] *n* (*AUT*) sobremarcha, superdirecta.
overdue [əuvə'djuː] *adj* retrasado; (*recognition*) tardío; (*bill*) vencido y no pagado; **that change was long ~** ese cambio tenía que haberse hecho hace tiempo.
overemphasis [əuvər'ɛmfəsɪs] *n*: **to put an ~ on** poner énfasis excesivo en.
overenthusiastic ['əuvərənθuːzɪ'æstɪk] *adj* demasiado entusiasta.
overestimate [əuvər'ɛstɪmeɪt] *vt* sobreestimar.
overexcited [əuvərɪk'saɪtɪd] *adj* sobreexcitado.
overexertion [əuvərɪg'zəːʃən] *n* agotamiento, fatiga.
overexpose [əuvərɪk'spəuz] *vt* (*PHOT*) sobreexponer.
overflow [əuvə'fləu] *vi* desbordarse ♦ *n* ['əuvəfləu] (*excess*) exceso; (*of river*) desbordamiento; (*also*: **~ pipe**) (cañería de) desagüe *m*.
overfly [əuvə'flaɪ] *vt* (*irreg*: *like* **fly**) sobrevolar.
overgenerous [əuvə'dʒɛnərəs] *adj* demasiado generoso.
overgrown [əuvə'grəun] *adj* (*garden*) cubierto de hierba; **he's just an ~ schoolboy** es un niño en grande.
overhang [əuvə'hæŋ] (*irreg*: *like* **hang**) *vt* sobresalir por encima de ♦ *vi* sobresalir.
overhaul *vt* [əuvə'hɔːl] revisar, repasar ♦ *n* ['əuvəhɔːl] revisión *f*.
overhead *adv* [əuvə'hɛd] por arriba *or* encima ♦ *adj* ['əuvəhɛd] (*cable*) aéreo; (*railway*) elevado, aéreo ♦ *n* ['əuvəhɛd] (*US*) = **overheads**.

overheads ['əuvəhɛdz] *npl* (*BRIT*) gastos *mpl* generales.
overhear [əuvə'hɪə*] *vt* (*irreg*: *like* **hear**) oír por casualidad.
overheat [əuvə'hiːt] *vi* (*engine*) recalentarse.
overjoyed [əuvə'dʒɔɪd] *adj* encantado, lleno de alegría.
overkill ['əuvəkɪl] *n* (*MIL*) capacidad *f* excesiva de destrucción; (*fig*) exceso.
overland ['əuvəlænd] *adj, adv* por tierra.
overlap *vi* [əuvə'læp] superponerse ♦ *n* ['əuvəlæp] superposición *f*.
overleaf [əuvə'liːf] *adv* al dorso.
overload [əuvə'ləud] *vt* sobrecargar.
overlook [əuvə'luk] *vt* (*have view of*) dar a, tener vistas a; (*miss*) pasar por alto; (*forgive*) hacer la vista gorda a.
overlord ['əuvəlɔːd] *n* señor *m*.
overmanning [əuvə'mænɪŋ] *n* exceso de mano de obra; (*in organization*) exceso de personal.
overnight [əuvə'naɪt] *adv* durante la noche; (*fig*) de la noche a la mañana ♦ *adj* de noche; **to stay** ~ pasar la noche.
overnight bag *n* fin *m* de semana, neceser *m* de viaje.
overnight stay *n* estancia de una noche.
overpass ['əuvəpɑːs] *n* (*US*) paso elevado *or* a desnivel.
overpay [əuvə'peɪ] *vt*: **to ~ sb by £50** pagar 50 libras de más a algn.
overplay [əuvə'pleɪ] *vt* exagerar; **to ~ one's hand** desmedirse.
overpower [əuvə'pauə*] *vt* dominar; (*fig*) embargar.
overpowering [əuvə'pauərɪŋ] *adj* (*heat*) agobiante; (*smell*) penetrante.
overproduction [əuvəprə'dʌkʃən] *n* superproducción *f*.
overrate [əuvə'reɪt] *vt* sobrevalorar.
overreach [əuvə'riːtʃ] *vt*: **to ~ o.s.** ir demasiado lejos, pasarse.
override [əuvə'raɪd] *vt* (*irreg*: *like* **ride**) (*order, objection*) no hacer caso de.
overriding [əuvə'raɪdɪŋ] *adj* predominante.
overrule [əuvə'ruːl] *vt* (*decision*) anular; (*claim*) denegar.
overrun [əuvə'rʌn] *vt* (*irreg*: *like* **run**) (*MIL*: *country*) invadir; (*time limit*) rebasar, exceder ♦ *vi* rebasar el límite previsto; **the town is ~ with tourists** el pueblo está inundado de turistas.
overseas [əuvə'siːz] *adv* en ultramar; (*abroad*) en el extranjero ♦ *adj* (*trade*) exterior; (*visitor*) extranjero.
oversee [əuvə'siː] *vt* supervisar.
overseer ['əuvəsɪə*] *n* (*in factory*) supervisor(a) *m/f*; (*foreman*) capataz *m*.
overshadow [əuvə'ʃædəu] *vt* (*fig*) eclipsar.
overshoot [əuvə'ʃuːt] *vt* (*irreg*: *like* **shoot**) excederse.
oversight ['əuvəsaɪt] *n* descuido; **due to an** ~ a causa de un descuido *or* una equivocación.
oversimplify [əuvə'sɪmplɪfaɪ] *vt* simplificar demasiado.
oversleep [əuvə'sliːp] *vi* (*irreg*: *like* **sleep**) dormir más de la cuenta, no despertarse a tiempo.
overspend [əuvə'spɛnd] *vi* gastar más de la cuenta; **we have overspent by 5 dollars** hemos excedido el presupuesto en 5 dólares.
overspill ['əuvəspɪl] *n* exceso de población.
overstaffed [əuvə'stɑːft] *adj*: **to be** ~ tener exceso de plantilla.
overstate [əuvə'steɪt] *vt* exagerar.
overstatement ['əuvəsteɪtmənt] *n* exageración *f*.
overstay [əuvə'steɪ] *vt*: **to ~ one's time** *or* **welcome** quedarse más de lo conveniente.
overstep [əuvə'stɛp] *vt*: **to ~ the mark** *or* **the limits** pasarse de la raya.
overstock [əuvə'stɔk] *vt* abarrotar.
overstretched [əuvə'strɛtʃt] *adj* utilizado por encima de su capacidad.
overstrike *n* ['əuvəstraɪk] (*on printer*) superposición *f* ♦ *vt* (*irreg*: *like* **strike**) [əuvə'straɪk] superponer.
oversubscribed [əuvəsəb'skraɪbd] *adj* suscrito en exceso.
overt [əu'vəːt] *adj* abierto.
overtake [əuvə'teɪk] *vt* (*irreg*: *like* **take**) sobrepasar; (*BRIT AUT*) adelantar.
overtax [əuvə'tæks] *vt* (*ECON*) exigir contribuciones *fpl* excesivas *or* impuestos *mpl* excesivos a; (*fig*: *strength, patience*) agotar, abusar de; **to ~ o.s.** fatigarse demasiado.
overthrow [əuvə'θrəu] *vt* (*irreg*: *like* **throw**) (*government*) derrocar.
overtime ['əuvətaɪm] *n* horas *fpl* extraordinarias; **to do** *or* **work** ~ hacer *or* trabajar horas extraordinarias *or* extras.
overtime ban *n* prohibición *f* de (hacer) horas extraordinarias.
overtone ['əuvətəun] *n* (*fig*) tono.
overture ['əuvətʃuə*] *n* (*MUS*) obertura; (*fig*) propuesta.
overturn [əuvə'təːn] *vt, vi* volcar.
overview ['əuvəvjuː] *n* visión *f* de conjunto.
overweight [əuvə'weɪt] *adj* demasiado

gordo *or* pesado.
overwhelm [əuvə'wɛlm] *vt* aplastar.
overwhelming [əuvə'wɛlmɪŋ] *adj* (*victory, defeat*) arrollador(a); (*desire*) irresistible; **one's ~ impression is of heat** lo que más impresiona es el calor.
overwhelmingly [əuvə'wɛlmɪŋlɪ] *adv* abrumadoramente.
overwork [əuvə'wəːk] *n* trabajo excesivo ♦ *vt* hacer trabajar demasiado ♦ *vi* trabajar demasiado.
overwrite [əuvə'raɪt] *vt* (*irreg: like* **write**) (*COMPUT*) sobreescribir.
ovulation [ɔvju'leɪʃən] *n* ovulación *f.*
owe [əu] *vt* deber; **to ~ sb sth, to ~ sth to sb** deber algo a algn.
owing to ['əuɪŋtuː] *prep* debido a, por causa de.
owl [aul] *n* (*long-eared* ~) búho; (*barn* ~) lechuza.
own [əun] *vt* tener, poseer ♦ *vi*: **to ~ to sth/ to having done sth** confesar *or* reconocer algo/haber hecho algo ♦ *adj* propio; **a room of my ~** mi propia habitación; **to get one's ~ back** tomarse la revancha; **on one's ~** solo, a solas; **can I have it for my (very) ~?** ¿puedo quedarme con él?; **to come into one's ~** llegar a realizarse.
►**own up** *vi* confesar.
own brand *n* (*COMM*) marca propia.
owner ['əunə*] *n* dueño/a.
owner-occupier ['əunər'ɔkjupaɪə*] *n* ocupante propietario/a *m/f.*
ownership ['əunəʃɪp] *n* posesión *f*; **it's under new ~** está bajo nueva dirección.
own goal *n* (*SPORT*) autogol *m*; **to score an ~** marcar un gol en propia puerta, marcar un autogol.
ox, *pl* **oxen** [ɔks, 'ɔksn] *n* buey *m.*
Oxbridge ['ɔksbrɪdʒ] *n* (*BRIT*) *universidades de Oxford y Cambridge*; *ver recuadro.*

OXBRIDGE

El término **Oxbridge** *es una fusión de Ox(ford) y (Cam)bridge, las dos universidades británicas más antiguas y con mayor prestigio académico y social. Muchos miembros destacados de la clase dirigente del país son antiguos alumnos de una de las dos. El mismo término suele aplicarse a todo lo que ambas representan en cuestión de prestigio y privilegios sociales.*

Oxfam ['ɔksfæm] *n abbr* (*BRIT*: = *Oxford Committee for Famine Relief*) OXFAM.
oxide ['ɔksaɪd] *n* óxido.
Oxon. ['ɔksn] *abbr* (*BRIT*: =*Oxoniensis*) = *of Oxford.*
oxtail ['ɔksteɪl] *n*: ~ **soup** sopa de rabo de buey.
oxygen ['ɔksɪdʒən] *n* oxígeno.
oxygen mask *n* máscara de oxígeno.
oxygen tent *n* tienda de oxígeno.
oyster ['ɔɪstə*] *n* ostra.
oz. *abbr* = **ounce(s)**.
ozone ['əuzəun] *n* ozono; ~ **layer** capa de ozono.

Pp

P, p [piː] *n* (*letter*) P, p *f*; **P for Peter** P de París.
P *abbr* = **president, prince.**
p *abbr* (= *page*) pág.; (*BRIT*) = **penny, pence.**
PA *n abbr see* **personal assistant, public address system** ♦ *abbr* (*US*) = *Pennsylvania.*
pa [pɑː] *n* (*col*) papá *m.*
p.a. *abbr* = **per annum.**
PAC *n abbr* (*US*) = *political action committee.*
pace [peɪs] *n* paso; (*rhythm*) ritmo ♦ *vi*: **to ~ up and down** pasearse de un lado a otro; **to keep ~ with** llevar el mismo paso que; (*events*) mantenerse a la altura de *or* al corriente de; **to set the ~** (*running*) marcar el paso; (*fig*) marcar la pauta; **to put sb through his ~s** (*fig*) poner a algn a prueba.
pacemaker ['peɪsmeɪkə*] *n* (*MED*) marcapasos *m inv.*
pacific [pə'sɪfɪk] *adj* pacífico ♦ *n*: **the P~ (Ocean)** el (Océano) Pacífico.
pacification [pæsɪfɪ'keɪʃən] *n* pacificación *f.*
pacifier ['pæsɪfaɪə*] *n* (*US*: *dummy*) chupete *m.*
pacifism ['pæsɪfɪzəm] *n* pacifismo.
pacifist ['pæsɪfɪst] *n* pacifista *m/f.*
pacify ['pæsɪfaɪ] *vt* (*soothe*) apaciguar; (*country*) pacificar.
pack [pæk] *n* (*packet*) paquete *m*; (*COMM*) embalaje *m*; (*of hounds*) jauría; (*of wolves*) manada; (*of thieves etc*) banda; (*of cards*) baraja; (*bundle*) fardo; (*US*: *of cigarettes*) paquete *m*, cajetilla ♦ *vt* (*wrap*) empaquetar; (*fill*) llenar; (*in suitcase etc*) meter, poner; (*cram*) llenar, atestar; (*fig*: *meeting etc*) llenar de partidarios; (*COMPUT*) comprimir; **to ~ (one's bags)**

hacer las maletas; **to ~ sb off** despachar a algn; **the place was ~ed** el local estaba (lleno) hasta los topes; **to send sb ~ing** (*col*) echar a algn con cajas destempladas.

►**pack in** *vi* (*break down*: *watch, car*) estropearse ♦ *vt* (*col*) dejar; **~ it in!** ¡para!, ¡basta ya!

►**pack up** *vi* (*col*: *machine*) estropearse; (*person*) irse ♦ *vt* (*belongings, clothes*) recoger; (*goods, presents*) empaquetar, envolver.

package ['pækɪdʒ] *n* paquete *m*; (*bulky*) bulto; (*also*: **~ deal**) acuerdo global ♦ *vt* (*COMM*: *goods*) envasar, embalar.

package holiday *n* viaje *m* organizado (con todo incluido).

package tour *n* viaje *m* organizado.

packaging ['pækɪdʒɪŋ] *n* envase *m*.

packed lunch [pækt-] *n* almuerzo frío.

packer ['pækə*] *n* (*person*) empacador(a) *m/f*.

packet ['pækɪt] *n* paquete *m*.

packet switching [-'swɪtʃɪŋ] *n* (*COMPUT*) conmutación *f* por paquetes.

packhorse ['pækhɔːs] *n* caballo de carga.

pack ice *n* banco de hielo.

packing ['pækɪŋ] *n* embalaje *m*.

packing case *n* cajón *m* de embalaje.

pact [pækt] *n* pacto.

pad [pæd] *n* (*of paper*) bloc *m*; (*cushion*) cojinete *m*; (*launching* ~) plataforma (de lanzamiento); (*col*: *flat*) casa ♦ *vt* rellenar.

padded cell ['pædɪd-] *n* celda acolchada.

padding ['pædɪŋ] *n* relleno; (*fig*) paja.

paddle ['pædl] *n* (*oar*) canalete *m*, pala; (*US*: *for table tennis*) pala ♦ *vt* remar ♦ *vi* (*with feet*) chapotear.

paddle steamer *n* vapor *m* de ruedas.

paddling pool ['pædlɪŋ-] *n* (*BRIT*) piscina para niños.

paddock ['pædək] *n* (*field*) potrero.

paddy field ['pædɪ-] *n* arrozal *m*.

padlock ['pædlɔk] *n* candado ♦ *vt* cerrar con candado.

padre ['pɑːdrɪ] *n* capellán *m*.

paediatrician, (*US*) **pediatrician** [piːdɪə'trɪʃən] *n* pediatra *m/f*.

paediatrics, (*US*) **pediatrics** [piːdɪ'ætrɪks] *n* pediatría.

paedophile, (*US*) **pedophile** ['piːdəufaɪl] *adj* de pedófilos ♦ *n* pedófilo/a.

pagan ['peɪgən] *adj, n* pagano/a *m/f*.

page [peɪdʒ] *n* página; (*also*: **~ boy**) paje *m* ♦ *vt* (*in hotel etc*) llamar por altavoz a.

pageant ['pædʒənt] *n* (*procession*) desfile *m*; (*show*) espectáculo.

pageantry ['pædʒəntrɪ] *n* pompa.

page break *n* límite *m* de la página.

pager ['peɪdʒə*] *n* busca *m*.

paginate ['pædʒɪneɪt] *vt* paginar.

pagination [pædʒɪ'neɪʃən] *n* paginación *f*.

pagoda [pə'gəudə] *n* pagoda.

paid [peɪd] *pt, pp of* **pay** ♦ *adj* (*work*) remunerado; (*official*) asalariado; **to put ~ to** (*BRIT*) acabar con.

paid-up ['peɪdʌp], (*US*) **paid-in** ['peɪdɪn] *adj* (*member*) con sus cuotas pagadas *or* al día; (*share*) liberado; **~ capital** capital *m* desembolsado.

pail [peɪl] *n* cubo, balde *m*.

pain [peɪn] *n* dolor *m*; **to be in ~** sufrir; **on ~ of death** so *or* bajo pena de muerte; *see also* **pains**.

pained [peɪnd] *adj* (*expression*) afligido.

painful ['peɪnful] *adj* doloroso; (*difficult*) penoso; (*disagreeable*) desagradable.

painfully ['peɪnfəlɪ] *adv* (*fig*: *very*) terriblemente.

painkiller ['peɪnkɪlə*] *n* analgésico.

painless ['peɪnlɪs] *adj* sin dolor; (*method*) fácil.

pains [peɪnz] *npl* (*efforts*) esfuerzos *mpl*; **to take ~ to do sth** tomarse trabajo en hacer algo.

painstaking ['peɪnzteɪkɪŋ] *adj* (*person*) concienzudo, esmerado.

paint [peɪnt] *n* pintura ♦ *vt* pintar; **a tin of ~** un bote de pintura; **to ~ the door blue** pintar la puerta de azul.

paintbox ['peɪntbɔks] *n* caja de pinturas.

paintbrush ['peɪntbrʌʃ] *n* (*artist's*) pincel *m*; (*decorator's*) brocha.

painter ['peɪntə*] *n* pintor(a) *m/f*.

painting ['peɪntɪŋ] *n* pintura.

paintwork ['peɪntwəːk] *n* pintura.

pair [pɛə*] *n* (*of shoes, gloves etc*) par *m*; (*of people*) pareja; **a ~ of scissors** unas tijeras; **a ~ of trousers** unos pantalones, un pantalón.

►**pair off** *vi*: **to ~ off (with sb)** hacer pareja (con algn).

pajamas [pɪ'dʒɑːməz] *npl* (*US*) pijama *msg*, piyama *msg* (*LAM*).

Pakistan [pɑːkɪ'stɑːn] *n* Paquistán *m*.

Pakistani [pɑːkɪ'stɑːnɪ] *adj, n* paquistaní *m/f*.

PAL [pæl] *n abbr* (*TV*) = *phase alternation line*.

pal [pæl] *n* (*col*) amiguete/a *m/f*, colega *m/f*.

palace ['pæləs] *n* palacio.

palatable ['pælɪtəbl] *adj* sabroso; (*acceptable*) aceptable.

palate ['pælɪt] *n* paladar *m*.

palatial [pə'leɪʃəl] *adj* (*surroundings, residence*) suntuoso, espléndido.

palaver [pə'lɑːvə*] *n* (*fuss*) lío.

pale [peɪl] *adj* (*gen*) pálido; (*colour*) claro

♦ *n*: **to be beyond the ~** pasarse de la raya ♦ *vi* palidecer; **to grow** *or* **turn ~** palidecer; **to ~ into insignificance (beside)** no poderse comparar (con).
paleness ['peɪlnɪs] *n* palidez *f*.
Palestine ['pælɪstaɪn] *n* Palestina.
Palestinian [pælɪs'tɪnɪən] *adj, n* palestino/a *m/f*.
palette ['pælɪt] *n* paleta.
paling ['peɪlɪŋ] *n* (*stake*) estaca; (*fence*) valla.
palisade [pælɪ'seɪd] *n* palizada.
pall [pɔːl] *n* (*of smoke*) cortina ♦ *vi* cansar.
pallbearer ['pɔːlbɛərə*] *n* portador *m* del féretro.
pallet ['pælɪt] *n* (*for goods*) pallet *m*.
palliative ['pælɪətɪv] *n* paliativo.
pallid ['pælɪd] *adj* pálido.
pallor ['pælə*] *n* palidez *f*.
pally ['pælɪ] *adj* (*col*): **to be very ~ with sb** ser muy amiguete de algn.
palm [pɑːm] *n* (*ANAT*) palma; (*also*: **~ tree**) palmera, palma ♦ *vt*: **to ~ sth off on sb** (*BRIT col*) endosarle algo a algn.
palmist ['pɑːmɪst] *n* quiromántico/a, palmista *m/f*.
Palm Sunday *n* Domingo de Ramos.
palpable ['pælpəbl] *adj* palpable.
palpably ['pælpəblɪ] *adv* obviamente.
palpitation [pælpɪ'teɪʃən] *n* palpitación *f*; **to have ~s** tener palpitaciones.
paltry ['pɔːltrɪ] *adj* (*amount etc*) miserable; (*insignificant*: *person*) insignificante.
pamper ['pæmpə*] *vt* mimar.
pamphlet ['pæmflət] *n* folleto; (*political*: *handed out in street*) panfleto.
pan [pæn] *n* (*also*: **sauce~**) cacerola, cazuela, olla; (*also*: **frying ~**) sartén *m*; (*of lavatory*) taza ♦ *vi* (*CINE*) tomar panorámicas; **to ~ for gold** cribar oro.
pan- [pæn] *pref* pan-.
panacea [pænə'sɪə] *n* panacea.
panache [pə'næʃ] *n* gracia, garbo.
Panama ['pænəmɑː] *n* Panamá *m*.
Panama Canal *n* el Canal de Panamá.
pancake ['pænkeɪk] *n* crepe *f*, panqueque *m* (*LAM*).
Pancake Day *n* martes *m* de carnaval.
pancake roll *n* rollito de primavera.
pancreas ['pæŋkrɪəs] *n* páncreas *m*.
panda ['pændə] *n* panda *m*.
panda car *n* (*BRIT*) coche *m* de la policía.
pandemonium [pændɪ'məunɪəm] *n* (*noise*): **there was ~** se armó un tremendo jaleo; (*mess*) caos *m*.
pander ['pændə*] *vi*: **to ~ to** complacer a.
p&h *abbr* (*US*: = *postage and handling*) gastos de envío.
P&L *abbr* = *profit and loss*.
p & p *abbr* (*BRIT*: = *postage and packing*) gastos de envío.
pane [peɪn] *n* cristal *m*.
panel ['pænl] *n* (*of wood*) panel *m*; (*of cloth*) paño; (*RADIO, TV*) panel *m* de invitados.
panel game *n* (*TV*) programa *m* concurso para equipos.
panelling, (*US*) **paneling** ['pænəlɪŋ] *n* paneles *mpl*.
panellist, (*US*) **panelist** ['pænəlɪst] *n* miembro del jurado.
pang [pæŋ] *n*: **~s of conscience** remordimientos *mpl*; **~s of hunger** dolores *mpl* del hambre.
panhandler ['pænhændlə*] *n* (*US col*) mendigo/a.
panic ['pænɪk] *n* pánico ♦ *vi* dejarse llevar por el pánico.
panic buying [-baɪɪŋ] *n compras masivas por miedo a futura escasez*.
panic-stricken ['pænɪkstrɪkən] *adj* preso del pánico.
pannier ['pænɪə*] *n* (*on bicycle*) cartera; (*on mule etc*) alforja.
panorama [pænə'rɑːmə] *n* panorama *m*.
panoramic [pænə'ræmɪk] *adj* panorámico.
pansy ['pænzɪ] *n* (*BOT*) pensamiento; (*col*: *pej*) maricón *m*.
pant [pænt] *vi* jadear.
panther ['pænθə*] *n* pantera.
panties ['pæntɪz] *npl* bragas *fpl*.
pantihose ['pæntɪhəuz] *n* (*US*) medias *fpl*, panties *mpl*.
panto ['pæntəu] *n* (*BRIT col*) = **pantomime**.
pantomime ['pæntəmaɪm] *n* (*BRIT*) representación *f* musical navideña; *ver recuadro*.

PANTOMIME

En época navideña los teatros británicos ponen en escena representaciones llamadas **pantomimes**, *versiones libres de cuentos tradicionales como Aladino o El gato con botas. En ella nunca faltan personajes como la dama ("dame"), papel que siempre interpreta un actor; el protagonista joven ("principal boy"), normalmente interpretado por una actriz, y el malvado ("villain"). Es un espectáculo familiar dirigido a los niños pero con grandes dosis de humor para adultos en el que se alienta la participación del público.*

pantry ['pæntrɪ] *n* despensa.
pants [pænts] *n* (*BRIT*: *underwear*: *woman's*) bragas *fpl*; (: *man's*) calzoncillos *mpl*; (*US*:

trousers) pantalones *mpl.*
pantsuit ['pæntsjuːt] *n* (*US*) traje *m* de chaqueta y pantalón.
papal ['peɪpəl] *adj* papal.
paparazzi [pæpə'rætsɪ] *npl* paparazzi *mpl.*
paper ['peɪpə*] *n* papel *m*; (*also*: **news~**) periódico, diario; (*study, article*) artículo; (*exam*) examen *m* ♦ *adj* de papel ♦ *vt* empapelar; **(identity) ~s** *npl* papeles *mpl*, documentos *mpl*; **a piece of ~** un papel; **to put sth down on ~** poner algo por escrito.
paper advance *n* (*on printer*) avance *m* de papel.
paperback ['peɪpəbæk] *n* libro de bolsillo.
paper bag *n* bolsa de papel.
paperboy ['peɪpəbɔɪ] *n* (*selling*) vendedor *m* de periódicos; (*delivering*) repartidor *m* de periódicos.
paper clip *n* clip *m.*
paper hankie *n* pañuelo de papel.
paper money *n* papel *m* moneda.
paper profit *n* beneficio no realizado.
paper shop *n* (*BRIT*) tienda de periódicos.
paperweight ['peɪpəweɪt] *n* pisapapeles *m inv.*
paperwork ['peɪpəwəːk] *n* trabajo administrativo; (*pej*) papeleo.
papier-mâché ['pæpɪeɪ'mæʃeɪ] *n* cartón *m* piedra.
paprika ['pæprɪkə] *n* pimentón *m.*
Pap test ['pæp-] *n* (*MED*) frotis *m* (cervical).
papyrus [pə'paɪərəs] *n* papiro.
par [pɑː*] *n* par *f*; (*GOLF*) par *m* ♦ *adj* a la par; **to be on a ~ with** estar a la par con; **at ~** a la par; **to be above/below ~** estar sobre/bajo par; **to feel under ~** sentirse en baja forma.
parable ['pærəbl] *n* parábola.
parachute ['pærəʃuːt] *n* paracaídas *m inv* ♦ *vi* lanzarse en paracaídas.
parachutist ['pærəʃuːtɪst] *n* paracaidista *m/f.*
parade [pə'reɪd] *n* desfile *m* ♦ *vt* (*gen*) recorrer, desfilar por; (*show off*) hacer alarde de ♦ *vi* desfilar; (*MIL*) pasar revista; **a fashion ~** un desfile de modelos.
parade ground *n* plaza de armas.
paradise ['pærədaɪs] *n* paraíso.
paradox ['pærədɔks] *n* paradoja.
paradoxical [pærə'dɔksɪkl] *adj* paradójico.
paradoxically [pærə'dɔksɪklɪ] *adv* paradójicamente.
paraffin ['pærəfɪn] *n* (*BRIT*): **~ (oil)** parafina.
paraffin heater *n* estufa de parafina.
paraffin lamp *n* quinqué *m.*
paragon ['pærəgən] *n* modelo.
paragraph ['pærəgrɑːf] *n* párrafo, acápite *m* (*LAM*); **new ~** punto y aparte, punto acápite (*LAM*).
Paraguay ['pærəgwaɪ] *n* Paraguay *m.*
Paraguayan [pærə'gwaɪən] *adj, n* paraguayo/a *m/f*, paraguayano/a *m/f.*
parallel ['pærəlɛl] *adj*: **~ (with/to)** en paralelo (con/a); (*fig*) semejante (a) ♦ *n* (*line*) paralela; (*fig, GEO*) paralelo.
paralysis [pə'rælɪsɪs] *n* parálisis *f inv.*
paralytic [pærə'lɪtɪk] *adj* paralítico.
paralyze ['pærəlaɪz] *vt* paralizar.
paramedic [pærə'mɛdɪk] *n* auxiliar *m/f* sanitario/a.
parameter [pə'ræmɪtə*] *n* parámetro.
paramilitary [pærə'mɪlɪtərɪ] *adj* (*organization, operations*) paramilitar.
paramount ['pærəmaunt] *adj*: **of ~ importance** de suma importancia.
paranoia [pærə'nɔɪə] *n* paranoia.
paranoid ['pærənɔɪd] *adj* (*person, feeling*) paranoico.
paranormal [pærə'nɔːml] *adj* paranormal.
parapet ['pærəpɪt] *n* parapeto.
paraphernalia [pærəfə'neɪlɪə] *n* parafernalia.
paraphrase ['pærəfreɪz] *vt* parafrasear.
paraplegic [pærə'pliːdʒɪk] *n* parapléjico/a.
parapsychology [pærəsaɪ'kɔlədʒɪ] *n* parasicología.
parasite ['pærəsaɪt] *n* parásito/a.
parasol ['pærəsɔl] *n* sombrilla, quitasol *m.*
paratrooper ['pærətruːpə*] *n* paracaidista *m/f.*
parcel ['pɑːsl] *n* paquete *m* ♦ *vt* (*also*: **~ up**) empaquetar, embalar; **to be part and ~ of** ser parte integrante de.
►**parcel out** *vt* parcelar, repartir.
parcel bomb *n* paquete *m* bomba.
parcel post *n* servicio de paquetes postales.
parch [pɑːtʃ] *vt* secar, resecar.
parched [pɑːtʃt] *adj* (*person*) muerto de sed.
parchment ['pɑːtʃmənt] *n* pergamino.
pardon ['pɑːdn] *n* perdón *m*; (*LAW*) indulto ♦ *vt* perdonar; indultar; **~ me!, I beg your ~!** ¡perdone usted!; **(I beg your) ~?**, (*US*) **~ me?** ¿cómo (dice)?
pare [pɛə*] *vt* (*nails*) cortar; (*fruit etc*) pelar.
parent ['pɛərənt] *n*: **~s** *npl* padres *mpl.*
parentage ['pɛərəntɪdʒ] *n* familia, linaje *m*; **of unknown ~** de padres desconocidos.
parental [pə'rɛntl] *adj* paternal/maternal.
parent company *n* casa matriz.
parenthesis, *pl* **parentheses** [pə'rɛnθɪsɪs, -θɪsiːz] *n* paréntesis *m inv*; **in parentheses** entre paréntesis.

parenthood ['pɛərənthud] *n* el ser padres.
parent ship *n* buque *m* nodriza.
Paris ['pærɪs] *n* París *m.*
parish ['pærɪʃ] *n* parroquia.
parish council *n* consejo parroquial.
parishioner [pə'rɪʃənə*] *n* feligrés/esa *m/f.*
Parisian [pə'rɪzɪən] *adj, n* parisino/a *m/f*, parisiense *m/f.*
parity ['pærɪtɪ] *n* paridad *f*, igualdad *f.*
park [pɑːk] *n* parque *m*, jardín *m* público ♦ *vt* aparcar, estacionar ♦ *vi* aparcar, estacionar.
parka ['pɑːkə] *n* parka.
parking ['pɑːkɪŋ] *n* aparcamiento, estacionamiento; **"no ~"** "prohibido aparcar *or* estacionarse".
parking lights *npl* luces *fpl* de estacionamiento.
parking lot *n* (*US*) parking *m*, aparcamiento, playa *f* de estacionamiento (*LAM*).
parking meter *n* parquímetro.
parking offence, (*US*) **parking violation** *n* ofensa por aparcamiento indebido.
parking place *n* sitio para aparcar, aparcamiento.
parking ticket *n* multa de aparcamiento.
Parkinson's *n* (*also*: **~ disease**) (enfermedad *f* de) Parkinson *m.*
parkway ['pɑːkweɪ] *n* (*US*) alameda.
parlance ['pɑːləns] *n* lenguaje *m*; **in common/modern ~** en lenguaje corriente/moderno.
parliament ['pɑːləmənt] *n* parlamento; (*Spanish*) las Cortes *fpl*; *ver recuadro.*

PARLIAMENT

El Parlamento británico (**Parliament**) *tiene como sede el palacio de Westminster, también llamado "Houses of Parliament". Consta de dos cámaras: la Cámara de los Comunes ("House of Commons") está formada por 650 diputados ("Members of Parliament") que acceden a ella tras ser elegidos por sufragio universal en su respectiva área o circunscripción electoral ("constituency"). Se reúne 175 días al año y sus sesiones son presididas y moderadas por el Presidente de la Cámara ("Speaker"). La cámara alta es la Cámara de los Lores ("House of Lords") y sus miembros son nombrados por el monarca o bien han heredado su escaño. Su poder es limitado, aunque actúa como tribunal supremo de apelación, excepto en Escocia.*

parliamentary [pɑːlə'mɛntərɪ] *adj* parlamentario.
parlour, (*US*) **parlor** ['pɑːlə*] *n* salón *m*, living *m* (*LAM*).
parlous ['pɑːləs] *adj* peligroso, alarmante.
Parmesan [pɑːmɪ'zæn] *n* (*also*: **~ cheese**) queso parmesano.
parochial [pə'rəukɪəl] *adj* parroquial; (*pej*) de miras estrechas.
parody ['pærədɪ] *n* parodia ♦ *vt* parodiar.
parole [pə'rəul] *n*: **on ~** en libertad condicional.
paroxysm ['pærəksɪzəm] *n* (*MED*) paroxismo, ataque *m*; (*of anger, laughter, coughing*) ataque *m*; (*of grief*) crisis *f.*
parquet ['pɑːkeɪ] *n*: **~ floor(ing)** parquet *m.*
parrot ['pærət] *n* loro, papagayo.
parrot fashion *adv* como un loro.
parsimonious [pɑːsɪ'məunɪəs] *adj* tacaño.
parsley ['pɑːslɪ] *n* perejil *m.*
parsnip ['pɑːsnɪp] *n* chirivía.
parson ['pɑːsn] *n* cura *m.*
part [pɑːt] *n* (*gen, MUS*) parte *f*; (*bit*) trozo; (*of machine*) pieza; (*THEAT etc*) papel *m*; (*of serial*) entrega; (*US*: *in hair*) raya ♦ *adv* = **partly** ♦ *vt* separar; (*break*) partir ♦ *vi* (*people*) separarse; (*roads*) bifurcarse; (*crowd*) apartarse; (*break*) romperse; **to take ~ in** participar *or* tomar parte en; **to take sb's ~** tomar partido por algn; **for my ~** por mi parte; **for the most ~** en su mayor parte; (*people*) en su mayoría; **for the better ~ of the day** durante la mayor parte del día; **~ of speech** (*LING*) categoría gramatical, parte *f* de la oración; **to take sth in good/bad ~** aceptar algo bien/tomarse algo a mal.
▸**part with** *vt fus* ceder, entregar; (*money*) pagar; (*get rid of*) deshacerse de.
partake [pɑː'teɪk] *vi* (*irreg*: *like* **take**) (*formal*): **to ~ of sth** (*food*) comer algo; (*drink*) tomar *or* beber algo.
part exchange *n* (*BRIT*): **in ~** como parte del pago.
partial ['pɑːʃl] *adj* parcial; **to be ~ to** (*like*) ser aficionado a.
partially ['pɑːʃəlɪ] *adv* en parte, parcialmente.
participant [pɑː'tɪsɪpənt] *n* (*in competition*) concursante *m/f.*
participate [pɑː'tɪsɪpeɪt] *vi*: **to ~ in** participar en.
participation [pɑːtɪsɪ'peɪʃən] *n* participación *f.*
participle ['pɑːtɪsɪpl] *n* participio.
particle ['pɑːtɪkl] *n* partícula; (*of dust*) mota; (*fig*) pizca.
particular [pə'tɪkjulə*] *adj* (*special*) particular; (*concrete*) concreto; (*given*) determinado; (*detailed*) detallado,

minucioso; (*fussy*) quisquilloso, exigente; ~**s** *npl* (*information*) datos *mpl*, detalles *mpl*; (*details*) pormenores *mpl*; **in** ~ en particular; **to be very** ~ **about** ser muy exigente en cuanto a; **I'm not** ~ me es *or* da igual.

particularly [pə'tɪkjuləlɪ] *adv* especialmente, en particular.

parting ['pɑːtɪŋ] *n* (*act of*) separación *f*; (*farewell*) despedida; (*BRIT*: *in hair*) raya ♦ *adj* de despedida; ~ **shot** (*fig*) golpe *m* final.

partisan [pɑːtɪ'zæn] *adj* partidista ♦ *n* partidario/a; (*fighter*) partisano/a.

partition [pɑː'tɪʃən] *n* (*POL*) división *f*; (*wall*) tabique *m* ♦ *vt* dividir; dividir con tabique.

partly ['pɑːtlɪ] *adv* en parte.

partner ['pɑːtnə*] *n* (*COMM*) socio/a; (*SPORT*, *at dance*) pareja; (*spouse*) cónyuge *m/f*; (*friend etc*) compañero/a ♦ *vt* acompañar.

partnership ['pɑːtnəʃɪp] *n* (*gen*) asociación *f*; (*COMM*) sociedad *f*; **to go into** ~ **(with)**, **form a** ~ **(with)** asociarse (con).

part payment *n* pago parcial.

partridge ['pɑːtrɪdʒ] *n* perdiz *f*.

part-time ['pɑːt'taɪm] *adj*, *adv* a tiempo parcial.

part-timer [pɑːt'taɪmə*] *n* trabajador(a) *m/f* a tiempo parcial.

party ['pɑːtɪ] *n* (*POL*) partido; (*celebration*) fiesta; (*group*) grupo; (*LAW*) parte *f*, interesado ♦ *adj* (*POL*) de partido; (*dress etc*) de fiesta, de gala; **to have** *or* **give** *or* **throw a** ~ organizar una fiesta; **dinner** ~ cena; **to be a** ~ **to a crime** ser cómplice *m/f* de un crimen.

party line *n* (*POL*) línea política del partido; (*TEL*) línea compartida.

party piece *n*: **to do one's** ~ hacer su numerito (de fiesta).

party political broadcast *n* ≈ espacio electoral.

pass [pɑːs] *vt* (*time, object*) pasar; (*place*) pasar por; (*exam, law*) aprobar; (*overtake, surpass*) rebasar; (*approve*) aprobar ♦ *vi* pasar; (*SCOL*) aprobar ♦ *n* (*permit*) permiso, pase *m*; (*membership card*) carnet *m*; (*in mountains*) puerto; (*SPORT*) pase *m*; (*SCOL*: *also*: ~ **mark**) aprobado; **to** ~ **sth through sth** pasar algo por algo; **to** ~ **the time of day with sb** pasar el rato con algn; **things have come to a pretty** ~! ¡hasta dónde hemos llegado!; **to make a** ~ **at sb** (*col*) insinuársele a algn.

►**pass away** *vi* fallecer.

►**pass by** *vi* pasar ♦ *vt* (*ignore*) pasar por alto.

►**pass down** *vt* (*customs, inheritance*) pasar, transmitir.

►**pass for** *vt fus* pasar por; **she could** ~ **for twenty-five** se podría creer que sólo tiene 25 años.

►**pass on** *vi* (*die*) fallecer, morir ♦ *vt* (*hand on*): **to** ~ **on (to)** transmitir (a); (*cold, illness*) pegar (a); (*benefits*) dar (a); (*price rises*) pasar (a).

►**pass out** *vi* desmayarse; (*MIL*) graduarse.

►**pass over** *vi* (*die*) fallecer ♦ *vt* omitir, pasar por alto.

►**pass up** *vt* (*opportunity*) dejar pasar, no aprovechar.

passable ['pɑːsəbl] *adj* (*road*) transitable; (*tolerable*) pasable.

passably ['pɑːsəblɪ] *adv* pasablemente.

passage ['pæsɪdʒ] *n* pasillo; (*act of passing*) tránsito; (*fare, in book*) pasaje *m*; (*by boat*) travesía.

passageway ['pæsɪdʒweɪ] *n* (*in house*) pasillo, corredor *m*; (*between buildings etc*) pasaje *m*, pasadizo.

passenger ['pæsɪndʒə*] *n* pasajero/a, viajero/a.

passer-by [pɑːsə'baɪ] *n* transeúnte *m/f*.

passing ['pɑːsɪŋ] *adj* (*fleeting*) pasajero; **in** ~ de paso.

passing place *n* (*AUT*) apartadero.

passion ['pæʃən] *n* pasión *f*.

passionate ['pæʃənɪt] *adj* apasionado.

passionately ['pæʃənɪtlɪ] *adv* apasionadamente, con pasión.

passion fruit *n* fruta de la pasión, granadilla.

passion play *n* drama *m* de la Pasión.

passive ['pæsɪv] *adj* (*also LING*) pasivo.

passive smoking *n efectos del tabaco en fumadores pasivos*.

passkey ['pɑːskiː] *n* llave *f* maestra.

Passover ['pɑːsəuvə*] *n* Pascua (de los judíos).

passport ['pɑːspɔːt] *n* pasaporte *m*.

passport control *n* control *m* de pasaporte.

password ['pɑːswəːd] *n* (*also COMPUT*) contraseña.

past [pɑːst] *prep* (*further than*) más allá de; (*later than*) después de ♦ *adj* pasado; (*president etc*) antiguo ♦ *n* (*time*) pasado; (*of person*) antecedentes *mpl*; **quarter/half** ~ **four** las cuatro y cuarto/media; **he's** ~ **forty** tiene más de cuarenta años; **I'm** ~ **caring** ya no me importa; **to be** ~ **it** (*col*: *person*) estar acabado; **for the** ~ **few/3 days** durante los últimos días/últimos 3 días; **to run** ~ pasar corriendo por; **in the** ~ en el pasado, antes.

pasta ['pæstə] *n* pasta.
paste [peɪst] *n* (*gen*) pasta; (*glue*) engrudo ♦ *vt* (*stick*) pegar; (*glue*) engomar; **tomato ~** tomate concentrado.
pastel ['pæstl] *adj* pastel; (*painting*) al pastel.
pasteurized ['pæstəraɪzd] *adj* pasteurizado.
pastille ['pæstl] *n* pastilla.
pastime ['pɑːstaɪm] *n* pasatiempo.
past master *n*: **to be a ~ at** ser un maestro en.
pastor ['pɑːstə*] *n* pastor *m*.
pastoral ['pɑːstərl] *adj* pastoral.
pastry ['peɪstrɪ] *n* (*dough*) pasta; (*cake*) pastel *m*.
pasture ['pɑːstʃə*] *n* (*grass*) pasto.
pasty *n* ['pæstɪ] empanada ♦ *adj* ['peɪstɪ] pastoso; (*complexion*) pálido.
pat [pæt] *vt* dar una palmadita a; (*dog etc*) acariciar ♦ *n* (*of butter*) porción *f* ♦ *adj*: **he knows it (off) ~** se lo sabe de memoria *or* al dedillo; **to give sb/o.s. a ~ on the back** (*fig*) felicitar a algn/felicitarse.
patch [pætʃ] *n* (*of material*) parche *m*; (*mended part*) remiendo; (*of land*) terreno; (*COMPUT*) ajuste *m* ♦ *vt* (*clothes*) remendar; **(to go through) a bad ~** (pasar por) una mala racha.
▸**patch up** *vt* (*mend temporarily*) reparar; **to ~ up a quarrel** hacer las paces.
patchwork ['pætʃwəːk] *n* labor *f* de retales.
patchy ['pætʃɪ] *adj* desigual.
pate [peɪt] *n*: **bald ~** calva.
pâté ['pæteɪ] *n* paté *m*.
patent ['peɪtnt] *n* patente *f* ♦ *vt* patentar ♦ *adj* patente, evidente.
patent leather *n* charol *m*.
patently ['peɪtntlɪ] *adv* evidentemente.
patent medicine *n* específico.
patent office *n* oficina de patentes y marcas.
patent rights *npl* derechos *mpl* de patente.
paternal [pə'təːnl] *adj* paternal; (*relation*) paterno.
paternalistic [pətəːnə'lɪstɪk] *adj* paternalista.
paternity [pə'təːnɪtɪ] *n* paternidad *f*.
paternity suit *n* (*LAW*) caso de paternidad.
path [pɑːθ] *n* camino, sendero; (*trail, track*) pista; (*of missile*) trayectoria.
pathetic [pə'θɛtɪk] *adj* (*pitiful*) penoso, patético; (*very bad*) malísimo; (*moving*) conmovedor(a).
pathetically [pə'θɛtɪklɪ] *adv* penosamente, patéticamente; (*very badly*) malísimamente mal, de pena.
pathological [pæθə'lɔdʒɪkəl] *adj* patológico.
pathologist [pə'θɔlədʒɪst] *n* patólogo/a.
pathology [pə'θɔlədʒɪ] *n* patología.
pathos ['peɪθɔs] *n* patetismo.
pathway ['pɑːθweɪ] *n* sendero, vereda.
patience ['peɪʃns] *n* paciencia; (*BRIT CARDS*) solitario; **to lose one's ~** perder la paciencia.
patient ['peɪʃnt] *n* paciente *m/f* ♦ *adj* paciente, sufrido; **to be ~ with sb** tener paciencia con algn.
patiently ['peɪʃəntlɪ] *adv* pacientemente, con paciencia.
patio ['pætɪəu] *n* patio.
patriot ['peɪtrɪət] *n* patriota *m/f*.
patriotic [pætrɪ'ɔtɪk] *adj* patriótico.
patriotism ['pætrɪətɪzəm] *n* patriotismo.
patrol [pə'trəul] *n* patrulla ♦ *vt* patrullar por; **to be on ~** patrullar, estar de patrulla.
patrol boat *n* patrullero, patrullera.
patrol car *n* coche *m* patrulla.
patrolman [pə'trəulmən] *n* (*US*) policía *m*.
patron ['peɪtrən] *n* (*in shop*) cliente *m/f*; (*of charity*) patrocinador(a) *m/f*; **~ of the arts** mecenas *m*.
patronage ['pætrənɪdʒ] *n* patrocinio, protección *f*.
patronize ['pætrənaɪz] *vt* (*shop*) ser cliente de; (*look down on*) tratar con condescendencia a.
patronizing ['pætrənaɪzɪŋ] *adj* condescendiente.
patron saint *n* santo/a patrón/ona.
patter ['pætə*] *n* golpeteo; (*sales talk*) labia ♦ *vi* (*rain*) tamborilear.
pattern ['pætən] *n* (*SEWING*) patrón *m*; (*design*) dibujo; (*behaviour, events*) esquema *m*; **~ of events** curso de los hechos; **behaviour ~s** modelos *mpl* de comportamiento.
patterned ['pætənd] *adj* (*material*) estampado.
paucity ['pɔːsɪtɪ] *n* escasez *f*.
paunch [pɔːntʃ] *n* panza, barriga.
pauper ['pɔːpə*] *n* pobre *m/f*.
pause [pɔːz] *n* pausa; (*interval*) intervalo ♦ *vi* hacer una pausa; **to ~ for breath** detenerse para tomar aliento.
pave [peɪv] *vt* pavimentar; **to ~ the way for** preparar el terreno para.
pavement ['peɪvmənt] *n* (*BRIT*) acera, vereda (*LAM*), andén *m* (*LAM*), banqueta (*LAM*); (*US*) calzada, pavimento.
pavilion [pə'vɪlɪən] *n* pabellón *m*; (*SPORT*) vestuarios *mpl*.
paving ['peɪvɪŋ] *n* pavimento.
paving stone *n* losa.
paw [pɔː] *n* pata; (*claw*) garra ♦ *vt* (*animal*) tocar con la pata; (*pej*: *touch*) tocar,

manosear.
pawn [pɔːn] *n* (*CHESS*) peón *m*; (*fig*) instrumento ♦ *vt* empeñar.
pawnbroker ['pɔːnbrəukə*] *n* prestamista *m/f*.
pawnshop ['pɔːnʃɔp] *n* casa de empeños.
pay [peɪ] *n* paga; (*wage etc*) sueldo, salario ♦ (*vb*: *pt, pp* **paid**) *vt* pagar; (*visit*) hacer; (*respect*) ofrecer ♦ *vi* pagar; (*be profitable*) rendir, compensar, ser rentable; **to be in sb's ~** estar al servicio de algn; **to ~ attention (to)** prestar atención (a); **I paid £5 for that record** pagué 5 libras por ese disco; **how much did you ~ for it?** ¿cuánto pagaste por él?; **to ~ one's way** (*contribute one's share*) pagar su parte; (*remain solvent*: *company*) ser solvente; **to ~ dividends** (*COMM*) pagar dividendos; (*fig*) compensar; **it won't ~ you to do that** no te merece la pena hacer eso; **to put paid to** (*plan, person*) acabar con.
►**pay back** *vt* (*money*) devolver, reembolsar; (*person*) pagar.
►**pay for** *vt fus* pagar.
►**pay in** *vt* ingresar.
►**pay off** *vt* liquidar; (*person*) pagar; (*debts*) liquidar, saldar; (*creditor*) cancelar, redimir; (*workers*) despedir; (*mortgage*) cancelar, redimir ♦ *vi* (*scheme, decision*) dar resultado; **to ~ sth off in instalments** pagar algo a plazos.
►**pay out** *vt* (*rope*) ir dando; (*money*) gastar, desembolsar.
►**pay up** *vt* pagar.
payable ['peɪəbl] *adj* pagadero; **to make a cheque ~ to sb** extender un cheque a favor de algn.
pay award *n* aumento de sueldo.
pay day *n* día *m* de paga.
PAYE *n abbr* (*BRIT*: = *pay as you earn*) *sistema de retención fiscal en la fuente de ingresos*.
payee [peɪ'iː] *n* portador(a) *m/f*.
pay envelope *n* (*US*) = **pay packet**.
paying ['peɪɪŋ] *adj*: **~ guest** huésped(a) *m/f* que la paga.
payload ['peɪləud] *n* carga útil.
payment ['peɪmənt] *n* pago; **advance ~** (*part sum*) anticipo, adelanto; (*total sum*) saldo; **monthly ~** mensualidad *f*; **deferred ~, ~ by instalments** pago a plazos *or* diferido; **on ~ of £5** mediante pago de *or* pagando £5; **in ~ for** (*goods, sum owed*) en pago de.
pay packet *n* (*BRIT*) sobre *m* (de la paga).
pay-phone ['peɪfəun] *n* teléfono público.
payroll ['peɪrəul] *n* nómina; **to be on a firm's ~** estar en la nómina de una compañía.
pay slip *n* hoja del sueldo.
pay station *n* (*US*) teléfono público.
PBS *n abbr* (*US*: = *Public Broadcasting Service*) *agrupación de ayuda a la realización de emisiones para la TV pública*.
PC *n abbr see* **personal computer**; (*BRIT*) = **police constable** ♦ *abbr* (*BRIT*) = *Privy Councillor* ♦ *adj abbr* = **politically correct**.
pc *abbr* = **per cent, postcard**.
p/c *abbr* = **petty cash**.
PCB *n abbr see* **printed circuit board**.
PD *n abbr* (*US*) = **police department**.
pd *abbr* = **paid**.
PDSA *n abbr* (*BRIT*) = *People's Dispensary for Sick Animals*.
PDT *n abbr* (*US*: = *Pacific Daylight Time*) *hora de verano del Pacífico*.
PE *n abbr* (= *physical education*) ed. física ♦ *abbr* (*Canada*) = *Prince Edward Island*.
pea [piː] *n* guisante *m*, chícharo (*LAM*), arveja (*LAM*).
peace [piːs] *n* paz *f*; (*calm*) paz *f*, tranquilidad *f*; **to be at ~ with sb/sth** estar en paz con algn/algo; **to keep the ~** (*policeman*) mantener el orden; (*citizen*) guardar el orden.
peaceable ['piːsəbl] *adj* pacífico.
peaceably [pɪːsəblɪ] *adv* pacíficamente.
peaceful ['piːsful] *adj* (*gentle*) pacífico; (*calm*) tranquilo, sosegado.
peacekeeping ['piːskiːpɪŋ] *adj* de pacificación ♦ *n* pacificación *f*.
peacekeeping force *n* fuerza de pacificación.
peace offering *n* (*fig*) prenda de paz.
peacetime ['piːstaɪm] *n*: **in ~** en tiempo de paz.
peach [piːtʃ] *n* melocotón *m*, durazno (*LAM*).
peacock ['piːkɔk] *n* pavo real.
peak [piːk] *n* (*of mountain*: *top*) cumbre *f*, cima; (: *point*) pico; (*of cap*) visera; (*fig*) cumbre *f*.
peak-hour ['piːkauə*] *adj* (*traffic etc*) de horas punta.
peak hours *npl*, **peak period** *n* horas *fpl* punta.
peak rate *n* tarifa máxima.
peaky ['piːkɪ] *adj* (*BRIT col*) pálido, paliducho; **I'm feeling a bit ~** estoy malucho, no me encuentro bien.
peal [piːl] *n* (*of bells*) repique *m*; **~ of laughter** carcajada.
peanut ['piːnʌt] *n* cacahuete *m*, maní *m* (*LAM*).
peanut butter *n* mantequilla de cacahuete.

pear ['pɛə*] *n* pera.
pearl [pə:l] *n* perla.
peasant ['pɛznt] *n* campesino/a.
peat [pi:t] *n* turba.
pebble ['pɛbl] *n* guijarro.
peck [pɛk] *vt* (*also*: ~ **at**) picotear; (*food*) comer sin ganas ♦ *n* picotazo; (*kiss*) besito.
pecking order ['pɛkɪŋ-] *n* orden *m* de jerarquía.
peckish ['pɛkɪʃ] *adj* (*BRIT col*): **I feel** ~ tengo ganas de picar algo.
peculiar [pɪ'kju:lɪə*] *adj* (*odd*) extraño, raro; (*typical*) propio, característico; (*particular: importance, qualities*) particular; ~ **to** propio de.
peculiarity [pɪkju:lɪ'ærɪtɪ] *n* peculiaridad *f*, característica.
peculiarly [pɪ'kju:lɪəlɪ] *adv* extrañamente; particularmente.
pedal ['pɛdl] *n* pedal *m* ♦ *vi* pedalear.
pedal bin *n* cubo de la basura con pedal.
pedant ['pɛdənt] *n* pedante *m/f*.
pedantic [pɪ'dæntɪk] *adj* pedante.
pedantry ['pɛdəntrɪ] *n* pedantería.
peddle ['pɛdl] *vt* (*goods*) ir vendiendo *or* vender de puerta en puerta; (*drugs*) traficar con; (*gossip*) divulgar.
peddler ['pɛdlə*] *n* vendedor(a) *m/f* ambulante.
pedestal ['pɛdəstl] *n* pedestal *m*.
pedestrian [pɪ'dɛstrɪən] *n* peatón *m* ♦ *adj* pedestre.
pedestrian crossing *n* (*BRIT*) paso de peatones.
pedestrian precinct *n* zona reservada para peatones.
pediatrics [pi:dɪ'ætrɪks] *n* (*US*) = **paediatrics**.
pedigree ['pɛdɪgri:] *n* genealogía; (*of animal*) pedigrí *m* ♦ *cpd* (*animal*) de raza, de casta.
pedlar ['pɛdlə*] *n* (*BRIT*) = **peddler**.
pee [pi:] *vi* (*col*) mear.
peek [pi:k] *vi* mirar a hurtadillas; (*COMPUT*) inspeccionar.
peel [pi:l] *n* piel *f*; (*of orange, lemon*) cáscara; (*: removed*) peladuras *fpl* ♦ *vt* pelar ♦ *vi* (*paint etc*) desconcharse; (*wallpaper*) despegarse, desprenderse.
▸**peel back** *vt* pelar.
peeler ['pi:lə*] *n*: **potato** ~ mondador *m or* pelador *m* de patatas, pelapatatas *m inv*.
peep [pi:p] *n* (*BRIT: look*) mirada furtiva; (*sound*) pío ♦ *vi* (*BRIT*) piar.
▸**peep out** *vi* asomar la cabeza.
peephole ['pi:phəul] *n* mirilla.
peer [pɪə*] *vi*: **to** ~ **at** escudriñar ♦ *n* (*noble*) par *m*; (*equal*) igual *m*.
peerage ['pɪərɪdʒ] *n* nobleza.
peerless ['pɪəlɪs] *adj* sin par, incomparable, sin igual.
peeved [pi:vd] *adj* enojado.
peevish ['pi:vɪʃ] *adj* malhumorado.
peevishness ['pi:vɪʃnɪs] *n* mal humor *m*.
peg [pɛg] *n* clavija; (*for coat etc*) gancho, colgador *m*; (*BRIT: also*: **clothes** ~) pinza; (*tent* ~) estaca ♦ *vt* (*clothes*) tender; (*groundsheet*) fijar con estacas; (*fig: wages, prices*) fijar.
pejorative [pɪ'dʒɔrətɪv] *adj* peyorativo.
Pekin [pi:'kɪn], **Peking** [pi:'kɪŋ] *n* Pekín *m*.
pekinese [pi:kɪ'ni:z] *n* pequinés/esa *m/f*.
pelican ['pɛlɪkən] *n* pelícano.
pelican crossing *n* (*BRIT AUT*) paso de peatones señalizado.
pellet ['pɛlɪt] *n* bolita; (*bullet*) perdigón *m*.
pell-mell ['pɛl'mɛl] *adv* en tropel.
pelmet ['pɛlmɪt] *n* galería.
pelt [pɛlt] *vt*: **to** ~ **sb with sth** arrojarle algo a algn ♦ *vi* (*rain: also*: ~ **down**) llover a cántaros ♦ *n* pellejo.
pelvis ['pɛlvɪs] *n* pelvis *f*.
pen [pɛn] *n* (*ballpoint* ~) bolígrafo; (*fountain* ~) pluma; (*for sheep*) redil *m*; (*US col: prison*) cárcel *f*, chirona; **to put** ~ **to paper** tomar la pluma.
penal ['pi:nl] *adj* penal; ~ **servitude** trabajos *mpl* forzados.
penalize ['pi:nəlaɪz] *vt* (*punish*) castigar; (*SPORT*) sancionar, penalizar.
penalty ['pɛnltɪ] *n* (*gen*) pena; (*fine*) multa; (*SPORT*) sanción *f*; ~ **(kick)** (*FOOTBALL*) penalty *m*.
penalty area *n* (*BRIT SPORT*) área de castigo.
penalty clause *n* cláusula de penalización.
penalty shoot-out [-'ʃu:taut] *n* (*FOOTBALL*) tanda de penaltis.
penance ['pɛnəns] *n* penitencia.
pence [pɛns] *pl of* **penny**.
penchant ['pɑ̃:ʃɑ̃:ŋ] *n* predilección *f*, inclinación *f*.
pencil ['pɛnsl] *n* lápiz *m*, lapicero (*esp LAM*) ♦ *vt* (*also*: ~ **in**) escribir con lápiz.
pencil case *n* estuche *m*.
pencil sharpener *n* sacapuntas *m inv*.
pendant ['pɛndnt] *n* pendiente *m*.
pending ['pɛndɪŋ] *prep* antes de ♦ *adj* pendiente; ~ **the arrival of** ... hasta que llegue ..., hasta llegar ... .
pendulum ['pɛndjuləm] *n* péndulo.
penetrate ['pɛnɪtreɪt] *vt* penetrar.
penetrating ['pɛnɪtreɪtɪŋ] *adj* penetrante.
penetration [pɛnɪ'treɪʃən] *n* penetración *f*.
penfriend ['pɛnfrɛnd] *n* (*BRIT*) amigo/a por

correspondencia.
penguin ['pɛŋgwɪn] *n* pingüino.
penicillin [pɛnɪ'sɪlɪn] *n* penicilina.
peninsula [pə'nɪnsjulə] *n* península.
penis ['pi:nɪs] *n* pene *m.*
penitence ['pɛnɪtns] *n* penitencia.
penitent ['pɛnɪtnt] *adj* arrepentido; (*REL*) penitente.
penitentiary [pɛnɪ'tɛnʃərɪ] *n* (*US*) cárcel *f*, presidio.
penknife ['pɛnnaɪf] *n* navaja.
Penn(a). *abbr* (*US*) = *Pennsylvania.*
pen name *n* seudónimo.
pennant ['pɛnənt] *n* banderola; banderín *m.*
penniless ['pɛnɪlɪs] *adj* sin dinero.
Pennines ['pɛnaɪnz] *npl* (Montes *mpl*) Peninos *mpl.*
penny, *pl* **pennies** *or* (*BRIT*) **pence** ['pɛnɪ, 'pɛnɪz, pɛns] *n* penique *m*; (*US*) centavo.
penpal ['pɛnpæl] *n* amigo/a por correspondencia.
penpusher ['pɛnpuʃə*] *n* (*pej*) chupatintas *m/f inv.*
pension ['pɛnʃən] *n* (*allowance, state payment*) pensión *f*; (*old-age*) jubilación *f.*
►**pension off** *vt* jubilar.
pensioner ['pɛnʃənə*] *n* (*BRIT*) jubilado/a.
pension fund *n* fondo de pensiones.
pensive ['pɛnsɪv] *adj* pensativo; (*withdrawn*) preocupado.
pentagon ['pɛntəgən] *n* pentágono; **the P~** (*US POL*) el Pentágono; *ver recuadro.*

> **PENTAGON**
>
> *Se conoce como el Pentágono* (**the Pentagon**) *al edificio de planta pentagonal que acoge las dependencias del Ministerio de Defensa estadounidense ("Department of Defense") en Arlington, Virginia. En lenguaje periodístico se aplica también a la dirección militar del país.*

Pentecost ['pɛntɪkɔst] *n* Pentecostés *m.*
penthouse ['pɛnthaus] *n* ático (de lujo).
pent-up ['pɛntʌp] *adj* (*feelings*) reprimido.
penultimate [pɛ'nʌltɪmət] *adj* penúltimo.
people ['pi:pl] *npl* gente *f*; (*citizens*) pueblo *sg*, ciudadanos *mpl* ♦ *n* (*nation, race*) pueblo, nación *f* ♦ *vt* poblar; **several ~ came** vinieron varias personas; **~ say that ...** dice la gente que ...; **old/young ~** los ancianos/jóvenes; **~ at large** la gente en general; **a man of the ~** un hombre del pueblo.
PEP *n abbr* (= *Personal Equity Plan*) *plan personal de inversión con desgravación fiscal.*
pep [pɛp] *n* (*col*) energía.
►**pep up** *vt* animar.
pepper ['pɛpə*] *n* (*spice*) pimienta; (*vegetable*) pimiento, ají *m* (*LAM*), chile *m* (*LAM*) ♦ *vt* (*fig*) salpicar.
peppermint ['pɛpəmɪnt] *n* menta; (*sweet*) pastilla de menta.
pepperoni [pɛpə'rəunɪ] *n* ≈ salchichón *m* picante.
pepperpot ['pɛpəpɔt] *n* pimentero.
peptalk ['pɛptɔ:k] *n* (*col*): **to give sb a ~** darle a algn una inyección de ánimo.
per [pə:*] *prep* por; **~ day/person** por día/persona; **as ~ your instructions** de acuerdo con sus instrucciones.
per annum *adv* al año.
per capita *adj, adv* per cápita.
perceive [pə'si:v] *vt* percibir; (*realize*) darse cuenta de.
per cent, (*US*) **percent** [pə'sɛnt] *n* por ciento; **a 20 ~ discount** un descuento del 20 por ciento.
percentage [pə'sɛntɪdʒ] *n* porcentaje *m*; **to get a ~ on all sales** percibir un tanto por ciento sobre todas las ventas; **on a ~ basis** a porcentaje.
percentage point *n* punto (porcentual).
perceptible [pə'sɛptəbl] *adj* perceptible; (*notable*) sensible.
perception [pə'sɛpʃən] *n* percepción *f*; (*insight*) perspicacia.
perceptive [pə'sɛptɪv] *adj* perspicaz.
perch [pə:tʃ] *n* (*fish*) perca; (*for bird*) percha ♦ *vi* posarse.
percolate ['pə:kəleɪt] *vt* (*coffee*) filtrar ♦ *vi* (*coffee, fig*) filtrarse.
percolator ['pə:kəleɪtə*] *n* cafetera de filtro.
percussion [pə'kʌʃən] *n* percusión *f.*
percussionist [pə'kʌʃənɪst] *n* percusionista *m/f.*
peremptory [pə'rɛmptərɪ] *adj* perentorio.
perennial [pə'rɛnɪəl] *adj* perenne.
perfect *adj* ['pə:fɪkt] perfecto ♦ *n* (*also*: **~ tense**) perfecto ♦ *vt* [pə'fɛkt] perfeccionar; **he's a ~ stranger to me** no le conozco de nada, me es completamente desconocido.
perfection [pə'fɛkʃən] *n* perfección *f.*
perfectionist [pə'fɛkʃənɪst] *n* perfeccionista *m/f.*
perfectly ['pə:fɪktlɪ] *adv* perfectamente; **I'm ~ happy with the situation** estoy muy contento con la situación; **you know ~ well** lo sabes muy bien *or* perfectamente.
perforate ['pə:fəreɪt] *vt* perforar.
perforation [pə:fə'reɪʃən] *n* perforación *f.*
perform [pə'fɔ:m] *vt* (*carry out*) realizar,

llevar a cabo; (*THEAT*) representar; (*piece of music*) interpretar ♦ *vi* (*THEAT*) actuar; (*TECH*) funcionar.
performance [pə'fɔːməns] *n* (*of task*) realización *f*; (*of a play*) representación *f*; (*of player etc*) actuación *f*; (*of engine*) rendimiento; (*of car*) prestaciones *fpl*; (*of function*) desempeño; **the team put up a good** ~ el equipo se defendió bien.
performer [pə'fɔːmə*] *n* (*actor*) actor *m*, actriz *f*; (*MUS*) intérprete *m/f*.
performing [pə'fɔːmɪŋ] *adj* (*animal*) amaestrado.
performing arts *npl*: **the** ~ las artes teatrales.
perfume ['pəːfjuːm] *n* perfume *m*.
perfunctory [pə'fʌŋktərɪ] *adj* superficial.
perhaps [pə'hæps] *adv* quizá(s), tal vez; ~ **so/not** puede que sí/no.
peril ['pɛrɪl] *n* peligro, riesgo.
perilous ['pɛrɪləs] *adj* peligroso.
perilously ['pɛrɪləslɪ] *adv*: **they came** ~ **close to being caught** por poco les cogen *or* agarran.
perimeter [pə'rɪmɪtə*] *n* perímetro.
period ['pɪərɪəd] *n* período, periodo; (*HISTORY*) época; (*SCOL*) clase *f*; (*full stop*) punto; (*MED*) regla, periodo; (*US SPORT*) tiempo ♦ *adj* (*costume, furniture*) de época; **for a** ~ **of three weeks** durante (un período de) tres semanas; **the holiday** ~ el período de vacaciones.
periodic [pɪərɪ'ɔdɪk] *adj* periódico.
periodical [pɪərɪ'ɔdɪkl] *adj* periódico ♦ *n* revista, publicación *f* periódica.
periodically [pɪərɪ'ɔdɪklɪ] *adv* de vez en cuando, cada cierto tiempo.
period pains *npl* dolores *mpl* de la regla *or* de la menstruación.
peripatetic [pɛrɪpə'tɛtɪk] *adj* (*salesman*) ambulante; (*teacher*) con trabajo en varios colegios.
peripheral [pə'rɪfərəl] *adj* periférico ♦ *n* (*COMPUT*) periférico, unidad *f* periférica.
periphery [pə'rɪfərɪ] *n* periferia.
periscope ['pɛrɪskəup] *n* periscopio.
perish ['pɛrɪʃ] *vi* perecer; (*decay*) echarse a perder.
perishable ['pɛrɪʃəbl] *adj* perecedero.
perishables ['pɛrɪʃəblz] *npl* productos *mpl* perecederos.
peritonitis [pɛrɪtə'naɪtɪs] *n* peritonitis *f*.
perjure ['pəːdʒə*] *vt*: **to** ~ **o.s.** perjurar.
perjury ['pəːdʒərɪ] *n* (*LAW*) perjurio.
perk [pəːk] *n* beneficio, extra *m*.
▸**perk up** *vi* (*cheer up*) animarse.
perky ['pəːkɪ] *adj* alegre, animado.
perm [pəːm] *n* permanente *f* ♦ *vt*: **to have one's hair** ~**ed** hacerse una permanente.
permanence ['pəːmənəns] *n* permanencia.
permanent ['pəːmənənt] *adj* permanente; (*job, position*) fijo; (*dye, ink*) indeleble; ~ **address** domicilio permanente; **I'm not** ~ **here** no estoy fijo aquí.
permanently ['pəːmənəntlɪ] *adv* (*lastingly*) para siempre, de modo definitivo; (*all the time*) permanentemente.
permeate ['pəːmɪeɪt] *vi* penetrar, trascender ♦ *vt* penetrar, trascender a.
permissible [pə'mɪsɪbl] *adj* permisible, lícito.
permission [pə'mɪʃən] *n* permiso; **to give sb** ~ **to do sth** autorizar a algn para que haga algo; **with your** ~ con su permiso.
permissive [pə'mɪsɪv] *adj* permisivo.
permit *n* ['pəːmɪt] permiso, licencia; (*entrance pass*) pase *m* ♦ *vt* [pə'mɪt] permitir; (*accept*) tolerar ♦ *vi* [pə'mɪt]: **weather** ~**ting** si el tiempo lo permite; **fishing** ~ permiso de pesca; **building/export** ~ licencia *or* permiso de construcción/exportación.
permutation [pəːmju'teɪʃən] *n* permutación *f*.
pernicious [pəː'nɪʃəs] *adj* nocivo; (*MED*) pernicioso.
pernickety [pə'nɪkɪtɪ] *adj* (*col*: *person*) quisquilloso; (: *task*) delicado.
perpendicular [pəːpən'dɪkjulə*] *adj* perpendicular.
perpetrate ['pəːpɪtreɪt] *vt* cometer.
perpetual [pə'pɛtjuəl] *adj* perpetuo.
perpetually [pə'pɛtjuəlɪ] *adv* (*eternally*) perpetuamente; (*continuously*) constantemente, continuamente.
perpetuate [pə'pɛtjueɪt] *vt* perpetuar.
perpetuity [pəːpɪ'tjuːɪtɪ] *n*: **in** ~ a perpetuidad.
perplex [pə'plɛks] *vt* dejar perplejo.
perplexed [pə'plɛkst] *adj* perplejo, confuso.
perplexing [pə'plɛksɪŋ] *adj* que causa perplejidad.
perplexity [pə'plɛksɪtɪ] *n* perplejidad *f*, confusión *f*.
perquisites ['pəːkwɪzɪts] *npl* (*also*: **perks**) beneficios *mpl*.
persecute ['pəːsɪkjuːt] *vt* (*pursue*) perseguir; (*harass*) acosar.
persecution [pəːsɪ'kjuːʃən] *n* persecución *f*.
perseverance [pəːsɪ'vɪərəns] *n* perseverancia.
persevere [pəːsɪ'vɪə*] *vi* perseverar.
Persia ['pəːʃə] *n* Persia.
Persian ['pəːʃən] *adj, n* persa *m/f* ♦ *n* (*LING*) persa *m*; **the** ~ **Gulf** el Golfo Pérsico.
Persian cat *n* gato persa.

persist [pə'sɪst] *vi* persistir; **to ~ in doing sth** empeñarse en hacer algo.
persistence [pə'sɪstəns] *n* empeño.
persistent [pə'sɪstənt] *adj* (*lateness, rain*) persistente; (*determined*) porfiado; (*continuing*) constante; **~ offender** (*LAW*) multirreincidente *m/f*.
persistently [pə'sɪstəntlɪ] *adv* persistentemente; (*continually*) constantemente.
persnickety [pə'snɪkətɪ] *adj* (*US col*) = **pernickety**.
person ['pə:sn] *n* persona; **in ~** en persona; **on** *or* **about one's ~** (*weapon, money*) encima; **a ~ to ~ call** (*TEL*) una llamada (de) persona a persona.
personable ['pə:snəbl] *adj* atractivo.
personal ['pə:snl] *adj* personal, individual; (*visit*) en persona; (*BRIT TEL*) persona a persona.
personal allowance *n* desgravación *f* personal.
personal assistant (PA) *n* ayudante *m/f* personal.
personal belongings *npl* efectos *mpl* personales.
personal column *n* anuncios *mpl* personales.
personal computer (PC) *n* ordenador *m* personal.
personal effects *npl* efectos *mpl* personales.
personal identification number (PIN) *n* (*COMPUT, BANKING*) número personal de identificación.
personality [pə:sə'nælɪtɪ] *n* personalidad *f*.
personal loan *n* préstamo personal.
personally ['pə:snəlɪ] *adv* personalmente.
personal organizer *n* agenda (profesional); (*electronic*) organizador *m* personal.
personal property *n* bienes *mpl* muebles.
personal stereo *n* walkman ® *m*.
personification [pə:sɔnɪfɪ'keɪʃən] *n* personificación *f*.
personify [pə:'sɔnɪfaɪ] *vt* encarnar, personificar.
personnel [pə:sə'nɛl] *n* personal *m*.
personnel department *n* departamento de personal.
personnel management *n* gestión *f* de personal.
personnel manager *n* jefe *m* de personal.
perspective [pə'spɛktɪv] *n* perspectiva; **to get sth into ~** ver algo en perspectiva *or* como es.
Perspex ® ['pə:spɛks] *n* (*BRIT*) vidrio acrílico, plexiglás *m* ®.
perspiration [pə:spɪ'reɪʃən] *n* transpiración *f*, sudor *m*.
perspire [pə'spaɪə*] *vi* transpirar, sudar.
persuade [pə'sweɪd] *vt*: **to ~ sb to do sth** persuadir a algn para que haga algo; **to ~ sb of sth/that** persuadir *or* convencer a algn de algo/de que; **I am ~d that ...** estoy convencido de que ....
persuasion [pə'sweɪʒən] *n* persuasión *f*; (*persuasiveness*) persuasiva; (*creed*) creencia.
persuasive [pə'sweɪsɪv] *adj* persuasivo.
persuasively [pə'sweɪsɪvlɪ] *adv* de modo persuasivo.
pert [pə:t] *adj* impertinente, fresco, atrevido.
pertaining [pə:'teɪnɪŋ]: **~ to** *prep* relacionado con.
pertinent ['pə:tɪnənt] *adj* pertinente, a propósito.
perturb [pə'tə:b] *vt* perturbar.
perturbing [pə'tə:bɪŋ] *adj* inquietante, perturbador(a).
Peru [pə'ru:] *n* el Perú.
perusal [pə'ru:zəl] *n* (*quick*) lectura somera; (*careful*) examen *m*.
peruse [pə'ru:z] *vt* (*examine*) leer con detención, examinar; (*glance at*) mirar por encima.
Peruvian [pə'ru:vɪən] *adj, n* peruano/a *m/f*.
pervade [pə'veɪd] *vt* impregnar; (*influence, ideas*) extenderse por.
pervasive [pə'veɪsɪv] *adj* (*smell*) penetrante; (*influence*) muy extendido; (*gloom, feelings, ideas*) reinante.
perverse [pə'və:s] *adj* perverso; (*stubborn*) terco; (*wayward*) travieso.
perversely [pə'və:slɪ] *adv* perversamente; tercamente; traviesamente.
perverseness [pə'və:snɪs] *n* perversidad *f*; terquedad *f*; travesura.
perversion [pə'və:ʃən] *n* perversión *f*.
pervert *n* ['pə:və:t] pervertido/a ♦ *vt* [pə'və:t] pervertir.
pessary ['pɛsərɪ] *n* pesario.
pessimism ['pɛsɪmɪzəm] *n* pesimismo.
pessimist ['pɛsɪmɪst] *n* pesimista *m/f*.
pessimistic [pɛsɪ'mɪstɪk] *adj* pesimista.
pest [pɛst] *n* (*insect*) insecto nocivo; (*fig*) lata, molestia; **~s** *npl* plaga.
pest control *n* control *m* de plagas.
pester ['pɛstə*] *vt* molestar, acosar.
pesticide ['pɛstɪsaɪd] *n* pesticida *m*.
pestilence ['pɛstɪləns] *n* pestilencia.
pestle ['pɛsl] *n* mano *f* de mortero *or* de almirez.
pet [pɛt] *n* animal *m* doméstico; (*favourite*) favorito/a ♦ *vt* acariciar ♦ *vi* (*col*)

besuquearse ♦ *cpd*: **my ~ aversion** mi manía.
petal ['pɛtl] *n* pétalo.
peter ['pi:tə*]: **to ~ out** *vi* agotarse, acabarse.
petite [pə'ti:t] *adj* menuda, chiquita.
petition [pə'tɪʃən] *n* petición *f* ♦ *vt* presentar una petición a ♦ *vi*: **to ~ for divorce** pedir el divorcio.
pet name *n* nombre *m* cariñoso, apodo.
petrified ['pɛtrɪfaɪd] *adj* (*fig*) pasmado, horrorizado.
petrochemical [pɛtrə'kɛmɪkl] *adj* petroquímico.
petrodollars ['pɛtrəudɔləz] *npl* petrodólares *mpl*.
petrol ['pɛtrəl] (*BRIT*) *n* gasolina; (*for lighter*) bencina; **two/four-star ~** gasolina normal/súper.
petrol bomb *n* cóctel *m* Molotov.
petrol can *n* bidón *m* de gasolina.
petrol engine *n* (*BRIT*) motor *m* de gasolina.
petroleum [pə'trəulɪəm] *n* petróleo.
petroleum jelly *n* vaselina.
petrol pump *n* (*BRIT*) (*in car*) bomba de gasolina; (*in garage*) surtidor *m* de gasolina.
petrol station *n* (*BRIT*) gasolinera.
petrol tank *n* (*BRIT*) depósito (de gasolina).
petticoat ['pɛtɪkəut] *n* combinación *f*, enagua(s) *f(pl)* (*LAM*).
pettifogging ['pɛtɪfɔgɪŋ] *adj* quisquilloso.
pettiness ['pɛtɪnɪs] *n* mezquindad *f*.
petty ['pɛtɪ] *adj* (*mean*) mezquino; (*unimportant*) insignificante.
petty cash *n* dinero para gastos menores.
petty cash book *n* libro de caja auxiliar.
petty officer *n* contramaestre *m*.
petulant ['pɛtjulənt] *adj* malhumorado.
pew [pju:] *n* banco.
pewter ['pju:tə*] *n* peltre *m*.
Pfc *abbr* (*US MIL*) = *private first class*.
PG *n abbr* (*CINE*) = *parental guidance*.
PGA *n abbr* = *Professional Golfers' Association*.
PH *n abbr* (*US MIL*: = *Purple Heart*) *decoración otorgada a los heridos de guerra*.
pH *n abbr* (= *pH value*) pH.
PHA *n abbr* (*US*) = *Public Housing Administration*.
phallic ['fælɪk] *adj* fálico.
phantom ['fæntəm] *n* fantasma *m*.
Pharaoh ['fɛərəu] *n* faraón *m*.
pharmaceutical [fɑ:mə'sju:tɪkl] *adj* farmaceútico.
pharmacist ['fɑ:məsɪst] *n* farmacéutico/a.
pharmacy ['fɑ:məsɪ] *n* (*US*) farmacia.
phase [feɪz] *n* fase *f* ♦ *vt*: **to ~ sth in/out** introducir/retirar algo por etapas; **~d withdrawal** retirada progresiva.
PhD *abbr* = **Doctor of Philosophy**.
pheasant ['fɛznt] *n* faisán *m*.
phenomenal [fɪ'nɔmɪnl] *adj* fenomenal, extraordinario.
phenomenally [fɪ'nɔmɪnlɪ] *adv* extraordinariamente.
phenomenon, *pl* **phenomena** [fə'nɔmɪnən, -nə] *n* fenómeno.
phial ['faɪəl] *n* ampolla.
philanderer [fɪ'lændərə*] *n* donjuán *m*, don Juan *m*.
philanthropic [fɪlən'θrɔpɪk] *adj* filantrópico.
philanthropist [fɪ'lænθrəpɪst] *n* filántropo/a.
philatelist [fɪ'lætəlɪst] *n* filatelista *m/f*.
philately [fɪ'lætəlɪ] *n* filatelia.
Philippines ['fɪlɪpi:nz] *npl*: **the ~** (las Islas) Filipinas.
philosopher [fɪ'lɔsəfə*] *n* filósofo/a.
philosophical [fɪlə'sɔfɪkl] *adj* filosófico.
philosophy [fɪ'lɔsəfɪ] *n* filosofía.
phlegm [flɛm] *n* flema.
phlegmatic [flɛg'mætɪk] *adj* flemático.
phobia ['fəubjə] *n* fobia.
phone [fəun] *n* teléfono ♦ *vt* telefonear, llamar por teléfono; **to be on the ~** tener teléfono; (*be calling*) estar hablando por teléfono.
►**phone back** *vt, vi* volver a llamar.
►**phone up** *vt, vi* llamar por teléfono.
phone book *n* guía telefónica.
phone box, phone booth *n* cabina telefónica.
phone call *n* llamada (telefónica).
phonecard ['fəunkɑ:d] *n* tarjeta telefónica.
phone-in ['fəunɪn] *n* (*BRIT RADIO, TV*) *programa de radio or televisión con las líneas abiertas al público*.
phone tapping [-tæpɪŋ] *n* escuchas telefónicas.
phonetics [fə'nɛtɪks] *n* fonética.
phon(e)y ['fəunɪ] *adj* falso ♦ *n* (*person*) farsante *m/f*.
phonograph ['fəunəgræf] *n* (*US*) fonógrafo, tocadiscos *m inv*.
phonology [fəu'nɔlədʒɪ] *n* fonología.
phosphate ['fɔsfeɪt] *n* fosfato.
phosphorus ['fɔsfərəs] *n* fósforo.
photo ['fəutəu] *n* foto *f*.
photo... ['fəutəu] *pref* foto....
photocall ['fəutəukɔ:l] *n* sesión *f* fotográfica para la prensa.
photocopier ['fəutəukɔpɪə*] *n* fotocopiadora.
photocopy ['fəutəukɔpɪ] *n* fotocopia ♦ *vt*

fotocopiar.
photoelectric [fəutəuɪ'lɛktrɪk] *adj*: ~ **cell** célula fotoeléctrica.
photo finish *n* resultado comprobado por fotocontrol.
Photofit ® ['fəutəufɪt] *n* (*also*: ~ **picture**) retrato robot.
photogenic [fəutəu'dʒɛnɪk] *adj* fotogénico.
photograph ['fəutəgræf] *n* fotografía ♦ *vt* fotografiar; **to take a** ~ **of sb** sacar una foto de algn.
photographer [fə'tɔgrəfə*] *n* fotógrafo.
photographic [fəutə'græfɪk] *adj* fotográfico.
photography [fə'tɔgrəfɪ] *n* fotografía.
photo opportunity *n oportunidad de salir en la foto.*
Photostat ® ['fəutəustæt] *n* fotóstato.
photosynthesis [fəutəu'sɪnθəsɪs] *n* fotosíntesis *f*.
phrase [freɪz] *n* frase *f* ♦ *vt* (*letter*) expresar, redactar.
phrase book *n* libro de frases.
physical ['fɪzɪkl] *adj* físico; ~ **examination** reconocimiento médico; ~ **exercises** ejercicios *mpl* físicos.
physical education *n* educación *f* física.
physically ['fɪsɪklɪ] *adv* físicamente.
physical training *n* gimnasia.
physician [fɪ'zɪʃən] *n* médico/a.
physicist ['fɪzɪsɪst] *n* físico/a.
physics ['fɪzɪks] *n* física.
physiological [fɪzɪə'lɔdʒɪkl] *adj* fisiológico.
physiology [fɪzɪ'ɔlədʒɪ] *n* fisiología.
physiotherapy [fɪzɪəu'θɛrəpɪ] *n* fisioterapia.
physique [fɪ'ziːk] *n* físico.
pianist ['pɪənɪst] *n* pianista *m/f*.
piano [pɪ'ænəu] *n* piano.
piano accordion *n* (*BRIT*) acordeón-piano *m*.
piccolo ['pɪkələu] *n* (*MUS*) flautín *m*.
pick [pɪk] *n* (*tool*: *also*: ~**-axe**) pico, piqueta ♦ *vt* (*select*) elegir, escoger; (*gather*) coger (*SP*), recoger (*LAM*); (*lock*) abrir con ganzúa; (*scab, spot*) rascar ♦ *vi*: **to** ~ **and choose** ser muy exigente; **take your** ~ escoja lo que quiera; **the** ~ **of** lo mejor de; **to** ~ **one's nose/teeth** hurgarse las narices/escarbarse los dientes; **to** ~ **pockets** ratear, ser carterista; **to** ~ **one's way through** andar a tientas, abrirse camino; **to** ~ **a fight/quarrel with sb** buscar pelea/camorra con algn; **to** ~ **sb's brains** aprovecharse de los conocimientos de algn.
▸**pick at** *vt fus*: **to** ~ **at one's food** comer con poco apetito.
▸**pick off** *vt* (*kill*) matar de un tiro.
▸**pick on** *vt fus* (*person*) meterse con.
▸**pick out** *vt* escoger; (*distinguish*) identificar.
▸**pick up** *vi* (*improve*: *sales*) ir mejor; (: *patient*) reponerse; (: *FINANCE*) recobrarse ♦ *vt* (*from floor*) recoger; (*buy*) comprar; (*find*) encontrar; (*learn*) aprender; (*RADIO, TV, TEL*) captar; **to** ~ **up speed** acelerarse; **to** ~ **o.s. up** levantarse; **to** ~ **up where one left off** reempezar algo donde lo había dejado.
pickaxe, (*US*) **pickax** ['pɪkæks] *n* pico, zapapico.
picket ['pɪkɪt] *n* (*in strike*) piquete *m* ♦ *vt* hacer un piquete en, piquetear; **to be on** ~ **duty** estar de piquete.
picketing ['pɪkɪtɪŋ] *n* organización *f* de piquetes.
picket line *n* piquete *m*.
pickings ['pɪkɪŋz] *npl* (*pilferings*): **there are good** ~ **to be had here** se pueden sacar buenas ganancias de aquí.
pickle ['pɪkl] *n* (*also*: ~**s**: *as condiment*) escabeche *m*; (*fig*: *mess*) apuro ♦ *vt* conservar en escabeche; (*in vinegar*) conservar en vinagre; **in a** ~ en un lío, en apuros.
pick-me-up ['pɪkmɪʌp] *n* reconstituyente *m*.
pickpocket ['pɪkpɔkɪt] *n* carterista *m/f*.
pickup ['pɪkʌp] *n* (*BRIT*: *on record player*) brazo; (*small truck*: *also*: ~ **truck**, ~ **van**) furgoneta.
picnic ['pɪknɪk] *n* picnic *m*, merienda ♦ *vi* merendar en el campo.
pictorial [pɪk'tɔːrɪəl] *adj* pictórico; (*magazine etc*) ilustrado.
picture ['pɪktʃə*] *n* cuadro; (*painting*) pintura; (*photograph*) fotografía; (*film*) película; (*TV*) imagen *f* ♦ *vt* pintar; **the** ~**s** (*BRIT*) el cine; **we get a good** ~ **here** captamos bien la imagen aquí; **to take a** ~ **of sb/sth** hacer *or* sacar una foto a algn/de algo; **the garden is a** ~ **in June** el jardín es una preciosidad en junio; **the overall** ~ la impresión general; **to put sb in the** ~ poner a algn al corriente *or* al tanto.
picture book *n* libro de dibujos.
picturesque [pɪktʃə'rɛsk] *adj* pintoresco.
piddling ['pɪdlɪŋ] *adj* insignificante.
pidgin ['pɪdʒɪn] *adj*: ~ **English** *lengua franca basada en el inglés.*
pie [paɪ] *n* (*of meat etc*: *large*) pastel *m*; (: *small*) empanada; (*sweet*) tarta.
piebald ['paɪbɔːld] *adj* pío.
piece [piːs] *n* pedazo, trozo; (*of cake*) trozo;

(*DRAUGHTS etc*) ficha; (*CHESS, part of a set*) pieza; (*item*): **a ~ of furniture/advice** un mueble/un consejo ♦ *vt*: **to ~ together** juntar; (*TECH*) armar; **to take to ~s** desmontar; **a ~ of news** una noticia; **a 10p ~** una moneda de 10 peniques; **a six-~ band** un conjunto de seis (músicos); **in one ~** (*object*) de una sola pieza; **~ by ~** pieza por *or* a pieza; **to say one's ~** decir su parecer.
piecemeal ['pi:smi:l] *adv* poco a poco.
piece rate *n* tarifa a destajo.
piecework ['pi:swə:k] *n* trabajo a destajo.
pie chart *n* gráfico de sectores *or* de tarta.
pier [pɪə*] *n* muelle *m*, embarcadero.
pierce [pɪəs] *vt* penetrar en, perforar; **to have one's ears ~d** hacerse los agujeros de las orejas.
piercing ['pɪəsɪŋ] *adj* (*cry*) penetrante.
piety ['paɪətɪ] *n* piedad *f*.
pig [pɪg] *n* cerdo, puerco, chancho (*LAM*); (*person: greedy*) tragón/ona *m/f*, comilón/ona *m/f*; (: *nasty*) cerdo/a.
pigeon ['pɪdʒən] *n* paloma; (*as food*) pichón *m*.
pigeonhole ['pɪdʒənhəul] *n* casilla.
piggy bank ['pɪgɪbæŋk] *n* hucha (*en forma de cerdito*).
pigheaded ['pɪg'hɛdɪd] *adj* terco, testarudo.
piglet ['pɪglɪt] *n* cerdito, cochinillo.
pigment ['pɪgmənt] *n* pigmento.
pigmentation [pɪgmən'teɪʃən] *n* pigmentación *f*.
pigmy ['pɪgmɪ] *n* = **pygmy**.
pigskin ['pɪgskɪn] *n* piel *f* de cerdo.
pigsty ['pɪgstaɪ] *n* pocilga.
pigtail ['pɪgteɪl] *n* (*girl's*) trenza; (*Chinese, TAUR*) coleta.
pike [paɪk] *n* (*spear*) pica; (*fish*) lucio.
pilchard ['pɪltʃəd] *n* sardina.
pile [paɪl] *n* (*heap*) montón *m*; (*of carpet*) pelo ♦ (*vb: also*: **~ up**) *vt* amontonar; (*fig*) acumular ♦ *vi* amontonarse; **in a ~** en un montón; **to ~ into** (*car*) meterse en.
▸**pile on** *vt*: **to ~ it on** (*col*) exagerar.
piles [paɪlz] *npl* (*MED*) almorranas *fpl*, hemorroides *mpl*.
pile-up ['paɪlʌp] *n* (*AUT*) accidente *m* múltiple.
pilfer ['pɪlfə*] *vt, vi* ratear, robar, sisar.
pilfering ['pɪlfərɪŋ] *n* ratería.
pilgrim ['pɪlgrɪm] *n* peregrino/a; **the Pilgrim Fathers** *or* **Pilgrims** *los primeros colonos norteamericanos*; *see also* **Thanksgiving (Day)**.
pilgrimage ['pɪlgrɪmɪdʒ] *n* peregrinación *f*, romería.
pill [pɪl] *n* píldora; **the ~** la píldora; **to be on the ~** tomar la píldora (anticonceptiva).
pillage ['pɪlɪdʒ] *vt* pillar, saquear.
pillar ['pɪlə*] *n* pilar *m*, columna.
pillar box *n* (*BRIT*) buzón *m*.
pillion ['pɪljən] *n* (*of motorcycle*) asiento trasero; **to ride ~** ir en el asiento trasero.
pillion passenger *n* pasajero que va detrás.
pillory ['pɪlərɪ] *vt* poner en ridículo.
pillow ['pɪləu] *n* almohada.
pillowcase ['pɪləukeɪs], **pillowslip** ['pɪləuslɪp] *n* funda (de almohada).
pilot ['paɪlət] *n* piloto *inv* ♦ *adj* (*scheme etc*) piloto ♦ *vt* pilotar; (*fig*) guiar, conducir.
pilot light *n* piloto.
pimento [pɪ'mɛntəu] *n* pimiento morrón.
pimp [pɪmp] *n* chulo, cafiche *m* (*LAM*).
pimple ['pɪmpl] *n* grano.
pimply ['pɪmplɪ] *adj* lleno de granos.
PIN *n abbr see* **personal identification number**.
pin [pɪn] *n* alfiler *m*; (*ELEC: of plug*) clavija; (*TECH*) perno; (: *wooden*) clavija; (*drawing ~*) chincheta; (*in grenade*) percutor *m* ♦ *vt* prender (con alfiler); sujetar con perno; **~s and needles** hormigueo *sg*; **to ~ sth on sb** (*fig*) cargar a algn con la culpa de algo.
▸**pin down** *vt* (*fig*): **there's something strange here, but I can't quite ~ it down** aquí hay algo raro pero no puedo precisar qué es; **to ~ sb down** hacer que algn concrete.
pinafore ['pɪnəfɔ:*] *n* delantal *m*.
pinafore dress *n* (*BRIT*) pichi *m*.
pinball ['pɪnbɔ:l] *n* (*also*: **~ machine**) millón *m*, fliper *m*.
pincers ['pɪnsəz] *npl* pinzas *fpl*, tenazas *fpl*.
pinch [pɪntʃ] *n* pellizco; (*of salt etc*) pizca ♦ *vt* pellizcar; (*col: steal*) birlar ♦ *vi* (*shoe*) apretar; **at a ~** en caso de apuro; **to feel the ~** (*fig*) pasar apuros *or* estrecheces.
pinched [pɪntʃt] *adj* (*drawn*) cansado; **~ with cold** transido de frío; **~ for money/space** mal *or* falto de dinero/espacio *or* sitio.
pincushion ['pɪnkuʃən] *n* acerico.
pine [paɪn] *n* (*also*: **~ tree**) pino ♦ *vi*: **to ~ for** suspirar por.
▸**pine away** *vi* morirse de pena.
pineapple ['paɪnæpl] *n* piña, ananá(s) (*LAM*) *m*.
pine cone *n* piña.
pine needle *n* aguja de pino.
ping [pɪŋ] *n* (*noise*) sonido agudo.
Ping-Pong ® ['pɪŋpɔŋ] *n* pingpong *m*.
pink [pɪŋk] *adj* (de color) rosa ♦ *n* (*colour*) rosa; (*BOT*) clavel *m*.

pinking shears ['pɪŋkɪŋ-] *npl* tijeras *fpl* dentadas.
pin money *n* dinero para gastos extra.
pinnacle ['pɪnəkl] *n* cumbre *f*.
pinpoint ['pɪnpɔɪnt] *vt* precisar.
pinstripe ['pɪnstraɪp] *adj*: ~ **suit** traje *m* a rayas.
pint [paɪnt] *n* pinta (*BRIT* = *0.57 l*; *US* = *0.47 l*); (*BRIT col*: *of beer*) pinta de cerveza, ≈ jarra (*SP*).
pin-up ['pɪnʌp] *n* (*picture*) *fotografía de mujer u hombre medio desnudos*; ~ **(girl)** ≃ chica de calendario.
pioneer [paɪə'nɪə*] *n* pionero/a ♦ *vt* promover.
pious ['paɪəs] *adj* piadoso, devoto.
pip [pɪp] *n* (*seed*) pepita; **the ~s** (*BRIT TEL*) la señal.
pipe [paɪp] *n* tubería, cañería; (*for smoking*) pipa, cachimba (*LAM*), cachimbo (*LAM*) ♦ *vt* conducir en cañerías; **(bag)~s** *npl* gaita *sg*.
▸**pipe down** *vi* (*col*) callarse.
pipe cleaner *n* limpiapipas *m inv*.
piped music [paɪpt-] *n* música ambiental.
pipe dream *n* sueño imposible.
pipeline ['paɪplaɪn] *n* tubería, cañería; (*for oil*) oleoducto; (*for natural gas*) gaseoducto; **it is in the** ~ (*fig*) está en trámite.
piper ['paɪpə*] *n* (*gen*) flautista *m/f*; (*with bagpipes*) gaitero/a.
pipe tobacco *n* tabaco de pipa.
piping ['paɪpɪŋ] *adv*: **to be ~ hot** estar calentito.
piquant ['pi:kənt] *adj* picante.
pique [pi:k] *n* pique *m*, resentimiento.
pirate ['paɪərət] *n* pirata *m/f* ♦ *vt* (*record, video, book*) hacer una copia pirata de.
pirated ['paɪərətɪd] *adj* (*book, record etc*) pirata *inv*.
pirate radio *n* (*BRIT*) emisora pirata.
pirouette [pɪru'ɛt] *n* pirueta ♦ *vi* piruetear.
Pisces ['paɪsi:z] *n* Piscis *m*.
piss [pɪs] *vi* (*col*) mear.
pissed [pɪst] *adj* (*col*: *drunk*) mamado.
pistol ['pɪstl] *n* pistola.
piston ['pɪstən] *n* pistón *m*, émbolo.
pit [pɪt] *n* hoyo; (*also*: **coal** ~) mina; (*in garage*) foso de inspección; (*also*: **orchestra** ~) foso de la orquesta; (*quarry*) cantera ♦ *vt* (*subj*: *chickenpox*) picar; (: *rust*) comer; **to ~ A against B** oponer A a B; **~s** *npl* (*AUT*) box *msg*; **~ted with** (*chickenpox*) picado de.
pitapat ['pɪtə'pæt] *adv*: **to go** ~ (*heart*) latir rápidamente; (*rain*) golpetear.
pitch [pɪtʃ] *n* (*throw*) lanzamiento; (*MUS*) tono; (*BRIT SPORT*) campo, terreno; (*tar*) brea; (*in market etc*) puesto; (*fig*: *degree*) nivel *m*, grado ♦ *vt* (*throw*) arrojar, lanzar ♦ *vi* (*fall*) caer(se); (*NAUT*) cabecear; **I can't keep working at this** ~ no puedo seguir trabajando a este ritmo; **at its (highest)** ~ en su punto máximo; **his anger reached such a ~ that** ... su ira *or* cólera llegó a tal extremo que ...; **to ~ a tent** montar una tienda (de campaña); **to ~ one's aspirations too high** tener ambiciones desmesuradas.
pitch-black ['pɪtʃ'blæk] *adj* negro como boca de lobo.
pitched battle [pɪtʃt-] *n* batalla campal.
pitcher ['pɪtʃə*] *n* cántaro, jarro.
pitchfork ['pɪtʃfɔ:k] *n* horca.
piteous ['pɪtɪəs] *adj* lastimoso.
pitfall ['pɪtfɔ:l] *n* riesgo.
pith [pɪθ] *n* (*of orange*) piel *f* blanca; (*fig*) meollo.
pithead ['pɪthɛd] *n* (*BRIT*) bocamina.
pithy ['pɪθɪ] *adj* jugoso.
pitiful ['pɪtɪful] *adj* (*touching*) lastimoso, conmovedor(a); (*contemptible*) lamentable.
pitifully ['pɪtɪfəlɪ] *adv*: **it's ~ obvious** es tan evidente que da pena.
pitiless ['pɪtɪlɪs] *adj* despiadado, implacable.
pitilessly ['pɪtɪlɪslɪ] *adv* despiadadamente, implacablemente.
pittance ['pɪtns] *n* miseria.
pity ['pɪtɪ] *n* (*compassion*) compasión *f*, piedad *f*; (*shame*) lástima ♦ *vt* compadecer(se de); **to have** *or* **take ~ on sb** compadecerse de algn; **what a ~!** ¡qué pena!; **it is a ~ that you can't come** ¡qué pena que no puedas venir!
pitying ['pɪtɪɪŋ] *adj* compasivo, de lástima.
pivot ['pɪvət] *n* eje *m* ♦ *vi*: **to ~ on** girar sobre; (*fig*) depender de.
pixel ['pɪksl] *n* (*COMPUT*) pixel *m*, punto.
pixie ['pɪksɪ] *n* duendecillo.
pizza ['pi:tsə] *n* pizza.
placard ['plækɑ:d] *n* (*in march etc*) pancarta.
placate [plə'keɪt] *vt* apaciguar.
place [pleɪs] *n* lugar *m*, sitio; (*rank*) rango; (*seat*) plaza, asiento; (*post*) puesto; (*in street names*) plaza; (*home*): **at/to his** ~ en/a su casa ♦ *vt* (*object*) poner, colocar; (*identify*) reconocer; (*find a post for*) dar un puesto a, colocar; (*goods*) vender; **to take** ~ tener lugar; **to be ~d** (*in race, exam*) colocarse; **out of** ~ (*not suitable*) fuera de lugar; **in the first** ~ (*first of all*) en primer lugar; **to change ~s with sb** cambiarse de sitio con algn; **from ~ to ~**

de un sitio a *or* para otro; **all over the ~** por todas partes; **he's going ~s** (*fig, col*) llegará lejos; **I feel rather out of ~ here** me encuentro algo desplazado; **to put sb in his ~** (*fig*) poner a algn en su lugar; **it is not my ~ to do it** no me incumbe a mí hacerlo; **to ~ an order with sb (for)** hacer un pedido a algn (de); **we are better ~d than a month ago** estamos en mejor posición que hace un mes.

placebo [plə'si:bəu] *n* placebo.

place mat *n* (*wooden etc*) salvamanteles *m inv*; (*in linen etc*) mantel *m* individual.

placement ['pleɪsmənt] *n* colocación *f*.

place name *n* topónimo.

placenta [plə'sɛntə] *n* placenta.

placid ['plæsɪd] *adj* apacible, plácido.

placidity [plæ'sɪdɪtɪ] *n* placidez *f*.

plagiarism ['pleɪdʒjərɪzm] *n* plagio.

plagiarist ['pleɪdʒjərɪst] *n* plagiario/a.

plagiarize ['pleɪdʒjəraɪz] *vt* plagiar.

plague [pleɪg] *n* plaga; (*MED*) peste *f* ♦ *vt* (*fig*) acosar, atormentar; **to ~ sb with questions** acribillar a algn a preguntas.

plaice [pleɪs] *n, pl inv* platija.

plaid [plæd] *n* (*material*) tela de cuadros.

plain [pleɪn] *adj* (*clear*) claro, evidente; (*simple*) sencillo; (*frank*) franco, abierto; (*not handsome*) poco atractivo; (*pure*) natural, puro ♦ *adv* claramente ♦ *n* llano, llanura; **in ~ clothes** (*police*) vestido de paisano; **to make sth ~ to sb** dejar algo en claro a algn.

plain chocolate *n* chocolate *m* oscuro *or* amargo.

plainly ['pleɪnlɪ] *adv* claramente, evidentemente; (*frankly*) francamente.

plainness ['pleɪnnɪs] *n* (*clarity*) claridad *f*; (*simplicity*) sencillez *f*; (*of face*) falta de atractivo.

plain speaking *n*: **there has been some ~** se ha hablado claro.

plaintiff ['pleɪntɪf] *n* demandante *m/f*.

plaintive ['pleɪntɪv] *adj* (*cry, voice*) lastimero, quejumbroso; (*look*) que da lástima.

plait [plæt] *n* trenza ♦ *vt* trenzar.

plan [plæn] *n* (*drawing*) plano; (*scheme*) plan *m*, proyecto ♦ *vt* (*think*) pensar; (*prepare*) proyectar, planear; (*intend*) pensar, tener la intención de ♦ *vi* hacer proyectos; **have you any ~s for today?** ¿piensas hacer algo hoy?; **to ~ to do** pensar hacer; **how long do you ~ to stay?** ¿cuánto tiempo piensas quedarte?; **to ~ (for)** planear, proyectar.

▸**plan out** *vt* planear detalladamente.

plane [pleɪn] *n* (*AVIAT*) avión *m*; (*tree*) plátano; (*tool*) cepillo; (*MATH*) plano.

planet ['plænɪt] *n* planeta *m*.

planetarium [plænɪ'tɛərɪəm] *n* planetario.

planetary ['plænɪtərɪ] *adj* planetario.

plank [plæŋk] *n* tabla.

plankton ['plæŋktən] *n* plancton *m*.

planned economy [plænd-] *n* economía planificada.

planner ['plænə*] *n* planificador(a) *m/f*; (*chart*) diagrama *m* de planificación; **town ~** urbanista *m/f*.

planning ['plænɪŋ] *n* (*POL, ECON*) planificación *f*; **family ~** planificación familiar.

planning committee *n* (*in local government*) comité *m* de planificación.

planning permission *n* licencia de obras.

plant [plɑ:nt] *n* planta; (*machinery*) maquinaria; (*factory*) fábrica ♦ *vt* plantar; (*field*) sembrar; (*bomb*) colocar.

plantain ['plæntеɪn] *n* llantén *m*.

plantation [plæn'teɪʃən] *n* plantación *f*; (*estate*) hacienda.

planter ['plɑ:ntə*] *n* hacendado.

plant pot *n* maceta, tiesto.

plaque [plæk] *n* placa.

plasma ['plæzmə] *n* plasma *m*.

plaster ['plɑ:stə*] *n* (*for walls*) yeso; (*also*: **~ of Paris**) yeso mate; (*MED*: *for broken leg etc*) escayola; (*BRIT*: *also*: **sticking ~**) tirita, esparadrapo ♦ *vt* enyesar; (*cover*): **to ~ with** llenar *or* cubrir de; **to be ~ed with mud** estar cubierto de barro.

plasterboard ['plɑ:stəbɔ:d] *n* cartón *m* yeso.

plaster cast *n* (*MED*) escayola; (*model, statue*) vaciado de yeso.

plastered ['plɑ:stəd] *adj* (*col*) borracho.

plasterer ['plɑ:stərə*] *n* yesero.

plastic ['plæstɪk] *n* plástico ♦ *adj* de plástico.

plastic bag *n* bolsa de plástico.

plastic bullet *n* bala de goma.

plastic explosive *n* goma 2 ®.

plasticine ® ['plæstɪsi:n] *n* (*BRIT*) plastilina ®.

plastic surgery *n* cirujía plástica.

plate [pleɪt] *n* (*dish*) plato; (*metal, in book*) lámina; (*PHOT, on door*) placa; (*AUT*: *number ~*) matrícula.

plateau, ~s *or* **~x** ['plætəu, -z] *n* meseta, altiplanicie *f*.

plateful ['pleɪtful] *n* plato.

plate glass *n* vidrio *or* cristal *m* cilindrado.

platen ['plætən] *n* (*on typewriter, printer*) rodillo.

plate rack *n* escurreplatos *m inv*.

platform ['plætfɔːm] *n* (*RAIL*) andén *m*; (*stage*) plataforma; (*at meeting*) tribuna; (*POL*) programa *m* (electoral); **the train leaves from ~ 7** el tren sale del andén número 7.
platform ticket *n* (*BRIT*) billete *m* de andén.
platinum ['plætɪnəm] *n* platino.
platitude ['plætɪtjuːd] *n* tópico, lugar *m* común.
platonic [plə'tɔnɪk] *adj* platónico.
platoon [plə'tuːn] *n* pelotón *m*.
platter ['plætə*] *n* fuente *f*.
plaudits ['plɔːdɪts] *npl* aplausos *mpl*.
plausibility [plɔːzɪ'bɪlɪtɪ] *n* verosimilitud *f*, credibilidad *f*.
plausible ['plɔːzɪbl] *adj* verosímil; (*person*) convincente.
play [pleɪ] *n* (*gen*) juego; (*THEAT*) obra ♦ *vt* (*game*) jugar; (*instrument*) tocar; (*THEAT*) representar; (: *part*) hacer el papel de; (*fig*) desempeñar ♦ *vi* jugar; (*frolic*) juguetear; **to ~ safe** ir a lo seguro; **to bring** *or* **call into ~** poner en juego; **to ~ a trick on sb** gastar una broma a algn; **they're ~ing at soldiers** están jugando a (los) soldados; **to ~ for time** (*fig*) tratar de ganar tiempo; **to ~ into sb's hands** (*fig*) hacerle el juego a algn; **a smile ~ed on his lips** una sonrisa le bailaba en los labios.
▸**play about, play around** *vi* (*person*) hacer el tonto; **to ~ about** *or* **around with** (*fiddle with*) juguetear con; (*idea*) darle vueltas a.
▸**play along** *vi*: **to ~ along with** seguirle el juego a ♦ *vt*: **to ~ sb along** (*fig*) jugar con algn.
▸**play back** *vt* poner.
▸**play down** *vt* quitar importancia a.
▸**play on** *vt fus* (*sb's feelings, credulity*) aprovecharse de; **to ~ on sb's nerves** atacarle los nervios a algn.
▸**play up** *vi* (*cause trouble*) dar guerra.
playact ['pleɪækt] *vi* (*fig*) hacer comedia *or* teatro.
play-acting ['pleɪæktɪŋ] *n* teatro.
playboy ['pleɪbɔɪ] *n* playboy *m*.
player ['pleɪə*] *n* jugador(a) *m/f*; (*THEAT*) actor *m*, actriz *f*; (*MUS*) músico/a.
playful ['pleɪful] *adj* juguetón/ona.
playground ['pleɪgraund] *n* (*in school*) patio de recreo.
playgroup ['pleɪgruːp] *n* jardín *m* de infancia.
playing card ['pleɪɪŋ-] *n* naipe *m*, carta.
playing field *n* campo de deportes.
playmaker ['pleɪmeɪkə*] *n* (*SPORT*) *jugador encargado de facilitar buenas jugadas a sus compañeros.*
playmate ['pleɪmeɪt] *n* compañero/a de juego.
play-off ['pleɪɔf] *n* (*SPORT*) (partido de) desempate *m*.
playpen ['pleɪpɛn] *n* corral *m*.
playroom ['pleɪruːm] *n* cuarto de juego.
playschool ['pleɪskuːl] *n* = **playgroup**.
plaything ['pleɪθɪŋ] *n* juguete *m*.
playtime ['pleɪtaɪm] *n* (*SCOL*) (hora de) recreo.
playwright ['pleɪraɪt] *n* dramaturgo/a.
plc *abbr* (= *public limited company*) S.A.
plea [pliː] *n* (*request*) súplica, petición *f*; (*excuse*) pretexto, disculpa; (*LAW*) alegato, defensa.
plea bargaining *n* (*LAW*) *acuerdo entre fiscal y defensor para agilizar los trámites judiciales.*
plead [pliːd] *vt* (*LAW*): **to ~ sb's case** defender a alguien; (*give as excuse*) poner como pretexto ♦ *vi* (*LAW*) declararse; (*beg*): **to ~ with sb** suplicar *or* rogar a algn; **to ~ guilty/not guilty** (*defendant*) declararse culpable/inocente; **to ~ for sth** (*beg for*) suplicar algo.
pleasant ['plɛznt] *adj* agradable.
pleasantly ['plɛzntlɪ] *adv* agradablemente.
pleasantries ['plɛzntrɪz] *npl* (*polite remarks*) cortesías *fpl*; **to exchange ~** conversar amablemente.
please [pliːz] *vt* (*give pleasure to*) dar gusto a, agradar ♦ *vi* (*think fit*): **do as you ~** haz lo que quieras *or* lo que te dé la gana; **to ~ o.s.** hacer lo que le parezca; **~!** ¡por favor!; **~ yourself!** ¡haz lo que quieras!, ¡como quieras!; **~ don't cry!** ¡no llores! te lo ruego.
pleased [pliːzd] *adj* (*happy*) alegre, contento; (*satisfied*): **~ (with)** satisfecho (de); **~ to meet you** (*col*) ¡encantado!, ¡tanto *or* mucho gusto!; **to be ~ (about sth)** alegrarse (de algo); **we are ~ to inform you that** ... tenemos el gusto de comunicarle que ....
pleasing ['pliːzɪŋ] *adj* agradable, grato.
pleasurable ['plɛʒərəbl] *adj* agradable, grato.
pleasurably ['plɛʒərəblɪ] *adv* agradablemente, gratamente.
pleasure ['plɛʒə*] *n* placer *m*, gusto; (*will*) voluntad *f* ♦ *cpd* de recreo; **"it's a ~"** "el gusto es mío"; **it's a ~ to see him** da gusto verle; **I have much ~ in informing you that** ... tengo el gran placer de comunicarles que ...; **with ~** con mucho *or* todo gusto; **is this trip for business or**

~? ¿este viaje es de negocios o de placer?
pleasure cruise *n* crucero de placer.
pleasure ground *n* parque *m* de atracciones.
pleasure-seeking ['plɛʒəsɪːkɪŋ] *adj* hedonista.
pleat [pliːt] *n* pliegue *m*.
pleb [plɛb] *n*: **the ~s** la gente baja, la plebe.
plebeian [plɪ'biːən] *n* plebeyo/a ♦ *adj* plebeyo; (*pej*) ordinario.
plebiscite ['plɛbɪsɪt] *n* plebiscito.
plectrum ['plɛktrəm] *n* plectro.
pledge [plɛdʒ] *n* (*object*) prenda; (*promise*) promesa, voto ♦ *vt* (*pawn*) empeñar; (*promise*) prometer; **to ~ support for sb** prometer su apoyo a algn; **to ~ sb to secrecy** hacer jurar a algn que guardará el secreto.
plenary ['pliːnərɪ] *adj*: **in ~ session** en sesión plenaria.
plentiful ['plɛntɪful] *adj* copioso, abundante.
plenty ['plɛntɪ] *n* abundancia; **~ of** mucho(s)/a(s); **we've got ~ of time to get there** tenemos tiempo de sobra para llegar.
plethora ['plɛθərə] *n* plétora.
pleurisy ['pluərɪsɪ] *n* pleuresía.
pliability [plaɪə'bɪlɪtɪ] *n* flexibilidad *f*.
pliable ['plaɪəbl] *adj* flexible.
pliers ['plaɪəz] *npl* alicates *mpl*, tenazas *fpl*.
plight [plaɪt] *n* condición *f or* situación *f* difícil.
plimsolls ['plɪmsəlz] *npl* (*BRIT*) zapatillas *fpl* de tenis.
plinth [plɪnθ] *n* plinto.
PLO *n abbr* (= *Palestine Liberation Organization*) OLP *f*.
plod [plɔd] *vi* caminar con paso pesado; (*fig*) trabajar laboriosamente.
plodder ['plɔdə*] *n trabajador(a) diligente pero lento/a*.
plodding ['plɔdɪŋ] *adj* (*student*) empollón(ona); (*worker*) más aplicado que brillante.
plonk [plɔŋk] (*col*) *n* (*BRIT*: *wine*) vino peleón ♦ *vt*: **to ~ sth down** dejar caer algo.
plot [plɔt] *n* (*scheme*) complot *m*, conjura; (*of story, play*) argumento; (*of land*) terreno, parcela ♦ *vt* (*mark out*) trazar; (*conspire*) tramar, urdir ♦ *vi* conspirar; **a vegetable ~** un cuadro de hortalizas.
plotter ['plɔtə*] *n* (*instrument*) trazador *m* (de gráficos); (*COMPUT*) trazador *m*.
plotting ['plɔtɪŋ] *n* conspiración *f*, intrigas *fpl*.
plough, (*US*) **plow** [plau] *n* arado ♦ *vt* (*earth*) arar.
▶**plough back** *vt* (*COMM*) reinvertir.
▶**plough through** *vt fus* (*crowd*) abrirse paso a la fuerza por.
ploughing ['plauɪŋ] *n* labranza.
ploughman ['plaumən] *n*: **~'s lunch** pan *m* con queso y cebolla.
plow [plau] (*US*) = **plough**.
ploy [plɔɪ] *n* truco, estratagema.
pluck [plʌk] *vt* (*fruit*) coger (*SP*), recoger (*LAM*); (*musical instrument*) puntear; (*bird*) desplumar ♦ *n* valor *m*, ánimo; **to ~ up courage** hacer de tripas corazón; **to ~ one's eyebrows** depilarse las cejas.
plucky ['plʌkɪ] *adj* valiente.
plug [plʌg] *n* tapón *m*; (*ELEC*) enchufe *m*, clavija; (*AUT*: *also*: **spark(ing) ~**) bujía ♦ *vt* (*hole*) tapar; (*col*: *advertise*) dar publicidad a; **to give sb/sth a ~** dar publicidad a algn/algo; **to ~ a lead into a socket** enchufar un hilo en una toma.
▶**plug in** *vt, vi* (*ELEC*) enchufar.
plughole ['plʌghəul] *n* desagüe *m*.
plum [plʌm] *n* (*fruit*) ciruela; (*also* **~ job**) chollo.
plumage ['pluːmɪdʒ] *n* plumaje *m*.
plumb [plʌm] *adj* vertical ♦ *n* plomo ♦ *adv* (*exactly*) exactamente, en punto ♦ *vt* sondar; (*fig*) sondear.
▶**plumb in** *vt* (*washing machine*) conectar.
plumber ['plʌmə*] *n* fontanero/a, plomero/a (*LAM*).
plumbing ['plʌmɪŋ] *n* (*trade*) fontanería, plomería (*LAM*); (*piping*) cañerías.
plume [pluːm] *n* (*gen*) pluma; (*on helmet*) penacho.
plummet ['plʌmɪt] *vi*: **to ~ (down)** caer a plomo.
plump [plʌmp] *adj* rechoncho, rollizo ♦ *vt*: **to ~ sth (down) on** dejar caer algo en.
▶**plump for** *vt fus* (*col*: *choose*) optar por.
▶**plump up** *vt* ahuecar.
plumpness ['plʌmpnɪs] *n* gordura.
plunder ['plʌndə*] *n* pillaje *m*; (*loot*) botín *m* ♦ *vt* saquear, pillar.
plunge [plʌndʒ] *n* zambullida ♦ *vt* sumergir, hundir ♦ *vi* (*fall*) caer; (*dive*) saltar; (*person*) arrojarse; (*sink*) hundirse; **to take the ~** lanzarse; **to ~ a room into darkness** sumir una habitación en la oscuridad.
plunger ['plʌndʒə*] *n* émbolo; (*for drain*) desatascador *m*.
plunging ['plʌndʒɪŋ] *adj* (*neckline*) escotado.
pluperfect [pluː'pəːfɪkt] *n* pluscuamperfecto.
plural ['pluərl] *n* plural *m*.
plus [plʌs] *n* (*also*: **~ sign**) signo más; (*fig*) punto a favor ♦ *adj*: **a ~ factor** (*fig*) un

factor *m* a favor ♦ *prep* más, y, además de; **ten/twenty** ~ más de diez/veinte.
plush [plʌʃ] *adj* de felpa.
plutonium [pluːˈtəunɪəm] *n* plutonio.
ply [plaɪ] *vt* (*a trade*) ejercer ♦ *vi* (*ship*) ir y venir; (*for hire*) ofrecerse (para alquilar); **three** ~ (*wool*) de tres cabos; **to ~ sb with drink** no dejar de ofrecer copas a algn.
plywood [ˈplaɪwud] *n* madera contrachapada.
PM *abbr* (*BRIT*) *see* **Prime Minister**.
p.m. *adv abbr* (= *post meridiem*) de la tarde *or* noche.
PMS *n abbr* (= *premenstrual syndrome*) SPM *m*.
PMT *n abbr* (= *premenstrual tension*) SPM *m*.
pneumatic [njuːˈmætɪk] *adj* neumático.
pneumatic drill *n* taladradora neumática.
pneumonia [njuːˈməunɪə] *n* pulmonía, neumonía.
PO *n abbr* (= *Post Office*) Correos *mpl*; (*NAUT*) = **petty officer**.
po *abbr* = **postal order**.
POA *n abbr* (*BRIT*) = *Prison Officers' Association*.
poach [pəutʃ] *vt* (*cook*) escalfar; (*steal*) cazar/pescar en vedado ♦ *vi* cazar/pescar en vedado.
poached [pəutʃt] *adj* (*egg*) escalfado.
poacher [ˈpəutʃə*] *n* cazador(a) *m/f* furtivo/a.
poaching [ˈpəutʃɪŋ] *n* caza/pesca furtiva.
PO Box *n abbr see* **Post Office Box**.
pocket [ˈpɔkɪt] *n* bolsillo; (*of air, GEO, fig*) bolsa; (*BILLIARDS*) tronera ♦ *vt* meter en el bolsillo; (*steal*) embolsarse; (*BILLIARDS*) entronerar; **breast** ~ bolsillo de pecho; ~ **of resistance** foco de resistencia; ~ **of warm air** bolsa de aire caliente; **to be out of** ~ salir perdiendo; **to be £5 in/out of** ~ salir ganando/perdiendo 5 libras.
pocketbook [ˈpɔkɪtbuk] *n* (*US*: *wallet*) cartera; (: *handbag*) bolso.
pocketful [ˈpɔkɪtful] *n* bolsillo lleno.
pocket knife *n* navaja.
pocket money *n* asignación *f*.
pockmarked [ˈpɔkmɑːkt] *adj* (*face*) picado de viruelas.
pod [pɔd] *n* vaina.
podgy [ˈpɔdʒɪ] *adj* gordinflón/ona.
podiatrist [pɔˈdiːətrɪst] *n* (*US*) podólogo/a.
podiatry [pɔˈdiːətrɪ] *n* (*US*) podología.
podium [ˈpəudɪəm] *n* podio.
POE *n abbr* = *port of embarkation, port of entry*.
poem [ˈpəuɪm] *n* poema *m*.
poet [ˈpəuɪt] *n* poeta *m/f*.
poetic [pəuˈɛtɪk] *adj* poético.
poet laureate [-ˈlɔːrɪɪt] *n* poeta *m* laureado; *ver recuadro*.

> **POET LAUREATE**
>
> *El poeta de la corte, denominado* **Poet Laureate**, *ocupa como tal un puesto vitalicio al servicio de la Casa Real británica. Era tradición que escribiera poemas conmemorativos para ocasiones oficiales, aunque hoy día esto es poco frecuente. El primer poeta así distinguido fue Ben Jonson, en 1616.*

poetry [ˈpəuɪtrɪ] *n* poesía.
poignant [ˈpɔɪnjənt] *adj* conmovedor(a).
poignantly [ˈpɔɪnjəntlɪ] *adv* de modo conmovedor.
point [pɔɪnt] *n* punto; (*tip*) punta; (*purpose*) fin *m*, propósito; (*BRIT ELEC*: *also*: **power** ~) toma de corriente, enchufe *m*; (*use*) utilidad *f*; (*significant part*) lo esencial; (*place*) punto, lugar *m*; (*also*: **decimal** ~): **2 ~ 3 (2.3)** dos coma tres (2,3) ♦ *vt* (*gun etc*): **to ~ sth at sb** apuntar con algo a algn ♦ *vi* señalar con el dedo; **~s** *npl* (*AUT*) contactos *mpl*; (*RAIL*) agujas *fpl*; **to be on the ~ of doing sth** estar a punto de hacer algo; **to make a ~ of doing sth** poner empeño en hacer algo; **to get the ~** comprender; **to come to the ~** ir al meollo; **there's no ~ (in doing)** no tiene sentido (hacer); ~ **of departure** (*also fig*) punto de partida; ~ **of order** cuestión *f* de procedimiento; ~ **of sale** (*COMM*) punto de venta; **~-of-sale advertising** publicidad *f* en el punto de venta; **the train stops at Carlisle and all ~s south** el tren para en Carlisle, y en todas las estaciones al sur; **when it comes to the ~** a la hora de la verdad; **in ~ of fact** en realidad; **that's the whole ~!** ¡de eso se trata!; **to be beside the ~** no venir al caso; **you've got a ~ there!** ¡tienes razón!
►**point out** *vt* señalar.
►**point to** *vt fus* indicar con el dedo; (*fig*) indicar, señalar.
point-blank [ˈpɔɪntˈblæŋk] *adv* (*also*: **at ~ range**) a quemarropa.
pointed [ˈpɔɪntɪd] *adj* (*shape*) puntiagudo, afilado; (*remark*) intencionado.
pointedly [ˈpɔɪntɪdlɪ] *adv* intencionadamente.
pointer [ˈpɔɪntə*] *n* (*stick*) puntero; (*needle*) aguja, indicador *m*; (*clue*) indicación *f*, pista; (*advice*) consejo.
pointless [ˈpɔɪntlɪs] *adj* sin sentido.
pointlessly [ˈpɔɪntlɪslɪ] *adv* inútilmente, sin

motivo.
point of view *n* punto de vista.
poise [pɔɪz] *n* (*of head, body*) porte *m*; (*calmness*) aplomo.
poised [pɔɪzd] *adj* (*in temperament*) sereno.
poison ['pɔɪzn] *n* veneno ♦ *vt* envenenar.
poisoning ['pɔɪznɪŋ] *n* envenenamiento.
poisonous ['pɔɪznəs] *adj* venenoso; (*fumes etc*) tóxico; (*fig: ideas, literature*) pernicioso; (*: rumours, individual*) nefasto.
poke [pəuk] *vt* (*fire*) hurgar, atizar; (*jab with finger, stick etc*) dar; (*COMPUT*) almacenar; (*put*): **to ~ sth in(to)** introducir algo en ♦ *n* (*jab*) empujoncito; (*with elbow*) codazo; **to ~ one's head out of the window** asomar la cabeza por la ventana; **to ~ fun at sb** ridiculizar a algn; **to give the fire a ~** atizar el fuego.
►**poke about** *vi* fisgonear.
poker ['pəukə*] *n* atizador *m*; (*CARDS*) póker *m*.
poker-faced ['pəukə'feɪst] *adj* de cara impasible.
poky ['pəukɪ] *adj* estrecho.
Poland ['pəulənd] *n* Polonia.
polar ['pəulə*] *adj* polar.
polar bear *n* oso polar.
polarization [pəulərаɪ'zeɪʃən] *n* polarización *f*.
polarize ['pəuləraɪz] *vt* polarizar.
Pole [pəul] *n* polaco/a.
pole [pəul] *n* palo; (*GEO*) polo; (*TEL*) poste *m*; (*flag ~*) asta; (*tent ~*) mástil *m*.
poleaxe ['pəulæks] *vt* (*fig*) desnucar.
pole bean *n* (*US*) judía trepadora.
polecat ['pəulkæt] *n* (*BRIT*) turón *m*; (*US*) mofeta.
Pol. Econ. ['pɔlɪkɔn] *n abbr* = *political economy*.
polemic [pɔ'lɛmɪk] *n* polémica.
polemicist [pɔ'lɛmɪsɪst] *n* polemista *m/f*.
pole star *n* estrella polar.
pole vault *n* salto con pértiga.
police [pə'liːs] *n* policía ♦ *vt* (*streets, city, frontier*) vigilar.
police car *n* coche-patrulla *m*.
police constable *n* (*BRIT*) guardia *m*, policía *m*.
police department *n* (*US*) policía.
police force *n* cuerpo de policía.
policeman [pə'liːsmən] *n* guardia *m*, policía *m*, agente *m* (*LAM*).
police officer *n* guardia *m*, policía *m*.
police record *n*: **to have a ~** tener antecedentes penales.
police state *n* estado policial.
police station *n* comisaría.
policewoman [pə'liːswumən] *n* mujer *f* policía.
policy ['pɔlɪsɪ] *n* política; (*also*: **insurance ~**) póliza; (*of newspaper, company*) política; **it is our ~ to do that** tenemos por norma hacer eso; **to take out a ~** sacar una póliza, hacerse un seguro.
policy holder *n* asegurado/a.
policy-making ['pɔlɪsɪmeɪkɪŋ] *n* elaboración *f* de directrices generales; **~ body** organismo encargado de elaborar las directrices generales.
polio ['pəulɪəu] *n* polio *f*.
Polish ['pəulɪʃ] *adj* polaco ♦ *n* (*LING*) polaco.
polish ['pɔlɪʃ] *n* (*for shoes*) betún *m*; (*for floor*) cera (de lustrar); (*for nails*) esmalte *m*; (*shine*) brillo, lustre *m*; (*fig: refinement*) refinamiento ♦ *vt* (*shoes*) limpiar; (*make shiny*) pulir, sacar brillo a; (*fig: improve*) perfeccionar, refinar.
►**polish off** *vt* (*work*) terminar; (*food*) despachar.
►**polish up** *vt* (*shoes, furniture etc*) limpiar, sacar brillo a; (*fig: language*) perfeccionar.
polished ['pɔlɪʃt] *adj* (*fig: person*) refinado.
polite [pə'laɪt] *adj* cortés, atento; (*formal*) correcto; **it's not ~ to do that** es de mala educación hacer eso.
politely [pə'laɪtlɪ] *adv* cortésmente.
politeness [pə'laɪtnɪs] *n* cortesía.
politic ['pɔlɪtɪk] *adj* prudente.
political [pə'lɪtɪkl] *adj* político.
political asylum *n* asilo político.
politically [pə'lɪtɪkəlɪ] *adv* políticamente.
politically correct *adj* políticamente correcto.
politician [pɔlɪ'tɪʃən] *n* político/a.
politics ['pɔlɪtɪks] *n* política.
polka ['pɔlkə] *n* polca.
polka dot *n* lunar *m*.
poll [pəul] *n* (*votes*) votación *f*, votos *mpl*; (*also*: **opinion ~**) sondeo, encuesta ♦ *vt* (*votes*) obtener; (*in opinion ~*) encuestar; **to go to the ~s** (*voters*) votar; (*government*) acudir a las urnas.
pollen ['pɔlən] *n* polen *m*.
pollen count *n* índice *m* de polen.
pollination [pɔlɪ'neɪʃən] *n* polinización *f*.
polling ['pəulɪŋ] *n* (*BRIT POL*) votación *f*; (*TEL*) interrogación *f*.
polling booth *n* cabina de votar.
polling day *n* día *m* de elecciones.
polling station *n* centro electoral.
pollster ['pəulstə*] *n* (*person*) encuestador(a) *m/f*; (*organization*) empresa de encuestas *or* sondeos.
poll tax *n* (*BRIT, formerly*) contribución *f* municipal (*no progresiva*).

pollutant [pə'luːtənt] *n* (agente *m*) contaminante *m*.
pollute [pə'luːt] *vt* contaminar.
pollution [pə'luːʃən] *n* contaminación *f*, polución *f*.
polo ['pəuləu] *n* (*sport*) polo.
polo-neck ['pəuləunɛk] *adj* de cuello vuelto ♦ *n* (*sweater*) suéter *m* de cuello vuelto.
poly ['pɔlɪ] *n abbr* (*BRIT*) = **polytechnic**.
poly... [pɔlɪ] *pref* poli....
poly bag *n* (*BRIT col*) bolsa de plástico.
polyester [pɔlɪ'ɛstə*] *n* poliéster *m*.
polyethylene [pɔlɪ'ɛθɪliːn] *n* (*US*) polietileno.
polygamy [pə'lɪgəmɪ] *n* poligamia.
polygraph ['pɔlɪgrɑːf] *n* polígrafo.
polymath ['pɔlɪmæθ] *n* erudito/a.
Polynesia [pɔlɪ'niːzɪə] *n* Polinesia.
Polynesian [pɔlɪ'niːzɪən] *adj, n* polinesio/a *m/f*.
polyp ['pɔlɪp] *n* (*MED*) pólipo.
polystyrene [pɔlɪ'staɪriːn] *n* poliestireno.
polytechnic [pɔlɪ'tɛknɪk] *n* escuela politécnica.
polythene ['pɔlɪθiːn] *n* (*BRIT*) polietileno.
polythene bag *n* bolsa de plástico.
polyurethane [pɔlɪ'juərɪθeɪn] *n* poliuretano.
pomegranate ['pɔmɪgrænɪt] *n* granada.
pommel ['pɔml] *n* pomo ♦ *vt* = **pummel**.
pomp [pɔmp] *n* pompa.
pompom ['pɔmpɔm] *n* borla.
pompous ['pɔmpəs] *adj* pomposo; (*person*) presumido.
pond [pɔnd] *n* (*natural*) charca; (*artificial*) estanque *m*.
ponder ['pɔndə*] *vt* meditar.
ponderous ['pɔndərəs] *adj* pesado.
pong [pɔŋ] *n* (*BRIT col*) peste *f* ♦ *vi* (*BRIT col*) apestar.
pontiff ['pɔntɪf] *n* pontífice *m*.
pontificate [pɔn'tɪfɪkeɪt] *vi* (*fig*): **to ~ (about)** pontificar (sobre).
pontoon [pɔn'tuːn] *n* pontón *m*; (*BRIT*: *card game*) veintiuna.
pony ['pəunɪ] *n* poney *m*, potro.
ponytail ['pəunɪteɪl] *n* coleta, cola de caballo.
pony trekking *n* (*BRIT*) excursión *f* a caballo.
poodle ['puːdl] *n* caniche *m*.
pooh-pooh [puː'puː] *vt* desdeñar.
pool [puːl] *n* (*natural*) charca; (*pond*) estanque *m*; (*also*: **swimming ~**) piscina, alberca (*LAM*); (*billiards*) billar *m* americano; (*COMM*: *consortium*) consorcio; (: *US*: *monopoly trust*) trust *m* ♦ *vt* juntar; **typing ~** servicio de mecanografía; **(football) ~s** *npl* quinielas *fpl*.
poor [puə*] *adj* pobre; (*bad*) malo ♦ *npl*: **the ~** los pobres.
poorly ['puəlɪ] *adj* mal, enfermo.
pop [pɔp] *n* ¡pum!; (*sound*) ruido seco; (*MUS*) (música) pop *m*; (*US col*: *father*) papá *m*; (*col*: *drink*) gaseosa ♦ *vt* (*burst*) hacer reventar ♦ *vi* reventar; (*cork*) saltar; **she ~ped her head out (of the window)** sacó de repente la cabeza (por la ventana).
►**pop in** *vi* entrar un momento.
►**pop out** *vi* salir un momento.
►**pop up** *vi* aparecer inesperadamente.
pop concert *n* concierto pop.
popcorn ['pɔpkɔːn] *n* palomitas *fpl* (de maíz).
pope [pəup] *n* papa *m*.
poplar ['pɔplə*] *n* álamo.
poplin ['pɔplɪn] *n* popelina.
popper ['pɔpə*] *n* corchete *m*, botón *m* automático.
poppy ['pɔpɪ] *n* amapola; *see also* **Remembrance Sunday**.
poppycock ['pɔpɪkɔk] *n* (*col*) tonterías *fpl*.
Popsicle ® ['pɔpsɪkl] *n* (*US*) polo.
populace ['pɔpjuləs] *n* pueblo.
popular ['pɔpjulə*] *adj* popular; **a ~ song** una canción popular; **to be ~ (with)** (*person*) caer bien (a); (*decision*) ser popular (entre).
popularity [pɔpju'lærɪtɪ] *n* popularidad *f*.
popularize ['pɔpjuləraɪz] *vt* popularizar; (*disseminate*) vulgarizar.
populate ['pɔpjuleɪt] *vt* poblar.
population [pɔpju'leɪʃən] *n* población *f*.
population explosion *n* explosión *f* demográfica.
populous ['pɔpjuləs] *adj* populoso.
porcelain ['pɔːslɪn] *n* porcelana.
porch [pɔːtʃ] *n* pórtico, entrada.
porcupine ['pɔːkjupaɪn] *n* puerco *m* espín.
pore [pɔː*] *n* poro ♦ *vi*: **to ~ over** enfrascarse en.
pork [pɔːk] *n* (carne *f* de) cerdo *or* chancho (*LAM*).
pork chop *n* chuleta de cerdo.
porn [pɔːn] *adj* (*col*) porno *inv* ♦ *n* porno.
pornographic [pɔːnə'græfɪk] *adj* pornográfico.
pornography [pɔː'nɔgrəfɪ] *n* pornografía.
porous ['pɔːrəs] *adj* poroso.
porpoise ['pɔːpəs] *n* marsopa.
porridge ['pɔrɪdʒ] *n* gachas *fpl* de avena.
port [pɔːt] *n* (*harbour*) puerto; (*NAUT*: *left side*) babor *m*; (*wine*) oporto; (*COMPUT*) puerta, puerto, port *m*; **~ of call** puerto de

escala.
portable ['pɔːtəbl] *adj* portátil.
portal ['pɔːtl] *n* puerta (grande), portalón *m.*
port authorities *npl* autoridades *fpl* portuarias.
portcullis [pɔːt'kʌlɪs] *n* rastrillo.
portend [pɔː'tɛnd] *vt* presagiar, anunciar.
portent ['pɔːtɛnt] *n* presagio, augurio.
porter ['pɔːtə*] *n* (*for luggage*) maletero; (*doorkeeper*) portero/a, conserje *m/f*; (*US RAIL*) mozo de los coches-cama.
portfolio [pɔːt'fəulɪəu] *n* (*case, of artist*) cartera, carpeta; (*POL, FINANCE*) cartera.
porthole ['pɔːthəul] *n* portilla.
portico ['pɔːtɪkəu] *n* pórtico.
portion ['pɔːʃən] *n* porción *f*; (*helping*) ración *f.*
portly ['pɔːtlɪ] *adj* corpulento.
portrait ['pɔːtreɪt] *n* retrato.
portray [pɔː'treɪ] *vt* retratar; (*in writing*) representar.
portrayal [pɔː'treɪəl] *n* representación *f.*
Portugal ['pɔːtjugl] *n* Portugal *m.*
Portuguese [pɔːtju'giːz] *adj* portugués/esa ♦ *n, pl inv* portugués/esa *m/f*; (*LING*) portugués *m.*
Portuguese man-of-war [-mænəu'wɔː*] *n* (*jellyfish*) *especie de medusa.*
pose [pəuz] *n* postura, actitud *f*; (*pej*) afectación *f*, pose *f* ♦ *vi* posar; (*pretend*): **to ~ as** hacerse pasar por ♦ *vt* (*question*) plantear; **to strike a ~** tomar *or* adoptar una pose *or* actitud.
poser ['pəuzə*] *n* problema *m*/pregunta difícil; (*person*) = **poseur**.
poseur [pəu'zəː*] *n* presumido/a, persona afectada.
posh [pɔʃ] *adj* (*col*) elegante, de lujo ♦ *adv* (*col*): **to talk ~** hablar con acento afectado.
position [pə'zɪʃən] *n* posición *f*; (*job*) puesto ♦ *vt* colocar; **to be in a ~ to do sth** estar en condiciones de hacer algo.
positive ['pɔzɪtɪv] *adj* positivo; (*certain*) seguro; (*definite*) definitivo; **we look forward to a ~ reply** (*COMM*) esperamos que pueda darnos una respuesta en firme; **he's a ~ nuisance** es un auténtico pelmazo; **~ cash flow** (*COMM*) flujo positivo de efectivo.
positively ['pɔzɪtɪvlɪ] *adv* (*affirmatively, enthusiastically*) de forma positiva; (*col: really*) absolutamente.
posse ['pɔsɪ] *n* (*US*) pelotón *m.*
possess [pə'zɛs] *vt* poseer; **like one ~ed** como un poseído; **whatever can have ~ed you?** ¿cómo se te ocurrió?
possessed [pə'zɛst] *adj* poseso, poseído.
possession [pə'zɛʃən] *n* posesión *f*; **to take ~ of sth** tomar posesión de algo.
possessive [pə'zɛsɪv] *adj* posesivo.
possessiveness [pə'zɛsɪvnɪs] *n* posesividad *f.*
possessor [pə'zɛsə*] *n* poseedor(a) *m/f*, dueño/a.
possibility [pɔsɪ'bɪlɪtɪ] *n* posibilidad *f*; **he's a ~ for the part** es uno de los posibles para el papel.
possible ['pɔsɪbl] *adj* posible; **as big as ~** lo más grande posible; **it is ~ to do it** es posible hacerlo; **as far as ~** en la medida de lo posible; **a ~ candidate** un(a) posible candidato/a.
possibly ['pɔsɪblɪ] *adv* (*perhaps*) posiblemente, tal vez; **I cannot ~ come** me es imposible venir; **could you ~ ...?** ¿podrías ...?
post [pəust] *n* (*BRIT: letters, delivery*) correo; (*job, situation*) puesto; (*trading ~*) factoría; (*pole*) poste *m* ♦ *vt* (*BRIT: send by ~*) mandar por correo; (*: put in mailbox*) echar al correo; (*MIL*) apostar; (*bills*) fijar, pegar; (*BRIT: appoint*): **to ~ to** destinar a; **by ~** por correo; **by return of ~** a vuelta de correo; **to keep sb ~ed** tener a algn al corriente.
post ... [pəust] *pref* post..., pos...; **~ 1950** pos(t) 1950.
postage ['pəustɪdʒ] *n* porte *m*, franqueo.
postage stamp *n* sello (de correo).
postal ['pəustl] *adj* postal, de correos.
postal order *n* giro postal.
postbag ['pəustbæg] *n* (*BRIT*) correspondencia, cartas *fpl.*
postbox ['pəustbɔks] *n* (*BRIT*) buzón *m.*
postcard ['pəustkaːd] *nf* (tarjeta) postal *f.*
postcode ['pəustkəud] *n* (*BRIT*) código postal.
postdate [pəust'deɪt] *vt* (*cheque*) poner fecha adelantada a.
poster ['pəustə*] *n* cartel *m*, afiche *m* (*LAM*).
poste restante [pəust'rɛstɔ̃nt] *n* (*BRIT*) lista de correos.
posterior [pɔs'tɪərɪə*] *n* (*col*) trasero.
posterity [pɔs'tɛrɪtɪ] *n* posteridad *f.*
poster paint *n* pintura al agua.
post-free [pəust'friː] *adj* (con) porte pagado.
postgraduate ['pəust'grædjuɪt] *n* posgraduado/a.
posthumous ['pɔstjuməs] *adj* póstumo.
posthumously ['pɔstjuməslɪ] *adv* póstumamente, con carácter póstumo.
posting ['pəustɪŋ] *n* destino.
postman ['pəustmən] *n* cartero.

postmark ['pəustmɑːk] *n* matasellos *m inv.*
postmaster ['pəustmɑːstə*] *n* administrador *m* de correos.
Postmaster General *n* director *m* general de correos.
postmistress ['pəustmɪstrɪs] *n* administradora de correos.
post-mortem [pəust'mɔːtəm] *n* autopsia.
postnatal ['pəust'neɪtl] *adj* postnatal, postparto.
post office *n* (*building*) (oficina de) correos *m*; (*organization*): **the P~ O~** Administración *f* General de Correos.
Post Office Box (PO Box) *n* apartado postal, casilla de correos (*LAM*).
post-paid ['pəust'peɪd] *adj* porte pagado.
postpone [pəs'pəun] *vt* aplazar, postergar (*LAM*).
postponement [pəs'pəunmənt] *n* aplazamiento.
postscript ['pəustskrɪpt] *n* posdata.
postulate ['pɔstjuleɪt] *vt* postular.
posture ['pɔstʃə*] *n* postura, actitud *f.*
postwar [pəust'wɔː*] *adj* de la posguerra.
posy ['pəuzɪ] *n* ramillete *m* (de flores).
pot [pɔt] *n* (*for cooking*) olla; (*for flowers*) maceta; (*for jam*) tarro, pote *m* (*LAM*); (*piece of pottery*) cacharro; (*col: marijuana*) costo ♦ *vt* (*plant*) poner en tiesto; (*conserve*) conservar (en tarros); **~s of** (*col*) montones de; **to go to ~** (*col: work, performance*) irse al traste.
potash ['pɔtæʃ] *n* potasa.
potassium [pə'tæsɪəm] *n* potasio.
potato, ~es [pə'teɪtəu] *n* patata, papa (*LAM*).
potato crisps, (*US*) **potato chips** *npl* patatas *fpl or* papas *fpl* (*LAM*) fritas.
potato peeler *n* pelapatatas *m inv.*
potbellied ['pɔtbɛlɪd] *adj* (*from overeating*) barrigón/ona; (*from malnutrition*) con el vientre hinchado.
potency ['pəutnsɪ] *n* potencia.
potent ['pəutnt] *adj* potente, poderoso; (*drink*) fuerte.
potentate ['pəutnteɪt] potentado.
potential [pə'tɛnʃl] *adj* potencial, posible ♦ *n* potencial *m*; **to have ~** prometer.
potentially [pə'tɛnʃəlɪ] *adv* en potencia.
pothole ['pɔthəul] *n* (*in road*) bache *m*; (*BRIT: underground*) gruta.
potholer ['pɔthəulə*] *n* (*BRIT*) espeleólogo/a.
potholing ['pɔthəulɪŋ] *n* (*BRIT*): **to go ~** dedicarse a la espeleología.
potion ['pəuʃən] *n* poción *f*, pócima.
potluck [pɔt'lʌk] *n*: **to take ~** conformarse con lo que haya.
pot roast *n* carne *f* asada.
potshot ['pɔtʃɔt] *n*: **to take a ~ at sth** tirar a algo sin apuntar.
potted ['pɔtɪd] *adj* (*food*) en conserva; (*plant*) en tiesto *or* maceta; (*fig: shortened*) resumido.
potter ['pɔtə*] *n* alfarero/a ♦ *vi*: **to ~ around, ~ about** entretenerse haciendo cosillas; **to ~ round the house** estar en casa haciendo cosillas; **~'s wheel** torno de alfarero.
pottery ['pɔtərɪ] *n* cerámica, alfarería; **a piece of ~** un objeto de cerámica.
potty ['pɔtɪ] *adj* (*col: mad*) chiflado ♦ *n* orinal *m* de niño.
potty-trained ['pɔtɪtreɪnd] *adj* que ya no necesita pañales.
pouch [pautʃ] *n* (*ZOOL*) bolsa; (*for tobacco*) petaca.
pouf(fe) [puːf] *n* (*stool*) pouf *m.*
poultry ['pəultrɪ] *n* aves *fpl* de corral; (*dead*) pollos *mpl.*
poultry farm *n* granja avícola.
poultry farmer *n* avicultor(a) *m/f.*
pounce [pauns] *vi*: **to ~ on** precipitarse sobre ♦ *n* salto, ataque *m.*
pound [paund] *n* libra; (*for dogs*) perrera; (*for cars*) depósito ♦ *vt* (*beat*) golpear; (*crush*) machacar ♦ *vi* (*beat*) dar golpes; **half a ~** media libra; **a one ~ note** un billete de una libra.
pounding ['paundɪŋ] *n*: **to take a ~** (*team*) recibir una paliza.
pound sterling *n* libra esterlina.
pour [pɔː*] *vt* echar; (*tea*) servir ♦ *vi* correr, fluir; (*rain*) llover a cántaros.
►**pour away, pour off** *vt* vaciar, verter.
►**pour in** *vi* (*people*) entrar en tropel; **to come ~ing in** (*water*) entrar a raudales; (*letters*) llegar a montones; (*cars, people*) llegar en tropel.
►**pour out** *vi* (*people*) salir en tropel ♦ *vt* (*drink*) echar, servir.
pouring ['pɔːrɪŋ] *adj*: **~ rain** lluvia torrencial.
pout [paut] *vi* hacer pucheros.
poverty ['pɔvətɪ] *n* pobreza, miseria; (*fig*) falta, escasez *f.*
poverty line *n*: **below the ~** por debajo del umbral de pobreza.
poverty-stricken ['pɔvətɪstrɪkn] *adj* necesitado.
poverty trap *n* trampa de la pobreza.
POW *n abbr* = **prisoner of war.**
powder ['paudə*] *n* polvo; (*face ~*) polvos *mpl*; (*gun~*) pólvora ♦ *vt* empolvar; **to ~ one's face** ponerse polvos; **to ~ one's nose** empolvarse la nariz, ponerse

polvos; (*euphemism*) ir al baño.
powder compact *n* polvera.
powdered milk ['paudəd-] *n* leche *f* en polvo.
powder keg *n* (*fig*) polvorín *m*.
powder puff *n* borla (para empolvarse).
powder room *n* aseos *mpl*.
powdery ['paudərɪ] *adj* polvoriento.
power ['pauə*] *n* poder *m*; (*strength*) fuerza; (*nation*) potencia; (*drive*) empuje *m*; (*TECH*) potencia; (*ELEC*) energía ♦ *vt* impulsar; **to be in ~** (*POL*) estar en el poder; **to do all in one's ~ to help sb** hacer todo lo posible por ayudar a algn; **the world ~s** las potencias mundiales.
powerboat ['pauəbəut] *n* lancha a motor.
power cut *n* (*BRIT*) apagón *m*.
powered ['pauəd] *adj*: **~ by** impulsado por; **nuclear-~ submarine** submarino nuclear.
power failure *n* = **power cut**.
powerful ['pauəful] *adj* poderoso; (*engine*) potente; (*strong*) fuerte; (*play, speech*) conmovedor(a).
powerhouse ['pauəhaus] *n* (*fig: person*) fuerza motriz; **a ~ of ideas** una cantera de ideas.
powerless ['pauəlɪs] *adj* impotente, ineficaz.
power line *n* línea de conducción eléctrica.
power of attorney *n* poder *m*, procuración *f*.
power point *n* (*BRIT*) enchufe *m*.
power station *n* central *f* eléctrica.
power steering *n* (*AUT*) dirección *f* asistida.
powwow ['pauwau] *n* conferencia ♦ *vi* conferenciar.
pp *abbr* (= *per procurationem: by proxy*) p.p.
PPE *n abbr* (*BRIT SCOL*) = *philosophy, politics and economics*.
PPS *abbr* (= *post postscriptum*) *posdata adicional*; (*BRIT*: = *Parliamentary Private Secretary*) *ayudante de un ministro*.
PQ *abbr* (*Canada*) = *Province of Quebec*.
PR *n abbr see* **proportional representation**; (= *public relations*) relaciones *fpl* públicas ♦ *abbr* (*US*) = *Puerto Rico*.
Pr. *abbr* (= *prince*) P.
practicability [præktɪkə'bɪlɪtɪ] *n* factibilidad *f*.
practicable ['præktɪkəbl] *adj* (*scheme*) factible.
practical ['præktɪkl] *adj* práctico.
practicality [præktɪ'kælɪtɪ] *n* (*of situation etc*) aspecto práctico.
practical joke *n* broma pesada.
practically ['præktɪklɪ] *adv* (*almost*) casi, prácticamente.
practice ['præktɪs] *n* (*habit*) costumbre *f*; (*exercise*) práctica; (*training*) adiestramiento; (*MED*) clientela ♦ *vt, vi* (*US*) = **practise**; **in ~** (*in reality*) en la práctica; **out of ~** desentrenado; **to put sth into ~** poner algo en práctica; **it's common ~** es bastante corriente; **target ~** práctica de tiro; **he has a small ~** (*doctor*) tiene pocos pacientes; **to set up in ~ as** establecerse como.
practise, (*US*) **practice** ['præktɪs] *vt* (*carry out*) practicar; (*profession*) ejercer; (*train at*) practicar ♦ *vi* ejercer; (*train*) practicar.
practised, (*US*) **practiced** ['præktɪst] *adj* (*person*) experto; (*performance*) bien ensayado; (*liar*) consumado; **with a ~ eye** con ojo experto.
practising, (*US*) **practicing** ['præktɪsɪŋ] *adj* (*Christian etc*) practicante; (*lawyer*) que ejerce; (*homosexual*) activo.
practitioner [præk'tɪʃənə*] *n* practicante *m/f*; (*MED*) médico/a.
pragmatic [præg'mætɪk] *adj* pragmático.
pragmatism ['prægmətɪzəm] *n* pragmatismo.
pragmatist ['prægmətɪst] *n* pragmatista *m/f*.
Prague [prɑːg] *n* Praga.
prairie ['prɛərɪ] *n* (*US*) pampa.
praise [preɪz] *n* alabanza(s) *f*(*pl*), elogio(s) *m*(*pl*).
praiseworthy ['preɪswəːðɪ] *adj* loable.
pram [præm] *n* (*BRIT*) cochecito de niño.
prance [prɑːns] *vi* (*horse*) hacer cabriolas.
prank [præŋk] *n* travesura.
prat [præt] *n* (*BRIT col*) imbécil *m/f*.
prattle ['prætl] *vi* parlotear; (*child*) balbucear.
prawn [prɔːn] *n* gamba.
pray [preɪ] *vi* rezar; **to ~ for forgiveness** pedir perdón.
prayer [prɛə*] *n* oración *f*, rezo; (*entreaty*) ruego, súplica.
prayer book *n* devocionario, misal *m*.
pre- ['priː] *pref* pre..., ante-; **~1970** pre 1970.
preach [priːtʃ] *vi* predicar.
preacher ['priːtʃə*] *n* predicador(a) *m/f*; (*US: minister*) pastor(a) *m/f*.
preamble [prɪ'æmbl] *n* preámbulo.
prearrange [priːə'reɪndʒ] *vt* organizar *or* acordar de antemano.
prearrangement [priːə'reɪndʒmənt] *n*: **by ~** por previo acuerdo.
precarious [prɪ'kɛərɪəs] *adj* precario.
precariously [prɪ'kɛərɪəslɪ] *adv* precariamente.
precaution [prɪ'kɔːʃən] *n* precaución *f*.

precautionary [prɪ'kɔːʃənrɪ] *adj* (*measure*) de precaución.
precede [prɪ'siːd] *vt, vi* preceder.
precedence ['prɛsɪdəns] *n* precedencia; (*priority*) preferencia.
precedent ['prɛsɪdənt] *n* precedente *m;* **to establish** *or* **set a ~** sentar un precedente.
preceding [prɪ'siːdɪŋ] *adj* precedente.
precept ['priːsɛpt] *n* precepto.
precinct ['priːsɪŋkt] *n* recinto; (*US: district*) distrito, barrio; **~s** *npl* recinto; **pedestrian ~** (*BRIT*) zona peatonal; **shopping ~** (*BRIT*) centro comercial.
precious ['prɛʃəs] *adj* precioso; (*treasured*) querido; (*stylized*) afectado ♦ *adv* (*col*): **~ little/few** muy poco/pocos; **your ~ dog** (*ironic*) tu querido perro.
precipice ['prɛsɪpɪs] *n* precipicio.
precipitate *adj* [prɪ'sɪpɪtɪt] (*hasty*) precipitado ♦ *vt* [prɪ'sɪpɪteɪt] precipitar.
precipitation [prɪsɪpɪ'teɪʃən] *n* precipitación *f.*
precipitous [prɪ'sɪpɪtəs] *adj* (*steep*) escarpado; (*hasty*) precipitado.
précis ['preɪsiː] *n* resumen *m.*
precise [prɪ'saɪs] *adj* preciso, exacto; (*person*) escrupuloso.
precisely [prɪ'saɪslɪ] *adv* exactamente, precisamente.
precision [prɪ'sɪʒən] *n* precisión *f.*
preclude [prɪ'kluːd] *vt* excluir.
precocious [prɪ'kəuʃəs] *adj* precoz.
preconceived [priːkən'siːvd] *adj* (*idea*) preconcebido.
preconception [priːkən'sɛpʃən] *n* (*idea*) idea preconcebida.
precondition [priːkən'dɪʃən] *n* condición *f* previa.
precursor [priː'kəːsə*] *n* precursor(a) *m/f.*
predate ['priː'deɪt] *vt* (*precede*) preceder.
predator ['prɛdətə*] *n* depredador *m.*
predatory ['prɛdətərɪ] *adj* depredador(a).
predecessor ['priːdɪsɛsə*] *n* antecesor(a) *m/f.*
predestination [priːdɛstɪ'neɪʃən] *n* predestinación *f.*
predestine [priː'dɛstɪn] *vt* predestinar.
predetermine [priːdɪ'təːmɪn] *vt* predeterminar.
predicament [prɪ'dɪkəmənt] *n* apuro.
predicate ['prɛdɪkɪt] *n* predicado.
predict [prɪ'dɪkt] *vt* predecir, pronosticar.
predictable [prɪ'dɪktəbl] *adj* previsible.
predictably [prɪ'dɪktəblɪ] *adv* (*behave, react*) de forma previsible; **~ she didn't arrive** como era de prever, no llegó.
prediction [prɪ'dɪkʃən] *n* pronóstico, predicción *f.*
predispose ['priːdɪs'pəuz] *vt* predisponer.
predominance [prɪ'dɔmɪnəns] *n* predominio.
predominant [prɪ'dɔmɪnənt] *adj* predominante.
predominantly [prɪ'dɔmɪnəntlɪ] *adv* en su mayoría.
predominate [prɪ'dɔmɪneɪt] *vi* predominar.
pre-eminent [priː'ɛmɪnənt] *adj* preeminente.
pre-empt [priː'ɛmt] *vt* (*BRIT*) adelantarse a.
pre-emptive [priː'ɛmtɪv] *adj*: **~ strike** ataque *m* preventivo.
preen [priːn] *vt*: **to ~ itself** (*bird*) limpiarse las plumas; **to ~ o.s.** pavonearse.
prefab ['priːfæb] *n* casa prefabricada.
prefabricated [priː'fæbrɪkeɪtɪd] *adj* prefabricado.
preface ['prɛfəs] *n* prefacio.
prefect ['priːfɛkt] *n* (*BRIT: in school*) monitor(a) *m/f.*
prefer [prɪ'fəː*] *vt* preferir; (*LAW: charges, complaint*) presentar; (*: action*) entablar; **to ~ coffee to tea** preferir el café al té.
preferable ['prɛfrəbl] *adj* preferible.
preferably ['prɛfrəblɪ] *adv* preferentemente, más bien.
preference ['prɛfrəns] *n* preferencia; **in ~ to sth** antes que algo.
preference shares *npl* acciones *fpl* privilegiadas.
preferential [prɛfə'rɛnʃəl] *adj* preferente.
prefix ['priːfɪks] *n* prefijo.
pregnancy ['prɛgnənsɪ] *n* embarazo.
pregnancy test *n* prueba del embarazo.
pregnant ['prɛgnənt] *adj* embarazada; **3 months ~** embarazada de tres meses; **~ with meaning** cargado de significado.
prehistoric ['priːhɪs'tɔrɪk] *adj* prehistórico.
prehistory [priː'hɪstərɪ] *n* prehistoria.
prejudge [priː'dʒʌdʒ] *vt* prejuzgar.
prejudice ['prɛdʒudɪs] *n* (*bias*) prejuicio; (*harm*) perjuicio ♦ *vt* (*bias*) predisponer; (*harm*) perjudicar; **to ~ sb in favour of/against** (*bias*) predisponer a algn a favor de/en contra de.
prejudiced ['prɛdʒudɪst] *adj* (*person*) predispuesto; (*view*) parcial, interesado; **to be ~ against sb/sth** estar predispuesto en contra de algn/algo.
prelate ['prɛlət] *n* prelado.
preliminaries [prɪ'lɪmɪnərɪz] *npl* preliminares *mpl*, preparativos *mpl.*
preliminary [prɪ'lɪmɪnərɪ] *adj* preliminar.
prelude ['prɛljuːd] *n* preludio.
premarital ['priː'mærɪtl] *adj* prematrimonial, premarital.

premature ['prɛmətʃuə*] *adj* (*arrival etc*) prematuro; **you are being a little ~** te has adelantado.
prematurely [prɛmə'tʃuəlɪ] *adv* prematuramente, antes de tiempo.
premeditate [priː'mɛdɪteɪt] *vt* premeditar.
premeditated [priː'mɛdɪteɪtɪd] *adj* premeditado.
premeditation [priːmɛdɪ'teɪʃən] *n* premeditación *f*.
premenstrual [priː'mɛnstruəl] *adj* premenstrual.
premenstrual tension *n* (*MED*) tensión *f* premenstrual.
premier ['prɛmɪə*] *adj* primero, principal ♦ *n* (*POL*) primer(a) ministro/a.
première ['prɛmɪɛə*] *n* estreno.
premise ['prɛmɪs] *n* premisa.
premises ['prɛmɪsɪs] *npl* local *msg*; **on the ~** en el lugar mismo; **business ~** locales *mpl* comerciales.
premium ['priːmɪəm] *n* prima; **to be at a ~** estar muy solicitado; **to sell at a ~** (*shares*) vender caro.
premium bond *n* (*BRIT*) *bono del estado que participa en una lotería nacional*.
premium deal *n* (*COMM*) oferta extraordinaria.
premium gasoline *n* (*US*) (gasolina) súper *m*.
premonition [prɛmə'nɪʃən] *n* presentimiento.
preoccupation [priːɔkju'peɪʃən] *n* preocupación *f*.
preoccupied [priː'ɔkjupaɪd] *adj* (*worried*) preocupado; (*absorbed*) ensimismado.
prep [prɛp] *adj abbr*: **~ school = preparatory school** ♦ *n abbr* (*SCOL*: = *preparation*) deberes *mpl*.
prepaid [priː'peɪd] *adj* porte pagado; **~ envelope** sobre *m* de porte pagado.
preparation [prɛpə'reɪʃən] *n* preparación *f*; **~s** *npl* preparativos *mpl*; **in ~ for sth** en preparación para algo.
preparatory [prɪ'pærətərɪ] *adj* preparatorio, preliminar; **~ to sth/to doing sth** como preparación para algo/para hacer algo.
preparatory school *n* (*BRIT*) *colegio privado de enseñanza primaria*; (*US*) *colegio privado de enseñanza secundaria*; *see also* **public school**.
prepare [prɪ'pɛə*] *vt* preparar, disponer ♦ *vi*: **to ~ for** prepararse *or* disponerse para; (*make preparations*) hacer preparativos para.
prepared [prɪ'pɛəd] *adj* (*willing*): **to be ~ to help sb** estar dispuesto a ayudar a algn.
preponderance [prɪ'pɔndərns] *n* preponderancia, predominio.
preposition [prɛpə'zɪʃən] *n* preposición *f*.
prepossessing [priːpə'zɛsɪŋ] *adj* agradable, atractivo.
preposterous [prɪ'pɔstərəs] *adj* absurdo, ridículo.
prerecorded ['priːrɪ'kɔːdɪd] *adj*: **~ broadcast** programa *m* grabado de antemano; **~ cassette** cassette *f* pregrabada.
prerequisite [priː'rɛkwɪzɪt] *n* requisito previo.
prerogative [prɪ'rɔgətɪv] *n* prerrogativa.
Presbyterian [prɛzbɪ'tɪərɪən] *adj, n* presbiteriano/a *m/f*.
presbytery ['prɛzbɪtərɪ] *n* casa parroquial.
preschool ['priː'skuːl] *adj* (*child, age*) preescolar.
prescribe [prɪ'skraɪb] *vt* prescribir; (*MED*) recetar; **~d books** (*BRIT SCOL*) libros *mpl* del curso.
prescription [prɪ'skrɪpʃən] *n* (*MED*) receta; **to make up** *or* (*US*) **fill a ~** preparar una receta; **only available on ~** se vende solamente con receta (médica).
prescription charges *npl* (*BRIT*) precio *sg* de las recetas.
prescriptive [prɪ'skrɪptɪv] *adj* normativo.
presence ['prɛzns] *n* presencia; (*attendance*) asistencia.
presence of mind *n* aplomo.
present *adj* ['prɛznt] (*in attendance*) presente; (*current*) actual ♦ *n* (*gift*) regalo; (*actuality*) actualidad *f*, presente *m* ♦ *vt* [prɪ'zɛnt] (*introduce*) presentar; (*expound*) exponer; (*give*) presentar, dar, ofrecer; (*THEAT*) representar; **to be ~ at** asistir a, estar presente en; **those ~** los presentes; **to give sb a ~, make sb a ~ of sth** regalar algo a algn; **at ~** actualmente; **to ~ o.s. for an interview** presentarse a una entrevista; **may I ~ Miss Clark** permítame presentarle *or* le presento a la Srta Clark.
presentable [prɪ'zɛntəbl] *adj*: **to make o.s. ~** arreglarse.
presentation [prɛzn'teɪʃən] *n* presentación *f*; (*gift*) obsequio; (*of case*) exposición *f*; (*THEAT*) representación *f*; **on ~ of the**

voucher al presentar el vale.
present-day ['prɛzntdeɪ] *adj* actual.
presenter [prɪ'zɛntə*] *n* (*RADIO, TV*) locutor(a) *m/f*.
presently ['prɛzntlɪ] *adv* (*soon*) dentro de poco; (*US: now*) ahora.
present participle *n* participio (de) presente.
present tense *n* (tiempo) presente *m*.
preservation [prɛzə'veɪʃən] *n* conservación *f*.
preservative [prɪ'zə:vətɪv] *n* conservante *m*.
preserve [prɪ'zə:v] *vt* (*keep safe*) preservar, proteger; (*maintain*) mantener; (*food*) conservar; (*in salt*) salar ♦ *n* (*for game*) coto, vedado; (*often pl: jam*) confitura.
preshrunk [pri:'ʃrʌŋk] *adj* inencogible.
preside [prɪ'zaɪd] *vi* presidir.
presidency ['prɛzɪdənsɪ] *n* presidencia.
president ['prɛzɪdənt] *n* presidente *m/f*; (*US: of company*) director(a) *m/f*.
presidential [prɛzɪ'dɛnʃl] *adj* presidencial.
press [prɛs] *n* (*tool, machine, newspapers*) prensa; (*printer's*) imprenta; (*of hand*) apretón *m* ♦ *vt* (*push*) empujar; (*squeeze*) apretar; (*grapes*) pisar; (*clothes: iron*) planchar; (*pressure*) presionar; (*doorbell*) apretar, pulsar, tocar; (*insist*): **to ~ sth on sb** insistir en que algn acepte algo ♦ *vi* (*squeeze*) apretar; (*pressurize*) ejercer presión; **to go to ~** (*newspaper*) entrar en prensa; **to be in the ~** (*being printed*) estar en prensa; (*in the newspapers*) aparecer en la prensa; **we are ~ed for time** tenemos poco tiempo; **to ~ sb to do** *or* **into doing sth** (*urge, entreat*) presionar a algn para que haga algo; **to ~ sb for an answer** insistir a algn para que conteste; **to ~ charges against sb** (*LAW*) demandar a algn.
▸**press ahead** *vi* seguir adelante.
▸**press on** *vi* avanzar; (*hurry*) apretar el paso.
press agency *n* agencia de prensa.
press clipping *n* = **press cutting**.
press conference *n* rueda de prensa.
press cutting *n* recorte *m* (de periódico).
pressing ['prɛsɪŋ] *adj* apremiante.
pressman ['prɛsmæn] *n* periodista *m*.
press officer *n* jefe/a *m/f* de prensa.
press release *n* comunicado de prensa.
press stud *n* (*BRIT*) botón *m* de presión.
press-up ['prɛsʌp] *n* (*BRIT*) flexión *f*.
pressure ['prɛʃə*] *n* presión *f*; (*urgency*) apremio, urgencia; (*influence*) influencia; **high/low ~** alta/baja presión; **to put ~ on sb** presionar a algn, hacer presión sobre algn.
pressure cooker *n* olla a presión.
pressure gauge *n* manómetro.
pressure group *n* grupo de presión.
pressurize ['prɛʃəraɪz] *vt* presurizar; **to ~ sb (into doing sth)** presionar a algn (para que haga algo).
pressurized ['prɛʃəraɪzd] *adj* (*container*) a presión.
Prestel ® ['prɛstɛl] *n* videotex *m*.
prestige [prɛs'ti:ʒ] *n* prestigio.
prestigious [prɛs'tɪdʒəs] *adj* prestigioso.
presumably [prɪ'zju:məblɪ] *adv* es de suponer que, cabe presumir que; **~ he did it** es de suponer que lo hizo él.
presume [prɪ'zju:m] *vt* suponer, presumir; **to ~ to do** (*dare*) atreverse a hacer.
presumption [prɪ'zʌmpʃən] *n* suposición *f*; (*pretension*) presunción *f*.
presumptuous [prɪ'zʌmptjuəs] *adj* presumido.
presuppose [pri:sə'pəuz] *vt* presuponer.
presupposition [pri:sʌpə'zɪʃən] *n* presuposición *f*.
pre-tax [pri:'tæks] *adj* anterior al impuesto.
pretence, (*US*) **pretense** [prɪ'tɛns] *n* (*claim*) pretensión *f*; (*pretext*) pretexto; (*make-believe*) fingimiento; **on** *or* **under the ~ of doing sth** bajo *or* con el pretexto de hacer algo; **she is devoid of all ~** no es pretenciosa.
pretend [prɪ'tɛnd] *vt* (*feign*) fingir ♦ *vi* (*feign*) fingir; (*claim*): **to ~ to sth** pretender a algo.
pretense [prɪ'tɛns] *n* (*US*) = **pretence**.
pretension [pri'tɛnʃən] *n* (*claim*) pretensión *f*; **to have no ~s to sth/to being sth** no engañarse en cuanto a algo/a ser algo.
pretentious [prɪ'tɛnʃəs] *adj* pretencioso.
pretext ['pri:tɛkst] *n* pretexto; **on** *or* **under the ~ of doing sth** con el pretexto de hacer algo.
prettily ['prɪtɪlɪ] *adv* encantadoramente, con gracia.
pretty ['prɪtɪ] *adj* (*gen*) bonito, lindo (*LAM*) ♦ *adv* bastante.
prevail [prɪ'veɪl] *vi* (*gain mastery*) prevalecer; (*be current*) predominar; (*persuade*): **to ~ (up)on sb to do sth** persuadir a algn para que haga algo.
prevailing [prɪ'veɪlɪŋ] *adj* (*dominant*) predominante.
prevalent ['prɛvələnt] *adj* (*dominant*) dominante; (*widespread*) extendido; (*fashionable*) de moda.
prevarication [prɪværɪ'keɪʃən] *n* evasivas *fpl*.
prevent [prɪ'vɛnt] *vt*: **to ~ (sb) from doing**

sth impedir (a algn) hacer algo.
preventable [prɪ'vɛntəbl] *adj* evitable.
preventative [prɪ'vɛntətɪv] *adj* preventivo.
prevention [prɪ'vɛnʃən] *n* prevención *f*.
preventive [prɪ'vɛntɪv] *adj* preventivo.
preview ['priːvjuː] *n* (*of film*) preestreno.
previous ['priːvɪəs] *adj* previo, anterior; **he has no ~ experience in that field** no tiene experiencia previa en ese campo; **I have a ~ engagement** tengo un compromiso anterior.
previously ['priːvɪəslɪ] *adv* antes.
prewar [priː'wɔː*] *adj* antes de la guerra.
prey [preɪ] *n* presa ♦ *vi*: **to ~ on** vivir a costa de; (*feed on*) alimentarse de; **it was ~ing on his mind** le obsesionaba.
price [praɪs] *n* precio; (*BETTING*: *odds*) puntos *mpl* de ventaja ♦ *vt* (*goods*) fijar el precio de; **to go up** *or* **rise in ~** subir de precio; **what is the ~ of ...?** ¿qué precio tiene ...?; **to put a ~ on sth** poner precio a algo; **what ~ his promises now?** ¿para qué sirven ahora sus promesas?; **he regained his freedom, but at a ~** recobró su libertad, pero le había costado caro; **to be ~d out of the market** (*article*) no encontrar comprador por ese precio; (*nation*) no ser competitivo.
price control *n* control *m* de precios.
price-cutting ['praɪskʌtɪŋ] *n* reducción *f* de precios.
priceless ['praɪslɪs] *adj* que no tiene precio; (*col*: *amusing*) divertidísimo.
price list *n* tarifa.
price tag *n* etiqueta.
price war *n* guerra de precios.
pricey ['praɪsɪ] *adj* (*BRIT col*) caro.
prick [prɪk] *n* pinchazo; (*with pin*) alfilerazo; (*sting*) picadura ♦ *vt* pinchar; picar; **to ~ up one's ears** aguzar el oído.
prickle ['prɪkl] *n* (*sensation*) picor *m*; (*BOT*) espina; (*ZOOL*) púa.
prickly ['prɪklɪ] *adj* espinoso; (*fig*: *person*) enojadizo.
prickly heat *n* sarpullido causado por exceso de calor.
pride [praɪd] *n* orgullo; (*pej*) soberbia ♦ *vt*: **to ~ o.s. on** enorgullecerse de; **to take (a) ~ in** enorgullecerse de; **her ~ and joy** su orgullo; **to have ~ of place** tener prioridad.
priest [priːst] *n* sacerdote *m*.
priestess ['priːstɪs] *n* sacerdotisa.
priesthood ['priːsthud] *n* (*practice*) sacerdocio; (*priests*) clero.
prim [prɪm] *adj* (*demure*) remilgado; (*prudish*) gazmoño.
primacy ['praɪməsɪ] *n* primacía.
prima donna ['priːmə'dɔnə] *n* primadonna.
primal ['praɪməl] *adj* original; (*important*) principal.
primarily ['praɪmərɪlɪ] *adv* (*above all*) ante todo, primordialmente.
primary ['praɪmərɪ] *adj* primario; (*first in importance*) principal ♦ *n* (*US*: *also*: **~ election**) (elección *f*) primaria; *ver recuadro*.

> **PRIMARY**
>
> *Las elecciones primarias* (**primaries**) *sirven para preseleccionar a los candidatos de los partidos Demócrata ("Democratic") y Republicano ("Republican") durante la campaña que precede a las elecciones a presidente de los Estados Unidos. Se inician en New Hampshire y tienen lugar en 35 estados de febrero a junio. El número de votos obtenidos por cada candidato determina el número de delegados que votarán en el congreso general ("National Convention") de julio y agosto, cuando se decide el candidato definitivo de cada partido.*

primary colour, (*US*) **primary color** *n* color *m* primario.
primary education *n* enseñanza primaria.
primary school *n* (*BRIT*) escuela primaria; *ver recuadro*.

> **PRIMARY SCHOOL**
>
> *En el Reino Unido la escuela a la que van los niños entre cinco y once años se llama* **primary school**, *a menudo dividida en "infant school" (entre cinco y siete años de edad) y "junior school" (entre siete y once).*

primate *n* ['praɪmɪt] (*REL*) primado ♦ *n* ['praɪmeɪt] (*ZOOL*) primate *m*.
prime [praɪm] *adj* primero, principal; (*basic*) fundamental; (*excellent*) selecto, de primera clase ♦ *n*: **in the ~ of life** en la flor de la vida ♦ *vt* (*gun, pump*) cebar; (*fig*) preparar.
Prime Minister (PM) *n* primer(a) ministro/a; *see also* **Downing Street**.
primer ['praɪmə*] *n* (*book*) texto elemental; (*paint*) capa preparatoria.
prime time *n* (*RADIO, TV*) horas *fpl* de mayor audiencia.
primeval [praɪ'miːvəl] *adj* primitivo.
primitive ['prɪmɪtɪv] *adj* primitivo; (*crude*) rudimentario; (*uncivilized*) inculto.
primly ['prɪmlɪ] *adv* remilgadamente; con

gazmoñería.

primrose ['prɪmrəuz] *n* primavera, prímula.

primus (stove) ® ['praɪməs-] *n* (*BRIT*) hornillo de camping.

prince [prɪns] *n* príncipe *m.*

prince charming *n* príncipe *m* azul.

princess [prɪn'sɛs] *n* princesa.

principal ['prɪnsɪpl] *adj* principal ♦ *n* director(a) *m/f*; (*in play*) protagonista principal *m/f*; (*COMM*) capital *m*, principal *m*; *see also* **pantomime**.

principality [prɪnsɪ'pælɪtɪ] *n* principado.

principle ['prɪnsɪpl] *n* principio; **in** ~ en principio; **on** ~ por principio.

print [prɪnt] *n* (*impression*) marca, impresión *f*; huella; (*letters*) letra de molde; (*fabric*) estampado; (*ART*) grabado; (*PHOT*) impresión *f* ♦ *vt* (*gen*) imprimir; (*on mind*) grabar; (*write in capitals*) escribir en letras de molde; **out of** ~ agotado.

▸print out *vt* (*COMPUT*) imprimir.

printed circuit ['prɪntɪd-] *n* circuito impreso.

printed circuit board (PCB) *n* tarjeta de circuito impreso (TCI).

printed matter *n* impresos *mpl.*

printer ['prɪntə*] *n* (*person*) impresor(a) *m/f*; (*machine*) impresora.

printhead ['prɪnthɛd] *n* cabeza impresora.

printing ['prɪntɪŋ] *n* (*art*) imprenta; (*act*) impresión *f*; (*quantity*) tirada.

printing press *n* prensa.

printout ['prɪntaut] *n* (*COMPUT*) printout *m.*

print wheel *n* rueda impresora.

prior ['praɪə*] *adj* anterior, previo ♦ *n* prior *m*; ~ **to doing** antes de *or* hasta hacer; **without** ~ **notice** sin previo aviso; **to have a** ~ **claim to sth** tener prioridad en algo.

prioress [praɪə'rɛs] *n* priora.

priority [praɪ'ɔrɪtɪ] *n* prioridad *f*; **to have** *or* **take** ~ **over sth** tener prioridad sobre algo.

priory ['praɪərɪ] *n* priorato.

prise, (*US*) **prize** [praɪz] *vt*: **to** ~ **open** abrir con palanca.

prism ['prɪzəm] *n* prisma *m.*

prison ['prɪzn] *n* cárcel *f*, prisión *f* ♦ *cpd* carcelario.

prison camp *n* campamento para prisioneros.

prisoner ['prɪznə*] *n* (*in prison*) preso/a; (*under arrest*) detenido/a; (*in dock*) acusado/a; **the** ~ **at the bar** el/la acusado/a; **to take sb** ~ hacer *or* tomar prisionero a algn.

prisoner of war *n* prisionero/a *or* preso/a de guerra.

prissy ['prɪsɪ] *adj* remilgado.

pristine ['prɪsti:n] *adj* pristino.

privacy ['prɪvəsɪ] *n* (*seclusion*) soledad *f*; (*intimacy*) intimidad *f*; **in the strictest** ~ con el mayor secreto.

private ['praɪvɪt] *adj* (*personal*) particular; (*confidential*) secreto, confidencial; (*intimate*) privado, íntimo; (*sitting etc*) a puerta cerrada ♦ *n* soldado raso; "~" (*on envelope*) "confidencial"; (*on door*) "privado"; **in** ~ en privado; **in (his)** ~ **life** en su vida privada; **to be in** ~ **practice** tener consulta particular.

private enterprise *n* la empresa privada.

private eye *n* detective *m/f* privado/a.

private hearing *n* (*LAW*) vista a puerta cerrada.

private limited company *n* (*BRIT*) sociedad *f* de responsabilidad limitada.

privately ['praɪvɪtlɪ] *adv* en privado; (*in o.s.*) en secreto.

private parts *npl* partes *fpl* pudendas.

private property *n* propiedad *f* privada.

private school *n* colegio privado.

privation [praɪ'veɪʃən] *n* (*state*) privación *f*; (*hardship*) privaciones *fpl*, estrecheces *fpl.*

privatize ['praɪvɪtaɪz] *vt* privatizar.

privet ['prɪvɪt] *n* alheña.

privilege ['prɪvɪlɪdʒ] *n* privilegio; (*prerogative*) prerrogativa.

privileged ['prɪvɪlɪdʒd] *adj* privilegiado; **to be** ~ **to do sth** gozar del privilegio de hacer algo.

privy ['prɪvɪ] *adj*: **to be** ~ **to** estar enterado de.

Privy Council *n* consejo privado (de la Corona); *ver recuadro.*

PRIVY COUNCIL

El consejo de asesores de la Corona conocido como **Privy Council** *tuvo su origen en la época de los normandos, y fue adquiriendo mayor importancia hasta ser substituido en 1688 por el actual Consejo de Ministros ("Cabinet"). Hoy día sigue existiendo con un carácter fundamentalmente honorífico y los ministros del gobierno y otras personalidades políticas, eclesiásticas y jurídicas adquieren el rango de "privy councillors" de manera automática.*

prize [praɪz] *n* premio ♦ *adj* (*first class*) de primera clase ♦ *vt* apreciar, estimar; (*US*) = **prise.**

prize fighter *n* boxeador *m* profesional.

prize fighting *n* boxeo *m* profesional.

prize-giving ['praɪzgɪvɪŋ] *n* distribución *f* de premios.
prize money *n* (*SPORT*) bolsa.
prizewinner ['praɪzwɪnə*] *n* premiado/a.
prizewinning ['praɪzwɪnɪŋ] *adj* (*novel, essay*) premiado.
PRO *n abbr* = **public relations officer.**
pro [prəu] *n* (*SPORT*) profesional *m/f*; **the ~s and cons** los pros y los contras.
pro- [prəu] *pref* (*in favour of*) pro, en pro de; **~Soviet** pro-soviético.
proactive [prəu'æktɪv] *adj*: **to be ~** impulsar la actividad.
probability [prɔbə'bɪlɪtɪ] *n* probabilidad *f*; **in all ~** lo más probable.
probable ['prɔbəbl] *adj* probable; **it is ~/ hardly ~ that** es probable/poco probable que.
probably ['prɔbəblɪ] *adv* probablemente.
probate ['prəubeɪt] *n* (*LAW*) legalización *f* de un testamento.
probation [prə'beɪʃən] *n*: **on ~** (*employee*) a prueba; (*LAW*) en libertad condicional.
probationary [prə'beɪʃənrɪ] *adj*: **~ period** período de prueba.
probationer [prə'beɪʃənə*] *n* (*LAW*) persona en libertad condicional; (*nurse*) ≈ ATS *m/f* (*SP*) *or* enfermero/a en prácticas.
probation officer *n persona a cargo de los presos en libertad condicional.*
probe [prəub] *n* (*MED, SPACE*) sonda; (*enquiry*) investigación *f* ♦ *vt* sondar; (*investigate*) investigar.
probity ['prəubɪtɪ] *n* probidad *f*.
problem ['prɔbləm] *n* problema *m*; **what's the ~?** ¿cuál es el problema?, ¿qué pasa?; **no ~!** ¡por supuesto!; **to have ~s with the car** tener problemas con el coche.
problematic(al) [prɔblə'mætɪk(l)] *adj* problemático.
problem-solving [prɔbləm'sɔlvɪŋ] *n* resolución *f* de problemas; **~ skills** técnicas de resolución de problemas.
procedural [prəu'siːdʒərəl] *adj* de procedimiento; (*LAW*) procesal.
procedure [prə'siːdʒə*] *n* procedimiento; (*bureaucratic*) trámites *mpl*; **cashing a cheque is a simple ~** cobrar un cheque es un trámite sencillo.
proceed [prə'siːd] *vi* proceder; (*continue*): **to ~ (with)** continuar (con); **to ~ against sb** (*LAW*) proceder contra algn; **I am not sure how to ~** no sé cómo proceder; *see also* **proceeds.**
proceedings [prə'siːdɪŋz] *npl* acto *sg*, actos *mpl*; (*LAW*) proceso *sg*; (*meeting*) función *fsg*; (*records*) actas *fpl*.
proceeds ['prəusiːdz] *npl* ganancias *fpl*, ingresos *mpl*.
process ['prəusɛs] *n* proceso; (*method*) método, sistema *m*; (*proceeding*) procedimiento ♦ *vt* tratar, elaborar ♦ *vi* [prə'sɛs] (*BRIT formal: go in procession*) desfilar; **in ~** en curso; **we are in the ~ of moving to ...** estamos en vías de mudarnos a ....
processed cheese ['prəusɛst-], (*US*) **process cheese** *n* queso fundido.
processing ['prəusɛsɪŋ] *n* elaboración *f*.
procession [prə'sɛʃən] *n* desfile *m*; **funeral ~** cortejo fúnebre.
pro-choice [prəu'tʃɔɪs] *adj* en favor del derecho de elegir de la madre.
proclaim [prə'kleɪm] *vt* proclamar; (*announce*) anunciar.
proclamation [prɔklə'meɪʃən] *n* proclamación *f*; (*written*) proclama.
proclivity [prə'klɪvɪtɪ] *n* propensión *f*, inclinación *f*.
procrastinate [prəu'kræstɪneɪt] *vi* demorarse.
procrastination [prəukræstɪ'neɪʃən] *n* dilación *f*.
procreation [prəukrɪ'eɪʃən] *n* procreación *f*.
Procurator Fiscal ['prɔkjureɪtə-] *n* (*Scottish*) fiscal *m/f*.
procure [prə'kjuə*] *vt* conseguir, obtener.
procurement [prə'kjuəmənt] *n* obtención *f*.
prod [prɔd] *vt* (*push*) empujar; (*with elbow*) dar un codazo a ♦ *n* empujoncito; codazo.
prodigal ['prɔdɪgl] *adj* pródigo.
prodigious [prə'dɪdʒəs] *adj* prodigioso.
prodigy ['prɔdɪdʒɪ] *n* prodigio.
produce *n* ['prɔdjuːs] (*AGR*) productos *mpl* agrícolas ♦ *vt* [prə'djuːs] producir; (*yield*) rendir; (*bring*) sacar; (*show*) presentar, mostrar; (*proof of identity*) enseñar, presentar; (*THEAT*) presentar, poner en escena; (*offspring*) dar a luz.
produce dealer *n* (*US*) verdulero/a.
producer [prə'djuːsə*] *n* (*THEAT*) director(a) *m/f*; (*AGR, CINE*) productor(a) *m/f*.
product ['prɔdʌkt] *n* producto.
production [prə'dʌkʃən] *n* (*act*) producción *f*; (*THEAT*) representación *f*, montaje *m*; **to put into ~** lanzar a la producción.
production agreement *n* (*US*) acuerdo de productividad.
production line *n* línea de producción.
production manager *n* jefe/jefa *m/f* de producción.
productive [prə'dʌktɪv] *adj* productivo.
productivity [prɔdʌk'tɪvɪtɪ] *n* productividad *f*.
productivity agreement *n* (*BRIT*) acuerdo

de productividad.
productivity bonus *n* bono de productividad.
Prof. [prɔf] *abbr* (= *professor*) Prof.
profane [prəˈfeɪn] *adj* profano.
profess [prəˈfɛs] *vt* profesar; **I do not ~ to be an expert** no pretendo ser experto.
professed [prəˈfɛst] *adj* (*self-declared*) declarado.
profession [prəˈfɛʃən] *n* profesión *f*.
professional [prəˈfɛʃnl] *n* profesional *m/f* ♦ *adj* profesional; (*by profession*) de profesión; **to take ~ advice** buscar un consejo profesional.
professionalism [prəˈfɛʃnəlɪzm] *n* profesionalismo.
professionally [prəˈfɛʃnəlɪ] *adv*: **I only know him ~** sólo le conozco por nuestra relación de trabajo.
professor [prəˈfɛsə*] *n* (*BRIT*) catedrático/a; (*US*: *teacher*) profesor(a) *m/f*.
professorship [prəˈfɛsəʃɪp] *n* cátedra.
proffer [ˈprɔfə*] *vt* ofrecer.
proficiency [prəˈfɪʃənsɪ] *n* capacidad *f*, habilidad *f*.
proficiency test *n* prueba de capacitación.
proficient [prəˈfɪʃənt] *adj* experto, hábil.
profile [ˈprəufaɪl] *n* perfil *m*; **to keep a high/low ~** tratar de llamar la atención/pasar inadvertido.
profit [ˈprɔfɪt] *n* (*COMM*) ganancia; (*fig*) provecho ♦ *vi*: **to ~ by** *or* **from** aprovechar *or* sacar provecho de; **~ and loss account** cuenta de ganancias y pérdidas; **with ~s endowment assurance** seguro dotal con beneficios; **to sell sth at a ~** vender algo con ganancia.
profitability [prɔfɪtəˈbɪlɪtɪ] *n* rentabilidad *f*.
profitable [ˈprɔfɪtəbl] *adj* (*ECON*) rentable; (*beneficial*) provechoso, útil.
profitably [ˈprɔfɪtəblɪ] *adv* rentablemente; provechosamente.
profit centre, (*US*) **profit center** *n* centro de beneficios.
profiteering [prɔfɪˈtɪərɪŋ] *n* (*pej*) explotación *f*.
profit-making [ˈprɔfɪtmeɪkɪŋ] *adj* rentable.
profit margin *n* margen *m* de ganancia.
profit-sharing [ˈprɔfɪtʃɛərɪŋ] *n* participación *f* de empleados en los beneficios.
profits tax *n* impuesto sobre los beneficios.
profligate [ˈprɔflɪgɪt] *adj* (*dissolute*: *behaviour, act*) disoluto; (: *person*) libertino; (*extravagant*): **he's very ~ with his money** es muy derrochador.
pro forma [ˈprəuˈfɔːmə] *adj*: **~ invoice** factura pro-forma.
profound [prəˈfaund] *adj* profundo.
profoundly [prəˈfaundlɪ] *adv* profundamente.
profusely [prəˈfjuːslɪ] *adv* profusamente.
profusion [prəˈfjuːʒən] *n* profusión *f*, abundancia.
progeny [ˈprɔdʒɪnɪ] *n* progenie *f*.
programme, (*US*) **program** [ˈprəugræm] *n* programa *m* ♦ *vt* programar.
program(m)er [ˈprəugræmə*] *n* programador(a) *m/f*.
program(m)ing [ˈprəugræmɪŋ] *n* programación *f*.
program(m)ing language *n* lenguaje *m* de programación.
progress *n* [ˈprəugrɛs] progreso; (*development*) desarrollo ♦ *vi* [prəˈgrɛs] progresar, avanzar; desarrollarse; **in ~** (*meeting, work etc*) en curso; **as the match ~ed** a medida que avanzaba el partido.
progression [prəˈgrɛʃən] *n* progresión *f*.
progressive [prəˈgrɛsɪv] *adj* progresivo; (*person*) progresista.
progressively [prəˈgrɛsɪvlɪ] *adv* progresivamente, poco a poco.
progress report *n* (*MED*) informe *m* sobre el estado del paciente; (*ADMIN*) informe *m* sobre la marcha del trabajo.
prohibit [prəˈhɪbɪt] *vt* prohibir; **to ~ sb from doing sth** prohibir a algn hacer algo; **"smoking ~ed"** "prohibido fumar".
prohibition [prəuɪˈbɪʃən] *n* (*US*) prohibicionismo.
prohibitive [prəˈhɪbɪtɪv] *adj* (*price etc*) prohibitivo.
project *n* [ˈprɔdʒɛkt] proyecto; (*SCOL, UNIV*: *research*) trabajo, proyecto ♦ (*vb*: [prəˈdʒɛkt]) *vt* proyectar ♦ *vi* (*stick out*) salir, sobresalir.
projectile [prəˈdʒɛktaɪl] *n* proyectil *m*.
projection [prəˈdʒɛkʃən] *n* proyección *f*; (*overhang*) saliente *m*.
projectionist [prəˈdʒɛkʃənɪst] *n* (*CINE*) operador(a) *m/f* de cine.
projection room *n* (*CINE*) cabina de proyección.
projector [prəˈdʒɛktə*] *n* proyector *m*.
proletarian [prəulɪˈtɛərɪən] *adj* proletario.
proletariat [prəulɪˈtɛərɪət] *n* proletariado.
pro-life [prəuˈlaɪf] *adj* pro-vida.
proliferate [prəˈlɪfəreɪt] *vi* proliferar, multiplicarse.
proliferation [prəlɪfəˈreɪʃən] *n* proliferación *f*.
prolific [prəˈlɪfɪk] *adj* prolífico.
prologue, (*US*) **prolog** [ˈprəulɔg] *n* prólogo.

prolong [prə'lɔŋ] *vt* prolongar, extender.
prom [prɔm] *n abbr* (*BRIT*) = **promenade, promenade concert** ♦ *n* (*US*: *ball*) baile *m* de gala; *ver recuadro*.

> **PROM**
>
> *Los conciertos de música clásica más conocidos en Inglaterra son los llamados* **Proms** (*o* **promenade concerts**), *que tienen lugar en el "Royal Albert Hall" de Londres, aunque también se llama así a cualquier concierto de esas características. Su nombre se debe al hecho de que en un principio el público paseaba durante las actuaciones; en la actualidad parte de la gente que acude a ellos permanece de pie. En Estados Unidos se llama* **prom** *a un baile de gala en un colegio o universidad.*

promenade [prɔmə'nɑːd] *n* (*by sea*) paseo marítimo ♦ *vi* (*stroll*) pasearse.
promenade concert *n* concierto (*en que parte del público permanece de pie*).
promenade deck *n* cubierta de paseo.
prominence ['prɔmɪnəns] *n* (*fig*) importancia.
prominent ['prɔmɪnənt] *adj* (*standing out*) saliente; (*important*) eminente, importante; **he is ~ in the field of ...** destaca en el campo de ....
prominently ['prɔmɪnəntlɪ] *adv* (*display, set*) muy a la vista; **he figured ~ in the case** desempeñó un papel destacado en el juicio.
promiscuity [prɔmɪs'kjuːɪtɪ] *n* promiscuidad *f*.
promiscuous [prə'mɪskjuəs] *adj* (*sexually*) promiscuo.
promise ['prɔmɪs] *n* promesa ♦ *vt, vi* prometer; **to make sb a ~** prometer algo a algn; **a young man of ~** un joven con futuro; **to ~ (sb) to do sth** prometer (a algn) hacer algo; **to ~ well** ser muy prometedor.
promising ['prɔmɪsɪŋ] *adj* prometedor(a).
promissory note ['prɔmɪsərɪ-] *n* pagaré *m*.
promontory ['prɔməntrɪ] *n* promontorio.
promote [prə'məut] *vt* promover; (*new product*) dar publicidad a, lanzar; (*MIL*) ascender; **the team was ~d to the second division** (*BRIT FOOTBALL*) el equipo ascendió a la segunda división.
promoter [prə'məutə*] *n* (*of sporting event*) promotor(a) *m/f*; (*of company, business*) patrocinador(a) *m/f*.
promotion [prə'məuʃən] *n* (*gen*) promoción *f*; (*MIL*) ascenso.
prompt [prɔmpt] *adj* pronto ♦ *adv*: **at 6 o'clock ~** a las seis en punto ♦ *n* (*COMPUT*) aviso, guía ♦ *vt* (*urge*) mover, incitar; (*THEAT*) apuntar; **to ~ sb to do sth** instar a algn a hacer algo; **to be ~ to do sth** no tardar en hacer algo; **they're very ~** (*punctual*) son muy puntuales.
prompter ['prɔmptə*] *n* (*THEAT*) apuntador(a) *m/f*.
promptly ['prɔmptlɪ] *adv* (*punctually*) puntualmente; (*rapidly*) rápidamente.
promptness ['prɔmptnɪs] *n* puntualidad *f*; rapidez *f*.
promulgate ['prɔməlgeɪt] *vt* promulgar.
prone [prəun] *adj* (*lying*) postrado; **~ to** propenso a.
prong [prɔŋ] *n* diente *m*, punta.
pronoun ['prəunaun] *n* pronombre *m*.
pronounce [prə'nauns] *vt* pronunciar; (*declare*) declarar ♦ *vi*: **to ~ (up)on** pronunciarse sobre; **they ~d him unfit to plead** le declararon incapaz de defenderse.
pronounced [prə'naunst] *adj* (*marked*) marcado.
pronouncement [prə'naunsmənt] *n* declaración *f*.
pronunciation [prənʌnsɪ'eɪʃən] *n* pronunciación *f*.
proof [pruːf] *n* prueba; **70° ~** graduación *f* del 70 por 100 ♦ *adj*: **~ against** a prueba de ♦ *vt* (*tent, anorak*) impermeabilizar.
proofreader ['pruːfriːdə*] *n* corrector(a) *m/f* de pruebas.
prop [prɔp] *n* apoyo; (*fig*) sostén *m* ♦ *vt* (*also*: **~ up**) apoyar; (*lean*): **to ~ sth against** apoyar algo contra.
Prop. *abbr* (*COMM*) = **proprietor**.
propaganda [prɔpə'gændə] *n* propaganda.
propagate ['prɔpəgeɪt] *vt* propagar.
propel [prə'pɛl] *vt* impulsar, propulsar.
propeller [prə'pɛlə*] *n* hélice *f*.
propelling pencil [prə'pɛlɪŋ-] *n* (*BRIT*) lapicero.
propensity [prə'pɛnsɪtɪ] *n* propensión *f*.
proper ['prɔpə*] *adj* (*suited, right*) propio; (*exact*) justo; (*apt*) apropiado, conveniente; (*timely*) oportuno; (*seemly*) correcto, decente; (*authentic*) verdadero; (*col*: *real*) auténtico; **to go through the ~ channels** (*ADMIN*) ir por la vía oficial.
properly ['prɔpəlɪ] *adv* (*adequately*) correctamente; (*decently*) decentemente.
proper noun *n* nombre *m* propio.
properties ['prɔpətɪz] *npl* (*THEAT*) accesorios *mpl*, atrezzo *msg*.
property ['prɔpətɪ] *n* propiedad *f*; (*estate*) finca; **lost ~** objetos *mpl* perdidos;

personal ~ bienes *mpl* muebles.
property developer *n* promotor(a) *m/f* de construcciones.
property owner *n* dueño/a de propiedades.
property tax *n* impuesto sobre la propiedad.
prophecy ['prɔfɪsɪ] *n* profecía.
prophesy ['prɔfɪsaɪ] *vt* profetizar; (*fig*) predecir.
prophet ['prɔfɪt] *n* profeta *m/f*.
prophetic [prə'fɛtɪk] *adj* profético.
proportion [prə'pɔːʃən] *n* proporción *f*; (*share*) parte *f*; **to be in/out of** ~ **to** *or* **with sth** estar en/no guardar proporción con algo; **to see sth in** ~ (*fig*) ver algo en su justa medida.
proportional [prə'pɔːʃənl] *adj* proporcional.
proportionally [prəpɔːʃnəlɪ] *adv* proporcionalmente, en proporción.
proportional representation (PR) *n* (*POL*) representación *f* proporcional.
proportional spacing *n* (*on printer*) espaciado proporcional.
proportionate [prə'pɔːʃənɪt] *adj* proporcionado.
proportionately [prə'pɔːʃnɪtlɪ] *adv* proporcionadamente, en proporción.
proportioned [prə'pɔːʃənd] *adj* proporcionado.
proposal [prə'pəuzl] *n* propuesta; (*offer of marriage*) oferta de matrimonio; (*plan*) proyecto; (*suggestion*) sugerencia.
propose [prə'pəuz] *vt* proponer; (*have in mind*): **to** ~ **sth/to do** *or* **doing sth** proponer algo/proponerse hacer algo ♦ *vi* declararse.
proposer [prə'pəuzə*] *n* (*of motion*) proponente *m/f*.
proposition [prɔpə'zɪʃən] *n* propuesta, proposición *f*; **to make sb a** ~ proponer algo a algn.
propound [prə'paund] *vt* (*theory*) exponer.
proprietary [prə'praɪətərɪ] *adj* (*COMM*): ~ **article** artículo de marca; ~ **brand** marca comercial.
proprietor [prə'praɪətə*] *n* propietario/a, dueño/a.
propriety [prə'praɪətɪ] *n* decoro.
propulsion [prə'pʌlʃən] *n* propulsión *f*.
pro rata [prəu'rɑːtə] *adv* a prorrata.
prosaic [prəu'zeɪɪk] *adj* prosaico.
Pros. Atty. *abbr* (*US*) = *prosecuting attorney*.
proscribe [prə'skraɪb] *vt* proscribir.
prose [prəuz] *n* prosa; (*SCOL*) traducción *f* inversa.
prosecute ['prɔsɪkjuːt] *vt* (*LAW*) procesar; **"trespassers will be ~d"** (*LAW*) "se procesará a los intrusos".
prosecution [prɔsɪ'kjuːʃən] *n* proceso, causa; (*accusing side*) acusación *f*.
prosecutor ['prɔsɪkjuːtə*] *n* acusador(a) *m/f*; (*also*: **public** ~) fiscal *m/f*.
prospect *n* ['prɔspɛkt] (*chance*) posibilidad *f*; (*outlook*) perspectiva; (*hope*) esperanza ♦ (*vb*: [prə'spɛkt]) *vt* explorar ♦ *vi* buscar; ~**s** *npl* (*for work etc*) perspectivas *fpl*; **to be faced with the** ~ **of** tener que enfrentarse a la posibilidad de que ...; **we were faced with the** ~ **of leaving early** se nos planteó la posibilidad de marcharnos pronto; **there is every** ~ **of an early victory** hay buenas perspectivas de una pronta victoria.
prospecting [prə'spɛktɪŋ] *n* prospección *f*.
prospective [prə'spɛktɪv] *adj* (*possible*) probable, eventual; (*certain*) futuro; (*buyer*) presunto; (*legislation, son-in-law*) futuro.
prospector [prə'spɛktə*] *n* explorador(a) *m/f*; **gold** ~ buscador *m* de oro.
prospectus [prə'spɛktəs] *n* prospecto.
prosper ['prɔspə*] *vi* prosperar.
prosperity [prɔ'spɛrɪtɪ] *n* prosperidad *f*.
prosperous ['prɔspərəs] *adj* próspero.
prostate ['prɔsteɪt] *n* (*also*: ~ **gland**) próstata.
prostitute ['prɔstɪtjuːt] *n* prostituta; **male** ~ prostituto.
prostitution [prɔstɪ'tjuːʃən] *n* prostitución *f*.
prostrate ['prɔstreɪt] *adj* postrado; (*fig*) abatido ♦ *vt*: **to** ~ **o.s.** postrarse.
protagonist [prə'tægənɪst] *n* protagonista *m/f*.
protect [prə'tɛkt] *vt* proteger.
protection [prə'tɛkʃən] *n* protección *f*; **to be under sb's** ~ estar amparado por algn.
protectionism [prə'tɛkʃənɪzəm] *n* proteccionismo.
protection racket *n* chantaje *m*.
protective [prə'tɛktɪv] *adj* protector(a); ~ **custody** (*LAW*) detención *f* preventiva.
protector [prə'tɛktə*] *n* protector(a) *m/f*.
protégé ['prəutɛʒeɪ] *n* protegido/a.
protein ['prəutiːn] *n* proteína.
pro tem [prəu'tɛm] *adv abbr* (= *pro tempore: for the time being*) provisionalmente.
protest *n* ['prəutɛst] protesta ♦ (*vb*: [prə'tɛst]) *vi* protestar ♦ *vt* (*affirm*) afirmar, declarar; **to do sth under** ~ hacer algo bajo protesta; **to** ~ **against/about** protestar en contra de/por.
Protestant ['prɔtɪstənt] *adj, n* protestante *m/f*.
protester, protestor [prə'tɛstə*] *n* (*in*

demonstration) manifestante *m/f.*
protest march *n* manifestación *f* or marcha (de protesta).
protocol ['prəutəkɔl] *n* protocolo.
prototype ['prəutətaɪp] *n* prototipo.
protracted [prə'træktɪd] *adj* prolongado.
protractor [prə'træktə*] *n* (*GEOM*) transportador *m.*
protrude [prə'tru:d] *vi* salir, sobresalir.
protuberance [prə'tju:bərəns] *n* protuberancia.
proud [praud] *adj* orgulloso; (*pej*) soberbio, altanero ♦ *adv*: **to do sb ~** tratar a algn a cuerpo de rey; **to do o.s. ~** no privarse de nada; **to be ~ to do sth** estar orgulloso de hacer algo.
proudly ['praudlɪ] *adv* orgullosamente, con orgullo; (*pej*) con soberbia, con altanería.
prove [pru:v] *vt* probar; (*verify*) comprobar; (*show*) demostrar ♦ *vi*: **to ~ correct** resultar correcto; **to ~ o.s.** ponerse a prueba; **he was ~d right in the end** al final se vio que tenía razón.
proverb ['prɔvə:b] *n* refrán *m.*
proverbial [prə'və:bɪəl] *adj* proverbial.
proverbially [prə'və:bɪəlɪ] *adv* proverbialmente.
provide [prə'vaɪd] *vt* proporcionar, dar; **to ~ sb with sth** proveer a algn de algo; **to be ~d with** ser provisto de.
▶**provide for** *vt fus* (*person*) mantener a; (*problem etc*) tener en cuenta.
provided [prə'vaɪdɪd] *conj*: **~ (that)** con tal de que, a condición de que.
Providence ['prɔvɪdəns] *n* Divina Providencia.
providing [prə'vaɪdɪŋ] *conj* a condición de que, con tal de que.
province ['prɔvɪns] *n* provincia; (*fig*) esfera.
provincial [prə'vɪnʃəl] *adj* provincial; (*pej*) provinciano.
provision [prə'vɪʒən] *n* provisión *f*; (*supply*) suministro, abastecimiento; **~s** *npl* provisiones *fpl*, víveres *mpl*; **to make ~ for** (*one's family, future*) atender las necesidades de.
provisional [prə'vɪʒənl] *adj* provisional, provisorio (*LAM*); (*temporary*) interino ♦ *n*: **P~** (*Irish POL*) Provisional *m* (*miembro de la tendencia activista del IRA*).
provisional driving licence *n* (*BRIT AUT*) carnet *m* de conducir provisional; *see also* **L-plates.**
proviso [prə'vaɪzəu] *n* condición *f*, estipulación *f*; **with the ~ that** a condición de que.
Provo ['prɔvəu] *n abbr* (*col*) = **Provisional.**
provocation [prɔvə'keɪʃən] *n* provocación *f.*
provocative [prə'vɔkətɪv] *adj* provocativo.
provoke [prə'vəuk] *vt* (*arouse*) provocar, incitar; (*cause*) causar, producir; (*anger*) enojar; **to ~ sb to sth/to do** *or* **into doing sth** provocar a algn a algo/a hacer algo.
provoking [prə'vəukɪŋ] *adj* provocador(a).
provost ['prɔvəst] *n* (*BRIT*: *of university*) rector(a) *m/f*; (*Scottish*) alcalde(sa) *m/f.*
prow [prau] *n* proa.
prowess ['prauɪs] *n* (*skill*) destreza, habilidad *f*; (*courage*) valor *m*; **his ~ as a footballer** (*skill*) su habilidad como futbolista.
prowl [praul] *vi* (*also*: **~ about, ~ around**) merodear ♦ *n*: **on the ~** de merodeo, merodeando.
prowler ['praulə*] *n* merodeador(a) *m/f.*
proximity [prɔk'sɪmɪtɪ] *n* proximidad *f.*
proxy ['prɔksɪ] *n* poder *m*; (*person*) apoderado/a; **by ~** por poderes.
PRP *n abbr* (= *performance related pay*) *retribución en función del rendimiento en el trabajo.*
prude [pru:d] *n* gazmoño/a, mojigato/a.
prudence ['pru:dns] *n* prudencia.
prudent ['pru:dnt] *adj* prudente.
prudently ['pru:dntlɪ] *adv* prudentemente, con prudencia.
prudish ['pru:dɪʃ] *adj* gazmoño.
prudishness [pru:dɪʃnɪs] *n* gazmoñería, ñoñería.
prune [pru:n] *n* ciruela pasa ♦ *vt* podar.
pry [praɪ] *vi*: **to ~ into** entrometerse en.
PS *abbr* (= *postscript*) P.D.
psalm [sɑ:m] *n* salmo.
PSAT *n abbr* (*US*) = *Preliminary Scholastic Aptitude Test.*
PSBR *n abbr* (*BRIT*: = *public sector borrowing requirement*) endeudamiento público.
pseud [sju:d] *n* (*BRIT col*: *intellectually*) farsante *m/f*; (: *socially*) pretencioso/a.
pseudo ... [sju:dəu] *pref* seudo....
pseudonym ['sju:dənɪm] *n* seudónimo.
PST *n abbr* (*US*: = *Pacific Standard Time*) *hora de invierno del Pacífico.*
PSV *n abbr* (*BRIT*) *see* **public service vehicle.**
psyche ['saɪkɪ] *n* psique *f.*
psychiatric [saɪkɪ'ætrɪk] *adj* psiquiátrico.
psychiatrist [saɪ'kaɪətrɪst] *n* psiquiatra *m/f.*
psychiatry [saɪ'kaɪətrɪ] *n* psiquiatría.
psychic ['saɪkɪk] *adj* (*also*: **~al**) psíquico.
psycho ['saɪkəu] *n* (*col*) psicópata *m/f*, pirado/a.
psychoanalyse, psychoanalyze [saɪkəu-'ænəlaɪz] *vt* psicoanalizar.
psychoanalysis, *pl* **psychoanalyses**

[saɪkəuə'nælɪsɪs, -siːz] *n* psicoanálisis *m inv*.
psychoanalyst [saɪkəu'ænəlɪst] *n* psicoanalista *m/f*.
psychological [saɪkə'lɔdʒɪkl] *adj* psicológico.
psychologically [saɪkə'lɔdʒɪklɪ] *adv* psicológicamente.
psychologist [saɪ'kɔlədʒɪst] *n* psicólogo/a.
psychology [saɪ'kɔlədʒɪ] *n* psicología.
psychopath ['saɪkəupæθ] *n* psicópata *m/f*.
psychosis, *pl* **psychoses** [saɪ'kəusɪs, -siːz] *n* psicosis *f inv*.
psychotherapy [saɪkəu'θɛrəpɪ] *n* psicoterapia.
psychotic [saɪ'kɔtɪk] *adj, n* psicótico/a.
PT *n abbr* (*BRIT*: = *Physical Training*) Ed. Fís.
pt *abbr* = **pint(s), point(s)**.
Pt. *abbr* (*GEO*: = *Point*) Pta.
PTA *n abbr* (*BRIT*: = *Parent-Teacher Association*) ≈ Asociación *f* de Padres de Alumnos.
Pte. *abbr* (*BRIT MIL*) = **private**.
PTO *abbr* (= *please turn over*) sigue.
PTV *n abbr* (*US*) = *pay television, public television*.
pub [pʌb] *n abbr* (= *public house*) pub *m*, bar *m*; *ver recuadro*.

PUB

En un **pub** (*o* **public house**) *se pueden consumir fundamentalmente bebidas alcohólicas, aunque en la actualidad también se sirven platos ligeros durante el almuerzo. Es, además, un lugar de encuentro donde se juega a los dardos o al billar, entre otras actividades. La estricta regulación sobre la venta de alcohol controla las horas de apertura, aunque éstas son más flexibles desde hace unos años. No se puede servir alcohol a los menores de 18 años.*

pub crawl *n* (*col*): **to go on a ~** ir a recorrer bares.
puberty ['pjuːbətɪ] *n* pubertad *f*.
pubic ['pjuːbɪk] *adj* púbico.
public ['pʌblɪk] *adj, n* público; **in ~** en público; **to make sth ~** revelar *or* hacer público algo; **to be ~ knowledge** ser del dominio público; **to go ~** (*COMM*) proceder a la venta pública de acciones.
public address system (PA) *n* megafonía, sistema *m* de altavoces.
publican ['pʌblɪkən] *n* dueño/a *or* encargado/a de un bar.
publication [pʌblɪ'keɪʃən] *n* publicación *f*.
public company *n* sociedad *f* anónima.
public convenience *n* (*BRIT*) aseos *mpl* públicos, sanitarios *mpl* (*LAM*).
public holiday *n* día *m* de fiesta, (día) feriado (*LAM*).
public house *n* (*BRIT*) bar *m*, pub *m*.
publicity [pʌb'lɪsɪtɪ] *n* publicidad *f*.
publicize ['pʌblɪsaɪz] *vt* publicitar; (*advertise*) hacer propaganda para.
public limited company (plc) *n* sociedad *f* anónima (S.A.).
publicly ['pʌblɪklɪ] *adv* públicamente, en público.
public opinion *n* opinión *f* pública.
public ownership *n* propiedad *f* pública; **to be taken into ~** ser nacionalizado.
Public Prosecutor *n* Fiscal *m/f* del Estado.
public relations (PR) *n* relaciones *fpl* públicas.
public relations officer *n* encargado/a de relaciones públicas.
public school *n* (*BRIT*) colegio privado; (*US*) instituto; *ver recuadro*.

PUBLIC SCHOOL

En Inglaterra el término **public school** *se usa para referirse a un colegio privado de pago, generalmente de alto prestigio social y en régimen de internado. Algunos de los más conocidos son Eton o Harrow. Muchos de sus alumnos estudian previamente hasta los 13 años en un centro privado de pago llamado "prep(aratory) school" y al terminar el bachiller pasan a estudiar en las universidades de Oxford y Cambridge. En otros lugares como Estados Unidos el mismo término se refiere a una escuela pública de enseñanza gratuita administrada por el Estado.*

public sector *n* sector *m* público.
public-spirited [pʌblɪk'spɪrɪtɪd] *adj* cívico.
public transport, (*US*) **public transportation** *n* transporte *m* público.
public works *npl* obras *fpl* públicas.
publish ['pʌblɪʃ] *vt* publicar.
publisher ['pʌblɪʃə*] *n* (*person*) editor(a) *m/f*; (*firm*) editorial *f*.
publishing ['pʌblɪʃɪŋ] *n* (*industry*) industria del libro.
publishing company *n* (casa) editorial *f*.
puce [pjuːs] *adj* de color pardo rojizo.
puck [pʌk] *n* (*ICE HOCKEY*) puck *m*.
pucker ['pʌkə*] *vt* (*pleat*) arrugar; (*brow etc*) fruncir.
pudding ['pudɪŋ] *n* pudín *m*; (*BRIT*: *sweet*) postre *m*; **black ~** morcilla; **rice ~** arroz *m* con leche.

puddle ['pʌdl] *n* charco.
puerile ['pjuəraɪl] *adj* pueril.
Puerto Rican ['pwəːtəu'riːkən] *adj, n* puertorriqueño/a *m/f*.
Puerto Rico [-'riːkəu] *n* Puerto Rico.
puff [pʌf] *n* soplo; (*of smoke*) bocanada; (*of breathing, engine*) resoplido; (*powder* ~) borla ♦ *vt*: **to ~ one's pipe** dar chupadas a la pipa; (*also*: ~ **out**: *sails, cheeks*) hinchar, inflar ♦ *vi* (*gen*) soplar; (*pant*) jadear; **to ~ out smoke** echar humo.
puffed [pʌft] *adj* (*col*: *out of breath*) sin aliento.
puffin ['pʌfɪn] *n* frailecillo.
puff pastry, (*US*) **puff paste** *n* hojaldre *m*.
puffy ['pʌfɪ] *adj* hinchado.
pull [pul] *n* (*tug*): **to give sth a ~** dar un tirón a algo; (*fig*: *advantage*) ventaja; (: *influence*) influencia ♦ *vt* tirar de, jalar (*LAM*); (*haul*) tirar, jalar (*LAM*), arrastrar; (*strain*): **to ~ a muscle** sufrir un tirón ♦ *vi* tirar, jalar (*LAM*); **to ~ to pieces** hacer pedazos; **to ~ one's punches** andarse con bromas; **to ~ one's weight** hacer su parte; **to ~ o.s. together** tranquilizarse; **to ~ sb's leg** tomar el pelo a algn; **to ~ strings (for sb)** enchufar (a algn).
▶**pull about** *vt* (*handle roughly*: *object*) manosear; (: *person*) maltratar.
▶**pull apart** *vt* (*take apart*) desmontar.
▶**pull down** *vt* (*house*) derribar.
▶**pull in** *vi* (*AUT*: *at the kerb*) parar (junto a la acera); (*RAIL*) llegar.
▶**pull off** *vt* (*deal etc*) cerrar.
▶**pull out** *vi* irse, marcharse; (*AUT*: *from kerb*) salir ♦ *vt* sacar, arrancar.
▶**pull over** *vi* (*AUT*) hacerse a un lado.
▶**pull round, pull through** *vi* salvarse; (*MED*) recobrar la salud.
▶**pull up** *vi* (*stop*) parar ♦ *vt* (*uproot*) arrancar, desarraigar; (*stop*) parar.
pulley ['pulɪ] *n* polea.
pull-out ['pulaut] *n* suplemento ♦ *cpd* (*pages, magazine*) separable.
pullover ['puləuvə*] *n* jersey *m*, suéter *m*.
pulp [pʌlp] *n* (*of fruit*) pulpa; (*for paper*) pasta; (*pej*: *also*: ~ **magazines** *etc*) prensa amarilla; **to reduce sth to ~** hacer algo papilla.
pulpit ['pulpɪt] *n* púlpito.
pulsate [pʌl'seɪt] *vi* pulsar, latir.
pulse [pʌls] *n* (*ANAT*) pulso; (*of music, engine*) pulsación *f*; (*BOT*) legumbre *f*; **to feel** *or* **take sb's ~** tomar el pulso a algn.
pulverize ['pʌlvəraɪz] *vt* pulverizar; (*fig*) hacer polvo.
puma ['pjuːmə] *n* puma *m*.
pumice (stone) ['pʌmɪs-] *n* piedra pómez.
pummel ['pʌml] *vt* aporrear.
pump [pʌmp] *n* bomba; (*shoe*) zapatilla de tenis ♦ *vt* sacar con una bomba; (*fig*: *col*) (son)sacar; **to ~ sb for information** (son)sacarle información a algn.
▶**pump up** *vt* inflar.
pumpkin ['pʌmpkɪn] *n* calabaza.
pun [pʌn] *n* juego de palabras.
punch [pʌntʃ] *n* (*blow*) golpe *m*, puñetazo; (*tool*) punzón *m*; (*for paper*) perforadora; (*for tickets*) taladro; (*drink*) ponche *m* ♦ *vt* (*hit*): **to ~ sb/sth** dar un puñetazo *or* golpear a algn/algo; (*make a hole in*) punzar; perforar.
punch-drunk ['pʌntʃdrʌŋk] *adj* (*BRIT*) grogui, sonado.
punch(ed) card [pʌntʃ(t)-] *n* tarjeta perforada.
punch line *n* (*of joke*) remate *m*.
punch-up ['pʌntʃʌp] *n* (*BRIT col*) riña.
punctual ['pʌŋktjuəl] *adj* puntual.
punctuality [pʌŋktju'ælɪtɪ] *n* puntualidad *f*.
punctually ['pʌŋktjuəlɪ] *adv*: **it will start ~ at 6** empezará a las 6 en punto.
punctuate ['pʌŋktjueɪt] *vt* puntuar; (*fig*) interrumpir.
punctuation [pʌŋktju'eɪʃən] *n* puntuación *f*.
punctuation mark *n* signo de puntuación.
puncture ['pʌŋktʃə*] (*BRIT*) *n* pinchazo ♦ *vt* pinchar; **to have a ~** tener un pinchazo.
pundit ['pʌndɪt] *n* experto/a.
pungent ['pʌndʒənt] *adj* acre.
punish ['pʌnɪʃ] *vt* castigar; **to ~ sb for sth/for doing sth** castigar a algn por algo/por haber hecho algo.
punishable ['pʌnɪʃəbl] *adj* punible, castigable.
punishing ['pʌnɪʃɪŋ] *adj* (*fig*: *exhausting*) agotador(a).
punishment ['pʌnɪʃmənt] *n* castigo; (*fig, col*): **to take a lot of ~** (*boxer*) recibir una paliza; (*car*) ser maltratado.
punitive ['pjuːnɪtɪv] *adj* punitivo.
punk [pʌŋk] *n* (*also*: ~ **rocker**) punki *m/f*; (*also*: ~ **rock**) música punk; (*US col*: *hoodlum*) matón *m*.
punt [pʌnt] *n* (*boat*) batea; (*IRELAND*) libra irlandesa ♦ *vi* (*bet*) apostar.
punter ['pʌntə*] *n* (*gambler*) jugador(a) *m/f*.
puny ['pjuːnɪ] *adj* enclenque.
pup [pʌp] *n* cachorro.
pupil ['pjuːpl] *n* alumno/a; (*of eye*) pupila.
puppet ['pʌpɪt] *n* títere *m*.
puppet government *n* gobierno títere.
puppy ['pʌpɪ] *n* cachorro, perrito.
purchase ['pəːtʃɪs] *n* compra; (*grip*) agarre *m*, asidero ♦ *vt* comprar.
purchase order *n* orden *f* de compra.

purchase price *n* precio de compra.
purchaser ['pəːtʃɪsə*] *n* comprador(a) *m/f.*
purchase tax *n* (*BRIT*) impuesto sobre la venta.
purchasing power ['pəːtʃɪsɪŋ-] *n* poder *m* adquisitivo.
pure [pjuə*] *adj* puro; **a ~ wool jumper** un jersey de pura lana; **it's laziness, ~ and simple** es pura vagancia.
purebred ['pjuəbrɛd] *adj* de pura sangre.
purée ['pjuəreɪ] *n* puré *m.*
purely ['pjuəlɪ] *adv* puramente.
purgatory ['pəːgətərɪ] *n* purgatorio.
purge [pəːdʒ] *n* (*MED, POL*) purga ♦ *vt* purgar.
purification [pjuərɪfɪ'keɪʃən] *n* purificación *f*, depuración *f.*
purify ['pjuərɪfaɪ] *vt* purificar, depurar.
purist ['pjuərɪst] *n* purista *m/f.*
puritan ['pjuərɪtən] *n* puritano/a.
puritanical [pjuərɪ'tænɪkl] *adj* puritano.
purity ['pjuərɪtɪ] *n* pureza.
purl [pəːl] *n* punto del revés.
purloin [pəː'lɔɪn] *vt* hurtar, robar.
purple ['pəːpl] *adj* morado.
purport [pəː'pɔːt] *vi*: **to ~ to be/do** dar a entender que es/hace.
purpose ['pəːpəs] *n* propósito; **on ~** a propósito, adrede; **to no ~** para nada, en vano; **for teaching ~s** con fines pedagógicos; **for the ~s of this meeting** para los fines de esta reunión.
purpose-built ['pəːpəs'bɪlt] *adj* (*BRIT*) construido especialmente.
purposeful ['pəːpəsful] *adj* resuelto, determinado.
purposely ['pəːpəslɪ] *adv* a propósito, adrede.
purr [pəː*] *n* ronroneo ♦ *vi* ronronear.
purse [pəːs] *n* monedero; (*US*: *handbag*) bolso ♦ *vt* fruncir.
purser ['pəːsə*] *n* (*NAUT*) comisario/a.
purse snatcher [-snætʃə*] *n* (*US*) *persona que roba por el procedimiento del tirón.*
pursue [pə'sjuː] *vt* seguir; (*harass*) perseguir; (*profession*) ejercer; (*pleasures*) buscar; (*inquiry, matter*) seguir.
pursuer [pə'sjuːə*] *n* perseguidor(a) *m/f.*
pursuit [pə'sjuːt] *n* (*chase*) caza; (*of pleasure etc*) busca; (*occupation*) actividad *f*; **in (the) ~ of sth** en busca de algo.
purveyor [pə'veɪə*] *n* proveedor(a) *m/f.*
pus [pʌs] *n* pus *m.*
push [puʃ] *n* empujón *m*; (*MIL*) ataque *m*; (*drive*) empuje *m* ♦ *vt* empujar; (*button*) apretar; (*promote*) promover; (*fig*: *press, advance*: *views*) fomentar; (*thrust*): **to ~ sth (into)** meter algo a la fuerza (en) ♦ *vi* empujar; (*fig*) hacer esfuerzos; **at a ~** (*col*) a duras penas; **she is ~ing 50** (*col*) raya en los 50; **to be ~ed for time/money** andar justo de tiempo/escaso de dinero; **to ~ a door open/shut** abrir/cerrar una puerta empujándola; **to ~ for** (*better pay, conditions*) reivindicar; **"~"** (*on door*) "empujar"; (*on bell*) "pulse".
▸**push aside** *vt* apartar con la mano.
▸**push in** *vi* colarse.
▸**push off** *vi* (*col*) largarse.
▸**push on** *vi* (*continue*) seguir adelante.
▸**push through** *vt* (*measure*) despachar.
▸**push up** *vt* (*total, prices*) hacer subir.
push-bike ['puʃbaɪk] *n* (*BRIT*) bicicleta.
push-button ['puʃbʌtn] *adj* con botón de mando.
pushchair ['puʃtʃɛə*] *n* (*BRIT*) silla de niño.
pusher ['puʃə*] *n* (*drug ~*) traficante *m/f* de drogas.
pushover ['puʃəuvə*] *n* (*col*): **it's a ~** está tirado.
push-up ['puʃʌp] *n* (*US*) flexión *f.*
pushy ['puʃɪ] *adj* (*pej*) agresivo.
puss [pus], **pussy(-cat)** ['pusɪ(kæt)] *n* minino.
put [put], *pt, pp* **put** *vt* (*place*) poner, colocar; (*~ into*) meter; (*express, say*) expresar; (*a question*) hacer; (*estimate*) calcular; (*cause to be*): **to ~ sb in a good/bad mood** poner a algn de buen/mal humor; **to ~ a lot of time into sth** dedicar mucho tiempo a algo; **to ~ money on a horse** apostar dinero en un caballo; **to ~ money into a company** invertir dinero en una compañía; **to ~ sb to a lot of trouble** causar mucha molestia a algn; **we ~ the children to bed** acostamos a los niños; **how shall I ~ it?** ¿cómo puedo explicarlo *or* decirlo?; **I ~ it to you that ...** le sugiero que ...; **to stay ~** no moverse.
▸**put about** *vi* (*NAUT*) virar ♦ *vt* (*rumour*) hacer correr.
▸**put across** *vt* (*ideas etc*) comunicar.
▸**put aside** *vt* (*lay down*: *book etc*) dejar *or* poner a un lado; (*save*) ahorrar; (*in shop*) guardar.
▸**put away** *vt* (*store*) guardar.
▸**put back** *vt* (*replace*) devolver a su lugar; (*postpone*) posponer; (*set back*: *watch, clock*) retrasar; **this will ~ us back 10 years** esto nos retrasará 10 años.
▸**put by** *vt* (*money*) guardar.
▸**put down** *vt* (*on ground*) poner en el suelo; (*animal*) sacrificar; (*in writing*) apuntar; (*suppress*: *revolt etc*) sofocar; (*attribute*) atribuir; **~ me down for £15** apúntame por 15 libras; **~ it down on my**

account (*COMM*) póngalo en mi cuenta.
▸**put forward** *vt* (*ideas*) presentar, proponer; (*date*) adelantar.
▸**put in** *vt* (*application, complaint*) presentar.
▸**put in for** *vt fus* (*job*) solicitar; (*promotion*) pedir.
▸**put off** *vt* (*postpone*) aplazar; (*discourage*) desanimar, quitar las ganas a.
▸**put on** *vt* (*clothes, lipstick etc*) ponerse; (*light etc*) encender; (*play etc*) presentar; (*brake*) echar; (*assume*: *accent, manner*) afectar, fingir; (*airs*) adoptar, darse; (*concert, exhibition etc*) montar; (*extra bus, train etc*) poner; (*col*: *kid, have on*: *esp US*) tomar el pelo a; (*inform, indicate*): **to ~ sb on to sb/sth** informar a algn de algn/algo; **to ~ on weight** engordar.
▸**put out** *vt* (*fire, light*) apagar; (*one's hand*) alargar; (*news, rumour*) hacer circular; (*tongue etc*) sacar; (*person*: *inconvenience*) molestar, fastidiar; (*dislocate*: *shoulder, vertebra, knee*) dislocar(se) ♦ *vi* (*NAUT*): **to ~ out to sea** hacerse a la mar; **to ~ out from Plymouth** salir de Plymouth.
▸**put through** *vt* (*call*) poner; **~ me through to Miss Blair** póngame *or* comuníqueme (*LAM*) con la Señorita Blair.
▸**put together** *vt* unir, reunir; (*assemble*: *furniture*) armar, montar; (*meal*) preparar.
▸**put up** *vt* (*raise*) levantar, alzar; (*hang*) colgar; (*build*) construir; (*increase*) aumentar; (*accommodate*) alojar; (*incite*): **to ~ sb up to doing sth** instar *or* incitar a algn a hacer algo; **to ~ sth up for sale** poner algo a la venta.
▸**put upon** *vt fus*: **to be ~ upon** (*imposed upon*) dejarse explotar.
▸**put up with** *vt fus* aguantar.
putrid ['pjuːtrɪd] *adj* podrido.
putsch [putʃ] *n* golpe *m* de estado.
putt [pʌt] *vt* hacer un putt ♦ *n* putt *m*, golpe *m* corto.
putter ['pʌtə*] *n* putter *m*.
putting green ['pʌtɪŋ-] *n* green *m*, minigolf *m*.
putty ['pʌtɪ] *n* masilla.
put-up ['putʌp] *adj*: **~ job** (*BRIT*) estafa.
puzzle ['pʌzl] *n* (*riddle*) acertijo; (*jigsaw*) rompecabezas *m inv*; (*also*: **crossword ~**) crucigrama *m*; (*mystery*) misterio ♦ *vt* dejar perplejo, confundir ♦ *vi*: **to ~ about** quebrar la cabeza por; **to ~ over** (*sb's actions*) quebrarse la cabeza por; (*mystery, problem*) devanarse los sesos sobre; **to be ~d about sth** no llegar a entender algo.
puzzling ['pʌzlɪŋ] *adj* (*question*) misterioso, extraño; (*attitude, set of instructions*) extraño.
PVC *n abbr* (= *polyvinyl chloride*) P.V.C. *m*.
Pvt. *abbr* (*US MIL*) = **private.**
PW *n abbr* (*US*) = **prisoner of war.**
pw *abbr* (= *per week*) por semana.
PX *n abbr* (*US*: = *post exchange*) *economato militar*.
pygmy ['pɪgmɪ] *n* pigmeo/a.
pyjamas, (*US*) **pajamas** [pɪ'dʒɑːməz] *npl* (*BRIT*) pijama *m*, piyama *m* (*LAM*); **a pair of ~** un pijama.
pylon ['paɪlən] *n* torre *f* de conducción eléctrica.
pyramid ['pɪrəmɪd] *n* pirámide *f*.
Pyrenean [pɪrə'niːən] *adj* pirenaico.
Pyrenees [pɪrə'niːz] *npl*: **the ~** los Pirineos.
Pyrex ® ['paɪreks] *n* pírex *m* ♦ *cpd*: **~ casserole** cazuela de pírex.
python ['paɪθən] *n* pitón *m*.

Q q

Q, q [kjuː] *n* (*letter*) Q, q *f*; **Q for Queen** Q de Quebec.
Qatar [kæ'tɑː] *n* Qatar *m*.
QC *n abbr* (*BRIT*: = *Queen's Council*) *título concedido a determinados abogados*.
QED *abbr* (= *quod erat demonstrandum*) Q.E.D.
QM *n abbr* = **quartermaster.**
q.t. *n abbr* (*col*: = *quiet*): **on the ~** a hurtadillas.
qty *abbr* (= *quantity*) ctdad.
quack [kwæk] *n* (*of duck*) graznido; (*pej*: *doctor*) curandero/a, matasanos *m inv* ♦ *vi* graznar.
quad [kwɔd] *abbr* = **quadrangle, quadruple, quadruplet.**
quadrangle ['kwɔdræŋgl] *n* (*BRIT*: *courtyard*: *abbr*: **quad**) patio.
quadruple [kwɔ'druːpl] *vt, vi* cuadruplicar.
quadruplet [kwɔ'druːplɪt] *n* cuatrillizo.
quagmire ['kwægmaɪə*] *n* lodazal *m*, cenegal *m*.
quail [kweɪl] *n* (*bird*) codorniz *f* ♦ *vi* amedrentarse.
quaint [kweɪnt] *adj* extraño; (*picturesque*) pintoresco.
quaintly ['kweɪntlɪ] *adv* extrañamente;

pintorescamente.
quake [kweɪk] *vi* temblar ♦ *n abbr* = **earthquake.**
Quaker ['kweɪkə*] *n* cuáquero/a.
qualification [kwɔlɪfɪ'keɪʃən] *n* (*reservation*) reserva; (*modification*) modificación *f*; (*act*) calificación *f*; (*paper* ~) título; **what are your ~s?** ¿qué títulos tienes?
qualified ['kwɔlɪfaɪd] *adj* (*trained*) cualificado; (*fit*) capacitado; (*limited*) limitado; (*professionally*) titulado; **~ for/to do sth** capacitado para/para hacer algo; **he's not ~ for the job** no está capacitado para ese trabajo; **it was a ~ success** fue un éxito relativo.
qualify ['kwɔlɪfaɪ] *vt* (*LING*) calificar a; (*capacitate*) capacitar; (*modify*) matizar; (*limit*) moderar ♦ *vi* (*SPORT*) clasificarse; **to ~ (as)** calificarse (de), graduarse (en), recibirse (de) (*LAM*); **to ~ (for)** reunir los requisitos (para); **to ~ as an engineer** sacar el título de ingeniero.
qualifying ['kwɔlɪfaɪɪŋ] *adj* (*exam, round*) eliminatorio.
qualitative ['kwɔlɪtətɪv] *adj* cualitativo.
quality ['kwɔlɪtɪ] *n* calidad *f*; (*moral*) cualidad *f*; **of good/poor ~** de buena *or* alta/poca calidad.
quality control *n* control *m* de calidad.
quality of life *n* calidad *f* de vida.
quality press *n* prensa seria; *ver recuadro.*

QUALITY PRESS

La expresión **quality press** *se refiere los periódicos que dan un tratamiento serio de las noticias, ofreciendo información detallada sobre un amplio espectro de temas y análisis en profundidad de la actualidad. Por su tamaño, considerablemente mayor que el de los periódicos sensacionalistas, se les llama también "broadsheets".*

qualm [kwɑːm] *n* escrúpulo; **to have ~s about sth** sentir escrúpulos por algo.
quandary ['kwɔndrɪ] *n*: **to be in a ~** verse en un dilema.
quango ['kwæŋgəu] *n abbr* (*BRIT*: = *quasi-autonomous non-governmental organization*) *organismo semi-autónomo de subvención estatal.*
quantifiable [kwɔntɪ'faɪəbl] *adj* cuantificable.
quantitative ['kwɔntɪtətɪv] *adj* cuantitativo.
quantity ['kwɔntɪtɪ] *n* cantidad *f*; **in ~** en grandes cantidades.
quantity surveyor *n* aparejador(a) *m/f*.
quantum leap ['kwɔntəm-] *n* (*fig*) avance *m* espectacular.
quarantine ['kwɔrntiːn] *n* cuarentena.
quark [kwɑːk] *n* cuark *m*.
quarrel ['kwɔrl] *n* riña, pelea ♦ *vi* reñir, pelearse; **to have a ~ with sb** reñir *or* pelearse con algn; **I can't ~ with that** no le veo pegas.
quarrelsome ['kwɔrəlsəm] *adj* pendenciero.
quarry ['kwɔrɪ] *n* (*for stone*) cantera; (*animal*) presa.
quart [kwɔːt] *n cuarto de galón = 1.136 l.*
quarter ['kwɔːtə*] *n* cuarto, cuarta parte *f*; (*of year*) trimestre *m*; (*district*) barrio; (*US, Canada: 25 cents*) cuarto de dólar ♦ *vt* dividir en cuartos; (*MIL: lodge*) alojar; **~s** *npl* (*barracks*) cuartel *m*; (*living ~s*) alojamiento *sg*; **a ~ of an hour** un cuarto de hora; **to pay by the ~** pagar trimestralmente *or* cada 3 meses; **it's a ~ to** *or* (*US*) **of 3** son las 3 menos cuarto; **it's a ~ past** *or* (*US*) **after 3** son las 3 y cuarto; **from all ~s** de todas partes; **at close ~s** de cerca.
quarterback ['kwɔːtəbæk] *n* (*US: football*) mariscal *m* de campo.
quarter-deck ['kwɔːtədɛk] *n* (*NAUT*) alcázar *m*.
quarter final *n* cuarto de final.
quarterly ['kwɔːtəlɪ] *adj* trimestral ♦ *adv* cada 3 meses, trimestralmente.
quartermaster ['kwɔːtəmɑːstə*] *n* (*MIL*) comisario, intendente *m* militar.
quartet(te) [kwɔː'tɛt] *n* cuarteto.
quarto ['kwɔːtəu] *n* tamaño holandés ♦ *adj* de tamaño holandés.
quartz [kwɔːts] *n* cuarzo.
quash [kwɔʃ] *vt* (*verdict*) anular, invalidar.
quasi- ['kweɪzaɪ] *pref* cuasi.
quaver ['kweɪvə*] *n* (*BRIT MUS*) corchea ♦ *vi* temblar.
quay [kiː] *n* (*also*: **~side**) muelle *m*.
Que. *abbr* (*Canada*) = *Quebec.*
queasiness ['kwiːzɪnɪs] *n* malestar *m*, náuseas *fpl*.
queasy ['kwiːzɪ] *adj*: **to feel ~** tener náuseas.
Quebec [kwɪ'bɛk] *n* Quebec *m*.
queen [kwiːn] *n* reina; (*CARDS etc*) dama.
queen mother *n* reina madre.
Queen's Speech *n ver recuadro.*

QUEEN'S SPEECH

Se llama **Queen's Speech** *(o "King's Speech") al discurso que pronuncia el monarca durante la sesión de apertura del*

Parlamento británico, en el que se expresan las líneas generales de la política del gobierno para la nueva legislatura. El Primer Ministro se encarga de redactarlo con la ayuda del Consejo de Ministros y es leído en la Cámara de los Lores ("House of Lords") ante los miembros de ambas cámaras.

queer ['kwɪə*] *adj* (*odd*) raro, extraño ♦ *n* (*pej: col*) marica *m*.
quell [kwɛl] *vt* calmar; (*put down*) sofocar.
quench [kwɛntʃ] *vt* (*flames*) apagar; **to ~ one's thirst** apagar la sed.
querulous ['kwɛruləs] *adj* (*person, voice*) quejumbroso.
query ['kwɪərɪ] *n* (*question*) pregunta; (*doubt*) duda ♦ *vt* preguntar; (*disagree with, dispute*) no estar conforme con, dudar de.
quest [kwɛst] *n* busca, búsqueda.
question ['kwɛstʃən] *n* pregunta; (*matter*) asunto, cuestión *f* ♦ *vt* (*doubt*) dudar de; (*interrogate*) interrogar, hacer preguntas a; **to ask sb a ~, put a ~ to sb** hacerle una pregunta a algn; **the ~ is ...** el asunto es ...; **to bring** *or* **call sth into ~** poner algo en (tela de) duda; **beyond ~** fuera de toda duda; **it's out of the ~** imposible, ni hablar.
questionable ['kwɛstʃənəbl] *adj* discutible; (*doubtful*) dudoso.
questioner ['kwɛstʃənə*] *n* interrogador(a) *m/f*.
questioning ['kwɛstʃənɪŋ] *adj* inquisitivo ♦ *n* preguntas *fpl*; (*by police etc*) interrogatorio.
question mark *n* punto de interrogación.
questionnaire [kwɛstʃə'nɛə*] *n* cuestionario.
queue [kju:] (*BRIT*) *n* cola ♦ *vi* hacer cola; **to jump the ~** colarse.
quibble ['kwɪbl] *vi* andarse con sutilezas.
quick [kwɪk] *adj* rápido; (*temper*) vivo; (*agile*) ágil; (*mind*) listo; (*eye*) agudo; (*ear*) fino ♦ *n*: **cut to the ~** (*fig*) herido en lo más vivo; **be ~!** ¡date prisa!; **to be ~ to act** obrar con prontitud; **she was ~ to see that** se dio cuenta de eso en seguida.
quicken ['kwɪkən] *vt* apresurar ♦ *vi* apresurarse, darse prisa.
quick-fire ['kwɪkfaɪə*] *adj* (*questions etc*) rápido, (hecho) a quemarropa.
quick fix *n* (*pej*) parche *m*.
quickly ['kwɪklɪ] *adv* rápidamente, de prisa; **we must act ~** tenemos que actuar cuanto antes.
quickness ['kwɪknɪs] *n* rapidez *f*; (*of temper*) viveza; (*agility*) agilidad *f*; (*of mind, eye etc*) agudeza.
quicksand ['kwɪksænd] *n* arenas *fpl* movedizas.
quickstep ['kwɪkstɛp] *n* *baile de ritmo rápido*.
quick-tempered [kwɪk'tɛmpəd] *adj* de genio vivo.
quick-witted [kwɪk'wɪtɪd] *adj* listo, despabilado.
quid [kwɪd] *n, pl inv* (*BRIT col*) libra.
quid pro quo ['kwɪdprəu'kwəu] *n* quid pro quo *m*, compensación *f*.
quiet ['kwaɪət] *adj* (*not busy: day*) tranquilo; (*silent*) callado; (*reserved*) reservado; (*discreet*) discreto; (*not noisy: engine*) silencioso ♦ *n* tranquilidad *f* ♦ *vt, vi* (*US*) = **quieten**; **keep ~!** ¡cállate!, ¡silencio!; **business is ~ at this time of year** hay poco movimiento en esta época.
quieten ['kwaɪətn] (*also*: **~ down**) *vi* (*grow calm*) calmarse; (*grow silent*) callarse ♦ *vt* calmar; hacer callar.
quietly ['kwaɪətlɪ] *adv* tranquilamente; (*silently*) silenciosamente.
quietness ['kwaɪətnɪs] *n* (*silence*) silencio; (*calm*) tranquilidad *f*.
quill [kwɪl] *n* (*of porcupine*) púa; (*pen*) pluma.
quilt [kwɪlt] *n* (*BRIT*) edredón *m*.
quin [kwɪn] *n abbr* = **quintuplet**.
quince [kwɪns] *n* membrillo.
quinine [kwɪ'ni:n] *n* quinina.
quintet(te) [kwɪn'tɛt] *n* quinteto.
quintuplet [kwɪn'tju:plɪt] *n* quintillizo.
quip [kwɪp] *n* ocurrencia ♦ *vi* decir con ironía.
quirk [kwə:k] *n* peculiaridad *f*; **by some ~ of fate** por algún capricho del destino.
quit *pt, pp* **quit** *or* **quitted** [kwɪt] *vt* dejar, abandonar; (*premises*) desocupar; (*COMPUT*) abandonar ♦ *vi* (*give up*) renunciar; (*go away*) irse; (*resign*) dimitir; **~ stalling!** (*US col*) ¡déjate de evasivas!
quite [kwaɪt] *adv* (*rather*) bastante; (*entirely*) completamente; **~ a few of them** un buen número de ellos; **~ (so)!** ¡así es!, ¡exactamente!; **~ new** bastante nuevo; **that's not ~ right** eso no está del todo bien; **not ~ as many as last time** no tantos como la última vez; **she's ~ pretty** es bastante guapa.
Quito ['ki:təu] *n* Quito.
quits [kwɪts] *adj*: **~ (with)** en paz (con); **let's call it ~** quedamos en paz.
quiver ['kwɪvə*] *vi* estremecerse ♦ *n* (*for arrows*) carcaj *m*.
quiz [kwɪz] *n* (*game*) concurso; (*: TV, RADIO*)

programa-concurso; (*questioning*) interrogatorio ♦ *vt* interrogar.
quizzical ['kwɪzɪkl] *adj* burlón(ona).
quoits [kwɔɪts] *npl* juego de aros.
quorum ['kwɔːrəm] *n* quórum *m*.
quota ['kwəutə] *n* cuota.
quotation [kwəu'teɪʃən] *n* cita; (*estimate*) presupuesto.
quotation marks *npl* comillas *fpl*.
quote [kwəut] *n* cita ♦ *vt* (*sentence*) citar; (COMM: *sum, figure*) cotizar ♦ *vi*: **to ~ from** citar de; **~s** *npl* (*inverted commas*) comillas *fpl*; **in ~s** entre comillas; **the figure ~d for the repairs** el presupuesto dado para las reparaciones; **~ ... unquote** (*in dictation*) comillas iniciales ... finales.
quotient ['kwəuʃənt] *n* cociente *m*.
qv *n abbr* (= *quod vide: which see*) q.v.
qwerty keyboard ['kwəːtɪ-] *n* teclado QWERTY.

R r

R, r [ɑː*] *n* (*letter*) R, r *f*; **R for Robert,** (*US*) **R for Roger** R de Ramón.
R *abbr* (= *right*) dcha.; (= *river*) R.; (= *Réaumur (scale)*) R; (*US CINE*: = *restricted*) *sólo mayores*; (*US POL*) = **republican**; (*BRIT*: = *Rex, Regina*) R.
RA *abbr* = *rear admiral* ♦ *n abbr* (*BRIT*) = **Royal Academy**, *Royal Academician*.
RAAF *n abbr* = *Royal Australian Air Force*.
Rabat [rə'bɑːt] *n* Rabat *m*.
rabbi ['ræbaɪ] *n* rabino.
rabbit ['ræbɪt] *n* conejo ♦ *vi*: **to ~ (on)** (*BRIT col*) hablar sin ton ni son.
rabbit hutch *n* conejera.
rabble ['ræbl] *n* (*pej*) chusma, populacho.
rabies ['reɪbiːz] *n* rabia.
RAC *n abbr* (*BRIT*: = *Royal Automobile Club*) ≈ RACE *m* (*SP*).
raccoon [rə'kuːn] *n* mapache *m*.
race [reɪs] *n* carrera; (*species*) raza ♦ *vt* (*horse*) hacer correr; (*person*) competir contra; (*engine*) acelerar ♦ *vi* (*compete*) competir; (*run*) correr; (*pulse*) latir a ritmo acelerado; **the arms ~** la carrera armamentista; **the human ~** el género humano; **he ~d across the road** cruzó corriendo la carretera; **to ~ in/out** entrar/salir corriendo.
race car *n* (*US*) = **racing car**.
race car driver *n* (*US*) = **racing driver**.
racecourse ['reɪskɔːs] *n* hipódromo.
racehorse ['reɪshɔːs] *n* caballo de carreras.
race meeting *n* concurso hípico.
race relations *npl* relaciones *fpl* raciales.
racetrack ['reɪstræk] *n* hipódromo; (*for cars*) circuito de carreras.
racial ['reɪʃl] *adj* racial.
racial discrimination *n* discriminación *f* racial.
racial integration *n* integración *f* racial.
racialism ['reɪʃəlɪzəm] *n* racismo.
racialist ['reɪʃəlɪst] *adj, n* racista *m/f*.
racing ['reɪsɪŋ] *n* carreras *fpl*.
racing car *n* (*BRIT*) coche *m* de carreras.
racing driver *n* (*BRIT*) corredor(a) *m/f* de coches.
racism ['reɪsɪzəm] *n* racismo.
racist ['reɪsɪst] *adj, n* racista *m/f*.
rack [ræk] *n* (*also*: **luggage ~**) rejilla (portaequipajes); (*shelf*) estante *m*; (*also*: **roof ~**) baca; (*clothes ~*) perchero ♦ *vt* (*cause pain to*) atormentar; **to go to ~ and ruin** venirse abajo; **to ~ one's brains** devanarse los sesos.
►**rack up** *vt* conseguir, ganar.
racket ['rækɪt] *n* (*for tennis*) raqueta; (*noise*) ruido, estrépito; (*swindle*) estafa, timo.
racketeer [rækɪ'tɪə*] *n* (*esp US*) estafador(a) *m/f*.
racoon [rə'kuːn] *n* = **raccoon**.
racquet ['rækɪt] *n* raqueta.
racy ['reɪsɪ] *adj* picante, subido.
RADA ['rɑːdə] *n abbr* (*BRIT*) = *Royal Academy of Dramatic Art*.
radar ['reɪdɑː*] *n* radar *m*.
radar trap *n* trampa radar.
radial ['reɪdɪəl] *adj* (*tyre*: *also*: **~-ply**) radial.
radiance ['reɪdɪəns] *n* brillantez *f*, resplandor *m*.
radiant ['reɪdɪənt] *adj* brillante, resplandeciente.
radiate ['reɪdɪeɪt] *vt* (*heat*) radiar, irradiar ♦ *vi* (*lines*) extenderse.
radiation [reɪdɪ'eɪʃən] *n* radiación *f*.
radiation sickness *n* enfermedad *f* de radiación.
radiator ['reɪdɪeɪtə*] *n* (*AUT*) radiador *m*.
radiator cap *n* tapón *m* de radiador.
radiator grill *n* (*AUT*) rejilla del radiador.
radical ['rædɪkl] *adj* radical.
radically ['rædɪkəlɪ] *adv* radicalmente.
radii ['reɪdɪaɪ] *npl of* **radius**.
radio ['reɪdɪəu] *n* radio *f or m* (*LAM*) ♦ *vi*: **to ~ to sb** mandar un mensaje por radio a algn ♦ *vt* (*information*) radiar, transmitir por radio; (*one's position*) indicar por

radio; (*person*) llamar por radio; **on the ~** en *or* por la radio.
radioactive [reɪdɪəu'æktɪv] *adj* radi(o)activo.
radioactivity [reɪdɪəuæk'tɪvɪtɪ] *n* radi(o)actividad *f*.
radio announcer *n* locutor(a) *m/f* de radio.
radio-controlled [reɪdɪəukən'trəuld] *adj* teledirigido.
radiographer [reɪdɪ'ɔgrəfə*] *n* radiógrafo/a.
radiography [reɪdɪ'ɔgrəfɪ] *n* radiografía.
radiology [reɪdɪ'ɔlədʒɪ] *n* radiología.
radio station *n* emisora.
radio taxi *n* radio taxi *m*.
radiotelephone [reɪdɪəu'tɛlɪfəun] *n* radioteléfono.
radiotelescope [reɪdɪəu'tɛlɪskəup] *n* radiotelescopio.
radiotherapist [reɪdɪəu'θɛrəpɪst] *n* radioterapeuta *m/f*.
radiotherapy ['reɪdɪəuθɛrəpɪ] *n* radioterapia.
radish ['rædɪʃ] *n* rábano.
radium ['reɪdɪəm] *n* radio.
radius, *pl* **radii** ['reɪdɪəs, -ɪaɪ] *n* radio; **within a ~ of 50 miles** en un radio de 50 millas.
RAF *n abbr see* **Royal Air Force**.
raffia ['ræfɪə] *n* rafia.
raffle ['ræfl] *n* rifa, sorteo ♦ *vt* (*object*) rifar.
raft [rɑːft] *n* (*craft*) balsa; (*also*: **life ~**) balsa salvavidas.
rafter ['rɑːftə*] *n* viga.
rag [ræg] *n* (*piece of cloth*) trapo; (*torn cloth*) harapo; (*pej*: *newspaper*) periodicucho; (*for charity*) *actividades estudiantiles benéficas* ♦ *vt* (*BRIT*) tomar el pelo a; **~s** *npl* harapos *mpl*; **in ~s** en harapos, hecho jirones.
rag-and-bone man [rægən'bəunmæn] *n* (*BRIT*) trapero.
rag doll *n* muñeca de trapo.
rage [reɪdʒ] *n* (*fury*) rabia, furor *m* ♦ *vi* (*person*) rabiar, estar furioso; (*storm*) bramar; **to fly into a ~** montar en cólera; **it's all the ~** es lo último.
ragged ['rægɪd] *adj* (*edge*) desigual, mellado; (*cuff*) roto; (*appearance*) andrajoso, harapiento; **~ left/right** (*text*) margen *m* izquierdo/derecho irregular.
raging ['reɪdʒɪŋ] *adj* furioso; **in a ~ temper** de un humor de mil demonios.
rag week *n ver recuadro*.

RAG WEEK

En la universidad los estudiantes suelen organizar cada año lo que llaman **rag week**. *Consiste en una serie de actos festivos y de participación general como teatro en la calle, marchas patrocinadas etc, para hacer colectas con fines benéficos. En ocasiones hacen también una revista ("rag mag"), que consiste básicamente en chistes más bien picantes para vender a los transeúntes, e incluso un baile de gala ("rag ball").*

raid [reɪd] *n* (*MIL*) incursión *f*; (*criminal*) asalto; (*by police*) redada, allanamiento (*LAM*) ♦ *vt* invadir, atacar; asaltar.
raider ['reɪdə*] *n* invasor(a) *m/f*.
rail [reɪl] *n* (*on stair*) barandilla, pasamanos *m inv*; (*on bridge*) pretil *m*; (*of balcony, ship*) barandilla; (*for train*) riel *m*, carril *m*; **~s** *npl* vía *sg*; **by ~** por ferrocarril, en tren.
railcard ['reɪlkɑːd] *n* (*BRIT*) *tarjeta para obtener descuentos en el tren*; **Young Person's ~** ≈ Tarjeta joven (*ESP*).
railing(s) ['reɪlɪŋz] *n*(*pl*) verja *sg*.
railway ['reɪlweɪ], (*US*) **railroad** ['reɪlrəud] *n* ferrocarril *m*, vía férrea.
railway engine *n* (máquina) locomotora.
railway line *n* (*BRIT*) línea (de ferrocarril).
railwayman ['reɪlweɪmən] *n* (*BRIT*) ferroviario.
railway station *n* (*BRIT*) estación *f* de ferrocarril.
rain [reɪn] *n* lluvia ♦ *vi* llover; **in the ~** bajo la lluvia; **it's ~ing** llueve, está lloviendo; **it's ~ing cats and dogs** está lloviendo a cántaros *or* a mares.
rainbow ['reɪnbəu] *n* arco iris.
raincoat ['reɪnkəut] *n* impermeable *m*.
raindrop ['reɪndrɔp] *n* gota de lluvia.
rainfall ['reɪnfɔːl] *n* lluvia.
rainforest ['reɪnfɔrɪst] *n* selva tropical.
rainproof ['reɪnpruːf] *adj* impermeable, a prueba de lluvia.
rainstorm ['reɪnstɔːm] *n* temporal *m* (de lluvia).
rainwater ['reɪnwɔːtə*] *n* agua de lluvia.
rainy ['reɪnɪ] *adj* lluvioso.
raise [reɪz] *n* aumento ♦ *vt* (*lift*) levantar; (*build*) erigir, edificar; (*increase*) aumentar; (*doubts*) suscitar; (*a question*) plantear; (*cattle, family*) criar; (*crop*) cultivar; (*army*) reclutar; (*funds*) reunir; (*loan*) obtener; (*end*: *embargo*) levantar; **to ~ one's voice** alzar la voz; **to ~ one's glass to sb/sth** brindar por algn/algo; **to ~ a laugh/a smile** provocar risa/una sonrisa; **to ~ sb's hopes** dar esperanzas a algn.
raisin ['reɪzn] *n* pasa de Corinto.

rake [reɪk] *n* (*tool*) rastrillo; (*person*) libertino ♦ *vt* (*garden*) rastrillar; (*fire*) hurgar; (*with machine gun*) barrer.
▸**rake in, rake together** *vt* sacar.
rake-off [ˈreɪkɔf] *n* (*col*) comisión *f*, tajada.
rakish [ˈreɪkɪʃ] *adj* (*dissolute*) libertino; **at a ~ angle** (*hat*) echado a un lado, de lado.
rally [ˈrælɪ] *n* reunión *f*; (*POL*) mitin *m*; (*AUT*) rallye *m*; (*TENNIS*) peloteo ♦ *vt* reunir ♦ *vi* reunirse; (*sick person, STOCK EXCHANGE*) recuperarse.
▸**rally round** *vt fus* (*fig*) dar apoyo a.
rallying point [ˈrælɪɪŋ-] *n* (*POL, MIL*) punto de reunión.
RAM [ræm] *n abbr* (= *random access memory*) RAM *f*.
ram [ræm] *n* carnero; (*TECH*) pisón *m* ♦ *vt* (*crash into*) dar contra, chocar con; (*tread down*) apisonar.
ramble [ˈræmbl] *n* caminata, excursión *f* en el campo ♦ *vi* (*pej*: *also*: **~ on**) divagar.
rambler [ˈræmblə*] *n* excursionista *m/f*; (*BOT*) trepadora.
rambling [ˈræmblɪŋ] *adj* (*speech*) inconexo; (*BOT*) trepador(a); (*house*) laberíntico.
rambunctious [ræmˈbʌŋkʃəs] *adj* (*US*) = **rumbustious.**
RAMC *n abbr* (*BRIT*) = *Royal Army Medical Corps.*
ramification [ræmɪfɪˈkeɪʃən] *n* ramificación *f*.
ramp [ræmp] *n* rampa; **on/off ~** *n* (*US AUT*) vía de acceso/salida; "**~**" (*AUT*) "rampa".
rampage [ræmˈpeɪdʒ] *n*: **to be on the ~** desmandarse.
rampant [ˈræmpənt] *adj* (*disease etc*): **to be ~** estar muy extendido.
rampart [ˈræmpɑːt] *n* terraplén *m*; (*wall*) muralla.
ram raid *vt* atracar (*rompiendo el escaparate con un coche*).
ramshackle [ˈræmʃækl] *adj* destartalado.
RAN *n abbr* = *Royal Australian Navy.*
ran [ræn] *pt of* **run.**
ranch [rɑːntʃ] *n* (*US*) hacienda, estancia.
rancher [ˈrɑːntʃə*] *n* ganadero.
rancid [ˈrænsɪd] *adj* rancio.
rancour, (*US*) **rancor** [ˈræŋkə*] *n* rencor *m*.
random [ˈrændəm] *adj* fortuito, sin orden; (*COMPUT, MATH*) aleatorio ♦ *n*: **at ~** al azar.
random access *n* (*COMPUT*) acceso aleatorio.
randy [ˈrændɪ] *adj* (*BRIT col*) cachondo, caliente.
rang [ræŋ] *pt of* **ring.**
range [reɪndʒ] *n* (*of mountains*) cadena de montañas, cordillera; (*of missile*) alcance *m*; (*of voice*) registro; (*series*) serie *f*; (*of products*) surtido; (*MIL*: *also*: **shooting ~**) campo de tiro; (*also*: **kitchen ~**) fogón *m* ♦ *vt* (*place*) colocar; (*arrange*) arreglar ♦ *vi*: **to ~ over** (*wander*) recorrer; (*extend*) extenderse por; **within (firing) ~** a tiro; **do you have anything else in this price ~?** ¿tiene algo más de esta gama de precios?; **intermediate-/short-~ missile** proyectil *m* de medio/corto alcance; **to ~ from ... to...** oscilar entre ... y...; **~d left/right** (*text*) alineado a la izquierda/derecha.
ranger [reɪndʒə*] *n* guardabosques *m inv*.
Rangoon [ræŋˈguːn] *n* Rangún *m*.
rangy [ˈreɪndʒɪ] *adj* alto y delgado.
rank [ræŋk] *n* (*row*) fila; (*MIL*) rango; (*status*) categoría; (*BRIT*: *also*: **taxi ~**) parada ♦ *vi*: **to ~ among** figurar entre ♦ *adj* (*stinking*) fétido, rancio; (*hypocrisy, injustice etc*) manifiesto; **the ~ and file** (*fig*) las bases; **to close ~s** (*MIL*) cerrar filas; (*fig*) hacer un frente común; **~ outsider** participante *m/f* sin probabilidades de vencer; **I ~ him 6th** yo le pongo en sexto lugar.
rankle [ˈræŋkl] *vi* (*insult*) doler.
ransack [ˈrænsæk] *vt* (*search*) registrar; (*plunder*) saquear.
ransom [ˈrænsəm] *n* rescate *m*; **to hold sb to ~** (*fig*) poner a algn entre la espada y la pared.
rant [rænt] *vi* despotricar.
ranting [ˈræntɪŋ] *n* desvaríos *mpl*.
rap [ræp] *vt* golpear, dar un golpecito en.
rape [reɪp] *n* violación *f*; (*BOT*) colza ♦ *vt* violar.
rape(seed) oil [ˈreɪp(siːd)-] *n* aceite *m* de colza.
rapid [ˈræpɪd] *adj* rápido.
rapidity [rəˈpɪdɪtɪ] *n* rapidez *f*.
rapidly [ˈræpɪdlɪ] *adv* rápidamente.
rapids [ˈræpɪdz] *npl* (*GEO*) rápidos *mpl*.
rapier [ˈreɪpɪə*] *n* estoque *m*.
rapist [ˈreɪpɪst] *n* violador *m*.
rapport [ræˈpɔː*] *n* entendimiento.
rapprochement [ræˈprɔʃmɑ̃ːŋ] *n* acercamiento.
rapt [ræpt] *adj* (*attention*) profundo; **to be ~ in contemplation** estar ensimismado.
rapture [ˈræptʃə*] *n* éxtasis *m*.
rapturous [ˈræptʃərəs] *adj* extático; (*applause*) entusiasta; **a ~ (party)** *macrofiesta con música máquina*; **~ music** música máquina.
rare [rɛə*] *adj* raro, poco común; (*CULIN*: *steak*) poco hecho; **it is ~ to find that ...** es raro descubrir que ....
rarefied [ˈrɛərɪfaɪd] *adj* (*air, atmosphere*)

enrarecido.
rarely ['rɛəlɪ] *adv* rara vez, pocas veces.
raring ['rɛərɪŋ] *adj*: **to be ~ to go** (*col*) tener muchas ganas de empezar.
rarity ['rɛərɪtɪ] *n* rareza.
rascal ['rɑːskl] *n* pillo/a, pícaro/a.
rash [ræʃ] *adj* imprudente, precipitado ♦ *n* (*MED*) salpullido, erupción *f* (cutánea); **to come out in a ~** salir salpullidos.
rasher ['ræʃə*] *n* loncha.
rashly ['ræʃlɪ] *adv* imprudentemente, precipitadamente.
rashness ['ræʃnɪs] *n* imprudencia, precipitación *f*.
rasp [rɑːsp] *n* (*tool*) escofina ♦ *vt* (*speak*: *also*: **~ out**) decir con voz áspera.
raspberry ['rɑːzbərɪ] *n* frambuesa.
rasping ['rɑːspɪŋ] *adj*: **a ~ noise** un ruido áspero.
Rastafarian [ræstə'fɛərɪən] *adj, n* rastafari *m/f*.
rat [ræt] *n* rata.
ratchet ['rætʃɪt] *n* (*TECH*) trinquete *m*.
rate [reɪt] *n* (*ratio*) razón *f*; (*percentage*) tanto por ciento; (*price*) precio; (: *of hotel*) tarifa; (*of interest*) tipo; (*speed*) velocidad *f* ♦ *vt* (*value*) tasar; (*estimate*) estimar; **to ~ as** ser considerado como; **~s** *npl* (*BRIT*) impuesto *sg* municipal; (*fees*) tarifa *sg*; **failure ~** porcentaje *m* de fallos; **pulse ~** pulsaciones *fpl* por minuto; **~ of pay** tipos *mpl* de sueldo; **at a ~ of 60 kph** a una velocidad de 60 kph; **~ of growth** ritmo de crecimiento; **~ of return** (*COMM*) tasa de rendimiento; **bank ~** tipo *or* tasa de interés bancario; **at any ~** en todo caso; **to ~ sb/sth highly** tener a algn/algo en alta estima; **the house is ~d at £84 per annum** (*BRIT*) la casa está tasada en 84 libras al año.
rateable value ['reɪtəbl-] *n* (*BRIT*) valor *m* impuesto.
rate-capping ['reɪtkæpɪŋ] *n* (*BRIT*) fijación *f* de las contribuciones.
ratepayer ['reɪtpeɪə*] *n* (*BRIT*) contribuyente *m/f*.
rather ['rɑːðə*] *adv* antes, más bien; (*somewhat*) algo, un poco; (*quite*) bastante; **it's ~ expensive** es algo caro; (*too much*) es demasiado caro; **there's ~ a lot** hay bastante; **I would** *or* **I'd ~ go** preferiría ir; **I'd ~ not** prefiero que no; **I ~ think he won't come** me inclino a creer que no vendrá; **or ~** (*more accurately*) o mejor dicho.
ratification [rætɪfɪ'keɪʃən] *n* ratificación *f*.
ratify ['rætɪfaɪ] *vt* ratificar.
rating ['reɪtɪŋ] *n* (*valuation*) tasación *f*; (*standing*) posición *f*; (*BRIT NAUT*: *sailor*) marinero; **~s** *npl* (*RADIO, TV*) clasificación *f*.
ratio ['reɪʃɪəu] *n* razón *f*; **in the ~ of 100 to 1** a razón de *or* en la proporción de 100 a 1.
ration ['ræʃən] *n* ración *f*; **~s** *npl* víveres *mpl* ♦ *vt* racionar.
rational ['ræʃənl] *adj* racional; (*solution, reasoning*) lógico, razonable; (*person*) cuerdo, sensato.
rationale [ræʃə'nɑːl] *n* razón *f* fundamental.
rationalism ['ræʃnəlɪzəm] *n* racionalismo.
rationalization [ræʃnəlaɪ'zeɪʃən] *n* racionalización *f*.
rationalize ['ræʃnəlaɪz] *vt* (*reorganize*: *industry*) racionalizar.
rationally ['ræʃnəlɪ] *adv* racionalmente; (*logically*) lógicamente.
rationing ['ræʃnɪŋ] *n* racionamiento.
ratpack ['rætpæk] *n* (*BRIT col*) *periodistas que persiguen a los famosos*.
rat race *n lucha incesante por la supervivencia*.
rattan [ræ'tæn] *n* rota, caña de Indias.
rattle ['rætl] *n* golpeteo; (*of train etc*) traqueteo; (*object*: *of baby*) sonaja, sonajero; (: *of sports fan*) matraca ♦ *vi* sonar, golpear; traquetear; (*small objects*) castañetear ♦ *vt* hacer sonar agitando; (*col*: *disconcert*) poner nervioso a.
rattlesnake ['rætlsneɪk] *n* serpiente *f* de cascabel.
ratty ['rætɪ] *adj* (*col*) furioso; **to get ~** mosquearse.
raucous ['rɔːkəs] *adj* estridente, ronco.
raucously ['rɔːkəslɪ] *adv* de modo estridente, roncamente.
raunchy ['rɔːntʃɪ] *adj* (*col*) lascivo.
ravage ['rævɪdʒ] *vt* hacer estragos en, destrozar; **~s** *npl* estragos *mpl*.
rave [reɪv] *vi* (*in anger*) encolerizarse; (*with enthusiasm*) entusiasmarse; (*MED*) delirar, desvariar ♦ *cpd*: **~ review** reseña entusiasta; **a ~ (party)** *macrofiesta con música máquina*; **~ music** música máquina.
raven ['reɪvən] *n* cuervo.
ravenous ['rævənəs] *adj*: **to be ~** tener un hambre canina.
ravine [rə'viːn] *n* barranco.
raving ['reɪvɪŋ] *adj*: **~ lunatic** loco de atar.
ravings ['reɪvɪŋz] *npl* desvaríos *mpl*.
ravioli [rævɪ'əulɪ] *n* ravioles *mpl*, ravioli *mpl*.
ravish ['rævɪʃ] *vt* (*charm*) encantar, embelesar; (*rape*) violar.
ravishing ['rævɪʃɪŋ] *adj* encantador(a).
raw [rɔː] *adj* (*uncooked*) crudo; (*not processed*) bruto; (*sore*) vivo;

(*inexperienced*) novato, inexperto.
Rawalpindi [rɔːl'pɪndɪ] *n* Rawalpindi *m.*
raw data *n* (*COMPUT*) datos *mpl* en bruto.
raw deal *n* (*col*: *bad deal*) mala pasada *or* jugada; (: *harsh treatment*) injusticia.
raw material *n* materia prima.
ray [reɪ] *n* rayo; ~ **of hope** (rayo de) esperanza.
rayon ['reɪɔn] *n* rayón *m.*
raze [reɪz] *vt* (*also*: ~ **to the ground**) arrasar, asolar.
razor ['reɪzə*] *n* (*open*) navaja; (*safety* ~) máquina de afeitar.
razor blade *n* hoja de afeitar.
razzle(-dazzle) ['ræzl('dæzl)] *n* (*BRIT col*): **to be/go on the** ~ estar/irse de juerga.
razzmatazz ['ræzmə'tæz] *n* (*col*) animación *f*, bullicio.
R & B *n abbr* = *rhythm and blues.*
RC *abbr* = **Roman Catholic.**
RCAF *n abbr* = *Royal Canadian Air Force.*
RCMP *n abbr* = *Royal Canadian Mounted Police.*
RCN *n abbr* = *Royal Canadian Navy.*
RD *abbr* (*US POST*) = *rural delivery.*
Rd *abbr* = **road.**
R & D *n abbr* (= *research and development*) I + D.
RDC *n abbr* (*BRIT*) = *rural district council.*
RE *n abbr* (*BRIT*) = *religious education*; (*BRIT MIL*) = *Royal Engineers.*
re [riː] *prep* con referencia a.
re ... [riː] *pref* re....
reach [riːtʃ] *n* alcance *m*; (*BOXING*) envergadura; (*of river etc*) extensión *f* entre dos recodos ♦ *vt* alcanzar, llegar a; (*achieve*) lograr ♦ *vi* extenderse; (*stretch out hand*: *also*: ~ **down,** ~ **over,** ~ **across** *etc*) tender la mano; **within** ~ al alcance (de la mano); **out of** ~ fuera del alcance; **to** ~ **out for sth** alargar *or* tender la mano para tomar algo; **can I** ~ **you at your hotel?** ¿puedo localizarte en tu hotel?; **to** ~ **sb by phone** comunicarse con algn por teléfono.
react [riː'ækt] *vi* reaccionar.
reaction [riː'ækʃən] *n* reacción *f.*
reactionary [riː'ækʃənrɪ] *adj, n* reaccionario/a *m/f.*
reactor [riː'æktə*] *n* reactor *m.*
read, *pt, pp* **read** [riːd, rɛd] *vi* leer ♦ *vt* leer; (*understand*) entender; (*study*) estudiar; **to take sth as read** (*fig*) dar algo por sentado; **do you** ~ **me?** (*TEL*) ¿me escucha?; **to** ~ **between the lines** leer entre líneas.
▸**read out** *vt* leer en alta voz.
▸**read over** *vt* repasar.
▸**read through** *vt* (*quickly*) leer rápidamente, echar un vistazo a; (*thoroughly*) leer con cuidado *or* detenidamente.
▸**read up** *vt*, **read up on** *vt fus* documentarse sobre.
readable ['riːdəbl] *adj* (*writing*) legible; (*book*) que merece la pena leer.
reader ['riːdə*] *n* lector(a) *m/f*; (*book*) libro de lecturas; (*BRIT*: *at university*) profesor(a) *m/f.*
readership ['riːdəʃɪp] *n* (*of paper etc*) número de lectores.
readily ['rɛdɪlɪ] *adv* (*willingly*) de buena gana; (*easily*) fácilmente; (*quickly*) en seguida.
readiness ['rɛdɪnɪs] *n* buena voluntad; (*preparedness*) preparación *f*; **in** ~ (*prepared*) listo, preparado.
reading ['riːdɪŋ] *n* lectura; (*understanding*) comprensión *f*; (*on instrument*) indicación *f.*
reading lamp *n* lámpara portátil.
reading matter *n* lectura.
reading room *n* sala de lectura.
readjust [riːə'dʒʌst] *vt* reajustar ♦ *vi* (*person*): **to** ~ **to** reajustarse a.
readjustment [riːə'dʒʌstmənt] *n* reajuste *m.*
ready ['rɛdɪ] *adj* listo, preparado; (*willing*) dispuesto; (*available*) disponible ♦ *n*: **at the** ~ (*MIL*) listo para tirar; ~ **for use** listo para usar; **to be** ~ **to do sth** estar listo para hacer algo; **to get** ~ *vi* prepararse ♦ *vt* preparar.
ready cash *n* efectivo.
ready-made ['rɛdɪ'meɪd] *adj* confeccionado.
ready money *n* dinero contante.
ready reckoner *n* tabla de cálculos hechos.
ready-to-wear ['rɛdɪtə'wɛə*] *adj* confeccionado.
reaffirm [riːə'fəːm] *vt* reafirmar.
reagent [riː'eɪdʒənt] *n* reactivo.
real [rɪəl] *adj* verdadero, auténtico; **in** ~ **terms** en términos reales; **in** ~ **life** en la vida real, en la realidad.
real ale *n* cerveza elaborada tradicionalmente.
real estate *n* bienes *mpl* raíces.
real estate agency *n* = **estate agency.**
realism ['rɪəlɪzəm] *n* (*also ART*) realismo.
realist ['rɪəlɪst] *n* realista *m/f.*
realistic [rɪə'lɪstɪk] *adj* realista.
realistically [rɪə'lɪstɪklɪ] *adv* de modo realista.
reality [riː'ælɪtɪ] *n* realidad *f*; **in** ~ en

realidad.
realization [rɪəlaɪ'zeɪʃən] *n* comprensión *f*; (*of a project*; *COMM*: *of assets*) realización *f*.
realize ['rɪəlaɪz] *vt* (*understand*) darse cuenta de; (*a project*; *COMM*: *asset*) realizar; **I ~ that ...** comprendo *or* entiendo que ....
really ['rɪəlɪ] *adv* realmente; **~?** ¿de veras?
realm [rɛlm] *n* reino; (*fig*) esfera.
real time *n* (*COMPUT*) tiempo real.
Realtor ® ['rɪəltɔː*] *n* (*US*) corredor(a) *m/f* de bienes raíces.
ream [riːm] *n* resma; **~s** (*fig, col*) montones *mpl*.
reap [riːp] *vt* segar; (*fig*) cosechar, recoger.
reaper ['riːpə*] *n* segador(a) *m/f*.
reappear [riːə'pɪə*] *vi* reaparecer.
reappearance [riːə'pɪərəns] *n* reaparición *f*.
reapply [riːə'plaɪ] *vi* volver a presentarse, hacer *or* presentar una nueva solicitud.
reappoint [riːə'pɔɪnt] *vt* volver a nombrar.
reappraisal [riːə'preɪzl] *n* revaluación *f*.
rear [rɪə*] *adj* trasero ♦ *n* parte *f* trasera ♦ *vt* (*cattle, family*) criar ♦ *vi* (*also*: **~ up**) (*animal*) encabritarse.
rear-engined ['rɪər'ɛndʒɪnd] *adj* (*AUT*) con motor trasero.
rearguard ['rɪəgɑːd] *n* retaguardia.
rearm [riː'ɑːm] *vt* rearmar ♦ *vi* rearmarse.
rearmament [riː'ɑːməmənt] *n* rearme *m*.
rearrange [riːə'reɪndʒ] *vt* ordenar *or* arreglar de nuevo.
rear-view ['rɪəvjuː]: **~ mirror** *n* (*AUT*) espejo retrovisor.
reason ['riːzn] *n* razón *f* ♦ *vi*: **to ~ with sb** tratar de que algn entre en razón; **it stands to ~ that** es lógico que; **the ~ for/why** la causa de/la razón por la cual; **she claims with good ~ that she's underpaid** dice con razón que está mal pagada; **all the more ~ why you should not sell it** razón de más para que no lo vendas.
reasonable ['riːznəbl] *adj* razonable; (*sensible*) sensato.
reasonably ['riːznəblɪ] *adv* razonablemente; **a ~ accurate report** un informe bastante exacto.
reasoned ['riːznd] *adj* (*argument*) razonado.
reasoning ['riːznɪŋ] *n* razonamiento, argumentos *mpl*.
reassemble [riːə'sɛmbl] *vt* volver a reunir; (*machine*) montar de nuevo ♦ *vi* volver a reunirse.
reassert [riːə'səːt] *vt* reafirmar, reiterar.
reassurance [riːə'ʃuərəns] *n* consuelo.
reassure [riːə'ʃuə*] *vt* tranquilizar; **to ~ sb that** tranquilizar a algn asegurándole que.
reassuring [riːə'ʃuərɪŋ] *adj* tranquilizador(a).
reawakening [riːə'weɪknɪŋ] *n* despertar *m*.
rebate ['riːbeɪt] *n* (*on product*) rebaja; (*on tax etc*) desgravación *f*; (*repayment*) reembolso.
rebel ['rɛbl] *n* rebelde *m/f* ♦ *vi* [rɪ'bɛl] rebelarse, sublevarse.
rebellion [rɪ'bɛljən] *n* rebelión *f*, sublevación *f*.
rebellious [rɪ'bɛljəs] *adj* rebelde; (*child*) revoltoso.
rebirth [riː'bəːθ] *n* renacimiento.
rebound [rɪ'baund] *vi* (*ball*) rebotar ♦ *n* ['riːbaund] rebote *m*.
rebuff [rɪ'bʌf] *n* desaire *m*, rechazo ♦ *vt* rechazar.
rebuild [riː'bɪld] *vt* (*irreg*: *like* **build**) reconstruir.
rebuilding [riː'bɪldɪŋ] *n* reconstrucción *f*.
rebuke [rɪ'bjuːk] *n* reprimenda ♦ *vt* reprender.
rebut [rɪ'bʌt] *vt* rebatir.
recalcitrant [rɪ'kælsɪtrənt] *adj* reacio.
recall [rɪ'kɔːl] *vt* (*remember*) recordar; (*ambassador etc*) retirar; (*COMPUT*) volver a llamar ♦ *n* recuerdo.
recant [rɪ'kænt] *vi* retractarse.
recap ['riːkæp] *vt, vi* recapitular.
recapitulate [riːkə'pɪtjuleɪt] *vt, vi* = **recap.**
recapture [riː'kæptʃə*] *vt* (*town*) reconquistar; (*atmosphere*) hacer revivir.
recd., rec'd *abbr* (= *received*) rbdo.
recede [rɪ'siːd] *vi* retroceder.
receding [rɪ'siːdɪŋ] *adj* (*forehead, chin*) hundido; **~ hairline** entradas *fpl*.
receipt [rɪ'siːt] *n* (*document*) recibo; (*act of receiving*) recepción *f*; **~s** *npl* (*COMM*) ingresos *mpl*; **to acknowledge ~ of** acusar recibo de; **we are in ~ of ...** obra en nuestro poder ....
receivable [rɪ'siːvəbl] *adj* (*COMM*) a cobrar.
receive [rɪ'siːv] *vt* recibir; (*guest*) acoger; (*wound*) sufrir; **"~ed with thanks"** (*COMM*) "recibí".
Received Pronunciation [rɪ'siːvd-] *n see* **RP**.
receiver [rɪ'siːvə*] *n* (*TEL*) auricular *m*; (*RADIO*) receptor *m*; (*of stolen goods*) perista *m/f*; (*LAW*) administrador *m* jurídico.
receivership [rɪ'siːvəʃɪp] *n*: **to go into ~** entrar en liquidación.
recent ['riːsnt] *adj* reciente; **in ~ years** en los últimos años.
recently ['riːsntlɪ] *adv* recientemente, recién (*LAM*); **~ arrived** recién llegado; **until ~** hasta hace poco.

receptacle [rɪ'sɛptɪkl] *n* receptáculo.
reception [rɪ'sɛpʃən] *n* (*in building, office etc*) recepción *f*; (*welcome*) acogida.
reception centre *n* (*BRIT*) centro de recepción.
reception desk *n* recepción *f*.
receptionist [rɪ'sɛpʃənɪst] *n* recepcionista *m/f*.
receptive [rɪ'sɛptɪv] *adj* receptivo.
recess [rɪ'sɛs] *n* (*in room*) hueco; (*for bed*) nicho; (*secret place*) escondrijo; (*POL etc: holiday*) período vacacional; (*US LAW: short break*) descanso; (*SCOL: esp US*) recreo.
recession [rɪ'sɛʃən] *n* recesión *f*, depresión *f*.
recharge [riː'tʃɑːdʒ] *vt* (*battery*) recargar.
rechargeable [riː'tʃɑːdʒəbl] *adj* recargable.
recipe ['rɛsɪpɪ] *n* receta.
recipient [rɪ'sɪpɪənt] *n* recibidor(a) *m/f*; (*of letter*) destinatario/a.
reciprocal [rɪ'sɪprəkl] *adj* recíproco.
reciprocate [rɪ'sɪprəkeɪt] *vt* devolver, corresponder a ♦ *vi* corresponder.
recital [rɪ'saɪtl] *n* (*MUS*) recital *m*.
recitation [rɛsɪ'teɪʃən] *n* (*of poetry*) recitado; (*of complaints etc*) enumeración *f*, relación *f*.
recite [rɪ'saɪt] *vt* (*poem*) recitar; (*complaints etc*) enumerar.
reckless ['rɛkləs] *adj* temerario, imprudente; (*speed*) peligroso.
recklessly ['rɛkləslɪ] *adv* imprudentemente; de modo peligroso.
recklessness ['rɛkləsnɪs] *n* temeridad *f*, imprudencia.
reckon ['rɛkən] *vt* (*count*) contar; (*consider*) considerar ♦ *vi*: **to ~ without sb/sth** dejar de contar con algn/algo; **he is somebody to be ~ed with** no se le puede descartar; **I ~ that** ... me parece que ..., creo que ....
▸**reckon on** *vt fus* contar con.
reckoning ['rɛkənɪŋ] *n* (*calculation*) cálculo.
reclaim [rɪ'kleɪm] *vt* (*land*) recuperar; (*: from sea*) rescatar; (*demand back*) reclamar.
reclamation [rɛklə'meɪʃən] *n* recuperación *f*; rescate *m*.
recline [rɪ'klaɪn] *vi* reclinarse.
reclining [rɪ'klaɪnɪŋ] *adj* (*seat*) reclinable.
recluse [rɪ'kluːs] *n* recluso/a.
recognition [rɛkəg'nɪʃən] *n* reconocimiento; **transformed beyond ~** irreconocible; **in ~ of** en reconocimiento de.
recognizable ['rɛkəgnaɪzəbl] *adj*: **~ (by)** reconocible (por).
recognize ['rɛkəgnaɪz] *vt* reconocer, conocer; **to ~ (by/as)** reconocer (por/como).
recoil [rɪ'kɔɪl] *vi* (*person*): **to ~ from doing sth** retraerse de hacer algo ♦ *n* (*of gun*) retroceso.
recollect [rɛkə'lɛkt] *vt* recordar, acordarse de.
recollection [rɛkə'lɛkʃən] *n* recuerdo; **to the best of my ~** que yo recuerde.
recommend [rɛkə'mɛnd] *vt* recomendar; **she has a lot to ~ her** tiene mucho a su favor.
recommendation [rɛkəmɛn'deɪʃən] *n* recomendación *f*.
recommended retail price (RRP) *n* (*BRIT*) precio (recomendado) de venta al público.
recompense ['rɛkəmpɛns] *vt* recompensar ♦ *n* recompensa.
reconcilable ['rɛkənsaɪləbl] *adj* (re)conciliable.
reconcile ['rɛkənsaɪl] *vt* (*two people*) reconciliar; (*two facts*) conciliar; **to ~ o.s. to sth** resignarse *or* conformarse a algo.
reconciliation [rɛkənsɪlɪ'eɪʃən] *n* reconciliación *f*.
recondite [rɪ'kɔndaɪt] *adj* recóndito.
recondition [riːkən'dɪʃən] *vt* (*machine*) reparar, reponer.
reconditioned [riːkən'dɪʃənd] *adj* renovado, reparado.
reconnaissance [rɪ'kɔnɪsns] *n* (*MIL*) reconocimiento.
reconnoitre, (*US*) **reconnoiter** [rɛkə'nɔɪtə*] *vt, vi* (*MIL*) reconocer.
reconsider [riːkən'sɪdə*] *vt* repensar.
reconstitute [riː'kɔnstɪtjuːt] *vt* reconstituir.
reconstruct [riːkən'strʌkt] *vt* reconstruir.
reconstruction [riːkən'strʌkʃən] *n* reconstrucción *f*.
reconvene [riːkən'viːn] *vt* volver a convocar ♦ *vi* volver a reunirse.
record *n* ['rɛkɔːd] (*MUS*) disco; (*of meeting etc*) relación *f*; (*register*) registro, partida; (*file*) archivo; (*also*: **police** *or* **criminal ~**) antecedentes *mpl* penales; (*written*) expediente *m*; (*SPORT*) récord *m*; (*COMPUT*) registro ♦ *vt* [rɪ'kɔːd] (*set down, also COMPUT*) registrar; (*relate*) hacer constar; (*MUS: song etc*) grabar; **in ~ time** en un tiempo récord; **public ~s** archivos *mpl* nacionales; **he is on ~ as saying that** ... hay pruebas de que ha dicho públicamente que ...; **Spain's excellent ~** el excelente historial de España; **off the ~** *adj* no oficial ♦ *adv* confidencialmente.
record card *n* (*in file*) ficha.

recorded delivery letter [rɪ'kɔːdɪd-] *n* (*BRIT POST*) carta de entrega con acuse de recibo.
recorded music *n* música grabada.
recorder [rɪ'kɔːdə*] *n* (*MUS*) flauta de pico; (*TECH*) contador *m*.
record holder *n* (*SPORT*) actual poseedor(a) *m/f* del récord.
recording [rɪ'kɔːdɪŋ] *n* (*MUS*) grabación *f*.
recording studio *n* estudio de grabación.
record library *n* discoteca.
record player *n* tocadiscos *m inv*.
recount *vt* [rɪ'kaunt] contar.
re-count ['riːkaunt] *n* (*POL*: *of votes*) segundo escrutinio, recuento ♦ *vt* [riː'kaunt] volver a contar.
recoup [rɪ'kuːp] *vt*: **to ~ one's losses** recuperar las pérdidas.
recourse [rɪ'kɔːs] *n* recurso; **to have ~ to** recurrir a.
recover [rɪ'kʌvə*] *vt* recuperar; (*rescue*) rescatar ♦ *vi* recuperarse.
recovery [rɪ'kʌvərɪ] *n* recuperación *f*; rescate *m*; (*MED*): **to make a ~** restablecerse.
recreate [riːkrɪ'eɪt] *vt* recrear.
recreation [rɛkrɪ'eɪʃən] *n* recreación *f*; (*amusement*) recreo.
recreational [rɛkrɪ'eɪʃənl] *adj* de recreo.
recreational drug *n* droga recreativa.
recreational vehicle *n* (*US*) caravana *or* roulotte *f* pequeña.
recrimination [rɪkrɪmɪ'neɪʃən] *n* recriminación *f*.
recruit [rɪ'kruːt] *n* recluta *m/f* ♦ *vt* reclutar; (*staff*) contratar.
recruitment [rɪ'kruːtmənt] *n* reclutamiento.
rectangle ['rɛktæŋgl] *n* rectángulo.
rectangular [rɛk'tæŋgjulə*] *adj* rectangular.
rectify ['rɛktɪfaɪ] *vt* rectificar.
rector ['rɛktə*] *n* (*REL*) párroco; (*SCOL*) rector(a) *m/f*.
rectory ['rɛktərɪ] *n* casa del párroco.
rectum ['rɛktəm] *n* (*ANAT*) recto.
recuperate [rɪ'kuːpəreɪt] *vi* reponerse, restablecerse.
recur [rɪ'kəː*] *vi* repetirse; (*pain, illness*) producirse de nuevo.
recurrence [rɪ'kəːrns] *n* repetición *f*.
recurrent [rɪ'kəːrnt] *adj* repetido.
recycle [riː'saɪkl] *vt* reciclar.
red [rɛd] *n* rojo ♦ *adj* rojo; **to be in the ~** (*account*) estar en números rojos; (*business*) tener un saldo negativo; **to give sb the ~ carpet treatment** recibir a algn con todos los honores.
red alert *n* alerta roja.
red-blooded ['rɛd'blʌdɪd] *adj* (*col*) viril.
redbrick university ['rɛdbrɪk-] *n ver recuadro*.

REDBRICK UNIVERSITY

El término **redbrick university** *se aplica a las universidades construidas en los grandes centros urbanos industriales como Birmingham, Liverpool o Manchester a finales del siglo XIX o principios del XX. Deben su nombre a que sus edificios son normalmente de ladrillo, a diferencia de las universidades tradicionales de Oxford y Cambridge, cuyos edificios suelen ser de piedra.*

Red Cross *n* Cruz *f* Roja.
redcurrant ['rɛdkʌrənt] *n* grosella.
redden ['rɛdn] *vt* enrojecer ♦ *vi* enrojecerse.
reddish ['rɛdɪʃ] *adj* (*hair*) rojizo.
redecorate [riː'dɛkəreɪt] pintar de nuevo; volver a decorar.
redecoration [riːdɛkə'reɪʃən] *n* renovación *f*.
redeem [rɪ'diːm] *vt* (*sth in pawn*) desempeñar; (*fig, also REL*) rescatar.
redeemable [rɪ'diːməbl] *adj* canjeable.
redeeming [rɪ'diːmɪŋ] *adj*: **~ feature** punto bueno *or* favorable.
redefine [riːdɪ'faɪn] *vt* redefinir.
redemption [rɪ'dɛmpʃən] *n* (*REL*) redención *f*; **to be past** *or* **beyond ~** no tener remedio.
redeploy [riːdɪ'plɔɪ] *vt* (*resources*) disponer de nuevo.
redevelop [riːdɪ'vɛləp] *vt* reorganizar.
redevelopment [riːdɪ'vɛləpmənt] *n* reorganización *f*.
red-handed [rɛd'hændɪd] *adj*: **he was caught ~** le pillaron con las manos en la masa.
redhead ['rɛdhɛd] *n* pelirrojo/a.
red herring *n* (*fig*) pista falsa.
red-hot [rɛd'hɔt] *adj* candente.
redirect [riːdaɪ'rɛkt] *vt* (*mail*) reexpedir.
rediscover [riːdɪs'kʌvə*] *vt* redescubrir.
rediscovery [riːdɪs'kʌvərɪ] *n* redescubrimiento.
redistribute [riːdɪs'trɪbjuːt] *vt* redistribuir, hacer una nueva distribución de.
red-letter day [rɛd'lɛtə-] *n* día *m* señalado, día *m* especial.
red light *n*: **to go through** *or* **jump a ~** (*AUT*) saltarse un semáforo.
red-light district *n* barrio chino, zona de

tolerancia.
red meat *n* carne *f* roja.
redness ['rɛdnɪs] *n* rojez *f.*
redo [riː'duː] *vt* (*irreg: like* **do**) rehacer.
redolent ['rɛdələnt] *adj:* ~ **of** (*smell*) con fragancia a; **to be ~ of** (*fig*) evocar.
redouble [riː'dʌbl] *vt:* **to ~ one's efforts** redoblar los esfuerzos.
redraft [riː'drɑːft] *vt* volver a redactar.
redress [rɪ'drɛs] *n* reparación *f* ♦ *vt* reparar, corregir; **to ~ the balance** restablecer el equilibrio.
Red Sea *n:* **the ~** el mar Rojo.
redskin ['rɛdskɪn] *n* piel roja *m/f.*
red tape *n* (*fig*) trámites *mpl*, papeleo (*col*).
reduce [rɪ'djuːs] *vt* reducir; (*lower*) rebajar; **to ~ sth by/to** reducir algo en/a; **to ~ sb to silence/despair/tears** hacer callar/ desesperarse/llorar a algn; **"~ speed now"** (*AUT*) "reduzca la velocidad".
reduced [rɪ'djuːst] *adj* (*decreased*) reducido, rebajado; **at a ~ price** con rebaja *or* descuento; **"greatly ~ prices"** "grandes rebajas".
reduction [rɪ'dʌkʃən] *n* reducción *f*; (*of price*) rebaja; (*discount*) descuento.
redundancy [rɪ'dʌndənsɪ] *n* despido; (*unemployment*) desempleo; **voluntary ~** baja voluntaria.
redundancy payment *n* indemnización *f* por desempleo.
redundant [rɪ'dʌndənt] *adj* (*BRIT: worker*) parado, sin trabajo; (*detail, object*) superfluo; **to be made ~** quedar(se) sin trabajo, perder el empleo.
reed [riːd] *n* (*BOT*) junco, caña; (*MUS: of clarinet etc*) lengüeta.
re-educate [riː'ɛdjukeɪt] *vt* reeducar.
reedy ['riːdɪ] *adj* (*voice, instrument*) aflautado.
reef [riːf] *n* (*at sea*) arrecife *m.*
reek [riːk] *vi:* **to ~ (of)** oler *or* apestar (a).
reel [riːl] *n* carrete *m*, bobina; (*of film*) rollo ♦ *vt* (*TECH*) devanar; (*also:* **~ in**) sacar ♦ *vi* (*sway*) tambalear(se); **my head is ~ing** me da vueltas la cabeza.
►**reel off** *vt* recitar de memoria.
re-election [riːɪ'lɛkʃən] *n* reelección *f.*
re-engage [riːɪn'geɪdʒ] *vt* contratar de nuevo.
re-enter [riː'ɛntə*] *vt* reingresar en, volver a entrar en.
re-entry [riː'ɛntrɪ] *n* reingreso, reentrada.
re-examine [riːɪg'zæmɪn] *vt* reexaminar.
re-export *vt* ['riːɪks'pɔːt] reexportar ♦ *n* [riː'ɛkspɔːt] reexportación *f.*
ref [rɛf] *n abbr* (*col*) = **referee.**
ref. *abbr* (*COMM:* = *with reference to*) Ref.
refectory [rɪ'fɛktərɪ] *n* comedor *m.*
refer [rɪ'fəː*] *vt* (*send*) remitir; (*ascribe*) referir a, relacionar con ♦ *vi:* **to ~ to** (*allude to*) referirse a, aludir a; (*apply to*) relacionarse con; (*consult*) remitirse a; **he ~red me to the manager** me envió al gerente.
referee [rɛfə'riː] *n* árbitro; (*BRIT: for job application*) persona que da referencias de otro ♦ *vt* (*match*) arbitrar en.
reference ['rɛfrəns] *n* (*mention, in book*) referencia; (*sending*) remisión *f*; (*relevance*) relación *f*; (*for job application: letter*) carta de recomendación; **with ~ to** con referencia a; (*COMM: in letter*) me remito a.
reference book *n* libro de consulta.
reference library *n* biblioteca de consulta.
reference number *n* número de referencia.
referendum, *pl* **referenda** [rɛfə'rɛndəm, -də] *n* referéndum *m.*
referral [rɪ'fəːrəl] *n* remisión *f.*
refill *vt* [riː'fɪl] rellenar ♦ *n* ['riːfɪl] repuesto, recambio.
refine [rɪ'faɪn] *vt* (*sugar, oil*) refinar.
refined [rɪ'faɪnd] *adj* (*person, taste*) refinado, culto.
refinement [rɪ'faɪnmənt] *n* (*of person*) cultura, educación *f.*
refinery [rɪ'faɪnərɪ] *n* refinería.
refit (*NAUT*) *n* ['riːfɪt] reparación *f* ♦ *vt* [riː'fɪt] reparar.
reflate [riː'fleɪt] *vt* (*economy*) reflacionar.
reflation [riː'fleɪʃən] *n* reflación *f.*
reflationary [riː'fleɪʃənrɪ] *adj* reflacionario.
reflect [rɪ'flɛkt] *vt* (*light, image*) reflejar ♦ *vi* (*think*) reflexionar, pensar; **it ~s badly/ well on him** le perjudica/le hace honor.
reflection [rɪ'flɛkʃən] *n* (*act*) reflexión *f*; (*image*) reflejo; (*discredit*) crítica; **on ~** pensándolo bien.
reflector [rɪ'flɛktə*] *n* (*AUT*) catafaros *m inv*; (*telescope*) reflector *m.*
reflex ['riːflɛks] *adj, n* reflejo.
reflexive [rɪ'flɛksɪv] *adj* (*LING*) reflexivo.
reform [rɪ'fɔːm] *n* reforma ♦ *vt* reformar.
reformat [riː'fɔːmæt] *vt* (*COMPUT*) recomponer.
Reformation [rɛfə'meɪʃən] *n:* **the ~** la Reforma.
reformatory [rɪ'fɔːmətərɪ] *n* (*US*) reformatorio.
reformer [rɪ'fɔːmə*] *n* reformador(a) *m/f.*
refrain [rɪ'freɪn] *vi:* **to ~ from doing** abstenerse de hacer ♦ *n* (*MUS etc*) estribillo.
refresh [rɪ'frɛʃ] *vt* refrescar.

refresher course [rɪ'frɛʃə-] *n* (*BRIT*) curso de repaso.
refreshing [rɪ'frɛʃɪŋ] *adj* (*drink*) refrescante; (*sleep*) reparador; (*change etc*) estimulante; (*idea, point of view*) estimulante, interesante.
refreshments [rɪ'frɛʃmənts] *npl* (*drinks*) refrescos *mpl*.
refrigeration [rɪfrɪdʒə'reɪʃən] *n* refrigeración *f*.
refrigerator [rɪ'frɪdʒəreɪtə*] *n* frigorífico, refrigeradora (*LAM*), heladera (*LAM*).
refuel [ri:'fjuəl] *vi* repostar (combustible).
refuelling, (*US*) **refueling** [ri:'fjuəlɪŋ] *n* reabastecimiento de combustible.
refuge ['rɛfju:dʒ] *n* refugio, asilo; **to take ~ in** refugiarse en.
refugee [rɛfju'dʒi:] *n* refugiado/a.
refugee camp *n* campamento para refugiados.
refund *n* ['ri:fʌnd] reembolso ♦ *vt* [rɪ'fʌnd] devolver, reembolsar.
refurbish [ri:'fə:bɪʃ] *vt* restaurar, renovar.
refurnish [ri:'fə:nɪʃ] *vt* amueblar de nuevo.
refusal [rɪ'fju:zəl] *n* negativa; **first ~** primera opción; **to have first ~ on sth** tener la primera opción a algo.
refuse *n* ['rɛfju:s] basura ♦ (*vb*: [rɪ'fju:z]) *vt* (*reject*) rehusar; (*say no to*) negarse a ♦ *vi* negarse; (*horse*) rehusar; **to ~ to do sth** negarse a *or* rehusar hacer algo.
refuse bin *n* cubo *or* bote *m* (*LAM*) *or* balde *m* (*LAM*) de la basura.
refuse collection *n* recogida de basuras.
refuse disposal *n* eliminación *f* de basuras.
refusenik [rɪ'fju:znɪk] *n* *judío/a que tenía prohibido emigrar de la ex-URSS*.
refuse tip *n* vertedero.
refute [rɪ'fju:t] *vt* refutar, rebatir.
regain [rɪ'geɪn] *vt* recobrar, recuperar.
regal ['ri:gl] *adj* regio, real.
regale [rɪ'geɪl] *vt* agasajar, entretener.
regalia [rɪ'geɪlɪə] *n* galas *fpl*.
regard [rɪ'gɑ:d] *n* (*gaze*) mirada; (*aspect*) respecto; (*esteem*) respeto, consideración *f* ♦ *vt* (*consider*) considerar; (*look at*) mirar; **to give one's ~s to** saludar de su parte a; **"(kind) ~s"** "muy atentamente"; **"with kindest ~s"** "con muchos recuerdos"; **~s to María, please give my ~s to María** recuerdos a María, dele recuerdos a María de mi parte; **as ~s, with ~ to** con respecto a, en cuanto a.
regarding [rɪ'gɑ:dɪŋ] *prep* con respecto a, en cuanto a.
regardless [rɪ'gɑ:dlɪs] *adv* a pesar de todo; **~ of** sin reparar en.
regatta [rɪ'gætə] *n* regata.
regency ['ri:dʒənsɪ] *n* regencia.
regenerate [rɪ'dʒɛnəreɪt] *vt* regenerar.
regent ['ri:dʒənt] *n* regente *m/f*.
reggae ['rɛgeɪ] *n* reggae *m*.
régime [reɪ'ʒi:m] *n* régimen *m*.
regiment *n* ['rɛdʒɪmənt] regimiento ♦ *vt* ['rɛdʒɪmɛnt] reglamentar.
regimental [rɛdʒɪ'mɛntl] *adj* militar.
regimentation [rɛdʒɪmɛn'teɪʃən] *n* regimentación *f*.
region ['ri:dʒən] *n* región *f*; **in the ~ of** (*fig*) alrededor de.
regional ['ri:dʒənl] *adj* regional.
regional development *n* desarrollo regional.
register ['rɛdʒɪstə*] *n* registro ♦ *vt* registrar; (*birth*) declarar; (*letter*) certificar; (*subj: instrument*) marcar, indicar ♦ *vi* (*at hotel*) registrarse; (*sign on*) inscribirse; (*make impression*) producir impresión; **to ~ a protest** presentar una queja; **to ~ for a course** matricularse *or* inscribirse en un curso.
registered ['rɛdʒɪstəd] *adj* (*design*) registrado; (*BRIT: letter*) certificado; (*student*) matriculado; (*voter*) registrado.
registered company *n* sociedad *f* legalmente constituida.
registered nurse *n* (*US*) enfermero/a titulado/a.
registered office *n* domicilio social.
registered trademark *n* marca registrada.
registrar ['rɛdʒɪstrɑ:*] *n* secretario/a (del registro civil).
registration [rɛdʒɪs'treɪʃən] *n* (*act*) declaración *f*; (*AUT: also*: **~ number**) matrícula.
registry ['rɛdʒɪstrɪ] *n* registro.
registry office *n* (*BRIT*) registro civil; **to get married in a ~** casarse por lo civil.
regret [rɪ'grɛt] *n* sentimiento, pesar *m*; (*remorse*) remordimiento ♦ *vt* sentir, lamentar; (*repent of*) arrepentirse de; **we ~ to inform you that ...** sentimos informarle que ....
regretful [rɪ'grɛtful] *adj* pesaroso, arrepentido.
regretfully [rɪ'grɛtfəlɪ] *adv* con pesar, sentidamente.
regrettable [rɪ'grɛtəbl] *adj* lamentable; (*loss*) sensible.
regrettably [rɪ'grɛtəblɪ] *adv* desgraciadamente.
regroup [ri:'gru:p] *vt* reagrupar ♦ *vi* reagruparse.
regt *abbr* = **regiment**.

regular ['rɛgjulə*] *adj* regular; (*soldier*) profesional; (*col: intensive*) verdadero; (*listener, reader*) asiduo, habitual ♦ *n* (*client etc*) cliente/a *m/f* habitual.
regularity [rɛgju'lærɪtɪ] *n* regularidad *f*.
regularly ['rɛgjuləlɪ] *adv* con regularidad.
regulate ['rɛgjuleɪt] *vt* (*gen*) controlar; (*TECH*) regular, ajustar.
regulation [rɛgju'leɪʃən] *n* (*rule*) regla, reglamento; (*adjustment*) regulación *f*.
rehabilitate [ri:ə'bɪlɪteɪt] *vt* rehabilitar.
rehabilitation ['ri:əbɪlɪ'teɪʃən] *n* rehabilitación *f*.
rehash [ri:'hæʃ] *vt* (*col*) hacer un refrito de.
rehearsal [rɪ'hə:səl] *n* ensayo; **dress ~** ensayo general *or* final.
rehearse [rɪ'hə:s] *vt* ensayar.
rehouse [ri:'hauz] *vt* dar nueva vivienda a.
reign [reɪn] *n* reinado; (*fig*) predominio ♦ *vi* reinar; (*fig*) imperar.
reigning ['reɪnɪŋ] *adj* (*monarch*) reinante, actual; (*predominant*) imperante.
reimburse [ri:ɪm'bə:s] *vt* reembolsar.
rein [reɪn] *n* (*for horse*) rienda; **to give sb free ~** dar rienda suelta a algn.
reincarnation [ri:ɪnkɑ:'neɪʃən] *n* reencarnación *f*.
reindeer ['reɪndɪə*] *n* (*pl inv*) reno.
reinforce [ri:ɪn'fɔ:s] *vt* reforzar.
reinforced concrete [ri:ɪn'fɔ:st-] *n* hormigón armado.
reinforcement [ri:ɪn'fɔ:smənt] *n* (*action*) refuerzo; **~s** *npl* (*MIL*) refuerzos *mpl*.
reinstate [ri:ɪn'steɪt] *vt* (*worker*) reintegrar (a su puesto).
reinstatement [ri:ɪn'steɪtmənt] *n* reintegración *f*.
reissue [ri:'ɪʃu:] *vt* (*record, book*) reeditar.
reiterate [ri:'ɪtəreɪt] *vt* reiterar, repetir.
reject *n* ['ri:dʒɛkt] (*thing*) desecho ♦ *vt* [rɪ'dʒɛkt] rechazar; (*proposition, offer etc*) descartar.
rejection [rɪ'dʒɛkʃən] *n* rechazo.
rejoice [rɪ'dʒɔɪs] *vi*: **to ~ at** *or* **over** regocijarse *or* alegrarse de.
rejoinder [rɪ'dʒɔɪndə*] *n* (*retort*) réplica.
rejuvenate [rɪ'dʒu:vəneɪt] *vt* rejuvenecer.
rekindle [ri:'kɪndl] *vt* volver a encender; (*fig*) despertar.
relapse [rɪ'læps] *n* (*MED*) recaída; (*into crime*) reincidencia.
relate [rɪ'leɪt] *vt* (*tell*) contar, relatar; (*connect*) relacionar ♦ *vi* relacionarse; **to ~ to** (*connect*) relacionarse *or* tener que ver con.
related [rɪ'leɪtɪd] *adj* afín; (*person*) emparentado; **~ to** con referencia a, relacionado con.
relating [rɪ'leɪtɪŋ]: **~ to** *prep* referente a.
relation [rɪ'leɪʃən] *n* (*person*) pariente *m/f*; (*link*) relación *f*; **in ~ to** en relación con, en lo que se refiere a; **to bear a ~ to** guardar relación con; **diplomatic/international ~s** relaciones *fpl* diplomáticas/internacionales.
relationship [rɪ'leɪʃənʃɪp] *n* relación *f*; (*personal*) relaciones *fpl*; (*also*: **family ~**) parentesco.
relative ['rɛlətɪv] *n* pariente *m/f*, familiar *m/f* ♦ *adj* relativo.
relatively ['rɛlətɪvlɪ] *adv* (*fairly, rather*) relativamente.
relative pronoun *n* pronombre *m* relativo.
relax [rɪ'læks] *vi* descansar; (*quieten down*) relajarse ♦ *vt* relajar; (*grip*) aflojar; **~!** (*calm down*) ¡tranquilo!
relaxation [ri:læk'seɪʃən] *n* (*rest*) descanso; (*easing*) relajación *f*, relajamiento *m*; (*amusement*) recreo; (*entertainment*) diversión *f*.
relaxed [rɪ'lækst] *adj* relajado; (*tranquil*) tranquilo.
relaxing [rɪ'læksɪŋ] *adj* relajante.
relay *n* ['ri:leɪ] (*race*) carrera de relevos ♦ *vt* [rɪ'leɪ] (*RADIO, TV, pass on*) retransmitir.
release [rɪ'li:s] *n* (*liberation*) liberación *f*; (*discharge*) puesta en libertad *f*; (*of gas etc*) escape *m*; (*of film etc*) estreno ♦ *vt* (*prisoner*) poner en libertad; (*film*) estrenar; (*book*) publicar; (*piece of news*) difundir; (*gas etc*) despedir, arrojar; (*free: from wreckage etc*) liberar; (*TECH: catch, spring etc*) desenganchar; (*let go*) soltar, aflojar.
relegate ['rɛləgeɪt] *vt* relegar; (*SPORT*): **to be ~d to** bajar a.
relent [rɪ'lɛnt] *vi* ceder, ablandarse; (*let up*) descansar.
relentless [rɪ'lɛntlɪs] *adj* implacable.
relentlessly [rɪ'lɛntlɪslɪ] *adv* implacablemente.
relevance ['rɛləvəns] *n* relación *f*.
relevant ['rɛləvənt] *adj* (*fact*) pertinente; **~ to** relacionado con.
reliability [rɪlaɪə'bɪlɪtɪ] *n* fiabilidad *f*; seguridad *f*; veracidad *f*.
reliable [rɪ'laɪəbl] *adj* (*person, firm*) de confianza, de fiar; (*method, machine*) seguro; (*source*) fidedigno.
reliably [rɪ'laɪəblɪ] *adv*: **to be ~ informed that ...** saber de fuente fidedigna que ....
reliance [rɪ'laɪəns] *n*: **~ (on)** dependencia (de).
reliant [rɪ'laɪənt] *adj*: **to be ~ on sth/sb**

depender de algo/algn.
relic ['rɛlɪk] *n* (*REL*) reliquia; (*of the past*) vestigio.
relief [rɪ'liːf] *n* (*from pain, anxiety*) alivio, desahogo; (*help, supplies*) socorro, ayuda; (*ART, GEO*) relieve *m*; **by way of light ~** a modo de diversión.
relief road *n* carretera de descongestionamiento.
relieve [rɪ'liːv] *vt* (*pain, patient*) aliviar; (*bring help to*) ayudar, socorrer; (*burden*) aligerar; (*take over from: gen*) sustituir a; (*: guard*) relevar; **to ~ sb of sth** quitar algo a algn; **to ~ sb of his command** (*MIL*) relevar a algn de su mando; **to ~ o.s.** hacer sus necesidades; **I am ~d to hear you are better** me alivia saber que estás *or* te encuentras mejor.
religion [rɪ'lɪdʒən] *n* religión *f*.
religious [rɪ'lɪdʒəs] *adj* religioso.
religious education *n* educación *f* religiosa.
religiously [rɪ'lɪdʒəslɪ] *adv* religiosamente.
relinquish [rɪ'lɪŋkwɪʃ] *vt* abandonar; (*plan, habit*) renunciar a.
relish ['rɛlɪʃ] *n* (*CULIN*) salsa; (*enjoyment*) entusiasmo; (*flavour*) sabor *m*, gusto ♦ *vt* (*food, challenge etc*) saborear; **to ~ doing** gozar haciendo.
relive [riː'lɪv] *vt* vivir de nuevo, volver a vivir.
relocate [riːləu'keɪt] *vt* trasladar ♦ *vi* trasladarse.
reluctance [rɪ'lʌktəns] *n* desgana, renuencia.
reluctant [rɪ'lʌktənt] *adj* reacio; **to be ~ to do sth** resistirse a hacer algo.
reluctantly [rɪ'lʌktəntlɪ] *adv* de mala gana.
rely [rɪ'laɪ]: **to ~ on** *vt fus* confiar en, fiarse de; (*be dependent on*) depender de; **you can ~ on my discretion** puedes contar con mi discreción.
remain [rɪ'meɪn] *vi* (*survive*) quedar; (*be left*) sobrar; (*continue*) quedar(se), permanecer; **to ~ silent** permanecer callado.
remainder [rɪ'meɪndə*] *n* resto.
remaining [rɪ'meɪnɪŋ] *adj* sobrante.
remains [rɪ'meɪnz] *npl* restos *mpl*.
remand [rɪ'mɑːnd] *n*: **on ~** detenido (bajo custodia) ♦ *vt*: **to ~ in custody** mantener bajo custodia.
remand home *n* (*BRIT*) reformatorio.
remark [rɪ'mɑːk] *n* comentario ♦ *vt* comentar; **to ~ on sth** hacer observaciones sobre algo.
remarkable [rɪ'mɑːkəbl] *adj* notable; (*outstanding*) extraordinario.
remarkably [rɪ'mɑːkəblɪ] *adv* extraordinariamente.
remarry [riː'mærɪ] *vi* casarse por segunda vez, volver a casarse.
remedial [rɪ'miːdɪəl] *adj*: **~ education** educación *f* de los niños atrasados.
remedy ['rɛmədɪ] *n* remedio ♦ *vt* remediar, curar.
remember [rɪ'mɛmbə*] *vt* recordar, acordarse de; (*bear in mind*) tener presente; **I ~ seeing it, I ~ having seen it** recuerdo haberlo visto; **she ~ed doing it** se acordó de hacerlo; **~ me to your wife and children!** ¡déle recuerdos a su familia!
remembrance [rɪ'mɛmbrəns] *n* (*memory, souvenir*) recuerdo; **in ~ of** en conmemoración de.
Remembrance Day, Remembrance Sunday *n* (*BRIT*) *ver recuadro*.

> **REMEMBRANCE DAY**
>
> *En el Reino Unido el domingo más cercano al 11 de noviembre es* **Remembrance Day** *o* **Remembrance Sunday**, *aniversario de la firma del armisticio de 1918 que puso fin a la Primera Guerra Mundial. Tal día se recuerda a todos aquellos que murieron en las dos guerras mundiales con dos minutos de silencio a las once de la mañana hora en que se firmó el armisticio durante los actos de conmemoración celebrados en los monumentos a los caídos. Allí se colocan coronas de amapolas, flor que también se suele llevar prendida en el pecho tras pagar un donativo para los inválidos de guerra.*

remind [rɪ'maɪnd] *vt*: **to ~ sb to do sth** recordar a algn que haga algo; **to ~ sb of sth** recordar algo a algn; **she ~s me of her mother** me recuerda a su madre; **that ~s me!** ¡a propósito!
reminder [rɪ'maɪndə*] *n* notificación *f*; (*memento*) recuerdo.
reminisce [rɛmɪ'nɪs] *vi* recordar (viejas historias).
reminiscent [rɛmɪ'nɪsnt] *adj*: **to be ~ of sth** recordar algo.
remiss [rɪ'mɪs] *adj* descuidado; **it was ~ of me** fue un descuido de mi parte.
remission [rɪ'mɪʃən] *n* remisión *f*; (*of sentence*) reducción *f* de la pena.
remit [rɪ'mɪt] *vt* (*send: money*) remitir, enviar.
remittance [rɪ'mɪtns] *n* remesa, envío.
remnant ['rɛmnənt] *n* resto; (*of cloth*) retal *m*, retazo; **~s** *npl* (*COMM*) restos de serie.

remonstrate ['rɛmənstreɪt] *vi* protestar.
remorse [rɪ'mɔːs] *n* remordimientos *mpl.*
remorseful [rɪ'mɔːsful] *adj* arrepentido.
remorseless [rɪ'mɔːslɪs] *adj* (*fig*) implacable, inexorable.
remorselessly [rɪ'mɔːslɪslɪ] *adv* implacablemente, inexorablemente.
remote [rɪ'məut] *adj* remoto; (*distant*) lejano; (*person*) distante; **there is a ~ possibility that ...** hay una posibilidad remota de que ....
remote control *n* mando a distancia.
remote-controlled [rɪ'məutkən'trəuld] *adj* teledirigido, con mando a distancia.
remotely [rɪ'məutlɪ] *adv* remotamente; (*slightly*) levemente.
remoteness [rɪ'məutnɪs] *n* alejamiento; distancia.
remould ['riːməuld] *n* (*BRIT*: *tyre*) neumático *or* llanta (*LAM*) recauchutado/a.
removable [rɪ'muːvəbl] *adj* (*detachable*) separable.
removal [rɪ'muːvəl] *n* (*taking away*) (el) quitar; (*BRIT*: *from house*) mudanza; (*from office*: *dismissal*) destitución *f*; (*MED*) extirpación *f*.
removal van *n* (*BRIT*) camión *m* de mudanzas.
remove [rɪ'muːv] *vt* quitar; (*employee*) destituir; (*name*: *from list*) tachar, borrar; (*doubt*) disipar; (*TECH*) retirar, separar; (*MED*) extirpar; **first cousin once ~d** (*parent's cousin*) tío/a segundo/a; (*cousin's child*) sobrino/a segundo/a.
remover [rɪ'muːvə*] *n*: **make-up ~** desmaquilladora.
remunerate [rɪ'mjuːnəreɪt] *vt* remunerar.
remuneration [rɪmjuːnə'reɪʃən] *n* remuneración *f*.
Renaissance [rɪ'neɪsɔ̃ns] *n*: **the ~** el Renacimiento.
rename [riː'neɪm] *vt* poner nuevo nombre a.
render ['rɛndə*] *vt* (*thanks*) dar; (*aid*) proporcionar; (*honour*) dar, conceder; (*assistance*) dar, prestar; **to ~ sth** + *adj* volver algo + *adj*.
rendering ['rɛndərɪŋ] *n* (*MUS etc*) interpretación *f*.
rendez-vous ['rɔndɪvuː] *n* cita ♦ *vi* reunirse, encontrarse; (*spaceship*) efectuar una reunión espacial.
rendition [rɛn'dɪʃən] *n* (*MUS*) interpretación *f*.
renegade ['rɛnɪgeɪd] *n* renegado/a.
renew [rɪ'njuː] *vt* renovar; (*resume*) reanudar; (*extend date*) prorrogar; (*negotiations*) volver a.
renewable [rɪ'njuːəbl] *adj* renovable; **~ energy, ~s** energías renovables.
renewal [rɪ'njuːəl] *n* renovación *f*; reanudación *f*; prórroga.
renounce [rɪ'nauns] *vt* renunciar a; (*right, inheritance*) renunciar.
renovate ['rɛnəveɪt] *vt* renovar.
renovation [rɛnə'veɪʃən] *n* renovación *f*.
renown [rɪ'naun] *n* renombre *m*.
renowned [rɪ'naund] *adj* renombrado.
rent [rɛnt] *n* alquiler *m*; (*for house*) arriendo, renta ♦ *vt* (*also*: **~ out**) alquilar.
rental ['rɛntl] *n* (*for television, car*) alquiler *m*.
rent boy *n* (*BRIT col*) chapero.
renunciation [rɪnʌnsɪ'eɪʃən] *n* renuncia.
reopen [riː'əupən] *vt* volver a abrir, reabrir.
reorder [riː'ɔːdə*] *vt* volver a pedir, repetir el pedido de; (*rearrange*) volver a ordenar *or* arreglar.
reorganization [riːɔːgənaɪ'zeɪʃən] *n* reorganización *f*.
reorganize [riː'ɔːgənaɪz] *vt* reorganizar.
rep [rɛp] *n abbr* (*COMM*) = **representative;** (*THEAT*) = **repertory.**
Rep. *abbr* (*US POL*) = **representative, republican.**
repair [rɪ'pɛə*] *n* reparación *f*, arreglo; (*patch*) remiendo ♦ *vt* reparar, arreglar; **in good/bad ~** en buen/mal estado; **under ~** en obras.
repair kit *n* caja de herramientas.
repair man *n* mecánico.
repair shop *n* taller *m* de reparaciones.
repartee [rɛpɑː'tiː] *n* réplicas *fpl* agudas.
repast [rɪ'pɑːst] *n* (*formal*) comida.
repatriate [riː'pætrɪeɪt] *vt* repatriar.
repay [riː'peɪ] *vt* (*irreg*: *like* **pay**) (*money*) devolver, reembolsar; (*person*) pagar; (*debt*) liquidar; (*sb's efforts*) devolver, corresponder a.
repayment [riː'peɪmənt] *n* reembolso, devolución *f*; (*sum of money*) recompensa.
repeal [rɪ'piːl] *n* revocación *f* ♦ *vt* revocar.
repeat [rɪ'piːt] *n* (*RADIO, TV*) reposición *f* ♦ *vt* repetir ♦ *vi* repetirse.
repeatedly [rɪ'piːtɪdlɪ] *adv* repetidas veces.
repeat order *n* (*COMM*): **to place a ~ for** renovar un pedido de.
repel [rɪ'pɛl] *vt* repugnar.
repellent [rɪ'pɛlənt] *adj* repugnante ♦ *n*: **insect ~** crema/loción *f* anti-insectos.
repent [rɪ'pɛnt] *vi*: **to ~ (of)** arrepentirse (de).
repentance [rɪ'pɛntəns] *n* arrepentimiento.
repercussion [riːpə'kʌʃən] *n* (*consequence*) repercusión *f*; **to have ~s** repercutir.

repertoire ['rɛpətwɑː*] *n* repertorio.
repertory ['rɛpətərɪ] *n* (*also*: ~ **theatre**) teatro de repertorio.
repertory company *n* compañía de repertorio.
repetition [rɛpɪ'tɪʃən] *n* repetición *f*.
repetitious [rɛpɪ'tɪʃəs] *adj* repetidor(a), que se repite.
repetitive [rɪ'pɛtɪtɪv] *adj* (*movement, work*) repetitivo, reiterativo; (*speech*) lleno de repeticiones.
rephrase [riː'freɪz] *vt* decir *or* formular de otro modo.
replace [rɪ'pleɪs] *vt* (*put back*) devolver a su sitio; (*take the place of*) reemplazar, sustituir.
replacement [rɪ'pleɪsmənt] *n* reemplazo; (*act*) reposición *f*; (*thing*) recambio; (*person*) suplente *m/f*.
replacement cost *n* costo de sustitución.
replacement part *n* repuesto.
replacement value *n* valor *m* de sustitución.
replay ['riːpleɪ] *n* (*SPORT*) partido de desempate; (*TV: playback*) repetición *f*.
replenish [rɪ'plɛnɪʃ] *vt* (*tank etc*) rellenar; (*stock etc*) reponer; (*with fuel*) repostar.
replete [rɪ'pliːt] *adj* repleto, lleno.
replica ['rɛplɪkə] *n* réplica, reproducción *f*.
reply [rɪ'plaɪ] *n* respuesta, contestación *f* ♦ *vi* contestar, responder; **in** ~ en respuesta; **there's no** ~ (*TEL*) no contestan.
reply coupon *n* cupón-respuesta *m*.
reply-paid [rɪ'plaɪ'peɪd] *adj*: ~ **postcard** tarjeta postal con respuesta pagada.
report [rɪ'pɔːt] *n* informe *m*; (*PRESS etc*) reportaje *m*; (*BRIT: also*: **school** ~) informe *m* escolar; (*of gun*) detonación *f* ♦ *vt* informar sobre; (*PRESS etc*) hacer un reportaje sobre; (*notify: accident, culprit*) denunciar ♦ *vi* (*make a* ~) presentar un informe; (*present o.s.*): **to** ~ **(to sb)** presentarse (ante algn); **annual** ~ (*COMM*) informe *m* anual; **to** ~ **(on)** hacer un informe (sobre); **it is** ~**ed from Berlin that ...** se informa desde Berlín que ....
report card *n* (*US, Scottish*) cartilla escolar.
reportedly [rɪ'pɔːtɪdlɪ] *adv* según se dice, según se informa.
reporter [rɪ'pɔːtə*] *n* (*PRESS*) periodista *m/f*, reportero/a; (*RADIO, TV*) locutor(a) *m/f*.
repose [rɪ'pəuz] *n*: **in** ~ (*face, mouth*) en reposo.
repossess [riːpə'zɛs] *vt* recuperar.
repossession order [riːpə'zɛʃən-] *n orden de devolución de la vivienda por el impago de la hipoteca.*
reprehensible [rɛprɪ'hɛnsɪbl] *adj* reprensible, censurable.
represent [rɛprɪ'zɛnt] *vt* representar; (*COMM*) ser agente de.
representation [rɛprɪzɛn'teɪʃən] *n* representación *f*; (*petition*) petición *f*; ~**s** *npl* (*protest*) quejas *fpl*.
representative [rɛprɪ'zɛntətɪv] *n* (*US POL*) representante *m/f*, diputado/a; (*COMM*) representante *m/f* ♦ *adj*: ~ **(of)** representativo (de).
repress [rɪ'prɛs] *vt* reprimir.
repression [rɪ'prɛʃən] *n* represión *f*.
repressive [rɪ'prɛsɪv] *adj* represivo.
reprieve [rɪ'priːv] *n* (*LAW*) indulto; (*fig*) alivio ♦ *vt* indultar; (*fig*) salvar.
reprimand ['rɛprɪmɑːnd] *n* reprimenda ♦ *vt* reprender.
reprint ['riːprɪnt] *n* reimpresión *f* ♦ *vt* [riː'prɪnt] reimprimir.
reprisal [rɪ'praɪzl] *n* represalia; **to take** ~**s** tomar represalias.
reproach [rɪ'prəutʃ] *n* reproche *m* ♦ *vt*: **to** ~ **sb with sth** reprochar algo a algn; **beyond** ~ intachable.
reproachful [rɪ'prəutʃful] *adj* de reproche, de acusación.
reproduce [riːprə'djuːs] *vt* reproducir ♦ *vi* reproducirse.
reproduction [riːprə'dʌkʃən] *n* reproducción *f*.
reproductive [riːprə'dʌktɪv] *adj* reproductor(a).
reproof [rɪ'pruːf] *n* reproche *m*.
reprove [rɪ'pruːv] *vt*: **to** ~ **sb for sth** reprochar algo a algn.
reptile ['rɛptaɪl] *n* reptil *m*.
republic [rɪ'pʌblɪk] *n* república.
republican [rɪ'pʌblɪkən] *adj*, *n* republicano/a *m/f*.
repudiate [rɪ'pjuːdɪeɪt] *vt* (*accusation*) rechazar; (*obligation*) negarse a reconocer.
repudiation [rɪpjuːdɪ'eɪʃən] *n* incumplimiento.
repugnance [rɪ'pʌgnəns] *n* repugnancia.
repugnant [rɪ'pʌgnənt] *adj* repugnante.
repulse [rɪ'pʌls] *vt* rechazar.
repulsion [rɪ'pʌlʃən] *n* repulsión *f*, repugnancia.
repulsive [rɪ'pʌlsɪv] *adj* repulsivo.
repurchase [riː'pəːtʃəs] *vt* volver a comprar, readquirir.
reputable ['rɛpjutəbl] *adj* (*make etc*) de renombre.
reputation [rɛpju'teɪʃən] *n* reputación *f*; **he has a** ~ **for being awkward** tiene fama de

difícil.
repute [rɪ'pjuːt] *n* reputación *f*, fama.
reputed [rɪ'pjuːtɪd] *adj* supuesto; **to be ~ to be rich/intelligent** *etc* tener fama de rico/inteligente *etc*.
reputedly [rɪ'pjuːtɪdlɪ] *adv* según dicen *or* se dice.
request [rɪ'kwɛst] *n* solicitud *f*, petición *f* ♦ *vt*: **to ~ sth of** *or* **from sb** solicitar algo a algn; **at the ~ of** a petición de; **"you are ~ed not to smoke"** "se ruega no fumar".
request stop *n* (*BRIT*) parada discrecional.
requiem ['rɛkwɪəm] *n* réquiem *m*.
require [rɪ'kwaɪə*] *vt* (*need*: *subj*: *person*) necesitar, tener necesidad de; (: *thing, situation*) exigir, requerir; (*want*) pedir; (*demand*) insistir en que; **to ~ sb to do sth/sth of sb** exigir que algn haga algo; **what qualifications are ~d?** ¿qué títulos se requieren?; **~d by law** requerido por la ley.
requirement [rɪ'kwaɪəmənt] *n* requisito; (*need*) necesidad *f*.
requisite ['rɛkwɪzɪt] *n* requisito ♦ *adj* necesario, requerido.
requisition [rɛkwɪ'zɪʃən] *n* solicitud *f*; (*MIL*) requisa ♦ *vt* (*MIL*) requisar.
reroute [riː'ruːt] *vt* desviar.
resale ['riːseɪl] *n* reventa.
resale price maintenance *n* mantenimiento del precio de venta.
rescind [rɪ'sɪnd] *vt* (*LAW*) abrogar; (*contract*) rescindir; (*order etc*) anular.
rescue ['rɛskjuː] *n* rescate *m* ♦ *vt* rescatar; **to come/go to sb's ~** ir en auxilio de uno, socorrer a algn; **to ~ from** librar de.
rescue party *n* equipo de salvamento.
rescuer ['rɛskjuə*] *n* salvador(a) *m/f*.
research [rɪ'səːtʃ] *n* investigaciones *fpl* ♦ *vt* investigar; **a piece of ~** un trabajo de investigación; **to ~ (into sth)** investigar (algo).
research and development (R & D) *n* investigación *f* y desarrollo.
researcher [rɪ'səːtʃə*] *n* investigador(a) *m/f*.
research work *n* investigación *f*.
resell [riː'sɛl] *vt* revender.
resemblance [rɪ'zɛmbləns] *n* parecido; **to bear a strong ~ to** parecerse mucho a.
resemble [rɪ'zɛmbl] *vt* parecerse a.
resent [rɪ'zɛnt] *vt* resentirse por, ofenderse por; **he ~s my being here** le molesta que esté aquí.
resentful [rɪ'zɛntful] *adj* resentido.
resentment [rɪ'zɛntmənt] *n* resentimiento.
reservation [rɛzə'veɪʃən] *n* reserva; (*BRIT*: *also*: **central ~**) mediana; **with ~s** con reservas.
reservation desk *n* (*US*: *in hotel*) recepción *f*.
reserve [rɪ'zəːv] *n* reserva; (*SPORT*) suplente *m/f* ♦ *vt* (*seats etc*) reservar; **~s** *npl* (*MIL*) reserva *sg*; **in ~** en reserva.
reserve currency *n* divisa de reserva.
reserved [rɪ'zəːvd] *adj* reservado.
reserve price *n* (*BRIT*) precio mínimo.
reserve team *n* (*SPORT*) equipo de reserva.
reservist [rɪ'zəːvɪst] *n* (*MIL*) reservista *m*.
reservoir ['rɛzəvwɑː*] *n* (*artificial lake*) embalse *m*, represa; (*small*) depósito.
reset [riː'sɛt] *vt* (*COMPUT*) reinicializar.
reshape [riː'ʃeɪp] *vt* (*policy*) reformar, rehacer.
reshuffle [riː'ʃʌfl] *n*: **Cabinet ~** (*POL*) remodelación *f* del gabinete.
reside [rɪ'zaɪd] *vi* residir.
residence ['rɛzɪdəns] *n* residencia; (*formal*: *home*) domicilio; (*length of stay*) permanencia; **in ~** (*doctor*) residente; **to take up ~** instalarse.
residence permit *n* (*BRIT*) permiso de residencia.
resident ['rɛzɪdənt] *n* vecino/a; (*in hotel*) huésped/a *m/f* ♦ *adj* residente; (*population*) permanente.
residential [rɛzɪ'dɛnʃəl] *adj* residencial.
residue ['rɛzɪdjuː] *n* resto, residuo.
resign [rɪ'zaɪn] *vt* (*gen*) renunciar a ♦ *vi*: **to ~ (from)** dimitir (de), renunciar (a); **to ~ o.s. to** (*endure*) resignarse a.
resignation [rɛzɪg'neɪʃən] *n* dimisión *f*; (*state of mind*) resignación *f*; **to tender one's ~** presentar la dimisión.
resigned [rɪ'zaɪnd] *adj* resignado.
resilience [rɪ'zɪlɪəns] *n* (*of material*) elasticidad *f*; (*of person*) resistencia.
resilient [rɪ'zɪlɪənt] *adj* (*person*) resistente.
resin ['rɛzɪn] *n* resina.
resist [rɪ'zɪst] *vt* resistirse a; (*temptation, damage*) resistir.
resistance [rɪ'zɪstəns] *n* resistencia.
resistant [rɪ'zɪstənt] *adj*: **~ (to)** resistente (a).
resolute ['rɛzəluːt] *adj* resuelto.
resolutely ['rɛzəluːtlɪ] *adv* resueltamente.
resolution [rɛzə'luːʃən] *n* (*gen*) resolución *f*; (*purpose*) propósito; (*COMPUT*) definición *f*; **to make a ~** tomar una resolución.
resolve [rɪ'zɔlv] *n* (*determination*) resolución *f*; (*purpose*) propósito ♦ *vt* resolver ♦ *vi* resolverse; **to ~ to do** resolver hacer.
resolved [rɪ'zɔlvd] *adj* resuelto.
resonance ['rɛzənəns] *n* resonancia.

resonant ['rɛzənənt] *adj* resonante.
resort [rɪ'zɔːt] *n* (*town*) centro turístico; (*recourse*) recurso ♦ *vi*: **to ~ to** recurrir a; **in the last ~** como último recurso; **seaside/winter sports ~** playa, estación *f* balnearia/centro de deportes de invierno.
resound [rɪ'zaund] *vi*: **to ~ (with)** resonar (con).
resounding [rɪ'zaundɪŋ] *adj* sonoro; (*fig*) clamoroso.
resource [rɪ'sɔːs] *n* recurso; **~s** *npl* recursos *mpl*; **natural ~s** recursos *mpl* naturales; **to leave sb to his/her own ~s** (*fig*) abandonar a algn/a a sus propios recursos.
resourceful [rɪ'sɔːsful] *adj* ingenioso.
resourcefulness [rɪ'sɔːsfulnɪs] *n* inventiva, iniciativa.
respect [rɪs'pɛkt] *n* (*consideration*) respeto; (*relation*) respecto; **~s** *npl* recuerdos *mpl*, saludos *mpl* ♦ *vt* respetar; **with ~ to** con respecto a; **in this ~** en cuanto a eso; **to have** *or* **show ~ for** tener *or* mostrar respeto a; **out of ~ for** por respeto a; **in some ~s** en algunos aspectos; **with due ~ I still think you're wrong** con el respeto debido, sigo creyendo que está equivocado.
respectability [rɪspɛktə'bɪlɪtɪ] *n* respetabilidad *f*.
respectable [rɪs'pɛktəbl] *adj* respetable; (*quite big*: *amount etc*) apreciable; (*passable*) tolerable; (*quite good*: *player, result etc*) bastante bueno.
respected [rɪs'pɛktɪd] *adj* respetado, estimado.
respectful [rɪs'pɛktful] *adj* respetuoso.
respectfully [rɪs'pɛktfulɪ] *adv* respetuosamente; **Yours ~** Le saluda atentamente.
respecting [rɪs'pɛktɪŋ] *prep* (con) respecto a, en cuanto a.
respective [rɪs'pɛktɪv] *adj* respectivo.
respectively [rɪs'pɛktɪvlɪ] *adv* respectivamente.
respiration [rɛspɪ'reɪʃən] *n* respiración *f*.
respiratory [rɛs'pɪrətərɪ] *adj* respiratorio.
respite ['rɛspaɪt] *n* respiro; (*LAW*) prórroga.
resplendent [rɪs'plɛndənt] *adj* resplandeciente.
respond [rɪs'pɔnd] *vi* responder; (*react*) reaccionar.
respondent [rɪs'pɔndənt] *n* (*LAW*) demandado/a.
response [rɪs'pɔns] *n* respuesta; (*reaction*) reacción *f*; **in ~ to** como respuesta a.
responsibility [rɪspɔnsɪ'bɪlɪtɪ] *n* responsabilidad *f*; **to take ~ for sth/sb** admitir responsabilidad por algo/uno.
responsible [rɪs'pɔnsɪbl] *adj* (*liable*): **~ (for)** responsable (de); (*character*) serio, formal; (*job*) de responsabilidad; **to be ~ to sb (for sth)** ser responsable ante algn (de algo).
responsibly [rɪs'pɔnsɪblɪ] *adv* con seriedad.
responsive [rɪs'pɔnsɪv] *adj* sensible.
rest [rɛst] *n* descanso, reposo; (*MUS*) pausa, silencio; (*support*) apoyo; (*remainder*) resto ♦ *vi* descansar; (*be supported*): **to ~ on** apoyarse en ♦ *vt* (*lean*): **to ~ sth on/against** apoyar algo en *or* sobre/contra; **the ~ of them** (*people, objects*) los demás; **to set sb's mind at ~** tranquilizar a algn; **to ~ one's eyes** *or* **gaze on** fijar la mirada en; **it ~s with him** depende de él; **~ assured that ...** tenga por seguro que ....
restaurant ['rɛstərɔŋ] *n* restaurante *m*.
restaurant car *n* (*BRIT*) coche-comedor *m*.
restaurant owner *n* dueño/a *or* propietario/a de un restaurante.
rest cure *n* cura de reposo.
restful ['rɛstful] *adj* descansado, tranquilo.
rest home *n* residencia de ancianos.
restitution [rɛstɪ'tjuːʃən] *n*: **to make ~ to sb for sth** restituir algo a algn; (*paying*) indemnizar a algn por algo.
restive ['rɛstɪv] *adj* inquieto; (*horse*) rebelón/ona.
restless ['rɛstlɪs] *adj* inquieto; **to get ~** impacientarse.
restlessly ['rɛstlɪslɪ] *adv* inquietamente, con inquietud *f*.
restlessness ['rɛstlɪsnɪs] *n* inquietud *f*.
restock [riː'stɔk] *vt* reaprovisionar.
restoration [rɛstə'reɪʃən] *n* restauración *f*; (*giving back*) devolución *f*, restitución *f*.
restorative [rɪ'stɔːrətɪv] *adj* reconstituyente, fortalecedor(a) ♦ *n* reconstituyente *m*.
restore [rɪ'stɔː*] *vt* (*building*) restaurar; (*sth stolen*) devolver, restituir; (*health*) restablecer.
restorer [rɪ'stɔːrə*] *n* (*ART etc*) restaurador(a) *m/f*.
restrain [rɪs'treɪn] *vt* (*feeling*) contener, refrenar; (*person*): **to ~ (from doing)** disuadir (de hacer).
restrained [rɪs'treɪnd] *adj* (*style*) reservado.
restraint [rɪs'treɪnt] *n* (*restriction*) freno, control *m*; (*of style*) reserva; **wage ~** control *m* de los salarios.
restrict [rɪs'trɪkt] *vt* restringir, limitar.
restricted [rɪs'trɪktɪd] *adj* restringido, limitado.
restriction [rɪs'trɪkʃən] *n* restricción *f*,

limitación *f.*
restrictive [rɪs'trɪktɪv] *adj* restrictivo.
restrictive practices *npl* (*INDUSTRY*) prácticas *fpl* restrictivas.
rest room *n* (*US*) aseos *mpl.*
restructure [riː'strʌktʃə*] *vt* reestructurar.
result [rɪ'zʌlt] *n* resultado ♦ *vi*: **to ~ in** terminar en, tener por resultado; **as a ~ of** a *or* como consecuencia de; **to ~ (from)** resultar (de).
resultant [rɪ'zʌltənt] *adj* resultante.
resume [rɪ'zjuːm] *vt* (*work, journey*) reanudar; (*sum up*) resumir ♦ *vi* (*meeting*) continuar.
résumé ['reɪzjuːmeɪ] *n* resumen *m.*
resumption [rɪ'zʌmpʃən] *n* reanudación *f.*
resurgence [rɪ'səːdʒəns] *n* resurgimiento.
resurrection [rɛzə'rɛkʃən] *n* resurrección *f.*
resuscitate [rɪ'sʌsɪteɪt] *vt* (*MED*) resucitar.
resuscitation [rɪsʌsɪ'teɪʃn] *n* resucitación *f.*
retail ['riːteɪl] *n* venta al por menor ♦ *cpd* al por menor ♦ *vt* vender al por menor *or* al detalle ♦ *vi*: **to ~ at** (*COMM*) tener precio de venta al público de.
retailer ['riːteɪlə*] *n* minorista *m/f*, detallista *m/f.*
retail outlet *n* punto de venta.
retail price *n* precio de venta al público, precio al detalle *or* al por menor.
retail price index *n* índice *m* de precios al por menor.
retain [rɪ'teɪn] *vt* (*keep*) retener, conservar; (*employ*) contratar.
retainer [rɪ'teɪnə*] *n* (*servant*) criado; (*fee*) anticipo.
retaliate [rɪ'tælɪeɪt] *vi*: **to ~ (against)** tomar represalias (contra).
retaliation [rɪtælɪ'eɪʃən] *n* represalias *fpl*; **in ~ for** como represalia por.
retaliatory [rɪ'tælɪətərɪ] *adj* de represalia.
retarded [rɪ'tɑːdɪd] *adj* retrasado.
retch [rɛtʃ] *vi* darle a algn arcadas.
retentive [rɪ'tɛntɪv] *adj* (*memory*) retentivo.
rethink [riː'θɪŋk] *vt* repensar.
reticence ['rɛtɪsns] *n* reticencia, reserva.
reticent ['rɛtɪsnt] *adj* reticente, reservado.
retina ['rɛtɪnə] *n* retina.
retinue ['rɛtɪnjuː] *n* séquito, comitiva.
retire [rɪ'taɪə*] *vi* (*give up work*) jubilarse; (*withdraw*) retirarse; (*go to bed*) acostarse.
retired [rɪ'taɪəd] *adj* (*person*) jubilado.
retirement [rɪ'taɪəmənt] *n* jubilación *f*; **early ~** jubilación *f* anticipada.
retiring [rɪ'taɪərɪŋ] *adj* (*departing: chairman*) saliente; (*shy*) retraído.
retort [rɪ'tɔːt] *n* (*reply*) réplica ♦ *vi* replicar.
retrace [riː'treɪs] *vt*: **to ~ one's steps** volver sobre sus pasos, desandar lo andado.
retract [rɪ'trækt] *vt* (*statement*) retirar; (*claws*) retraer; (*undercarriage, aerial*) replegar ♦ *vi* retractarse.
retractable [rɪ'træktəbl] *adj* replegable.
retrain [riː'treɪn] *vt* reciclar.
retraining [riː'treɪnɪŋ] *n* reciclaje *m*, readaptación *f* profesional.
retread ['riːtrɛd] *n* neumático *or* llanta (*LAM*) recauchutado/a.
retreat [rɪ'triːt] *n* (*place*) retiro; (*MIL*) retirada ♦ *vi* retirarse; (*flood*) bajar; **to beat a hasty ~** (*fig*) retirarse en desbandada.
retrial ['riːtraɪəl] *n* nuevo proceso.
retribution [rɛtrɪ'bjuːʃən] *n* desquite *m.*
retrieval [rɪ'triːvəl] *n* recuperación *f*; **information ~** recuperación *f* de datos.
retrieve [rɪ'triːv] *vt* recobrar; (*situation, honour*) salvar; (*COMPUT*) recuperar; (*error*) reparar.
retriever [rɪ'triːvə*] *n* perro cobrador.
retroactive [rɛtrəu'æktɪv] *adj* retroactivo.
retrograde ['rɛtrəgreɪd] *adj* retrógrado.
retrospect ['rɛtrəspɛkt] *n*: **in ~** retrospectivamente.
retrospective [rɛtrə'spɛktɪv] *adj* retrospectivo; (*law*) retroactivo ♦ *n* exposición *f* retrospectiva.
return [rɪ'təːn] *n* (*going or coming back*) vuelta, regreso; (*of sth stolen etc*) devolución *f*; (*recompense*) recompensa; (*FINANCE: from land, shares*) ganancia, ingresos *mpl*; (*COMM: of merchandise*) devolución *f* ♦ *cpd* (*journey*) de regreso; (*BRIT: ticket*) de ida y vuelta; (*match*) de vuelta ♦ *vi* (*person etc: come or go back*) volver, regresar; (*symptoms etc*) reaparecer ♦ *vt* devolver; (*favour, love etc*) corresponder a; (*verdict*) pronunciar; (*POL: candidate*) elegir; **~s** *npl* (*COMM*) ingresos *mpl*; **tax ~** declaración *f* de la renta; **in ~ (for)** a cambio (de); **by ~ of post** a vuelta de correo; **many happy ~s (of the day)!** ¡feliz cumpleaños!
returnable [rɪ'təːnəbl] *adj*: **~ bottle** envase *m* retornable.
returner [rɪ'təːnə*] *n* *mujer que vuelve a trabajar tras un tiempo dedicada a la familia.*
returning officer [rɪ'təːnɪŋ-] *n* (*BRIT POL*) escrutador(a) *m/f.*
return key *n* (*COMPUT*) tecla de retorno.
reunion [riː'juːnɪən] *n* reencuentro.
reunite [riːjuː'naɪt] *vt* reunir; (*reconcile*) reconciliar.
rev [rɛv] *n abbr* (*AUT*: = *revolution*) revolución *f* ♦ (*vb*: *also*: **~ up**) *vt* acelerar.

revaluation [riːvæljuːˈeɪʃən] *n* revalorización *f*.
revamp [riːˈvæmp] *vt* renovar.
Rev(d). *abbr* (= *reverend*) R., Rvdo.
reveal [rɪˈviːl] *vt* (*make known*) revelar.
revealing [rɪˈviːlɪŋ] *adj* revelador(a).
reveille [rɪˈvælɪ] *n* (*MIL*) diana.
revel [ˈrɛvl] *vi*: **to ~ in sth/in doing sth** gozar de algo/haciendo algo.
revelation [rɛvəˈleɪʃən] *n* revelación *f*.
reveller, (*US*) **reveler** [ˈrɛvlə*] *n* jaranero, juerguista *m/f*.
revelry [ˈrɛvlrɪ] *n* jarana, juerga.
revenge [rɪˈvɛndʒ] *n* venganza; (*in sport*) revancha; **to take ~ on** vengarse de; **to get one's ~ (for sth)** vengarse (de algo).
revengeful [rɪˈvɛndʒful] *adj* vengativo.
revenue [ˈrɛvənjuː] *n* ingresos *mpl*, rentas *fpl*.
revenue account *n* cuenta de ingresos presupuestarios.
revenue expenditure *n* gasto corriente.
reverberate [rɪˈvəːbəreɪt] *vi* (*sound*) resonar, retumbar.
reverberation [rɪvəːbəˈreɪʃən] *n* resonancia.
revere [rɪˈvɪə*] *vt* reverenciar, venerar.
reverence [ˈrɛvərəns] *n* reverencia.
Reverend [ˈrɛvərənd] *adj* (*in titles*): **the ~ John Smith** (*Anglican*) el Reverendo John Smith; (*Catholic*) el Padre John Smith; (*Protestant*) el Pastor John Smith.
reverent [ˈrɛvərənt] *adj* reverente.
reverie [ˈrɛvərɪ] *n* ensueño.
reversal [rɪˈvəːsl] *n* (*of order*) inversión *f*; (*of policy*) cambio de rumbo; (*of decision*) revocación *f*.
reverse [rɪˈvəːs] *n* (*opposite*) contrario; (*back*: *of cloth*) revés *m*; (: *of coin*) reverso; (: *of paper*) dorso; (*AUT*: *also*: **~ gear**) marcha atrás ♦ *adj* (*order*) inverso; (*direction*) contrario ♦ *vt* (*decision, AUT*) dar marcha atrás a; (*position, function*) invertir ♦ *vi* (*BRIT AUT*) poner en marcha atrás; **in ~ order** en orden inverso; **the ~** lo contrario; **to go into ~** dar marcha atrás.
reverse-charge call [rɪˈvəːstʃɑːdʒ-] *n* (*BRIT*) llamada a cobro revertido.
reverse video *n* vídeo inverso.
reversible [rɪˈvəːsəbl] *adj* (*garment, procedure*) reversible.
reversing lights [rɪˈvəːsɪŋ-] *npl* (*BRIT AUT*) luces *fpl* de marcha atrás.
revert [rɪˈvəːt] *vi*: **to ~ to** volver *or* revertir a.
review [rɪˈvjuː] *n* (*magazine, MIL*) revista; (*of book, film*) reseña; (*US*: *examination*) repaso, examen *m* ♦ *vt* repasar, examinar; (*MIL*) pasar revista a; (*book, film*) reseñar; **to come under ~** ser examinado.
reviewer [rɪˈvjuːə*] *n* crítico/a.
revile [rɪˈvaɪl] *vt* injuriar, vilipendiar.
revise [rɪˈvaɪz] *vt* (*manuscript*) corregir; (*opinion*) modificar; (*BRIT*: *study*: *subject*) repasar; (*look over*) revisar; **~d edition** edición *f* corregida.
revision [rɪˈvɪʒən] *n* corrección *f*; modificación *f*; (*of subject*) repaso; (*revised version*) revisión *f*.
revisit [riːˈvɪzɪt] *vt* volver a visitar.
revitalize [riːˈvaɪtəlaɪz] *vt* revivificar.
revival [rɪˈvaɪvəl] *n* (*recovery*) reanimación *f*; (*POL*) resurgimiento; (*of interest*) renacimiento; (*THEAT*) reestreno; (*of faith*) despertar *m*.
revive [rɪˈvaɪv] *vt* resucitar; (*custom*) restablecer; (*hope, courage*) reanimar; (*play*) reestrenar ♦ *vi* (*person*) volver en sí; (*from tiredness*) reponerse; (*business*) reactivarse.
revoke [rɪˈvəuk] *vt* revocar.
revolt [rɪˈvəult] *n* rebelión *f* ♦ *vi* rebelarse, sublevarse ♦ *vt* dar asco a, repugnar; **to ~ (against sb/sth)** rebelarse (contra algn/algo).
revolting [rɪˈvəultɪŋ] *adj* asqueroso, repugnante.
revolution [rɛvəˈluːʃən] *n* revolución *f*.
revolutionary [rɛvəˈluːʃənrɪ] *adj, n* revolucionario/a *m/f*.
revolutionize [rɛvəˈluːʃənaɪz] *vt* revolucionar.
revolve [rɪˈvɔlv] *vi* dar vueltas, girar.
revolver [rɪˈvɔlvə*] *n* revólver *m*.
revolving [rɪˈvɔlvɪŋ] *adj* (*chair, door etc*) giratorio.
revue [rɪˈvjuː] *n* (*THEAT*) revista.
revulsion [rɪˈvʌlʃən] *n* asco, repugnancia.
reward [rɪˈwɔːd] *n* premio, recompensa ♦ *vt*: **to ~ (for)** recompensar *or* premiar (por).
rewarding [rɪˈwɔːdɪŋ] *adj* (*fig*) gratificante; **financially ~** económicamente provechoso.
rewind [riːˈwaɪnd] *vt* (*watch*) dar cuerda a; (*wool etc*) devanar.
rewire [riːˈwaɪə*] *vt* (*house*) renovar la instalación eléctrica de.
reword [riːˈwəːd] *vt* expresar en otras palabras.
rewrite [riːˈraɪt] *vt* (*irreg*: *like* **write**) reescribir.
Reykjavik [ˈreɪkjəviːk] *n* Reykjavik *m*.
RFD *abbr* (*US POST*)= *rural free delivery*.
Rh *abbr* (= *rhesus*) Rh *m*.

rhapsody ['ræpsədɪ] *n* (*MUS*) rapsodia; (*fig*): **to go into rhapsodies over** extasiarse por.
rhesus negative ['ri:səs-] *adj* (*MED*) Rh negativo.
rhesus positive *adj* (*MED*) Rh positivo.
rhetoric ['rɛtərɪk] *n* retórica.
rhetorical [rɪ'tɔrɪkl] *adj* retórico.
rheumatic [ru:'mætɪk] *adj* reumático.
rheumatism ['ru:mətɪzəm] *n* reumatismo, reúma.
rheumatoid arthritis ['ru:mətɔɪd-] *n* reúma *m* articular.
Rhine [raɪn] *n*: **the ~** el (río) Rin.
rhinestone ['raɪnstəun] *n* diamante *m* de imitación.
rhinoceros [raɪ'nɔsərəs] *n* rinoceronte *m*.
Rhodes [rəudz] *n* Rodas *f*.
rhododendron [rəudə'dɛndrn] *n* rododendro.
Rhone [rəun] *n*: **the ~** el (río) Ródano.
rhubarb ['ru:bɑ:b] *n* ruibarbo.
rhyme [raɪm] *n* rima; (*verse*) poesía ♦ *vi*: **to ~ (with)** rimar (con); **without ~ or reason** sin ton ni son.
rhythm ['rɪðm] *n* ritmo.
rhythmic(al) ['rɪðmɪk(l)] *adj* rítmico.
rhythmically ['rɪðmɪklɪ] *adv* rítmicamente.
rhythm method *n* método (de) Ogino.
RI *n abbr* (*BRIT*: = *religious instruction*) ed. religiosa ♦ *abbr* (*US*) = *Rhode Island*.
rib [rɪb] *n* (*ANAT*) costilla ♦ *vt* (*mock*) tomar el pelo a.
ribald ['rɪbəld] *adj* escabroso.
ribbon ['rɪbən] *n* cinta; **in ~s** (*torn*) hecho trizas.
rice [raɪs] *n* arroz *m*.
ricefield ['raɪsfi:ld] *n* arrozal *m*.
rice pudding *n* arroz *m* con leche.
rich [rɪtʃ] *adj* rico; (*soil*) fértil; (*food*) pesado; (: *sweet*) empalagoso; **the ~** *npl* los ricos; **~es** *npl* riqueza *sg*; **to be ~ in sth** abundar en algo.
richly ['rɪtʃlɪ] *adv* ricamente.
richness ['rɪtʃnɪs] *n* riqueza; (*of soil*) fertilidad *f*.
rickets ['rɪkɪts] *n* raquitismo.
rickety ['rɪkɪtɪ] *adj* (*old*) desvencijado; (*shaky*) tambaleante.
rickshaw ['rɪkʃɔ:] *n* carro de culí.
ricochet ['rɪkəʃeɪ] *n* rebote *m* ♦ *vi* rebotar.
rid, *pt, pp* **rid** [rɪd] *vt*: **to ~ sb of sth** librar a algn de algo; **to get ~ of** deshacerse *or* desembarazarse de.
riddance ['rɪdns] *n*: **good ~!** ¡y adiós muy buenas!
ridden ['rɪdn] *pp of* **ride**.
-ridden ['rɪdn] *suff*: **disease~** plagado de enfermedades; **inflation~** minado por la inflación.
riddle ['rɪdl] *n* (*conundrum*) acertijo; (*mystery*) enigma *m*, misterio ♦ *vt*: **to be ~d with** ser lleno *or* plagado de.
ride [raɪd] *n* paseo; (*distance covered*) viaje *m*, recorrido ♦ *vb* (*pt* **rode**, *pp* **ridden**) *vi* (*horse*: *as sport*) montar; (*go somewhere*: *on horse, bicycle*) dar un paseo, pasearse; (*journey*: *on bicycle, motor cycle, bus*) viajar ♦ *vt* (*a horse*) montar a; (*distance*) viajar; **to ~ a bicycle** andar en bicicleta; **to ~ at anchor** (*NAUT*) estar fondeado; **can you ~ a bike?** ¿sabes montar en bici(cleta)?; **to go for a ~** dar un paseo; **to take sb for a ~** (*fig*) tomar el pelo a algn.
►**ride out** *vt*: **to ~ out the storm** (*fig*) capear el temporal.
rider ['raɪdə*] *n* (*on horse*) jinete *m*; (*on bicycle*) ciclista *m/f*; (*on motorcycle*) motociclista *m/f*.
ridge [rɪdʒ] *n* (*of hill*) cresta; (*of roof*) caballete *m*; (*wrinkle*) arruga.
ridicule ['rɪdɪkju:l] *n* irrisión *f*, burla ♦ *vt* poner en ridículo a, burlarse de; **to hold sth/sb up to ~** poner algo/a algn en ridículo.
ridiculous [rɪ'dɪkjuləs] *adj* ridículo.
ridiculously [rɪ'dɪkjuləslɪ] *adv* ridículamente, de modo ridículo.
riding ['raɪdɪŋ] *n* equitación *f*; **I like ~** me gusta montar a caballo.
riding habit *n* traje *m* de montar.
riding school *n* escuela de equitación.
rife [raɪf] *adj*: **to be ~** ser muy común; **to be ~ with** abundar en.
riffraff ['rɪfræf] *n* chusma, gentuza.
rifle ['raɪfl] *n* rifle *m*, fusil *m* ♦ *vt* saquear.
►**rifle through** *vt fus* saquear.
rifle range *n* campo de tiro; (*at fair*) tiro al blanco.
rift [rɪft] *n* (*fig*: *between friends*) desavenencia; (: *in party*) escisión *f*.
rig [rɪg] *n* (*also*: **oil ~**: *on land*) torre *f* de perforación; (: *at sea*) plataforma petrolera ♦ *vt* (*election etc*) amañar los resultados de.
►**rig out** *vt* (*BRIT*) ataviar.
►**rig up** *vt* improvisar.
rigging ['rɪgɪŋ] *n* (*NAUT*) aparejo.
right [raɪt] *adj* (*true, correct*) correcto, exacto; (*suitable*) indicado, debido; (*proper*) apropiado, propio; (*just*) justo; (*morally good*) bueno; (*not left*) derecho ♦ *n* (*title, claim*) derecho; (*not left*) derecha ♦ *adv* (*correctly*) bien, correctamente; (*straight*) derecho, directamente; (*not on the left*) a la derecha; (*to the ~*) hacia la

derecha ♦ *vt* (*put straight*) enderezar ♦ *excl* ¡bueno!, ¡está bien!; **to be** ~ (*person*) tener razón; **to get sth** ~ acertar en algo; **you did the** ~ **thing** hiciste bien; **let's get it** ~ **this time!** ¡a ver si esta vez nos sale bien!; **to put a mistake** ~ corregir un error; **the** ~ **time** la hora exacta; (*fig*) el momento oportuno; **by** ~**s** en justicia; ~ **and wrong** el bien y el mal; **film** ~**s** derechos *mpl* de la película; **on the** ~ a la derecha; **to be in the** ~ tener razón; ~ **now** ahora mismo; ~ **before/after** inmediatamente antes/después; ~ **in the middle** exactamente en el centro; ~ **away** en seguida; **to go** ~ **to the end of sth** llegar hasta el final de algo; ~**, who's next?** bueno, ¿quién sigue?; **all** ~! ¡vale!; **I'm/I feel all** ~ **now** ya estoy bien.

right angle *n* ángulo recto.

righteous ['raɪtʃəs] *adj* justo, honrado; (*anger*) justificado.

righteousness ['raɪtʃəsnɪs] *n* justicia.

rightful ['raɪtful] *adj* (*heir*) legítimo.

right-hand ['raɪthænd] *adj* (*drive, turn*) por la derecha.

right-handed [raɪt'hændɪd] *adj* (*person*) que usa la mano derecha.

right-hand man *n* brazo derecho.

right-hand side *n* derecha.

rightly ['raɪtlɪ] *adv* correctamente, debidamente; (*with reason*) con razón; **if I remember** ~ si recuerdo bien.

right-minded ['raɪt'maɪndɪd] *adj* (*sensible*) sensato; (*decent*) honrado.

right of way *n* (*on path etc*) derecho de paso; (*AUT*) prioridad *f* de paso.

rights issue *n* (*STOCK EXCHANGE*) emisión *f* gratuita de acciones.

right-wing [raɪt'wɪŋ] *adj* (*POL*) de derechas, derechista.

right-winger [raɪt'wɪŋə*] *n* (*POL*) persona de derechas, derechista *m/f*; (*SPORT*) extremo derecha.

rigid ['rɪdʒɪd] *adj* rígido; (*person, ideas*) inflexible.

rigidity [rɪ'dʒɪdɪtɪ] *n* rigidez *f*; inflexibilidad *f*.

rigidly ['rɪdʒɪdlɪ] *adv* rígidamente; (*inflexibly*) inflexiblemente.

rigmarole ['rɪgmərəul] *n* galimatías *m inv*.

rigor mortis ['rɪgə'mɔːtɪs] *n* rigidez *f* cadavérica.

rigorous ['rɪgərəs] *adj* riguroso.

rigorously ['rɪgərəslɪ] *adv* rigurosamente.

rigour, (*US*) **rigor** ['rɪgə*] *n* rigor *m*, severidad *f*.

rig-out ['rɪgaut] *n* (*BRIT col*) atuendo.

rile [raɪl] *vt* irritar.

rim [rɪm] *n* borde *m*; (*of spectacles*) montura, aro; (*of wheel*) llanta.

rimless ['rɪmlɪs] *adj* (*spectacles*) sin aros.

rimmed [rɪmd] *adj*: ~ **with** con un borde de, bordeado de.

rind [raɪnd] *n* (*of bacon, cheese*) corteza; (*of lemon etc*) cáscara.

ring [rɪŋ] *n* (*of metal*) aro; (*on finger*) anillo; (*of people*) corro; (*of objects*) círculo; (*gang*) banda; (*for boxing*) cuadrilátero; (*of circus*) pista; (*bull* ~) ruedo, plaza; (*sound of bell*) toque *m*; (*telephone call*) llamada ♦ *vb* (*pt* **rang**, *pp* **rung** [ræŋ, rʌŋ]) *vi* (*on telephone*) llamar por teléfono; (*large bell*) repicar; (*also*: ~ **out**: *voice, words*) sonar; (*ears*) zumbar ♦ *vt* (*BRIT TEL*: *also*: ~ **up**) llamar; (*bell etc*) hacer sonar; (*doorbell*) tocar; **that has the** ~ **of truth about it** eso suena a verdad; **to give sb a** ~ (*BRIT TEL*) llamar por teléfono a algn, dar un telefonazo a algn; **the name doesn't** ~ **a bell (with me)** el nombre no me suena; **to** ~ **sb (up)** llamar a algn.

►**ring back** *vt, vi* (*TEL*) devolver la llamada.

►**ring off** *vi* (*BRIT TEL*) colgar, cortar la comunicación.

ring binder *n* carpeta de anillas.

ring finger *n* (dedo) anular *m*.

ringing ['rɪŋɪŋ] *n* (*of bell*) toque *m*, tañido; (*louder*: *of large bell*) repique *m*; (*in ears*) zumbido.

ringing tone *n* (*TEL*) tono de llamada.

ringleader ['rɪŋliːdə*] *n* (*of gang*) cabecilla *m/f*.

ringlets ['rɪŋlɪts] *npl* tirabuzones *mpl*, bucles *mpl*.

ring road *n* (*BRIT*) carretera periférica *or* de circunvalación.

rink [rɪŋk] *n* (*also*: **ice** ~) pista de hielo; (*for roller-skating*) pista de patinaje.

rinse [rɪns] *n* (*of dishes*) enjuague *m*; (*of clothes*) aclarado; (*of hair*) reflejo ♦ *vt* enjuagar; aclarar; dar reflejos a.

Rio (de Janeiro) ['riːəu(dədʒə'nɪərəu)] *n* Río de Janeiro.

riot ['raɪət] *n* motín *m*, disturbio ♦ *vi* amotinarse; **to run** ~ desmandarse.

rioter ['raɪətə*] *n* amotinado/a.

riot gear *n* uniforme *m* antidisturbios *inv*.

riotous ['raɪətəs] *adj* alborotado; (*party*) bullicioso; (*uncontrolled*) desenfrenado.

riotously ['raɪətəslɪ] *adv* bulliciosamente.

riot police *n* policía antidisturbios.

RIP *abbr* (= *rest in peace*) q.e.p.d.

rip [rɪp] *n* rasgón *m*, desgarrón *m* ♦ *vt* rasgar, desgarrar ♦ *vi* rasgarse.

►**rip up** *vt* hacer pedazos.

ripcord ['rɪpkɔːd] *n* cabo de desgarre.

ripe [raɪp] *adj* (*fruit*) maduro.
ripen ['raɪpən] *vt, vi* madurar.
ripeness ['raɪpnɪs] *n* madurez *f*.
rip-off ['rɪpɔf] *n* (*col*): **it's a ~!** ¡es una estafa!, ¡es un timo!
riposte [rɪ'pɔst] *n* respuesta aguda, réplica.
ripple ['rɪpl] *n* onda, rizo; (*sound*) murmullo ♦ *vi* rizarse ♦ *vt* rizar.
rise [raɪz] *n* (*slope*) cuesta, pendiente *f*; (*hill*) altura; (*increase*: *in wages*: *Brit*) aumento; (: *in prices, temperature*) subida, alza; (*fig*: *to power etc*) ascenso; (: *ascendancy*) auge *m* ♦ *vi* (*pt* **rose**, *pp* **risen** [rəuz, 'rɪzn]) (*gen*) elevarse; (*prices*) subir; (*waters*) crecer; (*river*) nacer; (*sun*) salir; (*person*: *from bed etc*) levantarse; (*also*: **~ up**: *rebel*) sublevarse; (*in rank*) ascender; **~ to power** ascenso al poder; **to give ~ to** dar lugar *or* origen a; **to ~ to the occasion** ponerse a la altura de las circunstancias.
rising ['raɪzɪŋ] *adj* (*increasing*: *number*) creciente; (: *prices*) en aumento *or* alza; (*tide*) creciente; (*sun, moon*) naciente ♦ *n* (*uprising*) sublevación *f*.
rising damp *n* humedad *f* de paredes.
rising star *n* (*fig*) figura en alza.
risk [rɪsk] *n* riesgo, peligro ♦ *vt* (*gen*) arriesgar; (*dare*) atreverse a; **to take** *or* **run the ~ of doing** correr el riesgo de hacer; **at ~** en peligro; **at one's own ~** bajo su propia responsabilidad; **fire/health/security ~** peligro de incendio/para la salud/para la seguridad.
risk capital *n* capital *m* de riesgo.
risky ['rɪskɪ] *adj* arriesgado, peligroso.
risqué ['riːskeɪ] *adj* (*joke*) subido de color.
rissole ['rɪsəul] *n* croqueta.
rite [raɪt] *n* rito; **last ~s** últimos sacramentos *mpl*.
ritual ['rɪtjuəl] *adj* ritual ♦ *n* ritual *m*, rito.
rival ['raɪvl] *n* rival *m/f*; (*in business*) competidor(a) *m/f* ♦ *adj* rival, opuesto ♦ *vt* competir con.
rivalry ['raɪvlrɪ] *n* rivalidad *f*, competencia.
river ['rɪvə*] *n* río ♦ *cpd* (*port, traffic*) de río, del río; **up/down ~** río arriba/abajo.
riverbank ['rɪvəbæŋk] *n* orilla (del río).
riverbed ['rɪvəbɛd] *n* lecho, cauce *m*.
rivet ['rɪvɪt] *n* roblón *m*, remache *m* ♦ *vt* remachar; (*fig*) fascinar.
riveting ['rɪvɪtɪŋ] *adj* (*fig*) fascinante.
Riviera [rɪvɪ'ɛərə] *n*: **the (French) ~** la Costa Azul; **the Italian ~** la Riviera italiana.
Riyadh [rɪ'jɑːd] *n* Riyadh *m*.
RMT *n abbr* (=*Rail, Maritime and Transport*) *sindicato de transportes*.
RN *n abbr* (*BRIT*) *see* **Royal Navy**; (*US*) = **registered nurse**.
RNA *n abbr* (= *ribonucleic acid*) ARN *m*, RNA *m*.
RNLI *n abbr* (*BRIT*: = *Royal National Lifeboat Institution*) *servicio de lanchas de socorro*.
RNZAF *n abbr* = *Royal New Zealand Air Force*.
RNZN *n abbr* = *Royal New Zealand Navy*.
road [rəud] *n* (*gen*) camino; (*motorway etc*) carretera; (*in town*) calle *f*; **major/minor ~** carretera general/secundaria; **main ~** carretera; **it takes 4 hours by ~** se tarda 4 horas por carretera; **on the ~ to success** camino del éxito.
roadblock ['rəudblɔk] *n* barricada, control *m*, retén *m* (*LAM*).
road haulage *n* transporte *m* por carretera.
roadhog ['rəudhɔg] *n* loco/a del volante.
road map *n* mapa *m* de carreteras.
road rage *n conducta agresiva de los conductores*.
road safety *n* seguridad *f* vial.
roadside ['rəudsaɪd] *n* borde *m* (del camino) ♦ *cpd* al lado de la carretera; **by the ~** al borde del camino.
roadsign ['rəudsaɪn] *n* señal *f* de tráfico.
roadsweeper ['rəudswiːpə*] *n* (*BRIT*: *person*) barrendero/a.
road user *n* usuario/a de la vía pública.
roadway ['rəudweɪ] *n* calzada.
roadworks ['rəudwəːks] *npl* obras *fpl*.
roadworthy ['rəudwəːðɪ] *adj* (*car*) en buen estado para circular.
roam [rəum] *vi* vagar ♦ *vt* vagar por.
roar [rɔː*] *n* (*of animal*) rugido, bramido; (*of crowd*) clamor *m*, rugido; (*of vehicle, storm*) estruendo; (*of laughter*) carcajada ♦ *vi* rugir, bramar; hacer estruendo; **to ~ with laughter** reírse a carcajadas.
roaring ['rɔːrɪŋ] *adj*: **a ~ success** un tremendo éxito; **to do a ~ trade** hacer buen negocio.
roast [rəust] *n* carne *f* asada, asado ♦ *vt* (*meat*) asar; (*coffee*) tostar.
roast beef *n* rosbif *m*.
roasting ['rəustɪŋ] *n*: **to give sb a ~** (*col*) echar una buena bronca a algn.
rob [rɔb] *vt* robar; **to ~ sb of sth** robar algo a algn; (*fig: deprive*) quitar algo a algn.
robber ['rɔbə*] *n* ladrón/ona *m/f*.
robbery ['rɔbərɪ] *n* robo.
robe [rəub] *n* (*for ceremony etc*) toga; (*also*: **bath ~**) bata.
robin ['rɔbɪn] *n* petirrojo.
robot ['rəubɔt] *n* robot *m*.
robotics [rəu'bɔtɪks] *n* robótica.
robust [rəu'bʌst] *adj* robusto, fuerte.
rock [rɔk] *n* (*gen*) roca; (*boulder*) peña,

peñasco; (*BRIT*: *sweet*) ≈ pirulí *m* ♦ *vt* (*swing gently*) mecer; (*shake*) sacudir ♦ *vi* mecerse, balancearse; sacudirse; **on the ~s** (*drink*) con hielo; **their marriage is on the ~s** su matrimonio se está yendo a pique; **to ~ the boat** (*fig*) crear problemas.

rock and roll *n* rock and roll *m*, rocanrol *m*.

rock-bottom ['rɔk'bɔtəm] *adj* (*fig*) por los suelos; **to reach** *or* **touch rock bottom** (*price*) estar por los suelos; (*person*) tocar fondo.

rock cake *n* (*BRIT*) *bollito de pasas con superficie rugosa.*

rock climber *n* escalador(a) *m/f*.

rock climbing *n* (*SPORT*) escalada.

rockery ['rɔkərɪ] *n* cuadro alpino.

rocket ['rɔkɪt] *n* cohete *m* ♦ *vi* (*prices*) dispararse, ponerse por las nubes.

rocket launcher *n* lanzacohetes *m inv*.

rock face *n* pared *f* de roca.

rocking chair ['rɔkɪŋ-] *n* mecedora.

rocking horse *n* caballo de balancín.

rocky ['rɔkɪ] *adj* (*gen*) rocoso; (*unsteady*: *table*) inestable.

Rocky Mountains *npl*: **the ~** las Montañas Rocosas.

rococo [rə'kəukəu] *adj* rococó *inv* ♦ *n* rococó.

rod [rɔd] *n* vara, varilla; (*TECH*) barra; (*also*: **fishing ~**) caña.

rode [rəud] *pt of* **ride**.

rodent ['rəudnt] *n* roedor *m*.

rodeo ['rəudɪəu] *n* rodeo.

roe [rəu] *n* (*species: also:* **~ deer**) corzo; (*of fish*): **hard/soft ~** hueva/lecha.

rogue [rəug] *n* pícaro, pillo.

roguish ['rəugɪʃ] *adj* (*child*) travieso; (*smile etc*) pícaro.

role [rəul] *n* papel *m*, rol *m*.

role-model ['rəulmɔdl] *n* modelo a imitar.

role play *n* (*also*: **~ing**) juego de papeles *or* roles.

roll [rəul] *n* rollo; (*of bank notes*) fajo; (*also*: **bread ~**) panecillo; (*register*) lista, nómina; (*sound: of drums etc*) redoble *m*; (*movement*: *of ship*) balanceo ♦ *vt* hacer rodar; (*also*: **~ up**: *string*) enrollar; (: *sleeves*) arremangar; (*cigarettes*) liar; (*also*: **~ out**: *pastry*) aplanar ♦ *vi* (*gen*) rodar; (*drum*) redoblar; (*in walking*) bambolearse; (*ship*) balancearse; **cheese ~** panecillo de queso.

▸**roll about, roll around** *vi* (*person*) revolcarse.

▸**roll by** *vi* (*time*) pasar.

▸**roll in** *vi* (*mail, cash*) entrar a raudales.

▸**roll over** *vi* dar una vuelta.

▸**roll up** *vi* (*col*: *arrive*) presentarse, aparecer ♦ *vt* (*carpet, cloth, map*) arrollar; (*sleeves*) arremangar; **to ~ o.s. up into a ball** acurrucarse, hacerse un ovillo.

roll call *n*: **to take a ~** pasar lista.

rolled [rəuld] *adj* (*umbrella*) plegado.

roller ['rəulə*] *n* rodillo; (*wheel*) rueda.

roller blind *n* (*BRIT*) persiana (enrollable).

roller coaster *n* montaña rusa.

roller skates *npl* patines *mpl* de rueda.

rollicking ['rɔlɪkɪŋ] *adj*: **we had a ~ time** nos divertimos una barbaridad.

rolling ['rəulɪŋ] *adj* (*landscape*) ondulado.

rolling mill *n* taller *m* de laminación.

rolling pin *n* rodillo (de cocina).

rolling stock *n* (*RAIL*) material *m* rodante.

ROM [rɔm] *n abbr* (= *read only memory*) (memoria) ROM *f*.

Roman ['rəumən] *adj*, *n* romano/a *m/f*.

Roman Catholic *adj*, *n* católico/a *m/f* (romano/a).

romance [rə'mæns] *n* (*love affair*) amor *m*, idilio; (*charm*) lo romántico; (*novel*) novela de amor.

romanesque [rəumə'nɛsk] *adj* románico.

Romania [ruː'meɪnɪə] *n* = **Rumania**.

Romanian [ruː'meɪnɪən] *adj*, *n* = **Rumanian**.

Roman numeral *n* número romano.

romantic [rə'mæntɪk] *adj* romántico.

romanticism [rə'mæntɪsɪzəm] *n* romanticismo.

Romany ['rəumənɪ] *adj* gitano ♦ *n* (*person*) gitano/a; (*LING*) lengua gitana, caló (*SP*).

Rome [rəum] *n* Roma.

romp [rɔmp] *n* retozo, jugueteo ♦ *vi* (*also*: **~ about**) juguetear; **to ~ home** (*horse*) ganar fácilmente.

rompers ['rɔmpəz] *npl* pelele *m*.

roof [ruːf] *n* (*gen*) techo; (*of house*) tejado ♦ *vt* techar, poner techo a; **~ of the mouth** paladar *m*.

roofing ['ruːfɪŋ] *n* techumbre *f*.

roof rack *n* (*AUT*) baca.

rook [ruk] *n* (*bird*) graja; (*CHESS*) torre *f*.

rookie ['rukɪ] *n* (*col*) novato/a; (*MIL*) chivo.

room [ruːm] *n* (*in house*) cuarto, habitación *f*, pieza (*esp LAm*); (*also*: **bed~**) dormitorio; (*in school etc*) sala; (*space*) sitio; **~s** *npl* (*lodging*) alojamiento *sg*; **"~s to let"**, (*US*) **"~s for rent"** "se alquilan pisos *or* cuartos"; **single/double ~** habitación individual/doble *or* para dos personas; **is there ~ for this?** ¿cabe esto?; **to make ~ for sb** hacer sitio para algn; **there is ~ for improvement** podría mejorarse.

roominess ['ruːmɪnɪs] *n* amplitud *f*, espaciosidad *f*.

rooming house ['ruːmɪŋ-] *n* (*US*) pensión *f*.

roommate ['ru:mmeɪt] *n* compañero/a de cuarto.
room service *n* servicio de habitaciones.
room temperature *n* temperatura ambiente.
roomy ['ru:mɪ] *adj* espacioso.
roost [ru:st] *n* percha ♦ *vi* pasar la noche.
rooster ['ru:stə*] *n* gallo.
root [ru:t] *n* (*BOT, MATH*) raíz *f* ♦ *vi* (*plant, belief*) arraigar(se); **to take** ~ (*plant*) echar raíces; (*idea*) arraigar(se); **the** ~ **of the problem is that** ... la raíz del problema es que ....
►**root about** *vi* (*fig*) rebuscar.
►**root for** *vt fus* apoyar a.
►**root out** *vt* desarraigar.
root beer *n* (*US*) *refresco sin alcohol de extractos de hierbas.*
rooted ['ru:tɪd] *adj* enraizado; (*opinions etc*) arraigado.
rope [rəup] *n* cuerda; (*NAUT*) cable *m* ♦ *vt* (*box*) atar *or* amarrar con (una) cuerda; (*climbers: also:* ~ **together**) encordarse; **to** ~ **sb in** (*fig*) persuadir a algn a tomar parte; **to know the** ~**s** (*fig*) conocer los trucos (del oficio).
rope ladder *n* escala de cuerda.
ropey ['rəupɪ] *adj* (*col*) chungo.
rosary ['rəuzərɪ] *n* rosario.
rose [rəuz] *pt of* **rise** ♦ *n* rosa; (*also:* ~**bush**) rosal *m*; (*on watering can*) roseta ♦ *adj* color de rosa.
rosé ['rəuzeɪ] *n* vino rosado, clarete *m.*
rosebed ['rəuzbɛd] *n* rosaleda.
rosebud ['rəuzbʌd] *n* capullo de rosa.
rosebush ['rəuzbuʃ] *n* rosal *m.*
rosemary ['rəuzmərɪ] *n* romero.
rosette [rəu'zɛt] *n* rosetón *m.*
ROSPA ['rɔspə] *n abbr* (*BRIT*) = *Royal Society for the Prevention of Accidents.*
roster ['rɔstə*] *n*: **duty** ~ lista de tareas.
rostrum ['rɔstrəm] *n* tribuna.
rosy ['rəuzɪ] *adj* rosado, sonrosado; **the future looks** ~ el futuro parece prometedor.
rot [rɔt] *n* (*decay*) putrefacción *f*, podredumbre *f*; (*fig: pej*) tonterías *fpl* ♦ *vt* pudrir, corromper ♦ *vi* pudrirse, corromperse; **it has** ~**ted** está podrido; **to stop the** ~ (*fig*) poner fin a las pérdidas.
rota ['rəutə] *n* lista (de tareas).
rotary ['rəutərɪ] *adj* rotativo.
rotate [rəu'teɪt] *vt* (*revolve*) hacer girar, dar vueltas a; (*change round: crops*) cultivar en rotación; (*: jobs*) alternar ♦ *vi* (*revolve*) girar, dar vueltas.
rotating [rəu'teɪtɪŋ] *adj* (*movement*) rotativo.
rotation [rəu'teɪʃən] *n* rotación *f*; **in** ~ por turno.
rote [rəut] *n*: **by** ~ de memoria.
rotor ['rəutə*] *n* rotor *m.*
rotten ['rɔtn] *adj* (*decayed*) podrido; (*: wood*) carcomido; (*fig*) corrompido; (*col: bad*) pésimo; **to feel** ~ (*ill*) sentirse fatal; ~ **to the core** completamente podrido.
rotund [rəu'tʌnd] *adj* rotundo.
rouble, (*US*) **ruble** ['ru:bl] *n* rublo.
rouge [ru:ʒ] *n* colorete *m.*
rough [rʌf] *adj* (*skin, surface*) áspero; (*terrain*) accidentado; (*road*) desigual; (*voice*) bronco; (*person, manner: coarse*) tosco, grosero; (*weather*) borrascoso; (*treatment*) brutal; (*sea*) embravecido; (*cloth*) basto; (*plan*) preliminar; (*guess*) aproximado; (*violent*) violento ♦ *n* (*GOLF*): **in the** ~ en las hierbas altas; **to** ~ **it** vivir sin comodidades; **to sleep** ~ (*BRIT*) pasar la noche al raso; **the sea is** ~ **today** el mar está agitado hoy; **to have a** ~ **time (of it)** pasar una mala racha; ~ **estimate** cálculo aproximado.
roughage ['rʌfɪdʒ] *n* fibra(s) *f(pl)*, forraje *m.*
rough-and-ready ['rʌfən'rɛdɪ] *adj* improvisado, tosco.
rough-and-tumble ['rʌfən'tʌmbl] *n* pelea.
roughcast ['rʌfkɑ:st] *n* mezcla gruesa.
rough copy, rough draft *n* borrador *m.*
roughen ['rʌfn] *vt* (*a surface*) poner áspero.
roughly ['rʌflɪ] *adv* (*handle*) torpemente; (*make*) toscamente; (*approximately*) aproximadamente; ~ **speaking** más o menos.
roughness ['rʌfnɪs] *n* aspereza; tosquedad *f*; brutalidad *f.*
roughshod ['rʌfʃɔd] *adv*: **to ride** ~ **over** (*person*) pisotear a; (*objections*) hacer caso omiso de.
rough work *n* (*SCOL etc*) borrador *m.*
roulette [ru:'lɛt] *n* ruleta.
Roumania [ru:'meɪnɪə] *n* = **Rumania.**
round [raund] *adj* redondo ♦ *n* círculo; (*of policeman*) ronda; (*of milkman*) recorrido; (*of doctor*) visitas *fpl*; (*game: of cards, in competition*) partida; (*of ammunition*) cartucho; (*BOXING*) asalto; (*of talks*) ronda ♦ *vt* (*corner*) doblar ♦ *prep* alrededor de ♦ *adv*: **all** ~ por todos lados; **the long way** ~ por el camino menos directo; **all the year** ~ durante todo el año; **it's just** ~ **the corner** (*fig*) está a la vuelta de la esquina; **to ask sb** ~ invitar a algn a casa; **I'll be** ~ **at 6 o'clock** llegaré a eso de las 6; **she arrived** ~ **(about) noon** llegó alrededor del mediodía; ~ **the clock** *adv* las 24

horas; **to go ~ to sb's (house)** ir a casa de algn; **to go ~ the back** pasar por atrás; **to go ~ a house** visitar una casa; **enough to go ~** bastante (para todos); **in ~ figures** en números redondos; **to go the ~s** (*story*) divulgarse; **a ~ of applause** una salva de aplausos; **a ~ of drinks/ sandwiches** una ronda de bebidas/ bocadillos; **a ~ of toast** (*BRIT*) una tostada; **the daily ~** la rutina cotidiana.

►**round off** *vt* (*speech etc*) acabar, poner término a.

►**round up** *vt* (*cattle*) acorralar; (*people*) reunir; (*prices*) redondear.

roundabout ['raundəbaut] *n* (*BRIT: AUT*) glorieta, rotonda; (: *at fair*) tiovivo ♦ *adj* (*route, means*) indirecto.

rounded ['raundɪd] *adj* redondeado, redondo.

rounders ['raundəz] *n* (*BRIT: game*) *juego similar al béisbol*.

roundly ['raundlɪ] *adv* (*fig*) rotundamente.

round-robin ['raundrɔbɪn] *n* (*SPORT: also:* ~ **tournament**) liguilla.

round trip *n* viaje *m* de ida y vuelta.

roundup ['raundʌp] *n* rodeo; (*of criminals*) redada; **a ~ of the latest news** un resumen de las últimas noticias.

rouse [rauz] *vt* (*wake up*) despertar; (*stir up*) suscitar.

rousing ['rauzɪŋ] *adj* (*applause*) caluroso; (*speech*) conmovedor(a).

rout [raut] *n* (*MIL*) derrota; (*flight*) desbandada ♦ *vt* derrotar.

route [ruːt] *n* ruta, camino; (*of bus*) recorrido; (*of shipping*) rumbo, derrota; **the best ~ to London** el mejor camino *or* la mejor ruta para ir a Londres; **en ~ from ... to** en el viaje de ... a; **en ~ for** rumbo a, con destino en.

route map *n* (*BRIT: for journey*) mapa *m* de carreteras.

routine [ruː'tiːn] *adj* (*work*) rutinario ♦ *n* rutina; (*THEAT*) número; (*COMPUT*) rutina.

roving ['rəuvɪŋ] *adj* (*wandering*) errante; (*salesman*) ambulante; (*reporter*) volante.

row [rəu] *n* (*line*) fila, hilera; (*KNITTING*) vuelta; [rau] (*noise*) escándalo; (*dispute*) bronca, pelea; (*fuss*) jaleo; (*scolding*) reprimenda ♦ *vi* (*in boat*) remar; [rau] reñir(se) ♦ *vt* (*boat*) conducir remando; **4 days in a ~** 4 días seguidos; **to make a ~** armar un lío; **to have a ~** pelearse, reñir.

rowboat ['rəubəut] *n* (*US*) bote *m* de remos.

rowdy ['raudɪ] *adj* (*person: noisy*) ruidoso; (: *quarrelsome*) pendenciero; (*occasion*) alborotado ♦ *n* pendenciero.

row houses *npl* (*US*) casas *fpl* adosadas.

rowing ['rəuɪŋ] *n* remo.

rowing boat *n* (*BRIT*) bote *m or* barco de remos.

royal ['rɔɪəl] *adj* real.

Royal Academy (of Arts) *n* (*BRIT*) la Real Academia (de Bellas Artes); *ver recuadro*.

> **ROYAL ACADEMY (OF ARTS)**
>
> *La* **Royal Academy (of Arts)**, *fundada en 1768 durante el reinado de Jorge III, es una institución dedicada al fomento de la pintura, escultura y arquitectura en el Reino Unido. Además de dar cursos de arte, presenta una exposición anual de artistas contemporáneos en su sede de Burlington House, en el centro de Londres. No existe una institución equivalente a la Real Academia de la Lengua.*

Royal Air Force (RAF) *n* Fuerzas Aéreas Británicas *fpl*.

royal blue *n* azul *m* marino.

royalist ['rɔɪəlɪst] *adj, n* monárquico/a *m/f*.

Royal Navy (RN) *n* (*BRIT*) Marina Británica.

royalty ['rɔɪəltɪ] *n* (*royal persons*) (miembros *mpl* de la) familia real; (*payment to author*) derechos *mpl* de autor.

RP *n abbr* (= *Received Pronunciation*) *ver recuadro*.

> **RP**
>
> *El acento con el que suelen hablar las clases medias y altas de Inglaterra se denomina* **RP** (*o* **Received Pronunciation**). *Es el acento estándar, sin variaciones regionales, que aún usan los locutores en los informativos nacionales de la "BBC". También suele tomarse como norma en la enseñanza del inglés británico como lengua extranjera. Todavía conserva un gran prestigio, aunque la gran mayoría de la población habla con el acento de su región, que puede ser más o menos fuerte según su educación o clase social.*

rpm *abbr* (= *revs per minute*) r.p.m.

RR *abbr* (*US*) = **railroad**.

RSA *n abbr* (*BRIT*) = *Royal Society of Arts, Royal Scottish Academy*.

RSI *n abbr* (*MED*: = *repetitive strain injury*) *traumatismo producido por un esfuerzo continuado (como el de las mecanógrafas)*.

RSPB *n abbr* (*BRIT*) = *Royal Society for the Protection of Birds*.

RSPCA *n abbr* (*BRIT*) = *Royal Society for the*

Prevention of Cruelty to Animals.
R.S.V.P. *abbr* (= *répondez s'il vous plaît*) SRC.
RTA *n abbr* (= *road traffic accident*) accidente *m* de carretera.
Rt. Hon. *abbr* (*BRIT*: = *Right Honourable*) *tratamiento honorífico de diputado.*
Rt. Rev. *abbr* (= *Right Reverend*) Rvdo.
rub [rʌb] *vt* (*gen*) frotar; (*hard*) restregar ♦ *n* (*gen*) frotamiento; (*touch*) roce *m*; **to ~ sb up** *or* (*US*) **~ sb the wrong way** sacar de quicio a algn.
▸**rub down** *vt* (*body*) secar frotando; (*horse*) almohazar.
▸**rub in** *vt* (*ointment*) frotar.
▸**rub off** *vt* borrarse ♦ *vi* quitarse (frotando); **to ~ off on sb** influir en algn, pegársele a algn.
▸**rub out** *vt* borrar ♦ *vi* borrarse.
rubber ['rʌbə*] *n* caucho, goma; (*BRIT*: *eraser*) goma de borrar.
rubber band *n* goma, gomita.
rubber bullet *n* bala de goma.
rubber plant *n* ficus *m*.
rubber ring *n* (*for swimming*) flotador *m*.
rubber stamp *n* sello (de caucho) ♦ *vt*: **rubber-stamp** (*fig*) aprobar maquinalmente.
rubbery ['rʌbərɪ] *adj* (como) de goma.
rubbish ['rʌbɪʃ] (*BRIT*) *n* (*from household*) basura; (*waste*) desperdicios *mpl*; (*fig*: *pej*) tonterías *fpl*; (*trash*) basura, porquería ♦ *vt* (*col*) poner por los suelos; **what you've just said is ~** lo que acabas de decir es una tontería.
rubbish bin *n* cubo *or* bote *m* (*LAM*) de la basura.
rubbish dump *n* (*in town*) vertedero, basurero.
rubbishy ['rʌbɪʃɪ] *adj* de mala calidad, de pacotilla.
rubble ['rʌbl] *n* escombros *mpl*.
ruby ['ru:bɪ] *n* rubí *m*.
RUC *n abbr* (= *Royal Ulster Constabulary*) *fuerza de policía en Irlanda del Norte.*
rucksack ['rʌksæk] *n* mochila.
ructions ['rʌkʃənz] *npl*: **there will be ~** se va a armar la gorda.
ruddy ['rʌdɪ] *adj* (*face*) rubicundo; (*col*: *damned*) condenado.
rude [ru:d] *adj* (*impolite*: *person*) grosero, maleducado; (: *word, manners*) rudo, grosero; (*indecent*) indecente; **to be ~ to sb** ser grosero con algn.
rudeness ['ru:dnɪs] *n* grosería, tosquedad *f*.
rudiment ['ru:dɪmənt] *n* rudimento.
rudimentary [ru:dɪ'mentərɪ] *adj* rudimentario.
rue [ru:] *vt* arrepentirse de.
rueful ['ru:ful] *adj* arrepentido.
ruffian ['rʌfɪən] *n* matón *m*, criminal *m*.
ruffle ['rʌfl] *vt* (*hair*) despeinar; (*clothes*) arrugar; (*fig*: *person*) agitar.
rug [rʌg] *n* alfombra; (*BRIT*: *for knees*) manta.
rugby ['rʌgbɪ] *n* (*also*: **~ football**) rugby *m*.
rugged ['rʌgɪd] *adj* (*landscape*) accidentado; (*features*) robusto.
rugger ['rʌgə*] *n* (*BRIT col*) rugby *m*.
ruin ['ru:ɪn] *n* ruina ♦ *vt* arruinar; (*spoil*) estropear; **~s** *npl* ruinas *fpl*, restos *mpl*; **in ~s** en ruinas.
ruinous ['ru:ɪnəs] *adj* ruinoso.
rule [ru:l] *n* (*norm*) norma, costumbre *f*; (*regulation, ruler*) regla; (*government*) dominio; (*dominion etc*): **under British ~** bajo el dominio británico ♦ *vt* (*country, person*) gobernar; (*decide*) disponer; (*draw lines*) trazar ♦ *vi* gobernar; (*LAW*) fallar; **to ~ against/in favour of/on** fallar en contra de/a favor de/sobre; **to ~ that** ... (*umpire, judge*) fallar que ...; **it's against the ~s** está prohibido; **as a ~** por regla general, generalmente; **by ~ of thumb** por experiencia; **majority ~** (*POL*) gobierno mayoritario.
▸**rule out** *vt* excluir.
ruled [ru:ld] *adj* (*paper*) rayado.
ruler ['ru:lə*] *n* (*sovereign*) soberano; (*for measuring*) regla.
ruling ['ru:lɪŋ] *adj* (*party*) gobernante; (*class*) dirigente ♦ *n* (*LAW*) fallo, decisión *f*.
rum [rʌm] *n* ron *m*.
Rumania [ru:'meɪnɪə] *n* Rumanía.
Rumanian [ru:'meɪnɪən] *adj, n* rumano/a *m/f*.
rumble ['rʌmbl] *n* ruido sordo; (*of thunder*) redoble *m* ♦ *vi* retumbar, hacer un ruido sordo; (*stomach, pipe*) sonar.
rumbustious [rʌm'bʌstʃəs] *adj* (*person*) bullicioso.
rummage ['rʌmɪdʒ] *vi* revolverlo todo.
rumour, (*US*) **rumor** ['ru:mə*] *n* rumor *m* ♦ *vt*: **it is ~ed that** ... se rumorea que ...; **~ has it that** ... corre la voz de que ....
rump [rʌmp] *n* (*of animal*) ancas *fpl*, grupa.
rumple ['rʌmpl] *vt* (*clothes*) arrugar; (*hair*) despeinar.
rump steak *n* filete *m* de lomo.
rumpus ['rʌmpəs] *n* (*col*) lío, jaleo; (*quarrel*) pelea, riña; **to kick up a ~** armar un follón *or* armar bronca.
run [rʌn] *n* (*SPORT*) carrera; (*outing*) paseo, excursión *f*; (*distance travelled*) trayecto; (*series*) serie *f*; (*THEAT*) temporada; (*SKI*) pista; (*in tights, stockings*) carrera; ♦ *vb* (*pt*

ran, *pp* **run** [ræn, rʌn]) *vt* (*operate: business*) dirigir; (*: competition, course*) organizar; (*: hotel, house*) administrar, llevar; (*COMPUT: program*) ejecutar; (*to pass: hand*) pasar; (*bath*): **to ~ a bath** llenar la bañera ♦ *vi* (*gen*) correr; (*work: machine*) funcionar, marchar; (*bus, train: operate*) circular, ir; (*: travel*) ir; (*continue: play*) seguir en cartel; (*: contract*) ser válido; (*flow: river, bath*) fluir; (*colours, washing*) desteñirse; (*in election*) ser candidato; **to go for a ~** ir a correr; **to make a ~ for it** echar(se) a correr, escapar(se), huir; **to have the ~ of sb's house** tener el libre uso de la casa de algn; **a ~ of luck** una racha de suerte; **there was a ~ on** (*meat, tickets*) hubo mucha demanda de; **in the long ~** a la larga; **on the ~** en fuga; **I'll ~ you to the station** te llevaré a la estación en coche; **to ~ a risk** correr un riesgo; **to ~ errands** hacer recados; **it's very cheap to ~** es muy económico; **to be ~ off one's feet** estar ocupadísimo; **to ~ for the bus** correr tras el autobús; **we shall have to ~ for it** tendremos que escapar; **the train ~s between Gatwick and Victoria** el tren circula entre Gatwick y Victoria; **the bus ~s every 20 minutes** el autobús pasa cada 20 minutos; **to ~ on petrol/on diesel/off batteries** funcionar con gasolina/gasoil/ baterías; **my salary won't ~ to a car** mi sueldo no me da para comprarme un coche; **the car ran into the lamppost** el coche chocó contra el farol.

▸**run about, run around** *vi* (*children*) correr por todos lados.

▸**run across** *vt fus* (*find*) dar *or* topar con.

▸**run away** *vi* huir.

▸**run down** *vi* (*clock*) pararse ♦ *vt* (*reduce: production*) ir reduciendo; (*factory*) restringir la producción de; (*AUT*) atropellar; (*criticize*) criticar; **to be ~ down** (*person: tired*) encontrarse agotado.

▸**run in** *vt* (*BRIT: car*) rodar.

▸**run into** *vt fus* (*meet: person, trouble*) tropezar con; (*collide with*) chocar con; **to ~ into debt** contraer deudas, endeudarse.

▸**run off** *vt* (*water*) dejar correr ♦ *vi* huir corriendo.

▸**run out** *vi* (*person*) salir corriendo; (*liquid*) irse; (*lease*) caducar, vencer; (*money*) acabarse.

▸**run out of** *vt fus* quedar sin; **I've ~ out of petrol** se me acabó la gasolina.

▸**run over** *vt* (*AUT*) atropellar ♦ *vt fus* (*revise*) repasar.

▸**run through** *vt fus* (*instructions*) repasar.

▸**run up** *vt* (*debt*) incurrir en; **to ~ up against** (*difficulties*) tropezar con.

run-around ['rʌnəraund] *n*: **to give sb the ~** traer a algn al retortero.

runaway ['rʌnəweɪ] *adj* (*horse*) desbocado; (*truck*) sin frenos; (*person*) fugitivo.

rundown ['rʌndaun] *n* (*BRIT: of industry etc*) cierre *m* gradual.

rung [rʌŋ] *pp of* **ring** ♦ *n* (*of ladder*) escalón *m*, peldaño.

run-in ['rʌnɪn] *n* (*col*) altercado.

runner ['rʌnə*] *n* (*in race: person*) corredor(a) *m/f*; (*: horse*) caballo; (*on sledge*) patín *m*; (*wheel*) ruedecilla.

runner bean *n* (*BRIT*) judía escarlata.

runner-up [rʌnər'ʌp] *n* subcampeón/ona *m/f*.

running ['rʌnɪŋ] *n* (*sport*) atletismo; (*race*) carrera ♦ *adj* (*costs, water*) corriente; (*commentary*) en directo; **to be in/out of the ~ for sth** tener/no tener posibilidades de ganar algo; **6 days ~** 6 días seguidos.

running costs *npl* (*of business*) gastos *mpl* corrientes; (*of car*) gastos *mpl* de mantenimiento.

running head *n* (*TYP, WORD PROCESSING*) encabezamiento normal.

running mate *n* (*US POL*) candidato/a a la vice-presidencia.

runny ['rʌnɪ] *adj* derretido.

run-off ['rʌnɔf] *n* (*in contest, election*) desempate *m*; (*extra race*) carrera de desempate.

run-of-the-mill ['rʌnəvðə'mɪl] *adj* común y corriente.

runt [rʌnt] *n* (*also pej*) enano.

run-up ['rʌnʌp] *n*: **~ to** (*election etc*) período previo a.

runway ['rʌnweɪ] *n* (*AVIAT*) pista (de aterrizaje).

rupee [ruː'piː] *n* rupia.

rupture ['rʌptʃə*] *n* (*MED*) hernia ♦ *vt*: **to ~ o.s.** causarse una hernia.

rural ['ruərl] *adj* rural.

ruse [ruːz] *n* ardid *m*.

rush [rʌʃ] *n* ímpetu *m*; (*hurry*) prisa, apuro (*LAM*); (*COMM*) demanda repentina; (*BOT*) junco; (*current*) corriente *f* fuerte, ráfaga ♦ *vt* apresurar; (*work*) hacer de prisa; (*attack: town etc*) asaltar ♦ *vi* correr, precipitarse; **gold ~** fiebre *f* del oro; **we've had a ~ of orders** ha habido una gran demanda; **I'm in a ~ (to do)** tengo prisa *or* apuro (*LAM*) (por hacer); **is there any ~ for this?** ¿te corre prisa esto?; **to ~ sth off** hacer algo de prisa y corriendo.

▸**rush through** *vt fus* (*meal*) comer de prisa; (*book*) leer de prisa; (*work*) hacer de prisa; (*town*) atravesar a toda

velocidad; (*COMM*: *order*) despachar rápidamente.
rush hour *n* horas *fpl* punta.
rush job *n* (*urgent*) trabajo urgente.
rusk [rʌsk] *n* bizcocho tostado.
Russia ['rʌʃə] *n* Rusia.
Russian ['rʌʃən] *adj* ruso ♦ *n* ruso/a; (*LING*) ruso.
rust [rʌst] *n* herrumbre *f*, moho ♦ *vi* oxidarse.
rustic ['rʌstɪk] *adj* rústico.
rustle ['rʌsl] *vi* susurrar ♦ *vt* (*paper*) hacer crujir; (*US*: *cattle*) hurtar, robar.
rustproof ['rʌstpru:f] *adj* inoxidable.
rusty ['rʌstɪ] *adj* oxidado.
rut [rʌt] *n* surco; (*ZOOL*) celo; **to be in a ~** ser esclavo de la rutina.
ruthless ['ru:θlɪs] *adj* despiadado.
RV *abbr* (= *revised version*) *traducción inglesa de la Biblia de 1855* ♦ *n abbr* (*US*) = **recreational vehicle.**
rye [raɪ] *n* centeno.
rye bread *n* pan de centeno.

S s

S, s [ɛs] *n* (*letter*) S, s *f*; **S for Sugar** S de sábado.
S *abbr* (= *Saint*) Sto./a.; (*US SCOL*: *mark*: = *satisfactory*) suficiente; (= *south*) S; = **small.**
SA *n abbr* = **South Africa, South America.**
sabbath ['sæbəθ] *n* domingo; (*Jewish*) sábado.
sabbatical [sə'bætɪkl] *adj*: **~ year** año sabático.
sabotage ['sæbətɑ:ʒ] *n* sabotaje *m* ♦ *vt* sabotear.
sabre, (*US*) **saber** ['seɪbə*] *n* sable *m*.
saccharin(e) ['sækərɪn] *n* sacarina.
sachet ['sæʃeɪ] *n* sobrecito.
sack [sæk] *n* (*bag*) saco, costal *m* ♦ *vt* (*dismiss*) despedir, echar; (*plunder*) saquear; **to get the ~** ser despedido; **to give sb the ~** despedir *or* echar a algn.
sackful ['sækful] *n* saco.
sacking ['sækɪŋ] *n* (*material*) arpillera.
sacrament ['sækrəmənt] *n* sacramento.
sacred ['seɪkrɪd] *adj* sagrado, santo.
sacred cow *n* (*fig*) vaca sagrada.
sacrifice ['sækrɪfaɪs] *n* sacrificio ♦ *vt* sacrificar; **to make ~s (for sb)** sacrificarse (por algn).
sacrilege ['sækrɪlɪdʒ] *n* sacrilegio.
sacrosanct ['sækrəusæŋkt] *adj* sacrosanto.
sad [sæd] *adj* (*unhappy*) triste; (*deplorable*) lamentable.
sadden ['sædn] *vt* entristecer.
saddle ['sædl] *n* silla (de montar); (*of cycle*) sillín *m* ♦ *vt* (*horse*) ensillar; **to ~ sb with sth** (*col*: *task, bill, name*) cargar a algn con algo; (: *responsibility*) gravar a algn con algo; **to be ~d with sth** (*col*) quedar cargado con algo.
saddlebag ['sædlbæg] *n* alforja.
sadism ['seɪdɪzm] *n* sadismo.
sadist ['seɪdɪst] *n* sádico/a.
sadistic [sə'dɪstɪk] *adj* sádico.
sadly ['sædlɪ] *adv* tristemente; (*regrettably*) desgraciadamente; **~ lacking (in)** muy deficiente (en).
sadness ['sædnɪs] *n* tristeza.
sado-masochism [seɪdəu'mæsəkɪzɪm] *n* sadomasoquismo.
sae *abbr* (*BRIT*: = *stamped addressed envelope*) *sobre con las propias señas de uno y con sello.*
safari [sə'fɑ:rɪ] *n* safari *m*.
safari park *n* safari *m*.
safe [seɪf] *adj* (*out of danger*) fuera de peligro; (*not dangerous, sure*) seguro; (*unharmed*) ileso; (*trustworthy*) digno de confianza ♦ *n* caja de caudales, caja fuerte; **~ and sound** sano y salvo; **(just) to be on the ~ side** para mayor seguridad; **~ journey!** ¡buen viaje!; **it is ~ to say that** ... se puede decir con confianza que ....
safe bet *n* apuesta segura; **it's a ~ she'll turn up** seguro que viene.
safe-breaker ['seɪfbreɪkə*] *n* (*BRIT*) ladrón/ona *m/f* de cajas fuertes.
safe-conduct [seɪf'kɔndʌkt] *n* salvoconducto.
safe-cracker ['seɪfkrækə*] *n* (*US*) = **safe-breaker.**
safe-deposit ['seɪfdɪpɔzɪt] *n* (*vault*) cámara acorazada; (*box*) caja de seguridad *or* de caudales.
safeguard ['seɪfgɑ:d] *n* protección *f*, garantía ♦ *vt* proteger, defender.
safe haven *n* refugio.
safekeeping ['seɪf'ki:pɪŋ] *n* custodia.
safely ['seɪflɪ] *adv* seguramente, con seguridad; (*without mishap*) sin peligro; **I can ~ say** puedo decir *or* afirmar con toda seguridad.
safeness ['seɪfnɪs] *n* seguridad *f*.
safe passage *n* garantías *fpl* para

marcharse en libertad.
safe sex *n* sexo seguro *or* sin riesgo.
safety ['seɪftɪ] *n* seguridad *f* ♦ *cpd* de seguridad; **road ~** seguridad *f* en carretera; **~ first!** ¡precaución!
safety belt *n* cinturón *m* (de seguridad).
safety catch *n* seguro.
safety net *n* red *f* (de seguridad).
safety pin *n* imperdible *m*, seguro (*LAM*).
safety valve *n* válvula de seguridad *or* de escape.
saffron ['sæfrən] *n* azafrán *m*.
sag [sæg] *vi* aflojarse.
saga ['sɑːgə] *n* (*HISTORY*) saga; (*fig*) epopeya.
sage [seɪdʒ] *n* (*herb*) salvia; (*man*) sabio.
Sagittarius [sædʒɪ'tɛərɪəs] *n* Sagitario.
sago ['seɪgəu] *n* sagú *m*.
Sahara [sə'hɑːrə] *n*: **the ~ (Desert)** el Sáhara.
Sahel [sæ'hɛl] *n* Sahel *m*.
said [sɛd] *pt, pp of* **say**.
Saigon [saɪ'gɔn] *n* Saigón *m*.
sail [seɪl] *n* (*on boat*) vela ♦ *vt* (*boat*) gobernar ♦ *vi* (*travel*: *ship*) navegar; (: *passenger*) pasear en barco; (*set off*: *also*: **to set ~**) zarpar; **to go for a ~** dar un paseo en barco; **they ~ed into Copenhagen** arribaron a Copenhague.
►**sail through** *vt fus* (*exam*) aprobar fácilmente.
sailboat ['seɪlbəut] *n* (*US*) velero, barco de vela.
sailing ['seɪlɪŋ] *n* (*SPORT*) balandrismo; **to go ~** salir en balandro.
sailing ship *n* barco de vela.
sailor ['seɪlə*] *n* marinero, marino.
saint [seɪnt] *n* santo; **S~ John** San Juan.
saintliness ['seɪntlɪnɪs] *n* santidad *f*.
saintly ['seɪntlɪ] *adj* santo.
sake [seɪk] *n*: **for the ~ of** por; **for the ~ of argument** digamos, es un decir; **art for art's ~** el arte por el arte.
salad ['sæləd] *n* ensalada; **tomato ~** ensalada de tomate.
salad bowl *n* ensaladera.
salad cream *n* (*BRIT*) mayonesa.
salad dressing *n* aliño.
salad oil *n* aceite *m* para ensalada.
salami [sə'lɑːmɪ] *n* salami *m*, salchichón *m*.
salaried ['sælərɪd] *adj* asalariado.
salary ['sælərɪ] *n* sueldo.
salary earner *n* asalariado/a.
salary scale *n* escala salarial.
sale [seɪl] *n* venta; (*at reduced prices*) liquidación *f*, saldo; **"for ~"** "se vende"; **on ~** en venta; **on ~ or return** (*goods*) venta por reposición; **closing-down** *or* (*US*) **liquidation ~** liquidación *f*; **~ and lease back** venta y arrendamiento al vendedor.
saleroom ['seɪlruːm] *n* sala de subastas.
sales assistant *n* (*BRIT*) dependiente/a *m/f*.
sales campaign *n* campaña de venta.
sales clerk *n* (*US*) dependiente/a *m/f*.
sales conference *n* conferencia de ventas.
sales drive *n* promoción *f* de ventas.
sales figures *npl* cifras *fpl* de ventas.
sales force *n* personal *m* de ventas.
salesman ['seɪlzmən] *n* vendedor *m*; (*in shop*) dependiente *m*; (*representative*) viajante *m*.
sales manager *n* gerente *m/f* de ventas.
salesmanship ['seɪlzmənʃɪp] *n* arte *m* de vender.
sales meeting *n* reunión *f* de ventas.
sales tax *n* (*US*) = **purchase tax**.
saleswoman ['seɪlzwumən] *n* vendedora; (*in shop*) dependienta; (*representative*) viajante *f*.
salient ['seɪlɪənt] *adj* (*features, points*) sobresaliente.
saline ['seɪlaɪn] *adj* salino.
saliva [sə'laɪvə] *n* saliva.
sallow ['sæləu] *adj* cetrino.
sally forth, sally out *vi* salir, ponerse en marcha.
salmon ['sæmən] *n* (*pl inv*) salmón *m*.
salon ['sælɔn] *n* (*hairdressing ~, beauty ~*) salón *m*.
saloon [sə'luːn] *n* (*US*) bar *m*, taberna; (*BRIT AUT*) (coche *m* de) turismo; (*ship's lounge*) cámara, salón *m*.
SALT [sɔːlt] *n abbr* (= *Strategic Arms Limitation Treaty*) tratado SALT.
salt [sɔːlt] *n* sal *f* ♦ *vt* salar; (*put ~ on*) poner sal en; **an old ~** un lobo de mar.
►**salt away** *vt* (*col*: *money*) ahorrar.
salt cellar *n* salero.
salt mine *n* mina de sal.
saltwater ['sɔːlt'wɔːtə*] *adj* (*fish etc*) de agua salada, de mar.
salty ['sɔːltɪ] *adj* salado.
salubrious [sə'luːbrɪəs] *adj* sano; (*fig*: *district etc*) atractivo.
salutary ['sæljutərɪ] *adj* saludable.
salute [sə'luːt] *n* saludo; (*of guns*) salva ♦ *vt* saludar.
salvage ['sælvɪdʒ] *n* (*saving*) salvamento, recuperación *f*; (*things saved*) objetos *mpl* salvados ♦ *vt* salvar.
salvage vessel *n* buque *m* de salvamento.
salvation [sæl'veɪʃən] *n* salvación *f*.
Salvation Army *n* Ejército de Salvación.
salve [sælv] *n* (*cream etc*) ungüento,

bálsamo.
salver ['sælvə*] *n* bandeja.
salvo ['sælvəu] *n* (*MIL*) salva.
Samaritan [sə'mærıtən] *n*: **to call the ~s** llamar al teléfono de la esperanza.
same [seım] *adj* mismo ♦ *pron*: **the ~** el mismo/la misma; **the ~ book as** el mismo libro que; **on the ~ day** el mismo día; **at the ~ time** (*at the ~ moment*) al mismo tiempo; (*yet*) sin embargo; **all** *or* **just the ~** sin embargo, aun así; **they're one and the ~** (*person*) son la misma persona; (*thing*) son iguales; **to do the ~ (as sb)** hacer lo mismo (que otro); **and the ~ to you!** ¡igualmente!; **~ here!** ¡yo también!; **the ~ again** (*in bar etc*) otro igual.
sampan ['sæmpæn] *n* sampán *m*.
sample ['sɑːmpl] *n* muestra ♦ *vt* (*food, wine*) probar; **to take a ~** tomar una muestra; **free ~** muestra gratuita.
sanatorium, *pl* **-ria** [sænə'tɔːrıəm, -rıə] *n* (*BRIT*) sanatorio.
sanctify ['sæŋktıfaı] *vt* santificar.
sanctimonious [sæŋktı'məunıəs] *adj* santurrón/ona.
sanction ['sæŋkʃən] *n* sanción *f* ♦ *vt* sancionar; **to impose economic ~s on** *or* **against** imponer sanciones económicas a *or* contra.
sanctity ['sæŋktıtı] *n* (*gen*) santidad *f*; (*inviolability*) inviolabilidad *f*.
sanctuary ['sæŋktjuərı] *n* (*gen*) santuario; (*refuge*) asilo, refugio.
sand [sænd] *n* arena; (*beach*) playa ♦ *vt* (*also*: **~ down**: *wood etc*) lijar.
sandal ['sændl] *n* sandalia.
sandalwood ['sændlwud] *n* sándalo.
sandbag ['sændbæg] *n* saco de arena.
sandblast ['sændblɑːst] *vt* limpiar con chorro de arena.
sandbox ['sændbɔks] *n* (*US*) = **sandpit**.
sandcastle ['sændkɑːsl] *n* castillo de arena.
sand dune *n* duna.
sander ['sændə*] *n* pulidora.
S & M *n abbr* (= *sadomasochism*) sadomasoquismo.
sandpaper ['sændpeıpə*] *n* papel *m* de lija.
sandpit ['sændpıt] *n* (*for children*) cajón *m* de arena.
sands [sændz] *npl* playa *sg* de arena.
sandstone ['sændstəun] *n* piedra arenisca.
sandstorm ['sændstɔːm] *n* tormenta de arena.
sandwich ['sændwıtʃ] *n* bocadillo (*SP*), sandwich *m* (*LAM*) ♦ *vt* (*also*: **~ in**) intercalar; **to be ~ed between** estar apretujado entre; **cheese/ham ~** sandwich de queso/jamón.
sandwich board *n* cartelón *m*.
sandwich course *n* (*BRIT*) *programa que intercala períodos de estudio con prácticas profesionales.*
sandy ['sændı] *adj* arenoso; (*colour*) rojizo.
sane [seın] *adj* cuerdo, sensato.
sang [sæŋ] *pt of* **sing**.
sanitarium [sænı'tɛərıəm] *n* (*US*) = **sanatorium**.
sanitary ['sænıtərı] *adj* (*system, arrangements*) sanitario; (*clean*) higiénico.
sanitary towel, (*US*) **sanitary napkin** *n* paño higiénico, compresa.
sanitation [sænı'teıʃən] *n* (*in house*) servicios *mpl* higiénicos; (*in town*) servicio de desinfección.
sanitation department *n* (*US*) departamento de limpieza y recogida de basuras.
sanity ['sænıtı] *n* cordura; (*of judgment*) sensatez *f*.
sank [sæŋk] *pt of* **sink**.
San Marino ['sænmə'riːnəu] *n* San Marino.
Santa Claus [sæntə'klɔːz] *n* San Nicolás *m*, Papá Noel *m*.
Santiago [sæntı'ɑːgəu] *n* (*also*: **~ de Chile**) Santiago (de Chile).
sap [sæp] *n* (*of plants*) savia ♦ *vt* (*strength*) minar, agotar.
sapling ['sæplıŋ] *n* árbol nuevo *or* joven.
sapphire ['sæfaıə*] *n* zafiro.
Saragossa [særə'gɔsə] *n* Zaragoza.
sarcasm ['sɑːkæzm] *n* sarcasmo.
sarcastic [sɑː'kæstık] *adj* sarcástico; **to be ~** ser sarcástico.
sarcophagus, *pl* **sarcophagi** [sɑː'kɔfəgəs, -gaı] *n* sarcófago.
sardine [sɑː'diːn] *n* sardina.
Sardinia [sɑː'dınıə] *n* Cerdeña.
Sardinian [sɑː'dınıən] *adj, n* sardo/a *m/f*.
sardonic [sɑː'dɔnık] *adj* sardónico.
sari ['sɑːrı] *n* sari *m*.
SAS *n abbr* (*BRIT MIL*: = *Special Air Service*) *cuerpo del ejército británico encargado de misiones clandestinas.*
SASE *n abbr* (*US*: = *self-addressed stamped envelope*) *sobre con las propias señas de uno y con sello.*
sash [sæʃ] *n* faja.
Sask. *abbr* (*Canada*) = *Saskatchewan*.
SAT *n abbr* (*US*) = *Scholastic Aptitude Test*.
sat [sæt] *pt, pp of* **sit**.
Sat. *abbr* (= *Saturday*) sáb.
Satan ['seıtn] *n* Satanás *m*.
satanic [sə'tænık] *adj* satánico.
satchel ['sætʃl] *n* bolsa; (*child's*) cartera, mochila (*LAM*).
sated ['seıtıd] *adj* (*appetite, person*) saciado.

satellite ['sætəlaɪt] *n* satélite *m*.
satellite television *n* televisión *f* por satélite.
satiate ['seɪʃɪeɪt] *vt* saciar, hartar.
satin ['sætɪn] *n* raso ♦ *adj* de raso; **with a ~ finish** satinado.
satire ['sætaɪə*] *n* sátira.
satirical [sə'tɪrɪkl] *adj* satírico.
satirist ['sætɪrɪst] *n* (*writer etc*) escritor(a) *m/f* satírico/a; (*cartoonist*) caricaturista *m/f*.
satirize ['sætɪraɪz] *vt* satirizar.
satisfaction [sætɪs'fækʃən] *n* satisfacción *f*; **it gives me great ~** es para mí una gran satisfacción; **has it been done to your ~?** ¿se ha hecho a su satisfacción?
satisfactorily [sætɪs'fæktərɪlɪ] *adv* satisfactoriamente, de modo satisfactorio.
satisfactory [sætɪs'fæktərɪ] *adj* satisfactorio.
satisfied ['sætɪsfaɪd] *adj* satisfecho; **to be ~ (with sth)** estar satisfecho (de algo).
satisfy ['sætɪsfaɪ] *vt* satisfacer; (*pay*) liquidar; (*convince*) convencer; **to ~ the requirements** llenar los requisitos; **to ~ sb that** convencer a algn de que; **to ~ o.s. of sth** convencerse de algo.
satisfying ['sætɪsfaɪɪŋ] *adj* satisfactorio.
satsuma [sæt'suːmə] *n* satsuma.
saturate ['sætʃəreɪt] *vt*: **to ~ (with)** empapar *or* saturar (de).
saturated fat [sætʃəreɪtɪd-] *n* grasa saturada.
saturation [sætʃə'reɪʃən] *n* saturación *f*.
Saturday ['sætədɪ] *n* sábado.
sauce [sɔːs] *n* salsa; (*sweet*) crema; (*fig*: *cheek*) frescura.
saucepan ['sɔːspən] *n* cacerola, olla.
saucer ['sɔːsə*] *n* platillo.
saucily ['sɔːsɪlɪ] *adv* con frescura, descaradamente.
sauciness ['sɔːsɪnɪs] *n* frescura, descaro.
saucy ['sɔːsɪ] *adj* fresco, descarado.
Saudi Arabia ['saudɪ-] *n* Arabia Saudí *or* Saudita.
Saudi (Arabian) ['saudɪ-] *adj, n* saudí *m/f*, saudita *m/f*.
sauna ['sɔːnə] *n* sauna.
saunter ['sɔːntə*] *vi* deambular.
sausage ['sɔsɪdʒ] *n* salchicha; (*salami etc*) salchichón *m*.
sausage roll *n* empanadilla.
sauté ['səuteɪ] *adj* (*CULIN*: *potatoes*) salteado; (: *onions*) dorado, rehogado ♦ *vt* saltear; dorar.
savage ['sævɪdʒ] *adj* (*cruel, fierce*) feroz, furioso; (*primitive*) salvaje ♦ *n* salvaje *m/f* ♦ *vt* (*attack*) embestir.
savagely ['sævɪdʒlɪ] *adv* con ferocidad, furiosamente; de modo salvaje.
savagery ['sævɪdʒrɪ] *n* ferocidad *f*; salvajismo.
save [seɪv] *vt* (*rescue*) salvar, rescatar; (*money, time*) ahorrar; (*put by*) guardar; (*COMPUT*) salvar (y guardar); (*avoid*: *trouble*) evitar ♦ *vi* (*also*: **~ up**) ahorrar ♦ *n* (*SPORT*) parada ♦ *prep* salvo, excepto; **to ~ face** salvar las apariencias; **God ~ the Queen!** ¡Dios guarde a la Reina!, ¡Viva la Reina!; **I ~d you a piece of cake** te he guardado un trozo de tarta; **it will ~ me an hour** con ello ganaré una hora.
saving ['seɪvɪŋ] *n* (*on price etc*) economía ♦ *adj*: **the ~ grace of** el único mérito de; **~s** *npl* ahorros *mpl*; **to make ~s** economizar.
savings account *n* cuenta de ahorros.
savings bank *n* caja de ahorros.
saviour, (*US*) **savior** ['seɪvjə*] *n* salvador(a) *m/f*.
savoir-faire ['sævwɑː'fɛə*] *n* don *m* de gentes.
savour, (*US*) **savor** ['seɪvə*] *n* sabor *m*, gusto ♦ *vt* saborear.
savo(u)ry ['seɪvərɪ] *adj* sabroso; (*dish*: *not sweet*) salado.
savvy ['sævɪ] *n* (*col*) conocimiento, experiencia.
saw [sɔː] *pt of* **see** ♦ *n* (*tool*) sierra ♦ *vt* (*pt* **sawed,** *pp* **sawed** *or* **sawn** [sɔːn]) serrar; **to ~ sth up** (a)serrar algo.
sawdust ['sɔːdʌst] *n* (a)serrín *m*.
sawmill ['sɔːmɪl] *n* aserradero.
sawn [sɔːn] *pp of* **saw**.
sawn-off ['sɔːnɔf], (*US*) **sawed-off** ['sɔːdɔf] *adj*: **~ shotgun** escopeta de cañones recortados.
saxophone ['sæksəfəun] *n* saxófono.
say [seɪ] *n*: **to have one's ~** expresar su opinión; **to have a** *or* **some ~ in sth** tener voz y voto en algo ♦ *vt, vi* (*pt, pp* **said** [sɛd]) decir; **to ~ yes/no** decir que sí/no; **my watch ~s 3 o'clock** mi reloj marca las tres; **that is to ~** es decir; **that goes without ~ing** ni que decir tiene; **she said (that) I was to give you this** me pidió que te diera esto; **I should ~ it's worth about £100** yo diría que vale unas 100 libras; **~ after me** repite lo que yo diga; **shall we ~ Tuesday?** ¿quedamos, por ejemplo, el martes?; **that doesn't ~ much for him** eso no dice nada a su favor; **when all is said and done** al fin y al cabo, a fin de cuentas; **there is something** *or* **a lot to be said for it** hay algo *or* mucho que decir a su favor.
saying ['seɪɪŋ] *n* dicho, refrán *m*.
say-so ['seɪsəu] *n* (*col*) autorización *f*.

SBA *n abbr* (*US*) = *Small Business Administration.*
SC *n abbr* (*US*) = **Supreme Court** ♦ *abbr* (*US*) = *South Carolina.*
s/c *abbr* = **self-contained.**
scab [skæb] *n* costra; (*pej*) esquirol(a) *m/f.*
scaffold ['skæfəld] *n* (*for execution*) cadalso.
scaffolding ['skæfəldɪŋ] *n* andamio, andamiaje *m.*
scald [skɔːld] *n* escaldadura ♦ *vt* escaldar.
scalding ['skɔːldɪŋ] *adj* (*also*: ~ **hot**) hirviendo, que arde.
scale [skeɪl] *n* (*gen, MUS*) escala; (*of fish*) escama; (*of salaries, fees etc*) escalafón *m* ♦ *vt* (*mountain*) escalar; (*tree*) trepar; ~**s** *npl* (*small*) balanza *sg*; (*large*) báscula *sg*; **on a large** ~ a gran escala; ~ **of charges** tarifa, lista de precios; **pay** ~ escala salarial; **to draw sth to** ~ dibujar algo a escala.
▸**scale down** *vt* reducir.
scaled-down [skeɪld'daun] *adj* reducido proporcionalmente.
scale model *n* modelo a escala.
scallop ['skɔləp] *n* (*ZOOL*) venera; (*SEWING*) festón *m.*
scalp [skælp] *n* cabellera ♦ *vt* escalpar.
scalpel ['skælpl] *n* bisturí *m.*
scam [skæm] *n* (*col*) estafa, timo.
scamper ['skæmpə*] *vi*: **to** ~ **away,** ~ **off** escabullirse.
scampi ['skæmpɪ] *npl* gambas *fpl.*
scan [skæn] *vt* (*examine*) escudriñar; (*glance at quickly*) dar un vistazo a; (*TV, RADAR*) explorar, registrar ♦ *n* (*MED*) examen *m* ultrasónico.
scandal ['skændl] *n* escándalo; (*gossip*) chismes *mpl.*
scandalize ['skændəlaɪz] *vt* escandalizar.
scandalous ['skændələs] *adj* escandaloso.
Scandinavia [skændɪ'neɪvɪə] *n* Escandinavia.
Scandinavian [skændɪ'neɪvɪən] *adj, n* escandinavo/a *m/f.*
scanner ['skænə*] *n* (*RADAR, MED*) escáner *m.*
scant [skænt] *adj* escaso.
scantily ['skæntɪlɪ] *adv*: ~ **clad** *or* **dressed** ligero de ropa.
scantiness ['skæntɪnɪs] *n* escasez *f*, insuficiencia.
scanty ['skæntɪ] *adj* (*meal*) insuficiente; (*clothes*) ligero.
scapegoat ['skeɪpgəut] *n* cabeza de turco, chivo expiatorio.
scar [skɑː] *n* cicatriz *f* ♦ *vt* marcar con una cicatriz ♦ *vi* cicatrizarse.
scarce [skɛəs] *adj* escaso.
scarcely ['skɛəslɪ] *adv* apenas; ~ **anybody** casi nadie; **I can** ~ **believe it** casi no puedo creerlo.
scarceness ['skɛəsnɪs], **scarcity** ['skɛəsɪtɪ] *n* escasez *f.*
scarcity value *n* valor *m* de escasez.
scare [skɛə*] *n* susto, sobresalto; (*panic*) pánico ♦ *vt* asustar, espantar; **to** ~ **sb stiff** dar a algn un susto de muerte; **bomb** ~ amenaza de bomba.
▸**scare away, scare off** *vt* espantar, ahuyentar.
scarecrow ['skɛəkrəu] *n* espantapájaros *m inv.*
scared [skɛəd] *adj*: **to be** ~ asustarse, estar asustado.
scaremonger ['skɛəmʌŋgə*] *n* alarmista *m/f.*
scarf, *pl* **scarves** [skɑːf, skɑːvz] *n* (*long*) bufanda; (*square*) pañuelo.
scarlet ['skɑːlɪt] *adj* escarlata.
scarlet fever *n* escarlatina.
scarper ['skɑːpə*] *vi* (*BRIT col*) largarse.
scarred [skɑːd] *adj* lleno de cicatrices.
scarves [skɑːvz] *npl of* **scarf.**
scary ['skɛərɪ] *adj* (*col*) de miedo; **it's** ~ da miedo.
scathing ['skeɪðɪŋ] *adj* mordaz; **to be** ~ **about sth** criticar algo duramente.
scatter ['skætə*] *vt* (*spread*) esparcir, desparramar; (*put to flight*) dispersar ♦ *vi* desparramarse; dispersarse.
scatterbrained ['skætəbreɪnd] *adj* ligero de cascos.
scavenge ['skævɪndʒ] *vi*: **to** ~ **(for)** (*person*) revolver entre la basura (para encontrar); **to** ~ **for food** (*hyenas etc*) nutrirse de carroña.
scavenger ['skævɪndʒə*] *n* (*person*) *mendigo/a que rebusca en la basura*; (*ZOOL: animal*) animal *m* de carroña; (: *bird*) ave *f* de carroña.
SCE *n abbr* = *Scottish Certificate of Education.*
scenario [sɪ'nɑːrɪəu] *n* (*THEAT*) argumento; (*CINE*) guión *m*; (*fig*) escenario.
scene [siːn] *n* (*THEAT, fig etc*) escena; (*of crime, accident*) escenario; (*sight, view*) vista, perspectiva; (*fuss*) escándalo; **the political** ~ **in Spain** el panorama político español; **behind the** ~**s** (*also fig*) entre bastidores; **to appear** *or* **come on the** ~ (*also fig*) aparecer, presentarse; **to make a** ~ (*col: fuss*) armar un escándalo.
scenery ['siːnərɪ] *n* (*THEAT*) decorado; (*landscape*) paisaje *m.*
scenic ['siːnɪk] *adj* (*picturesque*) pintoresco.
scent [sɛnt] *n* perfume *m*, olor *m*; (*fig: track*) rastro, pista; (*sense of smell*) olfato ♦ *vt*

perfumar; (*suspect*) presentir; **to put** *or* **throw sb off the ~** (*fig*) despistar a algn.
sceptic, (*US*) skeptic ['skɛptɪk] *n* escéptico/a.
sceptical, (*US*) skeptical ['skɛptɪkl] *adj* escéptico.
scepticism, (*US*) skepticism ['skɛptɪsɪzm] *n* escepticismo.
sceptre, (*US*) scepter ['sɛptə*] *n* cetro.
schedule ['ʃɛdju:l, (*US*) 'skɛdju:l] *n* (*of trains*) horario; (*of events*) programa *m*; (*list*) lista ♦ *vt* (*timetable*) establecer el horario de; (*list*) catalogar; (*visit*) fijar la hora de; **on ~** a la hora, sin retraso; **to be ahead of/behind ~** estar adelantado/retrasado; **we are working to a very tight ~** tenemos un programa de trabajo muy apretado; **everything went according to ~** todo salió según lo previsto; **the meeting is ~d for 7** *or* **to begin at 7** la reunión está fijada para las 7.
scheduled ['ʃɛdju:ld, (*US*) 'skɛdju:ld] *adj* (*date, time*) fijado; (*visit, event, bus, train*) programado; (*stop*) previsto; **~ flight** vuelo regular.
schematic [skɪ'mætɪk] *adj* (*diagram etc*) esquemático.
scheme [ski:m] *n* (*plan*) plan *m*, proyecto; (*method*) esquema *m*; (*plot*) intriga; (*trick*) ardid *m*; (*arrangement*) disposición *f*; (*pension ~ etc*) sistema *m* ♦ *vt* proyectar ♦ *vi* (*plan*) hacer proyectos; (*intrigue*) intrigar; **colour ~** combinación *f* de colores.
scheming ['ski:mɪŋ] *adj* intrigante.
schism ['skɪzəm] *n* cisma *m*.
schizophrenia [skɪtsə'fri:nɪə] *n* esquizofrenia.
schizophrenic [skɪtsə'frɛnɪk] *adj* esquizofrénico.
scholar ['skɔlə*] *n* (*pupil*) alumno/a, estudiante *m/f*; (*learned person*) sabio/a, erudito/a.
scholarly ['skɔləlɪ] *adj* erudito.
scholarship ['skɔləʃɪp] *n* erudición *f*; (*grant*) beca.
school [sku:l] *n* (*gen*) escuela, colegio; (*in university*) facultad *f*; (*of fish*) banco ♦ *vt* (*animal*) amaestrar; **to be at** *or* **go to ~** ir al colegio *or* a la escuela.
school age *n* edad *f* escolar.
schoolbook ['sku:lbuk] *n* libro de texto.
schoolboy ['sku:lbɔɪ] *n* alumno.
schoolchild, *pl* **-children** ['sku:ltʃaɪld, -tʃɪldrən] *n* alumno/a.
schooldays ['sku:ldeɪz] *npl* años *mpl* del colegio.
schoolgirl ['sku:lgə:l] *n* alumna.
schooling ['sku:lɪŋ] *n* enseñanza.
school-leaver ['sku:lli:və*] *n* (*BRIT*) *joven que ha terminado la educación secundaria.*
schoolmaster ['sku:lma:stə*] *n* (*primary*) maestro; (*secondary*) profesor *m*.
schoolmistress ['sku:lmɪstrɪs] *n* (*primary*) maestra; (*secondary*) profesora.
schoolroom ['sku:lrum] *n* clase *f*.
schoolteacher ['sku:lti:tʃə*] *n* (*primary*) maestro/a; (*secondary*) profesor(a) *m/f*.
schoolyard ['sku:lja:d] *n* (*US*) patio del colegio.
schooner ['sku:nə*] *n* (*ship*) goleta.
sciatica [saɪ'ætɪkə] *n* ciática.
science ['saɪəns] *n* ciencia; **the ~s** las ciencias.
science fiction *n* ciencia-ficción *f*.
scientific [saɪən'tɪfɪk] *adj* científico.
scientist ['saɪəntɪst] *n* científico/a.
sci-fi ['saɪfaɪ] *n abbr* (*col*) = **science fiction.**
Scilly Isles ['sɪlɪ-], **Scillies** ['sɪlɪz] *npl*: **the ~** las Islas Sorlingas.
scintillating ['sɪntɪleɪtɪŋ] *adj* (*wit, conversation, company*) brillante, chispeante, ingenioso.
scissors ['sɪzəz] *npl* tijeras *fpl*; **a pair of ~** unas tijeras.
scoff [skɔf] *vt* (*BRIT col: eat*) engullir ♦ *vi*: **to ~ (at)** (*mock*) mofarse (de).
scold [skəuld] *vt* regañar.
scolding ['skəuldɪŋ] *n* riña, reprimenda.
scone [skɔn] *n pastel de pan.*
scoop [sku:p] *n* cucharón *m*; (*for flour etc*) pala; (*PRESS*) exclusiva ♦ *vt* (*COMM: market*) adelantarse a; (: *profit*) sacar; (*COMM, PRESS: competitors*) adelantarse a.
▸**scoop out** *vt* excavar.
▸**scoop up** *vt* recoger.
scooter ['sku:tə*] *n* (*motor cycle*) Vespa ®; (*toy*) patinete *m*.
scope [skəup] *n* (*of plan, undertaking*) ámbito; (*reach*) alcance *m*; (*of person*) competencia; (*opportunity*) libertad *f* (de acción); **there is plenty of ~ for improvement** hay bastante campo para efectuar mejoras.
scorch [skɔ:tʃ] *vt* (*clothes*) chamuscar; (*earth, grass*) quemar, secar.
scorcher ['skɔ:tʃə*] *n* (*col: hot day*) día *m* abrasador.
scorching ['skɔ:tʃɪŋ] *adj* abrasador(a).
score [skɔ:*] *n* (*points etc*) puntuación *f*; (*MUS*) partitura; (*reckoning*) cuenta; (*twenty*) veintena ♦ *vt* (*goal, point*) ganar; (*mark, cut*) rayar ♦ *vi* marcar un tanto; (*FOOTBALL*) marcar un gol; (*keep score*) llevar el tanteo; **to keep (the) ~** llevar la

cuenta; **to have an old ~ to settle with sb** (*fig*) tener cuentas pendientes con algn; **on that ~** en lo que se refiere a eso; **~s of people** (*fig*) muchísima gente, cantidad de gente; **to ~ 6 out of 10** obtener una puntuación de 6 sobre 10.

▸score out *vt* tachar.

scoreboard ['skɔːbɔːd] *n* marcador *m*.

scoreline ['skɔːlaɪn] *n* (*SPORT*) resultado final.

scorer ['skɔːrə*] *n* marcador *m*; (*keeping score*) encargado/a del marcador.

scorn [skɔːn] *n* desprecio ♦ *vt* despreciar.

scornful ['skɔːnful] *adj* desdeñoso, despreciativo.

scornfully ['skɔːnfulɪ] *adv* desdeñosamente, con desprecio.

Scorpio ['skɔːpɪəu] *n* Escorpión *m*.

scorpion ['skɔːpɪən] *n* alacrán *m*, escorpión *m*.

Scot [skɔt] *n* escocés/esa *m/f*.

Scotch [skɔtʃ] *n* whisky *m* escocés.

scotch [skɔtʃ] *vt* (*rumour*) desmentir; (*plan*) frustrar.

Scotch tape ® *n* (*US*) cinta adhesiva, celo, scotch ® *m*.

scot-free [skɔt'friː] *adv*: **to get off ~** (*unpunished*) salir impune; (*unhurt*) salir ileso.

Scotland ['skɔtlənd] *n* Escocia.

Scots [skɔts] *adj* escocés/esa.

Scotsman ['skɔtsmən] *n* escocés *m*.

Scotswoman ['skɔtswumən] *n* escocesa.

Scottish ['skɔtɪʃ] *adj* escocés/esa; **the ~ National Party** *partido político independista escocés*; **the ~ Parliament** el Parlamento escocés.

scoundrel ['skaundrəl] *n* canalla *m/f*, sinvergüenza *m/f*.

scour ['skauə*] *vt* (*clean*) fregar, estregar; (*search*) recorrer, registrar.

scourer ['skauərə*] *n* (*pad*) estropajo; (*powder*) limpiador *m*.

scourge [skəːdʒ] *n* azote *m*.

scout [skaut] *n* (*MIL*, *also*: **boy ~**) explorador *m*.

▸scout around *vi* reconocer el terreno.

scowl [skaul] *vi* fruncir el ceño; **to ~ at sb** mirar con ceño a algn.

scrabble ['skræbl] *vi* (*claw*): **to ~ (at)** arañar ♦ *n*: **S~** ® Intelect *m* ®; **to ~ about** *or* **around for sth** revolver todo buscando algo.

scraggy ['skrægɪ] *adj* flaco, delgaducho.

scram [skræm] *vi* (*col*) largarse.

scramble ['skræmbl] *n* (*climb*) subida (difícil); (*struggle*) pelea ♦ *vi*: **to ~ out/through** salir/abrirse paso con dificultad; **to ~ for** pelear por; **to go scrambling** (*SPORT*) hacer motocrós.

scrambled eggs ['skræmbld-] *npl* huevos *mpl* revueltos.

scrap [skræp] *n* (*bit*) pedacito; (*fig*) pizca; (*fight*) riña, bronca; (*also*: **~ iron**) chatarra, hierro viejo ♦ *vt* (*discard*) desechar, descartar ♦ *vi* reñir, armar (una) bronca; **~s** *npl* (*waste*) sobras *fpl*, desperdicios *mpl*; **to sell sth for ~** vender algo como chatarra.

scrapbook ['skræpbuk] *n* álbum *m* de recortes.

scrap dealer *n* chatarrero/a.

scrape [skreɪp] *n* (*fig*) lío, apuro ♦ *vt* raspar; (*skin etc*) rasguñar; (**~** *against*) rozar.

▸scrape through *vi* (*succeed*) salvarse por los pelos; (*exam*) aprobar por los pelos.

scraper ['skreɪpə*] *n* raspador *m*.

scrap heap *n* (*fig*): **on the ~** desperdiciado; **to throw sth on the ~** desechar *or* descartar algo.

scrap iron *n* chatarra.

scrap merchant *n* (*BRIT*) chatarrero/a.

scrap metal *n* chatarra, desecho de metal.

scrap paper *n* pedazos *mpl* de papel.

scrappy ['skræpɪ] *adj* (*essay etc*) deshilvanado; (*education*) incompleto.

scrap yard *n* depósito de chatarra; (*for cars*) cementerio de coches.

scratch [skrætʃ] *n* rasguño; (*from claw*) arañazo ♦ *adj*: **~ team** equipo improvisado ♦ *vt* (*record*) rayar; (*with claw, nail*) rasguñar, arañar; (*COMPUT*) borrar ♦ *vi* rascarse; **to start from ~** partir de cero; **to be up to ~** cumplir con los requisitos.

scratchpad ['skrætʃpæd] *n* (*US*) bloc *m* de notas.

scrawl [skrɔːl] *n* garabatos *mpl* ♦ *vi* hacer garabatos.

scrawny ['skrɔːnɪ] *adj* (*person, neck*) flaco.

scream [skriːm] *n* chillido ♦ *vi* chillar; **it was a ~** (*fig, col*) fue para morirse de risa; **he's a ~** (*fig, col*) es muy divertido *or* de lo más gracioso; **to ~ at sb (to do sth)** gritarle a algn (para que haga algo).

scree [skriː] *n* cono de desmoronamiento.

screech [skriːtʃ] *vi* chirriar.

screen [skriːn] *n* (*CINE, TV*) pantalla; (*movable*) biombo; (*wall*) tabique *m*; (*also*: **wind~**) parabrisas *m inv* ♦ *vt* (*conceal*) tapar; (*from the wind etc*) proteger; (*film*) proyectar; (*fig: person: for security*) investigar; (*: for illness*) hacer una exploración a.

screen editing *n* (*COMPUT*) corrección *f* en pantalla.

screening ['skri:nɪŋ] *n* (*of film*) proyección *f*; (*for security*) investigación *f*; (*MED*) exploración *f*.
screen memory *n* (*COMPUT*) memoria de la pantalla.
screenplay ['skri:npleɪ] *n* guión *m*.
screen saver [-seɪvə*] *n* salvapantallas *m inv*.
screen test *n* prueba de pantalla.
screw [skru:] *n* tornillo; (*propeller*) hélice *f* ♦ *vt* atornillar; **to ~ sth to the wall** fijar algo a la pared con tornillos.
▸**screw up** *vt* (*paper, material etc*) arrugar; (*col*: *ruin*) fastidiar; **to ~ up one's eyes** arrugar el entrecejo; **to ~ up one's face** torcer *or* arrugar la cara.
screwdriver ['skru:draɪvə*] *n* destornillador *m*.
screwed-up ['skru:d'ʌp] *adj* (*col*): **she's totally ~** está trastornada.
screwy ['skru:ɪ] *adj* (*col*) chiflado.
scribble ['skrɪbl] *n* garabatos *mpl* ♦ *vt* escribir con prisa; **to ~ sth down** garabatear algo.
script [skrɪpt] *n* (*CINE etc*) guión *m*; (*writing*) escritura, letra.
scripted ['skrɪptɪd] *adj* (*RADIO, TV*) escrito.
Scripture ['skrɪptʃə*] *n* Sagrada Escritura.
scriptwriter ['skrɪptraɪtə*] *n* guionista *m/f*.
scroll [skrəul] *n* rollo ♦ *vt* (*COMPUT*) desplazar.
scrotum ['skrəutəm] *n* escroto.
scrounge [skraundʒ] (*col*) *vt*: **to ~ sth off** *or* **from sb** gorronear algo a algn ♦ *vi*: **to ~ on sb** vivir a costa de algn.
scrounger ['skraundʒə*] *n* gorrón/ona *m/f*.
scrub [skrʌb] *n* (*clean*) fregado; (*land*) maleza ♦ *vt* fregar, restregar; (*reject*) cancelar, anular.
scrubbing brush ['skrʌbɪŋ-] *n* cepillo de fregar.
scruff [skrʌf] *n*: **by the ~ of the neck** por el pescuezo.
scruffy ['skrʌfɪ] *adj* desaliñado, desaseado.
scrum(mage) ['skrʌm(mɪdʒ)] *n* (*RUGBY*) melée *f*.
scruple ['skru:pl] *n* escrúpulo; **to have no ~s about doing sth** no tener reparos en *or* escrúpulos para hacer algo.
scrupulous ['skru:pjuləs] *adj* escrupuloso.
scrupulously ['skru:pjuləslɪ] *adv* escrupulosamente; **to be ~ fair/honest** ser sumamente justo/honesto.
scrutinize ['skru:tɪnaɪz] *vt* escudriñar; (*votes*) escrutar.
scrutiny ['skru:tɪnɪ] *n* escrutinio, examen *m*; **under the ~ of sb** bajo la mirada *or* el escrutinio de algn.
scuba ['sku:bə] *n* escafandra autónoma.
scuba diving *n* submarinismo.
scuff [skʌf] *vt* (*shoes, floor*) rayar.
scuffle ['skʌfl] *n* refriega.
scullery ['skʌlərɪ] *n* trascocina.
sculptor ['skʌlptə*] *n* escultor(a) *m/f*.
sculpture ['skʌlptʃə*] *n* escultura.
scum [skʌm] *n* (*on liquid*) espuma; (*pej*: *people*) escoria.
scupper ['skʌpə*] *vt* (*BRIT*: *boat*) hundir; (: *fig*: *plans etc*) acabar con.
scurrilous ['skʌrɪləs] *adj* difamatorio, calumnioso.
scurry ['skʌrɪ] *vi*: **to ~ off** escabullirse.
scurvy ['skə:vɪ] *n* escorbuto.
scuttle ['skʌtl] *n* (*also*: **coal ~**) cubo, carbonera ♦ *vt* (*ship*) barrenar ♦ *vi* (*scamper*): **to ~ away, ~ off** escabullirse.
scythe [saɪð] *n* guadaña.
SD, S. Dak. *abbr* (*US*) = *South Dakota*.
SDI *n abbr* (= *Strategic Defense Initiative*) IDE *f*.
SDLP *n abbr* (*BRIT POL*) = *Social Democratic and Labour Party*.
SDP *n abbr* (*BRIT POL*) = *Social Democratic Party*.
sea [si:] *n* mar *m/f*; **by ~** (*travel*) en barco; **on the ~** (*boat*) en el mar; (*town*) junto al mar; **to be all at ~** (*fig*) estar despistado; **out to** *or* **at ~** en alta mar; **to go by ~** ir en barco; **heavy** *or* **rough ~s** marejada; **by** *or* **beside the ~** (*holiday*) en la playa; (*village*) a orillas del mar; **a ~ of faces** una multitud de caras.
sea bed *n* fondo del mar.
sea bird *n* ave *f* marina.
seaboard ['si:bɔ:d] *n* litoral *m*.
sea breeze *n* brisa de mar.
seadog ['si:dɔg] *n* lobo de mar.
seafarer ['si:fɛərə*] *n* marinero.
seafaring ['si:fɛərɪŋ] *adj* (*community*) marinero; (*life*) de marinero.
seafood ['si:fu:d] *n* mariscos *mpl*.
sea front *n* paseo marítimo.
seagoing ['si:gəuɪŋ] *adj* (*ship*) de alta mar.
seagull ['si:gʌl] *n* gaviota.
seal [si:l] *n* (*animal*) foca; (*stamp*) sello ♦ *vt* (*close*) cerrar; (: *with ~*) sellar; (*decide*: *sb's fate*) decidir; (: *bargain*) cerrar; **~ of approval** sello de aprobación.
▸**seal off** *vt* obturar.
seal cull *n* matanza de crías de foca.
sea level *n* nivel *m* del mar.
sealing wax ['si:lɪŋ-] *n* lacre *m*.
sea lion *n* león *m* marino.
sealskin ['si:lskɪn] *n* piel *f* de foca.
seam [si:m] *n* costura; (*of metal*) juntura; (*of coal*) veta, filón *m*; **the hall was**

bursting at the ~s la sala rebosaba de gente.
seaman ['si:mən] *n* marinero.
seamanship ['si:mənʃɪp] *n* náutica.
seamless ['si:mlɪs] *adj* sin costura(s).
seance ['seɪɔns] *n* sesión *f* de espiritismo.
seaplane ['si:pleɪn] *n* hidroavión *m.*
seaport ['si:pɔ:t] *n* puerto de mar.
search [sə:tʃ] *n* (*for person, thing*) busca, búsqueda; (*of drawer, pockets*) registro; (*inspection*) reconocimiento ♦ *vt* (*look in*) buscar en; (*examine*) examinar; (*person, place*) registrar; (*COMPUT*) buscar ♦ *vi*: **to ~ for** buscar; **in ~ of** en busca de; **"~ and replace"** (*COMPUT*) "buscar y reemplazar".
▸search through *vt fus* registrar.
searcher ['sə:tʃə*] *n* buscador(a) *m/f.*
searching ['sə:tʃɪŋ] *adj* (*question*) penetrante.
searchlight ['sə:tʃlaɪt] *n* reflector *m.*
search party *n* equipo de salvamento.
search warrant *n* mandamiento judicial.
searing ['sɪərɪŋ] *adj* (*heat*) abrasador(a); (*pain*) agudo.
seashore ['si:ʃɔ*] *n* playa, orilla del mar; **on the ~** a la orilla del mar.
seasick ['si:sɪk] *adj* mareado; **to be ~** marearse.
seaside ['si:saɪd] *n* playa, orilla del mar; **to go to the ~** ir a la playa.
seaside resort *n* playa.
season ['si:zn] *n* (*of year*) estación *f*; (*sporting etc*) temporada; (*gen*) época, período ♦ *vt* (*food*) sazonar; **to be in/out of ~** estar en sazón/fuera de temporada; **the busy ~** (*for shops, hotels etc*) la temporada alta; **the open ~** (*HUNTING*) la temporada de caza *or* de pesca.
seasonal ['si:znl] *adj* estacional.
seasoned ['si:znd] *adj* (*wood*) curado; (*fig: worker, actor*) experimentado; (*troops*) curtido; **~ campaigner** veterano/a.
seasoning ['si:znɪŋ] *n* condimento.
season ticket *n* abono.
seat [si:t] *n* (*in bus, train: place*) asiento; (*chair*) silla; (*PARLIAMENT*) escaño; (*buttocks*) trasero; (*centre: of government etc*) sede *f* ♦ *vt* sentar; (*have room for*) tener cabida para; **are there any ~s left?** ¿quedan plazas?; **to take one's ~** sentarse, tomar asiento; **to be ~ed** estar sentado, sentarse.
seat belt *n* cinturón *m* de seguridad.
seating ['si:tɪŋ] *n* asientos *mpl.*
seating arrangements *npl* distribución *fsg* de los asientos.
seating capacity *n* número de asientos, aforo.
SEATO ['si:təu] *n abbr* (= *Southeast Asia Treaty Organization*) OTASE *f.*
sea water *n* agua *m* del mar.
seaweed ['si:wi:d] *n* alga marina.
seaworthy ['si:wə:ðɪ] *adj* en condiciones de navegar.
SEC *n abbr* (*US*: = *Securities and Exchange Commission*) *comisión de operaciones bursátiles.*
sec. *abbr* = **second(s)**.
secateurs [sɛkə'tə:z] *npl* podadera *sg.*
secluded [sɪ'klu:dɪd] *adj* retirado.
seclusion [sɪ'klu:ʒən] *n* retiro.
second ['sɛkənd] *adj* segundo ♦ *adv* (*in race etc*) en segundo lugar ♦ *n* (*gen*) segundo; (*AUT*: *also*: **~ gear**) segunda; (*COMM*) artículo con algún desperfecto; (*BRIT SCOL: degree*) título universitario de segunda clase ♦ *vt* (*motion*) apoyar; [sɪ'kɔnd] (*employee*) trasladar temporalmente; **~ floor** (*BRIT*) segundo piso; (*US*) primer piso; **Charles the S~** Carlos Segundo; **to ask for a ~ opinion** (*MED*) pedir una segunda opinión; **just a ~!** ¡un momento!; **to have ~ thoughts** cambiar de opinión; **on ~ thoughts** *or* (*US*) **thought** pensándolo bien; **~ mortgage** segunda hipoteca.
secondary ['sɛkəndərɪ] *adj* secundario.
secondary education *n* enseñanza secundaria.
secondary school *n* escuela secundaria; *ver recuadro.*

SECONDARY SCHOOL

En el Reino Unido se llama **secondary school** *a un centro educativo para alumnos de 11 a 18 años, si bien muchos estudiantes acaban a los 16, edad mínima de escolarización obligatoria. La mayor parte de estos centros funcionan como "comprehensive schools", aunque aún existen algunos de tipo selectivo.*

second-best [sɛkənd'bɛst] *n* segundo.
second-class ['sɛkənd'klɑ:s] *adj* de segunda clase ♦ *adv*: **to send sth ~** enviar algo por correo de segunda clase; **to travel ~** viajar en segunda; **~ citizen** ciudadano/a de segunda (clase).
second cousin *n* primo/a segundo/a.
seconder ['sɛkəndə*] *n* el/la que apoya una moción.
second-guess ['sɛkənd'gɛs] *vt* (*evaluate*) juzgar (a posteriori); (*anticipate*): **to ~ sth/sb** (intentar) adivinar algo/lo que va

a hacer algn.
secondhand ['sɛkənd'hænd] *adj* de segunda mano, usado ♦ *adv*: **to buy sth ~** comprar algo de segunda mano; **to hear sth ~** oír algo indirectamente.
second hand *n* (*on clock*) segundero.
second-in-command ['sɛkəndɪnkə'mɑːnd] *n* (*MIL*) segundo en el mando; (*ADMIN*) segundo/a, ayudante *m/f*.
secondly ['sɛkəndlɪ] *adv* en segundo lugar.
secondment [sɪ'kɔndmənt] *n* (*BRIT*) traslado temporal.
second-rate ['sɛkənd'reɪt] *adj* de segunda categoría.
secrecy ['siːkrəsɪ] *n* secreto.
secret ['siːkrɪt] *adj, n* secreto; **in ~** *adv* en secreto; **to keep sth ~ (from sb)** ocultarle algo (a algn); **to make no ~ of sth** no ocultar algo.
secret agent *n* agente *m/f* secreto/a, espía *m/f*.
secretarial [sɛkrɪ'tɛərɪəl] *adj* (*course*) de secretariado; (*staff*) de secretaría; (*work, duties*) de secretaria.
secretariat [sɛkrɪ'tɛərɪət] *n* secretaría.
secretary ['sɛkrətərɪ] *n* secretario/a; **S~ of State** (*BRIT POL*) Ministro (con cartera).
secretary-general ['sɛkrətərɪ'dʒɛnərl] *n* secretario/a general.
secretary pool *n* (*US*) = **typing pool**.
secrete [sɪ'kriːt] *vt* (*MED, ANAT, BIO*) secretar; (*hide*) ocultar, esconder.
secretion [sɪ'kriːʃən] *n* secreción *f*.
secretive ['siːkrətɪv] *adj* reservado, sigiloso.
secretly ['siːkrɪtlɪ] *adv* en secreto.
secret police *n* policía secreta.
secret service *n* servicio secreto.
sect [sɛkt] *n* secta.
sectarian [sɛk'tɛərɪən] *adj* sectario.
section ['sɛkʃən] *n* sección *f*; (*part*) parte *f*; (*of document*) artículo; (*of opinion*) sector *m*; **business ~** (*PRESS*) sección *f* de economía.
sectional ['sɛkʃənl] *adj* (*regional*) regional, local.
sector ['sɛktə*] *n* (*gen, COMPUT*) sector *m*.
secular ['sɛkjulə*] *adj* secular, seglar.
secure [sɪ'kjuə*] *adj* (*free from anxiety*) seguro; (*firmly fixed*) firme, fijo ♦ *vt* (*fix*) asegurar, afianzar; (*get*) conseguir; (*COMM*: *loan*) garantizar; **to make sth ~** afianzar algo; **to ~ sth for sb** conseguir algo para algn.
secured creditor [sɪ'kjuəd-] *n* acreedor(a) *m/f* con garantía.
securely [sɪ'kjuəlɪ] *adv* firmemente; **it is ~ fastened** está bien sujeto.
security [sɪ'kjuərɪtɪ] *n* seguridad *f*; (*for loan*) fianza; (: *object*) prenda; **securities** *npl* (*COMM*) valores *mpl*, títulos *mpl*; **~ of tenure** tenencia asegurada; **to increase/tighten ~** aumentar/estrechar las medidas de seguridad; **job ~** seguridad *f* en el empleo.
Security Council *n*: **the ~** el Consejo de Seguridad.
security forces *npl* fuerzas *fpl* de seguridad.
security guard *n* guardia *m/f* de seguridad.
security risk *n* riesgo para la seguridad.
secy. *abbr* (= *secretary*) Srio/a.
sedan [sɪ'dæn] *n* (*US AUT*) sedán *m*.
sedate [sɪ'deɪt] *adj* tranquilo ♦ *vt* administrar sedantes a, sedar.
sedation [sɪ'deɪʃən] *n* (*MED*) sedación *f*; **to be under ~** estar bajo sedación.
sedative ['sɛdɪtɪv] *n* sedante *m*, calmante *m*.
sedentary ['sɛdntrɪ] *adj* sedentario.
sediment ['sɛdɪmənt] *n* sedimento.
sedimentary [sɛdɪ'mɛntərɪ] *adj* (*GEO*) sedimentario.
sedition [sɪ'dɪʃən] *n* sedición *f*.
seduce [sɪ'djuːs] *vt* (*gen*) seducir.
seduction [sɪ'dʌkʃən] *n* seducción *f*.
seductive [sɪ'dʌktɪv] *adj* seductor(a).
see [siː] *vb* (*pt* **saw**, *pp* **seen** [sɔː, siːn]) *vt* (*gen*) ver; (*understand*) ver, comprender; (*look at*) mirar ♦ *vi* ver ♦ *n* sede *f*; **to ~ sb to the door** acompañar a algn a la puerta; **to ~ that** (*ensure*) asegurarse de que; **~ you soon/later/tomorrow!** ¡hasta pronto/luego/mañana!; **as far as I can ~** por lo visto *or* por lo que veo; **there was nobody to be ~n** no se veía a nadie; **let me ~** (*show me*) a ver; (*let me think*) vamos a ver; **to go and ~ sb** ir a ver a algn; **~ for yourself** compruébalo tú mismo; **I don't know what she ~s in him** no sé qué le encuentra.
▸**see about** *vt fus* atender a, encargarse de.
▸**see off** *vt* despedir.
▸**see through** *vt fus* calar ♦ *vt* llevar a cabo.
▸**see to** *vt fus* atender a, encargarse de.
seed [siːd] *n* semilla; (*in fruit*) pepita; (*fig*) germen *m*; (*TENNIS*) preseleccionado/a; **to go to ~** (*plant*) granar; (*fig*) descuidarse.
seedless ['siːdlɪs] *adj* sin semillas *or* pepitas.
seedling ['siːdlɪŋ] *n* planta de semillero.
seedy ['siːdɪ] *adj* (*person*) desaseado; (*place*) sórdido.
seeing ['siːɪŋ] *conj*: **~ (that)** visto que, en vista de que.

seek, *pt, pp* **sought** [siːk, sɔːt] *vt* (*gen*) buscar; (*post*) solicitar; **to ~ advice/help from sb** pedir consejos/solicitar ayuda a algn.
►**seek out** *vt* (*person*) buscar.
seem [siːm] *vi* parecer; **there ~s to be...** parece que hay ...; **it ~s (that)** ... parece que ...; **what ~s to be the trouble?** ¿qué pasa?; **I did what ~ed best** hice lo que parecía mejor.
seemingly ['siːmɪŋlɪ] *adv* aparentemente, según parece.
seen [siːn] *pp of* **see**.
seep [siːp] *vi* filtrarse.
seer [sɪə*] *n* vidente *m/f*, profeta *m/f*.
seersucker [sɪə'sʌkə*] *n* sirsaca.
seesaw ['siːsɔː] *n* balancín *m*, subibaja *m*.
seethe [siːð] *vi* hervir; **to ~ with anger** enfurecerse.
see-through ['siːθruː] *adj* transparente.
segment ['sɛgmənt] *n* segmento.
segregate ['sɛgrɪgeɪt] *vt* segregar.
segregation [sɛgrɪ'geɪʃən] *n* segregación *f*.
Seine [seɪn] *n* Sena *m*.
seismic ['saɪzmɪk] *adj* sísmico.
seize [siːz] *vt* (*grasp*) agarrar, asir; (*take possession of*) secuestrar; (: *territory*) apoderarse de; (*opportunity*) aprovecharse de.
►**seize up** *vi* (*TECH*) agarrotarse.
►**seize (up)on** *vt fus* valerse de.
seizure ['siːʒə*] *n* (*MED*) ataque *m*; (*LAW*) incautación *f*.
seldom ['sɛldəm] *adv* rara vez.
select [sɪ'lɛkt] *adj* selecto, escogido; (*hotel, restaurant, clubs*) exclusivo ♦ *vt* escoger, elegir; (*SPORT*) seleccionar; **a ~ few** una minoría selecta.
selection [sɪ'lɛkʃən] *n* selección *f*, elección *f*; (*COMM*) surtido.
selection committee *n* comisión *f* de nombramiento.
selective [sɪ'lɛktɪv] *adj* selectivo.
self [sɛlf] *n* (*pl* **selves** [sɛlvz]) uno mismo ♦ *pref* auto ...; **the ~** el yo.
self-addressed ['sɛlfə'drɛst] *adj*: **~ envelope** sobre *m* con la dirección propia.
self-adhesive [sɛlfəd'hiːzɪv] *adj* autoadhesivo, autoadherente.
self-appointed [selfə'pɔɪntɪd] *adj* autonombrado.
self-assurance [sɛlfə'ʃuərəns] *n* confianza en sí mismo.
self-assured [sɛlfə'ʃuəd] *adj* seguro de sí mismo.
self-catering [sɛlf'keɪtərɪŋ] *adj* (*BRIT*) sin pensión *or* servicio de comida; **~ apartment** apartamento con cocina propia.
self-centred, (*US*) **self-centered** [sɛlf'sɛntəd] *adj* egocéntrico.
self-cleaning [sɛlf'kliːnɪŋ] *adj* autolimpiador.
self-confessed [sɛlfkən'fɛst] *adj* (*alcoholic etc*) confeso.
self-confidence [sɛlf'kɔnfɪdns] *n* confianza en sí mismo.
self-confident [sɛlf'kɔnfɪdnt] *adj* seguro de sí (mismo), lleno de confianza en sí mismo.
self-conscious [sɛlf'kɔnʃəs] *adj* cohibido.
self-contained [sɛlfkən'teɪnd] *adj* (*gen*) independiente; (*BRIT*: *flat*) con entrada particular.
self-control [sɛlfkən'trəul] *n* autodominio.
self-defeating [sɛlfdɪ'fiːtɪŋ] *adj* contraproducente.
self-defence, (*US*) **self-defense** [sɛlfdɪ'fɛns] *n* defensa propia.
self-discipline [sɛlf'dɪsɪplɪn] *n* autodisciplina.
self-employed [sɛlfɪm'plɔɪd] *adj* que trabaja por cuenta propia, autónomo.
self-esteem [sɛlfɪ'stiːm] *n* amor *m* propio.
self-evident [sɛlf'ɛvɪdnt] *adj* patente.
self-explanatory [sɛlfɪks'plænətərɪ] *adj* que no necesita explicación.
self-financing [sɛlffaɪ'nænsɪŋ] *adj* autofinanziado.
self-governing [sɛlf'gʌvənɪŋ] *adj* autónomo.
self-help ['sɛlf'hɛlp] *n* autosuficiencia, ayuda propia.
self-importance [sɛlfɪm'pɔːtns] *n* presunción *f*, vanidad *f*.
self-important [sɛlfɪm'pɔːtnt] *adj* vanidoso.
self-indulgent [sɛlfɪn'dʌldʒənt] *adj* indulgente consigo mismo.
self-inflicted [sɛlfɪn'flɪktɪd] *adj* infligido a sí mismo.
self-interest [sɛlf'ɪntrɪst] *n* egoísmo.
selfish ['sɛlfɪʃ] *adj* egoísta.
selfishly ['sɛlfɪʃlɪ] *adv* con egoísmo, de modo egoísta.
selfishness ['sɛlfɪʃnɪs] *n* egoísmo.
selflessly ['sɛlflɪslɪ] *adv* desinteresadamente.
selfless ['sɛlflɪs] *adj* desinteresado.
self-made man ['sɛlfmeɪd-] *n hombre que ha triunfado por su propio esfuerzo.*
self-pity [sɛlf'pɪtɪ] *n* lástima de sí mismo.
self-portrait [sɛlf'pɔːtreɪt] *n* autorretrato.
self-possessed [sɛlfpə'zɛst] *adj* sereno, dueño de sí mismo.
self-preservation ['sɛlfprɛzə'veɪʃən] *n* propia conservación *f*.

self-propelled [sɛlfprə'pɛld] *adj* autopropulsado, automotor/triz.
self-raising [sɛlf'reɪzɪŋ], (*US*) **self-rising** [sɛlf'raɪzɪŋ] *adj*: ~ **flour** harina con levadura.
self-reliant [sɛlfrɪ'laɪənt] *adj* independiente, autosuficiente.
self-respect [sɛlfrɪ'spɛkt] *n* amor *m* propio.
self-respecting [sɛlfrɪ'spɛktɪŋ] *adj* que tiene amor propio.
self-righteous [sɛlf'raɪtʃəs] *adj* santurrón/ona.
self-rising [sɛlf'raɪzɪŋ] *adj* (*US*) = **self-raising.**
self-sacrifice [sɛlf'sækrɪfaɪs] *n* abnegación *f*.
self-same [sɛlfseɪm] *adj* mismo, mismísimo.
self-satisfied [sɛlf'sætɪsfaɪd] *adj* satisfecho de sí mismo.
self-service [sɛlf'sə:vɪs] *adj* de autoservicio.
self-styled ['sɛlfstaɪld] *adj* supuesto, sedicente.
self-sufficient [sɛlfsə'fɪʃənt] *adj* autosuficiente.
self-supporting [sɛlfsə'pɔ:tɪŋ] *adj* económicamente independiente.
self-tanning [sɛlf'tænɪŋ] *adj* autobronceador.
self-taught [sɛlf'tɔ:t] *adj* autodidacta.
self-test ['sɛlftɛst] *n* (*COMPUT*) autocomprobación *f*.
sell, *pt, pp* **sold** [sɛl, səuld] *vt* vender ♦ *vi* venderse; **to ~ at** *or* **for £10** venderse a 10 libras; **to ~ sb an idea** (*fig*) convencer a algn de una idea.
▶**sell off** *vt* liquidar.
▶**sell out** *vi* transigir, transar (*LAM*); **to ~ out (to sb/sth)** (*COMM*) vender su negocio (a algn/algo) ♦ *vt* agotar las existencias de, venderlo todo; **the tickets are all sold out** las entradas están agotadas.
▶**sell up** *vi* (*COMM*) liquidarse.
sell-by date ['sɛlbaɪ-] *n* fecha de caducidad.
seller ['sɛlə*] *n* vendedor(a) *m/f*; **~'s market** mercado de demanda.
selling price ['sɛlɪŋ-] *n* precio de venta.
Sellotape ® ['sɛləuteɪp] *n* (*BRIT*) cinta adhesiva, celo, scotch ® *m*.
sellout ['sɛlaut] *n* traición *f*; **it was a ~** (*THEAT etc*) fue un éxito de taquilla.
selves [sɛlvz] *npl of* **self.**
semantic [sɪ'mæntɪk] *adj* semántico.
semaphore ['sɛməfɔ:*] *n* semáforo.
semblance ['sɛmbləns] *n* apariencia.
semen ['si:mən] *n* semen *m*.
semester [sɪ'mɛstə*] *n* (*US*) semestre *m*.
semi ['sɛmɪ] *n* = **semidetached house.**
semi... [sɛmɪ] *pref* semi..., medio....
semicircle ['sɛmɪsə:kl] *n* semicírculo.
semicircular ['sɛmɪ'sə:kjulə*] *adj* semicircular.
semicolon [sɛmɪ'kəulən] *n* punto y coma.
semiconductor [sɛmɪkən'dʌktə*] *n* semiconductor *m*.
semiconscious [sɛmɪ'kɔnʃəs] *adj* semiconsciente.
semidetached (house) [sɛmɪdɪ'tætʃt-] *n* casa adosada.
semi-final [sɛmɪ'faɪnl] *n* semi-final *f*.
seminar ['sɛmɪnɑ:*] *n* seminario.
seminary ['sɛmɪnərɪ] *n* (*REL*) seminario.
semiprecious stone [sɛmɪ'prɛʃəs-] *n* piedra semipreciosa.
semiquaver ['sɛmɪkweɪvə*] *n* (*BRIT*) semicorchea.
semiskilled ['sɛmɪskɪld] *adj* (*work, worker*) semicualificado.
semi-skimmed *adj* semidesnatado.
semitone ['sɛmɪtəun] *n* semitono.
semolina [sɛmə'li:nə] *n* sémola.
SEN *n abbr* (*BRIT*) = *State Enrolled Nurse.*
Sen., sen. *abbr* = **senator, senior.**
senate ['sɛnɪt] *n* senado; *see also* **Congress.**
senator ['sɛnɪtə*] *n* senador(a) *m/f*.
send, *pt, pp* **sent** [sɛnd, sɛnt] *vt* mandar, enviar; **to ~ by post** mandar por correo; **to ~ sb for sth** mandar a algn a buscar algo; **to ~ word that ...** avisar *or* mandar aviso de que ...; **she ~s (you) her love** te manda *or* envía cariñosos recuerdos; **to ~ sb to sleep/into fits of laughter** dormir/hacer reír a algn; **to ~ sb flying** echar a algn; **to ~ sth flying** tirar algo.
▶**send away** *vt* (*letter, goods*) despachar.
▶**send away for** *vt fus* pedir.
▶**send back** *vt* devolver.
▶**send for** *vt fus* mandar traer; (*by post*) escribir pidiendo algo.
▶**send in** *vt* (*report, application*) mandar.
▶**send off** *vt* (*goods*) despachar; (*BRIT SPORT: player*) expulsar.
▶**send on** *vt* (*letter*) mandar, expedir; (*luggage etc: in advance*) facturar.
▶**send out** *vt* (*invitation*) mandar; (*emit: light, heat*) emitir, difundir; (*: signal*) emitir.
▶**send round** *vt* (*letter, document etc*) hacer circular.
▶**send up** *vt* (*person, price*) hacer subir; (*BRIT: parody*) parodiar.
sender ['sɛndə*] *n* remitente *m/f*.
send-off ['sɛndɔf] *n*: **a good ~** una buena despedida.
send-up ['sɛndʌp] *n* (*col*) parodia, sátira.

Senegal [sɛnɪ'gɔ:l] *n* Senegal *m*.
Senegalese [sɛnɪgə'li:z] *adj, n* senegalés/esa *m/f*.
senile ['si:naɪl] *adj* senil.
senility [sɪ'nɪlɪtɪ] *n* senilidad *f*.
senior ['si:nɪə*] *adj* (*older*) mayor, más viejo; (: *on staff*) más antiguo; (*of higher rank*) superior ♦ *n* mayor *m*; **P. Jones ~** P. Jones padre.
senior citizen *n* persona de la tercera edad.
senior high school *n* (*US*) ≈ instituto de enseñanza media; *see also* **high school**.
seniority [si:nɪ'ɔrɪtɪ] *n* antigüedad *f*; (*in rank*) rango superior.
sensation [sɛn'seɪʃən] *n* (*physical feeling, impression*) sensación *f*.
sensational [sɛn'seɪʃənl] *adj* sensacional.
sense [sɛns] *n* (*faculty, meaning*) sentido; (*feeling*) sensación *f*; (*good ~*) sentido común, juicio ♦ *vt* sentir, percibir; **~ of humour** sentido del humor; **it makes ~** tiene sentido; **there is no ~ in (doing) that** no tiene sentido (hacer) eso; **to come to one's ~s** (*regain consciousness*) volver en sí, recobrar el sentido; **to take leave of one's ~s** perder el juicio.
senseless ['sɛnslɪs] *adj* estúpido, insensato; (*unconscious*) sin conocimiento.
senselessly ['sɛnslɪslɪ] *adv* estúpidamente, insensatamente.
sensibility [sɛnsɪ'bɪlɪtɪ] *n* sensibilidad *f*; **sensibilities** *npl* delicadeza *sg*.
sensible ['sɛnsɪbl] *adj* sensato; (*reasonable*) razonable, lógico.
sensibly ['sɛnsɪblɪ] *adv* sensatamente; razonablemente, de modo lógico.
sensitive ['sɛnsɪtɪv] *adj* sensible; (*touchy*) susceptible; **he is very ~ about it** es muy susceptible acerca de eso.
sensitivity [sɛnsɪ'tɪvɪtɪ] *n* sensibilidad *f*; susceptibilidad *f*.
sensual ['sɛnsjuəl] *adj* sensual.
sensuous ['sɛnsjuəs] *adj* sensual.
sent [sɛnt] *pt, pp of* **send**.
sentence ['sɛntəns] *n* (*LING*) frase *f*, oración *f*; (*LAW*) sentencia, fallo ♦ *vt*: **to ~ sb to death/to 5 years** condenar a algn a muerte/a 5 años de cárcel; **to pass ~ on sb** (*also fig*) sentenciar *or* condenar a algn.
sentiment ['sɛntɪmənt] *n* sentimiento; (*opinion*) opinión *f*.
sentimental [sɛntɪ'mɛntl] *adj* sentimental.
sentimentality [sɛntɪmɛn'tælɪtɪ] *n* sentimentalismo, sensiblería.
sentinel ['sɛntɪnl] *n* centinela *m*.
sentry ['sɛntrɪ] *n* centinela *m*.
sentry duty *n*: **to be on ~** estar de guardia, hacer guardia.
Seoul [səul] *n* Seúl *m*.
separable ['sɛpərəbl] *adj* separable.
separate *adj* ['sɛprɪt] separado; (*distinct*) distinto ♦ (*vb*: ['sɛpəreɪt]) *vt* separar; (*part*) dividir ♦ *vi* separarse; **~ from** separado *or* distinto de; **under ~ cover** (*COMM*) por separado; **to ~ into** dividir *or* separar en; **he is ~d from his wife, but not divorced** está separado de su mujer, pero no (está) divorciado.
separately ['sɛprɪtlɪ] *adv* por separado.
separates ['sɛprɪts] *npl* (*clothes*) coordinados *mpl*.
separation [sɛpə'reɪʃən] *n* separación *f*.
sepia ['si:pɪə] *adj* color sepia *inv*.
Sept. *abbr* (= *September*) sep.
September [sɛp'tɛmbə*] *n* se(p)tiembre *m*.
septic ['sɛptɪk] *adj* séptico; **to go ~** ponerse séptico.
septicaemia, (*US*) **septicemia** [sɛptɪ'si:mɪə] *n* septicemia.
septic tank *n* fosa séptica.
sequel ['si:kwl] *n* consecuencia, resultado; (*of story*) continuación *f*.
sequence ['si:kwəns] *n* sucesión *f*, serie *f*; (*CINE*) secuencia; **in ~** en orden *or* serie.
sequential [sɪ'kwɛnʃəl] *adj*: **~ access** (*COMPUT*) acceso en serie.
sequin ['si:kwɪn] *n* lentejuela.
Serb [sə:b] *adj, n* = **Serbian**.
Serbia ['sə:bɪə] *n* Serbia.
Serbian ['sə:bɪən] *adj* serbio ♦ *n* serbio/a; (*LING*) serbio.
Serbo-Croat ['sə:bəu'krəuæt] *n* (*LING*) serbocroata *m*.
serenade [sɛrə'neɪd] *n* serenata ♦ *vt* dar serenata a.
serene [sɪ'ri:n] *adj* sereno, tranquilo.
serenely [sɪ'ri:nlɪ] *adv* serenamente, tranquilamente.
serenity [sə'rɛnɪtɪ] *n* serenidad *f*, tranquilidad *f*.
sergeant ['sɑ:dʒənt] *n* sargento.
sergeant major *n* sargento mayor.
serial ['sɪərɪəl] *n* novela por entregas; (*TV*) telenovela.
serial access *n* (*COMPUT*) acceso en serie.
serial interface *n* (*COMPUT*) interface *m* en serie.
serialize ['sɪərɪəlaɪz] *vt* publicar/televisar por entregas.
serial killer *n* asesino/a múltiple.
serial number *n* número de serie.
serial printer *n* (*COMPUT*) impresora en serie.
series ['sɪəri:z] *n, pl inv* serie *f*.

serious ['sɪərɪəs] *adj* serio; (*grave*) grave; **are you ~ (about it)?** ¿lo dices en serio?
seriously ['sɪərɪəslɪ] *adv* en serio; (*ill, wounded etc*) gravemente; (*col: extremely*) de verdad; **to take sth/sb ~** tomar algo/a algn en serio; **he's ~ rich** es una pasada de rico.
seriousness ['sɪərɪəsnɪs] *n* seriedad *f*; gravedad *f*.
sermon ['sə:mən] *n* sermón *m*.
serpent ['sə:pənt] *n* serpiente *f*.
serrated [sɪ'reɪtɪd] *adj* serrado, dentellado.
serum ['sɪərəm] *n* suero.
servant ['sə:vənt] *n* (*gen*) servidor(a) *m/f*; (*house* ~) criado/a.
serve [sə:v] *vt* servir; (*customer*) atender; (*subj: train*) tener parada en; (*apprenticeship*) hacer; (*prison term*) cumplir ♦ *vi* (*servant, soldier etc*) servir; (*TENNIS*) sacar ♦ *n* (*TENNIS*) saque *m*; **it ~s him right** se lo merece, se lo tiene merecido; **to ~ a summons on sb** entregar una citación a algn; **it ~s my purpose** me sirve para lo que quiero; **are you being ~d?** ¿le atienden?; **the power station ~s the entire region** la central eléctrica abastece a toda la región; **to ~ as/for/to do** servir de/para/para hacer; **to ~ on a committee/a jury** ser miembro de una comisión/un jurado.
►**serve out, serve up** *vt* (*food*) servir.
service ['sə:vɪs] *n* (*gen*) servicio; (*REL: Catholic*) misa; (*: other*) oficio (religioso); (*AUT*) mantenimiento; (*of dishes*) juego ♦ *vt* (*car, washing machine*) mantener; (*: repair*) reparar; **the S~s** las fuerzas armadas; **funeral ~** exequias *fpl*; **to hold a ~** celebrar un oficio religioso; **the essential ~s** los servicios esenciales; **medical/social ~s** servicios *mpl* médicos/sociales; **the train ~ to London** los trenes a Londres; **to be of ~ to sb** ser útil a algn.
serviceable ['sə:vɪsəbl] *adj* servible, utilizable.
service area *n* (*on motorway*) área de servicios.
service charge *n* (*BRIT*) servicio.
service industries *npl* industrias *fpl* del servicio.
serviceman ['sə:vɪsmən] *n* militar *m*.
service station *n* estación *f* de servicio.
servicing ['sə:vɪsɪŋ] *n* (*of car*) revisión *f*; (*of washing machine etc*) servicio de reparaciones.
serviette [sə:vɪ'ɛt] *n* (*BRIT*) servilleta.
servile ['sə:vaɪl] *adj* servil.
session ['sɛʃən] *n* (*sitting*) sesión *f*; **to be in ~** estar en sesión.
session musician *n* músico *m/f* de estudio.
set [sɛt] *n* juego; (*RADIO*) aparato; (*TV*) televisor *m*; (*of utensils*) batería; (*of cutlery*) cubierto; (*of books*) colección *f*; (*TENNIS*) set *m*; (*group of people*) grupo; (*CINE*) plató *m*; (*THEAT*) decorado; (*HAIRDRESSING*) marcado ♦ *adj* (*fixed*) fijo; (*ready*) listo; (*resolved*) resuelto, decidido ♦ (*vb: pt, pp* **set**) *vt* (*place*) poner, colocar; (*fix*) fijar; (*adjust*) ajustar, arreglar; (*decide: rules etc*) establecer, decidir; (*assign: task*) asignar; (*: homework*) poner ♦ *vi* (*sun*) ponerse; (*jam, jelly*) cuajarse; (*concrete*) fraguar; **a ~ of false teeth** una dentadura postiza; **a ~ of dining-room furniture** muebles *mpl* de comedor; **~ in one's ways** con costumbres arraigadas; **a ~ phrase** una frase hecha; **to be all ~ to do sth** estar listo para hacer algo; **to be ~ on doing sth** estar empeñado en hacer algo; **a novel ~ in Valencia** una novela ambientada en Valencia; **to ~ to music** poner música a; **to ~ on fire** incendiar, prender fuego a; **to ~ free** poner en libertad; **to ~ sth going** poner algo en marcha; **to ~ sail** zarpar, hacerse a la mar.
►**set about** *vt fus*: **to ~ about doing sth** ponerse a hacer algo.
►**set aside** *vt* poner aparte, dejar de lado.
►**set back** *vt* (*progress*): **to ~ back (by)** retrasar (por); **a house ~ back from the road** una casa apartada de la carretera.
►**set down** *vt* (*subj: bus, train*) dejar; (*record*) poner por escrito.
►**set in** *vi* (*infection*) declararse; (*complications*) comenzar; **the rain has ~ in for the day** parece que va a llover todo el día.
►**set off** *vi* partir ♦ *vt* (*bomb*) hacer estallar; (*cause to start*) poner en marcha; (*show up well*) hacer resaltar.
►**set out** *vi*: **to ~ out to do sth** proponerse hacer algo ♦ *vt* (*arrange*) disponer; (*state*) exponer; **to ~ out (from)** salir (de).
►**set up** *vt* (*organization*) establecer.
setback ['sɛtbæk] *n* (*hitch*) revés *m*, contratiempo; (*in health*) recaída.
set menu *n* menú *m*.
set phrase *n* frase *f* hecha.
set square *n* cartabón *m*.
settee [sɛ'ti:] *n* sofá *m*.
setting ['sɛtɪŋ] *n* (*scenery*) marco; (*of jewel*) engaste *m*, montadura.
setting lotion *n* fijador *m* (para el pelo).
settle ['sɛtl] *vt* (*argument, matter*) resolver; (*pay: bill, accounts*) pagar, liquidar; (*colonize: land*) colonizar; (*MED: calm*)

calmar, sosegar ♦ *vi* (*dust etc*) depositarse; (*weather*) estabilizarse; (*also*: ~ **down**) instalarse; (*calm down*) tranquilizarse; **to ~ for sth** convenir en aceptar algo; **to ~ on sth** decidirse por algo; **that's ~d then** bueno, está arreglado; **to ~ one's stomach** asentar el estómago.
►**settle in** *vi* instalarse.
►**settle up** *vi*: **to ~ up with sb** ajustar cuentas con algn.
settlement ['sɛtlmənt] *n* (*payment*) liquidación *f*; (*agreement*) acuerdo, convenio; (*village etc*) poblado; **in ~ of our account** (*COMM*) en pago *or* liquidación de nuestra cuenta.
settler ['sɛtlə*] *n* colono/a, colonizador(a) *m/f*.
setup ['sɛtʌp] *n* sistema *m*.
seven ['sɛvn] *num* siete.
seventeen [sɛvn'tiːn] *num* diez y siete, diecisiete.
seventh ['sɛvnθ] *adj* séptimo.
seventy ['sɛvntɪ] *num* setenta.
sever ['sɛvə*] *vt* cortar; (*relations*) romper.
several ['sɛvərl] *adj, pron* varios/as *m/fpl*, algunos/as *m/fpl*; ~ **of us** varios de nosotros; ~ **times** varias veces.
severance ['sɛvərəns] *n* (*of relations*) ruptura.
severance pay *n* indemnización *f* por despido.
severe [sɪ'vɪə*] *adj* severo; (*serious*) grave; (*hard*) duro; (*pain*) intenso.
severely [sɪ'vɪəlɪ] *adv* severamente; (*wounded, ill*) de gravedad, gravemente.
severity [sɪ'vɛrɪtɪ] *n* severidad *f*; gravedad *f*; intensidad *f*.
Seville [sə'vɪl] *n* Sevilla.
sew, *pt* **sewed**, *pp* **sewn** [səu, səud, səun] *vt, vi* coser.
►**sew up** *vt* coser.
sewage ['suːɪdʒ] *n* (*effluence*) aguas *fpl* residuales; (*system*) alcantarillado.
sewage works *n* estación *f* depuradora (de aguas residuales).
sewer ['suːə*] *n* alcantarilla, cloaca.
sewing ['səuɪŋ] *n* costura.
sewing machine *n* máquina de coser.
sewn [səun] *pp of* **sew**.
sex [sɛks] *n* sexo; **the opposite ~** el sexo opuesto; **to have ~ with sb** tener relaciones (sexuales) con algn.
sex act *n* acto sexual, coito.
sex appeal *n* sex-appeal *m*, gancho.
sex education *n* educación *f* sexual.
sexism ['sɛksɪzəm] *n* sexismo.
sexist ['sɛksɪst] *adj, n* sexista *m/f*.
sex life *n* vida sexual.
sex object *n* objeto sexual.
sextant ['sɛkstənt] *n* sextante *m*.
sextet [sɛks'tɛt] *n* sexteto.
sexual ['sɛksjuəl] *adj* sexual; ~ **assault** atentado contra el pudor; ~ **harassment** acoso sexual; ~ **intercourse** relaciones *fpl* sexuales.
sexually ['sɛksjuəlɪ] *adv* sexualmente.
sexy ['sɛksɪ] *adj* sexy.
Seychelles [seɪ'ʃɛlz] *npl*: **the ~** las Seychelles.
SF *n abbr* = **science fiction**.
SG *n abbr* (*US*: = *Surgeon General*) *jefe del servicio federal de sanidad*.
Sgt *abbr* (= *sergeant*) sgto.
shabbily ['ʃæbɪlɪ] *adv* (*treat*) injustamente; (*dressed*) pobremente.
shabbiness ['ʃæbɪnɪs] *n* (*of dress, person*) aspecto desharrapado; (*of building*) mal estado.
shabby ['ʃæbɪ] *adj* (*person*) desharrapado; (*clothes*) raído, gastado.
shack [ʃæk] *n* choza, chabola.
shackle ['ʃækl] *vt* encadenar; (*fig*): **to be ~d by sth** verse obstaculizado por algo.
shackles ['ʃæklz] *npl* grillos *mpl*, grilletes *mpl*.
shade [ʃeɪd] *n* sombra; (*for lamp*) pantalla; (*for eyes*) visera; (*of colour*) tono *m*, tonalidad *f*; (*US*: *window ~*) persiana ♦ *vt* dar sombra a; **~s** *npl* (*US*: *sunglasses*) gafas *fpl* de sol; **in the ~** a la sombra; (*small quantity*): **a ~ of** un poquito de; **a ~ smaller** un poquito más pequeño.
shadow ['ʃædəu] *n* sombra ♦ *vt* (*follow*) seguir y vigilar; **without** *or* **beyond a ~ of doubt** sin lugar a dudas.
shadow cabinet *n* (*BRIT POL*) gobierno en la oposición.
shadowy ['ʃædəuɪ] *adj* oscuro; (*dim*) indistinto.
shady ['ʃeɪdɪ] *adj* sombreado; (*fig*: *dishonest*) sospechoso; (: *deal*) turbio.
shaft [ʃɑːft] *n* (*of arrow, spear*) astil *m*; (*AUT, TECH*) eje *m*, árbol *m*; (*of mine*) pozo; (*of lift*) hueco, caja; (*of light*) rayo; **ventilator ~** chimenea de ventilación.
shaggy ['ʃægɪ] *adj* peludo.
shake [ʃeɪk] *vb* (*pt* **shook**, *pp* **shaken** [ʃuk, 'ʃeɪkn]) *vt* sacudir; (*building*) hacer temblar; (*perturb*) inquietar, perturbar; (*weaken*) debilitar; (*alarm*) trastornar ♦ *vi* estremecerse; (*tremble*) temblar ♦ *n* (*movement*) sacudida; **to ~ one's head** (*in refusal*) negar con la cabeza; (*in dismay*) mover *or* menear la cabeza, incrédulo; **to ~ hands with sb** estrechar la mano a

algn; **to ~ in one's shoes** (*fig*) temblar de miedo.
▸**shake off** *vt* sacudirse; (*fig*) deshacerse de.
▸**shake up** *vt* agitar.
shake-up ['ʃeɪkʌp] *n* reorganización *f*.
shakily ['ʃeɪkɪlɪ] *adv* (*reply*) con voz temblorosa *or* trémula; (*walk*) con paso vacilante; (*write*) con mano temblorosa.
shaky ['ʃeɪkɪ] *adj* (*unstable*) inestable, poco firme; (*trembling*) tembloroso; (*health*) delicado; (*memory*) defectuoso; (*person*: *from illness*) temblando; (*premise etc*) incierto.
shale [ʃeɪl] *n* esquisto.
shall [ʃæl] *aux vb*: **I ~ go** iré.
shallot [ʃə'lɔt] *n* (*BRIT*) cebollita, chalote *m*.
shallow ['ʃæləu] *adj* poco profundo; (*fig*) superficial.
shallows ['ʃæləuz] *npl* bajío *sg*, bajos *mpl*.
sham [ʃæm] *n* fraude *m*, engaño ♦ *adj* falso, fingido ♦ *vt* fingir, simular.
shambles ['ʃæmblz] *n* desorden *m*, confusión *f*; **the economy is (in) a complete ~** la economía está en un estado desastroso.
shambolic [ʃæm'bɔlɪk] *adj* (*col*) caótico.
shame [ʃeɪm] *n* vergüenza; (*pity*) lástima, pena ♦ *vt* avergonzar; **it is a ~ that/to do** es una lástima *or* pena que/hacer; **what a ~!** ¡qué lástima *or* pena!; **to put sth/sb to ~** (*fig*) ridiculizar algo/a algn.
shamefaced ['ʃeɪmfeɪst] *adj* avergonzado.
shameful ['ʃeɪmful] *adj* vergonzoso.
shamefully ['ʃeɪmfulɪ] *adv* vergonzosamente.
shameless ['ʃeɪmlɪs] *adj* descarado.
shampoo [ʃæm'puː] *n* champú *m* ♦ *vt* lavar con champú.
shampoo and set *n* lavado y marcado.
shamrock ['ʃæmrɔk] *n* trébol *m*.
shandy ['ʃændɪ], (*US*) **shandygaff** ['ʃændɪgæf] *n* clara, cerveza con gaseosa.
shan't [ʃɑːnt] = **shall not**.
shantytown ['ʃæntɪtaun] *n* barrio de chabolas.
SHAPE [ʃeɪp] *n abbr* (= *Supreme Headquarters Allied Powers, Europe*) *cuartel general de las fuerzas aliadas en Europa*.
shape [ʃeɪp] *n* forma ♦ *vt* formar, dar forma a; (*clay*) modelar; (*stone*) labrar; (*sb's ideas*) formar; (*sb's life*) determinar ♦ *vi* (*also*: **~ up**) (*events*) desarrollarse; (*person*) formarse; **to take ~** tomar forma; **to get o.s. into ~** ponerse en forma *or* en condiciones; **in the ~ of a heart** en forma de corazón; **I can't bear gardening in any ~ or form** no aguanto la jardinería de ningún modo.
-shaped *suff*: **heart~** en forma de corazón.
shapeless ['ʃeɪplɪs] *adj* informe, sin forma definida.
shapely ['ʃeɪplɪ] *adj* bien formado *or* proporcionado.
share [ʃɛə*] *n* (*part*) parte *f*, porción *f*; (*contribution*) cuota; (*COMM*) acción *f* ♦ *vt* dividir; (*fig*: *have in common*) compartir; **to have a ~ in the profits** tener una proporción de las ganancias; **he has a 50% ~ in a new business venture** tiene una participación del 50% en un nuevo negocio; **to ~ in** participar en; **to ~ out (among *or* between)** repartir (entre).
share capital *n* (*COMM*) capital *m* social en acciones.
share certificate *n* certificado *or* título de una acción.
shareholder ['ʃɛəhəuldə*] *n* (*BRIT*) accionista *m/f*.
share index *n* (*COMM*) índice *m* de la bolsa.
share issue *n* emisión *f* de acciones.
share price *n* (*COMM*) cotización *f*.
shark [ʃɑːk] *n* tiburón *m*.
sharp [ʃɑːp] *adj* (*razor, knife*) afilado; (*point*) puntiagudo; (*outline*) definido; (*pain*) intenso; (*MUS*) desafinado; (*contrast*) marcado; (*voice*) agudo; (*curve, bend*) cerrado; (*person*: *quick-witted*) avispado; (: *dishonest*) poco escrupuloso ♦ *n* (*MUS*) sostenido ♦ *adv*: **at 2 o'clock ~** a las 2 en punto; **to be ~ with sb** hablar a algn de forma brusca y tajante; **turn ~ left** tuerce del todo a la izquierda.
sharpen ['ʃɑːpn] *vt* afilar; (*pencil*) sacar punta a; (*fig*) agudizar.
sharpener ['ʃɑːpnə*] *n* (*gen*) afilador *m*; (*pencil ~*) sacapuntas *m inv*.
sharp-eyed [ʃɑːp'aɪd] *adj* de vista aguda.
sharpish ['ʃɑːpɪʃ] *adv* (*BRIT col*: *quickly*) prontito, bien pronto.
sharply ['ʃɑːplɪ] *adv* (*abruptly*) bruscamente; (*clearly*) claramente; (*harshly*) severamente.
sharp-tempered [ʃɑːp'tɛmpəd] *adj* de genio arisco.
sharp-witted [ʃɑːp'wɪtɪd] *adj* listo, despabilado.
shatter ['ʃætə*] *vt* hacer añicos *or* pedazos; (*fig*: *ruin*) destruir, acabar con ♦ *vi* hacerse añicos.
shattered ['ʃætəd] *adj* (*grief-stricken*) destrozado, deshecho; (*exhausted*) agotado, hecho polvo.
shattering ['ʃætərɪŋ] *adj* (*experience*) devastador(a), anonadante.
shatterproof ['ʃætəpruːf] *adj* inastillable.

shave [ʃeɪv] *vt* afeitar, rasurar ♦ *vi* afeitarse ♦ *n*: **to have a ~** afeitarse.
shaven ['ʃeɪvn] *adj* (*head*) rapado.
shaver ['ʃeɪvə*] *n* (*also*: **electric ~**) máquina de afeitar (eléctrica).
shaving ['ʃeɪvɪŋ] *n* (*action*) afeitado, **~s** *npl* (*of wood etc*) virutas *fpl*.
shaving brush *n* brocha (de afeitar).
shaving cream *n* crema (de afeitar).
shaving point *n* enchufe *m* para máquinas de afeitar.
shaving soap *n* jabón *m* de afeitar.
shawl [ʃɔːl] *n* chal *m*.
she [ʃiː] *pron* ella; **there ~ is** allí está; **~-cat** gata; *NB*: *for ships, countries follow the gender of your translation*.
sheaf, *pl* **sheaves** [ʃiːf, ʃiːvz] *n* (*of corn*) gavilla; (*of arrows*) haz *m*; (*of papers*) fajo.
shear [ʃɪə*] *vt* (*pt* **~ed**, *pp* **~ed** *or* **shorn** [ʃɔːn]) (*sheep*) esquilar, trasquilar.
▸**shear off** *vi* romperse.
shears ['ʃɪəz] *npl* (*for hedge*) tijeras *fpl* de jardín.
sheath [ʃiːθ] *n* vaina; (*contraceptive*) preservativo.
sheath knife *n* cuchillo de monte.
sheaves [ʃiːvz] *npl of* **sheaf**.
shed [ʃɛd] *n* cobertizo; (*INDUSTRY, RAIL*) nave *f* ♦ *vt* (*pt, pp* **shed**) (*skin*) mudar; (*tears*) derramar; **to ~ light on** (*problem, mystery*) aclarar, arrojar luz sobre.
she'd [ʃiːd] = **she had, she would**.
sheen [ʃiːn] *n* brillo, lustre *m*.
sheep [ʃiːp] *n* (*pl inv*) oveja.
sheepdog ['ʃiːpdɔg] *n* perro pastor.
sheep farmer *n* ganadero (de ovejas).
sheepish ['ʃiːpɪʃ] *adj* tímido, vergonzoso.
sheepskin ['ʃiːpskɪn] *n* piel *f* de carnero.
sheepskin jacket *n* zamarra.
sheer [ʃɪə*] *adj* (*utter*) puro, completo; (*steep*) escarpado; (*material*) diáfano ♦ *adv* verticalmente; **by ~ chance** de pura casualidad.
sheet [ʃiːt] *n* (*on bed*) sábana; (*of paper*) hoja; (*of glass, metal*) lámina.
sheet feed *n* (*on printer*) alimentador *m* de papel.
sheet lightning *n* relámpago (difuso).
sheet metal *n* metal *m* en lámina.
sheet music *n* hojas *fpl* de partitura.
sheik(h) [ʃeɪk] *n* jeque *m*.
shelf, *pl* **shelves** [ʃɛlf, ʃɛlvz] *n* estante *m*.
shelf life *n* (*COMM*) periodo de conservación antes de la venta.
shell [ʃɛl] *n* (*on beach*) concha, caracol (*LAM*); (*of egg, nut etc*) cáscara; (*explosive*) proyectil *m*, obús *m*; (*of building*) armazón *m* ♦ *vt* (*peas*) desenvainar; (*MIL*) bombardear.
▸**shell out** *vi* (*col*): **to ~ out (for)** soltar el dinero (para), desembolsar (para).
she'll [ʃiːl] = **she will, she shall**.
shellfish ['ʃɛlfɪʃ] *n* (*pl inv*) crustáceo; (*pl*: *as food*) mariscos *mpl*.
shellsuit ['ʃɛlsuːt] *n* chándal *m* (de tactel ®).
shelter ['ʃɛltə*] *n* abrigo, refugio ♦ *vt* (*aid*) amparar, proteger; (*give lodging to*) abrigar; (*hide*) esconder ♦ *vi* abrigarse, refugiarse; **to take ~ (from)** refugiarse *or* asilarse (de); **bus ~** parada de autobús cubierta.
sheltered ['ʃɛltəd] *adj* (*life*) protegido; (*spot*) abrigado.
shelve [ʃɛlv] *vt* (*fig*) dar carpetazo a.
shelves [ʃɛlvz] *npl of* **shelf**.
shelving ['ʃɛlvɪŋ] *n* estantería.
shepherd ['ʃɛpəd] *n* pastor *m* ♦ *vt* (*guide*) guiar, conducir.
shepherdess ['ʃɛpədɪs] *n* pastora.
shepherd's pie *n pastel de carne y puré de patatas*.
sherbert ['ʃəːbət] *n* (*BRIT*: *powder*) polvos *mpl* azucarados; (*US*: *water ice*) sorbete *m*.
sheriff ['ʃɛrɪf] *n* (*US*) sheriff *m*.
sherry ['ʃɛrɪ] *n* jerez *m*.
she's [ʃiːz] = **she is, she has**.
Shetland ['ʃɛtlənd] *n* (*also*: **the ~s, the ~ Isles**) las Islas *fpl* Shetland.
Shetland pony *n* pony *m* de Shetland.
shield [ʃiːld] *n* escudo; (*TECH*) blindaje *m* ♦ *vt*: **to ~ (from)** proteger (de).
shift [ʃɪft] *n* (*change*) cambio; (*at work*) turno ♦ *vt* trasladar; (*remove*) quitar ♦ *vi* moverse; (*change place*) cambiar de sitio; **the wind has ~ed to the south** el viento ha virado al sur; **a ~ in demand** (*COMM*) un desplazamiento de la demanda.
shift key *n* (*on typewriter*) tecla de mayúsculas.
shiftless ['ʃɪftlɪs] *adj* (*person*) vago.
shift work *n* (*BRIT*) trabajo por turnos; **to do ~** trabajar por turnos.
shifty ['ʃɪftɪ] *adj* tramposo; (*eyes*) furtivo.
Shiite ['ʃiːaɪt] *adj, n* shiíta *m/f*.
shilling ['ʃɪlɪŋ] *n* (*BRIT*) chelín *m* (= *12 old pence*; *20 in a pound*).
shilly-shally ['ʃɪlɪʃælɪ] *vi* titubear, vacilar.
shimmer ['ʃɪmə*] *n* reflejo trémulo ♦ *vi* relucir.
shimmering ['ʃɪmərɪŋ] *adj* reluciente; (*haze*) trémulo; (*satin etc*) lustroso.
shin [ʃɪn] *n* espinilla ♦ *vi*: **to ~ down/up a tree** bajar de/trepar un árbol.
shindig ['ʃɪndɪg] *n* (*col*) fiesta, juerga.
shine [ʃaɪn] *n* brillo, lustre *m* ♦ (*vb*: *pt, pp*

shone [ʃɔn]) *vi* brillar, relucir ♦ *vt* (*shoes*) lustrar, sacar brillo a; **to ~ a torch on sth** dirigir una linterna hacia algo.
shingle ['ʃɪŋgl] *n* (*on beach*) guijarras *fpl*.
shingles ['ʃɪŋglz] *n* (*MED*) herpes *msg*.
shining ['ʃaɪnɪŋ] *adj* (*surface, hair*) lustroso; (*light*) brillante.
shiny ['ʃaɪnɪ] *adj* brillante, lustroso.
ship [ʃɪp] *n* buque *m*, barco ♦ *vt* (*goods*) embarcar; (*oars*) desarmar; (*send*) transportar *or* enviar por vía marítima; **~'s manifest** manifiesto del buque; **on board ~** a bordo.
shipbuilder ['ʃɪpbɪldə*] *n* constructor(a) *m/f* naval.
shipbuilding ['ʃɪpbɪldɪŋ] *n* construcción *f* naval.
ship canal *n* canal *m* de navegación.
ship chandler [-'tʃɑːndlə*] *n* proveedor *m* de efectos navales.
shipment ['ʃɪpmənt] *n* (*act*) embarque *m*; (*goods*) envío.
shipowner ['ʃɪpəunə*] *n* naviero, armador *m*.
shipper ['ʃɪpə*] *n* compañía naviera.
shipping ['ʃɪpɪŋ] *n* (*act*) embarque *m*; (*traffic*) buques *mpl*.
shipping agent *n* agente *m/f* marítimo/a.
shipping company *n* compañía naviera.
shipping lane *n* ruta de navegación.
shipping line *n* = **shipping company**.
shipshape ['ʃɪpʃeɪp] *adj* en buen orden.
shipwreck ['ʃɪprɛk] *n* naufragio ♦ *vt*: **to be ~ed** naufragar.
shipyard ['ʃɪpjɑːd] *n* astillero.
shire ['ʃaɪə*] *n* (*BRIT*) condado.
shirk [ʃəːk] *vt* eludir, esquivar; (*obligations*) faltar a.
shirt [ʃəːt] *n* camisa; **in ~ sleeves** en mangas de camisa.
shirty ['ʃəːtɪ] *adj* (*BRIT col*): **to be ~** estar de malas pulgas.
shit [ʃɪt] (*col!*) *n* mierda; (*nonsense*) chorradas *fpl*; **to be a ~** ser un cabrón ♦ *excl* ¡mierda!; **tough ~!** ¡te jodes!
shiver ['ʃɪvə*] *vi* temblar, estremecerse; (*with cold*) tiritar.
shoal [ʃəul] *n* (*of fish*) banco.
shock [ʃɔk] *n* (*impact*) choque *m*; (*ELEC*) descarga (eléctrica); (*emotional*) conmoción *f*; (*start*) sobresalto, susto; (*MED*) postración *f* nerviosa ♦ *vt* dar un susto a; (*offend*) escandalizar; **to get a ~** (*ELEC*) sentir una sacudida eléctrica; **to give sb a ~** dar un susto a algn; **to be suffering from ~** padecer una postración nerviosa; **it came as a ~ to hear that ...** me (*etc*) asombró descubrir que ....
shock absorber [-əbsɔːbə*] *n* amortiguador *m*.
shocker ['ʃɔkə*] *n* (*col*): **it was a real ~** fue muy fuerte.
shocking ['ʃɔkɪŋ] *adj* (*awful*: *weather, handwriting*) espantoso, horrible; (*improper*) escandaloso; (*result*) inesperado.
shock therapy, shock treatment *n* (*MED*) terapia de choque.
shock wave *n* onda expansiva *or* de choque.
shod [ʃɔd] *pt, pp of* **shoe** ♦ *adj* calzado.
shoddiness ['ʃɔdɪnɪs] *n* baja calidad *f*.
shoddy ['ʃɔdɪ] *adj* de pacotilla.
shoe [ʃuː] *n* zapato; (*for horse*) herradura; (*brake ~*) zapata ♦ *vt* (*pt, pp* **shod** [ʃɔd]) (*horse*) herrar.
shoebrush ['ʃuːbrʌʃ] *n* cepillo para zapatos.
shoehorn ['ʃuːhɔːn] *n* calzador *m*.
shoelace ['ʃuːleɪs] *n* cordón *m*.
shoemaker ['ʃuːmeɪkə*] *n* zapatero/a.
shoe polish *n* betún *m*.
shoeshop ['ʃuːʃɔp] *n* zapatería.
shoestring ['ʃuːstrɪŋ] *n* (*shoelace*) cordón *m*; (*fig*): **on a ~** con muy poco dinero, a lo barato.
shone [ʃɔn] *pt, pp of* **shine**.
shoo [ʃuː] *excl* ¡fuera!; (*to animals*) ¡zape! ♦ *vt* (*also*: **~ away, ~ off**) ahuyentar.
shook [ʃuk] *pt of* **shake**.
shoot [ʃuːt] *n* (*on branch, seedling*) retoño, vástago; (*shooting party*) cacería; (*competition*) concurso de tiro; (*preserve*) coto de caza ♦ (*vb*: *pt, pp* **shot** [ʃɔt]) *vt* disparar; (*kill*) matar a tiros; (*execute*) fusilar; (*CINE*: *film, scene*) rodar, filmar ♦ *vi* (*FOOTBALL*) chutar; **to ~ (at)** tirar (a); **to ~ past** pasar como un rayo; **to ~ in/out** *vi* entrar corriendo/salir disparado.
▸**shoot down** *vt* (*plane*) derribar.
▸**shoot up** *vi* (*prices*) dispararse.
shooting ['ʃuːtɪŋ] *n* (*shots*) tiros *mpl*, tiroteo; (*HUNTING*) caza con escopeta; (*act*: *murder*) asesinato (a tiros); (*CINE*) rodaje *m*.
shooting star *n* estrella fugaz.
shop [ʃɔp] *n* tienda; (*workshop*) taller *m* ♦ *vi* (*also*: **go ~ping**) ir de compras; **to talk ~** (*fig*) hablar del trabajo; **repair ~** taller *m* de reparaciones.
▸**shop around** *vi* comparar precios.
shopaholic ['ʃɔpə'hɔlɪk] *n* (*col*) adicto/a a las compras.
shop assistant *n* (*BRIT*) dependiente/a *m/f*.
shop floor *n* (*BRIT fig*) taller *m*, fábrica.

shopkeeper ['ʃɔpkiːpə*] *n* (*BRIT*) tendero/a.
shoplift ['ʃɔplɪft] *vi* robar en las tiendas.
shoplifter ['ʃɔplɪftə*] *n* ratero/a.
shoplifting ['ʃɔplɪftɪŋ] *n* ratería, robo (en las tiendas).
shopper ['ʃɔpə*] *n* comprador(a) *m/f*.
shopping ['ʃɔpɪŋ] *n* (*goods*) compras *fpl*.
shopping bag *n* bolsa (de compras).
shopping centre, (*US*) **shopping center** *n* centro comercial.
shopping mall *n* centro comercial.
shop-soiled ['ʃɔpsɔɪld] *adj* (*BRIT*) deteriorado.
shop steward *n* (*BRIT INDUSTRY*) enlace *m/f* sindical.
shop window *n* escaparate *m*, vidriera (*LAM*).
shopworn ['ʃɔpwɔːn] *adj* (*US*) usado.
shore [ʃɔː*] *n* (*of sea, lake*) orilla ♦ *vt*: **to ~ (up)** reforzar; **on ~** en tierra.
shore leave *n* (*NAUT*) permiso para bajar a tierra.
shorn [ʃɔːn] *pp of* **shear**.
short [ʃɔːt] *adj* (*not long*) corto; (*in time*) breve, de corta duración; (*person*) bajo; (*curt*) brusco, seco ♦ *vi* (*ELEC*) ponerse en cortocircuito ♦ *n* (*also*: **~ film**) cortometraje *m*; **(a pair of) ~s** (unos) pantalones *mpl* cortos; **to be ~ of sth** estar falto de algo; **in ~** en pocas palabras; **a ~ time ago** hace poco (tiempo); **in the ~ term** a corto plazo; **to be in ~ supply** escasear, haber escasez de; **I'm ~ of time** me falta tiempo; **~ of doing...** a menos que hagamos *etc*...; **everything ~ of...** todo menos...; **it is ~ for** es la forma abreviada de; **to cut ~** (*speech, visit*) interrumpir, terminar inesperadamente; **to fall ~ of** no alcanzar; **to run ~ of sth** acabársele algo; **to stop ~** parar en seco; **to stop ~ of** detenerse antes de.
shortage ['ʃɔːtɪdʒ] *n* escasez *f*, falta.
shortbread ['ʃɔːtbrɛd] *n pasta de mantequilla*.
short-change [ʃɔːt'tʃeɪndʒ] *vt*: **to ~ sb** no dar el cambio completo a algn.
short-circuit [ʃɔːt'səːkɪt] *n* cortocircuito ♦ *vt* poner en cortocircuito ♦ *vi* ponerse en cortocircuito.
shortcoming ['ʃɔːtkʌmɪŋ] *n* defecto, deficiencia.
short(crust) pastry ['ʃɔːt(krʌst)-] *n* (*BRIT*) pasta quebradiza.
shortcut ['ʃɔːtkʌt] *n* atajo.
shorten ['ʃɔːtn] *vt* acortar; (*visit*) interrumpir.
shortfall ['ʃɔːtfɔːl] *n* déficit *m*, deficiencia.
shorthand ['ʃɔːthænd] *n* (*BRIT*) taquigrafía; **to take sth down in ~** taquigrafiar algo.
shorthand notebook *n* cuaderno de taquigrafía.
shorthand typist *n* (*BRIT*) taquimecanógrafo/a.
short list *n* (*BRIT*: *for job*) lista de candidatos pre-seleccionados.
short-lived ['ʃɔːt'lɪvd] *adj* efímero.
shortly ['ʃɔːtlɪ] *adv* en breve, dentro de poco.
shortness ['ʃɔːtnɪs] *n* (*of distance*) cortedad *f*; (*of time*) brevedad *f*; (*manner*) brusquedad *f*.
short-sighted [ʃɔːt'saɪtɪd] *adj* (*BRIT*) miope, corto de vista; (*fig*) imprudente.
short-sightedness [ʃɔːt'saɪtɪdnɪs] *n* miopía; (*fig*) falta de previsión, imprudencia.
short-staffed [ʃɔːt'stɑːft] *adj* falto de personal.
short story *n* cuento.
short-tempered [ʃɔːt'tɛmpəd] *adj* enojadizo.
short-term ['ʃɔːttəːm] *adj* (*effect*) a corto plazo.
short time *n*: **to work ~, be on ~** (*INDUSTRY*) trabajar con sistema de horario reducido.
short-time working ['ʃɔːttaɪm-] *n* trabajo de horario reducido.
short wave *n* (*RADIO*) onda corta.
shot [ʃɔt] *pt, pp of* **shoot** ♦ *n* (*sound*) tiro, disparo; (*person*) tirador(a) *m/f*; (*try*) tentativa; (*injection*) inyección *f*; (*PHOT*) toma, fotografía; (*shotgun pellets*) perdigones *mpl*; **to fire a ~ at sb/sth** tirar *or* disparar contra algn/algo; **to have a ~ at (doing) sth** probar suerte con algo; **like a ~** (*without any delay*) como un rayo; **a big ~** (*col*) un pez gordo; **to get ~ of sth/sb** (*col*) deshacerse de algo/algn, quitarse algo/a algn de encima.
shotgun ['ʃɔtgʌn] *n* escopeta.
should [ʃud] *aux vb*: **I ~ go now** debo irme ahora; **he ~ be there now** debe de haber llegado (ya); **I ~ go if I were you** yo en tu lugar me iría; **I ~ like to** me gustaría; **~ he phone** ... si llamara ..., en caso de que llamase ....
shoulder ['ʃəuldə*] *n* hombro; (*BRIT*: *of road*): **hard ~** arcén *m* ♦ *vt* (*fig*) cargar con; **to look over one's ~** mirar hacia atrás; **to rub ~s with sb** (*fig*) codearse con algn; **to give sb the cold ~** (*fig*) dar de lado a algn.
shoulder blade *n* omóplato.
shoulder bag *n* bolso de bandolera.
shoulder strap *n* tirante *m*.
shouldn't ['ʃudnt] = **should not**.

shout [ʃaut] *n* grito ♦ *vt* gritar ♦ *vi* gritar, dar voces.
▸**shout down** *vt* hundir a gritos.
shouting ['ʃautɪŋ] *n* griterío.
shouting match *n* (*col*) discusión *f* a voz en grito.
shove [ʃʌv] *n* empujón *m* ♦ *vt* empujar; (*col*: *put*): **to ~ sth in** meter algo a empellones; **he ~d me out of the way** me quitó de en medio de un empujón.
▸**shove off** *vi* (*NAUT*) alejarse del muelle; (*fig*: *col*) largarse.
shovel ['ʃʌvl] *n* pala; (*mechanical*) excavadora ♦ *vt* mover con pala.
show [ʃəu] *n* (*of emotion*) demostración *f*; (*semblance*) apariencia; (*COMM, TECH*: *exhibition*) exhibición *f*, exposición *f*; (*THEAT*) función *f*, espectáculo; (*organization*) negocio, empresa ♦ *vb* (*pt* **showed,** *pp* **shown** [ʃəun]) *vt* mostrar, enseñar; (*courage etc*) mostrar, manifestar; (*exhibit*) exponer; (*film*) proyectar ♦ *vi* mostrarse; (*appear*) aparecer; **on ~** (*exhibits etc*) expuesto; **to be on ~** estar expuesto; **it's just for ~** es sólo para impresionar; **to ask for a ~ of hands** pedir una votación a mano alzada; **who's running the ~ here?** ¿quién manda aquí?; **to ~ a profit/loss** (*COMM*) arrojar un saldo positivo/negativo; **I have nothing to ~ for it** no saqué ningún provecho (de ello); **to ~ sb to his seat/to the door** acompañar a algn a su asiento/a la puerta; **as ~n in the illustration** como se ve en el grabado; **it just goes to ~ that ...** queda demostrado que ...; **it doesn't ~** no se ve *or* nota.
▸**show in** *vt* (*person*) hacer pasar.
▸**show off** *vi* (*pej*) presumir ♦ *vt* (*display*) lucir; (*pej*) hacer alarde de.
▸**show out** *vt*: **to ~ sb out** acompañar a algn a la puerta.
▸**show up** *vi* (*stand out*) destacar; (*col*: *turn up*) presentarse ♦ *vt* descubrir; (*unmask*) desenmascarar.
showbiz ['ʃəubɪz] *n* (*col*) = **show business.**
show business *n* el mundo del espectáculo.
showcase ['ʃəukeɪs] *n* vitrina; (*fig*) escaparate *m*.
showdown ['ʃəudaun] *n* enfrentamiento *m*.
shower ['ʃauə*] *n* (*rain*) chaparrón *m*, chubasco; (*of stones etc*) lluvia; (*also*: **~ bath**) ducha ♦ *vi* llover ♦ *vt*: **to ~ sb with sth** colmar a algn de algo; **to have** *or* **take a ~** ducharse.
shower cap *n* gorro de baño.
showerproof ['ʃauəpru:f] *adj* impermeable.
showery ['ʃauərɪ] *adj* (*weather*) lluvioso.
showground ['ʃəugraund] *n* ferial *m*, real *m* (de la feria).
showing ['ʃəuɪŋ] *n* (*of film*) proyección *f*.
show jumping *n* hípica.
showman ['ʃəumən] *n* (*at fair, circus*) empresario (de espectáculos); (*fig*) actor *m* consumado.
showmanship ['ʃəumənʃɪp] *n* dotes *fpl* teatrales.
shown [ʃəun] *pp of* **show.**
show-off ['ʃəuɔf] *n* (*col*: *person*) fantasmón/ona *m/f*.
showpiece ['ʃəupi:s] *n* (*of exhibition etc*) objeto más valioso, joya; **that hospital is a ~** ese hospital es un modelo del género.
showroom ['ʃəuru:m] *n* sala de muestras.
show trial *n* juicio propagandístico.
showy ['ʃəuɪ] *adj* ostentoso.
shrank [ʃræŋk] *pt of* **shrink.**
shrapnel ['ʃræpnl] *n* metralla.
shred [ʃrɛd] *n* (*gen pl*) triza, jirón *m*; (*fig*: *of truth, evidence*) pizca, chispa ♦ *vt* hacer trizas; (*documents*) triturar; (*CULIN*) desmenuzar.
shredder ['ʃrɛdə*] *n* (*vegetable ~*) picadora; (*document ~*) trituradora (de papel).
shrewd [ʃru:d] *adj* astuto.
shrewdly ['ʃru:dlɪ] *adv* astutamente.
shrewdness ['ʃru:dnɪs] *n* astucia.
shriek [ʃri:k] *n* chillido ♦ *vt, vi* chillar.
shrill [ʃrɪl] *adj* agudo, estridente.
shrimp [ʃrɪmp] *n* camarón *m*.
shrine [ʃraɪn] *n* santuario, sepulcro.
shrink, *pt* **shrank,** *pp* **shrunk** [ʃrɪŋk, ʃræŋk, ʃrʌŋk] *vi* encogerse; (*be reduced*) reducirse ♦ *vt* encoger; **to ~ from (doing) sth** no atreverse a hacer algo.
▸**shrink away** *vi* retroceder, retirarse.
shrinkage ['ʃrɪŋkɪdʒ] *n* encogimiento; reducción *f*; (*COMM*: *in shops*) pérdidas *fpl*.
shrink-wrap ['ʃrɪŋkræp] *vt* empaquetar en envase termoretráctil.
shrivel ['ʃrɪvl] (*also*: **~ up**) *vt* (*dry*) secar; (*crease*) arrugar ♦ *vi* secarse; arrugarse.
shroud [ʃraud] *n* sudario ♦ *vt*: **~ed in mystery** envuelto en el misterio.
Shrove Tuesday ['ʃrəuv-] *n* martes *m* de carnaval.
shrub [ʃrʌb] *n* arbusto.
shrubbery ['ʃrʌbərɪ] *n* arbustos *mpl*.
shrug [ʃrʌg] *n* encogimiento de hombros ♦ *vt, vi*: **to ~ (one's shoulders)** encogerse de hombros.
▸**shrug off** *vt* negar importancia a; (*cold, illness*) deshacerse de.

shrunk [ʃrʌŋk] *pp of* **shrink**.
shrunken ['ʃrʌŋkn] *adj* encogido.
shudder ['ʃʌdə*] *n* estremecimiento, escalofrío ♦ *vi* estremecerse.
shuffle ['ʃʌfl] *vt* (*cards*) barajar; **to ~ (one's feet)** arrastrar los pies.
shun [ʃʌn] *vt* rehuir, esquivar.
shunt [ʃʌnt] *vt* (*RAIL*) maniobrar.
shunting yard ['ʃʌntɪŋ-] *n* estación *f* de maniobras.
shut, *pt, pp* **shut** [ʃʌt] *vt* cerrar ♦ *vi* cerrarse.
▸**shut down** *vt, vi* cerrar; (*machine*) parar.
▸**shut off** *vt* (*stop: power, water supply etc*) interrumpir, cortar; (*: engine*) parar.
▸**shut out** *vt* (*person*) excluir, dejar fuera; (*noise, cold*) no dejar entrar; (*block: view*) tapar; (*: memory*) tratar de olvidar.
▸**shut up** *vi* (*col: keep quiet*) callarse ♦ *vt* (*close*) cerrar; (*silence*) callar.
shutdown ['ʃʌtdaun] *n* cierre *m*.
shutter ['ʃʌtə*] *n* contraventana; (*PHOT*) obturador *m*.
shuttle ['ʃʌtl] *n* lanzadera; (*also*: **~ service**: *AVIAT*) puente *m* aéreo ♦ *vi* (*subj: vehicle, person*) ir y venir ♦ *vt* (*passengers*) transportar, trasladar.
shuttlecock ['ʃʌtlkɔk] *n* volante *m*.
shuttle diplomacy *n* viajes *mpl* diplomáticos.
shy [ʃaɪ] *adj* tímido ♦ *vi*: **to ~ away from doing sth** (*fig*) rehusar hacer algo; **to be ~ of doing sth** esquivar hacer algo.
shyly ['ʃaɪlɪ] *adv* tímidamente.
shyness ['ʃaɪnɪs] *n* timidez *f*.
Siam [saɪ'æm] *n* Siam *m*.
Siamese [saɪə'mi:z] *adj* siamés/esa ♦ *n* (*person*) siamés/esa *m/f*; (*LING*) siamés *m*; **~ cat** gato siamés; **~ twins** gemelos/as *m/fpl* siameses/as.
Siberia [saɪ'bɪərɪə] *n* Siberia.
sibling ['sɪblɪŋ] *n* (*formal*) hermano/a.
Sicilian [sɪ'sɪlɪən] *adj, n* siciliano/a *m/f*.
Sicily ['sɪsɪlɪ] *n* Sicilia.
sick [sɪk] *adj* (*ill*) enfermo; (*nauseated*) mareado; (*humour*) morboso; **to be ~** (*BRIT*) vomitar; **to feel ~** estar mareado; **to be ~ of** (*fig*) estar harto de; **a ~ person** un(a) enfermo/a; **to be (off) ~** estar ausente por enfermedad; **to fall** *or* **take ~** ponerse enfermo.
sickbag ['sɪkbæg] *n* bolsa para el mareo.
sick bay *n* enfermería.
sickbed ['sɪkbɛd] *n* lecho de enfermo.
sick building syndrome *n enfermedad causada por falta de ventilación y luz natural en un edificio.*
sicken ['sɪkn] *vt* dar asco a ♦ *vi* enfermar; **to be ~ing for** (*cold, flu etc*) mostrar síntomas de.
sickening ['sɪknɪŋ] *adj* (*fig*) asqueroso.
sickle ['sɪkl] *n* hoz *f*.
sick leave *n* baja por enfermedad.
sickle-cell anaemia ['sɪklsɛl-] *n* anemia de células falciformes, drepanocitosis *f*.
sick list *n*: **to be on the ~** estar de baja.
sickly ['sɪklɪ] *adj* enfermizo; (*taste*) empalagoso.
sickness ['sɪknɪs] *n* enfermedad *f*, mal *m*; (*vomiting*) náuseas *fpl*.
sickness benefit *n* subsidio de enfermedad.
sick pay *n prestación por enfermedad pagada por la empresa.*
sickroom ['sɪkru:m] *n* cuarto del enfermo.
side [saɪd] *n* (*gen*) lado; (*face, surface*) cara; (*of paper*) cara; (*slice of bread*) rebanada; (*of body*) costado; (*of animal*) ijar *m*, ijada; (*of lake*) orilla; (*part*) lado; (*aspect*) aspecto; (*team: SPORT*) equipo; (*: POL etc*) partido; (*of hill*) ladera ♦ *adj* (*door, entrance*) lateral ♦ *vi*: **to ~ with sb** ponerse de parte de algn; **by the ~ of** al lado de; **~ by ~** juntos/as; **from all ~s** de todos lados; **to take ~s (with)** tomar partido (por); **~ of beef** flanco de vaca; **the right/wrong ~** el derecho/revés; **from ~ to ~** de un lado a otro.
sideboard ['saɪdbɔ:d] *n* aparador *m*.
sideboards ['saɪdbɔ:dz] (*BRIT*), **sideburns** ['saɪdbə:nz] *npl* patillas *fpl*.
sidecar ['saɪdkɑ:*] *n* sidecar *m*.
side dish *n* entremés *m*.
side drum *n* (*MUS*) tamboril *m*.
side effect *n* efecto secundario.
sidekick ['saɪdkɪk] *n* compinche *m*.
sidelight ['saɪdlaɪt] *n* (*AUT*) luz *f* lateral.
sideline ['saɪdlaɪn] *n* (*SPORT*) línea lateral; (*fig*) empleo suplementario.
sidelong ['saɪdlɔŋ] *adj* de soslayo; **to give a ~ glance at sth** mirar algo de reojo.
side plate *n* platito.
side road *n* (*BRIT*) calle *f* lateral.
sidesaddle ['saɪdsædl] *adv* a la amazona.
side show *n* (*stall*) caseta; (*fig*) atracción *f* secundaria.
sidestep ['saɪdstɛp] *vt* (*question*) eludir; (*problem*) esquivar ♦ *vi* (*BOXING etc*) dar un quiebro.
side street *n* calle *f* lateral.
sidetrack ['saɪdtræk] *vt* (*fig*) desviar (de su propósito).
sidewalk ['saɪdwɔ:k] *n* (*US*) acera, vereda (*LAM*), andén *m* (*LAM*), banqueta (*LAM*).
sideways ['saɪdweɪz] *adv* de lado.
siding ['saɪdɪŋ] *n* (*RAIL*) apartadero, vía muerta.

sidle ['saɪdl] *vi*: **to ~ up (to)** acercarse furtivamente (a).

SIDS [sɪdz] *n abbr* (= *sudden infant death syndrome*) (síndrome *m* de la) muerte *f* súbita.

siege [si:dʒ] *n* cerco, sitio; **to lay ~ to** cercar, sitiar.

siege economy *n* economía de sitio *or* de asedio.

Sierra Leone [sɪ'ɛrəlɪ'əun] *n* Sierra Leona.

siesta [sɪ'ɛstə] *n* siesta.

sieve [sɪv] *n* colador *m* ♦ *vt* cribar.

sift [sɪft] *vt* cribar ♦ *vi*: **to ~ through** pasar por una criba; (*information*) analizar cuidadosamente.

sigh [saɪ] *n* suspiro ♦ *vi* suspirar.

sight [saɪt] *n* (*faculty*) vista; (*spectacle*) espectáculo; (*on gun*) mira, alza ♦ *vt* ver, divisar; **in ~** a la vista; **out of ~** fuera de (la) vista; **at ~** a la vista; **at first ~** a primera vista; **to lose ~ of sth/sb** perder algo/a algn de vista; **to catch ~ of sth/sb** divisar algo/a algn; **I know her by ~** la conozco de vista; **to set one's ~s on (doing) sth** aspirar a *or* ambicionar (hacer) algo.

sighted ['saɪtɪd] *adj* vidente, de vista normal; **partially ~** de vista limitada.

sightseer ['saɪtsi:ə*] *n* excursionista *m/f*, turista *m/f*.

sightseeing ['saɪtsi:ɪŋ] *n* excursionismo, turismo; **to go ~** visitar monumentos.

sign [saɪn] *n* (*with hand*) señal *f*, seña; (*trace*) huella, rastro; (*notice*) letrero; (*written*) signo; (*road ~*) indicador *m*; (: *with instructions*) señal *f* de tráfico ♦ *vt* firmar; **as a ~ of** en señal de; **it's a good/bad ~** es buena/mala señal; **plus/minus ~** signo de más/de menos; **to ~ one's name** firmar.

▸**sign away** *vt* (*rights etc*) ceder.

▸**sign off** *vi* (*RADIO, TV*) cerrar el programa.

▸**sign on** *vi* (*MIL*) alistarse; (*as unemployed*) apuntarse al paro; (*employee*) firmar un contrato ♦ *vt* (*MIL*) alistar; (*employee*) contratar; **to ~ on for a course** matricularse en un curso.

▸**sign out** *vi* firmar el registro (al salir).

▸**sign over** *vt*: **to ~ sth over to sb** traspasar algo a algn.

▸**sign up** *vi* (*MIL*) alistarse ♦ *vt* (*contract*) contratar.

signal ['sɪgnl] *n* señal *f* ♦ *vi* (*AUT*) señalizar ♦ *vt* (*person*) hacer señas a; (*message*) transmitir; **the engaged ~** (*TEL*) la señal de comunicando; **the ~ is very weak** (*TV*) no captamos bien el canal; **to ~ a left/right turn** (*AUT*) indicar que se va a doblar a la izquierda/derecha; **to ~ to sb (to do sth)** hacer señas a algn (para que haga algo).

signal box *n* (*RAIL*) garita de señales.

signalman ['sɪgnlmən] *n* (*RAIL*) guardavía *m*.

signatory ['sɪgnətərɪ] *n* firmante *m/f*.

signature ['sɪgnətʃə*] *n* firma.

signature tune *n* sintonía.

signet ring ['sɪgnət-] *n* (anillo de) sello.

significance [sɪg'nɪfɪkəns] *n* significado; (*importance*) trascendencia; **that is of no ~** eso no tiene importancia.

significant [sɪg'nɪfɪkənt] *adj* significativo; trascendente; **it is ~ that ...** es significativo que ....

significantly [sɪg'nɪfɪkəntlɪ] *adv* (*smile*) expresivamente; (*improve, increase*) sensiblemente; **and, ~ ...** y debe notarse que ....

signify ['sɪgnɪfaɪ] *vt* significar.

sign language *n* mímica, lenguaje *m* por *or* de señas.

signpost ['saɪnpəust] *n* indicador *m*.

silage ['saɪlɪdʒ] *n* ensilaje *m*.

silence ['saɪlns] *n* silencio ♦ *vt* hacer callar; (*guns*) reducir al silencio.

silencer ['saɪlnsə*] *n* (*on gun, BRIT AUT*) silenciador *m*.

silent ['saɪlnt] *adj* (*gen*) silencioso; (*not speaking*) callado; (*film*) mudo; **to keep** *or* **remain ~** guardar silencio.

silently ['saɪlntlɪ] *adv* silenciosamente, en silencio.

silent partner *n* (*COMM*) socio/a comanditario/a.

silhouette [sɪlu:'ɛt] *n* silueta; **~d against** destacado sobre *or* contra.

silicon ['sɪlɪkən] *n* silicio.

silicon chip *n* chip *m*, plaqueta de silicio.

silicone ['sɪlɪkəun] *n* silicona.

silk [sɪlk] *n* seda ♦ *cpd* de seda.

silky ['sɪlkɪ] *adj* sedoso.

sill [sɪl] *n* (*also*: **window~**) alféizar *m*; (*AUT*) umbral *m*.

silliness ['sɪlɪnɪs] *n* (*of person*) necedad *f*; (*of idea*) lo absurdo.

silly ['sɪlɪ] *adj* (*person*) tonto; (*idea*) absurdo; **to do sth ~** hacer una tontería.

silo ['saɪləu] *n* silo.

silt [sɪlt] *n* sedimento.

silver ['sɪlvə*] *n* plata; (*money*) moneda suelta ♦ *adj* de plata.

silver paper (*BRIT*), **silver foil** *n* papel *m* de plata.

silver plate *n* vajilla de plata.

silver-plated [sɪlvə'pleɪtɪd] *adj* plateado.

silversmith ['sɪlvəsmɪθ] *n* platero/a.
silverware ['sɪlvəwɛə*] *n* plata.
silver wedding (anniversary) *n* (*BRIT*) bodas *fpl* de plata.
silvery ['sɪlvrɪ] *adj* plateado.
similar ['sɪmɪlə*] *adj*: ~ **to** parecido *or* semejante a.
similarity [sɪmɪ'lærɪtɪ] *n* parecido, semejanza.
similarly ['sɪmɪləlɪ] *adv* del mismo modo; (*in a similar way*) de manera parecida; (*equally*) igualmente.
simile ['sɪmɪlɪ] *n* símil *m*.
simmer ['sɪmə*] *vi* hervir a fuego lento.
▸**simmer down** *vi* (*fig, col*) calmarse, tranquilizarse.
simpering ['sɪmpərɪŋ] *adj* afectado; (*foolish*) bobo.
simple ['sɪmpl] *adj* (*easy*) sencillo; (*foolish, COMM*) simple; **the** ~ **truth** la pura verdad.
simple interest *n* (*COMM*) interés *m* simple.
simple-minded [sɪmpl'maɪndɪd] *adj* simple, ingenuo.
simpleton ['sɪmpltən] *n* inocentón/ona *m/f*.
simplicity [sɪm'plɪsɪtɪ] *n* sencillez *f*; (*foolishness*) ingenuidad *f*.
simplification [sɪmplɪfɪ'keɪʃən] *n* simplificación *f*.
simplify ['sɪmplɪfaɪ] *vt* simplificar.
simply ['sɪmplɪ] *adv* (*in a simple way*: *live, talk*) sencillamente; (*just, merely*) sólo.
simulate ['sɪmjuleɪt] *vt* simular.
simulation [sɪmju'leɪʃən] *n* simulación *f*.
simultaneous [sɪməl'teɪnɪəs] *adj* simultáneo.
simultaneously [sɪməl'teɪnɪəslɪ] *adv* simultáneamente, a la vez.
sin [sɪn] *n* pecado ♦ *vi* pecar.
since [sɪns] *adv* desde entonces ♦ *prep* desde ♦ *conj* (*time*) desde que; (*because*) ya que, puesto que; ~ **then** desde entonces; ~ **Monday** desde el lunes; **(ever)** ~ **I arrived** desde que llegué.
sincere [sɪn'sɪə*] *adj* sincero.
sincerely [sɪn'sɪəlɪ] *adv* sinceramente; **yours** ~ (*in letters*) le saluda (afectuosamente); ~ **yours** (*US*: *in letters*) le saluda atentamente.
sincerity [sɪn'sɛrɪtɪ] *n* sinceridad *f*.
sinecure ['saɪnɪkjuə*] *n* chollo.
sinew ['sɪnju:] *n* tendón *m*.
sinful ['sɪnful] *adj* (*thought*) pecaminoso; (*person*) pecador(a).
sing, *pt* **sang,** *pp* **sung** [sɪŋ, sæŋ, sʌŋ] *vt* cantar ♦ *vi* (*gen*) cantar; (*bird*) trinar; (*ears*) zumbar.
Singapore [sɪŋə'pɔ:*] *n* Singapur *m*.
singe [sɪndʒ] *vt* chamuscar.
singer ['sɪŋə*] *n* cantante *m/f*.
Singhalese [sɪŋə'li:z] *adj* = **Sinhalese.**
singing ['sɪŋɪŋ] *n* (*of person, bird*) canto; (*songs*) canciones *fpl*; (*in the ears*) zumbido; (*of kettle*) silbido.
single ['sɪŋgl] *adj* único, solo; (*unmarried*) soltero; (*not double*) individual, sencillo ♦ *n* (*BRIT*: *also*: ~ **ticket**) billete *m* sencillo; (*record*) sencillo, single *m*; ~**s** *npl* (*TENNIS*) individual *msg*; **not a** ~ **one was left** no quedaba ni uno; **every** ~ **day** todos los días (sin excepción).
▸**single out** *vt* (*choose*) escoger; (*point out*) singularizar.
single bed *n* cama individual.
single-breasted [sɪŋgl'brɛstɪd] *adj* (*jacket, suit*) recto, sin cruzar.
single-density ['sɪŋgldɛnsɪtɪ] *adj* (*COMPUT*: *disk*) de densidad sencilla.
single-entry book-keeping ['sɪŋglɛntrɪ-] *n* contabilidad *f* por partida simple.
Single European Market *n*: **the** ~ el Mercado Único Europeo.
single file *n*: **in** ~ en fila de uno.
single-handed [sɪŋgl'hændɪd] *adv* sin ayuda.
single-minded [sɪŋgl'maɪndɪd] *adj* resuelto, firme.
single parent *n* (*mother*) madre *f* soltera; (*father*) padre *m* soltero.
single-parent family ['sɪŋglpɛərənt-] *n* familia monoparental.
single room *n* habitación *f* individual.
singles bar *n* (*esp US*) bar *m* para solteros.
single-sex school ['sɪŋglsɛks-] *n* escuela no mixta.
single-sided [sɪŋgl'saɪdɪd] *adj* (*COMPUT*: *disk*) de una cara.
single spacing *n* (*TYP*): **in** ~ a un espacio.
singlet ['sɪŋglɪt] *n* camiseta.
singly ['sɪŋglɪ] *adv* uno por uno.
singsong ['sɪŋsɔŋ] *adj* (*tone*) cantarín/ina ♦ *n* (*songs*): **to have a** ~ tener un concierto improvisado.
singular ['sɪŋgjulə*] *adj* singular, extraordinario; (*odd*) extraño; (*LING*) singular ♦ *n* (*LING*) singular *m*; **in the feminine** ~ en femenino singular.
singularly ['sɪŋgjuləlɪ] *adv* singularmente, extraordinariamente.
Sinhalese [sɪnhə'li:z] *adj* singhalese.
sinister ['sɪnɪstə*] *adj* siniestro.
sink [sɪŋk] *n* fregadero ♦ *vb* (*pt* **sank,** *pp* **sunk** [sæŋk, sʌŋk]) *vt* (*ship*) hundir, echar a pique; (*foundations*) excavar; (*piles etc*): **to** ~ **sth into** hundir algo en ♦ *vi* (*gen*)

hundirse; **he sank into a chair/the mud** se dejó caer en una silla/se hundió en el barro; **the shares** *or* **share prices have sunk to 3 dollars** las acciones han bajado a 3 dólares.
▸**sink in** *vi* (*fig*) penetrar, calar; **the news took a long time to ~ in** la noticia tardó mucho en hacer mella en él (*or* mí *etc*).
sinking ['sɪŋkɪŋ] *adj*: **that ~ feeling** la sensación esa de desmoralización.
sinking fund *n* fondo de amortización.
sink unit *n* fregadero.
sinner ['sɪnə*] *n* pecador(a) *m/f*.
Sinn Féin [ʃɪn'feɪn] *n partido político republicano de Irlanda del Norte*.
sinuous ['sɪnjuəs] *adj* sinuoso.
sinus ['saɪnəs] *n* (*ANAT*) seno.
sip [sɪp] *n* sorbo ♦ *vt* sorber, beber a sorbitos.
siphon ['saɪfən] *n* sifón *m* ♦ *vt* (*also*: **~ off**) (*funds*) desviar.
sir [səː*] *n* señor *m*; **S~ John Smith** el Señor John Smith; **yes ~** sí, señor; **Dear S~** (*in letter*) Muy señor mío, Estimado Señor; **Dear S~s** Muy señores nuestros, Estimados Señores.
siren ['saɪərn] *n* sirena.
sirloin ['səːlɔɪn] *n* solomillo; **~ steak** filete *m* de solomillo.
sisal ['saɪsəl] *n* pita, henequén *m* (*LAM*).
sissy ['sɪsɪ] *n* (*col*) marica *m*.
sister ['sɪstə*] *n* hermana; (*BRIT*: *nurse*) enfermera jefe.
sister-in-law ['sɪstərɪnlɔː] *n* cuñada.
sister organization *n* organización *f* hermana.
sister ship *n* barco gemelo.
sit, *pt, pp* **sat** [sɪt, sæt] *vi* sentarse; (*be sitting*) estar sentado; (*assembly*) reunirse; (*dress etc*) caer, sentar ♦ *vt* (*exam*) presentarse a; **that jacket ~s well** esa chaqueta sienta bien; **to ~ on a committee** ser miembro de una comisión *or* un comité.
▸**sit about, sit around** *vi* holgazanear.
▸**sit back** *vi* (*in seat*) recostarse.
▸**sit down** *vi* sentarse; **to be ~ting down** estar sentado.
▸**sit in on** *vt fus*: **to ~ in on a discussion** asistir a una discusión.
▸**sit up** *vi* incorporarse; (*not go to bed*) no acostarse.
sitcom ['sɪtkɔm] *n abbr* (= *situation comedy*) telecomedia.
sit-down ['sɪtdaun] *adj*: **~ strike** huelga de brazos caídos; **a ~ meal** una comida sentada.
site [saɪt] *n* sitio; (*also*: **building ~**) solar *m* ♦ *vt* situar.
sit-in ['sɪtɪn] *n* (*demonstration*) sentada *f*.
siting ['saɪtɪŋ] *n* (*location*) situación *f*, emplazamiento.
sitter ['sɪtə*] *n* (*ART*) modelo *m/f*; (*baby~*) canguro *m/f*.
sitting ['sɪtɪŋ] *n* (*of assembly etc*) sesión *f*; (*in canteen*) turno.
sitting member *n* (*POL*) titular *m/f* de un escaño.
sitting room *n* sala de estar.
sitting tenant *n inquilino con derechos de estancia en una vivienda*.
situate ['sɪtjueɪt] *vt* situar, ubicar (*LAM*).
situated ['sɪtjueɪtɪd] *adj* situado, ubicado (*LAM*).
situation [sɪtju'eɪʃən] *n* situación *f*; **"~s vacant"** (*BRIT*) "ofertas de trabajo".
situation comedy *n* (*TV, RADIO*) serie *f* cómica, comedia de situación.
six [sɪks] *num* seis.
six-pack ['sɪkspæk] *n* (*esp US*) paquete *m* de seis cervezas.
sixteen [sɪks'tiːn] *num* dieciséis.
sixth [sɪksθ] *adj* sexto; **the upper/lower ~** (*SCOL*) el séptimo/sexto año.
sixty ['sɪkstɪ] *num* sesenta.
size [saɪz] *n* (*gen*) tamaño; (*extent*) extensión *f*; (*of clothing*) talla; (*of shoes*) número; **I take ~ 5 shoes** calzo el número cinco; **I take ~ 14** mi talla es la 42; **I'd like the small/large ~** (*of soap powder etc*) quisiera el tamaño pequeño/grande.
▸**size up** *vt* formarse una idea de.
sizeable ['saɪzəbl] *adj* importante, considerable.
sizzle ['sɪzl] *vi* crepitar.
SK *abbr* (*Canada*) = *Saskatchewan*.
skate [skeɪt] *n* patín *m*; (*fish*: *pl inv*) raya ♦ *vi* patinar.
▸**skate over, skate round** *vt fus* (*problem, issue*) pasar por alto.
skateboard ['skeɪtbɔːd] *n* monopatín *m*.
skater ['skeɪtə*] *n* patinador(a) *m/f*.
skating ['skeɪtɪŋ] *n* patinaje *m*; **figure ~** patinaje *m* artístico.
skating rink *n* pista de patinaje.
skeleton ['skɛlɪtn] *n* esqueleto; (*TECH*) armazón *m*; (*outline*) esquema *m*.
skeleton key *n* llave *f* maestra.
skeleton staff *n* personal *m* reducido.
skeptic ['skɛptɪk] *etc* (*US*) = **sceptic**.
sketch [skɛtʃ] *n* (*drawing*) dibujo; (*outline*) esbozo, bosquejo; (*THEAT*) pieza corta ♦ *vt* dibujar; esbozar.
sketch book *n* bloc *m* de dibujo.
sketching ['skɛtʃɪŋ] *n* dibujo.
sketch pad *n* bloc *m* de dibujo.
sketchy ['skɛtʃɪ] *adj* incompleto.

skewer ['skjuːə*] *n* broqueta.
ski [skiː] *n* esquí *m* ♦ *vi* esquiar.
ski boot *n* bota de esquí.
skid [skɪd] *n* patinazo ♦ *vi* patinar; **to go into a ~** comenzar a patinar.
skid mark *n* señal *f* de patinazo.
skier ['skiːə*] *n* esquiador(a) *m/f*.
skiing ['skiːɪŋ] *n* esquí *m*; **to go ~** practicar el esquí, (ir a) esquiar.
ski instructor *n* instructor(a) *m/f* de esquí.
ski jump *n* pista para salto de esquí.
skilful, (*US*) **skillful** ['skɪlful] *adj* diestro, experto.
ski lift *n* telesilla *m*, telesquí *m*.
skill [skɪl] *n* destreza, pericia; (*technique*) arte *m*, técnica; **there's a certain ~ to doing it** se necesita cierta habilidad para hacerlo.
skilled [skɪld] *adj* hábil, diestro; (*worker*) cualificado.
skillet ['skɪlɪt] *n* sartén *f* pequeña.
skillful ['skɪlful] *etc* (*US*) = **skilful** *etc*.
skil(l)fully ['skɪlfulɪ] *adv* hábilmente, con destreza.
skim [skɪm] *vt* (*milk*) desnatar; (*glide over*) rozar, rasar ♦ *vi*: **to ~ through** (*book*) hojear.
skimmed milk [skɪmd-] *n* leche *f* desnatada *or* descremada.
skimp [skɪmp] *vt* (*work*) chapucear; (*cloth etc*) escatimar; **to ~ on** (*material etc*) economizar; (*work*) escatimar.
skimpy ['skɪmpɪ] *adj* (*meagre*) escaso; (*skirt*) muy corto.
skin [skɪn] *n* (*gen*) piel *f*; (*complexion*) cutis *m*; (*of fruit, vegetable*) piel *f*, cáscara; (*crust: on pudding, paint*) nata ♦ *vt* (*fruit etc*) pelar; (*animal*) despellejar; **wet** *or* **soaked to the ~** calado hasta los huesos.
skin cancer *n* cáncer *m* de piel.
skin-deep ['skɪn'diːp] *adj* superficial.
skin diver *n* buceador(a) *m/f*.
skin diving *n* buceo.
skinflint ['skɪnflɪnt] *n* tacaño/a, roñoso/a.
skinhead ['skɪnhɛd] *n* cabeza *m/f* rapada, skin(head) *m/f*.
skinny ['skɪnɪ] *adj* flaco, magro.
skintight ['skɪntaɪt] *adj* (*dress etc*) muy ajustado.
skip [skɪp] *n* brinco, salto; (*container*) contenedor *m* ♦ *vi* brincar; (*with rope*) saltar a la comba ♦ *vt* (*pass over*) omitir, saltar.
ski pants *npl* pantalones *mpl* de esquí.
ski pole *n* bastón *m* de esquiar.
skipper ['skɪpə*] *n* (*NAUT, SPORT*) capitán *m*.
skipping rope ['skɪpɪŋ-] *n* (*BRIT*) comba, cuerda (de saltar).
ski resort *n* estación *f* de esquí.
skirmish ['skəːmɪʃ] *n* escaramuza.
skirt [skəːt] *n* falda, pollera (*LAM*) ♦ *vt* (*surround*) ceñir, rodear; (*go round*) ladear.
skirting board ['skəːtɪŋ-] *n* (*BRIT*) rodapié *m*.
ski run *n* pista de esquí.
ski suit *n* traje *m* de esquiar.
skit [skɪt] *n* sátira, parodia.
ski tow *n* arrastre *m* (de esquí).
skittle ['skɪtl] *n* bolo; **~s** (*game*) boliche *m*.
skive [skaɪv] *vi* (*BRIT col*) gandulear.
skulk [skʌlk] *vi* esconderse.
skull [skʌl] *n* calavera; (*ANAT*) cráneo.
skullcap ['skʌlkæp] *n* (*worn by Jews*) casquete *m*; (*worn by Pope*) solideo.
skunk [skʌŋk] *n* mofeta.
sky [skaɪ] *n* cielo; **to praise sb to the skies** poner a algn por las nubes.
sky-blue [skaɪ'bluː] *adj* (azul) celeste.
skydiving ['skaɪdaɪvɪŋ] *n* paracaidismo acrobático.
sky-high ['skaɪ'haɪ] *adj* (*col*) por las nubes ♦ *adv* (*throw*) muy alto; **prices have gone ~** (*col*) los precios están por las nubes.
skylark ['skaɪlɑːk] *n* (*bird*) alondra.
skylight ['skaɪlaɪt] *n* tragaluz *m*, claraboya.
skyline ['skaɪlaɪn] *n* (*horizon*) horizonte *m*; (*of city*) perfil *m*.
skyscraper ['skaɪskreɪpə*] *n* rascacielos *m inv*.
slab [slæb] *n* (*stone*) bloque *m*; (*of wood*) tabla, plancha; (*flat*) losa; (*of cake*) trozo; (*of meat, cheese*) tajada, trozo.
slack [slæk] *adj* (*loose*) flojo; (*slow*) de poca actividad; (*careless*) descuidado; (*COMM: market*) poco activo; (*: demand*) débil; (*period*) bajo; **business is ~** hay poco movimiento en el negocio.
slacken ['slækn] (*also*: **~ off**) *vi* aflojarse ♦ *vt* aflojar; (*speed*) disminuir.
slackness ['slæknɪs] *n* flojedad *f*; negligencia.
slacks [slæks] *npl* pantalones *mpl*.
slag [slæg] *n* escoria, escombros *mpl*.
slag heap *n* escorial *m*, escombrera.
slain [sleɪn] *pp of* **slay**.
slake [sleɪk] *vt* (*one's thirst*) apagar.
slalom ['slɑːləm] *n* eslálom *m*.
slam [slæm] *vt* (*door*) cerrar de golpe; (*throw*) arrojar (violentamente); (*criticize*) vapulear, vituperar ♦ *vi* cerrarse de golpe.
slammer [slæmə*] *n* (*col*): **the ~** la trena, el talego.
slander ['slɑːndə*] *n* calumnia, difamación *f* ♦ *vt* calumniar, difamar.

slanderous ['slɑːndərəs] *adj* calumnioso, difamatorio.
slang [slæŋ] *n* argot *m*; (*jargon*) jerga.
slanging match ['slæŋɪŋ-] *n* (*BRIT col*) bronca gorda.
slant [slɑːnt] *n* sesgo, inclinación *f*; (*fig*) punto de vista; **to get a new ~ on sth** obtener un nuevo punto de vista sobre algo.
slanted ['slɑːntɪd], **slanting** ['slɑːntɪŋ] *adj* inclinado.
slap [slæp] *n* palmada; (*in face*) bofetada ♦ *vt* dar una palmada/bofetada a ♦ *adv* (*directly*) de lleno.
slapdash ['slæpdæʃ] *adj* chapucero.
slaphead ['slæphɛd] *n* (*BRIT col*) colgado/a.
slapstick ['slæpstɪk] *n*: **~ comedy** comedia de payasadas.
slap-up ['slæpʌp] *adj*: **a ~ meal** (*BRIT*) un banquetazo, una comilona.
slash [slæʃ] *vt* acuchillar; (*fig*: *prices*) quemar.
slat [slæt] *n* (*of wood, plastic*) tablilla, listón *m*.
slate [sleɪt] *n* pizarra ♦ *vt* (*BRIT*: *fig*: *criticize*) vapulear.
slaughter ['slɔːtə*] *n* (*of animals*) matanza; (*of people*) carnicería ♦ *vt* matar.
slaughterhouse ['slɔːtəhaus] *n* matadero.
Slav [slɑːv] *adj* eslavo.
slave [sleɪv] *n* esclavo/a ♦ *vi* (*also*: **~ away**) trabajar como un negro; **to ~ (away) at sth** trabajar como un negro en algo.
slave driver *n* (*col, pej*) tirano/a.
slave labour, (*US*) **slave labor** *n* trabajo de esclavos.
slaver ['slævə*] *vi* (*dribble*) babear.
slavery ['sleɪvərɪ] *n* esclavitud *f*.
slavish ['sleɪvɪʃ] *adj* (*devotion*) de esclavo; (*imitation*) servil.
slay, *pt* **slew**, *pp* **slain** [sleɪ, sluː, sleɪn] *vt* (*literary*) matar.
SLD *n abbr* (*BRIT POL*) = *Social and Liberal Democrats*.
sleazy ['sliːzɪ] *adj* (*fig*: *place*) sórdido.
sledge [slɛdʒ], (*US*) **sled** [slɛd] *n* trineo.
sledgehammer ['slɛdʒhæmə*] *n* mazo.
sleek [sliːk] *adj* (*shiny*) lustroso.
sleep [sliːp] *n* sueño ♦ *vb* (*pt, pp* **slept** [slɛpt]) *vi* dormir ♦ *vt*: **we can ~ 4** podemos alojar a 4, tenemos cabida para 4; **to go to ~** dormirse; **to have a good night's ~** dormir toda la noche; **to put to ~** (*patient*) dormir; (*animal*: *euphemism*: *kill*) sacrificar; **to ~ lightly** tener el sueño ligero; **to ~ with sb** (*euphemism*) acostarse con algn.
▸**sleep in** *vi* (*oversleep*) quedarse dormido.
sleeper ['sliːpə*] *n* (*person*) durmiente *m/f*; (*BRIT RAIL*: *on track*) traviesa; (: *train*) coche-cama *m*.
sleepiness ['sliːpɪnɪs] *n* somnolencia.
sleeping bag ['sliːpɪŋ-] *n* saco de dormir.
sleeping car *n* coche-cama *m*.
sleeping partner *n* (*COMM*) socio/a comanditario/a.
sleeping pill *n* somnífero.
sleeping sickness *n* enfermedad *f* del sueño.
sleepless ['sliːplɪs] *adj*: **a ~ night** una noche en blanco.
sleeplessness ['sliːplɪsnɪs] *n* insomnio.
sleepwalk ['sliːpwɔːk] *vi* caminar dormido; (*habitually*) ser sonámbulo.
sleepwalker ['sliːpwɔːkə*] *n* sonámbulo/a.
sleepy ['sliːpɪ] *adj* soñoliento; **to be** *or* **feel ~** tener sueño.
sleet [sliːt] *n* aguanieve *f*.
sleeve [sliːv] *n* manga; (*TECH*) manguito; (*of record*) funda.
sleeveless ['sliːvlɪs] *adj* (*garment*) sin mangas.
sleigh [sleɪ] *n* trineo.
sleight [slaɪt] *n*: **~ of hand** prestidigitación *f*.
slender ['slɛndə*] *adj* delgado; (*means*) escaso.
slept [slɛpt] *pt, pp of* **sleep**.
sleuth [sluːθ] *n* (*col*) detective *m/f*.
slew [sluː] *vi* (*veer*) torcerse ♦ *pt of* **slay**.
slice [slaɪs] *n* (*of meat*) tajada; (*of bread*) rebanada; (*of lemon*) rodaja; (*utensil*) paleta ♦ *vt* cortar, tajar; rebanar; **~d bread** pan *m* de molde.
slick [slɪk] *adj* (*skilful*) hábil, diestro ♦ *n* (*also*: **oil ~**) capa de aceite.
slid [slɪd] *pt, pp of* **slide**.
slide [slaɪd] *n* (*in playground*) tobogán *m*; (*PHOT*) diapositiva; (*microscope ~*) portaobjetos *m inv*, plaquilla de vidrio; (*BRIT*: *also*: **hair ~**) pasador *m* ♦ (*vb*: *pt, pp* **slid** [slɪd]) *vt* correr, deslizar ♦ *vi* (*slip*) resbalarse; (*glide*) deslizarse; **to let things ~** (*fig*) dejar que ruede la bola.
slide projector *n* (*PHOT*) proyector *m* de diapositivas.
slide rule *n* regla de cálculo.
sliding ['slaɪdɪŋ] *adj* (*door*) corredizo; **~ roof** (*AUT*) techo de corredera.
sliding scale *n* escala móvil.
slight [slaɪt] *adj* (*slim*) delgado; (*frail*) delicado; (*pain etc*) leve; (*trifling*) insignificante; (*small*) pequeño ♦ *n* desaire *m* ♦ *vt* (*offend*) ofender, desairar; **a ~ improvement** una ligera mejora; **not in the ~est** en absoluto; **there's not the**

~**est possibility** no hay la menor *or* más mínima posibilidad.
slightly ['slaɪtlɪ] *adv* ligeramente, un poco; ~ **built** delgado.
slim [slɪm] *adj* delgado, esbelto ♦ *vi* adelgazar.
slime [slaɪm] *n* limo, cieno.
slimming ['slɪmɪŋ] *n* adelgazamiento ♦ *adj* (*diet, pills*) adelgazante.
slimness ['slɪmnɪs] *n* delgadez *f*.
slimy ['slaɪmɪ] *adj* limoso; (*covered with mud*) fangoso; (*also fig: person*) adulón, zalamero.
sling [slɪŋ] *n* (*MED*) cabestrillo; (*weapon*) honda ♦ *vt* (*pt, pp* **slung** [slʌŋ]) tirar, arrojar; **to have one's arm in a** ~ llevar el brazo en cabestrillo.
slink, *pt, pp* **slunk** [slɪŋk, slʌŋk] *vi*: **to** ~ **away,** ~ **off** escabullirse.
slinky ['slɪŋkɪ] *adj* (*clothing*) pegado al cuerpo, superajustado.
slip [slɪp] *n* (*slide*) resbalón *m*; (*mistake*) descuido; (*underskirt*) combinación *f*; (*of paper*) papelito ♦ *vt* (*slide*) deslizar ♦ *vi* (*slide*) deslizarse; (*stumble*) resbalar(se); (*decline*) decaer; (*move smoothly*): **to** ~ **into/out of** (*room etc*) colarse en/salirse de; **to let a chance** ~ **by** dejar escapar la oportunidad; **to** ~ **sth on/off** ponerse/quitarse algo; **to** ~ **on a jumper** ponerse un jersey *or* un suéter; **it** ~**ped from her hand** se la cayó de la mano; **to give sb the** ~ dar esquinazo a algn; **wages** ~ (*BRIT*) hoja del sueldo; **a** ~ **of the tongue** un lapsus.
▸**slip away** *vi* escabullirse.
▸**slip in** *vt* meter ♦ *vi* meterse, colarse.
▸**slip out** *vi* (*go out*) salir (un momento).
slip-on ['slɪpɔn] *adj* de quita y pon; (*shoes*) sin cordones.
slipped disc [slɪpt-] *n* vértebra dislocada.
slipper ['slɪpə*] *n* zapatilla, pantufla.
slippery ['slɪpərɪ] *adj* resbaladizo.
slip road *n* (*BRIT*) carretera de acceso.
slipshod ['slɪpʃɔd] *adj* descuidado, chapucero.
slipstream ['slɪpstriːm] *n* viento de la hélice.
slip-up ['slɪpʌp] *n* (*error*) desliz *m*.
slipway ['slɪpweɪ] *n* grada, gradas *fpl*.
slit [slɪt] *n* raja; (*cut*) corte *m* ♦ *vt* (*pt, pp* **slit**) rajar, cortar; **to** ~ **sb's throat** cortarle el pescuezo a algn.
slither ['slɪðə*] *vi* deslizarse.
sliver ['slɪvə*] *n* (*of glass, wood*) astilla; (*of cheese, sausage*) lonja, loncha.
slob [slɔb] *n* (*col*) patán/ana *m/f*, palurdo/a.
slog [slɔg] (*BRIT*) *vi* sudar tinta ♦ *n*: **it was a** ~ costó trabajo (hacerlo).
slogan ['sləugən] *n* eslogan *m*, lema *m*.
slop [slɔp] *vi* (*also*: ~ **over**) derramarse, desbordarse ♦ *vt* derramar, verter.
slope [sləup] *n* (*up*) cuesta, pendiente *f*; (*down*) declive *m*; (*side of mountain*) falda, vertiente *f* ♦ *vi*: **to** ~ **down** estar en declive; **to** ~ **up** subir (en pendiente).
sloping ['sləupɪŋ] *adj* en pendiente; en declive.
sloppily ['slɔpɪlɪ] *adv* descuidadamente; con descuido *or* desaliño.
sloppiness ['slɔpɪnɪs] *n* descuido; desaliño.
sloppy ['slɔpɪ] *adj* (*work*) descuidado; (*appearance*) desaliñado.
slosh [slɔʃ] *vi*: **to** ~ **about** *or* **around** chapotear.
sloshed [slɔʃt] *adj* (*col: drunk*): **to get** ~ agarrar una trompa.
slot [slɔt] *n* ranura; (*fig: in timetable*) hueco; (*RADIO, TV*) espacio ♦ *vt*: **to** ~ **into** encajar en.
sloth [sləuθ] *n* (*vice*) pereza; (*ZOOL*) oso perezoso.
slot machine *n* (*BRIT: vending machine*) máquina expendedora, (*for gambling*) máquina tragaperras.
slot meter *n* contador *m*.
slouch [slautʃ] *vi*: **to** ~ **about,** ~ **around** (*laze*) gandulear.
Slovak ['sləuvæk] *adj* eslovaco ♦ *n* eslovaco/a; (*LING*) eslovaco; **the** ~ **Republic** Eslovaquia.
Slovakia [sləu'vækɪə] *n* Eslovaquia.
Slovakian [sləu'vækɪən] *adj, n* = **Slovak**.
Slovene [sləu'viːn] *adj* esloveno ♦ *n* esloveno/a; (*LING*) esloveno.
Slovenia [sləu'viːnɪə] *n* Eslovenia.
Slovenian [sləu'viːnɪən] *adj, n* = **Slovene**.
slovenly ['slʌvənlɪ] *adj* (*dirty*) desaliñado, desaseado; (*careless*) descuidado.
slow [sləu] *adj* lento; (*watch*): **to be** ~ estar atrasado ♦ *adv* lentamente, despacio ♦ *vt* (*also*: ~ **down,** ~ **up**) retardar; (*engine, machine*) reducir la marcha de ♦ *vi* (*also*: ~ **down,** ~ **up**) ir más despacio; "~" (*road sign*) "disminuir la velocidad"; **at a** ~ **speed** a una velocidad lenta; **the** ~ **lane** el carril derecho; **business is** ~ (*COMM*) hay poca actividad; **my watch is 20 minutes** ~ mi reloj lleva 20 minutos de retraso; **bake for two hours in a** ~ **oven** cocer *or* asar 2 horas en el horno a fuego lento; **to be** ~ **to act/decide** tardar en obrar/decidir; **to go** ~ (*driver*) conducir despacio; (*in industrial dispute*) trabajar a ritmo lento.
slow-acting [sləu'æktɪŋ] *adj* de efecto

retardado.
slowcoach ['sləukəutʃ] *n* (*BRIT col*) tortuga.
slowdown ['sləudaun] *n* (*US*) huelga de celo.
slowly ['sləulɪ] *adv* lentamente, despacio; **to drive** ~ conducir despacio; ~ **but surely** lento pero seguro.
slow motion *n*: **in** ~ a cámara lenta.
slow-moving ['sləu'mu:vɪŋ] *adj* lento.
slowpoke ['sləupəuk] *n* (*US col*) = **slowcoach**.
sludge [slʌdʒ] *n* lodo, fango.
slug [slʌg] *n* babosa; (*bullet*) posta.
sluggish ['slʌgɪʃ] *adj* (*slow*) lento; (*lazy*) perezoso; (*business, market, sales*) inactivo.
sluggishly ['slʌgɪʃlɪ] *adv* lentamente.
sluggishness ['slʌgɪʃnɪs] *n* lentitud *f*.
sluice [slu:s] *n* (*gate*) esclusa; (*channel*) canal *m* ♦ *vt*: **to** ~ **down** *or* **out** regar.
slum [slʌm] *n* (*area*) barrios *mpl* bajos; (*house*) casucha.
slumber ['slʌmbə*] *n* sueño.
slum clearance (programme) *n* (programa *m* de) deschabolización *f*.
slump [slʌmp] *n* (*economic*) depresión *f* ♦ *vi* hundirse; **the** ~ **in the price of copper** la baja repentina del precio del cobre; **he was** ~**ed over the wheel** se había desplomado encima del volante.
slung [slʌŋ] *pt, pp of* **sling**.
slunk [slʌŋk] *pt, pp of* **slink**.
slur [slə:*] *n* calumnia ♦ *vt* calumniar, difamar; (*word*) pronunciar mal; **to cast a** ~ **on sb** manchar la reputación de algn, difamar a algn.
slurp [slə:p] *vt, vi* sorber ruidosamente.
slurred [slə:d] *adj* (*pronunciation*) poco claro.
slush [slʌʃ] *n* nieve *f* a medio derretir.
slush fund *n* fondos *mpl* para sobornar.
slushy ['slʌʃɪ] *adj* (*col: poetry etc*) sentimentaloide.
slut [slʌt] *n* marrana.
sly [slaɪ] *adj* (*clever*) astuto; (*nasty*) malicioso.
slyly ['slaɪlɪ] *adv* astutamente; taimadamente.
slyness ['slaɪnɪs] *n* astucia.
smack [smæk] *n* (*slap*) manotada; (*blow*) golpe *m* ♦ *vt* dar una manotada a; golpear con la mano ♦ *vi*: **to** ~ **of** saber a, oler a ♦ *adv*: **it fell** ~ **in the middle** (*col*) cayó justo en medio.
smacker ['smækə*] *n* (*col: kiss*) besazo; (*: BRIT: pound note*) billete *m* de una libra; (*: US: dollar bill*) billete *m* de un dólar.
small [smɔ:l] *adj* pequeño, chico (*esp LAM*); (*in height*) bajo, chaparro (*LAM*); (*letter*) en minúscula ♦ *n*: ~ **of the back** región *f* lumbar; ~ **shopkeeper** pequeño/a comerciante *m/f*; **to get** *or* **grow** ~**er** (*stain, town*) empequeñecer; (*debt, organization, numbers*) reducir, disminuir; **to make** ~**er** (*amount, income*) reducir; (*garden, object, garment*) achicar.
small ads *npl* (*BRIT*) anuncios *mpl* por palabras.
small arms *npl* armas *fpl* cortas.
small business *n* pequeño negocio; ~**es** la pequeña empresa.
small change *n* suelto, cambio.
smallholder ['smɔ:lhəuldə*] *n* (*BRIT*) granjero/a, parcelero/a.
smallholding ['smɔ:lhəuldɪŋ] *n* parcela, minifundio.
small hours *npl*: **in the** ~ a altas horas de la noche.
smallish ['smɔ:lɪʃ] *adj* más bien pequeño.
small-minded [smɔ:l'maɪndɪd] *adj* mezquino, de miras estrechas.
smallness ['smɔ:lnɪs] *n* pequeñez *f*.
smallpox ['smɔ:lpɔks] *n* viruela.
small print *n* letra pequeña *or* menuda.
small-scale ['smɔ:lskeɪl] *adj* (*map, model*) a escala reducida; (*business, farming*) en pequeña escala.
small talk *n* cháchara.
small-time ['smɔ:ltaɪm] *adj* (*col*) de poca categoría *or* monta; **a** ~ **thief** un(a) ratero/a.
small-town ['smɔ:ltaun] *adj* de provincias.
smarmy ['smɑ:mɪ] *adj* (*BRIT pej*) pelotillero (*fam*).
smart [smɑ:t] *adj* elegante; (*clever*) listo, inteligente; (*quick*) rápido, vivo; (*weapon*) inteligente ♦ *vi* escocer, picar; **the** ~ **set** la gente de buen tono; **to look** ~ estar elegante; **my eyes are** ~**ing** me pican los ojos.
smartcard ['smɑ:tkɑ:d] *n* tarjeta inteligente.
smarten up ['smɑ:tn-] *vi* arreglarse ♦ *vt* arreglar.
smartness ['smɑ:tnɪs] *n* elegancia; (*cleverness*) inteligencia.
smash [smæʃ] *n* (*also*: ~**-up**) choque *m*; (*sound*) estrépito ♦ *vt* (*break*) hacer pedazos; (*car etc*) estrellar; (*SPORT: record*) batir ♦ *vi* hacerse pedazos; (*against wall etc*) estrellarse.
►**smash up** *vt* (*car*) hacer pedazos; (*room*) destrozar.
smash hit *n* exitazo.
smashing ['smæʃɪŋ] *adj* (*col*) cojonudo.
smattering ['smætərɪŋ] *n*: **a** ~ **of Spanish**

algo de español.

smear [smɪə*] *n* mancha; (*MED*) frotis *m inv* (cervical); (*insult*) calumnia ♦ *vt* untar; (*fig*) calumniar, difamar; **his hands were ~ed with oil/ink** tenía las manos manchadas de aceite/tinta.

smear campaign *n* campaña de calumnias.

smear test *n* (*MED*) citología, frotis *m inv* (cervical).

smell [smɛl] *n* olor *m*; (*sense*) olfato ♦ (*vb*: *pt, pp* **smelt** *or* **~ed** [smɛlt, smɛld]) *vt, vi* oler; **it ~s good/of garlic** huele bien/a ajo.

smelly ['smɛlɪ] *adj* maloliente.

smelt [smɛlt] *vt* (*ore*) fundir ♦ *pt, pp of* **smell**.

smile [smaɪl] *n* sonrisa ♦ *vi* sonreír.

smiling ['smaɪlɪŋ] *adj* sonriente, risueño.

smirk [smə:k] *n* sonrisa falsa *or* afectada.

smith [smɪθ] *n* herrero.

smithy ['smɪðɪ] *n* herrería.

smitten ['smɪtn] *adj*: **he's really ~ with her** está totalmente loco por ella.

smock [smɔk] *n* blusón; (*children's*) babi *m*; (*US*: *overall*) guardapolvo, bata.

smog [smɔg] *n* smog *m*.

smoke [sməuk] *n* humo ♦ *vi* fumar; (*chimney*) echar humo ♦ *vt* (*cigarettes*) fumar; **to go up in ~** (*house etc*) quemarse; (*fig*) quedar en agua de borrajas; **do you ~?** ¿fumas?

smoked [sməukt] *adj* (*bacon, glass*) ahumado.

smokeless fuel ['sməuklɪs-] *n* combustible *m* sin humo.

smokeless zone ['sməuklɪs-] *n* zona libre de humo.

smoker ['sməukə*] *n* (*person*) fumador(a) *m/f*; (*RAIL*) coche *m* de fumadores.

smoke screen *n* cortina de humo.

smoke shop *n* (*US*) estanco, tabaquería.

smoking ['sməukɪŋ] *n*: **"no ~"** "prohibido fumar"; **he's given up ~** ha dejado de fumar.

smoking compartment, (*US*) **smoking car** *n* departamento de fumadores.

smoky ['sməukɪ] *adj* (*room*) lleno de humo.

smolder ['sməuldə*] *vi* (*US*) = **smoulder**.

smoochy ['smu:tʃɪ] *adj* (*col*) blandengue.

smooth [smu:ð] *adj* liso; (*sea*) tranquilo; (*flavour, movement*) suave; (*person*: *pej*) meloso ♦ *vt* alisar; (*also*: **~ out**) (*creases*) alisar; (*difficulties*) allanar.

►**smooth over** *vt*: **to ~ things over** (*fig*) limar las asperezas.

smoothly ['smu:ðlɪ] *adv* (*easily*) fácilmente; **everything went ~** todo fue sobre ruedas.

smoothness ['smu:ðnɪs] *n* (*of skin, cloth*) tersura; (*of surface, flavour, movement*) suavidad *f*.

smother ['smʌðə*] *vt* sofocar; (*repress*) contener.

smoulder, (*US*) **smolder** ['sməuldə*] *vi* arder sin llama.

smudge [smʌdʒ] *n* mancha ♦ *vt* manchar.

smug [smʌg] *adj* engreído.

smuggle ['smʌgl] *vt* pasar de contrabando; **to ~ in/out** (*goods etc*) meter/sacar de contrabando.

smuggler ['smʌglə*] *n* contrabandista *m/f*.

smuggling ['smʌglɪŋ] *n* contrabando.

smugly ['smʌglɪ] *adv* con suficiencia.

smugness ['smʌgnɪs] *n* suficiencia.

smut [smʌt] *n* (*grain of soot*) carbonilla, hollín *m*; (*mark*) tizne *m*; (*in conversation etc*) obscenidades *fpl*.

smutty ['smʌtɪ] *adj* (*fig*) verde, obsceno.

snack [snæk] *n* bocado, tentempié *m*; **to have a ~** tomar un bocado.

snack bar *n* cafetería.

snag [snæg] *n* problema *m*; **to run into** *or* **hit a ~** encontrar inconvenientes, dar con un obstáculo.

snail [sneɪl] *n* caracol *m*.

snake [sneɪk] *n* (*gen*) serpiente *f*; (*harmless*) culebra; (*poisonous*) víbora.

snap [snæp] *n* (*sound*) chasquido; golpe *m* seco; (*photograph*) foto *f* ♦ *adj* (*decision*) instantáneo ♦ *vt* (*fingers etc*) castañetear; (*break*) partir, quebrar; (*photograph*) tomar una foto de ♦ *vi* (*break*) partirse, quebrarse; (*fig*: *person*) contestar bruscamente; **to ~ (at sb)** (*subj*: *person*) hablar con brusquedad (a algn); (: *dog*) intentar morder (a algn); **to ~ shut** cerrarse de golpe; **to ~ one's fingers at sth/sb** (*fig*) burlarse de algo/uno; **a cold ~** (*of weather*) una ola de frío.

►**snap off** *vi* (*break*) partirse.

►**snap up** *vt* agarrar.

snap fastener *n* (*US*) botón *m* de presión.

snappy ['snæpɪ] *adj* (*col*: *answer*) instantáneo; (*slogan*) conciso; **make it ~!** (*hurry up*) ¡date prisa!

snapshot ['snæpʃɔt] *n* foto *f* (instantánea).

snare [snɛə*] *n* trampa ♦ *vt* cazar con trampa; (*fig*) engañar.

snarl [snɑ:l] *n* gruñido ♦ *vi* gruñir; **to get ~ed up** (*wool, plans*) enmarañarse, enredarse; (*traffic*) quedar atascado.

snatch [snætʃ] *n* (*fig*) robo; **~es of** trocitos *mpl* de ♦ *vt* (**~ away**) arrebatar; (*grasp*) coger (*SP*), agarrar; **~es of conversation** fragmentos *mpl* de conversación; **to ~ a sandwich** comer un bocadillo a prisa; **to ~ some sleep** buscar tiempo para dormir; **don't ~!** ¡no me lo quites!

▸**snatch up** *vt* agarrar.
snazzy ['snæzɪ] *adj* (*col*) guapo.
sneak [sniːk] *vi*: **to ~ in/out** entrar/salir a hurtadillas ♦ *vt*: **to ~ a look at sth** mirar algo de reojo ♦ *n* (*fam*) soplón/ona *m/f*.
sneakers ['sniːkəz] *npl* (*US*) zapatos *mpl* de lona, zapatillas *fpl*.
sneaking ['sniːkɪŋ] *adj*: **to have a ~ feeling/suspicion that ...** tener la sensación/sospecha de que ....
sneaky ['sniːkɪ] *adj* furtivo.
sneer [snɪə*] *n* sonrisa de desprecio ♦ *vi* sonreír con desprecio; **to ~ at sth/sb** burlarse *or* mofarse de algo/uno.
sneeze [sniːz] *n* estornudo ♦ *vi* estornudar.
snide [snaɪd] *adj* (*col*: *sarcastic*) sarcástico.
sniff [snɪf] *vi* sorber (por la nariz) ♦ *vt* husmear, oler; (*glue, drug*) esnifar.
▸**sniff at** *vt fus*: **it's not to be ~ed at** no es de despreciar.
sniffer dog ['snɪfə-] *n* (*for drugs*) perro antidroga; (*for explosives*) perro antiexplosivos.
snigger ['snɪgə*] *n* risa disimulada ♦ *vi* reírse con disimulo.
snip [snɪp] *n* (*piece*) recorte *m*; (*bargain*) ganga ♦ *vt* tijeretear.
sniper ['snaɪpə*] *n* francotirador(a) *m/f*.
snippet ['snɪpɪt] *n* retazo.
snivelling, (*US*) **sniveling** ['snɪvlɪŋ] *adj* llorón/ona.
snob [snɔb] *n* (e)snob *m/f*.
snobbery ['snɔbərɪ] *n* (e)snobismo.
snobbish ['snɔbɪʃ] *adj* (e)snob.
snobbishness ['snɔbɪʃnɪs] *n* (e)snobismo.
snog [snɔg] *vi* (*BRIT col*) besuquearse, morrear; **to ~ sb** besuquear a algn.
snooker ['snuːkə*] *n* snooker *m*.
snoop [snuːp] *vi*: **to ~ about** fisgonear.
snooper ['snuːpə*] *n* fisgón/ona *m/f*.
snooty ['snuːtɪ] *adj* (e)snob.
snooze [snuːz] *n* siesta ♦ *vi* echar una siesta.
snore [snɔː*] *vi* roncar ♦ *n* ronquido.
snoring ['snɔːrɪŋ] *n* ronquidos *mpl*.
snorkel ['snɔːkl] *n* tubo de respiración.
snort [snɔːt] *n* bufido ♦ *vi* bufar ♦ *vt* (*col*: *drugs*) esnifar.
snotty ['snɔtɪ] *adj* (*col*) creído.
snout [snaut] *n* hocico, morro.
snow [snəu] *n* nieve *f* ♦ *vi* nevar ♦ *vt*: **to be ~ed under with work** estar agobiado de trabajo.
snowball ['snəubɔːl] *n* bola de nieve ♦ *vi* ir aumentándose.
snow-blind ['snəublaɪnd] *adj* cegado por la nieve.
snowbound ['snəubaund] *adj* bloqueado por la nieve.
snow-capped ['snəukæpt] *adj* (*peak*) cubierto de nieve, nevado.
snowdrift ['snəudrɪft] *n* ventisquero.
snowdrop ['snəudrɔp] *n* campanilla.
snowfall ['snəufɔːl] *n* nevada.
snowflake ['snəufleɪk] *n* copo de nieve.
snowline ['snəulaɪn] *n* límite *m* de las nieves perpetuas.
snowman ['snəumæn] *n* figura de nieve.
snowplough, (*US*) **snowplow** ['snəuplau] *n* quitanieves *m inv*.
snowshoe ['snəuʃuː] *n* raqueta (de nieve).
snowstorm ['snəustɔːm] *n* tormenta de nieve, nevasca.
Snow White *n* Blancanieves *f*.
snowy ['snəuɪ] *adj* de (mucha) nieve.
SNP *n abbr* (*BRIT POL*) = *Scottish National Party*.
snub [snʌb] *vt*: **to ~ sb** desairar a algn ♦ *n* desaire *m*, repulsa.
snub-nosed [snʌb'nəuzd] *adj* chato.
snuff [snʌf] *n* rapé *m* ♦ *vt* (*also*: **~ out**: *candle*) apagar.
snuffbox ['snʌfbɔks] *n* caja de rapé.
snuff movie *n* (*col*) película porno (*que acaba con un asesinato real*).
snug [snʌg] *adj* (*cosy*) cómodo; (*fitted*) ajustado.
snuggle ['snʌgl] *vi*: **to ~ down in bed** hacerse un ovillo *or* acurrucarse en la cama; **to ~ up to sb** acurrucarse junto a algn.
snugly ['snʌglɪ] *adv* cómodamente; **it fits ~** (*object in pocket etc*) cabe perfectamente; (*garment*) ajusta perfectamente.
SO *abbr* (*BANKING*) = **standing order.**

KEYWORD

so [səu] *adv* **1** (*thus, likewise*) así, de este modo; **if ~** de ser así; **I like swimming — ~ do I** a mí me gusta nadar — a mí también; **I've got work to do — ~ has Paul** tengo trabajo que hacer — Paul también; **it's 5 o'clock — ~ it is!** son las cinco — ¡pues es verdad!; **I hope/think ~** espero/creo que sí; **~ far** hasta ahora; (*in past*) hasta este momento; **~ to speak** por decirlo así
2 (*in comparisons etc*: *to such a degree*) tan; **~ quickly (that)** tan rápido (que); **~ big (that)** tan grande (que); **she's not ~ clever as her brother** no es tan lista como su hermano; **we were ~ worried** estábamos preocupadísimos
3: **~ much** *adj* tanto/a ♦ *adv* tanto; **~ many** tantos/as
4 (*phrases*): **10 or ~** unos 10, 10 o así; **~**

long! (*inf*: *goodbye*) ¡hasta luego!; **she didn't ~ much as send me a birthday card** no me mandó ni una tarjeta siquiera por mi cumpleaños; ~ **(what)?** (*col*) ¿y (qué)? ♦ *conj* **1** (*expressing purpose*): ~ **as to do** para hacer; ~ **(that)** para que +*sub*; **we hurried ~ (that) we wouldn't be late** nos dimos prisa para no llegar tarde **2** (*expressing result*) así que; ~ **you see, I could have gone** así que ya ves, (yo) podría haber ido; ~ **that's the reason!** ¡así que es por eso *or* por eso es!

soak [səuk] *vt* (*drench*) empapar; (*put in water*) remojar ♦ *vi* remojarse, estar a remojo.

▸**soak in** *vi* penetrar.

▸**soak up** *vt* absorber.

soaking ['səukɪŋ] *adj* (*also*: ~ **wet**) calado *or* empapado (hasta los huesos *or* el tuétano).

so-and-so ['səuənsəu] *n* (*somebody*) fulano/a de tal.

soap [səup] *n* jabón *m*.

soapbox ['saupbɔks] *n* tribuna improvisada.

soapflakes ['səupfleɪks] *npl* jabón *msg* en escamas.

soap opera *n* (*TV*) telenovela; (*RADIO*) radionovela.

soap powder *n* jabón *m* en polvo.

soapsuds ['səupsʌdz] *npl* espuma *sg*.

soapy ['səupɪ] *adj* jabonoso.

soar [sɔː*] *vi* (*on wings*) remontarse; (*building etc*) elevarse; (*price*) subir vertiginosamente; (*morale*) elevarse.

soaring ['sɔːrɪŋ] *adj* (*flight*) por lo alto; (*prices*) en alza *or* aumento; ~ **inflation** inflación *f* altísima *or* en aumento.

sob [sɔb] *n* sollozo ♦ *vi* sollozar.

s.o.b. *n abbr* (*US col!* = *son of a bitch*) hijo de puta (*!*).

sober ['səubə*] *adj* (*moderate*) moderado; (*serious*) serio; (*not drunk*) sobrio; (*colour, style*) discreto.

▸**sober up** *vi* pasársele a algn la borrachera.

soberly ['səubəlɪ] *adv* sobriamente.

sobriety [sə'braɪətɪ] *n* (*not being drunk*) sobriedad *f*; (*seriousness, sedateness*) seriedad *f*, sensatez *f*.

sob story *n* (*col, pej*) dramón *m*.

Soc. *abbr* (= *society*) S.

so-called ['səu'kɔːld] *adj* presunto, supuesto.

soccer ['sɔkə*] *n* fútbol *m*.

soccer pitch *n* campo *or* cancha (*LAM*) de fútbol.

soccer player *n* jugador(a) *m/f* de fútbol.

sociability [səuʃə'bɪlɪtɪ] *n* sociabilidad *f*.

sociable ['səuʃəbl] *adj* sociable.

social ['səuʃl] *adj* social ♦ *n* velada, fiesta.

social class *n* clase *f* social.

social climber *n* arribista *m/f*.

social club *n* club *m*.

Social Democrat *n* socialdemócrata *m/f*.

social insurance *n* (*US*) seguro social.

socialism ['səuʃəlɪzəm] *n* socialismo.

socialist ['səuʃəlɪst] *adj, n* socialista *m/f*.

socialite ['səuʃəlaɪt] *n persona que alterna con la buena sociedad*.

socialize ['səuʃəlaɪz] *vi* hacer vida social; **to ~ with** (*colleagues*) salir con.

social life *n* vida social

socially ['səuʃəlɪ] *adv* socialmente.

social science(s) *n(pl)* ciencias *fpl* sociales.

social security *n* seguridad *f* social.

social services *npl* servicios *mpl* sociales.

social welfare *n* asistencia social.

social work *n* asistencia social.

social worker *n* asistente/a *m/f* social.

society [sə'saɪətɪ] *n* sociedad *f*; (*club*) asociación *f*; (*also*: **high ~**) buena sociedad ♦ *cpd* (*party, column*) social, de sociedad.

socio-economic ['səusɪəuiːkə'nɔmɪk] *adj* socioeconómico.

sociological [səusɪə'lɔdʒɪkəl] *adj* sociológico.

sociologist [səusɪ'ɔlədʒɪst] *n* sociólogo/a.

sociology [səusɪ'ɔlədʒɪ] *n* sociología.

sock [sɔk] *n* calcetín *m*, media (*LAM*); **to pull one's ~s up** (*fig*) hacer esfuerzos, despabilarse.

socket ['sɔkɪt] *n* (*ELEC*) enchufe *m*.

sod [sɔd] *n* (*of earth*) césped *m*; (*col!*) cabrón/ona *m/f* (*!*) ♦ *excl*: ~ **off!** (*col!*) ¡vete a la porra!

soda ['səudə] *n* (*CHEM*) sosa; (*also*: ~ **water**) soda; (*US*: *also*: ~ **pop**) gaseosa.

sodden ['sɔdn] *adj* empapado.

sodium ['səudɪəm] *n* sodio.

sodium chloride *n* cloruro sódico *or* de sodio.

sofa ['səufə] *n* sofá *m*.

Sofia ['səufɪə] *n* Sofía.

soft [sɔft] *adj* (*teacher, parent*) blando; (*gentle, not loud*) suave; (*stupid*) bobo; ~ **currency** divisa blanda *or* débil.

soft-boiled ['sɔftbɔɪld] *adj* (*egg*) pasado por agua.

soft copy *n* (*COMPUT*) copia transitoria.

soft drink *n* bebida no alcohólica.

soft drugs *npl* drogas *fpl* blandas.

soften ['sɔfn] *vt* ablandar; suavizar ♦ *vi*

ablandarse; suavizarse.
softener ['sɔfnə*] *n* suavizante *m*.
soft fruit *n* bayas *fpl*.
soft furnishings *npl* tejidos *mpl* para el hogar.
soft-hearted [sɔft'hɑːtɪd] *adj* bondadoso.
softly ['sɔftlɪ] *adv* suavemente; (*gently*) delicadamente, con delicadeza.
softness ['sɔftnɪs] *n* blandura; suavidad *f*.
soft option *n* alternativa fácil.
soft sell *n* venta persuasiva.
soft target *n* blanco *or* objetivo fácil.
soft toy *n* juguete *m* de peluche.
software ['sɔftwɛə*] *n* (*COMPUT*) software *m*.
soft water *n* agua blanda.
soggy ['sɔgɪ] *adj* empapado.
soil [sɔɪl] *n* (*earth*) tierra, suelo ♦ *vt* ensuciar.
soiled [sɔɪld] *adj* sucio, manchado.
sojourn ['sɔdʒəːn] *n* (*formal*) estancia.
solace ['sɔlɪs] *n* consuelo.
solar ['səulə*] *adj* solar.
solarium, *pl* **solaria** [sə'lɛərɪəm, -rɪə] *n* solario.
solar panel *n* panel *m* solar.
solar plexus [-'plɛksəs] *n* (*ANAT*) plexo solar.
solar power *n* energía solar.
solar system *n* sistema *m* solar.
sold [səuld] *pt, pp of* **sell**.
solder ['səuldə*] *vt* soldar ♦ *n* soldadura.
soldier ['səuldʒə*] *n* (*gen*) soldado; (*army man*) militar *m* ♦ *vi*: **to ~ on** seguir adelante; **toy ~** soldadito de plomo.
sold out *adj* (*COMM*) agotado.
sole [səul] *n* (*of foot*) planta; (*of shoe*) suela; (*fish*: *pl inv*) lenguado ♦ *adj* único; **the ~ reason** la única razón.
solely ['səullɪ] *adv* únicamente, sólo, solamente; **I will hold you ~ responsible** le consideraré el único responsable.
solemn ['sɔləm] *adj* solemne.
sole trader *n* (*COMM*) comerciante *m/f* exclusivo/a.
solicit [sə'lɪsɪt] *vt* (*request*) solicitar ♦ *vi* (*prostitute*) abordar clientes.
solicitor [sə'lɪsɪtə*] *n* abogado/a; *see also* **barrister**.
solid ['sɔlɪd] *adj* sólido; (*gold etc*) macizo; (*line*) continuo; (*vote*) unánime ♦ *n* sólido; **we waited 2 ~ hours** esperamos 2 horas enteras; **to be on ~ ground** estar en tierra firme; (*fig*) estar seguro.
solidarity [sɔlɪ'dærɪtɪ] *n* solidaridad *f*.
solid fuel *n* combustible *m* sólido.
solidify [sə'lɪdɪfaɪ] *vi* solidificarse.
solidity [sə'lɪdɪtɪ] *n* solidez *f*.
solidly ['sɔlɪdlɪ] *adv* sólidamente; (*fig*) unánimemente.
solid-state ['sɔlɪdsteɪt] *adj* (*ELEC*) estado sólido.
soliloquy [sə'lɪləkwɪ] *n* soliloquio.
solitaire [sɔlɪ'tɛə*] *n* (*game, gem*) solitario.
solitary ['sɔlɪtərɪ] *adj* solitario, solo; (*isolated*) apartado, aislado; (*only*) único.
solitary confinement *n* incomunicación *f*; **to be in ~** estar incomunicado.
solitude ['sɔlɪtjuːd] *n* soledad *f*.
solo ['səuləu] *n* solo.
soloist ['səuləuɪst] *n* solista *m/f*.
Solomon Islands ['sɔləmən-] *npl*: **the ~** las Islas Salomón.
solstice ['sɔlstɪs] *n* solsticio.
soluble ['sɔljubl] *adj* soluble.
solution [sə'luːʃən] *n* solución *f*.
solve [sɔlv] *vt* resolver, solucionar.
solvency ['sɔlvənsɪ] *n* (*COMM*) solvencia.
solvent ['sɔlvənt] *adj* (*COMM*) solvente ♦ *n* (*CHEM*) solvente *m*.
solvent abuse *n* uso indebido de disolventes.
Som. *abbr* (*BRIT*) = *Somerset*.
Somali [sə'mɑːlɪ] *adj, n* somalí *m/f*.
Somalia [sə'mɑːlɪə] *n* Somalia.
Somaliland [sə'mɑːlɪlænd] *n* Somaliland *f*.
sombre, (*US*) **somber** ['sɔmbə*] *adj* sombrío.

KEYWORD

some [sʌm] *adj* **1** (*a certain amount or number of*): **~ tea/water/biscuits** té/agua/ (unas) galletas; **have ~ tea** tómese un té; **there's ~ milk in the fridge** hay leche en el frigo; **there were ~ people outside** había algunas personas fuera; **I've got ~ money, but not much** tengo algo de dinero, pero no mucho

2 (*certain: in contrasts*) algunos/as; **~ people say that ...** hay quien dice que ...; **~ films were excellent, but most were mediocre** hubo películas excelentes, pero la mayoría fueron mediocres

3 (*unspecified*): **~ woman was asking for you** una mujer estuvo preguntando por ti; **~ day** algún día; **~ day next week** un día de la semana que viene; **he was asking for ~ book (or other)** pedía no se qué libro; **in ~ way or other** de alguna que otra manera

4 (*considerable amount of*) bastante; **~ days ago** hace unos cuantos días; **after ~ time** pasado algún tiempo; **at ~ length** con mucho detalle

5 (*col*: *intensive*): **that was ~ party!** ¡menuda fiesta!

♦ *pron* **1** (*a certain number*): **I've got ~** (*books etc*) tengo algunos/as
2 (*a certain amount*) algo; **I've got ~** (*money, milk*) tengo algo; **would you like ~?** (*coffee etc*) ¿quiere un poco?; (*books etc*) ¿quiere alguno?; **could I have ~ of that cheese?** ¿me puede dar un poco de ese queso?; **I've read ~ of the book** he leído parte del libro
♦ *adv*: **~ 10 people** unas 10 personas, una decena de personas.

somebody ['sʌmbədɪ] *pron* alguien; **~ or other** alguien.
someday ['sʌmdeɪ] *adv* algún día.
somehow ['sʌmhau] *adv* de alguna manera; (*for some reason*) por una u otra razón.
someone ['sʌmwʌn] *pron* = **somebody**.
someplace ['sʌmpleɪs] *adv* (*US*) = **somewhere**.
somersault ['sʌməsɔːlt] *n* (*deliberate*) salto mortal; (*accidental*) vuelco ♦ *vi* dar un salto mortal; dar vuelcos.
something ['sʌmθɪŋ] *pron* algo ♦ *adv*: **he's ~ like me** es un poco como yo; **~ to do** algo que hacer; **it's ~ of a problem** es bastante problemático.
sometime ['sʌmtaɪm] *adv* (*in future*) algún día, en algún momento; **~ last month** durante el mes pasado; **I'll finish it ~** lo terminaré un día de éstos.
sometimes ['sʌmtaɪmz] *adv* a veces.
somewhat ['sʌmwɔt] *adv* algo.
somewhere ['sʌmwɛə*] *adv* (*be*) en alguna parte; (*go*) a alguna parte; **~ else** (*be*) en otra parte; (*go*) a otra parte.
son [sʌn] *n* hijo.
sonar ['səunɑː*] *n* sonar *m*.
sonata [sə'nɑːtə] *n* sonata.
song [sɔŋ] *n* canción *f*.
songwriter ['sɔŋraɪtə*] *n* compositor(a) *m/f* de canciones.
sonic ['sɔnɪk] *adj* (*boom*) sónico.
son-in-law ['sʌnɪnlɔː] *n* yerno.
sonnet ['sɔnɪt] *n* soneto.
sonny ['sʌnɪ] *n* (*col*) hijo.
soon [suːn] *adv* pronto, dentro de poco; **~ afterwards** poco después; **very/quite ~** muy/bastante pronto; **how ~ can you be ready?** ¿cuánto tardas en prepararte?; **it's too ~ to tell** es demasiado pronto para saber; **see you ~!** ¡hasta pronto!; *see also* **as**.
sooner ['suːnə*] *adv* (*time*) antes, más temprano; **I would ~ do that** preferiría hacer eso; **~ or later** tarde o temprano; **no ~ said than done** dicho y hecho; **the ~ the better** cuanto antes mejor; **no ~ had we left than ...** apenas nos habíamos marchado cuando ....
soot [sut] *n* hollín *m*.
soothe [suːð] *vt* tranquilizar; (*pain*) aliviar.
soothing ['suːðɪŋ] *adj* (*ointment etc*) sedante; (*tone, words etc*) calmante, tranquilizante.
SOP *n abbr* = *standard operating procedure.*
sophisticated [sə'fɪstɪkeɪtɪd] *adj* sofisticado.
sophistication [səfɪstɪ'keɪʃən] *n* sofisticación *f*.
sophomore ['sɔfəmɔː*] *n* (*US*) estudiante *m/f* de segundo año.
soporific [sɔpə'rɪfɪk] *adj* soporífero.
sopping ['sɔpɪŋ] *adj*: **~ (wet)** empapado.
soppy ['sɔpɪ] *adj* (*pej*) bobo, tonto.
soprano [sə'prɑːnəu] *n* soprano *f*.
sorbet ['sɔːbeɪ] *n* sorbete *m*.
sorcerer ['sɔːsərə*] *n* hechicero.
sordid ['sɔːdɪd] *adj* (*place etc*) sórdido; (*motive etc*) mezquino.
sore [sɔː*] *adj* (*painful*) doloroso, que duele; (*offended*) resentido ♦ *n* llaga; **~ throat** dolor *m* de garganta; **my eyes are ~, I have ~ eyes** me duelen los ojos; **it's a ~ point** es un asunto delicado *or* espinoso.
sorely *adv*: **I am ~ tempted to (do it)** estoy muy tentado a (hacerlo).
soreness ['sɔːnɪs] *n* dolor *m*.
sorrel ['sɔrəl] *n* (*BOT*) acedera.
sorrow ['sɔrəu] *n* pena, dolor *m*.
sorrowful ['sɔrəuful] *adj* afligido, triste.
sorrowfully ['sɔrəufulɪ] *adv* tristemente.
sorry ['sɔrɪ] *adj* (*regretful*) arrepentido; (*condition, excuse*) lastimoso; (*sight, failure*) triste; **~!** ¡perdón!, ¡perdone!; **I am ~** lo siento; **I feel ~ for him** me da lástima *or* pena; **I'm ~ to hear that ...** siento saber que ...; **to be ~ about sth** lamentar algo.
sort [sɔːt] *n* clase *f*, género, tipo; (*make*: *of coffee, car etc*) marca ♦ *vt* (*also*: **~ out**: *papers*) clasificar; (: *problems*) arreglar, solucionar; (*COMPUT*) clasificar; **what ~ do you want?** (*make*) ¿qué marca quieres?; **what ~ of car?** ¿qué tipo de coche?; **I shall do nothing of the ~** no pienso hacer nada parecido; **it's ~ of awkward** (*col*) es bastante difícil.
sortie ['sɔːtɪ] *n* salida.
sorting office ['sɔːtɪŋ-] *n* oficina de clasificación del correo.
SOS *n* SOS *m*.
so-so ['səusəu] *adv* regular, así así.
soufflé ['suːfleɪ] *n* suflé *m*.
sought [sɔːt] *pt, pp of* **seek**.
sought-after ['sɔːtɑːftə*] *adj* solicitado,

codiciado.
soul [səul] *n* alma *f*; **God rest his ~** Dios le reciba en su seno *or* en su gloria; **I didn't see a ~** no vi a nadie; **the poor ~ had nowhere to sleep** el pobre no tenía dónde dormir.
soul-destroying ['səuldıstrɔııŋ] *adj* (*work*) deprimente.
soulful ['səulful] *adj* lleno de sentimiento.
soulmate ['səulmeıt] *n* compañero/a del alma.
soul-searching ['səulsəːtʃıŋ] *n*: **after much ~** después de pensarlo mucho, después de darle muchas vueltas.
sound [saund] *adj* (*healthy*) sano; (*safe, not damaged*) en buen estado; (*valid*: *argument, policy, claim*) válido; (: *move*) acertado; (*dependable*: *person*) de fiar; (*sensible*) sensato, razonable ♦ *adv*: **~ asleep** profundamente dormido ♦ *n* (*noise*) sonido, ruido; (*GEO*) estrecho ♦ *vt* (*alarm*) sonar; (*also*: **~ out**: *opinions*) consultar, sondear ♦ *vi* sonar, resonar; (*fig*: *seem*) parecer; **to ~ like** sonar a; **to be of ~ mind** estar en su sano juicio; **I don't like the ~ of it** no me gusta nada; **it ~s as if** ... parece que ....
▶**sound off** *vi* (*col*): **to ~ off (about)** (*give one's opinions*) despotricar (contra).
sound barrier *n* barrera del sonido.
sound bite *n* cita jugosa.
sound effects *npl* efectos *mpl* sonoros.
sound engineer *n* ingeniero/a del sonido.
sounding ['saundıŋ] *n* (*NAUT etc*) sondeo.
sounding board *n* caja de resonancia.
soundly ['saundlı] *adv* (*sleep*) profundamente; (*beat*) completamente.
soundproof ['saundpruːf] *adj* insonorizado.
sound system *n* equipo de sonido.
soundtrack ['saundtræk] *n* (*of film*) banda sonora.
sound wave *n* (*PHYSICS*) onda sonora.
soup [suːp] *n* (*thick*) sopa; (*thin*) caldo; **in the ~** (*fig*) en apuros.
soup kitchen *n* comedor *m* de beneficencia.
soup plate *n* plato sopero.
soupspoon ['suːpspuːn] *n* cuchara sopera.
sour ['sauə*] *adj* agrio; (*milk*) cortado; **it's just ~ grapes!** (*fig*) ¡pura envidia!, ¡están verdes!; **to go** *or* **turn ~** (*milk*) cortarse; (*wine*) agriarse; (*fig*: *relationship*) agriarse; (: *plans*) irse a pique.
source [sɔːs] *n* fuente *f*; **I have it from a reliable ~ that** ... sé de fuente fidedigna que ....
source language *n* (*COMPUT*) lenguaje *m* fuente *or* de origen.
south [sauθ] *n* sur *m* ♦ *adj* del sur ♦ *adv* al sur, hacia el sur; **(to the) ~ of** al sur de; **the S~ of France** el Sur de Francia; **to travel ~** viajar hacia el sur.
South Africa *n* Sudáfrica.
South African *adj, n* sudafricano/a *m/f*.
South America *n* América del Sur, Sudamérica.
South American *adj, n* sudamericano/a *m/f*.
southbound ['sauθbaund] *adj* (con) rumbo al sur.
south-east [sauθ'iːst] *n* sudeste *m* ♦ *adj* (*counties etc*) (del) sudeste.
Southeast Asia *n* Sudeste *m* asiático.
southerly ['sʌðəlı] *adj* sur; (*from the south*) del sur.
southern ['sʌðən] *adj* del sur, meridional; **the ~ hemisphere** el hemisferio sur.
South Korea *n* Corea del Sur.
South Pole *n* Polo Sur.
South Sea Islands *npl*: **the ~** Oceanía.
South Seas *npl*: **the ~** los Mares del Sur.
South Vietnam *n* Vietnam *m* del Sur.
southward(s) ['sauθwəd(z)] *adv* hacia el sur.
south-west [sauθ'wɛst] *n* suroeste *m*.
souvenir [suːvə'nıə*] *n* recuerdo.
sovereign ['sɔvrın] *adj, n* soberano/a *m/f*.
sovereignty ['sɔvrıntı] *n* soberanía.
soviet ['səuvıət] *adj* soviético.
Soviet Union *n*: **the ~** la Unión Soviética.
sow [sau] *n* cerda, puerca ♦ *vt* [səu] (*pt* **~ed**, *pp* **~n** [səun]) (*gen*) sembrar; (*spread*) esparcir.
soya ['sɔıə], (*US*) **soy** [sɔı] *n* soja.
soy(a) bean *n* semilla de soja.
soy(a) sauce *n* salsa de soja.
sozzled ['sɔzld] *adj* (*BRIT col*) mamado.
spa [spɑː] *n* balneario.
space [speıs] *n* espacio; (*room*) sitio ♦ *vt* (*also*: **~ out**) espaciar; **to clear a ~ for sth** hacer sitio para algo; **in a confined ~** en un espacio restringido; **in a short ~ of time** en poco *or* un corto espacio de tiempo; **(with)in the ~ of an hour/three generations** en el espacio de una hora/tres generaciones.
space bar *n* (*on typewriter*) barra espaciadora.
spacecraft ['speıskrɑːft] *n* nave *f* espacial, astronave *f*.
spaceman ['speısmæn] *n* astronauta *m*, cosmonauta *m*.
spaceship ['speısʃıp] *n* = **spacecraft**.
space shuttle *n* transportador *m* espacial.
spacesuit ['speıssuːt] *n* traje *m* espacial.

spacewoman ['speɪswumən] *n* astronauta, cosmonauta.
spacing ['speɪsɪŋ] *n* espacio.
spacious ['speɪʃəs] *adj* amplio.
spade [speɪd] *n* (*tool*) pala; **~s** *npl* (*CARDS*: *British*) picas *fpl*; (: *Spanish*) espadas *fpl*.
spadework ['speɪdwəːk] *n* (*fig*) trabajo preliminar.
spaghetti [spə'gɛtɪ] *n* espaguetis *mpl*.
Spain [speɪn] *n* España.
span [spæn] *n* (*of bird, plane*) envergadura; (*of hand*) palmo; (*of arch*) luz *f*; (*in time*) lapso ♦ *vt* extenderse sobre, cruzar; (*fig*) abarcar.
Spaniard ['spænjəd] *n* español(a) *m/f*.
spaniel ['spænjəl] *n* perro de aguas.
Spanish ['spænɪʃ] *adj* español(a) ♦ *n* (*LING*) español *m*, castellano; **the** ~ *npl* (*people*) los españoles; ~ **omelette** tortilla española *or* de patata.
spank [spæŋk] *vt* zurrar, dar unos azotes a.
spanner ['spænə*] *n* (*BRIT*) llave *f* inglesa.
spar [spɑː*] *n* palo, verga ♦ *vi* (*BOXING*) entrenarse (en el boxeo).
spare [spɛə*] *adj* de reserva; (*surplus*) sobrante, de más ♦ *n* (*part*) pieza de repuesto ♦ *vt* (*do without*) pasarse sin; (*afford to give*) tener de sobra; (*refrain from hurting*) perdonar; (*details etc*) ahorrar; **to** ~ (*surplus*) sobrante, de sobra; **there are 2 going** ~ sobran *or* quedan 2; **to** ~ **no expense** no escatimar gastos; **can you** ~ **(me) £10?** ¿puedes prestarme *or* darme 10 libras?; **can you** ~ **the time?** ¿tienes tiempo?; **I've a few minutes to** ~ tengo unos minutos libres; **there is no time to** ~ no hay tiempo que perder.
spare part *n* pieza de repuesto.
spare room *n* cuarto de los invitados.
spare time *n* ratos *mpl* de ocio, tiempo libre.
spare tyre, (*US*) **spare tire** *n* (*AUT*) neumático *or* llanta (*LAM*) de recambio.
spare wheel *n* (*AUT*) rueda de recambio.
sparing ['spɛərɪŋ] *adj*: **to be** ~ **with** ser parco en.
sparingly ['spɛərɪŋlɪ] *adv* escasamente.
spark [spɑːk] *n* chispa; (*fig*) chispazo.
spark(ing) plug ['spɑːk(ɪŋ)-] *n* bujía.
sparkle ['spɑːkl] *n* centelleo, destello ♦ *vi* centellear; (*shine*) relucir, brillar.
sparkler ['spɑːklə*] *n* bengala.
sparkling ['spɑːklɪŋ] *adj* centelleante; (*wine*) espumoso.
sparring partner ['spɑːrɪŋ-] *n* sparring *m*; (*fig*) contrincante *m/f*.
sparrow ['spærəu] *n* gorrión *m*.
sparse [spɑːs] *adj* esparcido, escaso.
sparsely ['spɑːslɪ] *adv* escasamente; **a** ~ **furnished room** un cuarto con pocos muebles.
spartan ['spɑːtən] *adj* (*fig*) espartano.
spasm ['spæzəm] *n* (*MED*) espasmo; (*fig*) arranque *m*, ataque *m*.
spasmodic [spæz'mɔdɪk] *adj* espasmódico.
spastic ['spæstɪk] *n* espástico/a.
spat [spæt] *pt, pp of* **spit** ♦ *n* (*US*) riña.
spate [speɪt] *n* (*fig*): ~ **of** torrente *m* de; **in** ~ (*river*) crecido.
spatial ['speɪʃl] *adj* espacial.
spatter ['spætə*] *vt*: **to** ~ **with** salpicar de.
spatula ['spætjulə] *n* espátula.
spawn [spɔːn] *vt* (*pej*) engendrar ♦ *vi* desovar, frezar ♦ *n* huevas *fpl*.
SPCA *n abbr* (*US*) = *Society for the Prevention of Cruelty to Animals*.
SPCC *n abbr* (*US*) = *Society for the Prevention of Cruelty to Children*.
speak, *pt* **spoke,** *pp* **spoken** [spiːk, spəuk, 'spəukn] *vt* (*language*) hablar; (*truth*) decir ♦ *vi* hablar; (*make a speech*) intervenir; **to** ~ **one's mind** hablar claro *or* con franqueza; **to** ~ **to sb/of** *or* **about sth** hablar con algn/de *or* sobre algo; **to** ~ **at a conference/in a debate** hablar en un congreso/un debate; **he has no money to** ~ **of** no tiene mucho dinero que digamos; ~**ing!** ¡al habla!; ~ **up!** ¡habla más alto!
▸**speak for** *vt fus*: **to** ~ **for sb** hablar por *or* en nombre de algn; **that picture is already spoken for** (*in shop*) ese cuadro está reservado.
speaker ['spiːkə*] *n* (*in public*) orador(a) *m/f*; (*also*: **loud**~) altavoz *m*; (*for stereo etc*) bafle *m*; (*POL*): **the S**~ (*BRIT*) *el Presidente de la Cámara de los Comunes*; (*US*) *el Presidente del Congreso*; **are you a Welsh** ~**?** ¿habla Ud galés?
speaking ['spiːkɪŋ] *adj* hablante.
-speaking ['spiːkɪŋ] *suff* -hablante; **Spanish**~ **people** los hispanohablantes.
spear [spɪə*] *n* lanza; (*for fishing*) arpón *m* ♦ *vt* alancear; arponear.
spearhead ['spɪəhɛd] *vt* (*attack etc*) encabezar ♦ *n* punta de lanza, vanguardia.
spearmint ['spɪəmɪnt] *n* (*BOT etc*) menta verde.
spec [spɛk] *n* (*col*): **on** ~ por si acaso; **to buy on** ~ arriesgarse a comprar.
special ['spɛʃl] *adj* especial; (*edition etc*) extraordinario; (*delivery*) urgente ♦ *n* (*train*) tren *m* especial; **nothing** ~ nada de particular, nada extraordinario.
special agent *n* agente *m/f* especial.

special correspondent *n* corresponsal *m/f* especial.
special delivery *n* (*POST*): **by** ~ por entrega urgente.
special effects *npl* (*CINE*) efectos *mpl* especiales.
specialist ['spɛʃəlɪst] *n* especialista *m/f*; **a heart** ~ (*MED*) un(a) especialista del corazón.
speciality [spɛʃɪ'ælɪtɪ], (*US*) **specialty** ['spɛʃəltɪ] *n* especialidad *f*.
specialize ['spɛʃəlaɪz] *vi*: **to** ~ **(in)** especializarse (en).
specially ['spɛʃlɪ] *adv* especialmente.
special offer *n* (*COMM*) oferta especial.
special train *n* tren *m* especial.
specialty ['spɛʃəltɪ] *n* (*US*) = **speciality**.
species ['spi:ʃi:z] *n* especie *f*.
specific [spə'sɪfɪk] *adj* específico.
specifically [spə'sɪfɪklɪ] *adv* (*explicitly*: *state, warn*) específicamente, expresamente; (*especially*: *design, intend*) especialmente.
specification [spɛsɪfɪ'keɪʃən] *n* especificación *f*; ~**s** *npl* (*plan*) presupuesto *sg*; (*of car, machine*) descripción *f* técnica; (*for building*) plan *msg* detallado.
specify ['spɛsɪfaɪ] *vt, vi* especificar, precisar; **unless otherwise specified** salvo indicaciones contrarias.
specimen ['spɛsɪmən] *n* ejemplar *m*; (*MED*: *of urine*) espécimen *m*; (: *of blood*) muestra.
specimen copy *n* ejemplar *m* de muestra.
specimen signature *n* muestra de firma.
speck [spɛk] *n* grano, mota.
speckled ['spɛkld] *adj* moteado.
specs [spɛks] *npl* (*col*) gafas *fpl* (*SP*), anteojos *mpl*.
spectacle ['spɛktəkl] *n* espectáculo.
spectacle case *n* estuche *m or* funda (de gafas).
spectacles ['spɛktəklz] *npl* (*BRIT*) gafas *fpl* (*SP*), anteojos *mpl*.
spectacular [spɛk'tækjulə*] *adj* espectacular; (*success*) impresionante.
spectator [spɛk'teɪtə*] *n* espectador(a) *m/f*.
spectator sport *n* deporte *m* espectáculo.
spectra ['spɛktrə] *npl of* **spectrum**.
spectre, (*US*) **specter** ['spɛktə*] *n* espectro, fantasma *m*.
spectrum, *pl* **spectra** ['spɛktrəm, -trə] *n* espectro.
speculate ['spɛkjuleɪt] *vi* especular; (*try to guess*): **to** ~ **about** especular sobre.
speculation [spɛkju'leɪʃən] *n* especulación *f*.
speculative ['spɛkjulətɪv] *adj* especulativo.
speculator ['spɛkjuleɪtə*] *n* especulador(a) *m/f*.
sped [spɛd] *pt, pp of* **speed**.
speech [spi:tʃ] *n* (*faculty*) habla; (*formal talk*) discurso; (*words*) palabras *fpl*; (*manner of speaking*) forma de hablar; (*language*) idioma *m*, lenguaje *m*.
speech day *n* (*BRIT SCOL*) ≈ día de reparto de premios.
speech impediment *n* defecto del habla.
speechless ['spi:tʃlɪs] *adj* mudo, estupefacto.
speech therapy *n* logopedia.
speed [spi:d] *n* (*also*: *AUT, TECH*: *gear*) velocidad *f*; (*haste*) prisa; (*promptness*) rapidez *f* ♦ *vi* (*pt, pp* **sped** [spɛd]) (*AUT*: *exceed* ~ *limit*) conducir con exceso de velocidad; **at full** *or* **top** ~ a máxima velocidad; **at a** ~ **of 70 km/h** a una velocidad de 70 km por hora; **at** ~ a gran velocidad; **a five-**~ **gearbox** una caja de cambios de 5 velocidades; **shorthand/typing** ~ rapidez *f* en taquigrafía/mecanografía; **the years sped by** los años pasaron volando.
▸**speed up** *vi* acelerarse ♦ *vt* acelerar.
speedboat ['spi:dbəut] *n* lancha motora.
speedily ['spi:dɪlɪ] *adv* rápido, rápidamente.
speeding ['spi:dɪŋ] *n* (*AUT*) exceso de velocidad.
speed limit *n* límite *m* de velocidad, velocidad *f* máxima.
speedometer [spɪ'dɔmɪtə*] *n* velocímetro.
speed trap *n* (*AUT*) control *m* de velocidades.
speedway ['spi:dweɪ] *n* (*SPORT*) pista de carrera.
speedy ['spi:dɪ] *adj* (*fast*) veloz, rápido; (*prompt*) pronto.
spell [spɛl] *n* (*also*: **magic** ~) encanto, hechizo; (*period of time*) rato, período; (*turn*) turno ♦ *vt* (*pt, pp* **spelt** *or* ~**ed** [spɛlt, spɛld]) (*also*: ~ **out**) deletrear; (*fig*) anunciar, presagiar; **to cast a** ~ **on sb** hechizar a algn; **he can't** ~ no sabe escribir bien, comete faltas de ortografía; **can you** ~ **it for me?** ¿cómo se deletrea *or* se escribe?; **how do you** ~ **your name?** ¿cómo se escribe tu nombre?
spellbound ['spɛlbaund] *adj* embelesado, hechizado.
spelling ['spɛlɪŋ] *n* ortografía.
spelling mistake *n* falta de ortografía.
spelt [spɛlt] *pt, pp of* **spell**.
spend, *pt, pp* **spent** [spɛnd, spɛnt] *vt* (*money*) gastar; (*time*) pasar; (*life*) dedicar; **to** ~ **time/money/effort on sth** gastar tiempo/dinero/energías en algo.

spending ['spɛndɪŋ] *n*: **government ~** gastos *mpl* del gobierno.
spending money *n* dinero para gastos.
spending power *n* poder *m* adquisitivo.
spendthrift ['spɛndθrɪft] *n* derrochador(a) *m/f*, manirroto/a.
spent [spɛnt] *pt, pp of* **spend** ♦ *adj* (*cartridge, bullets, match*) usado.
sperm [spəːm] *n* esperma.
sperm bank *n* banco de esperma.
sperm whale *n* cachalote *m*.
spew [spjuː] *vt* vomitar, arrojar.
sphere [sfɪə*] *n* esfera.
spherical ['sfɛrɪkl] *adj* esférico.
sphinx [sfɪŋks] *n* esfinge *f*.
spice [spaɪs] *n* especia ♦ *vt* especiar.
spiciness ['spaɪsɪnɪs] *n* lo picante.
spicy ['spaɪsɪ] *adj* picante.
spick-and-span ['spɪkən'spæn] *adj* impecable.
spider ['spaɪdə*] *n* araña.
spider's web *n* telaraña.
spiel [ʃpiːl] *n* (*col*) rollo.
spike [spaɪk] *n* (*point*) punta; (*ZOOL*) pincho, púa; (*BOT*) espiga; (*ELEC*) pico parásito ♦ *vt*: **to ~ a quote** cancelar una cita; **~s** *npl* (*SPORT*) zapatillas *fpl* con clavos.
spiky ['spaɪkɪ] *adj* (*bush, branch*) cubierto de púas; (*animal*) erizado.
spill, *pt, pp* **spilt** *or* **~ed** [spɪl, spɪlt, spɪld] *vt* derramar, verter; (*blood*) derramar ♦ *vi* derramarse; **to ~ the beans** (*col*) descubrir el pastel.
▸**spill out** *vi* derramarse, desparramarse.
▸**spill over** *vi* desbordarse.
spillage ['spɪlɪdʒ] *n* (*event*) derrame *m*; (*substance*) vertidos.
spin [spɪn] *n* (*revolution of wheel*) vuelta, revolución *f*; (*AVIAT*) barrena; (*trip in car*) paseo (en coche) ♦ *vb* (*pt, pp* **spun** [spʌn]) *vt* (*wool etc*) hilar; (*wheel*) girar ♦ *vi* girar, dar vueltas; **the car spun out of control** el coche se descontroló y empezó a dar vueltas.
▸**spin out** *vt* alargar, prolongar.
spina bifida ['spaɪnə'bɪfɪdə] *n* espina *f* bífida.
spinach ['spɪnɪtʃ] *n* espinacas *fpl*.
spinal ['spaɪnl] *adj* espinal.
spinal column *n* columna vertebral.
spinal cord *n* médula espinal.
spindly ['spɪndlɪ] *adj* (*leg*) zanquivano.
spin doctor *n* (*col*) *informador(a) parcial al servicio de un partido político*.
spin-dry ['spɪn'draɪ] *vt* centrifugar.
spin-dryer [spɪn'draɪə*] *n* (*BRIT*) secadora centrífuga.
spine [spaɪn] *n* espinazo, columna vertebral; (*thorn*) espina.
spine-chilling ['spaɪntʃɪlɪŋ] *adj* terrorífico.
spineless ['spaɪnlɪs] *adj* (*fig*) débil, flojo.
spinet [spɪ'nɛt] *n* espineta.
spinning ['spɪnɪŋ] *n* (*of thread*) hilado; (*art*) hilandería.
spinning top *n* peonza.
spinning wheel *n* rueca, torno de hilar.
spin-off ['spɪnɔf] *n* derivado, producto secundario.
spinster ['spɪnstə*] *n* soltera; (*pej*) solterona.
spiral ['spaɪərl] *n* espiral *f* ♦ *adj* en espiral ♦ *vi* (*prices*) dispararse; **the inflationary ~** la espiral inflacionista.
spiral staircase *n* escalera de caracol.
spire ['spaɪə*] *n* aguja, chapitel *m*.
spirit ['spɪrɪt] *n* (*soul*) alma *f*; (*ghost*) fantasma *m*; (*attitude*) espíritu *m*; (*courage*) valor *m*, ánimo; **~s** *npl* (*drink*) alcohol *msg*, bebidas *fpl* alcohólicas; **in good ~s** alegre, de buen ánimo; **Holy S~** Espíritu *m* Santo; **community ~, public ~** civismo.
spirit duplicator *n* copiadora al alcohol.
spirited ['spɪrɪtɪd] *adj* enérgico, vigoroso.
spirit level *n* nivel *m* de aire.
spiritual ['spɪrɪtjuəl] *adj* espiritual ♦ *n* (*also*: **Negro ~**) canción *f* religiosa, espiritual *m*.
spiritualism ['spɪrɪtjuəlɪzəm] *n* espiritualismo.
spit [spɪt] *n* (*for roasting*) asador *m*, espetón *m*; (*spittle*) esputo, escupitajo; (*saliva*) saliva ♦ *vi* (*pt, pp* **spat** [spæt]) escupir; (*sound*) chisporrotear.
spite [spaɪt] *n* rencor *m*, ojeriza ♦ *vt* fastidiar; **in ~ of** a pesar de, pese a.
spiteful ['spaɪtful] *adj* rencoroso, malévolo.
spitting ['spɪtɪŋ] *n*: **"~ prohibited"** "se prohíbe escupir" ♦ *adj*: **to be the ~ image of sb** ser la viva imagen de algn.
spittle ['spɪtl] *n* saliva, baba.
splash [splæʃ] *n* (*sound*) chapoteo; (*of colour*) mancha ♦ *vt* salpicar de ♦ *vi* (*also*: **~ about**) chapotear; **to ~ paint on the floor** manchar el suelo de pintura.
splashdown ['splæʃdaun] *n* amaraje *m*, amerizaje *m*.
spleen [spliːn] *n* (*ANAT*) bazo.
splendid ['splɛndɪd] *adj* espléndido.
splendidly ['splɛndɪdlɪ] *adv* espléndidamente; **everything went ~** todo fue a las mil maravillas.
splendour, (*US*) **splendor** ['splɛndə*] *n* esplendor *m*; (*of achievement*) brillo, gloria.
splice [splaɪs] *vt* empalmar.
splint [splɪnt] *n* tablilla.

splinter ['splɪntə*] *n* astilla ♦ *vi* astillarse, hacer astillas.
splinter group *n* grupo disidente, facción *f*.
split [splɪt] *n* hendedura, raja; (*fig*) división *f*; (*POL*) escisión *f* ♦ (*vb*: *pt*, *pp* **split**) *vt* partir, rajar; (*party*) dividir; (*work, profits*) repartir ♦ *vi* (*divide*) dividirse, escindirse; **to ~ the difference** partir la diferencia; **to do the ~s** hacer el spagat; **to ~ sth down the middle** (*also fig*) dividir algo en dos.
▸**split up** *vi* (*couple*) separarse, romper; (*meeting*) acabarse.
split-level ['splɪtlɛvl] *adj* (*house*) dúplex.
split peas *npl* guisantes *mpl* secos.
split personality *n* doble personalidad *f*.
split second *n* fracción *f* de segundo.
splitting ['splɪtɪŋ] *adj* (*headache*) horrible.
splutter ['splʌtə*] *vi* chisporrotear; (*person*) balbucear.
spoil, *pt*, *pp* **spoilt** *or* **~ed** [spɔɪl, spɔɪlt, spɔɪld] *vt* (*damage*) dañar; (*ruin*) estropear, echar a perder; (*child*) mimar, consentir; (*ballot paper*) invalidar ♦ *vi*: **to be ~ing for a fight** estar con ganas de lucha, andar con ganas de pelea.
spoiled [spɔɪld] *adj* (*US*: *food*: *bad*) pasado, malo; (: *milk*) cortado.
spoils [spɔɪlz] *npl* despojo *sg*, botín *msg*.
spoilsport ['spɔɪlspɔːt] *n* aguafiestas *m inv*.
spoilt [spɔɪlt] *pt*, *pp of* **spoil** ♦ *adj* (*child*) mimado, consentido; (*ballot paper*) invalidado.
spoke [spəuk] *pt of* **speak** ♦ *n* rayo, radio.
spoken ['spəukn] *pp of* **speak**.
spokesman ['spəuksmən] *n* portavoz *m*, vocero (*LAM*).
spokesperson ['spəukspəːsn] *n* portavoz *m/f*, vocero/a (*LAM*).
spokeswoman ['spəukswumən] *n* portavoz *f*, vocera (*LAM*).
sponge [spʌndʒ] *n* esponja; (*CULIN*: *also*: **~ cake**) bizcocho ♦ *vt* (*wash*) lavar con esponja ♦ *vi*: **to ~ on** *or* (*US*) **off sb** vivir a costa de algn.
sponge bag *n* (*BRIT*) neceser *m*.
sponge cake *n* bizcocho, pastel *m*.
sponger ['spʌndʒə*] *n* gorrón/ona *m/f*.
spongy ['spʌndʒɪ] *adj* esponjoso.
sponsor ['spɔnsə*] *n* (*RADIO, TV*) patrocinador(a) *m/f*; (*for membership*) padrino/madrina; (*COMM*) fiador(a) *m/f*, avalador(a) *m/f* ♦ *vt* patrocinar; apadrinar; (*parliamentary bill*) apoyar, respaldar; (*idea etc*) presentar, promover; **I ~ed him at 3p a mile** (*in fund-raising race*) me apunté para darle 3 peniques la milla.
sponsorship ['spɔnsəʃɪp] *n* patrocinio.
spontaneity [spɔntə'neɪɪtɪ] *n* espontaneidad *f*.
spontaneous [spɔn'teɪnɪəs] *adj* espontáneo.
spontaneously [spɔn'teɪnɪəslɪ] *adv* espontáneamente.
spooky ['spuːkɪ] *adj* (*col*: *place, atmosphere*) espeluznante, horripilante.
spool [spuːl] *n* carrete *m*; (*of sewing machine*) canilla.
spoon [spuːn] *n* cuchara.
spoon-feed ['spuːnfiːd] *vt* dar de comer con cuchara a; (*fig*) dárselo todo mascado a.
spoonful ['spuːnful] *n* cucharada.
sporadic [spə'rædɪk] *adj* esporádico.
sport [spɔːt] *n* deporte *m*; (*person*) buen(a) perdedor(a) *m/f*; (*amusement*) juego, diversión *f*; **indoor/outdoor ~s** deportes *mpl* en sala cubierta/al aire libre; **to say sth in ~** decir algo en broma.
sport coat *n* (*US*) = **sports jacket**.
sporting ['spɔːtɪŋ] *adj* deportivo; **to give sb a ~ chance** darle a algn su oportunidad.
sports car *n* coche *m* sport.
sports coat *n* (*US*) = **sports jacket**.
sports ground *n* campo de deportes, centro deportivo.
sports jacket, (*US*) **sport jacket** *n* chaqueta deportiva.
sportsman ['spɔːtsmən] *n* deportista *m*.
sportsmanship ['spɔːtsmənʃɪp] *n* deportividad *f*.
sports pages *npl* páginas *fpl* deportivas.
sportswear ['spɔːtswɛə*] *n* ropa de deporte.
sportswoman ['spɔːtswumən] *n* deportista.
sporty ['spɔːtɪ] *adj* deportivo.
spot [spɔt] *n* sitio, lugar *m*; (*dot*: *on pattern*) punto, mancha; (*pimple*) grano; (*also*: **advertising ~**) spot *m*; (*small amount*): **a ~ of** un poquito de ♦ *vt* (*notice*) notar, observar ♦ *adj* (*COMM*) inmediatamente efectivo; **on the ~** en el acto, acto seguido; (*in difficulty*) en un aprieto; **to do sth on the ~** hacer algo en el acto; **to put sb on the ~** poner a algn en un apuro.
spot check *n* reconocimiento rápido.
spotless ['spɔtlɪs] *adj* (*clean*) inmaculado; (*reputation*) intachable.
spotlessly ['spɔtlɪslɪ] *adv*: **~ clean** limpísimo.
spotlight ['spɔtlaɪt] *n* foco, reflector *m*; (*AUT*) faro auxiliar.
spot-on [spɔt'ɔn] *adj* (*BRIT col*) exacto.
spot price *n* precio de entrega inmediata.
spotted ['spɔtɪd] *adj* (*pattern*) de puntos.
spotty ['spɔtɪ] *adj* (*face*) con granos.

spouse [spauz] *n* cónyuge *m/f.*
spout [spaut] *n* (*of jug*) pico; (*pipe*) caño ♦ *vi* chorrear.
sprain [spreɪn] *n* torcedura, esguince *m* ♦ *vt*: **to ~ one's ankle** torcerse el tobillo.
sprang [spræŋ] *pt of* **spring.**
sprawl [sprɔːl] *vi* tumbarse ♦ *n*: **urban ~** crecimiento urbano descontrolado; **to send sb ~ing** tirar a algn al suelo.
sprawling ['sprɔːlɪŋ] *adj* (*town*) desparramado.
spray [spreɪ] *n* rociada; (*of sea*) espuma; (*container*) atomizador *m*; (*of paint*) pistola rociadora; (*of flowers*) ramita ♦ *vt* rociar; (*crops*) regar ♦ *cpd* (*deodorant*) en atomizador.
spread [sprɛd] *n* extensión *f*; (*of idea*) diseminación *f*; (*col*: *food*) comilona; (*PRESS, TYP*: *two pages*) plana ♦ *vb* (*pt, pp* **spread**) *vt* extender; diseminar; (*butter*) untar; (*wings, sails*) desplegar; (*scatter*) esparcir ♦ *vi* extenderse; diseminarse; untarse; desplegarse; esparcirse; **middle-age ~** gordura de la mediana edad; **repayments will be ~ over 18 months** los pagos se harán a lo largo de 18 meses.
spread-eagled ['sprɛdiːgld] *adj*: **to be ~** estar despatarrado.
spreadsheet ['sprɛdʃiːt] *n* (*COMPUT*) hoja de cálculo.
spree [spriː] *n*: **to go on a ~** ir de juerga *or* farra (*LAM*).
sprightly ['spraɪtlɪ] *adj* vivo, enérgico.
spring [sprɪŋ] *n* (*season*) primavera; (*leap*) salto, brinco; (*coiled metal*) resorte *m*; (*of water*) fuente *f*, manantial *m*; (*bounciness*) elasticidad *f* ♦ *vb* (*pt* **sprang,** *pp* **sprung** [spræŋ, sprʌŋ]) *vi* (*arise*) brotar, nacer; (*leap*) saltar, brincar ♦ *vt*: **to ~ a leak** (*pipe etc*) empezar a hacer agua; **he sprang the news on me** de repente me soltó la noticia; **in (the) ~** en (la) primavera; **to walk with a ~ in one's step** andar dando saltos *or* brincos; **to ~ into action** lanzarse a la acción.
►**spring up** *vi* (*problem*) surgir.
springboard ['sprɪŋbɔːd] *n* trampolín *m.*
spring-clean [sprɪŋ'kliːn] *n* (*also*: **~ing**) limpieza general.
spring onion *n* cebolleta.
spring roll *n* rollito de primavera.
springtime ['sprɪŋtaɪm] *n* primavera.
springy ['sprɪŋɪ] *adj* elástico; (*grass*) mullido.
sprinkle ['sprɪŋkl] *vt* (*pour*) rociar; **to ~ water on, ~ with water** rociar *or* salpicar de agua.
sprinkler ['sprɪŋklə*] *n* (*for lawn*) aspersor *m*; (*to put out fire*) aparato de rociadura automática.
sprinkling ['sprɪŋklɪŋ] *n* (*of water*) rociada; (*of salt, sugar*) un poco de.
sprint [sprɪnt] *n* (e)sprint *m* ♦ *vi* (*gen*) correr a toda velocidad; (*SPORT*) esprintar; **the 200 metres ~** el (e)sprint de 200 metros.
sprinter ['sprɪntə*] *n* velocista *m/f.*
spritzer ['sprɪtsə*] *n* vino blanco con soda.
sprocket ['sprɔkɪt] *n* (*on printer etc*) rueda dentada.
sprocket feed *n* avance *m* por rueda dentada.
sprout [spraut] *vi* brotar, retoñar ♦ *n*: **(Brussels) ~s** *npl* coles *fpl* de Bruselas.
spruce [spruːs] *n* (*BOT*) pícea ♦ *adj* aseado, pulcro.
►**spruce up** *vt* (*tidy*) arreglar, acicalar; (*smarten up*: *room etc*) ordenar; **to ~ o.s. up** arreglarse.
sprung [sprʌŋ] *pp of* **spring.**
spry [spraɪ] *adj* ágil, activo.
SPUC *n abbr* (= *Society for the Protection of Unborn Children*) ≈ Federación *f* Española de Asociaciones Pro-vida.
spun [spʌn] *pt, pp of* **spin.**
spur [spəː*] *n* espuela; (*fig*) estímulo, aguijón *m* ♦ *vt* (*also*: **~ on**) estimular, incitar; **on the ~ of the moment** de improviso.
spurious ['spjuərɪəs] *adj* falso.
spurn [spəːn] *vt* desdeñar, rechazar.
spurt [spəːt] *n* chorro; (*of energy*) arrebato ♦ *vi* chorrear; **to put in** *or* **on a ~** (*runner*) acelerar; (*fig*: *in work etc*) hacer un gran esfuerzo.
sputter ['spʌtə*] *vi* = **splutter.**
spy [spaɪ] *n* espía *m/f* ♦ *vi*: **to ~ on** espiar a ♦ *vt* (*see*) divisar, lograr ver ♦ *cpd* (*film, story*) de espionaje.
spying ['spaɪɪŋ] *n* espionaje *m.*
Sq. *abbr* (*in address*: = *Square*) Plza.
sq. *abbr* (*MATH etc*) = **square.**
squabble ['skwɔbl] *n* riña, pelea ♦ *vi* reñir, pelear.
squad [skwɔd] *n* (*MIL*) pelotón *m*; (*POLICE*) brigada; (*SPORT*) equipo; **flying ~** (*POLICE*) brigada móvil.
squad car *n* (*POLICE*) coche-patrulla *m.*
squaddie ['skwɔdɪ] *n* (*MIL*: *col*) chivo.
squadron ['skwɔdrn] *n* (*MIL*) escuadrón *m*; (*AVIAT, NAUT*) escuadra.
squalid ['skwɔlɪd] *adj* miserable.
squall [skwɔːl] *n* (*storm*) chubasco; (*wind*) ráfaga.
squalor ['skwɔlə*] *n* miseria.
squander ['skwɔndə*] *vt* (*money*)

derrochar, despilfarrar; (*chances*) desperdiciar.
square [skwɛə*] *n* cuadro; (*in town*) plaza; (*US: block of houses*) manzana, cuadra (*LAM*) ♦ *adj* cuadrado ♦ *vt* (*arrange*) arreglar; (*MATH*) cuadrar; (*reconcile*): **can you ~ it with your conscience?** ¿cómo se justifica ante sí mismo? ♦ *vi* cuadrar, conformarse; **all ~** igual(es); **a ~ meal** una comida decente; **2 metres ~** 2 metros por 2; **1 ~ metre** un metro cuadrado; **to get one's accounts ~** dejar las cuentas claras; **I'll ~ it with him** (*col*) yo lo arreglo con él; **we're back to ~ one** (*fig*) hemos vuelto al punto de partida.
▸**square up** *vi* (*settle*): **to ~ up (with sb)** ajustar cuentas (con algn).
square bracket *n* (*TYP*) corchete *m.*
squarely ['skwɛəlɪ] *adv* (*fully*) de lleno; (*honestly, fairly*) honradamente, justamente.
square root *n* raíz *f* cuadrada.
squash [skwɔʃ] *n* (*vegetable*) calabaza; (*SPORT*) squash *m*; (*BRIT: drink*): **lemon/orange ~** zumo (*SP*) *or* jugo (*LAM*) de limón/naranja ♦ *vt* aplastar.
squat [skwɔt] *adj* achaparrado ♦ *vi* agacharse, sentarse en cuclillas; (*on property*) ocupar ilegalmente.
squatter ['skwɔtə*] *n* ocupante *m/f* ilegal, okupa *m/f.*
squawk [skwɔːk] *vi* graznar.
squeak [skwiːk] *vi* (*hinge, wheel*) chirriar, rechinar; (*shoe, wood*) crujir ♦ *n* (*of hinge, wheel etc*) chirrido, rechinamiento; (*of shoes*) crujir *m*; (*of mouse etc*) chillido.
squeaky ['skwiːkɪ] *adj* que cruje; **to be ~ clean** (*fig*) ser superhonrado.
squeal [skwiːl] *vi* chillar, dar gritos agudos.
squeamish ['skwiːmɪʃ] *adj* delicado, remilgado.
squeeze [skwiːz] *n* presión *f*; (*of hand*) apretón *m*; (*COMM: credit ~*) restricción *f* ♦ *vt* (*lemon etc*) exprimir; (*hand, arm*) apretar; **a ~ of lemon** unas gotas de limón; **to ~ past/under sth** colarse al lado de/por debajo de algo.
▸**squeeze out** *vt* exprimir; (*fig*) excluir.
▸**squeeze through** *vi* abrirse paso con esfuerzos.
squelch [skwɛltʃ] *vi* chapotear.
squid [skwɪd] *n* calamar *m.*
squiggle ['skwɪgl] *n* garabato.
squint [skwɪnt] *vi* entrecerrar los ojos ♦ *n* (*MED*) estrabismo; **to ~ at sth** mirar algo entornando los ojos.
squire ['skwaɪə*] *n* (*BRIT*) terrateniente *m.*
squirm [skwəːm] *vi* retorcerse, revolverse.
squirrel ['skwɪrəl] *n* ardilla.
squirt [skwəːt] *vi* salir a chorros.
Sr *abbr* = **senior, sister** (*REL*).
SRC *n abbr* (*BRIT*: = *Students' Representative Council*) *consejo de estudiantes.*
Sri Lanka [srɪ'læŋkə] *n* Sri Lanka *m.*
SRN *n abbr* (*BRIT*) = *State Registered Nurse.*
SRO *abbr* (*US*) = *standing room only.*
SS *abbr* (= *steamship*) M.V.
SSA *n abbr* (*US*: = *Social Security Administration*) ≈ Seguro Social.
SST *n abbr* (*US*) = *supersonic transport.*
ST *abbr* (*US*: = *Standard Time*) *hora oficial.*
St *abbr* (= *saint*) Sto./a.; (= *street*) c/.
stab [stæb] *n* (*with knife etc*) puñalada; (*of pain*) pinchazo; **to have a ~ at (doing) sth** (*col*) probar (a hacer) algo ♦ *vt* apuñalar; **to ~ sb to death** matar a algn a puñaladas.
stabbing ['stæbɪŋ] *n*: **there's been a ~** han apuñalado a alguien ♦ *adj* (*pain*) punzante.
stability [stə'bɪlɪtɪ] *n* estabilidad *f.*
stabilization [steɪbəlaɪ'zeɪʃən] *n* estabilización *f.*
stabilize ['steɪbəlaɪz] *vt* estabilizar ♦ *vi* estabilizarse.
stabilizer ['steɪbəlaɪzə*] *n* (*AVIAT, NAUT*) estabilizador *m.*
stable ['steɪbl] *adj* estable ♦ *n* cuadra, caballeriza; **riding ~s** escuela hípica.
staccato [stə'kɑːtəu] *adj, adv* staccato.
stack [stæk] *n* montón *m*, pila; (*col*) mar *f* ♦ *vt* amontonar, apilar; **there's ~s of time to finish it** hay cantidad de tiempo para acabarlo.
stacker ['stækə*] *n* (*for printer*) apiladora.
stadium ['steɪdɪəm] *n* estadio.
staff [stɑːf] *n* (*work force*) personal *m*, plantilla; (*BRIT SCOL: also*: **teaching ~**) cuerpo docente; (*stick*) bastón *m* ♦ *vt* proveer de personal; **to be ~ed by Asians/women** tener una plantilla asiática/femenina.
staffroom ['stɑːfruːm] *n* sala de profesores.
Staffs *abbr* (*BRIT*) = *Staffordshire.*
stag [stæg] *n* ciervo, venado; (*BRIT STOCK EXCHANGE*) especulador *m* con nuevas emisiones.
stage [steɪdʒ] *n* escena; (*point*) etapa; (*platform*) plataforma; **the ~** el escenario, el teatro ♦ *vt* (*play*) poner en escena, representar; (*organize*) montar, organizar; (*fig: perform: recovery etc*) efectuar; **in ~s** por etapas; **in the early/final ~s** en las primeras/últimas etapas; **to go through a difficult ~** pasar una fase

or etapa mala.
stagecoach ['steɪdʒkəutʃ] *n* diligencia.
stage door *n* entrada de artistas.
stagehand ['steɪdʒhænd] *n* tramoyista *m/f.*
stage-manage ['steɪdʒmænɪdʒ] *vt* (*fig*) manipular.
stage manager *n* director(a) *m/f* de escena.
stagger ['stægə*] *vi* tambalear ♦ *vt* (*amaze*) asombrar; (*hours, holidays*) escalonar.
staggering ['stægərɪŋ] *adj* (*amazing*) asombroso, pasmoso.
staging post ['steɪdʒɪŋ-] *n* escala.
stagnant ['stægnənt] *adj* estancado.
stagnate [stæg'neɪt] *vi* estancarse; (*fig: economy, mind*) quedarse estancado.
stagnation [stæg'neɪʃən] *n* estancamiento.
stag night, stag party *n* despedida de soltero.
staid [steɪd] *adj* (*clothes*) serio, formal.
stain [steɪn] *n* mancha; (*colouring*) tintura ♦ *vt* manchar; (*wood*) teñir.
stained glass window [steɪnd-] *n* vidriera de colores.
stainless ['steɪnlɪs] *adj* (*steel*) inoxidable.
stain remover *n* quitamanchas *m inv.*
stair [stɛə*] *n* (*step*) peldaño, escalón *m*; **~s** *npl* escaleras *fpl.*
staircase ['stɛəkeɪs], **stairway** ['stɛəweɪ] *n* escalera.
stairwell ['stɛəwɛl] *n* hueco *or* caja de la escalera.
stake [steɪk] *n* estaca, poste *m*; (*BETTING*) apuesta ♦ *vt* (*bet*) apostar; (*also*: **~ out**: *area*) cercar con estacas; **to be at ~** estar en juego; **to have a ~ in sth** tener interés en algo; **to ~ a claim to (sth)** presentar reclamación por *or* reclamar (algo).
stake-out ['steɪkaut] *n* vigilancia; **to be on a ~** estar de vigilancia.
stalactite ['stæləktaɪt] *n* estalactita.
stalagmite ['stæləgmaɪt] *n* estalagmita.
stale [steɪl] *adj* (*bread*) duro; (*food*) pasado.
stalemate ['steɪlmeɪt] *n* tablas *fpl*; **to reach ~** (*fig*) estancarse, alcanzar un punto muerto.
stalk [stɔːk] *n* tallo, caña ♦ *vt* acechar, cazar al acecho; **to ~ off** irse airado.
stall [stɔːl] *n* (*in market*) puesto; (*in stable*) casilla (de establo) ♦ *vt* (*AUT*) parar, calar ♦ *vi* (*AUT*) pararse, calarse; (*fig*) buscar evasivas; **~s** *npl* (*BRIT: in cinema, theatre*) butacas *fpl*; **a newspaper ~** un quiosco (de periódicos); **a flower ~** un puesto de flores.
stallholder ['stɔːlhəuldə*] *n* dueño/a de un puesto.
stallion ['stælɪən] *n* semental *m*, garañón *m.*
stalwart ['stɔːlwət] *n* partidario/a incondicional.
stamen ['steɪmən] *n* estambre *m.*
stamina ['stæmɪnə] *n* resistencia.
stammer ['stæmə*] *n* tartamudeo, balbuceo ♦ *vi* tartamudear, balbucir.
stamp [stæmp] *n* sello, estampilla (*LAM*); (*mark, also fig*) marca, huella; (*on document*) timbre *m* ♦ *vi* (*also*: **~ one's foot**) patear ♦ *vt* patear, golpear con el pie; (*letter*) poner sellos en; (*with rubber ~*) marcar con sello; **~ed addressed envelope (sae)** sobre *m* sellado con las señas propias.
►**stamp out** *vt* (*fire*) apagar con el pie; (*crime, opposition*) acabar con.
stamp album *n* álbum *m* para sellos.
stamp collecting *n* filatelia.
stamp duty *n* (*BRIT*) derecho de timbre.
stampede [stæm'piːd] *n* (*of cattle*) estampida.
stamp machine *n* máquina (expendedora) de sellos.
stance [stæns] *n* postura.
stand [stænd] *n* (*attitude*) posición *f*, postura; (*for taxis*) parada; (*music ~*) atril *m*; (*SPORT*) tribuna; (*at exhibition*) stand *m* ♦ *vb* (*pt, pp* **stood** [stud]) *vi* (*be*) estar, encontrarse; (*be on foot*) estar de pie; (*rise*) levantarse; (*remain*) quedar en pie ♦ *vt* (*place*) poner, colocar; (*tolerate, withstand*) aguantar, soportar; **to make a ~** resistir; (*fig*) mantener una postura firme; **to take a ~ on an issue** adoptar una actitud hacia una cuestión; **to ~ for parliament** (*BRIT*) presentarse (como candidato) a las elecciones; **nothing ~s in our way** nada nos lo impide; **to ~ still** quedarse inmóvil; **to let sth ~ as it is** dejar algo como está; **as things ~** tal como están las cosas; **to ~ sb a drink/meal** invitar a algn a una copa/a comer; **the company will have to ~ the loss** la empresa tendrá que hacer frente a las pérdidas; **I can't ~ him** no le aguanto, no le puedo ver; **to ~ guard** *or* **watch** (*MIL*) hacer guardia.
►**stand aside** *vi* apartarse, mantenerse aparte.
►**stand by** *vi* (*be ready*) estar listo ♦ *vt fus* (*opinion*) mantener.
►**stand down** *vi* (*withdraw*) ceder el puesto; (*MIL, LAW*) retirarse.
►**stand for** *vt fus* (*signify*) significar; (*tolerate*) aguantar, permitir.
►**stand in for** *vt fus* suplir a.
►**stand out** *vi* (*be prominent*) destacarse.
►**stand up** *vi* (*rise*) levantarse, ponerse de

pie.

▸**stand up for** *vt fus* defender.

▸**stand up to** *vt fus* hacer frente a.

stand-alone ['stændələun] *adj* (*COMPUT*) autónomo.

standard ['stændəd] *n* patrón *m*, norma; (*flag*) estandarte *m* ♦ *adj* (*size etc*) normal, corriente, estándar; **~s** *npl* (*morals*) valores *mpl* morales; **the gold ~** (*COMM*) el patrón oro; **high/low ~** de alto/bajo nivel; **below** *or* **not up to ~** (*work*) de calidad inferior; **to be** *or* **come up to ~** satisfacer los requisitos; **to apply a double ~** aplicar un doble criterio.

standardization [stændədaɪ'zeɪʃən] *n* normalización *f*.

standardize ['stændədaɪz] *vt* estandarizar.

standard lamp *n* (*BRIT*) lámpara de pie.

standard model *n* modelo stándard.

standard of living *n* nivel *m* de vida.

standard practice *n* norma, práctica común.

standard rate *n* tasa de imposición.

standard time *n* hora oficial.

stand-by ['stændbaɪ] *n* (*alert*) alerta, aviso; (*also*: **~ ticket**: *THEAT*) *entrada reducida de última hora*; (: *AVIAT*) billete *m* standby; **to be on ~** estar preparado; (*doctor*) estar listo para acudir; (*AVIAT*) estar en la lista de espera.

stand-by generator *n* generador *m* de reserva.

stand-by passenger *n* (*AVIAT*) pasajero/a en lista de espera.

stand-by ticket *n* (*AVIAT*) (billete *m*) standby *m*.

stand-in ['stændɪn] *n* suplente *m/f*; (*CINE*) doble *m/f*.

standing ['stændɪŋ] *adj* (*upright*) derecho; (*on foot*) de pie, en pie; (*permanent*: *committee*) permanente; (: *rule*) fijo; (: *army*) permanente, regular; (*grievance*) constante, viejo ♦ *n* reputación *f*; (*duration*): **of 6 months' ~** que lleva 6 meses; **of many years' ~** que lleva muchos años; **he was given a ~ ovation** le dieron una calurosa ovación de pie; **~ joke** motivo constante de broma; **a man of some ~** un hombre de cierta posición *or* categoría.

standing order *n* (*BRIT*: *at bank*) giro bancario; **standing orders** *npl* (*MIL*) reglamento *sg* general.

standing room *n* sitio para estar de pie.

stand-off ['stændɔf] *n* (*esp US*: *stalemate*) punto muerto.

stand-offish [stænd'ɔfɪʃ] *adj* distante.

standpat ['stændpæt] *adj* (*US*) inmovilista.

standpipe ['stændpaɪp] *n* tubo vertical.

standpoint ['stændpɔɪnt] *n* punto de vista.

standstill ['stændstɪl] *n*: **at a ~** paralizado, en un punto muerto; **to come to a ~** pararse, quedar paralizado.

stank [stæŋk] *pt of* **stink**.

staple ['steɪpl] *n* (*for papers*) grapa; (*product*) producto *or* artículo de primeva necesidad ♦ *adj* (*crop, industry, food etc*) básico ♦ *vt* grapar.

stapler ['steɪplə*] *n* grapadora.

star [stɑː*] *n* estrella; (*celebrity*) estrella, astro ♦ *vi*: **to ~ in** ser la estrella de; **four-~ hotel** hotel *m* de cuatro estrellas; **4-~ petrol** gasolina extra.

star attraction *n* atracción *f* principal.

starboard ['stɑːbəd] *n* estribor *m*.

starch [stɑːtʃ] *n* almidón *m*.

starchy ['stɑːtʃɪ] *adj* (*food*) feculento.

stardom ['stɑːdəm] *n* estrellato.

stare [stɛə*] *n* mirada fija ♦ *vi*: **to ~ at** mirar fijo.

starfish ['stɑːfɪʃ] *n* estrella de mar.

stark [stɑːk] *adj* (*bleak*) severo, escueto; (*simplicity, colour*) austero; (*reality, truth*) puro; (*poverty*) absoluto ♦ *adv*: **~ naked** en cueros.

starkers ['stɑːkəz] *adj* (*BRIT col*): **to be ~** estar en cueros.

starlet ['stɑːlɪt] *n* (*CINE*) actriz *f* principiante.

starling ['stɑːlɪŋ] *n* estornino.

starry ['stɑːrɪ] *adj* estrellado.

starry-eyed [stɑːrɪ'aɪd] *adj* (*gullible, innocent*) inocentón/ona, ingenuo; (*idealistic*) idealista; (*from wonder*) asombrado; (*from love*) enamoradísimo.

Stars and Stripes *npl*: **the ~** las barras y las estrellas, la bandera de EEUU.

star sign *n* signo del zodíaco.

star-studded ['stɑːstʌdɪd] *adj*: **a ~ cast** un elenco estelar.

start [stɑːt] *n* (*beginning*) principio, comienzo; (*departure*) salida; (*sudden movement*) sobresalto; (*advantage*) ventaja ♦ *vt* empezar, comenzar; (*cause*) causar; (*found*: *business, newspaper*) establecer, fundar; (*engine*) poner en marcha ♦ *vi* (*begin*) comenzar, empezar; (*with fright*) asustarse, sobresaltarse; (*train etc*) salir; **to give sb a ~** dar un susto a algn; **at the ~** al principio; **for a ~** en primer lugar; **to make an early ~** ponerse en camino temprano; **the thieves had 3 hours' ~** los ladrones llevaban 3 horas de ventaja; **to ~ a fire** provocar un incendio; **to ~ doing** *or* **to do sth** empezar a hacer algo; **to ~ (off) with ...**

(*firstly*) para empezar; (*at the beginning*) al principio.
▸**start off** *vi* empezar, comenzar; (*leave*) salir, ponerse en camino.
▸**start over** *vi* (*US*) volver a empezar.
▸**start up** *vi* comenzar; (*car*) ponerse en marcha ♦ *vt* comenzar; (*car*) poner en marcha.
starter ['stɑːtə*] *n* (*AUT*) botón *m* de arranque; (*SPORT: official*) juez *m/f* de salida; (*: runner*) corredor(a) *m/f*; (*BRIT CULIN*) entrada.
starting point ['stɑːtɪŋ-] *n* punto de partida.
starting price *n* (*COMM*) precio inicial.
startle ['stɑːtl] *vt* asustar, sobresaltar.
startling ['stɑːtlɪŋ] *adj* alarmante.
star turn *n* (*BRIT*) atracción *f* principal.
starvation [stɑː'veɪʃən] *n* hambre *f*, hambruna (*LAM*); (*MED*) inanición *f*.
starvation wages *npl* sueldo *sg* de hambre.
starve [stɑːv] *vi* pasar hambre; (*to death*) morir de hambre ♦ *vt* hacer pasar hambre; (*fig*) privar; **I'm starving** estoy muerto de hambre.
stash [stæʃ] *vt*: **to ~ sth away** (*col*) poner algo a buen recaudo.
state [steɪt] *n* estado; (*pomp*): **in ~** con mucha ceremonia ♦ *vt* (*say, declare*) afirmar; (*a case*) presentar, exponer; **~ of emergency** estado de excepción *or* emergencia; **~ of mind** estado de ánimo; **to lie in ~** (*corpse*) estar de cuerpo presente; **to be in a ~** estar agitado.
State Department *n* (*US*) Ministerio de Asuntos Exteriores.
state education *n* (*BRIT*) enseñanza pública.
stateless ['steɪtlɪs] *adj* desnacionalizado.
stately ['steɪtlɪ] *adj* majestuoso, imponente.
statement ['steɪtmənt] *n* afirmación *f*; (*LAW*) declaración *f*; (*COMM*) estado; **official ~** informe *m* oficial; **~ of account, bank ~** estado de cuenta.
state-of-the-art ['steɪtəvðɪ'ɑːt] *adj* (*technology etc*) puntero.
state-owned ['steɪtəund] *adj* estatal, del estado.
States [steɪts] *npl*: **the ~** los Estados Unidos.
state school *n* escuela *or* colegio estatal.
statesman ['steɪtsmən] *n* estadista *m*.
statesmanship ['steɪtsmənʃɪp] *n* habilidad *f* política, arte *m* de gobernar.
static ['stætɪk] *n* (*RADIO*) parásitos *mpl* ♦ *adj* estático.
static electricity *n* electricidad *f* estática.
station ['steɪʃən] *n* (*gen*) estación *f*; (*place*) puesto, sitio; (*RADIO*) emisora; (*rank*) posición *f* social ♦ *vt* colocar, situar; (*MIL*) apostar; **action ~s!** ¡a los puestos de combate!; **to be ~ed in** (*MIL*) estar estacionado en.
stationary ['steɪʃnərɪ] *adj* estacionario, fijo.
stationer ['steɪʃənə*] *n* papelero/a.
stationer's (shop) *n* (*BRIT*) papelería.
stationery ['steɪʃənərɪ] *n* (*writing paper*) papel *m* de escribir; (*writing materials*) artículos *mpl* de escritorio.
station master *n* (*RAIL*) jefe *m* de estación.
station wagon *n* (*US*) coche *m* familiar con ranchera.
statistic [stə'tɪstɪk] *n* estadística.
statistical [stə'tɪstɪkl] *adj* estadístico.
statistics [stə'tɪstɪks] *n* (*science*) estadística.
statue ['stætjuː] *n* estatua.
statuette [stætju'ɛt] *n* figurilla.
stature ['stætʃə*] *n* estatura; (*fig*) talla.
status ['steɪtəs] *n* condición *f*, estado; (*reputation*) reputación *f*, estatus *m*; **the ~ quo** el statu quo.
status line *n* (*COMPUT*) línea de situación *or* de estado.
status symbol *n* símbolo de prestigio.
statute ['stætjuːt] *n* estatuto, ley *f*.
statute book *n* código de leyes.
statutory ['stætjutrɪ] *adj* estatutario; **~ meeting** junta ordinaria.
staunch [stɔːntʃ] *adj* leal, incondicional ♦ *vt* (*flow, blood*) restañar.
stave [steɪv] *vt*: **to ~ off** (*attack*) rechazar; (*threat*) evitar.
stay [steɪ] *n* (*period of time*) estancia; (*LAW*): **~ of execution** aplazamiento de una sentencia ♦ *vi* (*remain*) quedar(se); (*as guest*) hospedarse; **to ~ put** seguir en el mismo sitio; **to ~ the night/5 days** pasar la noche/estar *or* quedarse 5 días.
▸**stay behind** *vi* quedar atrás.
▸**stay in** *vi* (*at home*) quedarse en casa.
▸**stay on** *vi* quedarse.
▸**stay out** *vi* (*of house*) no volver a casa; (*strikers*) no volver al trabajo.
▸**stay up** *vi* (*at night*) velar, no acostarse.
staying power ['steɪɪŋ-] *n* resistencia, aguante *m*.
STD *n abbr* (*BRIT: = subscriber trunk dialling*) *servicio de conferencias automáticas*; (*= sexually transmitted disease*) ETS *f*.
stead [stɛd] *n*: **in sb's ~** en lugar de algn; **to stand sb in good ~** ser muy útil a algn.
steadfast ['stɛdfɑːst] *adj* firme, resuelto.
steadily ['stɛdɪlɪ] *adv* (*firmly*) firmemente; (*unceasingly*) sin parar; (*fixedly*)

fijamente; (*walk*) normalmente; (*drive*) a velocidad constante.
steady ['stɛdɪ] *adj* (*fixed*) firme, fijo; (*regular*) regular; (*boyfriend etc*) formal, fijo; (*person, character*) sensato, juicioso ♦ *vt* (*hold*) mantener firme; (*stabilize*) estabilizar; (*nerves*) calmar; **to ~ o.s. on** *or* **against sth** afirmarse en algo.
steak [steɪk] *n* (*gen*) filete *m*; (*beef*) bistec *m*.
steal, *pt* **stole**, *pp* **stolen** [stiːl, stəul, 'stəuln] *vt, vi* robar.
▸**steal away**, **steal off** *vi* marcharse furtivamente, escabullirse.
stealth [stɛlθ] *n*: **by ~** a escondidas, sigilosamente.
stealthy ['stɛlθɪ] *adj* cauteloso, sigiloso.
steam [stiːm] *n* vapor *m*; (*mist*) vaho, humo ♦ *vt* (*CULIN*) cocer al vapor ♦ *vi* echar vapor; (*ship*): **to ~ along** avanzar, ir avanzando; **under one's own ~** (*fig*) por sus propios medios *or* propias fuerzas; **to run out of ~** (*fig: person*) quedar(se) agotado, quemarse; **to let off ~** (*fig*) desahogarse.
▸**steam up** *vi* (*window*) empañarse; **to get ~ed up about sth** (*fig*) ponerse negro por algo.
steam engine *n* máquina de vapor.
steamer ['stiːmə*] *n* (buque *m* de) vapor *m*; (*CULIN*) *recipiente para cocinar al vapor*.
steam iron *n* plancha de vapor.
steamroller ['stiːmrəulə*] *n* apisonadora.
steamship ['stiːmʃɪp] *n* = **steamer**.
steamy ['stiːmɪ] *adj* (*room*) lleno de vapor; (*window*) empañado.
steel [stiːl] *n* acero ♦ *adj* de acero.
steel band *n* banda de percusión del Caribe.
steel industry *n* industria siderúrgica.
steel mill *n* fábrica de acero.
steelworks ['stiːlwəːks] *n* acería, fundición *f* de acero.
steely ['stiːlɪ] *adj* (*determination*) inflexible; (*gaze*) duro; (*eyes*) penetrante; **~ grey** gris *m* metálico.
steelyard ['stiːljɑːd] *n* romana.
steep [stiːp] *adj* escarpado, abrupto; (*stair*) empinado; (*price*) exorbitante, excesivo ♦ *vt* empapar, remojar.
steeple ['stiːpl] *n* aguja, campanario.
steeplechase ['stiːpltʃeɪs] *n* carrera de obstáculos.
steeplejack ['stiːpldʒæk] *n* reparador(a) *m/f* de chimeneas *or* de campanarios.
steer [stɪə*] *vt* (*car*) conducir (*SP*), manejar (*LAM*); (*person*) dirigir, guiar ♦ *vi* conducir; **to ~ clear of sb/sth** (*fig*) esquivar a algn/evadir algo.
steering ['stɪərɪŋ] *n* (*AUT*) dirección *f*.
steering committee *n* comisión *f* directiva.
steering wheel *n* volante *m*.
stellar ['stɛlə*] *adj* estelar.
stem [stɛm] *n* (*of plant*) tallo; (*of glass*) pie *m*; (*of pipe*) cañón *m* ♦ *vt* detener; (*blood*) restañar.
▸**stem from** *vt fus* ser consecuencia de.
stench [stɛntʃ] *n* hedor *m*.
stencil ['stɛnsl] *n* (*typed*) cliché *m*, clisé *m*; (*lettering*) plantilla ♦ *vt* hacer un cliché de.
stenographer [stɛ'nɔgrəfə*] *n* (*US*) taquígrafo/a.
step [stɛp] *n* paso; (*sound*) paso, pisada; (*stair*) peldaño, escalón *m* ♦ *vi*: **to ~ forward** dar un paso adelante; **~s** *npl* (*BRIT*) = **~ladder**; **~ by ~** paso a paso; (*fig*) poco a poco; **to keep in ~ (with)** llevar el paso de; (*fig*) llevar el paso de, estar de acuerdo con; **to be in/out of ~ with** estar acorde con/estar en disonancia con; **to take ~s to solve a problem** tomar medidas para resolver un problema.
▸**step down** *vi* (*fig*) retirarse.
▸**step in** *vi* entrar; (*fig*) intervenir.
▸**step off** *vt fus* bajar de.
▸**step on** *vt fus* pisar.
▸**step over** *vt fus* pasar por encima de.
▸**step up** *vt* (*increase*) aumentar.
step aerobics *npl* step *m*.
stepbrother ['stɛpbrʌðə*] *n* hermanastro.
stepdaughter ['stɛpdɔːtə*] *n* hijastra.
stepfather ['stɛpfɑːðə*] *n* padrastro.
stepladder ['stɛplædə*] *n* escalera doble *or* de tijera.
stepmother ['stɛpmʌðə*] *n* madrastra.
stepping stone ['stɛpɪŋ-] *n* pasadera.
step Reebok ® [-'riːbɔk] *n* step *m*.
stepsister ['stɛpsɪstə*] *n* hermanastra.
stepson ['stɛpsʌn] *n* hijastro.
stereo ['stɛrɪəu] *n* estéreo ♦ *adj* (*also*: **~phonic**) estéreo, estereofónico; **in ~** en estéreo.
stereotype ['stɪərɪətaɪp] *n* estereotipo ♦ *vt* estereotipar.
sterile ['stɛraɪl] *adj* estéril.
sterilization [stɛrɪlaɪ'zeɪʃən] *n* esterilización *f*.
sterilize ['stɛrɪlaɪz] *vt* esterilizar.
sterling ['stəːlɪŋ] *adj* (*silver*) de ley ♦ *n* (*ECON*) libras *fpl* esterlinas; **a pound ~** una libra esterlina; **he is of ~ character** tiene un carácter excelente.
stern [stəːn] *adj* severo, austero ♦ *n* (*NAUT*) popa.
sternum ['stəːnəm] *n* esternón *m*.

steroid ['stɪərɔɪd] *n* esteroide *m*.
stethoscope ['stɛθəskəup] *n* estetoscopio.
stevedore ['sti:vədɔ:*] *n* estibador *m*.
stew [stju:] *n* cocido, estofado, guisado (*LAM*) ♦ *vt, vi* estofar, guisar; (*fruit*) cocer; **~ed fruit** compota de fruta.
steward ['stju:əd] *n* (*BRIT*: *gen*) camarero; (*shop* ~) enlace *m/f* sindical.
stewardess ['stjuədəs] *n* azafata.
stewardship ['stjuədʃɪp] *n* tutela.
stewing steak ['stju:ɪŋ-], (*US*) **stew meat** *n* carne *f* de vaca.
St. Ex. *abbr* = **stock exchange**.
stg *abbr* (= *sterling*) ester.
stick [stɪk] *n* palo; (*as weapon*) porra; (*walking* ~) bastón *m* ♦ *vb* (*pt, pp* **stuck** [stʌk]) *vt* (*glue*) pegar; (*col*: *put*) meter; (: *tolerate*) aguantar, soportar ♦ *vi* pegarse; (*come to a stop*) quedarse parado; (*get jammed*: *door, lift*) atascarse; **to get hold of the wrong end of the** ~ entender al revés; **to** ~ **to** (*word, principles*) atenerse a, ser fiel a; (*promise*) cumplir; **it stuck in my mind** se me quedó grabado; **to** ~ **sth into** clavar *or* hincar algo en.
►**stick around** *vi* (*col*) quedarse.
►**stick out** *vi* sobresalir ♦ *vt*: **to** ~ **it out** (*col*) aguantar.
►**stick up** *vi* sobresalir.
►**stick up for** *vt fus* defender.
sticker ['stɪkə*] *n* (*label*) etiqueta adhesiva; (*with slogan*) pegatina.
sticking plaster ['stɪkɪŋ-] *n* (*BRIT*) esparadrapo.
sticking point *n* (*fig*) punto de fricción.
stickler ['stɪklə*] *n*: **to be a** ~ **for** insistir mucho en.
stick shift *n* (*US AUT*) palanca de cambios.
stick-up ['stɪkʌp] *n* asalto, atraco.
sticky ['stɪkɪ] *adj* pegajoso; (*label*) adhesivo; (*fig*) difícil.
stiff [stɪf] *adj* rígido, tieso; (*hard*) duro; (*difficult*) difícil; (*person*) inflexible; (*price*) exorbitante; **to have a** ~ **neck/back** tener tortícolis/dolor de espalda; **the door's** ~ la puerta está atrancada.
stiffen ['stɪfn] *vt* hacer más rígido; (*limb*) entumecer ♦ *vi* endurecerse; (*grow stronger*) fortalecerse.
stiffness ['stɪfnɪs] *n* rigidez *f*.
stifle ['staɪfl] *vt* ahogar, sofocar.
stifling ['staɪflɪŋ] *adj* (*heat*) sofocante, bochornoso.
stigma, *pl* (*BOT, MED, REL*) **~ta**, (*fig*) **~s** ['stɪgmə, stɪg'mɑ:tə] *n* estigma *m*.
stile [staɪl] *n* escalera (*para pasar una cerca*).
stiletto [stɪ'lɛtəu] *n* (*BRIT*: *also*: ~ **heel**) tacón *m* de aguja.
still [stɪl] *adj* inmóvil, quieto; (*orange juice etc*) sin gas ♦ *adv* (*up to this time*) todavía; (*even*) aún; (*nonetheless*) sin embargo, aun así ♦ *n* (*CINE*) foto *f* fija; **keep** ~**!** ¡estate quieto!, ¡no te muevas!; **he** ~ **hasn't arrived** todavía no ha llegado.
stillborn ['stɪlbɔ:n] *adj* nacido muerto.
still life *n* naturaleza muerta.
stilt [stɪlt] *n* zanco; (*pile*) pilar *m*, soporte *m*.
stilted ['stɪltɪd] *adj* afectado, artificial.
stimulant ['stɪmjulənt] *n* estimulante *m*.
stimulate ['stɪmjuleɪt] *vt* estimular.
stimulating ['stɪmjuleɪtɪŋ] *adj* estimulante.
stimulation [stɪmju'leɪʃən] *n* estímulo.
stimulus, *pl* **-li** ['stɪmjuləs, -laɪ] *n* estímulo, incentivo.
sting [stɪŋ] *n* (*wound*) picadura; (*pain*) escozor *m*, picazón *m*; (*organ*) aguijón *m*; (*col*: *confidence trick*) timo ♦ *vb* (*pt, pp* **stung** [stʌŋ]) *vt* picar ♦ *vi* picar, escocer; **my eyes are** ~**ing** me pican *or* escuecen los ojos.
stingy ['stɪndʒɪ] *adj* tacaño.
stink [stɪŋk] *n* hedor *m*, tufo ♦ *vi* (*pt* **stank**, *pp* **stunk** [stæŋk, stʌŋk]) heder, apestar.
stinking ['stɪŋkɪŋ] *adj* hediondo, fétido; (*fig*: *col*) horrible.
stint [stɪnt] *n* tarea, destajo; **to do one's** ~ **at sth** hacer su parte (de algo), hacer lo que corresponde (de algo) ♦ *vi*: **to** ~ **on** escatimar.
stipend ['staɪpɛnd] *n* salario, remuneración *f*.
stipendiary [staɪ'pɛndɪərɪ] *adj*: ~ **magistrate** magistrado/a estipendiario/a.
stipulate ['stɪpjuleɪt] *vt* estipular.
stipulation [stɪpju'leɪʃən] *n* estipulación *f*.
stir [stə:*] *n* (*fig*: *agitation*) conmoción *f* ♦ *vt* (*tea etc*) remover; (*fire*) atizar; (*move*) agitar; (*fig*: *emotions*) conmover ♦ *vi* moverse; **to give sth a** ~ remover algo; **to cause a** ~ causar conmoción *or* sensación.
►**stir up** *vt* excitar; (*trouble*) fomentar.
stir-fry ['stə:fraɪ] *vt* sofreír removiendo ♦ *n* *plato preparado sofriendo y removiendo los ingredientes*.
stirrup ['stɪrəp] *n* estribo.
stitch [stɪtʃ] *n* (*SEWING*) puntada; (*KNITTING*) punto; (*MED*) punto (de sutura); (*pain*) punzada ♦ *vt* coser; (*MED*) suturar.
stoat [stəut] *n* armiño.
stock [stɔk] *n* (*COMM*: *reserves*) existencias *fpl*, stock *m*; (: *selection*) surtido; (*AGR*) ganado, ganadería; (*CULIN*) caldo; (*fig*: *lineage*) estirpe *f*, cepa; (*FINANCE*) capital *m*; (: *shares*) acciones *fpl*; (*RAIL*: *rolling* ~) material *m* rodante ♦ *adj* (*COMM*: *goods,*

size) normal, de serie; (*fig*: *reply etc*) clásico, trillado; (: *greeting*) acostumbrado ♦ *vt* (*have in* ~) tener existencias de; (*supply*) proveer, abastecer; **in** ~ en existencia *or* almacén; **to have sth in** ~ tener existencias de algo; **out of** ~ agotado; **to take** ~ **of** (*fig*) considerar, examinar; ~**s** *npl* (*HISTORY*: *punishment*) cepo *sg*; ~**s and shares** acciones y valores; **government** ~ papel *m* del Estado.

►**stock up with** *vt fus* abastecerse de.

stockbroker ['stɔkbrəukə*] *n* agente *m/f or* corredor(a) *m/f* de bolsa.

stock control *n* (*COMM*) control *m* de existencias.

stock cube *n* pastilla *or* cubito de caldo.

stock exchange *n* bolsa.

stockholder ['stɔkhəuldə*] *n* (*US*) accionista *m/f*.

Stockholm ['stɔkhəum] *n* Estocolmo.

stocking ['stɔkɪŋ] *n* media.

stock-in-trade ['stɔkɪn'treɪd] *n* (*tools etc*) herramientas *fpl*; (*stock*) existencia de mercancías; (*fig*): **it's his** ~ es su especialidad.

stockist ['stɔkɪst] *n* (*BRIT*) distribuidor(a) *m/f*.

stock market *n* bolsa (de valores).

stock phrase *n* vieja frase *f*.

stockpile ['stɔkpaɪl] *n* reserva ♦ *vt* acumular, almacenar.

stockroom ['stɔkru:m] *n* almacén *m*, depósito.

stocktaking ['stɔkteɪkɪŋ] *n* (*BRIT COMM*) inventario, balance *m*.

stocky ['stɔkɪ] *adj* (*strong*) robusto; (*short*) achaparrado.

stodgy ['stɔdʒɪ] *adj* indigesto, pesado.

stoical ['stəuɪkəl] *adj* estoico.

stoke [stəuk] *vt* atizar.

stole [stəul] *pt of* **steal** ♦ *n* estola.

stolen ['stəuln] *pp of* **steal**.

stolid ['stɔlɪd] *adj* (*person*) imperturbable, impasible.

stomach ['stʌmək] *n* (*ANAT*) estómago; (*belly*) vientre *m* ♦ *vt* tragar, aguantar.

stomach ache *n* dolor *m* de estómago.

stomach pump *n* bomba gástrica.

stomach ulcer *n* úlcera de estómago.

stomp [stɔmp] *vi*: **to** ~ **in/out** entrar/salir con pasos ruidosos.

stone [stəun] *n* piedra; (*in fruit*) hueso; (*BRIT*: *weight*) = *6.348 kg*; *14 pounds* ♦ *adj* de piedra ♦ *vt* apedrear; **within a** ~**'s throw of the station** a tiro de piedra *or* a dos pasos de la estación.

Stone Age *n*: **the** ~ la Edad de Piedra.

stone-cold ['stəun'kəuld] *adj* helado.

stoned [stəund] *adj* (*col*: *drunk*) trompa, borracho, colocado.

stone-deaf ['stəun'dɛf] *adj* sordo como una tapia.

stonemason ['stəunmeɪsən] *n* albañil *m*.

stonewall [stəun'wɔ:l] *vi* alargar la cosa innecesariamente ♦ *vt* dar largas a.

stonework ['stəunwə:k] *n* (*art*) cantería.

stony ['stəunɪ] *adj* pedregoso; (*glance*) glacial.

stood [stud] *pt*, *pp of* **stand**.

stooge [stu:dʒ] *n* (*col*) hombre *m* de paja.

stool [stu:l] *n* taburete *m*.

stoop [stu:p] *vi* (*also*: **have a** ~) ser cargado de espaldas; (*bend*) inclinarse, encorvarse; **to** ~ **to (doing) sth** rebajarse a (hacer) algo.

stop [stɔp] *n* parada, alto; (*in punctuation*) punto ♦ *vt* parar, detener; (*break off*) suspender; (*block*) tapar, cerrar; (*prevent*) impedir; (*also*: **put a** ~ **to**) poner término a ♦ *vi* pararse, detenerse; (*end*) acabarse; **to** ~ **doing sth** dejar de hacer algo; **to** ~ **sb (from) doing sth** impedir a algn hacer algo; **to** ~ **dead** pararse en seco; ~ **it!** ¡basta ya!, ¡párate!

►**stop by** *vi* pasar por.

►**stop off** *vi* interrumpir el viaje.

►**stop up** *vt* (*hole*) tapar.

stopcock ['stɔpkɔk] *n* llave *f* de paso.

stopgap ['stɔpgæp] *n* interino; (*person*) sustituto/a; (*measure*) medida provisional ♦ *cpd* (*situation*) provisional.

stoplights ['stɔplaɪts] *npl* (*AUT*) luces *fpl* de detención.

stopover ['stɔpəuvə*] *n* parada intermedia; (*AVIAT*) escala.

stoppage ['stɔpɪdʒ] *n* (*strike*) paro; (*temporary stop*) interrupción *f*; (*of pay*) suspensión *f*; (*blockage*) obstrucción *f*.

stopper ['stɔpə*] *n* tapón *m*.

stop press *n* noticias *fpl* de última hora.

stopwatch ['stɔpwɔtʃ] *n* cronómetro.

storage ['stɔ:rɪdʒ] *n* almacenaje *m*; (*COMPUT*) almacenamiento.

storage capacity *n* espacio de almacenaje.

storage heater *n* acumulador *m* de calor.

store [stɔ:*] *n* (*stock*) provisión *f*; (*depot*; *BRIT*: *large shop*) almacén *m*; (*US*) tienda; (*reserve*) reserva, repuesto ♦ *vt* (*gen*, *COMPUT*) almacenar; (*keep*) guardar; (*in filing system*) archivar; ~**s** *npl* víveres *mpl*; **who knows what is in** ~ **for us** quién sabe lo que nos espera; **to set great/little** ~ **by sth** dar mucha/poca importancia a algo, valorar mucho/poco algo.

►**store up** *vt* acumular.
storehouse ['stɔːhaus] *n* almacén *m*, depósito.
storekeeper ['stɔːkiːpə*] *n* (*US*) tendero/a.
storeroom ['stɔːruːm] *n* despensa.
storey, (*US*) **story** ['stɔːrɪ] *n* piso.
stork [stɔːk] *n* cigüeña.
storm [stɔːm] *n* tormenta; (*wind*) vendaval *m*; (*fig*) tempestad *f* ♦ *vi* (*fig*) rabiar ♦ *vt* tomar por asalto, asaltar; **to take a town by** ~ (*MIL*) tomar una ciudad por asalto.
storm cloud *n* nubarrón *m*.
storm door *n* contrapuerta.
stormy ['stɔːmɪ] *adj* tempestuoso.
story ['stɔːrɪ] *n* historia; (*PRESS*) artículo; (*joke*) cuento, chiste *m*; (*plot*) argumento; (*lie*) cuento; (*US*) = **storey.**
storybook ['stɔːrɪbuk] *n* libro de cuentos.
storyteller ['stɔːrɪtɛlə*] *n* cuentista *m/f*.
stout [staut] *adj* (*strong*) sólido; (*fat*) gordo, corpulento ♦ *n* cerveza negra.
stove [stəuv] *n* (*for cooking*) cocina; (*for heating*) estufa; **gas/electric** ~ cocina de gas/eléctrica.
stow [stəu] *vt* meter, poner; (*NAUT*) estibar.
stowaway ['stəuəweɪ] *n* polizón/ona *m/f*.
straddle ['strædl] *vt* montar a horcajadas.
straggle ['strægl] *vi* (*wander*) vagar en desorden; (*lag behind*) rezagarse.
straggler ['stræglə*] *n* rezagado/a.
straggling ['stræglɪŋ], **straggly** ['stræglɪ] *adj* (*hair*) desordenado.
straight [streɪt] *adj* (*direct*) recto, derecho; (*plain, uncomplicated*) sencillo; (*frank*) franco, directo; (*in order*) en orden; (*continuous*) continuo; (*THEAT: part, play*) serio; (*person: conventional*) recto, convencional; (*: heterosexual*) heterosexual ♦ *adv* derecho, directamente; (*drink*) solo; **to put** *or* **get sth** ~ dejar algo en claro; **10** ~ **wins** 10 victorias seguidas; **to be (all)** ~ (*tidy*) estar en orden; (*clarified*) estar claro; **I went** ~ **home** (me) fui directamente a casa; ~ **away,** ~ **off** (*at once*) en seguida.
straighten ['streɪtn] *vt* (*also:* ~ **out**) enderezar, poner derecho; **to** ~ **things out** poner las cosas en orden.
straight-faced [streɪt'feɪst] *adj* serio ♦ *adv* sin mostrar emoción, impávido.
straightforward [streɪt'fɔːwəd] *adj* (*simple*) sencillo; (*honest*) sincero.
strain [streɪn] *n* (*gen*) tensión *f*; (*TECH*) esfuerzo; (*MED*) distensión *f*, torcedura; (*breed*) raza; (*lineage*) linaje *m*; (*of virus*) variedad *f* ♦ *vt* (*back etc*) distender, torcerse; (*tire*) cansar; (*stretch*) estirar; (*filter*) filtrar; (*meaning*) tergiversar ♦ *vi* esforzarse; ~**s** *npl* (*MUS*) son *m*; **she's under a lot of** ~ está bajo mucha tensión.
strained [streɪnd] *adj* (*muscle*) torcido; (*laugh*) forzado; (*relations*) tenso.
strainer ['streɪnə*] *n* colador *m*.
strait [streɪt] *n* (*GEO*) estrecho; **to be in dire** ~**s** (*fig*) estar en un gran aprieto.
straitjacket ['streɪtdʒækɪt] *n* camisa de fuerza.
strait-laced [streɪt'leɪst] *adj* mojigato, gazmoño.
strand [strænd] *n* (*of thread*) hebra; (*of rope*) ramal *m*; **a** ~ **of hair** un pelo.
stranded ['strændɪd] *adj* (*person*) colgado.
strange [streɪndʒ] *adj* (*not known*) desconocido; (*odd*) extraño, raro.
stranger ['streɪndʒə*] *n* desconocido/a; (*from another area*) forastero/a; **I'm a** ~ **here** no soy de aquí.
strangle ['stræŋgl] *vt* estrangular.
stranglehold ['stræŋglhəuld] *n* (*fig*) dominio completo.
strangulation [stræŋgju'leɪʃən] *n* estrangulación *f*.
strap [stræp] *n* correa; (*of slip, dress*) tirante *m* ♦ *vt* atar con correa.
straphanging ['stræphæŋɪŋ] *n* viajar *m* de pie *or* parado (*LAM*).
strapless ['stræplɪs] *adj* (*bra, dress*) sin tirantes.
strapped [stræpt] *adj*: **to be** ~ **for cash** (*col*) andar mal de dinero.
strapping ['stræpɪŋ] *adj* robusto, fornido.
Strasbourg ['stræzbəːg] *n* Estrasburgo.
strata ['strɑːtə] *npl of* **stratum.**
stratagem ['strætɪdʒəm] *n* estratagema.
strategic [strə'tiːdʒɪk] *adj* estratégico.
strategy ['strætɪdʒɪ] *n* estrategia.
stratum, *pl* **strata** ['strɑːtəm, 'strɑːtə] *n* estrato.
straw [strɔː] *n* paja; (*drinking* ~) caña, pajita; **that's the last** ~! ¡eso es el colmo!
strawberry ['strɔːbərɪ] *n* fresa, frutilla (*LAM*).
stray [streɪ] *adj* (*animal*) extraviado; (*bullet*) perdido; (*scattered*) disperso ♦ *vi* extraviarse, perderse; (*wander: walker*) vagar, ir sin rumbo fijo; (*: speaker*) desvariar.
streak [striːk] *n* raya; (*fig: of madness etc*) vena ♦ *vt* rayar ♦ *vi*: **to** ~ **past** pasar como un rayo; **to have** ~**s in one's hair** tener vetas en el pelo; **a winning/losing** ~ una racha de buena/mala suerte.
streaker ['striːkə*] *n* corredor(a) *m/f* desnudo/a.
streaky ['striːkɪ] *adj* rayado.
stream [striːm] *n* riachuelo, arroyo; (*jet*)

chorro; (*flow*) corriente *f*; (*of people*) oleada ♦ *vt* (*SCOL*) dividir en grupos por habilidad ♦ *vi* correr, fluir; **to ~ in/out** (*people*) entrar/salir en tropel; **against the ~** a contracorriente; **on ~** (*new power plant etc*) en funcionamiento.

streamer ['stri:mə*] *n* serpentina.

stream feed *n* (*on photocopier etc*) alimentación *f* continua.

streamline ['stri:mlaɪn] *vt* aerodinamizar; (*fig*) racionalizar.

streamlined ['stri:mlaɪnd] *adj* aerodinámico.

street [stri:t] *n* calle *f* ♦ *adj* callejero; **the back ~s** las callejuelas; **to be on the ~s** (*homeless*) estar sin vivienda; (*as prostitute*) hacer la calle.

streetcar ['stri:tkɑ:] *n* (*US*) tranvía *m*.

street cred [-krɛd] *n* (*col*) *imagen de estar en la onda*.

street lamp *n* farol *m*.

street lighting *n* alumbrado público.

street market *n* mercado callejero.

street plan *n* plano callejero.

streetwise ['stri:twaɪz] *adj* (*col*) pícaro.

strength [strɛŋθ] *n* fuerza; (*of girder, knot etc*) resistencia; (*of chemical solution*) potencia; (*of wine*) graduación *f* de alcohol; **on the ~ of** a base de, en base a; **to be at full/below ~** tener/no tener completo el cupo.

strengthen ['strɛŋθn] *vt* fortalecer, reforzar.

strenuous ['strɛnjuəs] *adj* (*tough*) arduo; (*energetic*) enérgico; (*opposition*) firme, tenaz; (*efforts*) intensivo.

stress [strɛs] *n* (*force, pressure*) presión *f*; (*mental strain*) estrés *m*, tensión *f*; (*accent, emphasis*) énfasis *m*, acento; (*LING, POETRY*) acento; (*TECH*) tensión *f*, carga ♦ *vt* subrayar, recalcar; **to be under ~** estar estresado; **to lay great ~ on sth** hacer hincapié en algo.

stressful ['strɛsful] *adj* (*job*) estresante.

stretch [strɛtʃ] *n* (*of sand etc*) trecho; (*of road*) tramo; (*of time*) período, tiempo ♦ *vi* estirarse; (*extend*): **to ~ to** *or* **as far as** extenderse hasta; (*be enough*: *money, food*): **to ~ to** alcanzar para, dar de sí para ♦ *vt* extender, estirar; (*make demands of*) exigir el máximo esfuerzo a; **to ~ one's legs** estirar las piernas.

►**stretch out** *vi* tenderse ♦ *vt* (*arm etc*) extender; (*spread*) estirar.

stretcher ['strɛtʃə*] *n* camilla.

stretcher-bearer ['strɛtʃəbɛərə*] *n* camillero/a.

stretch marks *npl* estrías *fpl*.

strewn [stru:n] *adj*: **~ with** cubierto *or* sembrado de.

stricken ['strɪkən] *adj* (*person*) herido; (*city, industry etc*) condenado; **~ with** (*arthritis, disease*) afligido por; **grief-~** destrozado por el dolor.

strict [strɪkt] *adj* (*order, rule etc*) estricto; (*discipline, ban*) severo; **in ~ confidence** en la más absoluta confianza.

strictly ['strɪktlɪ] *adv* estrictamente; (*totally*) terminantemente; **~ confidential** estrictamente confidencial; **~ speaking** en (el) sentido estricto (de la palabra); **~ between ourselves ...** entre nosotros ....

stridden ['strɪdn] *pp of* **stride**.

stride [straɪd] *n* zancada, tranco ♦ *vi* (*pt* **strode**, *pp* **stridden** [strəud, 'strɪdn]) dar zancadas, andar a trancos; **to take in one's ~** (*fig*: *changes etc*) tomar con calma.

strident ['straɪdnt] *adj* estridente; (*colour*) chillón/ona.

strife [straɪf] *n* lucha.

strike [straɪk] *n* huelga; (*of oil etc*) descubrimiento; (*attack*) ataque *m*; (*SPORT*) golpe *m* ♦ *vb* (*pt, pp* **struck** [strʌk]) *vt* golpear, pegar; (*oil etc*) descubrir; (*obstacle*) topar con; (*produce*: *coin, medal*) acuñar; (: *agreement, deal*) concertar ♦ *vi* declarar la huelga; (*attack*: *MIL etc*) atacar; (*clock*) dar la hora; **on ~** (*workers*) en huelga; **to call a ~** declarar una huelga; **to go on** *or* **come out on ~** ponerse *or* declararse en huelga; **to ~ a match** encender una cerilla; **to ~ a balance** (*fig*) encontrar un equilibrio; **to ~ a bargain** cerrar un trato; **the clock struck 9 o'clock** el reloj dio las nueve.

►**strike back** *vi* (*MIL*) contraatacar; (*fig*) devolver el golpe.

►**strike down** *vt* derribar.

►**strike off** *vt* (*from list*) tachar; (*doctor etc*) suspender.

►**strike out** *vt* borrar, tachar.

►**strike up** *vt* (*MUS*) empezar a tocar; (*conversation*) entablar; (*friendship*) trabar.

strikebreaker ['straɪkbreɪkə*] *n* rompehuelgas *m/f inv*.

striker ['straɪkə*] *n* huelgista *m/f*; (*SPORT*) delantero.

striking ['straɪkɪŋ] *adj* (*colour*) llamativo; (*obvious*) notorio.

Strimmer ® ['strɪmə*] *n* cortacéspedes *m inv* (*especial para los bordes*).

string [strɪŋ] *n* (*gen*) cuerda; (*row*) hilera; (*COMPUT*) cadena ♦ *vt* (*pt, pp* **strung** [strʌŋ]): **to ~ together** ensartar; **to ~ out**

extenderse; **the ~s** *npl* (*MUS*) los instrumentos de cuerda; **to pull ~s** (*fig*) mover palancas; **to get a job by pulling ~s** conseguir un trabajo por enchufe; **with no ~s attached** (*fig*) sin compromiso.
string bean *n* judía verde, habichuela.
string(ed) instrument [strɪŋ(d)-] *n* (*MUS*) instrumento de cuerda.
stringent ['strɪndʒənt] *adj* riguroso, severo.
string quartet *n* cuarteto de cuerdas.
strip [strɪp] *n* tira; (*of land*) franja; (*of metal*) cinta, lámina ♦ *vt* desnudar; (*also*: ~ **down**: *machine*) desmontar ♦ *vi* desnudarse.
strip cartoon *n* tira cómica, historieta (*LAM*).
stripe [straɪp] *n* raya; (*MIL*) galón *m*; **white with green ~s** blanco con rayas verdes.
striped [straɪpt] *adj* a rayas, rayado.
strip lighting *n* alumbrado fluorescente.
stripper ['strɪpə*] *n* artista *m/f* de striptease.
strip-search ['strɪpsə:tʃ] *vt*: **to ~ sb** desnudar y registrar a algn.
striptease ['strɪpti:z] *n* striptease *m*.
strive, *pt* **strove**, *pp* **striven** [straɪv, strəuv, 'strɪvn] *vi*: **to ~ to do sth** esforzarse *or* luchar por hacer algo.
strobe [strəub] *n* (*also*: ~ **light**) luz *f* estroboscópica.
strode [strəud] *pt of* **stride**.
stroke [strəuk] *n* (*blow*) golpe *m*; (*MED*) apoplejía; (*caress*) caricia; (*of pen*) trazo; (*SWIMMING*: *style*) estilo; (*of piston*) carrera ♦ *vt* acariciar; **at a ~** de golpe; **a ~ of luck** un golpe de suerte; **two-~ engine** motor *m* de dos tiempos.
stroll [strəul] *n* paseo, vuelta ♦ *vi* dar un paseo *or* una vuelta; **to go for a ~, have** *or* **take a ~** dar un paseo.
stroller ['strəulə*] *n* (*US*: *pushchair*) cochecito.
strong [strɔŋ] *adj* fuerte; (*bleach, acid*) concentrado ♦ *adv*: **to be going ~** (*company*) marchar bien; (*person*) conservarse bien; **they are 50 ~** son 50.
strong-arm ['strɔŋɑ:m] *adj* (*tactics, methods*) represivo.
strongbox ['strɔŋbɔks] *n* caja fuerte.
strong drink *n* bebida cargada *or* fuerte.
stronghold ['strɔŋhəuld] *n* fortaleza; (*fig*) baluarte *m*.
strong language *n* lenguaje *m* fuerte.
strongly ['strɔŋlɪ] *adv* fuertemente, con fuerza; (*believe*) firmemente; **to feel ~ about sth** tener una opinión firme sobre algo.
strongman ['strɔŋmæn] *n* forzudo; (*fig*) hombre *m* robusto.
strongroom ['strɔŋru:m] *n* cámara acorazada.
stroppy ['strɔpɪ] *adj* (*BRIT col*) borde; **to get ~** ponerse borde.
strove [strəuv] *pt of* **strive**.
struck [strʌk] *pt, pp of* **strike**.
structural ['strʌktʃərəl] *adj* estructural.
structure ['strʌktʃə*] *n* estructura; (*building*) construcción *f*.
struggle ['strʌgl] *n* lucha ♦ *vi* luchar; **to have a ~ to do sth** esforzarse por hacer algo.
strum [strʌm] *vt* (*guitar*) rasguear.
strung [strʌŋ] *pt, pp of* **string**.
strut [strʌt] *n* puntal *m* ♦ *vi* pavonearse.
strychnine ['strɪkni:n] *n* estricnina.
stub [stʌb] *n* (*of ticket etc*) matriz *f*; (*of cigarette*) colilla ♦ *vt*: **to ~ one's toe on sth** dar con el dedo del pie contra algo.
▸**stub out** *vt* (*cigarette*) apagar.
stubble ['stʌbl] *n* rastrojo; (*on chin*) barba (incipiente).
stubborn ['stʌbən] *adj* terco, testarudo.
stucco ['stʌkəu] *n* estuco.
stuck [stʌk] *pt, pp of* **stick** ♦ *adj* (*jammed*) atascado.
stuck-up [stʌk'ʌp] *adj* engreído, presumido.
stud [stʌd] *n* (*shirt ~*) corchete *m*; (*of boot*) taco; (*of horses*) caballeriza; (*also*: ~ **horse**) caballo semental ♦ *vt* (*fig*): **~ded with** salpicado de.
student ['stju:dənt] *n* estudiante *m/f* ♦ *adj* estudiantil; **a law/medical ~** un(a) estudiante de derecho/medicina.
student driver *n* (*US AUT*) aprendiz(a) *m/f* de conductor.
students' union *n* (*BRIT*: *association*) sindicato de estudiantes; (: *building*) centro de estudiantes.
studio ['stju:dɪəu] *n* estudio; (*artist's*) taller *m*.
studio flat, (*US*) **studio apartment** *n* estudio.
studious ['stju:dɪəs] *adj* estudioso; (*studied*) calculado.
studiously ['stju:dɪəslɪ] *adv* (*carefully*) con esmero.
study ['stʌdɪ] *n* estudio ♦ *vt* estudiar; (*examine*) examinar, investigar ♦ *vi* estudiar; **to make a ~ of sth** realizar una investigación de algo; **to ~ for an exam** preparar un examen.
stuff [stʌf] *n* materia; (*cloth*) tela; (*substance*) material *m*, sustancia; (*things, belongings*) cosas *fpl* ♦ *vt* llenar; (*CULIN*)

rellenar; (*animal*: *for exhibition*) disecar; **my nose is ~ed up** tengo la nariz tapada; **~ed toy** juguete *m or* muñeco de trapo.
stuffing ['stʌfɪŋ] *n* relleno.
stuffy ['stʌfɪ] *adj* (*room*) mal ventilado; (*person*) de miras estrechas.
stumble ['stʌmbl] *vi* tropezar, dar un traspié.
►**stumble across** *vt fus* (*fig*) tropezar con.
stumbling block ['stʌmblɪŋ-] *n* tropiezo, obstáculo.
stump [stʌmp] *n* (*of tree*) tocón *m*; (*of limb*) muñón *m* ♦ *vt*: **to be ~ed** quedarse perplejo; **to be ~ed for an answer** quedarse sin saber qué contestar.
stun [stʌn] *vt* aturdir.
stung [stʌŋ] *pt, pp of* **sting**.
stunk [stʌŋk] *pp of* **stink**.
stunning ['stʌnɪŋ] *adj* (*fig*) pasmoso.
stunt [stʌnt] *n* (*AVIAT*) vuelo acrobático; (*publicity* ~) truco publicitario.
stunted ['stʌntɪd] *adj* enano, achaparrado.
stuntman ['stʌntmæn] *n* especialista *m*.
stupefaction [stju:pɪ'fækʃən] *n* estupefacción *f*.
stupefy ['stju:pɪfaɪ] *vt* dejar estupefacto.
stupendous [stju:'pɛndəs] *adj* estupendo, asombroso.
stupid ['stju:pɪd] *adj* estúpido, tonto.
stupidity [stju:'pɪdɪtɪ] *n* estupidez *f*.
stupor ['stju:pə*] *n* estupor *m*.
sturdy ['stə:dɪ] *adj* robusto, fuerte.
stutter ['stʌtə*] *n* tartamudeo ♦ *vi* tartamudear.
sty [staɪ] *n* (*for pigs*) pocilga.
stye [staɪ] *n* (*MED*) orzuelo.
style [staɪl] *n* estilo; (*fashion*) moda; (*of dress etc*) hechura; (*hair* ~) corte *m*; **in the latest** ~ en el último modelo.
stylish ['staɪlɪʃ] *adj* elegante, a la moda.
stylist ['staɪlɪst] *n* (*hair* ~) peluquero/a
stylus, *pl* **styli** *or* **styluses** ['staɪləs, -laɪ] *n* (*of record player*) aguja.
Styrofoam ® ['staɪrəfəum] *n* (*US*) poliestireno ♦ *adj* (*cup*) de poliestireno.
suave [swɑ:v] *adj* cortés, fino.
sub [sʌb] *n abbr* = **submarine, subscription**.
sub... [sʌb] *pref* sub....
subcommittee ['sʌbkəmɪtɪ] *n* subcomisión *f*.
subconscious [sʌb'kɔnʃəs] *adj* subconsciente ♦ *n* subconsciente *m*.
subcontinent [sʌb'kɔntɪnənt] *n*: **the Indian** ~ el subcontinente (de la India).
subcontract *n* ['sʌb'kɔntrækt] subcontrato ♦ *vt* ['sʌbkən'trækt] subcontratar.
subcontractor ['sʌbkən'træktə*] *n* subcontratista *m/f*.
subdivide [sʌbdɪ'vaɪd] *vt* subdividir.
subdue [səb'dju:] *vt* sojuzgar; (*passions*) dominar.
subdued [səb'dju:d] *adj* (*light*) tenue; (*person*) sumiso, manso.
sub-editor ['sʌb'ɛdɪtə*] *n* (*BRIT*) redactor(a) *m/f*.
subject *n* ['sʌbdʒɪkt] súbdito; (*SCOL*) tema *m*, materia ♦ *vt* [səb'dʒɛkt]: **to ~ sb to sth** someter a algn a algo ♦ *adj* ['sʌbdʒɪkt]: **to be ~ to** (*law*) estar sujeto a; **~ to confirmation in writing** sujeto a confirmación por escrito; **to change the ~** cambiar de tema.
subjective [səb'dʒɛktɪv] *adj* subjetivo.
subject matter *n* materia; (*content*) contenido.
sub judice [sʌb'dju:dɪsɪ] *adj* (*LAW*) pendiente de resolución.
subjugate ['sʌbdʒugeɪt] *vt* subyugar, sojuzgar.
subjunctive [səb'dʒʌŋktɪv] *adj, n* subjuntivo.
sublet [sʌb'lɛt] *vt, vi* subarrendar, realquilar.
sublime [sə'blaɪm] *adj* sublime.
subliminal [sʌb'lɪmɪnl] *adj* subliminal.
submachine gun ['sʌbmə'ʃi:n-] *n* metralleta.
submarine [sʌbmə'ri:n] *n* submarino.
submerge [səb'mə:dʒ] *vt* sumergir; (*flood*) inundar ♦ *vi* sumergirse.
submersion [səb'mə:ʃən] *n* submersión *f*.
submission [səb'mɪʃən] *n* sumisión *f*; (*to committee etc*) ponencia.
submissive [səb'mɪsɪv] *adj* sumiso.
submit [səb'mɪt] *vt* someter; (*proposal, claim*) presentar ♦ *vi* someterse; **I ~ that** ... me permito sugerir que ....
subnormal [sʌb'nɔ:məl] *adj* subnormal.
subordinate [sə'bɔ:dɪnət] *adj, n* subordinado/a *m/f*.
subpoena [səb'pi:nə] (*LAW*) *n* citación *f* ♦ *vt* citar.
subroutine [sʌbru:'ti:n] *n* (*COMPUT*) subrutina.
subscribe [səb'skraɪb] *vi* suscribir; **to ~ to** (*fund*) suscribir, aprobar; (*opinion*) estar de acuerdo con; (*newspaper*) suscribirse a.
subscribed capital [səb'skraɪbd-] *n* capital *m* suscrito.
subscriber [səb'skraɪbə*] *n* (*to periodical*) suscriptor(a) *m/f*; (*to telephone*) abonado/a.
subscript ['sʌbskrɪpt] *n* (*TYP*) subíndice *m*.
subscription [səb'skrɪpʃən] *n* (*to club*) abono; (*to magazine*) suscripción *f*; **to take**

out a ~ to suscribirse a.
subsequent ['sʌbsɪkwənt] *adj* subsiguiente, posterior; ~ **to** posterior a.
subsequently ['sʌbsɪkwəntlɪ] *adv* posteriormente, más tarde.
subservient [səb'səːvɪənt] *adj*: ~ **(to)** servil (a).
subside [səb'saɪd] *vi* hundirse; (*flood*) bajar; (*wind*) amainar.
subsidence [səb'saɪdns] *n* hundimiento; (*in road*) socavón *m*.
subsidiarity [səbsɪdɪ'ærɪtɪ] *n* (*POL*) subsidiariedad *f*.
subsidiary [səb'sɪdɪərɪ] *n* sucursal *f*, filial *f* ♦ *adj* (*UNIV: subject*) secundario.
subsidize ['sʌbsɪdaɪz] *vt* subvencionar.
subsidy ['sʌbsɪdɪ] *n* subvención *f*.
subsist [səb'sɪst] *vi*: **to ~ on sth** subsistir a base de algo, sustentarse con algo.
subsistence [səb'sɪstəns] *n* subsistencia.
subsistence allowance *n* dietas *fpl*.
subsistence level *n* nivel *m* de subsistencia.
subsistence wage *n* sueldo de subsistencia.
substance ['sʌbstəns] *n* sustancia; (*fig*) esencia; **to lack ~** (*argument*) ser poco convincente; (*accusation*) no tener fundamento; (*film, book*) tener poca profundidad.
substance abuse *n* uso indebido de sustancias tóxicas.
substandard [sʌb'stændəd] *adj* (*goods*) inferior; (*housing*) deficiente.
substantial [səb'stænʃl] *adj* sustancial, sustancioso; (*fig*) importante.
substantially [səb'stænʃəlɪ] *adv* sustancialmente; ~ **bigger** bastante más grande.
substantiate [səb'stænʃɪeɪt] *vt* comprobar.
substitute ['sʌbstɪtjuːt] *n* (*person*) suplente *m/f*; (*thing*) sustituto ♦ *vt*: **to ~ A for B** sustituir B por A, reemplazar A por B.
substitution [sʌbstɪ'tjuːʃən] *n* sustitución *f*.
subterfuge ['sʌbtəfjuːdʒ] *n* subterfugio.
subterranean [sʌbtə'reɪnɪən] *adj* subterráneo.
subtitle ['sʌbtaɪtl] *n* subtítulo.
subtle ['sʌtl] *adj* sutil.
subtlety ['sʌtltɪ] *n* sutileza.
subtly ['sʌtlɪ] *adv* sutilmente.
subtotal [sʌb'təutl] *n* subtotal *m*.
subtract [səb'trækt] *vt* restar; sustraer.
subtraction [səb'trækʃən] *n* resta; sustracción *f*.
suburb ['sʌbəːb] *n* barrio residencial; **the ~s** las afueras (de la ciudad).
suburban [sə'bəːbən] *adj* suburbano; (*train etc*) de cercanías.
suburbia [sə'bəːbɪə] *n* barrios *mpl* residenciales.
subversion [səb'vəːʃən] *n* subversión *f*.
subversive [səb'vəːsɪv] *adj* subversivo.
subway ['sʌbweɪ] *n* (*BRIT*) paso subterráneo *or* inferior; (*US*) metro.
sub-zero [sʌb'zɪərəu] *adj*: ~ **temperatures** temperaturas *fpl* por debajo del cero.
succeed [sək'siːd] *vi* (*person*) tener éxito; (*plan*) salir bien ♦ *vt* suceder a; **to ~ in doing** lograr hacer.
succeeding [sək'siːdɪŋ] *adj* (*following*) sucesivo; ~ **generations** generaciones *fpl* futuras.
success [sək'sɛs] *n* éxito; (*gain*) triunfo.
successful [sək'sɛsful] *adj* (*venture*) de éxito, exitoso (*esp LAM*); **to be ~ (in doing)** lograr (hacer).
successfully [sək'sɛsfulɪ] *adv* con éxito.
succession [sək'sɛʃən] *n* (*series*) sucesión *f*, serie *f*; (*descendants*) descendencia; **in ~** sucesivamente.
successive [sək'sɛsɪv] *adj* sucesivo, consecutivo; **on 3 ~ days** tres días seguidos.
successor [sək'sɛsə*] *n* sucesor(a) *m/f*.
succinct [sək'sɪŋkt] *adj* sucinto.
succulent ['sʌkjulənt] *adj* suculento ♦ *n* (*BOT*): **~s** plantas *fpl* carnosas.
succumb [sə'kʌm] *vi* sucumbir.
such [sʌtʃ] *adj* tal, semejante; (*of that kind*): ~ **a book** tal libro; ~ **books** tales libros; (*so much*): ~ **courage** tanto valor ♦ *adv* tan; ~ **a long trip** un viaje tan largo; ~ **a lot of** tanto; ~ **as** (*like*) tal como; **a noise ~ as to** un ruido tal que; ~ **books as I have** cuantos libros tengo; **I said no ~ thing** no dije tal cosa; **it's ~ a long time since we saw each other** hace tanto tiempo que no nos vemos; ~ **a long time ago** hace tantísimo tiempo; **as ~** *adv* como tal.
such-and-such ['sʌtʃənsʌtʃ] *adj* tal o cual.
suchlike ['sʌtʃlaɪk] *pron* (*col*): **and ~** y cosas por el estilo.
suck [sʌk] *vt* chupar; (*bottle*) sorber; (*breast*) mamar; (*subj: pump, machine*) aspirar.
sucker ['sʌkə*] *n* (*BOT*) serpollo; (*ZOOL*) ventosa; (*col*) bobo, primo.
sucrose ['suːkrəuz] *n* sacarosa.
suction ['sʌkʃən] *n* succión *f*.
suction pump *n* bomba aspirante *or* de succión.
Sudan [su'dæn] *n* Sudán *m*.
Sudanese [suːdə'niːz] *adj, n* sudanés/esa *m/f*.
sudden ['sʌdn] *adj* (*rapid*) repentino, súbito; (*unexpected*) imprevisto; **all of a ~** de

repente.
sudden-death [sʌdn'dɛθ] *n* (*also*: ~ **play off**) desempate *m* instantáneo, muerte *f* súbita.
suddenly ['sʌdnlı] *adv* de repente.
suds [sʌdz] *npl* espuma *sg* de jabón.
sue [su:] *vt* demandar; **to ~ (for)** demandar (por); **to ~ for divorce** solicitar *or* pedir el divorcio; **to ~ for damages** demandar por daños y perjuicios.
suede [sweıd] *n* ante *m*, gamuza (*LAM*).
suet ['suıt] *n* sebo.
Suez Canal ['su:ız-] *n* Canal *m* de Suez.
Suff. *abbr* (*BRIT*) = *Suffolk.*
suffer ['sʌfə*] *vt* sufrir, padecer; (*tolerate*) aguantar, soportar; (*undergo*: *loss, setback*) experimentar ♦ *vi* sufrir, padecer; **to ~ from** sufrir, tener; **to ~ from the effects of alcohol/a fall** sufrir los efectos del alcohol/resentirse de una caída.
sufferance ['sʌfərns] *n*: **he was only there on ~** estuvo allí sólo porque se lo toleraron.
sufferer ['sʌfərə*] *n* víctima *f*; (*MED*) **~ from** enfermo/a de.
suffering ['sʌfərıŋ] *n* (*hardship, deprivation*) sufrimiento; (*pain*) dolor *m*.
suffice [sə'faıs] *vi* bastar, ser suficiente.
sufficient [sə'fıʃənt] *adj* suficiente, bastante.
sufficiently [sə'fıʃəntlı] *adv* suficientemente, bastante.
suffix ['sʌfıks] *n* sufijo.
suffocate ['sʌfəkeıt] *vi* ahogarse, asfixiarse.
suffocation [sʌfə'keıʃən] *n* sofocación *f*, asfixia.
suffrage ['sʌfrıdʒ] *n* sufragio.
suffuse [sə'fju:z] *vt*: **to ~ (with)** (*colour*) bañar (de); **her face was ~d with joy** su cara estaba llena de alegría.
sugar ['ʃugə*] *n* azúcar *m* ♦ *vt* echar azúcar a, azucarar.
sugar basin *n* (*BRIT*) = **sugar bowl.**
sugar beet *n* remolacha.
sugar bowl *n* azucarero.
sugar cane *n* caña de azúcar.
sugar-coated [ʃugə'kəutıd] *adj* azucarado.
sugar lump *n* terrón *m* de azúcar.
sugar refinery *n* refinería de azúcar.
sugary ['ʃugərı] *adj* azucarado.
suggest [sə'dʒɛst] *vt* sugerir; (*recommend*) aconsejar; **what do you ~ I do?** ¿qué sugieres que haga?; **this ~s that ...** esto hace pensar que ....
suggestion [sə'dʒɛstʃən] *n* sugerencia; **there's no ~ of ...** no hay indicación *or* evidencia de ....
suggestive [sə'dʒɛstıv] *adj* sugestivo; (*pej*: *indecent*) indecente.
suicidal ['suısaıdl] *adj* suicida; (*fig*) suicida, peligroso.
suicide ['suısaıd] *n* suicidio; (*person*) suicida *m/f*; **to commit ~** suicidarse.
suicide attempt, suicide bid *n* intento de suicidio.
suit [su:t] *n* (*man's*) traje *m*; (*woman's*) traje de chaqueta; (*LAW*) pleito; (*CARDS*) palo ♦ *vt* convenir; (*clothes*) sentar bien a, ir bien a; (*adapt*): **to ~ sth to** adaptar *or* ajustar algo a; **to be ~ed to sth** (*suitable for*) ser apto para algo; **well ~ed** (*couple*) hechos el uno para el otro; **to bring a ~ against sb** entablar demanda contra algn; **to follow ~** (*CARDS*) seguir el palo; (*fig*) seguir el ejemplo (de algn); **that ~s me** me va bien.
suitable ['su:təbl] *adj* conveniente; (*apt*) indicado.
suitably ['su:təblı] *adv* convenientemente; (*appropriately*) en forma debida.
suitcase ['su:tkeıs] *n* maleta, valija (*LAM*).
suite [swi:t] *n* (*of rooms, MUS*) suite *f*; (*furniture*): **bedroom/dining room ~** (juego de) dormitorio/comedor *m*; **a three-piece ~** un tresillo.
suitor ['su:tə*] *n* pretendiente *m*.
sulfate ['sʌlfeıt] *n* (*US*) = **sulphate.**
sulfur ['sʌlfə*] *n* (*US*) = **sulphur.**
sulk [sʌlk] *vi* estar de mal humor.
sulky ['sʌlkı] *adj* malhumorado.
sullen ['sʌlən] *adj* hosco, malhumorado.
sulphate, (*US*) **sulfate** ['sʌlfeıt] *n* sulfato; **copper ~** sulfato de cobre.
sulphur, (*US*) **sulfur** ['sʌlfə*] *n* azufre *m*.
sulphur dioxide *n* dióxido de azufre.
sultan ['sʌltən] *n* sultán *m*.
sultana [sʌl'tɑ:nə] *n* (*fruit*) pasa de Esmirna.
sultry ['sʌltrı] *adj* (*weather*) bochornoso; (*seductive*) seductor(a).
sum [sʌm] *n* suma; (*total*) total *m*.
►**sum up** *vt* resumir; (*evaluate rapidly*) evaluar ♦ *vi* hacer un resumen.
Sumatra [su'mɑ:trə] *n* Sumatra.
summarize ['sʌməraız] *vt* resumir.
summary ['sʌmərı] *n* resumen *m* ♦ *adj* (*justice*) sumario.
summer ['sʌmə*] *n* verano ♦ *adj* de verano; **in (the) ~** en (el) verano.
summerhouse ['sʌməhaus] *n* (*in garden*) cenador *m*, glorieta.
summertime ['sʌmətaım] *n* (*season*) verano.
summer time *n* (*by clock*) hora de verano.

summery ['sʌmərɪ] *adj* veraniego.
summing-up [sʌmɪŋ'ʌp] *n* (*LAW*) resumen *m.*
summit ['sʌmɪt] *n* cima, cumbre *f.*
summit (conference) *n* (conferencia) cumbre *f.*
summon ['sʌmən] *vt* (*person*) llamar; (*meeting*) convocar; **to ~ a witness** citar a un testigo.
▸**summon up** *vt* (*courage*) armarse de.
summons ['sʌmənz] *n* llamamiento, llamada ♦ *vt* citar, emplazar; **to serve a ~ on sb** citar a algn ante el juicio.
sumo ['su:məu] *n* (*also:* **~ wrestling**) sumo.
sump [sʌmp] *n* (*BRIT AUT*) cárter *m.*
sumptuous ['sʌmptjuəs] *adj* suntuoso.
sun [sʌn] *n* sol *m*; **they have everything under the ~** no les falta nada, tienen de todo.
Sun. *abbr* (= *Sunday*) dom.
sunbathe ['sʌnbeɪð] *vi* tomar el sol.
sunbeam ['sʌnbi:m] *n* rayo de sol.
sunbed ['sʌnbɛd] *n* cama solar.
sunburn ['sʌnbə:n] *n* (*painful*) quemadura del sol; (*tan*) bronceado.
sunburnt ['sʌnbə:nt], **sunburned** ['sʌnbə:nd] *adj* (*tanned*) bronceado; (*painfully*) quemado por el sol.
sundae ['sʌndeɪ] *n helado con frutas y nueces.*
Sunday ['sʌndɪ] *n* domingo.
Sunday paper *n* (periódico) dominical *m.*
Sunday school *n* catequesis *f.*
sundial ['sʌndaɪəl] *n* reloj *m* de sol.
sundown ['sʌndaun] *n* anochecer *m*, puesta de sol.
sundries ['sʌndrɪz] *npl* géneros *mpl* diversos.
sundry ['sʌndrɪ] *adj* varios, diversos; **all and ~** todos sin excepción.
sunflower ['sʌnflauə*] *n* girasol *m.*
sung [sʌŋ] *pp of* **sing**.
sunglasses ['sʌnglɑ:sɪz] *npl* gafas *fpl* de sol.
sunk [sʌŋk] *pp of* **sink**.
sunken ['sʌŋkn] *adj* (*bath*) hundido.
sunlamp ['sʌnlæmp] *n* lámpara solar ultravioleta.
sunlight ['sʌnlaɪt] *n* luz *f* del sol.
sunlit ['sʌnlɪt] *adj* iluminado por el sol.
sunny ['sʌnɪ] *adj* soleado; (*day*) de sol; (*fig*) alegre; **it is ~** hace sol.
sunrise ['sʌnraɪz] *n* salida del sol.
sun roof *n* (*AUT*) techo corredizo *or* solar; (*on building*) azotea, terraza.
sunscreen ['sʌnskri:n] *n* protector *m* solar.
sunset ['sʌnsɛt] *n* puesta del sol.
sunshade ['sʌnʃeɪd] *n* (*over table*) sombrilla.
sunshine ['sʌnʃaɪn] *n* sol *m.*
sunstroke ['sʌnstrəuk] *n* insolación *f.*
suntan ['sʌntæn] *n* bronceado.
suntanned ['sʌntænd] *adj* bronceado.
suntan oil *n* aceite *m* bronceador.
super ['su:pə*] *adj* (*col*) bárbaro.
superannuation [su:pərænju'eɪʃən] *n* jubilación *f*, pensión *f.*
superb [su:'pə:b] *adj* magnífico, espléndido.
Super Bowl *n* (*US SPORT*) *super copa de fútbol americano.*
supercilious [su:pə'sɪlɪəs] *adj* (*disdainful*) desdeñoso; (*haughty*) altanero.
superconductor [su:pəkən'dʌktə*] *n* superconductor *m.*
superficial [su:pə'fɪʃəl] *adj* superficial.
superfluous [su'pə:fluəs] *adj* superfluo, de sobra.
superglue ['su:pəglu:] *n* cola de contacto, supercola.
superhighway ['su:pəhaɪweɪ] *n* (*US*) superautopista; **the information ~** la superautopista de la información.
superhuman [su:pə'hju:mən] *adj* sobrehumano.
superimpose ['su:pərɪm'pəuz] *vt* sobreponer.
superintend [su:pərɪn'tɛnd] *vt* supervisar.
superintendent [su:pərɪn'tɛndənt] *n* director(a) *m/f*; (*police ~*) subjefe/a *m/f.*
superior [su'pɪərɪə*] *adj* superior; (*smug*: *person*) altivo, desdeñoso; (: *smile, air*) de suficiencia; (: *remark*) desdeñoso ♦ *n* superior *m*; **Mother S~** (*REL*) madre *f* superiora.
superiority [supɪərɪ'ɔrɪtɪ] *n* superioridad *f*; desdén *m.*
superlative [su'pə:lətɪv] *adj, n* superlativo.
superman ['su:pəmæn] *n* superhombre *m.*
supermarket ['su:pəmɑ:kɪt] *n* supermercado.
supermodel ['su:pəmɔdl] *n* top model *f*, supermodelo *f.*
supernatural [su:pə'nætʃərəl] *adj* sobrenatural.
supernova [su:pə'nəuvə] *n* supernova.
superpower ['su:pəpauə*] *n* (*POL*) superpotencia.
supersede [su:pə'si:d] *vt* suplantar.
supersonic ['su:pə'sɔnɪk] *adj* supersónico.
superstar ['su:pəstɑ:*] *n* superestrella ♦ *adj* de superestrella.
superstition [su:pə'stɪʃən] *n* superstición *f.*
superstitious [su:pə'stɪʃəs] *adj* supersticioso.
superstore ['su:pəstɔ:*] *n* (*BRIT*) hipermercado.
supertanker ['su:pətæŋkə*] *n*

superpetrolero.

supertax ['su:pətæks] *n* sobretasa, sobreimpuesto.

supervise ['su:pəvaɪz] *vt* supervisar.

supervision [su:pə'vɪʒən] *n* supervisión *f*.

supervisor ['su:pəvaɪzə*] *n* (*gen, UNIV*) supervisor(a) *m/f*.

supervisory ['su:pəvaɪzərɪ] *adj* de supervisión.

supine ['su:paɪn] *adj* supino.

supper ['sʌpə*] *n* cena; **to have ~** cenar.

supplant [sə'plɑ:nt] *vt* suplantar, reemplazar.

supple ['sʌpl] *adj* flexible.

supplement *n* ['sʌplɪmənt] suplemento ♦ *vt* [sʌplɪ'mɛnt] suplir.

supplementary [sʌplɪ'mɛntərɪ] *adj* suplementario.

supplementary benefit *n* (*BRIT*) subsidio adicional de la seguridad social.

supplier [sə'plaɪə*] *n* suministrador(a) *m/f*; (*COMM*) distribuidor(a) *m/f*.

supply [sə'plaɪ] *vt* (*provide*) suministrar; (*information*) facilitar; (*fill*: *need, want*) suplir, satisfacer; (*equip*): **to ~ (with)** proveer (de) ♦ *n* provisión *f*; (*of gas, water etc*) suministro ♦ *adj* (*BRIT*: *teacher etc*) suplente; **supplies** *npl* (*food*) víveres *mpl*; (*MIL*) pertrechos *mpl*; **office supplies** materiales *mpl* para oficina; **to be in short ~** escasear, haber escasez de; **the electricity/water/gas ~** el suministro de electricidad/agua/gas; **~ and demand** la oferta y la demanda.

support [sə'pɔ:t] *n* (*moral, financial etc*) apoyo; (*TECH*) soporte *m* ♦ *vt* apoyar; (*financially*) mantener; (*uphold*) sostener; (*SPORT*: *team*) seguir, ser hincha de; **they stopped work in ~ (of)** pararon de trabajar en apoyo (de); **to ~ o.s.** (*financially*) ganarse la vida.

support buying [-'baɪɪŋ] *n* compra proteccionista.

supporter [sə'pɔ:tə*] *n* (*POL etc*) partidario/a; (*SPORT*) aficionado/a; (*FOOTBALL*) hincha *m/f*.

supporting [sə'pɔ:tɪŋ] *adj* (*wall*) de apoyo; **~ role** papel *m* secundario; **~ actor/actress** actor/actriz *m/f* secundario/a.

supportive [sə'pɔ:tɪv] *adj* de apoyo; **I have a ~ family/wife** mi familia/mujer me apoya.

suppose [sə'pəuz] *vt, vi* suponer; (*imagine*) imaginarse; **to be ~d to do sth** deber hacer algo; **I don't ~ she'll come** no creo que venga; **he's ~d to be an expert** se le supone un experto.

supposedly [sə'pəuzɪdlɪ] *adv* según cabe suponer.

supposing [sə'pəuzɪŋ] *conj* en caso de que; **always ~ (that) he comes** suponiendo que venga.

supposition [sʌpə'zɪʃən] *n* suposición *f*.

suppository [sə'pɔzɪtrɪ] *n* supositorio.

suppress [sə'prɛs] *vt* suprimir; (*yawn*) ahogar.

suppression [sə'prɛʃən] *n* represión *f*.

supremacy [su'prɛməsɪ] *n* supremacía.

supreme [su'pri:m] *adj* supremo.

Supreme Court *n* (*US*) Tribunal *m* Supremo, Corte *f* Suprema.

supremo [su'pri:məu] *n* autoridad *f* máxima.

Supt. *abbr* (*POLICE*) = **superintendent.**

surcharge ['sə:tʃɑ:dʒ] *n* sobretasa, recargo.

sure [ʃuə*] *adj* seguro; (*definite, convinced*) cierto; (*aim*) certero ♦ *adv*: **that ~ is pretty, that's ~ pretty** (*US*) ¡qué bonito es!; **to be ~ of sth** estar seguro de algo; **to be ~ of o.s.** estar seguro de sí mismo; **to make ~ of sth/that** asegurarse de algo/asegurar que; **I'm not ~ how/why/when** no estoy seguro de cómo/por qué/cuándo; **~!** (*of course*) ¡claro!, ¡por supuesto!; **~ enough** efectivamente.

sure-fire ['ʃuəfaɪə*] *adj* (*col*) infalible.

sure-footed [ʃuə'futɪd] *adj* de pie firme.

surely ['ʃuəlɪ] *adv* (*certainly*) seguramente; **~ you don't mean that!** ¡no lo dices en serio!

surety ['ʃuərətɪ] *n* fianza; (*person*) fiador(a) *m/f*; **to go** *or* **stand ~ for sb** ser fiador de algn, salir garante por algn.

surf [sə:f] *n* olas *fpl*.

surface ['sə:fɪs] *n* superficie *f* ♦ *vt* (*road*) revestir ♦ *vi* salir a la superficie ♦ *cpd* (*MIL, NAUT*) de (la) superficie; **on the ~ it seems that ...** (*fig*) a primera vista parece que ....

surface area *n* área de la superficie.

surface mail *n* vía terrestre.

surface-to-air ['sə:fɪstə'ɛə*] *adj* (*MIL*) tierra-aire.

surface-to-surface ['sə:fɪstə'sə:fɪs] *adj* (*MIL*) tierra-tierra.

surfboard ['sə:fbɔ:d] *n* plancha (de surf).

surfeit ['sə:fɪt] *n*: **a ~ of** un exceso de.

surfer ['sə:fə*] *n* súrfer *m/f*.

surfing ['sə:fɪŋ] *n* surf *m*.

surge [sə:dʒ] *n* oleada, oleaje *m*; (*ELEC*) sobretensión *f* transitoria ♦ *vi* avanzar a tropel; **to ~ forward** avanzar rápidamente.

surgeon ['sə:dʒən] *n* cirujano/a.

surgery ['sə:dʒərɪ] *n* cirugía; (*BRIT*: *room*)

consultorio; (: *POL*) *horas en las que los electores pueden reunirse personalmente con su diputado*; **to undergo ~** operarse; *see also* **constituency**.
surgery hours *npl* (*BRIT*) horas *fpl* de consulta.
surgical ['sə:dʒɪkl] *adj* quirúrgico.
surgical spirit *n* (*BRIT*) alcohol *m*.
surly ['sə:lɪ] *adj* hosco, malhumorado.
surmount [sə:'maunt] *vt* superar, vencer.
surname ['sə:neɪm] *n* apellido.
surpass [sə:'pɑ:s] *vt* superar, exceder.
surplus ['sə:pləs] *n* excedente *m*; (*COMM*) superávit *m* ♦ *adj* (*COMM*) excedente, sobrante; **to have a ~ of sth** tener un excedente de algo; **it is ~ to our requirements** nos sobra; **~ stock** saldos *mpl*.
surprise [sə'praɪz] *n* sorpresa ♦ *vt* sorprender; **to take by ~** (*person*) coger a algn desprevenido *or* por sorpresa, sorprender a algn; (*MIL*: *town, fort*) atacar por sorpresa.
surprising [sə'praɪzɪŋ] *adj* sorprendente.
surprisingly [sə'praɪzɪŋlɪ] *adv* (*easy, helpful*) de modo sorprendente; **(somewhat) ~, he agreed** para sorpresa de todos, aceptó.
surrealism [sə'rɪəlɪzəm] *n* surrealismo.
surrealist [sə'rɪəlɪst] *adj, n* surrealista *m/f*.
surrender [sə'rɛndə*] *n* rendición *f*, entrega ♦ *vi* rendirse, entregarse ♦ *vt* (*claim, right*) renunciar.
surrender value *n* valor *m* de rescate.
surreptitious [sʌrəp'tɪʃəs] *adj* subrepticio.
surrogate ['sʌrəgɪt] *n* (*BRIT*: *substitute*) sustituto/a ♦ *adj*: **~ coffee** sucedáneo de café.
surrogate mother *n* madre *f* de alquiler.
surround [sə'raund] *vt* rodear, circundar; (*MIL etc*) cercar.
surrounding [sə'raundɪŋ] *adj* circundante.
surroundings [sə'raundɪŋz] *npl* alrededores *mpl*, cercanías *fpl*.
surtax ['sə:tæks] *n* sobretasa, sobreimpuesto.
surveillance [sə:'veɪləns] *n* vigilancia.
survey *n* ['sə:veɪ] inspección *f*, reconocimiento; (*inquiry*) encuesta; (*comprehensive view*: *of situation etc*) vista de conjunto ♦ *vt* [sə:'veɪ] examinar, inspeccionar; (*SURVEYING*: *building*) inspeccionar; (: *land*) hacer un reconocimiento de, reconocer; (*look at*) mirar, contemplar; (*make inquiries about*) hacer una encuesta de; **to carry out a ~ of** inspeccionar, examinar.
surveyor [sə'veɪə*] *n* (*BRIT*) (*of building*) perito *m/f*; (*of land*) agrimensor(a) *m/f*.
survival [sə'vaɪvl] *n* supervivencia.
survival course *n* curso de supervivencia.
survival kit *n* equipo de emergencia.
survive [sə'vaɪv] *vi* sobrevivir; (*custom etc*) perdurar ♦ *vt* sobrevivir a.
survivor [sə'vaɪvə*] *n* superviviente *m/f*.
susceptibility [səsɛptə'bɪlɪtɪ] *n* (*to illness*) propensión *f*.
susceptible [sə'sɛptəbl] *adj* (*easily influenced*) influenciable; (*to disease, illness*): **~ to** propenso a.
suspect *adj, n* ['sʌspɛkt] sospechoso/a *m/f* ♦ *vt* [səs'pɛkt] sospechar.
suspected [səs'pɛktɪd] *adj* presunto; **to have a ~ fracture** tener una posible fractura.
suspend [səs'pɛnd] *vt* suspender.
suspended animation [səs'pɛndəd-] *n*: **in a state of ~** en (estado de) hibernación.
suspended sentence *n* (*LAW*) libertad *f* condicional.
suspender belt [səs'pɛndə*-] *n* (*BRIT*) liguero, portaligas *m inv* (*AM*).
suspenders [səs'pɛndəz] *npl* (*BRIT*) ligas *fpl*; (*US*) tirantes *mpl*.
suspense [səs'pɛns] *n* incertidumbre *f*, duda; (*in film etc*) suspense *m*.
suspension [səs'pɛnʃən] *n* (*gen, AUT*) suspensión *f*; (*of driving licence*) privación *f*.
suspension bridge *n* puente *m* colgante.
suspension file *n* archivador *m* colgante.
suspicion [səs'pɪʃən] *n* sospecha; (*distrust*) recelo; (*trace*) traza; **to be under ~** estar bajo sospecha; **arrested on ~ of murder** detenido bajo sospecha de asesinato.
suspicious [səs'pɪʃəs] *adj* (*suspecting*) receloso; (*causing suspicion*) sospechoso; **to be ~ of** *or* **about sb/sth** tener sospechas de algn/algo.
suss out [sʌs-] *vt* (*BRIT col*) calar.
sustain [səs'teɪn] *vt* sostener, apoyar; (*suffer*) sufrir, padecer.
sustainable [səs'teɪnəbl] *adj* sostenible.
sustained [səs'teɪnd] *adj* (*effort*) sostenido.
sustenance ['sʌstɪnəns] *n* sustento.
suture ['su:tʃə*] *n* sutura.
SW *abbr* = **short wave**.
swab [swɔb] *n* (*MED*) algodón *m*, frotis *m inv* ♦ *vt* (*NAUT*: *also*: **~ down**) limpiar, fregar.
swagger ['swægə*] *vi* pavonearse.
swallow ['swɔləu] *n* (*bird*) golondrina; (*of food*) bocado; (*of drink*) trago ♦ *vt* tragar.
►**swallow up** *vt* (*savings etc*) consumir.
swam [swæm] *pt of* **swim**.
swamp [swɔmp] *n* pantano, ciénaga ♦ *vt* abrumar, agobiar.
swampy ['swɔmpɪ] *adj* pantanoso.

swan [swɔn] *n* cisne *m*.
swank [swæŋk] (*col*) *n* (*vanity, boastfulness*) fanfarronada ♦ *vi* fanfarronear, presumir.
swan song *n* (*fig*) canto del cisne.
swap [swɔp] *n* canje *m*, trueque *m* ♦ *vt*: **to ~ (for)** canjear (por).
SWAPO ['swɑːpəu] *n abbr* (= *South-West Africa People's Organization*) SWAPO *f*.
swarm [swɔːm] *n* (*of bees*) enjambre *m*; (*fig*) multitud *f* ♦ *vi* (*fig*) hormiguear, pulular.
swarthy ['swɔːðɪ] *adj* moreno.
swashbuckling ['swɔʃbʌklɪŋ] *adj* (*person*) aventurero; (*film*) de capa y espada.
swastika ['swɔstɪkə] *n* esvástika, cruz *f* gamada.
swat [swɔt] *vt* aplastar ♦ *n* (*also*: **fly ~**) matamoscas *m inv*.
SWAT [swɔt] *n abbr* (*US*: = *Special Weapons and Tactics*) *unidad especial de la policía.*
swathe [sweɪð] *vt*: **to ~ in** (*blankets*) envolver en; (*bandages*) vendar en.
sway [sweɪ] *vi* mecerse, balancearse ♦ *vt* (*influence*) mover, influir en ♦ *n* (*rule, power*): **~ (over)** dominio (sobre); **to hold ~ over sb** dominar a algn, mantener el dominio sobre algn.
Swaziland ['swɑːzɪlænd] *n* Swazilandia.
swear, *pt* **swore,** *pp* **sworn** [swɛə*, swɔː*, swɔːn] *vi* jurar; (*with swearwords*) decir tacos ♦ *vt*: **to ~ an oath** prestar juramento, jurar; **to ~ to sth** declarar algo bajo juramento.
▸**swear in** *vt* tomar juramento (a).
swearword ['swɛəwəːd] *n* taco, palabrota.
sweat [swɛt] *n* sudor *m* ♦ *vi* sudar.
sweatband ['swɛtbænd] *n* (*SPORT*: *on head*) banda; (: *on wrist*) muñequera.
sweater ['swɛtə*] *n* suéter *m*.
sweatshirt ['swɛtʃəːt] *n* sudadera.
sweatshop ['swɛtʃɔp] *n* fábrica donde se explota al obrero.
sweaty ['swɛtɪ] *adj* sudoroso.
Swede [swiːd] *n* sueco/a.
swede [swiːd] *n* (*BRIT*) nabo.
Sweden ['swiːdn] *n* Suecia.
Swedish ['swiːdɪʃ] *adj, n* (*LING*) sueco.
sweep [swiːp] *n* (*act*) barrida; (*of arm*) manotazo *m*; (*curve*) curva, alcance *m*; (*also*: **chimney ~**) deshollinador(a) *m/f* ♦ *vb* (*pt, pp* **swept** [swɛpt]) *vt* barrer; (*disease, fashion*) recorrer ♦ *vi* barrer.
▸**sweep away** *vt* barrer; (*rub out*) borrar.
▸**sweep past** *vi* pasar rápidamente; (*brush by*) rozar.
▸**sweep up** *vi* barrer.
sweeper ['swiːpə*] *n* (*person*) barrendero/a; (*machine*) barredora; (*FOOTBALL*) líbero, libre *m*.
sweeping ['swiːpɪŋ] *adj* (*gesture*) dramático; (*generalized*) generalizado; (*changes, reforms*) radical.
sweepstake ['swiːpsteɪk] *n* lotería.
sweet [swiːt] *n* (*candy*) dulce *m*, caramelo; (*BRIT*: *pudding*) postre *m* ♦ *adj* dulce; (*sugary*) azucarado; (*charming*: *person*) encantador(a); (: *smile, character*) dulce, amable, agradable ♦ *adv*: **to smell/taste ~** oler/saber dulce.
sweet and sour *adj* agridulce.
sweetcorn ['swiːtkɔːn] *n* maíz *m* (dulce).
sweeten ['swiːtn] *vt* (*person*) endulzar; (*add sugar to*) poner azúcar a.
sweetener ['swiːtnə*] *n* (*CULIN*) edulcorante *m*.
sweetheart ['swiːthɑːt] *n* amor *m*, novio/a; (*in speech*) amor, cariño.
sweetness ['swiːtnɪs] *n* (*gen*) dulzura.
sweet pea *n* guisante *m* de olor.
sweet potato *n* batata, camote *m* (*LAM*).
sweetshop ['swiːtʃɔp] *n* (*BRIT*) confitería, bombonería.
swell [swɛl] *n* (*of sea*) marejada, oleaje *m* ♦ *adj* (*US*: *col*: *excellent*) estupendo, fenomenal ♦ *vb* (*pt* **~ed**, *pp* **swollen** *or* **~ed** ['swəulən]) *vt* hinchar, inflar ♦ *vi* hincharse, inflarse.
swelling ['swɛlɪŋ] *n* (*MED*) hinchazón *f*.
sweltering ['swɛltərɪŋ] *adj* sofocante, de mucho calor.
swept [swɛpt] *pt, pp of* **sweep**.
swerve [swəːv] *n* regate *m*; (*in car*) desvío brusco ♦ *vi* desviarse bruscamente.
swift [swɪft] *n* (*bird*) vencejo ♦ *adj* rápido, veloz.
swiftly ['swɪftlɪ] *adv* rápidamente.
swiftness ['swɪftnɪs] *n* rapidez *f*, velocidad *f*.
swig [swɪg] *n* (*col*: *drink*) trago.
swill [swɪl] *n* bazofia ♦ *vt* (*also*: **~ out, ~ down**) lavar, limpiar con agua.
swim [swɪm] *n*: **to go for a ~** ir a nadar *or* a bañarse ♦ *vb* (*pt* **swam**, *pp* **swum** [swæm, swʌm]) *vi* nadar; (*head, room*) dar vueltas ♦ *vt* pasar a nado; **to go ~ming** ir a nadar; **to ~ a length** nadar *or* hacer un largo.
swimmer ['swɪmə*] *n* nadador(a) *m/f*.
swimming ['swɪmɪŋ] *n* natación *f*.
swimming cap *n* gorro de baño.
swimming costume *n* bañador *m*, traje *m* de baño.
swimmingly ['swɪmɪŋlɪ] *adv*: **to go ~** (*wonderfully*) ir como una seda *or* sobre ruedas.
swimming pool *n* piscina, alberca (*LAM*).

swimming trunks *npl* bañador *msg.*
swimsuit ['swɪmsuːt] *n* = **swimming costume.**
swindle ['swɪndl] *n* estafa ♦ *vt* estafar.
swine [swaɪn] *n, pl inv* cerdo, puerco; (*col!*) canalla *m* (*!*).
swing [swɪŋ] *n* (*in playground*) columpio; (*movement*) balanceo, vaivén *m*; (*change of direction*) viraje *m*; (*rhythm*) ritmo; (*POL: in votes etc*): **there has been a ~ towards/ away from Labour** ha habido un viraje en favor/en contra del Partido Laborista ♦ *vb* (*pt, pp* **swung** [swʌŋ]) *vt* balancear; (*on a ~*) columpiar; (*also*: **~ round**) voltear, girar ♦ *vi* balancearse, columpiarse; (*also*: **~ round**) dar media vuelta; **a ~ to the left** un movimiento hacia la izquierda; **to be in full ~** estar en plena marcha; **to get into the ~ of things** meterse en situación; **the road ~s south** la carretera gira hacia el sur.
swing bridge *n* puente *m* giratorio.
swing door, (*US*) **swinging door** ['swɪŋɪŋ-] *n* puerta giratoria.
swingeing ['swɪndʒɪŋ] *adj* (*BRIT*) abrumador(a).
swipe [swaɪp] *n* golpe *m* fuerte ♦ *vt* (*hit*) golpear fuerte; (*col: steal*) guindar; (*credit card etc*) pasar.
swirl [swəːl] *vi* arremolinarse.
swish [swɪʃ] *n* (*sound: of whip*) chasquido; (*: of skirts*) frufrú *m*; (*: of grass*) crujido ♦ *adj* (*col: smart*) elegante ♦ *vi* chasquear.
Swiss [swɪs] *adj, n* (*pl inv*) suizo/a *m/f.*
switch [swɪtʃ] *n* (*for light, radio etc*) interruptor *m*; (*change*) cambio ♦ *vt* (*change*) cambiar de; (*invert: also*: **~ round, ~ over**) intercambiar.
▸**switch off** *vt* apagar; (*engine*) parar.
▸**switch on** *vt* (*AUT: ignition*) encender, prender (*LAM*); (*engine, machine*) arrancar; (*water supply*) conectar.
switchboard ['swɪtʃbɔːd] *n* (*TEL*) centralita (de teléfonos), conmutador *m* (*LAM*).
Switzerland ['swɪtsələnd] *n* Suiza.
swivel ['swɪvl] *vi* (*also*: **~ round**) girar.
swollen ['swəulən] *pp of* **swell.**
swoon [swuːn] *vi* desmayarse.
swoop [swuːp] *n* (*by police etc*) redada; (*of bird etc*) descenso en picado, calada ♦ *vi* (*also*: **~ down**) caer en picado.
swop [swɔp] = **swap.**
sword [sɔːd] *n* espada.
swordfish ['sɔːdfɪʃ] *n* pez *m* espada.
swore [swɔː*] *pt of* **swear.**
sworn [swɔːn] *pp of* **swear.**
swot [swɔt] (*BRIT*) *vt, vi* empollar ♦ *n* empollón/ona *m/f.*
swum [swʌm] *pp of* **swim.**
swung [swʌŋ] *pt, pp of* **swing.**
sycamore ['sɪkəmɔː*] *n* sicomoro.
sycophant ['sɪkəfænt] *n* adulador(a) *m/f,* pelotillero/a.
Sydney ['sɪdnɪ] *n* Sidney *m.*
syllable ['sɪləbl] *n* sílaba.
syllabus ['sɪləbəs] *n* programa *m* de estudios; **on the ~** en el programa de estudios.
symbol ['sɪmbl] *n* símbolo.
symbolic(al) [sɪm'bɔlɪk(l)] *adj* simbólico; **to be ~ of sth** simbolizar algo.
symbolism ['sɪmbəlɪzəm] *n* simbolismo.
symbolize ['sɪmbəlaɪz] *vt* simbolizar.
symmetrical [sɪ'mɛtrɪkl] *adj* simétrico.
symmetry ['sɪmɪtrɪ] *n* simetría.
sympathetic [sɪmpə'θɛtɪk] *adj* compasivo; (*understanding*) comprensivo; **to be ~ to a cause** (*well-disposed*) apoyar una causa; **to be ~ towards** (*person*) ser comprensivo con.
sympathize ['sɪmpəθaɪz] *vi*: **to ~ with sb** compadecerse de algn; (*understand*) comprender a algn.
sympathizer ['sɪmpəθaɪzə*] *n* (*POL*) simpatizante *m/f.*
sympathy ['sɪmpəθɪ] *n* (*pity*) compasión *f*; (*understanding*) comprensión *f*; **a letter of ~** un pésame; **with our deepest ~** nuestro más sentido pésame.
symphony ['sɪmfənɪ] *n* sinfonía.
symposium [sɪm'pəuzɪəm] *n* simposio.
symptom ['sɪmptəm] *n* síntoma *m*, indicio.
symptomatic [sɪmptə'mætɪk] *adj*: **~ (of)** sintomático (de).
synagogue ['sɪnəgɔg] *n* sinagoga.
sync [sɪŋk] *n* (*col*): **to be in/out of ~ (with)** ir/no ir al mismo ritmo (que); (*fig: people*) conectar/no conectar con.
synchromesh ['sɪŋkrəumɛʃ] *n* cambio sincronizado de velocidades.
synchronize ['sɪŋkrənaɪz] *vt* sincronizar ♦ *vi*: **to ~ with** sincronizarse con.
synchronized swimming ['sɪŋkrənaɪzd-] *n* natación *f* sincronizada.
syncopated ['sɪŋkəpeɪtɪd] *adj* sincopado.
syndicate ['sɪndɪkɪt] *n* (*gen*) sindicato; (*PRESS*) agencia (de noticias).
syndrome ['sɪndrəum] *n* síndrome *m.*
synonym ['sɪnənɪm] *n* sinónimo.
synonymous [sɪ'nɔnɪməs] *adj*: **~ (with)** sinónimo (con).
synopsis, *pl* **synopses** [sɪ'nɔpsɪs, -siːz] *n* sinopsis *f inv.*
syntax ['sɪntæks] *n* sintaxis *f.*
syntax error *n* (*COMPUT*) error *m* sintáctico.

synthesis, *pl* **syntheses** ['sɪnθəsɪs, -si:z] *n* síntesis *f inv.*
synthesizer ['sɪnθəsaɪzə*] *n* sintetizador *m.*
synthetic [sɪn'θɛtɪk] *adj* sintético ♦ *n* sintético.
syphilis ['sɪfɪlɪs] *n* sífilis *f.*
syphon ['saɪfən] = **siphon.**
Syria ['sɪrɪə] *n* Siria.
Syrian ['sɪrɪən] *adj, n* sirio/a *m/f.*
syringe [sɪ'rɪndʒ] *n* jeringa.
syrup ['sɪrəp] *n* jarabe *m*, almíbar *m.*
system ['sɪstəm] *n* sistema *m*; (*ANAT*) organismo; **it was quite a shock to his ~** fue un golpe para él.
systematic [sɪstə'mætɪk] *adj* sistemático; metódico.
system disk *n* (*COMPUT*) disco del sistema.
systems analyst *n* analista *m/f* de sistemas.

Tt

T, t [ti:] *n* (*letter*) T, t *f*; **T for Tommy** T de Tarragona.
TA *n abbr* (*BRIT*) = *Territorial Army.*
ta [tɑ:] *excl* (*BRIT col*) ¡gracias!
tab [tæb] *n abbr* = **tabulator** ♦ *n* lengüeta; (*label*) etiqueta; **to keep ~s on** (*fig*) vigilar.
tabby ['tæbɪ] *n* (*also*: **~ cat**) gato atigrado.
tabernacle ['tæbənækl] *n* tabernáculo.
table ['teɪbl] *n* mesa; (*chart*: *of statistics etc*) cuadro, tabla ♦ *vt* (*BRIT*: *motion etc*) presentar; **to lay** *or* **set the ~** poner la mesa; **to clear the ~** quitar *or* levantar la mesa; **league ~** (*FOOTBALL, RUGBY*) clasificación *f* del campeonato; **~ of contents** índice *m* de materias.
tablecloth ['teɪblklɔθ] *n* mantel *m.*
table d'hôte [tɑ:bl'dəut] *n* menú *m.*
table lamp *n* lámpara de mesa.
tablemat ['teɪblmæt] *n* salvamanteles *m inv*, posaplatos *m inv.*
tablespoon ['teɪblspu:n] *n* cuchara grande; (*also*: **~ful**: *as measurement*) cucharada.
tablet ['tæblɪt] *n* (*MED*) pastilla, comprimido; (*for writing*) bloc *m*; (*of stone*) lápida; **~ of soap** pastilla de jabón.
table talk *n* conversación *f* de sobremesa.
table tennis *n* ping-pong *m*, tenis *m* de mesa.
table wine *n* vino de mesa.
tabloid ['tæblɔɪd] *n* (*newspaper*) periódico popular sensacionalista.
tabloid press *n ver recuadro.*

> **TABLOID PRESS**
>
> *El término genérico* **tabloid press** *o "tabloids" se usa para referirse a los periódicos populares británicos, por su tamaño reducido. A diferencia de la llamada "quality press", estos periódicos se caracterizan por su lenguaje sencillo, presentación llamativa y contenido a menudo sensacionalista, con gran énfasis en noticias sobre escándalos financieros y sexuales de los famosos, por lo que también reciben el nombre peyorativo de "gutter press".*

taboo [tə'bu:] *adj, n* tabú *m.*
tabulate ['tæbjuleɪt] *vt* disponer en tablas.
tabulator ['tæbjuleɪtə*] *n* tabulador *m.*
tachograph ['tækəgrɑ:f] *n* tacógrafo.
tacit ['tæsɪt] *adj* tácito.
tacitly ['tæsɪtlɪ] *adv* tácitamente.
taciturn ['tæsɪtə:n] *adj* taciturno.
tack [tæk] *n* (*nail*) tachuela; (*stitch*) hilván *m*; (*NAUT*) bordada ♦ *vt* (*nail*) clavar con tachuelas; (*stitch*) hilvanar ♦ *vi* virar; **to ~ sth on to (the end of) sth** (*of letter, book*) añadir algo a(l final de) algo.
tackle ['tækl] *n* (*gear*) equipo; (*fishing ~, for lifting*) aparejo; (*FOOTBALL*) entrada, tackle *m*; (*RUGBY*) placaje *m* ♦ *vt* (*difficulty*) enfrentarse a; (*grapple with*) agarrar; (*FOOTBALL*) entrar a; (*RUGBY*) placar.
tacky ['tækɪ] *adj* pegajoso; (*fam*) hortera *inv.*
tact [tækt] *n* tacto, discreción *f.*
tactful ['tæktful] *adj* discreto, diplomático; **to be ~** tener tacto.
tactfully ['tæktfulɪ] *adv* diplomáticamente, con tacto.
tactical ['tæktɪkl] *adj* táctico.
tactical voting *n* voto útil.
tactician [tæk'tɪʃən] *n* táctico/a.
tactics ['tæktɪks] *n, npl* táctica *sg.*
tactless ['tæktlɪs] *adj* indiscreto.
tactlessly ['tæktlɪslɪ] *adv* indiscretamente, sin tacto.
tadpole ['tædpəul] *n* renacuajo.
taffy ['tæfɪ] *n* (*US*) melcocha.
tag [tæg] *n* (*label*) etiqueta; **price/name ~** etiqueta del precio/con el nombre.
▸**tag along** *vi*: **to ~ along with sb** engancharse a algn.
Tahiti [tɑ:'hi:tɪ] *n* Tahití *m.*
tail [teɪl] *n* cola; (*ZOOL*) rabo; (*of shirt, coat*)

faldón *m* ♦ *vt* (*follow*) vigilar a; **heads or ~s** cara o cruz; **to turn ~** volver la espalda.
▸**tail away, tail off** *vi* (*in size, quality etc*) ir disminuyendo.
tailback ['teɪlbæk] *n* (*BRIT AUT*) cola.
tail coat *n* frac *m*.
tail end *n* cola, parte *f* final.
tailgate ['teɪlgeɪt] *n* (*AUT*) puerta trasera.
tail light *n* (*AUT*) luz *f* trasera.
tailor ['teɪlə*] *n* sastre *m* ♦ *vt*: **to ~ sth (to)** confeccionar algo a medida (para); **~'s (shop)** sastrería.
tailoring ['teɪlərɪŋ] *n* (*cut*) corte *m*; (*craft*) sastrería.
tailor-made ['teɪlə'meɪd] *adj* (*also fig*) hecho a (la) medida.
tailwind ['teɪlwɪnd] *n* viento de cola.
taint [teɪnt] *vt* (*meat, food*) contaminar; (*fig: reputation*) manchar, tachar (*LAM*).
tainted ['teɪntɪd] *adj* (*water, air*) contaminado; (*fig*) manchado.
Taiwan [taɪ'wɑːn] *n* Taiwán *m*.
Tajikistan [tɑːdʒɪkɪ'stɑːn] *n* Tayikistán *m*.
take [teɪk] *vb* (*pt* **took**, *pp* **taken** [tuk, 'teɪkn]) *vt* tomar; (*grab*) coger (*SP*), agarrar (*LAM*); (*gain: prize*) ganar; (*require: effort, courage*) exigir; (*support weight of*) aguantar; (*hold: passengers etc*) tener cabida para; (*accompany, bring, carry*) llevar; (*exam*) presentarse a; (*conduct: meeting*) presidir ♦ *vi* (*fire*) prender; (*dye*) coger (*SP*), agarrar, tomar ♦ *n* (*CINE*) toma; **to ~ sth from** (*drawer etc*) sacar algo de; (*person*) coger (*SP*) algo a; **to ~ sb's hand** tomar de la mano a algn; **to ~ notes** tomar apuntes; **to be ~n ill** ponerse enfermo; **~ the first on the left** toma la primera a la izquierda; **I only took Russian for one year** sólo estudié ruso un año; **I took him for a doctor** le tenía por médico; **it won't ~ long** durará poco; **it will ~ at least 5 litres** tiene cabida por lo menos para 5 litros; **to be ~n with sb/sth** (*attracted*) tomarle cariño a algn/tomarle gusto a algo; **I ~ it that** ... supongo que ....
▸**take after** *vt fus* parecerse a.
▸**take apart** *vt* desmontar.
▸**take away** *vt* (*remove*) quitar; (*carry off*) llevar ♦ *vi*: **to ~ away from** quitar mérito a.
▸**take back** *vt* (*return*) devolver; (*one's words*) retractar.
▸**take down** *vt* (*building*) derribar; (*dismantle: scaffolding*) desmantelar; (*message etc*) apuntar, tomar nota de.
▸**take in** *vt* (*BRIT: deceive*) engañar; (*understand*) entender; (*include*) abarcar; (*lodger*) acoger, recibir; (*orphan, stray dog*) recoger; (*SEWING*) achicar.
▸**take off** *vi* (*AVIAT*) despegar, decolar (*LAM*) ♦ *vt* (*remove*) quitar; (*imitate*) imitar, remedar.
▸**take on** *vt* (*work*) emprender; (*employee*) contratar; (*opponent*) desafiar.
▸**take out** *vt* sacar; (*remove*) quitar; **don't ~ it out on me!** ¡no te desquites conmigo!
▸**take over** *vt* (*business*) tomar posesión de ♦*vi*: **to ~ over from sb** reemplazar a algn.
▸**take to** *vt fus* (*person*) coger cariño a (*SP*), encariñarse con (*LAM*); (*activity*) aficionarse a; **to ~ to doing sth** aficionarse a (hacer) algo.
▸**take up** *vt* (*a dress*) acortar; (*occupy: time, space*) ocupar; (*engage in: hobby etc*) dedicarse a; (*absorb: liquids*) absorber; (*accept: offer, challenge*) aceptar ♦ *vi*: **to ~ up with sb** hacerse amigo de algn.
▸**take upon** *vt*: **to ~ it upon o.s. to do sth** encargarse de hacer algo.
takeaway ['teɪkəweɪ] *adj* (*BRIT: food*) para llevar.
take-home pay ['teɪkhəum-] *n* salario neto.
taken ['teɪkən] *pp of* **take**.
takeoff ['teɪkɔf] *n* (*AVIAT*) despegue *m*, decolaje *m* (*LAM*).
takeover ['teɪkəuvə*] *n* (*COMM*) absorción *f*.
takeover bid *n* oferta pública de adquisición.
takings ['teɪkɪŋz] *npl* (*COMM*) ingresos *mpl*.
talc [tælk] *n* (*also*: **~um powder**) talco.
tale [teɪl] *n* (*story*) cuento; (*account*) relación *f*; **to tell ~s** (*fig*) contar chismes.
talent ['tælnt] *n* talento.
talented ['tæləntɪd] *adj* talentoso, de talento.
talisman ['tælɪzmən] *n* talismán *m*.
talk [tɔːk] *n* charla; (*gossip*) habladurías *fpl*, chismes *mpl*; (*conversation*) conversación *f* ♦ *vi* (*speak*) hablar; (*chatter*) charlar; **~s** *npl* (*POL etc*) conversaciones *fpl*; **to give a ~** dar una charla *or* conferencia; **to ~ about** hablar de; **to ~ sb into doing sth** convencer a algn para que haga algo; **to ~ sb out of doing sth** disuadir a algn de que haga algo; **to ~ shop** hablar del trabajo; **~ing of films, have you seen ...?** hablando de películas, ¿has visto ...?
▸**talk over** *vt* discutir.
talkative ['tɔːkətɪv] *adj* hablador(a).
talker ['tɔːkə*] *n* hablador(a) *m/f*.
talking point ['tɔːkɪŋ-] *n* tema *m* de conversación.
talking-to ['tɔːkɪŋtuː] *n*: **to give sb a good ~** echar una buena bronca a algn.

talk show *n* programa *m* magazine.
tall [tɔːl] *adj* alto; (*tree*) grande; **to be 6 feet** ~ ≈ medir 1 metro 80, tener 1 metro 80 de alto; **how ~ are you?** ¿cuánto mides?
tallboy ['tɔːlbɔɪ] *n* (*BRIT*) cómoda alta.
tallness ['tɔːlnɪs] *n* altura.
tall story *n* cuento chino.
tally ['tælɪ] *n* cuenta ♦ *vi*: **to ~ (with)** concordar (con), cuadrar (con); **to keep a ~ of sth** llevar la cuenta de algo.
talon ['tælən] *n* garra.
tambourine [tæmbə'riːn] *n* pandereta.
tame [teɪm] *adj* (*mild*) manso; (*tamed*) domesticado; (*fig*: *story, style, person*) soso, anodino.
tameness ['teɪmnɪs] *n* mansedumbre *f*.
Tamil ['tæmɪl] *adj* tamil ♦ *n* tamil *m/f*; (*LING*) tamil *m*.
tamper ['tæmpə*] *vi*: **to ~ with** (*lock etc*) intentar forzar; (*papers*) falsificar.
tampon ['tæmpən] *n* tampón *m*.
tan [tæn] *n* (*also*: **sun~**) bronceado ♦ *vt* broncear ♦ *vi* ponerse moreno ♦ *adj* (*colour*) marrón; **to get a ~** broncearse, ponerse moreno.
tandem ['tændəm] *n* tándem *m*.
tandoori [tæn'duərɪ] *adj, n* tandoori *m* (*asado a la manera hindú, en horno de barro*).
tang [tæŋ] *n* sabor *m* fuerte.
tangent ['tændʒənt] *n* (*MATH*) tangente *f*; **to go off at a ~** (*fig*) salirse por la tangente.
tangerine [tændʒə'riːn] *n* mandarina.
tangible ['tændʒəbl] *adj* tangible; **~ assets** bienes *mpl* tangibles.
Tangier [tæn'dʒɪə*] *n* Tánger *m*.
tangle ['tæŋgl] *n* enredo; **to get in(to) a ~** enredarse.
tango ['tæŋgəu] *n* tango.
tank [tæŋk] *n* (*water ~*) depósito, tanque *m*; (*for fish*) acuario; (*MIL*) tanque *m*.
tankard ['tæŋkəd] *n* bock *m*.
tanker ['tæŋkə*] *n* (*ship*) petrolero; (*truck*) camión *m* cisterna.
tankful ['tæŋkful] *n*: **to get a ~ of petrol** llenar el depósito de gasolina.
tanned [tænd] *adj* (*skin*) moreno, bronceado.
tannin ['tænɪn] *n* tanino.
tanning ['tænɪŋ] *n* (*of leather*) curtido.
tannoy ® ['tænɔɪ] *n*: **over the ~** por el altavoz.
tantalizing ['tæntəlaɪzɪŋ] *adj* tentador(a).
tantamount ['tæntəmaunt] *adj*: **~ to** equivalente a.
tantrum ['tæntrəm] *n* rabieta; **to throw a ~** coger una rabieta.
Tanzania [tænzə'nɪə] *n* Tanzania.
Tanzanian [tænzə'nɪən] *adj, n* tanzano/a *m/f*.
tap [tæp] *n* (*BRIT*: *on sink etc*) grifo, canilla (*LAM*); (*gentle blow*) golpecito; (*gas ~*) llave *f* ♦ *vt* (*table etc*) tamborilear; (*shoulder etc*) dar palmaditas en; (*resources*) utilizar, explotar; (*telephone conversation*) intervenir, pinchar; **on ~** (*fig*: *resources*) a mano; **beer on ~** cerveza de barril.
tap-dancing ['tæpdɑːnsɪŋ] *n* claqué *m*.
tape [teɪp] *n* cinta; (*also*: **magnetic ~**) cinta magnética; (*sticky ~*) cinta adhesiva ♦ *vt* (*record*) grabar (en cinta); **on ~** (*song etc*) grabado (en cinta).
tape deck *n* pletina.
tape measure *n* cinta métrica, metro.
taper ['teɪpə*] *n* cirio ♦ *vi* afilarse.
tape-record ['teɪprɪkɔːd] *vt* grabar (en cinta).
tape recorder *n* grabadora.
tape recording *n* grabación *f*.
tapered ['teɪpəd], **tapering** ['teɪpərɪŋ] *adj* terminado en punta.
tapestry ['tæpɪstrɪ] *n* (*object*) tapiz *m*; (*art*) tapicería.
tape-worm ['teɪpwəːm] *n* solitaria, tenia.
tapioca [tæpɪ'əukə] *n* tapioca.
tappet ['tæpɪt] *n* excéntrica.
tar [tɑː*] *n* alquitrán *m*, brea; **low/middle ~ cigarettes** cigarrillos con contenido bajo/medio de alquitrán.
tarantula [tə'ræntjulə] *n* tarántula.
tardy ['tɑːdɪ] *adj* (*late*) tardío; (*slow*) lento.
tare [tɛə*] *n* (*COMM*) tara.
target ['tɑːgɪt] *n* (*gen*) blanco; **to be on ~** (*project*) seguir el curso previsto.
target audience *n público al que va destinado un programa etc.*
target market *n* (*COMM*) *mercado al que va destinado un producto etc.*
target practice *n* tiro al blanco.
tariff ['tærɪf] *n* tarifa.
tariff barrier *n* (*COMM*) barrera arancelaria.
tarmac ['tɑːmæk] *n* (*BRIT*: *on road*) alquitranado; (*AVIAT*) pista (de aterrizaje).
tarn [tɑːn] *n* lago pequeño de montaña.
tarnish ['tɑːnɪʃ] *vt* deslustrar.
tarot ['tærəu] *n* tarot *m*.
tarpaulin [tɑː'pɔːlɪn] *n* alquitranado.
tarragon ['tærəgən] *n* estragón *m*.
tarry ['tærɪ] *vi* entretenerse, quedarse atrás.
tart [tɑːt] *n* (*CULIN*) tarta; (*BRIT col*: *pej*: *woman*) fulana ♦ *adj* (*flavour*) agrio, ácido.
►**tart up** *vt* (*room, building*) dar tono a.
tartan ['tɑːtn] *n* tartán *m* ♦ *adj* de tartán.
tartar ['tɑːtə*] *n* (*on teeth*) sarro.

tartar sauce *n* salsa tártara.
tartly ['tɑːtlɪ] *adv* (*answer*) ásperamente.
task [tɑːsk] *n* tarea; **to take to ~** reprender.
task force *n* (*MIL, POLICE*) grupo de operaciones.
taskmaster ['tɑːskmɑːstə*] *n*: **he's a hard ~** es muy exigente.
Tasmania [tæz'meɪnɪə] *n* Tasmania.
tassel ['tæsl] *n* borla.
taste [teɪst] *n* sabor *m*, gusto; (*also*: **after~**) dejo; (*sip*) sorbo; (*fig*: *glimpse, idea*) muestra, idea ♦ *vt* probar ♦ *vi*: **to ~ of** *or* **like** (*fish etc*) saber a; **you can ~ the garlic (in it)** se nota el sabor a ajo; **can I have a ~ of this wine?** ¿puedo probar este vino?; **to have a ~ for sth** ser aficionado a algo; **in good/bad ~** de buen/mal gusto; **to be in bad** *or* **poor ~** ser de mal gusto.
taste bud *n* papila gustativa *or* del gusto.
tasteful ['teɪstful] *adj* de buen gusto.
tastefully ['teɪstfulɪ] *adv* elegantemente, con buen gusto.
tasteless ['teɪstlɪs] *adj* (*food*) soso; (*remark*) de mal gusto.
tastelessly ['teɪstlɪslɪ] *adv* con mal gusto.
tastily ['teɪstɪlɪ] *adv* sabrosamente.
tastiness ['teɪstɪnɪs] *n* (buen) sabor *m*, lo sabroso.
tasty ['teɪstɪ] *adj* sabroso, rico.
ta-ta ['tæ'tɑː] *interj* (*BRIT col*) hasta luego, adiós.
tatters ['tætəz] *npl*: **in ~** (*also*: **tattered**) hecho jirones.
tattoo [tə'tuː] *n* tatuaje *m*; (*spectacle*) espectáculo militar ♦ *vt* tatuar.
tatty ['tætɪ] *adj* (*BRIT col*) cochambroso.
taught [tɔːt] *pt, pp of* **teach**.
taunt [tɔːnt] *n* pulla ♦ *vt* lanzar pullas a.
Taurus ['tɔːrəs] *n* Tauro.
taut [tɔːt] *adj* tirante, tenso.
tavern ['tævən] *n* (*old*) posada, fonda.
tawdry ['tɔːdrɪ] *adj* de mal gusto.
tawny ['tɔːnɪ] *adj* leonado.
tax [tæks] *n* impuesto ♦ *vt* gravar (con un impuesto); (*fig*: *test*) poner a prueba; (: *patience*) agotar; **before/after ~** impuestos excluidos/incluidos; **free of ~** libre de impuestos.
taxable ['tæksəbl] *adj* (*income*) imponible, sujeto a impuestos.
tax allowance *n* desgravación *f* fiscal.
taxation [tæk'seɪʃən] *n* impuestos *mpl*; **system of ~** sistema *m* tributario.
tax avoidance *n* evasión *f* de impuestos.
tax collector *n* recaudador(a) *m/f*.
tax disc *n* (*BRIT AUT*) pegatina del impuesto de circulación.
tax evasion *n* evasión *f* fiscal.
tax exemption *n* exención *f* de impuestos.
tax-free ['tæksfriː] *adj* libre de impuestos.
tax haven *n* paraíso fiscal.
taxi ['tæksɪ] *n* taxi *m* ♦ *vi* (*AVIAT*) rodar por la pista.
taxidermist ['tæksɪdəːmɪst] *n* taxidermista *m/f*.
taxi driver *n* taxista *m/f*.
tax inspector *n* inspector(a) *m/f* de Hacienda.
taxi rank (*BRIT*), **taxi stand** *n* parada de taxis.
tax payer *n* contribuyente *m/f*.
tax rebate *n* devolución *f* de impuestos, reembolso fiscal.
tax relief *n* desgravación *f* fiscal.
tax return *n* declaración *f* de la renta.
tax shelter *n* protección *f* fiscal.
tax year *n* año fiscal.
TB *n abbr* = **tuberculosis**.
TD *n abbr* (*US*) = **Treasury Department**; (: *FOOTBALL*) = **touchdown**.
tea [tiː] *n* té *m*; (*BRIT*: *snack*) ≈ merienda; **high ~** (*BRIT*) ≈ merienda-cena.
tea bag *n* bolsita de té.
tea break *n* (*BRIT*) descanso para el té.
teacake ['tiːkeɪk] *n* bollito, queque *m* (*LAM*).
teach, *pt, pp* **taught** [tiːtʃ, tɔːt] *vt*: **to ~ sb sth, ~ sth to sb** enseñar algo a algn ♦ *vi* enseñar; (*be a teacher*) ser profesor(a); **it taught him a lesson** (eso) le sirvió de escarmiento.
teacher ['tiːtʃə*] *n* (*in secondary school*) profesor(a) *m/f*; (*in primary school*) maestro/a; **Spanish ~** profesor(a) *m/f* de español.
teacher training college *n* (*for primary schools*) escuela normal; (*for secondary schools*) centro de formación del profesorado.
teach-in ['tiːtʃɪn] *n* seminario.
teaching ['tiːtʃɪŋ] *n* enseñanza.
teaching aids *npl* materiales *mpl* pedagógicos.
teaching hospital *n* hospital universitario.
tea cosy *n* cubretetera *m*.
teacup ['tiːkʌp] *n* taza de té.
teak [tiːk] *n* (madera de) teca.
tea leaves *npl* hojas *fpl* de té.
team [tiːm] *n* equipo; (*of animals*) pareja.
►**team up** *vi* asociarse.
team spirit *n* espíritu *m* de equipo.
teamwork ['tiːmwəːk] *n* trabajo en equipo.
tea party *n* té *m*.
teapot ['tiːpɔt] *n* tetera.
tear [tɛə*] *n* rasgón *m*, desgarrón *m*; [tɪə*] lágrima ♦ *vb* [tɛə*] (*pt* **tore**, *pp* **torn** [tɔː*,

tɔːn]) *vt* romper, rasgar ♦ *vi* rasgarse; **in ~s** llorando; **to burst into ~s** deshacerse en lágrimas; **to ~ to pieces** *or* **to bits** *or* **to shreds** (*also fig*) hacer pedazos, destrozar.
▸**tear along** *vi* (*rush*) precipitarse.
▸**tear apart** *vt* (*also fig*) hacer pedazos.
▸**tear away** *vt*: **to ~ o.s. away (from sth)** alejarse (de algo).
▸**tear out** *vt* (*sheet, cheque*) arrancar.
▸**tear up** *vt* (*sheet of paper etc*) romper.
tearaway ['tɛərəweɪ] *n* (*col*) gamberro/a.
teardrop ['tɪədrɔp] *n* lágrima.
tearful ['tɪəful] *adj* lloroso.
tear gas *n* gas *m* lacrimógeno.
tearing ['tɛərɪŋ] *adj*: **to be in a ~ hurry** tener muchísima prisa.
tearoom ['tiːruːm] *n* salón *m* de té.
tease [tiːz] *n* bromista *m/f* ♦ *vt* tomar el pelo a.
tea set *n* servicio de té.
teashop ['tiːʃɔp] *n* café *m*, cafetería.
Teasmaid ® ['tiːzmeɪd] *n* tetera automática.
teaspoon ['tiːspuːn] *n* cucharita; (*also*: **~ful**: *as measurement*) cucharadita.
tea strainer *n* colador *m* de té.
teat [tiːt] *n* (*of bottle*) boquilla, tetilla.
teatime ['tiːtaɪm] *n* hora del té.
tea towel *n* (*BRIT*) paño de cocina.
tea urn *n* tetera grande.
tech [tɛk] *n abbr* (*col*) = **technology; technical college.**
technical ['tɛknɪkl] *adj* técnico.
technical college *n* centro de formación profesional.
technicality [tɛknɪ'kælɪtɪ] *n* detalle *m* técnico; **on a legal ~** por una cuestión formal.
technically ['tɛknɪklɪ] *adv* técnicamente.
technician [tɛk'nɪʃn] *n* técnico/a.
technique [tɛk'niːk] *n* técnica.
techno ['tɛknəu] *n* (*MUS*) (música) tecno.
technocrat ['tɛknəkræt] *n* tecnócrata *m/f*.
technological [tɛknə'lɔdʒɪkl] *adj* tecnológico.
technologist [tɛk'nɔlədʒɪst] *n* tecnólogo/a.
technology [tɛk'nɔlədʒɪ] *n* tecnología.
teddy (bear) ['tɛdɪ-] *n* osito de peluche.
tedious ['tiːdɪəs] *adj* pesado, aburrido.
tedium ['tiːdɪəm] *n* tedio.
tee [tiː] *n* (*GOLF*) tee *m*.
teem [tiːm] *vi*: **to ~ with** rebosar de; **it is ~ing (with rain)** llueve a mares.
teenage ['tiːneɪdʒ] *adj* (*fashions etc*) juvenil.
teenager ['tiːneɪdʒə*] *n* adolescente *m/f*.
teens [tiːnz] *npl*: **to be in one's ~** ser adolescente.
tee-shirt ['tiːʃəːt] *n* = **T-shirt.**
teeter ['tiːtə*] *vi* balancearse.
teeth [tiːθ] *npl of* **tooth.**
teethe [tiːð] *vi* echar los dientes.
teething ring ['tiːðɪŋ-] *n* mordedor *m*.
teething troubles ['tiːðɪŋ-] *npl* (*fig*) dificultades *fpl* iniciales.
teetotal ['tiː'təutl] *adj* (*person*) abstemio.
teetotaller, (*US*) **teetotaler** ['tiː'təutlə*] *n* (*person*) abstemio/a.
TEFL ['tɛfl] *n abbr* = *Teaching of English as a Foreign Language*; **~ qualification** *título para la enseñanza del inglés como lengua extranjera.*
Teflon ® ['tɛflɔn] *n* teflón *m* ®.
Teheran [tɛə'rɑːn] *n* Teherán *m*.
tel. *abbr* (= *telephone*) tel.
Tel Aviv ['tɛlə'viːv] *n* Tel Aviv *m*.
telecast ['tɛlɪkɑːst] *vt, vi* transmitir por televisión.
telecommunications ['tɛlɪkəmjuːnɪ'keɪʃənz] *n* telecomunicaciones *fpl*.
teleconferencing [tɛlɪ'kɔnfərənsɪŋ] *n* teleconferencias *fpl*.
telefax ['tɛlɪfæks] *n* telefax *m*.
telegram ['tɛlɪgræm] *n* telegrama *m*.
telegraph ['tɛlɪgrɑːf] *n* telégrafo.
telegraphic [tɛlɪ'græfɪk] *adj* telegráfico.
telegraph pole *n* poste *m* telegráfico.
telegraph wire *n* hilo telegráfico.
telepathic [tɛlɪ'pæθɪk] *adj* telepático.
telepathy [tə'lɛpəθɪ] *n* telepatía.
telephone ['tɛlɪfəun] *n* teléfono ♦ *vt* llamar por teléfono, telefonear; **to be on the ~** (*subscriber*) tener teléfono; (*be speaking*) estar hablando por teléfono.
telephone booth, (*BRIT*) **telephone box** *n* cabina telefónica.
telephone call *n* llamada telefónica.
telephone directory *n* guía telefónica.
telephone exchange *n* central *f* telefónica.
telephone number *n* número de teléfono.
telephonist [tə'lɛfənɪst] *n* (*BRIT*) telefonista *m/f*.
telephoto ['tɛlɪ'fəutəu] *adj*: **~ lens** teleobjetivo.
teleprinter ['tɛlɪprɪntə*] *n* teletipo, teleimpresora.
teleprompter ® ['tɛlɪprɔmptə*] *n* teleapuntador *m*.
telesales ['tɛlɪseɪlz] *npl* televentas *fpl*.
telescope ['tɛlɪskəup] *n* telescopio.
telescopic [tɛlɪ'skɔpɪk] *adj* telescópico; (*umbrella*) plegable.
Teletext ® ['tɛlɪtɛkst] *n* teletexto *m*.
telethon ['tɛlɪθɔn] *n* telemaratón *m*,

maratón *m* televisivo (*con fines benéficos*).
televise ['tɛlɪvaɪz] *vt* televisar.
television ['tɛlɪvɪʒən] *n* televisión *f*; **to watch ~** mirar *or* ver la televisión.
television licence *n* impuesto por uso de televisor.
television set *n* televisor *m*.
teleworking ['tɛlɪˌwəːkɪŋ] *n* teletrabajo.
telex ['tɛlɛks] *n* télex *m* ♦ *vt* (*message*) enviar por télex; (*person*) enviar un télex a ♦ *vi* enviar un télex.
tell *pt, pp* **told** [tɛl, təuld] *vt* decir; (*relate: story*) contar; (*distinguish*): **to ~ sth from** distinguir algo de ♦ *vi* (*talk*): **to ~ (of)** contar; (*have effect*) tener efecto; **to ~ sb to do sth** decir a algn que haga algo; **to ~ sb about sth** contar algo a algn; **to ~ the time** dar *or* decir la hora; **can you ~ me the time?** ¿me puedes decir la hora?; **(I) ~ you what ...** fíjate ...; **I couldn't ~ them apart** no podía distinguirlos.
►**tell off** *vt*: **to ~ sb off** regañar a algn.
►**tell on** *vt fus*: **to ~ on sb** chivarse de algn.
teller ['tɛlə*] *n* (*in bank*) cajero/a.
telling ['tɛlɪŋ] *adj* (*remark, detail*) revelador(a).
telltale ['tɛlteɪl] *adj* (*sign*) indicador(a).
telly ['tɛlɪ] *n* (*BRIT col*) tele *f*.
temerity [tə'mɛrɪtɪ] *n* temeridad *f*.
temp [tɛmp] *n abbr* (*BRIT*: = *temporary office worker*) empleado/a eventual ♦ *vi* trabajar como empleado/a eventual.
temper ['tɛmpə*] *n* (*mood*) humor *m*; (*bad ~*) (mal) genio; (*fit of anger*) ira; (*of child*) rabieta ♦ *vt* (*moderate*) moderar; **to be in a ~** estar furioso; **to lose one's ~** enfadarse, enojarse (*LAM*); **to keep one's ~** contenerse, no alterarse.
temperament ['tɛmprəmənt] *n* (*nature*) temperamento.
temperamental [tɛmprə'mɛntl] *adj* temperamental.
temperance ['tɛmpərns] *n* moderación *f*; (*in drinking*) sobriedad *f*.
temperate ['tɛmprət] *adj* moderado; (*climate*) templado.
temperature ['tɛmprətʃə*] *n* temperatura; **to have** *or* **run a ~** tener fiebre.
tempered ['tɛmpəd] *adj* (*steel*) templado.
tempest ['tɛmpɪst] *n* tempestad *f*.
tempestuous [tɛm'pɛstjuəs] *adj* (*relationship, meeting*) tempestuoso.
tempi ['tɛmpiː] *npl of* **tempo.**
template ['tɛmplɪt] *n* plantilla.
temple ['tɛmpl] *n* (*REL*) templo; (*ANAT*) sien *f*.
templet ['tɛmplɪt] *n* = **template.**
tempo, *pl* **~s** *or* **tempi** ['tɛmpəu, 'tɛmpiː] *n* tempo; (*fig: of life etc*) ritmo.
temporal ['tɛmpərl] *adj* temporal.
temporarily ['tɛmpərərɪlɪ] *adv* temporalmente.
temporary ['tɛmpərərɪ] *adj* provisional, temporal; (*passing*) transitorio; (*worker*) eventual; **~ teacher** maestro/a interino/a.
tempt [tɛmpt] *vt* tentar; **to ~ sb into doing sth** tentar *or* inducir a algn a hacer algo; **to be ~ed to do sth** (*person*) sentirse tentado de hacer algo.
temptation [tɛmp'teɪʃən] *n* tentación *f*.
tempting ['tɛmptɪŋ] *adj* tentador(a).
ten [tɛn] *num* diez; **~s of thousands** decenas *fpl* de miles.
tenable ['tɛnəbl] *adj* sostenible.
tenacious [tə'neɪʃəs] *adj* tenaz.
tenaciously [tə'neɪʃəslɪ] *adv* tenazmente.
tenacity [tə'næsɪtɪ] *n* tenacidad *f*.
tenancy ['tɛnənsɪ] *n* alquiler *m*.
tenant ['tɛnənt] *n* (*rent-payer*) inquilino/a; (*occupant*) habitante *m/f*.
tend [tɛnd] *vt* (*sick etc*) cuidar, atender; (*cattle, machine*) vigilar, cuidar ♦ *vi*: **to ~ to do sth** tener tendencia a hacer algo.
tendency ['tɛndənsɪ] *n* tendencia.
tender ['tɛndə*] *adj* tierno, blando; (*delicate*) delicado; (*sore*) sensible; (*affectionate*) tierno, cariñoso ♦ *n* (*COMM: offer*) oferta; (*money*): **legal ~** moneda de curso legal ♦ *vt* ofrecer; **to put in a ~ (for)** hacer una oferta (para); **to put work out to ~** ofrecer un trabajo a contrata; **to ~ one's resignation** presentar la dimisión.
tenderize ['tɛndəraɪz] *vt* (*CULIN*) ablandar.
tenderly ['tɛndəlɪ] *adv* tiernamente.
tenderness ['tɛndənɪs] *n* ternura; (*of meat*) blandura.
tendon ['tɛndən] *n* tendón *m*.
tendril ['tɛndrɪl] *n* zarcillo.
tenement ['tɛnəmənt] *n* casa *or* bloque *m* de pisos *or* vecinos (*LAM*).
Tenerife [tɛnə'riːf] *n* Tenerife *m*.
tenet ['tɛnət] *n* principio.
Tenn. *abbr* (*US*) = *Tennessee*.
tenner ['tɛnə*] *n* (billete *m* de) diez libras *fpl*.
tennis ['tɛnɪs] *n* tenis *m*.
tennis ball *n* pelota de tenis.
tennis club *n* club *m* de tenis.
tennis court *n* cancha de tenis.
tennis elbow *n* (*MED*) sinovitis *f* del codo.
tennis match *n* partido de tenis.
tennis player *n* tenista *m/f*.
tennis racket *n* raqueta de tenis.
tennis shoes *npl* zapatillas *fpl* de tenis.
tenor ['tɛnə*] *n* (*MUS*) tenor *m*.
tenpin bowling ['tɛnpɪn-] *n* bolos *mpl*.
tense [tɛns] *adj* tenso; (*stretched*) tirante;

(*stiff*) rígido, tieso; (*person*) nervioso ♦ *n* (*LING*) tiempo ♦ *vt* (*tighten*: *muscles*) tensar.
tensely ['tɛnslɪ] *adv*: **they waited ~** esperaban tensos.
tenseness ['tɛnsnɪs] *n* tirantez *f*, tensión *f*.
tension ['tɛnʃən] *n* tensión *f*.
tent [tɛnt] *n* tienda (de campaña), carpa (*LAM*).
tentacle ['tɛntəkl] *n* tentáculo.
tentative ['tɛntətɪv] *adj* (*person*) indeciso; (*provisional*) provisional.
tentatively ['tɛntətɪvlɪ] *adv* con indecisión; (*provisionally*) provisionalmente.
tenterhooks ['tɛntəhuks] *npl*: **on ~** sobre ascuas.
tenth [tɛnθ] *adj* décimo.
tent peg *n* clavija, estaca.
tent pole *n* mástil *m*.
tenuous ['tɛnjuəs] *adj* tenue.
tenure ['tɛnjuə*] *n* posesión *f*, tenencia; **to have ~** tener posesión *or* título de propiedad.
tepid ['tɛpɪd] *adj* tibio.
term [tə:m] *n* (*limit*) límite *m*; (*COMM*) plazo; (*word*) término; (*period*) período; (*SCOL*) trimestre *m* ♦ *vt* llamar, calificar de; **~s** *npl* (*conditions*) condiciones *fpl*; (*COMM*) precio, tarifa; **in the short/long ~** a corto/largo plazo; **during his ~ of office** bajo su mandato; **to be on good ~s with sb** llevarse bien con algn; **to come to ~s with** (*problem*) aceptar; **in ~s of** ... en cuanto a ..., en términos de ....
terminal ['tə:mɪnl] *adj* terminal ♦ *n* (*ELEC*) borne *m*; (*COMPUT*) terminal *m*; (*also*: **air ~**) terminal *f*; (*BRIT*: *also*: **coach ~**) (estación *f*) terminal *f*.
terminate ['tə:mɪneɪt] *vt* poner término a; (*pregnancy*) interrumpir ♦ *vi*: **to ~ in** acabar en.
termination [tə:mɪ'neɪʃən] *n* fin *m*; (*of contract*) terminación *f*; **~ of pregnancy** interrupción *f* del embarazo.
termini ['tə:mɪnaɪ] *npl of* **terminus**.
terminology [tə:mɪ'nɔlədʒɪ] *n* terminología.
terminus, *pl* **termini** ['tə:mɪnəs, 'tə:mɪnaɪ] *n* término, (estación *f*) terminal *f*.
termite ['tə:maɪt] *n* termita, comején *m*.
term paper *n* (*US UNIV*) trabajo escrito trimestral *or* semestral.
Ter(r). *abbr* = **terrace**.
terrace ['tɛrəs] *n* terraza; (*BRIT*: *row of houses*) hilera de casas adosadas; **the ~s** (*BRIT SPORT*) las gradas *fpl*.
terraced ['tɛrəst] *adj* (*garden*) escalonado; (*house*) adosado.
terracotta ['tɛrə'kɔtə] *n* terracota.
terrain [tɛ'reɪn] *n* terreno.
terrible ['tɛrɪbl] *adj* terrible, horrible; (*fam*) malísimo.
terribly ['tɛrɪblɪ] *adv* terriblemente; (*very badly*) malísimamente.
terrier ['tɛrɪə*] *n* terrier *m*.
terrific [tə'rɪfɪk] *adj* fantástico, fenomenal, macanudo (*LAM*); (*wonderful*) maravilloso.
terrify ['tɛrɪfaɪ] *vt* aterrorizar; **to be terrified** estar aterrado *or* aterrorizado.
terrifying ['tɛrɪfaɪɪŋ] *adj* aterrador(a).
territorial [tɛrɪ'tɔ:rɪəl] *adj* territorial.
territorial waters *npl* aguas *fpl* jurisdiccionales.
territory ['tɛrɪtərɪ] *n* territorio.
terror ['tɛrə*] *n* terror *m*.
terrorism ['tɛrərɪzəm] *n* terrorismo.
terrorist ['tɛrərɪst] *n* terrorista *m/f*.
terrorize ['tɛrəraɪz] *vt* aterrorizar.
terse [tə:s] *adj* (*style*) conciso; (*reply*) brusco.
tertiary ['tə:ʃərɪ] *adj* terciario; **~ education** enseñanza superior.
Terylene ® ['tɛrəli:n] *n* (*BRIT*) terylene *m* ®.
TESL [tɛsl] *n abbr* = *Teaching of English as a Second Language*.
TESSA ['tɛsə] *n abbr* (*BRIT*: = *Tax Exempt Special Savings Account*) *plan de ahorro por el que se invierte a largo plazo a cambio de intereses libres de impuestos*.
test [tɛst] *n* (*trial, check*) prueba, ensayo; (: *of goods in factory*) control *m*; (*of courage etc, CHEM, MED*) prueba; (*of blood, urine*) análisis *m inv*; (*exam*) examen *m*, test *m*; (*also*: **driving ~**) examen *m* de conducir ♦ *vt* probar, poner a prueba; (*MED*) examinar; (: *blood*) analizar; **to put sth to the ~** someter algo a prueba; **to ~ sth for sth** analizar algo en busca de algo.
testament ['tɛstəmənt] *n* testamento; **the Old/New T~** el Antiguo/Nuevo Testamento.
test ban *n* (*also*: **nuclear ~**) suspensión *f* de pruebas nucleares.
test card *n* (*TV*) carta de ajuste.
test case *n* (*JUR*) juicio que sienta precedente.
testes ['tɛsti:z] *npl* testes *mpl*.
test flight *n* vuelo de ensayo.
testicle ['tɛstɪkl] *n* testículo.
testify ['tɛstɪfaɪ] *vi* (*LAW*) prestar declaración; **to ~ to sth** atestiguar algo.
testimonial [tɛstɪ'məunɪəl] *n* (*of character*) (carta de) recomendación *f*.
testimony ['tɛstɪmənɪ] *n* (*LAW*) testimonio, declaración *f*.
testing ['tɛstɪŋ] *adj* (*difficult*: *time*) duro.

test match *n* (*CRICKET, RUGBY*) partido internacional.
testosterone [tɛs'tɔstərəun] *n* testosterona.
test paper *n* examen *m*, test *m*.
test pilot *n* piloto *m/f* de pruebas.
test tube *n* probeta.
test-tube baby *n* bebé *m* probeta *inv*.
tetanus ['tɛtənəs] *n* tétano.
tetchy ['tɛtʃɪ] *adj* irritable.
tether ['tɛðə*] *vt* atar (con una cuerda) ♦ *n*: **to be at the end of one's ~** no aguantar más.
Tex. *abbr* (*US*) = *Texas*.
text [tɛkst] *n* texto.
textbook ['tɛkstbuk] *n* libro de texto.
textiles ['tɛkstaɪlz] *npl* tejidos *mpl*.
textual ['tɛkstjuəl] *adj* del texto, textual.
texture ['tɛkstʃə*] *n* textura.
TGWU *n abbr* (*BRIT*: = *Transport and General Workers' Union*) *sindicato de transportistas*.
Thai [taɪ] *adj, n* tailandés/esa *m/f*.
Thailand ['taɪlænd] *n* Tailandia.
Thames [tɛmz] *n*: **the ~** el (río) Támesis.
than [ðæn, ðən] *conj* que; (*with numerals*): **more ~ 10/once** más de 10/una vez; **I have more/less ~ you** tengo más/menos que tú; **it is better to phone ~ to write** es mejor llamar por teléfono que escribir; **no sooner did he leave ~ the phone rang** en cuanto se marchó, sonó el teléfono.
thank [θæŋk] *vt* dar las gracias a, agradecer; **~ you (very much)** muchas gracias; **~ heavens, ~ God!** ¡gracias a Dios!, ¡menos mal!
thankful ['θæŋkful] *adj*: **~ for** agradecido (por).
thankfully ['θæŋkfəlɪ] *adv* (*gratefully*) con agradecimiento; (*with relief*) por suerte; **~ there were few victims** afortunadamente hubo pocas víctimas.
thankless ['θæŋklɪs] *adj* ingrato.
thanks [θæŋks] *npl* gracias *fpl* ♦ *excl* ¡gracias!; **~ to** *prep* gracias a.
Thanksgiving (Day) ['θæŋksgɪvɪŋ-] *n* día *m* de Acción de Gracias; *ver recuadro*.

THANKSGIVING DAY

En Estados Unidos el cuarto jueves de noviembre es **Thanksgiving Day**, *fiesta oficial en la que se conmemora la celebración que tuvieron los primeros colonos norteamericanos ("Pilgrims" o "Pilgrim Fathers") tras la estupenda cosecha de 1621, por la que se dan gracias a Dios. En Canadá se celebra una fiesta semejante el segundo lunes de octubre, aunque no está relacionada con dicha fecha histórica.*

KEYWORD

that [ðæt](*pl* **those**) *adj* (*demonstrative*) ese/a, *pl* esos/as; (*more remote*) aquel/aquella, *pl* aquellos/as; **leave those books on the table** deja esos libros sobre la mesa; **~ one** ése/ésa; (*more remote*) aquél/aquélla; **~ one over there** ése/ésa de ahí; aquél/aquélla de allí

♦ *pron* **1** (*demonstrative*) ése/a, *pl* ésos/as; (*neuter*) eso; (*more remote*) aquél/aquélla, *pl* aquéllos/as; (*neuter*) aquello; **what's ~?** ¿qué es eso (*or* aquello)?; **who's ~?** ¿quién es?; (*when pointing etc*) ¿quién es ése/a?; **is ~ you?** ¿eres tú?; **will you eat all ~?** ¿vas a comer todo eso?; **~'s my house** ésa es mi casa; **~'s what he said** eso es lo que dijo; **~ is (to say)** es decir; **at** *or* **with ~ she ...** en eso, ella ...; **do it like ~** hazlo así

2 (*relative*: *subject, object*) que; (*with preposition*) (el/la) que, el/la cual; **the book (~) I read** el libro que leí; **the books ~ are in the library** los libros que están en la biblioteca; **all (~) I have** todo lo que tengo; **the box (~) I put it in** la caja en la que *or* donde lo puse; **the people (~) I spoke to** la gente con la que hablé; **not ~ I know of** que yo sepa, no

3 (*relative*: *of time*) que; **the day (~) he came** el día (en) que vino

♦ *conj* que; **he thought ~ I was ill** creyó que yo estaba enfermo

♦ *adv* (*demonstrative*): **I can't work ~ much** no puedo trabajar tanto; **I didn't realise it was ~ bad** no creí que fuera tan malo; **~ high** así de alto.

thatched [θætʃt] *adj* (*roof*) de paja; **~ cottage** casita con tejado de paja.
Thatcherism ['θætʃərɪzəm] *n* thatcherismo.
thaw [θɔː] *n* deshielo ♦ *vi* (*ice*) derretirse; (*food*) descongelarse ♦ *vt* (*food*) descongelar.

KEYWORD

the [ðiː, ðə] *def art* **1** (*gen*) el, *f* la, *pl* los, *fpl* las (*NB* = el *immediately before feminine noun beginning with stressed (h)a*; *a+el* = al; *de+el* = del); **~ boy/girl** el chico/la chica; **~ books/flowers** los libros/las flores; **to ~ postman/from ~ drawer** al cartero/del cajón; **I haven't ~ time/money** no tengo tiempo/dinero; **100 pesetas to ~ dollar**

100 pesetas por dólar; **paid by ~ hour** pagado por hora
2 (*+adj to form noun*) los; lo; ~ **rich and ~ poor** los ricos y los pobres; **to attempt ~ impossible** intentar lo imposible
3 (*in titles, surnames*): **Elizabeth ~ First** Isabel Primera; **Peter ~ Great** Pedro el Grande; **do you know ~ Smiths?** ¿conoce a los Smith?
4 (*in comparisons*): ~ **more he works ~ more he earns** cuanto más trabaja más gana.

theatre, (*US*) **theater** ['θɪətə*] *n* teatro.
theatre-goer, (*US*) **theater-goer** ['θɪətəgəuə*] *n* aficionado/a al teatro.
theatrical [θɪ'ætrɪkl] *adj* teatral.
theft [θɛft] *n* robo.
their [ðɛə*] *adj* su.
theirs [ðɛəz] *pron* (el) suyo/(la) suya *etc*; *see also* **my, mine.**
them [ðɛm, ðəm] *pron* (*direct*) los/las; (*indirect*) les; (*stressed, after prep*) ellos/ellas; **I see ~** los veo; **both of ~** ambos/as, los/las dos; **give me a few of ~** dame algunos/as; *see also* **me.**
theme [θi:m] *n* tema *m*.
theme park *n* parque *m* temático.
theme song *n* tema *m* (musical).
themselves [ðəm'sɛlvz] *pl pron* (*subject*) ellos mismos/ellas mismas; (*complement*) se; (*after prep*) sí (mismos/as); *see also* **oneself.**
then [ðɛn] *adv* (*at that time*) entonces; (*next*) pues; (*later*) luego, después; (*and also*) además ♦ *conj* (*therefore*) en ese caso, entonces ♦ *adj*: **the ~ president** el entonces presidente; **from ~ on** desde entonces; **until ~** hasta entonces; **and ~ what?** y luego, ¿qué?; **what do you want me to do, ~?** ¿entonces, qué quiere que haga?
theologian [θɪə'ləudʒən] *n* teólogo/a.
theological [θɪə'lɔdʒɪkl] *adj* teológico.
theology [θɪ'ɔlədʒɪ] *n* teología.
theorem ['θɪərəm] *n* teorema *m*.
theoretical [θɪə'rɛtɪkl] *adj* teórico.
theoretically [θɪə'rɛtɪklɪ] *adv* teóricamente, en teoría.
theorize ['θɪəraɪz] *vi* teorizar.
theory ['θɪərɪ] *n* teoría.
therapeutic(al) [θɛrə'pju:tɪk(l)] *adj* terapéutico.
therapist ['θɛrəpɪst] *n* terapeuta *m/f*.
therapy ['θɛrəpɪ] *n* terapia.

KEYWORD

there ['ðɛə*] *adv* **1**: ~ **is,** ~ **are** hay; ~ **is no-one here** no hay nadie aquí; ~ **is no bread left** no queda pan; ~ **has been an accident** ha habido un accidente
2 (*referring to place*) ahí; (*distant*) allí; **it's ~** está ahí; **put it in/on/up/down ~** ponlo ahí dentro/encima/arriba/abajo; **I want that book ~** quiero ese libro de ahí; ~ **he is!** ¡ahí está!; **~'s the bus** ahí *or* ya viene el autobús; **back/down ~** allí atrás/abajo; **over ~, through ~** por allí
3: ~, ~ (*esp to child*) ¡venga, venga!

thereabouts ['ðɛərə'bauts] *adv* por ahí.
thereafter [ðɛər'ɑ:ftə*] *adv* después.
thereby ['ðɛəbaɪ] *adv* así, de ese modo.
therefore ['ðɛəfɔ:*] *adv* por lo tanto.
there's [ðɛəz] = **there is; there has.**
thereupon [ðɛərə'pɔn] *adv* (*at that point*) en eso, en seguida.
thermal ['θə:ml] *adj* termal.
thermal paper *n* papel *m* térmico.
thermal printer *n* termoimpresora.
thermodynamics ['θə:mədaɪnæmɪks] *n* termodinámica.
thermometer [θə'mɔmɪtə*] *n* termómetro.
thermonuclear [θə:məu'nju:klɪə*] *adj* termonuclear.
Thermos ® ['θə:məs] *n* (*also*: ~ **flask**) termo.
thermostat ['θə:məustæt] *n* termostato.
thesaurus [θɪ'sɔ:rəs] *n* tesoro, diccionario de sinónimos.
these [ði:z] *pl adj* estos/as ♦ *pl pron* éstos/as.
thesis, *pl* **theses** ['θi:sɪs, -si:z] *n* tesis *f inv*; *see also* **doctorate.**
they [ðeɪ] *pl pron* ellos/ellas; ~ **say that ...** (*it is said that*) se dice que ....
they'd [ðeɪd] = **they had; they would.**
they'll [ðeɪl] = **they shall, they will.**
they're [ðɛə*] = **they are.**
they've [ðeɪv] = **they have.**
thick [θɪk] *adj* (*wall, slice*) grueso; (*dense: liquid, smoke etc*) espeso; (*vegetation, beard*) tupido; (*stupid*) torpe ♦ *n*: **in the ~ of the battle** en lo más reñido de la batalla; **it's 20 cm ~** tiene 20 cm de espesor.
thicken ['θɪkn] *vi* espesarse ♦ *vt* (*sauce etc*) espesar.
thicket ['θɪkɪt] *n* espesura.
thickly ['θɪklɪ] *adv* (*spread*) en capa espesa; (*cut*) en rebanada gruesa; (*populated*) densamente.
thickness ['θɪknɪs] *n* espesor *m*, grueso.
thickset [θɪk'sɛt] *adj* fornido.

thickskinned [θɪk'skɪnd] *adj* (*fig*) insensible.

thief, *pl* **thieves** [θi:f, θi:vz] *n* ladrón/ona *m/f*.

thieving ['θi:vɪŋ] *n* robo, hurto ♦ *adj* ladrón/ona.

thigh [θaɪ] *n* muslo.

thighbone ['θaɪbəun] *n* fémur *m*.

thimble ['θɪmbl] *n* dedal *m*.

thin [θɪn] *adj* delgado; (*wall, layer*) fino; (*watery*) aguado; (*light*) tenue; (*hair*) escaso; (*fog*) ligero; (*crowd*) disperso ♦ *vt*: **to ~ (down)** (*sauce, paint*) diluir ♦ *vi* (*fog*) aclararse; (*also*: **~ out**: *crowd*) dispersarse; **his hair is ~ning** se está quedando calvo.

thing [θɪŋ] *n* cosa; (*object*) objeto, artículo; (*contraption*) chisme *m*; (*mania*) manía; **~s** *npl* (*belongings*) cosas *fpl*; **the best ~ would be to...** lo mejor sería...; **the main ~ is ...** lo principal es ...; **first ~ (in the morning)** a primera hora (de la mañana); **last ~ (at night)** a última hora (de la noche); **the ~ is ...** lo que pasa es que ...; **how are ~s?** ¿qué tal van las cosas?; **she's got a ~ about mice** le dan no sé qué los ratones; **poor ~!** ¡pobre! *m/f*, ¡pobrecito/a!

think, *pt, pp* **thought** [θɪŋk, θɔ:t] *vi* pensar ♦ *vt* pensar, creer; (*imagine*) imaginar; **what did you ~ of it?** ¿qué te parece?; **what did you ~ of them?** ¿qué te parecieron?; **to ~ about sth/sb** pensar en algo/uno; **I'll ~ about it** lo pensaré; **to ~ of doing sth** pensar en hacer algo; **I ~ so/not** creo que sí/no; **~ again!** ¡piénsalo bien!; **to ~ aloud** pensar en voz alta; **to ~ well of sb** tener buen concepto de algn.

▸**think out** *vt* (*plan*) elaborar, tramar; (*solution*) encontrar.

▸**think over** *vt* reflexionar sobre, meditar; **I'd like to ~ things over** me gustaría pensármelo.

▸**think through** *vt* pensar bien.

▸**think up** *vt* imaginar.

thinking ['θɪŋkɪŋ] *n*: **to my (way of) ~** a mi parecer.

think tank *n* grupo de expertos.

thinly ['θɪnlɪ] *adv* (*cut*) en lonchas finas; (*spread*) en una capa fina.

thinness ['θɪnnɪs] *n* delgadez *f*.

third [θə:d] *adj* (*before nmsg*: **tercer**) tercero ♦ *n* tercero/a; (*fraction*) tercio; (*BRIT SCOL*: *degree*) *título universitario de tercera clase*.

third degree *adj* (*burns*) de tercer grado.

thirdly ['θə:dlɪ] *adv* en tercer lugar.

third party insurance *n* (*BRIT*) seguro a terceros.

third-rate ['θə:d'reɪt] *adj* de poca calidad.

Third World *n*: **the ~** el Tercer Mundo ♦ *cpd* tercermundista.

thirst [θə:st] *n* sed *f*.

thirsty ['θə:stɪ] *adj* (*person*) sediento; **to be ~** tener sed.

thirteen [θə:'ti:n] *num* trece.

thirteenth [θə:'ti:nθ] *adj* decimotercero ♦ *n* (*in series*) decimotercero/a; (*fraction*) decimotercio.

thirtieth ['θə:tɪəθ] *adj* trigésimo ♦ *n* (*in series*) trigésimo/a; (*fraction*) treintavo.

thirty ['θə:tɪ] *num* treinta.

KEYWORD

this [ðɪs] (*pl* **these**) *adj* (*demonstrative*) este/a; *pl* estos/as; (*neuter*) esto; **~ man/woman** este hombre/esta mujer; **these children/flowers** estos chicos/estas flores; **~ way** por aquí; **~ time last year** hoy hace un año; **~ one (here)** éste/a, esto (de aquí)

♦ *pron* (*demonstrative*) éste/a; *pl* éstos/as; (*neuter*) esto; **who is ~?** ¿quién es éste/ésta?; **what is ~?** ¿qué es esto?; **~ is where I live** aquí vivo; **~ is what he said** esto es lo que dijo; **~ is Mr Brown** (*in introductions*) le presento al Sr. Brown; (*photo*) éste es el Sr. Brown; (*on telephone*) habla el Sr. Brown; **they were talking of ~ and that** hablaban de esto y lo otro

♦ *adv* (*demonstrative*): **~ high/long** así de alto/largo; **~ far** hasta aquí.

thistle ['θɪsl] *n* cardo.

thong [θɔŋ] *n* correa.

thorn [θɔ:n] *n* espina.

thorny ['θɔ:nɪ] *adj* espinoso.

thorough ['θʌrə] *adj* (*search*) minucioso; (*knowledge*) profundo; (*research*) a fondo.

thoroughbred ['θʌrəbrɛd] *adj* (*horse*) de pura sangre.

thoroughfare ['θʌrəfɛə*] *n* calle *f*; **"no ~"** "prohibido el paso".

thoroughgoing ['θʌrəgəuɪŋ] *adj* a fondo.

thoroughly ['θʌrəlɪ] *adv* minuciosamente; a fondo.

thoroughness ['θʌrənɪs] *n* minuciosidad *f*.

those [ðəuz] *pl pron* ésos/ésas; (*more remote*) aquéllos/as ♦ *pl adj* esos/esas; aquellos/as.

though [ðəu] *conj* aunque ♦ *adv* sin embargo, aún así; **even ~** aunque; **it's not so easy, ~** sin embargo no es tan fácil.

thought [θɔ:t] *pt, pp of* **think** ♦ *n* pensamiento; (*opinion*) opinión *f*; (*intention*) intención *f*; **to give sth some ~**

pensar algo detenidamente; **after much ~** después de pensarlo bien; **I've just had a ~** se me acaba de ocurrir una idea.
thoughtful ['θɔːtful] *adj* pensativo; (*considerate*) atento.
thoughtfully ['θɔːtfəlɪ] *adv* pensativamente; atentamente.
thoughtless ['θɔːtlɪs] *adj* desconsiderado.
thoughtlessly ['θɔːtlɪslɪ] *adv* insensatamente.
thought-provoking ['θɔːtprəvəukɪŋ] *adj* estimulante.
thousand ['θauzənd] *num* mil; **two ~** dos mil; **~s of** miles de.
thousandth ['θauzəntθ] *num* milésimo.
thrash [θræʃ] *vt* dar una paliza a.
▸**thrash about** *vi* revolverse.
▸**thrash out** *vt* discutir a fondo.
thrashing ['θræʃɪŋ] *n*: **to give sb a ~** dar una paliza a algn.
thread [θrɛd] *n* hilo; (*of screw*) rosca ♦ *vt* (*needle*) enhebrar.
threadbare ['θrɛdbɛə*] *adj* raído.
threat [θrɛt] *n* amenaza; **to be under ~ of** estar amenazado de.
threaten ['θrɛtn] *vi* amenazar ♦ *vt*: **to ~ sb with sth/to do** amenazar a algn con algo/ con hacer.
threatening ['θrɛtnɪŋ] *adj* amenazador(a), amenazante.
three [θriː] *num* tres.
three-dimensional [θriːdɪ'mɛnʃənl] *adj* tridimensional.
threefold ['θriːfəuld] *adv*: **to increase ~** triplicar.
three-piece ['θriːpiːs]: **~ suit** *n* traje *m* de tres piezas; **~ suite** *n* tresillo.
three-ply [θriː'plaɪ] *adj* (*wood*) de tres capas; (*wool*) triple.
three-quarter [θriː'kwɔːtə*] *adj*: **~ length sleeves** mangas *fpl* tres cuartos.
three-quarters [θriː'kwɔːtəz] *npl* tres cuartas partes; **~ full** tres cuartas partes lleno.
three-wheeler [θriː'wiːlə*] *n* (*car*) coche *m* cabina.
thresh [θrɛʃ] *vt* (*AGR*) trillar.
threshing machine ['θrɛʃɪŋ-] *n* trilladora.
threshold ['θrɛʃhəuld] *n* umbral *m*; **to be on the ~ of** (*fig*) estar al borde de.
threshold agreement *n* convenio de nivel crítico.
threw [θruː] *pt of* **throw**.
thrift [θrɪft] *n* economía.
thrifty ['θrɪftɪ] *adj* económico.
thrill [θrɪl] *n* (*excitement*) emoción *f* ♦ *vt* emocionar; **to be ~ed** (*with gift etc*) estar encantado.
thriller ['θrɪlə*] *n* película/novela de suspense.
thrilling ['θrɪlɪŋ] *adj* emocionante.
thrive, *pt* **thrived, throve**, *pp* **thrived, thriven** [θraɪv, θrəuv, 'θrɪvn] *vi* (*grow*) crecer; (*do well*) prosperar.
thriving ['θraɪvɪŋ] *adj* próspero.
throat [θrəut] *n* garganta; **I have a sore ~** me duele la garganta.
throb [θrɔb] *n* (*of heart*) latido; (*of engine*) vibración *f* ♦ *vi* latir; vibrar; (*with pain*) dar punzadas; **my head is ~bing** la cabeza me da punzadas.
throes [θrəuz] *npl*: **in the ~ of** en medio de.
thrombosis [θrɔm'bəusɪs] *n* trombosis *f*.
throne [θrəun] *n* trono.
throng [θrɔŋ] *n* multitud *f*, muchedumbre *f* ♦ *vt, vi* apiñarse, agolparse.
throttle ['θrɔtl] *n* (*AUT*) acelerador *m* ♦ *vt* estrangular.
through [θruː] *prep* por, a través de; (*time*) durante; (*by means of*) por medio de, mediante; (*owing to*) gracias a ♦ *adj* (*ticket, train*) directo ♦ *adv* completamente, de parte a parte; de principio a fin; **(from) Monday ~ Friday** (*US*) de lunes a viernes; **to go ~ sb's papers** mirar entre los papeles de algn; **I am halfway ~ the book** voy por la mitad del libro; **the soldiers didn't let us ~** los soldados no nos dejaron pasar; **to put sb ~ to sb** (*TEL*) poner *or* pasar a algn con algn; **to be ~** (*TEL*) tener comunicación; (*have finished*) haber terminado; **"no ~ road"** (*BRIT*) "calle sin salida".
throughout [θruː'aut] *prep* (*place*) por todas partes de, por todo; (*time*) durante todo ♦ *adv* por *or* en todas partes.
throughput ['θruːput] *n* (*of goods, materials*) producción *f*; (*COMPUT*) capacidad *f* de procesamiento.
throve [θrəuv] *pt of* **thrive**.
throw [θrəu] *n* tiro; (*SPORT*) lanzamiento ♦ *vt* (*pt* **threw**, *pp* **thrown** [θruː, θrəun]) tirar, echar, botar (*LAM*); (*SPORT*) lanzar; (*rider*) derribar; (*fig*) desconcertar; **to ~ a party** dar una fiesta.
▸**throw about, throw around** *vt* (*litter etc*) tirar, esparcir.
▸**throw away** *vt* tirar.
▸**throw off** *vt* deshacerse de.
▸**throw open** *vt* (*doors, windows*) abrir de par en par; (*house, gardens etc*) abrir al público; (*competition, race*) abrir a todos.
▸**throw out** *vt* tirar, botar (*LAM*).
▸**throw together** *vt* (*clothes*) amontonar; (*meal*) preparar a la carrera; (*essay*) hacer sin cuidado.

▸**throw up** *vi* vomitar, devolver.
throwaway ['θrəuəweɪ] *adj* para tirar, desechable.
throwback ['θrəubæk] *n*: **it's a ~ to** (*fig*) eso nos lleva de nuevo a.
throw-in ['θrəuɪn] *n* (*SPORT*) saque *m* de banda.
thrown [θrəun] *pp of* **throw**.
thru [θru:] (*US*) = **through**.
thrush [θrʌʃ] *n* zorzal *m*, tordo; (*MED*) candiasis *f*.
thrust [θrʌst] *n* (*TECH*) empuje *m* ♦ *vt* (*pt, pp* **thrust**) empujar; (*push in*) introducir.
thrusting ['θrʌstɪŋ] *adj* (*person*) dinámico, con empuje.
thud [θʌd] *n* golpe *m* sordo.
thug [θʌg] *n* gamberro/a.
thumb [θʌm] *n* (*ANAT*) pulgar *m* ♦ *vt*: **to ~ a lift** hacer dedo; **to give sth/sb the ~s up/down** aprobar/desaprobar algo/a algn.
▸**thumb through** *vt fus* (*book*) hojear.
thumb index *n* uñero, índice *m* recortado.
thumbnail ['θʌmneɪl] *n* uña del pulgar.
thumbnail sketch *n* esbozo.
thumbtack ['θʌmtæk] *n* (*US*) chincheta, chinche *f*.
thump [θʌmp] *n* golpe *m*; (*sound*) ruido seco *or* sordo ♦ *vt, vi* golpear.
thumping ['θʌmpɪŋ] *adj* (*col*: *huge*) descomunal.
thunder ['θʌndə*] *n* trueno; (*of applause etc*) estruendo ♦ *vi* tronar; (*train etc*): **to ~ past** pasar como un trueno.
thunderbolt ['θʌndəbəult] *n* rayo.
thunderclap ['θʌndəklæp] *n* trueno.
thunderous ['θʌndərəs] *adj* ensordecedor(a), estruendoso.
thunderstorm ['θʌndəstɔ:m] *n* tormenta.
thunderstruck ['θʌndəstrʌk] *adj* pasmado.
thundery ['θʌndərɪ] *adj* tormentoso.
Thur(s). *abbr* (= *Thursday*) juev.
Thursday ['θə:zdɪ] *n* jueves *m inv*.
thus [ðʌs] *adv* así, de este modo.
thwart [θwɔ:t] *vt* frustrar.
thyme [taɪm] *n* tomillo.
thyroid ['θaɪrɔɪd] *n* tiroides *m inv*.
tiara [tɪ'ɑ:rə] *n* tiara, diadema.
Tiber ['taɪbə*] *n* Tíber *m*.
Tibet [tɪ'bɛt] *n* el Tibet.
Tibetan [tɪ'bɛtən] *adj* tibetano ♦ *n* tibetano/a; (*LING*) tibetano.
tibia ['tɪbɪə] *n* tibia.
tic [tɪk] *n* tic *m*.
tick [tɪk] *n* (*sound*: *of clock*) tictac *m*; (*mark*) señal *f* (de visto bueno), palomita (*LAM*); (*ZOOL*) garrapata; (*BRIT col*): **in a ~** en un instante; (*BRIT col*: *credit*): **to buy sth on ~** comprar algo a crédito ♦ *vi* hacer tictac ♦ *vt* marcar, señalar; **to put a ~ against sth** poner una señal en algo.
▸**tick off** *vt* marcar; (*person*) reñir.
▸**tick over** *vi* (*BRIT*: *engine*) girar en marcha lenta; (: *fig*) ir tirando.
ticker tape ['tɪkə-] *n* cinta perforada.
ticket ['tɪkɪt] *n* billete *m*, tíquet *m*, boleto (*LAM*); (*for cinema etc*) entrada, boleto (*LAM*); (*in shop*: *on goods*) etiqueta; (*for library*) tarjeta; (*US POL*) lista (de candidatos); **to get a parking ~** (*AUT*) ser multado por estacionamiento ilegal.
ticket agency *n* (*THEAT*) agencia de venta de entradas.
ticket collector *n* revisor(a) *m/f*.
ticket holder *n* poseedor(a) *m/f* de billete *or* entrada.
ticket inspector *n* revisor(a) *m/f*, inspector(a) *m/f* de boletos (*LAM*).
ticket office *n* (*THEAT*) taquilla, boletería (*LAM*); (*RAIL*) despacho de billetes *or* boletos (*LAM*).
ticking-off ['tɪkɪŋ'ɔf] *n* (*col*): **to give sb a ~** echarle una bronca a algn.
tickle ['tɪkl] *n*: **to give sb a ~** hacer cosquillas a algn ♦ *vt* hacer cosquillas a.
ticklish ['tɪklɪʃ] *adj* (*which tickles*: *blanket*) que pica; (: *cough*) irritante; **to be ~** tener cosquillas.
tidal ['taɪdl] *adj* de marea.
tidal wave *n* maremoto.
tidbit ['tɪdbɪt] (*US*) = **titbit**.
tiddlywinks ['tɪdlɪwɪŋks] *n* juego de la pulga.
tide [taɪd] *n* marea; (*fig*: *of events*) curso, marcha ♦ *vt*: **to ~ sb over** *or* **through (until)** sacar a algn del apuro (hasta); **high/low ~** marea alta/baja; **the ~ of public opinion** la tendencia de la opinión pública.
tidily ['taɪdɪlɪ] *adv* bien, ordenadamente; **to arrange ~** ordenar; **to dress ~** vestir bien.
tidiness ['taɪdɪnɪs] *n* (*order*) orden *m*; (*cleanliness*) aseo.
tidy ['taɪdɪ] *adj* (*room*) ordenado; (*drawing, work*) limpio; (*person*) (bien) arreglado; (: *in character*) metódico; (*mind*) claro, metódico ♦ *vt* (*also*: **~ up**) ordenar, poner en orden.
tie [taɪ] *n* (*string etc*) atadura; (*BRIT*: *neck~*) corbata; (*fig*: *link*) vínculo, lazo; (*SPORT*: *draw*) empate *m* ♦ *vt* atar ♦ *vi* (*SPORT*) empatar; **family ~s** obligaciones *fpl* familiares; **cup ~** (*SPORT*: *match*) partido de copa; **to ~ in a bow** hacer un lazo; **to ~ a knot in sth** hacer un nudo en algo.
▸**tie down** *vt* atar; (*fig*): **to ~ sb down to**

obligar a algn a.
▸**tie in** *vi*: **to ~ in (with)** (*correspond*) concordar (con).
▸**tie on** *vt* (*BRIT*: *label etc*) atar.
▸**tie up** *vt* (*parcel*) envolver; (*dog*) atar; (*boat*) amarrar; (*arrangements*) concluir; **to be ~d up** (*busy*) estar ocupado.
tie-break(er) ['taɪbreɪk(ə*)] *n* (*TENNIS*) tiebreak *m*, muerte *f* súbita; (*in quiz*) punto decisivo.
tie-on ['taɪɔn] *adj* (*BRIT*: *label*) para atar.
tie-pin ['taɪpɪn] *n* (*BRIT*) alfiler *m* de corbata.
tier [tɪə*] *n* grada; (*of cake*) piso.
tie tack *n* (*US*) alfiler *m* de corbata.
tiff [tɪf] *n* (*col*) pelea, riña.
tiger ['taɪgə*] *n* tigre *m*.
tight [taɪt] *adj* (*rope*) tirante; (*money*) escaso; (*clothes, budget*) ajustado; (*programme*) apretado; (*col*: *drunk*) borracho ♦ *adv* (*squeeze*) muy fuerte; (*shut*) herméticamente; **to be packed ~** (*suitcase*) estar completamente lleno; (*people*) estar apretados; **everybody hold ~!** ¡agárense bien!
tighten ['taɪtn] *vt* (*rope*) tensar, estirar; (*screw*) apretar ♦ *vi* estirarse; apretarse.
tight-fisted [taɪt'fɪstɪd] *adj* tacaño.
tight-lipped ['taɪt'lɪpt] *adj*: **to be ~** (*silent*) rehusar hablar; (*angry*) apretar los labios.
tightly ['taɪtlɪ] *adv* (*grasp*) muy fuerte.
tightness ['taɪtnɪs] *n* (*of rope*) tirantez *f*; (*of clothes*) estrechez *f*; (*of budget*) lo ajustado.
tightrope ['taɪtrəup] *n* cuerda floja.
tightrope walker *n* equilibrista *m/f*, funambulista *m/f*.
tights [taɪts] *npl* (*BRIT*) medias *fpl*, panties *mpl*.
tigress ['taɪgrɪs] *n* tigresa.
tilde ['tɪldə] *n* tilde *f*.
tile [taɪl] *n* (*on roof*) teja; (*on floor*) baldosa; (*on wall*) azulejo ♦ *vt* (*floor*) poner baldosas en; (*wall*) alicatar.
tiled [taɪld] *adj* (*floor*) embaldosado; (*wall, bathroom*) alicatado; (*roof*) con tejas.
till [tɪl] *n* caja (registradora) ♦ *vt* (*land*) cultivar ♦ *prep, conj* = **until**.
tiller ['tɪlə*] *n* (*NAUT*) caña del timón.
tilt [tɪlt] *vt* inclinar ♦ *vi* inclinarse ♦ *n* (*slope*) inclinación *f*; **to wear one's hat at a ~** llevar el sombrero echado a un lado *or* terciado; **(at) full ~** a toda velocidad *or* carrera.
timber [tɪmbə*] *n* (*material*) madera; (*trees*) árboles *mpl*.
time [taɪm] *n* tiempo; (*epoch*: *often pl*) época; (*by clock*) hora; (*moment*) momento; (*occasion*) vez *f*; (*MUS*) compás *m* ♦ *vt* calcular *or* medir el tiempo de; (*race*) cronometrar; (*remark etc*) elegir el momento para; **a long ~** mucho tiempo; **4 at a ~** 4 a la vez; **for the ~ being** de momento, por ahora; **at ~s** a veces, a ratos; **~ after ~, ~ and again** repetidas veces, una y otra vez; **from ~ to ~** de vez en cuando; **in ~** (*soon enough*) a tiempo; (*after some time*) con el tiempo; (*MUS*) al compás; **in a week's ~** dentro de una semana; **in no ~** en un abrir y cerrar de ojos; **any ~** cuando sea; **on ~** a la hora; **to be 30 minutes behind/ahead of ~** llevar media hora de retraso/adelanto; **to take one's ~** tomárselo con calma; **he'll do it in his own ~** (*without being hurried*) lo hará sin prisa; (*out of working hours*) lo hará en su tiempo libre; **by the ~ he arrived** cuando llegó; **5 ~s 5** 5 por 5; **what ~ is it?** ¿qué hora es?; **what ~ do you make it?** ¿qué hora es *or* tiene?; **to be behind the ~s** estar atrasado; **to carry 3 boxes at a ~** llevar 3 cajas a la vez; **to keep ~** llevar el ritmo *or* el compás; **to have a good ~** pasarlo bien, divertirse; **to ~ sth well/badly** elegir un buen/mal momento para algo; **the bomb was ~d to explode 5 minutes later** la bomba estaba programada para explotar 5 minutos más tarde.
time-and-motion expert ['taɪmənd'məuʃən-] *n* experto/a en la ciencia de la producción.
time-and-motion study ['taɪmənd'məuʃən-] *n* estudio de desplazamientos y tiempos.
time bomb *n* bomba de relojería.
time card *n* tarjeta de registro horario.
time clock *n* reloj *m* registrador.
time-consuming ['taɪmkənsjuːmɪŋ] *adj* que requiere mucho tiempo.
time frame *n* plazo.
time-honoured, (*US*) **time-honored** ['taɪmɔnəd] *adj* consagrado.
timekeeper ['taɪmkiːpə*] *n* (*SPORT*) cronómetro.
time lag *n* desfase *m*.
timeless ['taɪmlɪs] *adj* eterno.
time limit *n* (*gen*) límite *m* de tiempo; (*COMM*) plazo.
timely ['taɪmlɪ] *adj* oportuno.
time off *n* tiempo libre.
timer ['taɪmə*] *n* (*~ switch*) interruptor *m*; (*in kitchen, TECH*) temporizador *m*.
time-saving ['taɪmseɪvɪŋ] *adj* que ahorra tiempo.
time scale *n* escala de tiempo.

time sharing *n* (*COMPUT*) tiempo compartido.
time sheet *n* = **time card.**
time signal *n* señal *f* horaria.
time switch *n* (*BRIT*) interruptor *m* (horario).
timetable ['taɪmteɪbl] *n* horario; (*programme of events etc*) programa *m*.
time zone *n* huso horario.
timid ['tɪmɪd] *adj* tímido.
timidity [tɪ'mɪdɪtɪ] *n* timidez *f*.
timidly ['tɪmɪdlɪ] *adv* tímidamente.
timing ['taɪmɪŋ] *n* (*SPORT*) cronometraje *m*; **the ~ of his resignation** el momento que eligió para dimitir.
timpani ['tɪmpənɪ] *npl* tímpanos *mpl*.
tin [tɪn] *n* estaño; (*also*: **~ plate**) hojalata; (*BRIT*: *can*) lata.
tinfoil ['tɪnfɔɪl] *n* papel *m* de estaño.
tinge [tɪndʒ] *n* matiz *m* ♦ *vt*: **~d with** teñido de.
tingle ['tɪŋgl] *n* hormigueo ♦ *vi* (*cheeks, skin*: *from cold*) sentir comezón; (: *from bad circulation*) sentir hormigueo.
tinker ['tɪŋkə*] *n* calderero/a; (*gipsy*) gitano/a.
►**tinker with** *vt fus* jugar con, tocar.
tinkle ['tɪŋkl] *vi* tintinear.
tin mine *n* mina de estaño.
tinned [tɪnd] *adj* (*BRIT*: *food*) en lata, en conserva.
tinnitus ['tɪnɪtəs] *n* (*MED*) acufeno.
tinny ['tɪnɪ] *adj* (*sound, taste*) metálico; (*pej*: *car*) poco sólido, de pacotilla.
tin opener [-əupnə*] *n* (*BRIT*) abrelatas *m inv*.
tinsel ['tɪnsl] *n* oropel *m*.
tint [tɪnt] *n* matiz *m*; (*for hair*) tinte *m* ♦ *vt* (*hair*) teñir.
tinted ['tɪntɪd] *adj* (*hair*) teñido; (*glass, spectacles*) ahumado.
tiny ['taɪnɪ] *adj* minúsculo, pequeñito.
tip [tɪp] *n* (*end*) punta; (*gratuity*) propina; (*BRIT*: *for rubbish*) vertedero; (*advice*) consejo ♦ *vt* (*waiter*) dar una propina a; (*tilt*) inclinar; (*empty*: *also* **~ out**) vaciar, echar; (*predict*: *winner*) pronosticar; (: *horse*) recomendar; **he ~ped out the contents of the box** volcó el contenido de la caja.
►**tip off** *vt* avisar, poner sobreaviso a.
►**tip over** *vt* volcar ♦ *vi* volcarse.
tip-off ['tɪpɔf] *n* (*hint*) advertencia.
tipped [tɪpt] *adj* (*BRIT*: *cigarette*) con filtro.
Tipp-Ex ® ['tɪpɛks] *n* Tipp-Ex ® *m*.
tipple ['tɪpl] *n* (*BRIT*): **his ~ is Cointreau** bebe Cointreau.
tipster ['tɪpstə*] *n* (*RACING*) pronosticador(a) *m/f*.
tipsy ['tɪpsɪ] *adj* alegre, achispado.
tiptoe ['tɪptəu] *n* (*BRIT*): **on ~** de puntillas.
tiptop ['tɪptɔp] *adj*: **in ~ condition** en perfectas condiciones.
tirade [taɪ'reɪd] *n* diatriba.
tire ['taɪə*] *n* (*US*) = **tyre** ♦ *vt* cansar ♦ *vi* (*gen*) cansarse; (*become bored*) aburrirse.
►**tire out** *vt* agotar, rendir.
tired ['taɪəd] *adj* cansado; **to be ~ of sth** estar harto de algo; **to be/feel/look ~** estar/sentirse/parecer cansado.
tiredness ['taɪədnɪs] *n* cansancio.
tireless ['taɪəlɪs] *adj* incansable.
tirelessly ['taɪəlɪslɪ] *adv* incansablemente.
tiresome ['taɪəsəm] *adj* aburrido.
tiring ['taɪrɪŋ] *adj* cansado.
tissue ['tɪʃu:] *n* tejido; (*paper handkerchief*) pañuelo de papel, kleenex *m* ®.
tissue paper *n* papel *m* de seda.
tit [tɪt] *n* (*bird*) herrerillo común; **to give ~ for tat** dar ojo por ojo.
titbit ['tɪtbɪt], (*US*) **tidbit** ['tɪdbɪt] *n* (*food*) golosina; (*news*) pedazo.
titillate ['tɪtɪleɪt] *vt* estimular, excitar.
titillation [tɪtɪ'leɪʃən] *n* estimulación *f*, excitación *f*.
titivate ['tɪtɪveɪt] *vt* emperejilar.
title ['taɪtl] *n* título; (*LAW*: *right*): **~ (to)** derecho (a).
title deed *n* (*LAW*) título de propiedad.
title page *n* portada.
title role *n* papel *m* principal.
titter ['tɪtə*] *vi* reírse entre dientes.
tittle-tattle ['tɪtltætl] *n* chismes *mpl*.
titular ['tɪtjulə*] *adj* (*in name only*) nominal.
T-junction ['ti:dʒʌŋkʃən] *n* cruce *m* en T.
TM *abbr* (= *trademark*) marca de fábrica; = **transcendental meditation.**
TN *abbr* (*US*) = *Tennessee.*
TNT *n abbr* (= *trinitrotoluene*) TNT *m*.

KEYWORD

to [tu:, tə] *prep* **1** (*direction*) a; **to go ~ France/London/school/the station** ir a Francia/Londres/al colegio/a la estación; **to go ~ Claude's/the doctor's** ir a casa de Claude/al médico; **the road ~ Edinburgh** la carretera de Edimburgo; **~ the left/right** a la izquierda/derecha
2 (*as far as*) hasta, a; **from here ~ London** de aquí a *or* hasta Londres; **to count ~ 10** contar hasta 10; **from 40 ~ 50 people** entre 40 y 50 personas
3 (*with expressions of time*): **a quarter/twenty ~ 5** las 5 menos cuarto/veinte
4 (*for, of*): **the key ~ the front door** la llave de la puerta principal; **she is**

secretary ~ the director es la secretaria del director; **a letter ~ his wife** una carta a *or* para su mujer
5 (*expressing indirect object*) a; **to give sth ~ sb** darle algo a algn; **give it ~ me** dámelo; **to talk ~ sb** hablar con algn; **to be a danger ~ sb** ser un peligro para algn; **to carry out repairs ~ sth** hacer reparaciones en algo
6 (*in relation to*): **3 goals ~ 2** 3 goles a 2; **30 miles ~ the gallon** ≈ 9,4 litros a los cien (kilómetros); **8 apples ~ the kilo** 8 manzanas por kilo
7 (*purpose, result*): **to come ~ sb's aid** venir en auxilio *or* ayuda de algn; **to sentence sb ~ death** condenar a algn a muerte; **~ my great surprise** con gran sorpresa mía
♦ *with vb* **1** (*simple infin*): **~ go/eat** ir/comer
2 (*following another vb*): **to want/try/start ~ do** querer/intentar/empezar a hacer; *see also relevant vb*
3 (*with vb omitted*): **I don't want ~** no quiero
4 (*purpose, result*) para; **I did it ~ help you** lo hice para ayudarte; **he came ~ see you** vino a verte
5 (*equivalent to relative clause*): **I have things ~ do** tengo cosas que hacer; **the main thing is ~ try** lo principal es intentarlo
6 (*after adj etc*): **ready ~ go** listo para irse; **too old ~ ...** demasiado viejo (como) para ...
♦ *adv*: **pull/push the door ~** tirar de/empujar la puerta; **to go ~ and fro** ir y venir.

toad [təud] *n* sapo.
toadstool ['təudstu:l] *n* seta venenosa.
toady ['təudɪ] *n* pelota *m/f* ♦ *vi*: **to ~ to sb** hacer la pelota *or* dar coba a algn.
toast [təust] *n* (*CULIN*: *also*: **piece of ~**) tostada; (*drink, speech*) brindis *m inv* ♦ *vt* (*CULIN*) tostar; (*drink to*) brindar.
toaster ['təustə*] *n* tostador *m*.
toastmaster ['təustmɑ:stə*] *n persona que propone brindis y anuncia a los oradores en un banquete*.
toast rack *n* rejilla para tostadas.
tobacco [tə'bækəu] *n* tabaco; **pipe ~** tabaco de pipa.
tobacconist [tə'bækənɪst] *n* estanquero/a, tabaquero/a (*LAM*); **~'s (shop)** (*BRIT*) estanco, tabaquería (*LAM*).
tobacco plantation *n* plantación *f* de tabaco, tabacal *m*.
Tobago [tə'beɪgəu] *n see* **Trinidad and Tobago.**
toboggan [tə'bɔgən] *n* tobogán *m*.
today [tə'deɪ] *adv, n* (*also fig*) hoy *m*; **what day is it ~?** ¿qué día es hoy?; **what date is it ~?** ¿a qué fecha estamos hoy?; **~ is the 4th of March** hoy es el 4 de marzo; **~'s paper** el periódico de hoy; **a fortnight ~** de hoy en 15 días, dentro de 15 días.
toddle ['tɔdl] *vi* empezar a andar, dar los primeros pasos.
toddler ['tɔdlə*] *n* niño/a (que empieza a andar).
toddy ['tɔdɪ] *n* ponche *m*.
to-do [tə'du:] *n* (*fuss*) lío.
toe [təu] *n* dedo (del pie); (*of shoe*) punta ♦ *vt*: **to ~ the line** (*fig*) acatar las normas; **big/little ~** dedo gordo/pequeño del pie.
TOEFL *n abbr* = *Test(ing) of English as a Foreign Language*.
toehold ['təuhəuld] *n* punto de apoyo (para el pie).
toenail ['təuneɪl] *n* uña del pie.
toffee ['tɔfɪ] *n* caramelo.
toffee apple *n* (*BRIT*) manzana de caramelo.
tofu ['təufu:] *n* tofu *m*.
toga ['təugə] *n* toga.
together [tə'gɛðə*] *adv* juntos; (*at same time*) al mismo tiempo, a la vez; **~ with** *prep* junto con.
togetherness [tə'gɛðənɪs] *n* compañerismo.
toggle switch ['tɔgl-] *n* (*COMPUT*) conmutador *m* de palanca.
Togo ['təugəu] *n* Togo.
togs [tɔgz] *npl* (*col*: *clothes*) atuendo, ropa.
toil [tɔɪl] *n* trabajo duro, labor *f* ♦ *vi* esforzarse.
toilet ['tɔɪlət] *n* (*BRIT*: *lavatory*) servicios *mpl*, wáter *m* ♦ *cpd* (*bag, soap etc*) de aseo; **to go to the ~** ir al baño; *see also* **toilets.**
toilet bag *n* neceser *m*, bolsa de aseo.
toilet bowl *n* taza (de retrete).
toilet paper *n* papel *m* higiénico.
toiletries ['tɔɪlətrɪz] *npl* artículos *mpl* de aseo; (*make-up etc*) artículos *mpl* de tocador.
toilet roll *n* rollo de papel higiénico.
toilets ['tɔɪləts] *npl* (*BRIT*) servicios *mpl*.
toilet soap *n* jabón *m* de tocador.
toilet water *n* (agua de) colonia.
to-ing and fro-ing ['tuɪŋən'frəuɪŋ] *n* vaivén *m*.
token ['təukən] *n* (*sign*) señal *f*, muestra; (*souvenir*) recuerdo; (*voucher*) vale *m*; (*disc*) ficha ♦ *cpd* (*fee, strike*) nominal, simbólico; **book/record ~** (*BRIT*) vale *m* para comprar libros/discos; **by the same**

~ (*fig*) por la misma razón.
tokenism ['təukənɪzəm] *n* (*POL*) política simbólica *or* de fachada.
Tokyo ['təukjəu] *n* Tokio, Tokío.
told [təuld] *pt, pp of* **tell.**
tolerable ['tɔlərəbl] *adj* (*bearable*) soportable; (*fairly good*) pasable.
tolerably ['tɔlərəblɪ] *adv* (*good, comfortable*) medianamente.
tolerance ['tɔlərns] *n* (*also*: *TECH*) tolerancia.
tolerant ['tɔlərnt] *adj*: ~ **of** tolerante con.
tolerantly ['tɔlərntlɪ] *adv* con tolerancia.
tolerate ['tɔləreɪt] *vt* tolerar.
toleration [tɔlə'reɪʃən] *n* tolerancia.
toll [təul] *n* (*of casualties*) número de víctimas; (*tax, charge*) peaje *m* ♦ *vi* (*bell*) doblar.
toll bridge *n* puente *m* de peaje.
toll call *n* (*US TELEC*) conferencia, llamada interurbana.
toll-free *adj, adv* (*US*) gratis.
toll road *n* carretera de peaje.
tomato, ~es [tə'mɑːtəu] *n* tomate *m*.
tomato puree *n* puré *m* de tomate.
tomb [tuːm] *n* tumba.
tombola [tɔm'bəulə] *n* tómbola.
tomboy ['tɔmbɔɪ] *n* marimacho.
tombstone ['tuːmstəun] *n* lápida.
tomcat ['tɔmkæt] *n* gato.
tomorrow [tə'mɔrəu] *adv, n* (*also fig*) mañana; **the day after** ~ pasado mañana; ~ **morning** mañana por la mañana; **a week** ~ de mañana en ocho (días).
ton [tʌn] *n* (*BRIT* = *1016 kg*; *US*: *also* **short** ~ = *907,18 kg*) tonelada; ~**s of** (*col*) montones de.
tonal ['təunl] *adj* tonal.
tone [təun] *n* tono ♦ *vi* armonizar; **dialling** ~ (*TEL*) señal *f* para marcar.
▸**tone down** *vt* (*criticism*) suavizar; (*colour*) atenuar.
▸**tone up** *vt* (*muscles*) tonificar.
tone-deaf [təun'dɛf] *adj* sin oído musical.
toner ['təunə*] *n* (*for photocopier*) virador *m*.
Tonga ['tɔŋə] *n* Islas *fpl* Tonga.
tongs [tɔŋz] *npl* (*for coal*) tenazas *fpl*; (*for hair*) tenacillas *fpl*.
tongue [tʌŋ] *n* lengua; ~ **in cheek** *adv* en plan de broma.
tongue-tied ['tʌŋtaɪd] *adj* (*fig*) mudo.
tongue-twister ['tʌŋtwɪstə*] *n* trabalenguas *m inv*.
tonic ['tɔnɪk] *n* (*MED*) tónico; (*MUS*) tónica; (*also*: ~ **water**) (agua) tónica.
tonight [tə'naɪt] *adv, n* esta noche; **I'll see you** ~ nos vemos esta noche.
tonnage ['tʌnɪdʒ] *n* (*NAUT*) tonelaje *m*.
tonsil ['tɔnsl] *n* amígdala; **to have one's ~s out** sacarse las amígdalas *or* anginas.
tonsillitis [tɔnsɪ'laɪtɪs] *n* amigdalitis *f*; **to have** ~ tener amigdalitis.
too [tuː] *adv* (*excessively*) demasiado; (*very*) muy; (*also*) también; **it's** ~ **sweet** está demasiado dulce; **I'm not** ~ **sure about that** no estoy muy seguro de eso; **I went** ~ yo también fui; ~ **much** *adv, adj* demasiado; ~ **many** *adj* demasiados/as; ~ **bad!** ¡mala suerte!
took [tuk] *pt of* **take.**
tool [tuːl] *n* herramienta; (*fig*: *person*) instrumento.
tool box *n* caja de herramientas.
tool kit *n* juego de herramientas.
tool shed *n* cobertizo (para herramientas).
toot [tuːt] *n* (*of horn*) bocinazo; (*of whistle*) silbido ♦ *vi* (*with car horn*) tocar la bocina.
tooth, *pl* **teeth** [tuːθ, tiːθ] *n* (*ANAT, TECH*) diente *m*; (*molar*) muela; **to clean one's teeth** lavarse los dientes; **to have a** ~ **out** sacarse una muela; **by the skin of one's teeth** por un pelo.
toothache ['tuːθeɪk] *n* dolor *m* de muelas.
toothbrush ['tuːθbrʌʃ] *n* cepillo de dientes.
toothpaste ['tuːθpeɪst] *n* pasta de dientes.
toothpick ['tuːθpɪk] *n* palillo.
tooth powder *n* polvos *mpl* dentífricos.
top [tɔp] *n* (*of mountain*) cumbre *f*, cima; (*of head*) coronilla; (*of ladder*) (lo) alto; (*of cupboard, table*) superficie *f*; (*lid*: *of box, jar*) tapa; (: *of bottle*) tapón *m*; (*of list, table, queue, page*) cabeza; (*toy*) peonza; (*DRESS*: *blouse*) blusa; (: *T-shirt*) camiseta; (: *of pyjamas*) chaqueta ♦ *adj* de arriba; (*in rank*) principal, primero; (*best*) mejor ♦ *vt* (*exceed*) exceder; (*be first in*) encabezar; **on** ~ **of** sobre, encima de; **from** ~ **to bottom** de pies a cabeza; **the** ~ **of the milk** la nata; **at the** ~ **of the stairs** en lo alto de la escalera; **at the** ~ **of the street** al final de la calle; **at the** ~ **of one's voice** (*fig*) a voz en grito; **at** ~ **speed** a máxima velocidad; **a** ~ **surgeon** un cirujano eminente; **over the** ~ (*col*) excesivo, desmesurado; **to go over the** ~ pasarse.
▸**top up**, (*US*) **top off** *vt* volver a llenar.
topaz ['təupæz] *n* topacio.
top-class ['tɔp'klɑːs] *adj* de primera clase.
topcoat ['tɔpkəut] *n* sobretodo, abrigo.
topflight ['tɔpflaɪt] *adj* de primera (categoría *or* clase).
top floor *n* último piso.
top hat *n* sombrero de copa.
top-heavy [tɔp'hɛvɪ] *adj* (*object*) con más peso en la parte superior.

topic ['tɔpɪk] *n* tema *m*.
topical ['tɔpɪkl] *adj* actual.
topless ['tɔplɪs] *adj* (*bather etc*) topless.
top-level ['tɔplɛvl] *adj* (*talks*) al más alto nivel.
topmost ['tɔpməust] *adj* más alto.
top-notch ['tɔp'nɔtʃ] *adj* (*col*) de primerísima categoría.
topography [tə'pɔgrəfɪ] *n* topografía.
topping ['tɔpɪŋ] *n* (*CULIN*): **with a ~ of cream** con nata por encima.
topple ['tɔpl] *vt* volcar, derribar ♦ *vi* caerse.
top-ranking ['tɔpræŋkɪŋ] *adj* de alto rango.
top-secret [tɔp'siːkrɪt] *adj* de alto secreto.
top-security ['tɔpsɪ'kjuərɪtɪ] *adj* (*BRIT*) de máxima seguridad.
topsy-turvy ['tɔpsɪ'təːvɪ] *adj, adv* patas arriba.
top-up ['tɔpʌp] *n*: **would you like a ~?** ¿quiere que se lo vuelva a llenar?
top-up loan *n* (*BRIT*) préstamo complementario.
torch [tɔːtʃ] *n* antorcha; (*BRIT*: *electric*) linterna.
tore [tɔː*] *pt of* **tear**.
torment *n* ['tɔːmɛnt] tormento ♦ *vt* [tɔː'mɛnt] atormentar; (*fig*: *annoy*) fastidiar.
torn [tɔːn] *pp of* **tear**.
tornado, ~es [tɔː'neɪdəu] *n* tornado.
torpedo, ~es [tɔː'piːdəu] *n* torpedo.
torpedo boat *n* torpedero, lancha torpedera.
torpor ['tɔːpə*] *n* letargo.
torrent ['tɔrnt] *n* torrente *m*.
torrential [tɔ'rɛnʃl] *adj* torrencial.
torrid ['tɔrɪd] *adj* tórrido; (*fig*) apasionado.
torso ['tɔːsəu] *n* torso.
tortoise ['tɔːtəs] *n* tortuga.
tortoiseshell ['tɔːtəʃɛl] *adj* de carey.
tortuous ['tɔːtjuəs] *adj* tortuoso.
torture ['tɔːtʃə*] *n* tortura ♦ *vt* torturar; (*fig*) atormentar.
torturer ['tɔːtʃərə*] *n* torturador(a) *m/f*.
Tory ['tɔːrɪ] *adj, n* (*BRIT POL*) conservador(a) *m/f*.
toss [tɔs] *vt* tirar, echar; (*head*) sacudir ♦ *n* (*movement*: *of head etc*) sacudida; (*of coin*) tirada, echada (*LAM*); **to ~ a coin** echar a cara o cruz; **to ~ up for sth** jugar algo a cara o cruz; **to ~ and turn** (*in bed*) dar vueltas (en la cama); **to win/lose the ~** (*also SPORT*) ganar/perder (a cara o cruz).
tot [tɔt] *n* (*BRIT*: *drink*) copita; (*child*) nene/a *m/f*.
▸**tot up** *vt* sumar.
total ['təutl] *adj* total, entero ♦ *n* total *m*, suma ♦ *vt* (*add up*) sumar; (*amount to*) ascender a; **grand ~** cantidad *f* total; (*cost*) importe *m* total; **in ~** en total, en suma.
totalitarian [təutælɪ'tɛərɪən] *adj* totalitario.
totality [təu'tælɪtɪ] *n* totalidad *f*.
total loss *n* siniestra total.
totally ['təutəlɪ] *adv* totalmente.
tote [təut] *vt* (*col*) acarrear, cargar con.
tote bag *n* bolsa.
totem pole ['təutəm-] *n* poste *m* totémico.
totter ['tɔtə*] *vi* tambalearse.
touch [tʌtʃ] *n* (*sense*) tacto; (*contact*) contacto; (*FOOTBALL*) fuera de juego ♦ *vt* tocar; (*emotionally*) conmover; **a ~ of** (*fig*) una pizca *or* un poquito de; **to get in ~ with sb** ponerse en contacto con algn; **I'll be in ~** le llamaré/escribiré; **to lose ~** (*friends*) perder contacto; **to be out of ~ with events** no estar al corriente (de los acontecimientos); **the personal ~** el toque personal; **to put the finishing ~es to sth** dar el último toque a algo; **no artist in the country can ~ him** no hay artista en todo el país que le iguale.
▸**touch on** *vt fus* (*topic*) aludir (brevemente) a.
▸**touch up** *vt* (*paint*) retocar.
touch-and-go ['tʌtʃən'gəu] *adj* arriesgado.
touchdown ['tʌtʃdaun] *n* aterrizaje *m*; (*US FOOTBALL*) ensayo.
touched [tʌtʃt] *adj* conmovido; (*col*) chiflado.
touchiness ['tʌtʃɪnɪs] *n* susceptibilidad *f*.
touching ['tʌtʃɪŋ] *adj* conmovedor(a).
touchline ['tʌtʃlaɪn] *n* (*SPORT*) línea de banda.
touch-sensitive ['tʌtʃ'sɛnsɪtɪv] *adj* sensible al tacto.
touch-type ['tʌtʃtaɪp] *vi* mecanografiar al tacto.
touchy ['tʌtʃɪ] *adj* (*person*) quisquilloso.
tough [tʌf] *adj* (*meat*) duro; (*journey*) penoso; (*task, problem, situation*) difícil; (*resistant*) resistente; (*person*) fuerte; (: *pej*) bruto ♦ *n* (*gangster etc*) gorila *m*; **they got ~ with the workers** se pusieron muy duros con los trabajadores.
toughen ['tʌfn] *vt* endurecer.
toughness ['tʌfnɪs] *n* dureza; (*resistance*) resistencia; (*strictness*) inflexibilidad *f*.
toupée ['tuːpeɪ] *n* peluquín *m*.
tour ['tuə*] *n* viaje *m*; (*also*: **package ~**) viaje *m* con todo incluido; (*of town, museum*) visita ♦ *vt* viajar por; **to go on a ~ of** (*region, country*) ir de viaje por; (*museum, castle*) visitar; **to go on ~** partir *or* ir de gira.

touring ['tuərɪŋ] *n* viajes *mpl* turísticos, turismo.
tourism ['tuərɪzm] *n* turismo.
tourist ['tuərɪst] *n* turista *m/f* ♦ *cpd* turístico; **the ~ trade** el turismo.
tourist class *n* (*AVIAT*) clase *f* turista.
tourist office *n* oficina de turismo.
tournament ['tuənəmənt] *n* torneo.
tourniquet ['tuənɪkeɪ] *n* (*MED*) torniquete *m.*
tour operator *n* touroperador(a) *m/f*, operador(a) *m/f* turístico/a.
tousled ['tauzld] *adj* (*hair*) despeinado.
tout [taut] *vi*: **to ~ for business** solicitar clientes ♦ *n*: **ticket ~** revendedor(a) *m/f.*
tow [təu] *n*: **to give sb a ~** (*AUT*) remolcar a algn ♦ *vt* remolcar; **"on** *or* (*US*) **in ~"** (*AUT*) "a remolque".
toward(s) [tə'wɔːd(z)] *prep* hacia; (*of attitude*) respecto a, con; (*of purpose*) para; **~ noon** alrededor de mediodía; **~ the end of the year** hacia finales de año; **to feel friendly ~ sb** sentir amistad hacia algn.
towel ['tauəl] *n* toalla; **to throw in the ~** (*fig*) darse por vencido, renunciar.
towelling ['tauəlɪŋ] *n* (*fabric*) felpa.
towel rail, (*US*) **towel rack** *n* toallero.
tower ['tauə*] *n* torre *f* ♦ *vi* (*building, mountain*) elevarse; **to ~ above** *or* **over sth/sb** dominar algo/destacarse sobre algn.
tower block *n* (*BRIT*) bloque *m* de pisos.
towering ['tauərɪŋ] *adj* muy alto, imponente.
town [taun] *n* ciudad *f*; **to go to ~** ir a la ciudad; (*fig*) tirar la casa por la ventana; **in the ~** en la ciudad; **to be out of ~** estar fuera de la ciudad.
town centre *n* centro de la ciudad.
town clerk *n* secretario/a del Ayuntamiento.
town council *n* Ayuntamiento, consejo municipal.
town crier [-kraɪə*] *n* (*BRIT*) pregonero.
town hall *n* ayuntamiento.
townie ['taunɪ] *n* (*BRIT col*) persona de la ciudad.
town plan *n* plano de la ciudad.
town planner *n* urbanista *m/f.*
town planning *n* urbanismo.
township ['taunʃɪp] *n* *municipio habitado sólo por negros en Sudáfrica.*
townspeople ['taunzpiːpl] *npl* gente *f* de ciudad.
towpath ['təupɑːθ] *n* camino de sirga.
towrope ['təurəup] *n* cable *m* de remolque.
tow truck *n* (*US*) camión *m* grúa.
toxic ['tɔksɪk] *adj* tóxico.
toxin ['tɔksɪn] *n* toxina.
toy [tɔɪ] *n* juguete *m.*
▸**toy with** *vt fus* jugar con; (*idea*) acariciar.
toyshop ['tɔɪʃɔp] *n* juguetería.
toy train *n* tren *m* de juguete.
trace [treɪs] *n* rastro ♦ *vt* (*draw*) trazar, delinear; (*locate*) encontrar; **there was no ~ of it** no había ningún indicio de ello.
trace element *n* oligoelemento.
trachea [trə'kɪə] *n* (*ANAT*) tráquea.
tracing paper ['treɪsɪŋ-] *n* papel *m* de calco.
track [træk] *n* (*mark*) huella, pista; (*path: gen*) camino, senda; (*: of bullet etc*) trayectoria; (*: of suspect, animal*) pista, rastro; (*RAIL*) vía; (*COMPUT, SPORT*) pista; (*on record*) canción *f* ♦ *vt* seguir la pista de; **to keep ~ of** mantenerse al tanto de, seguir; **a 4-~ tape** una cinta de 4 pistas; **the first ~ on the record/tape** la primera canción en el disco/la cinta; **to be on the right ~** (*fig*) ir por buen camino.
▸**track down** *vt* (*person*) localizar; (*sth lost*) encontrar.
tracker dog ['trækə*-] *n* (*BRIT*) perro rastreador.
track events *npl* (*SPORT*) pruebas *fpl* en pista.
tracking station ['trækɪŋ-] *n* (*SPACE*) estación *f* de seguimiento.
track meet *n* (*US*) concurso de carreras y saltos.
track record *n*: **to have a good ~** (*fig*) tener un buen historial.
tracksuit ['træksuːt] *n* chandal *m.*
tract [trækt] *n* (*GEO*) región *f*; (*pamphlet*) folleto.
traction ['trækʃən] *n* (*AUT, power*) tracción *f*; **in ~** (*MED*) en tracción.
traction engine *n* locomotora de tracción.
tractor ['træktə*] *n* tractor *m.*
trade [treɪd] *n* comercio, negocio; (*skill, job*) oficio, empleo; (*industry*) industria ♦ *vi* negociar, comerciar; **foreign ~** comercio exterior.
▸**trade in** *vt* (*old car etc*) ofrecer como parte del pago.
trade barrier *n* barrera comercial.
trade deficit *n* déficit *m* comercial.
Trade Descriptions Act *n* (*BRIT*) *ley sobre descripciones comerciales.*
trade discount *n* descuento comercial.
trade fair *n* feria de muestras.
trade-in ['treɪdɪn] *adj*: **~ price/value** *precio/valor de un artículo usado que se descuenta del precio de otro nuevo.*
trademark ['treɪdmɑːk] *n* marca de fábrica.
trade mission *n* misión *f* comercial.

trade name *n* marca registrada.
trade-off *n*: **a ~ (between)** un equilibrio (entre).
trade price *n* precio al detallista.
trader ['treɪdə*] *n* comerciante *m/f*.
trade reference *n* referencia comercial.
trade secret *n* secreto profesional.
tradesman ['treɪdzmən] *n* (*shopkeeper*) comerciante *m/f*.
trade union *n* sindicato.
trade unionist [-'juːnjənɪst] *n* sindicalista *m/f*.
trade wind *n* viento alisio.
trading ['treɪdɪŋ] *n* comercio.
trading account *n* cuenta de compraventa.
trading estate *n* (*BRIT*) polígono industrial.
trading stamp *n* cupón *m*, sello de prima.
tradition [trə'dɪʃən] *n* tradición *f*.
traditional [trə'dɪʃənl] *adj* tradicional.
traditionally [trə'dɪʃənlɪ] *adv* tradicionalmente.
traffic ['træfɪk] *n* (*gen, AUT*) tráfico, circulación *f*, tránsito ♦ *vi*: **to ~ in** (*pej: liquor, drugs*) traficar en; **air ~** tráfico aéreo.
traffic calming [-'kɑːmɪŋ] *n* reducción *f* de la velocidad de la circulación.
traffic circle *n* (*US*) glorieta de tráfico.
traffic island *n* refugio, isleta.
traffic jam *n* embotellamiento, atasco.
trafficker ['træfɪkə*] *n* traficante *m/f*.
traffic lights *npl* semáforo *sg*.
traffic offence, (*US*) **traffic violation** *n* infracción *f* de tráfico.
traffic warden *n* guardia *m/f* de tráfico.
tragedy ['trædʒədɪ] *n* tragedia.
tragic ['trædʒɪk] *adj* trágico.
tragically ['trædʒɪkəlɪ] *adv* trágicamente.
trail [treɪl] *n* (*tracks*) rastro, pista; (*path*) camino, sendero; (*dust, smoke*) estela ♦ *vt* (*drag*) arrastrar; (*follow*) seguir la pista de; (*follow closely*) vigilar ♦ *vi* arrastrarse; **to be on sb's ~** seguir la pista de algn.
►**trail away, trail off** *vi* (*sound*) desvanecerse; (*interest, voice*) desaparecer.
►**trail behind** *vi* quedar a la zaga.
trailer ['treɪlə*] *n* (*AUT*) remolque *m*; (*caravan*) caravana; (*CINE*) trailer *m*, avance *m*.
trail truck *n* (*US*) trailer *m*.
train [treɪn] *n* tren *m*; (*of dress*) cola; (*series*): **~ of events** curso de los acontecimientos ♦ *vt* (*educate*) formar; (*teach skills to*) adiestrar; (*sportsman*) entrenar; (*dog*) amaestrar; (*point: gun etc*): **to ~ on** apuntar a ♦ *vi* (*SPORT*) entrenarse; (*be educated, learn a skill*) formarse; **to go by ~** ir en tren; **one's ~ of thought** el razonamiento de algn; **to ~ sb to do sth** enseñar a algn a hacer algo.
train attendant *n* (*US RAIL*) empleado/a de coches-cama.
trained [treɪnd] *adj* (*worker*) cualificado; (*animal*) amaestrado.
trainee [treɪ'niː] *n* trabajador(a) *m/f* en prácticas ♦ *cpd*: **he's a ~ teacher** (*primary*) es estudiante de magisterio; (*secondary*) está haciendo las prácticas del I.C.E.
trainer ['treɪnə*] *n* (*SPORT*) entrenador(a) *m/f*; (*of animals*) domador(a) *m/f*; **~s** *npl* (*shoes*) zapatillas *fpl* (de deporte).
training ['treɪnɪŋ] *n* formación *f*; entrenamiento; **to be in ~** (*SPORT*) estar entrenando; (: *fit*) estar en forma.
training college *n* (*gen*) colegio de formación profesional; (*for teachers*) escuela normal.
training course *n* curso de formación.
traipse [treɪps] *vi* andar penosamente.
trait [treɪt] *n* rasgo.
traitor ['treɪtə*] *n* traidor(a) *m/f*.
trajectory [trə'dʒɛktərɪ] *n* trayectoria, curso.
tram [træm] *n* (*BRIT: also*: **~car**) tranvía *m*.
tramline ['træmlaɪn] *n* carril *m* de tranvía.
tramp [træmp] *n* (*person*) vagabundo/a; (*col: offensive: woman*) puta ♦ *vi* andar con pasos pesados.
trample ['træmpl] *vt*: **to ~ (underfoot)** pisotear.
trampoline ['træmpəliːn] *n* trampolín *m*.
trance [trɑːns] *n* trance *m*; **to go into a ~** entrar en trance.
tranquil ['træŋkwɪl] *adj* tranquilo.
tranquillity, (*US*) **tranquility** [træŋ'kwɪlɪtɪ] *n* tranquilidad *f*.
tranquillizer, (*US*) **tranquilizer** ['træŋkwɪlaɪzə*] *n* (*MED*) tranquilizante *m*.
trans- [trænz] *pref* trans-, tras-.
transact [træn'zækt] *vt* (*business*) tramitar.
transaction [træn'zækʃən] *n* transacción *f*, operación *f*; **cash ~s** transacciones al contado.
transatlantic ['trænzət'læntɪk] *adj* transatlántico.
transcend [træn'sɛnd] *vt* rebasar.
transcendent [træn'sɛndənt] *adj* trascendente.
transcendental [trænsɛn'dɛntl] *adj*: **~ meditation** meditación *f* transcendental.
transcribe [træn'skraɪb] *vt* transcribir, copiar.
transcript ['trænskrɪpt] *n* copia.

transcription [træn'skrɪpʃən] *n* transcripción *f.*
transept ['trænsɛpt] *n* crucero.
transfer *n* ['trænsfə*] transferencia; (*SPORT*) traspaso; (*picture, design*) calcomanía ♦ *vt* [træns'fəː*] trasladar, pasar; **to ~ the charges** (*BRIT TEL*) llamar a cobro revertido; **by bank ~** por transferencia bancaria *or* giro bancario; **to ~ money from one account to another** transferir dinero de una cuenta a otra; **to ~ sth to sb's name** transferir algo al nombre de algn.
transferable [træns'fəːrəbl] *adj*: **not ~** intransferible.
transfix [træns'fɪks] *vt* traspasar; (*fig*): **~ed with fear** paralizado por el miedo.
transform [træns'fɔːm] *vt* transformar.
transformation [trænsfə'meɪʃən] *n* transformación *f.*
transformer [træns'fɔːmə*] *n* (*ELEC*) transformador *m.*
transfusion [træns'fjuːʒən] *n* transfusión *f.*
transgress [træns'grɛs] *vt* (*go beyond*) traspasar; (*violate*) violar, infringir.
tranship [træn'ʃɪp] *vt* trasbordar.
transient ['trænzɪənt] *adj* transitorio.
transistor [træn'zɪstə*] *n* (*ELEC*) transistor *m.*
transistorized [træn'zɪstəraɪzd] *adj* (*circuit*) transistorizado.
transistor radio *n* transistor *m.*
transit ['trænzɪt] *n*: **in ~** en tránsito.
transit camp *n* campamento de tránsito.
transition [træn'zɪʃən] *n* transición *f.*
transitional [træn'zɪʃənl] *adj* transitorio.
transition period *n* período de transición.
transitive ['trænzɪtɪv] *adj* (*LING*) transitivo.
transitively ['trænzɪtɪvlɪ] *adv* transitivamente.
transitory ['trænzɪtərɪ] *adj* transitorio.
transit visa *n* visado de tránsito.
translate [trænz'leɪt] *vt*: **to ~ (from/into)** traducir (de/a).
translation [trænz'leɪʃən] *n* traducción *f.*
translator [trænz'leɪtə*] *n* traductor(a) *m/f.*
translucent [trænz'luːsnt] *adj* traslúcido.
transmission [trænz'mɪʃən] *n* transmisión *f.*
transmit [trænz'mɪt] *vt* transmitir.
transmitter [trænz'mɪtə*] *n* transmisor *m*; (*station*) emisora.
transparency [træns'pɛərnsɪ] *n* (*BRIT PHOT*) diapositiva.
transparent [træns'pærnt] *adj* transparente.
transpire [træns'paɪə*] *vi* (*turn out*) resultar (ser); (*happen*) ocurrir, suceder; (*become known*): **it finally ~d that ...** por fin se supo que ....
transplant *vt* [træns'plɑːnt] transplantar ♦ *n* ['trænsplɑːnt] (*MED*) transplante *m*; **to have a heart ~** hacerse un transplante de corazón.
transport *n* ['trænspɔːt] transporte *m* ♦ *vt* [træns'pɔːt] transportar; **public ~** transporte *m* público.
transportable [træns'pɔːtəbl] *adj* transportable.
transportation [trænspɔː'teɪʃən] *n* transporte *m*; (*of prisoners*) deportación *f.*
transport café *n* (*BRIT*) bar-restaurante *m* de carretera.
transpose [træns'pəuz] *vt* transponer.
transsexual [trænz'sɛksjuəl] *adj, n* transexual *m/f.*
transverse ['trænzvəːs] *adj* transverso, transversal.
transvestite [trænz'vɛstaɪt] *n* travesti *m/f.*
trap [træp] *n* (*snare, trick*) trampa; (*carriage*) cabriolé *m* ♦ *vt* coger (*SP*) *or* agarrar (*LAM*) en una trampa; (*immobilize*) bloquear; (*jam*) atascar; **to set** *or* **lay a ~ (for sb)** poner(le) una trampa (a algn); **to ~ one's finger in the door** pillarse el dedo en la puerta.
trap door *n* escotilla.
trapeze [trə'piːz] *n* trapecio.
trapper ['træpə*] *n* trampero, cazador *m.*
trappings ['træpɪŋz] *npl* adornos *mpl.*
trash [træʃ] *n* basura; (*nonsense*) tonterías *fpl.*
trash can *n* (*US*) cubo, balde *m* (*LAM*) *or* bote *m* (*LAM*) de la basura.
trash can liner *n* (*US*) bolsa de basura.
trashy ['træʃɪ] *adj* (*col*) chungo.
trauma ['trɔːmə] *n* trauma *m.*
traumatic [trɔː'mætɪk] *adj* (*PSYCH, fig*) traumático.
travel ['trævl] *n* viaje *m* ♦ *vi* viajar ♦ *vt* (*distance*) recorrer; **this wine doesn't ~ well** este vino pierde con los viajes.
travel agency *n* agencia de viajes.
travel agent *n* agente *m/f* de viajes.
travel brochure *n* folleto turístico.
traveller, (*US*) **traveler** ['trævlə*] *n* viajero/a; (*COMM*) viajante *m/f.*
traveller's cheque, (*US*) **traveler's check** *n* cheque *m* de viaje.
travelling, (*US*) **traveling** ['trævlɪŋ] *n* los viajes, el viajar ♦ *adj* (*circus, exhibition*) ambulante ♦ *cpd* (*bag, clock*) de viaje.
travel(l)ing expenses *npl* dietas *fpl.*
travel(l)ing salesman *n* viajante *m.*
travelogue ['trævəlɔg] *n* (*book*) relación *f* de viajes; (*film*) documental *m* de viajes;

(*talk*) recuento de viajes.
travel sickness *n* mareo.
traverse ['trævəs] *vt* atravesar.
travesty ['trævəstɪ] *n* parodia.
trawler ['trɔːlə*] *n* pesquero de arrastre.
tray [treɪ] *n* (*for carrying*) bandeja; (*on desk*) cajón *m*.
treacherous ['trɛtʃərəs] *adj* traidor(a); **road conditions are ~** el estado de las carreteras es peligroso.
treachery ['trɛtʃərɪ] *n* traición *f*.
treacle ['triːkl] *n* (*BRIT*) melaza.
tread [trɛd] *n* paso, pisada; (*of tyre*) banda de rodadura ♦ *vi* (*pt* **trod**, *pp* **trodden** [trɔd, 'trɔdn]) pisar.
▶**tread on** *vt fus* pisar.
treas. *abbr* = **treasurer**.
treason ['triːzn] *n* traición *f*.
treasure ['trɛʒə*] *n* tesoro ♦ *vt* (*value*) apreciar, valorar.
treasure hunt *n* caza del tesoro.
treasurer ['trɛʒərə*] *n* tesorero/a.
treasury ['trɛʒərɪ] *n*: **the T~**, (*US*) **the T~ Department** ≈ el Ministerio de Economía y de Hacienda.
treasury bill *n* bono del Tesoro.
treat [triːt] *n* (*present*) regalo; (*pleasure*) placer *m* ♦ *vt* tratar; (*consider*) considerar; **to give sb a ~** hacer un regalo a algn; **to ~ sb to sth** invitar a algn a algo; **to ~ sth as a joke** tomar algo a broma.
treatise ['triːtɪz] *n* tratado.
treatment ['triːtmənt] *n* tratamiento; **to have ~ for sth** recibir tratamiento por algo.
treaty ['triːtɪ] *n* tratado.
treble ['trɛbl] *adj* triple ♦ *vt* triplicar ♦ *vi* triplicarse.
treble clef *n* (*MUS*) clave *f* de sol.
tree [triː] *n* árbol *m*.
tree-lined ['triːlaɪnd] *adj* bordeado de árboles.
tree trunk *n* tronco de árbol.
trek [trɛk] *n* (*long journey*) expedición *f*; (*tiring walk*) caminata.
trellis ['trɛlɪs] *n* enrejado.
tremble ['trɛmbl] *vi* temblar.
trembling ['trɛmblɪŋ] *n* temblor *m* ♦ *adj* tembloroso.
tremendous [trɪ'mɛndəs] *adj* tremendo; (*enormous*) enorme; (*excellent*) estupendo.
tremendously [trɪ'mɛndəslɪ] *adv* enormemente, sobremanera; **he enjoyed it ~** lo disfrutó de lo lindo.
tremor ['trɛmə*] *n* temblor *m*; (*also*: **earth ~**) temblor *m* de tierra.
trench [trɛntʃ] *n* zanja; (*MIL*) trinchera.
trench coat *n* trinchera.
trench warfare *n* guerra de trincheras.
trend [trɛnd] *n* (*tendency*) tendencia; (*of events*) curso; (*fashion*) moda; **~ towards/away from sth** tendencia hacia/en contra de algo; **to set the ~** marcar la pauta.
trendy ['trɛndɪ] *adj* de moda.
trepidation [trɛpɪ'deɪʃən] *n* inquietud *f*.
trespass ['trɛspəs] *vi*: **to ~ on** entrar sin permiso en; **"no ~ing"** "prohibido el paso".
trespasser ['trɛspəsə*] *n* intruso/a *m/f*; **"~s will be prosecuted"** "se procesará a los intrusos".
tress [trɛs] *n* guedeja.
trestle ['trɛsl] *n* caballete *m*.
trestle table *n* mesa de caballete.
tri- [traɪ] *pref* tri-.
trial ['traɪəl] *n* (*LAW*) juicio, proceso; (*test: of machine etc*) prueba; (*hardship*) desgracia; **~s** *npl* (*ATHLETICS, of horses*) pruebas *fpl*; **to bring sb to ~ (for a crime)** llevar a algn a juicio (por un delito); **~ by jury** juicio ante jurado; **to be sent for ~** ser remitido al tribunal; **by ~ and error** a fuerza de probar.
trial balance *n* balance *m* de comprobación.
trial basis *n*: **on a ~** a modo de prueba.
trial offer *n* oferta de prueba.
trial run *n* prueba.
triangle ['traɪæŋgl] *n* (*MATH, MUS*) triángulo.
triangular [traɪ'æŋgjulə*] *adj* triangular.
triathlon [traɪ'æθlən] *n* triatlón *m*.
tribal ['traɪbəl] *adj* tribal.
tribe [traɪb] *n* tribu *f*.
tribesman ['traɪbzmən] *n* miembro de una tribu.
tribulation [trɪbju'leɪʃən] *n* tribulación *f*.
tribunal [traɪ'bjuːnl] *n* tribunal *m*.
tributary ['trɪbjuːtərɪ] *n* (*river*) afluente *m*.
tribute ['trɪbjuːt] *n* homenaje *m*, tributo; **to pay ~ to** rendir homenaje a.
trice [traɪs] *n*: **in a ~** en un santiamén.
trick [trɪk] *n* trampa; (*conjuring ~, deceit*) truco; (*joke*) broma; (*CARDS*) baza ♦ *vt* engañar; **it's a ~ of the light** es una ilusión óptica; **to play a ~ on sb** gastar una broma a algn; **that should do the ~** eso servirá; **to ~ sb out of sth** quitarle algo a algn con engaños; **to ~ sb into doing sth** hacer que algn haga algo con engaños.
trickery ['trɪkərɪ] *n* engaño.
trickle ['trɪkl] *n* (*of water etc*) hilo ♦ *vi* gotear.
trick question *n* pregunta capciosa.

trickster ['trɪkstə*] *n* estafador(a) *m/f.*
tricky ['trɪkɪ] *adj* difícil; (*problem*) delicado.
tricycle ['traɪsɪkl] *n* triciclo.
tried [traɪd] *adj* probado.
trifle ['traɪfl] *n* bagatela; (*CULIN*) *dulce de bizcocho, gelatina, fruta y natillas* ♦ *adv*: **a ~ long** un pelín largo ♦ *vi*: **to ~ with** jugar con.
trifling ['traɪflɪŋ] *adj* insignificante.
trigger ['trɪgə*] *n* (*of gun*) gatillo.
►**trigger off** *vt* desencadenar.
trigonometry [trɪgə'nɔmətrɪ] *n* trigonometría.
trilby ['trɪlbɪ] *n* (*also*: ~ **hat**) sombrero flexible *or* tirolés.
trill [trɪl] *n* (*of bird*) gorjeo; (*MUS*) trino.
trilogy ['trɪlədʒɪ] *n* trilogía.
trim [trɪm] *adj* (*elegant*) aseado; (*house, garden*) en buen estado; (*figure*): **to be ~** tener buen talle ♦ *n* (*haircut etc*) recorte *m* ♦ *vt* (*neaten*) arreglar; (*cut*) recortar; (*decorate*) adornar; (*NAUT*: *a sail*) orientar; **to keep in (good) ~** mantener en buen estado.
trimmings ['trɪmɪŋz] *npl* (*extras*) accesorios *mpl*; (*cuttings*) recortes *mpl.*
Trinidad and Tobago ['trɪnɪdæd-] *n* Trinidad *f* y Tobago.
Trinity ['trɪnɪtɪ] *n*: **the ~** la Trinidad.
trinket ['trɪŋkɪt] *n* chuchería, baratija.
trio ['tri:əu] *n* trío.
trip [trɪp] *n* viaje *m*; (*excursion*) excursión *f*; (*stumble*) traspié *m* ♦ *vi* (*stumble*) tropezar; (*go lightly*) andar a paso ligero; **on a ~** de viaje.
►**trip over** *vt fus* tropezar con.
►**trip up** *vi* tropezar, caerse ♦ *vt* hacer tropezar *or* caer.
tripartite [traɪ'pɑ:taɪt] *adj* (*agreement, talks*) tripartito.
tripe [traɪp] *n* (*CULIN*) callos *mpl*; (*pej*: *rubbish*) bobadas *fpl.*
triple ['trɪpl] *adj* triple ♦ *adv*: **~ the distance/the speed** 3 veces la distancia/la velocidad.
triple jump *n* triple salto.
triplets ['trɪplɪts] *npl* trillizos/as *m/fpl.*
triplicate ['trɪplɪkət] *n*: **in ~** por triplicado.
tripod ['traɪpɔd] *n* trípode *m.*
Tripoli ['trɪpəlɪ] *n* Trípoli *m.*
tripper ['trɪpə*] *n* turista *m/f*, excursionista *m/f.*
tripwire ['trɪpwaɪə*] *n* cable *m* de trampa.
trite [traɪt] *adj* trillado.
triumph ['traɪʌmf] *n* triunfo ♦ *vi*: **to ~ (over)** vencer.
triumphal [traɪ'ʌmfl] *adj* triunfal.
triumphant [traɪ'ʌmfənt] *adj* triunfante.
triumphantly [traɪ'ʌmfəntlɪ] *adv* triunfalmente, en tono triunfal.
trivia ['trɪvɪə] *npl* trivialidades *fpl.*
trivial ['trɪvɪəl] *adj* insignificante, trivial.
triviality [trɪvɪ'ælɪtɪ] *n* insignificancia, trivialidad *f.*
trivialize ['trɪvɪəlaɪz] *vt* trivializar.
trod [trɔd] *pt of* **tread**.
trodden ['trɔdn] *pp of* **tread**.
trolley ['trɔlɪ] *n* carrito; (*in hospital*) camilla.
trolley bus *n* trolebús *m.*
trombone [trɔm'bəun] *n* trombón *m.*
troop [tru:p] *n* grupo, banda; *see also* **troops**.
►**troop in** *vi* entrar en tropel.
►**troop out** *vi* salir en tropel.
troop carrier *n* (*plane*) transporte *m* (militar); (*NAUT*: *also*: **troopship**) (buque *m* de) transporte *m.*
trooper ['tru:pə*] *n* (*MIL*) soldado (de caballería); (*US*: *policeman*) policía *m/f* montado/a.
trooping the colour ['tru:pɪŋ-] *n* (*ceremony*) presentación *f* de la bandera.
troopship ['tru:pʃɪp] *n* (buque *m* de) transporte *m.*
trophy ['trəufɪ] *n* trofeo.
tropic ['trɔpɪk] *n* trópico; **the ~s** los trópicos, la zona tropical; **T~ of Cancer/Capricorn** trópico de Cáncer/Capricornio.
tropical ['trɔpɪkl] *adj* tropical.
trot [trɔt] *n* trote *m* ♦ *vi* trotar; **on the ~** (*BRIT fig*) seguidos/as.
►**trot out** *vt* (*excuse, reason*) volver a usar; (*names, facts*) sacar a relucir.
trouble ['trʌbl] *n* problema *m*, dificultad *f*; (*worry*) preocupación *f*; (*bother, effort*) molestia, esfuerzo; (*unrest*) inquietud *f*; (*with machine etc*) fallo, avería; (*MED*): **stomach ~** problemas *mpl* gástricos ♦ *vt* molestar; (*worry*) preocupar, inquietar ♦ *vi*: **to ~ to do sth** molestarse en hacer algo; **~s** *npl* (*POL etc*) conflictos *mpl*; **to be in ~** estar en un apuro; (*for doing wrong*) tener problemas; **to have ~ doing sth** tener dificultad en *or* para hacer algo; **to go to the ~ of doing sth** tomarse la molestia de hacer algo; **what's the ~?** ¿qué pasa?; **the ~ is ...** el problema es ..., lo que pasa es ...; **please don't ~ yourself** por favor no se moleste.
troubled ['trʌbld] *adj* (*person*) preocupado; (*epoch, life*) agitado.
trouble-free ['trʌblfri:] *adj* sin problemas *or* dificultades.
troublemaker ['trʌblmeɪkə*] *n* agitador(a) *m/f.*
troubleshooter ['trʌblʃu:tə*] *n* (*in conflict*)

mediador(a) *m/f*.
troublesome ['trʌblsəm] *adj* molesto, inoportuno.
trouble spot *n* centro de fricción, punto caliente.
troubling ['trʌblɪŋ] *adj* (*thought*) preocupante; **these are ~ times** son malos tiempos.
trough [trɔf] *n* (*also:* **drinking ~**) abrevadero; (*also*: **feeding ~**) comedero; (*channel*) canal *m*.
trounce [trauns] *vt* dar una paliza a.
troupe [tru:p] *n* grupo.
trouser press *n* prensa para pantalones.
trousers ['trauzəz] *npl* pantalones *mpl*; **short ~** pantalones *mpl* cortos.
trouser suit *n* traje *m* de chaqueta y pantalón.
trousseau, *pl* **~x** *or* **~s** ['tru:səu, -z] *n* ajuar *m*.
trout [traut] *n* (*pl inv*) trucha.
trowel ['trauəl] *n* paleta.
truant ['truənt] *n*: **to play ~** (*BRIT*) hacer novillos.
truce [tru:s] *n* tregua.
truck [trʌk] *n* (*US*) camión *m*; (*RAIL*) vagón *m*.
truck driver *n* camionero/a.
trucker ['trʌkə*] *n* (*esp US*) camionero/a.
truck farm *n* (*US*) huerto de hortalizas.
trucking ['trʌkɪŋ] *n* (*esp US*) transporte *m* en camión.
trucking company *n* (*US*) compañía de transporte por carretera.
truckload ['trʌkləud] *n* camión *m* lleno.
truculent ['trʌkjulənt] *adj* agresivo.
trudge [trʌdʒ] *vi* caminar penosamente.
true [tru:] *adj* verdadero; (*accurate*) exacto; (*genuine*) auténtico; (*faithful*) fiel; (*wheel*) centrado; (*wall*) a plomo; (*beam*) alineado; **~ to life** verídico; **to come ~** realizarse, cumplirse.
truffle ['trʌfl] *n* trufa.
truly ['tru:lɪ] *adv* realmente; (*faithfully*) fielmente; **yours ~** (*in letter-writing*) atentamente.
trump [trʌmp] *n* (*CARDS*) triunfo; **to turn up ~s** (*fig*) salir *or* resultar bien.
trump card *n* triunfo; (*fig*) baza.
trumped-up ['trʌmptʌp] *adj* inventado.
trumpet ['trʌmpɪt] *n* trompeta.
truncated [trʌŋ'keɪtɪd] *adj* truncado.
truncheon ['trʌntʃən] *n* (*BRIT*) porra.
trundle ['trʌndl] *vt, vi*: **to ~ along** rodar haciendo ruido.
trunk [trʌŋk] *n* (*of tree, person*) tronco; (*of elephant*) trompa; (*case*) baúl *m*; (*US AUT*) maletero, baúl *m* (*LAM*); *see also* **trunks**.
trunk call *n* (*BRIT TEL*) llamada interurbana.
trunk road *n* carretera principal.
trunks [trʌŋks] *npl* (*also*: **swimming ~**) bañador *m*.
truss [trʌs] *n* (*MED*) braguero ♦ *vt*: **to ~ (up)** atar.
trust [trʌst] *n* confianza; (*COMM*) trust *m*; (*LAW*) fideicomiso ♦ *vt* (*rely on*) tener confianza en; (*entrust*): **to ~ sth to sb** confiar algo a algn; (*hope*): **to ~ (that)** esperar (que); **in ~** en fideicomiso; **you'll have to take it on ~** tienes que aceptarlo a ojos cerrados.
trust company *n* banco fideicomisario.
trusted ['trʌstɪd] *adj* de confianza, fiable, de fiar.
trustee [trʌs'ti:] *n* (*LAW*) fideicomisario.
trustful ['trʌstful] *adj* confiado.
trust fund *n* fondo fiduciario *or* de fideicomiso.
trusting ['trʌstɪŋ] *adj* confiado.
trustworthy ['trʌstwə:ðɪ] *adj* digno de confianza, fiable, de fiar.
trusty ['trʌstɪ] *adj* fiel.
truth, ~s [tru:θ, tru:ðz] *n* verdad *f*.
truthful ['tru:θfəl] *adj* (*person*) sincero; (*account*) fidedigno.
truthfully ['tru:θfulɪ] *adv* (*answer*) con sinceridad.
truthfulness ['tru:θfulnɪs] *n* (*of account*) verdad *f*; (*of person*) sinceridad *f*.
try [traɪ] *n* tentativa, intento; (*RUGBY*) ensayo ♦ *vt* (*LAW*) juzgar, procesar; (*test*: *sth new*) probar, someter a prueba; (*attempt*) intentar; (*strain*: *patience*) hacer perder ♦ *vi* probar; **to give sth a ~** intentar hacer algo; **to ~ one's (very) best** *or* **hardest** poner todo su empeño, esmerarse; **to ~ to do sth** intentar hacer algo.
▸**try on** *vt* (*clothes*) probarse.
▸**try out** *vt* probar, poner a prueba.
trying ['traɪɪŋ] *adj* cansado; (*person*) pesado.
tsar [zɑ:*] *n* zar *m*.
T-shirt ['ti:ʃə:t] *n* camiseta.
T-square ['ti:skwɛə*] *n* regla en T.
TT *adj abbr* (*BRIT col*) = **teetotal** ♦ *abbr* (*US*) = *Trust Territory*.
tub [tʌb] *n* cubo (*SP*), balde *m* (*LAM*); (*bath*) bañera, tina (*esp LAM*).
tuba ['tju:bə] *n* tuba.
tubby ['tʌbɪ] *adj* regordete.
tube [tju:b] *n* tubo; (*BRIT*: *underground*) metro; (*US col*: *television*) tele *f*.
tubeless ['tju:blɪs] *adj* (*tyre*) sin cámara.
tuber ['tju:bə*] *n* (*BOT*) tubérculo.
tuberculosis [tjubə:kju'ləusɪs] *n*

tuberculosis *f inv.*
tube station *n* (*BRIT*) estación *f* de metro.
tubing ['tju:bɪŋ] *n* tubería (*SP*), cañería; **a piece of ~** un trozo de tubo.
tubular ['tju:bjulə*] *adj* tubular.
TUC *n abbr* (*BRIT*: = *Trades Union Congress*) *federación nacional de sindicatos.*
tuck [tʌk] *n* (*SEWING*) pliegue *m* ♦ *vt* (*put*) poner.
▸**tuck away** *vt* esconder.
▸**tuck in** *vt* meter; (*child*) arropar ♦ *vi* (*eat*) comer con apetito.
▸**tuck up** *vt* (*child*) arropar.
tuck shop *n* (*SCOL*) tienda de golosinas.
Tue(s). *abbr* (= *Tuesday*) mart.
Tuesday ['tju:zdɪ] *n* martes *m inv*; **on ~** el martes; **on ~s** los martes; **every ~** todos los martes; **every other ~** cada dos martes, un martes sí y otro no; **last/next ~** el martes pasado/próximo; **a week/fortnight on ~, ~ week/fortnight** del martes en 8/15 días, del martes en una semana/dos semanas.
tuft [tʌft] *n* mechón *m*; (*of grass etc*) manojo.
tug [tʌg] *n* (*ship*) remolcador *m* ♦ *vt* remolcar.
tug-of-love [tʌgəv'lʌv] *n*: **~ children** *hijos envueltos en el litigio de los padres por su custodia.*
tug-of-war [tʌgəv'wɔ:*] *n* juego de la cuerda.
tuition [tju:'ɪʃən] *n* (*BRIT*) enseñanza; (: *private ~*) clases *fpl* particulares; (*US*: *school fees*) matrícula.
tulip ['tju:lɪp] *n* tulipán *m.*
tumble ['tʌmbl] *n* (*fall*) caída ♦ *vi* caerse, tropezar; **to ~ to sth** (*col*) caer en la cuenta de algo.
tumbledown ['tʌmbldaun] *adj* ruinoso.
tumble dryer *n* (*BRIT*) secadora.
tumbler ['tʌmblə*] *n* vaso.
tummy ['tʌmɪ] *n* (*col*) barriga, vientre *m.*
tumour, (*US*) **tumor** ['tju:mə*] *n* tumor *m.*
tumult ['tju:mʌlt] *n* tumulto.
tumultuous [tju:'mʌltjuəs] *adj* tumultuoso.
tuna ['tju:nə] *n* (*pl inv*) (*also*: **~ fish**) atún *m.*
tundra ['tʌndrə] *n* tundra.
tune [tju:n] *n* (*melody*) melodía ♦ *vt* (*MUS*) afinar; (*RADIO, TV, AUT*) sintonizar; **to be in/out of ~** (*instrument*) estar afinado/desafinado; (*singer*) afinar/desafinar; **to be in/out of ~ with** (*fig*) armonizar/desentonar con; **to the ~ of** (*fig*: *amount*) por (la) cantidad de.
▸**tune in** *vi* (*RADIO, TV*): **to ~ in (to)** sintonizar (con).
▸**tune up** *vi* (*musician*) afinar (su instrumento).
tuneful ['tju:nful] *adj* melodioso.
tuner ['tju:nə*] *n* (*radio set*) sintonizador *m*; **piano ~** afinador(a) *m/f* de pianos.
tungsten ['tʌŋstn] *n* tungsteno.
tunic ['tju:nɪk] *n* túnica.
tuning ['tju:nɪŋ] *n* sintonización *f*; (*MUS*) afinación *f.*
tuning fork *n* diapasón *m.*
Tunis ['tju:nɪs] *n* Túnez *m.*
Tunisia [tju:'nɪzɪə] *n* Túnez *m.*
Tunisian [tju:'nɪzɪən] *adj, n* tunecino/a *m/f.*
tunnel ['tʌnl] *n* túnel *m*; (*in mine*) galería ♦ *vi* construir un túnel/una galería.
tunnel vision *n* (*MED*) visión *f* periférica restringida; (*fig*) estrechez *f* de miras.
tunny ['tʌnɪ] *n* atún *m.*
turban ['tə:bən] *n* turbante *m.*
turbid ['tə:bɪd] *adj* turbio.
turbine ['tə:baɪn] *n* turbina.
turbo ['tə:bəu] *n* turbo.
turboprop ['tə:bəuprɔp] *n* turbohélice *m.*
turbot ['tə:bət] *n* (*pl inv*) rodaballo.
turbulence ['tə:bjuləns] *n* (*AVIAT*) turbulencia.
turbulent ['tə:bjulənt] *adj* turbulento.
tureen [tə'ri:n] *n* sopera.
turf [tə:f] *n* césped *m*; (*clod*) tepe *m* ♦ *vt* cubrir con césped.
▸**turf out** *vt* (*col*) echar a la calle.
turf accountant *n* corredor(a) *m/f* de apuestas.
turgid ['tə:dʒɪd] *adj* (*prose*) pesado.
Turin [tjuə'rɪn] *n* Turín *m.*
Turk [tə:k] *n* turco/a.
Turkey ['tə:kɪ] *n* Turquía.
turkey ['tə:kɪ] *n* pavo.
Turkish ['tə:kɪʃ] *adj* turco ♦ *n* (*LING*) turco.
Turkish bath *n* baño turco.
turmeric ['tə:mərɪk] *n* cúrcuma.
turmoil ['tə:mɔɪl] *n* desorden *m*, alboroto.
turn [tə:n] *n* turno; (*in road*) curva; (*THEAT*) número; (*MED*) ataque *m* ♦ *vt* girar, volver, voltear (*LAM*); (*collar, steak*) dar la vuelta a; (*shape*: *wood, metal*) tornear; (*change*): **to ~ sth into** convertir algo en ♦ *vi* volver, voltearse (*LAM*); (*person*: *look back*) volverse; (*reverse direction*) dar la vuelta, voltear (*LAM*); (*milk*) cortarse; (*change*) cambiar; (*become*): **to ~ into sth** convertirse *or* transformarse en algo; **a good ~** un favor; **it gave me quite a ~** me dio un susto; **"no left ~"** (*AUT*) "prohibido girar a la izquierda"; **it's your ~** te toca a ti; **in ~** por turnos; **to take ~s** turnarse; **at the ~ of the year/century** a fin de año/a finales de siglo; **to take a ~ for the worse** (*situation, patient*) empeorar; **they ~ed him against us** le pusieron en contra

nuestra; **the car ~ed the corner** el coche dobló la esquina; **to ~ left** (*AUT*) torcer *or* girar a la izquierda; **she has no-one to ~ to** no tiene a quién recurrir.
▸**turn away** *vi* apartar la vista ♦ *vt* (*reject: person, business*) rechazar.
▸**turn back** *vi* volverse atrás.
▸**turn down** *vt* (*refuse*) rechazar; (*reduce*) bajar; (*fold*) doblar.
▸**turn in** *vi* (*col: go to bed*) acostarse ♦ *vt* (*fold*) doblar hacia dentro.
▸**turn off** *vi* (*from road*) desviarse ♦ *vt* (*light, radio etc*) apagar; (*engine*) parar.
▸**turn on** *vt* (*light, radio etc*) encender, prender (*LAM*); (*engine*) poner en marcha.
▸**turn out** *vt* (*light, gas*) apagar; (*produce: goods, novel etc*) producir ♦ *vi* (*attend: troops*) presentarse; (*: doctor*) atender; **to ~ out to be** ... resultar ser ....
▸**turn over** *vi* (*person*) volverse ♦ *vt* (*mattress, card*) dar la vuelta a; (*page*) volver.
▸**turn round** *vi* volverse; (*rotate*) girar.
▸**turn to** *vt fus*: **to ~ to sb** acudir a algn.
▸**turn up** *vi* (*person*) llegar, presentarse; (*lost object*) aparecer ♦ *vt* (*radio*) subir, poner más alto; (*heat, gas*) poner más fuerte.
turnabout ['tə:nəbaut], **turnaround** ['tə:nəraund] *n* (*fig*) giro total.
turncoat ['tə:nkəut] *n* renegado/a.
turned-up ['tə:ndʌp] *adj* (*nose*) respingón/ona.
turning ['tə:nɪŋ] *n* (*side road*) bocacalle *f*; (*bend*) curva; **the first ~ on the right** la primera bocacalle a la derecha.
turning point *n* (*fig*) momento decisivo.
turnip ['tə:nɪp] *n* nabo.
turnkey system ['tə:nki:-] *n* (*COMPUT*) sistema *m* de seguridad.
turnout ['tə:naut] *n* asistencia, número de asistentes, público.
turnover ['tə:nəuvə*] *n* (*COMM: amount of money*) facturación *f*; (*: of goods*) movimiento; **there is a rapid ~ in staff** hay mucho movimiento de personal.
turnpike ['tə:npaɪk] *n* (*US*) autopista de peaje.
turnstile ['tə:nstaɪl] *n* torniquete *m*.
turntable ['tə:nteɪbl] *n* plato.
turn-up ['tə:nʌp] *n* (*BRIT: on trousers*) vuelta.
turpentine ['tə:pəntaɪn] *n* (*also:* **turps**) trementina.
turquoise ['tə:kwɔɪz] *n* (*stone*) turquesa ♦ *adj* color turquesa.
turret ['tʌrɪt] *n* torreón *m*.
turtle ['tə:tl] *n* tortuga (marina).
turtleneck (sweater) ['tə:tlnɛk-] *n* (jersey *m* de) cuello cisne.
Tuscany ['tʌskənɪ] *n* Toscana.
tusk [tʌsk] *n* colmillo.
tussle ['tʌsl] *n* lucha, pelea.
tutor ['tju:tə*] *n* profesor(a) *m/f*.
tutorial [tju:'tɔ:rɪəl] *n* (*SCOL*) seminario.
tuxedo [tʌk'si:dəu] *n* (*US*) smóking *m*, esmoquin *m*.
TV [ti:'vi:] *n abbr* (= *television*) televisión *f*.
TV dinner *n* cena precocinada.
TV licence *n licencia que se paga por el uso del televisor, destinada a financiar la BBC*.
twaddle ['twɔdl] *n* (*col*) tonterías *fpl*.
twang [twæŋ] *n* (*of instrument*) tañido; (*of voice*) timbre *m* nasal.
tweak [twi:k] *vt* (*nose, ear*) pellizcar; (*hair*) tirar.
tweed [twi:d] *n* tweed *m*.
tweezers ['twi:zəz] *npl* pinzas *fpl* (de depilar).
twelfth [twɛlfθ] *num* duodécimo.
Twelfth Night *n* (Día *m* de) Reyes *mpl*.
twelve [twɛlv] *num* doce; **at ~ o'clock** (*midday*) a mediodía; (*midnight*) a medianoche.
twentieth ['twɛntɪɪθ] *num* vigésimo.
twenty ['twɛntɪ] *num* veinte.
twerp [twə:p] *n* (*col*) idiota *m/f*.
twice [twaɪs] *adv* dos veces; **~ as much** dos veces más, el doble; **she is ~ your age** ella te dobla edad; **~ a week** dos veces a la *or* por semana.
twiddle ['twɪdl] *vt, vi*: **to ~ (with) sth** dar vueltas a algo; **to ~ one's thumbs** (*fig*) estar de brazos cruzados.
twig [twɪg] *n* ramita ♦ *vi* (*col*) caer en la cuenta.
twilight ['twaɪlaɪt] *n* crepúsculo; (*morning*) madrugada; **in the ~** en la media luz.
twill [twɪl] *n* sarga, estameña.
twin [twɪn] *adj, n* gemelo/a *m/f* ♦ *vt* hermanar.
twin(-bedded) room ['twɪn('bɛdɪd)-] *n* habitación *f* con dos camas.
twin beds *npl* camas *fpl* gemelas.
twin-carburettor ['twɪnkɑ:bju'rɛtə*] *adj* de dos carburadores.
twine [twaɪn] *n* bramante *m* ♦ *vi* (*plant*) enroscarse.
twin-engined [twɪn'ɛndʒɪnd] *adj* bimotor; **~ aircraft** avión *m* bimotor.
twinge [twɪndʒ] *n* (*of pain*) punzada; (*of conscience*) remordimiento.
twinkle ['twɪŋkl] *n* centelleo ♦ *vi* centellear; (*eyes*) parpadear.
twin town *n* ciudad *f* hermanada *or*

gemela.
twirl [twəːl] *n* giro ♦ *vt* dar vueltas a ♦ *vi* piruetear.
twist [twɪst] *n* (*action*) torsión *f*; (*in road, coil*) vuelta; (*in wire, flex*) doblez *f*; (*in story*) giro ♦ *vt* torcer, retorcer; (*roll around*) enrollar; (*fig*) deformar ♦ *vi* serpentear; **to ~ one's ankle/wrist** (*MED*) torcerse el tobillo/la muñeca.
twisted ['twɪstɪd] *adj* (*wire, rope*) trenzado, enroscado; (*ankle, wrist*) torcido; (*fig: logic, mind*) retorcido.
twit [twɪt] *n* (*col*) tonto.
twitch [twɪtʃ] *n* sacudida; (*nervous*) tic *m* nervioso ♦ *vi* moverse nerviosamente.
two [tuː] *num* dos; **~ by ~, in ~s** de dos en dos; **to put ~ and ~ together** (*fig*) atar cabos.
two-bit [tuː'bɪt] *adj* (*esp US col, pej*) de poca monta, de tres al cuarto.
two-door [tuː'dɔː*] *adj* (*AUT*) de dos puertas.
two-faced [tuː'feɪst] *adj* (*pej: person*) falso, hipócrita.
twofold ['tuːfəuld] *adv*: **to increase ~** duplicarse ♦ *adj* (*increase*) doble; (*reply*) en dos partes.
two-piece [tuː'piːs] *n* (*also*: **~ suit**) traje *m* de dos piezas; (*also*: **~ swimsuit**) dos piezas *m inv*, bikini *m*.
two-seater [tuː'siːtə*] *n* (*plane, car*) avión *m*/coche *m* de dos plazas, biplaza *m*.
twosome ['tuːsəm] *n* (*people*) pareja.
two-stroke ['tuːstrəuk] *n* (*also*: **~ engine**) motor *m* de dos tiempos ♦ *adj* de dos tiempos.
two-tone ['tuː'təun] *adj* (*colour*) bicolor, de dos tonos.
two-way ['tuːweɪ] *adj*: **~ traffic** circulación *f* de dos sentidos; **~ radio** radio *f* emisora y receptora.
TX *abbr* (*US*) = *Texas*.
tycoon [taɪ'kuːn] *n*: **(business) ~** magnate *m/f*.
type [taɪp] *n* (*category*) tipo, género; (*model*) modelo; (*TYP*) tipo, letra ♦ *vt* (*letter etc*) escribir a máquina; **what ~ do you want?** ¿qué tipo quieres?; **in bold/italic ~** en negrita/cursiva.
type-cast ['taɪpkɑːst] *adj* (*actor*) encasillado.
typeface ['taɪpfeɪs] *n* tipo de letra.
typescript ['taɪpskrɪpt] *n* texto mecanografiado.
typeset ['taɪpsɛt] *vt* (*irreg: like* **set**) componer.
typesetter ['taɪpsɛtə*] *n* cajista *m/f*.
typewriter ['taɪpraɪtə*] *n* máquina de escribir.
typewritten ['taɪprɪtn] *adj* mecanografiado.
typhoid ['taɪfɔɪd] *n* (fiebre *f*) tifoidea.
typhoon [taɪ'fuːn] *n* tifón *m*.
typhus ['taɪfəs] *n* tifus *m*.
typical ['tɪpɪkl] *adj* típico.
typically ['tɪpɪklɪ] *adv* típicamente.
typify ['tɪpɪfaɪ] *vt* tipificar.
typing ['taɪpɪŋ] *n* mecanografía.
typing pool *n* (*BRIT*) servicio de mecanógrafos.
typist ['taɪpɪst] *n* mecanógrafo/a.
typography [taɪ'pɔgrəfɪ] *n* tipografía.
tyranny ['tɪrənɪ] *n* tiranía.
tyrant ['taɪərənt] *n* tirano/a.
tyre, (*US*) **tire** ['taɪə*] *n* neumático, llanta (*LAM*).
tyre pressure *n* presión *f* de los neumáticos.
Tyrol [tɪ'rəul] *n* Tirol *m*.
Tyrolean [tɪrə'lɪən], **Tyrolese** [tɪrə'liːz] *adj* tirolés/esa.
Tyrrhenian Sea [tɪ'riːnɪən-] *n* Mar *m* Tirreno.
tzar [zɑː*] *n* = **tsar**.

U u

U, u [juː] *n* (*letter*) U, u *f*; **U for Uncle** U de Uruguay.
U *n abbr* (*BRIT CINE*: = *universal*) todos los públicos.
UB40 *n abbr* (*BRIT*: = *unemployment benefit form 40*) *número de referencia en la solicitud de inscripción en la lista de parados; por extensión, la tarjeta del paro o su beneficiario.*
U-bend ['juːbɛnd] *n* (*AUT, in pipe*) recodo.
ubiquitous [juː'bɪkwɪtəs] *adj* omnipresente, ubicuo.
UCAS ['juːkæs] *n abbr BRIT*: = *Universities and Colleges Admissions Service*.
UDA *n abbr* (*BRIT*: = *Ulster Defence Association*) *organización paramilitar protestante de Irlanda del Norte.*
UDC *n abbr* (*BRIT*) = *Urban District Council*.
udder ['ʌdə*] *n* ubre *f*.
UDI *n abbr* (*BRIT POL*) = *unilateral declaration of independence*.
UDR *n abbr* (*BRIT*: = *Ulster Defence Regiment*) *fuerza de seguridad de Irlanda del Norte.*

UEFA [juː'eɪfə] *n abbr* (= *Union of European Football Associations*) U.E.F.A. *f*.
UFO ['juːfəu] *n abbr* = (*unidentified flying object*) OVNI *m*.
Uganda [juː'gændə] *n* Uganda.
Ugandan [juː'gændən] *adj* de Uganda.
UGC *n abbr* (*BRIT*: = *University Grants Committee*) *entidad gubernamental que controla las finanzas de las universidades*.
ugh [əːh] *excl* ¡uf!
ugliness ['ʌglɪnɪs] *n* fealdad *f*.
ugly ['ʌglɪ] *adj* feo; (*dangerous*) peligroso.
UHF *abbr* (= *ultra-high frequency*) UHF *f*.
UHT *adj abbr* (= *ultra heat treated*): ~ **milk** leche *f* uperizada.
UK *n abbr* (= *United Kingdom*) Reino Unido, R.U.
Ukraine [juː'kreɪn] *n* Ucrania.
Ukrainian [juː'kreɪnɪən] *adj* ucraniano ♦ *n* ucraniano/a; (*LING*) ucraniano.
ulcer ['ʌlsə*] *n* úlcera; **mouth** ~ úlcera bucal.
Ulster ['ʌlstə*] *n* Ulster *m*.
ulterior [ʌl'tɪərɪə*] *adj* ulterior; ~ **motive** segundas intenciones *fpl*.
ultimate ['ʌltɪmət] *adj* último, final; (*greatest*) mayor ♦ *n*: **the** ~ **in luxury** el colmo del lujo.
ultimately ['ʌltɪmətlɪ] *adv* (*in the end*) por último, al final; (*fundamentally*) a fin de cuentas.
ultimatum, *pl* ~**s** *or* **ultimata** [ʌltɪ'meɪtəm, -tə] *n* ultimátum *m*.
ultra- ['ʌltrə] *pref* ultra-.
ultrasonic [ʌltrə'sɔnɪk] *adj* ultrasónico.
ultrasound ['ʌltrəsaund] *n* (*MED*) ultrasonido.
ultraviolet ['ʌltrə'vaɪəlɪt] *adj* ultravioleta.
um [ʌm] *interj*; (*col*: *in hesitation*) esto, este (*LAM*).
umbilical cord [ʌmbɪ'laɪkl-] *n* cordón *m* umbilical.
umbrage ['ʌmbrɪdʒ] *n*: **to take** ~ **(at)** ofenderse (por).
umbrella [ʌm'brɛlə] *n* paraguas *m inv*; **under the** ~ **of** (*fig*) bajo la protección de.
umlaut ['umlaut] *n* diéresis *f inv*.
umpire ['ʌmpaɪə*] *n* árbitro ♦ *vt* arbitrar.
umpteen [ʌmp'tiːn] *num* enésimos/as; **for the** ~**th time** por enésima vez.
UMW *n abbr* (= *United Mineworkers of America*) *sindicato de mineros*.
UN *n abbr* (= *United Nations*) ONU *f*.
un- [ʌn] *pref* in-; des-; no ...; poco ...; nada ....
unabashed [ʌnə'bæʃt] *adj* nada avergonzado.
unabated [ʌnə'beɪtɪd] *adj*: **to continue** ~ seguir con la misma intensidad.
unable [ʌn'eɪbl] *adj*: **to be** ~ **to do sth** no poder hacer algo; (*not know how to*) ser incapaz de hacer algo, no saber hacer algo.
unabridged [ʌnə'brɪdʒd] *adj* íntegro.
unacceptable [ʌnək'sɛptəbl] *adj* (*proposal, behaviour, price*) inaceptable; **it's** ~ **that** no se puede aceptar que.
unaccompanied [ʌnə'kʌmpənɪd] *adj* no acompañado; (*singing, song*) sin acompañamiento.
unaccountably [ʌnə'kauntəblɪ] *adv* inexplicablemente.
unaccounted [ʌnə'kauntɪd] *adj*: **two passengers are** ~ **for** faltan dos pasajeros.
unaccustomed [ʌnə'kʌstəmd] *adj*: **to be** ~ **to** no estar acostumbrado a.
unacquainted [ʌnə'kweɪntɪd] *adj*: **to be** ~ **with** (*facts*) desconocer, ignorar.
unadulterated [ʌnə'dʌltəreɪtɪd] *adj* (*gen*) puro; (*wine*) sin mezcla.
unaffected [ʌnə'fɛktɪd] *adj* (*person, behaviour*) sin afectación, sencillo; (*emotionally*): **to be** ~ **by** no estar afectado por.
unafraid [ʌnə'freɪd] *adj*: **to be** ~ no tener miedo.
unaided [ʌn'eɪdɪd] *adj* sin ayuda, por sí solo.
unanimity [juːnə'nɪmɪtɪ] *n* unanimidad *f*.
unanimous [juː'nænɪməs] *adj* unánime.
unanimously [juː'nænɪməslɪ] *adv* unánimemente.
unanswered [ʌn'ɑːnsəd] *adj* (*question, letter*) sin contestar; (*criticism*) incontestado.
unappetizing [ʌn'æpɪtaɪzɪŋ] *adj* poco apetitoso.
unappreciative [ʌnə'priːʃɪətɪv] *adj* desagradecido.
unarmed [ʌn'ɑːmd] *adj* (*person*) desarmado; (*combat*) sin armas.
unashamed [ʌnə'ʃeɪmd] *adj* desvergonzado.
unassisted [ʌnə'sɪstɪd] *adj, adv* sin ayuda.
unassuming [ʌnə'sjuːmɪŋ] *adj* modesto, sin pretensiones.
unattached [ʌnə'tætʃt] *adj* (*person*) soltero; (*part etc*) suelto.
unattended [ʌnə'tɛndɪd] *adj* (*car, luggage*) sin atender.
unattractive [ʌnə'træktɪv] *adj* poco atractivo.
unauthorized [ʌn'ɔːθəraɪzd] *adj* no autorizado.
unavailable [ʌnə'veɪləbl] *adj* (*article, room,*

book) no disponible; (*person*) ocupado.
unavoidable [ʌnə'vɔɪdəbl] *adj* inevitable.
unavoidably [ʌnə'vɔɪdəblɪ] *adv* (*detained*) por causas ajenas a su voluntad.
unaware [ʌnə'wɛə*] *adj*: **to be ~ of** ignorar.
unawares [ʌnə'wɛəz] *adv* de improviso.
unbalanced [ʌn'bælənst] *adj* desequilibrado; (*mentally*) trastornado.
unbearable [ʌn'bɛərəbl] *adj* insoportable.
unbeatable [ʌn'bi:təbl] *adj* (*gen*) invencible; (*price*) inmejorable.
unbeaten [ʌn'bi:tn] *adj* (*team*) imbatido; (*army*) invicto; (*record*) no batido.
unbecoming [ʌnbɪ'kʌmɪŋ] *adj* (*unseemly*: *language, behaviour*) indecoroso, impropio; (*unflattering*: *garment*) poco favorecedor(a).
unbeknown(st) [ʌnbɪ'nəun(st)] *adv*: **~ to me** sin saberlo yo.
unbelief [ʌnbɪ'li:f] *n* incredulidad *f*.
unbelievable [ʌnbɪ'li:vəbl] *adj* increíble.
unbelievingly [ʌnbɪ'li:vɪŋlɪ] *adv* sin creer.
unbend [ʌn'bɛnd] (*irreg*: *like* **bend**) *vi* (*fig*: *person*) relajarse ♦ *vt* (*wire*) enderezar.
unbending [ʌn'bɛndɪŋ] *adj* (*fig*) inflexible.
unbias(s)ed [ʌn'baɪəst] *adj* imparcial.
unblemished [ʌn'blɛmɪʃt] *adj* sin mancha.
unblock [ʌn'blɔk] *vt* (*pipe*) desatascar; (*road*) despejar.
unborn [ʌn'bɔ:n] *adj* que va a nacer.
unbounded [ʌn'baundɪd] *adj* ilimitado, sin límite.
unbreakable [ʌn'breɪkəbl] *adj* irrompible.
unbridled [ʌn'braɪdld] *adj* (*fig*) desenfrenado.
unbroken [ʌn'brəukən] *adj* (*seal*) intacto; (*series*) continuo, ininterrumpido; (*record*) no batido; (*spirit*) indómito.
unbuckle [ʌn'bʌkl] *vt* desabrochar.
unburden [ʌn'bə:dn] *vt*: **to ~ o.s.** desahogarse.
unbusinesslike [ʌn'bɪznɪslaɪk] *adj* (*trader*) poco profesional; (*transaction*) incorrecto; (*fig*: *person*) poco práctico; (: *without method*) desorganizado.
unbutton [ʌn'bʌtn] *vt* desabrochar.
uncalled-for [ʌn'kɔ:ldfɔ:*] *adj* gratuito, inmerecido.
uncanny [ʌn'kænɪ] *adj* extraño, extraordinario.
unceasing [ʌn'si:sɪŋ] *adj* incesante.
unceremonious ['ʌnsɛrɪ'məunɪəs] *adj* (*abrupt, rude*) brusco, hosco.
uncertain [ʌn'sə:tn] *adj* incierto; (*indecisive*) indeciso; **it's ~ whether** no se sabe si; **in no ~ terms** sin dejar lugar a dudas.
uncertainty [ʌn'sə:tntɪ] *n* incertidumbre *f*.
unchallenged [ʌn'tʃælɪndʒd] *adj* (*LAW etc*) incontestado; **to go ~** no encontrar respuesta.
unchanged [ʌn'tʃeɪndʒd] *adj* sin cambiar *or* alterar.
uncharitable [ʌn'tʃærɪtəbl] *adj* (*remark, behaviour*) demasiado duro.
uncharted [ʌn'tʃɑ:tɪd] *adj* inexplorado.
unchecked [ʌn'tʃɛkt] *adj* desenfrenado.
uncivil [ʌn'sɪvɪl] *adj* descortés, grosero.
uncivilized [ʌn'sɪvɪlaɪzd] *adj* (*gen*) inculto, poco civilizado; (*fig*: *behaviour etc*) bárbaro.
uncle ['ʌŋkl] *n* tío.
unclear [ʌn'klɪə*] *adj* poco claro; **I'm still ~ about what I'm supposed to do** todavía no tengo muy claro lo que tengo que hacer.
uncoil [ʌn'kɔɪl] *vt* desenrollar ♦ *vi* desenrollarse.
uncomfortable [ʌn'kʌmfətəbl] *adj* incómodo; (*uneasy*) inquieto.
uncomfortably [ʌn'kʌmfətəblɪ] *adv* (*uneasily*: *say*) con inquietud; (: *think*) con remordimiento *or* nerviosismo.
uncommitted [ʌnkə'mɪtɪd] *adj* (*attitude, country*) no comprometido; **to remain ~ to** (*policy, party*) no comprometerse a.
uncommon [ʌn'kɔmən] *adj* poco común, raro.
uncommunicative [ʌnkə'mju:nɪkətɪv] *adj* poco comunicativo, reservado.
uncomplicated [ʌn'kɔmplɪkeɪtɪd] *adj* sin complicaciones.
uncompromising [ʌn'kɔmprəmaɪzɪŋ] *adj* intransigente.
unconcerned [ʌnkən'sə:nd] *adj* indiferente; **to be ~ about** ser indiferente a, no preocuparse de.
unconditional [ʌnkən'dɪʃənl] *adj* incondicional.
uncongenial [ʌnkən'dʒi:nɪəl] *adj* desagradable.
unconnected [ʌnkə'nɛktɪd] *adj* (*unrelated*): **to be ~ with** no estar relacionado con.
unconscious [ʌn'kɔnʃəs] *adj* sin sentido; (*unaware*) inconsciente ♦ *n*: **the ~** el inconsciente; **to knock sb ~** dejar a algn sin sentido.
unconsciously [ʌn'kɔnʃəslɪ] *adv* inconscientemente.
unconsciousness [ʌn'kɔnʃəsnɪs] *n* inconsciencia.
unconstitutional [ʌnkɔnstɪ'tju:ʃənl] *adj* anti-constitucional.
uncontested [ʌnkən'tɛstɪd] *adj* (*champion*) incontestado; (*PARLIAMENT*: *seat*) ganado sin oposición.
uncontrollable [ʌnkən'trəuləbl] *adj* (*temper*)

indomable; (*laughter*) incontenible.
uncontrolled [ʌnkən'trəuld] *adj* (*child, dog, emotion*) incontrolado; (*inflation, price rises*) desenfrenado.
unconventional [ʌnkən'vɛnʃənl] *adj* poco convencional.
unconvinced [ʌnkən'vɪnst] *adj*: **to be** *or* **remain ~** seguir sin convencerse.
unconvincing [ʌnkən'vɪnsɪŋ] *adj* poco convincente.
uncork [ʌn'kɔːk] *vt* descorchar.
uncorroborated [ʌnkə'rɔbəreɪtɪd] *adj* no confirmado.
uncouth [ʌn'kuːθ] *adj* grosero, inculto.
uncover [ʌn'kʌvə*] *vt* (*gen*) descubrir; (*take lid off*) destapar.
undamaged [ʌn'dæmɪdʒd] *adj* (*goods*) en buen estado; (*fig: reputation*) intacto.
undaunted [ʌn'dɔːntɪd] *adj*: **~ by** sin dejarse desanimar por.
undecided [ʌndɪ'saɪdɪd] *adj* (*character*) indeciso; (*question*) no resuelto, pendiente.
undelivered [ʌndɪ'lɪvəd] *adj* no entregado al destinatario; **if ~ return to sender** en caso de no llegar a su destino devolver al remitente.
undeniable [ʌndɪ'naɪəbl] *adj* innegable.
undeniably [ʌndɪ'naɪəblɪ] *adv* innegablemente.
under ['ʌndə*] *prep* debajo de; (*less than*) menos de; (*according to*) según, de acuerdo con ♦ *adv* debajo, abajo; **~ there** ahí debajo; **~ construction** en construcción; en obras; **~ the circumstances** dadas las circunstancias; **in ~ 2 hours** en menos de dos horas; **~ anaesthetic** bajo los efectos de la anestesia; **~ discussion** en discusión, sobre el tapete.
under... [ʌndə*] *pref* sub....
under-age [ʌndər'eɪdʒ] *adj* menor de edad.
underarm ['ʌndərɑːm] *n* axila, sobaco ♦ *cpd*: **~ deodorant** desodorante *m* corporal.
undercapitalised [ʌndə'kæpɪtəlaɪzd] *adj* descapitalizado.
undercarriage ['ʌndəkærɪdʒ] *n* (*BRIT AVIAT*) tren *m* de aterrizaje.
undercharge [ʌndə'tʃɑːdʒ] *vt* cobrar de menos.
underclass ['ʌndəklɑːs] *n* clase *f* marginada.
underclothes ['ʌndəkləuðz] *npl* ropa *sg* interior *or* íntima (*LAM*).
undercoat ['ʌndəkəut] *n* (*paint*) primera mano.
undercover [ʌndə'kʌvə*] *adj* clandestino.
undercurrent ['ʌndəkʌrnt] *n* corriente *f* submarina; (*fig*) tendencia oculta.
undercut ['ʌndəkʌt] *vt* (*irreg: like* **cut**) vender más barato que; fijar un precio más barato que.
underdeveloped [ʌndədɪ'vɛləpt] *adj* subdesarrollado.
underdog ['ʌndədɔg] *n* desvalido/a.
underdone [ʌndə'dʌn] *adj* (*CULIN*) poco hecho.
underemployment [ʌndərɪm'plɔɪmənt] *n* subempleo.
underestimate [ʌndər'ɛstɪmeɪt] *vt* subestimar.
underexposed [ʌndərɪks'pəuzd] *adj* (*PHOT*) subexpuesto.
underfed [ʌndə'fɛd] *adj* subalimentado.
underfoot [ʌndə'fut] *adv*: **it's wet ~** el suelo está mojado.
underfunded [ʌndə'fʌndɪd] *adj* infradotado (económicamente).
undergo [ʌndə'gəu] *vt* (*irreg: like* **go**) sufrir; (*treatment*) recibir, someterse a; **the car is ~ing repairs** están reparando el coche.
undergraduate ['ʌndə'grædjuət] *n* estudiante *m/f* ♦ *cpd*: **~ courses** cursos *mpl* de licenciatura.
underground ['ʌndəgraund] *n* (*BRIT: railway*) metro; (*POL*) movimiento clandestino ♦ *adj* subterráneo.
undergrowth ['ʌndəgrəuθ] *n* maleza.
underhand(ed) [ʌndə'hænd(ɪd)] *adj* (*fig*) poco limpio.
underinsured [ʌndərɪn'ʃuəd] *adj* insuficientemente asegurado.
underlie [ʌndə'laɪ] *vt* (*irreg: like* **lie**) (*fig*) ser la razón fundamental de; **the underlying cause** la causa fundamental.
underline [ʌndə'laɪn] *vt* subrayar.
underling ['ʌndəlɪŋ] *n* (*pej*) subalterno/a.
undermanning [ʌndə'mænɪŋ] *n* falta de personal.
undermentioned [ʌndə'mɛnʃənd] *adj* abajo citado.
undermine [ʌndə'maɪn] *vt* socavar, minar.
underneath [ʌndə'niːθ] *adv* debajo ♦ *prep* debajo de, bajo.
undernourished [ʌndə'nʌrɪʃt] *adj* desnutrido.
underpaid [ʌndə'peɪd] *adj* mal pagado.
underpants ['ʌndəpænts] *npl* calzoncillos *mpl*.
underpass ['ʌndəpɑːs] *n* (*BRIT*) paso subterráneo.
underpin [ʌndə'pɪn] *vt* (*argument, case*) secundar, sostener.
underplay [ʌndə'pleɪ] *vt* (*BRIT*) minimizar.
underpopulated [ʌndə'pɔpjuleɪtɪd] *adj* poco poblado.

underprice [ʌndə'praɪs] *vt* vender demasiado barato.
underpriced [ʌndə'praɪst] *adj* con precio demasiado bajo.
underprivileged [ʌndə'prɪvɪlɪdʒd] *adj* desvalido.
underrate [ʌndə'reɪt] *vt* infravalorar, subestimar.
underscore ['ʌndəskɔː*] *vt* subrayar, sostener.
underseal [ʌndə'siːl] *vt* (*AUT*) proteger contra la corrosión.
undersecretary [ʌndə'sɛkrətrɪ] *n* subsecretario/a.
undersell [ʌndə'sɛl] *vt* (*competitors*) vender más barato que.
undershirt ['ʌndəʃəːt] *n* (*US*) camiseta.
undershorts ['ʌndəʃɔːts] *npl* (*US*) calzoncillos *mpl*.
underside ['ʌndəsaɪd] *n* parte *f* inferior, revés *m*.
undersigned ['ʌndəsaɪnd] *adj, n*: **the ~** el/la *etc* abajo firmante.
underskirt ['ʌndəskəːt] *n* (*BRIT*) enaguas *fpl*.
understaffed [ʌndə'stɑːft] *adj* falto de personal.
understand [ʌndə'stænd] (*irreg*: *like* **stand**) *vt, vi* entender, comprender; (*assume*) tener entendido; **to make o.s. understood** hacerse entender; **I ~ you have been absent** tengo entendido que (usted) ha estado ausente.
understandable [ʌndə'stændəbl] *adj* comprensible.
understanding [ʌndə'stændɪŋ] *adj* comprensivo ♦ *n* comprensión *f*, entendimiento; (*agreement*) acuerdo; **to come to an ~ with sb** llegar a un acuerdo con algn; **on the ~ that** a condición de que (+ *subjun*).
understate [ʌndə'steɪt] *vt* minimizar.
understatement [ʌndə'steɪtmənt] *n* subestimación *f*; (*modesty*) modestia (excesiva); **to say it was good is quite an ~** decir que estuvo bien es quedarse corto.
understood [ʌndə'stud] *pt, pp of* **understand** ♦ *adj* entendido; (*implied*): **it is ~ that** se sobreentiende que.
understudy ['ʌndəstʌdɪ] *n* suplente *m/f*.
undertake [ʌndə'teɪk] (*irreg*: *like* **take**) *vt* emprender; **to ~ to do sth** comprometerse a hacer algo.
undertaker ['ʌndəteɪkə*] *n* director(a) *m/f* de pompas fúnebres.
undertaking ['ʌndəteɪkɪŋ] *n* empresa; (*promise*) promesa.
undertone ['ʌndətəun] *n* (*of criticism*) connotación *f*; (*low voice*): **in an ~** en voz baja.
undervalue [ʌndə'væljuː] *vt* (*fig*) subestimar, infravalorar; (*COMM etc*) valorizar por debajo de su precio.
underwater [ʌndə'wɔːtə*] *adv* bajo el agua ♦ *adj* submarino.
underwear ['ʌndəwɛə*] *n* ropa interior *or* íntima (*LAM*).
underweight [ʌndə'weɪt] *adj* de peso insuficiente; (*person*) demasiado delgado.
underworld ['ʌndəwəːld] *n* (*of crime*) hampa, inframundo.
underwrite [ʌndə'raɪt] (*irreg*: *like* **write**) *vt* (*COMM*) suscribir; (*INSURANCE*) asegurar (*contra riesgos*).
underwriter ['ʌndəraɪtə*] *n* (*INSURANCE*) asegurador/a *m/f*.
undeserving [ʌndɪ'zəːvɪŋ] *adj*: **to be ~ of** no ser digno de.
undesirable [ʌndɪ'zaɪərəbl] *adj* indeseable.
undeveloped [ʌndɪ'vɛləpt] *adj* (*land, resources*) sin explotar.
undies ['ʌndɪz] *npl* (*col*) paños *mpl* menores.
undiluted [ʌndaɪ'luːtɪd] *adj* (*concentrate*) concentrado.
undiplomatic [ʌndɪplə'mætɪk] *adj* poco diplomático.
undischarged [ʌndɪs'tʃɑːdʒd] *adj*: **~ bankrupt** quebrado/a no rehabilitado/a.
undisciplined [ʌn'dɪsɪplɪnd] *adj* indisciplinado.
undiscovered [ʌndɪs'kʌvəd] *adj* no descubierto; (*unknown*) desconocido.
undisguised [ʌndɪs'gaɪzd] *adj* franco, abierto.
undisputed [ʌndɪ'spjuːtɪd] *adj* incontestable.
undistinguished [ʌndɪs'tɪŋgwɪʃt] *adj* mediocre.
undisturbed [ʌndɪs'təːbd] *adj* (*sleep*) ininterrumpido; **to leave sth ~** dejar algo tranquilo *or* como está.
undivided [ʌndɪ'vaɪdɪd] *adj*: **I want your ~ attention** quiero su completa atención.
undo [ʌn'duː] *vt* (*irreg*: *like* **do**) deshacer.
undoing [ʌn'duːɪŋ] *n* ruina, perdición *f*.
undone [ʌn'dʌn] *pp of* **undo** ♦ *adj*: **to come ~** (*clothes*) desabrocharse; (*parcel*) desatarse.
undoubted [ʌn'dautɪd] *adj* indudable.
undoubtedly [ʌn'dautɪdlɪ] *adv* indudablemente, sin duda.
undress [ʌn'drɛs] *vi* desnudarse, desvestirse (*esp LAM*).
undrinkable [ʌn'drɪŋkəbl] *adj* (*unpalatable*) imbebible; (*poisonous*) no potable.
undue [ʌn'djuː] *adj* indebido, excesivo.

undulating ['ʌndjuleɪtɪŋ] *adj* ondulante.
unduly [ʌn'djuːlɪ] *adv* excesivamente, demasiado.
undying [ʌn'daɪɪŋ] *adj* eterno.
unearned [ʌn'əːnd] *adj* (*praise, respect*) inmerecido; ~ **income** ingresos *mpl* no ganados, renta no ganada *or* salarial.
unearth [ʌn'əːθ] *vt* desenterrar.
unearthly [ʌn'əːθlɪ] *adj*: ~ **hour** (*col*) hora intempestiva.
unease [ʌn'iːz] *n* malestar *m*.
uneasy [ʌn'iːzɪ] *adj* intranquilo; (*worried*) preocupado; **to feel ~ about doing sth** sentirse incómodo con la idea de hacer algo.
uneconomic(al) ['ʌniːkə'nɔmɪk(l)] *adj* no económico.
uneducated [ʌn'ɛdjukeɪtɪd] *adj* ignorante, inculto.
unemployed [ʌnɪm'plɔɪd] *adj* parado, sin trabajo ♦ *n*: **the ~** los parados.
unemployment [ʌnɪm'plɔɪmənt] *n* paro, desempleo, cesantía (*LAM*).
unemployment benefit *n* (*BRIT*) subsidio de desempleo *or* paro.
unending [ʌn'ɛndɪŋ] *adj* interminable.
unenviable [ʌn'ɛnvɪəbl] *adj* poco envidiable.
unequal [ʌn'iːkwəl] *adj* (*length, objects etc*) desigual; (*amounts*) distinto; (*division of labour*) poco justo.
unequalled, (*US*) **unequaled** [ʌn'iːkwəld] *adj* inigualado, sin par.
unequivocal [ʌnɪ'kwɪvəkəl] *adj* (*answer*) inequívoco, claro; (*person*) claro.
unerring [ʌn'əːrɪŋ] *adj* infalible.
UNESCO [juː'nɛskəu] *n abbr* (= *United Nations Educational, Scientific and Cultural Organization*) UNESCO *f*.
unethical [ʌn'ɛθɪkəl] *adj* (*methods*) inmoral; (*doctor's behaviour*) que infringe la ética profesional.
uneven [ʌn'iːvn] *adj* desigual; (*road etc*) con baches.
uneventful [ʌnɪ'vɛntful] *adj* sin incidentes.
unexceptional [ʌnɪk'sɛpʃənl] *adj* sin nada de extraordinario, corriente.
unexciting [ʌnɪk'saɪtɪŋ] *adj* (*news*) sin interés; (*film, evening*) aburrido.
unexpected [ʌnɪk'spɛktɪd] *adj* inesperado.
unexpectedly [ʌnɪk'spɛktɪdlɪ] *adv* inesperadamente.
unexplained [ʌnɪks'pleɪnd] *adj* inexplicado.
unexploded [ʌnɪks'pləudɪd] *adj* sin explotar.
unfailing [ʌn'feɪlɪŋ] *adj* (*support*) indefectible; (*energy*) inagotable.
unfair [ʌn'fɛə*] *adj*: ~ **(to sb)** injusto (con algn); **it's ~ that ...** es injusto que ..., no es justo que ....
unfair dismissal *n* despido improcedente.
unfairly [ʌn'fɛəlɪ] *adv* injustamente.
unfaithful [ʌn'feɪθful] *adj* infiel.
unfamiliar [ʌnfə'mɪlɪə*] *adj* extraño, desconocido; **to be ~ with sth** desconocer *or* ignorar algo.
unfashionable [ʌn'fæʃnəbl] *adj* (*clothes*) pasado *or* fuera de moda; (*district*) poco elegante.
unfasten [ʌn'fɑːsn] *vt* desatar.
unfathomable [ʌn'fæðəməbl] *adj* insondable.
unfavourable, (*US*) **unfavorable** [ʌn'feɪvərəbl] *adj* desfavorable.
unfavo(u)rably [ʌn'feɪvrəblɪ] *adv*: **to look ~ upon** ser adverso a.
unfeeling [ʌn'fiːlɪŋ] *adj* insensible.
unfinished [ʌn'fɪnɪʃt] *adj* inacabado, sin terminar.
unfit [ʌn'fɪt] *adj* en baja forma; (*incompetent*) incapaz; ~ **for work** no apto para trabajar.
unflagging [ʌn'flægɪŋ] *adj* incansable.
unflappable [ʌn'flæpəbl] *adj* imperturbable.
unflattering [ʌn'flætərɪŋ] *adj* (*dress, hairstyle*) poco favorecedor.
unflinching [ʌn'flɪntʃɪŋ] *adj* impávido.
unfold [ʌn'fəuld] *vt* desdoblar; (*fig*) revelar ♦ *vi* abrirse; revelarse.
unforeseeable [ʌnfɔː'siːəbl] *adj* imprevisible.
unforeseen ['ʌnfɔː'siːn] *adj* imprevisto.
unforgettable [ʌnfə'gɛtəbl] *adj* inolvidable.
unforgivable [ʌnfə'gɪvəbl] *adj* imperdonable.
unformatted [ʌn'fɔːmætɪd] *adj* (*disk, text*) sin formatear.
unfortunate [ʌn'fɔːtʃnət] *adj* desgraciado; (*event, remark*) inoportuno.
unfortunately [ʌn'fɔːtʃnətlɪ] *adv* desgraciadamente, por desgracia.
unfounded [ʌn'faundɪd] *adj* infundado.
unfriendly [ʌn'frɛndlɪ] *adj* antipático.
unfulfilled [ʌnful'fɪld] *adj* (*ambition*) sin realizar; (*prophecy, promise, terms of contract*) incumplido; (*desire, person*) insatisfecho.
unfurl [ʌn'fəːl] *vt* desplegar.
unfurnished [ʌn'fəːnɪʃt] *adj* sin amueblar.
ungainly [ʌn'geɪnlɪ] *adj* (*walk*) desgarbado.
ungodly [ʌn'gɔdlɪ] *adj*: **at an ~ hour** a una hora intempestiva.
ungrateful [ʌn'greɪtful] *adj* ingrato.
unguarded [ʌn'gɑːdɪd] *adj* (*moment*) de descuido.

unhappily [ʌn'hæpɪlɪ] *adv* (*unfortunately*) desgraciadamente.
unhappiness [ʌn'hæpɪnɪs] *n* tristeza.
unhappy [ʌn'haepɪ] *adj* (*sad*) triste; (*unfortunate*) desgraciado; (*childhood*) infeliz; ~ **with** (*arrangements etc*) poco contento con, descontento de.
unharmed [ʌn'hɑːmd] *adj* (*person*) ileso.
UNHCR *n abbr* (= *United Nations High Commission for Refugees*) ACNUR *m*.
unhealthy [ʌn'hɛlθɪ] *adj* (*gen*) malsano, insalubre; (*person*) enfermizo; (*interest*) morboso.
unheard-of [ʌn'həːdɔv] *adj* inaudito, sin precedente.
unhelpful [ʌn'hɛlpful] *adj* (*person*) poco servicial; (*advice*) inútil.
unhesitating [ʌn'hɛzɪteɪtɪŋ] *adj* (*loyalty*) automático; (*reply, offer*) inmediato; (*person*) resuelto.
unholy [ʌn'həulɪ] *adj*: **an ~ alliance** una alianza nefasta; **he returned at an ~ hour** volvió a una hora intempestiva.
unhook [ʌn'huk] *vt* desenganchar; (*from wall*) descolgar; (*undo*) desabrochar.
unhurt [ʌn'həːt] *adj* ileso.
unhygienic [ʌnhaɪ'dʒiːnɪk] *adj* antihigiénico.
UNICEF ['juːnɪsɛf] *n abbr* (= *United Nations International Children's Emergency Fund*) UNICEF *f*.
unidentified [ʌnaɪ'dɛntɪfaɪd] *adj* no identificado; ~ **flying object (UFO)** objeto volante no identificado.
unification [juːnɪfɪ'keɪʃən] *n* unificación *f*.
uniform ['juːnɪfɔːm] *n* uniforme *m* ♦ *adj* uniforme.
uniformity [juːnɪ'fɔːmɪtɪ] *n* uniformidad *f*.
unify ['juːnɪfaɪ] *vt* unificar, unir.
unilateral [juːnɪ'lætərəl] *adj* unilateral.
unimaginable [ʌnɪ'mædʒɪnəbl] *adj* inconcebible, inimaginable.
unimaginative [ʌnɪ'mædʒɪnətɪv] *adj* falto de imaginación.
unimpaired [ʌnɪm'pɛəd] *adj* (*unharmed*) intacto; (*not lessened*) no disminuido; (*unaltered*) inalterado.
unimportant [ʌnɪm'pɔːtənt] *adj* sin importancia.
unimpressed [ʌnɪm'prɛst] *adj* poco impresionado.
uninhabited [ʌnɪn'hæbɪtɪd] *adj* desierto; (*country*) despoblado; (*house*) deshabitado, desocupado.
uninhibited [ʌnɪn'hɪbɪtɪd] *adj* nada cohibido, desinhibido.
uninjured [ʌn'ɪndʒəd] *adj* (*person*) ileso.
uninspiring [ʌnɪn'spaɪərɪŋ] *adj* anodino.
unintelligent [ʌnɪn'tɛlɪdʒənt] *adj* poco inteligente.
unintentional [ʌnɪn'tɛnʃənəl] *adj* involuntario.
unintentionally [ʌnɪn'tɛnʃnəlɪ] *adv* sin querer.
uninvited [ʌnɪn'vaɪtɪd] *adj* (*guest*) sin invitación.
uninviting [ʌnɪn'vaɪtɪŋ] *adj* (*place, offer*) poco atractivo; (*food*) poco apetecible.
union ['juːnjən] *n* unión *f*; (*also*: **trade ~**) sindicato ♦ *cpd* sindical; **the U~** (*US*) la Unión.
union card *n* carnet *m* de sindicato.
unionize ['juːnjənaɪz] *vt* sindicalizar.
Union Jack *n* bandera del Reino Unido.
Union of Soviet Socialist Republics (USSR) *n* Unión *f* de Repúblicas Socialistas Soviéticas.
union shop *n* (*US*) *empresa de afiliación sindical obligatoria*.
unique [juː'niːk] *adj* único.
unisex ['juːnɪsɛks] *adj* unisex.
Unison ['juːnɪsn] *n* (*trade union*) *gran sindicato de funcionarios*.
unison ['juːnɪsn] *n*: **in ~** en armonía.
unissued capital [ʌn'ɪʃuːd-] *n* capital *m* no emitido.
unit ['juːnɪt] *n* unidad *f*; (*team, squad*) grupo; **kitchen ~** módulo de cocina; **production ~** taller *m* de fabricación; **sink ~** fregadero.
unit cost *n* costo unitario.
unite [juː'naɪt] *vt* unir ♦ *vi* unirse.
united [juː'naɪtɪd] *adj* unido.
United Arab Emirates *npl* Emiratos *mpl* Árabes Unidos.
United Kingdom (UK) *n* Reino Unido.
United Nations (Organization) (UN, UNO) *n* Naciones Unidas *fpl* (ONU *f*).
United States (of America) (US, USA) *n* Estados Unidos *mpl* (de América) (EE.UU. *mpl*).
unit price *n* precio unitario.
unit trust *n* (*BRIT*) bono fiduciario.
unity ['juːnɪtɪ] *n* unidad *f*.
Univ. *abbr* = **university**.
universal [juːnɪ'vəːsl] *adj* universal.
universally [juːnɪ'vəːsəlɪ] *adv* universalmente.
universe ['juːnɪvəːs] *n* universo.
university [juːnɪ'vəːsɪtɪ] *n* universidad *f* ♦ *cpd* (*student, professor, education, degree*) universitario; (*year*) académico; **to be at/go to ~** estudiar en/ir a la universidad.
unjust [ʌn'dʒʌst] *adj* injusto.
unjustifiable [ʌndʒʌstɪ'faɪəbl] *adj* injustificable.

unjustified [ʌn'dʒʌstɪfaɪd] *adj* (*text*) no alineado *or* justificado.
unkempt [ʌn'kɛmpt] *adj* descuidado; (*hair*) despeinado.
unkind [ʌn'kaɪnd] *adj* poco amable; (*comment etc*) cruel.
unkindly [ʌn'kaɪndlɪ] *adv* (*speak*) severamente; (*treat*) cruelmente, mal.
unknown [ʌn'nəun] *adj* desconocido ♦ *adv*: ~ **to me** sin saberlo yo; ~ **quantity** (*MATH, fig*) incógnita.
unladen [ʌn'leɪdən] *adj* (*weight*) vacío, sin cargamento.
unlawful [ʌn'lɔːful] *adj* ilegal, ilícito.
unleaded [ʌn'lɛdɪd] *n* (*also*: ~ **petrol**) gasolina sin plomo.
unleash [ʌn'liːʃ] *vt* desatar.
unleavened [ʌn'lɛvənd] *adj* ácimo, sin levadura.
unless [ʌn'lɛs] *conj* a menos que; ~ **he comes** a menos que venga; ~ **otherwise stated** salvo indicación contraria; ~ **I am mistaken** si no mi equivoco.
unlicensed [ʌn'laɪsənst] *adj* (*BRIT*: *to sell alcohol*) no autorizado.
unlike [ʌn'laɪk] *adj* distinto ♦ *prep* a diferencia de.
unlikelihood [ʌn'laɪklɪhud] *n* improbabilidad *f*.
unlikely [ʌn'laɪklɪ] *adj* improbable.
unlimited [ʌn'lɪmɪtɪd] *adj* ilimitado; ~ **liability** responsabilidad *f* ilimitada.
unlisted [ʌn'lɪstɪd] *adj* (*US TEL*) que no figura en la guía; ~ **company** empresa sin cotización en bolsa.
unlit [ʌn'lɪt] *adj* (*room*) oscuro, sin luz.
unload [ʌn'ləud] *vt* descargar.
unlock [ʌn'lɔk] *vt* abrir (con llave).
unlucky [ʌn'lʌkɪ] *adj* desgraciado; (*object, number*) que da mala suerte; **to be** ~ (*person*) tener mala suerte.
unmanageable [ʌn'mænɪdʒəbl] *adj* (*unwieldy*: *tool, vehicle*) difícil de manejar; (: *situation*) incontrolable.
unmanned [ʌn'mænd] *adj* (*spacecraft*) sin tripulación.
unmannerly [ʌn'mænəlɪ] *adj* mal educado, descortés.
unmarked [ʌn'mɑːkt] *adj* (*unstained*) sin mancha; ~ **police car** vehículo policial camuflado.
unmarried [ʌn'mærɪd] *adj* soltero.
unmask [ʌn'mɑːsk] *vt* desenmascarar.
unmatched [ʌn'mætʃt] *adj* incomparable.
unmentionable [ʌn'mɛnʃnəbl] *adj* (*topic, vice*) indecible; (*word*) que no se debe decir.
unmerciful [ʌn'məːsɪful] *adj* despiadado.
unmistakable [ʌnmɪs'teɪkəbl] *adj* inconfundible.
unmistakably [ʌnmɪs'teɪkəblɪ] *adv* de modo inconfundible.
unmitigated [ʌn'mɪtɪgeɪtɪd] *adj* rematado, absoluto.
unnamed [ʌn'neɪmd] *adj* (*nameless*) sin nombre; (*anonymous*) anónimo.
unnatural [ʌn'nætʃrəl] *adj* (*gen*) antinatural; (*manner*) afectado; (*habit*) perverso.
unnecessary [ʌn'nɛsəsərɪ] *adj* innecesario, inútil.
unnerve [ʌn'nəːv] *vt* (*subj*: *accident*) poner nervioso; (: *hostile attitude*) acobardar; (: *long wait, interview*) intimidar.
unnoticed [ʌn'nəutɪst] *adj*: **to go** *or* **pass** ~ pasar desapercibido.
UNO ['juːnəu] *n abbr* = (*United Nations Organization*) ONU *f*.
unobservant [ʌnəb'zəːvnt] *adj*: **to be** ~ ser poco observador, ser distraído.
unobtainable [ʌnəb'teɪnəbl] *adj* inasequible; (*TEL*) inexistente.
unobtrusive [ʌnəb'truːsɪv] *adj* discreto.
unoccupied [ʌn'ɔkjupaɪd] *adj* (*house etc*) libre, desocupado.
unofficial [ʌnə'fɪʃl] *adj* no oficial; ~ **strike** huelga no oficial.
unopened [ʌn'əupənd] *adj* (*letter, present*) sin abrir.
unopposed [ʌnə'pəuzd] *adj* (*enter, be elected*) sin oposición.
unorthodox [ʌn'ɔːθədɔks] *adj* poco ortodoxo.
unpack [ʌn'pæk] *vi* deshacer las maletas, desempacar (*LAM*).
unpaid [ʌn'peɪd] *adj* (*bill, debt*) sin pagar, impagado; (*COMM*) pendiente; (*holiday*) sin sueldo; (*work*) sin pago, voluntario.
unpalatable [ʌn'pælətəbl] *adj* (*truth*) desagradable.
unparalleled [ʌn'pærəlɛld] *adj* (*unequalled*) sin par; (*unique*) sin precedentes.
unpatriotic [ʌnpætrɪ'ɔtɪk] *adj* (*person*) poco patriota; (*speech, attitude*) antipatriótico.
unplanned [ʌn'plænd] *adj* (*visit*) imprevisto; (*baby*) no planeado.
unpleasant [ʌn'plɛznt] *adj* (*disagreeable*) desagradable; (*person, manner*) antipático.
unplug [ʌn'plʌg] *vt* desenchufar, desconectar.
unpolluted [ʌnpə'luːtɪd] *adj* impoluto, no contaminado.
unpopular [ʌn'pɔpjulə*] *adj* poco popular; **to be** ~ **with sb** (*person, law*) no ser popular con algn; **to make o.s.** ~ **(with)**

hacerse impopular (con).
unprecedented [ʌn'prɛsɪdəntɪd] *adj* sin precedentes.
unpredictable [ʌnprɪ'dɪktəbl] *adj* imprevisible.
unprejudiced [ʌn'prɛdʒudɪst] *adj* (*not biased*) imparcial; (*having no prejudices*) sin prejuicio.
unprepared [ʌnprɪ'pɛəd] *adj* (*person*) desprevenido; (*speech*) improvisado.
unprepossessing [ʌnpriːpə'zɛsɪŋ] *adj* poco atractivo.
unprincipled [ʌn'prɪnsɪpld] *adj* sin escrúpulos.
unproductive [ʌnprə'dʌktɪv] *adj* improductivo; (*discussion*) infructuoso.
unprofessional [ʌnprə'fɛʃənl] *adj* poco profesional; ~ **conduct** negligencia.
unprofitable [ʌn'prɔfɪtəbl] *adj* poco provechoso, no rentable.
UNPROFOR *n abbr* (= *United Nations Protection Force*) FORPRONU *f*, Unprofor *f*.
unprotected ['ʌnprə'tɛktɪd] *adj* (*sex*) sin protección.
unprovoked [ʌnprə'vəukt] *adj* no provocado.
unpunished [ʌn'pʌnɪʃt] *adj*: **to go** ~ quedar sin castigo, salir impune.
unqualified [ʌn'kwɔlɪfaɪd] *adj* sin título, no cualificado; (*success*) total, incondicional.
unquestionably [ʌn'kwɛstʃənəblɪ] *adv* indiscutiblemente.
unquestioning [ʌn'kwɛstʃənɪŋ] *adj* (*obedience, acceptance*) incondicional.
unravel [ʌn'rævl] *vt* desenmarañar.
unreal [ʌn'rɪəl] *adj* irreal.
unrealistic [ʌnrɪə'lɪstɪk] *adj* poco realista.
unreasonable [ʌn'riːznəbl] *adj* irrazonable; **to make** ~ **demands on sb** hacer demandas excesivas a algn.
unrecognizable [ʌn'rɛkəgnaɪzəbl] *adj* irreconocible.
unrecognized [ʌn'rɛkəgnaɪzd] *adj* (*talent, genius*) ignorado; (*POL: regime*) no reconocido.
unrecorded [ʌnrɪ'kɔːdɪd] *adj* no registrado.
unrefined [ʌnrɪ'faɪnd] *adj* (*sugar, petroleum*) sin refinar.
unrehearsed [ʌnrɪ'həːst] *adj* (*THEAT etc*) improvisado; (*spontaneous*) espontáneo.
unrelated [ʌnrɪ'leɪtɪd] *adj* sin relación; (*family*) no emparentado.
unrelenting [ʌnrɪ'lɛntɪŋ] *adj* implacable.
unreliable [ʌnrɪ'laɪəbl] *adj* (*person*) informal; (*machine*) poco fiable.
unrelieved [ʌnrɪ'liːvd] *adj* (*monotony*) constante.
unremitting [ʌnrɪ'mɪtɪŋ] *adj* incesante.
unrepeatable [ʌnrɪ'piːtəbl] *adj* irrepetible.
unrepentant [ʌnrɪ'pɛntənt] *adj* (*smoker, sinner*) impenitente; **to be** ~ **about sth** no arrepentirse de algo.
unrepresentative [ʌnrɛprɪ'zɛntətɪv] *adj* (*untypical*) poco representativo.
unreserved [ʌnrɪ'zəːvd] *adj* (*seat*) no reservado; (*approval, admiration*) total.
unreservedly [ʌnrɪ'zəːvɪdlɪ] *adv* sin reserva.
unresponsive [ʌnrɪ'spɔnsɪv] *adj* insensible.
unrest [ʌn'rɛst] *n* inquietud *f*, malestar *m*; (*POL*) disturbios *mpl*.
unrestricted [ʌnrɪ'strɪktɪd] *adj* (*power, time*) sin restricción; (*access*) libre.
unrewarded [ʌnrɪ'wɔːdɪd] *adj* sin recompensa.
unripe [ʌn'raɪp] *adj* verde, inmaduro.
unrivalled, (*US*) **unrivaled** [ʌn'raɪvəld] *adj* incomparable, sin par.
unroll [ʌn'rəul] *vt* desenrollar.
unruffled [ʌn'rʌfld] *adj* (*person*) imperturbable; (*hair*) liso.
unruly [ʌn'ruːlɪ] *adj* indisciplinado.
unsafe [ʌn'seɪf] *adj* (*journey*) peligroso; (*car etc*) inseguro; (*method*) arriesgado; ~ **to drink/eat** no apto para el consumo humano.
unsaid [ʌn'sɛd] *adj*: **to leave sth** ~ dejar algo sin decir.
unsaleable, (*US*) **unsalable** [ʌn'seɪləbl] *adj* invendible.
unsatisfactory ['ʌnsætɪs'fæktərɪ] *adj* poco satisfactorio.
unsatisfied [ʌn'sætɪsfaɪd] *adj* (*desire, need etc*) insatisfecho.
unsavoury, (*US*) **unsavory** [ʌn'seɪvərɪ] *adj* (*fig*) repugnante.
unscathed [ʌn'skeɪðd] *adj* ileso.
unscientific [ʌnsaɪən'tɪfɪk] *adj* poco científico.
unscrew [ʌn'skruː] *vt* destornillar.
unscrupulous [ʌn'skruːpjuləs] *adj* sin escrúpulos.
unseat [ʌn'siːt] *vt* (*rider*) hacer caerse de la silla a; (*fig: official*) hacer perder su escaño a.
unsecured [ʌnsɪ'kjuəd] *adj*: ~ **creditor** acreedor(a) *m/f* común.
unseeded [ʌn'siːdɪd] *adj* (*SPORT*) no preseleccionado.
unseen [ʌn'siːn] *adj* (*person, danger*) oculto.
unselfish [ʌn'sɛlfɪʃ] *adj* generoso, poco egoísta; (*act*) desinteresado.
unsettled [ʌn'sɛtld] *adj* inquieto; (*situation*) inestable; (*weather*) variable.
unsettling [ʌn'sɛtlɪŋ] *adj* perturbador(a),

inquietante.
unshak(e)able [ʌn'ʃeɪkəbl] *adj* inquebrantable.
unshaven [ʌn'ʃeɪvn] *adj* sin afeitar.
unsightly [ʌn'saɪtlɪ] *adj* desagradable.
unskilled [ʌn'skɪld] *adj*: ~ **workers** mano *f* de obra no cualificada.
unsociable [ʌn'səuʃəbl] *adj* insociable.
unsocial [ʌn'səuʃl] *adj*: ~ **hours** horario nocturno.
unsold [ʌn'səuld] *adj* sin vender.
unsolicited [ʌnsə'lɪsɪtɪd] *adj* no solicitado.
unsophisticated [ʌnsə'fɪstɪkeɪtɪd] *adj* (*person*) sencillo, ingenuo; (*method*) poco sofisticado.
unsound [ʌn'saund] *adj* (*health*) malo; (*in construction*: *floor, foundations*) defectuoso; (*policy, advice, judgment*) erróneo; (*investment*) poco seguro.
unspeakable [ʌn'spiːkəbl] *adj* indecible; (*awful*) incalificable.
unspoken [ʌn'spəukn] *adj* (*words*) sobreententido; (*agreement, approval*) tácito.
unstable [ʌn'steɪbl] *adj* inestable.
unsteady [ʌn'stɛdɪ] *adj* inestable.
unstinting [ʌn'stɪntɪŋ] *adj* (*support etc*) pródigo.
unstuck [ʌn'stʌk] *adj*: **to come** ~ despegarse; (*fig*) fracasar.
unsubstantiated [ʌnsəb'stænʃɪeɪtɪd] *adj* (*rumour, accusation*) no comprobado.
unsuccessful [ʌnsək'sɛsful] *adj* (*attempt*) infructuoso; (*writer, proposal*) sin éxito; **to be** ~ (*in attempting sth*) no tener éxito, fracasar.
unsuccessfully [ʌnsək'sɛsfulɪ] *adv* en vano, sin éxito.
unsuitable [ʌn'suːtəbl] *adj* inconveniente, inapropiado; (*time*) inoportuno.
unsuited [ʌn'suːtɪd] *adj*: **to be** ~ **for** *or* **to** no ser apropiado para.
unsung ['ʌnsʌŋ] *adj*: **an** ~ **hero** un héroe desconocido.
unsupported [ʌnsə'pɔːtɪd] *adj* (*claim*) sin fundamento; (*theory*) sin base firme.
unsure [ʌn'ʃuə*] *adj* inseguro, poco seguro; **to be** ~ **of o.s.** estar poco seguro de sí mismo.
unsuspecting [ʌnsə'spɛktɪŋ] *adj* confiado.
unsweetened [ʌn'swiːtnd] *adj* sin azúcar.
unsympathetic [ʌnsɪmpə'θɛtɪk] *adj* (*attitude*) poco comprensivo; (*person*) sin compasión; ~ **(to)** indiferente (a).
untangle [ʌn'tæŋgl] *vt* desenredar.
untapped [ʌn'tæpt] *adj* (*resources*) sin explotar.
untaxed [ʌn'tækst] *adj* (*goods*) libre de impuestos; (*income*) antes de impuestos.
unthinkable [ʌn'θɪŋkəbl] *adj* inconcebible, impensable.
unthinkingly [ʌn'θɪŋkɪŋlɪ] *adv* irreflexivamente.
untidy [ʌn'taɪdɪ] *adj* (*room*) desordenado, en desorden; (*appearance*) desaliñado.
untie [ʌn'taɪ] *vt* desatar.
until [ən'tɪl] *prep* hasta ♦ *conj* hasta que; ~ **he comes** hasta que venga; ~ **now** hasta ahora; ~ **then** hasta entonces; **from morning** ~ **night** de la mañana a la noche.
untimely [ʌn'taɪmlɪ] *adj* inoportuno; (*death*) prematuro.
untold [ʌn'təuld] *adj* (*story*) nunca contado; (*suffering*) indecible; (*wealth*) incalculable.
untouched [ʌn'tʌtʃt] *adj* (*not used etc*) intacto, sin tocar; (*safe*: *person*) indemne, ileso; (*unaffected*): ~ **by** insensible a.
untoward [ʌntə'wɔːd] *adj* (*behaviour*) impropio; (*event*) adverso.
untrained [ʌn'treɪnd] *adj* (*worker*) sin formación; (*troops*) no entrenado; **to the** ~ **eye** para los no entendidos.
untrammelled, (*US*) **untrammeled** [ʌn'træməld] *adj* ilimitado.
untranslatable [ʌntrænz'leɪtəbl] *adj* intraducible.
untried [ʌn'traɪd] *adj* (*plan*) no probado.
untrue [ʌn'truː] *adj* (*statement*) falso.
untrustworthy [ʌn'trʌstwəːðɪ] *adj* (*person*) poco fiable.
unusable [ʌn'juːzəbl] *adj* inservible.
unused [ʌn'juːzd] *adj* sin usar, nuevo; **to be** ~ **to (doing) sth** no estar acostumbrado a (hacer) algo.
unusual [ʌn'juːʒuəl] *adj* insólito, poco común.
unusually [ʌn'juːʒuəlɪ] *adv*: **he arrived** ~ **early** llegó más temprano que de costumbre.
unveil [ʌn'veɪl] *vt* (*statue*) descubrir.
unwanted [ʌn'wɔntɪd] *adj* (*person, effect*) no deseado.
unwarranted [ʌn'wɔrəntɪd] *adj* injustificado.
unwary [ʌn'wɛərɪ] *adj* imprudente, incauto.
unwavering [ʌn'weɪvərɪŋ] *adj* inquebrantable.
unwelcome [ʌn'wɛlkəm] *adj* (*at a bad time*) inoportuno, molesto; **to feel** ~ sentirse incómodo.
unwell [ʌn'wɛl] *adj*: **to feel** ~ estar indispuesto, sentirse mal.
unwieldy [ʌn'wiːldɪ] *adj* difícil de manejar.
unwilling [ʌn'wɪlɪŋ] *adj*: **to be** ~ **to do sth** estar poco dispuesto a hacer algo.

unwillingly [ʌn'wılıŋlı] *adv* de mala gana.
unwind [ʌn'waınd] (*irreg: like* **wind**) *vt* desenvolver ♦ *vi* (*relax*) relajarse.
unwise [ʌn'waız] *adj* imprudente.
unwitting [ʌn'wıtıŋ] *adj* inconsciente.
unworkable [ʌn'wəːkəbl] *adj* (*plan*) impracticable.
unworthy [ʌn'wəːðı] *adj* indigno; **to be ~ of sth/to do sth** ser indigno de algo/de hacer algo.
unwrap [ʌn'ræp] *vt* deshacer.
unwritten [ʌn'rıtn] *adj* (*agreement*) tácito; (*rules, law*) no escrito.
unzip [ʌn'zıp] *vt* abrir la cremallera de.

KEYWORD

up [ʌp] *prep*: **to go/be ~ sth** subir/estar subido en algo; **he went ~ the stairs/the hill** subió las escaleras/la colina; **we walked/climbed ~ the hill** subimos la colina; **they live further ~ the street** viven más arriba en la calle; **go ~ that road and turn left** sigue por esa calle y gira a la izquierda
♦ *adv* **1** (*upwards, higher*) más arriba; **~ in the mountains** en lo alto (de la montaña); **put it a bit higher** ~ ponlo un poco más arriba *or* alto; **to stop halfway** ~ pararse a la mitad del camino *or* de la subida; **~ there** ahí *or* allí arriba; **~ above** en lo alto, por encima, arriba; **"this side ~"** "este lado hacia arriba"; **to live/go ~ North** vivir en el norte/ir al norte
2: **to be** ~ (*out of bed*) estar levantado; (*prices, level*) haber subido; (*building*) estar construido; (*tent*) estar montado; (*curtains, paper etc*) estar puesto; **time's** ~ se acabó el tiempo; **when the year was** ~ al terminarse el año; **he's well ~ in** *or* **on politics** (*BRIT: knowledgeable*) está muy al día en política; **what's up?** (*wrong*) ¿qué pasa?; **what's ~ with him?** ¿qué le pasa?; **prices are ~ on last year** los precios han subido desde el año pasado
3: **~ to** (*as far as*) hasta; **~ to now** hasta ahora *or* la fecha
4: **to be ~ to** (*depending on*): **it's ~ to you** depende de ti; **he's not ~ to it** (*job, task etc*) no es capaz de hacerlo; **I don't feel ~ to it** no me encuentro con ánimos para ello; **his work is not ~ to the required standard** su trabajo no da la talla; (*inf: be doing*): **what is he ~ to?** ¿qué estará tramando?
♦ *vi* (*col*): **she ~ped and left** se levantó y se marchó
♦ *vt* (*col: price*) subir
♦ *n*: **~s and downs** altibajos *mpl*.

up-and-coming [ʌpənd'kʌmıŋ] *adj* prometedor(a).
upbeat ['ʌpbiːt] *n* (*MUS*) tiempo no acentuado; (*in economy, prosperity*) aumento ♦ *adj* (*col*) optimista, animado.
upbraid [ʌp'breıd] *vt* censurar, reprender.
upbringing ['ʌpbrıŋıŋ] *n* educación *f*.
upcoming ['ʌpkʌmıŋ] *adj* próximo.
update [ʌp'deıt] *vt* poner al día.
upend [ʌp'ɛnd] *vt* poner vertical.
upfront [ʌp'frʌnt] *adj* claro, directo ♦ *adv* a las claras; (*pay*) por adelantado; **to be ~ about sth** admitir algo claramente.
upgrade [ʌp'greıd] *vt* ascender; (*COMPUT*) modernizar.
upheaval [ʌp'hiːvl] *n* trastornos *mpl*; (*POL*) agitación *f*.
uphill [ʌp'hıl] *adj* cuesta arriba; (*fig: task*) penoso, difícil ♦ *adv*: **to go** ~ ir cuesta arriba.
uphold [ʌp'həuld] (*irreg: like* **hold**) *vt* sostener.
upholstery [ʌp'həulstərı] *n* tapicería.
upkeep ['ʌpkiːp] *n* mantenimiento.
upmarket [ʌp'mɑːkıt] *adj* (*product*) de categoría.
upon [ə'pɔn] *prep* sobre.
upper ['ʌpə*] *adj* superior, de arriba ♦ *n* (*of shoe: also:* **~s**) pala.
upper case *n* (*TYP*) mayúsculas *fpl*.
upper-class [ʌpə'klɑːs] *adj* (*district, people, accent*) de clase alta; (*attitude*) altivo.
uppercut ['ʌpəkʌt] *n* uppercut *m*, gancho a la cara.
upper hand *n*: **to have the** ~ tener la sartén por el mango.
Upper House *n* (*POL*): **the** ~ la Cámara alta.
uppermost ['ʌpəməust] *adj* el más alto; **what was ~ in my mind** lo que me preocupaba más.
Upper Volta [-'vəultə] *n* Alto Volta *m*.
upright ['ʌpraıt] *adj* vertical; (*fig*) honrado.
uprising ['ʌpraızıŋ] *n* sublevación *f*.
uproar ['ʌprɔː*] *n* tumulto, escándalo.
uproarious [ʌp'rɔːrıəs] *adj* escandaloso; (*hilarious*) graciosísimo; (*exceptional*) espectacular.
uproot [ʌp'ruːt] *vt* desarraigar.
upset *n* ['ʌpsɛt] (*to plan etc*) revés *m*, contratiempo; (*MED*) trastorno ♦ *vt* [ʌp'sɛt] (*irreg: like* **set**) (*glass etc*) volcar; (*spill*) derramar; (*plan*) alterar; (*person*) molestar, perturbar ♦ *adj* [ʌp'sɛt] preocupado, perturbado; (*stomach*) revuelto; **to have a stomach ~** (*BRIT*) tener el estómago revuelto; **to get ~**

molestarse, llevarse un disgusto.
upset price *n* (*US, Scottish*) precio mínimo *or* de reserva.
upsetting [ʌp'sɛtɪŋ] *adj* (*worrying*) inquietante; (*offending*) ofensivo; (*annoying*) molesto.
upshot ['ʌpʃɔt] *n* resultado.
upside-down ['ʌpsaɪd'daun] *adv* al revés.
upstage ['ʌp'steɪdʒ] *vt* robar protagonismo a.
upstairs [ʌp'stɛəz] *adv* arriba ♦ *adj* (*room*) de arriba ♦ *n* el piso superior.
upstart ['ʌpstɑːt] *n* advenedizo.
upstream [ʌp'striːm] *adv* río arriba.
upsurge ['ʌpsəːdʒ] *n* (*of enthusiasm etc*) arrebato.
uptake ['ʌpteɪk] *n*: **he is quick/slow on the ~** es muy listo/torpe.
uptight [ʌp'taɪt] *adj* tenso, nervioso.
up-to-date ['ʌptə'deɪt] *adj* moderno, actual; **to bring sb ~ (on sth)** poner a algn al corriente/tanto (de algo).
upturn ['ʌptəːn] *n* (*in luck*) mejora; (*COMM*: *in market*) resurgimiento económico; (: *in value of currency*) aumento.
upturned ['ʌptəːnd] *adj*: **~ nose** nariz *f* respingona.
upward ['ʌpwəd] *adj* ascendente.
upwardly-mobile ['ʌpwədlɪ'məubaɪl] *adj*: **to be ~** mejorar socialmente.
upward(s) ['ʌpwəd(z)] *adv* hacia arriba.
URA *n abbr* (*US*) = *Urban Renewal Administration.*
Ural Mountains ['juərəl-] *npl*: **the ~** (*also*: **the Urals**) los Montes Urales.
uranium [juə'reɪnɪəm] *n* uranio.
Uranus [juə'reɪnəs] *n* (*ASTRO*) Urano.
urban ['əːbən] *adj* urbano.
urbane [əː'beɪn] *adj* cortés, urbano.
urbanization ['əːbənaɪ'zeɪʃən] *n* urbanización *f.*
urchin ['əːtʃɪn] *n* pilluelo, golfillo.
Urdu ['uəduː] *n* urdu *m.*
urge [əːdʒ] *n* (*force*) impulso; (*desire*) deseo ♦ *vt*: **to ~ sb to do sth** animar a algn a hacer algo.
►**urge on** *vt* animar.
urgency ['əːdʒənsɪ] *n* urgencia.
urgent ['əːdʒənt] *adj* (*earnest, persistent*: *plea*) insistente; (: *tone*) urgente.
urgently ['əːdʒəntlɪ] *adv* con urgencia, urgentemente.
urinal ['juərɪnl] *n* (*building*) urinario; (*vessel*) orinal *m.*
urinate ['juərɪneɪt] *vi* orinar.
urine ['juərɪn] *n* orina.
urn [əːn] *n* urna; (*also*: **tea ~**) tetera (grande).
Uruguay ['juerəgwaɪ] *n* el Uruguay.
Uruguayan [juərə'gwaɪən] *adj, n* uruguayo/a *m/f.*
US *n abbr* (= *United States*) EE.UU.
us [ʌs] *pron* nos; (*after prep*) nosotros/as; (*col*: *me*): **give ~ a kiss** dame un beso; *see also* **me**.
USA *n abbr see* **United States of America**; (*MIL*) = *United States Army.*
usable ['juːzəbl] *adj* utilizable.
USAF *n abbr* = *United States Air Force.*
usage ['juːzɪdʒ] *n* (*LING*) uso; (*utilization*) utilización *f.*
USCG *n abbr* = *United States Coast Guard.*
USDA *n abbr* = *United States Department of Agriculture.*
USDAW ['ʌzdɔː] *n abbr* (*BRIT*: = *Union of Shop, Distributive and Allied Workers*) *sindicato de empleados de comercio.*
USDI *n abbr* = *United States Department of the Interior.*
use *n* [juːs] uso, empleo; (*usefulness*) utilidad *f* ♦ *vt* [juːz] usar, emplear; **in ~** en uso; **out of ~** en desuso; **to be of ~** servir; **ready for ~** listo (para usar); **to make ~ of sth** aprovecharse *or* servirse de algo; **it's no ~** (*pointless*) es inútil; (*not useful*) no sirve; **what's this ~d for?** ¿para qué sirve esto?; **to be ~d to** estar acostumbrado a (*SP*), acostumbrar; **to get ~d to** acostumbrarse a; **she ~d to do it** (ella) solía *or* acostumbraba hacerlo.
►**use up** *vt* agotar.
used [juːzd] *adj* (*car*) usado.
useful ['juːsful] *adj* útil; **to come in ~** ser útil.
usefulness ['juːsfəlnɪs] *n* utilidad.
useless ['juːslɪs] *adj* inútil; (*unusable*: *object*) inservible.
uselessly ['juːslɪslɪ] *adv* inútilmente, en vano.
uselessness ['juːslɪsnɪs] *n* inutilidad *f.*
user ['juːzə*] *n* usuario/a; (*of petrol, gas etc*) consumidor(a) *m/f.*
user-friendly ['juːzə'frɛndlɪ] *adj* (*COMPUT*) fácil de utilizar.
USES *n abbr* = *United States Employment Service.*
usher ['ʌʃə*] *n* (*at wedding*) ujier *m*; (*in cinema etc*) acomodador *m* ♦ *vt*: **to ~ sb in** (*into room*) hacer pasar a algn; **it ~ed in a new era** (*fig*) inició una nueva era.
usherette [ʌʃə'rɛt] *n* (*in cinema*) acomodadora.
USIA *n abbr* = *United States Information Agency.*

USM *n abbr* = *United States Mail*; *United States Mint.*
USN *n abbr* = *United States Navy.*
USPHS *n abbr* = *United States Public Health Service.*
USPO *n abbr* = *United States Post Office.*
USS *abbr* = *United States Ship* (*or Steamer*).
USSR *n abbr*: **the** ~ la U.R.S.S.
usu. *abbr* = **usually**.
usual ['ju:ʒuəl] *adj* normal, corriente; **as** ~ como de costumbre, como siempre.
usually ['ju:ʒuəlɪ] *adv* normalmente.
usurer ['ju:ʒərə*] *n* usurero.
usurp [ju:'zə:p] *vt* usurpar.
usury ['ju:ʒərɪ] *n* usura.
UT *abbr* (*US*) = *Utah.*
utensil [ju:'tɛnsl] *n* utensilio; **kitchen ~s** batería de cocina.
uterus ['ju:tərəs] *n* útero.
utilitarian [ju:tɪlɪ'tɛərɪən] *adj* utilitario.
utility [ju:'tɪlɪtɪ] *n* utilidad *f.*
utility room *n* trascocina.
utilization [ju:tɪlaɪ'zeɪʃən] *n* utilización *f.*
utilize ['ju:tɪlaɪz] *vt* utilizar.
utmost ['ʌtməust] *adj* mayor ♦ *n*: **to do one's** ~ hacer todo lo posible; **it is of the ~ importance that** ... es de la mayor importancia que ....
utter ['ʌtə*] *adj* total, completo ♦ *vt* pronunciar, proferir.
utterance ['ʌtərns] *n* palabras *fpl*, declaración *f.*
utterly ['ʌtəlɪ] *adv* completamente, totalmente.
U-turn ['ju:'tə:n] *n* cambio de sentido; (*fig*) giro de 180 grados.
Uzbekistan [ʌzbɛkɪ'stɑ:n] *n* Uzbekistán *m.*

V v

V, v [vi:] (*letter*) V, v *f*; **V for Victor** V de Valencia.
v. *abbr* (= *verse*) vers.º (= *vide*: *see*) V, vid., vide; (= *versus*) vs.; = **volt**.
VA, Va. *abbr* (*US*) = *Virginia.*
vac [væk] *n abbr* (*BRIT col*) = **vacation.**
vacancy ['veɪkənsɪ] *n* (*BRIT*: *job*) vacante *f*; (*room*) cuarto libro; **have you any vacancies?** ¿tiene *or* hay alguna habitación *or* algún cuarto libre?
vacant ['veɪkənt] *adj* desocupado, libre; (*expression*) distraído.
vacant lot *n* (*US*) solar *m.*
vacate [və'keɪt] *vt* (*house*) desocupar; (*job*) dejar (vacante).
vacation [və'keɪʃən] *n* vacaciones *fpl* ; **on** ~ de vacaciones; **to take a** ~ (*esp US*) tomarse unas vacaciones.
vacation course *n* curso de vacaciones.
vacationer [və'keɪʃənə*], **vacationist** [və'keɪʃənɪst] *n* (*US*) turista *m/f.*
vaccinate ['væksɪneɪt] *vt* vacunar.
vaccination [væksɪ'neɪʃən] *n* vacunación *f.*
vaccine ['væksi:n] *n* vacuna.
vacuum ['vækjum] *n* vacío.
vacuum bottle *n* (*US*) = **vacuum flask**.
vacuum cleaner *n* aspiradora.
vacuum flask *n* (*BRIT*) termo.
vacuum-packed ['vækjum'pækt] *adj* envasado al vacío.
vagabond ['vægəbɔnd] *n* vagabundo/a.
vagary ['veɪgərɪ] *n* capricho.
vagina [və'dʒaɪnə] *n* vagina.
vagrancy ['veɪgrənsɪ] *n* vagabundeo.
vagrant ['veɪgrənt] *n* vagabundo/a.
vague [veɪg] *adj* vago; (*blurred*: *memory*) borroso; (*uncertain*) incierto, impreciso; (*person*) distraído; **I haven't the ~st idea** no tengo la más remota idea.
vaguely ['veɪglɪ] *adv* vagamente.
vagueness ['veɪgnɪs] *n* vaguedad *f*; imprecisión *f*; (*absent-mindedness*) despiste *m.*
vain [veɪn] *adj* (*conceited*) presumido; (*useless*) vano, inútil; **in** ~ en vano.
vainly ['veɪnlɪ] *adv* (*to no effect*) en vano; (*conceitedly*) vanidosamente.
valance ['væləns] *n* (*for bed*) *volante alrededor de la colcha o sábana que cuelga hasta el suelo.*
valedictory [vælɪ'dɪktərɪ] *adj* de despedida.
valentine ['væləntaɪn] *n* (*also*: ~ **card**) tarjeta del Día de los Enamorados.
valet ['væleɪ] *n* ayuda *m* de cámara.
valet service *n* (*for clothes*) planchado.
valiant ['væljənt] *adj* valiente.
valiantly ['væljəntlɪ] *adv* valientemente, con valor.
valid ['vælɪd] *adj* válido; (*ticket*) valedero; (*law*) vigente.
validate ['vælɪdeɪt] *vt* (*contract, document*) convalidar; (*argument, claim*) dar validez a.
validity [və'lɪdɪtɪ] *n* validez *f*; vigencia.
valise [və'li:z] *n* maletín *m.*
valley ['vælɪ] *n* valle *m.*
valour, (*US*) **valor** ['vælə*] *n* valor *m*, valentía.

valuable ['væljuəbl] *adj* (*jewel*) de valor; (*time*) valioso; **~s** *npl* objetos *mpl* de valor.
valuation [vælju'eɪʃən] *n* tasación *f*, valuación *f*.
value ['vælju:] *n* valor *m*; (*importance*) importancia ♦ *vt* (*fix price of*) tasar, valorar; (*esteem*) apreciar; **~s** *npl* (*moral*) valores *mpl* morales; **to lose (in) ~** (*currency*) bajar; (*property*) desvalorizarse; **to gain (in) ~** (*currency*) subir; (*property*) valorizarse; **you get good ~ (for money) in that shop** la relación calidad-precio es muy buena en esa tienda; **to be of great ~ to sb** ser de gran valor para algn; **it is ~d at £8** está valorado en ocho libras.
value added tax (VAT) *n* (*BRIT*) impuesto sobre el valor añadido *or* agregado (*LAM*) (IVA *m*).
valued ['vælju:d] *adj* (*appreciated*) apreciado.
valueless ['vælju:lɪs] *adj* sin valor.
valuer ['vælju:ə*] *n* tasador(a) *m/f*.
valve [vælv] *n* (*ANAT, TECH*) válvula.
vampire ['væmpaɪə*] *n* vampiro.
van [væn] *n* (*AUT*) furgoneta, camioneta (*LAM*); (*BRIT RAIL*) furgón *m* (de equipajes).
V and A *n abbr* (*BRIT*) = *Victoria and Albert Museum*.
vandal ['vændl] *n* vándalo/a.
vandalism ['vændəlɪzəm] *n* vandalismo.
vandalize ['vændəlaɪz] *vt* dañar, destruir, destrozar.
vanguard ['vængɑ:d] *n* vanguardia.
vanilla [və'nɪlə] *n* vainilla.
vanish ['vænɪʃ] *vi* desaparecer, esfumarse.
vanity ['vænɪtɪ] *n* vanidad *f*.
vanity case *n* neceser *m*.
vantage point ['vɑ:ntɪdʒ-] *n* posición *f* ventajosa.
vaporize ['veɪpəraɪz] *vt* vaporizar ♦ *vi* vaporizarse.
vapour, (*US*) **vapor** ['veɪpə*] *n* vapor *m*; (*on breath, window*) vaho.
vapo(u)r trail *n* (*AVIAT*) estela.
variable ['vɛərɪəbl] *adj* variable ♦ *n* variable *f*.
variance ['vɛərɪəns] *n*: **to be at ~ (with)** estar en desacuerdo (con), no cuadrar (con).
variant ['vɛərɪənt] *n* variante *f*.
variation [vɛərɪ'eɪʃən] *n* variación *f*.
varicose ['værɪkəus] *adj*: **~ veins** varices *fpl*.
varied ['vɛərɪd] *adj* variado.
variety [və'raɪətɪ] *n* variedad *f*, diversidad *f*; (*quantity*) surtido; **for a ~ of reasons** por varias *or* diversas razones.
variety show *n* espectáculo de variedades.
various ['vɛərɪəs] *adj* varios/as, diversos/as; **at ~ times** (*different*) en distintos momentos; (*several*) varias veces.
varnish ['vɑ:nɪʃ] *n* (*gen*) barniz *m*; (*nail ~*) esmalte *m* ♦ *vt* (*gen*) barnizar; (*nails*) pintar (con esmalte).
vary ['vɛərɪ] *vt* variar; (*change*) cambiar ♦ *vi* variar; (*disagree*) discrepar; **to ~ with** *or* **according to** variar según *or* de acuerdo con.
varying ['vɛərɪɪŋ] *adj* diversos/as.
vase [vɑ:z] *n* florero.
vasectomy [və'sɛktəmɪ] *n* vasectomía.
Vaseline ® ['væsɪli:n] *n* vaselina ®.
vast [vɑ:st] *adj* enorme; (*success*) abrumador(a), arrollador(a).
vastly ['vɑ:stlɪ] *adv* enormemente.
vastness ['vɑ:stnɪs] *n* inmensidad *f*.
VAT [væt] *n abbr* (*BRIT*: = *value added tax*) IVA *m*.
vat [væt] *n* tina, tinaja.
Vatican ['vætɪkən] *n*: **the ~** el Vaticano.
vatman ['vætmæn] *n* (*BRIT col*) inspector *m* *or* recaudador *m* del IVA; **"how to avoid the ~"** "cómo evitar pagar el IVA".
vaudeville ['vəudəvɪl] *n* (*US*) vodevil *m*.
vault [vɔ:lt] *n* (*of roof*) bóveda; (*tomb*) tumba; (*in bank*) cámara acorazada ♦ *vt* (*also*: **~ over**) saltar (por encima de).
vaunted ['vɔ:ntɪd] *adj*: **much ~** cacareado.
VC *n abbr* = **vice-chairman, vice-chancellor**; (*BRIT*: = *Victoria Cross*) *condecoración militar*.
VCR *n abbr* = **video cassette recorder**.
VD *n abbr see* **venereal disease**.
VDU *n abbr see* **visual display unit**.
veal [vi:l] *n* ternera.
veer [vɪə*] *vi* (*ship*) virar.
veg. [vɛdʒ] *n abbr* (*BRIT col*) = **vegetable(s)**.
vegan ['vi:gən] *n* vegetariano/a estricto/a.
vegeburger, veggieburger ['vɛdʒɪbə:gə*] *n* hamburguesa vegetal.
vegetable ['vɛdʒtəbl] *n* (*BOT*) vegetal *m*; (*edible plant*) legumbre *f*, hortaliza ♦ *adj* vegetal; **~s** *npl* (*cooked*) verduras *fpl*.
vegetable garden *n* huerta, huerto.
vegetarian [vɛdʒɪ'tɛərɪən] *adj, n* vegetariano/a *m/f*.
vegetate ['vɛdʒɪteɪt] *vi* vegetar.
vegetation [vɛdʒɪ'teɪʃən] *n* vegetación *f*.
vegetative ['vɛdʒɪtətɪv] *adj* vegetativo; (*BOT*) vegetal.
vehemence ['vi:ɪməns] *n* vehemencia; violencia.
vehement ['vi:ɪmənt] *adj* vehemente, apasionado; (*dislike, hatred*) violento.
vehicle ['vi:ɪkl] *n* vehículo; (*fig*) vehículo,

medio.
vehicular [vɪ'hɪkjulə*] *adj*: ~ **traffic** circulación *f* rodada.
veil [veɪl] *n* velo ♦ *vt* velar; **under a ~ of secrecy** (*fig*) en el mayor secreto.
veiled [veɪld] *adj* (*also fig*) disimulado, velado.
vein [veɪn] *n* vena; (*of ore etc*) veta.
Velcro ® ['vɛlkrəu] *n* velcro *m* ®.
vellum ['vɛləm] *n* (*writing paper*) papel *m* vitela.
velocity [vɪ'lɔsɪtɪ] *n* velocidad *f*.
velour [və'luə*] *n* terciopelo.
velvet ['vɛlvɪt] *n* terciopelo ♦ *adj* aterciopelado.
vendetta [vɛn'dɛtə] *n* vendetta.
vending machine ['vɛndɪŋ-] *n* máquina expendedora, expendedor *m*.
vendor ['vɛndə*] *n* vendedor(a) *m/f*; **street ~** vendedor(a) *m/f* callejero/a.
veneer [və'nɪə*] *n* chapa, enchapado; (*fig*) barniz *m*.
venereal [vɪ'nɪərɪəl] *adj*: ~ **disease (VD)** enfermedad *f* venérea.
Venetian blind [vɪ'ni:ʃən-] *n* persiana.
Venezuela [vɛnɛ'zweɪlə] *n* Venezuela.
Venezuelan [vɛnɛ'zweɪlən] *adj, n* venezolano/a *m/f*.
vengeance ['vɛndʒəns] *n* venganza; **with a ~** (*fig*) con creces.
vengeful ['vɛndʒful] *adj* vengativo.
Venice ['vɛnɪs] *n* Venecia.
venison ['vɛnɪsn] *n* carne *f* de venado.
venom ['vɛnəm] *n* veneno.
venomous ['vɛnəməs] *adj* venenoso.
venomously ['vɛnəməslɪ] *adv* con odio.
vent [vɛnt] *n* (*opening*) abertura; (*air-hole*) respiradero; (*in wall*) rejilla (de ventilación) ♦ *vt* (*fig*: *feelings*) desahogar.
ventilate ['vɛntɪleɪt] *vt* ventilar.
ventilation [vɛntɪ'leɪʃən] *n* ventilación *f*.
ventilation shaft *n* pozo de ventilación.
ventilator ['vɛntɪleɪtə*] *n* ventilador *m*.
ventriloquist [vɛn'trɪləkwɪst] *n* ventrílocuo/a.
venture ['vɛntʃə*] *n* empresa ♦ *vt* arriesgar; (*opinion*) ofrecer ♦ *vi* arriesgarse, lanzarse; **a business ~** una empresa comercial; **to ~ to do sth** aventurarse a hacer algo.
venture capital *n* capital *m* arriesgado.
venue ['vɛnju:] *n* (*meeting place*) lugar *m* de reunión; (*for concert*) local *m*.
Venus ['vi:nəs] *n* (*ASTRO*) Venus *m*.
veracity [və'ræsɪtɪ] *n* veracidad *f*.
veranda(h) [və'rændə] *n* terraza; (*with glass*) galería.
verb [və:b] *n* verbo.
verbal ['və:bl] *adj* verbal.
verbally ['və:bəlɪ] *adv* verbalmente, de palabra.
verbatim [və:'beɪtɪm] *adj, adv* al pie de la letra, palabra por palabra.
verbose [və:'bəus] *adj* prolijo.
verdict ['və:dɪkt] *n* veredicto, fallo; (*fig*: *opinion*) opinión *f*, juicio; ~ **of guilty/not guilty** veredicto de culpabilidad/ inocencia.
verge [və:dʒ] *n* (*BRIT*) borde *m*; **to be on the ~ of doing sth** estar a punto de hacer algo.
►**verge on** *vt fus* rayar en.
verger ['və:dʒə*] *n* sacristán *m*.
verification [vɛrɪfɪ'keɪʃən] *n* comprobación *f*, verificación *f*.
verify ['vɛrɪfaɪ] *vt* comprobar, verificar; (*COMPUT*) verificar; (*prove the truth of*) confirmar.
veritable ['vɛrɪtəbl] *adj* verdadero, auténtico.
vermin ['və:mɪn] *npl* (*animals*) bichos *mpl*; (*insects, fig*) sabandijas *fpl*.
vermouth ['və:məθ] *n* vermut *m*.
vernacular [və'nækjulə*] *n* lengua vernácula.
versatile ['və:sətaɪl] *adj* (*person*) polifacético; (*machine, tool etc*) versátil.
versatility [və:sə'tɪlɪtɪ] *n* versatilidad *f*.
verse [və:s] *n* versos *mpl*, poesía; (*stanza*) estrofa; (*in bible*) versículo; **in ~** en verso.
versed [və:st] *adj*: **(well-)~ in** versado en.
version ['və:ʃən] *n* versión *f*.
versus ['və:səs] *prep* contra.
vertebra, *pl* **~e** ['və:tɪbrə, bri:] *n* vértebra.
vertebrate ['və:tɪbrɪt] *n* vertebrado.
vertical ['və:tɪkl] *adj* vertical.
vertically ['və:tɪkəlɪ] *adv* verticalmente.
vertigo ['və:tɪgəu] *n* vértigo; **to suffer from ~** tener vértigo.
verve [və:v] *n* brío.
very ['vɛrɪ] *adv* muy ♦ *adj*: **the ~ book which** el mismo libro que; **the ~ last** el último (de todos); **at the ~ least** al menos; **~ much** muchísimo; **~ well/little** muy bien/ poco; **~ high frequency** (*RADIO*) frecuencia muy alta; **it's ~ cold** hace mucho frío; **the ~ thought (of it) alarms me** con sólo pensarlo me entra miedo.
vespers ['vɛspəz] *npl* vísperas *fpl*.
vessel ['vɛsl] *n* (*ANAT*) vaso; (*ship*) barco; (*container*) vasija.
vest [vɛst] *n* (*BRIT*) camiseta; (*US*: *waistcoat*) chaleco.
vested interests ['vɛstɪd-] *npl* (*COMM*) intereses *mpl* creados.

vestibule ['vɛstɪbju:l] *n* vestíbulo.
vestige ['vɛstɪdʒ] *n* vestigio, rastro.
vestry ['vɛstrɪ] *n* sacristía.
Vesuvius [vɪ'su:vɪəs] *n* Vesubio.
vet [vɛt] *n abbr* = **veterinary surgeon** ♦ *vt* revisar; **to ~ sb for a job** someter a investigación a algn para un trabajo.
veteran ['vɛtərn] *n* veterano/a ♦ *adj*: **she is a ~ campaigner for ...** es una veterana de la campaña de ... .
veteran car *n* coche *m* antiguo.
veterinarian [vɛtrɪ'nɛərɪən] *n* (*US*) = **veterinary surgeon.**
veterinary ['vɛtrɪnərɪ] *adj* veterinario.
veterinary surgeon *n* (*BRIT*) veterinario/a.
veto ['vi:təu] *n* (*pl* **~es**) veto ♦ *vt* prohibir, vedar; **to put a ~ on** vetar.
vetting ['vɛtɪŋ] *n*: **positive ~** *investigación gubernamental de los futuros altos cargos de la Administración.*
vex [vɛks] *vt* (*irritate*) fastidiar; (*make impatient*) impacientar.
vexed [vɛkst] *adj* (*question*) controvertido.
vexing ['vɛksɪŋ] *adj* molesto, engorroso.
VFD *n abbr* (*US*) = *voluntary fire department.*
VG *n abbr* (*BRIT SCOL etc*: = *very good*) S (= *sobresaliente*).
VHF *abbr* (= *very high frequency*) VHF *f.*
VI *abbr* (*US*) = *Virgin Islands.*
via ['vaɪə] *prep* por, por vía de.
viability [vaɪə'bɪlɪtɪ] *n* viabilidad *f.*
viable ['vaɪəbl] *adj* viable.
viaduct ['vaɪədʌkt] *n* viaducto.
vial ['vaɪəl] *n* frasco pequeño.
vibes [vaɪbz] *npl* (*col*): **I got good/bad ~** me dio buen/mal rollo.
vibrant ['vaɪbrənt] *adj* (*lively, bright*) vivo; (*full of emotion*: *voice*) vibrante; (*colour*) fuerte.
vibraphone ['vaɪbrəfəun] *n* vibráfono.
vibrate [vaɪ'breɪt] *vi* vibrar.
vibration [vaɪ'breɪʃən] *n* vibración *f.*
vibrator [vaɪ'breɪtə*] *n* vibrador *m.*
vicar ['vɪkə*] *n* párroco.
vicarage ['vɪkərɪdʒ] *n* parroquia.
vicarious [vɪ'kɛərɪəs] *adj* indirecto; (*responsibility*) delegado.
vice [vaɪs] *n* (*evil*) vicio; (*TECH*) torno de banco.
vice- [vaɪs] *pref* vice....
vice-chairman ['vaɪs'tʃɛəmən] *n* vicepresidente *m.*
vice-chancellor [vaɪs'tʃɑ:nsələ*] *n* (*BRIT UNIV*) rector(a) *m/f.*
vice-president [vaɪs'prɛzɪdənt] *n* vice-presidente/a *m/f.*
viceroy ['vaɪsrɔɪ] *n* virrey *m.*
vice versa ['vaɪsɪ'və:sə] *adv* viceversa.
vicinity [vɪ'sɪnɪtɪ] *n* (*area*) vecindad *f*; (*nearness*) proximidad *f*; **in the ~ (of)** cercano (a).
vicious ['vɪʃəs] *adj* (*remark*) malicioso; (*blow*) brutal; **a ~ circle** un círculo vicioso.
viciousness ['vɪʃəsnɪs] *n* brutalidad *f.*
vicissitudes [vɪ'sɪsɪtju:dz] *npl* vicisitudes *fpl*, peripecias *fpl.*
victim ['vɪktɪm] *n* víctima; **to be the ~ of** ser víctima de.
victimization [vɪktɪmaɪ'zeɪʃən] *n* persecución *f*; (*of striker etc*) represalias *fpl.*
victimize ['vɪktɪmaɪz] *vt* (*strikers etc*) tomar represalias contra.
victor ['vɪktə*] *n* vencedor(a) *m/f.*
Victorian [vɪk'tɔ:rɪən] *adj* victoriano.
victorious [vɪk'tɔ:rɪəs] *adj* vencedor(a).
victory ['vɪktərɪ] *n* victoria; **to win a ~ over sb** obtener una victoria sobre algn.
video ['vɪdɪəu] *cpd* de vídeo ♦ *n* vídeo ♦ *vt* grabar (en vídeo).
video camera *n* videocámara, cámara de vídeo.
video cassette *n* videocassette *f.*
video (cassette) recorder *n* vídeo, videocassette *f.*
videodisk ['vɪdɪəudɪsk] *n* videodisco.
video game *n* videojuego.
video nasty *n* vídeo de violencia y/o porno duro.
videophone ['vɪdɪəufəun] *n* videoteléfono, videófono.
video recording *n* videograbación *f.*
video tape *n* cinta de vídeo.
vie [vaɪ] *vi*: **to ~ with** competir con.
Vienna [vɪ'ɛnə] *n* Viena.
Viennese [vɪə'ni:z] *adj, n* vienés/esa *m/f.*
Vietnam, Viet Nam [vjɛt'næm] *n* Vietnam *m.*
Vietnamese [vjɛtnə'mi:z] *adj* vietnamita ♦ *n* (*pl inv*) vietnamita *m/f*; (*LING*) vietnamita *m.*
view [vju:] *n* vista; (*landscape*) paisaje *m*; (*opinion*) opinión *f*, criterio ♦ *vt* (*look at*) mirar; (*examine*) examinar; **on ~** (*in museum etc*) expuesto; **in full ~ of sb** a la vista de algn; **to be within ~ (of sth)** estar a la vista (de algo); **an overall ~ of the situation** una visión de conjunto de la situación; **in ~ of the fact that** en vista de que; **to take** *or* **hold the ~ that ...** opinar *or* pensar que ...; **with a ~ to doing sth** con miras *or* vistas a hacer algo.
viewdata ['vju:deɪtə] *n* (*BRIT*) videodatos *mpl.*
viewer ['vju:ə*] *n* (*small projector*) visionadora; (*TV*) televidente *m/f*,

telespectador(a) *m/f*.
viewfinder ['vju:faɪndə*] *n* visor *m* de imagen.
viewpoint ['vju:pɔɪnt] *n* punto de vista.
vigil ['vɪdʒɪl] *n* vigilia; **to keep ~** velar.
vigilance ['vɪdʒɪləns] *n* vigilancia.
vigilance committee *n* (*US*) comité *m* de autodefensa.
vigilant ['vɪdʒɪlənt] *adj* vigilante.
vigilante [vɪdʒɪ'læntɪ] *n vecino/a que se toma la justicia por su mano.*
vigorous ['vɪgərəs] *adj* enérgico, vigoroso.
vigorously ['vɪgərəslɪ] *adv* enérgicamente, vigorosamente.
vigour, (*US*) **vigor** ['vɪgə*] *n* energía, vigor *m*.
vile [vaɪl] *adj* (*action*) vil, infame; (*smell*) repugnante.
vilify ['vɪlɪfaɪ] *vt* denigrar, vilipendiar.
villa ['vɪlə] *n* (*country house*) casa de campo; (*suburban house*) chalet *m*.
village ['vɪlɪdʒ] *n* aldea.
villager ['vɪlɪdʒə*] *n* aldeano/a.
villain ['vɪlən] *n* (*scoundrel*) malvado/a; (*criminal*) maleante *m/f*; *see also* **pantomime**.
VIN *n abbr* (*US*) = *vehicle identification number*.
vinaigrette [vɪneɪ'grɛt] *n* vinagreta.
vindicate ['vɪndɪkeɪt] *vt* vindicar, justificar.
vindication [vɪndɪ'keɪʃən] *n*: **in ~ of** en justificación de.
vindictive [vɪn'dɪktɪv] *adj* vengativo.
vine [vaɪn] *n* vid *f*.
vinegar ['vɪnɪgə*] *n* vinagre *m*.
vine-growing ['vaɪngrəuɪŋ] *adj* (*region*) viticultor(a).
vineyard ['vɪnjɑ:d] *n* viña, viñedo.
vintage ['vɪntɪdʒ] *n* (*year*) vendimia, cosecha; **the 1970 ~** la cosecha de 1970.
vintage car *n* coche *m* antiguo *or* de época.
vintage wine *n* vino añejo.
vintage year *n*: **it's been a ~ for plays** ha sido un año destacado en lo que a teatro se refiere.
vinyl ['vaɪnl] *n* vinilo.
viola [vɪ'əulə] *n* (*MUS*) viola.
violate ['vaɪəleɪt] *vt* violar.
violation [vaɪə'leɪʃən] *n* violación *f*; **in ~ of sth** en violación de algo.
violence ['vaɪələns] *n* violencia; **acts of ~** actos *mpl* de violencia.
violent ['vaɪələnt] *adj* (*gen*) violento; (*pain*) intenso; **a ~ dislike of sb/sth** una profunda antipatía *or* manía a algn/algo.
violently ['vaɪələntlɪ] *adv* (*severely: ill, angry*) muy.
violet ['vaɪələt] *adj* violado, violeta ♦ *n* (*plant*) violeta.
violin [vaɪə'lɪn] *n* violín *m*.
violinist [vaɪə'lɪnɪst] *n* violinista *m/f*.
VIP *n abbr* (= *very important person*) VIP *m*.
viper ['vaɪpə*] *n* víbora.
viral ['vaɪərəl] *adj* vírico.
virgin ['və:dʒɪn] *n* virgen *m/f* ♦ *adj* virgen; **the Blessed V~** la Santísima Virgen.
virginity [və:'dʒɪnɪtɪ] *n* virginidad *f*.
Virgo ['və:gəu] *n* Virgo.
virile ['vɪraɪl] *adj* viril.
virility [vɪ'rɪlɪtɪ] *n* virilidad *f*.
virtual ['və:tjuəl] *adj* virtual.
virtually ['və:tjuəlɪ] *adv* (*almost*) prácticamente, virtualmente; **it is ~ impossible** es prácticamente imposible.
virtual reality *n* realidad *f* virtual.
virtue ['və:tju:] *n* virtud *f*; **by ~ of** en virtud de.
virtuosity [və:tju'ɔsɪtɪ] *n* virtuosismo.
virtuoso [və:tju'əusəu] *n* virtuoso.
virtuous ['və:tjuəs] *adj* virtuoso.
virulence ['vɪruləns] *n* virulencia.
virulent ['vɪrulənt] *adj* virulento, violento.
virus ['vaɪərəs] *n* virus *m*.
visa ['vi:zə] *n* visado, visa (*LAM*).
vis-à-vis [vi:zə'vi:] *prep* con respecto a.
viscount ['vaɪkaunt] *n* vizconde *m*.
viscous ['vɪskəs] *adj* viscoso.
vise [vaɪs] *n* (*US TECH*) = **vice**.
visibility [vɪzɪ'bɪlɪtɪ] *n* visibilidad *f*.
visible ['vɪzəbl] *adj* visible; **~ exports/imports** exportaciones *fpl*/importaciones *fpl* visibles.
visibly ['vɪzɪblɪ] *adv* visiblemente.
vision ['vɪʒən] *n* (*sight*) vista; (*foresight, in dream*) visión *f*.
visionary ['vɪʒənrɪ] *n* visionario/a.
visit ['vɪzɪt] *n* visita ♦ *vt* (*person*) visitar, hacer una visita a; (*place*) ir a, (ir a) conocer; **to pay a ~ to** (*person*) visitar a; **on a private/official ~** en visita privada/oficial.
visiting ['vɪzɪtɪŋ] *adj* (*speaker, professor*) invitado; (*team*) visitante.
visiting card *n* tarjeta de visita.
visiting hours *npl* (*in hospital etc*) horas *fpl* de visita.
visitor *n* (*gen*) visitante *m/f*; (*to one's house*) visita; (*tourist*) turista *m/f*; (*tripper*) excursionista *m/f*; **to have ~s** (*at home*) tener visita.
visitors' book *n* libro de visitas.
visor ['vaɪzə*] *n* visera.
VISTA ['vɪstə] *n abbr* (= *Volunteers In Service to America*) *programa de ayuda voluntaria a los necesitados.*
vista ['vɪstə] *n* vista, panorama.

visual ['vɪzjuəl] *adj* visual.
visual aid *n* medio visual.
visual arts *npl* artes *fpl* plásticas.
visual display unit (VDU) *n* unidad *f* de despliegue visual, monitor *m*.
visualize ['vɪzjuəlaɪz] *vt* imaginarse; (*foresee*) prever.
visually ['vɪzjuəlɪ] *adv*: ~ **handicapped** con visión deficiente.
vital ['vaɪtl] *adj* (*essential*) esencial, imprescindible; (*crucial*) crítico; (*person*) enérgico, vivo; (*of life*) vital; **of ~ importance (to sb/sth)** de suma importancia (para algn/algo).
vitality [vaɪ'tælɪtɪ] *n* energía, vitalidad *f*.
vitally ['vaɪtəlɪ] *adv*: ~ **important** de suma importancia.
vital statistics *npl* (*of population*) estadísticas *fpl* demográficas; (*col*: *woman's*) medidas *fpl* (corporales).
vitamin ['vɪtəmɪn] *n* vitamina.
vitamin pill *n* pastilla de vitaminas.
vitreous ['vɪtrɪəs] *adj* (*china, enamel*) vítreo.
vitriolic [vɪtrɪ'ɔlɪk] *adj* mordaz.
viva ['vaɪvə] *n* (*also*: ~ **voce**) examen *m* oral.
vivacious [vɪ'veɪʃəs] *adj* vivaz, alegre.
vivacity [vɪ'væsɪtɪ] *n* vivacidad *f*.
vivid ['vɪvɪd] *adj* (*account*) gráfico; (*light*) intenso; (*imagination*) vivo.
vividly ['vɪvɪdlɪ] *adv* (*describe*) gráficamente; (*remember*) como si fuera hoy.
vivisection [vɪvɪ'sɛkʃən] *n* vivisección *f*.
vixen ['vɪksn] *n* (ZOOL) zorra, raposa; (*pej*: *woman*) arpía, bruja.
viz *abbr* (= *videlicet*: *namely*) v.gr.
VLF *abbr* = *very low frequency*.
V-neck ['vi:nɛk] *n* cuello de pico.
VOA *n abbr* (= *Voice of America*) Voz *f* de América.
vocabulary [vəu'kæbjulərɪ] *n* vocabulario.
vocal ['vəukl] *adj* vocal; (*articulate*) elocuente.
vocal cords *npl* cuerdas *fpl* vocales.
vocalist ['vəukəlɪst] *n* cantante *m/f*.
vocation [vəu'keɪʃən] *n* vocación *f*.
vocational [vəu'keɪʃənl] *adj* vocacional; ~ **guidance** orientación *f* profesional; ~ **training** formación *f* profesional.
vociferous [və'sɪfərəs] *adj* vociferante.
vociferously [və'sɪfərəslɪ] *adv* a gritos.
vodka ['vɔdkə] *n* vodka *m*.
vogue [vəug] *n* boga, moda; **to be in ~, be the ~** estar de moda *or* en boga.
voice [vɔɪs] *n* voz *f* ♦ *vt* (*opinion*) expresar; **in a loud/soft ~** en voz alta/baja; **to give ~ to** expresar.
voice mail *n* fonobuzón *m*.
voice-over ['vɔɪsəuvə*] *n* voz *f* en off.
void [vɔɪd] *n* vacío; (*hole*) hueco ♦ *adj* (*invalid*) nulo, inválido; (*empty*): ~ **of** carente *or* desprovisto de.
voile [vɔɪl] *n* gasa.
vol. *abbr* (= *volume*) t.
volatile ['vɔlətaɪl] *adj* volátil; (COMPUT: *memory*) no permanente.
volcanic [vɔl'kænɪk] *adj* volcánico.
volcano, ~es [vɔl'keɪnəu] *n* volcán *m*.
volition [və'lɪʃən] *n*: **of one's own ~** por su propia voluntad.
volley ['vɔlɪ] *n* (*of gunfire*) descarga; (*of stones etc*) lluvia; (TENNIS *etc*) volea.
volleyball *n* voleibol *m*, balonvolea *m*.
volt [vəult] *n* voltio.
voltage ['vəultɪdʒ] *n* voltaje *m*; **high/low ~** alto/bajo voltaje, alta/baja tensión.
volte-face ['vɔlt'fɑ:s] *n* viraje *m*.
voluble ['vɔljubl] *adj* locuaz, hablador(a).
volume ['vɔlju:m] *n* (*of tank*) volumen *m*; (*book*) tomo; ~ **one/two** (*of book*) tomo primero/segundo; **~s** *npl* (*great quantities*) cantidad *fsg*; **his expression spoke ~s** su expresión (lo) decía todo.
volume control *n* (RADIO, TV) (botón *m* del) volumen *m*.
volume discount *n* (COMM) descuento por volumen de compras.
voluminous [və'lu:mɪnəs] *adj* (*large*) voluminoso; (*prolific*) prolífico.
voluntarily ['vɔləntrɪlɪ] *adv* libremente, voluntariamente.
voluntary ['vɔləntərɪ] *adj* voluntario, espontáneo.
voluntary liquidation *n* (COMM) liquidación *f* voluntaria.
voluntary redundancy *n* (BRIT) despido voluntario.
volunteer [vɔlən'tɪə*] *n* voluntario/a ♦ *vi* ofrecerse (de voluntario); **to ~ to do** ofrecerse a hacer.
voluptuous [və'lʌptjuəs] *adj* voluptuoso.
vomit ['vɔmɪt] *n* vómito ♦ *vt, vi* vomitar.
voracious [və'reɪʃəs] *adj* voraz; (*reader*) ávido.
vote [vəut] *n* voto; (*votes cast*) votación *f*; (*right to ~*) derecho a votar; (*franchise*) sufragio ♦ *vt* (*chairman*) elegir ♦ *vi* votar, ir a votar; ~ **of thanks** voto de gracias; **to put sth to the ~, to take a ~ on sth** someter algo a votación; ~ **for** *or* **in favour of/against** voto a favor de/en contra de; **to ~ to do sth** votar por hacer algo; **he was ~d secretary** fue elegido secretario por votación; **to pass a ~ of confidence/no confidence** aprobar un voto de confianza/de censura.
voter ['vəutə*] *n* votante *m/f*.

voting ['vəutɪŋ] *n* votación *f*.
voting paper *n* (*BRIT*) papeleta de votación.
voting right *n* derecho a voto.
vouch [vautʃ]: **to ~ for** *vt fus* garantizar, responder de.
voucher ['vautʃə*] *n* (*for meal, petrol*) vale *m*; **luncheon/travel ~** vale *m* de comida/de viaje.
vow [vau] *n* voto ♦ *vi* hacer voto; **to take** *or* **make a ~ to do sth** jurar hacer algo, comprometerse a hacer algo.
vowel ['vauəl] *n* vocal *f*.
voyage ['vɔɪɪdʒ] *n* (*journey*) viaje *m*; (*crossing*) travesía.
voyeur [vwɑː'jəː*] *n* voyeur *m/f*, mirón/ona *m/f*.
VP *n abbr* (= *vice-president*) V.P.
vs *abbr* (= *versus*) vs.
VSO *n abbr* (*BRIT*: = *Voluntary Service Overseas*) *organización que envía jóvenes voluntarios a trabajar y enseñar en los países del Tercer Mundo.*
VT, Vt. *abbr* (*US*) = *Vermont.*
vulgar ['vʌlgə*] *adj* (*rude*) ordinario, grosero; (*in bad taste*) de mal gusto.
vulgarity [vʌl'gærɪtɪ] *n* grosería; mal gusto.
vulnerability [vʌlnərə'bɪlɪtɪ] *n* vulnerabilidad *f*.
vulnerable ['vʌlnərəbl] *adj* vulnerable.
vulture ['vʌltʃə*] *n* buitre *m*, gallinazo (*LAM*).

Ww

W, w ['dʌbljuː] *n* (*letter*) W, w *f*; **W for William** W de Washington.
W *abbr* (= *west*) O; (*ELEC*: = *watt*) v.
WA *abbr* (*US*) = *Washington.*
wad [wɔd] *n* (*of cotton wool, paper*) bolita; (*of banknotes etc*) fajo.
wadding ['wɔdɪŋ] *n* relleno.
waddle ['wɔdl] *vi* andar como un pato.
wade [weɪd] *vi*: **to ~ through** caminar por el agua; (*fig*: *a book*) leer con dificultad.
wading pool ['weɪdɪŋ-] *n* (*US*) piscina para niños.
wafer ['weɪfə*] *n* (*biscuit*) barquillo; (*REL*) oblea; (: *consecrated*) hostia; (*COMPUT*) oblea, microplaqueta.
wafer-thin ['weɪfə'θɪn] *adj* finísimo.
waffle ['wɔfl] *n* (*CULIN*) gofre *m* ♦ *vi* meter el rollo.
waffle iron *n* molde *m* para hacer gofres.
waft [wɔft] *vt* llevar por el aire ♦ *vi* flotar.
wag [wæg] *vt* menear, agitar ♦ *vi* moverse, menearse; **the dog ~ged its tail** el perro meneó la cola.
wage [weɪdʒ] *n* (*also*: **~s**) sueldo, salario ♦ *vt*: **to ~ war** hacer la guerra; **a day's ~** el sueldo de un día.
wage claim *n* reivindicación *f* salarial.
wage differential *n* diferencia salarial.
wage earner *n* asalariado/a.
wage freeze *n* congelación *f* de salarios.
wage packet *n* sobre *m* de la paga.
wager ['weɪdʒə*] *n* apuesta ♦ *vt* apostar.
waggle ['wægl] *vt* menear, mover.
wag(g)on ['wægən] *n* (*horse-drawn*) carro; (*BRIT RAIL*) vagón *m*.
wail [weɪl] *n* gemido ♦ *vi* gemir.
waist [weɪst] *n* cintura, talle *m*.
waistcoat ['weɪstkəut] *n* (*BRIT*) chaleco.
waistline ['weɪstlaɪn] *n* talle *m*.
wait [weɪt] *n* espera; (*interval*) pausa ♦ *vi* esperar; **to lie in ~ for** acechar a; **I can't ~ to** (*fig*) estoy deseando; **to ~ for** esperar (a); **to keep sb ~ing** hacer esperar a algn; **~ a moment!** ¡un momento!, ¡un momentito!; **"repairs while you ~"** "reparaciones en el acto".
▸**wait behind** *vi* quedarse.
▸**wait on** *vt fus* servir a.
▸**wait up** *vi* esperar levantado.
waiter ['weɪtə*] *n* camarero.
waiting ['weɪtɪŋ] *n*: **"no ~"** (*BRIT AUT*) "prohibido estacionarse".
waiting list *n* lista de espera.
waiting room *n* sala de espera.
waitress ['weɪtrɪs] *n* camarera.
waive [weɪv] *vt* suspender.
waiver ['weɪvə*] *n* renuncia.
wake [weɪk] *vb* (*pt* **woke** *or* **waked**, *pp* **woken** *or* **waked** [wəuk, 'wəukn]) *vt* (*also*: **~ up**) despertar ♦ *vi* (*also*: **~ up**) despertarse ♦ *n* (*for dead person*) velatorio; (*NAUT*) estela; **to ~ up to sth** (*fig*) darse cuenta de algo; **in the ~ of** tras, después de; **to follow in sb's ~** (*fig*) seguir las huellas de algn.
waken ['weɪkn] *vt, vi* = **wake**.
Wales [weɪlz] *n* País *m* de Gales.
walk [wɔːk] *n* (*stroll*) paseo; (*hike*) excursión *f* a pie, caminata; (*gait*) paso, andar *m*; (*in park etc*) paseo ♦ *vi* andar, caminar; (*for pleasure, exercise*) pasearse ♦ *vt* (*distance*) recorrer a pie, andar; (*dog*) (sacar a) pasear; **to go for a ~** ir a dar un paseo; **10 minutes' ~ from here** a 10

minutos de aquí andando; **people from all ~s of life** gente de todas las esferas; **to ~ in one's sleep** ser sonámbulo/a; **I'll ~ you home** te acompañaré a casa.
►**walk out** *vi* (*go out*) salir; (*as protest*) marcharse, salirse; (*strike*) declararse en huelga; **to ~ out on sb** abandonar a algn.
walkabout ['wɔːkəbaut] *n*: **to go (on a) ~** darse un baño de multitudes.
walker ['wɔːkə*] *n* (*person*) paseante *m/f*, caminante *m/f*.
walkie-talkie ['wɔːkɪ'tɔːkɪ] *n* walkie-talkie *m*.
walking ['wɔːkɪŋ] *n* (el) andar; **it's within ~ distance** se puede ir andando *or* a pie.
walking shoes *npl* zapatos *mpl* para andar.
walking stick *n* bastón *m*.
Walkman ® *n* walkman *m* ®.
walk-on ['wɔːkɔn] *adj* (*THEAT: part*) de comparsa.
walkout ['wɔːkaut] *n* (*of workers*) huelga.
walkover ['wɔːkəuvə*] *n* (*col*) pan *m* comido.
walkway ['wɔːkweɪ] *n* paseo.
wall [wɔːl] *n* pared *f*; (*exterior*) muro; (*city ~ etc*) muralla; **to go to the ~** (*fig: firm etc*) quebrar, ir a la bancarrota.
►**wall in** *vt* (*garden etc*) cercar con una tapia.
walled [wɔːld] *adj* (*city*) amurallado; (*garden*) con tapia.
wallet ['wɔlɪt] *n* cartera, billetera (*esp LAM*).
wallflower ['wɔːlflauə*] *n* alhelí *m*; **to be a ~** (*fig*) comer pavo.
wall hanging *n* tapiz *m*.
wallop ['wɔləp] *vt* (*col*) zurrar.
wallow ['wɔləu] *vi* revolcarse; **to ~ in one's grief** sumirse en su pena.
wallpaper ['wɔːlpeɪpə*] *n* papel *m* pintado.
wall-to-wall ['wɔːltə'wɔːl] *adj*: **~ carpeting** moqueta.
wally ['wɔlɪ] *n* (*col*) majadero/a.
walnut ['wɔːlnʌt] *n* nuez *f*; (*tree*) nogal *m*.
walrus, *pl* **~** *or* **~es** ['wɔːlrəs] *n* morsa.
waltz [wɔːlts] *n* vals *m* ♦ *vi* bailar el vals.
wan [wɔn] *adj* pálido.
wand [wɔnd] *n* (*also*: **magic ~**) varita (mágica).
wander ['wɔndə*] *vi* (*person*) vagar; deambular; (*thoughts*) divagar; (*get lost*) extraviarse ♦ *vt* recorrer, vagar por.
wanderer ['wɔndərə*] *n* vagabundo/a.
wandering ['wɔndərɪŋ] *adj* (*tribe*) nómada; (*minstrel, actor*) ambulante; (*path, river*) sinuoso; (*glance, mind*) distraído.
wane [weɪn] *vi* menguar.
wangle ['wæŋgl] (*BRIT col*) *vt*: **to ~ sth** agenciarse *or* conseguir algo ♦ *n* chanchullo.
wanker ['wæŋkə*] *n* (*col!*) pajero/a (*!*); (*as insult*) mamón/ona (*!*) *m/f*.
want [wɔnt] *vt* (*wish for*) querer, desear; (*need*) necesitar; (*lack*) carecer de ♦ *n* (*poverty*) pobreza; **for ~ of** por falta de; **~s** *npl* (*needs*) necesidades *fpl*; **to ~ to do** querer hacer; **to ~ sb to do sth** querer que algn haga algo; **you're ~ed on the phone** te llaman al teléfono; **to be in ~** estar necesitado; **"cook ~ed"** "se necesita cocinero/a".
want ads *npl* (*US*) anuncios *mpl* por palabras.
wanting ['wɔntɪŋ] *adj*: **to be ~ (in)** estar falto (de); **to be found ~** no estar a la altura de las circunstancias.
wanton ['wɔntn] *adj* (*playful*) juguetón/ona; (*licentious*) lascivo.
war [wɔː*] *n* guerra; **to make ~** hacer la guerra; **the First/Second World W~** la primera/segunda guerra mundial.
warble ['wɔːbl] *n* (*of bird*) trino, gorjeo ♦ *vi* (*bird*) trinar.
war cry *n* grito de guerra.
ward [wɔːd] *n* (*in hospital*) sala; (*POL*) distrito electoral; (*LAW: child*) pupilo/a.
►**ward off** *vt* desviar, parar; (*attack*) rechazar.
warden ['wɔːdn] *n* (*BRIT: of institution*) director(a) *m/f*; (*of park, game reserve*) guardián/ana *m/f*; (*BRIT: also*: **traffic ~**) guardia *m/f*.
warder ['wɔːdə*] *n* (*BRIT*) guardián/ana *m/f*, carcelero/a.
wardrobe ['wɔːdrəub] *n* armario, guardarropa, ropero, clóset/closet *m* (*LAM*).
warehouse ['wɛəhaus] *n* almacén *m*, depósito.
wares [wɛəz] *npl* mercancías *fpl*.
warfare ['wɔːfɛə*] *n* guerra.
war game *n* juego de estrategia militar.
warhead ['wɔːhɛd] *n* cabeza armada; **nuclear ~s** cabezas *fpl* nucleares.
warily ['wɛərɪlɪ] *adv* con cautela, cautelosamente.
warlike ['wɔːlaɪk] *adj* guerrero.
warm [wɔːm] *adj* caliente; (*person, greeting, heart*) afectuoso, cariñoso; (*supporter*) entusiasta; (*thanks, congratulations, apologies*) efusivo; (*clothes etc*) que abriga; (*welcome, day*) caluroso; **it's ~** hace calor; **I'm ~** tengo calor; **to keep sth ~** mantener algo caliente.
►**warm up** *vi* (*room*) calentarse; (*person*) entrar en calor; (*athlete*) hacer ejercicios

de calentamiento; (*discussion*) acalorarse ♦ *vt* calentar.
warm-blooded ['wɔːm'blʌdɪd] *adj* de sangre caliente.
war memorial *n* monumento a los caídos.
warm-hearted [wɔːm'hɑːtɪd] *adj* afectuoso.
warmly ['wɔːmlɪ] *adv* afectuosamente.
warmonger ['wɔːmʌŋgə*] *n* belicista *m/f*.
warmongering ['wɔːmʌŋgrɪŋ] *n* belicismo.
warmth [wɔːmθ] *n* calor *m*.
warm-up ['wɔːmʌp] *n* (*SPORT*) ejercicios *mpl* de calentamiento.
warn [wɔːn] *vt* avisar, advertir; **to ~ sb not to do sth** *or* **against doing sth** aconsejar a algn que no haga algo.
warning ['wɔːnɪŋ] *n* aviso, advertencia; **gale ~** (*METEOROLOGY*) aviso de vendaval; **without (any) ~** sin aviso *or* avisar.
warning light *n* luz *f* de advertencia.
warning triangle *n* (*AUT*) triángulo señalizador.
warp [wɔːp] *vi* (*wood*) combarse.
warpath ['wɔːpɑːθ] *n*: **to be on the ~** (*fig*) estar en pie de guerra.
warped [wɔːpt] *adj* (*wood*) alabeado; (*fig*: *character, sense of humour etc*) pervertido.
warrant ['wɔrnt] *n* (*LAW*: *to arrest*) orden *f* de detención; (: *to search*) mandamiento de registro ♦ *vt* (*justify, merit*) merecer.
warrant officer *n* (*MIL*) brigada *m*; (*NAUT*) contramaestre *m*.
warranty ['wɔrəntɪ] *n* garantía; **under ~** (*COMM*) bajo garantía.
warren ['wɔrən] *n* (*of rabbits*) madriguera; (*fig*) laberinto.
warring ['wɔːrɪŋ] *adj* (*interests etc*) opuesto; (*nations*) en guerra.
warrior ['wɔrɪə*] *n* guerrero/a.
Warsaw ['wɔːsɔː] *n* Varsovia.
warship ['wɔːʃɪp] *n* buque *m* *or* barco de guerra.
wart [wɔːt] *n* verruga.
wartime ['wɔːtaɪm] *n*: **in ~** en tiempos de guerra, en la guerra.
wary ['wɛərɪ] *adj* cauteloso; **to be ~ about** *or* **of doing sth** tener cuidado con hacer algo.
was [wɔz] *pt of* **be**.
wash [wɔʃ] *vt* lavar; (*sweep, carry*: *sea etc*) llevar ♦ *vi* lavarse ♦ *n* (*clothes etc*) lavado; (*bath*) baño; (*of ship*) estela; **he was ~ed overboard** fue arrastrado del barco por las olas; **to have a ~** lavarse.
►**wash away** *vt* (*stain*) quitar lavando; (*subj*: *river etc*) llevarse; (*fig*) limpiar.
►**wash down** *vt* lavar.
►**wash off** *vt* quitar lavando.
►**wash up** *vi* (*BRIT*) fregar los platos; (*US*: *have a wash*) lavarse.
Wash. *abbr* (*US*) = *Washington*.
washable ['wɔʃəbl] *adj* lavable.
washbasin ['wɔʃbeɪsn], (*US*) **washbowl** ['wɔʃbəul] *n* lavabo.
washcloth ['wɔʃklɔθ] *n* (*US*) manopla.
washer ['wɔʃə*] *n* (*TECH*) arandela.
washing ['wɔʃɪŋ] *n* (*dirty*) ropa sucia; (*clean*) colada.
washing line *n* cuerda de (colgar) la ropa.
washing machine *n* lavadora.
washing powder *n* (*BRIT*) detergente *m* (en polvo).
Washington ['wɔʃɪŋtən] *n* (*city, state*) Washington *m*.
washing-up [wɔʃɪŋ'ʌp] *n* fregado; (*dishes*) platos *mpl* (para fregar); **to do the ~** fregar los platos.
washing-up liquid *n* lavavajillas *m inv*.
wash leather *n* gamuza.
wash-out ['wɔʃaut] *n* (*col*) fracaso.
washroom ['wɔʃrum] *n* servicios *mpl*.
wasn't ['wɔznt] = **was not**.
Wasp, WASP [wɔsp] *n abbr* (*US col*: = *White Anglo-Saxon Protestant*) *sobrenombre, en general peyorativo, que se da a los americanos de origen anglosajón, acomodados y de tendencia conservadora.*
wasp [wɔsp] *n* avispa.
waspish ['wɔspɪʃ] *adj* (*character*) irascible; (*comment*) mordaz, punzante.
wastage ['weɪstɪdʒ] *n* desgaste *m*; (*loss*) pérdida; **natural ~** desgaste natural.
waste [weɪst] *n* derroche *m*, despilfarro; (*misuse*) desgaste *m*; (*of time*) pérdida; (*food*) sobras *fpl*; (*rubbish*) basura, desperdicios *mpl* ♦ *adj* (*material*) de desecho; (*left over*) sobrante; (*energy, heat*) desperdiciado; (*land, ground*: *in city*) sin construir; (: *in country*) baldío ♦ *vt* (*squander*) malgastar, derrochar; (*time*) perder; (*opportunity*) desperdiciar; **~s** *npl* (*area of land*) tierras *fpl* baldías; **to lay ~** devastar, arrasar; **it's a ~ of money** es tirar el dinero; **to go to ~** desperdiciarse.
►**waste away** *vi* consumirse.
wastebasket ['weɪstbɑːskɪt] *n* (*esp US*) = **wastepaper basket**.
waste disposal (unit) *n* (*BRIT*) triturador *m* de basura.
wasteful ['weɪstful] *adj* derrochador(a); (*process*) antieconómico.
wastefully ['weɪstfulɪ] *adv*: **to spend money ~** derrochar dinero.
waste ground *n* (*BRIT*) terreno baldío.
wasteland ['weɪstlənd] *n* (*urban*)

descampados *mpl.*
wastepaper basket ['weɪstpeɪpə-] *n* papelera.
waste pipe *n* tubo de desagüe.
waste products *npl* (*INDUSTRY*) residuos *mpl.*
waster ['weɪstə*] *n* (*col*) gandul *m/f.*
watch [wɔtʃ] *n* reloj *m*; (*vigil*) vigilia; (*vigilance*) vigilancia; (*MIL: guard*) centinela *m*; (*NAUT: spell of duty*) guardia ♦ *vt* (*look at*) mirar, observar; (*: match, programme*) ver; (*spy on, guard*) vigilar; (*be careful of*) cuidar, tener cuidado de ♦ *vi* ver, mirar; (*keep guard*) montar guardia; **to keep a close ~ on sth/sb** vigilar algo/a algn de cerca; **~ how you drive/what you're doing** ten cuidado al conducir/con lo que haces.
▸**watch out** *vi* cuidarse, tener cuidado.
watch band *n* (*US*) pulsera (de reloj).
watchdog ['wɔtʃdɔg] *n* perro guardián; (*fig*) organismo de control.
watchful ['wɔtʃful] *adj* vigilante, sobre aviso.
watchfully ['wɔtʃfulɪ] *adv*: **to stand ~** permanecer vigilante.
watchmaker ['wɔtʃmeɪkə*] *n* relojero/a.
watchman *n* guardián *m*; (*also*: **night ~**) sereno, vigilante *m*; (*in factory*) vigilante *m* nocturno.
watch stem *n* (*US*) cuerda.
watch strap *n* pulsera (de reloj).
watchword ['wɔtʃwə:d] *n* consigna, contraseña.
water ['wɔ:tə*] *n* agua ♦ *vt* (*plant*) regar ♦ *vi* (*eyes*) llorar; **I'd like a drink of ~** quisiera un vaso de agua; **in British ~s** en aguas británicas; **to pass ~** orinar; **his mouth ~ed** se le hizo la boca agua.
▸**water down** *vt* (*milk etc*) aguar.
water closet *n* wáter *m.*
watercolour, (*US*) **watercolor** ['wɔ:təkʌlə*] *n* acuarela.
water-cooled ['wɔ:təku:ld] *adj* refrigerado (por agua).
watercress ['wɔ:təkrɛs] *n* berro.
waterfall ['wɔ:təfɔ:l] *n* cascada, salto de agua.
waterfront ['wɔ:təfrʌnt] *n* (*seafront*) parte *f* que da al mar; (*at docks*) muelles *mpl.*
water heater *n* calentador *m* de agua.
water hole *n* abrevadero.
watering can ['wɔ:tərɪŋ-] *n* regadera.
water level *n* nivel *m* del agua.
water lily *n* nenúfar *m.*
waterline ['wɔ:təlaɪn] *n* (*NAUT*) línea de flotación.
waterlogged ['wɔ:təlɔgd] *adj* (*boat*) anegado; (*ground*) inundado.
water main *n* cañería del agua.
watermark ['wɔ:təmɑ:k] *n* (*on paper*) filigrana.
watermelon ['wɔ:təmɛlən] *n* sandía.
water polo *n* waterpolo, polo acuático.
waterproof ['wɔ:təpru:f] *adj* impermeable.
water-repellent ['wɔ:tərɪ'pɛlənt] *adj* hidrófugo.
watershed ['wɔ:təʃɛd] *n* (*GEO*) cuenca; (*fig*) momento crítico.
water-skiing ['wɔ:təski:ɪŋ] *n* esquí *m* acuático.
water softener *n* ablandador *m* de agua.
water tank *n* depósito de agua.
watertight ['wɔ:tətaɪt] *adj* hermético.
water vapour, (*US*) **water vapor** *n* vapor *m* de agua.
waterway ['wɔ:təweɪ] *n* vía fluvial *or* navegable.
waterworks ['wɔ:təwə:ks] *npl* central *fsg* depuradora.
watery ['wɔ:tərɪ] *adj* (*colour*) desvaído; (*coffee*) aguado; (*eyes*) lloroso.
watt [wɔt] *n* vatio.
wattage ['wɔtɪdʒ] *n* potencia en vatios.
wattle ['wɔtl] *n* zarzo.
wave [weɪv] *n* ola; (*of hand*) señal *f* con la mano; (*RADIO, in hair*) onda; (*fig: of enthusiasm, strikes*) oleada ♦ *vi* agitar la mano; (*flag*) ondear ♦ *vt* (*handkerchief, gun*) agitar; **short/medium/long ~** (*RADIO*) onda corta/media/larga; **the new ~** (*CINE, MUS*) la nueva ola; **to ~ goodbye to sb** decir adiós a algn con la mano; **he ~d us over to his table** nos hizo señas (con la mano) para que nos acercásemos a su mesa.
▸**wave aside, wave away** *vt* (*person*): **to ~ sb aside** apartar a algn con la mano; (*fig: suggestion, objection*) rechazar; (*doubts*) desechar.
waveband ['weɪvbænd] *n* banda de ondas.
wavelength ['weɪvlɛŋθ] *n* longitud *f* de onda.
waver ['weɪvə*] *vi* oscilar; (*confidence*) disminuir; (*faith*) flaquear.
wavy ['weɪvɪ] *adj* ondulado.
wax [wæks] *n* cera ♦ *vt* encerar ♦ *vi* (*moon*) crecer.
waxen ['wæksn] *adj* (*fig: pale*) blanco como la cera.
waxworks ['wækswə:ks] *npl* museo *sg* de cera.
way [weɪ] *n* camino; (*distance*) trayecto, recorrido; (*direction*) dirección *f*, sentido; (*manner*) modo, manera; (*habit*) costumbre *f*; **which ~? — this ~** ¿por

dónde? *or* ¿en qué dirección? — por aquí; **on the ~** (*en route*) en (el) camino; (*expected*) en camino; **to be on one's ~** estar en camino; **you pass it on your ~ home** está de camino a tu casa; **to be in the ~** bloquear el camino; (*fig*) estorbar; **to keep out of sb's ~** esquivar a algn; **to make ~ (for sb/sth)** dejar paso (a algn/algo); (*fig*) abrir camino (a algn/algo); **to go out of one's ~ to do sth** desvivirse por hacer algo; **to lose one's ~** perderse, extraviarse; **to be the wrong ~ round** estar del *or* al revés; **in a ~** en cierto modo *or* sentido; **by the ~** a propósito; **by ~ of** (*via*) pasando por; (*as a sort of*) como, a modo de; **"~ in"** (*BRIT*) "entrada"; **"~ out"** (*BRIT*) "salida"; **the ~ back** el camino de vuelta; **the village is rather out of the ~** el pueblo está un poco apartado *or* retirado; **it's a long ~ away** está muy lejos; **to get one's own ~** salirse con la suya; **"give ~"** (*BRIT AUT*) "ceda el paso"; **no ~!** (*col*) ¡ni pensarlo!; **put it the right ~ up** ponlo boca arriba; **he's in a bad ~** está grave; **to be under ~** (*work, project*) estar en marcha.

waybill ['weɪbɪl] *n* (*COMM*) hoja de ruta, carta de porte.

waylay [weɪ'leɪ] *vt* (*irreg*: *like* **lay**) atacar.

wayside ['weɪsaɪd] *n* borde *m* del camino; **to fall by the ~** (*fig*) fracasar.

way station *n* (*US RAIL*) apeadero; (*fig*) paso intermedio.

wayward ['weɪwəd] *adj* díscolo, caprichoso.

WC ['dʌblju'siː] *n abbr* (*BRIT*: = *water closet*) wáter *m*.

WCC *n abbr* = *World Council of Churches*.

we [wiː] *pl pron* nosotros/as; **~ understand** (nosotros) entendemos; **here ~ are** aquí estamos.

weak [wiːk] *adj* débil, flojo; (*tea, coffee*) flojo, aguado; **to grow ~(er)** debilitarse.

weaken ['wiːkən] *vi* debilitarse; (*give way*) ceder ♦ *vt* debilitar.

weak-kneed [wiːk'niːd] *adj* (*fig*) sin voluntad *or* carácter.

weakling ['wiːklɪŋ] *n* debilucho/a.

weakly ['wiːklɪ] *adj* enfermizo, débil ♦ *adv* débilmente.

weakness ['wiːknɪs] *n* debilidad *f*; (*fault*) punto débil.

wealth [wɛlθ] *n* (*money, resources*) riqueza; (*of details*) abundancia.

wealth tax *n* impuesto sobre el patrimonio.

wealthy ['wɛlθɪ] *adj* rico.

wean [wiːn] *vt* destetar.

weapon ['wɛpən] *n* arma.

wear [wɛə*] *n* (*use*) uso; (*deterioration*) desgaste *m*; (*clothing*): **sports/baby~** ropa de deportes/de niños ♦ *vb* (*pt* **wore**, *pp* **worn** [wɔː*, wɔːn]) *vt* (*clothes, beard*) llevar; (*shoes*) calzar; (*look, smile*) tener; (*damage*) gastar, usar ♦ *vi* (*last*) durar; (*rub through etc*) desgastarse; **evening ~** (*man's*) traje *m* de etiqueta; (*woman's*) traje *m* de noche; **to ~ a hole in sth** hacer un agujero en algo.

▸**wear away** *vt* gastar ♦ *vi* desgastarse.

▸**wear down** *vt* gastar; (*strength*) agotar.

▸**wear off** *vi* (*pain, excitement etc*) pasar.

▸**wear out** *vt* desgastar; (*person, strength*) agotar.

wearable ['wɛərəbl] *adj* que se puede llevar, ponible.

wear and tear *n* desgaste *m*.

wearer ['wɛərə*] *n*: **the ~ of this jacket** el/la que lleva puesta esta chaqueta.

wearily ['wɪərɪlɪ] *adv* con cansancio.

weariness ['wɪərɪnɪs] *n* cansancio; abatimiento.

wearisome ['wɪərɪsəm] *adj* (*tiring*) cansado, pesado; (*boring*) aburrido.

weary ['wɪərɪ] *adj* (*tired*) cansado; (*dispirited*) abatido ♦ *vt* cansar ♦ *vi*: **to ~ of** cansarse de, aburrirse de.

weasel ['wiːzl] *n* (*ZOOL*) comadreja.

weather ['wɛðə*] *n* tiempo ♦ *vt* (*storm, crisis*) hacer frente a; **under the ~** (*fig*: *ill*) mal, pachucho; **what's the ~ like?** ¿qué tiempo hace?, ¿cómo hace?

weather-beaten ['wɛðəbiːtn] *adj* curtido.

weathercock ['wɛðəkɔk] *n* veleta.

weather forecast *n* boletín *m* meteorológico.

weatherman ['wɛðəmæn] *n* hombre *m* del tiempo.

weatherproof ['wɛðəpruːf] *adj* (*garment*) impermeable.

weather report *n* parte *m* meteorológico.

weather vane *n* = **weathercock**.

weave, *pt* **wove**, *pp* **woven** [wiːv, wəuv, 'wəuvn] *vt* (*cloth*) tejer; (*fig*) entretejer ♦ *vi* (*fig*: *pt, pp* **~d**: *move in and out*) zigzaguear.

weaver ['wiːvə*] *n* tejedor(a) *m/f*.

weaving ['wiːvɪŋ] *n* tejeduría.

web [wɛb] *n* (*of spider*) telaraña; (*on foot*) membrana; (*network*) red *f*; **the (World Wide) W~** el *or* la Web.

webbed [wɛbd] *adj* (*foot*) palmeado.

webbing ['wɛbɪŋ] *n* (*on chair*) cinchas *fpl*.

website ['wɛbsaɪt] *n* sitio web.

wed [wɛd] *vt* (*pt, pp* **wedded**) casar ♦ *n*: **the newly-~s** los recién casados.

Wed. *abbr* (= *Wednesday*) miérc.

we'd [wi:d] = **we had; we would.**
wedded ['wɛdɪd] *pt, pp of* **wed.**
wedding ['wɛdɪŋ] *n* boda, casamiento.
wedding anniversary *adj* aniversario de boda; **silver/golden ~** bodas *fpl* de plata/de oro.
wedding day *n* día *m* de la boda.
wedding dress *n* traje *m* de novia.
wedding present *n* regalo de boda.
wedding ring *n* alianza.
wedge [wɛdʒ] *n* (*of wood etc*) cuña; (*of cake*) trozo ♦ *vt* acuñar; (*push*) apretar.
wedge-heeled ['wɛdʒ'hi:ld] *adj* con suela de cuña.
wedlock ['wɛdlɔk] *n* matrimonio.
Wednesday ['wɛdnzdɪ] *n* miércoles *m inv*.
wee [wi:] *adj* (*Scottish*) pequeñito.
weed [wi:d] *n* mala hierba, maleza ♦ *vt* escardar, desherbar.
▸**weed out** *vt* eliminar.
weedkiller ['wi:dkɪlə*] *n* herbicida *m*.
weedy ['wi:dɪ] *adj* (*person*) debilucho.
week [wi:k] *n* semana; **a ~ today** de hoy en ocho días; **Tuesday ~, a ~ on Tuesday** del martes en una semana; **once/twice a ~** una vez/dos veces a la semana; **this ~** esta semana; **in 2 ~s' time** dentro de 2 semanas; **every other ~** cada 2 semanas.
weekday ['wi:kdeɪ] *n* día *m* laborable; **on ~s** entre semana, en días laborables.
weekend [wi:k'ɛnd] *n* fin *m* de semana.
weekend case *n* neceser *m*.
weekly ['wi:klɪ] *adv* semanalmente, cada semana ♦ *adj* semanal ♦ *n* semanario; **~ newspaper** semanario.
weep, *pt, pp* **wept** [wi:p, wɛpt] *vi, vt* llorar; (*MED: wound etc*) supurar.
weeping willow ['wi:pɪŋ-] *n* sauce *m* llorón.
weepy ['wi:pɪ] *n* (*col: film*) película lacrimógena; (*: story*) historia lacrimógena.
weft [wɛft] *n* (*TEXTILES*) trama.
weigh [weɪ] *vt, vi* pesar; **to ~ anchor** levar anclas; **to ~ the pros and cons** pesar los pros y los contras.
▸**weigh down** *vt* sobrecargar; (*fig: with worry*) agobiar.
▸**weigh out** *vt* (*goods*) pesar.
▸**weigh up** *vt* pesar.
weighbridge ['weɪbrɪdʒ] *n* báscula para camiones.
weighing machine ['weɪɪŋ-] *n* báscula, peso.
weight [weɪt] *n* peso; (*on scale*) pesa; **to lose/put on ~** adelgazar/engordar; **~s and measures** pesas y medidas.
weighting ['weɪtɪŋ] *n* (*allowance*): **(London) ~** *dietas fpl* (*por residir en Londres*).
weightlessness ['weɪtlɪsnɪs] *n* ingravidez *f*.
weight lifter *n* levantador(a) *m/f* de pesas.
weight limit *n* límite *m* de peso.
weight training *n* musculación *f* (con pesas).
weighty ['weɪtɪ] *adj* pesado.
weir [wɪə*] *n* presa.
weird [wɪəd] *adj* raro, extraño.
weirdo ['wɪədəu] *n* (*col*) tío/a raro/a.
welcome ['wɛlkəm] *adj* bienvenido ♦ *n* bienvenida ♦ *vt* dar la bienvenida a; (*be glad of*) alegrarse de; **to make sb ~** recibir *or* acoger bien a algn; **thank you — you're ~** gracias — de nada; **you're ~ to try** puede intentar cuando quiera; **we ~ this step** celebramos esta medida.
weld [wɛld] *n* soldadura ♦ *vt* soldar.
welding ['wɛldɪŋ] *n* soldadura.
welfare ['wɛlfɛə*] *n* bienestar *m*; (*social aid*) asistencia social; **W~** (*US*) subsidio de paro; **to look after sb's ~** cuidar del bienestar de algn.
welfare state *n* estado del bienestar.
welfare work *n* asistencia social.
well [wɛl] *n* pozo ♦ *adv* bien ♦ *adj*: **to be ~** estar bien (de salud) ♦ *excl* ¡vaya!, ¡bueno!; **as ~** (*in addition*) además, también; **as ~ as** además de; **you might as ~ tell me** más vale que me lo digas; **it would be as ~ to ask** más valdría preguntar; **~ done!** ¡bien hecho!; **get ~ soon!** ¡que te mejores pronto!; **to do ~** (*business*) ir bien; **I did ~ in my exams** me han salido bien los exámenes; **they are doing ~ now** les va bien ahora; **to think ~ of sb** pensar bien de algn; **I don't feel ~** no me encuentro *or* siento bien; **~, as I was saying ...** bueno, como decía ....
▸**well up** *vi* brotar.
we'll [wi:l] = **we will, we shall.**
well-behaved ['wɛlbɪ'heɪvd] *adj*: **to be ~** portarse bien.
well-being ['wɛl'bi:ɪŋ] *n* bienestar *m*.
well-bred ['wɛl'brɛd] *adj* bien educado.
well-built ['wɛl'bɪlt] *adj* (*person*) fornido.
well-chosen ['wɛl'tʃəuzn] *adj* (*remarks, words*) acertado.
well-deserved ['wɛldɪ'zə:vd] *adj* merecido.
well-developed ['wɛldɪ'vɛləpt] *adj* (*arm, muscle etc*) bien desarrollado; (*sense*) agudo, fino.
well-disposed ['wɛldɪs'pəuzd] *adj*: **~ to(wards)** bien dispuesto a.
well-dressed ['wɛl'drɛst] *adj* bien vestido.
well-earned ['wɛl'ə:nd] *adj* (*rest*) merecido.
well-groomed ['wɛl'gru:md] *adj* de apariencia cuidada.

well-heeled ['wɛl'hiːld] *adj (col: wealthy)* rico.
well-informed ['wɛlɪn'fɔːmd] *adj (having knowledge of sth)* enterado, al corriente.
Wellington ['wɛlɪŋtən] *n* Wellington *m.*
wellingtons ['wɛlɪŋtənz] *npl (also:* **Wellington boots**) botas *fpl* de goma.
well-kept ['wɛl'kɛpt] *adj (secret)* bien guardado; *(hair, house)* bien cuidado.
well-known ['wɛl'nəun] *adj (person)* conocido.
well-mannered ['wɛl'mænəd] *adj* educado.
well-meaning ['wɛl'miːnɪŋ] *adj* bienintencionado.
well-nigh ['wɛl'naɪ] *adv:* ~ **impossible** casi imposible.
well-off ['wɛl'ɔf] *adj* acomodado.
well-read ['wɛl'rɛd] *adj* culto.
well-spoken ['wɛl'spəukən] *adj* bienhablado.
well-stocked ['wɛl'stɔkt] *adj (shop, larder)* bien surtido.
well-timed ['wɛl'taɪmd] *adj* oportuno.
well-to-do ['wɛltə'duː] *adj* acomodado.
well-wisher ['wɛlwɪʃə*] *n* admirador(a) *m/f.*
well-woman clinic ['wɛlwumən-] *n centro de prevención médica para mujeres.*
Welsh [wɛlʃ] *adj* galés/esa ♦ *n (LING)* galés *m;* **the** ~ *npl* los galeses; **the** ~ **Assembly** el Parlamento galés.
Welshman ['wɛlʃmən] *n* galés *m.*
Welsh rarebit [-'rɛəbɪt] *n* pan *m* con queso tostado.
Welshwoman ['wɛlʃwumən] *n* galesa.
welter ['wɛltə*] *n* mescolanza, revoltijo.
went [wɛnt] *pt of* **go**.
wept [wɛpt] *pt, pp of* **weep**.
were [wəː*] *pt of* **be**.
we're [wɪə*] = **we are**.
weren't [wəːnt] = **were not**.
werewolf, *pl* **-wolves** ['wɪəwulf, -wulvz] *n* hombre *m* lobo.
west [wɛst] *n* oeste *m* ♦ *adj* occidental, del oeste ♦ *adv* al *or* hacia el oeste; **the W~** Occidente *m.*
westbound ['wɛstbaund] *adj (traffic, carriageway)* con rumbo al oeste.
West Country *n:* **the** ~ el suroeste de Inglaterra.
westerly ['wɛstəlɪ] *adj (wind)* del oeste.
western ['wɛstən] *adj* occidental ♦ *n (CINE)* película del oeste.
westerner ['wɛstənə*] *n (POL)* occidental *m/f.*
westernized ['wɛstənaɪzd] *adj* occidentalizado.
West German *(formerly) adj* de Alemania Occidental ♦ *n* alemán/ana *m/f* (de Alemania Occidental).
West Germany *n (formerly)* Alemania Occidental.
West Indian *adj, n* antillano/a *m/f.*
West Indies [-'ɪndɪz] *npl:* **the** ~ las Antillas.
Westminster ['wɛstmɪnstə*] *n el parlamento británico,* Westminster *m.*
westward(s) ['wɛstwəd(z)] *adv* hacia el oeste.
wet [wɛt] *adj (damp)* húmedo; *(~ through)* mojado; *(rainy)* lluvioso ♦ *vt:* **to** ~ **one's pants** *or* **o.s.** mearse; **to get** ~ mojarse; **"~ paint"** 'recién pintado'.
wet blanket *n:* **to be a** ~ *(fig)* ser un/una aguafiestas.
wetness ['wɛtnɪs] *n* humedad *f.*
wet rot *n* putrefacción *f* por humedad.
wet suit *n* traje *m* de buzo.
we've [wiːv] = **we have**.
whack [wæk] *vt* dar un buen golpe a.
whale [weɪl] *n (ZOOL)* ballena.
whaler ['weɪlə*] *n (ship)* ballenero.
whaling ['weɪlɪŋ] *n* pesca de ballenas.
wharf, *pl* **wharves** [wɔːf, wɔːvz] *n* muelle *m.*

KEYWORD

what [wɔt] *adj* **1** *(in direct/indirect questions)* qué; ~ **size is he?** ¿qué talla usa?; ~ **colour/shape is it?** ¿de qué color/forma es?; ~ **books do you need?** ¿qué libros necesitas?
2 *(in exclamations):* ~ **a mess!** ¡qué desastre!; ~ **a fool I am!** ¡qué tonto soy!
♦ *pron* **1** *(interrogative)* qué; ~ **are you doing?** ¿qué haces *or* estás haciendo?; ~ **is happening?** ¿qué pasa *or* está pasando?; ~ **is it called?** ¿cómo se llama?; ~ **about me?** ¿y yo qué?; ~ **about doing ...?** ¿qué tal si hacemos ...?; ~ **is his address?** ¿cuáles son sus señas?; ~ **will it cost?** ¿cuánto costará?
2 *(relative)* lo que; **I saw** ~ **you did/was on the table** vi lo que hiciste/había en la mesa; ~ **I want is a cup of tea** lo que quiero es una taza de té; **I don't know** ~ **to do** no sé qué hacer; **tell me** ~ **you're thinking about** dime en qué estás pensando
3 *(reported questions):* **she asked me** ~ **I wanted** me preguntó qué quería
♦ *excl (disbelieving)* ¡cómo!; ~, **no coffee!** ¡que no hay café!

whatever [wɔt'ɛvə*] *adj:* ~ **book you choose** cualquier libro que elijas ♦ *pron:* **do** ~ **is necessary** haga lo que sea necesario; **no reason** ~ ninguna razón en

absoluto; **nothing** ~ nada en absoluto; ~ **it costs** cueste lo que cueste.
wheat [wi:t] *n* trigo.
wheatgerm ['wi:tdʒə:m] *n* germen *m* de trigo.
wheatmeal ['wi:tmi:l] *n* harina de trigo.
wheedle ['wi:dl] *vt*: **to** ~ **sb into doing sth** engatusar a algn para que haga algo; **to** ~ **sth out of sb** sonsacar algo a algn.
wheel [wi:l] *n* rueda; (*AUT*: *also*: **steering** ~) volante *m*; (*NAUT*) timón *m* ♦ *vt* (*pram etc*) empujar ♦ *vi* (*also*: ~ **round**) dar la vuelta, girar; **four-~ drive** tracción *f* en las cuatro ruedas; **front-/rear-~ drive** tracción *f* delantera/trasera.
wheelbarrow ['wi:lbærəu] *n* carretilla.
wheelbase ['wi:lbeɪs] *n* batalla.
wheelchair ['wi:ltʃεə*] *n* silla de ruedas.
wheel clamp *n* (*AUT*) cepo.
wheeler-dealer ['wi:lə'di:lə*] *n* chanchullero/a.
wheelie-bin ['wi:lɪbɪn] *n* (*BRIT*) contenedor *m* de basura.
wheeling ['wi:lɪŋ] *n*: ~ **and dealing** (*col*) chanchullos *mpl*.
wheeze [wi:z] *vi* resollar.
wheezy ['wi:zɪ] *adj* silbante.

KEYWORD

when [wεn] *adv* cuando; ~ **did it happen?** ¿cuándo ocurrió?; **I know ~ it happened** sé cuándo ocurrió
♦ *conj* **1** (*at, during, after the time that*) cuando; **be careful ~ you cross the road** ten cuidado al cruzar la calle; **that was ~ I needed you** entonces era cuando te necesitaba; **I'll buy you a car ~ you're 18** te compraré un coche cuando cumplas 18 años
2 (*on, at which*): **on the day ~ I met him** el día en qué le conocí
3 (*whereas*) cuando; **you said I was wrong ~ in fact I was right** dijiste que no tenía razón, cuando en realidad sí la tenía.

whenever [wεn'εvə*] *conj* cuando; (*every time*) cada vez que; **I go ~ I can** voy siempre *or* todas las veces que puedo.
where [wεə*] *adv* dónde ♦ *conj* donde; **this is** ~ aquí es donde; ~ **possible** donde sea posible; ~ **are you from?** ¿de dónde es usted?
whereabouts ['wεərəbauts] *adv* dónde ♦ *n*: **nobody knows his** ~ nadie conoce su paradero.
whereas [wεər'æz] *conj* mientras.
whereby [wεə'baɪ] *adv* mediante el/la cual *etc*.
whereupon [wεərə'pɔn] *conj* con lo cual, después de lo cual.
wherever [wεər'εvə*] *adv* dondequiera que; (*interrogative*) dónde; **sit ~ you like** siéntese donde quiera.
wherewithal ['wεəwɪðɔ:l] *n* recursos *mpl*; **the ~ (to do sth)** los medios económicos (para hacer algo).
whet [wεt] *vt* estimular; (*appetite*) abrir.
whether ['wεðə*] *conj* si; **I don't know ~ to accept or not** no sé si aceptar o no; ~ **you go or not** vayas o no vayas.
whey [weɪ] *n* suero.

KEYWORD

which [wɪtʃ] *adj* **1** (*interrogative: direct, indirect*) qué; ~ **picture(s) do you want?** ¿qué cuadro(s) quieres?; ~ **one?** ¿cuál?; ~ **one of you?** ¿cuál de vosotros?; **tell me ~ one you want** dime cuál (es el que) quieres
2: **in ~ case** en cuyo caso; **we got there at 8 pm, by ~ time the cinema was full** llegamos allí a las 8, cuando el cine estaba lleno
♦ *pron* **1** (*interrogative*) cual; **I don't mind** ~ el/la que sea; ~ **do you want?** ¿cuál quieres?
2 (*relative: replacing noun*) que; (: *replacing clause*) lo que; (: *after preposition*) (el/la) que, el/la cual; **the apple ~ you ate/~ is on the table** la manzana que comiste/que está en la mesa; **the chair on ~ you are sitting** la silla en la que estás sentado; **he didn't believe it, ~ upset me** no se lo creyó, lo cual *or* lo que me disgustó; **after** ~ después de lo cual.

whichever [wɪtʃ'εvə*] *adj*: **take ~ book you prefer** coja el libro que prefiera; ~ **book you take** cualquier libro que coja.
whiff [wɪf] *n* bocanada; **to catch a ~ of sth** oler algo.
while [waɪl] *n* rato, momento ♦ *conj* durante; (*whereas*) mientras; (*although*) aunque ♦ *vt*: **to ~ away the time** pasar el rato; **for a** ~ durante algún tiempo; **in a** ~ dentro de poco; **all the** ~ todo el tiempo; **we'll make it worth your** ~ te compensaremos generosamente.
whilst [waɪlst] *conj* = **while.**
whim [wɪm] *n* capricho.
whimper ['wɪmpə*] *n* (*weeping*) lloriqueo; (*moan*) quejido ♦ *vi* lloriquear; quejarse.
whimsical ['wɪmzɪkl] *adj* (*person*) caprichoso.
whine [waɪn] *n* (*of pain*) gemido; (*of engine*)

zumbido ♦ *vi* gemir; zumbar.
whip [wɪp] *n* látigo; (*BRIT POL*) *diputado encargado de la disciplina del partido en el parlamento* ♦ *vt* azotar; (*snatch*) arrebatar; (*US CULIN*) batir; *ver recuadro*.
►**whip up** *vt* (*cream etc*) batir (rápidamente); (*col*: *meal*) preparar rápidamente; (: *stir up*: *support, feeling*) avivar.

WHIP

En el Parlamento británico la disciplina de partido (en concreto de voto y de asistencia a la Cámara de los Comunes) está a cargo de un grupo de parlamentarios llamados **whips**, *encabezados por el "Chief Whip". Por lo general todos ellos tienen también altos cargos en la Administración del Estado si pertenecen al partido en el poder.*

whiplash ['wɪplæʃ] *n* (*MED*: *also*: ~ **injury**) latigazo.
whipped cream [wɪpt-] *n* nata montada.
whipping boy ['wɪpɪŋ-] *n* (*fig*) cabeza de turco.
whip-round ['wɪpraund] *n* (*BRIT*) colecta.
whirl [wəːl] *n* remolino ♦ *vt* hacer girar, dar vueltas a ♦ *vi* (*dancers*) girar, dar vueltas; (*leaves, dust, water etc*) arremolinarse.
whirlpool ['wəːlpuːl] *n* remolino.
whirlwind ['wəːlwɪnd] *n* torbellino.
whirr [wəː*] *vi* zumbar.
whisk [wɪsk] *n* (*BRIT CULIN*) batidor *m* ♦ *vt* (*BRIT CULIN*) batir; **to ~ sb away** *or* **off** llevarse volando a algn.
whiskers [wɪskəz] *npl* (*of animal*) bigotes *mpl*; (*of man*) patillas *fpl*.
whisky, (*US, Ireland*) **whiskey** ['wɪskɪ] *n* whisky *m*.
whisper ['wɪspə*] *n* cuchicheo; (*rumour*) rumor *m*; (*fig*) susurro, murmullo ♦ *vi* cuchichear, hablar bajo; (*fig*) susurrar ♦ *vt* decir en voz muy baja; **to ~ sth to sb** decirle algo al oído a algn.
whispering ['wɪspərɪŋ] *n* cuchicheo.
whist [wɪst] *n* (*BRIT*) whist *m*.
whistle ['wɪsl] *n* (*sound*) silbido; (*object*) silbato ♦ *vi* silbar; **to ~ a tune** silbar una melodía.
whistle-stop ['wɪslstɔp] *adj*: ~ **tour** (*US POL*) gira electoral rápida; (*fig*) recorrido rápido.
Whit [wɪt] *n* Pentecostés *m*.
white [waɪt] *adj* blanco; (*pale*) pálido ♦ *n* blanco; (*of egg*) clara; **to turn** *or* **go ~** (*person*) palidecer, ponerse blanco; (*hair*) encanecer; **the ~s** (*washing*) la ropa blanca; **tennis ~s** ropa *f* de tenis.
whitebait ['waɪtbeɪt] *n* chanquetes *mpl*.
white coffee *n* (*BRIT*) café *m* con leche.
white-collar worker ['waɪtkɔlə-] *n* oficinista *m/f*.
white elephant *n* (*fig*) maula.
white goods *npl* (*appliances*) electrodomésticos *mpl* de línea blanca; (*linen etc*) ropa blanca.
white-hot [waɪt'hɔt] *adj* (*metal*) candente, calentado al (rojo) blanco.
white lie *n* mentirijilla.
whiteness ['waɪtnɪs] *n* blancura.
white noise *n* sonido blanco.
white paper *n* (*POL*) libro blanco.
whitewash ['waɪtwɔʃ] *n* (*paint*) cal *f*, jalbegue *m* ♦ *vt* encalar, blanquear; (*fig*) encubrir.
whiting ['waɪtɪŋ] *n* (*pl inv*) (*fish*) pescadilla.
Whit Monday *n* lunes *m* de Pentecostés.
Whitsun ['wɪtsn] *n* (*BRIT*) Pentecostés *m*.
whittle ['wɪtl] *vt*: **to ~ away, ~ down** ir reduciendo.
whizz [wɪz] *vi*: **to ~ past** *or* **by** pasar a toda velocidad.
whizz kid *n* (*col*) prodigio/a.
WHO *n abbr* (= *World Health Organization*) OMS *f*.

KEYWORD

who [huː] *pron* **1** (*interrogative*) quién; **~ is it?**, **~'s there?** ¿quién es?; **~ are you looking for?** ¿a quién buscas?; **I told her ~ I was** le dije quién era yo
2 (*relative*) que; **the man/woman ~ spoke to me** el hombre/la mujer que habló conmigo; **those ~ can swim** los que saben *or* sepan nadar.

whodun(n)it [huː'dʌnɪt] *n* (*col*) novela policíaca.
whoever [huː'ɛvə*] *pron*: **~ finds it** cualquiera *or* quienquiera que lo encuentre; **ask ~ you like** pregunta a quien quieras; **~ he marries** se case con quien se case.
whole [həul] *adj* (*complete*) todo, entero; (*not broken*) intacto ♦ *n* (*total*) total *m*; (*sum*) conjunto; **~ villages were destroyed** pueblos enteros fueron destruídos; **the ~ of the town** toda la ciudad, la ciudad entera; **on the ~, as a ~** en general.
wholehearted [həul'hɑːtɪd] *adj* (*support, approval*) total; (*sympathy*) todo.
wholeheartedly [həul'hɑːtɪdlɪ] *adv* con entusiasmo.
wholemeal ['həulmiːl] *adj* (*BRIT*: *flour, bread*) integral.

wholesale ['həulseɪl] *n* venta al por mayor ♦ *adj* al por mayor; (*destruction*) sistemático.

wholesaler ['həulseɪlə*] *n* mayorista *m/f*.

wholesome ['həulsəm] *adj* sano.

wholewheat ['həulwi:t] *adj* = **wholemeal**.

wholly ['həulɪ] *adv* totalmente, enteramente.

KEYWORD

whom [hu:m] *pron* **1** (*interrogative*): ~ **did you see?** ¿a quién viste?; **to ~ did you give it?** ¿a quién se lo diste?; **tell me from ~ you received it** dígame de quién lo recibiste

2 (*relative*) que; **to** ~ a quien(es); **of** ~ de quien(es), del/de la que; **the man ~ I saw** el hombre qui vi; **the man to ~ I wrote** el hombre a quien escribí; **the lady about ~ I was talking** la señora de (la) que hablaba; **the lady with ~ I was talking** la señora con quien *or* (la) que hablaba.

whooping cough ['hu:pɪŋ-] *n* tos *f* ferina.

whoops [wu:ps] *excl* (*also*: **~-a-daisy!**) ¡huy!

whoosh [wuʃ] *n*: **it came out with a ~** (*sauce etc*) salió todo de repente; (*air*) salió con mucho ruido.

whopper ['wɔpə*] *n* (*col*: *lie*) embuste *m*; (: *large thing*): **a** ~ uno/a enorme.

whopping ['wɔpɪŋ] *adj* (*col*) enorme.

whore [hɔ:*] *n* (*col*: *pej*) puta.

KEYWORD

whose [hu:z] *adj* **1** (*possessive*: *interrogative*) de quién; **~ book is this?**, **~ is this book?** ¿de quién es este libro?; **~ pencil have you taken?** ¿de quién es el lápiz que has cogido?; **~ daughter are you?** ¿de quién eres hija?

2 (*possessive: relative*) cuyo/a, *pl* cuyos/as; **the man ~ son they rescued** el hombre cuyo hijo rescataron; **the girl ~ sister he was speaking to** la chica con cuya hermana estaba hablando; **those ~ passports I have** aquellas personas cuyos pasaportes tengo; **the woman ~ car was stolen** la mujer a quien le robaron el coche

♦ *pron* de quién; **~ is this?** ¿de quién es esto?; **I know ~ it is** sé de quién es.

KEYWORD

why [waɪ] *adv* por qué; **~ not?** ¿por qué no?; **~ not do it now?** ¿por qué no lo haces (*or* hacemos) ahora?

♦ *conj*: **I wonder ~ he said that** me pregunto por qué dijo eso; **that's not ~ I'm here** no es por eso (por lo) que estoy aquí; **the reason ~** la razón por la que

♦ *excl* (*expressing surprise, shock, annoyance*) ¡hombre!, ¡vaya!; (*explaining*): **~, it's you!** ¡hombre, eres tú!; **~, that's impossible** ¡pero si eso es imposible!

whyever [waɪ'ɛvə*] *adv* por qué.

WI *n abbr* (*BRIT*: = *Women's Institute*) *asociación de amas de casa* ♦ *abbr* (*GEO*) = **West Indies**; (*US*) = *Wisconsin*.

wick [wɪk] *n* mecha.

wicked ['wɪkɪd] *adj* malvado, cruel.

wickedness ['wɪkɪdnɪs] *n* maldad *f*, crueldad *f*.

wicker ['wɪkə*] *n* mimbre *m*.

wickerwork ['wɪkəwɜ:k] *n* artículos *mpl* de mimbre.

wicket ['wɪkɪt] *n* (*CRICKET*) palos *mpl*.

wicket keeper *n* guardameta *m*.

wide [waɪd] *adj* ancho; (*area, knowledge*) vasto, grande; (*choice*) grande ♦ *adv*: **to open ~** abrir de par en par; **to shoot ~** errar el tiro; **it is 3 metres ~** tiene 3 metros de ancho.

wide-angle lens ['waɪdæŋgl-] *n* (objetivo) gran angular *m*.

wide-awake [waɪdə'weɪk] *adj* bien despierto.

wide-eyed [waɪd'aɪd] *adj* con los ojos muy abiertos; (*fig*) ingenuo.

widely ['waɪdlɪ] *adv* (*differing*) muy; **it is ~ believed that ...** existe la creencia generalizada de que ...; **to be ~ read** (*author*) ser muy leído; (*reader*) haber leído mucho.

widen ['waɪdn] *vt* ensanchar.

wideness ['waɪdnɪs] *n* anchura; amplitud *f*.

wide open *adj* abierto de par en par.

wide-ranging [waɪd'reɪndʒɪŋ] *adj* (*survey, report*) de gran alcance; (*interests*) muy diversos.

widespread ['waɪdsprɛd] *adj* (*belief etc*) extendido, general.

widow ['wɪdəu] *n* viuda.

widowed ['wɪdəud] *adj* viudo.

widower ['wɪdəuə*] *n* viudo.

width [wɪdθ] *n* anchura; (*of cloth*) ancho; **it's 7 metres in ~** tiene 7 metros de ancho.

widthways ['wɪdθweɪz] *adv* a lo ancho.

wield [wi:ld] *vt* (*sword*) manejar; (*power*) ejercer.
wife, *pl* **wives** [waɪf, waɪvz] *n* mujer *f*, esposa.
wig [wɪg] *n* peluca.
wigging ['wɪgɪŋ] *n* (*BRIT col*) rapapolvo, bronca.
wiggle ['wɪgl] *vt* menear ♦ *vi* menearse.
wiggly ['wɪglɪ] *adj* (*line*) ondulado.
wigwam ['wɪgwæm] *n* tipi *m*, tienda india.
wild [waɪld] *adj* (*animal*) salvaje; (*plant*) silvestre; (*rough*) furioso, violento; (*idea*) descabellado; (*col*: *angry*) furioso ♦ *n*: **the** ~ la naturaleza; ~**s** *npl* regiones *fpl* salvajes, tierras *fpl* vírgenes; **to be** ~ **about** (*enthusiastic*) estar *or* andar loco por; **in its** ~ **state** en estado salvaje.
wild card *n* (*COMPUT*) comodín *m*.
wildcat ['waɪldkæt] *n* gato montés.
wildcat strike *n* huelga salvaje.
wilderness ['wɪldənɪs] *n* desierto; (*jungle*) jungla.
wildfire ['waɪldfaɪə*] *n*: **to spread like** ~ correr como un reguero de pólvora.
wild-goose chase [waɪld'gu:s-] *n* (*fig*) búsqueda inútil.
wildlife ['waɪldlaɪf] *n* fauna.
wildly ['waɪldlɪ] *adv* (*roughly*) violentamente; (*foolishly*) locamente; (*rashly*) descabelladamente.
wiles [waɪlz] *npl* artimañas *fpl*, ardides *mpl*.
wilful, (*US*) **willful** ['wɪlful] *adj* (*action*) deliberado; (*obstinate*) testarudo.

KEYWORD

will [wɪl] *aux vb* **1** (*forming future tense*): **I** ~ **finish it tomorrow** lo terminaré *or* voy a terminar mañana; **I** ~ **have finished it by tomorrow** lo habré terminado para mañana; ~ **you do it? — yes I** ~**/no I won't** ¿lo harás? — sí/no; **you won't lose it,** ~ **you?** no lo vayas a perder *or* no lo perderás ¿verdad?
2 (*in conjectures, predictions*): **he** ~ *or* **he'll be there by now** ya habrá llegado, ya debe (de) haber llegado; **that** ~ **be the postman** será el cartero, debe ser el cartero
3 (*in commands, requests, offers*): ~ **you be quiet!** ¿quieres callarte?; ~ **you help me?** ¿quieres ayudarme?; ~ **you have a cup of tea?** ¿te apetece un té?; **I won't put up with it!** ¡no lo soporto!
4 (*habits, persistence*): **the car won't start** el coche no arranca; **accidents** ~ **happen** son cosas que pasan
♦ *vt* (*pt, pp* **willed**): **to** ~ **sb to do sth** desear que algn haga algo; **he** ~**ed himself to go on** con gran fuerza de voluntad, continuó
♦ *n* **1** (*desire*) voluntad *f*; **against sb's** ~ contra la voluntad de algn; **he did it of his own free** ~ lo hizo por su propia voluntad
2 (*LAW*) testamento; **to make a** *or* **one's** ~ hacer su testamento.

willful ['wɪful] *adj* (*US*) = **wilful.**
willing ['wɪlɪŋ] *adj* (*with goodwill*) de buena voluntad; complaciente; **he's** ~ **to do it** está dispuesto a hacerlo; **to show** ~ mostrarse dispuesto.
willingly ['wɪlɪŋlɪ] *adv* con mucho gusto.
willingness ['wɪlɪŋnɪs] *n* buena voluntad.
will-o'-the-wisp ['wɪləðə'wɪsp] *n* fuego fatuo; (*fig*) quimera.
willow ['wɪləu] *n* sauce *m*.
willpower ['wɪlpauə*] *n* fuerza de voluntad.
willy-nilly [wɪlɪ'nɪlɪ] *adv* quiérase o no.
wilt [wɪlt] *vi* marchitarse.
Wilts *abbr* (*BRIT*) = *Wiltshire.*
wily ['waɪlɪ] *adj* astuto.
wimp [wɪmp] *n* (*col*) enclenque *m/f*; (*character*) calzonazos *m inv*.
win [wɪn] *n* (*in sports etc*) victoria, triunfo ♦ *vb* (*pt, pp* **won** [wʌn]) *vt* ganar; (*obtain*: *contract etc*) conseguir, lograr ♦ *vi* ganar.
►**win over,** (*BRIT*) **win round** *vt* convencer a.
wince [wɪns] *vi* encogerse.
winch [wɪntʃ] *n* torno.
Winchester disk ® ['wɪntʃɪstə-] *n* (*COMPUT*) disco Winchester ®.
wind *n* [wɪnd] viento; (*MED*) gases *mpl*; (*breath*) aliento ♦ *vb* [waɪnd] (*pt, pp* **wound** [waund]) *vt* enrollar; (*wrap*) envolver; (*clock, toy*) dar cuerda a; [wɪnd] (*take breath away from*) dejar sin aliento a ♦ *vi* (*road, river*) serpentear; **into** *or* **against the** ~ contra el viento; **to get** ~ **of sth** enterarse de algo; **to break** ~ ventosear.
►**wind down** *vt* (*car window*) bajar; (*fig*: *production, business*) disminuir.
►**wind up** *vt* (*clock*) dar cuerda a; (*debate*) concluir, terminar.
windbreak ['wɪndbreɪk] *n* barrera contra el viento.
windcheater ['wɪndtʃi:tə*], (*US*) **windbreaker** ['wɪndbreɪkə*] *n* cazadora.
winder ['waɪndə*] *n* (*on watch*) cuerda.
wind erosion *n* erosión *f* del viento.
windfall ['wɪndfɔ:l] *n* golpe *m* de suerte.
winding ['waɪndɪŋ] *adj* (*road*) tortuoso.
wind instrument *n* (*MUS*) instrumento de viento.
windmill ['wɪndmɪl] *n* molino de viento.
window ['wɪndəu] *n* ventana; (*in car, train*)

ventana; (*in shop etc*) escaparate *m*, vitrina (*LAM*), vidriera (*LAM*); (*COMPUT*) ventana.
window box *n* jardinera (de ventana).
window cleaner *n* (*person*) limpiacristales *m inv*.
window dressing *n* decoración *f* de escaparates.
window envelope *n* sobre *m* de ventanilla.
window frame *n* marco de ventana.
window ledge *n* alféizar *m*, repisa.
window pane *n* cristal *m*.
window-shopping ['wɪndəu'ʃɔpɪŋ] *n*: **to go** ~ ir a ver *or* mirar escaparates.
windowsill ['wɪndəusɪl] *n* alféizar *m*, repisa.
windpipe ['wɪndpaɪp] *n* tráquea.
wind power *n* energía eólica.
windscreen ['wɪndskriːn], (*US*) **windshield** ['wɪndʃiːld] *n* parabrisas *m inv*.
windscreen washer, (*US*) **windshield washer** *n* lavaparabrisas *m inv*.
windscreen wiper, (*US*) **windshield wiper** *n* limpiaparabrisas *m inv*.
windsurfing ['wɪndsəːfɪŋ] *n* windsurf *m*.
windswept ['wɪndswɛpt] *adj* azotado por el viento.
wind tunnel *n* túnel *m* aerodinámico.
windy ['wɪndɪ] *adj* de mucho viento; **it's** ~ hace viento.
wine [waɪn] *n* vino ♦ *vt*: **to** ~ **and dine sb** agasajar *or* festejar a algn.
wine bar *n bar especializado en vinos*.
wine cellar *n* bodega.
wine glass *n* copa (de *or* para vino).
wine-growing ['waɪngrəuɪŋ] *adj* viticultor(a).
wine list *n* lista de vinos.
wine merchant *n* vinatero.
wine tasting *n* degustación *f* de vinos.
wine waiter *n* escanciador *m*.
wing [wɪŋ] *n* ala; (*BRIT AUT*) aleta; ~**s** *npl* (*THEAT*) bastidores *mpl*.
winger ['wɪŋə*] *n* (*SPORT*) extremo.
wing mirror *n* (espejo) retrovisor *m*.
wing nut *n* tuerca (de) mariposa.
wingspan ['wɪŋspaen], **wingspread** ['wɪŋsprɛd] *n* envergadura.
wink [wɪŋk] *n* guiño; (*blink*) pestañeo ♦ *vi* guiñar; (*blink*) pestañear; (*light etc*) parpadear.
winkle ['wɪŋkl] *n* bígaro, bigarro.
winner ['wɪnə*] *n* ganador(a) *m/f*.
winning ['wɪnɪŋ] *adj* (*team*) ganador(a); (*goal*) decisivo; (*charming*) encantador(a).
winning post *n* meta.
winnings ['wɪnɪŋz] *npl* ganancias *fpl*.
winsome ['wɪnsəm] *adj* atractivo.
winter ['wɪntə*] *n* invierno ♦ *vi* invernar.
winter sports *npl* deportes *mpl* de invierno.
wintry ['wɪntrɪ] *adj* invernal.
wipe [waɪp] *n*: **to give sth a** ~ pasar un trapo sobre algo ♦ *vt* limpiar; **to** ~ **one's nose** limpiarse la nariz.
▸**wipe off** *vt* limpiar con un trapo.
▸**wipe out** *vt* (*debt*) liquidar; (*memory*) borrar; (*destroy*) destruir.
▸**wipe up** *vt* limpiar.
wire ['waɪə*] *n* alambre *m*; (*ELEC*) cable *m* (eléctrico); (*TEL*) telegrama *m* ♦ *vt* (*house*) poner la instalación eléctrica en; (*also*: ~ **up**) conectar.
wire cutters *npl* cortaalambres *msg inv*.
wireless ['waɪəlɪs] *n* (*BRIT*) radio *f*.
wire mesh, wire netting *n* tela metálica.
wire service *n* (*US*) agencia de noticias.
wire-tapping ['waɪə'tæpɪŋ] *n* intervención *f* telefónica.
wiring ['waɪərɪŋ] *n* instalación *f* eléctrica.
wiry ['waɪərɪ] *adj* enjuto y fuerte.
Wis(c). *abbr* (*US*) = *Wisconsin*.
wisdom ['wɪzdəm] *n* sabiduría, saber *m*; (*good sense*) cordura.
wisdom tooth *n* muela del juicio.
wise [waɪz] *adj* sabio; (*sensible*) juicioso; **I'm none the** ~**r** sigo sin entender.
▸**wise up** *vi* (*col*): **to** ~ **up (to sth)** enterarse (de algo).
...wise [waɪz] *suff*: **time**~ en cuanto a *or* respecto al tiempo.
wisecrack ['waɪzkræk] *n* broma.
wish [wɪʃ] *n* (*desire*) deseo ♦ *vt* desear; (*want*) querer; **best** ~**es** (*on birthday etc*) felicidades *fpl*; **with best** ~**es** (*in letter*) saludos *mpl*, recuerdos *mpl*; **to** ~ **sb goodbye** despedirse de algn; **he** ~**ed me well** me deseó mucha suerte; **to** ~ **sth on sb** imponer algo a algn; **to** ~ **to do/sb to do sth** querer hacer/que algn haga algo; **to** ~ **for** desear.
wishbone ['wɪʃbəun] *n* espoleta (*de la que tiran dos personas; quien se quede con el hueso más largo pide un deseo*).
wishful ['wɪʃful] *n*: **it's** ~ **thinking** eso es hacerse ilusiones.
wishy-washy ['wɪʃɪwɔʃɪ] *adj* (*col*: *colour*) desvaído; (: *ideas, thinking*) flojo.
wisp [wɪsp] *n* mechón *m*; (*of smoke*) voluta.
wistful ['wɪstful] *adj* pensativo; (*nostalgic*) nostálgico.
wit [wɪt] *n* (*wittiness*) ingenio, gracia; (*intelligence*: *also*: ~**s**) inteligencia; (*person*) chistoso/a; **to have** *or* **keep one's**

~s about one no perder la cabeza.
witch [wɪtʃ] *n* bruja.
witchcraft ['wɪtʃkrɑːft] *n* brujería.
witch doctor *n* hechicero.
witch-hunt ['wɪtʃhʌnt] *n* (*POL*) caza de brujas.

KEYWORD

with [wɪð, wɪθ] *prep* **1** (*accompanying, in the company of*) con (*con+mí, ti, sí = conmigo, contigo, consigo*); **I was ~ him** estaba con él; **we stayed ~ friends** nos quedamos en casa de unos amigos
2 (*descriptive, indicating manner etc*) con; de; **a room ~ a view** una habitación con vistas; **the man ~ the grey hat/blue eyes** el hombre del sombrero gris/de los ojos azules; **red ~ anger** rojo de ira; **to shake ~ fear** temblar de miedo; **to fill sth ~ water** llenar algo de agua
3: **I'm ~ you/I'm not ~ you** (*understand*) ya te entiendo/no te entiendo; **I'm not really ~ it today** no doy pie con bola hoy.

withdraw [wɪθ'drɔː] *vb* (*irreg*: *like* **draw**) *vt* retirar ♦ *vi* retirarse; (*go back on promise*) retractarse; **to ~ money (from the bank)** retirar fondos (del banco); **to ~ into o.s.** ensimismarse.
withdrawal [wɪθ'drɔːəl] *n* retirada.
withdrawal symptoms *npl* síndrome *m* de abstinencia.
withdrawn [wɪθ'drɔːn] *adj* (*person*) reservado, introvertido ♦ *pp of* **withdraw**.
wither ['wɪðə*] *vi* marchitarse.
withered ['wɪðəd] *adj* marchito, seco.
withhold [wɪθ'həuld] *vt* (*irreg*: *like* **hold**) (*money*) retener; (*decision*) aplazar; (*permission*) negar; (*information*) ocultar.
within [wɪð'ɪn] *prep* dentro de ♦ *adv* dentro; **~ reach** al alcance de la mano; **~ sight of** a la vista de; **~ the week** antes de que acabe la semana; **to be ~ the law** atenerse a la legalidad; **~ an hour from now** dentro de una hora.
without [wɪð'aut] *prep* sin; **to go** *or* **do ~ sth** prescindir de algo; **~ anybody knowing** sin saberlo nadie.
withstand [wɪθ'stænd] *vt* (*irreg*: *like* **stand**) resistir a.
witness ['wɪtnɪs] *n* (*person*) testigo *m/f*; (*evidence*) testimonio ♦ *vt* (*event*) presenciar, ser testigo de; (*document*) atestiguar la veracidad de; **~ for the prosecution/defence** testigo de cargo/descargo; **to ~ to (having seen) sth** dar testimonio de (haber visto) algo.
witness box, (*US*) **witness stand** *n* tribuna de los testigos.
witticism ['wɪtɪsɪzm] *n* dicho ingenioso.
wittily ['wɪtɪlɪ] *adv* ingeniosamente.
witty ['wɪtɪ] *adj* ingenioso.
wives [waɪvz] *npl of* **wife**.
wizard ['wɪzəd] *n* hechicero.
wizened ['wɪznd] *adj* arrugado, marchito.
wk *abbr* = **week**.
Wm. *abbr* = *William*.
WO *n abbr* = **warrant officer**.
wobble ['wɔbl] *vi* tambalearse.
wobbly ['wɔblɪ] *adj* (*hand, voice*) tembloroso; (*table, chair*) tambaleante, cojo.
woe [wəu] *n* desgracia.
woeful ['wəuful] *adj* (*bad*) lamentable; (*sad*) apesadumbrado.
wok [wɔk] *n* wok *m*.
woke [wəuk] *pt of* **wake**.
woken ['wəukn] *pp of* **wake**.
wolf, *pl* **wolves** [wulf, wulvz] *n* lobo.
woman, *pl* **women** ['wumən, 'wɪmɪn] *n* mujer *f*; **young ~** (mujer *f*) joven *f*; **women's page** (*PRESS*) sección *f* de la mujer.
woman doctor *n* doctora.
woman friend *n* amiga.
womanize ['wumənaɪz] *vi* ser un mujeriego.
womanly ['wumənlɪ] *adj* femenino.
womb [wuːm] *n* (*ANAT*) matriz *f*, útero.
women ['wɪmɪn] *npl of* **woman**.
Women's (Liberation) Movement *n* (*also*: **women's lib**) Movimiento de liberación de la mujer.
won [wʌn] *pt, pp of* **win**.
wonder ['wʌndə*] *n* maravilla, prodigio; (*feeling*) asombro ♦ *vi*: **to ~ whether** preguntarse si; **to ~ at** asombrarse de; **to ~ about** pensar sobre *or* en; **it's no ~ that** no es de extrañar que.
wonderful ['wʌndəful] *adj* maravilloso.
wonderfully ['wʌndəfəlɪ] *adv* maravillosamente, estupendamente.
wonky ['wɔŋkɪ] *adj* (*BRIT col*: *unsteady*) poco seguro, cojo; (: *broken down*) estropeado.
wont [wɔnt] *n*: **as is his/her ~** como tiene por costumbre.
won't [wəunt] = **will not**.
woo [wuː] *vt* (*woman*) cortejar.
wood [wud] *n* (*timber*) madera; (*forest*) bosque *m* ♦ *cpd* de madera.
wood alcohol *n* (*US*) alcohol *m* desnaturalizado.
wood carving *n* tallado en madera.
wooded ['wudɪd] *adj* arbolado.
wooden ['wudn] *adj* de madera; (*fig*) inexpresivo.

woodland ['wudlənd] *n* bosque *m*.
woodpecker ['wudpɛkə*] *n* pájaro carpintero.
wood pigeon *n* paloma torcaz.
woodwind ['wudwɪnd] *n* (*MUS*) instrumentos *mpl* de viento de madera.
woodwork ['wudwəːk] *n* carpintería.
woodworm ['wudwəːm] *n* carcoma.
woof [wuf] *n* (*of dog*) ladrido ♦ *vi* ladrar; **~, ~!** ¡guau, guau!
wool [wul] *n* lana; **knitting ~** lana (de hacer punto); **to pull the ~ over sb's eyes** (*fig*) dar a algn gato por liebre.
woollen, (*US*) **woolen** ['wulən] *adj* de lana ♦ *n*: **~s** géneros *mpl* de lana.
woolly, (*US*) **wooly** ['wulɪ] *adj* de lana; (*fig: ideas*) confuso.
woozy ['wuːzɪ] *adj* (*col*) mareado.
word [wəːd] *n* palabra; (*news*) noticia; (*promise*) palabra (de honor) ♦ *vt* redactar; **~ for ~** palabra por palabra; **what's the ~ for "pen" in Spanish?** ¿cómo se dice "pen" en español?; **to put sth into ~s** expresar algo en palabras; **to have a ~ with sb** hablar (dos palabras) con algn; **in other ~s** en otras palabras; **to break/keep one's ~** faltar a la palabra/cumplir la promesa; **to leave ~ (with/for sb) that ...** dejar recado (con/para algn) de que ...; **to have ~s with sb** (*quarrel with*) discutir *or* reñir con algn.
wording ['wəːdɪŋ] *n* redacción *f*.
word-of-mouth [wəːdəv'mauθ] *n*: **by** *or* **through ~** de palabra, por el boca a boca.
word-perfect ['wəːd'pəːfɪkt] *adj* (*speech etc*) sin faltas de expresión.
word processing *n* procesamiento *or* tratamiento de textos.
word processor [-'prəusɛsə*] *n* procesador *m* de textos.
wordwrap ['wəːdræp] *n* (*COMPUT*) salto de línea automático.
wordy ['wəːdɪ] *adj* verboso, prolijo.
wore [wɔː*] *pt of* **wear**.
work [wəːk] *n* trabajo; (*job*) empleo, trabajo; (*ART, LIT*) obra ♦ *vi* trabajar; (*mechanism*) funcionar, marchar; (*medicine*) ser eficaz, surtir efecto ♦ *vt* (*shape*) trabajar; (*stone etc*) tallar; (*mine etc*) explotar; (*machine*) manejar, hacer funcionar; (*cause*) producir; **to go to ~** ir a trabajar *or* al trabajo; **to be at ~ (on sth)** estar trabajando (en algo); **to set to ~, start ~** ponerse a trabajar; **to be out of ~** estar parado, no tener trabajo; **his life's ~** el trabajo de su vida; **to ~ hard** trabajar mucho *or* duro; **to ~ to rule** (*INDUSTRY*) hacer una huelga de celo; **to ~ loose** (*part*) desprenderse; (*knot*) aflojarse; *see also* **works**.
►**work off** *vt*: **to ~ off one's feelings** desahogarse.
►**work on** *vt fus* trabajar en, dedicarse a; (*principle*) basarse en; **he's ~ing on the car** está reparando el coche.
►**work out** *vi* (*plans etc*) salir bien, funcionar; (*SPORT*) hacer ejercicios ♦ *vt* (*problem*) resolver; (*plan*) elaborar; **it ~s out at £100** asciende a 100 libras.
►**work up** *vt*: **he ~ed his way up in the company** ascendió en la compañía mediante sus propios esfuerzos.
workable ['wəːkəbl] *adj* (*solution*) práctico, factible.
workaholic [wəːkə'hɔlɪk] *n* adicto/a al trabajo.
workbench ['wəːkbɛntʃ] *n* banco *or* mesa de trabajo.
worked up [wəːkt-] *adj*: **to get ~** excitarse.
worker ['wəːkə*] *n* trabajador(a) *m/f*, obrero/a; **office ~** oficinista *m/f*.
work force *n* mano *f* de obra.
work-in ['wəːkɪn] *n* (*BRIT*) ocupación *f* (de la empresa) sin interrupción del trabajo.
working ['wəːkɪŋ] *adj* (*day, week*) laborable; (*tools, conditions, clothes*) de trabajo; (*wife*) que trabaja; (*partner*) activo.
working capital *n* (*COMM*) capital *m* circulante.
working class *n* clase *f* obrera ♦ *adj*: **working-class** obrero.
working knowledge *n* conocimientos *mpl* básicos.
working man *n* obrero.
working order *n*: **in ~** en funcionamiento.
working party *n* comisión *f* de investigación, grupo de trabajo.
working week *n* semana laboral.
work-in-progress ['wəːkɪn'prəugrɛs] *n* (*COMM*) trabajo en curso.
workload ['wəːkləud] *n* cantidad *f* de trabajo.
workman ['wəːkmən] *n* obrero.
workmanship ['wəːkmənʃɪp] *n* (*art*) hechura; (*skill*) habilidad *f*.
workmate ['wəːkmeɪt] *n* compañero/a de trabajo.
workout ['wəːkaut] *n* (*SPORT*) sesión *f* de ejercicios.
work permit *n* permiso de trabajo.
works [wəːks] *nsg* (*BRIT: factory*) fábrica ♦ *npl* (*of clock, machine*) mecanismo; **road ~** obras *fpl*.
works council *n* comité *m* de empresa.
worksheet ['wəːkʃiːt] *n* (*COMPUT*) hoja de trabajo; (*SCOL*) hoja de ejercicios.

workshop ['wəːkʃɔp] *n* taller *m*.
work station *n* estación *f* de trabajo.
work study *n* estudio del trabajo.
worktop ['wəːktɔp] *n* encimera.
work-to-rule ['wəːktə'ruːl] *n* (*BRIT*) huelga de celo.
world [wəːld] *n* mundo ♦ *cpd* (*champion*) del mundo; (*power, war*) mundial; **all over the ~** por todo el mundo, en el mundo entero; **the business ~** el mundo de los negocios; **what in the ~ is he doing?** ¿qué diablos está haciendo?; **to think the ~ of sb** (*fig*) tener un concepto muy alto de algn; **to do sb a ~ of good** sentar muy bien a algn; **W~ War One/Two** la primera/segunda Guerra Mundial.
World Cup *n* (*FOOTBALL*): **the ~** el Mundial, los Mundiales.
world-famous [wəːld'feɪməs] *adj* de fama mundial, mundialmente famoso.
worldly ['wəːldlɪ] *adj* mundano.
world music *n* música étnica.
World Series *n*: **the ~** (*US BASEBALL*) el campeonato nacional de béisbol de EEUU.
World Service *n see* **BBC**.
world-wide ['wəːldwaɪd] *adj* mundial, universal.
worm [wəːm] *n* gusano; (*earth~*) lombriz *f*.
worn [wɔːn] *pp of* **wear** ♦ *adj* usado.
worn-out ['wɔːnaut] *adj* (*object*) gastado; (*person*) rendido, agotado.
worried ['wʌrɪd] *adj* preocupado; **to be ~ about sth** estar preocupado por algo.
worrisome ['wʌrɪsəm] *adj* preocupante, inquietante.
worry ['wʌrɪ] *n* preocupación *f* ♦ *vt* preocupar, inquietar ♦ *vi* preocuparse; **to ~ about** *or* **over sth/sb** preocuparse por algo/algn.
worrying ['wʌrɪɪŋ] *adj* inquietante.
worse [wəːs] *adj, adv* peor ♦ *n* el peor, lo peor; **a change for the ~** un empeoramiento; **so much the ~ for you** tanto peor para ti; **he is none the ~ for it** se ha quedado tan fresco *or* tan tranquilo; **to get ~, to grow ~** empeorar.
worsen ['wəːsn] *vt, vi* empeorar.
worse off *adj* (*fig*): **you'll be ~ this way** de esta forma estarás peor que antes.
worship ['wəːʃɪp] *n* (*organized ~*) culto; (*act*) adoración *f* ♦ *vt* adorar; **Your W~** (*BRIT*: *to mayor*) su Ilustrísima; (: *to judge*) su señoría.
worshipper, (*US*) **worshiper** ['wəːʃɪpə*] *n* devoto/a.
worst [wəːst] *adj* (el/la) peor ♦ *adv* peor ♦ *n* lo peor; **at ~** en el peor de los casos; **to come off ~** llevar la peor parte; **if the ~ comes to the ~** en el peor de los casos.
worst-case ['wəːstkeɪs] *adj*: **the ~ scenario** el peor de los casos.
worsted ['wustɪd] *n*: **(wool) ~** estambre *m*.
worth [wəːθ] *n* valor *m* ♦ *adj*: **to be ~** valer; **how much is it ~?** ¿cuánto vale?; **it's ~ it** vale *or* merece la pena; **to be ~ one's while (to do)** merecer la pena (hacer); **it's not ~ the trouble** no vale *or* merece la pena.
worthless ['wəːθlɪs] *adj* sin valor; (*useless*) inútil.
worthwhile ['wəːθwaɪl] *adj* (*activity*) que merece la pena; (*cause*) loable.
worthy ['wəːðɪ] *adj* (*person*) respetable; (*motive*) honesto; **~ of** digno de.

KEYWORD

would [wud] *aux vb* **1** (*conditional tense*): **if you asked him he ~ do it** si se lo pidieras, lo haría; **if you had asked him he ~ have done it** si se lo hubieras pedido, lo habría *or* hubiera hecho
2 (*in offers, invitations, requests*): **~ you like a biscuit?** ¿quieres una galleta?; (*formal*) ¿querría una galleta?; **~ you ask him to come in?** ¿quiere hacerle pasar?; **~ you open the window please?** ¿quiere *or* podría abrir la ventana, por favor?
3 (*in indirect speech*): **I said I ~ do it** dije que lo haría
4 (*emphatic*): **it WOULD have to snow today!** ¡tenía que nevar precisamente hoy!
5 (*insistence*): **she ~n't behave** no quiso comportarse bien
6 (*conjecture*): **it ~ have been midnight** sería medianoche; **it ~ seem so** parece ser que sí
7 (*indicating habit*): **he ~ go there on Mondays** iba allí los lunes.

would-be ['wudbiː] *adj* (*pej*) presunto.
wouldn't ['wudnt] = **would not**.
wound *vb* [waund] *pt, pp of* **wind** ♦ *n, vt* [wuːnd] *n* herida ♦ *vt* herir.
wove [wəuv] *pt of* **weave**.
woven ['wəuvən] *pp of* **weave**.
WP *n abbr* = **word processing; word processor** ♦ *abbr* (*BRIT col*: = *weather permitting*) si lo permite el tiempo.
WPC *n abbr* (*BRIT*) = *woman police constable*.
wpm *abbr* (= *words per minute*) p.p.m.
WRAC *n abbr* (*BRIT*: = *Women's Royal Army Corps*) *cuerpo auxiliar femenino del ejército de tierra*.
WRAF *n abbr* (*BRIT*: = *Women's Royal Air*

Force) cuerpo auxiliar femenino del ejército del aire.

wrangle ['ræŋgl] *n* riña ♦ *vi* reñir.

wrap [ræp] *n* (*stole*) chal *m* ♦ *vt* (*also*: ~ **up**) envolver; **under ~s** (*fig*: *plan, scheme*) oculto, tapado.

wrapper ['ræpə*] *n* (*BRIT*: *of book*) sobrecubierta; (*on chocolate etc*) envoltura.

wrapping paper ['ræpɪŋ-] *n* papel *m* de envolver.

wrath [rɔθ] *n* cólera.

wreak [ri:k] *vt* (*destruction*) causar; **to ~ havoc (on)** hacer *or* causar estragos (en); **to ~ vengeance (on)** vengarse (en).

wreath, ~s [ri:θ, ri:ðz] *n* (*funeral* ~) corona; (*of flowers*) guirnalda.

wreck [rɛk] *n* (*ship*: *destruction*) naufragio; (: *remains*) restos *mpl* del barco; (*pej*: *person*) ruina ♦ *vt* destrozar; **to be ~ed** (*NAUT*) naufragar.

wreckage ['rɛkɪdʒ] *n* (*remains*) restos *mpl*; (*of building*) escombros *mpl*.

wrecker ['rɛkə*] *n* (*US*: *breakdown van*) camión-grúa *m*.

WREN [rɛn] *n abbr* (*BRIT*) *miembro del WRNS.*

wren [rɛn] *n* (*ZOOL*) reyezuelo.

wrench [rɛntʃ] *n* (*TECH*) llave *f* inglesa; (*tug*) tirón *m* ♦ *vt* arrancar; **to ~ sth from sb** arrebatar algo violentamente a algn.

wrest [rɛst] *vt*: **to ~ sth from sb** arrebatar *or* arrancar algo a algn.

wrestle ['rɛsl] *vi*: **to ~ (with sb)** luchar (con *or* contra algn).

wrestler ['rɛslə*] *n* luchador(a) *m/f* (de lucha libre).

wrestling ['rɛslɪŋ] *n* lucha libre.

wrestling match *n* combate *m* de lucha libre.

wretch [rɛtʃ] *n* desgraciado/a, miserable *m/f*; **little ~!** (*often humorous*) ¡granuja!

wretched ['rɛtʃɪd] *adj* miserable.

wriggle ['rɪgl] *vi* serpentear.

wring *pt, pp* **wrung** [rɪŋ, rʌŋ] *vt* torcer, retorcer; (*wet clothes*) escurrir; (*fig*): **to ~ sth out of sb** sacar algo por la fuerza a algn.

wringer ['rɪŋə*] *n* escurridor *m*.

wringing ['rɪŋɪŋ] *adj* (*also*: ~ **wet**) empapado.

wrinkle ['rɪŋkl] *n* arruga ♦ *vt* arrugar ♦ *vi* arrugarse.

wrinkled ['rɪŋkld], **wrinkly** ['rɪŋklɪ] *adj* (*fabric, paper, etc*) arrugado.

wrist [rɪst] *n* muñeca.

wristband ['rɪstbænd] *n* (*BRIT*: *of shirt*) puño; (: *of watch*) correa.

wrist watch *n* reloj *m* de pulsera.

writ [rɪt] *n* mandato judicial; **to serve a ~ on sb** notificar un mandato judicial a algn.

write, *pt* **wrote,** *pp* **written** [raɪt, rəut, 'rɪtn] *vt, vi* escribir; **to ~ sb a letter** escribir una carta a algn.

▸**write away** *vi*: **to ~ away for** (*information, goods*) pedir por escrito *or* carta.

▸**write down** *vt* escribir; (*note*) apuntar.

▸**write off** *vt* (*debt*) borrar (como incobrable); (*fig*) desechar por inútil; (*smash up*: *car*) destrozar.

▸**write out** *vt* escribir.

▸**write up** *vt* redactar.

write-off ['raɪtɔf] *n* siniestro total; **the car is a ~** el coche es pura chatarra.

write-protect ['raɪtprə'tɛkt] *vt* (*COMPUT*) proteger contra escritura.

writer ['raɪtə*] *n* escritor(a) *m/f*.

write-up ['raɪtʌp] *n* (*review*) crítica, reseña.

writhe [raɪð] *vi* retorcerse.

writing ['raɪtɪŋ] *n* escritura; (*hand~*) letra; (*of author*) obras; **in ~** por escrito; **to put sth in ~** poner algo por escrito; **in my own ~** escrito por mí; *see also* **writings**.

writing case *n* estuche *m* de papel de escribir.

writing desk *n* escritorio.

writing paper *n* papel *m* de escribir.

writings *npl* obras *fpl*.

written ['rɪtn] *pp of* **write**.

WRNS *n abbr* (*BRIT*: *= Women's Royal Naval Service*) *cuerpo auxiliar femenino de la armada.*

wrong [rɔŋ] *adj* (*wicked*) malo; (*unfair*) injusto; (*incorrect*) equivocado, incorrecto; (*not suitable*) inoportuno, inconveniente ♦ *adv* mal ♦ *n* mal *m*; (*injustice*) injusticia ♦ *vt* ser injusto con; (*hurt*) agraviar; **to be ~** (*answer*) estar equivocado; (*in doing, saying*) equivocarse; **it's ~ to steal, stealing is ~** es mal robar; **you are ~ to do it** haces mal en hacerlo; **you are ~ about that, you've got it ~** en eso estás equivocado; **to be in the ~** no tener razón; (*guilty*) tener la culpa; **what's ~?** ¿qué pasa?; **what's ~ with the car?** ¿qué le pasa al coche?; **there's nothing ~** no pasa nada; **you have the ~ number** (*TEL*) se ha equivocado de número; **to go ~** (*person*) equivocarse; (*plan*) salir mal; (*machine*) estropearse.

wrongdoer ['rɔŋduə*] *n* malhechor(a) *m/f*.

wrong-foot [rɔŋ'fut] *vt* (*SPORT*) hacer perder el equilibrio a; (*fig*) poner en un

aprieto a.
wrongful ['rɔŋful] *adj* injusto; ~ **dismissal** (*INDUSTRY*) despido improcedente.
wrongly ['rɔŋlɪ] *adv* (*answer, do, count*) incorrectamente; (*treat*) injustamente.
wrote [rəut] *pt of* **write**.
wrought [rɔːt] *adj*: ~ **iron** hierro forjado.
wrung [rʌŋ] *pt, pp of* **wring**.
WRVS *n abbr* (*BRIT*: = *Women's Royal Voluntary Service*) *cuerpo de voluntarias al servicio de la comunidad.*
wry [raɪ] *adj* irónico.
wt. *abbr* = **weight**.
WV, W. Va. *abbr* (*US*) = *West Virginia.*
WWW *n abbr* (= *World Wide Web*) WWW *m or f.*
WY, Wyo. *abbr* (*US*) = *Wyoming.*
WYSIWYG ['wɪzɪwɪg] *abbr* (*COMPUT*: = *what you see is what you get*) *tipo de presentación en un procesador de textos.*

X *x*

X, x [eks] *n* (*letter*) X, x *f*: (*BRIT CINE*: *formerly*) no apto para menores de 18 años; **X for Xmas** X de Xiquena; **if you earn X dollars a year** si ganas X dólares al año.
X-certificate ['ɛkssə'tɪfɪkɪt] *adj* (*BRIT*: *film*: *formerly*) no apto para menores de 18 años.
Xerox ® ['zɪərɔks] *n* (*also*: ~ **machine**) fotocopiadora; (*photocopy*) fotocopia ♦ *vt* fotocopiar.
XL *abbr* = *extra large.*
Xmas ['ɛksməs] *n abbr* = **Christmas**.
X-rated ['eks'reɪtɪd] *adj* (*US*: *film*) no apto para menores de 18 años.
X-ray [ɛks'reɪ] *n* radiografía; ~**s** *npl* rayos *mpl* X ♦ *vt* radiografiar.
xylophone ['zaɪləfəun] *n* xilófono.

Y *y*

Y, y [waɪ] *n* (*letter*) Y, y *f*; **Y for Yellow,** (*US*) **Y for Yoke** Y de Yegua.
Y2K [ˌwaɪtuː'keɪ] *abbr* (= *Year 2000*): **the ~ problem** (*COMPUT*) el efecto 2000.
yacht [jɔt] *n* yate *m.*
yachting ['jɔtɪŋ] *n* (*sport*) balandrismo.
yachtsman ['jɔtsmən] *n* balandrista *m.*
yachtswoman ['jɔtswumən] balandrista.
yam [jæm] *n* ñame *m*; (*sweet potato*) batata, camote *m* (*LAM*).
Yank [jæŋk], **Yankee** ['jæŋkɪ] *n* (*pej*) yanqui *m/f.*
yank [jæŋk] *vt* tirar de, jalar de (*LAM*) ♦ *n* tirón *m.*
yap [jæp] *vi* (*dog*) aullar.
yard [jɑːd] *n* patio; (*US*: *garden*) jardín *m*; (*measure*) yarda; **builder's ~** almacén *m.*
yardstick ['jɑːdstɪk] *n* (*fig*) criterio, norma.
yarn [jɑːn] *n* hilo; (*tale*) cuento (chino).
yawn [jɔːn] *n* bostezo ♦ *vi* bostezar.
yawning ['jɔːnɪŋ] *adj* (*gap*) muy abierto.
yd. *abbr* (= *yard*) yda.
yeah [jɛə] *adv* (*col*) sí.
year [jɪə*] *n* año; (*SCOL, UNIV*) curso; **this ~** este año; ~ **in,** ~ **out** año tras año; **a** *or* **per** ~ al año; **to be 8 ~s old** tener 8 años; **she's three ~s old** tiene tres años; **an eight-~-old child** un niño de ocho años (de edad).
yearbook ['jɪəbuk] *n* anuario.
yearling ['jɪəlɪŋ] *n* (*horse*) potro de un año.
yearly ['jɪəlɪ] *adj* anual ♦ *adv* anualmente, cada año; **twice ~** dos veces al año.
yearn [jəːn] *vi*: **to ~ for sth** añorar algo, suspirar por algo.
yearning ['jəːnɪŋ] *n* ansia; (*longing*) añoranza.
yeast [jiːst] *n* levadura.
yell [jɛl] *n* grito, alarido ♦ *vi* gritar.
yellow ['jɛləu] *adj, n* amarillo.
yellow fever *n* fiebre *f* amarilla.
yellowish ['jɛləuɪʃ] *adj* amarillento.
Yellow Pages ® *npl* páginas *fpl* amarillas.
Yellow Sea *n*: **the ~** el Mar Amarillo.
yelp [jɛlp] *n* aullido ♦ *vi* aullar.
Yemen ['jɛmən] *n* Yemen *m.*
Yemeni ['jɛmənɪ] *adj, n* yemení *m/f*, yemenita *m/f.*

yen [jɛn] *n* (*currency*) yen *m*.
yeoman ['jəumən] *n*: **Y~ of the Guard** *alabardero de la Casa Real*.
yes [jɛs] *adv, n* sí *m*; **to say/answer ~** decir/contestar que sí; **to say ~ (to)** decir que sí (a), conformarse (con).
yes man *n* pelotillero.
yesterday ['jɛstədɪ] *adv, n* ayer *m*; **~ morning/evening** ayer por la mañana/tarde; **all day ~** todo el día de ayer; **the day before ~** antes de ayer, anteayer.
yet [jɛt] *adv* todavía ♦ *conj* sin embargo, a pesar de todo; **~ again** de nuevo; **it is not finished ~** todavía no está acabado; **the best ~** el/la mejor hasta ahora; **as ~** hasta ahora, todavía.
yew [ju:] *n* tejo.
Y-fronts ® ['waɪfrʌnts] *npl* (*BRIT*) calzoncillos *mpl*, eslip *msg* tradicional.
YHA *n abbr* (*BRIT*: = *Youth Hostel Association*) ≈ Red *f* Española de Albergues Juveniles.
Yiddish ['jɪdɪʃ] *n* yiddish *m*.
yield [ji:ld] *n* producción *f*; (*AGR*) cosecha; (*COMM*) rendimiento ♦ *vt* producir, dar; (*profit*) rendir ♦ *vi* rendirse, ceder; (*US AUT*) ceder el paso; **a ~ of 5%** un rédito del 5 por ciento.
YMCA *n abbr* (= *Young Men's Christian Association*) Asociación *f* de Jóvenes Cristianos.
yob(bo) ['jɔb(bəu)] *n* (*BRIT col*) gamberro.
yodel ['jəudl] *vi* cantar a la tirolesa.
yoga ['jəugə] *n* yoga *m*.
yog(h)ourt, yog(h)urt ['jəugət] *n* yogur *m*.
yoke [jəuk] *n* (*of oxen*) yunta; (*on shoulders*) balancín *m*; (*fig*) yugo ♦ *vt* (*also*: **~ together**: *oxen*) uncir.
yolk [jəuk] *n* yema (de huevo).
yonder ['jɔndə*] *adv* allá (a lo lejos).
yonks [jɔŋks] *npl* (*col*): **I haven't seen him for ~** hace siglos que no lo veo.
Yorks *abbr* (*BRIT*) = *Yorkshire*.

KEYWORD

you [ju:] *pron* **1** (*subject*: *familiar*) tú, *pl* vosotros/as (*SP*), ustedes (*LAM*); (*polite*) usted, *pl* ustedes; **~ are very kind** eres/es *etc* muy amable; **~ French enjoy your food** a vosotros (*or* ustedes) los franceses os (*or* les) gusta la comida; **~ and I will go** iremos tú y yo
2 (*object*: *direct*: *familiar*) te, *pl* os (*SP*), les (*LAM*); (*polite*) lo *or* le, *pl* los *or* les, *f* la, *pl* las; **I know ~** te/le *etc* conozco
3 (*object*: *indirect*: *familiar*) te, *pl* os (*SP*), les (*LAM*); (*polite*) le, *pl* les; **I gave the letter to ~ yesterday** te/os *etc* di la carta ayer
4 (*stressed*): **I told YOU to do it** te dije a ti que lo hicieras, es a ti a quien dije que lo hicieras; *see also* **3**, **5**
5 (*after prep*: *NB*: *con+ti = contigo*: *familiar*) ti, *pl* vosotros/as (*SP*), ustedes (*LAM*); (: *polite*) usted, *pl* ustedes; **it's for ~** es para ti/vosotros *etc*
6 (*comparisons*: *familiar*) tú, *pl* vosotros/as (*SP*), ustedes (*LAM*); (: *polite*) usted, *pl* ustedes; **she's younger than ~** es más joven que tú/vosotros *etc*
7 (*impersonal*: *one*): **fresh air does ~ good** el aire puro (te) hace bien; **~ never know** nunca se sabe; **~ can't do that!** ¡eso no se hace!

you'd [ju:d] = **you had; you would.**
you'll [ju:l] = **you will, you shall.**
young [jʌŋ] *adj* joven ♦ *npl* (*of animal*) cría; (*people*): **the ~** los jóvenes, la juventud; **a ~ man/lady** un(a) joven; **my ~er brother** mi hermano menor *or* pequeño; **the ~er generation** la nueva generación.
youngster ['jʌŋstə*] *n* joven *m/f*.
your [jɔ:*] *adj* tu; (*pl*) vuestro; (*formal*) su; **~ house** tu *etc* casa; *see also* **my**.
you're [juə*] = **you are**.
yours [jɔ:z] *pron* tuyo; (: *pl*) vuestro; (*formal*) suyo; **a friend of ~** un amigo tuyo *etc*; *see also* **faithfully, mine, sincerely**.
yourself [jɔ:'sɛlf] *pron* (*reflexive*) tú mismo; (*complement*) te; (*after prep*) tí (mismo); (*formal*) usted mismo; (: *complement*) se; (: *after prep*) sí (mismo); **you ~ told me** me lo dijiste tú mismo; **(all) by ~** sin ayuda de nadie, solo; *see also* **oneself**.
yourselves [jɔ:'sɛlvz] *pl pron* vosotros mismos; (*after prep*) vosotros (mismos); (*formal*) ustedes (mismos); (: *complement*) se; (: *after prep*) sí mismos.
youth [ju:θ] *n* juventud *f*; (*young man*) (*pl* **~s** [ju:ðz]) joven *m*; **in my ~** en mi juventud.
youth club *n* club *m* juvenil.
youthful ['ju:θful] *adj* juvenil.
youthfulness ['ju:θfəlnɪs] *n* juventud *f*.
youth hostel *n* albergue *m* juvenil.
youth movement *n* movimiento juvenil.
you've [ju:v] = **you have**.
yowl [jaul] *n* (*of animal, person*) aullido ♦ *vi* aullar.
yr. *abbr* (= *year*) a.
YT *abbr* (*Canada*) = *Yukon Territory*.
Yugoslav ['ju:gəuslɑ:v] *adj, n* yugoslavo/a *m/f*.
Yugoslavia [ju:gəu'slɑ:vɪə] *n* Yugoslavia.
Yugoslavian [ju:gəu'slɑ:vɪən] *adj* yugoslavo/a.

yuppie ['jʌpɪ] (*col*) *adj*, *n* yuppie *m/f*.
YWCA *n abbr* (= *Young Women's Christian Association*) Asociación *f* de Jóvenes Cristianas.

Zz

Z, z [zɛd, (*US*) ziː] *n* (*letter*) Z, z *f*; **Z for Zebra** Z de Zaragoza.
Zaire [zɑːˈiːə*] *n* Zaire *m*.
Zambia [ˈzæmbɪə] *n* Zambia.
Zambian [ˈzæmbɪən] *adj*, *n* zambiano/a *m/f*.
zany [ˈzeɪnɪ] *adj* estrafalario.
zap [zæp] *vt* (*COMPUT*) borrar.
zeal [ziːl] *n* celo, entusiasmo.
zealot [ˈzɛlət] *n* fanático/a.
zealous [ˈzɛləs] *adj* celoso, entusiasta.
zebra [ˈziːbrə] *n* cebra.
zebra crossing *n* (*BRIT*) paso de peatones.
zenith [ˈzɛnɪθ] *n* (*ASTRO*) cénit *m*; (*fig*) apogeo.
zero [ˈzɪərəu] *n* cero; **5 degrees below** ~ 5 grados bajo cero.
zero hour *n* hora cero.
zero option *n* (*POL*) opción *f* cero.
zero-rated [ˈzɪərəureɪtɪd] *adj* (*BRIT*) de tasa cero.
zest [zɛst] *n* entusiasmo; ~ **for living** brío.
zigzag [ˈzɪgzæg] *n* zigzag *m* ♦ *vi* zigzaguear.
Zimbabwe [zɪmˈbɑːbwɪ] *n* Zimbabwe *m*.
Zimbabwean [zɪmˈbɑːbwɪən] *adj*, *n* zimbabuo/a *m/f*.
Zimmer ® [ˈzɪmə*] *n* (*also*: ~ **frame**) andador *m*, andaderas *fpl*.
zinc [zɪŋk] *n* cinc *m*, zinc *m*.
Zionism [ˈzaɪənɪzm] *n* sionismo.
Zionist [ˈzaɪənɪst] *adj*, *n* sionista *m/f*.
zip [zɪp] *n* (*also*: ~ **fastener**, (*US*) ~**per**) cremallera, cierre *m* relámpago (*LAM*); (*energy*) energía, vigor *m* ♦ *vt* (*also*: ~ **up**) cerrar la cremallera de ♦ *vi*: **to** ~ **along to the shops** ir de compras volando.
zip code *n* (*US*) código postal.
zither [ˈzɪðə*] *n* cítara.
zodiac [ˈzəudɪæk] *n* zodíaco.
zombie [ˈzɔmbɪ] *n* zombi *m*.
zone [zəun] *n* zona.
zonked [zɔŋkt] *adj* (*col*) hecho polvo.
zoo [zuː] *n* zoo, (parque *m*) zoológico.
zoological [zuːəˈlɔdʒɪkəl] *adj* zoológico.
zoologist [zuˈɔlədʒɪst] *n* zoólogo/a.
zoology [zuːˈɔlədʒɪ] *n* zoología.
zoom [zuːm] *vi*: **to** ~ **past** pasar zumbando; **to** ~ **in (on sth/sb)** (*PHOT*, *CINE*) enfocar (algo/a algn) con el zoom.
zoom lens *n* zoom *m*.
zucchini [zuːˈkiːnɪ] *n*(*pl*) (*US*) calabacín(ines) *m*(*pl*).

Grammar
Gramática

USING THE GRAMMAR

The Grammar section deals systematically and comprehensively with all the information you will need in order to communicate accurately in Spanish. The user-friendly layout explains the grammar point on a left hand page, leaving the facing page free for illustrative examples. The boxed numbers, (→ [1]) etc, direct you to the relevant example in every case. Another strong point of the Grammar section is its comprehensive treatment of verbs. Regular verbs are fully explained, and 80 major irregular verbs are conjugated in their simple tenses. The irregular verbs are given in alphabetical order and laid out in tables, making them easy and efficient to consult. In addition, a verb index lists over 2,800 Spanish verbs, each cross-referred to the appropriate conjugation model.

The Grammar section also provides invaluable guidance on the danger of translating English structures by identical structures in Spanish. Use of Numbers and Punctuation are important areas covered towards the end of the section. Finally, the index lists the main words and grammatical terms in both English and Spanish.

ABBREVIATIONS

algn	alguien	**masc**	masculine	**sing**	singular
cond	conditional	**p(p)**	page(s)	**sth**	something
fem	feminine	**plur**	plural	**subj**	subjunctive
ff	and following pages	**sb**	somebody		

Grammar

CONTENTS

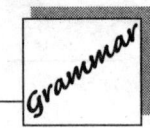

CONTENTS

❐ Simple Tenses: Formation

In Spanish the simple tenses are:

Present	→ 1
Imperfect	→ 2
Future	→ 3
Conditional	→ 4
Preterite	→ 5
Present Subjunctive	→ 6
Imperfect Subjunctive	→ 7

They are formed by adding endings to a verb stem. The endings show the number and person of the subject of the verb → 8

The stem and endings of regular verbs are totally predictable. The following sections show all the patterns for regular verbs. For irregular verbs see pp 80 ff.

Regular Verbs

There are three regular verb patterns (called conjugations), each identifiable by the ending of the infinitive:

- First conjugation verbs end in -**ar** e.g. **hablar** to speak.
- Second conjugation verbs end in -**er** e.g. **comer** to eat.
- Third conjugation verbs end in -**ir** e.g. **vivir** to live.

These three conjugations are treated in order on the following pages. The subject pronouns will appear in brackets because they are not always necessary in Spanish (see p 226).

Examples

1	**(yo) hablo**	I speak I am speaking I do speak
2	**(yo) hablaba**	I spoke I was speaking I used to speak
3	**(yo) hablaré**	I shall speak I shall be speaking
4	**(yo) hablaría**	I should/would speak I should/would be speaking
5	**(yo) hablé**	I spoke
6	**(que) (yo) hable**	(that) I speak
7	**(que) (yo) hablara** *or* **hablase**	(that) I speak
8	**(yo) hablo** **(nosotros) hablamos** **(yo) hablaría** **(nosotros) hablaríamos**	I speak we speak I would speak we would speak

❒ Simple Tenses: First Conjugation

◆ The stem is formed as follows:

TENSE	FORMATION	EXAMPLE
Present Imperfect Preterite Present Subjunctive Imperfect Subjunctive*	infinitive minus **-ar** * For irregular verbs see p 80	**habl-**
Future Conditional	infinitive	**hablar-**

◆ To the appropriate stem add the following endings:

		PRESENT → [1]	IMPERFECT → [2]	PRETERITE → [3]
	1st person	**-o**	**-aba**	**-é**
sing	2nd person	**-as**	**-abas**	**-aste**
	3rd person	**-a**	**-aba**	**-ó**
	1st person	**-amos**	**-ábamos**	**-amos**
plur	2nd person	**-áis**	**-abais**	**-asteis**
	3rd person	**-an**	**-aban**	**-aron**

		PRESENT SUBJUNCTIVE → [4]	IMPERFECT SUBJUNCTIVE → [5]
	1st person	**-e**	**-ara** *or* **-ase**
sing	2nd person	**-es**	**-aras** *or* **-ases**
	3rd person	**-e**	**-ara** *or* **-ase**
	1st person	**-emos**	**-áramos** *or* **-ásemos**
plur	2nd person	**-éis**	**-arais** *or* **-aseis**
	3rd person	**-en**	**-aran** *or* **-asen**

		FUTURE → [6]	CONDITIONAL → [7]
	1st person	**-é**	**-ía**
sing	2nd person	**-ás**	**-ías**
	3rd person	**-á**	**-ía**
	1st person	**-emos**	**-íamos**
plur	2nd person	**-éis**	**-íais**
	3rd person	**-án**	**-ían**

	1 PRESENT	2 IMPERFECT	3 PRETERITE
(yo)	habl**o**	habl**aba**	habl**é**
(tú)	habl**as**	habl**abas**	habl**aste**
(él/ella/Vd)	habl**a**	habl**aba**	habl**ó**
(nosotros/as)	habl**amos**	habl**ábamos**	habl**amos**
(vosotros/as)	habl**áis**	habl**abais**	habl**asteis**
(ellos/as/Vds)	habl**an**	habl**aban**	habl**aron**

	4 PRESENT SUBJUNCTIVE	5 IMPERFECT SUBJUNCTIVE
(yo)	habl**e**	habl**ara** *or* habl**ase**
(tú)	habl**es**	habl**aras** *or* habl**ases**
(él/ella/Vd)	habl**e**	habl**ara** *or* habl**ase**
(nosotros/as)	habl**emos**	habl**áramos** *or* habl**ásemos**
(vosotros/as)	habl**éis**	habl**arais** *or* habl**aseis**
(ellos/as/Vds)	habl**en**	habl**aran** *or* habl**asen**

	6 FUTURE	7 CONDITIONAL
(yo)	hablar**é**	hablar**ía**
(tú)	hablar**ás**	hablar**ías**
(él/ella/Vd)	hablar**á**	hablar**ía**
(nosotros/as)	hablar**emos**	hablar**íamos**
(vosotros/as)	hablar**éis**	hablar**íais**
(ellos/as/Vds)	hablar**án**	hablar**ían**

❒ Simple Tenses: Second Conjugation

◆ The stem is formed as follows:

TENSE	FORMATION	EXAMPLE
Present Imperfect Preterite Present Subjunctive Imperfect Subjunctive*	infinitive minus **-er** * For irregular verbs see p 80	**com-**
Future Conditional	infinitive	**comer-**

◆ To the appropriate stem add the following endings:

		PRESENT → 1	IMPERFECT → 2	PRETERITE → 3
sing	1st person	**-o**	**-ía**	**-í**
	2nd person	**-es**	**-ías**	**-iste**
	3rd person	**-e**	**-ía**	**-ió**
plur	1st person	**-emos**	**-íamos**	**-imos**
	2nd person	**-éis**	**-íais**	**-isteis**
	3rd person	**-en**	**-ían**	**-ieron**

		PRESENT SUBJUNCTIVE → 4	IMPERFECT SUBJUNCTIVE → 5
sing	1st person	**-a**	**-iera** *or* **-iese**
	2nd person	**-as**	**-ieras** *or* **-ieses**
	3rd person	**-a**	**-iera** *or* **-iese**
plur	1st person	**-amos**	**-iéramos** *or* **-iésemos**
	2nd person	**-áis**	**-ierais** *or* **-ieseis**
	3rd person	**-an**	**-ieran** *or* **-iesen**

		FUTURE → 6	CONDITIONAL → 7
sing	1st person	**-é**	**-ía**
	2nd person	**-ás**	**-ías**
	3rd person	**-á**	**-ía**
plur	1st person	**-emos**	**-íamos**
	2nd person	**-éis**	**-íais**
	3rd person	**-án**	**-ían**

Examples

	1 PRESENT	2 IMPERFECT	3 PRETERITE
(yo)	com**o**	com**ía**	com**í**
(tú)	com**es**	com**ías**	com**iste**
(él/ella/Vd)	com**e**	com**ía**	com**ió**
(nosotros/as)	com**emos**	com**íamos**	com**imos**
(vosotros/as)	com**éis**	com**íais**	com**isteis**
(ellos/as/Vds)	com**en**	com**ían**	com**ieron**

	4 PRESENT SUBJUNCTIVE	5 IMPERFECT SUBJUNCTIVE
(yo)	com**a**	com**iera** *or* com**iese**
(tú)	com**as**	com**ieras** *or* com**ieses**
(él/ella/Vd)	com**a**	com**iera** *or* com**iese**
(nosotros/as)	com**amos**	com**iéramos** *or* com**iésemos**
(vosotros/as)	com**áis**	com**ierais** *or* com**ieseis**
(ellos/as/Vds)	com**an**	com**ieran** *or* com**iesen**

	6 FUTURE	7 CONDITIONAL
(yo)	comer**é**	comer**ía**
(tú)	comer**ás**	comer**ías**
(él/ella/Vd)	comer**á**	comer**ía**
(nosotros/as)	comer**emos**	comer**íamos**
(vosotros/as)	comer**éis**	comer**íais**
(ellos/as/Vds)	comer**án**	comer**ían**

❒ Simple Tenses: Third Conjugation

- The stem is formed as follows:

TENSE	FORMATION	EXAMPLE
Present Imperfect Preterite Present Subjunctive Imperfect Subjunctive*	infinitive minus -**ir** * For irregular verbs see p 80	**viv-**
Future Conditional	infinitive	**vivir-**

- To the appropriate stem add the following endings:

		PRESENT → [1]	IMPERFECT → [2]	PRETERITE → [3]
sing	1st person	**-o**	**-ía**	**-í**
	2nd person	**-es**	**-ías**	**-iste**
	3rd person	**-e**	**-ía**	**-ió**
plur	1st person	**-imos**	**-íamos**	**-imos**
	2nd person	**-ís**	**-íais**	**-isteis**
	3rd person	**-en**	**-ían**	**-ieron**

		PRESENT SUBJUNCTIVE → [4]	IMPERFECT SUBJUNCTIVE → [5]
sing	1st person	**-a**	-**iera** *or* -**iese**
	2nd person	**-as**	-**ieras** *or* -**ieses**
	3rd person	**-a**	-**iera** *or* -**iese**
plur	1st person	**-amos**	-**iéramos** *or* -**iésemos**
	2nd person	**-áis**	-**ierais** *or* -**ieseis**
	3rd person	**-an**	-**ieran** *or* -**iesen**

		FUTURE → [6]	CONDITIONAL → [7]
sing	1st person	**-é**	**-ía**
	2nd person	**-ás**	**-ías**
	3rd person	**-á**	**-ía**
plur	1st person	**-emos**	**-íamos**
	2nd person	**-éis**	**-íais**
	3rd person	**-án**	**-ían**

Examples

	1 PRESENT	2 IMPERFECT	3 PRETERITE
(yo)	viv**o**	viv**ía**	viv**í**
(tú)	viv**es**	viv**ías**	viv**iste**
(él/ella/Vd)	viv**e**	viv**ía**	viv**ió**
(nosotros/as)	viv**imos**	viv**íamos**	viv**imos**
(vosotros/as)	viv**ís**	viv**íais**	viv**isteis**
(ellos/as/Vds)	viv**en**	viv**ían**	viv**ieron**

	4 PRESENT SUBJUNCTIVE	5 IMPERFECT SUBJUNCTIVE
(yo)	viv**a**	viv**iera** or viv**iese**
(tú)	viv**as**	viv**ieras** or viv**ieses**
(él/ella/Vd)	viv**a**	viv**iera** or viv**iese**
(nosotros/as)	viv**amos**	viv**iéramos** or viv**iésemos**
(vosotros/as)	viv**áis**	viv**ierais** or viv**ieseis**
(ellos/as/Vds)	viv**an**	viv**ieran** or viv**iesen**

	6 FUTURE	7 CONDITIONAL
(yo)	vivir**é**	vivir**ía**
(tú)	vivir**ás**	vivir**ías**
(él/ella/Vd)	vivir**á**	vivir**ía**
(nosotros/as)	vivir**emos**	vivir**íamos**
(vosotros/as)	vivir**éis**	vivir**íais**
(ellos/as/Vds)	vivir**án**	vivir**ían**

❐ The Imperative

The imperative is the form of the verb used to give commands or orders. It can be used politely, as in English 'Shut the door, please'.

In POSITIVE commands, the imperative forms for **Vd, Vds** and **nosotros** are the same as the subjunctive. The other forms are as follows:

tú (same as 3rd person singular present indicative)
vosotros (final **-r** of infinitive changes to **-d**) → [1]

(tú)	**habla** *speak*	**come** *eat*	**vive** *live*
(Vd)	**hable** *speak*	**coma** *eat*	**viva** *live*
(nosotros)	**hablemos** *let's speak*	**comamos** *let's eat*	**vivamos** *let's live*
(vosotros)	**hablad** *speak*	**comed** *eat*	**vivid** *live*
(Vds)	**hablen** *speak*	**coman** *eat*	**vivan** *live*

In NEGATIVE commands, all the imperative forms are exactly the same as the present subjunctive.

- The imperative of irregular verbs is given in the verb tables, pp 82 ff.

Position of object pronouns with the imperative

In POSITIVE commands: they follow the verb and are attached to it. An accent is needed to show the correct position for stress (see p 292) → [2]

In NEGATIVE commands: they precede the verb and are not attached to it → [3]

- For the order of object pronouns, see page 232.

Examples

1	**cantar** to sing	**cantad** sing
2	**Perdóneme** Excuse me	**Enviémoselos** Let's send them to him/her/them
	Elíjanos Choose us	**Explíquemelo** Explain it to me
	Esperémosla Let's wait for her/it	**Devuélvaselo** Give it back to him/her/them
3	**No me molestes** Don't disturb me	**No se la devolvamos** Let's not give it back to him/her/them
	No les castiguemos Let's not punish them	**No me lo mandes** Don't send it to me
	No las conteste Don't answer them	**No nos lo hagan** Don't do it to us

❐ The Imperative (Continued)

- For reflexive verbs – e.g. **levantarse** *to get up* – the object pronoun is the reflexive pronoun. It should be noted that the imperative forms need an accent to show the correct position for stress (see p 292). The forms **nosotros** and **vosotros** also drop the final **-s** and **-d** respectively before the pronoun → [1]

BUT: **idos (vosotros)** *go*

⚠ NOTE: For general instructions, the infinitive is used instead of the imperative →[2], but when it is preceded by **vamos a** it often translates *let's* … → [3]

Examples

Grammar

1	**Levántate** Get up	**No te levantes** Don't get up
	Levántese (Vd) Get up	**No se levante (Vd)** Don't get up
	Levantémonos Let's get up	**No nos levantemos** Let's not get up
	Levantaos Get up	**No os levantéis** Don't get up
	Levántense (Vds) Get up	**No se levanten (Vds)** Don't get up

2 **Ver pág ...**
See page
No pasar
Do not pass ...

3 **Vamos a ver**
Let's see
Vamos a empezar
Let's start

❐ Compound Tenses: Formation

In Spanish the compound tenses are:

Perfect → [1]
Pluperfect → [2]
Future Perfect → [3]
Conditional Perfect → [4]
Past Anterior → [5]
Perfect Subjunctive → [6]
Pluperfect Subjunctive → [7]

They consist of the past participle of the verb together with the auxiliary verb **haber**.

Compound tenses are formed in exactly the same way for both regular and irregular verbs, the only difference being that irregular verbs may have an irregular past participle.

The Past Participle

For all compound tenses you need to know how to form the past participle of the verb. For regular verbs this is as follows:

- 1st conjugation: replace the **-ar** of the infinitive by **-ado** → [8]
- 2nd conjugation: replace the **-er** of the infinitive by **-ido** → [9]
- 3rd conjugation: replace the **-ir** of the infinitive by **-ido** → [10]

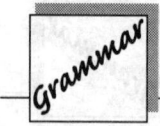

1 **(yo) he hablado**
I have spoken

2 **(yo) había hablado**
I had spoken

3 **(yo) habré hablado**
I shall have spoken

4 **(yo) habría hablado**
I should/would have spoken

5 **(yo) hube hablado**
I had spoken

6 **(que) (yo) haya hablado**
(that) I spoke, have spoken

7 **(que) (yo) hubiera/hubiese hablado**
(that) I had spoken

8	**cantar** to sing	→	**cantado** sung
9	**comer** to eat	→	**comido** eaten
10	**vivir** to live	→	**vivido** lived

❒ Compound Tenses: Formation (Continued)

Perfect tense:	the present tense of **haber** plus the past participle → [1]
Pluperfect tense:	the imperfect tense of **haber** plus the past participle → [2]
Future Perfect:	the future tense of **haber** plus the past participle → [3]
Conditional Perfect:	the conditional of **haber** plus the past participle → [4]

Examples

1 PERFECT	(yo) **he** habl**ado** (tú) **has** habl**ado** (él/ella/Vd) **ha** habl**ado** (nosotros/as) **hemos** habl**ado** (vosotros/as) **habéis** habl**ado** (ellos/as/Vds) **han** habl**ado**

2 PLUPERFECT	(yo) **había** habl**ado** (tú) **habías** habl**ado** (él/ella/Vd) **había** habl**ado** (nosotros/as) **habíamos** habl**ado** (vosotros/as) **habíais** habl**ado** (ellos/as/Vds) **habían** habl**ado**

3 FUTURE PERFECT	(yo) **habré** habl**ado** (tú) **habrás** habl**ado** (él/ella/Vd) **habrá** habl**ado** (nosotros/as) **habremos** habl**ado** (vosotros/as) **habréis** habl**ado** (ellos/as/Vds) **habrán** habl**ado**

4 CONDITIONAL PERFECT	(yo) **habría** habl**ado** (tú) **habrías** habl**ado** (él/ella/Vd) **habría** habl**ado** (nosotros/as) **habríamos** habl**ado** (vosotros/as) **habríais** habl**ado** (ellos/as/Vds) **habrían** habl**ado**

❒ Compound Tenses: Formation (Continued)

Past Anterior:	the preterite of **haber** plus the past participle → [1]
Perfect Subjunctive:	the present subjunctive of **haber** plus the past participle → [2]
Pluperfect Subjunctive:	the imperfect subjunctive of **haber** plus the past participle → [3]

- For how to form the past participle of regular verbs see p 18. The past participle of irregular verbs is given for each verb in the verb tables, pp 82 to 161.

Examples

Grammar

1 PAST ANTERIOR	(yo)	**hube** habl**ado**
	(tú)	**hubiste** habl**ado**
	(él/ella/Vd)	**hubo** habl**ado**
	(nosotros/as)	**hubimos** habl**ado**
	(vosotros/as)	**hubisteis** habl**ado**
	(ellos/as/Vds)	**hubieron** habl**ado**

2 PRESENT SUBJUNCTIVE	(yo)	**haya** habl**ado**
	(tú)	**hayas** habl**ado**
	(él/ella/Vd)	**haya** habl**ado**
	(nosotros/as)	**hayamos** habl**ado**
	(vosotros/as)	**hayáis** habl**ado**
	(ellos/as/Vds)	**hayan** habl**ado**

3 PLUPERFECT SUBJUNCTIVE	(yo)	**hubiera** or **hubiese** habl**ado**
	(tú)	**hubieras** or **hubieses** habl**ado**
	(él/ella/Vd)	**hubiera** or **hubiese** habl**ado**
	(nosotros/as)	**hubiéramos** or **hubiésemos** habl**ado**
	(vosotros/as)	**hubierais** or **hubieseis** habl**ado**
	(ellos/as/Vds)	**hubieran** or **hubiesen** habl**ado**

❐ Reflexive Verbs

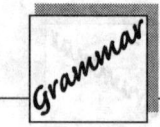

A reflexive verb is one accompanied by a reflexive pronoun. The infinitive of a reflexive verb ends with the pronoun **se**, which is added to the verb form e.g.

levantarse *to get up*; **lavarse** *to wash (oneself)*

The reflexive pronouns are:

PERSON	SINGULAR	PLURAL
1st	**me**	**nos**
2nd	**te**	**os**
3rd	**se**	**se**

- The reflexive pronoun 'reflects back' to the subject, but it is not always translated in English → [1]

  The plural pronouns are sometimes translated as *one another, each other* (the 'reciprocal' meaning) → [2]

  The reciprocal meaning may be emphasized by **el uno al otro/la una a la otra (los unos a los otros/las unas a las otras)** → [3]

- Both simple and compound tenses of reflexive verbs are conjugated in exactly the same way as those of non-reflexive verbs, except that the reflexive pronoun is always used.

  The only irregularity is in the 1st and 2nd person plural of the affirmative imperative (see p 16). A sample reflexive verb is conjugated in full on pp 28 to 31.

Position of reflexive pronouns

- Except with the infinitive, gerund and positive commands, the pronoun comes before the verb → [4]

- In the infinitive, gerund and positive commands, the pronoun follows the verb and is attached to it (but see also p 228) → [5]

Examples

1 **Me visto**
I'm dressing (myself)

Nos lavamos
We're washing (ourselves)

Se levanta
He gets up

2 **Nos queremos**
We love each other

Se parecen
They resemble one another

3 **Se miraban el uno al otro**
They were looking at each other

4 **Me acuesto temprano**
I go to bed early

No se ha despertado
He hasn't woken up

¿Cómo se llama Vd?
What is your name?

No te levantes
Don't get up

5 **Quiero irme**
I want to go away

Siéntense
Sit down

Estoy levantándome
I am getting up

Vámonos
Let's go

❒ Reflexive Verbs (Continued)

Some verbs have both a reflexive and non-reflexive form. When used reflexively, they have a different but closely related meaning, as shown in the following examples.

NON-REFLEXIVE	REFLEXIVE
acostar *to put to bed*	**acostarse** *to go to bed*
casar *to marry (off)*	**casarse** *to get married*
detener *to stop*	**detenerse** *to come to a halt*
dormir *to sleep*	**dormirse** *to go to sleep*
enfadar *to annoy*	**enfadarse** *to get annoyed*
hacer *to make*	**hacerse** *to become*
ir *to go*	**irse** *to leave, go away*
lavar *to wash*	**lavarse** *to get washed*
levantar *to raise*	**levantarse** *to get up*
llamar *to call*	**llamarse** *to be called*
poner *to put*	**ponerse** *to put on (clothing), to become*
sentir *to feel (something)*	**sentirse** *to feel (sick, tired, etc)*
vestir *to dress (someone)*	**vestirse** *to get dressed*
volver *to return*	**volverse** *to turn round*

◆ Some other verbs exist only in the reflexive:

arrepentirse *to repent* | **jactarse** *to boast*
atreverse *to dare* | **quejarse** *to complain*

◆ Some verbs acquire a different nuance when used reflexively:

caer *to fall* → [1] | **caerse** *to fall down (by accident)* → [2]
morir *to die, be killed (by accident or on purpose)* → [3] | **morirse** *to die (from natural causes)* → [4]

◆ Often a reflexive verb can be used:

— to avoid the passive (see p 34) → [5]

— in impersonal expressions (see p 40) → [6]

Examples

Grammar

1 **El agua caía desde las rocas**
Water fell from the rocks

2 **Me caí y me rompí el brazo**
I fell and broke my arm

3 **Tres personas han muerto en un accidente/atentado terrorista**
Three people were killed in an accident/a terrorist attack

4 **Mi abuelo se murió a los ochenta años**
My grandfather died at the age of eighty

5 **Se perdió la batalla**
The battle was lost

No se veían las casas
The houses could not be seen

6 **Se dice que ...**
(It is said that) People say that ...

No se puede entrar
You/One can't go in

No se permite
It is not allowed

❒ Reflexive Verbs (Continued)

Conjugation of: **lavarse** *to wash oneself*

I SIMPLE TENSES

PRESENT	
(yo)	**me** lav**o**
(tú)	**te** lav**as**
(él/ella/Vd)	**se** lav**a**
(nosotros/as)	**nos** lav**amos**
(vosotros/as)	**os** lav**áis**
(ellos/as/Vds)	**se** lav**an**
IMPERFECT	
(yo)	**me** lav**aba**
(tú)	**te** lav**abas**
(él/ella/Vd)	**se** lav**aba**
(nosotros/as)	**nos** lav**ábamos**
(vosotros/as)	**os** lav**abais**
(ellos/as/Vds)	**se** lav**aban**
FUTURE	
(yo)	**me** lavar**é**
(tú)	**te** lavar**ás**
(él/ella/Vd)	**se** lavar**á**
(nosotros/as)	**nos** lavar**emos**
(vosotros/as)	**os** lavar**éis**
(ellos/as/Vds)	**se** lavar**án**
CONDITIONAL	
(yo)	**me** lavar**ía**
(tú)	**te** lavar**ías**
(él/ella/Vd)	**se** lavar**ía**
(nosotros/as)	**nos** lavar**íamos**
(vosotros/as)	**os** lavar**íais**
(ellos/as/Vds)	**se** lavar**ían**

❐ Reflexive Verbs (Continued)

Conjugation of: **lavarse** *to wash oneself*

I SIMPLE TENSES

PRETERITE	
(yo)	**me** lavé
(tú)	**te** lav**aste**
(él/ella/Vd)	**se** lavó
(nosotros/as)	**nos** lav**amos**
(vosotros/as)	**os** lav**asteis**
(ellos/as/Vds)	**se** lav**aron**
PRESENT SUBJUNCTIVE	
(yo)	**me** lave
(tú)	**te** lav**es**
(él/ella/Vd)	**se** lave
(nosotros/as)	**nos** lav**emos**
(vosotros/as)	**os** lav**éis**
(ellos/as/Vds)	**se** lav**en**
IMPERFECT SUBJUNCTIVE	
(yo)	**me** lav**ara** *or* lav**ase**
(tú)	**te** lav**aras** *or* lav**ases**
(él/ella/Vd)	**se** lav**ara** *or* lav**ase**
(nosotros/as)	**nos** lav**áramos** *or* lav**ásemos**
(vosotros/as)	**os** lav**arais** *or* lav**aseis**
(ellos/as/Vds)	**se** lav**aran** *or* lav**asen**

❒ Reflexive Verbs (Continued)

Conjugation of: **lavarse** *to wash oneself*

II COMPOUND TENSES

PERFECT	
(yo)	**me he** lav**ado**
(tú)	**te has** lav**ado**
(él/ella/Vd)	**se ha** lav**ado**
(nosotros/as)	**nos hemos** lav**ado**
(vosotros/as)	**os habéis** lav**ado**
(ellos/as/Vds)	**se han** lav**ado**
PLUPERFECT	
(yo)	**me había** lav**ado**
(tú)	**te habías** lav**ado**
(él/ella/Vd)	**se había** lav**ado**
(nosotros/as)	**nos habíamos** lav**ado**
(vosotros/as)	**os habíais** lav**ado**
(ellos/as/Vds)	**se habían** lav**ado**
FUTURE PERFECT	
(yo)	**me habré** lav**ado**
(tú)	**te habrás** lav**ado**
(él/ella/Vd)	**se habrá** lav**ado**
(nosotros/as)	**nos habremos** lav**ado**
(vosotros/as)	**os habréis** lav**ado**
(ellos/as/Vds)	**se habrán** lav**ado**

❐ Reflexive Verbs (Continued)

Conjugation of: **lavarse** *to wash oneself*

II COMPOUND TENSES

PAST ANTERIOR

(yo)	**me hube** lavado
(tú)	**te hubiste** lavado
(él/ella/Vd)	**se hubo** lavado
(nosotros/as)	**nos hubimos** lavado
(vosotros/as)	**os hubisteis** lavado
(ellos/as/Vds)	**se hubieron** lavado

PERFECT SUBJUNCTIVE

(yo)	**me haya** lavado
(tú)	**te hayas** lavado
(él/ella/Vd)	**se haya** lavado
(nosotros/as)	**nos hayamos** lavado
(vosotros/as)	**os hayáis** lavado
(ellos/as/Vds)	**se hayan** lavado

PLUPERFECT SUBJUNCTIVE

(yo)	**me hubiera** *or* **hubiese** lavado
(tú)	**te hubieras** *or* **hubieses** lavado
(él/ella/Vd)	**se hubiera** *or* **hubiese** lavado
(nosotros/as)	**nos hubiéramos** *or* **hubiésemos** lavado
(vosotros/as)	**os hubierais** *or* **hubieseis** lavado
(ellos/as/Vds)	**se hubieran** *or* **hubiesen** lavado

❒ The Passive

In active sentences, the subject of a verb carries out the action of that verb, but in passive sentences the subject receives the action. Compare the following:

The car hit Jane (subject: *the car*)
Jane was hit by the car (subject: *Jane*)

- English uses the verb *'to be'* with the past participle to form passive sentences. Spanish forms them in the same way, i.e.:

  a tense of **ser** + past participle

  The past participle agrees in number and gender with the subject → [1]

  A sample verb is conjugated in the passive voice on pp 36 to 39.

- In English, the word *'by'* usually introduces the agent through which the action of a passive sentence is performed. In Spanish this agent is preceded by **por** → [2]

- The Passive voice is used much less frequently in Spanish than English. It is, however, often used in expressions where the identity of the agent is unknown or unimportant → [3]

Examples

1 **Pablo ha sido despedido**
Paul has been sacked
Su madre era muy admirada
His mother was greatly admired
El palacio será vendido
The palace will be sold
Las puertas habían sido cerradas
The doors had been closed

2 **La casa fue diseñada por mi hermano**
The house was designed by my brother

3 **La ciudad fue conquistada tras un largo asedio**
The city was conquered after a long siege
Ha sido declarado el estado de excepción
A state of emergency has been declared

❒ The Passive (Continued)

In English the indirect object in an active sentence can become the subject of the related passive sentence, e.g.

> *His mother gave him the book* (indirect object: *him*)
> He was given the book by his mother

This is not possible in Spanish. The indirect object remains as such, while the object of the active sentence becomes the subject of the passive sentence → [1]

Other ways to express a passive meaning

Since modern Spanish tends to avoid the passive, it uses various other constructions to replace it:

- If the agent (person or object performing the action) is known, the active is often preferred where English might prefer the passive → [2]
- The 3rd person plural of the active voice can be used. The meaning is equivalent to *they* + verb → [3]
- When the action of the sentence is performed on a person, the reflexive form of the verb can be used in the 3rd person singular, and the person becomes the object → [4]
- When the action is performed on a thing, this becomes the subject of the sentence and the verb is made reflexive, agreeing in number with the subject → [5]

Examples

1 **Su madre le regaló el libro**
His mother gave him the book
becomes
El libro le fue regalado por su madre
The book was given to him by his mother

2 **La policía interrogó al sospechoso**
The police questioned the suspect
rather than
El sospechoso fue interrogado por la policía

3 **Usan demasiada publicidad en la televisión**
Too much advertising is used on television

4 **Últimamente no se le/les ha visto mucho en público**
He has/they have not been seen much in public recently

5 **Esta palabra ya no se usa**
This word is no longer used
Todos los libros se han vendido
All the books have been sold

❐ The Passive (Continued)

Conjugation of: **ser amado** *to be loved*

PRESENT	
(yo)	**soy** amado(a)
(tú)	**eres** amado(a)
(él/ella/Vd)	**es** amado(a)
(nosotros/as)	**somos** amado(a)s
(vosotros/as)	**sois** amado(a)s
(ellos/as/Vds)	**son** amado(a)s
IMPERFECT	
(yo)	**era** amado(a)
(tú)	**eras** amado(a)
(él/ella/Vd)	**era** amado(a)
(nosotros/as)	**éramos** amado(a)s
(vosotros/as)	**erais** amado(a)s
(ellos/as/Vds)	**eran** amado(a)s
FUTURE	
(yo)	**seré** amado(a)
(tú)	**serás** amado(a)
(él/ella/Vd)	**será** amado(a)
(nosotros/as)	**seremos** amado(a)s
(vosotros/as)	**seréis** amado(a)s
(ellos/as/Vds)	**serán** amado(a)s
CONDITIONAL	
(yo)	**sería** amado(a)
(tú)	**serías** amado(a)
(él/ella/Vd)	**sería** amado(a)
(nosotros/as)	**seríamos** amado(a)s
(vosotros/as)	**seríais** amado(a)s
(ellos/as/Vds)	**serían** amado(a)s

❒ The Passive (Continued)

Conjugation of: **ser amado** *to be loved*

PRETERITE	
(yo)	**fui** am**ado(a)**
(tú)	**fuiste** am**ado(a)**
(él/ella/Vd)	**fue** am**ado(a)**
(nosotros/as)	**fuimos** am**ado(a)s**
(vosotros/as)	**fuisteis** am**ado(a)s**
(ellos/as/Vds)	**fueron** am**ado(a)s**
PRESENT SUBJUNCTIVE	
(yo)	**sea** am**ado(a)**
(tú)	**seas** am**ado(a)**
(él/ella/Vd)	**sea** am**ado(a)**
(nosotros/as)	**seamos** am**ado(a)s**
(vosotros/as)	**seáis** am**ado(a)s**
(ellos/as/Vds)	**sean** am**ado(a)s**
IMPERFECT SUBJUNCTIVE	
(yo)	**fuera** *or* **fuese** am**ado(a)**
(tú)	**fueras** *or* **fueses** am**ado(a)**
(él/ella/Vd)	**fuera** *or* **fuese** am**ado(a)**
(nosotros/as)	**fuéramos** *or* **fuésemos** am**ado(a)s**
(vosotros/as)	**fuerais** *or* **fueseis** am**ado(a)s**
(ellos/as/Vds)	**fueran** *or* **fuesen** am**ado(a)s**

❒ The Passive (Continued)

Conjugation of: **ser amado** *to be loved*

PERFECT	
(yo)	**he sido** amado(a)
(tú)	**has sido** amado(a)
(él/ella/Vd)	**ha sido** amado(a)
(nosotros/as)	**hemos sido** amado(a)s
(vosotros/as)	**habéis sido** amado(a)s
(ellos/as/Vds)	**han sido** amado(a)s
PLUPERFECT	
(yo)	**había sido** amado(a)
(tú)	**habías sido** amado(a)
(él/ella/Vd)	**había sido** amado(a)
(nosotros/as)	**habíamos sido** amado(a)s
(vosotros/as)	**habíais sido** amado(a)s
(ellos/as/Vds)	**habían sido** amado(a)s
FUTURE PERFECT	
(yo)	**habré sido** amado(a)
(tú)	**habrás sido** amado(a)
(él/ella/Vd)	**habrá sido** amado(a)
(nosotros/as)	**habremos sido** amado(a)s
(vosotros/as)	**habréis sido** amado(a)s
(ellos/as/Vds)	**habrán sido** amado(a)s
CONDITIONAL PERFECT	
(yo)	**habría sido** amado(a)
(tú)	**habrías sido** amado(a)
(él/ella/Vd)	**habría sido** amado(a)
(nosotros/as)	**habríamos sido** amado(a)s
(vosotros/as)	**habríais sido** amado(a)s
(ellos/as/Vds)	**habrían sido** amado(a)s

❒ The Passive (Continued)

Conjugation of: **ser amado** *to be loved*

PAST ANTERIOR	
(yo)	**hube sido** am**ado(a)**
(tú)	**hubiste sido** am**ado(a)**
(él/ella/Vd)	**hubo sido** am**ado(a)**
(nosotros/as)	**hubimos sido** am**ado(a)s**
(vosotros/as)	**hubisteis sido** am**ado(a)s**
(ellos/as/Vds)	**hubieron sido** am**ado(a)s**
PERFECT SUBJUNCTIVE	
(yo)	**haya sido** am**ado(a)**
(tú)	**hayas sido** am**ado(a)**
(él/ella/Vd)	**haya sido** am**ado(a)**
(nosotros/as)	**hayamos sido** am**ado(a)s**
(vosotros/as)	**hayáis sido** am**ado(a)s**
(ellos/as/Vds)	**hayan sido** am**ado(a)s**
PLUPERFECT SUBJUNCTIVE	
(yo)	**hubiera/-se sido** am**ado(a)**
(tú)	**hubieras/-ses sido** am**ado(a)**
(él/ella/Vd)	**hubiera/-se sido** am**ado(a)**
(nosotros/as)	**hubiéramos/-semos sido** am**ado(a)s**
(vosotros/as)	**hubierais/-seis sido** am**ado(a)s**
(ellos/as/Vds)	**hubieran/-sen sido** am**ado(a)s**

❒ Impersonal Verbs

Impersonal verbs are used only in the infinitive, the gerund, and in the 3rd person (usually singular); unlike English, Spanish does not use the subject pronoun with impersonal verbs, e.g.

llueve
it's raining

es fácil decir que ...
it's easy to say that ...

The most common impersonal verbs are:

INFINITIVE	CONSTRUCTION	
amanecer	**amanece/está amaneciendo** *it's daybreak*	
anochecer	**anochece/está anocheciendo** *it's getting dark*	
granizar	**graniza/está granizando** *it's hailing*	
llover	**llueve/está lloviendo** *it's raining*	→ 1
lloviznar	**llovizna/está lloviznando** *it's drizzling*	
nevar	**nieva/está nevando** *it's snowing*	
tronar	**truena/está tronando** *it's thundering*	

Some reflexive verbs are also used impersonally.
The most common are:

INFINITIVE	CONSTRUCTION
creerse	**se cree que*** + indicative → 2 *it is thought that; people think that*
decirse	**se dice que*** + indicative → 3 *it is said that; people say that*

Examples

1 **Llovía a cántaros**
It was raining cats and dogs
Estaba nevando cuando salieron
It was snowing when they left

2 **Se cree que llegarán mañana**
It is thought they will arrive tomorrow

3 **Se dice que ha sido el peor invierno en 50 años**
People say it's been the worst winter in 50 years

❐ Impersonal Verbs (Continued)

INFINITIVE	CONSTRUCTION
poderse	**se puede** + infinitive → [1] *one/people can, it is possible to*
tratarse de	**se trata de** + noun → [2] *it's a question/matter of something* *it's about something*
	se trata de + infinitive → [3] *it's a question/matter of doing;* *somebody must do*
venderse	**se vende*** + noun → [4] *to be sold; for sale*

* This impersonal construction conveys the same meaning as the 3rd person plural of these verbs; **creen que, dicen que, venden**

The following verbs are also commonly used in impersonal constructions:

INFINITIVE	CONSTRUCTION
bastar	**basta con** + infinitive → [5] *it is enough to do* **basta con** + noun → [6] *something is enough, it only takes something*
faltar	**falta** + infinitive → [7] *we still have to/one still has to*
haber	**hay** + noun → [8] *there is/are* **hay que** + infinitive → [9] *one has to/we have to*
hacer	**hace** + noun/adjective depicting weather/ dark/light etc → [10] *it is* **hace** + time expression + **que** + indicative → [11] *somebody has done* OR *been doing something since …* **hace** + time expression + **que** + negative indicative → [12] *it is … since*

Examples

1 **Aquí se puede aparcar**
One can park here

2 **No se trata de dinero**
It isn't a question/matter of money

3 **Se trata de poner fin al asunto**
We must put an end to the matter

4 **Se vende coche**
Car for sale

5 **Basta con telefonear para reservar un asiento**
You need only phone to reserve a seat

6 **Basta con un error para que todo se estropee**
One single error is enough to ruin everything

7 **Aún falta cerrar las maletas**
We/One still have/has to close the suitcases

8 **Hay una habitación libre**
There is one spare room

No había cartas esta mañana
There were no letters this morning

9 **Hay que cerrar las puertas**
We have/One has to shut the doors

10 **Hace calor/viento/sol**
It is hot/windy/sunny

Mañana hará bueno
It'll be nice (weather) tomorrow

11 **Hace seis meses que vivo/vivimos aquí**
I/We have lived *or* been living here for six months

12 **Hace tres años que no le veo**
It is three years since I last saw him

❒ Impersonal Verbs (Continued)

INFINITIVE	CONSTRUCTION
hacer falta	**hace falta** + noun object (+ indirect object) → [1] *(somebody) needs something, something is necessary (to somebody)* **hace falta** + infinitive (+ indirect object) → [2] *it is necessary to do* **hace falta que** + subjunctive → [3] *it is necessary to do, somebody must do*
parecer	**parece que** (+ indirect object) + indicative → [4] *it seems/appears that*
ser	**es/son** + time expression → [5] *it is* **es** + **de día/noche** → [6] *it is* **es** + adjective + infinitive → [7] *it is*
ser mejor	**es mejor** + infinitive → [8] *it's better to do* **es mejor que** + subjunctive → [9] *it's better if/that*
valer más	**más vale** + infinitive → [10] *it's better to do* **más vale que** + subjunctive → [11] *it's better to do/that somebody does*

Examples

1 **Hace falta valor para hacer eso**
One needs courage to do that, Courage is needed to do that

Me hace falta otro vaso más
I need an extra glass

2 **Hace falta volver**
It is necessary to return, We/I/You must return*

Me hacía falta volver
I had to return

3 **Hace falta que Vd se vaya**
You have to/must leave

4 **(Me) parece que estás equivocado**
It seems (to me) you are wrong

5 **Son las tres y media**
It is half past three

Ya es primavera
It is spring now

6 **Era de noche cuando llegamos**
It was night when we arrived

7 **Era inútil protestar**
It was useless to complain

8 **Es mejor no decir nada**
It's better to keep quiet

9 **Es mejor que lo pongas aquí**
It's better if/that you put it here

10 **Más vale prevenir que curar**
Prevention is better than cure

11 **Más valdría que no fuéramos**
It would be better if we didn't go/We'd better not go

* The translation here obviously depends on context

❐ The Infinitive

The infinitive is the form of the verb found in dictionary entries meaning *'to …'*, e.g. **hablar** *to speak*, **vivir** *to live*.

The infinitive is used in the following ways:

- After a preposition → [1]
- As a verbal noun → [2]
  In this use the article may precede the infinitive, especially when the infinitive is the subject and begins the sentence → [3]
- As a dependent infinitive, in the following verbal constructions:

  — with no linking preposition → [4]

  — with the linking preposition **a** → [5]
  (see also p 66)

  — with the linking preposition **de** → [6]
  (see also p 66)

  — with the linking preposition **en** → [7]
  (see also p 66)

  — with the linking preposition **con** → [8]
  (see also p 66)

  — with the linking preposition **por** → [9]
  (see also p 66)

- The following construction should also be noted: indefinite pronoun + **que** + infinitive → [10]
- The object pronouns generally follow the infinitive and are attached to it. For exceptions see p 228.

1 **Después de acabar el desayuno, salió de casa**
After finishing her breakfast she went out

Al enterarse de lo ocurrido se puso furiosa
When she found out what had happened she was furious

Me hizo daño sin saberlo
She hurt me without her knowing

2 **Su deporte preferido es montar a caballo**
Her favourite sport is horse riding

Ver es creer
Seeing is believing

3 **El viajar tanto me resulta cansado**
I find so much travelling tiring

4 **¿Quiere Vd esperar?**
Would you like to wait?

5 **Aprenderán pronto a nadar**
They will soon learn to swim

6 **Pronto dejará de llover**
It'll stop raining soon

7 **La comida tarda en hacerse**
The meal is taking a long time to cook

8 **Amenazó con denunciarles**
He threatened to report them (to the police)

9 **Comience Vd por decirme su nombre**
Please start by giving me your name

10 **Tengo algo que decirte**
I have something to tell you

❐ The Infinitive (Continued)

The verbs set out below are followed by the infinitive with no linking preposition.

- **deber, poder, saber, querer** and **tener que** (**hay que** in impersonal constructions) → 1
- **valer más, hacer falta:** see Impersonal Verbs, p 44.
- verbs of seeing or hearing, e.g. **ver** to see, **oír** to hear → 2
- **hacer** → 3
- **dejar** to let, allow → 3
- The following common verbs:

aconsejar	to advise → 4
conseguir	to manage to → 5
decidir	to decide
desear	to wish, want → 6
esperar	to hope → 7
evitar	to avoid → 8
impedir	to prevent → 9
intentar	to try → 10
lograr	to manage to → 5
necesitar	to need → 11
odiar	to hate
olvidar	to forget → 12
pensar	to think → 13
preferir	to prefer → 14
procurar	to try → 10
prohibir	to forbid → 15
prometer	to promise → 16
proponer	to propose → 17

Examples

1 **¿Quiere Vd esperar?**
Would you like to wait?
No puede venir
She can't come

2 **Nos ha visto llegar**
She saw us arriving
Se les oye cantar
You can hear them singing

3 **No me hagas reír**
Don't make me laugh
Déjeme pasar
Let me past

4 **Le aconsejamos dejarlo para mañana**
We advise you to leave it until tomorrow

5 **Aún no he conseguido/logrado entenderlo**
I still haven't managed to understand it

6 **No desea tener más hijos**
She doesn't want to have any more children

7 **Esperamos ir de vacaciones este verano**
We are hoping to go on holiday this summer

8 **Evite beber cuando conduzca**
Avoid drinking and driving

9 **No pudo impedirle hablar**
He couldn't prevent him from speaking

10 **Intentamos/procuramos pasar desapercibidos**
We tried not to be noticed

11 **Necesitaba salir a la calle**
I/he/she needed to go out

12 **Olvidó dejar su dirección**
He/she forgot to leave his/her address

13 **¿Piensan venir por Navidad?**
Are you thinking of coming for Christmas?

14 **Preferiría elegirlo yo mismo**
I'd rather choose it myself

15 **Prohibió fumar a los alumnos**
He forbade the pupils to smoke

16 **Prometieron volver pronto**
They promised to come back soon

17 **Propongo salir cuanto antes**
I propose to leave as soon as possible

❐ The Infinitive: Set Expressions

The following are set in Spanish with the meaning shown:

dejar caer	*to drop* → [1]
hacer entrar	*to show in* → [2]
hacer saber	*to let know, make known* → [3]
hacer salir	*to let out* → [4]
hacer venir	*to send for* → [5]
ir(se) a buscar	*to go for, go and get* → [6]
mandar hacer	*to order* → [7]
mandar llamar	*to send for* → [8]
oír decir que	*to hear it said that* → [9]
oír hablar de	*to hear of/about* → [10]
querer decir	*to mean* → [11]

The Perfect Infinitive

- The perfect infinitive is formed using the auxiliary verb **haber** with the past participle of the verb → [12]

- The perfect infinitive is found:
  — following certain prepositions, especially **después de** *after* → [13]
  — following certain verbal constructions → [14]

Examples

1 **Al verlo, dejó caer lo que llevaba en las manos**
When he saw him he dropped what he was carrying

2 **Haz entrar a nuestros invitados**
Show our guests in

3 **Quiero hacerles saber que no serán bien recibidos**
I want to let them know that they won't be welcome

4 **Hágale salir, por favor**
Please let him out

5 **Le he hecho venir a Vd porque ...**
I sent for you because ...

6 **Vete a buscar los guantes**
Go and get your gloves

7 **Me he mandado hacer un traje**
I have ordered a suit

8 **Mandaron llamar al médico**
They sent for the doctor

9 **He oído decir que está enfermo**
I've heard it said that he's ill

10 **No he oído hablar más de él**
I haven't heard anything more (said) of him

11 **¿Qué quiere decir eso?**
What does that mean?

12 **haber terminado** — to have finished
haberse vestido — to have got dressed

13 **Después de haber comprado el regalo, volvió a casa**
After buying/having bought the present, he went back home
Después de haber madrugado tanto, el taxi se retrasó
After she got up so early, the taxi arrived late

14 **perdonar a alguien por haber hecho**
to forgive somebody for doing/having done
dar las gracias a alguien por haber hecho
to thank somebody for doing/having done
pedir perdón por haber hecho
to be sorry for doing/having done

❒ The Gerund

Formation

- 1st conjugation
  Replace the **-ar** of the infinitive by **-ando** → [1]
- 2nd conjugation
  Replace the **-er** of the infinitive by **-iendo** → [2]
- 3rd conjugation
  Replace the **-ir** of the infinitive by **-iendo** → [3]
- For irregular gerunds, see irregular verbs, p 80 ff.

Uses

- After the verb **estar**, to form the continuous tenses → [4]
- After the verbs **seguir** and **continuar** *to continue,* and **ir** when meaning *to happen gradually* → [5]
- In time constructions, after **llevar** → [6]
- When the action in the main clause needs to be complemented by another action → [7]
- The position of object pronouns is the same as for the infinitive (see p 46).
- The gerund is invariable and strictly verbal in sense.

❒ The Present Participle

- It is formed by replacing the **-ar** of the infinitive of 1st conjugation verbs by **-ante**, and the **-er** and **-ir** of the 2nd and 3rd conjugations by **-iente** → [8]
- A very limited number of verbs have a present participle, which is either used as an adjective or a noun → [9]/[10]

Examples

1	**cantar → cantando** to sing singing	
2	**temer → temiendo** to fear fearing	
3	**partir → partiendo** to leave leaving	
4	**Estoy escribiendo una carta** I am writing a letter **Estaban esperándonos** They were waiting for us	
5	**Sigue viniendo todos los días** He/she is still coming every day **Continuarán subiendo los precios** Prices will continue to go up **El ejército iba avanzando poco a poco** The army was gradually advancing	
6	**Lleva dos años estudiando inglés** He/she has been studying English for two years	
7	**Pasamos el día tomando el sol en la playa** We spent the day sunbathing on the beach **Iba cojeando** He/she/I was limping **Salieron corriendo** They ran out	
8	**cantar → cantante** to sing singing/singer **pender → pendiente** to hang hanging **seguir → siguiente** to follow following	
9	**agua corriente** running water	
10	**un estudiante** a student	

❒ Use of Tenses

The Present

- Unlike English, Spanish often uses the same verb form for the simple present (e.g. *I smoke, he reads, we live*) and the continuous present (e.g. *I am smoking, he is reading, we are living*) → [1]
- Normally, however, the continuous present is used to translate the English:

  to be doing **estar haciendo** → [2]
- Spanish uses the present tense where English uses the perfect in the following cases:

  — with certain prepositions of time – notably **desde** *for/since* – when an action begun in the past is continued in the present → [3]

  ⚠ NOTE: The perfect can be used as in English when the verb is negative → [4]

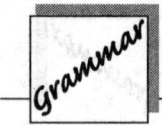

  — in the construction **acabar de hacer** *to have just done* → [5]
- Like English, Spanish often uses the present where a future action is implied → [6]

The Future

The future is generally used as in English → 7, but note the following:

- Immediate future time is often expressed by means of the present tense of **ir** + **a** + infinitive → [8]
- When *'will'* or *'shall'* mean *'wish to', 'are willing to'*, **querer** is used → [9]

The Future Perfect

- Used as in English *shall/will have done* → [10]
- It can also express conjecture, usually about things in the recent past → [11]

Examples

1 **Fumo** I smoke OR: I am smoking
Lee He reads OR: He is reading
Vivimos We live OR: We are living

2 **Está fumando**
He is smoking

3 **Linda estudia español desde hace seis meses**
Linda's been learning Spanish for six months (*and still is*)
Estoy de pie desde las siete
I've been up since seven
¿Hace mucho que esperan?
Have you been waiting long?
Ya hace dos semanas que estamos aquí
That's two weeks we've been here (now)

4 **No se han visto desde hace meses**
They haven't seen each other for months

5 **Isabel acaba de salir**
Isabel has just left

6 **Mañana voy a Madrid**
I am going to Madrid tomorrow

7 **Lo haré mañana**
I'll do it tomorrow

8 **Te vas a caer si no tienes cuidado**
You'll fall if you're not careful
Va a perder el tren
He's going to miss the train
Va a llevar una media hora
It'll take about half an hour

9 **¿Me quieres esperar un momento, por favor?**
Will you wait for me a second, please?

10 **Lo habré acabado para mañana**
I will have finished it for tomorrow

11 **Ya habrán llegado a casa**
They must have arrived home by now

❒ Use of Tenses (Continued)

The Imperfect

- The imperfect describes:
  - — an action or state in the past without definite limits in time → [1]
  - — habitual action(s) in the past (often expressed in English by means of *would* or *used to*) → [2]

- Spanish uses the imperfect tense where English uses the pluperfect in the following cases:
  - — with certain prepositions of time – notably **desde** *for/since* – when an action begun in the remoter past was continued in the more recent past → [3]

  ⚠ NOTE: The pluperfect is used as in English when the verb is negative or the action has been completed → [4]

  - — in the construction **acabar de hacer** *to have just done* → [5]

- Both the continuous and simple forms in English can be translated by the Spanish simple imperfect, but the continuous imperfect is used when the emphasis is on the fact that an action was going on at a precise moment in the past → [6]

The Perfect

- The perfect is generally used as in English → [7]

The Preterite

- The preterite generally corresponds to the English simple past in both written and spoken Spanish → [8]

  However, while English can use the simple past to describe habitual actions or settings, Spanish uses the imperfect (see above) → [9]

The Past Anterior

- This tense is only ever used in written, literary Spanish, to replace the pluperfect in time clauses where the verb in the main clause is in the preterite → [10]

Examples

1 **Todos mirábamos en silencio**
We were all watching in silence
Nuestras habitaciones daban a la playa
Our rooms overlooked the beach

2 **En su juventud se levantaba de madrugada**
In his youth he got up at dawn
Hablábamos sin parar durante horas
We would talk non-stop for hours on end
Mi hermano siempre me tomaba el pelo
My brother always used to tease me

3 **Hacía dos años que vivíamos en Irlanda**
We had been living in Ireland for two years
Estaba enfermo desde 1990
He had been ill since 1990
Hacía mucho tiempo que salían juntos
They had been going out together for a long time

4 **Hacía un año que no le había visto**
I hadn't seen him for a year
Hacía una hora que había llegado
She had arrived an hour before

5 **Acababa de encontrármelos**
I had just met them

6 **Cuando llegué, todos estaban fumando**
When I arrived, they were all smoking

7 **Todavía no han salido**
They haven't come out yet

8 **Me desperté y salté de la cama**
I woke up and jumped out of bed

9 **Siempre iban en coche al trabajo**
They always travelled to work by car

10 **Apenas hubo acabado, se oyeron unos golpes en la puerta**
She had scarcely finished when there was a knock at the door

❒ The Subjunctive: when to use it

(For how to form the subjunctive see pp 6 ff.)

- After verbs of:

  — 'wishing'

  querer que / **desear que** } to wish that, want → [1]

  — 'emotion' (e.g. regret, surprise, shame, pleasure, etc)

  sentir que to be sorry that → [2]
  sorprender que to be surprised that → [3]
  alegrarse de que to be pleased that → [4]

  — 'asking' and 'advising'

  pedir que to ask that → [5]
  aconsejar que to advise that → [6]

In all the above constructions, when the subject of the verbs in the main and subordinate clause is the same, the infinitive is used, and the conjunction **que** omitted → [7]

  — 'ordering', 'forbidding', 'allowing'

  mandar que* / **ordenar que** } to order that → [8]

  permitir que* / **dejar que*** } to allow that → [9]

  prohibir que* to forbid that → [10]
  impedir que* to prevent that → [11]

* With these verbs either the subjunctive or the infinitive is used when the object of the main verb is the subject of the subordinate verb → [12]

- Always after verbs expressing doubt or uncertainty, and verbs of opinion used negatively

  dudar que to doubt that → [13]
  no creer que / **no pensar que** } not to think that → [14]

59 Examples

1 **Queremos que esté contenta**
We want her to be happy (literally: We want that she is happy)
¿Desea Vd que lo haga yo?
Do you want me to do it?

2 **Sentí mucho que no vinieran**
I was very sorry that they didn't come

3 **Nos sorprendió que no les vieran Vds**
We were surprised you didn't see them

4 **Me alegro de que te gusten**
I'm pleased that you like them

5 **Solo les pedimos que tengan cuidado**
We're only asking you to take care

6 **Le aconsejé que no llegara tarde**
I advised him not to be late

7 **Quiero que lo termines pronto**
I want you to finish it soon
⚠ BUT: **Quiero terminarlo pronto**
I want to finish it soon

8 **Ha mandado que vuelvan**
He has ordered them to come back
Ordenó que fueran castigados
He ordered them to be punished

9 **No permitas que te tomen el pelo**
Don't let them pull your leg
No me dejó que la llevara a casa
She didn't allow me to take her home

10 **Te prohíbo que digas eso**
I forbid you to say that

11 **No les impido que vengan**
I am not preventing them from coming

12 **Les ordenó que salieran** OR: **Les ordenó salir**
She ordered them to go out

13 **Dudo que lo sepan hacer**
I doubt they can do it

14 **No creo que sean tan listos**
I don't think they are as clever as that

❒ The Subjunctive: when to use it (Continued)

◆ In impersonal constructions which express necessity, possibility, etc:

hace falta que **es necesario que**	*it is necessary that* → 1
es posible que	*it is possible that* → 2
más vale que	*it is better that* → 3
es una lástima que	*it is a pity that* → 4

⚠ NOTE: In impersonal constructions which state a fact or express certainty the indicative is used when the impersonal verb is affirmative. When it is negative, the subjunctive is used → 5

◆ After certain conjunctions

para que **a fin de que***	*so that* → 6
como si	*as if* → 7
sin que*	*without* → 8
a condición de que* **con tal (de) que*** **siempre que**	*provided that, on condition that* → 9
a menos que **a no ser que**	*unless* → 10
antes (de) que*	*before* → 11
no sea que	*lest/in case* → 12
mientras (que) **siempre que**	*as long as* → 13
(el) que	*the fact that* → 14

* When the subject of both verbs is the same, the infinitive is used, and the final **que** is omitted → 8

1 **¿Hace falta que vaya Jaime?**
Does James have to go?

2 **Es posible que tengan razón**
It's possible that they are right

3 **Más vale que se quede Vd en su casa**
It's better that you stay at home

4 **Es una lástima que haya perdido su perrito**
It's a shame/pity that she has lost her puppy

5 **Es verdad que va a venir**
It's true that he's coming

⚠ BUT: **No es verdad que vayan a hacerlo**
It's not true that they are going to do it

6 **Átalas bien para que no se caigan**
Tie them up tightly so that they won't fall

7 **Hablaba como si no creyera en sus propias palabras**
He talked as if he didn't believe in his own words

8 **Salimos sin que nos vieran**
We left without them seeing us

⚠ BUT: **Me fui sin esperarla**
I went without waiting for her

9 **Lo haré con tal de que me cuentes todo lo que pasó**
I'll do it provided you tell me all that happened

10 **Saldremos de paseo a menos que esté lloviendo**
We'll go for a walk unless it's raining

11 **Avísale antes de que sea demasiado tarde**
Warn him before it's too late

12 **Habla en voz baja, no sea que alguien nos oiga**
Speak softly in case anyone hears us

13 **Eso no pasará mientras yo sea el jefe aquí**
That won't happen as long as I am the boss here

14 **El que no me escribiera no me importaba demasiado**
The fact that he didn't write didn't matter to me too much

❒ The Subjunctive: when to use it (Continued)

- After the conjunctions

  de modo que
  de forma que
  de manera que
  } *so that* (indicating a purpose) → [1]

  ⚠ NOTE: When these conjunctions introduce a result and not a purpose the subjunctive is not used → [2]

- In relative clauses with an antecedent which is:

  — negative → [3]

  — indefinite → [4]

  — non-specific → [5]

- In main clauses, to express a wish or exhortation. The verb may be preceded by expressions like **ojalá** or **que** → [6]

- In the **si** clause of conditions where the English sentence contains a conditional tense → [7]

- In set expressions → [8]

- In the following constructions which translate *however*:

  — **por** + adjective + subjunctive → [9]

  — **por** + adverb + subjunctive → [10]

  — **por** + **mucho** + subjunctive → [11]

Examples

[1] **Vuélvanse de manera que les vea bien**
Turn round so that I can see you properly

[2] **No quieren hacerlo, de manera que tendré que hacerlo yo**
They won't do it, so I'll have to do it myself

[3] **No he encontrado a nadie que la conociera**
I haven't met anyone who knows her

No dijo nada que no supiéramos ya
He/she didn't say anything we didn't already know

[4] **Necesito alguien que sepa conducir**
I need someone who can drive

Busco algo que me distraiga
I'm looking for something to take my mind off it

[5] **Busca una casa que tenga calefacción central**
He/she's looking for a house which has central heating
(*subjunctive used since such a house may or may not exist*)

El que lo haya visto tiene que decírmelo
Anyone who has seen it must tell me
(*subjunctive used since it is not known who has seen it*)

[6] **¡Ojalá haga buen tiempo!**
Let's hope the weather will be good!

¡Que te diviertas!
Have a good time!

[7] **Si fuéramos en coche llegaríamos a tiempo**
If we went by car we'd be there in time

[8] **Diga lo que diga ...** Whatever he may say ... **Sea lo que sea ...** Be that as it may ...

Pase lo que pase ... Come what may ... **Sea como sea ...** One way or another ...

[9] **Por cansado que esté, seguirá trabajando**
No matter how/however tired he may be, he'll go on working

[10] **Por lejos que viva, iremos a buscarle**
No matter how/however far away he lives, we'll go and look for him

[11] **Por mucho que lo intente, nunca lo conseguirá**
No matter how/however hard he tries, he'll never succeed

❒ The Subjunctive: when to use it (Continued)

Clauses taking either a subjunctive or an indicative

In certain constructions, a subjunctive is needed when the action refers to future events or hypothetical situations, whereas an indicative is used when stating a fact or experience → [1]

The commonest of these are:

- The conjunctions

cuando	*when* → [1]
en cuanto / **tan pronto como**	*as soon as* → [2]
después (de) que*	*after* → [3]
hasta que	*until* → [4]
mientras	*while* → [5]
siempre que	*whenever* → [6]
aunque	*even though* → [7]

All conjunctions and pronouns ending in **-quiera** (*-ever*) → [8]

* ⚠ NOTE: If the subject of both verbs is the same, the subjunctive introduced by **después (de) que** may be replaced by **después de** + infinitive → [9]

Sequence of tenses in Subordinate Clauses

- If the verb in the main clause is in the present, future or imperative, the verb in the dependent clause will be in the present or perfect subjunctive → [10]

- If the verb in the main clause is in the conditional or any past tense, the verb in the dependent clause will be in the imperfect or pluperfect subjunctive → [11]

Examples

1 **Le aconsejé que oyera música cuando estuviera nervioso**
I advised him to listen to music when he felt nervous
Me gusta nadar cuando hace calor
I like to swim when it is warm

2 **Te devolveré el libro tan pronto como lo haya leído**
I'll give you back the book as soon as I have read it

3 **Te lo diré después de que te hayas sentado**
I'll tell you after you've sat down

4 **Quédate aquí hasta que volvamos**
Stay here until we come back

5 **No hablen en voz alta mientras estén ellos aquí**
Don't speak loudly while they are here

6 **Vuelvan por aquí siempre que quieran**
Come back whenever you wish to

7 **No le creeré aunque diga la verdad**
I won't believe him even if he tells the truth

8 **La encontraré dondequiera que esté**
I will find her wherever she might be

9 **Después de cenar nos fuimos al cine**
After dinner we went to the cinema

10 **Quiero que lo hagas** (*pres + pres subj*)
I want you to do it
Temo que no haya venido (*pres + perf subj*)
I fear he hasn't come (might not have come)
Iremos por aquí para que no nos vean (*future + pres subj*)
We'll go this way so that they won't see us

11 **Me gustaría que llegaras temprano** (*cond + imperf subj*)
I'd like you to arrive early
Les pedí que me esperaran (*preterite + imperf subj*)
I asked them to wait for me
Sentiría mucho que hubiese muerto (*cond + pluperf subj*)
I would be very sorry if he were dead

❒ Verbs governing a, de, con, en, por and para

The following lists (pp 66 to 73) contain common verbal constructions using the prepositions **a, de, con, en, por** and **para**.

Note the following abbreviations:

infin	infinitive
perf infin	perfect infinitive*
algn	alguien
sb	somebody
sth	something

* For formation see p 50

aburrirse de + infin	*to get bored with doing* → [1]
acabar con algo/algn	*to put an end to sth/finish with sb* → [2]
acabar de* + infin	*to have just done* → [3]
acabar por + infin	*to end up doing* → [4]
acercarse a algo/algn	*to approach sth/sb*
acordarse de algo/algn/de + infin	*to remember sth/sb/doing* → [5]
acostumbrarse a algo/algn/a + infin	*to get used to sth/sb/to doing* → [6]
acusar a algn de algo/de + perf infin	*to accuse sb of sth/of doing, having done* → [7]
advertir a algn de algo	*to notify, warn sb about sth* → [8]
aficionarse a algo/a + infin	*to grow fond of sth/of doing* → [9]
alegrarse de algo/de + perf infin	*to be glad about sth/of doing, having done* → [10]
alejarse de algn/algo	*to move away from sb/sth*
amenazar a algn con algo/con + infin	*to threaten sb with sth/to do* → [11]
animar a algn a + infin	*to encourage sb to do*
apresurarse a + infin	*to hurry to do* → [12]

* See also Use of Tenses, pp 54 and 56

Examples

Grammar

1	**Me aburría de no poder salir de casa** I used to get bored with not being able to leave the house
2	**Quiso acabar con su vida** He wanted to put an end to his life
3	**Acababan de llegar cuando ...** They had just arrived when ...
4	**El acusado acabó por confesarlo todo** The accused ended up by confessing everything
5	**Nos acordamos muy bien de aquellas vacaciones** We remember that holiday very well
6	**Me he acostumbrado a levantarme temprano** I've got used to getting up early
7	**Le acusó de haber mentido** She accused him of lying
8	**Advertí a mi amigo del peligro que corría** I warned my friend about the danger he was in
9	**Nos hemos aficionado a la música clásica** We've grown fond of classical music
10	**Me alegro de haberle conocido** I'm glad I met him
11	**Amenazó con denunciarles** He threatened to report them
12	**Se apresuraron a coger sitio** They hurried to find a seat

❒ Verbs governing a, de, con, en, por and para
(Continued)

aprender a + infin	*to learn to do* → 1
aprovecharse de algo/algn	*to take advantage of sth/sb*
aproximarse a algn/algo	*to approach sb/sth*
asistir a algo	*to attend sth, be at sth*
asomarse a/por	*to lean out of* → 2
asombrarse de + infin	*to be surprised at doing* → 3
atreverse a + infin	*to dare to do*
avergonzarse de algo/algn/de + perf infin	*to be ashamed of sth/sb/of doing, having done* → 4
ayudar a algn a + infin	*to help sb to do* → 5
bajarse de (+ place/vehicle)	*to get off/out of* → 6
burlarse de algn	*to make fun of sb*
cansarse de algo/algn/de + infin	*to tire of sth/sb/of doing*
carecer de algo	*to lack sth* → 7
cargar de algo	*to load with sth* → 8
casarse con algn	*to get married to sb* → 9
cesar de + infin	*to stop doing*
chocar con algo	*to crash/bump into sth* → 10
comenzar a + infin	*to begin to do*
comparar con algn/algo	*to compare with sb/sth*
consentir en + infin	*to agree to do*
consistir en + infin	*to consist of doing* → 11
constar de algo	*to consist of sth* → 12
contar con algn/algo	*to rely on sb/sth* → 13
convenir en + infin	*to agree to do* → 14
darse cuenta de algo	*to realize sth*
dejar de + infin	*to stop doing* → 15
depender de algo/algn	*to depend on sth/sb* → 16
despedirse de algn	*to say goodbye to sb*
dirigirse a + place/**a algn**	*to head for/address sb*
disponerse a + infin	*to get ready to do*
empezar a + infin	*to begin to do*
empezar por + infin	*to begin by doing* → 17

Examples

1 **Me gustaría aprender a nadar**
I'd like to learn to swim

2 **No te asomes a la ventana**
Don't lean out of the window

3 **Nos asombramos mucho de verles ahí**
We were very surprised at seeing them there

4 **No me avergüenzo de haberlo hecho**
I'm not ashamed of having done it

5 **Ayúdeme a llevar estas maletas**
Help me to carry these cases

6 **Se bajó del coche**
He got out of the car

7 **La casa carecía de jardín**
The house lacked (did not have) a garden

8 **El carro iba cargado de paja**
The cart was loaded with straw

9 **Se casó con Andrés**
She married Andrew

10 **Enciende la luz, o chocarás con la puerta**
Turn the light on, or you'll bump into the door

11 **Mi plan consistía en vigilarles de cerca**
My plan consisted of keeping a close eye on them

12 **El examen consta de tres partes**
The exam consists of three parts

13 **Cuento contigo para que me ayudes a hacerlo**
I rely on you to help me do it

14 **Convinieron en reunirse al día siguiente**
They agreed to meet the following day

15 **¿Quieres dejar de hablar?**
Will you stop talking?

16 **No depende de mí**
It doesn't depend on me

17 **Empieza por enterarte de lo que se trata**
Begin by finding out what it is about

❒ Verbs governing a, de, con, en, por and para
(Continued)

encontrarse con algn	*to meet sb (by chance)* → 1
enfadarse con algn	*to get annoyed with sb*
enseñar a algn a + infin	*to teach sb to* → 2
enterarse de algo	*to find out about sth* → 3
entrar en (+ place)	*to enter, go into*
esperar a + infin	*to wait until* → 4
estar de acuerdo con algn/algo	*to agree with sb/sth*
fiarse de algn/algo	*to trust sb/sth*
fijarse en algo/algn	*to notice sth/sb* → 5
hablar con algn	*to talk to sb* → 6
hacer caso a algn	*to pay attention to sb*
hartarse de algo/algn/de + infin	*to get fed up with sth/sb/with doing* → 7
interesarse por algo/algn	*to be interested in sth/sb* → 8
invitar a algn a + infin	*to invite sb to do*
jugar a (+ sports, games)	*to play*
luchar por algo/por + infin	*to fight, strive for/to do* → 9
llegar a (+ place)/**a** + infin	*to reach/to manage to do* → 10
llenar de algo	*to fill with sth*
negarse a + infin	*to refuse to do* → 11
obligar a algn a + infin	*to make sb do* → 12
ocuparse de algn/algo	*to take care of sb/attend to sth*
oler a algo	*to smell of sth* → 13
olvidarse de algo/algn/de + infin	*to forget sth/sb/to do* → 14
oponerse a algo/a + infin	*to be opposed to sth/to doing*
parecerse a algn/algo	*to resemble sb/sth*
pensar en algo/algn/en + infin	*to think about sth/sb/about doing* → 15
preguntar por algn	*to ask for/about sb*
preocuparse de *or* **por algo/algn**	*to worry about sth/sb* → 16

Examples

1 **Me encontré con ella al entrar en el banco**
I met her as I was entering the bank

2 **Le estoy enseñando a nadar**
I am teaching him to swim

3 **¿Te has enterado del sitio adonde hay que ir?**
Have you found out where we have to go?

4 **Espera a saber lo que quiere antes de comprar el regalo**
Wait until you know what he wants before buying the present

5 **Me fijé en él cuando subía a su coche**
I noticed him when he was getting into his car

6 **¿Puedo hablar con Vd un momento?**
May I talk to you for a moment?

7 **Me he hartado de escribirle**
I've got fed up with writing to him

8 **Me interesaba mucho por la arqueología**
I was very interested in archaeology

9 **Hay que luchar por mantener la paz**
One must strive to preserve peace

10 **Lo intenté sin llegar a conseguirlo**
I tried without managing to do it

11 **Se negó a hacerlo**
He refused to do it

12 **Le obligó a sentarse**
He made him sit down

13 **Este perfume huele a jazmín**
This perfume smells of jasmine

14 **Siempre me olvido de cerrar la puerta**
I always forget to shut the door

15 **No quiero pensar en eso**
I don't want to think about that

16 **Se preocupa mucho de/por su apariencia**
He worries a lot about his appearance

❒ Verbs governing a, de, con, en, por and para
(Continued)

preparase a + infin	*to prepare to do*
probar a + infin	*to try to do*
quedar en + infin	*to agree to do* → 1
quedar por + infin	*to remain to be done* → 2
quejarse de algo	*to complain of sth*
referirse a algo	*to refer to sth*
reírse de algo/algn	*to laugh at sth/sb*
rodear de	*to surround with* → 3
romper a + infin	*to (suddenly) start to do* → 4
salir de (+ place)	*to leave*
sentarse a (+ table etc)	*to sit down at*
subir(se) a (+ vehicle/place)	*to get on, into/to climb* → 5
servir de algo a algn	*to be useful to/serve sb as sth* → 6
servir para algo/para + infin	*to be good as sth/for doing* → 7
servirse de algo	*to use sth* → 8
soñar con algn/algo/con + infin	*to dream about/of sb/sth/of doing*
sorprenderse de algo	*to be surprised at sth*
tardar en + infin	*to take time to do* → 9
tener ganas de algo/de + infin	*to want sth/to do* → 10
tener miedo de algo	*to be afraid of sth* → 11
tener miedo a algn	*to be afraid of sb* → 12
terminar por + infin	*to end by doing*
tirar de algo/algn	*to pull sth/sb*
trabajar de (+ occupation)	*to work as* → 13
trabajar en (+ place of work)	*to work at/in* → 14
traducir a (+ language)	*to translate into*
tratar de + infin	*to try to do* → 15
tratarse de algo/algn/de + infin	*to be a question of sth/about sb/about doing* → 16
vacilar en + infin	*to hesitate to do* → 17
volver a + infin	*to do again* → 18

Examples

1 **Habíamos quedado en encontrarnos a las 8**
We had agreed to meet at 8

2 **Queda por averiguar dónde se ocultan**
It remains to be discovered where they are hiding

3 **Habían rodeado el jardín de un seto de cipreses**
They had surrounded the garden with a hedge of cypress trees

4 **Al apagarse la luz, el niño rompió a llorar**
When the lights went out, the little boy suddenly started to cry

5 **¡De prisa, sube al coche!**
Get into the car, quick!

6 **Esto me servirá de bastón**
This will serve me as a walking stick

7 **No sirvo para (ser) jardinero**
I'm no good as a gardener

8 **Se sirvió de un destornillador para abrirlo**
She used a screwdriver to open it

9 **Tardaron mucho en salir**
They took a long time to come out

10 **Tengo ganas de volver a España**
I want to go back to Spain

11 **Mi hija tiene miedo de la oscuridad**
My daughter is afraid of the dark

12 **Nunca tuvieron miedo a su padre**
They were never afraid of their father

13 **Pedro trabaja de camarero en Londres**
Peter works as a waiter in London

14 **Trabajaba en una oficina**
I used to work in an office

15 **No trates de engañarme**
Don't try to fool me

16 **Se trata de nuestro nuevo vecino**
It's about our new neighbour

17 **Nunca vacilaban en pedir dinero**
They never hesitated to borrow money

18 **No vuelvas a hacerlo nunca más**
Don't ever do it again

❐ Ser and Estar

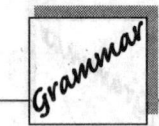

Spanish has two verbs – **ser** and **estar** – for *to be.*

They are not interchangeable and each one is used in defined contexts.

ser is used:

- With an adjective, to express a permanent or inherent quality → [1]
- To express occupation or nationality → [2]
- To express possession → [3]
- To express origin or the material from which something is made → [4]
- With a noun, pronoun or infinitive following the verb → [5]
- To express the time and date → [6]
- To form the passive, with the past participle (see p 32).

⚠ NOTE: This use emphasizes the action of the verb. If, however, the resultant state or condition needs to be emphasized, **estar** is used. The past participle then functions as an adjective (see p 204) and has to agree in gender and in number with the noun → [7]

estar is used:

- Always, to indicate place or location → [8]
- With an adjective or adjectival phrase, to express a quality or state seen by the speaker as subject to change or different from expected → [9]
- When speaking of a person's state of health → [10]
- To form the continuous tenses, used with the gerund (see p 52) → [11]
- With **de** + noun, to indicate a temporary occupation → [12]

Examples

[1] **Mi hermano es alto**
My brother is tall
María es inteligente
Mary is intelligent

[2] **Javier es aviador**
Javier is an airman
Sus padres son italianos
His parents are Italian

[3] **La casa es de Miguel**
The house belongs to Michael

[4] **Mi hermana es de Granada**
My sister is from Granada
Las paredes son de ladrillo
The walls are made of brick

[5] **Andrés es un niño travieso**
Andrew is a naughty boy
Soy yo, Enrique
It's me, Henry
Todo es proponérselo
It's all a question of putting your mind to it

[6] **Son las tres y media**
It's half past three
Mañana es sábado
Tomorrow is Saturday

[7] **Las puertas eran cerradas sigilosamente**
The doors were being silently closed
Las puertas estaban cerradas
The doors were closed (*resultant action*)

[8] **La comida está en la mesa**
The meal is on the table

[9] **Su amigo está enfermo**
Her friend is ill
Hoy estoy de mal humor
I'm in a bad mood today
El lavabo está ocupado
The toilet is engaged
Las tiendas están cerradas
The shops are closed

[10] **¿Cómo están Vds?**
How are you?
Estamos todos bien
We are all well

[11] **Estamos aprendiendo mucho**
We are learning a great deal

[12] **Mi primo está de médico en un pueblo**
My cousin works as a doctor in a village

❐ Ser and Estar (Continued)

With certain adjectives, both **ser** and **estar** can be used, although they are not interchangeable when used in this way:

— **ser** will express a permanent or inherent quality → [1]

— **estar** will express a temporary state or quality → [2]

Both **ser** and **estar** may also be used in set expressions.

The commonest of these are:

- With **ser**

Sea como sea	*Be that as it may*
Es igual/Es lo mismo	*It's all the same*
llegar a ser	*to become*
¿Cómo fue eso?	*How did that happen?*
¿Qué ha sido de él?	*What has become of him?*
ser para (with the idea of purpose)	*to be for* → [3]

- With **estar**

estar de pie/de rodillas	*to be standing/kneeling*
estar de viaje	*to be travelling*
estar de vacaciones	*to be on holiday*
estar de vuelta	*to be back*
estar de moda	*to be in fashion*
Está bien	*It's all right*
estar para	*to be about to do sth/to be in a mood for* → [4]
estar por	*to be inclined to/to be (all) for* → [5]
estar a punto de	*to be just about to do sth* → [6]

Examples

1 **Su hermana es muy joven/vieja**
His sister is very young/old
Son muy ricos/pobres
They are very rich/poor
Su amigo era un enfermo
His friend was an invalid
Es un borracho
He is a drunkard
Mi hijo es bueno/malo
My son is good/naughty
Viajar es cansado
Travelling is tiring

2 **Está muy joven/vieja con ese vestido**
She looks very young/old in that dress
Ahora están muy ricos/pobres
They have become very rich/poor lately
Estaba enfermo
He was ill
Está borracho
He is drunk
Está bueno/malo
He is well/ill
Hoy estoy cansada
I am tired today

3 **Este paquete es para Vd**
This parcel is for you
Esta caja es para guardar semillas
This box is for keeping seeds in

4 **Están para llegar**
They're about to arrive

5 **Estoy por irme a vivir a España**
I'm inclined to go and live in Spain

6 **Las rosas están a punto de salir**
The roses are about to come out

❐ Verbal Idioms

Special Intransitive Verbs

With the following verbs the Spanish construction is the opposite of the English. The subject in English becomes the indirect object of the Spanish verb, while the object in English becomes the subject of the Spanish verb.

Compare the following:

I like that house (subject: *I*, object: *that house*)
Esa casa me gusta (subject: **esa casa**, indirect object: **me**)

The commonest of these verbs are:

gustar	*to like* → [1]
gustar más	*to prefer* → [2]
encantar	(colloquial) *to love* → [3]
faltar	*to need/to be short of/to have missing* → [4]
quedar	*to be/have left* → [5]
doler	*to have a pain in/to hurt, ache* → [6]
interesar	*to be interested in* → [7]
importar	*to mind* → [8]

Examples

1 **Me gusta este vestido**
I like this dress (This dress pleases me)

2 **Me gustan más éstas**
I prefer these

3 **Nos encanta hacer deporte**
We love sport

4 **Me faltaban 100 pesetas**
I was short of 100 pesetas
Sólo le falta el toque final
It just needs the finishing touch
Le faltaban tres dientes
He/she had three teeth missing

5 **Sólo nos quedan dos kilómetros**
We only have two kilometres (left) to go

6 **Me duele la cabeza**
I have a headache

7 **Nos interesa mucho la política**
We are very interested in politics

8 **No me importa la lluvia**
I don't mind the rain

❒ Irregular Verbs

The verbs listed opposite and conjugated on pp 82 to 161 provide the main patterns for irregular verbs. The verbs are grouped opposite according to their infinitive ending and are shown in the following tables in alphabetical order.

In the tables, the most important irregular verbs are given in their most common simple tenses, together with the imperative and the gerund.

The past participle is also shown for each verb, to enable you to form all the compound tenses, as on pp 18 to 23.

The pronouns **ella** and **Vd** take the same verb endings as **él**, while **ellas** and **Vds** take the same endings as **ellos**.

- All the verbs included in the tables differ from the three conjugations set out on pp 8 to 13. Many – e.g. **contar** – serve as models for groups of verbs, while others – e.g. **ir** – are unique. On pp 162 to 186 you will find over 2,800 commonly used verbs listed alphabetically and cross-referred either to the relevant basic conjugation or to the appropriate model in the verb tables.

Imperfect Subjunctive of Irregular Verbs

For verbs with an irregular root form in the preterite tense – e.g. **andar → anduvieron** – the imperfect subjunctive is formed by using the root form of the 3rd person plural of the preterite tense, and adding the imperfect subjunctive endings **-iera/-iese** etc where the verb has an 'i' in the preterite ending – e.g. anduv**ieron** → anduv**iera/iese**. Where the verb has no 'i' in the preterite ending, add **-era/-ese** etc – e.g. produj**eron** → produj**era/ese**.

'-ar':

- actuar
- almorzar
- andar
- aunar
- avergonzar
- averiguar
- contar
- cruzar
- dar
- empezar
- enviar
- errar
- estar
- jugar
- negar
- pagar
- pensar
- rehusar
- rogar
- sacar
- volcar

'-er':

- caber
- caer
- cocer
- coger
- crecer
- entender
- haber
- hacer
- hay
- leer
- llover
- mover
- nacer
- oler
- poder
- poner
- querer
- resolver
- romper
- saber
- satisfacer
- ser
- tener
- torcer
- traer
- valer
- vencer
- ver
- volver

'-ir':

- abolir
- abrir
- adquirir
- bendecir
- conducir
- construir
- cubrir
- decir
- dirigir
- distinguir
- dormir
- elegir
- erguir
- escribir
- freír
- gruñir
- ir
- lucir
- morir
- oír
- pedir
- prohibir
- reír
- reñir
- reunir
- salir
- seguir
- sentir
- venir
- zurcir

abolir *to abolish*

PAST PARTICIPLE

abol**ido**

GERUND

abol**iendo**

IMPERATIVE

abol**id**

PRESENT*	PRESENT SUBJUNCTIVE
nosotros abol**imos** **vosotros** abol**ís** * Present tense only used in persons shown	*not used*

FUTURE	CONDITIONAL
yo abolir**é** **tú** abolir**ás** **él** abolir**á** **nosotros** abolir**emos** **vosotros** abolir**éis** **ellos** abolir**án**	**yo** abolir**ía** **tú** abolir**ías** **él** abolir**ía** **nosotros** abolir**íamos** **vosotros** abolir**íais** **ellos** abolir**ían**

IMPERFECT	PRETERITE
yo abol**ía** **tú** abol**ías** **él** abol**ía** **nosotros** abol**íamos** **vosotros** abol**íais** **ellos** abol**ían**	**yo** abol**í** **tú** abol**iste** **él** abol**ió** **nosotros** abol**imos** **vosotros** abol**isteis** **ellos** abol**ieron**

abrir *to open*

PAST PARTICIPLE	IMPERATIVE
abierto	abr**e**
	abri**d**

GERUND

abr**iendo**

PRESENT		PRESENT SUBJUNCTIVE	
yo	abr**o**	**yo**	abr**a**
tú	abr**es**	**tú**	abr**as**
él	abr**e**	**él**	abr**a**
nosotros	abr**imos**	**nosotros**	abr**amos**
vosotros	abr**ís**	**vosotros**	abr**áis**
ellos	abr**en**	**ellos**	abr**an**

FUTURE		CONDITIONAL	
yo	abrir**é**	**yo**	abrir**ía**
tú	abrir**ás**	**tú**	abrir**ías**
él	abrir**á**	**él**	abrir**ía**
nosotros	abrir**emos**	**nosotros**	abrir**íamos**
vosotros	abrir**éis**	**vosotros**	abrir**íais**
ellos	abrir**án**	**ellos**	abrir**ían**

IMPERFECT		PRETERITE	
yo	abr**ía**	**yo**	abr**í**
tú	abr**ías**	**tú**	abr**iste**
él	abr**ía**	**él**	abr**ió**
nosotros	abr**íamos**	**nosotros**	abr**imos**
vosotros	abr**íais**	**vosotros**	abr**isteis**
ellos	abr**ían**	**ellos**	abr**ieron**

actuar *to act*

PAST PARTICIPLE

actu**ado**

GERUND

actu**ando**

IMPERATIVE

actúa
actua**d**

PRESENT		PRESENT SUBJUNCTIVE	
yo	**actúo**	**yo**	**actúe**
tú	**actúas**	**tú**	**actúes**
él	**actúa**	**él**	**actúe**
nosotros	actu**amos**	**nosotros**	actu**emos**
vosotros	actu**áis**	**vosotros**	actu**éis**
ellos	**actúan**	**ellos**	**actúen**

FUTURE		CONDITIONAL	
yo	actuar**é**	**yo**	actuar**ía**
tú	actuar**ás**	**tú**	actuar**ías**
él	actuar**á**	**él**	actuar**ía**
nosotros	actuar**emos**	**nosotros**	actuar**íamos**
vosotros	actuar**éis**	**vosotros**	actuar**íais**
ellos	actuar**án**	**ellos**	actuar**ían**

IMPERFECT		PRETERITE	
yo	actu**aba**	**yo**	actu**é**
tú	actu**abas**	**tú**	actu**aste**
él	actu**aba**	**él**	actu**ó**
nosotros	actu**ábamos**	**nosotros**	actu**amos**
vosotros	actu**abais**	**vosotros**	actu**asteis**
ellos	actu**aban**	**ellos**	actu**aron**

adquirir *to acquire*

PAST PARTICIPLE	IMPERATIVE
adquir**ido**	**adquiere**
	adquiri**d**
GERUND	
adquir**iendo**	

PRESENT	PRESENT SUBJUNCTIVE
yo adquiero	**yo adquiera**
tú adquieres	**tú adquieras**
él adquiere	**él adquiera**
nosotros adquir**imos**	**nosotros** adquir**amos**
vosotros adquir**ís**	**vosotros** adquir**áis**
ellos adquieren	**ellos adquieran**

FUTURE	CONDITIONAL
yo adquirir**é**	**yo** adquirir**ía**
tú adquirir**ás**	**tú** adquirir**ías**
él adquirir**á**	**él** adquirir**ía**
nosotros adquirir**emos**	**nosotros** adquirir**íamos**
vosotros adquirir**éis**	**vosotros** adquirir**íais**
ellos adquirir**án**	**ellos** adquirir**ían**

IMPERFECT	PRETERITE
yo adquir**ía**	**yo** adquir**í**
tú adquir**ías**	**tú** adquir**iste**
él adquir**ía**	**él** adquir**ió**
nosotros adquir**íamos**	**nosotros** adquir**imos**
vosotros adquir**íais**	**vosotros** adquir**isteis**
ellos adquir**ían**	**ellos** adquir**ieron**

almorzar *to have lunch*

PAST PARTICIPLE	IMPERATIVE
almorz**ado**	**almuerza**
	almorza**d**
GERUND	
almorz**ando**	

PRESENT	PRESENT SUBJUNCTIVE
yo **almuerzo**	**yo** **almuerce**
tú **almuerzas**	**tú** **almuerces**
él **almuerza**	**él** **almuerce**
nosotros almorz**amos**	**nosotros** **almorcemos**
vosotros almorz**áis**	**vosotros** **almorcéis**
ellos **almuerzan**	**ellos** **almuercen**
FUTURE	CONDITIONAL
yo almorzar**é**	**yo** almorzar**ía**
tú almorzar**ás**	**tú** almorzar**ías**
él almorzar**á**	**él** almorzar**ía**
nosotros almorzar**emos**	**nosotros** almorzar**íamos**
vosotros almorzar**éis**	**vosotros** almorzar**íais**
ellos almorzar**án**	**ellos** almorzar**ían**
IMPERFECT	PRETERITE
yo almorz**aba**	**yo** **almorcé**
tú almorz**abas**	**tú** almorz**aste**
él almorz**aba**	**él** almorz**ó**
nosotros almorz**ábamos**	**nosotros** almorz**amos**
vosotros almorz**abais**	**vosotros** almorz**asteis**
ellos almorz**aban**	**ellos** almorz**aron**

andar *to walk*

PAST PARTICIPLE	IMPERATIVE
and**ado**	and**a**
	and**ad**
GERUND	
and**ando**	

PRESENT		PRESENT SUBJUNCTIVE	
yo	ando	**yo**	ande
tú	and**as**	**tú**	and**es**
él	and**a**	**él**	ande
nosotros	and**amos**	**nosotros**	and**emos**
vosotros	and**áis**	**vosotros**	and**éis**
ellos	and**an**	**ellos**	and**en**

FUTURE		CONDITIONAL	
yo	andar**é**	**yo**	andar**ía**
tú	andar**ás**	**tú**	andar**ías**
él	andar**á**	**él**	andar**ía**
nosotros	andar**emos**	**nosotros**	andar**íamos**
vosotros	andar**éis**	**vosotros**	andar**íais**
ellos	andar**án**	**ellos**	andar**ían**

IMPERFECT		PRETERITE	
yo	and**aba**	**yo**	**anduve**
tú	and**abas**	**tú**	**anduviste**
él	and**aba**	**él**	**anduvo**
nosotros	and**ábamos**	**nosotros**	**anduvimos**
vosotros	and**abais**	**vosotros**	**anduvisteis**
ellos	and**aban**	**ellos**	**anduvieron**

aunar *to join together*

PAST PARTICIPLE

aun**ado**

GERUND

aun**ando**

IMPERATIVE

aúna
auna**d**

PRESENT		PRESENT SUBJUNCTIVE	
yo	**aúno**	**yo**	**aúne**
tú	**aúnas**	**tú**	**aúnes**
él	**aúna**	**él**	**aúne**
nosotros	aun**amos**	**nosotros**	aun**emos**
vosotros	aun**áis**	**vosotros**	aun**éis**
ellos	**aúnan**	**ellos**	**aúnen**

FUTURE		CONDITIONAL	
yo	aunar**é**	**yo**	aunar**ía**
tú	aunar**ás**	**tú**	aunar**ías**
él	aunar**á**	**él**	aunar**ía**
nosotros	aunar**emos**	**nosotros**	aunar**íamos**
vosotros	aunar**éis**	**vosotros**	aunar**íais**
ellos	aunar**án**	**ellos**	aunar**ían**

IMPERFECT		PRETERITE	
yo	aun**aba**	**yo**	aun**é**
tú	aun**abas**	**tú**	aun**aste**
él	aun**aba**	**él**	aun**ó**
nosotros	aun**ábamos**	**nosotros**	aun**amos**
vosotros	aun**abais**	**vosotros**	aun**asteis**
ellos	aun**aban**	**ellos**	aun**aron**

avergonzar *to shame*

PAST PARTICIPLE

avergonz**ado**

GERUND

avergonz**ando**

IMPERATIVE

avergüenza
avergonza**d**

PRESENT		PRESENT SUBJUNCTIVE	
yo	**avergüenzo**	**yo**	**avergüence**
tú	**avergüenzas**	**tú**	**avergüences**
él	**avergüenza**	**él**	**avergüence**
nosotros	avergonz**amos**	**nosotros**	**avergoncemos**
vosotros	avergonz**áis**	**vosotros**	**avergoncéis**
ellos	**avergüenzan**	**ellos**	**avergüencen**

FUTURE		CONDITIONAL	
yo	avergonzar**é**	**yo**	avergonzar**ía**
tú	avergonzar**ás**	**tú**	avergonzar**ías**
él	avergonzar**á**	**él**	avergonzar**ía**
nosotros	avergonzar**emos**	**nosotros**	avergonzar**íamos**
vosotros	avergonzar**éis**	**vosotros**	avergonzar**íais**
ellos	avergonzar**án**	**ellos**	avergonzar**ían**

IMPERFECT		PRETERITE	
yo	avergonz**aba**	**yo**	**avergoncé**
tú	avergonz**abas**	**tú**	avergonz**aste**
él	avergonz**aba**	**él**	avergonz**ó**
nosotros	avergonz**ábamos**	**nosotros**	avergonz**amos**
vosotros	avergonz**abais**	**vosotros**	avergonz**asteis**
ellos	avergonz**aban**	**ellos**	avergonz**aron**

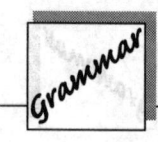

averiguar *to find out*

PAST PARTICIPLE	IMPERATIVE
averigu**ado**	averigu**a**
	averigua**d**
GERUND	
averigu**ando**	

PRESENT	PRESENT SUBJUNCTIVE
yo averiguo	**yo averigüe**
tú averigu**as**	**tú averigües**
él averigu**a**	**él averigüe**
nosotros averigu**amos**	**nosotros averigüemos**
vosotros averigu**áis**	**vosotros averigüéis**
ellos averigu**an**	**ellos averigüen**
FUTURE	**CONDITIONAL**
yo averigua**ré**	**yo** averigua**ría**
tú averigua**rás**	**tú** averigua**rías**
él averigua**rá**	**él** averigua**ría**
nosotros averigua**remos**	**nosotros** averigua**ríamos**
vosotros averigua**réis**	**vosotros** averigua**ríais**
ellos averigua**rán**	**ellos** averigua**rían**
IMPERFECT	**PRETERITE**
yo averigu**aba**	**yo averigüé**
tú averigu**abas**	**tú** averigu**aste**
él averigu**aba**	**él** averigu**ó**
nosotros averigu**ábamos**	**nosotros** averigu**amos**
vosotros averigu**abais**	**vosotros** averigu**asteis**
ellos averigu**aban**	**ellos** averigu**aron**

bendecir *to bless*

PAST PARTICIPLE

bendec**ido**

GERUND

bendiciendo

IMPERATIVE

bendice
bendeci**d**

PRESENT	PRESENT SUBJUNCTIVE
yo **bendigo**	**yo** **bendiga**
tú **bendices**	**tú** **bendigas**
él **bendice**	**él** **bendiga**
nosotros bendec**imos**	**nosotros** **bendigamos**
vosotros bendec**ís**	**vosotros** **bendigáis**
ellos **bendicen**	**ellos** **bendigan**

FUTURE	CONDITIONAL
yo bendecir**é**	**yo** bendecir**ía**
tú bendecir**ás**	**tú** bendecir**ías**
él bendecir**á**	**él** bendecir**ía**
nosotros bendecir**emos**	**nosotros** bendecir**íamos**
vosotros bendecir**éis**	**vosotros** bendecir**íais**
ellos bendecir**án**	**ellos** bendecir**ían**

IMPERFECT	PRETERITE
yo bendec**ía**	**yo** **bendije**
tú bendec**ías**	**tú** **bendijiste**
él bendec**ía**	**él** **bendijo**
nosotros bendec**íamos**	**nosotros** **bendijimos**
vosotros bendec**íais**	**vosotros** **bendijisteis**
ellos bendec**ían**	**ellos** **bendijeron**

caber *to fit*

PAST PARTICIPLE	IMPERATIVE
cab**ido**	cab**e**
	cabe**d**
GERUND	
cab**iendo**	

PRESENT		PRESENT SUBJUNCTIVE	
yo	**quepo**	**yo**	**quepa**
tú	cab**es**	**tú**	**quepas**
él	cab**e**	**él**	**quepa**
nosotros	cab**emos**	**nosotros**	**quepamos**
vosotros	cab**éis**	**vosotros**	**quepáis**
ellos	cab**en**	**ellos**	**quepan**

FUTURE		CONDITIONAL	
yo	**cabré**	**yo**	**cabría**
tú	**cabrás**	**tú**	**cabrías**
él	**cabrá**	**él**	**cabría**
nosotros	**cabremos**	**nosotros**	**cabríamos**
vosotros	**cabréis**	**vosotros**	**cabríais**
ellos	**cabrán**	**ellos**	**cabrían**

IMPERFECT		PRETERITE	
yo	cabí**a**	**yo**	**cupe**
tú	cabí**as**	**tú**	**cupiste**
él	cabí**a**	**él**	**cupo**
nosotros	cabí**amos**	**nosotros**	**cupimos**
vosotros	cabí**ais**	**vosotros**	**cupisteis**
ellos	cabí**an**	**ellos**	**cupieron**

caer *to fall*

PAST PARTICIPLE	IMPERATIVE
caído	**cae**
	caed
GERUND	
cayendo	

PRESENT	PRESENT SUBJUNCTIVE
yo caigo	**yo caiga**
tú caes	**tú caigas**
él cae	**él caiga**
nosotros ca**emos**	**nosotros caigamos**
vosotros ca**éis**	**vosotros caigáis**
ellos ca**en**	**ellos caigan**

FUTURE	CONDITIONAL
yo caer**é**	**yo** caer**ía**
tú caer**ás**	**tú** caer**ías**
él caer**á**	**él** caer**ía**
nosotros caer**emos**	**nosotros** caer**íamos**
vosotros caer**éis**	**vosotros** caer**íais**
ellos caer**án**	**ellos** caer**ían**

IMPERFECT	PRETERITE
yo ca**ía**	**yo caí**
tú ca**ías**	**tú caíste**
él ca**ía**	**él cayó**
nosotros ca**íamos**	**nosotros caímos**
vosotros ca**íais**	**vosotros caísteis**
ellos ca**ían**	**ellos cayeron**

cocer *to boil*

PAST PARTICIPLE

coc**ido**

GERUND

coc**iendo**

IMPERATIVE

cuece
coce**d**

PRESENT	PRESENT SUBJUNCTIVE
yo cuezo	**yo cueza**
tú cueces	**tú cuezas**
él cuece	**él cueza**
nosotros coc**emos**	**nosotros cozamos**
vosotros coc**éis**	**vosotros cozáis**
ellos cuecen	**ellos cuezan**

FUTURE	CONDITIONAL
yo coce**ré**	**yo** coce**ría**
tú coce**rás**	**tú** coce**rías**
él coce**rá**	**él** coce**ría**
nosotros coce**remos**	**nosotros** coce**ríamos**
vosotros coce**réis**	**vosotros** coce**ríais**
ellos coce**rán**	**ellos** coce**rían**

IMPERFECT	PRETERITE
yo coc**ía**	**yo** coc**í**
tú coc**ías**	**tú** coc**iste**
él coc**ía**	**él** coc**ió**
nosotros coc**íamos**	**nosotros** coc**imos**
vosotros coc**íais**	**vosotros** coc**isteis**
ellos coc**ían**	**ellos** coc**ieron**

coger *to catch*

PAST PARTICIPLE

cog**ido**

GERUND

cog**iendo**

IMPERATIVE

cog**e**
cog**ed**

PRESENT	PRESENT SUBJUNCTIVE
yo **cojo**	**yo** **coja**
tú cog**es**	**tú** **cojas**
él cog**e**	**él** **coja**
nosotros cog**emos**	**nosotros** **cojamos**
vosotros cog**éis**	**vosotros** **cojáis**
ellos cog**en**	**ellos** **cojan**

FUTURE	CONDITIONAL
yo coger**é**	**yo** coger**ía**
tú coger**ás**	**tú** coger**ías**
él coger**á**	**él** coger**ía**
nosotros coger**emos**	**nosotros** coger**íamos**
vosotros coger**éis**	**vosotros** coger**íais**
ellos coger**án**	**ellos** coger**ían**

IMPERFECT	PRETERITE
yo cog**ía**	**yo** cog**í**
tú cog**ías**	**tú** cog**iste**
él cog**ía**	**él** cog**ió**
nosotros cog**íamos**	**nosotros** cog**imos**
vosotros cog**íais**	**vosotros** cog**isteis**
ellos cog**ían**	**ellos** cog**ieron**

conducir *to drive, to lead*

PAST PARTICIPLE

conduc**ido**

GERUND

conduc**iendo**

IMPERATIVE

conduc**e**
conduc**id**

PRESENT	
yo	**conduzco**
tú	conduc**es**
él	conduc**e**
nosotros	conduc**imos**
vosotros	conduc**ís**
ellos	conduc**en**

PRESENT SUBJUNCTIVE	
yo	**conduzca**
tú	**conduzcas**
él	**conduzca**
nosotros	**conduzcamos**
vosotros	**conduzcáis**
ellos	**conduzcan**

FUTURE	
yo	conduc**iré**
tú	conduc**irás**
él	conduc**irá**
nosotros	conduc**iremos**
vosotros	conduc**iréis**
ellos	conduc**irán**

CONDITIONAL	
yo	conduc**iría**
tú	conduc**irías**
él	conduc**iría**
nosotros	conduc**iríamos**
vosotros	conduc**iríais**
ellos	conduc**irían**

IMPERFECT	
yo	conduc**ía**
tú	conduc**ías**
él	conduc**ía**
nosotros	conduc**íamos**
vosotros	conduc**íais**
ellos	conduc**ían**

PRETERITE	
yo	**conduje**
tú	**condujiste**
él	**condujo**
nosotros	**condujimos**
vosotros	**condujisteis**
ellos	**condujeron**

construir *to build*

PAST PARTICIPLE	IMPERATIVE
constru**ido**	**construye**
	construi**d**
GERUND	
construyendo	

PRESENT	PRESENT SUBJUNCTIVE
yo **construyo**	**yo** **construya**
tú **construyes**	**tú** **construyas**
él **construye**	**él** **construya**
nosotros constru**imos**	**nosotros** **construyamos**
vosotros constru**ís**	**vosotros** **construyáis**
ellos **construyen**	**ellos** **construyan**

FUTURE	CONDITIONAL
yo construir**é**	**yo** construir**ía**
tú construir**ás**	**tú** construir**ías**
él construir**á**	**él** construir**ía**
nosotros construir**emos**	**nosotros** construir**íamos**
vosotros construir**éis**	**vosotros** construir**íais**
ellos construir**án**	**ellos** construir**ían**

IMPERFECT	PRETERITE
yo constru**ía**	**yo** constru**í**
tú constru**ías**	**tú** constru**iste**
él constru**ía**	**él** **construyó**
nosotros constru**íamos**	**nosotros** constru**imos**
vosotros constru**íais**	**vosotros** constru**isteis**
ellos constru**ían**	**ellos** **construyeron**

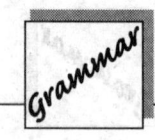

contar *to tell, to count*	
PAST PARTICIPLE	IMPERATIVE
cont**ado**	**cuenta**
	conta**d**
GERUND	
cont**ando**	

PRESENT	PRESENT SUBJUNCTIVE
yo **cuento**	**yo** **cuente**
tú **cuentas**	**tú** **cuentes**
él **cuenta**	**él** **cuente**
nosotros cont**amos**	**nosotros** cont**emos**
vosotros cont**áis**	**vosotros** cont**éis**
ellos **cuentan**	**ellos** **cuenten**
FUTURE	CONDITIONAL
yo contar**é**	**yo** contar**ía**
tú contar**ás**	**tú** contar**ías**
él contar**á**	**él** contar**ía**
nosotros contar**emos**	**nosotros** contar**íamos**
vosotros contar**éis**	**vosotros** contar**íais**
ellos contar**án**	**ellos** contar**ían**
IMPERFECT	PRETERITE
yo cont**aba**	**yo** cont**é**
tú cont**abas**	**tú** cont**aste**
él cont**aba**	**él** cont**ó**
nosotros cont**ábamos**	**nosotros** cont**amos**
vosotros cont**abais**	**vosotros** cont**asteis**
ellos cont**aban**	**ellos** cont**aron**

crecer *to grow*	
PAST PARTICIPLE	IMPERATIVE
crec**ido**	crec**e**
	crece**d**
GERUND	
crec**iendo**	

PRESENT	PRESENT SUBJUNCTIVE
yo **crezco**	**yo** **crezca**
tú crec**es**	**tú** **crezcas**
él crec**e**	**él** **crezca**
nosotros crec**emos**	**nosotros** **crezcamos**
vosotros crec**éis**	**vosotros** **crezcáis**
ellos crec**en**	**ellos** **crezcan**
FUTURE	CONDITIONAL
yo crecer**é**	**yo** crecer**ía**
tú crecer**ás**	**tú** crecer**ías**
él crecer**á**	**él** crecer**ía**
nosotros crecer**emos**	**nosotros** crecer**íamos**
vosotros crecer**éis**	**vosotros** crecer**íais**
ellos crecer**án**	**ellos** crecer**ían**
IMPERFECT	PRETERITE
yo crec**ía**	**yo** crec**í**
tú crec**ías**	**tú** crec**iste**
él crec**ía**	**él** crec**ió**
nosotros crec**íamos**	**nosotros** crec**imos**
vosotros crec**íais**	**vosotros** crec**isteis**
ellos crec**ían**	**ellos** crec**ieron**

cruzar *to cross*

PAST PARTICIPLE

cruz**ado**

GERUND

cruz**ando**

IMPERATIVE

cruz**a**
cruz**ad**

PRESENT	PRESENT SUBJUNCTIVE
yo cruz**o**	**yo** **cruce**
tú cruz**as**	**tú** **cruces**
él cruz**a**	**él** **cruce**
nosotros cruz**amos**	**nosotros** **crucemos**
vosotros cruz**áis**	**vosotros** **crucéis**
ellos cruz**an**	**ellos** **crucen**

FUTURE	CONDITIONAL
yo cruzar**é**	**yo** cruzar**ía**
tú cruzar**ás**	**tú** cruzar**ías**
él cruzar**á**	**él** cruzar**ía**
nosotros cruzar**emos**	**nosotros** cruzar**íamos**
vosotros cruzar**éis**	**vosotros** cruzar**íais**
ellos cruzar**án**	**ellos** cruzar**ían**

IMPERFECT	PRETERITE
yo cruz**aba**	**yo** **crucé**
tú cruz**abas**	**tú** cruz**aste**
él cruz**aba**	**él** cruz**ó**
nosotros cruz**ábamos**	**nosotros** cruz**amos**
vosotros cruz**abais**	**vosotros** cruz**asteis**
ellos cruz**aban**	**ellos** cruz**aron**

cubrir *to cover*

PAST PARTICIPLE	IMPERATIVE
cubierto	cubr**e** cubr**id**
GERUND	
cubr**iendo**	

PRESENT	PRESENT SUBJUNCTIVE
yo cubro	**yo** cubr**a**
tú cubres	**tú** cubr**as**
él cubre	**él** cubr**a**
nosotros cubr**imos**	**nosotros** cubr**amos**
vosotros cubr**ís**	**vosotros** cubr**áis**
ellos cubr**en**	**ellos** cubr**an**
FUTURE	CONDITIONAL
yo cubrir**é**	**yo** cubrir**ía**
tú cubrir**ás**	**tú** cubrir**ías**
él cubrir**á**	**él** cubrir**ía**
nosotros cubrir**emos**	**nosotros** cubrir**íamos**
vosotros cubrir**éis**	**vosotros** cubrir**íais**
ellos cubrir**án**	**ellos** cubrir**ían**
IMPERFECT	PRETERITE
yo cubr**ía**	**yo** cubr**í**
tú cubr**ías**	**tú** cubr**iste**
él cubr**ía**	**él** cubr**ió**
nosotros cubr**íamos**	**nosotros** cubr**imos**
vosotros cubr**íais**	**vosotros** cubr**isteis**
ellos cubr**ían**	**ellos** cubr**ieron**

dar *to give*

PAST PARTICIPLE

d**ado**

GERUND

d**ando**

IMPERATIVE

d**a**
da**d**

PRESENT	PRESENT SUBJUNCTIVE
yo **doy**	**yo** **dé**
tú das	**tú** des
él da	**él** **dé**
nosotros damos	**nosotros** demos
vosotros dais	**vosotros** deis
ellos dan	**ellos** den

FUTURE	CONDITIONAL
yo daré	**yo** daría
tú darás	**tú** darías
él dará	**él** daría
nosotros daremos	**nosotros** daríamos
vosotros daréis	**vosotros** daríais
ellos darán	**ellos** darían

IMPERFECT	PRETERITE
yo daba	**yo** **di**
tú dabas	**tú** **diste**
él daba	**él** **dio**
nosotros dábamos	**nosotros** **dimos**
vosotros dabais	**vosotros** **disteis**
ellos daban	**ellos** **dieron**

decir *to say*

PAST PARTICIPLE

dicho

GERUND

diciendo

IMPERATIVE

di
deci**d**

PRESENT	PRESENT SUBJUNCTIVE
yo **digo** **tú** **dices** **él** **dice** **nosotros** dec**imos** **vosotros** dec**ís** **ellos** **dicen**	**yo** **diga** **tú** **digas** **él** **diga** **nosotros** **digamos** **vosotros** **digáis** **ellos** **digan**
FUTURE	CONDITIONAL
yo **diré** **tú** **dirás** **él** **dirá** **nosotros** **diremos** **vosotros** **diréis** **ellos** **dirán**	**yo** **diría** **tú** **dirías** **él** **diría** **nosotros** **diríamos** **vosotros** **diríais** **ellos** **dirían**
IMPERFECT	PRETERITE
yo dec**ía** **tú** dec**ías** **él** dec**ía** **nosotros** dec**íamos** **vosotros** dec**íais** **ellos** dec**ían**	**yo** **dije** **tú** **dijiste** **él** **dijo** **nosotros** **dijimos** **vosotros** **dijisteis** **ellos** **dijeron**

dirigir *to direct*

PAST PARTICIPLE
dirig**ido**

GERUND
dirig**iendo**

IMPERATIVE
dirig**e**
dirigi**d**

PRESENT	PRESENT SUBJUNCTIVE
yo **dirijo**	**yo** **dirija**
tú dirig**es**	**tú** **dirijas**
él dirig**e**	**él** **dirija**
nosotros dirig**imos**	**nosotros** **dirijamos**
vosotros dirig**ís**	**vosotros** **dirijáis**
ellos dirig**en**	**ellos** **dirijan**

FUTURE	CONDITIONAL
yo dirigir**é**	**yo** dirigir**ía**
tú dirigir**ás**	**tú** dirigir**ías**
él dirigir**á**	**él** dirigir**ía**
nosotros dirigir**emos**	**nosotros** dirigir**íamos**
vosotros dirigir**éis**	**vosotros** dirigir**íais**
ellos dirigir**án**	**ellos** dirigir**ían**

IMPERFECT	PRETERITE
yo dirig**ía**	**yo** dirig**í**
tú dirig**ías**	**tú** dirig**iste**
él dirig**ía**	**él** dirig**ió**
nosotros dirig**íamos**	**nosotros** dirig**imos**
vosotros dirig**íais**	**vosotros** dirig**isteis**
ellos dirig**ían**	**ellos** dirig**ieron**

distinguir *to distinguish*

PAST PARTICIPLE

distingu**ido**

GERUND

distingu**iendo**

IMPERATIVE

disting**ue**
distingu**id**

PRESENT	PRESENT SUBJUNCTIVE
yo distingo	**yo distinga**
tú distingues	**tú distingas**
él distingue	**él distinga**
nosotros distingu**imos**	**nosotros distingamos**
vosotros distingu**ís**	**vosotros distingáis**
ellos disting**uen**	**ellos distingan**

FUTURE	CONDITIONAL
yo distinguir**é**	**yo** distinguir**ía**
tú distinguir**ás**	**tú** distinguir**ías**
él distinguir**á**	**él** distinguir**ía**
nosotros distinguir**emos**	**nosotros** distinguir**íamos**
vosotros distinguir**éis**	**vosotros** distinguir**íais**
ellos distinguir**án**	**ellos** distinguir**ían**

IMPERFECT	PRETERITE
yo distingu**ía**	**yo** distingu**í**
tú distingu**ías**	**tú** distingu**iste**
él distingu**ía**	**él** distingu**ió**
nosotros distingu**íamos**	**nosotros** distingu**imos**
vosotros distingu**íais**	**vosotros** distingu**isteis**
ellos distingu**ían**	**ellos** distingu**ieron**

dormir *to sleep*

PAST PARTICIPLE

dorm**ido**

GERUND

durmiendo

IMPERATIVE

duerme
dorm**id**

PRESENT		PRESENT SUBJUNCTIVE	
yo	**duermo**	**yo**	**duerma**
tú	**duermes**	**tú**	**duermas**
él	**duerme**	**él**	**duerma**
nosotros	dorm**imos**	**nosotros**	**durmamos**
vosotros	dorm**ís**	**vosotros**	**durmáis**
ellos	**duermen**	**ellos**	**duerman**

FUTURE		CONDITIONAL	
yo	dormir**é**	**yo**	dormir**ía**
tú	dormir**ás**	**tú**	dormir**ías**
él	dormir**á**	**él**	dormir**ía**
nosotros	dormir**emos**	**nosotros**	dormir**íamos**
vosotros	dormir**éis**	**vosotros**	dormir**íais**
ellos	dormir**án**	**ellos**	dormir**ían**

IMPERFECT		PRETERITE	
yo	dorm**ía**	**yo**	dorm**í**
tú	dorm**ías**	**tú**	dorm**iste**
él	dorm**ía**	**él**	**durmió**
nosotros	dorm**íamos**	**nosotros**	dorm**imos**
vosotros	dorm**íais**	**vosotros**	dorm**isteis**
ellos	dorm**ían**	**ellos**	**durmieron**

elegir *to choose*

PAST PARTICIPLE	IMPERATIVE
elegi**do**	**elige**
	elegi**d**

GERUND

eligiendo

PRESENT	PRESENT SUBJUNCTIVE
yo **elijo**	**yo** **elija**
tú **eliges**	**tú** **elijas**
él **elige**	**él** **elija**
nosotros elegi**mos**	**nosotros** **elijamos**
vosotros elegí**s**	**vosotros** **elijáis**
ellos **eligen**	**ellos** **elijan**

FUTURE	CONDITIONAL
yo elegir**é**	**yo** elegir**ía**
tú elegir**ás**	**tú** elegir**ías**
él elegir**á**	**él** elegir**ía**
nosotros elegir**emos**	**nosotros** elegir**íamos**
vosotros elegir**éis**	**vosotros** elegir**íais**
ellos elegir**án**	**ellos** elegir**ían**

IMPERFECT	PRETERITE
yo eleg**ía**	**yo** eleg**í**
tú eleg**ías**	**tú** eleg**iste**
él eleg**ía**	**él** **eligió**
nosotros eleg**íamos**	**nosotros** eleg**imos**
vosotros eleg**íais**	**vosotros** eleg**isteis**
ellos eleg**ían**	**ellos** **eligieron**

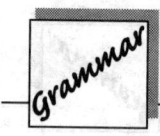

empezar *to begin*

PAST PARTICIPLE

empez**ado**

GERUND

empez**ando**

IMPERATIVE

empieza
empeza**d**

PRESENT		PRESENT SUBJUNCTIVE	
yo	**empiezo**	**yo**	**empiece**
tú	**empiezas**	**tú**	**empieces**
él	**empieza**	**él**	**empiece**
nosotros	empez**amos**	**nosotros**	**empecemos**
vosotros	empez**áis**	**vosotros**	**empecéis**
ellos	**empiezan**	**ellos**	**empiecen**

FUTURE		CONDITIONAL	
yo	empezar**é**	**yo**	empezar**ía**
tú	empezar**ás**	**tú**	empezar**ías**
él	empezar**á**	**él**	empezar**ía**
nosotros	empezar**emos**	**nosotros**	empezar**íamos**
vosotros	empezar**éis**	**vosotros**	empezar**íais**
ellos	empezar**án**	**ellos**	empezar**ían**

IMPERFECT		PRETERITE	
yo	empez**aba**	**yo**	**empecé**
tú	empez**abas**	**tú**	empez**aste**
él	empez**aba**	**él**	empez**ó**
nosotros	empez**ábamos**	**nosotros**	empez**amos**
vosotros	empez**abais**	**vosotros**	empez**asteis**
ellos	empez**aban**	**ellos**	empez**aron**

entender *to understand*

PAST PARTICIPLE	IMPERATIVE
entend**ido**	**entiende**
	entende**d**
GERUND	
entend**iendo**	

PRESENT	PRESENT SUBJUNCTIVE
yo entiendo	**yo entienda**
tú entiendes	**tú entiendas**
él entiende	**él entienda**
nosotros entend**emos**	**nosotros** entend**amos**
vosotros entend**éis**	**vosotros** entend**áis**
ellos entienden	**ellos entiendan**

FUTURE	CONDITIONAL
yo entender**é**	**yo** entender**ía**
tú entender**ás**	**tú** entender**ías**
él entender**á**	**él** entender**ía**
nosotros entender**emos**	**nosotros** entender**íamos**
vosotros entender**éis**	**vosotros** entender**íais**
ellos entender**án**	**ellos** entender**ían**

IMPERFECT	PRETERITE
yo entend**ía**	**yo** entend**í**
tú entend**ías**	**tú** entend**iste**
él entend**ía**	**él** entend**ió**
nosotros entend**íamos**	**nosotros** entend**imos**
vosotros entend**íais**	**vosotros** entend**isteis**
ellos entend**ían**	**ellos** entend**ieron**

enviar *to send*

PAST PARTICIPLE

envi**ado**

GERUND

envi**ando**

IMPERATIVE

envía
envia**d**

PRESENT		PRESENT SUBJUNCTIVE	
yo	**envío**	**yo**	**envíe**
tú	**envías**	**tú**	**envíes**
él	**envía**	**él**	**envíe**
nosotros	envi**amos**	**nosotros**	envi**emos**
vosotros	envi**áis**	**vosotros**	envi**éis**
ellos	**envían**	**ellos**	**envíen**

FUTURE		CONDITIONAL	
yo	enviar**é**	**yo**	enviar**ía**
tú	enviar**ás**	**tú**	enviar**ías**
él	enviar**á**	**él**	enviar**ía**
nosotros	enviar**emos**	**nosotros**	enviar**íamos**
vosotros	enviar**éis**	**vosotros**	enviar**íais**
ellos	enviar**án**	**ellos**	enviar**ían**

IMPERFECT		PRETERITE	
yo	envi**aba**	**yo**	envi**é**
tú	envi**abas**	**tú**	envi**aste**
él	envi**aba**	**él**	envi**ó**
nosotros	envi**ábamos**	**nosotros**	envi**amos**
vosotros	envi**abais**	**vosotros**	envi**asteis**
ellos	envi**aban**	**ellos**	envi**aron**

erguir *to erect*

PAST PARTICIPLE

ergu**ido**

GERUND

irguiendo

IMPERATIVE

yergue
ergui**d**

PRESENT	PRESENT SUBJUNCTIVE
yo yergo	**yo yerga**
tú yergues	**tú yergas**
él yergue	**él yerga**
nosotros ergu**imos**	**nosotros irgamos**
vosotros ergu**ís**	**vosotros irgáis**
ellos yerguen	**ellos yergan**

FUTURE	CONDITIONAL
yo erguir**é**	**yo** erguir**ía**
tú erguir**ás**	**tú** erguir**ías**
él erguir**á**	**él** erguir**ía**
nosotros erguir**emos**	**nosotros** erguir**íamos**
vosotros erguir**éis**	**vosotros** erguir**íais**
ellos erguir**án**	**ellos** erguir**ían**

IMPERFECT	PRETERITE
yo ergu**ía**	**yo** ergu**í**
tú ergu**ías**	**tú** ergu**iste**
él ergu**ía**	**él irguió**
nosotros ergu**íamos**	**nosotros** ergu**imos**
vosotros ergu**íais**	**vosotros** ergu**isteis**
ellos ergu**ían**	**ellos irguieron**

errar *to err*

PAST PARTICIPLE

err**ado**

GERUND

err**ando**

IMPERATIVE

yerra
erra**d**

PRESENT	PRESENT SUBJUNCTIVE
yo yerro	**yo yerre**
tú yerras	**tú yerres**
él yerra	**él yerre**
nosotros err**amos**	**nosotros** err**emos**
vosotros err**áis**	**vosotros** err**éis**
ellos yerran	**ellos yerren**

FUTURE	CONDITIONAL
yo erra**ré**	**yo** erra**ría**
tú erra**rás**	**tú** erra**rías**
él erra**rá**	**él** erra**ría**
nosotros erra**remos**	**nosotros** erra**ríamos**
vosotros erra**réis**	**vosotros** erra**ríais**
ellos erra**rán**	**ellos** erra**rían**

IMPERFECT	PRETERITE
yo err**aba**	**yo** err**é**
tú err**abas**	**tú** err**aste**
él err**aba**	**él** err**ó**
nosotros err**ábamos**	**nosotros** err**amos**
vosotros err**abais**	**vosotros** err**asteis**
ellos err**aban**	**ellos** err**aron**

escribir *to write*

PAST PARTICIPLE	IMPERATIVE
escrito	escrib**e**
	escribi**d**
GERUND	
escrib**iendo**	

PRESENT	PRESENT SUBJUNCTIVE
yo escrib**o**	**yo** escrib**a**
tú escrib**es**	**tú** escrib**as**
él escrib**e**	**él** escrib**a**
nosotros escrib**imos**	**nosotros** escrib**amos**
vosotros escrib**ís**	**vosotros** escrib**áis**
ellos escrib**en**	**ellos** escrib**an**
FUTURE	CONDITIONAL
yo escribir**é**	**yo** escribir**ía**
tú escribir**ás**	**tú** escribir**ías**
él escribir**á**	**él** escribir**ía**
nosotros escribir**emos**	**nosotros** escribir**íamos**
vosotros escribir**éis**	**vosotros** escribir**íais**
ellos escribir**án**	**ellos** escribir**ían**
IMPERFECT	PRETERITE
yo escrib**ía**	**yo** escrib**í**
tú escrib**ías**	**tú** escrib**iste**
él escrib**ía**	**él** escrib**ió**
nosotros escrib**íamos**	**nosotros** escrib**imos**
vosotros escrib**íais**	**vosotros** escrib**isteis**
ellos escrib**ían**	**ellos** escrib**ieron**

estar *to be*

PAST PARTICIPLE

est**ado**

GERUND

est**ando**

IMPERATIVE

está
esta**d**

PRESENT	PRESENT SUBJUNCTIVE
yo **estoy** **tú** **estás** **él** **está** **nosotros** est**amos** **vosotros** est**áis** **ellos** **están**	**yo** **esté** **tú** **estés** **él** **esté** **nosotros** est**emos** **vosotros** est**éis** **ellos** **estén**
FUTURE	**CONDITIONAL**
yo estar**é** **tú** estar**ás** **él** estar**á** **nosotros** estar**emos** **vosotros** estar**éis** **ellos** estar**án**	**yo** estar**ía** **tú** estar**ías** **él** estar**ía** **nosotros** estar**íamos** **vosotros** estar**íais** **ellos** estar**ían**
IMPERFECT	**PRETERITE**
yo est**aba** **tú** est**abas** **él** est**aba** **nosotros** est**ábamos** **vosotros** est**abais** **ellos** est**aban**	**yo** **estuve** **tú** **estuviste** **él** **estuvo** **nosotros** **estuvimos** **vosotros** **estuvisteis** **ellos** **estuvieron**

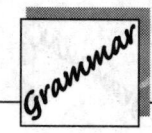

freír *to fry*

PAST PARTICIPLE	IMPERATIVE
frito	fríe
	freíd

GERUND
friendo

PRESENT		PRESENT SUBJUNCTIVE	
yo	frío	yo	fría
tú	fríes	tú	frías
él	fríe	él	fría
nosotros	freímos	nosotros	friamos
vosotros	freís	vosotros	friáis
ellos	fríen	ellos	frían

FUTURE		CONDITIONAL	
yo	freiré	yo	freiría
tú	freirás	tú	freirías
él	freirá	él	freiría
nosotros	freiremos	nosotros	freiríamos
vosotros	freiréis	vosotros	freiríais
ellos	freirán	ellos	freirían

IMPERFECT		PRETERITE	
yo	freía	yo	freí
tú	freías	tú	freíste
él	freía	él	frió
nosotros	freíamos	nosotros	freímos
vosotros	freíais	vosotros	freísteis
ellos	freían	ellos	frieron

gruñir *to grunt*

PAST PARTICIPLE

gruñ**ido**

GERUND

gruñendo

IMPERATIVE

gruñ**e**
gruñi**d**

PRESENT	PRESENT SUBJUNCTIVE
yo gruño	**yo** gruñ**a**
tú gruñ**es**	**tú** gruñ**as**
él gruñ**e**	**él** gruñ**a**
nosotros gruñ**imos**	**nosotros** gruñ**amos**
vosotros gruñ**ís**	**vosotros** gruñ**áis**
ellos gruñ**en**	**ellos** gruñ**an**

FUTURE	CONDITIONAL
yo gruñir**é**	**yo** gruñir**ía**
tú gruñir**ás**	**tú** gruñir**ías**
él gruñir**á**	**él** gruñir**ía**
nosotros gruñir**emos**	**nosotros** gruñir**íamos**
vosotros gruñir**éis**	**vosotros** gruñir**íais**
ellos gruñir**án**	**ellos** gruñir**ían**

IMPERFECT	PRETERITE
yo gruñ**ía**	**yo** gruñ**í**
tú gruñ**ías**	**tú** gruñ**iste**
él gruñ**ía**	**él** **gruñó**
nosotros gruñ**íamos**	**nosotros** gruñ**imos**
vosotros gruñ**íais**	**vosotros** gruñ**isteis**
ellos gruñ**ían**	**ellos** **gruñeron**

haber *to have (auxiliary)*

PAST PARTICIPLE	IMPERATIVE
hab**ido**	*not used*
GERUND	
hab**iendo**	

PRESENT	PRESENT SUBJUNCTIVE
yo he	**yo haya**
tú has	**tú hayas**
él ha	**él haya**
nosotros hemos	**nosotros hayamos**
vosotros hab**éis**	**vosotros hayáis**
ellos han	**ellos hayan**
FUTURE	CONDITIONAL
yo habré	**yo habría**
tú habrás	**tú habrías**
él habrá	**él habría**
nosotros habremos	**nosotros habríamos**
vosotros habréis	**vosotros habríais**
ellos habrán	**ellos habrían**
IMPERFECT	PRETERITE
yo hab**ía**	**yo hube**
tú hab**ías**	**tú hubiste**
él hab**ía**	**él hubo**
nosotros hab**íamos**	**nosotros hubimos**
vosotros hab**íais**	**vosotros hubisteis**
ellos hab**ían**	**ellos hubieron**

hacer *to do, to make*

PAST PARTICIPLE

hecho

GERUND

hac**iendo**

IMPERATIVE

haz
hace**d**

PRESENT	PRESENT SUBJUNCTIVE
yo **hago**	**yo** **haga**
tú hac**es**	**tú** **hagas**
él hac**e**	**él** **haga**
nosotros hac**emos**	**nosotros** **hagamos**
vosotros hac**éis**	**vosotros** **hagáis**
ellos hac**en**	**ellos** **hagan**

FUTURE	CONDITIONAL
yo **haré**	**yo** **haría**
tú **harás**	**tú** **harías**
él **hará**	**él** **haría**
nosotros **haremos**	**nosotros** **haríamos**
vosotros **haréis**	**vosotros** **haríais**
ellos **harán**	**ellos** **harían**

IMPERFECT	PRETERITE
yo hacía	**yo** **hice**
tú hacías	**tú** **hiciste**
él hacía	**él** **hizo**
nosotros hacíamos	**nosotros** **hicimos**
vosotros hacíais	**vosotros** **hicisteis**
ellos hacían	**ellos** **hicieron**

hay *there is, there are*

PAST PARTICIPLE

hab**ido**

GERUND

hab**iendo**

IMPERATIVE

not used

PRESENT	PRESENT SUBJUNCTIVE
hay	**haya**

FUTURE	CONDITIONAL
habrá	**habría**

IMPERFECT	PRETERITE
hab**ía**	**hubo**

ir *to go*

PAST PARTICIPLE

ido

GERUND

yendo

IMPERATIVE

ve
id

PRESENT		PRESENT SUBJUNCTIVE	
yo	**voy**	**yo**	**vaya**
tú	**vas**	**tú**	**vayas**
él	**va**	**él**	**vaya**
nosotros	**vamos**	**nosotros**	**vayamos**
vosotros	**vais**	**vosotros**	**vayáis**
ellos	**van**	**ellos**	**vayan**

FUTURE		CONDITIONAL	
yo	iré	**yo**	iría
tú	irás	**tú**	irías
él	irá	**él**	iría
nosotros	iremos	**nosotros**	iríamos
vosotros	iréis	**vosotros**	iríais
ellos	irán	**ellos**	irían

IMPERFECT		PRETERITE	
yo	**iba**	**yo**	**fui**
tú	**ibas**	**tú**	**fuiste**
él	**iba**	**él**	**fue**
nosotros	**íbamos**	**nosotros**	**fuimos**
vosotros	**ibais**	**vosotros**	**fuisteis**
ellos	**iban**	**ellos**	**fueron**

jugar *to play*

PAST PARTICIPLE	IMPERATIVE
jug**ado**	**juega**
	juga**d**
GERUND	
jug**ando**	

PRESENT	PRESENT SUBJUNCTIVE
yo **juego**	**yo** **juegue**
tú **juegas**	**tú** **juegues**
él **juega**	**él** **juegue**
nosotros jug**amos**	**nosotros** **juguemos**
vosotros jug**áis**	**vosotros** **juguéis**
ellos **juegan**	**ellos** **jueguen**
FUTURE	**CONDITIONAL**
yo jugar**é**	**yo** jugar**ía**
tú jugar**ás**	**tú** jugar**ías**
él jugar**á**	**él** jugar**ía**
nosotros jugar**emos**	**nosotros** jugar**íamos**
vosotros jugar**éis**	**vosotros** jugar**íais**
ellos jugar**án**	**ellos** jugar**ían**
IMPERFECT	**PRETERITE**
yo jug**aba**	**yo** **jugué**
tú jug**abas**	**tú** jug**aste**
él jug**aba**	**él** jug**ó**
nosotros jug**ábamos**	**nosotros** jug**amos**
vosotros jug**abais**	**vosotros** jug**asteis**
ellos jug**aban**	**ellos** jug**aron**

leer *to read*

PAST PARTICIPLE	IMPERATIVE
le**ído**	**lee**
	lee**d**
GERUND	
leyendo	

PRESENT	PRESENT SUBJUNCTIVE
yo leo	**yo** lea
tú lees	**tú** leas
él lee	**él** lea
nosotros leemos	**nosotros** leamos
vosotros leéis	**vosotros** leáis
ellos leen	**ellos** lean

FUTURE	CONDITIONAL
yo leeré	**yo** leería
tú leerás	**tú** leerías
él leerá	**él** leería
nosotros leeremos	**nosotros** leeríamos
vosotros leeréis	**vosotros** leeríais
ellos leerán	**ellos** leerían

IMPERFECT	PRETERITE
yo leía	**yo** **leí**
tú leías	**tú** **leíste**
él leía	**él** **leyó**
nosotros leíamos	**nosotros** **leímos**
vosotros leíais	**vosotros** **leísteis**
ellos leían	**ellos** **leyeron**

lucir *to shine*

PAST PARTICIPLE

luc**ido**

GERUND

luc**iendo**

IMPERATIVE

luc**e**
luci**d**

PRESENT		PRESENT SUBJUNCTIVE	
yo	**luzco**	**yo**	**luzca**
tú	luc**es**	**tú**	**luzcas**
él	luc**e**	**él**	**luzca**
nosotros	luc**imos**	**nosotros**	**luzcamos**
vosotros	luc**ís**	**vosotros**	**luzcáis**
ellos	luc**en**	**ellos**	**luzcan**

FUTURE		CONDITIONAL	
yo	lucir**é**	**yo**	lucir**ía**
tú	lucir**ás**	**tú**	lucir**ías**
él	lucir**á**	**él**	lucir**ía**
nosotros	lucir**emos**	**nosotros**	lucir**íamos**
vosotros	lucir**éis**	**vosotros**	lucir**íais**
ellos	lucir**án**	**ellos**	lucir**ían**

IMPERFECT		PRETERITE	
yo	luc**ía**	**yo**	luc**í**
tú	luc**ías**	**tú**	luc**iste**
él	luc**ía**	**él**	luc**ió**
nosotros	luc**íamos**	**nosotros**	luc**imos**
vosotros	luc**íais**	**vosotros**	luc**isteis**
ellos	luc**ían**	**ellos**	luc**ieron**

VERB TABLE

llover *to rain*

PAST PARTICIPLE	IMPERATIVE
llov**ido**	*not used*
GERUND	
llov**iendo**	

PRESENT	PRESENT SUBJUNCTIVE
llueve	**llueva**
FUTURE	**CONDITIONAL**
llover**á**	llover**ía**
IMPERFECT	**PRETERITE**
llov**ía**	llov**ió**

morir *to die*

PAST PARTICIPLE	IMPERATIVE
muerto	**muere**
	mori**d**
GERUND	
muriendo	

PRESENT		PRESENT SUBJUNCTIVE	
yo	**muero**	**yo**	**muera**
tú	**mueres**	**tú**	**mueras**
él	**muere**	**él**	**muera**
nosotros	mor**imos**	**nosotros**	**muramos**
vosotros	mor**ís**	**vosotros**	**muráis**
ellos	**mueren**	**ellos**	**mueran**

FUTURE		CONDITIONAL	
yo	morir**é**	**yo**	morir**ía**
tú	morir**ás**	**tú**	morir**ías**
él	morir**á**	**él**	morir**ía**
nosotros	morir**emos**	**nosotros**	morir**íamos**
vosotros	morir**éis**	**vosotros**	morir**íais**
ellos	morir**án**	**ellos**	morir**ían**

IMPERFECT		PRETERITE	
yo	mor**ía**	**yo**	mor**í**
tú	mor**ías**	**tú**	mor**iste**
él	mor**ía**	**él**	**murió**
nosotros	mor**íamos**	**nosotros**	mor**imos**
vosotros	mor**íais**	**vosotros**	mor**isteis**
ellos	mor**ían**	**ellos**	**murieron**

mover *to move*

PAST PARTICIPLE

mov**ido**

GERUND

mov**iendo**

IMPERATIVE

mueve
move**d**

PRESENT		PRESENT SUBJUNCTIVE	
yo	**muevo**	**yo**	**mueva**
tú	**mueves**	**tú**	**muevas**
él	**mueve**	**él**	**mueva**
nosotros	mov**emos**	**nosotros**	mov**amos**
vosotros	mov**éis**	**vosotros**	mov**áis**
ellos	**mueven**	**ellos**	**muevan**

FUTURE		CONDITIONAL	
yo	mover**é**	**yo**	mover**ía**
tú	mover**ás**	**tú**	mover**ías**
él	mover**á**	**él**	mover**ía**
nosotros	mover**emos**	**nosotros**	mover**íamos**
vosotros	mover**éis**	**vosotros**	mover**íais**
ellos	mover**án**	**ellos**	mover**ían**

IMPERFECT		PRETERITE	
yo	mov**ía**	**yo**	mov**í**
tú	mov**ías**	**tú**	mov**iste**
él	mov**ía**	**él**	mov**ió**
nosotros	mov**íamos**	**nosotros**	mov**imos**
vosotros	mov**íais**	**vosotros**	mov**isteis**
ellos	mov**ían**	**ellos**	mov**ieron**

nacer *to be born*

PAST PARTICIPLE	IMPERATIVE
nac**ido**	nac**e**
	nac**ed**
GERUND	
nac**iendo**	

PRESENT	PRESENT SUBJUNCTIVE
yo **nazco**	**yo** **nazca**
tú naces	**tú** **nazcas**
él nace	**él** **nazca**
nosotros nac**emos**	**nosotros** **nazcamos**
vosotros nac**éis**	**vosotros** **nazcáis**
ellos nac**en**	**ellos** **nazcan**

FUTURE	CONDITIONAL
yo nacer**é**	**yo** nacer**ía**
tú nacer**ás**	**tú** nacer**ías**
él nacer**á**	**él** nacer**ía**
nosotros nacer**emos**	**nosotros** nacer**íamos**
vosotros nacer**éis**	**vosotros** nacer**íais**
ellos nacer**án**	**ellos** nacer**ían**

IMPERFECT	PRETERITE
yo nac**ía**	**yo** nac**í**
tú nac**ías**	**tú** nac**iste**
él nac**ía**	**él** nac**ió**
nosotros nac**íamos**	**nosotros** nac**imos**
vosotros nac**íais**	**vosotros** nac**isteis**
ellos nac**ían**	**ellos** nac**ieron**

negar *to deny*

PAST PARTICIPLE

neg**ado**

GERUND

neg**ando**

IMPERATIVE

niega
nega**d**

PRESENT	PRESENT SUBJUNCTIVE
yo niego	**yo niegue**
tú niegas	**tú niegues**
él niega	**él niegue**
nosotros neg**amos**	**nosotros neguemos**
vosotros neg**áis**	**vosotros neguéis**
ellos niegan	**ellos nieguen**

FUTURE	CONDITIONAL
yo negar**é**	**yo** negar**ía**
tú negar**ás**	**tú** negar**ías**
él negar**á**	**él** negar**ía**
nosotros negar**emos**	**nosotros** negar**íamos**
vosotros negar**éis**	**vosotros** negar**íais**
ellos negar**án**	**ellos** negar**ían**

IMPERFECT	PRETERITE
yo neg**aba**	**yo negué**
tú neg**abas**	**tú** neg**aste**
él neg**aba**	**él** neg**ó**
nosotros neg**ábamos**	**nosotros** neg**amos**
vosotros neg**abais**	**vosotros** neg**asteis**
ellos neg**aban**	**ellos** neg**aron**

Grammar

oír *to hear*

PAST PARTICIPLE

oído

GERUND

oyendo

IMPERATIVE

oye
oíd

PRESENT	PRESENT SUBJUNCTIVE
yo oigo	**yo oiga**
tú oyes	**tú oigas**
él oye	**él oiga**
nosotros oímos	**nosotros oigamos**
vosotros oís	**vosotros oigáis**
ellos oyen	**ellos oigan**

FUTURE	CONDITIONAL
yo oiré	**yo oiría**
tú oirás	**tú oirías**
él oirá	**él oiría**
nosotros oiremos	**nosotros oiríamos**
vosotros oiréis	**vosotros oiríais**
ellos oirán	**ellos oirían**

IMPERFECT	PRETERITE
yo oía	**yo oí**
tú oías	**tú oíste**
él oía	**él oyó**
nosotros oíamos	**nosotros oímos**
vosotros oíais	**vosotros oísteis**
ellos oían	**ellos oyeron**

oler *to smell*

PAST PARTICIPLE

ol**ido**

GERUND

ol**iendo**

IMPERATIVE

huele
ole**d**

PRESENT	PRESENT SUBJUNCTIVE
yo huelo	**yo huela**
tú hueles	**tú huelas**
él huele	**él huela**
nosotros olemos	**nosotros** ol**amos**
vosotros ol**éis**	**vosotros** ol**áis**
ellos huelen	**ellos huelan**

FUTURE	CONDITIONAL
yo oler**é**	**yo** oler**ía**
tú oler**ás**	**tú** oler**ías**
él oler**á**	**él** oler**ía**
nosotros oler**emos**	**nosotros** oler**íamos**
vosotros oler**éis**	**vosotros** oler**íais**
ellos oler**án**	**ellos** oler**ían**

IMPERFECT	PRETERITE
yo ol**ía**	**yo** ol**í**
tú ol**ías**	**tú** ol**iste**
él ol**ía**	**él** ol**ió**
nosotros ol**íamos**	**nosotros** ol**imos**
vosotros ol**íais**	**vosotros** ol**isteis**
ellos ol**ían**	**ellos** ol**ieron**

pagar *to pay*

PAST PARTICIPLE	IMPERATIVE
pag**ado**	pag**a**
	paga**d**
GERUND	
pag**ando**	

PRESENT	PRESENT SUBJUNCTIVE
yo pago	**yo** **pague**
tú pag**as**	**tú** **pagues**
él pag**a**	**él** **pague**
nosotros pag**amos**	**nosotros** **paguemos**
vosotros pag**áis**	**vosotros** **paguéis**
ellos pag**an**	**ellos** **paguen**
FUTURE	**CONDITIONAL**
yo pagar**é**	**yo** pagar**ía**
tú pagar**ás**	**tú** pagar**ías**
él pagar**á**	**él** pagar**ía**
nosotros pagar**emos**	**nosotros** pagar**íamos**
vosotros pagar**éis**	**vosotros** pagar**íais**
ellos pagar**án**	**ellos** pagar**ían**
IMPERFECT	**PRETERITE**
yo pag**aba**	**yo** **pagué**
tú pag**abas**	**tú** pag**aste**
él pag**aba**	**él** pag**ó**
nosotros pag**ábamos**	**nosotros** pag**amos**
vosotros pag**abais**	**vosotros** pag**asteis**
ellos pag**aban**	**ellos** pag**aron**

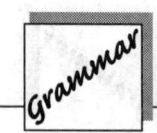

pedir *to ask for*

PAST PARTICIPLE	IMPERATIVE
ped**ido**	**pide**
	pedi**d**
GERUND	
pidiendo	

PRESENT		PRESENT SUBJUNCTIVE	
yo	**pido**	**yo**	**pida**
tú	**pides**	**tú**	**pidas**
él	**pide**	**él**	**pida**
nosotros	ped**imos**	**nosotros**	**pidamos**
vosotros	ped**ís**	**vosotros**	**pidáis**
ellos	**piden**	**ellos**	**pidan**

FUTURE		CONDITIONAL	
yo	pedir**é**	**yo**	pedir**ía**
tú	pedir**ás**	**tú**	pedir**ías**
él	pedir**á**	**él**	pedir**ía**
nosotros	pedir**emos**	**nosotros**	pedir**íamos**
vosotros	pedir**éis**	**vosotros**	pedir**íais**
ellos	pedir**án**	**ellos**	pedir**ían**

IMPERFECT		PRETERITE	
yo	ped**ía**	**yo**	ped**í**
tú	ped**ías**	**tú**	ped**iste**
él	ped**ía**	**él**	**pidió**
nosotros	ped**íamos**	**nosotros**	ped**imos**
vosotros	ped**íais**	**vosotros**	ped**isteis**
ellos	ped**ían**	**ellos**	**pidieron**

pensar *to think*

PAST PARTICIPLE

pens**ado**

GERUND

pens**ando**

IMPERATIVE

piensa
pensa**d**

PRESENT	PRESENT SUBJUNCTIVE
yo **pienso**	**yo** **piense**
tú **piensas**	**tú** **pienses**
él **piensa**	**él** **piense**
nosotros pens**amos**	**nosotros** pens**emos**
vosotros pens**áis**	**vosotros** pens**éis**
ellos **piensan**	**ellos** **piensen**

FUTURE	CONDITIONAL
yo pensar**é**	**yo** pensar**ía**
tú pensar**ás**	**tú** pensar**ías**
él pensar**á**	**él** pensar**ía**
nosotros pensar**emos**	**nosotros** pensar**íamos**
vosotros pensar**éis**	**vosotros** pensar**íais**
ellos pensar**án**	**ellos** pensar**ían**

IMPERFECT	PRETERITE
yo pens**aba**	**yo** pens**é**
tú pens**abas**	**tú** pens**aste**
él pens**aba**	**él** pens**ó**
nosotros pens**ábamos**	**nosotros** pens**amos**
vosotros pens**abais**	**vosotros** pens**asteis**
ellos pens**aban**	**ellos** pens**aron**

poder *to be able*

PAST PARTICIPLE

pod**ido**

GERUND

pudiendo

IMPERATIVE

puede
pode**d**

PRESENT	PRESENT SUBJUNCTIVE
yo puedo	**yo pueda**
tú puedes	**tú puedas**
él puede	**él pueda**
nosotros pod**emos**	**nosotros** pod**amos**
vosotros pod**éis**	**vosotros** pod**áis**
ellos pueden	**ellos puedan**

FUTURE	CONDITIONAL
yo podré	**yo podría**
tú podrás	**tú podrías**
él podrá	**él podría**
nosotros podremos	**nosotros podríamos**
vosotros podréis	**vosotros podríais**
ellos podrán	**ellos podrían**

IMPERFECT	PRETERITE
yo pod**ía**	**yo pude**
tú pod**ías**	**tú pudiste**
él pod**ía**	**él pudo**
nosotros pod**íamos**	**nosotros pudimos**
vosotros pod**íais**	**vosotros pudisteis**
ellos pod**ían**	**ellos pudieron**

poner *to put*

PAST PARTICIPLE

puesto

GERUND

pon**iendo**

IMPERATIVE

pon
pone**d**

PRESENT	PRESENT SUBJUNCTIVE
yo **pongo**	**yo** **ponga**
tú pones	**tú** **pongas**
él pone	**él** **ponga**
nosotros pon**emos**	**nosotros** **pongamos**
vosotros pon**éis**	**vosotros** **pongáis**
ellos ponen	**ellos** **pongan**

FUTURE	CONDITIONAL
yo **pondré**	**yo** **pondría**
tú **pondrás**	**tú** **pondrías**
él **pondrá**	**él** **pondría**
nosotros **pondremos**	**nosotros** **pondríamos**
vosotros **pondréis**	**vosotros** **pondríais**
ellos **pondrán**	**ellos** **pondrían**

IMPERFECT	PRETERITE
yo ponía	**yo** **puse**
tú ponías	**tú** **pusiste**
él ponía	**él** **puso**
nosotros poníamos	**nosotros** **pusimos**
vosotros poníais	**vosotros** **pusisteis**
ellos ponían	**ellos** **pusieron**

prohibir *to forbid*

PAST PARTICIPLE

prohibi**do**

GERUND

prohibi**endo**

IMPERATIVE

prohíbe
prohibi**d**

PRESENT		PRESENT SUBJUNCTIVE	
yo	**prohíbo**	**yo**	**prohíba**
tú	**prohíbes**	**tú**	**prohíbas**
él	**prohíbe**	**él**	**prohíba**
nosotros	prohib**imos**	**nosotros**	prohib**amos**
vosotros	prohib**ís**	**vosotros**	prohib**áis**
ellos	**prohíben**	**ellos**	**prohíban**

FUTURE		CONDITIONAL	
yo	prohibir**é**	**yo**	prohibir**ía**
tú	prohibir**ás**	**tú**	prohibir**ías**
él	prohibir**á**	**él**	prohibir**ía**
nosotros	prohibir**emos**	**nosotros**	prohibir**íamos**
vosotros	prohibir**éis**	**vosotros**	prohibir**íais**
ellos	prohibir**án**	**ellos**	prohibir**ían**

IMPERFECT		PRETERITE	
yo	prohib**ía**	**yo**	prohib**í**
tú	prohib**ías**	**tú**	prohib**iste**
él	prohib**ía**	**él**	prohib**ió**
nosotros	prohib**íamos**	**nosotros**	prohib**imos**
vosotros	prohib**íais**	**vosotros**	prohib**isteis**
ellos	prohib**ían**	**ellos**	prohib**ieron**

querer *to want*

PAST PARTICIPLE

queri**do**

GERUND

queri**endo**

IMPERATIVE

quiere
quere**d**

PRESENT	PRESENT SUBJUNCTIVE
yo **quiero**	**yo** **quiera**
tú **quieres**	**tú** **quieras**
él **quiere**	**él** **quiera**
nosotros quer**emos**	**nosotros** quer**amos**
vosotros quer**éis**	**vosotros** quer**áis**
ellos **quieren**	**ellos** **quieran**

FUTURE	CONDITIONAL
yo **querré**	**yo** **querría**
tú **querrás**	**tú** **querrías**
él **querrá**	**él** **querría**
nosotros **querremos**	**nosotros** **querríamos**
vosotros **querréis**	**vosotros** **querríais**
ellos **querrán**	**ellos** **querrían**

IMPERFECT	PRETERITE
yo quer**ía**	**yo** **quise**
tú quer**ías**	**tú** **quisiste**
él quer**ía**	**él** **quiso**
nosotros quer**íamos**	**nosotros** **quisimos**
vosotros quer**íais**	**vosotros** **quisisteis**
ellos quer**ían**	**ellos** **quisieron**

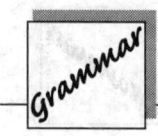

rehusar *to refuse*

PAST PARTICIPLE

rehus**ado**

GERUND

rehus**ando**

IMPERATIVE

rehúsa
rehusa**d**

PRESENT		PRESENT SUBJUNCTIVE	
yo	**rehúso**	**yo**	**rehúse**
tú	**rehúsas**	**tú**	**rehúses**
él	**rehúsa**	**él**	**rehúse**
nosotros	rehus**amos**	**nosotros**	rehus**emos**
vosotros	rehus**áis**	**vosotros**	rehus**éis**
ellos	**rehúsan**	**ellos**	**rehúsen**

FUTURE		CONDITIONAL	
yo	rehusar**é**	**yo**	rehusar**ía**
tú	rehusar**ás**	**tú**	rehusar**ías**
él	rehusar**á**	**él**	rehusar**ía**
nosotros	rehusar**emos**	**nosotros**	rehusar**íamos**
vosotros	rehusar**éis**	**vosotros**	rehusar**íais**
ellos	rehusar**án**	**ellos**	rehusar**ían**

IMPERFECT		PRETERITE	
yo	rehus**aba**	**yo**	rehus**é**
tú	rehus**abas**	**tú**	rehus**aste**
él	rehus**aba**	**él**	rehus**ó**
nosotros	rehus**ábamos**	**nosotros**	rehus**amos**
vosotros	rehus**abais**	**vosotros**	rehus**asteis**
ellos	rehus**aban**	**ellos**	rehus**aron**

reír *to laugh*

PAST PARTICIPLE

re**ído**

GERUND

riendo

IMPERATIVE

ríe
re**íd**

PRESENT	PRESENT SUBJUNCTIVE
yo río	**yo ría**
tú ríes	**tú rías**
él ríe	**él ría**
nosotros reímos	**nosotros riamos**
vosotros reís	**vosotros riáis**
ellos ríen	**ellos rían**

FUTURE	CONDITIONAL
yo reiré	**yo reiría**
tú reirás	**tú reirías**
él reirá	**él reiría**
nosotros reiremos	**nosotros reiríamos**
vosotros reiréis	**vosotros reiríais**
ellos reirán	**ellos reirían**

IMPERFECT	PRETERITE
yo reía	**yo reí**
tú reías	**tú reíste**
él reía	**él rió**
nosotros reíamos	**nosotros reímos**
vosotros reíais	**vosotros reísteis**
ellos reían	**ellos rieron**

reñir *to scold*

PAST PARTICIPLE

reñ**ido**

GERUND

riñendo

IMPERATIVE

riñe
reñi**d**

PRESENT	PRESENT SUBJUNCTIVE
yo **riño**	**yo** **riña**
tú **riñes**	**tú** **riñas**
él **riñe**	**él** **riña**
nosotros reñ**imos**	**nosotros** **riñamos**
vosotros reñ**ís**	**vosotros** **riñáis**
ellos **riñen**	**ellos** **riñan**

FUTURE	CONDITIONAL
yo reñir**é**	**yo** reñir**ía**
tú reñir**ás**	**tú** reñir**ías**
él reñir**á**	**él** reñir**ía**
nosotros reñir**emos**	**nosotros** reñir**íamos**
vosotros reñir**éis**	**vosotros** reñir**íais**
ellos reñir**án**	**ellos** reñir**ían**

IMPERFECT	PRETERITE
yo reñ**ía**	**yo** reñ**í**
tú reñ**ías**	**tú** reñ**iste**
él reñ**ía**	**él** **riñó**
nosotros reñ**íamos**	**nosotros** reñ**imos**
vosotros reñ**íais**	**vosotros** reñ**isteis**
ellos reñ**ían**	**ellos** **riñeron**

resolver *to solve*

PAST PARTICIPLE

resuelto

GERUND

resolv**iendo**

IMPERATIVE

resuelve
resolve**d**

PRESENT	PRESENT SUBJUNCTIVE
yo **resuelvo**	**yo** **resuelva**
tú **resuelves**	**tú** **resuelvas**
él **resuelve**	**él** **resuelva**
nosotros resolv**emos**	**nosotros** resolv**amos**
vosotros resolv**éis**	**vosotros** resolv**áis**
ellos **resuelven**	**ellos** **resuelvan**

FUTURE	CONDITIONAL
yo resolver**é**	**yo** resolver**ía**
tú resolver**ás**	**tú** resolver**ías**
él resolver**á**	**él** resolver**ía**
nosotros resolver**emos**	**nosotros** resolver**íamos**
vosotros resolver**éis**	**vosotros** resolver**íais**
ellos resolver**án**	**ellos** resolver**ían**

IMPERFECT	PRETERITE
yo resolv**ía**	**yo** resolv**í**
tú resolv**ías**	**tú** resolv**iste**
él resolv**ía**	**él** resolv**ió**
nosotros resolv**íamos**	**nosotros** resolv**imos**
vosotros resolv**íais**	**vosotros** resolv**isteis**
ellos resolv**ían**	**ellos** resolv**ieron**

reunir *to put together, to gather*

PAST PARTICIPLE	IMPERATIVE
reun**ido**	**reúne**
	reuni**d**
GERUND	
reun**iendo**	

PRESENT	PRESENT SUBJUNCTIVE
yo **reúno**	**yo** **reúna**
tú **reúnes**	**tú** **reúnas**
él **reúne**	**él** **reúna**
nosotros reun**imos**	**nosotros** reun**amos**
vosotros reun**ís**	**vosotros** reun**áis**
ellos **reúnen**	**ellos** **reúnan**
FUTURE	**CONDITIONAL**
yo reunir**é**	**yo** reunir**ía**
tú reunir**ás**	**tú** reunir**ías**
él reunir**á**	**él** reunir**ía**
nosotros reunir**emos**	**nosotros** reunir**íamos**
vosotros reunir**éis**	**vosotros** reunir**íais**
ellos reunir**án**	**ellos** reunir**ían**
IMPERFECT	**PRETERITE**
yo reun**ía**	**yo** reun**í**
tú reun**ías**	**tú** reun**iste**
él reun**ía**	**él** reun**ió**
nosotros reun**íamos**	**nosotros** reun**imos**
vosotros reun**íais**	**vosotros** reun**isteis**
ellos reun**ían**	**ellos** reun**ieron**

rogar *to beg*

PAST PARTICIPLE

rog**ado**

GERUND

rog**ando**

IMPERATIVE

ruega
roga**d**

PRESENT		PRESENT SUBJUNCTIVE	
yo	**ruego**	**yo**	**ruegue**
tú	**ruegas**	**tú**	**ruegues**
él	**ruega**	**él**	**ruegue**
nosotros	rog**amos**	**nosotros**	**roguemos**
vosotros	rog**áis**	**vosotros**	**roguéis**
ellos	**ruegan**	**ellos**	**rueguen**

FUTURE		CONDITIONAL	
yo	rogar**é**	**yo**	rogar**ía**
tú	rogar**ás**	**tú**	rogar**ías**
él	rogar**á**	**él**	rogar**ía**
nosotros	rogar**emos**	**nosotros**	rogar**íamos**
vosotros	rogar**éis**	**vosotros**	rogar**íais**
ellos	rogar**án**	**ellos**	rogar**ían**

IMPERFECT		PRETERITE	
yo	rog**aba**	**yo**	**rogué**
tú	rog**abas**	**tú**	rog**aste**
él	rog**aba**	**él**	rog**ó**
nosotros	rog**ábamos**	**nosotros**	rog**amos**
vosotros	rog**abais**	**vosotros**	rog**asteis**
ellos	rog**aban**	**ellos**	rog**aron**

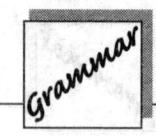

romper *to break*

PAST PARTICIPLE

roto

GERUND

romp**iendo**

IMPERATIVE

romp**e**
romp**ed**

PRESENT	PRESENT SUBJUNCTIVE
yo romp**o**	**yo** romp**a**
tú romp**es**	**tú** romp**as**
él romp**e**	**él** romp**a**
nosotros romp**emos**	**nosotros** romp**amos**
vosotros romp**éis**	**vosotros** romp**áis**
ellos romp**en**	**ellos** romp**an**

FUTURE	CONDITIONAL
yo romper**é**	**yo** romper**ía**
tú romper**ás**	**tú** romper**ías**
él romper**á**	**él** romper**ía**
nosotros romper**emos**	**nosotros** romper**íamos**
vosotros romper**éis**	**vosotros** romper**íais**
ellos romper**án**	**ellos** romper**ían**

IMPERFECT	PRETERITE
yo romp**ía**	**yo** romp**í**
tú romp**ías**	**tú** romp**iste**
él romp**ía**	**él** romp**ió**
nosotros romp**íamos**	**nosotros** romp**imos**
vosotros romp**íais**	**vosotros** romp**isteis**
ellos romp**ían**	**ellos** romp**ieron**

saber *to know*

PAST PARTICIPLE

sab**ido**

GERUND

sab**iendo**

IMPERATIVE

sab**e**
sabe**d**

PRESENT		PRESENT SUBJUNCTIVE	
yo	**sé**	**yo**	**sepa**
tú	sabes	**tú**	**sepas**
él	sabe	**él**	**sepa**
nosotros	sab**emos**	**nosotros**	**sepamos**
vosotros	sab**éis**	**vosotros**	**sepáis**
ellos	sab**en**	**ellos**	**sepan**

FUTURE		CONDITIONAL	
yo	**sabré**	**yo**	**sabría**
tú	**sabrás**	**tú**	**sabrías**
él	**sabrá**	**él**	**sabría**
nosotros	**sabremos**	**nosotros**	**sabríamos**
vosotros	**sabréis**	**vosotros**	**sabríais**
ellos	**sabrán**	**ellos**	**sabrían**

IMPERFECT		PRETERITE	
yo	sabía	**yo**	**supe**
tú	sabías	**tú**	**supiste**
él	sabía	**él**	**supo**
nosotros	sab**íamos**	**nosotros**	**supimos**
vosotros	sab**íais**	**vosotros**	**supisteis**
ellos	sab**ían**	**ellos**	**supieron**

sacar *to take out*

PAST PARTICIPLE

sac**ado**

GERUND

sac**ando**

IMPERATIVE

sac**a**
sac**ad**

PRESENT	PRESENT SUBJUNCTIVE
yo sac**o**	**yo** **saque**
tú sac**as**	**tú** **saques**
él sac**a**	**él** **saque**
nosotros sac**amos**	**nosotros** **saquemos**
vosotros sac**áis**	**vosotros** **saqueís**
ellos sac**an**	**ellos** **saquen**

FUTURE	CONDITIONAL
yo sacar**é**	**yo** sacar**ía**
tú sacar**ás**	**tú** sacar**ías**
él sacar**á**	**él** sacar**ía**
nosotros sacar**emos**	**nosotros** sacar**íamos**
vosotros sacar**éis**	**vosotros** sacar**íais**
ellos sacar**án**	**ellos** sacar**ían**

IMPERFECT	PRETERITE
yo sac**aba**	**yo** **saqué**
tú sac**abas**	**tú** sac**aste**
él sac**aba**	**él** sac**ó**
nosotros sac**ábamos**	**nosotros** sac**amos**
vosotros sac**abais**	**vosotros** sac**asteis**
ellos sac**aban**	**ellos** sac**aron**

salir *to go out*

PAST PARTICIPLE
sal**ido**

GERUND
sal**iendo**

IMPERATIVE
sal
sali**d**

PRESENT	PRESENT SUBJUNCTIVE
yo **salgo** **tú** sales **él** sale **nosotros** sal**imos** **vosotros** salís **ellos** salen	**yo** **salga** **tú** **salgas** **él** **salga** **nosotros** **salgamos** **vosotros** **salgáis** **ellos** **salgan**
FUTURE	CONDITIONAL
yo **saldré** **tú** **saldrás** **él** **saldrá** **nosotros** **saldremos** **vosotros** **saldréis** **ellos** **saldrán**	**yo** **saldría** **tú** **saldrías** **él** **saldría** **nosotros** **saldríamos** **vosotros** **saldríais** **ellos** **saldrían**
IMPERFECT	PRETERITE
yo salía **tú** salías **él** salía **nosotros** salíamos **vosotros** salíais **ellos** salían	**yo** salí **tú** saliste **él** salió **nosotros** salimos **vosotros** salisteis **ellos** salieron

satisfacer *to satisfy*

PAST PARTICIPLE

satisfecho

GERUND

satisfac**iendo**

IMPERATIVE

satisfaz/satisface
satisface**d**

PRESENT	PRESENT SUBJUNCTIVE
yo **satisfago**	**yo** **satisfaga**
tú satisface**s**	**tú** **satisfagas**
él satisface	**él** **satisfaga**
nosotros satisfac**emos**	**nosotros** **satisfagamos**
vosotros satisfac**éis**	**vosotros** **satisfagáis**
ellos satisface**n**	**ellos** **satisfagan**

FUTURE	CONDITIONAL
yo **satisfaré**	**yo** **satisfaría**
tú **satisfarás**	**tú** **satisfarías**
él **satisfará**	**él** **satisfaría**
nosotros **satisfaremos**	**nosotros** **satisfaríamos**
vosotros **satisfaréis**	**vosotros** **satisfaríais**
ellos **satisfarán**	**ellos** **satisfarían**

IMPERFECT	PRETERITE
yo satisfac**ía**	**yo** **satisfice**
tú satisfac**ías**	**tú** **satisficiste**
él satisfac**ía**	**él** **satisfizo**
nosotros satisfac**íamos**	**nosotros** **satisficimos**
vosotros satisfac**íais**	**vosotros** **satisficisteis**
ellos satisfac**ían**	**ellos** **satisficieron**

seguir *to follow*

PAST PARTICIPLE	IMPERATIVE
segu**ido**	**sigue**
	segui**d**
GERUND	
siguiendo	

PRESENT		PRESENT SUBJUNCTIVE	
yo	**sigo**	**yo**	**siga**
tú	**sigues**	**tú**	**sigas**
él	**sigue**	**él**	**siga**
nosotros	segu**imos**	**nosotros**	**sigamos**
vosotros	segu**ís**	**vosotros**	**sigáis**
ellos	**siguen**	**ellos**	**sigan**

FUTURE		CONDITIONAL	
yo	seguir**é**	**yo**	seguir**ía**
tú	seguir**ás**	**tú**	seguir**ías**
él	seguir**á**	**él**	seguir**ía**
nosotros	seguir**emos**	**nosotros**	seguir**íamos**
vosotros	seguir**éis**	**vosotros**	seguir**íais**
ellos	seguir**án**	**ellos**	seguir**ían**

IMPERFECT		PRETERITE	
yo	segu**ía**	**yo**	segu**í**
tú	segu**ías**	**tú**	segu**iste**
él	segu**ía**	**él**	**siguió**
nosotros	segu**íamos**	**nosotros**	segu**imos**
vosotros	segu**íais**	**vosotros**	segu**isteis**
ellos	segu**ían**	**ellos**	**siguieron**

sentir *to feel*

PAST PARTICIPLE

sent**ido**

GERUND

sintiendo

IMPERATIVE

siente
senti**d**

PRESENT		PRESENT SUBJUNCTIVE	
yo	**siento**	**yo**	**sienta**
tú	**sientes**	**tú**	**sientas**
él	**siente**	**él**	**sienta**
nosotros	sent**imos**	**nosotros**	**sintamos**
vosotros	sent**ís**	**vosotros**	**sintáis**
ellos	**sienten**	**ellos**	**sientan**

FUTURE		CONDITIONAL	
yo	sentir**é**	**yo**	sentir**ía**
tú	sentir**ás**	**tú**	sentir**ías**
él	sentir**á**	**él**	sentir**ía**
nosotros	sentir**emos**	**nosotros**	sentir**íamos**
vosotros	sentir**éis**	**vosotros**	sentir**íais**
ellos	sentir**án**	**ellos**	sentir**ían**

IMPERFECT		PRETERITE	
yo	sent**ía**	**yo**	sent**í**
tú	sent**ías**	**tú**	sent**iste**
él	sent**ía**	**él**	**sintió**
nosotros	sent**íamos**	**nosotros**	sent**imos**
vosotros	sent**íais**	**vosotros**	sent**isteis**
ellos	sent**ían**	**ellos**	**sintieron**

ser *to be*

PAST PARTICIPLE	IMPERATIVE
sido	**sé**
	se**d**
GERUND	
siendo	

PRESENT	PRESENT SUBJUNCTIVE
yo soy	**yo sea**
tú eres	**tú seas**
él es	**él sea**
nosotros somos	**nosotros seamos**
vosotros sois	**vosotros seáis**
ellos son	**ellos sean**

FUTURE	CONDITIONAL
yo seré	**yo** sería
tú serás	**tú** serías
él será	**él** sería
nosotros ser**emos**	**nosotros** ser**íamos**
vosotros ser**éis**	**vosotros** ser**íais**
ellos ser**án**	**ellos** ser**ían**

IMPERFECT	PRETERITE
yo era	**yo fui**
tú eras	**tú fuiste**
él era	**él fue**
nosotros éramos	**nosotros fuimos**
vosotros erais	**vosotros fuisteis**
ellos eran	**ellos fueron**

tener *to have*

PAST PARTICIPLE	IMPERATIVE
ten**ido**	**ten**
	tene**d**

GERUND

ten**iendo**

PRESENT		PRESENT SUBJUNCTIVE	
yo	**tengo**	**yo**	**tenga**
tú	**tienes**	**tú**	**tengas**
él	**tiene**	**él**	**tenga**
nosotros	ten**emos**	**nosotros**	**tengamos**
vosotros	ten**éis**	**vosotros**	**tengáis**
ellos	**tienen**	**ellos**	**tengan**

FUTURE		CONDITIONAL	
yo	**tendré**	**yo**	**tendría**
tú	**tendrás**	**tú**	**tendrías**
él	**tendrá**	**él**	**tendría**
nosotros	**tendremos**	**nosotros**	**tendríamos**
vosotros	**tendréis**	**vosotros**	**tendríais**
ellos	**tendrán**	**ellos**	**tendrían**

IMPERFECT		PRETERITE	
yo	ten**ía**	**yo**	**tuve**
tú	ten**ías**	**tú**	**tuviste**
él	ten**ía**	**él**	**tuvo**
nosotros	ten**íamos**	**nosotros**	**tuvimos**
vosotros	ten**íais**	**vosotros**	**tuvisteis**
ellos	ten**ían**	**ellos**	**tuvieron**

torcer *to twist*

PAST PARTICIPLE	IMPERATIVE
torc**ido**	**tuerce**
	torce**d**
GERUND	
torc**iendo**	

PRESENT	PRESENT SUBJUNCTIVE
yo **tuerzo**	**yo** **tuerza**
tú **tuerces**	**tú** **tuerzas**
él **tuerce**	**él** **tuerza**
nosotros torc**emos**	**nosotros** **torzamos**
vosotros torc**éis**	**vosotros** **torzáis**
ellos **tuercen**	**ellos** **tuerzan**
FUTURE	CONDITIONAL
yo torcer**é**	**yo** torcer**ía**
tú torcer**ás**	**tú** torcer**ías**
él torcer**á**	**él** torcer**ía**
nosotros torcer**emos**	**nosotros** torcer**íamos**
vosotros torcer**éis**	**vosotros** torcer**íais**
ellos torcer**án**	**ellos** torcer**ían**
IMPERFECT	PRETERITE
yo torc**ía**	**yo** torc**í**
tú torc**ías**	**tú** torc**iste**
él torc**ía**	**él** torc**ió**
nosotros torc**íamos**	**nosotros** torc**imos**
vosotros torc**íais**	**vosotros** torc**isteis**
ellos torc**ían**	**ellos** torc**ieron**

traer *to bring*

PAST PARTICIPLE

traído

GERUND

trayendo

IMPERATIVE

trae
traed

PRESENT	PRESENT SUBJUNCTIVE
yo traigo	**yo** traiga
tú traes	**tú** traigas
él trae	**él** traiga
nosotros traemos	**nosotros** traigamos
vosotros traéis	**vosotros** traigáis
ellos traen	**ellos** traigan

FUTURE	CONDITIONAL
yo traeré	**yo** traería
tú traerás	**tú** traerías
él traerá	**él** traería
nosotros traeremos	**nosotros** traeríamos
vosotros traeréis	**vosotros** traeríais
ellos traerán	**ellos** traerían

IMPERFECT	PRETERITE
yo traía	**yo** traje
tú traías	**tú** trajiste
él traía	**él** trajo
nosotros traíamos	**nosotros** trajimos
vosotros traíais	**vosotros** trajisteis
ellos traían	**ellos** trajeron

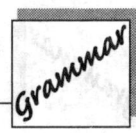

valer *to be worth*

PAST PARTICIPLE	IMPERATIVE
val**ido**	val**e**
	vale**d**
GERUND	
val**iendo**	

PRESENT	PRESENT SUBJUNCTIVE
yo **valgo**	**yo** **valga**
tú val**es**	**tú** **valgas**
él val**e**	**él** **valga**
nosotros val**emos**	**nosotros** **valgamos**
vosotros val**éis**	**vosotros** **valgáis**
ellos val**en**	**ellos** **valgan**

FUTURE	CONDITIONAL
yo **valdré**	**yo** **valdría**
tú **valdrás**	**tú** **valdrías**
él **valdrá**	**él** **valdría**
nosotros **valdremos**	**nosotros** **valdríamos**
vosotros **valdréis**	**vosotros** **valdríais**
ellos **valdrán**	**ellos** **valdrían**

IMPERFECT	PRETERITE
yo val**ía**	**yo** val**í**
tú val**ías**	**tú** val**iste**
él val**ía**	**él** val**ió**
nosotros val**íamos**	**nosotros** val**imos**
vosotros val**íais**	**vosotros** val**isteis**
ellos val**ían**	**ellos** val**ieron**

vencer *to win*

PAST PARTICIPLE

venc**ido**

GERUND

venc**iendo**

IMPERATIVE

venc**e**
vence**d**

PRESENT	PRESENT SUBJUNCTIVE
yo **venzo**	**yo** **venza**
tú vence**s**	**tú** **venzas**
él vence	**él** **venza**
nosotros vence**mos**	**nosotros** **venzamos**
vosotros venc**éis**	**vosotros** **venzáis**
ellos vence**n**	**ellos** **venzan**

FUTURE	CONDITIONAL
yo vencer**é**	**yo** vencer**ía**
tú vencer**ás**	**tú** vencer**ías**
él vencer**á**	**él** vencer**ía**
nosotros vencer**emos**	**nosotros** vencer**íamos**
vosotros vencer**éis**	**vosotros** vencer**íais**
ellos vencer**án**	**ellos** vencer**ían**

IMPERFECT	PRETERITE
yo venc**ía**	**yo** venc**í**
tú venc**ías**	**tú** venc**iste**
él venc**ía**	**él** venc**ió**
nosotros venc**íamos**	**nosotros** venc**imos**
vosotros venc**íais**	**vosotros** venc**isteis**
ellos venc**ían**	**ellos** venc**ieron**

venir *to come*

PAST PARTICIPLE

ven**ido**

GERUND

viniendo

IMPERATIVE

ven
veni**d**

PRESENT	PRESENT SUBJUNCTIVE
yo **vengo**	**yo** **venga**
tú **vienes**	**tú** **vengas**
él **viene**	**él** **venga**
nosotros ven**imos**	**nosotros** **vengamos**
vosotros ven**ís**	**vosotros** **vengáis**
ellos **vienen**	**ellos** **vengan**

FUTURE	CONDITIONAL
yo **vendré**	**yo** **vendría**
tú **vendrás**	**tú** **vendrías**
él **vendrá**	**él** **vendría**
nosotros **vendremos**	**nosotros** **vendríamos**
vosotros **vendréis**	**vosotros** **vendríais**
ellos **vendrán**	**ellos** **vendrían**

IMPERFECT	PRETERITE
yo ven**ía**	**yo** **vine**
tú ven**ías**	**tú** **viniste**
él ven**ía**	**él** **vino**
nosotros ven**íamos**	**nosotros** **vinimos**
vosotros ven**íais**	**vosotros** **vinisteis**
ellos ven**ían**	**ellos** **vinieron**

ver *to see*

PAST PARTICIPLE

visto

GERUND

viendo

IMPERATIVE

ve
ved

PRESENT	PRESENT SUBJUNCTIVE
yo veo	**yo** vea
tú ves	**tú** veas
él ve	**él** vea
nosotros vemos	**nosotros** veamos
vosotros veis	**vosotros** veáis
ellos ven	**ellos** vean

FUTURE	CONDITIONAL
yo veré	**yo** vería
tú verás	**tú** verías
él verá	**él** vería
nosotros veremos	**nosotros** veríamos
vosotros veréis	**vosotros** veríais
ellos verán	**ellos** verían

IMPERFECT	PRETERITE
yo veía	**yo** vi
tú veías	**tú** viste
él veía	**él** vio
nosotros veíamos	**nosotros** vimos
vosotros veíais	**vosotros** visteis
ellos veían	**ellos** vieron

volcar *to overturn*

PAST PARTICIPLE	IMPERATIVE
volc**ado**	**vuelca**
	volca**d**
GERUND	
volc**ando**	

PRESENT		PRESENT SUBJUNCTIVE	
yo	**vuelco**	**yo**	**vuelque**
tú	**vuelcas**	**tú**	**vuelques**
él	**vuelca**	**él**	**vuelque**
nosotros	volc**amos**	**nosotros**	**volquemos**
vosotros	volc**áis**	**vosotros**	**volquéis**
ellos	**vuelcan**	**ellos**	**vuelquen**
FUTURE		CONDITIONAL	
yo	volcar**é**	**yo**	volcar**ía**
tú	volcar**ás**	**tú**	volcar**ías**
él	volcar**á**	**él**	volcar**ía**
nosotros	volcar**emos**	**nosotros**	volcar**íamos**
vosotros	volcar**éis**	**vosotros**	volcar**íais**
ellos	volcar**án**	**ellos**	volcar**ían**
IMPERFECT		PRETERITE	
yo	volc**aba**	**yo**	**volqué**
tú	volc**abas**	**tú**	volc**aste**
él	volc**aba**	**él**	volc**ó**
nosotros	volc**ábamos**	**nosotros**	volc**amos**
vosotros	volc**abais**	**vosotros**	volc**asteis**
ellos	volc**aban**	**ellos**	volc**aron**

volver *to return*

PAST PARTICIPLE

vuelto

GERUND

volv**iendo**

IMPERATIVE

vuelve
volve**d**

PRESENT		PRESENT SUBJUNCTIVE	
yo	**vuelvo**	**yo**	**vuelva**
tú	**vuelves**	**tú**	**vuelvas**
él	**vuelve**	**él**	**vuelva**
nosotros	volv**emos**	**nosotros**	volv**amos**
vosotros	volv**éis**	**vosotros**	volv**áis**
ellos	**vuelven**	**ellos**	**vuelvan**

FUTURE		CONDITIONAL	
yo	volver**é**	**yo**	volver**ía**
tú	volver**ás**	**tú**	volver**ías**
él	volver**á**	**él**	volver**ía**
nosotros	volver**emos**	**nosotros**	volver**íamos**
vosotros	volver**éis**	**vosotros**	volver**íais**
ellos	volver**án**	**ellos**	volver**ían**

IMPERFECT		PRETERITE	
yo	volv**ía**	**yo**	volv**í**
tú	volv**ías**	**tú**	volv**iste**
él	volv**ía**	**él**	volv**ió**
nosotros	volv**íamos**	**nosotros**	volv**imos**
vosotros	volv**íais**	**vosotros**	volv**isteis**
ellos	volv**ían**	**ellos**	volv**ieron**

zurcir *to darn*

PAST PARTICIPLE	IMPERATIVE
zurc**ido**	zurc**e** zurci**d**
GERUND	
zurc**iendo**	

PRESENT	PRESENT SUBJUNCTIVE
yo **zurzo** **tú** zurc**es** **él** zurc**e** **nosotros** zurc**imos** **vosotros** zurc**ís** **ellos** zurc**en**	**yo** **zurza** **tú** **zurzas** **él** **zurza** **nosotros** **zurzamos** **vosotros** **zurzáis** **ellos** **zurzan**
FUTURE	CONDITIONAL
yo zurcir**é** **tú** zurcir**ás** **él** zurcir**á** **nosotros** zurcir**emos** **vosotros** zurcir**éis** **ellos** zurcir**án**	**yo** zurcir**ía** **tú** zurcir**ías** **él** zurcir**ía** **nosotros** zurcir**íamos** **vosotros** zurcir**íais** **ellos** zurcir**ían**
IMPERFECT	PRETERITE
yo zurc**ía** **tú** zurc**ías** **él** zurc**ía** **nosotros** zurc**íamos** **vosotros** zurc**íais** **ellos** zurc**ían**	**yo** zurc**í** **tú** zurc**iste** **él** zurc**ió** **nosotros** zurc**imos** **vosotros** zurc**isteis** **ellos** zurc**ieron**

VERBS INDEX

The following pages, 163 to 186, contain an index of over 2,800 commonly used verbs cross-referred to the appropriate conjugation model.

- Regular verbs belonging to the first, second and third conjugation are numbered 1, 2 and 3 respectively. For the regular conjugations see pp 6 to 13.
- Irregular verbs are numerically cross-referred to the appropriate model as conjugated on pp 82 to 161. Thus, **alzar** is cross-referred to p 100 where **cruzar**, the model for this verb group, is conjugated.
- Verbs which are most commonly used in the reflexive form – e.g. **amodorrarse** – have been cross-referred to the appropriate non-reflexive model. For the full conjugation of a reflexive verb, see pp 28 to 31.
- Verbs printed in **bold** – e.g. **abrir** – are themselves models.
- Superior numbers refer you to notes on p 187 which indicate how the verb differs from its model.

VERBS INDEX

amoldar	1
amonestar	1
amontonar	1
amordazar	100
amortajar	1
amortiguar	90
amortizar	100
amotinar	1
amparar	1
ampliar	110
amplificar	146
amputar	1
amueblar	1
amurallar	1
analizar	100
anclar	1
andar	87
anegar	131
anexionar	1
angustiar	1
anhelar	1
anidar	1
animar	1
aniquilar	1
anochecer[1]	199
anonadar	1
anotar	1
anquilosarse	1
ansiar	110
anteceder	2
anteponer	135
anticipar	1
antojarse	1
anudar	1
anular	1
anunciar	1
añadir	3
apabullar	1
apacentar	133
apaciguar	90
apadrinar	1
apagar	131
apalabrar	1
apalear	1
apañar	1
aparcar	146
aparecer	99
aparejar	1
aparentar	1
apartar	1
apasionarse	1
apearse	1
apedrear	1
apegarse	1
apelar	1
apellidar	1
apelotonarse	1
apenar	1
apercibir	3
apesadumbrar	1
apestar	1
apetecer	99
apiadarse	1
apiñarse	1
aplacar	146
aplanar	1
aplastar	1
aplaudir	3
aplazar	100
aplicar	146
apocar	146
apodar	1
apoderarse	1
aporrear	1
aportar	1
aposentarse	1
apostar	98
apoyar	1
apreciar	1
aprehender	2
apremiar	1
aprender	2
apresar	1
aprestarse	1
apresurarse	1
apretar	133
aprisionar	1
aprobar	98
apropiar	1
aprovechar	1
aproximar	1
apuntalar	1
apuntar	1
apuñalar	1
apurar	1
aquejar	1
aquietar	1
arañar	1
arar	1
arbitrar	1
arbolar	1
archivar	1
arder	2
arengar	1
argamasar	1
argüir	97
argumentar	1
armar	1
armonizar	100
arquear	1
arraigar	131
arrancar	146
arrasar	1
arrastrar	1
arrear	1
arrebatar	1
arreglar	1
arremangar	131
arremeter	2
arrendar	133

estrangular	1
estratificar	146
estrechar	1
estrellar	1
estremecer	99
estrenar	1
estreñir	140
estribar	1
estropear	1
estructurar	1
estrujar	1
estudiar	1
evacuar	1
evadir	3
evaluar	84
evaporar	1
evidenciar	1
evitar	1
evocar	146
evolucionar	1
exacerbar	1
exagerar	1
exaltar	1
examinar	1
exasperar	1
exceder	2
exceptuar	84
excitar	1
exclamar	1
excluir	97
excomulgar	131
excoriar	1
excusar	1
execrar	1
exhalar	1
exhibir	3
exhortar	1
exigir	104
eximir	3
existir	3
exonerar	1
exorcizar	100
expandir	3
expansionar	1
expatriarse	110
expedir	132
experimentar	1
expiar	110
expirar	1
explayar	1
explicar	146
explorar	1
explosionar	1
explotar	1
exponer	135
exportar	1
expresar	1
exprimir	3
expropiar	1
expugnar	1
expulsar	1
expurgar	131
extender	109
extenuar	84
exterminar	1
extinguir	105
extirpar	1
extraer	154
extralimitarse	1
extrañar	1
extraviar	110
extremar	1
eyacular	1
fabricar	146
facilitar	1
facturar	1
falsificar	146
faltar	1
fallar	1
fallecer	99
familiarizarse	100
fascinar	1
fastidiar	1
fatigar	131
favorecer	99
fecundar	1
felicitar	1
fermentar	1
fertilizar	100
festejar	1
fiar	110
fichar	1
figurar	1
fijar	1
filmar	1
filtrar	1
financiar	1
fingir	104
firmar	1
fisgar	131
flexibilizar	100
flirtear	1
florecer	99
flotar	1
fluctuar	84
fluir	97
fomentar	1
forcejear	1
forjar	1
formalizar	100
formar	1
forrar	1
fortalecer	99
forzar	86
fotocopiar	1
fotografiar	110
fracasar	1
fraccionar	1
fraguar	90
franquear	1

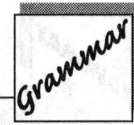

justificar	146
juzgar	131
labrar	1
lacerar	1
lacrar	1
lactar	1
ladear	1
ladrar	1
lagrimear	1
lamentar	1
lamer	2
laminar	1
languidecer	99
lanzar	100
lapidar	1
largar	131
lastimar	1
latir	3
lavar	1
leer	122
legalizar	100
legar	131
legislar	1
legitimar	1
lesionar	1
levantar	1
levar	1
liar	110
libar	1
liberar	1
libertar	1
librar	1
licenciar	1
licitar	1
licuar	84
lidiar	1
ligar	131
limar	1
limitar	1
limpiar	1
linchar	1
lindar	1
liquidar	1
lisiar	1
lisonjear	1
litigar	131
loar	1
localizar	100
lograr	1
lubricar	146
lubrificar	146
lucir	123
lucubrar	1
luchar	1
lustrar	1
llamar	1
llamear	1
llanear	1
llegar	131
llenar	1
llevar	1
llorar	1
lloriquear	1
llover[1]	124
lloviznar[1]	1
macerar	1
machacar	146
madrugar	131
madurar	1
magnetizar	100
magullar	1
maldecir	103
malear	1
malgastar	1
malograr	1
maltratar	1
malversar	1
malvivir	3
mamar	1
manar	1
mancomunar	1
manchar	1
mandar	1
manejar	1
mangonear	1
maniatar	1
manifestar	133
maniobrar	1
manipular	1
manosear	1
mantener	152
maquillar	1
maravillar	1
marcar	146
marchar	1
marchitar	1
marear	1
martillear	1
mascar	146
mascullar	1
masticar	146
masturbarse	1
medicar	146
medir	132
mentar	133
mentir	150
merendar	133
moler	126
morder	126
morir	125
motivar	1
motorizar	100
mover	126
movilizar	100
mudar	1
mugir	104
multar	1
multiplicar	146
murmurar	1
musitar	1

recomponer	135
reconciliar	1
reconfortar	1
reconocer	99
reconstruir	97
recopilar	1
recordar	98
recorrer	2
recortar	1
recostar	98
recrear	1
recriminar	1
recrudecer	99
rectificar	146
recubrir	83
recular	1
recuperar	1
recurrir	3
recusar	1
rechazar	100
rechinar	1
redactar	1
redescubrir	101
redimir	3
redoblar	1
redondear	1
reducir	96
reembolsar	1
reemplazar	100
referir	150
refinar	1
reflejar	1
reflexionar	1
refocilarse	1
reformar	1
reforzar	86
refractar	1
refrenar	1
refrendar	1
refrescar	146
refrigerar	1
refugiarse	1
refulgir	104
refundir	3
refunfuñar	1
refutar	1
regalar	1
regañar	1
regar	128
regatear	1
regenerar	1
regentar	1
regir	107
registrar	1
reglamentar	1
regocijar	1
regodearse	1
regresar	1
regular	1
regularizar	100
rehabilitar	1
rehacer	118
rehogar	131
rehuir[12]	97
rehusar	138
reinar	1
reincidir	3
reincorporarse	1
reintegrar	1
reír	139
reinvertir	3
reiterar	1
reivindicar	146
rejuvenecer	99
relacionar	1
relajar	1
relamer	2
relampaguear[1]	1
relanzar	100
relatar	1
relegar	131
relevar	1
relinchar	1
relucir	123
relumbrar	1
rellenar	1
remachar	1
remar	1
rematar	1
remedar	1
remediar	1
remendar	133
remeter	2
remitir	3
remojar	1
remolinar	1
remontar	1
remorder	126
remover	126
remozar	100
remunerar	1
renacer	127
rendir	132
renegar	128
renovar	98
rentar	1
renunciar	1
reñir	140
reorganizar	100
reorientar	1
reparar	1
repartir	3
repasar	1
repatriar	110
repeler	2
repensar	133
repercutir	3
repetir	132
repicar	146
replegar	128

replicar	146	resplandecer	99	revisar	1
repoblar	98	responder	2	revivir	3
reponer	135	resquebrajar	1	revocar	146
reportar	1	restablecer	99	revolcarse	159
reposar	1	restallar	1	revolotear	1
repostar	1	restar	1	revolucionar	1
reprender	2	restaurar	1	revolver	160
representar	1	restituir	97	rezagar	131
reprimir	3	restregar	131	rezar	100
reprobar	98	restringir	104	rezongar	131
reprochar	1	resucitar	1	rezumar	1
reproducir	96	resultar	1	ribetear	1
repudiar	1	resumir	3	ridiculizar	100
repugnar	1	retar	1	rifar	1
repujar	1	retardar	1	rimar	1
repulgar	131	retener	152	rivalizar	100
reputar	1	retirar	1	rizar	100
requerir	150	retocar	146	robar	1
resaltar	1	retorcer	153	robustecer	99
resarcir	161	retornar	1	rociar	110
resbalar	1	retozar	100	rodar	98
rescatar	1	retractar	1	rodear	1
rescindir	3	retraer	154	roer[13]	2
resecarse	146	retransmitir	3	**rogar**	143
resentirse	150	retrasar	1	**romper**	144
reseñar	1	retratar	1	roncar	146
reservar	1	retribuir	97	rondar	1
resfriarse	110	retroceder	2	ronquear	1
resguardar	1	retumbar	1	ronronear	1
residir	1	reunificar	146	rotular	1
resignarse	1	**reunir**	142	roturar	1
resistir	3	revalidar	1	rozar	100
resolver	141	revalorar	1	ruborizarse	100
resollar	98	revelar	1	rubricar	146
resonar	98	reventar	133	rugir	104
resoplar	1	reverberar	1	rumiar	1
respaldar	1	reverdecer	99	rumorearse	1
respetar	1	reverenciar	1	rutilar	1
respingar	131	revertir	150	**saber**	145
respirar	1	revestir	132	saborear	1

❑ Notes

The notes below indicate special peculiarities of individual verbs. When only some forms of a given tense are affected, all these are shown. When all forms of the tense are affected, only the 1st and 2nd persons are shown, followed by *etc.*

1 Gerund *2* Past Participle *3* Present *4* Preterite *5* Present Subjunctive *6* Imperfect Subjunctive

1) **acaecer, acontecer, amanecer, anochecer, competer, deshelar, escampar, granizar, helar, nevar, nublarse, relampaguear, tronar, verdear, verdecer:** used almost exclusively in infinitive and 3rd person singular

2) **asir** *3* asgo *5* asga, asgas *etc*

3) **atañer** *1* atañendo *4* atañó: see also 1) above

4) **balbucir** *3* balbuceo *5* balbucee, balbucees *etc*

5) **concernir** *3* concierne, conciernen *5* concierna, conciernan: only used in 3rd person

6) **degollar** *3* degüello, degüellas, degüella, degüellan *5* degüelle, degüelles, degüellen

7) **delinquir** *3* delinco *5* delinca, delincas *etc*

8) **desasir** *3* desasgo *5* desasga, desasgas *etc*

9) **discernir** *3* discierno, disciernes, discierne, disciernen *5* discierna, disciernas, disciernan

10) **enraizar** *3* enraízo, enraízas, enraíza, enraízan *5* enraíce, enraíces, enraícen

11) **pudrir** *2* podrido

12) **rehuir** *3* rehúyo, rehúyes, rehúye, rehúyen *5* rehúya, rehúyas, rehúyan

13) **roer** *4* royó, royeron *6* royera, royeras *etc*

14) **soler**: used only in present and imperfect indicative

15) **yacer** *3* yazgo *or* yazco *or* yago *5* yazga *etc or* yazca *etc or* yaga *etc*

❒ The Gender of Nouns

In Spanish, all nouns are either masculine or feminine, whether denoting people, animals or things. Gender is largely unpredictable and has to be learnt for each noun. However, the following guidelines will help you determine the gender for certain types of nouns.

◆ Nouns denoting male people and animals are usually – but not always – masculine, e.g.

un hombre	**un toro**
a man	*a bull*
un enfermero	**un semental**
a (male) nurse	*a stallion*

◆ Nouns denoting female people and animals are usually – but not always – feminine, e.g.

una niña	**una vaca**
a girl	*a cow*
una enfermera	**una yegua**
a nurse	*a mare*

◆ Some nouns are masculine *or* feminine depending on the sex of the person to whom they refer, e.g.

un camarada	**una camarada**
a (male) comrade	*a (female) comrade*
un belga	**una belga**
a Belgian (man)	*a Belgian (woman)*
un marroquí	**una marroquí**
a Moroccan (man)	*a Moroccan (woman)*

◆ Other nouns referring to either men or women have only one gender which applies to both, e.g.

una persona	**una visita**
a person	*a visitor*
una víctima	**una estrella**
a victim	*a star*

◆ Often the ending of a noun indicates its gender. Shown below are some of the most important to guide you.

Masculine endings

-o — **un clavo** *a nail,* **un plátano** *a banana*
EXCEPTIONS: **mano** *hand,* **foto** *photograph,* **moto(cicleta)** *motorbike.*

-l — **un tonel** *a barrel,* **un hotel** *a hotel*
EXCEPTIONS: **cal** *lime,* **cárcel** *prison,* **catedral** *cathedral,* col *cabbage,* **miel** *honey,* **piel** *skin,* **sal** *salt,* **señal** *sign*

-r — **un tractor** *a tractor,* **el altar** *the altar*
EXCEPTIONS: **coliflor** *cauliflower,* **flor** *flower,* **labor** *task*

-y — **el rey** *the king,* **un buey** *an ox*
EXCEPTION: **ley** *law*

Feminine endings

-a — **una casa** *a house,* **la cara** *the face*
EXCEPTIONS: **día** *day,* **mapa** *map,* **planeta** *planet,* **tranvía** *tram,* and most words ending in **-ma (tema** *subject,* **problema** *problem,* etc)

-ión — **una canción** *a song,* **una procesión** *a procession*
EXCEPTIONS: most nouns not ending in **-ción** or **-sión,** e.g. **avión** *aeroplane,* **camión** *lorry,* **gorrión** *sparrow*

-dad, -tad, -tud — **una ciudad** *a town,* **la libertad** *freedom,* **una multitud** *a crowd*

-ed — **una pared** *a wall,* **la sed** *thirst*
EXCEPTION: **césped** *lawn*

-itis — **una faringitis** *pharyngitis,* **la celulitis** *cellulitis*

-iz — **una perdiz** *a partridge,* **una matriz** *a matrix*
EXCEPTIONS: **lápiz** *pencil,* **maíz** *corn,* **tapiz** *tapestry*

-sis — **una tesis** *a thesis,* **una dosis** *a dose*
EXCEPTIONS: **análisis** *analysis,* **énfasis** *emphasis,* **paréntesis** *parenthesis*

-umbre — **la podredumbre** *rot,* **la muchedumbre** *crowd*

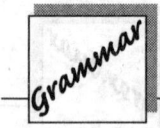

❒ Gender of nouns (Continued)

Some nouns change meaning according to gender. The most common are set out below:

	MASCULINE	FEMININE
capital	*capital* (money)	*capital* (city) → 1
clave	*harpsichord*	*clue*
cólera	*cholera*	*anger* → 2
cometa	*comet*	*kite*
corriente	*current month*	*current*
corte	*cut*	*court* (royal) → 3
coma	*coma*	*comma* → 4
cura	*priest*	*cure* → 5
frente	*front* (in war)	*forehead* → 6
guardia	*guard(sman)*	*guard* → 7
guía	*guide* (person)	*guide(book)* → 8
moral	*mulberry tree*	*morals*
orden	*order* (arrangement)	*order* (command) → 9
ordenanza	*office boy*	*ordinance*
papa	*Pope*	*potato*
parte	*dispatch*	*part* → 10
pendiente	*earring*	*slope*
pez	*fish*	*pitch*
policía	*policeman*	*police*
radio	*radius, radium*	*radio*

1 **Invirtieron mucho capital**
They invested a lot of capital
La capital es muy fea
The capital city is very ugly

2 **Es difícil luchar contra el cólera**
Cholera is difficult to combat
Montó en cólera
He got angry

3 **Me encanta tu corte de pelo**
I love your haircut
Se trasladó la corte a Madrid
The court was moved to Madrid

4 **Entró en un coma profundo**
He went into a deep coma
Aquí hace falta una coma
You need to put a comma here

5 **¿Quién es? – El cura**
Who is it? – The priest
No tiene cura
It's hopeless

6 **Han mandado a su hijo al frente**
Her son has been sent to the front
Tiene la frente muy ancha
She has a very broad forehead

7 **Vino un guardia de tráfico**
A traffic policeman came
Están relevando la guardia ahora
They're changing the guard now

8 **Nuestro guía nos hizo reír a carcajadas**
Our guide had us falling about laughing
Busco una guía turística
I'm looking for a guidebook

9 **Están en orden alfabético**
They're in alphabetical order
No hemos recibido la orden de pago
We haven't had the payment order

10 **Le mandó un parte al general**
He sent a dispatch to the general
En alguna parte debe estar
It must be somewhere or other

❐ Gender: the formation of feminines

As in English, male and female are sometimes differentiated by the use of two quite separate words, e.g.

mi marido	**mi mujer**
my husband	*my wife*
un toro	**una vaca**
a bull	*a cow*

There are, however, some words in Spanish which show this distinction by the form of their ending:

- Nouns ending in -**o** change to -**a** to form the feminine → 1
- If the masculine singular form already ends in -**a**, no further -**a** is added to the feminine → 2
- If the last letter of the masculine singular form is a consonant, an -**a** is normally added in the feminine* → 3

Feminine forms to note

MASCULINE	FEMININE	
el abad	**la abadesa**	*abbot/abbess*
un actor	**una actriz**	*actor/actress*
el alcalde	**la alcaldesa**	*mayor/mayoress*
el conde	**la condesa**	*count/countess*
el duque	**la duquesa**	*duke/duchess*
el emperador	**la emperatriz**	*emperor/empress*
un poeta	**una poetisa**	*poet/poetess*
el príncipe	**la princesa**	*prince/princess*
el rey	**la reina**	*king/queen*
un sacerdote	**una sacerdotisa**	*priest/priestess*
un tigre	**una tigresa**	*tiger/tigress*
el zar	**la zarina**	*tzar/tzarina*

* If the last syllable has an accent, it disappears in the feminine (see p 292) → 4

Examples

1	**un amigo** a (male) friend	**una amiga** a (female) friend
	un empleado a (male) employee	**una empleada** a (female) employee
	un gato a cat	**una gata** a (female) cat
2	**un deportista** a sportsman	**una deportista** a sportswoman
	un colega a (male) colleague	**una colega** a (female) colleague
	un camarada a (male) comrade	**una camarada** a (female) comrade
3	**un español** a Spaniard, a Spanish man	**una española** a Spanish woman
	un vendedor a salesman	**una vendedora** a saleswoman
	un jugador a (male) player	**una jugadora** a (female) player
4	**un lapón** a Laplander (man)	**una lapona** a Laplander (woman)
	un león a lion	**una leona** a lioness
	un neocelandés a New Zealander (man)	**una neocelandesa** a New Zealander (woman)

❒ The formation of plurals

- Nouns ending in an unstressed vowel add **-s** to the singular form → [1]

- Nouns ending in a consonant or a stressed vowel add **-es** to the singular form → [2]

⚠ BUT:

café	*coffee shop*	(plur: **cafés**)
mamá	*mummy*	(plur: **mamás**)
papá	*dad*	(plur: **papás**)
pie	*foot*	(plur: **pies**)
sofá	*sofa*	(plur: **sofás**)
té	*tea*	(plur: **tes**)

and words of foreign origin ending in a consonant, e.g.:

coñac	*brandy*	(plur: **coñacs**)
jersey	*jumper*	(plur: **jerseys**)

⚠ NOTE:

— nouns ending in **-n** or **-s** with an accent on the last syllable drop this accent in the plural (see p 292) → [3]

— nouns ending in **-n** with the stress on the second-last syllable in the singular add an accent to that syllable in the plural in order to show the correct position for stress (see p 292) → [4]

— nouns ending in **-z** change this to **c** in the plural → [5]

- Nouns with an unstressed final syllable ending in **-s** do not change in the plural → [6]

Examples

1	**la casa** the house **el libro** the book	**las casas** the houses **los libros** the books
2	**un rumor** a rumour **un jabalí** a boar	**unos rumores** (some) rumours **unos jabalíes** (some) boars
3	**la canción** the song **el autobús** the bus	**las canciones** the songs **los autobuses** the buses
4	**un examen** an exam **un crimen** a crime	**unos exámenes** (some) exams **unos crímenes** (some) crimes
5	**la luz** the light	**las luces** the lights
6	**un paraguas** an umbrella **la dosis** the dose **el lunes** Monday	**unos paraguas** (some) umbrellas **las dosis** the doses **los lunes** Mondays

❐ The Definite Article

	WITH MASC NOUN	WITH FEM NOUN	
SING	**el**	**la**	*the*
PLUR	**los**	**las**	*the*

- The gender and number of the noun determine the form of the article → [1]

  NOTE: However, if the article comes directly before a feminine singular noun which starts with a stressed **a-** or **ha-**, the masculine form **el** is used instead of the feminine **la** → [2]

- For uses of the definite article see p 199.
- **a** + **el** becomes **al** → [3]
- **de** + **el** becomes **del** → [4]

197 Examples

Grammar

1

el tren the train	**la estación** the station
el actor the actor	**la actriz** the actress
los hoteles the hotels	**las escuelas** the schools
los profesores the teachers	**las mujeres** the women

2

el agua the water	BUT:	**la misma agua** the same water
el hacha the axe	BUT:	**la mejor hacha** the best axe

3

al cine
to the cinema
al empleado
to the employee
al hospital
to the hospital

4

del departamento
from/of the department
del autor
from/of the author
del presidente
from/of the president

❒ Uses of the definite article

While the definite article is used in much the same way in Spanish as it is in English, its use is more widespread in Spanish. Unlike English the definite article is also used:

- with abstract nouns, except when following certain prepositions → [1]
- in generalizations, especially with plural or uncountable* nouns → [2]
- with parts of the body → [3]
  'Ownership' is often indicated by an indirect object pronoun or a reflexive pronoun → [4]
- with titles/ranks/professions followed by a proper name → [5]
  ⚠ EXCEPTIONS: with **Don/Doña, San/Santo(a)** → [6]
- before nouns of official, academic and religious buildings, and names of meals and games → [7]
- The definite article is NOT used with nouns in apposition unless those nouns are individualized → [8]

* An uncountable noun is one which cannot be used in the plural or with an indefinite article, e.g. **el acero** *steel*, **la leche** milk.

Examples

1 **Los precios suben**
Prices are rising
El tiempo es oro
Time is money

⚠ BUT:

con pasión — with passion
sin esperanza — without hope

2 **No me gusta el café**
I don't like coffee
Los niños necesitan ser queridos
Children need to be loved

3 **Vuelva la cabeza hacia la izquierda**
Turn your head to the left
No puedo mover las piernas
I can't move my legs

4 **La cabeza me da vueltas**
My head is spinning
Lávate las manos
Wash your hands

5 **El rey Jorge III** — King George III
el capitán Menéndez — Captain Menéndez
el doctor Ochoa — Doctor Ochoa
el señor Ramírez — Mr Ramírez

6 **Don Arturo Ruiz** — Mr Arturo Ruiz
Santa Teresa — Saint Teresa

7 **en la cárcel** — in prison
en la universidad — at university
en la iglesia — at church
la cena — dinner
el tenis — tennis
el ajedrez — chess

8 **Madrid, capital de España, es la ciudad que ...**
Madrid, the capital of Spain, is the city which ...

⚠ BUT:

Maria Callas, la famosa cantante de ópera ...
Maria Callas, the famous opera singer ...

❒ The Indefinite Article

	WITH MASC NOUN	WITH FEM NOUN	
SING	**un**	**una**	*a*
PLUR	**unos**	**unas**	*some*

The indefinite article is used in Spanish largely as it is in English.

⚠ BUT:

- There is no article when a person's profession is being stated → [1]

  The article is used, however, when the profession is qualified by an adjective → [2]

- The article is not used with the following words:

otro	*another*	→ [3]
cierto	*certain*	→ [4]
semejante	*such (a)*	→ [5]
tal	*such (a)*	→ [6]
cien	*a hundred*	→ [7]
mil	*a thousand*	→ [8]
sin	*without*	→ [9]
qué	*what a*	→ [10]

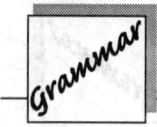

- There is no article with a noun in apposition → [11]. When an abstract noun is qualified by an adjective, the indefinite article is used, but is not translated in English → [12]

1 **Es profesor**
He's a teacher

Mi madre es enfermera
My mother is a nurse

2 **Es un buen médico**
He's a good doctor

Se hizo una escritora célebre
She became a famous writer

3 **otro libro**
another book

4 **cierta calle**
a certain street

5 **semejante ruido**
such a noise

6 **tal mentira**
such a lie

7 **cien soldados**
a hundred soldiers

8 **mil años**
a thousand years

9 **sin casa**
without a house

10 **¡Qué sorpresa!**
What a surprise!

11 **Baroja, gran escritor de la Generación del 98**
Baroja, a great writer of the 'Generación del 98'

12 **con una gran sabiduría/un valor admirable**
with great wisdom/admirable courage

Dieron pruebas de una sangre fría increíble
They showed incredible coolness

una película de un mal gusto espantoso
a film in appallingly bad taste

❒ The Article 'lo'

This is never used with a noun. Instead, it is used in the following ways:

- As an intensifier before an adjective or adverb in the construction

  lo + adjective/adverb + **que** → [1]

  ⚠ NOTE: The adjective agrees with the noun it refers to → [2]

- With an adjective or participle to form an abstract noun → [3]

- In the phrase **lo de** to refer to a subject of which speaker and listener are already aware. It can often be translated as *the business/affair of/about ...* → [4]

- In set expressions, the commonest of which are:

a lo mejor	*maybe, perhaps*	→ [5]
a lo lejos	*in the distance*	→ [6]
a lo largo de	*along, through*	→ [7]
por lo menos	*at least*	→ [8]
por lo tanto	*therefore, so*	→ [9]
por lo visto	*apparently*	→ [10]

Examples

1 **No sabíamos lo pequeña que era la casa**
We didn't know how small the house was
Sé lo mucho que te gusta la música
I know how much you like music

2 **No te imaginas lo simpáticos que son**
You can't imagine how nice they are
Ya sabes lo buenas que son estas manzanas
You already know how good these apples are

3 **Lo bueno de eso es que ...**
The good thing about it is that ...
Sentimos mucho lo ocurrido
We are very sorry about what happened

4 **Lo de ayer es mejor que lo olvides**
It's better if you forget what happened yesterday
Lo de tu hermano me preocupa mucho
The business about your brother worries me very much

5 **A lo mejor ha salido**
Perhaps he's gone out

6 **A lo lejos se veían unas casas**
Some houses could be seen in the distance

7 **A lo largo de su vida**
Throughout his life
A lo largo de la carretera
Along the road

8 **Hubo por lo menos cincuenta heridos**
At least fifty people were injured

9 **No hemos recibido ninguna instrucción al respecto, y por lo tanto no podemos ...**
We have not received any instructions about it, therefore we cannot ...

10 **Por lo visto, no viene**
Apparently he's not coming OR: He's not coming, it seems

❒ Adjectives

Most adjectives agree in number and in gender with the noun or pronoun.

⚠ NOTE that:

— if the adjective refers to two or more singular nouns of the same gender, a plural ending of that gender is required → [1]

— if the adjective refers to two or more singular nouns of different genders, a masculine plural ending is required → [2]

The formation of feminines

◆ Adjectives ending in **-o** change to **-a** → [3]

◆ Some groups of adjectives add **-a**:
  - adjectives of nationality or geographical origin → [4]
  - adjectives ending in **-or** (except irregular comparatives: see p 210), **-án, -ón, -ín** → [5]

⚠ NOTE: When there is an accent on the last syllable, it disappears in the feminine (see p 292).

◆ Other adjectives do not change → [6]

The formation of plurals

◆ Adjectives ending in an unstressed vowel add **-s** → [7]

◆ Adjectives ending in a stressed vowel or a consonant add **-es** → [8]

⚠ NOTE:

- if there is an accent on the last syllable of a word ending in a consonant, it will disappear in the plural (see p 292) → [9]
- if the last letter is a **z** it will become a **c** in the plural → [10]

205 Examples

1	**la lengua y la literatura españolas** (the) Spanish language and literature	
2	**Nunca había visto árboles y flores tan raros** I had never seen such strange trees and flowers	
3	**mi hermano pequeño** my little brother	**mi hermana pequeña** my little sister
4	**un chico español** a Spanish boy	**una chica española** a Spanish girl
	el equipo barcelonés the team from Barcelona	**la vida barcelonesa** the Barcelona way of life
5	**un niño encantador** a charming little boy	**una niña encantadora** a charming little girl
	un hombre holgazán an idle man	**una mujer holgazana** an idle woman
	un gesto burlón a mocking gesture	**una sonrisa burlona** a mocking smile
	un chico cantarín a boy fond of singing	**una chica cantarina** a girl fond of singing
6	**un final feliz** a happy ending	**una infancia feliz** a happy childhood
	mi amigo belga my Belgian (male) friend	**mi amiga belga** my Belgian (female) friend
	el vestido verde the green dress	**la blusa verde** the green blouse
7	**el último tren** the last train	**los últimos trenes** the last trains
	una casa vieja an old house	**unas casas viejas** (some) old houses
8	**un médico iraní** an Iranian doctor	**unos médicos iraníes** (some) Iranian doctors
	un examen fácil an easy exam	**unos exámenes fáciles** (some) easy exams
9	**un río francés** a French river	**unos ríos franceses** (some) French rivers
10	**un día feliz** a happy day	**unos días felices** (some) happy days

❐ Invariable Adjectives

Some adjectives and other parts of speech when used adjectivally never change in the feminine or plural.

The commonest of these are:

— nouns denoting colour → [1]
— compound adjectives → [2]
— nouns used as adjectives → [3]

Shortening of Adjectives

◆ The following drop the final **-o** before a masculine singular noun:

bueno *good* → [4]
malo *bad*
alguno* *some* → [5]
ninguno* *none*
uno *one* → [6]
primero *first* → [7]
tercero *third*
postrero *last* → [8]

* ⚠ NOTE: An accent is required to show the correct position for stress.

◆ **Grande** *big, great* is usually shortened to **gran** before a masculine *or* feminine singular noun → [9]

◆ **Santo** *Saint* changes to **San** except with saints' names beginning with **Do-** or **To-** → [10]

◆ **Ciento** *a hundred* is shortened to **cien** before a masculine *or* feminine plural noun → [11]

◆ **Cualquiera** drops the final **-a** before a masculine *or* feminine singular noun → [12]

1 **los vestidos naranja**
the orange dresses

2 **las chaquetas azul marino**
the navy blue jackets

3 **bebés probeta**
test-tube babies

mujeres soldado
women soldiers

4 **un buen libro**
a good book

5 **algún libro**
some book

6 **cuarenta y un años**
forty-one years

7 **el primer hijo**
the first child

8 **un postrer deseo**
a last wish

9 **un gran actor**
a great actor

una gran decepción
a great disappointment

10 **San Antonio**
Saint Anthony

Santo Tomás
Saint Thomas

11 **cien años**
a hundred years
cien millones
a hundred million

12 **cualquier día**
any day

a cualquier hora
any time

❒ Comparatives and Superlatives

Comparatives

These are formed using the following constructions:

más ... (que)		*more ... (than)*	→ 1
menos ... (que)		*less ... (than)*	→ 2
tanto ... como		*as ... as*	→ 3
tan ... como		*as ... as*	→ 4
tan ... que		*so ... that*	→ 5
demasiado ...	**para**	*too ...*	*to* → 6
bastante ...	**para**	*enough ...*	*to* → 6
suficiente ...	**para**	*enough ...*	*to* → 6

- *'Than'* followed by a clause is translated by **de lo que** → 7

Superlatives

These are formed using the following constructions:

el/la/los/las más ... (que)	*the most ... (that)*	→ 8
el/la/los/las menos ... (que)	*the least ... (that)*	→ 9

- After a superlative the preposition **de** is often translated as *in* → 10

- The absolute superlative (*very, most, extremely* + *adjective*) is expressed in Spanish by **muy** + adjective, or by adding **-ísimo/a/os/as** to the adjective when it ends in a consonant, or to its stem (adjective minus final vowel) when it ends in a vowel → 11

⚠ NOTE: It is sometimes necessary to change the spelling of the adjective when **-ísimo** is added, in order to maintain the same sound (see p 296) → 12

Examples

1 **una razón más seria**
a more serious reason
Es más alto que mi hermano
He's taller than my brother

2 **una película menos conocida**
a less well known film
Luis es menos tímido que tú
Luis is less shy than you

3 **Pablo tenía tanto miedo como yo**
Paul was as frightened as I was

4 **No es tan grande como creía**
It isn't as big as I thought

5 **El examen era tan difícil que nadie aprobó**
The exam was so difficult that nobody passed

6 **No tengo suficiente dinero para comprarlo**
I haven't got enough money to buy it

7 **Está más cansada de lo que parece**
She is more tired than she seems

8 **el caballo más veloz**
the fastest horse
los días más lluviosos
the wettest days
la casa más pequeña
the smallest house
las manzanas más maduras
the ripest apples

9 **el hombre menos simpático**
the least likeable man
los cuadros menos bonitos
the least attractive paintings
la niña menos habladora
the least talkative girl
las camisas menos viejas
the least old shirts

10 **la estación más ruidosa de Londres**
the noisiest station in London

11 **Este libro es muy interesante**
This book is very interesting
Era facilísimo de hacer
It was very easy to make
Tienen un coche rapidísimo
They have an extremely fast car

12 **Mi tío era muy rico**
My uncle was very rich
un león muy feroz
a very ferocious lion
Se hizo riquísimo
He became extremely rich
un tigre ferocísimo
an extremely ferocious tiger

❒ Comparatives and Superlatives (Continued)

Adjectives with irregular comparatives/superlatives

ADJECTIVE	COMPARATIVE	SUPERLATIVE
bueno *good*	**mejor** *better*	**el mejor** *the best*
malo *bad*	**peor** *worse*	**el peor** *the worst*
grande *big*	**mayor** OR: **más grande** *bigger; older*	**el mayor** OR: **el más grande** *the biggest; the oldest*
pequeño *small*	**menor** OR: **más pequeño** *smaller; younger; lesser*	**el menor** OR: **el más pequeño** *the smallest; the youngest; the least*

- The irregular comparative and superlative forms of **grande** and **pequeño** are used mainly to express:
  — age, in which case they come after the noun → 1
  — abstract size and degrees of importance, in which case they come before the noun → 2

  The regular forms are used mainly to express physical size → 3

- Irregular comparatives and superlatives have one form for both masculine and feminine, but always agree in number with the noun → 1

Examples

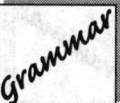

1 **mis hermanos mayores**
my older brothers
la hija menor
the youngest daughter

2 **el menor ruido**
the slightest sound
las mayores dificultades
the biggest difficulties

3 **Este plato es más grande que aquél**
This plate is bigger than that one
Mi casa es más pequeña que la tuya
My house is smaller than yours

❒ Demonstrative Adjectives

	MASCULINE	FEMININE	
SING	**este**	**esta**	*this*
	ese	**esa**	*that*
	aquel	**aquella**	
PLUR	**estos**	**estas**	*these*
	esos	**esas**	*those*
	aquellos	**aquellas**	

- Demonstrative adjectives normally precede the noun and always agree in number and in gender → [1]

- The forms **ese/a/os/as** are used:
  - — to indicate distance from the speaker but proximity to the person addressed → [2]
  - — to indicate a not too remote distance → [3]

- The forms **aquel/la/los/las** are used to indicate distance, in space or time → [4]

Examples

1 **Este bolígrafo no escribe**
This pen is not working
Esa revista es muy mala
That is a very bad magazine
Aquella montaña es muy alta
That mountain (over there) is very high
¿Conoces a esos señores?
Do you know those gentlemen?
Siga Vd hasta aquellos edificios
Carry on until you come to those buildings
¿Ves aquellas personas?
Can you see those people (over there)?

2 **Ese papel en donde escribes ...**
That paper you are writing on ...

3 **No me gustan esos cuadros**
I don't like those pictures

4 **Aquella calle parece muy ancha**
That street (over there) looks very wide
Aquellos años sí que fueron felices
Those were really happy years

❒ Interrogative Adjectives

	MASCULINE	FEMININE	
SING	**¿qué?**	**¿qué?**	*what?, which?*
	¿cuánto?	**¿cuánta?**	*how much?; how many?*
PLUR	**¿qué?**	**¿qué?**	*what?, which?*
	¿cuántos?	**¿cuántas?**	*how much?; how many?*

- Interrogative adjectives, when not invariable, agree in number and gender with the noun → [1]

- The forms shown above are also used in indirect questions → [2]

❒ Exclamatory Adjectives

	MASCULINE	FEMININE	
SING	**¡qué!**	**¡qué!**	*what (a)*
	¡cuánto!	**¡cuánta!**	*what (a lot of)*
PLUR	**¡qué!**	**¡qué!**	*what*
	¡cuántos!	**¡cuántas!**	*what (a lot of)*

- Exclamatory adjectives, when not invariable, agree in number and gender with the noun → [3]

Examples

1 **¿Qué libro te gustó más?**
Which book did you like most?
¿Qué clase de hombre es?
What type of man is he?
¿Qué instrumentos toca Vd?
What instruments do you play?
¿Qué ofertas ha recibido Vd?
What offers have you received?
¿Cuánto dinero te queda?
How much money have you got left?
¿Cuánta lluvia ha caído?
How much rain have we had?
¿Cuántos vestidos quieres comprar?
How many dresses do you want to buy?
¿Cuántas personas van a venir?
How many people are coming?

2 **No sé a qué hora llegó**
I don't know at what time she arrived
Dígame cuántas postales quiere
Tell me how many postcards you'd like

3 **¡Qué pena!**
What a pity!
¡Qué tiempo tan/más malo!
What lousy weather!
¡Cuánto tiempo!
What a long time!
¡Cuánta pobreza!
What poverty!
¡Cuántos autobuses!
What a lot of buses!
¡Cuántas mentiras!
What a lot of lies!

❐ Possessive Adjectives

Weak forms

WITH SING NOUN		WITH PLUR NOUN		
MASC	*FEM*	*MASC*	*FEM*	
mi	**mi**	**mis**	**mis**	*my*
tu	**tu**	**tus**	**tus**	*your*
su	**su**	**sus**	**sus**	*his; her; its; your (of* **Vd***)*
nuestro	**nuestra**	**nuestros**	**nuestras**	*our*
vuestro	**vuestra**	**vuestros**	**vuestras**	*your*
su	**su**	**sus**	**sus**	*their; your (of* **Vds***)*

- All possessive adjectives agree in number and (when applicable) in gender with the noun, NOT WITH THE OWNER → 1
- The weak forms always precede the noun → 1
- Since the form **su(s)** can mean *his, her, your (of* **Vd, Vds***)* or *their,* clarification is often needed. This is done by adding **de él, de ella, de Vds** etc to the noun, and usually (but not always) changing the possessive to a definite article → 2

Examples

1 **Pilar no ha traído nuestros libros**
Pilar hasn't brought our books
Antonio irá a vuestra casa
Anthony will go to your house
¿Han vendido su coche tus vecinos?
Have your neighbours sold their car?
Mi hermano y tu primo no se llevan bien
My brother and your cousin don't get on

2 **su casa → la casa de él**
his house
sus amigos → los amigos de Vd
your friends
sus coches → los coches de ellos
their cars
su abrigo → el abrigo de ella
her coat

❒ Possessive Adjectives (Continued)

Strong forms

WITH SING NOUN		WITH PLUR NOUN		
MASC	*FEM*	*MASC*	*FEM*	
mío	**mía**	**míos**	**mías**	*my*
tuyo	**tuya**	**tuyos**	**tuyas**	*your*
suyo	**suya**	**suyos**	**suyas**	*his; her; its; your* (*of* **Vd**)
nuestro	**nuestra**	**nuestros**	**nuestras**	*our*
vuestro	**vuestra**	**vuestros**	**vuestras**	*your*
suyo	**suya**	**suyos**	**suyas**	*their; your* (*of* **Vds**)

- The strong forms agree in the same way as the weak forms (see p 216).

- The strong forms always follow the noun, and they are used:
  — to translate the English *of mine, of yours,* etc → [1]
  — to address people → [2]

Examples

[1] **Es un capricho suyo**
It's a whim of hers
un amigo nuestro
a friend of ours
una revista tuya
a magazine of yours

[2] **Muy señor mío** (in letters)
Dear Sir
hija mía
my daughter
¡Dios mío!
My God!
Amor mío
Darling/My love

❒ Indefinite Adjectives

alguno(a)s	*some*
ambos(as)	*both*
cada	*each; every*
cierto(a)s	*certain; definite*
cualquiera, plur **cualesquiera**	*some; any*
los (las) demás	*the others; the remainder*
mismo(a)s	*same; -self*
mucho(a)s	*many; much*
ningún, ninguna plur **ningunos, ningunas**	*any; no*
otro(a)s	*other; another*
poco(a)s	*few; little*
tal(es)	*such (a)*
tanto(a)s	*so much; so many*
todo(a)s	*all; every*
varios(as)	*several; various*

Unless invariable, all indefinite adjectives agree in number and gender with the noun → [1]

- **alguno**

  Before a masculine singular noun it drops the final **-o** and adds an accent to show the correct position for stress → [2] (see also p 292)

- **ambos**

  Usually it is only used in written Spanish. The spoken language prefers the form **los dos/las dos** → [3]

- **cierto** and **mismo**

  They change their meaning according to their position in relation to the noun (see also **Position of Adjectives**, p 224) → [4]

- **cualquiera**

  It drops the final **-a** before a masculine *or* feminine noun → [5]

1	**el mismo día** the same day **mucha/poca gente** many/few people		**las mismas películas** the same films **mucho/poco dinero** much/little money
2	**algún día** some day		**alguna razón** some reason
3	**Me gustan los dos cuadros** I like both pictures **¿Conoces a las dos enfermeras?** Do you know both nurses?		
4	**cierto tiempo** a certain time	⚠ BUT:	**éxito cierto** sure success
	el mismo color the same colour	⚠ BUT:	**en la iglesia misma** in the church itself
5	**cualquier casa** any house	⚠ BUT:	**una revista cualquiera** any magazine

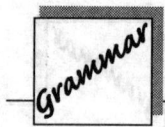

❒ Indefinite Adjectives (Continued)

- **ningún** is only used in negative sentences or phrases → [1]

- **otro**
  It is never preceded by an indefinite article → [2]

- **tal**
  It is never followed by an indefinite article → [3]

- **todo**
  It can be followed by a definite article, a demonstrative or possessive adjective or a place name → [4]

⚠ EXCEPTIONS:

— when **todo** in the singular means *any, every,* or *each* → [5]

— in some set expressions → [6]

Examples

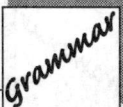

1 **No es ninguna tonta**
She's no fool
¿No tienes parientes? – No, ninguno
Haven't you any relatives? – No, none

2 **¿Me das otra manzana?**
Will you give me another apple?
Prefiero estos otros zapatos
I prefer these other shoes

3 **Nunca dije tal cosa**
I never said such a thing

4 **Estudian durante toda la noche**
They study all night
Ha llovido toda esta semana
It has rained all this week
Pondré en orden todos mis libros
I'll sort out all my books
Lo sabe todo Madrid
All Madrid knows it

5 **Podrá entrar toda persona que lo desee**
Any person who wishes to enter may do so

⚠ BUT:

Vienen todos los días
They come every day

6 **de todos modos**
anyway
a toda velocidad
at full/top speed
por todas partes
por todos lados
a/en todas partes
a/en todos lados
everywhere

❒ Position of Adjectives

- Spanish adjectives usually follow the noun → 1, 2
- Note that when used figuratively or to express a quality already inherent in the noun, adjectives can precede the noun → 3
- As in English, demonstrative, possessive (weak forms), numerical, interrogative and exclamatory adjectives precede the noun → 4
- Indefinite adjectives also usually precede the noun → 5

  ⚠ NOTE: **alguno** *some* in negative expressions follows the noun → 6

- Some adjectives can precede or follow the noun, but their meaning varies according to their position:

	BEFORE NOUN	AFTER NOUN	
antiguo	*former*	*old, ancient*	→ 7
diferente	*various*	*different*	→ 8
grande	*great*	*big*	→ 9
medio	*half*	*average*	→ 10
mismo	*same*	*-self, very/precisely*	→ 11
nuevo	*new, another, fresh*	*brand new*	→ 12
pobre	*poor (wretched)*	*poor (not rich)*	→ 13
puro	*sheer, mere*	*pure (clear)*	→ 14
varios	*several*	*various, different*	→ 15
viejo	*old (long known, etc)*	*old (aged)*	→ 16

- Adjectives following the noun are linked by **y** → 17

1	**la página siguiente** the following page	**la hora exacta** the right time	
2	**una corbata azul** a blue tie	**una palabra española** a Spanish word	
3	**un dulce sueño** a sweet dream		
	un terrible desastre (all disasters are terrible) a terrible disaster		
4	**este sombrero** this hat	**mi padre** my father	**¿qué hombre?** what man?
5	**cada día** every day	**otra vez** another time	**poco dinero** little money
6	**sin duda alguna** without any doubt		
7	**un antiguo colega** a former colleague	**la historia antigua** ancient history	
8	**diferentes capítulos** various chapters	**personas diferentes** different people	
9	**un gran pintor** a great painter	**una casa grande** a big house	
10	**medio melón** half a melon	**velocidad media** average speed	
11	**la misma respuesta** the same answer	**yo mismo** myself	**eso mismo** precisely that
12	**mi nuevo coche** my new car	**unos zapatos nuevos** (some) brand new shoes	
13	**esa pobre mujer** that poor woman	**un país pobre** a poor country	
14	**la pura verdad** the plain truth	**aire puro** fresh air	
15	**varios caminos** several ways/paths	**artículos varios** various items	
16	**un viejo amigo** an old friend	**esas toallas viejas** those old towels	
17	**una acción cobarde y falsa** a cowardly, deceitful act		

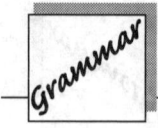

Personal Pronouns

SUBJECT PRONOUNS

PERSON	SINGULAR	PLURAL
1st	**yo** *I*	**nosotros** *we* (masc/masc + fem) **nosotras** *we* (all fem)
2nd	**tú** *you*	**vosotros** *you* (masc/masc + fem) **vosotras** *you* (all fem)
3rd	**él** *he; it* **ella** *she; it* **usted (Vd)** *you*	**ellos** *they* (masc/masc + fem) **ellas** *they* (all fem) **ustedes (Vds)** *you*

- Subject pronouns have a limited usage in Spanish. Normally they are only used:

  — for emphasis → [1]

  — for clarity → [2]

  ⚠ BUT: **Vd** and **Vds** should always be used for politeness, whether they are otherwise needed or not → [3]

- *It* as subject and *they,* referring to things, are never translated into Spanish → [4]

- **tú/usted**

  As a general rule, you should use **tú** (or **vosotros,** if plural) when addressing a friend, a child, a relative, someone you know well, or when invited to do so. In all other cases, use **usted** (or **ustedes**)

- **nosotros/as; vosotros/as; él/ella; ellos/ellas**

  All these forms reflect the number and gender of the noun(s) they replace. **Nosotros, vosotros** and **ellos** also replace a combination of masculine and feminine nouns.

Examples

1 **Ellos sí que llegaron tarde**
They really did arrive late
Tú no tienes por qué venir
There is no reason for you to come
Ella jamás creería eso
She would never believe that

2 **Yo estudio español pero él estudia francés**
I study Spanish but he studies French
Ella era muy deportista pero él prefería jugar a las cartas
She was a sporty type but he preferred to play cards
Vosotros saldréis primero y nosotros os seguiremos
You leave first and we will follow you

3 **Pase Vd por aquí**
Please come this way
¿Habían estado Vds antes en esta ciudad?
Had you been to this town before?

4 **¿Qué es? – Es una sorpresa**
What is it? – It's a surprise
¿Qué son? – Son abrelatas
What are they? – They are tin-openers

❐ Personal Pronouns (Continued)

DIRECT OBJECT PRONOUNS

PERSON	SINGULAR	PLURAL
1st	**me** *me*	**nos** *us*
2nd	**te** *you*	**os** *you*
3rd (masculine)	**lo** *him; it; you* (of **Vd**)	**los** *them; you* (of **Vds**)
(feminine)	**la** *her; it; you* (of **Vd**)	**las** *them; you* (of **Vds**)

- **lo** sometimes functions as a 'neuter' pronoun, referring to an idea or information contained in a previous statement or question. It is often not translated → [1]

Position of direct object pronouns

- In constructions other than the imperative affirmative, infinitive or gerund, the pronoun always comes before the verb → [2]

  In the imperative affirmative, infinitive and gerund, the pronoun follows the verb and is attached to it. An accent is needed in certain cases to show the correct position for stress (see also p 292) → [3]

- Where an infinitive or gerund depends on a previous verb, the pronoun may be used either after the infinitive or gerund, or before the main verb → [4]

  ⚠ NOTE: see how this applies to reflexive verbs → [4]

- For further information, see **Order of Object Pronouns**, p 232.

Reflexive Pronouns

These are dealt with under reflexive verbs, p 24.

Examples

1 **¿Va a venir María? – No lo sé**
Is Maria coming? – I don't know
Hay que regar las plantas – Yo lo haré
The plants need watering → I'll do it
Habían comido ya pero no nos lo dijeron
They had already eaten, but they didn't tell us
Yo conduzco de prisa pero él lo hace despacio
I drive fast but he drives slowly

2 **Te quiero**
I love you
¿Las ve Vd?
Can you see them?
¿No me oyen Vds?
Can't you hear me?
Tu hija no nos conoce
Your daughter doesn't know us
No los toques
Don't touch them

3 **Ayúdame**
Help me
Acompáñenos
Come with us
Quiero decirte algo
I want to tell you something
Estaban persiguiéndonos
They were coming after us

4 **Lo está comiendo** OR: **Está comiéndolo**
She is eating it
Nos vienen a ver OR: **Vienen a vernos**
They are coming to see us
No quería levantarse OR: **No se quería levantar**
He didn't want to get up
Estoy afeitándome OR: **Me estoy afeitando**
I'm shaving

❐ Personal Pronouns (Continued)

INDIRECT OBJECT PRONOUNS

PERSON	SINGULAR	PLURAL
1st	**me**	**nos**
2nd	**te**	**os**
3rd	**le**	**les**

- The pronouns shown in the above table replace the preposition **a** + noun → [1]

Position of indirect object pronouns

- In constructions other than the imperative affirmative, the infinitive or the gerund, the pronoun comes before the verb → [2]

  In the imperative affirmative, infinitive and gerund, the pronoun follows the verb and is attached to it. An accent is needed in certain cases to show the correct position for stress (see also p 292) → [3]

- Where an infinitive or gerund depends on a previous verb, the pronoun may be used either after the infinitive or gerund, or before the main verb → [4]

- For further information, see **Order of Object Pronouns**, p 232.

Reflexive Pronouns

These are dealt with under reflexive verbs, p 24.

Examples

1 **Estoy escribiendo a Teresa → Le estoy escribiendo**
I am writing to Teresa → I am writing to her
Da de comer al gato → Dale de comer
Give the cat some food → Give it some food

2 **Sofía os ha escrito** — **¿Os ha escrito Sofía?**
Sophie has written to you — Has Sophie written to you?
Carlos no nos habla
Charles doesn't speak to us
¿Qué te pedían?
What were they asking you for?
No les haga caso Vd
Don't take any notice of them

3 **Respóndame Vd** — **Díganos Vd la respuesta**
Answer me — Tell us the answer
No quería darte la noticia todavía
I didn't want to tell you the news yet
Llegaron diciéndome que ...
They came telling me that ...

4 **Estoy escribiéndole** OR: **Le estoy escribiendo**
I am writing to him/her
Les voy a hablar OR: **Voy a hablarles**
I'm going to talk to them

❐ Personal Pronouns (Continued)

Order of object pronouns

- When two object pronouns of different persons are combined, the order is: indirect before direct, i.e.

me **te** **nos** **os**	before	**lo** **la** **los** **las**	→ [1]

⚠ NOTE: When two 3rd person object pronouns are combined, the first (i.e. the indirect object pronoun) becomes **se** → [2]

Points to note on object pronouns

- As **le/les** can refer to either gender, and **se** to either gender, singular or plural, sometimes clarification is needed. This is done by adding **a él** *to him*, **a ella** *to her*, **a Vd** *to you* etc to the phrase, usually after the verb → [3]

- When a noun object precedes the verb, the corresponding object pronoun must be used too → [4]

- Indirect object pronouns are often used instead of possessive adjectives with parts of the body or clothing to indicate 'ownership', and also in certain common constructions involving reflexive verbs (see also **The Indefinite Article**, p 198) → [5]

- **Le** and **les** are often used in Spanish instead of **lo** and **los** when referring to people. Equally **la** is sometimes used instead of **le** when referring to a feminine person or animal, although this usage is considered incorrect by some speakers of Spanish → [6]

Examples

1 **Paloma os lo mandará mañana**
Paloma is sending it to you tomorrow
¿Te los ha enseñado mi hermana?
Has my sister shown them to you?
No me lo digas
Don't tell me (that)
Todos estaban pidiéndotelo
They were all asking you for it
No quiere prestárnosla
He won't lend it to us

2 **Se lo di ayer**
I gave it to him/her/them yesterday

3 **Le escriben mucho a ella**
They write to her often
Se lo van a mandar pronto a ellos
They will be sending it to them soon

4 **A tu hermano lo conozco bien**
I know your brother well
A María la vemos algunas veces
We sometimes see Maria

5 **La chaqueta le estaba ancha**
His jacket was too loose
Me duele el tobillo
My ankle is aching
Se me ha perdido el bolígrafo
I have lost my pen

6 **Le/lo encontraron en el cine**
They met him at the cinema
Les/los oímos llegar
We heard them coming
Le/la escribimos una carta
We wrote a letter to her

❒ Personal Pronouns (Continued)

Pronouns after prepositions

- These are the same as the subject pronouns, except for the forms **mí** *me,* **ti** *you* (sing), and the reflexive **sí** *himself, herself, themselves, yourselves* → 1

- **Con** *with* combines with **mí, ti** and **sí** to form

  conmigo *with me* → 2
  contigo *with you*
  consigo *with himself/herself etc*

- The following prepositions always take a subject pronoun:

  entre *between, among* → 3
  hasta / **incluso** *even, including* → 4
  salvo / **menos** *except* → 5
  según *according to* → 6

- These pronouns are used for emphasis, especially where contrast is involved → 7

- **Ello** *it, that* is used after a preposition when referring to an idea already mentioned, but never to a concrete noun → 8

- **A él, de él** NEVER contract → 9

Examples

1 **Pienso en ti**
I think about you

¿Son para mí?
Are they for me?

Es para ella
This is for her

Iban hacia ellos
They were going towards them

Volveréis sin nosotros
You'll come back without us

Volaban sobre vosotros
They were flying above you

Hablaba para si
He was talking to himself

2 **Venid conmigo**
Come with me

Lo trajeron consigo ⚠ BUT: **¿Hablaron con vosotros?**
They brought it/him with them — Did they talk to you?

3 **entre tú y ella**
between you and her

4 **Hasta yo puedo hacerlo**
Even I can do it

5 **todos menos yo**
everybody except me

6 **según tú**
according to you

7 **¿A ti no te escriben?**
Don't they write to you?

Me lo manda a mí, no a ti
She is sending it to me, not to you

8 **Nunca pensaba en ello**
He never thought about it

Por todo ello me parece que ...
For all those reasons it seems to me that ...

9 **A él no lo conozco**
I don't know him

No he sabido nada de él
I haven't heard from him

❒ Indefinite Pronouns

algo	*something, anything*	→ 1
alguien	*somebody, anybody*	→ 2
alguno/a/os/as	*some, a few*	→ 3
cada uno/a	*each (one)* *everybody*	→ 4
cualquiera	*anybody; any*	→ 5
los/las demás	*the others* *the rest*	→ 6
mucho/a/os/as	*many; much*	→ 7
nada	*nothing*	→ 8
nadie	*nobody*	→ 9
ninguno/a	*none, not any*	→ 10
poco/a/os/as	*few; little*	→ 11
tanto/a/os/as	*so much; so many*	→ 12
todo/a/os/as	*all; everything*	→ 13
uno ... (el) otro **una ... (la) otra**	*(the) one ... the other*	
		→ 14
unos ... (los) otros **unas ... (las) otras**	*some ... (the) others*	
varios/as	*several*	→ 15

◆ **algo, alguien, alguno**

They can never be used after a negative. The appropriate negative pronouns are used instead: **nada**, **nadie**, **ninguno** (see also negatives, p 272) → 16

Examples

1 **Tengo algo para ti** — I have something for you
¿Viste algo? — Did you see anything?

2 **Alguien me lo ha dicho** — Somebody said it to me
¿Has visto a alguien? — Have you seen anybody?

3 **Algunos de los niños ya sabían leer**
Some of the children could read already

4 **Le dió una manzana a cada uno**
She gave each of them an apple
!Cada uno a su casa!
Everybody go home!

5 **Cualquiera puede hacerlo**
Anybody can do it
Cualquiera de las explicaciones vale
Any of the explanations is a valid one

6 **Yo me fui, los demás se quedaron**
I went, the others stayed

7 **Muchas de las casas no tenían jardín**
Many of the houses didn't have a garden

8 **¿Qué tienes en la mano? – Nada**
What have you got in your hand? – Nothing

9 **¡A quién ves? – A nadie**
Who can you see? – Nobody

10 **¿Cuántas tienes? – Ninguna**
How many have you got? – None

11 **Había muchos cuadros, pero vi pocos que me gustaran**
There were many pictures, but I saw few I liked

12 **¿Se oía mucho ruido? – No tanto**
Was it very noisy? – Not so very

13 **Lo ha estropeado todo** — He has spoiled everything
Todo va bien — All is going well

14 **Unos cuestan 300 pesetas, los otros 400 pesetas**
Some cost 300 pesetas, the others 400 pesetas

15 **Varios de ellos me gustaron mucho**
I liked several of them very much

16 **Veo a alguien** — I can see somebody
No veo a nadie — I can't see anybody
Tengo algo que hacer — I have something to do
No tengo nada que hacer — I don't have anything to do

❒ Relative Pronouns

PEOPLE

SINGULAR	PLURAL	
que	**que**	*who, that* (subject) → [1]
que	**que**	*who(m), that* (direct object) → [2]
a quien	**a quienes**	
a quien	**a quienes**	*to whom, that* → [3]
de que	**de que**	*of whom, that* → [4]
de quien	**de quienes**	
cuyo/a	**cuyos/as**	*whose* → [5]

THINGS

SINGULAR AND PLURAL		
que	*which, that* (subject)	→ [6]
que	*which, that* (direct object)	→ [7]
a que	*to which, that*	→ [8]
de que	*of which, that*	→ [9]
cuyo	*whose*	→ [10]

⚠ NOTE: These forms can also refer to people.

- **cuyo** agrees with the noun it accompanies, NOT WITH THE OWNER → [5]/[10]

- You cannot omit the relative pronoun in Spanish as you can in English → [2]/[7]

1 **Mi hermano, que tiene veinte años, es el más joven**
My brother, who is twenty, is the youngest

2 **Los amigos que más quiero son ...**
The friends (that) I like best are ...

María, a quien Daniel admira tanto, es ...
Maria, whom Daniel admires so much, is ...

3 **Mis abogados, a quienes he escrito hace poco, están ...**
My lawyers, to whom I wrote recently, are ...

4 **La chica de que te hablé llega mañana**
The girl (that) I told you about is coming tomorrow

los niños de quienes se ocupa Vd
the children (that) you look after

5 **Vendrá la mujer cuyo hijo está enfermo**
The woman whose son is ill will be coming

6 **Hay una escalera que lleva a la buhardilla**
There's a staircase which leads to the loft

7 **La casa que hemos comprado tiene ...**
The house (which) we've bought has ...

Este es el regalo que me ha mandado mi amiga
This is the present (that) my friend has sent to me

8 **la tienda a que siempre va**
the shop (which) she always goes to

9 **las injusticias de que se quejan**
the injustices (that) they're complaining about

10 **la ventana cuyas cortinas están corridas**
the window whose curtains are drawn

❒ Relative Pronouns (Continued)

el cual, el que

- These are used when the relative is separated from the word it refers to, or when it would otherwise be unclear which word it referred to. The pronouns always agree in number and gender with the noun → [1]

  El cual may also be used when the verb in the relative clause is separated from the relative pronoun → [2]

lo que, lo cual

- The neuter form **lo** is normally used when referring to an idea, statement or abstract noun. In certain expressions, the form **lo cual** may also be used as the subject of the relative clause → [3]

Relative pronouns after prepositions

- **Que** and **quienes** are generally used after the prepositions:

a	*to*	→	[4]
con	*with*	→	[5]
de	*from, about, of*	→	[6]
en	*in, on, into*	→	[7]

  It should be noted that **en que** can sometimes be translated by:

  — *where.* In this case it can also be replaced by **en donde** or **donde** → [8]

  — *when.* Sometimes here it can be replaced by **cuando** → [9]

- **El que** or **el cual** are used after other prepositions, and they always agree → [10]

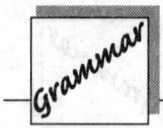

Examples

1 **El padre de Elena, el cual tiene mucho dinero, es ...**
Elena's father, who has a lot of money, is ...
(**el cual** is *used here since* **que** *or* **quien** *might equally refer to Elena*)
Su hermana, a la cual/la que hacía mucho que no veía, estaba también allí
His sister, whom I hadn't seen for a long time, was also there

2 **Vieron a su tio, el cual, después de levantarse, salió**
They saw their uncle, who, after having got up, went out

3 **No sabe lo que hace**
He doesn't know what he is doing
Lo que dijiste fue una tontería
What you said was foolish
Todo estaba en silencio, lo que (*or* **lo cual**) **me pareció muy raro**
All was silent, which I thought most odd

4 **las tiendas a (las) que íbamos**
the shops we used to go to

5 **la chica con quien** (*or* **la que**) **sale**
the girl he's going out with

6 **el libro de(l) que te hablé**
the book I told you about

7 **el lío en (el) que te has metido**
the trouble you've got yourself into

8 **el sitio en que (en donde/donde) se escondía**
the place where he/she was hiding

9 **el año en que naciste**
the year (when) you were born

10 **el puente debajo del que/cual pasa el río**
the bridge under which the river flows
las obras por las cuales/que es famosa
the plays for which she is famous

❒ Relative Pronouns (Continued)

el que, la que; los que, las que

These mean *the one(s) who/which, those who* → [1]

⚠ NOTE: **quien(es)** can replace **el que** *etc* when used in a general sense → [2]

todos los que, todas las que

These mean *all who, all those/the ones which* → [3]

todo lo que

This translates *all that, everything that* → [4]

el de, la de; los de, las de

These can mean:

— *the one(s) of, that/those of* → [5]

— *the one(s) with* → [6]

Examples

1 **Esa película es la que quiero ver**
That film is the one I want to see
¿Te acuerdas de ese amigo? El que te presenté ayer
Do you remember that friend? The one I introduced you to yesterday
Los que quieran entrar tendrán que pagar
Those who want to go in will have to pay

2 **Quien** (*or* **el que**) **llegue antes ganará el premio**
He who arrives first will win the prize

3 **Todos los que salían iban de negro**
All those who were coming out were dressed in black
¿Qué autobuses puedo tomar? – Todos los que pasen por aquí
Which buses can I take? – Any (All those) that come this way

4 **Quiero saber todo lo que ha pasado**
I want to know all that has happened

5 **Trae la foto de tu novio y la de tu hermano**
Bring the photo of your boyfriend and the one of your brother
Viajamos en mi coche y en el de María
We travelled in my car and Maria's
Te doy estos libros y también los de mi hermana
I'll give you these books and my sister's too

6 **Tu amigo, el de las gafas, me lo contó**
Your friend, the one with glasses, told me

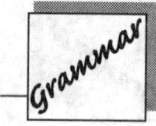

❐ Interrogative Pronouns

¿qué?	*what?; which?*
¿cuál(es)?	*which?; what?*
¿quién(es)?	*who?*

qué

It always translates *what* → 1

⚠ NOTE: **por** + **qué** is normally translated by *why* → 2

cuál

It normally implies a choice, and translates *which* → 3

⚠ EXCEPT when no choice is implied or more specific information is required → 4

⚠ NOTE: Whilst the pronoun **qué** can also work as an adjective, **cuál** only works as a pronoun → 5

quién

— **quién(es)** (subject or after preposition)	*who*	→ 6
— **a quién(es)** (object)	*whom*	→ 7
— **de quién(es)**	*whose*	→ 8

◆ All the forms shown above are also used in indirect questions → 9

Examples

1 **¿Qué estan haciendo?**
What are they doing?
¿Qué dices?
What are you saying?
¿Para qué lo quieres?
What do you want it for?

2 **¿Por qué no llegaron Vds antes?**
Why didn't you arrive earlier?

3 **¿Cuál de estos vestidos te gusta más?**
Which of these dresses do you like best?
¿Cuáles viste?
Which ones did you see?

4 **¿Cuál es la capital de España?**
What is the capital of Spain?
¿Cuál es tu consejo?
What is your advice?
¿Cuál es su fecha de nacimiento?
What is your date of birth?

5 **¿Qué libro es más interesante?**
Which book is more interesting?
¿Cuál (de estos libros) es más interesante?
Which (of these books) is more interesting?

6 **¿Quién ganó la carrera?**
Who won the race?
¿Con quiénes los viste?
Who did you see them with?

7 **¿A quiénes ayudaste?**
Who(m) did you help?
¿A quién se lo diste?
Who did you give it to?

8 **¿De quién es este libro?**
Whose is this book?

9 **Le pregunté para qué lo quería**
I asked him/her what he/she wanted it for
No me dijeron cuáles preferían
They didn't tell me which ones they preferred
No sabía a quién acudir
I didn't know who to turn to

❐ Possessive Pronouns

These are the same as the strong forms of the possessive adjectives, but they are always accompanied by the definite article.

SINGULAR

MASCULINE	FEMININE	
el mío	**la mía**	*mine*
el tuyo	**la tuya**	*yours* (of **tú**)
el suyo	**la suya**	*his; hers; its; yours* (of **Vd**)
el nuestro	**la nuestra**	*ours*
el vuestro	**la vuestra**	*yours* (of **vosotros**)
el suyo	**la suya**	*theirs; yours* (of **Vds**)

PLURAL

MASCULINE	FEMININE	
los míos	**las mías**	*mine*
los tuyos	**las tuyas**	*yours* (of **tú**)
los suyos	**las suyas**	*his; hers; its; yours* (of **Vd**)
los nuestros	**las nuestras**	*ours*
los vuestros	**las vuestras**	*yours* (of **vosotros**)
los suyos	**las suyas**	*theirs; yours* (of **Vds**)

- The pronoun agrees in number and gender with the noun it replaces, NOT WITH THE OWNER → [1]

- Alternative translations are *my own*, *your own*, etc → [2]

- After the prepositions **a** and **de** the article **el** is contracted in the normal way (see p 196)

  a + el mío → al mío → [3]

  de + el mío → del mío → [4]

1 **Pregunta a Cristina si este bolígrafo es el suyo**
Ask Christine if this pen is hers
¿Qué equipo ha ganado, el suyo o el nuestro?
Which team won – theirs or ours?
Mi perro es más joven que el tuyo
My dog is younger than yours
Daniel pensó que esos libros eran los suyos
Daniel thought those books were his
Si no tienes discos, te prestaré los míos
If you don't have any records, I'll lend you mine
Las habitaciones son menos amplias que las vuestras
The rooms are smaller than yours

2 **¿Es su familia tan grande como la tuya?**
Is his/her/their family as big as your own?
Sus precios son más bajos que los nuestros
Their prices are lower than our own

3 **¿Por qué prefieres este sombrero al mío?**
Why do you prefer this hat to mine?
Su coche se parece al vuestro
His/her/their car looks like yours

4 **Mi libro está encima del tuyo**
My book is on top of yours
Su padre vive cerca del nuestro
His/her/their father lives near ours

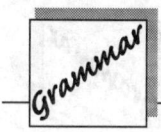

❒ Demonstrative Pronouns

	MASCULINE	FEMININE	NEUTER	
SING	**éste**	**ésta**	**esto**	*this*
	ése	**ésa**	**eso**	*that*
	aquél	**aquélla**	**aquello**	
PLUR	**éstos**	**éstas**		*these*
	ésos	**ésas**		*those*
	aquéllos	**aquéllas**		

- The pronoun agrees in number and gender with the noun it replaces → [1]

- The difference in meaning between the forms **ése** and **aquél** is the same as between the corresponding adjectives (see p 212)

- The masculine and feminine forms have an accent, which is the only thing that differentiates them from the corresponding adjectives.

- The neuter forms always refer to an idea or a statement or to an object when we want to identify it, etc, but never to specified nouns → [2]

- An additional meaning of **aquél** is *the former*, and of **éste** *the latter* → [3]

1 **¿Qué abrigo te gusta más? – Este de aquí**
Which coat do you like best? – This one here

Aquella casa era más grande que ésta
That house was bigger than this one

estos libros y aquéllos
these books and those (over there)

Quiero estas sandalias y ésas
I'd like these sandals and those ones

2 **No puedo creer que esto me esté pasando a mí**
I can't believe this is really happening to me

Eso de madrugar es algo que no le gusta
(This business of) getting up early is something she doesn't like

Aquello sí que me gustó
I really did like that

Esto es una bicicleta
This is a bicycle

3 **Hablaban Jaime y Andrés, éste a voces y aquél casi en un susurro**
James and Andrew were talking, the latter in a loud voice and the former almost in a whisper

❒ Adverbs

Formation

- Most adverbs are formed by adding **-mente** to the feminine form of the adjective. Accents on the adjective are not affected since the suffix **-mente** is stressed independently → [1]

  ⚠ NOTE: **-mente** is omitted:

  — in the first of two or more of these adverbs when joined by a conjunction → [2]
  — in **recientemente** *recently* when immediately preceding a past participle → [3]
  An accent is then needed on the last syllable (see p 292)

- The following adverbs are formed in an irregular way:

  bueno → **bien**
  good *well*
  malo → **mal**
  bad *badly*

Adjectives used as adverbs

Certain adjectives are used adverbially. These include:
alto, bajo, barato, caro, claro, derecho, fuerte and **rápido** → [4]

⚠ NOTE: Other adjectives used as adverbs agree with the subject, and can normally be replaced by the adverb ending in **-mente** or an adverbial phrase → [5]

Position of Adverbs

- When the adverb accompanies a verb, it may either immediately follow it or precede it for emphasis → [6]

  ⚠ NOTE: The adverb can never be placed between **haber** and the past participle in compound tenses → [7]

- When the adverb accompanies an adjective or another adverb, it generally precedes the adjective or adverb → [8]

1	FEM ADJECTIVE	ADVERB
	lenta slow	**lentamente** slowly
	franca frank	**francamente** frankly
	feliz happy	**felizmente** happily
	fácil easy	**fácilmente** easily

2 **Lo hicieron lenta pero eficazmente**
They did it slowly but efficiently

3 **El pan estaba recién hecho**
The bread had just been baked

4 **hablar alto/bajo**
to speak loudly/softly
costar barato/caro
to be cheap/expensive
ver claro
to see clearly
cortar derecho
to cut (in a) straight (line)
Habla muy fuerte
He talks very loudly
correr rápido
to run fast

5 **Esperaban impacientes** (*or* **impacientemente/con impaciencia**)
They were waiting impatiently
Vivieron muy felices (*or* **muy felizmente**)
They lived very happily

6 **No conocemos aún al nuevo médico**
We still haven't met the new doctor
Aún estoy esperando
I'm still waiting
Han hablado muy bien
They have spoken very well
Siempre le regalaban flores
They always gave her flowers

7 **Lo he hecho ya**
I've already done it
No ha estado nunca en Italia
She's never been to Italy

8 **un sombrero muy bonito**
a very nice hat
mañana temprano
early tomorrow
hablar demasiado alto
to talk too loud
hoy mismo
today

❐ Comparatives and Superlatives

Comparatives

These are formed using the following constructions:

más ... (que)	*more ... (than)*	→ 1
menos ... (que)	*less ... (than)*	→ 2
tanto como	*as much as*	→ 3
tan ... como	*as ... as*	→ 4
tan ... que	*so ... that*	→ 5
demasiado ... para	*too ... to*	→ 6
(lo) bastante ... / **(lo) suficientemente ...** } **para**	*enough to*	→ 7
cada vez más/menos	*more and more/ less and less*	→ 8

Superlatives

- These are formed by placing **más/menos** *the most/the least* before the adverb → 9
- **lo** is added before a superlative which is qualified → 10
- The absolute superlative (*very, most, extremely* + adverb) is formed by placing **muy** before the adverb. The form **-ísimo** (see also p 292) is also occasionally found → 11

Adverbs with irregular comparatives/superlatives

ADVERB	COMPARATIVE	SUPERLATIVE
bien	**mejor***	**(lo) mejor**
well	*better*	*(the) best*
mal	**peor**	**(lo) peor**
badly	*worse*	*(the) worst*
mucho	**más**	**(lo) más**
a lot	*more*	*(the) most*
poco	**menos**	**(lo) menos**
little	*less*	*(the) least*

* **más bien** also exists, meaning *rather* → 12

Examples

[1] **más de prisa** — more quickly
más abiertamente — more openly
Mi hermana canta más fuerte que yo
My sister sings louder than me

[2] **menos fácilmente** — less easily
menos a menudo — less often
Nos vemos menos frecuentemente que antes
We see each other less frequently than before

[3] **Daniel no lee tanto como Andrés**
Daniel doesn't read as much as Andrew

[4] **Hágalo tan rápido como le sea posible**
Do it as quickly as you can
Ganan tan poco como nosotros
They earn as little as we do

[5] **Llegaron tan pronto que tuvieron que esperarnos**
They arrived so early that they had to wait for us

[6] **Es demasiado tarde para ir al cine**
It's too late to go to the cinema

[7] **Eres (lo) bastante grande para hacerlo solo**
You're old enough to do it by yourself

[8] **Me gusta el campo cada vez más**
I like the countryside more and more

[9] **María es la que corre más rápido**
Maria is the one who runs fastest
El que llegó menos tarde fue Miguel
Miguel was the one to arrive the least late

[10] **Lo hice lo más de prisa que pude**
I did it as quickly as I could

[11] **muy lentamente** — very slowly
tempranísimo — extremely early
muchísimo — very much

[12] **Era un hombre más bien bajito**
He was a rather short man
Estaba más bien inquieta que impaciente
I was restless rather than impatient

❒ Common Adverbs and their usage

bastante	*enough; quite*	→ 1
bien	*well*	→ 2
cómo	*how*	→ 3
cuánto	*how much*	→ 4
demasiado	*too much; too*	→ 5
más	*more*	→ 6
menos	*less*	→ 7
mucho	*a lot; much*	→ 8
poco	*little, not much; not very*	→ 9
siempre	*always*	→ 10
también	*also, too*	→ 11
tan	*as*	→ 12
tanto	*as much*	→ 13
todavía/aún	*still; yet; even*	→ 14
ya	*already*	→ 15

- **bastante, cuánto, demasiado, mucho, poco** and **tanto** are also used as adjectives that agree with the noun they qualify (see indefinite adjectives, p 220 and interrogative adjectives, p 214)

1 **Es bastante tarde**
It's quite late

2 **¡Bien hecho!**
Well done!

3 **¡Cómo me ha gustado!**
How I liked it!

4 **¿Cuánto cuesta este libro?**
How much is this book?

5 **He comido demasiado**
I've eaten too much

Es demasiado caro
It's too expensive

6 **Mi hermano trabaja más ahora**
My brother works more now

Es más tímida que Sofía
She is shyer than Sophie

7 **Se debe beber menos**
One must drink less

Estoy menos sorprendida que tú
I'm less surprised than you are

8 **¿Lees mucho?**
Do you read a lot?

¿Está mucho más lejos?
Is it much further?

9 **Comen poco**
They don't eat (very) much

María es poco decidida
Maria is not very daring

10 **Siempre dicen lo mismo**
They always say the same (thing)

11 **A mí también me gusta**
I like it too

12 **Ana es tan alta como yo**
Ana is as tall as I am

13 **Nos aburrimos tanto como vosotros**
We got as bored as you did

14 **Todavía/aún tengo dos**
I've still got two

Todavía/aún no han llegado
They haven't arrived yet

Mejor aún/todavía
Even better

15 **Ya lo he hecho**
I've done it already

Grammar

PREPOSITIONS

256

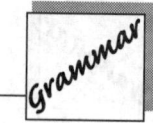

On the following pages you will find some of the most frequent uses of prepositions in Spanish. Particular attention is paid to cases where usage differs markedly from English. It is often difficult to give an English equivalent for Spanish prepositions, since usage *does* vary so much between the two languages. In the list below, the broad meaning of the preposition is given on the left, with examples of usage following. Prepositions are dealt with in alphabetical order, except **a**, **de**, **en** and **por** which are shown first.

a

at	**echar algo a algn**	*to throw sth at sb*
	a 50 pesetas el kilo	*(at) 50 pesetas a kilo*
	a 100 km por hora	*at 100 km per hour*
	sentarse a la mesa	*to sit down at the table*
in	**al sol**	*in the sun*
	a la sombra	*in the shade*
onto	**cayeron al suelo**	*they fell onto the floor*
	pegar una foto al álbum	*to stick a photo into the album*
to	**ir al cine**	*to go to the cinema*
	dar algo a algn	*to give sth to sb*
	venir a hacer	*to come to do*
from	**quitarle algo a algn**	*to take sth from sb*
	robarle algo a algn	*to steal sth from sb*
	arrebatarle algo a algn	*to snatch sth from sb*
	comprarle algo a algn	*to buy sth from/for sb**
	esconderle algo a algn	*to hide sth from sb*
means	**a mano**	*by hand*
	a caballo	*on horseback* (but note other forms of transport used with **en** and **por**)
	a pie	*on foot*

* The translation here obviously depends on the context.

manner	**a la inglesa**	*in the English manner*
	a pasos lentos	*with slow steps*
	poco a poco	*little by little*
	a ciegas	*blindly*
time, date: *at, on*	**a medianoche**	*at midnight*
	a las dos y cuarto	*at quarter past two*
	a tiempo	*on time*
	a final/fines de mes	*at the end of the month*
	a veces	*at times*
distance	**a 8 km de aquí**	*(at a distance of) 8 kms from here*
	a dos pasos de mi casa	*just a step from my house*
	a lo lejos	*in the distance*
with **el** + infin	**al levantarse**	*on getting up*
	al abrir la puerta	*on opening the door*
after certain adjectives	**dispuesto a todo**	*ready for anything*
	parecido a esto	*similar to this*
	obligado a ello	*obliged to (do) that*
after certain verbs	see p 66	

Personal a

When the direct object of a verb is a person or pet animal, **a** must always be placed immediately before it.

EXAMPLES: **querían mucho a sus hijos**
they loved their children dearly
el niño miraba a su perro con asombro
the boy kept looking at his dog in astonishment

⚠ EXCEPTION: **tener** *to have* — **tienen dos hijos** *they have two children*

de

from	**venir de Londres** **un médico de Valencia** **de la mañana a la noche** **de 10 a 15**	*to come from London* *a doctor from Valencia* *from morning till night* *from 10 to 15*
belonging to, of	**el sombrero de mi padre** **las lluvias de abril**	*my father's hat* *April showers*
contents, composition, material	**una caja de cerillas** **una taza de té** **un vestido de seda**	*a box of matches* *a cup of tea; a tea-cup* *a silk dress*
destined for	**una silla de cocina** **un traje de noche**	*a kitchen chair* *an evening dress*
descriptive	**la mujer del sombrero verde** **el vecino de al lad/lado**	*the woman with the green hat* *the next door neighbour*
manner	**de manera irregular** **de una puñalada**	*in an irregular way* *by stabbing*
quality	**una mujer de edad** **objetos de valor**	*an aged lady* *valuable items*
comparative + number	**había más/menos de 100 personas**	*there were more/fewer than 100 people*
after superlatives: *in*	**la ciudad más/menos bonita del mundo**	*the most/least beautiful city in the world*
after certain adjectives	**contento de ver** **fácil/difícil de entender** **capaz de hacer**	*pleased to see* *easy/difficult to understand* *capable of doing*
after certain verbs	see p 66	

en

in, at	**en el campo**	*in the country*
	en Londres	*in London*
	en la cama	*in bed*
	con un libro en la mano	*with a book in his hand*
	en voz baja	*in a low voice*
	en la escuela	*in/at school*
into	**entra en la casa**	*go into the house*
	metió la mano en su bolso	*she put her hand into her handbag*
on	**un cuadro en la pared**	*a picture on the wall*
	sentado en una silla	*sitting on a chair*
	en la planta baja	*on the ground floor*
time, dates, months: *at, in*	**en este momento**	*at this moment*
	en 1994	*in 1994*
	en enero	*in January*
transport: *by*	**en coche**	*by car*
	en avión	*by plane*
	en tren	*by train* (but see also **por**)
language	**en español**	*in Spanish*
duration	**lo haré en una semana**	*I'll do it in one week*
after certain adjectives	**es muy buena/mala en geografía**	*she is very good/bad at geography*
	fueron los primeros/ últimos/únicos en + infin	*they were the first/ last/only ones* + infin
after certain verbs	see p 66	

por

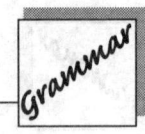

motion: *along, through, around*	**vaya por ese camino** **por el túnel** **pasear por el campo**	*go along that path* *through the tunnel* *to walk around the countryside*
vague location	**tiene que estar por aquí** **le busqué por todas partes**	*it's got to be somewhere around here* *I looked for him everywhere*
vague time	**por la tarde** **por aquellos días**	*in the afternoon* *in those days*
rate	**90 km por hora** **un cinco por ciento** **ganaron por 3 a 0**	*90 km per hour* *five per cent* *they won by 3 to 0*
agent of passive: *by*	**descubierto por unos niños** **odiado por sus enemigos**	*discovered by some children* *hated by his enemies*
by (means of)	**por barco** **por tren** **por correo aéreo** **llamar por teléfono**	*by boat* *by train (freight)* *by airmail* *to telephone*
cause, reason: *for, because*	**¿por qué?** **por todo eso** **por lo que he oído**	*why?, for what reason?* *because of all that* *judging by what I've heard*
+ infinitive: *to*	**libros por leer** **cuentas por pagar**	*books to be read* *bills to be paid*
equivalence	**¿me tienes por tonto?**	*do you think I'm stupid?*

+ adjective/ + adverb + **que**: *however*	**por buenos que sean**	*however good they are*
	por mucho que lo quieras	*however much you want it*
for	**¿cuanto me darán por este libro?**	*how much will they give me for this book?*
	te lo cambio por éste	*I'll swap you this one for it*
	no siento nada por ti	*I feel nothing for you*
	si no fuera por ti	*if it weren't for you*
	¡Por Dios!	*For God's sake!*
for the benefit of	**lo hago por ellos**	*I do it for their benefit*
on behalf of	**firma por mí**	*sign on my behalf*

por also combines with other prepositions to form double prepositions usually conveying the idea of movement. The commonest of these are:

over	**saltó por encima de la mesa**	*she jumped over the table*
under	**nadamos por debajo del puente**	*we swam under the bridge*
past	**pasaron por delante de Correos**	*they went past the post office*
behind	**por detrás de la puerta**	*behind the door*
through	**la luz entraba por entre las cortinas**	*light was coming in through the curtains*
+ donde	**¿por dónde has venido?**	*which way did you come?*

ante

faced with, before	**lo hicieron ante mis propios ojos**	*they did it before my very eyes*
	ante eso no se puede hacer nada	*one can't do anything when faced with that*
preference	**la salud ante todo**	*health above all things*

antes de

before (time)	**antes de las 5**	*before 5 o'clock*

bajo/debajo de

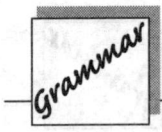

These are usually equivalent, although **bajo** is used more frequently in a figurative sense and with temperatures.

under	**bajo/debajo de la cama**	*under the bed*
	bajo el dominio romano	*under Roman rule*
below	**un grado bajo cero**	*one degree below zero*

con

with	**vino con su amigo**	*she came with her friend*
after certain adjectives	**enfadado con ellos**	*angry with them*
	magnánimo con sus súbditos	*magnanimous with his subjects*

contra

against	**no tengo nada contra ti**	*I've nothing against you*
	apoyado contra la pared	*leaning against the wall*

delante de

in front of	**iba delante de mí**	*she was walking in front of me*

desde

from	**desde aquí se puede ver**	*you can see it from here*
	llamaban desde España	*they were phoning from Spain*
	desde otro punto de vista	*from a different point of view*
	desde la 1 hasta las 6	*from 1 till 6*
	desde entonces	*from then onwards*
since	**desde que volvieron**	*since they returned*
for	**viven en esa casa desde hace 3 años**	*they've been living in that house for 3 years* ⚠ (NOTE TENSE)

detrás de

behind	**están detrás de la puerta**	*they are behind the door*

durante

during	**durante la guerra**	*during the war*
for	**anduvieron durante 3 días**	*they walked for 3 days*

entre

between	**entre 8 y 10**	*between 8 and 10*
among	**María y Elena, entre otras**	*Maria and Elena, among others*
reciprocal	**ayudarse entre sí**	*to help each other*

excepto

except (for)	**todos excepto tú**	*everybody except you*

hacia

towards	**van hacia ese edificio**	*they're going towards that building*
around (time)	**hacia las 3** **hacia fines de enero**	*at around 3 (o'clock)* *around the end of January*

Hacia can also combine with some adverbs to convey a sense of motion in a particular direction:

hacia arriba	*upwards*
hacia abajo	*downwards*
hacia adelante	*forwards*
hacia atrás	*backwards*
hacia adentro	*inwards*
hacia afuera	*outwards*

hasta

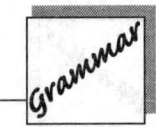

until	**hasta la noche**	*until night*
as far as	**viajaron hasta Sevilla**	*they travelled as far as Seville*
up to	**conté hasta 300 ovejas**	*I counted up to 300 lambs*
	hasta ahora no los había visto	*up to now I hadn't seen them*
even	**hasta un tonto lo entendería**	*even an imbecile would understand that*

para

for	**es para ti**	*it's for you*
	es para mañana	*it's for tomorrow*
	una habitación para dos noches	*a room for two nights*
	para ser un niño, lo hace muy bien	*for a child he is very good at it*
	salen para Cádiz	*they are leaving for Cádiz*
	se conserva muy bien para sus años	*he keeps very well for his age*
+ infin: *(in order) to*	**es demasiado torpe para comprenderlo**	*he's too stupid to understand*
+ **sí**: *to oneself*	**hablar para sí**	*to talk to oneself*
	reír para sí	*to laugh to oneself*
with time	**todavía tengo para 1 hora**	*I'll be another hour (at it) yet*

salvo

except (for)	**todos salvo él**	*all except him*
	salvo cuando llueve	*except when it's raining*
barring	**salvo imprevistos**	*barring the unexpected*
	salvo contraorden	*unless you hear to the contrary*

según

according to	**según su consejo**	*according to her advice*
	según lo que me dijiste	*according to what you told me*

sin

without	**sin agua/dinero**	*without water/money*
	sin mi marido	*without my husband*
+ infinitive	**sin contar a los otros**	*without counting the others*

sobre

on	**sobre la cama**	*on the bed*
	sobre el armario	*on (top of) the wardrobe*
on (to)	**póngalo sobre la mesa**	*put it on the table*
about, on	**un libro sobre Eva Perón**	*a book about Eva Perón*
above, over	**volábamos sobre el mar**	*we were flying over the sea*
	la nube sobre aquella montaña	*the cloud above that mountain*
approximately	**vendré sobre las 4**	*I'll come about 4 o'clock*
about	**Madrid tiene sobre 4 millones de habitantes**	*Madrid has about 4 million inhabitants*

tras

behind	**está tras el asiento**	*it's behind the seat*
after	**uno tras otro**	*one after another*
	día tras día	*day after day*
	corrieron tras el ladrón	*they ran after the thief*

❐ Conjunctions

There are conjunctions which introduce a main clause, such as **y** *and,* **pero** *but,* **si** *if,* **o** *or* etc, and those which introduce subordinate clauses like **porque** *because,* **mientras que** *while,* **después de que** *after* etc. They are used in much the same way as in English, but the following points are of note:

◆ Some conjunctions in Spanish require a following subjunctive, see pp 60 to 63.

◆ Some conjunctions are 'split' in Spanish like *both ... and, either ... or* in English:

tanto ... como	*both ... and*	→ 1
ni ... ni	*neither ... nor*	→ 2
o (bien) ... o (bien)	*either ... or (else)*	→ 3
sea ... sea	*either ... or, whether ... or*	→ 4

◆ **y**

— Before words beginning with **i-** or **hi-** + consonant it becomes **e** → 5

◆ **o**

— Before words beginning with **o-** or **ho-** it becomes **u** → 6
— Between numerals it becomes **ó** → 7

◆ **que**

— meaning *that* → 8
— in comparisons, meaning *than* → 9
— followed by the subjunctive, see p 58.

◆ **porque** (Not to be confused with **por qué** *why*)

— **como** should be used instead at the beginning of a sentence → 10

◆ **pero, sino**

— **pero** normally translates *but* → 11

— **sino** is used when there is a direct contrast after a negative → 12

[1] **Estas flores crecen tanto en verano como en invierno**
These flowers grow in both summer and winter

[2] **Ni él ni ella vinieron**
Neither he nor she came
No tengo ni dinero ni comida
I have neither money nor food

[3] **Debe de ser o ingenua o tonta**
She must be either naïve or stupid
O bien me huyen o bien no me reconocen
Either they're avoiding me or else they don't recognize me

[4] **Sea en verano, sea en invierno, siempre me gusta andar**
I always like walking, whether in summer or in winter

[5] **Diana e Isabel**
Diana and Isabel
madre e hija BUT: **árboles y hierba**
mother and daughter trees and grass

[6] **diez u once** **minutos u horas**
ten or eleven minutes or hours

[7] **37 ó 38**
37 or 38

[8] **Dicen que te han visto**
They say (that) they've seen you
¿Sabías que estábamos allí?
Did you know that we were there?

[9] **Le gustan más que nunca**
He likes them more than ever
María es menos guapa que su hermana
Maria is less attractive than her sister

[10] **Como estaba lloviendo no pudimos salir**
Because/As it was raining we couldn't go out
(Compare with: **No pudimos salir porque estaba lloviendo**)

[11] **Me gustaría ir, pero estoy muy cansada**
I'd like to go, but I am very tired

[12] **No es escocesa sino irlandesa**
She is not Scottish but Irish

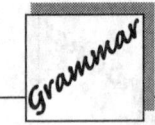

❒ Augmentative, diminutive and pejorative suffixes

These can be used after nouns, adjectives and some adverbs. They are attached to the end of the word after any final vowel has been removed

e.g. **puerta → puertita**
doctor → doctorcito

⚠ NOTE: Further changes sometimes take place (see p 296).

Augmentatives

These are used mainly to imply largeness, but they can also suggest clumsiness, ugliness or grotesqueness. The commonest augmentatives are:

ón/ona → [1]
azo/a → [2]
ote/a → [3]

Diminutives

These are used mainly to suggest smallness or to express a feeling of affection. Occasionally they can be used to express ridicule or contempt. The commonest diminutives are:

ito/a → [4]
(e)cito/a → [5]
(ec)illo/a → [6]
(z)uelo/a → [7]

Pejoratives

These are used to convey the idea that something is unpleasant or to express contempt. The commonest suffixes are:

ucho/a → [8]
acho/a → [9]
uzo/a → [10]
uco/a → [11]
astro/a → [12]

	ORIGINAL WORD	DERIVED FORM
1	**un hombre** a man	**un hombrón** a big man
2	**bueno** good	**buenazo** (person) easily imposed on
	un perro a dog	**un perrazo** a really big dog
	gripe flu	**un gripazo** a really bad bout of flu
3	**grande** big	**grandote** huge
	palabra word	**palabrota** swear word
	amigo friend	**amigote** old pal
4	**una casa** a house	**una casita** a cottage
	un poco a little	**un poquito** a little bit
	un rato a while	**un ratito** a little while
	mi hija my daughter	**mi hijita** my dear sweet daughter
	despacio slowly	**despacito** nice and slowly
5	**un viejo** an old man	**un viejecito** a little old man
	un pueblo a village	**un pueblecito** a small village
	una voz a voice	**una vocecita** a sweet little voice
6	**una ventana** a window	**una ventanilla** a small window (car, train etc)
	un chico a boy	**un chiquillo** a small boy
	una campana a bell	**una campanilla** a small bell
	un palo a stick	**un palillo** a toothpick
	un médico a doctor	**un mediquillo** a quack (doctor)
7	**los pollos** the chickens	**los polluelos** the little chicks
	hoyos hollows	**hoyuelos** dimples
	un ladrón a thief	**un ladronzuelo** a petty thief
	una mujer a woman	**una mujerzuela** a whore
8	**un animal** an animal	**un animalucho** a wretched animal
	un cuarto a room	**un cuartucho** a poky little room
	una casa a house	**una casucha** a shack
9	**rico** rich	**ricacho** nouveau riche
10	**gente** people	**gentuza** scum
11	**una ventana** a window	**un ventanuco** a miserable little window
12	**un político** a politician	**un politicastro** a third-rate politician

SENTENCE STRUCTURE

❒ Word order

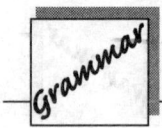

Word order in Spanish is much more flexible than in English. You can often find the subject placed after the verb or the object before the verb, either for emphasis or for stylistic reasons → [1]

There are some cases, however, where the order is always different from English. Most of these have already been dealt with under the appropriate part of speech, but are summarized here along with other instances not covered elsewhere.

- Object pronouns nearly always come before the verb → [2]
  For details, see pp 228 to 231.
- Qualifying adjectives nearly always come after the noun → [3]
  For details, see p 224.
- Following direct speech the subject always follows the verb → [4]

For word order in negative sentences, see p 272.

For word order in interrogative sentences, see p 276.

Examples

1 **Ese libro te lo di yo**
I gave you that book
No nos vio nadie
Nobody saw us

2 **Ya los veo**
I can see them now
Me lo dieron ayer
They gave it to me yesterday

3 **una ciudad española**
a Spanish town
vino tinto
red wine

4 **– Pienso que sí – dijo María**
'I think so,' said Maria
– No importa – replicó Daniel
'It doesn't matter,' Daniel replied

❐ Negatives

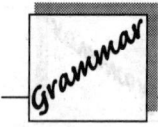

A sentence is made negative by adding **no** between the subject and the verb (and any preceding object pronouns) → [1]

There are, however, some points to note:

— in phrases like *not her, not now,* etc the Spanish **no** usually comes after the word it qualifies → [2]

— with verbs of saying, hoping, thinking etc *not* is translated by **que no** → [3]

Double negatives

no ... nada	*nothing*	*(not ... anything)*
no ... nadie	*nobody*	*(not ... anybody)*
no ... más	*no longer*	*(not ... any more)*
no ... nunca	*never*	*(not ... ever)*
no ... jamás	*never* (stronger)	*(not ... ever)*
no ... más que	*only*	*(not ... more than)*
no ... ningún(o)(a)	*no*	*(not any)*
no ... tampoco	*not ... either*	
no ... ni ... ni	*neither ... nor*	
no ... ni siquiera	*not even*	

Word order

- **No** precedes the verb (and any object pronouns) in both simple and compound tenses, and the second element follows the verb → [4]

- Sometimes the above negatives are placed before the verb (with the exception of **más** and **más que**), and **no** is then dropped → [5]

- For use of **nada, nadie** and **ninguno** as pronouns, see p 236.

Examples

	AFFIRMATIVE		NEGATIVE
1	**El coche es suyo**	→	**El coche no es suyo**
	The car is his		The car is not his
	Yo me lo pondré	→	**Yo no me lo pondré**
	I will put it on		I will not put it on

2 **¿Quién lo ha hecho? – Ella no**
Who did it? – Not her
¿Quieres un cigarrillo? – Ahora no
Do you want a cigarette? – Not now
Dame ese libro, el que está a tu lado no, el otro
Give me that book, not the one near you, the other one

3 **Opino que no** — **Dijeron que no**
I think not — They said not

4 **No dicen nada**
They don't say anything
No han visto a nadie
They haven't seen anybody
No me veréis más
You won't see me any more
No te olvidaré nunca/jamás
I'll never forget you
No habían recorrido más que 40 kms cuando ...
They hadn't travelled more than 40 kms when ...
No se me ha ocurrido ninguna idea
I haven't had any ideas
No les estaban esperando ni mi hijo ni mi hija
Neither my son nor my daughter were waiting for them
No ha venido ni siquiera Juan
Even John hasn't come

5 **Nadie ha venido hoy**
Nobody came today
Nunca me han gustado
I've never liked them
Ni mi hermano ni mi hermana fuman
Neither my brother nor my sister smokes

❐ Negatives (Continued)

Negatives in short replies

- **No**, *no* is the usual negative response to a question → [1]

⚠ NOTE: It is often translated as *not* → [2]
(see also p 272).

- Nearly all the other negatives listed on p 272 may be used without a verb in a short reply → [3]

Combinations of negatives

These are the most common combinations of negative particles:

no ... nunca más	→ [4]
no ... nunca a nadie	→ [5]
no ... nunca nada/nada nunca	→ [6]
no ... nunca más que	→ [7]
no ... ni ... nunca	→ [8]

1 **¿Quieres venir con nosotros? – No**
Do you want to come with us? – No

2 **¿Vienes o no?**
Are you coming or not?

3 **¿Ha venido alguien? – ¡Nadie!**
Has anyone come? – Nobody!
¿Has ido al Japón alguna vez? – Nunca
Have you ever been to Japan? – Never

4 **No lo haré nunca más**
I'll never do it again

5 **No se ve nunca a nadie por allí**
You never see anybody around there

6 **No cambiaron nada nunca**
They never changed anything

7 **No he hablado nunca más que con su mujer**
I've only ever spoken to his wife

8 **No me ha escrito ni llamado por teléfono nunca**
He/she has never written to me or phoned me

❒ Question forms

Direct

There are two ways of forming direct questions in Spanish:

- by inverting the normal word order so that
  subject + verb → *verb + subject* → [1]

- by maintaining the word order *subject + verb*, but by using a rising intonation at the end of the sentence → [2]

⚠ NOTE: In compound tenses the auxiliary may never be separated from the past participle, as happens in English → [3]

Indirect

An indirect question is one that is 'reported', e.g. he asked me *what the time was*, tell me *which way to go*. Word order in indirect questions can adopt one of the two following patterns:

- interrogative word + subject + verb → [4]

- interrogative word + verb + subject → [5]

¿verdad?, ¿no?

These are used wherever English would use *isn't it?, don't they?, weren't we?, is it?* etc tagged on to the end of a sentence → [6]

sí

Sí is the word for *yes* in answer to a question put either in the affirmative or in the negative → [7]

Examples

1 **¿Vendrá tu madre?**
Will your mother come?
¿Es posible eso?
Is it possible?
¿Lo trajo Vd?
Did you bring it?
¿Cuándo volverán Vds?
When will you come back?

2 **El gato, ¿se bebió toda la leche?**
Did the cat drink up all his milk?
Andrés, ¿va a venir?
Is Andrew coming?

3 **¿Lo ha terminado Vd?**
Have you finished it?
¿Había llegado tu amigo?
Had your friend arrived?

4 **Dime qué autobuses pasan por aquí**
Tell me which buses come this way
No sé cuántas personas vendrán
I don't know how many people will turn up

5 **Me preguntó dónde trabajaba mi hermano**
He asked me where my brother worked
No sabemos a qué hora empieza la película
We don't know what time the film starts

6 **Hace calor, ¿verdad?**
It's warm, isn't it?
No se olvidará Vd, ¿verdad?
You won't forget, will you?
Estaréis cansados, ¿no?
You will be tired, won't you?
Te lo dijo María, ¿no?
Maria told you, didn't she?

7 **¿Lo has hecho? – Sí**
Have you done it? – Yes (I have)
¿No lo has hecho? – Sí
Haven't you done it? – Yes (I have)

TRANSLATION PROBLEMS

Beware of translating word by word. While on occasions this is quite possible, quite often it is not. The need for caution is illustrated by the following:

- English phrasal verbs (i.e. verbs followed by a preposition), e.g. *to run away, to fall down*, are often translated by one word in Spanish → [1]
- English verbal constructions often contain a preposition where none exists in Spanish, or vice versa → [2]
- Two or more prepositions in English may have a single rendering in Spanish → [3]
- A word which is singular in English may be plural in Spanish, or vice versa → [4]
- Spanish has no equivalent of the possessive construction denoted by ...'s/...s' → [5]

❒ Specific problems

-ing

This is translated in a variety of ways in Spanish:

- *to be ... -ing* can sometimes be translated by a simple tense (see also pp 54 to 56) → [6]

  But, when a physical position is denoted, a past participle is used → [7]

- in the construction *to see/hear sb ... -ing*, use an infinitive → [8] *-ing* can also be translated by:
  - — an infinitive → [9]
    (see p 46)
  - — a perfect infinitive → [10]
    (see p 50)
  - — a gerund → [11]
    (see p 52)
  - — a noun → [12]

1	**huir** to run away	**caerse** to fall down	**ceder** to give in
2	**pagar** to pay for	**mirar** to look at	**escuchar** to listen to
	encontrarse con to meet	**fijarse en** to notice	**servirse de** to use
3	**extrañarse de** to be surprised at	**harto de** fed up with	
	soñar con to dream of	**contar con** to count on	
4	**unas vacaciones** a holiday	**sus cabellos** his/her hair	
	la gente people	**mi pantalón** my trousers	

5	**el coche de mi hermano** my brother's car *(literally: ... of my brother)*	**el cuarto de las niñas** the children's bedroom *(literally: ... of the children)*
6	**Se va mañana** He/she is leaving tomorrow	**¿Qué haces?** What are you doing?
7	**Está sentado ahí** He is sitting over there	**Estaba tendida en el suelo** She was lying on the ground
8	**Les veo venir** I can see them coming	**La he oído cantar** I've heard her singing
9	**Me gusta ir al cine** I like going to the cinema	**¡Deja de hablar!** Stop talking!
	En vez de contestar Instead of answering	**Antes de salir** Before leaving
10	**Después de haber abierto la caja, María ...** After opening the box, Maria ...	
11	**Pasamos la tarde fumando y charlando** We spent the afternoon smoking and chatting	
12	**El esquí me mantiene en forma** Skiing keeps me fit	

TRANSLATION PROBLEMS

to be

(See also **Verbal Idioms**, pp 74 to 76)

- In set expressions, describing physical and emotional conditions, **tener** is used:

tener calor/frío	*to be warm/cold*
tener hambre/sed	*to be hungry/thirsty*
tener miedo	*to be afraid*
tener razón	*to be right*

- Describing the weather, e.g. *what's the weather like?, it's windy/sunny,* use **hacer** → [1]

- For ages, e.g. *he is 6,* use **tener** (see also p 306) → [2]

there is/there are

- Both are translated by **hay** → [3]

can, be able

- Physical ability is expressed by **poder** → [4]

- If the meaning is *to know how to,* use **saber** → [5]

- *Can* + a 'verb of hearing or seeing etc' in English is not translated in Spanish → [6]

to

- Generally translated by **a** → [7]
- In time expressions, e.g. *10 to 6,* use **menos** → [8]
- When the meaning is *in order to,* use **para** → [9]
- Following a verb, as in *to try to do, to like to do,* see pp 46 and 48.
- *easy/difficult/impossible* etc *to do* are translated by **fácil/difícil/imposible** etc **de hacer** → [10]

Examples

1	**¿Qué tiempo hace?** What's the weather like?	**Hace bueno/malo/viento** It's lovely/miserable/windy
2	**¿Cuántos años tienes?** How old are you?	**Tengo quince (años)** I'm fifteen
3	**Hay un señor en la puerta** There's a gentleman at the door **Hay cinco libros en la mesa** There are five books on the table	
4	**No puedo salir contigo** I can't go out with you	
5	**¿Sabes nadar?** Can you swim?	
6	**No veo nada** I can't see anything	**¿Es que no me oyes?** Can't you hear me?
7	**Dale el libro a Isabel** Give the book to Isabel	
8	**las diez menos cinco** five to ten	**a las siete menos cuarto** at a quarter to seven
9	**Lo hice para ayudaros** I did it to help you **Se inclinó para atarse el cordón de zapato** He bent down to tie his shoe-lace	
10	**Este libro es fácil/difícil de leer** This book is easy/difficult to read	

Grammar

TRANSLATION PROBLEMS

must

- When *must* expresses an assumption, **deber de** is often used → [1]

  ⚠ NOTE: This meaning is also often expressed by **deber** directly followed by the infinitive → [2]

- When it expresses obligation, there are three possible translations:
  - — **tener que** → [3]
  - — **deber** → [4]
  - — **hay que** (impersonal) → [5]

may

- If *may* expresses possibility, it can be translated by:
  - — **poder**
  - — **puede (ser) que** + subjunctive } → [6]

- To express permission, use **poder** → [7]

will

- If *will* expresses willingness or desire rather than the future, the present tense of **querer** is used → [8]

would

- If *would* expresses willingness, use the preterite or imperfect of **querer** → [9]

- When a repeated or habitual action in the past is referred to, use
  - — the imperfect → [10]
  - — the imperfect of **soler** + infinitive → [11]

Examples

1 **Ha debido de mentir**
He must have lied
Debe de gustarle
She must like it

2 **Debe estar por aquí cerca**
It must be near here
Debo haberlo dejado en el tren
I must have left it on the train

3 **Tenemos que salir temprano mañana**
We must leave early tomorrow
Tengo que irme
I must go

4 **Debo visitarles**
I must visit them
Debéis escuchar lo que se os dice
You must listen to what is said to you

5 **Hay que entrar por ese lado**
One (We *etc*) must get in that way

6 **Todavía puede cambiar de opinión**
He may still change his mind
Creo que puede llover esta tarde
I think it may rain this afternoon
Puede (ser) que no lo sepa
She may not know

7 **¿Puedo irme?**
May I go?
Puede sentarse
You may sit down

8 **Quiere Vd esperar un momento, por favor?**
Will you wait a moment, please?
No quiere ayudarme
He won't help me

9 **No quisieron venir**
They wouldn't come

10 **Las miraba hora tras hora**
She would watch them for hours on end

11 **Últimamente solía comer muy poco**
Latterly he would eat very little

❒ Pronunciation of Vowels

Spanish vowels are always clearly pronounced and not relaxed in unstressed syllables as happens in English.

	EXAMPLES	HINTS ON PRONUNCIATION
[a]	c**a**sa	Between English *a* as in *hat* and *u* as in *hut*
[e]	p**e**nsar	Similar to English *e* in *pet*
[i]	f**i**lo	Between English *i* as in *pin* and *ee* as in *been*
[o]	l**o**c**o**	Similar to English *o* in *hot*
[u]	l**u**na	Between English *ew* as in *few* and *u* as in *put*

❒ Pronunciation of Diphthongs

All these diphthongs are shorter than similar English diphthongs.

[ai]	b**ai**le, h**ay**	Like *i* in *side*
[au]	c**au**sa	Like *ou* in *sound*
[ei]	p**ei**ne, r**ey**	Like *ey* in *grey*
[eu]	d**eu**da	Like the vowel sounds in English *may you*, but without the sound of the *y*
[oi]	b**oi**na, v**oy**	Like *oy* in *boy*

❒ Semi-consonants

[j]	hac**i**a, **y**a t**i**ene, **y**eso lab**i**o, **y**o	**i** following a consonant and preceding a vowel, and **y** preceding a vowel are pronounced as *y* in English *yet*
[w]	ag**u**a, b**u**eno ard**u**o, r**u**ido	**u** following a consonant and preceding a vowel is pronounced as *w* in English *walk*

⚠ EXCEPTIONS: **gue, gui** (see p 286)

❐ Pronunciation of Consonants

Some consonants are pronounced almost exactly as in English: [l, m, n, f, k, and in some cases g].

Others, listed below, are similar to English, but differences should be noted.

	EXAMPLES	
[p]	**p**adre	They are not aspirated, unlike English *p*ot, *c*ook and *t*en.
[k]	**c**o**c**o	
[t]	**t**an	
[t]	**t**odo, **t**ú	Pronounced with the tip of the tongue touching the upper front teeth and not the roof of the mouth as in English.
[d]	**d**oy, bal**d**e	

The following consonants are not heard in English:

	EXAMPLES	
[β]	la**b**io	This is pronounced between upper and lower lips, which do not touch, unlike English *b* as in *b*end.
[ɣo]	ha**g**a	Similar to English *g* as in *g*ate, but tongue does not touch the soft palate.
[ɲ]	a**ñ**o	Similar to *ni* in o*ni*on
[x]	**j**ota	Like the guttural *ch* in lo*ch*
[r]	pe**r**a	A single trill with the tip of the tongue against the teeth ridge.
[rr]	**r**ojo, pe**rr**o	A multiple trill with the tip of the tongue against the teeth ridge.

❒ From spelling to sounds

Note the pronunciation of the following (groups of) letters.

LETTER	PRONOUNCED	
b, v	[b]	These letters have the same value. At the start of a breath group, and after written **m** and **n**, the sound is similar to English *b*oy → [1]
	[β]	in all other positions, the sound is unknown in English (see p 285) → [2]
c	[k]	Before **a, o, u** or a consonant, like English *k*eep, but not aspirated → [3]
	[θ/s]	Before **e, i** like English *th*in, or, in Latin America and parts of Spain, like English *s*ame → [4]
ch	[tʃ]	Like English *ch*urch → [5]
d	[d]	At the start of the breath group and after **l** or **n**, it is pronounced similar to English *d*eep (see p 285) → [6]
	[ð]	Between vowels and after consonants (except **l** or **n**), it is pronounced very like English *th*ough → [7]
	[(ð)]	At the end of words, and in the verb ending **-ado**, it is often not pronounced → [8]
g	[x]	Before **e, i,** pronounced gutturally, similar to English lo*ch* → [9]
	[g]	At the start of the breath group and after **n,** it is pronounced like English *g*et → [10]
	[ɣ]	In other positions the sound is unknown in English → [11]
gue	[ge/ɣe]	The **u** is silent → [12]
gui	[gi/ɣi]	
güe	[gwe/ɣwe]	The **u** is pronounced like English
güi	[gwi/ɣwi]	*w*alk → [13]

Examples

1	**bomba** ['bomba]	**voy** [boi]	**vicio** ['biθjo]
2	**hubo** ['uβo]	**de veras** [de 'βeras]	**lavar** [la'βar]
3	**casa** ['kasa]	**coco** ['koko]	**cumbre** ['kumbre]
4	**cero** ['θero/'sero]	**cinco** ['θiŋko/'siŋko]	
5	**mucho** ['mutʃo]	**chuchería** [tʃutʃe'ria]	
6	**doy** [doi]	**balde** ['balde]	**bondad** [bon'dað]
7	**modo** ['moðo]	**ideal** [iðe'al]	
8	**Madrid** [ma'ðri(ð)]	**comprado** [kom'pra(ð)o]	
9	**gente** ['xente]	**giro** ['xiro]	**general** [xene'ral]
10	**ganar** [ga'nar]	**pongo** ['poŋgo]	
11	**agua** ['aɣwa]	**agrícola** [a'ɣrikola]	
12	**guija** ['gixa]	**guerra** ['gerra]	**pague** ['paɣe]
13	**agüero** [a 'ɣwero]	**argüir** [ar'ɣwir]	

❐ From spelling to sounds (Continued)

h	[-]	This is always silent → [1]
j	[x]	Like the guttural sound in English lo*ch*, but often aspirated at the end of a word → [2]
ll	[ʎ]	Similar to English *-ll-* in mi*ll*ion → [3]
	[j/ʒ]	In some parts of Spain and in Latin America, like English *y*et or plea*s*ure → [4]
-nv-	[mb]	This combination of letters is pronounced as in English *imb*ibe → [5]
ñ	[ɲ]	As in English on*i*on → [6]
q	[k]	Always followed by silent letter **u**, and pronounced as in English *k*eep, but not aspirated → [7]
s	[s]	Except where mentioned below, like English *s*ing → [8]
	[z]	When followed by **b**, **d**, **g**, **l**, **m**, **n** like English *z*oo → [9]
w	[w]	Like English *v*, *w* → [10]
x	[ks]	Between vowels, often like English e*x*it → [11]
	[s]	Before a consonant, and, increasingly, even between vowels, like English *s*end → [12]
y	[j]	Like English *y*es → [13]
	[ʒ]	In some parts of Latin America, like English lei*s*ure → [14]
z	[θ]	Like English *th*in → [15]
	[s]	In some parts of Spain and in Latin America, like English *s*end → [16]

1	**hombre** ['ombre]	**hoja** ['oxa]	**ahorrar** [ao'rrar]
2	**jota** ['xota]	**tejer** [te'xer]	**reloj** [re'lo(h)]
3	**calle** ['kaʎe]	**llamar** [ʎa'mar]	
4	**pillar** [pi'jar/pi'ʒar]	**olla** ['oja/'oʒa]	
5	**enviar** [em'bjar]	**sin valor** ['sim ba'lor]	
6	**uña** ['uɲa]	**bañar** [ba'ɲar]	
7	**aquel** [a'kel]	**querer** [ke'rer]	
8	**está** [es'ta]	**serio** ['serjo]	
9	**desde** ['dezðe]	**mismo** ['mizmo]	**asno** ['azno]
10	**wáter** ['bater]	**Walkman®** [wak'man]	
11	**éxito** ['eksito]	**máximo** ['maksimo]	
12	**extra** ['estra]	**sexto** ['sesto]	
13	**yo** [jo]	**yedra** ['jeðra]	
14	**yeso** ['ʒeso]	**yerno** ['ʒerno]	
15	**zapato** [θa'pato]	**zona** ['θona]	**luz** [luθ]
16	**zaguán** [sa'ɣwan]	**zueco** ['sweko]	**pez** [pes]

❒ Normal Word Stress

There are simple rules to establish which syllable in a Spanish word is stressed. When an exception to these rules occurs an acute accent (stress-mark) is needed (see p 292). These rules are as follows:

— words ending in a vowel or combination of vowels, or with the consonants **-s** or **-n** are stressed on the next to last syllable. The great majority of Spanish words fall into this category → [1]

— words ending in a consonant other than **-s** or **-n** bear the stress on the last syllable → [2]

— a minority of words bear the stress on the second to last syllable, and these always need an accent → [3]

— some nouns change their stress from singular to plural → [4]

❒ Stress in diphthongs

In the case of diphthongs there are rules to establish which of the vowels is stressed (see p 284 for pronunciation). These rules are as follows:

— diphthongs formed by the combination of a 'weak' vowel (**i**, **u**) and a 'strong' vowel (**a**, **e** or **o**) bear the stress on the strong vowel → [5]

— diphthongs formed by the combination of two 'weak' vowels bear the stress on the second vowel → [6]

⚠ NOTE: Two 'strong' vowels don't form a diphthong but are pronounced as two separate vowels. In these cases stress follows the normal rules → [7]

1	**ca**_sa_ house	**ca**_sas_ houses
	co_rre_ he runs	**co**_rren_ they run
	_pa_**la**_bra_ word	_pa_**la**_bras_ words
	cri_sis_ crisis	**cri**_sis_ crises
2	_re_**loj** watch	
	ver**dad** truth	
	bati**dor** beater	
3	_mur_**cié**_lago_ bat	
	pá_jaro_ bird	
4	_ca_**rác**_ter_ character	_carac_**te**_res_ characters
	ré_gimen_ regime	_re_**gí**_menes_ regimes
5	**bai**_le_ dance	
	boi_na_ beret	**pei**_ne_ comb
	cau_sa_ cause	**rei**_na_ queen
6	_fu_**i** I went	_vi_**u**_do_ widower
7	_me ma_**re**_o_ I feel dizzy	_ca_**er** to fall
	ca_os_ chaos	_co_**rre**_a_ leash

❐ The acute accent (´)

This is used in writing to show that a word is stressed contrary to the normal rules for stress (see p 290) → [1]

The following points should be noted:

- The same syllable is stressed in the plural form of adjectives and nouns as in the singular. To show this, it is necessary to
  - — add an accent in the case of unaccented nouns and adjectives ending in **-n** → [2]
  - — drop the accent from nouns and adjectives ending in **-n** or **-s** which have an accent on the last syllable → [3]

- The feminine form of accented nouns or adjectives does not have an accent → [4]

- When object pronouns are added to certain verb forms an accent is required to show that the syllable stressed in the verb form does not change. These verb forms are:
  - — the gerund → [5]
  - — the infinitive, when followed by two pronouns → [6]
  - — imperative forms, except for the 2nd person plural → [7]

- The absolute superlative forms of adjectives are always accented → [8]

- Accents on adjectives are not affected by the addition of the adverbial suffix **-mente** → [9]

1	**autobús** bus		**revolución** revolution
	relámpago lightning		**árboles** trees
2	**orden** order	→	**órdenes** orders
	examen examination	→	**exámenes** examinations
	joven young	→	**jóvenes** young
3	**revolución** revolution	→	**revoluciones** revolutions
	autobús bus	→	**autobuses** buses
	parlanchín chatty	→	**parlanchines** chatty
4	**marqués** marquis	→	**marquesa** marchioness
	francés French *(masc)*	→	**francesa** French *(fem)*
5	**comprando** buying	→	**comprándo(se)lo** buying it (for him/her/them)
6	**vender** to sell	→	**vendérselas** to sell them to him/her/them
7	**compra** buy	→	**cómpralo** buy it
	hagan do	→	**háganselo** do it for him/her/them
8	**viejo** old	→	**viejísimo** ancient
	caro expensive	→	**carísimo** very expensive
9	**fácil** easy	→	**fácilmente** easily

❒ The acute accent (Continued)

It is also used to distinguish between the written forms of words which are pronounced the same but have a different meaning or function. These are as follows:

- Possessive adjectives/personal pronouns → 1
- Demonstrative adjectives/demonstrative pronouns → 2
- Interrogative and exclamatory forms of adverbs, pronouns and adjectives → 3

⚠ NOTE: The accent is used in indirect as well as direct questions and exclamations → 4

- The pronoun **él** and the article **el** → 5
- A small group of words which could otherwise be confused. These are:

de	of, from	**dé**	give (pres subj)
mas	but	**más**	more
si	if	**sí**	yes; himself etc → 6
solo/a	alone	**sólo**	only → 7
te	you	**té**	tea

❒ The dieresis (¨)

This is used only in the combinations **güi** or **güe** to show that the **u** is pronounced as a semi-consonant (see p 284) → 8

1 **Han robado mi coche**
They've stolen my car
¿Te gusta tu trabajo?
Do you like your job?

A mí no me vio
He didn't see me
Tú, ¿que opinas?
What do you think?

2 **Me gusta esta casa**
I like this house
¿Ves aquellos edificios?
Can you see those buildings?

Me quedo con ésta
I'll take this one
Aquéllos son más bonitos
Those are prettier

3 **El chico con quien viajé**
The boy I travelled with
Donde quieras
Wherever you want

¿Con quién viajaste?
Who did you travel with?
¿Dónde encontraste eso?
Where did you find that?

4 **¿Cómo se abre?**
How does it open?

No sé cómo se abre
I don't know how it opens

5 **El puerto queda cerca**
The harbour's nearby

Él no quiso hacerlo
HE refused to do it

6 **si no viene**
if he doesn't come

Sí que lo sabe
Yes he DOES know

7 **Vino solo**
He came by himself

Sólo lo sabe él
Only he knows

8 **¡Qué vergüenza!**
How shocking!
En seguida averigüé dónde estaba
I found out straight away where it was

❒ Regular spelling changes

The consonants **c, g** and **z** are modified by the addition of certain verb or plural endings and by some suffixes. Most of the cases where this occurs have already been dealt with under the appropriate part of speech, but are summarized here along with other instances not covered elsewhere.

Verbs

The changes set out below occur so that the consonant of the verb stem is always pronounced the same as in the infinitive. For verbs affected by these changes see the list of verbs on p 81.

INFINITIVE	CHANGE			TENSES AFFECTED
-car	**c + e**	→	**-que**	Present subj, pret → [1]
-cer, -cir	**c + a, o**	→	**-za, -zo**	Present, pres subj → [2]
-gar	**g + e, i**	→	**-gue**	Present subj, pret → [3]
-guar	**gu + e**	→	**-güe**	Present subj, pret → [4]
-ger, -gir	**g + a, o**	→	**-ja, -jo**	Present, pres subj → [5]
-guir	**gu + a, o**	→	**-ga, -go**	Present, pres subj → [6]
-zar	**z + e**	→	**-ce**	Present subj, pret → [7]

Noun and adjective plurals

SINGULAR		PLURAL
vowel + **z**	→	**-ces** → [8]

Nouns and adjectives + suffixes

ENDING	SUFFIX	NEW ENDING
vowel + **z** +	**-cito**	**-cecito** → [9]
-go, -ga +	**-ito, -illo**	**-guito/a, -guillo/a** → [10]
-co, -ca +	**-ito, -illo**	**-quito/a, -quillo/a** → [11]

Adjective absolute superlatives

ENDING	SUPERLATIVE
-co	**-quísimo** → [12]
-go	**-guísimo** → [13]
vowel + **z**	**-císimo** → [14]

1 **Es inútil que lo busques aquí**
It's no good looking for it here
Saqué dos entradas
I got two tickets
2 **Hace falta que venzas tu miedo**
You must overcome your fear
3 **No creo que lleguemos antes**
I don't think we'll be there any sooner
Ya le pagué
I've already paid her
4 **Averigüé dónde estaba la casa**
I found out where the house was
5 **Cojo el autobús, es más barato**
I take the bus, it's cheaper
6 **¿Sigo?**
Shall I go on?
7 **No permiten que se cruce la frontera**
They don't allow people to cross the border
Nunca simpaticé mucho con él
I never got on very well with him

8	**voz → voces**		**luz → luces**	
	voice	voices	light	lights
	veloz → veloces		**capaz → capaces**	
	quick		capable	
9	**luz**	→	**lucecita**	
	light		little light	
10	**amigo**	→	**amiguito**	
	friend		chum	
11	**chico**	→	**chiquillo**	
	boy		little boy	
12	**rico**	→	**riquísimo**	
	rich		extremely rich	
13	**largo**	→	**larguísimo**	
	long		very, very long	
14	**feroz**	→	**ferocísimo**	
	fierce		extremely fierce	

THE ALPHABET

A, a	[a]	**J, j**	['xota]	**R, r**	['erre]
B, b	[be]	**K, k**	[ka]	**S, s**	['ese]
C, c	[θe]	**L, l**	['ele]	**T, t**	[te]
Ch, ch	[tʃe]	**Ll, ll**	['eʎe]	**U, u**	[u]
D, d	[de]	**M, m**	['eme]	**V, v**	['uβe]
E, e	[e]	**N, n**	['ene]	**W, w**	['uβe'doble]
F, f	['efe]	**Ñ, ñ**	['eɲe]	**X, x**	['ekis]
G, g	[xe]	**O, o**	[o]	**Y, y**	[i'ɣrjeɣa]
H, h	['atʃe]	**P, p**	[pe]	**Z, z**	['θeta]
I, i	[i]	**Q, q**	[ku]		

- The letters are feminine and you therefore talk of **una a**, or **la a**.

- Capital letters are used as in English except for the following:

— adjectives of nationality:

e.g. **una ciudad alemana** — a German town; **un autor español** — a Spanish author

— languages:

e.g. **¿Habla Vd inglés?** — Do you speak English? **Hablan español e italiano** — They speak Spanish and Italian

— days of the week:

lunes	Monday
martes	Tuesday
miércoles	Wednesday
jueves	Thursday
viernes	Friday
sábado	Saturday
domingo	Sunday

— months of the year:

enero	January	**julio**	July
febrero	February	**agosto**	August
marzo	March	**se(p)tiembre**	September
abril	April	**octubre**	October
mayo	May	**noviembre**	November
junio	June	**diciembre**	December

299 PUNCTUATION

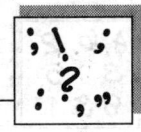

Spanish punctuation differs from English in the following ways:

Question marks

There are inverted question marks and exclamation marks at the beginning of a question or exclamation, as well as upright ones at the end.

Indications of dialogue

Dashes are used to indicate dialogue, and are equivalent to the English inverted commas:

– ¿Vendrás conmigo? – le preguntó María
'Will you come with me?' Maria asked him

⚠ NOTE: When no expression of saying, replying etc follows, only one dash is used at the beginning:

– Sí. 'Yes.'

Letter headings

At the beginning of a letter, a colon is used instead of the English comma:

Querida Cristina: Dear Cristina, **Muy Sr. mío**: Dear Sir,

Punctuation terms in Spanish

.	punto
,	coma
;	punto y coma
:	dos puntos
...	puntos suspensivos
¿ ?	interrogación
¿	se abre interrogación
?	se cierra interrogación
¡ !	admiración
¡	se abre admiración
!	se cierra admiración
" "	comillas (used as '...')
"	se abren comillas
"	se cierran comillas
( )	paréntesis
(	se abre paréntesis
)	se cierra paréntesis
–	guión
punto y aparte	new paragraph
punto final	last full stop

NUMBERS 300

❒ Cardinal numbers *(one, two, three etc)*

cero	0	**setenta**	70
uno (un, una)	1	**ochenta**	80
dos	2	**noventa**	90
tres	3	**cien (ciento)**	100
cuatro	4	**ciento uno(una)**	101
cinco	5	**ciento dos**	102
seis	6	**ciento diez**	110
siete	7	**ciento cuarenta y dos**	142
ocho	8	**doscientos(as)**	200
nueve	9	**doscientos(as) uno(una)**	201
diez	10	**doscientos(as) dos**	202
once	11	**trescientos(as)**	300
doce	12	**cuatrocientos(as)**	400
trece	13	**quinientos(as)**	500
catorce	14	**seiscientos(as)**	600
quince	15	**setecientos(as)**	700
dieciséis	16	**ochocientos(as)**	800
diecisiete	17	**novecientos(as)**	900
dieciocho	18	**mil**	1.000
diecinueve	19	**mil uno(una)**	1.001
veinte	20	**mil dos**	1.002
veintiuno	21	**mil doscientos veinte**	1.220
veintidós	22	**dos mil**	2.000
treinta	30	**cien mil**	100.000
treinta y uno	31	**doscientos(as) mil**	200.000
cuarenta	40	**un millón**	1.000.000
cincuenta	50	**dos millones**	2.000.000
sesenta	60	**un billón**	1.000.000.000.000

❒ Fractions

un medio; medio(a)	½
un tercio	⅓
dos tercios	⅔
un cuarto	¼
tres cuartos	¾
un quinto	⅕
cinco y tres cuartos	5¾

Others

cero coma cinco	0,5
uno coma tres	1,3
(el, un) diez por ciento	10%
dos más/y dos	2 + 2
dos menos dos	2 – 2
dos por dos	2 × 2
dos dividido por dos	2 ÷ 2

❒ Points to note on cardinals

- **uno** drops the **o** before masculine nouns, and the same applies when in compound numerals:

  un libro *1 book,* **treinta y un niños** *31 children*

- 1, 21, 31 etc and 200, 300, 400 etc have feminine forms:

  cuarenta y una pesetas *41 pesetas,* **quinientas libras** *£500*

- **ciento** is used before numbers smaller than 100, otherwise **cien** is used:

  ciento cuatro *104 but* **cien pesetas** *100 pesetas,* **cien mil** *100,000* (see also p 206)

- **millón** takes **de** before a noun:

  un millón de personas *1,000,000 people*

- **mil** is only found in the plural when meaning *thousands of:*

  miles de solicitantes *thousands of applicants*

- cardinals normally precede ordinals:

  los tres primeros pisos *the first three floors*

⚠ NOTE: The full stop is used with numbers over one thousand and the comma with decimals i.e. the opposite of English usage.

❐ Ordinal numbers *(first, second, third etc)*

primero (primer, primera)	1°,1ª	**undécimo(a)**	11°,11ª
segundo(a)	2°,2ª	**duodécimo(a)**	12°,12ª
tercero (tercer, tercera)	3°,3ª	**decimotercer(o)(a)**	13°,13ª
cuarto(a)	4°,4ª	**decimocuarto(a)**	14°,14ª
quinto(a)	5°,5ª	**decimoquinto(a)**	15°,15ª
sexto(a)	6°,6ª	**decimosexto(a)**	16°,16ª
séptimo(a)	7°,7ª	**decimoséptimo(a)**	17°,17ª
octavo(a)	8°,8ª	**decimoctavo(a)**	18°,18ª
noveno(a)	9°,9ª	**decimonoveno(a)**	19°,19ª
décimo(a)	10°,10ª	**vigésimo(a)**	20°,20ª

Points to note on ordinals

- They agree in gender and in number with the noun, which they normally precede, except with royal titles:

  la primera vez — the first time
  Felipe segundo — Philip II

- **primero** and **tercero** drop the **o** before a masculine singular noun:

  el primer premio — the first prize
  el tercer día — the third day

- Beyond **décimo** ordinal numbers are rarely used, and they are replaced by the cardinal number placed immediately after the noun:

  el siglo diecisiete — the seventeenth century
  Alfonso doce — Alfonso XII
  en el piso trece — on the 13th floor

⚠ BUT: **vigésimo(a)** 20th
(but not with royal titles or centuries)
centésimo(a) 100th
milésimo(a) 1,000th
millonésimo(a) 1,000,000th

❒ Numbers: Other Uses

- collective numbers:

un par	2, a couple
una decena (de personas)	about 10 (people)
una docena (de niños)	(about) a dozen (children)
una quincena (de hombres)	about fifteen (men)
una veintena* (de coches)	about twenty (cars)
un centenar, una centena (de casas)	about a hundred (houses)
cientos/centenares de personas	hundreds of people
un millar (de soldados)	about a thousand (soldiers)
miles/millares de moscas	thousands of flies

* 20, 30, 40, 50 can also be converted in the same way.

- measurements:

veinte metros cuadrados	20 square metres
veinte metros cúbicos	20 cubic metres
un puente de cuarenta metros de largo/longitud	a bridge 40 metres long

- distance:

De aquí a Madrid hay 400 km	Madrid is 400 km away
a siete km de aquí	7 km from here

❒ Telephone Numbers

Póngame con Madrid, el cuatro, cincuenta y ocho, veintidós, noventa y tres
I would like Madrid 458 22 93
Me da Valencia, el veinte, cincuenta y uno, setenta y tres
Could you get me Valencia 20 51 73
Extensión tres, tres, cinco/trescientos treinta y cinco
Extension number 335

⚠ NOTE: In Spanish telephone numbers may be read out individually, but more frequently they are broken down into groups of two. They are written in groups of two or three numbers (never four).

TIME 304

❑ The Time

¿Qué hora es? *What time is it?*
Es ... *(1 o'clock, midnight, noon)* } *It's ...*
Son las ... *(other times)* } *It's ...*
Es la una y cuarto *It's 1.15*
Son las diez menos cinco *It's 9.55*

00.00	**medianoche; las doce (de la noche)** *midnight, twelve o'clock*
00.10	**las doce y diez (de la noche)**
00.15	**las doce y cuarto**
00.30	**las doce y media**
00.45	**la una menos cuarto**
01.00	**la una (de la madrugada)** *one a.m., one o'clock in the morning*
01.10	**la una y diez (de la madrugada)**
02.45	**las tres menos cuarto**
07.00	**las siete (de la mañana)**
07.50	**las ocho menos diez**
12.00	**mediodía; las doce (de la mañana)** *noon, twelve o'clock*
13.00	**la una (de la tarde)** *one p.m., one o'clock in the afternoon*
19.00	**las siete (de la tarde)** *seven p.m., seven o'clock in the evening*
21.00	**las nueve (de la noche)** *nine p.m., nine o'clock at night*

⚠ NOTE: When referring to a timetable, the 24 hour clock is used:

las dieciséis cuarenta y cinco 16.45
las veintiuna quince 21.15

305 Examples

¿A qué hora vas a venir? – A las siete
What time are you coming? – At seven o'clock
Las oficinas cierran de dos a cuatro
The offices are closed from two until four
Vendré a eso de/hacia las siete y media
I'll come at around 7.30
a las seis y pico
just after 6 o'clock
a las cinco en punto
at 5 o'clock sharp
entre las ocho y las nueve
between 8 and 9 o'clock
Son más de las tres y media
It's after half past three
Hay que estar allí lo más tarde a las diez
You have to be there by ten o'clock at the latest
Tiene para media hora
He'll be half an hour (at it)
Estuvo sin conocimiento durante un cuarto de hora
She was unconscious for a quarter of an hour
Les estoy esperando desde hace una hora/desde las dos
I've been waiting for them for an hour/since two o'clock
Se fueron hace unos minutos
They left a few minutes ago
Lo hice en veinte minutos
I did it in twenty minutes
El tren llega dentro de una hora
The train arrives in an hour('s time)
¿Cuánto (tiempo) dura la película?
How long does the film last?
por la mañana/tarde/noche
in the morning/afternoon *or* evening/at night

mañana por la mañana
tomorrow morning

anoche
last night

anteayer
the day before yesterday

ayer por la tarde
yesterday afternoon *or* evening

pasado mañana
the day after tomorrow

15 CALENDAR 306

❒ Dates

¿Qué día es hoy? **¿A qué día estamos?**	What's the date today?
Es (el) ... **Estamos a ...**	It's the ...
uno/primero de mayo	Ist of May
dos de mayo	2nd of May
veintiocho de mayo	28th of May
lunes tres de octubre	Monday the 3rd of October
Vienen el siete de marzo	They're coming on the 7th of March

⚠ NOTE: Use cardinal numbers for dates. Only for the first of the month can the ordinal number sometimes be used.

❒ Years

Nací en 1970
I was born in 1970
el veinte de enero de mil novecientos setenta
(on) 20th January 1970

❒ Other expressions

en los años cincuenta	during the fifties
en el siglo veinte	in the twentieth century
en mayo	in May
lunes (quince)	Monday (the 15th)
el quince de marzo	on March the 15th
el/los lunes	on Monday/Mondays
dentro de diez días	in 10 days' time
hace diez días	10 days ago

❒ Age

¿Qué edad tiene? **¿Cuántos años tiene?**	How old is he/she?
Tiene 23 (años)	He/She is 23
Tiene unos 40 años	He/She is around 40
A los 21 años	At the age of 21

INDEX

Grammar

The following index lists comprehensively both grammatical terms and key words in English and Spanish.